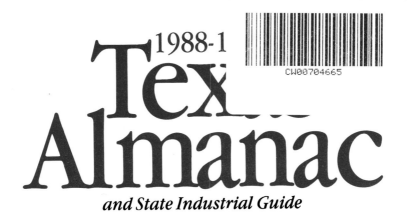

1988-1
Texas
Almanac
and State Industrial Guide

Published By

𝔗𝔥𝔢 𝔇𝔞𝔩𝔩𝔞𝔰 𝔐𝔬𝔯𝔫𝔦𝔫𝔤 𝔑𝔢𝔴𝔰

ISBN - 0-914511-04-1 *(hardback)*
ISBN - 0-914511-05-X *(paperback)*
Library of Congress Card No. 10-3390
Copyright 1987, A.H. Belo Corp., Communications Center, Dallas, TX 75265

Distributed by
Texas Monthly Press
P.O. Box 1569
Austin, TX 78767
512-476-7085

1988-1989
Texas Almanac

TABLE OF CONTENTS

MIKE KINGSTON, *Editor*

MARY G. CRAWFORD, *Associate Editor*

TOM ZIELINSKI, *Art Director*   GRAYSON MOODY, *Production*

SUE ELLEN BROWN, *Cover Illustration*   VIRGINIA GARDNER, *Production*

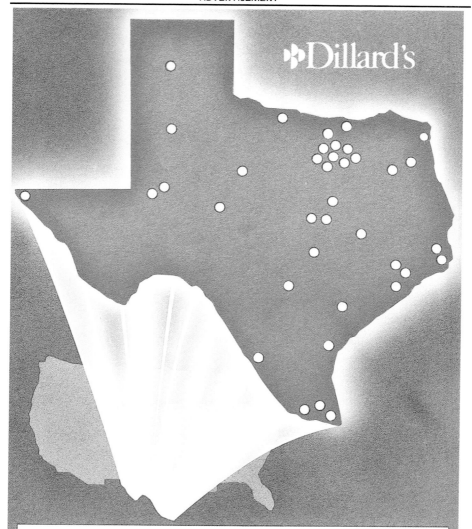

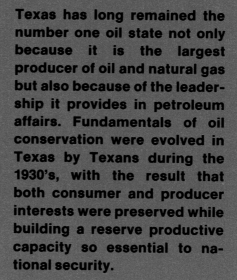

Building, maintaining, and operating Texas' basic transportation network

Scenic turnout on the Trans-Mountain Loop in El Paso.

The department assists local transit systems.

Bush peas on US 259 near Henderson.

New facilities to solve urban problems.

Good transportation is an essential element for every segment of our state's economy. The State Department of Highways and Public Transportation strives to give Texans everywhere beautiful, safe, efficient, and cost-effective mobility resources.

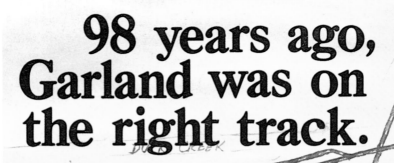

⬤ Cataract Surgery Center

- New Outpatient Facility
- Cataract & Lens Implant Surgery
- In Office Laser Surgery
- A Medicare Approved and Participating Provider
- Recorded Cataract Information 526-8288

CALL
214/528-8690

Texas Toll Free
1-800-442-5330

2801 Lemmon Avenue West
Dallas, Texas 75204

THE CHOICE IS SO CLEAR

Charles B. Key, M.D., F.A.C.S.   Jeffrey Whitman, M.D.

JCAH AND AAAHC APPROVED

THE

GULF COAST OF TEXAS

A HISTORY

By MIKE KINGSTON, *Editor, Texas Almanac*

Twenty-seven years after Christopher Columbus made initial contact with the New World, the first Spanish expeditions scouted Texas' Gulf Coast.

Francisco de Garay, governor of Jamaica, received permission to conduct a survey of the northern Gulf Coast from Florida to Mexico. At that time, the Spanish were seeking a passage through the North American continent to the Pacific Ocean.

Garay commissioned Alonso de Pinada to conduct a sea survey and prepare what became the first map of the region. When de Pinada conducted his survey in 1519, he found land, ports and rivers all along his route, describing them as "pleasing to the eye."

Based on Alvarez de Pinada's survey, Garay re-

(Continued on Page 17)

Dallas / Fort Worth International Airport

Your Passport To The World

Every year, more passengers enjoy the convenience of the DFW hub. More than 40 million passengers used Dallas/Fort Worth International Airport in 1986, making it the fourth busiest airport in the world.

Averaging 1,700 daily operations, DFW Airport offers scheduled service to 134 U.S. and 29 international destinations including every major city in North America.

Conveniently located 17 miles from downtown Dallas and Fort Worth, DFW Airport's layout provides easy access for the business and holiday traveler. Ample parking, rent-a-car facilities, and a Hyatt Regency Hotel are located on the Airport.

For a complimentary DFW Airport Guide or further airport information, please write the Public Information Office, Post Office Drawer DFW, DFW Airport, Texas 75261.

Dallas **Fort Worth International Airport**

Executive Director, Oris W. Dunham, Jr.
Post Office Drawer DFW
DFW Airport, Texas 75261
(214) 574-6701   Telex: 5101011662

Alonso Alvarez de Pineda in 1519 was the first European explorer to observe and map the Texas coastline. This statue was erected in Corpus Christi in his memory. Photo Courtesy the Corpus Christi Caller-Times.

ceived a grant from King Charles V to explore and colonize the region. As were most Spanish explorations, this one was privately financed. The governor in exchange received various concessions from the crown. Garay led an expedition in 1523 to establish a colony in the region he called "Amichel," the second of many names to be applied to Texas.

Alvarez de Pineda's reported activities (he was killed by Indians before writing a formal report, although he prepared the first complete map of the Gulf littoral) have resulted in confusion and uncertainty in the study of early Texas history. He sailed up the Rio Panuco to explore the country and to repair his ships. Texas historians have interpreted this river to be the Rio Grande, while American historians have held that the river was the Mississippi. In recent years, however, historians, such as Robert S. Weddle, have established that the Rio de las Palmas was the Soto la Marina in northern Mexico, a river about 100 miles south of the Rio Grande. It was so named by Garay in 1523, when he was blown to the river by a storm while attempting to reach a settlement on the Rio Panuco. Today a tributary of the Soto la Marina is still called the River of Palms.

Throughout much of the 16th century and most of the 17th, Spanish contact with the Texas coast was accidental. The exploits of Alvar Nunez Cabeza de Vaca, a survivor of the Panfilo de Narvaez expedition, are well known. The expedition set out from Florida to explore the northern Gulf region. Shipwrecked on Galveston or Follet Island in 1529, Cabeza de Vaca and his companions spent several years among the Indians of the coast.

The Karankawas, who inhabited the region from western Galveston Bay to Corpus Christi Bay, took Cabeza de Vaca into custody. Although they had a reputation for cannibalism, the Karankawas were appalled at the practice of surviving Spaniards' eating their companions who died during their first winter on the Texas coast. The Indians apparently practiced a form of exocannibalism in which portions of an enemy's body were eaten in an attempt to gain certain characteristics of that person such as courage, intelligence or physical prowess. The Karankawas did not eat members of their own tribe and did not understand why the Spaniards did.

These Indians and others along the coast were fierce and treacherous following contact with Spanish and French explorers. For two centuries, castaways and would-be explorers died at their hands. Cabeza de Vaca and his small party probably survived because they turned inland on their search for New Spain and traversed the Trans-Pecos in Texas on the way to the west coast of Mexico, where they found other Spaniards.

Other remnants of the Narvaez expedition were

shipwrecked farther south on the Texas coast and were tracked and killed by Indians, probably Coahuiltecans.

Two hundred and fifty Spaniards in 1554 met the same fate when three merchant ships laden with treasure were shipwrecked on Padre Island during a storm. Coastal Indians preyed on these unfortunate survivors as they tried to make their way to New Spain by way of the coast.

Survivors of the De Soto-Moscoso expedition were more fortunate. This group began a survey of the northern Gulf coast in 1539 under a grant to Hernando de Soto. He died in 1542 on the Mississippi River but named Luis de Moscoso Alvarado his successor. The expedition pushed into eastern Texas in search of New Spain and later retreated to the Mississippi, where seven brigantines were built. When the Spaniards sailed these ships to the Gulf in 1543, they stopped near the mouth of the Sabine River to caulk the vessels with pitch that came from an oil seep in the Gulf. Indians told the Spaniards that the pitch also could be used for medicine. It was the first mention of the use of a petroleum product that later made Texas famous.

Not all the early Spanish contact with the Texas coast was negative. In 1558, Guido de Lavazares was commissioned to survey the northern Gulf Coast in preparation for another colonization attempt. During the survey, Lavazares landed at Matagorda Bay and took possession in the name of King Charles V. The bay would not be "discovered" by the Frenchman Rene Robert Cavelier, Sieur de La Salle, for more than a century and a quarter.

Spanish contact with the Texas coast was only incidental during that time. Spain was the most powerful nation in Europe. And armed with a papal bull that gave it rights of discovery and colonization in the New World, Spain concentrated its attention on affairs in Europe. A series of Habsburg kings outdid one another in spending the treasure provided for royal coffers by New Spain and the rest of their empire. Dreams of instant wealth motivated most exploration, although the Roman Catholic Church provided a great impetus with its missionary zeal. But Texas offered neither quick wealth nor inhabitants easily converted to Christianity.

The fortunes of the Texas coast in the 17th century were tied directly to Spain's problems with Europe. The 16th century was the golden age of Spain. The Spanish developed a worldwide empire and in the New World created a European-Indian culture that exists today.

Success followed success under the leadership of Ferdinand and Isabella and the early Habsburg kings, Charles V and Philip II. The devout Spaniards interpreted these successes as confirmation by God of the justness of their cause. This confidence was shaken with the defeat, partly because of the intervention of the weather, of the Great Armada in 1588.

Despite the increasing wealth of Spain brought by the rich silver and gold deposits in the New World colonies, the nation's finances deteriorated under the Habsburgs. The wealth was dissipated in costly religious wars in Europe and in defense of Europe against the Turkish threat. Several times during the 16th century the government verged on bankruptcy.

Spanish colonial policy also changed. In 1573, Philip II promulgated several ordinances designed to correct abuses in earlier colonizing practices. Less emphasis was to be placed on military force, and more was to be laid on missionary effort. Mass baptisms with the recipients under duress were no longer acceptable. During the debate on treatment of Indians, the crown even briefly considered making the New World a spiritual haven without conquistadors or colonials. But the idea was quickly scuttled. Use of the word "conquest" in relation to the New World was banned, as Philip II preferred "pacification" or "discovery." The conquest and conversion of central Mexico to Christianity was completed by the mid-16th century, and the Inquisition began operating with renewed vigor Mexico in 1570-71.

Against this background, colonization in the northern Gulf was in limbo, except where needed to offset challenges by other Europeans. Florida's missions, for example, passed their golden age in the 17th century before missions were established in Texas. But the Florida missions were founded, in part, in response to French and English attempts to colonize the Atlantic coast. In the 17th century, the most zealous and competent missionaries went to New Spain's northern frontier, including Texas.

When other European powers became interested in Texas, Spain's attitude toward the vast unexplored area changed. Until the late 17th century, the Gulf was a Spanish lake; Spanish sovereignty was virtually unchallenged. But the Frenchman La Salle, changed that. In 1682, he completed an exploration of the Mississippi River to its mouth and claimed all the land drained by the river for the French king. Three years later, La Salle intended to reinforce the claim by establishing a colony at the mouth of the Mississippi. But through some confusion, La Salle's colonists ended up on Matagorda Bay.

The French in 1685 built Fort St. Louis on Garcitas Creek just above Lavaca Bay. Problems with Indians began almost immediately, and many supplies also were lost when one of the French ships sank. So morale of the small band of colonists was low. La Salle made several explorations of the region, once traveling as far as the Rio Grande. He was killed by one of his own men near the Trinity River while on an expedition to get relief for his colonists from French settlements on the Illinois River. Disease and raids by the fierce Karankawas took their toll on the colonists, and by 1689, most were scattered or dead.

Word of La Salle's intentions reached Spanish officials in late 1685 when crewmen on a French corsair captured off the coast of Yucatan told of the expedition. Texas Indians who encountered the French colonists confirmed the report the following year.

Six searches by land and five by sea to find La Salle's colony were initiated by Spanish officials in the next few years. One of the sea voyages visited Matagorda Bay in 1687 but failed to locate the French colony. Finally Alonso de Leon, governor of Coahuila and a seasoned frontiersman, found the French fort in 1689 and continued to look for survivors. Remnants of the fort were destroyed, although the Spanish returned more than 30 years later and established a presidio on the same site.

De Leon followed the trail of reported French activity to East Texas, and in 1690 established missions in the area. They were abandoned in 1693, however, and Texas again was forgotten by Spanish officials when the French threat eased. De Leon's explorations were the first official ventures by the Spanish government into eastern Texas. He named many landmarks, such as the Nueces and Trinity rivers.

Interest in Texas declined until 1716, when concern about the growing influence of French traders in East Texas prompted the re-establishment of the missions in the area. Missions also were founded at San Antonio in 1718 to provide a way station between the mission settlement of San Juan Bautista on the Rio Grande and the East Texas missions. San Juan Bautista was the Spanish gateway into Texas. Its ruins are located 35 miles below Eagle Pass at Guerrero, Coahuila.

French forces ousted Spaniards from East Texas in a comic war in 1719, but two years later, the Marquis of San Miguel de Aguayo, Joseph Azlor Virto de Vera, led an expedition to re-establish and reinforce the presidios in Texas. He dispatched troops to Lavaca Bay to establish a presidio. The facility was to defend against further French landings, and use of the bay as a port to cut shipping costs was considered. At the time, Veracruz was the port of entry for goods shipped to Texas, and high transportation costs were a continuing problem for settlers in colonial Spanish Texas.

French interest in the Texas coast continued, although it took bizarre twists. In 1719, for example, Simars de Bellisle and four shipmates from a French ship jumped ship in Galveston Bay. Then they were taken prisoner by Indians in the area. Only Bellisle survived, adding the first report of mounted Indians to the lore of the coast. Rescued by French traders, the seaman and Jean-Baptiste de la Harpe returned to Galveston Bay while seeking Matagorda Bay in 1721. Plans to establish a trading post failed to materialize, and the region was abandoned.

In early 1721 Spaniards occupied land for a presidio to be located on the site of the French Fort St. Louis. The presidio was named "Nuestra Senora de Loreto de la Bahia del Espiritu Santo." The first Indians attracted to the mission were Karankawas. These nomads were rebellious, however, and the padres soon asked that the mission be moved.

Four years later, the mission and presidio were relocated to the Guadalupe River in what today is called Mission Valley near Victoria. Efforts to dam the Guadalupe and to dig irrigation ditches were abandoned when it was determined that normal rainfall would support agriculture in the area. Tonkawas were the first Indians attracted to the mission, which remained at the site until mid-century.

Spanish influence in Europe declined rapidly in the final years of the 17th century. Charles II, the last of the Habsburgs and known as "the bewitched," was a mental defective incapable of leadership. Aware of this weakness, France began vigorous expansion in the New World. King Louis XIV chartered a trading company to colonize the land drained by the Mississippi River, as claimed by La Salle. In 1699, a settlement was established at Biloxi Bay, from which the Mississippi River was explored. The French insisted that they were protecting the Spanish from the English, who, it was argued, planned to establish a colony on the northern Gulf Coast and to acquire the rich silver mines in northern New Spain.

Charles II's death in 1700 provoked a crisis in Spain and in Europe. With no male heir in the Habsburg line, the throne was claimed by Philip V, whose grandmother, Maria Teresa, the daughter of Philip IV, married Louis XIV in 1660. Spanish leaders realized that the nation needed a strong monarch, and the French Bourbon seemed the solution.

Philip V's ascension to the throne prompted a civil war in Spain and the War of Spanish Succession that lasted until 1714 in Europe. Other countries feared that a close alliance between Spain and France would disrupt the balance of power in Europe. Philip established himself by beginning a reformation of the moribund government. Bourbon rule featured an efficient central government.

Texas in the 18th century had three centers of Spanish influence: San Antonio, Los Adaes and the La Bahia mission and presidio near Victoria. Each was a religious center, for the government used the missions to "civilize" the Indians and to convert them into useful Spanish citizens. Los Adaes, which is near present Robeline, La., and served as the capital of the province of Texas from 1721 to 1773, and La Bahia were bastions of defense against incursions by the French.

In 1727, Capt. Pedro de Rivera was ordered by the viceroy to conduct a survey of the missions and presidios in Texas. His recommendations in 1729 resulted in a reduction of the number of soldiers in the province and implementation of efficiencies in operation. As part of Rivera's recommendations, the governor of Texas also was ordered to initiate an annual reconnaissance of the Gulf Coast from Bahia del Espiritu Santo, which had been moved to Mission Valley near Victoria, to the Sabine River. One survey was made in 1727 by Francisco Alvarez Barreyro, an engineer who was sent by Rivera from La Bahia. Barreyro's expedition lasted 35 days, covered 363 leagues and examined the coast as far as the Neches River.

Indian problems increasingly bedeviled Spaniards on Texas' coast. The Comanches pushed their Apache enemies off the Great Plains. By mid-century, the

Apaches were raiding along the coast. The thinly manned presidios were hard pressed to protect the missions and the few settlers around them.

Xenophobia often motivated the exploration of the coast. After rumors were received in 1747 that Frenchmen were in the area, Joaquin de Orobio y Bazterra, commander of the presidio of La Bahia, was ordered to survey the area between the Guadalupe and Trinity Rivers. No Frenchmen were found, and shortly after Orobio's visit, Spanish traders from East Texas began visiting the area.

Spanish fears were realized in 1754 when the Frenchman Joseph Blancpain and a party of traders were caught in the area of the lower Trinity. The need for a military presence in the region became obvious, and it was coupled with efforts in 1756 to convert Atakapa Indians. The mission Nuestra Senora de la Luz was built on the Trinity River near present Wallisville, and the presidio San Agustin de Ahumada de Orcoquisac was located nearby. In 1766, both were damaged by a hurricane and later moved to higher ground.

Spanish officials also were aware that the eastern coast of Mexico was wide open to foreign adventurism, leaving the silver mines unprotected. In 1747, Jose de Escandon was selected to colonize today's Mexican state of Tamaulipas, which extended northward to the Nueces River.

Capt. Orobio again was ordered to survey the Texas coast, this time south from Matagorda Bay to the Rio Grande in preparation for Escandon's colonization effort. He made the first Spanish surveys of Corpus Christi Bay and the Nueces River in the area. Based on Orobio's information, Escandon recommended that a civil settlement be established at the Indian village of Santa Dorotea on the lower San Antonio River and that Presidio La Bahia and Mission Espiritu Santo be moved from near Victoria to the area of today's Goliad. These institutions were moved by 1749, but the civil settlement was not approved by Spanish officials.

By 1766, Escandon, who colonized the Lower Rio Grande Valley in Texas, reported to the viceroy that good progress was being made in settling the country between the Rio Grande and the Nueces River, which was the northern boundary of the colony that was called "Nuevo Santander" in honor of the great colonizer's home province in Spain. By then Blas Maria de la Garza Falcon, Captain of Camargo on the Rio Grande, had established the first settlement in present Nueces County. Called "Santa Petronila," the community was located five leagues (about 12 miles) from the Nueces River. During this period, an increasing number of cattle were being brought to the area.

The quality of missionary work improved during the period. In 1760, Father Bartolome Garcia published a manual for religious instruction in the Coahuiltecan language. About 20 Indian tribes represented at the missions on the lower Rio Grande and the San Antonio River used the publication. One of the first priorities of missionaries was to learn the native tongue so the neophytes could be trained in their own language. In many cases, these books are the only record of these languages available today.

A major change in colonial policy as applied to Texas took place after 1762. In anticipation of losing the huge Louisiana Territory to England in the settlement of the Seven Years' War, the French ceded the region to Spain, their ally late in the war. In turn, Spain lost western Florida, a strip of coastal land that ran to the east bank of the mouth of the Mississippi River, to the English. After the transfer of territory, Texas was no longer a buffer zone between New Spain and the French.

The change also allowed the crown to make economies in the administration of frontier government. Charles III, considered the greatest of Spanish Bourbon sovereigns, commissioned Jose de Galvez to study the adminstration of New Spain and to make recommendations for improvement. The king also appointed the Marquis de Rubi to study frontier defenses in 1767. Rubi recommended in 1773 that all the missions and presidios in Texas be closed except those at La Bahia and San Antonio. The missions on the Trinity had been abandoned in 1771 because of heavy Indian attacks, and the others were closed.

Efforts were made to gain more detailed information about Texas. Jose de Evia of the Spanish navy mapped the entire Gulf Coast from Florida to the Tampico in 1785 and 1786. Galveston Bay and the island were named for Bernardo de Galvez, governor of Louisiana and later viceroy of New Spain. But no attempt to settle the area was made. He also made the first detailed Spanish survey of Corpus Christi Bay.

Administration of the northern provinces was given to the office of the Internal Provinces, rather than the viceroy in Mexico City. Jose de Galvez's nephew, Bernardo, an experienced frontiersman and explorer, was named viceroy in 1785 and the office regained authority over the provinces. Bernardo developed a plan to control the Indians. No more truces would be offered; the Indians had the choice of either war or peace. In addition, the Indians were to be settled near presidios and were to be given supplies and firearms in an attempt to make them dependent on Spaniards. Unfortunately Bernardo de Galvez, whose career held so much potential for the development of the frontier, died of a mysterious illness in 1786. Between 1790 and 1810, the plan worked and the frontier towns prospered, churches were built and prospectors began exploring the territory for precious metals. The plan broke down during Mexico's war of independence when the government stopped making the annual gifts.

With the Louisiana Territory under Spanish control, Texas again fell into limbo. It was not until French treachery placed control of the territory in the hands of Anglo-Americans that Texas again became a center of concern.

Colonization

Texas' tranquillity that existed while Spain controlled the western Louisiana Territory ended abruptly with an act of duplicity and deceit by Napoleon Bonaparte. Under a secret treaty of 1800, Spain agreed to return the territory to France with the understanding that the French would not give the land to any country other than Spain.

Spain's Charles IV, however, was a weak king and failed to challenge Napoleon when in 1803 the French leader ignored the understanding and sold the huge Louisiana Territory west of the Mississippi River to the United States. Overnight, Texas was transformed into a quiet interior province to a frontier once again, and this time, the aggressive Anglo-Americans, not the undermanned French explorers, shared the border.

In addition, the American and French revolutions of the 18th century had created an atmosphere of change in the Spanish colony. Attempts to suppress the revolutionary writings and liberal ideas that formed the basis of these movements were dismal failures in Spanish America.

Of immediate concern was the boundary between Texas and the Louisiana Territory. Spain and France never agreed on a specific frontier, and after 1763, when the region was ceded to Spain by France, boundaries were not of concern. President Thomas Jefferson, however, initially claimed all of Texas to the Rio Grande based on La Salle's exploration of that region in 1685. Most maps of earlier periods had shown the territory as a French possession. But this was a result more of Spain's secrecy about its colonies than of a legitimate French claim to Texas.

Spain's initial response was to strengthen garrisons in Texas. In 1805, troops were sent to Orcoquisac and Atascosito in present-day Liberty County to control immigration into Southeast Texas. This military buildup also benefitted health care. In 1806, the province's first hospital was opened in San Antonio, and the first dentist came to the region. Smallpox vaccine, developed by William Jenner in 1798, also was introduced.

Texas' major problem, however, was underpopulation. Censuses in the early 19th century found about 4,000 people, excluding Indians, in the province. Spanish and later Mexican officials conceived many schemes for attracting settlers. In 1805, the British thwarted one colonial expedition from Spain by capturing four royal frigates that were to transfer 3,000 to 5,000 settlers from Cadiz to Texas. One can only speculate on the impact that these colonists, military veterans and their families, might have had on Texas' history if they had not been left at dockside.

Some population was moving into Texas from Mexico, however. In 1794, the Rancho de Santa Gertrudis, owned by Juan Barrera, was in operation on the north shore of Corpus Christi Bay, and by the turn of the century, ranchers from the Rio Grande were seeking grants for land in present-day Nueces County. Indian problems hampered some efforts. Martin de Leon, who later founded Victoria and settled a colony, began ranching on the Nueces River north of present-day Corpus Christi in 1809 but moved to San Antonio for protection from Indian harassment.

Political change was in the offing for Spain, as well as the rest of Europe. Charles IV took the throne in 1788 at the death of his father, Charles III, and Spain's brief regeneracy soon ended. The son had none of his father's skill as a ruler. Court life degenerated into a pursuit of pleasure, and governance of Spain's overseas territories suffered. By 1805, Charles IV was forced to abdicate in favor of his son, Ferdinand VII, who was no better a ruler. Napoleon Bonaparte took advantage of this weakness by luring the king and his father to France in 1808 and placing his brother, Joseph Bonaparte, on the Spanish throne in their absence. Civil war ensued in Spain, and colonists flexed their growing desire for self-government. Like other Spanish subjects, they rejected the rule of the usurper.

During the civil war, Spanish liberals gained control of the government and wrote a constitution in 1812 that increased the sovereignty of the people at the expense of the crown. The Cortes (legislature) moved from Madrid to Cadiz and considered many proposals for the colonization of Texas, which had become a hot item of interest. In 1813, the Cortes approved a plan by Col. Ricardo Reynal Keene to colonize the province with Irish Catholics from Spain. Keene's proposal included all the features that later made up the empresario system, but Ferdinand VII abrogated the plan, along with all legislation passed by the Cortes under the liberal constitution, when he regained the throne in 1814.

Mexico's war for independence began with Father Miguel Hidalgo's revolt at Dolores in September 1810, but the Texas Gulf Coast was little touched. In 1813, Augustus Magee, commander of the army of the insurgents, held the Presidio La Bahia. Most of the action during the days of the so-called Green Flag Republic of Texas occurred in the more populated parts of the province.

Galveston Island did play a major role, however. Don Jose Manuel de Herrera, a priest, was appointed an agent of Mexico during the war for independence. He appointed Don Luis Aury commodore of the navy of Mexico and directed him to occupy the island for use in action against Spanish shipping. Aury arrived in 1816 with 12-15 small vessels and in time almost swept Spanish commerce from the Gulf. When Aury left Galveston for action in Mexico, Jean Lafitte arrived in 1817 and swore fealty to Mexico. Lafitte had received amnesty from the United States for aid given against the British in the Battle of New Orleans in the War of 1812. But he was a character of mystery. The Mexican revolutionaries gave him control of the island to use as a base against the Spanish. Recent research had indicated that he also was a Spanish spy, even while preying on that country's shipping. American filibusters also tried in vain to get his support in their operations.

Whatever else was accomplished, Lafitte's occupation and operation in the Gulf brought prosperity to the island. By the end of 1817, there were 1,000 men from several nations at Galveston, some fugitives and others refugees. Gambling houses, pool parlors and drinking establishments sprang up, giving Galveston the appearance of a mining town. It also became quite a commercial center. The plunder from Spanish ships was sold at great discounts, and merchants from New Orleans and other Gulf ports were quick to take advantage of the bargains.

Importation of slaves into the United States was banned by law. But customers of Lafitte devised a scheme to circumvent the prohibition. Captured slaves were purchased for plantation owners and then declared as illegal imports to U.S. customs officials. Customs policy required that the contraband slaves be sold at auction. They were bought by the men who brought them to the mainland. These men also received half the auction price for turning in the contraband. Then the slaves were delivered to the slaveholders who had ordered them. Jim Bowie and his brothers were practitioners of the scheme and turned a $65,000 profit before retiring.

Lafitte also exercised tight discipline over those to whom he issued commissions to attack Spanish shipping. A "Captain Brown" violated his commission by raiding a plantation in Louisiana, and Lafitte hanged the man and turned his crew over to U.S. officials. In

Bernardo de Galvez was Viceroy of Mexico and one-time frontier Indian fighter. Galveston Bay was named for him. Photo Courtesy Archives Division, Texas State Library.

1820, some of Lafitte's charges plundered an American ship, and U.S. authorities insisted that he abandon Galveston Island. Karankawa Indians thereafter discouraged settlement on the island until the Texas Revolution.

The instability caused by the Mexican revolution also attracted adventurers, and New Orleans merchants had long been interested in opening trade with Texas. Spanish mercantile policy prohibited the establishment of ports in the province. All merchandise bound for Texas entered New Spain at Veracruz and was transported overland to its destination with costs greatly increased each step of the way. Smuggling and illicit trade with Louisiana, through many governments, thrived, providing lower priced and higher quality goods than were available through the official system of trade.

Filibusters from the United States entered Texas, though none was successful in taking advantage of the unsettled conditions. James Long centered one of his expeditions on the Gulf Coast after unsuccessfully seeking aid from Lafitte. Long was captured while attempting to hold the Presidio La Bahia in 1820 against government forces and died under mysterious circumstances after being released from official custody in Mexico City. His wife, Jane, remained in Texas after his death. For many years she was called the "mother of Texas" for giving birth to the first Anglo-American child in the province. Recent research, however, indicates that many Anglo-American children were born in Miller County, Arkansas, which later was recognized as part of Northeast Texas, some time before Mrs. Long gave birth to her second daughter.

Napoleonic exiles briefly settled in Texas. In 1818, Generals Charles Lallemand and Antoine Rigaud established the colony of Champ D'Asile on the Trinity River. The purpose of the settlement was to help Mexican insurgents overthrow the Spanish government and to place Joseph Bonaparte on the Mexican throne. Settlers left after only a brief stay, and Spanish troops were dispatched to destroy the settlement. Champ D'Asile served to accelerate U.S.-Spanish boundary negotiations, which were completed with the Adams-Onis Treaty of 1819. The United States gave up all claims to Texas in exchange for Spanish concession of western Florida — a strip of land on the Gulf running from the peninsula to the mouth of the Mississippi River.

Westerners in the United States were outraged that Texas had been given away, and illegal immigration into Texas gained momentum.

After the loss of the Louisiana Territory, Spanish immigration policy in Texas was loosened to give priority to former Spanish subjects from the territory who wanted to move. Efforts were made to keep Anglo-American immigrants away from the border near their fellow countrymen in the United States. But control of the Anglo-Americans who had been subjects of Spain in the Louisiana Territory was difficult. Attracted by Spain's and Mexico's liberal land grant policies, many started filtering into Southeast Texas even before colonists came to the province under the empresario programs. They later had land titles issued under the Imperial Colonization Law of 1823, although slowness of the procedure was one complaint levied against the Mexican government before the Texas Revolution.

In Spain in 1820, the army revolted against Ferdinand VII, who was forced to reinstate the Constitution of 1812 and the legislation that had been passed under its jurisdiction. In addition to re-establishing the colonization laws affecting Texas, the king also broke historical precedent: The usually secretive Spanish invited foreigners, not just former subjects, to settle on New Spain's northern frontier.

Moses Austin, who lived under Spanish rule in present-day Missouri, journeyed to Texas in 1820 to seek permission to settle 300 families under the new empresario program. Permission was granted, but Moses died before carrying through with the colonization. His son, Stephen F. Austin, accepted the responsibility. Before he could get settlers into Texas in 1821, however, Mexico gained its independence from Spain. The younger Austin had to renegotiate the grant with the new national government. He was ultimately successful, although the process took several months in the chaotic atmosphere in Mexico City shortly after independence. Austin scrupulously followed the terms of his contract with the government and became the most successful of the empresarios.

Mexico disposed of its public lands in a different manner than the United States. In 1824, the state governments — rather than the national as in the U.S. — were given the responsibility to develop the public lands. The national government did prohibit settlement by foreigners within 20 leagues (about 50 miles) of a national border. Also settlement within 10 leagues of the coast was prohibited in an attempt to curb smuggling.

Martin de Leon, who had earlier settled on the Aransas and Nueces rivers, got an informal grant in 1824 to settle families in an undefined area south of San Antonio. De Leon had seen the land during a cattle drive to New Orleans in 1823, and his grant predated the law authorizing the state to dispose of public land. Consequently, his grant and Green DeWitt's, which was approved in 1825 by the state of Coahuila y Texas, overlapped and caused a conflict.

De Leon reintroduced cattle raising into the region, where a century earlier large mission herds had grazed. He founded Guadalupe Victoria, named after the Mexican president, as capital of his colony and settled many families, including Americans and Irish, as well as Mexicans. De Leon died of cholera in 1833. Victoria was located in the middle of DeWitt's grant. De Leon's claim was recognized because he was a Mexican citizen and had established the town before DeWitt arrived.

DeWitt was the second most successful of the colonizers during the Mexican period. He received a grant southwest of Austin's in 1825 to settle 400 families and by year's end had laid out the town of Gonzales, which was named for the provisional governor of Coahuila y Texas, Rafael Gonzalez. The settlement was destroyed by Indians in 1826 and re-established the following year.

A second settlement called "Old Station" was established by DeWitt near the mouth of the Lavaca River. It was within the area near the coast in which settlement was prohibited and had to be abandoned in 1827 when Mexican officials suspected some colonists of dealing in contraband. Most residents moved to Gonzales.

A misunderstanding between Mexican officials and Anglo-American colonizers in Nacogdoches in 1826 resulted in the Fredonian Rebellion in which the Americans attempted to set up their own republic. Although the rebellion was short-lived and other Americans helped Mexican officials put it down, the revolt further fanned Mexican distrust. They knew that there was strong sentiment in the United States for the acquisition of Texas, and it was feared that the Americans might try to annex the Mexican province through subterfuge.

Therefore efforts were made to attract European colonists, especially Roman Catholics, to offset the large number of Anglo-Americans already in Texas. James Power, an Irishman, and James Hewetson of Monclova received a grant in June 1828 to settle 100

Mexican and 100 Irish families in an area between the Guadalupe and Lavaca rivers. The federal government allowed the colony to extend to the coast, and in 1829, the western boundary was moved to the Nueces River. Power and Hewetson had many problems attracting Irish settlers and asked to substitute English, German and American colonists.

The headquarters for the colony was the site of the old Refugio mission, which was still active in 1828. When it was abandoned a year later, Power and Hewetson bought the property and the buildings at auction from the government.

James McGloin and John McMullen, both Irish residents of Monclova, received a grant in August 1828 to settle 200 Irish families. The San Patricio grant covered a large area from just north of the Nueces River to the Rio Grande and southwest from a line running northeast from near Laredo to the Gulf, including the Lower Rio Grande Valley. (Only a small portion of present San Patricio County was within the grant.)

Many of their Irish families were recruited in the United States, and operations were suspended when the Law of 1830 prohibited immigration from the United States. McGloin and McMullen got an extension of their grant in 1834 and eventually gave 84 land titles to settlers.

The Atascosito District between the Trinity and Sabine rivers in Southeast Texas attracted many settlers prior to the colonization efforts of Austin. Empresario contracts were awarded to David G. Burnet in 1826, Joseph Vehlein in 1828 and Lorenzo de Zavala in 1829. But they had difficulty attracting colonists because independent settlers already had taken much of the choice land.

In addition to large land grants, settlers got other concessions, such as exemption from taxes and customs for seven years. As soon as the population of each colony was large enough, it was turned into a governmental unit with elected officials exercising authority.

Anglo-Texan towns sprang up shortly after colonization began. San Felipe de Austin was established on the Brazos River in July 1823. In addition to serving as the headquarters of the Austin colony, San Felipe also was the unofficial capital of the Anglo-Texan settlements.

Velasco was established in 1821 near the mouth of the Brazos. Through this community 25,000 colonists entered Texas between 1821 and 1836.

Washington-on-the-Brazos dates from 1822, when Andrew Robinson began operating a ferry on the Brazos just below the mouth of the Navasota River. This town served as the capital of Texas from 1842-45.

Anahuac was established in 1821 at the mouth of the Trinity River in eastern Galveston Bay. Originally called Perry's Point, the name was changed in 1825. In 1827, James Taylor White, one of the colony's major cattle raisers, settled nearby.

Columbia was settled in 1823 at the site of a former Indian village called Montezuma, and Brazoria, established on the Brazos River in 1828, was an important port and trade center for the Austin colony. Liberty was founded in 1821 and originally was called Atascosito.

John Richardson Harris was one of Austin's original colonists and, in 1824, was granted a league and labor of land. He took land at the junction of Buffalo and Bray's bayous and, in 1826, laid out the town of Harrisburg. Originally a steam-powered sawmill was erected, making Harrisburg a "timber town." The settlement also developed into a trade center for the Galveston Bay area, and, in 1830, Mexican officials allowed a crude road to be built to San Felipe. Harris did not live to see the success of his community; he died of yellow fever in New Orleans in August 1829. The town became a government center under the provisional government in December 1835 and was burned during the revolution.

These communities joined the older Spanish-Mexican settlements of San Antonio, La Bahia and Nacogdoches as the population centers for the fledgling province.

After the Fredonian Rebellion, Gen. Manuel Mier y Teran made a tour of Texas beginning in November 1827, ostensibly to survey the new eastern boundary with the United States. Recommendations based on his observations were incorporated into the Law of April 6, 1830, which greatly excited Anglo-Texans. Immigration from the United States was prohibited by the new law, garrisons were to be enlarged and new ones established, and other changes in the relations between citizens and government were made. One beneficial change was to allow foreign, especially American, ships to engage in coastal trade. The idea was to develop with Mexican ports the trade bonds that were tied to New Orleans at the time.

Cultural and political differences were at the root of many of the problems between the Anglo-Texans and Mexicans. Gen. Teran noted that the new colonists carried their political constitutions in their pockets. He foresaw a subtle movement from the United States in which peaceful penetration of the Mexican province by Americans would be followed by demands for political rights that the government was not prepared to extend and that would be taken through revolution.

Indeed, Anglo-Texans often failed to understand that Mexico did not extend the same guarantees of civil liberties as did the United States, or that those civil rights did not cross the national border.

Five new garrisons to enforce the provisions of the Law of 1830 were created under Gen. Teran's plan. Anahuac at the mouth of the Trinity River had been established in 1821; a fort was built in 1830. The other forts built in 1830 or 1831, included Lavaca on the river of the same name; Lipantitlan on the Nueces River near San Patricio; Tenoxtitlan on the Brazos River about half way between San Antonio and Nacogdoches; and Teran near Rockland on the Neches River in Tyler County. Teran's desire to "Mexicanize" Texas is reflected in the names of Anahuac, Lipantitlan and Tenoxtitlan that are Nahuatl, the Aztec language.

With all the changes, however, it was Mexico's attempt to begin collecting taxes and customs that finally sparked violence between the Anglo-Texans and their new government.

Prelude

Cultural differences between Anglos and Mexicans have been pointed out as a principle cause of the Texas Revolution. Political and economic differences were as important.

Mexico was a country in political turmoil. Once independence from Spain was secured, no consensus existed in Mexico as to the form of government that should be adopted. Liberals favored a federalist government, much like that in the United States. The Mexican constitution of 1824 adopted a federalist framework. Liberals soon learned that attitudes toward government were as important as the form. Political losers must subordinate their desires, but the lesson is difficult to practice. Conversely, Mexico was accustomed to a strong central government, as imposed during the long colonial period. Political power was distributed from the top of the government pyramid down, rather than from the grassroots up as in the federalist system. Centralists felt this was the only alternative since Mexico had no democratic tradition.

Federalists and centralists battled for control of government — and not always at the polls. Between May 1833 and August 1855, the presidency of Mexico changed hands 36 times, the average term being seven and one-half months. Revolt followed revolt. Chaos and anarchy were rules, not exceptions.

While Mexicans were still trying to determine the form their government should take, Anglo-Texans already had experience with a successful federal system before immigrating. They had little patience with the Mexicans, whose inexperience was interpreted as incompetence and, worse, dictatorial arrogance. The language difference aggravated the problem. Early Anglo settlers accepted the Mexican government and intended to become good citizens of their adopted country. As immigration grew, however, and empresarios like Stephen F. Austin lost direct control of the new settlers, loyalty to Mexico declined.

The Fredonian Rebellion in Nacogdoches in 1826 was the first incident that led to violent conflict. Empresario Haden Edwards misunderstood his responsibilities under Mexican law, and in a conflict with officials, he declared the independence of the Republic of Fredonia. Mexican officials, aided by Anglo colonists, quickly put down the insurgents. But government officials, never comfortable with Anglo-Americans, became more suspicious about their intentions.

Under the colonization law of 1824, new settlers were exempted from taxes and customs for seven years. By 1830, this period of grace was ending for many colonists, and one of the intents of the Law of April 6, 1830, was to tighten up tax collections. One of the state government's major problems was a lack of money to pay for the frontier defense and education system demanded by Anglo-Texans.

Two Americans in the service of the Mexican government figured prominently in the events that led to violence in 1832. George Fisher, a Serbian and naturalized American, was named collector of customs by Mexican officials. Fisher was to set up a customs office on Galveston Island, but in the interim, he opened shop in 1830 at the mouth of the Brazos River.

Texans were distressed with this turn of events. They thought the exemption from customs and taxes was permanent. Shippers claimed they were not given notice of the change in policy. Fisher was briefly removed from office, but returned the following year to stir up settlers even more.

About the same time, Col. John Davis Blackburn, who had entered Texas as a filibuster before joining the Mexican army of independence, was in 1830 put in command of a garrison at Anahuac at the mouth of the Trinity River in eastern Galveston Bay.

Both Fisher and Blackburn were soon at odds with Anglo-Texans. Fisher aggravated the situation by requiring ships to register at Point Bolivar near Anahuac more than 50 miles away from the customhouse on the Brazos. After a public uproar, Fisher resigned in 1832.

Blackburn's troubles were more complicated. Many settlers had entered Southeast Texas illegally after Mexico gained its independence. Although both state and federal governments agreed that titles should be issued, each claimed the authority to issue titles around Anahuac, since the area was within the 10-league prohibited area.

J. Francisco Madero, a land agent appointed by the state, was jailed by Blackburn for issuing land titles and setting up a local government at Liberty. Madero was later ordered released by Teran.

Then Blackburn arrested Patrick C. Jack, who had been elected captain of a militia unit formed by Anglo-Texans. Such units were illegal under Mexican law, a point not understood by the Anglos.

And finally, Blackburn took William B. Travis into custody, apparently for expressing disrespect for local officials. Travis was representing a Louisiana slaveholder who was trying to get two runaway slaves held by Blackburn returned from Texas.

A group of Anglos beseiged Anahuac, demanding the release of Jack and Travis. During the standoff, John Austin was sent to bring canons from San Felipe. He ignored the customs office at Velasco on the Brazos on the return trip, and a Mexican soldier was wounded in a brief firefight.

Jose de las Piedras, commander of the garrison at Nacogdoches, journeyed to Anahuac to defuse the situation. He convinced Blackburn to release Jack and Travis and to resign.

In the interim, Antonio Lopez de Santa Anna had revolted against the centralist government in Mexico and pledged to install a federalist regime. Texans supported Santa Anna and claimed to Mexican officials that their acts against Fisher and Blackburn, representatives of the centralist government, had been in support of Santa Anna's rebellion. Gen. Jose Antonio Mexia visited several hundred troops visited Brazoria in 1832, and he was convinced that the Anglo-Texans were not in revolt against Mexico.

Mexican troops at all Texas garrisons returned to Mexico to fight in Santa Anna's revolt. So the Texans had rebelled against Mexican authority and had suffered no retribution. With Santa Anna leading a reform movement, the Anglo-Texans felt it was time to carry their protests a step further. In 1832, officials at San Felipe called a convention to discuss grievances against the government. Petitions were drawn up but never presented to the national government. The following year, a second convention was called. Again petitions citing grievances were prepared. Texans wanted separation from the state of Coahuila, and a state constitution was drawn up. This was Sam Houston's first participation in Texas' political affairs. Stephen F. Austin agreed to present the Anglo-Texans' case to the national government in Mexico City.

While petitioning the national government directly was acceptable in the United States, it was improper in

Mexico, where business was to be conducted through channels. The Anglo-Texans inadvertently further aggravated the suspicions of Mexican officials concerning their intentions. And vice versa. On the return trip from Mexico City, Austin was arrested. He had written a letter to officials in San Antonio that was interpreted as calling for a revolution. During Austin's two years of imprisonment, settlers contained their complaints, fearing for his safety.

And the Mexican government was not insensitive to the Anglo-Texans' complaints. Col. Juan Nepomuceno Almonte toured Texas in 1834 with twofold instructions: to assure settlers that the government was moving to implement reforms and to determine the attitude of the colonists. Almonte found no unrest in Texas and advocated most of the reforms that Austin had requested in Mexico City.

Indeed, despite the turmoil, Texas was prospering. By 1834, 7,000 bales of cotton with a value of $315,000 were shipped to New Orleans. In the middle of the decade, Texas exports, including cotton and beaver, otter and deer skins, amounted to $500,000. Trade ratios were out of balance, however, because $630,000 in manufactured goods were imported. Almonte also found that there was little currency in Texas. Ninety percent of the business transactions were conducted in barter or credit, "which gives the country, in its trading relations, the appearance of a continued fair," he observed.

In 1833 and 1834, the legislature of Coahuila y Texas also was diligently trying to respond to the complaints of Texas colonists. The English language was recognized for official purposes. Religious toleration was approved. (Gen. Teran in 1828 had noted that freedom of religion was better than no religion at all, which was the case in Texas at the time.). And the court system was revised, providing Texas with an appellate court and trial by jury. Previously, the legislature had approved schools for the colonists, but this measure was not fully implemented because of a lack of funds and low population density. Texas also was divided into three departments, Bexar, Nacogdoches and Brazos, to facilitate administration.

In Mexico City, however, things were not going as well. Santa Anna, elected president in 1832 was revealing the duplicity that marked his career. Upon election, he turned the government over to Vice President Gomez Farias, a liberal, who instituted many reforms that drew opposition from the aristocracy, the clergy and the military. Santa Anna resumed power, exiled Farias, repudiated his federalist platform and began centralizing the national government. By October 1835, the Mexican Congress was subservient to Santa Anna. Liberals in the state of Zacatecas rebelled, and the revolt was ruthlessly put down. To make an example of the insurgents, troops were allowed to sack the state capital. The military also was sent into Coahuila to settle a dispute between centralists and federalists.

In January of 1835, the Mexican dictator sent troops to Anahuac to make another attempt at collecting taxes and customs. William B. Travis led a contingent of settlers that ousted the troops. Surprisingly, Travis found that the action was not universally popular among Anglo-Texans. Settlers were divided into two camps, the war party and the peace party. The war party was made up of generally newer colonists who had little time invested in Texas; it advocated a complete break with Mexico, seeking either independence or annexation to the United States. The peace party attracted longtime colonists, many of who had sincerely pledged allegiance to the Mexican government; its leaders counseled patience and wanted to ride out the current political storm, as had been done before.

Committees of correspondence, organized in 1832 and 1833, were reactivated, and a meeting was called at Washington-on-the-Brazos in October 1835. Because Mexican officials felt that the word "convention" sniffed of revolt and revolution, the Texans called the meeting a "consultation." Stephen F. Austin had been released from prison and had changed his position. Previously he advocated patience with the government; now he recommended war to defend freedom. Little was accomplished at the session. The peace party held control, and the representatives voted to defend the Mexican Constitution of 1824. Henry Smith was named governor of the provisional government. Sam Houston was appointed head of the armed forces, although he had no control over volunteers already in the field near San Antonio. Representatives were sent to the United States to raise money for the battle against Santa Anna. Another meeting was called for March 1836.

Military activity continued. In Gonzales in October, Mexican soldiers attempted to regain a cannon that had been issued to settlers to fight Indians. The settlers challenged the military, flying a flag proclaiming "come-and-take-it." After a brief skirmish, the Mexicans withdrew, but the first shots of the Texas revolution had been fired.

Gen. Martin Perfecto de Cos had entered Texas with a contingent of troops during the Gonzales incident and took command of San Antonio. Capt. George Collinsworth captured Goliad and a large store of supplies. And to force the Mexican military from Texas, an army of volunteers marched on San Antonio, which fell in December.

As 1835 ended, Anglo-Texans had removed all vestiges of the Mexican military from the region. So relatively simple had been the operation that no retaliation was feared. Most volunteers went home, their places filled by newcomers from the United States. A heavy price in blood was to be paid for the overconfidence.

Revolution

Santa Anna surprisingly entered Texas in early February 1836. Most Texans thought that if the Mexicans retaliated for the military defeats of the previous year it would come in the spring. A dry winter had destroyed forage between the Rio Grande and the Nueces River, and therefore food for the horses and pack animals had to be carried. Also, the Mexican army had suffered heavy losses in the battle of Zacatecas; it took time to train replacements.

And Texans also recalled that they had expelled the Mexican military in 1833 with no retaliation following. Perhaps the Mexicans would still be too busy with their infighting to worry with the troublesome Texans.

But Santa Anna had decided to make an example of Texas, not only for the colonists, but also for those Americans who thought they could take the Mexican territory by subterfuge or force. The Mexican president had fought against American frontiersmen in the Battle of Medina in 1813 and was unimpressed with their military prowess. Familiar with the highly trained, professional European military, Santa Anna simply did not feel that a volunteer fighting force could be effective.

In addition, both personal and national honor had been offended the previous December when Santa Anna's brother-in-law, Gen. Cos, had been expelled from Texas after losing San Antonio to insurgent Anglo-Texans. The overconfident Mexican dictator wanted to even the score for that affront, and then clear Texas of all Anglos.

Consequently, he took his army much farther north than ever dicated by military strategy. San Antonio could have been besieged with 1,000 men or less, while the rest of the Mexican army was concentrated on the populated regions along the Texas coast.

If Santa Anna had pursued a more conventional battle plan, Texas could had faced a disaster. No one was in charge of the military effort in early 1836. Sam Houston had been given command of the army, but not the volunteers. That command eventually was split among James Fannin, Frank W. Johnson and Dr. James Grant. Dr. Grant was a resident of northern Mexico and promoted an invasion of Mexico. He and Johnson felt that an attack on Matamoros would gain the support of Mexican liberals in a movement that could sweep across the entire nation. In January, Grant and Johnson had taken men and supplies from San Antonio and set up a base of operations at San Patricio. Fannin with some 400 volunteers occupied the Presidio La Bahia at Goliad. Houston had tried to discourage the proposed attack on Matamoros, and upon failure, he went to East Texas to treat with the Indians, whose neutrality, if not support, the Texans needed.

Not until independence was declared on March 2 did Texans begin to develop a coordinated military force. By that time, however, the stage was set for disasters at the Alamo and Goliad. Houston was given complete command, and a provisional government with David G. Burnet serving as interim president was organized.

Santa Anna entered Texas on Feb. 12 and laid siege

Continued on Page 25

The 'Yellow Stone'

Not all the gallant veterans of Texas' fight for independence were humans. One was a steamboat — a sidewheeler named the *Yellow Stone*.

The *Yellow Stone* was built in Louisville, Ky., in 1831 for John Jacob Astor's American Fur Company. The vessel was 120 feet long, with a 20-foot beam and a deep (six-foot) draft, constructed to specifications furnished by Pierre Chouteau Jr., western agent for Astor's fur trading company, for service on the Missouri and Yellowstone rivers. The boat's crew usually numbered about 21.

In summer, the *Yellow Stone* plied the waters of the upper Missouri, proudly displaying an oversize 12-foot by 18-foot American flag as it hauled furs, deerskins, buffalo robes and buffalo tongues downstream to market and returned with trade goods for the Indians. In winter, the *Yellow Stone* transported cotton and sugar cane among ports on the lower Mississippi until the spring thaw.

On a normal daylight run, the steamboat would burn 10 cords of wood, which meant that fuel itself was a considerable amount of its cargo. Ten cords of oak wood weigh 40 tons, of cottonwood 25 tons. In its six-and-a-half-year life, the *Yellow Stone* probably consumed 40,000 trees.

The *Yellow Stone's* last voyage on the Missouri was in July 1833. On that ill-fated journey, the crew was stricken with cholera, and all of them died except the captain and a young, semi-trained pilot named Joe LaBarge.

History Highlights

The next year and a half saw the *Yellow Stone* churning up the waters of the Mississippi under a succession of owners. In fall 1835, it was sold to the firm Thomas Toby and Brother of New Orleans, who had connections in Mexican Texas and who intended to employ the steamboat in intracoastal trade in the Gulf of Mexico.

The last day of December 1835 saw the *Yellow Stone* clearing the port of New Orleans headed for Texas under the command of Capt. Thomas Wigg Grayson, carrying 47 men of the Mobile Grays, volunteers looking for action in the Texas Revolution. These adventurous young men found their action: They all died at Goliad.

At that time, the Brazos and Trinity rivers were the only Texas waterways considered navigable by steamboats, but the *Yellow Stone*, intended for use in the deeper waters of the Missouri and the Mississippi, had trouble even with them. Sandbars, snags and droughts plagued the boat during its entire career on the Brazos.

On March 31, 1836, the *Yellow Stone* inadvertently stumbled into Texas history. Now under the command of Capt. John E. Ross, the vessel was taking on a load of cotton at Jared Groce's landing in present-day Waller County about 20 miles up the Brazos from San Felipe.

The Alamo had fallen on March 6. Even before that, settlers had begun leaving their homes to escape the advancing Mexican army, and after Sam Houston learned of the crushing defeat at the San Antonio mission, he left Gonzales and "advanced to the rear" toward the Colorado River with the Texas army, urging civilians along the way to flee. The trickle of refugees became a deluge; the mass exodus was called the Runaway Scrape.

Houston's retreat brought him to Groce's landing on March 31 facing a Brazos River swollen by spring rains. Desperate to cross, he commandeered the *Yellow Stone* to ferry men, horses and equipment to the opposite bank. Capt. Ross stacked his cargo of cotton bales in such a way as to protect the boat's boilers and pilothouse from snipers in case of hostilities. On April 12, Capt. Ross, finally satisfied with the cotton armor and the load of fuel, ferried Houston and his men across the river. Two days later, Ross guided the steamboat, under a full head of steam, on a wild, bumpy ride downriver past a Mexican army encamp-

The bell, the only remaining artifact from the steamboat "Yellow Stone," is housed at the Daughters of the Republic of Texas Museum at the Alamo in San Antonio. Photo Courtesy the Daughters of the Republic of Texas.

ment at Fort Bend. One over-eager Mexican soldier even tried in vain to lasso the smokestacks, the only parts of the superstructure peeking out from the tops of the cotton bales.

Capt. Ross proceeded to Galveston, picking up refugees along the way. On the island he found President Burnet, many other government officials and a large number of refugees. After the Texans' victory, the *Yellow Stone* transported Burnet and other officials to the battleground at San Jacinto at the request of Secretary of War Thomas J. Rusk. At Buffalo Bayou, the steamboat played host not only to Sam Houston, who needed medical treatment for a wounded ankle, but also Gen. Santa Anna, 47 of his officers and other Mexican soldiers. About 80 prisoners were taken to Galveston for incarceration. It is said that Burnet, never a fan of Houston's, refused to let Houston board the boat. But Capt. Ross would not budge until Houston was allowed on board.

A Mexican officer, writing of the voyage later, found it curious that, as the *Yellow Stone* passed the San Jacinto battleground, the Texas troops on board lined the rail and presented arms, accompanied by a solemn military drumbeat. "What was their object?" he wondered.

In the months that followed, the steamboat ran more errands for the army and the government of the new nation. Capt. Thomas Wigg Grayson, once more

Continued on Page 25

'Yellow Stone'

Continued From Page 24

in command, advertised in the *Telegraph and Texas Register* of Oct. 19, 1836, offering $3 a cord for wood along the route between Quintana and Washington-on-the-Brazos. It is not known whether the steamboat ever resumed regular Brazos runs.

It is also not known if the owners were ever able to collect the money owed by the government of the fledgling nation. Bills were sent to the Texas government several times. Sam Houston himself urged the Congress to authorize payment for the services of the *Yellow Stone*. But there is no firm evidence that the bills were ever paid.

The *Yellow Stone* was once again thrust into the Texas limelight when Stephen F. Austin died on Dec. 27, 1836, at the age of 43. The steamboat was summoned to Columbia to pick up the entourage and transport it a few miles downstream to Peach Point Plantation, home of Austin's sister and her husband, Emily and James F. Perry. Austin was interred in the plantation's burial ground, the Gulf Prairie Cemetery. Austin's body was later re-interred in the Texas State Cemetery in Austin.

Hauling freight and a few passengers around the Gulf occupied the steamboat's next several months. The vessel made two or three runs up Buffalo Bayou to the new village called Houston, but it was too long to turn around in Buffalo Bayou without first backing into White Oak Bayou — a tricky maneuver.

The spring of 1837 found the sturdy sidewheeler carrying to Houston a printing press meant for the *Telegraph and Texas Register*. Gail Borden Jr., the developer of condensed milk and part-owner of the paper, accompanied the press.

The *Yellow Stone* made a few more deliveries in the Galveston area; after that, there is no further evidence of its existence. Some historians think the steamboat literally dropped from sight: They believe that it hit a snag and sank in Buffalo Bayou. The last scrap of documentation is a bill to the Texas navy department dated June 2, 1837 — one last attempt to get paid for services rendered. What is generally accepted to be the bell of the *Yellow Stone* is on display at the Alamo.

One thing is certain, however: The *Yellow Stone* earned an important place in the history of Texas.
— *MARY G. CRAWFORD*

FOR FURTHER READING

Jackson, Donald, **Voyages of the Steamboat Yellow Stone**; Ticknor and Fields, New York, 1985.

Puryear, Pamela Ashworth and Nath Winfield Jr., **Sandbars and Sternwheelers, Steam Navigation on the Brazos**; Texas A&M University Press, College Station, 1976.

Webb, Walter Prescott and H. Bailey Carroll, eds., **The Handbook of Texas**, Vol. 2; Texas State Historical Association, Austin, 1952.

Continued From Page 23

to the Alamo for 13 days before attacking on March 6. Then his forces were tied down for several days, replacing the soldiers lost in the attack. Finally he split his forces with some troops following Houston across Texas in the Runaway Scrape.

A more successful operation was carried out, however, along the coast by Gen. Jose Urrea. Upon learning of the plans of Dr. Grant and Johnson to attack Matamoros, Santa Anna on Jan. 15 dispatched Gen. Urrea from Saltillo to Matamoros. Urrea learned that Grant and Johnson were approaching Matamoros, and he expected an attack. But the pair were hunting horses, and split up with Johnson returning to San Patricio.

Urrea trailed Johnson and surprised the Anglo-Texans in a pre-dawn attack on Feb. 27 at San Patricio. Johnson escaped but several insurgents were killed. A few days later, the Mexican general got word of Dr. Grant's approach and ambushed him at Agua Dulce Creek, killing the physician and several others. These two engagements were the first times that Mexican soldiers had defeated the Anglo-Texans. The news of the victories was celebrated at San Antonio.

Gen. Urrea continued to move up the coast. On March 20, he caught Fannin's command in an open prairie and captured nearly 400 men and supplies. The Texans claimed they thought they would get the honors of war, but papers held in Mexico reveal an unconditional surrender. Although aware of Santa Anna's threat to kill all insurgents, Urrea thought that the sheer number of prisoners would discourage a massacre. About 350 prisoners were executed on Santa Anna's direct order.

Mop-up operations consumed the next month of Urrea's campaign. He took Guadalupe Victoria, the small port at Linn's House and Matagorda. While camped on the Colorado River, "Dr. Harrison," the son of a United States general, was dispatched to upcoming settlements to offer guarantees of safety and protection to colonists who had not taken up arms against Mexico. Harrison, who Urrea said felt owed his life to the Mexican general, had some success.

When Urrea reached Brazoria on April 22, many colonists met him and expressed satisfaction with their treatment. Some said they were more concerned with Sam Houston's forces, which were made up of adventurers, than with the Mexican army. Aid was offered the Mexicans in taking Velasco at the mouth of the Brazos River and Galveston Island. History has given little note to these Texas Tories. Houston knew of the feelings of many, for letters from them to Santa Anna had been found among papers captured by the Texas army. Upon the Texans' victory at San Jacinto, Houston sent notes to the Tories to inform them that they were supporting a lost cause. Their names were never released.

Urrea was headed toward Velasco when word of Santa Anna's defeat reached him, and he was ordered to move northward to join with other Mexican forces in a retreat from Texas.

Santa Anna initially considered returning to Mexico after Dr. Grant's defeat and the fall of the Alamo. In his mind, the war was over, and he was fully aware of the fickle political tides that rocked Mexican government. The dictator wanted to return to Mexico City to consolidate his regime in the wake of the great victory. But his general staff talked him out of going.

While Texas' land forces were having problems dealing with the Mexican army, the new Republic's navy was providing a heroic defense of the coast. Initially, letters of marque were issued to privateers to provide protection for the shipping lanes to Texas. In early 1836, however, four ships — the *Independence*, the *Liberty*, the *Brutus* and the *Invincible* — were purchased and placed under the command of 29-year-old Charles E. Hawkins. The ships held off the Mexican navy and disrupted the army's sea supply lines. Between the work of the navy and Houston's scorched-earth policy during the Runaway Scrape, the Mexican army under Santa Anna's second in command, Vicente Filisola, was denied supplies after San Jacinto, and that was one factor leading to its withdrawal without a fight. Despite the successes, Houston was hostile to the navy. By late 1837, all four of the ships of Texas' first navy had been lost after carving out a unique and enviable place in the state's history.

Back on land, Santa Anna, after deciding to remain in Texas, hurried to rejoin the advance units. On April 7, he joined Gen. Ramirez y Sesma and entered San Felipe. Receiving intelligence that the rebel government was in Harrisburg, Santa Anna headed after the officials. Slowed by weather and sharpshooters, the Mexican contingent arrived in Harrisburg a week later, just in time to see Texas officials rowing to a schooner. While burning Harrisburg, Santa Anna got word that Houston and his army were headed for Lynch's ferry and escape into Louisiana.

Santa Anna wasted no time in chasing the rebel army, and that was his undoing, for he passed it and got cornered at San Jacinto. Early on April 21, 500 men joined Santa Anna's command, but the soldiers and officers settled down for their midday rest without posting sentries. Houston's forces attacked, and in less than 20 minutes, the Mexicans were routed and the battle was over. The Texans had won. Santa Anna was captured the next day dressed in a private's uniform.

Houston quickly got the Mexican leader to agree to a truce and then left for New Orleans for treatment of an ankle wound. President Burnet took charge of Santa Anna, and on May 14, the dictator signed two treaties at Velasco, a public document and a secret one. The public agreement declared hostilities would cease, that the Mexican army would withdraw to south of the Rio Grande and that Santa Anna would be shipped to Veracruz as soon as possible. In the secret treaty, Santa Anna agreed to recognize Texas' independence, to give diplomatic recognition, to negotiate a commercial treaty and to set the Rio Grande as the new Republic's southern boundary.

President Burnet had many problems with internal, as well as foreign, forces while trying to govern the young Republic. The army was in near revolt. Most Texans left the military after the battle of San Jacinto, and their ranks were filled by volunteers from the United States. Within months, the makeup of the army had changed to the extent that two-thirds of the soldiers had not been in Texas when the Republic seceded from Mexico. Santa Anna's release was delayed by a rebellious military, and threats were made against the civilian government. It was not until Houston was elected president in September that the problem was defused by furloughing most of the army. Thus Texas avoided a domestic military dictatorship, as well as a foreign one, in 1836.

The seat of government that had drifted from Washington-on-the-Brazos to Harrisburg to Galveston to Velasco during the revolution was moved to Columbia in October 1836 and then to the new village of Houston two months later.

Because of the transportation advantages, the Texas coast was to become the focal point of economic expansion in the coming years. Indians and Mexican soldiers still posed a threat on part of the coast, but Galveston and Houston were to present Texas' most urbane face to the world. Texas' Gulf Coast was to become the state's most progressive and most prosperous region.

The New Nation

After Texas gained independence from Mexico, the door was open for entrepreneurs to begin development of the rich territory. Unfortunately the Republic of Texas was caught in a worldwide recession that crippled many efforts at economic development. In the United States, the Panic of 1837, brought about by land speculation and poor, if not illegal, lending practices by banks, paralyzed economic activity. Access to credit, which the Republic had anticipated, was cut off. Attempts to rescue Texas' economy by circulating paper money proved disastrous.

Additionally, much of what appeared to glitter in the Republic's geography was not gold. Moses and Stephen F. Austin had envisioned development of the ports and a diversion of the Santa Fe trade from Independence, Mo., through Texas. The route across Texas brought the New Mexico city closer to the Gulf than did the Santa Fe Trail. But this potential was never developed, in part because fierce Indians blocked land access from the coast across Texas to Santa Fe.

As one historian noted, probably no state has fewer water transportation resources than Texas. But that was not the picture that early settlers had. They were impressed by the many bays and rivers emptying into the Gulf. These waterways offered the allure of cheap transportation for inland Texas. The markets of the world were thought to be at hand. Such was not to be. Texas' rivers were deceiving; they appeared navigable, but were not, settlers were to learn. The rivers were unreliable. They meandered too much. There was too much water available in the spring and too little at other times of the year. The rivers were full of log jams, snags, sand bars and muddy waters, none of which is conducive to navigation. The bays were shallow, subject to silting and, in most cases, unprotected from the seasonal storms that struck the coast regularly.

The Brazos and Trinity rivers held the highest hopes for navigation. But the truth of the river situation was not long in coming. Henry Austin, cousin of Stephen F. Austin, learned early of the vagaries of two of Texas' rivers. He sailed the first commercial steamboat up the Rio Grande in 1829. After discouragement on that stream, he repeated the distinction on the Brazos River a year later, where his luck was no better. His paddlewheeler, the *Ariel*, later was lost in a storm in the Gulf.

Despite the prohibition of settlement near the coast during the Mexican period, several coastal communities were established. Harrisburg was located on Buffalo Bayou, which fed into Galveston Bay. Galveston had a customhouse, as did Velasco at the mouth of the Brazos. Matagorda was established in 1827 by Stephen F. Austin, who received permission for a settlement at the mouth of the Colorado River. The community never realized the goal to become a major port, for sand bars prohibited ships from getting closer than four miles before they had to be unloaded and freight moved to shore by barges. The sites of today's Beaumont and Orange were occupied by small settlements that traced their beginnings to French and Spanish trappers and traders. Copano Bay had served as a port during the Mexican period and continued during the early years of the Republic.

Houston was established with some fanfare in the fall of 1836. The Allen brothers, Augustus C. and John K., migrated from New York to Texas in 1832 and engaged in land speculation around San Augustine and Nacogdoches. After the war of independence, they attempted to buy Harrisburg, which had been destroyed by Santa Anna, but the title was tied up in court. So they moved eight miles up Buffalo Bayou and bought half a league of land (about 2,200 acres) from Mrs. Elizabeth E. Parrott, the widow of John Austin, for $5,000. They paid $1,000 in cash and the remainder in notes.

Houston was not alone along the bayou. This was the era of "paper cities" that promoters envisioned to make themselves rich. Among the sister cities of Houston at the time were Powhattan, Scottsburg, Louisville, San Jacinto, Buffalo, Hamilton and others that shared great expectations, but few inhabitants.

Columbia in present-day Brazoria County had become the capital of the new Republic in September 1836, but the site had many shortcomings. Two months later, the Texas Congress, which included John Allen in its membership, moved the capital to the new city that the developers had named in honor of the hero of San Jacinto, Sam Houston.

The Allens claimed that Houston was at the head of navigation on Buffalo Bayou (a similar claim had been made by the developers of Harrisburg), but early shipping had difficulty negotiating the route. In 1839, the Buffalo Bayou Company was formed to clear the bayou for shipping. A year later, the Texas Congress authorized the city to build and maintain wharves, and in 1841, the Port of Houston was established by the city. Steamboat traffic along the bayou was common, if dangerous and unpredictable. It was not uncommon for the vessels to stop to allow passengers to hunt game along the way, and occasionally, ships' cooks killed a "beef" for supper. By the 1850s, both Harris County and Houston were providing money for dredging sand bars, and the State of Texas also was financing some projects.

Houston was successful because it was at a break in transportation — from water to ox train initially. The advantage was even more successfully exploited when railroad development proceeded.

Galveston also began its development with the Texas Revolution. Since 1830, a Mexican customhouse had been located on the island, but this was the only building when the government of the Republic took refuge there in mid-April 1836. After independence was declared in March, the interim government headed by President David Burnet had been on the move, sitting at Washington-on-the-Brazos and Harrisburg. The officials got out of Harrisburg shortly before Santa Anna's forces entered and put the town to the torch.

Crude battlements had been erected in the sand to stave off a Mexican attack, but on April 26, the Texans learned of the victory at San Jacinto. Burnet visited the battlefield and returned the prisoner Santa Anna, his entourage, the Texas cabinet and the wounded Sam Houston to Galveston. Mexican prisoners of war also were taken to the island. The government soon moved to more satisfactory accomodations at Velasco at the mouth of the Brazos.

Galveston, however, had an excellent port. In 1836, it was made the Republic's naval depot, and a year later it was designated a port of entry. Gail Borden Jr. was the first customs collector. In 1839, the facility received 228 commercial ships. Terrible storms often devastated the island, and were one reason the Mexicans and early Anglo settlers had stayed away. In 1837, Galveston was struck by one of these periodic catastrophes. Several ships were sunk by a hurricane and others grounded. Two of the grounded craft were never refloated. The *Perseverance* served as a customhouse for several years, and the *Elbe* was used first as a hotel and later as

This is an idyllic view of Houston, capital of the young Republic of Texas, presented to American readers in 1837. Photo Courtesy Archives Division, Texas State Library.

a jail by Galveston County.

In 1838, the Galveston City Co. was organized and began to sell lots in the townsite. Development was slow. John James Audubon, the naturalist, visited Galveston and Houston in 1837, and his descriptions flattered neither city.

Galveston's early status as Texas' leading port was tenuous. The storm of 1837 that devastated the few improvements on the island also deepened the channel at the island's west end. The island of San Luis, which had been used by the Mexican navy in its war against Spain, had an attractive harbor and easy access. A settlement was begun, and by 1841, 5,000 bales of cotton were shipped from the port. The harbor and channel eventually refilled with silt, driving shipping back to Galveston.

The commercial firm of McKinney & Williams brought maritime commerce to Texas. It operated the steamer *Ocean* in the New Orleans trade and the *Cayuga* on the Brazos. The Trinity River also was served by steamers. The *Columbia*, the pioneer ship of Charles Morgan's Morgan Lines reached Galveston in November 1837 and also provided service to Velasco. Morgan added the *New York*, another 150-ton steamer, a year later and soon faced competition from the *Cuba*, a 600-ton steam packet operated by Bogart & Hawthorne of New Orleans.

As ports, Galveston and Houston faced problems not experienced by Texas' fledgling inland cities. Yellow fever epidemics hit the two coastal cities in the summer of 1839. Dr. Ashbel Smith wrote a medical treatise on the epidemic, the first scientific paper written in Texas. Even though Galveston's city council quickly drew up quarantine regulations, another outbreak was suffered in 1844, and the fever visited regularly thereafter. Efforts also were made in Galveston to control gambling and other vice.

Galveston civic leaders were aware that the island's sole asset was its harbor, and attention was paid to deepening the channels and the harbor. The first railroad chartered by the Republic of Texas was the Galveston and Brazos in 1838, but no road was built because the charter was forfeited.

Galveston and Houston were growth areas, but other sections of the coast also were developing, if slowly. Jefferson County was established by the Texas Congress in 1837, and Beaumont was designated the county seat. Orange had a lumber mill by 1841. But otherwise the economic development of this southeast corner of Texas was delayed until after the Civil War because of the hazardous navigation conditions on the Neches River. Sabine City also was established at today's Sabine Pass in 1837. The city thrived early, but its importance sank after storms devastated the community on several occasions.

Brazoria and Fort Bend counties quickly moved into sugar production, which with cotton, was one of the two major cash crops in the new Republic. By 1843, Brazoria County had 29 steam-powered sugar mills, and by 1859, the two counties produced 80 percent of the sugar in Texas. When the industry fell on hard times after the Civil War, the Legislature adopted a program to allow planters to "rent" convicts from the prison system.

During this period, confusion crept into the name of the Republic's former capital, Columbia. Sometime after 1839, the community suffered economic difficulties and began to call itself "West Columbia." A second community to the east of the original settlement was known as "East Columbia," and tried for a time to adopt simply the name of "Columbia." But the railroads never acknowledged the name, and it did not stick. Today the towns are known as West Columbia, the former capital, and East Columbia.

While the eastern portion of Texas' Gulf Coast was settled and relatively civilized, the western section was not. Victoria was the southwestern military depot of the Republic. The Texas army was virtually disbanded in 1838, but prior to that time, it had used seven campsites near the community of Texana on the Navidad River above Lavaca Bay to defend against surprise Mexican attacks.

Though Texas was independent of Mexico, it was not free of its neighbor's problems. Federalists and Centralists were still battling for supremacy in Mexico. Much of the Federalist support came from the northern Mexican states, which being far from Mexico City were often ignored by the government. Consequently, they sought self-government through a federal system or even independence, such as Texas had gained. Although officially the Republic was neutral, most Texans backed the Federalists' cause and fought with them.

Between 1838-40, Mexican Federalists were supplied through Aransas and Nueces bays and at Brazos Santiago near the mouth of the Rio Grande. The soldiers headquartered at Fort Lipantitlan west of present-day Corpus Christi. Contraband trade thrived, and one trader taking advantage was Henry Lawrence Kinney, who in 1838 came to Texas from Illinois. With William P. Aubrey, Kinney set up trade at Live Oak Point in today's Aransas County. Kinney freighted goods to an old Indian trading grounds on the west bank of the Nueces River. In 1839, the trader built a permanent building on the site of what was to become Corpus Christi and set up trade with Mexican Federalists.

Kinney's settlement was important because it was Texas' sole claim to occupancy between the Nueces River and the Rio Grande. The Republic of Texas had claimed the Rio Grande as its southern boundary, although the Nueces and Medina rivers usually had been Texas' southern boundaries when it was a Spanish province. To develop a legal claim, Texas had to occupy the territory and exercise some jurisdiction. In 1842, with Corpus Christi little more than a camp, a post office was established with Aubrey the postmaster. When Texas gained annexation to the United States in 1845, the city had no more than 200 people and only one house.

The western frontier had other severe problems. In early 1840, a dozen Comanche chiefs were called to San Antonio to exchange prisoners and to discuss peace. When the Indians brought only one white prisoner, a girl who had been badly mistreated, the Texans attempted to take the chiefs into custody to hold hostage until other prisoners were released. The so-called Council House Fight ensued, and the chiefs and several braves and women were killed. In retaliation, 400 to 500 Comanches attacked Victoria and Linnville in August of the same year. Many men were away at the time fighting to establish the ill-fated Republic of the Rio Grande, leaving the region with little defense. Hundreds of head of horses and cattle were stolen, many settlers were killed, and at Linnville, a warehouse was plundered. The fledgling port, which had a customhouse, was not rebuilt after the raid. Settlers reported seeing the ludicrous sight of Indians riding away from Linnville wearing top hats and long-tailed coats taken in the raid. The Indians were soundly defeated at the battle of Plum Creek on their way north, however, and never raided so close to the coast again.

Another tragic story from the period concerned the founding of Indianola. When attempts to establish a German colony in the area were made, no provision was made for housing immigrants upon arrival. Prince Carl of Solms-Braunfels, a member of Adelsverein, a German immigration society, and commissioner-general of the organization's colonization effort, immediately began looking for a port site upon his arrival in Galveston in July 1844. The search settled on sites on the west banks of either Lavaca or Matagorda bays, and a location at the point where the two bays joined was selected. Prince Carl called it "Indian Point," although some immigrants called it "Carlshaven" or "Carl's Harbor." In 1849, the name was changed to "Indianola." The new port had water of sufficient depth for ships to anchor near the beach and have cargoes and passengers lightered.

John Meusebach replaced Prince Carl as commissioner-general in early 1845 and was immediately faced with a transportation problem. Heavy rains had made the hauling of goods and people to the inland colony almost impossible. In late 1845 and early 1846, 5,247 men, women and children arrived in 36 ships at Indian Point. Sanitary facilities were stretched past the breaking point. Teamsters hired by Meusebach deserted the task when the U.S. Army hired transportation at the beginning of the Mexican War. The stranded immigrants were struck by a series of epidemics of typhoid, cholera and meningitis. Estimates of deaths at Indian Point range between 400 and 2,000. The port thrived, however, and soon challenged Galveston for supremacy of the Gulf Coast.

The region between the Nueces and the Rio Grande was not so fortunate. It had become a no-man's-land with neither Texas nor Mexico exercising control. Outlaws from both countries roamed at will in the infamous Nueces Strip, as the region came to be called. In 1842, Lipan Apaches surprised the settlement of Corpus Christi, capturing men and horses. Kinney reported that the violence in the region in the early 1840s had killed or wounded 36 men and resulted in the loss of 1,353 horses to Indians.

Although the Texas Congress appropriated funds for frontier defense, the effort was was not totally successful. Anglo cowboys, organized to fight bandits, often attacked Mexican traders, and Mexican outlaws preyed on all merchants. It was not until a contingent of Texas Rangers under the legendary Capt. Jack C. Hays came to the area was peace temporarily brought to the region.

As Texas moved toward annexation to the United States, Corpus Christi flourished. In May 1845, Gen. Zachary Taylor brought the first U.S. troops to the city, and they were immediately put to work clearing the head-high grass that abounded in the region. Corpus

Gateways to Texas

Through the Spanish era, the interior of Texas received the most attention for development. The Gulf Coast was kept pristine, to protect against smuggling and infiltration by foreigners. Mexican administration loosened control of the coast, although efforts were made to prohibit settlement by foreigners, especially Americans.

Under the Republic of Texas, however, the region began to prosper and develop. The government gave the coast close attention for two reasons: The eastern portion was a population center, and the region was the primary source of revenue for the fledgling nation.

During the first four years of the Republic, customs collections represented 50 percent of the government's revenues; the figure grew to 80 percent in the last five years. Between 1835 and 1851, customs revenue represented almost 65 percent of the nearly $2.1 million collected by the Republic and the state government.

Customs were the almost sole source of hard money for the beleaguered Republic. Direct taxation was not accepted, and the Republic allowed taxes to be paid with scrip that had been issued by the government. In addition, Texas had a terrible balance of payments problem in its early years, importing many more goods than exported and losing hard currency in the bargain. These factors, compounded by lack of credit that dried up with the Panic of 1837, the worst economic recession in United States' history until that time, kept Texas on the financial ropes.

The Customs Service of the Republic of Texas was first authorized in December 1835 by the provisional government. Congress reaffirmed the service the following year and set up nine revenue districts: Galveston, Sabine, Brazos, Matagorda, Jackson, Aransas, La Bacca (Lavaca), Copano and Maximilian. Customhouses were maintained at Galveston, Aransas Pass, Linnville, Port Lavaca, Copano, Point Bolivar, Sabine Pass, Matagorda, Velasco, Sabine City (now Sabine Pass), San Augustine, Port Calhoun, San Luis and various river landings.

The United States was Texas' major trading partner, but by 1844, the Republic also was trading with ports in Europe that included Trieste, Antwerp, Cork, Dunkirk, London, Liverpool and Havre.

hristi was chosen as a camp site because it was south of the Nueces River and could be reached by sea.

The tent city of Corpus Christi flourished during the seven-and-one-half month tour of the Army of Occupation, which left for the Rio Grande on March 11, 1846. With its departure, the boom town died, but not for long.

Publicity that Corpus Christi received during the stay of the army made its name familiar, and Kinney took advantage of that with a promotion campaign on the U.S. Atlantic Coast and in Europe. The effort soon bore fruit.

Shipyards were built in 1848, and a contract to build wharfs was let the same year. By December of that year, the steamboat Fanny was making fortnightly runs to Port Lavaca and New Orleans.

Overland freighting soon boomed. Promoters boasted about the speed that goods could be shipped through Corpus Christi to San Antonio from New Orleans. Merchants from South Texas and Northern Mexico picked up goods for resale. On one trip, a ploughshare was pulled from Laredo to Corpus Christi to mark a trail, and agitation was underway for construction of a road over the route. And when the California gold rush began in 1849, Kinney increased his national advertising stressing the advantages of the Corpus Christi-to-San Diego road as the shortest way to "El Dorado." A trade caravan visited Chihuahua from Corpus Christi in 1849, opening a rich trade route from the Gulf to the interior of Mexico. Attention also was given to establishing a trade route through El Paso to the upper Rio Grande valley to supplant the Santa Fe Trail, but no action was taken to implement the idea.

Throughout this period of progress, however, Indian raids hardly abated. In 1850, a military camp — Fort Merrill — was erected on the Nueces more than 25 miles west of Corpus Christi.

As often to be its fortune, progress and turbulent times walked hand-in-hand along the Texas Gulf coast. But the early years of statehood brought an exciting period of development.

Age of Transportation

From the annexation by the United States to the Civil War, Texas' Gulf Coast concerned itself with transportation, both land and water. Most of the state's population was within 100 miles of the coast, and therefore, most of the economic activity was, too.

Annexation eased few problems. Today the federal government has assumed responsibility for internal improvements on rivers and highways, but that was not the case in the early 19th century. During the War of 1812, the government in Washington took responsibility for some internal improvements, but Southerners, citing state's rights, wanted to limit the responsibility. Consequently, from the beginning of Andrew Jackson's first administration in 1829 until the Civil War, improvements on a river wholly within a state were a state matter; the federal government would not be involved.

Until 1850, when the federal government paid Texas 10 million for land in New Mexico, Colorado, Wyoming, Kansas and Oklahoma that Texas brought into the Union, the state was no better prepared to pay for improvements than had been the Republic. In 1853, the Legislature appropriated $250,000 for improvements or navigation, and the figure rose to $350,000 three years later.

Most of the transportation debate in state government was centered around railroads. "Railroad fever" first struck Texas during the days of the Republic, and it was not far behind the rest of the nation. The first railroad to operate in the United States was the Baltimore & Ohio, a horse-pulled train, that began service in 1828. The first steam-powered train was the Charleston & Hamburg, which pulled its first load in 1830 and began regularly scheduled service on 136 miles of track in 1833. C&H also suffered the first locomotive explosion in 1831. By 1836, there were 1,098 miles of track in the United States. Nine years later, railroads with 5,000 miles of track operated in every state east of the Mississippi River, and people in virtually every community saw the iron horse as the economic savior.

The Republic of Texas chartered several railroad companies, but no track was laid. Indeed, the debate began during this period over whether railroads should be built and operated by the government or by private enterprise. A convention in Houston in 1842 endorsed government ownership. But the question was academic in Texas. The Republic had no money to invest in transportation — or anything else — and the financial Panic of 1837 had dried up credit and investment funds.

Ox teams and stagecoaches were the principal means of inland transportation in Texas prior to the 1850s. But roads were miserable. During dry seasons, there was excellent access to Houston by a series of roads fanning out in all directions. In wet periods, however — and there were many near the coast — these routes became quagmires. And the worse the roads became, the longer it took to get goods to market and the more expensive was the transportation. One historian noted that Houston's early economic development was probably retarded as much by the poor condition of the roads as by a lack of a deep-water port.

Road construction and maintenance were left to the counties during the republican and early statehood periods. And it was not until after the Civil War did counties begin building gravel roads. (Indeed, the state did not assume responsibility for highway construction until 1917.)

Even with the poor road system, however, ox-drawn freight wagons became general and profitable businesses. One estimate holds that there were 10,000 teams operating in Texas at the beginning of the Civil War. Communities saw them as necessities for prosperity, and freighters often could arouse public opposition to railroads, which were not universally popular. As late as 1850, the Houston *Telegram* inveighed against railroads and pointed out the advantages of plank roads and teaming. This position, no doubt, added fuel to the critics' argument that Houston dragged its feet on getting a railroad because of the vested freight interests in the city. Houston had improved some roads near the city with surplus funds supplied by the Port of Houston. Nevertheless, observers noted that the roads around Houston were in much the same condition as those used by Sam Houston when preparing to fight Santa Anna. Because of the condition of the roads, inland interests agitated with support from Galveston for routes to bypass Houston, and this fuss touched off a heated Houston-Galveston rivalry.

Galveston's leadership supported every attempt to improve transportation, to Houston's benefit or not. In 1850, the Galveston and Brazos Navigation Co. was chartered, and in 1855, a waterway to the Brazos was completed. The channel expedited the moving of Brazos cotton to Galveston and proved to be a thoroughfare for immigrants heading for the California gold rush. Although the route initially made money, the need for continued dredging later made it unprofitable.

The Texas Telegraph Co. brought the first communications improvement to the area. Financed in Louisiana, the company strung wire from Shreveport to Marshall, Henderson, Palestine, Montgomery and Houston in 1853 and 1854. A wire was laid under Galveston Bay to tie Galveston into the system in 1854. The one-man operation lasted only until 1855, when it closed. Edward Cushing re-established service in 1859-1860 to allow Houston to receive information on ship arrivals, weather and prices in New Orleans. Western Union acquired the company in 1869.

The Houston Navigation Co. dominated the bayou shipping during the 1850s, although wharf charges often drew complaints. These were dropped in 1860 so the city could remain competitive in water transportation. One of the most unusual cargos hauled during the period was a boatload of 40 camels that were shipped to the Francis R. Lubbock ranch on Sims Bayou.

Houston also got a leg up on Galveston in 1856 when the Legislature decided that the state's railroads should be developed by private enterprise. Galveston had wanted a state-built system with a series of railroads fanning out across Texas from the island city. Houston had supported the national plan of developing east-west railroads across Texas to tie into a continental system. The state was to provide generous land grants to attract railroad investors.

Neither Houston nor Galveston, however, had a hand in the state's first railroad, the Buffalo Bayou, Brazos and Colorado Railway Co. Gen. Sidney Sherman, a hero of San Jacinto, chartered the company in 1850, and by 1853, the 20-mile line began operating near

The General Sherman was the first locomotive to arrive in Texas and in 1852 became Engine No. 1 for the Buffalo Bayou, Brazos and Colorado Railroad. The engine was named for Gen. Sidney Sherman, a hero of the battle of San Jacinto. Illustration Courtesy Galveston Wharves.

Houston from Harrisburg to Stratford's Point. In 1856, Houston interests built a line to tap into the BBB&C, and another company, the Houston and Texas Central, began operation on 25 miles of track that ran north to Cypress. By 1860, the H&TC reached northward to Hockley, Hempstead and Millican.

In 1856, merchants in Brazoria County received a charter for the Houston Tap and Brazoria Railway Co. that was to connect the sugar-producing areas of the lower Brazos and Colorado river valleys with Houston. The initial efforts connected Columbia and Houston through a connection with the BBB&C. When completed in 1859, the line was popularly called "The Sugar Road." An eastward line that eventually was to connect New Orleans and Houston was started and by 1860 reached Orange. The line was one of two maintained by the Confederacy during the Civil War. The other was the H&CT.

Houston and Galveston merchants backed the Galveston, Houston and Henderson Railroad Co., which began construction at Virginia Point on the mainland across from Galveston and provided service to suburban Houston by 1859. In 1860, Galveston completed a railroad bridge, financed by $100,000 in bonds approved by voters, across the bay bringing rail service to the island. The Houston city council, however, would not let the GH&H connect with the Houston and Texas Central to give the Galveston line an outlet north of Houston. The connection finally was forced by John Magruder, the Confederate commander of Texas, during the Civil War and became permanent.

By the beginning of the Civil War, Houston was the railroad center of Texas with five lines radiating out from the city. Of the 450 miles of track in the state, more than 350 led to Houston. The city's prosperity could be measured in the amount of cotton handled, which jumped from 39,923 bales in 1854 to 115,010 in 1860.

Wharf owners in Galveston were organized into the Galveston Wharf and Cotton Press Co. in 1854 by Michel B. Menard and Samuel May Williams, and within five years had monopolistic control of the port. Because charges got so high, Houston interests suggested to shippers that they unload their vessels in the Gulf and barge goods to Houston, skipping Galveston altogether. When ships did this and landed at Galveston to reload for the return trip, however, the Galveston Wharf Co. levied an extra charge against the ship. This fledgling commercial fight was interrupted by the Civil War.

Competition for commercial supremacy on the Texas coast was not limited to Houston and Galveston. In Matagorda Bay, several small ports envisioned successful futures. Indianola was selected early as the depot for the U.S. Army's Quartermaster and Subsistence Departments. Supplies destined for outposts in Western Texas were shipped through Indianola and gave initial impetus for development of the port. A special wharf with a narrow-gauge railroad was built to warehouses at Indianola to facilitate unloading of supplies from ships.

As in other regions, transportation was the major concern through the 1850s. Railroads were out of the question at the time, so the best hopes for improved routes were all-weather roads. A new road shortened the distance from Indianola to New Braunfels by 25 miles in the late 1840s. The army helped open a new, shorter route from Victoria to San Antonio through Yorktown in 1850. But transportation, except for limited navigation of the Guadalupe River to Victoria, remained in the hands of ox-drawn carts and wagons.

Accessibility to not only Western Texas but also other trade areas in the United States was considered an early advantage in developing the ports. Dr. Levi Jones promoted development of a trade route from Matagorda Bay through El Paso to San Diego. The Victoria *Advocate* proposed opening a trade route to Santa Fe to siphon trade from Independence, Mo. Others saw trade with Chihuahua to be another potentially profitable enterprise.

In one head-to-head competition with rivals on the eastern Texas coast, the Matagorda ports fared favorably. Many merchants preferred to send goods to Austin and other communities on the upper Colorado River through Matagorda because roads to the interior were better from the western bay than they were at Houston. Better roads meant less travel time and lower costs.

Like the military, merchants used Indianola and other ports in Matagorda Bay to supply Western Texas. The appeal of the ports was the lower costs merchants paid because inventories could be reduced because more frequent deliveries could be made with trips also shorter. Cattle were the leading export for New Orleans during Indianola's early years, with animals driven from all over Western Texas for shipment. Lumber was the leading import.

The weather trouble that was to doom the region before the turn of the century made its presence felt early. A severe storm in 1851 destroyed all the wharfs in Port Lavaca, and three years later, the city was again devastated and the wharfs at Indianola were destroyed or severely damaged.

As coastal cities, the bay's ports enjoyed privileges and dangers not found in inland Texas at the time. The first New England ice, which became a regular import, arrived in Indianola in 1851, and yellow fever made its first appearance at the port in 1853. And unusual cargo also turned up occasionally. In 1856 and 1857, Indianola received shipments of camels that were to be part of Jefferson Davis' experiment in improved transportation in Western Texas. As U.S. Secretary of War, Davis thought camels, with their hardy constitution and ability to go long periods without water, would facilitate moving goods in rugged Western Texas. Such was not the case because the rugged terrain hurt the animals' feet, and the experiment was abandoned shortly before the Civil War began.

Though Indianola's economy thrived, improved transportation to the interior was still a necessity. In 1856, Port Lavaca got a leg up on its rival when construction of the San Antonio and Mexican Gulf Railroad began. But for Indianola's advantage as a deep-water port, the community's economy would have been in dire straits. By the end of the decade, however, the Indianola Railroad Co. had been chartered and had leveled grade for a line to tie into the SA&MG, which eventually absorbed the tap line.

The prosperity of the region was a two-edged sword when war broke out, for it attracted the attention of Union military leaders, and Indianola and Port Lavaca were to suffer more than other Texas cities during the Civil War.

Corpus Christi's growth was slower, although the

was not the fault of H.L. Kinney. The city's founder was a tireless promoter and advertised the advantages of Corpus Christi nationally and internationally.

Nueces County was established by the Legislature in 1846, and initially it encompassed an area running south of a line drawn between Corpus Christi and Laredo. The city was incorporated six years later. The first state representative from the Corpus Christi district was Mirabeau B. Lamar, former president of the Republic of Texas.

Business flourished with the influx of emigrants to California's gold rush, and Kinney widely advertised the advantage of the port at Corpus Christi. The port was first mentioned in the Federal Rivers and Harbor Act in 1852. Prior to this time, vessels had unloaded outside the breakwater, and goods were brought ashore by lighter. The Corpus Christi Ship Channel Co. was organized and launched a dredging operation to deepen a channel from the municipal docks to Aransas Pass in 1860.

In 1852, Richard King bought the ranch that was to become the world famous Santa Gertrudis Ranch. He had come to Texas during the Mexican War and served first as a steamboat captain on the Rio Grande before purchasing boats himself.

Kinney also organized the Lone Star Fair in 1852 to attract attention to Texas products. The fair is thought to be the first in the state, and later was moved to Houston and then Dallas.

Yellow fever continued its march down the Texas coast, reaching Corpus Christi in 1854. Accounts say that no family was spared a death in the first epidemic.

With the rest of the Gulf Coast, Corpus Christi bore the brunt of the Civil War in Texas. An era of fledgling prosperity was followed by a long bleak economic period that set the region back several years before recovery was realized.

Civil War

Though much of Texas was spared many of the difficulties of the Civil War, the Gulf Coast was on the front line of the battle. The Union blockade, which successfully stiffled Confederate shipping in the Eastern Gulf, put more pressure on Texas' ports to remain open so goods could be moved and war materiel imported.

The Union blockade reached Texas in the fall of 1862, forcing the Confederates to move cotton, their prime export, overland to Brownsville and Matamoros for shipment to European markets.

Galveston, the state's largest port, was the first target of Union conquest. On Oct. 4, 1862, Commander William B. Renshaw sailed into Galveston Bay and demanded that the island be surrendered to the Union. Confederate officials sought a truce to remove noncombatants from the island. The truce lasted until Dec. 24, when it was violated and Union forces took control of the city. Supplies were short, and Galveston residents had to depend on rations from the enemy to survive during the short-lived Union occupation.

Brigadier General Paul O. Hebert, Confederate commander of Texas, had been unpopular with both civilians and soldiers since assuming command in May 1862. The fall of Galveston prompted his removal and replacement in October with Major General John Bankhead Magruder. Regaining control of Galveston was one of Magruder's first objectives, and the second was to break the blockade. To battle for Galveston, he had two river steamers, the *Neptune* and the *Bayou City*, converted to gunships. Bales of cotton lining the ships' decks earned the vessels the title of "cottonclads." And they played a decisive role in retaking Galveston on Jan. 1, 1863.

Confederate land forces could make little headway against the Union defenses in Galveston. But the two plucky steamers took on the Union fleet, sinking one ship, grounding another, capturing six and sending others to sea to seek safety. The victory gave the Confederates control of the immediate Gulf. Union commander I. S. Burrell had no choice but to surrender. The Rebels had 300-400 prisoners.

Almost a month later, Magruder used similar tactics at Sabine Pass, equipping two river steamers as gunboats and putting two Union blockade vessels to flight. The victory reopened ports at Beaumont and Orange to Gulf shipping for the rest of the war and gave the cities an economic shot in the arm.

On Matagorda Bay in April 1861, Earl Van Dorn led Confederate forces in several successful operations against U.S. forces. Several Union ships, including the *Star of the West*, which as a U.S. Revenue Service cutter participated in the battle of Fort Sumter that opened the war, were captured. Union troops captured on Matagorda Island and Indianola, while awaiting transportation to withdraw, were paroled and left Texas by land.

Port Lavaca was shelled by federal gunships in October 1862.

The length of Texas' coastline proved a problem for the Union blockade. So Rear Admiral David G. Farragut devised a plan to reduce the number of ports available for Confederate use. In the fall of 1863, the Union mounted a major operation against the Texas coast, and the first objective, capturing Sabine Pass, provided one of the most dramatic stories of the war for the Confederacy. A fleet of ships and 5,000 troops were poised to attack the small Fort Griffin that protected the pass. Lt.

Richard "Dick" Dowling of the Davis Guards commanded only 42 men at the fort, which had but six cannon. Only the "cottonclad" steamer, *Uncle Ben*, was held in reserve up the river from the pass.

The battle opened with two Union gunships bombarding the tiny fort for an hour. After giving Dowling and his men what was thought to be time enough to retreat, the Union armada began moving through the pass, the gunboats followed by other ships. But Dowling and his crew didn't leave. With just the handful of cannons, the Confederates set up a withering line of fire. Both Union gunships were incapacitated, and they surrendered. Without the protection of these vessels, the other Union ships with 5,000 troops retreated to the Gulf and then to New Orleans.

Though Dowling's victory did not have the longstanding effects of the Battle of San Jacinto, it did boost sagging Confederate morale and damaged Union confidence for some time.

Confederate morale in Galveston sank as the war wore on. By 1864, the desertion rate among the soldiers was growing, and those that remained subjected the city to crime of every sort. One historian noted that the people who remained in Galveston probably wished that federal forces would return to restore order.

Residents of Victoria, Indianola and Port Lavaca could have felt the same way. Gen. Magruder was convinced that the Union would attempt an invasion of Texas at some point to cut the flow of cotton through the state to the Rio Grande. He ordered a scorched-earth policy that caused a bitter reaction by residents. The SA&MG railroad was to be destroyed, and the wharfs and warehouses at Indianola were marked for destruction. Residents argued that the destruction of the facilities was premature, for federal forces were not threatening. If they did threaten, there would be plenty of time for the destruction. The invasion never came, although the Union continued the blockade and took other measures.

The remainder of the Union's 1863 campaign in the Gulf was more successful than the attack on Sabine Pass. In early November, Brownsville and Brazos Santiago were taken, and the pass through the barrier island at Point (now Port) Isabel, was captured. Early in the war, small boats had used the waterways inside the barrier islands for part of the trip to transport cotton from the Brazos to the Rio Grande. These actions, along with the assignment of more ships to the blockade, stopped that traffic. But these losses did not stop the Confederates from using the Rio Grande to ship cotton to foreign markets, for cotton could still be shipped overland. Victoria was on one branch of the "Cotton Road" over which the precious cargo made its way to Mexico. And Union ships could not interfere with shipping from Mexican ports. But the Union action did slow down the movements of the goods that had to be routed to Laredo and then overland to Matamoros for shipment. Capt. John S. "Rip" Ford, commanding Texas state troops, later regained control of Brownsville, but the shipment of goods was still slowed because of the blockade.

Within two weeks after the taking of Brownsville and Brazos Santiago, Corpus Christi Pass and Port Aransas fell, along with Indianola, all of which were occupied or controlled for the remainder of the war. El Paso and the lower Texas coast were the only regions of the state held for any period of time by the Union during the Civil War.

Refugio County also felt the pain of war. Important salt works were operated in the county, but they were destroyed by a Union raiding party in 1862. And from time to time, the facilities were raided throughout the war, as were salt works in Brazoria County. St. Mary's, which was in Refugio County at the time although the site is in today's Aransas County, also was attacked. The small community's wharf and warehouses were destroyed in retaliation for the successful blockade-running operations headquartered there.

Corpus Christi had not been unanimous in its loyalty to the Confederacy. Edmund J. Davis, a former district attorney and district judge from the community, commanded Union forces in the area. And the commissioners court had declined to require residents of Nueces County to take a loyalty oath to the Confederacy. Although Corpus Christi was prostrate after the winter of 1863-64, Union forces did not occupy the city, though they could have with ease.

Even with Union forces controlling many ports, blockade running remained a profitable venture throughout the war. Both the Union and the blockade runners improved the quality of their ships as the conflict continued. At one time, for example, 10 schooners loaded with cotton were anchored near the mouth of the Brazos River seeking an opportunity to try their hand at outmaneuvering the federal ships that awaited in the Gulf. Even through the Union forces had set up a signal

system to notify authorities when blockaders were on the move, the potential profit of a successful run kept the ships and crews trying.

Houston's role in the war was not so colorful as Galveston's. The Bayou City was removed from the military action along the coast, but it did serve as an administrative and ordnance center. A Confederate shipyard was operated at Goose Creek just north of Morgan's Point. And refugees from nearby coastal towns, like Galveston, flocked to Houston to sit out the war. The city's residents, however, strongly supported the war effort to the extent, one newspaper reported, that an estimated 12 percent of the population joined the Confederate military. Once word of Lee's surrender reached Houston, an attitude of resistance sprang up, but it was quickly quelled by the city's leadership. Confederate soldiers stationed in Houston looted government warehouses when the war ended, seeking some compensation for their service. Soldiers passing through the city threatened to plunder private property until pleas by local officials discouraged them.

The war wound down in early 1865 with the last Confederate soldier leaving Galveston on May 24. The city also had been plundered by soldiers seeking compensation for service to the Confederacy. Reconstruction came to Texas through Galveston. On June 5, Union officials took possession of the city, and on June 18, General Gordon Granger, the U.S. commander of the District of Texas, arrived. A day later, on June 19, Granger read the proclamation freeing the slaves in Texas.

Progress and Problems

Reconstruction's ills struck the Texas coast after the Civil War, as they did all of the state. But the blow was softened somewhat by the concentration of most of the coast with economic growth.

All the railroads, built with such effort prior to the war, were destroyed or badly run down. For Houston and Galveston, the war was even more devastating. Galveston, as the state's major port, had achieved a level of prosperity that placed it well ahead of its sister cities in Texas; the city, however, was virtually depopulated by the war. In addition, both cities depended on the ship channels and wharfs for commerce that was their economic life blood, and these facilities, too, had not been maintained.

Early in the post-war period, repairs had to be made, and the credit of Texas' cities had to be re-established in national markets. This process was slowed by the depression that hit the nation in 1873.

Galveston, however, was so successful in regaining prosperity that upstate farmers criticized the city for allowing high freight charges and wharf fees. In 1874, the Galveston Wharf Co. lowered fees, and the city, which had challenged the company's monopoly, gained one-third interest in the firm in 1869. One study found that 11 of the 58 richest Texans (those with estates valued at $100,000 or more) were residents of Galveston. Business success also attracted the interest of organized labor. By 1872, a dozen unions were in operation in Galveston, and in 1877, the city suffered a series of strikes. Labor unions were hampered in their organization efforts throughout Texas by a lack of industrialization and by the failure of out-of-state unions to support them.

During Reconstruction, efforts were made to educate Galveston's newly freed slaves. The Freedman's Bureau operated several schools, although several city ordinances regulating the activities of blacks were passed. Indeed, Galveston's leading statewide politician of the day was a black, Norris Wright Cuney. The son of a plantation owner and his mistress, Cuney was educated in Pittsburgh, Pa., and returned to Texas in 1865. He became a customs collector and served on the city council from 1883-87. Cuney became a leader of the Republican Party in the latter part of the 19th century, helping to distribute patronage when the national party held the presidency. He also was chief collector of customs at the Port of Galveston for a time.

Transportation remained a major concern of Galveston's leadership. While its position as Texas' leading city was consolidated throughout the 1870s, efforts began in the 1880s to make Galveston's harbor a deepwater port. In 1880, railroad connections had been made from Galveston to Kansas City, and the federal government named Galveston as the Gulf port for the western states, which were clamoring for cheaper transporta-

tion. It became evident that ocean-going vessels must reach Galveston, and that meant deepening the channels that served the city. In 1881, the Deep Water Committee was organized, and the panel, led by William L. Moody, began a lobbying effort for federal funds in Washington. The goal was to acquire a 30-foot deep channel that would accommodate most ocean-going ships of the day.

After early rebuffs in Congress, the committee broadened its support by appealing to the western states to join their battle, since Galveston was designated to serve them. Leaders in these states responded. By 1890, the Galveston Harbor Bill was approved by Congress, and six years later, the *Algoa*, a British steamer drawing 21 feet of water tied up at a Galveston wharf. In 1885-86, Galveston shipped 22 percent of Texas' cotton exports; by 1897-98, 65 percent of these exports passed through the city, which had become the nation's leading cotton port.

Despite its desirable port facilities, Galveston was at a disadvantage to Houston because its railroad trade with the interior of Texas ran through the Bayou City. In 1873, John Sealy of Galveston led a drive to charter the Gulf, Colorado and Santa Fe Railway Co., which bypassed Houston. The line was completed to Fort Worth in 1881 and tied into the just completed Fort Worth and Denver Railroad.

Yellow fever continued to plague all Texas ports, and Galveston was hit particularly hard. Quarantines were effective when enforced, but too often local officials were more concerned with the economics of continuing trade with cities like New Orleans than with controlling the disease. Also quarantines often were used as economic weapons. Houston, for example, would quarantine Galveston during the yellow fever season, blocking the shipment of goods to Houston from its neighbor. The effect was to encourage shippers to send goods directly to Houston, bypassing Galveston. And Galveston also used the quarantine weapon. The state finally took over the responsibility for declaring and enforcing quarantines in the late 1870s.

The high incidence of yellow fever, however, has been credited with attracting the University of Texas Medical Branch to Galveston. Some of the city's leading physicians thought the disease might be associated with mosquitoes, but they had no scientific proof. With a medical facility, the disease could be studied more carefully. State voters approved separating the medical school from the main campus in 1881, and Galveston was selected as the home of the medical facility. The city previously had had two private medical schools. The medical branch opened in 1891.

Tourism also attracted the attention of the city's leadership. Galveston's beaches had been popular recreational facilities since the days of Aury and Lafitte.

To exploit this potential, a three-story, 200-room hotel, the Beach Hotel, was opened in 1883 and served as a focal point for social activity and tourism until it burned in 1898. Athletics played a role in community life. Galveston fielded a baseball team in the fledgling Texas League in 1887, and football came to the city in 1890. A black Galveston boxer, Jack Johnson, became world heavyweight champion in 1908.

As Texas' richest and most sophisticated city, Galveston aquired an impressive list of distinctions. In 1878, Col. A. H. Belo added the state's first telephone installed, connecting his home with the office of the *Galveston News*, his newspaper. The state's first telephone exchange was opened in Galveston in 1881, and service to Houston was connected in 1893. Long-distance service to St. Louis, Kansas City and Chicago was available in 1899. In 1885, the city provided the first professional fire department. Nicholas Clayton, Texas' first professional architect, designed much of the Victorian architecture for which Galveston is known today. Clayton dominated the city's architectural design during the last two decades of the 19th century. And as Galveston's prosperity increased, many of its frame buildings were replaced by handsome brick facilities. As the 20th century opened, Galveston had every reason to look to the future with optimism for continued economic growth and increased importance to Texas and the western states.

Houston was not far behind. In 1870, the federal government declared the city a port for the first time. And two years later, Congress made its first appropriation, $10,000, for upgrading the ship channel. At the time, Houston leaders began to warn that Galveston's harbor could not protect ships in a major storm.

Two companies, the Houston Direct Navigation Co. and the Buffalo Bayou Ship Channel Co., were organized to expedite improvement of the channel. In July 1874, one of the most important figures in Gulf Coast history, Charles Morgan, came to the aid of Houston. Morgan operated a fleet of steamships and had first provided service to Galveston in 1835. Before the Civil War, the Morgan Lines held a near monopoly on Texas coastwise shipping. During the conflict, Morgan suffered heavy losses as both Union and Confederate forces had commandeered his ships. Nevertheless, Morgan signed a contract to improve Houston's ship channel, and he acquired both the companies involved in the project. By 1876, the ship channel could handle a ship drawing nine and one-half feet of water. In 1877, a federal survey recommended construction of a ship channel from Bolivar Pass to Morgan's channel, despite reservations about using Morgan's facilities because of the toll charged.

Morgan's plans were more ambitious, however. At a point opposite the junction of Buffalo and Sims bayous, he established the town of Clinton, complete with wharf facilities and a rail line to Houston. Historians differ on Morgan's motives for helping Houston. Most think he was rebelling against Galveston's high wharf fees. (Indeed, he virtually built Indianola when Port Lavaca failed to heed complaints about high dock charges.) Others, however, feel that Morgan was simply biding time until east-west railroad connections were available through Texas from Louisiana. And that is what happened when rail service from New Orleans to Houston was completed in 1880. Steamer traffic to Clinton was curtailed in 1883, and freight was transported on Morgan's railroads. Nevertheless, traffic in the ship channel increased dramatically after Morgan's improvements were completed.

Houston, and most other cities served by Morgan, had a love-hate relation with the entrepreneur. After improving the ship channel, Morgan charged a toll for its use. Eventually a heavy iron chain was installed across the entrance of the waterway to ensure that no one evaded payment. As the chain grew more unpopular, the Morgan interests (Morgan died in 1878) offered to sell the improvements to the federal government. Although a proposal was accepted by Congress in 1879 and a contract drawn in 1881, the chain remained across the channel until the Morgan interests were paid $92,316 for the improvements in May 1892.

Railroads and Galveston's drive for a deep-water port put Houston's water facilities at a competitive disadvantage. And the city had little choice but to seek deep-water facilities, too. Houston had long argued that Galveston was an unsuitable port, for ships could not be protected from severe storms. The deep-water movement began in the 1890s in Houston, and it was eventually successful early in the 20th century.

Houston continued development begun before the war as a major rail center. The Houston and Texas Central line was still operating after the Civil War, and it immediately began construction toward northern Texas. In 1867, the H&TC reached Bryan, then Corsicana in 1871, Dallas in 1872 and Denison in 1873 when it tied into the Missouri, Kansas and Texas Railroad. The connection gave Houston a direct tie with Midwestern markets.

The Houston East and West Texas Narrow Gauge Railway line was started into East Texas in 1876 to tap the region's lumber industry. By 1878 the line had reached Cleveland and moved on to Livingston in 1879 and Moscow in 1880. The railroad was carrying 20 cars of lumber a day to Houston. And by 1880, with the completion of service to New Orleans, nine rail lines converged on Houston.

To aid in Houston's economic development, the Board of Trade was established in 1874 and later became the Board of Trade and Cotton Exchange. Once Houston had been called "a huddle of houses arranged on unoccupied lines of black mud," but civic improvements were begun, such as the paving of streets in 1882. Every avenue of development was pursued. From 1872-78, a state fair was promoted in Houston, and by the mid-1870s, there were five cotton compresses operating in the city.

Electric service came to the city when the Houston Electric Light and Power Co. was chartered in 1882, and efforts to create a sanitary water supply began soon thereafter. Phone service began with 40 subscribers in 1879, and long distance was added in 1895. By the 1890s, complaints about pollution of Buffalo Bayou arose, and federal officials put the city on notice that the waterway was to be cleaned up or funds from Washington for the ship channel would be cut. Houstonians also began to take more interest in their community, which had been called a "dirty village" and a "vagabond appearing city." The first 16 acres for Sam Houston Park were acquired in 1899. At the turn of the century, Houston had 45,000 people and listed 210 manufacturing plants.

Economic expansion was slower on the eastern Texas coast. Slavery had been the backbone of the economy of East Texas, and readjustment after the Civil War was difficult. Nevertheless, Beaumont became a major lumber shipping center early in its history and maintained that role well into the 20th century. Until displaced by petroleum in 1929, the timber industry was Texas' largest employer for 60 years. Efforts also were made to diversify the economy. The first experiments in irrigated rice farming were made in Jasper County in 1862. Prior to widespread irrigation, however, farmers planted rice in low, marshy areas. The Beaumont Rice Mill was founded in 1892 by J.E. Broussard, and other rice milling plants were located on the Trinity River.

Slavery had been limited in the western Texas Gulf, so the economic dislocations of Reconstruction and post-Civil War recovery were not as great as in East Texas. Also, Union sentiment had been stronger in Western Texas, especially among German immigrants, and the pangs of Reconstruction were not as great. Indeed, one of the top priorities of the military government was the rebuilding of the San Antonio and Mexican Gulf Railroad, which had been destroyed by the Confederates. The economy also was in transition. Cattle and sheep led the economic revival. Cattle had long been raised in the region from Matagorda Bay through the Coastal Bend. During both the Mexican and Civil wars, the absence of supervision had led to large increases in the number of cattle. Estimates vary from 5 million to 8 million head of cattle on the range following the Civil War. The glut soon destroyed prices on the New Orleans market.

Innovations restored profitability. First, cattlemen from the region began to trail the animals to Missouri and Kansas where prices made the long drives worthwhile. During this period, too, Texas' only two women trail drivers, Sally Scull of Refugio County and Margaret Hardy-Borland of the Victoria area, gained their reputations as being equals of their male counterparts.

Then the problem of waste was overcome. Packeries sprang up on both Corpus Christi and Matagorda bays to process hides and tallow that were exported to New York and New Orleans. Bone was ground into fertilizer. But the meat was wasted, for there was no way to preserve it to get it to market. The meat often was given away or left to rot. In July 1869, however, the Morgan Line ship, *Agnes*, transported 30 beef carcasses in a special refrigerated compartment to New Orleans from

Continued on Page 35

The Deadly Visitor

Now no longer a threat in the civilized world, yellow fever was for almost 75 years a regular and deadly visitor to Texas' Gulf Coast.

The name yellow fever comes from the deep jaundice that occurs during the latter stages of the disease, causing the patient's skin to take on an intense yellow hue. Other symptoms in severe cases of the viral disease include headache and backache, high fever, dizziness, nausea and vomiting. The disease attacks the major organs of the body with a general infection, causing fatty degeneration of the liver, kidneys and heart. Hemorrhaging from the mucous membranes leads to the "black vomit" that is characteristic of the final stages of yellow fever. Death may occur four to eight days after onset. Many cases are much milder, however, and are often mistaken for other fevers. Recovered cases are immune for life.

Yellow fever was also called "yellow jack" from the quarantine flag (or jack) raised on incoming ships by port inspection officers when suspicious signs were found in passengers or crew members. The dread disease is thought to have originated in Africa and to have come to the New World as a stowaway aboard merchant vessels, starting in the 17th century. The *aedes aegypti* mosquito, which carries the fever, could breed happily in the open barrels of drinking water that were carried on sailing ships in those days.

ASHBEL SMITH

History Highlights

According to Dr. Greensville Dowell's 1876 report on yellow fever and malarial diseases, the first outbreak of yellow fever in Texas occurred in 1833 in Columbia (now West Columbia) in present-day Brazoria County. From then until 1907, the unwelcome guest made almost-annual appearances in the state, mostly along the Gulf Coast, with an occasional sortie inland. Epidemics occurred in 1833, 1839, 1844, 1847, 1848, 1853, 1854, 1855, 1858, 1859, 1862, 1867, 1873, 1878, 1897, 1898, 1899, 1903 and 1907.

During the 1833 outbreak in Columbia, Dr. John Tinsley, a druggist, and a German physician named Jeager reported about 60 cases with 32 deaths. Asiatic cholera also was introduced that year, dealing coastal residents a double blow.

Details of the yellow fever epidemic of 1839 were minutely observed, recorded and published by Dr. Ashbel Smith in the first scientific paper published in Texas. Smith had been surgeon general of the Texas army and went on to serve the people of Texas as diplomat, state representative and agricultural scientist. He also was one of the major catalysts in the establishment of the University of Texas and the medical branch at Galveston.

In a letter to Dr. Casper Wistar Pennock written Oct. 21, 1839, Smith related, "About the first of this month the Yellow Fever made its appearance on the Strand (in Galveston)." He went on to describe the Strand — Galveston's major commercial street — as being located near a swampy "morass." Since yellow fever and malaria disappeared when cold weather arrived or when marshes or other areas of stagnant water were eliminated, many people concluded that "bad air" or "marshy emanations" caused the diseases. Smith generally agreed, but he also realized that yellow fever was not contagious and that minimal medication and maximum nursing care were better treatment than the harsher remedies employed by many other physicians of the day. He favored quinine and calomel, whereas others used, alone or in various combinations, castor oil, powdered charcoal, sulphate of zinc, oil of black pepper, chlorine water, Dover's powders, extract of dandelion, pulverized capsicum (red pepper), phosphate of lime, carbonate of lime and elixir of vitriol, not to mention bloodletting.

During the epidemic of 1847, Smith gained intimate personal knowledge of the disease. He described his case as "severe"; he could not sit up in

Dr. Greensville Dowell. Photo Courtesy Moody Medical Library, The University of Texas Medical Branch at Galveston.

bed for 11 days, and he fully expected to die. The physician recovered, however, and went on to treat victims of many subsequent outbreaks.

There were no trained nurses prior to the Civil War. Doctors helped as many victims as they could, but doctors were no more immune to yellow fever than their patients. Usually family members and neighbors had to nurse each other. Some of those who had survived bouts of the disease and were, therefore, immune organized into so-called Howard Associations to care for the sick, particularly around Galveston and Houston.

But the epidemics were not confined to Galveston and Houston. Publications of the period reported cases also in Brazoria, Richmond, Indianola, (Port) Lavaca, Liberty, Victoria, Brownsville, Matagorda, Sabine, Corpus Christi, Liverpool, Hockley, Cypress and La Grange, as well as other locations.

Contemporary descriptions of life during an epidemic are graphic. Amelia Barr, a novelist who lived in Texas from 1856 to 1868, described one outbreak in

Continued on Page 35

Deadly Visitor

Continued From Page 34

Galveston: "It was a terrible time. Little green frogs were everywhere and their croaking was incessant. The oleanders were sickeningly sweet and a terrible depression hung over the whole city. The cracking of ice, the moaning of the sick, the weeping for the dead or dying, the haggard faces of those well enough to nurse . . ." An account in an 1840 newspaper stated, "The sight of hearses dashing along at a gallop, without a mourner following the corpse, was horrible." A description of the 1867 epidemic in La Grange mentions mass burials in trenches at the site of the town's present cemetery, with no markers erected.

There were evidently sporadic attempts to use quarantines to control the spread of yellow fever during the 1840s, but enforcement was not effective.

On March 31, 1850, the voters of Galveston passed quarantine regulations, which were strengthened in 1853, when money was appropriated to build and staff the first quarantine station in Texas. The captain of a ship from the infected port of New Orleans circumvented this checkpoint by landing his passengers on the beach, from which they freely walked into the city. Clearly, more stringent measures were needed.

Statewide measures were passed by the Legislature in 1856, conferring authority on local governments to set up quarantine regulations within their jurisdictions. This is considered to be the nucleus that evolved into the Texas Department of Health.

Much stronger regulations were enacted by the Legislature in 1870, including authorizing the governor to declare a quarantine and to assess all incoming vessels a fee of 50 cents for every person on board.

Strict, sometimes vicious, enforcement of these 1870 quarantine laws provided the first ray of hope since the scourge first appeared on the Gulf Coast: The outbreak of yellow fever that year in Galveston resulted in only 16 deaths. In 1873, only seven people died. And in 1876, when yellow fever appeared in New Orleans, Texas' strict state quarantine officer refused to let any ships from the Louisiana city dock in Texas ports. Louisiana and Texas merchants alike complained bitterly, but the officer would not relent. There was no yellow fever in Texas that year.

Ironically, the very measures that made life along the Texas coast healthier caused development to suffer. With each quarantine, commerce was hobbled. Trade slowed to a crawl. Construction was postponed.

Building of the Galveston, Harrisburg and San Antonio Railway was delayed when yellow fever broke out in the construction camps west of Columbus.

As the effects of the stringent quarantine enforcement became evident, newspapers, local officials and merchants became increasingly reluctant to admit the presence of yellow fever, so that the life and commerce of their cities would not be disrupted. But courageous doctors such as Ashbel Smith and Greensville Dowell continued to publish factual accounts of each outbreak.

Although Texas scientists and physicians had observed that yellow fever occurred near marshy areas and disappeared with cold weather, none had connected it to mosquitoes. In 1848, an Alabama physician, Josiah Clark Knott, published a paper suggesting that yellow fever was of insect or animalcular origin. The mosquito was pinpointed as the culprit in Cuban physician Carlos Juan Finlay's paper that was read before the Royal Academy in Havana, Cuba, in 1881. But the mosquito as the carrier of the dreaded yellow jack was not proven until August 31, 1900, when a member of Dr. Walter Reed's Yellow Fever Commission, Dr. James Carroll, contracted the disease after being bitten by an infected mosquito on August 27. Antimosquito measures caused immediate improvement in cities, and the last recorded epidemic on the Texas Gulf Coast was in 1907. Finally, a vaccine was developed, which was made available around the world between 1940 and 1947.

But yellow jack is not dead. It lives on today in monkeys in the jungles of South America and Africa. And it would be possible for the disease to travel from monkey to jungle mosquito to traveler back to civilization to domestic mosquito to city dweller. There still is no specific treatment for the disease; prevention by eliminating the yellow fever mosquito is the best control.

— *MARY G. CRAWFORD*

FOR FURTHER READING
Bender, George A., **Great Moments in Medicine;** Northwood Institute Press, 1966.

Cox, George W., M. D., State Health Officer, **History of Public Health in Texas;** Texas State Department of Health, Austin, 1950.

Nixon, Pat Ireland, M.D., **The Medical Story of Early Texas, 1528-1853;** Mollie Bennett Lupe Memorial Fund, 1946.

Silverthorne, Elizabeth, **Ashbel Smith of Texas: Pioneer, Patriot, Statesman, 1805-1886;** Texas A&M University Press, College Station, 1982.

Continued From Page 33

Indianola in the first experiment of its type. The beef had been chilled after slaughter at a special refrigerated warehouse in Indianola. The problem of preservation was solved.

The weather lent a hand, too. Brutally cold winters in 1872 and 1873 diminished herds and raised prices to aid the economic recovery.

In addition to cattle, the open range also fostered development of a strong sheep market in Nueces and Duval counties, which were much larger geographically at the time. An estimated one million sheep were pastured in these two counties, and in the decade of the 1870s, sheep raising was their most profitable business. Corpus Christi became the largest wool market in the nation, and between 7 million and 12 million pounds of wool were bought and shipped through the port annually. But after 1880, the free range began to disappear behind wire fences. Sheep raising died with the profitability, and Corpus Christi lost its place as the top wool market.

Indianola also thrived as a military depot, and supplies for outposts in New Mexico and Arizona, as well as Western Texas, passed through its port. Steamship owner Charles Morgan also helped solve some inland transportation problems. He led a group of investors that acquired the SA&MG line in 1869 and connected it with the Indianola Railroad in 1871. The two lines were consolidated into the Gulf, Western Texas and Pacific Railway in 1871. Efforts to tie Matagorda Bay to Austin were stymied in December 1871 when the Houston and Texas Central reached the capital city, giving it an outlet to the Gulf. But Indianola still was a major port for trade with northern Mexico, as well as Western Texas, and often experienced traffic jams when carts engaged in the trade clogged the streets.

U.S. Army Capt. Randolph Marcy, who gained fame with explorations of West Texas, surveyed the coast in the 1850s and noted that Black Point on Copano Bay was the best port location on the western Gulf. The site was close to San Antonio and Chihuahua City. But the government never acted on the report.

Other communities, however, sprang up along the coast. In 1857, St. Mary's, located just north of present-day Bayside and near Black Point, was founded on Copano Bay by Joseph F. Smith, and for a time was the "metropolis of Refugio County." In 1867, a coeducational school, the Western Texas Institute, was established in the community. The small port became an export center for hides, tallow and cotton and imported primarily lumber and building materials. In 1868, the Morgan Line provided steamboat service, and wagons and carts dispersed goods over a wide area. There were no stagecoaches, however, and travelers had to ride mail hacks or rent horses. A lack of fresh water also was a problem.

St. Mary's future dimmed when the San Antonio and Aransas Railroad bypassed the city and connected with Rockport, which was established on Aransas Bay in 1867 and incorporated in 1870. This port was established because larger ships had trouble negotiating the reefs on the route to St. Mary's on Copano Bay. Morgan Line provided service. Hides and tallow also were shipped through Rockport, which had pens and warehouses. The post office opened in 1868. Rockport at the time was in Refugio County. But the city became the county seat of Aransas County when it was established in 1871 from part of Refugio County.

Electronic communications with the rest of the world came soon after the Civil War. Western Union brought telegraph service to Indianola in 1870 on a line extended westward from Houston to Columbus. A year later, the telegraph was extended to St. Mary's, Corpus Christi and Brownsville and then provided the first United States connection with Mexico. With the telegraph came a U.S. Army Signal Corps weather bureau station in Indianola. A second station on the Texas coast was operated at Galveston.

Indianola flourished, keenly competing with Galveston as the state's top port. But disaster struck with a great hurricane that ravaged the western Gulf city on Sept. 15-16, 1875. Three-quarters of the buildings of the town were destroyed, and the rest were damaged. At least 300 people died, and many bodies were never found. (For more on storms that struck Indianola see the next section, "Disaster.")

Indianola rebuilt, but its fate was probably already decided. Plans were to move the townsite to the edge of Power Horn Lake, where ground was higher and ships could be protected if the lake were dredged. But the Morgan Line flatly refused to spend any money on relocation. So the new town was rebuilt on the same site as the old.

Railroad construction north of the Gulf also was putting Indianola at a commercial disadvantage. In February 1877, the Galveston, Harrisburg and San Antonio Railroad reached San Antonio, giving the city its long-awaited tie to the Gulf. Much of the Western Texas trade that had come to Indianola could use the new line that made a transcontinental connection with the Southern Pacific at the Pecos River in 1883. Galveston reached into Indianola's trade area, and there was little the Matagorda port could do about the competition.

Like other coast cities, Indianola looked to develop tourism during the 1880s to diversify its economy. But in 1886 a second hurricane struck, destroying the town a second — and final — time. In November, the county seat was moved to Port Lavaca by voters, and Indianola all but ceased to exist. A special train was run to the ruins "to enable those who feel so inclined to inspect the ruins of that once prosperous city"; the train was sold out. The post office was closed in 1887.

Victoria's fortunes rose, especially after 1882. That summer, a rail line from the Rosenberg Junction on the New York, Texas and Mexico Railroad tied the city into transcontinental routes and made it a cattle center.

During the year in which Indianola suffered its first staggering setback, Corpus Christi solved a man-made problem. Since the Civil War, Mexican bandits had preyed on settlers and cattle herds in the notorious Nueces Strip between the Nueces River and the Rio Grande. The legendary Juan Cortina, who often claimed to be defending Mexicans against American injustice, led raids as far north as Refugio County. Richard King and Mifflin Kenedy began fencing their ranches in an attempt to cut losses to the rustlers. The roads to the Rio Grande were unsafe, and the rustlers were bold. In retaliation, Nueces Countians formed "minute companies" to fight the raiders, and the vigilante groups were often as brutal and rambunctious as the Mexican bandits.

Finally after a raid by outlaws on Nuecestown in March 1875, Gov. Richard Coke sent Capt. L. H. McNelly and a special company of Texas Rangers to Corpus Christi. The Rangers first disbanded the vigilante groups and then began to deal with the bandits. On one occasion in Brownsville, he lined up on the square the bodies of more than a dozen bandits killed during a cattle raid to send a message to Cortina. The Rangers soon had the trouble under control.

With the bandits subdued, construction on the Corpus Christi, San Diego and Rio Grande Railway, chartered in 1873, began in 1876. Five years later, the narrow-gauge line reached Laredo and linked with the National Mexican Railway. Uriah Lott, a Corpus Christi businessman, promoted the railroad.

Corpus Christi received its first steamer, the Morgan Line's *Gussie*, in 1874. The vessel used the newly dredged channel between Aransas and Corpus Christi bays. Previously steamers had to stop at the bar to be unloaded by lighters.

Texans on the Gulf Coast were dealing with problems within their control about as well as possible. But nature failed to cooperate and punctuated the history of the region with terrible disasters for the next quarter-century.

Disasters

Nature seldom allows beauty, serenity or utility of its handiwork to exist without exacting a price. On Texas' Gulf Coast, that price is the periodic storms that rake the region. The storms account in part for the sparse population of Indians that Europeans found in the 16th century. Spain, too, ignored the coast, except to keep other nations from gaining a foothold.

Hurricanes have buffeted the region since records have been kept. Serious storms lashed the thinly populated region in 1818 and 1837. It was not until the Anglo-American colonization increased its population that coastal storms could claim a high toll in life and property damage.

At least two communities — Indianola in Calhoun County and St. Mary's in Refugio County — have suffered death at the hands of serious Gulf storms, and the growth of a third — Galveston — was severely curtailed.

In the last quarter of the 19th century, Indianola was a thriving port, serving Western Texas, New Mexico and Arizona. Its population stood at an estimated 6,000 in 1875, and citizens saw no limit to its potential. Not 50 miles away, St. Mary's on Copano Bay faced similar prospects.

In September 1875, both communities suffered a near-fatal storm. It was the worst hurricane to strike the coast since the U.S. Weather Bureau, then a branch of the Army Signal Corps, began keeping records. But that was not long. The bureau had been created by Congress in 1870, and the chief signal officer was directed to warn stations of weather changes that could affect shipping, commerce and agriculture. A series of weather stations was created around the nation and linked by telegraph to report atmospheric conditions. Two weather stations were opened on the Texas coast, one at Galveston in 1871 and the other at Indianola in 1872.

The first signs of the 1875 storm occurred on the night of Sept. 14 when a wind change to the north resembling an ordinary norther took place. For 24 hours, the wind grew in intensity and pushed water inland. By the morning of Sept. 16, the water level was higher than the previous record at Indianola and eventually reached 15 feet above normal high tide. Water flooded the low-lying streets, and by noon, the wharves were being torn apart by wind. More people that usual were in town, many attending a spectacular murder trial. These people were trapped as water made roads impassable, and railroad schedules were canceled as high water undercut track.

The high winds pushed water as far as 20 miles inland. Then after midnight, the eye of the hurricane reached Indianola, and an eerie calm descended. As the eye passed, however, the intensity of the storm increased, and it entered its most destructive phase. The wind changed to the northwest, pushing the water back to the Gulf, and gravity increased the force of the flow of water. Water driven inland in 18 hours returned to the Gulf in just six. Millions of tons of water (salt water weighs 1,638 pounds per cubic yard) wreaked havoc on Indianola.

As dawn broke cool and cloudy on Sept. 17, the devastation was clearly visible. Three quarters of all buildings had simply vanished. Most of the others were knocked off their foundations and were damaged. In one 13-block stretch, 116 buildings were completely washed away, 90 were critically damaged, and only 36 were reparable. Throughout the town, only 12 buildings survived intact, and they were all located on higher elevations.

No one is sure how many died. Reports at the time said 270 bodies were recovered, but many victims were never found. Probably more than 300 lives were claimed by the storm. Many others were injured.

The Signal Corps devised new cautionary flags after the storm. An eight-by-10 foot red flag with a black rectangle in the middle was to signal approaching storms. But the flag was flown in November and December, causing a mild panic in Indianola, although only cold fronts were coming. So another flag, white with a red center, was added to denote a coming cold front.

Indianola rebuilt, albeit on a reduced scale. But life returned to near normal, residents apparently thinking that they had suffered a once-in-a-lifetime disaster. They were wrong.

North Texas suffered a devastating drought in 1886, and weather on the coast had been unusually hot and

Few buildings remained standing after Indianola was devastated by a storm in 1886. This second disaster in a decade killed the thriving port. Photo Courtesy Archives Division, Texas State Library.

dry. So Indianolans welcomed the brisk east breeze that came up on Aug. 18, but it was the prelude of another hurricane.

By the time the weather bureau at Indianola got orders to "up signals" on Aug. 19, the storm was well under way, and residents could not leave. Winds reached 102 miles per hour before the anemometer was destroyed, and water again was pushed inland. Many buildings that had withstood the 1875 catastrophe were destroyed, and fire added a deadly element. This time, only a few residents stayed, and most of them for less than a year. In April 1887, fire destroyed the remnants of the once-thriving business district. Soon thereafter, the railroad took up its tracks, and the post office closed. Indianola was no more.

St. Mary's experience was much the same, only it took an additional storm to seal its fate. In 1875, the wharves and warehouses of the "metropolis of Refugio County" were destroyed, and although the facilities were rebuilt, many merchants left for safer ground.

The 1886 storm was worse, attacking from two directions at once, observers said. It lasted from noon to sundown, and the damage was much more extensive. Indeed, the entire region suffered. Plank or lumber fences that had come into vogue on the surrounding prairies were scattered and replaced with barbed wire. Efforts were again made to rebuild, but these ended when another storm struck in 1887 and destroyed the repairs that had been made in the previous year. St. Mary's lingered longer than Indianola, however, for the community kept its post office until 1907.

Galveston, as Texas' premier city at the turn of the century, had much more to lose than its counterparts in the western Gulf. The census counted 37,789 people in 1900, and most residents had become casual about hurricanes. The city had taken few precautions. A line of salt cedars had been planted to stabilize the sand dunes on the beaches, and the elevation of the city had been increased some, but only to nine feet above sea level at the highest point.

The U.S. Weather Bureau, which in 1890 became a civilian agency in the Department of Agriculture, improved its reporting techniques and warning systems after Indianola's destruction. On Sept. 7, the bureau warned that a hurricane was in the Gulf. The storm passed over Florida and was somewhere at sea between the New Orleans and Galveston weather stations. Hurricane flags flew along the Texas coast and in Galveston.

Climatologist Isaac M. Cline of the weather bureau became so concerned about his instrument readings and the tide's running two feet above normal early on Sept. 8, 1900, that he personally warned people along the beach to take to higher ground. By mid-afternoon, as the tide continued to rise, Cline sent his brother to inform weather headquarters in Washington, D.C., that Galveston was going under and to send help. The message got through to Houston shortly before the telephone line went dead.

The storm struck with all its fury later in the day. Winds gusted to 120 miles an hour. The previous high-water record of 8.2 feet reached in 1875 was easily broken by a reading of 15.7 feet, as the sea surged across the island. When Sept. 9 dawned bright and clear, Galveston was devastated. Six thousand lives were lost, 3,600 homes destroyed and damage was estimated at $30 million. Across one edge of the city was a 30-block long line of debris, standing head high and four to five feet deep. Most brick buildings, including hospitals, and water service were unharmed. But telephone, telegraph and electric services were out. Mayor Walter C. Jones quickly appointed the Central Relief Committee to organize the early recovery.

A week after the disaster, martial law was declared for a short time, and the *Galveston News* reported that seven had been killed when caught looting.

Surprisingly, injuries were held to a minimum. Victims were either killed outright, or they survived virtually unscathed. The most serious immediate problem, however, was disposal of the dead. Trenches for mass burials were dug, but filled with water from the saturated ground before bodies could be interred. Seven hundred bodies were buried at sea at one time, but the practice was stopped when corpses washed onto the beach. Finally a policy was adopted to burn corpses where found. Funeral pyres burned into November, as an average of 70 bodies a day were found for about a month.

For much of the population, nothing was left, and no insurance was available. Relief was needed. Clara Barton and the Red Cross responded, as did generous citizens from around the world who donated more than $1.2 million. The funds aided the relief committee's work.

The disaster also attracted Albert E. Smith of Edison Co., who recorded the destruction and suffering with a new process known as moving pictures. This was one of the first documentaries, now so common on television, made of a catastrophe.

Within three weeks, freight began moving in the port, and municipal services were restored. A year later, 7,000 people attended a memorial service commemorating the disaster.

Unlike Indianola and St. Mary's, Galveston recovered, but its citizens never again saw black clouds boiling over the Gulf without concern. The age of innocence was over.

The New Century

Disaster and discovery set the tone for the development of Texas' Gulf Coast in the early 20th century. Galveston, as noted, was destroyed and spent the early years of the century in recovery. Houston, however, along with several other Southeast Texas communities, became a boom town as the discovery of Spindletop ushered Texas, the nation and the world into the oil age.

The presence of oil in Texas was well established. Indians had used oil seeps for medicinal purposes, and the Spanish used the petroleum to caulk boats on occasion. Immediately after the Civil War, contracts were made to allow for the exploration of oil and gas. And petroleum had been discovered at Nacogdoches and Corsicana. Indeed, Navarro was the leading oil-producing county in the state, and J. S. Cullinan built a refinery in the East Texas city and a pipeline to transport oil from nearby wells.

The conventional wisdom, however, was that oil in large commercial quantities simply did not exist in Texas. But men like Pattillo Higgins were not convinced when state and federal geologists counseled against drilling for oil around the salt domes near Beaumont. Beginning in 1892, three efforts were made to find oil near Beaumont. Only finances stopped Higgins, and in 1899, he sold his leases to Capt. Anthony F. Lucas, a mining engineer from Washington, D.C., who had experience in drilling salt domes in Louisiana.

One test well consumed Lucas' money, and he arranged an association with the firm of Guffey and Galey of Pittsburgh, Pa., which agreed to finance future drilling in return for a share of the profits, if any. The second well was started in October 1900. By Jan. 10, 1901, the crude rotary rig had reached a depth of 1,020 feet, and the well blew in, sending thousands of barrels of oil into the air. Texas' first oil boom was under way. It was more spectacular than anything else in the American experience except, perhaps, the California Gold Rush of 1849. The name "Spindletop," which was emblazoned in history, was taken from a nearby subdivision, Spindletop Heights. Despite all the legend that has developed around the monumental discovery, it might never have been made except for Lucas' wife, Caroline, who provided encouragement for her husband during particularly discouraging times.

Oil experts, investors, company executives and confidence men flocked to the area. By July 1901, there were 14 producing wells, three abandoned tests, 15 rigs drilling and 18 more preparing to drill — all on an 80-acre tract of land surrounding Spindletop. In the first year of operation, $630,753 worth of oil were sold at 25 cents a barrel, and another 1.5 million barrels of oil were held in stock.

Facilities for refining, storage and transportation of oil were lacking in the area. Within a year, 400 companies with capitalization of approximately $200 million were organized. Among these were today's Gulf, which was purchased recently by Chevron, and Texaco.

The first refinery was built at Port Arthur by the Guffey Oil Co., which had the facility in operation by July 13, 1901. This refinery was quickly followed by two more, one by Burt Refinery in Beaumont and another in Port Arthur by Texaco (the Texas Co.). In just over two and one-half years, $36 million was invested in Southeast Texas, one-third going to explorations and two-thirds to transportation, storage and refining.

Port Arthur was a new city, the brainchild of Arthur E. Stilwell, a promoter and president of the Kansas City Southern Railroad. Stilwell wanted a terminus and port for his railroad. So he bought 50,000 acres of land around the defunct community of Aurora on the northwest shore of Sabine Lake. Work began on the 4,000-acre townsite in 1895, and by 1899, a 25-foot deep channel that could handle ocean-going ships was complete. The vessels could come directly to Port Arthur's docks, and in 1906, the city became the port of entry for the Sabine District.

Spindletop's success encouraged drilling all along the Gulf Coast. By 1904, 650 wells were producing 21,674,111 barrels of oil a year in Southeast Texas. Discoveries had been made in Liberty, Hardin, Brazoria, Matagorda and Harris counties. Evidence of oil or gas, if not in commercial quantities, also had been found in Calhoun and San Patricio counties. By 1902, the Beaumont Oil Exchange and Board of Trade, the Houston Oil and Stock Exchange and the Galveston Oil and Stock Exchange were in operation.

In a brief time, Spindletop turned the world and nation askew. Russia had pioneered the use of fuel oil in steamships. But the United States soon put the fuel to work in locomotives, industry and the home. The Houston and Texas Central was probably the first railroad to try oil as a fuel, and Southern Pacific soon converted to oil at great savings over coal. Steamship lines soon followed suit, for oil was a great economy in both price and handling. Three barrels of oil provided the same energy as a ton of coal, but coal sold for $3.50 a ton, while three barrels of oil cost only 60 cents. In addition, one man could fuel a ship with oil, while more than 100 were needed to load it with coal.

Two monopolies also were broken by the discovery. Coal producers soon were faced with competition from cheaper fuel oil. And Standard Oil Co., which before Spindletop produced more than half the nation's oil, soon became only a competitor in the marketplace, although a formidable one. One fledgling Texas industry, lignite mining, became a casualty, however, being unable to meet the challenge of oil's economy.

To a great extent, eastern money was used to develop the transportation, storage and refining facilities. Texas investors were too small for the large outlays of capital needed. Exploration was within local reach; other functions were not. But to keep out-of-state interests from gaining too much power, Texas producers in 1905 defeated an attempt in the Legislature to allow one company to participate in all oil-industry functions.

Houston soon became the gateway to Beaumont. Immediately after Spindletop came in, six passenger trains a day, and many specials, too, were plying the 85 miles between the cities. Beaumont became a typical boom town. It is said that half of the whisky sold in Texas was consumed in Beaumont.

From a historical perspective, Houston probably benefited most from the oil strike. It added oil to the products that it shipped, and one of the world's largest refining and petrochemical complexes developed along the city's ship channel and the rest of the coast.

Galveston's disastrous storm paid dividends for Houston. For many years, leaders of the Bayou City argued that Galveston's harbor could not provide protection for ships during major storms. The hurricane of 1900 bore out the argument. So Congress looked more favorably on appropriations for an inland ship channel and port. Houston's drive to become a deep-water port was accomplished by 1908 when a channel 18 and one-half feet deep was completed and a turning basin was built at Harrisburg. The channel was deepened to 25 feet by 1914. A channel also was dredged to Texas City in 1904. The community, originally called Shoal Point, had been developed by a group of investors from Minnesota. A short railroad also was built, and the Mainland Co. purchased both townsite and railroad in 1898. In 1911, the city, which was located in Galveston County, but on the mainland, was incorporated.

During recovery from the devastating hurricane, Galveston's leadership — exercised through the Deep Water Committee — made basic changes in the community. The mayor-alderman form of municipal government was abandoned in favor of the innovative commission system. The panel included the mayor and a commissioner for each of four areas of concern: finance and revenue, fire and police, waterworks and sewage, and streets and public improvements. During the progressive era prior to World War I, the system was copied across the nation, but it proved inefficient. The tendency was for each commissioner to concentrate on only the office's particular responsibility, and there was little cooperation among the elected officials. Galveston used the commission system until 1960.

Technology was enlisted to protect the city from future storms. After a study, engineers recommended construction of a three-mile long seawall and elevation of the city. The city's part of the sea wall was completed in 1904, and Gov. Oscar Colquitt in 1911 rode in the first car to drive along the top of the wall after it was paved.

The city's elevation was raised in quarter-mile sections by dredging from the harbor and pumping the fluid sand to desired locations through pipes. By 1911, 500 city blocks had been elevated up to 11 feet with 16.3 million cubic yards of sand, and the double purpose was achieved of increasing the island's elevation while deepening the harbor.

Early dividends were received on the investments.

Like hundreds of other buildings, the Sacred Heart Catholic Church suffered severe damage in the disastrous Galveston Storm of 1900. Photo Courtesy Archives Division, Texas State Library.

Another big storm hit in 1909 causing only five deaths and minimal damage, and another storm in 1915 caused little damage.

Galveston's vulnerability to storms was an accepted fact after 1900, however, and the city paid a high price in lost development. As the rest of the eastern Gulf industrialized following Spindletop, Galveston stagnated. It remained a major cotton port. But the city received little of the valuable industrial growth that found its way to Houston and the smaller cities. Investors in Galveston had their money tied up in commerce, not industry. Even within Galveston County, Texas City became a major competitor with the island city.

And outside money was not attracted to Galveston. When Texaco (then the Texas Co.) began its search for a refinery site, it needed large acreage, fresh water, protection from storms and a deep-water port. Galveston and Texas City were rejected because of their hurricane potential. Houston got the facility.

Military installations, in part, helped both cities. Coast artillery was authorized for Fort Crockett in 1897, and a U.S. Coast Guard station was placed on Pelican Spit. In 1913, there were 7,000 soldiers stationed in Galveston and 8,000 in Texas City, providing a $450,000 monthly payroll. Texas City was named headquarters for the United States' expedition to Veracruz, and an army camp was set up in the city. With this base in the city, Congress appropriated $1.4 million so the channel to Texas City could be deepened to 30 feet and a dike could be built to keep the 300-foot wide channel from shoaling. When the camp was destroyed by the hurricane in 1915, it was not rebuilt, but the channel improvements stayed.

During the period, Galveston began to develop its image as a "sin city." Prostitution, gambling and alcohol became the city's major attractions, although all three were illegal in Texas at the time. But Galveston's leadership simply looked the other way while the vices flourished. Only occasional complaints by the military brought civic attempts at control of the illegal traffic.

Progress was not as fast in reaching the areas farther west on the Gulf Coast. One historian, for example, noted that Refugio County "went into a slumber" between 1886, when St. Mary's was destroyed, and 1906, the year after the first railroad appeared. In between, Refugio did get telephone service. The first line ran in 1892 from Balconia to Refugio. It did not provide service to Refugio, but only to ranches between the two communities. Finally in 1897, Refugio got telephone service when the line was extended to Corpus Christi.

The railroad was a real boon to Refugio County. Railroad construction in Texas slowed after 1882 when the state quit giving large land grants for new miles of line built. Therefore, the county had been disappointed on several occasions when it appeared that railroad service was imminent. Finally the St. Louis, Brownsville & Mexico Railroad arrived in 1905, bringing with it several hundred families in the following 12 years. Promoters subdivided several ranches and attracted settlers. Several communities were laid out for development including Woodsboro, Bonnie View, Bayside, Tivoli and Austwell. Lots in these towns were sold to investors across the nation and later resold by the county for back taxes.

Farther south, Aransas Pass, which was laid out in early 1885 with the construction of the San Antonio and

Aransas Pass Railroad, boomed in the 1890s. The pass is located in two counties, San Patricio and Aransas. Rockport got a boost when the San Antonio and Aransas Pass Railroad reached the community in 1888. The city began developing as a tourist resort at the turn of the century and did well until the beach property was destroyed by a hurricane in 1919. Rockport's hopes of becoming a deep-water port were scuttled by Corpus Christi, however, and the community became a commercial fishing center.

Much of the coast, however, lost importance, especially after the demise of Indianola. No other Matagorda Bay port took its place. Port Lavaca, an early competitor with Indianola and the apparent successor, was cut off by a reef that blocked deep-water ships, and lightering was too expensive. The goods that had entered Texas through Indianola were shipped to Galveston and Houston and then routed to Western Texas by railroad. Corpus Christi received some of the shipping because of its Texas-Mexico Railroad link with northern Mexico through Laredo.

The discovery of oil at Spindletop had an impact all along the coast, if even only upon the imaginations of residents. For example, legend held that oil had been discovered at St. Mary's during the 1870s when a water well became fouled with a black, scummy substance. Based in part on this tale, a Refugio newspaper saw the Spindletop discovery — 275 miles away — as irrefutable proof that oil in commercial quantities existed all along the coast. But 20 years passed and innumerable con men worked their wiles before the boast was proved correct.

There was other evidence of future riches, however. In 1885, natural gas flowed into a water well being drilled in Corpus Christi. The display was a preview of the large gas fields that would be discovered in the area, but at the time, no use could be found for the fuel.

Corpus Christi was in a period of transition as the 19th century ended. Col. E. H. Ropes of New York had hit town in 1889 and caused a land boom of sorts. He built a resort hotel, subdivided land and started dredging a channel. Land values rose. But the economic growth lasted only a couple of years, and Col. Ropes left town — to seek more money for his developments, he said — never to return. Some historians feel that the financial Panic of 1893 turned Ropes from a hero into a goat. Without this economic downturn, he could have been successful, and Corpus Christi would have benefited.

Changes were taking place, however. During the cattle boom following the Civil War, the ranges were overgrazed, and brush moved in. As the century closed, a few hardy farmers began clearing the brush from the land to plant crops. Nueces County's long growing season allowed harvesting two crops a year, and vegetables, followed by cotton, were planted. By 1903, an estimated 12,000 to 15,000 acres of land were under cultivation.

Corpus Christi's new mayor, Roy Miller, started a public improvement campaign in the first decade of the new century. Electricity and telephones already were in town, and streets were paved and sanitary sewer lines were laid. But Miller's major contribution may have been his attention to developing the city as a deepwater port. A young congressman, John Nance Garner, got the first appropriations for Corpus Christi's port in 1907. The port, along with oil discoveries and help from influential families of the region, like the Klebergs and the Kenedys, boosted Corpus Christi to maturity.

Two years later, President William Howard Taft was feted in the city while visiting his brother Charles' nearby ranch.

More indications of the natural gas potential of the region were displayed in 1913 when two gas wells blew out at White Point, 15 miles north of Corpus Christi in San Patricio County.

For most of the Texas coast, the new century promised to be a period of excitement and economic development, mixed with natural disaster and disappointment.

Boom to Bust

For the first four decades of the 20th century, Houston experienced an almost unbroken series of economic and civic successes. The city's leadership placed Houston in the right place at the right time and made sure that few opportunities for development and promotion slipped through their fingers.

The ship channel opened in 1908, but efforts to deepen it to 25 feet to attract the larger ocean-going vessels began almost immediately. In 1910, voters approved creation of the Harris County, Houston Ship Channel Navigation District. Bond issues of $1.25 million and $3 million also were approved to assure completion of the deepening project. And when banks were cautious about buying the navigation district bonds, Jesse H. Jones, a real estate developer and one of Texas' great leaders, convinced local institutions to buy the bonds.

In 1914, the Gulf Intracoastal Waterway, which runs from Florida to Brownsville, was completed to 200 miles below Galveston. Houston's ship channel was tied into the waterway. And the opening of the Panama Canal in the same year also aided development of Houston's port by giving it a convenient route to Pacific ports.

Even the shallow channel had begun to attract facilities for industries dependent on water transportation. By 1913, Houston had six cotton oil mills, seven compresses and 12 cotton warehouses and was one of the nation's top cotton ports. It also was a major lumber shipping center. Several railroads also operated maintenance shops in the city. In 1915, Gulf Refining Co. was operating a mixing plant on the channel with pipelines to Port Arthur and Goose Creek. By 1930, eight refineries were operating on the ship channel. Although early traffic on the channel was disappointing because World War I had disrupted trade, there still were 22 industries located below the Turning Basin and 16 above it. Houston's character was changing. Throughout its history, the city had been basically a commercial center, built on the transport of goods. With development of the ship channel, it was becoming more of an industrial center. In 1914, Houston had more than 50 labor unions, representing 21.5 percent of the white work force.

Houston lost one important battle to Dallas in 1914, however. Both cities had lobbied hard in Congress to get a Federal Reserve district bank. Dallas got the institution, and thereby got a leg up on Houston as a financial center. Houston got a branch of Dallas' Federal Reserve bank in 1919.

In 1917, Houston also suffered a major race riot when black troops stationed at Camp Logan went on a rampage after the arrest of a black soldier. Twenty people were killed and 11 wounded. In three courts martial, 13 black soldiers were given death sentences, and 63 were sentenced to life in prison.

Houston has benefited by the generosity of its residents. Rice Institute, endowed by William Marsh Rice, opened its doors in 1912, and in 1914, George Hermann donated the first 214 acres for Hermann Park. A decade later, the Hermann Hospital, endowed with Hermann's estate of almost $3 million, opened. The Houston Symphony Orchestra was organized in 1913, and in 1924, the Houston Museum of Fine Arts opened, becoming the first municipal museum of its type in Texas. During this period, Edna Saunders guided Houston's artistic affairs.

The decade of the 1920s was a period of unbroken growth and expansion. Congress had injected the vessels used in World War I into the nation's merchant marine, and money was invested in improving the nation's ports. By 1925, the ship channel had been deepened to 30 feet, and during the decade, Houston passed arch-rival Galveston in both tonnage and cargo value. During the same period, downtown development gave Houston a distinctive skyline that remained unchanged until the 1940s.

Attempts were made to give Houston's development some direction. A city plan commission was created in 1922, and in 1929, William C. Hogg, son of Gov. Jim Hogg, presented a comprehensive city plan to guide growth and to help avoid mistakes made in the past. An attempt to impose a zoning ordinance was turned down by city voters in 1938.

In 1922, the city's first radio station, WEV, went on the air, and three years later, Houston's most enduring station, KPRC, began operation.

The school district became independent during the decade, and in 1927, a local junior college was established to provide advanced education. The school later became the University of Houston. The first municipal airport opened in 1928 on Telephone Road.

And Jesse H. Jones also pulled off a coup for the

city. He single-handedly attracted the Democratic National Convention to Houston in 1928, despite the fact that he did not tell city officials about the effort or that a new coliseum had to be built to hold the 25,000 delegates and officials.

By 1930, Houston's port was surpassed in exports only by New York and Los Angeles. Tonnage did drop during the Depression, however. But the port was aided by competition provided by trucks for the railroads. Trucks had become such a factor that the state began to regulate them in 1932, and the federal government followed suit in 1935.

Debate always develops about the severity of the Depression in Texas. But Houston recovered quickly, after a low point in 1932 when the city quit taking applications for relief from blacks and Hispanics. Federal programs were quickly implemented, and in 1936, the high point of the Works Projects Administration, there were 12,000 people employed in 69 projects in Harris County that spent $2.1 million.

During the Depression, Jesse Jones organized a committee to counsel troubled banks, and as a consequence, no Houston bank failed. He took his talents to Washington as first a member and then chairman of the Reconstruction Finance Corp. Later Jones was federal loan administrator and secretary of the commerce department, ranking as one of the most powerful men in the Roosevelt administration.

As World War II approached, Houston stood at the threshhold of its most spectacular period of growth. The past was indeed prologue.

Although Galveston grew, it did not prosper as did Houston and other cities in the rich oil-producing sections of the coast. The island city turned its attention to other pursuits. In 1911, the Galvez Hotel opened on the beach front, enhancing the city's tourist facilities. Also as a tourist attraction, "Splash Day" was inaugurated in 1916 and continued as an annual event, attracting thousands of students, until 1965.

Labor problems erupted on Galveston's docks in 1920. Workers went on strike and closed the port. When local law-enforcement authorities sided with the strikers, Gov. William P. Hobby declared martial law and sent in the Texas National Guard. Through the 1920s, Galveston regained its preeminence as a cotton and grain shipping point and became a major port for sulphur, too.

The U.S. Army built an airfield on Galveston Island, and the Coast Guard installation was the largest between New Orleans and the Rio Grande. But otherwise Galveston had little defense responsibility, for it was considered vulnerable to bad weather and enemy attack in wartime.

Like Houston, Galveston was struck only a glancing blow by the Depression.

Other cities developing along the coast were more damaged. Freeport was founded in Brazoria County in 1912 by a group of investors interested in developing nearby sulphur deposits. The Brazos River was diverted in 1929 to accommodate large vessels, leaving the old channel as a tidal estuary. The Missouri-Pacific Railroad also provided transportation. The Freeport Sulphur Co. dominated the city's early economy, and the Stauffer Chemical plant opened in 1916.

Between Freeport and Corpus Christi, only oil and gas development shook the communities. Refugio, for example, was without municipal taxes from the 1880s until the administration of Mayor J. O. West from 1923 to 1932. But the city had no public improvements, either. Under Mayor West, streets were paved and water and sewer facilities installed.

The first commercial oil well in Calhoun County was discovered in 1934.

Corpus Christi was finding ways to grow. Farmers had redeemed brushland and made it bountiful. In 1918, Nueces County ginned 40,000 bales of cotton, the record for the county until that time, to aid the war effort. And when the United States entered World War I, North Beach, where Gen. Zachary Taylor's troops had camped prior to the Mexican War, became an army base again.

Although Corpus Christi had a port, ocean vessels could not reach the city. Harbor Island, 20 miles away at Aransas Pass, served as a port for most of the area. But on Sept. 14, 1919, another of the periodic hurricanes raked the coast. It was the worst storm to hit Corpus Christi, with tides reaching 10 and one-half feet. But Harbor Island was destroyed. Corpus Christi, like Houston, was aided by a quirk of weather.

In 1920, a federal survey of the coast to locate an adequate harbor was authorized and two years later, Corpus Christi was selected as the deep-water harbor site for the Southwest Texas coast. On Sept. 14, 1926, seven years to the day after the destructive hurricane, the new harbor was opened with access attained through a 25-foot deep channel running 21 miles to Aransas Pass. Through the next 20 years, Corpus Christi was to be transformed from a seaside town dependent on tourism and agriculture into a major industrial city.

The Depression hit Nueces County farmers hard, and they were glad to get federal help. When cotton acreage was retired under a federal program to reduce supply, grain sorghums were grown instead and became a major cash crop in the 1940s and 1950s. To solve the farmers' long-standing problem of access to short-term credit, the Coastal Bend Production Credit Association was created in 1934.

Corpus Christi began developing its airport by the clearing of land in 1928. Crop dusters originally used the airstrip, and Texas Air Transport inaugurated the city's first airline service in 1929, when the airport was officially opened.

In 1933, work began on a $7 million alkali plant, and by 1938, the port ranked fourth nationally in cotton shipments. Oil was discovered in 1930, to supplement previous natural gas production. Between 1936 and 1939, Nueces County added an average of one producing oil well per day. Refineries were attracted to the port facility.

On the eve of World War II, Congress authorized the Corpus Christi Naval Air Station, and construction began in 1940. Within 10 years, 32,000 naval aviators had trained at the facility, mostly during the war. Foster Field opened near Victoria in 1941, and the following year Aloe Field began training military pilots.

Texas' Gulf Coast was poised for its greatest era of growth, as war clouds darkened over Europe and Asia.

The Dynamo of Texas

World War II changed the character of Texas' Gulf Coast and pushed the region to the forefront of the state's economy. Houston became the largest city in the state in the 1930 U.S. Census, surpassing San Antonio and Dallas. The coast already was a factor in world trade and development. In 1930, for example, 57 percent of the world's sulphur supply was produced in Brazoria, Matagorda and Wharton counties.

In 1939-40, Dow Magnesium Corp. built a plant in Freeport to extract magnesium from seawater. And the Houston Ship Channel was well on its way to recovery from the effects of the Great Depression. Ellington Field in Houston also received its first contingent of airmen in 1941. The outbreak of World War II changed the coast forever.

Already the industrial center of Texas, the southeast corner of the state developed into an industrial giant in the 1940s because of war-related expansion. Two synthetic rubber plants were built along the ship channel, proving to be the forerunners of the giant petrochemical complex that marks the eastern Texas

coast. Refineries also expanded to help meet the demands of a world war. The San Jacinto Ordnance Depot was established on the ship channel by the U.S. Army, and a steel plant was built. In addition, two shipyards were built. The Houston Shipbuilding Corp., a subsidiary of Todd Shipbuilding of New York, turned out more than 200 cargo vessels and 14 tankers during the war. Brown Shipbuilding produced 300 vessels, including subchasers and escort ships. Shipyards also were operated in Orange and Galveston. As an industry, shipbuilding did not remain a major factor in employment after the war. But other industries, which had grown during the war, took up the slack.

During the conflict, $600 million were invested in chemical installations in Houston, and $300 million more were spent shortly after the war. In 1947, Phillips Petroleum Co. established a giant chemical installation. Texas City also became a petrochemical center. By 1965, the chemical industry in the so-called Golden Triangle of Freeport, Houston, Port Arthur-Orange employed 47,000 people at 187 installations. And after the

The Lyndon B. Johnson Space Center has had a major economic impact on Houston since opening in the mid-1960s. Photo Courtesy National Aeronautics and Space Administration.

war, the Houston ship channel began breaking tonnage records, handling 31.8 million tons in 1946 alone.

Houston also was expanding its transportation base. In 1946, the Civil Aeronautics Board designated Houston as an international air terminal. Eight years later, Houston International Airport, now William P. Hobby Airport, was opened, and in 1962, work began on the $100 million Houston Intercontinental Airport.

Tragedy marred the usually bright picture of development when in 1947 the Texas City port facility was struck by an explosion and subsequent fire that proved to be the worst man-made disaster in Texas history. Five hundred and twelve people died, 539 structures were destroyed and an estimated $200 million in damage was suffered.

While Houston and other coastal cities were growing during the post-war period, Galveston was only embellishing its reputation as a center of vice in the state. Although the Todd Shipyards operated the largest dry dock on the Gulf Coast, Galveston's economic base was tourism and vice. Local officials looked the other way — or even publicly touted the vices — as prostitution and gambling flourished. Finally in 1957, Texas Attorney General Will Wilson led a campaign to clean up the island city. Texas Rangers raided gambling establishments and warehouses and destroyed thousands of slot machines dumping the parts into the Gulf. The bad reputation gained as a sin center was in part dispelled when a civic cleanup campaign, headlined by attention to historic preservation, earned Galveston "All American City" recognition in 1962. The Moody Foundation, with a $440 million endowment, began operation in 1960 and gave the city a reputation for humanitarianism, which also helped dispel some of the previous bad image.

Houston's economic growth was diverse through the first six decades of the 20th century. Oil had provided a foundation, and by the mid-1960s, 10 major natural gas pipeline companies had headquarters in Houston. But the ship channel and the port played major roles. One study found in 1963 that the channel represented a $2.55 billion investment. Between 1910 and 1965, the federal government had invested $68 million in the channel and port, and in 1965 alone, $32.7 million in customs had been collected. A 1975 study by the University of Houston claimed that one-third of the money generated by the city was related to the port. The Texas Medical Center also is a major economic asset.

Houston's transportation matrix gained a new di-

mension in 1961 when the National Aeronautics and Space Administration announced that the new manned space craft center would be located 22 miles from Houston on land donated by Rice University. Within five years, the $60 million facility had more than 4,800 employees and a payroll of $50 million annually. Next to Spindletop, local observers contend, acquisition of the Lyndon B. Johnson Space Center has been the most important economic event in the city's history.

By 1976, Houston had gained a reputation as a true international city, attracting an estimated $200 million in foreign investment and hosting dozens of consuls and foreign branch banks.

Buoyed by spiraling oil prices, Houston continued spectacular growth through the 1970s. But when world oil prices dropped in the early 1980s, the city suffered a recession from which it is still recovering.

While many of the smaller coastal cities have become tourist and commercial fishing centers, Corpus Christi has had the most spectacular expansion outside Houston and the southeast Texas coast. As with the rest of the coast, Corpus Christi's industrial expansion began during the Second World War. Six refineries were built by 1951, and other industries expanded. Shipping was given a boost by the completion in 1949 of the Gulf Intracoastal Waterway from Corpus Christi to Brownsville. Manufacturing employment increased from 2,600 in 1940 to 6,500 in 1951. Shrimping gained importance in the early 1950s, with canneries established at Aransas Pass and Rockport, along with other coastal communities.

The deep-water port of Port Lavaca-Point Comfort was opened in 1963.

The petrochemical industry also boomed at Victoria and vicinity. Du Pont began a plant near Victoria in 1948, and soon Aluminum Company of America built a facility near Port Comfort and Union Carbide established a complex at Seadrift.

Tourism revived in Corpus Christi after the war, and in 1950, a four-mile causeway linking Corpus Christi and Padre Island was opened to traffic.

Texas' Gulf Coast has become a monument to man's ingenuity and determination to succeed. Beginning with modest physical assets that promised more potential than really existed, entrepreneurs have established 13 deep-water ports along the coast to attract trade and industry. None of the ports are natural, but were developed with vision and hard work, making Texas' coast the industrial cutting edge of the state's economy.

Bibliography

BOOKS

Allhands, James L., **Uriah Lott**; The Naylor Co., San Antonio, 1949.

Bender, George A., **Great Moments in Medicine**; Northwood Institute Press, 1966.

Bolton, Herbert Eugene, **Texas in the Middle Eighteenth Century: Studies in Spanish Colonial History and Administration**; University of California Publications in History, 1915 (rpt. University of Texas Press, Austin, 1970).

Boxer, C.R., **The Church Militant and Iberian Expansion, 1440-1770**; Johns Hopkins University Press, Baltimore, 1978.

Burke, James Wakefield, **A Forgotten Glory: The Missions of Old Texas**; Texian Press, Waco, 1979.

Castaneda, Carlos, **Our Catholic Heritage in Texas**, 7 volumes; Von Boeckmann-Jones Co., Publishers, Austin, 1936-1950.

Castaneda, Carlos, translator, **The Mexican Side of the Texas Revolution**; P.L. Turner Co., Austin, 1928 (rpt. Graphic Ideas, Inc., Austin, 1970).

Clark, James A., and Michel T. Halbouty, **Spindletop: The True Story of the Oil Discovery That Changed the World**; Gulf Publishing Co., Houston, 1952.

Clark, Joseph L., **The Texas Gulf Coast: Its History and Development**, 4 volumes; Lewis Historical Publishing Co., Inc., New York, 1955.

Connor, Seymour V., **Adventure in Glory**; Steck-Vaughn Co., Austin, 1965.

Corpus Christi Caller-Times, **Centennial History of Corpus Christi**; Corpus Christi Caller-Times, Corpus Christi, 1952.

Cox, George W., M.D., State Health Officer, **History of Public Health in Texas**; Texas State Department of Health, Austin, 1950.

Creighton, James A., **A Narrative History of Brazoria County**; Brazoria County Historical Commission, Angleton, 1975.

Crow, John A., **The Epic of Latin America**, Third Edition; University of California Press, Berkeley and Los Angeles, 1980.

Durant, Will, **The Reformation: Story of Civilization**, Part VI; Simon and Schuster, New York, 1957.

Durham, George, **Taming the Nueces Strip: The Story of McNelly's Rangers**; University of Texas Press, Austin, 1962.

Elliott, J.H., **Imperial Spain, 1469-1716**; New American Library, New York and Scarborough, Ontario.

Faculty and staff, UT Medical Branch at Galveston, **The University of Texas Medical Branch at Galveston: A 75-Year History**; University of Texas Press, Austin, 1967.

Fehrenbach, T.R., **Lone Star: A History of Texas and the Texans**; The MacMillan Co., New York, 1968.

Filisola, Don Vicente (translated by Wallace Woolsey), **Memoirs for the History of the War in Texas**; Eakin Press, Austin, 1985.

Fornell, Earl Wesley, **The Galveston Era: The Texas Crescent on the Eve of Seccession**; University of Texas Press, Austin, 1961.

Gouge, William M., **The Fiscal History of Texas**; Lippincott, Grambo, and Co., Philadelphia, 1852 (rpt. August M. Kelly, Publishers, New York, 1968).

Grimes, Roy, **300 Years in Victoria County**; Victoria Advocate Publishing Co., Victoria, 1968.

Harry, Jewel Horace, **A History of Chambers County**; Chambers County Historical Commission (Printed by Taylor Publishing Co., Dallas), 1981.

Hays, Charles W., **Galveston: History of the Island and the City**, 2 volumes; Jenkins Garrett Press, Austin, 1974.

Henson, Margaret Swett, **Juan Davis Blackburn: A Reappraisal of the Mexican Commander at Anahuac**; Texas A&M University Press, College Station, 1982.

Henson, Margaret Swett, **Samuel May Williams: Early Texas Entrepreneur**; Texas A&M University Press, College Station, 1976.

Holbrook, Stewart H., **The Story of American Railroads**; Bonanza Books, New York, 1947 (rpt. American Legacy Press, New York, 1981).

Hull, Anthony H., **Charles III and the Revival of Spain**; University Press of America, Washington, 1980.

Hurley, Marvin, **Decisive Years for Houston**; Houston Magazine, Houston Chamber of Commerce, Houston, 1966.

Huson, Hobart, **Refugio: A Comprehensive History of Refugio County from Aboriginal Times to 1955**, 2 volumes; The Rooke Foundation, Woodsboro, Texas, 1956.

Jackson, Donald, **Voyages of the Steamboat Yellow Stone**; Ticknor & Fields, New York, 1985.

Jensen, Oliver, **The American Heritage History of Railroads in America**; American Heritage Publishing Co., Inc, Bonanza Books, New York, 1975.

Jones, Billy M., **The Search for Maturity: The Saga of Texas, 1875-1900**; Steck-Vaughn Co., Austin, 1965.

Jordan, Terry G., **Trails to Texas: Southern Roots of Western Cattle Ranching**; University of Nebraska Press, Lincoln, 1981.

Larson, Henrietta M., and Kenneth W. Porter, **History of Humble Oil & Refining Company: A Study in Industrial Growth**; Harper & Brothers, New York, 1959.

Lynch, John, **Spain Under the Habsburgs**, 2 volumes; New York University Press, New York, 1984.

Malsch, Brownson, **Indianola: The Mother of Western Texas**; Shoal Creek Publishers, Inc., Austin, 1977.

Maril, Robert Lee, **Texas Shrimpers: Community, Capitalism and the Sea**; Texas A&M University Press, College Station, 1983.

Maxwell, Robert S., and Robert D. Baker, **Sawdust Empire: The Texas Lumber Industry, 1830-1940**; Texas A&M University Press, College Station, 1983.

McCampbell, Coleman, **Texas Seaport: The Story of the Growth of Corpus Christi and the Coastal Bend Area**; Exposition Press, New York, 1952.

McComb, David, **The Edge of Time: A History of Galveston**; University of Texas Press, Austin, 1986.

McComb, David, **Houston: A History**; University of Texas Press, Austin, 1981.

McDonald, Archie, **Travis**; Jenkins Publishing Co., The Pemberton Press, Austin, 1976.

McKay, Seth S., and Odie B. Faulk, **Texas After Spindletop, The Saga of Texas, 1901-1965**; Steck-Vaughn Co., Austin, 1965.

Miller, Ray, **Ray Miller's Galveston**; Cordovan Press, 1984.

Neill, Stephen, **A History of Christian Missions**; Pelican Books, New York, 1982.

Newcomb, W.W. Jr., **The Indians of Texas**; University of Texas Press, Austin, 1961.

Nixon, Pat Ireland, **The Medical Story of Early Texas, 1528-1853**; Mollie Bennett Lupe Memorial Fund, 1946.

Nueces County Historical Society, **The History of Nueces County**; Jenkins Publishing Co., Austin, 1972.

O'Connor, Kathryn Stoner, **Presidio La Bahia**; Von Boeckmann-Jones Co., Austin, 1966.

Partlow, Miriam, **Liberty, Liberty County and the Atascosito District**; The Pemberton Press, Jenkins Publishing Co., Austin, 1974.

Payne, Stanley G., **A History of Spain and Portugal**, 2 volumes; University of Wisconsin Press, Madison, 1973.

Puryear, Pamela Ashworth, and Nath Winfield Jr., **Sandbars and Sternwheelers: Steam Navigation on the Brazos**; Texas A&M University Press, College Station, 1976.

Reed, S.G., **A History of Texas Railroads**; St. Clair Publishing Co., Houston, 1941.

Refugio County History Book Committee of the Texas Extension Homemakers Council of Refugio County, **The History of Refugio County Texas**; Curtis Media Corp., Dallas, 1985.

Rister, Carl Coke, **Oil: Titan of the Southwest**; University of Oklahoma Press, Norman, 1949.

Robinson, Spencer W. (compiler and supervisor), **Spindletop: Where Oil Became an Industry**; Spindletop 50th Anniversary Commission, Beaumont, 1951.

Sibley, Marilyn McAdams, **The Port of Houston: A History**; University of Texas Press, Austin, 1968.

Siegel, Stanley E., **Houston: A Chronicle of the Supercity on Buffalo Bayou**; Harris County Historical Society, Houston, and Windsor Publications, Inc., Woodland Hills, Calif., 1983.

Silverthorne, Elizabeth, **Ashbel Smith of Texas: Pioneer, Patriot, Statesman, 1805-1886**; Texas A&M University Press, College Station, 1982.

Smyrl, Frank H., **Texas in Gray: The Civil War Years, 1861-1865**; American Press, Boston, 1983.

Smyrl, Frank H., **The Twenty-Eighth Star: Texas During the Period of Early Statehood, 1846-1851**; American Press, Boston, 1983.

Sowell, A.J., **History of Fort Bend County: Containing Biographical Sketches of Many Noted Characters**; W.H. Coyle & Co., Stationers and Printers, Houston, 1904.

Thonhoff, Robert H., **The Texas Connection**; Eakin Press, Burnet, 1981.

Houston's Astrodome, called the eighth wonder of the world when opened in 1965, has hosted major football, baseball and basketball games and is a major tourist attraction.

Victoria Advocate, **Indianola Scrap Book: History of a City That Once was the Gateway of Commerce for This Entire Section**; Victoria Advocate, Victoria, 1936.

Vigness, David, **The Revolutionary Decades: The Saga of Texas, 1810-1836**; Steck-Vaughn Co., Austin, 1965.

Wallace, Ernest, **Texas in Turmoil: The Saga of Texas, 1849-1875**; Steck-Vaughn, Austin, 1965.

Warner, C.A., **Texas Oil and Gas Since 1543**; Gulf Publishing Co., Houston, 1939.

Webb, Walter Prescott, and H. Bailey Carroll, editors, **The Handbook of Texas**, 2 volumes; Texas State Historical Association, Austin, 1952.

Weber, David, editor, **New Spain's Far Northern Frontier: Essays on Spain in the American West, 1540-1821**; University of New Mexico Press, Albuquerque, 1979.

Weddle, Robert S., **Spanish Sea: The Gulf of Mexico in North American Discovery, 1500-1685**; Texas A&M University Press, College Station, 1985.

Wheeler, Kenneth W., **To Wear a City's Crown: The Beginnings of Urban Growth in Texas, 1836-1865**; Harvard University Press, Cambridge, 1968.

Wintz, Cary D., **Reconstruction in Texas**; American Press, Boston, 1983.

ARTICLES

Biffle, Kent, **Nothing Lasts on the Coast's Shifting Sand**; The Dallas Morning News, Aug. 25, 1985.

Bolton, Herbert E., **The Location of LaSalle's Colony on the Gulf of Mexico**; Mississippi Valley Historical Review, September 1915.

Henson, Margaret Swett, **Tory Sentiment in Anglo-Texan Public Opinion, 1832-1836**; Southwestern Historical Quarterly, Vol. XC, No. 1, July 1986, Austin.

Scott, Bess, **Texians on the High Seas**; Texas Highways, February 1983.

Acknowledgements

Texas history begins on the Gulf Coast when Spaniards and other Europeans first began to map the region and to establish settlements. The numerous rivers emptying into the Gulf and the natural harbors first gave rise to dreams of riches. Only after the first Anglo-Americans settled, however, was it to be learned that the great economic potential of the region could be tapped only with a high investment of blood, sweat, tears and dollars.

The story of the development of the state's Gulf Coast, therefore, is a tale of man's conquest of nature. None of the 13 ports now functioning is natural; all had to be developed with foresight and energy.

Mike Kingston, editor of the Texas Almanac, prepared this brief history of the Gulf Coast. He wishes to thank the following historians for their help in gathering material and in presenting it accurately: Dr. Don Carleton, director, Eugene C. Barker Texas History Center, University of Texas at Austin; Dan Kilgore, Corpus Christi; Bob Nesbitt, Galveston; George Fred Rhodes, Port Lavaca; Dr. Stanley Siegel, professor of history, University of Houston; Dr. James Tinsley, professor of history University of Houston; Bill Walraven, Corpus Christi; and Robert S. Weddle, Bonham. Also appreciation is extended to Mary G. Crawford, associate editor of the Texas Almanac, for proofreading and editing.

Any errors, of course, are the author's alone.

An Economy in Transition—The Texas Gulf Coast

This article was prepared by Dr. Bernard L. Weinstein, director of the Center for Enterprising in the Edwin L. Cox School of Business at Southern Methodist University.

The economic history of both early and modern Texas is centered on the Gulf Coast. Because of its 600 miles of shoreline and numerous rivers, bays and estuaries, the Texas Gulf Coast was the first area of settlement. Small towns began dotting the crescent from Brownsville to Orange during the early 19th century, and many of these towns grew rapidly after the Republic of Texas was formed in 1836.

During the 19th century, the principal industries of the Gulf Coast were farming and shipping. The primary crops then, as now, were rice and cotton, with rice dominating the upper Gulf Coast and cotton the lower Gulf Coast. Texas' early ranching industry was also concentrated along the Gulf Coast.

Throughout the 19th century, Galveston was one of the busiest ports on the Gulf of Mexico. Major products exported from Galveston were foodstuffs, timber and fiber, while manufactured goods and "people" were the principal imports. In fact, in the late 19th century, Galveston became a major port of debarkation for European refugees who could not be processed at New York's overcrowded facilities.

The Gulf Coast was also the site of Texas' industrial revolution in the early 20th century. In 1901, oil was discovered at Spindletop near Beaumont, and the course of Texas' economic history was forever altered. Within two decades of the famous Anthony Lucas gusher, the entire Gulf Coast economy had been transformed from an agrarian to an industrial base. Crude oil helped to generate an elaborate industrial structure that supported the exploration, drilling, pumping, processing, distribution and marketing of petroleum products. Almost overnight, huge refineries and chemical plants sprang up along the Texas Gulf coastline. A huge steel and metal fabrication industry also evolved to serve the needs of the petrochemical sector for drilling pipe, pumps and other types of oil-field equipment.

A maze of pipelines was constructed up and down the Gulf Coast to bring crude oil to refineries and then to send finished products to America's industrial heartland. A great boom was underway that would transform cities like Beaumont, Port Arthur, Galveston, Houston and Corpus Christi into crowded, bustling and wealthy metropolises. Texas possessed in great abundance what America wanted most: energy to feed its growing industrial machine.

The growth of mining and manufacturing more or less signaled the demise of agriculture as the Gulf Coast's primary industry. Because coastal land values escalated rapidly during the early 20th century, Texas' crop and livestock industries migrated to the High Plains where land was cheap and abundant. Though the High Plains lacked adequate rainfall to support most crops, inexpensive natural gas permitted the tapping of underground aquifers to irrigate huge tracts of dry land.

By the 1920s, the Gulf Coast was starting to lose its pre-eminence as an energy-producing region, a result of the discovery of huge new fields in West Texas. Nonetheless, the Gulf Coast economy continued to expand in chemicals, refining, shipbuilding and repair, offshore services and oil-field and general manufacturing. This growth continued virtually without interruption until 1980.

Recent Economic and Population Trends in the Texas Gulf Coast

Until fairly recently, the economy of the Texas Gulf Coast was riding high. The dramatic escalation of oil prices during the 1970s, a result of embargos by the Organization of Petroleum Exporting Countries and worldwide shortages, created boom conditions along the Gulf Coast not seen since the beginning of the century. More than 1,800 petrochemical plants and petroleum refineries were providing thousands of jobs and billions of dollars in income to the area's work force. Shipbuilding, rig fabrication, metalworking and oil-field services also contributed greatly to regional prosperity.

Rapid population growth attended the economic boom of the 1970s. All of the metropolitan areas along the Texas Gulf Coast, with the exception of Beaumont-Port Arthur, recorded population gains in excess of the national average between 1970 and 1980 (see Table 1). Most spectacular was Houston's growth of 3.7 percent annually, a rate more than three times the national average. In Houston, and most other parts of the Gulf Coast, migration from outside of Texas accounted for a large part of the population gains.

During the first half of the 1980s, population growth slowed somewhat for the Gulf Coast while it picked up slightly in other parts of the state. Over the past two years, population growth in most Gulf Coast communities has probably ceased, a consequence of a sharp drop in net in-migration and the collapse of oil prices during 1985 and 1986, which wreaked havoc upon many sectors of the Texas economy and displaced several hundred thousand workers in key industries along the Gulf Coast.

The debacle of 1985-86 had been building up for several years. A decline in oil prices, a sluggish national economy and worldwide overcapacity in the region's basic industries eventually transpired to bring a halt to the Gulf Coast's economic expansion. Lately, employment, income and output have actually contracted, a situation that would have been inconceivable a mere five years ago. The pervasiveness of this decline is vividly illustrated in Table 2.

All five Gulf Coast metropolitan areas are posting lower total employment levels today than in 1984. As the numbers suggest, the upper Gulf Coast has been hit harder than the lower Gulf Coast, probably because of its heavier dependency on the petrochemical industry. The sharpest percentage decline in employment has been recorded in the Beaumont-Port Arthur area, while Corpus Christi and Victoria have remained relatively stable over the past seven years in terms of total employment.

A bleaker picture of the Gulf Coast economy develops if we concentrate on the manufacturing sector.

Table 1
Population Growth
1970-85
Texas Gulf Coast Metropolitan Areas

	1970	1980	1985	Average Annual Percent Change	
				1970-80	1980-85
Beaumont-Port Arthur	347,568	375,497	381,400	0.8%	0.3%
Houston	1,999,316	2,734,617	3,221,700	3.7	3.6
Galveston-Texas City	169,792	195,738	213,400	1.5	1.8
Victoria	53,766	68,807	75,500	2.8	1.9
Corpus Christi	284,830	326,228	358,800	1.4	2.0
Brazoria	N.A.	169,587	188,200	N.A.	2.2
State of Texas	11,198,655	14,228,383	16,385,000	2.7	3.0
U.S.	203,810,000	226,545,000	238,740,000	1.1	1.1

N.A.—Not available.

Source: Bureau of the Census.

Since 1980, tremendous job losses have been recorded in manufacturing in every Gulf Coast metropolitan area. In Beaumont-Port Arthur and Houston, nearly 40 percent of the manufacturing jobs have disappeared. In fact, the degree of contraction in Gulf Coast heavy industry far surpasses the experience of the Great Lakes region during the 1970s when large layoffs occurred in the automobile, steel, and rubber and tire industries.

The bulk of manufacturing employment losses in recent years has occurred in high-wage industries such as refining, chemicals, shipbuilding and metal fabrication.

Consequently, billions of dollars of purchasing power has been withdrawn from the regional economy. As Table 3 illustrates, average annual pay along the upper Texas Gulf Coast remains quite high. But many fewer workers are employed at these high wage rates as compared to five or six years ago.

Structural Change in the Oil Field and Its Impact on the Texas Gulf Coast Economy

Over the past six years, the Texas economy has diversified and restructured, though this diversification has occurred principally because of a sharp contraction in mining and manufacturing. Since 1981, Texas has lost nearly 234,000 jobs in these sectors, due mainly to the beleaguered energy industry. Employment in the primary and fabricated metals industries has declined at average annual rates of 8.6 percent and 4.8 percent respectively since 1981, while the oil-field equipment industry has lost jobs at the rate of 13.1 percent per year. As indicated above, a disproportionate share of these job losses has been recorded along the Texas Gulf Coast.

Texas' energy dependence has two important dimensions. First, nearly all of Texas' mining and much of the state's durable-goods manufacturing is highly sensitive to fluctuations in the price of oil. Second, a significant portion of non-durable manufacturing is concentrated in petroleum refining and petrochemicals. Both components of the energy sector—production and processing—are in the throes of structural change, and the effects are being felt across Texas and especially in the Gulf Coast.

In 1981, the price of a barrel of West Texas Intermediate (WTI) stood at roughly $35, and most energy economists were predicting even higher prices by mid-decade. But $35 oil encouraged exploration and drilling activity to an unprecedented degree, both in Texas and throughout the non-OPEC world. Very quickly, the world's energy "problem" became one of oversupply and not scarcity. North Sea producers in particular—the United Kingdom, Netherlands and Norway—began in late-1981 to flood world markets with comparatively inexpensive crude oil, effectively undercutting the OPEC cartel's, posted price of $35 per barrel.

Since 1981, oil prices have been on a roller-coaster ride, but the overall trend has been downward, so that in 1986 oil prices averaged only $15 per barrel. Lower prices have forced many small and independent producers to cut back drastically, and the demand for drilling equipment has plummeted. To illustrate, in 1981 the number of active drilling rigs in Texas topped 1,300. In May 1987, the rig count stood at a mere 265.

Particularly hard hit by falling oil prices have been the state's primary and fabricated metal, non-electrical machinery and shipbuilding industries, which produce pipe and valve, oil field machinery and drilling

Refineries along the Gulf Coast were among the victims of the drop in oil prices in the mid-1980s. Dallas Morning News Photo.

rigs for the oil companies. These industries dominate the Gulf Coast region and have been double whammied by declining demand and import competition from drilling equipment manufacturers in Europe and shipbuilders in Taiwan and Korea.

Equally strong forces are transforming the Texas Gulf Coast refiners and petrochemical processors, who account for a substantial proportion of the state's non-durable manufacturing and industrial construction employment. In 1980, for example, there were 56 active refineries in Texas with a combined capacity of nearly million barrels per calendar day (B/CD) (see Table 4) By 1985, the number of active refineries had fallen to 35 and capacity had been reduced by nearly 20 percent to just under 4 million B/CD. Naturally, refinery closures and capacity reductions have meant substantial layoff of refinery workers, and refinery construction activity has diminished to small, periodic maintenance and turnarounds.

Other forces are also at work to restructure Texas refining and petrochemical sectors and, concomitantly, the Gulf Coast region. Recent mergers and acquisitions among the major oil companies are being accompanied by the disposition of refinery assets, either to satisfy legal requirements or to raise cash to reduce debt burdens. It is also becoming cheaper to buy refined products and bulk petrochemicals abroad than to produce them domestically.

Within the context of declining mining and manufacturing employment statewide, the current wave of structural change in Texas is being followed by a transfer of vitality and power between two very distinct regional economies: North Central Texas, comprising largely the Dallas-Fort Worth metropolitan area, and the Gulf Coast. The former is characterized by a com

Table 2

Texas Gulf Coast Metropolitan Areas
Employment Changes, 1980-87

	Employment (000)						Percentage Change 1980-87	
	1980		1984		Feb. 1987			
	Total		Total		Total		Total	
	Non-Ag.	Mfg.	Non-Ag.	Mfg.	Non-Ag.	Mfg.	Non-Ag.	Mfg.
Beaumont-Port Arthur	148.7	38.5	141.0	30.5	127.2	24.1	—14.4%	—37.4%
Houston	1,439.3	240.2	1,539.7	197.2	1,371.9	147.5	—4.7	—38.6
Galveston-Texas City	70.3	11.4	72.0	10.1	69.2	9.0	—1.6	—21.1
Victoria	27.1	3.5	28.4	2.9	27.9	3.0	3.0	—14.3
Corpus Christi	124.7	16.1	131.0	14.7	128.1	11.8	2.7	—26.7

Source: Texas Employment Commission.

Table 3
Average Annual Pay
Gulf Coast Metropolitan Areas
1984-85

	1984	1985	Percent Change 1984-85
Beaumont-Port Arthur	$20,194	$20,349	0.8%
Houston	22,188	22,938	3.4
Galveston-Texas City	19,126	19,321	1.0
Victoria	17,513	17,804	1.7
Corpus Christi	17,741	18,387	3.6
Brazoria	21,922	22,569	2.9
U.S. Metropolitan Average	18,934	19,816	4.7

Source: Bureau of Labor Statistics.

paratively diversified, non-energy oriented, locally-controlled manufacturing base, while the Gulf Coast's economic base is externally controlled and highly susceptible to oil price shocks and the restructuring of energy processing.

Additional energy sector contraction in Texas is very likely, if not a virtual certainty, given continued pressure on oil prices and remaining overcapacity in the state's refineries and petrochemical plants. Though crude oil prices have trended upwards in recent months, it seems unlikely the OPEC cartel will be able to control prices as they did in the past. Moreover, any agreement by OPEC is probably superfluous, since non-OPEC producers can easily undercut the cartel through sales in the spot market.

With respect to the processing side of the oil industry, the Texas Gulf Coast should expect no relief. Despite plant closings and significant reductions in throughput, the refining industry nationwide remains characterized by overcapacity, a shrinking refined product market and increasing foreign competition. In fact, it is highly likely that by the end of the century the U.S. refining industry will employ 50,000 fewer workers than it does today, and many of those jobs will be lost in Texas.

Texas Gulf Coast
Metropolitan Area Profiles

Six metropolitan areas are found along the Texas Gulf Coast. All of these areas in mid-1987 were posting unemployment rates above the Texas statewide average, and several were witnessing a decline in the size of the local labor force (see Table 5). An analysis of the economic conditions and outlook for the Texas Gulf Coast metropolitan areas follows.

Beaumont-Port Arthur-Orange

Often referred to as the "Golden Triangle" or the "Triplex," the Beaumont-Port Arthur metropolitan area is the second largest on the Gulf Coast. It has also been the slowest-growing metropolitan area in Texas during the 1980s. According to the U.S. Bureau of the Census, the Triplex ranked 90th in size in 1985 among the nation's 317 statistically defined metropolitan areas with a population of 381,400. In 1980, it ranked 88th in the nation.

The industrial structure of the Beaumont-Port Arthur area is quite different from the state as a whole. Perhaps more than any other part of the state, heavy industry dominates the Golden Triangle. Manufacturing, construction and the transportation-communications-public utilities sectors account for 32 percent of the jobs in the area. By contrast, these sectors account for only 25 percent of total payroll employment statewide. Conversely, Beaumont-Port Arthur is significantly underrepresented in mining, finance-insurance-real estate, and government employment.

At present, there are about 250 manufacturing firms located in the Golden Triangle. Though companies such as Texaco, Mobil and Gulf States Utilities dominate the region, 70 percent of the manufacturing establishments in the Triplex employ fewer than 50 employees. Fabricated metal products and non-electrical machinery, typically small operations, are the most numerous industrial establishments in the area. Electronics, aerospace and other high-tech sectors are virtually absent.

The Golden Triangle has consistently posted the highest unemployment rate on the Gulf Coast for the past five years, due to its heavy dependence on petrochemicals and related industries. In recent years, the labor force has contracted, suggesting people are leaving the area in search of job opportunities elsewhere. On the plus side, workers in the Golden Triangle are typically well-paid, and both per-capita and median family income exceed the national norms. Retail sales also remain fairly strong.

The outlook for Beaumont-Port Arthur is less than rosy, and no substantial pickup can be anticipated until oil prices recover or the local economy diversifies. The area's refiners and chemical plants are unlikely to add employment, and the 75 percent drop in the rig count has caused the demand for machinery, pipe and oil field services to dry up. Other major industries in the Golden Triangle, such as steel, rubber and shipbuilding, are also in secular decline.

Houston

Houston is the largest metropolitan area on the Gulf Coast, with a current population of more than 3 million. Houston can rightly be called Energy City, U.S.A., and herein lies the explanation for its former strength and its current weakness.

Houston's population gains during the 1970s and early 1980s were remarkable. Growth between 1970 and 1980 averaged 3.7 percent annually, and between 1980 and 1982 Houston's population grew by an incredible 12 percent. Since 1982, however, population growth has slowed considerably. In fact, during 1986 the area's population actually dropped 1.6 percent. Migration has accounted for a large part of Houston's growth and decline over the past decade. As recently as 1982, Houston recorded net in-migration of 150,000 persons. A short four years later, in 1986, the Houston area recorded net out-migration of 94,000.

Job growth in Houston also was remarkable from the early 1970s through the early 1980s. From 1970 to 1980, nonagricultural employment in Houston grew at an average annual rate of 8.9 percent, faster than that recorded in any other large U.S. city. Between 1980 and 1984, however, job growth averaged a mere 0.6 percent per annum, slightly below the national and state averages. For the past three years, employment growth has

Table 4
Change in Refineries and Refining Capacity in Texas
1980-85 and 1975-1980

Active Refineries 1985	Active Refineries 1980	Active Refineries 1975	Total Capacity 1985 (B/CD)	Total Capacity 1980 (B/CD)	Total Capacity 1975 (B/CD)	Percent Chg. in Capacity 1980-1985	Percent Chg. in Capacity 1975-1980
35	56	45	3,936,124	4,878,875	3,929,430	−19.3%	19.2%

Source: U.S. Department of Energy, Energy Information Administration.

been negative, resulting in the loss of about 168,000 payroll jobs. While average wages and per-capita income remain high in Houston, the region has suffered considerable losses in total income and purchasing power in recent years.

In large part, Houston's industrial mix accounts for the recent pattern of job losses. The bulk of these losses, not surprisingly, is to be found in the area's once-booming energy sector, which encompasses a number of manufacturing industries and also greatly influences contract construction. Since 1980, approximately 93,000 manufacturing jobs have disappeared from the Houston area, or 38.6 percent of the industrial employment base. (During the 1970s, by contrast, Houston gained manufacturing employment at the rate of 7.1 percent per year.) In fact, Houston has lost manufacturing jobs more rapidly over the past seven years than either the nation or the state of Texas, a characteristic shared by most other Gulf Coast metropolitan areas.

Currently, there are about 3,000 manufacturing firms in Houston. Despite the prevalance of heavy industry in the area, only 23 firms employ more than 1,000 workers. Seventy-three percent of the manufacturing establishments in Houston employ less than 50 employees.

Though the past few years have been difficult ones for Houston, the worst may be over. Between mid-1986 and mid-1987, net out-migration from Houston has slowed and should reach only 38,000 in 1987. The number of unemployed persons in Houston has also declined over the past year, although this drop can be partly explained by out-migration. As with most other Gulf Coast areas, Houston's labor force has been contracting for the past two years.

Greater Houston is an integral part of a larger, energy-based regional economy experiencing major structural change. Through the changes in Houston's manufacturing employment base that have occurred over the past seven years, the area's economy is being permanently transformed. Economic diversification is being achieved, but the diversity has come about primarily by contraction. The major challenge to Houston's economic development community in the years ahead will be to revitalize the area's manufacturing sector so that growth in non-industrial sectors may be sustained.

Galveston-Texas City

The Galveston-Texas City metropolitan area, with a population of 213,400 in 1985, is really an economic subsidiary of Greater Houston. Not only is it contiguous to Houston, but its industrial structure is quite similar to that of Houston, especially the Texas City portion. And, like Houston, Galveston-Texas City has suffered from the fallout of lower oil prices in recent years.

In relative terms, Galveston-Texas City's job losses haven't been as severe as those in Houston, probably due to the positive influence of non-energy related employment on Galveston Island. Though traffic through the Port of Galveston has been depressed, the convention and tourism business has remained relatively strong. Galveston is also home to a medical school and a major complex of hospitals and other medical-care facilities that employ thousands of island and mainland residents.

The economic outlook for the Galveston-Texas City metropolitan area is uncertain. A real-estate boom that was underway in 1986 has collapsed, and local refineries and chemical plants continue to cut back. But Galveston's port and recreational facilities should prove to be

significant assets over the long term, especially if casino gambling is eventually approved.

Brazoria

Brazoria is also part of the Greater Houston conurbation. With a population of 188,000, it is the second-smallest metropolitan area on the Texas Gulf Coast. Located south of the city of Houston and west of Galveston, Brazoria is predominantly rural despite its metropolitan designation. The largest city in Brazoria County is Lake Jackson, with a population of 20,000. Alvin, the second largest city at 18,000, is actually a suburb of Houston.

Brazoria's major industries are refining, petrochemicals and oil-field equipment. As is the case in other parts of the state, these industries have been contracting for several years. But in recent months, energy-related employment has stabized, and the unemployment rate has dropped somewhat.

An economic rebound for Brazoria will be contingent upon a recovery of oil prices and increased rice exports. In this vein, American Rice is adding 300 permanent jobs to a new rice-processing facility.

Victoria

Victoria is the smallest metropolitan area in Texas, with a 1985 population of 75,500. The City of Victoria comprises about two-thirds of the county population. Population growth has occurred at a modest pace since 1970, and Victoria has been the least affected among the Texas Gulf Coast metropolitan areas by the collapse in the energy sector. Though employment in the region's petrochemical facilities has contracted in recent years, overall employment has continued to grow.

Income growth in Victoria has also been quite respectable. In 1983, the latest year for which substate data are available, per-capita income in Victoria was $9,398—just slightly below the Texas average of $9,443.

Recently, cogeneration construction projects have added several hundred jobs to the region's economy, though not enough to overcome the job losses in refining and petrochemicals. Victorians are currently attempting to diversify their economy by nurturing promising small companies rather than luring large industries to the region.

Corpus Christi

Located 320 miles southwest of Orange, Corpus Christi has the most diversified economy among the six Texas Gulf Coast metropolitan areas. With a 1985 population of 358,800, Corpus Christi is the 97th-largest urban area in the United States, up from 99th in 1980. Corpus Christi is the only area on the Gulf Coast still attracting migrants from other regions. Though the unemployment rate has risen slightly over the past year, the resident labor force and total employment continue to grow.

Corpus Christi differs from the rest of the Gulf Coast in that only 13 percent of its employment base was centered in manufacturing in 1980. By contrast, 17 percent of Houston's jobs and 26 percent of Beaumont-Port Arthur's jobs were concentrated in the manufacturing sector. Consequently, the drastic drop in energy-related manufacturing employment that occurred between 1980 and 1987 did not disrupt the Corpus Christi economy to the same degree as the upper Gulf Coast.

Agriculture, food processing, tourism and a large military presence also help to insulate Corpus Christi from the vicissitudes of the energy cycle and augur well for the future. Over the next few years, millions of federal dollars will pour into Nueces County to construct a new "home port" for the U.S.S. Wisconsin and various support vessels.

Table 5
Labor Force and Unemployment Rates
Texas Gulf Coast
March 1987 vs. March 1986

	Unemployment Rates		Labor Force	
	3/87	3/86	3/87	3/86
Beaumont-Port Arthur	12.2%	14.6%	157,700	161,900
Houston	9.0	9.3	1,570,700	1,606,000
Galveston-Texas City	10.3	10.9	104,300	106,600
Victoria	9.1	9.1	37,500	37,400
Corpus Christi	11.3	10.9	165,400	162,500
Brazoria	9.3	10.3	79,300	80,000
State of Texas	8.2	8.4	8,106,800	8,024,800

Source: Texas Employment Commission.

Bordering On...
The Majestic.

The sunsets are worth the move. The sky becomes a painter's palette of violet blues meshing with soft pinks and hues of yellow and orange. The colors slip behind a protective mountain range that guards two countries and over 400 years of history.

The accolades attributed to this expanding international metroplex don't stop with the explosions of colors that calm the senses. The twin cities of El Paso/Juarez combine urban with rural, ancient with new and a topography that blends deserts with mountains and valleys to herald it as one of the healthiest environments in the United States for industrial growth.

Year-round perfect weather encourages the joining of a potpourri of cultures in a variety of sports, entertainment, restaurants and annual events. The unlimited sunshine provides the energy for enhanced productivity.

Bordering on the majestic, the El Paso/Juarez mix can guarantee your business the highest quality of life through its active interest in the community's future growth.

For more information contact Denise Higgins, El Paso Industrial Development Corporation, 9 Civic Center Plaza, El Paso, Texas 79901, (915) 532-8281.

El Paso Electric

The blessing of the shrimp fleet in April is always a major event in Galveston and other ports along the Texas Gulf Coast. Photo Courtesy the Texas Department of Highways and Public Transportation.

Exploring The Texas Gulf Coast

This article was prepared for the Texas Almanac by Carol Barrington of Houston, a free-lance travel writer.

Exploring the entire Texas coast isn't an easy or short-term project — there's a lot of it, 624 tidewater miles to be exact. For more than 500 of those miles, it isn't one coast, it's two, with precious few connecting links.

A long string of barrier islands separates the Gulf of Mexico from most of the mainland, creating numerous quiet bays and long estuaries known in their totality as the Laguna Madre. Thrown up by wind and wave to blunt the brunt of storms that often blow in from June through September, these narrow strips of sand also nearly double the coastal recreational territory.

Some of those islands, such as Galveston and the north and south tips of Padre Island, are sandy playgrounds for thousands of vacationers every month. Others — Matagorda and San Jose are good examples — are far more wild and accessible only by boat. No condos, no beach umbrellas; just surf and gulls greet the occasional visitor.

Essentially, there are two major bases for exploring the coast: the resort city of Corpus Christi and the small communities sprinkled around its sparkling bay, and historic Galveston with its big city neighbor, Houston. Each is a destination in itself as well as being a gateway to the wildlife refuges, parks and open territory that make the Texas coast unique.

Corpus Christi Bay was named by Spanish explorers, but its namesake settlement didn't come to life as a frontier trading post until about 1839. Now a city of almost 260,000, Corpus Christi is booming with new hotels, restaurants and family-style fun. Within the past three years two new high-rise hotels have opened on its downtown waterfront, and nearby Mustang Island is a hotbed of condominium resort development.

Corpus Christi's cultural scene is thriving also, thanks to the Bayfront Plaza at the north end of palm-lined Shoreline Boulevard. The Art Museum of South Texas is part of that complex, as is the Corpus Christi Museum with its excellent "touching" exhibits for children.

"Old Irishtown" is a short walk away, a small plaza of period homes that has been preserved at Heritage Park. For another look at Corpus Christi's past, visit Centennial House, built in 1849 at what is now 411 N.

Broadway and thought to be the oldest structure in the city. Recently restored and furnished, it now flies a flag on the one day a week that it is open for tours.

Old houses and new hotels aside, Corpus Christi's big attraction is its beautiful and bountiful bay. Reveling in one of the least polluted environments in the country, this usually sunny city offers aquatic activities nearly year-round. Swimming is pleasant April through October, and nearly everything fun that floats — from aqua-trikes to jet skis — can be rented at the People's Street T-Head dock during the summer months.

This downtown waterfront also boasts an outstanding marina, plus there is rewarding year-round fishing from numerous municipal piers and jetties as well as aboard charter boats. An abundance of fish — more than 10 species — is regularly caught in Corpus Christi Bay.

A steady breeze is another blessing — sailing and windsurfing are ways of life here, and both lessons and rentals are offered at Corpus Christi Beach from May through September. Also called North Beach, this 1.4-mile-long strip of protected sand is across the Harbor Bridge at the north end of town. Families with small children also enjoy the shallow waters of McGee Beach on Shoreline Drive downtown.

"Must do's" in Corpus Christi include renting a pedal surrey for a cruise down the two-mile-long seawall and catching a close-up view of the city and its sailboats from the deck of Lighthouse Restaurant at the marina.

Other bits of fun include a sightseeing tour of the city's bay and boat harbor (the seventh largest in the nation) aboard the "Flagship" paddlewheeler and a day on the Tex-Mex Express, a five-car passenger train. This newly restored train is pulled by a diesel locomotive that makes the 157-mile round-trip between Corpus Christi and Laredo on Friday, Saturday and Sunday.

Annual celebrations in this resort city start with Buccaneer Days the last week of April, an 11-day festival featuring parades, fireworks, carnival, sailing regatta and assorted sporting and musical competitions.

Corpus Christi becomes a jazz enthusiast's paradise with a city-wide annual Jazz Festival the second week of

Bordering On...
The Abundant.

Without a doubt, the sunshine is replete. But the El Paso/Juarez Metroplex abounds in a variety of benefits that make it one of the most advantageous areas to live in the Southwest for growing companies.

A readily available work force, willing to work, insures high productivity within the industries, and low direct labor costs including benefits make employment attractive.

In addition, manufacturing and engineering consortiums offer companies a vast arena of talent from which to select professional personnel. Jointly, the cities provide a variety of technical and managerial training institutions as well as universities and a community college which interface closely with the industrial community.

Consider the El Paso/Juarez mix when you want your profit and productivity to abound.

For more information contact Denise Higgins, El Paso Industrial Development Corporation, 9 Civic Center Plaza, El Paso, Texas 79901, (915) 532-8281.

El Paso Electric

July. Bayfest in late September brings thousands to the waterfront, and the Harbor Lights celebration in early December lights the masts of nearly every sailboat in the marina.

Corpus Christi is the gateway to three satellite vacation areas on the Gulf: North Padre Island National Seashore, Port Aransas and Mustang Island, and Rockport-Fulton Beach.

North Padre Island National Seashore is a 20-minute drive south of the city via South Padre Island Drive and the John F. Kennedy Causeway. Day visitors to this barrier island should bypass the commercial and condominium development near the south end of the bridge and continue south to the Padre Island National Seashore.

PINS, with some 80 miles of open sand, is considered by environmentalists to be the largest and best natural beach left in America. Visitors can stop first at the Malaquite Beach visitors' area for information and then head for the sand. Beachcombing and shelling are rewarding — glass fishing floats still wash up on shore occasionally — and body surfing can be a thrill.

A second recreation area on North Padre Island, Balli Park, has the 1,240-foot-long Bob Hall Fishing Pier and a complete concession area. During peak tourist months a special municipal bus known as the Beach-B runs between Corpus Christi's major hotels and Padre Island Beach. Coolers, surfboards, chairs and such are welcome and the bus is air-conditioned, a lifesaver in summer.

Further information on the area is available from the Corpus Christi Convention & Tourist Bureau, Box 2664, Corpus Christi, TX 78403-2664; (512) 882-5603.

Surfers and real solitude seekers should swing left (north) at the end of the JFK Causeway and explore Mustang Island, another beautiful legacy from centuries of storms. The new J. P. Luby Youth Park has a scientifically designed surfing beach — those pilings offshore have been strategically placed to form waves — and farther up the road, the Mustang Island State Park has excellent sun-and-fun visitor facilities.

Port Aransas, at the northern tip of Mustang Island, is a ramshackle fishing town, well-known for its old relic of a hotel, the Tarpon Inn. The lobby walls are covered with thousands of tarpon scales autographed by successful fishermen, one of whom was President Franklin D. Roosevelt. Once a common catch in the deeper waters of the gulf and then nearly fished out, the giant tarpon are returning in greater numbers each year.

Two special treats in Port Aransas include charter-boat fishing from Fisherman's Wharf and riding the inexpensive passenger ferry, picnic in hand, to spend a day on deserted San Jose Island. The ferry has 10 departures daily, and visitors can stay as long as they like on the island, which provides real solitude. There are no facilities on this large island, however, so basic toiletries, water, sun lotion and umbrella, as well as fishing gear and a seine for gathering shrimp from the surf must be provided by the visitor.

Summer means fishing tournaments in Port Aransas, where everyone is welcome. The Deep Sea Round-Up in early July brings record catches of sailfish, marlin, redfish and shark to the town docks, and the Outboard Fishing Tournament follows later that month, limited to record fish caught from boats with outboard motors only. Then follows a shark-catching competition the end of the month, with the Dean Hawn Memorial Billfish Tournament in early August, a major international competition, completing the schedule.

Direct requests for information to the Port Aransas Chamber of Commerce, Box 356, Port Aransas, TX 78373; phone (800) 242-3084 in Texas; (800) 221-9198 elsewhere.

A second ferry links Port Aransas with the mainland, a free ride that often has leaping porpoises as escorts. Following Texas 361 and Texas 35 north soon brings visitors to the twin towns of Rockport and Fulton Beach. Both have become artists' havens. There is the first-rate Rockport Art Center near the harbor and the galleries scattered along Austin Street. Rockport's crescent beach on Aransas Bay is one of the most beautiful on the coast and perfect for family outings and picnics. Nearby in the turning basin, the Texas Parks and Wildlife Marine Lab and Aquarium is free and open for tours on weekdays, and the adjacent boat basin thrives with fishing charters and shrimp boats unloading their catches. Camera buffs love the harbor at sunset, one of the most picturesque locales on the entire coast.

Just a short jog north of Rockport on the coast road

The midway at the South Texas Fair in Beaumont is a colorful sight each year. Photo Courtesy the Texas Department of Highways and Public Transportation.

is neighboring Fulton Beach. Smaller and more funky than Rockport, this weathered community sports two popular restaurants on its bayfront — Schrenkeisen's and Charlotte Plummer's Seafare — as well as the handsome Fulton Mansion, built in 1874 and recently restored and opened for tours as an official state historic structure.

Both Rockport and Fulton Beach annually celebrate the Fulton Oysterfest on the first weekend of March, the Rockport Art Festival on the Fourth of July weekend and Rockport Seafair on the weekend preceding Columbus Day. For area information, contact the Rockport-Fulton Area Chamber of Commerce, Box 1055, Rockport, TX 78382; (512) 729-6445 or (800) 242-0071 in Texas; (800) 826-6441 elsewhere.

Nature's treasures flourish in the Rockport-Fulton Beach area. Beautiful oak trees, gnarled and twisted by sea winds into striking shapes, are common sights; one protected example in nearby Goose Island State Park is officially the largest live oak in Texas and is estimated to be 2,000 years old.

Major portions of Aransas Bay are protected as wildlife sanctuaries. Brown pelicans often survey the passing traffic from their perches on Rockport's road signs and thousands of migrating waterfowl winter here, a paradise for bird watchers as well as birds.

An extensive review of area birding is available from the Rockport Chamber of Commerce, Box 1055, Rockport, TX 78382. If a visitor's timing is right, he can catch the 2:55 p.m. tour on Thursdays of the Welder Wildlife Refuge, a private, 7,800-acre preserve 30 miles west via Farm-to-Market Road 881; (512) 364-2643.

On Texas 35 north of Fulton Beach is Goose Island State Park, Copano Bay Causeway State Park (with outstanding pier fishing) and a 54,829-acre wilderness known as Aransas National Wildlife Refuge. Home to nearly 300 species of birds, including a winter flock of rare whooping cranes, the wildlife refuge has a 16-mile driving loop, a large observation tower and numerous birding and nature trails. Boat tours also are available

Bordering On...
The Rewards.

Success is often based upon the power to compete. The El Paso/Juarez metroplex has provided this advantage to numerous companies through a variety of growth opportunities.

Honeywell, Tonka, TDK, Allen Bradley, GE, Rockwell International, GM, General Instruments, RCA, Ford, Chrysler, Allied Signal, Westinghouse, Mitsubishi, 3M Corporation and more have all reaped the rewards of the Southwest location.

Plentiful energy sources, educational opportunities, picture book climate, extensive banking and financial incentives, accessible transportation systems, willing labor and low costs only begin to whet the appetite for serious industrial and manufacturing concerns anxious to profit.

Insure your company's success with the strength of the ElPaso/Juarez metroplex.

For more information contact Denise Higgins, El Paso Industrial Development Corporation, 9 Civic Center Plaza, El Paso, Texas 79901, (915) 532-8281.

El Paso Electric

Colorful scenes abound on the Texas Gulf Coast. This shrimp boat at Aransas Pass provides a haunting subject at dusk. Photo Courtesy the Texas Department of Highways and Public Transportation.

from the nearby Sea Gun Marina and from the Rockport Harbor.

The next major stop on the Texas Coast is Galveston Island, but one can make interesting detours enroute via farm-to-market roads to small settlements like Seadrift, Port O'Connor, Indianola, Palacios and Matagorda. Each is a window on the real Texas.

Seadrift, Port O'Connor and Palacios primarily are fishing villages, and as such, they have attracted a significant number of the latest immigrant wave to Texas, the Vietnamese. If visitors want to overnight enroute, they should call for reservations at the venerable Luther Hotel in Palacios, built in 1903 and treasured by Texans as a low-key getaway. The number is (512) 972-2313.

Matagorda has a few historic homes, some mom-and-pop fishing and lodging operations, and a wild, 20-mile-long peninsula that shelters Lavaca and Matagorda bays. If a storm is brewing in the Gulf, Matagorda's mighty waves are an incredible sight.

Indianola is a ghost town. One of the great ports on the Gulf of Mexico from 1840-1875, it was the prime point of entry for thousands of early immigrants to Texas.

Then Mother Nature turned fickle. The town rebuilt after furious hurricanes in 1866 and 1875, although the latter killed some 500 people. A third violent storm, in 1886, left only sand, which is what visitors find today. Even road signs to Indianola are few and far between. From Texas 35 south of Port Lavaca, follow Texas 316 about 11 miles to and through Magnolia Beach until it ends at the Gulf and a historic marker.

Storms also have figured mightily in the history of Galveston Island, but with a happier outcome. For centuries the happy hunting and fishing grounds of the Karankawa Indians, it became an ideal home for pirate Jean Lafitte in the early 19th century. Then came the settling of Texas, and Galveston began to grow, thanks to its extensive and natural deepwater harbor. The 1880s began the city's golden period — its Strand boomed with commerce as the "Wall Street of the West," and its streets were lined with some of the most extravagant architecture in the country. But 1900 was not only the turn of the century, it was the turn of Galveston's fortunes.

A major hurricane literally swept the city away, killing more than 6,000 persons and devastating its economy. The opening of the Houston Ship Channel in 1915 was a second major economic blow, and Galveston never again was a financial mover and shaker in Texas circles.

Today's visitors, however, get a historical bonanza

in addition to good beaches and extensive recreational fun. The first stop should be The Strand Visitors Center, 2016 Strand, for maps, brochures, audio-guide equipment (fee) and general advice.

The Strand has been undergoing redevelopment for the past decade and now sports four blocks of shops, galleries and restaurants behind vintage facades. The *Elissa*, a square-rigged barque that called on the port of Galveston in the 1880s, rides at anchor one block north at Pier 21, and the historic and handsome Tremont House Hotel is one block south at 2300 Ship's Mechanic Row, (800) 874-2300.

Other major historic sights include The Bishop's Palace, an 1880s home designed by Nicholas Clayton and considered one of the 100 most outstanding residential structures in America; Ashton Villa, built in 1879 in Italianate style (an outstanding film on Galveston and the 1900 storm is shown in the Carriage House as part of the tour); and the 1839 Samuel May Williams Home, with audio dramas about the Williams family in every room.

Carriage rides, tour trains and a trolley cover the highlights of the city's three historic districts, and three museums offer additional looks at the past. The Center for Transportation and Commerce — better known as the Railroad Museum — just beyond the west end of The Strand is a feature that should not be missed. With advance reservations, dinner can be eaten in the diner, a deja vu experience for those who remember when trains were the major mode of travel across the U.S.

Contemporary Galveston is equally rich to explore. The 32 miles of beachfront vary in style from Stewart's Beach with its lifeguards, concessions and (usually) crowds on the eastern end of the island to the long undeveloped stretches of West Beach. Three "pocket parks," west of town via Seawall Boulevard and FM 3005, mix the best of those two worlds — just enough development (changing rooms, showers, snacks and picnic tables) to make them comfortable, with little disturbance of the natural beauty of the shore.

Nor are the finer things in life overlooked in Galveston. Overnight visitors should check the playbill at the 1894 Grand Opera House, now restored to its former grandeur. It's a year-round showcase for major-league performers, an elegant evening on the town. Less formal is the Mary Moody Northen Amphitheatre at Galveston Island State Park, where Broadway favorites alternate with historical dramas on summer weekend evenings. An inexpensive barbecue dinner is available just prior to the performance, an ideal family outing.

Festivals are as constant to Galveston as seagulls,

The National Aeronautics and Space Administration's Johnson Space Center has proved a popular tourist attraction in Houston. Photo Courtesy the Texas Department of Highways and Public Transportation.

but the highlights of the year are a full-scale Mardi Gras in February and March, the Blessing of the Fleet in April, the historical homes tour the first weekend of May, a major Fourth of July celebration at Ashton Villa and Dickens on the Strand the first week of December. For information, contact the Galveston Island Convention and Visitors' Bureau, 2106 Seawall Blvd., Galveston, TX 77550; (800) 351-4236 in Texas; (800) 351-4237 elsewhere.

Galveston can be used as a base to explore the last stretch of the Texas coast as a day-trip before heading north to Houston. The northeastern tip of Galveston Island is connected by free, 24-hour ferry to the Bolivar Peninsula and Texas 87, then flirts with the surf almost all the way to the Louisiana border.

One tip for travelers: The lines for the Bolivar ferry can be long, particularly on good weather weekends, so snacks, drinks, suntan lotion, some portable shade and a good book would be good companions.

Of interest: Texas 87 is the only coast road in the state, and keeping it in passable repair is a continuing engineering challenge for the Texas Department of Highways and Public Transportation. Shown as a shell trace on old Civil War maps, Texas 87 was not paved until 1932. Since then, however, hurricanes Carla, David and Alicia have closed the road with major washouts, and large sections have been relocated several times to accommodate the ever-changing profile of the coast. Even now, if the wind is from the south and the moon is full, portions of the road are submerged at high tide. Not to worry, however, the road is passable 98 percent of the time.

Once off the Bolivar ferry, directional signs on the right point to Fort Travis Seashore Park, the first stop. Now operated as a Galveston County park, this is historic sand. An old fort that dates from the late 1800s has been renovated and provides protected swimming beaches and shore fishing areas.

Shortly beyond Fort Travis, Bolivar's open beach begins. Those seeking solitude will find it here. Driving on the beach remains legal on Bolivar, however, so sunbathers should use caution.

During the reconstruction of Texas 87 after Hurricane Carla in the 1960s, highway workers found countless arrowheads, fossilized horse and camel bones, and

even mastodon teeth in Bolivar's changing sands. Thanks to a fossil bed offshore, beachcombers still uncover such treasures, particularly after storms. Best hunting grounds are between High Island and Sea Rim State Park, 23 miles southwest of metropolitan Port Arthur.

Sea Rim is a destination in itself, more than 15,000 acres of natural coastal beach and wetlands divided into two units. The beach section offers not only the usual beachside sun and fun, complete with comfort concessions, but also an interpretive center and a 3,640-foot-long boardwalk through natural wetlands behind the beach dunes. The unique marsh unit can be accessed only by small power boat (less than 30 hp) or canoe (bring your own; none are available for rental at this writing). Sneaking up on wildlife by canoe is by far the more memorable experience. Although Sea Rim no longer has a naturalist on the staff or airboat rides into the marsh, a slide show on the park's unspoiled ecology is available on summer evenings.

Of interest: Natural wetlands comprise much of the upper Texas coast, making duck and geese hunting excellent November through January. For area information, contact Sea Rim State Park, (409) 971-2909.

Birding, as noted in the Rockport information, is rewarding year-round but particularly outstanding in winter, thanks to the fact that the Mississippi Flyway and Central Flyway both cross the upper Texas coast. Large numbers of migratory waterfowl and birds thrive at San Bernard National Wildlife Refuge, 10 miles west of Freeport, and at Anahuac National Wildlife Refuge on the upper reaches of Galveston Bay. Both are open to the public. Sidney Island, another protected habitat at the north end of Sabine Lake near Port Arthur, is restricted to authorized boat entry, largely because its harbors the rare roseate spoonbill; binocular viewing from shore is possible. Sidney Island also is a rest station for migrating monarch butterflies in October.

Less than an hour's drive north of Galveston via Interstate 45, Houston is another good hub for exploring the upper reaches of the Texas Gulf Coast. Glistening with contemporary skyscrapers, the nation's fourth-largest city soars from the flat coastal plain like a sentinel to the good life.

Begun as a real estate promotion in 1836 shortly after Gen. Sam Houston's army won Texas' independence from Mexico at nearby San Jacinto Battleground, Houston today sports the most outstanding collection of urban architecture in America. Major works by I. M. Pei, Philip Johnson and other world-renowned architects dot downtown's neat blocks, and visitors love getting lost in the labyrinth of tunnels that link many of those buildings one level below the busy city streets.

The arts ride high in Houston. Outstanding sculptures dominate many corporate courtyards downtown, and the $72 million Gus W. Wortham Theatre Center, opened in early 1987, brings two outstanding new theatres for the performing arts to the central business district. Nearby, Jones Hall is home to the Houston Symphony, and the Nina Vance Alley Theatre is one of the three oldest professional repertory companies in America. Both play to packed houses nearly year-round.

In strong visual contrast, tiny Sam Houston Park lies tucked in the sunrise shadow of downtown. Here docents provide guided tours of several historic homes, including the Kellum-Noble House (1847), the Nichols-Rice-Cherry House (1850), the San Felipe Cottage (1875) and the Old Place (1824); the latter is the oldest structure in Harris County. An adjacent museum, the Gallery of Texas History, exhibits artifacts from 1519 to present. For those who feel like a picnic in the park, the tea room in the Yesteryear Shop, operated weekdays by the Harris County Heritage Society, makes a great sandwich.

Other "don't miss" places in Houston include the Hermann Park Zoo (free, and noted for its outstanding children's petting area, nocturnal animals exhibit and walk-through aviary); the Museum of Fine Arts (check the bookstore for a list of "must sees" if time is limited); and the Galleria (west of downtown at Westheimer and Post Oak roads).

The latter is the glitzy nucleus of Houston's second "downtown," a three-part shopping center thriving with upscale shops; major department stores like Neiman-Marcus, Lord and Taylor and Marshall Field; an indoor ice rink; office buildings; and several major hotels. The often-expensive shopping is outstanding and the people-watching is world class. Many of the stores

The old lighthouse at Matagorda Island provided many a camera enthusiast with a lovely and thoughtful subject. Photo Courtesy the Texas Department of Highways and Public Transportation.

require their clerks to be multilingual, so heavy is the influx of foreign shoppers here.

The general surrounding area also is loosely referred to as the Galleria, dotted with corporate skyscrapers, fashionable shopping centers, hotels and restaurants and usually plagued by traffic.

If plotting a course from downtown to the Galleria, visitors should detour through the ritzy River Oaks residential area via Allen Parkway/Kirby Drive. Houston's equivalent of Southern California's Beverly Hills, River Oaks is home to society mavens and oil magnates alike, plus an Arab sheik or two has a mansion here.

Several of the most outstanding homes and gardens are open for visitors during the annual Azalea Trail, sponsored annually in mid-to-late March by the River Oaks Garden Club. With advance reservations one also can try on the neighborhood for size at Bayou Bend, the John Staub-designed home of the late Miss Ima Hogg. Sited on 14 oak-studded acres in the most exclusive section of River Oaks, Bayou Bend now showcases an outstanding collection of American antiques as an extension of the Museum of Fine Arts.

Nearly everyone who comes to Houston for the first time wants to see two things: the Astrodome and the Johnson Space Center. The first is south of downtown via either Main or Fannin street, and is best seen in action. If no sporting event is scheduled, the three guided tours given daily (fee) are well done and include a multimedia presentation.

The NASA/Lyndon B. Johnson Space Center, usually just called JSC or NASA, is a 1,620-acre complex 25 miles south of metro Houston via I-45 (Gulf Freeway) and NASA Road One. Open daily except Christmas Day and free, it offers guided tours of Mission Control (sign up at Information Desk in the Visitor Information Center as soon as you arrive), self-guiding tours of four other buildings and an outdoor display of space hardware in Rocket Park.

Rumors to the contrary, one can't experience weightlessness in an anti-gravity machine at JSC — there is no such thing. But a visitor can, among other things, walk through Skylab, check out moon rocks and play "guess who is an astronaut?" when lunching in the JSC cafeteria. Don't look for men and women in moon suits, however; in their work-a-day clothes the astronauts look just like the folks next door.

Of interest: Plans for a new $40 million visitors center are underway, with an opening tentatively set for 1989.

Houston's port is the third largest in America, surprising in a city located 50 miles inland from the Gulf of Mexico. Huge tankers and cargo ships follow a 40-foot-deep channel dredged out of Galveston Bay and the San Jacinto River to end up within a foot of downtown. The free 90-minute tours aboard the M/V Sam Houston take travelers into the heart of the action. Departures are at specific times five days a week and reservations as far in advance as possible are recommended.

Visitors should know that Houston has two major airports and that several of the major airlines operate flights from both. Travelers should confirm which airport they will be using. William P. Hobby Airport is south of downtown via the Gulf Freeway or Texas 35, and Houston Intercontinental Airport is north via either I-45, U.S. 59 or North Belt. There is scheduled surface transportation by bus, van and helicopter from the airports to various locations throughout the city. Houston also is served by Amtrak from New Orleans, San Antonio and Los Angeles.

When to explore Houston depends on one's tolerance for heat and humidity. Winters generally are mild, spring and fall are prime times and summer can be steamy. May-through-September visitors should pack sweaters for inside use, however; Houston is the most air-conditioned city in the world, and the transition from the exterior to interior climate can be a chiller.

If one likes special events, don't miss the Houston Livestock Show and Rodeo during the last week of February and the first week of March, or the blaze of azaleas that brightens the city the rest of that month. Early April brings the Houston Festival to various venues around town, and the wildflowers begin to bloom along the roadsides, an outstanding show of bluebonnets, Indian paintbrush, etc.

The Greater Houston Convention & Visitors Council is an excellent source of information on events, accommodations, tours, sightseeing and commercial suppliers. Contact them at 3300 Main St., Houston, TX 77002; (800) 392-7722 in Texas; (800) 231-7799 elsewhere.

Religion in Texas

This replica of Daniel Parker's first Pilgrim Baptist Church in Anderson County was built in 1949. The original church was moved to Texas from Illinois in 1833 and was the first Baptist Church in Texas. Texas Almanac Photo.

Religion in Early Texas

This article was written by Mike Kingston, editor of the Texas Almanac. Special thanks are extended to Dr. John W. Storey, Lamar University, Beaumont; Rev. Walter N. Vernon, retired Methodist minister and historian, Dallas; Dr. Eugene W. Baker, Baylor University, Waco; and Dr. James T. Moore, North Harris County College, Houston, for their advice. Any errors are the author's alone.

Though Texas today has about 8 million church members and adherents, organized religion developed slowly in the state.

The Indian tribes that inhabited the territory of Texas prior to the coming of Europeans in the 16th century engaged in a variety of religious practices. Most embraced, however vaguely, a concept of a supreme being. They were not monotheistic, however, believing instead in a variety of supernatural powers, organized in a hierarchy. For agricultural Indians, various ceremonies accompanied planting and harvesting of crops, and nomadic Indians sought the help of spirits in hunts.

Roman Catholic missionaries brought Christianity to Texas. The missions now commonly called Ysleta and Socorro were established in the El Paso area in 1680, when Spanish colonists were expelled from Pueblo Indian communities in the upper Rio Grande valley. Friendly Tigua Indians and others, who accompanied the settlers in their flights, were housed at the missions.

In 1690, the Mission San Francisco de los Tejas was established near present-day Weches in Houston County in East Texas. Concern that the French were planning to colonize the vast expanse of Texas in the wake of LaSalle's unsuccessful effort prompted Spanish authorities to locate missions in this part of the state. The missions were withdrawn three years later, but re-established in 1716. The first mission in the San Antonio area, San Antonio de Valero (now known as the Alamo), was established in 1718.

Missions had religious and civic responsibilities. They were to convert natives to Christianity, to civilize them, to teach them trades and to make useful Spanish citizens of them. The approach worked among the settled Indians of Mexico, but the nomadic tribes of Texas resisted the efforts. Although many Indians were attracted by the protection provided by nearby Spanish

presidios and by food during lean years, the complete civilizing process usually was not successful. Up to 40 missions were established across Texas during the Spanish period, meeting varying degrees of success. Some lasted only a few months, while others are active today as churches.

Missions were supported by the Spanish crown, and as financial difficulties deepened in Spain, funding declined. Lacking funds, the missions often could not fulfill promises made to proselytes, and this angered them.

Attempts to secularize the missions — to convert them into regular churches supported by their congregations — began in the late 18th century but were not successful.

Through the later Spanish colonial period and the early Mexican era, the missions and churches were in a state of decline. Morale and discipline among the priests were low, and two in San Antonio ignored their vows by taking wives, starting families and failing to adequately minister to their congregations.

Roman Catholicism was the traditional state religion for Spain and its colonies. When Texas was opened to Anglo-American immigration in 1820, Spain, and later Mexico, stipulated Catholicism as the state religion and required all newcomers to embrace it. Religious-civil rites, like marriage, were not recognized by the government unless performed by priests.

Other religions were prohibited by the state. From the beginning, authorities were hard pressed to enforce the ban. There were simply too few priests available to service the tide of Anglo settlers that came to the province. And few priests spoke English. What developed was not religious persecution, but an apathy toward religion altogether. Stephen F. Austin in 1823 and 1824 petitioned Mexican authorities without success to send English-speaking priests. When the Mexican war for independence began in 1810, immigration of priests from Spain was stopped, and seminaries in Mexico soon closed during the turbulence, some of which was aimed

Continued on Page 61

The color cover picture of this section was made in St. Olaf's Kierke near Cranfill's Gap in Bosque County by Mary G. Crawford of the Texas Almanac. The church was built by Norwegian pioneers who settled the area in the 1850s.

Missions on the Frontier

One of the unique institutions of the Spanish colonial frontier in Texas was the mission. It combined the evangelical zeal and idealism of the Holy Orders of the Roman Catholic Church with the political necessity of civilizing native peoples and defending national boundaries.

The evangelical movement within the Christian church began upon the death of Jesus Christ. Most religions retain a local character, but Christianity did not. The Apostles and other early believers fanned out from Jerusalem to spread word of the new faith. Though most of the first evangelists remained in the Mediterranean region, St. Thomas founded churches in India, and Nestorian Christians established churches in China in early missionary efforts. As the Middle Ages closed, the missionary effort centered in Northern Europe and Africa.

Spain made contributions to early missionary work. Ramon Lull, a Catalan priest born in 1235, is considered one of the great missionaries. Working with Moslems, he proposed a plan for spreading the Christian religion. Lull advocated a missionary effort that would incorporate:

• A comprehensive and accurate knowledge of the initiates' language.

• A book in which the truth of the Christian religion was demonstrated.

• A willingness of the faithful to witness their religion even at the cost of their lives.

History Highlights

When Pope Alexander VI divided the unexplored New World between the Spanish and Portuguese in 1493, he emphasized the responsibility of the Christian nations to take the religion to the newly discovered lands.

The Spanish church was in a unique position to take advantage of the challenge. In the closing years of the 15th century, Spain's church, like others in Europe, suffered from abuses. Absenteeism among the clergy existed, as did low standards of morality and learning. Queen Isabella, a devout Christian, wanted the quality of the clergy improved. She convinced Pope Alexander to allow Cardinal Francisco Jimenez de Cisneros, her confessor, to institute reforms among the friars and nuns. He began with his own order, the Franciscans, and later expanded his work to other orders. As a result of these reforms, the upheavals of the Protestant reformation were avoided in Spain. The Spanish church emanated a new vigor and readily accepted the evangelical challenge in the lands across the Atlantic Ocean.

The physical and spiritual conquests of Mexico, Central America and Peru were completed by the mid-16th century. But the methods of religious conversion and the treatment of the Indians were questioned by many of the missionaries.

After a lengthy debate, Spanish colonial policy changed. King Philip II issued new ordinances in 1573 limiting the role of the military in the pacification of new lands. No longer were mass baptisms under force of arms acceptable. And no longer was the word "conquest" acceptable when discussing the conversion of New World natives. Better treatment for the natives was mandated.

The policy change was inopportune in New Spain. The missionaries now were dealing with a different type of primitive people. While the Incas, Aztecs and Mayas were settled Indians with well-defined cultures and traditional hierarchies, the Chichimecs, as all Indians north of the Valley of Mexico were called, were nomadic and disinclined to the settled life proposed by the missionaries.

With the "spiritual conquest" of the rest of the New World complete, however, the most zealous and competent of the missionaries migrated to New Spain's northern frontiers. They were charged with the pacification, as well as the conversion, of the natives. And this was the crux of the mission system:

The San Elizario mission and presidio were among many such institutions established in the El Paso area during the Spanish colonial period. Photo Courtesy the Texas Department of Highways and Public Transportation.

Spain could not populate the vast lands it claimed in the New World, so the strategy was to convert the Indians into Spanish citizens through the institution of the mission.

The mission concept gained impetus from Sir Thomas More's *Utopia*, published in 1516. Proponents sought to create a moral community with Christ as the model of perfection. Work was to be the criterion for citizenship, and cooperation, not competition, was to be the foundation of the economy. Though the missions fell short of the ideal in practice, they were built on good intentions and an effort to transmit Christian moral values to New World natives.

As conceived, the missionaries would enter a new area, congregate receptive Indians around a church and instruct them in the faith and a trade. Farming and cattle raising were the most important of the initial trades, for they fed the community. Several missions might be located in a general area, and nearby would be established a presidio, or fort, for protection. Within 10 years, under the theory, the Indians should be converted to Christianity, trained in a trade and ready to become productive, taxpaying Spanish citizens. The missions would be converted into secular churches to be supported by the new converts; the missionaries would move forward on the frontier to their next challenge. In practice, however, few Texas missions were voluntarily secularized.

The priests were the shock troops in this struggle. And to a great extent, they were successful. By the time the English landed at Jamestown in 1607, there were 200 Iberian cities in the New World, but none in Texas at the time.

The first Texas missions were established in 1680,

Continued on Next Page

Missions

Continued from Previous Page

as a result of a revolt by Pueblo Indians against the Spanish in the upper Rio Grande valley. San Antonio de la Isleta, later called Corpus Christi de la Isleta, was established in today's El Paso for the Tigua Indians. The second mission, Nuestra Senora de la Concepcion del Socorro, was established within days of the first, and it was settled by Piro, Tano and Jemez Indians. Both missions sheltered Indians that had become friendly with the Spanish and could not stay in the area of the puebloes. Franciscans administered both missions.

Eight years later, the first East Texas mission, San Francisco de los Tejas, was established near the present-day community of Weches, and a second mission, Santisimo Nombre de Maria, was soon founded nearby. San Antonio de Valero, commonly known as the Alamo, was moved from the Rio Grande to San Antonio in 1716. The last mission established in Texas was Nuestra Senora del Refugio in 1793. It was moved to the site of present-day Refugio in 1795.

Missions were more than a chapel, usually comprising a complex of buildings. Included were small houses for Indians, workshops and classrooms, shops for carpenters, blacksmiths and tailors, kilns, a granary, houses for soldiers, a cemetery, and a garden and an orchard. Most were surrounded by fortified walls to protect against hostile Indians, and outside the walls were cultivated fields and pastures.

Because of the nomadic lifestyle of most Texas Indians, missionaries had to get groups to agree to submit to instruction in religious life and training in an occupation in exchange for food and protection from enemies. Education and training were slow processes, for often Indians would take advantage of the missionaries' generosity and stay only long enough to get food or clothing. When Indians ran away, they often were tracked down and returned to the mission by soldiers.

The crown supported the missions in early years. But as the Spanish government's financial position worsened, funds became scarce. Often money was not available to provide food, seed and tools as promised to Indians, and the neophytes rebelled, killing the missionaries.

The goal was to have the Indians trained in a trade and to turn the missions over to secular priests for use as churches within a decade. Then missionaries would move to new areas. But few Texas missions were voluntarily secularized, with their lands distributed to the neophytes.

No one is sure how many missions were established in Texas during the Spanish era. Estimates range up to 40. And the merits of the mission system are still debated: Was it a failure or a success? Cer-

Our Lady of Mount Carmel parish in El Paso was established as Mission Corpus Christi de la Ysleta in 1680. The mission was the center of the oldest settlement in Texas. Photo courtesy of the Texas Department of Highways and Public Transportation.

tainly many of the missions were unsuccessful. But six former missions established in the state during the colonial period are still active churches. These former missions include Our Lady of Mount Carmel (formerly Mission Corpus Christi de la Ysleta) in El Paso and Nuestra Senora de la Purisima (formerly Mission Nuestra Senora del Socorro) in Socorro, and in San Antonio, Mission Concepcion, Mission San Juan Capistrano, Mission San Francisco de la Espada and Mission San Jose. That is a good record for a 300-year government program.

Continued from Page 59

at the church. Priests for Texas simply were not available.

A major problem arose over marriage. Many couples wanted to wed, but could not for a lack of priests. To alleviate the problem, Austin was given authority to register marriage contracts. Under these, couples could marry in a civil ceremony and promise, under contract, to have the union blessed when Catholic clergy was available.

A handful of priests still tended the faithful at the old missions, and the military garrison at Nacogdoches had a chaplain. However, the army used the church as a barracks, and civilians attended mass in a private residence. In 1832, a Dominican priest from Ireland and two nuns arrived to serve the Irish colonists on the Nueces River.

Despite these problems, Austin continued to enforce the prohibition against other religions, expressing particular concern about the "Methodist excitement" that reached San Felipe. Efforts to liberalize the religion ban could be crippled if outsiders antagonized Mexican authorities, Austin feared.

Briefly in 1831 and 1832, Father Michael Muldoon served the Austin colony. Though he may never have said mass, the cleric attended to some religious duties. But his conduct was too impious for many colonists, who were relieved when he returned to Mexico.

The state of religion during this period therefore was not healthy. Gen. Manuel Mier y Teran, after touring Texas in 1828 and 1829, observed that freedom of religion would be preferable to no religion at all, which seemed to be the case at the time. Church members who had immigrated to Texas complained of a lack of respect for the Sabbath, when Texans paid more attention to recreation than to church-related activities.

The Awakening or Revival movement in American religion was a century old as Texas moved toward independence. Religious freedom had given people a broader choice of beliefs or non-belief. In the 1730s in America and England came a new response to the challenge of attracting new members.

It was one thing to inspire Christians, but quite another to convert non-believers for the first time. American Protestants had a large field of potential converts to religion including those who had not previously practiced religion, the young and those from other religions. A new emphasis on the emotions evolved in preaching, and mass meetings inspired crowd response and vibrant singing. Today, it is called the Old-Time Religion, but then it was young.

The First Awakening began in the 1730s and died down during the period of the American Revolution and early years of nationhood. At the turn of the 19th century, the Second Awakening was kindled, as a new generation saw in revivals and camp meetings fresh approaches to attract new Christians. Methodists, Presbyterians and Baptists were the most active denominations, but others worked with faith and dedication. From this atmosphere had most Texans emigrated.

Prior to Texas' independence, only isolated individual preachers came from the United States to the Mexican province. With the advent of the Second Great Awakening early in the 19th century, evangelical churches and preachers were in the forefront of the westward movement. Their goal was to see that the gospel was carried with the Anglo-American advance across the continent. Texas was in the path of the movement.

Protestantism made its first inroads into Texas between 1815 and 1817. In extreme Northeast Texas, which was considered to be part of Arkansas at the time, Methodist preachers made their first appearance. Circuit riders from Arkansas made trips into the region. Methodist William Stevenson in 1815 began preaching in private residences. Soon thereafter a small Methodist church, the first Protestant church in Texas, was organized at Jonesborough in present-day Red River County.

In 1820, Joseph Bays, a Baptist preacher, camped on the American side of the Sabine River with other colonists who answered Moses Austin's call for settlers. Bays ventured into Spanish territory to preach at a private residence, until ordered to stop by authorities. Three years later, Bays was arrested at San Felipe for preaching, but he escaped while being transported to San Antonio for trial.

Ministers like Sumner Bacon, an unofficial Cumberland Presbyterian missionary, arrived in Texas in 1825. Bacon preached where he could find worshipers, fought alongside Sam Houston in the revolution and, in 1833, became an official agent of the American Bible Society. The Cumberland branch of the Presbyterian church was organized in 1810, developing out of a schism during the evangelical revival that opened the century. A Cumberland church was organized in Red River County as early as 1833.

Daniel Parker, another Baptist preacher, brought the first of the denomination's churches to Texas. After a visit to the Mexican province, Parker decided that the ban extended only to establishing churches in the territory. Returning to Caldwell, Ill., Parker organized the Pilgrim Church of Predestination Baptists with seven members. On July 26, 1833, the small congregation, which grew by 11 on the trip, began its journey to Texas. Parker reasoned that the ban did not cover organized churches that moved into the territory. The congregation held its first conference in Austin Colony in January 1834. Although Parker was an antimissionary Baptist, historians have traced at least nine churches in East Texas that grew from efforts of his Pilgrim church in Anderson County.

The Providence Church in Bastrop County in 1834 was the first Baptist church organized in Texas, and Moses Gage, who served the church, was the first man licensed to preach in the territory.

Mexican authorities apparently were not zealous in their enforcement of the prohibition against Protestant meetings. A meeting conducted in Sabine County in 1832 by Needham J. Alford, a Methodist, and Sumner Bacon was reported to Col. Jose Piedras, commander of the garrison at Nacogdoches. "Are they stealing anything?" the officer asked. "Are they killing anybody? Are they doing anything bad?" When the answer to all the questions was negative, Piedras simply let the worshipers alone.

The first sparks of the Texas Revolution flared in 1832. After disputes with colonists, the Mexican military left the state, showing more interest in participating in Santa Anna's revolt in Mexico than in policing Texas. Thereafter, Protestant groups held regular camp meetings. This unique institution was initiated by James McGready on the Gasper River in Kentucky in 1800 or 1801. It quickly spread westward with revivalist preachers and remained a colorful part of frontier life into the 20th century.

As developed in Texas, camp meetings usually began on Thursdays and ended on Sundays, although some lasted up to two weeks. Families for miles around attended. Several worship services were held daily, leading up to the big evening service. Often preachers from several denominations were on hand. Camp meetings filled many needs. First, they drew together the otherwise scattered population that was so difficult for preachers to reach. And the sessions also congregated

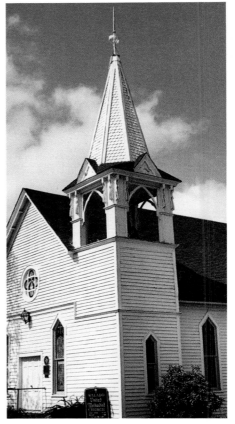

Originally served by circuit riders, the Saledo United Methodist Church was built in 1890. The architecture is typical of the period. Texas Almanac Photo.

people for socializing, as well as preaching. The religious message was basic and directed toward the future: Repent now, quit your sinning and avoid hellfire.

Once churches became established in Texas society, they became leaders in the educational movement. The trend began early. T. J. Pilgrim, a Baptist, in 1829 organized the first Sunday school in Texas at San Felipe, and about the same time, another was established at Matagorda by Baptists from New York.

In 1834, Austin was successful in obtaining a measure of religious tolerance. A state law provided that no person should be molested on account of his religious or political opinion, if he did not disturb public order. While Anglo-American colonists continued to complain about a lack of religious freedom, the Mexican state government liberalized the law as far as the national constitution allowed — and perhaps further.

Once the turmoil of the Texas Revolution receded, the major denominations took a serious interest in missionary work in the new republic.

Efforts had been made to attract missionaries prior to the rebellion. In the most celebrated case, Col. William B. Travis, who soon would die in the Alamo, wrote a New York newspaper in August 1835 lamenting the lack of a Methodist organization in Texas. He wrote, "I regret that the Methodist church, with its excellent itinerant system, has hitherto sent pioneers of the Gospel into almost every destitute portion of the globe, should have neglected so long this interesting country." He asked for five ministers for Texas.

Although the Mississippi Conference appointed

This historic synagogue, Temple Beth-El in Corsicana built in 1900, is one of many unique buildings constructed by Jewish congregations in Texas. Texas Almanac Photo.

Henry Stephenson as a missionary to Texas in 1834, the first official Methodist missionaries came in 1837 when Martin Ruter, Littleton Fowler and Robert Alexander were named by the Missionary Society of the Methodist Episcopal Church of the United States. Ruter was superintendent of the mission activity but lived only six months. His influence on education lasted long after his death.

Ruter divided Texas into three circuits. Circuit riders fanned out through the republic, led by Ruter who covered more than 2,200 miles on horseback in his short service in Texas. These ministers visited neighborhoods, determined if the people wanted a worship service and, if so, provided one. When sufficient interest was aroused, a church was organized. By 1839, there were 20 Methodist churches with 350 members in Texas, and two years later, the aggressive Methodists enlarged that number to 1,878 members. The first separate Methodist conference for Texas was authorized in 1840 and organized by Bishop Beverly Waugh.

Circuit riders carried the message of virtually every denomination across the sparsely inhabited territory. Bad weather, a lack of roads, sickness and, not least, hostile Indians were constant challenges. Their courage and dedication were similar to that of the Roman Catholic missionaries who first faced the fierce Indian tribes of the territory of Texas. Both groups contributed martyrs to the evangelical effort.

Disciples of Christ, or Christian, churches were established at Clarksville and Antioch in 1836, and others may have existed. The denomination did not have organizations at that time, and each church was freestanding.

James Huckins was the first official Baptist missionary, being appointed by the Home Missionary Society in 1840. After arrival, he asked for 15 missionaries to cover the large, sparsely settled region.

The mission board of the General Presbyterian Assembly appointed Rev. W. C. Blair missionary to Texas in 1839 and located him in Victoria. A decade later, the Presbyterian Church U.S.A. showed 10 ministers, 15 churches and 329 members in the state.

The first Episcopal services were held at Matagorda on Christmas Day 1838, and the first parish was organized a month later. Episcopal churches also were established in Houston and Galveston in 1838 and 1839. The Episcopal Diocese of Texas was formed in December 1849 with parishes in Galveston, Houston, Matagorda, Brazoria, San Augustine and Nacogdoches participating. Congregations also existed in San Antonio and Austin.

The Roman Catholic Church, which was in dire straits after years of neglect, despite its position as the state church, began rebuilding in 1838. Texas was placed under the authority of the Bishop Antonio Blanc of New Orleans. Rev. John Timon and Rev. Juan Francisco Llebaria were sent to the new republic to determine the state of the church. They got no farther than Houston, where they gathered information from around the republic. Poor roads, bad weather and Indians kept the priests from touring the new republic. In 1842, Rev. John Odin was named Vicar Apostolic of Texas to continue the work of rebuilding the church that Father Timon started. By 1846, 10 churches or chapels were completed. The Diocese of Galveston was erected in 1847 to include the new state of Texas.

Many of the early German immigrants were Lutherans. In 1850, the Lutheran Synod of South Carolina sent Pastor G. F. Guebner to Texas to analyze missionary needs. The same year, Pastor Casper Braun organized a congregation in Houston, which he served for 30 years. In Nov. 1851, the First Evangelical Lutheran Synod of Texas was formed, and from that time, the church moved forward in the state.

Jews were among the early immigrants to Texas. But they came in increasing numbers from Europe following the abortive political revolutions of 1848. As their numbers increased, Jewish institutions — benevolent associations, cemeteries, synagogues and community centers — were established. The first Jewish cemetery in Texas was founded in Houston in 1844, followed by the establishment of the first synagogue in 1854. Before the Civil War, a Jewish cemetery was founded in Galveston in 1852, and two years later, one was established in San Antonio, where religious services were initiated by the Hebrew Benevolent Society in 1856.

Although most preachers in early Texas were sincere, some came whose lives "did not tally with their professions." Initially, none of the Protestant denominations had official organizations to provide credentials, and the Ecclesiastical Committee for Vigilance for Texas, formed by Methodist, Baptist and Presbyterian ministers in Houston to certify newly arrived preachers, was only partly effective. Baptist Huckins lamented the preacher on the Gulf Coast whose sermons were attended by ruffians and scoundrels who cheered and stamped their feet. After the preaching, the minister and his boisterous congregation adjourned to the groghouse to imbibe in strong spirits.

Such performances, and others by charlatans who preyed on the desire for religion, brought all ministers into disrespect. And they gave early Texans an excuse to treat ministers as slightly comical figures. One preacher, for example, delivered a sermon at a small settlement in which he announced the death of the devil. Afterward, a public meeting passed a resolution lamenting the demise of the preacher's father and appointing a local citizen to oversee the devil's estate. Z.N. Morrell, a legendary Baptist preacher who arrived in Texas in 1836, once caned a heckler who disrupted services. Few challenged the preacher again.

Texas politicians went even further when writing the Constitution of 1836, prohibiting preachers from serving in Congress or holding executive office in the republic. Rationale was that the preachers needed to spend their time saving souls. The prohibition was not unusual in American politics, with the first such noted in the constitution of New York State in 1777, which eliminated ministers from consideration for military, as well as civil, offices. Louisiana and other states also banned preachers from some offices. In Texas, the prohibition was carried over into the state constitutions of 1845 and 1866 after Texas joined the Union.

Despite the politicians' opinion of preachers, the Senate chamber in the Capitol in Houston was the scene of almost weekly interdenominational preaching with Protestants and Catholics sharing the lectern.

As if the frontier life was not challenging enough,

intradenominational disagreements often flared. Each denomination had to some degree factions of "old religion" and new, of traditionalists and revivalists. Presbyterians split long before coming to the new republic.

Texas Baptists seem to have had the most difficulty early. Antimissionaries — also called "primitives" and "hardshell" — organized first with the arrival of Daniel Parker's Pilgrim Church. This group opposed creation of missions, because, it was argued, they were man-made institutions, not authorized in the Bible. Antimissionaries were strongest in East Texas, where they had a major voice in early Baptist associations. At one point, antimissionaries wanted to make their belief an article of faith. Missionary Baptists eventually prevailed, but the disagreement hindered early evangelical efforts.

Judaism was reshaping its institutions as Jews experienced the new freedom of the United States. Early congregations in Texas, though small, still had fierce debates over the maintenance of the orthodox ritual or adoption of reforms. Released from the peer and community pressures of the European ghettos, Jewish immigrants practiced their religion with a new independence.

As a benchmark of the impact of organized religion in Texas, the U.S. Census of 1850 found there were 328 churches in the state with an aggregate capacity of 60,000 persons. By denomination, the church numbers broke down like this: 173 were Methodist; 70, Baptist; 47, Presbyterian; 13, Roman Catholic; five, Episcopal; five, Christian, and 15 of smaller groups. Church property was valued at $206,930.

A failure to provide education facilities was one complaint Texas revolutionaries had against the Mexican government. But after independence, the government of the Republic, lacking money, did no better. So the early responsibility for education fell to private and religious groups. The church denominations were interested in training ministers, as well as providing a general education. Dr. Frederick Eby, an education historian, calculated there were 19 educational institutions chartered by the Republic of Texas, including Baylor University and a forerunner of Southwestern University of Georgetown, the state's two oldest educational institutions. Between annexation in 1845 and the Civil War, another 117 institutions were chartered, including seven universities, 30 colleges, 40 academies, 27 institutes, three high schools, two seminaries, an orphan asylum and a medical college. The leaders in the number of institutions organized were the Masons, Methodists, Baptists, Presbyterians, Roman Catholics, Lutherans and Episcopalians.

Washington County was one of the religious and educational centers of early Texas by virtue of one of the capitals of the Republic being located there. At Chappell Hill, the Methodists founded Soule University in 1856, one of the forerunners to Southwestern University. Presbyterians had a co-educational school at nearby Gay Hill, and Baylor University was chartered in 1845 and opened in 1846 at Independence. In adjacent Fayette County, Rutersville College was founded as a non-sectarian school by Methodists in 1840. The Texas Congress, in the interest of keeping church and state separate, declined to charter a religious school, hence the non-sectarian nature of another forerunner of Southwestern University.

Poor roads and equally bad mail service made communication facilities almost nil in the infant Republic. The first denominational newspaper in the Republic was the *Texas Christian Advocate and Brenham Advertiser*, published by Methodists in 1847. Although the publication had several name changes, it is the forerunner of today's *United Methodist Reporter*.

Texas Baptists were allotted space in 1841 in the *Baptist Banner and Western Pioneer*, published in Louisville, Ky., and, in 1847, in the *Southwestern Baptist* of New Orleans. In January 1855, the *Texas Baptist* published its first edition, and the circulation rose to 2,600 before a shortage of newsprint during the Civil War forced suspension of publication.

Like others across the South, Texas' denominations broke with their counterparts in the North over the question of slavery. Methodists separated from the General Conference in 1844, and the Southern Baptist Convention was founded in 1845. Episcopalians split only during the war, and Roman Catholics did not break up before or during the war.

Most churches ministered to black slaves, many of whom became church members, though always in an inferior status to whites. They usually were required to

Which School Is the Oldest In the State?

A hot debate can be stirred between Texas Methodists and Baptists over the question of which university is the state's oldest. Baylor University, a Baptist school in Waco, and Southwestern University, a Methodist institution in Georgetown, are the competitors.

Baylor's lineage is simple. The school was chartered as a Baptist institution by the Congress of the Republic of Texas in 1845. For the next 40 years, Baylor, which was named for Baptist educator R.E.B. Baylor, operated in Independence in Washington County. In 1886, after years of Baptist bickering, the school was moved to Waco and merged with Waco University. Waco and Baylor have lived happily ever after.

The history of Southwestern University is more complex. Four predecessor schools provide the background for the Georgetown institution. Rutersville College was chartered in 1840 as a non-sectarian school. The Texas Congress was adamant about maintaining the separation of church and state and refused to charter a sectarian institution. Recognizing the practical politics of the situation, the Methodists accepted a non-sectarian charter. When a charter was sought by Baptists for Baylor five years later, the mood of the Congress had changed.

All the trustees and the president of Rutersville College were Methodists, however, and considered the school to be a Methodist institution. Rutersville College, inspired by its namesake, Martin Ruter, the first Methodist missionary to Texas, had a turbulent history, and by 1854, the Methodist Conference was making provision to abandon its operation. Control of a co-educational school at Chappell Hill was transferred to the conference, and Soule University came into existence on Feb. 2, 1856. Property of Rutersville College was given to the state in 1858.

Two other schools were operated by Methodists for a short time. Wesleyan College in San Augustine was chartered in 1844 and lasted only three years. McKenzie College near Clarksville became a Methodist school in 1860 but was mortally wounded by the Civil War and closed its doors in 1868.

Francis Asbury Mood, president of Soule University, led a movement to consolidate the higher educational efforts of Texas' five Methodist conferences into a single institution. The result was that Southwestern University (originally called Texas University) began operation on Oct. 6, 1873, in Georgetown.

The charter of Southwestern holds this provision that ties its lineage into that of its predecessors:

> The right to confer degrees, regular and honorary, in the arts and sciences, heretofore conveyed through the Legislature of the State of Texas in the charters of Rutersville College, Rutersville; Wesleyan College, San Augustine; Soule University, Chappell Hill; and to McKenzie College, Clarksville, Red River county, are hereby transferred and perpetuated and retained to said Curators; and the graduates of said colleges and University shall be entitled to all the literary privileges and honors inuring (sic) to other graduates of Southwestern University.

Both Baylor and Southwestern have served Texas and their denominations with distinction throughout their histories.

sit in designated areas and were not allowed to participate in church deliberations. Black churches also were established when the membership justified. According to one source, a Methodist conference purchased a particularly effective black minister from a Masonic Lodge to give him more freedom in preaching to blacks and whites. Churches reflected the society of the times. Texans begrudgingly gave blacks their freedom, but few whites would accept the former slaves as social equals or associate with them above menial contact. To remain in white churches, blacks would have to accept an unequal status, which most would not do. Therefore most blacks formed churches within existing denominations but with separate governing bodies.

During the days of the Republic, no more than one Texan in eight — and probably even a smaller segment — was affiliated with a church. Church expansion far exceeded population growth between 1850 and 1860. Population grew 184 percent in the decade, but the number of churches increased from 341 in 1850 to 1,034, according to the 1860 U.S. Census. Methodists and Baptists were by far the largest denominations in the state. Accommodations rather than membership apparently were counted by the census to avoid having the state

seem to investigate church membership. The aggregate accommodations in Methodist churches expanded from 33,045 in 1850 to 103,799 a decade later. Baptists could accommodate 10,680 in 1850 and 77,435 ten years later. By 1860, there were 410 Methodist churches in Texas, 280 Baptist, 72 Presbyterian and 52 Cumberland Presbyterian. Other denominations also expanded, but on a smaller scale than the three major evangelistic denominations.

Despite all this activity, organized religion did not reach parts of Texas until after the Civil War. During the conflict, Sam Newcomb at a private civilian fort on the Brazos River wrote in his diary, "There are men and women here, with grown children, who have never heard a preaching."

Once established, however, churches carried out their traditional roles as civilizing forces, moral and ethical leaders, and as major supporters of education.

Bibliography

BOOKS

Ahlstrom, Sidney E., **A Religious History of the American People;** Yale University Press, New Haven, 1972.

Boxer, C.R., **The Church Militant and Iberian Expansion, 1440-1770;** Johns Hopkins University Press, Baltimore, 1978.

Carroll, J.M., (edited by J.B. Cranfill), **A History of Texas Baptists;** Baptist Standard Publishing Co., Dallas, 1923.

Castanada, Carlos, **Our Catholic Heritage in Texas,** seven volumes; Von Boeckmann-Jones Co., Publishers, Austin, 1937-1958.

Cohen, Henry, David Lefkowitz and Ephraim Frisch, **One Hundred Years of Jewry in Texas;** Jewish Advisory Committee for the Texas Centennial Religious Program, Dallas, 1936.

Crow, John A., **The Epic of Latin America, Third Edition;** University of California Press, Berkeley, 1980.

Elliott, J.H., **Imperial Spain;** New American Library, New York.

Hall, Colby D., **Texas Disciples;** Texas Christian University Press, Fort Worth, 1953.

Hogan, William Ransom, **The Texas Republic: A Social and Economic History;** University of Oklahoma Press, Norman, 1946 (rpt University of Texas Press, Austin, 1980).

Institute of Texan Cultures, **The Jewish Texans;** University of Texas at San Antonio, Institute of Texan Cultures, San Antonio, 1974.

Jones, Ralph Wood, **Southwestern University 1840-1961;** Jenkins Publishing Co., San Felipe Press, Austin, 1973.

Marty, Martin E., **Pilgrims in Their Own Land: 500 Years of Religion in America;** Little, Brown and Co., Boston, 1984.

Matthews, Harlan J., chairman, et al., **Centennial Story of Texas Baptists;** Baptist General Convention of Texas, Dallas, 1936.

Murphy, DuBose, **A Short History of the Protestant Episcopal Church in Texas;** Turner Co., 1935.

Neill, Stephen, **A History of Christian Missions;** Pelican Books, New York, 1982.

Obst, Martin H., et al., **Our God is Marching On: A Centennial History of Bethlehem Lutheran Church, Round Top, Texas;** Bethlehem Lutheran Church, Round Top, 1966.

Reichley, A. James, **Religion In American Public Life;** The Brookings Institution, Washington, D.C., 1985.

Richardson, Rupert, Ernest Wallace and Adrian Anderson, **Texas: The Lone Star State,** Third Edition; Prentice-Hall, Inc., Englewood Cliffs, N.J., 1970.

Richardson, Willard, editor, **The Texas Almanac of 1857;** The Galveston News Publishing Co., Galveston, 1856.

Nail, Olin W., editor, **Texas Methodist Centennial Yearbook;** Olin W. Nail, publisher, Elgin, 1934.

Newcomb, W.W., Jr., **The Indians of Texas: From Prehistoric to Modern Times;** University of Texas Press, Austin, 1961.

Red, William Stuart, **The Texas Colonists and Religion, 1821-1836;** E.L. Shettles, Publisher, Austin, 1924.

Smith, Jesse Guy, **Heroes of the Saddle Bags: A History of Christian Denominations in the Republic of Texas;** The Naylor Co., San Antonio, 1951.

Thrall, Homer S., **History of Methodism in Texas;** Publishing House of the Methodist Episcopal Church, South, Nashville, 1889.

Vernon, Walter N., et al., **The Methodist Excitement in Texas: A History;** Texas United Methodist Historical Society, Bridwell Library, SMU, Dallas, 1984.

Vernon, Walter N., **William Stevenson, Riding Preacher;** Southern Methodist University Press, Dallas, 1964.

Several Texas Groups Pursue Religious History

Religious history in Texas has attracted the interest of many groups representing several denominations. Among the religious history associations, their chief officers and their permanent addresses are the following:

• Texas Baptist Historical Society: Dr. Charles S. McIlvenne, Lufkin, president; Dr. Robert Phillips, Fort Worth, secretary-treasurer; address, P.O. Box 22000, Fort Worth, TX 76122.

• Texas Catholic Historical Society: Dr. Patrick Foley, Fort Worth, president; address, Catholic Archives of Texas, Diocese of Austin, P.O. Box 13327, Austin, TX 78711.

• Texas Jewish Historical Society: Ginger-Jacobs, Dallas, president; Cathy Schechter, Austin, executive secretary, Austin; address, P.O. Box 50501, Austin, TX 78763.

• Texas United Methodist Historical Society: Rev. John C. Johnson, Weatherford, president; address, Mr. Roger Loyd, Bridwell Library, Southern Methodist University, Dallas, TX 75275.

ARTICLES

Baker, Eugene W., **Baylor's Beginnings;** Baylor: The Magazine of Baylor University, June-July 1985, Waco.

Brown, Lawrence L., **A loving look at two prominent Episcopalians;** Houston Chronicle, March 1, 1986.

Eudy, John Carroll, **Methodist arrived with missionary spirit and goals;** Houston Chronicle, March 1, 1986.

Moore, James T., **The Revolution was a setback for Catholicism;** Houston Chronicle, March 1, 1986.

Moore, Louis, **State's religious history colorful;** Houston Chronicle, March 1, 1986.

Owens, Estelle, **Baptists reflected Southern ways, interests, attitudes;** Houston Chronicle, March 1, 1986.

Pearsal, Joan, **A New Role for San Antonio's Missions;** Texas Parks and Wildlife Magazine, January 1984.

Turner, Thomas E., **Baylor: Texas' Oldest University in Continuous Existence;** Baylor University Report, September 1982, Waco.

West, John O., **Pueblos, Adobe, and El Paso's Mission Trail;** Heritage Magazine, Winter 1986.

Church Calendar for 1988-1989

This calendar presents for a two-year period the major days of religious observance for Christians, Jews and Muslims and, within the Christian community, major dates observed by Roman Catholic, Orthodox, Episcopal and Lutheran churches. Within each of these communions many other days of observance, such as saints' days, exist, but only those regarded as major are listed.

Many days of observance, such as Christmas and Easter, do not carry the list of communions observing them since it is assumed that practically all Christian bodies do. In certain cases, a religious observance will be named differently by various communions and this is noted.

In the Orthodox dates, immovable observances are listed in accordance wih the Gregorian calendar. Movable dates (those depending on the date of Easter) will differ often from Western dates, since Pascha (Easter) in the Orthodox communions does not always fall on the same day as in the Western churches. For Orthodox churches that use the old Julian calendar, observances are held 13 days later than listed here.

Ecumenical dates, such as World Communion Sunday, are also included.

For Jews and Muslims, who follow differing lunar calendars, the dates of major observances are translated into Gregorian dates. For Muslim observances, the festivals are dated according to astronomical calculations that have been published in Paris, not the United States, and this could lead to slight variations. Since the actual beginning of a new month in the Islamic calendar is determined by the appearance of the new moon, the corresponding dates given here on the Gregorian calendar may vary slightly. It is also possible for a festival to occur twice in the same Gregorian year. Only 'Id al-Fitr and the 'Id al-Adha are religious holidays that are prescribed by the texts of Islam. Other Islamic dates are nevertheless key moments in the lives of Muslim believers.

(Note: In the calendar, "RC" stands for Roman Catholic, "O" for Orthodox, "E" for Episcopal, "L" for Lutheran, "ECU" for Ecumenical.) From YEARBOOK OF AMERICAN AND CANADIAN CHURCHES, 1986 by Constant H. Jacquet. Copyright © 1986 by The National Council of the Churches of Christ in the USA. Used by permission of the publisher, Abingdon Press.

	1988	1989
New Year's Day (RC—Solemnity of Mary; O—Circumcision of Jesus Christ; E—Feast of the Holy Name; L—Name of Jesus)	Jan. 1	Jan. 1
Epiphany (Armenian Christmas)	Jan. 6	Jan. 6
Feast Day of St. John the Baptist (O)	Jan. 7	Jan. 7
1st Sunday After Epiphany (Feast of the Baptism of Our Lord)	Jan. 10	Jan. 8
Week of Prayer for Christian Unity (ECU)	Jan. 18 to 25	Jan. 18 to 25
Presentation of Jesus in the Temple (O—The Meeting of Our Lord and Savior Jesus Christ)	Feb. 2	Feb. 2
Last Sunday After Epiphany	Feb. 14	Feb. 5
Ash Wednesday (Western churches)	Feb. 17	Feb. 8
Brotherhood Week (Interfaith)	Feb. 21 to 27	Feb. 19 to 25
Easter Lent Begins (Eastern Orthodox)	Feb. 22	Mar. 13
Purim (Jewish)	Mar. 3	Mar. 21
World Day of Prayer (ECU)	Mar. 4	Mar. 3
Joseph, Husband of Mary (RC, E, L)	Mar. 19	Mar. 19
The Annunciation (RC, O, E, L)	Mar. 25	Mar. 25
Sunday of the Passion (Palm Sunday) (Western churches)	Mar. 27	Mar. 19
Holy Week (Western churches)	Mar. 27 to Apr. 2	Mar. 19 to 25
Maundy Thursday (Western churches)	Mar. 31	Mar. 23
Good Friday (Friday of the Passion of Our Lord) (Western churches)	Apr. 1	Mar. 24
1st Day of Passover (Jewish, 8 days)	Apr. 2	Apr. 20
Palm Sunday (Eastern Orthodox)	Apr. 3	Apr. 23
Easter (Western churches)	Apr. 3	Mar. 26
Holy Week (Eastern Orthodox)	Apr. 3 to 9	Apr. 23 to 29
Holy Thursday (Eastern Orthodox)	Apr. 7	Apr. 27
Holy (Good) Friday, Burial of Jesus Christ (Eastern Orthodox)	Apr. 8	Apr. 28
Pascha (Eastern Orthodox Easter)	Apr. 10	Apr. 30
First Day of the Month of Ramadan	Apr. 18	Apr. 8
May Fellowship Day (ECU)	May 6	May 5
Rural Life Sunday (ECU)	May 8	May 14
Ascension Day (Western churches)	May 12	May 4
Ascension Day (Eastern Orthodox)	May 19	June 8
'Id al-Fitr (Festival of the End of Ramadan, celebrated on the first day of the month of Shawwal)	May 20	May 8
1st Day of Shavuot (Jewish, 2 days)	May 22	June 9
Pentecost (Whitsunday) (Western churches)	May 22	May 14
Holy Trinity (RC, E, L)	May 29	May 21
Pentecost (Eastern Orthodox)	May 29	May 18
Visitation of the Blessed Virgin Mary (RC, E, L)	May 31	May 31
Corpus Christi (RC)	June 5	May 28
Sacred Heart of Jesus (RC)	June 10	June 2
Nativity of St. John the Baptist (RC, E, L)	June 24	June 24
Saint Peter and Saint Paul, Apostles (RC, O, E, L)	June 29	June 29
Feast Day of the Twelve Apostles of Christ (O)	June 30	June 30
'Id al-Adha (Festival of Sacrifice at time of annual pilgrimage to Mecca)	July 24	July 15
The Transfiguration of Our Lord Jesus Christ (RC, O, E, L)	Aug. 6	Aug. 6
First Day of the Month of Muharram (beginning of Muslim liturgical year)	Aug. 13	Aug. 4
Feast of the Blessed Virgin Mary (RC—Assumption of Blessed Mary, the Virgin; O—Falling Asleep (Dormition) of the Blessed Virgin Mary; E—Feast of the Blessed Virgin Mary; L—Mary, Mother of Our Lord)	Aug. 15	Aug. 15
The Birth of the Blessed Virgin (RC, O)	Sept. 8	Sept. 8
1st Day of Rosh Hashanah (Jewish, 2 days)	Sept. 12	Sept. 30
Holy Cross Day (O—The Adoration of the Holy Cross; RC—Triumph of the Cross)	Sept. 14	Sept. 14
Yom Kippur (Jewish)	Sept. 21	Oct. 9
1st Day of Sukkot (Jewish, 7 days)	Sept. 26	Oct. 14
World Communion Sunday (ECU)	Oct. 2	Oct. 1
Shemini Atzeret (Jewish)	Oct. 3	Oct. 21
Simhat Torah (Jewish)	Oct. 4	Oct. 22
Laity Sunday (ECU)	Oct. 9	Oct. 8

	1988	1989
Mawlid al-Nabi (Anniversary of Prophet Muhammad's birthday)	Oct. 24	Oct. 14
Reformation Sunday (L).	Oct. 30	Oct. 29
Reformation Day (L)	Oct. 31	Oct. 31
All Saints Day (RC, E, L).	Nov. 1	Nov. 1
World Community Day (ECU).	Nov. 4	Nov. 3
Stewardship Day (ECU)	Nov. 13	Nov. 12
Bible Sunday (ECU)	Nov. 20	Nov. 19
Last Sunday After Pentecost (RC, L—Feast of Christ the King)	Nov. 20	Nov. 26
Thanksgiving Sunday (U.S.)	Nov. 20	Nov. 19
Presentation of the Blessed Virgin Mary in the Temple (Also Presentation of the Theotokos) (O)	Nov. 21	Nov. 21
Thanksgiving Day (U.S.)	Nov. 24	Nov. 23
1st Sunday of Advent.	Nov. 27	Dec. 3
Feast Day of St. Andrew the Apostle (RC, O, E, L)	Nov. 30	Nov. 30
1st Day of Hanukkah (Jewish, 8 days)	Dec. 4	Dec. 23
Immaculate Conception of the Blessed Virgin Mary (RC)	Dec. 8	Dec. 8
4th Sunday of Advent (Sunday before Christmas)	Dec. 18	Dec. 24
Christmas	Dec. 25	Dec. 25

Church Membership in Texas

Below is given the number of churches, number of full members (confirmed communicants) and number of total adherents of the different denominations in Texas in 1980 (latest year for which data available). These data are taken from "Churches and Church Membership in the United States 1980," authors Bernard Quinn, Herman Anderson, Martin Bradley, Paul Goetting and Peggy Shriver. This is an enumeration by region, state and county based on data reported by 111 church bodies with 112,538,310 adherents. It was copyrighted in 1982 by the National Council of the Churches of Christ in the U.S.A. It was published by the Glenmary Research Center, Atlanta, Ga. and is reprinted here with their written permission. Further use not sanctioned without written permission from the above-named source. For various reasons, some small groups did not participate.

Church Name—	No. of Churches	Full Members (Confirmed Communicants)	No. Total Adherents
Advent Christian....	4	299	*364
A.M.E. Zion	7	1,752	2,095
American Baptist Assn.	340	45,361	45,361
Am. Baptist U.S.A. ...	59	17,787	*21,770
American Lutheran..	257	85,286	106,657
Assemblies of God...	1,134	117,957	162,232
Baptist Missionary Assn.	517	97,351	*118,643
Brethren in Christ ...	1	57	86
Catholic	1,227	N.A.	2,340,162
Ch. & Missionary Alliance........	23	1,160	2,239
Chris. Ch. (Disciples of Christ)	448	84,295	120,296
Chr. Churches & Chs. of Christ......	149	22,090	*27,255
C.M.E.	312	68,825	*83,932
Christian Reformed .	3	105	165
Church God (ABR) ..	3	86	*107
Church God (Anderson)	84	5,550	16,650
Church God (Cleveland)	192	12,824	*15,708
Church God (7th Day) (Denver)	20	644	*804
Ch. God in Christ (Mennonite)	4	207	207
Ch. of Jes. Christ (Bickertonite) ..	1	13	13
Latter-Day Saints ...	212	N.A.	68,375
Church of Brethren ..	4	310	*377
Ch. Lutheran Confession	3	147	201
Church of Nazarene..	309	24,670	39,479
Churches of Christ...	2,222	278,820	355,396
Congregational Christian	3	633	*782
Congregational Holiness.........	2	60	*73
Conservative Congregational ...	1	74	*92
Cumberland Presbyterian	51	4,969	8,408
Episcopal	395	136,416	174,581
Evangelical Ch. of N.A...........	1	46	46
Evangelical Congregational ...	1	38	*50
Evangelical Covenant Ch. Am.........	1	59	*77
Evangelical Free Church	15	1,142	*1,394

Church Name—	No. of Churches	Full Members (Confirmed Communicants)	No. Total Adherents
Evan. Lutheran Assn.	4	657	925
Evan. Lutheran Synod	2	39	157
Evan. Methodist	17	1,686	*2,050
Free Methodist	18	564	1,857
Friends-U.S.A.	15	1,525	*1,867
Gen. Conf. Mennonite Brethren	9	358	*461
Grace Brethren.....	1	13	*16
Internatl. Foursquare Gospel........	49	5,674	*6,988
Conservative Judaism	16	6,136	*7,557
Reformed Judaism ..	30	18,592	*22,857
Luth. Ch. America...	106	27,934	36,670
Lutheran-Missouri Synod	311	88,377	117,074
Mennonite	10	564	*712
Mennonite Gen. Conference	1	60	84
Metro Community...	7	1,004	2,008
N. Am. Baptist Conf.	11	798	*981
Orthodox Presbyterian	2	244	*299
Pentecostal Holiness.	70	3,353	*4,190
Christian Brethren ..	32	2,015	3,520
Presbyterian Ch. Am.	15	1,309	1,543
†Presbyterian Ch., U.S.	519	106,566	*130,895
Protestant Reformed	1	10	26
Ref. Presbyterian-Evan..	3	355	454
Salvation Army.....	44	4,379	14,720
Seventh Day Adventists	178	18,974	*23,354
S-D Baptist Gen. Conf.	2	18	*22
Southern Baptist Con.	3,896	2,172,997	*2,659,894
Southern Methodist..	6	229	315
Syrian Antioch	2	800	*976
Unitarian-Universal .	34	3,838	*4,701
United Ch. of Christ..	71	16,889	*20,626
United Methodist ...	2,257	761,290	*932,488
†United Presby. Ch., U.S.A.	348	53,278	*65,150
Wisconsin Evan. Lutheran	19	1,701	2,453
Total.	16,111	4,311,259	*7,781,967

N.A. Not applicable. *Total adherents estimated from known number of communicant, confirmed, full members. †Presbyterian Church, U.S. (Southern) and United Presbyterian Church, U.S.A., united after this census was taken and are now known as Presbyterian Church, (U.S.A.).

Environment

Water Supplies and Needs

The 69th Legislature separated the state's single water agency, the Texas Department of Water Resources, into two agencies: the Texas Water Commission and the Texas Water Development Board. In addition, the three-member Texas Water Commission was retained to handle judicial matters, and a six-member Texas Water Development Board was retained to establish board policy.

Texas, through its river authorities, municipalities, water districts and state-level agencies, exercises the dominant role in development of municipal and industrial water supplies. Approximately 80 percent of the money invested in the state's water projects has been provided by Texas entities of government.

Ground-Water Supplies and Use

Aquifers underlie more than half of the area of Texas. This ground water has long been the principal source of municipal supplies, but cities now increasingly depend upon surface reservoirs due to depletion of water in aquifer storage. More than half of Texas' total agricultural crop value is produced utilizing **ground water** for irrigation, mainly from the **High Plains (Ogallala) aquifer,** which underlies most of the Panhandle.

Declining water levels, mining and exhaustion of ground water, coupled with increasing energy costs, are major problems facing the state's water managers today.

Major aquifers in Texas follow (see map):

High Plains (Ogallala) — This formation furnishes practically the only usable quality water on the High Plains. It is composed of unconsolidated, fine- to coarse-grained, gray to red sand, clay, silt and gravel. Effective recharge from precipitation is small, averaging less than one-quarter inch yearly, whereas pumping is heavy, averaging about 5.3 million acre-feet yearly. Depletion at the present pumping rate threatens this as a water source for irrigation. The High Plains (Ogallala) aquifer supplies Texas' largest irrigated farming region, which produces most of Texas' cotton, grain sorghum and other crops.

Alluvium and Bolson Deposits — These water-bearing deposits are scattered throughout many areas in the state. They include the **Hueco and Mesilla Bolsons,** the **Cenozoic Alluvium** of West Texas, the alluviums of North Central Texas, the **Leona Alluvium** of Tom Green County and the **Brazos River Alluvium** of Southeast Texas. These deposits consist generally of sand, gravel, silt and clay. The quality of the water can range from fresh to saline.

In the westernmost Texas region, the Mesilla and Hueco Bolsons are the primary source of water supply for the **El Paso area,** where serious problems exist regarding ground-water depletion and quality degradation. Other sources of ground-water supply are from the **Salt Bolson** (Wildhorse Draw, Michigan Flat, Lobo Flat and Ryan Flat areas), the **Red Light Draw Bolson,** the **Green River Valley Bolson** and the **Presidio and Redford Bolsons.** In the Cenozoic Alluvium region, the **Coyonosa** area of northwest Pecos and northeast Reeves counties and northeastern Ward County are the most productive areas of usable quality ground water. Supplies are produced from the **Seymour aquifer** in North Central Texas.

Edwards-Trinity (Plateau) — This aquifer underlies the Edwards Plateau region of Southwest Texas. It consists of saturated sediments of the **Lower Cretaceous Comanchean Series** made up of sand, sandstone, gravel and conglomerate of the **Trinity Group (Antlers Sand);** and cherty, gypseous, argillaceous, cavernous limestones and dolomites of the **Comanche Peak, Edwards and Georgetown formations.** The ground water generally flows southeasterly, and near the edge of the Plateau, movement is toward the main streams where the water issues from springs. The water ranges in quality from

fresh to slightly saline and is hard. Most of the municipalities on the Plateau depend on this aquifer for their water supply. Where the land is arable and yield from wells is sufficient, irrigated farming is possible. Problems exist in those areas where development has exceeded the capabilities of the aquifer.

Edwards (Balcones Fault Zone) — Ground water occurs in fractures, honeycomb zones and solution channels in this aquifer that underlies an area along the **Balcones Fault Zone** from **Kinney County** on the west through **Bexar County** to **Bell County** on the north. Geologically, it is made up of the **Edwards and associated limestones** of Cretaceous age and consists of massive to thin-bedded, nodular, cherty, gypseous, argillaceous, white to gray limestone and dolomite of the **Comanche Peak, Edwards** and **Georgetown formations,** which have been downset from the Edwards Plateau due to faulting. The aquifer is recharged rapidly by water discharged from springs along the edge of the Edwards Plateau, which then flows in streams that traverse the many faults along the Balcones. The ground water moves through the aquifer generally in an easterly, northeasterly direction to points of discharge, notable of which are **Leona, San Antonio, San Pedro, Comal, San Marcos, Barton** and **Salado springs,** plus numerous smaller springs. In **Bexar County,** wells pumping from this aquifer are among the world's largest. The water is generally of good quality and it is used for public supply, irrigation, industrial, domestic and livestock watering purposes. Hydrologically, the aquifer is unique and is one of the state's most valuable natural resources. In the past, the aquifer was adequate to meet **San Antonio's** water needs, but increased growth and development in this area necessitate additional surface water supplies.

Trinity Group — These basal Cretaceous-age rocks extend over a large area of North and Central Texas and are composed primarily of sand with interbedded clays, limestone, dolomite, gravel and conglomerates. The Trinity Group is made up of the **Twin Mountains, Glen Rose** and **Paluxy formations;** however, to the west and north where the Glen Rose Formation thins or pinches out, the **Twin Mountains** and **Paluxy formations** coalesce and are called the **Antlers Formation.** The water quality is acceptable for most municipal and industrial purposes. Extensive irrigation occurs in **Comanche, Eastland** and **Erath** counties. The aquifer has been overdeveloped in the **Dallas-Fort Worth metropolitan** area and in the vicinity of **Waco,** where water levels have declined to near 1,200 feet below the land surface.

Carrizo-Wilcox — This aquifer of Eocene age is one of the most extensive water-bearing formations in Texas as geographically, and it furnishes water to wells in a wide belt extending from the Rio Grande northeastward into Arkansas and Louisiana. It consists of hydrologically connected ferruginous, cross-bedded sand with clay, sandstone, silt, lignite and gravel of the **Wilcox Group** and overlying **Carrizo Formation.** Throughout

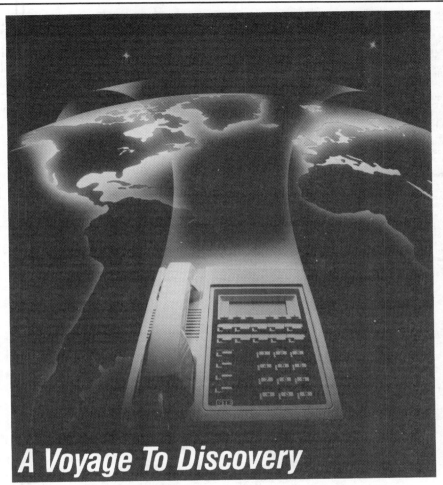

most of Texas, the Carrizo-Wilcox aquifer yields fresh to slightly saline water which is acceptable for most irrigation, public supply and industrial uses. Because of excessive pumping, the water levels have been significantly lowered, particularly in the **Winter Garden District of Dimmit and Zavala counties** and in the municipal and industrial areas located north of **Lufkin** in **Angelina** and **Nacogdoches counties**. However, water-level declines in the Winter Garden area have been significantly arrested during the past 10 years.

Gulf Coast Aquifer — Geologically, the Gulf Coast aquifer ranges in age from Miocene to Holocene, and it is collectively composed of the **Catahoula, Oakville, Lagarto, Goliad, Willis, Lissie and Beaumont formations**. Lithologically, it consists of alternating beds of clay, silt, sand and gravel which are hydrologically connected. The principal water-bearing units are the Goliad, Willis and Lissie formations. It parallels the Texas Gulf Coast from Mexico to Louisiana. Normally, fresh to slightly saline ground water occurs in the aquifer from the San Antonio River basin northeastward to Louisiana. In this area, large quantities are pumped for municipal, industrial and irrigation use. Ground-water quality tends to deteriorate in the San Antonio River basin and southwestward to Mexico, where there are areas in which no appreciable amounts of fresh to slightly saline water can be found. Problems of land-surface subsidence in the Houston area are well documented. Additionally, withdrawal of ground water from the Gulf Coast aquifer can cause increased chloride content, especially in the southwest portion, and salt-water encroachment along the coast. Therefore, management of future withdrawals from the aquifer is necessary in order to alleviate serious ground-water problems.

Water Budget

Average annual precipitation in Texas is estimated at 413,000,000 acre-feet. (One acre-foot is 325,851 gallons.) The **Average Annual Water Budget for Texas**, which follows, was compiled by the **Texas Water Development Board**.

This shows that more water is lost through evaporation, consumption by useless weeds and brush and discharge into the Gulf of Mexico than is used by Texas municipalities, industries and agriculture. In addition to these losses, precipitation is very unevenly distributed in Texas, with abundant supplies in the eastern half of the state contrasting with scarcities in the western portion. Also, it shows that the total outgo exceeds the income, which is the result of mining ground water.

Average Annual Water Budget for Texas

	Million Acre-Ft.	Per Cent
INCOME		
All precipitation	413	100.0
OUTGO		
Evaporation	174	42.0
From plant cover	52	12.5
From soil surface	122	29.5
Transpiration	193	47.0
From non-economic plants	154	37.5
Cultivated crops	16	4.0
Range and pasture plants	13	3.0
Commercial forests	10	2.5
Addition to ground-water storage	5	1.0
Surface Runoff	49	12.0
Industrial, municipal and irrigation consumption	2	0.5
Evaporation from water surface	8	2.0
Discharged into sea	39	9.5
Total Outgo	421	102.0

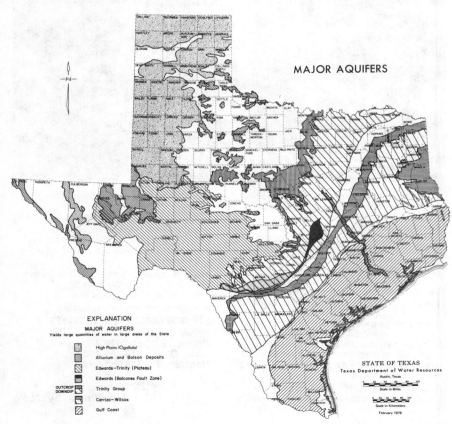

MAJOR AQUIFERS

EXPLANATION

MAJOR AQUIFERS

Yields large quantities of water in large areas of the State

High Plains (Ogallala)

Alluvium and Bolson Deposits

Edwards–Trinity (Plateau)

Edwards (Balcones Fault Zone)

OUTCROP DOWNDIP Trinity Group

Carrizo–Wilcox

Gulf Coast

STATE OF TEXAS

Texas Department of Water Resources

Austin, Texas

Scale in Miles

Scale in Kilometers

February 1979

Lakes and Reservoirs

The large increase in the number of reservoirs in Texas during the past half-century has greatly improved water conservation and supplies. As late as 1913, Texas had only eight major reservoirs with a total storage capacity of 376,000 acre-feet. Most of this capacity was in **Medina Lake**, with 254,000 acre-feet capacity, created by a dam completed in May 1913.

By 1920, Texas had 11 major reservoirs with combined storage capacity of 449,710 acre-feet. The state water agency reported 32 reservoirs and 1,284,520 acre-feet capacity in 1930; 47 reservoirs with 5,369,550 acre-feet capacity in 1940; 66 with 9,623,870 acre-feet capacity by 1950; 105 with total capacity of 22,746,200 in 1960; 149 with total capacity of 51,086,200 in 1970; 168 with total capacity of 53,302,400 in 1980. In January 1983, Texas had 189 major reservoirs existing or under construction, with a total capacity near 58.6 million acre-feet, of which 38.4 million acre-feet was conservation storage, 17.8 million acre-feet was flood control storage and 2.4 million acre-feet was considered inactive.

According to the U.S. Statistical Abstract of 1987, Texas ranks second behind Minnesota in inland water area among the continental states. Texas has 4,790 square miles of inland water, according to this survey, compared to Minnesota's 4,854 square miles.

The following table lists reservoirs in Texas having more than 5,000 acre-feet capacity. A few locally significant reservoirs of less capacity are not included. With few exceptions, the listed reservoirs are those that were completed by Jan. 1, 1987 and in use. An asterisk (*) indicates those that are under construction.

There are about 5,700 reservoirs in Texas with surface areas of 10 acres or larger; however, conservation water storage capacity in the listed reservoirs represents about 97 percent of total conservation water storage capacity in all Texas reservoirs.

Conservation storage capacity is used in the table below; the **surface area** used is that area at conservation elevation only. (Different methods of computing capacity are used; detailed information may be obtained from Texas Water Development Board, Austin; U.S. Army Corps of Engineers or local sources.) Also, it should be noted that boundary reservoir capacities include water designated for Texas use and non-Texas water.

In the list below, information is given in the following order: (1) Name of lake or reservoir; (2) county or counties in which located; (3) river or creek on which located; (4) location with respect to some city or town; (5) purpose of reservoir; (6) owner of reservoir. Some of these items, when not listed, are not available. For the larger lakes and reservoirs, the dam impounding water to form the lake bears the same name, unless otherwise indicated. Abbreviations in list below are as follows: L., lake; R., river; Co., county; Cr., creek; (C) conservation; (FC) flood control; (R) recreation; (P) power; (M) municipal; (D) domestic; (Ir.) irrigation; (In.) industry; (Mi.) mining including oil production; (FH) fish hatchery; USAE, United States Army Corps of Engineers; WC&ID, Water Control and Improvement District; WID, Water Improvement District; USBR, United States Bureau of Reclamation.

Lakes and Reservoirs	Conservation Surface Area (Acres)	Conservation Storage Capacity (Acre-Ft.)
Abilene L.—Taylor Co.; Elm Cr.; 6 mi. NW Tuscola; (M-In.-R); City of Abilene	595	7,900
Addicks Reservoir—Harris Co.; S. Mayde and Langham Crs.; 1 mi. E. Addicks; (for flood control only); USAE.	0	0
Alcoa L.—Milam Co.; Sandy Cr.; 7 mi. SW Rockdale; (In.-R); Aluminum Co. of America	880	14,750
Amistad Reservoir—Val Verde Co.; Rio Grande, dam between Del Rio and confluence of Rio Grande and Devils River; an international project of the U.S. and Mexico; 12 mi. NW Del Rio; (C-R-Ir.-P-FC); International Boundary and Water Com. (Texas' share of conservation capacity is 56.2 percent.)	64,900	3,383,900
Amon G. Carter, L.—Montague Co.; Big Sandy Cr.; 6 mi. S Bowie; (M-In.); City of Bowie	1,540	20,050
Anahuac L.—Chambers Co.; Turtle Bayou; near Anahuac; (Ir.-In.-Mi.); Chambers-Liberty counties Navigation District.	5,300	35,300
Aquilla L.—Hill Co.; Aquilla Cr.; 10.2 mi. SW of Hillsboro; (FC-M-Ir.-In.-R); USAE-Brazos R. Auth.	3,280	52,400
Arlington L.—Tarrant Co.; Village Cr.; 7 mi. W Arlington; (M-In.); City of Arlington. . . .	2,275	45,710
Arrowhead, L.—Clay Co.; Little Wichita R.; 13 mi. SE Wichita Falls; (M); City of Wichita Falls	16,200	262,100
Athens, L.—Henderson Co.; 8 mi. E Athens; (M-FC-R); Athens Mun. Water Authority (formerly **Flat Creek Reservoir**)	1,520	32,690
Aubrey L.—(See Ray Roberts L.)		
Austin, L.—Travis Co.; Colorado R.; W Austin city limits; (M-In.-P); City of Austin, leased to LCRA (impounded by **Tom Miller Dam**)	1,830	21,000
Balmorhea, L.—Reeves Co.; Sandia Cr.; 3 mi. SE Balmorhea; (Ir.); Reeves Co. WID No. 1	573	6,350
Bardwell L.—Ellis Co.; Waxahachie Cr.; 3 mi. SE Bardwell; (FC-C-R); USAE	3,570	53,580
Barker R.—Harris-Fort Bend counties; Buffalo Bayou; 1 mi. S Addicks; (for flood control only); USAE	0	0
Barney M. Davis Cooling Reservoir—Nueces Co.; off-channel storage reservoir of Laguna Madre arm of Gulf; 14 mi. SE Corpus Christi; (In.); Central Power & Light Co. . . .	1,100	6,600
Bastrop, L.—Bastrop Co.; Spicer Cr.; 3 mi. NE Bastrop; (In.); LCRA	906	16,590
Baylor Creek Lake—Childress Co.; 10 mi. NW Childress; (M-R); City of Childress	610	9,220
Belton L.—Bell-Coryell counties; Leon R.; 3 mi. N. Belton; (M-FC-In.-Ir.); USAE-Brazos R. Auth	12,300	457,300
Benbrook L.—Tarrant Co.; Clear Fk. Trinity R.; 10 mi. SW Fort Worth; (FC-R); USAE . .	3,770	88,200
Big Brown Creek Reservoir—Freestone Co. (See Fairfield L.).		
Big Hill Reservoir—Jefferson Co. (See J. D. Murphree Area Impoundments.).		
Bivins L.—Randall Co.; Palo Duro Cr.; 8 mi. NW Canyon; (M); Amarillo (also known as **Amarillo City Lake**); City of Amarillo.	379	5,120
Blackburn Crossing L.—(See Lake Palestine.).		
Bonham, L.—Fannin Co.; Timber Cr.; 5 mi. NE Bonham; (M); Bonham Mun. Water Auth..	1,020	12,000
Bowie L.—(See Amon G. Carter, L.)		
Brady Creek Reservoir—McCulloch Co.; Brady Cr.; 3 mi. W Brady; (M-In.); City of Brady	2,020	29,110
Brandy Branch Reservoir—Harrison Co.; Brandy Br.; 10 mi. SW Marshall; (In.); Southwestern Electric Power Co.	1,240	29,500
Brazoria Reservoir—Brazoria Co.; off-channel reservoir; 1 mi. NE Brazoria; (In.); Dow Chemical Co..	1,865	21,970
Bridgeport, L.—Wise-Jack counties; W. Fk. of Trinity R.; 4 mi. W Bridgeport; (M-In.-FC-R); Tarrant Co. WC&ID Dist. No. 1	13,000	386,420

Name		
Brownwood, L.—Brown Co.; Pecan Bayou; 8 mi. N Brownwood; (M-In.-Ir.); Brown Co. WC&ID No. 1	7,300	143,400
Brushy Creek Reservoir—(See Valley L.).		
Bryan Utilities L.—Brazos Co.; unnamed stream; 6 mi. NW Bryan; (R-In.); City of Bryan	829	15,227
Buchanan, L.—Burnet-Llano-San Saba counties; Colorado R.; 13 mi. W Burnet; (M-Ir.-Mi.-P); LCRA	23,060	955,200
Buffalo Springs L.—Lubbock Co.; Double Mtn.Fk. Brazos R.; 9 mi. SE Lubbock; (M-In.-R); Lubbock Co. WC & ID No. 1; (impounded by W. G. McMillan Sr. Dam)	200	3,950
Buffalo L.—Randall Co.; Tierra Blanca Cr.; 2 mi. S Umbarger; (R); U.S. Fish & Wildlife Service (impounded by Umbarger Dam).	1,900	18,150
Caddo L.—Harrison-Marion counties, Texas and Caddo Parish, La. An original natural lake, whose surface and capacity were increased by the construction of a dam on Cypress Creek near Mooringsport, La.	25,400	59,800
Calaveras L.—Bexar Co.; Calaveras Cr.; 15 mi. SE San Antonio; (In.); City Public Service Bd. of San Antonio.	3,450	61,800
Camp Creek L.—Robertson Co.; 13 mi. E Franklin; (R); Camp Creek Water Co.	750	8,550
Canyon L.—Comal Co.; Guadalupe R.; 12 mi. NW New Braunfels; (M-In.-P-FC); Guadalupe-Blanco R. Authority & USAE.	8,240	385,600
Casa Blanca L.—Webb Co.; Chacon Cr.; 3 mi. NE Laredo; (R); Webb County (impounded by Country Club Dam)	1,656	20,000
Cedar Bayou Cooling Reservoir—Chambers Co.; Cedar Bayou; 15 mi. SW Anahuac; (In.); Houston Lighting & Power Co.	2,600	20,000
Cedar Creek Reservoir—Henderson-Kaufman counties; Cedar Cr.; 3 mi. NE Trinidad; (sometimes called Joe B. Hogsett L.); (M-R); Tarrant Co. WC&ID No. 1.	33,750	679,200
Cedar Creek Reservoir—Fayette Co.; Cedar Cr.; 8.5 mi. E. La Grange; (In.); LCRA.	2,420	71,400
Champion Creek Reservoir—Mitchell Co.; 7 mi. S. Colorado City; (M-In.); Tex. Elec. Service Co.	1,560	41,600
Cherokee L.—Gregg-Rusk counties; Cherokee Bayou; 12 mi. SE Longview; (M-In.-R); Cherokee Water Co.	3,987	46,700
Choke Canyon Reservoir—Live Oak-McMullen counties; Frio R.; 4 mi. W Three Rivers; (M-In.-R-FC); City of Corpus Christi-USBR.	26,000	690,400
Cisco, L.—Eastland Co.; Sandy Cr.; 4 mi. N. Cisco; (M); City of Cisco (impounded by Williamson Dam)	445	8,800
Cleburne, L. Pat—Johnson Co.; Nolan R.; 4 mi. S. Cleburne; (M); City of Cleburne	1,550	25,300
Clyde, L.—Callahan Co.; N. Prong Pecan Bayou; 6 mi. S. Clyde; (M); City of Clyde and USDA Soil Conservation Service.	449	5,748
Coffee Mill L.—Fannin Co.; Coffee Mill Cr.; 12 mi. NW Honey Grove; (R); U.S. Forest Service	650	8,000
Coleman L.—Coleman Co.; Jim Ned Cr.; 14 mi. N. Coleman; (M-In.); City of Coleman.	2,000	40,000
Coleto Creek Reservoir—Goliad-Victoria counties; Coleto Cr.; 12 mi. SW Victoria; (In); Guadalupe-Blanco River Auth.	3,100	35,080
Colorado City, L.—Mitchell Co.; Morgan Cr.; 4 mi. SW Colorado City; (M-In.-P); Texas Elec. Service Co.	1,612	30,800
Conroe, L.—Montgomery-Walker counties; W. Fk. San Jacinto R.; 7 mi. NW Conroe; (M-In.-Mi.); San Jacinto River Authority, City of Houston and Texas Water Dev. Bd.	20,985	429,900
*Cooper L.—Delta-Hopkins counties; Sulphur R.; 3 mi. SE Cooper; (FC-M-R); USAE	19,305	310,000
Corpus Christi, L.—Live Oak-San Patricio-Jim Wells counties; Nueces R.; 4 mi. SW Mathis; (P-M-In.-Ir.-Mi.-R.); Lower Nueces River WSD (impounded by Wesley E. Seale Dam)	19,336	269,900
Crook, L.—Lamar Co.; Pine Cr.; 5 Mi. N. Paris; (M); City of Paris	1,226	9,964
Cypress Springs, L.—Franklin Co.; Big Cypress Cr.; 8 mi. SE Mount Vernon; (In-M); Franklin Co. WD and Texas Water Development Board (formerly Franklin Co. L.); impounded by Franklin Co. Dam.	3,400	66,800
Dallas L.—(See Lewisville L.).		
Dam B Reservoir—(See Steinhagen L., B.A.).		
Daniel, L.—Stephens Co.; Gunsolus Cr.; 7 mi. S Breckenridge; (M-In.); City of Breckenridge; (impounded by Gunsolus Creek Dam)	924	9,515
Davis L.—Knox Co.; Double Dutchman Cr.; 5 mi. SE Benjamin; (Ir); League Ranch	585	5,395
Decker L.—(See Walter E. Long, Lake.)		
DeCordova Bend Reservoir—(See Lake Granbury.)		
Delta Lake Res. Units 1 and 2—Hidalgo Co.; Rio Grande (off channel); 4 mi. N. Monte Alto; (Ir.); Hidalgo-Willacy counties WC&ID No. 1 (formerly Monte Alto Reservoir).	2,371	25,000
Diablo Reservoir—(See Amistad Reservoir.)		
Diversion, L.—Archer-Baylor counties; Wichita R.; 14 mi. W Holliday; (M-In.); City of Wichita Falls and Wichita Co. WID No. 2	3,419	40,000
Dunlap, L.—Guadalupe Co.; Guadalupe R.; 9 mi. NW Seguin; (P); Guadalupe-Blanco R. Authority; (impounded by TP-1 Dam)	410	3,550
Eagle L.—Colorado Co.; Colorado R. (off channel); in Eagle Lake; (Ir.); Lakeside Irrigation Co.	1,200	9,600
Eagle Mountain Lake—Tarrant-Wise counties; W. Fk. Trinity R.; 14 mi. NW Fort Worth; (M-In.-Ir.); Tarrant Co. WC&ID No. 1	9,200	190,300
East L.—(See Victor Braunig Lake.)		
Eddleman L.—(See Lake Graham.).		
Electra City L.—Wilbarger Co.; Camp Cr. and Beaver Cr.; 7 mi. SW Electra; (In.-M); City of Electra	660	8,055
Ellison Creek Reservoir—Morris Co.; Ellison Cr.; 8 mi. S. Daingerfield; (P-In.); Lone Star Steel	1,516	24,700
Fairfield L.—Freestone Co.; Big Brown Cr.; 11 mi. NE Fairfield; (In.); TP&L, Texas Elec. Service Co., DP&L and Industrial Generating Co. (formerly Big Brown Creek Reservoir).	2,350	50,600
Falcon Reservoir—Starr-Zapata counties; Rio Grande; (International—U.S.-Mexico); 3 mi. W Falcon Heights; (M-In.-Ir.-FC-P-R); International Boundary and Water Com.; (Texas' share of total conservation capacity is 58.6 per cent)	87,210	2,667,600
Farmers Creek Reservoir—Montague Co.; 8 mi. NE Nocona; (M-In.-Mi.) N Montague County Water Supply District (also known as Lake Nocona)	1,470	25,400
Ferrell's Bridge Dam Reservoir—(See Lake O' the Pines.)		
Flat Creek Reservoir—(See Athens Lake.).		
Forest Grove Reservoir—Henderson Co.; Caney Cr.; 7 mi. NW Athens; (In.); Texas Utilities Services, Inc., Agent	1,502	20,038
Forney Reservoir—(See Ray Hubbard Lake.)		

Fort Phantom Hill, Lake—Jones Co.; Elm Cr.; 5 mi. S. Nugent; (M-R); City of Abilene . . .	4,246	74,300
Franklin County L.—(See **Cypress Springs Lake**.)		
Galveston County Industrial Water Reservoir—Galveston Co.; off-channel storage Dickinson Bayou; 16 mi. S La Porte; (In.-M.); Galveston Co. Water Auth.	812	7,308
Garza-Little Elm—(See **Lewisville L.**)		
Georgetown, L.—Williamson Co.; N. Fk. San Gabriel R.; 3.5 mi. W Georgetown; (FC-M-In.); USAE (formerly **North Fork L.**)	1,310	37,050
Gibbons Creek Reservoir—Grimes Co.; Gibbons Cr.; 9.5 mi NW Anderson; (In.); Texas Mun. Power Agency	2,490	26,824
Gladewater, L.—Upshur Co.; Glade Cr.; in Gladewater; (M-R); City of Gladewater	800	6,950
Graham L.—Young Co.; Flint and Salt Creeks; 2 mi. NW Graham; (M-In.); City of Graham	2,550	45,000
Granbury L.—Hood-Parker counties; Brazos R.; 8 mi. SE Granbury; (M-In.-Ir.-P); Brazos River Authority (impounded by **DeCordova Bend Dam**)	8,700	151,300
Granger L.—Williamson Co.; San Gabriel R.; 10 mi. NE Taylor; (FC-M-In.); USAE (formerly **Laneport Lake**)	4,400	64,540
Granite Shoals L.—(See **Johnson L.**)		
Grapevine L.—Tarrant-Denton counties; Denton Cr.; 2 mi. NE Grapevine; (M-FC-In.-R.); USAE	7,380	187,700
Greenbelt L.—Donley Co.; Salt Fk. Red R.; 5 mi. N Clarendon; (M-In.); Greenbelt M&I Water Auth..	1,990	58,200
H-4 Reservoir—Gonzales Co.; Guadalupe R.; 4.5 mi. SE Belmont; (P); Guadalupe-Blanco R. Auth. (also called **Guadalupe Reservoir H-4**)	696	5,200
Halbert, L.—Navarro Co.; Elm Cr.; 4 mi. SE Corsicana; (M-In-R); City of Corsicana	650	7,420
Harris Reservoir—Brazoria Co.; off-channel between Brazos R. and Oyster Cr.; 8 mi. NW Angleton; (In.); Dow Chemical Co.	1,663	12,000
Hawkins, L.—Wood Co.; Little Sandy Cr.; 3 mi. NW Hawkins; (FC-R); Wood County; (impounded by **Wood Co. Dam No. 3**)	776	11,570
Holbrook L.—Wood Co.; Keys Cr.; 4 mi. NW Mineola; (FC-R); Wood County; (impounded by **Wood Co. Dam No. 2**)	653	7,770
Honea Reservoir—(See **Conroe Lake**.)		
Hords Creek L.—Coleman Co.; Hords Cr.; 5 mi. NW Valera; (M-FC); City of Coleman and USAE	510	8,600
Houston County L.—Houston Co.; Little Elkhart Cr.; 10 mi. NW Crockett; (M-In.); Houston Co. WC&ID No. 1.	1,282	19,500
Houston, L.—Harris Co.; San Jacinto R.; 4 mi. N Sheldon; (M-In.-Ir.-Mi.-R); City of Houston; (impounded by **Lake Houston Dam**)	12,240	140,500
Hubbard Creek Reservoir—Stephens Co.; 6 mi. NW Breckenridge; (M-In.-Mi.); West Central Texas Mun. Water Authority	15,250	317,800
Imperial Reservoir—Reeves-Pecos counties; Pecos R.; 35 mi. N Fort Stockton; (Ir.); Pecos County WC&ID No. 2.	1,530	6,000
Inks L.—Burnet-Llano counties; Colorado R.; 12 mi. W Burnet; (M-Ir.-Mi.-P); Lower Colorado River Authority	803	17,540
Iron Bridge Dam L.—(See **Lake Tawakoni**.)		
Jacksonville, L.—Cherokee Co.; Gum Cr.; 5 mi. SW Jacksonville; (M-R); City of Jacksonville; (impounded by **Buckner Dam**)	1,320	30,500
J. B. Thomas, L.—Scurry-Borden counties; Colorado R.; 16 mi. SW Snyder; (M-In.-R); Colorado River Mun. Water Dist.; (impounded by **Colorado R. Dam**)	7,820	202,300
J. D. Murphree Wildlife Management Area Impoundments—Jefferson Co.; off-channel reservoirs between Big Hill and Taylor Bayous; at Port Acres; (FH-R); State Park & Wildlife Dept. (formerly **Big Hill Reservoir**)	6,881	13,500
Joe B. Hogsett, L.—(See **Cedar Creek Reservoir**.).		
Joe Pool Reservoir—Dallas-Tarrant-Ellis counties; Mountain Cr.; 14 mi. SW Dallas; (FC-M-R); USAE-Trinity River Auth.	7,470	176,900
Johnson Creek Reservoir—Marion Co.; 13 mi. NW Jefferson; (In.); Southwestern Electric Co.	650	10,100
Johnson L., Lyndon B.—Burnet-Llano counties; (formerly **Granite Shoals L.**); Colorado R.; 5 mi. SW Marble Falls; (P); LCRA; (impounded by **Alvin Wirtz Dam**)	6,375	138,500
Kemp, L—Baylor Co.; Wichita R.; 6 mi. N Mabelle; (M-P-Ir.); City of Wichita Falls; Wichita Co. WID No. 2	16,540	319,600
Kemp Diversion Dam—(See **Diversion Lake**.)		
Kickapoo, L.—Archer Co.; N. Fk. Little Wichita R.; 10 mi. NW Archer City; (M); City of Wichita Falls	6,200	106,000
Kiowa, L.—Cooke Co.; Indian Cr.; 8 mi. SE Gainesville; (R); Lake Kiowa, Inc.	560	7,000
Kirby L.—Taylor Co.; Cedar Cr.; 5 mi. S. Abilene; (M); City of Abilene	740	7,620
Kurth, L.—Angelina Co.; off-channel reservoir; 8 mi. N Lufkin; (In.); Southland Paper Mills, Inc.	770	16,200
Lake Creek L.—McLennan Co.; Manos Cr.; 4 mi. SW Riesel; (In.); Texas P&L Co.	550	8,400
Lake Fork Reservoir—Wood-Rains counties; Lake Fork Cr.; 5 mi. W Quitman; (M-In.); SRA	27,690	635,200
Lake O' the Pines—Marion-Upshur-Harrison-Morris-Camp counties; Cypress Cr.; 9 mi. W Jefferson; (FC-C-R-In.-M); USAE. (Lake impounded by **Ferrell's Bridge Dam**.)	18,700	252,000
Lakeview L.—(See **Joe Pool Reservoir**.)		
Lampasas Reservoir—(See **Stillhouse Hollow Reservoir**.)		
Laneport L.—(See **Granger Lake**.)		
Lavon L. (Enlargement)—Collin Co.; East Fk. Trinity R.; 2 mi. W Lavon; (M-FC-In.); USAE	21,400	443,800
Leon, Lake—Eastland Co.; Leon R.; 7 mi. S Ranger; (M-In.); Eastland Co. Water Supply Dist.	1,590	26,420
Lewis Creek Reservoir—Montgomery Co.; Lewis Cr.; 10 mi. NW Conroe; (In.) Gulf States Utilities Co.	1,010	16,400
Lewisville L.—Denton Co.; Elm Fk. Trinity R.; 2 mi. NE Lewisville; (M-FC-In.-R.); USAE; (called also **Lake Dallas** and **Garza-Little Elm**)	23,280	464,500
Limestone, L.—Leon-Limestone-Robertson counties; Navasota R.; 7 mi. NW Marquez; (M-In.-Ir.); BRA	14,200	225,400
Livingston L.—Polk-San Jacinto-Trinity-Walker counties; Trinity R.; 6 mi. SW Livingston; (M-In.-Ir.); City of Houston and Trinity River Authority	82,600	1,750,000
Loma Alta Lake—Cameron Co.; off-channel Rio Grande; 8 mi. NE Brownsville; (M-In.); Brownsville Navigation Dist.	2,490	26,500

Lone Star Reservoir—(See **Ellison Creek Lake**.)		
Los Fresnos, Resaca de—(See **Resacas**.)		
McGee Bend Reservoir—(See **Sam Rayburn Reservoir**.)		
McQueeney, L.—Guadalupe Co.; Guadalupe R.; 5 mi. W Seguin; (P); Guadalupe-Blanco R. Authority; (impounded by **Abbott Dam**)	396	5,000
Mackenzie Reservoir—Briscoe Co.; Tule Cr.; 9 mi. NW Silverton; (M); Mackenzie Mun. Water Auth	910	46,250
Marble Falls L.—Burnet County; Colorado R.; (impounded by **Max Starcke Dam**); 1.25 mi. SE Marble Falls; (P); LCRA	780	8,760
Martin L.—Rusk-Panola counties; Martin Cr.; 17 mi. NE Henderson; (P); Texas Utilities Service Co., Inc.	5,020	77,620
Max Starcke Dam—(See **Marble Falls Lake**.)		
Medina L.—Medina-Bandera counties; Medina R.; 8 mi. W Rio Medina; (Ir.); Bexar-Medina-Atascosa Co. WID No. 1.	5,575	254,000
Meredith, L.—Moore-Potter-Hutchinson counties; Canadian R.; 10 mi. NW Borger; (M-In.-FC-R); cooperative project for municipal water supply by Amarillo, Lubbock and other High Plains Cities. Canadian R. Municipal Water Authority-USBR; (impounded by **Sanford Dam**)	16,504	821,300
Mexia, L.—Limestone Co.; Navasota R.; 7 mi. SW Mexia; (M-In); Bistone Mun. Water Dist.; (impounded by **Bistone Dam**)	1,200	10,000
Millers Creek Reservoir—Baylor Co.; Millers Cr.; 9 mi. SE Goree; (M); No. Central Tex. Mun. Water Auth. and Texas Water Development Board	2,350	30,700
Mineral Wells L.—Parker Co.; Rock Cr.; 4 mi. E Mineral Wells; (M); Palo Pinto Co. Mun. WD No. 1	646	6,760
Monte Alto Reservoir—(See **Delta Lake Res. Units 1 and 2.**)		
Monticello Reservoir—Titus Co.; Blundell Cr.; 2.5 mi. E. Monticello; (In.); Industrial Generating Co.	2,000	40,100
Moss L., Hubert H.—Cooke Co.; Fish Cr.; 10 mi. NW Gainesville; (M-In.); City of Gainesville	1,125	23,210
Mountain Creek L.—Dallas Co.; Mountain Cr.; 4 mi. SE Grand Prairie; (In.); Dallas P&L Co.	2,710	22,840
Mud Creek Dam L.—(See **Tyler Lake, East**.)		
Murphree, J. D. Area Impoundments.—(See **J. D. Murphree**.)		
Murvaul L.—Panola Co.; Murvaul Bayou; 10 mi. SW Carthage; (M-In.-R); Panola Co. Fresh Water Supply Dist. No. 1	3,820	45,815
Nacogdoches, L.—Nacogdoches Co.; Bayo Loco Cr.; 10 mi. W Nacogdoches; (M); City of Nacogdoches	2,210	41,140
Nasworthy, L.—Tom Green Co.; S Concho R.; 6 mi. SW San Angelo; (M-In.-Ir.); City of San Angelo	1,596	12,390
Navarro Mills L.—Navarro-Hill counties; Richland Cr.; 16 mi. SW Corsicana; (M-FC); USAE	5,070	60,900
Nocona L. — (See **Farmers Creek Reservoir**.)		
North Fk. Buffalo Creek Reservoir—Wichita Co.; 5 mi. NW Iowa Park; (M); Wichita Co. WC&ID No. 3	1,500	15,400
North Fork L.—(See **Georgetown L**.)		
North L.—Dallas Co.; S. Fork Grapevine Cr.; 2 mi. SE Coppell; (In.); Dallas P&L Co. . . .	800	17,000
Oak Creek Reservoir—Coke Co.; 5 mi. SE Blackwell; (M-In.); City of Sweetwater	2,375	39,360
O. C. Fisher L.—Tom Green Co.; N. Concho R.; 3 mi. NW San Angelo; (M-FC-C-Ir.-R-In.-Mi); USAE — Upper Colo. Auth. (formerly **San Angelo L**.)	5,440	119,200
Olmos Reservoir—Bexar Co.; Olmos Cr.; in San Antonio city limits; (exclusively for flood control); maximum capacity 12,600 acre-feet; City of San Antonio	0	0
Palestine, L.—Anderson-Cherokee-Henderson-Smith counties; Neches R.; 4 mi. E Frankston; (M-In.-R); Upper Neches R. MWA (impounded by **Blackburn Crossing Dam**)	25,560	411,300
Palmetto Bend Reservoir—(See **Texana, L**.)		
Palo Alto Resaca—(See **Resacas** in this list.)		
Palo Pinto, L.—Palo Pinto Co.; 15 mi. SW Mineral Wells; (M-In.); Palo Pinto Co. Municipal Water Dist. No. 1	2,661	42,200
Panola L.—(See **Murvaul L**.)		
Pat Mayse L.—Lamar Co.; Sanders Cr.; 2 mi. SW Arthur City; (M-In.-FC); USAE	5,993	124,500
Pinkston Reservoir—Shelby Co.; Sandy Cr.; 12.5 mi. SW Center; (M); City of Center; (formerly **Sandy Creek Reservoir**).	523	7,380
Possum Kingdom L.—Palo Pinto-Young-Stephens-Jack counties; Brazos R.; 11 mi. SW Graford; (M-In.-Ir.-Mi.-P-R); Brazos R. Authority; (impounded by **Morris Sheppard Dam**)	17,700	569,380
Proctor L.—Comanche Co.; Leon R.; 9 mi. NE Comanche; (M-In.-Ir.-FC); USAE-Brazos River Authority	4,610	59,300
Quarters Resaca.—(See **Resacas**.)		
Quitman, L.—Wood Co.; Dry Cr.; 4 mi. N Quitman; (FC-R); Wood County (impounded by **Wood Co. Dam No. 1**).	814	7,440
Randall, L.—Grayson Co.; Shawnee Cr.; 4 mi. NW Denison; (M); City of Denison	311	6,290
Ray Hubbard, L.—Collin-Dallas-Kaufman-Rockwall counties; (formerly called **Forney Reservoir**); E. Fk. Trinity R.; 15 mi. E Dallas; (M); City of Dallas	22,745	490,000
*Ray Roberts L.—Denton-Cooke-Grayson counties; Elm Fk. Trinity R.; 11 mi. NE Denton; (FC-M-D); City of Denton, Dallas, USAE; (also known as **Aubrey Reservoir**). . .	29,350	799,600
Red Bluff Reservoir—Loving-Reeves counties, Texas; and Eddy Co., N.M.; Pecos R.; 5 mi. N Orla; (Ir.-P); Red Bluff Water Power Control District	11,700	307,000
Resacas—Cameron-Hidalgo-Willacy counties; Rio Grande; these reservoirs are primarily for storage of water during periods of normal or above-normal flow in the river for use when the river's water volume is low. Some of these are old loops and bends in the river that have been isolated by the river's changing its channel. They are known by the Spanish name of resacas. Also a number of reservoirs have been constructed and connected with the main channel of the river by ditches through which the reservoirs are filled either by gravity flow or by pumping. This is reserve irrigation water for use during periods of low flow in the river channel. Most of these reservoirs are near the main channel of the river, but some of them are 20 or 25 miles distant.		
Reservoir No. 1 & No. 2—Cameron Co.; off-channel Rio Grande R.; 7 mi. SW San Benito; (Ir.-M-In.); Cameron Co. WID No. 2	900	14,200
*Richland Creek Reservoir—Freestone-Navarro counties; Richland Cr.; 23 mi. SE Corsicana; (M); Tarrant Co. WCID No. 1.	38,850	1,135,000

Rita Blanca L.—Hartley Co.; Rita Blanca Cr.; 2 mi. S Dalhart; (R); City of Dalhart	524	12,100
River Crest L.—Red River County; off-channel reservoir; 7 mi. SE Bogata; (In.); Texas P&L	555	7,000
Robert Lee Reservoir.—(See **Spence Reservoir.**)		
Salt Creek L.—(See **Graham L.**)		
Sam Rayburn Reservoir—Jasper-Angelina-Sabine-Nacogdoches-San Augustine counties; Angelina R.; (formerly **McGee Bend**); (FC-P-M-In.-Ir.-R); USAE	114,500	2,876,300
San Angelo L.—(See **O. C. Fisher L.**)		
Sandlin, L. Bob—Titus-Wood-Camp-Franklin counties; Big Cypress Cr.; 5 mi. SW Mount Pleasant; (In.-M-R); Titus Co. FWSD No. 1 (impounded by **Fort Sherman Dam**).	9,460	202,300
Sandow L.—(See **Alcoa Lake.**)		
Sandy Creek Reservoir—(See **Pinkston Reservoir.**)		
San Estaban L.—Presidio Co.; Alamito Cr.; 10 mi. S Marfa; (R); Wm. B. Blakemore	762	18,770
Sanford Reservoir.—(See **Meredith Lake.**)		
Santa Rosa L.—Wilbarger Co.; Beaver Cr.; 15 mi. S Vernon; (Mi.); W. T. Waggoner Estate	1,500	11,570
Sheldon Reservoir—Harris Co.; Carpenters Bayou; 2 mi. SW Sheldon; (R-FH); State Parks & Wildlife Com.	1,700	5,420
Smithers L.—Fort Bend Co.; Dry Creek; 10 mi. SE Richmond; (In.); Houston Lighting & Power Co.	2,480	18,700
Somerville L.—Burleson-Washington counties; Yegua Cr.; 2 mi. S Somerville; (M-In.-Ir.-FC); USAE-Brazos River Authority	11,460	160,100
Southland Paper Mills Reservoir.—(See **Kurth Lake.**)		
South Texas Project Reservoir—Matagorda Co.; off-channel Colorado R.; 16 mi. S Bay City; (In.); Houston Lighting & Power.	7,000	187,000
Spence Reservoir, E.V.—Coke Co.; Colorado R.; 2 mi. W. Robert Lee; (M-In.-Mi.); Colorado R. Mun. Water Dist.; (impounded by **Robert Lee Dam**)	14,950	484,800
Squaw Creek Reservoir—Somervell-Hood counties; Squaw Cr.; 4.5 mi. N Glen Rose; (In.); Texas Utilities Services, Inc.	3,228	151,047
Stamford, L.—Haskell Co.; Paint Cr.; 10 mi. SE Haskell; (M-In.); City of Stamford	4,690	52,700
Steinhagen L., B. A.—(Also called **Town Bluff Reservoir** and **Dam B. Reservoir**); Tyler-Jasper counties; Neches R.; ½ mi. N Town Bluff; (FC-R-C); (impounded by **Town Bluff Dam**)	13,700	94,200
Stillhouse Hollow L.—Bell Co.; Lampasas R.; 5 mi. SW Belton; (M-In.-Ir.-FC); USAE-Brazos R. Authority; (sometimes called **Lampasas Reservoir**)	6,430	234,900
Striker Creek Reservoir—Rusk-Cherokee counties; Striker Cr.; 18 mi. SW Henderson; (M-In.); Angelina-Nacogdoches WC&ID No. 1	2,400	26,960
Sulphur Springs L.—Hopkins Co.; White Oak Cr.; 2 mi. N Sulphur Springs; (M); Sulphur Springs WD; (impounded by **Lake Sulphur Springs Dam** and formerly called **White Oak Creek Reservoir**)	1,910	17,710
Swauano Creek Reservoir—(See **Welsh Reservoir.**)		
Sweetwater L.—Nolan Co.; Bitter and Cottonwood Creeks; 6 mi. SE Sweetwater; (M-In.); City of Sweetwater.	630	11,900
Tawakoni, L.—Rains-Van Zandt-Hunt counties; Sabine R.; 9 mi. NE Wills Point; (M-In.-Ir.-R); Sabine River Authority; (impounded by **Iron Bridge Dam**)	36,700	936,200
Terrell City L., New—Kaufman Co.; Muddy Cedar Cr.; 6 mi. E Terrell; (M-R); City of Terrell	830	8,712
Texana, L.—Jackson Co.; Navidad R. and Sandy Cr.; 6.8 mi. SE Edna; (M-Ir); USBR, Lavaca-Navidad R. Auth., Texas Water Dev. Bd.; (formerly **Palmetto Bend Reservoir**)	11,000	157,900
Texarkana L.—(See **Wright Patman Lake.**)		
Texoma L.—Grayson-Cooke counties, Texas; Bryan-Marshall-Love counties, Okla.; impounded by **Denison Dam** on Red R. short distance below confluence of Red and Washita Rivers; (P-FC-C-R); USAE	89,000	2,722,000
Thomas L.—(See **J. B. Thomas L.**)		
Toledo Bend Reservoir—Newton-Panola-Sabine-Shelby counties; Sabine R.; 14 mi. NE Burkeville; (M-In.-Ir.-P-R); Sabine River Authority. (Texas' share of capacity is half amount shown.)	181,600	4,472,900
Town Bluff Reservoir—(See **Steinhagen, Lake B. A.**)		
Tradinghouse Creek Reservoir—McLennan Co.; Tradinghouse Cr.; 9 mi. E Waco; (In.); Texas P&L	2,010	35,124
Travis, L.—Travis-Burnet counties; Colorado R.; 13 mi. NW Austin; (M-In.-Ir.-Mi.-P-FC-R); LCRA; (impounded by **Mansfield Dam**)	18,930	1,144,100
Trinidad L.—Henderson Co.; off-channel reservoir Trinity R.; 2 mi. S Trinidad; (P); Texas P&L Co.	740	7,450
Truscott Brine L.—Knox Co.; Bluff Cr.; 26 mi. NNW Knox City; (Chlorine Control); Red River Auth. of Texas	2,978	107,000
Turtle Bayou Reservoir—(See **Anahuac Lake.**).		
Twin Buttes Reservoir—Tom Green Co.; Concho R.; 8 mi. SW San Angelo; (M-In.-FC-Ir.-R.); City of San Angelo-USBR-Tom Green Co. WC&ID No. 1	9,080	177,800
Twin Oaks Reservoir—Robertson-Leon Co.; Duck Cr.; 12 mi. N Franklin; (In); Texas P&L . . .	2,300	30,319
Tyler L.—Smith Co.; Prairie and Mud Crs.; 12 mi. SE Tyler; (M-In); City of Tyler; (impounded by **Whitehouse and Mud Creek Dams**)	4,800	73,700
Upper Nueces Reservoir—Zavala Co.; Nueces R.; 6 mi. N Crystal City; (Ir.); Zavala-Dimmit Co. WID No. 1.	316	7,590
Valley Acres Reservoir—Hidalgo Co.; off-channel Rio Grande; 7 mi. N Mercedes; (Ir-M-FC); Valley Acres Water Dist.	906	7,840
Valley L.—Fannin-Grayson counties; 2.5 mi. N Savoy; (P); TP&L; (formerly **Brushy Creek Reservoir**)	1,080	16,400
Victor Braunig L.—Bexar Co.; Arroyo Seco; 15 mi. SE San Antonio; (In.); City Public Service Bd. of San Antonio	1,350	26,500
Waco L.—McLennan Co.; Bosque R.; 2 mi. W Waco; (M-FC-C-R); City of Waco-USAE-Brazos River Authority	7,270	151,900
***Wallisville L.**—Liberty-Chambers counties; Trinity R.; 2 mi. S Wallisville; (M-In.-Ir.); USAE	19,700	58,000
Walter E. Long L.—Travis Co.; Decker Cr.; 9 mi. E of capital, Austin; (M-In.-R); City of Austin; (formerly **Decker Lake**)	1,269	33,940
Waxahachie L.—Ellis Co.; S Prong Waxahachie Cr.; 4 mi. SE Waxahachie; (M-In); Ellis County WC&ID No. 1; (impounded by **S. Prong Dam**)	690	13,500
Weatherford L.—Parker Co.; Clear Fork Trinity River; 7 mi. E Weatherford; (M-In.); City of Weatherford	1,210	19,470

Welsh Reservoir—Titus Co.; Swauano Cr.; 11 mi. SE Mount Pleasant; (R-In.); Southwestern Electric Power Co.; (formerly **Swauano Creek Reservoir**.)	1,365	23,587
White Oak Creek Reservoir.—(See **Sulphur Springs Lake**.)		
White River L.—Crosby Co.; 16 mi. SE Crosbyton; (M-In.-Mi.); White River Municipal Water Dist.	2,020	44,300
White Rock L.—Dallas Co.; White Rock Cr.; within NE Dallas city limits; (R); City of Dallas	1,119	10,740
Whitney L.—Hill-Bosque-Johnson counties; Brazos R.; 5.5 mi. SW Whitney; (FC-P); USAE	23,560	622,800
Wichita, L.—Wichita Co.; Holliday Cr.; 6 mi. SW Wichita Falls; (M-P-R); City of Wichita Falls	2,200	9,000
Winnsboro, L.—Wood Co.; Big Sandy Cr.; 6 mi. SW Winnsboro; (FC-R); Wood County; (impounded by **Wood Co. Dam No. 4**)	806	8,100
Winters L.—Runnels Co.; Elm Cr.; 4.5 mi. E. Winters; (M); City of Winters	640	8,370
Worth, L.—Tarrant Co.; W. Fk. Trinity R.; in NW Fort Worth; (M); City of Fort Worth	3,560	38,130
Wright Patman L.—Bowie-Cass-Morris-Titus-Red River counties; Sulphur R.; 8 mi. SW Texarkana; (FC-M); USAE; (formerly **Texarkana Lake**.)	20,300	142,700

*Reservoir under construction.

Streams and Drainage Basins

Some 11,247 named streams are identified in the **U.S. Geological Survey Geographic Names Information System**. Their combined length is about 80,000 miles, and they drain 263,513 square miles within Texas. The following discussion describes 13 major rivers.

Rio Grande

The Pueblo Indians called this river **Posoge**, "river of great water." In 1582, Antonio de Espejo of Nueva Vizcaya, Mexico, followed the course of the Rio Conchos to its confluence with a great river, which Espejo named **Rio de Norte** (River of the North). The name **Rio Grande** was first given the stream apparently by the explorer Juan de Onate, who arrived on its banks near present day El Paso in 1598.

Thereafter the names were often consolidated, as **Rio Grande del Norte**. (It has its counterpart in the Portuguese Rio Grande do Sul in the state of that name in Brazil.) It was shown also on early Spanish maps as **Rio San Buenaventura** and **Rio Ganapetuan**. In its lower course it early acquired the name **Rio Bravo**, and it is called by that name today by many Mexicans living in its valley. At times it has also been known as **Rio Turbio**, probably because of its appearance during its frequent rises.

From source to mouth, the Rio Grande drops 12,000 feet to sea level as a snow-fed mountain torrent, carver of canyons, desert stream and meandering coastal river. Along its banks and in its valley Indian civilizations developed, and the white man made some of his first North American settlements.

This river rises in Colorado, flows the north-south length of New Mexico and forms the boundary of Texas and international U.S.-Mexican boundary for 889 or 1,248 miles, depending upon method of measurement. (See Texas Boundary Line.) The length of the Rio Grande, as of other rivers, depends on method of measurement and varies yearly as its course changes. Latest International Boundary and Water Commission figure is 1,896 miles, which is considerably below the 2,200-mile figure often used. Depending upon methods of measurement, the Rio Grande is the fourth- or fifth-longest North American river, exceeded only by the Missouri-Mississippi, McKenzie-Peace, St. Lawrence and possibly Yukon. Since all of these except the Missouri-Mississippi are partly in Canada, the Rio Grande is the second-longest river entirely within or bordering the United States. It is Texas' longest river.

The snow-fed flow of the Rio Grande is used for irrigation in Colorado below the San Juan Mountains, where the river rises at the Continental Divide. Turning south, it flows through a canyon in northern New Mexico and again irrigates a broad valley of central New Mexico. Dating from the 1600s, this is the oldest irrigated area of the United States, where Spanish missionaries encouraged Indian irrigation. Southern New Mexico impounds Rio Grande waters in Elephant Butte Reservoir for irrigation for 150 miles of valley above and below El Paso. Here is the oldest irrigated area in Texas and one of the oldest in the United States. Extensive irrigation practically exhausts the water supply. In this valley are situated the three oldest towns in Texas — Ysleta, Socorro and San Elizario. At the lower end of the El Paso irrigated valley, the upper Rio Grande, a snow-fed mountain stream, virtually ends except in seasons of above-normal flow.

It starts as a perennially flowing stream again where the Rio Conchos of Mexico flows into it at Presidio-Ojinaga. Through the Big Bend the Rio Grande flows through three successive canyons, the Santa Elena, the Mariscal and the Boquillas. The Santa Elena has a river bed elevation of 2,145 feet and a canyon rim elevation of 3,661. Corresponding figures for the Mariscal are 1,925 and 3,625, those for the Boquillas, 1,850 and 3,490. The river here flows around the base of the great Chisos Mountains. For about 100 miles the river is the southern boundary of the **Big Bend National Park**.

Below the Big Bend, the Rio Grande gradually emerges from mountains onto the Coastal Plains. At the confluence of the Rio Grande and the Devils River, the U.S. and Mexico have built **Amistad Dam**, to impound 3,383,900 acre-feet of water, of which Texas' share is 56.2 percent. **Falcon Reservoir**, also an international project, impounds 2,667,600 acre-feet of water, of which Texas' share in Zapata and Starr counties is 58.6 percent. Finally, the Rio Grande has created a fertile delta where it joins the Gulf of Mexico, called the **Lower Rio Grande Valley**, that is a major vegetable-fruit area.

The Rio Grande drains over 40,000 square miles of Texas.

Principal tributaries flowing from the Texas side of the Rio Grande are the Pecos and the Devils rivers. On the Mexican side are the **Rio Conchos**, the **Rio Salado** and the **Rio San Juan**. About three-fourths of the water running into the Rio Grande below El Paso comes from the Mexican side.

Nueces River

The Nueces River rises in Edwards County and flows 315 miles to Nueces Bay on the Gulf near Corpus Christi. Draining 17,000 square miles, it is a beautiful, spring-fed stream flowing through canyons until it issues from the Balcones Escarpment onto the Coastal Plain in northern Uvalde County. Alonso de Leon, in 1689, gave it its name. (Nueces, plural of nuez, means nuts in Spanish.) Much earlier, Cabeza de Vaca had referred to a Rio de las Nueces in this region, probably the same stream. Its original Indian name seems to have been Chotilapacquen. Crossing Texas in 1691, Teran de los Rios named the river San Diego. The Nueces was the boundary line between the Spanish provinces of Texas and Nuevo Santander. After the Revolution of 1836, both Texas and Mexico claimed the territory between the Nueces and the Rio Grande, a dispute which was settled by the Treaty of Guadalupe Hidalgo in 1848, which fixed the international boundary at the Rio Grande. Nueces runoff is about 620,000 acre-feet a year in its lower course. Principal water conservation project is **Lake Corpus Christi**. Principal tributaries of the Nueces are the **Frio** and the **Atascosa**.

San Antonio River

The San Antonio River has its source in large springs within and near the corporate limits of San Antonio. It flows 180 miles across the Coastal Plain to a junction with the Guadalupe near the Gulf Coast. Its channel through San Antonio has been developed into a parkway. Its principal tributaries are the **Medina River** and **Cibolo Creek**, both spring-fed streams and this, with its own origin in springs, gives it a remarkably steady flow of clear water.

This stream was first named the Leon by Alonso de Leon during his trip across Texas in 1689. (De Leon was not naming the stream for himself, but called it "lion" because its channel was filled with a rampaging flood.)

Because of its limited and rather arid drainage

area (4,200 square miles) the average runoff of the San Antonio River is relatively small, about 350,000 acre-feet annually near its mouth, but its flow, because of its springs, is one of the steadiest of Texas rivers.

Guadalupe River

The Guadalupe rises in its north and south prongs in the west central part of Kerr County. A spring-fed stream, it flows eastward through the Hill Country until it issues from the Balcones Escarpment near New Braunfels. It then meanders across the Coastal Plain to San Antonio Bay. Its total length is about 250 miles, and its drainage area is about 6,000 square miles. Its principal tributaries are the **San Marcos**, another spring-fed stream, which flows into it in Gonzales County, the **San Antonio**, which flows into it just above its mouth on San Antonio Bay and the **Comal**, which joins it at New Braunfels. The **Comal River** has its source in large springs within the city limits of New Braunfels and flows only about 2.5 miles to the Guadalupe. It is the **shortest river in Texas** and also the shortest river in the United States carrying an equivalent amount of water. There has been power development on the Guadalupe near Gonzales and Cuero for many years. Because of its springs, and its considerable drainage area, it has an annual runoff of more than 1 million acre-feet in its lower course.

The name Guadalupe is derived from Nuestra Senora de Guadalupe, the name given the stream by Alonso de Leon.

Lavaca River

The Lavaca is considered a primary stream in the Texas Basin because it flows directly into the Gulf, through Lavaca Bay. Without a spring water source and with only a small watershed, including that of its principal tributary, the **Navidad**, its flow is intermittent. The Spanish called it the Lavaca (cow) River because of the numerous bison they found. It is the principal stream running to the Gulf between the Guadalupe and the Colorado. Runoff averages about 600,000 acre-feet yearly into the Gulf.

Colorado River

Measured by length and drainage area, the Colorado is the largest river wholly in Texas. (This comparison excludes the Brazos, whose drainage basin extends into New Mexico.) Rising in Dawson County, the Colorado flows about 600 miles to Matagorda Bay on the Gulf. Its drainage area is 39,900 square miles. Its runoff reaches a volume of more than 2 million acre-feet near the Gulf. Its name is a Spanish word meaning "reddish." There is evidence that the name, Colorado, was given originally by Spanish explorers to the muddy Brazos, and Spanish mapmakers later transposed the two names. The river flows through a rolling, usually prairie terrain to the vicinity of San Saba County, where it enters the rugged Hill Country and Burnet-Llano Basin. It passes through a picturesque series of canyons until it issues from the Balcones Escarpment at Austin and flows across the Coastal Plain to the Gulf. In this area the most remarkable series of reservoirs in Texas has been built. There are two large reservoirs, **Lake Buchanan** in Burnet and Llano counties and Lake **Travis** in Travis County. Between these, in Burnet County, are three smaller reservoirs: Inks, Johnson (formerly **Granite Shoals**) and **Marble Falls**, built to aid power production from water running over the Buchanan Lake spillway. Below Lake Travis is the older Lake **Austin**, largely filled with silt, whose dam maintains a head for production of power from waters flowing down from the lakes above. Town Lake is in the city of Austin. This area is known as the **Highland Lakes Country**.

As early as the 1820s, Anglo-Americans settled on the banks of the lower Colorado, and in 1839 the **Capital Commission** of the Republic of Texas chose the picturesque area where the river flows from the Balcones Escarpment as the site of a new capital of the Republic — now **Austin**, capital of the state. The early colonists encouraged navigation along the lower channel with some success and boats occasionally ventured as far upstream as Austin. However, a natural log "raft" in the channel near the Gulf blocked river traffic. Conservation and utilization of the waters of the Colorado are under jurisdiction of three agencies created by the state Legislature, the **Lower, Central** and **Upper Colorado River Authorities.**

The principal tributaries of the Colorado are the several prongs of the **Concho River** on its upper course, the **Pecan Bayou (farthest west "bayou" in the United States)** and the Llano, San Saba and Pedernales Rivers. All except the Pecan Bayou flow into the Colorado from the Edwards Plateau and are spring-fed, perennially flowing. In the numerous mussels found along these streams occasional pearls have been found. The Middle Concho was designated on early Spanish maps as **Rio de las Perlas.**

Brazos River

The Brazos is the largest river between the Rio Grande and the Red River and is third in size of all rivers in Texas. It rises in three upper forks, the **Double Mountain, Salt** and **Clear forks** of the Brazos. The Brazos River proper is considered as beginning where the Double Mountain and Salt Forks flow together in Stonewall County. The Clear Fork joins this main stream in Young County, just above Lake Possum Kingdom. The Brazos crosses most of the main physiographic regions of Texas — High Plains, West Texas Lower Rolling Plains, West Cross Timbers, Grand Prairie and Gulf Coastal Plain.

The total length from the source of its longest upper prong, the Double Mountain Fork, to the mouth of the main stream at the Gulf, is about 840 miles, and the drainage area is about 42,800 square miles.

It flows directly into the Gulf near Freeport. Its annual runoff at places along its lower channel exceeds 5 million acre-feet.

The original name of this river was **Brazos de Dios,** meaning **"Arms of God."** There are several legends as to why. One is that the Coronado expedition, wandering on the trackless Llano Estacado, exhausted its water and was threatened with death from thirst. Arriving at the bank of the river they gave it the name of Brazos de Dios in thankfulness. Another is that a ship exhausted its water supply and its crew was saved when they found the mouth of the Brazos. Still another story is that miners on the San Saba were forced by drouth to seek water near present-day Waco and called it Brazos de Dios in thankfulness. There is also the theory that the early Spanish cartographers called the river "Arms of God" because of the great spread of its tributaries.

Much early Anglo-American colonization of Texas took place in the Brazos Valley. Along its channel were **San Felipe de Austin,** capital of Austin's colony, **Washington-on-the-Brazos,** where Texans declared independence, and other historic settlements. There was some navigation of the lower channel of the Brazos in this period. Near its mouth it intersects the Gulf Intracoastal Waterway, which provides connection with the commerce on the Mississippi.

Most of the Brazos Valley lies within the boundaries of the **Brazos River Authority,** which conducts a multipurpose program for development. A large reservoir on the Brazos is **Lake Whitney** (622,800 acre-feet capacity) on the main channel, where it is the boundary line between Hill and Bosque counties. Another large reservoir is **Lake Possum Kingdom** in Palo Pinto, Stephens, Young and Jack counties. **Lake Waco** on the Bosque and **Belton Lake** on the Leon are among the principal reservoirs on its tributaries. In addition to its three upper forks, other chief tributaries are the **Paluxy, Little** and **Navasota rivers.**

San Jacinto River

A short river with a drainage basin of 3,976 square miles and nearly 2 million acre-feet runoff, the San Jacinto runs directly to the Gulf through Galveston Bay. It is formed by the junction of its East and West forks in the northeastern part of Harris County. Its total length, including the East Fork, is about 85 miles. There are two stories of the origin of its name. One is that when early explorers discovered it, its channel was choked with hyacinth ("Jacinto" is the Spanish word for hyacinth). The other is that it was discovered on Aug. 17, St. Hyacinth's Day. Through the lower course of the San Jacinto and its tributary, Buffalo Bayou, runs the Houston Ship Channel connecting the Port of Houston with the Gulf. On the shore of the San Jacinto was fought the **Battle of San Jacinto,** April 21, 1836, in which Texas won its independence from Mexico. The **San Jacinto State Park** and monument are there.

Trinity River

The Trinity rises in its East Fork, Elm Fork, West Fork and Clear Fork in Grayson, Montague, Archer and Parker counties, respectively. The main stream begins with the junction of the Elm and West forks at Dallas. Its length is 550 river miles and its drainage area, 17,969 square miles. Because of moderate to heavy rainfall over its drainage area, it has a flow of 5,800,000 acre-feet near its mouth on the Gulf, exceeded only by the Neches, Red and Sabine River basins.

The Trinity derives its name from the Spanish "Trinidad." Alonso de Leon named it La Santisima Trinidad (the Most Holy Trinity).

Navigation was developed along its lower course with several riverport towns, such as Sebastopol in Trinity County. For many years there has been a basin-wide movement for navigation, conservation and utilization of its water. The Trinity River Authority is a state agency and the Trinity Improvement Association is a publicly supported nonprofit organization advocating its development.

The Trinity has in its valley more large cities, greater population and more industrial development than any other river basin in Texas. On the Lower Coastal Plain there is large use of its waters for rice irrigation. Largest reservoir on the Elm Fork is Lewisville Lake (formerly Garza-Little Elm and Lake Dallas). There are four reservoirs above Fort Worth—Lake Worth, Eagle Mountain and Bridgeport on the West Fork and Lake Benbrook on the Clear Fork. Lake Lavon in southeast Collin County and Lake Ray Hubbard in Collin-Dallas-Kaufman-Rockwall counties are on the East Fork.

Neches River

The Neches is in East Texas with total length of about 416 miles and drainage area of 10,011 square miles. Abundant rainfall over its entire basin gives it a flow near the Gulf of about 6 million acre-feet a year. The river takes its name from the Neches Indians that the early Spanish explorers found living along its banks. Principal tributary of the Neches, and comparable with the Neches in length and flow above their confluence, is the Angelina River, so named from Angelina (Little Angel), a Hainai Indian girl who converted to Christianity and played an important role in the early development of this region.

Both the Neches and the Angelina run most of their courses in the Piney Woods and there was much settlement along them as early as the 1820s. Sam Rayburn (McGee Bend) Reservoir, near Jasper on the Angelina River, was completed and dedicated in 1965.

Sabine River

The Sabine River is formed by three forks rising in Collin and Hunt counties. From its sources to its mouth on Sabine Lake, it flows approximately 360 miles and drains 9,733 square miles. Sabine comes from the Spanish word for cypress, as does the name of the Sabinal River, which flows into the Frio in Southwest Texas. The Sabine has the largest water discharge (6,800,000 acre-feet) at its mouth of any Texas river. Throughout most of Texas history the lower Sabine has been the eastern Texas boundary line, though for a while there was doubt as to whether the Sabine or the Arroyo Hondo, east of the Sabine in Louisiana, was the boundary. For a number of years the outlaw-infested neutral ground lay between them. There was also a boundary dispute in which it was alleged that the Neches was really the Sabine and, therefore, the boundary.

Travelers over the Camino Real, or Old San Antonio Road, crossed the Sabine at the famous Gaines Ferry, and there were famous crossings for the Atascosito Road and other travel and trade routes of that day.

Two of Texas' larger man-made reservoirs have been created by dams constructed on the Sabine River. The first of these is Lake Tawakoni, in Hunt, Rains and Van Zandt counties, with a capacity of 936,200 acre-feet. Toledo Bend Reservoir impounds 4,472,900 acre-feet of water on the Sabine in Newton, Panola, Sabine and Shelby counties. This is a joint project of Texas and Louisiana, through the Sabine River Authority.

Red River

The Red River (1,360 miles) is exceeded in length only by the Rio Grande among rivers associated with

Texas. Its original source is water in Curry County, New Mexico, near the Texas boundary, forming a definite channel as it crosses Deaf Smith County, Texas, in tributaries that flow into Prairie Dog Town Fork of the Red River. These waters carve the spectacular Palo Duro Canyon of the High Plains before the Red River leaves the Cap Rock Escarpment, flowing eastward.

Where the Red River crosses the 100th meridian, the river becomes the Texas-Oklahoma boundary and is soon joined by the Salt Fork to form the main channel. Its length across the Panhandle is about 200 miles and, from the Panhandle east, it is the Texas-Oklahoma boundary line for 440 miles and thereafter the Texas-Arkansas boundary for 40 miles before it flows into Arkansas, where it swings south to flow through Louisiana. The Red River is a part of the Mississippi drainage basin, and at one time it emptied all of its water into the Mississippi. In recent years, however, part of its water, especially at flood stage, has flowed to the Gulf via the Atchafalaya. The Red River takes its name from the red color of the current. This caused every explorer who came to its banks to call it "red" regardless of the language he spoke — Rio Rojo or Rio Roxo in Spanish, Riviere Rouge in French and Red River in English. The Spanish and French names were often found on maps until the middle of the last century when the English, Red River, came to be generally accepted. At an early date, the river became the axis for French advance from Louisiana northwestward as far as present-day Montague County. There was consistent early navigation of the river from its mouth on the Mississippi to Shreveport, above which navigation was blocked by a natural log raft. A number of important gateways into Texas from the North were established along the stream such as Pecan Point and Jonesborough in Red River County, Colbert Ferry and Preston in Grayson County and, later, Doan's Store Crossing in Wilbarger County. The river was a menace to the early traveler because of both its variable current and its quicksands which brought disaster to many a trail herd cow as well as ox team and covered wagon.

The largest water conservation project on the Red River is Lake Texoma, which is the largest lake lying wholly or partly in Texas and the tenth largest reservoir (in capacity) in the United States. Its capacity is 5,382,000 acre feet. Texas' share is 2,722,000.

Red River water's high content of salt and other minerals limits its usefulness along its upper reaches. Ten salt springs and tributaries in Texas and Oklahoma contribute most of these minerals.

The uppermost tributary of the Red River in Texas is the Tierra Blanca Creek, which rises in Curry County, N.M., and flows easterly across Deaf Smith and Randall counties to become the Prairie Dog Town Fork a few miles east of Canyon. Other principal tributaries in Texas are the Pease and the Wichita in North Central Texas and the Sulphur in Northeast Texas, which flows into the Red River after it has crossed the boundary line into Arkansas. From Oklahoma the principal tributary is the Washita. The Ouachita, a river with the same pronunciation of its name, though spelled differently, is the principal tributary to its lower course.

Canadian River

The Canadian River heads near Raton Pass in northern New Mexico near the Colorado boundary line and flows into Texas on the west line of Oldham County. It crosses the Texas Panhandle into Oklahoma and there flows into the Arkansas. Most of its course across the Panhandle is in a deep gorge. A tributary dips into Texas' North Panhandle and then flows to a confluence with the main channel in Oklahoma. One of several theories as to how the Canadian got its name is that some early explorers thought it flowed into Canada. Lake Meredith, formed by Sanford Dam on the Canadian, provides water for 11 Panhandle cities.

Because of the deep gorge and the quicksand at many places, the Canadian has been a peculiarly difficult stream to bridge. It is known especially in its lower course in Oklahoma as outstanding among the streams of the country for great amount of quicksand in its channel.

Texas Wildlife

Texas has many native animals and birds, plus species introduced on game preserves.

More than 540 species of **birds** — about three fourths of all different species found in the United States — have been identified in Texas.

Some 142 species of **animals,** including some that today are extremely rare, are found in Texas.

Through efforts of the **Texas Parks and Wildlife Department** and many individual landowners involved in conservation practices, our wildlife should be a permanent resource.

Hunting and Fishing

Texas offers a wide variety of hunting and fishing and ranks among the leading states in this form of recreation.

In the federal fiscal year of 1985, 1,309,391 hunters held licenses in Texas, ranking the state fifth in the nation; and there were 1,682,501 fishing licenses issued, ranking Texas fourth nationally.

In 1984, there were 1,362,501 hunting licenses issued in Texas, 1,866,909 fishing licenses.

Hunting, Fishing Licenses

A hunting license is required of Texas residents and nonresidents of Texas who hunt any wild bird or animal. Hunting licenses and stamps are valid during the period September 1 through the following August 31 of each year. A hunting license (except the non-resident small-game hunting license) is valid for taking all legal species of wildlife in Texas including deer, turkey, javelina, antelope, aoudad sheep and all small game and migratory game birds. Special licenses and tags are required for taking alligators, and a trapper's license is required to hunt fur-bearing animals.

All sport fishing licenses and stamps are valid only during the period September 1 through August 31, except those issued for a specific number of days and lifetime licenses.

In addition to sports hunting and fishing licenses, hunting/fishing stamps are required for special hunting/fishing privileges.

Detailed information concerning licenses, stamps, seasons, regulations and related information can be obtained from: Texas Parks and Wildlife Department, 4200 Smith School Road, Austin, Texas 78744 (1-800-792-1112).

Licenses Sold During FY 1986

Type of License	Fee (FY 1986)	Number Sold
Resident Hunting	$10.00	297,261
Special Resident Hunting (Exempt)	6.00	143,210
Resident Lifetime Hunting	300.00	New Lics.
Resident Comb. Hunting & Fishing	15.00	670,786
Resident Lifetime Comb. Hunting & Fishing	500.00	New Lics.
Resident Alligator Hunter's	25.00	418
Resident Trapper's	10.75	32,155
Nonresident General Hunting . . .	200.00	10,710
Nonresident Small Game	75.00	8,615
White-Winged Dove Stamp	6.00	15,207
Archery Hunting Stamp	6.00	61,666
Texas Waterfowl Stamp	5.00	145,683
Resident Fishing	8.00	1,110,436
Temporary Resident Fishing (14-Day)	5.00	58,052
Special Resident Fishing	1.50	4,190
Nonresident Fishing.	15.00	34,478
Temporary Nonresident Fishing (5-Day)	8.00	56,866
Freshwater Trout Stamp	5.00	13,560
Saltwater Sportfishing Stamp . . .	5.00	251,897

There were 383,500 whitetail deer killed in the 1985-86 hunting season, the most killed in 10 years and up 3 percent over the 1984-85 season. **Wild turkey killed** in 1985-86 estimated at 45,286, down from record high harvest of 54,624 in 1982-83. There were 4,544 mule deer killed in 1985-86, compared to 4,411 the year before. The javelina harvest dropped from 20,636 in 1984-85 to 17,482 in 1985-86.

The Texas Parks and Wildlife Department reported revenue of $30.9 million from sales of all licenses during fiscal 1986, an increase of some $6 million over fiscal 1984. In excess of 3 million licenses were sold. Various types of sports hunting and fishing licenses with fees and number sold during fiscal year 1986 are listed above.

Groups Boost Conservation

The protection of the state's natural areas is primarily the job of the Texas Parks and Wildlife Department. But there are many agencies, companies and individuals who also contribute to the conservation of Texas lands. A few large-scale cooperative government and private efforts are explained below:

Texas Natural Heritage Program: Identification of the finest remaining endangered natural areas in the state is the critical first step to the conservation of those resources. The Texas Natural Heritage Program was established in September 1983 as a cooperative venture between the Texas General Land Office and The Nature Conservancy, a national non-profit organization dedicated to the preservation of biological diversity. The program maintains a comprehensive computerized inventory of Texas' ecological resources. Information stored in this centralized database at the General Land Office includes status and distribution of rare, threatened or endangered plants, animals and natural communities. This information previously was scattered among academic institutions, state and federal agencies, private conservation groups, individuals and unpublished reports throughout the state and the nation. The continually updated and refined information is available to public and private users and is complemented by maps and manual files.

The Texas Conservation Foundation: The Texas Conservation Foundation is an agency created in 1969 by the Legislature to act as a trustee for gifts of land, money or other valuables donated to the state. These gifts are used for the benefit of the Texas system of parks, historical sites, and wildlife and natural areas, as the donors wish. The foundation, representing the parks and wildlife department, as well as the Texas Historical Commission and the General Land Office, accepts and maintains properties until such time as they

can be transferred to the the proper agency. The foundation also works with private organizations and citizens groups on identification, acquisition and protection of sites and resources.

The Nature Conservancy: Working through its state affiliate, the Texas Nature Conservancy, The Nature Conservancy, a national, private, non-profit organization, uses its resources to preserve unique and significant natural areas. Since 1966, the Texas conservancy, working in cooperation with government agencies and private groups, has acquired more than 158,000 acres in 29 projects, ranging from the Trans-Pecos to the Gulf Coast, from the Edwards Plateau to the Rio Grande Valley. The conservancy identifies areas that should be protected; it preserves the land through gift, lease, trade or outright purchase; and it manages and maintains some of the preserves itself, while holding others until an appropriate agency can be found to acquire and care for the properties. Membership in the Texas Nature Conservancy as of January 1986 was 7,100.

Conservancy projects in Texas are listed below. Information includes name of the area, agency managing the property as of January 1986, county, number of acres, and the date acquired by the conservancy. Abbreviations used in the list are: USFWS (U.S. Fish and Wildlife Service), TNC (Texas Nature Conservancy), TPWD (Texas Parks and Wildlife Department), NWR (national wildlife refuge), NP (natural preserve), SNA (state natural area) and WMA (wildlife management area). The projects are: Attwater's Prairie Chicken NWR, USFWS, Colorado, 3,468, 1965; Barrow Ranch/Anahuac NWR, USFWS, Chambers, 12,670, 1981; Beech Creek Woods/Big Thicket NP, USFWS, Tyler, 1, 1978; Big Thicket Bogs and Pineland, TNC, Tyler, 49, 1971; Clymer Meadow, TNC, Hunt, 113, 1986; Enchanted Rock SNA, TPWD, Llano, 1,641, 1978; Ezell's Cave, TNC, Hays,

2, 1967; Gunsight Mountain Ranch (Mgt. Agreement), Owner, Bandera, 740, 1983; Gypsum Dunes, TNC, Hudspeth, 226, 1980; Honey Creek Ranch SNA/WMA, TPWD, Comal, 1,825, 1981; Hookswood (Conservation Easement), Owner/TNC, Harris, 102, 1983.

Also included in the conservancy's acquisitions are: Little Rocky, Owner/TNC, Jasper, 84, 1977; Mares Woods/Armand's Bayou NP, Private, Galveston, 8, 1976; Leonhardt Prairie, TNC, Falls, 40, 1981; Marysee Prairie, TNC, Liberty, 3, 1973; McFaddin NWR, USFWS, Jefferson, 42,102, 1979; Mesquite Brushland (part interest), Owner, Duval, 683, 1980; North Rosillos Mountains

Preserve, TNC, Brewster, 67,000, 1984; Peach Point Marsh WMA, TPWD, Brazoria, 8,525, 1984; Roy E. Larsen Sandyland Sanctuary, TNC, Hardin, 2,178, 1977; Sabal Palm Woods Lower Rio Grande NWR, USFWS, Cameron, 367, 1980; San Bernard NWR, USFWS, Brazoria, 2,495, 1977; Schaleben Ranch Lower Rio Grande NWR, USFWS, Hidalgo, 568, 1983; Sea Rim/Texas Point NWR, USFWS, Jefferson, 8,971, 1978; Sheff's Woods, TNC, Smith, 75, 1969; Slop Bowl Marsh/Brazoria NWR, TNC/USFWS, Brazoria, 1,905, 1984; Smith Marsh/San Bernard NWR, USFWS, Matagorda, 2,375, 1977; Tridens Prairie, TNC, Lamar, 97, 1982; Wilson Preserve, TNC, Jefferson, 43, 1977.

The 1987 Texas Waterfowl Stamp and Print depicts White-fronted geese as painted by artist Gary Moss. Photo courtesy Collectors Covey.

Artist Al Barnes painted the 1987 Saltwater Stamp and Print, with spotted seatrout as his subjects. Photo courtesy Collectors Covey.

Wildlife Stamps and Prints

Information in the following article was furnished by the Texas Parks and Wildlife Dept., 4200 Smith School Road, Austin, TX 78744, and Collectors Covey, Box 57306, Dallas, TX 75207.

Since 1981, the Texas Parks and Wildlife Department has funded some of its acquisition, development and management of natural areas with the sale of wildlife stamps and matching art prints, designed by leading wildlife artists. There are currently three types of state-issued wildlife stamps, as described below. (There are various other stamps issued and sold by nonprofit organizations for the benefit of wildlife habitats. Because of space limitations, only the state-authorized stamps and prints are discussed here.)

Waterfowl Stamp: Commonly called a "Duck Stamp," the waterfowl stamp has been required of all waterfowl hunters since Fiscal Year 1982. Funds from the sale of waterfowl stamps and prints may be used for research, management and protection of waterfowl, for the acquisition, lease or development of waterfowl habitats in the state and for grants to international nonprofit organizations for the purpose of acquiring, developing and maintaining waterfowl propagation areas

in Canada. Subjects of waterfowl stamp artwork and artists are: 1981, Mallards, Larry Hayden; 1982, Pintails, Ken Carlson; 1983, American Widgeons, Maynard Reece; 1984, Wood Ducks, David Maass; 1985, Lesser Snow Geese, John P. Cowan; 1986, Green-winged Teal, Herb Booth; 1987, White-fronted Geese, Gary Moss.

Saltwater Stamp: Funds from the saltwater stamp, which has been required of all saltwater fishermen since 1986, may be used for coastal fisheries and management. In 1986, the featured fish was the redfish as depicted by artist John P. Cowan; in 1987, the spotted seatrout, by Al Barnes.

Non-game and Endangered Species Stamp: A non-game and endangered species stamp, the only one of the three wildlife stamps that is not a user stamp, was offered for the first time in 1985. Funds from sale of the non-game stamps and art prints are used for acquisition and development of habitats for, surveys of, research and management of, protection and restoration of, and dissemination of information about non-game and endangered species. The 1985 non-game stamp and art subject was the whooping crane by artist Ken Carlson; 1986, Attwater's prairie chicken by John P. Cowan; 1987, the bald eagle by artist Bob Kuhn.

Mammals

A few of the leading native mammals of Texas are described here. More complete information is found in "The Mammals of Texas," by William B. Davis, Bulletin 41 of the Texas Parks and Wildlife Department, Austin.

ARMADILLO—The nine-banded armadillo (Dasypus novemcinctus Linnaeus) is one of Texas' most interesting mammals. It has migrated north and east and is now common as far north and east as Oklahoma and Mississippi. There has been limited commercialization of the armadillo's shell in the manufacture of curios.

BADGER—The badger (Taxidea taxus Schreber) is found through West Texas, but in greatly reduced numbers since wholesale eradication of the prairie dog on which the badger preyed. It is a predator, but its pelt is valuable. The range of the badger includes the Texas Panhandle and South Texas, where it is common.

BAT—Twenty-nine species of these winged mammals have been found in Texas, but most of them are rare. The Brazilian bat (Tadarida brasiliensis) and the cave myotis (Myotis velifer Allen) constitute most of the bat population of the caves of Southwest and West Tex-

as. They have some economic value for their deposits of guano. Some commercial guano has been produced from Mason Bat Cave, Mason County; Beaver Creek Cavern, Burnet County; and from large deposits in other caves including Devil's Sink Hole in Edwards County, Blowout Cave in Blanco County and Bandera Bat Cave, Bandera County. The big brown bat (Eptesicus fuscus Beauvois), the red bat (Lasiurus borealis Muller) and the evening bat (Nycticeius humeralis Rafinesque) are found in East and Southeast Texas. The evening and big brown bats are forest and woodland dwelling mammals. Most of the rarer species of Texas bats have been found along the Rio Grande and in the Trans-Pecos.

BEAR—The black bear (Ursus americanus Pallas) was formerly common throughout most of the state. It is now almost extinct, with only small pockets of animals surviving in the inaccessible river bottoms of eastern Texas and in the higher portions of the Trans-Pecos.

BEAVER—Two subspecies of beaver are found in Texas, the Mexican beaver (Castor canadensis mexicanus) ranging along the Rio Grande and Devils River and the **Texas beaver** (Castor canadensis texensis) which has been brought back from the verge of extinction to abundance through restocking.

BIGHORN—(See **Sheep**.)

BISON—The largest of native terrestrial wild mammals of North America, the **American bison**, or **buffalo** (Bison bison Linnaeus) is found today on a few ranches and in zoos. This fine animal became rare about 1885 as the result of slaughter for hides, reaching a peak about the year 1875. Estimates of the number of buffalo killed vary, but as many as 200,000 hides sold in Fort Worth at a two-day sale. Except for the interest of the late **Col. Charles Goodnight** and a few other forevisioned men, the bison might be extinct.

CAT—The **jaguar** (Felis onca Linnaeus) is probably now extinct in Texas and, along with the **ocelot, jaguarundi** and **margay**, is listed as rare and endangered by both federal and state wildlife agencies. The **cougar** (Felis concolor Linnaeus), which is also known as **mountain lion, puma, panther, Mexican cougar**, etc., is found occasionally in the broken country of the Edwards Plateau and in the Trans-Pecos Mountains and the South Texas brush country. The former **panther** of the East Texas forest, which was closely related, may be extinct in Texas but still exists in a few areas of Southeastern U.S. The **ocelot** (Felis pardalis Linnaeus), also known as the **leopard cat**, is found usually along the border. The **red-and-gray cat**, or **jaguarundi** (Felis yagouaroundi Geoffroy) is found in extreme South Texas. The **margay** (Felis Wiedii Schinz) was reported in 1884 near Eagle Pass. The **bobcat** (Felis rufus Schreber) is found over the state in large numbers. The **feral housecat** has become a destroyer of game in many parts of Texas.

CHIPMUNK—The **gray-footed chipmunk** (Tamias canipes Bailey) is found at high altitudes in the Guadalupe and Sierra Diablo ranges of the Trans-Pecos. (See "Ground Squirrel," with which it is often confused in public reference.)

COATI—The **coati** (Nasua narica Linnaeus), a relative of the raccoon, is occasionally found in southern Texas. It inhabits woodland areas and feeds both on the ground and in trees. The species is also found occasionally in Big Bend National Park.

COYOTE—The **coyote** (Canis latrans Say), great in number, is the most destructive Texas predator of livestock. On the other hand, it is probably the most valuable predator in the balance of nature. It is a protection to crops and range lands by its control of rodents, rabbits, etc. It is found throughout the state, but is most numerous in the brush country of Southwest Texas.

DEER—The **white-tailed deer** (Odocoileus virginianus Boddaert) is an important Texas game animal. Its number in Texas is estimated at 3 million. It thrives best in the wooded and broken areas of the Edwards Plateau and south of San Antonio where it often competes for feed with domestic animals. Texas Parks and Wildlife Department has had success in transplanting deer to East Texas, the timbered sections of North Central Texas, and even in the thinly populated areas of Northwest Texas the white-tailed deer population has increased greatly. The **mule deer**, (Odocoileus hemionus Rafinesque) is found principally in the Trans-Pecos and in smaller numbers in the less thickly settled parts of the Staked Plains. It has increased in number in recent years. The little **Del Carmen deer** (white-tailed subspecies) is found in limited numbers in the high valleys of the Chisos Mountains in the Big Bend. The **American elk** (Cervus canadensis Erxleben), though not the original subspecies found in Texas, has been introduced into the Guadalupe and Davis Mountains.

FERRET—The **black-footed ferret** (Mustela nigripes Audubon and Bachman) was formerly found widely ranging through the West Texas country of the prairie dog on which it preyed. It is now considered extinct in Texas. It is of the same genus as the weasel and mink.

FOX—Most common is the **gray fox** (Urocyon cinereoargenteus Schreber) found in the forested area of East Texas and throughout most of the state where there is cover, notably in the broken parts of the Edwards Plateau and the rough country at the foot of the Staked Plains. The **kit** or **swift fox** (Vulpes velox Say) is found in the plains country of Northwest Texas. A second species of kit fox (Vulpes macrotis Merriam) is found in the Trans-Pecos and is fairly numerous in some localities. The **red fox** (Vulpes vulpes) is not a native but was introduced for sport.

GOPHER—Six species of pocket gophers occur in Texas. The **Botta's pocket gopher** (Thomomys bottae,

Eydoux and Gervais) is found in West Texas south of the High Plains, notably along the Rio Grande. The **plains pocket gopher** (Geomys bursarius Shaw) is found in the Panhandle and throughout North Central and East Texas. The **desert pocket gopher** (Geomys arenarius Merriam) and the **yellow-faced pocket gopher** (Pappogeomys castanops Baird) are found in the Trans-Pecos. The **Texas pocket gopher** (Geomys personatus True) is found in the sandy soils of the lower coastal region.

GROUND SQUIRREL—There are five or more species, living usually in the western part of the state. The **rock squirrel** (Spermophilus variegatus) is found throughout the Edwards Plateau and Trans-Pecos. The **Mexican ground squirrel** (Spermophilus mexicanus) is found in the Mexican border country from Brownsville to the Davis Mountains. The **spotted ground squirrel** (Spermophilus spilosoma) is found generally in favorable localities throughout the western half of the state. The **thirteen-lined ground squirrel** (Spermophilus tridecemlineatus Mitchill) is found in the Panhandle and in a narrow strip from Red River to the Gulf between Dallas and Corpus Christi. The **Texas antelope squirrel** (Ammospermophilus interpres Merriam) is found along the Rio Grande from El Paso to Val Verde County.

JAVELINA—The **javelina** or **collared peccary** (Tayassu tajacu Dicotyles) is found in the border country of Southwest Texas. It is fairly numerous. Its meat is edible if properly prepared, and there is limited use of its hide for the manufacture of gloves and other leather articles. Hunting it with dogs is a favorite sport of that region. A scrappy animal, it is the subject of many tall tales.

MINK—The **mink** (Mustela vison Schreber) is found in East Texas and along the Coastal Belt, usually in forested river bottoms. It yields a considerable fur crop. It is akin to the otter and weasel. Mink farming, partly with native and partly with introduced species, is found on a limited scale, usually in East Texas.

MOLE—The **mole** (Scalopus aquaticus Linnaeus) is found generally throughout the eastern half of the state.

MUSKRAT—There are three subspecies of muskrat in Texas, the **muskrat** (Ondatra zibethica rivalicia Bangs), which is found in Southeast Texas near Beaumont where it is commercially produced on muskrat ranges; the **Pecos River muskrat** (Ondatra zibethica ripensis) of Western Texas; and the **Great Plains muskrat** (Ondatra zibethica cinnamonia) of the Panhandle region. The muskrat is one of the most valuable of Texas' fur-bearing animals. Production of pelts comes largely from the coastal area near Beaumont.

NUTRIA—This introduced species (Myocastor coypus Molina) is found in Texas, except the Panhandle and extreme western portions. The fur is not valued too highly and, since they are in competition with muskrats, their spread is discouraged. They are used widely in Texas as a cure-all for ponds choked with vegetation.

OPOSSUM—This Texas marsupial, the Virginia opossum (Didelphis virginiana) is found in nearly all parts of the state. The opossum has economic value for its pelt, and its meat is considered a delicacy by some. It is one of the chief contributors to the Texas fur crop.

OTTER—A few **river otter** (Lutra canadensis Schreber) are found along East Texas rivers and coastal marshes. Although it is a prized fur-bearing animal, there is no evidence that the river otter can be considered either rare or endangered. The species is numerous in Liberty County where biologists have determined that its numbers have increased in recent years. While excess populations of this species, like other forms of wildlife, can be harvested with no danger to the species, loss of habitat through encroaching civilization presents the most formidable threat to its continued existence.

PORCUPINE—The **yellow-haired porcupine** (Erethizon dorsatum Linnaeus) is found in small numbers in higher mountain ranges of the Trans-Pecos and has recently moved into the eastern portion of the Panhandle along the Caprock.

PRAIRIE DOG—Until recent years probably no sight was so universal in West Texas as the **black-tailed prairie dog** (Cynomys ludovicianus Ord) and its burrow. Naturalists estimated its population in the hundreds of millions. Its destruction of range grasses, plus its peculiar susceptibility to eradication (usually by the introduction of the fumes of carbon disulphide into its burrow) have caused a great reduction of its numbers over its past range. However, it is making a comeback. **Prairie dog towns** often covered many acres with thickly spaced burrows or **prairie dog holes**. It is being propagated in several public zoos, notably in the prairie dog town in **Mackenzie Park** at Lubbock. It has been accorded its monument in Texas in the name of the **Prairie Dog Town Fork** of the Red River, along one segment of which is located the beautiful Palo Duro Canyon.

PRONGHORN—The **Pronghorn** is primarily a plains animal. It almost became extinct, but a continuous closed season and sound management program raised its numbers and there have been limited open seasons since 1944. Specifically, these animals inhabit the plains and basin regions of Brewster, Presidio, Jeff Davis, Culberson and Hudspeth counties. They have also sufficiently increased in numbers in the Permian Basin and Panhandle to permit open seasons in recent years.

RABBIT—The **black-tailed jack rabbit** (Lepus californicus Gray) is found throughout Texas except in the East Texas forest area. It breeds rapidly, and its long hind legs make it one of the world's faster-running animals. The **Eastern cottontail** (Sylvilagus floridanus Allen) is found throughout Texas except in Trans-Pecos region. The **desert cottontail** (Sylvilagus auduboni Baird) is found in South and West Texas, usually on the open range. The **swamp rabbit** (Sylvilagus aquaticus Bachman) is found in East Texas and the coastal area.

RACCOON—The **raccoon** (Procyon lotor Linnaeus) is found along streams throughout Texas.

RATS AND MICE—There are 40 or 50 species of rats and mice in Texas of varying characteristics, habitats and economic destructiveness. The **Norway rat** (Rattus norvegicus Berkenhout) and the **black rat** (Rattus rattus Linnaeus) are probably the most common and the most destructive. Some of the species are native, and others, notably the Norway rat, are invaders. The common **house mouse** (Mus musculis Linnaeus) is estimated in the hundreds of millions annually. The rare **Guadalupe Mountain vole** (Microtus mexicanus guadalupensis Bailey) is found only in the **Guadalupe Mountains National Park** and just over the border into New Mexico.

RINGTAIL—The **ringtail** (Bassariscus astutus Lichtenstein) is found generally in wooded areas west of the Trinity and in the broken sections of the Edwards Plateau. It is a valuable fur-bearing mammal.

SHEEP—The **barbary**, or **Aoudad, sheep** (Ammotragus lervia Pallas), first introduced to the Palo Duro Canyon area in 1957-58, have become firmly established. Barbary sheep have been introduced into many areas of Texas, but are designated as game animals in only eight counties of the Panhandle surrounding Palo Duro Canyon. Efforts are now under way by the Texas Parks and Wildlife Department to establish the **desert bighorn** (Ovis canadensis Shaw) in range formerly occupied.

SHREW—Three species are found in Texas, the **northern short-tailed shrew** (Blarina brevicauda Say), the **least shrew** (Cryptotis parva Say) and the **desert shrew** (Notiosorex crawfordi Coues). The first-mentioned is rarer, occurring in the Big Thicket. The least shrew is found generally in South Central and East Texas. The gray shrew is found in very limited numbers in the semiarid areas of West Texas and along the border.

SKUNK—There are six species of skunk in Texas. The **Eastern spotted skunk** (Spilogale putorius Rafinesque) is found throughout North Texas. A small skunk, it is often erroneously called civet cat. This skunk also is found in East Texas and the Gulf area. The **Western spotted skunk** (Spilogale gracilis Merriam) is found in the central, western and southern parts of the state. The **long-tailed**, or **broad-striped skunk** (Mephitis mephitis Schreber) is found in many parts of the state, usually along streams or in wooded areas. The **hooded skunk** (Mephitis macroura Lichtenstein) is found in limited numbers in the Trans-Pecos mountains. The **Gulf Coast hog-nosed skunk** (Conepatus leuconotus Lichtenstein), found in the Brownsville area, ranges southward into Mexico. The **mountain hog-nosed skunk** (Conepatus mesoleucus Lichtenstein) is found in sparsely timbered areas of Edwards Plateau, Central Texas, Trans-Pecos.

SQUIRREL—The **fox squirrel** (Sciurus niger Linnaeus) is found throughout East, Central and West Central Texas. The **gray, or cat, squirrel** (Sciurus carolinensis Gmelin) is found generally in the eastern third of the state. The **flying squirrel** (Glaucomys volans Linnaeus) is widely distributed in the Piney Woods and the East Texas Post Oak Belt.

WEASEL—The **brindled or long-tailed weasel** (Mustela frenata Lichtenstein), akin to the mink, is found in the Panhandle-Plains and South Texas.

WOLF—The **red wolf** (Canis rufus Audubon) was once found over a wide range in Eastern and Central Texas. It is now considered extirpated from the wild, with the only known remnants of the population now in captive propagation. The **gray wolf** (Canis lupus Linnaeus) once had a wide range over Central, Southern and Western Texas. It has been reduced almost to extinction. The **red wolf** and **gray wolf** are listed on the federal and state rare and endangered species lists; the few gray wolves which may be encountered in Texas are believed to be occasional individuals crossing over from Mexico.

Reptiles

Most of the more than 100 species of **snakes** found in Texas are beneficial as also are other reptiles. There are 15 **poisonous species** and subspecies and there are more cases of snakebite reported in Texas than any other state. Principal **poisonous reptiles** include three kinds of **copperheads** (Southern, Broadbanded and Trans-Pecos); one kind of **cottonmouth**; 10 kinds of **rattlesnakes** (western massasauga, desert massasauga, western pigmy, western diamondback, timber, banded rock, mottled rock, blacktailed, Mojave and prairie); and the **Texas coral snake**.

Also noteworthy are the **horned lizard; the vinegarroon,** a type of **whip scorpion,** also harmless; **tarantulas,** a hairy spider; and **alligators.**

Freshwater Fishing

During the 1985-86 fiscal year an estimated 3.2 million Texas fishermen spent more than 11 million days fishing on our 1.5 million acres of public impoundments and 80,000 miles of rivers, streams and bayous. These anglers fished for sport and food, avidly seeking such longtime favorites as largemouth bass, crappie, white bass, sunfish and the various species of catfish. Considerable time was spent seeking introduced species such as smallmouth bass, walleye, striped bass and the striped/white bass hybrid.

Freshwater recreational fishing is big business in Texas. During the fiscal year, these fishermen, both residents and visitors, spent an estimated $2.8 billion on the purchase of goods and services related to recreational fishing, according to Texas Parks and Wildlife Department officials.

The year 1986 marked the beginning of a new era of freshwater fishing in Texas. New, more restrictive regulations on the two most popular sport fishes, largemouth bass and crappie, reflected the state's commitment to maintaining and improving the quality of fishing in Texas.

The increasing number of fishermen is straining some fishery resources. New and better fishing equipment is adding to this increased pressure. Catch-and-release fishing has emerged on the Texas scene as the conservation theme of fishermen who desire continued quality fishing.

TP&WD has continued its programs of stocking fish in public waters to increase fish numbers and species diversity. Among the most successful introductions are:

• **Florida bass,** a subspecies of largemouth bass, grows heavier than native bass. The Florida bass has been stocked in almost every Texas reservoir and has forever changed the face of bass fishing in Texas. The 17-pound, 10-ounce bass caught in Texas in 1986 is among the 10 largest bass ever captured in the United States and places Texas among the top states in trophy bass fishing. Eight- to 12-pound bass, once a rare catch anywhere, are now commonly taken in Texas. Of the top 30 largemouth bass ever caught in Texas, all but one have been caught since the introduction of Florida bass in 1972.

• **Striped bass** were once native to Texas' coastal areas, and efforts to re-establish the species on the coast are underway. They also have been introduced successfully in fresh water. Reproducing populations have been established in Lakes Whitney and Texoma, and excellent striper fishing can be found at Lakes Buchanan, E. V. Spence, Possum Kingdom, Amistad and Livingston. A hybrid between the striped bass and white bass has added another sport fish for many smaller Texas reservoirs.

• **Walleyes,** native to the northern United States, have been stocked in many Texas reservoirs in the western half of the state. They adapt well to clear, rocky lakes that provide only sparse habitat for largemouth bass.

• **Smallmouth bass** also are doing well in many reservoirs in the western half of the state, where they have built sustained populations through natural reproduction. The state record smallmouth bass, caught in 1985, weighed six pounds, seven ounces, and many lakes have produced smallmouths weighing more than five pounds.

• **Saltwater red drum** have been introduced into some Texas freshwater reservoirs, and they are doing especially well in Lake Braunig at San Antonio.

In addition, rainbow trout are stocked during the winter months on a put-and-take basis in the Guadalupe River below Canyon Reservoir Dam, the Brazos River below the Morris Sheppard Dam, Possum Kingdom Lake, Foster County Park at San Angelo, Boykin Springs in Angelina County, the San Gabriel River below Lake Georgetown, the Clear Fork of the Trinity River in Fort Worth, and in several small lakes in state parks.

Commercial Fisheries

Shrimp made up 82 percent of the pounds landed and 91 percent of the value of all reported commercial marine products during 1985. Almost 10 million pounds of blue crabs valued at $3.3 million and 5 million pounds of oysters valued at $8.6 million demonstrate the increasing importance of these species in the commercial fishery.

Commercial Landings*
(Jan. 1, 1985 to Dec. 31, 1985)
Source: Texas Parks and Wildlife Department

Species	Pounds	Value
Finfish		
Drum, Black.............	633,100	$419,800
Flounder	437,900	439,500
Sheepshead	182,500	40,900
Snapper, Red	632,400	1,175,800
Other.................	1,252,400	550,800
Total Finfish	3,138,300	$2,626,800
Shellfish		
Shrimp (Heads On):		
Brown and Pink.....	57,432,100	$113,421,200
White	24,202,300	47,796,600
Other	606,100	164,900
Crabs................	9,705,700	3,304,000
Oysters..............	5,044,200	8,590,800
Other................	171,300	127,600
Total Shellfish	97,161,600	$173,405,100
Grand Total...........	100,299,900	$176,031,900

*Preliminary data.

Saltwater Fishing

The Coastal Fisheries Branch of the Texas Parks and Wildlife Department is responsible for making management recommendations regarding the state's saltwater fishery resources within the bays and estuaries and out to nine nautical miles in the Gulf of Mexico. More than $400 million is spent annually in Texas' 4 million acres of saltwater by approximately 15,000 commercial and over 1 million recreational fishermen. The economic value of the coastal fishery exceeds $1.7 billion annually.

The goal of the coastal fisheries program is to develop management plans within the concept of optimum yield for selected fisheries that include harvest regulations, resource stock enhancements or habitat enhancements based on monitoring programs and the best scientific information available. The objectives of the Coastal Fisheries Branch are: (1) to recommend management strategies for the aquatic marine resources based on the results of research and the best scientific information available; (2) to determine the sizes and changes in the sizes of finfish and shellfish populations caused by environmental conditions and fishing; (3) to determine the landings of marine species and the associated social and economic characteristics of the fisheries; (4) to develop mariculture techniques for selected species and make the information available to commercial mariculturists in Texas; (5) to educate the consumer regarding high quality, wholesome seafood products. In fiscal year 1986, a total of 31 technical reports, 14 scientific journal articles and two magazine articles about various aspects of the Texas coastal fishery resources were completed to aid in meeting the objectives.

Effective management of finfish and shellfish re-

sources must be based on a thorough knowledge of the population dynamics and status of the resources. Long-term trend data based on routine monitoring are necessary to assess changes in abundance and stability. Landings information from both sport and commercial fishermen is necessary to assess the impact of user groups on the fisheries and to determine the economic importance of the fisheries to the state.

The **Perry R. Bass Marine Fisheries Research Station** at Palacios was established to provide information and techniques necessary for the improvement of Texas fisheries management plans. Research effort is directed toward methods for spawning and rearing marine fish and shellfish. Once developed, such techniques will be used to provide animals for stocking coastal bays and freshwater reservoirs, and information on techniques will be made available to commercial mariculturists in Texas. Coastal fisheries personnel exchange information with their counterparts in other states.

As directed by the Texas Legislature, the Seafood Marketing Program was initiated to increase the utilization and value of seafood products. This charge is aimed at all functional levels within the marketing channel. The Seafood Marketing Program has functioned through an interagency contract with Texas A&M University, the Texas Agricultural Extension Service, the Sea Grant College Program's Marine Advisory Service and the Texas Department of Agriculture. Several fisheries development foundations nationwide have also supported various work completed by the Seafood Marketing Program.

Activities in Fiscal 1986

Regulations were modified to protect king mackerel by requiring a two-fish daily bag and possession limit for retention in Texas waters. These regulations conformed to those approved by the Gulf of Mexico Fishery Management Council for federal waters.

The closure period for Gulf shrimping in state waters was coordinated with the National Marine Fisheries Service for closure of the Exclusive Economic Zone (EEZ) to increase yield and value for the shrimping industry. The season was closed 30 minutes after sunset on May 10 and opened 30 minutes after sunset on July 2. The EEZ was closed to 15 nautical miles instead of 200 miles.

There was no change in the November 1-April 30 oystering season. The oyster program was expanded to provide coverage and increased efficiency coastwide.

Development of a state red drum management plan was continued as part of the 6-year plan for Coastal Fisheries programs approved by the commission. Fishery management plans were initiated for shrimp and oysters. The Branch also participated in the development, review and revision of 10 Gulf Council management plans, requiring 2,880 manhours.

There were 760 gill net samples, 1,080 bag seine samples, 3,840 trawl samples, 4,492 oyster dredge samples and 80 Southeast Area Monitoring and Assessment Program samples collected. A total of 1,144 survey days were spent to estimate landings and pressure of the recreational boat fishermen.

Gulf of Mexico waters from Alabama to the Rio Grande were sampled to a depth of 270 feet during June-July and October-November with other Gulf states and the National Marine Fisheries Service (NMFS). This effort was coordinated by the Gulf States Marine Fisheries Commission through SEAMAP. Results of sampling were used by the National Marine Fisheries Service to evaluate the closure of Gulf waters to shrimping.

A statewide mail survey of over 6,000 holders of the saltwater sport fishing stamp was initiated. The survey examines species preference, participation and socio-economic aspects of saltwater fishermen in Texas.

Routine collection of commercial landings data continued through a formal cooperative statistics agreement with NMFS. TP&WD collected commercial landings statistics on crabs, oysters and finfishes, while NMFS continued to gather landings statistics on shrimp.

The special studies of spotted seatrout and snook, culture and reproduction, and spotted seatrout/orangemouth corvina hybridization that were initiated in 1985 were continued. Methods for artificially inducing sexual maturity and spawning in orangemouth corvina, snook and Southern flounder were examined. Pond-cultured fry and fingerling of several fish species were stocked in Texas bays and inland reservoirs.

National Wildlife Refuges

In addition to the many state and national parks that can be reached from most major cities in Texas, there are 10 national wildlife refuges that may be visited at different times of the year for bird watching and wildlife viewing. It is best to write before visiting to check on facilities available and to be sure the refuge is open to visitors at that time. Addresses are given at the end of the description of each refuge.

Texas has more than 177,500 acres set aside in its 10 national wildlife refuges. Short sketches of each are given below:

Anahuac

The 24,293 acres of this refuge are managed primarily for migrating and wintering waterfowl, but the threatened **American alligator** also resides within its boundaries. As many as 30 species of **ducks** and **geese** have been sighted; in fact, waterfowl may be observed there year around. Of the 253 species listed in the refuge checklist, birders will find 42 species that actually nest at Anahuac. Many shorebirds also enjoy sanctuary here. Visitors may observe wildlife, sightsee, take photographs or engage in crabbing, fishing and floundering. Overnight camping is permitted only along bay shore and is limited to three days. Write directly to the refuge for information concerning public recreational uses and regulations. Address: Box 278, Anahuac 77514. Phone (409)267-3337.

Aransas

The 54,829 acres of this refuge furnish a home for **whooping cranes** in Texas. Its primary function is to provide a wintering area for waterfowl, wading birds and the endangered whoopers, but many other birds and mammals live in its diverse habitats. An archery hunt is held each year to help control the deer herd. More than 350 species of birds have been observed at Aransas. Birding is enhanced by a U.S. Fish and Wildlife leaflet that describes the birding spots and tells what to look for and when. **Deer, raccoons, armadillos, opossums** and many kinds of birds can be seen throughout the day. November through March is the most popular time to visit Aransas because many migratory waterfowl and the whoopers are present. Address: Box 100, Austwell 77950. Phone (512) 286-3559.

Attwater's Prairie Chicken

The refuge was established on July 1, 1972, to preserve habitat for the endangered Attwater's Prairie Chicken. The refuge comprises 7,980 acres of land. Ninety percent of the land is native prairie, and the remainder is cultivated croplands with a narrow strip of riparian woodlands. The refuge is open to the public from dawn to dusk daily, except during the period from Feb. 15 until May 1, when entrance is authorized by reservation only. The refuge is open to the public for wildlife/wildlands observations, photography and wildlife research. During the winter, large numbers of ducks, geese and sandhill cranes concentrate on the refuge fields and marshes to feed and rest. Address: Refuge Manager, Box 518, Eagle Lake 77434. Phone (409) 234-3021.

Brazoria

The 11,000 acres of this refuge serve as nesting area for mottled ducks, and its coastal salt marshes are part of ancestral wintering grounds of the **snow goose**. Fishing, crabbing and oystering are allowed in public waters on and around the refuge, and waterfowl hunting is permitted in specified areas. Access for these sports is by boat only. Since the refuge was established in 1966, 247 species of birds have been identified here. Freeport Christmas Bird Count always records one of highest number of species observed in nation. Prospective birders should check on refuge conditions in advance of planning trip, because access is poor and roads often muddy. Address: P.O. Drawer 1088, Angleton 77515. Phone (409) 849-6062.

Buffalo Lake

Known originally as **Tierra Blanca Water Conservation Project**, this has been one of major waterfowl refuges in the Central Flyway. At present, the lake is dry, with the dam and spillway needing major rehabilitation. Portions of refuge are open from March through October for picnicking, sightseeing, birding, nature study, photography and camping. When water is available, its 7,677 acres provide winter refuge for 1 million ducks and 80,000 geese, and summer refuge for 500,000 people. Checklist indicates 275 species of birds sighted at Buffalo Lake, with 44 species nesting. Address: Box 228, Umbarger 79091. Phone (806) 499-3382.

Hagerman

When **Denison Dam** was built creating **Lake Texoma**, 11,000 acres were set aside to provide food and safe resting place for migrating waterfowl and assure survival of all plant and animal species using area. Hagerman serves as winter home for several thousand ducks and geese. The 3,000-acre marsh and water area hosts large numbers of **Canada geese** and lesser flights of **snow** and white-fronted **geese**. Open meadows to dense stands of pecan, oak, ash and juniper comprise refuge's upland habitat and provide homes for songbirds, **quail, doves, squirrels, foxes, opossums, skunks, armadillos, rabbits, deer** and many other animals. **Beavers, raccoons** and **mink** favor stream and marsh banks.

Oil was discovered on refuge lands in 1951, and about 160 producing wells are presently operating. More than 35,000 people visit Hagerman each year to enjoy birding, sightseeing, nature study, photography, fishing and frogging. Hunting is restricted to dove and is closely regulated. Fishing is permitted from April 1 to Sept. 30. Overnight camping not allowed. Address: Route 3, Box 123, Sherman 75090. Phone (214) 786-2826.

Laguna Atascosa

Established 1946 as southernmost waterfowl refuge in Central Flyway, this refuge contains 46,000 acres, 7,000 of which are marsh and open water. It supports substantial numbers of wintering ducks, including one of larger concentrations of **redheads** and also home for rare **ocelot** and **jaguarundi**. Winter months are most popular for visitors. Birding is popular year around because of migratory birds in fall and winter, and exotic Mexican birds in summer. There are 354 bird species and 31 mammal species considered part of the refuge fauna. Walking trails and auto tours are provided, and fishing is permitted in Harlingen Ship Channel. Archery deer season and controlled gun hunt held most years on 27,000 acres. No other hunting allowed. Address: Box 450, Rio Hondo 78583. Phone (512) 748-3607.

McFaddin

Purchased in 1979 and 1980 with duck stamp revenues, McFaddin's 42,956 acres were acquired for their importance to wintering population of migratory waterfowl in the Central Flyway and for their estuarine values for marine organisms. McFaddin contains one of the densest populations of **American alligators** in Texas. In addition, there are **wintering ducks** and **geese, resident mottled duck, muskrat, river otter**, mink, raccoon, striped skunk, opossum, armadillo, gray fox, marsh wading birds, shore birds, freshwater and saltwater fish, shrimp, crabs and other marine organisms. Public activities include wildlife observation, photography, fishing, crabbing and waterfowl hunting. Twelve miles of beach provide opportunities for swimming, fishing, camping, picnicking and beachcombing. Address: Refuge Manager, P.O. Box J, Sabine Pass 77655. Phone (409) 971-2909.

Muleshoe

Oldest of national refuges in Texas, more than 5,000 acres of the 5,809 acres are composed of short-grass rangeland with scattered mesquite. As many as 700,000 migrating waterfowl are in residence by end of December. Also serves as roosting area for **sandhill cranes**. Birding is best during October and November, when 213 species are present. The five miles of road suitable for automobile travel reveal **rabbits, scaled quail, prairie dogs, burrowing owls** and occasionally **coyote, badger** or **skunk**. Visitor activities are limited to birding, nature study, photography and sightseeing. Address: Box 549, Muleshoe 79347. Phone (806)946-3341.

San Bernard

More than 80,000 **snow and blue geese** use the 24,000 acres as wintering area; **mottled ducks** nest here. **Shorebirds, gulls** and **terns** use mud flats, and **herons, egrets** and **ibis** are common on lower marsh area ponds. Bird checklist contains 245 species. Waterfowl hunting allowed and temporary blinds may be used in public hunting areas. No permits necessary for public hunting areas, but "Special Permit Waterfowl Hunt" held on refuge with participating hunters phoning in reservations just prior to the season. Information about special permit hunt should be obtained from refuge manager. Write P.O. Drawer 1088, Angleton 77515. Phone (409) 849-6062.

Santa Ana

Established in 1943 and referred to as **"gem of the National Wildlife Refuge System,"** these 2,080 acres of subtropical forest and native brushland provide habitat for more than 300 species of birds, 30 species of mammals, 50 species of reptiles and amphibians and 450 plant species. The refuge benefits more endangered and threatened species than any other refuge in the system. Bird watchers come from all over the United States and many foreign countries to view many Mexican bird species that reach the northern edge of their ranges in South Texas. Five trees on the refuge are classified as national champions: **Berlandier ash, brazil, honey mesquite, guayacan** and **Texas ebony**. This credits them as being the largest of their species in the United States. A Texas ebony natural area is set aside for scientific and educational purposes. Public facilities include Visitor Center, over 14 miles of foot trails, photography blinds and a 6.7-mile one-way tour road. Tour road is closed to private vehicles during winter months and an interpretive tram is available. Foot access is permitted from sunrise to sunset; vehicles permitted on tour road from 9:00 a.m. to 4:30 p.m. when tram is not operating. Address: Refuge Manager, Route 1, Box 202A, Alamo 78516. Phone (512) 787-3079.

Texas Point

Purchased in 1979 and 1980 with duck stamp revenues, Texas Point's 8,952 acres were acquired for their importance to wintering population of migratory waterfowl in the Central Flyway and for their estuarine values for marine organisms. Fauna found in the Texas Point refuge include **muskrat, river otter,** mink, raccoon, striped skunk, armadillo, gray fox, bobcat, nutria, coyote, **resident mottled duck, wintering ducks** and **geese,** marsh wading birds, shore birds, freshwater and saltwater fish, shrimp, crabs and other marine organisms. There is no public access to the beach; vehicular roads are non-existent. A cattle walk, located at the refuge parking lot along Highway 87 and for which rubber boots are often necessary, provides access by foot into the marsh for wildlife observation, hunting and crabbing. For information on waterfowl hunting at no charge, contact the McFaddin NWR manager, P.O. Box J, Sabine Pass 77655. Phone (409) 971-2909.

State Wildlife Areas

In addition to the above national refuges in Texas, there are **28 wildlife management areas** administered by the Texas Parks and Wildlife Department. A brief description of each is given below. Research concerning the preservation, management and wise use of wildlife and our other natural resources is conducted on these study areas. Many of the wildlife management areas are open to the public for nature study, hiking, camping, hunting and fishing. Hunting is regulated by one of three permit systems: self-registration, first-come-first-served or computer selection.

For further information concerning public use opportunities on state wildlife management areas, write to the **Texas Parks and Wildlife Department,** 4200 Smith School Road, Austin 78744, or phone toll-free 1-800-792-1112.

Alabama Creek Wildlife Management Area (Trinity County)—Approximately 14,500 acres of national forest land south of Apple Springs. Cooperative management program with U.S. Forest Service. Camping permitted at Forest Service campground on Neches River Feb. 1 through Sept. 30; from Oct. 1 to Jan. 31, camping limited to designated campsites. Deer gun hunting participants selected by computer drawing. Other hunting allowed by self-registration.

Angelina-Neches Scientific Area (Combined with Dam B Unit. See listing below.)

Bannister WMA (San Augustine County)—Contains 20,700 acres of national forest land east of Lufkin managed in a cooperative program with the U.S. Forest Service. Camping permitted anywhere on area from Feb. 1 through Sept. 30; from Oct. 1 to Jan. 31, camping limited to designated campsites. Deer gun hunting participants selected by computer drawing. Other hunting allowed by self-registration.

Black Gap WMA (Brewster County along Rio Grande)—Contains 77,805 acres owned plus 23,073 acres leased from General Land Office. Research conducted on desert mule deer, desert bighorn sheep, javelina, cougar and scaled quail. Black bear occasionally present. Primitive camping along river for fishermen and at designated sites for hunters. Fishing permitted from March 15 through June 15. Javelina hunting participants selected by computer drawing. Other hunting allowed by self-registration.

Caddo WMA (Fannin County)—Contains 16,140 acres of national forest land east of Bonham managed in a cooperative program with the U.S. Forest Service. The 13,360-acre **Bois d'Arc Unit** offers fishing and designated campsites on **Coffee Mill Lake** and **Lake Davy Crockett** Feb. 1 through Sept. 30; from Oct. 1 to Jan. 31, camping limited to designated campsites. This WMA is predominantly hardwood and pine forest. The 2,780-acre **Ladonia Unit** contains grassland prairie. Deer gun hunting participants selected by computer drawing. Other hunting allowed by self-registration.

Chaparral WMA (La Salle and Dimmit counties)—Research on brush country vegetation and wildlife conducted on 15,200 acres enclosed by high fence west of Artesia Wells. No public use facilities. Deer and javelina hunting participants selected by computer drawing. Other hunting on first-come-first-served basis.

Dam B-Angelina-Neches Unit of Eastern WMA (Jasper and Tyler counties)—Access primarily by boat to 13,445 acres west of Jasper adjacent to **B. A. Steinhagen Lake** at confluence of Angelina and Neches Rivers. Hunting for deer, feral hog and other legal wildlife species by self-registration. Permit from U.S. Corps of Engineers required for camping.

Elephant Mountain WMA (Brewster County)—Contains 23,000 acres of mountainous terrain and Chihuahuan desert. Acquired during 1985 for use in the restoration, development and management of native wildlife species. Not open for general public visitation or camping, but development of nature trails is underway. Experimental release of desert bighorn sheep broodstock initiated during early 1987. Participants in deer gun and archery hunts, pronghorn hunts and javelina hunts selected by drawing. Hunting for mourning dove and scaled quail by self-registration.

Gene Howe WMA (Hemphill County)—Research conducted on wildlife management on 5,821 acres of upper and rolling plains habitat east of Canadian on the south fork of the Canadian River. Contains remnant population of lesser prairie chicken. Deer and turkey hunters selected by computer drawing. Other hunting by self-registration.

Granger Unit of Eastern WMA (Williamson County)—Contains 6,716 acres of land and 4,400 acres of water on **Lake Granger** northeast of Taylor. Pheasant hunters selected by computer drawing. Other hunting allowed by self-registration.

Guadalupe Delta WMA (Calhoun County)—Contains 3,597 acres of coastal delta marsh along the perimeter of **Mission Lake** northwest of Seadrift used as a waterfowl refuge and for wildlife management research. Area is in initial phases of development and no public use facilities are present. Hunting on first-come-first-served basis.

Gus Engeling WMA (Anderson County)—Contains 10,941 acres of woodland west of Palestine used for wildlife management research. Fishing available on Catfish Creek and two small impoundments. Public use facilities include two nature trails and designated campsites. Deer, feral hog and turkey hunters selected by computer drawing. Other hunting on first-come-first-served basis.

Honey Creek WMA (Comal County)—Contains 1,500 acres of hill country terrain containing limestone formations vegetated with live oak and ash juniper. Acquired during 1985 from the Texas Nature Conservancy for preservation as a natural area. Not open to general public visitation or camping; however, public use facilities available at the adjacent Guadalupe River State Park. Participants in deer gun and archery hunts and turkey hunts selected by drawing.

James E. Daughtrey WMA (Live Oak and McMullen counties)—Contains approximately 25,000 acres located on perimeter of **Choke Canyon Reservoir** northwest of Three Rivers. Park and recreation facilities being developed on a portion of the area. Deer, javelina and turkey hunters selected by computer drawing. Other hunting on first-come-first-served basis.

J.D. Murphree WMA (Jefferson County)—Contains 12,389 acres of coastal marsh on Taylor's Bayou southwest of Port Arthur used as a waterfowl refuge for wildlife management research. Free access for fishing. Boat

ramps available for use during public hunts. Alligators are numerous. Hunting for waterfowl and other legal wildlife species is on first-come-first-served basis.

Keechi Creek WMA (Leon County)—Contains 1,500 acres of bottomland acquired during 1986 for development of waterfowl habitat. Not open to general public visitation or camping. Participants in deer gun and archery hunts selected by drawing. Hunting for squirrel and waterfowl on first-come-first-served basis.

Kerr WMA (Kerr County)—Research conducted on wildlife management and habitat development on 6,493 acres of Edwards Plateau juniper-oak habitat under high fence west of Kerrville. Intensive studies conducted on white-tailed deer genetics. Free fishing access to north fork of Guadalupe River. **Golden-cheeked warbler** is summer resident. Computer selection of hunters for deer and turkey hunts. Area open to public on scheduled field days with demonstration of habitat management procedures.

Las Palomas WMA (Cameron, Hidalgo, Presidio, Starr and Willacy counties)—Fourteen tracts comprising 3,513 acres in the Rio Grande Valley of south and west Texas. Primary use is to provide nesting habitat for white-winged dove. Ocelot, jaguarundi and cougar are present. Computer selection of hunters for white-winged dove and chachalaca hunts.

Matador WMA (Cottle County) — Contains 28,183 acres of upper and rolling plains northwest of Paducah. Research conducted on wildlife habitat development and upland game bird management. Small population of pronghorn present on area. Turkey hunters selected by computer drawing. Production of both bobwhite and scaled quail is generally high and draws many hunters. Hunting for quail is on first-come-first-served basis. Mourning dove hunting allowed by self-registration.

Matagorda Island WMA (Calhoun County)—Approximately 36,568 acres of marsh and island uplands south of Port O'Connor and accessible only by boat. Operated under cooperative agreement with the U.S. Fish and Wildlife Service and the General Land Office. Primary objective is to conserve habitats for endangered species and other migratory and resident wildlife species. **Whooping cranes** winter in the area and regularly utilize the southern portion of the island. Free access for marine fishing, nature study, hiking and beachcombing. Camping only in designated areas. Deer hunters selected by computer drawing. Hunting for waterfowl, quail and mourning dove on first-come-first-served basis.

M. O. Neasloney WMA (Gonzales County)—Contains 100 acres of post oak woodland acquired during 1984 for preservation as a natural area and nature study site for use by educational and wildlife conservation organizations through prior arrangement.

Moore Plantation WMA (Sabine County)—Includes 22,800 acres of national forest land east of Pineland under cooperative management agreement with U.S. Forest Service. Also contains 2,100 acres leased from Temple-Eastex, Inc. Camping permitted anywhere Feb. 1 through Sept. 30; from Oct. 1 to Jan. 31, camping limited to designated campsites. Deer gun hunting participants selected by computer drawing. Other hunting by self-registration.

North Toledo Bend Unit of Eastern WMA (Shelby County)—Composed of 3,600 acres of land and water along the Sabine River east of Center. Primary use is as a waterfowl management area and refuge. No camping permitted on area. No regular gun season for deer. Other hunting allowed by self-registration.

Pat Mayse Unit of Eastern WMA (Lamar County)—Contains approximately 8,925 acres of land and water adjacent to Pat Mayse Reservoir northwest of Paris. Contains wooded uplands and bottomland hardwood habitats. No camping on area, but allowed on designated campsite at adjacent U.S. Corps of Engineers facility at Lamar Point. Fishing allowed by self-registration. Participants for deer gun hunts selected by computer drawing. Other hunting by self-registration.

Peach Point WMA (Brazoria County)—Contains 8,580 acres of coastal marsh acquired from the Texas Nature Conservancy during 1985 for development of waterfowl habitat and use as a public hunting area. Not open to general public visitation or camping. Hunting for waterfowl on first-come-first-served basis.

Sheldon WMA (Harris County)—Contains 2,503 acres on **Carpenter's Bayou** east of Houston utilized primarily as a waterfowl and shorebird sanctuary. Composed largely of **Sheldon Reservoir** with adjacent levees and shoreline marsh. Cropland areas managed for production of wildlife foods. Public use facilities include two boat ramps with parking areas, five T-head fishing piers and 5.5 miles of levees. Free access for fishing. No hunting permitted.

Sierra Diablo WMA (Culberson County)—Includes 8,431 acres in the **Sierra Diablo Mountains** northwest of Van Horn. Utilized primarily for research concerning reintroduction of desert bighorn sheep to native ranges and management of desert mule deer. Mule deer hunt participants selected by computer drawing. Area closed to public except for mule deer hunts.

Somerville Unit of Eastern WMA (Burleson and Lee counties)—Approximately 3,500 acres in two units, the **Yegua Creek Unit** and the **Nails Creek Unit**, near **Lake Somerville** south of Caldwell. No camping on the area. Public use facilities are available nearby at U.S. Army Corps of Engineers Recreation Areas and at Lake Somerville State Recreation Areas. Deer gun hunt participants selected by computer drawing. Other hunting and fishing by self-registration.

Walter Buck WMA (Kimble County)—Contains approximately 2,123 acres of juniper-oak habitat in limestone escarpment southwest of Junction. Adjacent to the **South Llano River State Park**, which is in initial phase of development. Participants in deer and javelina hunts selected by computer drawing. Area not open to the public except for public hunts.

RESEARCH FACILITIES, FISH HATCHERIES

The **Texas Parks and Wildlife Department** operates a number of fish hatcheries and a research facility to support the conservation and management of fishery resources.

In the list below, the fish hatcheries have no public facilities, but scheduled tours are available by letter request for groups of 20 or more. There are no rates or charges. Write to individual hatchery for information.

Research Facilities

Heart of the Hills—Junction Star Route, Box 62, Ingram. Fishery management techniques that will enhance the conservation and management of freshwater reservoirs and streams are tested in the laboratory and pond facilities. Sophisticated laboratory and data analysis equipment provides fishery scientists with the capability to investigate most fishery problems.

Fish Hatcheries

Dundee—Archer County below the dam on Lake Diversion. Total acreage 141; pond acreage 78. Consists of 94 earthen ponds; fishes raised include striped bass, hybrid striped bass and smallmouth bass.

Eagle Mountain—Tarrant County below Eagle Mountain Reservoir Dam. Total acreage 70; pond acreage 46.1. Consists of 30 earthen ponds; fishes raised include smallmouth bass, channel catfish and blue catfish.

Huntsville—Walker County off State 19. Total acreage 247; pond acreage 32.51. Consists of 39 earthen ponds; fishes raised are Kemp's largemouth bass and Florida bass.

Jasper—Jasper County off State 63. Total acreage 227; pond acreage 64. Consists of 63 earthen ponds; fishes raised include Florida bass, Kemp's largemouth bass, blue catfish and crappie.

John Wilson Marine—Nueces County near Corpus Christi. Total area 30 acres with 20 acres of pond; expansion will add 19 acres of ponds and two buildings with laboratory and spawning capabilities. Red drum, common snook and spotted seatrout fry and fingerlings raised for stocking Texas bays. Facility, only one of its kind in world, resulted from cooperative effort by TP&WD, Gulf Coast Conservation Association and Central Power & Light Co. of Corpus Christi.

Possum Kingdom—Palo Pinto County below Possum Kingdom Reservoir Dam on State 16. Total acreage 103; pond acreage 28.98. Consists of 44 earthen ponds; fishes raised are striped bass and hybrid striped bass.

San Angelo No. 1—Tom Green County on US 87 at South Concho River. Total acreage 160; pond acreage 40. Consists of 40 earthen ponds; fishes raised are blue catfish, channel catfish and sunfish.

San Angelo No. 2—Tom Green County off US 277 at Lake Nasworthy. Total acreage 170; pond acreage 42. Consists of 31 earthen ponds. Fishes raised include channel catfish, sunfish and hybrid striped bass.

A. E. Wood—Hays County south of San Marcos. Under renovation. When completed in 1988, the facility will produce smallmouth bass, Florida bass, channel catfish, blue catfish, sunfish and grow out rainbow trout.

Tyler—Smith County off State 31. Total acreage 42; pond acreage 15. Consists of 35 earthen ponds; fishes produced are Kemp's largemouth bass and Florida bass.

Coastal Fisheries Branch

These facilities are mainly leased from private owners for office space and boat dockage. There are no public facilities.

Corpus Christi Field Station—Nueces County in Corpus Christi. Headquarters for personnel assigned to Cor-

These three whooping cranes are from the flock at Sundown Bay near Rockport. The birds migrate between Canada and Texas each year, and the number of birds in the flock at the Aransas National Wildlife Refuge is increasing. Associated Press Photo.

pus Christi Bay and upper Laguna Madre research programs.

Olmito Field Station—Cameron County, 3 mi. N. of Brownsville. Headquarters for personnel assigned to lower Laguna Madre and Gulf of Mexico research programs.

Palacios Field Station—Calhoun County in Palacios. Headquarters for personnel assigned to research programs in East Matagorda, Matagorda and Lavaca Bay areas.

Perry R. Bass Marine Fisheries Research Station—Calhoun County 3.5 mi. on Will Point Rd. Has 21 ponds, total acreage 40; pond acreage 22.8. Experimental marine research.

Port Arthur Field Station—Jefferson County on Pleasure Island. Serves as area headquarters for personnel

assigned to Sabine Lake and Gulf of Mexico fishery programs.

Port O'Connor Field Station—Calhoun County in Port O'Connor. Area headquarters for personnel assigned to San Antonio Bay system and Gulf of Mexico fishery programs.

Rockport Marine Laboratory—Aransas County, on Rockport boat basin. Headquarters for field program administrators and personnel assigned to Aransas Bay, Corpus Christi Bay and Gulf of Mexico biological programs. Complete marine ways and repair facility for departmental vessels and vehicles.

Seabrook Marine Laboratory—Harris County, on Seabrook waterfront. Headquarters for Coastal Fisheries research on Galveston Bay and Gulf of Mexico and Resource Protection Division chemist and biologist.

Vegetational Areas

(Editor's note: This article was updated for this edition of The Texas Almanac by Stephan L. Hatch, Curator, S.M. Tracy Herbarium and Associate Professor, Dept. of Range Science, Texas A&M University.)

Difference in amount and frequency of rainfall, in soils and in frost-free days gives Texas a great variety of vegetation. From the forests of East Texas to the deserts of West Texas, from the grassy plains of North Texas to the semi-arid brushlands of South Texas, plant species change continuously.

The following discussion of Texas' 10 vegetational areas (see map) and rangeland resources was prepared for the Texas Almanac by authorities at Texas A&M University.

Sideoats grama, which occurs on more different soils in Texas than any other native grass, was officially designated as the state grass of Texas by the Texas Legislature in 1971.

The 10 principal plant life areas of Texas, starting in the east, are:

1. **Piney Woods.** Most of this area of some 16 million acres ranges from about 50 to 500 feet above sea level and receives 40 to 60 inches of rain yearly. Many rivers, creeks and bayous drain the region. Nearly all of Texas' commercial timber comes from this area. Pine is the principal timber. There are three native species — the **longleaf, shortleaf** and **loblolly pine.** An introduced species, the slash pine, also is widely grown. Hardwoods include a variety of **oaks, elm, hickory, magnolia, sweet** and **black gum, tupelo** and others.

The area is interspersed with native and improved grasslands. Cattle are the primary grazing animals.

Deer and quail are abundant in properly managed localities. Primary forage plants, under proper grazing management, include species of the bluestems, rossettegrass, panicums, paspalums, blackseed needlegrass, Canada and Virginia wildryes, purpletop, broadleaf and spike woodoats, switchcane, lovegrasses, Indiangrass and legume species.

Highly disturbed areas have understory and overstory of undesirable woody plants that suppress growth of pine and desirable grasses. The primary forage grasses have been reduced and the grasslands invaded by threeawns, annual grasses, weeds, broomsedge bluestem, red lovegrass and shrubby woody species.

2. **Gulf Prairies and Marshes.** The gulf prairies and marshes cover approximately 10 million acres. There are two subunits: (a) **The marsh and salt grasses** immediately at tidewater, and (b) a little farther inland, a strip of **bluestems** and **tall grasses,** with some **gramas** in the western part. These grasses, except salt and marsh grasses, make excellent grazing. Oaks, elm and other hardwoods grow to some extent, especially along streams, and the area has some post oak and brushy extensions along its borders. Much of the Gulf Prairies is fertile farmland. The area is well suited for cattle.

Principal grasses of the Gulf Prairies are tall bunchgrasses, including big bluestem, little bluestem, seacoast bluestem, Indiangrass, eastern gamagrass, Texas wintergrass, switchgrass and gulf cordgrass. Seashore

Buffalograss
(Buchloe dactyloides)

Blue grama
(Bouteloua gracilis)

saltgrass occurs on moist saline sites. Heavy grazing has changed the range vegetation in many cases so that the predominant grasses are the less desirable broomsedge bluestem, smutgrass, threeawns, tumblegrass and many other inferior grasses. The other plants that have invaded the productive grasslands include oak underbrush, Macartney rose, huisache, mesquite, prickly pear, ragweed, bitter sneezeweed, broomweed and others.

Vegetation of the Gulf Marshes consists primarily of sedges, bullrush, flat-sedges, beakrush and other rushes, smooth cordgrass, marshhay cordgrass, marsh millet and maidencane. The marshes are grazed best during winter.

3. Post Oak Savannah. This secondary forest region, also called the Post Oak Belt, covers some 9 million acres. It is immediately west of the primary forest region, with less annual rainfall and a little higher elevation. Principal trees are post oak, blackjack oak and elm. Along streams are growths of pecans, walnuts and other kinds of water-demanding trees. The southwestern extension of this belt is often poorly defined, with large areas of prairie.

The upland soils are sandy and sandy loam, while the bottomlands are sandy loams and clays.

The original vegetation consisted mainly of little bluestem, big bluestem, Indiangrass, switchgrass, purpletop, silver bluestem, Texas wintergrass, spike woodoats, longleaf woodoats, post oak and blackjack oak. The area is still largely native or improved grasslands, with small farms located throughout. Intensive grazing has caused much of this area to degenerate to dense stands of a woody understory of yaupon, greenbriar and oak brush. Mesquite has become a serious problem. Good forage plants have been replaced by such inferior plants as splitbeard bluestem, red lovegrass, broomsedge bluestem, broomweed, bullnettle and western ragweed.

4. Blackland Prairies. This area of about 11 million acres, while called a "prairie," has much timber along the streams, including a variety of oaks, pecan, elm, horse-apple (bois d'arc) and mesquite. In its native state it was largely a grassy plain — the first native grassland in the westward extension of the Southern Forest Region.

Most of this fertile area has been cultivated, and only small acreages of meadowland remain in original vegetation. In heavily grazed pastures, the tall bunchgrass has been replaced by buffalograss, Texas grama and other less productive grasses. Mesquite, lotebush and other woody plants have invaded the grasslands.

The original grass vegetation includes big and little bluestem, Indiangrass, switchgrass, sideoats grama, hairy grama, tall dropseed, Texas wintergrass and buffalograss. Nongrass vegetation is largely legumes and composites.

5. Cross Timbers and Prairies. Approximately 16.5 million acres of alternating woodlands, often called the West Cross Timbers, and prairies constitute this region. Sharp changes in the vegetational cover are asso-

ciated with different soils and topography, but the grass composition is rather uniform.

The prairie-type grasses are big bluestem, little bluestem, Indiangrass, switchgrass, Canada wildrye, sideoats grama, hairy grama, tall grama, tall dropseed, Texas wintergrass, blue grama and buffalograss.

On the Cross Timbers soils, the grasses are composed of big bluestem, little bluestem, hooded windmillgrass, sand lovegrass, Indiangrass, switchgrass and many species of legumes. The woody vegetation includes shinnery, blackjack, post and live oaks.

The entire area has been invaded heavily by woody brush plants of oaks, mesquite, juniper and other unpalatable plants that furnish little forage for livestock.

6. South Texas Plains. South of San Antonio, between the coast and the Rio Grande, are some 20 million acres of subtropical dryland vegetation, consisting of small trees, shrubs, cactus, weeds and grasses. The area is noteworthy for extensive brushlands, known as the brush country, or the Spanish equivalents of chaparral or monte. Principal plants are mesquite, small live oak, post oak, prickly pear (Opuntia) cactus, catclaw, blackbrush, whitebrush, huajillo, huisache, cenizo and others which often grow very densely. The original vegetation was mainly perennial warm-season bunchgrasses in post oak, live oak and mesquite savannahs. Other brush species form dense thickets on the ridges and along streams. Long-continued grazing caused the region to be densely covered with a mixture of brush. Most of the desirable grasses have persisted under the protection of brush and cacti.

There are distinct differences in the original plant communities on various soils. Dominant grasses on the sandy loam soils are seacoast bluestem, bristlegrass, paspalum, windmillgrass, trichloris, silver bluestem, big sandbur and tanglehead. Dominant grasses on the clay and clay loams are silver bluestem, Arizona cottontop, buffalograss, common curlymesquite, bristlegrass, pappusgrass, gramas, plains lovegrass, Texas cupgrass, vinemesquite, other panicums and Texas wintergrass. Low saline soils are characterized by gulf cordgrass, seashore saltgrass, alkali sacaton and switchgrass. In the post oak and live oak savannahs, the grasses are mainly seacoast bluestem, Indiangrass, switchgrass, crinkleawn, paspalums and panicums. Today much of the area has been reseeded to buffelgrass.

7. Edwards Plateau. These 24 million acres are rolling to mountainous, with woodlands in the eastern part and grassy prairies in the west. There is a good deal of brushy growth in the central and eastern parts. The combination of grasses, weeds and small trees is ideal for cattle, sheep, goats, deer and wild turkey.

This limestone-based area is characterized by the large number of springfed, perennially flowing streams which originate in its interior and flow across the Balcones Escarpment, which bounds it on the south and east. The soils are shallow, ranging from sands to

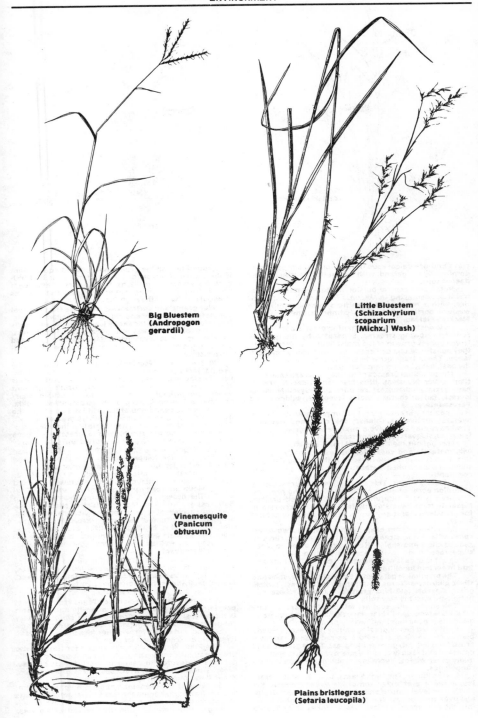

Big Bluestem
(Andropogon
gerardii)

Little Bluestem
(Schizachyrium
scoparium
[Michx.] Wash)

Vinemesquite
(Panicum
obtusum)

Plains bristlegrass
(Setaria leucopila)

Tobosa
(Chilaria Mutica)

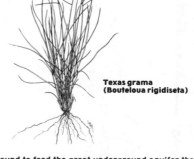

Texas grama
(Bouteloua rigidiseta)

clays and are calcareous in reaction. This area is pre-dominantly rangeland, with cultivation confined to the deeper soils.

In the east central portion is the well-marked Central Basin centering in Mason, Llano and Burnet counties, with a mixture of granitic and sandy soils. The western portion of the area comprises the semi-arid Stockton Plateau.

Noteworthy is the growth of cypress along the perennially flowing streams. Separated by many miles from cypress growth of the moist Southern Forest Belt, they constitute one of Texas' several "islands" of vegetation. These trees grow to stately proportions and, in the past, have been commercialized.

The principal grasses of the clay soils are cane bluestem, silver bluestem, little bluestem, sideoats grama, hairy grama, Indiangrass, common curlymesquite, buffalograss, fall witchgrass, plains lovegrass, wildryes and Texas wintergrass.

The rocky areas support tall or mid-grasses with an overstory of live oak, shinnery oak, cedar and mesquite. The heavy clay soils have a mixture of tobosagrass, buffalograss, sideoats grama and mesquite.

Throughout the Edwards Plateau, live oak, shinnery oak, mesquite and cedar dominate the woody vegetation. Woody plants have invaded to the degree that they should be controlled before range forage plants can re-establish.

8. Rolling Plains. This is a region of approximately 24 million acres of alternating woodlands and prairies. The area is half mesquite woodland and half prairie. Mesquite trees have steadily invaded and increased in the grasslands for many years, despite constant control efforts.

Soils range from coarse sands along outwash terraces adjacent to streams to tight or compact clays on redbed clays and shales. Rough broken lands on steep slopes are found in the western portion. About two-thirds of the area is rangeland. But cultivation is important in certain localities.

The original vegetation includes big, little, sand and silver bluestems, Texas wintergrass, Indiangrass, switchgrass, sideoats and blue gramas, wildryes, tobosa and buffalograss on the clay soils.

The sandy soils support tall bunchgrasses, mainly sand bluestem. Sand shinnery oak, sand sagebrush and mesquite are the dominant woody plants.

Continued heavy grazing causes increase in woody plants, low-value grasses such as red grama, red lovegrass, tumblegrass, gummy lovegrass, Texas grama, sand dropseed and sand bur; and western ragweed, croton and many other weeds. Yucca is a problem plant on certain rangelands.

9. High Plains. The High Plains, some 20 million treeless acres, are an extension of the Great Plains to the north. The level nature and porous soils prevent drainage over wide areas. The relatively light rainfall flows into the numerous shallow "playa" lakes or sinks into

the ground to feed the great underground aquifer that is the source of water for the countless wells that irrigate the surface of the plains. A large part of this area is under irrigated farming, but native grassland remains in about one-half of the High Plains.

Blue grama and buffalograss comprise the principal vegetation on the clay and clay loam "hardland" soils. Important grasses on the sandy loam "sandy land" soils are little bluestem, western wheatgrass, Indiangrass, switchgrass and sand reedgrass. Sand shinnery oak, sand sagebrush, mesquite and yucca are conspicuous invading brushy plants.

10. Trans-Pecos, Mountains and Basins. With as little as eight inches of annual rainfall, long hot summers and usually cloudless skies to encourage evaporation, this 18-million-acre area produces only drouth-resistant vegetation without irrigation. Grass is usually short and sparse. The principal growth consists of lechuguilla, ocotillo, yucca, cenizo and other arid land plants. In the more arid areas, yeso, chino and tobosa grasses prevail. There is some mesquite. The vegetation includes creosote-tarbush, desert shrub, grama grassland, yucca and juniper savannahs, pine oak forest and saline flats.

The mountains are 3,000 to 8,000 feet in elevation and support pinon pine, juniper and some ponderosa pine and other forest vegetation on a few of the higher slopes.

The grass vegetation, especially on the higher mountain slopes, includes many southwestern and Rocky Mountain species not present elsewhere in Texas. On the desert flats, black grama, burrograss and fluffgrass are frequent. More productive sites have numerous species of grama, muhly, Arizona cottontop, dropseed and perennial threeawn grasses. At the higher elevations, plains bristlegrass, little bluestem, Texas bluestem, sideoats grama, chino grama, blue grama, pinon ricegrass, wolftail and several species of needlegrass are frequent.

The common invaders on all depleted ranges are woody plants, burrograss, fluffgrass, hairy erioneuron, ear muhly, sand muhly, red grama, broom snakeweed, croton, cacti and several poisonous plants.

Range Resources

More than 100 million acres of Texas are devoted to providing grazing for domestic and wild animals. This is the largest single use for land in the state. Primary range uses include: watershed for streams, springs, lakes; food and cover for wildlife; forage for domestic livestock; and recreation for man.

The Piney Woods, primarily valued for timber, also provide significant grazing. More than 80 percent of the acreage is devoted to range in the Edwards Plateau, Cross Timbers and Prairies, South Texas Plains and Trans-Pecos Mountains and Basins.

Because it is perennial, range is a renewable resource. Range management seeks to perpetuate plants and methods which yield maximum returns, while controlling or eliminating competitive, undesirable plants.

Physical Features

Texas is at the crossroads of five major physiographic regions of North America: the **Gulf Coastal Plain;** the **Great Plains;** the **Interior Lowlands;** the **Rocky Mountain System;** and the **Basin and Range Province.**

A special thanks to Dr. William M. Holmes, chairman of the Department of Geography at North Texas State University, for his assistance in revising this section.

Physical Regions

Principal physical regions of Texas usually are listed as follows: (See also Plant Life and Soils.)

THE GULF COASTAL PLAINS

Texas' Gulf Coastal Plains are the western extension of the coastal plain extending from the Atlantic to beyond the Rio Grande. Its characteristic rolling to hilly surface covered with a heavy growth of pine and hardwoods extends into East Texas, but in the increasingly arid west its forests become secondary in nature, consisting largely of post oaks and, farther west, prairies and brush lands.

The interior limit of the Gulf Coastal Plains in Texas is the line of the **Balcones Fault and Escarpment.** This geologic fault or shearing of underground strata extends eastward from a point on the Rio Grande near Del Rio. It extends to the northwestern part of Bexar County where it turns northeastward and extends through Comal, Hays and Travis counties, intersecting the Colorado River immediately above Austin. The fault line is a single, definite geologic feature, accompanied by a line of southward- and eastward-facing hills. The resemblance of the hills to balconies when viewed from the plain below accounts for the Spanish name, balcones. North of Travis County the subterranean fault line and the surface line of hills become less distinct, the fault itself breaking into several irregularly parallel lines which extend all the way to the Red River. This northern subterranean extension of the Balcones fault line is approximately along the western margin of the Blackland Belt.

This fault line is usually accepted as the boundary between lowland and upland Texas. Below this fault line the surface is characteristically coastal plains. Above the Balcones Fault the surface is characteristically interior rolling plains.

Pine Belt or "Piney Woods"

The Pine Belt (often called locally the "Piney Woods") extends into Texas from the east 75 to 125 miles. From north to south it extends from the Red River to within about 25 miles of the Gulf Coast. Interspersed among the pines are some hardwood timbers, usually in valleys of rivers and creeks. This area is the source of practically all of Texas' large commercial timber production. (See index for chapter on forest resources.) It was settled early in Texas history and is an older farming area of the state. This area's soils and climate are adaptable to production of a variety of fruit and vegetable crops. Cattle raising has increased greatly, accompanied by the development of pastures planted to improved grasses. Lumber production is the principal manufacturing industry. There is a large iron and steel industry near Daingerfield in Morris County based on nearby iron deposits. Iron deposits are also worked in Rusk and one or two other counties.

A great oil field discovered in Gregg, Rusk and Smith counties in 1931 has done more than anything else to contribute to the economic growth of the area. This area has a variety of clays, lignite and other minerals as potentials for development.

Post Oak Belt

The main Post Oak Belt of Texas is wedged between the Pine Belt on the east, Blacklands on the west, and the Coastal Prairies on the south, covering a considerable area in East Central Texas. Principal industry is diversified farming and livestock raising.

Throughout, it is spotty in character with some insular areas of blackland soil, and some that closely resemble those of the Pine Belt. There is a small isolated area of pines in Bastrop County known as the **Lost Pines.** The Post Oak Belt has lignite, commercial clays and some other minerals.

Blackland Belt

The Blackland Belt stretches from the Rio Grande to the Red River, lying just below the line of the Balcones Fault, and varying in width from 15 to 70 miles. It is narrowest below the segment of the Balcones Fault from the Rio Grande to Bexar County and gradually widens as it runs northeast to the Red River. Its rolling prairie, easily turned by the plow, developed rapidly as a farming area until the 1930s and was the principal cotton-producing area of Texas. Now, however, other Texas irrigated, mechanized areas lead in farming. Because of the early growth, the Blackland Belt is still the most thickly populated area in the state and contains within it and along its border more of the state's large and middle-sized cities than any other area. Primarily because of this concentration of population, this belt has the most diversified manufacturing industry of the state.

Coastal Prairies

The Texas Coastal Prairies extend westward along the coast from the Sabine River, reaching inland 30 to 60 miles. Between the Sabine and Galveston Bay the line of demarcation between the prairies and the Pine Belt forests to the north is very distinct. The Coastal Prairie in varying character extends along the Gulf from the Sabine to the Lower Rio Grande Valley; the eastern half is covered with a heavy growth of grass; the western half, in a more arid area, is covered with short grass, and in some places with small timber and brush. The soil is heavy clay. Grass supports the densest cattle population in Texas, and cattle ranching is the principal agricultural industry. Rice is a major crop, grown under irrigation from wells and rivers. Cotton, grain sorghum and truck crops are grown.

Coastal Prairie areas have seen the greatest industrial development in Texas history since World War II. Chief concentration has been from Orange and Beaumont to Houston, and much of the development has been in **petrochemicals,** or chemicals derived from petroleum.

Corpus Christi, and the surrounding **Coastal Bend** region, and, south of the coastal plains, Brownsville, with its adjacent **Lower Rio Grande Valley** area, are rapidly developing seaports, agricultural and industrial sections. Cotton, grain, vegetables and citrus fruits are the principal crops. Cattle production is significant, with the famed **King Ranch** and other large ranches located here.

Lower Rio Grande Valley

The deep alluvial soils and distinctive economy cause the Lower Rio Grande Valley to be classified as a subregion of the Gulf Coastal Plain. Here is concentrated Texas' greatest citrus-winter vegetable area because of the normal absence of freezing weather and the rich delta soils of the Rio Grande. Despite occasional **damaging freezes,** as in 1951 and 1961, the Lower Valley ranks high among the nation's intensified fruit-and-truck regions. Much of the acreage is irrigated from the Rio Grande, although dryland farming also is practiced.

Rio Grande Plain

This may be roughly defined as lying south of San Antonio and between the Rio Grande and the Gulf Coast. The Rio Grande Plain shows characteristics of both the Texas Gulf Coastal Plain and the North Mexico Plains because there is similarity of topography, climate and plant life all the way from the Balcones Escarpment in Texas to the Sierra Madre Oriental in Mexico, which runs past Monterrey about 160 miles south of Laredo.

The Rio Grande Plain is part prairie, but much of it is covered with a dense growth of **prickly pear, cactus, mesquite, dwarf oak, catclaw, huajillo, huisache, blackbrush, cenizo** and other wild shrubs. This country is devoted primarily to raising cattle, sheep and goats. The Texas Angora goat and mohair industry centers in this area and on the Edwards Plateau, which borders it on the north. San Antonio and Laredo are its chief commercial centers, with San Antonio dominating trade.

There is some farming and the **Winter Garden,** centering in Dimmit and Zavala counties north of Laredo, is irrigated from wells and streams to produce vegetables in late winter and early spring. Primarily, however, the central and western part of the Rio Grande Plain is devoted to livestock raising. The rainfall is less than 25 inches annually and the hot summers bring heavy evaporation so that cultivation without irrigation is limited. Over a large area in the central and western parts of the Rio Grande Plain, the growth of **small oaks, mesquite, prickly pear (Opuntia) cactus** and a variety of wild shrubs is very dense and it is often called the **Brush Country.** It is also referred to as the **Chaparral** and the **monte.** (Monte is a Spanish word meaning mountain, also heavy forest or dense brush.)

INTERIOR LOWLAND

The North Central Plains of Texas are a southwestern extension into Texas of the interior lowlands that extend northward to the Canadian border, paralleling the Great Plains to the west. The North Central Plains of Texas extend from the Blackland Belt on the east to the **Cap Rock Escarpment** on the west. From north to south they extend from the Red River to the Colorado.

West Texas Rolling Plains

The West Texas Rolling Plains, approximately the western two-thirds of the North Central Plains in Texas, rise from east to west in altitude from about 750 feet to 2,000 feet at the base of the Cap Rock Escarpment. Annual rainfall ranges from about 30 inches on the east to 20 on the west. Temperature varies rather widely between summer's heat and winter's cold.

This area still has a large cattle-raising industry with many of the state's largest ranches. However, there is much level cultivable land.

Grand Prairie

Near the eastern edge of the North Central Plains is the Grand Prairie, extending south from the Red River in an irregular band through Cooke, Montague, Wise, Denton, Tarrant, Parker, Hood, Johnson, Bosque, Coryell and some adjacent counties. It is a limestone-based area, usually treeless except along the numerous streams, and adapted primarily to livestock raising and staple crop growing.

Sometimes called the **Fort Worth Prairie**, it has an agricultural economy and largely rural population, with no large cities except Fort Worth on its eastern boundary.

East and West Cross Timbers

Hanging over the top of the Grand Prairie and dropping down on each side are the East and West Cross Timbers. The two southward-extending bands are connected by a narrow strip along the Red River. The East Cross Timbers extend southward from the Red River through eastern Denton County and along the Dallas-Tarrant County boundary, then through Johnson County to the Brazos River and into Hill County. The much larger **West Cross Timbers** extend from the Red River south through Clay, Montague, Jack, Wise, Parker, Palo Pinto, Hood, Erath, Eastland, Comanche, Brown and Mills counties to the Colorado, where they meet the Edwards Plateau. Their soils are adapted to fruit and vegetable crops, which reach considerable commercial production in some areas in Parker, Erath, Eastland and Comanche counties.

GREAT PLAINS

The Great High Plains which lie to the east of the base of the Rocky Mountains extend into Northwest Texas. This Texas area is known as the **Staked Plains** or the Spanish equivalent, **Llano Estacado.***

*Historians differ as to the origin of this name. Some think that it came from the fact that the Coronado expedition, crossing the trackless sea of grass, staked its route so that it would be guided on its return trip. Others think that the "estacado" refers to the palisaded appearance of the Cap Rock in many places, especially the west-facing escarpment in New Mexico.

The **Cap Rock Escarpment** is the dividing line between the High Plains and the Lower Rolling Plains of West Texas. Like the Balcones Escarpment, the Cap Rock Escarpment is an outstanding natural boundary line. Unlike the Balcones Escarpment, the Cap Rock Escarpment is caused by surface erosion. In many places this escarpment is a striking physical feature, rising abruptly 200, 500 and in some places almost 1,000 feet above the plains at its base. Where rivers issue from the eastern face of this escarpment there frequently are notable canyons, such as the **Palo Duro Canyon** on the Prairie Dog Town Fork (main channel) of the Red River and the breaks along the Canadian as it crosses the Panhandle north of Amarillo.

Along the eastern edge of the Panhandle there is a gradual descent of the earth's surface from high to low plains, but at the Red River the Cap Rock Escarpment becomes a striking surface feature. It continues as an east-facing wall south through Briscoe, Floyd, Motley, Dickens, Crosby, Garza and Borden counties, gradually decreasing in elevation. South of Borden County the escarpment turns west to the vicinity of Winkler County, then turns north through the eastern part of New Mexico.

Stretching over the largest level plain of its kind in the United States, the High Plains rise gradually from about 2,700 feet on the east to more than 4,000 in spots along the New Mexico border.

Chiefly because of climate and the resultant agriculture, subdivisions are called the **North Plains** and **South Plains.** The North Plains, from Hale County north, has primarily wheat and grain sorghum farming, but with significant ranching and petroleum developments. Amarillo is the largest city, with Plainview on the south and Borger on the north as important commercial centers. The South Plains, also a leading grain sorghum region, leads Texas in cotton production. Lubbock is the principal city, and Lubbock County is the state's largest cotton producer. Irrigation from underground reservoirs, centered around Lubbock and Plainview, waters much of the crop acreage.

Edwards Plateau

Geographers usually consider the Great Plains at the foot of the Rocky Mountains continuing southward from the High Plains of Northwest Texas to the Rio Grande and the Balcones Escarpment. This southern and lower extension of the Great Plains in Texas is known as the Edwards Plateau.

It lies between the Rio Grande and the Colorado River. Its southeastern border is the Balcones Escarpment from the Rio Grande at Del Rio eastward to San Antonio and thence to Austin on the Colorado. Its upper boundary is the Pecos River, though the **Stockton Plateau** in the Trans-Pecos region is geologically and topographically classed with the Edwards Plateau. The Edwards Plateau varies from about 750 feet high at its southern and eastern borders to about 2,700 feet in places. Almost the entire surface is a thin, limestone-based soil covered with a medium to thick growth of cedar, small oak and mesquite with a varying growth of prickly pear. Grass for cattle, weeds for sheep and tree foliage for the browsing goats, support three industries—cattle, goat and sheep raising—upon which the area's economy depends. It is the nation's leading Angora goat and mohair producing region and one of the nation's leading sheep and wool areas. A few crops are grown.

Pecos Valley-Stockton Plateau

The eastern third of the Trans-Pecos is a rolling to rough country lying in the valley of the Pecos River and on the Stockton Plateau at the eastern base of the Davis Mountains. With only 10 to 12 inches of rainfall annually, this was exclusively ranching country until relatively recent times, when the discovery of great quantities of groundwater brought irrigation of cotton, alfalfa and other crops.

The Hill Country

The Hill Country is a popular name for an area of hills and spring-fed streams along the edge of the Balcones Escarpment. It is popular with tourists who visit the dude ranches and other attractions. Notable large springs include **Barton Springs** at Austin, **San Marcos Springs** at San Marcos, **Comal Springs** at New Braunfels, several springs at San Antonio, and a number of others.

The Burnet-Llano Basin

The Burnet-Llano Basin lies at the junction of the Colorado and Llano rivers in Burnet and Llano counties. Earlier this was known as the **"Central Mineral Region,"** because of the evidence there of a large number of minerals.

On the Colorado River in this area a succession of dams impounds two large and four small reservoirs. Uppermost is **Lake Buchanan,** one of the two large reservoirs, between Burnet and Llano counties. Below it in the western part of Travis County is **Lake Travis.** Between these two large reservoirs are three smaller ones, **Inks, L. B. Johnson** (formerly **Granite Shoals**) and **Marble Falls** reservoirs, used primarily for maintaining heads to produce electric power from the overflow from Lake Buchanan. **Lake Austin** is just above the city of Austin. Still another small lake is formed by a low-water dam in Austin.

A name for this recreational area is the **Highland Lakes Country.** Geologically this is an interesting area with Precambrian and Paleozoic rocks found on the surface.

BASIN AND RANGE PROVINCE

The Basin and Range province, with its center in Nevada, surrounds the Colorado Plateau on the west and south and enters far West Texas from southern New Mexico. It consists of broad interior drainage basins interspersed with scattered fault-block mountain ranges. Although this is the only part of Texas regarded as mountainous, these should not be confused with the Rockies. Of all the independent ranges in West Texas, only the Davis Mountains resemble the Rockies, and there is much debate about this.

Texas west of the Edwards Plateau is bounded on the north by New Mexico and on the south by the Rio Grande is distinctive in its physical and economic conditions. Traversed from north to south by an eastern range of the Rockies, it contains all of Texas' true mountains and also is very interesting geologically.

Highest of the Trans-Pecos Mountains is the **Guadalupe Range**, which enters the state from New Mexico. It comes to an abrupt end about 20 miles south of the boundary line, where are situated **Guadalupe Peak**, (8,749 feet, highest in Texas) and **El Capitan** (8,085 feet), which, because of perspective, appears to the observer on the plain below to be higher than Guadalupe and was for many years thought to be the highest mountain in Texas. Lying just west of the Guadalupe range and extending to the **Hueco Mountains** a short distance east of El Paso is the **Diablo Plateau** or basin. It has no drainage outlet to the sea. The runoff from the scant rain that falls on its surface drains into a series of salt lakes that lie just west of the Guadalupe Mountains. These lakes are entirely dry during periods of low rainfall, exposing bottoms of solid salt, and for years they were a source of commercial salt.

Davis Mountains

The **Davis Mountains** are principally in Jeff Davis County. The highest peak, **Mount Livermore**, (8,206 feet) is one of the highest in Texas. There are a number of mountains more than 7,000 feet high. These mountains intercept the moisture-bearing winds and receive more precipitation than elsewhere in the Trans-Pecos. They are greener with the growth of grass and forest trees than the other Trans-Pecos mountains. Noteworthy are the **San Solomon Springs** at the northern base of these mountains.

Big Bend

South of the Davis Mountains lies the **Big Bend**

Texas' Highs, Lows

Though most of Texas is located on flat plains or rolling prairies, there are substantial mountains in the Trans-Pecos region of far West Texas. The highest point in the state is **Guadalupe Peak** at 8,749 feet above sea level. Its twin, **El Capitan** stands at 8,085 feet and also is located in Culberson County near the New Mexico state line. Both are in the **Guadalupe Mountains National Park**, which includes scenic McKittrick Canyon. These elevations and the others in this article have been determined by the U.S. Geological Survey, unless otherwise noted.

In addition to Guadalupe and El Capitan, other peaks standing more than 8,000 feet above sea level include: **Shumard**, 8,615; **Bartlett**, 8,508; **Bush Mountain**, 8,631; **Hunter Peak** (also known as **Pine Top Mountain**), 8,368; **Baldy Peak**, 8,378, and **Mount Livermore**, 8,206. **Emory Peak** in the Chisos Mountains at 7,825 feet is another well-known elevation.

Fort Davis in Jeff Davis County is the **highest town of** any size in Texas at 5,050 feet, and the county has the highest average elevation. The **highest state highway point** also is in the county at McDonald Observatory at the end of a tap from State Highway 118 on Mount Locke. The observatory stands at 6,781 feet, as determined by the Texas Department of Highways and Public Transportation.

The **highest railway point** is **Paisano** on the Southern Pacific in Presidio County.

Sea level is the lowest elevation determined in Texas, and it can be found in all the coastal counties. No point in the state has been found by the geological survey to be below sea level.

The following is a list of the 10 highest peaks in Texas and their locations:

The 10 Highest Peaks in Texas

Name	County	Elevation
Guadalupe Peak	Culberson	8,749
Bush Mountain	Culberson	8,631
Shumard Peak	Culberson	8,615
Bartlett Peak	Culberson	8,508
Baldy Peak	Jeff Davis	8,378
Hunter Peak (Pine Top Mtn.)	Culberson	8,368
Mount Livermore	Jeff Davis	8,206
El Capitan	Culberson	8,085
Lost Peak	Culberson	7,830
Emory Peak	Brewster	7,825

country, so called because it is encompassed on three sides by a great southward swing of the Rio Grande. It is a mountainous country of scant rainfall and sparse population. Its principal mountains, the **Chisos**, rise to 7,825 feet in **Mount Emory**. Along the Rio Grande are the **Santa Elena**, **Mariscal** and **Boquillas** canyons with rim elevations of 3,500 to 3,775 feet. They are among the noteworthy canyons of the North American continent. Because of its remarkable topography, and plant and animal life, the southern part of this region along the Rio Grande is home to the **Big Bend National Park**, with headquarters in a deep valley in the Chisos Mountains. It is a favorite recreation area.

Upper Rio Grande Valley

The Upper Rio Grande (El Paso) Valley is a narrow strip of irrigated land running down the river from El Paso for a distance of 75 miles or more. In this area are the historic towns and missions of **Ysleta**, **Socorro** and **San Elizario**, oldest in Texas. Cotton is the chief product of the valley, much of it long-staple variety. This limited area has a dense urban and rural population in marked contrast to the territory surrounding it.

Area of Texas

Texas occupies about 7 percent of the total water and land area of the United States. **Second in size** among the states, Texas, according to the revised 1980 U.S. Census Bureau figures, has a land and water area of 266,807 square miles as compared with Alaska's 591,004 square miles. California, third largest state, has 158,706 square miles. Texas is as large as all of New England, New York, Pennsylvania, Ohio and Illinois combined.

The state's area consists of 262,017 square miles of land and 4,790 square miles of inland water, or 167,690,880 acres of land area and 3,065,600 acres of inland water.

The area given here differs from that given by the State Land Office in the chapter on State Government.

LENGTH AND BREADTH

The longest straight-line distance in a general north-south direction is 801 miles from the northwest corner of the Panhandle to the extreme southern tip of Texas on the Rio Grande below Brownsville. The greatest east-west distance is 773 miles from the extreme eastward bend in the Sabine River in Newton County to the extreme western bulge of the Rio Grande just above El Paso. The **geographic center** of Texas is southwest of Mercury in the northern portion of McCulloch County.

LATITUDE, LONGITUDE—ELEVATION

The extremes of latitude and longitude are as follows: From Latitude 25° 50′ N. at the extreme southern turn of the Rio Grande on the south line of Cameron County to Latitude 36° 30′ N. along the north line of the Panhandle, and from Longitude 93° 31′ W. at the extreme eastern point on the Sabine River on the east line of Newton County to Longitude 106° 38′ W. on the extreme westward point on the Rio Grande above El Paso.

In elevation the surface of the state varies from sea level along the Gulf Coast to 8,749 feet at the summit of Guadalupe Mountain in Culberson County.

TEXAS BOUNDARY LINE

The boundary of Texas by segments, including only larger river bends and only the great arc of the coast line, is as follows:

	Miles
Rio Grande	889.0
Coast line	367.0
Sabine River, Lake and Pass	180.0
Sabine River to Red River	106.5
Red River	480.0
East Panhandle line	133.6
North Panhandle line	167.0
West Panhandle line	310.2
Along 32nd parallel	209.0
Total	2,842.3

Following the smaller meanderings of the rivers and the tidewater coast line, the following are the boundary measurements:

	Miles
Rio Grande	1,248
Coast line (tidewater)	624
Sabine River, Lake and Pass	292
Red River	726
The five line segments given above	926
Total, including line segments given in table above.	3,816

For Further Reading: "Texas: A Geography," by Terry G. Jordan with John L. Bean Jr. and William M. Holmes; Westview Press, Boulder and London, 1984.

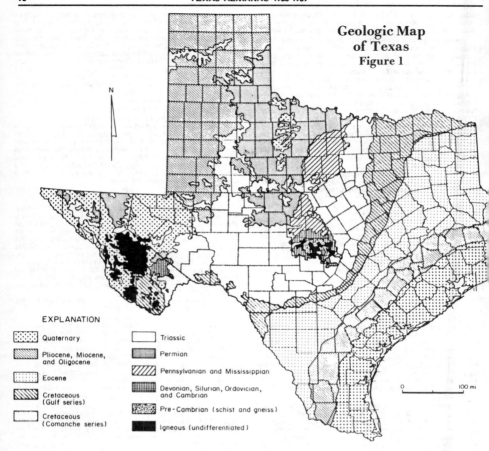

Geologic Map of Texas

Figure 1

EXPLANATION

- ░ Quaternary
- ▨ Pliocene, Miocene, and Oligocene
- ⋮ Eocene
- ▨ Cretaceous (Gulf series)
- ☐ Cretaceous (Comanche series)
- ☐ Triassic
- ▦ Permian
- ▨ Pennsylvanian and Mississippian
- ▦ Devonian, Silurian, Ordovician, and Cambrian
- ▨ Pre-Cambrian (schist and gneiss)
- ■ Igneous (undifferentiated)

0 ____ 100 mi

Geology of Texas

This article on the geology of Texas was prepared by the Bureau of Economic Geology at The University of Texas at Austin.

History in the Rocks

The fascinating geologic history of Texas is recorded in rocks — both those exposed at the surface and those penetrated by holes drilled in search of oil and natural gas. The rocks reveal a dynamic, ever-changing earth — ancient mountains, seas, volcanoes, earthquake belts, rivers, hurricanes and winds. Today, the volcanoes and great earthquake belts are no longer active, but rivers and streams, wind and rain, and the slow, inexorable alterations of rocks at or near the surface continue to change the face of Texas. The geologic history of Texas, as documented by the rocks, began more than a billion years ago; its legacy is the mineral wealth and varied land forms of modern Texas.

Geologic Time Travel

The story preserved in the rocks requires an understanding of the origin of the strata and how they have been deformed. **Stratigraphy** is the study of the composition, sequence and origin of the rocks: of what the rocks are made, how they were formed and the order in which the layers were formed. Structural geology reveals the architecture of the rocks: the locations of the mountains, volcanoes, sedimentary basins and earthquake belts. Figure 1 is a map of rocks of various geologic ages at the surface of Texas today. Figure 2 shows the major structural features of the state.

History concerns events through time, but geologic time is such a grandiose concept that most of us find it difficult to comprehend. So, geologists have named the various chapters of earth history. Figure 3, a generalized geologic time scale, shows the ages of the principal geologic units in Texas.

Precambrian Eon

Precambrian rocks, more than 600 million years old, are exposed at the surface in the Llano Uplift of Central Texas and in scattered outcrops in West Texas, around and north of Van Horn and near El Paso (Fig. 1). These rocks, some more than a billion years old, include complexly deformed rocks that were originally formed by cooling from a liquid state as well as rocks that were altered from pre-existing rocks.

Precambrian rocks, often called the "basement complex," are thought to form the foundation of continental masses. Precambrian rocks underlie all of Texas, and the outcrop in Central Texas is only the exposed part of the Texas Craton (Fig. 2), which is primarily buried by younger rocks.

Paleozoic Era

During the early part of the **Paleozoic Era** (approximately 600 million to 350 million years ago), broad, relatively shallow seas repeatedly inundated the Texas Craton and much of North and West Texas. The evidence for these events is the sandstones, shales and lime-

stones, similar to sediments that form in seas today, and fossils of animals, similar to modern crustaceans — the brachiopods, clams, snails and related organisms that live in modern marine environments. Early Paleozoic rocks are now exposed (Fig. 1) around the Llano Uplift and in far West Texas near Van Horn and El Paso and exist in the subsurface over most of West and North Texas.

By late Paleozoic (approximately 350 million to 240 million years ago), the Texas Craton was bordered on the east and south by a long, deep marine basin, called the Ouachita Trough. Sediments slowly accumulated in this trough until late in the Paleozoic Era. Plate-tectonic theory postulates that the collision of the North American Plate (upon which the Texas Craton is located) with the European and African-South American plates uplifted the thick sediments that had accumulated in the trough to form the Ouachita Mountains, which at that time extended across Texas. Today, in Texas that old mountain range is entirely buried by younger rocks and all that remains at the surface of the once majestic Ouachita Mountain chain is exposed only in southeastern Oklahoma and southwestern Arkansas.

During the **Pennsylvanian Period**, however, the Ouachita Mountains bordered the eastern margin of shallow inland seas that covered most of West Texas. Rivers flowed westward from the mountains to the sea bringing sediment to form deltas along an ever-changing coastline, and the sediments were then reworked by waves and currents of the inland sea. Today, these fluvial, delta and shallow marine deposits compose the late Paleozoic rocks that crop out and underlie the surface of North Central Texas.

Broad marine shelves divided the West Texas seas into several sub-basins, or deeper areas that received more sediments than accumulated on the limestone shelves. Limestone reefs rimmed the deeper basins. Today, these reef limestones are important oil reservoirs in West Texas. These seas gradually withdrew from Texas, and by the late **Permian Period**, all that was left in West Texas were shallow basins and wide tidal flats in which salt, gypsum and red muds accumulated in a hot, arid land. Strata deposited during the Permian Period are exposed today along the edge of the Panhandle as far east as Wichita Falls and south to Concho County and in the Trans-Pecos (Fig. 1).

Mesozoic Era

Approximately 240 million years ago, the major geologic events in Texas shifted from West Texas to East and Southeast Texas. The European and African-South American plates, which had collided with the North American plate to form the Ouachita Mountains, began to separate from North America. A series of faulted basins, or rifts, extending from Mexico to Nova Scotia were formed. These rifted basins received sediments from adjacent uplifts, and as Europe and the southern continents continued to drift away from North America, the Texas basins were eventually buried beneath thick deposits of marine salt within the newly formed East Texas and Gulf Coast basins (Fig. 2). Jurassic and Cretaceous rocks in East and Southeast Texas document a sequence of broad limestone shelves at the edge of the developing Gulf of Mexico. From time to time, the shelves were buried beneath deltaic sandstones and shales, which built the northwestern margin of the widening Gulf of Mexico to the south and southeast. As the underlying salt was buried more deeply by dense sediments, the salt became unstable and moved toward areas of least pressure. As the salt moved, it arched or pierced overlying sediments forming, in some cases, columns known as "salt domes." In some cases, these salt domes moved to the surface; others remain beneath a sedimentary overburden. This mobile salt formed numerous structures that would later serve to trap oil and natural gas.

By the early **Cretaceous** (approximately 140 million years ago), the shallow Mesozoic seas covered a large part of Texas, eventually extending west to the Trans-Pecos area and north almost to the present-day state boundaries. Today, the limestones deposited in those seas are exposed in the walls of the magnificent canyons of the Rio Grande in the Big Bend National Park area and in the canyons and headwaters of streams that drain the Edwards Plateau, as well as in Central Texas from San Antonio to Dallas.

Animals of many types lived in the shallow Mesozoic seas, tidal pools and coastal swamps. Today these lower Cretaceous rocks are some of the most fossiliferous in the state. Tracks of dinosaurs occur in several localities, and remains of terrestrial, aquatic and flying reptiles have been collected from Cretaceous rocks in many parts of Texas.

During most of the late Cretaceous, much of Texas lay beneath marine waters that were deeper than those of the early Cretaceous seas, except where rivers, deltas and shallow marine shelves existed. River delta and strandline sandstones are the reservoir rocks for the most prolific oil field in Texas. When discovered in 1930, this East Texas oil field contained recoverable reserves estimated at 5.6 billion barrels. The chalky rock that we now call the "Austin Chalk" was deposited when the Texas seas became deeper. Today, the chalk (and other Upper Cretaceous rocks) crops out in a wide band that extends from near Eagle Pass on the Rio Grande, east to San Antonio, north to Dallas and eastward to the Texarkana area (Fig. 1). The Austin Chalk and other upper Cretaceous rocks dip southeastward beneath the East Texas and Gulf Coast basins (Fig. 2). The late Cretaceous was the time of the last major seaway across Texas, because mountains were forming in the western United States that influenced areas as far away as Texas.

A chain of volcanoes formed beneth the late Cretaceous seas in an area roughly parallel to and south and east of the old, buried Ouachita Mountains. The eruptions of these volcanoes were primarily on the sea floor and great clouds of steam and ash likely accompanied them. Between eruptions, invertebrate marine animals built reefs on the shallow volcanic cones. Pilot Knob, located southeast of Austin, is one of these old volcanoes that is now exposed at the surface.

Cenozoic Era

At the dawn of the **Cenozoic Era**, approximately 65 million years ago, the northern and northwestern margins of the East Texas Basin were sites of deltas fed by rivers flowing eastward that drained areas to the north and west. Although there were minor incursions of the seas, the Cenozoic rocks principally document extensive seaward building by broad deltas, marshy lagoons, sandy barrier islands and embayments. Thick vegetation covered the levees and areas between the streams. Coastal plains were taking shape, under the same processes still at work today.

The Mesozoic marine salt became buried by thick sediments in the coastal plain area, and the salt began to form ridges and domes in the Houston and Rio Grande areas. The heavy load of sand, silt and mud deposited by the deltas eventually caused some areas of the coast to subside and form large fault systems, essentially parallel to the coast. Many of these coastal faults moved slowly and probably generated little earthquake activity. However, movement along the Balcones and Luling-Mexia-Talco Zones (Fig. 2), a complex system of faults along the western and northern edge of the basins, likely generated large earthquakes millions of years ago.

Glossary

The following words are used in the discussion of Texas geology. Brief definitions are given for non-specialists.

Alluvial — Materials, such as clay, silt, sand and gravel, that are deposited by moving water.

Caldera — A volcanic crater whose diameter is many times as large as the volcanic vent because of the collapse of the central part of the volcano.

Craton — A stable almost immovable portion of the earth's crust that forms the nuclear mass of a continent.

Deltaic — Pertaining to river deltas.

Dimension stone — Stone cut to specific dimensions, usually for construction purposes.

Embayment — A bay or a bay-like depression.

Evaporite — Sedimentary deposits of salts precipitated out of solution by the evaporation of water.

Fluvial — Pertaining to rivers.

Igneous — Rocks formed by cooling from molten material.

Metamorphic — Rocks changed by chemical processes or physical pressures.

Rip-rap — A foundation wall or supporting structure of stone thrown together in no particular order.

Sedimentary — Rocks laid down in strata by wind, water or ice erosion.

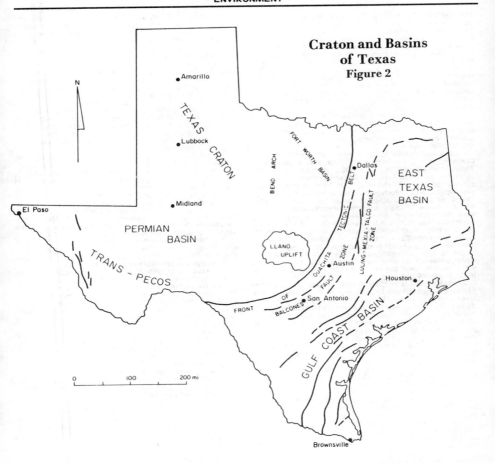

Craton and Basins of Texas
Figure 2

Predecessors of modern animals roamed the Texas Cenozoic coastal plains and woodlands. Bones and teeth of horses, camels, sloths, giant armadillos, mammoths, mastodons, bats, rats, large cats and other modern or extinct mammals have been dug from coastal plain deposits. Vegetation in the area included varieties of plants and trees both similar and dissimilar to modern ones. Fossil palmwood, the Texas "state stone," is found in sediments of early Cenozoic age.

The Cenozoic Era in Trans-Pecos Texas was entirely different. There extensive volcanic eruptions formed great calderas and lava flows. These eruptions ejected great clouds of volcanic ash and rock particles into the air — many times the amount of material ejected by the Mount St. Helens eruption. Ash from the eruptions drifted eastward and is found in many of the sand-and-siltstones of the Gulf Coastal Plains. Lava flowed over the older Paleozoic and Mesozoic rocks, and igneous intrusions melted their way upward into the crustal rocks. These volcanic and intrusive igneous rocks are well exposed in the arid areas of Trans-Pecos Texas today.

In the Texas Panhandle, streams originating in the recently elevated southern Rocky Mountains brought floods of gravel and sand into Texas and formed great alluvial fans as the braided streams crisscrossed the area. These fans were deposited on the older Paleozoic and Mesozoic rocks and occur from northwestern Texas into Nebraska. Between 1 million and 2 million years ago, the streams of the Texas Panhandle were isolated from their Rocky Mountain source, and the eastern edge of this sheet of alluvial material began to retreat westward, forming the caprock of the modern High Plains of Texas.

During the latter part of the Cenozoic Era, a great Ice Age descended upon the northern part of the North American continent. For more than 2 million years, there were successive advances and retreats of the thick sheets of glacial ice. Four periods of extensive glaciation were separated by warmer interglacial periods. Although the glaciers never reached as far south as Texas, the state's climate and sea level underwent major changes with each period of glacial advance and retreat. Sea level during times of glacial advance was 300 to 450 feet lower than during the warmer interglacial periods because so much sea water was captured in the ice sheets. The climate was both more humid and cooler than today, and the major Texas rivers carried more water and more sand and gravel to the sea. These deposits underlie the outer 50 miles or more of the Gulf Coastal Plain.

Approximately 3,000 years ago, sea level reached its modern position, and the rivers, deltas, lagoons, beaches and barrier islands that we know as coastal Texas have formed since that time.

Mineral Wealth
Fuel Minerals

Oil and natural gas are the most valuable minerals produced in Texas, contributing 28 percent of the oil production and 33 percent of the gas production in the United States in 1984. Oil and gas have been produced from most areas of Texas and from rocks of all geologic eras except the Precambrian. All of the major sedimentary basins of Texas (Fig. 2), have produced some oil or gas. The well-known Permian Basin of West Texas (Fig. 2) has yielded large quantities of oil since 1921, and it is an area of considerable promise for future production as well. Although large quantities of petroleum have been produced from rocks of Permian age, production in the area also occurs from older Paleozoic rocks. Production from rocks of Paleozoic age occurs primarily from North Central Texas westward to New Mexico and southwestward to the Rio Grande (Paleozoic outcrop area and west, Fig. 1), but there is also significant Paleozoic production in North Texas in Tarrant, Grayson and Cooke counties.

Mesozoic rocks are the primary hydrocarbon reservoirs of the East Texas Basin and the area south and east of the Balcones Fault Zone. Cenozoic sandstones are the main reservoirs along the Gulf Coast and offshore state waters.

Coal and lignite occur in rocks of Pennsylvanian, Cretaceous and Tertiary ages. Coal was produced in Texas from about 1850 to the 1940s, when petroleum became the common fuel. Significant production of coal did not resume until the mid-1970s. Most of the pre-1940 production was bituminous coal from North Central Texas, an area near Eagle Pass or from near Laredo. North Central Texas production was from Pennsylvanian rocks. Thurber, Newcastle and Bridgeport all had viable coal industries in the early 1900s. As early as 1850, soldiers from Fort Duncan near Eagle Pass are reported to have mined coal from the Cretaceous rocks. Commercial mining of coal from Eocene rocks near Laredo began in 1881. In addition to the commercial mining, small amounts of coal occurring in the Trans-Pecos were used to roast the ore in mercury mining districts in the Big Bend.

Small amounts of "brown coal" or lignite have been produced throughout the history of the state. It was mined by many early settlers for family and small industry use, and it was used to generate "coal gas" or "producer gas" for Texas cities around the turn of the century. Today, Texas ranks sixth nationally in coal production, and lignite accounts for most of this. Almost all of the lignite is consumed by mine-mouth electrical generating plants. Approximately 20 percent of the electricity generated in the state in 1986 was from plants fired by Texas lignite.

Uranium occurs in several widely separated Texas localities, but production has been limited to the Cenozoic sandstones along the coastal plains of south-central Texas, roughly from Karnes County southwest to Webb County. The surface mines, active from 1959 to the mid-1970s, have largely been abandoned and reclaimed, and production today is all from *in-situ* leaching. This requires the injection of a leaching fluid into the uranium-bearing strata, reaction of the fluid with the uranium ore and return of the fluid to the surface for stripping of the uranium. The fluid is then re-used.

Non-Fuel Minerals

In 1985, the value of non-fuel minerals produced was more than $1.9 billion dollars, ranking Texas second nationally. The non-fuel minerals found in Texas are summarized below in terms of geologic setting:

Igneous and metamorphic rocks are favorable sites for mineralization and the outcrops of Precambrian rocks provide occurrences of many metals and some rare earths. There is no mining of these at this time. The area around Llano has occurrences of several metals and is commonly referred to as the "Central Mineral Region," reflecting a history of complex mineralization. In the past, the Central Mineral Region had commercial production of such minerals as graphite and vermiculite, and it has enough varied mineral occurrences to make it a hunting ground for gem and mineral collectors. The Precambrian rocks of the Trans-Pecos also have complex mineralization suites. Copper and other metals have been produced from this area.

Igneous rocks occur primarily in Llano and adjacent counties and in the Trans-Pecos area. The Precambrian granites of the Llano area long have been utilized as dimension stones. Our state capitol and capitol-complex office buildings are built of this stone, which is shipped nationally. The Cenozoic igneous activity in the Trans-Pecos provided solutions rich with many metals, and metals now occur in host rocks of several different geologic time periods. Most of the gold and silver production recorded for the state was from this region. Other metals, including mercury and some lead and zinc, were produced from this area.

Most of the value of Texas non-fuel minerals is in the non-metallics. Crushed stone and sand and gravel are mixed with cement for all types of construction and, in addition, provide the roadbed for highways. Stone also is stacked to provide rip-rap for dams and jetties, and some is used to face buildings. There are numerous other uses of crushed stone, such as pigments, fillers, carriers, ceramics and bricks. Crushed limestone is used to manufacture cement and to produce lime. It is also used in agriculture and in the abatement of acidic gases produced by the burning of some fossil fuels. Limestone constitutes more than 95 percent of all the crushed stone produced in Texas and comes primarily from rocks of Cretaceous age. Outcrops of Paleozoic limestones and Cenozoic limestones and caliche also provide some crushed stone.

The rocks deposited in West and North Central Texas by the vanishing Permian seas left vast deposits of evaporitic rocks, such as gypsum, anhydrite and rock salt. The gypsum is now an important source material for the manufacture of wallboard. Gypsum also occurs in the area around Fredericksburg, in the Finlay Mountains east of El Paso, and overlying many salt domes as a "caprock."

The Permian salt beds and the salt domes of East and Gulf Coast Texas are a source of brine, produced primarily for use in the oil industry, but it also has other industrial and manufacturing applications. Rock salt is mined from two salt domes.

The clays of Texas, particularly those of the Pennsylvanian and Tertiary periods, have a number of uses including ceramics, bricks and refractory products. Some clays and shales expand when subjected to heat and are used as lightweight aggregate.

Texas is one of the few states that produce significant quantities of helium. The gas is produced in the Panhandle from Permian rocks, but the source of the helium is considered to be from Precambrian igneous rocks.

Native sulfur occurs in caprock over some of the Gulf Coast salt domes, and in bedded Permian rocks of far West Texas. Some crude oils and gases contain substantial amounts of sulfur, which is removed during processing. Texas is an important source of this secondary sulfur.

Physiography of Texas

Mountains, seas, coastal plains, rocky plateaus, high plains, forests — all this physiographic variety in Texas is controlled by the varied rocks and structures that underlie and crop out in Texas. State and national parks set aside glimpses of this variation so that Texans and visitors may enjoy the beauty of our state. Parks and the physical features of Texas are discussed elsewhere in this volume.

Soil Conservation and Use

The following discussion was prepared especially for the Texas Almanac by the **Soil Conservation Service,** U. S. Department of Agriculture, Temple, Texas. Additional information may be obtained from that source.

The vast expanse of Texas soils encouraged wasteful use of soil and water throughout much of the state's history. Some **1,000 different soils series** are recognized in the state. Settlers were attracted by these rich soils and the abundant water of the eastern half of the region, used them to build an agriculture and agribusiness of vast proportions, then found their abuse had created critical problems.

In the 1930s, interest in soil and water conservation began to mount. In 1935, the Soil Conservation Service was created in the U. S. Department of Agriculture. In 1939, the **Texas Soil Conservation Law** made it possible for landowners to organize local soil and water conservation districts.

The state as of Jan. 1, 1987, had **206 conservation districts** which manage the various conservation functions within the district. A subdivision of state government, each district is governed by a board of five elected landowners. Technical assistance in planning and applying conservation work is provided through the USDA Soil Conservation Service. State funds for districts are administered through the **Texas State Soil and Water Conservation Board.** (See Index.)

A recent national erosion inventory showed that more than twice as much soil is being lost to wind erosion each year than to sheet and rill erosion. The inventory also showed that about one-fourth of all land in Texas is "prime farmland."

Soil Subdivisions

Most authorities divide Texas into 20 major subdivisions that have similar or related soils, vegetation, topography, climate and land uses. These are called Major Land Resource Areas. Brief descriptions of these subdivisions follow.

1. TRANS-PECOS SOILS

The 18 million acres of the Trans-Pecos, mostly west of the Pecos River, are diverse plains and valleys intermixed with mountains — quite different from other Texas areas. (See also section on physiography.)

Upland soils are light reddish brown to brown clay loams, clays and sands, (mostly high in lime, some saline) and many areas of shallow soils and rock lands. Main series: Hoban, Reeves, Reagan (lower basins); Brewster, Lozier, Verhalen, Musquiz (mountains and valleys); Hueco, Wink, Kermit (sandy soils); Orla (gypsic soils). Bottomland soils are dark grayish brown to reddish brown, silt loams to clayey, alluvial soils (some saline). Main series: Harkey, Glendale, Saneli (Rio Grande); Pecos, Arno (Pecos River).

Rainfall is sparse, and vegetative cover is as thin and as variable as the topography, soils and drainage conditions. In general it is of two types: short grasses and shrubs on the flat soils of the basins and valleys, and a mixture of mid and short grasses and species of oak, pine, juniper and semiarid plants and shrubs on the rough and mountainous lands. Alkali sacaton and other salt-tolerant plants occur in the basin.

2. HIGH PLAINS SOILS

The High Plains area comprises the vast high plateau of more than 19 million acres in Northwestern Texas. It lies in the southern part of the Great Plains province that includes large similar areas in Oklahoma and New Mexico. The flat, nearly level surface of very large areas has few streams of any dissection to cause local relief. However, several major rivers originate in the High Plains or cross the area. The largest is the Canadian River which has cut a deep valley across the Panhandle section.

Playas, small intermittent lakes scattered through the area, lie up to 20 feet below the surrounding flat plains. Early estimates were that playas numbered 37,000; a 1965 survey indicated more than 19,000 in 44 counties, occupying some 340,000 acres. They received most of the runoff, with less than 10 percent of this water percolating back to the aquifer. In 1969 there were only limited numbers being utilized for recharge wells to return water to aquifers.

Soils are brown to reddish, mostly deep, clay loams, sandy loams and sands. Free lime is present under many soils at various depths. Main series: Pullman, Olton, Sherm (hardlands); Amarillo, Portales (mixed lands); Brownfield, Tivoli (sandy lands); Potter (loamy soils, shallow over caliche). The Guadalupe, Spur and Bippus series are the main soils on bottomlands, but are minor in extent.

The soils are moderately productive and the flat surface encourages irrigation and mechanization. Limited rainfall and constant danger of wind erosion are handicaps; but the region is Texas' leading producer of three most important crops — cotton, grain sorghums and wheat.

The native vegetation is of three distinct kinds. In the northern part and on the fine-textured soils south of the Canadian River, the vegetation is short grasses, mainly buffalo with some grama. In the southern part on the sandy loam soils it is largely grama and threeawn. On the deep sands it is mainly little bluestem, sand dropseed, sideoats grama and threeawn grasses. In places these sands support a thick growth of shinoak and sand sage (Artemisia).

3. ROLLING PLAINS SOILS

The Rolling Plains comprise an eastern section of the Great Plains in Northwestern Texas. The area lies west of the North Central Prairies and extends from the edge of the Edwards Plateau in Tom Green County northward into Oklahoma. It includes about 23 million acres. The Red Beds and associated reddish soils led to use of the name Red Plains by some.

Upland soils are pale brown through reddish brown to dark grayish brown sandy loams, clay loams and clays. Most soils have free lime in the lower part and are saline in places; some are shallow and stony; some are deep sands. Main series: Miles, Woodward, Springer, Vernon, Tillman (northern two-thirds); Abilene, Rowena, Mereta, Lueders (southern one-third).

Bottomland soils include minor areas of reddish brown, sandy to clayey, alluvial soils. Main series: Lincoln, Yahola, Guadalupe, Clairemont, Spur, Bippus and Mangum.

The native vegetation varies with soils and surface conditions. On the finer-textured soils curly mesquite, buffalo and grama grasses are dominant, with some scattered shrubs in places. On the coarser-textured soils the principal grasses are little bluestem, sideoats grama and threeawn grasses with sand sage and shinnery on areas of deep sand.

4. ROLLING RED PRAIRIES SOILS

The Rolling Red Prairies occupy about 1 million acres in North Central Texas adjoining Oklahoma. The area is dominantly prairie. The principal soils are of the Anocon, Bluegrove, Kamay, Kirkland and Stoneburg series. Bottomland soils are of the Gaddy, Yomont and Mangum.

Native vegetation is mainly little bluestem, sideoats, hairy and blue grama, Indian and buffalo grass. The area is mainly used for cattle ranching and growing small grains.

5. NORTH CENTRAL PRAIRIE SOILS

The North Central Prairies occupy about 5 million acres in Central North Texas. The area lies between the Western Cross Timbers and Rolling Plains and was heretofore often referred to as the Reddish Prairie. The area is dominantly prairie, but numerous small wooded areas are intermixed. The principal soils are of the Truce, Thurber, Bonti and Owens series. Narrow strips of alluvial soils, mainly of the Elandco and Frio series, occur in the flood plains of local streams. Small areas of other soils similar to those of the West Cross Timbers and Grand Prairie are intermixed. They are best suited for growing small grains and native grasses.

Native vegetation is mainly little bluestem, sideoats, hairy and blue grama, Indian and buffalo grass. Scrubby trees and shrubs, mainly post oak and mesquite, and cacti grow rather thickly in places.

6. EDWARDS PLATEAU SOILS

The 23 million acres of the Edwards Plateau are on an extensive tableland of Southwest Texas. Many of the soils are shallow over limestone, and streams have cut many valleys and canyons. Upland soils are dark, calcareous clays and clay loams, mostly gravelly and stony. Some deeper, less stony soils occur on the flat divides. Main series: Tarrant, Eckrant, Brackett and Tobosa (eastern two-thirds); Ector, Upton, Reagan (western one-third). Bottomland soils include minor areas of dark, calcareous, clayey alluvial soils. Main series: Frio, Oakalla and Dev.

This is principally a livestock, ranching region, the center of Texas' and the nation's mohair and wool production. Except where there is limited irrigation, cropping is largely confined to such drought-resistant crops as grain sorghums and grasses. Grasses, shrubs and scrubby trees dominate the native vegetation. There are many cedar brakes.

7. CENTRAL BASIN SOILS

The Central Basin, also known as the Llano Basin, occupies a relatively small area in Central Texas. It includes parts or all of Llano, Mason, Gillespie and adjoining counties. The total area is about 1.5 million acres.

Upland soils are reddish brown to brown, mostly gravelly and stony, sandy loams shallow over granite, limestone, gneiss and schist; deeper, less stony, sandy loam soils in the valleys. Main series: Pontotoc, Pedernales, Ligon, Castell, Katemcy, Hensley and Voca. Bottomland soils are minor areas of dark gray, alluvial soils. Main series: Frio, Gowen and Oakalla.

The native vegetation consists of grass and small oak and mesquite trees. On some rocky slopes, juniper forms the principal growth. Ranching is the main enterprise, with some farms producing peaches, grain sorghum and wheat.

8. NORTHERN RIO GRANDE PLAIN SOILS

The Northern Rio Grande Plain comprises about 5 million acres in an area of Southern Texas extending from Uvalde to Beeville. The main soils are deep, reddish brown or dark grayish brown, loamy, and of the Clareville, Elmendorf, Floresville, Miguel and Webb series in the eastern part. Native range is grassland, thorny brush and cacti. Most of the area is range grazed by beef cattle. Grain sorghum, cotton, corn, flax and small grain are grown in the eastern part. Irrigated cropland is in the Winter Garden area of the western part and produces corn, cotton, grain sorghum and truck crops such as spinach, carrots and cabbage.

9. WESTERN RIO GRANDE PLAIN SOILS

The Western Rio Grande Plain comprises about 6 million acres in an area of Southwestern Texas from Del Rio to Rio Grande City. The main upland soils are clayey, saline and of the Catarina and Montell series.

The vegetation is mid and short grasses with low thorny brush and cacti. Soils along the Rio Grande are mainly the Laredo, Rio Grande and Zalla series. Most of the soils along the river are used for growing vegetables and sorghums. The upland soils are used for grazing beef cattle.

10. CENTRAL RIO GRANDE PLAIN SOILS

The Central Rio Grande Plain comprises about 6 million acres in an area of Southern Texas from Live Oak to Hidalgo County. The main soils are Nueces and Sarita series (sandy); Delfina, Delmita and Duval (loamy); Randado and Zapata series (shallow). The vegetation is tall and mid grasses with scattered trees and shrubs. Much of the area is in large ranches used for raising beef cattle. A few areas are used for growing grain sorghum, cotton and small grain.

11. LOWER RIO GRANDE VALLEY SOILS

The Lower Rio Grande Valley comprises about 1.5 million acres in extreme Southern Texas. The main soils are deep, loamy and clayey, and of the Brennan, Hidalgo, Harlingen, Raymondville and Rio Grande series. Most of the soils are used for growing irrigated vegetables and citrus, along with cotton, grain sorghum and sugar cane. Some areas are in range and used for growing beef cattle.

12. WEST CROSS TIMBERS SOILS

The West Cross Timbers comprises a total of about 2.7 million acres. The area includes the wooded section west of the Grand Prairie and extends from the Red River southward to the north edge of Brown County. Small areas also occur intermixed or interlaced with soils of the western part of the Grand Prairie. The principal series are Windthorst, Nimrod and Duffau. Narrow areas of alluvial soils, mainly of the Gowen series, occur in the flood plains of local streams. Soils of the Ships, Yahola and Weswood series occur in the flood plains of the throughflowing rivers.

The native vegetation is mainly shinnery oak and post oak trees and a few other hardwoods. The trees are scrubby, of small size and unsuited for most uses other than firewood or fence posts. In places, grasses, including little bluestem, grama and threeawn, and scattered mesquite trees form a thick ground cover where the oak overstory is thin. Rangeland and pastures are used for grazing beef and dairy cattle. Crops are peanuts, grain sorghum, small grains, peaches, pecans and vegetables.

13. EAST CROSS TIMBERS SOILS

The East Cross Timbers includes a long narrow strip of wooded soils that separates the northern parts of the Blackland Prairie and Grand Prairie. This strip is only a few miles wide and extends from the Red River southward into Hill County and includes a total area of about 1 million acres. The soils are mainly of the Callisburg, Crosstell, Silstid and Gasil series.

The native vegetation is mainly post oak trees and a few other hardwoods. The trees are scrubby, of small size and unsuited for most uses other than firewood or fence posts. In places, grasses, including little bluestem, grama and threeawn, and scattered mesquite trees form a thick ground cover where the oak overstory is thin. Rangelands and pastures are used for grazing beef and dairy cattle. Crops are peanuts, grain sorghums, small grains, peaches, pecans and vegetables.

14. GRAND PRAIRIE SOILS

The Grand Prairie includes the prairie just west of the Blackland Prairie in North Central Texas. It extends south from the Red River to about the Colorado River and comprises about 7 million acres.

The principal soils of the Grand Prairie are of the Eckrant, Slidell and Denton series. Small areas of soils of the Crawford, Brackett, Krum and Lewisville series occur also on the uplands. Alluvial soils, mainly of the Frio and Bosque series, occur in the flood plains of streams.

The native vegetation is mainly short grasses with some mid and tall grasses on the deeper soils. Buffalo and grama grasses, little bluestem and Indian grass are the most widespread. In many places, especially on rocky slopes of shallow soils, small oak and juniper trees form a thick cover, and scattered mesquite trees occur throughout the area. The area is mainly used for growing beef cattle. Some small grain, grain sorghum and corn are grown.

15. BLACKLAND PRAIRIE SOILS

An almost treeless area, the Blackland Prairies consist of about 13 million acres of East Central Texas extending southwestwardly from the Red River to Bexar County. There are smaller, similar areas to the southeast.

The soils of the greater portion of the Blackland Prairie proper are mainly of the Houston Black, Heiden and Austin series with smaller areas of Lewisville, Altoga and Eddy soils. Bottomland soils are mainly Tinn and Trinity clays.

The native vegetation consists of bunch and short grasses. The main species are little and big bluestems, grama, Indian, buffalo and threeawn grasses. In places, scattered mesquite trees, cacti and other shrubs form a rather thick cover. Hardwood trees — mainly elm, hackberry and pecan — occur in stream bottoms. The main crops are grain sorghum, wheat, cotton, corn and hay. Pastures are used for beef and dairy cattle.

16. CLAYPAN AREA SOILS

The Claypan Area is a nearly level to gently rolling moderately dissected woodland savannah to brushy area (Post Oak Belt) with moderate surface drainage. The area is more than 3.5 million acres.

Upland soils are sandy loams, commonly thin over gray, mottled or red, firm, clayey subsoils. Some deep, sandy soils with less clayey subsoils exist. Main series: Lufkin, Axtell, Tabor (thin-surface claypan soils); Freestone and Padina (thick-surface sandy and loamy soils). Bottomlands are reddish brown to dark gray, to loamy to clayey alluvial soils. Main series: Ships, Weswood (Brazos and Colorado Rivers); Kaufman, Trinity, Gladewater, Nahatche (Trinity River and other smaller streams).

Vegetation consists of scattered stands of post oak and blackjack oak with tall bunchgrasses in the uplands; yaupon and other underbrush prevalent in places. In the bottomlands, hardwoods are predominant but pecans occur in some areas. The land is woodland and brushy range. A few areas are used for tame pasture and cool-season forage crops.

17. EAST TEXAS TIMBERLAND SOILS

The East Texas Timberlands comprise the forested eastern part of the state, about 14 million acres.

The principal soil series are the Woodtell, Kirvin, Cuthbert, Bowie, Lilbert and Tonkawa soils in the northern and central parts; Nacogdoches and Elrose soils in the "Redland" section; and Diboll, Kisatche, Rayburn, Tehran, Doucette, Pinetucky and Shankler soils in the southern part of the area. Alluvial soils, mainly Mantachie, Iuka, Severn, Oklared and Urbo are on flood plains of streams.

The native vegetation is a pine-hardwood forest. It is mainly loblolly pine, shortleaf pine, sweetgum and red oak trees with an understory of grasses and shrubs. Forestry and pastures are the main uses.

18. COAST PRAIRIE SOILS

The Coast Prairie includes the nearly flat strip that is near the Gulf Coast in Southeast Texas in the humid and subhumid zones. It ranges from 30 to 80 miles in width and parallels the coast from the Sabine River in Orange County to Baffin Bay in Kleberg County. Total area of the Coast Prairie is about 9 million acres. The principal soils in the eastern portion from about the San Antonio River to the Sabine River are Lake Charles, Bernard, Edna, Morey and Beaumont soils near the coast, comprising more than 4 million acres.

The more inland soils in the eastern section are Hockley, Katy and Crowley series, comprising nearly 2 million acres. The portions west and south of the San Antonio River are Victoria, Orelia, Papalote and Clareville soils, comprising some 2 million acres. Other important soils, which occur in the bottomlands, are Brazoria, Norwood, Pledger, Kaman and Urbo. The nearly level topography and productive soils encourage farming. Rice, grain sorghum, cotton and soybeans are main crops. The native vegetation is tall prairie grasses, mainly species of andropogon, paspalum and panicum, with a narrow fringe of trees along the streams.

19. COAST SALINE PRAIRIES SOILS

The Coast Saline Prairies include a narrow strip of wet lowlands adjacent to the coast and the barrier islands that extend from Mexico to Louisiana. The surface is at or only a few feet above sea level and it ranges from 3 to 20 miles wide. The total area is about 3 million acres. Important soil series are the Harris, Tatton, Veston and Galveston series in the eastern part, and the Mustang, Aransas, Placedo, Francitas, Barrada and Galveston in the southern part. Cattle grazing is the chief economic use of the various salt tolerant cordgrasses and sedges. Recreation is an important use of the barrier islands.

20. FLATWOODS SOILS

The Flatwoods area includes the flat, rather poorly drained forested area in humid Southeast Texas. Total area is about 2.5 million acres. Most soils have a water table near the surface at least part of the year. Soils are mainly fine sandy loam with loamy or clayey subsoils. Important soil series are the Segno, Sorter, Splendora, Kirbyville, Malbis and Evadale.

The land is mainly used for forest. The typical vegetation is a pine-hardwood forest that is longleaf pine, loblolly pine, sweetgum and various oak species.

Texas Forest Resources

This information was compiled and prepared by Sam D. Logan, director of Information and Education for the Texas Forest Service in the Texas A&M University System.

In the late 1970s, Texas harvested more timber than it grew for the first time since the early 1900s. This was a surprising increase in harvest volume considering the relatively low profits of the forest products industry. The recession of the early 1980s slowed the demand for timber products and gave the forests a temporary rest. Most experts, however, are predicting that during the latter part of this decade timber harvesting will again exceed growth.

There had been a significant variation in the production trends of most forest products by 1985, however. Pine veneer logs, hardwood chips and sawdust, pilings, paperboard and treated products, all exhibited strong growth. Poles, posts and paper output declined sharply, according to a Texas Forest Service report gleaned with the assistance of 121 Texas mills and 16 out-of-state mills in Louisiana, Arkansas and Oklahoma.

There was virtually no change from 1984 in the number of U.S. housing starts. In earlier years, the 1.73 million starts experienced in 1985 would have translated into a good year for the forest products industry. However, increased imports of softwood lumber from Canada took a substantial portion of the U.S. market, resulting in lower operating levels and production prices. The construction picture in Texas was markedly worse than in most of the U.S., as total value of all construction permits issued declined by 16 percent. In addition, pine timber killed by record epidemics of southern pine beetle in East Texas from 1983 into 1986 flooded the timber markets with lower value salvage logs that kept prices lower than normal.

Perhaps the greatest economic gain of the 20th century since the 1930s has been reforestation, both in protecting existing timber and in planting new forests. This reforestation commitment has been even more intensely renewed in recent years as most experts agree that the "nation's woodbasket" is shifting from the Pacific Northwest to the Southern forests, which extend from East Texas to the Atlantic Ocean. While both public and private cooperation has reduced fires and pests and has increased tree planting and fostered natural regrowth, the resource is still hard-pressed to keep pace with increasing demands. Many private nonindustrial landowners fail to replant after timber harvests.

The 22,032,000 million acres of forests in Texas—an area larger than the states of Massachusetts, Connecticut, New Hampshire, Rhode Island and Vermont combined—form the land base for this important renewable resource. There are two timber producing counties in

Texas (Harris and Houston) that are each larger than the entire state of Rhode Island.

Estimated market value of harvested timber (delivered value) was approximately $547.8 million in 1984. At the same time, recreational opportunities among forests have been expanded. The Texas Forestry Association Woodlands Trails program provides public hiking through designated scenic portions of privately owned timberland. (Information is available from Texas Forestry Association, P.O. Box 1488, Lufkin, TX 75901; the Texas Department of Highways and Public Transportation and other sources.) State and national forests in East Texas are also being improved for recreational purposes and to provide habitat and forage for wildlife. Trees are also valuable for prevention and control of pollution and erosion.

The following information was supplied largely by Texas Forest Service, Texas Forestry Association and federal agencies. Texas' forested area, including some secondary woodland and forest areas, totals an estimated 22.032 million acres. The principal forest and woodlands regions are: pine-hardwood, 10,901,500 acres; post oak, 2,993,600; East and West Cross Timbers, 2,226,310; cedar brakes, 4,561,053; coastal forests, 575,071, and miscellaneous, 774,442.

The most important forest area of the state, pro-

Estimated Timber Income
East Texas, 1984

Because of rounding of odd cents, columns don't add up.

County	Total value paid for delivered timber products (Dollars)	Industrial private nonfarm and public timberlands (Dollars)	Farm and misc. timberlands (Dollars)
Anderson . . .	$8,145,471	$2,362,186	$5,783,284
Angelina. . . .	20,393,249	13,051,679	7,341,570
Bowie	6,271,786	1,567,947	4,703,840
Camp	1,815,741	18,157	1,797,584
Cass	17,220,952	4,477,448	12,743,505
Chambers . . .	2,259,285	293,707	1,965,578
Cherokee . . .	20,243,152	6,275,377	13,967,775
Franklin	288,218	2,882	285,336
Gregg	895,106	8,951	886,155
Grimes	2,897,522	1,680,563	1,216,959
Hardin	23,126,468	16,188,528	6,937,941
Harris	2,737,575	219,006	2,518,569
Harrison	9,780,686	880,262	8,900,425
Houston	10,699,765	3,744,918	6,954,847
Jasper	24,661,248	18,495,936	6,165,312
Jefferson . . .	1,159,166	0	1,159,166
Leon	200,582	40,116	160,465
Liberty	15,844,388	7,129,975	8,714,414
Marion	7,991,267	1,598,253	6,393,014
Montgomery. . .	17,560,988	2,809,758	14,751,230
Morris	2,825,444	28,254	2,797,190
Nacogdoches . .	17,094,822	5,812,239	11,282,582
Newton	26,298,344	20,249,725	6,048,619
Orange	3,194,075	1,373,452	1,820,623
Panola	10,921,245	1,856,612	9,064,633
Polk	37,085,981	29,668,785	7,417,196
Red River . . .	1,929,750	443,842	1,485,907
Rusk	11,841,029	828,872	11,012,157
Sabine	13,781,036	10,060,156	3,720,880
San Augustine	15,709,242	11,467,747	4,241,495
San Jacinto . .	13,189,683	6,199,151	6,990,532
Shelby	17,138,144	5,141,443	11,996,701
Smith	7,042,024	70,420	6,971,604
Titus	1,104,676	11,047	1,093,629
Trinity	19,780,138	14,043,898	5,736,240
Tyler	29,406,918	21,761,119	7,645,799
Upshur	5,013,788	50,138	4,963,650
Walker	16,877,417	3,881,806	12,995,611
Waller.	1,317,247	487,381	829,865
Wood	2,640,198	79,206	2,560,992
Other counties. . .	1,676,954	1,291,255	385,699
State Totals. .	$450,060,770	$215,652,198	$234,408,571

Annual Growth and Annual Harvest of Growing Stock in East Texas 1975-1985

Year	Species	Growth (Millions Cu. Ft.)	Harvest (Millions Cu. Ft.)	Harvest Per Cent of Growth
1975	Pine	458.4	389.3	85
	Hardwood	208.5	72.6	35
1976	Pine	461.2	432.8	94
	Hardwood	215.7	80.6	37
1977	Pine	461.9	453.9	98
	Hardwood	222.7	89.1	40
1978	Pine	461.6	475.4	103
	Hardwood	229.1	103.1	45
1979	Pine	461.3	465.1	100
	Hardwood	236.4	102.4	43
1980	Pine	461.5	446.8	97
	Hardwood	243.5	109.6	45
1981	Pine	463.2	418.3	90
	Hardwood	251.1	99.6	40
1982	Pine	466.5	397.9	85
	Hardwood	259.5	89.2	34
1983	Pine	467.8	490.1	105
	Hardwood	267.2	148.3	56
1984	Pine	470.4	426.8	91
	Hardwood	275.4	118.2	43
1985	Pine	472.8	434.0	92
	Hardwood	284.0	117.5	41

ducing nearly all of the commercial timber, is the East Texas pine-hardwood region known as the **Piney Woods**. It extends over all or part of 43 counties.

Forest Conservation

Many agencies, companies, associations and others cooperate in the **conservation of Texas forest resources**. Among them are federal and state agencies, district and city and county governments, timber producers, processors and wood products manufacturers. Only a few major programs can be listed here.

Texas Reforestation Foundation

One of the most successful new programs is the Texas Reforestation Foundation (TRe), which is a landowner-assistance, forestry-incentives program designed to help regenerate and improve Texas' timberlands. Unlike other assistance programs, TRe is wholly financed by private interests through voluntary contributions. The money is distributed to private nonindustrial Texas landowners on a matching basis with operations directed from the TFA office in Lufkin, with technical assistance from the Texas Forest Service. TRe is a nonprofit foundation, operating with its own elected board of directors.

Since TRe began in 1981, more than $1.6 million in cost-share funds from the foundation have helped to reforest nearly 48,788 acres of Texas land.

Tree Farms

A tree farm is a privately owned, taxpaying woodland dedicated to continuing growth of forest crops and officially recognized by the **Texas Forestry Association** in cooperation with **American Forest Council**, the national sponsor. Tree farmers agree to manage their timber for the growth and harvest of forest products, and to protect their timber from fires, insects, disease and destructive overgrazing. Any landowner with 10 or more acres of forest land on which the trees are more than one year of age or land with a stand of viable tree seedlings may qualify.

On Jan. 1, 1986, there were 2,761 officially recognized tree farms in Texas, according to the Texas Forestry Association. Total area was 4,224,578 acres. **Texas ranked sixth** in the nation in number of tree farms and ninth in number of acres in them.

Texas Forest Service

In 1915, the Legislature created a **State Department of Forestry** and placed it under the direction of the **Agricultural & Mechanical College of Texas**.

In 1926, it was reorganized as the **Texas Forest Service (TFS)** under the board of the A&M College. Today the office of the director, the **Forest Management Department, Reforestation Department, Forest Genetics Laboratory** and the **Information and Education Section** are located on the campus of Texas A&M University in College Station.

The **Forest Fire Control Department, Forest Products Laboratory** and **Forest Pest Control Section** are located in the **Cudlipp Forestry Center** at Lufkin. Five area offices and 13 districts are located throughout East Texas, with area offices headquartered at Linden, Henderson, Lufkin, Woodville and Conroe.

In 1971, a staff silviculturist was stationed in Lubbock to assist landowners in establishing and maintaining windbreaks to protect their homesteads and fields from the high, drying winds in that region. In 1973, an urban forestry program was established to assist the public and city governments with developing land to maintain the urban forests, with TFS foresters in Fort Worth and San Antonio.

Forest Protection From Pests

Insects and diseases affecting forest trees cost landowners millions of dollars annually. The **TFS Pest Control Section**, established in 1962, is responsible for monitoring pest activity on 12 million acres of state and private forest lands in East Texas. The section also conducts applied research on major insect and disease pests of pine seed orchards, plantations and natural forest stands. The major insect pest of Texas forests is the **southern pine beetle**. Other important insect pests include seed and cone destroying insects, leaf-cutting ants, pine tip moths and pine sawflies. The most important disease in East Texas pine forests is fusiform rust. In Central Texas, oak diseases are causing considerable concern.

In the South southern pine beetles kill more timber annually than forest fires. The Texas Forest Service coordinates all beetle control activity in Texas, which includes detecting infestations from the air, notifying landowners and assisting them in controlling the infes-

tations. The most severe outbreak of southern pine beetles known in Texas occurred in 1985 when an estimated 78.7 million cubic feet of timber was killed.

Valuable seeds carrying superior genetic qualities must be protected from insect pests in southern pine seed orchards. Without control measures insects will usually reduce potential seed crops by more than 50 percent. **Coneworms** and **seedbugs** are the major insect pests in southern pine seed orchards. The TFS is involved in a research program directed toward developing improved measures for controlling these insect pests.

Pests of young pine plantations are increasing in importance with the acceleration of reforestation in East Texas. Texas leaf-cutting ants often cause serious mortality when present in or near newly planted pine plantations. These ants prefer deep, sandy soils and damage pine seedlings by removing needles and buds, particularly in the winter when other green vegetation is unavailable. This insect pest must be controlled in new plantations to prevent economic losses. Other pests in pine plantations include **pine tip moth, pine sawflies, gophers** and **rabbits**.

Fusiform rust has been recognized for many years as a severe problem on both slash and loblolly pines in the southeastern United States. The disease has its greatest impact in nurseries, seed orchards and young pine plantations. The TFS has been involved in periodic surveys, initiated in Texas in 1969, which have indicated that fusiform rust is most severe in slash pine plantations in Southeast Texas. Loblolly pine is not seriously damaged. The severity of the disease increased dramatically between 1969-1980, but appears to be static since 1980. The TFS also is evaluating forest manage-

Primary Forest Products By Species Group, 1953-85

Year	*Pulpwood Production Softwood	*Pulpwood Production Hardwood	Lumber Production Softwood	Lumber Production Hardwood	Plywood Production Softwood	**Paper & Paperboard Production Softwood
	(Cords)		(Thd. bd. ft.)		(Thd. sq. ft.)	(Thd. tons)
1953	1,159,261	51,443	...	...	...	...
1954	1,003,561	50,772	...	...	...	...
1955	1,119,486	84,289	798,200	359,200	...	...
1956	1,339,239	119,776	625,500	314,200	...	...
1957	1,260,390	160,528	569,900	266,600	...	...
1958	1,208,400	177,600	499,000	218,000	...	...
1959	1,185,300	230,300	465,800	283,500	...	...
1960	1,192,700	233,700	454,800	302,800	...	...
1961	1,195,700	245,800	430,200	275,000	...	...
1962	1,162,900	266,700	497,000	260,640	...	...
1963	1,172,500	271,100	567,800	271,440	...	...
1964	1,294,695	281,345	676,982	251,286	...	...
1965	1,294,535	362,087	700,250	355,190	93,000	...
1966	1,495,090	397,080	701,000	331,030	120,000	...
1967	1,657,495	319,669	632,353	160,447	120,000	...
1968	1,831,204	288,987	682,097	148,343	193,300	...
1969	1,996,144	331,781	788,471	183,027	221,300	...
1970	2,046,056	302,779	746,408	152,154	248,676	...
1971	2,215,913	306,033	805,989	149,370	447,003	...
1972	2,814,025	387,131	842,865	148,660	690,808	...
1973	3,081,143	412,355	807,995	120,879	767,688	...
1974	3,294,200	553,100	684,602	171,093	782,615	...
1975	3,164,200	384,100	704,572	147,359	959,649	...
1976	3,070,000	515,000	844,095	146,366	1,225,513	...
1977	3,143,045	486,845	848,253	191,686	1,352,527	...
1978	3,216,900	643,776	867,759	214,118	1,455,139	...
1979	3,286,800	582,013	845,830	204,536	1,299,282	...
1980	3,574,000	656,000	755,078	292,221	1,481,944	...
1981	3,443,000	572,000	707,311	275,591	1,553,345	2,339
1982	3,345,000	630,000	752,727	160,235	1,604,102	2,405
1983	4,216,000	1,386,000	862,378	152,350	1,898,556	2,497
1984	3,457,000	959,000	898,212	165,460	1,881,071	2,477
1985	3,492,000	1,178,000	856,157	175,254	1,985,699	2,499

*Includes both roundwood and residues.
**Reporting change made this information available starting in 1981.

ment practices and rust-resistant seedlings that will reduce losses caused by this disease.

Extensive mortality of oaks in the hill country of Central Texas is creating increasing public concern. The vascular wilt organism, "oak wilt," has been cited as the major causal agent of live oak disease in Central Texas. The incidence of oak wilt is poorly understood. Oak wilt appears to be responsible for much of the live oak mortality.

In an 11.3 million-acre area of Central Texas, the TFS is actively involved in a cooperative project to estimate the amount of total oak mortality, determine the relative incidence and severity of oak wilt, measure rates of disease spread, pilot test available prevention/suppression methods and develop procedures for reforesting the area of tree mortality. Without a better understanding of oak wilt involved, the future of live oak as a landscape or forest tree in Central Texas may be threatened.

Texas Forest Service entomologists are also asked to evaluate insect and disease problems in other areas of the state. Assistance has been provided regarding windbreak trees in the High Plains area and problems in coniferous forests in the mountains of West Texas.

The **gypsy moth** has been a serious defoliator of hardwood trees in the Northeast United States for many years. In the past decade this insect pest has been transported to many other areas of the country, including the West Coast, the Great Lakes States and various parts of the South. During the summer of 1984, male gypsy moths were trapped for the first time in Texas. Although no established gypsy moth populations are known to occur in Texas, more intensive monitoring with moth traps will be conducted in 1985 and beyond. A task force of leading entomologists in the state has been formed, to coordinate trapping efforts in Texas and prevent gypsy moth from becoming a serious tree pest in Texas.

Forest Fire Protection

Organized fire protection is provided by the TFS with some financial assistance from the federal government and from landowners. Texas first qualified for federal assistance in protection against forest fires in 1916. A division of forest protection, now the **Forest Fire Control Department**, was established at Lufkin in 1925.

From 1925 through 1986, 165,161 **forest fires** were reported and suppressed in East Texas by TFS. In 1986, 1,482 fires burned 19,317 acres, averaging 13 acres per fire. For the past five years, the average annual acreage loss to wildfire was 0.10 percent of the area protected.

Causes of the 1,482 fires in 1986 were: debris burning, 53 percent; incendiary, 31 percent; smokers, 3 percent; campfires, 3 percent; and miscellaneous, equipment use, railroads and children amounted to 9 percent. Lightning caused one percent of all forest fires.

For 57 years, from 1916 to 1975, basic rural fire fighting responsibility was confined to 48 counties, or the commercial forest area of East Texas.

The backbone of the TFS fire operations is a two-man fire crew with a crawler tractor equipped with a fire plow. This unit and its transport vehicle are both equipped with two-way radios. There are 85 such units in the 48-county area. These crewmen are trained at the **Texas Forest Service Ground Cover Training Facility** in Lufkin.

In 1973, the TFS was given the responsibility by State legislation for rural wildland fire defense in the whole state. The law authorized the TFS to develop rural fire protection plans and to provide training and equipment to organized groups throughout the state. It did not expand the operational area of the TFS fire units beyond the 48 counties of East Texas.

Rural Fire Protection In Texas

Of the huge loss annually caused by fire in the United States, much occurs in towns and villages with fewer than 10,000 residents. In general, most of these towns can ill afford fire equipment necessary for their protection. The **Rural Community Fire Protection Program (RCFP)**, administered in Texas through the Texas Forest Service, is helping meet this need.

Based on data collected by the Texas Forest Service from towns under 10,000 population, there are more than 38,000 rural fires annually. Twenty thousand of these are ground cover fires that burn an estimated one million acres each year. The next two highest categories of rural fires are single story residence and vehicular that account for 7,100 and 5,300 fires respectively.

Some counties have received increased requests

for operating funds from local communities whose main fire business has been in areas outside of corporate limits. There is an understandable but unfortunate tendency for city fire departments to refuse to make rural runs, and the smaller communities with established, well-organized departments are finding it increasingly expensive to take up the slack.

TFS began, in September 1973, an equipment development and testing program to assist rural communities in acquiring basic fire trucks at affordable prices. Testimony to the unqualified popularity of this equipment phase is that TFS has, through 1984, modified and delivered more than 700 complete rural fire trucks to small communities all over the state — with more than 100 active requests on hand at all times.

TFS is field-testing a new type of suppression equipment that may well evolve into a family of systems with wide applicability and effectiveness. The system is basically an air-injection, foam-generating unit that combines a foaming agent in water under pressure. Expansion rates vary from 5-to-1 as high as 20-to-1, depending upon equipment and operating characteristics. The equipment has practical use on standard tractor-plow units for safety and tractor operator protection. On pumper units used by volunteer fire departments, it greatly extends pumping time.

The TFS established courses to provide basic, intermediate and advanced training to VFD cooperators and to other interested groups. The courses comprise segments on equipment operation and maintenance, fire behavior, tactics and ground fire organization.

In 1976, the original training team included a chief training officer and two assistants. Inordinate travel costs and difficult scheduling problems for the team quickly necessitated a different approach. Contractual arrangements have been made with 10 certified fire

Texas Lumber Production, 1975-1985

Year—	*Lumber production		Tie production	
	Pine	Hardwood	Pine	Hardwood
	Thd. bd. ft.		Thd. pieces	
1975	704,572	147,359	352	978
1976	844,253	146,333	502	878
1977	848,253	191,686	259	1,366
1978	867,759	214,118	297	1,314
1979	845,830	204,536	305	1,214
1980	755,078	292,221	173	1,475
1981	707,311	275,591	172	1,756
1982	752,727	160,235	154	971
1983	862,378	152,350	155	866
1984	898,212	165,460	337	1,001
1985	856,157	175,254	101	926

*Includes tie volumes.

Texas Plywood Production, 1975-1985

Year—	Pine	Year—	Pine
	Thd. sq. ft.		Thd. sq. ft.
1975	959,649	1980	1,481,944
1976	1,225,513	1981	1,553,345
1977	1,352,527	1982	1,604,102
1978	1,455,139	1983	1,898,556
1979	1,299,282	1984	1,881,071
		1985	1,985,699

Texas Pulpwood Production, 1975-1985

	Roundwood		Chips & Sawdust		All Species Total Pulpwood Production
	Pine	Hardwood	Pine	Hardwood	
	Thousand cords				
1975	2,051	295	1,114	89	3,549
1976	1,982	404	1,088	111	3,585
1977	2,028	401	1,115	86	3,630
1978	2,068	458	1,118	185	3,829
1979	2,128	453	1,131	128	3,868
1980	2,196	473	1,378	183	4,230
1981	2,114	395	1,329	177	4,016
1982	1,900	495	1,445	135	3,975
1983	2,444	1,124	1,772	262	5,602
1984	1,890	731	1,567	228	4,416
1985	1,901	716	1,591	462	4,670

trainers in various regions of Texas to deliver the standard courses to local volunteers. All Texas Forest Service training is certified by the **Texas Firemen's and Fire Marshal's Association** and counts toward fireman certification.

As of December 1986, the Texas Forest Service trainers have conducted more than 2,700 classes and trained 41,000 firefighters. Plans are to continue to offer the course at the request of local fire departments. All trainer expense is paid by the Texas Forest Service.

Tree Seedlings

Pine seedlings are required for reforestation where natural seeding is delayed or unavailable. The **Indian Mound Nursery**, near Alto, Cherokee County, with an area of 120 acres, has a capacity for producing 40 million pine seedlings annually. Seedlings are sold at cost. Applications for seedlings are obtained from the TFS, county agricultural agents and Soil Conservation Service district supervisors.

A major proportion of the seedlings are raised from genetically improved seed produced by the TFS seed orchard. Varieties available include loblolly pine selected for growth rate and form, loblolly pine selected for drought resistance, slash pine selected for resistance to fusiform rust and longleaf pine. The nursery also raises a number of hardwood species for use in a windbreak.

Conifer and hardwood seedlings for the High Plains are grown at the West Texas Nursery in Lubbock. Two crops of conifer seedlings are grown in a climate-controlled greenhouse and shipped in styrofoam containers to planters in about 105 counties each spring. A variety of bare-root hardwood seedlings is also produced. Distribution is made through Soil and Water Conservation Districts.

State Forests

The first state forest, now known as the **E. O. Siecke State Forest** in Newton County, was purchased by the state in 1924. It contains 1,722 acres of pine land. An additional 100 acres were added by a 99-year lease in 1946.

The **W. Goodrich Jones State Forest**, south of Conroe in Montgomery County, containing 1,725 acres, was purchased in 1926. A 20-acre adjunct was given to the state in 1969.

The **I. D. Fairchild State Forest**, Texas' largest, is located west of Rusk in Cherokee County. This forest was transferred from the state prison system in 1925. An additional 536 acres were added to the original 2,360 acres in 1963 from the Texas State Hospitals and Special Schools, bringing the combined acreage total to 2,896.

The **John Henry Kirby State Forest** of 626 acres was donated by the late lumberman, **John Henry Kirby**, in 1929, and later donors. Revenue from this forest is given to the Association of Former Students of Texas A&M University for student loan purposes. All of the state forests are used primarily for demonstration and research.

The newest state forest, the **Paul N. Masterson Memorial Forest** of 520 acres, was donated in the fall of 1984. Mrs. Leonora O'Neal Masterson of Beaumont donated the land in Jasper County in honor of her husband, an active member of the Texas Forestry Association and a tree farmer.

Forest Industry and Harvest Trends

Timber is the second most valuable agricultural crop in the state and provides the raw materials for the ninth largest manufacturing industry. The timber producing-region of Texas, known as the Piney Woods, is in the eastern portion of the state. There are about 40 counties from which large amounts of timber are harvested. These trees are principally used to make paper products, lumber and plywood.

Texas' forest industry is large. It ranks third southwide in payroll, at $958.1 million and annually ships $5.5 billion in products.

The 1985 Harvest

The 1985 Texas timber harvest totalled 551.5 million cubic feet, an increase of 1.2 percent from the 1984 harvest. The three top producing counties were Polk, Angelina and Jasper. The pine harvest rose 1.7 percent to 434 million cubic feet, whereas the hardwood cut slipped less than 1 percent to 117.5 million cubic feet.

The total sawlog harvest was 996 million board feet, a decline of 2 percent from the 1984 mark. The pine sawlog harvest was 791 million board feet, or 80 percent of the total. Veneer logs harvested totalled 728 million board feet, of which 99 percent was pine.

Pulpwood, the highest volume product group, was stable at 2.6 million cords in 1985. Pine pulpwood totalled 1.9 million cords. In addition to this roundwood pulpwood, Texas pulp and paper operations consumed 2.1 million cords of chips and sawdust from mill residues.

Production of posts was off 31 percent in 1985, totalling just under 1.1 million pieces. Pole production was down 14 percent. Production of pilings, however, increased 31 percent.

Texas was a net exporter of raw wood fiber to the adjacent states of Louisiana, Arkansas and Oklahoma. Texas exported 60 million cubic feet of products and imported 45 million cubic feet from other states.

Primary Forest Products

Pine lumber production slipped 5 percent after setting a 30-year high in 1984. Production was 856 million board feet, compared with 898 million in 1984. Hardwood lumber production climbed 6 percent to 175 million board feet in 1985. Texas production of plywood and waferboard showed a 6 percent gain in 1985, reaching a record 1,986 million square feet. Texas' 10 panel plants accounted for 9 percent of the national production. Paper and paperboard production continued an upward trend. Total production was 2.5 million tons, representing about 4 percent of total U.S. paper and paperboard production.

Total production of treated wood products increased 13 percent between 1984 and 1985. The 43.5 million cubic feet of wood treated set a new high in Texas production. Spurred by consumer demand for do-it-yourself outdoor wood products, a 39 percent increase in treated lumber offset declines in most other treated products. Lumber accounts for 61 percent of total volume treated.

The pine harvest was 92 percent of growth in 1985, indicating that slightly more wood was grown than was cut. However, it is expected that, with an improved housing market, timber harvests will again begin to exceed the amount grown annually in Texas.

Approximately 144,243 acres were planted with pine seedlings in 1985. Most, 119,285 acres, was on forest industry owned land. About 22,528 acres of nonindustrial private land and 2,430 acres of public land were also planted. Most nonindustrial private reforestation and timber stand improvement (TSI) activities were funded by the cost-sharing programs available to Texas forest landowners. The federally funded Forestry Incentives Program (FIP) provided cost-shares of $389,259, which helped defray the expense of 10,844 acres of tree planting and 2,282 acres of TSI. The Texas Reforestation Foundation, Inc., provided cost-shares of $423,760, which helped fund 8,533 acres of tree planting and 377 acres of TSI. There were 3,151 acres of tree planting and 2,493 acres of TSI accomplished by nonindustrial private forest landowners with no cost-share assistance.

National Forests in Texas

There are four national forests and all or part of five national grasslands in Texas. These federally owned lands are administered by the U.S. Department of Agriculture-Forest Service. These units cover 782,681 acres in parts of 18 Texas counties, as follows:

ANGELINA NATIONAL FOREST—Angelina County, 58,842 acres; Jasper, 19,733; Nacogdoches, 9,542; San Augustine, 66,799. Total, 154,916.

DAVY CROCKETT NATIONAL FOREST—Houston County, 93,583 acres; Trinity, 67,910. Total, 161,493.

SABINE NATIONAL FOREST—Jasper County, 64 acres; Sabine, 114,498; San Augustine, 4,317; Shelby, 67,762; Newton, 1,579. Total, 188,220.

SAM HOUSTON NATIONAL FOREST—Montgomery County, 47,358 acres; San Jacinto, 59,596; Walker, 53,490. Total, 160,444.

BLACK KETTLE NATIONAL GRASSLAND—Hemphill County, 576 acres; Roger Mills County, Okla., 31,000 acres. Total, 31,576.

CADDO NATIONAL GRASSLAND—Fannin County, 17,796 acres. Total, 17,796.

LYNDON B. JOHNSON NATIONAL GRASSLAND—Montague County, 61 acres; Wise, 20,263. Total, 20,324.

McCLELLAN CREEK NATIONAL GRASSLAND—Gray County, 1,449 acres. Total, 1,449.

RITA BLANCA NATIONAL GRASSLAND—Dallam County, 78,027 acres; Cimarron County, Okla., 15,736 acres. Total, 93,763.

Administrative Units

The four National Forests and two National Grasslands (Caddo and Lyndon B. Johnson) in East Texas are administered by the Forest Supervisor with headquarters in Lufkin. This division is known as the National Forests in Texas and is locally administered by eight District Rangers, as follows:

Angelina National Forest, Angelina District at Lufkin. Sabine National Forest, Tenaha District at San Augustine; Yellowpine District at Hemphill. Davy Crockett National Forest, Neches District at Crockett; Trinity District at Apple Springs. Sam Houston National Forest, Raven District at New Waverly; San Jacinto District at Cleveland. Caddo-Lyndon B. Johnson District at Decatur. The three National Grasslands (Black Kettle, McClellan Creek and Rita Blanca) in West Texas are administered by the Forest Supervisor in Albuquerque, New Mexico, as units of the Cibola National Forest. The Black Kettle and McClellan Creek National Grasslands are administered locally by a District Ranger in Cheyenne, Okla., and the Rita Blanca by a District Ranger at Texline.

National Forests in Texas were established by invitation of the Texas Legislature by an Act of 1933, authorizing the purchase of lands in Texas for the establishment of national forests. President Franklin D. Roosevelt proclaimed these purchases of national forests on Oct. 15, 1936. Acquisition authority for purchase of the National Grasslands are primarily the Bankhead-Jones Farm Tenant Act (1937).

Timber Management

Each national forest constitutes a timber management working circle. All work is done under a detailed prescription prepared by a trained forester. Over 80,000 acres have been reforested artificially and thousands of additional acres have been treated to increase the quantity and quality of the timber.

Sales of sawtimber, pulpwood and other forest products are made at regular intervals.

The estimated net growth is over 200 million board feet per year and is valued at $20 million. About one-third of this growth is removed by cutting. The balance is left to grow. By the year 2000, growth is expected to exceed 300 million board feet per year.

Fire Protection

U.S. Forest Service cooperates with the Texas Forest Service in the protection of private and forest service lands inside the national forest boundaries. Detection of forest fires is done from airplanes.

Grazing Permits

Permits to graze cattle on national forests and national grasslands are granted to local residents for an annual fee. In calendar year 1986, approximately 4,700 head of cattle were grazed on national forests and 2,000 head of cattle were grazed on the Caddo-Lyndon B. Johnson area. On the Rita Blanca NG, 5,417 cattle are grazed each year — 4,531 in Texas and 886 in Oklahoma.

Hunting and Fishing

The Forest Service manages the home of many varieties of wildlife.

State hunting and fishing laws and regulations apply to all national forest land. Game law enforcement is carried out by Texas Parks and Wildlife Department.

The Angelina, Sabine, Neches and San Jacinto rivers, Sam Rayburn and Toledo Bend reservoirs, Lake Conroe and many small streams provide a wide variety of fishing opportunities.

Recreation Facilities

An estimated 2 million people visited the national forests in Texas for recreation in 1984. Many of these used established recreation areas. These areas are primarily for the purpose of picnicking, swimming, fishing, camping, boating and nature enjoyment and are: **Ratcliff Lake**, 25 miles west of Lufkin on Highway 7, has a 45-acre lake and facilities for picnicking, swimming, boating, fishing, camping and a 250-seat capacity campfire theater. **Double Lake**, 3 miles south of Coldspring on FM Road 2025, has a 30-acre lake and facilities for picnicking, camping, swimming and fishing. **Stubblefield Lake**, 15 miles west-northwest of New Waverly on the shores of **Lake Conroe**, has facilities for camping, picnicking and fishing. **Scotts Ridge Boat Ramp**, 8 miles west of Willis, provides a boat ramp and parking lot on **Lake Conroe**. **Boykin Springs**, 15 miles southeast of Zavalla, has a 6-acre lake and facilities for swimming, picnicking, fishing and camping. **Red Hills Lake**, 4 miles north of Milam on Highway 87, has a 17-acre lake and facilities for fishing, swimming, camping and picnicking. **Bouton Lake**, 7 miles southeast of Zavalla off Texas Highway 63, has a 9-acre natural lake with facilities for camping, picnicking and fishing.

Several areas have been built on the shores of **Sam Rayburn Reservoir**, which has 100 miles of national forest shoreline. These areas provide camping, picnicking, nature enjoyment, boating and fishing. Recreation areas are: **Sandy Creek** on Forest Service Road 333, 25 miles northwest of Jasper; **Caney Creek**, 10 miles southeast of Zavalla off FM 2743, in addition to the facilities mentioned above, has a 500-seat capacity campfire theater for evening campfire programs; **Harvey Creek**, 10 miles south of Broaddus on FM 2390, and **Townsend**, 7 miles north off FM 1277.

The recreational areas at **Toledo Bend Reservoir** include the following: **Willow Oak Recreation Area**, located 14 miles south of Hemphill off State Highway 87, has facilities for picnicking and camping and a boat ramp; **Indian Mounds Recreation Area**, accessible by FM 83 and FM 3382 a total distance of 15 miles east of Hemphill, has camping facilities and a boat launch ramp; **Ragtown**, 25 miles southeast of Center and accessible by State Highways 87 and 139, County Highway 3184 and Forest Service Road 132, has facilities for camping and boat launching; **Lakeview**, a primitive campground 12 miles southeast of Hemphill, can be reached via State Highway 87, County Highway 2928 and Forest Service Road 120.

Hiking Trails in National Forests

The **Lone Star Hiking Trail**, approximately 140 miles long, is located in the **Sam Houston National Forest** in Montgomery, Walker and San Jacinto counties. Twenty-six miles of the trail in San Jacinto County has been designated as national recreation trail.

The **4Cs National Recreation Trail** is 19 miles long and goes from **Ratcliff Recreation Area** to the Neches Bluff overlook in the **Davy Crockett National Forest**.

The **Saw Mill Trail** is 5½ miles long and goes from the old Aldrich Saw Mill site to **Boykin Springs Recreation Area** in the **Angelina National Forest**.

National Grasslands

The submarginal Dust Bowl project lands, purchased by the federal government under the Bankhead-Jones Farm Tenant Act, are today well covered with grasses and native shrubs. They are administered much like the national forests under a policy of multiple use for range, watershed, recreation and wildlife.

Recreation on the National Grasslands

Lake Davy Crockett Recreation Area, 11 miles north of Honey Grove on FM 100, is operated by a concessionaire who charges fees for certain facilities and services. There is a lodge, rental cabin, marina, boat launch ramp, small cafe and camping sites on a 450-acre lake. **Coffee Mill Lake Recreation Area** has picnic facilities on a 750-acre lake. This area is 4 miles west of Lake Davy Crockett Recreation Area. **Black Creek Lake Picnic Area** is located 8 miles southeast of Alvord. It has picnic facilities and a boat launch ramp. This site is on a 30-acre lake.

Lake McClellan in Gray County and **Lake Marvin**, which is part of the Black Kettle National Grassland in Hemphill County, created for flood control and recreation, receive over 28,000 recreation visitors annually. These lake areas provide camping, picnicking, fishing and boating facilities. Concessionaires operate facilities at both lakes and a nominal fee is charged for use of the areas. A limited amount of wildlife provides for public hunting under state game laws. At the **Rita Blanca National Grassland**, about 2,500 visitors a year enjoy picnicking and hunting.

Weather Highlights, 1985 and 1986

The following summary was prepared for this edition by John F. Griffiths and Janine M. Bryan, Office of State Climatologist, Department of Meteorology, Texas A&M University.

Jan. 12-13, 1985: A record-breaking snowstorm struck West and South Central Texas with up to 15 inches of snow that fell at many locations between San Antonio and the Rio Grande. San Antonio recorded 13.2 inches of snow for Jan. 12 (the greatest in a day) and 13.5 inches for the two-day total. Eagle Pass reported 14.5 inches of snow.

April 21, 1985: A massive multiple-vortex tornado touched down in the eastern part of Throckmorton County, where it destroyed a home and surrounding buildings and killed three people. A second tornado developed soon after in western Young County. Two people were injured.

April 27-28, 1985: Intense thunderstorms covered much of North Texas. Some of the most intense rainfall occurred near Rockwall, where approximately 10 inches fell from 9 to 11 p.m. on April 27. Eight people drowned.

May 13, 1985: A tornado touched down in Greenville in Hunt County. At least 100 buildings were damaged and 23 people were injured as the tornado passed through the densely populated area.

June 5-6, 1985: Heavy rains in the Hill Country resulted in serious flash flooding in Bexar, Blanco, Comal and Hays counties. The heaviest rains occurred in southern Blanco County near Twin Sisters, where an unofficial report of near 15 inches was measured. Damage estimates were in the millions of dollars.

Oct. 18-19, 1985: Heavy rainfall in much of North Texas and in eastern sections of the Edwards Plateau to the San Antonio area resulted in serious flooding. Three people drowned. Highest rainfall totals were in the Hill Country, where 10.75 inches of rain was reported at Mountain Home and 10.3 inches at the Kerr Wildlife Management Area.

Nov. 11, 1985: Very heavy rains fell over a broad area of Southeast Texas generally from Lavaca County on the west, eastward to Harris County and from Walker County southward to Brazoria County. Serious flooding resulted that covered about 10 counties. The heaviest rain fell from near Garwood (21 inches) in Colorado County east to East Bernard and to Rosenberg in Fort Bend County.

Feb. 5, 1986: A line of severe thunderstorms developed in eastern Texas producing four tornadoes, damaging microburst winds and up to tennis ball-sized hail. Tomball, northeast of Houston, was hit with a tornado that caused two deaths and devastated a mobile home park and an airport southeast of Tomball.

April 19, 1986: A severe thunderstorm spawned a multiple-vortex tornado 1.5 miles southwest of Sweetwater. It traveled northeast and hit the city, resulting in one fatality and 100 injuries. Many homes were destroyed.

May 7, 1986: A severe thunderstorm produced five tornadoes and up to baseball-size hail in the northeast corner of the Texas Panhandle near Canadian.

May 14, 1986: A tornado moved through the Archer City-Windthorst area of North Central Texas.

May 17, 1986: Intense thunderstorm winds associated with a gust front passage disrupted activities on Lake Livingston in San Jacinto County, where hundreds of boaters were engaged in a fishing tournament and sailing contest. Five persons drowned, as dozens of boats were capsized by winds estimated at 90 m.p.h.

May 24, 1986: A thunderstorm system went through Fort Worth producing damaging downburst winds measured at up to 95 m.p.h., hail up to three inches in diameter, and about four inches of rain in less than an hour. A probable combination of water loading and wind caused the collapse of a bowling alley and damage was sustained by a hotel and scores of nearby homes as well. Two people drowned in street flooding.

June 2-4, 1986: On the evening of June 2 up to two inches of rain fell over northern parts of San Antonio. On June 4, a record 24-hour rainfall of 6.5 inches at the National Weather Service Forecast Office, along with amounts close to 10 inches at other locations, resulted in widespread flash flooding and subsequent river flooding that lasted for several days along the Medina and San Antonio rivers. Up to 11.5 inches of rain fell in Medina County in and around Yancey.

June 26, 1986: Hurricane Bonnie made landfall between High Island and Sabine Pass around 3:45 a.m. The highest wind measured in the area was a gust to 97 m.p.h., which was recorded at the Sea Rim State Park. As much as 13 inches of rain fell in Ace in southern Polk County. There were several reports of funnel clouds, but no confirmed tornadoes. While the storm caused no major structural damage, there was widespread minor damage. Numerous injuries were reported.

Sept. 6, 1986: Up to 12 inches of rain fell over the south-east part of Travis County near Elroy.

Sept. 22-23, 1986: Moisture associated with the remnants of eastern Pacific Hurricane Newton combined with daytime heating of highly unstable air to bring torrential rains to the South Plains. Severe storms brought hail, numerous funnel clouds and at least two tornadoes.

Oct. 2-5, 1986: A slow-moving cold front combined with moisture associated with the remnants of eastern Pacific Hurricane Paine produced widespread, heavy rainfall over most of southwestern Texas. Many rain totals over the period exceeded six inches, some surpassed 10 inches, and a gauge at McCamey in Upton County collected 16.21 inches within a 24-hour period. Up to 15 inches of rain caused serious flooding over the northern part of Val Verde County on the watersheds of the Devils and Dry Devils rivers.

Nov. 22-24, 1986: An upper-level disturbance triggered heavy thunderstorms over eastern Texas. Some areas around Sour Lake, near Port Arthur, received 10 to 14 inches of rain.

In 1985 there were 90 reported tornadoes. Of these, two were killer tornadoes, one with three deaths and one with one death.

In 1986, 131 tornadoes were reported in Texas. Two were killer tornadoes, one with two deaths and one with one death.

Weather Summary—1985

The year 1985 featured a winter snowstorm that hit portions of South Central Texas beginning late on Jan. 11 and continuing until the early morning hours of Jan. 13. Snowfall amounts ranged from six to 14 inches in South Central Texas, with the area from Eagle Pass to north of Uvalde to San Antonio receiving the heaviest amounts. All previous snowfall records were broken at many locations including San Antonio, Rocksprings, Stockdale, Eagle Pass, Yorktown and Beeville. The southern boundary of snow cover was from northern Webb County eastward to Mathes and northeast to the Houston area. The most accumulation on the ground at the National Weather Service Office in San Antonio at any one time was 10 inches, while the total snowfall was 13.5 inches. This was also true at many other locations. Eagle Pass reported 14.5 inches of snowfall, but there were several depth reports up to 15 inches.

January and February brought lower-than-average temperatures throughout the state, with January precipitation above the mean in all areas except the Low Rolling Plains, North Central Texas and East Texas. Except for below-the-mean amounts in the Edwards Plateau region, February precipitation was above average for the state. March began a warming trend that lasted through May, with nearly all areas experiencing temperatures above their means. In April, however, the Southern and Lower Rio Grande Valley regions recorded average and slightly below-average temperatures. Above-average precipitation occurred throughout Texas in March, especially in the Upper Coast and Southern regions. April brought slightly higher-than-expected precipitation to the High Plains, Low Rolling Plains, South Central and Southern regions, while the rest of the state received below-average amounts. Nearly all of Texas experienced a very dry May, with only the Southern and Lower Valley regions receiving above-average precipitation. Temperatures in June and July were lower than usual across the state, except for June in East Texas and the Upper Coast regions. All areas of the state received above-average precipitation in June, except for below-the-mean amounts in East Texas. July brought precipitation that was slightly above the mean for most of Texas; however, the High Plains, North Central and Trans-Pecos regions were drier than average. August brought hot and dry conditions to all areas of Texas. The South Central and Southern regions received only 19 and 17 percent of their mean August precipitation. September through November brought higher-than-usual temperatures for all areas of Texas except for the High Plains and the Low Rolling Plains regions, where temperatures were below the mean. East Texas and the Southern region remained dry through September, but the remainder of the state received nearly average or above-average amounts of rain. October brought precipitation amounts that were above the mean to nearly all areas. Only the Lower Valley region received below average amounts. November precipitation amounts were below the mean in the High

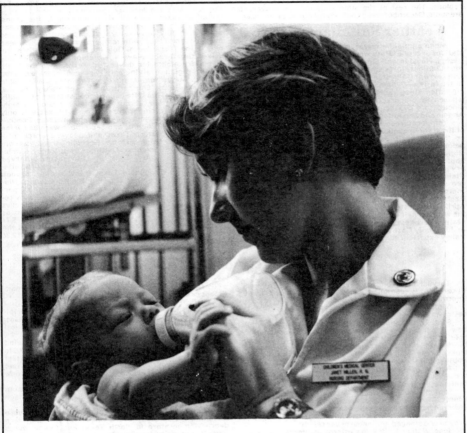

Plains, Low Rolling Plains, Trans-Pecos and Lower Valley regions. The rest of the state received above-average amounts. December was a cool, dry month for all of Texas.

Weather Summary—1986

Mean annual temperatures in 1986 for all first order stations except El Paso were above average. Austin, Galveston, Houston and San Antonio recorded their highest mean temperatures since before 1974. All first order stations except Galveston recorded above-average precipitaiton in 1986. Midland recorded its greatest annual precipitation since records began in 1930. Other stations whose 1986 total precipitation amounts were the greatest since before 1975 include Abilene, Amarillo, Lubbock, San Angelo and San Antonio.

Temperatures were higher-than-usual in all sections of the state in January, and the warm conditions persisted through April. January precipitation amounts were below the mean in all areas, except with average and slightly above-average amounts in the Trans-Pecos and Southern regions, respectively. Precipitation in February was above the mean in the High Plains, Low Rolling Plains, North Central and Lower Valley regions, while the remainder of Texas received below-average amounts. March and April were dry months across the state except East Texas received slightly above its mean amount in April. May brought higher-than-usual temperatures to the western half of the state and the Lower Valley, while eastern Texas experienced below-average temperatures. In June, only East Texas, the Upper Coast and the Lower Valley experienced temperatures above the mean, while

below-average temperatures were observed in the rest of the state. May and June precipitation was above average for all of Texas and well above average in the Trans-Pecos, which in June received 298 percent of its mean amount. In July, above-average temperatures prevailed over most of Texas, with temperatures below the mean only in the Trans-Pecos. Only the Low Rolling Plains received slightly above-average precipitation in July. July was a dry month for the rest of Texas, with the South Central region receiving only 10 percent of the expected amount. August temperatures were higher than usual in the Trans-Pecos, Southern and Lower Valley regions, while the rest of the state experienced average or slightly below-average temperatures. September brought higher-than-average temperatures to most of Texas, with only the Panhandle reporting average temperatures. Precipitation amounts in August and September were below the mean in southeastern Texas and above average elsewhere. October began a statewide cooling trend that continued through December. Only the Lower Valley in October and the Upper Coast in November observed temperatures above the mean. Above-average precipitation occurred throughout Texas from October through December. In December, the High Plains, Edwards Plateau and Southern regions received more than 300 percent of their mean amounts, while the Trans-Pecos recorded 634 percent of its mean. In Midland, the 3.30 inches recorded is the all-time record rainfall for December, as was San Antonio's 7.11 inches. Austin reported 5.77 inches, the second-greatest December rainfall; and the third-highest December rainfall in the Del Rio area (2.36 inches) was recorded.

Destructive Weather

This list of exceptionally destructive weather in Texas since 1766 is compiled from ESSA-Weather Bureau information:

Sept., 4, 1766: **Hurricane. Galveston Bay.** A mission destroyed.

Sept. 12, 1818: **Hurricane. Galveston Island.** Salt water flowed four feet deep. Only six buildings remained habitable. Of the six vessels and two barges in the harbor, even the two not seriously damaged were reduced to dismasted hulks. Pirate **Jean Lafitte** moved to one hulk so his **Red House** might serve as a hospital.

Aug. 6, 1844: **Hurricane.** Mouth of Rio Grande. All houses destroyed at the mouth of the river and at **Brazos Santiago,** eight miles north; 70 lives lost.

Sept. 16, 1875: **Hurricane.** Struck **Indianola,** Calhoun County. Three-fourths of town swept away; 176 lives lost. Flooding from the bay caused nearly all destruction.

Aug. 19-21, 1886: **Hurricane. Indianola.** Every house destroyed or damaged. Indianola never rebuilt.

June 27-July 1, 1899: **Rainstorm.** A storm, centered over the Brazos River watershed, precipitated an average of 17 inches over an area of 7,000 square miles. At **Hearne** the gage overflowed at 24 inches, and there was an estimated total rainfall of 30 inches. At **Turnersville,** Coryell County, 33 inches were recorded in three days. This rain caused the worst **Brazos River** flood on record. Between 30 and 35 lives were lost. Property damage was estimated at $9 million.

Sept. 8-9, 1900: **Hurricane. Galveston.** The **Great Galveston Storm** was the worst natural disaster in U.S. history. Loss of life at Galveston has been estimated at 6,000 to 8,000, but the exact number has never been definitely ascertained. The island was completely inundated, and not a single structure escaped damage. Most of the loss of life was due to drowning by storm tides that reached 15 feet or more. The anemometer blew away when the wind reached 100 miles per hour at 6:15 p.m. on the 8th. Wind reached an estimated maximum velocity of 120 miles per hour between 7:30 and 8:30 p.m. Property damage has been estimated at $30 to $40 million.

May 22-25, 1908: **Rainstorm;** unique because it originated on the Pacific Coast. It moved first into North Texas and southern Oklahoma and thence to Central Texas, precipitating as much as 10 inches. Heaviest floods were in the upper Trinity basin, but flooding was general as far south as the Nueces. Property damage exceeded $5 million and 11 lives were lost in the Dallas vicinity.

July 21, 1909: **Hurricane. Velasco,** Brazoria County. One-half of town destroyed, 41 lives lost; damage $2,000,000.

Dec. 1-5, 1913: **Rainstorm.** This caused the second major **Brazos River flood,** and caused more deaths than the storm of 1899. It formed over Central Texas and spread both southwest and northeast with precipitation

of 15 inches at **San Marcos** and 11 inches at **Kaufman.** Floods caused loss of 177 lives and $8,541,000 damage.

April 20-26, 1915: **Rainstorm.** Originated over Central Texas and spread into North and East Texas with precipitation up to 17 inches, causing floods in Trinity, Brazos, Colorado, and Guadalupe rivers. More than 40 lives lost and $2,330,000 damage.

Aug. 16-19, 1915: **Hurricane. Galveston.** Peak wind gusts of 120 miles recorded at **Galveston;** tide ranged 9.5 to 14.3 feet above mean sea level in the city, and up to 16.1 feet near the causeway. Business section flooded with 5 to 6 feet of water. At least 275 lives lost, damage $56 million. A new seawall prevented a repetition of the 1900 disaster.

Aug. 18, 1916: **Hurricane. Corpus Christi.** Maximum wind speed 100 miles per hour. 20 Lives lost; damage $1,600,000.

Jan. 10-12, 1918: **Blizzard.** This was the most severe since that of February, 1899; it was accompanied by zero degree temperature in North Texas and temperatures from 7° to 12° below freezing along the lower coast.

Sept. 14, 1919: **Hurricane.** Near **Corpus Christi.** Center moved inland south of **Corpus Christi;** tides 16 feet above normal in that area and 8.8 feet above normal at **Galveston.** Extreme wind at Corpus Christi measured at 110 miles per hour; 284 lives lost; damage $20,272,000.

Sept. 8-10, 1921: **Rainstorm.** Probably the **greatest rainstorm in Texas history,** it entered Mexico as a hurricane from the Gulf. Torrential rains fell as the storm moved northeasterly across Texas. Record floods occurred in **Bexar, Travis, Williamson, Bell** and **Milam counties,** killing 215 persons, with property losses over $19 million. Five to nine feet of water stood in downtown San Antonio. A total of 23.98 inches was measured at the U.S. Weather Bureau station at **Taylor** during a period of 35 hours, with a 24-hour maximum of 23.11 on September 9-10. The **greatest rainfall recorded in United States history** during 18 consecutive hours fell at Thrall, Williamson County, 36.40 inches fell on Sept. 9.

April 23-28, 1922: **Rainstorm.** An exceptional storm that entered Texas from the west and moved from the Panhandle to North Central and East Texas. Rains up to 12.6 inches over **Parker, Tarrant,** and **Dallas counties** caused severe floods in the Upper Trinity at **Fort Worth;** 11 lives were lost; damage was estimated at $1 million.

April 12, 1927: **Tornado.** Edwards, **Real** and **Uvalde counties;** 74 killed, 205 injured; damage $1,230,000. Most of damage was in Rocksprings where 72 deaths occurred and town was practically destroyed.

May 9, 1927: **Tornado. Garland;** eleven killed; damage $100,000.

May 9, 1927: **Tornado. Nevada,** Collin County; **Wolfe City,** Hunt County; and **Tigertown,** Lamar County; 28 killed, over 200 injured; damage $900,000.

May 6, 1930: **Tornado. Bynum, Irene and Mertens** in

Hill County; **Ennis,** Ellis County; and **Frost,** Navarro County; 41 killed; damage $2,100,000.

Aug. 13, 1932: **Hurricane.** Near **Freeport,** Brazoria County. Wind speed at **East Columbia** estimated at 100 miles per hour; 40 lives lost, 200 injured; damage $7,500,000.

July 22-25, 1933: **Tropical Storm.** One of the greatest U.S. storms in area and general rainfall. The storm reached the vicinity of **Freeport** late on July 22 and moved very slowly overland across eastern Texas, July 22-25. The storm center moved into northern Louisiana on the 25th. Rainfall averaged 12.50 inches over an area of about 25,000 square miles. Twenty inches or more fell in a small area of eastern Texas and western Louisiana surrounding **Logansport, La.** The 4-day total at Logansport was 22.30 inches. Property damage was estimated at $1,114,790.

July 25, 1934: **Hurricane.** Near **Seadrift,** Calhoun County, 19 lives lost, many minor injuries; damage $4.5 million. About 85 percent of damage was in crops.

April 28, 1942: **Tornado. Crowell,** Foard County; 11 killed, 250 injured; damage $1,500,000.

July 27, 1943: **Hurricane.** Near **Galveston.** Center moved inland across Bolivar Peninsula and Trinity Bay. A wind gust of 104 miles per hour was recorded at **Texas City;** 19 lives lost; damage estimated at $16,550,000.

Jan. 4, 1946: **Tornado.** Near **Lufkin,** Angelina County and **Nacogdoches,** Nacogdoches County; 13 killed, 250 injured; damage $2,050,000.

April 9, 1947: **Tornado. White Deer,** Carson County; **Glazier,** Hemphill County; and **Higgins,** Lipscomb County; 68 killed, 201 injured; damage $1,550,000. Glazier completely destroyed. One of the largest tornadoes on record. Width of path, 1½ miles at Higgins; length of path, 221 miles across portions of Texas, Oklahoma and Kansas. This tornado also struck **Woodward, Okla.**

May 15, 1949: **Tornado. Amarillo** and vicinity; six killed, 83 injured. Total damage from tornado, wind and hail, $5,310,000. Total destruction over one-block by three-block area in southern part of city; airport and 45 airplanes damaged; 28 railroad boxcars blown off track.

May 11, 1953: **Tornado.** Near **San Angelo,** Tom Green County; eleven killed, 159 injured; damage $3,239,000.

May 11, 1953: **Tornado. Waco,** McLennan County; 114 killed, 597 injured; damage $41,150,000. One of two most disastrous tornadoes; 150 homes destroyed, 900 homes damaged; 185 other buildings destroyed; 500 other buildings damaged.

April 2, 1957: **Tornado. Dallas,** Dallas County; 10 killed, 200 injured; damage $4 million. Moving through Oak Cliff and West Dallas, it damaged 574 buildings, largely homes.

June 27, 1957: **Hurricane Audrey.** Center crossed the Gulf coast near the Texas-Louisiana line. **Orange** was in the western portion of the eye between 9 and 10 a.m. In Texas, nine lives were lost, 450 persons injured; property damage was $8 million. Damage was extensive in Jefferson and Orange counties, with less in Chambers and Galveston counties. Maximum wind reported in Texas, 85 m.p.h. at Sabine Pass, with gusts to 100 m.p.h.

1985 Weather Extremes

Lowest Temp.—Sterling City, Sterling County, Feb. 2	−13°F
Highest Temp.—Boquillas Ranger Station, Brewster County, May 30	112°F
24-hr. Precip.—San Marcos, Hays County, Nov. 24	9.07″
Monthly Precip.—Alto, Cherokee County, Oct.	16.60″
Least Annual Precip.—Imperial, Pecos County	7.56″
Greatest Annual Precip.—Port Authur, Jefferson County	68.22″

1986 Weather Extremes

Lowest Temp.—Amarillo, Potter County; Perryton, Ochiltree County, Feb. 12+	−12°F
Highest Temp.—Henrietta, Clay County, July 31	113°F
24-hr. Precip.—Matagorda, Matagorda County, Oct. 23	9.80″
Monthly Precip.—McCamey, Upton County, Oct.	21.13″

(Least and Greatest Annual Precipitation for 1986 not available when this section went to press.)

Oct. 28, 1960: **Rainstorm.** Rains of 7-10 inches fell in South Central Texas; 11 died from drowning in flash floods. In Austin about 300 families were driven from their homes. Damage in Austin was estimated at $2.5 million.

Sept. 8-14, 1961: **Hurricane Carla. Port O'Connor;** maximum wind gust at **Port Lavaca** estimated at 175 miles per hour. Highest tide was 18.5 feet at **Port Lavaca.** Most damage was to coastal counties between **Corpus Christi** and **Port Arthur** and inland Jackson, Harris and Wharton counties. In Texas, 34 persons died; seven in a tornado that swept across Galveston Island; 465 persons were injured. Property and crop damage conservatively estimated at $300 million. The evacuation of an estimated 250,000 persons kept loss of life low. Hurricane Carla was the **largest hurricane** of record.

April 3, 1964: **Tornado. Wichita Falls.** Seven killed, 111 injured; damage $15 million; 225 homes destroyed, 50 with major damage, and 200 with minor damage. Sixteen other buildings received major damage.

April 22-29, 1966: **Flooding.** Northeast Texas. Twenty to 26 inches of rain fell in portions of Wood, Smith, Morris, Upshur, Gregg, Marion and Harrison counties. Nineteen persons drowned in the rampaging rivers and creeks that swept away bridges, roads and dams, and caused an estimated $12 million damage.

April 28, 1966: **Dallas County. Flash flooding** from torrential rains in Dallas County resulted in 14 persons drowned and property losses estimated at $15 million.

Sept. 18-23, 1967: **Hurricane Beulah.** Near **Brownsville.** The third largest hurricane of record, Hurricane Beulah moved inland near the mouth of the Rio Grande on the 20th. Wind gusts of 136 miles per hour were reported during Beulah's passage. Rains 10 to 20 inches over much of the area south of San Antonio resulted in record-breaking floods. An unofficial gaging station at Falfurrias registered the highest accumulated rainfall, 36 inches. The resultant stream overflow and surface runoff inundated 1.4 million acres. Beulah spawned 115 tornadoes, all in Texas; the greatest number on record

Extreme Texas Weather Records

NOAA Environmental Data Service lists the following recorded extremes of weather in Texas:

TEMPERATURE

Lowest—Tulia, February 12, 1899		−23° F
Seminole, February 8, 1933.		−23° F
Highest—Seymour, August 12, 1936.		120° F
Coldest Winter		1898-1899

RAINFALL

Wettest year—entire state	1941	42.62 in.
Driest year—entire state	1917	14.30 in.
Greatest annual—Clarksville	1873	109.38 in.
Least annual—Wink	1956	1.76 in.
†Greatest in 24 hours—Thrall September 9-10, 1921		38.20 in.

SNOWFALL

Greatest seasonal—Romero 1923-1924.	65.0 in.
Greatest monthly—Hale Center February, 1956	36.0 in.
Greatest single storm—Hale Center Feb. 2-5, 1956	33.0 in.
Greatest in 24 Hours—Plainview Feb. 3-4, 1956	24.0 in.
Maximum depth on ground—Hale Center Feb. 5, 1956	33.0 in.

WIND VELOCITY

Highest sustained wind (fastest mile)		
*Matagorda—Sept. 11, 1961	SE	145 mph
*Port Lavaca—Sept. 11, 1961	NE	145 mph
Highest peak gust (instantaneous velocity)		
*Aransas Pass—Aug. 3, 1970 (est.)	SW	180 mph
*Robstown—Aug. 3, 1970 (est.)	WSW	180 mph

*These velocities occurred during hurricanes. Theoretically, much higher velocities are possible within the vortex of a tornado, but no measurement with an anemometer has ever been made. The U.S. Weather Bureau's experimental Doppler radar equipment, a device which permits direct measurement of the high speeds in a spinning tornado funnel, received its first big test in the Wichita Falls tornado of April 2, 1958. This was the first tornado tracked by the Doppler radar, and for the first time in history, rotating winds up to 280 mph were clocked.

†Greatest 24-hour rainfall ever recorded in Texas at an official observing site occurred at Albany (Shackelford County) on Aug. 4, 1978 — 29.05 inches.

for any hurricane. Hurricane Beulah caused 13 deaths and 37 injuries, of which five deaths and 34 injuries were attributed to tornadoes. Property losses were estimated at $100 million and crop losses at $50 million.

April 18, 1970: **Tornado.** Near **Clarendon**, Donley County. Seventeen killed, 42 injured; damage $2,100,000. Fourteen persons were killed at a resort community at Green Belt Reservoir, 7½ miles north of Clarendon.

May 11, 1970: **Tornado. Lubbock**, Lubbock County. Twenty-six killed, 500 injured; damage $135 million. Fifteen square miles, almost one-quarter of the city of Lubbock, suffered damage.

Aug. 3-5, 1970: **Hurricane Celia. Corpus Christi.** Hurricane Celia was a unique but severe storm. Measured in dollars, it was the costliest in the state's history to that time. Sustained wind speeds reached 130 miles per hour, but it was great bursts of kinetic energy of short duration that appeared to cause the severe damage. Wind gusts of 161 miles per hour were measured at the Corpus Christi National Weather Service Office. At Aransas Pass, peak wind gusts were estimated as high as 180 miles per hour, after the wind equipment had been blown away. Celia caused 11 deaths in Texas, at least 466 injuries, and total property and crop damage in Texas estimated at $453,773,000. Hurricane Celia crossed the Texas coastline midway between Corpus Christi and Aransas Pass about 3:30 p.m. CST on Aug. 3. Hardest hit was the metropolitan area of Corpus Christi, including Robstown, Aransas Pass, Port Aransas and small towns on the north side of Corpus Christi Bay.

June 12-13, 1973: **Rainstorm.** Southeastern Texas. Ten drowned. Over $50 million in property and crop damage. From 10-15 inches of rain recorded.

Nov. 23-24, 1974: **Flash Flooding.** Central Texas. Over $1 million in property damage. Thirteen people killed, ten in Travis County.

June 15, 1976: **Rainstorm.** Harris County. Rains in excess of 13 inches caused damage estimated at near $25 million. Eight deaths were storm-related, including three drownings.

Aug. 1-4, 1978: **Heavy Rains, Flooding.** Edwards Plateau, Low Rolling Plains. Remnants of **Tropical Storm Amelia** caused some of the worst flooding of this century. As much as 30 inches of rain fell near **Albany** in Shackelford County, where six drownings were reported. **Bandera, Kerr, Kendall** and **Gillespie counties** were hit hard, as 27 people drowned and the damage total was at least $50 million.

Dec. 30-31, 1978: **Ice Storm.** North Central Texas. Possibly the **worst ice storm** in 30 years hit Dallas County particularly hard. Damage estimates reached $14 million, and six deaths were storm-related.

April 10, 1979: The worst single **tornado** in Texas' history hit **Wichita Falls.** Earlier on the same day, several tornadoes hit farther west. The destruction in Wichita Falls resulted in 42 dead, 1,740 injured, over 3,000 homes destroyed and damage of approximately $400 million. An estimated 20,000 persons were left homeless by this storm.

In all, the tornadoes on April 10 killed 53 people, injured 1,812 and caused over $500 million damages.

May 24-25, 1981: Severe **flooding** in Austin claimed 13 lives, injured about 100 and caused $40 million in damages. Up to 5.5 inches of rain fell in one hour just west of the city.

April 2, 1982: A **tornado** outbreak in Northeast Texas. The most severe **tornado struck Paris;** 10 people were killed, 170 injured and 1,000 left homeless. Over $50 million in damages resulted. A total of 7 tornadoes that day left 11 dead and 174 injured.

Aug. 15-21, 1983: **Hurricane Alicia** was the first hurricane to make landfall in the continental U.S. in three years (Aug. 18), and one of the costliest in Texas history ($3 billion). Alicia caused widespread damage to a large section of Southeast Texas, including coastal areas near **Galveston** and the entire **Houston** area. Alicia spawned 22 tornadoes, and highest winds were estimated near 130 mph. In all, 18 people in South Texas were killed and 1,800 injured as a result of the tropical storm.

Storms in 1985 and 1986 can be found in Weather Highlights for those years.

Meteorological Data

Source: NOAA, Environmental Data Service, Local Climatological Data.

Additional data for these locations are listed in the table of Texas temperature, freeze, growing season, and precipitation records, by counties.

	Temperature						Precipitation					Relative Humidity		Wind			
	Record Highest	Month and Yr.	Record Lowest	Month and Yr.	No. Days Max. 90° and Above	No. Days Min. 32° and Below	Maximum in 24 Hours	Month and Year	Snowfall Mean Annual	Max. Snowfall in 24 Hours	Month and Year	6:00 A.M. CST	Noon CST	Speed, MPH Mean Annual	Highest Miles Per Hour	Month and Year	Percent Possible Sunshine
Abilene	111	8-43	−9	1-47	96	55	6.78	5-08	4.9	8.0	†1-19	74	50	12.2	109	6-51	71
Amarillo	108	6-53	−16	2-99	65	110	6.75	5-51	14.9	20.6	3-34	72	45	13.7	84	5-49	73
Austin	109	†7-54	−2	1-49	104	23	19.03	9-21	1.1	9.7	11-37	83	56	9.3	57	2-47	61
Brownsville	106	3-84	12	2-99	117	2	12.19	9-67	‡‡	‡‡	†11-76	88	60	11.6	106	9-33	61
Corpus Christi	105	7-34	11	2-99	102	7	8.92	8-80	0.1	5.0	1-97	90	63	12.0	161	8-70	63
Dallas-Fort Worth	113	6-80	−8	†2-99	95	41	9.57	9-32	3.2	12.1	1-64	82	56	10.8	77	7-36	66
Del Rio	111	†7-60	11	2-51	125	16	8.88	6-35	0.9	8.6	1-85	79	54	9.9	62	3-35	70
El Paso	112	7-79	−8	1-62	106	62	6.50	7-1881	5.4	8.8	4-83	55	35	9.2	70	†5-50	83
Galveston	101	7-32	8	2-99	12	4	14.35	7-00	0.2	15.4	2-95	83	72	11.0	*100	9-00	63
***Houston	108	8-09	5	†1-40	92	24	15.65	8-45	0.4	4.4	2-60	91	60	7.8	84	3-26	56
Lubbock	109	†7-40	−17	2-33	79	96	5.82	10-83	10.5	16.3	1-83	74	46	12.5	70	5-52	73
Midland-Odessa	109	6-51	−11	2-85	97	63	5.99	7-61	4.1	6.8	1-74	73	42	11.1	67	2-60	75
Prt. Arthur-Beaumont	107	8-62	11	1-30	82	17	17.76	7-43	0.4	††20.0	2-95	91	64	10.0	91	8-40	58
San Angelo	111	†7-60	−1	2-85	108	53	11.75	9-36	3.3	7.4	1-78	78	49	10.5	75	4-69	70
San Antonio	107	8-09	0	1-49	111	23	7.28	9-73	0.8	13.2	1-85	83	55	9.4	74	8-42	60
Victoria	110	7-39	9	1-30	102	13	9.30	6-77	0.2	2.1	1-85	89	60	10.0	§150	9-61	62
Waco	112	8-69	−5	1-49	106	35	7.18	5-53	1.5	7.0	1-49	83	57	11.3	69	6-61	63
Wichita Falls	117	6-80	−12	1-47	107	69	6.22	9-80	6.0	8.1	1-85	82	51	11.7	92	6-45	68
**Shreveport, La.	110	8-09	−5	2-99	88	37	7.17	4-53	1.3	5.6	1-82	87	58	8.6	52	4-75	63

*100 mph recorded at 6:15 p.m. Sept. 8 just before anemometer blew away. Maximum velocity estimated 120 mph from NE between 7:30 p.m. and 8:30 p.m.

†Also recorded on earlier dates, months or years.

‡Anemometer damaged.

§Highest sustained wind estimated 110 mph. Highest gust estimated 150 mph at 5:55 p.m., Sept. 11, 1961.

**This station is included because it is near the boundary line and its data can be considered representative of the eastern border of Texas.

††Measured at Orange, Texas, near Port Arthur.

‡‡Trace, an amount too small to measure.

***The official Houston station was moved from near downtown to Intercontinental Airport, located 12 miles north of the old station.

Number Texas Tornadoes 1951-1986

Source: State Climatologist for Texas

Year	Jan.	Feb.	Mar.	April	May	June	July	Aug.	Sept.	Oct.	Nov.	Dec.	Annual
1951 ..	0	0	1	1	5	7	1	0	0	0	0	0	15
1952 ..	0	1	3	4	2	1	0	1	0	0	0	1	13
1953 ..	0	2	2	3	6	2	3	5	0	2	1	6	32
1954 ..	0	3	1	23	21	14	5	1	4	5	0	0	77
1955 ..	0	0	7	15	42	32	1	5	2	9	2	0	104
1956 ..	0	3	5	3	17	5	6	4	2	9	2	0	56
1957 ..	0	1	21	69	33	5	0	3	2	6	5	0	145
1958 ..	2	0	7	12	15	13	10	7	0	0	8	0	74
1959 ..	0	0	8	4	32	14	10	3	4	5	6	0	86
1960 ..	4	1	0	8	29	14	3	4	2	11	1	0	77
1961 ..	0	1	21	15	24	30	9	2	12	0	10	0	124
1962 ..	0	4	12	9	25	56	12	15	7	2	0	1	143
1963 ..	0	0	3	9	19	24	8	4	6	4	5	0	82
1964 ..	0	1	6	22	15	11	9	7	3	1	3	0	78
1965 ..	2	5	3	7	43	24	2	9	4	6	0	3	108
1966 ..	0	0	4	1	21	22	15	3	8	3	0	0	77
1967 ..	0	2	11	17	34	22	10	5	124	2	0	5	232
1968 ..	2	1	3	13	47	21	4	8	5	8	11	16	139
1969 ..	0	1	1	16	65	16	6	7	6	8	1	0	127
1970 ..	1	3	5	23	23	9	5	20	9	20	0	3	121
1971 ..	0	20	10	24	27	33	7	20	7	16	4	23	191
1972 ..	1	0	19	13	43	12	19	13	8	9	7	0	144
1973 ..	14	1	29	25	21	24	4	8	5	3	9	4	147
1974 ..	2	1	8	19	18	26	3	9	6	22	2	0	116
1975 ..	5	2	9	12	50	18	10	3	3	1	1	1	117
1976 ..	1	1	8	53	63	11	16	6	13	4	0	0	176
1977 ..	0	0	3	34	50	4	5	5	12	0	6	4	123
1978 ..	0	0	0	34	65	10	13	6	6	1	2	0	137
1979 ..	1	2	24	33	39	14	12	10	4	15	3	0	157
1980 ..	2	2	7	26	44	21	2	34	10	5	0	2	153
1981 ..	0	7	7	9	71	26	5	20	5	23	3	0	176
1982 ..	0	0	6	27	123	36	4	0	3	0	3	1	203
1983 ..	5	7	24	1	62	35	4	22	5	0	7	14	186
1984 ..	0	13	9	18	19	19	0	4	1	5	2	5	95
1985 ..	0	0	5	41	28	5	3	1	1	3	1	2	90
1986 ..	0	12	4	21	50	24	3	5	4	7	1	0	131
Total .	40	101	293	684	1,292	653	217	284	288	205	104	91	4,252

Tornadoes

An average of 118 tornadoes touch Texas soil each year. The annual total varies considerably, and certain areas are struck more often than others. Tornadoes occur with greatest frequency in the Red River Valley.

While tornadoes may occur in any month, and at any hour of the day, they occur with greatest frequency during the late spring and early summer months, and between the hours of 4 p.m. and 8 p.m. In the period 1951-1986, nearly 62 percent of all Texas tornadoes occurred within the 3-month period of April, May and June. Slightly more than one-fourth of the total occurred in May.

Partly due to the state's size, more tornadoes have been recorded in Texas than in any other state. Between 1951 and 1986, 4,252 funnel clouds reached the ground, thus becoming tornadoes. In the density of tornadoes, Texas ranks eleventh among the 50 states, with an average of 4.4 tornadoes per 10,000 square miles per year during this period.

The greatest outbreak of tornadoes on record in Texas was associated with **Hurricane Beulah** in September, 1967; 115 tornadoes, all in Texas, are known to have occurred with this great hurricane within a 5-day period, Sept. 19-23. Sixty-seven occurred on Sept. 20, a Texas record for a single day. As a result of Hurricane Beulah, September 1967, had 124 tornadoes, a Texas record for a single month. The greatest number in Texas in a single year was 232, also in 1967. The second-highest number in a single year was in 1982, when 203 tornadoes occurred in Texas, 123 of them in May, making it the worst outbreak of spring tornadoes in Texas.

An accompanying table, compiled by Environmental Data Service, National Oceanic and Atmospheric Administration, lists tornado occurrences in Texas, by months, for the period 1951-1986.

Texas Droughts, 1892-1986

The following table shows the duration and extent of Texas droughts by major areas, 1892-1986. For this purpose, droughts are arbitrarily defined as when the division has less than 75 per cent of the 1931-1960 average precipitation. The 1931-60 average precipitation is shown at the bottom of the table for each area, in inches. A short table which follows shows the frequency of droughts in each area and the total years of droughts in the area. No climatic subdivision has had less than 75 percent of average rainfall since 1964, except the High Plains, the Low Rolling Plains and the Edwards Plateau in 1970.

Year	High Plains	Low Rolling Plains	North Central	East Texas	Trans-Pecos	Edwards Plateau	South Central	Upper Coast	Southern	Lower Valley
1892 ..				68				73		
1893 ..			67	70		49	56	64	53	59
1894 ..				68						
1897 ..								73	72	
1898 ..									69	51
1901 ..		71	70				60	62	70	44
1902 ..									65	73
1907 ..										65
1909 ..			72	68	67	74	70			
1910 ..	59	59	64	69	43	65	69	74	59	
1911 ..										70
1916 ..		73		74	70		73	69		
1917 ..	58	50	63	59	44	46	42	50	32	48
1920 ..									71	
1921 ..				72						73
1922 ..				68						
1924 ..		73	73			71		72		
1925 ..		72						72		
1927 ..									74	74
1933 ..	72				62	68				
1934 ..	66				46	69				
1937 ..									72	
1939 ..										72
1943 ..			72							
1948 ..			73	74	62		73	67		
1950 ..							68		74	64
1951 ..					61	53				
1952 ..	68	66			73				56	70
1953 ..	69				49	73				
1954 ..	70	71	68	73		50	50	57	71	
1956 ..	51	57	61	68	44	43	55	62	53	53
1962 ..				68			67			65
1963 ..			63	68			65	61	73	
1964 ..	74						69			63
1970 ..	65	63					72			

1931-1960 Normal (inches) — 18.51, 22.99, 32.93, 45.96, 12.03, 25.91, 33.24, 46.19, 22.33, 24.27.

1941-1970 Normal (inches) — 18.59, 23.18, 32.94, 45.37, 11.57, 23.94, 33.03, 46.43, 21.95, 23.44.

1951-1980 Normal (inches) — 17.73, 22.80, 32.14, 44.65, 11.65, 23.52, 34.03, 45.93, 22.91, 24.73.

DROUGHT FREQUENCY

This table shows the number of years of drought and the number of separate droughts. For example, the High Plains has had 10 drought years, consisting of five 1-year droughts, one 2-year drought and one 3-year drought, for a total of seven droughts.

Years	High Plains	Low Rolling Plains	North Central	East Texas	Trans-Pecos	Edwards Plateau	South Central	Upper Coast	Southern	Lower Valley
1	5	6	8	6	5	7	10	8	9	13
2	1	1	2	2	4	4	2	2	2	1
3	1				1					
Total Droughts .	7	7	10	8	10	11	12	10	11	14
Drought Years	10	8	12	10	16	15	14	12	13	15

Texas Annual Average Precipitation, 1892-1986

Source: State Climatologist for Texas

Year—	Inches	Year—	Inches
1892.	26.32	1940.	32.70
1893.	18.50	**1941	42.62
1894.	25.61	1942.	30.68
1895.	29.83	1943.	24.28
1896.	25.15	1944.	34.08
1897.	24.21	1945.	30.06
1898.	24.56	1946.	35.16
1899.	27.57	1947.	24.75
1900.	36.87	1948.	21.79
1901.	20.13	1949.	35.08
1902.	28.28	1950.	24.48
1903.	29.64	1951.	21.99
1904.	26.78	1952.	23.27
1905.	35.98	1953.	24.76
1906.	29.19	1954.	19.03
1907.	28.51	1955.	23.59
1908.	29.06	1956.	16.17
1909.	21.58	1957.	36.93
1910.	19.52	1958.	32.71
1911.	26.83	1959.	31.29
1912.	24.92	1960.	33.78
1913.	33.25	1961.	30.20
1914.	35.19	1962.	24.05
1915.	28.79	1963.	20.95
1916.	23.05	1964.	24.11
*1917	14.30	1965.	27.55
1918.	26.03	1966.	28.68
1919.	42.15	1967.	28.44
1920.	29.90	1968.	34.54
1921.	25.18	1969.	29.85
1922.	29.83	1970.	26.36
1923.	37.24	1971.	29.58
1924.	22.32	1972.	28.73
1925.	25.37	1973.	38.37
1926.	32.97	1974.	32.78
1927.	24.32	1975.	29.07
1928.	27.56	1976.	33.37
1929.	29.47	1977.	24.04
1930.	28.44	1978.	27.00
1931.	28.37	1979.	31.43
1932.	32.76	1980.	24.49
1933.	26.15	1981.	32.65
1934.	25.59	1982.	26.97
1935.	35.80	1983.	25.75
1936.	30.32	1984.	26.08
1937.	25.89	1985.	29.97
1938.	25.35	1986.	34.11
1939.	23.52		

95-year mean 28.17 inches.
*Driest year, 1917.
**Wettest year, 1941.

Texas Weather

Mark Twain's observation that many people talk about the weather, but few do much about it, really applies to Texas weather. One common joke is that if you don't like Texas weather, wait a few minutes and it will change.

Two entertaining and informative books on Texas weather have been published in recent years. They are listed below.

FOR FURTHER READING—
Bomar, George W., **Texas Weather;** University of Texas Press, Austin, 1983.
Weems, John Edward, **"If You Don't Like the Weather. . .";** Texas Monthly Press, Austin, 1986.

How Cold Does It Feel?

Many factors enter into the feeling of coolness or extreme cold, the temperature and wind speed being most important. The following simplified table is based upon more complex "Wind-Chill" indexes available from the National Oceanic and Atmospheric Administration (National Weather Service).

Thermometer readings are listed in the figures across the top of the chart; the wind speeds are shown down the left side. To determine how chilly it really feels, get the proper column for each. Note the figure where they cross.

Thus, a 20-degree temperature with a 20-mile-an-hour wind is equal in chill to 1.8 degrees above zero. A temperature of 10 degrees with a 15 mph wind is equal to 5.3 degrees below.

A 10-mile-an-hour wind sets twigs dancing in the trees. A 25-mile-an-hour wind sets big branches moving, and if the temperature is even cool, it sets teeth chattering.

A chill effect of anything below 25 below zero creates the danger of freezing for persons not properly clothed.

Windchill Chart

ACTUAL THERMOMETER READING(°F)

Estimated Wind Speed MPH	50	40	30	20	10	0	—10
			APPARENT TEMPERATURE (°F)				
Calm	50	40	30	20	10	0	—10
5	48.3	38.0	27.8	17.5	7.1	—3.2	—13.5
10	44.6	33.5	22.5	11.5	0.5	—10.5	—21.4
15	41.3	29.6	18.0	6.3	—5.3	—16.7	—28.1
20	38.5	26.2	14.0	1.8	—10.4	—22.3	—34.2
25	36.1	23.3	10.6	—2.1	—14.8	—27.2	—39.5
30	34.1	20.9	7.8	—5.3	—18.3	—31.0	—43.7
40	30.9	17.1	3.2	—10.6	—24.0	—37.4	—50.7

The table above was devised by Dr. Robert G. Steadman, Texas Tech University, and was furnished to the Texas Almanac by the National Oceanic and Atmospheric Administration.

How Hot Does It Feel?

In the 40-year period from 1936 to 1975, nearly 20,000 people were killed in the United States by the effects of excessive heat. The overall effect of excessive heat on the body is known as heat stress. Important factors contributing to heat stress are: (1) air temperature; (2) humidity; (3) air movement; (4) radiant heat from incoming solar radiation (insolation), bright lights, stove or other source; (5) atmospheric pressure; (6) physiological factors which vary among people; (7) physical activity; and (8) clothing.

Of the above factors, temperature and humidity can be controlled by air conditioning. Air movement may be controlled by fans; even a slight breeze is usual-

Heat Discomfort Chart

Actual Thermometer Reading (°F)	RELATIVE HUMIDITY(%)										
	0	10	20	30	40	50	60	70	80	90	100
				APPARENT TEMPERATURE (°F)							
70	64.8	65.6	66.4	67.3	68.1	68.8	69.6	70.4	71.1	71.8	72.5
75	70.1	71.2	72.1	73.0	73.7	74.6	75.3	76.1	77.1	78.2	79.2
80	75.6	76.6	77.5	78.4	79.4	80.5	81.7	83.0	84.7	86.4	88.3
85	79.9	81.0	82.2	83.6	85.0	86.7	88.7	91.0	93.7	96.8	100.6
90	84.0	85.5	87.1	89.0	91.2	94.1	97.0	101.0	105.4	110.8	
95	88.0	90.0	92.4	95.3	98.4	102.6	107.4	113.9			
100	91.8	94.6	97.8	101.7	106.6	112.7	120.4				

	RELATIVE HUMIDITY (%)										
	0	5	10	15	20	25	30	35	40	45	50
105	95.8	97.5	99.4	101.5	103.8	106.4	109.3	112.4	116.5	121.1	126.0
110	99.7	101.9	104.2	107.0	110.3	113.8	118.0	121.8	128.6		
115	103.6	106.4	109.6	113.3	117.6	122.6	128.4				
120	107.4	111.1	115.2	120.1	125.7	132.2					

The table above was devised by Dr. Robert G. Steadman, Texas Tech University, and was furnished to the Texas Almanac by NOAA.

ly effective in reducing heat stress in hot, muggy weather. However, at very high temperatures (above normal body temperature of about 98.6° F.), winds above 10 miles per hour can increase heat stress in a shaded area by adding more heat to the body, whereas when the body is exposed to direct sunlight the effect of wind is nearly always to reduce heat stress. Radiant heating can be mitigated by shielding or by moving away from the source (for example, seeking shade). Atmospheric pressure is not usually a significant factor; however, at very high elevations, decreased pressure (and therefore decreased air supply) can contribute to heat exhaustion.

General Heat Stress Index

Danger Category	Apparent Temperature (°F)	Heat Syndrome
1. Caution	80°-90°	Fatigue possible with prolonged exposure and physical activity.
2. Extreme Caution	90°-105°	Sunstroke, heat cramps and heat exhaustion possible with prolonged exposure and physical activity.
3. Danger	105°-130°	Sunstroke, heat cramps or heat exhaustion likely. Heatstroke possible with prolonged exposure and physical activity.
4. Extreme Danger	Greater Than 130°	Heatstroke or sunstroke imminent.

NOTE: Degree of heat stress may vary with age, health and body characteristics.

Texas' Record Cold Wave

The "Winter of '99" was long remembered by Texans. It brought the most intense cold wave on record throughout the state on Feb. 11-12-13, 1899.

Minimum temperatures ranged from 6 to 23 degrees below zero over the northern portion of the state to about 12 above over the southern portion. Lowest temperatures occurred on the morning of Feb. 12 except at a few locations where the minimum was observed the next day. The Weather Bureau Office at Galveston recorded a temperature of 7.5 degrees, the lowest of record since the opening of this station in 1871. The next morning, Galveston Bay was covered over with thin ice except in the main channel or tide current. The lowest temperature ever recorded in Texas (−23 degrees) occurred at Tulia on Feb. 12 — a record which was later equalled at Seminole on Feb. 8, 1933.

Winter weather hit Texas early in February, 1899. Cold Polar Canadian air entered Texas Feb. 4, reaching Central Texas on Feb. 6. Temperatures moderated a little, in advance of a second surge of cold air that entered the Texas Panhandle during the early morning of Feb. 8. As this mass of cold air reached Brownsville at about 6 a.m. on Feb. 10, the third and most frigid mass of Polar Canadian air was poised over Alberta and Saskatchewan ready to plunge southward. This chilling outbreak reached Texas very early in the morning of Feb. 11, and by 7 a.m. the next day, was centered over portions of Northwest Texas, Oklahoma and Kansas. By now, the leading edge of the air mass had plunged as far south as the Isthmus of Tehuantepec in southern Mexico. By Feb. 13, the air mass was centered over the Texas coast, while the cold front (the leading edge of the air mass) had reached San Salvador in Central America. The highest barometric pressure (reduced to sea level) recorded in Texas during the cold wave was 31.06 inches of mercury (1051.8 millibars) at Abilene. At Galveston, the highest barometric pressure recorded was 30.73 inches (1040.6 millibars).

Precipitation (Inches) 1985

	High Plains	Low Rolling Plains	North Central	East Texas	Trans-Pecos	Edwards Plateau	South Central	Upper Coast	Southern	Lower Valley
Jan	0.57	0.50	1.33	2.77	0.84	1.28	2.71	3.28	2.06	1.63
Feb	0.99	1.81	2.32	4.32	0.51	1.19	2.68	4.90	1.35	1.42
Mar	1.93	2.63	3.83	3.92	0.52	1.89	2.95	6.34	2.00	1.03
Apr	1.62	2.82	3.42	3.65	0.29	1.46	3.76	3.09	3.64	1.25
May	2.41	2.56	3.31	3.41	0.88	2.85	2.64	2.07	4.05	3.95
Jun	4.50	5.06	4.20	1.94	1.90	3.28	4.73	4.78	4.03	3.65
July	1.99	2.16	1.93	3.48	1.60	1.82	2.05	3.98	1.57	1.61
Aug	1.60	1.29	0.59	1.03	1.29	0.67	0.53	2.82	0.41	1.36
Sept	4.91	3.32	3.52	3.14	3.24	3.56	5.32	6.02	3.17	5.56
Oct	3.97	3.96	6.02	8.02	1.63	3.13	4.37	5.79	5.26	2.71
Nov	0.33	0.72	3.04	6.92	0.28	1.43	5.66	3.65	2.04	0.67
Dec	0.20	0.18	1.61	3.72	0.01	0.40	1.18	2.67	0.26	0.94
Ann	25.02	27.01	35.12	46.32	12.99	22.96	38.58	49.39	29.84	25.78

Precipitation (Inches) 1986

	High Plains	Low Rolling Plains	North Central	East Texas	Trans-Pecos	Edwards Plateau	South Central	Upper Coast	Southern	Lower Valley
Jan	0.01	0.01	0.14	0.62	0.40	0.52	1.36	1.52	1.08	0.69
Feb	0.87	1.25	1.33	3.46	0.32	1.17	1.54	2.02	0.76	1.42
Mar	0.29	0.50	1.00	1.02	0.14	0.35	0.96	1.41	0.24	0.25
Apr	0.66	1.61	3.28	5.34	0.27	0.78	0.99	1.60	1.37	0.82
May	2.86	3.94	6.64	6.92	1.21	5.05	6.39	5.94	3.94	4.19
Jun	4.52	3.95	6.14	7.55	3.76	4.57	5.11	8.13	3.56	3.16
July	1.67	2.23	1.31	1.00	1.56	0.78	0.20	1.00	0.35	0.50
Aug	4.46	3.86	2.22	2.69	3.17	2.89	2.65	3.48	0.81	1.50
Sept	3.72	5.11	4.92	4.47	2.43	4.09	4.16	5.09	2.32	1.99
Oct	3.45	6.90	5.06	5.01	4.02	7.59	6.58	9.60	6.01	2.88
Nov	2.06	1.99	3.50	6.41	1.02	1.71	3.02	7.71	1.41	3.67
Dec	1.42	1.46	3.24	4.73	2.41	3.63	5.79	6.31	3.73	3.93
Ann	25.99	32.81	40.92	49.22	20.71	33.13	38.75	53.81	25.58	25.00

Temperatures 1985

	High Plains	Low Rolling Plains	North Central	East Texas	Trans-Pecos	Edwards Plateau	South Central	Upper Coast	Southern	Lower Valley
Jan	34.1	37.0	38.8	40.1	40.9	41.2	45.6	47.0	47.9	52.9
Feb	38.5	41.9	44.2	45.8	47.0	46.7	50.9	50.8	53.7	57.4
Mar	51.1	55.9	59.9	61.8	58.9	60.2	65.5	65.1	67.7	70.7
Apr	61.1	65.2	66.9	67.2	66.4	68.0	70.5	70.7	73.3	75.2
May	68.8	73.4	73.5	72.7	74.9	75.6	76.5	76.7	79.0	79.8
Jun	74.1	77.7	79.1	79.6	78.6	78.7	80.9	81.1	81.9	82.7
July	78.9	81.8	82.9	82.1	80.1	81.0	82.6	82.0	84.0	83.2
Aug	79.8	84.4	86.1	84.6	81.5	84.4	85.8	84.3	87.3	85.4
Sept	70.3	74.9	77.5	77.3	74.3	76.9	80.4	79.8	83.0	83.3
Oct	58.6	63.6	67.2	68.6	64.4	67.8	72.2	72.5	74.2	76.5
Nov	46.9	51.0	56.8	60.6	57.1	59.9	65.3	67.1	67.6	72.5
Dec	36.1	39.4	42.7	44.2	45.3	44.8	50.5	51.7	52.6	58.9
Ann	58.2	62.2	64.6	65.4	64.1	65.4	68.9	69.1	71.0	73.2

Temperatures 1986

	High Plains	Low Rolling Plains	North Central	East Texas	Trans-Pecos	Edwards Plateau	South Central	Upper Coast	Southern	Lower Valley
Jan	43.3	46.3	48.6	49.2	47.6	48.7	54.3	54.9	56.0	60.1
Feb	43.1	49.1	52.4	54.6	53.7	54.7	58.9	59.8	61.7	65.1
Mar	53.9	58.4	59.8	59.5	59.1	60.9	63.4	63.3	66.6	69.4
Apr	61.9	66.7	67.6	67.2	70.0	71.3	72.4	71.6	77.0	77.7
May	67.3	72.0	71.8	71.9	73.3	73.8	74.8	75.6	78.3	79.5
Jun	74.1	78.3	79.5	79.7	77.8	78.8	81.2	81.4	82.7	83.7
July	80.2	84.0	85.0	84.2	80.3	83.1	84.6	84.5	86.4	85.6
Aug	76.6	81.3	82.6	81.8	79.6	81.9	83.8	83.2	86.5	85.6
Sept	70.5	75.0	79.2	79.3	75.1	78.5	81.9	82.0	84.5	84.5
Oct	57.4	62.0	65.3	65.8	63.5	65.0	69.5	70.3	72.4	76.5
Nov	45.3	49.5	52.8	55.9	52.5	54.6	60.7	62.9	61.8	66.3
Dec	38.7	42.7	45.4	46.7	44.4	46.7	51.7	52.6	53.8	58.5
Ann	59.4	63.8	65.8	66.3	64.7	66.5	69.8	70.2	72.3	74.4

TEXAS TEMPERATURE, FREEZE, GROWING SEASON AND PRECIPITATION RECORDS, BY COUNTIES

Data in the table below are from the office of the State Climatologist for Texas, College Station. Because of the small change in averages, data are revised only at intervals of several years. Data below are the latest compilations, as of Jan. 1, 1987.

Table shows temperature, freeze, growing season and precipitation for each county in Texas. Data for counties where a National Weather Service Station has not been maintained long enough to establish a reliable mean are interpolated from isoline charts prepared from mean values from stations with long-established records. Mean maximum temperature for July is computed from the sum of the daily maxima. Mean minimum January is computed from the sum of the daily minima. Mean monthly temperature for July is the sum of mean maximum and mean minimum (for July) divided by 2. For stations where precipitation "Length of Record" has been left blank, data are based on the 30-year normal period 1941-70. Stations which have a specified precipitation "Length of Record" are based on data mainly from the period 1931-60.

County and Station	Temperature — tLength of record (Yr.)	Mean Max. July (°F.)	Mean Min. January (°F.)	Record Highest (°F.)	Record Lowest (°F.)	Avg. Freeze — Last in Spring	First in Fall	Growing Season (Days)	Precip. tLength of Record (Yr.)	Jan. (In.)	Feb. (In.)	Mar. (In.)	Apr. (In.)	May (In.)	June (In.)	July (In.)	Aug. (In.)	Sept. (In.)	Oct. (In.)	Nov. (In.)	Dec. (In.)	Annual (In.)
Anderson, Palestine	82	94	37	114	-6	Mar. 8	Nov. 27	264	—	3.32	3.16	3.42	4.31	5.09	3.36	1.96	2.51	3.34	3.16	3.26	3.62	40.51
†Andrews, Andrews	14	96	30	106	0	Apr. 6	Nov. 13	213	—	0.70	0.49	0.42	0.89	2.15	1.40	1.90	1.50	1.82	2.05	0.44	0.61	14.37
Angelina, Lufkin	65	94	39	110	-2	Mar. 14	Nov. 13	244	—	3.65	3.64	3.48	4.53	5.09	3.24	2.85	3.50	3.24	2.97	3.73	4.04	42.99
Aransas, Rockport	17	92	48	100	10	Feb. 7	Dec. 16	312	14	2.12	2.12	1.87	2.53	3.20	3.00	1.94	3.48	4.80	2.93	1.85	2.35	33.19
†Archer, Archer City	12	98	28	112	4	Mar. 31	Nov. 6	220	31	1.24	1.48	1.87	2.12	4.19	2.87	1.56	2.39	2.39	2.93	1.47	1.49	25.26
†Armstrong, Claude	14	92	19	105	-9	Apr. 5	Nov. 5	213	8	0.68	0.64	0.83	1.45	3.50	2.90	2.40	2.45	1.85	1.85	0.10	1.38	19.98
Atascosa, Poteet	34	97	42	110	-1	Feb. 24	Dec. 3	282	—	1.53	2.12	1.24	2.74	3.44	2.69	1.87	1.83	3.61	2.52	1.61	1.38	26.58
Austin, Sealy	50	95	40	110	9	Feb. 26	Dec. 6	282	—	3.10	3.34	2.49	3.80	4.65	2.49	3.00	2.10	3.88	3.75	3.00	3.51	42.04
Bailey, Muleshoe	48	92	20	105	-21	Apr. 22	Oct. 20	181	—	0.55	0.47	0.53	0.93	2.42	2.65	2.91	2.10	1.99	1.67	0.52	0.55	17.29
†Bandera, Medina	11	94	32	105	9	Mar. 26	Nov. 6	235	10	1.69	1.77	1.68	2.65	3.02	2.35	2.35	2.10	3.70	1.67	1.28	1.88	28.82
Bastrop, Smithville	54	96	40	111	-1	Mar. 6	Nov. 29	268	—	2.54	3.01	2.16	4.12	4.07	3.66	2.18	2.59	4.37	2.94	2.78	2.40	36.82
Baylor, Seymour	20	98	28	120	-14	Apr. 3	Nov. 2	214	—	1.11	1.31	1.40	2.38	3.94	3.40	2.04	2.32	3.11	2.67	1.29	1.15	26.36
Bee, Beeville	78	95	45	111	5	Feb. 22	Dec. 4	285	—	1.67	2.01	1.49	2.57	3.53	2.76	2.33	2.32	4.12	2.51	1.79	1.64	28.90
Bell, Temple	84	96	38	112	-4	Mar. 11	Nov. 24	258	—	2.39	2.82	2.17	3.94	4.87	2.98	1.61	2.10	3.26	2.89	2.44	2.42	34.00
†Bexar, San Antonio	91	94	42	107	0	Mar. 6	Nov. 26	265	—	1.66	2.06	1.54	3.07	4.87	2.79	1.69	2.41	3.71	2.89	1.77	2.42	27.54
Blanco, Blanco	74	96	32	110	-6	Mar. 26	Nov. 15	234	—	2.12	3.05	2.10	3.55	3.98	2.00	1.99	2.21	4.65	3.60	2.09	2.20	34.39
†Borden, Gail	13	96	30	106	-6	Apr. 6	Nov. 6	214	37	0.75	0.75	0.67	1.38	2.85	1.38	2.40	1.70	2.15	2.51	0.78	0.82	18.20
Bosque, Whitney Dam	26	96	36	111	-3	Mar. 23	Nov. 21	243	25	2.43	2.57	2.29	4.08	4.43	3.02	2.62	2.42	2.95	2.51	2.31	2.71	33.20
Bowie, Texarkana Dam	13	95	35	107	-3	Mar. 21	Nov. 11	235	25	4.50	4.65	4.50	4.00	5.00	3.45	3.05	3.05	2.50	2.50	4.30	4.50	47.59
Brazoria, Angleton	61	91	46	105	10	Mar. 5	Nov. 28	268	—	3.66	3.93	3.18	3.31	4.48	5.01	4.96	5.20	5.98	4.02	3.89	4.55	52.17
Brazos, College Station	24	95	42	106	-2	Mar. 1	Nov. 30	274	—	2.56	2.72	2.58	4.15	4.37	3.64	2.56	2.63	4.19	3.02	3.15	3.23	39.21
Brewster, Alpine	45	89	32	106	-1	Mar. 31	Nov. 9	223	—	0.74	0.38	0.35	0.49	1.18	2.72	2.72	2.55	2.23	1.33	0.50	0.52	15.53
Briscoe, Silverton	48	94	28	108	-9	Apr. 6	Nov. 6	214	—	0.72	0.56	0.76	1.18	3.01	3.67	2.62	2.42	2.23	1.67	0.61	0.75	20.50
Brooks, Falfurrias	68	98	48	112	9	Feb. 10	Dec. 10	303	—	1.46	1.68	1.68	1.46	3.16	3.13	1.17	2.40	4.93	1.67	0.98	1.16	24.18
Brown, Brownwood	98	98	33	112	-2	Mar. 22	Nov. 19	242	—	1.69	1.88	1.66	3.05	4.23	3.13	1.60	1.48	3.10	2.83	1.38	1.39	27.42
†Burleson, Somerville	11	94	38	105	11	Mar. 1	Dec. 1	275	7	3.00	2.62	2.62	4.20	4.20	3.58	2.75	2.60	2.80	2.80	3.30	3.50	37.45
Burnet, Burnet	81	96	37	114	-4	Mar. 29	Nov. 14	230	—	1.87	2.16	1.91	3.48	3.99	2.61	1.46	2.68	3.61	2.67	1.89	1.91	29.81
Caldwell, Luling	88	96	41	110	-3	Mar. 27	Nov. 29	275	—	1.99	2.62	1.77	3.73	3.56	3.91	2.03	2.08	3.89	2.88	2.38	2.80	32.65
Calhoun, Port Lavaca	35	92	47	107	10	Feb. 19	Dec. 16	300	32	2.50	2.75	2.35	3.45	3.88	3.60	3.60	2.95	4.50	2.88	2.38	1.91	36.83
†Callahan, Putnam	13	96	33	107	3	Mar. 28	Nov. 11	228	—	1.34	1.15	1.30	2.72	3.88	2.68	1.84	1.99	2.73	2.74	1.45	1.10	24.92
Cameron, Harlingen	60	95	51	108	21	Feb. 4	Dec. 12	341	—	1.44	1.37	0.84	1.51	2.99	2.38	1.40	2.55	4.67	2.95	1.47	1.12	25.13
Camp, Pittsburg (near)	14	93	36	109	-10	Mar. 21	Nov. 14	238	33	4.00	3.70	4.40	4.85	5.40	3.25	3.25	2.60	2.60	4.15	4.15	4.45	45.25
†Carson, Panhandle	7	92	21	109	-10	Apr. 17	Oct. 25	191	—	0.61	0.90	0.90	3.20	3.20	3.25	2.82	2.95	1.86	1.90	0.64	0.76	20.92
†Cass, Linden	14	93	31	103	-10	Mar. 19	Nov. 11	237	32	4.40	4.40	4.40	5.00	5.25	3.25	3.25	2.95	2.50	1.90	4.30	4.60	46.90
Castro, Dimmitt	44	93	22	104	-8	Apr. 16	Oct. 26	193	—	0.46	0.47	0.66	1.04	2.17	3.11	2.08	2.08	1.83	1.95	0.53	0.64	17.72
Chambers, Anahuac (near)	44	91	44	110	11	Mar. 1	Nov. 21	261	—	3.94	3.79	2.83	4.15	4.62	4.67	5.87	5.32	5.27	4.04	4.13	4.04	52.84
Cherokee, Rusk	33	94	38	110	-1	Mar. 8	Nov. 21	258	30	3.85	3.79	3.62	4.30	3.00	3.00	1.78	2.80	2.95	3.10	4.70	4.70	44.26
†Childress, Childress	60	98	26	115	-13	Apr. 3	Nov. 6	217	—	0.78	0.82	1.00	1.95	3.54	3.06	1.89	2.06	2.24	3.33	0.70	0.85	20.67
†Clay, Henrietta	98	98	30	116	-6	Mar. 27	Nov. 14	232	—	1.37	1.59	2.07	3.35	4.87	3.73	2.13	2.06	3.57	1.72	1.72	1.61	31.40
†Cochran, Morton	14	92	23	105	-12	Apr. 18	Oct. 24	189	26	0.60	0.39	0.40	0.89	2.45	1.90	2.37	2.00	2.10	1.85	0.30	0.37	15.62

Texas Temperature, Frost, Growing Season and Precipitation Records, by Counties. — (continued.)

County and Station	Temperature — Length of Record (Yr.)	Mean Max. July (°F)	Mean Min. January (°F)	Record Highest (°F)	Record Lowest (°F)	Average Freeze Dates — Last in Spring	Average Freeze Dates — First in Fall	Growing Season (Days)	Precip. — Length of Record (Yr.)	January (In.)	February (In.)	March (In.)	April (In.)	May (In.)	June (In.)	July (In.)	August (In.)	September (In.)	October (In.)	November (In.)	December (In.)	Annual (In.)
‡Coke, Robert Lee	14	97	29	109	−5	Mar. 31	Nov. 12	226	32	0.94	0.92	1.05	1.92	3.45	2.10	2.00	1.38	2.60	2.10	0.90	1.12	20.48
Coleman, Coleman	84	96	34	111	−6	Mar. 26	Nov. 16	235		1.62	1.30	1.26	2.86	4.27	2.89	1.86	2.09	3.35	2.54	1.51	1.27	26.82
Collin, McKinney	59	96	34	118	−7	Mar. 26	Nov. 11	230	25	2.15	2.61	3.16	4.82	5.17	3.68	2.54	2.18	3.99	2.51	2.64	2.15	38.10
Collingsworth, Wellington	16	96	26	110	−4	Apr. 5	Nov. 5	212		0.77	0.84	1.05	2.00	4.30	3.05	2.10	3.14	2.10	2.15	0.63	0.99	22.03
‡Colorado, Columbus	14	86	39	106	13	Mar. 1	Dec. 6	280		2.78	3.55	2.53	4.24	4.58	4.01	2.59	2.47	4.43	3.02	3.02	3.22	41.32
Comal, New Braunfels	89	95	40	110	2	Mar. 6	Nov. 26	265	12	2.13	2.73	1.83	3.00	3.92	3.29	3.00	2.47	3.93	3.50	2.42	2.42	33.19
Comanche, Proctor Reservoir	13	95	32	108	9	Mar. 27	Nov. 20	238		1.90	1.83	1.68	3.12	4.45	2.93	2.09	1.44	2.74	2.73	1.74	1.80	28.45
Concho, Paint Rock	13	96	35	109	8	Mar. 29	Nov. 8	228		1.78	1.07	1.68	2.40	4.76	3.82	2.12	1.93	2.34	2.85	1.09	1.01	22.28
Cooke, Gainesville	85	96	35	114	−12	Mar. 27	Nov. 27	226		2.12	2.29	2.58	3.65	4.62	2.94	2.12	2.34	3.39	3.19	2.05	1.80	33.88
Coryell, Gatesville	59	96	36	112	−6	Mar. 25	Nov. 21	241		2.12	2.73	2.58	4.62	3.68	2.94	1.55	2.09	3.39	3.39	2.17	2.11	32.58
Cottle, Paducah	21	97	29	111	−4	Apr. 1	Nov. 11	219	11	0.76	0.81	1.00	1.96	3.68	3.39	2.13	1.83	2.27	2.46	0.85	0.98	22.12
‡Crane, Crane	14	96	29	112	−5	Mar. 31	Nov. 11	225	11	0.85	0.58	0.46	0.80	1.83	1.50	1.70	1.10	1.65	1.50	0.35	0.65	12.97
Crockett, Ozona	25	94	28	108	8	Mar. 26	Nov. 11	233	50	0.80	0.80	0.44	1.12	1.83	2.00	1.67	1.60	1.60	1.67	0.56	0.72	14.90
Crosby, Crosbyton	64	94	26	110	−14	Apr. 10	Nov. 11	206		0.73	0.71	0.99	1.47	3.33	2.63	1.55	1.82	2.44	2.55	0.82	0.86	21.01
Culberson, Van Horn	33	95	30	107	−7	Apr. 2	Nov. 11	224		0.54	0.29	0.29	0.35	0.59	0.92	1.55	1.52	1.82	0.97	0.54	0.51	10.22
‡Dallam, Dalhart	28	95	21	107	−21	Apr. 23	Oct. 18	178		0.36	0.48	0.73	1.21	2.78	2.28	3.24	2.53	1.48	1.44	0.40	0.45	17.38
Dallas, Dallas	95	96	36	115	−10	Mar. 23	Nov. 13	235		1.96	2.57	3.04	4.72	4.85	3.27	1.80	1.31	3.25	3.18	2.05	2.60	35.94
Dawson, Lamesa	48	95	29	111	−12	Apr. 8	Nov. 6	212		0.65	0.38	0.60	1.00	2.39	1.87	2.39	1.31	2.36	2.05	0.67	0.59	16.09
Deaf Smith, Hereford	44	93	22	107	−17	Apr. 20	Oct. 22	185	22	0.46	0.49	0.60	1.13	2.35	2.86	2.65	2.22	1.63	1.94	0.45	0.59	17.37
Delta, Cooper		96	34			Mar. 25	Nov. 13	233	28	3.40	3.40	3.05	4.80	4.90	4.10	3.05	2.55	3.79	3.22	3.22	3.07	43.67
Denton, Denton	61	96	34	113	−3	Mar. 27	Nov. 8	226		1.57	2.35	2.55	4.24	4.90	3.30	1.88	2.62	3.79	2.52	2.29	2.01	33.29
De Witt, Cuero	22	96	44	109	5	Mar. 3	Nov. 29	270		2.05	2.46	1.52	3.12	4.07	3.28	2.22	2.12	4.25	2.20	2.29	2.08	33.37
‡Dickens, Dickens	12	96	30	110	−9	Apr. 4	Nov. 7	217	11	0.69	0.85	0.79	1.52	3.03	2.60	2.22	2.34	2.53	2.20	0.84	0.91	20.24
Dimmit, Carrizo Springs	49	99	42	114	13	Feb. 19	Dec. 6	290	21	0.86	1.16	0.99	1.91	3.41	2.18	1.21	2.30	3.32	2.52	0.86	0.86	21.50
Donley, Clarendon	20	96	26	117	−11	Apr. 13	Nov. 1	206	21	0.72	0.70	0.70	1.63	3.85	3.00	3.00	2.30	1.95	1.95	0.58	0.90	20.74
‡Duval, Freer	14	97		109	12	Feb. 16	Dec. 11	298	32	1.40	1.35	1.00	1.85	3.05	2.44	1.62	2.11	3.65	2.20	0.99	1.50	23.15
Eastland, Eastland	66	96	32	115	−5	Mar. 27	Nov. 10	229	31	1.58	1.52	1.51	3.09	4.05	2.64	1.80	2.11	2.78	2.94	1.75	1.39	27.09
‡Ector, Penwell	13	96	30	108		Apr. 2	Nov. 6	217	31	0.80	0.55	0.55	0.83	1.85	1.55	1.85	1.80	1.75	2.15	0.40	0.65	13.77
Edwards, Rocksprings	37	94	38	107	−9	Mar. 16	Nov. 21	250	40	0.99	1.12	1.12	1.85	3.13	2.80	1.94	2.44	3.60	2.15	0.80	1.05	21.19
Ellis, Waxahachie	21	96	34	115		Mar. 20	Nov. 21	246		2.02	2.38	2.13	4.36	4.90	3.33	1.53	2.11	1.16	3.11	2.53	2.53	35.95
El Paso, El Paso	98	94	32	112	−8	Mar. 9	Nov. 12	248		0.39	0.42	0.39	0.24	0.32	0.60	1.40	1.16	0.78	0.60	0.32	0.50	7.77
Erath, Dublin	74	96	32	114	−7	Mar. 27	Nov. 19	238		1.89	2.09	2.60	3.68	4.79	2.60	1.47	2.11	2.13	3.08	1.99	1.64	31.24
Falls, Marlin	31	96	38	112	−5	Mar. 13	Nov. 25	257		2.48	2.73	2.60	3.99	4.90	2.22	3.16	2.51	3.18	2.93	2.96	2.81	35.34
Fannin, Bonham	71	94	33	115		Mar. 27	Nov. 10	228		2.42	3.11	3.06	5.26	5.62	4.54	4.54	2.92	2.92	3.19	2.92	3.00	43.62
Fayette, Flatonia	67	94	41	111		Mar. 4	Dec. 4	277		2.11	2.42	1.94	1.86	3.79	3.80	2.09	2.17	4.53	2.88	2.58	2.53	35.67
‡Fisher, Rotan	14	98	31	111	3	Apr. 2	Nov. 6	218		0.89	0.90	0.76	1.60	3.35	2.71	1.91	2.10	2.36	2.35	1.01	1.01	21.21
Floyd, Floydada	36	94	28	109	−9	Apr. 2	Nov. 7	213	25	0.85	1.05	1.25	1.25	4.33	3.35	2.50	2.50	1.78	1.95	0.60	0.88	20.18
Foard, Crowell	28	94	28			Apr. 2	Nov. 7	219		0.96	1.05	2.47	2.12	4.69	2.83	2.31	3.98	4.23	2.71	1.09	1.09	23.93
Fort Bend, Sugar Land	70	94	44	108	16	Feb. 14	Dec. 14	296		3.33	3.33	3.71	4.07	5.25	3.71	3.50	2.60	4.67	4.07	3.20	3.63	45.07
Franklin, Mount Vernon	10	94	35	105	10	Mar. 23	Nov. 12	234	7	3.70	3.58	3.90	4.90	5.25	3.45	3.50	2.60	2.90	3.20	3.90	3.90	44.78
‡Freestone, Fairfield	14	94	36	111	8	Mar. 11	Nov. 29	218	31	3.20	3.59	3.05	3.90	4.90	2.20	2.20	2.04	2.99	2.38	3.35	3.60	38.53
Frio, Dilley	58	98	42	111		Feb. 23	Dec. 2	281	49	1.23	1.59	1.07	1.07	2.40	2.73	1.91	1.90	2.04	2.00	1.99	1.18	23.36
Gaines, Seminole	51	87	26	113	−23	Apr. 11	Dec. 25	210		0.55	0.60	0.60	1.44	2.40	2.63	1.62	4.40	2.00	2.83	0.54	0.54	15.83
Galveston, Galveston	104	87	49	101	8	Jan. 24	Dec. 25	335		3.02	2.63	2.63	2.88	4.05	4.05	2.36	1.68	1.94	2.11	2.11	3.67	42.20
‡Garza, Post	14	95	28	109	0	Apr. 1	Nov. 6	216		0.68	0.65	0.81	1.44	3.06	2.71	1.38	2.60	1.68	1.94	0.74	0.73	18.91
Gillespie, Fredericksburg	67	95	36	109	−5	Apr. 1	Nov. 6	219		1.38	1.81	1.55	2.88	3.33	2.90	1.38	2.60	3.72	3.04	1.54	1.32	27.45

Texas Temperature, Frost, Growing Season and Precipitation Records, by Counties.—(continued.)

County and Station	Temp †Len (Yr.)	Mean Max. July (°F)	Mean Min. Jan. (°F)	Highest Record (°F)	Lowest Record (°F)	Last in Spring	First in Fall	Growing Season (Days)	Precip †Len (Yr.)	Jan. (In.)	Feb. (In.)	March (In.)	April (In.)	May (In.)	June (In.)	July (In.)	August (In.)	September (In.)	October (In.)	November (In.)	December (In.)	Annual (In.)
‡Glasscock, Garden City	12	94	22	110	7	Apr. 2	Nov. 10	222	—	.66	.60	.69	1.24	2.38	1.67	2.04	1.41	1.87	1.80	.64	.81	15.81
Goliad, Goliad	37	94	46	112	7	Feb. 24	Dec. 6	285	—	1.92	2.62	1.78	2.60	5.07	3.15	2.53	2.88	4.22	2.14	2.14	1.95	33.79
Gonzales, Gonzales	11	96	42	104	18	Feb. 28	Dec. 1	276	—	1.93	2.56	1.74	3.61	3.46	1.76	1.76	2.37	4.16	2.76	2.14	2.03	32.07
Gray, Pampa	40	94	23	109	-12	Apr. 15	Oct. 27	195	—	.47	.71	.71	1.83	3.12	3.47	2.74	2.40	1.88	1.97	.58	.69	20.14
Grayson, Sherman	87	96	32	113	-2	Mar. 27	Nov. 9	227	—	1.92	3.03	2.99	4.89	5.76	3.85	2.51	2.63	4.18	3.07	2.68	2.32	39.83
Gregg, Longview	87	96	38	113	-7	Mar. 14	Nov. 16	247	—	3.92	3.75	3.84	5.63	6.07	3.62	3.14	2.51	3.70	3.09	3.84	4.07	47.18
‡Grimes, Anderson	10	96	46	108	4	Mar. 1	Dec. 1	278	—	3.12	3.33	2.76	4.31	4.31	3.44	3.05	2.82	4.10	3.39	3.39	3.36	40.52
Guadalupe, Seguin	47	93	42	110	-8	Mar. 6	Nov. 28	267	—	1.80	2.46	1.77	3.21	3.40	2.94	1.78	2.13	4.09	3.37	2.08	1.64	30.67
Hale, Plainview	77	93	26	108	-11	Apr. 10	Nov. 6	211	—	.71	.60	.75	1.38	2.90	3.03	1.78	1.89	1.76	1.92	.50	.76	19.34
Hall, Memphis	68	98	26	117	-1	Apr. 4	Nov. 4	213	—	.75	.83	.83	1.86	3.82	2.98	1.97	1.96	2.27	1.92	.60	.74	20.53
Hamilton, Hamilton	14	96	34	109	-7	Mar. 27	Nov. 2	239	—	1.82	1.98	1.86	3.53	4.34	2.58	1.42	2.36	3.22	1.85	1.77	1.58	29.61
Hansford, Spearman	63	94	20	111	-22	Apr. 22	Oct. 25	186	—	.56	.72	.93	1.49	3.29	3.35	3.58	2.79	1.94	1.86	.76	.68	22.16
Hardeman, Quanah (near)	111	99	28	119	-9	Mar. 31	Nov. 7	221	—	.77	.93	1.29	2.39	3.92	3.10	2.15	2.11	2.98	2.70	.97	1.01	24.32
Hardin, Kountze	—	93	19	108	5	Mar. 13	Nov. 14	246	—	4.75	4.45	4.45	4.50	5.20	4.25	5.22	2.98	3.75	2.70	4.50	4.60	53.00
Harris, Houston	51	93	45	108	—	Feb. 14	Dec. 11	300	6	3.57	3.54	2.68	3.54	5.10	4.52	4.12	2.17	4.65	4.05	4.03	4.04	48.19
Harrison, Marshall	71	92	37	112	-10	Mar. 16	Nov. 17	245	—	4.16	3.84	4.24	5.27	5.32	4.24	2.55	2.62	3.46	3.14	3.66	4.18	46.19
Hartley, Channing	9	92	20	104	-7	Apr. 22	Oct. 19	180	—	.58	.50	.68	1.35	2.88	2.30	2.55	2.75	1.53	1.60	.62	.66	18.00
Haskell, Haskell	21	96	30	115	-7	Mar. 28	Nov. 15	232	—	.93	1.21	1.10	2.26	3.62	2.73	2.25	2.31	2.65	2.46	1.30	1.07	24.14
Hays, San Marcos	82	96	40	111	-14	Mar. 14	Nov. 23	254	—	2.00	2.93	3.84	3.29	3.68	3.56	1.77	2.31	4.52	3.61	2.23	2.01	33.75
Hemphill, Canadian	65	95	23	112	-6	Apr. 9	Oct. 30	204	64	.62	.70	.90	1.57	4.09	3.05	2.44	2.17	1.84	1.78	.59	.75	20.50
Henderson, Athens	22	97	34	109	18	Mar. 11	Nov. 26	260	24	3.10	3.30	3.25	4.40	5.25	3.20	2.55	1.68	2.85	3.18	3.50	3.80	40.40
Hidalgo, Mission	58	97	49	110	18	Feb. 7	Dec. 8	327	—	1.22	1.13	.68	1.66	2.30	2.51	.81	1.68	3.62	2.62	.94	.73	19.90
Hill, Hillsboro	71	96	36	113	-1	Mar. 19	Nov. 21	247	—	2.16	2.74	2.52	4.36	4.92	3.31	1.80	3.31	3.00	2.62	2.28	2.28	34.47
Hockley, Levelland	35	93	24	109	-16	Apr. 15	Oct. 28	196	—	.61	.47	.52	1.00	2.70	2.10	1.90	1.70	2.25	2.00	.50	.50	16.60
Hood, Granbury	32	96	34	110	-6	Mar. 26	Nov. 13	232	—	2.05	1.89	1.90	3.55	5.20	2.90	2.05	2.17	2.78	3.18	1.95	2.30	31.78
Hopkins, Sulphur Springs	47	95	38	109	-10	Mar. 23	Nov. 16	238	—	2.76	3.47	2.73	5.48	5.75	3.67	2.55	2.57	2.85	4.02	3.45	3.15	45.29
‡Houston, Crockett	21	95	38	114	-7	Mar. 6	Nov. 26	265	—	3.58	3.35	3.25	4.38	4.75	3.37	2.34	2.57	3.71	3.33	3.91	3.61	41.72
Howard, Big Spring	73	93	34	113	-10	Apr. 4	Nov. 7	217	—	.60	.58	.20	1.22	4.75	1.58	1.80	1.71	1.83	.97	.74	.74	15.88
‡Hudspeth, Sierra Blanca	14	93	34	102	-16	Mar. 26	Nov. 12	231	32	.46	.26	.20	.30	.53	.60	2.25	1.30	1.25	.33	.41	.50	7.86
Hunt, Greenville (near)	74	94	34	116	-4	Mar. 21	Nov. 13	237	29	2.36	3.21	3.19	3.55	6.22	3.97	3.04	2.07	3.75	3.20	3.20	2.88	43.08
Hutchinson, Borger	27	93	22	107	-12	Apr. 20	Oct. 24	187	21	.64	.62	.90	1.40	3.35	2.87	2.55	2.62	1.75	1.75	.65	.81	19.91
‡Irion, Mertzon	13	96	32	108	-4	Apr. 27	Nov. 14	232	—	1.08	1.14	.98	2.37	2.92	2.51	1.31	2.01	3.33	2.08	1.04	.83	21.33
Jack, Jacksboro	34	96	32	112	-3	Apr. 1	Nov. 5	218	—	1.64	1.55	2.24	3.76	4.17	3.02	2.32	3.05	3.09	2.91	1.45	1.29	29.78
‡Jackson, Edna	8	93	40	105	18	Feb. 19	Nov. 6	290	—	2.40	2.92	2.24	2.98	4.47	4.37	2.71	3.43	5.20	3.92	2.69	2.46	39.65
Jasper, Jasper	20	93	40	107	6	Mar. 23	Nov. 6	229	—	4.94	4.50	4.17	4.56	6.22	4.37	4.17	3.43	3.63	4.69	4.39	4.69	51.03
Jeff Davis, Mount Locke	40	82	31	97	-10	—	—	—	—	.83	.48	.46	.46	1.49	2.47	3.77	2.62	2.75	1.51	.56	.54	18.74
Jefferson, Port Arthur	31	91	44	107	11	Mar. 11	Nov. 16	250	65	4.06	4.24	3.05	4.19	4.94	4.81	5.89	4.94	5.34	3.45	4.26	4.89	55.07
Jim Hogg, Hebbronville	15	99	47	107	-3	Feb. 15	Dec. 15	303	—	1.35	1.15	1.10	1.70	3.09	2.28	1.88	2.13	4.32	1.90	.92	1.30	20.78
Jim Wells, Alice	22	96	47	107	13	Feb. 18	Dec. 6	289	—	1.33	1.61	.93	1.97	3.09	2.96	1.96	2.52	4.93	2.84	1.30	1.29	27.04
Johnson, Cleburne	68	96	35	114	-2	Mar. 25	Nov. 14	233	—	1.80	2.57	1.87	4.07	4.75	3.33	1.67	2.57	4.35	2.93	1.61	2.04	33.04
Jones, Anson	18	97	30	110	-4	Mar. 31	Nov. 9	223	15	.90	1.28	.92	1.89	4.15	2.96	1.97	1.55	2.55	2.55	.56	1.32	23.37
Karnes, Kenedy	26	96	35	113	—	Feb. 24	Dec. 2	281	25	2.05	1.89	1.58	2.50	4.07	2.99	2.39	2.82	4.32	2.82	4.26	2.20	31.93
Kaufman, Kaufman	76	95	35	113	-3	Mar. 18	Nov. 21	248	—	2.45	3.06	1.80	5.00	3.84	3.45	1.56	2.13	4.35	3.53	2.95	2.93	39.82
Kendall, Boerne	83	95	38	108	-4	Mar. 25	Dec. 18	231	—	1.76	2.49	1.82	2.88	3.84	2.57	1.56	2.50	5.16	3.09	1.76	1.82	30.39
Kenedy, Armstrong	17	95	42	114	14	Feb. 2	Dec. 18	319	14	1.91	1.62	1.62	1.68	3.21	2.18	2.31	2.31	2.50	2.31	1.12	1.49	26.61
Kent, Jayton	14	97	28	110	-2	Apr. 4	Nov. 6	216	8	.84	.93	.79	1.75	3.50	2.38	2.10	2.10	2.25	2.20	.96	.95	20.75

Texas Temperature, Frost, Growing Season and Precipitation Records, by Counties. — (continued.)

County and Station	Temp. †Length of Record (Yr.)	July Mean Max. (°F.)	January Mean Min. (°F.)	Record Highest (°F.)	Record Lowest (°F.)	Last in Spring	First in Fall	Growing Season (Days)	Precip. †Length of Record (Yr.)	Jan. (In.)	Feb. (In.)	Mar. (In.)	Apr. (In.)	May (In.)	June (In.)	July (In.)	Aug. (In.)	Sept. (In.)	Oct. (In.)	Nov. (In.)	Dec. (In.)	Annual (In.)
Kerr, Kerrville	78	94	34	110	-7	Apr. 5	Nov. 7	216		1.57	2.24	1.98	3.08	3.75	2.61	1.66	2.05	4.05	3.54	1.56	1.66	29.75
‡Kimble, Junction	12	97	33	110	-11	Apr. 3	Nov. 3	213		1.24	1.37	1.13	2.22	2.82	2.53	1.71	2.50	2.89	1.90	1.03	0.99	22.33
‡King, Guthrie		97	27	114	-11	Apr. 8	Nov. 8	219		0.89	0.95	0.88	1.88	3.55	2.60	2.25	2.12	2.53	2.25	0.98	1.00	21.60
Kinney, Brackettville	18	96	39	109	8	Mar. 1	Nov. 26	270	26	0.92	1.28	0.92	1.99	2.80	3.09	1.07	1.83	3.16	2.25	0.75	0.79	20.85
Kleberg, Kingsville	26	96	48	108	11	Feb. 5	Dec. 16	314	23	1.50	1.50	0.90	2.05	2.80	2.30	1.38	2.50	3.58	2.45	1.38	1.62	26.50
Knox, Munday	37	98	28	116	-9	Apr. 3	Nov. 6	217		0.95	1.13	1.23	2.43	3.76	2.85	2.33	2.05	2.93	2.52	1.29	1.17	24.64
Lamar, Paris	87	94	33	115	-10	Mar. 25	Nov. 14	235		2.60	3.54	3.61	5.43	5.52	3.90	3.54	2.99	4.13	3.43	3.33	3.15	45.17
Lamb, Littlefield	22	93	24	110	-14	Apr. 16	Oct. 27	194		0.57	0.47	0.47	1.22	2.81	3.07	1.37	1.96	2.55	1.84	0.51	0.51	18.04
Lampasas, Lampasas	83	96	34	112	-12	Apr. 1	Nov. 10	223		1.73	2.14	1.95	3.46	4.21	2.70	1.37	2.30	3.27	2.77	1.95	1.95	29.80
La Salle, Cotulla	26	99	43	116	-7	Feb. 20	Dec. 6	288		1.00	1.40	0.82	2.05	2.87	2.24	1.69	1.80	3.22	2.21	1.06	1.06	20.72
Lavaca, Hallettsville	83	95	44	111	5	Mar. 1	Dec. 6	280		2.38	2.86	2.17	3.36	4.67	3.55	2.35	2.79	4.07	2.89	2.60	2.58	36.27
‡Lee, Lexington	14	96	38	105	2	Mar. 1	Nov. 29	273	17	2.90	2.90	2.40	3.75	4.00	3.65	2.50	2.38	3.22	2.55	3.00	3.00	35.88
Leon, Centerville	36	95	38	111	-3	Mar. 6	Dec. 1	270		3.35	3.39	2.85	4.45	4.56	3.19	1.79	2.65	3.54	3.54	3.24	3.25	39.48
Liberty, Liberty	72	93	40	108	8	Mar. 9	Dec. 19	261		3.91	4.25	2.84	4.29	4.84	4.18	4.60	3.87	4.45	3.97	3.92	4.73	49.75
Limestone, Mexia	70	96	37	112	-2	Mar. 15	Nov. 26	255		2.96	2.99	2.98	4.44	4.87	3.25	1.69	2.10	3.58	2.93	2.81	4.75	37.59
Lipscomb, Follett	40	95	23	110	-12	Apr. 10	Oct. 29	202		0.58	0.87	1.26	1.62	3.43	3.29	3.38	2.57	1.84	1.94	0.77	0.68	22.16
Live Oak, George West		97	45	115		Feb. 20	Dec. 6	289		1.43	1.82	1.74	2.05	3.43	2.50	2.10	2.50	3.72	2.68	1.43	1.43	25.64
Llano, Llano	83	97	34	111	-7	Mar. 29	Nov. 13	229	26	1.37	1.92	1.47	3.16	3.80	2.14	1.20	1.91	3.79	2.57	1.50	1.37	26.20
Loving, Mentone	11	96	29	112	-7	Apr. 2	Nov. 3	222		0.50	0.28	0.24	0.65	1.10	1.10	1.50	1.51	2.19	1.50	1.27	1.37	10.31
Lubbock, Lubbock	61	92	25	109	-17	Apr. 4	Nov. 3	208		0.55	0.50	0.89	1.08	3.17	2.78	2.23	1.87	2.19	2.05	0.49	0.61	18.41
Lynn, Tahoka	47	94	28	109	-15	Apr. 4	Nov. 7	217	14	0.62	0.59	0.81	1.12	3.09	2.33	2.29	1.52	2.35	1.93	0.65	0.58	17.88
McCulloch, Brady	47	96	34	108	-5	Mar. 31	Nov. 12	226		1.36	1.49	1.44	2.59	3.24	2.34	2.05	1.61	3.72	2.34	1.14	1.14	23.46
McLennan, Waco	93	96	36	111	-5	Mar. 16	Nov. 24	253	41	1.87	2.38	2.36	4.02	4.60	2.73	1.47	1.81	3.19	2.55	2.27	2.01	31.26
McMullen, Tilden	17	98	44	114		Mar. 13	Nov. 24	296		1.15	1.04	0.73	2.15	3.60	2.75	1.90	3.60	6.03	2.56	1.80	1.80	27.25
Madison, Madisonville	33	98	37	110	-2	Mar. 5	Dec. 2	272		3.50	3.35	2.98	4.30	4.60	3.50	2.90	2.21	3.25	2.80	3.70	3.90	41.50
Marion, Jefferson		94	36			Mar. 18	Nov. 7	236		3.78	3.74	3.93	5.29	5.09	3.72	2.72	2.43	3.37	3.06	3.73	4.05	44.83
Martin, Lenorah		95	30			Apr. 5	Nov. 9	215	31	0.75	0.64	0.57	1.05	2.35	1.70	2.05	1.50	1.95	1.70	0.70	0.76	15.72
Mason, Mason	19	95	34	109	-11	Apr. 3	Nov. 6	217		1.34	1.65	1.34	2.54	3.64	2.46	1.65	1.61	3.05	2.34	1.26	1.15	24.68
Matagorda, Matagorda	48	88	48	103	11	Feb. 17	Dec. 10	296		3.05	3.04	2.23	2.31	3.82	3.56	1.82	4.49	6.03	3.03	2.97	3.06	42.29
Maverick, Eagle Pass	82	100	40	115	-4	Mar. 5	Dec. 2	285		0.95	1.04	0.73	1.91	3.25	2.47	1.58	2.21	3.13	2.80	0.69	0.74	19.74
Medina, Hondo	72	96	42	112	4	Mar. 6	Nov. 24	263	14	1.67	1.48	1.48	2.77	3.66	2.72	1.65	2.43	3.89	2.87	1.41	1.50	28.43
‡Menard, Menard	14	95	30	109	-11	Mar. 31	Nov. 6	220		1.08	1.14	0.98	2.37	2.92	2.23	1.31	2.02	3.33	2.08	1.04	0.83	21.33
Midland, Midland	21	95	31	113	-11	Apr. 1	Nov. 6	218		0.59	0.56	0.56	0.85	1.92	1.49	1.82	1.52	1.54	1.38	0.49	0.52	13.51
Milam, Cameron	64	97	39	114	-7	Mar. 13	Nov. 24	256		2.49	2.82	2.31	3.22	3.72	2.88	1.24	1.95	3.67	3.03	2.79	2.77	33.87
‡Mills, Goldthwaite	15	87	34	110		Mar. 31	Nov. 16	230		1.63	1.78	1.64	3.20	3.98	2.47	1.32	2.21	3.12	2.80	1.92	1.57	27.52
Mitchell, Colorado City	55	96	30	115	-7	Apr. 3	Nov. 6	217		0.77	0.80	0.87	1.83	3.16	2.09	2.19	2.37	1.98	1.98	1.00	0.94	19.68
Montague, Bowie	20	96	32	112		Mar. 27	Nov. 12	229		1.63	1.88	2.13	3.05	4.70	3.68	2.05	1.75	2.85	2.85	1.75	2.03	29.39
Montgomery, Conroe	55	96	40	109	-18	Mar. 20	Nov. 26	270		3.63	3.64	3.61	4.67	4.86	3.20	3.29	3.61	3.92	3.89	3.89	2.03	45.53
‡Moore, Dumas	36	94	30	109	-4	Apr. 20	Oct. 22	185	35	0.60	0.54	0.78	1.30	2.95	2.45	2.60	2.67	1.55	1.60	0.64	0.70	18.33
‡Morris, Daingerfield (near)	16	94	30	109	-4	Mar. 21	Nov. 12	236	28	3.85	3.85	4.85	4.85	5.35	3.50	3.25	2.62	2.60	4.25	4.25	3.15	46.12
Motley, Matador	28	96	26	112	-4	Apr. 3	Nov. 13	218		0.63	0.67	0.81	1.67	3.30	3.40	2.34	1.86	2.16	2.32	0.76	0.89	20.35
Nacogdoches, Nacogdoches	75	96	36	112	-4	Mar. 15	Nov. 13	243		4.20	3.73	3.92	4.83	5.50	3.97	3.29	2.53	3.78	3.53	3.82	4.68	47.53
Navarro, Corsicana	96	95	36	113	-7	Mar. 13	Nov. 27	259		2.56	2.94	2.81	4.69	5.45	3.00	1.75	2.53	3.20	3.53	2.79	3.77	37.74
Newton, Kirbyville	46	93	40	107	-7	Mar. 23	Nov. 9	228		4.73	4.57	4.69	4.66	5.55	4.31	5.87	4.25	3.24	2.86	4.58	5.96	54.16
Nolan, Roscoe	38	96	30	110	-11	Apr. 2	Nov. 9	221		0.91	0.97	1.05	2.16	3.53	2.35	1.88	2.91	2.51	2.77	1.14	1.02	22.19
Nueces, Corpus Christi	88	94	47	105	11	Feb. 9	Dec. 15	309		1.58	1.95	1.10	2.15	3.17	2.67	1.88	3.20	4.90	2.77	1.63	1.53	28.53

Texas Temperature, Frost, Growing Season and Precipitation Records, by Counties. — (continued.)

County and Station	+Length of Record (Yr.)	July Mean Max (°F.)	January Mean Min (°F.)	Record Highest (°F.)	Record Lowest (°F.)	Last in Spring	First in Fall	*Growing Season (Days)	†Length of Record (Yr.)	Jan (In.)	Feb (In.)	Mar (In.)	Apr (In.)	May (In.)	Jun (In.)	Jul (In.)	Aug (In.)	Sep (In.)	Oct (In.)	Nov (In.)	Dec (In.)	Annual (In.)
‡Ochiltree, Perryton	93	92	18	106	−12	Apr. 18	Oct. 26	191	21	.54	.70	1.09	1.33	3.03	3.05	3.33	2.43	1.90	1.66	.70	.72	20.48
Oldham, Vega	52	92	19	108	−17	Apr. 19	Oct. 21	186		.55	.66	.82	1.29	2.56	3.02	3.17	2.85	1.77	1.54	.56	.75	19.54
‡Orange, Orange	91	91	41	99	19	Mar. 16	Nov. 11	240	18	4.28	4.94	3.47	4.91	4.85	5.04	6.70	5.43	6.76	3.70	4.24	5.60	59.92
Palo Pinto, Mineral Wells	14	96	33	112	9	Mar. 31	Nov. 7	221	21	1.80	2.05	2.00	2.00	5.15	3.20	1.88	2.78	2.75	2.75	1.80	2.05	30.13
Panola, Carthage	24	95	38	108	6	Mar. 16	Nov. 11	240		4.50	4.15	4.20	4.65	5.45	3.40	3.50	2.78	2.75	3.15	4.45	5.10	48.08
Parker, Weatherford	86	96	34	113	−11	Mar. 29	Nov. 9	225	42	1.89	2.39	2.16	4.08	4.90	3.06	1.99	1.94	3.44	3.05	1.72	1.75	32.37
Parmer, Friona	14	96	21	108	−15	Apr. 20	Oct. 20	183		.61	.45	.42	1.08	2.80	2.38	2.55	1.26	1.85	1.85	.52	.63	17.50
Pecos, Fort Stockton	21	93	29	114	−7	Mar. 31	Nov. 10	224		.65	.57	.42	.42	1.57	1.47	1.39	1.47	1.38	1.31	.58	.47	11.85
Polk, Livingston	38	94	39	108	11	Mar. 11	Nov. 16	250		4.04	4.04	3.31	4.78	4.77	3.73	3.73	2.93	3.66	3.66	4.13	4.17	47.19
Potter, Amarillo	83	92	24	108	−16	Apr. 17	Oct. 24	190		.54	.56	.77	1.23	2.83	3.45	2.95	2.93	1.93	1.83	.53	.73	20.28
Presidio, Presidio	48	100	33	117	4	Mar. 20	Nov. 18	238	26	.41	.20	.15	.21	.50	.89	1.24	.89	1.51	.72	.34	.33	8.47
Rains, Emory	13	93	35	110	3	Mar. 21	Nov. 11	242		3.10	3.40	3.60	4.70	5.50	3.60	3.10	3.10	2.85	3.70	3.70	3.65	45.95
Randall, Canyon	21	93	23	107	−14	Apr. 15	Oct. 27	195	7	.62	.52	.67	.57	2.74	3.45	3.01	1.13	1.82	1.62	.55	.72	20.16
Reagan, Big Lake	13	96	36	106	10	Mar. 28	Nov. 11	229		.85	.70	1.08	2.00	2.30	1.80	1.65	1.65	1.75	1.00	.56	.78	14.72
Real, Prade Ranch	19	94	38	104	5	Mar. 26	Nov. 17	236	17	1.25	1.30	1.30	1.30	3.50	2.87	1.12	2.76	2.88	2.35	1.00	1.38	23.88
Red River, Clarksville	72	94	34	115	−7	Mar. 23	Nov. 12	234		2.97	3.52	.44	5.73	5.67	3.43	3.12	3.50	3.50	1.25	3.54	3.31	45.29
Reeves, Balmorhea	52	94	32	112	−9	Apr. 1	Nov. 12	226	25	.63	.49	.27	2.97	1.50	1.47	1.59	2.61	1.64	.53	.53	.49	11.99
‡Refugio, Refugio	18	94	44	106	14	Feb. 14	Dec. 11	304		2.03	2.06	.93	2.97	2.95	2.75	2.90	2.61	4.83	1.83	1.83	1.37	33.76
Roberts, Miami	67	94	23	114	−15	Apr. 16	Oct. 25	192	11	.58	.77	.41	1.79	3.66	3.35	2.90	2.62	2.11	2.03	.68	.82	21.91
Robertson, Franklin	14	96	40	106	11	Mar. 6	Nov. 6	268		2.85	2.94	2.48	3.88	4.88	3.02	4.00	2.82	2.62	3.16	3.16	3.19	35.80
Rockwall, Rockwall	7	96	34	109	−11	Mar. 23	Nov. 14	236		2.29	2.92	3.14	5.16	5.45	3.86	2.16	2.18	3.16	3.18	2.75	2.43	38.68
Runnels, Ballinger	78	96	34	116	−9	Mar. 30	Nov. 13	228		1.23	1.04	1.05	4.05	3.84	2.04	1.41	2.82	2.66	2.26	1.14	.97	21.85
Rusk, Henderson	33	96	34	108	6	Mar. 11	Nov. 16	250		3.77	3.82	3.83	4.94	5.79	3.53	3.30	3.77	3.77	3.65	3.65	4.15	46.22
Sabine, Bronson	29	93	35	114	6	Mar. 21	Nov. 12	236		5.50	4.60	4.05	4.80	5.60	3.34	4.10	2.90	2.90	4.95	4.95	5.45	51.94
‡San Augustine, Jackson Hill	14	94	35	106	12	Mar. 19	Nov. 12	238	48	4.40	4.40	3.20	4.80	5.40	3.65	4.00	2.88	2.90	4.80	5.25	5.25	50.23
‡San Jacinto, Coldspring (near)	13	94	38	104	14	Mar. 5	Nov. 21	261	30	4.40	4.05	3.20	4.40	4.70	4.15	4.15	3.00	3.45	3.45	4.50	4.70	48.25
‡San Patricio, Sinton	18	95	44	107	8	Feb. 14	Dec. 14	303	18	1.49	1.80	1.59	3.00	3.25	2.60	2.50	3.80	4.65	2.54	1.85	1.42	30.60
‡San Saba, San Saba	13	94	34	108	−8	Mar. 28	Nov. 11	227	49	.87	1.50	1.80	3.00	3.68	2.27	1.37	1.65	3.29	1.64	1.80	1.42	26.19
‡Schleicher, Eldorado (near)	9	96	38	107	−6	Mar. 7	Nov. 21	259		.63	.91	.75	1.78	2.42	2.07	1.50	1.61	2.78	.81	.73	.73	18.19
Scurry, Snyder	63	96	30	115	−10	Apr. 4	Nov. 4	214		.63	.60	.75	1.61	3.50	2.22	2.22	1.61	1.95	2.22	.91	.91	19.32
Shackelford, Albany	92	97	31	114	−8	Mar. 30	Nov. 9	224		1.29	1.50	1.18	2.99	4.08	2.57	2.38	3.80	3.21	3.45	1.42	1.42	26.57
Shelby, Center	35	93	38	110	10	Mar. 17	Nov. 12	240		4.15	4.30	3.08	4.06	5.51	3.96	5.06	2.91	3.63	3.40	3.96	4.20	49.94
Sherman, Stratford	55	93	19	108	−20	Apr. 23	Oct. 22	182	18	.36	.45	.83	.83	2.81	2.47	3.57	2.91	1.57	1.42	.54	.47	18.36
Smith, Tyler	21	97	37	108	8	Mar. 7	Nov. 21	259		3.88	3.67	3.26	4.89	5.06	3.27	2.47	2.00	2.74	2.75	4.21	4.77	46.19
‡Somervell, Glen Rose	13	98	32	110	−1	Mar. 25	Nov. 16	236	10	2.15	2.40	2.13	3.75	5.00	2.90	2.12	1.95	3.00	2.75	2.05	2.04	32.65
Starr, Rio Grande City	92	98	48	115	7	Feb. 16	Dec. 16	314		.90	.96	.72	1.50	2.21	2.06	.90	1.95	3.97	1.75	.86	.62	18.87
Stephens, Breckenridge	49	98	38	114	5	Mar. 31	Nov. 8	222		.83	1.50	.97	2.98	2.69	2.69	1.84	1.95	3.15	2.68	1.62	1.26	26.33
Sterling, Sterling City	13	99	33	108	5	Apr. 7	Nov. 17	224		.68	.79	.97	1.80	2.61	1.85	2.14	1.86	2.38	1.96	.87	.94	19.00
‡Stonewall, Aspermont	14	99	38	110	6	Apr. 7	Nov. 16	224		.70	1.07	1.07	2.18	2.61	2.89	1.73	1.91	1.75	1.95	.84	.84	22.36
Sutton, Sonora	27	94	38	105	−1	Mar. 26	Nov. 16	235	43	.70	.95	.69	1.54	2.90	2.35	1.73	1.76	1.43	2.70	.67	2.04	17.59
Swisher, Tulia	21	93	24	109	−23	Apr. 10	Nov. 1	205	18	1.80	2.36	2.40	2.47	3.47	2.75	1.84	2.10	2.26	2.60	2.03	.79	18.94
Tarrant, Fort Worth	76	96	35	112	−8	Mar. 26	Nov. 17	230		1.02	1.50	2.54	3.86	4.47	3.05	2.34	2.05	3.15	2.69	1.20	1.82	32.30
Taylor, Abilene	89	93	33	109	−9	Mar. 31	Nov. 11	225		.59	.97	.97	2.47	3.86	2.34	1.19	.95	1.94	1.99	1.00	1.02	23.59
‡Terrell, Sanderson	14	96	26	110	−8	Mar. 21	Nov. 13	237	22	.44	.50	.27	.73	1.63	1.26	2.38	1.81	2.12	1.99	.35	.51	11.21
Terry, Brownfield	22	93	29	111	−8	Apr. 10	Nov. 2	206	10	.59	.84	.84	1.08	2.53	2.41	2.05	1.76	3.11	2.70	.47	.49	17.21
Throckmorton, Throckmorton	50	98	29	119	−9	Mar. 31	Nov. 6	220		1.16	1.34	1.33	2.95	4.05	2.98	2.05	1.76	3.11	2.70	1.23	1.16	25.82

Texas Temperature, Frost, Growing Season and Precipitation Records, by Counties.—(continued.)

County and Station	Temp Length of Record (Yr.)	Mean Max July (°F.)	Mean Min January (°F.)	Record Highest (°F.)	Record Lowest (°F.)	Last in Spring	First in Fall	Growing Season (Days)	Precip Length of Record (Yr.)	Jan (In.)	Feb (In.)	Mar (In.)	Apr (In.)	May (In.)	June (In.)	July (In.)	Aug (In.)	Sept (In.)	Oct (In.)	Nov (In.)	Dec (In.)	Annual (In.)
Titus, Mount Pleasant	59	95	35	118	-5	Mar. 23	Nov. 12	233	—	3.26	3.62	3.97	5.32	5.58	3.45	2.86	3.05	3.95	3.61	3.78	3.54	45.99
Tom Green, San Angelo	65	98	34	111		Mar. 25	Nov. 15	235	—	.81	.79	.87	1.66	2.70	1.88	1.23	1.44	2.74	1.86	.85	.70	17.53
Travis, Austin	79	95	41	109	-2	Mar. 3	Nov. 28	270	—	1.88	2.00	1.89	3.49	3.97	3.13	2.20	1.88	3.68	3.00	2.04	2.22	32.49
Trinity, Groveton	9	94	39	102	17	Mar. 6	Nov. 21	260	—	4.20	4.00	3.40	4.50	4.80	3.75	3.50	2.80	3.70	3.00	4.50	4.50	45.95
Tyler, Rockland	11	94	38	106	-3	Mar. 16	Nov. 12	241	29	4.50	4.17	3.33	4.50	5.70	4.19	3.58	2.79	3.70	3.61	4.34	4.34	48.37
Upshur, Gilmer	59	96	37	114	-4	Mar. 16	Nov. 16	245	—	3.30	3.62	3.84	6.03	5.47	3.56	2.68	2.70	3.49	3.06	3.85	4.14	45.74
Upton, McCamey	43	96	33	113	-2	Mar. 26	Nov. 12	232	—	.64	.51	.48	.77	1.91	1.49	1.64	1.42	1.34	1.39	.53	.58	12.70
Uvalde, Uvalde	72	96	40	108	-7	Mar. 10	Nov. 21	255	—	1.20	1.15	1.15	2.06	2.96	2.53	1.63	1.22	3.10	2.84	.98	.93	23.23
Val Verde, Del Rio	71	94	40	111	-12	Feb. 12	Dec. 9	300	—	.60	1.02	.72	1.57	2.41	2.03	1.02	1.22	3.01	2.07	.65	.52	16.88
Van Zandt, Wills Point	52	94	35	115	-1	Mar. 16	Nov. 21	250	—	2.92	3.35	3.35	5.76	5.86	3.31	2.27	1.22	3.45	3.71	3.53	3.34	43.09
Victoria, Victoria	30	92	46	110	-2	Feb. 19	Dec. 6	290	—	1.76	2.28	1.89	2.65	3.96	3.31	2.79	3.15	4.61	3.63	2.31	1.95	34.29
‡Walker, Huntsville	91	91	41	107	-9	Mar. 7	Nov. 27	265	—	3.51	3.73	3.12	4.63	4.61	4.05	3.24	3.01	4.15	3.39	3.62	3.93	44.99
‡Waller, Hempstead	13	95	39	107	13	Feb. 24	Dec. 4	283	67	3.50	3.73	2.87	3.85	4.30	3.10	3.45	3.10	3.40	3.10	3.93	4.00	41.67
Ward, Monahans	16	90	30	108	-9	Apr. 1	Nov. 10	223	—	.80	.40	.33	.76	1.60	1.20	1.75	1.40	1.38	1.50	.35	.57	12.04
Washington, Brenham	91	95	43	115	5	Mar. 3	Dec. 4	277	13	2.84	3.87	2.70	4.41	4.41	3.87	2.31	2.44	3.85	3.71	3.82	3.22	39.94
Webb, Laredo	40	99	47	115	5	Feb. 7	Dec. 26	322	—	.81	1.05	.50	1.68	2.25	2.03	.94	1.95	3.14	1.63	1.02	.87	17.87
Wharton, Pierce	68	93	48	108	-8	Mar. 5	Nov. 26	266	—	2.77	3.11	2.49	3.06	4.09	4.45	3.28	3.63	4.37	4.32	2.47	2.93	41.46
‡Wheeler, Shamrock	12	97	26	108	-17	Apr. 7	Nov. 1	208	—	.65	.69	1.09	2.03	3.95	3.62	2.57	3.63	2.37	2.56	.70	.83	23.70
Wichita, Wichita Falls	57	97	31	113	-14	Mar. 27	Nov. 11	229	—	1.07	1.16	1.62	3.16	4.58	3.39	2.16	1.77	3.19	2.68	1.35	1.28	27.22
Wilbarger, Vernon	42	98	29	119	-17	Mar. 31	Nov. 7	221	—	.96	1.12	1.41	2.40	4.68	3.22	2.12	1.40	2.73	3.02	1.18	1.06	25.65
‡Willacy, Raymondville	60	96	50	107	19	Feb. 6	Dec. 11	331	—	1.60	1.28	.85	1.52	3.73	2.68	1.30	2.73	5.13	2.66	1.37	.95	25.80
Williamson, Taylor	73	96	39	112	-14	Mar. 1	Nov. 24	258	—	2.25	2.94	2.01	3.61	3.63	3.25	1.56	2.23	4.01	3.21	2.47	2.72	33.98
Wilson, Floresville	14	96	42	106	-1	Feb. 24	Dec. 1	280	—	1.83	2.06	1.33	2.66	3.60	2.72	1.64	1.51	3.79	2.79	1.58	1.58	28.68
Winkler, Wink	35	96	29	114	-14	Apr. 1	Nov. 8	219	—	.54	.33	.72	.75	1.27	1.21	1.62	1.51	1.27	1.18	.36	.37	10.81
Wise, Bridgeport	40	96	33	115	-9	Mar. 31	Nov. 6	220	—	1.67	1.83	2.19	3.73	4.19	2.68	1.79	1.84	3.04	2.86	1.77	1.77	29.74
Wood, Mineola	10	94	36	107	-12	Mar. 17	Nov. 18	246	7	3.50	3.55	3.75	4.75	5.40	3.35	3.20	2.70	2.75	3.25	4.00	4.10	44.30
Yoakum, Plains	20	98	24	108	-9	Apr. 15	Oct. 31	199	32	.58	.39	.40	.80	2.30	1.81	2.25	1.75	2.13	2.00	.28	.30	14.99
Young, Graham	69	98	31	112	-8	Apr. 2	Nov. 4	216	—	1.37	1.52	1.73	3.47	4.12	2.97	2.01	1.65	3.35	2.67	1.64	1.33	28.03
‡Zapata, Zapata	14	100	46	112	21	Feb. 14	Dec. 5	304	11	.94	.80	.68	1.50	2.25	1.95	1.30	1.65	2.90	1.60	.76	.90	17.23
Zavala, Crystal City	21	99	41	109	11	Feb. 24	Dec. 1	280	21	.93	1.28	.88	1.67	3.46	2.27	1.19	2.44	3.21	2.48	.93	.80	21.54

Weather Reduces Pollution

Urbanization, industrialization and agribusiness practices are increasing air pollution problems in Texas, as in other states. But frequent changes in air mass and regional-scale weather disturbances in Texas do not favor objectionable concentrations of air pollutants much of the time.

There are significant seasonal and geographical variations. Statewide, most serious pollution is likely to occur in December and January (also in November in the Northeast). Conditions in warmer months are less conducive to pollution.

On a yearly basis, West Texas has less potential for air pollution than East Texas. The frequency of light winds and temperature inversions at night tend to create pollution problems.

Few high-pressure systems stagnate over Texas for any length of time; therefore, the meteorological situation most favorable for serious air-pollution episodes rarely is present. In Texas stagnation is more likely to occur over the East Texas Pine Belt and in the El Paso area than elsewhere.

Calendar For 1988 and 1989

The subsequent calendars were calculated principally from basic data in the U.S. Naval Observatory's publication, **Astronomical Phenomena.** Data were adapted for use in Texas on the basis of **Central Standard Time,** except for the period from 2 a.m. on the first Sunday in April until 2 a.m. on the last Sunday in October, when **Daylight Saving Time,** which is one hour later than Central Standard Time, is in effect.

All of Texas is in the CST zone except El Paso and Hudspeth counties and the northwest corner of Culberson County, which observe **Mountain Standard Time.** See accompanying map. MST is one hour earlier than CST.

All times here are figured for the intersection of meridian 99° 10' West and parallel 31° 23' North, which is about 15 miles northeast of Brady, McCulloch County. This point is the geographical center of the state. **Please note that this is a different point than was used in previous Almanacs.**

To get the time of sunrise or sunset, moonrise or moonset for any point in Texas, apply the following rules: Add to the time given in this calendar four minutes for each degree of longitude that any given place lies west of the 99th meridian, and subtract four minutes for each degree of longitude such place lies east of the 99th meridian.

At times there will also be considerable variation for distances north and south of the line of latitude 31 degrees 23 minutes north, but the rule for calculating it would be complicated. Procedure given above will get sufficiently close results.

An accompanying map shows the intersection for which all time is calculated, with some Texas major cities and their longitude. These make it convenient to calculate time at any given point.

Planetary Configurations and Phenomena

In the center column of the calendar on following pages are given the phenomena and planetary configurations of heavens for 1988 and 1989. Below is an explanation of the signs of the Sun, Moon and planets, and symbols used in the tables:

☉ The Sun.	⊕ The Earth.	♅ Uranus.
☾ The Moon.	♂ Mars.	Ψ Neptune.
☿ Mercury.	♃ Jupiter.	♇ Pluto.
♀ Venus.	♄ Saturn.	

Aspects

♂ This symbol appearing before the symbols for heavenly bodies means they are "in conjunction," that is having the same longitude as applies to the sky and appearing near each other.

♊ This symbol means that the two heavenly bodies are in "opposition," or differ by 180 degrees of longitude.

Common Astronomical Terms

Aphelion — Point at which a planet's orbit is farthest from the sun.

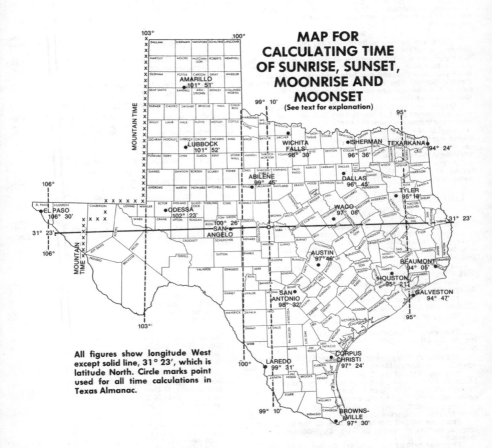

MAP FOR CALCULATING TIME OF SUNRISE, SUNSET, MOONRISE AND MOONSET
(See text for explanation)

All figures show longitude West except solid line, 31° 23', which is latitude North. Circle marks point used for all time calculations in Texas Almanac.

Perihelion — Point at which a planet's orbit is nearest the sun.

Apogee — That point of the moon's orbit farthest from the earth.

Perigee — That point of the moon's orbit nearest the earth.

Aspect — Apparent situation of a planet with respect to another body.

Eclipses: 1988 and 1989

1988

There will be four eclipses during 1988, two of the Sun and two of the Moon, as follows:

March 3—Partial eclipse of the Moon, visible in Asia, Central and eastern Europe, northeast Africa, Wilkes Land of Antarctica, Australia, New Zealand, Alaska, Hawaii, the Arctic regions, the Indian Ocean and the west half of the Pacific Ocean.

March 17-18—Total eclipse of the Sun, visible in eastern Asia, Indonesia, northwest Australia, New Guinea, Micronesia, extreme northwest of North America, western Hawaiian islands.

Aug. 27—Partial eclipse of the Moon, beginning visible on the east coast of Asia, most of Antarctica, Australia, New Zealand, eastern half of South America, Central America, North America except east of Hudson Bay, and the Pacific Ocean; end visible in eastern Asia, most of Antarctica, Australia, New Zealand, northern Central America, central and western North America and the Pacific Ocean.

Sept. 11—Annular eclipse of the Sun, visible in extreme eastern Africa, southern Asia, Indonesia, Australia except extreme northeast, New Zealand, part of Antarctica.

1989

There will be four eclipses during 1989, two of the Sun and two of the Moon as follows:

February 20—Total eclipse of the Moon, visible in the western half of North America, the Pacific Ocean, Australia, New Zealand and Asia; end visible in western Pacific Ocean, New Zealand, Australia, Asia, Europe except the Iberian peninsula, Africa except the west, and the Indian Ocean.

March 7—Partial eclipse of the Sun, visible in Hawaii, northwest part of North America, Greenland, extreme northeast Asia and the Arctic regions.

August 17—Total eclipse of the Moon, visible in extreme western Asia, Europe except the northeast, Africa, Iceland, south of Greenland, the Americas except northwest, Antarctica.

August 31—Partial eclipse of the Sun, visible in extreme southeast Africa, Madagascar and part of Antarctica.

Chronological Eras and Cycles, 1988 and 1989

The year 1988 of the Christian era comprises the latter part of the 212th and the beginning of the 213th year of the independence of the United States of America, and corresponds to the year 6701 of the Julian period.

Jan. 1, 1988, Julian calendar, corresponds to Jan. 14, 1988, Gregorian calendar.

The year 7497 of the Byzantine era begins on Sept. 14, 1988, Gregorian calendar.

The year 5749 of the Jewish era begins at sunset on Sept. 11, 1988, Gregorian calendar.

The year 4625 of the Chinese era begins Feb. 17, 1988.

The year 2741 since the foundation of Rome, according to VARRO, begins on Jan. 14, 1988, Gregorian calendar.

The year 2737 of the era of NABONASSAR begins on April 26, 1988, Gregorian calendar.

The year 2300 of the Grecian era, or the era of the SELEUCIDAE, begins in the present-day usage of the Syrians on Oct. 14, 1988, or on Sept. 14, 1988, Gregorian calendar, according to different sects.

The year 1705 of the era of DIOCLETIAN begins on Sept. 11, 1988, Gregorian calendar.

The year 1409 of the Islamic era, or the era of the Hegira, begins at sunset on Aug. 13, 1988, Gregorian calendar.

The year 1910 of the Saka era begins on March 21,

1988, Gregorian calendar, in the reformed Indian calendar.

The year 2648 of the Japanese era begins on Jan. 1, 1988, Gregorian calendar.

CHRONOLOGICAL CYCLES, 1988

Dominical Letter	CB	Julian Period	6701
Epact	11	Roman Indiction	11
Golden Number or		Solar Cycle	9
Lunar Cycle	XIII		

CHRONOLOGICAL ERAS, 1989

The year 1989 of the Christian era comprises the latter part of the 213th and the beginning of the 214th year of the independence of the United States of America, and corresponds to the year 6702 of the Julian period.

Jan. 1, 1989, Julian calendar, corresponds to Jan. 14, 1989, Gregorian calendar.

The year 7498 of the Byzantine era begins on Sept. 14, 1989, Gregorian calendar.

The year 5750 of the Jewish era begins at sunset on Sept. 29, 1989, Gregorian calendar.

The year 4626 of the Chinese era begins Feb. 6, 1989.

The year 2742 since the foundation of Rome, according to VARRO, begins on Jan. 14, 1989, Gregorian calendar.

The year 2738 of the era of NABONASSAR begins on April 26, 1989, Gregorian calendar.

The year 2301 of the Grecian era, or the era of the SELEUCIDAE, begins in the present-day usage of the Syrians on Sept. 14 (or Oct. 14), Gregorian calendar, according to different sects.

The year 1706 of the era of DIOCLETIAN begins on Sept. 11, 1989, Gregorian calendar.

The year 1410 of the Islamic era, or the era of the Hegira, begins at sunset on Aug. 3, 1989, Gregorian calendar.

The year 1911 of the Saka era begins on March 22, 1989, Gregorian calendar, in the reformed Indian calendar.

The year 2649 of the Japanese era begins on Jan. 1, 1989, Gregorian calendar.

CHRONOLOGICAL CYCLES, 1989

Dominical Letter	A	Julian Period	6702
Epact	22	Roman Indiction	12
Golden Number or		Solar Cycle	10
Lunar Cycle	XIV		

The Seasons, 1988 and 1989

The seasons of 1988 begin as follows, **Central Standard Time** (Daylight Saving Time, April 3-Oct. 30): **Spring**, March 20, 3:39 a.m.; **Summer**, June 20, 10:57 p.m.; **Fall**, Sept. 22, 2:29 p.m.; **Winter**, Dec. 21, 9:28 a.m.

1989

The seasons of 1989 begin as follows, **Central Standard Time** (Daylight Saving Time, April 2-Oct. 29): **Spring**, March 20, 9:28 p.m.; **Summer**, June 21, 3:53 a.m.; **Fall**, Sept. 22, 7:20 p.m.; **Winter**, Dec. 21, 3:22 p.m.

Morning and Evening Stars, 1988 and 1989

Morning Stars, 1988

Venus—June 20-Dec. 31.
Mars—Jan. 1-Sept. 28.
Jupiter—May 17-Nov. 23.
Saturn—Jan. 2-June 20.

Evening Stars, 1988

Venus—Jan. 1-June 6.
Mars—Sept. 28-Dec. 31.
Jupiter—Jan. 1-Apr. 19; Nov. 23-Dec. 31.
Saturn—June 20-Dec. 9.

Morning Stars, 1989

Venus—Jan. 1-Feb. 24.
Mars—Nov. 14-Dec. 31.
Jupiter—June 24-Dec. 27.
Saturn—Jan. 13-July 2.

Evening Stars, 1989

Venus—May 14-Dec. 31.
Mars—Jan. 1-Aug. 15.
Jupiter—Jan. 1-May 26; Dec. 27-Dec. 31.
Saturn—July 2-Dec. 21.

Holidays, Anniversaries and Festivals, 1988 and 1989

Bank Holidays — By act of the Sixty-second Legislature, 1971, legally prescribed (compulsory) bank holidays in Texas, in addition to Sundays, are New Year's Day, Washington's Birthday, Memorial Day, Independence Day, Labor Day, Columbus Day, Veterans Day, Thanksgiving and Christmas. The 69th Legislature, 1985–1986, established Martin Luther King's birthday as an official bank holiday. Should New Year's Day, Independence Day or Christmas fall on Saturday, banks close the preceding Friday. Should any of the three fall on Sunday banks close the next Monday. At their option, banks may close one day a week besides Sunday, usually Saturday, but on any day selected by individual banks. Prior to this act, permitting a 5-day banking week, bank holidays included all holidays in the list below marked with asterisk (*), double asterisk (**) or dagger (†).

1988		1989	
*New Year's Day	Friday, Jan. 1	*New Year's Day	Sunday, Jan. 1
Epiphany	Wednesday, Jan. 6	Epiphany	Friday, Jan. 6
§Arbor Day (Third Friday in January)	Friday, Jan. 15	‡‡Martin Luther King's Birthday	Monday, Jan. 16
‡‡Martin Luther King's Birthday	Monday, Jan. 18	**Confederate Heroes Day	Thursday, Jan. 19
**Confederate Heroes Day	Tuesday, Jan. 19	§Arbor Day (Third Friday in January)	Friday, Jan. 20
*Lincoln's Birthday	Friday, Feb. 12	Ash Wednesday	Wednesday, Feb. 8
‡‡Washington's Birthday (President's Day)		*Lincoln's Birthday	Sunday, Feb. 12
	Monday, Feb. 15	‡‡Washington's Birthday (President's Day)	
Ash Wednesday	Wednesday, Feb. 17		Monday, Feb. 20
†Texas Independence Day	Wednesday, March 2	†Texas Independence Day	Thursday, March 2
‡Sam Houston Day	Wednesday, March 2	‡Sam Houston Day	Thursday, March 2
‡Texas Flag Day	Wednesday, March 2	‡Texas Flag Day	Thursday, March 2
Palm Sunday	Sunday, March 27	Palm Sunday	Sunday, March 19
Good Friday	Friday, April 1	Good Friday	Friday, March 24
First Day of Passover (Pesach)	Saturday, April 2	Easter Sunday	Sunday, March 26
Easter Sunday	Sunday, April 3	First Day of Ramadan (Tabular)	Tuesday, April 18
First Day of Ramadan (Tabular)	Monday, April 18	First Day of Passover (Pesach)	Thursday, April 20
†San Jacinto Day	Thursday, April 21	†San Jacinto Day	Friday, April 21
Ascension Day	Thursday, May 12	Ascension Day	Thursday, May 4
Armed Forces Day	Saturday, May 21	Whitsunday — Pentecost	Sunday, May 14
Feast of Weeks (Shavuot)	Sunday, May 22	Armed Forces Day	Saturday, May 20
Whitsunday — Pentecost	Sunday, May 22	Trinity Sunday	Sunday, May 21
Trinity Sunday	Sunday, May 29	‡‡Memorial Day	Monday, May 29
‡‡Memorial Day	Monday, May 30	U.S. Flag Day	Wednesday, June 14
U.S. Flag Day	Tuesday, June 14	†Emancipation Day (in Texas)	Monday, June 19
†Emancipation Day (in Texas)	Sunday, June 19	Feast of Weeks (Shavuot)	Tuesday, June 19
*Independence Day	Monday, July 4	*Independence Day	Tuesday, July 4
‡Texas Pioneers' Day	Friday, Aug. 12	Islamic New Year (Tabular)	Saturday, Aug. 5
Islamic New Year (Tabular)	Sunday, Aug. 14	‡Texas Pioneers' Day	Saturday, Aug. 12
†Lyndon B. Johnson's Birthday	Saturday, Aug. 27	†Lyndon B. Johnson's Birthday	Sunday, Aug. 27
*Labor Day	Monday, Sept. 5	*Labor Day	Monday, Sept. 4
Jewish New Year (Rosh Hashanah)	Monday, Sept. 12	Constitution and Citizenship Day	Sunday, Sept. 17
Constitution and Citizenship Day	Saturday, Sept. 17	Jewish New Year (Rosh Hashanah)	Saturday, Sept. 30
Day of Atonement (Yom Kippur)	Wednesday, Sept. 21	Day of Atonement (Yom Kippur)	Saturday, Oct. 9
First Day of Tabernacles (Succoth)	Monday, Sept. 26	‡‡Columbus Day	Monday, Oct. 9
‡‡Columbus Day	Monday, Oct. 10	First Day of Tabernacles (Succoth)	Saturday, Oct. 14
‡§Poetry Day	Saturday, Oct. 15	‡§Poetry Day	Sunday, Oct. 15
‡Father of Texas Day	Thursday, Nov. 3	‡Father of Texas Day	Friday, Nov. 3
*General Election Day	Tuesday, Nov. 8	*Veterans Day	Saturday, Nov. 11
*Veterans Day	Friday, Nov. 11	*Thanksgiving Day †† (Fourth Thursday)	
*Thanksgiving Day †† (Fourth Thursday)			Thursday, Nov. 23
	Thursday, Nov. 24	First Sunday in Advent	Sunday, Dec. 3
First Sunday in Advent	Sunday, Nov. 27	First Day of Hanukkah (Feast of Lights)	
First Day of Hanukkah (Feast of Lights)	Friday, Dec. 23		Saturday, Dec. 23
*Christmas Day	Sunday, Dec. 25	*Christmas Day	Monday, Dec. 25

*National holidays which are also state holidays by act of the Texas Legislature, except Lincoln's Birthday, Feb. 12, which was exclusively a bank holiday, until the number of bank holidays was restricted by state law in 1955, providing a 5-day week and restricting the number of bank holidays.

†Legal holiday in Texas only.

‡"Special observance days," set aside by Texas Legislature. They are not legal holidays, though two of them fall on March 2, which is otherwise designated as a state legal holiday, except for bank closing.

§A "special observance day" by resolution of the Texas Legislature but also observed by legislative enactment in many other states.

In 1973, the Texas Legislature made Lyndon B. Johnson's Birthday, Aug. 27, a state holiday and made Jan. 19 **Confederate Heroes Day, combining the birthdays of Robert E. Lee (Jan. 19) and Jefferson Davis (June 3).

††**THANKSGIVING DAY IN TEXAS** was designated as the "fourth Thursday in November" by the Fifty-fifth Legislature, 1957. This made the state Thanksgiving coincide with the national holiday in all years. Prior to that Texas had, beginning with 1939, celebrated separate national and state Thanksgiving Days in all Novembers having five Thursdays. Texas, first by governor's proclamation, and by legislative resolution after 1951, continued to observe the last Thursday, until changed in 1957 to coincide in all years with the national holiday.

‡‡Starting in 1971, these changes were made in official holidays by the U.S. and Texas governments to give employees 3-day holiday weekends: Columbus Day made national holiday and set for second Monday in October; Washington's Birthday will be observed on third Monday in February; Memorial Day will be observed on last Monday in May. The addition of Martin Luther King Jr's. birthday to this list was effective in 1986.

Texas Special Observance Weeks, 1988 and 1989

Texas Week in 1988 will be the week of Tuesday, March 1 to Monday, March 7, inclusive; in 1989, it will be observed the week of Wednesday, March 1 to Tuesday, March 7, inclusive. This week includes **Texas Independence Day**, March 2.

Texas Conservation and Beautification Week includes the period beginning two days before San Jacinto Day, April 21, and ending two days after **National Wildflower Day**, April 24.

Calendar For 1988

Time given in this calendar is according to **Central Standard Time,** except for the period from April 3 to Oct. 30, during which **Daylight Saving Time** is observed. See page 123 for explanation of how to get exact time at any certain Texas point. Boldface figures for moonrise and moonset indicate p.m. **Times are figured for the point 99° 10′ West and 31° 23′ North. This is a different point than that used in previous Almanacs.**

1st Month JANUARY, 1988 31 Days

Moon's Phases—Full, Jan. 3, 7:40 p.m.; Last Qr., Jan. 12, 1:04 a.m.; New, Jan. 18, 11:26 p.m.; First Qr., Jan. 25, 3:53 p.m.

Day of			Planetary Configurations —Phenomena	*Hour of			
Year	Month	Week		Sunrise	Sunset	Moonrise	Moonset
1	1	Fr.		7:36	5:45	**3:40**	5:40
2	2	Sa.		7:36	5:46	**4:31**	6:38
3	3	Su.	⊕ at Perihelion	7:36	5:46	**5:26**	7:31
4	4	Mo.		7:36	5:47	**6:24**	8:18
5	5	Tu.		7:37	5:48	**7:22**	8:58
6	6	We.		7:37	5:49	**8:20**	9:33
7	7	Th.	☾ at Apogee	7:37	5:50	**9:15**	10:03
8	8	Fr.		7:37	5:50	**10:10**	10:30
9	9	Sa.		7:37	5:51	**11:04**	10:55
10	10	Su.		7:37	5:52	**11:58**	11:20
11	11	Mo.		7:37	5:53	...	11:45
12	12	Tu.		7:37	5:54	12:55	**12:00**
13	13	We.		7:37	5:55	1:55	**12:44**
14	14	Th.		7:37	5:55	2:59	**1:22**
15	15	Fr.		7:36	5:56	4:07	**2:08**
16	16	Sa.		7:36	5:57	5:16	**3:04**
17	17	Su.	♄☌☾	7:36	5:58	6:23	**4:11**
18	18	Mo.		7:36	5:59	7:24	**5:25**
19	19	Tu.	☾ at Perigee	7:35	6:00	8:16	**6:42**
20	20	We.	☿☌☾	7:35	6:01	8:59	**7:57**
21	21	Th.	♀☌☾	7:35	6:02	9:36	**9:08**
22	22	Fr.		7:34	6:03	10:09	**10:16**
23	23	Sa.		7:34	6:04	10:40	**11:22**
24	24	Su.	♃☌☾	7:34	6:04	11:10	...
25	25	Mo.		7:33	6:05	11:41	12:26
26	26	Tu.	☿ Gr. elong. E.	7:33	6:06	**12:15**	1:29
27	27	We.		7:32	6:07	**12:53**	2:33
28	28	Th.		7:32	6:08	**1:37**	3:35
29	29	Fr.		7:31	6:09	**2:26**	4:34
30	30	Sa.		7:31	6:10	**3:20**	5:28
31	31	Su.		7:30	6:11	**4:17**	6:16

2nd Month FEBRUARY, 1988 29 Days

Moon's Phases—Full, Feb. 2, 2:51 p.m.; Last Qr., Feb. 10, 5:01 p.m.; New, Feb. 17, 9:54 a.m.; First Qr., Feb. 24, 6:15 a.m.

Day of			Planetary Configurations —Phenomena	*Hour of			
Year	Month	Week		Sunrise	Sunset	Moonrise	Moonset
32	1	Mo.	☿ Stationary	7:29	6:12	**5:15**	6:58
33	2	Tu.		7:29	6:13	**6:13**	7:34
34	3	We.		7:28	6:13	**7:09**	8:05
35	4	Th.		7:27	6:14	**8:04**	8:33
36	5	Fr.		7:27	6:15	**8:58**	8:59
37	6	Sa.		7:26	6:16	**9:52**	9:23
38	7	Su.		7:25	6:17	**10:48**	9:48
39	8	Mo.		7:24	6:18	**11:45**	10:14
40	9	Tu.		7:24	6:19	...	10:43
41	10	We.		7:23	6:20	12:46	11:17
42	11	Th.		7:22	6:20	1:50	11:58
43	12	Fr.		7:21	6:21	2:57	**12:47**
44	13	Sa.	♂☌☾	7:20	6:22	4:03	**1:47**
45	14	Su.		7:19	6:23	5:05	**2:57**
46	15	Mo.		7:18	6:24	6:00	**4:12**
47	16	Tu.		7:17	6:25	6:48	**5:28**
48	17	We.	☾ at Perigee	7:17	6:25	7:28	**6:42**
49	18	Th.	♇ Stationary	7:16	6:26	8:03	**7:53**
50	19	Fr.		7:15	6:27	8:36	**9:02**
51	20	Sa.	♀☌☾	7:14	6:28	9:07	**10:10**
52	21	Su.	♃☌☾	7:13	6:29	9:39	**11:16**
53	22	Mo.	☿ Stationary	7:12	6:29	10:13	
54	23	Tu.	♂☌♄	7:10	6:30	10:51	12:22
55	24	We.		7:09	6:31	11:33	1:26
56	25	Th.		7:08	6:32	**12:21**	2:27
57	26	Fr.		7:07	6:33	**1:14**	3:24
58	27	Sa.		7:06	6:33	**2:11**	4:14
59	28	Su.		7:05	6:34	**3:09**	4:58
60	29	Mo		7:04	6:35	**4:06**	5:35

*See text before January calendar for explanation.

3rd Month MARCH, 1988 31 Days

Moon's Phases—Full, March 3, 10:01 a.m.; Last. Qr., March 11, 4:56 a.m.; New, March 17, 8:02 p.m.; First Qr., March 24, 10:41 p.m.

Day of			Planetary Configurations —Phenomena	*Hour of			
Year	Month	Week		Sunrise	Sunset	Moonrise	Moonset
61	1	Tu.	☾ at Apogee	7:03	6:36	**5:03**	6:08
62	2	We.		7:02	6:36	**5:58**	6:36
63	3	Th.	Eclipse ☾	7:00	6:37	**6:53**	7:03
64	4	Fr.		6:59	6:38	**7:47**	7:28
65	5	Sa.		6:58	6:38	**8:43**	7:53
66	6	Su.	♀☌♃	6:57	6:39	**9:39**	8:18
67	7	Mo.	♂☌♆	6:56	6:40	**10:39**	8:46
68	8	Tu.	☿ Gr. elong. W.	6:54	6:41	**11:41**	9:18
69	9	We.		6:53	6:41	...	9:55
70	10	Th.		6:52	6:42	12:46	10:40
71	11	Fr.	♂☌☾	6:51	6:43	1:51	11:34
72	12	Sa.	♂☌☾	6:50	6:43	2:53	**12:38**
73	13	Su.		6:48	6:44	3:49	**1:48**
74	14	Mo.		6:47	6:45	4:38	**3:02**
75	15	Tu.	☿☌☾	6:46	6:45	5:20	**4:15**
76	16	We.	☾ at Perigee	6:45	6:46	5:57	**5:27**
77	17	Th.	Eclipse ☉	6:43	6:47	6:30	**6:37**
78	18	Fr.		6:42	6:47	7:02	**7:46**
79	19	Sa.		6:41	6:48	7:34	**8:55**
80	20	Su.	Spring Begins	6:40	6:49	8:08	**10:03**
81	21	Mo.	♀☌☾	6:38	6:49	8:45	**11:10**
82	22	Tu.		6:37	6:50	9:27	...
83	23	We.		6:36	6:51	10:14	12:15
84	24	Th.		6:34	6:51	11:06	1:15
85	25	Fr.		6:33	6:52	**12:02**	2:09
86	26	Sa.		6:32	6:53	**1:00**	2:55
87	27	Su.		6:31	6:53	**1:59**	3:35
88	28	Mo.	☾ at Apogee	6:29	6:54	**2:56**	4:09
89	29	Tu.		6:28	6:55	**3:52**	4:39
90	30	We.		6:27	6:55	**4:46**	5:06
91	31	Th.		6:26	6:56	**5:41**	5:31

4th Month APRIL, 1988 30 Days

Moon's Phases—Full, April 2, 3:21 a.m.; Last Qr., April 9, 2:21 p.m.; New, April 16, 7:00 a.m.; First Qr., April 23, 5:32 p.m.

Day of			Planetary Configurations —Phenomena	*Hour of			
Year	Month	Week		Sunrise	Sunset	Moonrise	Moonset
92	1	Fr.		6:24	6:57	**6:36**	5:56
93	2	Sa.		6:23	6:57	**7:33**	6:22
94	3	†Su.	♀ Gr. elong E.	7:22	7:58	**9:32**	7:49
95	4	Mo.	♂ Stationary	7:21	7:59	**10:34**	8:20
96	5	Tu.		7:19	7:59	**11:39**	8:56
97	6	We.		7:18	8:00	...	9:39
98	7	Th.		7:17	8:01	12:44	10:30
99	8	Fr.	♄☌☾	7:16	8:01	1:46	11:29
100	9	Sa.		7:15	8:02	2:43	**12:36**
101	10	Su.	♂☌☾	7:13	8:03	3:33	**1:46**
102	11	Mo.	♆ Stationary	7:12	8:03	4:16	**2:57**
103	12	Tu.		7:11	8:04	4:53	**4:07**
104	13	We.	☾ at Perigee	7:10	8:05	5:27	**5:16**
105	14	Th.		7:09	8:05	5:58	**6:24**
106	15	Fr.		7:08	8:06	6:30	**7:32**
107	16	Sa.		7:06	8:07	7:02	**8:40**
108	17	Su.		7:05	8:07	7:38	**9:49**
109	18	Mo.		7:04	8:08	8:18	**10:56**
110	19	Tu.	♀☌☾	7:03	8:09	9:03	...
111	20	We.	☿ Superior	7:02	8:09	9:55	12:00
112	21	Th.		7:01	8:10	10:51	12:58
113	22	Fr.		7:00	8:11	11:49	1:49
114	23	Sa.		6:59	8:11	**12:48**	2:32
115	24	Su.		6:58	8:12	**1:46**	3:08
116	25	Mo.	☾ at Apogee	6:57	8:13	**2:43**	3:40
117	26	Tu.		6:56	8:13	**3:38**	4:08
118	27	We.		6:55	8:14	**4:32**	4:34
119	28	Th.		6:54	8:15	**5:27**	4:59
120	29	Fr.		6:53	8:15	**6:23**	5:24
121	30	Sa.		6:52	8:16	**7:22**	5:51

†Daylight Saving Time begins at 2 a.m.

Calendar For 1988

5th Month **MAY, 1988** **31 Days**

Moon's Phases—Full, May 1, 6:41 p.m.; Last Qr., May 8, 8:23 p.m.; New, May 15, 5:11 p.m.; First Qr., May 23, 11:49 a.m.; Full, May 31, 5:53 a.m.

Day of Year	Day of Month	Day of Week	Planetary Configurations —Phenomena	*Hour of Sunrise	*Hour of Sunset	*Hour of Moonrise	*Hour of Moonset
122	1	Su.	♇☍	6:51	8:17	8:24	6:21
123	2	Mo.	♃☌☉	6:50	8:17	9:29	6:55
124	3	Tu.		6:49	8:18	10:35	7:36
125	4	We.		6:48	8:19	11:39	8:26
126	5	Th.	♄☌☾	6:47	8:20	...	9:23
127	6	Fr.	♀Gr.Brilliancy	6:47	8:20	12:39	10:28
128	7	Sa.		6:46	8:21	1:31	11:38
129	8	Su.		6:45	8:22	2:15	12:48
130	9	Mo.	♂☌☾	6:44	8:22	2:53	1:56
131	10	Tu.	☾at Perigee	6:43	8:23	3:27	3:04
132	11	We.		6:43	8:24	3:58	4:09
133	12	Th.		6:42	8:24	4:28	5:15
134	13	Fr.		6:41	8:25	5:00	6:22
135	14	Sa.		6:41	8:26	5:33	7:29
136	15	Su.		6:40	8:26	6:11	8:37
137	16	Mo.		6:39	8:27	6:54	9:43
138	17	Tu.	☿☌☾	6:39	8:28	7:43	10:44
139	18	We.	♀☌☾	6:38	8:28	8:38	11:39
140	19	Th.		6:38	8:29	9:36	...
141	20	Fr.		6:37	8:30	10:36	12:26
142	21	Sa.		6:37	8:30	11:35	1:05
143	22	Su.	♀Stationary	6:36	8:31	12:32	1:39
144	23	Mo.	☾at Apogee	6:36	8:32	1:28	2:08
145	24	Tu.		6:35	8:32	2:22	2:35
146	25	We.		6:35	8:33	3:17	3:00
147	26	Th.		6:34	8:33	4:12	3:25
148	27	Fr.		6:34	8:34	5:09	3:51
149	28	Sa.		6:34	8:35	6:09	4:19
150	29	Su.		6:33	8:35	7:13	4:52
151	30	Mo.		6:33	8:36	8:20	5:31
152	31	Tu.	☿Stationary	6:33	8:36	9:27	6:17

6th Month **JUNE, 1988** **30 Days**

Moon's Phases—Last Qr., June 7, 1:21 a.m.; New, June 14, 4:14 a.m.; First Qr., June 22, 5:23 a.m.; Full, June 29, 2:46 p.m.

Day of Year	Day of Month	Day of Week	Planetary Configurations —Phenomena	*Hour of Sunrise	*Hour of Sunset	*Hour of Moonrise	*Hour of Moonset
153	1	We.	♄☌☾	6:33	8:37	10:30	7:13
154	2	Th.	♆☌☾	6:32	8:37	11:26	8:18
155	3	Fr.		6:32	8:38	...	9:28
156	4	Sa.	☾at Perigee	6:32	8:38	12:14	10:39
157	5	Su.		6:32	8:39	12:54	11:49
158	6	Mo.	♂☌☾	6:32	8:39	1:29	12:57
159	7	Tu.		6:32	8:40	2:01	2:02
160	8	We.		6:32	8:40	2:31	3:07
161	9	Th.		6:32	8:41	3:01	4:11
162	10	Fr.		6:32	8:41	3:33	5:17
163	11	Sa.	♃☌☾	6:32	8:42	4:08	6:23
164	12	Su.		6:32	8:42	4:48	7:29
165	13	Mo.		6:32	8:42	5:34	8:31
166	14	Tu.		6:32	8:43	6:27	9:29
167	15	We.		6:32	8:43	7:24	10:19
168	16	Th.		6:32	8:43	8:24	11:01
169	17	Fr.		6:32	8:44	9:24	11:37
170	18	Sa.		6:32	8:44	10:22	...
171	19	Su.		6:32	8:44	11:18	12:08
172	20	Mo.	Summer Begins	6:33	8:44	12:13	12:36
173	21	Tu.		6:33	8:44	1:07	1:01
174	22	We.		6:33	8:45	2:01	1:26
175	23	Th.		6:33	8:45	2:56	1:51
176	24	Fr.	☿Stationary	6:34	8:45	3:54	2:18
177	25	Sa.		6:34	8:45	4:56	2:48
178	26	Su.	♄☌♅	6:34	8:45	6:01	3:24
179	27	Mo.		6:35	8:45	7:08	4:06
180	28	Tu.	♄☌☾	6:35	8:45	8:14	4:58
181	29	We.	♆☌☾	6:35	8:45	9:14	6:00
182	30	Th.	♆☍	6:36	8:45	10:06	7:10

*See text before January calendar for explanation.

7th Month **JULY, 1988** **31 Days**

Moon's Phases—Last Qr., July 6, 6:36 a.m.; New, July 13, 4:53 p.m.; First Qr., July 21, 9:14 p.m.; Full, July 28, 10:25 p.m.

Day of Year	Day of Month	Day of Week	Planetary Configurations —Phenomena	*Hour of Sunrise	*Hour of Sunset	*Hour of Moonrise	*Hour of Moonset
183	1	Fr.		6:36	8:45	10:51	8:23
184	2	Sa.	☾at Perigee	6:36	8:45	11:29	9:36
185	3	Su.		6:37	8:45	...	10:46
186	4	Mo.	♀Stationary	6:37	8:45	12:02	11:54
187	5	Tu.	⊕at Aphelion	6:38	8:45	12:33	1:00
188	6	We.	☿Gr. elong. W.	6:38	8:45	1:03	2:05
189	7	Th.		6:39	8:44	1:35	3:10
190	8	Fr.		6:39	8:44	2:08	4:15
191	9	Sa.	♃☌☾	6:40	8:44	2:46	5:20
192	10	Su.		6:40	8:44	3:30	6:23
193	11	Mo.		6:41	8:43	4:20	7:22
194	12	Tu.		6:41	8:43	5:15	8:14
195	13	We.		6:42	8:43	6:14	8:58
196	14	Th.		6:43	8:42	7:14	9:36
197	15	Fr.		6:43	8:42	8:13	10:09
198	16	Sa.		6:44	8:42	9:10	10:38
199	17	Su.	☾at Apogee	6:44	8:41	10:05	11:04
200	18	Mo.		6:45	8:41	10:59	11:28
201	19	Tu.	♀Gr. Brilliancy	6:45	8:40	11:52	11:53
202	20	We.		6:46	8:40	12:47	...
203	21	Th.		6:47	8:39	1:43	12:18
204	22	Fr.		6:47	8:39	2:42	12:46
205	23	Sa.		6:48	8:38	3:44	1:18
206	24	Su.		6:49	8:37	4:49	1:57
207	25	Mo.	♇Stationary	6:49	8:37	5:54	2:43
208	26	Tu.	♄☌☾	6:50	8:36	6:57	3:40
209	27	We.		6:50	8:36	7:53	4:46
210	28	Th.		6:51	8:35	8:42	5:59
211	29	Fr.		6:52	8:34	9:24	7:13
212	30	Sa.	☾at Perigee	6:52	8:33	10:00	8:27
213	31	Su.		6:53	8:33	10:33	9:38

8th Month **AUGUST, 1988** **31 Days**

Moon's Phases—Last Qr., Aug. 4, 1:22 p.m.; New, Aug. 12, 7:31 a.m.; First Qr., Aug. 20, 10:51 a.m.; Full, Aug. 27, 5:56 a.m.

Day of Year	Day of Month	Day of Week	Planetary Configurations —Phenomena	*Hour of Sunrise	*Hour of Sunset	*Hour of Moonrise	*Hour of Moonset
214	1	Mo.		6:54	8:32	11:04	10:47
215	2	Tu.	☿Superior	6:54	8:31	11:36	11:54
216	3	We.		6:55	8:30	...	1:01
217	4	Th.		6:56	8:29	12:09	2:08
218	5	Fr.		6:56	8:28	12:46	3:14
219	6	Sa.	♃☌☾	6:57	8:28	1:28	4:18
220	7	Su.		6:57	8:27	2:16	5:17
221	8	Mo.		6:58	8:26	3:09	6:11
222	9	Tu.		6:59	8:25	4:07	6:57
223	10	We.		6:59	8:24	5:07	7:37
224	11	Th.		7:00	8:23	6:06	8:11
225	12	Fr.		7:01	8:22	7:03	8:40
226	13	Sa.		7:01	8:21	7:59	9:07
227	14	Su.	☾at Apogee	7:02	8:20	8:53	9:32
228	15	Mo.		7:03	8:19	9:47	9:56
229	16	Tu.		7:03	8:18	10:40	10:21
230	17	We.		7:04	8:17	11:35	10:48
231	18	Th.		7:04	8:16	12:32	11:17
232	19	Fr.		7:05	8:15	1:32	11:52
233	20	Sa.		7:06	8:13	2:34	...
234	21	Su.		7:06	8:12	3:38	12:34
235	22	Mo.	♄☌☾	7:07	8:11	4:40	1:24
236	23	Tu.	♆☌☾	7:08	8:10	5:38	2:25
237	24	We.		7:08	8:09	6:30	3:33
238	25	Th.		7:09	8:08	7:14	4:46
239	26	Fr.	♂Stationary	7:09	8:07	7:53	6:01
240	27	Sa.	Eclipse ☾	7:10	8:05	8:28	7:14
241	28	Su.		7:11	8:04	9:01	8:25
242	29	Mo.		7:11	8:03	9:33	9:36
243	30	Tu.	♄Stationary	7:12	8:02	10:07	10:45
244	31	We.		7:12	8:00	10:44	11:54

Calendar For 1988

9th Month — SEPTEMBER, 1988 — 30 Days

Moon's Phases—Last Qr., Sept. 2, 10:50 p.m.; New, Sept. 10, 11:49 p.m.; First Qr., Sept. 18, 10:18 p.m.; Full, Sept. 25, 2:07 p.m.

Day of Year	Day of Month	Day of Week	Planetary Configurations —Phenomena	*Hour of Sunrise	*Hour of Sunset	*Hour of Moonrise	*Hour of Moonset
245	1	Th.		7:13	7:59	**11:25**	**1:03**
246	2	Fr.	♃☌☾	7:14	7:58	...	**2:09**
247	3	Sa.		7:14	7:57	12:12	**3:12**
248	4	Su.		7:15	7:55	1:04	**4:08**
249	5	Mo.	♅ Stationary	7:15	7:54	2:01	**4:56**
250	6	Tu.	♀☌☾	7:16	7:53	3:00	**5:38**
251	7	We.		7:17	7:52	4:00	**6:13**
252	8	Th.		7:17	7:50	4:58	**6:44**
253	9	Fr.		7:18	7:49	5:54	**7:11**
254	10	Sa.	☾ at Apogee	7:18	7:48	6:48	**7:36**
255	11	Su.	Eclipse ☉	7:19	7:47	7:42	**8:01**
256	12	Mo.		7:19	7:45	8:36	**8:26**
257	13	Tu.	☿☌☾	7:20	7:44	9:30	**8:52**
258	14	We.		7:21	7:43	10:26	**9:20**
259	15	Th.	☿ Gr. elong. E	7:21	7:41	11:24	**9:53**
260	16	Fr.		7:22	7:40	12:25	**10:31**
261	17	Sa.		7:22	7:39	**1:27**	**11:17**
262	18	Su.	♄☌☾	7:23	7:37	**2:29**	...
263	19	Mo.	♆☌☾	7:24	7:36	**3:27**	12:12
264	20	Tu.		7:24	7:35	**4:19**	1:15
265	21	We.	♂ Closest Approach	7:25	7:34	**5:06**	2:24
266	22	Th.	Fall Begins	7:25	7:32	**5:46**	3:36
267	23	Fr.		7:26	7:31	**6:22**	4:48
268	24	Sa.	☾ at Perigee	7:27	7:30	**6:55**	6:00
269	25	Su.		7:27	7:28	**7:28**	7:10
270	26	Mo.		7:28	7:27	**8:02**	8:21
271	27	Tu.	♂☍	7:28	7:26	**8:38**	9:32
272	28	We.	☿ Stationary	7:29	7:24	**9:18**	10:43
273	29	Th.		7:30	7:23	**10:04**	11:53
274	30	Fr.	♃☌☾	7:30	7:22	**10:56**	**12:59**

10th Month — OCTOBER, 1988 — 31 Days

Moon's Phases—Last Qr., Oct. 2, 1:58 p.m.; New, Oct. 10, 4:49 p.m.; First Qr., Oct. 18, 8:01 a.m.; Full, Oct. 24, 11:35 p.m.

Day of Year	Day of Month	Day of Week	Planetary Configurations —Phenomena	*Hour of Sunrise	*Hour of Sunset	*Hour of Moonrise	*Hour of Moonset
275	1	Sa.		7:31	7:21	**11:53**	**2:00**
276	2	Su.		7:32	7:19	...	**2:52**
277	3	Mo.		7:32	7:18	12:52	**3:37**
278	4	Tu.		7:33	7:17	1:52	**4:14**
279	5	We.		7:33	7:16	2:51	**4:46**
280	6	Th.	♀☌☾	7:34	7:14	3:48	**5:15**
281	7	Fr.	☾ at Apogee	7:35	7:13	4:43	**5:41**
282	8	Sa.		7:35	7:12	5:37	**6:05**
283	9	Su.		7:36	7:11	6:30	**6:30**
284	10	Mo.		7:37	7:10	7:24	**6:56**
285	11	Tu.		7:37	7:08	8:20	**7:24**
286	12	We.		7:38	7:07	9:18	**7:55**
287	13	Th.		7:39	7:06	10:19	**8:32**
288	14	Fr.		7:40	7:05	11:21	**9:15**
289	15	Sa.		7:40	7:04	**12:22**	**10:07**
290	16	Su.	♄☌☾	7:41	7:03	**1:21**	**11:06**
291	17	Mo.	♆☌☾	7:42	7:02	**2:14**	...
292	18	Tu.		7:42	7:01	**3:01**	12:11
293	19	We.	☿ Stationary	7:43	6:59	**3:41**	1:20
294	20	Th.		7:44	6:58	**4:18**	2:29
295	21	Fr.		7:45	6:57	**4:51**	3:38
296	22	Sa.	♂☌☾	7:45	6:56	**5:23**	4:47
297	23	Su.	☾ at Perigee	7:46	6:55	**5:55**	5:56
298	24	Mo.		7:47	6:54	**6:30**	7:06
299	25	Tu.		7:48	6:53	**7:09**	8:17
300	26	We.	☿ Gr. elong. W	7:48	6:52	**7:53**	9:29
301	27	Th.	♃☌☾	7:49	6:51	**8:43**	10:39
302	28	Fr.		7:50	6:50	**9:40**	11:44
303	29	Sa.		7:51	6:50	**10:40**	**12:42**
304	30	†Su.	♂ Stationary	6:52	5:49	**10:41**	**12:31**
305	31	Mo.		6:52	5:48	**11:41**	**1:12**

†Daylight Saving Time ends at 2 a.m. *See text before January calendar for explanation.

11th Month — NOVEMBER, 1988 — 30 Days

Moon's Phases—Last Qr., Nov. 1, 4:11 a.m.; New, Nov. 9, 8:20 a.m.; First Qr., Nov. 16, 3:35 p.m.; Full, Nov. 23, 9:53 a.m.

Day of Year	Day of Month	Day of Week	Planetary Configurations —Phenomena	*Hour of Sunrise	*Hour of Sunset	*Hour of Moonrise	*Hour of Moonset
306	1	Tu.		6:53	5:47	...	**1:46**
307	2	We.		6:54	5:46	12:39	**2:16**
308	3	Th.		6:55	5:45	1:35	**2:43**
309	4	Fr.	☾ at Apogee	6:56	5:45	2:29	**3:08**
310	5	Sa.		6:56	5:44	3:23	**3:33**
311	6	Su.	♀☌☾	6:57	5:43	4:17	**3:58**
312	7	Mo.		6:58	5:42	5:12	**4:25**
313	8	Tu.		6:59	5:42	6:10	**4:56**
314	9	We.		7:00	5:41	7:10	**5:31**
315	10	Th.		7:01	5:40	8:13	**6:13**
316	11	Fr.		7:02	5:40	9:15	**7:03**
317	12	Sa.	♄☌☾	7:02	5:39	10:16	**8:01**
318	13	Su.	♆☌☾	7:03	5:39	11:11	**9:04**
319	14	Mo.		7:04	5:38	11:59	**10:12**
320	15	Tu.		7:05	5:38	**12:41**	**11:20**
321	16	We.		7:06	5:37	**1:18**	...
322	17	Th.		7:07	5:37	**1:51**	12:27
323	18	Fr.		7:08	5:36	**2:22**	1:33
324	19	Sa.	♂☌☾	7:08	5:36	**2:53**	2:40
325	20	Su.	☾ at Perigee	7:09	5:36	**3:25**	3:47
326	21	Mo.		7:10	5:35	**4:01**	4:55
327	22	Tu.	♃☍	7:11	5:35	**4:42**	6:05
328	23	We.	♃☌☾	7:12	5:35	**5:29**	7:16
329	24	Th.		7:13	5:34	**6:24**	8:24
330	25	Fr.		7:14	5:34	**7:23**	9:26
331	26	Sa.		7:14	5:34	**8:26**	10:20
332	27	Su.		7:15	5:34	**9:28**	11:06
333	28	Mo.		7:16	5:34	**10:28**	11:43
334	29	Tu.		7:17	5:34	**11:25**	**12:16**
335	30	We.		7:18	5:33	...	**12:44**

12th Month — DECEMBER, 1988 — 31 Days

Moon's Phases— Last Qr., Dec. 1, 12:49 a.m.; New, Dec. 8, 11:36 p.m.; First Qr., Dec. 15, 11:40 p.m.; Full, Dec. 22, 11:29 p.m.; Last Qr., Dec. 30, 10:57 p.m.

Day of Year	Day of Month	Day of Week	Planetary Configurations —Phenomena	*Hour of Sunrise	*Hour of Sunset	*Hour of Moonrise	*Hour of Moonset
336	1	Th.	☿ Superior	7:19	5:33	12:20	**1:09**
337	2	Fr.	☾ at Apogee	7:19	5:33	1:14	**1:34**
338	3	Sa.		7:20	5:33	2:07	**1:59**
339	4	Su.		7:21	5:33	3:02	**2:25**
340	5	Mo.		7:22	5:34	3:58	**2:54**
341	6	Tu.	♀☌☾	7:23	5:34	4:57	**3:28**
342	7	We.		7:23	5:34	5:59	**4:08**
343	8	Th.		7:24	5:34	7:03	**4:55**
344	9	Fr.		7:25	5:34	8:05	**7:51**
345	10	Sa.	♆☌☾	7:25	5:34	9:04	**6:55**
346	11	Su.		7:26	5:35	9:56	**8:03**
347	12	Mo.		7:27	5:35	10:41	**9:12**
348	13	Tu.		7:28	5:35	11:19	**10:20**
349	14	We.		7:28	5:35	11:53	**11:27**
350	15	Th.	☾ at Perigee	7:29	5:36	**12:24**	...
351	16	Fr.		7:29	5:36	**12:54**	12:32
352	17	Sa.	♂☌☾.	7:30	5:37	**1:25**	1:37
353	18	Su.		7:31	5:37	**1:59**	2:43
354	19	Mo.		7:31	5:37	**2:36**	3:50
355	20	Tu.	♃☌☾	7:32	5:38	**3:20**	4:59
356	21	We.	Winter Begins	7:32	5:38	**4:10**	6:07
357	22	Th.	♅☌☉	7:33	5:39	**5:07**	7:11
358	23	Fr.		7:33	5:40	**6:09**	8:08
359	24	Sa.		7:33	5:40	**7:12**	8:57
360	25	Su.		7:34	5:41	**8:13**	9:38
361	26	Mo.	♄☌☉	7:34	5:41	**9:13**	10:13
362	27	Tu.		7:35	5:42	**10:09**	10:43
363	28	We.		7:35	5:43	**11:03**	11:10
364	29	Th.	☾ at Apogee	7:35	5:43	**11:57**	11:35
365	30	Fr.		7:36	5:44	...	11:59
366	31	Sa.	♆☌☉	7:36	5:45	12:51	**12:25**

Calendar For 1989

Time given in this calendar is according to **Central Standard Time**, except for the period from April 2 to Oct. 29, during which **Daylight Saving Time** is observed. See page 123 for explanation of how to get exact time at any certain Texas point. Boldface figures for moonrise and moonset indicate p.m. **Times are figured for the point 99° 10′ West and 31° 23′ North. This is a different point than that used in previous Almanacs.**

1st Month **JANUARY, 1989** **31 Days**

Moon's Phases—New, Jan. 7, 1:22 p.m.; First Qr., Jan. 14, 7:58 a.m.; Full, Jan. 21, 3:33 p.m.; Last Qr., Jan. 29, 8:02 p.m.

Day of Year	Day of Month	Day of Week	Planetary Configurations —Phenomena	*Hour of Sunrise	*Hour of Sunset	*Hour of Moonrise	*Hour of Moonset
1	1	Su.	⊕ at Perihelion	7:36	5:45	1:45	**12:52**
2	2	Mo.		7:36	5:46	2:43	**1:23**
3	3	Tu.		7:36	5:46	3:43	**2:00**
4	4	We.		7:36	5:47	4:45	**2:44**
5	5	Th.		7:37	5:48	5:49	**3:36**
6	6	Fr.	♀☌☾	7:37	5:49	6:50	**4:38**
7	7	Sa.		7:37	5:50	7:46	**5:46**
8	8	Su.	☿☌☾	7:37	5:50	8:34	**6:57**
9	9	Mo.		7:37	5:51	9:17	**8:08**
10	10	Tu.	☾ at Perigee	7:37	5:52	9:53	**9:17**
11	11	We.		7:37	5:53	10:26	**10:24**
12	12	Th.	♀☌♅	7:37	5:54	10:57	**11:30**
13	13	Fr.		7:37	5:55	11:28	...
14	14	Sa.		7:37	5:55	**12:00**	12:36
15	15	Su.	☿ Stationary	7:36	5:56	**12:36**	1:43
16	16	Mo.	♀☌♄	7:36	5:57	**1:17**	2:50
17	17	Tu.		7:36	5:58	**2:04**	3:57
18	18	We.		7:36	5:59	**2:58**	5:01
19	19	Th.		7:35	6:00	**3:57**	6:00
20	20	Fr.	♃ Stationary	7:35	6:01	**4:59**	6:51
21	21	Sa.		7:35	6:02	**6:01**	7:34
22	22	Su.		7:34	6:03	**7:01**	8:11
23	23	Mo.		7:34	6:04	**7:58**	8:43
24	24	Tu.		7:34	6:04	**8:54**	9:11
25	25	We.		7:33	6:05	**9:48**	9:36
26	26	Th.		7:33	6:06	**10:41**	10:01
27	27	Fr.	☾ at Apogee	7:32	6:07	**11:35**	10:26
28	28	Sa.		7:32	6:08	...	10:52
29	29	Su.		7:31	6:09	12:31	11:21
30	30	Mo.		7:31	6:10	1:29	11:54
31	31	Tu.	☿☌♀	7:30	6:11	2:29	**12:34**

2nd Month **FEBRUARY, 1989** **28 Days**

Moon's Phases—New, Feb. 6, 1:37 a.m.; First Qr., Feb. 12, 5:15 p.m.; Full, Feb. 20, 9:32 a.m.; Last Qr., Feb. 28, 2:08 p.m.

Day of Year	Day of Month	Day of Week	Planetary Configurations —Phenomena	*Hour of Sunrise	*Hour of Sunset	*Hour of Moonrise	*Hour of Moonset
32	1	We.		7:29	6:12	3:31	**1:21**
33	2	Th.		7:29	6:13	4:32	**2:17**
34	3	Fr.	♄☌☾	7:28	6:13	5:30	**3:22**
35	4	Sa.	☿☌☾	7:27	6:14	6:22	**4:32**
36	5	Su.		7:27	6:15	7:08	**5:45**
37	6	Mo.		7:26	6:16	7:48	**6:57**
38	7	Tu.	☾ at Perigee	7:25	6:17	8:23	**8:07**
39	8	We.		7:24	6:18	8:56	**9:17**
40	9	Th.		7:24	6:19	9:28	**10:25**
41	10	Fr.		7:23	6:20	10:01	**11:34**
42	11	Sa.		7:22	6:20	10:37	...
43	12	Su.	♅☌☾	7:21	6:21	11:16	12:42
44	13	Mo.	♃☌☾	7:20	6:22	**12:02**	1:50
45	14	Tu.		7:19	6:23	**12:53**	2:56
46	15	We.		7:18	6:24	**1:50**	3:55
47	16	Th.		7:17	6:25	**2:51**	4:48
48	17	Fr.		7:17	6:25	**3:52**	5:33
49	18	Sa.	☿ Gr. elong. W.	7:16	6:26	**4:52**	6:12
50	19	Su.		7:15	6:27	**5:50**	6:44
51	20	Mo.	Eclipse ☾	7:14	6:28	**6:46**	7:13
52	21	Tu.		7:13	6:29	**7:40**	7:39
53	22	We.		7:12	6:29	**8:34**	8:04
54	23	Th.	☾ at Apogee	7:10	6:30	**9:27**	8:29
55	24	Fr.		7:09	6:31	**10:22**	8:54
56	25	Sa.		7:08	6:32	**11:19**	9:22
57	26	Su.		7:07	6:33	...	9:53
58	27	Mo.		7:06	6:33	12:17	10:29
59	28	Tu.		7:05	6:34	1:18	11:12

3rd Month **MARCH, 1989** **31 Days**

Moon's Phases—New, March 7, 12:19 p.m.; First Qr., March 14, 4:11 a.m.; Full, March 22, 3:58 a.m.; Last Qr., March 30, 4:21 a.m.

Day of Year	Day of Month	Day of Week	Planetary Configurations —Phenomena	*Hour of Sunrise	*Hour of Sunset	*Hour of Moonrise	*Hour of Moonset
60	1	We.		7:04	6:35	2:18	**12:02**
61	2	Th.	♄☌♆	7:03	6:36	3:16	**1:02**
62	3	Fr.	♄☌☾	7:02	6:36	4:09	**2:08**
63	4	Sa.		7:00	6:37	4:57	**3:18**
64	5	Su.	☿☌☾	6:59	6:38	5:39	**4:30**
65	6	Mo.		6:58	6:38	6:16	**5:42**
66	7	Tu.	Eclipse ☉	6:57	6:39	6:51	**6:53**
67	8	We.	☾ at Perigee	6:56	6:40	7:24	**8:04**
68	9	Th.		6:54	6:41	7:57	**9:15**
69	10	Fr.		6:53	6:41	8:33	**10:26**
70	11	Sa.		6:52	6:42	9:12	**11:37**
71	12	Su.	♃☌☾	6:51	6:43	9:57	...
72	13	Mo.		6:50	6:43	10:48	12:46
73	14	Tu.		6:48	6:44	11:44	1:50
74	15	We.		6:47	6:45	**12:45**	2:45
75	16	Th.		6:46	6:45	**1:46**	3:33
76	17	Fr.		6:45	6:46	**2:46**	4:13
77	18	Sa.		6:43	6:47	**3:44**	4:47
78	19	Su.		6:42	6:47	**4:40**	5:17
79	20	Mo.	Spring Begins	6:41	6:48	**5:35**	5:43
80	21	Tu.		6:40	6:49	**6:28**	6:08
81	22	We.	☾ at Apogee	6:38	6:49	**7:22**	6:33
82	23	Th.		6:37	6:50	**8:16**	6:58
83	24	Fr.		6:36	6:51	**9:12**	7:25
84	25	Sa.		6:34	6:51	**10:10**	7:55
85	26	Su.		6:33	6:52	**11:09**	8:29
86	27	Mo.		6:32	6:53	...	9:09
87	28	Tu.		6:31	6:53	12:09	9:56
88	29	We.		6:29	6:54	1:06	10:50
89	30	Th.	♄☌☾	6:28	6:55	2:00	11:52
90	31	Fr.		6:27	6:55	2:49	**12:58**

4th Month **APRIL, 1989** **30 Days**

Moon's Phases—New, April 5, 9:33 p.m.; First Qr., April 12, 5:13 p.m.; Full, April 20, 9:13 p.m.; Last Qr., April 28, 2:46 p.m.

Day of Year	Day of Month	Day of Week	Planetary Configurations —Phenomena	*Hour of Sunrise	*Hour of Sunset	*Hour of Moonrise	*Hour of Moonset
91	1	Sa.		6:26	6:56	3:31	**2:07**
92	2	†Su.		7:24	7:57	5:09	**4:17**
93	3	Mo.		7:23	7:57	5:44	**5:27**
94	4	Tu.		7:22	7:58	6:17	**6:37**
95	5	We.	☾ at Perigee	7:21	7:59	6:51	**7:48**
96	6	Th.		7:19	7:59	7:25	**9:01**
97	7	Fr.		7:18	8:00	8:04	**10:14**
98	8	Sa.		7:17	8:01	8:47	**11:27**
99	9	Su.	♃☌☾	7:16	8:01	9:37	...
100	10	Mo.	♅☌☾	7:15	8:02	10:34	12:35
101	11	Tu.		7:13	8:03	11:35	1:37
102	12	We.		7:12	8:03	**12:37**	2:29
103	13	Th.		7:11	8:04	**1:39**	3:12
104	14	Fr.		7:10	8:05	**2:38**	3:49
105	15	Sa.		7:09	8:05	**3:35**	4:20
106	16	Su.		7:08	8:06	**4:30**	4:47
107	17	Mo.		7:06	8:07	**5:23**	5:13
108	18	Tu.	☾ at Apogee	7:05	8:07	**6:17**	5:37
109	19	We.		7:04	8:08	**7:11**	6:02
110	20	Th.		7:03	8:09	**8:06**	6:29
111	21	Fr.		7:02	8:09	**9:04**	6:58
112	22	Sa.	♄ Stationary	7:01	8:10	**10:03**	7:31
113	23	Su.		7:00	8:11	**11:02**	8:09
114	24	Mo.		6:59	8:11	...	8:54
115	25	Tu.		6:58	8:12	12:01	9:46
116	26	We.	♄☌☾	6:57	8:13	12:55	10:44
117	27	Th.		6:56	8:13	1:45	11:48
118	28	Fr.		6:55	8:14	2:28	**12:54**
119	29	Sa.		6:54	8:15	3:07	**2:01**
120	30	Su.	☿ Gr. elong. E.	6:53	8:15	3:41	**3:08**

†Daylight Saving Time begins at 2 a.m.

Calendar For 1989

5th Month MAY, 1989 31 Days

Moon's Phases—New, May 5, 5:46 a.m.; First Qr., May 12, 8:19 a.m.; Full, May 20, 12:16 p.m.; Last Qr., May 27, 10:01 p.m.

Day of			Planetary Configurations —Phenomena	*Hour of			
Year	Month	Week		Sunrise	Sunset	Moonrise	Moonset
121	1	Mo.		6.52	8:16	4:14	**4:15**
122	2	Tu.		6.51	8:17	4:46	**5:24**
123	3	We.	☾ at Perigee	6.50	8:17	5:19	**6:35**
124	4	Th.		6:49	8:18	5:55	**7:47**
125	5	Fr.		6:48	8:19	6:36	**9:01**
126	6	Sa.	☿☌☾	6:47	8:20	7:23	**10:13**
127	7	Su.	♃☌☾	6:47	8:20	8:18	**11:20**
128	8	Mo.	♂☌☾	6:46	8:21	9:18	...
129	9	Tu.		6:45	8:22	10:23	12:18
130	10	We.		6:44	8:22	11:27	1:06
131	11	Th.		6:43	8:23	**12:29**	1:46
132	12	Fr.	☿ Stationary	6:43	8:24	**1:27**	2:20
133	13	Sa.		6:42	8:24	**2:23**	2:49
134	14	Su.		6:41	8:25	**3:17**	3:15
135	15	Mo.		6:41	8:26	**4:11**	3:40
136	16	Tu.	☾ at Apogee	6:40	8:26	**5:04**	4:05
137	17	We.		6:39	8:27	**5:59**	4:31
138	18	Th.		6:39	8:28	**6:56**	5:00
139	19	Fr.		6:38	8:28	**7:55**	5:31
140	20	Sa.		6:38	8:29	**8:55**	6:08
141	21	Su.		6:37	8:30	**9:54**	6:51
142	22	Mo.	♀☌♃	6:37	8:30	**10:51**	7:42
143	23	Tu.	♄☌☾	6:36	8:31	**11:42**	8:39
144	24	We.		6:36	8:32	...	9:42
145	25	Th.		6:35	8:32	12:27	10:47
146	26	Fr.		6:35	8:33	1:07	11:53
147	27	Sa.		6:34	8:33	1:42	**12:58**
148	28	Su.		6:34	8:34	2:14	**2:03**
149	29	Mo.		6:34	8:35	2:45	**3:09**
150	30	Tu.		6:33	8:35	3:16	**4:16**
151	31	We.	☾ at Perigee	6:33	8:36	3:50	**5:26**

6th Month JUNE, 1989 30 Days

Moon's Phases—New, June 3, 1:53 p.m.; First Qr., June 11, 12:59 a.m.; Full, June 19, 12:57 a.m.; Last Qr., June 26, 3:09 a.m.

Day of			Planetary Configurations —Phenomena	*Hour of			
Year	Month	Week		Sunrise	Sunset	Moonrise	Moonset
152	1	Th.		6:33	8:36	4:27	**6:37**
153	2	Fr.		6:33	8:37	5:11	**7:50**
154	3	Sa.		6:32	8:37	6:02	**8:59**
155	4	Su.	♀☌☾	6:32	8:38	7:00	**10:02**
156	5	Mo.		6:32	8:38	8:04	**10:56**
157	6	Tu.	♂☌☾	6:32	8:39	9:09	**11:40**
158	7	We.		6:32	8:39	10:14	...
159	8	Th.		6:32	8:40	11:15	12:17
160	9	Fr.	♃☌☉	6:32	8:40	**12:13**	12:49
161	10	Sa.		6:32	8:41	**1:09**	1:17
162	11	Su.		6:32	8:41	**2:03**	1:42
163	12	Mo.	☾ at Apogee	6:32	8:42	**2:56**	2:07
164	13	Tu.		6:32	8:42	**3:51**	2:33
165	14	We.		6:32	8:42	**4:47**	3:00
166	15	Th.		6:32	8:43	**5:45**	3:30
167	16	Fr.		6:32	8:43	**6:45**	4:05
168	17	Sa.		6:32	8:43	**7:45**	4:46
169	18	Su.	☿ Gr. elong. W.	6:32	8:44	**8:43**	5:35
170	19	Mo.	♂☌☾	6:32	8:44	**9:37**	6:31
171	20	Tu.	♄☌☾	6:32	8:44	**10:25**	7:33
172	21	We.	Summer Begins	6:33	8:44	**11:07**	8:38
173	22	Th.		6:33	8:44	**11:44**	9:45
174	23	Fr.		6:33	8:45	...	10:51
175	24	Sa.	♄☌♆	6:33	8:45	12:16	11:57
176	25	Su.		6:34	8:45	12:47	**1:01**
177	26	Mo.		6:34	8:45	1:18	**2:07**
178	27	Tu.	☾ at Perigee	6:34	8:45	1:50	**3:14**
179	28	We.		6:35	8:45	2:25	**4:22**
180	29	Th.		6:35	8:45	3:05	**5:33**
181	30	Fr.		6:35	8:45	3:51	**6:42**

*See text before January calendar for explanation.

7th Month JULY, 1989 31 Days

Moon's Phases—New, July 2, 8:59 p.m.; First Qr., July 10, 6:19 p.m.; Full, July 18, 11:42 a.m.; Last Qr., July 25, 7:31 a.m.

Day of			Planetary Configurations —Phenomena	*Hour of			
Year	Month	Week		Sunrise	Sunset	Moonrise	Moonset
182	1	Sa.	♃☌☾	6:36	8:45	4:46	**7:47**
183	2	Su.	♄☍	6:36	8:45	5:47	**8:44**
184	3	Mo.		6:36	8:45	6:52	**9:32**
185	4	Tu.	⊕ at Aphelion	6:37	8:45	7:57	**10:13**
186	5	We.	♂☌☾	6:37	8:45	9:01	**10:47**
187	6	Th.		6:38	8:45	10:01	**11:16**
188	7	Fr.		6:38	8:45	10:58	**11:43**
189	8	Sa.		6:39	8:44	11:53	...
190	9	Su.		6:39	8:44	**12:47**	12:09
191	10	Mo.	☾ at Apogee	6:40	8:44	**1:41**	12:34
192	11	Tu.		6:40	8:44	**2:36**	1:00
193	12	We.	♀☌♂	6:41	8:43	**3:33**	1:29
194	13	Th.		6:41	8:43	**4:32**	2:02
195	14	Fr.		6:42	8:43	**5:32**	2:40
196	15	Sa.		6:43	8:42	**6:31**	3:25
197	16	Su.		6:43	8:42	**7:27**	4:18
198	17	Mo.	♄☌☾	6:44	8:42	**8:18**	5:18
199	18	Tu.		6:44	8:41	**9:03**	6:24
200	19	We.		6:45	8:41	**9:42**	7:32
201	20	Th.		6:45	8:40	**10:17**	8:40
202	21	Fr.		6:46	8:40	**10:50**	9:47
203	22	Sa.		6:47	8:39	**11:21**	10:54
204	23	Su.	☾ at Perigee	6:47	8:39	**11:52**	11:59
205	24	Mo.		6:48	8:38	...	**1:06**
206	25	Tu.		6:49	8:37	12:26	**2:14**
207	26	We.		6:49	8:37	1:04	**3:23**
208	27	Th.		6:50	8:36	1:47	**4:32**
209	28	Fr.	♇ Stationary	6:50	8:36	2:38	**5:37**
210	29	Sa.	♃☌☾	6:51	8:35	3:35	**6:36**
211	30	Su.		6:52	8:34	4:38	**7:26**
212	31	Mo.		6:52	8:33	5:43	**8:09**

8th Month AUGUST, 1989 31 Days

Moon's Phases—New, Aug. 1, 10:06 a.m.; First Qr., Aug. 9, 11:28 a.m.; Full, Aug. 16, 9:07 p.m.; Last Qr., Aug. 23, 12:40 p.m.; New, Aug. 30, 11:44 p.m.

Day of			Planetary Configurations —Phenomena	*Hour of			
Year	Month	Week		Sunrise	Sunset	Moonrise	Moonset
213	1	Tu.		6:53	8:33	6:47	**8:45**
214	2	We.	☿☌☾	6:54	8:32	7:48	**9:17**
215	3	Th.	♂☌☾	6:54	8:31	8:47	**9:44**
216	4	Fr.	♀☌☾	6:55	8:30	9:43	**10:10**
217	5	Sa.	☿☌♂	6:56	8:29	10:38	**10:36**
218	6	Su.		6:56	8:28	11:32	**11:01**
219	7	Mo.	☾ at Apogee	6:57	8:28	**12:26**	**11:29**
220	8	Tu.		6:57	8:27	**1:22**	**11:59**
221	9	We.		6:58	8:26	**2:20**	...
222	10	Th.		6:59	8:25	**3:19**	12:35
223	11	Fr.		6:59	8:24	**4:18**	1:17
224	12	Sa.		7:00	8:23	**5:15**	2:05
225	13	Su.	♄☌☾	7:01	8:22	**6:08**	3:02
226	14	Mo.		7:01	8:21	**6:55**	4:05
227	15	Tu.		7:02	8:20	**7:37**	5:12
228	16	We.	Eclipse ☾	7:03	8:19	**8:14**	6:21
229	17	Th.		7:03	8:18	**8:48**	7:30
230	18	Fr.		7:04	8:17	**9:21**	8:39
231	19	Sa.	☾ at Perigee	7:04	8:16	**9:53**	9:47
232	20	Su.		7:05	8:15	**10:27**	10:55
233	21	Mo.		7:06	8:13	**11:04**	**12:04**
234	22	Tu.		7:06	8:12	**11:46**	**1:15**
235	23	We.		7:07	8:11	...	**2:24**
236	24	Th.		7:08	8:10	12:34	**3:31**
237	25	Fr.		7:08	8:09	1:29	**4:31**
238	26	Sa.	♃☌☾	7:09	8:08	2:30	**5:23**
239	27	Su.		7:09	8:07	3:34	**6:08**
240	28	Mo.		7:10	8:05	4:37	**6:46**
241	29	Tu.	☿ Gr. elong. E.	7:11	8:04	5:39	**7:18**
242	30	We.		7:11	8:03	6:38	**7:47**
243	31	Th.	Eclipse ☉	7:12	8:02	7:34	**8:13**

Calendar For 1989

9th Month SEPTEMBER, 1989 30 Days
Moon's Phases—First Qr., Sept. 8, 3:49 a.m.; Full, Sept. 15, 5:51 a.m.; Last Qr., Sept. 21, 8:10 p.m.; New, Sept. 29, 3:47 p.m.

Day of			Planetary Configurations —Phenomena	*Hour of			
Year	Month	Week		Sunrise	Sunset	Moonrise	Moonset
244	1	Fr.		7:12	8:00	8:29	**8:39**
245	2	Sa.	☿☌☾	7:13	7:59	9:24	**9:04**
246	3	Su.	♀☌☾	7:14	7:58	10:18	**9:31**
247	4	Mo.	☾ at Apogee	7:14	7:57	11:13	**10:00**
248	5	Tu.		7:15	7:55	**12:10**	**10:33**
249	6	We.		7:15	7:54	**1:08**	**11:11**
250	7	Th.		7:16	7:53	**2:06**	**11:56**
251	8	Fr.		7:17	7:52	**3:03**	...
252	9	Sa.	♄☌☾	7:17	7:50	**3:57**	12:48
253	10	Su.	♄ Stationary	7:18	7:49	**4:45**	1:47
254	11	Mo.	☿ Stationary	7:18	7:48	**5:29**	2:51
255	12	Tu.		7:19	7:47	**6:08**	3:59
256	13	We.		7:19	7:45	**6:43**	5:07
257	14	Th.		7:20	7:44	**7:16**	6:16
258	15	Fr.		7:21	7:43	**7:49**	7:26
259	16	Sa.	☾ at Perigee	7:21	7:41	**8:23**	8:35
260	17	Su.		7:22	7:40	**9:00**	9:47
261	18	Mo.		7:22	7:39	**9:42**	10:59
262	19	Tu.		7:23	7:37	**10:29**	**12:11**
263	20	We.	♆ Stationary	7:24	7:36	**11:24**	**1:21**
264	21	Th.		7:24	7:35	...	**2:25**
265	22	Fr.	Falls Begins	7:25	7:34	12:24	**3:21**
266	23	Sa.		7:25	7:32	1:27	**4:08**
267	24	Su.		7:26	7:31	2:31	**4:47**
268	25	Mo.		7:27	7:30	3:32	**5:20**
269	26	Tu.		7:27	7:28	4:32	**5:50**
270	27	We.		7:28	7:27	5:28	**6:17**
271	28	Th.		7:28	7:26	6:23	**6:42**
272	29	Fr.	♂☌☉	7:29	7:24	7:17	**7:08**
273	30	Sa.		7:30	7:23	8:12	**7:34**

10th Month OCTOBER, 1989 31 Days
Moon's Phases—First Qr., Oct. 7, 6:52 p.m.; Full, Oct. 14, 2:32 p.m.; Last Qr., Oct. 21, 7:19 a.m.; New, Oct. 29, 11:27 a.m.

Day of			Planetary Configurations —Phenomena	*Hour of			
Year	Month	Week		Sunrise	Sunset	Moonrise	Moonset
274	1	Su.	☾ at Apogee	7:30	7:22	9:07	**8:03**
275	2	Mo.		7:31	7:21	10:03	**8:34**
276	3	Tu.	♀☌☾	7:32	7:19	11:00	**9:11**
277	4	We.		7:32	7:18	11:58	**9:53**
278	5	Th.		7:33	7:17	**12:54**	**10:41**
279	6	Fr.		7:33	7:16	**1:48**	**11:36**
280	7	Sa.	♄☌☾	7:34	7:14	**2:38**	...
281	8	Su.		7:35	7:13	**3:22**	12:36
282	9	Mo.		7:35	7:12	**4:01**	1:40
283	10	Tu.	☿ Gr. elong. W.	7:36	7:11	**4:37**	2:46
284	11	We.		7:37	7:10	**5:11**	3:53
285	12	Th.		7:37	7:08	**5:43**	5:01
286	13	Fr.		7:38	7:07	**6:17**	6:10
287	14	Sa.	☾ at Perigee	7:39	7:06	**6:53**	7:21
288	15	Su.		7:40	7:05	**7:33**	8:34
289	16	Mo.		7:40	7:04	**8:19**	9:49
290	17	Tu.		7:41	7:03	**9:13**	11:02
291	18	We.		7:42	7:02	**10:13**	**12:12**
292	19	Th.	♃☌☾	7:41	7:01	**11:17**	**1:13**
293	20	Fr.		7:43	6:59	...	**2:04**
294	21	Sa.		7:44	6:58	12:23	**2:47**
295	22	Su.		7:45	6:57	1:26	**3:22**
296	23	Mo.		7:45	6:56	2:26	**3:53**
297	24	Tu.		7:46	6:55	3:23	**4:20**
298	25	We.		7:47	6:54	4:19	**4:46**
299	26	Th.		7:48	6:53	5:13	**5:12**
300	27	Fr.		7:48	6:52	6:06	**5:38**
301	28	Sa.	☾ at Apogee	7:49	6:51	7:01	**6:06**
302	29	†Su.		6:50	5:50	6:57	**5:36**
303	30	Mo.		6:51	5:50	7:54	**6:11**
304	31	Tu.		6:52	5:49	8:51	**6:52**

†Daylight Saving Time ends at 2 a.m. *See text before January calendar for explanation.

11th Month NOVEMBER, 1989 30 Days
Moon's Phases—First Qr., Nov. 6, 8:11 a.m.; Full, Nov. 12, 11:51 p.m.; Last Qr., Nov. 19, 10:44 p.m.; New, Nov. 28, 3:41 a.m.

Day of			Planetary Configurations —Phenomena	*Hour of			
Year	Month	Week		Sunrise	Sunset	Moonrise	Moonset
305	1	We.		6:52	5:48	9:49	**7:38**
306	2	Th.	♀☌☾	6:53	5:47	10:43	**8:31**
307	3	Fr.	♄☌☾	6:54	5:46	11:33	**9:28**
308	4	Sa.		6:55	5:45	**12:18**	**10:30**
309	5	Su.		6:56	5:45	**12:58**	**11:33**
310	6	Mo.		6:56	5:44	**1:34**	...
311	7	Tu.	♇☌☉	6:57	5:43	**2:07**	12:37
312	8	We.	♀ Gr. elong. E.	6:58	5:42	**2:39**	1:42
313	9	Th.		6:59	5:42	**3:11**	2:48
314	10	Fr.		7:00	5:41	**3:44**	3:55
315	11	Sa.		7:01	5:40	**4:22**	5:06
316	12	Su.	☾ at Perigee	7:02	5:40	**5:05**	6:20
317	13	Mo.		7:02	5:39	**5:56**	7:35
318	14	Tu.		7:03	5:39	**6:54**	8:48
319	15	We.	♀☌♄	7:04	5:38	**7:59**	9:55
320	16	Th.	♃☌☾	7:05	5:38	**9:07**	10:53
321	17	Fr.		7:06	5:37	**10:13**	11:41
322	18	Sa.		7:07	5:37	**11:16**	**12:21**
323	19	Su.		7:08	5:36	...	**12:54**
324	20	Mo.		7:08	5:36	12:16	**1:23**
325	21	Tu.		7:09	5:36	1:13	**1:49**
326	22	We.		7:10	5:35	2:07	**2:15**
327	23	Th.		7:11	5:35	3:01	**2:40**
328	24	Fr.	☾ at Apogee	7:12	5:35	3:55	**3:08**
329	25	Sa.		7:13	5:34	4:50	**3:38**
330	26	Su.		7:14	5:34	5:47	**4:12**
331	27	Mo.		7:14	5:34	6:45	**4:50**
332	28	Tu.		7:15	5:34	7:42	**5:35**
333	29	We.		7:16	5:34	8:38	**6:27**
334	30	Th.	♅☌☾	7:17	5:34	9:30	**7:24**

12th Month DECEMBER, 1989 31 Days
Moon's Phases—First Qr., Dec. 5, 7:26 p.m.; Full, Dec. 12, 10:30 a.m.; Last Qr., Dec. 19, 5:54 p.m.; New, Dec. 27, 9:20 p.m.

Day of			Planetary Configurations —Phenomena	*Hour of			
Year	Month	Week		Sunrise	Sunset	Moonrise	Moonset
335	1	Fr.	♄☌☾	7:18	5:33	10:17	**8:24**
336	2	Sa.	♀☌☾	7:19	5:33	10:59	**9:27**
337	3	Su.		7:19	5:33	11:35	**10:29**
338	4	Mo.		7:20	5:33	**12:08**	**11:32**
339	5	Tu.		7:21	5:33	**12:39**	...
340	6	We.		7:22	5:34	**1:09**	12:35
341	7	Th.		7:23	5:34	**1:41**	1:39
342	8	Fr.		7:23	5:34	**2:15**	2:46
343	9	Sa.		7:24	5:34	**2:54**	3:56
344	10	Su.	☾ at Perigee	7:25	5:34	**3:40**	5:08
345	11	Mo.		7:25	5:34	**4:34**	6:22
346	12	Tu.		7:26	5:35	**5:36**	7:32
347	13	We.	♃☌☾	7:27	5:35	**6:44**	8:35
348	14	Th.	♀ Gr. Brilliancy	7:28	5:35	**7:53**	9:29
349	15	Fr.		7:28	5:35	**8:59**	10:14
350	16	Sa.	☿☌♄	7:29	5:36	**10:02**	10:50
351	17	Su.		7:29	5:36	**11:02**	11:22
352	18	Mo.		7:30	5:37	**11:58**	11:50
353	19	Tu.		7:31	5:37	...	**12:16**
354	20	We.		7:31	5:37	12:53	**12:42**
355	21	Th.	Winter Begins	7:32	5:38	1:47	**1:09**
356	22	Fr.	☾ at Apogee	7:32	5:38	2:42	**1:38**
357	23	Sa.	☿ Gr. elong. E.	7:33	5:39	3:38	**2:10**
358	24	Su.		7:33	5:40	4:35	**2:47**
359	25	Mo.	♂☌☾	7:33	5:40	5:33	**3:30**
360	26	Tu.		7:34	5:41	6:30	**4:20**
361	27	We.	♅☌☉	7:34	5:41	7:24	**5:16**
362	28	Th.		7:35	5:42	8:14	**6:16**
363	29	Fr.	☿☌☾	7:35	5:43	8:58	**7:19**
364	30	Sa.	♀☌☾	7:35	5:43	9:36	**8:23**
365	31	Su.		7:36	5:44	10:11	**9:26**

Counties

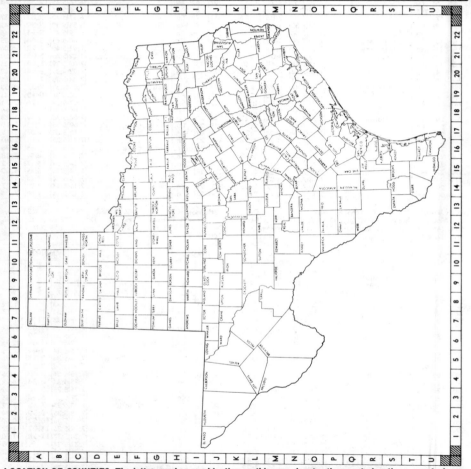

LOCATION OF COUNTIES: The letter-number combination on this map denotes the county locations; e.g. Anderson County (J-19) can be located by using the horizontal and vertical scales at top and bottom of this map.

Texas Counties and Towns

These pages describe Texas' 254 counties and hundreds of towns. Descriptions are based on reports from chambers of commerce, Texas Agricultural Extension Service, federal and state agencies and many others. Consult the index for other county information.

County maps are based on those of the Texas Highway Department and are copyrighted, 1987, as are the entire contents.

LETTER-NUMBER COMBINATIONS in parentheses with each county denote location on the map on this page. For example, Anderson County (J-19) means that Anderson County can be found near the intersection of lines J and 19 on the larger map.

AREA: Revised 1980 U.S. Census land area; excludes land submerged by water.

TOPOGRAPHY: Descriptions are from U.S. Geological Survey and local sources.

HISTORY, ORGANIZATION, COUNTY NAMES: From Texas Statutes, Fulmore's History and Geography of Texas as Told in County Names, WPA Historical Records Survey and Texas Centennial Commission Report.

COURTS, CONGRESSIONAL DISTRICTS, ETC.: The following abbreviations are used: Cong. Dist., Congressional District; St. Sen. Dist., State Senatorial District; St. Rep. Dist., State Representative District; St. Dist. Cts., State District Courts; U.S. Jud. Dist., U.S. Judicial District; Ct. Appeals, Court of Appeals; Admin. Jud. Dist., Administrative Judicial District.

The designations used in the following counties were districts as constituted in 1987.

Texas is divided into four U.S. Judicial Districts: Northern, Southern, Eastern and Western. These abbreviations are used to designate the city in which the court sits: N-Ab: Abilene; N-Am: Amarillo; N-Dl: Dallas; N-FW: Fort Worth; N-Lb: Lubbock; N-SAng: San Angelo; N-WF: Wichita Falls; S-Br: Brownsville; S-CC: Corpus Christi; S-Gn: Galveston; S-Hn: Houston; S-La: Laredo; S-Va: Victoria; E-Bt: Beaumont; E-Ml: Marshall; E-Ps: Paris; E-Sh: Sherman; E-Tx: Texarkana; E-Ty: Tyler; W-An: Austin; W-DR: Del Rio; W-EP: El Paso; W-Pe: Pecos; W-SAnt; San Antonio; W-Wa: Waco; W-M-O: Midland-Odessa.

VITAL STATISTICS: These vital statistics by county for 1985 were compiled by the Texas Department of Health.

AGRICULTURE: 1985 Texas County Statistics; County Agents' reports for 1986 are included when available.

Much additional Texas agricultural information will be found in the Texas Almanac section devoted to crops and livestock. This includes total cash receipts and production of major livestock and their products, and crops; along with discussions of leading commodities.

That information was obtained largely from Texas Crop and Livestock Reporting Service of the Texas Department of Agriculture and U.S. Department of Agriculture.

POPULATION: Revised July 1, 1985, U.S. Census figures are used for counties; revised July 1, 1984, Census figures are used for incorporated cities and towns. Texas Almanac estimates, based on reports from county agents, chambers of commerce and others, used where no official Census figures available. In some cases late adjustments in county totals will cause breakdowns not to add up.

ALTITUDES: The altitude extremes have been determined by the U.S. Geological Survey. Other elevation has been provided by the Texas Department of Highways and Public Transportation and Texas Railroad Commission.

WEATHER: From NOAA State Climatologist, College Station.

MINERALS: Oil value, 1986, State Comptroller.

SOILS: Texas Agricultural Experiment Station, U.S. Soil Conservation Service.

HIGHWAYS: Texas Department of Highways and Public Transportation.

TAX VALUE: 1986 Total assessed valuation, (before exemptions), State Property Tax Board. N.A. indicates information not available June 1, 1987.

FEDERAL EXPENDITURES: U.S. Census for Office of Management and Budget, 1986.

VOTER REGISTRATION: Voters eligible on Nov. 4, 1986, office of Secretary of State's Election Division.

INCOME: Per capita income (PCI) figures compiled by U.S. Bureau of the Census in 1983 and made available by the Texas State Data Center, Austin.

BUYING POWER: Effective Buying Income, 1986, Sales Management Magazine, (further reproduction prohibited without written permission from Sales Management).

RAILROADS: Texas Railroad Commission records as of 1986 used on county maps.

EMPLOYEES: This is the number of employees reported by the Texas Employment Commission for the third quarter of 1986. It includes all persons covered under the Texas Unemployment Compensation Act.

WAGES: These wages are based on the reported wages for the third quarter of 1986. These quarterly wages, as prepared by the Texas Employment Commission, are then multiplied by four to obtain an estimate of annual wages.

AVERAGE WEEKLY PAY: This figure is provided for 1986 third quarter wages by the Texas Employment Commission.

TAX RATIO: The tax ratio is the percentage of market value upon which the tax rate is levied in each taxing authority. The ratio for 1986 is determined by the State Property Tax Board.

BUS. ESTAB.: This is the number of business establishments in each county as determined by the U.S. Bureau of the Census in its 1984 County Business Patterns report. It includes all businesses, service establishments and industries covered by the Social Security law.

LEGEND FOR MAPS

Following is explanation of signs and symbols used:

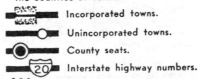

	Paved road of all types.
	Indicates divided roads.
	Surfaced roads—all-weather gravel, shell, etc.
	Roads under construction.

(With few exceptions roads shown on these maps are state and federal highways. Local roads of all types of improvement thread the counties of Texas.)

	Incorporated towns.
	Unincorporated towns.
	County seats.
20	Interstate highway numbers.
2	U.S. highway numbers.
2A	Alternate U.S. highway numbers.
2	State highway numbers.
2	Farm to market roads.
2	Park roads, temporary designations.
LR	County or local roads.
	Railroads.

Airports.

Notable parks.

Anderson

LOCATION: East Texas (J-19).

HISTORY: First settled in 1830s; created from Houston County and organized in 1846; named for **K. L. Anderson,** last vice-president, Texas Republic.

Cong. Dist.	2	U.S. Jud. Dist.	E-Tyler
St. Sen. Dist.	3	Ct. Appeals	12
St. Rep. Dist	11	Admin. Jud. Dist.	1
St. Dist. Cts.	3, 87, 349		

PHYSICAL FEATURES: Hilly, slopes to Trinity and Neches Rivers; sandy, clay, black soils; pines, hardwoods used commercially.

RECREATION. Fishing, hunting, many streams, lakes; **Dogwood Trails;** historic sites; **Engeling Wildlife Refuge; Texas State Railroad Park** for tourists; **Museum for East Texas Culture;** professional bicycle racing; civic auditorium; county fair; arts, crafts festival; tour of old homes. Tourist information center in restored 1890 depot.

MINERALS: Oil and gas.

1985 Pop.	46,400	Tax Ratio	0.97
Area (sq. mi.)	1,077	Oil value	$24,963,111
Altitude (ft.)	198-624	No. employed	11,846
Ann. rainfall (in.)	40.51	Avg. weekly wage	$321.75
Jan. temp. min.	37	Annual wages	$198,200,932
July temp. max.	94	1983 PCI	$7,445
Growing season (da.)	264	Buying pwr.	$410,227,000
Voters reg.	19,056	Tax value	$1,574,784,114
Businesses	912	Fed. expend.	$89,284,000

VITAL STATISTICS 1985: Births, 711; Deaths, 427; Marriages, 504; Divorces, 48.

AGRICULTURE: Annual agricultural receipts average about $35.5 million, with almost 90% from livestock and products. Hay, peas, watermelon and peanuts principal crops; over 50% of land in forests and about $2.9 million worth of timber products sold.

BUSINESS: Manufacturing, distribution, agribusiness, tourism; hunting and fishing leases; three Texas Department of Corrections units.

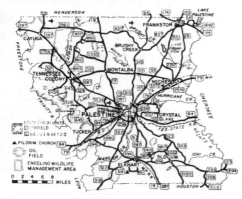

PALESTINE (18,153) county seat; wholesale meats, automotive parts, clothing, metal, wood products manufactured; large aluminum smelting plant; transportation center; agribusiness center; shipping center; **Scientific Balloon Station;** hospital; library; vocational-technical facilities; **Trinity Valley Community College.**

Other towns include **Frankston** (1,459), **Elkhart** (1,542), **Tennessee Colony,** which is site of **Coffield** and **Beto** Units, **Texas Department of Corrections.**

Andrews

LOCATION: Borders New Mexico (I-7).

HISTORY: Created 1876 from Bexar Territory; organized 1910; named for Texas Revolutionary soldier, **Richard Andrews.**

Cong. Dist.	19	U.S. Jud. Dist	W:M-O
St. Sen. Dist.	28	Ct. Appeals	8
St. Rep. Dist.	77	Admin. Jud. Dist.	7
St. Dist. Cts.	109		

PHYSICAL FEATURES: Plains, drain to playas;

grass, mesquite, shin oak; red clay, sandy soils.

RECREATION: Prairie dog town, oil museum, local arts and crafts and other events, camper facilities.

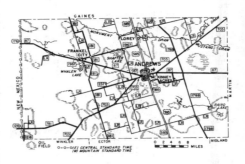

MINERALS: A leading producer of oil and gas.

1985 Pop.	16,500	Tax Ratio	0.91
Area (sq. mi.)	1,501	Oil value	$480,827,429
Altitude (ft.)	2,915-3,397	No. employed	5,069
Ann. rainfall (in.)	14.37	Avg. weekly wage	$414.33
Jan. temp. min.	30	Annual wages	$109,212,464
July temp. max.	96	1983 PCI	$9,156
Growing season (da.)	213	Buying pwr.	$181,268,000
Voters reg.	6,236	Tax value	$2,841,587,579
Businesses	388	Fed. expend.	$19,116,000

VITAL STATISTICS 1985: Births, 379; Deaths, 86; Marriages, 225; Divorces, 134.

AGRICULTURE: Income averages $11.8 million, about 50% from cattle, remainder cotton, sorghums; small grains, corn, hay; 15,000 acres irrigated.

BUSINESS: Chiefly oil related; vacuum cleaner manufacturing, fiberglass tank manufacturing; agribusiness.

ANDREWS (13,036) county seat; oil marketing center; amphitheatre; hospital, rest home, mental health center; parks.

Angelina

LOCATION: In east (K-21).

HISTORY: Created, organized 1846, from Nacogdoches County; named for **Angelina River.**

Cong. Dist.	2	U.S. Jud. Dist.	E.-Tyler
St. Sen. Dist.	3	Ct. Appeals	9
St. Rep. Dist.	17	Admin. Jud. Dist.	2
St. Dist. Cts.	159, 217		

PHYSICAL FEATURES: Rolling, hilly; black, red, gray soils; **Angelina National Forest;** much lumbering.

RECREATION: Lake Sam Rayburn; national, state forests, parks; historic sites; Texas Forest Festival third Saturday in May; Forestry Association Museum and historical locomotive exhibit; historical and creative arts museum; woodland trails; Ellen Trout Park and Zoo; county rodeo.

MINERALS: Limited output natural gas, oil.

1985 Pop.	68,900	Tax Ratio	0.91
Area (sq. mi.)	807	Oil value	$17,785
Altitude (ft.)	139-404	No. employed	26,277
Ann. rainfall (in.)	42.99	Avg. weekly wage	$309.37
Jan. temp. min.	39	Annual wages	$422,736,072
July temp. max.	94	1983 PCI	$7,721
Growing season (da.)	244	Buying pwr.	$698,604,000
Voters reg.	32,529	Tax value	$2,105,424,493
Businesses	1,616	Fed. expend.	$141,664,000

VITAL STATISTICS 1985: Births, 1,042; Deaths, 603; Marriages, 834; Divorces, 464.

AGRICULTURE: Leading timber-producing county with 70% of land in commercial forests; about $12 million average annual income from beef cattle, poultry; some hay, vegetables marketed.

BUSINESS: Many plants make oil field pumping units, newsprint, other paper products; wood products, iron and steel castings, truck trailers; mobile home units, horse stables.

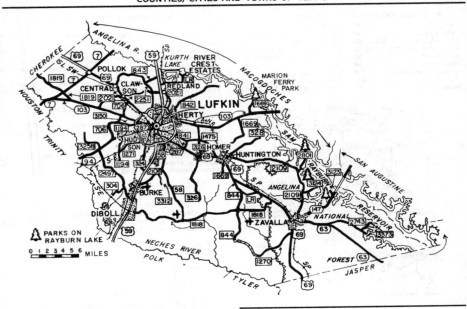

LUFKIN (30,616) county seat, a leading manufacturing center; **Angelina College;** two hospitals; **Lufkin State School** (mentally retarded); **Texas Forest Service Cudlipp Forestry Center; U.S. Forest Service; Ellen Trout Park Zoo; Historical and Creative Arts Center.** Other towns include **Diboll** (5,134), **Huntington** (1,996), **Burke** (319), **Hudson** (1,800), **Zavalla** (804), **Herty.**

Aransas

LOCATION: On Coast (Q-17).

HISTORY: Created, organized, 1871, from Refugio County; named for **Rio Nuestra Senora de Aranzazu,** derived from a Spanish palace.

Cong. Dist. 14	U.S. Jud. Dist. . . . . . S-CC
St. Sen. Dist. 18	Ct. Appeals 13
St. Rep. Dist. 36	Admin. Jud. Dist. 4
St. Dist. Cts. . . 36, 156, 343	

PHYSICAL FEATURES: Flat; sandy loam, coastal clay soils; many bays, inlets; mesquites, live oaks.

RECREATION: Many fishing, hunting, tourist facilities: **Fulton Mansion; Goose Island State Park; Aransas National Wildlife Refuge; State Marine Lab;** marine aquarium; many resort homes, Rockport Art Center.

MINERALS: Oil and gas produced, also oyster shell and sand.

1985 Pop.	17,500	Tax Ratio	0.95
Area (sq. mi.)	280	Oil value	$8,600,491
Altitude (ft.)	6-24	No. employed	4,063
Ann. rainfall (in.) . .	33.19	Avg. weekly wage	$266.82
Jan. temp. min.	48	Annual wages	$56,374,056
July temp. max. . . .	92	1983 PCI	$8,348
Growing season (da.)	312	Buying pwr. .	$213,767,000
Voters reg.	7,862	Tax value . .	$894,441,797
Businesses	414	Fed. expend. . .	$32,900,000

VITAL STATISTICS 1985: Births, 321; Deaths, 122; Marriages, 264; Divorces, 120.

AGRICULTURE: Average income of $2 million from livestock, chiefly beef cattle; grains and cotton.

BUSINESS: Tourism, fishing and shrimping; oil production; refining; shipbuilding, offshore equipment fabricated; carbon plant.

ROCKPORT (4,714) county seat; fishing; tourist center; art festival; oyster fest; sea fair in October; library.

Aransas Pass (8,176 in Aransas, Nueces and San Patricio counties) deepwater port on **Intracoastal Waterway,** oil producing; refining; industrial plants; shrimping, fishing, tourism; hospital, nursing home; art festival in July, Shrimporee in October. Other towns include **Fulton** (1,002), **Lamar.**

Archer

LOCATION: North Central (F-14).

HISTORY: Created from Fannin Land District, 1858; organized, 1880. Named for **Dr. B. T. Archer,** Republic of Texas commissioner to U.S.

Cong. Dist. 13	U.S. Jud. Dist. . . . . . N-WF
St. Sen. Dist. 30	Ct. Appeals 2
St. Rep. Dist. 80	Admin. Jud. Dist. 8
St. Dist. Cts. 97	

PHYSICAL FEATURES: Rolling, hilly, drained by Wichita River forks; black, red loams, sandy soils; mesquites, post oaks.

RECREATION: Lakes Arrowhead, Kickapoo, Diversion; rattlesnake roundup in spring; local events; quail hunting.

MINERALS: Oil, gas, stone produced.

1985 Pop.	7,900	Tax Ratio	0.96
Area (sq. mi.)	907	Oil value	$3,606,945
Altitude (ft.)	934-1,286	No. employed	1,597
Ann. rainfall (in.)	25.26	Avg. weekly wage	$287.04
Jan. temp. min.	28	Annual wages	$23,837,700
July temp. max.	98	1983 PCI	$8,642
Growing season (da.)	220	Buying pwr.	$80,701,000
Voters reg.	4,613	Tax value	$521,178,503
Businesses	177	Fed. expend.	$22,270,000

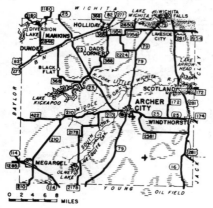

VITAL STATISTICS 1985: Births, 131; Deaths, 62; Marriages, 89; Divorces, 37.

AGRICULTURE: Income averages $37 million, 85% from beef and dairy cattle; wheat, other grains.

BUSINESS: Cattle and oil field services.

ARCHER CITY: (2,052) county seat; hospital, nursing home, library, County Museum. Other towns include **Holliday** (1,495), **Windthorst** (396), **Megargel** (403), **Lakeside City** (690), **Scotland** (386) and part of **Wichita Falls.**

Armstrong

LOCATION: Northwest, in Panhandle (D-9).

HISTORY: Created from Bexar District, 1876; organized 1890. Name honors pioneer family.

Cong. Dist.	13	U.S. Jud. Dist.	N-Am.
St. Sen. Dist.	31	Ct. Appeals	7
St. Rep. Dist.	84	Admin. Jud. Dist.	9
St. Dist. Cts.	47		

PHYSICAL FEATURES: Plain, broken by **Palo Duro Canyon, Cap Rock.** Chocolate loam, gray soils.

MINERALS: Sand, gravel produced.

RECREATION: **Palo Duro Canyon State Park;** pioneer **Goodnight Ranch home** Caprock Celebration in July.

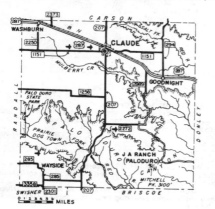

1985 Pop.	1,900	Tax Ratio	0.92
Area (sq. mi.)	910	Oil value	0
Altitude (ft.)	2,829-3,512	No. employed	338
Ann. rainfall (in.)	19.98	Avg. weekly wage	$265.89
Jan. temp. min.	19	Annual wages	$4,673,332
July temp. max.	92	1983 PCI	$8,365
Growing season (da.)	213	Buying pwr.	$28,688,000
Voters reg.	1,334	Tax value	$163,832,020
Businesses	41	Fed. expend.	$6,911,000

VITAL STATISTICS 1985: Births, 20; Deaths, 19; Marriages, 21; Divorces, 8.

AGRICULTURE: $15.5 million average income, 50% from beef cattle; wheat, sorghums, chief crops. About 15,000 acres irrigated.

BUSINESS: Agribusiness center.

CLAUDE (1,077) county seat; ranching, farming supplies; plow manufacturing; medical center; convalescent home; spring trade fair.

Atascosa

LOCATION: South, near San Antonio (P-14).

HISTORY: Created, organized from Bexar District, 1856. **Atascosa** is boggy in Spanish.

Cong. Dist.	15	U.S. Jud. Dist.	W-SAnt.
St. Sen. Dist.	21	Ct. Appeals	4
St. Rep. Dist.	45	Admin. Jud. Dist.	4
St. Dist. Cts.	81, 218		

PHYSICAL FEATURES: Grassy prairie, drained by Atascosa River, tributaries. Mesquites, other brush.

RECREATION: Local events; quail, deer hunting; Longhorn Museum; river park; little theater group; county fair; strawberry festival at Poteet in April; home of the cowboy homecoming in August.

MINERALS: Oil, gas, lignite.

1985 Pop.	28,500	Tax Ratio	0.96
Area (sq. mi.)	1,218	Oil value	$8,791,425
Altitude (ft.)	241-725	No. employed	5,222
Ann. rainfall (in.)	26.58	Avg. weekly wage	$278.90
Jan. temp. min.	42	Annual wages	$75,736,236
July temp. max.	97	1983 PCI	$6,430
Growing season (da.)	282	Buying pwr.	$248,499,000
Voters reg.	14,379	Tax value	$1,597,960,141
Businesses	493	Fed. expend.	$47,015,000

VITAL STATISTICS 1985: Births, 555; Deaths, 254; Marriages, 263; Divorces, 102.

AGRICULTURE: About $45 million average income, 60% from cattle, dairy products, hogs; peanuts, grain, hay; pecans, strawberries; 40,000 acres irrigated.

BUSINESS: Agribusinesses, oil well supplies, services; coal plant; light manufacturing; shipping.

JOURDANTON (3,543) county seat; hospital, rest home. **Pleasanton** (7,095) hospitals, nursing homes; "home of the cowboy"; peanut processing; power plant. Other towns include **Poteet** (3,519) "strawberry capital", **Lytle** (1,759), **Christine** (381), **Charlotte** (1,604).

Austin

LOCATION: Southeast (N-18).

HISTORY: Birthplace of Anglo-American colonization, named for **Stephen F. Austin**, colonists' leader; county created, organized 1837.

Cong. Dist. 14
St. Sen. Dist. 5
St. Rep. Dist. 30
St. Dist. Cts. 155
U.S. Jud. Dist. . . . . . S-Hn.
Ct. Appeals 1, 14
Admin. Jud. Dist. 3

PHYSICAL FEATURES: Level to hilly, drained by San Bernard, Brazos Rivers. Black prairie to sandy upland soils.

RECREATION: Fishing, hunting; local events; **Stephen F. Austin State Park**, other historic sites; bluebonnet trails in spring.

MINERALS: Oil, gas.

1985 Pop. 20,800	Tax Ratio 0.93
Area (sq. mi.) 656	Oil value $8,153,661
Altitude (ft.) 23-263	No. employed 5,675
Ann. rainfall (in.) . . 42.04	Avg. weekly wage $292.69
Jan. temp. min. 44	Wages paid $86,372,900
July temp. max. 95	1983 PCI $8,983
Growing season (da.) 282	Buying pwr. $250,438,000
Voters reg. 9,704	Tax value . . $1,458,591,940
Businesses 563	Fed. expend. . . $37,745,000

VITAL STATISTICS 1985: Births, 315; Deaths, 251; Marriages, 205; Divorces, 83.

AGRICULTURE: About $40 million average yearly income, 80% from livestock, poultry; sorghums, small grains, rice, corn, peanuts, cotton.

BUSINESS: Agribusiness center, steel, other manufacturing.

BELLVILLE (3,461) county seat; clothing, furniture, trailers, tubing, food products manufactured; oil production; hospital. Other towns include **Sealy** (4,868) oil field manufacturing, picturesque downtown; **Wallis** (1,312); **San Felipe** (675) colonial capital of Texas.

Bailey

LOCATION: Northwest (E-7).
HISTORY: Created from Bexar District, 1876, organized 1917. Named for Alamo hero, **Peter J. Bailey.**

Cong. Dist. 19
St. Sen. Dist. 31
St. Rep. Dist. 85
St. Dist. Cts. 287
U.S. Jud. Dist. . . . . . N-Lb.
Ct. Appeals 7
Admin. Jud. Dist. 9

PHYSICAL FEATURES: Plain; mostly sandy loam soils; mesquite brush; drains to Brazos, playas.
RECREATION: Muleshoe National Wildlife Refuge; museum; local events; hunting.
MINERALS: Insignificant.

1985 Pop. 8,300	Tax Ratio 0.97
Area (sq. mi.) 827	Oil value 0
Altitude (ft.) . . 3,790-4,060	No. employed 1,801
Ann. rainfall (in.) . . 17.29	Avg. weekly wage $285.57
Jan. temp. min. 20	Annual wages . $26,744,388
July temp. max. 92	1983 PCI $7,046
Growing season (da.) 181	Buying pwr. . . $60,379,000
Voters reg. 3,469	Tax value . . . $306,843,172
Businesses 211	Fed. expend. . . $24,780,000

VITAL STATISTICS 1985: Births, 133; Deaths, 55; Marriages, 99; Divorces, 42.

AGRICULTURE: About $75 million farm receipts annually, 60% from crops, 40% from livestock; crops include sorghums, corn, cotton, wheat, alfalfa, vegetables, sunflowers; about 150,000 acres irrigated; cattle, hogs, sheep; feedlots.

BUSINESS: Farm supply manufacturing, food processing plants, other agribusinesses.

MULESHOE (5,048) county seat; feed processing, farm tools manufacturing; **National Mule Memorial.**

Bandera

LOCATION: Southwest (N-13.)
HISTORY: Created, organized from Bexar, Uvalde counties, 1856; named for Bandera (flag) Mts.
Cong. Dist. 21
St. Sen. Dist. 25
U.S. Jud. Dist. . . . W-SAnt.
Ct. Appeals 4

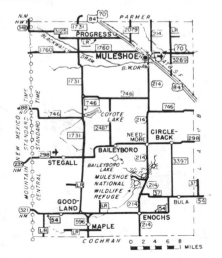

OIL FIELDS

STEPHEN F. AUSTIN STATE PARK

0 1 2 3 4 5 6 MILES

St. Rep. Dist. 45   Admin. Jud. Dist. 6
St. Dist. Cts. 216

PHYSICAL FEATURES: Hilly, plateau; Medina River, Lake; limestone, sandy soils; dominated by various species of oaks, walnuts, native cherry and Uvalde maple.

RECREATION: Dude and resort ranches, RV parks; hunting, leases, fishing; **Frontier Times Museum; Lost Maples State Park; Bandera Downs Race Track;** Fun-tier Days celebration, youth rodeo.

MINERALS: Not significant.

1985 Pop.	8,900	Tax Ratio	0.95
Area (sq. mi.)	793	Oil value	0
Altitude (ft.) . .	1,175-2,185	No. employed	1,277
Ann. rainfall (in.) .	28.82	Avg. weekly wage	$262.37
Jan. temp. min.	32	Annual wages .	$17,422,484
July temp. max.	94	1983 PCI	$8,340
Growing season (da.)	235	Buying pwr. . .	$97,959,000
Voters reg.	5,630	Tax value . .	$814,348,525
Businesses	174	Fed. expend. . .	$34,541,000

VITAL STATISTICS 1985: Births, 120; Deaths, 91; Marriages, 122; Divorces, 46.

AGRICULTURE: Over 95% of $6.8 million yearly agricultural income from beef cattle, sheep, goats, poultry and post cedar.

BUSINESS: Tourism, hunting, fishing, purse factory, ranching supplies, marketing, forest products.

BANDERA (1,012) county seat; cedar mill, cedar shingle factory, purse factory; hunting, guest ranching center; girls camp; museums; local events; nursing home. Other towns include **Medina, Lakehills, Pipe Creek, Vanderpool** and **Tarpley.**

Bastrop

LOCATION: Near Austin (M-16).

HISTORY: First settled 1829; county created 1836, organized 1837; named for **Baron de Bastrop,** who aided colonists.

Cong. Dist. 10   U.S. Jud. Dist. . . . . W-An.
St. Sen. Dist. 18   Ct. Appeals 3
St. Rep. Dist. 30   Admin. Jud. Dist. 2
St. Dist. Cts. 21, 335

PHYSICAL FEATURES: Rolling, alluvial, sandy, loam soils; varied timber, **"Lost Pines";** bisected by Colorado River.

RECREATION: Center of "Lost Pines" region; fishing, hunting; **Bastrop, Buescher State Parks; Lake Bastrop;** historic sites; museum; Elgin Western Days in July; Smithville Jamboree in April; Texas State Championship BBQ Cookoff in July.

MINERALS: Clay, oil, gas and lignite.

1985 Pop.		Tax Ratio	0.94
Area (sq. mi.)	895	Oil value	$229,702
Altitude (ft.)	356-729	No. employed	5,258
Ann. rainfall (in.) . .	36.82	Avg. weekly wage	$276.55
Jan. temp. min.	40	Annual wages	$75,613,728
July temp. max.	96	1983 PCI	$7,650
Growing season (da.)	268	Buying pwr. .	$321,670,000
Voters reg.	21,643	Tax value . .	$1,773,833,780
Businesses	513	Fed. expend. . .	$70,071,000

VITAL STATISTICS 1985: Births, 631; Deaths, 293; Marriages, 316; Divorces, 169.

AGRICULTURE: Average farm income $28 million, 90% from beef, dairy cattle, hogs, poultry. Crops include grain sorghums, pecans, corn, wheat, oats; fruit production beginning.

BUSINESS: Agribusiness, brick, electronic equipment, other manufacturing; tourism attracting residents from Austin.

BASTROP (3,789) county seat; oil well supply, agribusinesses, furniture manufacturing; hospital; **University of Texas Cancer research center;** federal correctional center. **Elgin** (4,535) famous for sausages; brick plants, cottonseed mill, food processing, furniture plant, agribusinesses; research instruments; leather works; hospital, nursing home. **Smithville** (3,470) cedar products, manufacturing, trading center; Environmental Science Park for Cancer Research; hospital, nursing home, medical clinics.

Baylor

LOCATION: North central (F-13).

HISTORY: Created from Fannin County, 1858, organized 1879. Named for **H. W. Baylor,** Texas Ranger surgeon.

Cong. Dist. 13   U.S. Jud. Dist. . . . . N-WF
St. Sen. Dist. 30   Ct. Appeals 11
St. Rep. Dist. 80   Admin. Jud. Dist. 9
St. Dist. Cts. 50

PHYSICAL FEATURES: Level to hilly; drains to Brazos, Wichita Rivers; sandy, loam, red soils; grassy, mesquites, cedars.

RECREATION: Lake Kemp; Millers Creek Reservoir; Fish Day in May, Settlers reunion and rodeo in July; hunting and fishing.

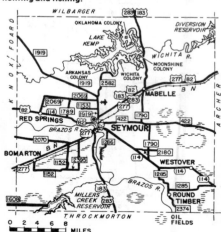

MINERALS: Oil, gas produced.

1985 Pop.	4,900	Tax Ratio	0.91
Area (sq. mi.)	862	Oil value	$2,422,891
Altitude (ft.)	1,053-1,394	No. employed	1,283
Ann. rainfall (in.)	26.36	Avg. weekly wage	$264.10
Jan. temp. min.	28	Annual wages	$17,619,864
July temp. max.	98	1983 PCI	$7,530
Growing season (da.)	214	Buying pwr.	$45,306,000
Voters reg.	3,245	Tax value	$303,523,485
Businesses	194	Fed. expend.	$17,177,000

VITAL STATISTICS 1985: Births, 75; Deaths, 78; Marriages, 45; Divorces, 13.

AGRICULTURE: About $13 million average annual income; livestock, mainly stocker cattle; wheat, cotton raised. 5,000 acres irrigated.

BUSINESS: Chiefly agribusiness; oil, gas production; light manufacturing.

SEYMOUR (3,754) county seat; agribusiness center; clothes manufacturing; metal works; hospital, nursing home; city park.

Bee

LOCATION: Southeast (P-15).

HISTORY: Created from Karnes, Live Oak, Goliad, Refugio, San Patricio counties, 1857; organized 1858; named for **Gen. Barnard Bee.**

Cong. Dist.	14	U.S. Jud. Dist.	S-CC
St. Sen. Dist.	21	Ct. Appeals	13
St. Rep. Dist.	33	Admin. Jud. Dist.	4
St. Dist. Cts.	36, 156, 343		

PHYSICAL FEATURES: Level to rolling; black clay, sandy, loam soils; brushy.

RECREATION: Hunting leases, camping, historical sites, western week in October, junior livestock show.

MINERALS: Considerable oil, gas produced.

1985 Pop.	27,300	Tax Ratio	0.85
Area (sq. mi.)	880	Oil value	$1,519,054
Altitude (ft.)	87-422	No. employed	6,372
Ann. rainfall (in.)	28.90	Avg. weekly wage	$273.19
Jan. temp. min.	45	Annual wages	$90,522,500
July temp. max.	95	1983 PCI	$6,945
Growing season (da.)	285	Buying pwr.	$252,237,000
Voters reg.	13,652	Tax value	$907,053,391
Businesses	567	Fed. expend.	$92,764,000

VITAL STATISTICS 1985: Births, 556; Deaths, 220; Marriages, 338; Divorces, 162.

AGRICULTURE: More than $30 million average income, from beef cattle, hogs, grain sorghums, small grains, cotton.

BUSINESS: Oil supplies, agribusiness; small feed lots; military installations provide major income source.

BEEVILLE (15,977) county seat; **Naval Air Station;** oil field services; agribusiness center; community college, hospital, nursing homes.

Bell

LOCATION: Central (K-16).

HISTORY: Created from Milam County and organized, 1850; named for **Gov. P. H. Bell.**

Cong. Dist.	11	U.S. Jud. Dist.	W-Waco
St. Sen. Dist.	24	Ct. Appeals	3
St. Rep. Dist.	53, 54	Admin. Jud. Dist.	3
St. Dist. Cts.	27, 146, 169, 264		

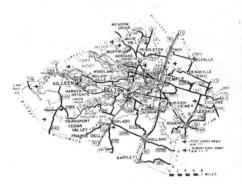

PHYSICAL FEATURES: Level to hilly; black to light soils; mixed timber.

RECREATION: Fishing, hunting; **Fort Hood Community Festival; Belton, Stillhouse Hollow Lakes;** historic sites include **Stagecoach Inn** at Salado; rattlesnake roundup at Belton in March; Salado art fair in August; gathering of Scottish clans at Salado in November.

MINERALS: Stone, sand, gravel.

1985 Pop.	170,800	Tax Ratio	0.91
Area (sq. mi.)	1,055	Oil value	0
Altitude (ft.)	429-1,245	No. employed	53,090
Ann. rainfall (in.)	34.00	Avg. weekly wage	$294.20
Jan. temp. min.	37	Annual wages	$812,213,532
July temp. max.	96	1983 PCI	$8,052
Growing season (da.)	258	Buying pwr.	$1,627,888,000
Voters reg.	57,843	Tax value	$3,738,043,759
Businesses	3,202	Fed. expend.	$1,244,511,000

VITAL STATISTICS 1985: Births, 5,017; Deaths, 1,164; Marriages, 3,475; Divorces, 2,257.

AGRICULTURE: About $33 million average farm income; 60% from cattle, sheep, goats, hogs, horses, poultry; a leading turkey-producing county; grain sorghums, cotton, hay, pecans, wheat, corn and cedar.

BUSINESS: Diversified manufacturers include computer equipment, plastic goods, furniture, clothing; agribusiness; distribution center; **Fort Hood;** tourism.

BELTON (11,904) county seat; **Mary Hardin-Baylor University;** school furniture, insulation, mobile home manufacturing; clinics, nursing home.

Killeen (55,666); site of **Fort Hood** military installation; **Central Texas College** and **American Education Complex;** varied manufacturing; medical center.

Temple (45,044); hub of one of nation's fastest growing urban areas; diversified industries; rail center; marketing and distribution center; market for large area; convention and exposition centers. **Temple Junior College;** one of nation's leading medical centers, **Scott and White Clinic and Hospital; Olin E. Teague VA Center.**

Other towns include **Harker Heights** (8,444), **Rogers** (1,367), **Nolanville** (1,726), **Bartlett** (1,556, mostly Williamson County) leading soil conservation center; **Holland** (1,006), **Troy** (1,581), **Little River-Academy** (1,150), **Morgans Point Resort** (1,277). Salado is historic town with **Central Texas Area Museum, Stagecoach Inn** and arts, crafts and antique shops.

Bexar

LOCATION: South (N-14).

HISTORY: Created 1836, organized 1837, from Spanish municipality named for **Duke de Bexar;** many historic sites.

Cong. Dist. 20, 21, 23	U.S. Jud. Dist. . . W-SAnt.
St. Sen. Dist. . 19, 21, 25, 26	Ct. Appeals 4
St. Rep. Dist. . . . 115-124	Admin. Jud. Dist. 4

St. Dist. Cts. 37, 45, 57, 73, 131, 144, 150, 166, 175, 186, 187, 224, 225, 226, 227, 285, 288, 289, 290

PHYSICAL FEATURES: Hilly; heavy black to thin limestone soils; springfed streams; underground water; mesquite, other brush.

1985 Pop.	1,134,900	Tax Ratio	0.93
Area (sq. mi.)	1,248	Oil value	$159,995
Altitude (ft.)	486-1,892	No. employed	418,034
Ann. rainfall (in.) . .	27.54	Avg. weekly wage	$324.79
Jan. temp. min.	42	Ann. wages . $7,060,304,644
July temp. max.	94	1983 PCI	$8,280
Growing season (da.)	265	Buying pwr.$11,402,335,000
Voters reg.	464,206	Tax value . $36,136,006,092
Businesses	23,962	Fed. expend. $4,613,330,000

VITAL STATISTICS 1985: Births, 22,236; Deaths, 7,824; Marriages, 14,136; Divorces, 7,705.

RECREATION: Major tourist and retirement area; **Alamo,** missions, other historic sites; river walk; Hertzberg circus collection; Water Park U.S.A.; Brackenridge Park; zoo; symphony orchestra; HemisFair Plaza; Folk Life Festival; Fiesta San Antonio; Institute of Texan Cultures; many military posts; parks; museums; deer, turkey, other hunting; fishing; many special events; major livestock show.

MINERALS: Cement, stone, oil, gas, sand and gravel, lime, clays.

EDUCATION: San Antonio College, St. Philips College, junior colleges; senior, Incarnate Word College, Our Lady of the Lake University, St. Mary's University, Trinity University, University of Texas at San Antonio, UT Health Science Center at San Antonio (five divisions), University of Mexico at San Antonio, Oblate School of Theology and Texas Lutheran College.

AGRICULTURE: About $60 million yearly farm income, from beef, dairy cattle, poultry, sheep, goats; sorghums, vegetables, hay, corn, nursery plant production, peanuts; about 15,000 acres irrigated.

BUSINESS: Large federal payrolls; federal expenditure a major factor; tourist business; varied manufactures; distribution center for large area; education and industrial biotechnological center.

SAN ANTONIO (842,779) county seat; Texas' third

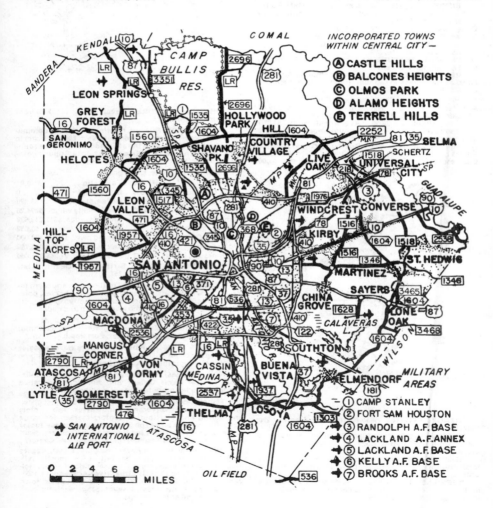

largest city; state's largest military center; varied manufacturing with emphasis on high-tech industries, construction equipment, concrete, dairy products, soft drinks, clothing, aircraft; mild climate; Alamo, other historic sites attract many tourists; HemisFair Plaza; Folk Life Festival; popular retirement area; **Institute of Texan Cultures.**

Other towns include **Balcones Heights** (2,912), **Alamo Heights,** (6,489), **Castle Hills** (5,312), **China Grove** (565), **Converse** (7,690), **Elmendorf** (527), **Grey Forest** (403), **Helotes** (1,564), **Hill Country Village** (1,356), **Hollywood Park** (3,996), **Kirby** (7,836), **Leon Valley** (10,837), **Live Oak** (8,734), **Lytle** (1,594, mostly in Atascosa County), **Olmos Park** (2,028), **Saint Hedwig** (1,101), **Schertz** (7,548 mostly Guadalupe County), **Selma** (449, partly in Guadalupe County), **Shavano Park** (1,626), **Somerset** (1,251), **Terrell Hills** (4,954), **Universal City** (11,676), **Windcrest** (6,733).

Blanco

LOCATION: Central (M-14).
HISTORY: Created, organized, 1858, from Burnet, Comal, Gillespie, Hays Counties; named for **Blanco** (white) **River.**

Cong. Dist.	10	U.S. Jud. Dist.	W-An.
St. Sen. Dist.	25	Ct. Appeals	3
St. Rep. Dist.	47	Admin. Jud. Dist.	3
St. Dist. Cts.	33		

PHYSICAL FEATURES: Hilly; Blanco, Pedernales Rivers; cedars, pecans, other trees.
RECREATION: President Lyndon B. Johnson boyhood home. **Blanco State Park; Pedernales Falls State Park;** hunting, fishing; scenic drives; county fair; fajita cookoff in June.
MINERALS: Insignificant.

1985 Pop.	5,300	Tax Ratio	0.96
Area (sq. mi.)	714	Oil value	0
Altitude (ft.)	978-1,801	No. employed	1,576
Ann. rainfall (in.)	34.39	Avg. weekly wage	$272.47
Jan. temp. min.	36	Annual wages	$22,330,240
July temp. max.	96	1983 PCI	$8,306
Growing season (da.)	234	Buying pwr.	$62,393,000
Voters reg.	3,488	Tax value	$868,235,977
Businesses	143	Fed. expend.	$14,201,000

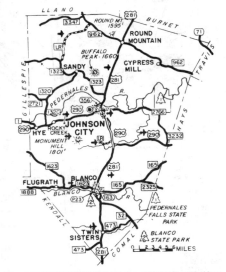

VITAL STATISTICS 1985: Births, 86; Deaths, 62; Marriages, 67; Divorces, 26.
AGRICULTURE: About $11 million yearly income, mostly from cattle, sheep, goats, hogs, hunting leases; peaches, grapes, hay.
BUSINESS: Trailer manufacturing, tourism, ranch supplies, marketing.
JOHNSON CITY (914) county seat; tourist center; nursing home. **Blanco** (1,353) ranch supply center; horticultural products; distribution; two nursing homes.

Borden

LOCATION: West (H-9).
HISTORY: Created, 1876, from Bexar District, organized, 1891; named for **Gail Borden,** pioneer patriot, inventor, editor.

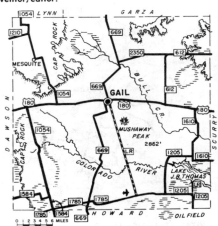

Cong. Dist.	17	U.S. Jud. Dist.	N-Lb.
St. Sen. Dist.	28	Ct. Appeals	11
St. Rep. Dist.	69	Admin. Jud. Dist.	7
St. Dist. Cts.	132		

PHYSICAL FEATURES: Rolling, broken by **Cap Rock** Escarpment; drains to Colorado River, **Lake J. B. Thomas;** sandy loam, clay soils.
RECREATION: Fishing; hunting; Lake J. B. Thomas; museum; junior livestock show and rodeo.
MINERALS: Oil, gas, sand and gravel.

1985 Pop.	1,000	Tax Ratio	0.89
Area (sq. mi.)	900	Oil value	$99,266,594
Altitude (ft.)	1,247-2,964	No. employed	133
Ann. rainfall (in.)	18.20	Avg. weekly wage	$370.01
Jan. temp. min.	32	Annual wages	$2,559,012
July temp. max.	96	1983 PCI	$8,417
Growing season (da.)	214	Buying pwr.	$6,043,000
Voters reg.	573	Tax value	$419,006,460
Businesses	6	Fed. expend.	$2,399,000

VITAL STATISTICS 1985: Births, 8; Deaths, 6; Marriages, 3; Divorces, 1.
AGRICULTURE: About $7.5 million annual income mostly from beef and stocker cattle, sheep, horses; cotton, wheat, sorghums, hay.
BUSINESS: Oil, agribusiness; new service station.
GAIL (est. 189) county seat; county museum; ambulance service.

Bosque

LOCATION: Central (J-15).
HISTORY: Created, organized, 1854, from Milam District, McLennan County; named for **Bosque** (woods) River.

Cong. Dist.	11	U.S. Jud. Dist.	W-Waco
St. Sen. Dist.	22	Ct. Appeals	10
St. Rep. Dist.	57	Admin. Jud. Dist.	3
St. Dist. Cts.	220		

PHYSICAL FEATURES: Hilly, broken by Bosque, Brazos Rivers; limestone to alluvial soils; cedars, oaks, mesquites.
RECREATION: **Lake Whitney, Meridian State Park, Bosque Memorial Museum** at Clifton; fishing; hunting; scenic routes; golf course; **Norwegian** smorgasbord at Norse community in November; Central Texas Youth Fair in Clifton in August; **Texas Safari** wildlife park in Clifton.
MINERALS: Lime, stone.

1985 Pop.	14,200	Tax Ratio	0.85
Area (sq. mi.)	989	Oil value	$16,619
Altitude (ft.)	503-1,221	No. employed	3,120
Ann. rainfall (in.)	33.20	Avg. weekly wage	$272.59

Jan. temp. min.	36	Annual wages	$44,225,392
July temp. max.	96	1983 PCI	$7,780
Growing season (da.)	243	Buying pwr.	$157,198,000
Voters reg.	8,008	Tax value	$795,286,538
Businesses	295	Fed. expend.	$38,300,000

VITAL STATISTICS 1985: Births, 200; Deaths, 235; Marriages, 174; Divorces, 78.

AGRICULTURE: About $28 million average annual income, nearly all from cattle, goats, sheep, poultry, hogs; peanuts, cotton, pecans, peaches, wheat, sorghums; cedar for posts, Christmas trees added.

BUSINESS: Agribusiness, tourism, small industries; tree supplier.

MERIDIAN (1,366) county seat; distribution center; varied manufacturing.

Clifton (3,215) area trade center; light manufacturing; hospital, rest home.

Other towns include **Valley Mills** (1,359, part McLennan County) with several small industries; **Iredell** (384), **Cranfills Gap** (386), **Morgan** (467) and **Walnut Springs** (625).

Bowie

LOCATION: Northeast (F-21).

HISTORY: Created 1840 from Red River County, organized 1841; named for Alamo hero, **James Bowie**.

Cong. Dist.	1	U.S. Jud. Dist.	E-Tx.
St. Sen. Dist.	1	Ct. Appeals	6
St. Rep. Dist.	1	Admin. Jud. Dist.	1
St. Dist. Cts.	5, 102, 202		

PHYSICAL FEATURES: Hilly, forested; clay, sandy, alluvial soils; drained by Red and Sulphur Rivers.

RECREATION: Lake Wright Patman, other lakes; hunting, fishing, historic sites, pioneer days.

MINERALS: Oil, gas, sand, gravel.

1985 Pop.	80,500	Tax Ratio	0.97
Area (sq. mi.)	891	Oil value	$687,455
Altitude (ft.)	225-437	No. employed	25,381
Ann. rainfall (in.)	47.59	Avg. weekly wage	$311.09
Jan. temp. min.	35	Annual wages	$410,587,652
July temp. max.	95	1983 PCI	$8,140
Growing season (da.)	235	Buying pwr.	$754,411,000
Voters reg.	41,512	Tax value	$1,970,262,976
Businesses	1,911	Fed. expend.	$469,796,000

VITAL STATISTICS 1985: Births, 1,205; Deaths, 746; Marriages, 1,016; Divorces, 665.

AGRICULTURE: About $40 million annual income mostly from beef, dairy cattle; crops include wheat, soybeans, milo, corn, rice; timber harvested; 4,000 acres irrigated.

BUSINESS: Manufacturing, agribusiness, government employment, tourism, **U.S. Army Depot,** ordnance plant.

BOSTON county seat.

Texarkana (est. 78,813 in Texas-Arkansas; 32,912 in Texas); distribution, **Red River Army Depot,** manufacturing center; medical center; **Texarkana Community College, East Texas State University at Texarkana;** hospitals; federal correctional unit; state line tourist attractions; Four States Fair in October and Piney Woods Rendezvous in April.

New Boston (4,758) paper mill, county courthouse.

Other towns include **De Kalb** (2,225), **Hooks** (2,512), **Leary** (310), **Maud** (1,126), **Nash** (2,202), **Wake Village** (3,866).

Brazoria

LOCATION:
On coast (O-20).

HISTORY: Created 1836, organized 1837 from Municipality of Brazoria, name derived from Brazos River. Settled by **Stephen F. Austin** colonists.

Cong. Dist.	14, 22	U.S. Jud. Dist.	S-Gn.
St. Sen. Dist.	17, 18	Ct. Appeals	1, 14
St. Rep. Dist.	27, 28, 29	Admin. Jud. Dist.	2
St. Dist. Cts.	23, 149, 239, 300		

PHYSICAL FEATURES: Flat, coastal soils, drained by Brazos and San Bernard Rivers.

RECREATION: Water sports, 20 miles natural beach; fishing, hunting; many historic sites; **Varner-Hogg State Park;** replica of first capitol of Republic of Texas at **West Columbia;** San Jacinto Day festival.

MINERALS: Oil, gas, magnesium, salt, sand and gravel.

1985 Pop.	188,200	Tax Ratio	0.90
Area (sq. mi.)	1,407	Oil value	$76,129,393
Altitude (ft.)	5-146	No. employed	54,549
Ann. rainfall (in.)	52.17	Avg. weekly wage	$451.09
Jan. temp. min.	46	Ann. wages	$1,279,557,644
July temp. max.	91	1983 PCI	$10,160
Growing season (da.)	268	Buying pwr.	$2,607,219,000
Voters reg.	79,247	Tax value	$9,998,350,040
Businesses	3,420	Fed. expd.	$356,630,000

VITAL STATISTICS 1985: Births, 3,467; Deaths, 1,072; Marriages, 2,062; Divorces, 1,269.

AGRICULTURE: About $45 million average annual income, 55% from rice, sorghum, soybeans; commercial turf; 45% from livestock; 30,000 acres of rice irrigated.

BUSINESS: Extensive petroleum and chemical industry; fishing; tourism; agribusiness.

ANGLETON (15,174) county seat; government center, banking and distribution center for large oil, chemical, agricultural area, rice, livestock operations; state's largest county fair; hospital, nursing home.

Brazosport: A community of nine cities. Community has world's largest basic chemical complex, deepwater seaport, shrimp and other commercial fishing; tourism; **Brazosport College;** hospital; school district. Brazosport cities include:

Brazoria (3,349), **Clute** (9,554), **Freeport** (12,411), **Jones Creek** (2,373), **Lake Jackson** (20,206), **Oyster Creek** (1,462), **Quintana** (30), **Richwood** (3,057), **Surfside Beach** (604).

Other county towns include **Alvin** (18,484) chemical plants, rice farming center, hospital, nursing home, **Alvin Community College; Pearland** (14,912) general manufacturing, **West Columbia** (4,415), **Sweeny** (3,699), **Baileys Prairie** (410), **Bonney** (99), **Brookside Village** (1,538), **Danbury** (1,529), **Hillcrest** (825), **Iowa Colony** (661), **Liverpool** (627), **Manvel** (4,441), **Holiday Lake** (628).

Brazos

LOCATION: Southeast (L-18).

HISTORY: Created 1841 from Robertson, Washington Counties, named **Navasota;** renamed for Brazos River in 1842, organized 1843; fastest growing SMSA in state in 1980 census.

Cong. Dist.	6	U.S. Jud. Dist.	S-Hn.
St. Sen. Dist.	5	Ct. Appeals	1, 10, 14
St. Rep. Dist.	14	Admin. Jud. Dist.	2
St. Dist. Cts.	85, 272, 361		

PHYSICAL FEATURES: Between Brazos, Navasota Rivers; rich bottom soils, sandy, clays on rolling uplands; mostly oak trees.

1985 Pop.	119,500	Tax Ratio	0.88
Area (sq. mi.)	588	Oil value	$11,699,291
Altitude (ft.)	197-312	No. employed	44,530
Ann. rainfall (in.)	39.21	Avg. weekly wage	$306.17
Jan. temp. min.	42	Annual wages	$708,972,768
July temp. max.	95	1983 PCI	$7,994

Growing season (da.)	274	Buying pwr.	$1,270,827,000
Voters reg.	50,691	Tax value	$3,656,141,607
Businesses	2,573	Fed. expend.	$198,346,000

VITAL STATISTICS 1985: Births, 1,974; Deaths, 552; Marriages, 1,105; Divorces, 459.

RECREATION: Fishing, hunting; Texas World Speedway, many springtime festivals, Texas A&M events.

MINERALS: Sand and gravel, lignite, gas, oil.

AGRICULTURE: About 80% of over $42 million annual income from cattle, hogs; sorghums, corn, cotton, wheat, oats, pecans chief crops.

BUSINESS: Agribusiness center; computers, research and development; offshore technology; four industrial parks. **Texas A&M University** enterprises major economic factor.

BRYAN (58,991) county seat; university enterprises; business forms, defense electronics, aluminum buildings, furniture, shoe products, other varied manufacturing; agribusiness center; hospitals, psychiatric facilities.

College Station (45,756); home of **Texas A&M University System;** mini-computers; offshore technology; other research and development. Other town, **Wixon Valley** (230).

Brewster

LOCATION: In Rio Grande's Big Bend (N-6).

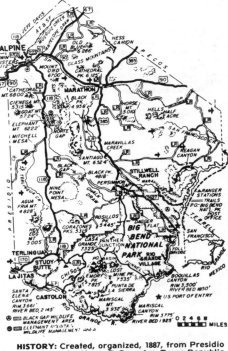

HISTORY: Created, organized, 1887, from Presidio County; named for Henry P. Brewster, Texas Republic Secretary of War.

Cong. Dist.	21	U.S. Jud. Dist.	W-Pe.
St. Sen. Dist.	25	Ct. Appeals	8
St. Rep. Dist.	68	Admin. Jud. Dist.	6
St. Dist. Cts.	83		

PHYSICAL FEATURES: Largest Texas county, area equal to Connecticut plus Rhode Island; mountains and deep canyons, distinctive geology, plant life, animals.

RECREATION: Many tourist attractions; **Big Bend National Park;** ghost mining towns; scenic drives, canyons, mountains; among last U.S. unspoiled "frontier" areas; **Museum of the Big Bend at Sul Ross State University;** annual **Chili Cook-Off at Terlingua;** retirement area;

Big Bend summer theater at Alpine; cavalry post at Lajitas; hunting leases.

MINERALS: Sand and gravel, fluorspar.

1985 Pop.	8,100	Tax Ratio	0.94
Area (sq. mi.)	6,169	Oil value	$58,383
Altitude (ft.)	1,355-7,825	No. employed	2,533
Ann. rainfall (in.)	15.53	Avg. weekly wage	$242.32
Jan. temp. min.	32	Annual wages	$31,917,932
July temp. max.	89	1983 PCI	$6,442
Growing season (da.)	223	Buying pwr.	$64,675,000
Voters reg.	4,746	Tax value	$466,941,355
Businesses	231	Fed. expd.	$16,375,000

VITAL STATISTICS 1985: Births, 118; Deaths, 63; Marriages, 79; Divorces, 37.

AGRICULTURE: About $10 million average income, nearly all from cattle, sheep, goats; pecans.

BUSINESS: Sul Ross State University; ranching; tourism; retirement developments; hunting leases; some curio manufacturing.

ALPINE (6,033) county seat; center for ranch trade, tourism; **Sul Ross State University;** hospital; local events; varied manufacturing.

Marathon, ranching center, tourism, gateway to **Big Bend National Park.**

Briscoe

LOCATION: Northwest (D-9).

HISTORY: Created from Bexar District, 1876, organized 1892; named for **Andrew Briscoe,** Texas Republic soldier.

Cong. Dist.	13	U.S. Jud. Dist.	N-Am.
St. Sen. Dist.	31	Ct. Appeals	7
St. Rep. Dist.	84	Admin. Jud. Dist.	9
St. Dist. Cts.	110		

PHYSICAL FEATURES: Partly on High Plains, broken by **Cap Rock Escarpment,** fork of Red River; sandy, loam soils.

RECREATION: Hunting, fishing; scenic drives; local events; **Briscoe County Museum; Caprock Canyon State Park, Mackenzie Reservoir.**

MINERALS: Insignificant.

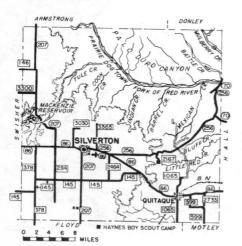

1985 Pop.	2,300	Tax Ratio	0.98
Area (sq. mi.)	887	Oil value	0
Altitude (ft.)	2,174-3,316	No. employed	323
Ann. rainfall (in.)	20.50	Avg. weekly wage	$238.05
Jan. temp. min.	26	Annual wages	$3,998,332
July temp. max.	94	1983 PCI	$6,229
Growing season (da.)	214	Buying pwr.	$19,162,000

Voters reg. .... 1,321 Tax value ... $111,962,289
Businesses .... 54 Fed. expend. $10,550,000

VITAL STATISTICS 1985: Births, 31; Deaths, 34; Marriages, 12; Divorces, 5.

AGRICULTURE: About $15.5 million average annual income from wheat, grain sorghums, cotton; beef cattle, cattle feeding increasing; over 50,000 acres irrigated.

BUSINESS: Agribusinesses.

SILVERTON (775) county seat; agribusiness center; irrigation supplies manufactured; county clinic.

Quitaque (700) trade center.

Brooks

LOCATION: South (S-15).

HISTORY: Created from Hidalgo, Starr, Zapata Counties, 1911, organized same year. Named for **J. A. Brooks,** Ranger-legislator.

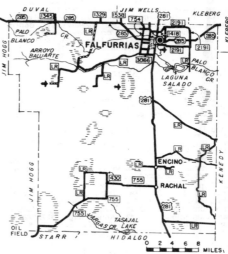

Cong. Dist.	15	U.S. Jud. Dist.	S-CC
St. Sen. Dist.	20	Ct. Appeals	4
St. Rep. Dist.	37	Admin. Jud. Dist.	5
St. Dist. Cts.	79		

PHYSICAL FEATURES: Level to rolling; brushy; light to dark sandy loam soils.

MINERALS: Oil, gas production.

1985 Pop.	9,300	Tax Ratio	0.88
Area (sq. mi.)	942	Oil value	$10,541,529
Altitude (ft.)	46-367	No. employed	1,737
Ann. rainfall (in.)	24.18	Avg. weekly wage	$281.97
Jan. temp. min.	48	Annual wages	$25,468,940
July temp. max.	98	1983 PCI	$5,621
Growing season (da.)	303	Buying pwr.	$56,738,000
Voters reg.	6,247	Tax value	$876,759,753
Businesses	163	Fed. expd.	$16,841,000

VITAL STATISTICS 1985: Births, 179; Deaths, 77; Marriages, 97; Divorces, 17.

RECREATION: Hunting, fishing; **Texas Ranger Museum, Don Pedrito Shrine.**

AGRICULTURE: Over $16.5 million average annual income mostly from beef, dairy cattle; grain, corn, hay, watermelons, vegetables.

BUSINESS: Chiefly oil, gas, cattle raising.

FALFURRIAS (6,555) county seat; retail center; agribusinesses, dairy center; baby apparel manufacturing; hospital, nursing home, museum, library.

Brown

LOCATION: Central (J-13).

HISTORY: Named for Indian fighter, **Henry S. Brown**; created 1856 from Comanche, Travis counties, organized 1857.

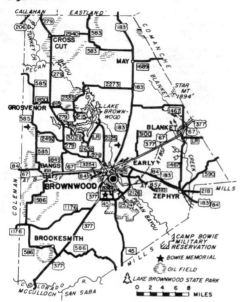

Cong. Dist.	11	U.S. Jud. Dist.	N-SAng.
St. Sen. Dist.	24	Ct. Appeals	11
St. Rep. Dist.	65	Admin. Jud. Dist.	7
St. Dist. Cts.	35		

PHYSICAL FEATURES: Rolling, hilly; drains to Colorado River; varied soils, timber.

RECREATION: Lake Brownwood State Park; MacArthur Academy of Freedom; fishing, hunting; Brown County Youth Fair in January; other local events.

MINERALS: Stone, oil, gas, clays.

1985 Pop.	35,100	Tax Ratio	0.97
Area (sq. mi.)	936	Oil value	$5,649
Altitude (ft.)	1,321-1,894	No. employed	11,660
Ann. rainfall (in.)	27.42	Avg. weekly wage	$308.16
Jan. temp. min.	33	Annual wages	$186,848,312
July temp. max.	96	1983 PCI	$7,694
Growing season (da.)	242	Buying pwr.	$377,870,000
Voters reg.	16,395	Tax value	$1,071,459,689
Businesses	937	Fed. expend.	$76,874,000

VITAL STATISTICS 1985: Births, 497; Deaths, 417; Marriages, 466; Divorces, 176.

AGRICULTURE: About 85% of $25 million average income from beef cattle, sheep, goats, hogs; wheat, grain sorghums, peanuts chief crops; about 6,000 acres irrigated.

BUSINESS: Agribusinesses, general manufacturing plants, distribution center.

BROWNWOOD (19,761) county seat; retail trade center; varied industries; distribution center; **Howard Payne University, MacArthur Academy of Freedom; State Home and School; Mental Health/Mental Retardation Center;** State 4-H club center; hospitals.

Other towns include **Bangs** (1,869), **Blanket** (388), **Early** (3,094).

Burleson

LOCATION: East central (L-17).

HISTORY: Created, organized, 1846, from Milam, Washington counties; named for **Edward Burleson** of Texas Revolution.

Cong. Dist.	14	U.S. Jud. Dist.	W-An.
St. Sen. Dist.	5	Ct. Appeals	1, 14
St. Rep. Dist.	13	Admin. Jud. Dist.	2
St. Dist. Cts.	21, 335		

PHYSICAL FEATURES: Rolling to hilly; drains to Brazos, Yegua Creek, **Somerville Lake;** loam and heavy bottom soils; oaks, other trees.

RECREATION: Fishing, limited hunting; **Somerville Lake** recreation; Birch Creek Park; Big Creek Park; historic sites.

MINERALS: Oil, gas, sand and gravel.

1985 Pop.	15,000	Tax Ratio	0.93
Area (sq. mi.)	668	Oil value	$29,536,233
Altitude (ft.)	221-417	No. employed	2,549
Ann. rainfall (in.)	34.45	Avg. weekly wage	$268.96
Jan. temp. min.	38	Annual wages	$35,650,416
July temp. max.	94	1983 PCI	$7,995
Growing season (da.)	275	Buying pwr.	$130,373,000
Voters reg.	7,167	Tax value	$1,109,248,845
Businesses	302	Fed. expend.	$39,811,000

VITAL STATISTICS 1985: Births, 239; Deaths, 174; Marriages, 163; Divorces, 95.

AGRICULTURE: About $25 million average annual income, about 85% from beef cattle, hogs, horses. Cotton, grain sorghum major crops; about 5,000 acres irrigated.

BUSINESS: Agribusiness, oil and natural gas; varied manufacturing.

CALDWELL (3,605) county seat; plants make aluminum furniture, other products; oil field tool and servicing; hospital, nursing home; annual fair, arts and crafts show.

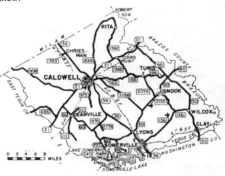

Somerville (2,410) has furniture factory; museum, heritage park, local events. Other towns are **Snook** (533) and **Clay** (61).

Burnet

LOCATION: Central (L-15).

HISTORY: Created from Bell, Travis, Williamson counties, 1852; organized 1854; named for **David G. Burnet,** provisional president, Texas Republic.

Cong. Dist.	10	U.S. Jud. Dist.	W-An.
St. Sen. Dist.	24	Ct. Appeals	3
St. Rep. Dist.	52	Admin. Jud. Dist.	3
St. Dist. Cts.	33		

PHYSICAL FEATURES: Many lakes; hilly; caves; sandy, red, black waxy soils; cedars, other trees.

RECREATION: Water sports on lakes; sites of historic forts; **Granite Mt.** furnished stone for **Texas Capitol;** deer, other hunting; major tourist center; **Longhorn Cavern** and **Inks Lake State Parks; Bluebonnet Trail** in spring.

MINERALS: Stone, graphite, sand and gravel

1985 Pop.	22,900	Tax Ratio	0.75
Area (sq. mi.)	994	Oil value	0
Altitude (ft.)	779-1,585	No. employed	5,839
Ann. rainfall (in.)	29.81	Avg. weekly wage	$271.73
Jan. temp. min.	37	Annual wages	$82,505,004
July temp. max.	96	1983 PCI	$8,007
Growing season (da.)	230	Buying pwr.	$256,482,000
Voters reg.	11,991	Tax value	$1,292,540,524
Businesses	679	Fed. expend.	$75,760,000

VITAL STATISTICS 1985: Births, 355; Deaths, 254;

Marriages, 295; Divorces, 160.

AGRICULTURE: About 95% of $15.8 million average income from cattle, sheep, goats; income from cedar posts, pecans, hay; some grains.

BUSINESS: Stone processing, manufacturing, agri-businesses, tourist trade, hunting leases.

BURNET (3,794) county seat; stone, graphite products; agribusiness; tourism; 2 hospitals, nursing homes.

Marble Falls (4,235) ranching, manufacturing of precision instruments, sporting goods; stone quarrying and tourist center; nursing home. Other towns are **Bertram** (1,002) ranching center; rest home; **Granite Shoals** (1,125), **Meadowlakes** (250).

Caldwell

LOCATION: South Central (N-16).

HISTORY: Created, organized from Bastrop, Gonzales counties, 1848. Named for Indian fighter, **Mathew Caldwell.**

Cong. Dist.	10	U.S. Jud. Dist.	W-An.
St. Sen. Dist.	18	Ct. Appeals	3
St. Rep. Dist.	31	Admin. Jud. Dist.	3
St. Dist. Cts.	22, 207, 274		

PHYSICAL FEATURES: Varied soils ranging from black clay to waxy; level, draining to San Marcos River.

RECREATION: Fishing, hunting; **Lockhart State Park; Luling Watermelon Thump;** Chisholm Trail round-

up at Lockhart; Plum Creek battle reenactment; oldest library in Texas, museums, nature trails; rodeo.

MINERALS: Oil, gas, sand, gravel.

1985 Pop.	27,400	Tax Ratio	0.79
Area (sq. mi.)	546	Oil value	$9,614,470
Altitude (ft.)	388-705	No. employed	5,241
Ann. rainfall (in.)	32.65	Avg. weekly wage	$277.21
Jan. temp. min.	41	Annual wages	$75,551,320
July temp. max.	96	1983 PCI	$6,461
Growing season (da.)	275	Buying pwr.	$215,613,000
Voters reg.	11,377	Tax value	$837,769,450
Businesses	510	Fed. expend.	$44,410,000

VITAL STATISTICS 1985: Births, 405; Deaths, 238; Marriages, 225; Divorces, 134.

AGRICULTURE: About $29 million average annual income, mostly from beef cattle, hogs, poultry; cotton, sorghums, wheat, corn, watermelons are leading crops.

BUSINESS: Petroleum, agribusiness, varied manufacturing.

LOCKHART (9,045) county seat; varied manufacturing plants, tourism; hospital, rest home.

Luling (5,397) oil industry center; concrete, poultry processing plants, iron works; other manufacturing; hospital, nursing homes; **Martindale** (1,068), **Uhland** (291).

Calhoun

LOCATION: On coast (P-18).

HISTORY: Created, organized from Jackson, Matagorda, Victoria counties, 1846. Named for **John C. Calhoun,** U.S. statesman.

Cong. Dist.	14	U.S. Jud. Dist.	S-Va.
St. Sen. Dist.	18	Ct. Appeals	13
St. Rep. Dist.	32	Admin. Jud. Dist.	4
St. Dist. Cts.	24, 135, 267		

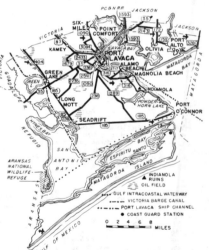

PHYSICAL FEATURES: Sandy; broken by bays; partly on Matagorda Island.

RECREATION: Beaches, fishing, water sports, historic sites, **Indianola State Park,** county park, **Matagorda Island, Green Lake;** Labor Day aircraft show and fishing festival, LaSalle Days in April, county fair.

MINERALS: Gas, oil.

1985 Pop.	21,700	Tax Ratio	0.94
Area (sq. mi.)	540	Oil value	$6,441,113
Altitude (ft.)	4-27	No. employed	8,057
Ann. rainfall (in.)	36.83	Avg. weekly wage	$463.86
Jan. temp. min.	47	Annual wages	$194,344,708
July temp. max.	92	1983 PCI	$8,350
Growing season (da.)	300	Buying pwr.	$226,639,000
Voters reg.	10,538	Tax value	$2,015,662,124
Businesses	439	Fed. expd.	$33,252,000

VITAL STATISTICS 1985: Births, 371; Deaths, 166; Marriages, 226; Divorces, 125.

AGRICULTURE: About 65% of $17.5 million average income from rice, grain sorghum, soybeans, corn; about 15,000 acres irrigated; beef cattle.

BUSINESS: Manufacturing, agribusinesses; petroleum, tourism, fishing and fish processing.

PORT LAVACA (12,349) county seat; commercial seafood operations, shipping, tourist center, chemical, offshore drilling rig, other manufacturing, tourism; hospital, nursing home.

Point Comfort (1,147) aluminum and plastic plants, deepwater port. Other towns include **Seadrift** (1,599), **Port O'Connor,** a fishing and resort center and offshore drilling supply base; library.

Callahan

LOCATION: West central (I-13).

HISTORY: Created 1858 from Bexar, Bosque, Travis counties; organized 1877; named for Texas Ranger, J. H. **Callahan.**

Cong. Dist.	17	U.S. Jud. Dist.	N-Ab.
St. Sen. Dist.	30	Ct. Appeals	11
St. Rep. Dist.	64	Admin. Jud. Dist.	7
St. Dist. Cts.	42		

PHYSICAL FEATURES: On divide between Brazos, Colorado River watersheds; level to rolling.

RECREATION: Hunting, local events, **Clyde Lake,** county museum, old settler reunion in July.

MINERALS: Oil and gas.

1985 Pop.	12,600	Tax Ratio	0.92
Area (sq. mi.)	899	Oil value	$432,375
Altitude (ft.)	1,604-2,204	No. employed	1,526
Ann. rainfall (in.)	24.92	Avg. weekly wage	$260.79
Jan. temp. min.	33	Annual wages	$20,694,508
July temp. max.	96	1983 PCI	$7,269
Growing season (da.)	228	Buying pwr.	$118,286,000
Voters reg.	6,566	Tax value	$446,432,192
Businesses	246	Fed. expd.	$25,261,000

VITAL STATISTICS 1985: Births, 170; Deaths, 146; Marriages, 105; Divorces, 76.

AGRICULTURE: About 75% of $11 million average income from beef cattle, sheep and hogs; wheat, peanuts, grain sorghums chief crops.

BUSINESS: Oil field services, agribusiness; county in Abilene SMSA.

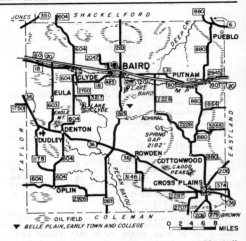

—·—·— OIL FIELD

▼ BELLE PLAIN, EARLY TOWN AND COLLEGE

BAIRD (1,737) county seat; center for ranching, oil field supplies; window manufacturer and candy packing, shipping; county hospital, clinic, nursing home.

Other towns include **Clyde** (3,053) metal products, helicopter parts, other small manufacturing; many work in Abilene; **Cross Plains** (1,201), **Putnam** (131).

Cameron

LOCATION: Southern tip (U-16).

HISTORY: Created, organized from Nueces County, 1848; named for **Capt. Ewen Cameron** of Mier Expedition.

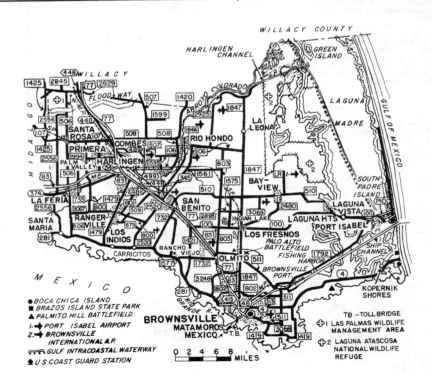

● BOCA CHICA ISLAND
■ BRAZOS ISLAND STATE PARK
▲ PALMITO HILL BATTLEFIELD
1.✈ PORT ISABEL AIRPORT
2.✈ BROWNSVILLE
    INTERNATIONAL A.P.
〰✕〰 GULF INTRACOASTAL WATERWAY
⚓ US COAST GUARD STATION

TB —TOLL BRIDGE
✛1 LAS PALMAS WILDLIFE MANAGEMENT AREA
✛2 LAGUNA ATASCOSA NATIONAL WILDLIFE REFUGE

Cong. Dist. 15	U.S. Jud. Dist. . . . . . S-Br.
St. Sen. Dist. 27	Ct. Appeals 13
St. Rep. Dist. . . . 37, 38, 39	Admin. Jud. Dist. 5
St. Dist. Cts. 103, 107, 138, 197, 357	

PHYSICAL FEATURES: Rich Rio Grande Valley soils; flat; semitropical climate.

RECREATION: Year-round resort; fishing, hunting, water sports; historical sites; Mexican gateway; **South Padre Island; Laguna-Atascosa Wildlife Refuge;** numerous local events; recreational vehicle center; Confederate Air Force Museum, air shows at Harlingen; Iwo Jima Monument.

MINERALS: Natural gas, oil.

1985 Pop. 249,800	Tax Ratio 0.78
Area (sq. mi.) 905	Oil value 0
Altitude (ft.) 3-67	No. employed 64,020
Ann. rainfall (in.) . . 25.13	Avg. weekly wage $259.46
Jan. temp. min. 51	Annual wages $863,756,816
July temp. max. 95	1983 PCI $5,375
Growing season (da.) 341	Buying pwr. $1,677,039,000
Voters reg. 91,499	Tax value . . $4,421,417,014
Businesses 4,613	Fed. expd. . . . $434,858,000

VITAL STATISTICS 1985: Births, 5,306; Deaths, 1,418; Marriages, 2,191; Divorces, 953.

AGRICULTURE: One of state's leading counties in total farm income amounting to about $91 million annually; cotton, sorghums, citrus, vegetables, sugarcane; some cattle, hogs, goats; more than 170,000 acres irrigated.

BUSINESS: Fruit, vegetables, seafood processing; fishing, shipping, tourism; agribusiness; manufacturing.

BROWNSVILLE (94,677) county seat; varied industries, shipping, **Port of Brownsville**, fishing, extensive tourism, agribusiness; **Texas Southmost College;** hospitals, nursing homes, crippled children health center; **Gladys Porter Zoo** for endangered species.

Harlingen (51,863) agribusiness and tourist center; varied manufacturing; port; wholesale and distribution center; recreational vehicle rally and pads; **Texas State Technical Institute;** Valley Baptist Medical Center; **Mental Health/Mental Retardation Center; South Texas Hospital; Confederate Air Force Flying Museum;** air show in October.

San Benito (20,695) agribusiness, tourism, varied manufacturing; hospital.

Other towns include **Bayview** (303), **Combes** (1,894), **Indian Lake** (196), **La Feria** (4,016), **Laguna Vista** (778), **Los Fresnos** (2,675), **Palm Valley** (820), **Rancho Viejo** (340), **Port Isabel** (4,243), **Primera** (1,675), **Rio Hondo** (1,970), **Santa Rosa** (2,121), **South Padre Island** (1,012) shipyard, **Indian Lake** (196), **Rangerville** (80).

Camp

LOCATION: Northeast (G-20).

HISTORY: 3rd smallest county; created, organized from Upshur County, 1874; named for jurist-legislator, J. L. Camp.

Cong. Dist. 1	U.S. Jud. Dist. . . . . E-MI.
St. Sen. Dist. 1	Ct. Appeals 6
St. Rep. Dist. 8	Admin. Jud. Dist. 1
St. Dist. Cts. 76, 276	

PHYSICAL FEATURES: Hilly, forested; drains to Cypress Creek on north; **Lake O' the Pines, Lake Bob Sandlin.**

RECREATION: Water sports, fishing on six lakes within 20 miles of Pittsburg; local events.

MINERALS: Oil, gas, clays, coal.

AGRICULTURE: More than $60 million annual income

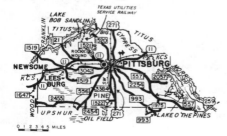

Carson

LOCATION: Northwestern (C-9).

HISTORY: Created from Bexar District, 1876; organized 1888; named for Republic of Texas Secretary of State, **S. P. Carson.**

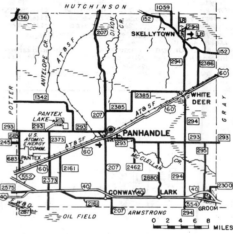

Cong. Dist. 13	U.S. Jud. Dist. . . . . N-Am.
St. Sen. Dist. 31	Ct. Appeals 7
St. Rep. Dist. 88	Admin. Jud. Dist. 9
St. Dist. Cts. 100	

PHYSICAL FEATURES: Level, some broken land; loam soils.

RECREATION: Museum, local events, sausage festivals.

MINERALS: Oil, gas production.

1985 Pop. 6,900	Tax Ratio 0.84
Area (sq. mi.) 924	Oil value $6,252,024
Altitude (ft.) . . 3,204-3,536	No. employed 4,177
Ann. rainfall (in.) . . 20.92	Avg. weekly wage $509.16
Jan. temp. min. 21	Annual wages $110,592,876
July temp. max. 93	1983 PCI $8,971
Growing season (da.) 191	Buying pwr. . . $78,816,000
Voters reg. 4,380	Tax value . . . $729,434,233
Businesses 150	Fed. expd. . . . $19,305,000

VITAL STATISTICS 1985: Births, 101; Deaths, 50; Marriages, 74; Divorces, 30.

AGRICULTURE: $33 million average annual income from hay, wheat, corn, beef cattle; 92,500 acres irrigated.

BUSINESS: Agribusinesses, oil field services.

PANHANDLE (2,368) county seat; agribusiness, petroleum center; nursing homes; airport; varied manufacturing.

Other towns include **White Deer** (1,369), **Skellytown** (944), **Groom** (725).

---

come, with 90% from livestock, dairy, poultry; peaches, vegetables, hay chief crops; 500 acres of horticulture crops irrigated; timber harvested.

1985 Pop. 10,000	Tax Ratio 0.98
Area (sq. mi.) 203	Oil value $19,812,657
Altitude (ft.) 277-538	No. employed 2,629
Ann. rainfall (in.) . . 45.25	Avg. weekly wage $274.39
Jan. temp. min. 36	Annual wages . $37,511,852
July temp. max. 95	1983 PCI $7,535
Growing season (da.) 238	Buying pwr. . $113,587,000
Voters reg. 5,959	Tax value . . $336,451,366
Businesses 262	Fed. expd. . . . $21,913,000

VITAL STATISTICS 1985: Births, 174; Deaths, 91; Marriages, 96; Divorces, 34.

BUSINESS: Agribusiness, timber industries; light manufacturing, food processing; retirement center.

PITTSBURG (4,561) county seat; several industries manufacture furniture, clothing, oil field products, metal buildings, air filters, steel castings, brick, process feed; hospital, nursing homes; community college under construction; **Rocky Mound** (127).

Cass

LOCATION: Northeast (G-21).
HISTORY: Named for **U. S. Sen. Lewis Cass;** created, organized 1846 from Bowie County.

Cong. Dist.	1	U.S. Jud. Dist.	E-MI.
St. Sen. Dist.	1	Ct. Appeals.	6
St. Rep. Dist.	8	Admin. Jud. Dist.	1
St. Dist. Cts.	5		

PHYSICAL FEATURES: Rolling, forested; timber produced; drained by Cypress Bayou, Sulphur River.
RECREATION: Fishing, water sports, county park; **Lake Wright Patman, Atlanta State Park,** Wildflower Trails in spring, forest festival.
MINERALS: Gas, oil, iron ore.

1985 Pop.	30,600	Tax Ratio	0.91
Area (sq. mi.)	937	Oil value	$5,944,473
Altitude (ft.)	219-486	No. employed	6,520
Ann. rainfall (in.)	46.90	Avg. weekly wage	$335.06
Jan. temp. min.	31	Annual wages	$113,598,944
July temp. max.	92	1983 PCI	$6,925
Growing season (da.)	237	Buying pwr.	$303,744,000
Voters reg.	16,457	Tax value	$1,201,420,335
Businesses	549	Fed. expd.	$66,069,000

VITAL STATISTICS 1985: Births, 468; Deaths, 382; Marriages, 342; Divorces, 183.
AGRICULTURE: More than $17 million average income with 85% from beef cattle, hogs; hay, watermelons, fruits and vegetables; timber income about 40% of total.

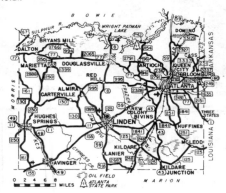

Musicians playing a hammered dulcimer and a guitar entertain visitors to the Edom Craft Fair, held each September in that Van Zandt County town. Texas Almanac photo.

Growing season (da.)	193	Buying pwr.	$69,270,000
Voters reg.	4,367	Tax value	$497,916,442
Businesses	222	Fed. expd.	$31,539,000

VITAL STATISTICS 1985: Births, 200; Deaths, 75; Marriages, 88; Divorces, 30.
AGRICULTURE: More than $160 million average annual income makes county one of state's leading agricultural producers; major crops are corn, wheat, sorghums, cotton, vegetables; more than 300,000 acres irrigated; feedlots with 225,000 head capacity.
BUSINESS: Varied agribusinesses.

BUSINESS: Paper mill, wood products, steel products, varied manufacturing; agribusinesses, sawmill.
LINDEN (2,473) county seat; oil tank manufacturing, wood treating plant, boat factory, garment manufacturing, other small plants; hospital, nursing home.
Atlanta (6,507) paper mill, clothing, computer terminals, other varied manufacturing; oil field servicing; agribusinesses; hospitals.
Other towns include **Avinger** (719), **Bloomburg** (387), **Domino** (258), **Douglassville** (226), **Hughes Springs** (2,501) warehousing, varied manufacturing, **Marietta** (191), **Queen City** (1,745).

Castro

LOCATION: Northwest (D-8).
HISTORY: Created 1876 from Bexar District, organized 1891. Named for **Henri Castro,** Texas colonizer.

Cong. Dist.	19	U.S. Jud. Dist.	N-Am.
St. Sen. Dist.	31	Ct. Appeals	7
St. Rep. Dist.	85	Admin. Jud. Dist.	9
St. Dist. Cts.	64, 242		

PHYSICAL FEATURES: Flat, drains to creeks, draws and playas; underground water.
RECREATION: Local events; pheasant hunting.
MINERALS: Not significant.

1985 Pop.	10,300	Tax Ratio	0.92
Area (sq. mi.)	899	Oil value	$136,502
Altitude (ft.)	3,731-3,942	No. employed	2,716
Ann. rainfall (in.)	17.72	Avg. weekly wage	$246.16
Jan. temp. min.	22	Annual wages	$34,765,956
July temp. max.	93	1983 PCI	$5,576

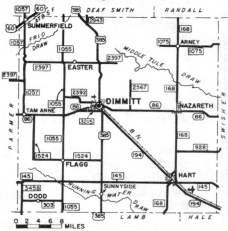

DIMMITT (4,875) county seat; corn-milling and starch plants; farm equipment, fertilizer manufacturing, food processing, other agribusinesses; library; hospital. Other towns are **Hart** (969) and **Nazareth** (257).

Said to be the nation's longest footbridge, this 546-foot span in the city of Rusk was originally built in 1861 so early citizens could get across the valley to town when the creek flooded. Texas Almanac photo.

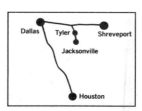

Chambers

LOCATION: On Galveston, other bays (M-21).

HISTORY: Named for **Gen. T. J. Chambers** surveyor; created, organized 1858 from Liberty, Jefferson counties.

Cong. Dist. 9
St. Sen. Dist. 4
St. Rep. Dist. 21
St. Dist. Cts. 253, 344
U.S. Jud. Dist. . . . . S-Gn.
Ct. Appeals 1, 14
Admin. Jud. Dist. 2

PHYSICAL FEATURES: Level, coastal soils; some forests.

RECREATION: Fishing, hunting; all water sports; camping facilities; 10 county parks; **Anahuac National Wildlife Refuge;** historic sites; **Texas Rice Festival.**

MINERALS: Oil, gas, salt, clays, sand and gravel.

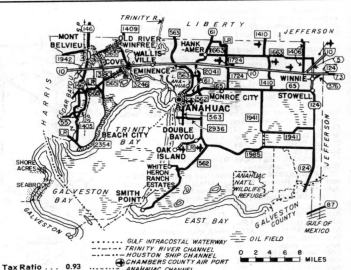

.... GULF INTRACOSTAL WATERWAY
-·-·-·- TRINITY RIVER CHANNEL
----- HOUSTON SHIP CHANNEL
⊙ CHAMBERS COUNTY AIR PORT
.... ANAHUAC CHANNEL
≈≈≈ OIL FIELD

0 2 4 6 8
MILES

1985 Pop.	19,400	Tax Ratio . . . 0.93
Area (sq. mi.)	616	Oil value $71,281,449
Altitude (ft.)	2-73	No. employed . 6,357
Ann. rainfall (in.) . .	52.84	Avg. weekly wage $472.06
Jan. temp. min.	44	Annual wages $156,046,764
July temp. max. .	91	1983 PCI $8,658
Growing season (da.)	261	Buying pwr. . $28,857,000
Voters reg.	10,340	Tax value . . $3,092,235,305
Businesses	331	Fed. expd. . . . $118,837,000

VITAL STATISTICS 1985: Births, 331; Deaths, 131; Marriages, 487; Divorces, 158.

AGRICULTURE: About $25 million income; about 85% from rice, soybeans; beef cattle; 44,000 acres irrigated; 15,000 acres timber.

BUSINESS: Petroleum, chemicals, steel plants, agribusinesses, varied manufacturing, tourism.

ANAHUAC (1,869) county seat; canal connects with Houston Ship Channel; agribusiness; hospital.

Other towns include **Mont Belvieu (1,807), Beach City** (1,062), **Cove** (627), **Old River-Winfree (1,255).**

Cherokee

LOCATION: East (J-20).
HISTORY: Named for Indians; created, organized 1846 from Nacogdoches County.

Cong. Dist. 1   U.S. Jud. Dist. . . . . E-Ty.
St. Sen. Dist. 3   Ct. Appeals 12
St. Rep. Dist. 11   Admin. Jud. Dis. 1
St. Dist. Cts. 2

PHYSICAL FEATURES: Hilly, partly forested; drains to Angelina, Neches Rivers; many streams, lakes; sandy, clay soils.

RECREATION: Water activities; fishing, hunting on many lakes; numerous historical sites, homes; Texas State Railroad excursion train; state parks.

Among points of interest are **Love's Lookout Park, Jim Hogg State Park,** birthplace of **first native Texan to become Governor; Caddoan Mounds State Park** near Alto; site of **ghost town** of **New Birmingham; I. D. Fairchild State Forest;** Nature Trails through forests; and several lakes.

MINERALS: Oil, gas, iron ore.

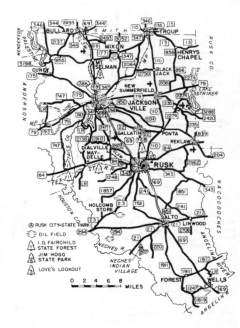

1985 Pop.	39,800	Tax Ratio 0.90
Area (sq. mi.)	1,052	Oil value $18,529,329
Altitude (ft.)	204-708	No. employed 12,316
Ann. rainfall (in.) . .	44.26	Avg. weekly wage $279.67
Jan. temp. min.	38	Annual wages $179,114,900
July temp. max.	91	1983 PCI $7,295
Growing season (da.)	258	Buying pwr. . $367,990,000
Voters reg.	18,552	Tax value . . $1,295,486,995
Businesses	793	Fed. expd. . . . $84,962,000

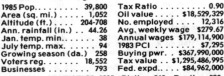

Ⓐ RUSK CITY-STATE PARK
≈≈ OIL FIELD
🌲 I. D. FAIRCHILD STATE FOREST
🌲 JIM HOGG STATE PARK
🌲 LOVE'S LOOKOUT

0 2 4 6 8
MILES

VITAL STATISTICS 1985: Births, 569; Deaths, 530; Marriages, 444; Divorces, 250.

AGRICULTURE: More than $55 million average income, about 65% from cattle, poultry; greenhouse plants, hay, vegetables, fruits; timber production including Christmas trees.

BUSINESS: Wood and plastics industries, other factories; agribusinesses.

RUSK (4,612) county seat; pulpwood shipping center; milk processor; other factories; **Rusk State Hospital,** other hospitals; state railroad, Rusk state park with camping.

Jacksonville (12,827), more than 60 industrial firms

make wood, plastic products, metal buildings, baskets; vegetable and hothouse floral production; hospitals, clinic; **Lon Morris College, Jacksonville College, Baptist M.A. Theological Seminary.**

Other towns include **Wells** (927), **Troup** (2,015, partly in Smith County), **Bullard** (887, partly in Smith County), **Alto** (1,209), **New Summerfield** (371), **Reklaw** (328, part Rusk County), **Gallatin** (278), **Cuney** (191).

Childress

LOCATION: Northwest (D-11).
HISTORY: Created 1876 from Bexar, Young Districts; organized 1887; named for **author of Texas Declaration of Independence, George C. Childress.**

Cong. Dist.	13	U.S. Jud. Dist. . . . N-Am.
St. Sen. Dist.	30	Ct. Appeals	7
St. Rep. Dist.	84	Admin. Jud. Dist.	9
St. Dist. Cts.	100		

PHYSICAL FEATURES: Rolling prairie, draining to Prairie Dog Town Fork of Red River; mixed soils.
RECREATION: Water recreation on **Lakes Childress** and **Baylor,** fishing, hunting; parks; county museum; July 4th ice cream freeze, other events.
MINERALS: Small production oil, gas.

1985 Pop.	6,500	Tax Ratio	0.86
Area (sq. mi.)	707	Oil value	$23,069
Altitude (ft.) . . 1,782-1,934		No. employed	1,660
Ann. rainfall (in.) . . 20.67		Avg. weekly wage $240.84
Jan. temp. min.	26	Annual wages . $20,789,896
July temp. max.	99	1983 PCI	$7,218
Growing season (da.) 217		Buying pwr. . . $57,543,000
Voters reg.	3,332	Tax value . . $151,117,006
Businesses	205	Fed. expd. . . $23,089,000

VITAL STATISTICS 1985: Births, 95; Deaths, 112; Marriages, 65; Divorces, 30.
AGRICULTURE: About $12 million average income from cotton, wheat, sorghums, cattle; 2,000 acres irrigated for cotton.
BUSINESS: Agribusinesses; varied manufacturing.

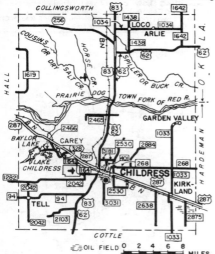

CHILDRESS (5,510) county seat; has more than 80% of county's population; plants make apparel, mobile homes, fences, wood products; hospital, nursing homes; home of Greenbelt Bowl, high school football all-star game.

Clay

LOCATION: North central (F-14).
HISTORY: Created, organized from Cooke County, 1857; Indians forced disorganization, 1862; reorganized, 1873; named for **Henry Clay,** U.S. statesman.

Cong. Dist.	13	U.S. Jud. Dist. . . . . N-WF
St. Sen. Dist.	30	Ct. Appeals	2

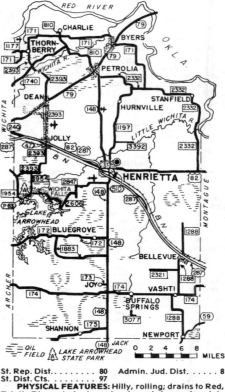

St. Rep. Dist.	80	Admin. Jud. Dist.	8
St. Dist. Cts.	97		

PHYSICAL FEATURES: Hilly, rolling; drains to Red, Trinity Rivers, Lake Arrowhead; sandy loam, chocolate soils; mesquites, post oaks.
RECREATION: Fishing, water sports at **Lake Arrowhead;** local events.
MINERALS: Oil and gas, stone.

1985 Pop.	9,700	Tax Ratio	0.91
Area (sq. mi.)	1,085	Oil value $1,503,050
Altitude (ft.) . . . 862-1,083		No. employed	1,228
Ann. rainfall (in.) . . 31.40		Avg. weekly wage $286.55
Jan. temp. min.	30	Annual wages . $18,298,256
July temp. max.	98	1983 PCI	$8,117
Growing season (da.) 232		Buying pwr. . $113,101,000
Voters reg.	5,920	Tax value . . $571,920,935
Businesses	155	Fed. expd. . . $20,561,000

VITAL STATISTICS 1985: Births, 111; Deaths, 102; Marriages, 134; Divorces, 52.
AGRICULTURE: Most of $38 million average income from livestock, chiefly beef and dairy cattle, swine; wheat, cotton, grain sorghums.
BUSINESS: Oil; agribusinesses; varied manufacturing.
HENRIETTA (3,213) county seat; plants make trophies, flatbed and livestock trailers, other products; hospital, rest homes; Pioneer Reunion and Rodeo in September.

Other towns include **Petrolia** (787), **Bellevue** (378), **Byers** (620), **Jolly** (179), **Dean** (223).

Cochran

LOCATION: Adjoins New Mexico (F-7).
HISTORY: Created from Bexar, Young Districts, 1876; organized 1924; named for **Robert Cochran,** who died in Alamo.

Cong. Dist.	19	U.S. Jud. Dist. . . . . N-Lb.
St. Sen. Dist.	28	Ct. Appeals	7
St. Rep. Dist.	77	Admin. Jud. Dist.	9
St. Dist. Cts.	286		

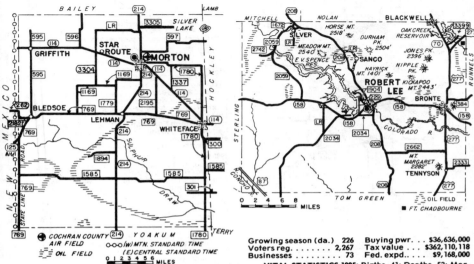

PHYSICAL FEATURES: Many small lakes (playas); level prairie; underground water; loam, sandy loam soils.

RECREATION: Rodeo, county fair, museum.

MINERALS: Oil, gas.

1985 Pop.	4,600	Tax Ratio	1.00
Area (sq. mi.)	775	Oil value	$86,461,732
Altitude (ft.)	3,687-3,965	No. employed	1,008
Ann. rainfall (in.)	15.62	Avg. weekly wage	$288.99
Jan. temp. min.	23	Annual wages	$15,147,980
July temp. max.	92	1983 PCI	$6,721
Growing season (da.)	189	Buying pwr.	$34,552,000
Voters reg.	2,308	Tax value	$867,974,693
Businesses	77	Fed. expd.	$13,743,000

VITAL STATISTICS 1985: Births, 84; Deaths, 42; Marriages, 37; Divorces, 9.

AGRICULTURE: More than $35 million average income from cotton, sorghums, wheat; cattle, extensive cattle feeding; 108,000 acres irrigated.

BUSINESS: Agribusinesses; feedlots.

MORTON (2,578) county seat; hospital, center for oil, agricultural trade, meat packing; **Whiteface** (517).

Coke

LOCATION: West central (J-11).

HISTORY: Created, organized 1889 from Tom Green County; named for **Gov. Richard Coke.**

Cong. Dist.	17	U.S. Jud. Dist.	N-SAng.
St. Sen. Dist.	25	Ct. Appeals	3
St. Rep. Dist.	66	Admin. Jud. Dist.	7
St. Dist Cts	51		

PHYSICAL FEATURES: Prairie, hills, Colorado River valley; sandy loam, red soils. E. V. Spence Reservoir (formerly Robert Lee).

RECREATION: Hunting, fishing; **E. V. Spence Reservoir; Oak Creek Reservoir;** historic sites, county museum, local events.

MINERALS: Oil, gas, sand and gravel.

1985 Pop.	3,600	Tax Ratio	0.94
Area (sq. mi.)	908	Oil value	$20,925,663
Altitude (ft.)	1,758-2,608	No. employed	834
Ann. rainfall (in.)	20.48	Avg. weekly wage	$306.10
Jan. temp. min.	29	Annual wages	$13,274,992
July temp. max.	97	1983 PCI	$8,801

Growing season (da.)	226	Buying pwr.	$36,636,000
Voters reg.	2,267	Tax value	$362,110,118
Businesses	73	Fed. expd.	$9,168,000

VITAL STATISTICS 1985: Births, 41; Deaths, 53; Marriages, 36; Divorces, 18.

AGRICULTURE: More than 90% of $10.2 million annual farm income from cattle, sheep, goats; cotton, sorghums, small grains, hay leading crops.

BUSINESS: Oil well supplies, agribusinesses, tourism.

ROBERT LEE (1,391) county seat; ranching; oil, gas center; hospital, nursing home; **Bronte** (1,083) and **Blackwell** (307, partly in Nolan County).

Coleman

LOCATION: West central (J-12).

HISTORY: Created 1858 from Brown, Travis counties; organization began 1862, completed 1864; named for Houston's aide, **R. M. Coleman.**

Cong. Dist.	17	U.S. Jud. Dist.	N-SAng.
St. Sen. Dist.	24	Ct. Appeals	11
St. Rep. Dist.	65	Admin. Jud. Dist.	7
St. Dist. Cts.	35, 42		

PHYSICAL FEATURES: Hilly, rolling; drains to Colorado River, Pecan Bayou; lakes; some mesquite, oaks.

RECREATION: Fishing, hunting; water sports; local events; historic sites; **Lake Coleman, Lake Scarborough, Hord's Creek Reservoir, other lakes; Santa Anna Peak.**

MINERALS: Oil, gas, coal, stone, clays.

1985 Pop.	10,600	Tax Ratio	0.69
Area (sq. mi.)	1,277	Oil value	$600,484
Altitude (ft.)	1,488-2,173	No. employed	2,221
Ann. rainfall (in.)	26.52	Avg. weekly wage	$232.40
Jan. temp. min.	34	Annual wages	$26,841,132
July temp. max.	96	1983 PCI	$6,884
Growing season (da.)	235	Buying pwr.	$102,834,000
Voters reg.	6,147	Tax value	$408,922,485
Businesses	272	Fed. expd.	$30,224,000

VITAL STATISTICS 1985: Births, 145; Deaths, 158; Marriages, 115; Divorces, 47.

AGRICULTURE: In excess of 80% of $24 million average annual income from cattle, sheep, hogs; wheat, oats, grain sorghums, cotton.

BUSINESS: Agribusinesses, petroleum, tile, brick plants, other manufacturers.

COLEMAN (6,070) county seat; bottling company, varied manufacturing and agribusinesses; hospital, nursing homes; city park, museum. **Santa Anna** (1,446), clay industry; **Novice** (202).

Coleman County (Cont'd.)

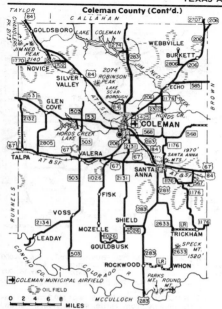

Collin

LOCATION: North central (G-17).

HISTORY: Created from Fannin County and organized, 1846. Named for pioneer there, **Collin McKinney.**

Cong. Dist.	3, 4, 26	U.S. Jud. Dist.	E-Sh.
St. Sen. Dist.	2, 8	Ct. Appeals	5
St. Rep. Dist.	60, 61, 62	Admin. Jud. Dist.	1
St. Dist. Cts.	199, 219, 296		

PHYSICAL FEATURES: Heavy, black clay soil; level to rolling; drains to Trinity, Lake Lavon.

RECREATION: Fishing, water sports on **Lavon,** other lakes; historic sites; old homes restoration, tours; Heard Natural Science Museum, McKinney Historical District, Old Collin County Post Office, Bolin Wildlife Exhibit; South Fork Ranch of Dallas TV series near Wylie; hot air balloon festival in September and local events in Plano.

MINERALS: Limited stone production.

1985 Pop.	196,900	Tax Ratio	0.95
Area (sq. mi.)	851	Oil value	0
Altitude (ft.)	472-753	No. employed	56,335
Ann. rainfall (in.)	38.10	Avg. weekly wage	$374.50
Jan. temp. min.	34	Ann. wages	$1,097,088,740
July temp. max.	96	1983 PCI	$12,028
Growing season (da.)	230	Buying pwr.	$2,934,989,000
Voters reg.	98,281	Tax value	$18,709,349,333
Businesses	4,248	Fed. expd.	$286,059,000

VITAL STATISTICS 1985: Births, 3,760; Deaths, 893; Marriages, 2,202; Divorces, 1,197.

AGRICULTURE: More than $45 million average annual income equally divided between crops, livestock; sorghums, wheat, hay, cotton, chief crops; beef cattle, horses.

BUSINESS: Varied manufacturing plants, agribusinesses, retail and wholesale center. Many work in Dallas.

McKINNEY (18,231) county seat; agribusiness,

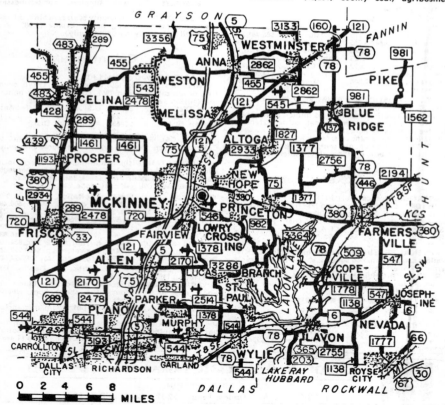

trade center; varied industries; hospitals, nursing homes; fashion outlet; three museums.

Plano (92,094), one of nation's fastest growing cities; compact disc, metals, newspaper printing, computer forms, satellite communications, bakery equipment, other manufacturing; research center, growing commercial and financial center; hospital, nursing homes, medical and psychiatric centers.

Other towns include **Addison** (5,553, mostly in Dallas County), **Allen** (11,226), **Altoga** (326), **Anna** (1,078), **Blue Ridge** (551), **Celina** (1,667), **Dallas** (974,239, mostly Dallas County), **Fairview** (1,287), **Farmersville** (2,622) livestock, cotton center, small industry, **Frisco** (4,254), **Josephine** (574), **Lavon** (222), **Lowry Crossing** (548), **Lucas** (1,592), **Melissa** (773), **Murphy** (1,114), **New Hope** (447), **Parker** (1,407), **Princeton** (3,918) varied manufacturing, printing, **Prosper** (791), **Richardson** (76,891, mostly in Dallas County), **Royse City** (1,606, mostly in Rockwall County), **Sachse** (2,311, mostly in Dallas County), **Saint Paul** (492), **Westminster** (320), **Weston** (468) and **Wylie** (3,972).

Collingsworth

LOCATION: In Panhandle (D-11).

HISTORY: Created, 1876, from Bexar and Young Districts, organized 1890. Named for Republic of Texas' first Chief Justice, James Collinsworth; name misspelled in law.

Cong. Dist.	13	U.S. Jud. Dist.	N-Am.
St. Sen. Dist.	31	Ct. Appeals	7
St. Rep. Dist.	84	Admin. Jud. Dist.	9
St. Dist. Cts.	100		

PHYSICAL FEATURES: Rolling, broken terrain, draining to Red River forks; sandy and loam soils.

RECREATION: Children's camp, county museum, Pioneer park.

MINERALS: Gas, oil production.

1985 Pop.	4,100	Tax Ratio	0.84
Area (sq. mi.)	909	Oil value	0
Altitude (ft.)	1,789-2,389	No. employed	894
Ann. rainfall (in.)	22.03	Avg. weekly wage	$226.55
Jan. temp. min.	26	Annual wages	$10,532,084
July temp. max.	99	1983 PCI	$6,820

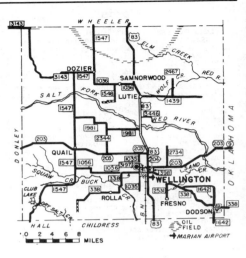

Growing season (da.)	212	Buying pwr.	$42,262,000
Voters reg.	2,837	Tax value	$143,577,970
Businesses	101	Fed. expd.	$14,250,000

VITAL STATISTICS 1985: Births, 54; Deaths, 60; Marriages, 85; Divorces, 19.

AGRICULTURE: About $18 million average income from cotton, grains, peanuts, beef cattle; 12,000 acres irrigated.

BUSINESS: Chiefly agribusinesses; railroad manufacturing, light industry.

WELLINGTON (2,653) county seat; feedlots, other agribusinesses; rail spike factory; hospital, nursing home; **Dodson** (168).

Colorado

LOCATION: Southeast (N-18).

HISTORY: Created 1836, an original county, organized 1837. Named for **Colorado River.**

Cong. Dist.	14	U.S. Jud. Dist.	S-Hn.
St. Sen. Dist.	5	Ct. Appeals	1, 14
St. Rep. Dist.	30	Admin. Jud. Dist.	3
St. Dist. Cts.	25, 2D25		

PHYSICAL FEATURES: 3 soil areas; level to rolling; bisected by Colorado River; oaks leading timber.

RECREATION: Hunting, many historic sites, homes; **Attwater's Prairie Chicken Refuge,** local events

MINERALS: Gas, oil, sand and gravel, stone.

1985 Pop.	20,100	Tax Ratio	0.91
Area (sq. mi.)	964	Oil value	$3,801,257
Altitude (ft.)	151-450	No. employed	5,291
Ann. rainfall (in.)	41.32	Avg. weekly wage	$287.63
Jan. temp. min.	39	Annual wages	$79,137,760
July temp. max.	86	1983 PCI	$7,843
Growing season (da.)	280	Buying pwr.	$196,655,000
Voters reg.	9,535	Tax value	$1,245,206,504
Businesses	569	Fed. expd.	$47,655,000

VITAL STATISTICS 1985: Births, 303; Deaths, 257; Marriages, 202; Divorces, 90.

AGRICULTURE: About $60 million average income from beef, dairy cattle; chief crops are rice, corn, grains, cotton, hay, soybeans; 35,000 acres irrigated, mostly rice.

BUSINESS: Agribusinesses; oil field services and equipment manufacturing. Plants process minerals.

COLUMBUS (4,250) county seat; agribusiness center; sand, gravel industries; oil, gas servicing, processing; oil field and clothing manufacturing; hospital, nursing home, many historical sites, old homes. Art show and antique sale in **May.**

Other towns include **Eagle Lake,** (4,158) farming center; concrete products; **Weimar** (2,125) varied manufacturing; hospital, nursing home.

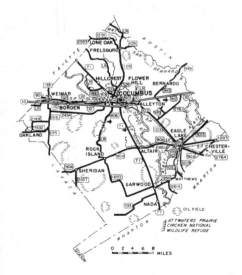

Comal

LOCATION: South central (N-14).

HISTORY: Created and organized from Bexar, Gonzales, Travis counties, 1846; named for Comal River.

Cong. Dist.	21	U.S. Jud. Dist.	W-SAnt.
St. Sen. Dist.	21	Ct. Appeals	3
St. Rep. Dist.	46	Admin. Jud. Dist.	3
St. Dist. Cts.	22, 207, 274		

PHYSICAL FEATURES: Hilly, spring-fed streams; 2½-mile-long Comal called "**shortest U.S. river**"; Guadalupe River; Canyon Lake.

1985 Pop.	46,200	Tax Ratio	0.88
Area (sq. mi.)	555	Oil value	0
Altitude (ft.)	623-1,473	No. employed	14,633
Ann. rainfall (in.)	33.19	Avg. weekly wage	$269.65
Jan. temp. min.	40	Annual wages	$205,187,420
July temp. max.	96	1983 PCI	$9,545
Growing season (da.)	265	Buying pwr.	$563,835,000
Voters reg.	23,778	Tax value	$2,912,943,379
Businesses	1,214	Fed. expd.	$102,321,000

VITAL STATISTICS 1985: Births, 686; Deaths, 411; Marriages, 579; Divorces, 217.

RECREATION: Tourist center; fishing, hunting; historic sites, museum; scenic drives; **Canyon Lake** facilities; **Landa Park** with 76 species of trees; **Prince Solms Park**, other county parks; **Natural Bridge Cavern;** river resorts, lodges, river sports; Wurstfest in November, other local events, old homes.

This hearth, typical of those found in the homes of early German settlers in Central Texas, is in the Pioneer Museum complex in Fredericksburg. Texas Almanac photo.

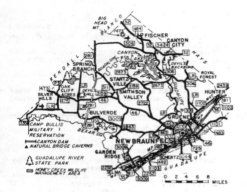

MINERALS: Stone, lime, sand and gravel.

AGRICULTURE: About 85% of $6.5 million farm income from beef cattle, sheep and Angora goats; some sorghum, wheat, oats.

BUSINESS: Plants make textiles, apparel, furniture, metal products, mineral, electrical manufacturing, concrete products; tourist business; county in San Antonio MSA, see metro page.

NEW BRAUNFELS (25,306) county seat; textile, furniture, metal products factories; tourist center; hospital, nursing homes, center for retarded.

Other towns include **Garden Ridge** (783) and **Schertz** (7,576, mostly in Guadalupe County).

Comanche

LOCATION: Central (J-14).

HISTORY: Created, organized, 1856, from Bosque, Coryell counties; named for **Indians.**

Cong. Dist.	17	U.S. Jud. Dist.	N-FW
St. Sen. Dist.	22	Ct. Appeals	11
St. Rep. Dist.	65	Admin Jud. Dist.	3
St. Dist. Cts.	220		

PHYSICAL FEATURES: Rolling, hilly; sandy, loam, waxy soils; drains to Leon River, Proctor Lake; pecans, oaks, mesquites, cedars.

RECREATION: Hunting, fishing, **Proctor Lake;** parks, museums, local events.

MINERALS: Limited gas, oil, stone, clay.

1985 Pop.	12,900	Tax Ratio	0.88
Area (sq. mi.)	930	Oil value	0
Altitude (ft.)	1,056-1,847	No. employed	2,974
Ann. rainfall (in.)	28.45	Avg. weekly wage	$235.98
Jan. temp. min.	32	Annual wages	$36,494,796
July temp. max.	95	1983 PCI	$7,509
Growing season (da.)	238	Buying pwr.	$117,702,000
Voters reg.	6,946	Tax value	$555,837,228
Businesses	319	Fed. expd.	$34,156,000

VITAL STATISTICS 1985: Births, 194; Deaths, 212; Marriages, 128; Divorces, 65.

AGRICULTURE: About $62 million average annual income, 75% from beef, dairy cattle, swine, sheep and goats; peanuts, grains, hay leading crops; pecans, fruit also produced; 44,000 acres irrigated, mostly peanuts.

BUSINESS: Peanut and pecan shelling plants; other agribusinesses; food processing; leather factory, pottery, livestock feed, varied other plants.

COMANCHE (4,151) county seat; plants make livestock feed, pecan and peanut products, leather, ceramic goods; agribusinesses; hospital, nursing home; public library; oldest courthouse on display on town square.

DeLeon (2,336) marketing center for peanuts, pecans, peaches; **Gustine** (488).

Concho

LOCATION: Central (K-12).

HISTORY: Created from Bexar District, 1858, organized 1879. Named for **Concho River.**

Cong. Dist. 17	U.S. Jud. Dist. . . . N-SAng.
St. Sen. Dist. 24	Ct. Appeals 3
St. Rep. Dist. 67	Admin. Jud. Dist. 7
St. Dist. Cts. 119, 198	

PHYSICAL FEATURES: Rough, broken area to south; level in north; sandy, loam and dark soils; drains to creeks and Colorado River.

RECREATION: Famed for 1,500 Indian **pictographs,** largest collection known; local events.

MINERALS: Oil, gas, stone produced.

1985 Pop. 2,800	Tax Ratio 0.86
Area (sq. mi.) 992	Oil value $35,410
Altitude (ft.) . . 1,631-2,083	No. employed 546
Ann. rainfall (in.) . . 22.28	Avg. weekly wage $233.98
Jan. temp. min. 35	Annual wages . $6,643,368
July temp. max. 96	1983 PCI $7,173
Growing season (da.) 228	Buying pwr. . . $26,731,000
Voters reg. 1,806	Tax value . . $288,802,214
Businesses 54	Fed. expd. . . . $11,739,000

VITAL STATISTICS 1985: Births, 29; Deaths, 40; Marriages, 25; Divorces, 11.

AGRICULTURE: More than $15 million farm income, 60% from sheep, cattle, goats; leading sheep producing county; grains, cotton chief crops.

BUSINESS: Chiefly agribusinesses.

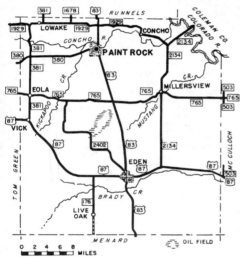

PAINT ROCK (290) county seat; named for **Indian pictographs;** ranching, farming center. **Eden** (1,308) is largest town, hospital, nursing home.

Cooke

LOCATION: North central, adjoins Oklahoma (F-16).

HISTORY: Created, organized, 1848, from Fannin County; named for **Capt. W. G. Cooke** of Texas Revolution.

Cong. Dist. 17, 26	U.S. Jud. Dist. . . . . E-Sh.
St. Sen. Dist. 30	Ct. Appeals 2
St. Rep. Dist. 63	Admin. Jud. Dist. 8
St. Dist. Cts. 235	

PHYSICAL FEATURES: Drains to Red, Trinity Rivers; **Lake Texoma** in northeast corner; sandy, red, loam soils.

RECREATION: Water sports; **Lake Ray Roberts** under construction; hunting, fishing; **Frank Buck Zoo;** museum; park; local events.

MINERALS: Oil, gas, sand and gravel.

1985 Pop. 29,000	Tax Ratio 0.80
Area (sq. mi.) 893	Oil value $25,067,530
Altitude (ft.) . . . 636-1,007	No. employed 8,919
Ann. rainfall (in.) . . 33.88	Avg. weekly wage $309.37
Jan. temp. min. 32	Annual wages $143,483,468
July temp. max. 96	1983 PCI $7,899
Growing season (da.) 226	Buying pwr. . $302,999,000
Voters reg. 15,072	Tax value . $1,094,174,192
Businesses 798	Fed. expd. . . . $55,314,000

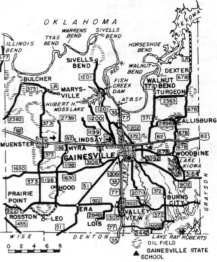

VITAL STATISTICS 1985: Births, 475; Deaths, 292; Marriages, 1,280; Divorces, 164.

AGRICULTURE: About 80% of $43 million average annual income from beef, dairy cattle, poultry, hogs, horses; crops include wheat, oats, grain sorghum, peanuts, hay; some irrigation.

BUSINESS: Agribusinesses, oil industries, varied manufacturing.

GAINESVILLE (14,066) county seat; factories make pipe, garments, boots, fishing lures, metal products, aircraft equipment; agribusinesses; **Cooke County College;** hospitals, nursing homes; **Gainesville State School; Camp Sweeney** for diabetic children.

Muenster (1,339) is a dairy center with Associated Milk Producers plant, cheese factory; REA headquarters, oil production center, feed processing, dress factory, other industries; hospital.

Other towns include **Callisburg** (329), **Lindsay** (638) and **Valley View** (574).

Coryell

LOCATION: Central (K-15).

HISTORY: Created from Bell County, organized, 1854; named for local pioneer, **James Coryell.**

Cong. Dist. 11	U.S. Jud. Dist. . . . . W-Wa.
St. Sen. Dist. 24	Ct. Appeals 10
St. Rep. Dist. 57	Admin. Jud. Dist. 3
St. Dist. Cts. 52	

PHYSICAL FEATURES: Leon Valley in center, remainder rolling, hilly.

RECREATION: **Mother Neff State Park;** hunting, nearby lakes and Leon River. **Fort Hood** brings many visitors; historic homes; log jail; local events.

MINERALS: Small stone, sand and gravel production.

1985 Pop. 57,200	Tax Ratio 0.83
Area (sq. mi.) 1,057	Oil value $112,747
Altitude (ft.) . . . 1,365-1,839	No. employed 6,771
Ann. rainfall (in.) . . 32.58	Avg. weekly wage $267.48
Jan. temp. min. 36	Annual wages . $94,178,352
July temp. max. 96	1983 PCI $7,092

Growing season (da.)　241
Voters reg. . . . . . .　15,805
Businesses . . . .　562
Buying pwr. . $673,930,000
Tax value . . . $840,933,640
Fed. expd.. . . . $78,796,000

VITAL STATISTICS
1985: Births, 894; Deaths, 252; Marriages, 509; Divorces, 209.

AGRICULTURE:
About 75% of $28 million average annual income from beef cattle, horses, sheep, goats; grains, hay, pecans produced; cedar posts.

BUSINESS: Fort Hood military business, agribusinesses, plastics and other manufacturing. Part of Killeen-Temple MSA.

GATESVILLE (6,931) county seat; agribusinesses; plants make boats, trailers, clothing, plastic medical products; **Mountain View** and **Gatesville** prisons for women; hospitals, nursing homes.

Copperas Cove (21,097), business center for **Fort Hood**, apparel, varied manufacturing; **Central Texas College;** hospital. Other towns include **Evant** (422), **Fort Gates** (755) and **Oglesby** (515).

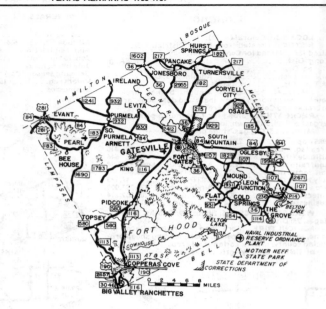

Cottle

LOCATION: Northwest (E-11).

HISTORY: Created, 1876, from Fannin County; organized 1892; named for **George W. Cottle,** Alamo hero.

Cong. Dist. . . . . 13　U.S. Jud. Dist. . . . . N-WF
St. Sen. Dist. . . . . . . 30　Ct. Appeals 7
St. Rep. Dist. . . . . . . 78　Admin. Jud. Dist. 9
St. Dist. Cts. 50

PHYSICAL FEATURES: Rough in west, level in east; gray, black, sandy and loam soils; drains to Pease River.

RECREATION: Settlers reunion in April; hunting;

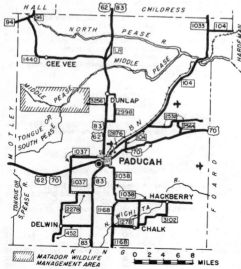

Matador Wildlife Management Area.

MINERALS: Not significant.

1985 Pop. 2,700	Tax Ratio 1.00
Area (sq. mi.) 895	Oil value $14,931
Altitude (ft.) . . 1,605-2,149	No. employed 607
Ann. rainfall (in.) . . 22.12	Avg. weekly wage $318.18
Jan. temp. min. 27	Annual wages . $10,043,112
July temp. max. 97	1983 PCI $7,627
Growing season (da.) 219	Buying pwr. . $30,482,000
Voters reg. 1,751	Tax value . . $168,204,263
Businesses 79	Fed. expd.. . . $10,297,000

VITAL STATISTICS 1985: Births, 41; Deaths, 29; Marriages, 22; Divorces, 11.

AGRICULTURE: About $15 million average income, from cotton, grains, guar, beef cattle, alfalfa; 6,000 acres irrigated.

BUSINESS: Chiefly agribusinesses and gasoline manufacturing.

PADUCAH (2,067) county seat; farm and ranch trading center; oil and gas center; hospital.

Crane

LOCATION: Southwest (J-7).

HISTORY: Created from Tom Green County, 1887, organized 1927; named for Baylor U. President **W. C. Crane.**

Cong. Dist. . . . . 21　U.S. Jud. Dist. . . . . W-M-O
St. Sen. Dist. . . . . 25　Ct. Appeals 8
St. Rep. Dist. . . . . 69　Admin. Jud. Dist. 7
St. Dist. Cts. 109

PHYSICAL FEATURES: Rolling prairie, Pecos Valley, some hills; sandy, loam soils; **Juan Cordona Lake.**

RECREATION: Local events; sites of pioneer trails and historic Horsehead Crossing on Pecos River; camping park.

MINERALS: Among county leaders in oil, gas production.

AGRICULTURE: Cattle ranching brings about $1.2 million yearly; very little farming.

BUSINESS: Oil-based economy.

1985 Pop. 5,200	Tax Ratio 0.78
Area (sq. mi.) 782	Oil value $280,091,609
Altitude (ft.) . . 2,475-2,902	No. employed 1,680
Ann. rainfall (in.) . . 12.97	Avg. weekly wage $416.87
Jan. temp. min. 29	Annual wages . $36,418,052
July temp. max. 96	1983 PCI $8,087

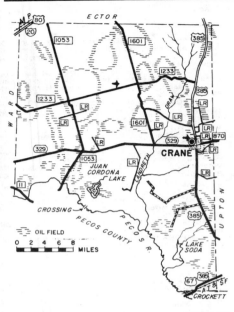

OIL FIELD

0 2 4 6 8 MILES

Growing season (da.)	225	Buying pwr. . . .	$57,265,000
Voters reg.	2,869	Tax value . .	$1,877,700,645
Businesses	134	Fed. expd.	$5,171,000

VITAL STATISTICS 1985: Births, 114; Deaths, 42; Marriages, 66; Divorces, 24.

CRANE (4,143) county seat; oil well servicing, production; hospital, nursing home.

Growing season (da.)	233	Buying pwr. . . .	$49,650,000
Voters reg.	2,661	Tax value . .	$827,097,743
Businesses	163	Fed. expd.	$8,292,000

VITAL STATISTICS 1985: Births, 87; Deaths, 35; Marriages, 51; Divorces, 12.

AGRICULTURE: A major sheep producing county; more than $20 million average income from cattle, sheep, goats, horses.

BUSINESS: Oil, ranching businesses.

OZONA (est. 3,500) county seat; trade center for large ranching area; hunting leases; tourism; hospital, nursing home.

Crosby

LOCATION: Northwest (F-9).

HISTORY: Created from Bexar District, 1876, organized 1886; named for Texas Land Commissioner **Stephen Crosby.**

Cong. Dist.	17	U.S. Jud. Dist.	N-Lb.
St. Sen. Dist.	28	Ct. Appeals	7
St. Rep. Dist.	84	Admin. Jud. Dist.	9
St. Dist. Cts.	72		

PHYSICAL FEATURES: Flat, rich soil above Cap Rock, broken below; drains into Brazos forks and playas.

RECREATION: White River Reservoir; Silver Falls Park; Crosby County Pioneer Museum at Crosbyton and Ralls Historical Museum have many Indian artifacts; Crosbyton Solar Power Plant; settlers reunion in August, outdoor theater, musical.

MINERALS: Sand, gravel, oil, gas.

1985 Pop.	8,400	Tax Ratio	0.86
Area (sq. mi.)	898	Oil value	$2,774,639
Altitude (ft.) . . 2,369-3,167		No. employed	2,213
Ann. rainfall (in.) . .	21.01	Avg. weekly wage	$269.21
Jan. temp. min.	26	Annual wages .	$30,979,940
July temp. max.	94	1983 PCI	$6,030
Growing season (da.)	206	Buying pwr. . . .	$52,574,000
Voters reg.	3,960	Tax value . .	$296,651,460
Businesses	165	Fed. expd. . . .	$25,982,000

VITAL STATISTICS 1985: Births, 142; Deaths, 78; Marriages, 57; Divorces, 38.

AGRICULTURE: About $48 million annual average income from cotton, sorghums, wheat, soybeans, sunflowers, cattle, hogs, poultry; 125,000 acres irrigated.

Crockett

LOCATION: Southwest (L-9).

HISTORY: Created 1875, from Bexar, organized 1891; named for Alamo hero, **David Crockett.**

Cong. Dist.	21
St. Sen. Dist.	25
St. Rep. Dist.	67
St. Dist. Cts.	112
U.S. Jud. Dist. . . .	N-SAng.
Ct. Appeals	8
Admin. Jud. Dist.	6

PHYSICAL FEATURES: Level to rough, hilly terrain; drains to Pecos River on south; rocky soils.

RECREATION: Hunting; historic sites, **Fort Lancaster State Park;** county museum; Davy Crockett statue in park.

MINERALS: Oil, gas.

1985 Pop.	4,700
Area (sq. mi.)	2,806
Altitude (ft.) . . 1,824-3,058	
Ann. rainfall (in.) . .	14.90
Jan. temp. min.	38
July temp. max.	95
Tax Ratio	0.73
Oil value	$36,644,568
No. employed	1,350
Avg. weekly wage	$304.62
Annual wages	$21,384,776
1983 PCI	$8,542

OIL FIELD

0 3 6 9 12 MILES

Crosby County (Cont'd.)

```
≡≡ OIL FIELD          0  2  4  6  8
                           MILES
```

BUSINESS: Agribusinesses, manufacturing, gasohol and solar plants; tourism; drug and alcohol treatment center.

CROSBYTON (2,234) county seat; agribusiness, trade center; hospital; nursing home.

Other towns include **Ralls** (2,263), **Lorenzo** (1,332).

Culberson

LOCATION: Far west (J-4).

HISTORY: Created from El Paso County, 1911, organized 1912; named for **D. B. Culberson,** Texas congressman.

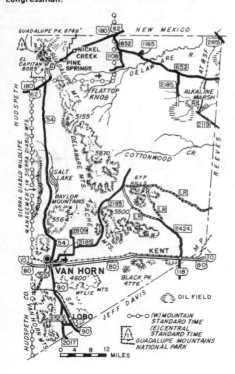

```
≡≡ OIL FIELD

○—○—○ (W) MOUNTAIN
        STANDARD TIME
○—○—○ (E) CENTRAL
        STANDARD TIME
      GUADALUPE MOUNTAINS
      NATIONAL PARK
0   4   8   12
       MILES
```

Cong. Dist.	16	U.S. Jud. Dist.	W-Pe.
St. Sen. Dist.	25	Ct. Appeals	8
St. Rep. Dist.	69	Admin. Jud. Dist.	6
St. Dist. Cts.	. . 34, 205, 210		

PHYSICAL FEATURES: Texas' highest mountains, entire county over 3,000 feet; slopes toward Pecos Valley on east, Diablo Bolson on west; salt lakes; unique vegetation in canyons.

RECREATION: Guadalupe Mountains National Park; Guadalupe and **El Capitan,** twin peaks; scenic canyons and mountains; historical museum at Van Horn; historical salt deposits.

MINERALS: Oil, gas, marble, stone.

1985 Pop.	3,500	Tax Ratio	0.82
Area (sq. mi.)	3,185	Oil value	$3,658,778
Altitude (ft.)	3,021-8,749	No. employed	1,319
Ann. rainfall (in.)	10.22	Avg. weekly wage	$365.96
Jan. temp. min.	30	Annual wages	$25,100,976
July temp. max.	95	1983 PCI	$4,567
Growing season (da.)	224	Buying pwr.	$18,469,000
Voters reg.	1,708	Tax value	$408,063,774
Businesses	100	Fed. expd.	$7,678,000

VITAL STATISTICS 1985: Births, 78; Deaths, 24; Marriages, 30; Divorces, 14.

AGRICULTURE: Almost $8 million average income from cattle, cotton, grains, pecans, vegetables; 20,000 acres irrigated.

BUSINESS: Agribusinesses, tourism, some mineral processing, oil production.

VAN HORN (2,882) county seat; convention center; ranching; rock crushing; hospital.

Dallam

LOCATION: Northwestern corner (A-7).

HISTORY: Created from Bexar District, 1876, organized 1891. Named for lawyer-editor **James W. Dallam.**

Cong. Dist.	13	U.S. Jud. Dist.	N-Am.
St. Sen. Dist.	31	Ct. Appeals	7
St. Rep. Dist.	88	Admin. Jud. Dist.	9
St. Dist. Cts.	69		

PHYSICAL FEATURES: Prairie, over 3,800 ft. elevation, broken by creeks; playas; sandy, loam soils. Rita Blanca National Grasslands.

RECREATION: Local events, **XIT Museum; XIT Rodeo,** and **Reunion** in August; **Lake Rita Blanca,** in Hartley County.

MINERALS: Not significant.

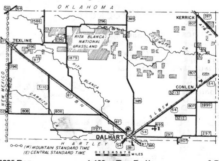

```
○—○—○ (W) MOUNTAIN STANDARD TIME
      (E) CENTRAL STANDARD TIME
0  1  2  3  4  5  6 MILES
```

1985 Pop.	6,600	Tax Ratio	0.79
Area (sq. mi.)	1,505	Oil value	0
Altitude (ft.)	3,869-4,693	No. employed	2,132
Ann. rainfall (in.)	17.38	Avg. weekly wage	$293.72
Jan. temp. min.	19	Annual wages	$32,563,872
July temp. max.	92	1983 PCI	$6,529
Growing season (da.)	178	Buying pwr.	$53,434,000
Voters reg.	2,761	Tax value	$254,189,768
Businesses	246	Fed. expd.	$24,019,000

VITAL STATISTICS 1985: Births, 132; Deaths, 61; Marriages, 79; Divorces, 37.

AGRICULTURE: About $59 million annual average income from beef cattle; corn, wheat, sorghums, alfalfa; 158,400 acres irrigated.

BUSINESS: Agribusinesses, tourism, small manufacturing.

DALHART (6,930, in Dallam and Hartley) county seat; agribusiness center for wide area of Texas, Oklahoma, New Mexico; railroad; cattle feedlots; small manufacturing; bottling plant; hospital; nursing home; Frank Phillips Junior College provides microwave night classes; **Texline** (413).

Dallas

LOCATION: North central (H-17).

HISTORY: Created, organized, 1846, from Nacogdoches, Robertson counties; named for U.S. Vice-President **George Mifflin Dallas.**

Cong. Dist. 3, 5, 6, 24	St. Dist. Cts. . . . 14, 44, 68,
St. Sen. Dist. . . . 2, 8, 9, 10,	95, 101, 116, 134, 160, 162,
16, 23	191, 192, 193, 194, 195, 203,
Rep. Dist. 98-114	204, 254, 255, 256, 265, 282,
U.S. Jud. Dist. . . . . N-DI.	283, 291, 292, 298, 301, 302,
Ct. Appeals 5	303, 304, 305, 330, Cr.,
Admin. Jud. Dist. 1	Cr. 2, Cr. 3, Cr. 4, Cr. 5

PHYSICAL FEATURES: Mostly flat, heavy Blackland soils, sandy clays in west; drains to Trinity River, tributaries.

RECREATION: Dallas County leads all other Texas recreation points as a destination for visitors. Its major attractions include cultural, athletic and special events, the **State Fair of Texas,** conventions and trade shows. Year-round attractions include the **Hall of State, Museum of Art, Science Place, Museum of Natural History, SMU Owen Arts Center, Biblical Arts Center; Dallas Zoo, Dallas Theater Center, Wax World;** also symphonies, professional and amateur sports, dinner playhouses, Texas broadcast museum; many restored historical buildings; special shows, and many lakes with full recreational facilities in the vicinity. (See also Tarrant County.)

MINERALS: Production of sand, gravel, cement, stone, clays.

EDUCATION: Within Dallas County are the following colleges and universities: **Southern Methodist University** (University Park), **University of Dallas** (Irving), **Dallas Baptist College, University of Texas at Dallas** (Richardson), **University of Texas Health Science Center at Dallas,** with three schools — **Southwestern Medical School,** School of Allied Health Sciences and Graduate School of Bio-Medical Sciences — Wadley Research Institute, Baylor University Dental College, Texas Woman's University — Dallas Center with two campuses, Bishop College, Dallas County Community College System, with seven colleges; Northwood Institute, (Cedar

Big Tex, mechanical host to the State Fair of Texas since 1952, is reassembled before the fair each October. When he is put together, he stands 52 feet tall and wears size 70 boots along with a 75-gallon hat.

TEXAS BRAGS

about the

STATE FAIR OF TEXAS

Always has...Always will!

FOR INFORMATION ABOUT THIS YEAR'S EXPOSITION, WRITE TO:

State Fair of Texas
P.O. Box 26010
Dallas, Tx. 75226

Hill), Amber University (Garland), East Texas State University Metroplex Commuter Facility (Garland), Dallas Bible College, Dallas Christian College, Dallas Theological Seminary and others.

1985 Pop.	1,781,700	Tax Ratio	0.96
Area (sq. mi.)	880	Oil value	0
Altitude (ft.)	450-750	No. employed	1,148,159
Ann. rainfall (in.)	35.94	Avg. weekly wage	$439.27
Jan. temp. min.	36	Ann. wages	$26,226,701,632
July temp. max.	95	1983 PCI	$11,648
Growing season (da.)	235	Buying pwr.	$24,600,118,000
Voters reg.	772,268	Tax value	$104,811,736,414
Businesses	55,817	Fed. expd.	$4,673,413,000

VITAL STATISTICS 1985: Births, 35,349; Deaths, 11,954; Marriages, 22,821; Divorces, 13,027.

AGRICULTURE: More than $35 million average annual farm income from beef cattle, horses, hogs and dairy products; nursery crops, cotton, wheat, oats, sorghums. Dallas is a leading center for agribusinesses, agricultural publications and trade associations.

BUSINESS: A national center for insurance, banking, transportation, electronics manufacturing, data processing, conventions and trade shows. More than 3,000 manufacturing plants make apparel, building material, food, oil field supply, electronic and many other products. Tourism is a major industry.

DALLAS (974,239, partly Collin, Denton and Kaufman counties) county seat; second largest city in Texas, seventh largest in U.S. Center for commerce, transportation, banking, insurance, retail and wholesale trade, manufacturing, distribution, data processing; conventions and trade shows. A favorite destination for tourists. Large banks; one of nation's busiest transportation hubs; headquarters of more than 650 firms with net worth of $1 million or more, ranking third nationally in this category; served by nation's largest airport; Dallas has home offices of more insurance firms than any other U.S. city; world headquarters for **U.S. Army and Air Force Exchange Service; Naval Air Station;** a leading cotton market and center for farm implements, trade associations, graphic arts and motion picture production; one of nation's leading fashion and computer centers; outstanding medical centers; **American Heart Associ-**

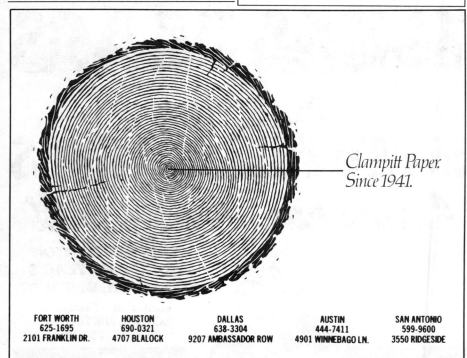

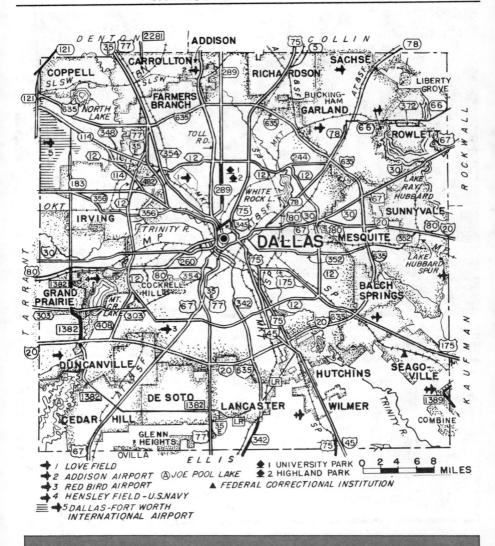

+ 1 LOVE FIELD
+ 2 ADDISON AIRPORT Ⓐ JOE POOL LAKE
+ 3 RED BIRD AIRPORT ▲ FEDERAL CORRECTIONAL INSTITUTION
+ 4 HENSLEY FIELD – U.S. NAVY
≡+ 5 DALLAS-FORT WORTH INTERNATIONAL AIRPORT

♠ 1 UNIVERSITY PARK
♠ 2 HIGHLAND PARK

0 2 4 6 8 MILES

The 60-acre Arts District in downtown Dallas, a planned mixed-use development area, includes arts facilities, such as the Dallas Museum of Art, the Morton H. Meyerson Symphony Center (slated to open with the fall season in 1989) and the Arts Magnet High School; commercial projects, such as the LTV Center, and historic buildings, such as the Belo Mansion (c. 1900) and the 1927 St. Paul United Methodist Church. Festivals, performances and other special events regularly enliven the public areas of the Arts District. Photo Courtesy of the Central Dallas Association.

ation headquarters; **Boy Scouts of America** headquarters; consular offices of many countries; plants make or process electronic, food, apparel, paper, chemical, furniture, plastic, stone, clay and glass, metal products; scientific goods and controlling instruments made.

Dallas ranks as one of the nation's top three cities in numbers of conventions, trade and market shows. **Dallas Convention Center,** located in the downtown area, has 1.9 million square feet under one roof with more than 600,000 square feet of exhibit space and 75 meeting rooms; **Dallas Market Hall** offers 202,000 square feet of exhibit space, 17 meeting rooms and a seating capacity of approximately 27,000. Facilities also at State Fair grounds. **World Trade Center** is international market center with 1.4 million square feet. **Infomart,** a giant computer sales complex, recently opened. **Reunion Are-**

na has up to 30,000 square feet of space, seats up to 20,000, and has parking space for 5,000 cars.

Other cities of Dallas County where much growth has occurred in recent years include: **Garland** (160,208) county's second largest city; center for industry and agriculture; more than 300 industrial plants; attractive residential areas; near lakes; **Amber University** and **East Texas State University** branch; medical centers.

Irving (120,057) manufacturing and distribution; service industries; leading residential center; **University of Dallas; North Lake College,** unit of community college system; **Texas Stadium,** home of **Dallas Cowboys** professional football team; hospitals; parks; adjacent to Dallas-Fort Worth International Airport.

Mesquite (77,255) residential city with varied industries and distribution center; popular rodeo; **Eastfield**

College of community college system.

Richardson (76,981, partly Collin County) extensive electronic manufacturing, varied other science-oriented manufacturing, research firms; corporate and division headquarters of major firms; residential city; **University of Texas at Dallas;** near **Texas A&M Research Center;** parks; hospitals.

Grand Prairie (86,076, partly in Tarrant) aircraft, aerospace, concrete, chemical manufacturing; other plants; distribution center; major recreation center with wax museum; **Traders Village;** wildlife park; go-cart racing; **Joe Pool Lake;** other attractions; medical center, nursing homes.

Farmers Branch (26,464) distribution center, varied manufacturing; residential city; **Brookhaven College** of community college system.

Carrollton (53,621, partly Denton County) residential city with many plants, distribution center.

Duncanville (31,892) varied manufacturing; residential city; industrial development; recreation with **Joe Pool Lake** nearing completion.

Lancaster (17,465) industrial and agricultural center; plants make hydraulic and plumbing equipment, swimming pools, chemicals, many other products; warehouse and distribution facilities; rebuilt old town area; **Cedar Valley College,** a campus of community college system; a residential city.

DeSoto (19,589) rapidly growing residential city for many employed in metro area.

Other towns include **Highland Park** (8,830) residential city; **University Park** (22,878) residential city with **Southern Methodist University; Balch Springs** (17,077).

Also **Addison** (6,618, partly Collin County) retail and restaurant city; **Buckingham** (188), **Cedar Hill** (9,665), **Cockrell Hill** (3,748), **Combine** (815, mostly Kaufman County), **Coppell** (6,172), **Glenn Heights** (1,131), **Grapevine** (16,792, mostly Tarrant County), **Hutchins** (3,690), **Rowlett** (10,573, partly Rockwall County), **Sachse** (2,311, partly Collin County), **Seagoville** (8,626), **Sunnyvale** (1,783), **Wilmer** (3,049).

Dawson

LOCATION: West (H-8).

HISTORY: Created from Bexar District, 1876, organized 1905; named for **Nicholas M. Dawson**, San Jacinto veteran.

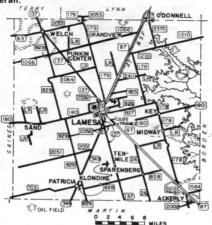

Cong. Dist.	19	U.S. Jud. Dist.	N-Lb.
St. Sen. Dist.	28	Ct. Appeals	11
St. Rep. Dist.	77	Admin. Jud. Dist.	7
St. Dist. Cts.	106		

PHYSICAL FEATURES: Rolling prairie, broken on east; drains to playas; sandy and loam soils.

RECREATION: Local parks, Dawson County Museum; campground; local events.

MINERALS: Production of gas, oil.

1985 Pop.	16,200	Tax Ratio	0.93
Area (sq. mi.)	903	Oil value	$68,521,681
Altitude (ft.)	2,860-3,095	No. employed	3,593
Ann. rainfall (in.)	16.09	Avg. weekly wage	$267.10
Jan. temp. min.	28	Annual wages	$49,905,240
July temp. max.	94	1983 PCI	$7,537
Growing season (da.)	212	Buying pwr.	$143,900,000
Voters reg.	8,654	Tax value	$926,427,009
Businesses	395	Fed. expd.	$40,010,000

VITAL STATISTICS 1985: Births, 332; Deaths, 130; Marriages, 186; Divorces, 60.

AGRICULTURE: About $45 million average annual income, 90% from crops; a major cotton producing county; also sorghums, wheat, other grains; cattle, hogs; 15,000 acres irrigated for cotton.

BUSINESS: Agribusinesses, oil industries; manufacturing.

LAMESA (12,303) county seat; agribusinesses, food processing, oil field services, textiles, clothing, farm and gin equipment manufactured, new computerized cotton classing office; hospital, nursing homes; library, museum, campus of **Howard County Junior College**.

Other towns include **Ackerly** (341, partly in Martin County) and **O'Donnell** (1,076, partly in Lynn County), **Los Ybanez** (156).

Deaf Smith

LOCATION: Northwest (C-7).

HISTORY: Created, 1876, from Bexar District; organized 1890. Named for famed scout, **Erastus (Deaf) Smith**.

Cong. Dist.	19	U.S. Jud. Dist.	N-Am.
St. Sen. Dist.	31	Ct. Appeals	7
St. Rep. Dist.	86	Admin. Jud. Dist.	9
St. Dist. Cts.	222		

PHYSICAL FEATURES: Level plain, partly broken; chocolate and sandy loam soils; drains to playas, **Palo Duro** and **Tierra Blanca Creeks**.

RECREATION: Local events, museum, tours; National Cowgirl Hall of Fame.

MINERALS: Not significant.

1985 Pop.	20,400	Tax Ratio	0.95
Area (sq. mi.)	1,497	Oil value	0
Altitude (ft.)	3,789-4,362	No. employed	6,625
Ann. rainfall (in.)	17.37	Avg. weekly wage	$256.09
Jan. temp. min.	22	Annual wages	$88,225,212
July temp. max.	93	1983 PCI	$6,640
Growing season (da.)	185	Buying pwr.	$157,353,000
Voters reg.	8,873	Tax value	$652,800,963
Businesses	528	Fed. expd.	$46,745,000

VITAL STATISTICS 1985: Births, 438; Deaths, 113; Marriages, 212; Divorces, 50.

AGRICULTURE: One of state's leading farm-producing counties with more than $317 million annual average income, 80% from livestock; large feedlot operations; crops include sorghums, wheat, oats, barley, sugar beets, corn, cotton, onions, other vegetables, sunflowers; 205,000 acres irrigated.

BUSINESS: Sugar refinery; meat packers; offset printing; other varied industries, mostly agribusinesses.

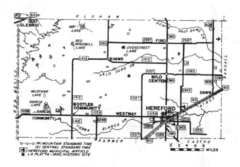

HEREFORD (15,365) county seat; agribusinesses, sugar refining, food processing, varied manufacturing; hospital, nursing home.

Delta

LOCATION: Northeast (F-19).

HISTORY: Created from Lamar, Hopkins counties, and organized, 1870. Greek letter **delta** origin of name, because of shape.

Cong. Dist.	1	U.S. Jud. Dist.	E-Ps.
St. Sen. Dist.	1	Ct. Appeals	6
St. Rep. Dist.	2	Admin. Jud. Dist.	1
St. Dist. Cts.	8, 62		

PHYSICAL FEATURES: Between two forks of Sulphur River; black, sandy, loam soils.

RECREATION: Fishing, hunting, local events; **Big Creek Lake** and **Lake Cooper** under construction.

MINERALS: Not significant.

1985 Pop.	4,800	Tax Ratio	1.00
Area (sq. mi.)	278	Oil value	0

Altitude (ft.)	396-536	
Ann. rainfall (in.) . .	43.67	
Jan. temp. min.	34	
July temp. max.	94	
Growing season (da.)	233	
Voters reg.	2,891	
Businesses	77	

No. employed	621
Avg. weekly wage	$200.96
Annual wages .	$6,489,508
1983 PCI	$6,987
Buying pwr. . .	$40,907,000
Tax value . .	$185,248,613
Fed. expd. . . .	$14,936,000

VITAL STATISTICS 1985: Births, 63; Deaths, 85; Marriages, 57; Divorces, 20.

AGRICULTURE: About $18 million annual average income from beef, dairy cattle, cotton, wheat, sorghums, other grains; some firewood.

BUSINESS: Agribusinesses, tourism, manufacturing.

COOPER (2,397) county seat; industrial park; manufacturing, agribusinesses; county museum. **Pecan Gap** (296, partly Fannin County).

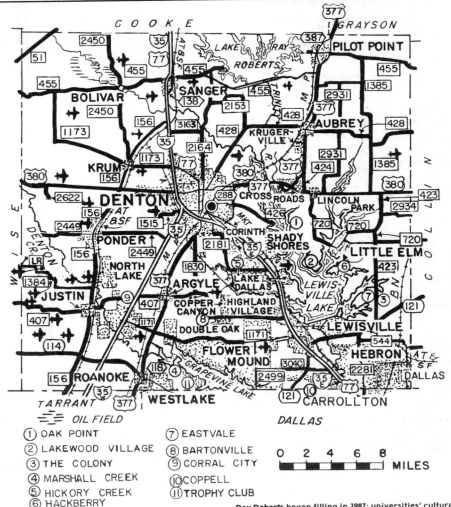

- (1) OAK POINT
- (2) LAKEWOOD VILLAGE
- (3) THE COLONY
- (4) MARSHALL CREEK
- (5) HICKORY CREEK
- (6) HACKBERRY
- (7) EASTVALE
- (8) BARTONVILLE
- (9) CORRAL CITY
- (10) COPPELL
- (11) TROPHY CLUB

0 2 4 6 8 MILES

Denton

LOCATION: North central (G-16).

HISTORY: Created, organized out of Fannin County, 1846; named for **John B. Denton**, pioneer preacher.

Cong. Dist.	26
St. Sen. Dist. . . .	10, 22, 30
St. Rep. Dist. . . .	59, 61
St. Dist. Cts. . .	16, 158, 211

U.S. Jud. Dist.	E-Sh.
Ct. Appeals	2
Admin. Jud. Dist.	8

PHYSICAL FEATURES: Partly hilly, draining to Trinity River, two lakes; Blackland and Grand Prairie soils.

RECREATION: Water activities at **Lewisville**, **Grapevine Lakes**, seven U.S. Corps of Engineers' parks; **Lake Ray Roberts** began filling in 1987; universities' cultural, athletic activities including "Texas Women: a Celebration of History" exhibit in the TWU library; State D.A.R. Museum "First Ladies of Texas" collection of gowns and memorabilia, Little Chapel-in-the-Woods, Botanical Gardens and other events; local events; annual Denton Jazzfest in September; (see also Dallas, Tarrant Counties).

MINERALS: Limited output oil, sand, gravel, gas, clay.

1985 Pop.	189,700	Tax Ratio	0.90
Area (sq. mi.)	911	Oil value	0
Altitude (ft.)	515-844	No. employed	58,437
Ann. rainfall (in.) . .	33.29	Avg. weekly wage	$331.96
Jan. temp. min.	34	Ann. wages .	$1,008,760,716
July temp. max.	96	1983 PCI	$11,003

Growing season (da.)   226
Voters reg.   91,530
Businesses   3,506
Buying pwr. $2,706,200,000
Tax value . . $10,076,993,546
Fed. expd.. . . $874,076,000

VITAL STATISTICS 1985: Births, 4,357; Deaths, 928; Marriages, 2,192; Divorces, 1,168.

AGRICULTURE: About $54 million average farm income, 75% from horses, cattle, poultry, dairy products; grains, cotton, hay, peanuts principal crops.

BUSINESS: Varied industries, colleges, tourism; part of Dallas-Fort Worth CMSA.

DENTON (46,075) county seat; **North Texas State University, Texas Woman's University, Denton State School** (for mentally retarded); civil defense center; plants make food products, apparel, brick, trucks, oil tools, heating and cooling equipment, many other products; hospital, nursing homes; women's museum.

Lewisville (23,812), electronics and varied industries, near **D/FW International Airport, Lewisville Lake.**

Other towns include **Carrollton** (53,621, part Dallas), **Pilot Point** (2,228) with varied manufacturing and antique shops, **Argyle** (1,246), **Aubrey** (1,147), **Bartonville** (565), **Copper Canyon** (589), **Corinth** (1,633), **Corral City** (104), **Cross Roads** (376), **Double Oak** (865), **Eastvale** (550), **Flower Mound** (6,422), **Hackberry** (95), **Hebron** (453), **Hickory Creek** (1,708), **Highland Village** (3,382), **Justin** (1,178), **Krugerville** (561), **Krum** (1,158), **Lake Dallas** (3,499), **Lakewood Village** (169), **Lincoln Park** (38), **Little Elm** (1,125), **Marshall Creek** (486), **Northlake** (169), **Oak Point** (487), **Ponder** (348), **Roanoke** (1,166), **Sanger** (3,140) varied manufacturing, hospital, tourism; **Shady Shores** (852), **Southlake** (3,612, mostly in Tarrant County), **Trophy Club** (2,800), **The Colony** (21,600) and **Westlake** (253, partly in Tarrant County).

DeWitt

LOCATION: South (O-16).
HISTORY: Created from Gonzales, Goliad, Victoria counties and organized, 1846; named for **Green De Witt,** colonizer.

Cong. Dist. 14
St. Sen. Dist. 18
St. Rep. Dist.. 31
St. Dist. Cts. . . 24, 135, 267
U.S. Jud. Dist. . . . . S-Va.
Ct. Appeals 13
Admin. Jud. Dist. 4

PHYSICAL FEATURES: Drained by Guadalupe and tributaries; rolling to level; waxy, loam, sandy soils.
RECREATION: Hunting, fishing, local events; historic homes, museum.
MINERALS: Production of oil and gas.

1985 Pop.. 20,200
Area (sq. mi.) 163-462
Altitude (ft.) 163-462
Ann. rainfall (in.) . . 33.37
Jan. temp. min.. 44
July temp. max. 96
Growing season (da.)   270
Voters reg. 9,020
Businesses 433
Tax Ratio 0.85
Oil value $1,751,099
No. employed 5,615
Avg. weekly wage $261.87
Annual wages $76,461,688
1983 PCI $7,356
Buying pwr. . $183,031,000
Tax value . . $910,689,808
Fed. expd.. . . $39,080,000

VITAL STATISTICS 1985: Births, 301; Deaths, 259; Marriages, 166; Divorces, 50.

AGRICULTURE: About $43 million annual farm income, mostly from beef cattle, dairy products, hogs, poultry; crops include sorghums, corn, oats, wheat, pecans.

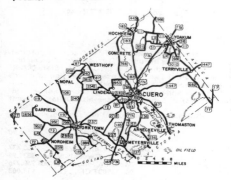

BUSINESS: Wood, furniture plants, textile mill, varied manufacturing, agribusinesses.

CUERO (7,576) county seat; turkey hatcheries, furniture, wood products, other manufacturing; agribusinesses, soft drink bottling; hospital, nursing homes; annual Turkeyfest. Other towns include **Yoakum** (6,355, part Lavaca), **Yorktown** (2,596) hospital, nursing home, historical museum, oil well servicing; **Nordheim** (429).

Dickens

LOCATION: Northwest (F-10).
HISTORY: Created, 1876, from Bexar District; organized 1891; named for Alamo hero who is variously listed as James R. Dimkins, James R. Dimpkins and J. Dickens. (According to noted authority Dr. Amelia Williams, writing in the Southwestern Historical Quarterly.)

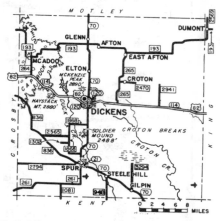

Cong. Dist. 13
St. Sen. Dist. 30
St. Rep. Dist.. 84
St. Dist. Cts. 110
U.S. Jud. Dist. . . . N-Lb.
Ct. Appeals 7
Admin. Jud. Dist. 9

PHYSICAL FEATURES: Broken land, Cap Rock in northwest; sandy, chocolate, red soils; drains to Croton, Duck Creeks.
RECREATION: Hunting, fishing, local events.
MINERALS: Small oil, gas output.

1985 Pop.. 3,100
Area (sq. mi.) 907
Altitude (ft.) . . 1,900-3,000
Ann. rainfall (in.) . . 20.24
Jan. temp. min.. 28
July temp. max. 95
Growing season (da.)   217
Voters reg. 1,872
Businesses 64
Tax Ratio 0.79
Oil value $1,227,846
No. employed 448
Avg. weekly wage $268.41
Annual wages $6,252,988
1983 PCI $5,568
Buying pwr. . $20,881,000
Tax value . . $96,708,525
Fed. expd.. . . $12,216,000

VITAL STATISTICS 1985: Births, 44; Deaths, 47; Marriages, 28; Divorces, 7.

AGRICULTURE: Crop-livestock income averages about $14 million, mostly from beef cattle, cotton, wheat, sorghums; 14,000 acres irrigated.

BUSINESS: Chiefly ranching, farming supplies, some manufacturing.

DICKENS (458) county seat.
Spur (1,579) principal agribusiness center.

Dimmit

LOCATION: Southwest (Q-12).
HISTORY: Named for **Philip Dimitt** of Texas Revolution; law misspelled name; created 1858 from Bexar, Maverick, Uvalde, Webb counties; organized 1880.

Cong. Dist. 23
St. Sen. Dist. 21
St. Rep. Dist.. 44
St. Dist. Cts. 293
U.S. Jud. Dist. . . . W-SAnt.
Ct. Appeals 4
Admin. Jud. Dist. 4

PHYSICAL FEATURES: Level to rolling; much brush; sandy, loam, red soils; drained by Nueces and tributaries.

RECREATION: Hunting, fishing, lake campsites; local events; mild climate makes area "Winter Garden" for tourists.

MINERALS: Oil, gas production.

1985 Pop.	11,900	Tax Ratio	0.94
Area (sq. mi.)	1,307	Oil value	$25,848,729
Altitude (ft.)	461-591	No. employed	2,501
Ann. rainfall (in.)	21.50	Avg. weekly wage	$245.12
Jan. temp. min.	42	Annual wages	$31,879,268
July temp. max.	99	1983 PCI	$4,753
Growing season (da.)	290	Buying pwr.	$64,858,000
Voters reg.	7,085	Tax value	$720,757,366
Businesses	189	Fed. expd.	$19,999,000

VITAL STATISTICS 1985: Births, 245; Deaths, 84; Marriages, 95; Divorces, 38.

AGRICULTURE: About $16.5 million annual average income from cotton, corn, vegetables; beef cattle; pecan trees; among leading irrigated vegetable growing counties since early in century; 10,000 acres irrigated.

BUSINESS: Agribusinesses, petroleum products, other varied manufacturing; tourism.

CARRIZO SPRINGS (7,553) county seat; agribusiness center, feedlot, food processing, garment manufacturing; oil and gas processing; hunting center; pecan shelling plant; hospitals, nursing home. Other towns include **Asherton** (1,609), **Big Wells** (938).

Donley

LOCATION: Northwest (D-10).

HISTORY: Created, 1876, organized 1882, out of Bexar District; named for Texas Supreme Court Justice S. P. Donley.

Cong. Dist.	13	U.S. Jud. Dist.	N-Am.
St. Sen. Dist.	31	Ct. Appeals	7
St. Rep. Dist.	84	Admin. Jud. Dist.	9
St. Dist. Cts.	100		

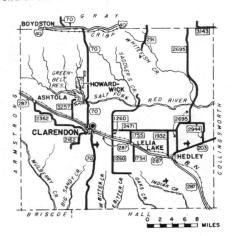

PHYSICAL FEATURES: Bisected by Red River Salt Fork; rolling to level; clay, loam, sandy soils.

RECREATION: Greenbelt Lake, hunting, fishing, camping, water sports; local events.

MINERALS: Small amount natural gas.

1985 Pop.	4,100	Tax Ratio	0.93
Area (sq. mi.)	929	Oil value	0
Altitude (ft.)	2,388-3,213	No. employed	845
Ann. rainfall (in.)	20.74	Avg. weekly wage	$266.12
Jan. temp. min.	26	Annual wages	$11,693,404
July temp. max.	96	1983 PCI	$7,694
Growing season (da.)	206	Buying pwr.	$35,297,000
Voters reg.	2,463	Tax value	$164,267,307
Businesses	117	Fed. expd.	$11,283,000

VITAL STATISTICS 1985: Births, 42; Deaths, 54; Marriages, 36; Divorces, 13.

AGRICULTURE: About $19 million average annual income, 66% from beef cattle, hogs, horses; cotton, sorghums, wheat, peanuts; 8,000 acres irrigated.

BUSINESS: Agribusinesses; distribution; varied manufacturing.

CLARENDON (2,316) county seat; **Clarendon Junior College; Burton Memorial Library;** agribusinesses, farm, road equipment, leather goods manufacturing; tourism; medical center; other towns include **Hedley** (405) and **Howardwick** (155).

Duval

LOCATION: South (R-15).

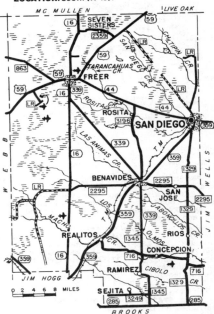

HISTORY: Created from Live Oak, Nueces, Starr counties, 1858, organized 1876; named for **B. H. Duval**, Goliad martyr.

Cong. Dist.	15	U.S. Jud. Dist.	S-CC
St. Sen. Dist.	21	Ct. Appeals	4
St. Rep. Dist.	44	Admin. Jud. Dist.	5
St. Dist. Cts.	229		

PHYSICAL FEATURES: Level to hilly, brushy in most areas; varied soils.

RECREATION: Hunting, tourist crossroads, rattlesnake roundup, local events.

MINERALS: Production of oil, gas, salt, uranium, sand and gravel.

1985 Pop.	13,300	Tax Ratio	0.87
Area (sq. mi.)	1,795	Oil value	$24,414,319
Altitude (ft.)	244-783	No. employed	2,799
Ann. rainfall (in.)	23.15	Avg. weekly wage	$314.21

Jan. temp. min.	42	Annual wages	$45,733,004
July temp. max.	97	1983 PCI	$5,422
Growing season (da.)	298	Buying pwr.	$98,229,000
Voters reg.	8,863	Tax value	$1,200,185,078
Businesses	181	Fed. expd.	$27,629,000

VITAL STATISTICS 1985: Births, 260; Deaths, 135; Marriages, 126; Divorces, 37.

AGRICULTURE: About $33 million annual average income, 75% from beef cattle, remainder from grains, cotton, vegetables, hay.

BUSINESS: Ranching, petroleum, tourism.

SAN DIEGO (5,695, part in Jim Wells) county seat; ranching, oil field, tourist center; hospital. Other towns include **Benavides** (2,005), **Freer** (3,735) U.S. Border Patrol Station, oil and cattle center, tourism.

Eastland

LOCATION: Central (I-13).

HISTORY: Created from Bosque, Coryell, Travis counties, 1858, organized 1873; named for **W. M. Eastland,** Mier Expedition martyr.

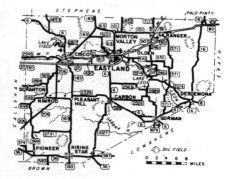

Cong. Dist.	17	U.S. Jud. Dist.	N-Ab.
St. Sen. Dist.	22	Ct. Appeals	11
St. Rep. Dist.	65	Admin. Jud. Dist.	8
St. Dist. Cts.	91		

PHYSICAL FEATURES: Hilly, rolling; sandy, loam soils; drained to Leon River forks.

RECREATION: Fishing, **Lake Leon, Lake Cisco;** water sports; hunting; festivals; historic sites and displays.

MINERALS: Production of oil, gas, stone, clays, sand and gravel.

1985 Pop.	20,700	Tax Ratio	0.94
Area (sq. mi.)	924	Oil value	$7,762,010
Altitude (ft.)	1,303-1,882	No. employed	4,982
Ann. rainfall (in.)	27.09	Avg. weekly wage	$253.12
Jan. temp. min.	32	Annual wages	$65,576,636
July temp. max.	96	1983 PCI	$6,942
Growing season (da.)	229	Buying pwr.	$183,472,000
Voters reg.	10,883	Tax value	$794,963,229
Businesses	587	Fed. expd.	$50,649,000

VITAL STATISTICS 1985: Births, 284; Deaths, 274; Marriages, 203; Divorces, 16.

AGRICULTURE: About $23 million average annual income with 60% from beef cattle, sheep, horses; peanuts, wheat, sorghums major crops; 10,000 acres irrigated.

BUSINESS: Agribusinesses, petroleum industries, varied manufacturing.

EASTLAND (4,193) county seat; plants make clothing, building stones, steel tanks, portable buildings, oil-field equipment; agribusinesses; printing; mental health center, hospital, nursing homes.

Cisco (4,676) plants make clothing, steel tanks, oil-field equipment, other products; Conrad Hilton's first hotel renovated; **Cisco Junior College;** hospitals.

Ranger (3,439) agribusinesses, varied manufacturing, oil field center; **Ranger Junior College;** hospital, nursing home. Other towns include **Gorman** (1,390) peanut processing, other agribusinesses; hospital, nursing home; **Rising Star** (1,254) farming center; **Carbon** (269).

Ector

LOCATION: West (J-7).

HISTORY: Created from Tom Green County, 1887; organized, 1891; named for Texas legislator-jurist, **M. D. Ector.**

Cong. Dist.	16, 19	U.S. Jud. Dist.	W: M-O
St. Sen. Dist.	28	Ct. Appeals	8
St. Rep. Dist.	75, 76	Admin. Jud. Dist.	7
St. Dist. Cts. 70, 161, 244, 358			

PHYSICAL FEATURES: Level to rolling, some sand dunes; **meteor crater;** limited vegetation.

RECREATION: Metropolitan cultural events; 2nd largest **U.S. meteor crater; Globe Theatre replica; Odessa College Museum.**

MINERALS: Leading oil-producing county with more than 2 billion barrels since 1926; gas, cement, stone.

1985 Pop.	134,700	Tax Ratio	0.96
Area (sq. mi.)	903	Oil value	$551,699,533
Altitude (ft.)	2,817-3,275	No. employed	41,744
Ann. rainfall (in.)	13.77	Avg. weekly wage	$369.04
Jan. temp. min.	30	Annual wages	$801,075,628
July temp. max.	96	1983 PCI	$9,778
Growing season (da.)	217	Buying pwr.	$1,735,538,000
Voters reg.	51,698	Tax value	$5,212,977,059
Businesses	3,955	Fed. expd.	$138,676,000

VITAL STATISTICS 1985: Births, 2,902; Deaths, 819; Marriages, 1,710; Divorces, 1,173.

AGRICULTURE: Average farm income more than $4.5 million, from beef cattle, poultry; pecans, hay.

BUSINESS: Oil-based economy. Center for Permian Basin oil field operations.

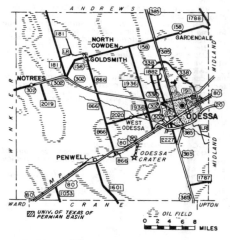

ODESSA (108,690) county seat; Odessa College, University of Texas of Permian Basin; hospital; cultural center; oil field services, supplies; large petrochemical complex; medical center; other industries; **Goldsmith** (522).

Edwards

LOCATION: Southwest (M-11).

HISTORY: Created from Bexar District, 1858; organized 1883; named for Nacogdoches empresario, **Hayden Edwards.**

Cong. Dist.	21	U.S. Jud. Dist.	W-Del Rio
St. Sen. Dist.	25	Ct. Appeals	4
St. Rep. Dist.	67	Admin. Jud. Dist.	6
St. Dist. Cts.	63		

PHYSICAL FEATURES: Rolling, hilly; caves; spring-fed streams; rocky, thin soils; drained by Llano, Nueces Rivers; varied timber.

RECREATION: Leading deer, turkey hunting area; fishing; scenic drives; local events; state park planned.

MINERALS: Oil, gas.

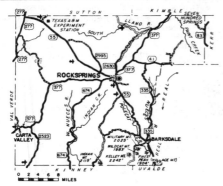

1985 Pop.	2,100	Tax Ratio	0.87
Area (sq. mi.)	2,120	Oil value	0
Altitude (ft.)	1,507-2,410	No. employed	382
Ann. rainfall (in.)	21.19	Avg. weekly wage	$253.56
Jan. temp. min.	38	Annual wages	$5,036,856
July temp. max.	94	1983 PCI	$5,739
Growing season (da.)	250	Buying pwr.	$15,910,000
Voters reg.	1,233	Tax value	$506,061,319
Businesses	52	Fed. expd.	$6,236,000

VITAL STATISTICS 1985: Births, 33; Deaths, 16; Marriages, 22; Divorces, 12.

AGRICULTURE: About $13 million average income, almost entirely from Angora goats, sheep, cattle; center of nation's goat-mohair production.

BUSINESS: Ranching economy; revenue also from hunting leases, tourism, oil, gas production.

ROCKSPRINGS (1,454) county seat; ranching, hunting center; tourism; hospital.

Ellis

LOCATION: Central (I-17).

HISTORY: Created 1849, organized 1850, from Navarro County. Named for **Richard Ellis,** president of Convention of 1836.

Cong. Dist.	6	U.S. Jud. Dist.	N-Dallas
St. Sen. Dist.	9	Ct. Appeals	10
St. Rep. Dist.	4	Admin. Jud. Dist.	1
St. Dist. Cts.	40		

PHYSICAL FEATURES: Rich Blackland soils; level to rolling; Chambers Creek, Trinity River.

RECREATION: National polka festival at Ennis; Gingerbread Trail homes tour, medieval fair and Charles Dickens festival at Waxahachie; cabrito cookoff; Italian Festival in Italy; Bluebonnet Trails; hunting.

MINERALS: Oil, gas and limestone.

1985 Pop. 73,300   Tax Ratio 0.93

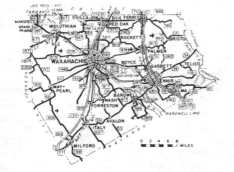

Area (sq. mi.)	939	Oil value	0
Altitude (ft.)	395-755	No. employed	19,811
Ann. rainfall (in.)	35.95	Avg. weekly wage	$339.94
Jan. temp. min.	35	Annual wages	$350,200,184
July temp. max.	96	1983 PCI	$8,530
Growing season (da.)	246	Buying pwr.	$746,878,000
Voters reg.	35,887	Tax value	$3,075,915,515
Businesses	1,368	Fed. expd.	$143,826,000

VITAL STATISTICS 1985: Births, 1,283; Deaths, 655; Marriages, 980; Divorces, 401.

AGRICULTURE: About $50 million average annual income. Crops, including cotton, sorghums, other grains, nursery operations are leading products; livestock production follows.

BUSINESS: Varied manufacturing, agribusinesses; many employed in Dallas.

WAXAHACHIE (15,758) county seat; varied manufacturing includes furniture, oil field equipment, apparel, commercial refrigeration, cottonseed products, millwork, fiberglass insulation, glass containers, monuments, business stationery, plastic piping, fertilizers, concrete and other products; **Southwestern Assemblies of God College** and branch of **Navarro Junior College;** motion picture production; tourism; hospital; nursing homes.

Ennis (12,653) agribusinesses; plants produce business forms, apparel, roofing, mobile home; plants process meat, paints, fertilizer and chemicals; Texas Motorplex Speedway; tourism; hospitals; nursing home; branch of Navarro Junior College; national polka festival in May.

Midlothian (4,323) cement plants, clothing, other factories.

Ferris (2,224, part in Dallas) large brick plant; other industries. Other towns include **Italy** (1,433) garment factory and varied manufacturing; **Palmer** (1,505), **Red Oak** (2,425), **Alma** (213), **Bardwell** (348), **Garrett** (212), **Glenn Heights** (1,131, mostly in Dallas County), **Grand Prairie** (86,076, mostly in Dallas County), **Maypearl** (729), **Milford** (710), **Ovilla** (1,307), **Oakleaf** (338), **Pecan Hill** (50), **Rice** (511).

El Paso

LOCATION: Most western county (J-1).

HISTORY: Created from Bexar District, 1849; organized 1850; named for historic northern pass **(Paso del Norte).**

PHYSICAL FEATURES: Fertile Rio Grande Valley; 7,000-ft. mountains; desert vegetation except where irrigated.

Cong. Dist.	16	U.S. Jud. Dist.	W-El Paso
St. Sen. Dist.	25, 29	Ct. Appeals	8
St. Rep. Dist.	70-74	Admin. Jud. Dist.	6
St. Dist. Cts.	34, 41, 65, 120, 168, 171, 205, 210, 243, 327, 346		

RECREATION: Gateway to Mexico; varied U.S.-Mexican metropolitan events, **Chamizal Museum;** major tourist center; December **Sun Carnival** with annual Sun Bowl football game; El Paso Festival in July; Border Folk Festival in October; missions and other historic sites; near Carlsbad Caverns, White Sands, bullfighting, horse and dog racing; amusement park.

MINERALS: Production of cement, stone, sand and gravel.

1985 Pop.	545,000	Tax Ratio	0.94
Area (sq. mi.)	1,014	Oil value	0
Altitude (ft.)	3,582-7,192	No. employed	167,903
Ann. rainfall (in.)	7.77	Avg. weekly wage	$287.07
Jan. temp. min.	32	Ann. wages	$2,506,461,232
July temp. max.	94	1983 PCI	$6,798
Growing season (da.)	248	Buying pwr.	$4,562,671,000
Voters reg.	179,527	Tax value	$11,203,235,633
Businesses	9,778	Fed. expd.	$1,723,578,000

VITAL STATISTICS 1985: Births, 11,617; Deaths, 2,912; Marriages, 7,575; Divorces, 2,946.

AGRICULTURE: About $41 million average annual income from dairy and beef cattle, hogs; cotton, grain, pecans, hay; 50,000 acres irrigated, mostly cotton.

BUSINESS: Government is major economic factor with wages and salaries exceeding $138.7 million annually; wholesale, retail distribution center; tourism; varied manufacturers; ore smelting, refining, cotton, food processing.

EL PASO (463,809) county seat (see metro page); fourth-largest Texas city; lowest altitude all-weather pass through Rocky Mountains; a center for government operations, manufacturing, trade and distribution; refining and processing of ore, oil, food, cotton and other farm and ranch products; plants make apparel, electronics products, footwear, building materials, other products; **University of Texas at El Paso; El Paso Community College; UT School of Nursing at El Paso; Texas Tech University Health Science Center;** home of **U.S. Army Air Defense Command;** 16 hospitals; museums. Numerous tourist attractions, convention, civic center, community theater, symphony orchestra, gateway to Mexico and largest U.S. city on Mexican border.

Federal installations include **Fort Bliss, Wm. Beaumont General Hospital** and **La Tuna** correction institution.

Ysleta, oldest Texas town, now in El Paso. Other towns include **Anthony** (3,129), **Clint** (1,703), **Vinton** (434), **San Elizario.**

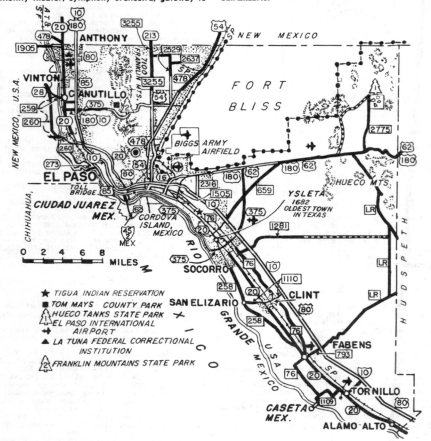

Erath

LOCATION: North central (I-14).

HISTORY: Created from Bosque, Coryell counties, 1856, organized same year; named for **George B. Erath,** Texas Revolution figure.

Cong. Dist.	17	U.S. Jud. Dist.	N-FW
St. Sen. Dist.	22	Ct. Appeals	11
St. Rep. Dist.	58	Admin. Jud. Dist.	8
St. Dist. Cts.	266		

PHYSICAL FEATURES: Hilly, rolling plains; clay loam, sandy soils; drains to Bosque River, Paluxy Creek.

RECREATION: Tarleton State University with fine arts center; Historical House museum; old courthouse; log cabins; Cross Timbers Country Opry; **Thurber,** ghost town; museums; nearby lakes, Bosque River Park; Dublin Community Fall Fair.

MINERALS: Gas, oil.

1985 Pop.	25,000	Tax Ratio	0.94
Area (sq. mi.)	1,080	Oil value	0
Altitude (ft.)	943-1,558	No. employed	7,460
Ann. rainfall (in.)	31.24	Avg. weekly wage	$264.02

Jan. temp. min.	34	Annual wages	$102,419,176
July temp. max.	96	1983 PCI	$8,781
Growing season (da.)	238	Buying pwr.	$274,044,000
Voters reg.	11,987	Tax value	$1,174,030,397
Businesses	636	Fed. Expend.	$52,813,000

VITAL STATISTICS 1985: Births, 306; Deaths, 261; Marriages, 318; Divorces, 274.

AGRICULTURE: Over 80% of $103 million average annual income from dairy, beef cattle, other livestock, poultry; state's second leading county in milk production; peanuts, the major cash crop, small grains, fruit, sorghums chief crops; horticulture industry, especially tree growing and greenhouses, expanding; 8,000 acres irrigated, mostly peanuts.

BUSINESS: Agricultural, industrial and educational enterprises.

STEPHENVILLE (12,691) county seat; **Tarleton State University of Texas A&M;** plants make coated abrasives, automotive parts, clothing, gratings and fasteners, mobile homes, steel products, feeds; electrical products; hospital, clinics, mental health-mental retardation center; **Texas A&M** research and extension center.

Dublin (2,883) agribusiness center; clothing; food products manufactured; hospital, nursing home.

mally heated hospital; apparel, rug manufacturing; printing; veterans hospital; tourism, Marlin festival, Stocker Cattle Conference.

Rosebud (2,102), **Lott** (957), **Bruceville-Eddy** (1,132, mostly McLennan County) and **Golinda** (372, partly McLennan County) are other towns.

Fannin

LOCATION: Borders Oklahoma (F-18).
HISTORY: Created from Red River County, 1837, organized, 1838; named for **James W. Fannin,** Goliad martyr.

Cong. Dist. 4	U.S. Jud. Dist . . . E-Paris
St. Sen. Dist. 2	Ct. Appeals 6
St. Rep. Dist. 2	Admin. Jud. Dist. 1
St. Dist. Cts. 6, 336	

MINERALS: Not significant; some sand produced.

1985 Pop. 24,600	Tax Ratio 0.91
Area (sq. mi.) 895	Oil value 0
Altitude (ft.) 478-767	No. employed 4,682
Ann. rainfall (in.) . . 43.62	Avg. weekly wage $266.63
Jan. temp. min. 33	Annual wages . $64,916,864
July temp. max. 94	1983 PCI $7,645
Growing season (da.) 228	Buying pwr. . $233,177,000
Voters reg. 13,968	Tax value . . . $813,905,002
Businesses 462	Fed. expd. $78,192,000

Falls

LOCATION: Central (K-17).
HISTORY: Created and organized, 1850 from Limestone, Milam counties; named for Brazos River falls.

Cong. Dist. 11	U.S. Jud. Dist. . . . W-Wa.
St. Sen. Dist. 9	Ct. Appeals 10
St. Rep. Dist. 55	Admin. Jud. Dist. 3
St. Dist. Cts. 82	

PHYSICAL FEATURES: Level to rolling; bisected by Brazos; Blackland, red, sandy loam soils; mineral springs.
RECREATION: Fishing, camping, mineral baths attract visitors; Falls County Youth Fair at Marlin; Highland Mansion and Falls on the Brazos.
MINERALS: Gas, small oil output; stone.

1985 Pop. 18,200	Tax Ratio 0.92
Area (sq. mi.) 770	Oil value 0
Altitude (ft.) 314-590	No. employed 3,205
Ann. rainfall (in.) . . 35.34	Avg. weekly wage $239.44
Jan. temp. min. 38	Annual wages . $39,905,928
July temp. max. 96	1983 PCI $6,616
Growing season (da.) 257	Buying pwr. . $161,761,000
Voters reg. 9,499	Tax value . . . $537,740,142
Businesses 320	Fed. expd. $54,037,000

VITAL STATISTICS 1985: Births, 228; Deaths, 263; Marriages, 150; Divorces, 66.
AGRICULTURE: More than $27 million average annual income; 75% from beef cattle, hogs, turkeys, eggs; crops include sorghums, hay, cotton, wheat, oats; 3,000 acres of cotton irrigated.
BUSINESS: Varied manufacturing; agribusinesses.
MARLIN (6,512) county seat; agribusinesses; small industries; noted for mineral water and spas; geother-

VITAL STATISTICS 1985: Births, 305; Deaths, 360; Marriages, 246; Divorces, 124.
PHYSICAL FEATURES: Rolling prairie, drained by Red River, Bois d'Arc Creek; mostly Blackland soils. Caddo National Grassland.
RECREATION: Sam Rayburn home, Sam Rayburn Memorial Library; Bonham State Park; lake activities on several area lakes; hunting; Ivanhoe Winery.
AGRICULTURE: About $33 million average annual income from beef cattle, hogs, sorghums, small grains, corn, soybeans, peanuts, hay, cotton, grapes; 3,900 acres irrigated; forest products marketed.
BUSINESS: Varied manufacturing, agribusinesses, distribution, meat packing, timber.
BONHAM (7,203) county seat; plants make clothing, mobile homes, fertilizers, other products; hospitals.

Other towns include **Bailey** (220), **Dodd City** (301), **Ector** (650), **Honey Grove** (1,861), **Ladonia** (667), **Leonard** (1,409) ladders manufactured, **Pecan Gap** (296, mostly Delta County), **Ravenna** (186), **Savoy** (818), **Trenton** (682) and **Windom** (285).

Fayette

LOCATION: South (N-17).

HISTORY: Created from Bastrop, Colorado counties, 1837; organized, 1838; named for French hero of U.S. Revolution, **Marquis de Lafayette.**

Cong. Dist.	14	U.S. Jud. Dist.	S-Hn.
St. Sen. Dist.	18	Ct. Appeals	3
St. Rep. Dist.	30	Admin. Jud. Dist.	3
St. Dist. Cts.	155		

PHYSICAL FEATURES: Rolling to level, bisected by Colorado River; sandy loam, black waxy soils.

RECREATION: Many historical restorations at **Round Top** and **Winedale,** including **Winedale Inn;** museums; **Monument Hill State Park, Faison Home Museum,** other historic sites; hunting, fishing, Fayette Power Project Lake; piano festival at **Round Top;** Czech chili cookoff at **Flatonia;** Fayette County Fair and Heritage Days at LaGrange.

MINERALS: Oil, gas, clays, sand and gravel.

1985 Pop.	20,200	Tax Ratio	0.99
Area (sq. mi.)	950	Oil value	$11,916,856
Altitude (ft.)	245-590	No. employed	7,402
Ann. rainfall (in.)	35.67	Avg. weekly wage	$278.46
Jan. temp. min.	42	Annual wages	$107,181,972
July temp. max.	96	1983 PCI	$7,841
Growing season (da.)	277	Buying pwr.	$213,906,000
Voters reg.	11,173	Tax value	$1,719,360,809
Businesses	693	Fed. expd.	$51,315,000

VITAL STATISTICS 1985: Births, 271; Deaths, 292; Marriages, 196; Divorces, 79.

AGRICULTURE: About $55 million annual average income, about 80% from beef, dairy cattle, hogs, poultry; crops include corn, sorghums, hay, peanuts, pecans.

BUSINESS: Agribusinesses, oil production, manufacturing includes steel fencing; and tourism.

LA GRANGE (4,194) county seat; laminated timber, monuments, wholesale nursery, other products; feed processing; power generation; hospital, rest home, clinics.

Schulenburg (2,414), steel, aluminum products, meat processing; rest home, clinics.

Other towns include **Round Top** (100) of historical interest; **Flatonia** (1,307), varied manufacturing; **Fayetteville** (338) and **Carmine** (294).

Fisher

LOCATION: West central (H-11).

HISTORY: Created from Bexar District, 1876; organized, 1886; named for **S. R. Fisher,** Texas Republic Secretary of Navy.

Cong. Dist.	17	U.S. Jud. Dist.	N-Ab.
St. Sen. Dist.	30	Ct. Appeals	11
St. Rep. Dist.	78	Admin. Jud. Dist.	7
St. Dist. Cts.	32		

PHYSICAL FEATURES: Rolling; red, sandy loam soils; drains to forks of Brazos River.

RECREATION: Hunting, fishing; local events.

MINERALS: Production of oil, gas, gypsum.

1985 Pop.	5,600	Tax Ratio	0.80
Area (sq. mi.)	897	Oil value	$26,326,564
Altitude (ft.)	1,723-2,235	No. employed	1,021
Ann. rainfall (in.)	21.21	Avg. weekly wage	$321.66
Jan. temp. min.	31	Annual wages	$17,077,740
July temp. max.	98	1983 PCI	$8,732
Growing season (da.)	218	Buying pwr.	$49,721,000
Voters reg.	3,299	Tax value	$387,463,875
Businesses	106	Fed. expd.	$17,682,000

VITAL STATISTICS 1985: Births, 73; Deaths, 59; Marriages, 44; Divorces, 19.

AGRICULTURE: The $27 million average income is from cattle, hogs, dairy products, sheep, cotton, grains.

BUSINESS: Oil, gypsum, agribusinesses, electric co-op.

ROBY (898) county seat; agribusinesses; electric co-op headquarters.

Rotan (2,273) gypsum plant, oil mill, agribusinesses.

Hamlin (3,235, mostly in Jones County) is farming center.

Floyd

LOCATION: Northwest (E-9).

HISTORY: Created from Bexar District, 1876; organized 1890. Named for **D. W. Floyd,** Alamo martyr.

Cong. Dist.	13	U.S. Jud. Dist.	N-Lb.
St. Sen. Dist.	30	Ct. Appeals	7
St. Rep. Dist.	84	Admin. Jud. Dist.	9
St. Dist. Cts.	110		

PHYSICAL FEATURES: Flat, broken by Cap Rock on east and by White River on south; many playas; red, black loam soils.

RECREATION: Hunting, fishing; museum; local events; county fair at Lockney.

MINERALS: Not significant.

1985 Pop.	9,100	Tax Ratio	0.83
Area (sq. mi.)	992	Oil value	0
Altitude (ft.)	2,574-3,316	No. employed	1,944
Ann. rainfall (in.)	20.18	Avg. weekly wage	$240.34
Jan. temp. min.	26	Annual wages	$24,295,492
July temp. max.	94	1983 PCI	$6,307
Growing season (da.)	213	Buying pwr.	$64,409,000
Voters reg.	4,793	Tax value	$331,408,128
Businesses	216	Fed. expd.	$33,712,000

VITAL STATISTICS 1985: Births, 155; Deaths, 87; Marriages, 83; Divorces, 31.

AGRICULTURE: More than $85 million average annual income from cotton, wheat, beef and stocker cattle; 250,000 acres irrigated.

BUSINESS: Livestock feeds, farm machinery and oilfield manufacturing; other agribusinesses; metal products; printing.

FLOYDADA (3,769) county seat; plants make farm products, race cars, sheet metal goods, oilfield equip-

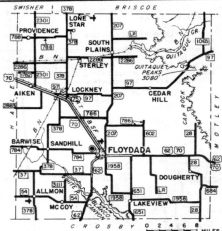

ment; meat and vegetable processing; trade, distribution, medical center; **Texas A&M Engineering Extension Service.**

Lockney (2,169) agribusiness center; plants make farm, oilfield equipment, bird houses; hospital, nursing home.

Foard

LOCATION: Northwest (E-12).
HISTORY: Created out of Cottle, Hardeman, King, Knox counties, 1891, and organized same year. Named for **Maj. Robert L. Foard** of Confederacy.

Cong. Dist.	13	U.S. Jud. Dist.	N-WF
St. Sen. Dist.	30	Ct. Appeals	7
St. Rep. Dist.	80	Admin. Jud. Dist.	9
St. Dist. Cts.	46		

PHYSICAL FEATURES: Drains to N. Wichita, Pease Rivers; sandy, loam soils, rolling surface.
RECREATION: Copper Breaks State Park across county line eight miles north of Crowell; local events.
MINERALS: Oil, gas.

1985 Pop.	1,800	Tax Ratio	0.92
Area (sq. mi.)	703	Oil value	$3,203,956
Altitude (ft.)	1,300-1,784	No. employed	464
Ann. rainfall (in.)	23.93	Avg. weekly wage	$212.54
Jan. temp. min.	28	Annual wages	$5,128,260
July temp. max.	98	1983 PCI	$6,750
Growing season (da.)	219	Buying pwr.	$17,102,000
Voters reg.	1,310	Tax value	$133,206,475
Businesses	47	Fed. expd.	$8,632,000

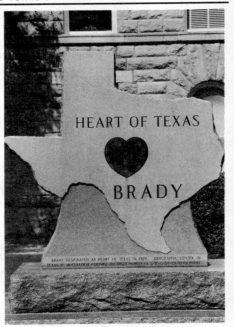

This monument in front of the McCulloch County courthouse in Brady commemorates Brady's designation as the "Heart of Texas" in 1923. The geographic center of the state is 20 miles north, 14½° east of this marker. Texas Almanac Photo.

VITAL STATISTICS 1985: Births, 33; Deaths, 45; Marriages, 16; Divorces, 7.
AGRICULTURE: $8.5 million average farm income from grains, cotton; beef and stocker cattle; more than 3,500 acres irrigated.
BUSINESS: Agribusiness, oil economy.
CROWELL (1,355) county seat; agribusiness center, factories make sportswear; hospital, nursing home.

Fort Bend

LOCATION: Southeast (N-19).
HISTORY: Named for river bend where Austin's colonists settled, among state's more historic counties; created 1837 from Austin County, organized 1838; scene of early **Jaybird-Woodpecker War.**

Cong. Dist.	22	U.S. Jud. Dist.	S-Hn.
St. Sen. Dist.	13, 17, 18	Ct. Appeals	1, 14
St. Rep. Dist.	26, 27	Admin. Jud. Dist.	2
St. Dist. Cts.	240, 268, 328		

PHYSICAL FEATURES: Drained by Brazos, San Bernard Rivers; level to rolling; rich alluvial soils; some loams, clays.
RECREATION: Many historic sites, museum, memorials; fishing, hunting; Czech Fest at Rosenberg first weekend in May, county fair in October.
MINERALS: Production of oil, gas, sulphur, salt, clays, sand and gravel.

1985 Pop.	188,200	Tax Ratio	0.93
Area (sq. mi.)	876	Oil value	$76,459,005
Altitude (ft.)	46-127	No. employed	37,045
Ann. rainfall (in.)	45.07	Avg. weekly wage	$401.61
Jan. temp. min.	44	Annual wages	$773,643,212
July temp. max.	94	1983 PCI	$11,720
Growing season (da.)	296	Buying pwr.	$2,633,568,000
Voters reg.	78,172	Tax value	$10,911,283,547
Businesses	2,460	Fed. expd.	$142,802,000

VITAL STATISTICS 1985: Births, 3,925; Deaths, 727; Marriages, 1,852; Divorces, 901.
AGRICULTURE: More than $90 million average an-

nual income, about 75% from rice, cotton, sorghums, soybeans, corn; cattle, poultry, hogs; vegetables produced; 28,000 acres irrigated, mostly rice, nursery crops.

BUSINESS: Petrochemicals, sulphur, sugar refinery; many residents work in Houston plants; county is part of Houston metro area.

RICHMOND (15,927) county seat; **Richmond State School** (for mentally retarded); adjoins larger **Rosenberg** (19,526) which has varied industries including food processing; annual Czech festival; **Wharton County Junior College** Annex.

Sugar Land (14,898) has sugar refinery, prison farm. Other towns include **Katy** (9,886, part Harris and Waller counties), **Missouri City** (31,054, part Harris), **Stafford** (5,723, part Harris), **Needville** (1,571), **Houston** (1,705,697, mostly Harris County), **Beasley** (539), **Kendleton** (664), **Meadows** (5,895), **Orchard** (481), **Fulshear** (623), **Pleak** (725), **Arcola** (896), **Simonton** (616) and **Thompsons** (263).

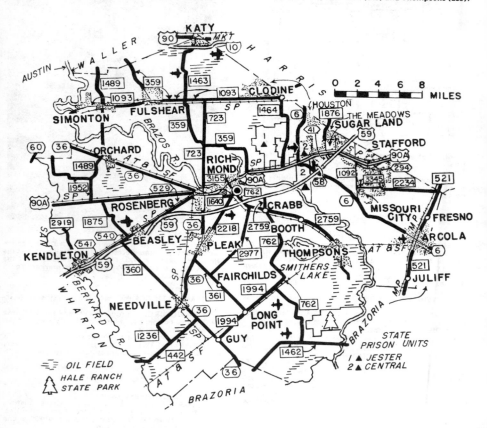

Franklin

LOCATION: Northeast (C-21).

HISTORY: Created, organized 1875 from Titus County; named for **Judge B. C. Franklin** of Texas.

Cong. Dist. 1	U.S. Jud. Dist. . . . . E-Tx.
St. Sen. Dist. 1	Ct. Appeals 6
St. Rep. Dist. 8	Admin. Jud. Dist. 1
St. Dist. Cts. 8, 62	

MINERALS: Oil, gas and lignite produced.

AGRICULTURE: More than 90% of $31 million average annual income from dairy and beef cattle, poultry; hay is principal crop; timber, Christmas trees marketed.

BUSINESS: Agribusinesses, oil.

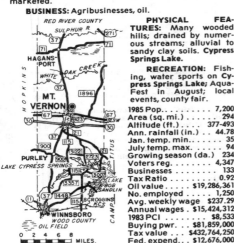

PHYSICAL FEATURES: Many wooded hills; drained by numerous streams; alluvial to sandy clay soils. **Cypress Springs Lake.**

RECREATION: Fishing, water sports on **Cypress Springs Lake;** Aqua-Fest in August; local events, county fair.

1985 Pop. 7,200	
Area (sq. mi.) 294	
Altitude (ft.) 377-493	
Ann. rainfall (in.) . . 44.78	
Jan. temp. min. 35	
July temp. max. 94	
Growing season (da.) 234	
Voters reg. 4,347	
Businesses 133	
Tax Ratio 0.92	
Oil value $19,286,361	
No. employed 1,250	
Avg. weekly wage $237.29	
Annual wages . $15,424,312	
1983 PCI $8,533	
Buying pwr. . . $81,859,000	
Tax value . . . $432,764,250	
Fed. expend. . . $12,676,000	

VITAL STATISTICS 1985: Births, 112; Deaths, 99; Marriages, 78; Divorces, 41.

MOUNT VERNON (2,084) county seat; furniture, clothing factories; livestock market, supply center; hospital; airport; **Winnsboro** (3,666, mostly in Wood, also Hopkins).

Freestone

LOCATION: East central (J-18).

HISTORY: Named for indigenous stone; created 1850 from Limestone County, organized 1851.

Cong. Dist. 6	U.S. Jud. Dist. . . . W-Wa.
St. Sen. Dist. 9	Ct. Appeals 10
St. Rep. Dist. 11	Admin. Jud. Dist. 2
St. Dist. Cts. 77, 87	

PHYSICAL FEATURES: Rolling, drains to Trinity River; Blackland, sandy, loam soils.

RECREATION: Fishing, hunting; **Fairfield Lake** recreation area; local events; historic sites, railroad museum at Teague; Coon Hunters championship in September.

MINERALS: Stone, gas, coal, oil, iron ore.

1985 Pop. 17,100	Tax Ratio 0.94
Area (sq. mi.) 888	Oil value $1,987,331
Altitude (ft.) 209-608	No. employed 3,931
Ann. rainfall (in.) . . 38.53	Avg. weekly wage $367.28
Jan. temp. min. 36	Annual wages . $75,077,672
July temp. max. 94	1983 PCI $7,944
Growing season (da.) 263	Buying pwr. . $168,100,000
Voters reg. 8,738	Tax value . . $1,476,393,117
Businesses 325	Fed. expd. . . . $34,062,000

VITAL STATISTICS 1985: Births, 219; Deaths, 177; Marriages, 151; Divorces, 83.

AGRICULTURE: About $20 million average annual income, mostly from cattle, hogs; hardwood timber; peaches, berries, pecans; oats for grazing.

BUSINESS: Mining, stone quarry, brick plant, varied manufacturing plants, agribusinesses; new electricity generating station.

FAIRFIELD (4,093) county seat; headquarters Continental Telephone Co.; lignite mining; sewing factory;

stone quarry; trading center; hospital, nursing home; Freestone County Museum.

Teague (3,620), has brick plant, metal fabrication, oil field tanks; railroad museum; hospital, nursing home.

Other towns include **Wortham** (1,336), **Streetman** (378, part Navarro), **Kirvin** (84).

Frio

LOCATION: South (P-13).

HISTORY: Created, organized, 1871, from Atascosa, Bexar, Uvalde counties; named for **Frio** (cold) **River.**

Cong. Dist. 15	U.S. Jud. Dist. . . . W-SAnt.
St. Sen. Dist. 21	Ct. Appeals 4
St. Rep. Dist. 45	Admin. Jud. Dist. 4
St. Dist. Cts. 81, 218	

PHYSICAL FEATURES: Rolling, much brush; bisected by Frio River; sandy, red sandy loam soils.

RECREATION: Hunting; local events; Big Foot Wallace Museum, other museums; in Winter Garden area; potato fest in June.

MINERALS: Production of oil, gas, stone.

1985 Pop. 14,200	Tax Ratio 0.95
Area (sq. mi.) 1,133	Oil value $21,790,674
Altitude (ft.) 435-763	No. employed 2,559
Ann. rainfall (in.) . . 23.36	Avg. weekly wage $237.04
Jan. temp. min. 42	Annual wages . $31,542,740
July temp. max. 98	1983 PCI $5,002
Growing season (da.) 281	Buying pwr. . $93,316,000
Voters reg. 7,894	Tax value . . $672,042,604
Businesses 260	Fed. expd. . . . $23,632,000

VITAL STATISTICS 1985: Births, 260; Deaths, 103; Marriages, 127; Divorces, 28.

AGRICULTURE: About $47.5 million average annual income; leading county for peanut production; also grain sorghums, corn; melons, vegetables; about 50,000

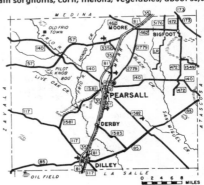

acres irrigated; beef cattle, swine; revenue from hunting leases.

BUSINESS: Chiefly agribusinesses, oil field services.

PEARSALL (7,879) county seat; oil, ranching center; food processing; melon, vegetable, livestock shipping; hospital, rest homes. Other towns include **Dilly** (2,773), **Moore.**

Gaines

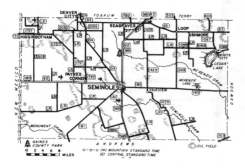

LOCATION: Adjoins New Mexico (H-7).

HISTORY: Created from Bexar District, 1876, organized 1905; named for **James Gaines,** signer of Texas Declaration of Independence.

Cong. Dist.	19	U.S. Jud. Dist.	N-Lb.
St. Sen. Dist.	28	Ct. Appeals	8
St. Rep. Dist.	77	Admin. Jud. Dist.	7
St. Dist. Cts.	106		

PHYSICAL FEATURES: Flat, drains to playas and draws; underground water supply.

RECREATION: Local events.

MINERALS: Production of oil, gas, sodium sulphate; one of leading oil-producing counties.

1985 Pop.	14,300	Tax Ratio	0.91
Area (sq. mi.)	1,504	Oil value	$471,687,074
Altitude (ft.)	3,039-3,581	No. employed	3,319
Ann. rainfall (in.)	15.83	Avg. weekly wage	$339.59
Jan. temp. min.	26	Annual wages	$58,609,664
July temp. max.	94	1983 PCI	$7,580
Growing season (da.)	210	Buying pwr.	$129,886,000
Voters reg.	5,598	Tax value	$3,964,663,659
Businesses	320	Fed. expd.	$33,760,000

VITAL STATISTICS 1985: Births, 326; Deaths, 92; Marriages, 447; Divorces, 68.

AGRICULTURE: State's second largest cotton-producing county; more than $95 million average annual income from cotton, sorghums, wheat, vegetables, peanuts, sunflowers, peaches, pecans; cattle, sheep, hogs; 400,000 acres irrigated.

BUSINESS: Major oil-producing county; oil field activities, agribusinesses, varied manufacturing.

SEMINOLE (6,794) county seat; market for farmers, oil field workers; petrochemical plants; cotton delinting plant; hospital. **Seagraves** (2,643) is market for three-county area; fertilizer and delinting plants; sewing factory; state mental health clinic.

Galveston

LOCATION: On coast, island (N-21).

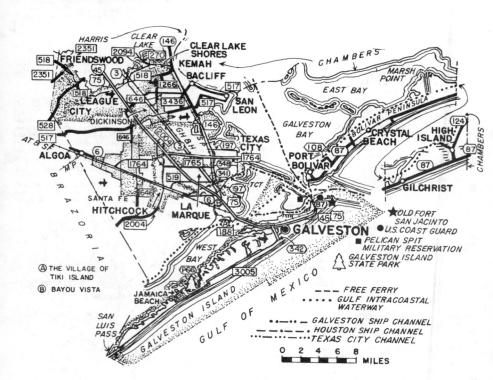

HISTORY: Among most historic counties; created from Brazoria County, 1838; organized, 1839; named for Spanish governor of Louisiana, **Count Bernardo de Galvez.**

Cong. Dist.	9	U.S. Jud. Dist.	S-Gn.
St. Sen. Dist.	4, 11	Ct. Appeals	1, 14
St. Rep. Dist.	24, 25	Admin. Jud. Dist.	2
St. Dist. Cts.	10, 56, 122, 212, 306		

PHYSICAL FEATURES: Partly island, partly coastal; flat, artificial drainage; sandy, loam, clay soils; broken by bays.

RECREATION: One of Texas' most historic cities; popular tourist and convention center; fishing, surfing, boating, sailing and other water sports on 32-mile Gulf beach, bay, tributaries; mild climate; Spring Historical District tour includes many homes, sites; **Sea-Arama; Rosenberg Library; Salt Water Fishing Hall of Fame;** museums; Shrimp Festival; strawberry festival at Dickinson; drama **"Lone Star"** presented in outdoor amphitheater in summer; restored sailing ship, railroad museum, Sports fest in Texas City.

MINERALS: Production of oil, gas, clays, sand and gravel.

1985 Pop.	213,400	Tax Ratio	0.92
Area (sq. mi.)	399	Oil value	$34,977,531
Altitude (ft.)	8-23	No. employed	66,433
Ann. rainfall (in.)	42.20	Avg. weekly wage	$367.64
Jan. temp. min.	49	Ann. wages	$1,270,033,476
July temp. max.	87	1983 PCI	$10,198
Growing season (da.)	335	Buying pwr.	$2,679,724,000
Voters reg.	103,161	Tax value	$8,516,071,621
Businesses	4,121	Fed. expd.	$568,111,000

VITAL STATISTICS 1985: Births, 3,834; Deaths, 1,735; Marriages, 2,523; Divorces, 596.

AGRICULTURE: About $6 million average annual income from beef cattle, horses; rice, soybeans, grain sorghums, corn, honey; 6,000 acres irrigated for rice.

BUSINESS: Port activities dominate economy; varied manufacturing; tourism; medical education center; oceanographic research center; ship building; fishing.

GALVESTON (62,379) county seat; shipping; tourist business; shipyard; other industries; port container facility; **University of Texas Medical Branch; National Maritime Research Center; Texas A&M Maritime Academy; Galveston College;** hospitals.

Texas City (43,551) refining, petrochemical plants; seaport; **College of the Mainland;** hospitals; varied local events.

Other towns include **LaMarque** (15,697) petrochemicals; **League City** (22,934), **Clear Lake Shores** (880), **Crystal Beach** (1,069), **Friendswood** (17,582), Hitchcock (6,405) hospital; oil field service, petrochemicals; **Jamaica Beach** (446), **Kemah** (1,591), **Dickinson** (8,656) with mineral oil plant, hospitals; **Santa Fe** (7,077), **Bayou Vista** (1,030) and **Tiki Island** (195).

Garza

LOCATION: Northwest (G-9).

HISTORY: Created from Bexar District, 1876; organized 1907; named for early Texas family.

Cong. Dist.	17	U.S. Jud. Dist.	N-Lb.
St. Sen. Dist.	28	Ct. Appeals	7
St. Rep. Dist.	78	Admin. Jud. Dist.	7
St. Dist. Cts.	106		

PHYSICAL FEATURES: Rough, broken land, with playas, gullies, canyons, Brazos River forks; sandy, loam, clay soils; Cap Rock on West.

RECREATION: Local events; historical markers; scenic areas; Post-Garza Museum; White River Lake.

MINERALS: Production of oil, gas.

1985 Pop.	5,500	Tax Ratio	0.95
Area (sq. mi.)	895	Oil value	$43,687,598
Altitude (ft.)	2,176-2,986	No. employed	1,218
Ann. rainfall (in.)	18.91	Avg. weekly wage	$282.22
Jan. temp. min.	28	Annual wages	$17,875,172
July temp. max.	95	1983 PCI	$8,058
Growing season (da.)	219	Buying pwr.	$51,017,000
Voters reg.	2,698	Tax value	$631,799,989
Businesses	141	Fed. expd.	$12,740,000

VITAL STATISTICS 1985: Births, 100; Deaths, 55; Marriages, 74; Divorces, 24.

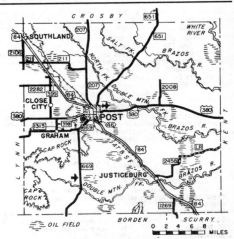

≡ OIL FIELD

0 2 4 6 8 MILES

AGRICULTURE: About $15 million average annual income, 50% from crops, mostly from cotton, grains; remainder from cattle, egg production, some hogs; 4,000 acres irrigated.

BUSINESS: Economy based on oil, farming.

POST (4,162) county seat; founded by C. W. Post, cereal manufacturer; oil, agribusiness center; hospital, nursing home.

Gillespie

LOCATION: West central (M-13).

HISTORY: Created and organized, 1848, from Bexar, Travis counties; named for Texas Ranger Capt. R. A. Gillespie; historic German settlement in heart of Comanche country, birthplace of President Lyndon B. Johnson and Fleet Admiral Chester W. Nimitz.

Cong. Dist.	21	U.S. Jud. Dist.	W-An.
St. Sen. Dist.	25	Ct. Appeals	4
St. Rep. Dist.	67	Admin. Jud. Dist.	6
St. Dist. Cts.	216		

PHYSICAL FEATURES: Plateau and hills, broken by spring-fed streams.

RECREATION: Among leading deer hunting areas; fishing; numerous historic sites and tourist attractions include **Lyndon B. Johnson National Historic Park, LBJ Ranch** and **Lyndon B. Johnson State Park, Admiral Nimitz State Historical Park; Pioneer Museum Complex, Enchanted Rock State Park;** many festivals and celebrations including Oktoberfest in October, Night in Old Fredericksburg in July.

MINERALS: Sand, gravel, granite, gypsum.

1985 Pop.	15,500	Tax Ratio	0.97
Area (sq. mi.)	1,061	Oil value	0
Altitude (ft.)	1,477-2,244	No. employed	4,624
Ann. rainfall (in.)	27.45	Avg. weekly wage	$234.97
Jan. temp. min.	36	Annual wages	$56,498,888
July temp. max.	95	1983 PCI	$7,853

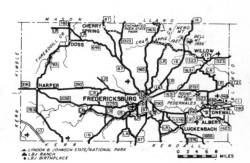

▲ LYNDON B JOHNSON STATE/NATIONAL PARK
■ LBJ RANCH
● LBJ BIRTHPLACE

0 2 4 6 8 MILES

Growing season (da.)	219
Voters reg.	8,911
Businesses	535

Buying pwr.	$152,608,000
Tax value	$1,718,583,075
Fed. expd.	$40,593,000

VITAL STATISTICS 1985: Births, 220; Deaths, 217; Marriages, 177; Divorces, 64.

AGRICULTURE: About $32 million average annual income, 90% from cattle, sheep, goats, hogs, turkeys; crops include hay, sorghums, oats, wheat; largest peach producing county in state.

BUSINESS: Agribusinesses, tourism, food processing, hunting leases, small manufacturing; granite for markers.

FREDERICKSBURG (7,243) county seat; plants make leather goods, trailers; food processing, foundry, agribusinesses; apparel manufacturing; limited wine production; museum, tourist attractions; hospital.

Other towns include **Harper, Stonewall.**

Glasscock

LOCATION: West (J-9).

HISTORY: Created, 1887, from Tom Green County; organized, 1893; named for Texas pioneer, **George W. Glasscock.**

Cong. Dist.	17
St. Sen. Dist.	25
St. Rep. Dist.	69
St. Dist. Cts.	118

U.S. Jud. Dist.	N-SAng.
Ct. Appeals	8
Admin. Jud. Dist.	7

PHYSICAL FEATURES: Level, broken by several small streams; sandy, loam soils.

RECREATION: Local events.

MINERALS: Production of oil, gas.

1985 Pop.	1,200	Tax Ratio	0.93
Area (sq. mi.)	900	Oil value	$38,281,394
Altitude (ft.)	2,495-2,727	No. employed	290
Ann. rainfall (in.)	15.81	Avg. weekly wage	$328.69
Jan. temp. min.	22	Annual wages	$4,956,680
July temp. max.	94	1983 PCI	$7,210
Growing season (da.)	222	Buying pwr.	$9,382,000
Voters reg.	692	Tax value	$481,954,195
Businesses	12	Fed. expd.	$4,119,000

VITAL STATISTICS 1985: Births, 21; Deaths, 4; Marriages, 12; Divorces, 3.

AGRICULTURE: About $15 million average income chiefly from cotton, grain sorghums, wheat, beef cattle, sheep; 40,000 acres irrigated.

BUSINESS: Economy based on oil, farming and ranching.

GARDEN CITY (pop. est. 293) county seat; serves sparsely settled ranching, oil area.

Goliad

LOCATION: South (P-16).

HISTORY: Among most historic areas; created 1836 from Spanish municipality; organized 1837; name is anagram of (H)idalgo.

Cong. Dist.	14
St. Sen. Dist.	18
St. Rep. Dist.	31
St. Dist. Cts.	24, 135, 267

U.S. Jud. Dist.	S-Va.
Ct. Appeals	13
Admin. Jud. Dist.	4

PHYSICAL FEATURES: Rolling, brushy; bisected by San Antonio River; sandy, loam, alluvial soils.

RECREATION: Many historic sites including missions, restored **Presidio La Bahia, Fannin Battleground; Goliad State Park; Gen. Ignacio Zaragoza** statue, **Mission Espiritu Santo de Zuniga; Old Market House** museum; fishing, hunting, camping; horse races, golf courses.

MINERALS: Production of oil, gas.

1985 Pop.	5,600	Tax Ratio	0.94
Area (sq. mi.)	859	Oil value	$4,016,040
Altitude (ft.)	63-242	No. employed	1,027
Ann. rainfall (in.)	33.79	Avg. weekly wage	$298.77
Jan. temp. min.	46	Annual wages	$15,955,748
July temp. max.	94	1983 PCI	$6,857
Growing season (da.)	285	Buying pwr.	$52,602,000
Voters reg.	3,754	Tax value	$893,846,501
Businesses	105	Fed. expd.	$11,544,000

VITAL STATISTICS 1985: Births, 78; Deaths, 62; Marriages, 57; Divorces, 21.

AGRICULTURE: About $25 million average annual income, more than 90% from cattle, hogs, sheep, poultry, horses; crops include sorghums, corn.

BUSINESS: Primarily based on oil; agribusiness, tourist income, electricity generating plant.

GOLIAD (2,089) county seat; a historic city with many sites of interest; tourism; oil; agribusinesses; hospital; library.

Gonzales

LOCATION: South central (N-16).

HISTORY: Among most historic areas and first Anglo-American settlements; original county, created 1836, organized 1837; named for Texas and Coahuila Gov. **Rafael Gonzales.**

Cong. Dist.	14, 15
St. Sen. Dist.	18
St. Rep. Dist.	31
St. Dist. Cts.	25, 2D25

U.S. Jud. Dist.	W-SAnt.
Ct. Appeals	13
Admin. Jud. Dist.	3

PHYSICAL FEATURES: Rolling, rich bottom soils along Guadalupe and its tributaries; some sandy areas; many oaks, pecans.

RECREATION: Historic sites, homes; 86 officially recognized homes or historical markers; **Palmetto State Park; Gonzales Museum, Gonzales County** jail and museum, **Independence Park;** other historical attractions. "Come and Take It" festival in Gonzales.

MINERALS: Production of gas, oil, clay, gravel.

1985 Pop.	18,800	Tax Ratio	0.91
Area (sq. mi.)	1,068	Oil value	$3,702,186
Altitude (ft.)	201-504	No. employed	5,206
Ann. rainfall (in.)	32.07	Avg. weekly wage	$241.14
Jan. temp. min.	42	Annual wages	$65,281,144
July temp. max.	96	1983 PCI	$6,471
Growing season (da.)	276	Buying pwr.	$148,917,000
Voters reg.	9,758	Tax value	$981,684,676
Businesses	466	Fed. expd.	$72,014,000

At the Brockett-Tyree Christmas Tree Farm east of Quitman, Andy Brockett inspects a Virginia pine for tipworm damage. Christmas trees are grown commercially at several locations in Texas. Texas Almanac Photo.

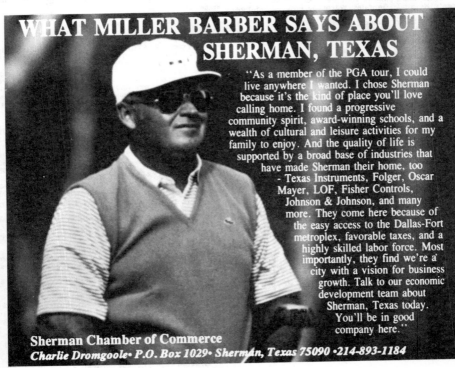

Gonzales County (Cont'd.)

VITAL STATISTICS 1985: Births, 315; Deaths, 212; Marriages, 175; Divorces, 86.

AGRICULTURE: More than $170 million average annual income. Top poultry and egg producing county in state, cattle; crops include grain, corn, peanuts, melons, pecans.

BUSINESS: Agribusinesses, poultry processing; feed plants; tile, clay plants.

GONZALES (7,977) county seat; "Lexington of Texas," poultry shipping, processing center; feed mills, boot manufacturing, food processing, steel fabrication; hospital, nursing home; museum; children's rehabilitation hospitals.

Ottine has **Palmetto State Park, Elks Crippled Children's Hospital; Gonzales Warm Springs Foundation Hospital.**

Other towns include **Waelder** (945), **Nixon** (2,211) poultry processing and livestock center and **Smiley** (546).

Gray

LOCATION: In Panhandle (C-10).

HISTORY: Created, 1876, from Bexar District; organized, 1902; named for **Peter W. Gray,** member first State Legislature.

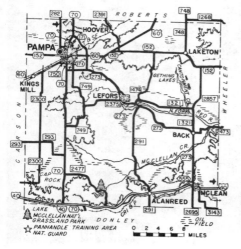

Cong. Dist.	13	U.S. Jud. Dist.	N-Am.
St. Sen. Dist.	31	Ct. Appeals	7
St. Rep. Dist.	84	Admin. Jud. Dist.	9
St. Dist. Cts.	31, 223		

PHYSICAL FEATURES: Level, broken by Red River forks, tributaries; sandy loam, waxy soils.

RECREATION: Water sports, **Lake McClellan National Grasslands Park; White Deer Land Museum;** golf tournaments, rodeos, other local events.

MINERALS: Production of oil, gas, sand, gravel.

1985 Pop.	27,100	Tax Ratio	0.88
Area (sq. mi.)	921	Oil value	$32,184,448
Altitude (ft.)	2,558-3,296	No. employed	8,704
Ann. rainfall (in.)	20.14	Avg. weekly wage	$348.45
Jan. temp. min.	23	Annual wages	$157,712,952
July temp. max.	94	1983 PCI	$9,770
Growing season (da.)	195	Buying pwr.	$311,549,000
Voters reg.	14,589	Tax value	$1,307,676,474
Businesses	934	Fed. expd.	$64,282,000

VITAL STATISTICS 1985: Births, 409; Deaths, 266; Marriages, 246; Divorces, 161.

AGRICULTURE: About $40 million average annual income, over 80% from feed and stocker cattle, hogs; sorghums, wheat, hay chief crops; 22,000 acres irrigated; large feedlots.

BUSINESS: Economy based on petroleum, agriculture, feed lot operations, chemical plant, other manufacturing.

PAMPA (22,275) county seat; chemical plants; petroleum processing; feedlots; meat packers; apparel, furniture plants, laminated windshields and tempered window glass manufactured; other industries; hospitals, nursing homes; **Clarendon College, Pampa Center.**

Other towns include **McLean** (1,127) and **Lefors** (781).

Grayson

LOCATION: North; adjoins Oklahoma (F-17).

HISTORY: Created, organized, 1846, from Fannin County; named for Republic of Texas **Atty. Gen. Peter W. Grayson.**

Cong. Dist.	4	U.S. Jud. Dist.	E-Sh.
St. Sen. Dist.	30	Ct. Appeals	5
St. Rep. Dist.	62	Admin. Jud. Dist.	1
St. Dist. Cts.	15, 59, 336		

PHYSICAL FEATURES: Level, some low hills; sandy loam, Blackland soils; drains to Red River on north and to tributaries of the Trinity River on the south.

RECREATION: Lake Texoma is a leading fishing, tourist attraction; annual striper fishing derby on lake and Red River; **Lake Ray Roberts** under construction; Western Week; **Pres. Dwight D. Eisenhower** birthplace; **Eisenhower State Park;** varied cultural activities; **Hagerman Wildlife Refuge;** many local events.

MINERALS: Production of oil, gas, stone.

1985 Pop.	96,700	Tax Ratio	0.78
Area (sq. mi.)	934	Oil value	$28,025,093
Altitude (ft.)	535-867	No. employed	35,222
Ann. rainfall (in.)	39.83	Avg. weekly wage	$351.16
Jan. temp. min.	32	Annual wages	$643,174,368
July temp. max.	96	1983 PCI	$9,190
Growing season (da.)	227	Buying pwr.	$1,120,259,000
Voters reg.	45,270	Tax value	$3,065,674,868
Businesses	2,329	Fed. expd.	$227,243,000

VITAL STATISTICS 1985: Births, 1,454; Deaths, 1,071; Marriages, 1,415; Divorces, 834.

AGRICULTURE: About $31 million average annual income, 65% beef, dairy cattle, hogs, horses, poultry; crops include wheat, sorghums, peanuts, hay, horticultural crops; 1,500 acres irrigated.

BUSINESS: Primarily a manufacturing, distribution and trade center for northern Texas and southern Oklahoma; tourism, minerals, agribusinesses significant.

SHERMAN (31,217) county seat; plants manufacture foods, meat products, livestock trailers, clothing, fishing lures, electronic products, ferrous and aluminum castings, truck bodies, cable reels, laminated windshields, boats, office equipment, surgical supplies, other products; many processors and distributors for major companies; **Austin College;** hospitals.

Denison (24,234); electronics manufacturing, transportation center; plants process foods, make clothing, furniture, plastics, many other products; tourist center; hospitals.

Grayson County College between Sherman-Denison.

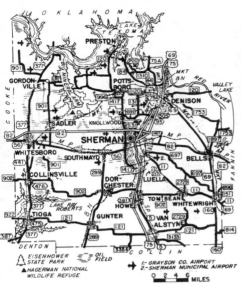

Whitewright (1,719) clothing, sausage manufacturing; clinics, nursing home.

Other towns include **Bells** (1,014), **Collinsville** (911), **Dorchester** (222), **Gunter** (882), **Howe** (2,300), **Knollwood** (241), **Luella** (441), **Pottsboro** (1,130), **Sadler** (348), **Southmayd** (348), **Tom Bean** (926), **Van Alstyne** (1,990), **Whitesboro** (3,289).

Gregg

LOCATION: Northeast (H-20).

HISTORY: Created, organized, 1873, from Rusk, Upshur counties; named for **Confederate Gen. John Gregg.**

Cong. Dist.	4	U.S. Jud. Dist.	E-Ty.
St. Sen. Dist.	1	Ct. Appeals	6, 12
St. Rep. Dist.	7	Admin. Jud. Dist.	1
St. Dist. Cts.	124, 188, 307		

PHYSICAL FEATURES: Hilly, timbered; some commercial lumbering; sandy, clay, alluvial soils; bisected by Sabine River.

RECREATION: Water activities on area lakes; hunting; varied cultural events; **East Texas Oil Museum,** tourism, East Texas Gusher Days in May at Gladewater; Shakespearean Festival in Kilgore.

MINERALS: Leading oil-producing county with over 2.5 billion bbl. production since 1931, mostly from East Texas field; gas, sand and gravel.

1985 Pop.	112,300
Area (sq. mi.)	273
Altitude (ft.)	289-436
Ann. rainfall (in.)	47.18
Jan. temp. min.	38
July temp. max.	96
Growing season (da.)	247
Voters reg.	53,150
Businesses	3,882
Tax Ratio	0.99
Oil value	$464,587,418
No. employed	46,195
Avg. weekly wage	$335.35
Annual wages	$805,580,788
1983 PCI	$9,361
Buying pwr.	$1,316,473,000
Tax value	$6,305,997,942
Fed. expd.	$203,806,000

VITAL STATISTICS 1985: Births, 1,880; Deaths, 1,016; Marriages, 1,561; Divorces, 621.

AGRICULTURE: About $4.5 million average income from beef cattle, hay production, race horse breeding, timber, Christmas tree production; crops negligible.

BUSINESS: Oil-based economy, but with significant other manufacturing; tourism, conventions; agribusinesses and lignite coal production; part of Longview-Marshall MSA.

LONGVIEW (73,263, partly Harrison County) county seat; center for East Texas oil industry; plants make aircraft components, plastics, chemicals, heavy equipment, recreational vehicles, metal cans, metal buildings, brewery products, paints, hats, steel products, mobile homes, railway equipment; many other products; convention center; **LeTourneau College** and **Kilgore College Longview Center;** hospitals.

Kilgore (12,138, in Gregg and Rusk counties) oil center; plants make ceramic products, boats, valves, other products; **Kilgore College;** hospitals; **East Texas Treatment Center.**

Other towns include **Gladewater** (7,381, part Upshur) with apparel, boat, oil field equipment manufacturers; hospital; developing tourism; **White Oak** (5,394), **Clarksville City** (542), **Easton** (375, partly Rusk), **Lakeport** (924), **Liberty City** (1,121), **Rolling Meadows** (268) and **Warren City** (329, partly Upshur).

Grimes

LOCATION: Southeast (L-18).

HISTORY: Created from Montgomery County and organized, 1846; named for **Jesse Grimes,** who signed Texas Declaration of Independence.

PHYSICAL FEATURES: Rich bottom soils along Brazos, Navasota Rivers; remainder hilly, partly forested.

RECREATION: Hunting, fishing; historic sites; renaissance festival in October; county fair.

AGRICULTURE: About $36.5 million average annual income; over 90% from beef, dairy cattle, hogs; crops include grains, corn, soybeans, watermelons, Christmas trees, some timber.

BUSINESS: Varied manufacturing, agribusinesses.

Cong. Dist.	6	U.S. Jud. Dist.	S-Hn.
St. Sen. Dist.	5	Ct. Appeals	1, 14
St. Rep. Dist.	15	Admin. Jud. Dist.	2
St. Dist. Cts.	12, 278		

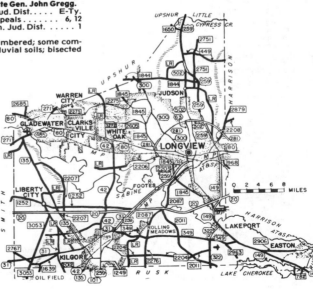

Grimes County (Cont'd.)

MINERALS: Some oil, gas, coal production.

1985 Pop.	18,800
Area (sq. mi.)	799
Altitude (ft.)	193-415
Ann. rainfall (in.)	40.52
Jan. temp. min.	40
July temp. max.	96
Growing season (da.)	278
Voters reg.	8,556
Businesses	334
Tax Ratio	0.98
Oil value	$562,370
No. employed	4,084
Avg. weekly wage	$358.57
Annual wages	$76,150,488
1983 PCI	$7,785
Buying pwr.	$136,930,000
Tax value	$1,100,580,898
Fed. expend.	$34,855,000

VITAL STATISTICS 1985: Births, 333; Deaths, 224; Marriages, 188; Divorces, 66.

ANDERSON (est. 320) county seat; rural center.

Navasota (6,808) agribusiness center for parts of three counties; plants make steel products, mobile homes, cheese, furniture, oil field supplies; food, wood processing; hospitals. **Todd Mission** (64) home of Texas Renaissance Festival in October.

Guadalupe

LOCATION: South central (N-15).
HISTORY: Created, organized, 1846, from Bexar, Gonzales counties; named for river.

Cong. Dist.	14
St. Sen. Dist.	21
St. Rep. Dist.	46
St. Dist. Cts.	25, 2D25, 274

U.S. Jud. Dist.	W-SAnt.
Ct. Appeals	4
Admin. Jud. Dist.	3

PHYSICAL FEATURES: Bisected by Guadalupe River; level to slightly rolling surface; sandy, loam, Blackland soils.
RECREATION: Fishing, hunting; historic sites; high school rodeo, festivals, other local events.
MINERALS: Production of oil, gas, sand and gravel, clays.

1985 Pop.	54,600	Tax Ratio	0.70
Area (sq. mi.)	713	Oil value	$10,705,740
Altitude (ft.)	372-726	No. employed	14,449
Ann. rainfall (in.)	30.67	Avg. weekly wage	$300.48
Jan. temp. min.	42	Annual wages	$225,767,708
July temp. max.	96	1983 PCI	$8,055
Growing season (da.)	267	Buying pwr.	$634,000,000
Voters reg.	26,220	Tax value	$1,530,378,667
Businesses	1,048	Fed. expd.	$105,216,000

VITAL STATISTICS 1985: Births, 955; Deaths, 425; Marriages, 632; Divorces, 283.

AGRICULTURE: About $28 million average annual income, 65% from beef, dairy cattle, hogs, poultry; crops include sorghums, corn, wheat, oats, cotton, peanuts, pecans, Christmas trees, peaches.

BUSINESS: Agribusinesses, varied manufacturing, many employed in San Antonio; county in San Antonio metro area.

SEGUIN (18,904) county seat; plants make aircraft parts, car radios, livestock feed, furniture, millwork, steel processing, fiberglass products, cotton goods, other products; **Texas Lutheran College;** hospital, clinics, nursing home.

Other towns include **Schertz** (7,546, part Bexar), **Cibolo** (657), **Marion** (835), **New Berlin** (269), **Selma** (543, partly in Bexar County).

Hale

LOCATION: Northwest (E-8).
HISTORY: Created from Bexar District, 1876; organized 1888; named for **Lt. J. C. Hale,** who died at San Jacinto.

Cong. Dist.	19
St. Sen. Dist.	31
St. Rep. Dist.	85
St. Dist. Cts.	64, 242

U.S. Jud. Dist.	N-Lb.
Ct. Appeals	7
Admin. Jud. Dist.	9

PHYSICAL FEATURES: Level; fertile sandy, loam soils; many playas; large underground water supply.
RECREATION: Local events; Llano Estacado Museum; Panhandle Parade of Breeds.
MINERALS: Production of oil, gas.

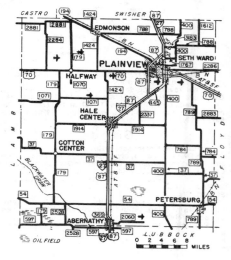

1985 Pop.	37,500	Tax Ratio	0.94
Area (sq. mi.)	1,005	Oil value	$56,731,150
Altitude (ft.)	3,500-3,600	No. employed	11,943
Ann. rainfall (in.)	19.34	Avg. weekly wage	$270.13
Jan. temp. min.	26	Annual wages	$167,761,416
July temp. max.	93	1983 PCI	$6,887
Growing season (da.)	211	Buying pwr.	$299,735,000
Voters reg.	14,183	Tax value	$1,122,674,006
Businesses	909	Fed. expd.	$106,234,000

VITAL STATISTICS 1985: Births, 675; Deaths, 321; Marriages, 377; Divorces, 194.

AGRICULTURE: About $123 million average annual income, one of leading farm-producing counties; cotton, major crop; others include corn, soybeans, sorghums, wheat, vegetables; beef cattle, swine, sheep; 400,000 acres irrigated.

BUSINESS: Many agribusinesses, food processing plants, manufacturing.

PLAINVIEW (22,414) county seat; meat packing plants, distribution center, other industries; **Wayland Baptist University;** hospitals, mental health/mental retardation center; international occupational center.

Other towns include **Abernathy** (2,849, part Lubbock) textile mill; **Hale Center** (2,136), **Petersburg** (1,548), **Edmonson** (268).

Hall

LOCATION: Northwest (D-10).

HISTORY: Created 1876, from Bexar, Young Districts; organized 1890; named for Republic of Texas Secretary of War W. D. C. Hall.

Cong. Dist. 13	U.S. Jud. Dist. . . . . N-Am.
St. Sen. Dist. 31	Ct. Appeals 7
St. Rep. Dist. 84	Admin. Jud. Dist. 9
St. Dist. Cts. 100	

MINERALS: Not significant.

PHYSICAL FEATURES: Rolling to hilly, broken by Red River forks, tributaries; red and black sandy loam soils.

RECREATION: Fishing, hunting; museum; local events.

1985 Pop. 4,800	Tax Ratio 0.87
Area (sq. mi.) 876	Oil value 0
Altitude (ft.) . . 2,238-3,315	No. employed 1,022
Ann. rainfall (in.) . 20.53	Avg. weekly wage $243.70
Jan. temp. min. 26	Annual wages . $12,951,248
July temp. max. 98	1983 PCI $6,465
Growing season (da.) 213	Buying pwr. . . $31,082,000
Voters reg. 2,933	Tax value . . . $183,904,177
Businesses 139	Fed. expd. $19,723,000

VITAL STATISTICS 1985: Births, 47; Deaths, 64; Marriages, 44; Divorces, 21.

AGRICULTURE: About $20 million average annual income, 80% from crops including cotton, sorghums, peanuts, wheat, vegetables; also beef cattle, hogs; 20,000 acres irrigated.

BUSINESS: Textiles; grain, cotton processing; farm, ranch supplies, marketing for large rural area.

MEMPHIS (3,114) county seat; foundry, cotton gins, food processing; grain elevators, irrigation equipment; hospital, nursing home.

Other towns include **Estelline** (254), **Lakeview** (211), **Turkey** (560).

Hamilton

LOCATION: Central (J-14).

HISTORY: Created 1842; then re-created, organized, 1858, from Bosque, Comanche, Lampasas counties; named for South Carolinian, **Gov. James Hamilton**, who aided Texas Revolution and Republic.

Cong. Dist. 11	U.S. Jud. Dist. . . . . W-Wa.
St. Sen. Dist. 22	Ct. Appeals 10
St. Rep. Dist. 54	Admin. Jud. Dist. 3
St. Dist. Cts. 220	

PHYSICAL FEATURES: Hilly, broken by scenic valleys; loam soils.

RECREATION: Deer, quail, dove, duck hunting; dove festival in September; Old Settlers Reunion in Hico.

MINERALS: Limited gas, oil, gravel.

1985 Pop. 8,100	Tax Ratio 0.90
Area (sq. mi.) 836	Oil value 0
Altitude (ft.) . . . 967-1,590	No. employed 1,787
Ann. rainfall (in.) . . 29.61	Avg. weekly wage $247.57
Jan. temp. min. 34	Annual wages . $23,006,052
July temp. max. 96	1983 PCI $7,426
Growing season (da.) 239	Buying pwr. . . $88,614,000
Voters reg. 4,469	Tax value . . . $442,774,600
Businesses 234	Fed. expd. . . . $22,412,000

VITAL STATISTICS 1985: Births, 93; Deaths, 155; Marriages, 94; Divorces, 52.

AGRICULTURE: More than $34 million average annual production; 90% from cattle, hogs, sheep, goats, poultry; crops include sorghums, small grains, cotton, hay, pecans.

BUSINESS: Agribusiness including more than 40 dairies; varied manufacturing; hunting leases, many residents commute to cities to work.

HAMILTON (3,005) county seat; plants make garments, wood molding, steel products, machine parts; hospital, nursing homes; library. **Hico** (1,422) is other principal town.

Hansford

LOCATION: Top of Panhandle (A-9).

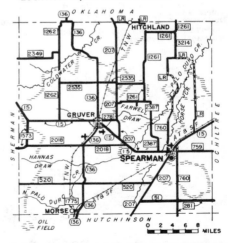

HISTORY: Created, 1876, from Bexar, Young Districts; organized 1889; named for **Judge J. M. Hansford**.

Cong. Dist. 13	U.S. Jud. Dist. . . . . N-Am.
St. Sen. Dist. 31	Ct. Appeals 7
St. Rep. Dist. 88	Admin. Jud. Dist. 9
St. Dist. Cts. 84	

1985 Pop.	6,500	Tax Ratio	0.96
Area (sq. mi.)	921	Oil value	$1,433,233
Altitude (ft.)	2,986-3,237	No. employed	1,824
Ann. rainfall (in.)	22.16	Avg. weekly wage	$372.62
Jan. temp. min.	20	Annual wages	$35,342,852
July temp. max.	94	1983 PCI	$10,153
Growing season (da.)	186	Buying pwr.	$63,473,000
Voters reg.	3,269	Tax value	$492,614,725
Businesses	210	Fed. expd.	$20,621,000

VITAL STATISTICS 1985: Births, 107; Deaths, 55; Marriages, 72; Divorces, 24.

PHYSICAL FEATURES: Level, drains to playas, creeks, draws; sandy, loam, black soils; underground water.

RECREATION: Stationmasters House Museum, hunting; county fair in October, roundup in June.

MINERALS: Production of gas, oil, stone, helium.

AGRICULTURE: More than $140 million average annual income, 65% from livestock; large cattle feeding operations; crops include sorghums, wheat, corn; 190,000 acres irrigated.

BUSINESS: Agribusinesses; mineral operations.

SPEARMAN (3,590) county seat; feedlots; center for grain marketing, storage; gas processing; hospital, retirement center; municipal airport. **Gruver** (1,199) is other principal town.

Hardeman

LOCATION: Borders Oklahoma (E-12).

HISTORY: Created, 1858, from Fannin; re-created, 1876, organized, 1884; named for pioneer Texas brothers, **Bailey** and **T. J. Hardeman.**

Cong. Dist.	13	U.S. Jud. Dist.	N-WF
St. Sen. Dist.	30	Ct. Appeals	7
St. Rep. Dist.	80	Admin. Jud. Dist.	9
St. Dist. Cts.	46		

PHYSICAL FEATURES: Rolling, broken area on divide between Pease, Red River forks; sandy, sandy loam soils.

RECREATION: Copper Breaks State Park; Lake Pauline activities; museum; Quanah Parker Pageant in June and other local events.

MINERALS: Production of oil, gas, gypsum.

1985 Pop.	6,400	Tax Ratio	0.88
Area (sq. mi.)	688	Oil value	$5,647,643
Altitude (ft.)	1,287-1,749	No. employed	1,632
Ann. rainfall (in.)	24.32	Avg. weekly wage	$279.03
Jan. temp. min.	28	Annual wages	$23,680,288
July temp. max.	99	1983 PCI	$8,159
Growing season (da.)	221	Buying pwr.	$64,668,000
Voters reg.	3,179	Tax value	$342,883,655
Businesses	167	Fed. expd.	$20,101,000

VITAL STATISTICS 1985: Births, 102; Deaths, 102; Marriages, 59; Divorces, 37.

AGRICULTURE: About $18 million average annual income, 65% from wheat, cotton, other crops; beef cattle, horses; about 8,600 acres irrigated, mostly cotton.

BUSINESS: Agribusinesses, some manufacturing.

QUANAH (3,963) county seat; agribusinesses, gypsum plant makes wall board; cotton oil mill, sheet metal works, sportswear, other plants; hospital, rest homes. **Chillicothe** (1,045) is other principal town.

Hardin

LOCATION: Southeast (L-21).

HISTORY: Created, organized, 1858, from Jefferson, Liberty counties. Named for Texas Revolutionist William Hardin.

Cong. Dist.	2	U.S. Jud. Dist.	E-Bt.
St. Sen. Dist.	3	Ct. Appeals	9
St. Rep. Dist.	20	Admin. Jud. Dist.	2
St. Dist. Cts.	88, 356		

PHYSICAL FEATURES: Heavily timbered; many streams; sandy, loam soils; **Big Thicket** covers much of area.

RECREATION: Big Thicket with rare plant, animal life; part of Big Thicket National Preserve; Big Thicket Museum at Saratoga; Red Cloud Water Park; hunting, fishing; local events.

MINERALS: Production of oil, gas, sand and gravel.

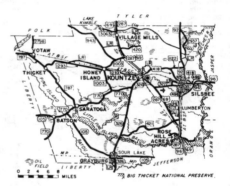

BIG THICKET NATIONAL PRESERVE.

1985 Pop.	43,400	Tax Ratio	0.91
Area (sq. mi.)	898	Oil value	$24,070,853
Altitude (ft.)	29-126	No. employed	7,667
Ann. rainfall (in.)	53.00	Avg. weekly wage	$289.52
Jan. temp. min.	42	Annual wages	$115,430,884
July temp. max.	93	1983 PCI	$8,366
Growing season (da.)	246	Buying pwr.	$469,430,000
Voters reg.	27,014	Tax value	$1,470,561,990
Businesses	655	Fed. expd.	$82,432,000

VITAL STATISTICS 1985: Births, 668; Deaths, 318; Marriages, 605; Divorces, 338.

AGRICULTURE: Almost $4.8 million average annual income, most of it from forestry products; over 85% of county forested; beef cattle, leading livestock; crops include hay, Christmas trees.

BUSINESS: Paper making, wood processing, minerals, food processing; county in Beaumont-Port Arthur-Orange MSA (see metro page).

KOUNTZE (2,782) county seat; tourism.

Silsbee (7,827) is trade, manufacturing center; lumber, paper, particle board, sawmills; rubber plant; oil, gas processing; rail division point; hospital, nursing home. Other towns include **Lumberton** (3,098) hospital; **Rose Hill Acres** (540), **Sour Lake** (2,045), Saratoga and Grayburg (159).

Harris

LOCATION: Southeast (M-20).

HISTORY: Created, 1836, organized, 1837; named for John R. Harris, 1824 founder of Harrisburg.

PHYSICAL FEATURES: Level; typically coastal surface and soils; many bayous, lakes, canals for artificial drainage; partly forested.

Cong. Dist. 7, 8, 9, 18, 22, 25	
St. Sen.	
Dist. 4, 5, 6, 7, 11, 13, 15, 17	
St. Rep. Dist. 125-150	
U.S. Jud. Dist. . . . . S-Hn.	
Ct. Appeals 1, 14	
Admin. Jud. Dist. 2	

St. Dist. Cts. . . . 11, 55, 61,
80, 113, 125, 127, 129, 133,
151, 152, 157, 164, 165, 174,
176, 177, 178, 179, 180, 182,
183, 184, 185, 189, 190, 208,
209, 215, 228, 230, 232, 234,
245, 246, 247, 248, 257, 262,
263, 269, 270, 280, 281, 295,
308, 309, 310, 311, 312, 313,
314, 315, 333, 334, 337, 338,
339, 351

MINERALS: Among leading oil, gas, petrochemical areas; production of petroleum, cement, natural gas liquids, natural gas, salt, lime, sand and gravel, clays, stone; approximately 1 billion bbls. oil produced since 1905; center of multicounty petrochemicals developments that are the world's largest (see Minerals section).

RECREATION: Fishing, boating, other freshwater and saltwater activities; **Astroworld** and **Waterworld** amusement parks and adjacent domed stadium; numerous athletic and cultural events associated with universities and colleges; professional baseball, football, basketball, other sports; **Jones Hall for the Performing Arts, Nina Vance Alley Theatre, Houston Theatre Center, Music Hall, coliseum, Convention Center, The Summit** — a 17,000-seat sports and entertainment center, **Sam Houston Park** with restored early Houston homes, church, stores; **Museum of Fine Arts, Contemporary Arts Museum, Rice Museum; Sarah Campbell Blaffer Gallery** at University of Houston; museum of natural science, planetarium, zoological gardens in Hermann Park; **San Jacinto Battleground State Park** with museum, Battleship Texas; **Lyndon B. Johnson Space Center;** annual Livestock Show and Rodeo; Houston Festival in spring; Azalea Trail, numerous art shows, cultural events, other tourist attractions. (Consult chambers of commerce or Greater Houston Convention and Visitors Council for details and dates.)

EDUCATION: Houston is a university center: more than 140,000 students are enrolled in 28 colleges and universities in Harris County. Senior colleges and universities: **Rice University, University of Houston** (three branches in Harris County), **Texas Southern University, University of St. Thomas, Houston Baptist University, Houston Baptist University Nursing School, South Texas College of Law, Hispanic International University.** Junior

colleges: **Houston Community College System, Lee College, San Jacinto College, North Harris County Junior College.** Medical schools and colleges: **University of St. Thomas Nursing School, University of Texas Health Science Center at Houston** (seven branches. See index for Universities and Colleges for individual schools therein), **Baylor College of Medicine, Institute of Religion and Human Development, Texas Chiropractic College, Texas Woman's University-Houston Center.** Theological schools: **St. Mary's Seminary, Texas Bible College.** Houston also has many business, technical and trade schools.

1985 Pop. 2,794,700		Tax Ratio 1.00
Area (sq. mi.) 1,734		Oil value $126,504,563
Altitude (ft.) 6-171		No. employed . . 1,247,865
Ann. rainfall (in.) . . 48.19		Avg. weekly wage $439.85
Jan. temp. min. 45		Ann. wages $28,542,019,808
July temp. max. 93		1983 PCI $11,699
Growing season (da.) 300		Buying pwr. $37,181,326,000
Voters reg. 1,142,582		Tax value $130,428,297,398
Businesses 73,052		Fed. expd. . . $5,492,886,000

VITAL STATISTICS 1985: Births, 54,488; Deaths, 15,687; Marriages, 31,246; Divorces, 19,404.

AGRICULTURE: $67.1 million annual income, about 25% from cattle, hogs, horses, poultry, dairy products; crops include rice, nursery crops, soybeans, grains, hay, corn, vegetables; some 50,000 acres irrigated, mostly rice.

BUSINESS: Highly industrialized county, with more than 3,800 manufacturing plants; corporate management center; nation's largest concentration of petrochemical plants; largest U.S. wheat-exporting port, the 2nd largest U.S. port in value of foreign trade and 3rd largest U.S. port in total tonnage; petroleum refining, chemicals, food and kindred products, fabricated metal products, non-electrical machinery, primary metals, scientific instruments; paper and allied products, printing and publishing, numerous other products manufactured; center of energy, space and medical research; center of international business, with 64 foreign banks and 5th largest consular corps in U.S.; increasing convention, tourist business; see Houston metro page for data on metropolitan area; see also sections on minerals, manufacturing, etc.

HOUSTON (1,705,697, in Harris, Fort Bend, Montgomery counties, most populous Texas city, and 4th in U.S.); county seat; ranks first in manufacture of petro-

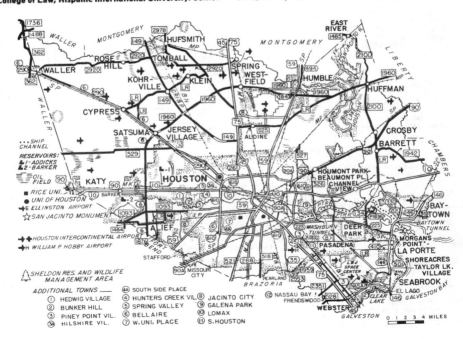

ADDITIONAL TOWNS ——
① HEDWIG VILLAGE
② BUNKER HILL
③ PINEY POINT VIL.
③A HILSHIRE VIL.
④A SOUTH SIDE PLACE
④ HUNTERS CREEK VIL.
⑤ SPRING VALLEY
⑥ BELLAIRE
⑦ W. UNI. PLACE
⑧ JACINTO CITY
⑨ GALENA PARK
⑩ LOMAX
⑪ S. HOUSTON
⑫ NASSAU BAY

leum equipment, agricultural chemicals, fertilizers, pesticides, oil and gas pipeline transmission; ranks high in commercial bank demand deposits, wholesale sales, retail sales, value added by manufacture and manufacturing payrolls; 61 foreign bank branches; 57 foreign consular offices; 29 foreign trade, investment and tourism offices; a leading scientific center; ranks fifth in manufacture of machinery, sixth in fabricated metals; a major distribution and shipping center; engineering and research center; food processing, textile mills; plants make apparel, lumber and wood products, furniture, paper, publications, chemical, petroleum and coal products, stone, clay and glass products, electrical and electronic products, many others; major medical and educational center; 7th largest public school system in U.S.; prominent corporate center, with more than 200 firms locating corporate headquarters, divisions or subsidiaries since 1970.

Pasadena (119,303) residential city with large industrial area manufacturing chemical and other petroleum-related products; civic center; retail mall; **San Jacinto College, Texas Chiropractic College;** 4 hospitals; historical museum; strawberry festival; Gilley's, the famous Western nightspot.

Bellaire (14,873) residential city, with several major office buildings.

The Clear Lake area includes: **Seabrook** (4,788), **Nassau Bay** (4,739), **El Lago** (3,170), **Webster** (3,001), **Taylor Lake Village** (3,524), **Lyndon B. Johnson Space Center, University of Houston-Clear Lake.** Bayport industrial complex includes Port of Bayport; 12 major marinas; 2 hospitals.

Baytown (60,676) refining, petrochemical center; steel manufacturing; **Lee College;** major shopping mall; hospital center; historical homes tour.

Tomball (6,228) petrochemicals; retail center; hospital, sports medicine center.

Humble (11,435) manufactures oil field equipment, gaskets; retail center; hospital.

Other towns include **Bunker Hill Village** (3,668), **Deer Park** (24,537) shipping, tourism, San Jacinto College Central, hospital; **Galena Park** (9,957), **Hedwig Village** (2,820), **Hilshire Village** (556), **Jersey Village** (5,143), **Hunters Creek Village** (4,523), **Jacinto City** (10,402), **Katy** (9,886, part Waller and Fort Bend), **La Porte** (23,851), **Morgan's Point** (557), **Missouri City** (31,054, part Fort Bend), **Piney Point Village** (3,250), **Shore Acres** (1,432), **South Houston** (14,525), **Southside Place** (1,560), **Spring Valley** (3,179), **Stafford** (5,723, mostly Fort Bend), **Waller** (1,750, mostly Waller), **West University Place** (12,965), **Friendswood** (4,305, in Harris County) and **Pearland** (15,688). (See also information on Fort Bend, Montgomery, Waller and Liberty counties; also see Galveston County.)

Harrison

LOCATION: Northeast (H-21).

HISTORY: Created, 1839, from Shelby County; organized, 1842; named for eloquent advocate of Texas Revolution, **Jonas Harrison.**

Cong. Dist.	1	U.S. Jud. Dist.	E-MI.
St. Sen. Dist.	1	Ct. Appeals	6
St. Rep. Dist.	9	Admin. Jud. Dist.	1
St. Dist. Cts.	71		

PHYSICAL FEATURES: Hilly, rolling; over half forested; Sabine River; **Caddo Lake.**

1985 Pop.	57,900	Tax Ratio	0.88
Area (sq. mi.)	908	Oil value	$4,196,759
Altitude (ft.)	168-417	No. employed	17,648
Ann. rainfall (in.)	46.19	Avg. weekly wage	$373.41
Jan. temp. min.	37	Annual wages	$342,683,792
July temp. max.	95	1983 PCI	$7,702
Growing season (da.)	245	Buying pwr.	$598,044,000
Voters reg.	30,617	Tax value	$2,795,328,276
Businesses	1,041	Fed. expd.	$134,166,000

VITAL STATISTICS 1985: Births, 855; Deaths, 580; Marriages, 1,589; Divorces, 320.

RECREATION: Fishing, other water activities; hunting; many plantation homes, many historic sites; Stagecoach Days in May; Old Courthouse Museum; Old World Store; **Caddo Lake and State Park, Lake O' The Pines,** Pirkey Lake.

MINERALS: Production of oil, gas, coal, clays, sand and gravel.

AGRICULTURE: About $18 million average annual

income, 90% from cattle, hogs, poultry; crops include wheat, oats, grains, corn, hay; timber.

BUSINESS: Oil, gas processing; lumbering; pottery manufacturing; varied manufacturing.

MARSHALL (24,954) county seat; petroleum, lumber processing; chemicals, steel products; tile, pottery, aluminum products; plants make a range of products; civic center; **Wiley College; East Texas Baptist University;** historic sites; hospital, nursing home.

Other towns include **Hallsville** (2,096) power plant, **Longview** (73,263, mostly Gregg County), **Nesbitt** (141), **Scottsville** (327), **Uncertain** (189) and **Waskom** (2,182).

Hartley

LOCATION: Borders New Mexico (B-8).

HISTORY: Created, 1876, from Bexar, Young Districts; organized, 1891; named for Texas pioneers, **O. C.** and **R. K. Hartley.**

Cong. Dist.	13	U.S. Jud. Dist.	N-Am.
St. Sen. Dist.	31	Ct. Appeals	7
St. Rep. Dist.	88	Admin. Jud. Dist.	9
St. Dist. Cts.	69		

PHYSICAL FEATURES: Level; drains to playas, Canadian River, tributaries; sandy, loam, chocolate soils; **Lake Rita Blanca.**

RECREATION: Lake Rita Blanca activities; ranch museum; local events; XIT Rodeo and Reunion at Dalhart.

MINERALS: Natural gas.

1985 Pop.	3,500	Tax Ratio	0.71
Area (sq. mi.)	1,462	Oil value	$5,431,017
Altitude (ft.)	3,439-4,397	No. employed	455
Ann. rainfall (in.)	18.00	Avg. weekly wage	$283.49
Jan. temp. min.	20	Annual wages	$6,707,408
July temp. max.	92	1983 PCI	$10,000
Growing season (da.)	180	Buying pwr.	$46,225,000
Voters reg.	2,236	Tax value	$194,226,442
Businesses	56	Fed. expd.	$9,800,000

VITAL STATISTICS 1985: Births, 45; Deaths, 31; Marriages, 33; Divorces, 16.

AGRICULTURE: About $81 million average annual income from sorghums, wheat, corn; cattle; about 100,000 acres irrigated.

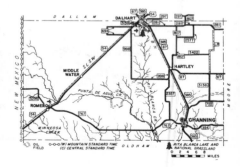

BUSINESS: Economy based on agriculture, gas production; varied manufacturing.

CHANNING (280) county seat.

Dalhart (6,930, in Dallam and Hartley counties) has feedlots, feed and meat processing plants, other industries.

Haskell

LOCATION: West central (G-12).

HISTORY: Created, 1858, from Milam, Fannin counties; re-created, 1876; organized, 1885; named for Goliad martyr, **C. R. Haskell.**

Cong. Dist.	17	U.S. Jud. Dist.	N-Ab.
St. Sen. Dist.	30	Ct. Appeals	11
St. Rep. Dist.	64	Admin. Jud. Dist.	7
St. Dist. Cts.	39		

PHYSICAL FEATURES: Rolling; broken areas; drained by Brazos tributaries; **Lake Stamford**; sandy loam, gray, black soils.

RECREATION: Lake Stamford activities; local events; hunting.

MINERALS: Production of oil and gas.

1985 Pop.	7,300	Tax Ratio	0.95
Area (sq. mi.)	901	Oil value	$4,295,871
Altitude (ft.)	1,416-1,681	No. employed	1,483
Ann. rainfall (in.)	24.14	Avg. weekly wage	$246.50
Jan. temp. min.	30	Annual wages	$19,009,164
July temp. max.	97	1983 PCI	$7,233
Growing season (da.)	232	Buying pwr.	$58,610,000
Voters reg.	4,656	Tax value	$434,960,234
Businesses	200	Fed. expd.	$25,978,000

VITAL STATISTICS 1985: Births, 116; Deaths, 115; Marriages, 61; Divorces, 26.

AGRICULTURE: About $25 million average annual income, 85% from cotton, grains; remainder from beef cattle, hogs; about 20,000 acres irrigated.

BUSINESS: Agribusinesses, oil field operations.

HASKELL (3,831) county seat; farm trading center. **O'Brien** (184), **Rochester** (459), **Rule** (1,016) **Stamford** (4,525, mostly Jones County) and **Weinert** (232) other principal towns.

Hays

LOCATION: South central (M-15).
HISTORY: Created 1843 from Travis County; orga-

nized same year; named for **Capt. Jack Hays,** famous Texas Ranger.

Cong. Dist.	10	U.S. Jud. Dist.	W-An.
St. Sen. Dist.	14	Ct. Appeals	3
St. Rep. Dist.	47	Admin. Jud. Dist.	3
St. Dist. Cts.	22, 207, 274		

PHYSICAL FEATURES: Partly hilly, partly Blackland.

RECREATION: Major tourist center; retirement area; fine fishing, hunting; **Aquarena; Pioneer Town; Wonder World;** university cultural, athletic events, **Cypress Creek** and **Blanco River** resorts and recreation, guest ranches; antique shops at Wimberley; "Chilympiad" men's cookoff in September.

MINERALS: Sand and gravel, cement produced.

1985 Pop.	56,000	Tax Ratio	0.94
Area (sq. mi.)	678	Oil value	0
Altitude (ft.)	582-1,501	No. employed	16,049
Ann. rainfall (in.)	33.75	Avg. weekly wage	$282.04
Jan. temp. min.	40	Annual wages	$235,382,688
July temp. max.	96	1983 PCI	$7,414
Growing season (da.)	254	Buying pwr.	$489,204,000
Voters reg.	27,289	Tax value	$3,520,824,560
Businesses	1,131	Fed. expd.	$91,710,000

VITAL STATISTICS 1985: Births, 953; Deaths, 279; Marriages, 628; Divorces, 254.

AGRICULTURE: About $13 million average annual income, 85% from cattle; crops include sorghums, hay, wheat, corn, cotton, some peaches and cedar posts.

BUSINESS: Tourism, education, retirement village, some manufacturing; county part of Austin SMSA.

SAN MARCOS (25,286) county seat; recreational-educational center; **Southwest Texas State University, San Marcos Baptist Academy, Gary Job Corps Training Center; Scheib Center** for mentally handicapped; **Aquarena, Wonder World;** varied manufacturing, printing and distribution center; hospital. "Chilympiad" and "Cinco de Mayo" cookoffs.

Wimberley (est. 3,065) tourism, retirement area; antique shops; cement plant; "First Saturday" market days April-November, Hillaceous 10,000 Run in April. Other towns include **Buda** (954), **Hays** (438), **Kyle** (3,033), **Dripping Springs** (779), **Mountain City** (350), **Woodcreek** (399).

Hemphill

LOCATION: Eastern Panhandle (B-11).

HISTORY: Created from Bexar, Young Districts, 1876; organized 1887; named for Republic of Texas Justice **John Hemphill.**

Cong. Dist.	13	U.S. Jud. Dist.	N-Am.
St. Sen. Dist.	31	Ct. Appeals	7
St. Rep. Dist.	88	Admin. Jud. Dist.	9
St. Dist. Cts.	31		

PHYSICAL FEATURES: Sloping surface, broken by Canadian, Washita Rivers, Lake Marvin; sandy, red, dark soils.

RECREATION: Lake Marvin activities; fall foliage tours; hunting, fishing; **Buffalo Wallow Indian Battleground, Gene Howe Wildlife Management Area,** golf course.

MINERALS: Production of oil and gas.

1985 Pop.	5,500	Tax Ratio	0.97
Area (sq. mi.)	903	Oil value	$3,460,935
Altitude (ft.)	2,185-2,843	No. employed	1,305
Ann. rainfall (in.)	20.50	Avg. weekly wage	$348.14
Jan. temp. min.	23	Annual wages	$23,624,968
July temp. max.	95	1983 PCI	$8,796
Growing season (da.)	204	Buying pwr.	$59,171,000
Voters reg.	2,870	Tax value	$1,056,298,328
Businesses	173	Fed. expd.	$6,338,000

VITAL STATISTICS 1985: Births, 93; Deaths, 38; Marriages, 69; Divorces, 28.

AGRICULTURE: More than 85% of $21 million average farm income from beef and stocker cattle, hogs; wheat, hay, sorghums principal crops.

BUSINESS: Economy based on petroleum production and refining, livestock production.

CANADIAN (4,098) county seat; oil and gas production; feedlot; hospital, nursing home; golf course.

Henderson

LOCATION: East (I-19).

HISTORY: Created and organized, 1846, from Houston, Nacogdoches counties; named for **Gov. J. Pinckney Henderson.**

Cong. Dist.	1	U.S. Jud. Dist.	E-Ty.
St. Sen. Dist.	9	Ct. Appeals	12
St. Rep. Dist.	12	Admin. Jud. Dist.	1
St. Dist. Cts.	3, 173		

PHYSICAL FEATURES: Hilly, rolling; one-third forested; bounded by Neches, Trinity Rivers; sandy, loam, clay soils; commercial timber; **Cedar Creek,** other lakes.

RECREATION: Cedar Creek Reservoir, Lake Palestine, Lake Athens, other public, private lakes; hunting, fishing; annual Black-eyed Pea Jamboree in July, fiddlers' reunion in May.

MINERALS: Production of oil, gas, clays, lignite, sulphur, sand and gravel.

1985 Pop.	52,100	Tax Ratio	0.94
Area (sq. mi.)	888	Oil value	$36,085,460
Altitude (ft.)	256-763	No. employed	10,071
Ann. rainfall (in.)	40.40	Avg. weekly wage	$286.45
Jan. temp. min.	37	Annual wages	$150,011,664
July temp. max.	95	1983 PCI	$8,136
Growing season (da.)	260	Buying pwr.	$608,514,000
Voters reg.	28,541	Tax value	$2,652,092,360
Businesses	913	Fed. expd.	$85,824,000

VITAL STATISTICS 1985: Births, 690; Deaths, 562; Marriages, 662; Divorces, 133.

AGRICULTURE: About 85% of almost $48 million income from cattle, hogs, horses, poultry; crops include grain, hay, fruits, vegetables, melons, nursery crops; hardwood timber marketed.

BUSINESS: Varied manufacturing; agribusinesses; minerals; recreation.

ATHENS (10,899) county seat; plants make radio-TV combinations, mobile homes, clothing, brick, clay products, medical and other products; **Trinity Valley Community College;** hospital.

Trinidad (1,316) has methane, power plants. **Mala-**

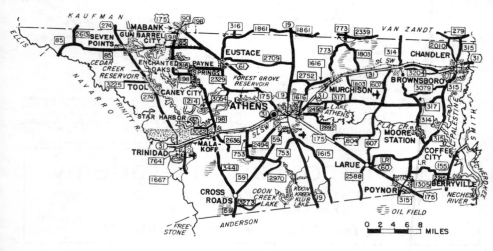

koff (2,193) has brick factory, tourism; lignite festival in October. **Seven Points** (925) center of lake activity. Other towns include **Chandler** (1,679), **Eustace** (652) gas producing plant, **Murchison** (639), **Tool** (1,838), **Berryville** (740), **Brownsboro** (697), **Caney City** (372), **Coffee City** (295), **Enchanted Oaks** (234), **Gun Barrel City** (2,816), **Moore Station** (400), **Payne Springs** (590), **Poynor** (259) and **Star Harbor** (361).

Hidalgo

LOCATION: Extreme south (U-15).
HISTORY: Settled early by Spaniards; created, organized, 1852, from Cameron, Starr Counties; named for Mexican leader, **Miguel Hidalgo y Costillo.**

Cong. Dist.	15
St. Sen. Dist.	20, 27
St. Rep. Dist	40-42, 206,275,332
St. Dist. Cts.	92, 93, 139,
U.S. Jud. Dist.	S-Br.
Ct. Appeals	13
Admin. Jud. Dist.	5

PHYSICAL FEATURES: Rich alluvial soils along Rio Grande; sandy, loam soils in north; semitropical vegetation.

RECREATION: Winter resort, retirement area; fishing, hunting; gateway to Mexico; historical sites; live steam museum at Alamo, Weslaso Bicultural Museum, other museums; many attractions; Rio Grande Valley livestock show at Mercedes; South Texas Lamb and Sheep show at Donna, Citrus Fiesta at Mission; Fiesta Hidalgo in March and annual Spring Arts and Plant Sale in April at Edinburg; consult chambers of commerce for special events.

MINERALS: Production of oil, gas, sand and gravel, stone.

1985 Pop.	352,200	Tax Ratio	0.88
Area (sq. mi.)	1,569	Oil value	$2,632,264
Altitude (ft.)	28-325	No. employed	83,834
Ann. rainfall (in.)	19.90	Avg. weekly wage	$255.85
Jan. temp. min.	49	Ann. wages	$1,115,363,612
July temp. max.	97	1983 PCI	$5,001
Growing season (da.)	327	Buying pwr.	$2,156,484,000
Voters reg.	134,756	Tax value	$7,181,050,782
Businesses	5,442	Fed. expd.	$622,201,000

VITAL STATISTICS 1985: Births, 7,725; Deaths, 1,848; Marriages, 3,739; Divorces, 95.

AGRICULTURE: $255 million average annual income makes county a leader in farm product sales; 90% of farm cash receipts from crops, principally from cotton, grain, vegetables, citrus, sugar cane; livestock includes cattle; 340,000 acres irrigated.

BUSINESS: Food processing, shipping; other agribusinesses; tourism; mineral operations; diversified metro area.

EDINBURG (30,031) county seat; vegetable processors, packers; agribusinesses; petroleum operations; clothing; tourist center; **Pan American University;** planetarium; hospitals; South Texas High School for special education, **Tropical Texas Center for Mental Health-Mental Retardation;** museum, fiestas.

McAllen (77,062) is a popular tourist center and has numerous agribusinesses; petroleum processing, plants make rubber products, medical equipment, hospital furniture, electronics, food equipment, apparel, other products; food processing, packing and shipping; trade center; major port of entry into Mexico; foreign trade zone.

Pharr (24,151) is an agribusiness, trucking and trading center; hospital.

Mission (28,618) is center for Valley citrus industry; candle manufacturer; Screwworm Eradication Center; fiberglass auto parts; agribusiness, tourism center.

Weslaco (22,683) is a food processing center; numerous other agribusinesses; clothing manufacturing; steel fabricator; tourist center; bicultural museum; citrus and vegetable research; hospital, nursing home; sugar cane festival in February.

Donna (11,386) agribusiness center; canning plants; furniture factory; tourism. Numerous other trading centers include **Alamo (8,257), Edcouch (3,550), Elsa (5,554), Hidalgo (2,728), La Joya (3,019), La Villa (1,665), Mercedes (13,267), Palmhurst (426), Palmview (805), Alton (3,726), San Juan (9,318)** and **Progreso Lakes (219).**

Hill

LOCATION: Central (I-16).
HISTORY: Created from Navarro County, organized, 1853; named for **G. W. Hill,** Republic of Texas official.

Cong. Dist. 6	U.S. Jud. Dist. . . . . W-Wa.
St. Sen. Dist. 9	Ct. Appeals 10
St. Rep. Dist. 57	Admin. Jud. Dist. 3
St. Dist. Cts. 66	

PHYSICAL FEATURES: Level to rolling; Blackland soils, some sandy loams; drains to Brazos; Lake Whitney, Navarro Mills Reservoir.

RECREATION: Lake Whitney, Aquilla Lake, Navarro Mills Lake activities; excursion boat on Lake Whitney; **Hill College; Confederate Museum,** historic structures; art festival in June; motorcycle track, varied activities.

MINERALS: Limestone, gas, oil.

1985 Pop.	27,400
Area (sq. mi.)	968
Altitude (ft.)	481-864
Ann. rainfall (in.) . .	34.47
Jan. temp. min.	36
July temp. max.	96
Growing season (da.)	247
Voters reg.	13,998
Businesses	596
Tax Ratio	0.85
Oil value	0
No. employed	5,536
Avg. weekly wage .	$278.55
Annual wages .	$80,187,084
1983 PCI	$7,430
Buying pwr. .	$257,491,000
Tax value . . .	$813,491,846
Fed. expd.	$71,930,000

VITAL STATISTICS 1985: Births, 387; Deaths, 416; Marriages, 337; Divorces, 133.

AGRICULTURE: About $60 million average annual income, 60% from crops including wheat, sorghum, hay, cotton, corn, peanuts; beef and dairy cattle, hogs, horses, poultry.

BUSINESS: Agribusinesses, varied manufacturing, tourism.

HILLSBORO (7,373) county seat; agricultural, manufacturing and retail center; **Hill College,** hospital, old courthouse and depot restoration; **Aquilla Lake.**

Whitney (1,887) is tourist center; varied manufacturing; hospital, nursing homes. Other towns include **Abbott (364), Aquilla (169), Blum (373), Bynum (298), Covington (273), Hubbard (1,782), Itasca (1,637), Malone (348), Mertens (118), Mount Calm (445), Penelope (222), Carl's Corner (230).**

Hockley

LOCATION: Northwest (F-7).
HISTORY: Created, 1876, from Bexar, Young Districts; organized 1921; named for Republic of Texas Secretary of War, **Gen. G. W. Hockley.**

Cong. Dist. 19	U.S. Jud. Dist. . . . . N-Lb.
St. Sen. Dist. 31	Ct. Appeals 7
St. Rep. Dist. 77	Admin. Jud. Dist. 9
St. Dist. Cts. 286	

MINERALS: Production of oil, gas, stone; one of leading oil-producing counties with more than 1 billion barrels produced.

1985 Pop. 25,400	Tax Ratio 0.95
Area (sq. mi.) 908	Oil value $417,410,689
Altitude (ft.) . . 3,388-3,633	No. employed 6,720
Ann. rainfall (in.) . . 16.60	Avg. weekly wage $322.22
Jan. temp. min. 24	Annual wages $112,597,848
July temp. max. 93	1983 PCI $7,546
Growing season (da.) 196	Buying pwr. . $222,216,000
Voters reg. 11,685	Tax value . $2,720,912,123
Businesses 541	Fed. expd. $53,374,000

VITAL STATISTICS 1985: Births, 563; Deaths, 183; Marriages, 268; Divorces, 161.

PHYSICAL FEATURES: Flat, draining to numerous playas, **Yellow House River, Lake;** loam, sandy loam soils.

RECREATION: Local events, Early Settlers' Day in July.

AGRICULTURE: More than 70% of $49 million income from crops, principally cotton, sorghums, wheat, soybeans, corn, hay, sunflowers; livestock includes cattle. 165,000 acres irrigated.

BUSINESS: Economy based on extensive oil, gas

FORT GRAHAM
LAKE WHITNEY STATE PARK
LAKE WHITNEY RECREATIONAL AREA
AQUILLA LAKE

0 2 4 6 8 MILES

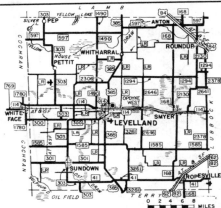

production and services, manufacturing, varied agribusinesses.

LEVELLAND (14,625) county seat; petroleum processing; oilfield equipment made; agribusinesses include vegetable oil mill, cattle feeding, other enterprises; cotton gins; **South Plains College**; hospital; art museum.

Other towns include **Anton** (1,198) with rabbit processing plant; **Sundown** (1,763), **Smyer** (487) and **Ropesville** (492).

Hood

LOCATION: Central (I-15).
HISTORY: Created, organized, 1866, from Johnson County; named for **Confederate Gen. John B. Hood.**

Cong. Dist.	6	U.S. Jud. Dist.	N-FW
St. Sen. Dist.	22	Ct. Appeals	2
St. Rep. Dist.	64	Admin. Jud. Dist.	8
St. Dist. Cts.	355		

PHYSICAL FEATURES: Hilly; broken by Paluxy, Brazos Rivers; sandy, sandy loam soils.
RECREATION: Fishing; scenic areas; summer theater; Lake Granbury; **Acton State Park**; harvest of arts in October.

MINERALS: Gas, stone, oil.

1985 Pop.	25,600	Tax Ratio	0.84
Area (sq. mi.)	425	Oil value	0
Altitude (ft.)	722-1,230	No. employed	4,966
Ann. rainfall (in.)	31.78	Avg. weekly wage	$312.66
Jan. temp. min.	34	Annual wages	$80,739,176
July temp. max.	96	1983 PCI	$10,561
Growing season (da.)	232	Buying pwr.	$359,887,000
Voters reg.	12,664	Tax value	$964,171,060
Businesses	509	Fed. expd.	$48,897,000

VITAL STATISTICS 1985: Births, 349; Deaths, 215; Marriages, 367; Divorces, 146.
AGRICULTURE: About $15 million average annual

income, 60% from beef cattle; crops include peanuts, pecans, hay; 3,000 acres irrigated.
BUSINESS: Agribusinesses; tourism, gas production.
GRANBURY (4,673) county seat; nuclear power plant; agribusinesses; tourism; historic buildings; hospital, nursing homes. Other towns are **Lipan** (512), **Tolar** (459), **Cresson** and **Acton.**

Hopkins

LOCATION: Northeast (G-19).
HISTORY: Created, organized, 1846, from Lamar, Nacogdoches counties; named for the pioneer **Hopkins Family.**

Cong. Dist.	1	U.S. Jud. Dist.	E-Ps.
St. Sen. Dist.	1	Ct. Appeals	6, 12
St. Rep. Dist.	2	Admin. Jud. Dist.	1
St. Dist. Cts.	8, 62		

PHYSICAL FEATURES: Drains northward to S. Sulphur River; light, sandy to heavier black soils; varied timber, including pines.
RECREATION: Fishing, hunting; **Lake Sulphur Springs** activities; museum; indoor rodeo, dairy festival in May.
MINERALS: Production of oil, gas and lignite.

1985 Pop.	28,700	Tax Ratio	1.01
Area (sq. mi.)	789	Oil value	$7,955,518
Altitude (ft.)	420-649	No. employed	8,185
Ann. rainfall (in.)	45.29	Avg. weekly wage	$303.95
Jan. temp. min.	34	Annual wages	$129,370,144
July temp. max.	94	1983 PCI	$8,020
Growing season (da.)	238	Buying pwr.	$263,883,000
Voters reg.	13,232	Tax value	$1,223,184,210
Businesses	610	Fed. expd.	$60,041,000

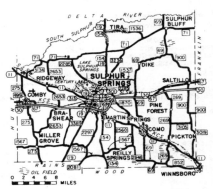

VITAL STATISTICS 1985: Births, 488; Deaths, 343; Marriages, 336; Divorces, 205.
AGRICULTURE: Leading dairy county in Texas and Southwest; about 465 Grade A dairies; also leader in beef cattle production; 95% of $135 million average annual farm income from cattle, hogs; hay, grains, soybeans leading crops; timber.
BUSINESS: Dairies, large milk processing plants; agribusinesses; varied manufacturing.
SULPHUR SPRINGS (13,817) county seat; milk plants; factories make candy, clothing, brick, valves, doors, other products; trading center; hospital, nursing homes; heritage museum. Other towns are **Como** (625), **Cumby** (691) and **Tira** (273).

Houston

LOCATION: East (K-19).
HISTORY: Created, organized, 1837 from Nacogdoches County, by Republic of Texas; named for **Sam Houston.**

Cong. Dist.	2	U.S. Jud. Dist.	E-Ty.
St. Sen. Dist.	5	Ct. Appeals	12
St. Rep. Dist.	15	Admin. Jud. Dist.	1
St. Dist. Cts.	3, 349		

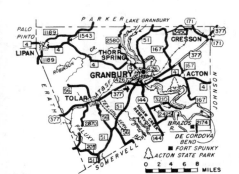

Houston County (Cont'd.)

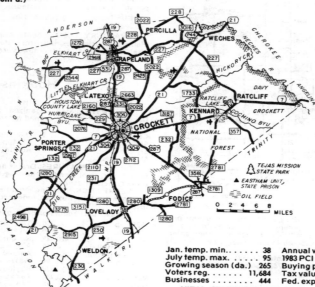

Jan. temp. min. 38	Annual wages $147,135,708
July temp. max. 95	1983 PCI $6,013
Growing season (da.) 265	Buying pwr. . $216,424,000
Voters reg. 11,684	Tax value . . $1,066,008,012
Businesses 444	Fed. expd. $50,134,000

VITAL STATISTICS 1985: Births, 264; Deaths, 286; Marriages, 234; Divorces, 43.

PHYSICAL FEATURES: Rolling, draining to Neches, Trinity Rivers; over half forested; commercial timber production.

RECREATION: Fishing, hunting; **Davy Crockett National Forest; Tejas Mission State Park;** 75 historical markers; **Houston County Lake;** many local events.

MINERALS: Production of oil, gas, sand and gravel.

AGRICULTURE: About $47 million average annual income, 80% from cattle, poultry; crops include cotton, peanuts, coastal hay; also timber sales.

BUSINESS: Economy based on livestock, timber, manufacturing, tourism.

CROCKETT (7,550) county seat; plants make concrete, wood products, steel joists, plastics, woodworks, furniture, clothing, mobile homes, process foods; hospitals, nursing homes; **Crockett State School;** 5th oldest Texas town; many historic sites. **Grapeland** (1,770), **Kennard** (490), **Latexo** (355), **Lovelady** (697) other principal towns.

1985 Pop. 22,700	Tax Ratio 0.93
Area (sq. mi.) 1,234	Oil value $6,587,511
Altitude (ft.) 167-552	No. employed 7,743
Ann. rainfall (in.) . . 41.72	Avg. weekly wage $365.43

Howard

LOCATION: West (I-9).

HISTORY: Named for **V. E. Howard,** Texas legislator; created, 1876, from Bexar, Young Districts; organized, 1882.

Cong. Dist. 17	U.S. Jud. Dist. . . . . N-Ab.
St. Sen. Dist. 28	Ct. Appeals 11
St. Rep. Dist. 69	Admin. Jud. Dist. 7
St. Dist. Cts. 118	

PHYSICAL FEATURES: On southern edge Llano Estacado; sandy, sandy loam soils.

RECREATION: Big Spring State Park; campground in **Comanche Trail Park;** several small parks; **Moss Creek Reservoir;** various other area lakes; museum; historical sites; county fair.

MINERALS: Production of oil, gas, sand, gravel and stone.

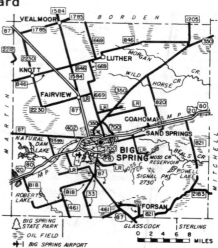

1985 Pop. 36,300	Tax Ratio 0.87
Area (sq. mi.) 901	Oil value $97,296,740
Altitude (ft.) . . 2,271-2,776	No. employed 10,589
Ann. rainfall (in.) . . 15.88	Avg. weekly wage $318.49
Jan. temp. min. 30	Annual wages $175,369,740
July temp. max. 95	1983 PCI $8,786
Growing season (da.) 217	Buying pwr. . $353,739,000
Voters reg. 16,129	Tax value . . $1,581,837,128
Businesses 935	Fed. expd. . . . $88,705,000

VITAL STATISTICS 1985: Births, 607; Deaths, 310; Marriages, 414; Divorces, 67.

AGRICULTURE: About $28 million average annual income, 90% from crops, principally cotton, wheat and sorghum; beef cattle; some 4,000 acres of irrigated land.

BUSINESS: Oil, gas operations; agribusinesses; varied manufacturing, including clothing.

BIG SPRING (27,459) county seat; plants make petrochemicals, carbon black, fiberglass pipe, plastics,

teaching aids, clothing; medical center with 6 hospitals; **Howard College;** school for the deaf; federal prison unit.

Other principal towns are **Coahoma** (1,168) a farming center; **Forsan** (284).

Hudspeth

LOCATION: Far west (K-2).

HISTORY: Named for Texas political leader, **Claude B. Hudspeth**; created, organized, 1917, from El Paso County.

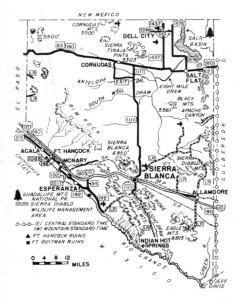

Cong. Dist.	16	U.S. Jud. Dist.	W-Pe.
St. Sen. Dist.	25	Ct. Appeals	8
St. Rep. Dist.	69	Admin. Jud. Dist.	6
St. Dist. Cts.	34,205,210		

PHYSICAL FEATURES: Plateau, basin terrain, draining to salt lakes, Rio Grande; mostly rocky, alkaline, clay soils, except alluvial along Rio Grande; desert, mountain vegetation.

RECREATION: Part of **Guadalupe Mountains National Park** containing unique plant life, canyons; scenic drives; fort ruins; hot springs; salt basin; white sands; hunting; many local events.

MINERALS: Talc, stone, gypsum produced.

1985 Pop.	2,600	Tax Ratio	0.94
Area (sq. mi.)	4,566	Oil value	0
Altitude (ft.)	3,492-7,484	No. employed	728
Ann. rainfall (in.)	7.86	Avg. weekly wage	$267.72
Jan. temp. min.	27	Annual wages	$10,135,144
July temp. max.	93	1983 PCI	$5,226
Growing season (da.)	231	Buying pwr.	$17,370,000
Voters reg.	1,198	Tax value	$308,567,397
Businesses	37	Fed. expd.	$7,000,000

VITAL STATISTICS 1985: Births, 45; Deaths, 14; Marriages, 32; Divorces, 4.

AGRICULTURE: About $20 million average annual income from cotton, alfalfa, vegetables, pecans; 25,000 acres irrigated; feed lot; cattle, hogs.

BUSINESS: Agribusiness, mining, tourism, hunting leases.

SIERRA BLANCA (est. 700) county seat; ranching center; tourist stop on interstate highway; land development. **Dell City** (548) feed lots; clinic, trading center.

Hunt

LOCATION: North (G-18).

HISTORY: Named for **Memucan Hunt**, Republic of Texas Secretary of Navy; created, organized, 1846, from Fannin, Nacogdoches counties.

Cong. Dist.	1, 4	U.S. Jud. Dist.	N-DI.
St. Sen. Dist.	2	Ct. Appeals	5, 6
St. Rep. Dist.	3	Admin. Jud. Dist.	1
St. Dist. Cts.	196, 354		

PHYSICAL FEATURES: Mostly heavy Blackland soil, some loam, sandy loams; level to rolling; Sabine, Sulphur Rivers; **Lake Tawakoni.**

RECREATION: Lake Tawakoni; **East Texas State University** events; local events; county fair.

MINERALS: Gas, oil, sand and gravel.

AGRICULTURE: About $30 million average annual income, 60% from cattle, horses, dairy products; hay, cotton, sorghums, wheat, oats; some timber.

1985 Pop.	65,200	Tax Ratio	0.96
Area (sq. mi.)	840	Oil value	0
Altitude (ft.)	688-1,553	No. employed	19,832
Ann. rainfall (in.)	43.08	Avg. weekly wage	$343.95
Jan. temp. min.	34	Annual wages	$354,705,704
July temp. max.	94	1983 PCI	$8,306
Growing season (da.)	237	Buying pwr.	$685,531,000
Voters reg.	29,132	Tax value	$1,795,000,853
Businesses	1,279	Fed. expd.	$201,798,000

VITAL STATISTICS 1985: Births, 983; Deaths, 603; Marriages, 707; Divorces, 438.

BUSINESS: Agribusinesses, education, varied manufacturing; many residents employed in Dallas metro area.

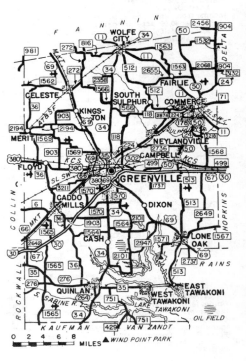

GREENVILLE (24,213) county seat; plants process foods, make electronic parts, clothing, plastics, drill bits, aircraft modification; hospital, nursing homes.

Commerce (7,716) East Texas State University major economic factor; plants make wood products, mobile homes, medical products; hospital, nursing homes. Other towns include **Caddo Mills** (1,302), **Campbell** (616), **Celeste** (863), **Lone Oak** (630), **Neylandville** (196), **Quinlan** (1,602), **West Tawakoni** (1,210) and **Wolfe City** (1,643) cottonseed milling, printing, sweaters and cheerleading supplies.

Hutchinson

LOCATION: North Panhandle (B-9).

HISTORY: Created, 1876, from Bexar Territory; organized 1901; named for pioneer jurist, **Anderson Hutchinson.**

Cong. Dist.	13	U.S. Jud. Dist.	N-Am.
St. Sen. Dist.	31	Ct. Appeals	7
St. Rep. Dist.	88	Admin. Jud. Dist.	9
St. Dist. Cts.	84, 316		

PHYSICAL FEATURES: Plain, broken by Canadian River and tributaries, **Lake Meredith;** many fertile valleys along streams.

RECREATION: Lake Meredith activities; fishing, camping, boating; **Alibates Flint Quarries** (in nearby Potter County); **Adobe Walls,** historic Indian battle site, ''world's largest'' fish fry in June.

MINERALS: Production of gas, oil, salt, sand and gravel.

1985 Pop.	28,100	Tax Ratio	0.95
Area (sq. mi.)	871	Oil value	$8,861,784
Altitude (ft.)	2,736-3,313	No. employed	9,169
Ann. rainfall (in.)	19.91	Avg. weekly wage	$406.04
Jan. temp. min.	22	Annual wages	$193,595,800
July temp. max.	93	1983 PCI	$9,934
Growing season (da.)	187	Buying pwr.	$376,438,000
Voters reg.	14,254	Tax value	$1,735,171,382
Businesses	718	Fed. expd.	$52,755,000

VITAL STATISTICS 1985: Births, 477; Deaths, 237; Marriages, 289; Divorces, 185.

AGRICULTURE: About $13 million average annual income from wheat, corn, sorghums; beef and stocker cattle; over 40,000 acres irrigated.

BUSINESS: Oil, gas, petrochemicals; agribusiness; varied manufacturing; tourism.

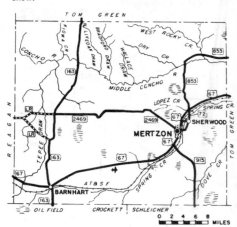

STINNETT (2,596) county seat; petroleum, gas refining, farm center. **Borger** (17,236), petroleum operating center; petrochemical plants; (Phillips Petroleum Co. operates world's largest inland refinery); varied manufacturing, tourism; machine, welding shops; **Frank Phillips College;** hospital, nursing homes.

Other towns are **Fritch** (2,912 part Moore) and **Sanford** (314).

Irion

LOCATION: Southwest (K-10).

HISTORY: Named for Republic of Texas leader, **R. A. Irion;** created, organized, 1889, from Tom Green County.

Cong. Dist.	21	U.S. Jud. Dist.	N-SAng.
St. Sen. Dist.	25	Ct. Appeals	3
St. Rep. Dist.	67	Admin. Jud. Dist.	7
St. Dist. Cts.	51		

PHYSICAL FEATURES: Hilly, broken by Middle Concho, tributaries; clay, sandy soils.

RECREATION: Hunting; historic sites; old Sherwood courthouse established in 1860; county fair, horse show.

MINERALS: Production of oil, gas.

1985 Pop.	2,000	Tax Ratio	0.75
Area (sq. mi.)	1,052	Oil value	$9,721,801
Altitude (ft.)	2,084-2,725	No. employed	402
Ann. rainfall (in.)	21.33	Avg. weekly wage	$373.30
Jan. temp. min.	32	Annual wages	$7,803,512
July temp. max.	96	1983 PCI	$8,906
Growing season (da.)	232	Buying pwr.	$14,776,000
Voters reg.	1,065	Tax value	$425,963,807
Businesses	40	Fed. expd.	$3,317,000

VITAL STATISTICS 1985: Births, 37; Deaths, 13; Marriages, 17; Divorces, 11.

AGRICULTURE: About $8 million annual average income, about 95% from cattle, sheep, goats; crops include sorghums, wheat, cotton.

BUSINESS: Ranching; oil, gas production.

MERTZON (837) county seat; ranching and wool warehouse center.

Jack

LOCATION: North (G-14).

HISTORY: Named for brothers, **P.C.** and **W. H. Jack,** leaders in Texas' independence effort; created 1856, from Cooke County; organized, 1857.

Cong. Dist.	17	U.S. Jud. Dist.	N-FW
St. Sen. Dist.	30	Ct. Appeals	2
St. Rep. Dist.	80	Admin. Jud. Dist.	8
St. Dist. Cts.	271		

PHYSICAL FEATURES: Rolling, broken by West Fork of the Trinity, other streams; sandy, dark brown, loam soils; **Lake Bridgeport; Lake Jacksboro.**

RECREATION: Lake activities; **Fort Richardson State Park,** other historic sites; rattlesnake hunt, rodeo, golf tournaments; Weekend in Old Mesquiteville Festival in June.

MINERALS: Production of oil, gas.

1985 Pop.	7,700	Tax Ratio	0.96
Area (sq. mi.)	920	Oil value	$6,031,799
Altitude (ft.)	976-1,297	No. employed	1,683
Ann. rainfall (in.)	29.78	Avg. weekly wage	$306.24
Jan. temp. min.	32	Annual wages	$26,801,320
July temp. max.	97	1983 PCI	$8,797
Growing season (da.)	218	Buying pwr.	$78,020,000
Voters reg.	4,117	Tax value	$696,921,358
Businesses	202	Fed. expd.	$15,523,000

VITAL STATISTICS 1985: Births, 114; Deaths, 103; Marriages, 93; Divorces, 49.

AGRICULTURE: About $12 million average annual income, over 90% from beef cattle; crops include wheat, oats, hay; firewood.

BUSINESS: Economy based on petroleum production, oil field services, livestock, manufacturing, tourism and recreation.

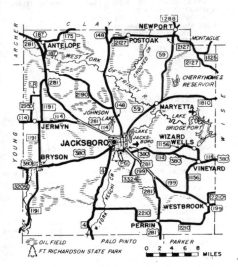

JACKSBORO (3,970) county seat; agribusinesses; oil well servicing, supplies; hospital, nursing home; airport.

Bryson (690) other leading town.

Jackson

LOCATION: On coast (O-18).

HISTORY: Mexican municipality, created 1835, became original county next year; named for U.S. President Andrew Jackson.

Cong. Dist.	14	U.S. Jud. Dist.	S-Va.
St. Sen. Dist.	18	Ct. Appeals	13
St. Rep. Dist.	31	Admin. Jud. Dist.	4
St. Dist. Cts.	24, 135, 267		

PHYSICAL FEATURES: Loam, clay, black soils; drains to creek, rivers, bays; prairie and motts of trees.

RECREATION: Hunting, fishing; historic sites; Texana Museum; Lake Texana activities; county fair.

MINERALS: Production of oil, gas.

1985 Pop.	13,600
Area (sq. mi.)	844
Altitude (ft.)	11-109
Ann. rainfall (in.)	39.65
Jan. temp. min.	42
July temp. max.	94
Growing season (da.)	290
Voters reg.	7,251
Businesses	329

Tax Ratio	0.91
Oil value	$72,682,938
No. employed	3,015
Avg. weekly wage	$303.03
Annual wages	$47,509,832
1983 PCI	$7,769
Buying pwr.	$135,707,000
Tax value	$1,376,165,980
Fed. expd.	$34,663,000

VITAL STATISTICS 1985: Births, 211; Deaths, 150; Marriages, 131; Divorces, 44.

AGRICULTURE: About $50 million average annual income, 85% from rice, sorghums, corn, cotton, other crops; a leading rice county; 26,000 acres irrigated for rice; beef cattle.

BUSINESS: Petroleum production and operation; metal fabrication and tooling, sheet metal works, other manufacturing; agribusiness; lake recreation.

EDNA (5,771) county seat; oil industry and agribusiness center; hospitals, nursing homes. **Ganado** (1,751) and **La Ward** (204) are other principal towns.

Jasper

LOCATION: Southeast (L-22).

HISTORY: Created, 1836, organized, 1837, from Mexican municipality; named for Sgt. William Jasper of U.S. Revolution.

1985 Pop.	32,400
Area (sq. mi.)	921
Altitude (ft.)	68-438
Ann. rainfall (in.)	51.03
Jan. temp. min.	40
July temp. max.	93
Growing season (da.)	229
Voters reg.	18,245
Businesses	647

Tax Ratio	0.87
Oil value	$837,089
No. employed	8,167
Avg. weekly wage	$325.09
Annual wages	$138,062,632
1983 PCI	$7,197
Buying pwr.	$329,179,000
Tax value	$1,305,715,780
Fed. expd.	$66,127,000

VITAL STATISTICS 1985: Births, 505; Deaths, 338; Marriages, 476; Divorces, 276.

BUSINESS: Economy based on timber industries, oil, tourism, fishing, agriculture.

Cong. Dist.	2	U.S. Jud. Dist.	E-Bt.
St. Sen. Dist.	3	Ct. Appeals	9
St. Rep. Dist.	20	Admin. Jud. Dist.	2
St. Dist. Cts.	1, 1A		

PHYSICAL FEATURES: Angelina and **Sabine National Forests; Sam Rayburn, Steinhagen Lakes; Neches River.**

RECREATION: Lake activities; hunting; **Martin Dies State Park;** azalea trail in spring; rodeo.

MINERALS: Oil, gas produced.

AGRICULTURE: $25 million average annual income, about 90% from cattle, hogs, poultry, horses; crops include vegetables, fruit, pecans, 87% of area forested, timber is major income producer with annual sale of $13 million.

JASPER (7,104) county seat; wood industries; plywood mill, sawmills, poultry processing plants, feed mills.

Other towns include **Buna, Browndell** (235), **Kirbyville** (2,036) lumber, livestock center; clinic, nursing home.

Jeff Davis

LOCATION: Southwest (I-5).

HISTORY: Named for **Jefferson Davis,** U.S. War Secretary, Confederate president; created, organized, 1887, from Presidio County.

PHYSICAL FEATURES: Highest average elevation in Texas, one mile or higher; peaks, canyons, plateaus; intermountain wash, clay, loam soils; cedars, oaks in highlands.

RECREATION: Scenic drives; hunting; **Fort Davis National Historic Site; Davis Mountains State Park; McDonald Observatory; Prude Ranch** summer camp.

MINERALS: Not significant.

Cong. Dist.	16	St. Dist. Cts.	83
St. Sen. Dist.	25	U.S. Jud. Dist.	W-Pe.
St. Rep. Dist.	69	Ct. Appeals	8
		Admin. Jud. Dist.	6

1985 Pop.	1,700	Tax Ratio	0.80
Area (sq. mi.)	2,258	Oil value	$11,960
Altitude (ft.)	3,871-8,378	Avg. weekly wage	$265.79
Ann. rainfall (in.)	18.74	Annual wages	$5,611,424
Jan. temp. min.	31	1983 PCI	$7,250
July temp. max.	82	Buying pwr.	$13,294,000
Growing season (da.)	209	Tax value	$146,014,390
Voters reg.	1,084	Fed. expend.	$3,960,000
Businesses	31		

VITAL STATISTICS 1985: Births, 20; Deaths, 11; Marriages, 23; Divorces, 2.

AGRICULTURE: Cattle yield $4.1 million; hunting leases significant; wine grapes, feed grains, alfalfa; about 3,000 acres irrigated.

BUSINESS: Ranching, tourism.

FORT DAVIS (est. 900) county seat; trade, scenic tourist center. **Valentine** (316) other town.

Jefferson

LOCATION: Southeast (M-22).

HISTORY: Created, 1836, from Mexican municipality; organized, 1837; named for **U.S. President Thomas Jefferson.**

Cong. Dist.	9	U.S. Jud. Dist.	E-Bt.
St. Sen. Dist.	4	Ct. Appeals	9
St. Rep. Dist.	20-23	Admin. Jud. Dist.	2
St. Dist. Cts.	58, 60, 136,		
	172, 252, 279, 317, Cr. 1		

PHYSICAL FEATURES: Grassy plain, with timber in northwest; beach sands, sandy loams, black clay soils; drains to Neches River, Gulf of Mexico.

MINERALS: Large producer of oil, gas, sulphur, salt, sand and gravel; **Spindletop,** first major Texas oil field; large petrochemical industry.

RECREATION: Beaches, fresh and saltwater fishing; duck, goose hunting; water activities; **Dick Dowling Monument and Park; Spindletop** site and boom town restoration; museum; saltwater lake; **Murphree Wildlife Refuge; Lamar University;** other events; historic sites; CavOILcade at Port Arthur, South Texas Fair, many festivals; **"Tex" Ritter** memorial and park at Nederland, also Dutch and French museums.

1985 Pop.	254,700	Tax Ratio	0.94
Area (sq. mi.)	937	Oil value	$26,509,680
Altitude (ft.)	3-42	No. employed	97,255
Ann. rainfall (in.)	55.07	Avg. weekly wage	$382.69
Jan. temp. min.	44	Ann. wages	$1,935,403,192
July temp. max.	91	1983 PCI	$9,713
Growing season (da.)	250	Buying pwr.	$3,096,535,000
Voters reg.	131,701	Tax value	$11,024,671,753
Businesses	6,172	Fed. expd.	$873,956,000

VITAL STATISTICS 1985: Births, 4,033; Deaths, 2,462; Marriages, 2,827; Divorces, 1,615.

AGRICULTURE: About $25 million average income, over 80% from crops, chiefly rice and soybeans; beef cattle; 33,000 acres irrigated, mostly rice; timber.

BUSINESS: Petrochemicals, other chemical plants; shipbuilding; steel mill; port activity; oil field supplies dominate economy.

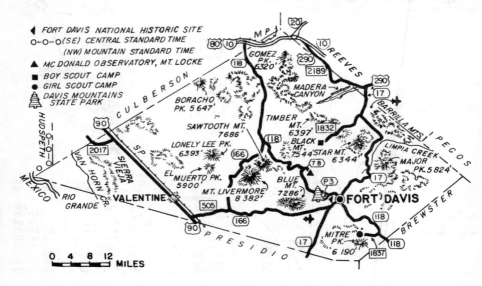

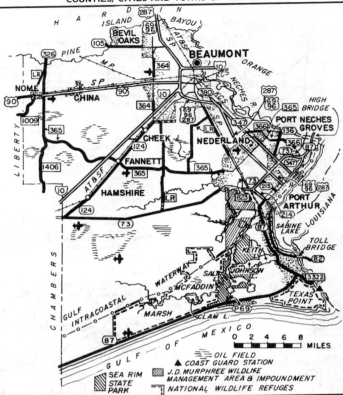

Legend:
- ▲ OIL FIELD
- COAST GUARD STATION
- J.D. MURPHREE WILDLIFE MANAGEMENT AREA & IMPOUNDMENT
- NATIONAL WILDLIFE REFUGES

BEAUMONT (123,356) county seat; varied chemical, petrochemical plants; oil refinery; shipbuilding; extensive port activities; rice milling center; steel mill; **Lamar University**; many hospitals, nursing homes; South Texas State Fair.

Port Arthur (64,092) center for oil, chemical activities; shipping, drydock; food processing; rice milling; tourism; **Lamar University** branch.

Nederland (17,005) oil and chemical plants; hospital. **Groves** (16,865) oil and chemical industry, engine service; hospital; library; tourism. Other towns include **Bevil Oaks** (1,481), **China** (1,397), **Nome** (610), **Port Neches** (14,333).

Jim Hogg

LOCATION: South (S-14).
HISTORY: Named for **Texas Gov. James Stephen Hogg;** created, organized, 1913, from Brooks, Duval counties.

Cong. Dist.	15	U.S. Jud. Dist.	S-La.
St. Sen. Dist.	21	Ct. Appeals	4
St. Rep. Dist.	44	Admin. Jud. Dist.	5
St. Dist. Cts.	229		

PHYSICAL FEATURES: Rolling plain, with heavy brush cover; white blow soil and sandy loam; parts hilly, broken.
RECREATION: Center of whitetail deer and bobwhite quail hunting; local events.
MINERALS: Oil, gas.

1985 Pop.	5,400	Tax Ratio	0.97
Area (sq. mi.)	1,136	Oil value	$2,938,246
Altitude (ft.)	249-742	No. employed	1,148
Ann. rainfall (in.)	20.78	Avg. weekly wage	$227.37
Jan. temp. min.	47	Annual wages	$13,573,272
July temp. max.	99	1983 PCI	$5,934
Growing season (da.)	303	Buying pwr.	$36,421,000
Voters reg.	4,002	Tax value	$496,781,760
Businesses	112	Fed. expd.	$10,050,000

VITAL STATISTICS 1985: Births, 123; Deaths, 35; Marriages, 58; Divorces, 0.
AGRICULTURE: More than $15 million average annual income, 80% from cattle ranching; sorghum principal crop; 2,000 acres irrigated.
BUSINESS: Oil, cattle operations.
HEBBRONVILLE (est. 4,050) county seat; center for ranching, oil field activities.

See Map on Page 202

Jim Wells

LOCATION: South (R-5).

Cong. Dist.	15	U.S. Jud. Dist.	S-CC
St. Sen. Dist.	20	Ct. Appeals	4
St. Rep. Dist.	44	Admin. Jud. Dist.	5
St. Dist. Cts.	79		

HISTORY: Created, 1911, from Nueces County; organized 1912; named for developer, **J. B. Wells Jr.**

PHYSICAL FEATURES: Level to rolling; sandy to dark soils; grassy, mesquite brush.
RECREATION: Hunting; fiestas, other local events, wildflower tour at Premont in March; oil and gas exposition in April.
MINERALS: Production of oil, gas, caliche.

1985 Pop.	40,300	Tax Ratio	0.91
Area (sq. mi.)	867	Oil value	$21,046,161
Altitude (ft.)	62-314	No. employed	9,989
Ann. rainfall (in.)	27.04	Avg. weekly wage	$273.19
Jan. temp. min.	47	Annual wages	$141,905,000
July temp. max.	97	1983 PCI	$6,806
Growing season (da.)	289	Buying pwr.	$292,119,000
Voters reg.	21,199	Tax value	$1,191,899,367
Businesses	944	Fed. expd.	$69,074,000

VITAL STATISTICS 1985: Births, 799; Deaths, 291; Marriages, 373; Divorces, 167.
AGRICULTURE: About $35 million average annual income from beef cattle; cotton, sorghums, wheat,

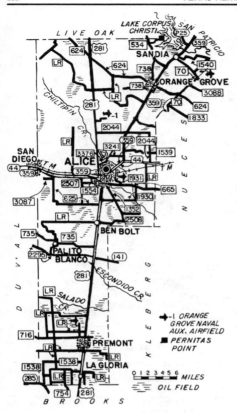

Jim Wells County (Cont'd.)

corn, vegetables, watermelons; estimated 5,000 acres irrigated.

BUSINESS: Oil, gas production, cotton and cattle dominate economy.

ALICE (22,273) county seat; oil field servicing center; agribusinesses; hospital, nursing home; Fiesta Bandana; **Bee County Junior College** extension.

Other towns include **Alice Southwest, Orange Grove** (1,536), **Premont** (3,149) hunting center, watermelon shipping, petroleum recycling plant; **San Diego** (5,695, part Duval).

Johnson

LOCATION: North (I-16).

HISTORY: Named for **Col. M. T. Johnson** of Mexican War, Confederacy; created, organized, 1854, out of Ellis, Hill, Navarro counties.

Cong. Dist. 6	U.S. Jud. Dist. . . . . N-DI.
St. Sen. Dist. 22	Ct. Appeals 10
St. Rep. Dist. 58	Admin. Jud. Dist. 3
St. Dist. Cts. 18, 249	

PHYSICAL FEATURES: Hilly, rolling, many soil types; Brazos, Trinity Rivers; **Lake Pat Cleburne.**

RECREATION: Excellent bird, deer hunting; water activities on **Lake Pat Cleburne, Lake Whitney** and at **Cleburne State Recreation Area;** museum; local events.

MINERALS: Limestone, sand, gravel.

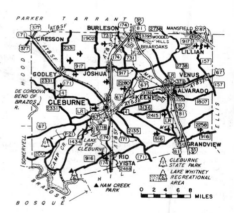

1985 Pop. 87,700	Tax Ratio 0.83
Area (sq. mi.) 731	Oil value 0
Altitude (ft.) . . . 651-1,065	No. employed 18,659
Ann. rainfall (in.) . . 33.04	Avg. weekly wage $288.03
Jan. temp. min. 35	Annual wages $279,474,200
July temp. max. 96	1983 PCI $9,098
Growing season (da.) 233	Buying pwr. . $989,141,000
Voters reg. 38,206	Tax value . . $2,512,138,830
Businesses 1,540	Fed. expd. . . . $133,751,000

VITAL STATISTICS 1985: Births, 1,407; Deaths, 735; Marriages, 1,094; Divorces, 270.

AGRICULTURE: A leading dairy county; 85% of an estimated $50 million annual income from cattle, horses, hogs and dairy products; crops include sorghums, cotton, peanuts, oats, wheat, hay, corn, truck crops, horticultural crops.

BUSINESS: Agribusinesses; railroad shops; manufacturing; distribution; lake activities; employment in Fort Worth and other parts of its metro area (see metro page).

CLEBURNE (21,413) county seat; dairy center; rail shipping terminal; railroad shops; varied manufacturing including wall components, agribusinesses; hospital.

Burleson (14,597, part Tarrant), light industry. Other towns include **Alvarado** (4,129), **Briaroaks** (628), **Godley** (654), **Grandview** (1,301), **Joshua** (2,349), **Keene** (3,094), **Mansfield** (10,733 mostly Tarrant), **Rio Vista** (657), **Venus** (950), **Wooded Hills** (266).

Jones

LOCATION: West Central (H-12).

HISTORY: Named for last Republic of Texas president, **Anson Jones**; created 1858, from Bexar, Bosque counties; re-created, 1876; organized, 1881.

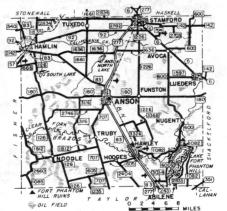

Cong. Dist. 17	U.S. Jud. Dist. ..... N-Ab.
St. Sen. Dist. 30	Ct. Appeals 11
St. Rep. Dist. 78	Admin. Jud. Dist. 7
St. Dist. Cts. 259	

PHYSICAL FEATURES: Level to rolling prairie; drained by Brazos River fork, tributaries; **Lake Stamford.**

RECREATION: Lake activities; **Ft. Phantom Hill** site; **Cowboys Christmas Ball; Cowboy Reunion** July 4th weekend; old courthouse, art show.

MINERALS: Oil, gas, sand and gravel, stone.

1985 Pop.	18,200	Tax Ratio	0.83
Area (sq. mi.)	931	Oil value	$3,997,222
Altitude (ft.) .. 1,560-1,855		No. employed	3,816
Ann. rainfall (in.) .. 23.37		Avg. weekly wage	$275.73
Jan. temp. min.	30	Annual wages .	$54,714,208
July temp. max.	97	1983 PCI	$7,677
Growing season (da.)	223	Buying pwr. .	$164,282,000
Voters reg.	8,745	Tax value ...	$559,435,006
Businesses	400	Fed. expd. ...	$74,333,000

VITAL STATISTICS 1985: Births, 259; Deaths, 212; Marriages, 174; Divorces, 75.

AGRICULTURE: About $29 million annual income, 75% from cotton, wheat, milo; beef cattle, hogs, horses, sheep; about 7,500 acres irrigated for peanuts, hay.

BUSINESS: Agribusinesses; clothing manufacturing; plants make a variety of products.

ANSON (3,065) county seat; farming center, trailer manufacturing, apparel factory; hospital, rest home.

Stamford (4,525, part Haskell), agribusinesses; apparel manufacturing, cotton gin and compress; hospital, mental health center, rest homes. **Hamlin** (3,235, part in Fisher), farming center; varied manufacturing; hospital, rest home. Other towns include **Hawley** (884), **Lueders** (473) limestone quarry. Also includes part of **Abilene.**

Karnes

LOCATION: South (O-15).

HISTORY: Created, organized, 1854, from Bexar, Goliad, San Patricio counties; named for Texas Revolutionary figure, **Henry W. Karnes.**

Cong. Dist. 15	U.S. Jud. Dist. ... W-SAnt.
St. Sen. Dist. 18	Ct. Appeals 4
St. Rep. Dist. 33	Admin. Jud. Dist. 4
St. Dist. Cts. 81, 218	

PHYSICAL FEATURES: Sandy loam, dark clay, alluvial soils in rolling terrain, traversed by San Antonio River; mesquite, oak trees.

RECREATION: Historic sites include **Old Helena;**

Panna Maria, Texas' oldest Polish settlement; bird hunting; local events, golf course and tennis courts; Bluebonnet Days at Kenedy in April; town and country days in Karnes City in September; restored courthouse and museum at Helena.

MINERALS: Oil, gas, stone; **uranium producing plant** at Falls City.

1985 Pop.	13,400	Tax Ratio	0.88
Area (sq. mi.)	753	Oil value	$1,417,811
Altitude (ft.) 225-525		No. employed	3,304
Ann. rainfall (in.) . 31.93		Avg. weekly wage	$267.19
Jan. temp. min.	44	Annual wages .	$45,905,412
July temp. max.	96	1983 PCI	$6,868
Growing season (da.)	281	Buying pwr. .	$114,158,000
Voters reg.	7,441	Tax value ...	$680,012,400
Businesses	356	Fed. expd. ...	$29,626,000

VITAL STATISTICS 1985: Births, 223; Deaths, 158; Marriages, 95; Divorces, 11.

AGRICULTURE: About $35 million average income, 80% from beef, dairy cattle, hogs; crops include sorghums, wheat, oats, corn.

BUSINESS: Agribusiness, mineral production, tourism; varied manufacturing.

KARNES CITY (3,251) county seat; farm-trading, processing center; oil producing and servicing; fiberglass products; farm, oil field equipment, other products; livestock sale; uranium ore processing; hospitals, nursing homes, library.

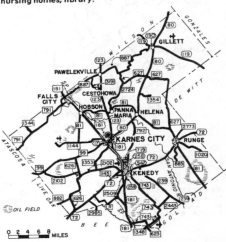

Kenedy (4,425), livestock sales, food processing, other agribusinesses; varied manufacturing; hunting center; rest homes, library.

Other towns include **Runge** (1,285), **Falls City** (547) farming center.

Kaufman

LOCATION: North (H-18).

HISTORY: Created from Henderson County and organized, 1848; named for member of Texas and U.S. Congresses, **D. S. Kaufman.**

Cong. Dist. 4	U.S. Jud. Dist. ..... N-Dl.
St. Sen. Dist. 2	Ct. Appeals 5, 12
St. Rep. Dist. 4	Admin. Jud. Dist. 1
St. Dist. Cts. 86	

PHYSICAL FEATURES: Largely Blackland prairie, draining to Trinity River, Cedar Creek and Lake.

RECREATION: Activities at **Cedar Creek** and **Ray Hubbard Lakes; Porter Farm** near Terrell is historic site of origin of **U.S.-Texas Agricultural Extension program;** historical homes at Terrell.

MINERALS: Oil, stone, gas.

1985 Pop.	49,300	Tax Ratio	0.95
Area (sq. mi.)	788	Oil value	$695,052
Altitude (ft.) 359-539		No. employed	12,809
Ann. rainfall (in.) . 39.82		Avg. weekly wage	$295.74
Jan. temp. min.	35	Annual wages	$196,984,572
July temp. max.	95	1983 PCI	$8,422

Growing season (da.) 248	Buying pwr. . $495,577,000
Voters reg. 23,235	Tax value . . $1,515,131,201
Businesses 1,094	Fed. expd. . . . $120,982,000

VITAL STATISTICS 1985: Births, 855; Deaths, 464; Marriages, 806; Divorces, 267.

AGRICULTURE: About $27 million average annual income, 80% from cattle, hogs, poultry, horses, crawfish; crops include cotton, grain, hay, oats, wheat.

BUSINESS: Varied manufacturing; trade center; part of Dallas metro area.

KAUFMAN (5,318) county seat; plants make steel power lines and other products; furniture, clothing.

Terrell (13,953), agribusinesses; plants make athletic uniforms, dresses, plastic goods, school supplies, machine parts, other products; **Terrell State Hospital; Southwestern Christian College.**

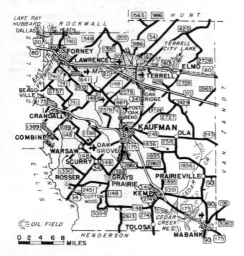

Other towns include **Forney** (4,008), **Mabank** (1,988), **Kemp** (1,206), **Combine** (815, partly Dallas County), **Cottonwood** (200), **Crandall** (1,207), **Heath** (1,647, mostly Rockwall County), **Oak Grove** (387), **Oak Ridge** (168), **Post Oak Bend** (353), **Grays Prairie** (208), **Rosser** (255).

Kendall

LOCATION: South central (M-14).

HISTORY: Created, organized from Blanco, Kerr counties, 1862; named for pioneer journalist-sheepman, contributor to Texas Almanac, **George W. Kendall.**

Cong. Dist.	21	U.S. Jud. Dist. . . .	W.-SAnt.
St. Sen. Dist.	25	Ct. Appeals.	4
St. Rep. Dist.	46	Admin. Jud. Dist.	6
St. Dist. Cts.	216		

PHYSICAL FEATURES: Hilly, plateau, with springfed streams, caves, scenic drives.

RECREATION: Hunting, fishing, Guadalupe River; tourist center; **Cascade Caverns;** historic sites; festival, other local celebrations.

MINERALS: Natural gas discovered.

1985 Pop.	14,000	Tax Ratio	0.97
Area (sq. mi.)	663	Oil value	0
Altitude (ft.) . .	1,159-2,011	No. employed	3,225
Ann. rainfall (in.) . .	30.39	Avg. weekly wage $248.86	
Jan. temp. min.	38	Annual wages . $41,734,620	
July temp. max.	94	1983 PCI	$9,865
Growing season (da.)	231	Buying pwr. . $150,433,000	
Voters reg.	7,097	Tax value . . $1,480,285,083	
Businesses	431	Fed. expd. $31,447,000	

VITAL STATISTICS 1985: Births, 205; Deaths, 138; Marriages, 179; Divorces, 46.

AGRICULTURE: About $8 million average income, 90% from cattle, sheep, Angora goats, horses; some sorghums, wheat, oats.

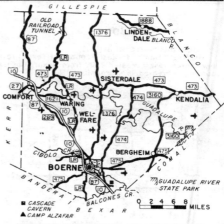

BUSINESS: Agribusinesses, some manufacturing.

BOERNE (4,396) county seat; livestock, tourism, varied manufacturing; nursing homes. **Comfort** has "True to the Union" Civil War monument; developing tourism; livestock center; hospital. **Sisterdale** is other principal town.

Kenedy

LOCATION: Southern, coastal (S-16).

HISTORY: Among last counties created, organized, 1921, from Cameron, Hidalgo, Willacy; named for pioneer ranchman, **Capt. Mifflin Kenedy.**

Cong. Dist.	27	U.S. Jud. Dist.	S-CC
St. Sen. Dist.	20	Ct. Appeals	13
St. Rep. Dist.	37	Admin. Jud. Dist.	5
St. Dist. Cts.	105		

PHYSICAL FEATURES: Typical coastal flat, sandy terrain, some loam soils; motts of live oaks.

MINERALS: Oil, gas.

1985 Pop.	600	Tax Ratio	1.00
Area (sq. mi.)	1,389	Oil value $12,713,919	
Altitude (ft.)	9-79	No. employed	290
Ann. rainfall (in.) . .	26.61	Avg. weekly wage $342.25	
Jan. temp. min.	48	Annual wages . $5,161,144	
July temp. max.	95	1983 PCI	$5,825
Growing season (da.)	319	Buying pwr. . $7,686,000	
Voters reg.	323	Tax value . $898,546,093	
Businesses	4	Fed. expd. $651,000	

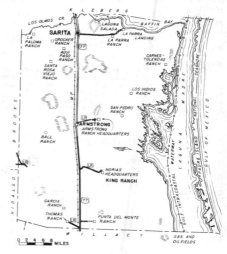

VITAL STATISTICS 1985: Births, 7; Deaths, 3; Marriages, 3; Divorces, 2.

AGRICULTURE: About $10 million average income, nearly all from cattle on large ranches.

BUSINESS: Oil-ranching economy.

SARITA (est. 185) county seat of one of the state's least populated counties; cattle shipping point; headquarters for large ranch enterprises; gas processing. Other town is **Armstrong**.

Kent

LOCATION: West (G-10).

HISTORY: Created, 1876, from Bexar, Young Territories; organized 1892. Name honors **Andrew Kent**, one of "Immortal 32" from Gonzales who died in Alamo.

Cong. Dist. 13   U.S. Jud. Dist. . . . . N-Lb.
St. Sen. Dist. 30   Ct. Appeals 7
St. Rep. Dist. 78   Admin. Jud. Dist. 7
St. Dist. Cts. 39

PHYSICAL FEATURES: Rolling, broken terrain; drains to Salt and Double Mountain forks Brazos River; sandy, loam soils.

RECREATION: Hunting, local events; scenic croton breaks and salt flat.

MINERALS: Oil, gas, sand and gravel.

1985 Pop. 1,300	Tax Ratio 0.95
Area (sq. mi.) 878	Oil value . . . $192,939,285
Altitude (ft.) . . 1,823-2,830	No. employed 270
Ann. rainfall (in.) . . 20.75	Avg. weekly wage $300.99
Jan. temp. min. 28	Annual wages $4,226,024
July temp. max. 97	1983 PCI $7,900
Growing season (da.) 216	Buying pwr. . $8,359,000
Voters reg. 886	Tax value . . . $795,071,093
Businesses 16	Fed. expd. $3,749,000

VITAL STATISTICS 1985: Births, 19; Deaths, 18; Marriages, 10; Divorces, 3.

AGRICULTURE: About $6 million average income, largely from cattle, sheep; cotton, wheat, sorghums, peanuts, grain produced.

BUSINESS: Agribusinesses, oil field operations.

JAYTON (607) county seat; oil field services, farm trade center.

Kerr

LOCATION: Southwest central (M-13).

HISTORY: Created, organized, 1856, from Bexar County; named for member of Austin's Colony, **James Kerr**.

Cong. Dist. 21   U.S. Jud. Dist. . . W-SAnt.
St. Sen. Dist. 25   Ct. Appeals 4
St. Rep. Dist. 67   Admin. Jud. Dist. 6
St. Dist. Cts. 198, 216

PHYSICAL FEATURES: Hills, spring-fed streams are scenic attractions. New dam and lake on Guadalupe River.

RECREATION: Very popular area for tourists, hunters, fishermen; dude ranches; **Kerrville State Park;** wildlife management area; hatchery; Texas Arts and Crafts Fair in Kerrville; Experimental aircraft fly-in; Cowboy Artists Museum; Kerrville Music Festival.

MINERALS: Limited sand, gravel.

1985 Pop. 34,600	Tax Ratio 0.91
Area (sq. mi.) 1,107	Oil value 0
Altitude (ft.) . . 1,524-2,303	No. employed 11,696
Ann. rainfall (in.) . . 29.75	Avg. weekly wage $257.41
Jan. temp. min. 34	Annual wages $156,557,656
July temp. max. 94	1983 PCI $9,819
Growing season (da.) 216	Buying pwr. . . $449,147,000
Voters reg. 18,531	Tax value . . $2,018,026,500
Businesses 1,006	Fed. expd. . . . $115,511,000

VITAL STATISTICS 1985: Births, 493; Deaths, 471; Marriages, 404; Divorces, 235.

AGRICULTURE: An estimated $6.5 million average income, 90% from cattle, sheep, goats; cedar posts sold; hay, oats, milo, wheat, pecans.

BUSINESS: Tourism; agribusinesses; manufacturing; medical services.

KERRVILLE (17,002) county seat; tourist center; many camps for recreation nearby; plants make aircraft, boats, recreational equipment, jewelry, glass; **Schreiner College,** now a four-year school; **Kerrville State Hospital; Veterans Hospital,** also local hospital. Other major town, **Ingram** (1,441).

Kimble

LOCATION: Central southwest (L-12).

HISTORY: Created from Bexar County, 1858; organized 1876; named for **George C. Kimble,** among Gonzales' **"Immortal 32"** who died in Alamo.

Cong. Dist.	21	U.S. Jud. Dist.	W-An.
St. Sen. Dist.	25	Ct. Appeals	4
St. Rep. Dist.	67	Admin. Jud. Dist.	6
St. Dist. Cts.	198		

PHYSICAL FEATURES: Broken, rolling plain; drains to Llano River; sandy, gray, chocolate loam soils.

RECREATION: Hunting, fishing in spring-fed streams; among leading deer counties; **Lake Junction;** Kimble Kow Kick, other local events; state park under development.

MINERALS: Limited sand, gravel, gas, oil.

1985 Pop.	4,300	Tax Ratio	0.61
Area (sq. mi.)	1,250	Oil value	$4,570
Altitude (ft.)	1,783-2,372	No. employed	1,131
Ann. rainfall (in.)	22.33	Avg. weekly wage	$233.80
Jan. temp. min.	33	Annual wages	$13,750,544
July temp. max.	97	1983 PCI	$7,081
Growing season (da.)	213	Buying pwr.	$33,510,000
Voters reg.	2,359	Tax value	$370,996,522
Businesses	136	Fed. expd.	$10,088,000

VITAL STATISTICS 1985: Births, 57; Deaths, 54; Marriages, 53; Divorces, 27.

AGRICULTURE: About $10 million average income, 90% from sheep, goats, cattle, hogs, horses; crops include pecans, fruit.

BUSINESS: Livestock producing, wool, mohair, tourism, hunting, fishing dominate economy. Cedar oil and wood products sold.

JUNCTION (2,761) county seat; cedar oil plant; ranching, tourism center; **Texas Tech University Center;** hospital, nursing home; library.

King

LOCATION: Northwest (F-11).

HISTORY: Created, 1876, from Bexar District; organized 1891; named for **William P. King** of **"Immortal 32"** from Gonzales who died in Alamo.

Cong. Dist.	13	U.S. Jud. Dist.	N-WF
St. Sen. Dist.	30	Ct. Appeals	7
St. Rep. Dist.	78	Admin. Jud. Dist.	9
St. Dist. Cts.	50		

PHYSICAL FEATURES: Hilly, broken by Wichita and Brazos tributaries; extensive grassland; dark loam to red soils.

RECREATION: Local events.

MINERALS: Oil, gas.

1985 Pop.	400	Tax Ratio	0.85
Area (sq. mi.)	914	Oil value	$8,155,277
Altitude (ft.)	1,739-2,081	No. employed	152
Ann. rainfall (in.)	21.60	Avg. weekly wage	$284.19
Jan. temp. min.	27	Annual wages	$2,246,252
July temp. max.	99	1983 PCI	$6,257
Growing season (da.)	219	Buying pwr.	$4,160,000
Voters reg.	307	Tax value	$313,367,845
Businesses	5	Fed. expd.	$1,316,000

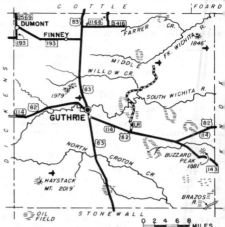

VITAL STATISTICS 1985: Births, 7; Deaths, 2; Marriages, 5; Divorces, 0.

AGRICULTURE: $10 million average income, over 90 percent from beef cattle, horses; cotton, grains produced.

BUSINESS: Minerals, ranching provide most income.

GUTHRIE (est. 140) county seat; ranch supply center.

Kinney

LOCATION: Southwest (O-11).

HISTORY: Created from Bexar County, 1850; organized, 1874; named for **H. L. Kinney,** founder of Corpus Christi.

Cong. Dist.	23	U.S. Jud. Dist.	W-DR
St. Sen. Dist.	21	Ct. Appeals	4
St. Rep. Dist.	68	Admin. Jud. Dist.	6
St. Dist. Cts.	63		

PHYSICAL FEATURES: Hilly, broken by many Rio Grande tributaries; **Anacacho Mountains; Nueces Canyon.**

RECREATION: Hunting; **Alamo Village guest ranch; Seminole Cemetery; Fort Clark Springs;** frontier fair in March.

MINERALS: Not significant.

1985 Pop.	2,500	Tax Ratio	0.85
Area (sq. mi.)	1,359	Oil value	0
Altitude (ft.)	909-1,981	No. employed	523

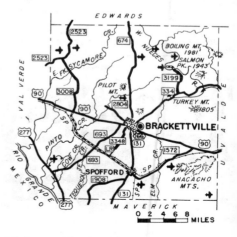

Ann. rainfall (in.) . . 20.85	Avg. weekly wage $231.26
Jan. temp. min. 39	Annual wages . $6,289,376
July temp. max. 94	1983 PCI $6,022
Growing season (da.) 270	Buying pwr. . . $15,876,000
Voters reg. 1,822	Tax value . . $330,908,690
Businesses 36	Fed. expd. $9,426,000

VITAL STATISTICS 1985: Births, 27; Deaths, 31; Marriages, 30; Divorces, 8.

AGRICULTURE: About $11 million average income, 85% from cattle, sheep, goats; grains, corn, onions produced. About 5,000 acres irrigated for grass, sorghums, vegetables.

BUSINESS: Agribusinesses, tourist trade.

BRACKETTVILLE (1,816) county seat; tourist center; local market; clinic; **Spofford** (77).

Kleberg

LOCATION: Southern coast (R-16).

HISTORY: Created, organized, 1913, from Nueces County; named for San Jacinto veteran-rancher, **Robert Kleberg.**

Cong. Dist. 27	U.S. Jud. Dist. . . . . . S-CC
St. Sen. Dist. 20	Ct. Appeals 13
St. Rep. Dist. 37	Admin. Jud. Dist. 5
St. Dist. Cts. 105	

PHYSICAL FEATURES: Coastal plain, broken by bays; sandy, loam, clay soils; tree motts.

RECREATION: Fishing, water activities, park on Baffin Bay; wildlife sanctuary; **Texas A&I** events, museum; **King Ranch** headquarters; livestock show and other local events.

MINERALS: Production of oil, gas; stone.

1985 Pop. 34,500	Tax Ratio 0.94
Area (sq. mi.) 853	Oil value $22,947,201
Altitude (ft.) 3-151	No. employed 8,687
Ann. rainfall (in.) . . 26.50	Avg. weekly wage $258.95
Jan. temp. min. 48	Annual wages $116,977,828
July temp. max. 96	1983 PCI $7,074
Growing season (da.) 314	Buying pwr. . $287,514,000
Voters reg. 13,122	Tax value . . $2,304,772,822
Businesses 654	Fed. expd. . . . $239,884,000

VITAL STATISTICS 1985: Births, 754; Deaths, 214; Marriages, 378; Divorces, 167.

AGRICULTURE: An estimated $46 million average annual income, 65% from cattle, hogs, poultry, horses; wheat, sorghums, cotton, corn, vegetables grown.

BUSINESS: Economy based on petroleum, cattle ranching; some manufacturing; some mesquite timber, products.

KINGSVILLE (29,949) county seat; industrial plants; food processing; petroleum processing; **Texas A&I University;** headquarters of **King Ranch, Santa Gertrudis Breeders International; Naval Air Station;** hospital.

Knox

LOCATION: Northwest (F-12).

HISTORY: Created from Bexar, Young Territories, 1858; re-created, 1876; organized 1886, named for U.S. Secretary of War, **Gen. Henry Knox.**

Cong. Dist. 13	U.S. Jud. Dist. . . . . . N-WF
St. Sen. Dist. 30	Ct. Appeals 11
St. Rep. Dist. 78	Admin. Jud. Dist. 9
St. Dist. Cts. 50	

PHYSICAL FEATURES: Eroded breaks on rolling plains; Brazos, Wichita Rivers; sandy, loam soils.

RECREATION: Lake activities, local events; centennial celebration during Sesquicentennial.

MINERALS: Oil, gas.

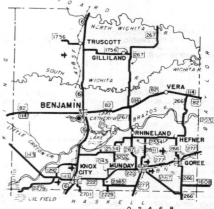

1985 Pop. 5,600	Tax Ratio 0.83
Area (sq. mi.) 845	Oil value $6,312,182
Altitude (ft.) . . . 1,401-1,646	No. employed 1,327
Ann. rainfall (in.) . . 24.64	Avg. weekly wage $224.38
Jan. temp. min. 28	Annual wages . $15,483,152
July temp. max. 98	1983 PCI $7,559
Growing season (da.) 217	Buying pwr. . . $40,202,000
Voters reg. 2,863	Tax value . . $219,878,391
Businesses 143	Fed. expd. $20,088,000

VITAL STATISTICS 1985: Births, 96; Deaths, 63; Marriages, 39; Divorces, 17.

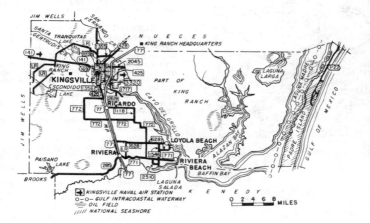

AGRICULTURE: About $23 million average income, 70% from crops that include cotton, wheat, sorghums, guar, corn, potatoes; beef cattle, sheep; about 33,000 acres irrigated.

BUSINESS: Agribusinesses, petroleum operations.

BENJAMIN (237) county seat; trade, market center; hospital, nursing home.

Munday (1,751) vegetable shipping center; portable offices, buildings manufactured; vegetable festival; **Texas A&M Experiment Vegetable Research Station;** center of irrigation from Seymour aquifer; library, nursing home.

Knox City (1,695) agribusiness, petroleum center; county hospital, nursing home; cap company; plant materials research center; **Goree** (520).

Lamar

LOCATION: Northeast (F-19).

HISTORY: Created, 1840, from Red River County; organized, 1841; named for Republic of Texas president, **Mirabeau B. Lamar.**

Cong. Dist.	1	U.S. Jud. Dist.	E-Ps.
St. Sen. Dist.	1	Ct. Appeals	6
St. Rep. Dist.	2	Admin. Jud. Dist.	1
St. Dist. Cts.	6, 62		

PHYSICAL FEATURES: On divide between Red, Sulphur Rivers; soils chiefly Blackland, except along Red; pines, hardwoods.

RECREATION: Pat Mayse Lake activities; **Gambill** goose refuge; hunting, fishing; Flying Tigers Air Museum, A.M. Aikin Archives; other museums; arts fair; Red River Valley Exposition; antique auto rally; other local events.

MINERALS: Negligible.

1985 Pop.	44,700	Tax Ratio	0.95
Area (sq. mi.)	919	Oil value	0
Altitude (ft.)	390-602	No. employed	16,134
Ann. rainfall (in.)	45.17	Avg. weekly wage	$326.89
Jan. temp. min.	34	Annual wages	$274,257,940
July temp. max.	94	1983 PCI	$7,379
Growing season (da.)	235	Buying pwr.	$435,352,000
Voters reg.	23,330	Tax value	$1,252,728,195
Businesses	1,041	Fed. expd.	$117,131,000

VITAL STATISTICS 1985: Births, 644; Deaths, 528; Marriages, 717; Divorces, 348.

AGRICULTURE: About $40 million average income, 80% from beef, dairy cattle; chief crops are hay, peanuts, sorghums, soybeans; a leading hay-producing county; timber marketed.

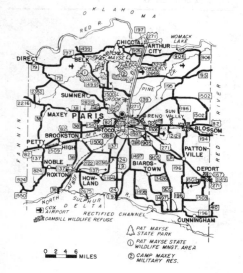

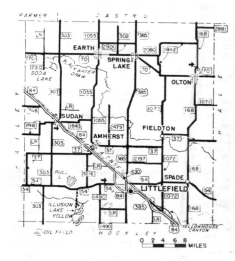

BUSINESS: Varied manufacturing; agribusinesses; tourism.

PARIS (26,176) county seat; plants make canned soups, steam generating equipment, apparel, food products, farm supplies, other products; medical center, nursing homes; **Paris Junior College.**

Other towns include **Blossom** (1,737), **Deport** (680, part Red River), **Reno** (1,144), **Roxton** (747), **Sun Valley** (83) and **Toco** (152).

Lamb

LOCATION: Northwest (E-8).

HISTORY: Created 1876, from Bexar District; organized, 1908; named for San Jacinto Battle victim, **Lt. G. A. Lamb.**

Cong. Dist.	19	U.S. Jud. Dist.	N-Lb.
St. Sen. Dist.	31	Ct. Appeals	7
St. Rep. Dist.	85	Admin. Jud. Dist.	9
St. Dist. Cts.	154		

PHYSICAL FEATURES: Rich, red, brown soils on plain; some hills; drains to numerous playas, Brazos Double Mountain Fork.

RECREATION: Local events; Sandhills celebration.

MINERALS: Production oil, stone, gas.

1985 Pop.	17,100	Tax Ratio	0.95
Area (sq. mi.)	1,013	Oil value	$206,419
Altitude (ft.)	3,486-3,849	No. employed	4,507
Ann. rainfall (in.)	18.04	Avg. weekly wage	$271.83
Jan. temp. min.	24	Annual wages	$63,708,708
July temp. max.	93	1983 PCI	$7,123
Growing season (da.)	194	Buying pwr.	$133,845,000
Voters reg.	8,814	Tax value	$1,144,454,084
Businesses	389	Fed. expd.	$51,732,000

VITAL STATISTICS 1985: Births, 293; Deaths, 184; Marriages, 151; Divorces, 92.

AGRICULTURE: About $115 million average income, evenly split among sorghums, cotton, wheat, other crops; cattle, hogs, sheep, horses; 265,000 acres irrigated.

BUSINESS: Agribusinesses.

LITTLEFIELD (7,088) county seat; agribusinesses, trade center; textile mill; plants make fertilizer, irrigation, other farm products; hospitals, nursing homes; airport.

Other towns include **Earth** (1,392) grain, cotton center, **Olton** (2,107) farm and feed lot center, food processing, **Sudan** (1,041), **Amherst** (847) and **Springlake** (180).

Lampasas

LOCATION: Central (K-14).

HISTORY: Name is Spanish for lilies, found in nearby streams; county created, organized, 1856, from Bell, Travis.

Cong. Dist. 11	U.S. Jud. Dist. . . . . W-An.
St. Sen. Dist. 24	Ct. Appeals 3
St. Rep. Dist. 54	Admin. Jud. Dist. 3
St. Dist. Cts. 27	

PHYSICAL FEATURES: Rolling, hilly; Colorado, Lampasas Rivers; cedars, oaks, pecans.

RECREATION: Hunting, fishing in streams; Spring Ho Festival, local events.

MINERALS: Sand and gravel, building stone.

1985 Pop. 13,600	Tax Ratio 0.95
Area (sq. mi.) 714	Oil value 0
Altitude (ft.) . . . 339-1,190	No. employed 2,430
Ann. rainfall (in.) . . 29.80	Avg. weekly wage $244.68
Jan. temp. min. 36	Annual wages . $30,918,948
July temp. max. 96	1983 PCI $7,941
Growing season (da.) 223	Buying pwr. . $129,054,000
Voters reg. 6,648	Tax value . . . $586,574,128
Businesses 294	Fed. expd. $34,103,000

VITAL STATISTICS 1985: Births, 230; Deaths, 138; Marriages, 231; Divorces, 39.

AGRICULTURE: About $11 million average income, 90% from cattle, hogs, sheep, goats; crops include oats, wheat, fruit, pecans.

BUSINESS: Many employed at **Fort Hood;** several industrial plants; tourism; agribusinesses.

LAMPASAS (6,749) county seat; ranching, hunting center; plants make feeds, western boots, apparel, nut harvesters, building trusses, rubber products, brooms, mops; food processing; hospital, nursing homes. **Lometa (722)** other principal town.

La Salle

LOCATION: South (Q-13).

HISTORY: Created from Bexar County, 1858; organized 1880; named for **Robert Cavalier Sieur de la Salle,** French explorer who died in Texas.

Cong. Dist. 15	U.S. Jud. Dist. . . . . S-La.
St. Sen. Dist. 21	Ct. Appeals 4
St. Rep. Dist. 44	Admin. Jud. Dist. 4
St. Dist. Cts. 81, 218	

PHYSICAL FEATURES: Brushy plain, broken by Nueces, Frio and their tributary streams; chocolate, dark gray, sandy loam soils.

RECREATION: Nature trails; **Chaparral Wildlife Management Area;** deer, bird, javelina hunting; wild hog cookoff; fishing; Cotulla school where the late **Pres. Lyndon B. Johnson** taught attracts tourists.

MINERALS: Production of oil, gas.

1985 Pop. 5,800	Tax Ratio 0.62
Area (sq. mi.) 1,517	Oil value $1,725,836
Altitude (ft.) 326-558	No. employed 950
Ann. rainfall (in.) . . 20.72	Avg. weekly wage $231.02
Jan. temp. min. 43	Annual wages . $11,412,864
July temp. max. 99	1983 PCI $5,202
Growing season (da.) 288	Buying pwr. . . $39,191,000
Voters reg. 3,619	Tax value . . . $307,064,485
Businesses 102	Fed. expd. $12,978,000

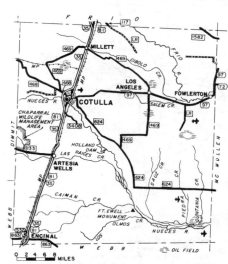

VITAL STATISTICS 1985: Births, 105; Deaths, 48; Marriages, 44; Divorces, 8.

AGRICULTURE: An estimated $18 million average income, 90% from beef and stocker cattle; crops include guar, sorghums, wheat, oats, peanuts, vegetables, melons; some mesquite sold, processed.

BUSINESS: Agribusinesses, hunting leases.

COTULLA (4,305) county seat; welding and steel fabrication; agribusiness center; clinics; **Encinal (720)** other major town.

Lavaca

LOCATION: South (N-17).

HISTORY: Named for Spanish word for cow, la vaca, from name of river; created, organized, 1846, from Colorado, Jackson, Gonzales, Victoria counties.

Cong. Dist. 14	U.S. Jud. Dist. . . . . S-Va.
St. Sen. Dist. 18	Ct. Appeals 13
St. Rep. Dist. 31	Admin. Jud. Dist. 3
St. Dist. Cts. 25, 2D25	

PHYSICAL FEATURES: North rolling, south plains; sandy loam, black waxy soils; drains to Lavaca, Navidad Rivers.

RECREATION: Deer, other hunting, fishing; Yoakum Tom-Tom June celebration; spring flower trails, fiddlers frolic, domino tournaments; other events.

MINERALS: Oil, gas.

1985 Pop. 18,500	Tax Ratio 0.96
Area (sq. mi.) 971	Oil value $2,699,037
Altitude (ft.) 133-503	No. employed 4,290
Ann. rainfall (in.) . . 36.27	Avg. weekly wage $245.88
Jan. temp. min. 44	Annual wages . $54,852,156
July temp. max. 95	1983 PCI $7,412
Growing season (da.) 280	Buying pwr. . $190,678,000
Voters reg. 10,637	Tax value . . $1,205,235,481
Businesses 549	Fed. expd. $48,739,000

VITAL STATISTICS 1985: Births, 260; Deaths, 283; Marriages, 198; Divorces, 57.

AGRICULTURE: About $50 million average income, 80% from cattle, hogs, poultry; crops include sorghums, small grains, corn, rice, hay, peaches, pecans, legumes. Nearly 4,200 acres irrigated, mostly rice.

BUSINESS: Varied manufacturing; leather goods center; agribusinesses; oil and gas production.

HALLETTSVILLE (2,589) county seat; plants make plastic products, furniture, portable buildings, other products; Lavaca Medical Center, nursing home.

Yoakum (6,355, part in De Witt County) plants make leather goods, furniture, process foods; hospital, nursing homes.

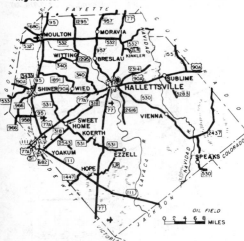

Shiner (2,150) brewery, wire products, saddle factory; hospital, nursing home.

Moulton (1,001) plants make boots, other leather products; feed mills, machine shop; other agribusinesses; clinic, nursing home; Czech, German polka, waltz fest.

Lee

LOCATION: Southeast (M-17).

HISTORY: Created from Bastrop, Burleson, Fayette, Washington counties and organized in 1874; named for **Confederate Gen. Robert E. Lee.**

Cong. Dist.	14	U.S. Jud. Dist.	W-An.
St. Sen. Dist.	18	Ct. Appeals	3
St. Rep. Dist.	30	Admin. Jud. Dist.	2
St. Dist. Cts.	21, 335		

PHYSICAL FEATURES: Rolling, broken by Yegua and its tributaries; red to black soils, sandy to heavy loams.

RECREATION: Fishing, hunting, pioneer village, Wendish museum and structures; new motels; local events; historic sites.

MINERALS: Oil, gas, lignite.

1985 Pop.	13,700	Tax Ratio	0.88
Area (sq. mi.)	631	Oil value	$10,419,124
Altitude (ft.)	238-513	No. employed	3,981
Ann. rainfall (in.)	35.88	Avg. weekly wage	$296.65

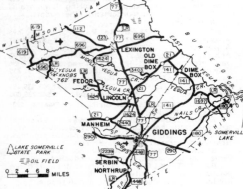

Jan. temp. min.	38	Annual wages	$61,410,904
July temp. max.	94	1983 PCI	$7,350
Growing season (da.)	273	Buying pwr.	$111,303,000
Voters reg.	6,430	Tax value	$936,537,862
Businesses	442	Fed. expd.	$19,435,000

VITAL STATISTICS 1985: Births, 222; Deaths, 138; Marriages, 150; Divorces, 65.

AGRICULTURE: Nearly $32 million average income, 85% from cattle, hogs; peanuts, wheat, oats.

BUSINESS: Varied manufacturing; agribusinesses; oil and gas operations.

GIDDINGS (4,841) county seat; oil field services and trucking; plants make boats, furniture, plastic products; livestock auctions; process meats; hospital, nursing homes; **Blinn College** extension; **Giddings State School and Home;** Geburtstag celebration.

Other towns include **Lexington** (1,284) livestock marketing center, nursery, peanut drying plant, many work at aluminum plant; **Serbin,** Wendish museum.

Leon

LOCATION: East central (K-18).

HISTORY: Created, organized, 1846, from Robertson County; named for Spanish founder of Victoria, **Martin de Leon.**

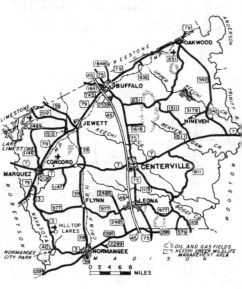

Cong. Dist.	6	U.S. Jud. Dist.	W-Wa.
St. Sen. Dist.	5	Ct. Appeals	10
St. Rep. Dist.	15	Admin. Jud. Dist.	2
St. Dist. Cts.	12, 87, 278		

PHYSICAL FEATURES: Hilly, rolling, almost half covered by timber; drains to Navasota, Trinity and tributaries; sandy, dark, alluvial soils.

RECREATION: Hilltop Lakes resort area; sites of Camino Real, Fort Boggy; deer hunting.

MINERALS: Oil, gas, iron ore, lignite.

1985 Pop.	12,600	Tax Ratio	0.89
Area (sq. mi.)	1,078	Oil value	$4,137,307
Altitude (ft.)	190-496	No. employed	2,972
Ann. rainfall (in.)	39.48	Avg. weekly wage	$328.44
Jan. temp. min.	38	Annual wages	$50,759,756
July temp. max.	95	1983 PCI	$7,190
Growing season (da.)	270	Buying pwr.	$114,962,000
Voters reg.	8,120	Tax value	$1,136,571,194
Businesses	246	Fed. expd.	$33,007,000

VITAL STATISTICS 1985: Births, 211; Deaths, 197; Marriages, 131; Divorces, 46.

AGRICULTURE: About $44 million average income, over 90% from livestock, principally beef cattle, hogs, poultry, horses; crops include hay, corn, sorghum, vegetables; timber estimated $2 million.

BUSINESS: Agribusinesses; oil production.

CENTERVILLE (854) county seat; steel products; farming center; clinic, nursing home.

Buffalo (1,921) farming center; electricity generating plant; hospital, nursing home.

Other towns include **Normangee** (581, partly Madison County), **Oakwood**(576), **Jewett** (816), **Leona** (188), **Marquez** (279).

Liberty

LOCATION: Southeast (M-20).

HISTORY: Named for Spanish municipality, **Libertad,** from which it was created in 1836; organized, 1837.

Cong. Dist.	2	U.S. Jud. Dist.	E-Bt.
St. Sen. Dist.	4	Ct. Appeals	9
St. Rep. Dist.	21	Admin. Jud. Dist.	2
St. Dist. Cts.	75, 253		

PHYSICAL FEATURES: Rolling; 60 percent in pine, hardwood timber; bisected by Trinity River; sandy, loam, black soils; Wallisville Reservoir; Big Thicket.

RECREATION: Big Thicket; hunting, fishing; historic sites; Trinity Valley exposition in October.

MINERALS: Oil, gas, sulphur, sand and gravel.

1985 Pop.	54,500	Tax Ratio	0.95
Area (sq. mi.)	1,174	Oil value	$34,067,772
Altitude (ft.)	23-261	No. employed	10,378
Ann. rainfall (in.)	49.75	Avg. weekly wage	$316.54
Jan. temp. min.	43	Annual wages	$170,825,828
July temp. max.	93	1983 PCI	$7,878
Growing season (da.)	261	Buying pwr.	$591,236,000
Voters reg.	24,401	Tax value	$2,101,461,994
Businesses	1,075	Fed. expd.	$100,663,000

VITAL STATISTICS 1985: Births, 930; Deaths, 542; Marriages, 741; Divorces, 332.

AGRICULTURE: About $26 million average income, ¾ from crops, principally rice, soybeans; beef cattle; timber marketed; 32,000 acres irrigated for rice; pulpwood, lumber, Christmas trees.

BUSINESS: Agribusinesses; chemical plants; varied manufacturing; tourism; forest industries; many work in Houston; part of Houston PMSA.

LIBERTY (8,377) county seat; port on barge canal; sulphur, oil, chemicals, timber, steel processed, shipped; farm products processed, shipped; nursing homes; library, museum; regional historical resources depository; oil pipe manufacturing and oil field services; liberty bell tower and plaza.

Other towns include **Cleveland** (6,691) forest products processed, shipped; farm, petroleum products shipped, herb farm; tourism; library, museum; hospital, nursing home; **Dayton** (6,576); **Daisetta** (1,252) man-

ufacturing; oil, food processing; **Ames** (1,344), **Devers** (433), **Hardin** (928), **Kenefick** (788), **North Cleveland** (301), **Plum Grove** (648) and **Dayton Lakes.**

Limestone

LOCATION: East central (J-17).

HISTORY: Created from Robertson County and organized, 1846; named for indigenous rock.

Cong. Dist.	6	U.S. Jud. Dist.	W-Wa.
St. Sen. Dist.	9	Ct. Appeals	10
St. Rep. Dist.	12	Admin. Jud. Dist.	2
St. Dist. Cts.	77, 87		

PHYSICAL FEATURES: Borders Blacklands, level to rolling; drained by Navasota and tributaries; on divide between Brazos and Trinity; **Lake Mexia, Lake Springfield, Lake Limestone.**

RECREATION: Fishing, water activities; restored **Fort Parker, Fort Parker State Park;** Confederate reunion ground, other historic sites; museum; hunting; Red Stocking Follies, fiddle festival, arts and crafts, other events.

MINERALS: Production of oil, gas, sand and gravel, clay, stone, lignite.

1985 Pop.	21,300	Tax Ratio	0.90
Area (sq. mi.)	931	Oil value	$24,632
Altitude (ft.)	375-665	No. employed	6,926
Ann. rainfall (in.)	37.59	Avg. weekly wage	$324.99
Jan. temp. min.	37	Annual wages	$117,046,056
July temp. max.	96	1983 PCI	$6,643
Growing season (da.)	255	Buying pwr.	$204,896,000
Voters reg.	10,028	Tax value	$1,892,853,885
Businesses	429	Fed. expd.	$49,286,000

VITAL STATISTICS 1985: Births, 341; Deaths, 298; Marriages, 292; Divorces, 152.

AGRICULTURE: About $32 million average annual income, 90% from cattle, hogs, horses; crops include sorghums, cotton, peaches, oats, wheat, corn, commercial vegetables.

BUSINESS: Varied manufacturing; agribusinesses; tourism; mineral operations.

GROESBECK (3,847) county seat; livestock market; plants make fiber material, trailers, concrete brick, industrial products; food processing; hospital, nursing home.

Mexia (7,121) agribusiness center; wholesale grocery distribution; furniture, sportswear, other products; **Mexia State School;** hospital.

Other towns include **Coolidge** (864), **Kosse** (519), **Tehuacana** (287) and **Thornton** (473).

Lipscomb

LOCATION: Northeast corner of Panhandle (A-11).
HISTORY: Created, 1876, from Bexar District; organized, 1887; named for **A. S. Lipscomb**, Republic of Texas leader.

Cong. Dist.	13	U.S. Jud. Dist.	N-Am.
St. Sen. Dist.	31	Ct. Appeals	7
St. Rep. Dist.	88	Admin. Jud. Dist.	9
St. Dist. Cts.	31		

PHYSICAL FEATURES: Plain, broken in east; drains to tributaries of Canadian, Wolf Creek; sandy loam, black soils.
RECREATION: Darrouzett festival and other local events.
MINERALS: Production of oil, gas.

1985 Pop.	4,000	Tax Ratio	0.84
Area (sq. mi.)	933	Oil value	$3,495,339
Altitude (ft.)	2,506-2,834	No. employed	849
Ann. rainfall (in.)	22.16	Avg. weekly wage	$354.21
Jan. temp. min.	23	Annual wages	$15,637,884
July temp. max.	95	1983 PCI	$8,932
Growing season (da.)	202	Buying pwr.	$40,133,000
Voters reg.	2,220	Tax value	$671,358,451
Businesses	130	Fed. expd.	$8,844,000

VITAL STATISTICS 1985: Births, 60; Deaths, 26; Marriages, 54; Divorces, 25.
AGRICULTURE: About $17 million average annual income, 65% from beef cattle, hogs; crops include wheat, sorghums, corn, alfalfa; about 10,000 acres irrigated.
BUSINESS: Agribusinesses; oil, gas operations.

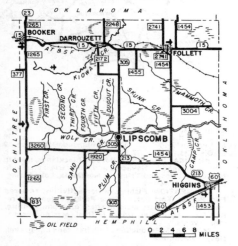

LIPSCOMB (est. 190) county seat.
Other towns include **Booker** (1,506, part in Ochiltree County), **Darrouzett** (511), **Follett** (605) and **Higgins** (679).

Live Oak

LOCATION: South (Q-15).
HISTORY: Named for predominant tree; created, organized, 1856, from Nueces, San Patricio Counties.

Cong. Dist.	15	U.S. Jud. Dist.	S-CC
St. Sen. Dist.	21	Ct. Appeals	13
St. Rep. Dist.	45	Admin. Jud. Dist.	4
St. Dist. Cts.	36, 156, 343		

PHYSICAL FEATURES: Brushy plains, partly broken by Nueces and tributaries; black waxy, gray sandy, other soils.
RECREATION: Lake Corpus Christi activities; **Mathis lake, Choke Canyon Reservoir**; hunting; Tips State Park, county fair.
MINERALS: Production of gas, oil, sand and gravel, uranium.

1985 Pop.	9,500	Tax Ratio	0.83
Area (sq. mi.)	1,057	Oil value	$2,439,208
Altitude (ft.)	96-479	No. employed	2,029

Ann. rainfall (in.)	25.64	Avg. weekly wage	$296.80
Jan. temp. min.	45	Annual wages	$31,315,172
July temp. max.	97	1983 PCI	$8,056
Growing season (da.)	289	Buying pwr.	$89,765,000
Voters reg.	6,568	Tax value	$1,096,071,150
Businesses	251	Fed. expd.	$38,733,000

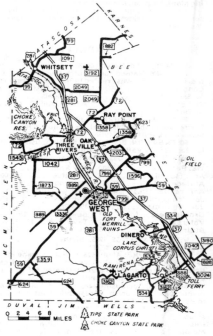

VITAL STATISTICS 1985: Births, 138; Deaths, 87; Marriages, 89; Divorces, 42.
AGRICULTURE: Some $25 million average yearly income, 70% from beef cattle, hogs; crops include milo, cotton, corn, wheat, hay.
BUSINESS: Oil activities, agribusinesses dominate economy.
GEORGE WEST (2,795) county seat; agribusinesses; petroleum refineries; uranium mining. **Three Rivers (2,177)** has refineries, boat factory.

Llano

LOCATION: West Central (L-14).
HISTORY: Name is Spanish for plains; created, organized, 1856, from Bexar District, Gillespie County.

Cong. Dist.	21	U.S. Jud. Dist.	W-An.
St. Sen. Dist.	24	Ct. Appeals	3
St. Rep. Dist.	47	Admin. Jud. Dist.	3
St. Dist. Cts.	33		

PHYSICAL FEATURES: Drains to Colorado, Llano Rivers; rolling to hilly; **Buchanan, Inks, Lyndon B. Johnson lakes.**
RECREATION: No. 1 deer hunting county; fishing, Highland Lakes activities; major tourist area; **Enchanted Rock State Park;** Spring Bluebonnet festival; hang gliding.
MINERALS: Stone, vermiculite.

1985 Pop.	12,100	Tax Ratio	0.92
Area (sq. mi.)	939	Oil value	0
Altitude (ft.)	1,038-1,867	No. employed	2,503
Ann. rainfall (in.)	26.20	Avg. weekly wage	$264.01
Jan. temp. min.	34	Annual wages	$34,363,108
July temp. max.	98	1983 PCI	$10,071
Growing season (da.)	229	Buying pwr.	$131,257,000
Voters reg.	7,552	Tax value	$1,406,964,346
Businesses	298	Fed. expd.	$40,670,000

VITAL STATISTICS 1985: Births, 105; Deaths, 220; Marriages, 131; Divorces, 45.

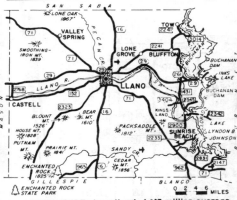

AGRICULTURE: An estimated $17 million average yearly income, more than 90% from beef cattle, hogs, goats; crops include peanuts, oats, hay.

BUSINESS: Tourism; ranch trading center; granite mined.

LLANO (3,244) county seat; tourist, hunting center; granite processing, rock crushing, winery, feed processing; hospital, nursing home; library. **Kingsland,** tourism, light manufacturing, nursing home. Other towns include **Buchanan Dam, Sunrise Beach** (509).

Loving

LOCATION: New Mexico line (J-6).

HISTORY: Last county organized; created 1887 from Tom Green; organized 1931; named for **Oliver Loving,** trail driver. Loving is Texas' least populous county.

Cong. Dist.	16	U.S. Jud. Dist.	W-Pe.
St. Sen. Dist.	25	Ct. Appeals	8
St. Rep. Dist.	69	Admin. Jud. Dist.	7
St. Dist. Cts.	143		

PHYSICAL FEATURES: Rolling prairies drain to Pecos River; **Red Bluff Lake;** sandy, loam, clay soils.

MINERALS: Production of oil, gas.

1985 Pop.	100	Tax Ratio	0.99
Area (sq. mi.)	671	Oil value	$21,359,466
Altitude (ft.)	2,685-3,311	No. employed	25
Ann. rainfall (in.)	10.31	Avg. weekly wage	$357.44
Jan. temp. min.	29	Annual wages	$464,676
July temp. max.	96	1983 PCI	$32,505
Growing season (da.)	222	Buying pwr.	$2,342,000
Voters reg.	113	Tax value	$315,315,540
Businesses	5	Fed. expd.	$198,000

VITAL STATISTICS 1985: Births, 0; Deaths, 1; Marriages, 4; Divorces, 0.

AGRICULTURE: About $500,000 income from beef cattle; no crops.

BUSINESS: Petroleum operations.

MENTONE (est. 50) county seat; supply center for oil fields; only town.

The falls for which Wichita Falls was named, and which had been virtually destroyed in 1886 by a flood, were reconstructed in 1987. Twenty-five thousand residents donated half the $400,000 cost, and the city provided the other half of the funds. Dallas Morning News Photo.

Lubbock

LOCATION: Northwest (F-8).

HISTORY: Named for **Col. Tom S. Lubbock,** an organizer of **Confederate Terry's Rangers;** county created, 1876, from Bexar District; organized, 1891.

Cong. Dist.	19	U.S. Jud. Dist.	N-Lb.
St. Sen. Dist.	28	Ct. Appeals	7
St. Rep. Dist.	82-84	Admin. Jud. Dist.	9
St. Dist. Cts.	72, 99,		
	137, 140, 237		

PHYSICAL FEATURES: Level plains, broken by 1,500 playas, Yellow House River; rich soils, with underground water.

RECREATION: Lubbock Lake archaeological site and park; lake activities; **Texas Tech** events; Lubbock Civic Center, Museum of Texas Tech and Moody Planetarium; Mackenzie State Park; Ranching Heritage Center; Panhandle-South Plains Fair; Lubbock Arts Festival in April; Buffalo Springs Lake.

MINERALS: Oil, gas, stone, sand and gravel.

1985 Pop.	222,800	Tax Ratio	0.94
Area (sq. mi.)	900	Oil value	$3,742,132
Altitude (ft.)	3,015-3,402	No. employed	85,779
Ann. rainfall (in.)	18.41	Avg. weekly wage	$321.36
Jan. temp. min.	25	Ann. wages	$1,433,447,788
July temp. max.	92	1983 PCI	$8,937
Growing season (da.)	208	Buying pwr.	$2,306,797,000
Voters reg.	94,160	Tax value	$5,601,240,888
Businesses	6,005	Fed. expd.	$459,171,000

VITAL STATISTICS 1985: Births, 4,528; Deaths, 1,421; Marriages, 2,736; Divorces, 1,604.

AGRICULTURE: $100 million average yearly income, about 75% from crops, including cotton, sorghums, wheat, corn, sunflowers; 225,000 acres irrigated, mostly cotton; feedlot cattle, poultry, hogs.

BUSINESS: World's largest cottonseed processing center; Texas' leading agribusiness center; headquarters for large cotton cooperative; cattle feedlots; manufacturing. See metro page.

LUBBOCK (178,529) county seat; center for large agricultural area; major electronics company's consumer products headquarters for making, servicing calculators; other large plants process oilseeds, make earthmoving equipment, mobile homes, food containers,

fire protection equipment, clothing, other products; distribution center for South Plains; large feedlots; medical center, psychiatric hospital; museum; **Texas Tech University** with law and medical schools; **Lubbock Christian College, South Plains College, Wayland Baptist College** campus; **Reese Air Force Base**; numerous hospi-

tals, nursing homes; state school for mentally retarded.

Other towns include **Abernathy** (2,849, part Hale County) cotton spinning mill; **Idalou** (2,453), **Shallowater** (2,107), **Slaton** (6,950) cotton, rail, manufacturing center; **Wolfforth** (2,271), **Ransom Canyon** (620) and **New Deal** (691).

Lynn

LOCATION: Northwest (G-8).

HISTORY: Created, 1876, from Bexar District; organized, 1903; named for Alamo martyr, W. Lynn (or Linn).

Cong. Dist.	17	U.S. Jud. Dist.	N-Lb.
St. Sen. Dist.	28	Ct. Appeals	7
St. Rep. Dist.	78	Admin. Jud. Dist.	7
St. Dist. Cts.	106		

PHYSICAL FEATURES: Plain, broken by Cap Rock Escarpment, playas and draws; sandy loam, black, gray soils.

RECREATION: Local events.

MINERALS: Oil, gas, stone.

1985 Pop.	7,800	Tax Ratio	0.95
Area (sq. mi.)	888	Oil value	$2,795,601
Altitude (ft.) . .	2,881-3,274	No. employed	1,082
Ann. rainfall (in.) . .	17.88	Avg. weekly wage	$290.46
Jan. temp. min.	27	Annual wages	$16,342,776
July temp. max.	94	1983 PCI	$6,105
Growing season (da.)	217	Buying pwr. .	$51,430,000
Voters reg.	4,067	Tax value . .	$330,502,414
Businesses	121	Fed. expd. . . .	$265,799,000

VITAL STATISTICS 1985: Births, 130; Deaths, 59; Marriages, 93; Divorces, 33.

AGRICULTURE: About $50 million average income, 90% from cotton, sorghums, wheat; cattle, hogs, sheep; 50,000 acres irrigated, mostly cotton.

BUSINESS: Cotton, grain sorghum industries.

TAHOKA (3,058) county seat; cotton center; cotton compress; farm equipment manufacturing; hospital, nursing home. Other towns include **O'Donnell** (1,076, part Dawson County), **Wilson** (552), **New Home** (243).

(For McCulloch County see next page.)

McLennan

LOCATION: Central (J-16).

HISTORY: Created from Milam County and organized in 1850; named for an original settler, **Neil McLennan Sr.**

PHYSICAL FEATURES: Mostly Blackland prairie, but rolling hills in west; drains to Bosque, Brazos Rivers and **Lake Waco;** heavy, loam, sandy soils.

Cong. Dist. 11	U.S. Jud. Dist. . . . . W-Wa.	
St. Sen. Dist. 9	Ct. Appeals 10	
St. Rep. Dist. 55, 56	Admin. Jud. Dist. 3	
St. Dist Cts. . 19, 54, 74, 170		

RECREATION: Varied metropolitan activities (see chamber of commerce for dates); **Fort Fisher Park** with camping facilities; **Homer Garrison Jr. Texas Ranger Museum; Texas Ranger Hall of Fame; Cameron Park; Lake Waco;** Brazos River festival and local events; zoo; historic sites and homes; museums; libraries; art center; symphony orchestra; civic theater; private telephone museum in McGregor; college university events; **Heart o' Texas Fair Rodeo, Brazos festival.** Westfest in West in September; Central Texas Fair.

MINERALS: Sand and gravel, stone, clays, oil, gas.

AGRICULTURE: $70 million average yearly income, 65% from cattle, dairy products; large producer of turkeys; cotton, sorghums, wheat, corn, hay principal crops.

BUSINESS: A leading distribution center for Central Texas; diversified manufacturing; government employment; agribusiness; education.

1985 Pop.	184,100	Tax Ratio	0.86
Area (sq. mi.)	1,031	Oil value	0
Altitude (ft.)	381-734	No. employed	70,705
Ann. rainfall (in.) . .	31.26	Avg. weekly wage	$312.68
Jan. temp. min.	38	Ann. wages . $1,149,642,840	
July temp. max.	96	1983 PCI	$8,309
Growing season (da.)	253	Buying pwr. $1,907,771,000	
Voters reg.	89,502	Tax value . . $4,491,682,943	
Businesses	4,529	Fed. expd. . . . $464,476,000	

VITAL STATISTICS 1985: Births, 3,104; Deaths, 1,755; Marriages, 2,369; Divorces, 1,044.

WACO (104,133) county seat; see metro page; center for manufacturing, tourism, conventions, agribusinesses; plants make glass products, health care products, food products, lumber, batteries, apparel, steel products, many other products; **Baylor University; Paul Quinn College; McLennan Community College; Texas State Technical Institute;** Veterans Administration regional office and hospital; other hospitals, nursing homes.

Other towns include **Bellmead** (8,025), **Beverly Hills** (2,316), **Bruceville-Eddy** (1,132, partly Falls County), **Crawford** (638), **Gholson** (294), **Golinda** (372, partly Falls County), **Hallsburg** (528), **Hewitt** (7,474), **Lacy-Lakeview** (2,878), **Leroy** (322), **Lorena** (887), **McGregor** (4,682) rocket motors, fuel devices, other products manufactured, nursing home; **Mart** (2,445) plastics, concrete services; **Moody** (1,502), **Northcrest** (2,057), **Riesel** (786), **Robinson** (6,426), **Ross** (261), **Valley Mills** (1,370, mostly Bosque County), **West** (2,519) and **Woodway** (7,580).

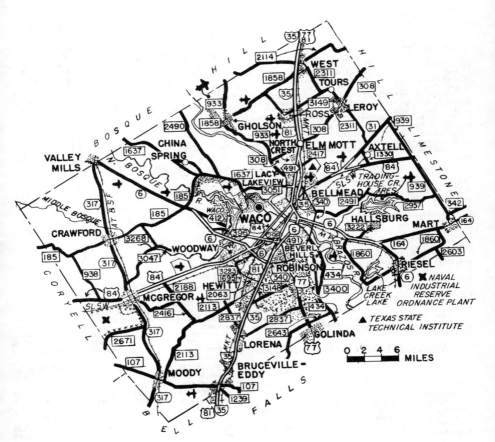

McCulloch

LOCATION: Texas' **geographical center** in county (K-13).

HISTORY: Created from Bexar District, 1856; organized, 1876; named for Texas pioneer, **Gen. Ben McCulloch.**

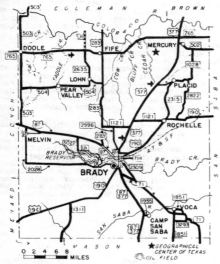

Cong. Dist.	21	U.S. Jud. Dist.	W-An.
St. Sen. Dist.	24	Ct. Appeals	3
St. Rep. Dist.	65	Admin. Jud. Dist.	7
St. Dist. Cts.	198		

PHYSICAL FEATURES: Hilly and rolling; drains to Colorado, Brady Creek and lake, San Saba River; black loams to sandy soils.

RECREATION: Hunting; **Brady Reservoir** activities; muzzle loading rifle association state championship, horse racing, world championship barbecue goat cook-off, sheep dog classic; other local events.

MINERALS: Production oil, sand, gravel, stone, gas.

1985 Pop.	9,000	Tax Ratio	0.86
Area (sq. mi.)	1,071	Oil value	0
Altitude (ft.)	1,442-2,021	No. employed	2,212
Ann. rainfall (in.)	23.46	Avg. weekly wage	$246.61
Jan. temp. min.	34	Annual wages	$28,366,436
July temp. max.	96	1983 PCI	$6,916
Growing season (da.)	226	Buying pwr.	$78,494,000
Voters reg.	4,501	Tax value	$447,837,940
Businesses	243	Fed. expd.	$24,784,000

VITAL STATISTICS 1985: Births, 137; Deaths, 150; Marriages, 106; Divorces, 61.

AGRICULTURE: About $15 million average income, 80% from beef cattle, sheep, goats, hogs, horses; crops include oats, wheat, sorghums, cotton, peanuts, hay. About 2,000 acres irrigated.

BUSINESS: Agribusinesses, manufacturing, tourism, hunting leases.

BRADY (5,925) county seat; ranching and tourist headquarters; plants process mohair and wool, peanuts, sand, make trailers, farm equipment, other products; hospital, nursing homes; **Central Texas College. Melvin** (213) other principal town.

(For McLennan County see previous page.)

McMullen

LOCATION: South (Q-14).

HISTORY: Created from Atascosa, Bexar, Live Oak Counties, 1858; organized, 1862, reorganized, 1877; named for Irish empresario, **John McMullen.**

RECREATION: Deer hunting; Lions Club Rodeo, August-September; 4-H Livestock show and sale in April; **Choke Canyon Reservoir** and wildlife management area.

MINERALS: Production of gas, oil and coal.

Cong. Dist.	15	U.S. Jud. Dist.	S-La.
St. Sen. Dist.	21	Ct. Appeals	4
St. Rep. Dist.	44	Admin. Jud. Dist.	4
St. Dist. Cts.	36, 156, 343		

PHYSICAL FEATURES: Brushy plain, sloping to Frio, Nueces and tributaries; saline clay soils.

1985 Pop.	1,000	Growing season (da.)	291
Area (sq. mi.)	1,163	Voters reg.	623
Altitude (ft.)	230-642	Businesses	22
Ann. rainfall (in.)	25.27	Tax Ratio	0.64
Jan. temp. min.	44	Oil value	$5,518,465
July temp. max.	98	No. employed	221
Avg. weekly wage	$326.59	Buying pwr.	$9,191,000
Annual wages	$3,753,200	Tax value	$522,673,759
1983 PCI	$10,439	Fed. expd.	$1,195,000

VITAL STATISTICS 1985: Births, 13; Deaths, 8; Marriages, 4; Divorces, 2.

AGRICULTURE: About $9 million average annual income, more than 90% from beef cattle; crops are corn, milo.

BUSINESS: Oil, gas production, cattle raising dominate economy.

TILDEN (est. 500) county seat; ranching, oil, gas center; manufcturing includes kitty litter, food processing and natural gas plant.

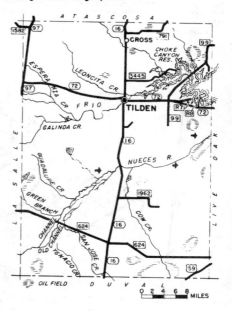

Madison

LOCATION: East Central (K-18).

HISTORY: Named for U.S. President James Madison; created from Grimes, Leon, Walker Counties, 1853; organized, 1854.

Cong. Dist.	6	U.S. Jud. Dist.	S-Hn.
St. Sen. Dist.	5	Ct. Appeals	10
St. Rep. Dist.	15	Admin. Jud. Dist.	2
St. Dist. Cts.	12, 278		

PHYSICAL FEATURES: Hilly, draining to Trinity, Navasota Rivers, Bedias Creek on boundaries; fifth of area timbered; alluvial, loam, sandy soils.

RECREATION: Fishing, hunting; water activities at **Lake Madison; Madisonville Sidewalk Cattlemen's** celebration in June; historic sites.

MINERALS: Production of oil, gas and gravel.

1985 Pop.	12,200	Tax Ratio	0.82
Area (sq. mi.)	473	Oil value	$5,484,465

TEXAS DEPT. OF CORRECTIONS
▲ FERGUSON UNIT
✦ OIL FIELD
✛ SITE OF SPANISH BLUFF

Altitude (ft.)	213-364	No. employed	3,157
Ann. rainfall (in.) . .	41.50	Avg. weekly wage	$313.63
Jan. temp. min. . .	40	Annual wages .	$51,486,940
July temp. max. .	94	1983 PCI	$6,392
Growing season (da.)	272	Buying pwr. .	$107,108,000
Voters reg.	5,289	Tax value . . .	$557,339,170
Businesses	192	Fed. expd.	$18,560,000

VITAL STATISTICS 1985: Births, 141; Deaths, 153; Marriages, 110; Divorces, 49.

AGRICULTURE: More than $40 million average annual income, about evenly split between cattle, horses, hogs and sorghums, oats, pecans.

BUSINESS: Agribusinesses, oil production, manufacturing.

MADISONVILLE (3,973) county seat; farm trading center; mushroom processing; plants make clothes, fiberglass products; hospital, nursing home, library; **Midway (300); Normangee (581,** mostly Leon County).

Marion

LOCATION: Northeast (G-21).

HISTORY: Created, organized, 1860, from Cass County; named for U.S. **Gen. Francis Marion.**

Cong. Dist.	1	U.S. Jud. Dist.	E-MI.
St. Sen. Dist.	1	Ct. Appeals	6
St. Rep. Dist.	8	Admin. Jud. Dist. . . .	1
St. Dist. Cts.	115, 276		

PHYSICAL FEATURES: Hilly, three-fourths forested with pines, hardwoods; drains to **Caddo Lake, Lake O' the Pines, Cypress Bayou.**

RECREATION: Lake O' the Pines, Caddo activities; hunting; **Excelsior Hotel;** 84 medallions on historic sites including **Jay Gould railroad car, House of Four Seasons; Freeman plantation;** historical museum; historical pilgrimage in May.

MINERALS: Oil, gas, clays, lignite.

1985 Pop.	10,200	Tax Ratio	0.94
Area (sq. mi.)	385	Oil value	$396,426
Altitude (ft.) . . .	168-379	No. employed	1,432
Ann. rainfall (in.) . .	44.83	Avg. weekly wage	$243.41
Jan. temp. min. . .	36	Annual wages .	$18,125,644
July temp. max. . .	94	1983 PCI	$5,913
Growing season (da.)	236	Buying pwr. . .	$92,333,000
Voters reg.	5,966	Tax value . . .	$391,148,113
Businesses	151	Fed. expd.	$22,015,000

VITAL STATISTICS 1985: Births, 144; Deaths, 120; Marriages, 193; Divorces, 48.

AGRICULTURE: About $3 million average income, 90% from beef cattle and some poultry, swine and horses; hay, vegetables are top crops; estimated $11 million in timber sales.

BUSINESS: Oil, timber industries; recreation; syrup plant.

JEFFERSON (2,519) county seat; one of state's oldest and most historic towns; once a major river port; sawmills; plants make syrup, reels, plate glass, oil field equipment and other products; antique shops; hospitals, nursing homes; historic pilgrimage each May, festival in October.

Martin

LOCATION: West (I-8).

HISTORY: Created from Bexar District, 1876; organized, 1884; named for **Republic of Texas Sen. Wylie Martin.**

Cong. Dist.	17	U.S. Jud. Dist. . . .	W:M-O
St. Sen. Dist.	28	Ct. Appeals	8
St. Rep. Dist.	77	Admin. Jud. Dist.	7
St. Dist. Cts.	118		

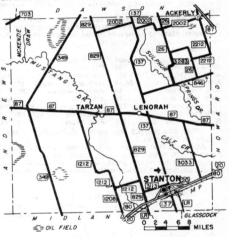

OIL FIELD

PHYSICAL FEATURES: Sandy, loam soils on plain, broken by playas, creeks.

RECREATION: Museum, Settlers reunion, local events.

MINERALS: Oil, gas.

1985 Pop.	5,300	Tax Ratio	0.93
Area (sq. mi.)	914	Oil value	$40,301,890
Altitude (ft.) . . .	2,518-2,888	No. employed	918
Ann. rainfall (in.) . .	15.72	Avg. weekly wage	$330.17
Jan. temp. min.	30	Annual wages .	$15,761,024
July temp. max. . .	95	1983 PCI	$9,067
Growing season (da.)	215	Buying pwr. .	$47,646,000
Voters reg.	2,523	Tax value . . .	$684,587,707
Businesses	92	Fed. expd.	$14,847,000

OIL FIELD

0 2 4 6 MILES

VITAL STATISTICS 1985: Births, 98; Deaths, 37; Marriages, 67; Divorces, 17.

AGRICULTURE: About $32 million average annual income, 90% from cotton, small grains, remainder from cattle; sheep, goat raising increasing; about 18,000 acres irrigated.

BUSINESS: Petroleum production, agribusinesses dominate economy.

STANTON (2,684) county seat; center for oil, ranching business; cotton compress; county hospital. **Ackerly** (341, partly Dawson County).

Mason

LOCATION: Central (L-13).

HISTORY: Created from Bexar, Gillespie counties, organized, 1858; named for Mexican War victim, **Lt. G. T. Mason.**

Cong. Dist.	21	U.S. Jud. Dist.	W-An.
St. Sen. Dist.	25	Ct. Appeals	4
St. Rep. Dist.	67	Admin. Jud. Dist.	3
St. Dist. Cts.	33		

PHYSICAL FEATURES: Hilly, draining to Llano, San Saba and tributaries; limestone, red soils; varied timber.

RECREATION: Major tourist area; outstanding deer, turkey hunting, river fishing; camping; bluebonnet trails; historic homes; restored town; **Ft. Mason Museum;** local events; golf course.

MINERALS: Topaz.

1985 Pop.	3,600	Tax Ratio	0.85
Area (sq. mi.)	934	Oil value	0
Altitude (ft.)	1,258-1,981	No. employed	688
Ann. rainfall (in.)	24.68	Avg. weekly wage	$218.79
Jan. temp. min.	34	Annual wages	$7,827,676
July temp. max.	95	1983 PCI	$6,476
Growing season (da.)	217	Buying pwr.	$30,529,000
Voters reg.	2,499	Tax value	$570,887,608
Businesses	105	Fed. expd.	$9,643,000

VITAL STATISTICS 1985: Births, 48; Deaths, 63; Marriages, 34; Divorces, 5.

AGRICULTURE: Some $21 million average yearly income, 80% from cattle, hogs, sheep, goats; peanuts, hay, coastal bermuda grass, wheat, oats, watermelon produced. Some 9,000 acres irrigated, mostly peanuts, hay.

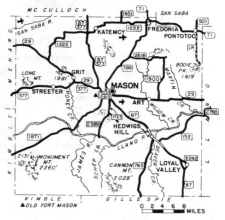

BUSINESS: Ranching, hunting, tourism, soft drink bottling.

MASON (2,094) county seat; tourist, ranching center; candy manufacturing; museum.

Matagorda

LOCATION: On coast (O-19).

HISTORY: An original county, created 1836 from Spanish municipality, named for canebrake; organized 1837; settled by Stephen F. Austin colonists.

Cong. Dist.	14	U.S. Jud. Dist.	S-Gn.
St. Sen. Dist.	18	Ct. Appeals	13
St. Rep. Dist.	29	Admin. Jud. Dist.	2
St. Dist. Cts.	23, 130		

PHYSICAL FEATURES: Flat, broken by bays; contains part of **Matagorda Island;** many different soils; drains to Colorado River, creeks, coast.

RECREATION: Coastal activities, including fishing, water sports, hunting; historic sites, museums; Rice Festival, local events.

MINERALS: Production of gas, oil, salt.

1985 Pop.	40,200	Tax Ratio	0.90
Area (sq. mi.)	1,127	Oil value	$19,288,015
Altitude (ft.)	2-56	No. employed	18,228
Ann. rainfall (in.)	42.29	Avg. weekly wage	$513.27
Jan. temp. min.	48	Annual wages	$486,507,552
July temp. max.	90	1983 PCI	$9,450
Growing season (da.)	296	Buying pwr.	$525,400,000
Voters reg.	18,394	Tax value	$3,420,287,926
Businesses	853	Fed. expd.	$72,489,000

VITAL STATISTICS 1985: Births, 815; Deaths, 341; Marriages, 493; Divorces, 249.

AGRICULTURE: About $75 million average annual income, 80% from rice, cotton, sorghums, soybeans, other crops; beef cattle produced. Estimated 42,000 acres irrigated, mostly for rice and turf.

BUSINESS: Petroleum operations, petrochemicals, agribusinesses dominate the economy; varied manufacturing; tourism significant.

BAY CITY (17,795) county seat; petrochemical, plastics, fertilizer plants, nuclear power plant; gas, oil processing, commercial fishing; tourist center; hospital, nursing homes; rice festival in October, fair and rodeo in March. Other towns include **Palacios** (4,603) tourism, seafood processing, petrochemical; hospital, library, airport. Other towns are **Van Vleck, Matagorda, Markham** and **Blessing.**

Maverick

LOCATION: On Rio Grande (P-11).

HISTORY: Named for pioneer, **Sam A. Maverick,** whose name is synonym for unbranded cattle; created 1856, from Kinney County; organized 1871.

Cong. Dist.	23	U.S. Jud. Dist.	W-DR
St. Sen. Dist.	21	Ct. Appeals	4
St. Rep. Dist.	68	Admin. Jud. Dist.	4
St. Dist. Cts.	293		

PHYSICAL FEATURES: Broken, rolling surface, with dense brush; clay, sandy, alluvial soils.

at Castroville; special tourist events; county fair; St. Louis Day celebration in August.

MINERALS: Oil, gas, clay, sand, gravel.

1985 Pop.	25,100	Tax Ratio	0.98
Area (sq. mi.)	1,331	Oil value	$137,871
Altitude (ft.)	635-1,995	No. employed	5,778
Ann. rainfall (in.)	28.43	Avg. weekly wage	$239.90
Jan. temp. min.	42	Annual wages	$72,082,252
July temp. max.	96	1983 PCI	$6,703
Growing season (da.)	263	Buying pwr.	$218,659,000
Voters reg.	13,209	Tax value	$1,493,710,658
Businesses	471	Fed. expd.	$58,098,000

VITAL STATISTICS 1985: Births, 454; Deaths, 218; Marriages, 189; Divorces, 76.

AGRICULTURE: $45 million average yearly income, 60% from cattle, hogs, sheep; crops include sorghum, small grains, corn, peanuts, hay, soybeans, guar, cotton, vegetables; 32,000 acres irrigated.

BUSINESS: Agribusinesses, tourism, varied manufacturing.

HONDO (6,152) county seat; plants make bathroom fixtures, brick and tile, metal buildings, oil field tanks, aircraft parts and accessories, other products; hospital, nursing homes; U.S. Air Force flight screening center.

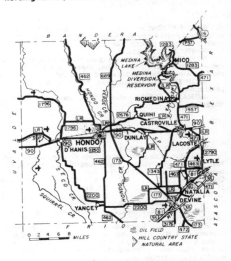

RECREATION: Tourist gateway to Mexico; white-tail deer, bird hunting; fishing; International Friendship Festival at Eagle Pass; annual events.

MINERALS: Production of oil, gas, sand and gravel.

AGRICULTURE: A $36.3 million average annual income, 90% from beef cattle, feedlots; crops include oats, sorghums, wheat, pecans, vegetables. About 16,000 acres irrigated from Rio Grande.

BUSINESS: Oil production, operations; agribusinesses; feedlots; tourist trade with Mexico.

1985 Pop.	34,200	Tax Ratio	0.97
Area (sq. mi.)	1,287	Oil value	$17,399,980
Altitude (ft.)	550-1,000	No. employed	6,316
Ann. rainfall (in.)	19.74	Avg. weekly wage	$232.11
Jan. temp. min.	40	Annual wages	$76,235,244
July temp. max.	100	1983 PCI	$
Growing season (da.)	285	Buying pwr.	$175,508,000
Voters reg.	11,166	Tax value	$919,965,135
Businesses	510	Fed. expd.	$60,754,000

VITAL STATISTICS 1985: Births, 755; Deaths, 165; Marriages, 520; Divorces, 87.

EAGLE PASS (24,097) county seat; varied manufacturing; tourism center; major rail and highway entry point into Mexico; hospital.

Medina

LOCATION: Southwest (O-13).

HISTORY: Created, organized, 1848, from Bexar; settled by Alsatians led by **Henri Castro** and named for river, probably for Spanish engineer, **Pedro Medina**.

Cong. Dist.	23	U.S. Jud. Dist.	W-SAnt.
St. Sen. Dist.	21	Ct. Appeals	4
St. Rep. Dist.	45	Admin. Jud. Dist.	6
St. Dist. Cts.	38		

PHYSICAL FEATURES: Scenic hills in north; south has fertile valleys, rolling surface; Medina River, lake.

RECREATION: A leading deer area; scenic drives; camping, fishing; historic sites, museum; **Landmark Inn**

Devine (4,016) peanut storage, shipping center; tire testing; 2 cattle feedlots; clothing factory; nurseries; nursing homes. Other towns include **Castroville** (2,037) Alsatian events, bakery, tourism, livestock genetics; **Lytle** (2,143, mostly in Atascosa County); **Natalia** (1,514) carpet underlaying manufactured; **La Coste** (942).

Menard

LOCATION: Central (L-12).

HISTORY: Created from Bexar, 1858, organized, 1871; named for Galveston's founder, **Michel B. Menard.**

Cong. Dist.	21	U.S. Jud. Dist.	N-SAng.
St. Sen. Dist.	25	Ct. Appeals	4
St. Rep. Dist.	67	Admin. Jud. Dist.	7
St. Dist. Cts.	198		

PHYSICAL FEATURES: Rolling, draining to San Saba and tributaries; limestone soils.

1985 Pop.	2,300	Tax Ratio	0.94
Area (sq. mi.)	902	Oil value	$157,147
Altitude (ft.)	1,690-2,346	No. employed	451
Ann. rainfall (in.)	21.33	Avg. weekly wage	$239.13
Jan. temp. min.	33	Annual wages	$5,608,304
July temp. max.	96	1983 PCI	$5,427
Growing season (da.)	220	Buying pwr.	$14,739,000
Voters reg.	1,614	Tax value	$261,688,530
Businesses	52	Fed. expd.	$7,316,000

VITAL STATISTICS 1985: Births, 33; Deaths, 29; Marriages, 21; Divorces, 10.

Menard County (Cont'd.)

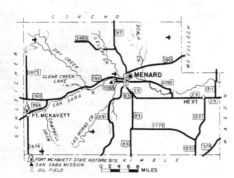

Jan. temp. min...... 31	Annual wages $971,451,708
July temp. max. 95	1983 PCI $13,409
Growing season (da.) 218	Buying pwr. $1,716,154,000
Voters reg. 47,991	Tax value . $4,727,576,440
Businesses 3,782	Fed. expd.... $129,866,000

VITAL STATISTICS 1985: Births, 2,424; Deaths, 588; Marriages, 1,345; Divorces, 701.

AGRICULTURE: About $13 million average annual income from swine, sheep; cotton, sorghums, small grains, pecans; about 15,000 acres irrigated.

BUSINESS: Among leading petroleum-producing counties; distributing, administrative center for oil industry; manufacturing including computer and telecommunications (see metro page).

MIDLAND (97,148) county seat; center for petroleum, petrochemical operations; plants make clothing, oil field and other petroleum-related equipment, plastics, electronic calculators, other products; livestock sale center; **Midland College;** hospitals.

RECREATION: Hunting, fishing; historic sites include **Real Presidio de San Saba, Ft. McKavett State Park;** museum, country store, **San Saba River.**

MINERALS: Oil, gas.

AGRICULTURE: About $13 million average annual income, 90% from beef cattle, sheep, goats; crops include grains, pecans; 2,000 acres irrigated.

BUSINESS: Agribusinesses, tourism, oil and gas production.

MENARD (1,715) county seat; ranching center; hospital.

Milam

LOCATION: East central (L-16).

HISTORY: Created, 1836, from municipality named for **Ben Milam,** 1835 leader in capture of San Antonio; organized, 1837.

Cong. Dist. 11	U.S. Jud. Dist.... W-Wa.
St. Sen. Dist. 5	Ct. Appeals 3
St. Rep. Dist........ 13	Admin. Jud. Dist. 3
St. Dist. Cts. 20	

PHYSICAL FEATURES: Partly level Blackland; southeast rolling; Brazos, Little Rivers.

RECREATION: Fishing, hunting; historic sites include Ft. Sullivan, Indian battlegrounds, mission sites; Milam County Museum in old jail at Cameron; festivals, other local events; **Alcoa Lake;** chili cookoff in August.

MINERALS: Large lignite deposits; limited oil, gas.

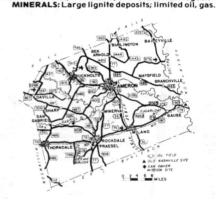

Midland

LOCATION: West (J-8).

HISTORY: Created from Tom Green, organized, 1885; name came from midway location on railroad between El Paso and Fort Worth.

Cong. Dist. 21	U.S. Jud. Dist.... W:M-O
St. Sen. Dist. 25	Ct. Appeals 8
St. Rep. Dist........ 76	Admin. Jud. Dist. 7
St. Dist. Cts. .. 142, 238, 318	

PHYSICAL FEATURES: Flat, broken by draws; sandy, loam soils.

RECREATION: Permian Basin Petroleum Museum, Library and Hall of Fame; Museum of the Southwest; Pliska Aviation Museum; zoo; polo; golf, tennis, professional baseball, community theater, metropolitan events (ask chamber of commerce for dates).

MINERALS: Production of oil, gas, stone.

1985 Pop........ 109,200	Tax Ratio 0.97
Area (sq. mi.) 902	Oil value $96,388,225
Altitude (ft.) . . 2,613-2,936	No. employed 42,887
Ann. rainfall (in.) . . 13.51	Avg. weekly wage $435.60

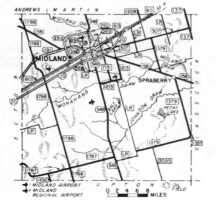

1985 Pop........ 23,700	Tax Ratio 0.90
Area (sq. mi.) 1,019	Oil value $309,460
Altitude (ft.) 306-648	No. employed 5,857
Ann. rainfall (in.) . . 33.87	Avg. weekly wage $447.45
Jan. temp. min...... 39	Annual wages $136,277,984
July temp. max. 96	1983 PCI $7,222
Growing season (da.) 256	Buying pwr. . $228,358,000
Voters reg. 11,824	Tax value . $1,495,922,127
Businesses 496	Fed. expd..... $52,197,000

VITAL STATISTICS 1985: Births, 339; Deaths, 303; Marriages, 290; Divorces, 89.

AGRICULTURE: About $55 million average annual income, 70% from cattle, hogs, poultry; crops include sorghums, cotton, wheat, hay, corn.

BUSINESS: Many employed at aluminum plant; varied manufacturing; lignite mining; agribusinesses.

CAMERON (5,817) county seat; plants make doors, furniture, steel products, pipe and fertilizer; power generation; other products; hospitals, nursing homes, library.

Rockdale (5,810) has large aluminum plant; lignite mining center; hospital, nursing homes. **Thorndale** (1,338) has cotton oil mill; manufactures cans, electricity; **Buckholts** (429), **Milano** (495).

Mills

LOCATION: Central (J-14).

HISTORY: Created, organized, 1887, from Brown, Comanche, Hamilton, Lampasas counties; named for pioneer jurist, **John T. Mills.**

Cong. Dist.	11	U.S. Jud. Dist.	N-SAng.
St. Sen. Dist.	24	Ct. Appeals	3
St. Rep. Dist.	54	Admin. Jud. Dist.	7
St. Dist. Cts.	35		

PHYSICAL FEATURES: Hills, plateau draining to Colorado River on southwest; sandy, loam soils.

RECREATION: Fishing, deer, dove and turkey hunting; historic suspension bridge, fiddlers' contest in May.

MINERALS: Not significant.

1985 Pop.	4,500	Tax Ratio	0.80
Area (sq. mi.)	748	Oil value	0
Altitude (ft.)	1,250-1,762	No. employed	1,075
Ann. rainfall (in.)	27.52	Avg. weekly wage	$224.70
Jan. temp. min.	34	Annual wages	$12,560,968
July temp. max.	87	1983 PCI	$6,607
Growing season (da.)	230	Buying pwr.	$48,523,000
Voters reg.	2,680	Tax value	$358,133,670
Businesses	95	Fed. expd.	$13,108,000

VITAL STATISTICS 1985: Births, 52; Deaths, 64; Marriages, 47; Divorces, 19.

AGRICULTURE: About $23 million average yearly income, 90% from sheep, beef cattle, Angora goats; crops principally hay, oats and sorghums.

BUSINESS: Chiefly agribusiness, hunting leases.

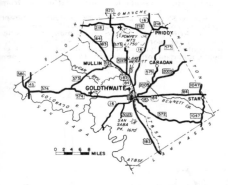

GOLDTHWAITE (1,858) county seat; center for farming, ranching activity; plants make farming equipment; metal products; hospital, nursing homes. **Mullin** (221).

Mitchell

LOCATION: West (I-10).

HISTORY: Created, 1876, from Bexar District; organized, 1881; named for pioneer brothers, **Asa and Eli Mitchell.**

Cong. Dist.	17	U.S. Jud. Dist.	N-Ab.
St. Sen. Dist.	30	Ct. Appeals	11
St. Rep. Dist.	66	Admin. Jud. Dist.	7
St. Dist. Cts.	32		

PHYSICAL FEATURES: Rolling, draining to Colorado and tributaries; sandy, red, dark soils; **Colorado and Champion Creek Lakes.**

RECREATION: Lake activities; **Lake Colorado City State Park;** museum, playhouse; hunting; local events.

MINERALS: Production of oil, gas.

1985 Pop.	9,000	Tax Ratio	0.90
Area (sq. mi.)	912	Oil value	$49,179,327
Altitude (ft.)	2,004-2,616	No. employed	2,193
Ann. rainfall (in.)	19.68	Avg. weekly wage	$260.67
Jan. temp. min.	30	Annual wages	$29,725,880
July temp. max.	96	1983 PCI	$7,427
Growing season (da.)	217	Buying pwr.	$80,007,000
Voters reg.	4,304	Tax value	$614,051,626
Businesses	250	Fed. expd.	$22,891,000

VITAL STATISTICS 1985: Births, 145; Deaths, 159; Marriages, 85; Divorces, 11.

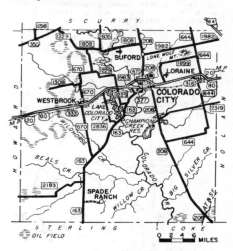

AGRICULTURE: Some $14 million annual average income from beef cattle, hogs, sheep, horses, dairy products, poultry; cotton, sorghums, small grains; 4,000 acres irrigated.

BUSINESS: Chiefly oil, agribusinesses; some manufacturing.

COLORADO CITY (5,549) county seat; plants make clothing, farm implements, carpet pads, process cotton, cottonseed, furs; electric service center; hospital, nursing homes. Other towns include **Loraine** (925) retirement center and **Westbrook** (328).

Montague

LOCATION: North (F-15).

HISTORY: Created from Cooke, 1857, organized, 1858; named for pioneer, **Daniel Montague.**

Cong. Dist.	17	U.S. Jud. Dist.	N-WF
St. Sen. Dist.	30	Ct. Appeals	2
St. Rep. Dist.	80	Admin. Jud. Dist.	8
St. Dist. Cts.	97		

PHYSICAL FEATURES: Rolling, draining to tributaries of Trinity, Red Rivers; sandy loams, red, black soils; **Lake Nocona, Lake Amon G. Carter; Lyndon B. Johnson National Grasslands.**

RECREATION: Lake activities; quail, turkey, deer hunting; scenic drives, museums; historical sites; Jim Bowie Days, "Chism Trail" scenic drive; other local events.

MINERALS: Production of oil, gas, stone.

1985 Pop.	18,500	Tax Ratio	0.91
Area (sq. mi.)	928	Oil value	$6,453,047
Altitude (ft.)	766-1,314	No. employed	4,233
Ann. rainfall (in.)	29.39	Avg. weekly wage	$245.10
Jan. temp. min.	32	Annual wages	$53,951,796
July temp. max.	96	1983 PCI	$7,503
Growing season (da.)	229	Buying pwr.	$164,626,000
Voters reg.	10,104	Tax value	$634,962,726
Businesses	493	Fed. expd.	$46,379,000

VITAL STATISTICS 1985: Births, 250; Deaths, 250; Marriages, 243; Divorces, 105.

AGRICULTURE: $23 million average annual income, 80% from livestock, chiefly beef, dairy cattle; crops include wheat, sorghums, peanuts, pasture grasses, peaches, apples, grapes, pecans, vegetables, some firewood.

BUSINESS: Agribusinesses; oil production; varied manufacturing.

MONTAGUE (est. 400) county seat; farm and cattle trade center.

Bowie (5,818) agribusiness center; apparel, boats, farm equipment, insulation, business uniforms, metal products manufactured; livestock sales; hospital, nursing home; library; Jim Bowie Days in June; historical museum. **Nocona** (3,206) is a major boot and leather goods, sporting goods, clothing manufacturing center; also uniforms, helicopter parts; hospital. **Saint Jo** (1,219) is farm trade center.

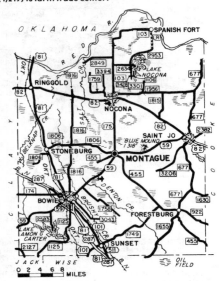

Montgomery

LOCATION: Southeast (M-19).

HISTORY: Created, organized, 1837, from Washington County; named for **U.S. Revolutionary Gen. Richard Montgomery.**

Cong. Dist. 2, 6, 8	U.S. Jud. Dist. . . . . S-Hn.
St. Sen. Dist. 3, 4, 5	Ct. Appeals 9
St. Rep. Dist. 15, 16	Admin. Jud. Dist. 2
St. Dist. Cts. . . 9, 2D9, 221, 284, 359	

PHYSICAL FEATURES: Rolling, over three-fourths timbered; **Sam Houston National Forest** over large area; loam, sandy, alluvial soils.

RECREATION: Hunting, fishing; **Lake Conroe** activities; **Sam Houston National Forest; W. G. Jones State Forest;** county fair, Heritage Museum, New Caney State Park.

MINERALS: Production of oil, gas, sand and gravel.

1985 Pop. 160,700	Tax Ratio 0.93
Area (sq. mi.) 1,047	Oil value $86,484,306
Altitude (ft.) 86-380	No. employed 31,737
Ann. rainfall (in.) . . 45.53	Avg. weekly wage $346.43
Jan. temp. min. 40	Annual wages $571,725,380
July temp. max. 94	1983 PCI $10,279
Growing season (da.) 270	Buying pwr. $2,066,589,000
Voters reg. 73,782	Tax value . . $7,531,484,848
Businesses 2,781	Fed. expd. . . . $254,674,000

VITAL STATISTICS 1985: Births, 2,886; Deaths, 1,027; Marriages, 1,965; Divorces, 991.

AGRICULTURE: About $103 million average annual income from horses, cattle; hay, nursery and greenhouse products, vegetables; substantial income from timber products.

BUSINESS: Many people work in Houston; center for lumber, oil production; part of Houston PMSA.

CONROE (18,943) county seat; many residential communities; workers employed in Houston; distribution center; plants make oil, wood, metal containers, oil field equipment, other products; food processing; new

hospital, nursing home; **Conroe College.**

Other towns include **Chateau Woods** (555), **Cut and Shoot** (678), **Magnolia** (1,132), **Montgomery** (281), **Oak Ridge** (2,483), **Panorama Village** (1,526), **Patton** (1,318), **Roman Forest** (1,022), **Shenandoah** (2,024), **Splendora** (722), **Stagecoach** (406), **Woodloch** (328), **Willis** (2,486), **Woodbranch** (991) and small part of Houston.

Moore

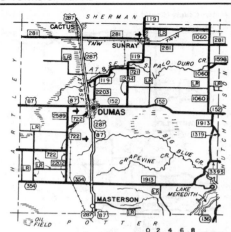

LOCATION: Northwest (B-8).

HISTORY: Created, 1876, from Bexar District; organized 1892; named for Republic of Texas Navy Commander, E. W. Moore.

Cong. Dist.	13	U.S. Jud. Dist. N-Am.
St. Sen. Dist.	31	Ct. Appeals. 7
St. Rep. Dist.	88	Admin. Jud. Dist. 9
St. Dist. Cts.	69	

PHYSICAL FEATURES: Flat to rolling, broken by creeks; sandy loams; **Lake Meredith.**

RECREATION: Lake Meredith activities; Dumas Dogie Days in June; historical museum; local events, art exhibits.

MINERALS: Production of natural gas, helium, oil.

1985 Pop.	17,400	Tax Ratio	0.87
Area (sq. mi.)	905	Oil value	$1,759,581
Altitude (ft.)	3,221-3,770	No. employed	6,602
Ann. rainfall (in.)	18.33	Avg. weekly wage	$368.95
Jan. temp. min.	20	Annual wages	$126,662,608
July temp. max.	93	1983 PCI	$8,850
Growing season (da.)	195	Buying pwr.	$176,831,000
Voters reg.	7,881	Tax value	$1,295,467,240
Businesses	450	Fed. expd.	$34,458,000

VITAL STATISTICS 1985: Births, 379; Deaths, 104; Marriages, 251; Divorces, 114.

AGRICULTURE: About $125 million average annual income, 75% from cattle; custom feedlots; crops include sorghums, wheat, corn; 200,000 acres irrigated.

BUSINESS: Extensive petroleum operations; major natural gas producing county; commercial tannery; beef processing, sorghum seed production, other agribusinesses.

DUMAS (12,900) county seat; tourism; regional retail center; petrochemical, refining, gas processing plants; feedlots; grain elevators; beef packers; fertilizer plants, leather tannery; hospital, nursing home.

Other towns include **Fritch** (2,912, mostly in Hutchinson County), **Sunray** (1,933), **Cactus** (1,041) large beef packing facility.

Morris

LOCATION: Northeast (G-20).

HISTORY: Named for legislator-jurist **W. W. Morris;** created from Titus County and organized in 1875.

Cong. Dist.	1
St. Sen. Dist.	1
St. Rep. Dist.	8
St. Dist. Cts.	76, 276
U.S. Jud. Dist.	E-Mi.
Ct. Appeals.	6
Admin. Jud. Dist.	1

MINERALS: Iron ore.

1985 Pop.	14,700		
Area (sq. mi.)	256		
Altitude (ft.)	268-537		
Ann. rainfall (in.)	46.12		
Jan. temp. min.	30		
July temp. max.	95		
Growing season (da.)	236		
Voters reg.	8,644		
Businesses	323		
Tax Ratio	1.00		
Oil value	0	1983 PCI	$7,056
No. employed	4,237	Buying pwr.	$135,050,000
Avg. weekly wage	$371.38	Tax value	$802,343,054
Annual wages	$81,825,764	Fed. expd.	$31,992,000

VITAL STATISTICS 1985: Births, 207; Deaths, 150; Marriages, 188; Divorces, 87.

PHYSICAL FEATURES: Rolling, forested hills; drains to streams, **Lone Star** and **Daingerfield Lakes.**

RECREATION: Activities on **Lake O' The Pines,** many small lakes; fishing, hunting; **Daingerfield State Park;** museum in Daingerfield; local events.

AGRICULTURE: An estimated $13 million average yearly income, 70% from beef cattle, poultry; crops include peanuts, peaches, corn, sorghums, vegetables; pine and hardwood timber sales.

BUSINESS: Steel mill; manufacturing; tourism; livestock, timber production.

DAINGERFIELD (3,008) county seat; plants make garments, chemicals, roofing products; process pipe, other steel products; hospital, clinics, nursing home, library.

Other towns include **Lone Star** (2,358) site of steel mill; **Naples** (1,906) and **Omaha** (1,000) commercial plant farm.

Motley

LOCATION: Northwest (E-10).

HISTORY: Created out of Bexar District, 1876; organized 1891; named for **Dr. J. W. Mottley,** Texas Declaration of Independence signer, but name misspelled in law.

Cong. Dist.	13	U.S. Jud. Dist. N-Lb.
St. Sen. Dist.	30	Ct. Appeals. 7
St. Rep. Dist.	84	Admin. Jud. Dist. 9
St. Dist. Cts.	110	

PHYSICAL FEATURES: Rough terrain, broken by Pease tributaries; sandy to red clay soils.

RECREATION: Local events; quail, dove, deer hunting; Matador Ranch headquarters; spring-fed pool at Roaring Springs; settlers reunion.

MINERALS: Oil, sand and gravel, gas.

1985 Pop.	1,800	Tax Ratio	0.81
Area (sq. mi.)	959	Oil value	0
Altitude (ft.)	1,928-3,034	No. employed	234
Ann. rainfall (in.)	20.35	Avg. weekly wage	$266.65
Jan. temp. min.	26	Annual wages	$3,244,668
July temp. max.	96	1983 PCI	$6,423
Growing season (da.)	218	Buying pwr.	$14,747,000
Voters reg.	1,181	Tax value	$124,067,399
Businesses	41	Fed. expd.	$7,717,000

VITAL STATISTICS 1985: Births, 21; Deaths, 29; Marriages, 10; Divorces, 8.

AGRICULTURE: About $14 million average yearly income, 65% from beef cattle, horses; crops include cotton, peanuts, wheat, guar, other grains; 6,000 acres irrigated, peanuts.

BUSINESS: Economy based on livestock, oil production.

MATADOR (1,019) county seat; farm trading center; clinic; **Roaring Springs** (282) plastic pipe, jewelry manufacturing; food processing.

See Map on next page.

Motley County (Cont'd.)

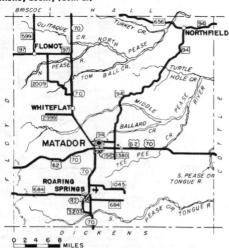

Nacogdoches

LOCATION: East (J-21).

HISTORY: Original county; created, 1836, organized, 1837; named for Indians; one of most historic areas.

Cong. Dist.	2	U.S. Jud. Dist.	E-Ty.
St. Sen. Dist.	3	Ct. Appeals	12
St. Rep. Dist.	10	Admin. Jud. Dist.	1
St. Dist. Cts.	145		

PHYSICAL FEATURES: On divide between streams; hilly; two-thirds forested; red, gray, sandy soils; **Sam Rayburn Reservoir.**

RECREATION: Lake, river activities; **Stephen F. Austin University events; Angelina National Forest;** historic sites major tourist attraction, including **Old Stone Fort,** pioneer homes, museums, Piney Woods Fair in October.

MINERALS: First Texas oil found here, 1866; production of gas, oil, clay, stone.

1985 Pop.	49,800	Tax Ratio	0.55
Area (sq. mi.)	939	Oil value	$46,448
Altitude (ft.)	182-655	No. employed	16,374
Ann. rainfall (in.)	47.53	Avg. weekly wage	$259.02
Jan. temp. min.	39	Annual wages	$220,545,596
July temp. max.	94	1983 PCI	$7,550
Growing season (da.)	243	Buying pwr.	$469,422,000
Voters reg.	23,962	Tax value	$1,285,160,370
Businesses	1,191	Fed. expd.	$95,954,000

The Carnegie Library building in Belton, first occupied in 1905, was used as a library until 1975. Texas Almanac photo.

VITAL STATISTICS 1985: Births, 738; Deaths, 427; Marriages, 569; Divorces, 126.

AGRICULTURE: About $160 million average annual income, 90% from cattle, poultry, dairy products; a leading broiler producing county; timber sales an estimated $8 million.

BUSINESS: Agribusinesses, manufacturing, education and tourism are leading economic factors.

NACOGDOCHES (28,744) county seat; plants make valves, feed, fertilizers, aluminum furniture, wood products, business forms, transformers, candy, dresses, motor homes; poultry processing center, other agribusinesses; trade, tourism center; **Stephen F. Austin State University;** hospitals, nursing homes; many historic sites, homes; museum.

Other towns include **Garrison** (1,024), **Cushing** (581), **Appleby** (497), **Chireno** (422).

Navarro

LOCATION: North central (I-17).

HISTORY: Created from Robertson County, organized in 1846; named for Republic of Texas leader, **Jose Antonio Navarro.**

Cong. Dist.	6	U.S. Jud. Dist.	N-Dl.
St. Sen. Dist.	9	Ct. Appeals	10
St. Rep. Dist.	12	Admin. Jud. Dist.	3
St. Dist. Cts.	13		

PHYSICAL FEATURES: Level Blackland, some rolling; Chambers, Richland Creeks, Trinity River; **Navarro Mills Lake, Richland Creek Reservoir.**

RECREATION: **Navarro Mills Lake** activities; Pioneer Village; historic sites, homes; Richland-Chambers Lake; Derrick Days in April.

MINERALS: Longest continuous Texas oil flow; over 200 million bbls. since 1895; production of oil, gas, sand and gravel.

1985 Pop.	39,100	Tax Ratio	0.93
Area (sq. mi.)	1,068	Oil value	$1,251,610
Altitude (ft.)	293-536	No. employed	12,624
Ann. rainfall (in.)	37.74	Avg. weekly wage	$293.85
Jan. temp. min.	36	Annual wages	$192,899,280
July temp. max.	96	1983 PCI	$7,980
Growing season (da.)	259	Buying pwr.	$387,834,000
Voters reg.	18,999	Tax value	$1,383,492,438
Businesses	928	Fed. expd.	$86,853,000

VITAL STATISTICS 1985: Births, 645; Deaths, 498; Marriages, 476; Divorces, 244.

AGRICULTURE: About $36 million average yearly income, ⅔ from beef, stocker dairy cattle, horses;

crops include cotton, sorghums, wheat, oats, hay, corn.

BUSINESS: Diversified manufacturing, agribusinesses, oil field operations, distribution.

CORSICANA (23,449) county seat; major industrial growth; large bakery; plants make hats, clothing, bottles, flat glass; oil field specialties, chemicals, plastic pipe, architectural metal products, railroad products, insulation; meat packing; other products; distribution center; **Navarro College;** new hospital.

Kerens (1,704) has fertilizer and petrochemical complex, other manufacturing; nursing home.

Other towns include **Angus** (229), **Barry** (196), **Blooming Grove** (854), **Dawson** (789), **Emhouse** (250), **Eureka** (257), **Frost** (647), **Goodlow** (378), **Mildred** (312), **Mustang** (15), **Navarro** (180), **Powell** (130), **Retreat** (280), **Rice** (511), **Richland** (247), **Streetman** (378, mostly Freestone County), **Oak Valley** (204).

Newton

LOCATION: Easternmost county (L-22).

HISTORY: Created, organized, 1846, from Jasper County; was named for **U.S. Revolutionary Corp. John Newton.**

RECREATION: Water sports; fishing, hunting, tourism, E. O. Siecke State Forest; Azalea Canyons.

PHYSICAL FEATURES: Densely forested hills, valleys; **Sabine National Forest;** spring-fed streams; highest Texas rainfall; **Toledo Bend Reservoir;** Sabine River; mostly sandy soils.

Cong. Dist.	2
St. Sen. Dist.	3
St. Rep. Dist.	19
St. Dist. Cts.	1, 1-A
U.S. Jud. Dist.	E-Bt.
Ct. Appeals	9
Admin. Jud. Dist.	2

MINERALS: Oil, gas.

1985 Pop.	13,400
Area (sq. mi.)	935
Altitude (ft.)	23-510
Ann. rainfall (in.)	54.16
Jan. temp. min.	40
July temp. max.	93
Growing season (da.)	228
Voters reg.	8,993
Businesses	168
Tax Ratio	0.93
Oil value	$8,688,581
No. employed	1,863
Avg. wkly. wage	$285.27
Annual wages	$27,635,832
1983 PCI	$5,920
Buying pwr.	$137,185,000
Tax value	$736,108,880
Fed. expd.	$24,175,000

VITAL STATISTICS 1985: Births, 212; Deaths, 157; Marriages, 229; Divorces, 81.

AGRICULTURE: About $2 million average yearly income from beef cattle, poultry, peaches, vegetables. Substantial timber production.

BUSINESS: Forestry activities, beef cattle production, tourism main economic factors. Crawfish production beginning.

NEWTON (1,646) county seat; lumber manufacturing; plywood mill; hospital; tourism; airport.

Nolan

LOCATION: West central (I-11).

HISTORY: Created from Bexar, Young Districts, 1876; organized 1881; named for adventurer **Philip Nolan.**

Cong. Dist.	17	U.S. Jud. Dist.	N-Ab.
St. Sen. Dist.	24	Ct. Appeals	11
St. Rep. Dist.	78	Admin. Jud. Dist.	7
St. Dist. Cts.	32		

PHYSICAL FEATURES: On divide between Brazos, Colorado watersheds; mostly red sandy loams, some waxy, sandy soils; **Sweetwater, Trammell, Oak Creek Lakes.**

RECREATION: Sweetwater and Oak Creek Lakes; hunting; rattlesnake roundup in March; pioneer museum; rodeos, other local events.

MINERALS: Production of oil, gas, cement, gypsum, stone, sand and gravel, clays.

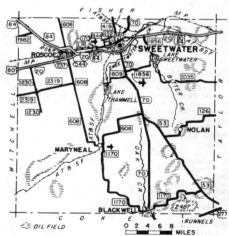

1985 Pop.	17,600	Tax Ratio	0.90
Area (sq. mi.)	915	Oil value	$20,411,413
Altitude (ft.)	1,990-2,603	No. employed	5,241
Ann. rainfall (in.)	22.19	Avg. weekly wage	$294.68
Jan. temp. min.	30	Annual wages	$80,310,568

July temp. max. 96	1983 PCI $8,077	
Growing season (da.) 221	Buying pwr. . . $180,988,000	
Voters reg. 7,985	Tax value . . $613,162,072	
Businesses 484	Fed. expd.. . . . $37,738,000	

VITAL STATISTICS 1985: Births, 258; Deaths, 185; Marriages, 268; Divorces, 99.

AGRICULTURE: An estimated $20 million average annual income from cattle, sheep and cotton, grains;

about 4,000 acres irrigated for cotton.

BUSINESS: Varied manufacturing; agribusinesses; oil and gas production.

SWEETWATER (12,744) county seat; plants make gypsum products, cement, cotton oil products, metal detectors; oil field service; **Texas State Technical Institute;** hospital, nursing homes, colosseum renovated.

Roscoe (1,636) is trade center; **Blackwell** (307, partly Coke County).

Nueces

LOCATION: Southern coast (R-16).

HISTORY: Name is Spanish for nuts, from river; created, organized, 1846, out of San Patricio County.

Cong. Dist. 15, 27	U.S. Jud. Dist. . . . . . S-CC
St. Sen. Dist. 20	Ct. Appeals 13
St. Rep. Dist. 34-36	Admin. Jud. Dist. 5
St. Dist. Cts. 28, 94,	
105, 117, 148, 214, 319, 347	

CORPUS CHRISTI (258,067) county seat; major seaport; petrochemical, aluminum plants; clothing manufacturing; seafood processing, electronics, telecommunications; offshore drilling equipment, zinc processing, corn products, other plants; **Naval Air Station; Army depot; Corpus Christi State University; Del Mar College;** hospitals; museums; recreation centers, gateway to **Padre Island National Seashore;** near **Aransas Wildlife Refuge.**

Other towns include **Agua Dulce** (996), **Aransas Pass**

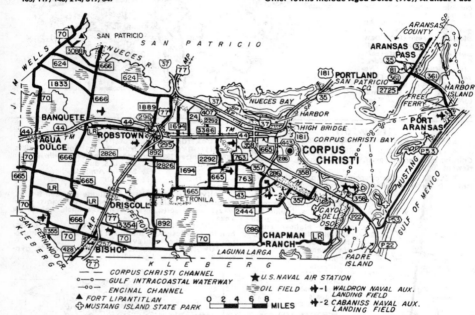

PHYSICAL FEATURES: Flat, rich soils, broken by bays, Nueces River, Petronila Creek; includes **Mustang Island,** north tip of **Padre Island.**

RECREATION: Major resort area; fishing, water sports; **Padre Island National Seashore; Mustang Island State Park; Art Museum of South Texas, Corpus Christi Museum; Buccaneer Days,** jazz festival, deep sea roundup, other metropolitan events.

MINERALS: Production of oil, gas, cement, lime, sand and gravel.

1985 Pop. 297,000	Tax Ratio 0.96	
Area (sq. mi.) 847	Oil value $18,547,275	
Altitude (ft.) 6-129	No. employed . . . 104,424	
Ann. rainfall (in.) . . 28.53	Avg. weekly wage $345.24	
Jan. temp. min. 47	Ann. wages . $1,874,699,748	
July temp. max. 94	1983 PCI $8,599	
Growing season (da.) 309	Buying pwr. $3,088,029,000	
Voters reg. 134,870	Tax value . $11,646,014,298	
Businesses 7,777	Fed. expd.. . . $967,103,000	

VITAL STATISTICS 1985: Births, 5,584; Deaths, 1,916; Marriages, 3,458; Divorces, 1,880.

AGRICULTURE: About $60 million average annual income, over 80% from a leading producer of grain sorghums, also produce corn, cotton; leading sorghum county; livestock includes beef, dairy cattle, horses.

BUSINESS: Diversified economy includes petroleum, agriculture, tourism, coastal shipping, manufacturing; military complex.

(8,176, part Aransas, San Patricio counties), **Bishop** (3,879) chemical plants, **Driscoll** (748), **Petronia** (185), **Port Aransas** (2,218) sea research institute, resort accommodations for fishing, hunting, **Portland** (12,722, mostly San Patricio County), **Robstown** (13,325) clothing plant, hospital, agribusiness, **San Patricio** (231, mostly San Patricio County).

Ochiltree

LOCATION: Extreme Northwest (A-10).

HISTORY: Created from Bexar District, 1876, organized, 1889; named for Republic of Texas leader, **W. B. Ochiltree.**

Cong. Dist. 13	U.S. Jud. Dist. . . . . N-Am.
St. Sen. Dist. 31	Ct. Appeals 7
St. Rep. Dist. 88	Admin. Jud. Dist. 9
St. Dist. Cts. 84	

PHYSICAL FEATURES: Level, broken by creeks; deep loam, clay soils.

RECREATION: Local events; Wheatheart of the Nation celebration in August; Museum of the Plains; Wolf Creek Park; Indian **"Buried City"** site.

MINERALS: Oil, gas.

1985 Pop. 11,000	Tax Ratio 0.79	
Area (sq. mi.) 919	Oil value $16,925,027	
Altitude (ft.) . . 2,642-3,007	No. employed 3,282	
Ann. rainfall (in.) . . 20.48	Avg. weekly wage $348.69	

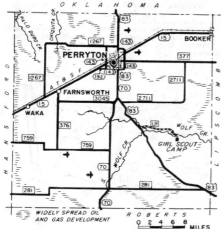

WIDELY SPREAD OIL AND GAS DEVELOPMENT

ROBERTS

0 2 4 6 8
MILES

Jan. temp. min.	18	Annual wages	$59,510,016
July temp. max.	93	1983 PCI	$10,377
Growing season (da.)	191	Buying pwr.	$121,253,000
Voters reg.	4,994	Tax value	$736,807,027
Businesses	368	Fed. expd.	$20,550,000

VITAL STATISTICS 1985: Births, 227; Deaths, 77; Marriages, 168; Divorces, 90.

AGRICULTURE: About $60 million average annual income, from beef cattle; crops include wheat, sorghums, corn, alfalfa. About 52,000 acres irrigated for wheat and sorghum.

BUSINESS: Oil, agribusinesses, center of large feedlot operations.

PERRYTON (9,266) county seat; oil field services and equipment manufacturing, cattle feeding, grain center; plastic fittings made; hospital, nursing home.

Oldham

LOCATION: Northwest (C-7).

HISTORY: Created 1876, from Bexar District, organized, 1880; named for editor-Confederate Senator, **W. S. Oldham.**

Cong. Dist.	13	U.S. Jud. Dist.	N-Am.
St. Sen. Dist.	31	Ct. Appeals	7
St. Rep. Dist.	88	Admin. Jud. Dist.	9
St. Dist. Cts.	222		

PHYSICAL FEATURES: Level, broken by Canadian River and tributaries.

RECREATION: Old Tascosa, with **Boot Hill Cemetery,** pioneer cowboy towns.

MINERALS: Sand and gravel, oil, gas, stone.

1985 Pop.	2,300	Tax Ratio	0.83
Area (sq. mi.)	1,485	Oil value	$1,312,240
Altitude (ft.)	3,200-4,200	No. employed	697
Ann. rainfall (in.)	19.54	Avg. weekly wage	$313.25
Jan. temp. min.	22	Annual wages	$11,353,772

July temp. max.	92	1983 PCI	$6,119
Growing season (da.)	186	Buying pwr.	$15,295,000
Voters reg.	1,061	Tax value	$155,620,092
Businesses	42	Fed. expd.	$5,604,000

VITAL STATISTICS 1985: Births, 35; Deaths, 14; Marriages, 35; Divorces, 11.

AGRICULTURE: About $35 million average yearly income, 80% from beef cattle; crops include sorghums, wheat; 25,000 acres irrigated.

BUSINESS: Ranching center.

VEGA (916) county seat; ranching trade center; **Cal Farley's Boys Ranch** on U.S. Highway 385; **Adrian** (216).

Orange

LOCATION: Extreme Southeast (M-22).

HISTORY: Created from Jefferson County, organized in 1852; named for early orange grove.

Cong. Dist.	2	U.S. Jud. Dist.	E-Bt.
St. Sen. Dist.	4	Ct. Appeals	9
St. Rep. Dist.	19	Admin. Jud. Dist.	2
St. Dist. Cts.	128, 163, 260		

PHYSICAL FEATURES: Bounded by Sabine, Neches, **Sabine Lake;** coastal soils; two-thirds timbered.

RECREATION: Fishing, hunting; other water sports; county park, museums, historical homes, crawfish promotion day, gumbo cookoff in May, metropolitan area events.

MINERALS: Production of oil, gas, clays, sand and gravel.

1985 Pop.	83,200	Tax Ratio	0.87
Area (sq. mi.)	362	Oil value	$3,306,909
Altitude (ft.)	16-25	No. employed	20,795
Ann. rainfall (in.)	59.92	Avg. weekly wage	$414.12
Jan. temp. min.	41	Annual wages	$447,806,048
July temp. max.	91	1983 PCI	$8,895
Growing season (da.)	240	Buying pwr.	$1,050,002,000
Voters reg.	40,306	Tax value	$3,102,658,970
Businesses	1,342	Fed. expd.	$127,005,000

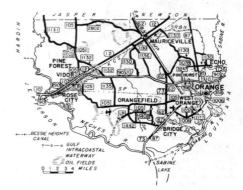

VITAL STATISTICS 1985: Births, 1,320; Deaths, 587; Marriages, 1,464; Divorces, 668.

AGRICULTURE: About $2 million from forest products, including Christmas trees; rice, soybeans, nursery stock, cattle; crawfish production.

BUSINESS: Petrochemicals; shipbuilding, shipping, agribusinesses, tourism; lumber processing; see Beaumont-Port Arthur metro page.

ORANGE: (25,974) county seat; seaport; plants make petrochemicals, container board, ships, cement, carbon black, steel, plastics, marble products; rice, soybean, timber processing and shipping; also crawfish farming, tree farms, papermill; **Lamar University branch,** hospital, theater, museum.

Other towns include **Bridge City** (7,818), **Pinehurst** (3,128), **Vidor** (13,134) steel plant, **West Orange** (5,005), **Pine Forest** (755), **Rose City** (967).

Palo Pinto

LOCATION: North central (H-14).

HISTORY: Created, 1856, from Bosque, Navarro counties; organized, 1857; named for creek, Spanish for painted stick.

Cong. Dist.	17	U.S. Jud. Dist.	N-FW
St. Sen. Dist.	22	Ct. Appeals	11
St. Rep. Dist.	64	Admin. Jud. Dist.	8
St. Dist. Cts.	29		

PHYSICAL FEATURES: Broken, hilly, wooded in parts; **Possum Kingdom Lake; Palo Pinto Creek Reservoir;** sandy, gray, black soils.

RECREATION: Tourist center; lake activities; hunting, fishing, water sports; **Possum Kingdom Lake, State Park; Mineral Wells State Park; Lake Palo Pinto;** Crazy Water Festival in June.

MINERALS: Oil, gas, clays, sand and gravel.

1985 Pop.	26,300	Tax Ratio	0.89
Area (sq. mi.)	949	Oil value	$710,883
Altitude (ft.)	782-1,470	No. employed	7,129
Ann. rainfall (in.)	30.13	Avg. weekly wage	$273.39
Jan. temp. min.	33	Annual wages	$101,347,904
July temp. max.	96	1983 PCI	$8,629
Growing season (da.)	221	Buying pwr.	$266,119,000
Voters reg.	12,674	Tax value	$1,010,259,527
Businesses	662	Fed. expd.	$57,526,000

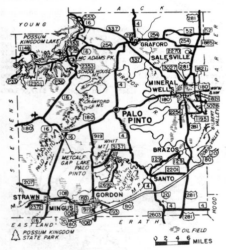

VITAL STATISTICS 1985: Births, 414; Deaths, 314; Marriages, 316; Divorces, 173.

AGRICULTURE: About $27 million average annual income, more than 80% from beef cattle, hogs, goats, sheep, horses; peanuts, vegetables, grains; cedar posts, firewood marketed.

BUSINESS: Varied manufacturing, tourism, agribusinesses.

PALO PINTO (est. 350) county seat (unincorporated community); annual old settlers reunion; farm trade center.

Mineral Wells (15,684, partly in Parker) plants make clay pipe, plastics, electronic products, brick, feeds, clothes, many other products; county hospital; tourist center; Weatherford College extension.

Other towns include **Strawn** (771), **Graford** (568), **Gordon** (541), **Mingus** (252).

Panola

LOCATION: On Louisiana line (I-21).

HISTORY: Name is Indian word for cotton; created from Harrison, Shelby Counties and organized, 1846.

Cong. Dist.	1	U.S. Jud. Dist.	E-Ty.
St. Sen. Dist.	1	Ct. Appeals	6, 12
St. Rep. Dist.	10	Admin. Jud. Dist.	1
St. Dist. Cts.	123		

PHYSICAL FEATURES: Three-fifths forested, rolling plain; broken by Sabine, **Murvaul Creek and Lake, Toledo Bend Reservoir.**

RECREATION: Lake Murvaul fishing, other water activities; hunting; scenic drives; Jim Reeves memorial; historic sites, homes; museum; **Pirtle Boy Scout Reservation.**

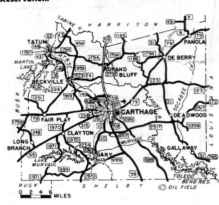

MINERALS: Gas, oil, coal.

1985 Pop.	22,000	Tax Ratio	0.89
Area (sq. mi.)	812	Oil value	$3,974,847
Altitude (ft.)	200-500	No. employed	6,226
Ann. rainfall (in.)	48.08	Avg. weekly wage	$301.47
Jan. temp. min.	38	Annual wages	$97,601,652
July temp. max.	95	1983 PCI	$8,042
Growing season (da.)	240	Buying pwr.	$226,669,000
Voters reg.	12,220	Tax value	$1,920,829,082
Businesses	459	Fed. expd.	$50,646,000

VITAL STATISTICS 1985: Births, 296; Deaths, 227; Marriages, 286; Divorces, 127.

AGRICULTURE: About $40 million average yearly income, 90% from cattle, hogs, poultry; among leading broiler counties; timber sales significant.

BUSINESS: Agribusinesses; varied manufacturing; forest industries; gas processing, oil field operation.

CARTHAGE (6,963) county seat; plants process petroleum, make oil field equipment; poultry processing, supplies; sawmills; **Panola Junior College;** county hospital, clinics, nursing homes. **Beckville** (1,026), **Gary** (351), **Tatum** (1,531, mostly Rusk County) other principal towns.

Parker

LOCATION: North central (H-15).

HISTORY: Named for pioneer legislator, **Isaac Parker;** created, organized, 1855, from Bosque, Navarro Counties.

Cong. Dist.	17	U.S. Jud. Dist.	N-FW
St. Sen. Dist.	22	Ct. Appeals	2
St. Rep. Dist.	63	Admin. Jud. Dist.	8
St. Dist. Cts.	43		

PHYSICAL FEATURES: Hilly, broken by Brazos, Trinity tributaries; varied soils; **Lake Weatherford and Lake Granbury.**

RECREATION: Railroad museum; park; water sports; nature trails; hunting; homes tour; festival in spring; first Monday trade days monthly.

MINERALS: Production of gas, oil, stone, sand and gravel, clays.

1985 Pop.	56,200	Tax Ratio	0.96
Area (sq. mi.)	902	Oil value	$192,022
Altitude (ft.)	718-966	No. employed	9,944
Ann. rainfall (in.)	32.37	Avg. weekly wage	$286.73
Jan. temp. min.	34	Annual wages	$148,267,652
July temp. max.	96	1983 PCI	$9,005
Growing season (da.)	225	Buying pwr.	$636,194,000
Voters reg.	25,775	Tax value	$2,339,806,335
Businesses	929	Fed. expd.	$79,025,000

VITAL STATISTICS 1985: Births, 847; Deaths, 464; Marriages, 1,001; Divorces, 368.

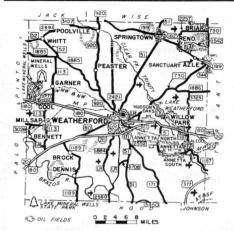

AGRICULTURE: About $41 million average yearly income, 80% from beef cattle, horses; crops chiefly peanuts, peaches and new vineyards, hay; $1 million in timber marketed.

BUSINESS: Primarily agribusinesses; varied manufacturing; many work in Fort Worth; county part of Fort Worth-Arlington PMSA. See metro page.

WEATHERFORD (14,050) county seat; agribusiness center; plants make plastics, rubber products, oil field equipment; **Weatherford College**; hospital, nursing homes.

Other towns include **Azle** (7,825 mostly Tarrant County), **Springtown** (2,336), **Mineral Wells** (15,684, mostly Palo Pinto County), **Aledo** (1,299), **Reno** (1,519), **Briar** (1,810, mostly Wise County), **Cool** (234), **Willow Park** (1,436), **Anneta** (247), **Anneta North** (273), **Anneta South** (271), **Hudson Oaks** (623), **Sanctuary** (262) and **Millsap** (412).

Parmer

LOCATION: Northwest (D-7).
HISTORY: Named for Republic of Texas figure, **Martin Parmer**; created from Bexar District, 1876, organized, 1907.

Cong. Dist.	19	U.S. Jud. Dist. . . . . N-Am.
St. Sen. Dist.	31	Ct. Appeals 7
St. Rep. Dist.	85	Admin. Jud. Dist. 9
St. Dist. Cts.	287	

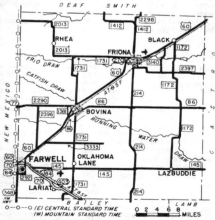

PHYSICAL FEATURES: Level, broken by draws, playas; sandy, clay, loam soils.
RECREATION: Maize Days in September; other local events.

MINERALS: Not significant.

1985 Pop.	10,900	Tax Ratio	0.87
Area (sq. mi.)	885	Oil value	0
Altitude (ft.) . . 3,926-4,163		No. employed	3,705
Ann. rainfall (in.) . .	17.50	Avg. weekly wage	$319.26
Jan. temp. min.	21	Annual wages .	$61,510,524
July temp. max.	92	1983 PCI	$5,745
Growing season (da.)	183	Buying pwr. . .	$67,463,000
Voters reg.	3,998	Tax value . . .	$411,444,747
Businesses	223	Fed. expd.	$38,319,000

VITAL STATISTICS 1985: Births, 177; Deaths, 72; Marriages, 204; Divorces, 44.

AGRICULTURE: About $190 million average yearly income from cattle, hogs, sheep, crops; among leading counties in total farm income; large cattle feeding operations; a leading producer of cattle, cattle on feed, corn, sugar beets, sunflowers, potatoes; crops also include sorghums, cotton, wheat, barley, vegetables, soybeans; 260,000 acres irrigated.

BUSINESS: Cattle feeding; grain elevators; meat packing plant; varied other agribusinesses.

FARWELL (1,365) county seat, agribusiness and trade center on New Mexico line; grain elevators; well drilling services; plants make farm and irrigation equipment, cattle feed, apparel, other products.

Friona (3,733) grain elevators; fertilizer processing; meat packing plant; large feedlots; other agribusinesses; hospital, nursing home. **Bovina** (1,580) is farm trade center.

See Pecos County on next page.

Polk

LOCATION: Southeast (K-20).
HISTORY: Named for U.S. President James K. Polk; created from Liberty County, organized, 1846.

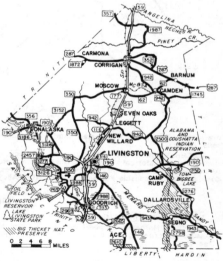

Cong. Dist.	2	U.S. Jud. Dist. . . . . S-Hn.
St. Sen. Dist.	3	Ct. Appeals 9
St. Rep. Dist.	18	Admin. Jud. Dist. 2
St. Dist. Cts. . . 9, 2D9, 258		

PHYSICAL FEATURES: Rolling; densely forested, with Big Thicket, unique plant, animal-life area; Neches, Trinity River, tributaries.

RECREATION: Tourist center; **Livingston Reservoir** fishing, other water activities; hunting; **Alabama-Coushatta Indian Reservation, Museum; Big Thicket;** woodlands trails, champion trees; historic homes; local events.

MINERALS: Oil, gas, sand and gravel.

1985 Pop.	30,000	Tax Ratio	0.78
Area (sq. mi.)	1,061	Oil value	$4,425,106
Altitude (ft.)	68-404	No. employed	6,671
Ann. rainfall (in.) . .	47.19	Avg. weekly wage	$298.06

Jan. temp. min.	39	Annual wages	$103,396,636
July temp. max.	93	1983 PCI	$6,713
Growing season (da.)	250	Buying pwr.	$281,361,000
Voters reg.	16,674	Tax value	$1,116,472,103
Businesses	557	Fed. expd.	$73,806,000

VITAL STATISTICS 1985: Births, 399; Deaths, 334; Marriages, 384; Divorces, 73.

AGRICULTURE: Leading Texas county in timber products delivered to mill and rail sidings, Christmas trees; $8 million from livestock, poultry; crops include peaches, blueberries, vegetables, soybeans.

BUSINESS: Timber, lumber production, tourism, oil.

LIVINGSTON (6,160) county seat; center for lumbering, tourism, oil.

Corrigan (1,970) plywood plant, **Goodrich** (429), **Onalaska** (562), **Seven Oaks** (373) other towns.

Pecos

LOCATION: West (L-7).

HISTORY: Second-largest county; created from Presidio, 1871; organized, 1872; named for **Pecos River**, name origin uncertain.

PHYSICAL FEATURES: High, broken plateau;

draining to Pecos and tributaries; sandy, clay, loam soils.

RECREATION: A major tourist area for recreational, scenic, historical attractions; **Old Fort Stockton, Annie Riggs Museum,** stage coach stop; scenic drives; **Dinosaur Track Roadside Park;** cattle trail sites; **Alley Oop Park** at **Iraan;** archaeological museum with oil, ranch heritage collections.

MINERALS: A leading petroleum producing county; gas, oil.

AGRICULTURE: $21 million average yearly income, 75% from cattle, sheep, goats; crops include cotton, grains, vegetables, alfalfa, pecans, grapes; 25,000 acres irrigated, all crops.

BUSINESS: Oil, gas chief factor in economy; agribusiness center; some manufacturing; tourism.

Cong. Dist.	21
St. Sen Dist	25
St. Rep. Dist	68
St. Dist. Cts.	83, 112
U.S. Jud. Dist	W-Pe.
Ct. Appeals	8
Admin. Jud. Dist	6

1985 Pop.	17,300
Area (sq. mi.)	4,776
Altitude (ft.)	2,168-4,797
Ann. rainfall (in.)	11.85
Jan. temp. min.	33
July temp. max.	94
Growing season (da.)	224
Voters Reg.	7,840
Businesses	486
Tax Ratio	0.94
Oil value	$512,913,553
No. employed	5,097
Avg. weekly wage	$321.86
Annual wages	$85,308,612
1983 PCI	$7,136
Buying pwr.	$139,548,000
Tax value	$6,070,405,569
Fed. expd.	$19,482,000

VITAL STATISTICS 1985: Births, 390; Deaths, 82; Marriages, 144; Divorces, 3.

FORT STOCKTON (9,957) county seat; distribution center for petroleum industry; tire test center; oil, gas processing; sulphur production; garment plant, new winery, varied manufacturing; hospital, nursing home; water carnival in July.

Iraan (1,849) is oil, gas center with ranching, tourist business; hospital.

Potter

LOCATION: Northwest (C-8).

HISTORY: Named for **Robert Potter,** Republic of Texas leader; created, 1876, from Bexar District; organized, 1887.

Cong. Dist.	13	U.S. Jud. Dist.	N-Am.
St. Sen. Dist.	31	Ct. Appeals	7
St. Rep. Dist.	87	Admin. Jud. Dist.	9
St. Dist. Cts.	47, 108, 181, 251, 320		

PHYSICAL FEATURES: Mostly level, part rolling; broken by Canadian River and tributaries; sandy, sandy loam, chocolate loam, clay soils; **Lake Meredith.**

RECREATION: Metropolitan events (ask chamber of commerce); **Lake Meredith** activities; **Alibates Flint Quarries National Monument;** hunting, fishing; Tri-State Fair.

MINERALS: Gas, oil, cement, stone, clays, sand and gravel.

1985 Pop.	107,200	Tax Ratio	0.77
Area (sq. mi.)	902	Oil value	$4,401,666
Altitude (ft.)	3,047-3,824	No. employed	58,665
Ann. rainfall (in.)	20.28	Avg. weekly wage	$348.93
Jan. temp. min.	24	Ann. wages	$1,064,464,900
July temp. max.	92	1983 PCI	$8,601
Growing season (da.)	190	Buying pwr.	$1,043,776,000
Voters reg.	34,531	Tax value	$3,051,228,782
Businesses	3,905	Fed. expd.	$543,545,000

VITAL STATISTICS 1985: Births, 2,147; Deaths, 963; Marriages, 1,682; Divorces, 864.

AGRICULTURE: About $10 million average yearly income, 80% from beef cattle; wheat, sorghums, chief crops. More than 6,700 acres irrigated.

BUSINESS: Transportation, distribution hub for large area; feedlot operations; petrochemicals; gas processing; agribusinesses; see metro page.

AMARILLO (162,863, part in Randall County) county seat; urban hub for North Panhandle oil, ranching area; distribution, marketing center for portions of five states; plants make many products; food processing; copper refinery; **Amarillo College; Northwest Hospital School of Nursing; Texas State Technical Institute** branch; nine hospitals, nursing homes; airport; museum; varied cultural, athletic and other recreational events.

See Map on next page.

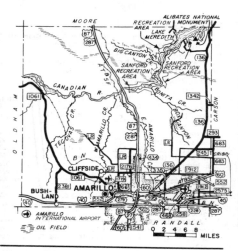

RECREATION: Tourist center; near **Big Bend National Park;** mild climate and scenic surroundings; extensive hunting; scenic drives along Rio Grande, in mountains; ghost towns, Mysterious Marfa Lights; **Fort D. A. Russell; Fort Leaton State Park;** gateway to Mexico West Coast by rail; **Kingston hot springs.**

MINERALS: Sand and gravel.

1985 Pop.	5,500	Tax Ratio	0.85
Area (sq. mi.)	3,857	Oil value	0
Altitude (ft.)	2,518-7,728	No. employed	1,213
Ann. rainfall (in.)	8.47	Avg. weekly wage	$199.70
Jan. temp. min.	33	Annual wages	$12,596,792
July temp. max.	100	1983 PCI	$4,467
Growing season (da.)	238	Buying pwr.	$29,340,000
Voters reg.	2,900	Tax value	$271,164,606
Businesses	131	Fed. expd.	$16,453,000

VITAL STATISTICS 1985: Births, 73; Deaths, 43; Marriages, 49; Divorces, 6.

AGRICULTURE: About 65% of $10 million average farm income from cattle, sheep, goat ranching; cantaloupes, onions, alfalfa chief crops; 4,000 acres irrigated.

BUSINESS: Ranching, income from hunting leases, tourism major economic factors.

MARFA (2,503) county seat; ranching supply and tourist center for large area; major gateway to mountainous area on Rio Grande in Texas and Mexico; many nearby tourist attractions, including scenic rail route to Mexican West Coast; U.S. Border Patrol sector headquarters.

Presidio (1,671) international bridge opened in 1985.

Presidio

LOCATION: Extreme Southwest (M-5).

HISTORY: Created, 1850, from Bexar District; organized, 1875; now 4th largest county; named for Spanish **Presidio del Norte** (fort of the north).

Cong. Dist.	21	U.S. Jud. Dist.	W-Pe.
St. Sen. Dist.	25	Ct. Appeals	8
St. Rep. Dist.	68	Admin. Jud. Dist.	6
St. Dist. Cts.	83		

PHYSICAL FEATURES: Rugged, mountainous; some of Texas' tallest mountains; many scenic drives; clays, loams, sandy loams on uplands; intermountain wash; timber sparse; **Capote Falls,** state's highest.

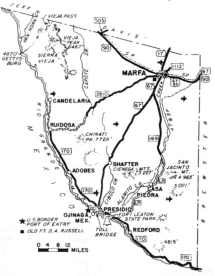

Rains

LOCATION: Northeast (G-18).

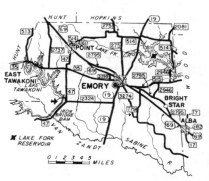

HISTORY: County, county seat named for **Emory Rains,** Republic of Texas leader; county created, organized, 1870, from Hopkins, Hunt, Wood.

PHYSICAL FEATURES: Rolling; partly Blackland, sandy loams, sandy soils; Sabine River, **Lake Tawakoni.**

RECREATION: Lake Tawakoni and **Lake Fork Reservoir** activities, local events.

Minerals: Gas, oil, coal.

Cong. Dist.	4	U.S. Jud. Dist.	E-Ty.
St. Sen. Dist.	2	Ct. Appeals	12
St. Rep. Dist.	3	Admin. Jud. Dist.	1
St. Dist. Cts.	8, 354		

1985 Pop.	5,900	Tax Ratio	0.94
Area (sq. mi.)	243	Oil value	0
Altitude (ft.)	406-491	No. employed	1,060
Ann. rainfall (in.)	42.95	Avg. weekly wage	$288.84
Jan. temp. min.	35	Annual wages	$15,920,940
July temp. max.	94	1983 PCI	$8,523
Growing season (da.)	242	Buying pwr.	$58,373,000
Voters reg.	3,794	Tax value	$412,984,250
Businesses	101	Fed. expd.	$11,272,000

VITAL STATISTICS 1985: Births, 70; Deaths, 75; Marriages, 84; Divorces, 34.

AGRICULTURE: About $15 million average yearly income, 90% from beef, dairy cattle, hogs; wheat, cotton, hay chief crops.

BUSINESS: Economy based upon oil, tourism, agribusinesses, some manufacturing.

EMORY (974) county seat; center for local trade, tourism; some manufacturing including clothing factory and cabinet shop; clinic. **East Tawakoni (494)** and **Point (520)** are centers for **Lake Tawakoni** tourist activities; **Alba (594,** most in Wood County).

Randall

LOCATION: Northwest (C-8).

HISTORY: Created, 1876, from Bexar District; organized, 1889; named for **Confederate Gen. Horace Randal** (county name misspelled when created).

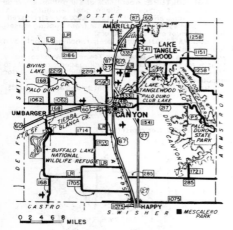

Cong. Dist.	13	U.S. Jud. Dist.	N-Am.
St. Sen. Dist.	31	Ct. Appeals	7
St. Rep. Dist.	86	Admin. Jud. Dist.	9
St. Dist. Cts. . .	47, 181, 251		

PHYSICAL FEATURES: Level, but broken by scenic **Palo Duro Canyon, Tierra Blanca (Buffalo) Lake;** silty clay, loam soils.

RECREATION: Palo Duro Canyon State Park, with **"Texas"** drama, **"A Day in the Old West"** celebration, major tourist attraction (ask chamber of commerce for dates); **Panhandle-Plains Historical Museum; West Texas State University** events; Aoudad sheep, migratory water fowl hunting in season; **Buffalo Lake National Wildlife Refuge.**

MINERALS: Not significant.

1985 Pop.	85,600	Tax Ratio	0.91
Area (sq. mi.)	917	Oil value	0
Altitude (ft.) . .	3,158-3,748	No. employed	15,232
Ann. rainfall (in.) . .	20.16	Avg. weekly wage	$302.79
Jan. temp. min.	23	Annual wages	$239,834,828
July temp. max.	93	1983 PCI	$11,697
Growing season (da.)	195	Buying pwr.	$1,308,207,000
Voters reg.	46,614	Tax value . . .	$2,123,540,158
Businesses	1,464	Fed. expd.	$42,948,000

VITAL STATISTICS 1985: Births, 1,352; Deaths, 472; Marriages, 745; Divorces, 626.

AGRICULTURE: About $70 million average yearly income, 75% from beef, dairy cattle, horses; wheat, sorghums, principal crops; more than 61,000 acres irrigated.

BUSINESS: Agribusinesses, education, some manufacturing, tourism; part of Amarillo metro area (see metro page).

CANYON (11,153) county seat; **West Texas University** major economic influence; **Amarillo College;** ranching, feedlots, farming center; gateway to **Palo Duro Canyon State Park** (see recreation, above); hospital. **Amarillo** is partly in Randall County (see Potter County). **Happy (710,** mostly Swisher County), **Lake Tanglewood (517), Timbercreek (170).**

Reagan

LOCATION: Southwest (K-9).

HISTORY: Named for **Sen. John H. Reagan,** first chairman, **Texas Railroad Commission;** county created, organized, 1903, from Tom Green.

PHYSICAL FEATURES: Level to hilly, broken by draws, **Big Lake;** sandy, loam, clay soils.

RECREATION: Lake fishing, local events.

MINERALS: Gas oil.

Cong. Dist.	21	U.S. Jud. Dist. . . .	N-SAng.
St. Sen. Dist.	25	Ct. Appeals	8
St. Rep. Dist.	69	Admin. Jud. Dist.	6
St. Dist. Cts.	83, 112		
1985 Pop.	5,000	Tax Ratio	0.77
Area (sq. mi.)	1,173	Oil value	$35,832,991
Altitude (ft.) . .	2,406-2,953	No. employed	1,201
Ann. rainfall (in.) . .	14.72	Avg. weekly wage	$361.83
Jan. temp. min.	36	Annual wages	$22,597,076
July temp. max.	96	1983 PCI	$8,071
Growing season (da.)	229	Buying pwr. . . .	$43,396,000
Voters reg.	2,055	Tax value . . .	$671,268,530
Businesses	112	Fed. expd.	$5,540,000

VITAL STATISTICS 1985: Births, 135; Deaths, 15; Marriages, 53; Divorces, 20.

AGRICULTURE: About $7.5 million average annual income, 65% from beef cattle, goats, sheep; cotton, grains principal crops; grapes introduced; 20,000 acres irrigated.

BUSINESS: Economy based on large oil production, natural gas, ranching.

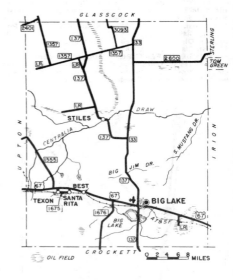

BIG LAKE (4,001) county seat; center for oil activities, ranching trade; hospital, nursing home; airport.

Real

LOCATION: Southwest central (N-12).

Cong. Dist.	21	U.S. Jud. Dist. . . .	W-SAnt.
St. Sen. Dist.	25	Ct. Appeals	4
St. Rep. Dist.	67	Admin. Jud. Dist.	6
St. Dist. Cts.	38		

MINERALS: Not significant.

1985 Pop......... 2,700	Tax Ratio 0.75
Area (sq. mi.) 697	Oil value 0
Altitude (ft.) .. 1,494-2,381	No. employed 511
Ann. rainfall (in.) .. 23.88	Avg. weekly wage $227.89
Jan. temp. min...... 38	Annual wages . $6,055,536
July temp. max..... 94	1983 PCI $5,795
Growing season (da.) 236	Buying pwr. . $16,737,000
Voters reg. 1,900	Tax value ... $295,077,753
Businesses 50	Fed. expd...... $7,032,000

HISTORY: Created, organized, 1913, from Bandera, Edwards, Kerr counties; named for legislator-ranchman Julius Real.

PHYSICAL FEATURES: Hilly, spring-fed streams, scenic canyons; Frio River; Nueces River; cedars, pecans, many live-oak, including second largest oak in state; walnut trees, other vegetation.

RECREATION: Major tourist, hunting center; many deer killed each season; fishing; Frio River; Nueces River; camping; artists' haven; Spanish mission site, **Camp Wood;** scenic drives.

VITAL STATISTICS 1985: Births, 29; Deaths, 33; Marriages, 30; Divorces, 13.

AGRICULTURE: A leading mohair-producing county; cattle, sheep, goats produce practically all of $6 million average farm income; income also from hunting leases.

BUSINESS: Tourism, hunting leases major source of income; ranch supplies; cedar sales; popular area for artists, recreational "second homes."

LEAKEY (516) county seat; center for ranching, tourism; medical facilities; cedar oil mill; **Camp Wood** (806) serves as tourist, ranching hub for parts of three counties.

Red River

LOCATION: Northeast (F-20).

HISTORY: Created 1836, as original county; organized, 1837; named for **Red River,** its northern boundary.

Cong. Dist. 1	U.S. Jud. Dist..... E-Ps.
St. Sen. Dist. 1	Ct. Appeals 6
St. Rep. Dist.......... 1	Admin. Jud. Dist. 1
St. Dist. Cts. 6, 102	

PHYSICAL FEATURES: On Red River-Sulphur divide; 39 different soil types; half timbered.

RECREATION: Historical sites; water activities; hunting; outstanding county fair in September.

MINERALS: Small oil flow, gas.

1985 Pop......... 15,500	Tax Ratio 0.81
Area (sq. mi.) 1,054	Oil value $129,584
Altitude (ft.) 287-525	No. employed 3,129
Ann. rainfall (in.) .. 45.29	Avg. weekly wage $236.00
Jan. temp. min...... 34	Annual wages . $38,399,376
July temp. max..... 94	1983 PCI $6,218
Growing season (da.) 234	Buying pwr. . $122,749,000
Voters reg........ 8,625	Tax value ... $448,923,245
Businesses 256	Fed. expd..... $42,547,000

VITAL STATISTICS 1985: Births, 181; Deaths, 230; Marriages, 269; Divorces, 83.

AGRICULTURE: About $28 million average yearly income, 65% from cattle, hogs, poultry; crops include soybeans, cotton, sorghums, wheat; timber sales substantial.

BUSINESS: Agribusinesses; lumbering; manufacturing.

CLARKSVILLE (4,787) county seat; plants make wood, aluminum products, boats, brushes, furniture, other products; hospital, nursing home, library, vocational school.

Other towns include Bogata (1,596), Detroit (720), Deport (680, mostly Lamar County), Annona (439), Avery (431).

Reeves

LOCATION: Southwest (K-6).

HISTORY: Created, 1883, from Pecos County; organized, 1884; named for **Confederate Col. George R. Reeves.**

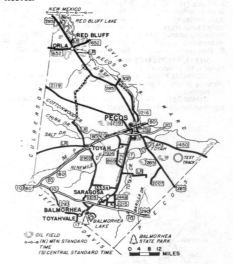

Cong. Dist. 16	U.S. Jud. Dist..... W-Pe.
St. Sen. Dist. 25	Ct. Appeals 8
St. Rep. Dist........ 69	Admin. Jud. Dist. 7
St. Dist. Cts. 143	

PHYSICAL FEATURES: Rolling plains, broken by many draws, Pecos River tributaries, **Balmorhea,**

Toyah, Red Bluff Lakes; Davis Mountains on south; chocolate loam, clay, sandy, mountain wash soils.

RECREATION: A major "western" tourist area; replica of **Judge Roy Bean Store, "Law West of Pecos";** western museum; park with javelina, prairie dogs, other animals; scenic drives; annual rodeo (celebrated centennial of first rodeo in 1983); water activities; **Balmorhea State Park** and lake.

MINERALS: Production of oil, gas, sand, gravel.

1985 Pop.	16,100	Tax Ratio	0.86
Area (sq. mi.)	2,626	Oil value	$16,385,873
Altitude (ft.)	2,538-4,210	No. employed	4,084
Ann. rainfall (in.)	11.99	Avg. weekly wage	$279.21
Jan. temp. min.	32	Annual wages	$59,297,020
July temp. max.	94	1983 PCI	$6,252
Growing season (da.)	226	Buying pwr.	$123,875,000
Voters reg.	8,388	Tax value	$502,603,540
Businesses	366	Fed. expd.	$23,304,000

VITAL STATISTICS 1985: Births, 369; Deaths, 115; Marriages, 183; Divorces, 69.

AGRICULTURE: About $35 million average annual income, 80% from beef, dairy cattle; crops include cotton, grains, alfalfa; 14,000 acres irrigated.

BUSINESS: Petroleum production; agribusinesses; tourism; feedlots; some manufacturing

PECOS (13,105) county seat; ranching, oil industry center; vegetables, pecans, cotton marketing, shipping, other agribusinesses; automotive proving grounds; hospital, nursing home; tourism.

Other towns include **Balmorhea** (528), **Toyah** (162).

Refugio

LOCATION: Southern coast (Q-17).

HISTORY: Original county, created 1836, organized, 1837; named for **Mission Our Lady of Refuge.**

Cong. Dist.	14	U.S. Jud. Dist.	S-Va.
St. Sen. Dist.	18	Ct. Appeals	13
St. Rep. Dist.	32	Admin. Jud. Dist.	4
St. Dist. Cts.	24, 135, 267		

PHYSICAL FEATURES: Coastal plain, broken by streams, bays; sandy, loam, black soils; mesquite, oak, huisache motts.

RECREATION: Water activities; hunting, fishing; historic sites; **Aransas National Wildlife Refuge,** "home of the whooping crane."

MINERALS: Production of oil, gas.

1985 Pop.	8,700	Tax Ratio	0.70
Area (sq. mi.)	771	Oil value	$225,325,733
Altitude (ft.)	7-78	No. employed	2,574
Ann. rainfall (in.)	33.76	Avg. weekly wage	$315.86
Jan. temp. min.	44	Annual wages	$42,277,948
July temp. max.	94	1983 PCI	$7,981
Growing season (da.)	304	Buying pwr.	$96,454,000
Voters reg.	5,420	Tax value	$1,512,986,569
Businesses	240	Fed. expd.	$30,527,000

VITAL STATISTICS 1985: Births, 131; Deaths, 92; Marriages, 74; Divorces, 38.

AGRICULTURE: About $23.5 million average yearly income from sorghums, cotton, corn, wheat; beef cattle, horses.

BUSINESS: Petroleum, petrochemical production, agribusinesses, tourism main economic factors.

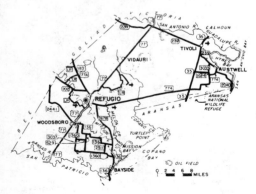

REFUGIO (3,707) county seat; center for petroleum producing, agribusiness activities; hospital, nursing home.

Other towns include **Woodsboro** (2,006), **Austwell** (276) and **Bayside** (383).

Roberts

LOCATION: Northwestern Panhandle (B-10).

HISTORY: Created, 1876, from Bexar District; organized, 1889; named for Texas leaders, **John S. Roberts** and **Gov. O. M. Roberts.**

Cong. Dist.	13	U.S. Jud. Dist.	N-Am.
St. Sen. Dist.	31	Ct. Appeals	7
St. Rep. Dist.	88	Admin. Jud. Dist.	9
St. Dist. Cts.	31		

PHYSICAL FEATURES: Rolling, broken by Canadian and many tributaries; Red Deer Creek; black, sandy loam, alluvial soils.

RECREATION: National cow-calling contest; scenic drives; county museum.

MINERALS: Production of gas, oil.

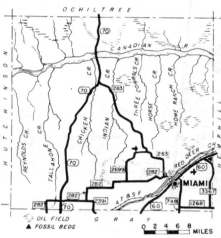

1985 Pop.	1,000	Tax Ratio	0.92
Area (sq. mi.)	915	Oil value	$5,564,894
Altitude (ft.)	2,467-3,219	No. employed	219
Ann. rainfall (in.)	21.91	Avg. weekly wage	$317.37
Jan. temp. min.	23	Annual wages	$3,614,280
July temp. max.	94	1983 PCI	$9,009
Growing season (da.)	192	Buying pwr.	$12,084,000
Voters reg.	830	Tax value	$358,982,025
Businesses	25	Fed. expd.	$2,683,000

VITAL STATISTICS 1985: Births, 14; Deaths, 10; Marriages, 16; Divorces, 0.

AGRICULTURE: About $8 million average yearly income, 75% from beef cattle; crops include wheat, milo, corn; about 6,000 acres irrigated for grains.

BUSINESS: Agribusinesses, oil field operations.

MIAMI (699) county seat; center for ranching, oil industry activities; some oil field equipment manufacturing.

Robertson

LOCATION: East central (K-17).

HISTORY: Among first counties, created 1837, organized 1838, subdivided into many others later; named for pioneer, **Sterling Clack Robertson.**

Cong. Dist.	6	U.S. Jud. Dist.	W-Wa.
St. Sen. Dist.	5	Ct. Appeals	10
St. Rep. Dist.	13	Admin Jud. Dist.	2
St. Dist. Cts.	82		

PHYSICAL FEATURES: Drains to Brazos, Navasota Rivers; sandy soils, heavy in bottoms.

RECREATION: Hunting, fishing; historic sites; historic homes tour; Country Music Jamboree; county fair

at Hearne; dogwood trails, wildlife preserves.
MINERALS: Gas, oil, lignite.

1985 Pop.	15,900	Tax Ratio	0.95
Area (sq. mi.)	864	Oil value	$353,228
Altitude (ft.)	277-491	No. employed	2,843
Ann. rainfall (in.)	35.80	Avg. weekly wage	$259.20
Jan. temp. min.	40	Annual wages	$38,320,152
July temp. max.	96	1983 PCI	$7,134

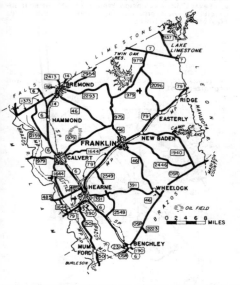

Growing season (da.) 268   Buying pwr. . . $130,635,000
Voters reg. 9,359   Tax value . . . $965,070,918
Businesses 242   Fed. expd. . . . $39,737,000

VITAL STATISTICS 1985: Births, 291; Deaths, 217; Marriages, 158; Divorces, 63.

AGRICULTURE: About $38 million average yearly income, 75% from beef cattle, dairy products, hogs, horses, poultry; crops include cotton, sorghums, small grains, watermelons, corn; 15,000 acres irrigated, mostly cotton.

BUSINESS: Agribusinesses, brick manufacturing, electricity generating plant under construction.

FRANKLIN (1,637) county seat; farm trade center, new vineyard, power plants.

Other towns include **Hearne** (5,711), some manufacturing; hospital, nursing home; library, airport. **Bremond** (1,244), **Calvert** (1,715) antique shops; annual pilgrimage in April.

Rockwall

LOCATION North central (G-17).
HISTORY: Created, organized, 1873, from Kaufman; smallest county; named for wall-like rock formation.
PHYSICAL FEATURES: Rolling prairie, mostly Blackland soil; Trinity River; Lake Ray Hubbard.
MINERALS: Not significant.

Cong. Dist. 4   U.S. Jud. Dist. . . . . N-DI.
St. Sen. Dist. 2   Ct. Appeals 5
St. Rep. Dist. 3   Admin. Jud. Dist. 1
St. Dist. Cts. 86
RECREATION: Lake Ray Hubbard activities (also see Dallas County); unusual rock outcropping.

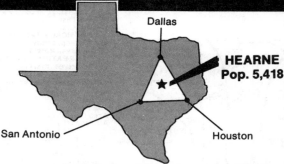

1985 Pop.	20,800	Tax Ratio	0.90
Area (sq. mi.)	128	Oil value	0
Altitude (ft.)	489-588	No. employed	5,785
Ann. rainfall (in.)	38.68	Avg. weekly wage	$283.22
Jan. temp. min.	34	Annual wages	$85,199,308
July temp. max.	96	1983 PCI	$12,466
Growing season (da.)	236	Buying pwr.	$324,896,000
Voters reg.	12,086	Tax value	$1,047,772,874
Businesses	441	Fed. expd.	$20,651,000

VITAL STATISTICS 1985: Births, 363; Deaths, 126; Marriages, 1,419; Divorces, 131.

AGRICULTURE: About $6 million average yearly farm income from beef cattle, horses; crops including wheat, sorghums.

BUSINESS: Industrial employment in local plants, Dallas; in Dallas metro area; tourist and residential development around **Lake Ray Hubbard;** varied manufacturing.

ROCKWALL (8,331) county seat; plants make aluminum, leather goods, windows; apparel, steel products; hospital, clinics, nursing home.

Royse City (1,578, part in Collin County), plants produce typewriter ribbons, elevators, clothing. Other towns include **Heath (1,647,** part Kaufman County), **Fate (378), McLendon-Chisholm (480), Rowlett (10,391,** part Dallas County), and small part of **Dallas** and **Garland.**

Runnels

LOCATION: Central (J-11).

HISTORY: Named for planter-legislator, **H. G. Runnels;** created, 1858, from Bexar, Travis Counties; organized, 1880.

Cong. Dist.	17	U.S. Jud. Dist.	N-SAng.
St. Sen. Dist.	24	Ct. Appeals	3
St. Rep. Dist.	65	Admin. Jud. Dist.	7
St. Dist. Cts.	119		

PHYSICAL FEATURES: Level to rolling; bisected by Colorado and tributaries; sandy loam, black waxy soils.

RECREATION: Deer and turkey hunting, fishing; Festival of Ethnic Cultures of Ballinger in April; 47 historical markers in county.

MINERALS: Production of oil, gas, sand and gravel.

1985 Pop.	12,500	Tax Ratio	0.78
Area (sq. mi.)	1,056	Oil value	$1,944,287
Altitude (ft.)	1,628-2,301	No. employed	3,191
Ann. rainfall (in.)	21.85	Avg. weekly wage	$249.01
Jan. temp. min.	34	Annual wages	$41,320,096
July temp. max.	96	1983 PCI	$7,547
Growing season (da.)	228	Buying pwr.	$114,186,000
Voters reg.	6,326	Tax value	$517,975,146
Businesses	331	Fed. expd.	$33,539,000

VITAL STATISTICS 1985: Births, 210; Deaths, 163; Marriages, 116; Divorces, 66.

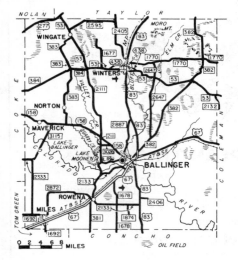

AGRICULTURE: About $36 million average yearly income, 60% from beef and stocker cattle, sheep; crops include cotton, sorghums, wheat.

BUSINESS: Agribusinesses, oil activity, manufacturing.

BALLINGER (4,536) county seat; Carnegie Library; plants make garments, communications equipment, bumpers, livestock feed, cotton compress; metal products; oil field services; meat processor; hospital; **Western Texas College** extension. **Winters (3,145)** varied manufacturing; museum; nursing home, hospital; **Miles (775)** other major towns.

Rusk

LOCATION: East (I-20).

HISTORY: Named for Republic of Texas, state leader, **T. J. Rusk;** created from Nacogdoches County and organized, 1843.

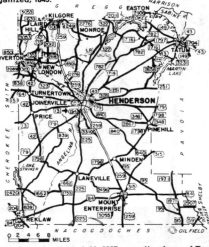

New London, March 18, 1937, was site of one of Texas' worst disasters, when a school explosion killed 293 students and faculty.

Cong. Dist.	1	U.S. Jud. Dist.	E-Ty.
St. Sen. Dist.	3	Ct. Appeals	6, 12
St. Rep. Dist.	9	Admin. Jud. Dist.	1
St. Dist. Cts.	4		

PHYSICAL FEATURES: On Sabine-Angelina divide; varied deep, sandy soils; over half in pines, hardwoods; **Striker Creek Reservoir; Lake Cherokee.**

RECREATION: Water sports; historic homes, sites; scenic drives; marked site of East Texas Field discovery oil well; golf tournaments.

MINERALS: A leading oil county; over 1.5 billion bbls. since 1930; part of East Texas field; gas, lignite, clays also produced.

1985 Pop.	43,200	Tax Ratio	0.93
Area (sq. mi.)	932	Oil value	$148,282,001
Altitude (ft.)	280-662	No. employed	11,256
Ann. rainfall (in.)	46.22	Avg. weekly wage	$380.19
Jan. temp. min.	38	Annual wages	$222,535,192
July temp. max.	94	1983 PCI	$8,259
Growing season (da.)	250	Buying pwr.	$506,034,000
Voters reg.	26,746	Tax value	$2,928,742,151
Businesses	813	Fed. expd.	$78,604,000

VITAL STATISTICS 1985: Births, 613; Deaths, 503; Marriages, 436; Divorces, 276.

AGRICULTURE: About $25 million average annual income, 90% from cattle, dairy products, hogs, poultry, horses; crops include watermelons, vegetables, hay, grains, corn; timber income estimated at $3 million.

BUSINESS: Economy based on oil, lumbering, agribusinesses, tourism.

HENDERSON (11,972) county seat; center for agribusiness, oil industry activities; plants make bricks, clothing, fiberglass, other products; hospital.

Overton (2,463, part Smith County) oil, lumbering center; petroleum production, processing; crosstie milling; **Texas A&M Research and Extension Center;** nursing home. Other towns are Kilgore (12,138 most in Gregg County), **New London (1,084), Tatum (1,531, part Panola County), Easton (375, part Gregg County), Mount Enterprise (520), Reklaw (328, part Cherokee County).**

Sabine

LOCATION: Borders Louisiana (J-22).
HISTORY: An original county, created 1836; organized, 1837; name is cypress in Spanish.

Cong. Dist.	2	U.S. Jud. Dist.	E-Bt.
St. Sen. Dist.	3	Ct. Appeals	12
St. Rep. Dist.	17	Admin. Jud. Dist.	2
St. Dist. Cts.	1, 273		

PHYSICAL FEATURES: Four-fifths forested; 114,498 acres in **Sabine National Forest; Sabine River, Toledo Bend Reservoir** on east; **Sam Rayburn Reservoir** on southwest.

RECREATION: Toledo Bend, Sam Rayburn Reservoir activities; many camp sites, marinas; **McMahan's Chapel,** pioneer Protestant Church; **Sabine National Forest;** hunting.

MINERALS: Not significant.

1985 Pop.	9,800	Tax Ratio	0.89
Area (sq. mi.)	486	Oil value	0
Altitude (ft.)	174-590	No. employed	1,726
Ann. rainfall (in.)	51.94	Avg. weekly wage	$296.43
Jan. temp. min.	38	Annual wages	$26,605,800
July temp. max.	94	1983 PCI	$6,577
Growing season (da.)	236	Buying pwr.	$86,454,000
Voters reg.	5,826	Tax value	$400,706,144
Businesses	157	Fed. expd.	$29,689,000

VITAL STATISTICS 1985: Births, 112; Deaths, 122; Marriages, 185; Divorces, 28.

AGRICULTURE: About $6 million average yearly income from beef cattle, poultry; vegetables; among leading broiler producers; significant timber

▲ SAM RAYBURN RESERVOIR
▲ MC MAHAN CHAPEL

marketing.
BUSINESS: Economy based on tourism, broilers, timber industries.
HEMPHILL (1,530) county seat; center for timber, poultry industries; tourism; **Pineland (1,118)** has plywood mill, other timber industries; **Bronson (292).**

San Augustine

LOCATION: East (J-21).
HISTORY: Among most historic counties; created and named for Mexican municipality in 1836, an original county; organized 1837.
PHYSICAL FEATURES: Hilly; four-fifths forested, with 6,799 acres in **Angelina National Forest, 4,317 in Sabine National Forest; Sam Rayburn Reservoir;** varied soils, sandy to black alluvial.
RECREATION: Lake activities; annual tour of antiques, arts, crafts show; many historic homes; **McMahan's Chapel,** pioneer Protestant Church in nearby Sabine County; tourist facilities in national forests.
MINERALS: Small amount oil.

▲ PARKS AND RECREATION SITES

Cong. Dist.	1	U.S. Jud. Dist.	E-Bt.
St. Sen. Dist.	3	Ct. Appeals	12
St. Rep. Dist.	17	Admin. Jud. Dist.	2
St. Dist. Cts.	1, 273		

AGRICULTURE: About $16 million average annual income, mostly from beef cattle; hay; timber sales significant.
BUSINESS: Lumbering; shipping; varied manufacturing.

1985 Pop.	8,800	Tax Ratio	0.85
Area (sq. mi.)	524	Oil value	0
Altitude (ft.)	156-502	No. employed	1,539
Ann. rainfall (in.)	50.23	Avg. weekly wage	$262.98
Jan. temp. min.	35	Annual wages	$21,045,808
July temp. max.	93	1983 PCI	$6,195
Growing season (da.)	238	Buying pwr.	$74,077,000
Voters reg.	6,461	Tax value	$300,230,346
Businesses	162	Fed. expd.	$20,820,000

VITAL STATISTICS 1985: Births, 120; Deaths, 123; Marriages, 114; Divorces, 19.

SAN AUGUSTINE (2,983) county seat; tourism; livestock, make fiberglass products, lumber and other wood products, metal fabrication, transformers and meters. Deep East Texas Electric Cooperative; lumbering; hospital; "Oldest Anglo-Saxon Town in Texas" with many historic homes; **Broaddus (245).**

San Jacinto

LOCATION: Southeast (L-20).
HISTORY: Created from Liberty, Montgomery, Polk, Walker Counties, 1869; re-created, organized,

▲ DOUBLE LAKE RECREATION AREA

1870; named for **Battle of San Jacinto.**

Cong. Dist.	2	U.S. Jud. Dist.	S-Hn.
St. Sen. Dist.	3	Ct. Appeals	9
St. Rep. Dist.	18	Admin. Jud. Dist.	2
St. Dist. Cts.	9, 2D9, 258		

PHYSICAL FEATURES: Rolling hills; four-fifths forested; 58,625 acres in **Sam Houston National Forest;** Trinity, San Jacinto Rivers.

RECREATION: **Livingston Reservoir** water activities; **Double Lake; Wolf Creek Park;** hunting; county fair; **Sam Houston National Forest;** old courthouse and jail are tourist attractions. Approximatey 60% of county in national forest.

MINERALS: Oil, gas and iron ore.

1985 Pop.	14,000	Tax Ratio	0.94
Area (sq. mi.)	572	Oil value	$85,324
Altitude (ft.)	74-386	No. employed	1,180
Ann. rainfall (in.)	48.25	Avg. weekly wage	$272.31
Jan. temp. min.	38	Annual wages	$16,709,456
July temp. max.	94	1983 PCI	$6,650
Growing season (da.)	261	Buying pwr.	$128,508,000
Voters reg.	8,772	Tax value	$845,647,082
Businesses	138	Fed. expd.	$29,498,000

VITAL STATISTICS 1985: Births, 182; Deaths, 132; Marriages, 176; Divorces, 86.

AGRICULTURE: Some $6.5 million average annual income from beef cattle, horses, hay; timber sales.

BUSINESS: Economy based on timber and oil.

COLDSPRING (704) county seat; center for lumbering, farm trade; historic sites. **Shepherd (1,983), Pointblank (429), Oakhurst (297)** other towns.

San Patricio

LOCATION: Southern coast (Q-16).

HISTORY: Created from, named for earlier municipality in 1836; organized, 1837, reorganized, 1847.

Cong. Dist.	15	U.S. Jud. Dist.	S-CC
St. Sen. Dist.	20	Ct. Appeals	13
St. Rep. Dist.	33	Admin. Jud. Dist.	4
St. Dist. Cts.	36, 156, 343		

PHYSICAL FEATURES: Between Aransas, Nueces Rivers, draining to them and bays; sandy loam, clay, black loam soils; **Lake Corpus Christi.**

RECREATION: Water activities; hunting; Corpus Christi Bay; **Lake Corpus Christi State Park; Welder Wildlife Refuge; Welder Park;** festivals, fishing tournament at Mathis; shrimporee in October; local events.

MINERALS: Production of oil, gas, stone, clays.

1985 Pop.	61,800	Tax Ratio	0.93
Area (sq. mi.)	693	Oil value	$22,173,512
Altitude (ft.)	11-137	No. employed	13,065
Ann. rainfall (in.)	30.60	Avg. weekly wage	$337.34
Jan. temp. min.	44	Annual wages	$229,183,380
July temp. max.	95	1983 PCI	$7,380
Growing season (da.)	303	Buying pwr.	$567,833,000
Voters reg.	30,027	Tax value	$2,199,973,366
Businesses	1,068	Fed. expd.	$102,636,000

VITAL STATISTICS 1985: Births, 1,110; Deaths, 470; Marriages, 479; Divorces, 262.

AGRICULTURE: About $51 million average annual income from sorghums, cotton, vegetables, corn, hay; beef cattle, hogs, goats, horses, poultry; cattle feedlots; 5,000 acres irrigated.

BUSINESS: Oil center; petrochemicals; agribusinesses; manufacturing; tourism; in Corpus Christi metro area.

SINTON (6,382) county seat; oil, agribusiness center; zoo, fiddlers' festival; 18-hole golf course.

Aransas Pass (8,176, part in Aransas, Nueces counties) shrimping and tourist center; offshore well servicing; aluminum and chemical plants; hospitals.

Other towns include **Gregory (2,979), Ingleside (6,048)** offshore oil services; **Lake City (450), Lakeside (289), Mathis (5,910)** varied manufacturing; medical clinics. **Odem (2,770)** petroleum processing, steel fabrication; **Portland (12,722,** part Nueces County), **Taft (3,598) Blackland Museum,** manufacture tanks, fertilizers; nursing homes; and **San Patricio (231,** part Nueces County).

San Saba

LOCATION: Central (K-14).

HISTORY: Created from Bexar and organized, 1856; named for river.

Cong. Dist.	11	U.S. Jud. Dist.	W-An.
St. Sen. Dist.	24	Ct. Appeals	3
St. Rep. Dist.	54	Admin. Jud. Dist.	3
St. Dist. Cts.	33		

PHYSICAL FEATURES: Hilly, rolling; bisected by San Saba River; Colorado River on east; black, gray sandy loam, alluvial soils.

RECREATION: A leading deer hunting area; annual rodeos, pecan festival; historic sites; log cabin museum, fishing; scenic drives; Gorman Falls.

MINERALS: Limited stone production.

1985 Pop.	5,700	Tax Ratio	0.86
Area (sq. mi.)	1,136	Oil value	0
Altitude (ft.)	1,100-1,900	No. employed	1,417
Ann. rainfall (in.)	26.19	Avg. weekly wage	$230.64
Jan. temp. min.	34	Annual wages	$16,995,112
July temp. max.	96	1983 PCI	$6,430
Growing season (da.)	227	Buying pwr.	$55,859,000
Voters reg.	3,054	Tax value	$440,978,650
Businesses	151	Fed. expd.	$15,746,000

VITAL STATISTICS 1985: Births, 65; Deaths, 89; Marriages, 33; Divorces, 33.

AGRICULTURE: About 80% of $20 million average farm income from cattle, hogs, sheep, goats, turkeys; crops include oats, wheat, peanuts, hay; about 5,000 acres irrigated.

BUSINESS: Agribusinesses; pecans; stone processing; tourist and hunting lease income.

SAN SABA (2,877) county seat; "Pecan capital of the world," agribusinesses; stone quarries, rock crushing plant; airplanes refurbished; manufacturing includes caps, feed, fertilizer; hospital, nursing homes; **Richland Springs (401)** another town.

Schleicher

LOCATION: Southwest (L-11).
HISTORY: Named for **Gustav Schleicher,** founder of German colony; county created from Crockett, 1887, organized, 1901.

Cong. Dist.	21	U.S. Jud. Dist.	N-SAng.
St. Sen. Dist.	25	Ct. Appeals	3
St. Rep. Dist.	67	Admin. Jud. Dist.	7
St. Dist. Cts.	51		

PHYSICAL FEATURES: Plateau, broken by Devils River, Concho, San Saba tributaries; part hilly; black soils.
RECREATION: Hunting; livestock show in January, youth rodeo in April, open rodeo in August.
MINERALS: Production of oil, gas.

1985 Pop.	3,200	Tax Ratio	0.80
Area (sq. mi.)	1,309	Oil value	$6,655,911
Altitude (ft.)	2,125-2,467	No. employed	624
Ann. rainfall (in.)	18.19	Avg. weekly wage	$374.01
Jan. temp. min.	30	Annual wages	$12,135,912
July temp. max.	94	1983 PCI	$7,819
Growing season (da.)	229	Buying pwr.	$27,680,000
Voters reg.	1,562	Tax value	$417,770,510
Businesses	62	Fed. expd.	$7,581,000

VITAL STATISTICS 1985: Births, 59; Deaths, 16; Marriages, 30; Divorces, 14.
AGRICULTURE: An estimated $10 million average annual income, 80% from cattle, sheep, Angora goats; crops include cotton, small grains, hay.

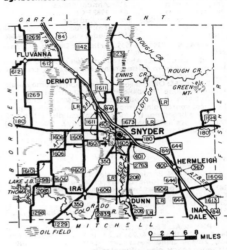

BUSINESS: Oil and ranching economy.
ELDORADO (2,418) county seat; center for livestock, woolen mill, mohair marketing; oil activities; medical center.

Scurry

LOCATION: West (H-10).
HISTORY: Created from Bexar, 1876; organized 1884; named for **Confederate Gen. W. R. Scurry.**

Cong. Dist.	17	U.S. Jud. Dist.	N-Lb.
St. Sen. Dist.	30	Ct. Appeals	11
St. Rep. Dist.	78	Admin. Jud. Dist.	7
St. Dist. Cts.	132		

PHYSICAL FEATURES: Drained by Colorado, Brazos tributaries; Lake J. B. Thomas; prairie, some hills; sandy, loam soils.
RECREATION: Lake J. B. Thomas water recreation; **Sandstone Canyon Indian** pictographs; **Towle Memorial Park;** museums, national finals, American Junior Rodeo Association in August; white buffalo days in October.
MINERALS: Nation's leading oil-producing county; also gas, stone.

1985 Pop.	19,800	Tax Ratio	0.97
Area (sq. mi.)	900	Oil value	$181,272,888
Altitude (ft.)	2,129-2,822	No. employed	6,334
Ann. rainfall (in.)	19.32	Avg. weekly wage	$342.12
Jan. temp. min.	28	Annual wages	$112,684,196
July temp. max.	96	1983 PCI	$9,524
Growing season (da.)	214	Buying pwr.	$231,888,000
Voters reg.	8,983	Tax value	$1,672,880,034
Businesses	630	Fed. expd.	$31,169,000

VITAL STATISTICS 1985: Births, 410; Deaths, 161; Marriages, 175; Divorces, 121.
AGRICULTURE: Some $16 million average annual income from cattle, hogs, sheep, cotton, sorghums, small grains; 1,400 acres irrigated for cotton, pastures.

BUSINESS: Oil production major economic factor; agribusinesses; manufacturing.

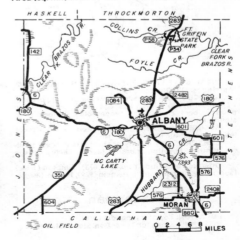

SNYDER (14,164) county seat; plants process oil, gas, magnesium; make apparel, wax, brick, other products; **Western Texas College;** hospital, nursing homes.

Shackelford

LOCATION: Central (H-13).
HISTORY: Created from Bosque County, 1858; organized, 1874; named for **Dr. Jack Shackelford** (sometimes referred to as John), Texas Revolutionary hero.

Cong. Dist.	17	U.S. Jud. Dist.	N-Ab.
St. Sen. Dist.	30	Ct. Appeals	11
St. Rep. Dist.	64	Admin. Jud. Dist.	7
St. Dist. Cts.	259		

PHYSICAL FEATURES: Rolling, hilly, numerous tributaries of Brazos; sandy and chocolate loam soils; **McCarty Lake.**
RECREATION: **Fort Griffin State Park** (in National Register of Historic Places), June **Fandangle** major tourist attractions; courthouse historical district; lake activities; hunting.
MINERALS: Production of oil, gas.

1985 Pop.	4,000	Tax Ratio	0.98
Area (sq. mi.)	915	Oil value	$1,809,878

Altitude (ft.) ..	1,217-1,788	No. employed	896
Ann. rainfall (in.) ..	26.57	Avg. weekly wage	$283.67
Jan. temp. min......	31	Annual wages .	$13,216,948
July temp. max. ..	97	1983 PCI	$8,584
Growing season (da.)	224	Buying pwr. ..	$46,843,000
Voters reg.	2,317	Tax value ..	$311,784,838
Businesses	150	Fed. expd....	$8,089,000

VITAL STATISTICS 1985: Births, 59; Deaths, 44; Marriages, 46; Divorces, 19.

AGRICULTURE: About $12 million average annual income, 85% from cattle, sheep, horses, hogs; crops include cotton, wheat.

BUSINESS: Oil and ranching economy; some manufacturing; June **"Fandangle"** is tourist attraction.

ALBANY (2,438) county seat; tourism; oil and agribusiness center; plants make oil field equipment; quarter-horse breeding, training; historical district; hospital; **Lueders** (473, part Jones County), **Moran** (404) major towns.

Shelby

LOCATION: Borders Louisiana (I-21).
HISTORY: Original county, created 1836; organized, 1837; named for **Isaac Shelby** of American Revolution.

Cong. Dist.	1	U.S. Jud. Dist.....	E-Ty.
St. Sen. Dist.	3	Ct. Appeals	12
St. Rep. Dist........	10	Admin. Jud. Dist.	1
St. Dist. Cts.	123, 273		

PHYSICAL FEATURES: Partly hills, much bottomland; much timber; 67,762 acres in **Sabine National Forest; Toledo Bend Reservoir;** Sabine, Attoyac, other streams; sandy, clay, alluvial soils.

RECREATION: **Toledo Bend Reservoir** activities; **Sabine National Forest;** hunting, fishing; camping; historic sites; poultry festival in October.

MINERALS: Gas, oil.

1985 Pop........	23,900	Tax Ratio	0.83
Area (sq. mi.)	791	Oil value	$343,380
Altitude (ft.)..	213-630	No. employed	5,189
Ann. rainfall (in.) ..	49.94	Avg. weekly wage	$267.63
Jan. temp. min......	38	Annual wages .	$72,214,728
July temp. max. ..	94	1983 PCI	$6,888
Growing season (da.)	240	Buying pwr. ..	$217,263,000
Voters reg.	13,069	Tax value ..	$666,268,656
Businesses	459	Fed. expd...	$61,234,000

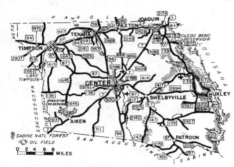

VITAL STATISTICS 1985: Births, 289; Deaths, 302; Marriages, 313; Divorces, 150.

AGRICULTURE: A leader in broiler and egg production; most of $80 million average yearly income from poultry, beef cattle; hay, vegetables; timber sales significant.

BUSINESS: Broiler, egg production, cattle, timber leading economic factors; tourism.

CENTER (5,839) county seat; plants process poultry, lumber; hospitals; nursing homes; **Shelby College Center.**

Other towns include **Tenaha** (1,073), **Timpson** (1,106) food processing, feed mill; **Joaquin** (969), **Huxley** (366).

Sherman

LOCATION: Top of Panhandle (A-8).
HISTORY: Named for Texas Gen. **Sidney Sherman;**

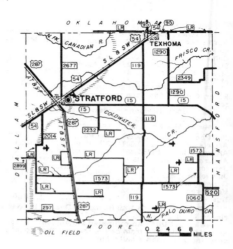

county created from Bexar District, 1876; organized 1889.

Cong. Dist.	13	U.S. Jud. Dist.....	N-Am.
St. Sen. Dist.	31	Ct. Appeals	7
St. Rep. Dist........	88	Admin. Jud. Dist.	9
St. Dist. Cts.	69		

PHYSICAL FEATURES: Level, broken by creeks, playas; sandy to dark loam soils; underground water.

RECREATION: Local events; pheasant hunting.

MINERALS: Production of gas, oil.

1985 Pop......	3,100	Tax Ratio	0.97
Area (sq. mi.)	923	Oil value	$7,043,824
Altitude (ft.) ..	3,485-3,743	No. employed	967
Ann. rainfall (in.) ..	18.36	Avg. weekly wage	$279.58
Jan. temp. min......	19	Annual wages .	$14,058,872
July temp. max. ..	93	1983 PCI	$13,076
Growing season (da.)	182	Buying pwr. ..	$47,574,000
Voters reg.	1,860	Tax value ..	$432,128,737
Businesses	75	Fed. expd...	$16,371,000

VITAL STATISTICS 1985: Births, 38; Deaths, 28; Marriages, 40; Divorces, 8.

AGRICULTURE: An estimated $100 million average annual income, 65% from beef and stocker cattle, much cattle feeding; crops chiefly wheat, sorghums, corn; 200,000 acres irrigated.

BUSINESS: Agribusinesses, large feedlot operations.

STRATFORD (1,993) county seat; agribusiness center; large feedlots and feed production; steel fabrication; tannery; industrial authority; nursing home. **Texhoma** (351) other principal town.

Smith

LOCATION: Northeast (H-19).
HISTORY: Named for Texas Revolutionary **Gen. James Smith;** county created, organized, 1846, from Nacogdoches.

Con. Dist.	4	U.S. Jud. Dist.....	E-Ty.
St. Sen. Dist.	2	Ct. Appeals	12
St. Rep. Dist........	5, 6	Admin. Jud. Dist.	1
St. Dist. Cts.	7, 114, 241,321		

PHYSICAL FEATURES: Rolling hills, many timbered; Sabine, Neches, other streams; **Lakes Tyler, Palestine;** alluvial, gray, sandy loam, clay soils.

RECREATION: Activities on **Lakes Palestine, Tyler,** other lakes; famed **Tyler Rose Garden; Texas Rose Festival** in October; Azalea Trail in spring; **Tyler State Park;** Goodman Museum; East Texas Fair in fall; collegiate events.

MINERALS: Production of oil, gas, clays, sand and gravel, stone.

1985 Pop.......	150,100	Tax Ratio	0.98
Area (sq. mi.)	932	Oil value	$33,881,130

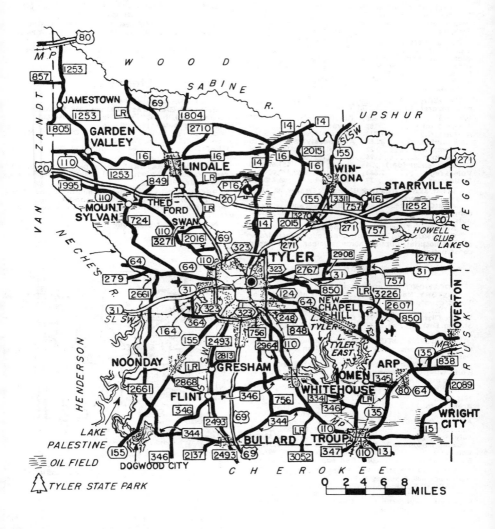

Altitude (ft.) 52-631
Ann. rainfall (in.) . . 46.19
Jan. temp. min. 37
July temp. max. 94
Growing season (da.) 259
Voters reg. 72,529
Businesses 4,353

No. employed 60,020
Avg. weekly wage $364.78
1983 PCI $9,504
Ann. wages . $1,138,501,788
Buying pwr. $1,830,375,000
Tax value . . $5,615,736,087
Fed. expd. . . . $297,023,000

VITAL STATISTICS 1985: Births, 2,541; Deaths, 1,315; Marriages, 1,856; Divorces, 783.

AGRICULTURE: A major producer of rose bushes and horticultural crops with sales of over $78 million annually. Livestock include beef, dairy cattle, horses; roses; blueberries, peaches, pecans, vegetables; timber sales estimated at $3 million.

BUSINESS: Varied manufacturing; agribusinesses; rose production center; oil production; tourism. See metro page.

TYLER (73,021) county seat; "Rose Capital of the World"; administrative, operations center for oil production; manufacturers and processors make tires, pipe, heating and cooling systems, refrigeration equipment, clothing, boxes, gas compressors, fertilizers, oth-

er products; **Texas College, University of Texas at Tyler, Tyler Junior College; University of Texas Health Center;** medical center; school of nursing.

Other towns include **Lindale** (2,671), **Troup** (2,015, part Cherokee County) manufacture clay products, steel buildings, trailers; **Whitehouse** (3,411), **New Chapel Hill** (670), **Arp** (1,045), **Bullard** (887, part Cherokee County), **Overton** (2,466, part Rusk County), **Winona** (514), **Noonday** (428), **Dogwood City.**

Somervell

LOCATION: North central (I-15).

HISTORY: 2nd smallest county in land area in Texas; created, organized as **Somerville County,** 1875, from Hood, Bosque; name changed to proper spelling 1876; named for Texas Republic **Gen. Alexander Somervell.**

Cong. Dist. 17
St. Sen. Dist. 22
St. Rep. Dist. 58
St. Dist. Cts. 18, 249

U.S. Jud. Dist. . . . . W-Wa.
Ct. Appeals 10
Admin. Jud. Dist. 3

PHYSICAL FEATURES: Hilly; Brazos, Paluxy Rivers; gray, dark, alluvial soils.

RECREATION: Fishing, hunting; unique geological formations; **Dinosaur Valley State Park**; Glen Rose Big Rock Park; nature trails, museum.

MINERALS: Limited sand, gravel.

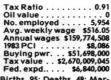

1985 Pop......... 4,600	Tax Ratio 0.91
Area (sq. mi.) 188	Oil value 0
Altitude (ft.) ... 627-1,013	No. employed 5,954
Ann. rainfall (in.) .. 32.65	Avg. weekly wage $516.05
Jan. temp. min..... 32	Annual wages $159,774,508
July temp. max. 98	1983 PCI $8,086
Growing season (da.) 236	Buying pwr.. $51,698,000
Voters reg........ 2,884	Tax value .. $2,670,009,045
Businesses 79	Fed. expd.... $6,840,000

VITAL STATISTICS 1985: Births, 95; Deaths, 48; Marriages, 93; Divorces, 12.

AGRICULTURE: About $3 million average yearly income, ¾ from beef cattle, hogs; crops include hay, peanuts, small grains, pecans.

BUSINESS: Tourism, agribusinesses.

GLEN ROSE (2,108) county seat; tourist, farm trade center; hospital, nursing home; nuclear plant under construction.

Starr

LOCATION: Far south (U-14).

HISTORY: Named for **Dr. J. H. Starr** of Republic of Texas; county created from Nueces, organized 1848.

Cong. Dist. 15	U.S. Jud. Dist. ...... S-Br.
St. Sen. Dist. 21	Ct. Appeals 4
St. Rep. Dist. 37	Admin. Jud. Dist. 5
St. Dist. Cts. 229	

PHYSICAL FEATURES: Rolling, some hills; dense brush; clay, loam, sandy soils, alluvial on Rio Grande; **Falcon Reservoir.**

RECREATION: Falcon Reservoir activities; deer, white wing dove hunting; access to Mexico; historic houses; grotto at Rio Grande City.

MINERALS: Production of oil, gas, sand and gravel.

1985 Pop......... 34,500	Tax Ratio 0.65
Area (sq. mi.) ... 1,226	Oil value..... $15,417,363
Altitude (ft.) 143-531	No. employed 4,467
Ann. rainfall (in.) .. 18.87	Avg. weekly wage $220.99
Jan. temp. min...... 48	Annual wages $51,334,676
July temp. max. 98	1983 PCI $3,100
Growing season (da.) 314	Buying pwr. $152,297,000
Voters reg....... 15,241	Tax value ... $927,991,669
Businesses 306	Fed. expd.... $57,895,000

VITAL STATISTICS 1985: Births, 742; Deaths, 189; Marriages, 448; Divorces, N.A.

AGRICULTURE: About $75 million average annual income, 66% from crops, including sorghums, cotton, vegetables; beef cattle, hogs, sheep, horses; 30,000 acres irrigated for vegetables.

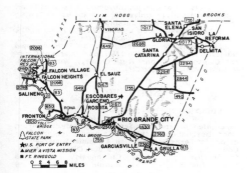

BUSINESS: Vegetable packing, shipping, other agribusinesses; oil processing; tourism.

RIO GRANDE CITY (est. 5,720) county seat; agribusiness center; food processing; exports to Mexico; hospital.

Other towns include **La Grulla** (1,484), **Roma** (3,955).

Stephens

LOCATION: North central (H-13).

HISTORY: Created as **Buchanan**, 1858, from Bosque; renamed, 1861, for Confederate Vice-President, **Alexander H. Stephens;** organized 1876.

Cong. Dist. 17	U.S. Jud. Dist .... N-Ab.
St. Sen. Dist. 22	Ct. Appeals 11
St. Rep. Dist 64	Admin. Jud. Dist...... 8
St. Dist. Cts. 90	

PHYSICAL FEATURES: Broken, hilly; **Hubbard Creek, Possum Kingdom, Daniel Lakes;** Brazos River; loam, sandy soils.

RECREATION: Lake activities; hunting; camp sites; historical points; **Swenson Museum;** Sandefer Oil Museum; aviation museum and annual air show; local events.

MINERALS: Oil, gas, stone.

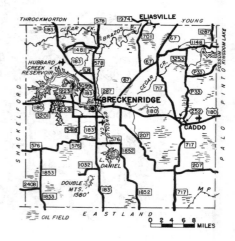

1985 Pop......... 10,400	Tax Ratio 0.88
Area (sq. mi.) 894	Oil value.... $62,507,045
Altitude (ft.) .. 1,127-1,578	No. employed 3,239
Ann. rainfall (in.) .. 26.33	Avg. weekly wage $293.08
Jan. temp. min...... 31	Annual wages . $49,363,728
July temp. max. 98	1983 PCI $7,822
Growing season (da.) 222	Buying pwr. . $107,925,000
Voters reg....... 5,769	Tax value ... $799,206,923
Businesses 397	Fed. expd.... $20,086,000

VITAL STATISTICS 1985: Births, 191; Deaths, 118; Marriages, 146; Divorces, 52.

AGRICULTURE: $8 million average annual income, 90% from beef cattle, horses, hogs, sheep; crops include wheat, oats, hay, peanuts, sorghums, cotton.

BUSINESS: Oil, agribusinesses, recreation, manufacturing of mobil homes, furniture, electronic equipment; aircraft parts, petrochemicals, oil field equipment.

BRECKENRIDGE (7,429) county seat; oil and agribusiness center; plants make clothing, petrochemicals, mobile homes, furniture, oil field equipment, aircraft parts, plaques and trophies, other products; hospital, nursing homes; airport; arts center and library.

Sterling

LOCATION: Southwest (J-10).

HISTORY: Named for buffalo hunter, **W. S. Sterling;** created, organized, 1891, from Tom Green County.

PHYSICAL FEATURES: Central prairie, surrounded by hills, broken by Concho and tributaries; sandy to black soils.

RECREATION: Hunting; local events.

MINERALS: Oil, gas.

AGRICULTURE: Some $5 million average annual income, nearly all from beef cattle, sheep.

Cong. Dist.	17	U.S. Jud. Dist.	N-SAng.
St. Sen. Dist.	25	Ct. Appeals	3
St. Rep. Dist	66	Admin. Jud. Dist	7
St. Dist. Cts.	51		

1985 Pop.	1,600	Tax Ratio	0.89
Area (sq. mi.)	923	Oil value	$14,859,293
Altitude (ft.)	2,167-2,623	No. employed	417
Ann. rainfall (in.)	19.00	Avg. weekly wage	$301.91
Jan. temp. min.	33	Annual wages	$6,546,760
July temp. max.	95	1983 PCI	$7,802
Growing season (da.)	224	Buying pwr.	$9,911,000
Voters reg.	909	Tax value	$549,045,680
Businesses	37	Fed. expd.	$3,111,000

VITAL STATISTICS 1985: Births, 38; Deaths, 10; Marriages, 17; Divorces, 4.

BUSINESS: Oil and ranging economy; hunting leases.

STERLING CITY (1,178) county seat; ranching trade center; oil field services; hospital, nursing home.

Stonewall

LOCATION: Northwest, below Cap Rock (G-11).

HISTORY: Named for **Confederate Gen. T. J. (Stonewall) Jackson;** created from Bexar, 1876, organized 1888.

Cong. Dist.	17	U.S. Jud. Dist.	N-Ab.
St. Sen. Dist.	30	Ct. Appeals	11
St. Rep. Dist	78	Admin. Jud. Dist	7
St. Dist. Cts	39		

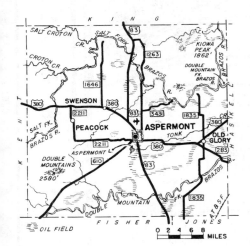

PHYSICAL FEATURES: Level, bisected by Brazos forks; sandy loam, sandy, other soils; some hills.

RECREATION: Local events.

MINERALS: Production of oil, gas, gypsum.

1985 Pop.	2,500	Tax Ratio	0.79
Area (sq. mi.)	925	Oil value	$25,650,977
Altitude (ft.)	1,659-1,964	No. employed	535
Ann. rainfall (in.)	22.36	Avg. weekly wage	$274.72
Jan. temp. min.	30	Annual wages	$7,642,740
July temp. max.	99	1983 PCI	$7,653
Growing season (da.)	220	Buying pwr.	$26,218,000
Voters reg.	1,610	Tax value	$270,131,027
Businesses	63	Fed. expd.	$6,749,000

VITAL STATISTICS 1985: Births, 33; Deaths, 38; Marriages, 26; Divorces, 11.

AGRICULTURE: An estimated $10 million average yearly income from beef cattle, hogs; cotton, sorghums, small grains, peanuts; 5,000 acres irrigated.

BUSINESS: Oil, agribusinesses leading economic factors.

ASPERMONT (1,388) county seat; center for oil field, ranching operations.

Sutton

LOCATION: Southwest (L-11).

HISTORY: Created from Crockett, 1887; organized, 1890; named for Confederate soldier, **Col. John S. Sutton.**

Cong. Dist.	21	U.S. Jud. Dist.	N-SAng.
St. Sen. Dist.	25	Ct. Appeals	4
St. Rep. Dist	67	Admin. Jud. Dist	6
St. Dist. Cts.	112		

PHYSICAL FEATURES: Level, broken by tributaries of Devils, Llano Rivers; black, red loam soils.

RECREATION: Among leading hunting counties; Meirs Museum; **Caverns of Sonora;** local events; county park, rodeo, goat cook-off.

MINERALS: Production of oil, gas, stone.

1985 Pop.	5,400	Tax Ratio	0.86
Area (sq. mi.)	1,455	Oil value	$461
Altitude (ft.)	1,942-2,461	No. employed	1,493
Ann. rainfall (in.)	17.59	Avg. weekly wage	$314.20
Jan. temp. min.	38	Annual wages	$24,393,532
July temp. max.	94	1983 PCI	$10,335
Growing season (da.)	235	Buying pwr.	$55,484,000
Voters reg.	2,429	Tax Value	$756,297,790
Businesses	163	Fed. expd.	$7,293,000

VITAL STATISTICS 1985: Births, 92; Deaths, 41; Marriages, 43; Divorces, 38.

AGRICULTURE: About $13 million average annual income, almost all from cattle, sheep, Angora goats.

BUSINESS: Agribusinesses, oil, tourism; hunting leases.

SONORA (4,387) county seat; oil field services; cattle, wool, mohair marketing center; **Texas A&M Agricultural Research Substation;** hospital, nursing home.

Swisher

LOCATION: Northwest (D-8).

HISTORY: Named for **J. G. Swisher** of Texas Revolution; county created from Bexar, Young Territories, 1876; organized, 1890; among last Indian strongholds.

Cong. Dist.	13	U.S. Jud. Dist	N-Am.
St. Sen. Dist.	31	Ct. Appeals	7
St. Rep. Dist	85	Admin. Jud. Dist	9
St. Dist. Cts.	64, 242		

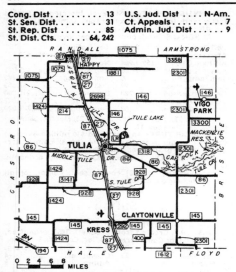

PHYSICAL FEATURES: Level, broken by Tule Canyon and Creek; playas; large underground water supply; rich soils.

RECREATION: Mackenzie Reservoir, Tule Lake activities; museum; local events.

MINERALS: Not significant.

1985 Pop.	8,800	Tax Ratio	0.93
Area (sq. mi.)	902	Oil value	0
Altitude (ft.)	3,354-3,604	No. employed	2,081
Ann. rainfall (in.)	18.94	Avg. weekly wage	$250.22

Jan. temp. min.	24	Annual wages	$27,077,688
July temp. max.	93	1983 PCI	$6,358
Growing season (da.)	205	Buying pwr.	$64,653,000
Voters reg.	4,299	Tax value	$517,116,513
Businesses	221	Fed. expd.	$34,455,000

VITAL STATISTICS 1985: Births, 177; Deaths, 97; Marriages, 85; Divorces, 44.

AGRICULTURE: Among leading counties in farm income; about $125 million average annual income, 60% fed cattle; crops include sorghums, wheat, cotton, corn, soybeans; 189,000 acres irrigated.

BUSINESS: Large feedlots, grain storage, other agribusinesses; varied manufacturing; tourism.

TULIA (4,477) county seat; center for farming activities; plants make a variety of products; grain storage; meat processors; hospital, nursing home; library, museum.

Other towns include **Happy** (710, part Randall County), **Kress** (757).

Tarrant

LOCATION: North (H-16).

HISTORY: Named for **Gen. Edward H. Tarrant,** who helped drive Indians from area; county created, 1849, from Navarro County; organized 1850.

Cong. Dist.	12, 24, 26	U.S. Jud. Dist	N-FW
St. Sen. Dist.	10, 12, 22, 23	Ct. Appeals	2
St. Rep. Dist	89-97	St. Dist. Cts.	17, 48, 67,
Admin. Jud. Dist.	8		96, 141, 153, 213, 231, 233,
			236, 297, 322, 323, 324, 325,
			342, 348, 352, 360,
			Cr. 1, Cr. 2, Cr. 3, Cr. 4

PHYSICAL FEATURES: Part Blackland, level to rolling; drains to Trinity; **Worth, Grapevine, Eagle Mountain, Benbrook Lakes.**

RECREATION: Numerous metropolitan events (ask chambers of commerce); **Scott Theatre; Amon G. Carter Museum; Kimbell Art Museum; Fort Worth Art Museum; Museum of Science and History; Casa Manana; famed Botanic Gardens; Forest Park Zoo; Log Cabin Village; Six Flags Over Texas at Arlington; Southwestern Exposition, Fat Stock show; Convention center; Stockyards Historical**

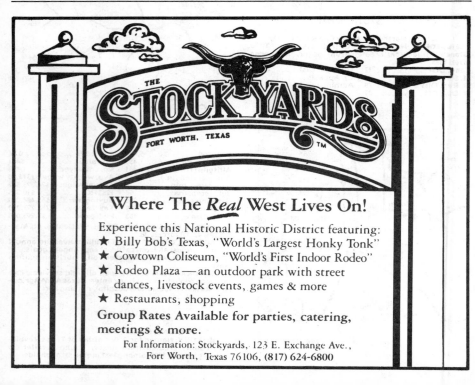

District; Colonial National Golf Tournament; Texas Rangers baseball at Arlington, other major athletic events.

MINERALS: Production of cement, sand, gravel, stone, gas.

EDUCATION: Among leading educational centers; schools include **Texas Christian University, Texas Wesleyan College, Southwestern Baptist Theological Seminary, Tarrant County Junior College System** (three campuses), **Texas College of Osteopathic Medicine** (merged with North Texas State University in 1975) all in Fort Worth; **University of Texas at Arlington, Arlington Baptist College, Bauder Fashion College** in Arlington.

1985 Pop.	1,056,000	Tax Ratio	0.92
Area (sq. mi.)	868	Oil value	0
Altitude (ft.)	484-864	No. employed	454,470
Ann. rainfall (in.)	32.30	Avg. weekly wage	$375.25
Jan. temp. min.	35	Ann. wages	$8,868,218,524
July temp. max.	96	1983 PCI	$10,649
Growing season (da.)	230	Buying pwr.	$13,475,386,000
Voters reg.	463,256	Tax value	$43,369,788,322
Businesses	25,979	Fed. expd.	$6,672,091,000

VITAL STATISTICS 1985: Births, 20,588; Deaths, 7,192; Marriages, 12,609; Divorces, 7,793.

AGRICULTURE: $21.2 million average farm income; dairy and beef cattle, hogs and poultry; headquarters for large dairy producers' organization at Arlington; large production eggs, milk; horses; major nursery stock production; crops include grain sorghums, small grains, cotton, pecans, vegetables.

BUSINESS: Diversified urban economy; planes, helicopters, foods, mobile homes, electronic equipment, chemicals, plastics among products of more than 1,100 factories; large federal expenditure due to defense industries; Dallas-Fort Worth Airport nation's largest; 4th most-populous Texas county; economy closely associated with Dallas urban area; in 1973 the Fort Worth and Dallas PMSAs were combined to form the most populous metro area in Texas and the 10th ranking nationally.

FORT WORTH (414,562) county seat; mercantile, commercial, banking and finance, insurance, manufacturing and wholesale trade center for much of West Texas; a leader in aerospace activities with large plane, helicopter and other plants; educational center (see Education, above); outstanding cultural center; museums; many conventions, other activities; serves as dis-

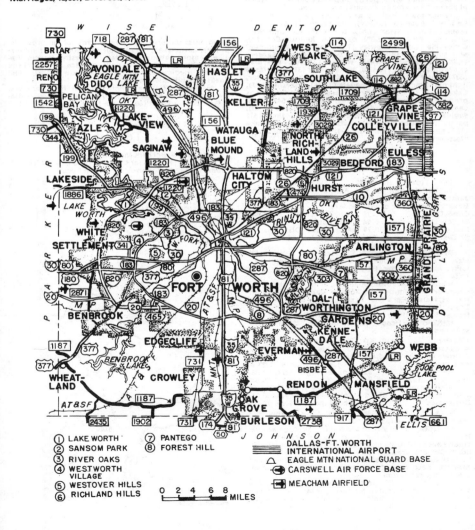

① LAKE WORTH
② SANSOM PARK
③ RIVER OAKS
④ WESTWORTH VILLAGE
⑤ WESTOVER HILLS
⑥ RICHLAND HILLS
⑦ PANTEGO
⑧ FOREST HILL

DALLAS-FT. WORTH INTERNATIONAL AIRPORT
⌂ EAGLE MTN NATIONAL GUARD BASE
CARSWELL AIR FORCE BASE
MEACHAM AIRFIELD

0 2 4 6 8 MILES

tribution center for wide area; agribusiness center for large area of state with large grain storage facilities and feed milling operations; **Dallas-Fort Worth International Airport. Billy Bob's Texas** night club, **Johnnie High's Music Revue;** hospitals, nursing homes; **Log Cabin Village.**

Arlington (213,832) 350 firms in large industrial district; industries make and distribute autos, food products, farm, oil field equipment, electronic components, aircraft and parts, rubber and plastic products; many other products; **University of Texas at Arlington; Arlington Baptist College; Bauder Fashion College;** medical and psychiatric hospitals, nursing homes; a leading recreation center with **Six Flags Over Texas** amusement park, other attractions; **Texas Rangers** baseball club; water park.

Grand Prairie (86,076, mostly in Dallas County).

Grapevine (16,792, partly Dallas County) has light manufacturing plants, Grapevine Lake-oriented tourist trade, air freight handling; **Grapevine Opry;** hospital; near D/FW International Airport.

White Settlement (15,590) adjacent to large plane plant, **Carswell Air Force Base;** hospital, nursing homes.

Mansfield (10,733, partly Johnson County) industrial parks; plants make various products; hospital.

Other towns include **Azle** (7,825, partly in Parker County), **Bedford** (31,029), **Benbrook** (16,690), **Blue Mound** (2,670), **Briar** (1,810, partly Parker and Wise counties), **Burleson** (1,398, partly in Johnson County), **Colleyville** (8,032), **Crowley** (7,001) oil field equipment and supplies manufactured, **Dalworthington Gardens** (1,281), **Edgecliff** (3,049), **Euless** (27,890), **Everman** (5,624), **Forest Hill** (13,173), **Haltom City** (31,505), **Haslet** (337), **Hurst** (34,402), **Keller** (5,459) distribution center, light manufacturing, **Kennedale** (2,876), **Lakeside** (997), **Lake Worth** (4,939), **North Richland Hills** (36,962) firms produce containers, mattresses, **Pantego** (2,543), **Pelican Bay** (1,015), **Richland Hills** (9,132), **River Oaks** (7,740), **Saginaw** (7,185), **Sansom Park** (4,132), **Southlake** (3,612 partly in Denton County), **Watauga** (16,800), **Westlake** (177, partly in Denton County), **Westover Hills** (717), **Westworth** (4,478).

Taylor

LOCATION: Central (I-12).

HISTORY: Named for Alamo heroes, **Edward, James, George Taylor,** brothers; county created from Bexar, Travis, 1858; organized 1878.

Cong. Dist. 17	U.S. Jud. Dist. . . . . N-Ab.
St. Sen. Dist. 24	Ct. Appeals 11
St. Rep. Dist. 78, 79	Admin. Jud. Dist. 7
St. Dist. Cts. 42, 104, 326, 350	

PHYSICAL FEATURES: Prairies, with **Callahan Divide,** draining to Colorado tributaries, Brazos forks; **Lakes Abilene, Kirby, Fort Phantom Hill;** mostly loam soils.

RECREATION: Metropolitan, school events (ask chambers of commerce); **Abilene State Park;** lake activities; **Nelson Park Zoo; Texas Cowboy Reunion,** West Texas Fair; **Fort Phantom Hill; Buffalo Gap** historical tour and art festival; rodeo, other events.

MINERALS: Production of oil, gas, stone, clays, sand and gravel.

1985 Pop. 122,200	Tax Ratio 0.96
Area (sq. mi.) 917	Oil value . . . $2,600,860
Altitude (ft.) . . 1,672-2,410	No. employed 46,027
Ann. rainfall (in.) . . 23.59	Avg. weekly wage $323.80
Jan. temp. min. 33	Annual wages $774,998,264
July temp. max. 94	1983 PCI $8,830
Growing season (da.) 225	Buying pwr. $1,275,362,000
Voters reg. 55,272	Tax value . . $3,744,230,533
Businesses 3,616	Fed. expd. . . . $669,476,000

VITAL STATISTICS 1985: Births, 2,484; Deaths, 959; Marriages, 1,635; Divorces, 909.

AGRICULTURE: About $48 million average annual income, 80% from cattle, hogs, sheep, horses; crops chiefly are cotton, sorghums, wheat; 5,000 acres irrigated, mostly pasture.

BUSINESS: Major economic factors include **Dyess Air Force Base,** feedlots, agribusiness, diversified manufacturing; education.

ABILENE (108,157, partly in Jones County) county seat; distribution center for large area; plants make apparel, trailers, building materials, aircraft parts, consumer electronics, plumbing fixtures, musical in-

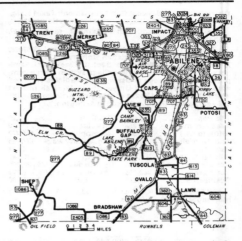

struments, uniforms, beverage cans, other products; process cottonseed, meats, dairy products; oil field service center; **Abilene Christian University, Hardin-Simmons University, McMurry College; Cisco Junior College** branch; medical center; **Abilene State School; West Texas Rehabilitation Center.**

Merkel (3,071) manufacturing; oil field services; feedlot; nursing home. **Tye** (1,974), **Tuscola** (793), **Buffalo Gap** (506), **Impact** (60), **Lawn** (445), **Trent** (335) other principal towns.

Terrell

LOCATION: Borders Mexico (M-8).

HISTORY: Named for **Confederate Gen. A. W. Terrell;** county created, organized 1905, from Pecos.

Cong. Dist. 21	U.S. Jud. Dist. . . . . W-DR
St. Sen. Dist. 25	Ct. Appeals 8
St. Rep. Dist. 68	Admin. Jud. Dist. 6
St. Dist. Cts. 63	

PHYSICAL FEATURES: Semimountainous, many canyons; rocky; limestone soils.

RECREATION: Hunting; lower canyons of Rio Grande accessible by boat; local events.

MINERALS: Production of gas, oil.

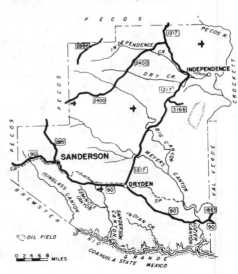

1985 Pop.	1,500	Tax Ratio	0.99
Area (sq. mi.)	2,357	Oil value	$1,511,079
Altitude (ft.)	1,668-2,792	No. employed	349
Ann. rainfall (in.)	11.21	Avg. weekly wage	$254.13
Jan. temp. min.	30	Annual wages	$4,611,976
July temp. max.	93	1983 PCI	$7,804
Growing season (da.)	237	Buying pwr.	$16,909,000
Voters reg.	1,084	Tax value	$350,410,095
Businesses	36	Fed. expd.	$4,929,000

VITAL STATISTICS 1985: Births, 31; Deaths, 14; Marriages, 22; Divorces, 3.

AGRICULTURE: Some $11 million average annual income, nearly all from sheep, goats, beef cattle; among leading counties in sheep, goat production.

BUSINESS: Ranching economy; oil and natural gas exploration increasing.

SANDERSON (est. 1,500) county seat; center for ranching, petroleum operations; rail terminal.

Terry

LOCATION: West (G-7).

HISTORY: Named for head of famed Texas Ranger troop, **Col. B. F. Terry.** County created from Bexar District, 1876; organized, 1904.

Cong. Dist.	19	U.S. Jud. Dist.	N-Lb.
St. Sen. Dist.	28	Ct. Appeals	7
St. Rep. Dist.	77	Admin. Jud. Dist.	9
St. Dist. Cts.	121		

PHYSICAL FEATURES: Level, broken by draws, playas; sandy, sandy loam, loam soils.

RECREATION: Local events; Terry County Heritage Museum, fall harvest festival.

MINERALS: Production of oil, gas, sodium sulphate.

1985 Pop.	15,400	Tax Ratio	0.97
Area (sq. mi.)	886	Oil value	$77,319,143
Altitude (ft.)	3,183-3,447	No. employed	3,472
Ann. rainfall (in.)	17.21	Avg. weekly wage	$351.96
Jan. temp. min.	26	Annual wages	$63,545,816
July temp. max.	93	1983 PCI	$7,563
Growing season (da.)	206	Buying pwr.	$135,537,000
Voters reg.	8,352	Tax value	$1,275,554,760
Businesses	346	Fed. expd.	$40,086,000

VITAL STATISTICS 1985: Births, 312; Deaths, 126; Marriages, 182; Divorces, 66.

AGRICULTURE: Among leading cotton counties; about $50 million average annual income, 90% from cotton, sorghums, wheat; some stocker and beef cattle, hogs; 250,000 acres irrigated, mostly cotton.

BUSINESS: Petroleum, agribusinesses.

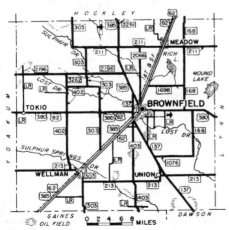

BROWNFIELD (10,846) county seat; oil field services; plants make irrigation equipment, fertilizers, process minerals; hospital, medical center, nursing homes.

Other towns include **Meadow** (609) and **Wellman** (266).

Throckmorton

LOCATION: North central (G-13).

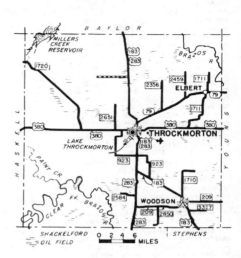

HISTORY: Named for **Dr. W. E. Throckmorton,** father of Gov. J. W. Throckmorton; county created from Fannin, 1858; organized, 1879.

Cong. Dist.	17	U.S. Jud. Dist.	N-Ab.
St. Sen. Dist.	30	Ct. Appeals	11
St. Rep. Dist.	64	Admin. Jud. Dist.	7
St. Dist. Cts.	39		

PHYSICAL FEATURES: Rolling, between Brazos forks; red to black soils.

RECREATION: Hunting, fishing; historic sites include **Camp Cooper, Camp Wilson,** site of former Comanche reservation; restored ranch home; Miller's Creek Lake.

MINERALS: Production of gas, oil.

1985 Pop.	2,300	Tax Ratio	0.76
Area (sq. mi.)	912	Oil value	$2,248,018
Altitude (ft.)	1,153-1,583	No. employed	438
Ann. rainfall (in.)	25.82	Avg. weekly wage	$287.86
Jan. temp. min.	29	Annual wages	$6,556,412
July temp. max.	98	1983 PCI	$7,364
Growing season (da.)	220	Buying pwr.	$14,833,000
Voters reg.	1,397	Tax value	$194,785,485
Businesses	75	Fed. expd.	$6,937,000

VITAL STATISTICS 1985: Births, 24; Deaths, 30; Marriages, 11; Divorces, 12.

AGRICULTURE: About $17 million average annual income, 75% from cattle, sheep, horses; crops include wheat, oats, cotton, sorghums, hay.

BUSINESS: Oil and agribusiness economy.

THROCKMORTON (1,381) county seat; plants make oil field equipment, other products; hospital, nursing home; oil field services. **Woodson** (325) other principal town.

Titus

LOCATION: Northeast (G-20).

HISTORY: Named for pioneer settler, **A. J. Titus;** county created from Bowie, Red River and organized 1846.

PHYSICAL FEATURES: Small and hilly; drains to Big Cypress Creek, Sulphur River; timbered.

RECREATION: Fishing, hunting; activities on **Monticello Reservoir, Lake Bob Sandlin, Welsh Reservoir,** other area lakes; railroad museum; riverboat; local events, county fair in September.

MINERALS: Production of oil, gas, lignite.

Cong. Dist. 1
St. Sen. Dist. 1
St. Rep. Dist. 8
St. Dist. Cts. . 76, 276
U.S. Jud. Dist. E-Tx.
Ct. Appeals 6
Admin. Jud. Dist. . 1

1985 Pop. 23,000
Area (sq. mi.) 412
Altitude (ft.) 301-462
Ann. rainfall (in.) . 45.99
Jan. temp. min. . . . 35
July temp. max. 95
Growing season (da.) 233
Voters reg. 12,241
Businesses 573
Tax Ratio 0.92
Oil value $16,007,510
No. employed 9,524
Avg. weekly wage $345.20
Annual wages $170,962,384
1983 PCI $8,195
Buying pwr. . $257,173,000
Tax value . . $1,631,683,380
Fed. expd. $52,050,000

VITAL STATISTICS 1985: Births, 381; Deaths, 255; Marriages, 304; Divorces, 71.

AGRICULTURE: About $30 million average annual income, over 90% from cattle, dairy products, poultry; among leading counties in broilers; crops include corn, watermelons, sorghums, hay, peanuts.

BUSINESS: Economy based largely on oil, agribusinesses, tourism; lignite mining and power generation.

MOUNT PLEASANT (11,682) county seat; tourism; plants make cables, furniture, other products; beef, poultry processing plants; hospital; nursing homes. **Northeast Texas Community College.**

Talco (816), **Monticello** (40), **Winfield** (435), **Miller's Cove** (52).

Travis

LOCATION: Central (M-15).

HISTORY: Created, 1840, when Austin became Texas Capital, from Bastrop County; organized, 1843; named for Alamo commander, **Col. Wm. B. Travis;** many other counties created from original area.

Cong. Dist. 10   U. S. Jud. Dist . . . . W-An.
St. Sen. Dist. 14   Ct. Appeals 3
St. Rep. Dist 47-51   Admin. Jud. Dist 3
St. Dist. Cts. . . 53, 98, 126,
    147, 167, 200, 201,250,
    261, 299, 331, 345, 353

PHYSICAL FEATURES: Scenic hills, broken by Colorado River and lakes; cedars, pecans, other trees; diverse soils, mineral deposits.

RECREATION: Major tourist center; 95 miles of Colorado River lakes from Austin northwestward; hunting, fishing; Austin Aqua Festival; livestock exposition; many collegiate, metropolitan, governmental events; (ask chamber of commerce, Texas Highway Department, Tourist Development Agency).

1985 Pop. 533,200   Tax Ratio 0.96
Area (sq. mi.) 989   Oil value 0
Altitude (ft.) . . . 444-1,330   No. employed 294,066
Ann. rainfall (in.) . . 32.49   Avg. weekly wage $375.65
Jan. temp. min. 41   Ann. wages . $5,744,268,284
July temp. max. 95   1983 PCI $10,532
Growing season (da.) 270   Buying pwr. $6,991,998,000
Voters reg. 271,742   Tax value . $36,219,718,283
Businesses 15,405   Fed. expd. . $2,318,956,000

VITAL STATISTICS 1985: Births, 10,562; Deaths, 2,836; Marriages, 7,049; Divorces, 3,704.

MINERALS: Production of lime, stone, sand, gravel, oil and gas.

EDUCATION: University of Texas main campus, South's largest university; **St. Edward's University, Maryhill College, Concordia Lutheran College, Huston-Tillotson College, Austin Community College;** many state eleemosynary schools, institutions.

Tom Green

LOCATION: West central (K-11).

HISTORY: Created from Bexar District, 1874, named for **Gen. Tom Green** of Texas Revolution; organized, 1875; 12 other counties created from this original area.

PHYSICAL FEATURES: Plains, rolling hills, broken by Concho forks; loams in basin, stony hillsides; **Nasworthy, Twin Buttes, O. C. Fisher Lakes.**

Cong. Dist. 21
St. Sen. Dist. 25
St. Rep. Dist. 66
St. Dist. Cts. . 51, 119, 340
U.S. Jud. Dist. . . . N-SAng.
Ct. Appeals 3
Admin. Jud. Dist. 7

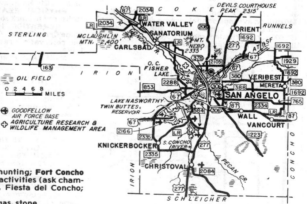

RECREATION: Water sports; hunting; **Fort Concho Museum;** metropolitan, collegiate activities (ask chamber of commerce); roping fiesta, Fiesta del Concho; stock show and rodeo.

MINERALS: Production of oil, gas, stone.

1985 Pop. 96,700   Tax Ratio 0.95
Area (sq. mi.) 1,515   Oil value $13,668,011
Altitude (ft.) . . 1,717-2,480   No. employed 35,035
Ann. rainfall (in.) . 17.53   Avg. weekly wage $311.29
Jan. temp. min. 34   Annual wages $567,122,508
July temp. max. 98   1983 PCI $8,987
Growing season (da.) 235   Buying pwr. $1,095,732,000
Voters reg. 40,247   Tax value . . $2,899,530,830
Businesses 2,683   Fed. expd. . . $261,921,000

VITAL STATISTICS 1985: Births, 1,714; Deaths, 858; Marriages, 1,224; Divorces, 895.

AGRICULTURE: An estimated $45 million average annual income from beef, dairy cattle, sheep, goats; a leading producer of wool, mohair; cotton, wheat, oats, sorghums; 15,000 acres irrigated.

BUSINESS: "Sheep and Wool Capital"; economy

based on varied agribusinesses, manufacturing; trade center for large area, educational center, medical center.

SAN ANGELO (84,350) county seat; varied agribusinesses; livestock feeding, packing center; plants make sportswear, footwear, surgical supplies, millwork, aircraft parts, oilfield equipment, other products; hospital; **Angelo State University; Texas A&M Research and Extension Center.**

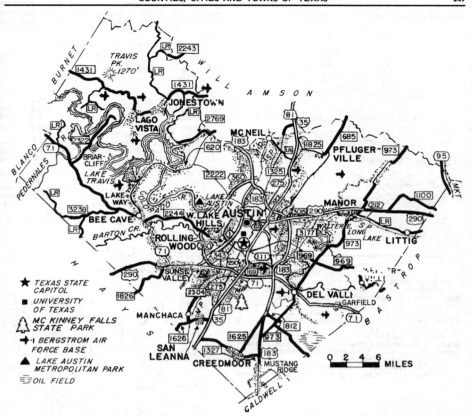

AGRICULTURE: Almost $27 million average annual income from beef, dairy cattle, horses, hogs; crops include sorghums, cotton, small grains, pecans.

BUSINESS: Urbanized area with economy based on education, state government, tourism, research and industry; many conventions.

AUSTIN: (397,001) county seat and state capital; large state and federal payrolls; **University of Texas, Austin Community College,** other schools (see **Education** above); a leading convention, tourism city; **Lyndon B. Johnson Presidential Library;** many research and science-oriented industries; hospitals, including state in-

stitutions; popular retirement area; **Bergstrom Air Force Base,** other federal activities; plants make electronic, business equipment, boats, many other products.

Other growing suburban towns include **Briarcliff** (129), **Garfield** (745), **Highland Country Club** (200), **Highland Lake Estates** (200), **Jonestown** (683), **West Lake Hills** (3,192), **Lakeway** (1,170), **Manor** (1,233), **Mustang Ridge** (435), **Pflugerville** (996), **Rollingwood** (1,376), **San Leanna** (297), **Sunset Valley** (503) and **Lago Vista** (2,500) resort community on **Lake Travis.**

Trinity

LOCATION: Southeast (K-20).

HISTORY: Named for river; county created, organized, 1850, out of Houston County.

Cong. Dist.	2	U.S. Jud. Dist	S-Hn.
St. Sen. Dist.	5	Ct. Appeals	1, 14
St. Rep. Dist	17	Admin. Jud. Dist	2
St. Dist. Cts.	2D9, 258		

MINERALS: Limited oil, gas, lignite, sand and gravel.

PHYSICAL FEATURES: Heavily forested hills, between Neches and Trinity; rich alluvial soils, sandy upland; 67,910 acres in **Davy Crockett National Forest.**

RECREATION: Livingston Reservoir activities; fishing, hiking, hunting; **Davy Crockett National Forest;** Timberfest in March; historic sites.

1985 Pop.	11,800	Tax Ratio	0.90
Area (sq. mi.)	692	Oil value	0
Altitude (ft.)	169-362	No. employed	1,994
Ann. rainfall (in.)	45.95	Avg. weekly wage	$250.06
Jan. temp. min.	39	Annual wages	$25,928,688
July temp. max.	94	1983 PCI	$6,879

Growing season (da.)	260	Buying pwr.	$99,528,000
Voters reg.	8,900	Tax value	$629,770,074
Businesses	214	Fed. expd.	$28,914,000

VITAL STATISTICS 1985: Births, 143; Deaths, 144; Marriages, 129; Divorces, 20.

AGRICULTURE: Timber sales produce income of more than $19 million; more than $11 million other farm income from beef cattle, poultry, hogs; hay, vegetables, peaches, pecans.

BUSINESS: Forestry, tourism, cattle chief sources income.

GROVETON (1,286) county seat; gateway to Davy Crockett National Forest recreation areas; lumbering center; clothing and oil field chemical manufacturing; nursing home; airport.

Other principal town is **Trinity** (3,371) steel fabrication; hospital, nursing home; a forest industries center near **Livingston Reservoir.**

See Map on next page.

Trinity County (Cont'd.)

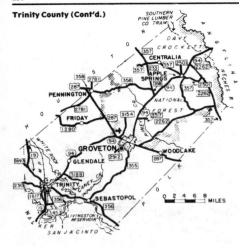

Tyler

LOCATION: Southeast (K-21).

HISTORY: Named for U.S. president, **John Tyler;** county created, organized, 1846, from Liberty.

Cong. Dist. 2	U.S. Jud. Dist . . . . E-Bt.
St. Sen. Dist. 3	Ct. Appeals 9
St. Rep. Dist 18	Admin. Jud. Dist. 2
St. Dist. Cts. 88, 1-A	

PHYSICAL FEATURES: Hilly, densely timbered; drains to Neches, Angelina, other streams; **B. A. Steinhagen Lake** (formerly **Town Bluff and Dam B**); **Big Thicket** is unique plant-animal area.

RECREATION: Big Thicket National Preserve; guest ranch; Heritage Village; lake activities; Allan Shivers

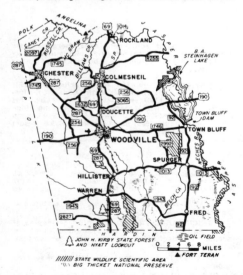

Museum; John Henry Kirby State Forest; historic sites; near **Alabama-Coushatta Indian Reservation;** dogwood festival in April; rodeo, arts and crafts fair, other local events.

MINERALS: Production of oil, gas.

1985 Pop.	18,600	Tax Ratio	0.86
Area (sq. mi.)	922	Oil value	$865,713
Altitude (ft.)	109-443	No. employed	2,976
Ann. rainfall (in.) . .	48.37	Avg. weekly wage	$261.63
Jan. temp. min.	38	Annual wages .	$40,487,916
July temp. max.	94	1983 PCI	$7,062
Growing season (da.)	241	Buying pwr. .	$196,871,000
Voters reg.	10,043	Tax value . . .	$902,501,376
Businesses	282	Fed. expd.	$43,049,000

VITAL STATISTICS 1985: Births, 233; Deaths, 206; Marriages, 178; Divorces, 114.

AGRICULTURE: Timber sales major income source; $7 million additional annual average farming income from cattle, hogs, poultry, horses; vegetables, fruit.

BUSINESS: Lumbering, poultry processing, some manufacturing; tourism, catfish production.

WOODVILLE (3,027) county seat; center for lumber manufacturing, livestock marketing; plants make aluminum products, windows, wood products, industrial products; tourist center; hospital, nursing homes.

Other towns include **Chester** (409) and **Colmesneil** (607).

Upshur

LOCATION: Northeast (H-20).

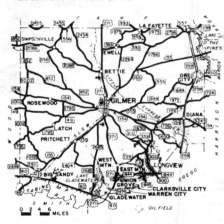

HISTORY: Created from Harrison, Nacogdoches counties, 1846; organized same year; named for U.S. Secretary of State, **A. P. Upshur.**

Cong. Dist. 1	U.S. Jud. Dist. . . . . E-Mk.
St. Sen. Dist. 1	Ct. Appeals . . . . . . 6, 1.
St. Rep. Dist. 5	Admin. Jud. Dist. . . . . .
St. Dist. Cts. 115	

PHYSICAL FEATURES: Rolling to hilly, over half forested; drains to Sabine, Cypress Creek, **Lake O' the Pines, Lake Gladewater.**

RECREATION: Scenic trails; hunting, fishing; East Texas October "Yamboree"; Cherokee rose festival in May, other local events.

MINERALS: Production of oil, gas, sand and gravel.

1985 Pop.	32,700	Tax Ratio	0.9
Area (sq. mi.)	587	Oil value	$3,857,13
Altitude (ft.)	225-685	No. employed	4,39
Ann. rainfall (in.) . .	45.74	Avg. weekly wage	$279.6
Jan. temp. min.	37	Annual wages .	$63,902,06
July temp. max.	96	1983 PCI	$7,32

Growing season (da.)	245	Buying pwr.	$322,048,000
Voters reg.	16,880	Tax value	$992,589,154
Businesses	403	Fed. expd.	$56,004,000

VITAL STATISTICS 1985: Births, 482; Deaths, 335; Marriages, 323; Divorces, 152.

AGRICULTURE: About $40 million average yearly income, 90% from beef, dairy cattle, hogs, poultry; among leading broiler and dairy producing counties; timber, vegetable crops, hay, peaches; timber a major product.

BUSINESS: Manufacturing, agribusinesses, petroleum production and lumber mill are leading economic factors; many work at nearby steel mills and other area plants.

GILMER (5,618) county seat; plants make electrical conduits and fittings, ceramic bathroom accessories, dresses, other products; process meat, vegetables, lumber; hospital, nursing homes.

Big Sandy (1,809) **Ambassador College; Gladewater** (7,381, mostly in Gregg County), **Ore City** (1,053), **Warren City** (331, mostly Gregg County), **East Mountain** (888), **Union Grove** (341) and **West Mountain** (448) are other principal towns.

Upton

LOCATION: West (K-8).

HISTORY: Created in 1887 from Tom Green County, not organized until 1910; name honors brothers, **John** and **William Upton**, Confederate colonels.

PHYSICAL FEATURES: North flat, south rolling, hilly; limestone, sandy loam soils, drains to creeks.

RECREATION: Historic sites, **Mendoza Trail Museum;** scenic areas; local events.

MINERALS: Production of oil, gas.

Cong. Dist.	21	U.S. Jud. Dist	W:M-0
St. Sen. Dist.	25	Ct. Appeals	8
St. Rep. Dist.	69	Admin. Jud. Dist	6
St. Dist. Cts.	83, 112		

1985 Pop.	5,600	Tax Ratio	0.93
Area (sq. mi.)	1,243	Oil value	$104,522,110
Altitude (ft.)	2,441-3,141	No. employed	1,416
Ann. rainfall (in.)	12.70	Avg. weekly wage	$404.04
Jan. temp. min.	33	Annual wages	$29,750,428
July temp. max.	96	1983 PCI	$7,423
Growing season (da.)	232	Buying pwr.	$48,072,000
Voters reg.	2,747	Tax value	$930,876,532
Businesses	112	Fed. expd.	$6,476,000

VITAL STATISTICS 1985: Births, 117; Deaths, 32; Marriages, 74; Divorces, 20.

AGRICULTURE: About $5.3 million average yearly income equally divided among sheep, goats, cattle and cotton; wheat, pecan production; 10,000 acres irrigated for cotton, pecans.

BUSINESS: Petroleum production, ranching, tourism.

RANKIN (1,494) county seat, and **McCamey** (2,880) are centers for oil and ranching activities; hospitals, nursing home; annual pecan show.

Uvalde

LOCATION: Southwest (O-12).

HISTORY: Created from Bexar, 1850; organized, 1853; re-created, organized, 1856; named for **Gov. Juan de Ugalde** of Coahuila, with name Anglicized.

Cong. Dist.	23	U.S. Jud. Dist	W-DR
St. Sen. Dist.	21	Ct. Appeals	4
St. Rep. Dist	67	Admin. Jud. Dist	6
St. Dist. Cts.	38		

PHYSICAL FEATURES: Part on Edwards Plateau, most is rolling hills below escarpment; spring-fed Sa-

O UVALDE TEST TRACK
▲ UVALDE NATIONAL FISH HATCHERY

0 4 8 12 MILES

binal, Frio, Leona, Nueces Rivers; cypress, cedar, other trees; unique **maple groves.**

RECREATION: Major deer, turkey hunting area; **Garner State Park;** water activities on scenic rivers; **John N. Garner Museum;** Uvalde Memorial Park; scenic trails; historic sites; local events; recreational homes.

MINERALS: Production asphalt, stone, sand and gravel.

1985 Pop.	24,700	Tax Ratio	0.91
Area (sq. mi.)	1,564	Oil value	0
Altitude (ft.)	699-1,957	No. employed	7,141
Ann. rainfall (in.)	23.23	Avg. weekly wage	$239.30
Jan. temp. min.	40	Annual wages	$88,860,204
July temp. max.	96	1983 PCI	$5,817
Growing season (da.)	255	Buying pwr.	$184,275,000
Voters reg.	11,626	Tax value	$980,948,265
Businesses	524	Fed. expd.	$44,259,000

VITAL STATISTICS 1985: Births, 418; Deaths, 183; Marriages, 229; Divorces, 68.

AGRICULTURE: About $53 million average annual income, from beef cattle, hogs, sheep, goats; crops include wheat, corn, oats, grain sorghums, cotton, vegetables; 56,000 acres irrigated.

BUSINESS: Agribusinesses; light manufacturing; tourism; hunting leases.

UVALDE (14,908) county seat; plants make clothes, asphalt products, pipe, process vegetables, wool, mohair; **Southwest Texas Junior College; Texas A&M Research and Extension Center;** hospital.

Sabinal (2,002) center for ranching, farming area; gateway to **Frio** and **Sabinal Canyons;** tourist, recreational, retirement areas.

Val Verde

LOCATION: Southwest (N-10).

HISTORY: Named for Civil War battle, **Val Verde** (green valley); county created, organized, 1885, from Crockett, Kinney, Pecos Counties.

Cong. Dist.	21	U.S. Jud. Dist.	W-DR
St. Sen. Dist.	25	Ct. Appeals	4
St. Rep. Dist.	68	Admin. Jud. Dist.	6
St. Dist. Cts.	63		

PHYSICAL FEATURES: Rolling, hilly; brushy; Devils, Pecos Rivers, **Amistad Lake;** limestone, alluvial soils.

RECREATION: Mexican gateway; deer hunting; **Amistad Lake** activities; Langtry restoration of **Judge Roy Bean's saloon;** San Felipe Springs.

MINERALS: Production sand and gravel, gas, oil.

1985 Pop.	39,400	Tax Ratio	0.96
Area (sq. mi.)	3,150	Oil value	0
Altitude (ft.)	900-2,200	No. employed	7,458
Ann. rainfall (in.)	16.88	Avg. weekly wage	$250.95
Jan. temp. min.	40	Annual wages	$97,325,600
July temp. max.	94	1983 PCI	$5,587

Val Verde County (Cont'd.)

Growing season (da.)   300   Buying pwr. . $302,445,000
Voters reg.   13,595   Tax value . . . $852,029,864
Businesses   699   Fed. expd.. . . $150,203,000

VITAL STATISTICS 1985: Births, 959; Deaths, 236; Marriages, 525; Divorces, 170.

AGRICULTURE: More than $16 million average yearly income, nearly all from sheep, Angora goats, cattle.

BUSINESS: Agribusiness; tourism; area trade center; large military, other U.S. expenditures.

DEL RIO (34,401) county seat; center for tourism and trade with Mexico; plants make clothing, electronic equipment; hospital; nursing homes.

Van Zandt

LOCATION: Northeast (H-18).

HISTORY: Named for Republic of Texas leader, **Isaac Van Zandt;** county created, organized from Henderson, 1848.

Cong. Dist. 4   U.S. Jud. Dist. . . . . E-Ty.
St. Sen. Dist. 2   Ct. Appeals 5, 12
St. Rep. Dist. 5   Admin. Jud. Dist. 1
St. Dist. Cts. 294

PHYSICAL FEATURES: In three soil belts; level to rolling, Sabine, Neches Rivers; **Lake Tawakoni;** partly forested.

RECREATION: Lake activities; historic sites; Canton "First Monday" trades day, county fair, salt festival, bluegrass festival.

MINERALS: Production of oil, gas, salt, iron ore, clays.

1985 Pop. 37,300   Tax Ratio 0.93
Area (sq. mi.) 855   Oil value $57,293,831
Altitude (ft.) 421-573   No. employed . . . 5,992
Ann. rainfall (in.) . . 43.09   Avg. weekly wage $274.58
Jan. temp. min. 35   Annual wages . $85,555,064
July temp. max. 94   1983 PCI $7,815
Growing season (da.)   250   Buying pwr. . $387,355,000
Voters reg. 20,619   Tax value . $1,483,671,915
Businesses 616   Fed. expd.. . . . $78,573,000

VITAL STATISTICS 1985: Births, 447; Deaths, 437; Marriages, 373; Divorces, 253.

AGRICULTURE: An estimated $51 million average annual income, 70% from cattle, hogs, dairy products; a leading county in beef cows and calves; a leading hay and sweet potatoe producer, also nursery stock, vegetables, grains, cotton.

BUSINESS: Economy based on oil, tourism, agribusinesses, light manufacturing; many commute to jobs in Dallas.

CANTON (2,975) county seat; popular "Trades Day"

each first Monday; agribusiness center; greeting cards printed; apparel factory, trailer plants; health care center, nursing homes.

Wills Point (3,125) plants make clothing, mobile homes, aluminum products, other products; nurseries; many work in Dallas, Greenville; livestock marketing center; clinic, nursing home.

Van (1,970) oil activity center; agribusinesses; concrete mixing plant; nursing homes, clinic.

Grand Saline (2,842) salt plant; oil field equipment and apparel manufacturers; steel sinks made; hospital; salt festival in June.

Edgewood (1,452) has oil, gas refineries, hat, rope manufacturing, steel fabrication; clinic; jamboree in April.

Other towns include **Edom** (277) and **Fruitvale** (395).

Victoria

LOCATION: South (P-17).

HISTORY: An original county, created 1836 from Mexican municipality named for Mexican president, **Guadalupe Victoria.**

Cong. Dist. 14   U.S. Jud. Dist. . . . . S-Va
St. Sen. Dist. 18   Ct. Appeals 13
St. Rep. Dist. 32   Admin. Jud. Dist. 4
St. Dist. Cts. . . 24, 135, 267

PHYSICAL FEATURES: Rolling, intersected by many streams; sandy loams, clays, alluvial soils.

RECREATION: Fishing, hunting; saltwater activities; many historic homes, sites; recreational park; zoo; Bach Festival in May, Armadillo Festival in August; Super Bowl of Chili, International Food Fair, Czech Heritage Festival in October; ask chamber of commerce.

MINERALS: Production of oil, gas, sand and gravel.

1985 Pop. 75,500   Tax Ratio 0.9
Area (sq. mi.) 887   Oil value $11,909,958
Altitude (ft.) 38-205   No. employed . . . 26,817
Ann. rainfall (in.) . . 34.29   Avg. weekly wage $334.59
Jan. temp. min. 46   Annual wages $466,464,653
July temp. max. 92   1983 PCI $9,397
Growing season (da.)   290   Buying pwr. . $852,222,000
Voters reg. 41,300   Tax value . $3,423,730,247
Businesses 2,253   Fed. expd.. . $110,960,000

VITAL STATISTICS 1985: Births, 1,486; Deaths, 572; Marriages, 884; Divorces, 513.

AGRICULTURE: More than $28 million average farm income from sorghums, corn, alfalfa; beef cattle, hogs, poultry; fish farming.

BUSINESS: Income from oil, manufacturing, petrochemical plants, agribusiness, tourism.

VICTORIA (55,113) county seat; tourism, agribusiness center; on barge canal; plants make petrochemicals, aluminum, steel products, boats, oil field equipment; foundry equipment; **Victoria College, University of Houston at Victoria;** Community Theater, Symphony; hospitals.

Bloomington is other principal town.

See Map on next page

Ann. rainfall (in.) .. 44.99	Avg. weekly wage $333.02
Jan. temp. min....... 41	Annual wages $285,046,552
July temp. max. 94	1983 PCI $7,319
Growing season (da.) 265	Buying pwr. . $503,415,000
Voters reg. 16,931	Tax value .. $1,146,605,740
Businesses 811	Fed. expd..... $81,526,000

VITAL STATISTICS 1985: Births, 592; Deaths, 285; Marriages, 493; Divorces, 255.

AGRICULTURE: About $15 million average yearly income, 60% from cattle, horses, hogs; crops include hay, some cotton, grains; estimated $15 million from timber sales.

BUSINESS: Economy based on education, state employment, agribusiness, lumbering, tourism.

HUNTSVILLE (30,152) county seat; Texas Department of Corrections headquarters; **Sam Houston State University** and adjoining museum; plants make wood products, valves, tools; oil, gas, lignite exploration; hospital.

Other towns include **New Waverly (962)** and **Riverside (390).**

Walker

LOCATION: Southeast (L-19).

HISTORY: Created, organized 1846, from Montgomery County; first named for U.S. Secretary of Treasury, **R. J. Walker;** renamed, 1863, for Texas Ranger **Capt. S. H. Walker.**

Cong. Dist. 2	U.S. Jud. Dist..... S-Hn.
St. Sen. Dist. 5	Ct. Appeals 1, 14
St. Rep. Dist........ 18	Admin. Jud. Dist. 2
St. Dist. Cts. 12, 278	

PHYSICAL FEATURES: Rolling hills; over 70 percent forested; **Sam Houston National Forest; San Jacinto, Trinity Rivers; large Texas prison units.**

RECREATION: Fishing, hunting; **Livingston Reservoir** activities; **Sam Houston museum, homes, grave;** other historic sites; **Huntsville State Park; Sam Houston National Forest;** county fair.

MINERALS: Clays, gas, oil, sand and gravel, stone.

1985 Pop......... 51,700	Tax Ratio 0.91
Area (sq. mi.) 786	Oil value $11,351
Altitude (ft.) 140-404	No. employed 16,460

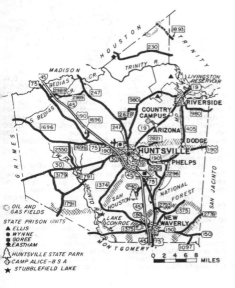

Waller

LOCATION: Southeast (M-18).

Cong. Dist. 14	
St. Sen. Dist. 5	
St. Rep. Dist........ 13	
St. Dist. Cts. 9, 155	
U.S. Jud. Dist...... S-Hn.	
Ct. Appeals 1, 14	
Admin. Jud. Dist. 2	

HISTORY: Named for **Edwin Waller,** Republic of Texas leader; county created, organized, 1873, from Austin, Grimes.

PHYSICAL FEATURES: Rolling prairie; drains to Brazos and San Jacinto Rivers; alluvial soils; almost one-fifth forested.

RECREATION: Fishing, hunting; historic sites; historical museum; county fair.

MINERALS: Oil, gas, sand and gravel.

1985 Pop....... 23,500	Tax Ratio 0.97
Area (sq. mi.) 514	Oil value $1,084,538
Altitude (ft.).... 110-249	No. employed 5,701
Ann. rainfall (in.) .. 41.67	Avg. weekly wage $307.83
Jan. temp. min. 39	Annual wages . $91,256,840
July temp. max. 95	1983 PCI $7,542
Growing season (da.) 283	Buying pwr. . $226,150,000
Voters reg. 11,407	Tax value .. $2,199,599,896
Businesses 371	Fed. expd.... $49,806,000

VITAL STATISTICS 1985: Births, 318; Deaths, 193; Marriages, 274; Divorces, 103.

AGRICULTURE: About $35 million average annual income from beef cattle, hogs, goats, sheep; rice, corn, peanuts, soybeans, vegetables; 14,000 acres irrigated for rice; timber marketed.

BUSINESS: Economy based on oil, agribusiness, Houston area growth; manufacturing; county part of Houston PMSA.

HEMPSTEAD (3,782) county seat; agribusiness center; varied manufacturing; hospital, clinic, nursing home.

Prairie View (3,715) site of **Prairie View A&M University.** Other towns include **Katy (9,886, partly in Fort Bend, Harris counties); Waller (1,750, part in Harris County); Brookshire (2,993); Pattison (448); Pine Island (425).**

Ward

LOCATION: Far west (J-6).

HISTORY: Named for Republic of Texas leader, **Thomas W. Ward;** county created from Tom Green, 1887; organized, 1892.

Cong. Dist. 16	U.S. Jud. Dist..... W-Pe.
St. Sen. Dist. 25	Ct. Appeals 8
St. Rep. Dist......... 69	Admin. Jud. Dist. 7
St. Dist. Cts. 143	

PHYSICAL FEATURES: Plain, sloping to Pecos River; sandy, loam soils.

RECREATION: Monahans Sandhills State Park, Museum; Pyote Rattlesnake Museum; Million Barrel Museum; county park; local events.

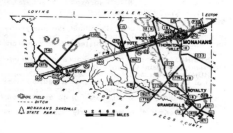

OIL FIELD
---- DITCH
△ MONAHANS SANDHILLS STATE PARK   0 2 4 6 8 MILES

MINERALS: Production of oil, gas, sand and gravel.

1985 Pop.	15,900	Tax Ratio	0.87
Area (sq. mi.)	836	Oil value	$103,196,681
Altitude (ft.)	2,467-2,799	No. employed	4,198
Ann. rainfall (in.)	12.04	Avg. weekly wage	$374.76
Jan. temp. min.	30	Annual wages	$81,809,028
July temp. max.	96	1983 PCI	$7,648
Growing season (da.)	223	Buying pwr.	$148,976,000
Voters reg.	6,628	Tax value	$1,170,731,449
Businesses	399	Fed. expd.	$20,366,000

VITAL STATISTICS 1985: Births, 307; Deaths, 125; Marriages, 180; Divorces, 84.

AGRICULTURE: About $2.7 million average annual income, more than 95% from beef cattle; alfalfa, hay; 300 acres of alfalfa irrigated.

BUSINESS: Oil, gas, other minerals dominate economy.

MONAHANS (9,450) county seat; center for oil, agribusiness activities; oil field equipment; gasoline plant; pecan shelling; county hospital, **West Texas Children's Home,** nursing home.

Other towns include **Barstow** (679), **Grandfalls** (786), **Pyote** (519) **Odessa College** extension; **Thorntonville** (784) and **Wickett** (769).

Washington

LOCATION: Southeast (M-18).

HISTORY: Named for **George Washington;** an original county created in 1836; organized, 1837.

Cong. Dist.	10	U.S. Jud. Dist.	W-An.
St. Sen. Dist.	5	Ct. Appeals	1, 14
St. Rep. Dist.	13	Admin. Jud. Dist.	2
St. Dist. Cts.	21,335		

PHYSICAL FEATURES: Rolling prairie of sandy loam, alluvial soils; Brazos and tributaries.

RECREATION: Many historic sites; **Washington-on-the-Brazos State Park; Texas Baptist Historical Museum; Star of Republic Museum; Somerville Lake;** fishing, hunting; old homes; bluebonnet trails in spring; Maifest.

MINERALS: Oil, gas and stone.

1985 Pop.	25,500	Tax Ratio	0.95
Area (sq. mi.)	610	Oil value	$2,057,890

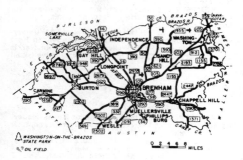

△ WASHINGTON-ON-THE-BRAZOS STATE PARK
OIL FIELD   0 2 4 6 8 MILES

Altitude (ft.)	343-460	No. employed	9,959
Ann. rainfall (in.)	39.94	Avg. weekly wage	$297.66
Jan. temp. min.	43	Annual wages	$154,151,780
July temp. max.	95	1983 PCI	$8,805
Growing season (da.)	277	Buying pwr.	$275,991,000
Voters reg.	12,754	Tax value	$1,552,637,200
Businesses	724	Fed. expd.	$59,222,000

VITAL STATISTICS 1985: Births, 419; Deaths, 308; Marriages, 248; Divorces, 123.

AGRICULTURE: Over $30 million average annual income, 90% from cattle, hogs, horses, dairy products, poultry; crops chiefly sorghums, corn, oats, hay, nursery stock, vegetables, pecans.

BUSINESS: Agribusinesses, oil, tourism, manufacturing.

BRENHAM (12,796) county seat; plants process cotton, make furniture, ice cream, mattresses, other products; **Blinn College;** hospitals; **Brenham State School. Burton** (365) another principal town.

Webb

LOCATION: Southwest (R-13).

HISTORY: Named for Republic of Texas leader, **James Webb;** created, organized, 1848, from Nueces and Bexar.

Cong. Dist.	23	U.S. Jud. Dist.	S-La.
St. Sen. Dist.	21	Ct. Appeals	4
St. Rep. Dist.	43	Admin. Jud. Dist.	4
St. Dist. Cts.	49, 111,341		

PHYSICAL FEATURES: Rolling, some hills; much brush; sandy, gray soils; alluvial along Rio Grande.

RECREATION: Major tourist gateway to Mexico; hunting, fishing; **Lake Casa Blanca,** water recreation, golf; **Border Olympics** in March; Rio Grande art festival in April; Washington Birthday celebration; historic sites; museum; **Fort McIntosh.**

MINERALS: Production of gas, oil, sand and gravel, stone.

OIL FIELD
0 2 4 6 8 10 MILES

1985 Pop.	118,100	Tax Ratio	0.94
Area (sq. mi.)	3,363	Oil value	$7,825,905
Altitude (ft.)	372-899	No. employed	33,203
Ann. rainfall (in.)	17.87	Avg. weekly wage	$261.16
Jan. temp. min.	47	Annual wages	$450,911,524
July temp. max.	99	1983 PCI	$4,816
Growing season (da.)	322	Buying pwr.	$709,915,000
Voters reg.	42,267	Tax value	$4,431,773,230
Businesses	2,210	Fed. expd.	$223,483,000

VITAL STATISTICS 1985: Births, 2,837; Deaths, 608; Marriages, 1,661; Divorces, 4.

AGRICULTURE: Among leading beef cattle counties; more than $37.5 million average annual income, mostly from calf production, horses, goats; crops include vegetables, sorghums, small grains, cotton.

BUSINESS: International trade, tourism, oil and gas operations, government center; manufacturing, agribusinesses; a major gateway for trade and tourism with Mexico.

LAREDO (108,676) county seat; town founded in 1755; plants make brick, clothing, shoes, electronics, other products; meat packing; major rail and highway gateway to Mexico; **Laredo Junior College; Laredo State University;** mental health-retardation center, hospitals, nursing homes; many tourist accommodations.

Wharton

LOCATION: Southeast (O-18).

HISTORY: Named for **John A., William H. Wharton,** brothers active in Texas Revolution; county created, organized, 1846, from Jackson, Matagorda.

Cong. Dist. 14	U.S. Jud. Dist. . . . . . S-Hn.
St. Sen. Dist. 5	Ct. Appeals 13
St. Rep. Dist. 29	Admin. Jud. Dist. 2
St. Dist. Cts. 23, 329	

PHYSICAL FEATURES: Prairie; bisected by Colorado River; alluvial, black, sandy loam soils.

RECREATION: Hunting, fishing; big game trophy, art and historical museums; historic sites; festivals.

MINERALS: Production of oil, gas, sulphur.

1985 Pop. 41,500	Tax Ratio 0.98
Area (sq. mi.) 1,086	Oil value $31,601,030
Altitude (ft.) 71-148	No. employed 11,327
Ann. rainfall (in.) . . 41.46	Avg. weekly wage $309.27
Jan. temp. min. 44	Annual wages $182,166,544
July temp. max. 93	1983 PCI $7,863
Growing season (da.) 266	Buying pwr. . . $411,577,000
Voters reg. 19,303	Tax value . . . $2,465,713,816
Businesses 1,042	Fed. expd. $84,960,000

VITAL STATISTICS 1985: Births, 734; Deaths, 386; Marriages, 394; Divorces, 169.

AGRICULTURE: About $130 million average annual income, 80% from crops; leading rice-producing county; other crops are sorghums, cotton, peaches, soybeans; beef cattle, hogs, poultry; about 100,000 acres irrigated.

BUSINESS: Economy based on oil, sulphur, other minerals; agribusinesses, varied manufacturing.

WHARTON (9,443) county seat; plants process minerals, rice, hides, pipe, farm equipment, beverage packing; **Wharton County Junior College;** hospitals, clinics, nursing homes.

El Campo (10,690) plants process aluminum, make plastic and metal products, clothing; rice drying, storage; hospital, nursing homes; **East Bernard** has agribusinesses, varied manufacturing; **Louise,** rice mill, agribusiness.

Wheeler

LOCATION: Eastern Panhandle (C-11).

HISTORY: Named for pioneer jurist, **R. T. Wheeler;** county created from Bexar, Young Districts, 1876; organized 1879.

Cong. Dist. 13	U.S. Jud. Dist. . . . . N-Am.
St. Sen. Dist. 31	Ct. Appeals 7
St. Rep. Dist. 88	Admin. Jud. Dist. 9
St. Dist. Cts. 31	

PHYSICAL FEATURES: Plain, on edge of Cap Rock; Red River, Sweetwater Creek; some canyons; red sandy loam, black clay soils.

RECREATION: Shamrock St. Patrick's Day event, Pioneer West museum at Shamrock; historic sites, **Old Mobeetie, Fort Elliott.**

MINERALS: Production of oil, gas.

1985 Pop. 7,300	Tax Ratio 1.00
Area (sq. mi.) 905	Oil value $6,818,118
Altitude (ft.) . . 2,127-2,869	No. employed 1,786
Ann. rainfall (in.) . . 23.70	Avg. weekly wage $284.41
Jan. temp. min. 26	Annual wages . $26,414,148
July temp. max. 97	1983 PCI $8,778
Growing season (da.) 208	Buying pwr. . . $85,050,000
Voters reg. 4,135	Tax value . . . $851,659,653
Businesses 214	Fed. expd. $35,334,000

VITAL STATISTICS 1985: Births, 109; Deaths, 84; Marriages, 282; Divorces, 36.

AGRICULTURE: About $34 million average annual income, 90% from beef and stocker cattle; crops include wheat, sorghums, cotton, alfalfa; 7,000 acres irrigated, mostly wheat, grain sorghum.

BUSINESS: Oil-agribusiness economy.

WHEELER (1,998) county seat; large feedlots; agribusiness, petroleum center; tourism; slaughter plant; hospital, nursing home.

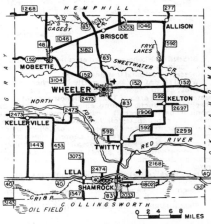

Shamrock (3,087) agribusiness, oil, gas processing plants; chemical plant; tourist center; hospital, nursing home. **Mobeetie (360)** other principal town.

Wichita

LOCATION: North (E-14).

HISTORY: Named for Indian tribe; county created from Young Territory, 1858; organized, 1882.

Cong. Dist. 13	U.S. Jud. Dist. . . . . N-WF
St. Sen. Dist. 30	Ct. Appeals 2
St. Rep. Dist. 80, 81	Admin. Jud. Dist. 8
St. Dist. Cts. . . 30, 78, 89	

PHYSICAL FEATURES: Prairie; Red, Wichita Rivers; **N. Fork Buffalo Creek, Wichita Lakes;** sandy, loam soils.

RECREATION: Metropolitan events (ask chamber of commerce); museums; historic Kell House, historic tour; Oil Bowl football game in August; collegiate activities; water sports on several lakes; **Lake Arrowhead State Park.**

MINERALS: Production of oil, gas, sand, gravel, stone.

1985 Pop. 125,600	Tax Ratio 0.98
Area (sq. mi.) 606	Oil value . . . $23,968,194
Altitude (ft.) . . . 954-1,225	No. employed 46,065
Ann. rainfall (in.) . . 27.22	Avg. weekly wage $317.96
Jan. temp. min. 31	Annual wages $761,651,292
July temp. max. 97	1983 PCI $9,120
Growing season (da.) 229	Buying pwr. $1,368,871,000
Voters reg. 55,661	Tax value . . $3,556,917,315
Businesses 3,669	Fed. expd. . . . $453,325,000

VITAL STATISTICS 1985: Births, 2,274; Deaths, 1,133; Marriages, 2,706; Divorces, 1,028.

AGRICULTURE: Some $20 million average yearly income from beef cattle, hogs, horses, dairy products; cotton, sorghum, wheat, other grains, hay; 22,000 acres irrigated for cotton and coastal bermuda pastures.

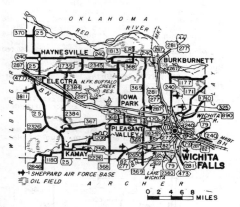

BUSINESS: Economy based on retail trade for large area, government, manufacturing, oil and agribusinesses; vocational training center.

WICHITA FALLS (98,899, partly in Archer and Clay counties) county seat; centennial in 1982; distribution center for large area of Texas, Oklahoma; plants make fiberglass products, clothing, electric components, mechanical parts, aircraft turbine components, hand tools, other products; oil field services; **Midwestern State University; Vernon Regional Junior College** nearby; vocational technical training center; **Sheppard Air Force Base; Wichita Falls State Hospital,** other hospitals.

Burkburnett (11,025) plants make chemical products, plastics, machinery, other products; nursing home.

Iowa Park (6,428) plants make fertilizers, oil field equipment; clinic, nursing home.

Electra (3,599) agribusiness, oil center; varied manufacturing; hospital, clinic, nursing home.

Pleasant Valley (343); **Lakeside City** (690).

Wilbarger

LOCATION: North (E-13).
HISTORY: Named for **Josiah** and **Mathias Wilbarger;** created from Bexar District, 1858; organized 1881.
PHYSICAL FEATURES: Rolling; Red, Pease Rivers, tributaries; sandy, loam, waxy soils; **Santa Rosa Lake.**

Cong. Dist. 13	U.S. Jud. Dist. . . . . N-WF
St. Sen. Dist. 30	Ct. Appeals 7
St. Rep. Dist. 80	Admin. Jud. Dist. 9
St. Dist. Cts. 46	

RECREATION: Santa Rosa Roundup, rodeo, parade in May; **Doan's Crossing,** site of cattle drive; other historic sites; Red River Valley Museum; hunting, fishing.
MINERALS: Production of oil, gas.

1985 Pop. 17,000	Tax Ratio 0.86
Area (sq. mi.) 947	Oil value $14,044,997
Altitude (ft.) . . 1,099-1,361	No. employed 6,299
Ann. rainfall (in.) . . 25.65	Avg. weekly wage $297.18
July temp. min. 29	Annual wages . $97,342,812
July temp. max. 98	1983 PCI $8,333
Growing season (da.) 221	Buying pwr. . $164,774,000
Voters reg. 7,663	Tax value . . . $822,668,860
Businesses 406	Fed. expd. $41,215,000

VITAL STATISTICS 1985: Births, 267; Deaths, 223; Marriages, 469; Divorces, 132.
AGRICULTURE: About $33 million average farm income from cotton, wheat, alfalfa; cattle, hogs, horses; 25,000 acres irrigated for alfalfa.
BUSINESS: Agribusinesses and oil.
VERNON (13,362) county seat; agribusiness and oil center; plants make clothes, guar products, meat processing; electricity generating plant; **Vernon Regional Junior College;** mental health center, hospital. **Lockett** is site of **Texas A&M Research and Extension Center.**

Willacy

LOCATION: South (T-16).
HISTORY: Named for Texas legislator, **John G. Willacy;** county created, organized, 1911 from Cameron, Hidalgo; reorganized 1921.

Cong. Dist. 27	U.S. Jud. Dist. . . . . . S-Br.
St. Sen. Dist. 20	Ct. Appeals 13
St. Rep. Dist. 37	Admin. Jud. Dist. 5
St. Dist. Cts. 103, 107, 138, 197, 357	

PHYSICAL FEATURES: Flat, sloping to Laguna Madre; alluvial, sandy, marshy soils; **Padre Island; La Sal Vieja, salt lake; Laguna Atascosa Wildlife Refuge.**
RECREATION: Fresh and salt water fishing, hunting; local events; mild climate attracts many winter tourists; Port Mansfield fishing tournament in July; winter fun festival; Raymondville ranch roundup.
MINERALS: Production of oil, gas.

1985 Pop. 18,800	Tax Ratio 0.85
Area (sq. mi.) 589	Oil value . . . $22,691,086
Altitude (ft.) 7-55	No. employed 3,689
Ann. rainfall (in.) . . 25.80	Avg. weekly wage $232.99
Jan. temp. min. 50	Annual wages . $44,695,056
July temp. max. 96	1983 PCI $4,786
Growing season (da.) 331	Buying pwr. . $101,286,000
Voters reg. 8,692	Tax value . . . $645,005,321
Businesses 268	Fed. expd. $38,292,000

VITAL STATISTICS 1985: Births, 372; Deaths, 127; Marriages, 209; Divorces, 52.
AGRICULTURE: About $44 million average yearly income, 90% from crops, chiefly cotton, sorghums, sugarcane, corn, vegetables; cattle, hogs, horses. 35,000 acres irrigated.
BUSINESS: Primarily oil, agribusinesses; tourism; shipping from **Port Mansfield.**
RAYMONDVILLE (10,082) county seat; agribusiness and oil center; clothing, fiberglass products manufactured; vegetables, seafood processed, shipped; tourist center; hospital. **Lyford** (1,747), **San Perlita** (441) other principal towns. **Port Mansfield** is popular Gulf Coast fishing port; shrimp processing.

See Map on next page.

Williamson

LOCATION: Central (L-16).

HISTORY: Named for **Robert M. Williamson,** pioneer leader; county created from Milam, organized 1848.

Cong. Dist. 11, 14	U.S. Jud. Dist. . . . . W-An.
St. Sen. Dist. 5, 18	Ct. Appeals 3
St. Rep. Dist. 52	Admin. Jud. Dist. 3
St. Dist. Cts. 26, 277	

PHYSICAL FEATURES: Level to rolling; mostly Blackland soil, some loam, sand; drained by San Gabriel, tributaries.

RECREATION: San Gabriel Park; water recreation on lakes; **Inner Space Cavern;** historic sites; hunting; **Dan Moody Museum** at Taylor; rattlesnake sacking; barbecue cookoff.

MINERALS: Building stone, sand and gravel, oil.

1985 Pop.	106,300	Tax Ratio	0.95
Area (sq. mi.)	1,137	Oil value	$46,890
Altitude (ft.) . . .	454-1,265	No. employed	25,289
Ann. rainfall (in.) . .	33.98	Avg. weekly wage	$288.66
Jan. temp. min.	39	Annual wages	$379,600,612
July temp. max.	96	1983 PCI	$9,546
Growing season (da.)	258	Buying pwr.	$1,232,627,000
Voters reg.	51,925	Tax value . .	$7,192,091,542
Businesses	2,153	Fed. expd. . . .	$130,016,000

VITAL STATISTICS 1985: Births, 2,165; Deaths, 632; Marriages, 1,074; Divorces, 616.

AGRICULTURE: More than $60 million average yearly income, divided among sorghums, wheat, corn, cotton; cattle, hogs, poultry, sheep, goats; income from deer leases, cedar posts.

BUSINESS: Agribusinesses, varied manufacturing, education are main economic factors; part of Austin MSA.

GEORGETOWN (12,332) county seat; agribusiness center; **Southwestern University; Inner Space Cavern;** plants make electric motors, structural products, electronic products, many other products; hospital, nursing homes.

Taylor (11,047) rapidly growing industrial, agribusiness and publishing center; Granger Lake; plants make furniture, clothing, bedding, machine shop products, fertilizers, many other products; process cottonseed, meats; barbecue catering; central newspaper printing plant; hospital, nursing homes; **Temple Junior College** extension.

Round Rock (17,904) plants make electronic equipment, generators, electric motors, lime, tools; **Texas Baptist Children's Home;** hospital, nursing homes. Other towns include **Bartlett** (1,556, part Bell County) first rural electrification in nation in 1933; clinic, rest home, library; **Granger** (1,137), **Cedar Park** (4,915), **Florence** (857) farm, retail center; manufacture candy, cabinets, fertilizer, **Hutto** (829), **Thrall** (593), **Leander** (2,963) and **Austin** (397,001, mostly in Travis County).

Wilson

LOCATION: South (O-15).

HISTORY: Created from Bexar, Karnes Counties and organized, 1860; named for **James C. Wilson,** member of Mier Expedition.

Cong. Dist. 15	U.S. Jud. Dist. . . . W-SAnt.
St. Sen. Dist. 21	Ct. Appeals 4
St. Rep. Dist. 45	Admin. Jud. Dist. 4
St. Dist. Cts. 81, 218	

PHYSICAL FEATURES: Rolling plains; mostly sandy soils, some heavier; San Antonio River, Cibolo Creek.

RECREATION: Stockdale watermelon festival in June; Floresville peanut festival in October; Wilson County Junior Livestock Show in January; arts, craft show in May.

MINERALS: Production of oil, gas, clays.

1985 Pop.	18,900	Tax Ratio	0.88
Area (sq. mi.)	807	Oil value	$3,479,367
Altitude (ft.)	362-781	No. employed	2,488

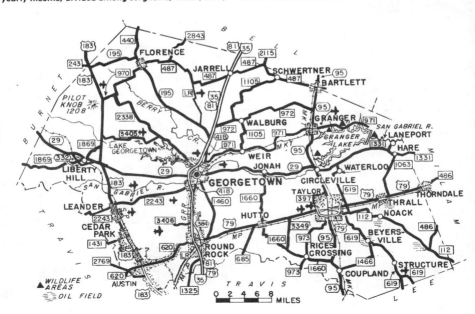

Wilson County (Cont'd.)

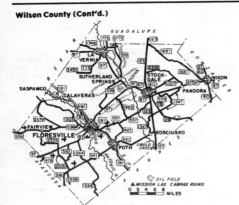

Ann. rainfall (in.) . . 28.68	Avg. weekly wage $247.29
Jan. temp. min. 42	Annual wages . $31,994,364
July temp. max. 96	1983 PCI $6,663
Growing season (da.) 280	Buying pwr. . $149,939,000
Voters reg. 11,868	Tax value . . . $784,464,730
Businesses 305	Fed. expd. . . . $30,836,000

VITAL STATISTICS 1985: Births, 270; Deaths, 134; Marriages, 173; Divorces, 59.

AGRICULTURE: About $45 million average annual income, 60% from beef, dairy cattle, hogs, poultry; crops include peanuts, sorghums, corn, small grains, vegetables, melons, sunflowers, fruit; 7,000 acres irrigated.

BUSINESS: Chiefly agribusinesses; some employed in San Antonio.

FLORESVILLE (4,952) county seat; agribusiness center; hospital, nursing home; shopping mall.

Stockdale (1,265) peanut drying plant, meat processing; medical center, nursing home, city park, pool. Other towns include **Poth** (1,516) and **La Vernia** (897).

Winkler

LOCATION: West (J-7).
HISTORY: Named for **Confederate Col. C. M.**

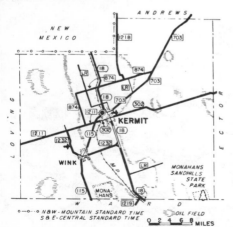

Winkler

Winkler; county created from Tom Green, 1887; organized, 1910.

Cong. Dist. 16		U.S. Jud. Dist. . . . . W-Pe.
St. Sen. Dist. 25		Ct. Appeals 8
St. Rep. Dist. 69		Admin. Jud. Dist. 7
St. Dist. Cts. 109		

PHYSICAL FEATURES: Plains, partly sandy hills.

RECREATION: Monahans Sandhills State Park in nearby Ward County; museum; zoo; wooden oil derrick; local events.

MINERALS: A leading petroleum producing county; gas, salt also produced.

1985 Pop. 10,800	Tax Ratio 0.93
Area (sq. mi.) 840	Oil value $71,832,940
Altitude (ft.) . . 2,671-3,193	No. employed 2,252
Ann. rainfall (in.) . . 10.81	Avg. weekly wage $325.51
Jan. temp. min. 29	Annual wages . $38,118,812
July temp. max. 96	1983 PCI $7,548
Growing season (da.) 219	Buying pwr. . $100,554,000
Voters reg. 4,377	Tax value . . . $980,231,429
Businesses 262	Fed. expd. . . . $13,693,000

VITAL STATISTICS 1985: Births, 187; Deaths, 99; Marriages, 160; Divorces, 43.

AGRICULTURE: About $1.5 million average yearly income, nearly all from beef cattle; 1,000 acres irrigated pasture.

BUSINESS: Oil and natural gas economy, among leading petroleum producing counties.

KERMIT (8,633) county seat, and **Wink** (1,612) are oil activity centers; hospital, nursing homes.

Wise

LOCATION: North (G-15).

HISTORY: Created, organized, 1856, from Cooke County; named for Virginian, **U.S. Sen. Henry A. Wise,** who favored Texas annexation.

Cong. Dist. 17		U.S. Jud. Dist. . . . . N-FW
St. Sen. Dist. 22		Ct. Appeals 2
St. Rep. Dist. 63		Admin. Jud. Dist. 8
St. Dist. Cts. 271		

PHYSICAL FEATURES: Rolling, hilly; clay, loam, sandy soils; **Lake Bridgeport; Eagle Mountain Lake.**

RECREATION: Lake Bridgeport activities; hunting; exotic deer preserve; historical sites; **Lyndon B. Johnson National Grasslands;** museum, little theater; Chisholm Trail Days in June; Sheriff's Posse rodeo; old courthouse; old settlers reunion; Butterfield Stage days, rodeo in July.

MINERALS: Production of gas, oil, stone, clays, sand, gravel.

1985 Pop. 32,000	Tax Ratio 0.97
Area (sq. mi.) 902	Oil value $16,240,956
Altitude (ft.) . . . 693-1,180	No. employed 7,124
Ann. rainfall (in.) . . 29.74	Avg. weekly wage $354.20
Jan. temp. min. 33	Annual wages $131,213,648
July temp. max. 96	1983 PCI $8,771
Growing season (da.) 220	Buying pwr. . $362,815,000
Voters reg. 15,856	Tax value . . $2,007,063,034
Businesses 522	Fed. expd. . . . $44,790,000

VITAL STATISTICS 1985: Births, 573; Deaths, 264; Marriages, 388; Divorces, 160.

AGRICULTURE: More than $54.5 million average annual income, 85% from dairy, beef cattle, horses, sheep, poultry; a leading dairy county; crops include sorghums, small grains, peanuts, vegetables, cantaloupes, watermelons, pecans.

BUSINESS: Agribusinesses, petroleum, recreation leading economic factors. Many work in Fort Worth.

DECATUR (4,523) county seat; center for petroleum production, dairying, cattle marketing; plants make clothing, glass, graphite, other products; hospital, nursing homes.

Bridgeport (3,997) trade center for lake resort; gas, oil production; agribusinesses; plants make brick, crushed limestone, metal fabrication, other products; hospital, rest home.

Other towns include **Alvord** (918), **Aurora** (458), **Boyd** (1,090), **Chico** (1,156), **Fairview** (211), **Lake Bridgeport** (266), **Newark** (581), **Rhome** (634), **Runaway Bay** (639).

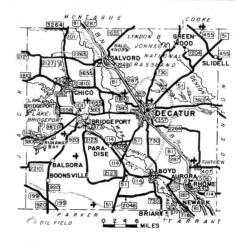

Wood

LOCATION: Northeast (G-19).

HISTORY: Created from Van Zandt County and organized, 1850; named for **Gov. George T. Wood.**

Cong. Dist. 4	U.S. Jud. Dist. . . . . E-Ty.
St. Sen. Dist. 2	Ct. Appeals 6, 12
St. Rep. Dist. 3	Admin. Jud. Dist. 1
St. Dist. Cts. . . . 114, 294	

PHYSICAL FEATURES: Hilly, almost half forested; sandy to alluvial soils; drained by Sabine and tributaries; 4 county lakes; many private lakes.

RECREATION: Activities at **Lake Fork Reservoir;** hunting; **Gov. Hogg Shrine State Park and museum;** historic sites; scenic drives; annual Autumn Trails, dogwood fiesta in April, settlers reunion in August, other local events.

MINERALS: A leading petroleum producing county; gas, sand, gravel, clays also produced.

1985 Pop. 28,200	Tax Ratio 0.95
Area (sq. mi.) 689	Oil value $156,789,168
Altitude (ft.) 299-630	No. employed 6,281
Ann. rainfall (in.) . . 44.30	Avg. weekly wage $276.33
Jan. temp. min. 36	Annual wages . . $90,254,356
July temp. max. 94	1983 PCI $7,797
Growing season (da.) 246	Buying pwr. . $294,895,000
Voters reg. 14,340	Tax value . . $1,956,904,971
Businesses 596	Fed. expd. . . . $69,577,000

VITAL STATISTICS 1985: Births, 381; Deaths, 369; Marriages, 326; Divorces, 212.

AGRICULTURE: About $50 million average yearly income, more than 80% from dairy, beef cattle, hogs, horses, broilers; truck crops, hay, corn, small grains; some Christmas trees, timber sold.

BUSINESS: Minerals, agribusinesses, tourism.

QUITMAN (1,994) county seat; agribusiness center; food processing; plants make boats, fence posts, fishing lines; hospital, nursing homes; dogwood fiesta in spring.

Mineola (4,774) farm trade, tourism center; railroad center; plants make clothing, livestock feeds, other farm products; manufacturing includes precision machinery, electronics, metal finishing; nursing home; railroad museum.

Other towns include **Winnsboro** (3,666, part Franklin), **Hawkins** (1,242) Jarvis Christian College, **Alba** (594), **Yantis** (209).

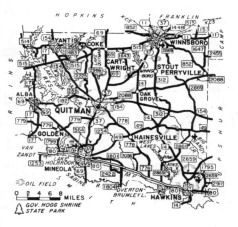

Yoakum

LOCATION: Borders New Mexico (G-7).

HISTORY: Named for **Henderson Yoakum,** pioneer historian; created from Bexar District, 1876; organized, 1907.

PHYSICAL FEATURES: Level to rolling; playas, draws; sandy, loam, chocolate soils.

RECREATION: Local events; Tsa Mo Ga Museum at Plains; settlers reunion in August.

MINERALS: Production of oil, gas, salt makes this a leading minerals producing county.

Cong. Dist. 19	U.S. Jud. Dist. . . . . N-Lb.
St. Sen. Dist. 28	Ct. Civil Appeals 7
St. Rep. Dist. 77	Admin. Jud. Dist. 9
St. Dist. Cts. 121	

1985 Pop. 9,600	Tax Ratio 1.00
Area (sq. mi.) 800	Oil value . . . $344,186,925
Altitude (ft.) . . 3,490-3,891	No. employed 3,008
Ann. rainfall (in.) . . 14.99	Avg. weekly wage $386.28
Jan. temp. min. 24	Annual wages . $60,421,316
July temp. max. 92	1983 PCI $8,481
Growing season (da.) 199	Buying pwr. . $111,376,000
Voters reg. 4,204	Tax value . $3,318,198,800
Businesses 260	Fed. expd. . . $16,246,000

VITAL STATISTICS 1985: Births, 193; Deaths, 57; Marriages, 139; Divorces, 46.

AGRICULTURE: About $28 million average yearly income, 90% from grains, cotton, sorghums, wheat, peanuts; beef cattle; 40,000 acres irrigated.

BUSINESS: Oil, agriculture dominate economy.

PLAINS (1,424) county seat; oil and agribusiness center; hospital planned.

Denver City (5,583) center for oil, farming activities in two counties; hospital, library.

Young

LOCATION: North (G-14).

HISTORY: Named for early Texan, **Col. W. C. Young;** county created, organized from Bosque, Fannin, 1856; reorganized, 1874.

Cong. Dist. 17	U.S. Jud. Dist. . . . . N-WF
St. Sen. Dist. 30	Ct. Appeals 2
St. Rep. Dist. 64	Admin. Jud. Dist. 8
St. Dist. Cts. 90	

PHYSICAL FEATURES: Hilly, broken; drained by Brazos and tributaries; **Possum Kingdom, Lake Graham.**

RECREATION: Fishing, boating and water sports at **Possum Kingdom** and **Lake Graham; Fort Belknap State Park;** site of former large **Indian reservation;** marker at oak tree in Graham where ranchmen formed forerunner of **Texas and Southwestern Cattle Raisers' Association;** one-arm dove hunt at Olney.

Young County (Cont'd.)

Cong. Dist.	15	U.S. Jud. Dist.	S-La.
St. Sen. Dist.	21	Ct. Appeals	4
St. Rep. Dist.	44	Admin. Jud. Dist.	4
St. Dist. Cts.	49		

1985 Pop.	8,500	Tax Ratio	0.79
Area (sq. mi.)	999	Oil value	$2,507,780
Altitude (ft.)	327-562	No. employed	1,315
Ann. rainfall (in.)	17.23	Avg. weekly wage	$260.71
Jan. temp. min.	46	Annual wages	$17,827,620
July temp. max.	100	1983 PCI	$5,453
Growing season (da.)	304	Buying pwr.	$45,944,000
Voters reg.	5,024	Tax value	$1,160,296,913
Businesses	92	Fed. expd.	$16,097,000

VITAL STATISTICS 1985: Births, 176; Deaths, 75; Marriages, 76; Divorces, 0.

BUSINESS: Economy based on oil, ranching, **Falcon Reservoir** activities.

ZAPATA (est. 3,500) county seat; tourist, agribusiness, oil center, developing as a retirement center, tourism; clinic.

Zavala

LOCATION: Southwest (P-12).

HISTORY: Created from Maverick, Uvalde Counties, 1858; organized, 1884; named for Texas Revolutionary leader, **Lorenzo de Zavala.**

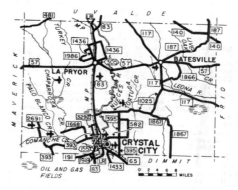

Cong. Dist.	23	U.S. Jud. Dist.	W-DR
St. Sen. Dist.	21	Ct. Appeals	4
St. Rep. Dist.	44	Admin. Jud. Dist.	4
St. Dist. Cts	293		

PHYSICAL FEATURES: Level to rolling; much brush; Nueces, Leona, other streams.

RECREATION: Hunting, fishing; annual spinach festival; local events.

MINERALS: Production of oil, gas.

1985 Pop.	12,000	Tax Ratio	0.91
Area (sq. mi.)	1,298	Oil value	$675,054
Altitude (ft.)	540-956	No. employed	2,140
Ann. rainfall (in.)	21.54	Avg. weekly wage	$238.77
Jan. temp. min.	41	Annual wages	$26,570,840
July temp. max.	99	1983 PCI	$3,908
Growing season (da.)	280	Buying pwr.	$61,157,000
Voters reg.	7,016	Tax value	$546,285,678
Businesses	147	Fed. expd.	$23,023,000

VITAL STATISTICS 1985: Births, 856; Deaths, 82; Marriages, 85; Divorces, 38.

AGRICULTURE: About $32 million average annual income from cotton, sorghums, small grains, corn, pecans, vegetables; beef, dairy cattle, sheep, goats, poultry; 38,000 acres irrigated.

BUSINESS: Chiefly agribusinesses, leading county in Winter Garden truck area; oil, gas, hunting income.

CRYSTAL CITY (8,496) county seat; varied agribusinesses including packing plants for vegetables; oil field services; cotton gin; hospital; spinach capital, "Home of Popeye."

MINERALS: Production of oil, gas, sand and gravel.

1985 Pop.	19,400	Tax Ratio	0.85
Area (sq. mi.)	919	Oil value	$2,017,194
Altitude (ft.)	1,038-1,389	No. employed	6,346
Ann. rainfall (in.)	28.03	Avg. weekly wage	$320.84
Jan. temp. min.	31	Annual wages	$105,876,924
July temp. max.	98	1983 PCI	$9,921
Growing season (da.)	216	Buying pwr.	$251,633,000
Voters reg.	9,890	Tax value	$754,262,040
Businesses	732	Fed. expd.	$42,095,000

VITAL STATISTICS 1985: Births, 357; Deaths, 279; Marriages, 253; Divorces, 117.

AGRICULTURE: About 60% of $20 million average farm income from beef cattle, hogs, sheep, goats; wheat chief crop, also cotton, sorghums; hunting leases.

BUSINESS: Oil, agribusinesses, tourism.

GRAHAM (9,852) county seat; plants make computer products, apparel, fences, fiberglass products, aluminum, floral products; hospital, nursing homes, mental health clinic, **Ranger Junior College** extension.

Olney (3,916) agribusiness center; plants make apparel, recreational vehicles, aluminum products, rubber hose, agricultural airplanes, other products; hospital, nursing homes.

Newcastle (771) other principal town.

Zapata

LOCATION: South (S-13).

HISTORY: Named for **Col. Antonio Zapata,** pioneer Mexican rancher; county created, organized, 1858, from Starr, Webb.

PHYSICAL FEATURES: Rolling; brushy; broken by tributaries of Rio Grande; **Falcon Reservoir.**

AGRICULTURE: About $18 million average yearly income, 90% from beef cattle; crops not significant.

RECREATION: Falcon Reservoir is tourist attraction; historic sites; winter tourist center.

MINERALS: Production of gas, oil.

Crime and Punishment

Crime in Texas

Crime has reasserted itself as Texas' No. 1 social problem. Since the early 1970s the state's crime rate has moved in an almost endless upward spiral, frustating the criminal justice system and citizens alike. In 1986, the crime rate took a leap of almost 14.9 percent, one of the highest one-year increases in a decade. The crimes themselves represent a significant loss in property, personal injury and lives. Beyond that, however, prison reform as administered by the federal courts will cost the state millions of dollars in new construction to house the swelling ranks of prisoners.

No population sector has escaped the effect of crime, as reflected in the report on index crime made to the Federal Bureau of Investigation by the Texas Department of Public Safety. Index crimes include murder, rape, aggravated assault, armed robbery, burglary, theft and motor vehicle theft. The state's six largest counties — Bexar, Dallas, El Paso, Harris, Tarrant and Travis — have a total crime rate of 9,894.2 index crimes per 100,000 population.

Individually, Potter County in the Panhandle had the highest crime rate in 1986, reaching 13,202.8, an increase of 27 percent over the previous year. Potter is one of 23 counties included in the metro category of counties with populations between 100,000 and 500,000. Two urban counties, Dallas County with 12,352.19 crimes per 100,000 and Tarrant County with 11,425.19, followed Potter. Overall, the metro counties suffered a crime rate of 7,053.7 offenses per 100,000, well below both the urban rate and the average state rate of 7,546.9.

Two hundred and twenty five rural counties registered a crime rate of 3,860.7 offenses per 100,000 population. Terrell County in the Big Bend was the only county

in the state not to register a single index crime in 1986. Terrell officials in early 1987 noted that the county had not suffered a burglary in three years. Although there was a drug bust in 1986, it was not an index crime. Twenty-six counties registered crime rates of less than 1,000 per 100,000 population. All were rural, sparsely populated counties. Following Terrell with the smallest crime rates were Dimmit, Jeff Davis and Concho, all in West Texas. Despite the increase in violent crime, 87 Texas counties did not register a murder in 1986.

Various theories concerning the cause of the increase in crime have failed to stand the test of time. Early in the 1970s, the unpopularity of the war in Vietnam often was cited as a cause of the growing lawlessness. The relatively young average age of the nation — under 28 years — also had proponents, as did the economic recessions of the period. As each proposed cause evaporated, the crime rate continued to rise, and did so steadily in Texas even through the boom period brought about by the oil crisis in the mid-1970s.

Most recently Jim Adams, the former director of the DPS, blamed the failure to require offenders to serve a larger part of the sentence given them by courts for increasing crime and for low morale among law-enforcement officers. And critics historically have blamed a "softness on crime" by the courts.

In the following pages, the crime statistics of 1986 for each county are reviewed, and this is followed by a review of the history of criminal corrections, probably the least understood element of the criminal justice system. These articles were written by Mike Kingston, editor of the Texas Almanac.

Texas Crime History 1974-1986*

Year—	Murder	Rape	Robbery	Aggravated Assault	Burglary	Theft	Car Theft	Rate Per 100,000 Population
1974	1,646	3,521	19,420	21,931	184,562	289,900	44,787	4,695.2
1975	1,639	3,430	20,076	22,658	203,821	362,665	47,386	5,407.2
1976	1,519	3,666	17,352	21,885	193,208	400,767	43,871	5,464.4
1977	1,705	4,338	19,552	26,714	205,672	383,451	51,018	5,397.1
1978	1,853	4,927	21,395	28,475	209,770	398,923	57,821	5,556.8
1979	2,226	6,028	25,636	33,909	239,263	411,555	72,687	5,911.7
1980	2,389	6,694	29,532	39,251	262,332	450,209	79,032	6,135.7
1981	2,438	6,816	28,516	40,673	275,652	454,210	83,244	6,042.4
1982	2,463	6,814	33,603	45,221	285,757	501,312	87,090	6,297.5
1983	2,238	6,334	29,769	42,195	262,214	503,555	82,522	5,907.1
1984	2,091	7,340	28,537	42,764	266,032	529,469	87,781	6,029.2
1985	2,124	8,367	31,693	47,868	289,913	596,130	99,561	6,570.9
1986	2,255	8,605	40,018	59,002	341,560	664,832	119,095	7,546.5

*Crime figures provided by Texas Department of Public Safety, Austin, the Federal Bureau of Investigation, Washington. Population figures used to determine crime rate per 100,000 population based on U.S. Bureau of Census estimates, except in 1980 when actual count used. The population figure used in determining the crime rate for 1986 in Texas was 16,369,571.

Crime in Texas Counties, 1986

	Murder	Rape	Armed Robbery	Aggravated Assault	Burglary	Theft	Motor Vehicle Theft	Total Crime	Crime Index Per 100,000
Anderson	10	13	31	222	677	1,250	100	2,303	4,963.36
Andrews	0	1	3	56	133	314	31	538	3,260.61
Angelina	6	29	27	241	792	1,939	168	3,202	4,647.31
Aransas	2	8	7	68	268	597	57	1,007	5,754.29
Archer	0	0	2	8	98	82	3	193	2,443.04
Armstrong	0	0	0	1	14	4	1	20	1,052.63
Atascosa	2	5	8	44	197	395	27	678	2,378.95
Austin	2	0	2	38	101	157	32	332	1,596.15
Bailey	1	1	2	34	86	131	6	261	3,144.58
Bandera	1	0	1	7	124	65	15	213	2,393.26
Bastrop	3	7	14	136	633	560	85	1,438	4,204.68
Baylor	0	0	0	8	45	59	3	115	2,346.94
Bee	2	2	5	67	314	443	39	872	3,194.14
Bell	14	150	200	326	3,254	6,511	544	10,999	6,439.70
Bexar	185	910	3,430	2,365	32,842	64,699	9,056	113,487	9,999.74
Blanco	1	2	0	5	34	7	4	53	1,000.00
Borden	0	0	0	0	8	11	0	19	1,900.00
Bosque	0	3	4	22	129	160	13	331	2,330.99
Bowie	10	39	68	253	1,435	2,806	238	4,849	6,023.60
Brazoria	21	52	87	318	2,175	4,743	517	7,913	4,204.57
Brazos	7	60	115	435	2,192	5,886	408	9,103	7,617.57
Brewster	2	1	0	8	73	121	5	210	2,592.59
Briscoe	0	0	0	2	16	25	2	45	1,956.52
Brooks	0	0	1	0	105	115	1	222	2,387.10
Brown	3	13	10	63	444	1,309	70	1,912	5,447.29
Burleson	0	4	5	63	156	163	21	412	2,746.67
Burnet	2	8	1	77	195	428	33	744	3,248.91
Caldwell	0	1	7	55	237	396	29	725	2,645.99
Calhoun	0	2	9	39	223	516	25	814	3,751.15
Callahan	1	0	0	7	43	46	11	108	857.14
Cameron	15	45	228	1,583	4,830	9,394	1,599	17,694	7,083.27
Camp	4	1	2	18	101	170	17	313	3,130.00
Carson	0	3	0	7	35	34	4	83	1,202.90
Cass	1	0	0	48	231	237	25	542	1,771.24
Castro	0	0	0	10	71	81	15	177	1,718.45
Chambers	5	9	17	23	264	279	30	627	3,231.96
Cherokee	7	2	14	84	369	742	70	1,288	3,236.18
Childress	0	0	2	33	65	118	8	226	3,476.92
Clay	1	0	3	31	137	161	13	346	3,567.01
Cochran	0	2	1	9	37	93	11	153	3,326.09
Coke	0	0	0	1	17	8	3	29	805.56
Coleman	1	0	1	24	115	102	3	246	2,320.75
Collin	10	44	84	256	2,470	6,155	579	9,598	4,874.56
Collingsworth	0	2	0	7	31	67	6	113	2,756.10
Colorado	3	3	3	41	182	269	30	531	2,641.79
Comal	6	4	38	184	844	1,664	93	2,833	6,132.03
Comanche	0	0	4	16	63	103	6	192	1,488.37
Concho	0	0	0	0	8	1	1	10	357.14
Cooke	2	3	9	43	335	650	107	1,149	3,962.07
Coryell	4	10	13	67	397	888	69	1,448	2,531.47
Cottle	0	2	1	12	5	5	2	27	1,000.00
Crane	0	0	0	8	39	82	4	133	2,557.69
Crockett	0	0	2	20	26	75	4	127	2,702.13
Crosby	1	0	0	2	55	30	10	98	1,166.67
Culberson	0	0	0	3	19	14	31	67	1,914.29
Dallam	0	3	2	24	49	146	9	233	3,530.30
Dallas	415	1,580	10,635	10,399	55,147	119,960	21,943	220,079	12,352.19
Dawson	1	0	9	30	245	512	17	814	5,024.69
DeWitt	1	0	2	35	89	101	15	243	1,202.97
Deaf Smith	4	6	2	109	241	804	45	1,211	5,936.27
Delta	0	0	0	5	27	10	5	47	979.17
Denton	11	60	128	447	3,386	8,461	921	13,414	7,071.16
Dickens	0	1	2	7	40	51	2	103	3,322.58
Dimmit	0	0	1	3	18	4	1	27	226.89
Donley	1	0	0	16	21	34	7	79	1,926.83
Duval	0	3	2	31	130	130	14	310	2,330.83
Eastland	1	1	3	60	220	341	36	662	3,198.07
Ector	19	92	175	460	3,589	7,746	557	12,638	9,382.33
Edwards	0	0	0	6	38	9	9	62	2,952.38
El Paso	52	225	1,073	3,616	9,884	22,521	2,733	40,104	7,358.53
Ellis	7	14	51	242	1,275	2,014	267	3,870	5,279.67
Erath	0	8	6	26	293	562	40	935	3,740.00
Falls	1	1	4	30	94	140	1	271	1,489.01
Fannin	1	1	0	30	180	357	20	589	2,394.31
Fayette	1	1	1	4	75	38	15	135	668.32
Fisher	1	0	1	0	21	16	3	42	750.00
Floyd	0	1	1	14	112	139	8	275	3,021.98
Foard	0	0	0	2	10	7	1	20	1,111.11

(Crime in Texas Counties, 1986, Continued)

	Murder	Rape	Armed Robbery	Aggravated Assault	Burglary	Theft	Motor Vehicle Theft	Total Crime	Crime Index Per 100,000
Fort Bend	7	22	126	342	2,515	3,957	643	7,612	4,044.63
Franklin	0	0	0	2	84	67	17	170	2,361.11
Freestone	2	3	3	28	168	248	41	493	2,883.04
Frio	1	2	2	47	166	193	23	434	3,056.34
Gaines	1	1	2	8	93	289	10	404	2,825.17
Galveston	24	104	527	1,046	4,334	8,911	1,114	16,060	7,525.77
Garza	0	0	1	13	45	47	4	110	2,000.00
Gillespie	1	0	0	13	104	161	8	287	1,851.61
Glasscock	0	0	0	0	9	11	3	23	1,916.67
Goliad	0	0	0	0	35	23	3	61	1,089.29
Gonzales	3	1	3	45	146	301	31	530	2,819.15
Gray	0	15	13	106	370	944	58	1,506	5,557.20
Grayson	9	32	82	428	1,772	4,374	360	7,057	7,297.83
Gregg	21	51	136	254	2,400	5,081	455	8,398	7,478.18
Grimes	2	0	5	68	198	293	73	639	3,398.94
Guadalupe	5	8	24	268	781	1,470	76	2,632	4,820.51
Hale	1	9	19	139	486	1,243	55	1,952	5,205.33
Hall	1	0	0	3	15	16	0	35	729.17
Hamilton	3	0	3	27	93	83	19	228	2,814.81
Hansford	0	0	0	12	47	108	7	174	2,676.92
Hardeman	0	0	0	3	59	108	7	177	2,765.62
Hardin	4	8	11	35	240	365	48	711	1,638.25
Harris	497	1,930	12,660	9,895	63,583	98,212	42,982	229,759	8,221.24
Harrison	7	27	26	126	543	1,260	111	2,100	3,626.94
Hartley	0	0	1	1	9	9	2	22	628.57
Haskell	0	0	2	3	44	42	3	94	1,287.67
Hays	4	16	38	224	921	2,377	154	3,734	6,667.86
Hemphill	0	0	0	5	33	40	4	82	1,490.91
Henderson	8	13	22	168	969	1,262	112	2,554	4,902.11
Hidalgo	33	84	178	1,146	6,403	12,303	1,528	21,675	6,154.17
Hill	0	10	22	52	369	528	68	1,049	3,828.47
Hockley	0	0	3	36	339	697	48	1,123	4,421.26
Hood	1	2	3	17	194	362	29	608	2,393.70
Hopkins	1	6	7	41	303	522	91	971	3,383.28
Houston	3	6	3	34	169	225	30	470	2,070.48
Howard	5	10	22	353	720	1,347	96	2,553	7,033.06
Hudspeth	0	0	2	7	10	11	2	32	1,230.77
Hunt	6	23	54	573	1,270	2,227	181	4,334	6,647.24
Hutchinson	3	3	7	33	238	444	41	769	2,736.65
Irion	0	1	0	2	6	6	0	15	750.00
Jack	0	0	1	3	57	107	14	182	2,363.64
Jackson	1	0	2	15	112	122	9	261	1,919.12
Jasper	2	0	10	36	167	453	37	705	2,175.93
Jeff Davis	0	0	0	0	3	1	0	4	333.33
Jefferson	33	145	607	868	5,433	9,760	808	17,654	6,931.29
Jim Hogg	0	0	0	8	27	8	2	45	833.33
Jim Wells	4	14	19	86	1,044	1,475	61	2,703	6,707.20
Johnson	7	7	38	95	1,006	1,938	297	3,388	3,863.17
Jones	1	4	2	15	178	148	21	369	2,027.47
Karnes	1	0	1	8	74	35	6	125	932.84
Kaufman	8	14	38	115	784	1,000	175	2,134	4,328.60
Kendall	2	0	4	20	122	152	23	323	2,307.14
Kenedy	0	0	0	0	1	0	2	3	500.00
Kent	0	0	1	3	8	5	0	17	1,307.69
Kerr	5	6	24	120	477	779	36	1,447	4,182.08
Kimble	0	0	0	0	17	22	4	43	1,000.00
King	0	0	2	3	4	5	1	15	3,750.00
Kinney	0	0	1	4	22	22	13	62	2,480.00
Kleberg	5	8	19	161	554	1,320	53	2,120	6,144.93
Knox	0	0	0	4	21	20	2	47	839.29
La Salle	0	1	0	10	72	60	12	155	2,672.41
Lamar	2	22	45	377	782	2,415	172	3,815	8,534.68
Lamb	0	2	4	57	135	249	7	454	2,654.97
Lampasas	1	3	3	16	137	247	25	432	3,176.47
Lavaca	2	1	3	8	115	164	7	300	1,621.62
Lee	0	0	3	26	104	159	13	305	2,226.28
Leon	3	0	1	1	95	39	19	158	1,253.97
Liberty	5	5	47	281	811	1,414	229	2,792	5,122.94
Limestone	5	4	8	102	251	404	56	830	3,896.71
Lipscomb	0	2	1	4	12	18	4	41	1,025.00
Live Oak	2	0	2	8	42	60	9	123	1,294.74
Llano	0	3	0	10	99	184	15	311	2,570.25
Loving	0	0	0	0	3	3	1	7	7,000.00
Lubbock	30	133	339	1,419	6,851	11,893	996	21,661	9,721.17
Lynn	2	1	0	12	47	72	10	144	1,846.15
Madison	1	4	2	89	132	172	13	413	3,385.25
Marion	1	0	4	59	118	138	2	322	3,156.86
Martin	0	1	0	9	33	72	2	117	2,207.55
Mason	0	0	0	0	15	6	3	24	666.67
Matagorda	6	11	22	255	683	1,572	154	2,703	6,723.88
Maverick	1	1	3	92	390	1,115	83	1,685	4,566.40
McCulloch	1	2	0	27	88	109	16	243	2,700.00

(Crime in Texas Counties, 1986, Continued)

	Murder	Rape	Armed Robbery	Aggravated Assault	Burglary	Theft	Motor Vehicle Theft	Total Crime	Crime Index Per 100,000
McLennan	21	85	299	724	5,023	8,913	784	15,849	8,608.91
McMullen	0	0	0	0	10	6	3	19	1,900.00
Medina	2	2	8	82	206	371	37	708	2,820.72
Menard	0	0	0	3	22	2	1	28	1,217.39
Midland	2	47	56	442	2,180	2,736	336	5,799	5,310.44
Milam	1	3	2	29	180	341	38	594	2,506.33
Mills	0	0	0	6	6	11	2	25	555.56
Mitchell	0	1	6	34	79	156	22	299	3,322.22
Montague	1	2	3	35	271	300	45	657	3,551.35
Montgomery	15	53	94	521	2,566	4,300	639	8,188	5,095.21
Moore	0	0	0	3	86	225	9	323	1,856.32
Morris	2	1	2	33	160	256	13	467	3,176.87
Motley	0	0	0	1	2	3	1	7	388.89
Nacogdoches	4	13	26	243	561	1,438	129	2,414	4,847.39
Navarro	9	20	58	55	666	1,384	116	2,308	5,902.81
Newton	3	3	6	9	86	63	13	183	1,365.67
Nolan	0	4	4	84	172	401	31	696	3,954.55
Nueces	36	215	371	847	6,861	15,602	1,318	25,250	8,501.68
Ochiltree	0	4	1	27	54	240	5	331	3,009.09
Oldham	0	0	4	1	12	24	4	45	1,956.52
Orange	8	28	135	245	1,748	2,629	238	5,031	6,046.88
Palo Pinto	1	3	12	55	456	649	91	1,267	4,817.49
Panola	3	0	5	101	126	249	19	503	2,255.61
Parker	2	12	21	67	888	1,168	189	2,347	4,176.16
Parmer	2	1	2	22	74	140	29	270	2,477.06
Pecos	3	1	7	51	123	333	40	558	3,225.43
Polk	2	2	8	92	461	569	61	1,195	3,983.33
Potter	21	86	277	522	3,742	8,797	682	14,127	13,178.17
Presidio	1	1	0	2	21	6	3	34	618.18
Rains	1	1	0	20	47	58	9	137	2,322.03
Randall	2	1	1	18	149	333	44	548	640.19
Reagan	1	1	0	3	43	61	0	109	2,180.00
Real	0	0	0	4	9	0	0	13	481.48
Red River	1	3	4	30	161	198	27	424	2,735.48
Reeves	2	5	8	76	317	626	22	1,056	6,559.01
Refugio	0	1	4	32	66	100	8	211	2,425.29
Roberts	0	0	0	0	8	6	0	14	1,400.00
Robertson	4	4	12	96	311	326	14	767	4,823.90
Rockwall	3	5	9	43	263	444	74	841	4,043.27
Runnels	1	1	0	2	40	67	0	111	888.00
Rusk	2	0	14	43	588	915	102	1,664	3,851.85
Sabine	0	0	0	0	42	44	1	87	887.76
San Augustine	0	0	1	10	42	148	3	204	2,318.18
San Jacinto	2	2	8	69	258	209	50	598	4,271.43
San Patricio	8	7	23	157	672	1,227	97	2,191	3,545.31
San Saba	1	0	1	12	53	48	4	119	2,087.72
Schleicher	1	0	0	0	24	22	1	48	1,500.00
Scurry	2	4	3	40	84	370	22	525	2,651.52
Shackelford	4	0	1	8	42	19	8	82	2,050.00
Shelby	3	5	7	45	189	291	37	577	2,414.23
Sherman	0	0	0	0	8	20	5	33	1,064.52
Smith	16	157	185	472	3,349	7,168	640	11,987	7,986.01
Somervell	0	1	2	6	80	70	21	180	3,913.04
Starr	3	3	7	24	215	239	47	538	1,559.42
Stephens	3	3	3	16	93	183	13	314	3,019.23
Sterling	0	0	0	0	17	4	1	22	1,375.00
Stonewall	0	0	0	1	10	14	3	29	1,160.00
Sutton	1	0	1	13	23	70	6	114	2,111.11
Swisher	0	2	2	30	59	174	7	274	3,113.64
Tarrant	251	797	4,382	5,295	30,763	65,021	14,141	120,650	11,425.19
Taylor	14	52	184	296	2,554	4,395	378	7,873	6,442.72
Terrell	0	0	0	0	0	0	0	0	0.00
Terry	0	6	5	83	201	477	32	804	5,220.78
Throckmorton	0	0	0	0	9	6	0	15	652.17
Titus	2	2	9	49	238	639	66	1,005	4,369.57
Tom Green	3	42	63	388	1,226	3,698	224	5,644	5,836.61
Travis	53	424	1,174	1,531	14,513	31,891	2,536	52,122	9,775.32
Trinity	0	1	1	4	86	104	10	206	1,745.76
Tyler	0	0	1	33	169	134	15	352	1,892.47
Upshur	6	13	11	74	438	514	57	1,113	3,403.67
Upton	2	1	0	33	36	81	1	154	2,750.00
Uvalde	1	0	3	43	242	396	62	747	3,024.29
Val Verde	4	7	17	179	638	1,330	156	2,331	5,916.24
Van Zandt	1	2	8	43	474	637	101	1,266	3,394.10
Victoria	3	25	63	399	1,426	2,828	197	4,941	6,544.37
Walker	4	21	23	171	515	1,398	179	2,311	4,470.02
Waller	1	13	11	75	332	420	76	928	3,948.94
Ward	2	6	4	25	200	487	38	762	4,792.45
Washington	4	3	3	15	150	510	19	704	2,760.78
Webb	22	14	143	449	2,593	5,069	700	8,990	7,612.19
Wharton	4	4	17	95	485	1,213	61	1,879	4,527.71

(Crime in Texas Counties, 1986, Continued)

	Murder	Rape	Armed Robbery	Aggravated Assault	Burglary	Theft	Motor Vehicle Theft	Total Crime	Crime Index Per 100,000
Wheeler	1	1	0	2	14	22	5	45	616.44
Wichita	17	72	290	370	2,896	5,945	535	10,125	8,061.31
Wilbarger	1	3	14	61	232	411	34	756	4,447.06
Willacy	3	1	1	70	213	198	15	501	2,664.89
Williamson	5	72	45	294	1,160	2,984	200	4,760	4,477.89
Wilson	1	3	4	40	273	176	19	516	2,730.16
Winkler	1	1	1	5	58	185	12	264	2,444.44
Wise	1	0	1	38	267	355	66	728	2,275.00
Wood	4	2	4	46	257	303	41	657	2,329.79
Yoakum	0	0	1	16	57	197	5	276	2,875.00
Young	5	3	3	13	208	314	35	581	2,994.85
Zapata	1	0	0	15	57	79	3	155	1,823.53
Zavala	1	3	5	22	94	82	10	217	1,808.33
Total	2,255	8,605	40,018	59,001	341,560	664,832	119,095	1,235,367	7,546.53

Corrections in Texas

As the crime rate has spiraled in Texas and the United States, attention has focused on apprehending and convicting the criminal. In popular culture — TV shows and crime novels — emphasis is placed on the chase, the capture and the courtroom drama. Hence, the public perception of the criminal justice system is out of balance, for once the guilt of an offender is determined, several alternative punishments are available.

A criminal can be placed on probation, if he is a first offender or if the crime is nonviolent. Or the offender can be sent briefly to prison for a taste of life behind bars. In both cases, he remains under the jurisdiction of the court in which the trial took place. The probationary period can be as short as a few months or as long as several years.

If the defendant has a long criminal record or if the crime was violent, a prison term will be given. Today, all persons incarcerated in the Texas Department of Corrections are placed under mandatory supervision or parole for their release. Parole procedures theoretically select the best risks among the prisoners for a successful return to the free society. Mandatory supervision requires even the most serious offender to be released a few months early, so he too can be kept under supervision. These offenders stay at halfway houses and report to parole officers for a period of time. The theory is that even hardened criminals have a better

ADULTS UNDER CORRECTION SUPERVISION—1984

	Total	Jail	Prison	Parole	Probation
U.S. (1000s)	2,665.4	221.8	463.9	268.5	1,711.2
Rate per 10,000 people 18 and over	154	13	27	15	99
Texas (1000s)	328.2	15.2	36.7	40.8	235.6
Rate per 10,000 people 18 and over	291	13	33	36	209

Source: Statistical Abstract of the United States, 1987.

chance to "go straight" if thy have counsel and supervision during the important re-entry period.

These elements of the criminal justice system seldom get public attention until they break down — i.e., a probationer or parolee commits a heinous crime. Yet the success of the justice system ultimately rests on the ability of these elements to successfully rehabilitate offenders. Rehabilitation often has a low priority is the struggle to maintain a well-supervised and orderly system.

—*Mike Kingston*

Prisons

Texas, no less than other states, has been concerned with both punishment and rehabilitation of criminal offenders. Until a century and a half ago in Europe and England, capital punishment was decreed for hundreds of crimes, and the alternative was corporal punishment, which included flogging, as well as lopping off hands and feet in some cases.

The modern prison system is a development of the United States that has been adopted worldwide. Texas has shared, sometimes with reluctance, in the American tradition of treating prisoners humanely while attempting rehabilitation. Until the late 18th century, jails or prisons were holding facilities, housing criminal offenders or debtors until punishment was meted out. Forced public labor by those incarcerated as an act of humiliation also was a feature. Crowded and unsanitary, the facilities often were the targets of social critics who sought improved treatment for society's flotsam.

Many penologists date the birth of the modern prison system as May 8, 1787, when Dr. Benjamin Rush, a signer of the Declaration of Independence, delivered a critique of the existing system to a small group meeting at the home of Benjamin Franklin in Philadelphia. Rush proposed useful work, instead of public degradation, and indeterminate sentences to be determined by the offender's progress toward regeneration as appropriate punishments.

American Quakers led a reform movement in Pennsylvania. The colony had approved hard labor as the chief form of punishment in 1682 in response to horrible conditions and punishments in existing jails.

The 18th century Enlightenment philosophers supported humane treatment of prisoners with their recognition of man's essential dignity and imperfections. One of the most influencial writings of the period was an essay written in 1764 by Cesare Bonesana, Marchese de Beccaria, an Italian. Among other reforms, he suggested that imprisonment should be widely used as a punishment with improved quarters for the prisoners and with offenders being separated by a classification system to include age, sex and degree of criminality. Later in the century, Jeremy Bentham, a reformer of British criminal law, introduced the concept of the indeterminate sentence to make the punishment fit the crime.

William Penn brought the concept of humanitarian treatment of prisoners to the Americas. With Quaker support, the cradle of modern prisons — the so-called "Penitentiary House" — was built within the Walnut Street Jail in Philadelphia. The facility was to be used exclusively for the "correction" of criminals. To that end, prisoners were to be kept in complete solitude, so in the goal of the reformers, offenders would have no choice but to consider their acts. Individual cells had thick walls to prohibit communication between prisoners, and great care was taken to keep the inmates separate and silent. Soon it was apparent that the solitude had undesirable physical and psychological effects. So an eight-to-10 hour daily work schedule was initiated, with prisoners doing piece work or handicrafts in their cells. The sex, alcohol and idleness that characterized earlier jails was missing.

The first complete modern prison was the Western Penitentiary, which opened near Pittsburgh, Pa., in

1826. In addition to work and solitude, prisoners were given Bibles for meditation.

The twofold philosophy of these early prisons is reflected in modern institutions. First, men were expected to act in enlightened self interest, and it was felt they could achieve progress through a combination of materialistic philosophy and religious ethic.

In addition, the industrial revolution fostered the idea that prisons should be self-supporting; society should not be burdened with the upkeep of those who had broken its laws. A facility in Auburn, N.Y., opened in 1823, was the first to incorporate this approach. Prisoners were allowed to congregate for work and other activities, but they were to remain completely silent. The military regimen was designed to make prisoners silently reflect on the "errors of their lives." The facility served as a model for more than 30 state prisons in the next half century. Attempts to provide basic education for offenders in the 1830s and 1840s were token and sporadic.

Discipline was strict in these early prisons. Silence was an absolute requirement, and flogging was the most common punishment. Prisoners were required to walk in lock-step, in which they touched the shoulder or side of the inmate in front of them and walked in unison.

While early Texans may have been in sympathy with these experiments, a lack of money prohibited any attempt to incorporate them into a system of corrections, or, indeed, to establish a prison system. The Republic reimbursed sheriffs for keeping offenders who had been sentenced to prison. Rehabilitation was not considered in the agreement. Although the Texas Congress authorized construction of a prison in 1842, no action was taken because the $2,000 appropriation was too small.

At statehood, the framers of the Constitution of 1845 stipulated that the Legislature would create a prison system. The First Legislature attempted to establish a prison, but the Mexican War intervened; so it was up to the Second Legislature in 1848 to build Texas' first prison. The governor was authorized to appoint three commissioners to select a site and to superintend the construction of a prison. Initially, $10,000 was appropriated to operate the system, but this was later cut to $5,000. The state's first chain gang, made up of prisoners who had been held by sheriffs, built the initial prison in Huntsville. On Oct. 1, 1849, William G. Sansom, serving three years for cattle theft from Fayette County, was designated prisoner No. 1 in the Texas prison system. Two other offenders joined him that day. The prison was not completed for several years, however, because of a lack of funds.

In the 1850s, the Legislature appropriated $35,000 for construction of a cotton and wool mill within the prison walls. Though never as profitable as hoped, the facility provided satisfactory work for inmates. During the Civil War, the mill was a major asset for it turned out cloth for the Confederate military and for disadvantaged Texans. Some of the production also found its way into the black market of the day.

The prison population declined during the war, and for a time, Union prisoners of war were housed in the facility. They were moved, however, when officers complained that it was against the rules of war to house military prisoners in penitentiaries. Gen. Sam Houston, living out his days in Huntsville after being deposed as governor because he of opposition to secession, regularly visited the Union prisoners.

As the end of the Civil War introduced a lawless period in Texas, the prison population jumped from 134 in 1866 to 356 a year later and continued to climb. The concept of profitable prison industries developed in the Eastern states to the extent that after the Civil War, it replaced rehabilitation as the goal of the prison systems. Texas, like most Southern states, ignored these models, while seeking ways to minimize the costs of prisons. More work had to be found for the prisoners, and, of course, the system had to turn a profit. First the superintendent of prisons was authorized by the Legislature to find gainful employment for the inmates. Then the lease period in the history of Texas prisons began.

Kentucky in 1825 was the first state to lease its prison system to a private contractor, who would care for the prisoners and profit from their labor. Several other Southern states tried the approach. After one false start three years earlier, the Texas Legislature in 1871 directed the governor to lease the prison system to a private contractor. A.J. Cunningham, the first contractor, agreed to pay the state $3 per prisoner per month.

As the prison population continued to grow, the lease system became more unsatisfactory. The contractors began to sublease convicts to planters, tanners, bricklayers and as railroad work crews. Abuses abounded. Prisoners were physically mistreated, inadequately fed, poorly clothed and often were required to work well into chilly weather without shoes. Escapes rose from 50 in 1871 to 382 in 1876, and many convicts were never recaptured. Deaths also increased alarmingly. The Legislature first mandated a change of contractors, but even then, abuses continued. Contractors could not be counted on to see after the basic needs of the inmates or to treat them humanely.

Investigations regularly spotlighted abuses, and public opinion demanded reform. Finally, in 1883, the Legislature replaced the lease system with the contract system. Again, the state sought to put the prisons on a pay-as-you-go basis. Under the new system, however, the state retained responsibility for the basic treatment of inmates, seeing that they were fed and clothed. But the inmates' labor was contracted to employers who operated shops within the prison walls. The prison superintendent also was authorized to hire out chain gangs of convicts for construction labor to railroads, public utilities and other employers. This system was not notably successful. From the beginning, critics complained that the products produced were inferior and that the state was putting itself in unfair competition with private industry. Boycotts ruined sales.

In addition to the contract system, Texas prison officials looked into other means of keeping convicts busy and profitable. In 1885, the first prison farm — the Harlem farm (now the Jester Unit) in Fort Bend County — was purchased. Problems soon cropped up. Most prisoners were not from farms. They knew nothing of farm work and cared less about learning to do it. Encouraging their cooperation was difficult.

At the same time, a factory to produce all the brick for the prison system was opened on the Harlem farm. A smelter opened at Rusk to test the profitability of East Texas iron ore. Cast-iron pipe and other products were produced for state agencies, but the operation was not as successful as hoped.

Life was never easy for Texas' convicts, despite the repeated reforms. Charles A. Favor, convicted of swindling in Navarro County in the early 1890s, wrote of his experiences at the turn of the century. Prisoners were gathered from county jails by transfer agents, who took them to prison by train. The convicts were chained by the neck in pairs on the trip. Favor went to Rusk, where he first shoveled iron ore and later moved to a "coaling camp" to make charcoal.

Prisoners were dressed in striped suits and were provided poor food. The state provided no underwear and only two pairs of socks a year. The inmates were housed in single cells, and for overtime work on Sunday, they were paid five cents an hour. Favor said the prison had a good library, containing mostly religious literature. In 1875, the state had made its first gesture toward an education program by providing $500 for books to establish a library. All inmates were expected to attend religious services "and to pay good attention." Once a week, usually on Sunday, the prisoners were shaved.

Discipline was built on the principle that the prisoner "has no rights at all, and but few privileges." The "strap" was the severest form of punishment. This was a leather strap about 18 inches long and three inches wide, connected to a wooden handle. Prisoners were whipped on bare skin. Favor said the law limited punishment to "39 licks," one less than under Mosaic Law. After his release, the writer said he had "never yet met a man who was whipped who is doing any good for himself or the world." Most grew to hate the state's authority because of the humiliating treatment.

Upon release, a convict got a cheap suit of clothes, a hat and shoes. In addition, he received $5 in cash and railroad fare, not to exceed $15, to the town in which he was convicted.

Favor apparently saw the error of his ways while in prison, for much of the booklet is devoted to imploring young people to consider their actions and to stay out of trouble.

Convict morale predictably was low. Between 1883-1909, 2,300 convicts escaped, and many were not recaptured. Unlike today, offenders were expected to serve every day of their sentence. But the governor did have the power to pardon inmates, and in many cases, this

Field work has long been a feature of life in the Texas Department of Corrections. This historic photo reflects an era before modern equipment was introduced. Photo courtesy of TDC.

action shortened sentences. During the same period of the escapes, 3,600 were pardoned.

Over time changes were made in the prisons. Under the leadership of the chaplains, educational opportunities were improved. The library was increased from 705 books in 1884 to 8,000 in 1910. A separate farm for women prisoners (known as the Goree Unit) was opened during this period, and youthful offenders were sent to a new facility at Gatesville. (Children as young as nine years old previously had been sent to the state penitentiary. Texas set the age of criminal responsibility at seven in 1836 and raised it to nine in 1856.)

Health care was improved. The prison hospital was modernized in 1892, and the number of medical personnel was increased. (Favor noted that inmates with medical training were utilized, such as the pharmacist who screened convicts on sick call before sending them to a doctor.) In 1899, a camp for prisoners with tuberculosis opened at the Wynne farm, where they received treatment and a lighter work schedule. After 1900, mentally ill convicts, who had been treated as if they were just mean and left in the general prison population, were sent to state hospitals.

The contract era ended in 1910, after yet another legislative study uncovered continued abuses. One lawmaker pleaded that the "organized hell" and "Black Hole of Calcutta" of Texas prisons be eliminated through legislative reform to become "only a ghostly memory in the minds of the people." More attention was directed to the prison system's agricultural operation. Attempts to improve discipline also were made by offering "good time" allowances so inmates could earn early release. For a time, too, the superintendent was allowed to parole inmates to employers, but the system developed trappings of peonage and fell into disuse after 1911.

Prison reform has had many starts and stops in Texas, as in the nation. Prisons hold a low priority in the legislative appropriation process. No alumni groups support improvements, as in the case of colleges, nor are there influential citizens backing reform in most cases. Consequently, unless conditions grow completely intolerable and inhumane, only minimum funding is available. And the treatment of prisoners declines. During the Progressive Era of the late-19th and early 20th centuries, the state's prisons, as did those nationally, received more attention than usual. Prison sanitation, treatment of prisoners, food, clothing and disci-

pline came under review. As this era waned, so did attention to prisons.

Before 1924, each county hanged its own offenders. In 1923, the Legislature gave that responsibility to the prison system, selecting the electric chair as the method of execution. "Old Sparky," as the inmates referred to the chair, was first used in Huntsville on Feb. 8, 1924. A total of 365 persons died by this method of execution before its use was halted by the U.S. Supreme Court in 1964. Brazoria County claims the last legal hanging in Texas, executing a man convicted of murder on Aug. 31, 1923, in Angleton.

Texas' prison population grew, but the system stagnated after World War I. Though the prison system made a profit of $1.5 million in 1917, the treatment of inmates did not improve. Efforts were made to encourage reform. To emphasize the poor conditions, one former convict of this period wrote:

"I helped dig twenty-six graves while I was in the pen, and only three of these men died from natural causes; the others were beaten to death or run over and killed or died from wading and working in the water. When anyone did die they (prison officials) would write their people and state that they (the prisoners) died of heart trouble or consumpion(sic).''

By 1925, the prison system merited another legislative study. The prisons owed $700,000, and the inmate count had grown 35 percent over a two-year period. But the Legislature adjourned before the committee report was complete. Two years later, however, the three-man prison board was abolished in favor of a Board of Prison Commissioners. A new prison manager was named. Not until 1930 was a progressive manager, Lee Simmons, hired, however. For the next seven years, many changes were implemented. The shoe factory was remodeled to enable the facility to provide shoes for all state institutions. A modern print shop was set up, and a woodyard to supply fuel for the prison power plant established up. Surplus fuel was sold in Walker County to offset prison expenses. The agricultural program was expanded, and in 1931, the prison rodeo, which gained national attention, was inaugurated. Under Simmons' administration, the number of escapes decreased, although the prison population increased.

From 1937 to 1948, however, was a period of decay in Texas prisons. More prisoners were crammed into existing buildings. For example, 1,500 prisoners were housed at the Huntsville unit, which had been built for

1,200. Along with the crowding, the system became permeated with brutality, self-mutilation, sexual perversion, incompetency and petty graft. Prison farms in 1947 were not as productive as they should have been, nor were most of the system's factories. Only the license plate factory worked at full capacity. During that year, prison records show that 87 inmates cut their heel tendons in acts of self-mutilation. The system was a mess.

The media took note of the situation, and some reporters went beyond the guided tours provided by prison officials. Wrote one journalist:

"(Those) who have seen and smelled the tanks of the prison farms, the filth, and idleness and hopelessness of life behind bars, and who have seen the stubs of hands and limbs of men who have maimed themselves, may wonder why the system can possibly have any supporters."

On Nov. 27, 1947, the nine-man prison board announced the hiring of O.B. Ellis of the Shelby County (Memphis) Tennessee Penal Farm as general manager of Texas' prisons. A new era began.

Ellis faced major problems. The prison system was in debt, and its operations were outdated. The agricultural program was in bad condition. Of the 73,000 acres of land owned, only 20,000 were in cultivation. Fields were worked with Georgia stock plows and 1,400 mules; less than 20 mechanized farm implements were on hand. Despite owning some of the best pasture land on the Gulf Plains, the system spent a half-million dollars a year purchasing beef on the open market. And no attempt was being made to raise vegetables for the convicts' meals.

Early in his administration, Ellis learned that there was food on hand for only 90 days, with no money to buy more. Gov. Beauford H. Jester transferred $179,000 from the highway fund to cover this contingency. When wardens reported that inmates would not work, Ellis instituted a no-work-no-eat rule, and cooperation quickly improved significantly.

The media aided the new manager by publicizing the prison system's problems and Ellis' proposed solutions. A program was announced calling for a modernization of the agricultural operations, improvement of food and living conditions of the inmates, upgraded pay and standards for guards and institution of a rehabilitation program.

The Legislature was called upon for larger appropriations for the system. Results were soon apparent. By 1951, the cattle herd had almost doubled to 10,288 head. Enough vegetables were grown to satisfy the prison system's needs and to sell $60,000 worth to other state institutions. A building program alleviated overcrowding, and recreational facilities were improved.

Inmate morale was raised to the point that when Ellis asked for volunteers at the Huntsville Unit to help save the system's cotton crop that was threatened by a hurricane, 1,500 men responded.

Medical care improved. In 1959, a psychiatric treatment center for mentally disturbed inmates was opened on the Wynne Unit, near Huntsville. Renewed emphasis was placed on education. The state required compulsory schooling for prisoners who could not pass a third-grade test, and in 1956, the General Educational Development program was instituted that allowed inmates to gain the equivalent of a high-school degree. As early as 1949, Alcoholics Anonymous programs were established, and a full-time alcoholic counselor program was instituted in 1959.

The many reforms that Ellis brought to the system in 12 years moved it from being one of the worst to one of the best in the nation. When Ellis died suddenly in 1961, Texas' prison system had become a source of pride to the state.

George J. Beto replaced Ellis and continued his predecessor's policies. Beto, an ordained Lutheran minister, was a former member of the Texas Board of Corrections and a former president of Concordia College in Austin. The new director was called "Walking George," by inmates because he maintained close contact with the prisoners and their families. When he took office in January 1962, the Texas Department of Corrections had 12,000 inmates on 13 units.

During Beto's administration improvements were made in both housing and rehabilitation of prisoners. The Ferguson Unit for first offenders ages 17-22 was opened in 1962, providing an opportunity to segregate young inmates from the more hardened criminals. A pre-release program was established in 1963 on the Jester Unit, formerly the Harlem farm, to ease offenders'

re-entry into the free world. The Diagnostic Center was opened near Huntsville in 1964; each new convict spends four to six weeks at this facility for comprehensive medical, mental, educational and aptitude testing.

Education programs also expanded. College level courses began in cooperation with local community colleges began in 1965. Three years later, the Windham School District, which operates solely within the prison system, was established by the Legislature; the district offers offenders an opportunity to gain basic educational and vocational skills with which to function upon release.

The Legislature also authorized TDC to sell products to other state agencies and political subdivisions as long as quality was satisfactory. By 1972, the system had 22 industrial facilities with sales of $6 million annually.

Beto retired in 1972 to teach at the Institute of Contemporary Corrections at Sam Houston State University. The institute was authorized by the Legislature to provide training for TDC personnel and to conduct continuing research into penal and criminal statistics.

W.J. Estelle Jr. succeeded Beto and guided TDC through its most turbulent years. The system had 16,100 prisoners on 14 units when he took control and 36,600 convicts when he left in 1983. The reason is simple: Crime began an unabated increase — in Texas, and nationally — in the 1960s, and in response, the federal government funneled millions of dollars into the criminal justice systems of the states. Law enforcement agencies and the court system were the major beneficiaries. With more efficient police work and speedier disposition of criminal cases, the prison system soon severely overcrowded. With the glut of inmates, prison facilities such as medical care and recreation, among others, suffered.

At the same time, federal courts began redefining and reinforcing the rights of the accused before trial and of prisoners after conviction. Against this background, inmate David Ruiz quietly filed a handwritten 45-page suit against TDC in 1972, claiming that incarceration in the system was "cruel and unusual punishment," which is prohibited by the U.S. Constitution. Ruiz contended that medical care was so bad as to be nonexistent and that a shortage of guards forced the use of prisoners to provide discipline. The so-called "building tenders" had broad authority over other inmates. The situation was compared to a World War II concentration camp.

Seven other inmates also filed suits against the prison system, and in 1974, U.S. District Judge William W. Justice of Tyler combined the cases into a class-action suit, which meant it would affect all TDC inmates, not just those who had brought action. William Bennett Turner of San Francisco was appointed attorney for the plaintiffs by Judge Justice. Attorneys took four years to prepare their cases.

Estelle continued the policies of Ellis and Beto, expanding many programs including the prison industries and educational opportunities. The director emphasized discipline, asserting that when prisons are clean and safe for guards and prisoners, many strides can be taken toward rehabilitation.

A breakdown in security in 1974 brought TDC national attention and its greatest tragedy. Inmate Fred Gomez Carrasco, a notorious drug dealer and gang leader, was housed at the Central Unit in Huntsville. A gun was smuggled to Carrasco, and with two other inmates, Rudy Dominguez and Ignacio Cuevas, he held 11 prison employees hostage for 11 days in the unit library. When the convicts, behind a rolling barricade that included human shields, tried to reach an armored car, law officers blocked the escape. Two hostages, prison employees Elizabeth Yvonne Beseda and Judith Stanley, were killed by the convicts. Carrasco and Dominguez took their own lives, a Walker County justice of the peace ruled. A chaplain, Father Joseph O'Brien, was wounded, but the other seven hostages were not hurt. Cuevas was convicted for his part in the standoff and murder.

The Ruiz case came to trial in the fall of 1978, lasting 159 days while 349 witnesses testified and 1,565 exhibits were presented. Judge Justice ruled that incarceration in TDC, the nation's largest prison system at the time, was unconstitutional. Among the findings were that TDC was overcrowded, health and safety standards were inadequate, there were too few guards, brutality toward prisoners existed, phyciatric and medical care was poor, inmates were denied due process in disciplinary hearings, and that inmates had too little access to courts. Sweeping and expensive changes were ordered.

After this ruling money dominated the relations between TDC spokesmen and the Legislature during the 1980s. To meet many of the standards that the federal judge required, the state would have to launch a massive building program and spend hundreds of millions of dollars for new personnel, including doctors. In 1983, Estelle asked for $1.5 billion for the two-year budget period and received a little over half that amount.

Citizens groups, usually uninterested in prison affairs, became a factor in the 1980s. Citizens United for the Rehabilitation of Errants (CURE), under the direction of Charles Sullivan, a former Roman Catholic priest, began monitoring the system and proposed changes, often opposed by prison officials, to the Legislature. Also, other citizen groups in several parts of Texas opposed plans to build new prisons in their areas, slowing, if not halting, efforts to ease overcrowding. A site in Grimes County was acquired in 1981, and a new prison was built near Palestine.

To ease overcrowding in 1982, some inmates were housed in tents. But even this measure did not stop the prison system from temporarily closing its doors to new convicts when the population limit set by the court was surpassed in the spring of 1982. The action forced many counties to keep prisoners in their jails, although many of these facilities also were overcrowded.

Estelle resigned as director in October 1983. Daniel McKastle served as interim director into 1984 until succeeded by Ray Procunier, the former director of the California prison system. Two other men have served as director since Procunier left in 1985. O. L. McCotter replaced Procunier, serving until December 1986. In May 1987, James A. Lynaugh was named director.

A wave of violence also struck the prison system when the prisoner-guards — the building tenders — were withdrawn and gangs of convicts began feuding. In 1984, 25 prisoners were killed and 404 injured in prison violence, and in 1985, 27 died and 215 were injured.

Judge Justice ruled TDC in contempt of his court order and threatened to begin fining the State of Texas up to $800,500 a day if the pace of prison changes was not increased in 1987. Faced with this pressure from the judge and with more closures because of overcrowding of the prison system in early 1987, the Legislature and Gov. Bill Clements made reform a top item during the legislative session.

But Texas' crime rate shows no sign of declining, and citizens reject most proposals that would place offenders in diversionary programs rather than prisons. The troubles of TDC appear to be far from over.

Adult Supervision in Texas, 1986

County	Probation[1]	Parole[2]	Prison[3]	Jail[4]	County	Probation[1]	Parole[2]	Prison[3]	Jail[4]
Anderson	2,199	56	43	32	Delta	0	3	12	3
Andrews	331	21	31	17	Denton.	2,327	255	246	59
Angelina	1,611	135	188	50	Dickens	0	3	3	5
Aransas	0	38	47	22	Dimmit	0	5	8	5
Archer	0	8	16	8	Donley	0	4	3	5
Armstrong	0	4	3	2	Duval.	811	21	11	9
Atascosa	0	40	74	20	Eastland	358	27	39	14
Austin	0	26	32	16	Ector	1,924	433	400	160
Bailey	275	12	12	7	Edwards	0	4	1	0
Bandera	0	5	4	12	El Paso.	10,960	910	835	905
Bastrop	1,967	38	38	19	Ellis.	655	163	107	83
Baylor	269	6	7	9	Erath	454	30	50	19
Bee	0	49	77	25	Falls	617	29	32	9
Bell	5,827	275	487	139	Fannin	0	42	31	21
Bexar.	23,499	2,061	2,210	1,005	Fayette	1,043	11	20	32
Blanco	0	7	5	3	Fisher	0	6	5	12
Borden.	0	0	0	0	Floyd.	280	14	13	6
Bosque.	0	17	21	7	Foard.	0	2	3	3
Bowie.	1,191	169	150	162	Fort Bend.	1,918	258	181	150
Brazoria.	2,648	297	218	274	Franklin	0	6	20	7
Brazos	1,856	218	261	113	Freestone	0	34	70	17
Brewster	0	7	8	13	Frio	0	31	28	25
Briscoe	0	1	0	0	Gaines	0	23	35	16
Brooks	0	18	25	8	Galveston.	2,963	575	484	295
Brown	688	67	72	42	Garza	0	11	14	4
Burleson	0	31	49	10	Gillespie	0	13	19	9
Burnet	0	30	20	24	Glasscock	0	1	1	2
Caldwell.	2,693	51	79	30	Goliad.	0	9	18	4
Calhoun	0	34	26	24	Gonzales	0	27	37	15
Callahan	0	11	16	6	Gray	705	49	43	12
Cameron	7,684	320	336	400	Grayson	1,438	142	110	65
Camp.	0	20	18	8	Gregg	2,659	231	261	147
Carson	0	5	12	7	Grimes.	0	20	31	12
Cass	463	53	59	25	Guadalupe	1,798	63	116	35
Castro	0	17	10	13	Hale	920	86	103	73
Chambers	0	35	48	38	Hall	375	14	8	7
Cherokee	752	61	62	33	Hamilton	0	13	14	6
Childress	0	12	14	8	Hansford	0	10	3	3
Clay	0	2	12	6	Hardeman	0	6	4	5
Cochran	0	2	6	3	Hardin	729	88	50	21
Coke	0	5	6	1	Harris	43,053	11,452	9,285	4,450
Coleman	0	19	12	5	Harrison	714	94	130	47
Collin	3,412	227	239	155	Hartley	0	8	1	2
Collingsworth. .	0	5	5	5	Haskell.	0	9	15	8
Colorado	0	24	29	10	Hays	0	74	51	53
Comal	0	53	80	110	Hemphill	0	4	6	3
Comanche	456	21	24	13	Henderson	0	89	124	40
Concho	0	3	4	0	Hidalgo	6,687	291	278	275
Cooke	474	38	62	15	Hill.	637	44	44	30
Coryell	625	47	45	14	Hockley	484	27	32	42
Cottle.	0	6	2	2	Hood	799	48	73	31
Crane.	82	7	10	13	Hopkins	893	68	71	38
Crockett.	0	2	7	4	Houston	0	41	36	17
Crosby	0	13	6	7	Howard	693	58	85	17
Culberson	0	2	7	6	Hudspeth	0	5	7	19
Dallam	0	18	12	9	Hunt	942	122	111	64
Dallas	33,729	7,454	6,811	2,623	Hutchinson. . . .	706	67	29	39
Dawson	751	43	36	11	Irion	0	2	2	0
DeWitt	0	29	52	14	Jack.	648	12	15	10
Deaf Smith. . . .	499	41	59	52	Jackson	0	32	57	20

County	Probation[1]	Parole[2]	Prison[3]	Jail[4]
Jasper	1,382	44	37	10
Jeff Davis	0	2	1	0
Jefferson	3,457	952	774	368
Jim Hogg	0	5	7	4
Jim Wells	849	67	87	25
Johnson	2,054	110	113	73
Jones	528	25	36	17
Karnes	0	31	40	10
Kaufman	916	103	110	23
Kendall	0	7	16	6
Kenedy	0	0	2	1
Kent	0	0	3	0
Kerr	1,104	45	63	47
Kimble	0	7	11	6
King	0	0	0	0
Kinney	0	6	4	22
Kleberg	779	46	43	24
Knox	0	8	11	9
La Salle	0	9	10	4
Lamar	1,332	118	167	65
Lamb	293	23	25	22
Lampasas	0	18	40	12
Lavaca	0	21	20	9
Lee	0	19	19	7
Leon	0	19	17	7
Liberty	1,532	153	153	84
Limestone	1,508	50	58	20
Lipscomb	0	3	3	2
Live Oak	0	13	22	14
Llano	0	2	12	10
Loving	0	3	0	0
Lubbock	3,667	624	493	344
Lynn	0	4	13	7
Madison	0	21	14	5
Marion	0	16	13	8
Martin	0	2	4	7
Mason	721	2	2	1
Matagorda	1,363	66	82	50
Maverick	490	12	28	15
McCulloch	317	12	15	14
McLennan	2,796	538	443	292
McMullen	0	3	1	0
Medina	0	19	27	12
Menard	0	5	4	1
Midland	2,086	284	303	78
Milam	443	45	37	16
Mills	0	1	0	5
Mitchell	0	17	16	15
Montague	451	27	20	12
Montgomery	3,153	346	303	77
Moore	439	34	25	24
Morris	719	27	26	8
Motley	0	0	4	0
Nacogdoches	1,208	84	96	36
Navarro	564	95	157	41
Newton	0	34	18	7
Nolan	603	44	63	41
Nueces	4,364	642	628	336
Ochiltree	0	21	17	18
Oldham	0	4	5	3
Orange	1,189	246	154	55
Palo Pinto	406	44	65	31
Panola	744	39	38	9
Parker	1,096	72	72	59
Parmer	0	8	7	4
Pecos	956	20	25	20
Polk	1,067	74	46	29
Potter	2,915	408	302	285
Presidio	0	4	8	29
Rains	0	18	11	14
Randall	0	42	98	56
Reagan	0	2	6	7
Real	0	1	6	7
Red River	300	30	38	10
Reeves	473	37	27	558
Refugio	0	11	19	9
Roberts	0	1	0	1
Robertson	0	42	57	15
Rockwall	0	17	27	6
Runnels	0	16	24	13
Rusk	523	64	75	12
Sabine	0	10	16	11
San Augustine	0	15	11	4
San Jacinto	0	25	23	10
San Patricio	2,641	127	117	55
San Saba	0	5	6	3
Schleicher	0	5	2	3
Scurry	426	55	63	38
Shackelford	0	7	8	11

One In Every 43 Texans Is Under Supervision for Crime

Texas' high crime rate has brought about another phenomenon: An average of one in every 43 of the state's citizens is under some sort of supervision by the criminal justice system. This includes the number of people on felony or misdemeanor probation, on parole, in prison or in local jails.

The state's six urban counties (those with 500,000 and more population) have an average of one in every 40 citizens under supervision. In metropolitan counties (with populations between 100,000 and 500,000) one in every 44 citizens is under supervision, and in rural areas, the average drops to one citizen in every 47.

Among urban areas, Dallas has one of every 35 persons under supervision. In metropolitan counties, Bell has one in 25, Potter one in 27 and Cameron one in 29.

County	Probation[1]	Parole[2]	Prison[3]	Jail[4]
Shelby	0	54	45	7
Sherman	0	1	1	4
Smith	3,167	347	277	205
Somervell	0	5	11	13
Starr	0	29	14	9
Stephens	0	7	15	15
Sterling	0	2	2	1
Stonewall	0	0	6	3
Sutton	0	1	6	17
Swisher	0	23	24	10
Tarrant	14,327	2,884	2,098	1,400
Taylor	2,052	253	273	204
Terrell	0	2	0	1
Terry	643	29	40	14
Throckmorton	0	1	4	0
Titus	0	56	31	26
Tom Green	2,356	259	232	115
Travis	11,237	1,214	1,374	548
Trinity	0	31	31	4
Tyler	291	23	33	13
Upshur	539	47	25	14
Upton	0	3	5	5
Uvalde	541	30	22	28
Val Verde	749	45	52	124
Van Zandt	430	59	61	21
Victoria	3,739	159	178	103
Walker	1,545	295	84	32
Waller	0	45	44	17
Ward	0	22	18	60
Washington	0	45	43	8
Webb	938	68	119	450
Wharton	0	93	66	32
Wheeler	259	8	3	5
Wichita	1,637	235	187	111
Wilbarger	0	30	22	11
Willacy	0	32	28	8
Williamson	2,051	147	256	120
Wilson	0	17	31	8
Winkler	177	14	24	13
Wise	0	42	45	25
Wood	718	33	58	20
Yoakum	0	11	9	10
Young	527	58	23	20
Zapata	0	2	9	5
Zavala	0	18	7	30
Total	282,948	41,697	39,045	20,815

1. Probation figures are for Jan. 31, 1986, as provided by the Texas Adult Probation Commission. Statistics for rural areas are given for the home county of the district court; these figures, therefore, represent the several counties in the judicial district.

2. Parole figures are from the annual report of the Board of Pardons and Paroles of Aug. 31, 1986.

3. Prison figures reflect the inmate population of the Texas Department of Corrections as of March 31, 1987. The statistics were provided by TDC. A total of 772 prisoners had not been classified as to county of origin when this report was compiled, so the state total by county is out of balance by that number.

4. Jail figures represent the average daily population of the jails in Texas, as reflected in the annual report of the Texas Commission on Jail Standards on Aug. 31, 1986.

Pardons and Paroles

Texas has never been a leader in the clemency movement in corrections. Texans usually want offenders to serve their time in prison. But the state has grudgingly followed other states in providing means for shortening sentences and for releasing offenders from prison early.

Parole is the conditional release from prison under supervision after a portion of the offender's regular sentence has been served. A pardon is the state's forgiveness for a crime, which is expunged from an individual's criminal record by the act.

Clemency in various forms has been a feature of most legal systems. Mosaic law, for example, created sanctuary cities in which an accused murderer was safe from the passions of a victim's family. After trial in the temple court, an offender could live under the protection of the high priest. When the priest died, those under his protection could be granted amnesty and return home.

Christianity and clemency were introduced in England in the 6th century. As the British crown tried to strengthen the central government by consolidating control over the judiciary, the pardon power became a symbol of royal authority.

Antecedents of today's system of parole and clemency began in England in 1597 in response to a labor shortage in the colonies. The law was changed to allow banishment "beyond the seas" of rogues. Twenty years later, the Privy Council passed an order granting reprieves and stays of execution to persons convicted of robbery and who were strong enough to be employed in the colonies. When sent to the colonies, these prisoners were auctioned as indentured servants. Banishment, or transportation, of prisoners lasted until the American Revolution in North America and continued until 1867 to Australia.

Parole has long been used by the military to release prisoners of war on the condition that they no longer fight. The term "parole" apparently was coined by Dr. S. G. Howe of Boston in 1846 in a letter to the Prison Association of New York.

The first attempt to let prisoners earn early release came in New York in 1817 when the initial "good time" law was passed. Prisoners were allowed to shorten their sentences by no more than one-fourth through proper behavior that earned them extra credit for days served. In practice, this system was little better than the pardon procedure that was used to reduce excessively long sentences. By the end of the century, 44 states had some form of good-time law.

Our present parole system grew from the efforts of Captain Alexander Maconochie, governor of the penal colony of Norfolk Island off Australia from 1840 to 1844. The "father" of modern parole devised a system of rewards that could shorten the period before a "ticket of leave" was issued. Under the system, the offender earned marks for favorable conduct. These could be used to reduce the period served before release or to buy extra food.

The prisoners moved through a graded system in preparation for release. First they served strict imprisonment, followed by a period of hard labor on a chain gang. In the final two steps, a period of freedom within a confined area preceeded release on a ticket of leave. An offender with a ticket had to report regularly to the constabulary where he lived for the remainder of his sentence.

Maconochie was considered too lenient by Australians and was removed from office, but his reforms were incorporated into the legal system.

Indeterminate sentences, which were being assessed in the United States by 1832, were another step toward today's system of paroles. True indeterminate sentences had no maximum or minimum length of service but depended solely on a prisoner's performance and attitude. At first, judges were reluctant to give up full sentencing authority, as were chief excutives protective of the clemency power of pardons. But tentative steps were taken toward this type of sentencing in some states in the 19th century.

Clemency in the state of Texas began with the Constitution of 1845, which gave the governor power to grant reprieves and pardons, except in cases of treason or impeachment. In treason cases, clemency could be extended only with the consent of the state Senate. In 1876, the chief executive was given authority to commute — to shorten or change — sentences. The Legisla-

Gov. James E. Ferguson aroused public antagonism with his liberal policy of pardons. Between 1915-1917, he granted 1,774 full pardons and 479 conditional pardons. Photo courtesy Archives Division, Texas State Library.

ture created the Board of Pardons Advisors in 1893 to help the governor review cases. Although late in the 19th and early in the 20th century many states were giving advisory boards authority in clemency cases, the Texas governor's power was not curbed until a constitutional amendment was approved by voters in 1936. Some governors were too liberal in the use of pardons, many Texans thought. Gov. James E. Ferguson granted 1,774 pardons and 479 conditional pardons between 1915 and 1917, and Gov. William P. Hobby approved 1,319 pardons and 199 conditional pardons during his four-year tenure following Ferguson. Between 1925 and 1927, Gov. Miriam A. Ferguson extended 384 pardons and 777 conditional pardons. The 1936 amendment created a constitutional Board of Pardons and Paroles that was to recommend clemency before the governor could act.

Zebulon Brockway, superintendent of the Elmira, N.Y., Reformatory is called the "father" of parole in the United States. Building on work by Captain Manconochie and Sir William Crofton, who refined parole while head of the Irish prison system in 1854, Brockway in 1877 made provisions for parole of prisoners on parole when the offender was considered fit to re-enter free society. Texas passed its first parole law in 1905, and by 1922, 45 states had adopted the procedure.

Legislation passed in 1911 gave the Board of Prison Commissioners, with approval of the governor, authority to make rules and regulations governing parole. But no system of supervision of paroled offenders existed. Two years later, with the addition of an indeterminate sentence law that increased the use of parole, the governor was given sole power to grant paroles, though the prison board still wrote the rules.

In 1929, the pardons board was revitalized and a third member added by the Legislature to create the Board of Pardons and Paroles, which was to recommend prisoners for parole to the governor, as well as to advise in clemency cases. Parole could be granted only to prisoners who had never before been convicted of a crime punishable by sentence to the penitentiary. The law in 1930 was changed to exclude from parole only prisoners who had previously served time in prison.

The reform of 1936 gave the Board of Pardons and Paroles exclusive power to recommend paroles. The authority was exercised if the board felt the prisoner would stay out of trouble and not endanger society. There were no parole officers, but a supervisor of parolees was to keep records. If a parolee violated conditions of his release or committed a new crime, his parole was to be revoked by the governor. A sentence for a crime committed while on parole was not to begin until the offender completed serving time for his initial crime.

Gov. James V. Allred in 1937 called for formation of voluntary parole boards. Voluntary parole supervisors, who received no compensation, were appointed in 242 of 254 counties in Texas. They assisted parolees in obtaining jobs and required the offenders to make reports.

The present general framework for the operation of Adult Probation and Parole in Texas was established in 1947, but the system was not funded. Supervision continued to be conducted by volunteers. Finally in 1957, a Division of Parole Supervision was created, and Vincent O'Leary of Washington state came to Texas to set up a supervision system. Originally the system was manned by a director, four area supervisors and a staff of 40 parole officers.

A six-member parole commission to assist the board was created in 1975, and in 1977, Texas adopted a system of mandatory supervision of released convicts. Previously only the best risks were placed under parole supervision. Today, all convicts are under supervision for a time after release from Texas prisons.

Parole and mandatory supervision were separated from probation under Texas law in 1985, and the Legislature imposed the state's first supervision fee on pris-

on releasees. The governor was removed from the parole process in 1985 when the board was increased from three to six members. Also a controversial element in parole was eliminated when the Legislature allowed juries to be told about the conditions of early release. Under law, an offender is eligible for parole when he has credit for serving one-third of his sentence or 20 years, whichever is less. (This does not mean that an offender is automatically parolled, but that he is eligible for consideration.)

Pressure was increased on the parole board when the prison system became overcrowded. On one hand, the board was critized for not paroling eligible offenders quickly enough to make room for new prisoners and, on the other hand, for releasing too many offenders who subsequently committed new crimes. In 1986, the average offender to receive parole served 2.09 years of a 9.99 year sentence, or about 20.9 percent, while the average time served for all inmates was 25.4 percent of an average 7.7 year sentence.

Through February 1987, the Board of Pardons and Paroles had nearly 1,000 employees, including 500 parole officers and caseworkers supervising more than 44,290 released offenders. The parole officials operated from 42 regional and district offices covering all of Texas' 254 counties.

Probation

Probation is an American contribution to corrections. There are historical precedents, however. In the Middle Ages, the church offered sanctuary to persons accused of breaking secular laws that bore heavy penalties. In the 17th century, a form of suspended sentence called "benefit of clergy" was developed in England that allowed an offender to move freely within society.

John Augustus, a Boston cobbler, is credited with being the "father" of probation. In 1841, he attended court sessions and was appalled that drunks could be sentenced to jail for failure to pay their fines. The cobbler's interest in the temperance movement led him to get the courts to release offenders to him after he paid their fines. Between 1841 and 1848, he handled almost 2,000 persons, and his success rate was reported to be high. Only 10 of his charges absconded before the end of their probation.

Augustus provided the important characteristic element of probation: supervision. Massachusetts had experimented in 1836 with a recognizance law, which had many features of probation. The state passed the nation's first probation law in 1876, and by the turn of the century, four other states had similar laws.

Probation gained popularity after the first juvenile court was created in 1899. Several states, including Texas in 1907, adopted juvenile probation laws long before they extended the leniency to adults, although Texas did not pay juvenile probation officers until 1919. While the federal government adopted probation in 1925, Mississippi in 1956 was the last state to adopt the policy.

In 1913, Texas passed the Suspended Sentence Law that was the first step toward probation. Under the law, the offender was simply released under his own recognizance. No supervision was provided, and the person remained free while on "good behavior," which meant as long as no new felony was committed. Originally only juries could assess a suspended sentence, but in 1931, the law was amended to allow judges to use the provision. Suspended sentences remained part of state law until 1965.

Diversionary programs that kept offenders out of prison have long been scapegoats. Gov. Pat Neff blamed the Suspended Sentence Act for a perceived crime problem in the state, and in 1922, he disbanded the Board of Pardons.

Texas was one of the last states to provide statutory authority for probation. The Legislature passed the Adult Probation and Parole Law in 1947, incorporating most of the elements of a model law. Initially, only the court, not the jury, could extend probation, and the defendant was eligible only if there was no previous felony conviction on his record and if the punishment for the crime for which he was convicted did not exceed 10 years.

Under the law, the Board of Pardons and Paroles also became the state Board of Probation. And a supervision system was set up. However, this provision of the law was never put into effect because the Legislature failed to appropriate funds. Probation services were

made available by sheriffs, ministers and others on a voluntary basis. Some counties schemed to provide the services. In 1953, for example, Dallas County hired two probation officers and called them "grand jury bailiffs."

In 1957, the Legislature separated probation and parole in the law and made supervision of probationers a function of county government. Otherwise there was no change in provisions.

Because counties had a choice of whether to adopt adult probation, some did and others did not. Basically, the larger counties did. In 1965, district judges were given responsiblity for administration of the adult probation program, but county commissioners courts had to provide funding.

Under the 1965 changes, both judges and juries could grant probation, although juries were limited to extending it to first-time offenders. And for the first time, misdemeanants could be given probation. In 1967, the Legislature allowed counties to levy a $10 monthly supervision fee on each probationer to finance the program.

A study in 1971 found that probation supervision of some type was provided in 210 of Texas' 254 counties, and about $8 million in local and federal funds was spent on probation administration. The average caseload of each officer was 113 felony probationers, about twice the recommended level.

Full state operation of the probation program began in 1977, and today probation gets more attention because of the overcrowding of the prison system. Modest attempts to set up community corrections programs also are moving ahead. Supporters say probation has many advantages. It is cheaper than incarceration, and probationers can be required to reimburse victims for losses. In addition, probationers can continue to support their family. About three-quarters of those sentenced successfully complete probation, although some are sent to prison for violating terms of their release or for committing new crimes.

Soaring costs of imprisoning offenders brought about greater interest in probation in the 1980s. Several programs aimed at diverting criminals from prisons have been initiated. Basically, they put the probationer under close supervision of probation officers. In some cases, they live in a special home. Advocates point out that with probation, offenders can repay their victims, continue to support their families and remain taxpayers, not tax burdens.

In 1986, Texas had 117 local adult probation departments with just over 1,400 professional probation officers supervising 282,879 probationers. The cost per probationer per day for operating the system was 77 cents, according to state probation officials; to house a inmate in prison costs $24.84 a day, excluding construction costs.

Though most Texans would prefer that offenders serve prison time, probation is becoming more attractive because of the state's continuing problems with the prison system.

Gallows were provided with trap doors, like this one in Brownwood, for hanging offenders in Texas prior to 1924. Brownwood Bulletin Photo by Robert Tindol.

Executions In Texas

When other methods of corrections and rehabilitation have failed, the death penalty is used to remove particularly heinous offenders from society. The death penalty has been a feature of the various legal systems that have ruled Texas through history.

Early European explorers found that Indian groups executed prisoners of war and practiced cannibalism on the victims. Some Indian groups allowed families of victims of murder and other crimes to take vengeance on the perpetrators, including taking their lives.

Both the Spanish and Mexican legal systems provided for capital punishment, and the Republic of Texas and the early state government also spelled out capital crimes.

Unitl 1924, hanging was the method of execution in Texas. The sentence usually was carried out in public. Often a carnival atmosphere developed around public executions. J. W. Thomas of Rogers was so appalled at a hanging in 1922 that he ran for the state Senate on a platform of changing the manner in which Texas handled executions. He was successful in changing the method of execution to electrocution and closeting the proceedings.

Counties had been responsible for executing their own criminals. Under the new law, the state became the executioner. The last legal hanging in Texas took place on Aug. 31, 1923, at Angleton in Brazoria County when Nathan Lee was hanged for murder. On Feb. 8, 1924, the electric chair was used for the first time in Texas. (New York first used electrocution for execution in 1890.) Between 1924 and 1964, when executions were suspended by the U.S. Supreme Court, 365 persons were executed in Texas. Twenty were electrocuted in 1935, the busiest year, and 18 offenders were killed in 1938.

When the Supreme Court lifted the moratorium in 1976, Texas reinstated the death penalty in 1978. The

The electric chair — called "Old Sparky" — was used to execute 365 persons in Texas between 1924 and 1964. Dallas Morning News Photo.

means of execution was changed to the lethal injection of chemicals into the victim. Charles Brooks on Dec. 6, 1982, became the first offender in the United States to die of lethal injection.

Texas led the nation in executions in 1986 with nine. Between 1982 and 1986, 19 persons were executed in Texas, the most of any state.

—MIKE KINGSTON

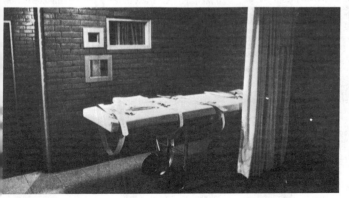

Since 1982, criminals have been strapped to a gurney in this chamber and injected with lethal chemicals. Associated Press Photo.

Population

Texas Population at Mid-Decade

The authors of this article written for the Texas Almanac are Dr. Steve H. Murdock, professor and head, and Rita R. Hamm, research associate, in the Department of Rural Sociology in the Texas Agricultural Experiment Station of the Texas A&M University System.

Patterns of Population Growth

The preliminary U.S. Bureau of the Census estimate of Texas population as of July 1, 1986, was 16,685,000. This represented an increase of 296,000 or 1.8 percent from 1985 when the state's population was 16,389,000 and an increase of nearly 2.5 million persons since 1980 when the state's population was 14,229,000. From 1980 to 1986, Texas' numerical increase in population exceeded that in all other states, except California, which experienced a population increase of 3.3 million, and Texas' percentage change of 17.3 percent was exceeded by only four other states (Alaska with 32.8 percent, Arizona with 22.1 percent, Nevada with 20.3 percent and Florida with 19.8 percent). Texas continued to be the nation's third largest state in 1986, behind California with 26.9 million in 1986 and New York with 17.8 million in 1986, but its present rate of growth could make it the second largest state by the early 1990s. When the entire 1980 to 1986 time period is examined, then, it is evident that Texas experienced very rapid population growth.

The reason for this growth clearly lies in a substantial increase in net in-migration to the state. During the decade of the 1970s, Texas experienced net in-migration of 1.7 million persons (which accounted for 58 percent of the state's growth during the decade) and from 1980 to 1986, 1.3 million persons or roughly 52 percent of all population growth in the state was due to net in-migration. The rate of in-migration was particularly rapid during the initial part of the 1980s. From 1980 to 1981, 329,000 (61 percent) of the 537,000 increase in the state's population was due to net in-migration from other states. From 1981-82, 429,000 (70 percent) of the 609,000 increase was due to net in-migration and from 1982-83, 257,000 (58 percent) of the 442,000 increase was due to net in-migration. Beginning in 1982, in-migration began to slow and since 1983-84 has averaged only about 100,000 per year. Thus, net in-migration to the state increased from an annual rate of 1.6 percent in the 1970s to 2.9 percent from 1981-82 and then declined to roughly 0.6 percent by 1985-86. Natural increase (the excess of births over deaths), on the other hand, has remained relatively constant at from 1.1 to 1.5 percent per year throughout the 1980s. As a result of such patterns, the proportion of population growth due to migration has declined from 70 percent in 1981-82 to less than 37 percent by 1985-86, a proportion similar to that observed in earlier decades.

In sum, after growing rapidly in the first two years of the 1980s, Texas' rate of population growth has slowed substantially since 1982. While still growing nearly twice as rapidly as the nation as a whole, the nation's population increased by 1.0 percent from 1985-86, while the Texas population increased by 1.8 percent), Texas' rate of population growth since 1983 has been approximately one-half of that experienced during the 1980-83 time period and approximately two-thirds of the rate experienced during the 1970s.

Although estimates for areas smaller than the state as a whole have not been released for 1986 (and revised county-level estimates for 1981-83 that will include, for the first time, a census bureau estimate of undocumented aliens have not yet been released), existing U.S. Bureau of the Census estimates for 1981-1985 suggest that the slowdown in Texas' population growth is pervasive in both the cities and counties of the state.

Population Growth in Metropolitan Areas

Texas' metropolitan areas experienced patterns of rapid population growth during the 1970s, with annual growth rates of more than 4 percent per year occurring in Austin, Brownsville-Harlingen-San Benito, Bryan-College Station, Houston and McAllen-Pharr-Edinburg. Patterns of population growth and net migration for metropolitan areas in the 1980s show dramatically different patterns, however (see Table 2). Although all 26 of the state's Metropolitan Statistical Areas experienced population growth from 1970-80 and from 1980-82, by 1982-84 three metropolitan areas — Beaumont-Port Arthur-Orange, Odessa and Wichita Falls — were experiencing population decline. From 1984-85, a total of six metropolitan areas — Abilene, Beaumont-Port Arthur-Orange, Killeen-Temple, Lubbock, San Angelo and Wichita Falls — declined in population. For another 15 areas, annualized rates of growth for the period from 1984-85 were slower than for the period from 1982-84, and for 22 areas, annualized rates of growth for 1984-85 were slower than those from 1980-82. Thus, most of the state's metropolitan areas are experiencing patterns of population change that are significantly different from those that occurred during the 1970s and early 1980s.

Such differences are even more evident when patterns of net migration are examined. During the 1970s, all metropolitan areas in the state experienced net in-migration. By 1980-82, however, two areas, Killeen-Temple and Lubbock were experiencing net out-migration. From 1982-84, the number of metropolitan areas experiencing net out-migration increased to four — Beaumont-Port Arthur-Orange, Lubbock, Victoria and Wichita Falls. During 1984-85, the effects of the slowdown became very evident. For this period, 17 of the state's 26 metropolitan areas experienced net out-migration with annual rates of net out-migration of more than 1 percent being evident in Abilene, Beaumont-Port Arthur-Orange, Killeen-Temple, Lubbock, Odessa, San Angelo and Wichita Falls. By 1984-85, 65 percent of the state's 26 major cities were experiencing net out-migration. For those 11 areas that were experiencing net out-migration but not population decline, natural increase was sufficiently large to compensate for the loss of population due to net out-migration. The data on net migration for Texas' Metropolitan Statistical Areas thus clearly suggest that the slowdown in Texas' net in-migration has permeated nearly all regions of the state.

Several areas of the state, however, continued to have relatively rapid growth and significant rates of net in-migration through 1985. The two most rapidly growing areas of the state continued to be Austin and Dallas-Fort Worth. Austin's estimated annual rate of

Figure 1
Counties in Texas With Population Decline for Alternative Time Periods

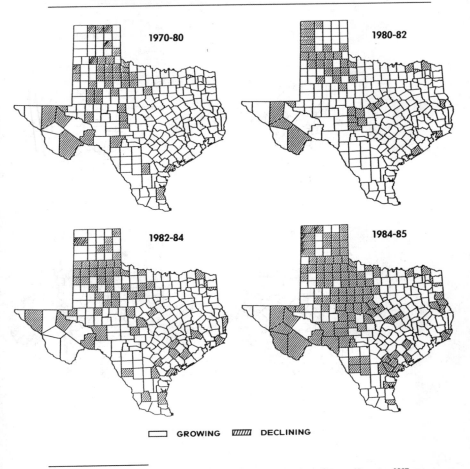

GROWING   ▨ DECLINING

Source: Steve H. Murdock, Kenneth Backman, and Sean-Shong Hwang. 1987. Update 1987—The Continued Slowdown in Texas Population Growth: 1980-1985 Population Change in Texas Counties. Austin: Texas State Data Center.

population growth from 1984-85 was 6.9 percent, and its annual rate of net migration from 1984-85 was 5.6 percent. Comparable figures for Dallas-Fort Worth were a population growth rate of 3.9 percent and a net migration rate of 2.7 percent. According to these estimates, other metropolitan areas in the state continuing to experience population growth of more than 2 percent per year and net in-migration of more than 1 percent during 1984-85 were Midland (2.9 percent population growth and 1.3 percent net migration), San Antonio (2.5 percent and 1.3 percent) and Tyler (2.7 percent and 1.9 percent). Although when county data become available for the periods after 1985, it may be evident that these patterns have changed, the most rapid population growth from 1984-85 continued to be in the central corridor of Texas.

County Population Growth and Net Migration

Data for Texas counties suggest that the slowdown in Texas population growth is producing patterns of change similar to those that occurred in the 1960s, a period of relatively slow population growth in the state. The number of counties in the state experiencing both population decline and net out-migration by 1985 was similar to the number experiencing such patterns during the 1960s. In the 1960s, 146 counties experienced population decline, and 180 had net out-migration, with growth occurring primarily in the state's metropolitan areas. By 1980-82, the number of counties showing population decline had dropped to only 41, and the number with net out-migration was only 57. But from 1984-85, 110 counties again showed population decline, and 147 were experiencing net out-migration. An examination of such data for central-city counties in metropolitan areas, suburban metropolitan counties, nonmetropolitan counties that are adjacent to metropolitan counties and nonmetropolitan counties that are not adjacent to metropolitan counties further suggests that the patterns of the 1960s were again evident for 1984-85. That is, population declined in the state's most rural counties and grew most rapidly in suburban counties. By 1985, nonmetropolitan nonadjacent counties were experienc-

Figure 2
Counties in Texas Having Net Out-migration for Alternative Time Periods

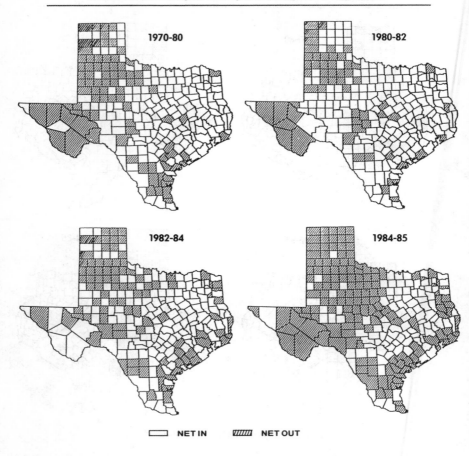

□ NET IN   ▨ NET OUT

Source: Steve H. Murdock, Kenneth Backman, and Sean-Shong Hwang. 1987.
Update 1987—The Continued Slowdown in Texas Population Growth: 1980-1985
Population Change in Texas Counties. Austin: Texas State Data Center.

ing mean rates of population growth and net migration that indicated both net out-migration and population decline, and nonmetropolitan counties adjacent to a metropolitan county were growing very slowly (by less than 1 percent per year). Within metropolitan areas by 1984-85, population growth had declined to less than one-half the 1980-82 rate in central-city counties, while growth rates remained relatively strong in suburban counties of the state.

The pervasiveness of the slowdown in Texas population growth and in the rate of net migration is particularly evident when viewed graphically (see Figures 1 and 2). By 1984-85, the number of counties that showed patterns of population decline and net out-migration not only increased but had also became evident in nearly all parts of the state. Except for central Texas, very few parts of the state were not experiencing a slowdown in population growth by 1985.

A slowdown in Texas' population growth was occurring by the middle of the 1980s. The annualized rate of growth for 1985-86 was only 1.8 percent compared with 4.1 percent from 1981 to 1982, and 1.2 percent of the 1.8 percent rate of growth from 1985 to 1986 was due to natural increase. By 1986, the state's rate of population growth had declined to a level reminiscent of the 1960s, when the annualized rate of growth was 1.7 percent and a majority of the state's counties were showing patterns of net out-migration. Only relatively high rates of natural increase in the 1980s have offset net out-migration to produce population growth in a majority of the state's counties. For the state's metropolitan areas, the patterns have no recent historical precedent; for even during the 1960s, most of the metropolitan areas experienced net in-migration. By 1985 however, 65 percent of the state's metropolitan areas were showing net out-migration, although only six did not have rates of natural increase that were sufficiently high to offset net out-migration and thus to enable the areas to show population growth rather than decline. The state's most rural counties are experiencing population loss, with only suburban counties retaining patterns of relatively rapid growth. Finally, nearly all regions are experienc-

Table 1

Annual Population Change and Net Migration and Annualized Rates of Population Change, Net Migration and Natural Increase for Texas, 1980-86

**Year	Population	Numercial Change From Preceding Year	Time Period	Net Migration	Net Migration Rate (%)	Natural Increase Rate (%)	Percent Population Change
1980	14,229,000	*303,000	1970-80	*177,000	*1.6	*1.1	*2.7
1981	14,766,000	537,286	1980-81	329,585	2.3	1.5	3.8
1982	15,376,000	609,059	1981-82	429,032	2.9	1.2	4.1
1983	15,818,000	441,999	1982-83	256,902	1.7	1.2	2.9
1984	16,083,000	265,142	1983-84	87,328	0.5	1.2	1.7
1985	16,389,000	306,243	1984-85	118,869	0.7	1.2	1.9
1986	16,685,000	296,438	1985-86	109,521	0.6	1.2	1.8

*Annualized for 1970-80.

**All post-1980 estimates are for July 1 of the year noted. Population values for 1980 are for April 1, 1980. Values for 1980 are from the 1980 Census of Population and post-1980 estimates were obtained from the U.S. Bureau of the Census, Local Population Estimates Branch (December 19, 1986).

ing both patterns of slowdown in population growth and an increasing rate of net out-migration.

Although, we must caution the reader that the trends described are based on census bureau population estimates, not on actual population counts, and that trends for only a few years may be misleading, there appears to be little doubt that the slowdown in Texas' population growth is real, extensive and pervasive. The causes for these patterns appear to be largely economic, and it appears that such growth will return to the levels of the 1970s and early 1980s only when the Texas economy shows a substantial recovery.

Population Characteristics at Mid-Decade

Although data on the characteristics of the population are collected in a comprehensive manner only at the time of the census, data from the Current Population Survey conducted monthly by the U.S. Bureau of the Census provides information indicating the direction of trends in key characteristics for intercensal periods. Using such survey data, trends in selected population characteristics in Texas from 1980 to 1985 can be described.

As with the U.S. population as a whole, the Texas population is aging as the baby-boom generation enters middle-age. In Texas, as in the United States as a whole, this generation (made up of persons born between 1946 and 1964) makes up one-third of the population. The first members of this generation entered their 40s in 1986. As a result of the aging of this group, the median age of the Texas population increased by 1.3 years, from 28.0 in 1980 to roughly 29.3 years in 1985. This change compares to a change of 1.2 years from 1940 to 1980 and an expected increase of more than five years by the turn of the century.

The Texas population is diverse, with one-third of all Texans being of either black (12 percent in 1980) or Hispanic (21 percent in 1980). Due to substantially higher birth rates, the proportion of Hispanics in the population is expected to increase in the coming years. From 1980 to 1985, for example, the U.S. Bureau of the Census estimates that, although the total population of the state increased by 15.1 percent, the black population increased by 12 percent and the Hispanic population by 23.2 percent. By the year 2000, it is estimated that the Hispanic population will account for at least 26 percent of the total population and blacks for 12 percent, and by the year 2030 Hispanics could account for nearly one-third of the state's population and blacks, Hispanics and other racial/ethnic minorities together for as much as 50 percent of the population.

During the first half of the 1980s, households and families in Texas have continued to display the trends of the 1970s. The average size of households has declined and the number of one- and two-person households has continued to increase. In like manner, the proportion of households consisting of nonfamily households also continued to increase from 1980 to 1985, and the proportion of adult Texans who were single continued to increase. From 1980 to 1985, the average size of households in Texas decreased from 2.82 to 2.76 (a decline of 2.2 percent), the proportion of one- and two-person households increased from 52.5 percent in 1980 to 53.1 percent in 1985, and the percent of all households that were nonfamily

households increased from 25.4 percent in 1980 to 27.1 percent in 1985. Within family households, the proportion of married-couple households continued to decline from 84.0 percent of all family households in 1980 to 81.4 percent of such households in 1985, while male and female householder families both increased as a proportion of family households. The proportion of Texans choosing to remain single or who became single again also continued to increase. Whereas in 1980, 23.9 percent of persons 15 years of age or older have never married and 9.0 percent were separated or divorced, by 1985, 25.8 percent of the population of this age had never married and another 10.6 percent were divorced or separated.

As a result of these household and family patterns, the number of households in the state continued to increase from 4.9 million in 1980 to 5.8 million in 1985. As in the 1970s, when the number of households in Texas increased by 44 percent while the population increased by 27 percent, from 1980 to 1985, the number of households increased more rapidly than the population (by 18.4 percent compared to 15.1 percent for population). Although the aging of the population with its subsequent decline in the rate of new household formation is reducing the rate of household growth relative to population growth, the rate of increase in households continued to outpace the rate of increase in population during the first five years of 1980s. These patterns in the state reflect similar patterns in the nation as a whole.

The Future of Texas' Population Growth

Although the rate of Texas' population growth since 1982 has been relatively slow compared to recent historical patterns, most population analysts see a return to at least moderate rates of population growth during the remainder of this century. Projections of the population of the state made by the Texas Water Development Board indicate a population of between 16.9 and 17.8 million persons by 1990 and between 19.6 and 21.3 million by the year 2000. Annual growth rates of between 0.7 and 1.8 percent through 1990 and 1.6 percent to 2.0 percent from 1990 to 2000 are anticipated.

Similarly, the Texas Department of Health projects a population of 17.6 million by 1990 and 20.3 million by the year 2000 (indicating annual rates of growth of 1.5 percent from 1985 to 2000). Projections by the authors suggest that the state's future rate of growth and total population could vary widely, depending on when the state's economy recovers, but that a population of between 17.7 million and 18.2 million by 1990, and between 20.1 and 21.9 million by the year 2000, seems likely (implying an annual growth rate of between 1.4 and 2.0 percent between 1985 and 2000).

These projections point to a population that is likely to exceed 20 million by the turn of the century, meaning that at least another 3.3 million persons will likely be added between 1986 and 2000 and that the population will increase by nearly another 20 percent between 1986 to 2000. This compares to a projected growth of only 11 percent for the nation as a whole between 1986 and 2000. The long-term future of the Texas' population is thus likely to be one of relatively continuous and rapid growth.

Metropolitan Texas

The federal government, effective June 30, 1983, adopted a three-tier system of defining the geographic units it uses to gather statistics in metropolitan areas in the United States.

The **Metropolitan Statistical Areas (MSA)** are free-standing metropolitan areas composed of one or more counties. **Primary Metropolitan Statistical Areas (PMSA)** are sub-units of a larger classification, **Consolidated Metropolitan Statistical Areas (CMSA)**. CMSAs are metropolitan areas with more than 1 million population and are made up of two or more PMSAs. Texas has five PMSAs, comprising two CMSAs, and 23 MSAs.

Metropolitan Statistical Areas (MSA) In Texas

July 1, 1986
Population

Consolidated Metropolitan Statistical Areas (CMSA):

Dallas-Fort Worth CMSA (Dallas PMSA and Fort Worth-Arlington PMSA)	3,655,300
Houston-Galveston-Brazoria CMSA (Houston PMSA, Galveston-Texas City PMSA and Brazoria PMSA)	3,634,300

Metropolitan Statistical Areas (MSA) and Primary Metropolitan Statistical Areas (PMSA):

Level A — Population 1,000,000 or More

Houston PMSA (Fort Bend, Harris, Liberty, Montgomery and Waller Counties)	3,230,700
Dallas PMSA (Collin, Dallas, Denton, Ellis, Kaufman and Rockwall Counties)	2,401,400
San Antonio MSA (Bexar, Comal and Guadalupe Counties)	1,276,400
Fort Worth-Arlington PMSA (Johnson, Parker and Tarrant Counties)	1,253,900

Level B — Population 250,000 to 1,000,000

Austin MSA (Hays, Travis and Williamson Counties)	726,400
El Paso MSA (El Paso County)	561,500
Beaumont-Port Arthur MSA (Hardin, Jefferson and Orange Counties)	375,800
McAllen-Edinburg-Mission MSA (Hidalgo County)	365,900
Corpus Christi MSA (Nueces and San Patricio Counties)	363,300

Level C — Population 100,000 to 250,000

Brownsville-Harlingen MSA (Cameron County)	257,300
Killeen-Temple MSA (Bell and Coryell Counties)	233,700
Lubbock MSA (Lubbock County)	224,800
Galveston-Texas City PMSA (Galveston County)	214,800
Amarillo MSA (Potter and Randall Counties)	195,200
Brazoria PMSA (Brazoria County)	188,700
Waco MSA (McLennan County)	187,600
Longview-Marshall MSA (Gregg and Harrison Counties)	170,300
Tyler MSA (Smith County)	152,100
Odessa MSA (Ector County)	133,100
Wichita Falls MSA (Wichita County)	127,100
Abilene MSA (Taylor County)	125,900
Bryan-College Station MSA (Brazos County)	120,800
Laredo MSA (Webb County)	120,800
*Texarkana MSA (Bowie County, Tx. and Miller County, Ark.)	119,900
Midland MSA (Midland County)	111,300

Level D — Population Under 100,000

Sherman-Denison MSA (Grayson County)	98,300
San Angelo MSA (Tom Green County)	98,100
Victoria MSA (Victoria County)	76,000

Texas Metropolitan Areas Most Numerous in Nation

Texas leads the nation in the number of metropolitan statistical areas — five primary metropolitan statistical areas and 23 metropolitan statistical areas — with 28. Three of the state's cities, Houston, Dallas and San Antonio, are among the top 10 largest municipalities in the nation.

The state's metropolitan areas, however, do not rank as high as the cities in comparative size with others in the United States. Based on 1986 population estimates, the Dallas-Fort Worth CMSA passed the Houston-Galveston-Brazoria CMSA to rank as the eighth largest in the nation. Houston-Galveston-Brazoria ranked ninth. There was only a difference of 21,000 population between the two CMSAs. The diversified economy of Dallas-Fort Worth was credited with helping the area weather the economic slump that has afflicted Texas. Houston's oil-based economy was hit harder by the drop in world oil prices in 1986.

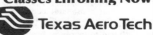

Population of Cities and Towns

Population: Population of **incorporated places** is from the U.S. Census Bureau Estimates of Population of July 1984. Places incorporated before 1980 are printed in lightface capital letters, e.g., "ABBOTT." Places incorporated since 1980 are printed in boldface type, e.g., "**Altoga.**" Population figures for towns incorporated since July 1984 are local estimates.

Population of **unincorporated places** is not enumerated by the Census Bureau; the population figure given here for unincorporated towns is an estimate of the number of persons considered locally as living in that community. The names are printed in lightface type, e.g., "Acton." In some cases we could not obtain a reliable population estimate; these places show "NA" (Not Available) in place of population.

Metropolitan Statistical Area population for 1985 is from U.S. Census Bureau estimates, July 1985.

County Seats: County seats are marked with a section mark (§). If more than one county is listed, the town is the county seat of the first-named county.

Post Offices: Places with post offices are marked with an asterisk (*) e.g., "*Ace."

Banking Towns: Towns with one or more banks as of December 31, 1986, are marked with a dagger (†), e.g., "†ALAMO." (This includes national, state and private banking institutions.) Information from **Federal Reserve Bank,** Dallas.

Number of Business Establishments: The number following the name of the county in the list below indicates the number of rated business establishments in the given town or city, e.g., "Adamsville, Lampasas, 1" means that Adamsville in Lampasas County has one business establishment given a credit rating by **Dun & Bradstreet.**

Location: County in which town is located immediately follows name of town, e.g., "Aberfoyle, Hunt," meaning Aberfoyle in Hunt County. If town is in more than one county, the county names are separated with hyphens.

Town and County—	Pop.
A	
*ABBOTT, Hill, 6	364
Aberfoyle, Hunt	35
*†ABERNATHY, Hale-Lubbock, 49	2,849
Abex, Navarro	NA
§*†ABILENE, Taylor-Jones, 2,400	108,157
1985 metro. pop.	122,200
Ables Springs, Kaufman	NA
Abner, Kaufman	NA
Abram, Hidalgo	NA
Acala, Hudspeth	25
*Ace, Polk	40
*ACKERLY, Dawson-Martin, 5	341
Acme, Hardeman	14
Acton, Hood	450
Acuff, Lubbock	30
Acworth, Red River	52
A & D Acres, Llano	NA
Adams, Lamar	NA
Adams Acres, Montgomery	NA
Adams Gardens, Cameron	200
Adams Hill, Bexar	NA
Adams Oaks, Montgomery	NA
Adams Store, Panola	NA
Adamsville, Lampasas, 1	28
*†Addicks, Harris	150
Addielou, Red River	31
*†ADDISON, Dallas, 251	6,618
Addran, Hopkins	NA
Adell, Parker	NA
*Adkins, Bexar, 45	241
Admiral, Callahan	18
Adobes, Presidio	NA
*ADRIAN, Oldham, 5	216
Advance, Parker	NA
*Afton, Dickens, 4	100
Afton Park, Montgomery	NA
Agnes, Parker	NA
*AGUA DULCE, Nueces, 9	996
Agua Nueva, Jim Hogg	20
Agua Verde, Travis	NA
Aguilares, Webb	10
*Aiken, Floyd	60
Aiken, Shelby	75
Aikin Grove, Red River	26
Air Country Estates, Williamson	NA
Airport City, Bexar	106
Airville, Bell	10
Alabama-Coushatta Indian Res., Polk	603
Alabama Creek, Trinity	20
*†ALAMO, Hidalgo, 98	8,257
Alamo Alto, El Paso	25
Alamo Beach, Calhoun	NA
*ALAMO HEIGHTS, Bexar, 22	6,489
*Alanreed, Gray	60
Alazan, Nacogdoches	NA
*ALBA, Wood-Rains, 15	594
§†ALBANY, Shackelford, 111	2,438
*Albert, Gillespie, 2	25

Town and County—	Pop.
Albion, Red River	50
Alderbranch, Anderson	NA
Aldine, Harris	12,623
*†ALEDO, Parker, 48	1,299
Aleman, Hamilton	60
Alethia, Montgomery	NA
Alexander, Erath	40
Alexanders Store, Shelby	NA
Aley, Henderson	NA
Alfred, Jim Wells	10
Algerita, San Saba	48
Algoa, Galveston	135
§*†ALICE, Jim Wells, 623	22,273
*†Alief, Harris, 12	1,400
Allamoore, Hudspeth	NA
*†ALLEN, Collin, 137	11,226
Allendale, Montgomery	NA
Allenfarm, Brazos	30
Allenhurst, Matagorda	NA
Allen's Chapel, Fannin	41
Allen's Point, Fannin	76
*Alleyton, Colorado, 4	165
*Allison, Wheeler, 4	135
Allison, Wise	NA
Allmon, Floyd	NA
Allred, Yoakum	NA
ALMA, Ellis, 1	213
Almeda, Harris	NA
Almira, Cass	NA
Almont, Bowie	NA
§*†ALPINE, Brewster, 134	6,033
Alpine Village, Travis	NA
Alsa, Van Zandt	30
Alsdorf, Ellis	NA
*Altair, Colorado, 3	30
Altavista, Jim Hogg	NA
*†ALTO, Cherokee, 38	1,209
Alto Bonito, Starr	70
Altoga, Collin	326
*ALTON, Hidalgo	3,726
Alum, Wilson	NA
Alum Creek, Bastrop	NA
*†ALVARADO, Johnson, 84	4,129
*†ALVIN, Brazoria, 556	18,484
*†ALVORD, Wise, 33	923
§*†AMARILLO, Potter-Randall, 3,248	162,863
1985 metro. pop.	192,800
Ambia, Lamar	20
Ambrose, Grayson	41
Ames, Coryell	NA
*AMES, Liberty	1,344
Amherst, Lamar	NA
*†AMHERST, Lamb, 10	847
Amity, Comanche	NA
Ammannsville, Fayette	42
Amphion, Atascosa	NA
Amsterdam, Brazoria	NA
Anadarko, Rusk	NA
*†ANAHUAC, Chambers, 81	1,860
Anchorage, Atascosa	NA
Ander, Goliad	35
§*†Anderson, Grimes, 15	320
Anderson Mill, Williamson	NA
*Andice, Williamson, 2	25

Town and County—	Pop.
§*†ANDREWS, Andrews, 290	13,036
§*†ANGLETON, Brazoria, 275	15,174
ANGUS, Navarro	229
Anhalt, Comal	NA
*†ANNA, Collin, 11	1,078
Annarose, Live Oak	NA
ANNETTA, Parker	247
ANNETTA NORTH, Parker	273
ANNETTA SOUTH, Parker	271
*ANNONA, Red River, 3	439
§*†ANSON, Jones, 49	3,065
*Antelope, Jack, 1	65
*ANTHONY, El Paso, 30	3,129
(On boundary line of El Paso County, TX and Dona Ana County, NM.)	
Anthony, Fannin	10
Anthony Harbor, San Augustine	NA
Antioch, Cass	29
Antioch, Delta	25
Antioch, Madison	20
Antioch, Panola	121
Antioch, Shelby	NA
Antioch, Smith	NA
*†ANTON, Hockley, 14	1,198
Apache Shores, Travis	NA
APPLEBY, Nacogdoches	497
*Apple Springs, Trinity, 9	130
April Sound, Montgomery	NA
*AQUILLA, Hill, 1	169
Arah, Scurry	NA
*†ARANSAS PASS, San Patricio-Aransas-Nueces, 172	8,176
Arbala, Hopkins	41
Arcadia, Shelby	20
§*†ARCHER CITY, Archer, 51	2,052
Arcola, Fort Bend	896
Arden, Irion	1
Argo, Titus	26
*ARGYLE, Denton, 24	1,294
Arizona, Walker	NA
Arkadelphia, Bowie	NA
Arkansas Colony, Baylor	NA
Arlie, Childress	NA
*†ARLINGTON, Tarrant, 4,105	213,832
Fort Worth-Arlington 1985 metro. pop.	1,199,900
Armstrong, Bell	22
*Armstrong, Kenedy	20
Arneckeville, DeWitt	50
Arnett, Coryell	NA
Arnett, Hockley	26
Arney, Castro	NA
*†ARP, Smith, 19	1,045
Arrowhead Lake, Montgomery	NA
Arrowhead Shores, Hood	NA
Arrowhead Village, Comal	NA
Arroyo City, Cameron	NA
*Art, Mason	18

Town and County—	Pop.	Town and County—	Pop.	Town and County—	Pop.
Artesian Lakes Estates, Montgomery	NA	*BARSTOW, Ward, 3	679	Bennett, Parker	85
*Artesia Wells, La Salle, 4	30	*†BARTLETT, Williamson-Bell, 15	1,556	Bennett Estates, Montgomery	NA
*Arthur City, Lamar, 5	200	Bartley Woods, Fannin	30	Benoit, Runnels	NA
Arvana, Dawson	25	Bartons Chapel, Jack	NA	Ben-Roy Bay, Smith	NA
Asa, McLennan	46	BARTONVILLE, Denton	587	Bentonville, Jim Wells	15
Ash, Houston	NA	Barwise, Floyd	30	Bentwood Acres, Grayson	NA
Ashby, Matagorda	NA	Bascom, Smith	NA	*†Ben Wheeler, Van Zandt, 22	400
*ASHERTON, Dimmit, 1	1,609	Bassett, Bowie	373	*Berclair, Goliad, 2	70
Ashland, Upshur	20	§*†BASTROP, Bastrop, 120	4,802	Berea, Houston	NA
Ashmore, Gaines	25	Bastrop Bayou Acres, Brazoria	NA	Berea, Marion	74
Ashtola, Donley	20	Bastrop Beach, Brazoria	NA	*Bergheim, Kendall, 5	22
Ashwood, Matagorda	NA	Bateman, Bastrop	NA	*Bergstrom Air Force Base, Travis	2,945
Asia, Polk	NA	Batesville, Red River	14	Berlin, Washington	NA
§*†ASPERMONT, Stonewall, 37	1,388	*Batesville, Zavala, 12	203	Bernard Acres, Brazoria	NA
Astro Hills, Comal	NA	*Batson, Hardin, 5	140	Bernardo, Colorado	155
*Atascosa, Bexar, 6	300	Battle, McLennan	NA	Berryhill, Shackelford	NA
Ater, Coryell	NA	Bavarian Hills, Bexar	NA	Berry's Creek, Williamson	50
§*†ATHENS, Henderson, 317	10,899	Baxter, Henderson	20	BERRYVILLE, Henderson	740
*†ATLANTA, Cass, 145	6,507	§*†BAY CITY, Matagorda, 398	17,795	*†BERTRAM, Burnet, 19	1,002
Atlas, Lamar	20	Bay Harbor, Galveston	NA	Bess, Duval	20
Atoy, Cherokee	NA	Baylake, Angelina	NA	Bessmay, Jasper	NA
Attoyac, Nacogdoches	NA	Baylor Lake, Childress	27	*Best, Reagan	25
Attoyac Village, Nacogdoches	NA	Bayou Village, Angelina	NA	Bethany, Panola	50
Atwell, Callahan	NA	Bayou Vista, Galveston	1,030	Bethel, Anderson	31
*AUBREY, Denton, 48	1,191	*BAYSIDE, Refugio, 3	383	Bethel, Ellis	NA
Auburn, Ellis	12	Bayside Terrace, Harris	NA	Bethel, Henderson	NA
Augusta, Houston	20	*†BAYTOWN, Harris-Chambers, 815	60,676	Bethel, Runnels	NA
AURORA, Wise	458	*BAYVIEW, Cameron	303	Bethlehem, Upshur	25
§*†AUSTIN, Travis-Williamson, 9,522	397,001	Baywood Estates, Henderson	NA	Bettie, Upshur	110
1985 metro. pop.	695,500	Bazette, Navarro	30	Beulah, Limestone	NA
Austin Lake Estates, Travis	NA	Beach, Montgomery	NA	Beverly Hill, Collin	NA
Austonio, Houston, 1	37	BEACH CITY, Chambers	1,062	Beverly Hills, Bexar	NA
*AUSTWELL, Refugio, 7	276	Beans, Jasper	NA	BEVERLY HILLS, McLennan	2,316
*Avalon, Ellis, 5	130	Bear Creek Oaks, Hays	NA	BEVIL OAKS, Jefferson	1,481
*AVERY, Red River, 4	431	Bear Creek Park, Travis	NA	Bevilport, Jasper	NA
*†AVINGER, Cass, 13	719	Bear Creek Ranch, Montgomery	NA	Beyersville, Williamson	75
*Avoca, Jones, 1	121	*BEASLEY, Fort Bend, 3	539	Biardstown, Lamar	75
*Axtell, McLennan, 9	105	Beattie, Comanche	50	*Big Bend National Park, Brewster, 2	105
*†AZLE, Tarrant-Parker, 185	7,825	Beaukiss, Williamson	20	Bigby Corner, Glasscock	NA
B		§*†BEAUMONT, Jefferson, 2,551	123,356	Big Creek, Burleson	NA
Babyhead, Llano	20	Beaumont-Port Arthur		Big Creek, Franklin	NA
Back, Gray	14	1985 metro. pop.	381,300	*Bigfoot, Frio, 4	75
*†Bacliff, Galveston, 18	4,851	Beaumont Place, Harris	NA	*Biggs Field, El Paso	4,226
Bagby, Fannin	NA	Beaux Art Gardens, Jefferson	NA	Big Hill, Limestone	3
*Bagwell, Red River, 2	150	Beaver Dams, Bowie	NA	§*†BIG LAKE, Reagan, 96	4,001
*BAILEY, Fannin, 1	220	*Bebe, Gonzales	52	Big Oaks, Marion	NA
Baileyboro, Bailey	NA	Beck, Lamb	NA	Big Oaks Estates, Montgomery	NA
BAILEY'S PRAIRIE, Brazoria	410	Becker, Kaufman	NA	*†BIG SANDY, Upshur, 28	1,809
Baileyville, Milam	45	*†BECKVILLE, Panola, 18	1,026	§*†BIG SPRING, Howard, 542	27,459
Bainer, Lamb	NA	Becton, Lubbock	125	Big Square, Castro	NA
Bainville, Karnes	NA	*†BEDFORD, Tarrant, 381	31,029	Big Thicket, Liberty	NA
§*†BAIRD, Callahan, 16	1,737	*†Bedias, Grimes, 6	301	Big Thicket Lake Estates, Polk	NA
Baker, Floyd	NA	Bee Cave, Travis	50	Big Valley, Mills	35
Bakersfield, Pecos	30	Beechwood, Sabine	NA	Big Valley Ranchettes, Coryell	NA
Balboa Acres, Hidalgo	NA	*Bee House, Coryell	40	*BIG WELLS, Dimmit, 3	938
*†BALCH SPRINGS, Dallas	17,077	§*†BEEVILLE, Bee, 233	15,977	Bila Hora, Lavaca	NA
BALCONES HEIGHTS, Bexar	2,934	Beeville Naval Air Station, Bee	1,250	Biloxi, Newton	NA
Balcones Village, Travis-Williamson	NA	Behrnville, Williamson	30	Birch, Burleson	NA
Bald Hill, Angelina	NA	Belcherville, Montague	34	Birch Creek, Burleson	NA
Bald Prairie, Robertson	31	Belfalls, Bell	20	*Birome, Hill	31
Baldwin, Harrison	NA	Belgrade, Newton	NA	Birthright, Hopkins	40
§*†BALLINGER, Runnels, 106	4,536	Belk, Lamar	55	Biry, Medina	NA
*BALMORHEA, Reeves, 4	528	*†BELLAIRE, Harris, 438	14,826	*†BISHOP, Nueces, 32	3,879
Balsora, Wise	50	Bell Branch, Ellis	NA	Bishop Hills, Potter	250
Bammel, Harris	NA	*BELLEVUE, Clay, 12	378	*Bivins, Cass, 4	105
§*†BANDERA, Bandera, 70	1,012	*BELLMEAD, McLennan, 23	8,025	Bivouac Estates, Kerr	NA
Bandera Falls, Bandera	NA	*†BELLS, Grayson, 14	1,014	*Black, Parmer, 1	100
*†BANGS, Brown, 25	1,869	§*†BELLVILLE, Austin, 137	3,461	Black Flat, Archer	NA
Bankersmith, Kendall	NA	Belmena, Milam	15	Blackfoot, Anderson	33
*Banquete, Nueces, 6	449	*Belmont, Gonzales, 2	60	Black Hill, Atascosa	NA
Barbarosa, Guadalupe	25	Belott, Houston	NA	Black Hills, Navarro	NA
Barclay, Falls	72	§*†BELTON, Bell, 221	11,904	Black Jack, Cherokee	47
*BARDWELL, Ellis, 3	348	*Ben Arnold, Milam, 1	148	Black Jack, Robertson	NA
*Barker, Harris, 11	160	*BENAVIDES, Duval, 14	2,005	Blackjack, Smith	NA
*Barksdale, Edwards, 6	617	*Ben Bolt, Jim Wells, 3	110	Blackland, Rockwall	49
Barnes, Polk	NA	*†BENBROOK, Tarrant	16,960	Black Oak, Hopkins	NA
Barnes Switch, Trinity	15	(Businesses included in Fort Worth count.)		*BLACKWELL, Nolan-Coke, 5	307
*Barnhart, Irion	135	Benchley, Robertson	110	Blair, Taylor	25
*Barnum, Polk, 2	29	*Bend, San Saba, 1	115	Blanchard, Polk	50
*Barrett, Harris	2,750	*Ben Franklin, Delta, 2	75	*†BLANCO, Blanco, 42	1,353
*BARRY, Navarro, 1	196	Ben Hur, Limestone	100	Blanconia, Bee	15
		§*BENJAMIN, Knox, 1	237	Bland Lake, San Augustine	25
				*BLANKET, Brown, 5	388
				Blanton, Hill	NA

Town and County—	Pop.	Town and County—	Pop.	Town and County—	Pop.
Bieakwood, Newton.	300	Bradshaw, Taylor	61	Broyles Chapel, Anderson	NA
*Bledsoe, Cochran, 4	125	§*†BRADY, McCulloch, 142	5,925	*BRUCEVILLE-EDDY,	
*Bleiblerville, Austin, 2	71	*Brady, Shelby	NA	McLennan-Falls, 6	1,132
*Blessing, Matagorda, 12.	571	Branch, Collin	447	(Bruceville and Eddy share	
Blevins, Falls	36	Branchville, Milam	200	city government.)	
Blewett, Uvalde	25	*Brandon, Hill	80	Brundage, Dimmit	50
Block House, Williamson	NA	Brangus Ranch, Williamson.	NA	*Bruni, Webb, 12	698
Blodgett, Titus	NA	Branom, Hopkins	NA	Brunswick, Cherokee	50
*†BLOOMBURG, Cass, 3	387	*Brashear, Hopkins, 1	280	Brushie Prairie, Navarro.	NA
Bloomdale, Collin	NA	*†BRAZORIA, Brazoria, 83.	3,349	Brushy, Hood	NA
*†BLOOMING GROVE,		1985 metro. pop.	188,200	Brushy Bend Park, Williamson	NA
Navarro, 8	854	Brazos, Palo Pinto	47	Brushy Creek, Anderson	50
*Bloomington, Victoria, 3	1,864	Brazos Country, Austin	NA	Brushy Creek, Brazos	NA
*BLOSSOM, Lamar, 9	1,737	Brazos Point, Bosque.	NA	Brushy Creek, Williamson	NA
Blowout, Blanco	NA	Brazosport, Brazoria	53,046	Brushy Creek North,	
Blue, Lee	50	(This is the group city name		Williamson	NA
Blueberry Hill, Montgomery	NA	applied to the industrial and		§*†BRYAN, Brazos, 1,091	58,991
*Bluegrove, Clay, 1	125	port area including Freeport,		Bryan-College Station	
Blue Haven Estates, Hunt	NA	Clute, Quintana, Richwood,		1985 metro. pop.	119,500
Blue Hills Estates, Travis.	NA	Brazoria, Lake Jackson, Jones		Bryan Beach, Brazoria	NA
Blue Lake Estates, Llano.	300	Creek, Oyster Creek and		Bryans Mill, Cass	71
BLUE MOUND, Tarrant	2,670	Surfside and having a joint		Bryarly, Red River	5
Blue Mountain, Mason	NA	Brazosport Independent School		Bryce, Rusk	NA
*BLUE RIDGE, Collin, 5.	551	District and joint Brazosport		Bryden, Moore	NA
Blue Ridge, Falls.	NA	Chamber of Commerce.)		*†BRYSON, Jack, 7	690
Bluetown, Cameron	40	Breakaway Park, Williamson	NA	*†Buchanan Dam, Llano, 21	1,011
Bluett, Wise	NA	§*†BRECKENRIDGE, Stephens,		Buchanan Lake Village, Llano.	NA
*Bluff Dale, Erath, 1	123	301.	7,429	Buchel, DeWitt	NA
Bluff Springs, Travis.	50	*†BREMOND, Robertson, 14 .	1,244	Buck, Polk	NA
*Bluffton, Llano, 1.	75	§*†BRENHAM, Washington,		Buck Creek, Cottle	69
*BLUM, Hill, 21	373	465.	12,796	Buckeye, Matagorda.	25
Bluntzer, Nueces.	150	Breslau, Lavaca	65	Buck Hills, Montgomery	NA
Boardhouse, Blanco	NA	Briar, Tarrant-Wise-Parker.	1,810	*†BUCKHOLTS, Milam, 6	429
Bobo, Shelby	NA	Briarcliff, Travis-Hays.	129	Buckhorn, Austin	20
Bob Town, Jack.	NA	BRIAROAKS, Johnson.	628	Buckhorn, Newton	NA
Boddle, Grayson	NA	Briarwick, Bexar	NA	BUCKINGHAM, Dallas	188
§*†BOERNE, Kendall, 248	4,396	Brice, Hall	37	Buckner, Parker	NA
*†BOGATA, Red River, 9	1,596	*†BRIDGE CITY, Orange,		*†BUDA, Hays, 81	954
Bois d'Arc, Anderson.	NA	106.	7,818	Buell Park, Williamson	NA
Bois d'Arc, Rains.	10	*†BRIDGEPORT, Wise, 153	3,997	Buena Vista, Bexar	NA
Bold Springs, Polk.	100	Bridges Chapel, Titus	NA	Buena Vista, Burnet	NA
Boldtville, Bexar	NA	Brierwood Bay, Henderson	NA	Buena Vista, Cameron.	NA
*†Boling, Wharton, 17	720	*Briggs, Burnet, 1	92	*†BUFFALO, Leon, 61	1,921
Bolivar, Denton	40	Bright Star, Rains	75	*BUFFALO GAP, Taylor, 10.	506
*Bomarton, Baylor	23	Brinker, Hopkins	NA	Buffalo Gap, Travis.	NA
*Bonanza, Hill	NA	Brinwood Shores, Hunt	NA	Buffalo Mop, Limestone	NA
Bonanza, Hopkins	26	*Briscoe, Wheeler, 4	135	Buffalo Springs, Clay.	51
Bonanza Beach, Burnet	NA	Bristol, Ellis	94	Buford, El Paso	NA
Bonanza Beach Estates,		Britton, Ellis.	30	Buford, Mitchell	25
Henderson	NA	*BROADDUS, San Augustine,		Bugbee Heights, Hutchinson	75
§*†BONHAM, Fannin, 116	7,203	6	245	Bug Tussle, Fannin	15
Bonita, Montague	15	Broadway, Crosby.	NA	*Bula, Bailey, 5	105
Bonnerville, Freestone	NA	Broadway, Lamar.	25	Bulcher, Cooke	NA
BONNEY, Brazoria	99	Broadway Junction, Lamar.	NA	*†BULLARD, Smith-	
Bonnie View, Refugio	25	Brock, Parker	51	Cherokee, 22	887
Bono, Johnson	NA	Brock Junction, Parker.	NA	Bull Run, Newton	NA
Bonus, Wharton	42	Brogado, Reeves.	122	*Bulverde, Comal	25
*Bon Wier, Newton, 6.	475	Bronco, Yoakum	30	Bulverde Estates, Comal	NA
*BOOKER, Lipscomb-		*BRONSON, Sabine, 4	292	Bulverde Hills, Comal	NA
Ochiltree, 48.	1,506	*†BRONTE, Coke, 13	1,083	*†Buna, Jasper, 61.	1,669
Boonsville, Wise	52	*Brookeland, Sabine, 6	220	Buncombe, Panola	87
*Booth, Fort Bend, 2	60	*Brookesmith, Brown, 5.	61	Bunger, Young	26
Bootleg, Deaf Smith	NA	Brook Forest, Montgomery	NA	BUNKER HILL, Harris	3,668
Borden, Colorado	NA	Brooks, Panola	40	Bunker Hill, Jasper	NA
*†BORGER, Hutchinson,		*Brooks Air Force Base, Bexar	720	Bunker Hill, Lamar	NA
454.	17,236	Brookshier, Runnels	NA	Bunns Bluff, Orange	NA
Bosqueville, McLennan.	72	*BROOKSHIRE, Waller, 101.	2,993	Bunyan, Erath	20
§*Boston, Bowie, 1.	200	BROOKSIDE VILLAGE,		*†BURKBURNETT, Wichita,	
Boudreaux Estates, Harris	NA	Brazoria	1,538	125.	11,025
*†BOVINA, Parmer, 19	1,580	*Brookston, Lamar, 3	70	BURKE, Angelina	319
Bowers, Polk.	NA	Broom City, Anderson	NA	*Burkett, Coleman, 3	30
Bowers City, Gray.	26	Broome, Panola	21	*Burkeville, Newton, 3.	515
*†BOWIE, Montague, 160.	5,818	Brown Chapel, Navarro.	NA	Burleigh, Austin	69
Bowser, San Saba	NA	Brown College, Washington.	NA	*†BURLESON, Johnson-	
Box Church, Limestone	45	BROWNDELL, Jasper.	235	Tarrant, 326.	14,597
Boxelder, Red River	258	§*†BROWNFIELD, Terry,		*Burlington, Milam, 2	140
Boxwood, Upshur	NA	187.	10,846	§*†BURNET, Burnet, 141.	3,794
Boyce, Ellis.	75	Browning, Smith	25	Burns, Bowie	NA
Boyd, Fannin	40	Brownsboro, Caldwell	NA	Burns City, Cooke	61
*†BOYD, Wise, 41	1,090	*†BROWNSBORO, Henderson,		Burrantown, Houston	NA
*Boys' Ranch, Oldham.	435	11.	710	Burroughsville, Victoria	NA
Boz, Ellis.	15	§*†BROWNSVILLE, Cameron,		Burrow, Hunt	NA
Bozar, Mills	NA	1,254.	94,677	*†BURTON, Washington, 16.	365
Brachfield, Rusk	30	Brownsville-Harlingen		Busby, Fisher	12
Bracken, Comal	76	1985 metro. pop.	249,800	*Bushland, Potter, 6	130
§*†BRACKETTVILLE, Kinney,		§*†BROWNWOOD, Brown,		Bushwhacker Peninsula,	
23.	1,816	494.	19,761	Henderson	NA
Brad, Palo Pinto	26			Bustamante, Zapata	25
Bradford, Anderson	22			Busterville, Hockley	NA

Town and County—	Pop.
Butler, Bastrop	NA
Butler, Freestone	67
*†BYERS, Clay, 12	620
*BYNUM, Hill, 1	298
Byrd, Ellis	15
Byrds, Brown	NA
Byrdtown, Lamar	NA
C	
Cabot Kingsmill, Gray	62
*CACTUS, Moore, 11	1,041
Caddell Cove, San Augustine	NA
*Caddo, Stephens, 3	40
Caddo Camp, Hunt	NA
Caddo Lake Estates, Marion	NA
*†CADDO MILLS, Hunt, 16	1,302
Cade Chapel, Navarro	NA
Cade Lake, Burleson	NA
Cadiz, Bee	15
Cain City, Gillespie	NA
Calaveras, Wilson	100
§*†CALDWELL, Burleson, 157	3,605
Caledonia, Rusk	NA
Calf Creek, McCulloch	23
Calina, Limestone	NA
*Call, Jasper-Newton, 5	170
*Calliham, McMullen	90
CALLISBURG, Cooke	329
Call Junction, Jasper	50
*†CALVERT, Robertson, 16	1,715
Cambridge Shores, Grayson	NA
*Camden, Polk, 2	1,200
Camelot, Travis	NA
§*†CAMERON, Milam, 105	5,817
Camilla, San Jacinto	70
Camp Air, Mason	15
*CAMPBELL, Hunt, 14	616
*Campbellton, Atascosa, 3	275
Camp Creek Lake, Robertson	241
Camp Dale Robertson, Marion	NA
Campo Alto, Hidalgo	NA
Camp Ruby, Polk	35
Camp San Saba, McCulloch	36
Camp Scenic, Kerr	NA
Camp Seale, Polk	NA
Camp Springs, Scurry	10
Camp Swift, Bastrop	NA
Camp Switch, Gregg	70
Campti, Shelby	NA
*Camp Verde, Kerr, 1	41
*CAMP WOOD, Real, 12	806
Camp Worth, San Augustine	NA
Canada Verde, Wilson	123
§*†CANADIAN, Hemphill, 110	4,098
Canal City, Galveston	NA
Canary, Leon	NA
Candelaria, Presidio	55
Caney, Matagorda	296
CANEY CITY, Henderson	372
Caney Creek, Henderson	NA
Caney Creek Estates, Matagorda	NA
Caney Creek Estates, Montgomery	NA
Cannon, Grayson	75
Canterbury Estates, Smith	NA
§*†CANTON, Van Zandt, 93	2,975
Cantu, Hidalgo	NA
*Canutillo, El Paso, 38	1,800
Canyon, Lubbock	40
§*†CANYON, Randall, 147	11,153
Canyon City, Comal	100
Canyon Creek Estates, Comal	NA
*†Canyon Lake, Comal	100
Canyon Lake Acres, Comal	NA
Canyon Lake Estates, Comal	NA
Canyon Lake Forest, Comal	NA
Canyon Lake Hills, Comal	NA
Canyon Lake Island, Comal	NA
Canyon Lake Mobile Home Est., Comal	NA
Canyon Lake Shores, Comal	NA
Canyon Lake Village, Comal	NA
Canyon Lake Village West, Comal	NA
Canyon Park Estates, Comal	NA
Canyon Springs Resort, Comal	NA
Canyon Valley, Crosby	NA
Canyon View Acres, Comal	NA

Town and County—	Pop.
Cape Conroe, Montgomery	NA
Cape Malibu, Montgomery	NA
Cape Tranquility, Henderson	NA
Capitola, Fisher	NA
Caplen, Galveston	30
Capps Addition, Montgomery	NA
Capps Corner, Montague	NA
Cap Rock, Crosby	NA
Caps, Taylor	100
Cara Blanca, Baylor	NA
Caradan, Mills	20
Carancahua, Jackson	NA
*CARBON, Eastland, 5	269
Carbondale, Bowie	30
Cardinal Hills, Travis	NA
*Carey, Childress	60
Carl, Travis	NA
Carlisle, Rusk	161
Carlisle, Trinity	95
Carlos, Grimes	NA
*Carlsbad, Tom Green, 3	100
Carl's Corner, Hill	230
Carlson, Travis	61
*Carlton, Hamilton, 3	70
*†CARMINE, Fayette, 8	294
Carmona, Polk	50
Caro, Nacogdoches	113
Carpenter, Wilson	NA
Carpenters Bluff, Grayson	NA
Carriage Hills, Montgomery	NA
Carricitos, Cameron	25
Carrizo Creek Estates, Nacogdoches	NA
§*†CARRIZO SPRINGS, Dimmit, 109	7,553
Carroll, Smith	60
Carroll Springs, Anderson	NA
*†CARROLLTON, Dallas-Denton-Collin, 1,349	53,621
Carson, Fannin	22
*Carswell Air Force Base, Tarrant	3,162
*Carta Valley, Edwards	20
Carter Lake, Brazos	NA
Carterville, Cass	25
Carterville, Harrison	NA
§*†CARTHAGE, Panola, 177	6,963
Cartwright, Kaufman	NA
Cartwright, Wood	61
Carver, Leon	NA
Carver Park, Bexar	NA
Casa Piedra, Presidio	21
Casey, El Paso	115
Cash, Hunt	56
*Cason, Morris, 4	173
Cass, Cass	NA
Cassie, Burnet	NA
Cassin, Bexar	NA
*Castell, Llano, 1	72
†CASTLE HILLS, Bexar	5,312
Castle Terrace, Burnet	NA
Castlewood Forest, Travis	NA
*†CASTROVILLE, Medina, 33	2,037
*Catarina, Dimmit, 3	45
*Cat Spring, Austin, 2	76
Causeway Beach, Henderson	NA
Cavazos, Cameron	NA
Cave Creek, Gillespie	NA
Caviness, Lamar	80
Cawthon, Brazos	75
Cayote, Bosque	NA
*Cayuga, Anderson, 2	56
Cedar Bay, Smith	NA
Cedar Bayou, Harris-Chambers	1,287
Cedar Branch Park, Henderson	NA
Cedar Creek, Anderson	NA
*Cedar Creek, Bastrop, 13	145
Cedar Creek, Waller	NA
Cedar Creek Park, Hill	NA
*†CEDAR HILL, Dallas-Ellis, 170	9,667
Cedar Hill, Floyd	NA
Cedar Lake, Matagorda	148
*Cedar Lane, Matagorda	85
Cedar Mills, Grayson	NA
*†CEDAR PARK, Williamson, 166	4,915

Town and County—	Pop.
Cedar Point, Llano	NA
Cedar Shores Estates, Bosque	170
Cedar Springs, Falls	90
Cedar Springs, Upshur	NA
Cedarvale, Kaufman	NA
Cedar Valley, Bell	4
Cedar Valley, Travis	70
*Cee Vee, Cottle, 1	71
Cego, Falls	98
Cele, Travis	NA
*†CELESTE, Hunt, 1	863
*†CELINA, Collin, 30	1,667
Celotex, Fisher	NA
Centennial, Coleman	NA
Center, Fisher	NA
Center, Limestone	76
§*†CENTER, Shelby, 213	5,839
Center City, Mills	15
Center Grove, Franklin	NA
Center Grove, Houston	NA
Center Grove, Titus	NA
Center Hill, Houston	NA
Center Line, Burleson	NA
Center Mill, Hood	NA
Center Plains, Swisher	NA
Center Point, Camp	NA
Center Point, Ellis	NA
Centerpoint, Hays	NA
Center Point, Howard	NA
Center Point, Hunt	NA
*Center Point, Kerr, 14	623
Center Point, Panola	NA
Center Point, Upshur	NA
Centerview, Leon	NA
§*†CENTERVILLE, Leon, 31	854
Centerville, Trinity	40
Center Vine, Morris	NA
Central, Angelina	105
Central Gardens, Jefferson	NA
Central Heights, Nacogdoches	NA
Central High, Cherokee	NA
*Centralia, Trinity	26
Cestohowa, Karnes	110
Chaille, Grimes	20
*Chalk, Cottle	45
Chalk Bluff Estates, McLennan	NA
Chalk Hill, Rusk	NA
Chalk Mountain, Erath	25
Chambersville, Collin	40
Chambliss, Collin	25
Champion, Nolan	16
Chances Store, Burleson	NA
*†CHANDLER, Henderson, 40	1,679
Chaney, Eastland	35
*†Channelview, Harris, 246	8,227
§*CHANNING, Hartley, 6	280
Chaparral Estates, Liberty	NA
Chapel Hill, Smith	NA
Chapman, Rusk	20
Chapman Lakeside, San Augustine	NA
*Chapman Ranch, Nueces, 3	100
Chapparal Park, Hays	NA
Chappel, San Saba	25
*†Chappell Hill, Washington, 12	310
Charco, Goliad	68
Charleston, Delta	120
Charlie, Clay	65
*†CHARLOTTE, Atascosa, 20	1,604
CHATEAU WOODS, Montgomery	555
*Chatfield, Navarro, 1	40
Chatt, Hill	NA
*Cheapside, Gonzales	31
Cheek, Jefferson	62
Cheneyboro, Navarro	NA
*Cherokee, San Saba, 7	175
Cherokee Club Estates, Cherokee	NA
Cherokee Cove, Hunt	NA
Cherokee Hill, Smith	NA
Cherry Spring, Gillespie	75
*†CHESTER, Tyler, 6	409
Chesterville, Colorado	NA
*†CHICO, Wise, 29	1,156
*Chicota, Lamar	125

Town and County—	Pop.
Chihuahua, Hidalgo	NA
Chihuahua Farm, Zapata	NA
§*†CHILDRESS, Childress, 137	5,510
*†CHILLICOTHE, Hardeman, 15	1,045
*†Chilton, Falls, 10	310
*CHINA, Jefferson, 15	1,397
CHINA GROVE, Bexar	565
China Grove, Scurry	15
*China Spring, McLennan, 11	181
Chinati, Presidio	NA
Chinquapin, Matagorda	NA
*†CHIRENO, Nacogdoches, 4	422
Chisholm, Rockwall (See McLendon-Chisholm)	
Chita, Trinity	75
Choate, Karnes	NA
Chocolate Bayou, Brazoria	60
Choice, Shelby	21
*Chriesman, Burleson, 1	30
*CHRISTINE, Atascosa, 1	381
*Christoval, Tom Green, 6	216
C.H. Rouse Estates, Montgomery	NA
Church Hill, Rusk	15
Churchill Bridge, Brazoria	NA
*†CIBOLO, Guadalupe, 35	657
Cipres, Hidalgo	20
Circle, Cherokee	NA
Circle, Lamb	NA
Circleback, Bailey	10
Circleville, Travis	NA
Circleville, Williamson	42
*CISCO, Eastland, 97	4,676
Cistern, Fayette	75
Citrus City, Hidalgo	NA
Citrus Grove, Matagorda	NA
Clairemont, Kent	15
Clairette, Erath	55
Clara, Wichita	100
Clardy, Lamar	NA
§*†CLARENDON, Donley, 51	2,316
Clareville, Bee	23
Clark, Liberty	NA
Clark, Victoria	NA
Clarkson, Milam	10
§*†CLARKSVILLE, Red River, 107	4,787
CLARKSVILLE CITY, Gregg-Upshur	542
§*†CLAUDE, Armstrong, 16	1,077
Clauene, Hockley	24
Clawson, Angelina	195
*Clay, Burleson, 1	61
Clays Corner, Parmer	NA
*Clayton, Panola, 1	79
Claytonville, Fisher	21
Claytonville, Swisher	116
Clear Creek, Burnet	NA
Clear Creek, Henderson	NA
Clear Creek Forest, Montgomery	NA
Clear Lake, Collin	50
Clear Lake City, Harris (Annexed by Houston)	
CLEAR LAKE SHORES, Galveston	880
Clear Springs, Guadalupe	60
Clearview Estates, Henderson	NA
Clearview Point, Henderson	NA
Clearwater, Franklin	NA
Clear Water Bay, Henderson	NA
Clear Water Cove, San Patricio	NA
§*†CLEBURNE, Johnson, 429	21,413
Clegg, Live Oak	25
Clemons, Waller	NA
*Clemville, Matagorda	54
Cleo, Kimble	3
Cleveland, Austin	78
*†CLEVELAND, Liberty, 219	6,691
Cliffside, Potter	206
*†CLIFTON, Bosque, 106	3,215
Clifton, Van Zandt	NA
Climax, Collin	40
Cline, Uvalde	10
*CLINT, El Paso, 21	1,703
Clinton, Hunt	NA

Town and County—	Pop.
Clopton, Franklin	15
Close City, Garza	107
Cloverleaf, Harris	NA
Club Lake, Collingsworth	NA
Club Lakeview, Waller	NA
*†CLUTE, Brazoria, 231	9,554
*†CLYDE, Callahan, 45	3,053
*†COAHOMA, Howard, 24	1,168
Cobb, Archer	NA
Cobbs, Kaufman	NA
Coble, Hockley	NA
Cochran, Austin	116
*COCKRELL HILL, Dallas	3,748
COFFEE CITY, Henderson	295
Coffeeville, Upshur	50
Cofferville, Lamb	NA
Coit, Limestone	NA
Coke, Wood	105
§*†COLDSPRING, San Jacinto, 30	704
Cold Springs, Coryell	NA
Coldwater, Dallam	NA
§*†COLEMAN, Coleman, 123	6,070
Coleman Cove, San Augustine	NA
Colfax, Van Zandt	35
Colita, Polk	NA
College Hill, Bowie	116
College Mound, Kaufman	350
*Collegeport, Matagorda, 1	91
*†COLLEGE STATION, Brazos, 698	45,756
Bryan-College Station 1985 metro. pop.	119,500
*†COLLEYVILLE, Tarrant, 154	8,032
*†COLLINSVILLE, Grayson, 16	911
*†COLMESNEIL, Tyler, 14	607
Cologne, Goliad	85
Colony, Fayette	NA
Colony, Rains	70
Colorado, Jim Hogg	23
§*†COLORADO CITY, Mitchell, 122	5,549
Colorado River Ranchettes, Travis	NA
Colquitt, Kaufman	NA
Coltexo, Gray	5
Coltharp, Houston	NA
Colton, Travis	50
Columbia Lakes, Brazoria	NA
§*†COLUMBUS, Colorado, 123	4,250
Comal, Comal	40
Comal Hills, Comal	NA
§*†COMANCHE, Comanche, 111	4,151
Comanche Cove, Hood	560
Comanche Harbor, Hood	250
Comanche Pass, Travis	NA
Comanche Rancheros, Llano	NA
*COMBES, Cameron, 10	1,894
COMBINE, Kaufman-Dallas	815
Cometa, Zavala	NA
*†Comfort, Kendall, 32	1,460
*†COMMERCE, Hunt, 122	7,716
*COMO, Hopkins, 13	625
Compton, Rusk	NA
*Comstock, Val Verde, 1	375
Comyn, Comanche	27
*Concan, Uvalde, 5	71
*Concepcion, Duval, 1	25
Concho, Concho	NA
Concord, Cherokee	NA
Concord, Hunt	30
Concord, Johnson	NA
*Concord, Leon	28
Concord, Liberty	26
Concord, Madison	50
Concord, Rusk	23
Concordia, Nueces	NA
Concrete, DeWitt	46
*Cone, Crosby	110
Conlen, Dallam	61
Connor, Madison	50
§*†CONROE, Montgomery, 1,390	18,943
Conroe Bay, Montgomery	NA
Content, Bell	25

Town and County—	Pop.
*†CONVERSE, Bexar, 79	7,690
Conway, Carson	50
Cooks Point, Burleson	60
Cooks Store, Anderson	NA
*Cookville, Titus, 4	105
COOL, Parker	236
Cool Crest, Bexar	NA
*†COOLIDGE, Limestone, 11	864
Coon Creek, Bosque	NA
§*†COOPER, Delta, 23	2,397
Cooper, Houston	NA
Copano Village, Aransas	210
Copeland, Montgomery	NA
Copeland, Smith	NA
Copeland Creek, Marion	NA
*Copeville, Collin, 7	106
*†COPPELL, Dallas-Denton, 83	6,172
*†COPPERAS COVE, Coryell-Lampasas, 135	21,070
COPPER CANYON, Denton	612
Corbet, Navarro	80
Cordele, Jackson	74
CORINTH, Denton	1,696
Corinth, Jones	25
Corinth, Leon	NA
Corinthian Point, Montgomery	NA
Corley, Bowie	35
Cornersville, Hopkins	NA
Cornett, Cass	30
Corn Hill, Williamson	NA
Cornudas, Hudspeth	NA
§*†CORPUS CHRISTI, Nueces-San Patricio-Kleberg, 4,559	258,067
1985 metro. pop.	358,800
Corpus Christi Naval Air Station, Nueces	500
CORRAL CITY, Denton	108
*†CORRIGAN, Polk, 30	1,970
Corry, Lamb	NA
§*†CORSICANA, Navarro, 524	23,449
Coryell City, Coryell	125
*Cost, Gonzales, 5	62
Cotton Center, Fannin, 8	5
*Cotton Center, Hale, 9	205
Cottondale, Wise	NA
Cotton Flat, Midland	NA
Cotton Gin, Freestone	28
Cotton Patch, DeWitt	NA
Cottonwood, Brazos	NA
Cottonwood, Callahan	65
Cottonwood, Erath	23
Cottonwood, Kaufman	200
Cottonwood, McLennan	NA
Cottonwood, Madison	40
Cottonwood, Somervell	24
Cottonwood-Concord, Freestone	61
Cottonwood Shores, Burnet	NA
§*†COTULLA, La Salle, 51	4,305
Couch, Karnes	NA
Coughran, Atascosa	NA
Council Creek Village, Burnet	NA
Country Campus, Walker	60
Country Colony, Montgomery	NA
Country Estates, Hays	NA
Country Manor Estates, Smith	NA
Country Pines, Montgomery	NA
Country Place, Smith	NA
Country Place Acres, Montgomery	NA
Country Squire Estates, Orange	NA
County Glen, Williamson	NA
County Line, Hale	30
County Line, Lubbock	30
County Line, Rains	40
County Living, Williamson	NA
*†Coupland, Williamson, 6	135
Courtney, Grimes	55
COVE, Chambers	627
Cove Springs, Cherokee	NA
*COVINGTON, Hill, 1	270
Cow Creek, Erath	14
Cox, Upshur	NA
Coxville, Travis	NA
*Coyanosa, Pecos, 1	270
*Coy City, Karnes	30

Town and County—	Pop.
Crabb, Fort Bend	125
Crabbs Prairie, Walker	NA
Craft, Cherokee	21
Crafton, Wise	20
Craig, Rusk	NA
*†CRANDALL, Kaufman, 15	1,207
§*†CRANE, Crane, 81	4,143
Cranes Mill, Comal	NA
*†CRANFILLS GAP, Bosque, 9	386
*CRAWFORD, McLennan, 10	638
Creath, Houston	NA
Crecy, Trinity	NA
Creechville, Ellis	NA
*CREEDMOOR, Travis, 3	261
Creekmore Village, Liberty-Polk	NA
Creekwood Addition, Montgomery	NA
Crenneland, Galveston	NA
Crescent Heights, Henderson	NA
Crescent Oaks Beach Estates, Denton	NA
*Cresson, Hood-Johnson, 8	208
Crestonia, Duval	NA
Crestwood, Llano	NA
Crestwood, Marion	NA
Crestwood Acres, Bexar	NA
Crestwood Farms, Montgomery	NA
Crete, Trinity	NA
Crews, Runnels	NA
Crims Chapel, Rusk	NA
Cripple Creek Farms, Montgomery	NA
Cripple Creek Farms West, Montgomery	NA
Cripple Creek North, Montgomery	NA
Crisp, Ellis	90
§*†CROCKETT, Houston, 206	7,550
*†Crosby, Harris, 140	2,500
§*†CROSBYTON, Crosby, 44	2,234
Cross, Grimes	49
Cross, McMullen	50
*†CROSS PLAINS, Callahan, 27	1,201
Crossroads, Cass	NA
Cross Roads, Comanche	NA
Crossroads, Delta	10
CROSS ROADS, Denton	390
Crossroads, Harrison	NA
Cross Roads, Henderson	135
Crossroads, Hopkins	NA
Crossroads, Jackson	NA
Cross Roads, Milam	35
Cross Roads, Rusk	NA
Crow, Wood	25
§*†CROWELL, Foard, 25	1,355
*†CROWLEY, Tarrant, 106	7,001
Crown, Atascosa	NA
Cruz Calle, Duval	NA
Cryer Creek, Navarro	15
*†Crystal Beach, Galveston	1,069
§*†CRYSTAL CITY, Zavala, 63	8,496
Crystal Creek Forest, Montgomery	NA
Crystal Falls, Stephens	10
Crystal Forest, Montgomery	NA
Crystal Lake, Anderson	NA
Crystal Lake Estates, Polk	NA
Crystal Lake Park, Montgomery	NA
Cuadrilla, El Paso	40
Cuba, Johnson	NA
§*†CUERO, DeWitt, 130	7,576
Cuevitas, Hidalgo	NA
Cuevitas, Jim Hogg	12
Culebra, Bexar	NA
Culleoka, Collin	NA
Cumberland Estates, Smith	NA
Cumberland Ridge, Smith	NA
*CUMBY, Hopkins, 13	691
Cundiff, Jack	45
*Cuney, Cherokee, 1	191
*Cunningham, Lamar, 2	110
Currie, Navarro	25
Curtis, Jasper	NA
*†CUSHING, Nacogdoches, 23	581

Town and County—	Pop.
Cusseta, Cass	30
*CUT AND SHOOT, Montgomery	678
Cuthand, Red River	116
Cuthbert, Mitchell	NA
Cyclone, Bell	45
Cypress, Franklin	20
*†Cypress, Harris, 174	260
Cypress Bend, Montgomery	NA
Cypress Cove, Comal	NA
Cypress Creek, Kerr	200
Cypress Creek Acres, Hays	NA
Cypress Gardens, Comal	NA
*Cypress Mill, Blanco	56
Cyril, Rusk	NA

D

Town and County—	Pop.
Dabney, Uvalde	30
Dacosta, Victoria	89
Dacus, Montgomery	161
Dads Corner, Archer	NA
Daffan, Travis	NA
§*†DAINGERFIELD, Morris, 77	3,008
*DAISETTA, Liberty, 15	1,252
Dalby Springs, Bowie	141
*Dale, Caldwell, 6	126
§*†DALHART, Dallam-Hartley, 190	6,930
*Dallardsville, Polk	350
§*†DALLAS, Dallas-Collin-Denton-Kaufman, 26,621	974,239
Dallas-Fort Worth 1985 CMSA pop.	3,511,600
Dalton, Cass	NA
DALWORTHINGTON GARDENS, Tarrant	1,281
Dam B (Dogwood Station), Tyler	56
*Damon, Brazoria, 16	375
*†DANBURY, Brazoria, 15	1,529
*Danciger, Brazoria, 1	314
*Danevang, Wharton, 3	61
Daniels, Panola	NA
Danville, Collin	NA
Danville, Gregg	NA
Daphne, Franklin	NA
Darby Hill, San Jacinto	NA
Darco, Harrison	85
Darden, Polk	NA
*DARROUZETT, Lipscomb, 17	511
Datura, Limestone	NA
*Davilla, Milam	200
Davis, Atascosa	NA
Davis Hill, Liberty	NA
Davis Prairie, Limestone	NA
Davisville, Angelina	NA
Davy, DeWitt	NA
*Dawn, Deaf Smith, 4	94
*†DAWSON, Navarro, 7	789
*†DAYTON, Liberty, 164	6,576
Dayton Lakes, Liberty	NA
Deadwood, Panola	106
DEAN, Clay	223
Dean, Hockley	18
*†Deanville, Burleson, 3	130
*DeBerry, Panola, 10	191
§*†DECATUR, Wise, 141	4,523
Decker Estates, Montgomery	NA
†Decker Prairie, Montgomery	NA
Deep Water Point Estates, Collin	NA
Deer Acres, Smith	NA
Deerfield Estates, Brazos	NA
Deer Haven, Llano	NA
Deer Lake Lodge, Montgomery	NA
*†DEER PARK, Harris, 292	24,537
Deerwood, Montgomery	NA
Deerwood East, Waller	NA
Deerwood Lakes, Waller	NA
Deerwood North, Waller	NA
*†DEKALB, Bowie, 65	2,225
Delaware Bend, Cooke	NA
Delba, Fannin	20
*†DELEON, Comanche, 64	2,536
Delhi, Caldwell	NA
Delia, Limestone	NA
*DELL CITY, Hudspeth, 15	548

Town and County—	Pop.
Dellwood, Webb	2,000
Del Mar Heights, Cameron	NA
*Delmita, Starr, 1	99
Delray, Panola	40
§*†DEL RIO, Val Verde, 389	34,401
Delrose, Upshur	NA
*Del Valle, Travis, 40	300
Delwin, Cottle	70
Demi-John Island, Brazoria	NA
Denhawken, Wilson	46
*†DENISON, Grayson, 427	24,234
Sherman-Denison 1985 metro. pop.	96,700
Denman Crossroads, Van Zandt	NA
Denning, San Augustine	361
*Dennis, Parker, 1	86
Denson Springs, Anderson	NA
Denton, Callahan	NA
§*†DENTON, Denton, 837	51,172
Denton, Franklin	NA
*†DENVER CITY, Yoakum, 153	5,583
*†DEPORT, Lamar-Red River, 7	680
Derby, Frio	50
*Dermott, Scurry	5
Dernal, Victoria	NA
*Desdemona, Eastland, 4	180
Desert, Collin	25
*†DESOTO, Dallas, 360	19,589
Dessau, Travis	NA
*†DETROIT, Red River, 8	720
*†DEVERS, Liberty, 14	433
*†DEVINE, Medina, 87	4,016
Dew, Freestone	71
Dewalt, Fort Bend, 1	25
DeWees, Wilson	35
Deweesville, Karnes	NA
*Deweyville, Newton, 8	850
Dewville, Gonzales	15
Dexter, Cooke	NA
Dextra, Nacogdoches	NA
*†D'Hanis, Medina, 6	548
Dial, Fannin	76
Dial, Hutchinson	20
*Dialville, Cherokee	200
Diamondhead, Montgomery	NA
*Diana, Upshur, 14	200
*†DIBOLL, Angelina, 48	5,134
Dicey, Parker	NA
§*†DICKENS, Dickens, 4	458
*†DICKINSON, Galveston, 151	8,656
Dies, Tyler	NA
*Dike, Hopkins, 7	170
*†DILLEY, Frio, 51	2,773
Dilworth, Gonzales	15
Dilworth, Red River	22
*Dime Box, Lee, 13	313
§*†DIMMITT, Castro, 103	4,875
Dimple, Red River	60
*Dinero, Live Oak, 1	35
Ding Dong, Bell	22
Direct, Lamar	70
Dirgin, Rusk	12
Divide, Hopkins	NA
Divot, Frio	28
Dixie, Grayson	25
Dixie Isle, Henderson	NA
Dixon, Hunt	31
Dixon-Hopewell, Houston	NA
Doak Springs, Lee	NA
Doans, Wilbarger	20
*Dobbin, Montgomery, 6	170
Dobrowolski, Atascosa	10
Dodd, Castro	35
*DODD CITY, Fannin, 3	301
*Dodge, Walker, 1	150
*DODSON, Collingsworth, 1	168
Dodson Prairie, Palo Pinto	NA
Dog Ridge, Bell	125
*Dogwood, Tyler	NA
Dogwood City, Smith	NA
Dogwood Forest, Montgomery	NA
Dogwood Forest, Nacogdoches	NA
Dogwood Point, Sabine	NA
Dolen, Liberty	NA
Dolores, Webb	20

Town and County—	Pop.	Town and County—	Pop.	Town and County—	Pop.
DOMINO, Cass	258	*EASTON, Gregg-Rusk	375	*Elm Mott, McLennan, 20	190
Donall Estates, Burnet	NA	East Point, Wood	NA	*Elmo, Kaufman, 2	90
*†Donie, Freestone, 5	206	East River, Harris-Montgomery	NA	Elmont, Grayson	41
*DONNA, Hidalgo, 89	11,386	East Sweden, McCulloch	NA	Elm Ridge, Milam	25
*Doole, McCulloch, 1	74	EAST TAWAKONI, Rains	494	Elmtown, Anderson	NA
*DORCHESTER, Grayson, 4	222	East Tempe, Polk	100	Elm Valley Park, Bexar	NA
Dorras, Stonewall	NA	EASTVALE, Denton	571	Eloise, Falls	41
Doss, Cass	NA	Eastview Terrace, Bexar	NA	El Oso, Karnes	NA
*Doss, Gillespie, 4	75	East Village, Bexar	NA	§*†EL PASO, El Paso,	
Dot, Falls	21	Eaton, Robertson	NA	5,138	463,809
Dothan, Eastland	20	Ebenezer, Camp	55	1985 metro. pop.	545,000
Dotson, Panola	40	Ebenezer, Jasper	NA	El Pinion Estates, San	
Double Bayou, Chambers	400	Echo, Coleman	16	Augustine	NA
Double Diamond Estates,		Echo, Orange	25	Elroy, Travis	125
Hutchinson-Moore	175	Echo Forest, Orange	NA	*ELSA, Hidalgo, 28	5,554
DOUBLE OAK, Denton	898	Echols, Limestone	NA	*El Sauz, Starr	85
*Doucette, Tyler, 3	131	*Ecleto, Karnes	22	El Tacalote, Jim Wells	100
*Dougherty, Floyd, 2	100	Eclipse, Jasper	NA	El Toro, Jackson	NA
Dougherty, Rains	75	*ECTOR, Fannin, 3	650	Elwood, Fannin	31
Douglas, Smith	NA	*EDCOUCH, Hidalgo, 13	3,550	Elwood, Madison	28
*Douglass, Nacogdoches, 2	75	*Eddy, Falls-McLennan		Ely, Fannin	15
Dove Meadows, Harris	NA	(See Bruceville-Eddy), 10		*†Elysian Fields, Harrison, 3	300
Downing, Comanche	20	*†EDEN, Concho, 22	1,308	Elysium, Bastrop	NA
Downsville, McLennan	35	Eden, Nacogdoches	NA	Emberson, Lamar	80
Doyle, Limestone	10	Eden Heights, Polk	NA	Emblem, Hopkins	52
Dozier, Collingsworth	30	Edgar, DeWitt	NA	Emerald Bay, Smith	NA
Drane, Navarro	16	Edge, Brazos	100	*EMHOUSE, Navarro, 1	250
Draper Addition (Also called		EDGECLIFF, Tarrant	3,049	Emille, Tyler	NA
Hippie Ridge), Wise	NA	*Eddy, Falls-McLennan		Emmett, Navarro	100
Drasco, Runnels	NA	Edgewater, San Augustine	NA	§*†EMORY, Rains, 38	974
Draw, Lynn	39	Edgewater Beach, Travis	NA	Enchanted Forest,	
Dreka, Shelby	NA	Edgewater Estates,		Montgomery	NA
Dresden, Navarro	25	San Patricio	NA	ENCHANTED OAKS,	
Dreyer, Gonzales	20	*†EDGEWOOD, Van Zandt,		Henderson	234
*Driftwood, Hays, 8	21	22	1,452	Enchanted Valley, Burnet	NA
Driftwood, Henderson	NA	Edgeworth, Bell	20	*ENCINAL, La Salle, 11	720
*†Dripping Springs, Hays, 55	779	Edhube, Fannin	25	*Encino, Brooks, 3	110
*DRISCOLL, Nueces, 4	748	§*†EDINBURG, Hidalgo,		*Energy, Comanche	65
Drivers, Nacogdoches	NA	374	30,031	Engle, Fayette	106
Drumright, Glasscock	NA	McAllen-Edinburg-Mission		English, Red River	92
*Dryden, Terrell	13	1985 metro. pop.	352,200	*†Enloe, Delta, 2	113
Dubina, Fayette	NA	*EDMONSON, Hale, 6	268	*†ENNIS, Ellis, 292	12,653
*†DUBLIN, Erath, 59	2,883	§*†EDNA, Jackson, 126	5,771	Ennis, Scurry	3
Dudley, Callahan	25	Edna Hill, Erath	32	Enoch, Upshur	NA
*Duffau, Erath	76	EDOM, Van Zandt, 3	277	*Enochs, Bailey, 1	164
Dugger, Guadalupe	10	*Edroy, San Patricio, 6	200	Enright, Brazos	NA
Dull, La Salle	NA	Egan, Johnson	21	Ensign, Ellis	10
§*†DUMAS, Moore, 260	12,900	Egypt, Leon	NA	Enterprise, Van Zandt	90
*Dumont, King-Dickens, 1	85	Egypt, Montgomery	NA	*Eola, Concho, 4	218
Dunbar, Rains	40	*Egypt, Wharton, 1	26	Eolian, Stephens	9
*†DUNCANVILLE, Dallas,		Elam Springs, Upshur	NA	Equestrian Estates, Brazos	NA
463	31,892	El Arroyo, Starr	NA	*Era, Cooke, 1	200
Dundee, Archer	40	*Elbert, Throckmorton, 5	150	Ericksdahl, Jones	75
Dunlap, Cottle	30	Elbow, Howard	NA	Erin, Jasper	40
Dunlap, Travis	80	El Calaboz, Cameron	NA	Ernies Acres, Brazoria	NA
*Dunlay, Medina, 1	119	El Camino, Sabine	NA	Erwin, Grimes	NA
*Dunn, Scurry, 1	75	El Campo Club, Calhoun	NA	Escobares, Starr	216
Dunstan, Bastrop	NA	*†EL CAMPO, Wharton, 336	10,690	Escobas, Zapata	25
Duplex, Fannin	25	El Carro, Jim Wells	NA	Eskota, Fisher	NA
Duran, Mills	NA	§*†ELDORADO, Schleicher,		Esperanza, Hudspeth	75
Durango, Falls	54	43	2,418	Espey, Atascosa	NA
Durham Park, Williamson	NA	Eldorado Center, Navarro	NA	Esquire Estates, Henderson	NA
Duster, Comanche	NA	Eldorado Country, Matagorda	NA	Esseville, Live Oak	NA
Duval, Travis	NA	Eldridge, Colorado	NA	Estacado, Lubbock	80
Dye, Montague	NA	*†ELECTRA, Wichita, 77	3,599	*ESTELLINE, Hall, 6	254
Dyersdale, Harris	NA	Electric City, Hutchinson	350	Estes, Aransas	50
*Dyess Air Force Base, Taylor	4,676	Elevation, Milam	12	Ethel, Grayson	25
E		El Gato, Hidalgo	NA	*Etoile, Nacogdoches, 2	70
Eagle, Chambers	50	*†ELGIN, Bastrop, 82	4,984	Etter, Moore	160
*†EAGLE LAKE, Colorado,		Eli, Hall	30	Eubank Acres, Travis	NA
88	4,158	*Eliasville, Young, 1	116	Eula, Callahan	125
§*†EAGLE PASS, Maverick,		*El Indio, Maverick, 2	148	*†EULESS, Tarrant, 475	27,890
321	24,097	Elk, McLennan	NA	Eulogy, Bosque	45
Eanes, Travis	NA	*†ELKHART, Anderson, 22	1,542	Eunice, Leon	NA
*EARLY, Brown	3,094	Elkton, Smith	NA	Eureka, Franklin	NA
Earlywine, Washington	NA	EL LAGO, Harris	3,170	Eureka, Navarro	257
*†EARTH, Lamb, 18	1,392	*Ellinger, Fayette, 4	200	Eureka, Stephens	NA
*†East Bernard, Wharton, 63	1,500	Elliott, Robertson	NA	*†EUSTACE, Henderson, 11	652
East Caney, Hopkins	NA	Elliott, Wilbarger	50	*Evadale, Jasper, 16	715
East Columbia, Brazoria	95	Ellis, Austin	NA	*EVANT, Coryell-	
East Delta, Delta	50	*Elmaton, Matagorda	165	Hamilton, 9	422
East Direct, Lamar	NA	Elmdale, Taylor	NA	Evergreen, Hamilton	NA
Easter, Castro	91	*ELMENDORF, Bexar, 16	527	Evergreen, San Jacinto	50
Easterly, Robertson, 1	61	Elm Grove, Caldwell	NA	Evergreen Park, Orange	NA
Eastgate, Liberty	NA	Elm Grove, Cherokee	NA	*EVERMAN, Tarrant	5,624
Eastham, Shelby	NA	Elm Grove, Fayette	NA	(Businesses included in	
§*†EASTLAND, Eastland, 159	4,193	Elm Grove, San Saba	NA	Fort Worth count.)	
EAST MOUNTAIN, Upshur	888	Elm Grove Camp, Guadalupe	110	Ewell, Upshur	100
		Elmina, Walker	NA	Eylau, Bowie	2,962

Town and County—	Pop.
Ezzell, Lavaca	55
F	
*†Fabens, El Paso, 36	3,400
Fails, Walker	NA
Fairbanks, Harris	1,050
Fairchilds, Fort Bend	150
§*†FAIRFIELD, Freestone, 120	4,093
Fairland, Burnet	NA
Fairlie, Hunt	80
Fairmont, Sabine	NA
Fair Oaks, Bexar	NA
Fair Oaks, Freestone	23
Fair Oaks, Limestone	NA
Fair Play, Panola	80
Fairview, Angelina	NA
Fairview, Armstrong	NA
Fairview, Brazos	NA
Fairview, Cass	NA
FAIRVIEW, Collin	1,287
Fairview, Comanche	NA
Fairview, Crosby	NA
Fairview, Gaines	NA
Fairview, Hockley	10
Fairview, Hood	NA
Fairview, Howard	85
Fairview, Rusk	NA
Fairview, Wilson	322
FAIRVIEW, Wise	211
Fairy, Hamilton	31
Falcon, Zapata	50
*Falcon Heights, Starr, 1	361
Falcon Village, Starr	NA
§*†FALFURRIAS, Brooks, 67	6,555
Fallon, Limestone	NA
*†FALLS CITY, Karnes, 21	547
Fambrough, Stephens	NA
Famuliner, Cochran	NA
Fannett, Jefferson	105
*Fannin, Goliad, 1	105
Fargo, Wilbarger	161
Farmers Academy, Titus	NA
*†FARMERS BRANCH, Dallas	26,464
(Businesses included in Dallas count.)	
Farmers Valley, Wilbarger	50
*†FARMERSVILLE, Collin, 53	2,622
Farmington, Grayson	20
*Farnsworth, Ochiltree, 5	149
Farr, Ward	NA
Farrar, Limestone	51
Farrsville, Newton	NA
§*†FARWELL, Parmer, 52	1,365
*Fashing, Atascosa	50
*FATE, Rockwall, 4	378
Faught, Lamar	25
Faulkner (or Pinhook), Lamar	48
Fawil, Newton	NA
Fayburg, Collin	NA
*†FAYETTEVILLE, Fayette, 15	338
Fays Corner, Hidalgo	NA
Faysville, Hidalgo	300
Fedor, Lee	76
*Fentress, Caldwell, 2	85
*†FERRIS, Ellis, 33	2,224
Fetzer, Waller	NA
Field Schoolhouse, Erath	12
Field Senate, Jack	NA
Fields Store, Waller	NA
*Fieldton, Lamb, 3	126
*Fife, McCulloch	32
Files Valley, Hill	50
Fincastle, Henderson	NA
Finney, Hale	15
Finney, King	70
First Colony, Fort Bend	NA
*Fischer, Comal, 4	20
Fisk, Coleman	40
Five Notch, Harrison	NA
Five Points, Ellis	NA
Flaccus, Karnes	NA
Flagg, Castro	50
Flamingo Isles, Galveston	NA
Flamingo Lake, Montgomery	NA
*Flat, Coryell, 1	210
Flat Fork, Shelby	NA

Town and County—	Pop.
*†FLATONIA, Fayette, 53	1,307
Flat Prairie, Trinity	NA
Flats, Rains	100
Flat Top, Stonewall	NA
Flatwoods, Eastland	56
*Flint, Smith, 37	150
Flint Rock Hills, Travis	NA
Flo, Leon	20
*Flomot, Motley, 2	181
Flora, Hopkins	NA
Flora Bluff, Franklin	NA
*†FLORENCE, Williamson, 18	857
§*†FLORESVILLE, Wilson, 80	4,952
Florey, Andrews	25
Flower Hill, Colorado	NA
†FLOWER MOUND, Denton	6,669
Floy, Fayette	NA
Floyd, Hunt	220
§*†FLOYDADA, Floyd, 79	3,769
Flugrath, Blanco	NA
*Fluvanna, Scurry, 8	180
Fly Gap, Mason	NA
*Flynn, Leon, 3	81
Foard City, Foard	10
Fodice, Houston	49
*†FOLLETT, Lipscomb, 20	605
Folsom, Shelby	NA
Foncine, Collin	20
Foot, Collin	20
Footes, Gregg	NA
Ford, Deaf Smith	NA
Ford Oaks, Travis	NA
Fords Corner, San Augustine	NA
Fordtran, Victoria	18
*Forest, Cherokee	85
*Forestburg, Montague, 3	200
Forest Chapel, Lamar	NA
Forest Cove, Montgomery	NA
Forest Creek, Bexar	NA
Forest Glade, Bexar	NA
Forest Glade, Limestone	340
Forest Grove, Collin	20
Forest Grove, Milam	60
Forest Heights, Orange	250
Forest Hill, Lamar	NA
†FOREST HILL, Tarrant	13,173
Forest Hill, Wood	NA
Forest Hill Estates, Coryell	125
Forest Hills, Montgomery	NA
Forest Lake, Brazos	NA
Forest Lake, Gregg	NA
Forest North Estates, Williamson	NA
Forest Park, Henderson	NA
Forest Trail, Montgomery	NA
Forest View North, Comal	NA
*†FORNEY, Kaufman, 101	4,008
*Forreston, Ellis, 11	300
*FORSAN, Howard, 9	284
*Fort Bliss, El Paso	22,000
Fort Clark Springs, Kinney	1,070
§*†Fort Davis, Jeff Davis, 16	1,212
FORT GATES, Coryell	755
Fort Griffin, Shackelford	96
*Fort Hancock, Hudspeth, 5	400
*†Fort Hood, Bell-Coryell, 10	32,963
*Fort McKavett, Menard, 1	45
Fort Parker, Limestone	2
Fort Parker State Park, Limestone	30
*Fort Sam Houston, Bexar	10,000
Fort Spunky, Hood	15
Fort Stanley Creek, Angelina	NA
§*†FORT STOCKTON, Pecos, 192	9,957
§*†FORT WORTH, Tarrant, 10,836	414,562
Dallas-Fort Worth 1985 CMSA pop.	3,511,600
Foster, Fort Bend	NA
Foster, Terry	NA
Fosters Store, Burleson	NA
Fostoria, Montgomery	NA
Fouke, Wood	NA
Four Corners, Brazoria	NA
Four Corners, Chambers	NA
Four Corners, Harris	NA

Town and County—	Pop.
Four Corners, Montgomery	NA
Four Points, Travis	NA
Four Way, Moore	NA
*Fowlerton, La Salle, 1	100
Fox Run, Bexar	NA
Foxwood, Montgomery	NA
Frame Switch, Williamson	20
*Francitas, Jackson	30
Frank, Fannin	3
*Frankel City, Andrews	NA
Frankell, Stephens	NA
§*†FRANKLIN, Robertson, 28	1,637
Franklin Center, Scurry	NA
*†FRANKSTON, Anderson, 55	1,459
*Fred, Tyler, 2	239
§*†FREDERICKSBURG, Gillespie, 294	7,243
Fredonia, Gregg	NA
*Fredonia, Mason, 1	50
Freedom, Rains	60
Freeneytown, Rusk	NA
*†FREEPORT, Brazoria, 405	12,411
*†FREER, Duval, 103	3,735
Freestone, Freestone	35
Freeway Forest, Montgomery	NA
Freeway Oaks Estates, Montgomery	NA
Freheit, Comal	NA
Frelsburg, Colorado	75
Frenstat, Burleson	NA
Fresno, Collingsworth	NA
*Fresno, Fort Bend, 27	300
Freyburg, Fayette	45
Friday, Trinity	41
Friendly, Van Zandt	NA
Friendship, Dawson	5
Friendship, Lamb	NA
Friendship, Leon	NA
Friendship, Smith	NA
Friendship, Trinity	NA
Friendship, Upshur	NA
Friendship, Williamson	48
Friendship Village, Bowie	NA
*†FRIENDSWOOD, Galveston-Harris, 315	17,582
Frio, Castro	60
*†FRIONA, Parmer, 95	3,733
Frio Town, Frio	38
*†FRISCO, Collin-Denton, 126	4,254
*†FRITCH, Hutchinson-Moore, 33	2,912
Frog, Kaufman	NA
Frognot, Collin	NA
Front, Panola	NA
Frontier Lakes, Montgomery	NA
*Fronton, Starr	110
*†FROST, Navarro, 8	647
Fruitland, Montague	20
*FRUITVALE, Van Zandt, 8	395
Frydek, Austin	150
Fulbright, Red River	150
FULLER SPRINGS, Angelina	1,464
*†FULSHEAR, Fort Bend, 12	623
*†FULTON, Aransas, 43	1,002
Funston, Jones	76
Furrh, Panola	40
G	
Gadston, Lamar	NA
Gafford, Hopkins	NA
§*Gail, Borden, 4	202
§*†GAINESVILLE, Cooke, 410	14,066
Galena, Smith	NA
*†GALENA PARK, Harris, 101	9,957
Galilee, Smith	NA
Galilee, Walker	NA
*GALLATIN, Cherokee, 2	278
Galle, Guadalupe	80
Galleon Bay, Nueces	NA
Galloway, Panola	71
§*†GALVESTON, Galveston, 1,057	62,379
Galveston-Texas City 1985 metro. pop.	213,400

Town and County—	Pop.
Hamon, Gonzales	15
Hampton, Nacogdoches	NA
*Hamshire, Jefferson, 6	350
Hancock Oak Hills, Comal	NA
*Hankamer, Chambers, 5	189
Hannibal, Erath	NA
Hanover, Milam	27
Hansford, Hansford	NA
*†HAPPY, Swisher-Randall, 19	710
Happy Hill, Johnson	NA
Happy Landing, Shelby	NA
Happy Union, Hale	15
Happy Valley, Taylor	NA
Haralson Lakes, Tyler	NA
Harbin, Erath	21
Harborlight, Sabine	NA
Harbor Point, Henderson	NA
Harborview, Brazoria	NA
Hardin, Coleman	NA
Hardin, Hardin	NA
*HARDIN, Liberty, 14	928
Hardy, Montague	NA
Hare, Williamson	70
*Hargill, Hidalgo, 1	550
*†HARKER HEIGHTS, Bell	8,444
Harkeyville, San Saba	12
*Harleton, Harrison, 5	260
*†HARLINGEN, Cameron, 857	51,863
Brownsville-Harlingen 1985 metro. pop.	249,800
Harlow, Hunt	NA
Harmon, Lamar	35
Harmony, Floyd	NA
Harmony, Grimes	12
Harmony, Limestone	NA
Harmony, Nacogdoches	NA
Harmony Hall, Austin	NA
*†Harper, Gillespie, 17	383
Harpersville, Stephens	NA
Harriet, Tom Green	NA
Harris Chapel, Panola	180
Harrison, McLennan	25
*Harrold, Wilbarger, 4	320
*†HART, Castro, 34	969
Hartburg, Newton	275
Hart Camp, Lamb	NA
*Hartley, Hartley, 6	370
Harvard Switch, Camp	NA
Harvest Acres, Montgomery	NA
Harvey, Brazos	310
Harwell Point, Burnet	NA
*Harwood, Gonzales, 2	112
§*†HASKELL, Haskell, 86	3,831
Haslam, Shelby	101
*HASLET, Tarrant, 12	337
*Hasse, Comanche	43
Hatchel, Runnels	16
Hatchetville, Hopkins	NA
Havana, Hidalgo	NA
*†HAWKINS, Wood, 31	1,242
*HAWLEY, Jones, 15	884
Hawthorne, Shelby	NA
Hawthorne, Walker	NA
Hawthorn Ridge, Montgomery	NA
Haynesville, Wichita	60
Haynie Flat, Travis-Burnet	NA
HAYS, Hays	438
Hays City, Hays	NA
Hays Country Oaks, Hays	NA
Hazeldell, Comanche	NA
Hazy Hollow, Montgomery	NA
Headsville, Robertson	NA
*†HEARNE, Robertson, 87	5,711
*HEATH, Rockwall-Kaufman	1,647
Heatherstone, Harris	NA
§*†Hebbronville, Jim Hogg, 51	4,050
HEBRON, Denton	470
Heckville, Lubbock	NA
*†HEDLEY, Donley, 7	405
Hedwigs Hill, Mason	10
HEDWIG VILLAGE, Harris	2,820
Hefner, Knox	76
Hegar, Waller	NA
Heidelberg, Hidalgo	NA
*Heidenheimer, Bell, 2	144
Helena, Karnes	35
Helmic, Trinity	NA

Town and County—	Pop.
*†Helotes, Bexar, 53	1,564
§*†HEMPHILL, Sabine, 76	1,530
§*†HEMPSTEAD, Waller, 78	3,782
§*†HENDERSON, Rusk, 306	11,972
Henderson Chapel, Concho	NA
Hendricks, Hunt	NA
Henly, Hays	55
§*†HENRIETTA, Clay, 55	3,213
Henry's Chapel, Cherokee	75
§*†HEREFORD, Deaf Smith, 384	15,365
Heritage Farm, Bexar	NA
Heritage Hills, Hays	NA
Heritage Oaks, Hays	NA
Heritage Oaks, Montgomery	NA
Hermits Cove, Rains	40
*Hermleigh, Scurry, 2	200
Herty, Angelina	605
Hester, Navarro	35
*†HEWITT, McLennan, 97	7,474
*Hext, Menard	64
HICKORY CREEK, Denton	1,774
Hickory Creek, Fort Bend	NA
Hickory Creek, Houston	NA
Hickory Creek, Hunt	NA
Hickory Forrest, Guadalupe	300
Hickory Hills, Montgomery	NA
Hickory Hills, Sabine	NA
Hickory Hollow, Hunt	NA
Hickory Hollow, San Augustine	NA
Hicksbaugh, Tyler	NA
*†HICO, Hamilton, 27	1,422
*†HIDALGO, Hidalgo, 91	2,728
Hidden Acres, Henderson	NA
Hidden Acres, Williamson	NA
Hidden Forest Estates, Montgomery	NA
Hidden Hill Lakes, Smith	NA
Hidden Hills, Travis	NA
Hidden Hills Harbor, Henderson	NA
Hidden Meadows, Williamson	NA
Hidden Valley, Travis	NA
Hide Away, Brazoria	NA
Hideaway, Comal	NA
Hide-Away Bay, Smith	NA
Hide-A-Way Lake, Smith	NA
Higginbotham, Gaines	210
*†HIGGINS, Lipscomb, 15	679
High, Lamar	55
Highbank, Falls	126
High Chaparral, Williamson	NA
High Chapparal, Montgomery	NA
High Gabriel East, Williamson	NA
High Gabriel West, Williamson	NA
High Hill, Fayette	116
*High Island, Galveston, 9	500
Highland, Erath	NA
Highland, Smith	NA
Highland Acres, Hunt	NA
Highland Addition, Parker	NA
Highland Bayou, Galveston	NA
Highland Haven, Burnet	NA
Highland Hollow, Montgomery	NA
†HIGHLAND PARK, Dallas	8,830
(Businesses included in Dallas count.)	
Highland Park, Nacogdoches	NA
*†Highlands, Harris, 188	5,000
†HIGHLAND VILLAGE, Denton	3,512
High Point, Collin	NA
High Point, Grimes	15
Highsaw, Henderson	NA
Hightower, Liberty	30
Hightown, Polk	NA
Hilda, Mason	NA
Hilger, Fannin	NA
Hill and Dale Acres, Montgomery	NA
Hill Country Ranches, Hays	NA
HILL COUNTRY VILLAGE, Bexar	1,356
Hillcrest, Colorado	25

Town and County—	Pop.
HILLCREST VILLAGE, Brazoria	825
*Hillister, Tyler, 3	200
Hillje, Wharton	51
Hills, Lee	20
§*†HILLSBORO, Hill, 183	7,373
Hillside Estates, Henderson	NA
Hills Prairie, Bastrop	35
Hilltop Acres, Bexar	NA
Hilltop Acres, Kaufman	NA
*Hilltop Lakes, Leon	300
HILSHIRE VILLAGE, Harris	556
Hinckley, Lamar	40
Hindes, Atascosa	14
Hines, Johnson	NA
Hinkles Ferry, Brazoria	35
Hippie Ridge (Also called Draper Addition), Wise	NA
Hiram, Kaufman	34
*†HITCHCOCK, Galveston, 67	6,405
Hitchland, Hansford	27
Hitson, Fisher	NA
Hix, Burleson	35
Hoard, Wood	NA
Hobbs, Fisher	91
*Hobson, Karnes, 4	135
*Hochheim, DeWitt, 1	70
*Hockley, Harris, 18	300
Hodges, Jones	250
Hogan Acres, Johnson	NA
Hogansville, Rains	200
Hogg, Burleson	NA
Holcomb Store, Cherokee	NA
Holiday Beach, Aransas	1,000
Holiday Estates, Hunt	NA
Holiday Forest, Sabine	NA
Holiday Harbor, Marion	NA
Holiday Hills, Smith	NA
Holiday Hills Estates, Stephens	NA
Holiday Lake Estates, Polk	NA
Holiday Lakes, Brazoria	628
Holiday Oaks, Montgomery	NA
Holiday Shores, Brazoria	NA
Holiday Shores, Collin	NA
*†HOLLAND, Bell, 10	1,014
Holland Quarters, Panola	40
*HOLLIDAY, Archer, 28	1,495
Holly, Houston	NA
Holly Acres, Angelina	NA
Holly Beach, Cameron	NA
Holly Grove, Polk	NA
Holly Hills, Polk	NA
Holly Springs, Jasper	50
Holly Terrace, Montgomery	NA
HOLLYWOOD PARK, Bexar	3,996
Holman, Fayette	116
Homer, Angelina	360
§*†HONDO, Medina, 105	6,152
Honea Forrest Estates, Montgomery	NA
*†HONEY GROVE, Fannin, 25	1,861
Honey Island, Hardin	401
Hood, Cooke	75
Hooker Ridge, Rains	250
*†HOOKS, Bowie, 25	2,512
Hoop and Holler, Liberty	NA
Hoover, Gray	5
Hoover, Lamar	NA
Hope, Lavaca	45
Hopewell, Franklin	35
Hopewell, Houston	NA
Hopewell, Leon	NA
Hopewell, Red River	150
Horizon City, El Paso	500
Hornsby Bend, Travis	20
*Horseshoe Bay, Llano	500
Horseshoe Bay South, Burnet	NA
Horseshoe Bay West, Llano	NA
Horseshoe Bend, Liberty	NA
Horseshoe Falls, Comal	NA
Horseshoe Lake, Smith	NA
Hortense, Polk	25
Horton, Delta	25
Horton, Panola	NA
Hostetter Creek Estates, Montgomery	NA
Houmont Park, Harris	NA

Town and County—	Pop.	Town and County—	Pop.	Town and County—	Pop.
§*†HOUSTON, Harris-Fort Bend-Montgomery, 42,916.	1,705,697	Indian Lake, Newton	NA	Jonah, Williamson, 1	60
1985 PMSA pop.	3,221,600	Indian Lodge, Bosque	NA	Jones, Van Zandt	NA
Howard, Ellis	26	Indian Mound Estates, Sabine .	NA	*Jonesboro, Coryell-Hamilton, 4	200
HOWARDWICK, Donley	155	Indian Oaks, Henderson	NA	JONES CREEK, Brazoria	2,373
*†HOWE, Grayson, 16	2,300	Indian Oaks, Waller	NA	Jones Prairie, Milam	35
Howellville, Harris	36	Indian Oaks, Williamson	NA	*Jonestown, Travis	683
Howland, Lamar	90	Indianola, Calhoun	200	*Jonesville, Harrison, 2	28
Howth, Waller	65	Indian Rock, Upshur	NA	Joplin, Jack	NA
Hoxie, Williamson	50	Indian Springs Lake Estates, Polk	NA	Joppa, Burnet	NA
Hoyte, Milam	20	Indian Woods, Montgomery	NA	Jordans Store, Shelby	NA
Hub, Parmer	NA	Indio, Presidio	NA	*JOSEPHINE, Collin, 1	574
Hubbard, Bowie	269	*†Industry, Austin, 15	475	*†JOSHUA, Johnson, 67	2,349
*†HUBBARD, Hill, 23	1,782	*†Inez, Victoria, 14	309	Josselet, Haskell	NA
Huber, Shelby	NA	*†INGLESIDE, San Patricio, 60	6,048	Josserand, Trinity	NA
Huckabay, Erath	150	Ingleside-on-the-Bay, San Patricio	NA	Jot-Em-Down, Hunt-Delta	10
Hudd, Scurry	NA	*†Ingram, Kerr, 43	1,441	§*†JOURDANTON, Atascosa, 67	3,543
Huddleston, Montague	NA	Inks Lake Village, Llano	NA	Joy, Clay	150
HUDSON, Angelina	1,800	Inverness Point, Travis	NA	Joyce, Webb	20
Hudson Bend, Travis	NA	*†Iola, Grimes, 12	331	Jud, Haskell	40
HUDSON OAKS, Parker	623	IOWA COLONY, Brazoria	661	*Judson, Gregg, 7	650
Hudsons Chapel, Cherokee	NA	*†IOWA PARK, Wichita, 90.	6,428	Jumbo, Castro	NA
Hudsonville, Fannin	5	*Ira, Scurry, 15	250	Jumbo, Panola	NA
Huff, Archer	NA	*†IRAAN, Pecos, 25	1,849	Junction, Coleman	NA
Huffines, Cass	90	Irby, Haskell	NA	§*†JUNCTION, Kimble, 71	2,761
*†Huffman, Harris, 32	50	*†IREDELL, Bosque, 7	384	Juno, Val Verde	10
*Hufsmith, Harris	250	Ireland, Coryell	60	*Justiceburg, Garza	76
*HUGHES SPRINGS, Cass, 67	2,501	*Irene, Hill, 1	160	*†JUSTIN, Denton, 28	1,223
Hughey, Gregg	NA	Irish Meadows, Smith	NA	**K**	
*†Hull, Liberty, 12	1,800	Ironton, Cherokee	110	Kalgary, Crosby	140
Hulon Lakes, Montgomery	NA	*†IRVING, Dallas, 2,911	120,057	*Kamay, Wichita, 13	642
*†HUMBLE, Harris, 872	11,435	Isla, Scurry	29	Kamey, Calhoun	NA
Humble Colorado Camp, Jim Hogg	NA	Island Village, Llano	NA	Kanawha, Red River	149
Humble Government Wells Camp, Duval	NA	Israel, Polk	25	*Karnack, Harrison, 12	775
Hume, Cherokee	NA	*†ITALY, Ellis, 15	1,433	§*†KARNES CITY, Karnes, 48	3,251
*Hungerford, Wharton, 14	178	*†ITASCA, Hill, 17	1,650	Karon, Live Oak	20
*Hunt, Kerr, 11	708	Ivan, Stephens	15	*Katemcy, Mason, 1	90
Hunter, Comal	30	*Ivanhoe, Fannin, 2	110	*†KATY, Harris-Waller-Fort Bend, 501	9,886
HUNTERS CREEK VILLAGE, Harris	4,523	Iverson, Hill	NA	§*†KAUFMAN, Kaufman, 120	5,318
Hunters Glen, Hays	NA	*Izoro, Lampasas, 1	31	Kaufman Estates, Kaufman	240
Hunters Retreat, Montgomery	NA	**J**		Keechi, Leon	67
*†HUNTINGTON, Angelina, 37	1,996	*†JACINTO CITY, Harris	10,402	*†KEENE, Johnson, 32	3,094
Huntoon, Ochiltree	21	§*†JACKSBORO, Jack, 157.	3,970	Keeter, Wise	NA
§*†HUNTSVILLE, Walker, 506	30,152	Jackson, Marion	NA	Keith, Grimes	NA
Hurley, Wood	NA	Jackson, Shelby	NA	Keith Lake, Jefferson	NA
*Hurlwood, Lubbock	115	Jackson, Van Zandt	NA	*†KELLER, Tarrant, 170	5,459
Hurnville, Clay	15	*†JACKSONVILLE, Cherokee, 326	12,827	Kellers Corner, Cameron	NA
Huron, Hill	NA	Jacobia, Hunt	60	*Kellerville, Wheeler	50
*†HURST, Tarrant, 754	34,402	Jacobs, Rusk	NA	Kellogg, Hunt	NA
Hurstown, Shelby	NA	Jakes Colony, Guadalupe	30	Kelly, Collin	NA
Hurst Springs, Coryell	NA	JAMAICA BEACH, Galveston	446	*Kelly Air Force Base, Bexar	2,363
*†HUTCHINS, Dallas, 63.	3,690	James, Shelby	NA	Kellyville, Marion	NA
*†HUTTO, Williamson, 17.	842	James, Upshur	NA	Kelsey, Upshur	50
HUXLEY, Shelby	366	Jamestown, Newton	70	Kelton, Wheeler	75
Huxley Bay, Shelby	NA	Jamestown, Smith	75	*Keltys, Angelina	800
*Hye, Blanco	105	JA Ranch, Armstrong	20	*KEMAH, Galveston, 66.	1,591
Hylton, Nolan	28	Jardin, Hunt	22	*†KEMP, Kaufman, 75.	1,206
Hynds City, Montague	NA	*†Jarrell, Williamson, 15	410	Kemper City, Victoria	16
I		§*†JASPER, Jasper, 286.	7,104	*Kempner, Lampasas, 6	420
Iago, Wharton	56	§*†JAYTON, Kent, 10.	607	Ken Brook Valley, Montgomery	NA
Ibex, Shackelford	25	Jean, Young	91	*Kendalia, Kendall, 1	76
Ida, Grayson	50	Jeddo, Bastrop	NA	*KENDLETON, Fort Bend, 1 .	664
*†IDALOU, Lubbock, 35.	2,453	§*†JEFFERSON, Marion, 83 .	2,519	*†KENEDY, Karnes, 105	4,425
Idle Hour Acres, Travis	NA	Jenkins, Morris	NA	KENEFICK, Liberty	788
Ike, Ellis	10	Jennings, Lamar	NA	*†KENNARD, Houston, 6	490
Illinois Bend, Montague	NA	Jericho, Shelby	NA	*†KENNEDALE, Tarrant, 83 .	2,876
IMPACT, Taylor	60	*Jermyn, Jack	75	*Kenney, Austin	200
Impala Point, Henderson	NA	Jerrys Quarters, Washington.	NA	Kenser, Hunt	NA
Impala Woods, Polk	NA	JERSEY VILLAGE, Harris	5,143	Kensing, Delta	35
*Imperial, Pecos, 8	720	*†JEWETT, Leon, 37	816	*Kent, Culberson, 1	60
Imperial Valley, Travis	NA	Jiba, Kaufman	NA	Kentucky Town, Grayson	NA
Inadale, Scurry	8	*†JOAQUIN, Shelby, 15	969	*†KERENS, Navarro, 23	1,704
Independence, Washington	140	Joe Lee, Bell	2	§*†KERMIT, Winkler, 148	8,633
India, Ellis	12	Johnson, Anderson	NA	*Kerrick, Dallam, 2	60
Indian Creek, Smith	NA	Johnson, Terry	NA	§*†KERRVILLE, Kerr, 560.	17,002
Indian Gap, Hamilton	36	§*†JOHNSON CITY, Blanco, 39.	914	Kerrville South, Kerr	6,600
Indian Harbor Estates, Hood	691	Johnson Creek, Marion	NA	Key, Dawson	20
Indian Hill, Newton	NA	Johnston Store, Nacogdoches .	NA	Key Allegro, Aransas	600
Indian Hills, Bexar	NA	Johnsville, Erath	25	Key Ranch Estates, Henderson	NA
Indian Hills, Comal	NA	Johntown, Red River	175	Kiam, Polk	NA
Indian Hills, Llano	NA	Joiner, Fayette	NA	Kicaster, Wilson	100
INDIAN LAKE, Cameron	196	*Joinerville, Rusk, 1	140	Kiesling, Tom Green	NA
		Joliet, Caldwell	NA	*Kildare, Cass, 3	49
		JOLLY, Clay	179		
		Jolly Oaks, Williamson	NA		
		Jollyville, Williamson	150		

Town and County—	Pop.	Town and County—	Pop.	Town and County—	Pop.
Kildare Junction, Cass	NA	Laceola, Madison	10	Lakeshore Estates, Marion	NA
Kilgore, Goliad	120	*Lackland Air Force Base,		Lake Shore Estates, Stephens	NA
*†KILGORE, Gregg-Rusk,		Bexar	2,655	Lakeshore Estates West,	
486	12,138	*†LACOSTE, Medina, 16	942	Marion	NA
*†KILLEEN, Bell, 608	55,666	Lacy, Trinity	24	Lakeshore Gardens,	
Killeen-Temple		LACY-LAKEVIEW, McLennan	2,878	San Patricio	NA
1985 metro. pop.	228,000	*†LADONIA, Fannin, 9	677	Lakeshore Ranch, Travis	NA
Kimball, Bosque	NA	LaFayette, Upshur	80	LAKESIDE, San Patricio	289
Kimbro, Travis	50	*†LA FERIA, Cameron, 41	4,016	LAKESIDE, Tarrant	997
King, Coryell	25	Lagarto, Live Oak	80	Lakeside Acres, Bexar	NA
King Ranch Headquarters,		La Gloria, Jim Wells	NA	Lakeside Beach, Burnet	NA
Kleberg	NA	La Gloria, Starr	102	LAKESIDE CITY, Archer-	
*Kingsbury, Guadalupe, 6	200	Lago, Cameron	NA	Wichita	690
Kings Country, Franklin	NA	*Lago Vista, Travis, 17	2,500	Lakeside Estates, Angelina	NA
Kings Cove, Burnet	NA	§*†LA GRANGE, Fayette, 229	4,194	Lakeside Estates, Bexar	NA
Kings Highway, Brazos	NA	*LA GRULLA, Starr, 3	1,484	Lakeside Heights, Llano	NA
*†Kingsland, Llano, 53	1,500	Laguna, Uvalde	NA	Lakeside Village, Bosque	226
Kingsland Cove, Burnet	NA	Laguna Heights, Cameron	740	Lake Splendora, Montgomery	NA
Kingsland Estates, Llano	NA	*Laguna Park, Bosque	550	LAKE TANGLEWOOD,	
Kingsland Hills, Burnet	NA	Laguna Tres Estates, Hood	280	Randall	517
Kingsmill, Gray	65	Laguna Vista, Burnet	NA	Lake Tejas, San Jacinto	NA
Kings Point, Bexar	NA	LAGUNA VISTA, Cameron	778	Laketon, Gray	12
Kingston, Hunt	140	Laguna Vista Estates,		Lake Victor, Burnet	215
Kings Village, Travis	NA	Henderson	NA	Lakeview, Floyd	NA
§*†KINGSVILLE, Kleberg,		La Hacienda Estates, Travis	NA	Lakeview, Franklin	NA
280	29,949	Lahey, Terry	NA	*LAKEVIEW, Hall, 3	211
*Kingsville Naval Air Station,		Laird, Montgomery	NA	Lakeview, Lynn	NA
Kleberg	323	*Laird Hill, Rusk, 1	405	Lakeview, Marion	NA
Kingtown, Nacogdoches	NA	La Isla, El Paso	29	Lakeview, Orange	75
*†Kingwood, Harris, 170	50	Lajitas, Brewster	50	Lakeview, Swisher	NA
Kinkler, Lavaca	75	*LA JOYA, Hidalgo, 10	3,019	Lakeview, Tarrant	NA
Kinney Point, Franklin	NA	La Junta, Parker	NA	Lakeview Estates, Johnson	NA
Kinwood, Harris	NA	Lake, Wise	NA	Lakeview Estates, Orange	NA
Kiomatia, Red River	61	Lake Arrowhead, Clay	75	Lakeview Estates, Wise	NA
Kiowa Village, Hunt	NA	Lake Austin Lodges, Travis	NA	Lakeview Heights, Kaufman	240
*†KIRBY, Bexar	7,836	Lake Bonanza, Montgomery	NA	Lakeview Hills, Travis	NA
Kirby Town, Hardin	NA	LAKE BRIDGEPORT, Wise	266	Lakeview Manor, Montgomery	NA
*†KIRBYVILLE, Jasper, 91	2,036	Lake Cisco, Eastland	105	Lake View Park, Comal	NA
Kirk, Limestone	NA	LAKE CITY, San Patricio	450	*LAKEWAY, Travis	1,170
*Kirkland, Childress	102	Lake Conroe Forest,		Lake Whitney Estates, Hill	NA
Kirtley, Fayette	43	Montgomery	NA	Lake Wildwood, Montgomery	NA
*KIRVIN, Freestone	84	Lake Conroe Heights,		Lakewood, Henderson	NA
Kitsee Ridge, Hunt	NA	Montgomery	NA	Lakewood, San Augustine	NA
*†Klein, Harris	NA	Lake Conroe Hills,		Lakewood, Travis	NA
Klondike, Dawson	20	Montgomery	NA	Lakewood Colony, Montgomery	NA
*Klondike, Delta	135	Lake Conroe Terrace,		Lakewood Estates, Burnet	NA
Klump, Washington	NA	Montgomery	NA	Lakewood Estates,	
Knapp, Scurry	10	Lake Conroe West,		Montgomery	NA
*Knickerbocker, Tom Green	50	Montgomery	NA	Lakewood Estates, Travis	NA
Knight, Polk	NA	*Lake Creek, Delta, 1	60	Lakewood Forest, Llano	NA
Knights Forest, Liberty	NA	Lake Creek Falls, Montgomery	NA	Lakewood Harbor, Hill	NA
*Knippa, Uvalde, 13	360	Lake Crockett Estates, Fannin	5	Lakewood Hills, Comal	NA
Knobbs Springs, Lee	20	*†LAKE DALLAS, Denton, 66	3,634	LAKEWOOD VILLAGE,	
Knob Hill, Denton	NA	Lake Dunlap, Guadalupe	500	Denton	176
Knolle, Nueces-Jim Wells	NA	Lake Forest Falls, Montgomery	NA	*†LAKE WORTH, Tarrant	4,939
Knoll Ridge Acres, Bexar	NA	Lake Forest Lodge,		La Leona, Cameron	NA
Knollwood, Grayson	241	Montgomery	NA	La Lomita, Hidalgo	NA
Knollwood, Smith	NA	Lake Gardens, Tom Green	NA	Lamar, Aransas	1,600
Knollwood, Travis	NA	Lake Haven, Smith	NA	Lamar, Shelby	NA
*Knott, Howard, 2	685	*Lakehills, Bandera	300	*LA MARQUE, Galveston,	
Knox Acres, Montgomery	NA	Lake Hyatt Estates, Tyler	NA	150	15,697
*†KNOX CITY, Knox, 37	1,696	*†LAKE JACKSON, Brazoria,		Lamasco, Fannin	32
Koerth, Lavaca	45	247	20,206	§*†LAMESA, Dawson, 226	12,303
Kohrville, Harris	NA	Lake Jackson Farms, Brazoria	NA	Lamkin, Comanche	88
Kokomo, Eastland	25	Lake James, Hidalgo	NA	§*†LAMPASAS, Lampasas,	
Komensky, Lavaca	NA	*LAKE KIOWA, Cooke	1,200	145	6,749
Kona Kai, Galveston	NA	Lakeland, Montgomery	NA	Lanark, Cass	NA
Koocksville, Mason	NA	Lake Lavon Lodges, Collin	NA	*†LANCASTER, Dallas, 290	17,465
Kopernik Shores, Cameron	26	Lake Leon, Eastland	75	Landrum Station, Cameron	125
*Kopperl, Bosque, 1	225	Lake Livingston Estates, Polk	NA	*Lane City, Wharton, 2	111
Kosciusko, Wilson	390	Lake Lorraine, Montgomery	NA	Laneley, Freestone	27
*†KOSSE, Limestone, 11	519	Lake Louise, Montgomery	NA	Laneport, Williamson	60
§*†KOUNTZE, Hardin, 46	2,782	Lake Meredith Estates,		*Laneville, Rusk, 7	200
Kovar, Bastrop	NA	Hutchinson	262	Langford Place, Orange	NA
*†KRESS, Swisher, 29	757	Lake Mount Pleasant,		*Langtry, Val Verde, 1	145
Kreutsberg, Kendall	NA	Montgomery	NA	Lanham, Hamilton	NA
Kristenstad, Hood	NA	Lake Nueces, Uvalde	15	Lanier, Cass	40
Krohn Ranchettes,		Lake Oak, Henderson	NA	Lannius, Fannin	79
Montgomery	NA	Lake Placid, Brazos	NA	Lansing, Harrison	NA
KRUGERVILLE, Denton	583	Lake Placid, Guadalupe	300	Lantana, Cameron	NA
*†KRUM, Denton, 11	1,203	LAKEPORT, Gregg	924	La Paloma, Cameron	110
*Kurten, Brazos, 7	150	Lake Rayburn Shores,		La Parita, Atascosa	NA
*†KYLE, Hays, 38	3,033	Angelina	NA	*†LA PORTE, Harris, 311	23,851
Kyote, Atascosa	25	Lakeridge Estates, Smith	NA	*†La Pryor, Zavala, 19	550
L		Lakeridge Heights, Stephens	NA	§*†LAREDO, Webb, 1,445	108,676
LaBelle, Jefferson	NA	Lake Rolling Wood,		1985 metro. pop.	118,100
*La Blanca, Hidalgo	150	Montgomery	NA	La Reforma, Starr	45
Lacasa, Stephens	NA	Lake Sam Rayburn Estates,		*Lariat, Parmer, 2	200
La Casita, Starr	NA	Sabine	NA	Lark, Carson	NA

Town and County—	Pop.
La Rose, Nueces	20
*Larue, Henderson, 11	160
*LaSalle, Jackson	75
LaSalle Estates, Montgomery	NA
*Lasara, Willacy, 3	100
Las Escobas, Starr	NA
Las Milpas, Hidalgo	NA
Las Playas, Brazoria	NA
Las Rusias, Cameron	NA
Lassater, Marion	48
Las Yescas, Cameron	NA
Latch, Upshur	50
Latex, Harrison	NA
*LATEXO, Houston, 3	355
La Tina, Cameron	NA
Latium, Washington	30
Lauback, Guadalupe	13
*Laughlin Air Force Base, Val Verde	2,005
La Union, Cameron	20
Laurel, Newton	125
Laureles, Cameron	20
Laurel Estates, Hays	NA
Lavada, Franklin	NA
Lavender, Limestone	NA
*†LA VERNIA, Wilson, 32	847
*LA VILLA, Hidalgo, 3	1,665
*LAVON, Collin, 3	222
Lavon Beach Estates, Collin	NA
Lavon Shores Estates, Collin	NA
Law, Brazos	NA
*LA WARD, Jackson, 8	204
*LAWN, Taylor, 6	445
Lawrence, Kaufman	113
Lawsonville, Rusk	NA
Lazare, Cottle-Hardeman	26
*Lazbuddie, Parmer, 9	248
Lazy Acres, Nacogdoches	NA
Lazy Caney Pines, Montgomery	NA
Lazy Forest, Montgomery	NA
Lazy River Resort, Austin	NA
*Leaday, Coleman	55
League, Crosby	NA
*†LEAGUE CITY, Galveston, 265	22,934
Leagueville, Henderson	NA
§*†LEAKEY, Real, 23	516
*†LEANDER, Williamson, 117	2,963
Leander Heights, Williamson	NA
LEARY, Bowie	310
Lebanon, Collin	50
*Leesburg, Camp, 2	115
Lee Spring, Smith	NA
*Leesville, Gonzales, 2	150
*LEFORS, Gray, 7	781
*Leggett, Polk, 4	375
Legion, Kerr	NA
Lehman, Cochran	NA
Leigh, Harrison	100
Leisure Acres, Coryell	25
Leisure Land, Henderson	NA
Lela, Wheeler	135
*Lelia Lake, Donley, 3	125
*Leming, Atascosa, 3	250
*Lenorah, Martin, 3	70
Lenz, Karnes	NA
Leo, Cooke	80
Leo, Lee	NA
*LEONA, Leon, 3	188
*†LEONARD, Fannin, 26	1,409
Leona Schroder, Nueces	40
Leonidas, Montgomery	NA
*Leon Junction, Coryell	25
Leon Springs, Bexar	137
*LEON VALLEY, Bexar	10,837
*LEROY, McLennan, 2	322
Lesley, Hall	45
§*†LEVELLAND, Hockley, 329	14,625
Leverett's Chapel, Rusk	450
Levi, McLennan	50
Levita, Coryell	70
*†LEWISVILLE, Denton, 750	24,728
*†LEXINGTON, Lee, 16	1,284

Town and County—	Pop.
Liberty, Coleman	NA
Liberty, Freestone	75
Liberty, Hopkins	NA
§*†LIBERTY, Liberty, 268	8,377
Liberty, Lubbock	10
Liberty, Milam	40
Liberty, Newton	NA
Liberty, Rusk	NA
Liberty Chapel, Johnson	NA
†Liberty City, Gregg	1,121
Liberty Hill, Houston	NA
Liberty Hill, Milam	25
*Liberty Hill, Williamson, 20	300
Liberty Oaks, Williamson	NA
Lilbert, Nacogdoches	NA
*Lillian, Johnson, 4	105
*Lincoln, Lee, 3	276
*†LINDALE, Smith, 113	2,671
§*†LINDEN, Cass, 45	2,473
Lindendale, Kendall	NA
Lindenau, DeWitt	50
*LINDSAY, Cooke, 8	638
*Lingleville, Erath	100
*Linn, Hidalgo, 6	450
Linn Flat, Nacogdoches	NA
Linwood, Cherokee	40
*†LIPAN, Hood, 14	512
§*Lipscomb, Lipscomb, 2	45
*Lissie, Wharton, 4	70
Littig, Travis	37
Little Cypress, Orange	1,050
*LITTLE ELM, Denton, 13	1,168
§*†LITTLEFIELD, Lamb, 124.	7,088
Little Hope, Wood	NA
Little Midland, Burnet	NA
Little New York, Gonzales	20
Little Ridge Estates, Collin	NA
*LITTLE RIVER-ACADEMY, Bell, 7	1,150
Littleville, Hamilton	NA
Lively, Kaufman	NA
LIVE OAK, Bexar	8,734
Live Oak, Concho	NA
Liveoak, Newton	NA
Live Oak Bend, Matagorda	NA
Liveoak Estates, Montgomery	NA
Live Oak Ranchettes, Williamson	NA
Live Oak Resorts, Hill	NA
*LIVERPOOL, Brazoria, 7	627
§*†LIVINGSTON, Polk, 289.	6,160
§*†LLANO, Llano, 91	3,244
Lobo, Culberson	40
Loch Ness Cove, Montgomery	NA
Lochridge, Brazoria	NA
Locker, San Saba	16
Lockett, Wilbarger	200
Lockettville, Hockley	20
§*†LOCKHART, Caldwell, 126	9,045
*†LOCKNEY, Floyd, 59	2,169
Loco, Childress	NA
Locust, Grayson	NA
*Lodi, Marion, 2	164
Lodwick, Marion	NA
Loeb, Hardin	NA
Loebau, Lee	20
Logan, Panola	40
Log Cabin Estates, Henderson	NA
*Lohn, McCulloch, 2	149
Loire, Wilson	50
Lois, Cooke	60
Lolaville, Collin	NA
*Lolita, Jackson, 5	300
Lollipop, Henderson	NA
Loma, Walker	NA
Loma Alta, McMullen	25
Loma Alta, Val Verde	30
Lomax, Howard	NA
*†LOMETA, Lampasas, 13	722
*London, Kimble, 2	180
London, Rusk	NA
Londonderry, Harris	NA
Lone Camp, Palo Pinto	32
Lone Cedar, Ellis	18
Lone Elm, Ellis	20
Lone Elm, Kaufman	NA
*Lone Grove, Llano	50
Lone Oak, Bexar	NA

Town and County—	Pop.
Lone Oak, Colorado	NA
Lone Oak, Erath	NA
*†LONE OAK, Hunt, 15	630
Lone Oak Estates, Bexar	NA
Lone Pine, Houston	NA
Lone Star, Cherokee	NA
Lone Star, Floyd	NA
Lone Star, Franklin	NA
Lone Star, Kaufman	NA
Lone Star, Lamar	NA
*†LONE STAR, Morris, 71	2,358
*Long Branch, Panola, 1	181
Long Hollow, Leon	NA
Long Lake, Anderson	NA
Long Lake Estates, Montgomery	NA
*Long Mott, Calhoun, 5	76
Long Mountain, Mason	NA
Longpoint, Washington	80
§*†LONGVIEW, Gregg- Harrison-Upshur, 1,857	73,263
Longview-Marshall 1985 metro. pop.	170,200
Longworth, Fisher	65
Lonnie, Childress	NA
Loon Bay, Henderson	NA
Looneyville, Nacogdoches	NA
*Loop, Gaines, 8	315
*Lopeno, Zapata, 1	100
Lopezville, Hidalgo	NA
*LORAINE, Mitchell, 4	925
*†LORENA, McLennan, 46	887
*†LORENZO, Crosby, 15	1,338
*Los Angeles, La Salle	140
Los Barreras, Starr	125
Los Coyotes, Willacy	NA
*Los Ebanos, Hidalgo	100
Los Escondidos, Burnet	NA
*†LOS FRESNOS, Cameron, 42	2,675
*Los Indios, Cameron, 1	206
Losoya, Bexar	322
Los Saenz, Starr (See Roma-Los Saenz)	
Lost Creek, Coleman	NA
Lost Hollow Creek, Llano	NA
Lost Lakes, Montgomery	NA
Lost Prairie, Limestone	2
Lost River Estates, Williamson	NA
Los Ybanez, Dawson	156
*†LOTT, Falls, 14	957
Lotta, Harrison	10
*Louise, Wharton, 12	310
Lovelace, Hill	NA
*†LOVELADY, Houston, 8	697
Loves Lookout, Cherokee	NA
*Loving, Young, 10	240
*Lowake, Concho, 1	40
Lowman, Lamar	NA
LOWRY CROSSING, Collin	548
Loyal Valley, Mason	50
Loyola Beach, Kleberg	NA
*Lozano, Cameron	200
§*†LUBBOCK, Lubbock, 3,631	178,529
1985 metro. pop.	222,800
LUCAS, Collin	1,592
Luckenbach, Gillespie	25
*LUEDERS, Jones- Shackelford, 4	473
LUELLA, Grayson	441
§*†LUFKIN, Angelina, 818	30,616
*†LULING, Caldwell, 146	5,397
Lull, Hidalgo	NA
*†LUMBERTON, Hardin, 28.	3,098
Lumkins, Ellis	20
Lums Chapel, Lamb	NA
Lund, Travis	50
Lusk, Throckmorton	NA
Luther, Howard	335
Lutie, Collingsworth	35
Lydia, Red River	109
*LYFORD, Willacy, 18	1,747
Lynchburg, Harris	100
Lynn Grove, Grimes	NA
Lynnwood Lakes, Waller	NA
*Lyons, Burleson, 4	360
*†LYTLE, Atascosa-Medina- Bexar, 22	2,143

Town and County—	Pop.
Lytton Springs, Caldwell	76
Mc	
*McAdoo, Dickens, 1	169
*†MCALLEN, Hidalgo, 1,496.	77,062
McAllen-Edinburg-Mission 1985 metro. pop.	352,200
*†MCCAMEY, Upton, 51	2,880
*McCaulley, Fisher, 1	96
McClanahan, Falls	60
McClelland, Shelby	NA
McCollum, Montague	NA
McCook, Hidalgo	91
*McCoy, Atascosa, 1	25
McCoy, Floyd	NA
McCoy, Kaufman	20
McCoy, Panola	NA
McCoy, Red River	175
McCullough, Ellis	NA
*McDade, Bastrop, 4	345
McDade Estates, Montgomery	NA
McDaniels, Brown	NA
*McFaddin, Victoria	320
McGee Landing, Sabine	NA
McGirk, Hamilton	NA
*†MCGREGOR, McLennan, 85.	4,682
§*†MCKINNEY, Collin, 458.	18,231
McKinney Acres, Andrews	NA
McKnight, Rusk	NA
*†MCLEAN, Gray, 26.	1,127
MCLENDON-CHISHOLM, Rockwall	480
*McLeod, Cass, 1	50
McMahan, Caldwell	125
McMillan, San Saba	NA
McNair, Harris	2,039
*McNary, Hudspeth	250
McNeel, Brazoria	NA
McNeil, Caldwell	NA
*McNeil, Travis	70
*McQueeney, Guadalupe, 23	640
M	
*†MABANK, Kaufman-Henderson, 179.	1,988
Mabelle, Baylor	6
Mabry, Red River	60
*Macdona, Bexar, 4	297
Macedonia, Harrison	NA
Macey, Brazos	NA
Macon, Franklin	NA
Macune, San Augustine	100
Madero, Hidalgo	NA
§*†MADISONVILLE, Madison, 142.	3,973
Madras, Red River	61
Mae, Jim Wells	NA
Magnet, Wharton	42
*†MAGNOLIA, Montgomery, 124.	1,132
Magnolia, San Jacinto	30
Magnolia Beach, Calhoun	NA
Magnolia Bend, Montgomery	NA
Magnolia Gardens, Harris	NA
Magnolia Hills, Montgomery	NA
Magnolia Lake, Montgomery	NA
Magnolia Oaks, Montgomery	NA
*Magnolia Springs, Jasper	80
Maha, Travis	NA
Mahl, Nacogdoches	NA
Mahomet, Burnet	47
Mahoney, Hopkins	NA
Majors, Franklin	NA
*†MALAKOFF, Henderson, 57.	2,203
Mallard, Montague	NA
*MALONE, Hill, 4	352
Malta, Bowie	297
Malvern, Leon	NA
Mambrino, Hood	74
*Manchaca, Travis, 41	4,700
Manchester, Red River	185
Mangum, Eastland	15
Mangus Corner, Bexar	NA
Manheim, Lee	40
Mankin, Henderson	NA
Mankins, Archer	45
*MANOR, Travis, 62	1,233

Town and County—	Pop.
*†MANSFIELD, Tarrant-Johnson, 267.	10,733
*†MANVEL, Brazoria, 68	4,441
*Maple, Bailey, 2	130
Maple, Red River	30
Maple Spring, Titus	NA
Mapleton, Houston	NA
*Marathon, Brewster, 7	800
*†MARBLE FALLS, Burnet, 271.	4,235
§*†MARFA, Presidio, 31	2,503
Margaret, Foard	51
Marie, Runnels	NA
*MARIETTA, Cass, 1	191
*†MARION, Guadalupe, 28.	835
Marion Ferry Park, Angelina	NA
*Markham, Matagorda, 10.	603
Mark Heights, Smith	NA
Markley, Young	31
Markout, Kaufman	80
Marlboro Country, Hays	NA
§*†MARLIN, Falls, 94.	6,512
Marlow, Milam	45
*MARQUEZ, Leon, 6	279
Mars, Van Zandt	NA
§*†MARSHALL, Harrison, 415.	24,954
Longview-Marshall 1985 metro. pop.	170,200
Marshall Creek Estates, Denton	505
Marshall Ford, Travis	NA
Marshall Northeast, Harrison	1,500
Marston, Polk	25
*†MART, McLennan, 38.	2,445
*Martindale, Caldwell, 11	1,068
Martinez, Bexar	NA
Martin Prairie, Grimes	75
Martins Mills, Van Zandt	125
Martin Springs, Hopkins	115
*Martinsville, Nacogdoches	126
Marvin, Lamar	NA
Maryetta, Jack	7
*Maryneal, Nolan, 2	75
Marys Creek, Baylor	NA
Marysville, Cooke	NA
§*†MASON, Mason, 50	2,094
Mason Lake Estates, Liberty	NA
Massey, Hill	NA
Massey Lake, Anderson	NA
Masters, Throckmorton	NA
*Masterson, Moore, 4	15
§*†MATADOR, Motley, 19	1,019
*Matagorda, Matagorda, 10.	605
*†MATHIS, San Patricio, 75	5,910
Matthews, Colorado	NA
Matthey Estate, Bexar	NA
*MAUD, Bowie, 9.	1,126
*†Mauriceville, Orange, 15	6,500
Maverick, Runnels	31
Maxdale, Bell	4
Maxey, Lamar	55
*Maxwell, Caldwell, 9	185
*May, Brown, 1	285
*Maydelle, Cherokee	250
Mayfield, Hale	NA
Mayfield, Hill	NA
Mayflower, Newton	100
Mayhill, Denton	150
Maynard, San Jacinto	25
*†MAYPEARL, Ellis, 5	729
*Maysfield, Milam, 1	140
*MEADOW, Terry, 6	609
Meadowbrook, Montgomery	NA
Meadowbrook, Smith	NA
Meadowcreek, Kaufman	240
Meadow Grove, Bell	10
Meadow Lake, Guadalupe	250
Meadowlakes, Burnet	250
Meadowood Acres, Bexar	NA
Meadows, Fort Bend	5,895
Meadowview, Hunt	NA
Meadow Village, Bexar	NA
Mecca, Madison	6
Medicine Mound, Hardeman	50
Medill, Lamar	50
*Medina, Bandera, 7	515
*Medina Base, Bexar	NA
Meeker, Jefferson	NA

Town and County—	Pop.
Meek Estates, Henderson	NA
Meeks, Bell	15
*MEGARGEL, Archer, 7	403
Meldrum, Shelby	NA
*†MELISSA, Collin, 13	773
Mellon, Frio	14
Melrose, Nacogdoches	150
*MELVIN, McCulloch, 6	213
§*†MEMPHIS, Hall, 63	3,114
§*†MENARD, Menard, 19	1,715
Mendoza, Caldwell	50
Menlow, Hill	10
§*Mentone, Loving, 2	50
Mentz, Colorado	NA
*†MERCEDES, Hidalgo, 93	13,267
Mercers Gap, Comanche	NA
Mercury, McCulloch	166
*Mereta, Tom Green, 1	75
§*†MERIDIAN, Bosque, 53.	1,366
*Merit, Hunt, 2	215
*†MERKEL, Taylor, 43	3,071
Merle, Burleson	NA
Merriam, Eastland	14
*MERTENS, Hill, 1	118
§*†MERTZON, Irion, 19	837
Mesa, El Paso	50
*†MESQUITE, Dallas, 1,115	77,255
Mesquite Acres Island, San Patricio	NA
Metcalf Gap, Palo Pinto	NA
*†MEXIA, Limestone, 172	7,121
Mexico, Hunt	NA
*Meyersville, DeWitt, 2	110
§*†MIAMI, Roberts, 18.	699
*Mico, Medina, 2	98
Midcity, Lamar	NA
Middle Gabriel Estates, Williamson	NA
Middleton, Leon	26
*Middle Water, Hartley	10
Midessa Heights, Midland	NA
*Midfield, Matagorda	70
*Midkiff, Upton, 9	68
Midlake Village, Sabine	NA
§*†MIDLAND, Midland, 2,948.	97,148
1985 metro. pop.	109,200
*†MIDLOTHIAN, Ellis, 120	4,323
Midville, Brazos	NA
Midway, Bell	122
Midway, Bexar	NA
Midway, Dawson	20
Midway, Fannin	7
Midway, Franklin	NA
Midway, Hill	NA
Midway, Howard	NA
Midway, Jim Wells	NA
Midway, Lavaca	NA
Midway, Limestone	NA
*Midway, Madison, 8	300
Midway, Montgomery	NA
Midway, Red River	40
Midway, Scurry	2
Midway, Smith	NA
Midway, Titus	NA
Midway, Upshur	NA
Midway, Van Zandt	31
Midyett, Panola	NA
Mikesta, Live Oak	NA
*Milam, Sabine, 7	177
*MILANO, Milam, 7.	495
Milburn, McCulloch	NA
Mildred, Navarro	312
*†MILES, Runnels, 12	775
*†MILFORD, Ellis, 12	710
Mill Creek, Waller	NA
Mill Creek, Washington	40
Mill Creek Forest, Montgomery	NA
Miller Grove, Camp	NA
Miller Grove, Hopkins	115
MILLER'S COVE, Titus	52
*Millersview, Concho, 1	75
Millett, La Salle	90
Millheim, Austin	150
*Millican, Brazos, 1	100
Milligan, Collin	NA
*MILLSAP, Parker, 13.	412
Millsville, San Patricio	NA

Town and County—	Pop.	Town and County—	Pop.	Town and County—	Pop.
Milo Center, Deaf Smith	NA	Mossy Grove, Walker	NA	Navidad, Jackson	NA
Milton, Lamar	80	Mostyn, Montgomery	NA	Navo, Denton	35
Mims, Brazoria	NA	*†MOULTON, Lavaca, 37.	1,001	*NAZARETH, Castro, 9	257
Mims Chapel, Marion	NA	*Mound, Coryell, 1.	75	Necessity, Stephens.	10
*Minden, Rusk, 1.	350	Mound City, Anderson-		Nechanitz, Fayette	21
*†MINEOLA, Wood, 146.	4,774	Houston.	NA	*Neches, Anderson, 2.	114
*Mineral, Bee, 1	50	**Mountain City, Hays.	350	*†NEDERLAND, Jefferson,	
*†MINERAL WELLS,		Mountain Community, Coryell	300	364.	17,005
Palo Pinto-Parker, 394	15,684	*Mountain Home, Kerr, 2.	96	Needmore, Bailey	98
Minerva, Milam	60	Mountain Peak, Ellis.	20	*†NEEDVILLE, Fort Bend,	
Mings Chapel, Upshur	NA	Mountain Springs, Cooke	100	43.	1,571
*MINGUS, Palo Pinto, 4	252	Mountain Springs, Hill	NA	Neely Ward, Cochran	NA
Mink Branch Valley,		Mountain Top, Eastland	22	Negley, Red River.	136
Montgomery	NA	Mountain Valley Estates,		Neinda, Jones	31
Minter, Lamar	78	Johnson.	NA	Nell, Live Oak	NA
*Mirando City, Webb, 4	559	Mountain View, Smith.	NA	Nelleva, Brazos.	NA
*†MISSION, Hidalgo, 276	28,618	Mountain View, Travis	393	Nelson City, Kendall	NA
McAllen-Edinburg-Mission		Mountain View Estates, Hunt	NA	Nelsonville, Austin	110
1985 metro. pop.	352,200	Mount Bethel, Panola	62	Nelta, Hopkins	36
Mission Bend, Fort Bend	NA	Mount Blanco, Crosby	NA	*Nemo, Somervell, 4	56
Mission Hills, Bexar	NA	*MOUNT CALM, Hill, 6	445	NESBITT, Harrison	141
Mission Valley, Comal.	NA	Mount Calm, Limestone	5	Nesbitt, Robertson	NA
Mission Valley, Victoria	208	*†MOUNT ENTERPRISE, Rusk,		Neuville, Shelby	43
*†MISSOURI CITY, Fort Bend-		16.	520	*Nevada, Collin, 5	400
Harris, 250	31,054	Mount Gainor, Hays	NA	*NEWARK, Wise, 8	581
Misty Oaks, Bexar.	NA	Mount Haven, Cherokee	NA	*New Baden, Robertson, 1	105
Mitchell, Eastland.	46	Mount Hermon, Shelby	56	NEW BERLIN, Guadalupe	269
Mitchell Hill, Tyler	NA	Mount Lookout, Comal	NA	Newberry Hollow, Kerr	NA
Mixon, Cherokee.	50	Mount Pleasant, Grimes	12	New Bethel, Jefferson	NA
*†MOBEETIE, Wheeler, 8	360	§*†MOUNT PLEASANT, Titus,		New Bielau, Colorado	NA
Modern, Jim Wells	NA	311.	11,682	New Birthright, Hopkins	NA
Moffat, Bell.	150	Mount Rose, Falls.	NA	New Blox, Jasper	NA
Moffett, Angelina	NA	Mount Selman, Cherokee	200	*†NEW BOSTON, Bowie, 69	4,758
Moistown, Cameron	25	Mount Sharp, Hays	NA	§*†NEW BRAUNFELS, Comal-	
Moline, Lampasas.	40	Mount Sylvan, Smith, 1	181	Guadalupe, 762.	25,337
§*†MONAHANS, Ward-		Mount Union, Jasper.	NA	New Bremen, Austin	NA
Winkler, 254	9,455	§*†MOUNT VERNON, Franklin,		Newburg, Comanche.	35
Monaville, Waller	180	74.	2,084	Newby, Leon.	40
Monkeyville, Hays	NA	Mount Vernon, Houston	NA	New Camp Ruby, Polk	NA
Monkstown, Fannin	35	Mouth of Pedernales, Travis	NA	*†New Caney, Montgomery,	
Monroe, Rusk.	96	Mozelle, Cochran	NA	93.	2,771
*Monroe City, Chambers	90	Mozelle, Coleman	NA	New Caney Heights,	
Mont, Lavaca	30	Mozo, Williamson	NA	Montgomery	NA
Montadale, Williamson	NA	Muddig, Hunt	NA	*†NEWCASTLE, Young, 4	771
§*Montague, Montague, 4	400	Muellersville, Washington	40	NEW CHAPEL HILL, Smith	670
Montague Village, Coryell	1,275	*†MUENSTER, Cooke, 68.	1,339	New Colony, Bell	4
*Montalba, Anderson, 2	110	Mulberry, Fannin	17	New Colony, Cass	NA
*†MONT BELVIEU, Chambers,		Mulberry Cove, Hunt.	NA	New Corn Hill, Williamson	NA
57.	1,807	Mulberry Creek Estates,		*NEW DEAL, Lubbock, 10	691
*Monte Alto, Hidalgo	525	Taylor	NA	*Newgulf, Wharton, 3	963
Monte Grande, Cameron	NA	Mulberry Ridge, Angelina	NA	New Harmony, Shelby	NA
Montell, Uvalde	10	*Muldoon, Fayette, 4.	98	New Harmony, Smith	NA
Monte Oaks, Montgomery	NA	§*†MULESHOE, Bailey, 149	5,048	New Harp, Montague	NA
Monte Robles Park, Bexar.	NA	*MULLIN, Mills, 8	221	*NEW HOME, Lynn, 2	243
Montfort, Navarro	NA	Mullins Prairie, Fayette	NA	New Hope, Cherokee	NA
*MONTGOMERY, Montgomery,		*Mumford, Robertson, 1	170	NEW HOPE, Collin	447
95.	281	*†MUNDAY, Knox, 33	1,751	New Hope, Franklin	NA
Monthalia, Gonzales	65	Munger, Limestone.	NA	New Hope, Freestone	85
MONTICELLO, Titus	40	Mungerville, Dawson	NA	New Hope, Jones	25
*†MOODY, McLennan, 26	1,502	Munson, Rockwall.	64	New Hope, Rusk	NA
Moonshine Colony, Baylor.	NA	*MURCHISON, Henderson, 12	639	New Hope, San Augustine	NA
Moore, Brazos.	NA	MURPHY, Collin.	1,114	New Hope, Smith	NA
*Moore, Frio, 3	230	Murray, Cameron	NA	New Hope, Wood	NA
Moore Hill, Polk	NA	Murray, Young.	29	Newlin, Hall	31
Moore's Crossing, Travis.	25	Murvaul, Panola	110	*NEW LONDON, Rusk, 15	1,084
MOORE STATION, Henderson	400	Musgrove, Wood	NA	New Lynn, Lynn	18
Mooreville, Falls.	91	Musfang, Denton	NA	Newman, El Paso	60
Mooring, Brazos	80	MUSTANG, Navarro.	15	New Mesquite, Collin	NA
Morales, Jackson	25	Mustang Mott, DeWitt.	NA	New Moore, Lynn	NA
*†MORAN, Shackelford, 8	404	**Mustang Ridge,**		New Mountain, Upshur	NA
Moravia, Lavaca.	165	Travis-Caldwell	435	*Newport, Clay-Jack.	70
*MORGAN, Bosque, 1	467	*Myra, Cooke	70	New Prospect, Rusk	NA
Morgan Bluff, Orange.	NA	Myrtle Springs, Van Zandt, 1	131	New River Lake Estates,	
Morgan Creek, Burnet	NA	Mystic Oak, Travis	NA	Liberty	NA
*Morgan Mill, Erath, 3.	206	**N**		New Salem, Palo Pinto	NA
MORGAN'S POINT, Harris	557	Nacalina, Nacogdoches.	NA	New Salem, Rusk	31
MORGAN'S POINT RESORT,		§*†NACOGDOCHES, Nacogdoches,		Newsome, Camp	100
Bell.	1,277	678.	28,744	*NEW SUMMERFIELD,	
Morrill, Cherokee	NA	*Nada, Colorado, 6	165	Cherokee, 9	371
Morris Ranch, Gillespie.	NA	*†NAPLES, Morris, 26	1,906	New Sweden, Travis	60
*Morse, Hansford, 6	150	Naruna, Burnet.	45	Newt, Fannin	2
§*†MORTON, Cochran, 47	2,578	*NASH, Bowie, 28.	2,202	§*†NEWTON, Newton, 53.	1,646
Morton, Harrison	NA	Nash, Ellis	25	*†New Ulm, Austin, 10	650
Morton Valley, Eastland	46	*NASSAU BAY, Harris.	4,739	*†NEW WAVERLY, Walker,	
*Moscow, Polk, 3.	170	Nat, Nacogdoches.	25	23.	962
Mosheim, Bosque	75	*NATALIA, Medina, 12	1,514	New Wehdem, Austin	100
Moss Bluff, Liberty	65	*Navarro, Navarro.	180	New Willard, Polk	160
Moss Hill, Liberty	49	Navarro Mills, Navarro	50	†New York, Henderson	NA
Mosswood, Montgomery	NA	*†NAVASOTA, Grimes, 131	6,808	NEYLANDVILLE, Hunt	196

Town and County—	Pop.	Town and County—	Pop.	Town and County—	Pop.
Nickel Creek, Culberson	16	Oak Grove, Bowie	294	Old Sabinetown, Sabine	NA
Nickleberry, Cass	NA	Oak Grove, Colorado	NA	Old Salem, Bowie	NA
Nickleville, Wise	NA	Oak Grove, Ellis	10	Old Snake River, Liberty	NA
Niederwald, Hays-Caldwell	79	Oak Grove, Hopkins	NA	Old Town Meadows,	
Nigton, Trinity	34	OAK GROVE, Kaufman	387	Williamson	NA
Nimrod, Eastland	85	Oak Grove, Wood	74	Old Union, Bowie	238
Nineveh, Leon	101	Oak Harbor, Henderson	NA	Old Union, Limestone	25
Nix, Lampasas	NA	Oak Heights, Kerr	NA	Oletha, Limestone	NA
*†NIXON, Gonzales-		Oak Hill, Hood	NA	Olfen, Runnels	NA
Wilson, 28	2,211	Oak Hill, Rusk	24	Olin, Hamilton	12
Noack, Williamson	60	Oakhill Ranches, Bexar	NA	Olivia, Calhoun	215
Nob Hill, Llano	NA	Oak Island, Chambers	NA	Ollie, Polk	NA
Nobility, Fannin	21	Oaklake, McLennan	60	*†Olmito, Cameron, 11	200
Noble, Lamar	40	Oakland, Brazoria	NA	Olmos, Guadalupe	30
Nockenut, Wilson	10	Oakland, Cherokee	NA	OLMOS PARK, Bexar	2,028
*†NOCONA, Montague, 103	3,206	*Oakland, Colorado, 1	80	*†OLNEY, Young, 93	3,916
Nogalus Prairie, Trinity	41	Oakland, Jack	NA	*†OLTON, Lamb, 43	2,107
*Nolan, Nolan, 1	131	Oakland, Van Zandt	26	*†OMAHA, Morris, 17	1,000
*NOLANVILLE, Bell, 3	1,726	Oak Lane, Montgomery	NA	Omega, Gregg	NA
Nolte, Guadalupe	25	Oak Leaf, Ellis	338	Omen, Smith	150
*NOME, Jefferson, 13	610	Oak Manor, Brazoria	NA	*†ONALASKA, Polk, 58	562
Noodle, Jones	40	Oak Meadows Estates,		One Seventy-Seven Lake	
Noonday, Smith	428	Montgomery	NA	Estates, Montgomery	NA
Nopal, DeWitt	25	Oak Moss, Bexar	NA	Onion Creek, Travis	NA
*†NORDHEIM, DeWitt, 7	429	Oak Park, Travis	NA	Opdyke, Hockley	20
Norman, Williamson	20	OAK POINT, Denton	506	Opdyke West, Hockley	NA
Normandy, Maverick	98	Oak Ridge, Fannin	90	Open Air Estates, Smith	NA
*†NORMANGEE, Leon-		Oak Ridge, Grayson	NA	Oplin, Callahan	75
Madison, 20	581	OAK RIDGE, Kaufman	168	O'Quinn, Fayette	25
*Normanna, Bee, 1	75	Oak Ridge, Llano	NA	Oran, Palo Pinto	NA
Norse, Bosque	110	Oak Ridge, Nacogdoches	NA	§*†ORANGE, Orange, 555	25,974
North Alamo, Hidalgo	NA	Oak Ridge Estates, Marion	NA	Beaumont-Port Arthur	
North Cedar, Trinity	NA	OAK RIDGE NORTH,		1985 metro. pop.	381,300
NORTH CLEVELAND, Liberty	301	Montgomery	2,483	Orangedale, Bee	35
Northcliff, Guadalupe	1,800	Oak Shade, Polk	NA	*Orangefield, Orange, 16	725
North Country, Montgomery	NA	Oaks North, Bexar	NA	*†ORANGE GROVE, Jim Wells,	
North Cowden, Ector	80	Oak Springs, Hill	NA	29	1,536
NORTHCREST, McLennan	2,057	Oak Terrace, Montgomery	NA	Orangeville, Fannin	23
*Northfield, Motley	15	Oak Terrace Estates, Polk	NA	*ORCHARD, Fort Bend, 9	481
North Groesbeck, Hardeman	NA	Oak Trail Shores, Hood	3,500	*†ORE CITY, Upshur, 31	1,053
North Hopkins, Hopkins	NA	OAK VALLEY, Navarro	204	Orient, Tom Green	40
North Houston, Harris	NA	Oak Valley Park, Travis	NA	*Orla, Reeves, 6	183
North Jericho, Shelby	NA	Oakview, Comal	NA	Osage, Coryell	30
NORTHLAKE, Denton	176	Oak Village, Bexar	NA	Oscar, Bell	40
Northlake Estates, Williamson	NA	Oak Village North, Comal	NA	Osceola, Hill	90
North Line Oaks, Williamson	NA	*Oakville, Live Oak, 1	260	Oslo, Hansford	NA
North Oaks, Travis	NA	*†OAKWOOD, Leon, 8	576	Otey, Brazoria	318
North Orange Heights, Orange	NA	Oakwood Acres, Bexar	NA	Otis Chalk, Howard	79
North Park Estates, Travis	NA	Oatmeal, Burnet	20	*Ottine, Gonzales	90
*†NORTH RICHLAND HILLS,		*O'BRIEN, Haskell, 2	184	*Otto, Falls, 1	85
Tarrant	36,962	Oceanshore, Galveston	NA	*Ovalo, Taylor	225
Northrup, Lee	71	Ocee, McLennan	35	*†OVERTON, Rusk-Smith,	
North San Antonio Hills,		Ochiltree, Ochiltree	NA	57	2,463
Bexar	NA	Odds, Limestone	NA	†OVILLA, Ellis-Dallas	1,307
North Shore Colony, Travis	NA	*Odell, Wilbarger	131	Owens, Brown	NA
North Star, Archer	NA	*†ODEM, San Patricio, 36	2,770	Owens, Crosby	75
Northwest Oaks, Burnet	NA	§*†ODESSA, Ector-		Owensville, Robertson	NA
Northwest Woods,		Midland, 2,872	108,690	Owentown, Smith	NA
Williamson	NA	1985 metro. pop.	134,700	Owl Creek, Bell	45
North Woods, Montgomery	NA	*†O'DONNELL, Lynn-		OYSTER CREEK, Brazoria	1,462
*North Zulch, Madison, 3	100	Dawson, 21	1,076	§*†Ozona, Crockett, 72	3,500
*Norton, Runnels, 2	76	Oenaville, Bell	120	**P**	
Notla, Ochiltree	20	O'Farrell, Cass	20	Pacio, Delta	15
*Notrees, Ector, 2	338	Ogburn, Wood	NA	Padgett, Young	23
Nottingham Forest, Orange	NA	*†OGLESBY, Coryell, 1	515	Padre Island, Nueces	NA
Nottingham Woods, Houston	NA	*Oilton, Webb	458	§*†PADUCAH, Cottle, 48	2,067
*NOVICE, Coleman, 2	202	Oklahoma, Montgomery	NA	*Paige, Bastrop, 4	275
Novice, Lamar	NA	Oklahoma Flat, Hockley	NA	§*†PAINT ROCK, Concho, 8	290
Noxville, Kimble	3	Oklahoma Lane, Parmer	64	*†PALACIOS, Matagorda, 77	4,603
Nubia, Taylor	NA	*Oklaunion, Wilbarger, 1	138	Palava, Fisher	12
Nugent, Jones	41	Okra, Eastland	20	Paleface Lake Country Estates,	
Nunelee, Fannin	25	Ola, Kaufman	50	Travis	NA
*Nursery, Victoria, 4	106	Old Boston, Bowie	NA	§*†PALESTINE, Anderson,	
O		Old Bowling, Leon	20	398	18,153
Oak, Ellis	NA	Old Center, Panola	83	Palito Blanco, Jim Wells	35
Oakalla, Burnet	45	Old Diana, Upshur	NA	*†PALMER, Ellis, 14	1,505
Oak Bend, Brazoria	NA	Old Dime Box, Lee	200	Palm Harbor, Aransas	125
Oak Branch, Ellis	NA	*Olden, Eastland, 1	110	PALMHURST, Hidalgo	426
Oak Cliff Acres, Comal	NA	Oldenburg, Fayette	54	Palm Park, Bexar	NA
Oak Creek, Bexar	NA	Old Ferry, Travis	NA	PALM VALLEY, Cameron	820
Oak Crest Estates, Williamson		*Old Glory, Stonewall, 1	125	PALMVIEW, Hidalgo	805
	NA	Oldham, Tyler	NA	Palo Alto, Nueces	15
Oakdale, Hopkins	NA	Old Larissa, Cherokee	NA	Palo Alto Park, Bexar	NA
Oakdale, Polk	25	Old Midway, Leon	NA	Paloduro, Armstrong	NA
Oak Flat, Nacogdoches	NA	*Old Ocean, Brazoria, 10	915	Palomino Park, Travis	NA
Oak Flats, Rusk	NA	Old River Lake, Liberty	NA	§*Palo Pinto, Palo Pinto, 8	350
Oak Forest, Gonzales	25	OLD RIVER-WINFREE,		*Paluxy, Hood	76
Oak Forest, Montgomery	NA	Chambers	1,255	§*†PAMPA, Gray, 566	22,275
Oak Forest Haven, Hunt	NA			Pancake, Coryell	NA

Town and County—	Pop.
*†PORT ARTHUR, Jefferson, 635.	64,092
Beaumont-Port Arthur 1985 metro. pop.	381,300
Port-Au-Prince, Brazoria	NA
*Port Bolivar, Galveston, 20.	1,200
Port Brownsville, Cameron	NA
*†Porter, Montgomery, 112	2,146
Porter Heights, Montgomery	NA
Porter Springs, Houston	50
Porterville Timbers, Montgomery	NA
*†PORT ISABEL, Cameron, 120.	4,243
*†PORTLAND, San Patricio-Nueces, 114	12,722
§*†PORT LAVACA, Calhoun, 224.	12,349
*Port Mansfield, Willacy, 6	731
*†PORT NECHES, Jefferson, 157.	14,333
*Port O'Connor, Calhoun, 15.	810
Port Sullivan, Milam	15
Porvenir, Presidio	NA
Posey, Hopkins	NA
Posey, Lubbock	125
§*†POST, Garza, 90	4,162
Post Oak, Blanco	NA
Postoak, Jack	79
Postoak, Lamar	NA
Post Oak, Lee	NA
Post Oak, Robertson	NA
POST OAK BEND, Kaufman	353
Post Oak Point, Austin	NA
*†POTEET, Atascosa, 28	3,519
*†POTH, Wilson, 20	1,516
Potosi, Taylor	149
*†POTTSBORO, Grayson, 35	1,130
*Pottsville, Hamilton, 2	312
*Powderly, Lamar, 9	185
*†POWELL, Navarro, 3	130
*POYNOR, Henderson, 4	259
Praesel, Milam	115
Praha, Fayette	25
Prairie Center, Matagorda	NA
Prairie Chapel, McLennan	NA
Prairie Dell, Bell	12
Prairie Grove, Franklin	NA
*Prairie Hill, Limestone	150
Prairie Hill, Washington	NA
*Prairie Lea, Caldwell	100
Prairie Mountain, Llano	NA
Prairie Point, Cooke	30
Prairieview, Hale	NA
*PRAIRIE VIEW, Waller, 3.	3,715
Prairieville, Kaufman	50
*†PREMONT, Jim Wells, 44	3,149
*†Presidio, Presidio, 22	1,671
Preston, Grayson	250
*Price, Rusk, 1	275
*Priddy, Mills, 4	215
PRIMERA, Cameron	1,675
Primrose, Van Zandt	24
*†PRINCETON, Collin, 31	3,918
Pringle, Hutchinson	40
Pritchett, Upshur	125
*Proctor, Comanche, 5	220
*Progreso, Hidalgo, 15.	185
Progreso Lakes, Hidalgo	219
Progress, Bailey	49
Prospect, Rains	40
*†PROSPER, Collin, 12	791
*Providence, Floyd	NA
Providence, Polk	NA
Pruitt, Cass.	NA
Pruitt, Van Zandt	NA
Pueblo, Callahan	NA
Pueblo, Eastland.	46
Pueblo Nuevo, Webb	130
Puerto Rico, Hidalgo.	91
Pullman, Potter	31
Pumphrey, Runnels	NA
Pumpkin, San Jacinto	20
Pumpville, Val Verde	21
Punkin Center, Dawson	NA
Punkin Center, Eastland	12
Punkin Center, Hardeman	NA

Town and County—	Pop.
*Purdon, Navarro, 2	133
Purley, Franklin	81
*Purmela, Coryell, 1	61
Pursley, Navarro	40
Purves, Erath	50
*PUTNAM, Callahan, 6	131
*PYOTE, Ward, 1	519
Q	
*Quail, Collingsworth, 1.	92
Quail Valley, Williamson	NA
§*†QUANAH, Hardeman, 91.	3,963
Quarry, Washington	NA
Quarterway, Hale	12
*QUEEN CITY, Cass, 24.	1,745
*Quemado, Maverick, 6.	426
Quicksand, Newton	NA
Quihi, Medina.	104
*†QUINLAN, Hunt, 72	1,602
QUINTANA, Brazoria	30
*†QUITAQUE, Briscoe, 11	700
§*†QUITMAN, Wood, 87	1,994
R	
Rabb, Nueces	20
Rabbit Hollow, Williamson	NA
Rabbs Prairie, Fayette	31
Raccoon Bend, Austin	NA
Rachal, Brooks	36
Radium, Jones	26
Ragtown, Lamar	25
*Rainbow, Somervell, 5	76
Rainbow Hills, Bexar.	NA
Raintree Country, Montgomery	NA
Raisin, Victoria.	50
Raleigh, Navarro	NA
*†RALLS, Crosby, 42	2,263
Ralph, Randall	NA
Ramireno, Zapata	NA
Ramirez, Duval.	40
Ranch Branch, Mason	NA
Ranch Harbor Estates, Hill	NA
Ranchito, Cameron	NA
Ranchland Acres, Midland	NA
Rancho Alegre, Jim Wells	1,950
Rancho de la Parita, Jim Wells.	NA
RANCHO VIEJO, Cameron	340
Rand, Kaufman	NA
Randado, Jim Hogg.	15
*Randolph, Fannin	70
*†Randolph Air Force Base, Bexar	3,015
*†RANGER, Eastland, 56	3,439
Ranger Country, Williamson	NA
Rangerville, Cameron	80
Rankin, Ellis	12
§*†RANKIN, Upton, 16	1,494
*Ransom Canyon, Lubbock	620
*Ratcliff, Houston, 2	106
Ratibor, Bell	10
Rattan, Delta	10
*Ravenna, Fannin, 1	186
Ravenwood, Brazos.	NA
Ray, Grayson	NA
Rayburn, Liberty	30
Rayburn Country, Jasper	600
Rayburn Hideaway, Nacogdoches	NA
Rayford Forest, Montgomery	NA
Raylake, Angelina	NA
Rayland, Foard	30
§*†RAYMONDVILLE, Willacy, 103.	10,082
Ray Point, Live Oak	75
*Raywood, Liberty, 16	231
Razor, Lamar	15
*Reagan, Falls, 3	200
Reagan Wells, Uvalde	20
Reagor Springs, Ellis.	45
*Realitos, Duval, 1.	250
Reata Trails, Williamson	NA
Rebecca Creek Park, Comal	NA
Red Bank, Bowie.	NA
Red Bluff, Jackson	NA
Red Bluff, Reeves.	40
Red Branch, Grayson	NA
Red Branch, Leon	NA
Redbud Acres, Williamson.	NA
Red Cut Heights, Bowie	563

Town and County—	Pop.
Redfield, Nacogdoches	NA
*Redford, Presidio	107
Red Gate, Hidalgo.	NA
Red Hill, Cass	20
Red Hill, Limestone.	NA
Red Lake, Freestone	NA
Redland, Angelina	NA
Redland, Leon	35
Redland, Van Zandt	NA
Redlawn, Cherokee	NA
Red Lick, Bowie	NA
*†RED OAK, Ellis, 93	2,425
*Red Ranger, Bell.	12
*Red Rock, Bastrop, 1	100
*Red Springs, Baylor, 2	81
Red Springs, Smith	NA
Redtown, Angelina	NA
*†Redwater, Bowie, 4	958
Redwood, Guadalupe	400
Reeds Settlement, Red River	50
Reedville, Caldwell	NA
Reese, Cherokee	75
*Reese Air Force Base, Lubbock	1,563
Reese Village, Lubbock	2,600
Reeves, Hardin	NA
Refuge, Houston	NA
§*†REFUGIO, Refugio, 99	3,707
Regency, Mills	25
Rehburg, Washington	NA
Reilly Springs, Hopkins	44
Rek Hill, Fayette.	NA
*REKLAW, Cherokee-Rusk, 5	328
Relampago, Hidalgo	NA
Reliance, Brazos.	NA
Rendon, Tarrant.	90
RENO, Lamar.	1,144
RENO, Parker	1,519
Reservation, Kerr.	NA
Retreat, Grimes	NA
Retreat, Hill	NA
RETREAT, Navarro	280
Retta, Johnson	NA
Reyes, Duval.	NA
Reynard, Houston	NA
Rhea, Parmer.	98
Rhea Mills, Collin	47
Rhineland, Knox	196
*†RHOME, Wise, 15.	634
Rhonesboro, Upshur	40
Ricardo, Kleberg	120
*†RICE, Navarro-Ellis, 7	511
Rices Crossing, Williamson	100
*Richards, Grimes, 8	296
*†RICHARDSON, Dallas-Collin, 2,054	76,981
*RICHLAND, Navarro, 1	247
Richland, Rains	100
Richland, Travis	NA
RICHLAND HILLS, Tarrant	9,132
*RICHLAND SPRINGS, San Saba, 11	401
§*†RICHMOND, Fort Bend, 187	15,927
†RICHWOOD, Brazoria	3,057
Rico Ranchos, Travis	NA
Riderville, Panola	50
Ridge, Mills	NA
*Ridge, Robertson	67
Ridgeheights, Midland	NA
Ridgemar Landing, Williamson	NA
Ridgeway, Hopkins	54
Ridgewood, Midland	NA
Ridings, Fannin	10
*†RIESEL, McLennan, 4	786
Rimwick Forest, Montgomery	NA
Rincon, Starr	NA
*Ringgold, Montague	100
Rio Bravo, Webb	4,000
Rio del Sol, Cameron	NA
*Rio Frio, Real	50
§*†Rio Grande City, Starr, 98.	5,720
*RIO HONDO, Cameron, 24	1,970
Rio Llano Ranch, Llano	NA
*Riomedina, Medina, 2	53
Rios, Duval	75
*†RIO VISTA, Johnson, 8	657

Town and County—	Pop.	Town and County—	Pop.	Town and County—	Pop.
*†RISING STAR, Eastland, 23.	1,254	Rogers Hill, McLennan	NA	Rush Prairie, Navarro.	NA
Rita, Burleson.	50	Rogers Plantation, Brazos.	NA	§*†RUSK, Cherokee, 71	4,612
River, Zavala	NA	Roland, Collin	NA	Russell, Leon	27
River Acres, Tyler.	NA	Rolling Hills, Hunt.	NA	Russelltown, Cameron	NA
River Bend, Newton	NA	Rolling Hills, Potter.	1,000	Rustic Acres, Angelina	NA
River Bend, Sabine	NA	Rolling Hills, Waller	NA	Rutersville, Fayette	72
Riverbend Oaks, Williamson	NA	Rolling Hills Shores, Hood	NA	Ruth Springs, Henderson.	NA
Riverbrook, Montgomery	NA	ROLLING MEADOWS, Gregg	268	*Rye, Liberty, 6.	76
Riverby, Fannin	15	Rolling Oaks, Hays	NA		
River Club Estates, Montgomery	NA	ROLLINGWOOD, Travis	1,376	S	
River Crest Estates, Travis	NA	*†ROMA, Starr, 44.	3,955	Sabanna, Eastland	12
River Crest Estates, Angelina	NA	ROMAN FOREST, Montgomery	1,022	*†SABINAL, Uvalde, 18	2,002
River Hill, Panola	NA	Roman Hills, Montgomery	NA	Sabine, Gregg.	750
River Hills, Travis.	NA	*Romayor, Liberty	96	Sabine Farms, Harrison	NA
River Meadows, Hays	NA	Romero, Hartley	25	Sabine Sands, Newton	NA
River Oaks, Brazos	NA	Romney, Eastland.	12	†SACHSE, Dallas-Collin	2,311
River Oaks, Burnet	NA	*Roosevelt, Kimble, 2	98	*Sacul, Nacogdoches, 1	170
River Oaks, Hays	NA	Roosevelt, Lubbock, 1	3,500	Saddle and Surrey, Montgomery	NA
RIVER OAKS, Tarrant	7,740	*ROPESVILLE, Hockley, 9	492	*SADLER, Grayson, 4	348
River Oaks, Travis	NA	R.O. Ranch Estates, Travis	NA	*Sagerton, Haskell, 2	115
River Oaks, Williamson	NA	Rosalie, Red River	100	*†SAGINAW, Tarrant, 9.	7,185
River Oaks Estates, Montgomery	NA	*Rosanky, Bastrop, 3.	210	St. Clair Cove, Galveston	NA
River Plantation, Montgomery	NA	Rosborough Springs, Harrison	NA	St. Elmo, Freestone.	NA
River Ridge, Montgomery.	NA	*†ROSCOE, Nolan, 22.	1,636	St. Francis, Potter.	30
Rivers End, Brazoria.	NA	*†ROSEBUD, Falls, 36	2,102	*ST. HEDWIG, Bexar, 3	1,111
*RIVERSIDE, Walker, 10	390	ROSE CITY, Orange	697	St. Holland, Grimes.	50
Riverside Estates, Brazoria	NA	Rose Hill, Harris	NA	*†ST. JO, Montague, 22	1,219
River Terrace, Harris	NA	Rose Hill, San Jacinto	10	St. John, Harrison	NA
River Trail, Nueces	NA	ROSE HILL ACRES, Hardin.	540	St. John Colony, Caldwell.	NA
Riverwood, Montgomery	NA	*†ROSENBERG, Fort Bend, 380.	19,526	St. Lawrence, Glasscock	NA
*Riviera, Kleberg, 21.	550	Rosevine, Sabine	50	ST. PAUL, Collin	492
Riviera Beach, Kleberg.	NA	Rosewood, Upshur	100	St. Paul, San Patricio.	180
Riviera Estates, Polk	NA	Rosewood Hill, Harris	NA	*†Salado, Bell, 42.	1,500
Roach, Cass	NA	*Rosharon, Brazoria, 27.	435	Salem, Cherokee.	NA
Roane, Navarro	120	Rosita, Duval	NA	Salem, Grimes	50
*†ROANOKE, Denton, 116	1,211	Rosita, Starr	220	Salem, Newton	85
*Roans Prairie, Grimes, 3	56	*ROSS, McLennan, 3	261	Salem, Victoria	25
*ROARING SPRINGS, Motley, 6	282	Ross City, Howard.	81	Salesville, Palo Pinto.	40
Robbins, Leon	20	*Rosser, Kaufman, 2	255	Saline, Menard	58
§*†ROBERT LEE, Coke, 25	1,391	*Rosston, Cooke	110	*Salineno, Starr, 1	155
Robertson, Crosby	35	Rossville, Atascosa	47	Salmon Lake, Anderson.	20
*†ROBINSON, McLennan	6,476	*†ROTAN, Fisher, 27	2,273	*Salt Flat, Hudspeth	35
Robinson Arms Landing, Reeves	21	Rough Creek, San Saba	NA	Salt Gap, McCulloch	25
*†ROBSTOWN, Nueces, 188	13,325	Round House, Navarro	NA	*Saltillo, Hopkins, 2	200
§*†ROBY, Fisher, 12	898	*†Round Mountain, Blanco, 3.	73	Samaria, Navarro	NA
*Rochelle, McCulloch, 4.	163	Round Mountain, Travis	NA	Sam Fordyce, Hidalgo.	85
*†ROCHESTER, Haskell, 8.	459	Round Prairie, Navarro	40	Sam Houston Lake Estates, Liberty	NA
Rock Bluff, Burnet	NA	Round Prairie, Robertson	NA	*Samnorwood, Collingsworth	110
Rock Creek, McLennan	25	*†ROUND ROCK, Williamson-Travis, 475	17,904	Sample, Gonzales	25
Rock Creek, Somervell	36	Round Timber, Baylor.	8	*Sam Rayburn, Jasper	NA
*†ROCKDALE, Milam, 130.	5,810	*†ROUND TOP, Fayette, 5.	100	Sanaloma Estates, Williamson	NA
Rockett, Ellis	124	Round Top, Fisher	NA	§*†SAN ANGELO, Tom Green, 1,435.	84,350
Rockford, Lamar	NA	Roundup, Hockley.	27	1985 metro. pop.	96,700
Rock Harbor, Hood	NA	Rowden, Callahan.	30	§*†SAN ANTONIO, Bexar, 13,466.	842,779
Rockhill, Collin	25	*†Rowena, Runnels, 7	466	1985 metro. pop.	1,235,700
Rock Hill, Franklin	NA	Rowland, Montague	NA	San Antonio Prairie, Burleson	NA
Rock Hill, Wood.	21	*†ROWLETT, Dallas-Rockwall, 218	10,573	Sanatorium, Tom Green	450
Rockhouse, Austin	NA	*†ROXTON, Lamar, 5	747	§*†SAN AUGUSTINE, San Augustine, 77	2,983
Rock House, Williamson	NA	Royal Forest, Comal	NA	*†SAN BENITO, Cameron, 190	20,695
*Rock Island, Colorado, 3.	160	Royal Forest, Montgomery	NA	San Carlos, Hidalgo.	100
Rock Island, Marion	NA	Royal Oaks, Henderson	NA	San Carlos, Starr.	NA
*Rockland, Tyler	105	Royal Oaks, Kerr	NA	Sanco, Coke	30
*Rockne, Bastrop	400	Royal Oaks, Llano	NA	Sanctuary, Parker	262
§*†ROCKPORT, Aransas, 237.	4,714	Royal Oaks, Montgomery	NA	Sand, Dawson	20
§*†ROCKSPRINGS, Edwards, 26.	1,454	Royal Oaks, Orange	NA	Sandbranch, Dallas.	NA
§*†ROCKWALL, Rockwall, 257.	5,939	Royal Oaks, Smith	NA	§*†Sanderson, Terrell, 15.	1,250
*Rockwood, Coleman	80	*Royalty, Ward, 2	196	Sand Flat, Johnson	NA
Rocky Branch, Morris	135	Royal View, Bexar.	NA	Sand Flat, Rains	100
Rocky Creek, Angelina	NA	Royder, Brazos	NA	Sand Flat, Smith	NA
Rocky Creek, Blanco	NA	*†ROYSE CITY, Rockwall-Collin, 56	1,800	Sandhill, Floyd	NA
Rocky Hill, Angelina	NA	Royston, Fisher	30	Sand Hill, Upshur	NA
ROCKY MOUND, Camp	127	Rucker, Comanche	NA	*Sandia, Jim Wells, 7	215
Rocky Point, Burnet	NA	Rucker's Bridge, Lamar	20	§*†SAN DIEGO, Duval-Jim Wells, 33	5,695
Rocky Point, Rains	80	Rugby, Red River	24	Sand Lake, Ellis	NA
Roddy, Van Zandt	NA	Ruidosa, Presidio	43	Sandlin, Stonewall	NA
Rodney Calm, Navarro	NA	*†RULE, Haskell, 15	1,016	Sandoval, Williamson	50
Roeder, Titus	NA	Rumley, Lampasas	NA	Sand Ridge, Houston	NA
*Roganville, Jasper	100	RUNAWAY BAY, Wise.	639	Sand Springs, Howard	903
*†ROGERS, Bell, 15	1,367	*†RUNGE, Karnes, 11	1,285	Sandusky, Grayson	NA
Rogers, Taylor	NA	Runn, Hidalgo.	NA	*Sandy, Blanco, 1	25
		Running Water, Hale.	NA	Sandy, Limestone	5
		Rural Shade, Navarro	30	Sandy Acres, Burnet	NA
		Rushing, Navarro	NA		

Town and County—	Pop.	Town and County—	Pop.	Town and County—	Pop.
Sandy Acres, Midland	NA	*SCOTTSVILLE, Harrison, 7	327	Shaws Bend, Colorado	NA
Sandy Harbor, Llano	85	Scranton, Eastland	40	*Sheffield, Pecos, 5	600
Sandy Hill, Washington	50	Scrappin Valley, Newton	NA	Shelby, Austin	175
Sandy Hills, Montgomery	NA	*Scroggins, Franklin, 4	125	*Shelbyville, Shelby, 5	215
Sandy Point, Brazoria	30	*Scurry, Kaufman, 9	315	Sheldon, Harris	1,665
*San Elizario, El Paso, 1	1,100	*†SEABROOK, Harris-		Shell Camp, Gregg	225
*SAN FELIPE, Austin, 2	675	Chambers-Galveston, 236	4,788	Shell Shore, Smith	NA
*SANFORD, Hutchinson, 6	314	*†SEADRIFT, Calhoun, 18	1,599	Shelter Cove, Polk	NA
Sanford Estates, Hutchinson	70	*†SEAGOVILLE, Dallas-		SHENANDOAH,	
San Gabriel, Milam, 1	100	Kaufman, 114	8,632	Montgomery	2,024
San Gabriel Heights,		*†SEAGRAVES, Gaines, 52	2,643	Shep, Taylor	60
Williamson	NA	Seale, Robertson	26	*†SHEPHERD, San Jacinto,	
San Gabriel River Ranch,		*†SEALY, Austin, 155	4,868	27	1,983
Williamson	NA	Seaton, Bell	60	*Sheppard Air Force Base,	
*†SANGER, Denton, 72	3,261	Seawillow, Caldwell	NA	Wichita	3,825
San Geronimo, Bexar	NA	*Sebastian, Willacy, 9	404	*Sheridan, Colorado, 8	225
*San Isidro, Starr, 9	130	Sebastopol, Trinity	31	§*†SHERMAN, Grayson,	
San Jacinto, Walker	NA	Seco Mines, Maverick	NA	615	31,217
San Jose, Duval	15	Security, Montgomery	24	Sherman-Denison 1985	
*†SAN JUAN, Hidalgo, 77	9,318	Sedalia, Collin	25	metro. pop.	96,700
SAN LEANNA, Travis	297	Sedwick, Shackelford	NA	Sherry, Red River	15
*San Leon, Galveston	100	*Segno, Polk	80	Sherwood, Irion	73
San Manuel, Hidalgo	NA	Segovia, Kimble	25	Sherwood Forest, Bexar	NA
§*†SAN MARCOS, Hays-		*†SEGUIN, Guadalupe,		Sherwood Shores, Bell	600
Caldwell, 493	25,288	508	18,904	Sherwood Shores, Burnet	NA
SAN PATRICIO, San Patricio-		Sejita, Duval	22	Sherwood Shores, Grayson	NA
Nueces	231	Selden, Erath	71	Sherwood Shores #3, Burnet	NA
San Pedro, Cameron	NA	Selfs, Fannin	30	Shields, Coleman	13
San Pedro, Zapata	25	SELMA, Bexar-Guadalupe-		Shiloh, Bastrop	NA
*SAN PERLITA, Willacy, 1	441	Comal	545	Shiloh, Lavaca	NA
San Roman, Starr	NA	*Selman City, Rusk, 5	271	Shiloh, Leon	NA
§*†SAN SABA, San Saba, 69	2,877	§*†SEMINOLE, Gaines, 201	6,794	Shiloh, Limestone	110
SANSOM PARK, Tarrant	4,132	Sempronius, Austin	NA	Shiloh, Williamson	NA
*†SANTA ANNA, Coleman,		Senior, Bexar	NA	*†SHINER, Lavaca, 60	2,150
26	1,446	Sentinel Oaks, Montgomery	NA	Shinnery Lake, Stonewall	NA
Santa Anna, Coleman	30	Serbin, Lee	90	Shire, Rusk	200
Santa Catarina, Starr	48	Serenada Country, Williamson	NA	Shirley, Hopkins	NA
*Santa Elena, Starr, 1	64	Serene Hills, Bexar	NA	Shirley Creek, Nacogdoches	NA
*SANTA FE, Galveston, 87	7,077	Seth Ward, Hale	1,600	*†Shiro, Grimes, 2	205
Santa Margarita, Willacy	NA	Settlers Village, Harris	NA	Shive, Hamilton	61
*Santa Maria, Cameron, 1	210	Seven Coves, Montgomery	NA	SHOREACRES, Harris-	
Santa Monica, Willacy	NA	SEVEN OAKS, Polk	373	Chambers	1,432
Santa Rita, Reagan	NA	Seven Pines, Gregg-Upshur	NA	Shore Acres, Hunt	NA
*SANTA ROSA, Cameron, 16	2,121	*†SEVEN POINTS, Henderson	925	Shore Ridge, Kerr	NA
*†Santo, Palo Pinto, 14	312	Seven Sisters, Duval	60	Short, Shelby	NA
*San Ygnacio, Zapata, 3	895	Seward Junction, Williamson	NA	Shovel Mountain, Burnet	NA
*Saragosa, Reeves	185	Sexton, Sabine	27	*Sidney, Comanche, 2	196
*Saratoga, Hardin, 3	1,000	Sexton City, Rusk	NA	§*†Sierra Blanca, Hudspeth,	
Sarber, Marion	NA	Seymore, Hopkins	NA	5	700
Sarco, Goliad	40	§*†SEYMOUR, Baylor, 105	3,754	Siesta Shores, Travis	NA
Sardis, Cass	NA	Seymour Colony, Baylor	NA	Siesta Verde, Hays	NA
Sardis, Ellis	NA	Shadow Bay, Montgomery	NA	Signal Peak, Culberson	NA
Sardis, Fisher	12	Shadow Lake Estates,		Silas, Shelby	NA
*Sargent, Matagorda	76	Montgomery	NA	Siloam, Bowie	50
§*Sarita, Kenedy, 1	185	Shadowland Retreat,		*†SILSBEE, Hardin, 208	7,827
Saron, Trinity	NA	Montgomery	NA	*Silver, Coke, 4	60
*Saspamco, Wilson, 2	443	Shadowood Estates, Smith	NA	Silver City, Fannin	NA
*Satin, Falls, 1	138	Shady Acres, Burnet	NA	Silver City, Milam	25
Satsuma, Harris	NA	Shady Brook Acres,		Silver City, Montgomery	NA
Sattler, Comal	30	Montgomery	NA	Silver City, Navarro	NA
Saturn, Gonzales	15	Shady Creek Ranch, Burnet	NA	Silver City, Red River	25
Sauney Stand, Washington	NA	Shady Dale, Montgomery	NA	Silver Creek Village #1,	
Savage, Crosby	NA	Shady Grove, Burnet	NA	Burnet	NA
*SAVOY, Fannin, 6	818	Shady Grove, Cherokee	20	Silver Creek Village #2,	
Sayers, Bexar	NA	Shady Grove, Franklin	NA	Burnet	NA
Sayersville, Bastrop	NA	Shady Grove, Houston	NA	Silver Hills, Comal-Kendall	NA
Scatter Branch, Hunt	NA	Shady Grove, Kerr	NA	Silver Lake, Van Zandt	42
Scenic Brook, Travis	NA	Shady Grove, Panola	NA	Silver Pines, Smith	NA
Scenic Brook West, Travis	NA	Shady Grove, Smith	NA	§*†SILVERTON, Briscoe, 18	775
Scenic Hills, Guadalupe	150	Shady Grove, Upshur	NA	Silver Valley, Coleman	20
Scenic Terrace, Comal	NA	Shady Meadow, Montgomery	NA	Simmons, Live Oak	35
Scharbauer City, Ector	20	Shady Oaks, Brazoria	NA	Simmons Bottom, Liberty	NA
Schattel, Frio	130	SHADY SHORES, Denton	885	*Simms, Bowie, 6	240
*†SCHERTZ, Guadalupe-		Shady Shores, Henderson	NA	Simms, Deaf Smith	NA
Comal-Bexar, 86	7,576	Shady Shores, Marion	NA	*SIMONTON, Fort Bend, 17	616
Schicke Point, Calhoun	NA	*Shafter, Presidio	31	Simpsonville, Matagorda	NA
Schoolerville, Hamilton	NA	*†SHALLOWATER, Lubbock,		Simpsonville, Upshur	100
School Hill, Erath	22	17	2,107	Sims, Brazos	NA
Schoolland, Gonzales	NA	*†SHAMROCK, Wheeler, 68	3,087	Simsboro, Freestone	NA
Schroeder, Goliad	350	Shamrock Estates, Collin	NA	Sinclair City, Smith	NA
*†SCHULENBURG, Fayette,		Shamrock Shores, Sabine	NA	Singing Sands, Galveston	NA
93	2,414	Shangri La, Burnet	NA	Singletary Sites, Newton	NA
Schumannsville, Guadalupe	400	Shankleville, Newton	NA	*Singleton, Grimes	44
Schwab City, Polk	NA	Shannon, Clay	23	§*†SINTON, San Patricio, 90	6,382
*†Schwertner, Williamson, 1	150	Sharp, Milam	75	Sion, Walker	NA
Science Hall, Jasper	NA	SHAVANO PARK, Bexar	1,626	Sipe Springs, Comanche	75
Scissors, Hidalgo	NA	Shawnee Prairie, Angelina	NA	*Sisterdale, Kendall, 3	63
*SCOTLAND, Archer-		Shawnee Shores, Hunt	NA	Sivells Bend, Cooke	100
Clay, 8	388	Shawnee Shores, Sabine	NA	Six Lakes, Liberty-Polk	NA

Town and County—	Pop.
Sixmile, Calhoun	NA
Skeeterville, San Saba	NA
*SKELLYTOWN, Carson, 8	944
Skellyville, Travis	NA
*Skidmore, Bee, 10	500
Sky Harbor, Hood	NA
Sky Lakes, Waller	NA
Skyline Acres, Comal	NA
Skyline Acres, Hays	NA
Slabtown, Lamar	NA
Slate Shoals, Lamar	NA
*†SLATON, Lubbock, 92.	6,950
Slaughter Creek Acres, Travis	NA
Slay, Ellis	NA
Slayden, Gonzales	15
Sleepy Hollow, Hays	NA
Sleepy Hollow, Montgomery	NA
Slide, Lubbock	44
*Slidell, Wise, 2	175
Sloan, San Saba	NA
Slocum, Anderson	125
Smetana, Brazos	80
*†SMILEY, Gonzales, 16	546
Smithfield, Tarrant, 3	1,000
Smith Grove, Houston	NA
*Smithland, Marion	179
Smith Oaks, Grayson	50
Smith Point, Chambers	150
Smiths Bluff, Jefferson	NA
Smithson Valley, Comal	15
*†SMITHVILLE, Bastrop, 68.	4,206
Smithwick, Burnet	NA
*SMYER, Hockley, 3	487
Smyrna, Cass	NA
Smyrna, Harrison	NA
Smyrna, Rains	25
*†SNOOK, Burleson, 9	533
Snow Hill, Collin	20
Snow Hill, Upshur	NA
Snuff Ridge, Liberty	NA
Snug Harbor, Brazoria	NA
Snyder, Hale	NA
§*†SNYDER, Scurry, 372	14,164
SOCORRO, El Paso	18,000
Solms, Comal	40
*†SOMERSET, Bexar, 15	1,251
*†SOMERVILLE, Burleson, 23.	2,410
Sommers Mill, Bell	6
§*†SONORA, Sutton, 103.	4,387
Sorghumville, Houston	NA
*†SOUR LAKE, Hardin, 35	2,045
*South Bend, Young, 1	100
South Bosque, McLennan	80
South Brice, Hall	15
South Camp, King	20
Southern Oaks, Montgomery	NA
South Franklin, Franklin	30
South Gale, Grayson	NA
South Groveton, Trinity	175
South Haven, Howard	NA
*†SOUTH HOUSTON, Harris, 344.	14,525
South Jonestown Hills, Travis	NA
*†SOUTHLAKE, Denton-Tarrant, 89.	3,612
*Southland, Garza, 1	168
Southland Plantation, Polk	NA
*SOUTHMAYD, Grayson, 2	348
South Mountain, Coryell	NA
*†SOUTH PADRE ISLAND, Cameron, 111	1,012
*South Plains, Floyd, 4	25
South Purmela, Coryell	3
Southridge Estates, Guadalupe	100
South San Gabriel Ranches, Williamson	NA
South San Pedro, Nueces	3,065
South Shore, Bell	40
SOUTHSIDE PLACE, Harris	1,560
South Sulphur, Hunt	60
South Texarkana, Bowie	370
Southton, Bexar	113
Sowells Bluff, Fannin	5
*Spade, Lamb, 2	174

Town and County—	Pop.
Spanish Fort, Montague	50
Spanish Oak Estates, Williamson	NA
Spanish Oak Terrace, Williamson	NA
Spanish Shores, Henderson	NA
Spanish Trail, Hood	400
Sparenberg, Dawson	20
Sparks, Bell	30
*Speaks, Lavaca	60
§*†SPEARMAN, Hansford, 103.	3,590
Specht Store, Bexar	NA
Speegleville, McLennan	111
Spencer, Montague	NA
*Spicewood, Burnet, 21	110
Spicewood Beach, Burnet	NA
Spicewood Springs, Travis	NA
Spider Mountain, Burnet	NA
Spillers Store, Leon	NA
Spillview Estates, Henderson	NA
*SPLENDORA, Montgomery, 37.	722
Splendora Estates, Montgomery	NA
Splendora Farms, Montgomery	NA
*SPOFFORD, Kinney	70
Spoke Hills, Hays	NA
Sportsman Village, Marion	NA
Spraberry, Midland	46
*†Spring, Harris, 1,245	15,000
*Spring Branch, Comal, 19	200
Spring Branch, Smith	NA
Spring Creek, Hutchinson	139
Spring Creek, San Saba	NA
Spring Creek, Throckmorton	NA
Spring Creek Estates, Montgomery	NA
Springdale, Cass	30
Springfield, Anderson	20
Springfield, Jim Wells	NA
Spring Forest, Montgomery	NA
Spring Hill, Bowie	209
†Spring Hill, Guadalupe	400
Spring Hill, Navarro	60
Spring Hill, San Jacinto	NA
Spring Hills, Montgomery	NA
Spring Hills, Sabine	NA
Spring Hills North, Montgomery	NA
*SPRINGLAKE, Lamb, 9	180
Spring Lake Estates, Montgomery	NA
Spring Oaks, Montgomery	NA
Spring Place, Franklin	NA
*†SPRINGTOWN, Parker, 77.	2,336
†SPRING VALLEY, Harris	3,179
Spring Valley, McLennan	NA
Spring Valley, Travis	NA
Spring Woods, Montgomery	NA
Sprinkle, Travis	NA
*†SPUR, Dickens, 25	1,579
*Spurger, Tyler, 2	472
Stacy, McCulloch	20
Staff, Eastland	65
*†STAFFORD, Fort Bend-Harris, 603	5,723
Stag Creek, Comanche	50
STAGECOACH, Montgomery	400
Stage Coach Farms, Montgomery	NA
Stage Coach Hills, Bexar	NA
Stage Coach Hills Estates, Bexar	NA
Stairtown, Caldwell	35
Staley, San Jacinto	30
*†STAMFORD, Jones-Haskell, 71	4,525
Stampede, Bell	10
Stamps, Upshur	NA
Stanfield, Clay	25
§*†STANTON, Martin, 41	2,684
*Staples, Guadalupe, 1	75
*Star, Mills, 3	85
STAR HARBOR, Henderson	361
Star Route, Cochran	NA
Starrville, Smith	75

Town and County—	Pop.
Startzville, Comal	30
State Line, Culberson	18
Steep Creek, San Augustine	NA
Steep Hollow, Brazos	NA
Steiner, Bosque	20
Stephens Creek, San Jacinto	135
§*†STEPHENVILLE, Erath, 322.	12,691
Sterley, Floyd	10
§*†STERLING CITY, Sterling, 26.	1,178
Sterrett, Ellis	28
Stewards Mill, Freestone	22
Stewart, Rusk	NA
Stiles, Reagan	16
Stillwell Crossing, Brewster	3
§*†STINNETT, Hutchinson, 28.	2,596
Stith, Jones	18
*†STOCKDALE, Wilson, 29.	1,264
Stockholm, Hidalgo	50
Stockman, Shelby	52
Stoneburg, Montague	51
Stone City, Brazos	NA
Stone Creek, Harris	NA
Stoneham, Grimes	12
Stonehurst, Williamson	NA
Stone Point, Van Zandt	32
Stone Ridge, Smith	NA
*Stonewall, Gillespie, 5	245
Stony, Denton	25
Stout, Wood	86
*Stowell, Chambers, 12	1,592
Stranger, Falls	27
§*†STRATFORD, Sherman, 61.	1,993
Stratton, DeWitt	25
*†STRAWN, Palo Pinto, 10	771
Streeter, Mason	100
*STREETMAN, Freestone-Navarro, 7	378
Strickland Crossing, Sabine	NA
String Prairie, Bastrop	75
Stringtown, Hunt	NA
Stringtown, Newton	NA
Strong, Shelby	NA
Structure, Williamson	60
Stuart Place, Cameron	NA
Stubblefield, Houston	NA
Stubbs, Kaufman	NA
Study Butte, Brewster	120
Styx, Kaufman	NA
*Sublime, Lavaca	75
*†SUDAN, Lamb, 23.	1,041
*†SUGAR LAND, Fort Bend, 423.	14,898
Sugar Valley, Matagorda	NA
*Sullivan City, Hidalgo, 4	350
*Sulphur Bluff, Hopkins, 1	280
Sulphur Springs, Angelina	NA
§*†SULPHUR SPRINGS, Hopkins, 365.	13,817
Summerall, Henderson	NA
*Summerfield, Castro, 8	60
Summerfield, Cherokee	25
Summer Hill, Henderson	NA
Summerville, Gonzales	NA
Summit Oaks, Bexar	NA
*Sumner, Lamar, 5	80
*†SUNDOWN, Hockley, 32	1,763
Sunniland, Live Oak	75
Sunnyside, Castro	106
Sunnyside, Waller	120
Sunnyside, Wilson	300
SUNNYVALE, Dallas.	1,783
Sun Oil Camp, Starr	100
*†SUNRAY, Moore, 43	1,933
Sunrise, Falls	1,220
*SUNRISE BEACH, Llano	509
*Sunset, Montague, 4.	200
Sunset Oaks, Burnet	NA
Sunset Ridge, Montgomery	NA
SUNSET VALLEY, Travis	503
SUN VALLEY, Lamar	83
Sunview, Marion	NA
SURFSIDE BEACH, Brazoria.	604
*Sutherland Springs, Wilson, 10.	362

Town and County—	Pop.
Swamp City, Gregg	8
Swan, Smith	150
Swannerland, Franklin	NA
*†SWEENY, Brazoria, 49	3,699
Sweet Farms, Williamson	NA
Sweet Home, Guadalupe, 1	40
*Sweet Home, Lavaca, 3	360
Sweet Home, Lee	NA
Sweet Union, Cherokee	20
§*†SWEETWATER, Nolan, 272	12,738
Swenson, Stonewall	185
Swift, Nacogdoches	125
Swiftex, Bastrop	NA
Swinneytown, Smith	NA
Swiss Alp, Fayette	46
Swiss Village, Burnet	NA
Sylvan, Lamar	68
*Sylvester, Fisher, 2	79
Sylvester, Trinity	29
T	
Tabor, Brazos	150
Tadmor, Houston	NA
*†TAFT, San Patricio, 45	3,598
§*†TAHOKA, Lynn, 44	3,058
Taiton, Wharton	24
*†TALCO, Titus, 22	816
Tall Timbers, Montgomery	NA
Tall Tree, Franklin	NA
*Talpa, Coleman, 1	122
Talty, Kaufman	32
Tam Anne, Castro	NA
Tamina, Montgomery	NA
Tamina Manor, Montgomery	NA
Tanglewilde Farms, Montgomery	NA
Tanglewood, Lee	48
Tanglewood Beach, Kaufman	NA
Tanglewood Island, Stephens	NA
Tanglewood Manor, Montgomery	NA
Tankersley, Tom Green	20
Tara, Fort Bend	NA
Tarkington Prairie, Liberty	NA
*Tarpley, Bandera, 2	30
*Tarzan, Martin, 3	80
Tascosa Hills, Potter	NA
*†TATUM, Rusk-Panola, 16	1,531
*†TAYLOR, Williamson, 208	11,047
Taylor Lake Estates, Polk	NA
TAYLOR LAKE VILLAGE, Harris	3,524
Taylorsville, Caldwell	NA
Taylor Town, Lamar	40
Tazewell, Hopkins	NA
*†TEAGUE, Freestone, 52	3,620
Teaselville, Smith	NA
Tecula, Cherokee	NA
*TEHUACANA, Limestone	287
Tejas Village, Hunt	NA
Tejas Village, Marion	NA
*Telegraph, Kimble	3
*Telephone, Fannin, 7	210
*Telferner, Victoria, 9	304
*Telico, Ellis	95
*Tell, Childress, 1	63
*†TEMPLE, Bell, 862	45,044
Killeen-Temple 1985 metro. pop.	228,000
Temple Springs, Jasper	NA
*†TENAHA, Shelby, 14	1,073
Tenmile, Dawson	NA
Tennessee, Shelby	NA
*Tennessee Colony, Anderson, 5	120
*Tennyson, Coke	35
*Terlingua, Brewster, 4	25
Terminal, Midland	421
Terrace, Bexar	NA
Terrace Park, Llano	NA
Terramar Beach, Galveston	NA
*†TERRELL, Kaufman, 251	13,953
TERRELL HILLS, Bexar	4,954
Terry Chapel, Falls	NA
Terryville, DeWitt	40
*†TEXARKANA (Texas portion), Bowie, 884	32,912
(Combined population of	

Town and County—	Pop.
Texarkana, Texas-Arkansas is about 55,335.)	
1985 metro. pop. (excluding Ark. portion)	80,500
*†TEXAS CITY, Galveston, 496	43,551
Galveston-Texas City 1985 metro. pop.	213,400
Texas National, Montgomery	NA
*TEXHOMA, Sherman	351
(Combined population of Texhoma, Texas and Oklahoma is about 1,098; post office and banks are in Oklahoma.)	
*†TEXLINE, Dallam, 14	413
*Texon, Reagan	35
Thalia, Foard, 1	104
*†THE COLONY, Denton	22,431
Thedford, Smith	65
*The Grove, Coryell	65
The Heights, Brazoria	NA
Thelma, Limestone	NA
The Oaks, Comal	NA
Theon, Williamson	20
Thermo, Hopkins	NA
The Settlement, Hays	NA
The Villages, Smith	NA
The Willows, Burnet	NA
The Woodlands, Brazos	NA
*†The Woodlands, Montgomery	100
*Thicket, Hardin, 1	306
Thomas, Upshur	NA
*Thomaston, DeWitt	45
Thompson, Harris	NA
*THOMPSONS, Fort Bend, 2	263
Thompsonville, Gonzales	30
Thompsonville, Jim Hogg	NA
Thornberry, Clay	60
*†THORNDALE, Milam-Williamson, 16	1,338
*†THORNTON, Limestone, 5	473
THORNTONVILLE, Ward	784
Thorp Spring, Hood	184
Thousand Oaks, Williamson	NA
*THRALL, Williamson, 4	593
Three Oaks, Wilson	150
Three Points, Travis	NA
*†THREE RIVERS, Live Oak, 47	2,177
Three States, Cass	NA
Three Way, Erath	NA
Thrifty, Brown	NA
§*†THROCKMORTON, Throckmorton, 25	1,381
Thunderbird Shores, Henderson	NA
Thurber, Erath	8
Tidewater Oaks, Matagorda	NA
Tidwell, Hunt	NA
Tidwell Prairie, Robertson	NA
Tigertown, Lamar	NA
Tiki Island Village, Galveston	195
§*†Tilden, McMullen, 11	500
Tilmon, Caldwell	25
Timber Creek, Bexar	NA
Timber Creek, Smith	NA
Timbercreek Canyon, Randall	170
Timberdale Estates, Smith	NA
Timberhill Village, Hidalgo	NA
Timber Lake, Burnet	NA
Timberlake, Sabine	NA
Timber Lake Acres, Montgomery	NA
Timber Lake Estates, Liberty	NA
Timber Lake Estates, Montgomery	NA
Timber Land, Smith	NA
Timberline Park, Bexar	NA
Timberline West, Williamson	NA
Timber Ridge, Bexar	NA
Timber Ridge, Montgomery	NA
Timberwilde, Brazos	NA
Timesville, Leon	NA
*†TIMPSON, Shelby, 27	1,106
Tin Top, Parker	25
*Tioga, Grayson, 6	551
TIRA, Hopkins	273
*Tivoli, Refugio, 9	540

Town and County—	Pop.
Tivy, Kerr	NA
Tobacco Patch, Polk	NA
TOCO, Lamar	152
Todd City, Anderson	NA
TODD MISSION, Grimes	64
Tokio, McLennan	NA
*Tokio, Terry, 2	60
*TOLAR, Hood, 6	459
Tolbert, Wilbarger	30
Toledo Beach, Sabine	NA
Toledo Village, Newton	NA
Toledo Village, Sabine	NA
Tolette, Lamar	NA
Tolosa, Kaufman	58
*†TOMBALL, Harris, 312	6,228
*†TOM BEAN, Grayson, 4	926
Tomlinson Hill, Falls	NA
Tonkawa Springs, Williamson	NA
Tonkowon Country, Williamson	NA
TOOL, Henderson	1,838
Topsey, Coryell	20
*Tornillo, El Paso, 1	241
Tours, McLennan	100
*Tow, Llano, 5	305
Towering Pines, Sabine	NA
Tower Lake, Wilson	100
Town Bluff, Tyler	26
Townsend, San Augustine	NA
Tow Village, Llano	NA
*TOYAH, Reeves, 1	162
*Toyahvale, Reeves	60
Tradewinds, Henderson	NA
Traildust, Denton	39
Trailwood, Bexar	NA
Travis, Falls	60
Travis Oaks, Travis	NA
Travis Peak, Travis	NA
Trawick, Nacogdoches	100
Treasure Island, Brazoria	NA
Treasure Island, Guadalupe	500
*†TRENT, Taylor, 2	335
*†TRENTON, Fannin, 20	682
Tres Palacios Oaks, Matagorda	NA
Tri-Lake Estates, Montgomery	NA
Triangle, Falls	NA
Trickham, Coleman	12
Trimmier, Bell	90
*TRINIDAD, Henderson, 10	1,316
*†TRINITY, Trinity, 88	3,371
Trinity River Lake Estates, Liberty	NA
Triple Peak Ranch Estates, Comal	NA
Trophy Club, Denton	2,800
*†TROUP, Smith-Cherokee, 41	2,015
Trout Creek, Newton	NA
Trout Creek Lodge, Jasper	NA
*†TROY, Bell, 8	1,581
Truby, Jones	26
Trukton, Rusk	NA
Trumbull, Ellis	65
*Truscott, Knox, 3	187
Tucker, Anderson	304
*Tuleta, Bee, 4	98
§*†TULIA, Swisher, 108	4,445
Tulip, Fannin	10
Tulsita, Bee	25
Tundra, Van Zandt	34
Tunis, Burleson	150
*†TURKEY, Hall, 19	560
Turlington, Freestone	27
Turnbaugh Corner, Ector	NA
*Turnersville, Coryell	155
Turnersville, Travis	90
Turnertown, Rusk	76
Turney, Cherokee	100
Turtle Bayou, Chambers	42
Turtle Cove, Brazoria	NA
Turtle Creek, Montgomery	NA
*†TUSCOLA, Taylor, 8	793
Tuxedo, Jones	42
Twichell, Ochiltree	22
Twin Cedar Retreat, Sabine	NA
Twin Creek, Bexar	NA

Town and County—	Pop.
Twin Isles, Burnet	NA
Twin Lake Estates, Montgomery	NA
Twin Lakes, Smith	NA
Twin Shores, Montgomery	NA
Twin Sisters, Blanco	78
Twin Valley Terrace, Bexar	NA
*Twitty, Wheeler	60
§*†TYE, Taylor, 29	1,974
§*†TYLER, Smith, 2,414	73,021
1985 metro. pop.	150,100
*Tynan, Bee, 4	200
Type, Williamson	40
Tyson, Hill	NA

U

Town and County—	Pop.
Uhland, Caldwell-Hays	291
*Umbarger, Randall, 4	327
UNCERTAIN, Harrison	189
Union, Brazos	NA
Union, San Augustine	NA
Union, Scurry	20
Union, Terry	85
Union, Wilson	22
Union Bluff, Hill	NA
Union Center, Eastland	NA
Union Flat, Childress	NA
Union Grove, Bell	4
Union Grove, Erath	12
UNION GROVE, Upshur	341
Union High, Navarro	NA
Union Valley, Hunt	25
Unity, Lamar	NA
*†UNIVERSAL CITY, Bexar, 152	11,676
University Acres, Brazos	NA
†UNIVERSITY PARK, Dallas	22,878
(Businesses are included in Dallas count.)	
Upper Meyersville, DeWitt	NA
Upshaw, Nacogdoches	NA
Upton, Bastrop	25
Urbana, San Jacinto	10
Utley, Bastrop	30
*Utopia, Uvalde, 6	360
§*†UVALDE, Uvalde, 291	14,908
Uz, Montague	40
Valdasta, Collin	40
*VALENTINE, Jeff Davis, 3	316
*Valera, Coleman, 1	80
Valley Creek, Fannin	12
Valley Grove, Rusk	NA
Valley Hi, Bexar	NA
*†VALLEY MILLS, Bosque-McLennan, 22	1,370
Valley Ridge, Brazos	NA
*Valley Spring, Llano, 1	50
Valley View, Comal	NA
*†VALLEY VIEW, Cooke, 17	574
Valley View, Cottle	20
Valley View, Mitchell	NA
Valley View, Runnels	NA
Valley View, Upshur	200
Valley View, Wichita	NA
Valley View, Williamson	NA
Valleyview Acres, Smith	NA
Valley Wells, Dimmit	25
Valley Wood Acres, Montgomery	NA
Val Verde, Hidalgo	NA
Val Verde, Milam	25
*†VAN, Van Zandt, 36	1,970
*†VAN ALSTYNE, Grayson, 35	1,990
Vance, Real	20
*Vancourt, Tom Green, 3	125
Vandalia, Red River	35
*Vanderbilt, Jackson, 5	667
*Vanderpool, Bandera, 1	20
Vandyke, Comanche	20
§*†VAN HORN, Culberson, 62	2,882
Van Raub, Bexar	NA
Van Sickle, Hunt	NA
*Van Vleck, Matagorda, 12	1,051
Vasco, Delta	20
Vashti, Clay	140
Vattmannville, Kleberg	NA

Town and County—	Pop.
Vaughan, Hill	70
Veach, San Augustine	NA
*Vealmoor, Howard, 3	179
§*†VEGA, Oldham, 22	916
*VENUS, Johnson, 8	950
*Vera, Knox, 3	276
Verde Mills, Bexar	NA
Verdi, Atascosa	NA
*Verhalen, Reeves	52
*Veribest, Tom Green, 4	40
§*†VERNON, Wilbarger, 231	13,362
Verona, Collin	NA
Vessey, Red River	14
Veterans, Ward	NA
*Viboras, Starr	22
Vick, Concho	20
Vicksburg, Montgomery	NA
Victoria, Limestone	25
§*†VICTORIA, Victoria, 1,312	55,113
1985 metro. pop.	75,500
Victory City, Bowie	NA
Vidauri, Refugio	NA
*†VIDOR, Orange, 207	13,134
Vienna, Lavaca	40
View, Taylor, 3	75
Viewpoint, Lamar	NA
*Vigo Park, Swisher	31
Villa Cavazos, Cameron	NA
*Village Mills, Hardin, 8	300
Village Oaks, Williamson	NA
Village Shores, Comal	NA
Village West, Travis	NA
Villa Nueva, Cameron	NA
Villareales, Starr	NA
Vincent, Howard	500
Vinegarone, Val Verde	NA
*Vineyard, Jack	37
Vinton, El Paso	434
Violet, Nueces	160
Virginia Estates, Montgomery	NA
Vista, Hamilton	NA
Vistula, Houston	NA
Vivian, Foard	NA
*Voca, McCulloch, 3	56
Volente, Travis	NA
Volga, Houston	NA
*Von Ormy, Bexar, 28	264
*Von Ormy Heights, Bexar	NA
Vontress, Haskell	NA
*Voss, Coleman	20
*Votaw, Hardin, 1	160
Vsetin, Lavaca	NA
Vysehrad, Lavaca	NA

W

Town and County—	Pop.
§*†WACO, McLennan, 2,131	104,133
1985 metro. pop.	184,100
*Wadsworth, Matagorda, 7	152
*WAELDER, Gonzales, 8	945
Wagner, Hunt	NA
*Waka, Ochiltree, 3	145
Wakefield, Polk	NA
*WAKE VILLAGE, Bowie	3,866
*Walburg, Williamson, 4	250
Walco Hills, Montgomery	NA
Waldeck, Fayette	35
Walden, Montgomery	NA
Waldrip, McCulloch	NA
Walhalla, Fayette	37
Walkers Mill, Harrison	NA
*Wall, Tom Green, 5	200
Wallace, Van Zandt	NA
Wallace Prairie, Grimes	75
*†WALLER, Harris-Waller, 93	1,750
Walling, Hill	NA
*†WALLIS, Austin, 15	1,312
*Wallisville, Chambers, 2	377
Walnut Bend, Cooke	100
Walnut Creek, Montgomery	NA
Walnut Forest, Travis	NA
Walnut Grove, Collin	200
Walnut Grove, Smith	NA
Walnut Hills, Montgomery	NA
Walnut Hills, Potter	60
Walnut Place, Travis	NA

Town and County—	Pop.
Walnut Ridge, Angelina	NA
*WALNUT SPRINGS, Bosque, 8	627
Walnut Springs, Ellis	NA
Walnut Springs, Montgomery	NA
Walton, Van Zandt	35
Wamba, Bowie	70
Waneta, Houston	NA
Waples, Hood	NA
*Warda, Fayette, 5	67
Wards Creek, Bowie	164
*Waring, Kendall, 1	73
Warlock, Marion	NA
Warner Junction, Grayson	NA
*Warren, Tyler, 7	304
WARREN CITY, Gregg-Upshur	331
*Warrenton, Fayette, 2	50
Warsaw, Kaufman	58
Warwick, Smith	NA
Washburn, Armstrong	104
*Washington, Washington, 6	265
*†WASKOM, Harrison, 36	2,182
Wastella, Nolan	13
WATAUGA, Tarrant	16,800
Water Front Park, Comal	NA
Waterloo, Williamson	60
Waterman, Shelby	53
Waters Bluff, Smith	NA
Waters Park, Travis	NA
*Water Valley, Tom Green	120
Watkins, Van Zandt	NA
Watson, Burnet	NA
Watt, Limestone	NA
Watterson, Bastrop	NA
Watts, Marion	NA
Waverly, San Jacinto	50
§*†WAXAHACHIE, Ellis, 336	15,758
Wayland, Stephens	15
Wayne, Cass	NA
*Wayside, Armstrong, 3	40
Wayside, Lynn	NA
Wealthy, Leon	NA
§*†WEATHERFORD, Parker, 452	14,050
Weatherly, Hall	20
Weaver, Hopkins	35
Webb, Shelby	NA
Webb, Webb	40
Webberville, Travis	50
Webbville, Coleman	50
*†WEBSTER, Harris, 331	3,001
Weches, Houston	26
Weedhaven, Jackson	NA
Weekend Retreats, Montgomery	NA
Weeping Mary, Cherokee	NA
*Weesatche, Goliad, 4	525
*†WEIMAR, Colorado, 80	2,125
Weinert, Guadalupe	10
*WEINERT, Haskell, 4	232
Weir, Hopkins	NA
*Weir, Williamson, 3	100
Weiss Bluff, Jasper	NA
*Welch, Dawson, 9	110
Welcome, Austin	150
Weldon, Houston	131
*Welfare, Kendall, 1	36
*Wellborn, Brazos, 3	100
Wellborn Oaks, Brazos	NA
§*†WELLINGTON, Collingsworth, 66	2,653
*Wellman, Terry, 3	266
*†WELLS, Cherokee, 10	927
Wells, Lynn	NA
Wells Creek, Anderson	NA
Wellswood, San Augustine	NA
Wentworth, Van Zandt	32
Wesco, Gray	7
Weser, Goliad	50
*†WESLACO, Hidalgo, 263	22,683
Wesley, Washington	60
Wesley Grove, Walker	NA
*†WEST, McLennan, 73	2,519
West Bluff, Orange	NA
Westbrook, Jack	NA
*WESTBROOK, Mitchell, 6	328

Constitution of Texas

Following is the complete text of the Constitution of Texas. It includes the original document which was adopted on Feb. 15, 1876, plus the 287 amendments approved through the election of Nov. 4, 1986.

Each amendment is accompanied by a footnote explaining when it was adopted. This text, with footnotes, of the Constitution is copyrighted by the A. H. Belo Corporation and may not be reprinted without written permission from the publisher.

Amendment of the Texas Constitution requires a two-thirds favorable vote by both the Texas House of Representatives and the Senate, followed by a majority vote of approval by voters in a statewide election.

Prior to 1973, amendments to the constitution could not be submitted by a special session of the Legislature. But the constitution was amended in 1972 to allow submission of amendments if the special session were opened to the subject by the governor.

Constitutional amendments are not subject to a gubernatorial veto. Once submitted, voters have the final decision on whether to change the constitution as proposed.

The following table lists the total number of amendments submitted to voters by the Texas Legislature and shows the year in which the Legislature approved them for submission to voters; e.g., the Sixty-ninth Legislature in 1985 approved 18 amendments to be submitted to voters — 14 in 1985 and four in 1986.

Year	No.	Year	No.	Year	No.
1879	1	1919	13	1957	12
1881	2	1921	5	1959	4
1883	5	1923	2	1961	14
1887	6	1925	4	1963	7
1889	2	1927	8	1965	27
1891	5	1929	7	1967	20
1893	2	1931	9	1969	16
1895	5	1933	12	1971	18
1897	5	1935	13	1973	9
1899	1	1937	7	1975	12
1901	1	1939	4	1977	15
1903	3	1941	5	1978	1
1905	3	1943	3	1979	12
1907	9	1945	8	1981	10
1909	4	1947	9	1982	3
1911	5	1949	10	1983	19
1913	7	1951	7	1985	17
1915	7	1953	11	1986	1
1917	3	1955	9	1987	23

Amendments, 1985

Fourteen amendments were voted on Nov. 5, 1985:

HJR 6 (two amendments) — Authorizing issuance of additional Texas water development bonds to create special water funds for conservation and development. First approved 705,878 to 251,031; second approved 651,699 to 284,552.

HJR 19 — Authorizing issuance of general obligation bonds to provide financing assistance for purchase of farm and ranch land. Approved 498,902 to 425,698.

HJR 27 — Relating to number of precincts in Chambers County. Approved 628,246 to 299,020.

HJR 54 — Authorizing Legislature to enact laws permitting a city or town to spend public funds and levy assessments for relocation or replacement of water laterals on private property. Approved 524,151 to 396,943.

HJR 72 — Authorizing Legislature to require prior approval of expenditure or emergency transfer of other appropriated funds. Approved 663,478 to 274,527.

HJR 89 — Relating to authority of Legislature to regulate provision of health care by hospital districts. Approved 544,991 to 302,288.

SJR 6 — Relating to placement of state inmates in penal or correctional facilities of other states. Approved 600,117 to 328,834.

SJR 9 — Providing additional bonding authority for veterans' housing assistance program and changing definition of those veterans eligible to participate. Approved 518,021 to 384,987.

SJR 10 — Granting Supreme Court and Court of Criminal Appeals jurisdiction to answer questions of state law certified from federal appellate courts. Approved 461,483 to 442,407.

SJR 14 — Creating Judicial Districts Board and providing for reapportionment of judicial districts by that board or by the Legislative Redistricting Board. Approved 606,333 to 278,595.

SJR 16 — Relating to manner in which a person is charged with criminal offense and to jurisdiction of courts in criminal cases. Approved 647,276 to 238,802.

SJR 21 — Authorizing use of proceeds from sale of permanent school fund land to acquire other land as part of permanent school fund. Approved 496,189 to 360,555.

SJR 27 — Abolishing office of county treasurer in Andrews and El Paso counties and abolishing office of county surveyor in Collin, Dallas, Denton, El Paso, Henderson and Randall counties. Approved 584,641 to 251,483.

Amendments, 1986

Four amendments were voted on Nov. 4, 1986:

HJR 73 — Allowing political subdivisions to purchase certain mutual insurance. Approved 1,544,815 to 855,032.

SJR 4 — Permitting branch banking under certain circumstances. Approved 1,942,095 to 707,818.

SJR 15 — Relating to apportionment of value of railroad rolling stock among counties for purpose of property taxation. Approved 1,409,714 to 977,823.

SJR 33 — Relating to statutory revision and to requirement that each bill have a title expressing subject of bill. Approved 1,811,414 to 651,146.

Amendments, 1987

Twenty-three amendments were to be voted on Nov. 3, 1987:

HJR 2 — Relating to the establishment of an economic stabilization fund in the state treasury.

HJR 4 — Authorizing the Legislature to provide for the issuance of bonds and state financing of development and production of Texas products and businesses.

HJR 5 — Authorizing the Legislature to provide assistance to encourage economic development in the state.

HJR 18 — Relating to the creation, operation and financing of jail districts.

HJR 35 — Abolishing the office of county treasurer in Gregg, Fayette and Nueces counties.

HJR 48 — Limiting school tax increases on the residence homestead of the surviving spouse of an elderly person.

HJR 60 — Raising the maximum property tax rate that may be adopted by certain rural fire prevention districts after an election.

HJR 65 — Aiding turnpikes, toll roads and toll bridges.

HJR 83 — Permitting a county to perform work without compensation for another governmental entity.

HJR 88 — Allowing the issuance of general obligation bonds for undertakings related to a superconducting super collider research facility.

HJR 96 — Authorizing the Legislature to provide ad valorem tax relief for certain offshore drilling equipment that is not in use.

HJR 104 — Relating to the establishment of a self-insurance pool for grain storage facilities and permitting the use of public funds as surety.

SJR 9 — Relating to the eligibility of a member of the Legislature for another office.

SJR 12 — Relating to the exemption from ad valorem taxation of certain tangible personal property located in the state.

SJR 17 — Permitting the Legislature to include members of more than one department of the state government in the membership of an agency or committee.

SJR 26 — Relating to the immunity of a city or town from liability for damages arising from its proprietary functions.

SJR 27 — Authorizing the creation of emergency medical services districts and authorizing those districts to levy an ad valorem tax on property located in the district.

SJR 34 — Giving the state a limited right to appeal in criminal cases.

SJR 35 — Permitting spouses to hold community property with right of survivorship.

SJR 53 — Allowing the Legislature to limit the authority of a governor to fill vacancies in state and district offices if the governor is not re-elected.

SJR 54 — Authorizing the issuance of additional Texas Water Development Bonds for water supply, water quality and flood control purposes.

SJR 55 — Providing for the issuance of general obligation bonds to finance certain local public facilities.

SJR 56 — Providing for the issuance of general obligation bonds for certain construction projects.

Index to State Constitution

The following index to the Texas State Constitution includes all amendments voted on through the election of Nov. 4, 1986. In some instances, reference may be to a section that has been deleted from the text of the Constitution as carried here. However, these references are included when it is clear in the note telling that a section has been deleted that the reference was once a part of the text.

In some instances, an article number is given after the main heading and then there may be references to other articles under the heading (See **Courts, Art. V:** and then under **Impeachment of judges: XV, Secs. 2, 6**).

We trust that this index will be helpful to readers in finding particular sections they are looking for. The Texas Almanac welcomes any suggestions for improving this index, or any criticisms that might help us make this index more useful to our readers.

Text of Texas Constitution

The following is a complete text of the Constitution of Texas, containing all amendments adopted through Nov. 2, 1982, with explanatory footnotes:

Preamble

Humbly invoking the blessings of Almighty God, the people of the State of Texas do ordain and establish this Constitution.

ARTICLE I — BILL OF RIGHTS

That the general, great and essential principles of liberty and free government may be recognized and established, we declare:

Sec. 1. Texas Free and Independent — Texas is a free and independent State, subject only to the Constitution of the United States, and the maintenance of our free institutions and the perpetuity of the Union depend upon the preservation of the right of local self-government, unimpaired to all the states.

Sec. 2. All Political Power Is Inherent in the People — All political power is inherent in the people, and all free governments are founded on their authority, and instituted for their benefit. The faith of the people of Texas stands pledged to the preservation of a republican form of government, and subject to this limitation only, they have at all times the inalienable right to alter, reform or abolish their government in such manner as they may think expedient.

Sec. 3. All Free Men Have Equal Rights — All free men, when they form a social compact, have equal rights, and no man, or set of men, is entitled to exclusive separate public emoluments or privileges but in consideration of public services.

**Sec. 3-a. Equality under the law shall not be denied or abridged because of sex, race, color, creed or national origin. This amendment is self-operative.

[Note — Sec. 3-a of Art. I is an added amendment setting forth civil rights for all. Submitted by the Sixty-second Legislature (1971) and adopted in an election Nov. 7, 1972.]

Sec. 4. There Shall Be No Religious Test for Office — No religious test shall ever be required as a qualification to any office or public trust in this State; nor shall anyone be excluded from holding office on account of his religious sentiments, provided he acknowledge the existence of a Supreme Being.

Sec. 5. How Oaths Shall Be Administered — No person shall be disqualified to give evidence in any of the courts of this State on account of his religious opinions, or for want of any religious belief, but all oaths or affirmations shall be administered in the mode most binding upon the conscience, and shall be taken subject to the pains and penalties of perjury.

Sec. 6. Freedom in Religious Worship Guaranteed — All men have a natural and indefeasible right to worship Almighty God according to the dictates of their own consciences. No man shall be compelled to attend, erect or support any place of worship, or to maintain any ministry against his consent. No human authority ought, in any case whatever, to control or interfere with the rights of conscience in matters of religion, and no preference shall ever be given by law to any religious society or mode of worship. But it shall be the duty of the Legislature to pass such laws as may be necessary to protect equally every religious denomination in the peaceable enjoyment of its own mode of public worship.

Sec. 7. No Appropriation for Sectarian Purposes — No money shall be appropriated or drawn from the Treasury for the benefit of any sect, or religious society, theological or religious seminary, nor shall property belonging to the State be appropriated for any such purposes.

Sec. 8. Liberty of Speech and Press Guaranteed; Libel. Every person shall be at liberty to speak, write or publish his opinions, on any subject, being responsible for the abuse of that privilege; and no law shall ever be passed curtailing the liberty of speech or of the press. In prosecutions for the publication of papers, investigating the conduct of officers or men in public capacity, or when the matter published is proper for public information, the truth thereof may be given in evidence. And in all indictments for libels, the jury shall have the right to determine the law and the facts, under the direction of the court, as in other cases.

Sec. 9. No Unreasonable Seizures and Searches Allowed — The people shall be secure in their persons, houses, papers and possessions from all unreasonable seizures or searches, and no warrant to search any place, or to seize any person or thing, shall issue without describing them as near as may be, or without probable cause, supported by oath or affirmation.

Sec. 10. Rights of Accused Persons in Criminal Prosecutions — In all criminal prosecutions the accused shall have a speedy public trial by an impartial jury. He shall have the right to demand the nature and cause of the accusation against him, and to have a copy thereof. He shall not be compelled to give evidence against himself and shall have the right of being heard by himself or counsel, or both; shall be confronted by the witnesses against him and shall have compulsory process for obtaining witnesses in his favor, except that when the witness resides out of the State and the offense charged is a violation of any of the antitrust laws of this State, the defendant and the State shall have the right to produce and have the evidence admitted by deposition, under such rules and laws as the Legislature may hereafter provide; and no person shall be held to answer for a criminal offense, unless on an indictment of a grand jury, except in cases in which the punishment is by fine or imprisonment, otherwise than in the penitentiary; in cases of impeachment and in cases arising in the army or navy, or in the militia, when in actual service in time of war or public danger.

[Note — The foregoing is an amended section, the amendment consisting of the addition of that clause relating to depositions of witnesses resident outside of the State in antitrust suits. Submitted by the Thirty-fifth Legislature (1917) and adopted at election on Nov. 5, 1918.]

Sec. 11. Bail — All prisoners shall be bailable by sufficient sureties, unless for capital offenses, when the proof is evident; but this provision shall not be so construed as to prevent bail after indictment found upon examination of the evidence, in such manner as may be prescribed by law.

Sec. 11-a. Multiple Convictions; Denial of Bail — Any person (1) accused of a felony less than capital in this State, who has been theretofore twice convicted of a felony, the second conviction being subsequent to the first, both in point of time of commission of the offense and conviction therefor, (2) accused of a felony less than capital in this State, committed while on bail for a prior felony for which he has been indicted, or (3) accused of a felony less than capital in this State involving the use of a deadly weapon after being convicted of a prior felony, after a hearing, and upon evidence substantially showing the guilt of the accused of the offense in (1) or (3) above or of the offense committed while on bail in (2) above, may be denied bail pending trial, by a district judge in this State, if said order denying bail pending trial is issued within seven calendar days subsequent to the time of incarceration of the accused; provided, however, that if the accused is not accorded a trial upon the accusation under (1) or (3) above or the accusation and indictment used under (2) above within sixty (60) days from the time of his incarceration upon the accusation, the order denying bail shall be automatically set aside, unless a continuance is obtained upon the motion or request of the accused; provided, further, that the right of appeal to the Court of Criminal Appeals of this State is expressly accorded the accused for a review of any judgment or order made hereunder, and said appeal shall be given preference by the Court of Criminal Appeals.

[Note — Sec. 11-a of Art. I is an added amendment permitting denial of bail to a person charged with a felony less than capital who has been theretofore twice convicted of a felony. Submitted by the Fifty-fourth Legislature (1955) and adopted in election Nov. 6, 1956. This section was amended to provide for further denial of bail under circumstances (2) and (3) above, and providing for 60-day limit to that person's incarceration without trial; and providing for that person's right of appeal. Submitted by the Sixty-fifth Legislature (1977) and adopted in election Nov. 8, 1977.]

Sec. 12. The Writ of Habeas Corpus — The writ of habeas corpus is a writ of right, and shall never be suspended. The Legislature shall enact laws to render the remedy speedy and effectual.

Sec. 13. Excessive Bail and Fine and Unusual Punishment Prohibited; Courts Open — Excessive bail shall not be required, nor excessive fines imposed, nor cruel or unusual punishment inflicted. All courts shall be open, and every person for an injury done him in his lands, goods, person or reputation, shall have due course of law.

Sec. 14. No Person Shall Be Put Twice in Jeopardy — No person, for the same offense, shall be twice put in jeopardy of life or liberty, nor shall a person be again put upon trial for the same offense after a verdict of not guilty in a court of competent jurisdiction.

Sec. 15. Right of Trial by Jury — The right of trial by jury shall remain inviolate. The Legislature shall pass such laws as may be needed to regulate the same, and to maintain its purity and efficiency. Provided, that the Legislature may provide for the temporary commitment, for observation and/or treatment, of mentally ill persons not charged with a criminal offense, for a period of time not to exceed ninety (90) days, by order of the County Court without the necessity of a trial by jury.

[Note — The original Sec. 15 of Art. I was amended to add the last sentence. Submitted by the Forty-fourth Legislature (1935) and adopted in an election Aug. 24, 1935.]

Section 15-a. No person shall be committed as a person of unsound mind except on competent medical or psychiatric testimony. The Legislature may enact all laws necessary to provide for the trial, adjudication of insanity and com-

Article I — (Cont'd.); Article II and III

mitment of persons of unsound mind and to provide for a method of appeal from judgments rendered in such cases. Such laws may provide for a waiver of trial by jury. In cases where the person under inquiry has not been charged with the commission of a criminal offense, by the concurrence of the person under inquiry, or his next of kin, and an attorney ad litem appointed by a judge of either the County or Probate Court of the county where the trial is being held, and shall provide for a method of service of notice of such trial upon the person under inquiry and of his right to demand a trial by jury.

[Note — Sec. 15-a of Art. I is an added amendment relating to requiring medical or psychiatric testimony for commitment of persons of unsound mind and authorizing Legislature to provide for trial and commitment of such persons and for waiver of trial by jury where the person under inquiry has not been charged with commission of a criminal offense. Submitted by the Fifty-fourth Legislature (1955) and adopted in election Nov. 6, 1956.]

Sec. 16. **There Shall Be No Bill of Attainder or Ex-Post Facto Laws** — No bill of attainder or ex post facto law, retroactive law, or any other law impairing the obligation of contracts shall be made.

Sec. 17. **Privileges and Franchises: Eminent Domain** — No person's property shall be taken, damaged or destroyed for or applied to public use without adequate compensation being made, unless by the consent of such person; and when taken, except for the use of the State, such compensation shall be first made or secured by a deposit of money; and no irrevocable or uncontrollable grant of special privileges or immunities shall be made; but all privileges and franchises granted by the Legislature, or created under its authority, shall be subject to the control thereof.

Sec. 18. **No Imprisonment for Debt** — No person shall ever be imprisoned for debt.

Sec. 19. **Due Course of Law** — No citizen of this State shall be deprived of life, liberty, property, privileges or immunities, or in any manner disfranchised, except by the due course of the law of the land.

Sec. 20. **No Outlawry or Deportations** — No citizen shall be outlawed. No person shall be transported out of the State for any offense committed within the same. This section does not prohibit an agreement with another state providing for the confinement of inmates of this State in the penal or correctional facilities of that state.

[Note — The foregoing Sec. 20 of Art. I was amended to permit state prisoners to be placed in penal facilities of another state pursuant to an interstate agreement. Submitted by the Sixty-ninth Legislature (1985) and adopted in an election Nov. 5, 1985.]

Sec. 21. **Corruption of Blood, Forfeiture; Suicide** — No conviction shall work corruption of blood or forfeiture of estate, and the estates of those who destroy their own lives shall descend or vest as in the case of natural death.

Sec. 22. **Treason** — Treason against the State shall consist only in levying war against it, or adhering to its enemies, giving them aid and comfort; and no person shall be convicted of treason except on the testimony of two witnesses to the same overt act or on confession in open court.

Sec. 23. **Right to Bear Arms** — Every citizen shall have the right to keep and bear arms in the lawful defense of himself or the State; but the Legislature shall have power, by law, to regulate the wearing of arms, with a view to prevent crime.

Sec. 24. **Military Subordinate to Civil Authority** — The military shall at all times be subordinate to the civil authority.

Sec. 25. **Quartering Soldiers** — No soldier shall in time of peace be quartered in the house of any citizen without the consent of the owner, nor in time of war but in a manner prescribed by law.

Sec. 26. **Perpetuities; Monopolies; Primogeniture; Entailments** — Perpetuities and monopolies are contrary to the genius of a free government, and shall never be allowed, nor shall the law of primogeniture or entailments ever be in force in this State.

Sec. 27. **Right of Petition Guaranteed** — The citizens shall have the right, in a peaceable manner, to assemble together for their common good and apply to those invested with the powers of government for redress of grievances or other purposes, by petition, address or remonstrance.

Sec. 28. **Power to Suspend Laws** — No power of suspending laws in this State shall be exercised except by the Legislature.

Sec. 29. **"Bill of Rights" Inviolate** — To guard against transgressions of the high powers being delegated, we declare that everything in this "Bill of Rights" is excepted out of the general powers of government, and shall forever remain inviolate, and all laws contrary thereto, or to the following provisions, shall be void.

ARTICLE II — THE POWERS OF GOVERNMENT

Sec. 1. **Departments of Government to Be Kept Distinct** —

The powers of the government of the State of Texas shall be divided into three distinct departments, each of which shall be confined to a separate body of magistracy, to wit: Those which are legislative to one, those which are executive to another, and those which are judicial to another; and no person, or collection of persons, being of one of these departments shall exercise any power properly attached to either of the others, except in the instances herein expressly permitted.

ARTICLE III — LEGISLATIVE DEPARTMENT

Sec. 1. **The Legislature: House and Senate** — The legislative power of this State shall be vested in a Senate and House of Representatives, which together shall be styled "The Legislature of the State of Texas."

Sec. 2. **Number of Members Limited** — The Senate shall consist of thirty-one members, and shall never be increased above this number. The House of Representatives shall consist of ninety-three members until the first apportionment after the adoption of this Constitution, when or at any apportionment thereafter the number of Representatives may be increased by the Legislature, upon the ratio of not more than one Representative for every 15,000 inhabitants; provided, the number of Representatives shall never exceed 150.

Sec. 3. **Election of Senators; New Apportionment** — The Senators shall be chosen by the qualified electors for the term of four years; but a new Senate shall be chosen after every apportionment, and the Senators elected after each apportionment shall be divided by lot into two classes. The seats of the Senators of the first class shall be vacated at the expiration of the first two years, and those of the second class at the expiration of four years, so that one half of the Senators shall be chosen biennially thereafter. Senators shall take office following their election, on the day set by law for the convening of the regular session of the Legislature, and shall serve thereafter for the full term of years to which elected and until their successors shall have been elected and qualified.

[Note — The foregoing Sec. 3 of Art. III was amended to establish the date on which newly elected members of the Senate shall qualify and take office. Submitted by the Fifty-ninth Legislature (1965) and adopted in election Nov. 8, 1966.]

Sec. 4. **Election of Representatives; Term of Office** — The members of the House of Representatives shall be chosen by the qualified electors for the term of two years. Representatives shall take office following their election, on the day set by law for the convening of the regular session of the Legislature, and shall serve thereafter for the full term of years to which elected and until their successors shall have been elected and qualified.

[Note—The foregoing Sec. 4 of Art. III was amended to provide for the date on which newly elected members of the House of Representatives shall qualify and take office. Submitted by the Fifty-ninth Legislature (1965) and adopted in an election Nov. 8, 1966.]

Sec. 5. **Time of Meeting; Method of Procedure** — The Legislature shall meet every two years at such time as may be provided by law and at other times when convened by the Governor. When convened in regular session, the first thirty days thereof shall be devoted to the introduction of bills and resolutions, acting upon emergency appropriations, passing upon the confirmation of the recess appointees of the Governor and such emergency matters as may be submitted by the Governor in special messages to the Legislature; provided, that during the succeeding thirty days of the regular session of the Legislature the various committees of each house shall hold hearings to consider all bills and resolutions and other matters then pending; and such emergency matters as may be submitted by the Governor; provided, further that during the following sixty days the Legislature shall act upon such bills and resolutions as may be then pending and upon such emergency matters as may be submitted by the Governor in special messages to the Legislature; provided, however, either house may otherwise determine its order of business by an affirmative vote of four fifths of its membership.

[Note — Sec. 5 of Art. III has been amended once, to provide for a 120-day session. It was submitted together with the amendment of Sec. 24 of Art. III. Submitted by the Forty-first Legislature (1929); ratified Nov. 4, 1930.]

Sec. 6. **Qualifications of Senators** — No person shall be a Senator unless he be a citizen of the United States, and, at the time of his election, a qualified elector of this State, and shall have been a resident of this State five years next preceding his election and the last year thereof a resident of the district for which he shall be chosen, and shall have attained the age of twenty-six years.

Sec. 7. **Qualifications of Representatives** — No person shall be a Representative unless he be a citizen of the United States, and, at the time of his election, a qualified elector of this State, and shall have been a resident of this State two years preceding his election, the last year thereof a resi-

Article III — (Cont'd.)

dent of the district for which he shall be chosen, and shall have attained the age of twenty-one years.

Sec. 8. Each House to Judge Qualifications of Its Own Members — Each house shall be the judge of the qualifications and election of its own members; but contested elections shall be determined in such manner as shall be provided by law.

Sec. 9. President Pro Tem of the Senate; Speaker of the House; Officers — (a) The Senate shall, at the beginning and close of each session, and at such other times as may be necessary, elect one of its members President pro tempore, who shall perform the duties of the Lieutenant Governor in any case of absence or disability of that officer. If the said office of Lieutenant Governor becomes vacant, the President pro tempore of the Senate shall convene the Committee of the Whole Senate within 30 days after the vacancy occurs. The Committee of the Whole shall elect one of its members to perform the duties of the Lieutenant Governor in addition to his duties as Senator until the next general election. If the Senator so elected ceases to be a Senator before the election of a new Lieutenant Governor, another Senator shall be elected in the same manner to perform the duties of the Lieutenant Governor until the next general election. Until the Committee of the Whole elects one of its members for this purpose, the President pro tempore shall perform the duties of the Lieutenant Governor as provided by this subsection.

(b) The House of Representatives shall, when it first assembles, organize temporarily, and thereupon proceed to the election of a Speaker from its own members.

(c) Each House shall choose its other officers.

[Note — Sec. 9 of Art. III was amended to provide for method of filling a vacancy in the office of Lieutenant Governor. Submitted by the Sixty-eighth Legislature (1983) and approved in election Nov. 6, 1984.]

Sec. 10. Quorum — Two thirds of each house shall constitute a quorum to do business, but a smaller number may adjourn from day to day and compel the attendance of absent members, in such manner and under such penalties as each house may provide.

Sec. 11. Rules: Power to Punish and Expel — Each house may determine the rules of its own proceedings, punish members for disorderly conduct, and, with the consent of two thirds, expel a member, but not a second time for the same offense.

Sec. 12. Journal: Yeas and Nays — Each house shall keep a journal of its proceedings, and publish the same; and the yeas and nays of the members of either house on any question shall, at the desire of any three members present, be entered on the journals.

Sec. 13. Vacancies, How Filled — When vacancies occur in either house, the Governor, or the person exercising the power of the Governor, shall issue writs of election to fill such vacancies; and should the Governor fail to issue a writ of election to fill any such vacancy within twenty days after it occurs, the returning officer of the district in which such vacancy may have happened shall be authorized to order an election for that purpose.

Sec. 14. Members of Legislature Privileged From Arrest — Senators and Representatives shall, except in cases of treason, felony or breach of the peace, be privileged from arrest during the session of the Legislature, and in going to or returning from the same, allowing one day for every twenty miles such member may reside from the place at which the Legislature is convened.

Sec. 15. Each House May Punish Disorderly Conduct — Each house may punish, by imprisonment, during its sessions, any person not a member for disrespectful or disorderly conduct in its presence, or for obstructing any of its proceedings; provided, such imprisonment shall not, at any one time, exceed forty-eight hours.

Sec. 16. Sessions to Be Open — The sessions of each house shall be open, except the Senate when in executive session.

Sec. 17. Adjournments — Neither house shall, without the consent of the other, adjourn for more than three days, nor to any other place than that where the Legislature may be sitting.

Sec. 18. Ineligibility of Members to Certain Offices; Not to Be Interested in Contracts — No Senator or Representative shall, during the term for which he was elected, be eligible to (1) any civil office of profit under this State which shall have been created, or the emoluments of which may have been increased, during such term, or (2) any office or place, the appointment to which may be made, in whole or in part, by either branch of the Legislature; provided, however, the fact that the term of office of Senators and Representatives does not end precisely on the last day of December but extends a few days into January of the succeeding year shall be considered as de minimis, and the ineligibility herein created shall terminate on the last day in December of the last full calendar year of the term for which he was elected. No member of either House shall vote for any other member for any office whatever, which may be filled by a vote of the Legislature, except in such cases as are in this Constitution provided, nor shall any member of the Legislature be interested, either directly or indirectly, in any contract with the State, or any county thereof, authorized by any law passed during the term for which he was elected.

[Note — Sec. 18 of Art. III was amended to fix the time during which members of Legislature shall be ineligible to hold other office. Submitted by the Sixtieth Legislature (1967) and adopted in election Nov. 5, 1968.]

Sec. 19. What Officers Ineligible to Membership in Legislature — No judge of any court, Secretary of State, Attorney General, clerk of any court of record, or any person holding a lucrative office under the United States, or this State, or any foreign government, shall, during the term for which he is elected or appointed, be eligible to the Legislature.

Sec. 20. Receivers or Disbursers of Public Funds Not Eligible to Membership in the Legislature Until Discharge Received — No person who at any time may have been a collector of taxes or who may have been otherwise entrusted with public money, shall be eligible to the Legislature, or to any office of profit or trust under the State Government, until he shall have obtained a discharge for the amount of such collections, or for all public moneys with which he may have been entrusted.

Sec. 21. Freedom in Debate — No member shall be questioned in any other place for words spoken in debate in either house.

Sec. 22. Personal Interest in Measure or Bill — A member who has a personal or private interest in any measure or bill, proposed or pending before the Legislature, shall disclose the fact to the house of which he is a member, and shall not vote thereon.

Sec. 23. Removal Vacates Office — If any Senator or Representative remove his residence from the district or county for which he was elected, his office shall thereby become vacant, and the vacancy shall be filled as provided in Sec. 13 of this article.

Sec. 23-a. John Tarleton Contract Validated — The Legislature is authorized to appropriate so much money as may be necessary, not to exceed seventy-five thousand ($75,000) dollars, to pay claims incurred by John Tarleton Agricultural College for the construction of a building on the campus of such college pursuant to deficiency authorization by the Governor of Texas on Aug. 31, 1937.

[Note — Sec. 23-a. of Art. III is an added amendment to provide for payment of a contractor whose contract had been annulled. Submitted by the Forty-ninth Legislature (1945) and ratified in election Nov. 5, 1946.]

Sec. 24. Mileage and Per Diem — Members of the Legislature shall receive from the Public Treasury a salary of Six Hundred Dollars ($600) per month. Each member shall also receive a per diem of Thirty Dollars ($30) for each day during each Regular and Special Session of the Legislature. No Regular Session shall be of longer duration than one hundred and forty (140) days.

In addition to the per diem the Members of each House shall be entitled to mileage at the same rate as prescribed by law for employees of the State of Texas. This amendment takes effect on April 22, 1975.

[Note — Sec. 24 of Art. III has been amended four times, first raising the per diem and decreasing the mileage. It was submitted with the amendment of Sec. 5 of Art. III. Submitted by Forty-first Legislature (1929); ratified Nov. 4, 1930. Further amended to raise per diem to $25 for first 120 days only. Submitted by Fifty-third Legislature (1953) and adopted in election Nov. 2, 1954. Further amended to fix the salary at $4,800 per year and setting the per diem at $12 per day for first 120 days of regular session and 30 days of each special session. Submitted by Fifty-sixth Legislature (1959) and adopted in election Nov. 8, 1960. It was amended to set salaries of members of Legislature at $600 per month and set per diem of $30 per day during legislative sessions and a mileage allowance at the same rate provided by law for state employees. Submitted by Sixty-fourth Legislature (1975) and adopted in election April 22, 1975.]

Sec. 25. Senatorial Districts, How Apportioned — The State shall be divided into senatorial districts of contiguous territory according to the number of qualified electors, as nearly as may be, and each district shall be entitled to elect one Senator; and no single county shall be entitled to more than one Senator.

Sec. 26. Representative Districts, How Apportioned — The members of the House of Representatives shall be apportioned among the several counties, according to the number of population in each, as nearly as may be, on a ratio obtained by dividing the population of the State, as ascertained by the most recent United States census, by the number of members of which the House is composed; provided that whenever a single county has sufficient population to be entitled to a Representative, such county shall be formed into a separate representative district, and when two or more counties are required to make up the ratio of representation, such counties shall be contiguous to each

Article III — (Cont'd.)

other; and when any one county has more than sufficient population to be entitled to one or more Representatives, such Representative or Representatives shall be apportioned to such county, and for any surplus of population it may be joined in a representative district with any other contiguous county or counties.

Sec. 26-a. **Redistricting According to Population** — Provided, however, that no county shall be entitled to or have under any apportionment more than seven (7) Representatives unless the population of such county shall exceed seven hundred thousand (700,000) people as ascertained by the most recent United States census, in which event such county shall be entitled to one additional Representative for each one hundred thousand (100,000) population in excess of seven hundred thousand (700,000) population as shown by the latest United States census; nor shall any district be created which would permit any county to have more than seven (7) Representatives except under the conditions set forth above.

[Note — Sec. 26-a of Art. III is an added amendment, to place limitation on representation of counties with large population. Adopted in election Nov. 3, 1936.]

Sec. 27. **Election of Members** — Elections for Senators and Representatives shall be general throughout the State, and shall be regulated by law.

Sec. 28. **Reapportionment After Each Census** — The Legislature shall, at its first regular session after the publication of each United States decennial census, apportion the State into senatorial and representative districts, agreeable to the provisions of Sections 25, 26 and 26-a of this Article. In the event the Legislature shall at any such first regular session following the publication of a United States decennial census, fail to make such apportionment, same shall be done by the Legislative Redistricting Board of Texas, which is hereby created, and shall be composed of five (5) members, as follows: The Lieutenant Governor, the Speaker of the House of Representatives, the Attorney General, the Comptroller of Public Accounts and the Commissioner of the General Land Office, a majority of whom shall constitute a quorum. Said board shall assemble in the City of Austin within ninety (90) days after the final adjournment of such regular session. The board shall, within sixty (60) days after assembling, apportion the State into senatorial and representative districts, or into senatorial or representative districts, as the failure of action of such Legislature may make necessary. Such apportionment shall be in writing and signed by three (3) or more of the members of the board duly acknowledged as the act and deed of such board, and when so executed and filed with the Secretary of State, shall have force and effect of law. Such apportionment shall become effective at the next succeeding statewide general election. The Supreme Court of Texas shall have jurisdiction to compel such commission to perform its duties in accordance with the provisions of this section by writ of mandamus or other extraordinary writs conformable to the usages of law. The Legislature shall provide necessary funds for clerical and technical aid and for other expenses incidental to the work of the board, and the Lieutenant Governor and the Speaker of the House of Representatives shall be entitled to receive per diem and travel expense during the board's session in the same manner and amount as they would receive while attending a special session of the Legislature. This amendment shall become effective Jan. 1, 1951.

[Note — The foregoing Section 28 of Art. III was amended to provide for the Legislative Redistricting Board of Texas, this action being taken because of failure of past Legislatures to obey the mandate in the original Sec. 28 to redistrict the state after each decennial census. Submitted by the Fiftieth Legislature (1947) and adopted Nov. 2, 1948.]

Proceedings

Sec. 29. **Enacting Clause** — The enacting clause of all laws shall be: "Be it enacted by the Legislature of the State of Texas."

Sec. 30. **Laws to Be Passed by Bill: Amendments** — No law shall be passed, except by bill, and no bill shall be so amended in its passage through either house as to change its original purpose.

Sec. 31. **Bills May Originate in Either House and May Be Amended or Rejected by the Other House** — Bills may originate in either house, and when passed by such house may be amended, altered or rejected by the other.

Sec. 32. **Bills to Be Read on Three Several Days: Suspension of Rule** — No bill shall have the force of a law until it has been read on three several days in each house, and free discussion allowed thereon; but in cases of imperative public necessity (which necessity shall be stated in a preamble or in the body of the bill) four fifths of the house in which the bill may be pending may suspend this rule, the yeas and nays being taken on the question of suspension and entered upon the journals.

Sec. 33. **Bills for Raising Revenue** — All bills for raising revenue shall originate in the House of Representatives, but the Senate may amend or reject them as other bills.

Sec. 34. **Bill or Resolution Defeated, Not to Be Considered Again** — After a bill has been considered and defeated by either house of the Legislature, no bill containing the same substance shall be passed into a law during the same session. After a resolution has been acted on and defeated, no resolution containing the same substance shall be considered at the same session.

Sec. 35. **Bills to Contain but One Subject, Which Must Be Expressed in Title** — (a) No bill (except general appropriation bills, which may embrace the various subjects and accounts for and on account of which moneys are appropriated) shall contain more than one subject.

(b) The rules of procedure of each house shall require that the subject of each bill be expressed in its title in a manner that gives the Legislature and the public reasonable notice of that subject. The Legislature is solely responsible for determining compliance with the rule.

(c) A law, including a law enacted before the effective date of this subsection, may not be held void on the basis of an insufficient title.

[Note — The foregoing Sec. 35 of Art. III was amended to require each house to include in its rules of procedure a rule that each bill contain title expressing bill's subject. Submitted by Sixty-ninth Legislature (1985) and adopted in an election Nov. 4, 1986.]

Sec. 36. **Reviving or Amending Laws** — No law shall be revived or amended by reference to its title; but in such case the act revived, or the section or sections amended, shall be re-enacted and published at length.

Sec. 37. **Reference to Committees** — No bill shall be considered unless it has been first referred to a committee and reported thereon, and no bill shall be passed which has not been presented and referred to and reported from a committee at least three days before the final adjournment of the Legislature.

Sec. 38. **Signing Bills** — The presiding officer of each house shall, in the presence of the house over which he presides, sign all bills and joint resolutions passed by the Legislature, after their titles have been publicly read before signing, and the fact of signing shall be entered on the journals.

Sec. 39. **When Laws Take Effect** — No law passed by the Legislature, except the general appropriation act, shall take effect or go into force until ninety days after the adjournment of the session at which it was enacted, unless in case of an emergency, which emergency must be expressed in a preamble or in the body of the act, the Legislature shall, by a vote of two thirds of all the members elected to each house, otherwise direct; said vote to be taken by yeas and nays, and entered upon the journals.

Sec. 40. **Business and Duration of Special Sessions** — When the Legislature shall be convened in special session, there shall be no legislation upon subjects other than those designated in the proclamation of the Governor calling such session, or presented to them by the Governor; and no such session shall be of longer duration than thirty days.

Sec. 41. **Elections: Votes, How Taken** — In all elections by the Senate and House of Representatives, jointly or separately, the vote shall be given viva voce, except in the election of their officers.

[Note — Sec. 42 of Art. III, relating to passage of laws, was deleted by constitutional amendment in election Aug. 5, 1969.]

Requirements and Limitations

Sec. 43. **Revision and Publication of Laws** — (a) The Legislature shall provide for revising, digesting and publishing the laws, civil and criminal; provided, that in the adoption of and giving effect to any such digest or revision the Legislature shall not be limited by Secs. 35 and 36 of this article.

(b) In this section, "revision" includes a revision of the statutes on a particular subject and any enactment having the purpose, declared in the enactment, of codifying without substantive change statutes that individually relate to different subjects.

[Note — The foregoing Sec. 43 of Art. III was amended to provide for the continuing revision of state laws. Submitted by the Sixty-ninth Legislature (1985) and adopted in an election Nov. 4, 1986.]

Sec. 44. **Compensation of Officers: Payment of Claims** — The Legislature shall provide by law for the compensation of all officers, servants, agents and public contractors, not provided for in this Constitution, but shall not grant extra compensation to any officer, agent, servant or public contractors, after such public service shall have been performed or contract entered into for the performance of the same; nor grant, by appropriation or otherwise, any amount of money out of the Treasury of the State, to any individual, on a claim, real or pretended, when the same shall not have been provided for by pre-existing law; nor employ anyone in the name of the State, unless authorized by pre-existing law.

Article III — (Cont'd.)

Sec. 45. **Change of Venue** — The power to change the venue in civil and criminal cases shall be vested in the courts, to be exercised in such manner as shall be provided by law; and the Legislature shall pass laws for that purpose.

[Note — Sec. 46 of Art. III, relating to vagrant laws, was deleted by constitutional amendment in election Aug. 5, 1969.]

Sec. 47. **Lotteries Shall Be Prohibited** — (a) The Legislature shall pass laws prohibiting lotteries and gift enterprises in this State.

(b) The Legislature by law may authorize and regulate bingo games conducted by a church, synagogue, religious society, volunteer fire department, nonprofit veterans organization, fraternal organization, or nonprofit organization supporting medical research or treatment programs. A law enacted under this subsection must permit the qualified voters of any county, justice precinct, or incorporated city or town to determine from time to time by a majority vote of the qualified voters voting on the question at an election whether bingo games may be held in the county, justice precinct, or city or town. The law must also require that:

(1) all proceeds from the games are spent in Texas for charitable purposes of the organizations;

(2) the games are limited to one location as defined by law on property owned or leased by the church, synagogue, religious society, volunteer fire department, nonprofit veterans organization, fraternal organization, or nonprofit organization supporting medical research or treatment programs; and

(3) the games are conducted, promoted, and administered by members of the church, synagogue, religious society, volunteer fire department, nonprofit veterans organization, fraternal organization, or nonprofit organization supporting medical research or treatment programs.

(c) The law enacted by the Legislature authorizing bingo games must include:

(1) a requirement that the entities conducting the games report quarterly to the Comptroller of Public Accounts about the amount of proceeds that the entities collect from the games and the purposes for which the proceeds are spent; and

(2) criminal or civil penalties to enforce the reporting requirement.

[Note — The foregoing Sec. 47 of Art. III was amended to authorize bingo games on local option basis if games are conducted by religious society or other charitable society and proceeds are to be spent in Texas for charitable purposes of the organization. Submitted by the Sixty-sixth Legislature (1979) and adopted in election Nov. 4, 1980.]

[Note — Sec. 48 of Art. III, relating to power to levy taxes, was deleted by constitutional amendment in election Aug. 5, 1969.]

[Note — Sec. 48a and Sec. 48b, relating to the Teachers' Retirement Fund and Teachers' Retirement System, respectively, were deleted by constitutional amendment in an election April 22, 1975. See also note under Art. III, Sec. 51e and Sec. 51f; Art. XVI, Sec. 62 and Sec. 63. See also Art. XVI, Sec. 67, which replaces the foregoing Sections.]

Sec. 48-d. **Rural Fire Prevention Districts** — The Legislature shall have the power to provide for the establishment and creation of rural fire-prevention districts and to authorize a tax on the ad valorem property situated in said districts not to exceed three (3c) cents on the one hundred ($100) dollars valuation for the support thereof; provided that no tax shall be levied in support of said districts until approved by vote of the people residing therein.

[Note — The foregoing Sec. 48-d of Art. III was submitted as an amendment by the Fifty-first Legislature (1949) and ratified in an election Nov. 8, 1949. The absence of Section 48-c is explained by the fact that such section was proposed as an amendment but failed to carry.]

Sec. 49. **Purpose for Which Debts May Be Created** — No debt shall be created by or on behalf of the State, except to supply casual deficiencies of revenue, repel invasion, suppress insurrection, defend the State in war or pay existing debt; and the debt created to supply deficiencies in the revenue shall never exceed in the aggregate at any one time $200,000.

Sec. 49-a. **Limiting Appropriations to Anticipated Revenue; Comptroller's Certification Required; Issuance of Certain General Revenue Bonds Authorized** — It shall be the duty of the Comptroller of Public Accounts in advance of each regular session of the Legislature to prepare and submit to the Governor and to the Legislature upon its convening a statement under oath showing fully the financial condition of the State Treasury at the close of the last fiscal period and an estimate of the probable receipts and disbursements for the then current fiscal year. There shall also be contained in said statement an itemized estimate of the anticipated revenue based on the laws then in effect that will be received by and for the State from all sources showing the fund accounts to be credited during the succeeding biennium and said statement shall contain such other information as may be required by law. Supplemental statements shall be submitted at any special session of the Legislature and at such other times as may be necessary to show probable changes.

From and after Jan. 1, 1945, save in the case of emergency and imperative public necessity and with a four-fifths vote of the total membership of each house, no appropriation in excess of the cash and anticipated revenue of the funds from which such appropriation is to be made shall be valid. From and after Jan. 1, 1945, no bill containing an appropriation shall be considered as passed or be sent to the Governor for consideration until and less the Comptroller of Public Accounts endorses his certificate thereon showing that the amount appropriated is within the amount estimated to be available in the affected funds. When the Comptroller finds an appropriation bill exceeds the estimated revenue he shall endorse such finding thereon and return to the house in which same originated. Such information shall be immediately made known to both the House of Representatives and the Senate, and the necessary steps shall be taken to bring such appropriation to within the revenue, either by providing additional revenue or reducing the appropriation.

For the purpose of financing the outstanding obligations of the general revenue fund of the State and placing its current accounts on a cash basis the Legislature of the State of Texas is hereby authorized to provide for the issuance, sale and retirement of serial bonds equal in principal to the total outstanding, valid and approved obligations owing by said fund on Sept. 1, 1943, provided such bonds shall not draw interest in excess of 2 per cent per annum and shall mature within twenty years from date.

[Note — The foregoing Sec. 49-a of Art. III is an amendment added to provide for Comptroller's estimates of receipts and disbursements and limit legislative appropriations, as stated. Adopted in an election Nov. 3, 1942.]

Sec. 49-b. **Veterans' Land Board; Bonds Authorized for Creation of Veterans' Land Fund; Purchase of Land by State and Sales to Veterans** — By virtue of prior amendments to this Constitution, there has been created a governmental agency of the State of Texas performing governmental duties which has been designated the Veterans' Land Board. Said Board shall continue to function for the purposes specified in all of the prior Constitutional Amendments except as modified herein. Said Board shall be composed of the Commissioner of the General Land Office and two (2) citizens of the State of Texas, one (1) of whom shall be well versed in veterans' affairs and one (1) of whom shall be well versed in finances. One (1) such citizen member shall, with the advice and consent of the Senate, be appointed biennially by the Governor to serve for a term of four (4) years; but the members serving on said Board on the date of adoption hereof shall complete the terms to which they were appointed. In the event of the resignation or death of any such citizen member, the Governor shall appoint a replacement to serve for the unexpired portion of the term to which the deceased or resigning member had been appointed. The compensation for said citizen members shall be as is now or may hereafter be fixed by the Legislature; and each shall make bond in such amount as is now or may hereafter be prescribed by the Legislature.

The Commissioner of the General Land Office shall act as Chairman of said Board and shall be the administrator of the Veterans' Land Program under such terms and restrictions as are now or may hereafter be provided by law. In the absence or illness of said Commissioner, the Chief Clerk of the General Land Office shall be the Acting Chairman of said Board with the same duties and powers that said Commissioner would have if present.

The Veterans' Land Board may provide for, issue and sell not to exceed Nine Hundred and Fifty Million Dollars ($950,000,000) in bonds or obligations of the State of Texas for the purpose of creating a fund to be known as the Veterans' Land Fund, Seven Hundred Million Dollars ($700,000,000) of which have heretofore been authorized. Such bonds or obligations shall be sold for not less than par value and accrued interest; shall be issued in such forms, denominations, and upon such terms as are now or may hereafter be provided by law; shall be issued and sold at such times, at such places, and in such installments as may be determined by said Board; and shall bear a rate or rates of interest as may be fixed by said Board but the weighted average annual interest rate, as that phrase is commonly and ordinarily used and understood in the municipal-bond market, of all the bonds issued and sold in any installment of any bonds may not exceed the rate specified in Sec. 65 of this article. All bonds or obligations issued and sold hereunder shall, after execution by the Board, approval by the Attorney General of Texas, registration by the Comptroller of Public Accounts of the State of Texas, and delivery to the

Article III — (Cont'd.)

purchaser or purchasers, be incontestable and shall constitute general obligations of the State of Texas under the Constitution of Texas; and all bonds heretofore issued and sold by said Board are hereby in all respects validated and declared to be general obligations of the State of Texas. In order to prevent default in the payment of principal or interest on any such bonds, the Legislature shall appropriate a sufficient amount to pay the same.

In the sale of any such bonds or obligations, a preferential right of purchase shall be given to the administrators of the various Teacher Retirement Funds, the Permanent University Funds, and the Permanent School Funds.

Said Veterans' Land Fund shall consist of any lands heretofore or hereafter purchased by said Board, until the sale price thereof, together with any interest and penalties due, have been received by said Board (although nothing herein shall be construed to prevent said Board from accepting full payment for a portion of any tract), and of the moneys attributable to any bonds heretofore or hereafter issued and sold by said Board which moneys so attributable shall include but shall not be limited to: the proceeds from the issuance and sale of such bonds; the moneys received from the sale or resale of any lands, or rights therein, purchased with such proceeds; the moneys received from the sale or resale of any lands, or rights therein, purchased with other moneys attributable to such bonds; the interest and penalties received from the sale or resale of such lands, or rights therein; the bonuses, income, rents, royalties, and any other pecuniary benefit received by said Board from any such lands; sums received by way of indemnity or forfeiture for the failure of any bidder for the purchase of any such bonds to comply with his bid and accept and pay for such bonds or for the failure of any bidder for the purchase of any lands comprising a part of said Fund to comply with his bid and accept and pay for any such lands; and interest received from investments of any such moneys. The principal and interest on the bonds heretofore and hereafter issued by said Board shall be paid out of the moneys of said Fund in conformance with the Constitutional provisions authorizing such bonds; but the moneys of said Fund which are not immediately committed to the payment of principal and interest on such bonds, the purchase of lands as herein provided, or the payment of expenses as herein provided may be invested in bonds or obligations of the United States until such funds are needed for such purposes.

All moneys comprising a part of said Fund and not expended for the purposes herein provided shall be a part of said Fund until there are sufficient moneys therein to retire fully all of the bonds heretofore or hereafter issued and sold by said Board, at which time all such moneys remaining in said Fund, except such portion thereof as may be necessary to retire all such bonds which portion shall be set aside and retained in said Fund for the purpose of retiring all such bonds, shall be deposited to the credit of the General Revenue Fund to be appropriated to such purposes as may be prescribed by law. All moneys becoming a part of said Fund thereafter shall likewise be deposited to the credit of the General Revenue Fund.

When a Division of said Fund (each Division consisting of the moneys attributable to the bonds issue and sold pursuant to a single Constitutional authorization, and the lands purchased therewith) contains sufficient moneys to retire all of the bonds secured by such Division, the moneys thereof, except such portion as may be needed to retire all of the bonds secured by such Division which portion shall be set aside and remain a part of such Division for the purpose of retiring all such bonds, may be used for the purpose of paying the principal and the interest thereon, together with the expenses herein authorized, or any other bonds heretofore or hereafter issued and sold by said Board. Such use shall be a matter for the discretion and direction of said Board; but there may be no such use of any such moneys contrary to the rights of any holder of any of the bonds issued and sold by said Board or violative of any contract to which said Board is a party.

The Veterans' Land Fund shall be used by said Board for the purpose of purchasing lands situated in the State of Texas owned by the United States or any governmental agency thereof, owned by the Texas Prison System or any other governmental agency of the State of Texas, or owned by any person, firm, or corporation. All lands thus purchased shall be acquired at the lowest price obtainable, to be paid for in cash, and shall be a part of such Fund. Such lands heretofore or hereafter purchased and comprising a part of said Fund are hereby declared to be held for a governmental purpose, although the individual purchasers thereof shall be subject to taxation to the same extent and in the same manner as are purchasers of lands dedicated to the Permanent Free Public School Fund.

The lands of the Veterans' Land Fund shall be sold by said Board in such quantities, on such terms, at such prices, at such rates of interest and under such rules and regulations as are now or may hereafter be provided by law to veterans as they are now or may hereafter be defined by the laws of the State of Texas. The foregoing notwithstanding, any lands in the Veterans' Land Fund which have been first offered for sale to veterans and which have not been sold may be sold or resold to such purchasers, in such quantities, and on such terms, and at such prices and rates of interest, and under such rules and regulations as are now or may hereafter be provided by law.

Said Veterans' Land Fund, to the extent of the moneys attributable to any bonds hereafter issued and sold by said Board may be used by said Board, as is now or may hereafter be provided by law, for the purpose of paying the expenses of surveying, monumenting, road construction, legal fees, recordation fees, advertising and other like costs necessary or incidental to the purchase and sale, or resale, of any lands purchased with any of the moneys attributable to such additional bonds, such expenses to be added to the price of such lands when sold, or resold, by said Board; for the purpose of paying the expenses of issuing, selling, and delivering any such additional bonds; and for the purpose of meeting the expenses of paying the interest or principal due or to become due on any such additional bonds.

All of the moneys attributable to any series of bonds hereafter issued and sold by said Board (a 'series of bonds' being all of the bonds issued and sold in a single transaction as a single installment of bonds) may be used for the purchase of lands as herein provided, to be sold as herein provided, for a period ending eight (8) years after the date of sale of such series of bonds; provided, however, that so much of such moneys as may be necessary to pay interest on bonds hereafter issued and sold shall be set aside for that purpose in accordance with the resolution adopted by said Board authorizing the issuance and sale of such series of bonds. After such eight (8) year period, all of such moneys shall be set aside for the retirement of any bonds hereafter issued and sold and to pay interest thereon, together with any expenses as provided herein, in accordance with the resolution or resolutions authorizing the issuance and sale of such additional bonds, until there are sufficient moneys to retire all of the bonds hereafter issued and sold, at which time all such moneys then remaining a part of said Veterans' Land Fund and thereafter becoming a part of said Fund shall be governed as elsewhere provided herein.

This amendment being intended only to establish a basic framework and not to be a comprehensive treatment of the Veterans' Land Program, there is hereby reposed in the Legislature full power to implement and effectuate the design and objects of this amendment, including the power to delegate such duties, responsibilities, functions, and authority to the Veterans' Land Board as it believes necessary.

Should the Legislature enact any enabling laws in anticipation of this amendment, no such law shall be void by reason of its anticipatory nature.

[Note — The foregoing Sec. 49-b of Art. III has been amended ten times: First, for the purpose of aiding war veterans in land purchases. Submitted by Forty-ninth Legislature (1945), and ratified in a special election Nov. 7, 1946. (It was by error that the date was set as Nov. 7 instead of Nov. 5, which was the general election date.) Second, it was amended to increase the authorized bond issue from $25,000,000 to $100,000,000 and to make minor changes. Submitted by Fifty-second Legislature (1951), and ratified in an election Nov. 13, 1951. Third, it was amended to change membership of the Veterans' Land Board and to raise the total of bonds authorized to $200,000,000. Submitted by Fifty-fourth Legislature (1955) and adopted in election Nov. 6, 1956. Fourth, it was amended to fix the rate of interest not to exceed 3½ per cent per annum. Submitted by Fifty-sixth Legislature (1959) and adopted in election Nov. 8, 1960. Fifth, it was amended to provide for offering land in the Veterans' Land Fund to nonveteran purchasers after land has first been offered to veterans. Submitted by Fifty-seventh Legislature (1961) and adopted in election Nov. 6, 1962. Sixth, to extend Veterans' Land Program by authorizing sale of bonds to increase Veterans' Land Fund for purchasing land to be sold to Texas veterans who served between Sept. 16, 1940, and date of formal withdrawal of U.S. troops from Viet Nam; and providing for additional $200,000,000 in bonds for this program. Submitted by Sixtieth Legislature (1967) and adopted in election Nov. 11, 1967. Seventh, to provide for additional $100 million in bonds for the Veterans' Land Fund and to make all veterans eligible to participate who served in armed forces after Sept. 16, 1940. Submitted by Sixty-third Legislature (1973) and adopted in election Nov. 6, 1973. Eighth, to provide for additional $200 million in bonds for the Veterans' Land Fund and to extend the right to apply to purchase land to unmarried surviving spouses of veterans who meet requirements set out herein. Submitted by Sixty-fifth Legislature (1977) and adopted in election Nov. 8, 1977. Ninth, to raise to $950 million the amount of bonds authorized for the Veterans' Land Fund. Submitted by Sixty-seventh Legislature (1981) and adopted in election Nov. 3, 1981. Tenth, to define an eligible veteran for purposes of this program. Submitted by Sixty-ninth Legislature (1985) and adopted in an election Nov. 5, 1985.]

Sec. 49-b-1. Bonds Authorized to Finance Veterans' Land Program and Veterans' Housing Assistance Program — (a) In

Article III — (Cont'd.)

addition to the general obligation bonds authorized to be issued and to be sold by the Veterans' Land Board by Sec. 49-b of this article, the Veterans' Land Board may provide for, issue, and sell not to exceed $1.3 billion in bonds of the State of Texas, $800 million of which have heretofore been authorized to provide financing to veterans of the state in recognition of their service to their state and country.

(b) For purposes of this section, "veteran" means a person who satisfies the definition of "veteran" as is now or may hereafter be set forth by the laws of the State of Texas.

(c) The bonds shall be sold for not less than par value and accrued interest; shall be issued in such forms and denominations, upon such terms, at such times and places, and in such installments as may be determined by the board; and, notwithstanding the rate of interest specified by any other provision of this Constitution, shall bear a rate or rates of interest fixed by the board. All bonds issued and sold pursuant to Subsections (a) through (f) of this section shall, after execution by the board, approval by the Attorney General of Texas, registration by the Comptroller of Public Accounts of the State of Texas, and delivery to the purchaser or purchasers, be incontestable and shall constitute general obligations of the state under the Constitution of Texas.

(d) Three hundred million dollars of the state bonds authorized by this section shall be used to augment the Veterans' Land Fund. The Veterans' Land Fund shall be used by the board for the purpose of purchasing lands situated in the State of Texas owned by the United States government or any agency thereof, the State of Texas or any subdivision or agency thereof, or any person, firm, or corporation. The lands shall be sold to veterans in such quantities, on such terms, at such prices, at such rates of interest, and under such rules and regulations as may be authorized by law. The expenses of the board in connection with the issuance of the bonds and the purchase and sale of the lands may be paid from money in the fund. The Veterans' Land Fund shall continue to consist of any lands purchased by the board until the sale price therefor, together with any interest and penalties due, have been received by the board (although nothing herein shall prevent the board from accepting full payment for a portion of any tract) and of the money attributable to any bonds issued and sold by the board for the Veterans' Land Fund, which money so attributable shall include but shall not be limited to the proceeds from the issuance and sale of such bonds; the money received from the sale or resale of any lands, or rights therein, purchased from such proceeds; the money received from the sale or resale of any lands, or rights therein, purchased with other money attributable to such bonds; the interest and penalties received from the sale or resale of such lands, or rights therein; the bonuses, income, rents, royalties, and any other pecuniary benefit received by the board from any such lands; sums received by way of indemnity or forfeiture for the failure of any bidder for the purchase of any such bonds to comply with his bid and accept and pay for such bonds or for the failure of any bidder for the purchase of any lands comprising a part of the fund to comply with his bid and accept and pay for any such lands; and interest received from investments of any such money. The principal of and interest on the general obligation bonds previously authorized by Sec. 49-b of this Constitution shall be paid out of the money of the fund in conformance with the constitutional provisions authorizing such bonds. The principal of and interest on the general obligation bonds authorized by this section for the benefit of the Veterans' Land Fund shall be paid out of the money of the fund, but the money of the fund which is not immediately committed to the payment of principal and interest on such bonds, the purchase of lands as herein provided, or the payment of expenses as herein provided may be invested in bonds or obligations of the United States until the money is needed for such purposes.

(e) The Veterans' Housing Assistance Fund is created, and $1 billion of the state bonds authorized by this section shall be used for the Veterans' Housing Assistance Fund, $500 million of which have heretofore been authorized. Money in the Veterans' Housing Assistance Fund shall be administered by the Veterans' Land Board and shall be used for the purpose of making home mortgage loans to veterans for housing within the State of Texas in such quantities, on such terms, at such rates of interest, and under such rules and regulations as may be authorized by law. The expenses of the board in connection with the issuance of the bonds and the making of the loans may be paid from money in the fund. The Veterans' Housing Assistance Fund shall consist of any interest of the board in all home mortgage loans made to veterans by the board pursuant to a Veterans' Housing Assistance Program which the Legislature may establish by appropriate legislation until, with respect to any such home mortgage loan, the principal amount, together with any interest and penalties due, have been received by the board; the money attributable to any bonds issued and sold by the board to provide money for the fund, which money so attributable shall include but shall

not be limited to the proceeds from the issuance and sale of such bonds; income, rents, and any other pecuniary benefit received by the board as a result of making such loans; sums received by way of indemnity or forfeiture for the failure of any bidder for the purchase of any such bonds to comply with his bid and accept and pay for such bonds; and interest received from investments of any such money. The principal of and interest on the general obligation bonds authorized by this section for the benefit of the Veterans' Housing Assistance Fund shall be paid out of the money of the fund, but the money of the fund which is not immediately committed to the payment of principal and interest on such bonds, the making of home mortgage loans as herein provided, or the payment of expenses as herein provided may be invested in bonds or obligations of the United States until the money is needed for such purposes.

(f) To the extent there is not money in either the Veterans' Land Fund or the Veterans' Housing Assistance Fund, as the case may be, available for payment of principal of and interest on the general obligation bonds authorized by this section to provide money for either of the funds, there is hereby appropriated out of the first money coming into the treasury in each fiscal year, not otherwise appropriated by this Constitution, an amount which is sufficient to pay the principal of and interest on such general obligation bonds that mature or become due during that fiscal year.

(g) Receipt of all kinds of the funds determined by the board not to be required for the payment of principal of and interest on the general obligation bonds herein authorized, heretofore authorized, or hereafter authorized by this Constitution to be issued by the board to provide money for either of the funds may be used by the board, to the extent not inconsistent with the proceedings authorizing such bonds, to pay the principal of and interest on general obligation bonds issued to provide money for the other fund, or to pay the principal of and interest on revenue bonds of the board issued for the purposes of providing funds for the purchasing of lands and making the sale thereof to veterans or making home mortgage loans to veterans as provided by this section. The revenue bonds shall be special obligations and payable only from the receipt of the funds and shall not constitute indebtedness of the state or the Veterans' Land Board. The board is authorized to issue such revenue bonds from time to time which shall not exceed an aggregate principal amount that can be fully retired from the receipts of the funds and other revenues pledged to the retirement of the revenue bonds. The revenue bonds shall be issued in such forms and denominations, upon such terms, at such times and places, and in such installments as may be determined by the board; and, notwithstanding the rate of interest specified by any other provision of the Constitution, shall bear a rate or rates of interest fixed by the board.

[Note — The foregoing Sec. 49-b-1 of Art. III was added to provide financial assistance to veterans and to authorize issuance of bonds to finance the Veterans' Land Program and the Veterans' Housing Assistance Program. Submitted by Sixty-eighth Legislature (1983) and adopted in election Nov. 8, 1983. It was further amended to provide $500 million additional bonding authority for the veterans' housing assistance program and changing definition of veterans eligible to participate in veterans' land program and veterans' housing program. Submitted by Sixty-ninth Legislature (1985) and adopted in an election Nov. 5, 1985.]

Sec. 49-c. Texas Water Development Board, Fund; Purpose — There is hereby created as an agency of the State of Texas the Water Development Board to exercise such powers as necessary under this provision together with such other duties and restrictions as may be prescribed by law. The qualifications, compensation and number of members of said Board shall be determined by law. They shall be appointed by the Governor with the advice and consent of the Senate in the manner and for such terms as may be prescribed by law.

The Texas Water Development Board shall have the authority to provide for, issue and sell general obligation bonds of the State of Texas in an amount not to exceed One Hundred Million Dollars ($100,000,000). The Legislature of Texas, upon two-thirds (⅔) vote of the elected Members of each House, may authorize the Board to issue additional bonds in an amount not exceeding One Hundred Million Dollars ($100,000,000). The bonds authorized herein or permitted to be authorized by the Legislature shall be called "Texas Water Development Bonds," shall be executed in such form, denominations and upon such terms as may be prescribed by law, provided, however, that the bonds shall not bear more than four percent (4%) interest per annum; they may be issued in such installments as the Board finds feasible and practical in accomplishing the purpose set forth herein.

All moneys received from the sale of State bonds shall be deposited in a fund hereby created in the State Treasury to be known as the Texas Water Development Fund to be administered (without further appropriation) by the Texas Water Development Board in such manner as prescribed by law.

Such fund shall be used only for the purpose of aiding or

Article III — (Cont'd.)

making funds available upon such terms and conditions as the Legislature may prescribe, to the various political subdivisions or bodies politic and corporate of the State of Texas including river authorities, conservation and reclamation districts and districts created or organized or authorized to be created or organized under Article XVI, Section 59 or Article III, Section 52, of this Constitution, interstate compact commissions to which the State of Texas is a party and municipal corporations, in the conservation and development of the water resources of this State, including the control, storing and preservation of its storm and flood waters and the waters of its rivers and streams, for all useful and lawful purposes by the acquisition, improvement, extension, or construction of dams, reservoirs and other water storage projects, including any system necessary for the transportation of water from storage to points of treatment and/or distribution, including facilities for transporting water therefrom to wholesale purchasers, or for any one or more of such purposes or methods.

Any or all financial assistance as provided herein shall be repaid with interest upon such terms, conditions and manner of repayment as may be provided by law.

While any of the bonds authorized by this provision or while any of the bonds that may be authorized by the Legislature under this provision, or any interest on any of such bonds, is outstanding and unpaid, there is hereby appropriated out of the first moneys coming into the Treasury in each fiscal year, not otherwise appropriated by this Constitution, an amount which is sufficient to pay the principal and interest on such bonds that mature or become due during such fiscal year, less the amount in the sinking fund at the close of the prior fiscal year.

The Legislature may provide for the investment of moneys available in the Texas Water Development Fund, and the interest and sinking funds established for the payment of bonds issued by the Texas Water Development Board. Income from such investment shall be used for the purposes prescribed by the Legislature. The Legislature may also make appropriations from the General Revenue Fund for paying administrative expenses of the Board.

From the moneys received by the Texas Water Development Board as repayment of principal for financial assistance or as interest thereon, there shall be deposited in the interest and sinking fund for the bonds authorized by this Section sufficient moneys to pay the interest and principal to become due during the ensuing year and sufficient to establish and maintain a reserve in said fund equal to the average annual principal and interest requirements on all outstanding bonds issued under this Section. If any year prior to December 31, 1982 moneys are received in excess of the foregoing requirements then such excess shall be deposited to the Texas Water Development Fund, and may be used for administrative expenses of the Board and for the same purposes and upon the same terms and conditions prescribed for the proceeds derived from the sale of such State bonds. No grant of financial assistance shall be made under the provisions of this Section after December 31, 1982, and all moneys thereafter received as repayment of principal for financial assistance or as interest thereon shall be deposited in the interest and sinking fund for the State bonds; except that such amount as may be required to meet the administrative expenses of the Board may be annually set aside; and provided, that after all State bonds have been fully paid with interest, or after there are on deposit in the interest and sinking fund sufficient moneys to pay all future maturities of principal and interest, additional moneys so received shall be deposited to the General Revenue Fund.

All bonds issued hereunder shall after approval by the Attorney General, registration by the Comptroller of Public Accounts of the State of Texas, and delivery to the purchasers, be incontestable and shall constitute general obligations of the State of Texas under the Constitution of Texas.

[Note — The foregoing Sec. 49-c of Art. III, an amendment, was added, setting up the Texas Water Development Board and Fund and providing for supervision thereof. Submitted by the Fifty-fifth Legislature (1957) and adopted in election Nov. 5, 1957.]

Sec. 49-d. **Development and Conservation of Public Waters** — It is hereby declared to be the policy of the State of Texas to encourage the optimum development of the limited number of feasible sites available for the construction or enlargement of dams and reservoirs for the conservation of the public waters of the state, which waters are held in trust for the use and benefit of the public, and to encourage the optimum regional development of systems built for the filtration, treatment, and transmission of water and wastewater. The proceeds from the sale of the additional bonds authorized hereunder deposited in the Texas Water Development Fund and the proceeds of bonds previously authorized by Art. III, Sec. 49-c of this Constitution, may be used by the Texas Water Development Board, under such provisions as the Legislature may prescribe by general law, including the requirement of a permit for storage or benefi-

cial use, for the additional purposes of acquiring and developing storage facilities, and any system or works necessary for the filtration, treatment and transportation of water or wastewater, or for any one or more of such purposes or methods, whether or not such a system or works is connected with a reservoir in which the state has a financial interest; provided however, the Texas Water Development Fund or any other state fund provided for water development, transmission, transfer or filtration shall not be used to finance any project which contemplates or results in the removal from the basin of origin of any surface water necessary to supply the reasonably foreseeable future water requirements for the next ensuing fifty-year period within the river basin of origin, except on a temporary, interim basis.

Under such provisions as the Legislature may prescribe by general law the Texas Water Development Fund may be used for the conservation and development of water for useful purposes by construction or reconstruction or enlargement of reservoirs constructed or to be constructed or enlarged within the State of Texas or on any stream constituting a boundary of the State of Texas, together with any system or works necessary for the filtration, treatment and/or transportation of water, by any one or more of the following governmental agencies; by the United States of America or any agency, department or instrumentality thereof; by the State of Texas or any agency, department or instrumentality thereof; by political subdivisions or bodies politic and corporate of the state; by interstate compact commissions to which the State of Texas is a party; and by municipal corporations. The Legislature shall provide terms and conditions under which the Texas Water Development Board may sell, transfer or lease, in whole or in part, any reservoir and associated system or works which the Texas Water Development Board has financed in whole or in part.

Under such provisions as the Legislature may prescribe by general law, the Texas Water Development Board may also execute long-term contracts with the United States or any of its agencies for the acquisition and development of storage facilities in reservoirs constructed or to be constructed by the Federal Government. Such contracts when executed shall constitute general obligations of the State of Texas in the same manner and with the same effect as state bonds issued under the authority of the preceding Sec. 49-c of this Constitution, and the provisions in said Sec. 49-c with respect to payment of principal and interest on state bonds issued shall likewise apply with respect to payment of principal and interest required to be paid by such contracts. If storage facilities are acquired for a term of years, such contracts shall contain provisions for renewal that will protect the state's investment.

The aggregate of the bonds authorized hereunder shall not exceed $200,000,000 and shall be in addition to the aggregate of the bonds previously authorized by said Sec. 49-c of Art. III of this Constitution. The Legislature upon two-thirds (⅔) vote of the elected members of each House, may authorize the board to issue all or any portion of such $200,000,000 in additional bonds herein authorized.

The Legislature shall provide terms and conditions for the Texas Water Development Board to sell, transfer or lease, in whole or in part, any acquired facilities or the right to use such facilities at a price not less than the direct cost of the board in acquiring same; and the Legislature may provide terms and conditions for the board to sell any unappropriated public waters of the state that might be stored in such facilities. As a prerequisite to the purchase of such storage or water, the applicant therefor shall have secured a valid permit from the Texas Water Commission or its successor authorizing the acquisition of such storage facilities or the water impounded therein. The money received from any sale, transfer or lease of facilities shall be used to pay principal and interest on state bonds issued or contractual obligations incurred by the Texas Water Development Board, provided that when moneys are sufficient to pay the full amount of indebtedness then outstanding and the full amount of interest to accrue thereon, any further sums received from the sale, transfer or lease of such facilities shall be deposited and used as provided by law. Money received from the sale of water, which shall include standby service, may be used for the operation and maintenance of acquired facilities, and for the payment of principal and interest on debt incurred.

Should the Legislature enact enabling laws in anticipation of the adoption of this amendment, such acts shall not be void by reason of their anticipatory character.

[Note — The foregoing Sec. 49-d of Art. III, an amendment, was added to authorize the Texas Water Development Board to acquire and develop storage facilities in reservoirs and to dispose of such storage facilities and water upon such terms as Legislature shall prescribe. Submitted by the Fifty-seventh Legislature (1961) and adopted in election Nov. 6, 1962. It was further amended to provide for optimum development of water reservoirs and investment of the Texas Water Development Fund. Submitted by the Fifty-ninth Legislature (1965) and adopted in an election Nov. 8, 1966. It was again amended to encourage optimum

Article III — (Cont'd.)

regional development of systems built for filtration, treatment and transmission of water and wastewater. Submitted by the Sixty-ninth Legislature (1985) and adopted in an election Nov. 5, 1985.]

Sec. 49-d-1. **Water Development Bonds** — (a) The Texas Water Development Board shall upon direction of the Texas Water Quality Board, or any successor agency designated by the Legislature, issue additional Texas Water Development Bonds up to an additional aggregate principal amount of Two Hundred Million Dollars ($200,000,000) to provide grants, loans, or any combination of grants and loans for water quality enhancement purposes as established by the Legislature. The Texas Water Quality Board or any successor agency designated by the Legislature may make such grants and loans to political subdivisions or bodies politic and corporate of the State of Texas, including municipal corporations, river authorities, conservation and reclamation districts, and districts created or organized or authorized to be created or organized under Art. XVI, Sec. 59, or Art. III, Sec. 52, of this Constitution, State agencies, and interstate agencies and compact commissions to which the State of Texas is a party, and upon such terms and conditions as the Legislature may authorize by general law. The bonds shall be issued for such terms, in such denominations, form and installments, and upon such conditions as the Legislature may authorize.

(b) The proceeds from the sale of such bonds shall be deposited in the Texas Water Development Fund to be invested and administered as prescribed by law.

(c) The bonds authorized in this Sec. 49-d-1 and all bonds authorized by Sections 49-c and 49-d of Art. III shall bear interest at not more than 6 percent per annum and mature as the Texas Water Development Board shall prescribe, subject to the limitations as may be imposed by the Legislature.

(d) The Texas Water Development Fund shall be used for the purposes heretofore permitted by, and subject to the limitations in Sections 49-c, 49-d and 49-d-1; provided, however, that the financial assistance may be made pursuant to the provisions of Sections 49-c, 49-d and 49-d-1 subject only to the availability of funds and without regard to the provisions in Sec. 49-c that such financial assistance shall terminate after Dec. 31, 1982.

(e) Texas Water Development Bonds are secured by the general credit of the State and shall after approval by the Attorney General, registration by the Comptroller of Public Accounts of the State of Texas, and delivery to the purchasers, be incontestable and shall constitute general obligations of the State of Texas under the Constitution of Texas.

(f) Should the Legislature enact enabling laws in anticipation of the adoption of this amendment, such acts shall not be void by reason of their anticipatory character.

[Note — The foregoing Sec. 49-d-1, an amendment, was added to provide for an additional $100 million for grants and loans for water improvement; also to raise the interest rate on water bonds to 6 percent. Submitted by the Sixty-second Legislature (1971) and adopted in an election May 18, 1971. It was amended to increase to $200 million the amount available for water quality enhancement. Submitted by the Sixty-fourth Legislature (1975) and adopted in an election Nov. 2, 1976.]

Sec. 49-d-2. (a) The Texas Water Development Board may issue additional Texas Water Development Bonds up to an additional aggregate principal amount of $980 million. Of the additional bonds authorized to be issued, $590 million of those bonds are dedicated for use for the purposes provided by Sec. 49-c and Sec. 49-d of this article with $400 million of those bonds to be used for state participation in the acquisition and development of facilities for the storage, transmission, transportation, and treatment of water and wastewater as authorized by Sec. 49-d of this article. The Legislature may set limits on the extent of state participation in projects in each fiscal year through the General Appropriations Act or other law, and state participation is limited to 50 percent of the funding for any single project. Of the additional bonds authorized, $190 million are dedicated for use for the purposes provided by Sec. 49-d-1 of this article and $200 million are dedicated exclusively for flood control projects and may be made available for any acquisition or construction necessary to achieve structural and nonstructural flood control purposes.

(b) The Texas Water Development Board shall issue the additional bonds authorized by this section for the terms, in the denominations, form, and installments, on the conditions, and subject to the limitations provided by Sec. 49-c, Sec. 49-d, and Sec. 49-d-1 of this article and by laws adopted by the Legislature implementing those sections.

(c) Proceeds from the sale of the bonds authorized by this section shall be deposited in the Texas water development fund to be administered and invested as provided by law.

(d) Financial assistance made available for the pur-

poses provided by this section is subject only to availability of funds. The requirement of Sec. 49-c of this article that financial assistance terminate on Dec. 31, 1982, does not apply to financial assistance made available under this section.

(e) Bonds issued under this section shall bear interest as provided by Sec. 65 of this article.

[Note — The foregoing Sec. 49-d-2 Art. III, an amendment, was added to authorize issuance of an additional $980 million of Texas Water Development Bonds. Submitted by the Sixty-ninth Legislature (1985) and adopted in an election Nov. 5, 1985.]

Sec. 49-d-3. (a) The Legislature by law may create one or more special funds in the state treasury for use for or in aid of water conservation, water development, water quality enhancement, flood control, drainage, subsidence control, recharge, chloride control, agricultural soil and water conservation, desalinization or any combination of those purposes, may make money in a special fund available to cities, counties, special governmental districts and authorities, and other political subdivisions of the state for use for the purposes for which the fund was created by grants, loans, or any other means, and may appropriate money to any of the special funds to carry out the purposes of this section.

(b) Money deposited in a special fund created under this section may not be used to finance or aid any project that contemplates or results in the removal from the basin of origin of any surface water necessary to supply the reasonably foreseeable water requirements for the next ensuing 50-year period within the river basin of origin, except on a temporary, interim basis.

[Note — The foregoing Sec. 49-d-3, of Art. III, an amendment, was added to create special water funds for water conservation, development, quality enhancement, flood control, drainage, subsidence control, recharge, chloride control, agricultural soil and water conservation and desalinization of water. Submitted by Sixty-ninth Legislature (1985) and adopted in an election Nov. 5, 1985.]

Sec. 49-d-4. (a) In addition to other programs authorized by this constitution, the Legislature by law may provide for the creation, administration, and implementation of a bond insurance program to which the state pledges its general credit in an amount not to exceed $250 million to insure the payment in whole or in part of the principal of and interest on bonds or other obligations that are issued by cities, counties, special governmental districts and authorities, and other political subdivisions of the state as defined by law for use for or in aid of water conservation, water development, water quality enhancement, flood control, drainage, recharge, chloride control, desalinization, or any combination of those purposes.

(b) The Legislature by law shall designate the state agency to administer the bond insurance program and may authorize that agency to execute insurance contracts that bind the state to pay the principal of and interest on the bonds if the bonds are in default or the bonds are subject to impending default, subject to the limits provided by this section and by law.

(c) The payment by the state of any insurance commitment made under this section must be made from the first money coming into the state treasury that is not otherwise dedicated by this constitution.

(d) Notwithstanding the total amount of bonds insured under this section, the total amount paid and not recovered by the state under this section, excluding the costs of administration, may not exceed $250 million.

(e) Except on a two-thirds vote of the members elected to each house of the Legislature, the ratio of bonds insured to the total liability of the state must be two to one.

(f) Except on a two-thirds vote of the members elected to each house of the Legislature, the state agency administering the bond insurance program may not authorize bond insurance coverage under the program in any state fiscal year that exceeds a total of $100 million.

(g) Unless authorized to continue by a two-thirds vote of the members elected to each house, this section and the bond insurance program authorized by this section expire on the sixth anniversary of the date on which this section becomes a part of the constitution. However, bond insurance issued before the expiration of this section and the program is not affected by the expiration of this section and the program and remains in effect according to its terms, and the state is required to fulfill all of the terms of that previously issued insurance.

[Note — The foregoing Sec. 49-d-4 of Art. III, an amendment, was added to authorize a bond insurance program. Submitted by the Sixty-ninth Legislature (1985) and adopted in an election Nov. 5, 1985.]

Sec. 49-d-5. For the purpose of any program established or authorized by Sec. 49-c, Sec. 49-d, Sec. 49-d-1, Sec. 49-d-2, or Sec. 49-d-4 of this article, the Legislature by law may extend any benefits to nonprofit water supply corporations

Article III — (Cont'd.)

that it may extend to a district created or organized under Art. XVI, Sec. 59, of this constitution.

[Note — The foregoing Sec. 49-d-5 of Art. III, an amendment, was added to clarify the purpose for which Texas Water Development Bonds may be issued. Submitted by Sixty-ninth Legislature (1985) and adopted in an election Nov. 5, 1985.]

Sec. 49-e. **Texas Park Development Bonds** — The Parks and Wildlife Department, or its successor vested with the powers, duties, and authority which deals with the operation, maintenance, and improvement of State Parks, shall have the authority to provide for, issue and sell general obligation bonds of the State of Texas in an amount not to exceed Seventy-Five Million Dollars ($75,000,000). The bonds authorized herein shall be called "Texas Park Development Bond," shall be executed in such form, denominations, and upon such terms as may be prescribed by law, provided, however, that the bonds shall bear a rate or rates of interest as may be fixed by the Parks and Wildlife Department or its successor, but the weighted average annual interest rate, as that phrase is commonly and ordinarily used and understood in the municipal bond market, of all the bonds issued and sold in any installment of any bonds, shall not exceed four and one-half percent (4½%) interest per annum; they may be issued in such installments as said Parks and Wildlife Department, or its said successor, finds feasible and practical in accomplishing the purpose set forth herein.

All moneys received from the sale of said bonds shall be deposited in a fund hereby created with the State Treasurer to be known as the Texas Park Development Fund to be administered (without further appropriation) by the said Parks and Wildlife Department, or its said successor, in such manner as prescribed by law.

Such fund shall be used by said Parks and Wildlife Department, or its said successor, under such provisions as the Legislature may prescribe by general law, for the purposes of acquiring lands from the United States, or any governmental agency thereof, from any governmental agency of the State of Texas, or from any person, firm, or corporation, for State Park Sites and for developing said sites as State Parks.

While any of the bonds authorized by this provision, or any interest on any such bonds, is outstanding and unpaid, there is hereby appropriated out of the first moneys coming into the Treasury in each fiscal year, not otherwise appropriated by this Constitution, an amount which is sufficient to pay the principal and interest on such bonds that mature or become due during such fiscal year, less the amount in the interest and sinking fund at the close of the prior fiscal year, which includes any receipts derived during the prior fiscal year by said Parks and Wildlife Department, or its said successor, from admission charges to State Parks, as the Legislature may prescribe by general law.

The Legislature may provide for the investment of moneys available in the Texas Park Development Fund and the interest and sinking fund established for the payment of bonds issued by said Parks and Wildlife Department, or its said successor. Income from such investment shall be used for the purposes prescribed by the Legislature.

From the moneys received by said Parks and Wildlife Department, or its said successor, from the sale of the bonds issued hereunder, there shall be deposited in the interest and sinking fund for the bonds authorized by this section sufficient moneys to pay the interest to become due during the State fiscal year in which the bonds were issued. After all bonds have been fully paid with interest, or after there are on deposit in the interest and sinking fund sufficient moneys to pay all future maturities of principal and interest, additional moneys received from admission charges to State Parks shall be deposited to the State Parks Fund, or any successor fund which may be established by the Legislature as a depository for Park revenue earned by said Parks and Wildlife Department, or its said successor.

All bonds issued hereunder shall after approval by the Attorney General, registration by the Comptroller of Public Accounts of the State of Texas, and delivery to the purchasers, be incontestable and shall constitute general obligations of the State of Texas under the Constitution of Texas.

Should the Legislature enact enabling laws in anticipation of the adoption of this amendment, such acts shall not be void by reason of their anticipatory nature.

[Note — The foregoing Sec. 49-e of Art. III, an amendment, was added to authorize issuance and sale of $75,000,000 in bonds to create the Texas Park Development Fund to acquire lands for State Park sites and to develop State Parks. Submitted by the Sixtieth Legislature (1967) and adopted in election Nov. 11, 1967.]

Sec. 49-f. (a) The Legislature by general law may provide for the issuance of general obligation bonds of the state, the proceeds of which shall be used to make loans and provide other financing assistance for the purchase of farm and ranch land.

(b) All money received from the sale of the bonds shall be deposited in a fund created with the state treasurer to be known as the farm and ranch finance program fund. This fund shall be administered by the Veterans' Land Board in the manner prescribed by law.

(c) Sec. 65(b) of this article applies to the payment of interest on the bonds.

(d) The principal amount of bonds outstanding at one time may not exceed $500 million.

(e) While any of the bonds authorized by this section or any interest on those bonds is outstanding and unpaid, there is appropriated out of the first money coming into the treasury in each fiscal year not otherwise appropriated by this constitution an amount that is sufficient to pay the principal and interest on the bonds that mature or become due during the fiscal year less the amount in the interest and sinking fund at the close of the prior fiscal year.

(f) The bonds shall be approved by the attorney general and registered with the comptroller of public accounts. The bonds, when approved and registered, are general obligations of the state and are incontestable.

[Note — The foregoing Sec. 49-f of Art. III, an amendment, was added to authorize the issuance of general obligation bonds to provide financing for purchase of farm and ranch land. Submitted by Sixty-ninth Legislature (1985) and adopted in an election Nov. 5, 1985.]

Sec. 50. **Credit of State Not to Be Pledged** — The Legislature shall have no power to give or to lend or to authorize the giving or lending of the credit of the State in aid of, or to any person, association or corporation, whether municipal or other, or to pledge the credit of the State in any manner whatsoever, for the payment of the liabilities, present or prospective, of any individual, association of individuals, municipal or other corporation whatsoever.

Sec. 50-a. **State Medical Education Board, Fund; Purpose** — The Legislature shall create a State Medical Education Board to be composed of not more than six (6) members whose qualifications, duties and terms of office shall be prescribed by law. The Legislature shall also establish a State Medical Education Fund and make adequate appropriations therefor to be used by the State Medical Education Board to provide grants, loans or scholarships to students desiring to study medicine and agreeing to practice in the rural areas of this State, upon such terms and conditions as shall be prescribed by law. The term "rural areas" as used in this section shall be defined by law.

[Note — The foregoing Sec. 50-a of Art. III, an amendment, was added for the stated purpose of providing scholarships and to set up a State Medical Education Board. Submitted by the Fifty-second Legislature and adopted in an election Nov. 4, 1952.]

Sec. 50-b. **Student Loans** — (a) The Legislature may provide that the Coordinating Board, Texas College and University System, or its successor or successors, shall have the authority to provide for, issue and sell general obligation bonds of the State of Texas in an amount not to exceed Eighty-five Million Dollars ($85,000,000). The bonds authorized herein, shall be called "Texas College Student Loan Bonds," shall be executed in such form, denominations and upon such terms as may be prescribed by law, provided, however, that the bonds shall not bear more than four per cent (4%) interest per annum; they may be issued in such installments as the Board finds feasible and practical in accomplishing the purposes of this section.

(b) All moneys received from the sale of such bonds shall be deposited in a fund hereby created in the State Treasury to be known as the Texas Opportunity Plan Fund to be administered by the Coordinating Board, Texas College and University System, or its successor or successors to make loans to students who have been admitted to attend any institution of higher education within the State of Texas, public or private, including Junior Colleges, which are recognized or accredited under terms and conditions prescribed by the Legislature, and to pay interest and principal on such bonds and provide a sinking fund therefor under such conditions as the Legislature may prescribe.

(c) While any of the bonds, or interest on said bonds authorized by this section is outstanding and unpaid, there is hereby appropriated out of the first moneys coming into the Treasury in each fiscal year, not otherwise appropriated by this Constitution, an amount sufficient to pay the principal and interest on such bonds that mature or become due during such fiscal year, less the amount in the sinking fund at the close of the prior fiscal year.

(d) The Legislature may provide for the investment of moneys available in the Texas Opportunity Plan Fund, and the interest and sinking funds established for the payment of bonds issued by the Coordinating Board, Texas College and University System, or its successor or successors. Income from such investment shall be used for the purposes prescribed by the Legislature.

(e) All bonds issued hereunder shall, after approval by the Attorney General, registration by the Comptroller of Public Accounts of the State of Texas, and delivery to the

Article III — (Cont'd.)

purchasers, be incontestable and shall constitute general obligations of the State of Texas under this Constitution.

(f) Should the Legislature enact enabling laws in anticipation of the adoption of this amendment, such acts shall not be void because of their anticipatory nature.

[Note — The foregoing Sec. 50-b of Art. III, an amendment, was added to provide a system of student loans at institutions of higher education and to provide for creation of the Texas Opportunity Plan Fund. Submitted by the Fifty-ninth Legislature (1965) and adopted in an election Nov. 2, 1965.]

Sec. 50-b-1. (a) The Legislature may provide that the Coordinating Board, Texas College and University System, or its successor or successors, shall have authority to provide for, issue and sell general obligation bonds of the State of Texas in an amount not to exceed Two Hundred Million Dollars ($200,000,000) in addition to those heretofore authorized to be issued pursuant to Sec. 50-b of the Constitution. The bonds authorized herein shall be executed in such form, upon such terms and be in such denomination as may be prescribed by law and shall bear interest, and be issued in such installments as shall be prescribed by the Board provided that the maximum net effective interest rate to be borne by such bonds may be fixed by law.

(b) The moneys received from the sale of such bonds shall be deposited to the credit of the Texas Opportunity Plan Fund created by Sec. 50-b of the Constitution and shall otherwise be handled as provided in Sec. 50-b of the Constitution and the laws enacted pursuant thereto.

(c) The said bonds shall be general obligations of the state and shall be payable in the same manner and from the same sources as bonds heretofore authorized pursuant to Sec. 50-b.

(d) All bonds issued hereunder shall, after approval by the Attorney General, registration by the Comptroller of Public Accounts of the State of Texas, and delivery to the purchasers, be incontestable and shall constitute general obligations of the State of Texas under this Constitution.

(e) Should the Legislature enact enabling laws in anticipation of the adoption of this amendment such acts shall not be void because of their anticipatory nature.

[Note—The foregoing Sec. 50-b-1 of Art. III, an amendment, was added to provide for additional loans to students at higher educational institutions under the Texas Opportunity Plan. Submitted by the Sixty-first Legislature (1969) and adopted in election Aug. 5, 1969.]

Sec. 50-c. **Farm and Ranch Loan Security Fund** — (a) The Legislature may provide that the commissioner of agriculture shall have the authority to provide for, issue, and sell general obligation bonds of the State of Texas in an amount not to exceed $10 million. The bonds shall be called "Farm and Ranch Loan Security Bonds" and shall be executed in such form, denominations, and on such terms as may be prescribed by law. The bonds shall bear interest rates fixed by the Legislature of the State of Texas.

(b) All money received from the sale of Farm and Ranch Loan Security Bonds shall be deposited in a fund hereby created with the State Treasurer to be known as the "Farm and Ranch Loan Security Fund." This fund shall be administered without further appropriation by the commissioner of agriculture in the manner prescribed by law.

(c) The Farm and Ranch Loan Security Fund shall be used by the commissioner of agriculture under provisions prescribed by the Legislature for the purpose of guaranteeing loans used for the purchase of farm and ranch real estate, for acquiring real estate mortgages or deeds of trust on lands purchased with guaranteed loans, and to advance to the borrower a percentage of the principal and interest due on those loans; provided that the commissioner shall require at least six percent interest be paid by the borrower on any advance of principal and interest. The Legislature may authorize the commissioner to sell at foreclosure any land acquired in this manner, and proceeds from that sale shall be deposited in the Farm and Ranch Loan Security Fund.

(d) The Legislature may provide for the investment of money available in the Farm and Ranch Loan Security Fund and the interest and sinking fund established for the payment of bonds issued by the commissioner of agriculture. Income from the investment shall be used for purposes prescribed by the Legislature.

(e) While any of the bonds authorized by this section or any interest on those bonds is outstanding and unpaid, there is hereby appropriated out of the first money coming into the treasury in each fiscal year not otherwise appropriated by this constitution an amount that is sufficient to pay the principal and interest on the bonds that mature or become due during the fiscal year less the amount in the interest and sinking fund at the close of the prior fiscal year.

[Note — Sec. 50-c of Art. III, an amendment, was added to provide for the guarantee of loans for purchase of farm

and ranch real estate for qualified borrowers by the sale of general obligation bonds of the State of Texas. Submitted by the Sixty-sixth Legislature (1979) and adopted in election Nov. 6, 1979.]

Sec. 50-d. (a) On a two-thirds vote of the members elected to each house of the Legislature, the Texas Water Development Board may issue and sell Texas agricultural water conservation bonds in an amount not to exceed $200 million.

(b) The proceeds from the sale of Texas agricultural water conservation bonds shall be deposited in a fund created in the state treasury to be known as the agricultural water conservation fund.

(c) Texas agricultural water conservation bonds are general obligations of the State of Texas. During the time that Texas agricultural water conservation bonds or any interest on those bonds is outstanding or unpaid, there is appropriated out of the first money coming into the state treasury in each fiscal year, not otherwise appropriated by this constitution, an amount that is sufficient to pay the principal of and interest on those bonds that mature or become due during that fiscal year, less the amount in the sinking fund at the close of the prior fiscal year.

(d) The terms, conditions, provisions, and procedures for issuance and sale and management of proceeds of Texas agricultural water conservation bonds shall be provided by law.

(e) The Legislature may not approve and the Texas Water Development Board may not issue and sell Texas agricultural water conservation bonds on or after the fourth anniversary of the date on which this section becomes a part of the constitution.

[Note — The foregoing Sec. 50-d of Art. III, an amendment, was added to authorize issuance and sale of $200 million of Texas agricultural water conservation bonds. Submitted by the Sixty-ninth Legislature (1985) and adopted in an election Nov. 5, 1985.]

Sec. 51. **Tax Levy Authorized for Confederate Soldiers and Sailors and Their Widows** — The Legislature shall have no power to make any grant or authorize the making of any grant of public moneys to any individual, association of individuals, municipal or other corporations whatsoever; provided, however, the Legislature may grant aid to indigent and disabled Confederate soldiers and sailors under such regulations and limitations as may be deemed by the Legislature as expedient, and to their widows in indigent circumstances under such regulations and limitations as may be deemed by the Legislature as expedient; provided that the provisions of this Section shall not be construed so as to prevent the grant of aid in cases of public calamity.

[Note—The foregoing Sec. 51 of Art. III, in its present form, is the result of much amendment. The original Sec. 51, which prohibited all grants of public money to individuals, associations, etc., with the single exception of cases of "public calamity," has been amended nine times, as follows: (1) Establishing Confederate Home. Submitted by Twenty-third Legislature (1893) and ratified at election, Nov. 6, 1894, and proclaimed adopted Dec. 21, 1894. (2) Providing for pensions for Confederate veterans from appropriations not to exceed $250,000 annually. Submitted by Twenty-fifth Legislature (1897), adopted at election, Nov. 1, 1898, and proclaimed Dec. 22, 1898. (3) Raising amount that might be appropriated for Confederate pensions from $250,000 to $500,000 annually. Submitted by Twenty-eighth Legislature (1903), adopted in election, Nov. 8, 1904, and proclaimed Dec. 29, 1904. (4) Increasing authorized maximum appropriations for Confederate Home from $100,000 to $150,000 annually. Submitted by Thirty-first Legislature (1909), adopted in election, Nov. 8, 1910, and declared adopted Dec. 31, 1910. (5) Authorizing 5c ad valorem tax for Confederate pension fund—also omitting "public calamity" clause. Submitted by Thirty-second Legislature (1911), adopted Nov. 3, 1912, and proclaimed Dec. 30, 1912. (6) Authorizing 7c ad valorem tax for Confederate pension fund — also reinstating "public calamity" clause. Submitted by Thirty-eighth Legislature (1923) and adopted Nov. 4, 1924. (7) Eliminating specific restrictions upon grants of aid to Confederate soldiers, sailors and others with respect to date of removal to Texas, etc.; and conferring such authority upon the Legislature. Submitted by Fortieth Legislature (1927); ratified Nov. 6, 1928; proclaimed Feb. 6, 1929. (8) Cutting tax from 7c to 2c by addition of Sec. 17 of Art. VII, which was deleted by Constitutional amendment in 1982. (9) Further amended to provide for abolition of the two cents ad valorem tax for this purpose by Dec. 31, 1976, but making provision for aiding these veterans and their widows. (See also Art. VIII, Sec. 1-e.) Submitted by Sixtieth Legislature (1967) and adopted in election Nov. 5, 1968.]

Sec. 51-a—**Assistance and Medical Care to Needy Aged, Needy Blind, Needy Children and Totally Disabled; Limitation on Expenditures for Same** — The Legislature shall have the power, by General Laws, to provide, subject to limitations herein contained, and such other limitations, restrictions and regulations as may be by the Legislature be deemed expedient, for assistance grants to dependent children and the

Article III — (Cont'd.)

caretakers of such children, needy persons who are totally and permanently disabled because of a mental or physical handicap, needy aged persons and needy blind persons.

The Legislature may provide by General Law for medical care, rehabilitation and other similar services for needy persons. The Legislature may prescribe such other eligibility requirements for participation in these programs as it deems appropriate and may make appropriations out of state funds for such purposes. The maximum amount paid out of state funds for assistance grants to or on behalf of needy dependent children and their caretakers shall not exceed the amount of Eighty Million Dollars ($80,000,000) during any fiscal year, except that the limit shall be One Hundred Sixty Million Dollars ($160,000,000) for the two years of the 1982-1983 biennium. For the two years of each subsequent biennium, the maximum amount shall not exceed one percent of the state budget. The Legislature by general statute shall provide for the means for determining the state budget amounts, including state and other funds appropriated by the Legislature, to be used in establishing the biennial limit.

Provided further, that if the limitations and restrictions herein contained are found to be in conflict with the provisions of appropriate federal statutes, as they now are or as they may be amended to the extent that federal matching money is not available to the state for these purposes, then and in that event the Legislature is specifically authorized and empowered to prescribe such limitations and restrictions and enact such laws as may be necessary in order that such federal matching money will be available for assistance and/or medical care for or on behalf of needy persons.

Nothing in this section shall be construed to amend, modify or repeal Sec. 31 of Art. XVI of this Constitution; provided further, however, that such medical care, services or assistance shall also include the employment of objective or subjective means, without the use of drugs, for the purpose of ascertaining and measuring the powers of vision of the human eye, and fitting lenses or prisms to correct or remedy any defect or abnormal condition of vision. Nothing herein shall be construed to permit optometrists to treat the eyes for any defect whatsoever in any manner nor to administer nor to prescribe any drug or physical treatment whatsoever, unless such optometrist is a regularly licensed physician or surgeon under the laws of this state.

[Note—The foregoing Sec. 51-a of Art. III, an amendment, was first submitted by Forty-ninth Legislature and adopted in an election Aug. 25, 1945. It supplanted four earlier amendments, as follows: An original Sec. 51-a which provided for issuance of $20,000,000 in state bonds for relief (the so-called "Bread bonds") this amendment having been submitted by Forty-third Legislature and adopted Aug. 26, 1933; and also Secs. 51-b, 51-c and 51-d, which originally provided for old-age pensions and other welfare measures, adopted in elections Aug. 24, 1935 and Aug. 23, 1937. Because of this consolidation, the Constitution did skip from Sec. 51-a to Sec. 51-e until a Sec. 51-b was added in election Nov. 2, 1954, and a Subsection 51a-a was added in election Nov. 5, 1957. It was further amended to raise the limit from $35,000,000 to $42,000,000. Submitted by Fifty-third Legislature (1953) and adopted in election Nov. 2, 1954. It was again amended to raise the limit from $42,000,000 to $47,000,000 and authorizing legislative appropriations to raise the needed money. Submitted by Fifty-fifth Legislature (1957) and adopted in election Nov. 5, 1957. It was further amended to raise the total amount of assistance to $52,000,000 per year. Submitted by Fifty-seventh Legislature (1961) and adopted in election Nov. 6, 1962. It was further amended to combine the former Sections 51-a and 51-b-1 of Art. III into one section to be known as Sec. 51-a; further raising the total amount of assistance to $60,000,000 per year and providing that Legislature shall prescribe the residence requirements. Submitted by Fifty-eighth Legislature (1963) and adopted in election Nov. 9, 1963. It was further amended in 1965 to create a new Sec. 51-a which consolidates the old Sec. 51-a and Subsections 51-a-1 and 51-a-2. The new Sec. 51-a enables the State of Texas to cooperate with the U.S. government in providing assistance and medical care for the needy aged, needy blind, needy children and needy totally disabled; expands age categories of those eligible for blind assistance and of needy children; and extends eligibility for the aged to citizens of the U.S. or noncitizens who have resided in the U.S. for 25 years. Submitted by Fifty-ninth Legislature (1965) and adopted in election Nov. 2, 1965. It was again amended to raise the limit on amount to be expended from $60,000,000 to $80,000,000 a year. It further provided that certain amounts be allocated out of the Omnibus Tax Clearance Fund for aid to permanently and totally disabled, families with dependent children and for old-age assistance. Submitted by Sixty-first Legislature (1969) and adopted in an election Aug. 5, 1969. The regular session of the Sixty-seventh Legislature (1981) submitted an amendment to raise the amount to be expended on Aid for Depen-

dent Children in the 1982-1983 biennium to a maximum of $160 million and, for each subsequent biennium, the maximum amount would not exceed one percent of the state budget. This proposed amendment inadvertently cut out other needy recipients and SJR 10 of the Called Session of the Sixty-seventh Legislature (1982) amended the proposed amendment to include other needy recipients in this fund. Adopted in election Nov. 2, 1982.]

[Note — Sec. 51-b of Art. III, creating the State Building Commission and the State Building Fund, was eliminated by a constitutional amendment in an election Nov. 7, 1978.]

Sec. 51-c. **False Imprisonment** — The Legislature may grant aid and compensation to any person who has heretofore paid a fine or served a sentence in prison, or who may hereafter pay a fine or serve a sentence in prison, under the laws of this State for an offense for which he or she is not guilty, under such regulations and limitations as the Legislature may deem expedient.

[Note — Sec. 51-c of Art. III was added to provide that Legislature may grant aid and compensation to persons who have been fined or imprisoned under laws of this state for offenses of which they are not guilty. Submitted by the Fifty-fourth Legislature (1955) and adopted in election Nov. 6, 1956.]

Sec. 51-d. **Assistance to Survivors of Law Enforcement Officers Killed on Duty** — The Legislature shall have the power, by general law, to provide for the payment of assistance by the State of Texas to the surviving spouse, minor children, and surviving dependent parents, brothers, and sisters of officers, employees and agents, including members of organized volunteer fire departments and members of organized police reserve or auxiliary units with authority to make an arrest, of the state or of any city, county, district, or other political subdivision who, because of the hazardous nature of their duties, suffer death in the course of the performance of those official duties. Should the Legislature enact any enabling laws in anticipation of this amendment, no such law shall be void by reason of its anticipatory nature.

[Note — The foregoing Sec. 51-d, an amendment, was added to provide assistance for survivors of law enforcement officers killed in performance of their duty. Submitted by the Fifty-ninth Legislature (1965), and adopted in election Nov. 8, 1966. It was further amended to provide for assistance to survivors of members of volunteer fire departments and organized police reserve, or auxiliary units with authority to make arrests, of political subdivisions of the state. Submitted by the Sixty-first Legislature (1969) and adopted in election Aug. 5, 1969. It was again amended to provide compensation for dependent parents, brothers and sisters of officers killed in performing their duties. Submitted by the Sixty-eighth Legislature (1983) and adopted in election Nov. 6, 1984.]

[Note — Sec. 51e and Sec. 51f, relating to City and Town Pension System and Local Pension Plans, respectively, were deleted by a constitutional amendment election April 22, 1975. See also note under Art. III, Sec. 48a and Sec. 48b; Art. XVI, Sec. 62 and Sec. 63. See also Art. XVI, Sec. 67, which replaces the foregoing Sections.]

Sec. 51-g. **Social Security Coverage for Municipal Employees** — The Legislature shall have the power to pass such laws as may be necessary to enable the State to enter into agreements with the Federal Government to obtain for proprietary employees of its political subdivisions coverage under the old-age and survivors insurance provisions of Title II of the Federal Social Security Act as amended. The Legislature shall have the power to make appropriations and authorize all obligations necessary to the establishment of such Social Security coverage program.

[Note — The foregoing Sec. 51-g of Art.III, an amendment, was added for the stated purpose of extending Social Security coverage to municipal employees. Submitted by the Fifty-third Legislature (1953) and adopted in an election Nov. 2, 1954.]

Sec. 52. **Counties, Cities, Etc., Not Authorized to Grant Money or Become Stockholders; Exceptions** — (a) Except as otherwise provided by this section, the Legislature shall have no power to authorize any county, city, town or other political corporation or subdivision of the State to lend its credit or to grant public money or thing of value in aid of, or to any individual, association or corporation whatsoever, or to become a stockholder in such corporation, association or company. However, this section does not prohibit the use of public funds or credit for the payment of premiums on nonassessable life, health, or accident insurance policies and annuity contracts issued by a mutual insurance company authorized to do business in this State.

[Note — Sec. 52(a) was amended to allow political subdivisions the opportunity to engage in and transact business with authorized mutual insurance companies in same

Article III — (Cont'd.)

manner as with other insurance companies. Submitted by Sixty-ninth Legislature (1985) and adopted in an election Nov. 4, 1986.]

(b) Under legislative provision any county, any political subdivision of a county, any number of adjoining counties or any political subdivision of the State or any defined district now or hereafter to be described and defined within the State of Texas, and which may or may not include towns, villages or municipal corporations, upon a vote of a two-thirds majority of the resident property taxpayers voting thereon who are qualified electors of such district or territory, to be affected thereby, in addition to all other debts, may issue bonds or otherwise lend its credit in any amount not to exceed one fourth of the assessed valuation of the real property of such district or territory, except that the total bonded indebtedness of any city or town shall never exceed the limits imposed by other provisions of this Constitution, and levy and collect taxes to pay the interest thereon and provide a sinking fund for the redemption thereof, as the Legislature may authorize, and in such manner as it may authorize the same, for the following purposes, to wit:

(1) The improvement of rivers, creeks and streams to prevent overflows and to permit of navigation thereof or irrigation thereof, or in aid of such purposes.

(2) The construction and maintenance of pools, lakes, reservoirs, dams, canals and waterways for the purposes of irrigation, drainage or navigation, or in aid thereof.

(3) The construction, maintenance and operation of macadamized, graveled or paved roads and turnpikes or in aid thereof.

(c) Notwithstanding the provisions of Subsection (b) of this section, bonds may be issued by any county in an amount not to exceed one fourth of the assessed valuation of the real property in the county, for the construction, maintenance, and operation of macadamized, graveled, or paved roads and turnpikes, or in aid thereof, upon a vote of a majority of the resident property taxpayers voting thereon who are qualified electors of the county, and without the necessity of further or amendatory legislation. The county may levy and collect taxes to pay the interest on the bonds as it becomes due and to provide a sinking fund for redemption of the bonds.

(d) Any defined district created under this section that is authorized to issue bonds or otherwise lend its credit for the purposes stated in Subdivisions (1) and (2) of Subsection (b) of this section may engage in fire-fighting activities and may issue bonds or otherwise lend its credit for fire-fighting purposes as provided by law and this constitution.

[Note — The foregoing Sec. 52 of Art. III, is an amended section, the amendment authorizing formation of districts for issuance of bonds for leveeing, drainage, irrigation, highway construction and other public improvements. Submitted by the Twenty-eighth Legislature (1903), adopted in election, Nov. 8, 1904, and proclaimed Dec. 29, 1904. It was further amended to permit any county, on vote of a majority of qualified property taxpaying electors, to issue road bonds in an amount not exceeding one fourth of assessed valuation of the real property in the county. Submitted by the Sixty-first Legislature (1969) and adopted in election Nov. 3, 1970. It was further amended by adding Subsection (d) to authorize certain districts to engage in fire-fighting activities and to issue bonds or otherwise lend their credit for fire-fighting purposes. (See also Subsection (f) of Sec. 59, Art. XVI.) Submitted by the Sixty-fifth Legislature (1977) and adopted in election Nov. 7, 1978.]

Sec. 52-b. **Legislature Prohibited to Lend Credit of State in Building or Maintaining Toll Roads and Turnpikes** — The Legislature shall have no power or authority to in any manner lend the credit of the State or grant any public money to, or assume any indebtedness, present or future, bonded or otherwise, of any individual, person, firm, partnership, association, corporation, public corporation, public agency, or political subdivision of the State, or anyone else, which is now or hereafter authorized to construct, maintain or operate toll roads and turnpikes within this State.

[Note — The foregoing Sec. 52-b of Art. III, an amendment, was added for the stated purpose of prohibiting Legislature from lending credit of State in building or maintaining toll roads and turnpikes. Submitted by the Fifty-third Legislature (1953) and adopted in an election Nov. 2, 1954.]

Sec. 52-d. **Harris County Road Districts** — Upon the vote of a majority of the resident qualified electors owning rendered taxable property therein so authorizing, a county or road district may collect an annual tax for a period not exceeding five (5) years to create a fund for constructing lasting and permanent roads and bridges or both. No contract involving the expenditure of any of such fund shall be valid unless, when it is made, money shall be on hand in such fund.

At such election, the Commissioners Court shall submit for adoption a road plan and designate the amount of special tax to be levied; the number of years said tax is to be levied; the location, description and character of the roads and bridges; and the estimated cost thereof. The funds raised by such taxes shall not be used for purposes other than those specified in the plan submitted to the voters. Elections may be held from time to time to extend or discontinue said plan or to increase or diminish said tax. The Legislature shall enact laws prescribing the procedure hereunder.

The provisions of this section shall apply only to Harris County and road districts therein.

[Note — The foregoing Sec. 52-d of Art. III, an amendment, was added for the stated purpose of giving special local tax powers to Harris County. Adopted in an election Aug. 23, 1937.]

Note that Secs. 52-a and 52-c are omitted. Such sections never existed. The Fifty-third Legislature (1953) submitted an amendment to be numbered 52-b, and same was adopted in an election Nov. 2, 1954. Obviously, the designation, "Sec. 52-d," in Senate Joint Resolution No. 16 of the Forty-fifth Legislature resulted from confusion of a new section number with the sequence of paragraphs "a, b and c" under section 52 immediately above. Some published texts of the State Constitution give this as "Paragraph d," under Sec. 52, as it might properly have been designated, but SJR No. 16 of the Fifty-third Legislature definitely gave it as a separate "Sec. 52-d." Since Sec. 52-b was added in 1954, Secs. 52-a and 52-c are still missing.

Sec. 52-e. **Dallas County Road Bonds** — Bonds to be issued by Dallas County under Sec. 52 of Art. III of this Constitution for the construction, maintenance and operation of macadamized, graveled or paved roads and turnpikes, or in aid thereof, may, without the necessity of further or amendatory legislation, be issued upon a vote of a majority of the resident property taxpayers voting thereon who are qualified electors of said county, and bonds heretofore or hereafter issued under Subsections (a) and (b) of said Sec. 52 shall not be included in determining the debt limit prescribed in said Section.

[Note — The foregoing Sec. 52-e of Art. III, an amendment, was added to allow Dallas County to issue bonds for construction of roads upon majority vote of resident property taxpayers. Submitted by the Sixtieth Legislature (1967) and adopted in election Nov. 5, 1968.]

Note: As in the case of Sec. 52-d above, this section might more properly have been designated as paragraph "e" under Sec. 52, but the Sixtieth Legislature designated it as Sec. 52-e, which resulted in there being two Sections 52-e, as they also designated the section below, relating to payment of medical expenses for county and precinct officials, as Sec. 52-e.

Sec. 52-e. **Payment of Medical Expenses for County and Precinct Officials** — Each county in the State of Texas is hereby authorized to pay all medical expenses, all doctor bills and all hospital bills for Sheriffs, Deputy Sheriffs, Constables, Deputy Constables and other county and precinct law enforcement officials who are injured in the course of their official duties; providing that while said Sheriff, Deputy Sheriff, Constable, Deputy Constable or other county or precinct law enforcement official is hospitalized or incapacitated that the county shall continue to pay his maximum salary; providing, however, that said payment of salary shall cease on the expiration of the term of office to which such official was elected or appointed. Provided, however, that no provision contained herein shall be construed to amend, modify, repeal or nullify Art. XVI, Sec. 31, of the Constitution of the State of Texas.

[Note — The foregoing Sec. 52-e of Art. III, an amendment, was added to authorize counties to pay medical bills for county and precinct law enforcement officials who are injured in line of duty; and the county shall continue to pay maximum salary for duration of term to which they were elected or appointed. Submitted by the Sixtieth Legislature (1967) and adopted in election Nov. 11, 1967.]

Sec. 52-f. **Private Roads in County** — A county with a population of 5,000 or less, according to the most recent federal census, may construct and maintain private roads if it imposes a reasonable charge for the work. The Legislature by general law may limit this authority. Revenue received from private road work may be used only for the construction, including right-of-way acquisition, or maintenance of public roads.

[Note — Sec. 52-f of Art. III, an amendment, was added to authorize counties with population of 5,000 or less to perform private road work. Submitted by the Sixty-sixth Legislature (1979) and adopted in election Nov. 4, 1980.]

Sec. 53. **Extra Compensation by Municipal Corporations** — The Legislature shall have no power to grant or to authorize any county or municipal authority to grant any extra com-

Article III — (Cont'd.)

pensation, fee or allowance to a public officer, agent, servant or contractor, after service has been rendered or a contract has been entered into and performed in whole or in part; nor pay, nor authorize the payment of any claim created against any county or municipality of the State under any agreement or contract made without authority of law.

Sec. 54. **Liens on Railroads** — The Legislature shall have no power to release or alienate any lien held by the State upon any railroad, or in anywise change the tenor or meaning or pass any act explanatory thereof; but the same shall be enforced in accordance with the original terms upon which it was acquired.

Sec. 55. **Power of Legislature to Release Debt** — The Legislature shall have no power to release or extinguish, or to authorize the releasing or extinguishing, in whole or in part, the indebtedness, liability or obligation of any corporation or individual, to this State or to any county or defined subdivision thereof, or other municipal corporation therein, except delinquent taxes which have been due for a period of at least ten years.

[Note—The foregoing Sec. 55 of Art. III is an amendment of an original section, the amendment having been adopted to include the clause "except delinquent taxes which have been due for a period of at least ten years." Submitted by the Forty-second Legislature (1931) and adopted in an election Nov. 8, 1932. Proclaimed Jan. 9, 1933.]

Sec. 56. **Special Laws; Limitations** — The Legislature shall not, except as otherwise provided in this Constitution, pass any local or special law authorizing:

The creation, extension or impairing of liens;

Regulating the affairs of counties, cities, towns, wards or school districts;

Changing the names of persons or places;

Changing the venue in civil or criminal cases;

Authorizing the laying out, opening, altering or maintaining of roads, highways, streets or alleys;

Relating to ferries or bridges, or incorporating ferry or bridge companies, except for the erection of bridges crossing streams which form boundaries between this and any other State;

Vacating roads, town plats, streets or alleys;

Relating to cemeteries, graveyards or public grounds not of the states;

Authorizing the adoption or legitimation of children;

Locating or changing county seats;

Incorporating cities, towns or villages, or changing their charter;

For the opening and conducting of election or fixing or changing the places of voting;

Granting divorces;

Creating offices, or prescribing the powers and duties of officers in counties, cities, towns, election or school districts;

Changing the law of descent or succession;

Regulating the practice or jurisdiction of, or changing the rules of evidence in any judicial proceeding or inquiry before courts, justices of the peace, sheriffs, commissioners, arbitrators or other tribunals, or providing or changing methods for the collection of debts or the enforcing of judgments or prescribing the effect of judicial sales of real estate;

Regulating the fees or extending the powers and duties of aldermen, justices of the peace, magistrates or constables;

Regulating the management of public schools, the building or repairing of schoolhouses, and the raising of money for such purposes;

Fixing the rate of interest;

Affecting the estates of minors or persons under disability;

Remitting fines, penalties and forfeitures and refunding moneys legally paid into the Treasury;

Exempting property from taxation;

Regulating labor, trade, mining and manufacturing;

Declaring any named person of age;

Extending the time for the assessment or collection of taxes, or otherwise relieving any assessor or collector of taxes from the due performance of his official duties or his securities from liability;

Giving effect to informal or invalid wills or deeds;

Summoning or impaneling grand or petit juries;

For limitation of civil or criminal actions;

For incorporating railroads or other works of internal improvements;

And in all other cases where a general law can be made applicable no local or special law shall be enacted; provided, that nothing herein contained shall be construed to prohibit the Legislature from passing special laws for the preservation of the game and fish of this State in certain localities.

Sec. 57. **Notice of Local or Special Laws** — No local or special law shall be passed unless notice of the intention to apply therefor shall have been published in the locality where the matter or thing to be affected may be situated, which notice shall state the substance of the contemplated law, and shall be published at least thirty days prior to the introduction into the Legislature of such bill and in the manner to be provided by law. The evidence of such notice having been published shall be exhibited in the Legislature before such act shall be passed.

Sec. 58. **Sessions to Be Held at Austin, Seat of Government** — The Legislature shall hold its sessions at the City of Austin, which is hereby declared to be the seat of government.

Sec. 59. **Workmen's Compensation for State Employees** — The Legislature shall have power to pass such laws as may be necessary to provide for workmen's compensation insurance for such State employees, as in its judgment is necessary or required; and to provide for the payment of all costs, charges and premiums on such policies of insurance; providing, the state shall never be required to purchase insurance for any employee.

[Note — The foregoing Sec. 59 of Art. III, an amendment, was added for the stated purpose of providing for workmen's compensation for state employees. Adopted in an election, Nov. 3, 1936.]

Sec. 60. **Workmen's Compensation Insurance for County Employees** — The Legislature shall have the power to pass such laws as may be necessary to enable all counties and other political subdivisions of this State to provide Workmen's Compensation insurance, including the right to provide its own insurance risk, for all employees of the county or political subdivision as in its judgment is necessary or required; and the Legislature shall provide suitable laws for the administration of such insurance in the counties or political subdivisions of this State and for the payment of the costs, charges and premiums on such policies of insurance and the benefits to be paid thereunder.

[Note — The foregoing Sec. 60 of Art. III was first added for the stated purpose of providing workmen's compensation insurance for county employees. Adopted in election Nov. 2, 1948. Further amended to include all political subdivisions. Submitted by the Fifty-seventh Legislature (1961) and adopted in election Nov. 6, 1962.]

Sec. 61. The Legislature shall have the power to enact laws to enable cities, towns and villages of this state to provide Workmen's Compensation Insurance, including the right to provide their own insurance risk for all employees; and the Legislature shall provide suitable laws for the administration of such insurance in the said municipalities and for payment of the costs, charges, and premiums on policies of insurance and the benefits to be paid thereunder.

[Note — The foregoing Sec. 61 of Art. III, an amendment, was added for the stated purpose of providing workmen's compensation insurance for municipal employees. Submitted by the Fifty-second Legislature and adopted in an election Nov. 4, 1952.]

Sec. 61-a. **Salary of Governor, Attorney General, Comptroller of Public Accounts, Treasurer, Commissioner of General Land Office and Secretary of State** — The Legislature shall not fix the salary of the Governor, Attorney General, Comptroller of Public Accounts, the Treasurer, Commissioner of the General Land Office or Secretary of State at a sum less than that fixed for such officials in the Constitution on Jan. 1, 1953.

[Note — The foregoing Sec. 61-a of Art. III, an amendment, was added to fix the salaries of the aforementioned officials. Submitted by the Fifty-third Legislature (1953) and adopted in an election Nov. 2, 1954; as submitted in SJR 5, this amendment was designated merely as "Section 61" duplicating the number of an existing section. To distinguish between the two, it is here designated as "Section 61-a."]

Sec. 62. **Continuity of State and Local Governmental Operations** — (a) The Legislature, in order to insure continuity of state and local governmental operations in periods of emergency resulting from disasters caused by enemy attack, shall have the power and the immediate duty to provide for prompt and temporary succession to the powers and duties of public offices, of whatever nature and whether filled by election or appointment, the incumbents of which may become unavailable for carrying on the powers and duties of such offices. Provided, however, that Article I of the Constitution of Texas, known as the "Bill of Rights" shall not be in any manner affected, amended, impaired, suspended, repealed or suspended hereby.

(b) When such a period of emergency or the immediate threat of enemy attack exists, the Legislature may suspend procedural rules imposed by this Constitution that relate to:

(1) the order of business of the Legislature;

(2) the percentage of each house of the Legislature necessary to constitute a quorum;

(3) the requirement that a bill must be read on three

Article III — (Cont'd.); Article IV

days in each house before it has the force of law;

(4) the requirement that a bill must be referred to and reported from committee before its consideration; and

(5) the date on which laws passed by the Legislature take effect.

(c) When such a period of emergency or the immediate threat of enemy attack exists, the Governor, after consulting with the Lieutenant Governor and the Speaker of the House of Representatives, may suspend the constitutional requirement that the Legislature hold its sessions in Austin, the seat of government. When this requirement has been suspended, the Governor shall determine a place other than Austin at which the Legislature will hold its sessions during such period of emergency or immediate threat of enemy attack. The Governor shall notify the Lieutenant Governor and the Speaker of the House of Representatives of the place and time at which the Legislature will meet. The Governor may take security precautions, consistent with the state of emergency, in determining the extent to which that information may be released.

(d) To suspend the constitutional rules specified by Subsection (b) of this section, the Governor must issue a proclamation and the House of Representatives and the Senate must concur in the proclamation as provided by this section.

(e) The Governor's proclamation must declare that a period of emergency resulting from disasters caused by enemy attack exists, or that the immediate threat of enemy attack exists, and that suspension of constitutional rules relating to legislative procedure is necessary to assure continuity of state government. The proclamation must specify the period, not to exceed two years, during which the constitutional rules specified by Subsection (b) of this section are suspended.

(f) The House of Representatives and the Senate, by concurrent resolution approved by the majority of the members present, must concur in the Governor's proclamation. A resolution of the House of Representatives and the Senate concurring in the Governor's proclamation suspends the constitutional rules specified by Subsection (b) of this section for the period of time specified by the Governor's proclamation.

(g) The constitutional rules specified by Subsection (b) of this section may not be suspended for more than two years under a single proclamation. A suspension may be renewed, however, if the Governor issues another proclamation as provided by Subsection (e) of this section and the House of Representatives and the Senate, by concurrent resolution, concur in that proclamation.

[Note — The foregoing Sec. 62 of Art. III, an amendment, was added to provide for temporary succession to powers and duties of public offices in periods of emergency resulting from disaster caused by enemy attack. Submitted by the Fifty-seventh Legislature (1961) and adopted in election Nov. 6, 1962. It was further amended to authorize suspension of certain constitutional rules relating to legislative procedure during disasters or during immediate threat of enemy attack. Submitted by Sixty-eighth Legislature (1983) and adopted in election Nov. 8, 1983.]

Sec. 63. **Consolidation of Governmental Functions in Counties of 1,200,000 or More Inhabitants** — (1) The Legislature may by statute provide for the consolidation of some functions of government of any one or more political subdivisions comprising or located within any county in this state having one million, two hundred thousand (1,200,000) or more inhabitants. Any such statute shall require an election to be held within the political subdivisions affected thereby with approval by a majority of the voters in each of these political subdivisions, under such terms and conditions as the Legislature may require.

(2) The county government, or any political subdivision(s) comprising or located therein, may contract one with another for the performance of governmental functions required or authorized by this Constitution or the laws of this state, under such terms and conditions as the Legislature may prescribe. The term "governmental functions," as it relates to counties, includes all duties, activities and operations of statewide importance in which the county acts for the state, as well as of local importance, whether required or authorized by this Constitution or the laws of this state.

[Note — The foregoing Sec. 63 of Art. III, an amendment, was added to provide for consolidation of governmental functions between political subdivisions within counties of 1,200,000 or more inhabitants. Submitted by the Fifty-ninth Legislature (1965) and adopted in election Nov. 8, 1966.]

Sec. 64. **Consolidation of Governmental Offices and Functions in Counties** — (a) The Legislature may by special statute provide for consolidation of governmental offices and functions of government of any one or more political subdivisions comprising or located within any county. Any such statute shall require an election to be held within the political subdivisions affected thereby with approval by a majority of the voters in each of these subdivisions, under such terms and conditions as the Legislature may require.

(b) The county government, or any political subdivision(s) comprising or located therein, may contract one with another for the performance of governmental functions required or authorized by this Constitution or the Laws of this State, under such terms and conditions as the Legislature may prescribe. No person acting under a contract made pursuant to this Subsection (b) shall be deemed to hold more than one office of honor, trust or profit or more than one civil office of emolument. The term "governmental functions," as it relates to counties, includes all duties, activities and operations of statewide importance in which the county acts for the State, as well as of local importance, whether required or authorized by this Constitution or the Laws of this State.

[Note — The foregoing Sec. 64 of Art. III, an amendment, was first added to provide for consolidation of governmental functions in El Paso and Tarrant Counties. Submitted by the Sixtieth Legislature (1967) and adopted in election Nov. 5, 1968. It was further amended to provide for consolidation of governmental functions in any county. Submitted by the Sixty-first Legislature (1969) and adopted in election Nov. 3, 1970.]

Sec. 65. **Interest Rate on State Bonds** — (a) Wherever the Constitution authorizes an agency, instrumentality, or subdivision of the State to issue bonds and specifies the maximum rate of interest which may be paid on such bonds issued pursuant to such constitutional authority, such bonds may bear interest at rates not to exceed a weighted average annual interest rate of 12 percent unless otherwise provided by Subsection (b) of this section. All Constitutional provisions specifically setting rates in conflict with this provision are hereby repealed.

(b) Bonds issued by the Veterans' Land Board after the effective date of this subsection bear interest at a rate or rates determined by the board, but the rate or rates may not exceed a net effective interest rate of 10 percent per year unless otherwise provided by law. A statute that is in effect on the effective date of this subsection and that sets as a maximum interest rate payable on bonds issued by the Veterans' Land Board a rate different from the maximum rate provided by this subsection is ineffective unless reenacted by the Legislature after that date.

[Note — Sec. 65 of Art. III is an added amendment to set the interest rate on state bonds not to exceed a weighted average annual interest of 6 per cent. Submitted by the Sixty-second Legislature (1971) and adopted in an election Nov. 7, 1972. The interest rate was raised to 12 percent in an amendment submitted by a special session of the Sixty-seventh Legislature (1982) and adopted in election Nov. 2, 1982.]

ARTICLE IV — EXECUTIVE DEPARTMENT

Sec. 1. **Officers of Executive Department** — The executive department of the State shall consist of a Governor, who shall be the chief executive officer of the State; a Lieutenant Governor, Secretary of State, Comptroller of Public Accounts, Treasurer, Commissioner of the General Land Office and Attorney General.

Sec. 2. **Election of Executive Officers** — All the above officers of the executive department (except Secretary of State) shall be elected by the qualified voters of the State at the time and places of election for members of the Legislature.

Sec. 3. **Election Results; Ties; Contests** — The returns of every election for said executive officers, until otherwise provided by law, shall be made out, sealed up and transmitted by the returning officers prescribed by law, to the seat of government, directed to the Secretary of State, who shall deliver the same to the Speaker of the House of Representatives as soon as the Speaker shall be chosen, and the said Speaker shall, during the first week of the session of the Legislature, open and publish them in the presence of both houses of the Legislature. The person voted for at said election having the highest number of votes for each of said offices, respectively, and being constitutionally eligible, shall be declared by the Speaker, under sanction of the Legislature, to be elected to said office. But if two or more persons shall have the highest and an equal number of votes for either of said offices, one of them shall be immediately chosen to such office by a joint vote of both houses of the Legislature. Contested elections for either of said offices shall be determined by both houses of the Legislature in joint session.

Sec. 3-a. **Gubernatorial Succession** — If, at the time the Legislature shall canvass the election returns for the offices of Governor and Lieutenant Governor, the person receiving the highest number of votes for the office of Governor, as declared by the Speaker, has died, then the person having the highest number of votes for the office of Lieutenant Governor shall act as Governor until after the next general election. It is further provided that in the event the person with the highest number of votes for the Office of Governor

Article IV — (Cont'd.)

as declared by the Speaker, shall become disabled, or fail to qualify, then the Lieutenant Governor shall act as Governor until a person has qualified for the office of Governor or until after the next general election. Any succession to the governorship not otherwise provided for in this Constitution may be provided for by law; provided, however, that any person succeeding to the office of Governor shall be qualified as otherwise provided in this Constitution, and shall, during the entire term to which he may succeed, be under all the restrictions and inhibitions imposed in this Constitution on the Governor.

[Note — An added amendment, for the purpose stated therein. Submitted by the Fiftieth Legislature (1947) and adopted in election, Nov. 2, 1948.]

Sec. 4. **Governor, When Installed; Term; Qualifications** — The Governor elected at the general election in 1974, and thereafter, shall be installed on the first Tuesday after the organization of the Legislature, or as soon thereafter as practicable, and shall hold his office for the term of four years, or until his successor shall be duly installed. He shall be at least thirty years of age, a citizen of the United States, and shall have resided in this State at least five years immediately preceding his election.

[Note — Sec. 4 of Art. IV was amended to raise to four years the term of office of Governor. Submitted by the Sixty-second Legislature (1971) and adopted in an election Nov. 7, 1972.]

Sec. 5. **Governor's Salary and Mansion** — The Governor shall, at stated times, receive as compensation for his service an annual salary in an amount to be fixed by the Legislature, and shall have the use and occupation of the Governor's Mansion, fixtures and furniture.

[Note — The foregoing Sec. 5 of Art. IV was first amended to raise Governor's salary from $4,000 to $12,000. Adopted in an election Nov. 3, 1936. Further amended to give Legislature authority to fix salary. Submitted by the Fifty-third Legislature (1953) and adopted in election Nov. 2, 1954.]

Sec. 6. **Governor to Hold No Other Office, Etc.** — During the time he holds the office of Governor he shall not hold any other office, civil, military or corporate; nor shall he practice any profession or receive compensation, reward, fee or the promise thereof for the same; nor receive any salary, reward or compensation or the promise thereof from any person or corporation for any service rendered or performed during the time he is Governor or to be thereafter rendered or performed.

Sec. 7. **Commander in Chief; May Call Out Militia** — He shall be commander in chief of the military forces of the State, except when they are called into actual service of the United States. He shall have power to call forth the militia to execute the laws of the State, to suppress insurrections, repel invasions and protect the frontier from hostile incursions by Indians or other predatory bands.

Sec. 8. **Governor May Convene Legislature** — The Governor may, on extraordinary occasions, convene the Legislature at the seat of government or at a different place in case that should be in possession of the public enemy, or in case of the prevalence of disease threat. His proclamation therefor shall state specifically the purpose for which the Legislature is convened.

Sec. 9. **Governor's Message; to Account for Moneys; Present Estimates, Etc.** — The Governor shall, at the commencement of each session of the Legislature, and at the close of his term of office, give to the Legislature information, by message, of the condition of the State; and he shall recommend to the Legislature such measures as he may deem expedient. He shall account to the Legislature for all public moneys received and paid out by him from any funds subject to his order, with vouchers; and shall accompany his message with a statement of the same. And at the commencement of each regular session he shall present estimates of the amount of money required to be raised by taxation for all purposes.

Sec. 10. **Governor Shall Cause the Laws to Be Executed; Intercourse With Other States** — He shall cause the laws to be faithfully executed and shall conduct, in person, or in such manner as shall be prescribed by law, all intercourse and business of the State with other States and with the United States.

Sec. 11. **Board of Pardons and Paroles: Advisory Authority to Governor in Granting Reprieves, Paroles, Pardons, Etc.** — The Legislature shall by law establish a Board of Pardons and Paroles and shall require it to keep record of its actions and the reasons for its actions. The Legislature shall have authority to enact parole laws.

In all criminal cases, except treason and impeachment, the Governor shall have power, after conviction, on the written signed recommendation and advice of the Board of Pardons and Paroles, or a majority thereof, to grant reprieves and commutations of punishment and pardons; and under such rules as the Legislature may prescribe, and upon the written recommendation and advice of a majority of the Board of Pardons and Paroles, he shall have the power to remit fines and forfeitures. The Governor shall have the power to grant one reprieve in any capital case for a period not to exceed thirty (30) days; and he shall have the power to revoke conditional pardons. With the advice and consent of the Legislature, he may grant reprieves, commutations of punishment and pardons in cases of treason.

[Note—The foregoing Sec. 11 of Art. IV was amended from the original to establish the stated procedure for granting pardons and paroles, which was originally vested exclusively in the Governor's office. Submitted by the Forty-fourth Legislature (1935) and adopted in an election Nov. 3, 1936. It was again amended to make the Board of Pardons and Paroles a statutory agency and to give the board power to revoke paroles. Submitted by the Sixty-eighth Legislature (1983) and adopted in election Nov. 8, 1983.]

Sec. 11-a. **Suspension of Sentences; Probation** — The courts of the State of Texas having original jurisdiction of criminal actions shall have the power, after conviction, to suspend the imposition or execution of sentence and to place the defendant upon probation and to reimpose such sentence, under such conditions as the Legislature may prescribe.

[Note — The foregoing Sec. 11-a of Art. IV, an amendment, was added for the stated purpose of providing suspended sentences. Submitted by the Forty-fourth Legislature (1935) and adopted in an election Aug. 24, 1935.]

Sec. 12. **Governor to Fill Vacancies in State and District Offices** — All vacancies in State or district offices, except members of the Legislature, shall be filled, unless otherwise provided by law, by appointment of the Governor, which appointment, if made during its session, shall be with the advice and consent of two thirds of the Senate present. If made during the recess of the Senate, the said appointee, or some other person to fill such vacancy, shall be nominated to the Senate during the first ten days of its session. If rejected, said office shall immediately become vacant, and the Governor shall, without delay, make further nominations until a confirmation takes place. But should there be no confirmation during the session of the Senate, the Governor shall not thereafter appoint any person to fill such vacancy who has been rejected by the Senate, but may appoint some other person to fill the vacancy until the next session of the Senate or until the regular election to said office, should it sooner occur. Appointments to vacancies in offices elective by the people shall only continue until the first general election thereafter.

Sec. 13. **Where Governor Shall Reside** — During the session of the Legislature the Governor shall reside where its sessions are held and at all other times at the seat of government, except when, by act of the Legislature, he may be required or authorized to reside elsewhere.

Sec. 14. **Approval of Bills; Veto Bill Not Returned to Become a Law** — Every bill which shall have passed both houses of the Legislature shall be presented to the Governor for his approval. If he approve, he shall sign it, but if he disapprove it, he shall return it with his objections to the house in which it originated, which house shall enter the objections at large upon its journal, and proceed to reconsider it. If, after such reconsideration, two thirds of the members present agree to pass the bill, it shall be sent, with the objections, to the other house, by which likewise it shall be reconsidered, and if approved by two thirds of the members of that house, it shall become a law; but in such cases the votes of both houses shall be determined by yeas and nays; and the names of the members voting for and against the bill shall be entered on the journal of each house, respectively. If any bill shall not be returned by the Governor with his objections within ten days (Sundays excepted) after it shall have been presented to him, the same shall be a law in like manner as if he had signed it, unless the Legislature, by its adjournment, prevent its return, in which case it shall be a law, unless he shall file the same, with his objections, in the office of the Secretary of State and give notice thereof by public proclamation within twenty days after such adjournment. If any bill presented to the Governor contains several items of appropriation he may object to one or more of such items, and approve the other portion of the bill. In such case he shall append to the bill, at the time of signing it, a statement of the items to which he objects, and no item so objected to shall take effect. If the Legislature be in session he shall transmit to the house in which the bill originated a copy of such statement, and the items objected to shall be separately considered. If, on reconsideration, one or more of such items be approved by two thirds of the members present, of each house, the same shall be part of the law, notwithstanding the objections of the Governor. If any such bill containing several items of appropriation not having been presented to the Governor ten days (Sundays excepted) prior to adjournment, be in the hands of the Governor at the time of adjournment, he shall have twenty days from such adjournment within which to file

Article IV — (Cont'd.); Article V

objections to any items thereof and make proclamation of the same, and such item or items shall not take effect.

Sec. 15. **What to Be Presented for Approval** — Every order, resolution or vote to which the concurrence of both houses of the Legislature may be necessary except on questions of adjournment shall be presented to the Governor, and before it shall take effect shall be approved by him; or, being disapproved, shall be repassed by both houses, and all the rules, provisions and limitations shall apply thereto as prescribed in the last preceding section in the case of a bill.

Sec. 16. **Lieutenant Governor; Election; Term; Powers and Duties** — There shall also be a Lieutenant Governor, who shall be chosen at every election for Governor by the same electors, in the same manner, continue in office for the same time and possess the same qualifications. The electors shall distinguish for whom they vote as Governor and for whom as Lieutenant Governor. The Lieutenant Governor shall, by virtue of his office, be President of the Senate and shall have, when in committee of the whole, a right to debate, and vote on all questions; and when the Senate is equally divided, to give the casting vote. In case of the death, resignation, removal from office, inability or refusal of the Governor to serve, or of his impeachment or absence from the State, the Lieutenant Governor shall exercise the powers and authority appertaining to the office of Governor until another be chosen at the periodical election, and be duly qualified; or until the Governor, impeached, absent or disabled, shall be acquitted, return or his disability be removed.

Sec. 17. **Vacancy in Office; Compensation** — If, during the vacancy in the office of Governor, the Lieutenant Governor should die, resign, refuse to serve or be removed from office or be unable to serve; or if he shall be impeached or absent from the State, the President of the Senate, for the time being, shall, in like manner, administer the government until he shall be superseded by a Governor or Lieutenant Governor. The Lieutenant Governor shall, while he acts as President of the Senate, receive for his services the same compensation and mileage which shall be allowed to the members of the Senate, and no more; and during the time he administers the government as Governor, he shall receive in like manner the same compensation which the Governor would have received had he been employed in the duties of his office, and no more. The President, for the time being, of the Senate, shall, during the time he administers the government, receive in like manner the same compensation which the Governor would have received had he been employed in the duties of his office.

Sec. 18. **Succession to Governorship** — The Lieutenant Governor, or President of the Senate, succeeding to the office of Governor shall, during the entire terms to which he may succeed, be under all the restrictions and inhibitions imposed in this Constitution on the Governor.

Sec. 19. **Seal of State; Secretary of State to Keep, Etc.** — There shall be a seal of the State which shall be kept by the Secretary of State and used by him officially under the direction of the Governor. The seal of the State shall be a star of five points, encircled by olive and live oak branches, and the words "The State of Texas."

Sec. 20. **Commissions to Be Signed and Sealed** — All commissions shall be in the name and by the authority of the State of Texas, sealed with the State seal, signed by the Governor, and attested by the Secretary of State.

Sec. 21. **Secretary of State; Term; Duties; Compensation** — There shall be a Secretary of State, who shall be appointed by the Governor, by and with the advice and consent of the Senate, and who shall continue in office during the term of service of the Governor. He shall authenticate the publication of the laws and keep a fair register of all official acts and proceedings of the Governor, and shall, when required, lay the same and all papers, minutes and vouchers relative thereto, before the Legislature or either house thereof, and shall perform such other duties as may be required of him by law. He shall receive for his services an annual salary in an amount to be fixed by the Legislature.

[Note — The foregoing Sec. 21 of Art. IV was first amended from the original to raise the salary of the Secretary of State from $2,000 to $6,000 a year. Amendment adopted in an election Nov. 3, 1936. Further amended to give Legislature authority to fix salary. Submitted by the Fifty-third Legislature (1953) and adopted in election Nov. 2, 1954.]

Sec. 22. **Attorney General; Term; Duties; Residence; Salary** — The Attorney General elected at the general election in 1974, and thereafter, shall hold his office for four years and until his successor is duly qualified. He shall represent the State in all suits and pleas in the Supreme Court of the State in which the state may be a party, and shall especially inquire into the charter rights of all private corporations, and from time to time in the name of the State, take such action in the courts as may be proper and necessary to prevent any private corporation from exercising any power or demanding or collecting any species of taxes, tolls, freight or wharfage not authorized by law. He shall whenever sufficient cause exists, seek a judicial forfeiture of such charters, unless otherwise expressly directed by law, and give legal advice in writing to the Governor and other executive officers, when requested by them, and perform such other duties as may be required by law. He shall reside at the seat of government during his continuance in office. He shall receive for his services an annual salary in an amount to be fixed by the Legislature.

[Note — The foregoing Sec. 22 of Art. IV was amended from the original to raise the Attorney General's fixed salary from $2,000 to $10,000 a year and to eliminate provisions for fees not to exceed $2,000 a year. Amendment adopted in an election Nov. 3, 1936. Further amended to give Legislature authority to fix salary. Submitted by the Fifty-third Legislature (1953) and adopted in election Nov. 2, 1954. It was further amended to lengthen the term of office from two to four years. Submitted by the Sixty-second Legislature (1971) and adopted in an election Nov. 7, 1972.]

Sec. 23. **Comptroller; Treasurer, and Commissioner of the General Land Office; Terms; Salaries; Residence; Fees** — The Comptroller of Public Accounts, the Treasurer and the Commissioner of the General Land Office and any statutory state officer who is elected by the electorate of Texas at large, unless a term of office is otherwise specifically provided in this Constitution, shall each hold office for the term of four years and until his successor is qualified. The four-year term applies to these officers who are elected at the general election in 1974 or thereafter. Each shall receive an annual salary in an amount to be fixed by Legislature; reside at the capital of the State during his continuance in office, and perform such duties as are or may be required by law. They and the Secretary of State shall not receive to their own use any fees, costs or perquisites of office. All fees that may be payable by law for any service performed by any officer specified in this section, or in his office, shall be paid, when received into the State Treasury.

[Note — The foregoing Sec. 23 of Art. IV was first amended from the original to raise salaries of three state officials mentioned from $2,500 each to $6,000 each annually. Amendment adopted in an election Nov. 3, 1936. Further amended to give Legislature authority to fix salary. Submitted by the Fifty-third Legislature (1953) and adopted in election Nov. 2, 1954. It was further amended to raise to four years the term of office of the above-named officials. Submitted by the Sixty-second Legislature (1971) and adopted in an election Nov. 7, 1972.]

Sec. 24. **Officers to Account to the Governor; Duty of Governor; False Reports** — An account shall be kept by the officers of the executive department and by all officers and managers of State institutions of all moneys and choses in action received and disbursed or otherwise disposed of by them, severally, from all sources, and for every service performed; and a semi-annual report thereof shall be made to the Governor, under oath. The Governor may, at any time, require information in writing from any and all of said officers or managers upon any subject relating to the duties, conditions, management and expenses of their respective offices and institutions, which information shall be required by the Governor under oath, and the Governor may also inspect their books, accounts, vouchers and public funds; and any officer or manager who, at any time shall willfully make a false report or give false information, shall be guilty of perjury and so adjudged and punished accordingly and removed from office.

Sec. 25. **Laws for Investigation of Breaches of Trust** — The Legislature shall pass efficient laws facilitating the investigation of breaches of trust and duty by all custodians of public funds and providing for their suspensions from office on reasonable cause shown, and for the appointment of temporary incumbents of their offices during such suspensions.

Sec. 26. **Notaries Public** — (a) The Secretary of State shall appoint a convenient number of notaries public for the state who shall perform such duties as now are or may be prescribed by law. The qualifications of notaries public shall be prescribed by law.

(b) The terms of office of notaries public shall not be less than two years nor more than four years as provided by law.

[Note — The foregoing Sec. 26 of Art. IV was amended from the original to give the Secretary of State the authority, formerly held by the Governor, to appoint notaries public, and to include the stated contents of paragraphs (b) and (c). Submitted by the Forty-sixth Legislature (1939), and adopted in an election Nov. 5, 1940. It was further amended to establish terms of notaries public for not less than two years nor more than four years; did away with old sections (b) and (c) and provided for terms of office for notaries. Submitted by the Sixty-sixth Legislature (1979) and adopted in election Nov. 6, 1979.]

ARTICLE V — JUDICIAL DEPARTMENT

Temporary Provision. (a) This temporary provision

Article V — (Cont'd.)

applies to the constitutional amendment proposed by S.J.R. No. 14, 69th Legislature, Regular Session, 1985, and expires Jan. 1, 1992.

(b) Courts of Appeals Districts and Judges. The supreme judicial districts of the state become courts of appeals districts. Associate justices of the courts of appeals become justices of the courts of appeals.

(c) County Courts and County Judges. Unless otherwise provided by law, all county courts in existence under the Constitution continue in effect with jurisdiction as provided by law. The judges of those courts remain as county court judges and as presiding officers of the county commissioners courts.

(d) Municipal Courts, County Courts at Law, and Justice of the Peace Courts. Unless otherwise provided by law, order, charter, or ordinance, these courts and judges of them remain as they exist at the time of adoption of the amendments, including any new courts authorized by law but not taking effect until after the date of adoption of these amendments.

(e) Judicial Districts and Judges. Unless otherwise provided by law, judicial districts in existence at the time of adoption of these amendments remain in effect, including any districts authorized by law but not taking effect until after the date of adoption of these amendments.

(f) Laws and Rules Continued. Except to the extent inconsistent with the provisions of these amendments, all laws and rules of court in force on the effective date of these amendments continue in effect until otherwise provided by law.

(g) Other Provisions. In the event a transfer or transition has not been provided for by these amendments or other law, the Supreme Court shall provide by rule for the orderly transfer or transition.

(h) The initial term of the member of the Judicial Districts Board appointed by the governor expires on Dec. 31, 1990.

[Note — The foregoing Temporary Provision to Art. V was added to provide for reapportionment of judicial districts by the Judicial Districts Board or by the Legislative Redistricting Board, and to provide for administration and jurisdiction of constitutional courts. It will expire Jan. 1, 1992. Submitted by Sixty-ninth Legislature (1985) and adopted in election Nov. 5, 1985.]

Sec. 1. **The Several Courts; Criminal Courts** — The judicial power of this State shall be vested in one Supreme Court, in one Court of Criminal Appeals, in Courts of Appeals, in District Courts, in County Courts, in Commissioners' Courts, in courts of Justices of the Peace and in such other courts as may be provided by law.

The Legislature may establish such other courts as it may deem necessary and prescribe the jurisdiction and organization thereof and may conform the jurisdiction of the district and other inferior courts thereto.

[Note — The foregoing Sec. 1 of Art. V is an amended section, being a general revision of the original, to provide for "Courts of Civil Appeals" and a "Court of Criminal Appeals" in place of the old "Court of Appeals," making minor changes. Submitted by the Twenty-second Legislature (1891), ratified at an election Aug. 11, 1891, and declared adopted Sept. 22, 1891. It was amended to provide for a Court of Criminal Appeals with nine judges and to permit the court to sit in panels of three judges. (See also note under Sec. 4 below.) Submitted by the Sixty-fifth Legislature (1977) and adopted in election Nov. 8, 1977. It was further amended to change Courts of Civil Appeals to Courts of Appeal. Submitted by the Sixty-sixth Legislature (1979) and adopted in election Nov. 4, 1980.]

Sec. 1-a. **Retirement and Compensation of Judges** — (1) Subject to the further provisions of this section, the Legislature shall provide for the retirement and compensation of justices and judges of the Appellate Courts and District and Criminal District Courts on account of length of service, age and disability, and for their reassignment to active duty where and when needed. The office of every such justice and judge shall become vacant when the incumbent reaches the age of seventy-five (75) years or such earlier age, not less than seventy (70) years, as the Legislature may prescribe; but, in the case of an incumbent whose term of office includes the effective date of this Amendment, this provision shall not prevent him from serving the remainder of said term nor be applicable to him before his period or periods of judicial service shall have reached a total of ten (10) years.

(2) The name of the State Judicial Qualifications Commission is changed to the State Commission on Judicial Conduct. The Commission consists of eleven (11) members, to wit: (i) one (1) Justice of a Court of Appeals; (ii) one (1) District Judge; (iii) two (2) members of the State Bar, who have respectively practiced as such for over ten (10) consecutive years next preceding their selection; (iiii) four (4) citizens, at least thirty (30) years of age, not licensed to

practice law nor holding any salaried public office or employment; (v) one (1) Justice of the Peace; (vi) one (1) Judge of a Municipal Court; and, (vii) one (1) Judge of a County Court at Law; provided that no person shall be or remain a member of the Commission, who does not maintain physical residence within this state, or who resides in, or holds a judgeship within or for, the same Supreme Judicial District as another member of the Commission, or who shall have ceased to retain the qualifications above specified for his respective class of membership, except that the Justice of the Peace and the Judges of a Municipal Court and/or a County Court at Law shall be selected at large without regard to whether they reside or hold a judgeship in the same Supreme Judicial District as another member of the Commission. Commissioners of classes (i), (ii), and (vii) above shall be chosen by the Supreme Court with advice and consent of the Senate, those of class (iii) by the Board of Directors of the State Bar under regulations to be prescribed by the Supreme Court with advice and consent of the Senate, those of class (iiii) by appointment of the Governor with advice and consent of the Senate, and the commissioners of classes (v) and (vi) by appointment of the Supreme Court as provided by law, with the advice and consent of the Senate.

(3) The regular term of office of Commissioners shall be six (6) years; but the initial members of each of classes (i), (ii) and (iii) shall respectively be chosen for terms of four (4) and six (6) years, and the initial members of class (iiii) for respective terms of two (2), four (4) and six (6) years. Interim vacancies shall be filled in the same manner as vacancies due to expiration of a full term, but only for the unexpired portion of the term in question. Commissioners may succeed themselves in office only if having served less than three (3) consecutive years.

(4) Commissioners shall receive no compensation for their services as such. The Legislature shall provide for the payment of the necessary expense for the operation of the Commission.

(5) The Commission may hold its meetings, hearings and other proceedings at such times and places as it shall determine but shall meet at Austin at least once each year. It shall annually select one of its members as chairman. A quorum shall consist of six (6) members. Proceedings shall be by majority vote of those present, except that recommendations for retirement, censure, suspension, or removal of any person holding an office named in paragraph A of Subsection (6) of this section shall be by affirmative vote of at least six (6) members.

(6) A. Any justice or judge of the courts established by this Constitution or created by the Legislature as provided in Sec. 1, Art. V, of this Constitution, may, subject to the other provisions hereof, be removed from office for willful or persistent violation of rules promulgated by the Supreme Court of Texas, incompetence in performing the duties of the office, willful violation of the Code of Judicial Conduct, or willful or persistent conduct that is clearly inconsistent with the proper performance of his duties or casts public discredit upon the judiciary or administration of justice. Any person holding such office may be disciplined or censured, in lieu of removal from office, as provided by this subsection. Any person holding an office specified in this subsection may be suspended from office with or without pay by the Commission immediately on being indicted by a State or Federal grand jury for a felony offense or charged with a misdemeanor involving official misconduct. On the filing of a sworn complaint charging a person holding such office with willful or persistent violation of rules promulgated by the Supreme Court of Texas, incompetence in performing the duties of the office, willful violation of the Code of Judicial Conduct, or willful and persistent conduct that is clearly inconsistent with the proper performance of his duties or casts public discredit on the judiciary or on the administration of justice, the Commission, after giving the person notice and an opportunity to appear and be heard before the Commission, may recommend to the Supreme Court the suspension of such person from office. The Supreme Court, after considering the record of such appearance and the recommendation of the Commission, may suspend the person from office with or without pay, pending final disposition of the charge.

B. Any person holding an office named in paragraph A of this subsection who is eligible for retirement benefits under the laws of this state providing for judicial retirement may be involuntarily retired, and any person holding an office named in that paragraph who is not eligible for retirement benefits under such laws may be removed from office, for disability seriously interfering with the performance of his duties, which is, or is likely to become, permanent in nature.

C. The law relating to the removal, discipline, suspension, or censure of a Justice or Judge of the courts established by this Constitution or created by the Legislature as provided in this Constitution applies to a master or magistrate appointed as provided by law to serve a trial court of this State and to a retired or former Judge who continues as a judicial officer subject to an assignment to sit on a court of this State. Under the law relating to the removal of an ac-

Article V — (Cont'd.)

tive Justice or Judge, the Commission and the review tribunal may prohibit a retired or former Judge from holding judicial office in the future or from sitting on a court of this State by assignment.

(7) The Commission shall keep itself informed as fully as may be of circumstances relating to the misconduct or disability of particular persons holding an office named in paragraph A of Subsection (6) of this section, receive complaints or reports, formal or informal, from any source in this behalf and make such preliminary investigations as it may determine. Its orders for the attendance or testimony of witnesses or for the production of documents at any hearing or investigation shall be enforceable by contempt proceedings in the District Court or by a Master.

(8) After such investigation as it deems necessary, the Commission may in its discretion issue a private or public admonition, warning, reprimand, or requirement that the person obtain additional training or education, or if the Commission determines that the situation merits such action, it may institute formal proceedings and order a formal hearing to be held before it concerning the public censure, removal, or retirement of a person holding an office or position specified in Subsection (6) of this section, or it may in its discretion request the Supreme Court to appoint an active or retired District Judge or Justice of a Court of Appeals, or retired Judge or Justice of the Court of Criminal Appeals or the Supreme Court, as a Master to hear and take evidence in any such matter, and to report thereon to the Commission. The Master shall have all the power of a District Judge in the enforcement of orders pertaining to witnesses, evidence, and procedure. If, after formal hearing, or after considering the record and report of a Master, the Commission finds good cause therefor, it shall issue an order of public censure or it shall recommend to a review tribunal the removal or retirement, as the case may be, of the person in question holding an office or position specified in Subsection (6) of this section and shall thereupon file with the tribunal the entire record before the Commission.

(9) A tribunal to review the Commission's recommendation for the removal or retirement of a person holding an office or position specified in Subsection (6) of this section is composed of seven (7) Justices or Judges of the Courts of Appeals who are selected by lot by the Chief Justice of the Supreme Court. Each Court of Appeals shall designate one of its members for inclusion in the list from which the selection is made. Service on the tribunal shall be considered part of the official duties of a judge, and no additional compensation may be paid for such service. The review tribunal shall review the record of the proceedings on the law and facts and in its discretion may, for good cause shown, permit the introduction of additional evidence. Within 90 days after the date on which the record is filed with the review tribunal, it shall order public censure, retirement or removal, as it finds just and proper, or wholly reject the recommendation. A Justice, Judge, Master, or Magistrate may appeal a decision of the review tribunal to the Supreme Court under the substantial evidence rule. Upon an order for involuntary retirement for disability or an order for removal, the office in question shall become vacant. The review tribunal, in an order for involuntary retirement for disability or an order for removal, may prohibit such person from holding judicial office in the future. The rights of an incumbent so retired to retirement benefits shall be the same as if his retirement had been voluntary.

(10) All papers filed with and proceedings before the Commission or a Master shall be confidential, unless otherwise provided by law, and the filing of papers with, and the giving of testimony before the Commission or a Master shall be privileged, unless otherwise provided by law. However, the Commission may issue a public statement through its executive director or its Chairman at any time during any of its proceedings under this Section when sources other than the Commission cause notoriety concerning a Judge or the Commission itself and the Commission determines that the best interests of a Judge or of the public will be served by issuing the statement.

(11) The Supreme Court shall by rule provide for the procedure before the Commission, Masters, review tribunal, and the Supreme Court. Such rule shall provide the right of discovery of evidence to a Justice, Judge, Master, or Magistrate after formal proceedings are instituted and shall afford to any person holding an office or position specified in Subsection (6) of this section, against whom a proceeding is instituted to cause his retirement or removal, due process of law for the procedure before the Commission, Masters, review tribunal, and the Supreme Court in the same manner that any person whose property rights are in jeopardy in an adjudicatory proceeding is entitled to due process of law, regardless of whether or not the interest of the person holding an office or position specified in Subsection (6) of this section in remaining in active status is considered to be a right or a privilege. Due process shall include the right to notice, counsel, hearing, confrontation of his accusers, and all such other incidents of due process as are ordinarily available in proceedings whether or not mis-

feasance is charged, upon proof of which a penalty may be imposed.

(12) No person holding an office specified in Subsection (6) of this section shall sit as a member of the Commission in any proceeding involving his own suspension, discipline, censure, retirement or removal.

(13) This Sec. 1-a is alternative to and cumulative of, the methods of removal of persons holding an office named in paragraph A of Subsection (6) of this section provided elsewhere in this Constitution.

(14) The Legislature may promulgate laws in furtherance of this Section that are not inconsistent with its provisions.

TEMPORARY PROVISION. (a) This temporary provision applies to the constitutional amendment proposed by H.J.R. No. 4, Sixty-eighth Legislature, Regular Session, 1983, and expires Jan. 1, 1988.

(b) The consitutional amendment takes effect Jan. 1, 1985.

(c) The initial term of the commissioner of class (v) added by amendment in 1977 expired on Nov. 19, 1979. The initial term of the commissioner of class (vi) and (vii) expires on Nov. 19, 1985.

(d) Each person holding office as a member of the Commission on Judicial Conduct on Jan. 1, 1985, continues to hold the office for the term for which he was appointed.

(e) The offices of the first commissioner of class (i) and the first commissioner of class (ii) whose terms expire after Jan. 1, 1985, are abolished on the expiration of the terms.

(f) Changes made in the constitution by this amendment do not apply to investigations and formal proceedings where the investigation of judicial conduct by the commission began before Jan. 1, 1985.

[Note — The foregoing Sec. 1-a was added to provide for retirement and compensation of judges. Submitted by Fiftieth Legislature (1947) and adopted in election, Nov. 2, 1948. It was amended to provide for automatic retirement of district and appellate judges for old age; to create the State Judicial Qualifications Commission and defining its functions; and empowering the Supreme Court to remove district and appellate judges for misconduct and to retire such judges in cases of disability. Submitted by Fifty-ninth Legislature (1965) and adopted in election Nov. 2, 1965. It was further amended to specifically name those offices under the jurisdiction of the Commission and to broaden the Commission's duties and powers. Submitted by Sixty-first Legislature (1969) and adopted in election Nov. 3, 1970. It was further amended to change the name of the State Judicial Qualifications Commission to the State Commission on Judicial Conduct; raise the number of members of the Commission to eleven; set out specific qualifications for membership; and provide for the suspension, censure, removal or involuntary retirement of a justice under certain circumstances. Submitted by Sixty-fifth Legislature (1977) and adopted in election Nov. 8, 1977. It was again amended to specify ways to discipline active judges, certain retired and former judges, and certain masters and magistrates of courts. Submitted by Sixty-eighth Legislature (1983) and adopted in election Nov. 6, 1984.]

Sec. 2. Supreme Court; Quorum; Qualifications; Election; Salary; Vacancy — The Supreme Court shall consist of the Chief Justice and eight Justices, any five of whom shall constitute a quorum, and the concurrence of five shall be necessary to a decision of a case; provided, that when the business of the court may require, the court may sit in sections as designated by the court to hear argument of causes and to consider applications for writs of error or other preliminary matters. No person shall be eligible to serve in the office of Chief Justice or Justice of the Supreme Court unless the person is licensed to practice law in this state and is, at the time of election, a citizen of the United States and of this State and has attained the age of thirty-five years and has been a practicing lawyer or a lawyer and judge of a court of record together at least ten years. Said Justices shall be elected (three of them each two years) by the qualified voters of the State at a general election; shall hold their offices six years or until their successors are elected and qualified; and shall each receive such compensation as shall be provided by law. In case of a vacancy in the office of the Chief Justice or any Justice of the Supreme Court, the Governor shall fill the vacancy until the next general election for State officers, and at such general election the vacancy for the unexpired term shall be filled by election by the qualified voters of the State. The Justices of the Supreme Court who may be in office at the time this amendment takes effect shall continue in office until the expiration of their terms of office under the present Constitution and until their successors are elected and qualified.

[Note — The foregoing Sec. 2 of Art. V has been thrice amended: (1) To raise salaries and make minor adjustments, by amendment submitted by the Twenty-second Legislature, ratified in an election Aug. 11, 1891, and declared adopted Sept. 22, 1891; (2) to raise the number of justices on the Supreme Court from three to nine and make other adjustments, by amendment submitted by the Forty-

Article V — (Cont'd.)

ninth Legislature and adopted in an election Aug. 25, 1945; and (3) to change name of Commission of Appeals and qualifications of Supreme Court Justices. Submitted by the Sixty-sixth Legislature (1979) and adopted in election Nov. 4, 1980.]

Sec. 3. **Jurisdiction; Terms of Court** — The Supreme Court shall exercise the judicial power of the state except as otherwise provided in this Constitution. Its jurisdiction shall be co-extensive with the limits of the State and its determinations shall be final except in criminal law matters. Its appellate jurisdiction shall be final and shall extend to all cases except in criminal law matters and as otherwise provided in this Constitution or by law. The Supreme Court and the Justices thereof shall have power to issue writs of habeas corpus, as may be prescribed by law; and under such regulations as may be prescribed by law, the said courts and the Justices thereof may issue the writs of mandamus, procedendo, certiorari and such other writs as may be necessary to enforce its jurisdiction. The Legislature may confer original jurisdiction on the Supreme Court to issue writs of quo warranto and mandamus in such cases as may be specified, except as against the Governor of the State.

The Supreme Court shall also have power, upon affidavit or otherwise as by the court may be determined to ascertain such matters of fact as may be necessary to the proper exercise of its jurisdiction.

The Supreme Court shall appoint a clerk, who shall give bond in such manner as is now or may hereafter be required by law, and he may hold his office for four years and shall be subject to removal by said court for good cause entered of record on the minutes of said court, who shall receive such compensation as the Legislature may provide.

[Note—The foregoing Sec. 3 of Art. V has been thrice amended, as follows: (1) To readjust jurisdiction of the Supreme Court to that of the Courts of Civil Appeals which were established by amendment of the same date, and also to consolidate the original Sec. 4, providing for a clerk of the court, with Sec. 3, by amendment submitted by the Twenty-second Legislature (1891), ratified Aug. 11, 1891, and proclaimed Sept. 22, 1891; (2) to eliminate provisions that the Supreme Court "sit from first Monday in October of each year until the last Saturday in June of the next year," by amendment submitted as part of the amendment, which added Sec. 3-a. See note of that section; and (3) redefining the jurisdiction of the Supreme Court. Submitted by the Sixty-sixth Legislature (1979) and adopted in election Nov. 4, 1980.]

Sec. 3-a. **Time of Sitting** — The Supreme Court may sit at any time during the year at the seat of government for the transaction of business and each term thereof shall begin and end with each calendar year.

[Note—The foregoing Sec. 3-a of Art. V was added to make the time of sitting of the Supreme Court discretionary with that court. It was substituted for a provision formerly incorporated in Sec. 3. (See note on Sec. 3.) Submitted by the Forty-first Legislature (1929), ratified in an election Nov. 4, 1930, and proclaimed Dec. 17, 1930.]

Sec. 3-b. **Direct Appeal** — The Legislature shall have the power to provide by law, for an appeal direct to the Supreme Court of this State from an order of any trial court granting or denying an interlocutory or permanent injunction on the grounds of the constitutionality or unconstitutionality of any statute of this State, or on the validity or invalidity of any administrative order issued by any state agency under any statute of this State.

[Note—The foregoing Sec. 3-b of Art. V was added for the stated purpose of providing for direct appeals. Submitted by the Forty-sixth Legislature and adopted in an election Nov. 5, 1940.]

Sec. 3-c. (a) The supreme court and the court of criminal appeals have jurisdiction to answer questions of state law certified from a federal appellate court.

(b) The supreme court and the court of criminal appeals shall promulgate rules of procedure relating to the review of those questions.

[Note — The foregoing Sec. 3-c of Art. V, an amendment, was added to grant the Supreme Court and the Court of Criminals Appeals jurisdiction to answer questions of state law certified from a federal appellate court. Submitted by the Sixty-ninth Legislature (1985) and adopted in an election Nov. 5, 1985.]

Sec. 4. **Court of Criminal Appeals** — The Court of Criminal Appeals shall consist of eight Judges and one Presiding Judge. The Judges shall have the same qualifications and receive the same salaries as the Associate Justices of the Supreme Court, and the Presiding Judge shall have the same qualifications and receive the same salary as the Chief Justice of the Supreme Court. The Presiding Judge and the Judges shall be elected by the qualified voters of the state at a general election and shall hold their offices for a term of six years. In case of a vacancy in the office of a Judge of the Court of Criminal Appeals, the Governor shall, with the advice and consent of the Senate, fill said vacancy by appointment until the next succeeding general election.

For the purpose of hearing cases, the Court of Criminal Appeals may sit in panels of three Judges, the designation thereof to be under rules established by the court. In a panel of three Judges, two Judges shall constitute a quorum and the concurrence of two Judges shall be necessary for a decision. The Presiding Judge, under rules established by the court, shall convene the court en banc for the transaction of all other business and may convene the court en banc for the purpose of hearing cases. The court must sit en banc during proceedings involving capital punishment and other cases as required by law. When convened en banc, five Judges shall constitute a quorum and the concurrence of five Judges shall be necessary for a decision. The Court of Criminal Appeals may appoint Commissioners in aid of the Court of Criminal Appeals as provided by law.

[Note—The foregoing Sec. 4 of Art. V is an amendment, superseding, in part, the original Sec. 5 which provided for the former "Court of Appeals." The original Sec. 4 provided for the appointment of Supreme Court clerks, and was absorbed in the amended Sec. 3. Submitted by the Twenty-second Legislature (1891); ratified Aug. 11, 1891, and adopted Sept. 22, 1891. It was further amended to raise number of judges from three to five and define their terms of office. Submitted by the Fifty-ninth Legislature (1965) and adopted in election Nov. 8, 1966. It was again amended to raise the number of judges from five to nine and to provide that the Court of Criminal Appeals may sit in panels of three judges. Submitted by the Sixty-fifth Legislature (1977) and adopted in election Nov. 8, 1977.]

Sec. 5. **Jurisdiction; Power; Terms; Clerk, Etc.** — The Court of Criminal Appeals shall have final appellate jurisdiction coextensive with the limits of the State and its determinations shall be final in all criminal cases of whatever grade, with such exceptions and under such regulations as may be provided in this Constitution or as prescribed by law.

The appeal of all cases in which the death penalty has been assessed shall be to the Court of Criminal Appeals. The appeal of all other criminal cases shall be to the Courts of Appeal as prescribed by law. In addition, the Court of Criminal Appeals may, on its own motion, review a decision of a Court of Appeals in a criminal case as provided by law. Discretionary review by the Court of Criminal Appeals is not a matter of right, but of sound judicial discretion.

Subject to such regulations as may be prescribed by law, the Court of Criminal Appeals and the Judges thereof shall have the power to issue the writ of habeas corpus, and in criminal law matters, the writs of mandamus, procedendo, prohibition, and certiorari. The court and the judges thereof shall have the power to issue such other writs as may be necessary to protect its jurisdiction or enforce its judgments. The court shall have the power upon affidavit or otherwise to ascertain such matters of fact as may be necessary to the exercise of its jurisdiction.

The Court of Criminal Appeals may sit for the transaction of business at any time during the year and each term shall begin and end with each calendar year. The Court of Criminal Appeals shall appoint a clerk of the court who shall give bond in such manner as is now or may hereafter be required by law, and who shall hold his office for a term of four years unless sooner removed by the court for good cause entered of record on the minutes of said court.

The clerk of the Court of Criminal Appeals who may be in office at the time when this amendment takes effect shall continue in office for the term of his appointment.

[Note—The foregoing Sec. 5 of Art. V is an amendment, superseding primarily the original Sec. 6, which defined jurisdiction, powers, etc. of the old "Court of Appeals." (See also note on Sec. 6 below.) Submitted by Twenty-second Legislature (1891); ratified at an election Aug. 11, 1891, and declared adopted Sept. 22, 1891. It was further amended to redefine jurisdiction, powers and terms of office. Submitted by Fifty-ninth Legislature (1965) and adopted in election Nov. 8, 1966. (See note under Sec. 4 above.) It was again amended to enlarge the court's jurisdiction and to redefine its term of office. Submitted by Sixty-fifth Legislature (1977) and adopted in election Nov. 8, 1977. It was again amended to redefine jurisdiction of Courts of Criminal Appeals. Submitted by Sixty-sixth Legislature (1979) and adopted in election Nov. 4, 1980.]

Sec. 6. **Supreme Judicial Districts; Courts of Civil Appeals; Jurisdiction; Term; Justices; Election; Salary; Clerk** — The state shall be divided into courts of appeals districts, with each district having a Chief Justice, two or more other Justices, and such other officials as may be provided by law. The Justices shall have the qualifications prescribed for Justices of the Supreme Court. The Court of Appeals may sit in sections as authorized by law. The concurrence of a majority of the judges sitting in a section is necessary to decide a case. Said Court of Appeals shall have appellate jurisdiction

Article V — (Cont'd.)

coextensive with the limits of their respective districts, which shall extend to all cases of which the District Courts or County Courts have original or appellate jurisdiction under such restrictions and regulations as may be prescribed by law. Provided, that the decisions of said courts shall be conclusive on all questions of fact brought before them on appeal or error. Said courts shall have such other jurisdiction, original and appellate, as may be prescribed by law.

Each of said Courts of Appeals shall hold its sessions at a place in its district to be designated by the Legislature and at such time as may be prescribed by law. Said justices shall be elected by the qualified voters of their respective districts at a general election for a term of six years and shall receive for their services the sum provided by law. Each Court of Appeals shall appoint a clerk in the same manner as the clerk of the Supreme Court, which clerk shall receive such compensation as may be fixed by law.

All constitutional and statutory references to the Courts of Civil Appeals shall be construed to mean the Courts of Appeals.

[Note—The foregoing Sec. 6 of Art. V, establishing the Courts of Civil Appeals, is an amendment, superseding parts of the original Secs. 5 and 6, which provided for the old "Court of Appeals," and defined its jurisdiction, powers, etc. Submitted by the Twenty-second Legislature (1891), ratified at an election Aug. 11, 1891, and declared adopted Sept. 22, 1891. It was further amended to increase the number of justices on a Court of Civil Appeals, permitting a Court of Civil Appeals to sit in sections and requiring a concurrence of a majority of justices to decide a case. Submitted by the Sixty-fifth Legislature (1977) and adopted in election Nov. 7, 1978. It was again amended to change the name of the Courts of Civil Appeals to the Courts of Appeal and to redefine the jurisdiction of said courts. Submitted by the Sixty-sixth Legislature (1979) and adopted in election Nov. 4, 1980. It was again amended to redefine the membership and duties of the Courts of Appeals. Submitted by the Sixty-ninth Legislature (1985) and adopted in an election Nov. 5, 1985.]

Sec. 7. Judicial Districts; Judges; Their Qualifications; Residence; Term of Office; Salary; Terms of Court — The State shall be divided into judicial districts, with each district having one or more Judges as may be provided by law or by this Constitution. Each district judge shall be elected by the qualified voters at a General Election and shall be a citizen of the United States and of this State, who is licensed to practice law in this State and has been a practicing lawyer or a Judge of a Court in this State, or both combined, for four (4) years next preceding his election, who has resided in the district in which he was elected for two (2) years next preceding his election, and who shall reside in his district during his term of office and hold his office for the period of four (4) years, and who shall receive for his services an annual salary to be fixed by the Legislature. The Court shall conduct its proceedings at the county seat of the county in which the case is pending, except as otherwise provided by law. He shall hold the regular terms of his Court at the County Seat of each County in his district in such manner as may be prescribed by law. The Legislature shall have power by General or Special Laws to make such provisions concerning the terms or sessions of each Court as it may deem necessary.

The Legislature shall also provide for the holding of District Court when the Judge thereof is absent, or is from any cause disabled or disqualified from presiding.

[Note—The foregoing Sec. 7 of Art. V has been amended three times: (1) Effecting a general revision of the original Sec. 7 to eliminate specification that judge must be "twenty-five years of age" and making minor changes. Submitted by the Twenty-second Legislature (1891) and ratified in election Aug. 11, 1891. (2) Providing that the District Court shall conduct its proceedings in the county seat of the county in which the case is pending "except as otherwise provided by law." Submitted by the Fifty-first Legislature (1949) and adopted in election Nov. 8, 1949. (3) It was again amended to redefine the membership and terms of office of the district courts. Submitted by the Sixty-ninth Legislature (1985) and adopted in an election Nov. 5, 1985.]

Sec. 7a. (a) The Judicial Districts Board is created to reapportion the judicial districts authorized by Art. V, Sec. 7, of this constitution.

(b) The membership of the board consists of the Chief Justice of the Texas Supreme Court who serves as chairman, the presiding judge of the Texas Court of Criminal Appeals, the presiding judge of each of the administrative judicial districts of the state, the president of the Texas Judicial Council, and one person who is licensed to practice law in this state appointed by the governor with the advice and consent of the senate for a term of four years. In the event of a vacancy in the appointed membership, the vacancy is filled for the unexpired term in the same manner as the original appointment.

(c) A majority of the total membership of the board constitutes a quorum for the transaction of business. The adoption of a reapportionment order requires a majority vote of the total membership of the board.

(d) The reapportionment powers of the board shall be exercised in the interims between regular sessions of the Legislature, except that a reapportionment may not be ordered by the board during an interim immediately following a regular session of the Legislature in which a valid and subsisting statewide apportionment of judicial districts is enacted by the Legislature. The board has other powers and duties as provided by the Legislature and shall exercise its powers under the policies, rules, standards, and conditions, not inconsistent with this section, that the Legislature provides.

(e) Unless the Legislature enacts a statewide reapportionment of the judicial districts following each federal decennial census, the board shall convene not later than the first Monday of June of the third year following the year in which the federal decennial census is taken to make a statewide reapportionment of the districts. The board shall complete its work on the reapportionment and file its order with the secretary of state not later than Aug. 31 of the same year. If the Judicial Districts Board fails to make a statewide apportionment by that date, the Legislative Redistricting Board established by Art. III, Sec. 28, of this constitution shall make a statewide reapportionment of the judicial districts not later than the 150th day after the final day for the Judicial Districts Board to make the reapportionment.

(f) In addition to the statewide reapportionment, the board may reapportion the judicial districts of the state as the necessity for reapportionment appears by redesignating, in one or more reapportionment orders, the county or counties that comprise the specific judicial districts affected by those reapportionment orders. In modifying any judicial district, no county having a population as large or larger than the population of the judicial district being reapportioned shall be added to the judicial district.

(g) Except as provided by Subsection (i) of this section, this section does not limit the power of the Legislature to reapportion the judicial districts of the state, to increase the number of judicial districts, or to provide for consequent matters on reapportionment. The Legislature may provide for the effect of a reapportionment made by the board on pending cases or the transfer of pending cases, for jurisdiction of a county court where county court jurisdiction has been vested by law in a district court affected by the reapportionment, for terms of the courts upon existing officers and their duties, and for all other matters affected by the reapportionment. The Legislature may delegate any of these powers to the board. The Legislature shall provide for the necessary expenses of the board.

(h) Any judicial reapportionment order adopted by the board must be approved by a record vote of the majority of the membership of both the senate and house of representatives before such order can become effective and binding.

(i) The Legislature, the Judicial Districts Board, or the Legislative Redistricting Board may not redistrict the judicial districts to provide for any judicial district smaller in size than an entire county except as provided by this section. Judicial districts smaller in size than the entire county may be created subsequent to a general election where a majority of the persons voting on the proposition adopt the proposition "to allow the division of _____County into judicial districts composed of parts of _____County." No redistricting plan may be proposed or adopted by the Legislature, the Judicial Districts Board, or the Legislative Redistricting Board in anticipation of a future action by the voters of any county.

[Note — The foregoing Sec. 7a of Art. V, an amendment, was added to create the Judicial Districts Board and to define its membership and duties. Submitted by the Sixty-ninth Legislature (1985) and adopted in an election Nov. 5, 1985.]

Sec. 8. **Jurisdiction and Powers of the District Courts** — District Court jurisdiction consists of exclusive, appellate, and original jurisdiction of all actions, proceedings, and remedies, except in cases where exclusive, appellate, or original jurisdiction may be conferred by this Constitution or other law on some other court, tribunal, or administrative body. District Court judges shall have the power to issue writs necessary to enforce their jurisdiction. The District Court shall have appellate jurisdiction and general supervisory control over the County Commissioners' Court with such exceptions and under such regulations as may be prescribed by law.

[Note—The foregoing Sec. 8 of Art. V is an amendment of the original Sec. 8, including the words "of contested elections" in the first paragraph and adding the last sentence in the second paragraph. Submitted by the Twenty-second Legislature (1891), ratified at an election Aug. 11, 1891, and declared adopted Sept. 22, 1891. It was further amended to give District and County Courts general jurisdiction over probate matters; and further provided that

Article V — (Cont'd.)

Legislature may increase, diminish or eliminate jurisdiction of District Court or County Court in probate matters; and further provided that Legislature may provide that all appeals in such matters be to Courts of Civil Appeals. Submitted by the Sixty-third Legislature (1973) and adopted in election Nov. 6, 1973. It was again amended to define the exact duties of the judges of the district courts. Submitted by the Sixty-ninth Legislature (1985) and adopted in an election Nov. 5, 1985.]

Sec. 9. **Clerk of the District Court; Term of Office; How Removed; How Vacancy Is Filled** — There shall be a Clerk for the District Court of each county, who shall be elected by the qualified voters for state and county officers, and who shall hold his office for four years, subject to removal by information, or by indictment of a grand jury and conviction by a petit jury. In case of vacancy the judge of a District Court shall have the power to appoint a Clerk, who shall hold until the office can be filled by election.

[Note—The foregoing Sec. 9 of Art. V has been amended to change the term of office from two to four years. Submitted by the Fifty-third Legislature (1953) and adopted in election Nov. 2, 1954.]

Sec. 10. **Jury Trial; by Whom Fee Is to Be Paid** — In the trial of all cases in the District Courts, the plaintiff or defendant shall, upon application made in open court, have the right of trial by jury; but no jury shall be impaneled in any civil case unless demanded by a party to the case, and a jury fee be paid by the party demanding a jury, for such sum and with such exceptions as may be prescribed by the Legislature.

Sec. 11. **Disqualification of Judges; Special Judges; Exchange of Districts; Vacancies** — No judge shall sit in any case wherein he may be interested, or where either of the parties may be connected with him either by affinity or consanguinity, within such a degree as may be prescribed by law, or when he shall have been counsel in the case. When the Supreme Court, the Court of Criminal Appeals, the Court of Civil Appeals, or any member of either, shall be thus disqualified to hear and determine any case or cases in said court, the same shall be certified to the Governor of the State, who shall immediately commission the requisite number of persons, learned in the law, for the trial and determination of such cause or causes. When a Judge of the District Court is disqualified by any of the causes above stated, the parties may, by consent, appoint a proper person to try said case; or, upon their failing to do so, a competent person may be appointed to try the same in the county where it is pending in such manner as may be prescribed by law.

And the District Judges may exchange districts or hold courts for each other when they may deem it expedient, and shall do so when required by law. This disqualification of Judges of inferior tribunals shall be remedied, and vacancies in their offices filled, as may be prescribed by law.

[Note — The foregoing Sec. 11 of Art. V is an amended section, having been amended to use correct references to courts as established in amended Secs. 1, 3, 4, 5 and 6. Submitted by the Twenty-second Legislature (1891), ratified at an election Aug. 11, 1891, and declared adopted Sept. 22, 1891.]

Sec. 12. **Judges Conservators of Peace; Style of Writs; Prosecution by State** — (a) All judges of courts of this State, by virtue of their office, are conservators of the peace throughout the State.

(b) An indictment is a written instrument presented to a court by a grand jury charging a person with the commission of an offense. An information is a written instrument presented to a court by an attorney for the State charging a person with the commission of an offense. The practice and procedures relating to the use of indictments and informations, including their contents, amendment, sufficiency, and requisites, are as provided by law. The presentment of an indictment or information to a court invests the court with jurisdiction of the cause.

[Note — The foregoing Sec. 12 of Art. V has been amended from the original to substitute "Courts of the State" for enumeration of kinds of courts contained in original sections and applying to courts before general revision of judiciary in 1891. Submitted by the Twenty-second Legislature (1891), ratified at an election Aug. 11, 1891, and declared adopted Sept. 22, 1891. It was further amended to explain the manner in which a person is charged with a criminal offense and certain requirements applicable to state writs and processes. Submitted by the Sixty-ninth Legislature (1985) and adopted in election Nov. 5, 1985.]

Sec. 13. **Jurors, Grand and Petit; Number Required to Return Verdict** — Grand and petit juries in the District Courts shall be composed of twelve men; but nine members of a grand jury shall be a quorum to transact business and present bills. In trials of civil cases and in trials of criminal cases below the grade of felony in the District Courts, nine members of the jury concurring may render a verdict, but when the verdict shall be rendered by less than the whole number, it shall be signed by every member of the jury concurring in it. When, pending the trial of any case, one or more jurors, not exceeding three, may die, or be disabled from sitting, the remainder of the jury shall have the power to render the verdict; provided, that the Legislature may change or modify the rule authorizing less than the whole number of the jury to render a verdict.

[Note — Sec. 14 of Art. V, defining judicial districts and time of holding courts therein was deleted by constitutional amendment in an election Nov. 5, 1985.]

Sec. 15. **County Court; Election; Term of Office of County Judges; Fees** — There shall be established in each county in this State, a County Court, which shall be a court of record; and there shall be elected in each county by the qualified voters a County Judge, who shall be well informed in the law of the state, shall be a conservator of the peace, and shall hold his office for four years and until his successor shall be elected and qualified. He shall receive as compensation for his services such fees and perquisites as may be prescribed by law.

[Note — The foregoing Sec. 15 of Art. V has been amended to change the term of office from two to four years. Submitted by the Fifty-third Legislature (1953) and adopted in election Nov. 2, 1954.]

Sec. 16. **Jurisdiction of County Court; Appeals; Probate Jurisdiction; May Issue Writs; Judge Disqualified, When** — The County Court has jurisdiction as provided by law. The County Judge is the presiding officer of the County Court and has judicial functions as provided by law. County court judges shall have the power to issue writs necessary to enforce their jurisdiction.

County Courts in existence on the effective date of this amendment are continued unless otherwise provided by law. When the Judge of the County Court is disqualified in any case pending in the County Court the parties interested may, by consent, appoint a proper person to try said case, or upon their failing to do so a competent person may be appointed to try the same in the county where it is pending in such manner as may be prescribed by law.

[Note — The foregoing Sec. 16 of Art. V is an amendment from the original to make changes relating to appeals to the county court, relating to disqualification of the judge, and minor changes. Submitted by the Twenty-second Legislature (1891), ratified at an election Aug. 11, 1891, and declared adopted Sept. 22, 1891. It was further amended to extend jurisdiction of Justices of Peace in civil cases. (See also Sec. 19 of Art. V.) Submitted by the Sixty-fifth Legislature (1977) and adopted in election Nov. 7, 1978. It was amended again to redefine jurisdiction of appellate courts. Submitted by the Sixty-sixth Legislature (1979) and adopted in election Nov. 4, 1980. It was again amended to define the jurisdiction of the County Judge and his duties. Submitted by the Sixty-ninth Legislature (1985) and adopted in an election Nov. 5, 1985.]

[Note — Sec. 16-a of Art. V, providing for probate courts, was deleted by constitutional amendment in an election Nov. 5, 1985.]

Sec. 17. **Terms of County Court for Criminal Business; Prosecution Commenced by Information; Grand Jury to Inquire Into Misdemeanors; Quashing of Grand Jury Indictments; Jury** — The County Court shall hold terms as provided by law. Prosecutions may be commenced in said court by information filed by the County Attorney, or by affidavit, as may be provided by law. Grand juries empaneled in the District Courts shall inquire into misdemeanors, and all indictments therefor returned into the District Courts shall forthwith be certified to the County Courts, or other inferior courts having jurisdiction to try them, for trial; and if such indictment be quashed in the county, or other inferior court, the person charged shall not be discharged if there is probable cause of guilt, but may be held by such court or magistrate to answer an information or affidavit. A jury in the County Court shall consist of six men; but no jury shall be empaneled to try a civil case, unless demanded by one of the parties, who shall pay such jury fee therefor in advance as may be prescribed by law, unless he makes affidavit that he is unable to pay the same.

[Note — The foregoing Sec. 17 of Art. V was amended to redefine the terms of office of county judges. Submitted by the Sixty-ninth Legislature (1985) and adopted in an election Nov. 5, 1985.]

Sec. 18. **Terms of Justices of the Peace; County Commissioners and Commissioners' Court** — (a) Each county in the state, with a population of 30,000 or more, according to the most recent federal census, from time to time, for the convenience of the people, shall be divided into not less than four and not more than eight precincts. Each county in the State with a population of 18,000 or more but less than 30,000

Article V — (Cont'd.)

according to the most recent federal census, from time to time, for the convenience of the people, shall be divided into not less than two and not more than five precincts. Each county in the State with a population of less than 18,000, according to the most recent federal census, from time to time, for the convenience of the people, shall be designated as a single precinct or, if the Commissioners Court determines that the county needs more than one precinct, shall be divided into not more than four precincts. Notwithstanding the population requirements of this subsection, Chambers County, from time to time, for the convenience of the people, shall be divided into not less than two and not more than six precincts. A division or designation under this subsection shall be made by the Commissioners Court provided for by this Constitution. In each such precinct there shall be elected one Justice of the Peace and one Constable, each of whom shall hold his office for four years and until his successor shall be elected and qualified; provided that in any precinct in which there may be a city of 18,000 or more inhabitants, there shall be elected two Justices of the Peace.

(b) Each county shall, in the manner provided for justice of the peace and constable precincts, be divided into four Commissioners' precincts in each of which there shall be elected by the qualified voters thereof one County Commissioner, who shall hold his office for four years and until his successor shall be elected and qualified. The County Commissioners so chosen, with the County Judge as presiding officer, shall compose the County Commissioners Court, which shall exercise such powers and jurisdiction over all county business as is conferred by this Constitution and the laws of the state, or as may be hereafter prescribed.

(c) When the boundaries of justice of the peace and constable precincts are changed, each Justice and Constable in office on the effective date of the change, or elected to a term of office beginning on or after the effective date of the change, shall serve in the precinct in which the person resides for the term to which each was elected or appointed, even though the change in boundaries places the person's residence outside the precinct for which he was elected or appointed, abolishes the precinct for which he was elected or appointed, or temporarily results in extra Justices or Constables serving in a precinct. When, as a result of a change of precinct boundaries, a vacancy occurs in the office of Justice of the Peace or Constable, the Commissioners Court shall fill the vacancy by appointment until the next general election.

(d) When the boundaries of commissioners precincts are changed, each commissioner in office on the effective date of the change, or elected to a term of office beginning on or after the effective date of the change, shall serve in the precinct to which each was elected or appointed for the entire term to which each was elected or appointed, even though the change in boundaries places the person's residence outside the precinct for which he was elected or appointed.

[Note — The foregoing Sec. 18 of Art. V was first amended to change the term of office for Justices of the Peace and Constables from two to four years. Submitted by the Fifty-third Legislature (1953) and adopted in election Nov. 2, 1954. It was again amended to authorize fewer justice of the peace and constable precincts in counties with populations of less than 30,000 and to provide for continuous service by Justices of Peace, Constables and County Commissioners when precinct boundaries are changed. Submitted by Sixty-eighth Legislature (1983) and adopted in election Nov. 8, 1983. It was again amended to allow Chambers County to be divided into two to six precincts. Submitted by Sixty-ninth Legislature (1985) and adopted in an election Nov. 5, 1985.]

Sec. 19. Criminal Jurisdiction of Justices of the Peace; Appeals; Justices of the Peace ex-Officio Notaries — Justice of the peace courts shall have original jurisdiction in criminal matters of misdemeanor cases punishable by fine only, exclusive jurisdiction in civil matters where the amount in controversy is two hundred dollars or less, and such other jurisdiction as may be provided by law. Justices of the peace shall be ex officio notaries public.

[Note — The foregoing Sec. 19 of Art. V was amended to extend jurisdiction of Justices of Peace and to give them jurisdiction in civil matters involving $200 or less. (See also Sec. 16 of Art. V.) Submitted by the Sixty-fifth Legislature (1977) and adopted in election Nov. 7, 1978. It was again amended to redefine the duties of Justices of the Peace and to make them ex officio notaries public. Submitted by the Sixty-ninth Legislature (1985) and adopted in an election Nov. 5, 1985.]

Sec. 20. County Clerk; Election; Terms; Duties; Vacancies — There shall be elected for each county, by the qualified voters, a County Clerk, who shall hold his office for four years, who shall be clerk of the County and Commissioners' Courts and recorder of the county, whose duties, perqui-

sites and fees of office shall be prescribed by the Legislature, and a vacancy in whose office shall be filled by the Commissioners' Court until the next general election; provided, that in counties having a population of less than 8,000 persons there may be an election of a single clerk, who shall perform the duties of District and County Clerks.

[Note — The foregoing Sec. 20 of Art. V has been amended to change the term of office from two to four years. Submitted by the Fifty-third Legislature (1953) and adopted in election Nov. 2, 1954.]

Sec. 21. County and District Attorneys; Duties; Vacancies; Fees — A County Attorney, for counties in which there is not a resident Criminal District Attorney, shall be elected by the qualified voters of each county, who shall be commissioned by the Governor and hold his office for the term of four years. In case of vacancy the Commissioners' Court of the county shall have power to appoint a County Attorney until the next general election. The County Attorneys shall represent the State in all cases in the District and inferior courts in their respective counties; but if any county shall be included in a district in which there shall be a District Attorney, the respective duties of District Attorneys and County Attorneys shall, in such counties, be regulated by the Legislature. The Legislature may provide for the election of District Attorneys in such districts as may be deemed necessary, and make provisions for the compensation of District Attorneys and County Attorneys. District Attorneys shall hold office for a term of four years, and until their successors have qualified.

[Note — The foregoing Sec. 21 of Art. V has been amended to change the term of office from two to four years; also leaves solely to Legislature provision for annual salary to be paid by State to District and County Attorneys. Submitted by the Fifty-third Legislature (1953) and adopted in election Nov. 2, 1954.]

[Note — Sec. 22 of Art. V, giving Legislature power to change jurisdiction of county courts, was deleted by constitutional amendment in an election Nov. 5, 1985.]

Sec. 23. Sheriff; Term of Office; Vacancy — There shall be elected by the qualified voters of each county a Sheriff, who shall hold his office for the term of four years, whose duties and perquisites and fees of office shall be prescribed by the Legislature, and vacancies in whose office shall be filled by the Commissioners' Court until the next general election.

[Note — The foregoing Sec. 23 of Art. V has been amended to change the term of office from two to four years. Submitted by the Fifty-third Legislature (1953) and adopted in election Nov. 2, 1954.]

Sec. 24. Certain Officers Removed by District Courts for Drunkenness, Incompetency, Official Misconduct, Etc. — County Judges, County Attorneys, Clerks of the District and County Courts, Justices of the Peace, Constables and other county officers may be removed by the Judges of the District Courts for incompetency, official misconduct, habitual drunkenness or other causes defined by law, upon the cause therefor being set forth in writing, and the finding of its truth by a jury.

[Note — Sec. 25 of Art. V, giving the Supreme Court power to make rules of procedure was deleted by constitutional amendment in an election Nov. 5, 1985.]

Sec. 26. No Appeal in Criminal Cases by the State — The State shall have no right of appeal in criminal cases.

Sec. 27. Transfer of Cases by the Legislature — The Legislature shall, at its first session provide for the transfer of all business, civil and criminal, pending in District Courts, over which jurisdiction is given by this Constitution to the County Courts or other inferior courts, to such county or inferior courts, and for the trial or disposition of all such causes by such county or other inferior courts.

Sec. 28. Vacancies in Offices of Judges of Superior Courts to Be Filled by the Governor — Vacancies in the office of the Judges of the Supreme Court, the Court of Criminal Appeals, the Court of Civil Appeals and District Courts shall be filled by the Governor until the next succeeding general election, and vacancies in the office of County Judge and Justices of the Peace shall be filled by the Commissioners' Court until the next succeeding general election.

[Note — The foregoing Sec. 28 of Art. V has been amended from the original to make names of courts harmonize with names in amended Secs. 1, 3, 4, 5 and 6. Submitted by the Twenty-second Legislature (1891), ratified in an election Aug. 11, 1891, and declared adopted Sept. 22, 1891. This section was again amended to provide that appointments to the offices of County Judge and Justice of the Peace should be filled only to the next succeeding general election instead of for the full elected term. Submitted by the Fifty-fifth Legislature (1957) and adopted in election Nov. 4, 1958.]

Sec. 29. Terms of County Courts; Probate Business; Prosecutions — The County Court shall hold at least four terms

Article V — (Cont'd.); Article VI

for both civil and criminal business annually, as may be provided by the Legislature, or by the Commissioners' Court of the county under authority of law, and such other terms each year as may be fixed by the Commissioners' Court; provided, the Commissioners' Court of any county having fixed the times and number of terms of the County Court shall not change the same again until the expiration of one year. Said court shall dispose of probate business either in term time or vacation, under such regulations as may be prescribed by law. Prosecutions may be commenced in said courts in such manner as is or may be provided by law, and a jury therein shall consist of six men. Until otherwise provided, the terms of the County Court shall be held on the first Mondays in February, May, August and November, and may remain in session three weeks.

[Note — Sec. 29 of Art. V, an amendment, was added for stated purpose of prescribing county court terms. Submitted by the Eighteenth Legislature (1883), ratified in an election Aug. 14, 1883, and proclaimed adopted Sept. 25, 1883.]

Sec. 30. **County Judges and Criminal District Attorneys; Terms** — The Judges of all courts of county-wide jurisdiction heretofore or hereafter created by the Legislature of this State, and all Criminal District Attorneys now or hereafter authorized by the laws of this State, shall be elected for a term of four years, and shall serve until their successors have qualified.

[Note — Sec. 30 of Art. V, an amendment, was added for purpose of prescribing term of office of County Judges and Criminal District Attorneys. Submitted by the Fifty-third Legislature (1953) and adopted in election Nov. 2, 1954.]

Sec. 31. **Court Administration and Rule-making Authority** — (a) The Supreme Court is responsible for the efficient administration of the judicial branch and shall promulgate rules of administration not inconsistent with the laws of the state as may be necessary for the efficient and uniform administration of justice in the various courts.

(b) The Supreme Court shall promulgate rules of civil procedure for all courts not inconsistent with the laws of the state as may be necessary for the efficient and uniform administration of justice in the various courts.

(c) The Legislature may delegate to the Supreme Court or Court of Criminal Appeals the power to promulgate such other rules as may be prescribed by law or this Constitution, subject to such limitations and procedures as may be provided by law.

[Note — The foregoing Sec. 31 of Art. V, an amendment, was added to provide for the administration and jurisdiction of constitutional courts. Submitted by the Sixty-ninth Legislature (1985) and adopted in an election Nov. 5, 1985.]

[Note — For further clarification of rules of procedure for the different courts, see Temporary Provision at the beginning of Article V.]

ARTICLE VI. — SUFFRAGE

Sec. 1. **Persons Who Cannot Vote** — The following classes of persons shall not be allowed to vote in this State, to wit:

*First: Persons under eighteen (18) years of age.

Second: Idiots and lunatics.

Third: All paupers supported by any county.

Fourth: All persons convicted of any felony, subject to such exceptions as the Legislature may make.

[Note — The foregoing Sec. 1 of Art. VI has been twice amended from the original to give privilege of ballot to officers and enlisted men of National Guard, National Guard Reserves, Officers Reserve Corps, Organized Reserves and retired officers and enlisted men of Army, Navy and Marine Corps. Submitted by the Forty-second Legislature (1931) and adopted in an election Nov. 8, 1932. Proclaimed Jan. 9, 1933. It was further amended by HJR 10 submitted by the Fifty-third Legislature (1953) and adopted in an election Nov. 2, 1954, to remove restrictions against members of the Armed Forces. This amendment also repealed the original Sec. 2-a of Art. VI which provided for poll tax exemption for war veterans. See also note under Sec. 2 and new Sec. 2-a.* Texas on April 27, 1971, became the twenty-first state to ratify an amendment to the U.S. Constitution lowering the voting age to 18 from 21. When Ohio ratified the amendment in July, 1971, it was the 38th state to do so, the number required to change the voting age.]

Sec. 2. **Annual Registration; Absentee Voting** — Every person subject to none of the foregoing disqualifications, who shall have attained the age of *21 years and who shall be a citizen of the United States and who shall have resided in this State one year next preceding an election and the last six months within the district or county in which such person offers to vote, shall be deemed a qualified elector; provided, however, that before offering to vote at an election a voter shall have registered annually, but such requirement

for registration shall not be considered a qualification of an elector within the meaning of the term "qualified elector" as used in any other Article of this Constitution in respect to any matter except qualification and eligibility to vote at an election. Any legislation enacted in anticipation of the adoption of this Amendment shall not be invalid because of its anticipatory nature. The Legislature may authorize absentee voting. And this provision of the Constitution shall be self-enacting without the necessity of further legislation.

[Note — The foregoing Sec. 2 of Art. VI has been amended six times, as follows: (1) To include provision that declaration of foreigner must be filed at least six months before election to enable him to vote in such election. Submitted by Twenty-fourth Legislature (1895), ratified in an election Nov. 3, 1896, and declared adopted Dec. 18, 1896. (2) To make poll tax receipt certificate of registration for voting. Submitted by Twenty-seventh Legislature (1901), ratified in an election Nov. 4, 1902, and declared adopted Dec. 26, 1902. (3) To limit suffrage to citizens; allowing husband or wife to pay poll tax for other; authorizing absentee voting. Submitted by Thirty-seventh Legislature (1921) and ratified in election July 23, 1921. (4) To extend suffrage to members of the Armed Forces of the United States. Submitted by Fifty-third Legislature (1953) and adopted in an election Nov. 2, 1954. (5) To omit the requirement that members of armed services may vote only in county in which they resided at time of entering the service. Submitted by Fifty-ninth Legislature (1965) and adopted in election Nov. 8, 1966. (6) To repeal the poll tax as a voting requirement and substituting therefor annual registration. Submitted by Fifty-ninth Legislature (1965), adopted in election Nov. 8, 1966. *See also note under Sec. 1 above.]

Sec. 2-a. **Vote for Electors for President and Vice President and Statewide Offices** — (a) Notwithstanding any other provision of this Constitution, the Legislature may enact laws and provide a method of registration, including the time of such registration, permitting any person who is qualified to vote in this state except for the residence requirements within a county or district, as set forth in Sec. 2 of this article, to vote for (1) electors for president and vice president of the United States and (2) all offices, questions or propositions to be voted on by all electors throughout this state.

(b) Notwithstanding any other provision of this Constitution, the Legislature may enact laws and provide for a method of registration, including the time for such registration, permitting any person (1) who is qualified to vote in this state except for the residence requirements of Sec. 2 of this article, and (2) who shall have resided anywhere within this state at least thirty (30) days next preceding a general election in a presidential election year, and (3) who shall have been a qualified elector in another state immediately prior to his removal to this state or would have been eligible to vote in such other state had he remained there until such election, to vote for electors for president and vice president of the United States in that election.

(c) Notwithstanding any other provision of this Constitution, the Legislature may enact laws and provide for a method of registration, including the time for such registration, permitting absentee voting for electors for president and vice president of the United States in this state by former residents of this state (1) who have removed to another state, and (2) who meet all qualifications, except residence requirements, for voting for electors for president and vice president in this state at the time of the election, but the privileges of suffrage so granted shall be only for such period of time as would permit a former resident of this state to meet the residence requirements for voting in his new state of residence, and in no case for more than twenty-four (24) months.

[Note — The foregoing Sec. 2-a, an amendment, was added to provide for voting on electors for president and vice president and on all statewide offices. Submitted by the Fifty-ninth Legislature (1965) and adopted in election Nov. 8, 1966.]

Sec. 3. **Electors in Towns and Cities; Only Property Taxpayers to Vote in Certain Instances** — All qualified electors of the State, as herein described, who shall have resided for six months immediately preceding an election within the limits of any city or corporate town, shall have the right to vote for Mayor and all other elective officers; but in all elections to determine expenditure of money or assumption of debt, only those shall be qualified to vote who pay taxes on property in said city or incorporated town; provided, that no poll tax for the payment of debts thus incurred shall be levied upon the persons debarred from voting in relation thereto.

Sec. 3-a. **Only Those Who Have Rendered Property for Taxation May Vote in Bond Elections** — When an election is held by any county, or any number of counties, or any political subdivision of the State, or any political subdivision of a county, or any defined district now or hereafter to be described and defined within the State and which may or may not include towns, villages or municipal corporations,

Article VI — (Cont'd.); Article VII

or any city, town or village, for the purpose of issuing bonds or otherwise lending credit, or expending money or assuming any debt, only qualified electors who own taxable property in the State, county, political subdivision, district, city, town or village where such election is held, and who have duly rendered the same for taxation, shall be qualified to vote and all electors shall vote in the election precinct of their residence.

[Note — The foregoing Sec. 3-a of Art. VI, an amendment, was added for the purpose of limiting voters participating in bond elections to those who have rendered property for taxation. Submitted by the Forty-second Legislature (1931) and adopted in an election Nov. 8, 1932; proclaimed Jan. 9, 1933.]

Sec. 4. Voter Registration — In all elections by the people the vote shall be by ballot, and the Legislature shall provide for the numbering of tickets and make such other regulations as may be necessary to detect and punish fraud and preserve the purity of the ballot box; and the Legislature shall provide by law for the registration of all voters.

[Note — The foregoing Sec. 4 of Art. VI has been amended twice as follows: A provision for the registration of voters in cities of 10,000 or more population was added by amendment submitted by the Twenty-second Legislature (1891), ratified in election Aug. 11, 1891, and declared adopted Sept. 22, 1891. It was further amended to delete this provision for registration of voters in cities of 10,000 or more population. (See also note under Sec. 2, Art. VI.) Submitted by the Fifty-ninth Legislature (1965) and adopted in election Nov. 8, 1966.]

Sec. 5. Voters Privileged From Arrest — Voters shall, in all cases except treason, felony or breach of the peace, be privileged from arrest during their attendance at elections and in going to and returning therefrom.

ARTICLE VII. — EDUCATION—
THE PUBLIC FREE SCHOOLS

Sec. 1. Public Schools to Be Established — A general diffusion of knowledge being essential to the preservation of the liberties and rights of the people, it shall be the duty of the Legislature of the State to establish and make suitable provision for the support and maintenance of an efficient system of public free schools.

Sec. 2. Provisions Governing the Levy and Collection of Taxes for the Support of the Public Free Schools — All funds, lands and other property heretofore set apart and appropriated for the support of public schools, all the alternate sections of land reserved by the State out of grants heretofore made or that may hereafter be made to railroads or other corporations, of any nature whatsoever, one half of the public domain of the State, and all sums of money that may come to the State from the sale of any portion of the same shall constitute a perpetual public school fund.

Sec. 3. School Taxes — One fourth of the revenue derived from the State occupation taxes and a poll tax of one ($1.00) dollar on every inhabitant of this State, between the ages of 21 and 60 years, shall be set apart annually for the benefit of the public free schools; and in addition thereto, there shall be levied and collected an annual ad valorem State tax of such an amount not to exceed 35c on the one hundred ($100.00) dollars valuation, as, with the available school fund arising from all other sources, will be sufficient to maintain and support the public schools of this State for a period of not less than six months in each year, and it shall be the duty of the State Board of Education to set aside a sufficient amount out of the said tax to provide free textbooks for the use of children attending the public free schools of this State; provided, however, that should the limit of taxation herein named be insufficient the deficit may be met by appropriation from the general funds of the State, and the Legislature may also provide for the formation of school districts by general laws, and all such school districts may embrace parts of two or more counties. And the Legislature shall be authorized to pass laws for the assessment and collection of taxes in all said districts and for the management and control of the public school or schools of such districts, whether such districts are composed of territory wholly within a county or in parts of two or more counties. And the Legislature may authorize an additional ad valorem tax to be levied and collected within all school districts heretofore formed or hereafter formed, for the further maintenance of public free schools, and for the erection and equipment of school buildings therein; provided, that a majority of the qualified property taxpaying voters of the district voting at an election to be held for that purpose shall vote such tax not to exceed in any one year $1 on the $100 valuation of the property subject to taxation in such district, but the limitation upon the amount of school district tax herein authorized shall not apply to incorporated cities or towns constituting separate and independent school districts, nor to independent or common school districts created by general or special law.

[Note — The foregoing Sec. 3 of Art. VII is an amended

section, having been altered six times: (1) To authorize a State ad valorem school tax of not more than 20c, and further to authorize creation by Legislature of school districts for local taxation not to exceed 20c. Submitted by Eighteenth Legislature (1883), ratified in election Aug. 14, 1883, and declared adopted Sept. 25, 1883. (2) To authorize maximum tax in school districts of 50c. Submitted by Thirtieth Legislature (1907), ratified in an election Nov. 3, 1908, and declared adopted Feb. 2, 1909. (3) To authorize intercounty school districts and authorizing Legislature to pass laws for management and control of districts. Submitted by Thirty-first Legislature (1909), ratified in an election Aug. 3, 1909. See note on 3-a below. (4) To increase maximum tax for State school purposes from 20c to 35c and provide for free textbooks. Submitted by Thirty-fifth Legislature (1917) and adopted at election of Nov. 5, 1918. (5) To remove 50c limit on school district tax submitted by Thirty-sixth Legislature (1919) and adopted at election of Nov. 2, 1920. (6) To eliminate the provision authorizing the Legislature to create districts by special law. Submitted by Thirty-ninth Legislature (1925) and ratified in an election Nov. 2, 1926, and proclaimed Jan. 20, 1927.]

See Sec. 1-e of Art. VIII for provisions to gradually abolish the ad valorem tax as a source for state school support.

[Note — Sec. 3-a of Art. VII, relating to county line districts, validation, bonds and taxation, was deleted by constitutional amendment in election Aug. 5, 1969.]

Sec. 3-b. County School Districts — No tax for the maintenance of public free schools voted in any independent school district and no tax for the maintenance of a junior college voted by a junior college district, nor any bonds voted in any such district, but unissued, shall be abrogated, canceled or invalidated by change of any kind in the boundaries thereof. After any change in boundaries, the governing body of any such district, without the necessity of an additional election, shall have the power to assess, levy and collect ad valorem taxes on all taxable property within the boundaries of the district as changed, for the purposes of the maintenance of public free schools or the maintenance of a junior college, as the case may be, and the payment of principal of and interest on all bonded indebtedness outstanding against, or attributable, adjusted or allocated to, such district or any territory therein, in the amount, at the rate, or not to exceed the rate, and in the manner authorized in the district prior to the change in its boundaries, and further in accordance with the laws under which all such bonds, respectively, were voted; and such governing body also shall have the power, without the necessity of an additional election, to sell and deliver any unissued bonds voted in the district prior to any such change in boundaries, and to assess, levy and collect ad valorem taxes on all taxable property in the district as changed, for the payment of principal of and interest on such bonds in the manner permitted by the laws under which such bonds were voted. In those instances where the boundaries of any such independent school district are changed by the annexation of, or consolidation with, one or more whole school districts, the taxes to be levied for the purposes herein-above authorized may be in the amount or at not to exceed the rate theretofore voted in the district having at the time of such change the greatest scholastic population according to the latest scholastic census and only the unissued bonds of such district voted prior to such change, may be subsequently sold and delivered and any voted, but unissued, bonds of other school districts involved in such annexation or consolidation shall not thereafter be issued.

[Note. The foregoing Sec. 3-b of Art. VII, an amendment, was added originally for the purpose of allowing independent school districts in Dallas County to work out adjustment of boundaries without abrogating, canceling or invalidating existing tax rates and bonds. Submitted by the Fifty-seventh Legislature (1961) and adopted in election Nov. 6, 1962. Further amended to include school districts in any county of Texas. Submitted by the Fifty-ninth Legislature (1965) and adopted in election Nov. 8, 1966.]

Sec. 4. Sale of School Lands; No Release to Purchasers; the Investment of Proceeds — The lands herein set apart to the public free school fund shall be sold under such regulations, at such times and on such terms as may be prescribed by law; and the Legislature shall not have power to grant any relief to purchasers thereof. The proceeds of such sales must be used to acquire other land for the Public Free School fund as provided by law or the proceeds shall be invested by the comptroller, as may be directed by the Board of Education herein provided for, in the bonds of the United States, the State of Texas, or counties in said State, or in such other securities and under such restrictions as may be prescribed by law; and the State shall be responsible for all investments.

[Note — The foregoing Sec. 4 of Art. VII is an amended section, the amendment authorizing investment of money from sale of State public school lands in securities other

Article VII — (Cont'd.)

than State and United States bonds, as was required by the original section. The amendment also added the clause making the State responsible for such investments. Submitted by the Eighteenth Legislature (1883), ratified in an election Aug. 14, 1883, and declared adopted Sept. 25, 1883. It was again amended to authorize proceeds from sale of land dedicated to permanent school fund to be used to acquire other land for that fund. Submitted by Sixty-ninth Legislature (1985) and adopted in an election Nov. 5, 1985.]

Sec. 4A. **Patents Issued for Free Public School Lands** — (a) On application to the School Land Board, a natural person is entitled to receive a patent to land from the commissioner of the General Land Office if:

(1) the land is surveyed public free school land, either surveyed or platted according to records of the General Land Office;

(2) the land was not patentable under the law in effect immediately before adoption of this section;

(3) the person acquired the land without knowledge of the title defect out of the State of Texas or Republic of Texas and held the land under color of title, the chain of which dates from at least as early as January 1, 1932; and

(4) the person, in conjunction with his predecessors in interest:

(A) has a recorded deed on file in the respective county courthouse and has claimed the land for a continuous period of at least 50 years as of November 15, 1981; and

(B) for at least 50 years has paid taxes on the land together with all interest and penalties associated with any period of delinquency of said taxes; provided, however, that in the event that public records concerning the tax payments on the land are unavailable for any period within the past 50 years, the tax assessors-collectors of the taxing jurisdictions in which the land is located shall provide the School Land Board with a sworn certificate stating that, to the best of their knowledge, all taxes have been paid for the past 50 years and there are no outstanding taxes nor interest or penalties currently due against the property.

(b) The applicant for the patent must submit to the School Land Board certified copies of his chain of title and a survey of the land for which a patent is sought, if requested to do so by the board. The board shall determine the qualifications of the applicant to receive a patent under this section. Upon a finding by the board that the applicant meets the requirements of Subsection (a) of this section, the commissioner of the General Land Office shall award the applicant a patent. If the applicant is denied a patent, he may file suit against the board in a district court of the county in which the land is situated within 60 days from the date of the denial of the patent under this section. The trial shall be de novo and not subject to the Administrative Procedure and Texas Register Act, and the burden of proof is on the applicant.

(c) This section does not apply to beach land, submerged land, or islands, and may not be used by an applicant to resolve a boundary dispute. This section does not apply to land that, previous to the effective date of this section, was found by a court of competent jurisdiction to be state owned or to land on which the state has given a mineral lease that on the effective date of this section was productive.

(d) Application for a patent under this section must be filed with the School Land Board within five years from the effective date of this section.

(e) This section is self-executing.

(f) This section expires on January 1, 1990.

[Note — The foregoing Sec. 4A of Art. VII, an amendment, was added to authorize the Commissioner of the General Land Office to issue patents for certain public free school fund land held in good faith under color of title for at least 50 years as of Nov. 15, 1981. Submitted by the Sixty-seventh Legislature (1981) and adopted in election Nov. 3, 1981.]

Sec. 5. **Permanent School Fund; Interest; Alienation; Sectarian Schools** — (a) The principal of all bonds and other funds, and the principal arising from the sale of the lands hereinbefore set apart to said school fund, shall be the permanent school fund, and all the interest derivable therefrom and the taxes herein authorized and levied shall be the available school fund. The available school fund shall be applied annually to the support of the public free schools. Except as provided by this section, no law shall ever be enacted appropriating any part of the permanent or available school fund to any other purpose whatever; nor shall the same or any part thereof ever be appropriated to or used for the support of any sectarian school; and the available school fund herein provided shall be distributed to the several counties according to their scholastic population and applied in such manner as may be provided by law.

(b) The Legislature by law may provide for using the permanent school fund and the income from the permanent school fund to guarantee bonds issued by school districts.

(c) The Legislature may appropriate part of the available school fund for administration of the permanent school fund or of a bond guarantee program established under this section.

[Note — The foregoing Sec. 5 of Art. VII is an amended section. It was first amended to allow Legislature to add not exceeding 1 per cent annually of the total value of the permanent school fund to the available school fund. Submitted by the Twenty-second Legislature (1891), ratified in an election Aug. 11, 1891, and declared adopted Sept. 22, 1891. It was further amended to delete this provision. Submitted by the Fifty-eighth Legislature (1963), and adopted in election Nov. 3, 1964. It was again amended to authorize use of the permanent school fund to guarantee bonds issued by school districts. Submitted by Sixty-eighth Legislature (1983) and adopted in election Nov. 8, 1983.]

Sec. 6. **County School Lands; Limitations; Settlers; Proceeds** — All lands heretofore or hereafter granted to the several counties of this State for educational purposes are of right the property of said counties respectively to which they were granted, and title thereto is vested in said counties, and no adverse possession or limitation shall ever be available against the title of any county. Each county may sell or dispose of its lands in whole or in part in manner to be here provided by the Commissioners' Court of the county. Actual settlers residing on said land shall be protected in the prior right of purchasing the same to the extent of their settlement, not to exceed 160 acres, at the price fixed by said court, which price shall not include the value of existing improvements made thereon by such settlers. Said lands, and the proceeds thereof, when sold, shall be held by said counties alone as a trust for the benefit of public schools therein; said proceeds to be invested in bonds of the United States, the State of Texas, or counties in said State, or in such other securities and under such restrictions as may be prescribed by law; and the counties shall be responsible for all investments; the interest thereon and other revenue, except principal, shall be available fund.

[Note — The foregoing Sec. 6 of Art. VII is an amended section, the amendment authorizing the investment of money from sale of county public school lands in securities other than State and United States bonds (as was required in the original section), and making counties responsible for such investments. Submitted by the Eighteenth Legislature (1883), ratified in an election August 14, 1883, and declared adopted Sept. 25, 1883.]

Sec. 6-a. **Taxation of County School Lands** — All agriculture or grazing school land mentioned in Sec. 6 of this article owned by any county shall be subject to taxation except for State purposes to the same extent as lands privately owned.

[Note — The foregoing Sec. 6-a of Art. VII, an amendment, was added for the stated purpose of providing taxation of lands mentioned in Sec. 6. Submitted by the Thirty-ninth Legislature (1925), ratified in an election Nov. 2, 1926, and proclaimed Jan. 20, 1927.]

Sec. 6-b. Notwithstanding the provisions of Sec. 6, Art. VII, Constitution of the State of Texas, any county, acting through the commissioners court, may reduce the county permanent school fund of that county and may distribute the amount of the reduction to the independent and common school districts of the county on a per scholastic basis to be used solely for the purpose of reducing bonded indebtedness of those districts or for making permanent improvements. The commissioners court shall, however, retain a sufficient amount of the corpus of the county permanent school fund to pay ad valorem taxes on school lands or royalty interests owned at the time of the distribution. Nothing in this Section affects financial aid to any school district by the State.

[Note — Sec. 6-b of Art VII is an added amendment to allow a county to reduce its county permanent school fund and distribute the money to independent and common school districts on a per capita basis. Submitted by the Sixty-second Legislature (1971) and adopted in an election Nov. 7, 1972.]

[Note — Sec. 7 of Art. VII, relating to separate schools for white and colored, was deleted by constitutional amendment in election Aug. 5, 1969.]

Sec. 8. **Board of Education; Terms and Duties** — The Legislature shall provide by law for a State Board of Education, whose members shall be appointed or elected in such manner and by such authority and shall serve for such terms as the Legislature shall prescribe not to exceed six years. The said board shall perform such duties as may be prescribed by law.

[Note — The foregoing Sec. 8 of Art. VII is an amended section, reconstituting the State Board of Education. The original text provided for a Board of Education consisting of Governor, Comptroller and Secretary of State, serving ex officio. Submitted by the Fortieth Legislature (1927);

Article VII — (Cont'd.)

ratified Nov. 6, 1928; proclaimed Feb. 6, 1929.]

Asylums

Sec. 9. **Lands of Asylums; Sale**. All lands heretofore granted for the benefit of the lunatic, blind, deaf and dumb, and orphan asylums, together with such donations as may have been or may hereafter be made to either of them, respectively, as indicated in the several grants, are hereby set apart to provide a permanent fund for the support, maintenance and improvement of said asylums. And the Legislature may provide for the sale of the lands and the investment of the proceeds in the manner as provided for the sale and investment of school lands in Sec. 4 of this article.

University

Sec. 10. **University Lands and Funds** — The Legislature shall, as soon as practicable, establish, organize and provide for the maintenance, support and direction of a University of the first class, to be located by a vote of the people of this State and styled "The University of Texas," for the promotion of literature and the arts and sciences, including an agricultural, and mechanical department.

Sec. 11. **University Funds; How Invested** — In order to enable the Legislature to perform the duties set forth in the foregoing section, it is hereby declared all lands and other property heretofore set apart and appropriated for the establishment and maintenance of the University of Texas, together with all the proceeds of sales of the same, heretofore made or hereafter to be made, and all grants, donations and appropriations that may hereafter be made by the State of Texas, or from any other source, except donations limited to specific purposes, shall constitute and become a permanent university fund. And the same as realized and received into the treasury of the State (together with such sums belonging to the fund, as may now be in the treasury) shall be invested in bonds of the United States, the State of Texas, or counties of said State, or in school bonds of municipalities or in bonds of any city of this State or in bonds issued under and by virtue of the Federal Farm Loan Act approved by the President of the United States July 17, 1916, and amendments thereto; and the interest accruing thereon shall be subject to appropriation by the Legislature to accomplish the purpose declared in the foregoing section; provided, that the one tenth of the alternate sections of the lands granted to railroads reserved by the State, which were set apart and appropriated to the establishment of the University of Texas by an act of the Legislature of Feb. 11, 1858, entitled "An act to establish the University of Texas" shall not be included in or constitute a part of, the permanent university fund.

[Note — The foregoing Sec. 11 of Art. VII has been twice amended as follows: (1) Adding a clause giving the Board of Regents of the University of Texas latitude in expending part of the permanent fund for buildings. Submitted by the Forty-first Legislature (1929); ratified Nov. 4, 1930. (2) Eliminating this latitude allowed the Board of Regents and restoring the original provisions of the Constitution which limited investments to bonds of the United States, State or civil subdivisions. This last amendment added also the clause "except donations limited to specific purposes." Submitted by the Forty-second Legislature (1931); adopted Nov. 8, 1932. Proclaimed Jan. 9, 1933.]

Sec. 11-a. In addition to the bonds enumerated in Section 11 of Article VII of the Constitution of the State of Texas, the Board of Regents of The University of Texas may invest the Permanent University Fund in securities, bonds or other obligations issued, insured, or guaranteed in any manner by the United States Government, or any of its agencies, and in such bonds, debentures, or obligations, and preferred and common stocks issued by corporations, associations, and other institutions as the Board of Regents of The University of Texas System may deem to be proper investments for said funds; provided, however, that not more than one per cent (1%) of said fund shall be invested in the securities of any one (1) corporation, nor shall more than five per cent (5%) of the voting stock of any one corporation be owned; provided, further, that stocks eligible for purchase shall be restricted to stocks of companies incorporated within the United States which have paid dividends for five (5) consecutive years or longer immediately prior to the date of purchase and which, except for bank stocks and insurance stocks, are listed upon an exchange registered with the Securities and Exchange Commission or its successors.

In making each and all of such investments said Board of Regents shall exercise the judgment and care under the circumstances then prevailing which men of ordinary prudence, discretion, and intelligence exercise in the management of their own affairs, not in regard to speculation but in regard to the permanent disposition of their funds, considering the probable income therefrom as well as the probable safety of their capital.

The interest, dividends and other income accruing from the investments of the Permanent University Fund, except the portion thereof which is appropriated by the operation of Sec. 18 of Art. VII for the payment of principal and interest on bonds or notes issued thereunder, shall be subject to appropriation by the Legislature to accomplish the purposes declared in Sec. 10 of Article VII of this Constitution.

This amendment shall be self-enacting, and shall become effective upon its adoption, provided, however, that the Legislature shall provide by law for full disclosure of all details concerning the investments in corporate stocks and bonds and other investments authorized herein.

[Note — Sec.11-a of Art. VII was added to provide for broader investment of the Permanent University Fund in corporate bonds and stocks under certain conditions and limitations. Submitted by the Fifty-fourth Legislature (1955) and adopted in election Nov. 6, 1956. It was further amended to increase the types of securities available for investment to the Permanent University Fund by allowing securities, bonds or other obligations issued, insured or guaranteed in any manner by the federal government. Submitted by the Sixtieth Legislature (1967) and adopted in election Nov.5, 1968.]

Sec. 12. **Lands to Be Sold; No Relief of Purchasers** — The land herein set apart to the university fund shall be sold under such regulations at such times and on such terms as may be provided by law, and the Legislature shall provide for the prompt collection, at maturity, of all debts due on account of university lands heretofore sold, or that may hereafter be sold, and shall in neither event have the power to grant relief to the purchasers.

Sec. 13. **Agricultural and Mechanical College; Appropriations** — The Agricultural and Mechanical College of Texas, established by an act of the Legislature passed April 17, 1871, located in the County of Brazos, is hereby made and constituted a branch of the University of Texas, for instruction in agriculture, the mechanic arts and the natural sciences connected therewith. And the Legislature shall at its next session make an appropriation not to exceed $40,000 for the construction and completion of the buildings and improvements, and for providing the furniture necessary to put said college in immediate and successful operation.

Sec. 14. **Prairie View A&M** — Prairie View A&M University in Waller County is an institution of the first class under the direction of the same governing board as Texas A&M University referred to in Article VII, Section 13, of this constitution as the Agricultural and Mechanical College of Texas.

[Note — The foregoing Sec. 14 of Art. VII was substituted for an earlier Sec. 14. It sets out that Prairie View A&M University is an institution of the first class under direction of Texas A&M University governing board. (See also Sections 17 and 18 of Art. VII.) Submitted by the Sixty-eighth Legislature (1983) and adopted in election Nov. 6, 1984.]

Sec. 15. **Land Appropriated for University; How Sold** — In addition to the lands heretofore granted to the University of Texas, there is hereby set apart and appropriated, for the endowment, maintenance and support of said university and its branches, 1,000,000 acres of the unappropriated public domain of the State, to be designated and surveyed as may be provided by law; and said lands shall be sold under the same regulations and the proceeds invested in the same manner as is provided for the sale and investment of the permanent university fund; and the Legislature shall not have the power to grant any relief to the purchasers of said lands.

Sec. 16. **Terms of Office in School Systems** — The Legislature shall fix by law the terms of all offices of the public school system and of the State institutions of higher education, inclusive, and the terms of members of the respective boards, not to exceed six years.

[Note — The foregoing Sec. 16 of Art. VII is the first of two amendments numbered 16. (See following section and note thereon.) This amendment was added for the stated purpose of providing for fixing of terms of office in public school system. Submitted by the Fortieth Legislature (1927); ratified Nov. 6, 1928; proclaimed Feb. 6, 1929.]

Sec. 16 [a.] **Taxation of University Lands** — All land mentioned in Secs. 11, 12 and 15 of Article VII of the Constitution of the State of Texas, now belonging to the University of Texas, shall be subject to the taxation for county purpose to the same extent as lands privately owned; provided, they shall be rendered for taxation upon values fixed by the State Tax Board; and providing, that the State shall remit annually to each of the counties in which said lands are located an amount equal to the tax imposed upon said land for county purposes.

[Note — The foregoing section, which obviously should have been numbered either 16-a or 17, was designated as No. 16 in H.J.R. No. 11 of the Forty-first Legislature (1929) in which the amendment was submitted. It is customarily printed in legal references as Sec. 16 [a.] This amendment

Article VII — (Cont'd.)

was added for the stated purpose of providing for taxation of University of Texas lands. It was ratified Nov. 4, 1930. Declared adopted Dec. 17, 1930.]

Sec. 17. **Support for Higher Education** — (a) In the fiscal year beginning September 1, 1985, and each fiscal year thereafter, there is hereby appropriated out of the first money coming into the state treasury not otherwise appropriated by the constitution $100 million to be used by eligible agencies and institutions of higher education for the purpose of acquiring land either with or without permanent improvements, constructing and equipping buildings or other permanent improvements, major repair or rehabilitation of buildings or other permanent improvements, and acquisition of capital equipment, library books and library materials. During the regular session of the legislature that is nearest, but preceding, the beginning of each fifth fiscal year dating from September 1, 1985, the legislature may by two-thirds vote of the membership of each house adjust the amount of the constitutional appropriation for the ensuing five years but may not adjust the appropriation in such a way as to impair any obligation created by the issuance of bonds or notes in accordance with this section.

(b) The funds appropriated under Subsection (a) of this section shall be for the use of the following eligible agencies and institutions of higher education (even though their names may be changed):

(1) East Texas State University including East Texas State University at Texarkana; (2) Lamar University including Lamar University at Orange and Lamar University at Port Arthur; (3) Midwestern State University; (4) North Texas State University; (5) Pan American University including Pan American University at Brownsville; (6) Stephen F. Austin State University; (7) Texas College of Osteopathic Medicine; (8) Texas State University System Administration and the following component institutions: (9) Angelo State University; (10) Sam Houston State University; (11) Southwest Texas State University; (12) Sul Ross State University including Uvalde Study Center; (13) Texas Southern University; (14) Texas Tech University; (15) Texas Tech University Health Sciences Center; (16) Texas Woman's University; (17) University of Houston System Administration and the following component institutions: (18) University of Houston — University Park; (19) University of Houston — Victoria; (20) University of Houston — Clear Lake; (21) University of Houston — Downtown; (22) University System of South Texas System Administration and the following component institutions: (23) Corpus Christi State University; (24) Laredo State University; (25) Texas A&I University; and (26) West Texas State University.

(c) Pursuant to a two-thirds vote of the membership of each house of the legislature, institutions of higher education may be created at a later date by general law, and, when created, such an institution shall be entitled to participate in the funding provided by this section if it is not created as a part of The University of Texas System or The Texas A&M University System. An institution that is entitled to participate in dedicated funding provided by Article VII, Section 18, of this constitution may not be entitled to participate in the funding provided by this section.

(d) In the year 1985 and every 10 years thereafter, the legislature or an agency designated by the legislature no later than August 31 of such year shall allocate by equitable formula the annual appropriations made under Subsection (a) of this section to the governing boards of eligible agencies and institutions of higher education. The legislature shall review, or provide for a review, of the allocation formula at the end of the fifth year of each 10-year allocation period. At that time adjustments may be made in the allocation formula, but no adjustment that will prevent the payment of outstanding bonds and notes, both principal and interest, may be made.

(e) Each governing board authorized to participate in the distribution of money under this section is authorized to expend all money distributed to it for any of the purposes enumerated in Subsection (a). In addition, unless a single bonding agency is designated as hereinafter provided, such governing board may issue bonds and notes for the purposes of refunding bonds or notes issued under this section or prior law, acquiring land either with or without permanent improvements, constructing and equipping buildings or other permanent improvements, and for major repair and rehabilitation of buildings or other permanent improvements, and may pledge up to 50 percent of the money allocated to such governing board pursuant to this section to secure the payment of the principal and interest of such bonds or notes. Proceeds from the issuance of bonds or notes under this subsection shall be maintained in a local depository selected by the governing board issuing the bonds or notes. The bonds and notes issued under this subsection shall be payable solely out of the money appropriated by this section and shall mature serially or otherwise in not more than 10 years from their respective dates. All bonds issued under this section shall be sold only through competitive bidding and are subject to approval by the at-

torney general. Bonds approved by the attorney general shall be incontestable. The permanent university fund may be invested in the bonds and notes issued under this section. In lieu of the authority granted to each governing board herein, the legislature by general law may designate a single agency to issue bonds and notes authorized under this section and transfer to that agency the authority to collect and pledge money to the payment of such bonds and notes for the purposes, to the extent, and subject to the restrictions of this section. Provided, that such agency shall be authorized to issue such bonds and notes for the benefit of an eligible institution and pledge money collected hereunder only as directed by the governing board of each eligible institution.

(f) The funds appropriated by this section may not be used for the purpose of constructing, equipping, repairing, or rehabilitating buildings or other permanent improvements that are to be used for student housing, intercollegiate athletics, or auxiliary enterprises.

(g) Except for that portion of the allocated funds that may be required to be transferred to a single bonding agency, if one is created, the comptroller of public accounts shall make annual transfers of the funds allocated pursuant to Subsection (d) directly to the governing boards of the eligible institutions.

(h) To assure efficient use of construction funds and the orderly development of physical plants to accommodate the state's real need, the legislature may provide for the approval or disapproval of all new construction projects at the eligible agencies and institutions entitled to participate in the funding provided by this section.

(i) The legislature by general law may dedicate portions of the state's revenues to the creation of a dedicated fund ("the higher education fund") for the purposes expressed in Subsection (a) of this section. The legislature shall provide for administration of the fund, which shall be invested in the manner provided for investment of the permanent university fund. The income from the investment of the higher education fund shall be credited to the higher education fund until such time as the fund totals $2 billion. The principal of the higher education fund shall never be expended. At the beginning of the fiscal year after the fund reaches $2 billion, as certified by the comptroller of public accounts, the dedication of general revenue funds provided for in Subsection (a) of this section shall cease. At the beginning of the fiscal year after the fund reaches $2 billion, and each year thereafter, 10 percent of the interest, dividends, and other income accruing from the investments of the higher education fund during the previous fiscal year shall be deposited and become part of the principal of the fund, and out of the remainder of the annual income from the investment of the principal of the fund there shall be appropriated an annual sum sufficient to pay the principal and interest due on the bonds and notes issued under this section and the balance of the income shall be allocated, distributed, and expended as provided for the appropriations made under Subsection (a).

(j) The state systems and institutions of higher education designated in this section may not receive any additional funds from the general revenue of the state for acquiring land with or without permanent improvements, for constructing or equipping buildings or other permanent improvements, or for major repair and rehabilitation of buildings or other permanent improvements except that:

(1) in the case of fire or natural disaster the legislature may appropriate from the general revenue an amount sufficient to replace the uninsured loss of any building or other permanent improvement; and

(2) the legislature, by two-thirds vote of each house, may, in cases of demonstrated need, which need must be clearly expressed in the body of the act, appropriate additional general revenue funds for acquiring land with or without permanent improvements, for constructing or equipping buildings or other permanent improvements, or for major repair and rehabilitation of buildings or other permanent improvements.

This subsection does not apply to legislative appropriations made prior to the adoption of this amendment.

(k) Without the prior approval of the legislature, appropriations under this section may not be expended for acquiring land with or without permanent improvements, or for constructing and equipping buildings or other permanent improvements, for a branch campus or educational center that is not a separate degree-granting institution created by general law.

(l) This section is self-enacting upon the issuance of the governor's proclamation declaring the adoption of the amendment, and the state comptroller of public accounts and the state treasurer shall do all things necessary to effectuate this section. This section does not impair any obligation created by the issuance of any bonds and notes in accordance with prior law, and all outstanding bonds and notes shall be paid in full, both principal and interest, in accordance with their terms. If the provisions of this section conflict with any other provisions of this constitution, then the provisions of this section shall prevail, notwithstanding all such conflicting provisions.

Article VII — (Cont'd.)

[Note — The foregoing Sec. 17 of Art. VII is an added amendment that supersedes the old Sec. 17 which provided for a confederate pension fund tax, college building fund tax and reduced the ad valorem ceiling for general purposes. That section was deleted in an election Nov. 2, 1982. This added Sec. 17 was proposed to create from general revenue a special higher education assistance fund for construction and related activities, to restructure the permanent university fund and to increase the number of institutions eligible to benefit from the permanent university fund. (See also Sections 14 and 18 of Art. VII.) Submitted by the Sixty-eighth Legislature (1983) and adopted in election Nov. 6, 1984.]

Sec. 18. **Building Bonds Authorized for the University of Texas and Texas A&M University; Retired From Income From the Permanent University Fund; Etc.** — (a) The Board of Regents of The Texas A&M University System may issue bonds and notes not to exceed a total amount of 10 percent of the cost value of the investments and other assets of the permanent university fund (exclusive of real estate) at the time of the issuance thereof, and may pledge all or any part of its one-third interest in the available university fund to secure the payment of the principal and interest of those bonds and notes, for the purpose of acquiring land either with or without permanent improvements, constructing and equipping buildings or other permanent improvements, major repair and rehabilitation of buildings and other permanent improvements, acquiring capital equipment and library books and library materials, and refunding bonds or notes issued under this Section or prior law, at or for The Texas A&M University System administration and the following component institutions of the system:

(1) Texas A&M University, including its medical college which the legislature may authorize as a separate medical institution; (2) Prairie View A&M University, including its nursing school in Houston; (3) Tarleton State University; (4) Texas A&M University at Galveston; (5) Texas Forest Service; (6) Texas Agricultural Experiment Stations; (7) Texas Agricultural Extension Service; (8) Texas Engineering Experiment Stations; (9) Texas Transportation Institute; and (10) Texas Engineering Extension Service.

(b) The Board of Regents of The University of Texas System may issue bonds and notes not to exceed a total amount of 20 percent of the cost value of investments and other assets of the permanent university fund (exclusive of real estate) at the time of issuance thereof, and may pledge all or any part of its two-thirds interest in the available university fund to secure the payment of the principal and interest of those bonds and notes, for the purpose of acquiring land either with or without permanent improvements, constructing and equipping buildings or other permanent improvements, major repair and rehabilitation of buildings and other permanent improvements, acquiring capital equipment and library books and library materials, and refunding bonds or notes issued under this section or prior law, at or for The University of Texas System administration and the following component institutions of the system:

(1) The University of Texas at Arlington; (2) The University of Texas at Austin; (3) The University of Texas at Dallas; (4) The University of Texas at El Paso; (5) The University of Texas of the Permian Basin; (6) The University of Texas at San Antonio; (7) The University of Texas at Tyler; (8) The University of Texas Health Science Center at Dallas; (9) The University of Texas Medical Branch at Galveston; (10) The University of Texas Health Science Center at Houston; (11) The University of Texas Health Science Center at San Antonio; (12) The University of Texas System Cancer Center; (13) The University of Texas Health Center at Tyler; and (14) The University of Texas Institute of Texan Cultures at San Antonio.

(c) Pursuant to a two-thirds vote of the membership of each house of the legislature, institutions of higher education may be created at a later date as a part of The University of Texas System or The Texas A&M University System by general law, and, when created, such an institution shall be entitled to participate in the funding provided by this section for the system in which it is created. An institution that is entitled to participate in dedicated funding provided by Article VII, Section 17, of this constitution may not be entitled to participate in the funding provided by this section.

(d) The proceeds of the bonds or notes issued under Subsection (a) or (b) of this section may not be used for the purpose of constructing, equipping, repairing, or rehabilitating buildings or other permanent improvements that are to be used for student housing, intercollegiate athletics, or auxiliary enterprises.

(e) The available university fund consists of the dividends, interest and other income from the permanent university fund (less administrative expenses) including the net income attributable to the surface of permanent university fund land. Out of one-third of the available university fund, there shall be appropriated an annual sum sufficient to pay the principal and interest due on the bonds and notes

issued by the Board of Regents of The Texas A&M University System under this section and prior law, and the remainder of that one-third of the available university fund shall be appropriated to the Board of Regents of The Texas A&M University System which shall have the authority and duty in turn to appropriate an equitable portion of the same for the support and maintenance of The Texas A&M University System administration, Texas A&M University, and Prairie View A&M University. The Board of Regents of The Texas A&M University System, in making just and equitable appropriations to Texas A&M University and Prairie View A&M University, shall exercise its discretion with due regard to such criteria as the board may deem appropriate from year to year, taking into account all amounts appropriated from Subsection (f) of this section. Out of the other two-thirds of the available university fund there shall be appropriated an annual sum sufficient to pay the principal and interest due on the bonds and notes issued by the Board of Regents of The University of Texas System under this section and prior law, and the remainder of such two-thirds of the available university fund, shall be appropriated for the support and maintenance of The University of Texas at Austin and The University of Texas System administration.

(f) It is provided, however, that, for 10 years beginning upon the adoption of this amendment, before any other allocation is made of The University of Texas System's two-thirds share of the available university fund, remaining after payment of principal and interest on its bonds and notes issued under this section and prior law, $6 million per year shall be appropriated out of that share to the Board of Regents of The Texas A&M University System for said board's use in making appropriations to Prairie View A&M University. This subsection expires and is deleted from this constitution 10 years from the adoption of this amendment.

(g) The bonds and notes issued under this section shall be payable solely out of the available university fund, mature serially or otherwise in not more than 30 years from their respective dates, and, except for refunding bonds, be sold only through competitive bidding. All of these bonds and notes are subject to approval by the attorney general and when so approved are incontestable. The permanent university fund may be invested in these bonds and notes.

(h) To assure efficient use of construction funds and the orderly development of physical plants to accommodate the state's real need, the legislature may provide for the approval or disapproval of all new construction projects at the eligible agencies and institutions entitled to participate in the funding provided by this section except The University of Texas at Austin, Texas A&M University in College Station, and Prairie View A&M University.

(i) The state systems and institutions of higher education designated in this section may not receive any funds from the general revenue of the state for acquiring land with or without permanent improvements, for constructing or equipping buildings or other permanent improvements, or for major repair and rehabilitation of buildings or other permanent improvements except that:

(1) In the case of fire or natural disaster the legislature may appropriate from the general revenue an amount sufficient to replace the uninsured loss of any building or other permanent improvement; and

(2) The legislature, by two-thirds vote of each house, may, in cases of demonstrated need, which need must be clearly expressed in the body of the act, appropriate general revenue funds for acquiring land with or without permanent improvements, for constructing or equipping buildings or other permanent improvements, or for major repair and rehabilitation of buildings or other permanent improvements.

This subsection does not apply to legislative appropriations made prior to the adoption of this amendment.

(j) This section is self-enacting on the issuance of the governor's proclamation declaring the adoption of this amendment, and the state comptroller of public accounts and the state treasurer shall do all things necessary to effectuate this section. This section does not impair any obligation created by the issuance of bonds or notes in accordance with prior law, and all outstanding bonds and notes shall be paid in full, both principal and interest, in accordance with their terms, and the changes herein made in the allocation of the available university fund shall not affect the pledges thereof made in connection with such bonds or notes heretofore issued. If the provisions of this section conflict with any other provision of this constitution, then the provisions of this section shall prevail, notwithstanding any such conflicting provisions.

[Note — Sec. 18 and Sec. 17 of Art. VII were originally added to the Constitution as a single amendment to provide for funding of construction at Texas universities and colleges. Submitted by the Fiftieth Legislature (1947) and adopted in election Aug. 23, 1947. It was further amended in election Nov. 6, 1956 and again in an election Nov. 8, 1968. Sec. 17 was repealed in election Nov. 2, 1982. A new Sec. 17 and Sec. 18 were submitted by the Sixty-eighth Legislature (1983) and adopted in election Nov. 6, 1984. (See also notes under Sec. 14 and Sec. 17.)]

Article VIII

ARTICLE VIII — TAXATION AND REVENUE

Sec. 1. Taxation to Be Equal and Uniform; Occupation and Income Taxes; Exemptions; Limitations Upon Counties, Cities, Etc. — Taxation shall be equal and uniform. All real property and tangible personal property in this State, whether owned by natural persons or corporations, other than municipal, shall be taxed in proportion to its value, which shall be ascertained as may be provided by law. The Legislature may provide for the taxation of intangible property and may also impose occupation taxes, both upon natural persons and upon corporations, other than municipal, doing any business in this State. It may also tax incomes of both natural persons and corporations, other than municipal, except that persons engaged in mechanical and agricultural pursuits shall never be required to pay an occupation tax. The Legislature by general law shall exempt household goods not held or used for production of income and personal effects not held or used for the production of income, and the Legislature by general law may exempt all or part of the personal property homestead of a family or single adult, "personal property homestead" meaning that personal property exempt by law from forced sale for debt, from ad valorem taxation. The occupation tax levied by any county, city or town, for any year, on persons or corporations pursuing any profession or business, shall not exceed one half of the tax levied by the State for the same period on such profession or business.

[Note — Sec. 1 of Art. VIII was amended to provide tax relief for residential homesteads and to provide personal property exemptions. (See also Sec. 1-b, and Sec. 23 of Art. VIII.) Submitted by the Sixty-fifth Legislature, (1977) and adopted in election Nov. 7, 1978.]

Sec. 1-a. Abolishing Ad Valorem Tax for State's General Fund Purposes; Providing Local Tax Rate, Etc. — From and after Jan 1, 1951, no State ad valorem tax shall be levied upon any property within this State for general revenue purposes. From and after January 1, 1951, the several counties of the State are authorized to levy ad valorem taxes upon all property within their respective boundaries for county purposes, except the first three thousand dollars ($3,000) value of residential homesteads of married or unmarried adults, male or female, including those living alone, to not exceed thirty cents (30c) on each one hundred dollars ($100) valuation, in addition to all other ad valorem taxes authorized by the Constitution of this State, provided the revenue derived therefrom shall be used for construction and maintenance of farm-to-market roads or for flood control, except as herein otherwise provided.

Provided that in those counties or political subdivisions or areas of the State from which tax donations have heretofore been granted, the State Automatic Tax Board shall continue to levy the full amount of the State ad valorem tax for the duration of such donation, or until all legal obligations heretofore authorized by the law granting such donation or donations heretofore authorized by the law granting such donation or donations shall have been fully discharged, whichever shall first occur; provided that if such donation to any such county or political subdivision for less than the full amount of State ad valorem taxes so levied, the portion of such taxes remaining over and above such donation shall be retained by said county or subdivision.

[Note — Sec. 1-a of Art. VIII was first added and then amended, as follows: (1) Giving homesteads $3,000 exemption from State taxes. Submitted by the Forty-second Legislature (1931), and adopted in an election Nov. 8, 1932. (2) Making more definite the provision for extending the exemption to counties and subdivisions having tax remission as soon as tax remission ceased, whether by expiration of the period designated in the act granting remission or voluntarily by action of local authorities. The original amendment failed to make provision for the latter contingency. Submitted by the Forty-third Legislature (1933), and adopted in an election Aug. 26, 1933. (3) Reducing maximum ad valorem tax for general revenue from 35c to 30c. (4) Abolishing ad valorem tax for state general fund purposes and providing for local taxation as indicated in text of section. (See also Sec. 1-b immediately below and note thereon.) Submitted by the Fiftieth Legislature (1947) and adopted in election Nov. 2, 1948. (5) Extending the $3,000 ad valorem tax exemption to homesteads of unmarried adults. Submitted by the Sixty-third Legislature (1973) and adopted in election Nov. 6, 1973.]

Sec. 1-b. Homestead Exemption Under State Tax — (a) Three thousand dollars ($3,000) of the assessed taxable value of all residence homesteads of married or unmarried adults, male or female, including those living alone, shall be exempt from all taxation for all State purposes.

(b) From and after January 1, 1973, the governing body of any county, city, town, school district, or other political subdivision of the State may exempt by its own action not less than three thousand dollars ($3,000) of the market value of residence homesteads of persons, married or unmarried, including those living alone, who are under a disability for purposes of payment of disability insurance benefits

under Federal Old-Age, Survivors, and Disability Insurance or its successor or of married or unmarried persons sixty-five (65) years of age or older, including those living alone, from all ad valorem taxes thereafter levied by the political subdivision. As an alternative, upon receipt of a petition signed by twenty per cent (20%) of the voters who voted in the last preceding election held by the political subdivision, the governing body of the subdivision shall call an election to determine by majority vote whether an amount not less than three thousand dollars ($3,000) as provided in the petition, of the market value of residence homesteads of disabled persons or of persons sixty-five (65) years of age or over shall be exempt from ad valorem taxes thereafter levied by the political subdivision. An eligible disabled person who is sixty-five (65) years of age or older may not receive both exemptions from the same political subdivision in the same year but may choose either if the subdivision has adopted both. Where any ad valorem tax has theretofore been pledged for the payment of any debt, the taxing officers of the political subdivision shall have authority to continue to levy and collect the tax against the homestead property at the same rate as the tax so pledged until the debt is discharged, if the cessation of the levy would impair the obligation of the contract by which the debt was created.

An exemption adopted under this subsection based on assessed value is increased, effective January 1, 1979, to an amount that, when converted to market value, provides the same reduction in taxes, except that the market value exemption shall be rounded to the nearest $100.

(c) Five Thousand Dollars ($5,000) of the market value of the residence homestead of a married or unmarried adult, including one living alone, is exempt from ad valorem taxation for general elementary and secondary public school purposes. In addition to this exemption, the Legislature by general law may exempt an amount not to exceed Ten Thousand Dollars ($10,000) of the market value of the residence homestead of a person who is disabled as defined in Subsection (b) of this section and of a person sixty-five (65) years of age or older from ad valorem taxation for general elementary and secondary public school purposes. The Legislature by general law may base the amount of and condition eligibility for the additional exemption authorized by this subsection for disabled persons and for persons sixty-five (65) years of age or older on economic need. An eligible disabled person who is sixty-five (65) years of age or older may not receive both exemptions from a school district but may choose either. An eligible person is entitled to receive both the exemption required by this subsection for all residence homesteads and any exemption adopted pursuant to Subsection (b) of this section, but the Legislature shall provide by general law whether an eligible disabled or elderly person may receive both the additional exemption for the elderly and disabled authorized by this subsection and any exemption for the elderly or disabled adopted pursuant to Subsection (b) of this section. Where ad valorem tax has previously been pledged for the payment of debt, the taxing officers of a school district may continue to levy and collect the tax against the value of homesteads exempted under this subsection until the debt is discharged if the cessation of the levy would impair the obligation of the contract by which the debt was created. The Legislature shall provide for formulas to protect school districts against all or part of the revenue loss incurred by the implementation of Article VIII, Sections 1-b(c), 1-b(d), and 1-d-1, of this constitution. The Legislature by general law may define residence homestead for purposes of this section.

(d) Except as otherwise provided by this subsection, if a person receives the residence homestead exemption prescribed by Subsection (c) of this section for homesteads of persons sixty-five (65) years of age or older, the total amount of ad valorem taxes imposed on that homestead for general elementary and secondary public school purposes may not be increased while it remains the residence homestead of that person or that person's spouse who receives the exemption. However, those taxes may be increased to the extent the value of the homestead is increased by improvements other than repairs or improvements made to comply with governmental requirements.

(e) The governing body of a political subdivision may exempt from ad valorem taxation a percentage of the market value of the residence homestead of a married or unmarried adult, including one living alone. The percentage may not exceed forty percent (40%) for the years 1982 through 1984, thirty percent (30%) for the years 1985 through 1987, and twenty percent (20%) in 1988 and each subsequent year. However, the amount of an exemption authorized pursuant to this subsection may not be less than Five Thousand Dollars ($5,000) unless the Legislature by general law prescribes other monetary restrictions on the amount of the exemption. An eligible adult is entitled to receive other applicable exemptions provided by law. Where ad valorem tax has previously been pledged for the payment of debt, the governing body of a political subdivision may continue to levy and collect the tax against the value of the homesteads exempted under this subsection

Article VIII — (Cont'd.)

until the debt is discharged if the cessation of the levy would impair the obligation of the contract by which the debt was created. The Legislature by general law may prescribe procedures for the administration of residence homestead exemptions.

[Note — Sec. 1-b of Art. VIII was amended to allow county, city, school district or other political subdivision to exempt not less than $3,000 of the assessed value of residence homesteads of persons 65 years and older from all ad valorem taxes levied by the subdivision. Submitted by Sixty-second Legislature (1971) and adopted in election Nov. 7, 1972. See also note under 1-c below. It was further amended to extend to unmarried persons the $3,000 ad valorem exemption on homesteads. Submitted by Sixty-third Legislature (1973) and adopted in election Nov. 6, 1973. See also Art. XVI, Secs. 50, 51 and 52. It was further amended to give added tax relief to disabled persons and persons over sixty-five and to provide for administration of property tax. It also added Subsections (c) and (d). (See also Sec. 1, Sec. 21, and Sec. 23 of Art. VIII.) Submitted by Sixty-fifth Legislature (1977) and adopted in election Nov. 7, 1978. It was again amended to add subsection (e) to authorize political subdivisions to provide property tax relief for owners of residence homesteads and changing certain property tax administrative procedures. (See also Sec. 21, Subsection (c) of Art. VIII.) Submitted by Sixty-seventh Legislature (1981) and adopted in election Nov. 3, 1981.]

Sec. 1-c. Optional Provisions Relating to Sec. 1-a and Sec. 1-b — Provided, however, the terms of this resolution shall not be effective unless House Joint Resolution No. 24 is adopted by the people and in no event shall this resolution go into effect until January 1, 1951.

[Note — Sec. 1-b and Sec. 1-c were added because of an oversight in writing the text of Sec. 1-a (adopted by joint resolution at an earlier date) which would have abolished the $3,000 homestead exemption under the state school tax on adoption of Sec. 1-a by the people. Submitted by the Fiftieth Legislature (1947) and adopted in election Nov. 2, 1948.]

Sec. 1-d. Taxation of Agricultural Land — (a) All land owned by natural persons which is designated for agricultural use in accordance with the provisions of this section shall be assessed for all tax purposes on the consideration of only those factors relative to such agricultural use. "Agricultural use" means the raising of livestock or growing of crops, fruit, flowers, and other products of the soil under natural conditions as a business venture for profit, which business is the primary occupation and source of income of the owner.

(b) For each assessment year the owner wishes to qualify his land under provisions of this section as designated for agricultural use he shall file with the local tax assessor a sworn statement in writing describing the use to which the land is devoted.

(c) Upon receipt of the sworn statement in writing the local tax assessor shall determine whether or not such land qualifies for the designation as to agricultural use as defined herein and in the event it so qualifies he shall designate such land as being for agricultural use and assess the land accordingly.

(d) Such local tax assessor may inspect the land and require such evidence of use and source of income as may be necessary or useful in determining whether or not the agricultural use provision of this article applies.

(e) No land may qualify for the designation provided for in this act unless for at least three (3) successive years immediately preceding the assessment date the land has been devoted exclusively for agricultural use, or unless the land has been continuously developed for agriculture during such time.

(f) Each year during which the land is designated for agricultural use, the local tax assessor shall note on his records the valuation which would have been made had the land not qualified for such designation under this section. If designated land is subsequently diverted to a purpose other than that of agricultural use, or is sold, the land shall be subject to an additional tax. The additional tax shall equal the difference between taxes paid or payable, hereunder, and the amount of tax payable for the preceding three years had the land been otherwise assessed. Until paid, there shall be a lien for additional taxes and interest on land assessed under the provisions of this section.

(g) The valuation and assessment of any minerals or subsurface rights to minerals shall not come within the provisions of this section.

[Note — The foregoing Sec. 1-d of Art. VIII, an amendment, was added for the stated purpose of providing that all land designated for agricultural use be assessed only as such. Submitted by the Fifty-ninth Legislature (1965) and adopted in an election Nov. 8, 1966.]

Sec. 1-d-1. Open-Space Land Taxation — (a) To promote the preservation of open-space land, the legislature shall provide by general law for taxation of open-space land devoted to farm or ranch purposes on the basis of its productive capacity and may provide by general law for taxation of open-space land devoted to timber production on the basis of its productive capacity. The legislature by general law may provide eligibility limitations under this section and may impose sanctions in furtherance of the taxation policy of this section.

(b) If a property owner qualifies his land for designation for agricultural use under Section 1-d of this article, the land is subject to the provisions of Section 1-d for the year in which the designation is effective and is not subject to a law enacted under this Section 1-d-1 in that year.

[Note — The foregoing Sec. 1-d-1 of Art. VIII is an amendment to promote preservation of open-space land and to provide for taxation of production of timber thereon; also redefines use of open land for agricultural purposes and taxation thereon. Submitted by the Sixty-fifth Legislature (1977) and adopted in election Nov. 7, 1978.]

Sec. 1-e. Gradual Abolition of Ad Valorem Tax — (1) No State ad valorem taxes shall be levied upon any property within this State.

(2) All receipts from previously authorized State ad valorem taxes that are collected on or after the effective date of the 1982 amendment to this section shall be deposited to the credit of the general fund of the county collecting the taxes and may be expended for county purposes. Receipts from taxes collected before that date shall be distributed by the Legislature among institutions eligible to receive distributions under prior law. Those receipts and receipts distributed under prior law may be expended for the purposes provided under prior law or for repair and renovation of existing permanent improvements.

[Note — Sec. 1-e of Art. VIII was added to provide for the gradual abolition of the ad valorem tax for all state purposes except those that were listed under Art. VII, Sec. 17 (which was repealed by constitutional amendment in an election Nov. 2, 1982) for certain institutions of higher education and for pension funds for Confederate veterans and their widows, and for Texas Rangers and their widows. Submitted by the Sixtieth Legislature (1967) and adopted in an election Nov. 5, 1968. Sec. 1-e was amended to abolish the state property tax and to add Subsection (2), which is self-explanatory. Submitted by Called Session of the Sixty-seventh Legislature (1982) and adopted in election Nov. 2, 1982. (See also Art. III, Sec. 51 and Art. XVI, Sec. 66.)]

Sec. 1-f. Ad Valorem Tax Relief — The legislature by law may provide for the preservation of cultural, historical, or natural history resources by:

(1) granting exemptions or other relief from state ad valorem taxes on appropriate property so designated in the manner prescribed by law; and

(2) authorizing political subdivisions to grant exemptions or other relief from ad valorem taxes on appropriate property so designated by the political subdivision in the manner prescribed by general law.

[Note — Sec. 1-f of Art. VIII was added to authorize tax relief to preserve certain cultural, historical or natural history resources. Submitted by the Sixty-fifth Legislature (1977) and adopted in election Nov. 8, 1977.]

Sec. 1-g. Tax Relief to Encourage Development and Improvement of Property — (a) The legislature by general law may authorize cities, towns, and other taxing units to grant exemptions or other relief from ad valorem taxes on property located in a reinvestment zone for the purpose of encouraging development or redevelopment and improvement of the property.

(b) The Legislature by general law may authorize an incorporated city or town to issue bonds or notes to finance the development or redevelopment of an unproductive, underdeveloped, or blighted area within the city or town and to pledge for repayment of those bonds or notes increases in ad valorem tax revenues imposed on property in the area by the city or town and other political subdivisions.

[Note — Sec. 1-g of Art. VIII was added to encourage development and improvement of certain areas through tax relief. Submitted by the Sixty-seventh Legislature (1981) and adopted in election Nov. 3, 1981.]

Sec. 1-h. Validation of Assessment Ratio — Sec. 26.03, Tax Code, is validated as of January 1, 1980.

[Note — Sec. 1-h of Art. VIII, an amendment, was added to give validation date of Sec. 26.03 of the Tax Code. Submitted by Called Session of the Sixty-seventh Legislature (1982) and adopted in election Nov. 2, 1982.]

Sec. 2. Occupation Taxes Equal and Uniform; Exemptions Therefrom — (a) All occupation taxes shall be equal and uniform upon the same class of subjects within the limits of the authority levying the tax; but the Legislature may, by general laws, exempt from taxation public property used

Article VIII — (Cont'd.)

for public purposes; actual places of religious worship, also any property owned by a church or by a strictly religious society for the exclusive use as a dwelling place for the ministry of such church or religious society, and which yields no revenue whatever to such church or religious society; provided that such exemption shall not extend to more property than is reasonably necessary for a dwelling place and in no event more than one acre of land; places of burial not held for private or corporate profit; solar or wind-powered energy devices; all buildings used exclusively and owned by persons or associations of persons for school purposes and the necessary furniture of all schools and property used exclusively and reasonably necessary in conducting any association engaged in promoting the religious, educational and physical development of boys, girls, young men or young women operating under a State or National organization of like character; also, the endowment funds of such institutions of learning and religion not used with a view to profit; and when the same are invested in bonds or mortgages, or in land or other property which has been and shall hereafter be bought in by such institutions under foreclosure sales made to satisfy or protect such bonds or mortgages, that such exemption of such land and property shall continue only for two years after the purchase of the same at such sale by such institutions and no longer, and institutions of purely public charity; and all laws exempting property from taxation other than the property mentioned in this Section shall be null and void.

(b) The Legislature may, by general law, exempt property owned by a disabled veteran or by the surviving spouse and surviving minor children of a disabled veteran. A disabled veteran is a veteran of the armed services of the United States who is classified as disabled by the Veterans Administration or by a successor to that agency; or the military service in which he served. A veteran who is certified as having a disability of less than 10 per cent is not entitled to an exemption. A veteran having a disability rating of not less than 10 per cent nor more than 30 per cent may be granted an exemption from taxation for property valued at up to $1,500. A veteran having a disability rating of more than 30 per cent but not more than 50 per cent may be granted an exemption from taxation for property valued at up to $2,000. A veteran having a disability rating of more than 50 per cent but not more than 70 per cent may be granted an exemption from taxation for property valued at up to $2,500. A veteran who has a disability rating of more than 70 per cent, or a veteran who has a disability rating of not less than 10 per cent and has attained the age of 65, or a disabled veteran whose disability consists of the loss or loss of use of one or more limbs, total blindness in one or both eyes, or paraplegia, may be granted an exemption from taxation for property valued at up to $3,000. The spouse and children of any member of the United States Armed Forces who loses his life while on active duty will be granted an exemption from taxation for property valued at up to $2,500. A deceased disabled veteran's surviving spouse and children may be granted an exemption which in the aggregate is equal to the exemption to which the decedent was entitled at the time he died.

[Note — Sec. 2 of Art. VIII has been amended four times as follows: (1) Adding clause with reference to endowment fund. Submitted by the Twenty-ninth Legislature (1905); ratified Nov. 6, 1906, and proclaimed adopted Jan. 7, 1907. (2) Permitting exemption of ministers' dwellings and certain other property of religious organizations, the original amendment having provided only for exemption for "actual places of worship." Submitted by the Fortieth Legislature (1927); ratified Nov. 6, 1928; proclaimed Feb. 6, 1929. (3) To allow certain tax exemptions to disabled veterans, their surviving spouses and surviving minor children and to survivors of members of the armed forces who lose their life while on active duty. Submitted by the Sixty-second Legislature (1971) and adopted in an election Nov. 7, 1972. (4) Authorizing Legislature to exempt from taxation solar and wind-powered energy devices. Submitted by the Sixty-fifth Legislature (1977) and adopted in election Nov. 7, 1978.]

Sec. 3. **Taxes to Be Collected for Public Purposes Only** — Taxes shall be levied and collected by general laws and for public purposes only.

Sec. 4. **Power to Tax Corporations Not to Be Surrendered** — The power to tax corporations and corporate property shall not be surrendered or suspended by act of the Legislature, by any contract or grant to which the State shall be a party.

Sec. 5. **Railroad Taxes Due Cities and Towns** — All property of railroad companies, of whatever description lying or being within the limits of any city or incorporated town within this State, shall bear its proportionate share of municipal taxation, and if any such property shall not have been heretofore rendered, the authorities of the city or town within which it lies shall have power to require its rendition and collect the usual municipal tax thereon, as on other property lying within said municipality.

Sec. 6. **Appropriations; How Made and for What Period** —

No money shall be drawn from the Treasury but in pursuance of specific appropriations made by law; nor shall any appropriation of money be made for a longer term than two years, except by the First Legislature to assemble under this Constitution, which may make the necessary appropriations to carry on the government until the assembling of the Sixteenth Legislature.

Sec. 7. **Special Funds Not to Be Borrowed or Diverted** — The Legislature shall not have power to borrow, or in any manner divert from its purpose any special fund that may, or ought to, come into the Treasury; and shall make it penal for any person or persons to borrow, withhold or in any manner to divert from its purpose, any special fund or any part thereof.

Sec. 7-a. **Net Motor License Fees and Motor Fuel Tax Revenues Restricted, Except One Fourth of Fuel Taxes to Schools, to Highway Improvement Policing and Administration** — Subject to legislative appropriation, allocation and direction, all net revenues remaining after payment of all refunds allowed by law and expenses of collection derived from motor vehicle registration fees, and all taxes, except gross production and ad valorem taxes, on motor fuels and lubricants used to propel motor vehicles over public roadways, shall be used for the sole purpose of acquiring rights of way, constructing, maintaining, and policing such public roadways and for the administration of such laws as may be prescribed by the Legislature pertaining to the supervision of traffic and safety on such roads; and for the payment of the principal and interest on county and road district bonds or warrants voted or issued prior to January 2, 1939, and declared eligible prior to January 2, 1945, for payment out of the County and Road District Highway Fund under existing law, provided, however, that one fourth (¼) of such net revenue from the motor fuel tax shall be allocated to the Available School Fund; and, provided, however, that the net revenue derived by counties from motor vehicle registration fees shall never be less than the maximum amounts allowed to be retained by each county and the percentage allowed to be retained by each county under the laws in effect on January 1, 1945. Nothing contained herein shall be construed as authorizing the pledging of the State's credit for any purpose.

[Note — Sec. 7-a of Art. VIII is an amendment, restricting revenues from motor vehicle registration and motor fuel taxes to the stated purposes of highway improvement, policing and administration. Submitted by the Forty-ninth Legislature (1945), ratified in an election Nov. 5, 1946.]

Sec. 8. **Railroad Property; How Assessed** — All property of railroad companies shall be assessed, and the taxes collected in the several counties in which said property is situated, including so much of the roadbed and fixtures as shall be in each county. The rolling stock may be assessed in gross in the county where the principal office of the company is located, and the county tax paid upon it shall be apportioned as provided by general law in proportion to the distance such road may run through any such county, among the several counties through which the road passes, as part of their tax assets.

[Note — The foregoing Sec. 8 of Art. VIII, an amendment, was added to allow Legislature to provide by general law for apportionment of value of railroad rolling stock among counties for purposes of property taxation. Submitted by Sixty-ninth Legislature (1985) and adopted in an election Nov. 4, 1986.]

Sec. 9. **Rate of State and Municipal Taxation** — The State tax on property, exclusive of the tax necessary to pay the public debt, and of the taxes provided for the benefit of the public free school, shall never exceed thirty-five cents (35c) on the One Hundred Dollars ($100) valuation; and no county, city or town shall levy a tax rate in excess of Eighty Cents (80c) on the One Hundred Dollars ($100) valuation in any one (1) year for general fund, permanent improvement fund, road and bridge fund and jury fund purposes; provided further that at the time the Commissioners Court meets to levy the annual tax rate for each county it shall levy whatever tax rate may be needed for the four (4) constitutional purposes; namely, general fund, permanent improvement fund, road and bridge fund and jury fund so long as the Court does not impair any outstanding bonds or other obligations and so long as the total of the foregoing tax levies does not exceed Eighty Cents (80c) on the One Hundred Dollars ($100) valuation in any one (1) year. Once the Court has levied the annual tax rate, the same shall remain in force and effect during that taxable year; and the Legislature may also authorize an additional annual ad valorem tax to be levied and collected for the further maintenance of the public roads; provided that a majority of the qualified property tax-paying voters of the county voting at an election to be held for that purpose shall vote such tax, not to exceed fifteen cents (15c) on the One Hundred Dollars ($100) valuation of the property subject to taxation in such county. Any county may put all tax money collected by the county into one general fund, without regard to the purpose or source of each tax. And the Legislature may

Article VIII — (Cont'd.)

pass local laws for the maintenance of the public roads and highways, without the local notice required for special or local laws. This section shall not be construed as a limitation of powers delegated to counties, cities or towns by any other section or sections of this Constitution.

[Note — The foregoing Sec. 9 of Art. VIII has been amended seven times as follows: (1) To lower State tax rate from 50c to 35c, a separate State school tax having been provided by companion amendment, Sec. 3 of Art. VII. Submitted by Eighteenth Legislature (1883), ratified in an election Aug. 14, 1883, and declared adopted Sept. 25, 1883. (2) To authorize Legislature to provide for a 15c local road tax. Submitted by Twenty-first Legislature (1889), ratified in an election Nov. 3, 1890, and declared adopted Dec. 19, 1890. (3) To authorize 15c tax for jurors. Submitted by Twenty-ninth Legislature (1905), ratified in an election Nov. 6, 1906, and declared adopted Jan. 7, 1907. (4) Providing that County Commissioners "may re-allocate the foregoing county taxes by changing the rates provided for any of the foregoing purposes" if approved by "a majority of the qualified property taxpaying voters," but restricting the period to six years, and restricting total to 80c on the $100 valuation. Submitted by Forty-eighth Legislature and adopted in an election Nov. 7, 1944. (5) Abolishing ad valorem tax for State general revenue fund purposes, and making other provisions. (See Sec. 1-a of Art. VIII and note thereon.) Submitted by Fiftieth Legislature (1947) and adopted in election Nov. 2, 1948. (6) Giving Commissioners Court authority to levy whatever sums may be necessary for general fund purposes, permanent improvement fund purposes, road and bridge purposes and jury purposes, so long as total of these tax rates does not exceed 80c on the $100 valuation in any one year. Submitted by Fifty-fourth Legislature (1955) and adopted in election Nov. 6, 1956. (7) To allow counties to put all county taxes into one general fund. Submitted by Sixtieth Legislature (1967) and adopted in election Nov. 11, 1967.]

Sec. 10. Taxes Not to Be Released Except by Two-Thirds Vote of Each House — The Legislature shall have no power to release the inhabitants of, or property in, any county, city or town, from the payment of taxes levied for State or county purposes, unless in case of great public calamity in any such county, city or town, when such release may be made by a vote of two-thirds of each house of the Legislature.

Sec. 11. Where Property Is to Be Assessed — All property, whether owned by persons or corporations, shall be assessed for taxation and the taxes paid in the county where situated, but the Legislature may by a two-thirds vote authorize the payment of taxes of non-residents of counties to be made at the office of the Comptroller of Public Accounts. And all lands and other property not rendered for taxation by the owner thereof shall be assessed at its fair value by the proper officer.

[Note — Sec. 12 of Art. VIII, relating to unorganized counties, was deleted by constitutional amendment in election Aug. 5, 1969.]

Sec. 13. Tax Sales; Tax Deeds; Redemptions — Provision shall be made by the first Legislature for the speedy sale, without the necessity of a suit in court, of a sufficient portion of all lands and other property for the taxes due thereon, and every year thereafter for the sale, in like manner, of all lands and other property upon which the taxes have not been paid; and the deed of conveyance to the purchaser for all lands and other property thus sold shall be held to vest a good and perfect title in the purchaser thereof, subject to be impeached only for actual fraud; provided, that the former owner shall within two years from date of filing for record of purchaser's deed have the right to redeem the land upon the following basis:

(1) Within the first year of the redemption period upon the payment of the amount of money paid for the land, including one ($1) dollar tax deed recording fee and all taxes, penalties, interest and costs plus not exceeding twenty-five (25%) percent of the aggregate total;

(2) Within the last year of the redemption period upon the payment of the amount of money paid for the land, including one ($1) dollar tax deed recording fee and all taxes, penalties, interest and costs paid plus not exceeding fifty (50%) percent of the aggregate total.

[Note — The foregoing Sec. 13 of Art. VIII was amended to insert the provisions for redemption given above for the original clause, which provided for "double the amount of money paid for the land" to be paid by the original owner for redemption. Submitted by the Forty-second Legislature (1931), and adopted in an election Nov. 8, 1932. Proclaimed July 26, 1933.]

Sec. 14. County Tax Assessor and Collector — Except as provided in Sec. 16 of this Article, there shall be elected by the qualified electors of each county an Assessor and Collector of Taxes, who shall hold his office for four years and until his successor is elected and qualified; and such Asses-

sor and Collector of Taxes shall perform all the duties with respect to assessing property for the purpose of taxation and of collecting taxes as may be prescribed by the Legislature.

[Note — Sec. 14 of Art. VIII was first amended to consolidate offices of Tax Assessor and Tax Collector. (See also Sec. 16.) Submitted by the Forty-second Legislature (1931), and adopted in an election Nov. 8, 1932. Proclaimed Jan. 9, 1933. It was again amended to change term of office from two to four years. Submitted by the Fifty-third Legislature (1953) and adopted in election Nov. 2, 1954.]

Sec. 15. Tax Liens and Sales — The annual assessment made upon landed property shall be a special lien thereon; and all property, both real and personal, belonging to any delinquent taxpayer shall be liable to seizure and sale for the payment of all the taxes and penalties due by such delinquent, and such property may be sold for the payment of the taxes and penalties due by such delinquent, under such regulations as the Legislature may provide.

Sec. 16. Sheriff to Be County Tax Assessor-Collector in Some Counties — The Sheriff of each county, in addition to his other duties, shall be the Assessor and Collector of Taxes therefor. But in counties having ten thousand (10,000) or more inhabitants, to be determined by the last preceding census of the United States, an Assessor and Collector of Taxes shall be elected, as provided in Sec. 14 of this Article and shall hold office for four years and until his successor shall be elected and qualified.

[Note — Sec. 16 of Art. VIII was first amended to harmonize with section consolidating offices of Assessor and Collector of Taxes. (See also Sec. 14.) Submitted by the Forty-second Legislature (1931) and adopted in an election Nov. 8, 1932. Proclaimed Jan. 9, 1933. It was again amended to change term of office from two to four years. Submitted by the Fifty-third Legislature (1953) and adopted in election Nov. 2, 1954.]

Sec. 16-a. Assessor-Collector of Taxes in Counties of Less Than Ten Thousand — In any county having a population of less than ten thousand (10,000) inhabitants, as determined by last preceding census of the United States, the Commissioners' Court may submit to the qualified property taxpaying voters of such county at an election the question of adding an Assessor-Collector of Taxes to the list of authorized county officials. If a majority of such voters voting in such election shall approve of adding an Assessor-Collector of Taxes to such list, then such official shall be elected at the next General Election for such Constitutional term of office as is provided for other Tax Assessor-Collectors in this State.

[Note — The foregoing Sec. 16-a of Art. VIII, an amendment, was added for the stated purpose of providing for a Tax Assessor-Collector in counties of less than 10,000 population. Submitted by the Fifty-third Legislature (1953) and adopted in an election Nov. 2, 1954.]

Sec. 17. Power of Legislature as to Taxes — The specification of the objects and subjects of taxation shall not deprive the Legislature of the power to require other subjects or objects to be taxed, in such manner as may be consistent with the principles of taxation fixed in this Constitution.

Sec. 18. Equalization of Taxes — (a) The Legislature shall provide for equalizing, as near as may be, the valuation of all property subject to or rendered for taxation and may also provide for the classification of all lands with reference to their value in the several counties.

(b) A single appraisal within each county of all property subject to ad valorem taxation by the county and all other taxing units located therein shall be provided by general law. The Legislature, by general law, may authorize appraisals outside a county when political subdivisions are situated in more than one county or when two or more counties elect to consolidate appraisal services.

(c) The Legislature, by general law, shall provide for a single board of equalization for each appraisal entity consisting of qualified persons residing within the territory appraised by that entity. Members of the board of equalization may not be elected officials of the county or of the governing body of a taxing unit.

(d) The Legislature shall prescribe by general law the methods, timing and administrative process for implementing the requirements of this section.

[Note — Sec. 18 of Art. VIII was amended to provide for a single appraisal and a single board of equalization for ad valorem tax purposes. Submitted by the Sixty-sixth Legislature (1979) and adopted in election Nov. 4, 1980.]

Sec. 19. Farm Products in the Hands of the Producer Exempt From All Taxation — Farm products, livestock, and poultry in the hands of the producer, and family supplies for home and farm use, are exempt from all taxation until otherwise directed by a two-thirds vote of all the members *elect to both houses of the Legislature.

Article VIII — (Cont'd.); Article IX

*Explanatory Note — Expressed thus in official draft of Constitution.

[Note — The foregoing Sec. 19 of Art. VIII, an amendment, was added for the stated purpose of exempting farm products from taxation. Submitted by the Sixteenth Legislature (1879); ratified in an election Sept. 2, 1879, and declared adopted Oct. 14, 1879. It was amended to change the wording to include livestock and poultry with farm products as exempt from taxation. Submitted by the Sixty-seventh Legislature (1981) and adopted in election Nov. 3, 1981.]

Sec. 19-a. **Farm Implements Exempt From Taxation** — Implements of husbandry that are used in the production of farm or ranch products are exempt from ad valorem taxation.

[Note — The foregoing Sec. 19-a of Art. VIII, an amendment, was added to exempt implements of farm husbandry from ad valorem taxation. Submitted by Called Session of the Sixty-seventh Legislature (1982) and adopted in election Nov. 2, 1982.]

Sec. 20. **Limiting Ad Valorem Tax Assessment; Discount for Prompt Payment of Taxes** — No property of any kind in this State shall ever be assessed for ad valorem taxes at a greater value than its fair cash market value nor shall any Board of Equalization of any governmental or political subdivision or taxing district within this State fix the value of any property for tax purposes at more than its fair cash market value; provided, that in order to encourage the prompt payment of taxes, the Legislature shall have the power to provide that the taxpayer shall be allowed by the State and all governmental and political subdivisions and taxing districts of the State a three per cent discount on ad valorem taxes due the State or due any governmental or political subdivision or taxing district of the State if such taxes are paid ninety days before the date when they would otherwise become delinquent; and the taxpayer shall be allowed a two per cent discount on said taxes if paid sixty days before said taxes would become delinquent; and the taxpayer shall be allowed a one per cent discount if said taxes are paid thirty days before they would otherwise become delinquent. This amendment shall be effective Jan. 1, 1939. The Legislature shall pass necessary laws for the proper administration of this Section.

[Note — The foregoing Sec. 20 of Art. VIII, an amendment, was added (1) to restrict assessed value to true market value, and (2) to provide for stated discounts for prepayment of taxes. Adopted in an election Aug. 23, 1937.]

Sec. 21. **Limitation on Property Taxes** — (a) Subject to any exceptions prescribed by general law, the total amount of property taxes imposed by a political subdivision in any year may not exceed the total amount of property taxes imposed by that subdivision in the preceding year unless the governing body of the subdivision gives notice of its intent to consider an increase in taxes and holds a public hearing on the proposed increase before it increases those total taxes. The legislature shall prescribe by law the form, content, timing, and methods of giving the notice and the rules for the conduct of the hearing.

(b) In calculating the total amount of taxes imposed in the current year for the purposes of Subsection (a) of this section, the taxes on property in territory added to the political subdivision since the preceding year and on new improvements that were not taxable in the preceding year are excluded. In calculating the total amount of taxes imposed in the preceding year for the purposes of Subsection (a) of this section, the taxes imposed on real property that is not taxable by the subdivision in the current year are excluded.

(c) The Legislature by general law shall require that, subject to reasonable exceptions, a property owner be given notice of a revaluation of his property and a reasonable estimate of the amount of taxes that would be imposed on his property if the total amount of property taxes for the subdivision were not increased according to any law enacted pursuant to Subsection (a) of this section. The notice must be given before the procedures required in Subsection (a) are instituted.

[Note—The foregoing Sec. 21 of Art. VIII, an amendment, was added to limit increases in property revaluation and to prescribe method of giving notice before property revaluated. (See also Sec. 1, Sec. 1-b and Sec. 23 of Art. VIII.) Submitted by the Sixty-fifth Legislature (1977) and adopted in election Nov. 7, 1978. It was further amended to change wording of administrative procedures in notifying property owners. (See also Subsection (e) of Section 1-b of Art. VIII.) Submitted by the Sixty-seventh Legislature (1981) and adopted in election Nov. 3, 1981.]

Sec. 22. **State Tax Revenues** — (a) In no biennium shall the rate of growth of appropriations from state tax revenues not dedicated by this constitution exceed the estimat-ed rate of growth of the state's economy. The Legislature shall provide by general law procedures to implement this subsection.

(b) If the Legislature by adoption of a resolution approved by a record vote of a majority of the members of each house finds that an emergency exists and identifies the nature of the emergency, the Legislature may provide for appropriations in excess of the amount authorized by Subsection (a) of this section. The excess authorized under this subsection may not exceed the amount specified in the resolution.

(c) In no case shall appropriations exceed revenues as provided in Article III, Sec. 49-a, of this constitution. Nothing in this section shall be construed to alter, amend, or repeal Article III, Sec. 49-a, of this constitution.

[Note—The foregoing Sec. 22 of Art. VIII, an amendment, was added to limit the rate of growth of appropriations from state tax revenues; and to provide for emergency spending by state. (See also Sec. 49-a of Art. III. Submitted by the Sixty-fifth Legislature (1977) and adopted in election Nov. 7, 1978.]

Sec. 23. **No Statewide Real Property Appraisal** — (a) There shall be no statewide appraisal of real property for ad valorem tax purposes; however, this shall not preclude formula distribution of tax revenues to political subdivisions of the state.

(b) Administrative and judicial enforcement of uniform standards and procedures for appraisal of property for ad valorem tax purposes, as prescribed by general law, shall originate in the county where the tax is imposed, except that the Legislature may provide by general law for political subdivisions with boundaries extending outside the county.

[Note — The foregoing Sec. 23 of Art. VIII, an amendment, was added to prohibit a statewide appraisal of real property for ad valorem tax purposes; but allows local subdivisions to administer tax rate. (See also Sec. 1, Sec. 1-b, Sec. 21 of Art. VIII.) Submitted by the Sixty-fifth Legislature (1977) and adopted in election Nov. 7, 1978.]

ARTICLE IX — COUNTIES

Sec. 1. **Creation and Organization of Counties; Changing of County Lines** — The Legislature shall have power to create counties for the convenience of the people, subject to the following provisions:

First. In the territory of the State exterior to all counties now existing, no new counties shall be created with a less area than 900 square miles in a square form, unless prevented by pre-existing boundary lines. Should the State lines render this impracticable in border counties, the area may be less. The territory referred to may, at any time, in whole or in part, be divided into counties in advance of population and attached for judicial and land surveying purposes to the most convenient organized county or counties.

Second. Within the territory of any county or counties now existing, no new county shall be created with a less area than 700 square miles, nor shall any such county now existing be reduced to a less area than 700 square miles. No new counties shall be created so as to approach nearer than twelve miles of the county seat of any county from which it may, in whole or in part, be taken. Counties of a less area than 900, but of 700 or more square miles, within counties now existing, may be created by a two-thirds vote of each house of the Legislature, taken by yeas and nays, and entered on the journals. Any county now existing may be reduced to an area of not less than 700 square miles by a like two-thirds vote. When any part of a county is stricken off and attached to or created into another county, the part stricken off shall be holden for and obliged to pay its proportion of all the liabilities then existing of the county from which it was taken, in such manner as may be prescribed by law.

Third. No part of any existing county shall be detached from it and attached to another existing county until the proposition for such change shall have been submitted, in such manner as may be provided by law, to a vote of the electors of both counties, and shall have received a majority of those voting on the question in each.

Sec. 1-a. **Regulation of Travel on Gulf Coast Beaches** — The Legislature may authorize the governing body of any county bordering on the Gulf of Mexico or the tidewater limits thereof to regulate and restrict the speed, parking and travel of motor vehicles on beaches available to the public by virtue of public right and the littering of such beaches.

Nothing in this amendment shall increase the rights of any riparian or littoral landowner with regard to beaches available to the public by virtue of public right or submerged lands.

The Legislature may enact any laws not inconsistent with this Section which it may deem necessary to permit said counties to implement, enforce and administer the provisions contained herein.

Article IX — (Cont'd.)

[Note — The foregoing Sec. 1-a of Art. IX, an amendment, was added to authorize regulation of travel on Gulf Coast beaches open to the public. Submitted by the Fifty-seventh Legislature (1961) and adopted in election Nov. 6, 1962.]

County Seats

Sec. 2. **How County Seats Are Created and Changed** — The Legislature shall pass laws regulating the manner of removing county seats, but no county seat situated within five miles of the geographical center of the county shall be removed except by a vote of two-thirds of all electors voting on the subject. A majority of such electors, however, voting at such election, may remove a county seat from a point more than five miles from a geographical center of the county to a point within five miles of such center, in either case the center to be determined by a certificate from the Commissioner of the General Land Office.

[Note — Sec. 3 of Art. IX, relating to home rule, was deleted by constitutional amendment in election Aug. 5, 1969.]

Sec. 4. **County-Wide Hospital Districts** — The Legislature may by law authorize the creation of county-wide Hospital Districts in counties having a population in excess of 190,000 and in Galveston County, with power to issue bonds for the purchase, acquisition, construction, maintenance and operation of any county-owned hospital, or where the hospital system is jointly operated by a county and city within the county, and to provide for the transfer to the county-wide hospital district of the title to any land, buildings or equipment, jointly or separately owned, and for the assumption by the district of any outstanding bonded indebtedness theretofore issued by any county or city for the establishment of hospitals or hospital facilities; to levy a tax not to exceed seventy-five (75c) cents on the One Hundred ($100.00) Dollars valuation of all taxable property within such district, provided, however, that such district shall be approved at an election held for that purpose, and that only qualified, property taxpaying voters in such county shall vote therein; provided further, that such hospital district shall assume full responsibility for providing medical and hospital care to needy inhabitants of the county, and thereafter such county and cities therein shall not levy any other tax for hospital purposes; and provided further that should the Legislature enact enabling laws in anticipation of the adoption of this amendment, such acts shall not be invalid because of their anticipatory character.

[Note — The foregoing Sec. 4 of Art. IX, an amendment, was added to the Constitution for the purpose of providing for county-wide hospital districts. Submitted by the Fifty-third Legislature (1953) and adopted in election Nov. 2, 1954.]

Sec. 5 (a). The Legislature may by law authorize the creation of two hospital districts, one to be coextensive with and have the same boundaries as the incorporated City of Amarillo, as such boundaries now exist or as they may hereafter be lawfully extended, and the other to be coextensive with Wichita County.

If such district or districts are created, they may be authorized to levy a tax not to exceed Seventy-five Cents (75c) on the One Hundred Dollars ($100.00) valuation of taxable property within the district; provided, however no tax may be levied until approved by a majority vote of the participating resident qualified property taxpaying voters who have duly rendered their property for taxation. The maximum rate of tax may be changed at subsequent elections so long as obligations are not impaired, and not to exceed the maximum limit of Seventy-five Cents (75c) per One Hundred Dollars ($100.00) valuation, and no election shall be required by subsequent changes in the boundaries of the City of Amarillo.

If such tax is authorized, no political subdivision or municipality within or having the same boundaries as the district may levy a tax for medical or hospital care for needy individuals, nor shall they maintain or erect hospital facilities, but the district shall by resolution assume all such responsibilities and shall assume all of the liabilities and obligations (including bonds and warrants) of such subdivisions or municipalities or both. The maximum tax rate submitted shall be sufficient to discharge such obligations, liabilities, and responsibilities, and to maintain and operate the hospital system, and the Legislature may authorize the district to issue tax bonds for the purpose of the purchase, construction, acquisition, repair or renovation of improvements and initially equipping the same, and such bonds shall be payable from said Seventy-five Cents (75c) tax. The Legislature shall provide for transfer of title to properties to the district.

b. The Legislature may by law permit the County of Potter (in which the City of Amarillo is partially located) to render financial aid to that district by paying a part of the expenses of operating and maintaining the system and paying a part of the debts of the district (whether assumed or created by the district) and may authorize the levy of a tax not to exceed Ten Cents (10c) per One Hundred Dollars ($100.00) valuation (in addition to other taxes permitted by this Constitution) upon all property within the county but without the City of Amarillo at the time such levy is made for such purposes. If such tax is authorized, the district shall by resolution assume the responsibilities, obligations, and liabilities of the county in the manner and to the extent hereinabove provided for political subdivisions having boundaries coextensive with the district, and the county shall not thereafter levy taxes (other than herein provided) for hospital purposes nor for providing hospital care for needy individuals of the county.

c. The Legislature may by law authorize the creation of a hospital district within Jefferson County, the boundaries of which shall include only the area comprising the Jefferson County Drainage District No. 7 and the Port Arthur Independent School District, as such boundaries existed on the first day of January, 1957, with the power to issue bonds for the sole purpose of purchasing a site for, and the construction and initial equipping of, a hospital system, and with the power to levy a tax of not to exceed Seventy-five Cents (75c) on the One Hundred Dollars ($100) valuation of property therein for the purpose of paying the principal and interest on such bonds.

The creation of such hospital district shall not be final until approved at an election by a majority of the resident property taxpaying voters voting at said election who have duly rendered their property for taxation upon the tax rolls of either said Drainage or said School District, nor shall such bonds be issued or such tax be levied until so approved by such voters.

The district shall not have the power to levy any tax for maintenance or operation of the hospital or facilities, but shall contract with other political subdivisions of the state or private individuals, associations, or corporations for such purposes.

If the district hereinabove authorized is finally created, no other hospital district may be created embracing any part of the territory within its boundaries, but the Legislature by law may authorize the creation of a hospital district incorporating herein the remainder of Jefferson County, having the powers and duties and with the limitations presently provided by Art. IX, Section 4, of the Constitution of Texas, except that such district shall be confirmed at an election wherein the resident qualified property taxpaying voters who have duly rendered their property within such proposed district for taxation on the county rolls, shall be authorized to vote. A majority of those participating in the election voting in favor of the district shall be necessary for its confirmation and for bonds to be issued.

[Note — The foregoing Sec. 5 of Art. IX, an amendment, was added to provide for the creation of special hospital districts and authorizing the levying of taxes for their support. Submitted by the Fifty-fifth Legislature (1957) and adopted in an election Nov. 4, 1958.]

Sec. 6. **Lamar County Hospital District Abolished** — On the effective date of this Amendment, the Lamar County Hospital District is abolished. The Commissioners Court of Lamar County may provide for the transfer or for the disposition of the assets of the Lamar County Hospital District.

[Note — the foregoing Sec. 6 of Art. IX, an amendment, was added to authorize creation of a hospital district in Lamar County and authorizing the levying of taxes for its support. Submitted by the Fifty-sixth Legislature (1959) and adopted in an election Nov. 8, 1960. It was amended to abolish the hospital district. Submitted by the Sixty-second Legislature (1971) and adopted in an election Nov. 7, 1972.]

Sec. 7. **Hidalgo County Hospital District; Creation, Tax Rate**— The Legislature may by law authorize the creation of a Hospital District coextensive with Hidalgo County, having the powers and duties and with the limitations presently provided in Art. IX, Sec. 5 (a), of the Constitution of Texas, as it applies to Hidalgo County, except that the maximum rate of tax that the said Hidalgo County Hospital District may be authorized to levy shall be ten cents (10c) per One Hundred Dollars ($100) valuation of taxable property within the District subject to district taxation.

[Note — The foregoing Sec. 7 of Art. IX, an amendment, was added to authorize creation of a hospital district in Hidalgo County and authorizing the levying of taxes for its support. Submitted by the Fifty-sixth Legislature (1959) and adopted in an election Nov. 8, 1960.]

Sec. 8. **Comanche County Hospital District; Creation, Tax Rate** — The Legislature may by law authorize the creation of a Hospital District to be coextensive with the limits of County Commissioners Precinct No. 4 of Comanche County, Texas.

If such District is created, it may be authorized to levy a tax not to exceed seventy-five cents (75c) on the One Hun-

Article IX — (Cont'd.)

dred Dollar ($100) valuation of taxable property within the District; provided, however, no tax may be levied until approved by a majority vote of the participating resident qualified property taxpaying voters who have duly rendered their property for taxation. The maximum rate of tax may be changed at subsequent elections so long as obligations are not impaired, and not to exceed the maximum limit of seventy-five cents (75c) per One Hundred Dollar ($100) valuation, and no election shall be required by subsequent changes in the boundaries of the Commissioners Precinct No. 4 of Comanche County.

If such tax is authorized, no political subdivision or municipality within or having the same boundaries as the District may levy a tax for medical or hospital care for needy individuals, nor shall they maintain or erect hospital facilities, but the District shall by resolution assume all such responsibilities and shall assume all of the liabilities and obligations (including bonds and warrants) of such subdivisions or municipalities or both. The maximum tax rate submitted shall be sufficient to discharge such obligations, liabilities, and responsibilities and to maintain and operate the hospital system, and the Legislature may authorize the District to issue tax bonds for the purpose of the purchase, construction, acquisition, repair or renovation of improvements and initially equipping the same, and such bonds shall be payable from said seventy-five cents (75c) tax. The Legislature shall provide for transfer of title to properties to the District.

(b) The Legislature may by law permit the County of Comanche to render financial aid to that District by paying a part of the expenses of operating and maintaining the system and paying a part of the debts of the District (whether assumed or created by the District) and may authorize the levy of a tax not to exceed ten cents (10c) per One Hundred Dollar ($100) valuation (in addition to other taxes permitted by this Constitution) upon all property within the County but without the County Commissioners Precinct No. 4 of Comanche County at the time such levy is made for such purposes. If such tax is authorized, the District shall by resolution assume the responsibilities, obligations and liabilities of the County in the manner and to the extent hereinabove provided for political subdivisions having boundaries coextensive with the District, and the County shall not hereafter levy taxes (other than herein provided) for hospital purposes nor for providing hospital care for needy individuals of the county.

(c) Should the Legislature enact enabling laws in anticipation of the adoption of this amendment, such Acts shall not be invalid because of their anticipatory character.

[Note — The foregoing Sec. 8 of Art. IX, an amendment, was added to authorize creation of a hospital district in Comanche County and authorizing the levying of taxes for its support. Submitted by the Fifty-sixth Legislature (1959) and adopted in an election Nov. 8, 1960.]

Sec. 9. The Legislature may by law provide for the creation, establishment, maintenance and operation of hospital districts composed of one or more counties or all or any part of one or more counties with power to issue bonds for the purchase, construction, acquisition, repair or renovation of buildings and improvements and equipping same, for hospital purposes; providing for the transfer to the hospital district of the title to any land, buildings, improvements and equipment located wholly within the district which may be jointly or separately owned by any city, town or county, providing that any district so created shall assume full responsibility for providing medical and hospital care for its needy inhabitants and assume the outstanding indebtedness incurred by cities, towns and counties for hospital purposes prior to the creation of the district, if same are located wholly within its boundaries, and a pro rata portion of such indebtedness based upon the then last approved tax assessment rolls of the included cities, towns and counties if less than all the territory thereof is included within the district boundaries; providing that after its creation no other municipality or political subdivision shall have the power to levy taxes or issue bonds or other obligations for hospital purposes or for providing medical care within the boundaries of the district; providing for the levy of annual taxes at a rate not to exceed seventy-five cents (75c) on the one hundred dollar valuation of all taxable property within such district for the purpose of meeting the requirements of the district's bonds, the indebtedness assumed by it and its maintenance and operating expenses, providing that such district shall not be created or such tax authorized unless approved by a majority of the qualified property taxpaying electors thereof voting at an election called for the purpose; and providing further that the support and maintenance of the district's hospital system shall never become a charge against or obligation of the State of Texas nor shall any direct appropriation be made by the Legislature for the construction, maintenance or improvement of any of the facilities of such district.

Provided, however, that no district shall be created except by act of the Legislature and then only after thirty (30)

days' public notice to the district affected, and in no event may the Legislature provide for a district to be created without the affirmative vote of a majority of the taxpaying voters in the district concerned.

The Legislature may also provide for the dissolution of hospital districts provided that a process is afforded by statute for:

(1) Determining the desire of a majority of the qualified voters within the district to dissolve it;

(2) Disposing of or transferring the assets, if any, of the district; and

(3) Satisfying the debts and bond obligations, if any, of the district, in such manner as to protect the interest of the citizens within the district, including their collective property rights in the assets and property of the district, provided, however, that any grant from federal funds, however dispensed, shall be considered an obligation to be repaid in satisfaction and provided that no election to dissolve shall be held more often than once each year. In such connection, the statute shall provide against disposal or transfer of the assets of the district except for due compensation unless such assets are transferred to another governmental agency, such as a county, embracing such district and using such transferred assets in such a way as to benefit citizens formerly within the district.

[Note—The foregoing Sec. 9 of Art. IX, an amendment, was added to provide for the creation of special hospital districts and authorizing the levying of taxes for their support. Submitted by the Fifty-seventh Legislature (1961) and adopted in an election Nov. 6, 1962. It was further amended to provide method of dissolution of hospital districts. Submitted by the Fifty-ninth Legislature (1965) and adopted in election Nov. 8, 1966.]

Sec. 9A. The Legislature by law may determine the health care services a hospital district is required to provide, the requirements a resident must meet to qualify for services, and any other relevant provisions necessary to regulate the provision of health care to residents.

[Note — Sec. 9a of Art. IX, an amendment, was added to authorize Legislature to regulate the provision of health care by hospital districts. Submitted by Sixty-ninth Legislature (1985) and adopted in an election Nov. 5, 1985.]

[Note — Sec. 10 of Art. IX is blank.]

Sec. 11. The Legislature may by law authorize the creation of hospital districts in Ochiltree, Castro, Hansford and Hopkins Counties, each district to be coextensive with the limits of such county.

If any such district is created, it may be authorized to levy a tax not to exceed Seventy-five Cents (75c) on the One Hundred Dollar ($100) valuation of taxable property within the district; provided, however, no tax may be levied until approved by a majority of the participating resident qualified property taxpaying voters who have duly rendered their property for taxation. The maximum rate of tax may be changed at subsequent elections so long as obligations are not impaired, and not to exceed the maximum limit of Seventy-five Cents (75c) per One Hundred Dollar ($100) valuation.

If such tax is authorized, no political subdivision or municipality within or having the same boundaries as the district may levy a tax for medical or hospital care for needy individuals, nor shall they maintain or erect hospital facilities, but the district shall by resolution assume all such responsibilities and shall assume all of the liabilities and obligations (including bonds and warrants) of such subdivisions or municipalities or both. The maximum tax rate submitted shall be sufficient to discharge obligations, liabilities, and responsibilities, and to maintain and operate the hospital system, and the Legislature may authorize the district to issue tax bonds for the purpose of the purchase, construction, acquisition, repair or renovation of improvements and initially equipping the same, and such bonds shall be payable from said Seventy-five Cent (75c) tax. The Legislature shall provide for transfer of title to properties to the district.

[Note—The foregoing Sec. 11 of Art. IX, an amendment, was added to provide for the creation of special hospital districts and to authorize the levying of taxes for their support. It is obviously misnumbered, as there is no Sec. 10 of Art. IX. Submitted by the Fifty-seventh Legislature (1961) and adopted in an election Nov. 6, 1962.]

Sec. 12. **Establishment of Airport Authorities** — The Legislature may by law provide for the creation, establishment, maintenance and operation of Airport Authorities composed of one or more counties, with power to issue general obligation bonds, revenue bonds, either or both of them, for the purchase, acquisition by the exercise of the power of eminent domain or otherwise, construction, reconstruction, repair or renovation of any airport or airports, landing fields and runways, airport buildings, hangars, facilities, equipment, fixtures, and any and all property, real or personal, necessary to operate, equip and maintain an airport; shall provide for the option by the governing body of the city or cities whose airport facilities are served by certificated airlines and whose facility or some interest therein, is proposed to be or has been acquired by the authority, to either appoint or elect a board of directors of said authority; if the directors are appointed such appointment shall be made by the County Commissioners Court after consultation with and consent of the governing body or bodies of such city or cities, and if the board of directors is elected they shall be elected by the qualified taxpaying voters of the county which chooses to elect the directors to represent that county, such directors shall serve without compensation for a term fixed by the Legislature not to exceed six (6) years, and shall be selected on the basis of the proportionate population of each county based upon the last preceding federal census, and shall be a resident or residents of such county; provide that no county shall have less than one (1) member on the board of directors; provide for the holding of an election in each county proposing the creation of an authority to be called by the Commissioners Court or Commissioners Courts, as the case may be, upon petition of five percent (5%) of the qualified taxpaying voters within the county or counties, said elections to be held on the same day if more than one county is included, provided that no more than one (1) such election may be called in a county until after the expiration of one (1) year; in the event such an election has failed, and thereafter only upon a petition of ten percent (10%) of the qualified taxpaying voters being presented to the Commissioners Court or Commissioners Courts of the county or counties in which such an election has failed, and in the event that two or more counties vote on the proposition of the creation of an authority therein, the proposition shall not be deemed to carry unless the majority of the qualified taxpaying voters in each county voting thereon vote in favor thereof; provided, however, that an Airport Authority may be created and be composed of the county or counties that vote in favor of its creation if separate propositions are submitted to the voters of each county so that they may vote for a two or more county authority or a single county authority; provide for the appointment by the board of directors of an assessor and collector of taxes in the authority, whether constituted of one or more counties, whose duty it shall be to assess all taxable property, both real and personal, and collect the taxes thereon, based upon the tax rolls approved by the board of directors, the tax to be levied not to exceed seventy-five cents (75c) per one hundred dollars ($100) assessed valuation of the property, provided, however, that the property of state regulated common carriers required by law to pay a tax upon intangible assets shall not be subject to taxation by the authority, said taxable property shall be assessed on a valuation not to exceed the market value and shall be equal and uniform throughout the authority as is otherwise provided by the Constitution; the Legislature shall authorize the purchase or acquisition by the authority of any existing airport facility publicly owned and financed and served by certificated airlines, in fee or of or any interest therein, or to enter into any lease agreement therefor, upon such terms and conditions as may be mutually agreeable to the authority and the owner of such facilities, or authorize the acquisition of same through the exercise of the power of eminent domain, and in the event such acquisition, if there are any general obligation bonds that the owner of the publicly owned airport facility has outstanding, the same shall be fully assumed by the authority and sufficient taxes levied by the authority to discharge said outstanding indebtedness; and likewise any city or owner that has outstanding revenue bonds where the revenues of the airport have been pledged or said bonds constitute a lien against the airport facilities, the authority shall assume and discharge all the obligations of the city under the ordinances and bond indentures under which said revenue bonds have been issued and sold. Any city which owns airport facilities not serving certificated airlines which are not purchased or acquired or taken over as herein provided by such authority, shall have the power to operate the same under the existing laws or as the same may hereafter be amended. Any such authority when created may be granted the power and authority to promulgate, adopt and enforce appropriate zoning regulations to protect the airport from hazards and obstructions which would interfere with the use of the airport and its facilities for landing and takeoff; an additional county or counties may be added to an existing authority if a petition of five percent (5%) of the qualified taxpaying voters is filed with and an election is called by the Commissioners Court of the county or counties seeking admission to an authority and the vote is favorable, then admission may be granted to such county or counties by the board of directors of the then existing authority upon such terms and conditions as they may agree upon and evidenced by a resolution approved by two-thirds (⅔) of the then existing board of directors, provided, however, the county or counties that may be so added to the then existing authority shall be given representation on the board of directors by adding additional directors in proportion to their population according to the last preceding federal census.

[Note—The foregoing Sec. 12 was added to provide by law for the establishment of airport authorities. Submitted by the Fifty-ninth Legislature (1965) and adopted in election Nov. 8, 1966.]

Sec. 13. **Mental Health Services** — Notwithstanding any other section of this article, the Legislature in providing for the creation, establishment, maintenance, and operation of a hospital district, shall not be required to provide that such district shall assume full responsibility for the establishment, maintenance, support, or operation of mental health services or mental retardation services including the operation of any community mental health centers, community mental retardation centers or community health and mental retardation centers which may exist or be thereafter established within the boundaries of such district, nor shall the Legislature be required to provide that such district shall assume full responsibility of public health department units and clinics and related public health activities or services, and the Legislature shall not be required to restrict the power of any municipality or political subdivision to levy taxes or issue bonds or other obligations or to expend public moneys for the establishment, maintenance, support, or operation of mental health services, mental retardation services, public health units or clinics or related public health activities or services or the operation of such community mental health or mental retardation centers within the boundaries of the hospital districts; and unless a statute creating a hospital district shall expressly prohibit participation by any entity other than the hospital district in the establishment, maintenance, or support of mental health services, mental retardation services, public health units or clinics or related public health activities within or partly within the boundaries of any hospital district, any municipality or any other political subdivision or state-supported entity within the hospital district may participate in the establishment, maintenance, and support of mental health services, mental retardation services, public health units and clinics and related public health activities and may levy taxes, issue bonds or other obligations, and expend public moneys for such purposes as provided by law.

[Note—The foregoing Sec. 13 of Art. IX, an amendment, was added to permit municipalities and other political subdivisions within hospital districts to participate in establishment, maintenance, support or operation of mental health, mental retardation or public health services. Submitted by the Sixtieth Legislature (1967) and adopted in election Nov. 11, 1967.]

ARTICLE X — RAILROADS

[Note—All of Art. X relating to railroads, except Sec. 2, was deleted by constitutional amendment in election Aug. 5, 1969.]

*Article [Sec.] 2. **Public Highways; Common Carriers; Duty of the Legislature; Fixing Rates** — Railroads heretofore constructed or which may hereafter be constructed in this State are hereby declared public highways and railroad companies common carriers. The Legislature shall pass laws to regulate railroad freight and passenger tariffs to correct abuses, and prevent unjust discrimination and extortion in the rates of freight and passenger tariffs on the different railroads in this State, and enforce the same by adequate penalties; and to the further accomplishments of these objects and purposes may provide and establish all requisite means and agencies invested with such powers as may be deemed adequate and advisable.

[Note—The foregoing *"Article Sec. 2" of Art. X is an amended section, the amendment being in the last clause which permitted establishment of the Railroad Commission of Texas. Submitted by the Twenty-first Legislature (1889), ratified in an election Nov. 4, 1890, and declared adopted Dec. 19, 1890.]

*Explanatory Note—The legislative resolution submitting this amendment erroneously used the word, "Article," instead of the usual abbreviation, "Sec." Order used above is according to official draft of the Constitution.

ARTICLE XI — MUNICIPAL CORPORATIONS

Sec. 1. **Counties Are Legal Subdivisions of the State** — The several counties of this State are hereby recognized as legal subdivisions of the State.

Sec. 2. **Public Buildings and Roads** — The construction of jails, courthouses and bridges and the establishment of county poorhouses and farms and the laying out, construction and repairing of county roads shall be provided for by general laws.

Sec. 3. **No County or Municipal Corporation Shall Become a Subscriber to the Capital Stock of Any Private Corporation or Make Any Donation to the Same** — No county, city or other municipal corporation shall hereafter become a subscriber to the capital of any private corporation or association, or make any appropriation or donation to the same, or in anywise loan its credit; but this shall not be construed to in any

Article XI — (Cont'd.); Article XII

way affect any obligation heretofore undertaken pursuant to law.

Sec. 4. Cities and Towns Having a Population of 5,000 or Less Inhabitants to Be Chartered by General Laws; Dues to Be Collected in Current Money — Cities and towns having a population of 5,000 or less may be chartered alone by general laws. They may levy, assess and collect such taxes as may be authorized by law, but no tax for any purpose shall ever be lawful for any one year which shall exceed 1½ percent of the taxable property of such city; and all taxes shall be collectible only in current money, and all licenses and occupation taxes levied, and all fines, forfeitures and penalties accruing to said cities and towns shall be collectible only in current money.

[Note—The foregoing Sec. 4 of Art. XI has been twice amended, as follows: (1) To provide that towns of 5,000 or less (instead of 10,000 or less, as provided by the original section) may be chartered alone by general law. Submitted by the Thirty-first Legislature (1909), ratified in an election Aug. 3, 1909, and declared adopted Sept. 24, 1909. (2) To authorize a maximum tax rate, in towns of 5,000 or less, of 1½ percent of taxable values in lieu of the originally specified maximum of one fourth of 1 percent. Submitted by the Thirty-sixth Legislature (1919) and adopted at election of Nov. 2, 1920.]

Sec. 5. Cities of More Than 5,000 Inhabitants May by a Majority Vote of the Qualified Voters Adopt Their Own Charter; Limitation as to Taxation and Debt — Cities having more than five thousand (5,000) inhabitants may, by a majority vote of the qualified voters of said city, at an election held for that purpose, adopt or amend their charters, subject to such limitations as may be prescribed by the Legislature, and providing that no charter or any ordinance passed under said charter shall contain any provision inconsistent with the Constitution of the State or of the general laws enacted by the Legislature of this State; said cities may levy, assess and collect such taxes as may be authorized by law or by their charters; but no tax for any purpose shall ever be lawful for any one year which shall exceed 2½ percent of the taxable property of such city, and no debt shall ever be created by any city unless at the same time provision be made to assess and collect annually a sufficient sum to pay the interest thereon and creating a sinking fund of at least 2 percent thereon; and provided, further, that no city charter shall be altered, amended or repealed oftener than every two years.

[Note—The foregoing Sec. 5 of Art. XI has been twice amended, as follows: (1) To authorize towns of more than 5,000 population (instead of more than 10,000, as provided in the original section) to be chartered by special act, and allowing in such cities a maximum tax rate of 2½ percent. Submitted by the Thirty-first Legislature (1909), ratified in an election Aug. 3, 1909, and proclaimed Sept. 24, 1909. (2) To grant home rule to cities of more than 5,000 population. Submitted by the Thirty-second Legislature (1911), adopted at election of Nov. 5, 1912, and proclaimed Dec. 30, 1912.]

Sec. 6. Municipal Taxation — Counties, cities, and towns are authorized, in such mode as may now or may hereafter be provided by law, to levy, assess and collect the taxes necessary to pay the interest and provide a sinking fund to satisfy any indebtedness heretofore legally made and undertaken; but all such taxes shall be assessed and collected separately from that levied, assessed and collected for current expenses of municipal government and shall, when levied, specify in the act of levying the purpose therefor; and such taxes may be paid in the coupons, bonds or other indebtedness for the payment of which such tax may have been levied.

Sec. 7. Taxation of Seawalls, Etc.; Restrictions and Limitations; Eminent Domain — All counties and cities bordering on the coast of the Gulf of Mexico are hereby authorized upon a vote of the majority of the resident property taxpayers voting thereon at an election called for such purpose, to levy and collect such tax for construction of seawalls, breakwaters or sanitary purposes, as may now or may hereafter be authorized by law, and may create a debt for such works and issue bonds in evidence thereof. But no debt for any purpose shall ever be incurred in any manner by any city or county unless provision is made at the time of creating the same, for levying and collecting a sufficient tax to pay the interest thereon and provide at least 2 percent as a sinking fund; and the condemnation of the right of way for the erection of such work shall be fully provided for.

[Note—The foregoing Sec. 7 of Art. XI was amended to simplify language describing electors' qualifications. Submitted by the Forty-second Legislature (1931), adopted in election Nov. 8, 1932. Proclaimed Jan. 9, 1933. Further amended to provide that a majority of resident property taxpayers may vote to issue bonds for construction of seawalls and breakwaters. Submitted by the Sixty-third Legislature (1973) and adopted in election Nov. 6, 1973.]

Sec. 8. State Aid for Seawalls, Etc. — The counties and cities on the Gulf Coast being subject to calamitous overflows, and a very large proportion of the general revenue being derived from those otherwise prosperous localities.* The Legislature is specially authorized to aid, by donation of such portion of the public domain as may be deemed proper, and in such mode as may be provided by law, the construction of seawalls or breakwaters, such aid to be proportioned to the extent and value of the works constructed, or to be constructed, in any locality.

*Explanatory Note—The starting of a new sentence at this point follows the official draft of the Constitution, but it is evident that the foregoing phrase ending with "localities" was meant to modify the following sentence.

Sec. 9. Public Buildings, Etc. — The property of counties, cities and towns owned and held only for public purposes, such as public buildings and the sites therefor, fire engines and the furniture thereof, and all property used or intended for extinguishing fires, public grounds and all other property devoted exclusively to the use and benefit of the public, shall be exempt from forced sale and from taxation; provided, nothing herein shall prevent the enforcement of the vendor's lien, the mechanic's or builder's lien, or other liens now existing.

[Note—Sec. 10 of Art. XI, relating to special taxes and school districts, was deleted by constitutional amendment in election Aug. 5, 1969.]

Sec. 11. Term of Office for City Officials — A home rule city may provide by charter or charter amendment, and a city, town or village operating under the general laws may provide by majority vote of the qualified voters voting at an election called for that purpose, for a longer term of office than two (2) years for its officers, either elective or appointive, or both, but not to exceed four (4) years; provided, however, that tenure under Civil Service shall not be affected hereby.

Provided, however, if any of such officers, elective or appointive, shall announce their candidacy, or shall in fact become a candidate, in any general, special or primary election, for any office of profit or trust under the laws of this State or the United States other than the office then held, at any time when the unexpired term of the office then held shall exceed one (1) year, such announcement or such candidacy shall constitute an automatic resignation of the office then held, and the vacancy thereby created shall be filled pursuant to law in the same manner as other vacancies for such office are filled.

A municipality so providing a term exceeding two (2) years but not exceeding four (4) years for any of its non-civil service officers must elect all of the members of its governing body by majority vote of the qualified voters in such municipality, and any vacancy or vacancies occurring on such governing body shall not be filled by appointment but must be filled by majority vote of the qualified voters at a special election called for such purpose within one hundred and twenty (120) days after such vacancy or vacancies occur.

[Note—The foregoing Sec. 11 of Art. XI, an amendment, was added to provide four-year terms for city officials. Submitted by the Fifty-fifth Legislature (1957), adopted in election Nov. 4, 1958.]

Sec. 12. Sanitation Sewer Lines — The Legislature by general law may authorize a city or town to expend public funds for the relocation or replacement of sanitation sewer laterals or water laterals on private property if the relocation or replacement is done in conjunction with or immediately following the replacement or relocation of sanitation sewer mains or water mains serving the property. The law must authorize the city or town to affix, with the consent of the owner of the private property, a lien on the property for the cost of relocating or replacing the sewer laterals on the property and must provide that the cost shall be assessed against the property with repayment by the property owner to be amortized over a period not to exceed five years at a rate of interest to be set as provided by the law. The lien may not be enforced until after five years have expired since the date the lien was affixed.

[Note — The foregoing Sec. 12 of Art. XI, an amendment, was added to permit a city or town to expend public funds and levy assessments for relocation or replacement of sanitation sewer laterals on private property. Submitted by Sixty-eighth Legislature (1983) and adopted in election Nov. 8, 1983. It was again amended to allow Legislature to enact laws permitting a city or town to spend public funds for the relocation or replacement of water laterals on private property. Submitted by the Sixty-ninth Legislature (1985) and adopted in an election Nov. 5, 1985.]

ARTICLE XII — PRIVATE CORPORATIONS

Sec. 1. Corporations Created by General Laws — No private corporation shall be created except by general laws.

Sec. 2. General Laws to be Enacted — General laws shall

Article XII — (Cont'd.); Article XIII, XIV, XV and XVI

be enacted providing for the creation of private corporations, and shall therein provide fully for the adequate protection of the public and of the individual stockholders.

[Note—Sections 3, 4, 5 and 7 of Art. XII—relating to franchises, and wharfage and freight tolls—were deleted by constitutional amendment in election Aug. 5, 1969.]

Sec. 6. The Issuance of Stocks and Bonds by Corporations Prohibited Except for Money Paid and Labor Done, Etc. — No corporation shall issue stock or bonds except for money paid, labor done, or property actually received, and all fictitious increase of stock or indebtedness shall be void.

ARTICLE XIII — SPANISH AND MEXICAN LAND TITLES

[Note—The entire Art. XIII, relating to Spanish and Mexican Land Titles, was deleted by constitutional amendment in election Aug. 5, 1969.]

ARTICLE XIV — PUBLIC LANDS AND LAND OFFICE

Sec. 1. General Land Office; Grants to Be Registered in; Land Office to Be Self-Sustaining — There shall be one General Land Office in the State, which shall be at the seat of government, where all land titles which have emanated or may hereafter emanate from the State shall be registered, except those titles the registration of which may be prohibited by this Constitution. It shall be the duty of the Legislature at the earliest practicable time to make the Land Office self-sustaining, and from time to time the Legislature may establish such subordinate offices as may be deemed necessary.

[Note—All of Art. XIV relating to public lands and the Land Office, except Sec. 1, was deleted by constitutional amendment in election Aug. 5, 1969.]

ARTICLE XV — IMPEACHMENT

Sec. 1. Power of Impeachment Vested in the House of Representatives — The power of impeachment shall be vested in the House of Representatives.

Sec. 2. Trial by Senate — Impeachment of the Governor, Lieutenant Governor, Attorney General, Treasurer, Commissioner of the General Land Office, Comptroller, and the Judges of the Supreme Court, Courts of Appeal and District Courts shall be tried by the Senate.

Sec. 3. Oath of Senators — When the Senate is sitting as a court of impeachment, the Senators shall be on oath, or affirmation, impartially to try the party impeached, and no person shall be convicted without the concurrence of two thirds of the Senators present.

Sec. 4. Judgment; Party Convicted Subject to Indictment Under the Criminal Laws — Judgment in cases of impeachment shall extend only to removal from office and disqualification from holding any office of honor, trust or profit under this State. A party convicted on impeachment shall also be subject to indictment, trial and punishment, according to law.

Sec. 5. Officers Suspended During Pending Proceedings — All officers against whom articles of impeachment may be preferred shall be suspended from the exercise of the duties of their office during the pendency of such impeachment. The Governor may make a provisional appointment to fill the vacancy occasioned by the suspension of an officer until the decision on the impeachment.

Sec. 6. Removal of District Judges — Any Judge of the District Courts of the State who is incompetent to discharge the duties of his office, or who shall be guilty of partiality, or oppression, or other official misconduct, or whose habits and conduct are such as to render him unfit to hold such office or who shall negligently fail to perform his duties as Judge, or who shall fail to execute in a reasonable measure the business in his courts, may be removed by the Supreme Court. The Supreme Court shall have original jurisdiction to hear and determine the causes aforesaid when presented in writing, upon the oaths, taken before some Judge of a court of record, of not less than ten lawyers, practicing in the courts held by such Judge, and licensed to practice in the Supreme Court; said presentment to be founded either upon the knowledge of the persons making it or upon the written oaths as to facts of creditable witnesses. The Supreme Court may issue all needful process and prescribe all needful rules to give effect to this section. Causes of this kind shall have precedence and be tried as soon as practicable.

Sec. 7. Trial and Removal of Other Officers — The Legislature shall provide by law for the trial and removal from office of all officers of this State, the modes for which have not been provided in this Constitution.

Address

Sec. 8. Removal of Judges of Supreme Court and Courts of Appeals and of District Courts — The Judges of the Supreme Court, Courts of Appeals and District Courts shall be removed by the Governor on the address of two thirds of each house of the Legislature, for willful neglect of duty, incompetency, habitual drunkenness, oppression in office,

or other reasonable cause which shall not be sufficient ground for impeachment; provided, however that the cause or causes for which such removal shall be required shall be stated at length in such address and entered on the journals of each house; and provided, further, that the cause or causes shall be notified to the Judge so intended to be removed, and he shall be admitted to a hearing in his own defense before any vote for such address shall pass; and in all such cases the vote shall be taken by yeas and nays and entered on the journals of each house, respectively.

Sec. 9. Removal of Appointed Officials by Governor; Special Session of Senate for This Purpose — (a) In addition to the other procedures provided by law for removal of public officers, the governor who appoints an officer may remove the officer with the advice and consent of two-thirds of the members of the senate present.

(b) If the Legislature is not in session when the governor desires to remove an officer, the governor shall call a special session of the senate for consideration of the proposed removal. The session may not exceed two days in duration.

[Note — The foregoing Sec. 9 of Art. XV, an amendment, was added to authorize the governor to remove appointed officers with the advice and consent of the senate. Submitted by the Sixty-sixth Legislature (1979) and adopted in election Nov. 4, 1980.]

ARTICLE XVI — GENERAL PROVISIONS

Sec. 1. Official Oaths — Members of the Legislature, and all other elected officers, before they enter upon the duties of their offices, shall take the following Oath or Affirmation:

"I,   , do solemnly swear (or affirm), that I will faithfully execute the duties of the office of   of the State of Texas, and will to the best of my ability preserve, protect, and defend the Constitution and laws of the United States and of this State; and I furthermore solemnly swear (or affirm), that I have not, directly nor indirectly paid, offered, or promised to pay, contributed, nor promised to contribute any money, or valuable thing, or promised any public office or employment, as a reward for the giving or withholding a vote at the election at which I was elected. So help me God."

The Secretary of State, and all other appointed officers, before they enter upon the duties of their offices, shall take the following Oath or Affirmation:

"I,   , do solemnly swear (or affirm), that I will faithfully execute the duties of the office of   of the State of Texas, and will to the best of my ability preserve, protect, and defend the Constitution and laws of the United States and of this State; and I furthermore solemnly swear (or affirm), that I have not directly nor indirectly paid, offered, or promised to pay, contributed, or promised to contribute any money, or valuable thing, or promised any public office or employment, as a reward to secure my appointment or the confirmation thereof. So help me God.''

[Note—The foregoing Sec. 1 of Art. XVI was twice amended from the original text to eliminate that part of the oath stating that the incoming official had not fought a duel or sent or accepted a challenge to a duel or acted as a second in a duel. Submitted by the Forty-fifth Legislature (1937) and adopted in an election Nov. 8, 1938. It was further amended to change the form of the oath of office to include appointive officers of the State. Submitted by the Fifty-fourth Legislature (1955) and adopted in an election Nov. 6, 1956.]

Sec. 2. Right of Suffrage to Be Protected; Criminals Disfranchised — Laws shall be made to exclude from office, serving on juries, and from the right of suffrage, those who may have been or shall hereafter be convicted of bribery, perjury, forgery or other high crimes. The privilege of free suffrage shall be protected by laws, regulating elections and prohibiting, under adequate penalties, all undue influence therein from power, bribery, tumult, or other improper practice.

[Note—Sections 3 and 4 of Art. XVI—relating to fines, and dueling—were deleted by constitutional amendment in election Aug. 5, 1969.]

Sec. 5. Bribery in Elections Disqualification for Holding Office — Every person shall be disqualified from holding any office of profit or trust in this State who shall have been convicted of having given or offered a bribe to procure his election or appointment.

Sec. 6. Appropriations for Private Purposes Prohibited; Expenditures to Be Published — (a) No appropriation for private or individual purposes shall be made, unless authorized by this Constitution. A regular statement, under oath, and an account of the receipts and expenditures of all public money shall be published annually, in such manner as shall be prescribed by law.

(b) State agencies charged with the responsibility of providing services to those who are blind, crippled, or otherwise physically or mentally handicapped may accept money from private or federal sources, designated by the

Article XVI — (Cont'd.)

private or federal source as money to be used in and establishing and equipping facilities for assisting those who are blind, crippled, or otherwise physically or mentally handicapped in becoming gainfully employed, in rehabilitating and restoring the handicapped, and in providing other services determined by the state agency to be essential for the better care and treatment of the handicapped. Money accepted under this subsection is state money. State agencies may spend money accepted under this subsection, and no other money, for specific programs and projects to be conducted by local level or other private, nonsectarian associations, groups, and nonprofit organizations, in establishing and equipping facilities for assisting those who are blind, crippled, or otherwise physically or mentally handicapped in becoming gainfully employed, in rehabilitating and restoring the handicapped, and in providing other services determined by the state agency to be essential for the better care or treatment of the handicapped.

The state agencies may deposit money accepted under this subsection either in the state treasury or in other secure depositories. The money may not be expended for any purpose other than the purpose for which it was given. Notwithstanding any other provision of this Constitution, the state agencies may expend money accepted under this subsection without the necessity of an appropriation, unless the Legislature, by law, requires that the money be expended only on appropriation. The Legislature may prohibit state agencies from accepting money under this subsection or may regulate the amount of money accepted, the way the acceptance and expenditure of the money is administered, and the purposes for which the state agencies may expend the money. Money accepted under this subsection for a purpose prohibited by the Legislature shall be returned to the entity that gave the money.

This subsection does not prohibit state agencies authorized to render services to the handicapped from contracting with privately-owned or local facilities for necessary and essential services, subject to such conditions, standards, and procedures as may be prescribed by law.

[Note—The foregoing Sec. 6 of Art. XVI was amended to authorize public grants to private groups for assistance to the blind, crippled or otherwise physically and mentally handicapped. Submitted by the Fifty-ninth Legislature (1965) and adopted in election Nov. 8, 1966.]

[Note—Sec. 7 of Art. XVI, relating to paper money, was deleted by constitutional amendment in election Aug. 5, 1969.]

Sec. 8. **Counties May Provide Workhouses, Poorhouses and Farms** — Each county in the State may provide, in such manner as may be prescribed by law, a manual labor poorhouse and farm, for taking care of, managing, employing and supplying the wants of its indigent and poor inhabitants.

Sec. 9. **Absence on Business of the State or United States Shall Not Forfeit a Residence Once Obtained** — Absence on business of the State or of the United States shall not forfeit a residence once obtained, so as to deprive anyone of the right of suffrage, or of being elected or appointed to any office, under the exceptions contained in this Constitution.

Sec. 10. **Deductions From Salaries to be Provided for** — The Legislature shall provide for deductions from the salaries of public officers who may neglect the performance of any duty that may be assigned them by law.

Sec. 11. **Usurious Interest Prohibited** — The Legislature shall have authority to classify loans and lenders, license and regulate lenders, define interest and fix maximum rates of interest; provided, however, in the absence of legislation fixing maximum rates of interest all contracts for a greater rate of interest than ten per centum (10%) per annum shall be deemed usurious; provided, further, that in contracts where no rate of interest is agreed upon, the rate shall not exceed six per centum (6%) per annum. Should any regulatory agency, acting under the provisions of this Section, cancel or refuse to grant any permit under any law passed by the Legislature; then such applicant or holder shall have the right of appeal to the courts and granted a trial de novo as that term is used in appealing from the justice of peace court to the county court.

[Note—The foregoing Sec. 11 of Art. XVI has been twice amended—first setting 10 percent and 6 percent as interest rates, in place of original provision for 12 percent and 8 percent. Submitted by the Twenty-second Legislature (1891), ratified in election Aug. 11, 1891, and declared adopted Sept. 22, 1891. Further amended to grant right of appeal from justice of peace court to county court. Submitted by the Fifty-sixth Legislature (1959) and adopted in election Nov. 8, 1960.]

Sec. 12. **Officers Not Eligible** — No member of Congress, nor person holding or exercising any office of profit or trust under the United States, or either of them, or under any foreign power, shall be eligible as a member of the Legislature or hold or exercise any office of profit or trust under this State.

[Note—Sec. 13 of Art. XVI, relating to arbitration laws, was deleted by constitutional amendment in election Aug. 5, 1969.]

Sec. 14. **Residence of Officers** — All civil officers shall reside within the State, and all district or county officers within their districts or counties, and shall keep their offices at such places as may be required by law; and failure to comply with this condition shall vacate the office so held.

Sec. 15. **Community Property of Husband and Wife; Partition Thereof** — All Property, both real and personal, of a spouse owned or claimed before marriage, and that acquired afterward by gift, devise or descent, shall be the separate property of that spouse; and laws shall be passed more clearly defining the rights of the spouses, in relation to separate and community property; provided that persons about to marry and spouses, without the intention to defraud pre-existing creditors, may by written instrument from time to time partition between themselves all or part of their property, then existing or to be acquired, or exchange between themselves the community interest of one spouse or future spouse in any property for the community interest of the other spouse or future spouse in other community property then existing or to be acquired, whereupon the portion or interest set aside to each spouse shall be and constitute a part of the separate property and estate of such spouse or future spouse; and the spouses may from time to time, by written instrument, agree between themselves that the income or property from all or part of the separate property then owned by one of them, or which thereafter might be acquired, shall be the separate property of that spouse; and if one spouse makes a gift of property to the other that gift is presumed to include all the income or property which might arise from that gift of property.

[Note—Sec. 15 of Art. XVI originally had no provision for partition of community property of husband and wife. Provision for partition was the purpose of the amended section. Submitted by the Fiftieth Legislature (1947) and adopted in election Nov. 2, 1948. It was further amended to allow spouses to agree that income or property arising from separate property is to be separate property. Submitted by the Sixty-sixth Legislature (1979) and adopted in election Nov. 4, 1980.]

Sec. 16. **Banking Corporations** — (a) The Legislature shall, by general laws, authorize the incorporation of state banks and savings and loan associations and shall provide for a system of state supervision, regulation and control of such bodies which will adequately protect and secure the depositors and creditors thereof.

No state bank shall be chartered until all of the authorized capital stock has been subscribed and paid in full in cash. Except as may be permitted by the Legislature pursuant to subsections (b), (d), and (e) of this Section 16, state bank shall not be authorized to engage in business at more than one place, which shall be designated in its charter; however, this restriction shall not apply to any other type of financial institution chartered under the laws of this state.

No foreign corporation, other than the national banks of the United States domiciled in this State, shall be permitted to exercise banking or discounting privileges in this State.

(b) If it finds that the convenience of the public will be served thereby, the Legislature may authorize state and national banks to establish and operate unmanned teller machines within the county or city of their domicile. Such machines may perform all banking functions. Banks which are domiciled within a city lying in two or more counties may be permitted to establish and operate unmanned teller machines within both the city and the county of their domicile. The Legislature shall provide that a bank shall have the right to share in the use of these teller machines, not situated at a banking house, which are located within the county or the city of the bank's domicile, on a reasonable, nondiscriminatory basis, consistent with anti-trust laws. Banks may share the use of such machines within the county or city of their domicile with savings and loan associations and credit unions which are domiciled in the same county or city.

(c) A state bank created by virtue of the power granted by this section, notwithstanding any other provision of this section, has the same rights and privileges that are or may be granted to national banks of the United States domiciled in this State.

Should the Legislature enact legislation in anticipation of the adoption of this amendment, such law shall not be invalid because of its anticipatory character.

(d) The Legislature may authorize a state bank or national bank of the United States domiciled in this State to engage in business at more than one place if it does so through the purchase and assumption of certain assets and liabilities of a failed state bank or a failed national bank of the United States domiciled in this State.

(e) The Legislature shall authorize a state bank or national bank of the United States domiciled in this State to

Article XVI — (Cont'd.)

establish and operate banking facilities at locations within the county or city of its domicile, subject to limitations the Legislature imposes. The Legislature may permit a bank domiciled within a city located in two or more counties to establish and operate branches within both the city and the county of its domicile, subject to limitations the Legislature imposes.

(f) A bank may not be considered a branch or facility of another bank solely because it is owned or controlled by the same stockholders as the other bank, has common accounting and administrative systems with the other bank, or has a name similar to the other bank's or because of a combination of those factors.

[Note—The foregoing Sec. 16 of Art. XVI has been amended from the original, as follows: (1) To eliminate the original provision that "No corporate body shall hereafter be created, renewed or extended with banking or discounting privileges," and making possible the establishment of the present state banking system. Submitted by the Twenty-eighth Legislature (1903), ratified in an election Nov. 8, 1904, and declared adopted Dec. 29, 1904. (2) Eliminating a provision, contained in the amendment of 1904, making shareholders of banks liable to the extent of twice the par value of the shares owned. Submitted by the Forty-fifth Legislature (1937), and adopted in an election Aug. 23, 1937. (3) Authorizing banks to use unmanned teller machines within the county or city of their domicile on a shared basis. Submitted by the Sixty-sixth Legislature (1979) and adopted in election Nov. 4, 1980. (4) Adding Subsection (c), providing state banks same rights and privileges as national banks. Submitted by the Sixty-eighth Legislature (1983) and adopted in election Nov. 6, 1984. (5) Amending sections (a) and (c) and adding sections (d), (e) and (f) to provide that a bank may offer full service banking at more than one location within the city or county where its principal facility is located, subject to limitations and restrictions provided by law. Submitted by the Sixty-ninth Legislature (1986) and adopted in an election Nov. 4, 1986.]

Sec. 17. **Officers to Perform Duties Until Successor Qualified** — All officers within this State shall continue to perform the duties of their offices until their successors shall be duly qualified.

Sec. 18. **Vested Rights** — The rights of property and of action, which have been acquired under the Constitution and the laws of the Republic and State, shall not be divested; nor shall any rights or actions, which have been divested, barred or declared null and void by the Constitution of the Republic and State be reinvested, renewed or reinstated by this Constitution; but the same shall remain precisely in the situation which they were before the adoption of this Constitution, unless otherwise herein provided; and provided, further, that no cause of action heretofore barred shall be revived.

Sec. 19. **Qualifications of Jurors** — The Legislature shall prescribe by law the qualifications of grand and petit jurors; provided that neither the right nor the duty to serve on grand and petit juries shall be denied or abridged by reason of sex. Whenever in the Constitution the term "men" is used in reference to grand or petit juries, such term shall include persons of the female as well as the male sex.

[Note—The foregoing Sec. 19 of Art. XVI was amended to include women jurors. Submitted by the Fifty-third Legislature (1953) and adopted in an election Nov. 2, 1954.]

Sec. 20. **Manufacture and Sale of Intoxicants** — (a) The Legislature shall have the power to enact a Mixed Beverage Law regulating the sale of mixed alcoholic beverages on a local option election basis. The Legislature shall also have the power to regulate the manufacture, sale, possession and transportation of intoxicating liquors, including the power to establish a state monopoly on the sale of distilled liquors.

Should the Legislature enact any enabling laws in anticipation of this amendment, no such law shall be void by reason of its anticipatory nature.

(b) The Legislature shall enact a law or laws whereby the qualified voters of any county, justices precinct or incorporated town or city may, by a majority vote of those voting, determine from time to time whether the sale of intoxicating liquors for beverage purposes shall be prohibited or legalized within the prescribed limits; and such laws shall contain provisions for voting on the sale of intoxicating liquors of various types and various alcoholic content.

(c) In all counties, justices precincts or incorporated towns or cities wherein the sale of intoxicating liquors had been prohibited by local option elections held under the laws of the State of Texas and in force at the time of the taking effect of Section 20, Article XVI of the Constitution of Texas, it shall continue to be unlawful to manufacture, sell, barter or exchange in any such county, justices precinct or incorporated town or city, any spiritous, vinous or malt liquors or medicated bitters capable of producing intoxication or any other intoxicants whatsoever, for beverage pur-

poses, unless and until a majority of the qualified voters in such county or political subdivision thereof voting in an election held for such purposes shall determine such to be lawful; provided that this subsection shall not prohibit the sale of alcoholic beverages containing not more than 3.2 percent alcohol by weight in cities, counties or political subdivisions thereof in which the qualified voters have voted to legalize such sale under the provisions of Chapter 116, Acts of the Regular Session of the Forty-third Legislature.

[Note—The foregoing Sec. 20 of Art. XVI has been amended from the original (which merely provided for local option elections in "any county, justices precinct, town or city") five times, as follows: (1) To insert a clause in original section "or such subdivision of a county as may be designated by Commissioners' Court of said county," with reference to local option elections. Submitted by Twenty-second Legislature (1891), ratified in an election Aug. 11, 1891, and declared adopted Sept. 22, 1891. (2) To declare state-wide prohibition. Submitted by Thirty-sixth Legislature (1919), and declared adopted May 24, 1919. (3) To legalize sale of vinous and malt liquors of not more than 3.2 percent alcohol. Submitted by Forty-third Legislature (1933), and adopted in an election Aug. 26, 1933. (4) To legalize sale of all liquors, as stated in the section printed above. Submitted by Forty-fourth Legislature (1935), and adopted in an election Aug. 24, 1935. (5) To give Legislature power to enact a Mixed Beverage Law regulating sale of mixed drinks on local option election basis. Submitted by Sixty-first Legislature (1969) and adopted in election Nov. 3, 1970.]

Sec. 21. **Stationery; Public Printing** — All stationery, printing, fuel used in the Legislature and departments of the government other than the judicial department, printing and binding of the laws, journals, and department reports, and all other printing and binding and the repairing and furnishing of the halls and rooms used during meetings of the Legislature and in committees, except proclamations and such products and services as may be done by handicapped individuals employed in nonprofit rehabilitation facilities providing sheltered employment to the handicapped in Texas, shall be performed under contract, to be given to the lowest responsible bidder, below such maximum price and under such regulations as shall be prescribed by law. No member or officer of any department of the government shall in any way have a financial interest in such contracts, and all such contracts or programs involving the state use of the products and services of handicapped individuals shall be subject to such requirements as might be established by the Legislature.

[Note—The foregoing Sec. 21 of Art. XVI was amended to eliminate reference to the Deaf and Dumb Asylum; to allow certain products and services of handicapped persons to be used by agencies of state government; to require other products and services required for operation of state government be acquired under bids by lowest responsible bidder; and to eliminate requirement that Governor, Secretary of State and Comptroller of Public Accounts be personally involved with such transactions. Submitted by the Sixty-fifth Legislature (1977) and adopted in election Nov. 7, 1978.]

Sec. 22. **Fence Laws** — The Legislature shall have the power to pass such fence laws, applicable to any subdivision of the State or county, as may be needed to meet the wants of the people.

Sec. 23. **Stock Laws** — The Legislature may pass laws for the regulation of livestock and the protection of stock raisers in the stock raising portion of the State, and exempt from the operation of such laws other portions, sections or counties; and shall have power to pass general and special laws for the inspection of cattle, stock and hides, and for the regulation of brands; provided, that any local law thus passed shall be submitted to the freeholders of the section to be affected thereby, and approved by them before it shall go into effect.

Sec. 24. **Roads; Convict Labor** — The Legislature shall make provision for laying out and working public roads, for the building of bridges, and for utilizing fines, forfeitures, and convict labor to all these purposes.

Sec. 25. **Drawbacks and Rebates in Freight Insurance, Transportation, Storage, Etc., Prohibited** — That all drawbacks and rebatement of insurance, freight, transportation, carriage, wharfage, storage, compressing, bailing, repairing, or for any other kind of labor or service of, or to any cotton, grain or any other produce or article of commerce in this State, paid or allowed or contracted for to any common carrier, shipper, merchant, commission merchant, factor, agent or middleman of any kind not the true and absolute owner thereof, are forever prohibited; and it shall be the duty of the Legislature to pass effective laws punishing all persons in this State who pay, receive or contract for or respecting the same.

Sec. 26. **Homicide: Civil Action For** — Every person, corporation or company that may commit a homicide, through willful act or omission or gross neglect, shall be responsible in exemplary damages to the surviving husband, widow,

Article XVI — (Cont'd.)

heirs of his or her body, or such of them as there may be, without regard to any criminal proceeding that may or may not be had in relation to the homicide.

Sec. 27. Vacancies in Offices Filled for Unexpired Term Only — In all elections to fill vacancies of office in this State, it shall be to fill the unexpired term only.

Sec. 28. Wages Exempt From Garnishment — No current wages for personal service shall ever be subject to garnishment, except for the enforcement of court-ordered child support payments.

[Note — The foregoing Sec. 28 of Art. XVI was amended to allow Legislature to provide for additional remedies to enforce court-ordered child support payments. Submitted by Sixty-eighth Legislature (1983) and adopted in election Nov. 8, 1983.]

[Note—Sec. 29 of Art. XVI, relating to barratry, was deleted by constitutional amendment in election Aug. 5, 1969.]

Sec. 30. Duration of Offices; Term of Railroad Commissioner — (a) The duration of all offices not fixed by this Constitution shall never exceed two years.

(b) When a Railroad Commission is created by law it shall be composed of three Commissioners, who shall be elected by the people at a general election for state officers, and their term of office shall be six years. Railroad Commissioners first elected after this amendment goes into effect shall hold office as follows: One shall serve two years, and one four years, and one six years; their terms to be decided by lot immediately after they shall have qualified. And one Railroad Commissioner shall be elected every two years thereafter. In case of vacancy in said office the Governor of the State shall fill said vacancy by appointment until the next general election.

(c) The Legislature may provide that members of the governing board of a district or authority created by authority of Art. III, Sec. 52(b) (1) or (2), or Art. XVI, Sec. 59, of this Constitution serve terms not to exceed four years.

[Note — The foregoing Sec. 30 of Art. XVI was amended from the original to permit six-year terms for the newly created offices of the three-place Railroad Commission of Texas. The original section consisted only of the first clause of the amendment as printed above. Submitted by the Twenty-third Legislature (1893), ratified in an election Nov. 6, 1894, and declared adopted Dec. 21, 1894. It was further amended to provide four-year terms for members of governing boards of certain water districts and conservation and reclamation districts. Submitted by the Sixty-seventh Legislature (1981) and adopted in an election Nov. 2, 1982.]

Sec. 30-a. Board of Regents, Trustees, Managers, Etc.; Term of Office — The Legislature may provide by law that the members of the Board of Regents of the State University and boards of trustees or managers of the educational, eleemosynary and penal institutions of this State, and such boards as have been or may hereafter be established by law, may hold their respective offices for the term of six (6) years, one third of the members of such boards to be elected or appointed every two years in such manner as the Legislature may determine; vacancies in such offices to be filled as may be provided by law, and the Legislature shall enact suitable laws to give effect to this section.

[Note—The foregoing Sec. 30-a of Art. XVI, an amendment, was added to give the Legislature authority to provide official terms of more than two years. (See Sec. 30 above and note thereunder.) Submitted by the Thirty-second Legislature (1911), ratified at an election Nov. 5, 1912, and declared adopted Dec. 30, 1912.]

Sec. 30-b. Tenure Under Municipal Civil Service — Wherever by virtue of statute or charter provisions appointive officers of any municipality are placed under the terms and provisions of Civil Service and rules are set up governing appointment to and removal from such offices, the provisions of Article 16, Section 30, of the Texas Constitution limiting the duration of all offices not fixed by the Constitution to two (2) years shall not apply, but the duration of such offices shall be governed by the provisions of the Civil Service law or charter provisions applicable thereto.

[Note—The foregoing Sec. 30-b of Art. XVI, an amendment, was added to extend to local officials terms under the Civil Service exemption from the two-year restriction in the first clause of Sec. 30. (See Secs. 30 and 30-a and notes thereunder.) Submitted by the Forty-sixth Legislature; ratified in an election Nov. 5, 1940.]

Sec. 31. Qualifications of Physicians to Be Prescribed — The Legislature may pass laws prescribing the qualifications of practitioners of medicine in this State, and to punish persons for malpractice, but no preference shall ever be given by law to any schools of medicine.

[Note—Sec. 32 of Art. XVI, relating to Board of Health

and Vital Statistics, was deleted by constitutional amendment in election Aug. 5, 1969.]

Sec. 33. Condition Under Which a Person Can Not Receive Compensation From the State — The accounting officers in this State shall neither draw nor pay a warrant or check on funds of the State of Texas, whether in the treasury or otherwise, to any person for salary or compensation who holds at the same time more than one civil office of emolument, in violation of Sec. 40.

[Note—The foregoing Sec. 33 of Art. XVI has been amended four times, as follows: (1) To release National Guard of Texas, National Guard Reserve and Officers' Reserve Corps and United States Organized Reserves from the prohibition against holding remunerative office. Submitted by Thirty-ninth Legislature (1925), and adopted in an election Nov. 2, 1926. Proclaimed Jan. 20, 1927. (2) To add to those released from the prohibition against holding remunerative office all retired officers and enlisted men of the United States Army, Navy and Marine Corps. Submitted by Forty-second Legislature (1931), and adopted in an election Nov. 8, 1932. Proclaimed Jan. 9, 1933. (3) To allow nonelective state officers and employees to serve in other nonelective offices under this state or the U.S. until Sept. 1, 1969, and thereafter only if authorized by Legislature, if the offices are of benefit to Texas or are required by state or federal law and there is no conflict of interest; prohibiting elected officers from holding any other office under this state; and adding members of Air National Guard, Air National Guard Reserve, Air Force Reserve and retired members of Air Force to list of persons exempted. Submitted by Sixtieth Legislature (1967) and adopted in election Nov. 11, 1967. (4) It was amended to delete the old Sec. 33 of Art. XVI and substitute the foregoing therefor. (See also note under Sec. 40 of Art. XVI.) Submitted by the Sixty-second Legislature (1971) and adopted in election Nov. 7, 1972.]

[Note—Sections 34, 35, 36 and 38 of Art. XVI—relating to military forts, laborers on public works, payments to schoolteachers, and a Commissioner of Insurance, Statistics and History—were deleted by constitutional amendment in election Aug. 5, 1969.]

Sec. 37. Mechanic's Liens to Be Enforced — Mechanics, artisans and material men of every class shall have a lien upon the buildings and articles made or repaired by them, for the value of their labor done thereon, or material furnished therefor; and the Legislature shall provide by law for the speedy and efficient enforcement of said liens.

Sec. 39. Memorials of Texas History — The Legislature may, from time to time, make appropriations for preserving and perpetuating memorials of the history of Texas, by means of monuments, statues, paintings and documents of historical value.

Sec. 40. Provision Against Holding More Than One Office; Exceptions — No person shall hold or exercise at the same time, more than one civil office of emolument, except that of Justice of the Peace, County Commissioner, Notary Public and Postmaster, Officer of the National Guard, the National Guard Reserve, and the Officers Reserve Corps of the United States and enlisted men of the National Guard, the National Guard Reserve, and the Organized Reserves of the United States, and retired officers of the United States Army, Air Force, Navy, Marine Corps, and Coast Guard, and retired warrant officers, and retired enlisted men of the United States Army, Air Force, Navy, Marine Corps, and Coast Guard, and the officers and directors of soil and water conservation districts, unless otherwise specially provided herein. Provided, that nothing in this Constitution shall be construed to prohibit an officer or enlisted man of the National Guard, and the National Guard Reserve, or an officer in the Officers Reserve Corps of the United States, or an enlisted man in the Organized Reserves of the United States, or retired officers of the United States Army, Air Force, Navy, Marine Corps, and Coast Guard, and retired warrant officers, and retired enlisted men of the United States Army, Air Force, Navy, Marine Corps, and Coast Guard, and officers of the State soil and water conservation districts, from holding at the same time any other office or position of honor, trust or profit, under this State or the United States, or from voting at any election, general, special or primary in this State when otherwise qualified. State employees or other individuals who receive all or part of their compensation either directly or indirectly from funds of the State of Texas and who are not State officers, shall not be barred from serving as members of the governing bodies of school districts, cities, towns, or other local governmental districts; provided, however, that such State employees or other individuals shall receive no salary for serving as members of such governing bodies. It is further provided that a non-elective State officer may hold other non-elective offices under the State or the United States, if the other office is of benefit to the State of Texas or is required by the State or Federal law, and there is no conflict with the original office for which he receives salary or compensation. No member of the Legislature of this State may hold any other office or position of profit under

Article XVI — (Cont'd.)

this State, or the United States, except as a notary public if qualified by law.

[Note—The foregoing Sec. 40 of Art. XVI has been amended three times as follows: (1) To release National Guard, National Guard Reserve and Officers' Reserve Corps and United States Organized Reserves from the prohibition against holding remunerative office. Submitted by Thirty-ninth Legislature (1925), and adopted in an election Nov. 2, 1926. Proclaimed Jan. 20, 1927. (2) To add to those released from the prohibition against holding remunerative office all retired officers and enlisted men of the United States Army, Navy and Marine Corps. Submitted by Forty-second Legislature (1931) and adopted in an election Nov. 8, 1932. Proclaimed Jan. 9, 1933. (3) To add to those released from the prohibition against holding remunerative office retired officers or enlisted men of the Air Force and Coast Guard; and officers and directors of soil and water conservation districts, unless otherwise specially prohibited; also certain other state employees who are not officers of the state. Submitted by Sixty-second Legislature (1971) and adopted in an election Nov. 7, 1972.]

Sec. 41. **Bribery of Certain Officials to Be Prohibited** — Any person who shall, directly or indirectly, offer, give or promise any money or thing of value, testimonial, privilege or personal advantage to any executive or judicial officer or member of the Legislature, to influence him in the performance of any of his public or official duties, shall be guilty of bribery and be punished in such manner as shall be provided by law. And any member of the Legislature, or executive or judicial officer, who shall solicit, demand or receive, or consent to receive, directly or indirectly, for himself or for another, from any company, corporation or person any money, appointment, employment testimonial, reward, thing of value or employment, or of personal advantage or promise thereof, for his vote or official influence, or for withholding the same, or with any understanding, expressed or implied, that his vote or official action shall be in any way influenced thereby, or who shall solicit, demand and receive any such money or other advantage, matter or thing aforesaid, for another, as the consideration of his vote or official influence, in consideration of the payment or promise of such money, advantage, matter or thing to another, shall be held guilty of bribery within the meaning of the Constitution, and shall incur the disabilities provided for said offenses, with a forfeiture of the office they may hold, and such other additional punishment as is or shall be provided by law.

[Note—Sec. 42 of Art. XVI, relating to an asylum for inebriates, was deleted by constitutional amendment in election Aug. 5, 1969.]

Sec. 43. **Exemption From Public Service** — No man or set of men shall ever be exempted, relieved or discharged from the performance of any public duty or service imposed by general law, by any special law. Exemptions from the performance of such public duty or service shall only be made by general law.

Sec. 44. **County Treasurer and Surveyor** — (a) Except as otherwise provided by this section, the Legislature shall prescribe the duties and provide for the election by the qualified voters of each county in this State, of a County Treasurer and a County Surveyor, who shall have an office at the county seat, and hold their office for four years, and until their successors are qualified; and shall have such compensation as may be provided by law.

(b) The office of County Treasurer in the counties of Tarrant and Bee is abolished and all the powers, duties, and functions of the office in each of these counties are transferred to the County Auditor or to the officer who succeeds to the auditor's functions. The office of County Treasurer in the counties of Bexar and Collin are abolished and all the powers, duties, and functions of the office in each of these counties are transferred to the County Clerk. However, the office of County Treasurer shall be abolished in the counties covered by this subsection only after a local election has been held in each county and the proposition "to abolish the elective office of county treasurer" has passed by a majority of those persons voting in said election.

(c) The office of County Treasurer in Andrews County is abolished and all the powers, duties, and functions of that office are transferred to the County Auditor of that county or to the officer who succeeds to the auditor's functions.

(d) The office of County Treasurer in El Paso County is abolished. The Commissioners Court of the county may employ or contract with a qualified person or may designate another county officer to perform any of the functions that would have been performed by the County Treasurer if the office had not been abolished. However, the office of County Treasurer in El Paso County is abolished under this subsection only if, at the statewide election at which this amendment is submitted to the voters, a majority of the voters of El Paso County voting on the question at that election favor the amendment.

(e) The office of County Surveyor in the counties of Denton, Randall, Collin, Dallas, El Paso, and Henderson is abolished upon the approval of the abolition by a majority of the qualified voters of the respective county voting on the question at an election that the Commissioners Court of the county may call. If the election is called, the Commissioners Court shall order the ballot at the election to be printed to provide for voting for or against the proposition: "Abolishing the office of county surveyor." Each qualified voter of the county is entitled to vote in the election. If the office of County Surveyor is abolished under this subsection, the maps, field notes, and other records in the custody of the County Surveyor are transferred to the County Clerk of the county. After abolition, the Commissioners Court may employ or contract with a qualified person to perform any of the functions that would have been performed by the County Surveyor if the office had not been abolished.

(f) The office of County Treasurer in Andrews County is abolished under Subsection (c) of this section on the adoption of the constitutional amendment that added that subsection, and that was proposed by Senate Joint Resolution 27 of the 69th Legislature, Regular Session, 1985. The office of County Treasurer in El Paso County is abolished under Subsection (d) of this section on Jan. 1, 1986, if the conditions of that subsection are met. If that office in El Paso County is not abolished, Subsection (d) of this section expires Jan. 1, 1986. This subsection expires Jan. 2, 1986.

[Note—The foregoing Sec. 44 of Art. XVI was amended to raise term of office from two to four years. Submitted by the Fifty-third Legislature (1953) and adopted in election Nov. 2, 1954. It was further amended to abolish the office of County Treasurer in Tarrant and Bee counties. Submitted by the Sixty-seventh Legislature (1981) and adopted in election Nov. 2, 1982. It was amended again to abolish the office of County Treasurer in Bexar and Collin counties. Submitted by Sixty-eighth Legislature (1983) and adopted in election Nov. 6, 1984. It was again amended to abolish the office of county treasurer in Andrews and El Paso counties; to abolish the office of county surveyor in Collin, Dallas, Denton, El Paso, Henderson and Randall counties. Submitted by the Sixty-ninth Legislature (1985) and adopted in an election Nov. 5, 1985.]

[Note—Sections 45 and 46 of Art. XVI—relating to records of the history of Texas and organization of a militia — were deleted by constitutional amendment in election Aug. 5, 1969.]

Sec. 47. **Scruples Against Bearing Arms** — Any person who conscientiously scruples to bear arms shall not be compelled to do so, but shall pay an equivalent for personal service.

Sec. 48. **Laws to Remain in Force** — All laws and parts of laws now in force in the State of Texas which are not repugnant to the Constitution of the United States or to this Constitution shall continue and remain in force as the laws of this State until they expire by their own limitation or shall be amended or repealed by the Legislature.

Sec. 49. **Exemptions From Forced Sales** — The Legislature shall have power, and it shall be its duty, to protect by law from forced sale a certain portion of the personal property of all heads of families, and also of unmarried adults, male and female.

Sec. 50. **Homestead Exemptions; Encumbrances, Pretended Sales** — The homestead of a family, or of a single adult person, shall be, and is hereby protected from forced sale, for the payment of all debts except for the purchase money thereof, or a part of such purchase money, the taxes due thereon, or for work and material used in constructing improvements thereon, and in this last case only when the work and material are contracted for in writing, with the consent of both spouses, in the case of a family homestead, given in the same manner as is required in making a sale and conveyance of the homestead; nor may the owner or claimant of the property claimed as homestead, if married, sell or abandon the homestead without the consent of the other spouse, given in such manner as may be prescribed by law. No mortgage, trust deed, or other lien on the homestead shall ever be valid, except for the purchase money therefor, or improvements made thereon, as hereinbefore provided, whether such mortgage, or trust deed, or other lien, shall have been created by the owner alone, or together with his or her spouse, in case the owner is married. All pretended sales of the homestead involving any condition of defeasance shall be void.

[Note—The foregoing Sec. 50 of Art. XVI was amended to include single persons under the homestead exemption provision; and it further made the wife an equal partner under the homestead provision. Submitted by the Sixty-third Legislature (1973) and adopted in election Nov. 6, 1973.]

Sec. 51. **Homestead Defined** — The homestead, not in a town or city, shall consist of not more than two hundred acres of land, which may be in one or more parcels, with the improvements thereon; the homestead in a city, town or village, shall consist of lot or lots amounting to not more

Article XVI — (Cont'd.)

than one acre of land, together with any improvements on the land; provided, that the same shall be used for the purposes of a home, or as a place to exercise the calling or business of the homestead claimant, whether a single adult person, or the head of a family; provided also, that any temporary renting of the homestead shall not change the character of the same, when no other homestead has been acquired.

[Note—The foregoing Sec. 51 was amended to raise the value of lots, exclusive of improvements, from $5,000 to $10,000 when designated as homesteads. Submitted by the Sixty-first Legislature (1969) and adopted in election Nov. 3, 1970. It was further amended to provide that family homesteads may not be abandoned except with consent of both spouses. Submitted by the Sixty-third Legislature (1973) and adopted in election Nov. 6, 1973. It was again amended to replace the limitation on the value of an urban homestead with a limitation based on size. Submitted by Sixty-eighth Legislature (1983) and adopted in election Nov. 8, 1983.]

Sec. 52. **Descent of Homestead** — On the death of the husband or wife, or both, the homestead shall descend and vest in like manner as other real property of the deceased, and shall be governed by the same laws of descent and distribution, but it shall not be partitioned among the heirs of the deceased during the lifetime of the surviving husband or wife, or so long as the survivor may elect to use or occupy the same as a homestead, or so long as the guardian of the minor children of the deceased may be permitted, under the order of the proper court having jurisdiction, to use and occupy the same.

Sec. 53. **Declaration Validating Process and Writs** — That no inconvenience may arise from the adoption of this Constitution, it is declared that all process and writs of all kinds which have been or may be issued and not returned or executed when this Constitution is adopted shall remain valid, and shall not be in any way affected by the adoption of this Constitution.

[Note—Sections 54 and 55 of Art. XVI—relating to pensions, and the indigent lunatics—were deleted by constitutional amendment in election Aug. 5, 1969.]

Sec. 56. **Advertising Texas' Resources** — The Legislature of the State of Texas shall have the power to appropriate money and establish the procedure necessary to expend such money for the purpose of developing information about the historical, natural, agricultural, industrial, educational, marketing, recreational and living resources of Texas, and for the purpose of informing persons and corporations of other states through advertising in periodicals having national circulation, and the dissemination of factual information about the advantages and economic resources offered by the State of Texas; providing, however, that neither the name nor the picture of any living state official shall ever be used in any of said advertising, and providing that the Legislature may require that any sum of money appropriated hereunder shall be matched by an equal sum paid into the State Treasury from private sources before any of said money may be expended.

[Note—The foregoing Sec. 56 of Art. XVI is substituted for the original Section 56 which prohibited the expenditure of state funds for attracting immigrants. Submitted by the Fifty-fifth Legislature (1957) and adopted in an election Nov. 4, 1958.]

[Note—Sections 57, 58 and 60 of Art. XVI—relating to land for state capitol, management of the prison system and the Texas Centennial—were deleted by constitutional amendment in election Aug. 5, 1969.]

*Sec. 59-a. **Conservation and Development of Natural Resources** — The conservation and development of all the natural resources of this State, including the control, storing, preservation and distribution of its storm and flood waters, the waters of its rivers and streams, for irrigation, power and all other useful purposes, the reclamation and irrigation of its arid, semi-arid and other lands needing irrigation, the reclamation and drainage of its overflowed lands, and other lands needing drainage, the conservation and development of its forests, water and hydro-electric power, the navigation of its inland and coastal waters, and the preservation and conservation of all such natural resources of the State are each and all hereby declared public rights and duties; and the Legislature shall pass all such laws as may be appropriate thereto.

*The resolution submitting this amendment was headed "Sec. 59-a," followed by paragraphs "(b)" and "(c)." Obviously, the first heading should have been "Sec. 59 (a)," the parenthetical (a) referring only to the first paragraph.

(b) There may be created within the State of Texas or the State may be divided into, such number of conservation and reclamation districts as may be determined to be essential to the accomplishment of the purposes of this amendment to the Constitution, which districts shall be governmental agencies and bodies politic and corporate with such powers of government and with the authority to exercise such rights, privileges and functions concerning the subject matter of this amendment as may be conferred by law.

(c) The Legislature shall authorize all such indebtedness as may be necessary to provide all improvements and the maintenance thereof requisite to the achievement of the purposes of this amendment, and all such indebtedness may be evidenced by bonds of such conservation and reclamation districts, to be issued under such regulations as may be prescribed by law and shall, also, authorize the levy and collection within such districts of all such taxes, equitably distributed, as may be necessary for the payment of the interest and the creation of a sinking fund for payment of such bonds; and also for the maintenance of such districts and improvements, and such indebtedness shall be a lien upon the property assessed for the payment thereof; provided, the Legislature shall not authorize the issuance of any bonds or provide for any indebtedness against any reclamation district unless such proposition shall first be submitted to the qualified property taxpaying voters of such district and the proposition adopted.

(d) No law creating a conservation and reclamation district shall be passed unless notice of the intention to introduce such a bill setting forth the general substance of the contemplated law shall have been published at least thirty (30) days and not more than ninety (90) days prior to the introduction thereof in a newspaper or newspapers having general circulation in the county or counties in which said district or any part thereof is or will be located and by delivering a copy of such notice and such bill to the Governor who shall submit such notice and bill to the Texas Water Commission, or its successor, which shall file its recommendation as to such bill with the Governor, Lieutenant Governor and Speaker of the House of Representatives within thirty (30) days from date notice was received by the Texas Water Commission. Such notice and copy of bill shall also be given of the introduction of any bill amending a law creating or governing a particular conservation and reclamation district if such bill (1) adds additional land to the district, (2) alters the taxing authority of the district, (3) alters the authority of the district with respect to the issuance of bonds, or (4) alters the qualifications or terms of office of the members of the governing body of the district.

(e) No law creating a conservation and reclamation district shall be passed unless, at the time notice of the intention to introduce a bill is published as provided in Subsection (d) of this section, a copy of the proposed bill is delivered to the commissioners court of each county in which said district or any part thereof is or will be located and to the governing body of each incorporated city or town in whose jurisdiction said district or any part thereof is or will be located. Each such commissioners court and governing body may file its written consent or opposition to the creation of the proposed district with the governor, lieutenant governor, and speaker of the house of representatives. Each special law creating a conservation and reclamation district shall comply with the provisions of the general laws then in effect relating to consent by political subdivisions to the creation of conservation and reclamation districts and to the inclusion of land within the district.

(f) A conservation and reclamation district created under this section to perform any or all of the purposes of this section may engage in fire-fighting activities and may issue bonds or other indebtedness for fire-fighting purposes as provided by law and this constitution.

[Note—The foregoing Sec. 59-a, obviously meant to be Sec. 59 (see footnote), was added to establish a conservation policy. Submitted by Thirty-fifth Legislature (1917), and adopted in an election of Aug. 21, 1917, and proclaimed Oct. 2, 1917. It was amended by adding paragraph (d) to require notice at both the local level and state level through publication in a newspaper having general circulation in county in which district is to be set up at least 30 days prior to introduction of bill in Legislature. Submitted by Fifty-eighth Legislature (1963) and adopted in election Nov. 3, 1964. It was further amended to establish certain requirements relative to enactment of laws creating certain conservation and reclamation districts. Submitted by Sixty-third Legislature (1973) and adopted in election Nov. 6, 1973. It was further amended by adding Subsection (f), authorizing certain districts to engage in fire-fighting activities and to issue bonds or otherwise lend their credit for fire-fighting purposes. (See also Subsection (d), Sec. 52, Art. III.) Submitted by Sixty-fifth Legislature (1977) and adopted in election Nov. 7, 1978.]

[Note—See note after Sec. 56 for Sec. 60.]

Sec. 61. **Compensation of District and County Officials** — All district officers in the State of Texas and all county officers in counties having a population of twenty thousand (20,000) or more, according to the then last preceding Federal Census, shall be compensated on a salary basis. In all

Article XVI — (Cont'd.)

counties in this State, the Commissioners Courts shall be authorized to determine whether precinct officers shall be compensated on a fee basis or on a salary basis, with the exception that it shall be mandatory upon the Commissioners Courts to compensate all justices of the peace, constables, deputy constables and precinct law enforcement officers on a salary basis beginning January 1, 1973; and in counties having a population of less than twenty thousand (20,000), according to the then last preceding Federal Census, the Commissioners Court shall also have the authority to determine whether county officers shall be compensated on a fee basis or on a salary basis, with the exception that it shall be mandatory upon the Commissioners Courts to compensate all sheriffs, deputy sheriffs, county law enforcement officers, including sheriffs who also perform the duties of assessor and collector of taxes, and their deputies, on a salary basis beginning January 1, 1949.

All fees earned by district, county and precinct officers shall be paid into the county treasury where earned for the account of the proper fund, provided that fees incurred by the State, county and any municipality, or in case where a pauper's oath is filed, shall be paid into the county treasury when collected and provided that where any officer is compensated wholly on a fee basis such fees may be retained by such officer or paid into the treasury of the county as the Commissioners Court may direct. All notaries public, county surveyors and public weighers shall continue to be compensated on a fee basis.

[Note—The foregoing Sec. 61 of Art. XVI has been amended three times, as follows: (1) To put all district and county officials in counties of more than 20,000 population on a salary basis, substituting for fee basis, and making it optional with the Commissioners Courts whether precinct officers in counties of less than 20,000 should be on salary or fee basis and optional with reference to county officers in counties of less than 20,000. Submitted by the Forty-fourth Legislature (1935), and adopted in an election Aug. 24, 1935. (2) To make mandatory a salary basis for constables and precinct enforcement officers in counties of more than 20,000 and making it mandatory, in counties of less than 20,000 population, that all sheriffs, deputy sheriffs and other county enforcement officers, be on salary basis. Submitted by the Fiftieth Legislature (1947) and adopted in election Nov. 2, 1948. (3) To include justices of the peace with those to be compensated on salary basis beginning Jan. 1, 1973. Submitted by the Sixty-second Legislature (1971) and adopted in an election Nov. 7, 1972.]

[Note—Sec. 62 and Sec. 63 of Art. XVI, pertaining to **Retirement, Disability and Death Compensation Funds and Teacher and State Employee Retirement System**, respectively, were repealed in a constitutional amendment election April 22, 1975. See also note under Art. III, Sec. 48-a, 48-b, 51-e and 51-f; also see Sec. 67 of Art. XVI, which replaces the foregoing Sections.]

Sec. 64. Inspector of Hides and Animals; Elective District, County and Precinct Offices; Terms of Office — The office of Inspector of Hides and Animals, the elective district, county and precinct offices which have heretofore had terms of two years, shall hereafter have terms of four years; and the holders of such terms shall serve until their successors are qualified.

[Note — The foregoing Sec. 64 of Art. XVI, an amendment, was added for the purpose of setting term of office for these officials. Submitted by the Fifty-third Legislature (1953) and adopted in election Nov. 2, 1954.]

Sec. 65. District and County Officials; Terms of Office — The following officers elected at the general election in November, 1954, and thereafter, shall serve for the full terms provided in this Constitution.

(a) District Clerks; (b) County Clerks; (c) County Judges; (d) Judges of County Courts-at-Law, County Criminal Courts, County Probate Courts, and County Domestic Relations Courts; (e) County Treasurers; (f) Criminal District Attorneys; (g) County Surveyors; (h) Inspectors of Hides and Animals; (i) County Commissioners for Precincts Two and Four; (j) Justices of the Peace.

Notwithstanding other provisions of this Constitution, the following officers elected at the general election in November, 1954, shall serve only for terms of two years: (a) Sheriffs; (b) Assessors and Collectors of Taxes; (c) District Attorneys; (d) County Attorneys; (e) Public Weighers; (f) County Commissioners for Precincts One and Three; (g) Constables. At subsequent elections, such officers shall be elected for the full terms provided in this Constitution.

In any district, county or precinct where any of the aforementioned offices is of such nature that two or more persons hold such office, with the result that candidates file for "Place No. 1," "Place No. 2," etc., the officers elected at the general election in November, 1954, shall serve for a term of two years if the designation of their office is an uneven number, and for a term of four years, if the designation of their office is an even number. Thereafter, all such officers shall be elected for the term provided in this Constitution.

Provided, however, if any of the officers named herein shall announce their candidacy, or shall in fact become a candidate, in any General, Special or Primary Election, for any office of profit or trust under the laws of this state or the United States other than the office then held, at any time when the unexpired term of the office then held shall exceed one (1) year, such announcement or such candidacy shall constitute an automatic resignation of the office then held, and the vacancy thereby created shall be filled pursuant to law in the same manner as other vacancies for such office are filled.

[Note — The foregoing Sec. 65 of Art. XVI, an amendment, was added for the purpose of setting the terms of office of the aforementioned officers. Submitted by the Fifty-third Legislature (1953) and adopted in an election Nov. 2, 1954. This section was further amended by adding the provision that a person must resign his present term of office if same has more than a year to run when he becomes a candidate for another office. Submitted by the Fifty-fifth Legislature (1957) and adopted in an election Nov. 4, 1958.]

Sec. 66. Pensions for Texas Rangers — The Legislature shall have authority to provide for a system of retirement and disability pensions for retiring Texas Rangers who have not been eligible at any time for membership in the Employees Retirement System of Texas as that retirement system was established by Chapter 352, Acts of the Fiftieth Legislature, Regular Session, 1947, and who have had as much as two (2) years service as a Texas Ranger, and to their widows; providing that no pension shall exceed Eighty Dollars ($80) per month to any such Texas Ranger or his widow, provided that such widow was legally married prior to January 1, 1957, to a Texas Ranger qualifying for such pension.

These pensions may be paid only from the special fund created by *Sec. 17, Art. VII for a payment of pensions for services in the Confederate army and navy, frontier organizations, and the militia of the State of Texas, and for widows of such soldiers serving in said armies, navies, organizations or militia.

*Sec. 17, Art. VII was repealed by amendment adopted in election Nov. 2, 1982. No provision has been made for deletion of this reference in Art. XVI to Sec. 17, Art. VII. (See Art. VIII, Sec. 1-e.)

[Note — The foregoing Sec. 66 of Art. XVI, an amendment, was added to provide for retirement pensions for Texas Rangers and their widows. Submitted by the Fifty-fifth Legislature (1957), adopted in an election Nov. 4, 1958. (See also Art. VIII, Sec. 1-e.)]

Sec. 67. State Retirement Systems — (a) General Provisions. (1) The Legislature may enact general laws establishing systems and programs of retirement and related disability and death benefits for public employees and officers. Financing of benefits must be based on sound actuarial principles. The assets of a system are held in trust for the benefit of members and may not be diverted.

(2) A person may not receive benefits from more than one system for the same service, but the Legislature may provide by law that a person with service covered by more than one system or program is entitled to a fractional benefit from each system or program based on service rendered under each system or program calculated as to amount upon the benefit formula used in that system or program. Transfer of service credit between the Employees Retirement System of Texas and the Teacher Retirement System of Texas also may be authorized by law.

(3) Each statewide benefit system must have a board of trustees to administer the system and to invest the funds of the system in such securities as the board may consider prudent investments. In making investments, a board shall exercise the judgment and care under the circumstances then prevailing that persons of ordinary prudence, discretion, and intelligence exercise in the management of their own affairs, not in regard to speculation, but in regard to the permanent disposition of their funds, considering the probable income therefrom as well as the probable safety of their capital. The Legislature by law may further restrict the investment discretion of a board.

(4) General laws establishing retirement systems and optional retirement programs for public employees and officers in effect at the time of the adoption of this section remain in effect, subject to the general powers of the Legislature established in this subsection.

(b) **State Retirement Systems.** (1) The Legislature shall establish by law a Teacher Retirement System of Texas to provide benefits for persons employed in the public schools, colleges, and universities supported wholly or partly by the state. Other employees may be included under the system by law.

(2) The Legislature shall establish by law an Employees Retirement System of Texas to provide benefits for officers and employees of the state and such state-compensated of-

Article XVI — (Cont'd.); Article XVII

ficers and employees of appellate courts and judicial districts as may be included under the system by law.

(3) The amount contributed by a person participating in the Employees Retirement System of Texas or the Teacher Retirement System of Texas shall be established by the Legislature but may not be less than six percent of current compensation. The amount contributed by the state may not be less than six percent nor more than 10 percent of the aggregate compensation paid to individuals participating in the system. In an emergency, as determined by the governor, the Legislature may appropriate such additional sums as are actuarially determined to be required to fund benefits authorized by law.

(c) **Local Retirement Systems.** (1) The Legislature shall provide by law for:

(A) The creation by any city or county of a system of benefits for its officers and employees;

(B) A statewide system of benefits for the officers and employees of counties or other political subdivisions of the state in which counties or other political subdivisions may voluntarily participate; and

(C) A statewide system of benefits for officers and employees of cities in which cities may voluntarily participate.

(2) Benefits under these systems must be reasonably related to participant tenure and contributions.

(d) **Judicial Retirement System.** (1) Notwithstanding any other provision of this section, the system of retirement, disability, and survivors' benefits heretofore established in the constitution or by law for justices, judges, and commissioners of the appellate courts and judges of the district and criminal district courts is continued in effect. Contributions required and benefits payable are to be as provided by law.

(2) General administration of the Judicial Retirement System of Texas is by the Board of Trustees of the Employees Retirement System of Texas under such regulations as may be provided by law.

(e) **Anticipatory Legislation.** Legislation enacted in anticipation of this amendment is not void because it is anticipatory.

[Note — The foregoing Sec. 67 of Art. XVI, an amendment, was added to revise and consolidate provisions relating to state and local retirement systems and programs, and providing for a maximum state contribution to state systems of 10 percent of aggregate compensation paid to individuals. Submitted by the Sixty-fourth Legislature (1975) and adopted in an election April 22, 1975. See also notes under Art. III, Sections 48-a, 48-b, 51-e and 51-f; and Art. XVI, Sections 62 and 63.]

Sec. 68. **Promoting, Marketing Agricultural Products** — The Legislature may provide for the advancement of food and fiber in this state by providing representative associations of agricultural producers with authority to collect such refundable assessments on their product sales as may be approved by referenda of producers. All revenue collected shall be used solely to finance programs of marketing, promotion, research, and education relating to that commodity.

[Note — The foregoing Sec. 68 of Art. XVI, an amendment, was added to provide for the advancement of food and fiber production and marketing through research, education and promotion, financed by producers of agricultural products. Submitted by Sixty-eighth Legislature (1983) and adopted in election Nov. 8, 1983.]

Sec. 69. The Legislature may require, by rider in the General Appropriations Act or by separate statute, the prior approval of the expenditure or the emergency transfer of any funds appropriated by the agencies of state government.

[Note — The foregoing Sec. 69 of Art. XVI, an amendment, was added to protect public funds by authorizing prior approval of expenditure or emergency transfer of state appropriations. Submitted by Sixty-ninth Legislature (1985) and adopted in an election Nov. 5, 1985.]

ARTICLE XVII — MODE OF AMENDING THE CONSTITUTION OF THIS STATE

Sec. 1. **How the Constitution Is to Be Amended** — The Legislature, at any regular session, or at any special session when the matter is included within the purposes for which the session is convened, may propose amendments revising the Constitution, to be voted upon by the qualified electors for statewide offices and propositions, as defined in the Constitution and statutes of this State. The date of the elections shall be specified by the Legislature. The proposal for submission must be approved by a vote of two-thirds of all the members elected to each House, entered by yeas and nays on the journals.

A brief explanatory statement of the nature of a proposed amendment, together with the date of the election and the wording of the proposition as it is to appear on the ballot, shall be published twice in each newspaper in the State which meets requirements set by the Legislature for the publication of official notices of officers and departments of the state government. The explanatory statement shall be prepared by the Secretary of State and shall be approved by the Attorney General. The Secretary of State shall send a full and complete copy of the proposed amendment or amendments to each county clerk who shall post the same in a public place in the courthouse at least 30 days prior to the election on said amendment. The first notice shall be published not more than 60 days nor less than 50 days before the date of the election, and second notice shall be published on the same day in the succeeding week. The Legislature shall fix the standards for the rate of charge for the publication, which may not be higher than the newspaper's published national rate for advertising per column inch.

The election shall be held in accordance with procedures prescribed by the Legislature, and the returning officer in each county shall make returns to the Secretary of State of the number of legal votes cast at the election for and against each amendment. If it appears from the returns that a majority of the votes cast have been cast in favor of an amendment, it shall become a part of this Constitution, and proclamation thereof shall be made by the Governor.

[Note—Sec. 1 of Art. XVII was amended to revise provisions on time and method of proposing amendments to State Constitution and publishing notice of proposed amendments. Submitted by the Sixty-second Legislature (1971) and adopted in an election Nov. 7, 1972.]

Sec. 2. **Rewriting State Constitution** — (a) When the Legislature convenes in regular session in January, 1973, it shall provide by concurrent resolution for the establishment of a constitutional revision commission. The Legislature shall appropriate money to provide an adequate staff, office space, equipment, and supplies for the commission.

(b) The commission shall study the need for constitutional change and shall report its recommendations to the members of the Legislature not later than November 1, 1973.

(c) The members of the Sixty-third Legislature shall be convened as a constitutional convention at noon on the second Tuesday in January, 1974. The Lieutenant Governor shall preside until a chairman of the convention is elected. The convention shall elect other officers it deems necessary, adopt temporary and permanent rules, and publish a journal of its proceedings. A person elected to fill a vacancy in the Sixty-third Legislature before dissolution of the convention becomes a member of the convention on taking office as a member of the Legislature.

(d) Members of the convention shall receive compensation, mileage, per diem as determined by a five-member committee, to be composed of the Governor, Lieutenant Governor, Speaker of the House, Chief Justice of the Supreme Court, and Chief Justice of the Court of Criminal Appeals. This shall not be held in conflict with Art. XVI, Sec. 33 of the Texas Constitution. The convention may provide for the expenses of its members and for the employment of a staff for the convention, and for these purposes may by resolution appropriate money from the general revenue fund of the State Treasury. Warrants shall be drawn pursuant to vouchers signed by the chairman or by a person authorized by him in writing to sign them.

(e) The convention, by resolution adopted on the vote of at least two-thirds of its members, may submit for a vote of the qualified electors of this State a new Constitution which may contain alternative articles or sections, or may submit revisions of the existing Constitution which may contain alternative articles or sections. Each resolution shall specify the date of the election, the form of the ballots, and the method of publicizing the proposals to be voted on. To be adopted, each proposal must receive the favorable vote of the majority of those voting on the proposal. The conduct of the election, the canvassing of the votes, and the reporting of the returns shall be as provided for elections under Sec. 1 of this article.

(f) The convention may be dissolved by resolution adopted on the vote of at least two thirds of its members; but it is automatically dissolved at 11:59 p.m. on May 31, 1974, unless its duration is extended for a period not to exceed 60 days by resolution adopted on the vote of at least two thirds of its members.

(g) The Bill of Rights of the present Texas Constitution shall be retained in full.

[Note—The foregoing Sec. 2 of Art. XVII is an added amendment, providing for a constitutional convention for the purpose of submitting to the voters a new constitution or revisions of the existing state constitution. Submitted by the Sixty-second Legislature (1971) and adopted in an election Nov. 7, 1972.]

A Concise History of Texas

THIS short history of Texas from prehistoric times to the present was prepared especially for the Sesquicentennial by Mike Kingston, editor of the Texas Almanac. As in any project of this magnitude, Kingston had the help of many people. He particularly wants to thank Ruth Harris, Mary Crawford and Paula LaRocque of The Dallas Morning News for proofreading and editing the material.

Several professionals critiqued the manuscript, and their comments and suggestions were invaluable. Included among these were: Dr. Alan Skinner, an independent professional archaeologist of Dallas; Bob Forrester, an amateur archaeologist of Fort Worth; Dr. David Weber, chairman of the Department of History, Southern Methodist University; Dr. Archie P. McDonald, professor of history, Stephen F. Austin University; Dr. Fane Downs, professor of history, McMurry College; Dr. Paul Lack, professor of history, McMurry College; Dr. Alwyn Barr, chairman of the Department of History, Texas Tech University; Dr. Adrian N. Anderson, chairman of the Department of History, Lamar University; and the late Dr. Ernest Wallace of Texas Tech University. Any errors, of course, are those of the author alone.

Table of Contents

Prehistoric Texas

MANY factors make the once-simple picture of early humanity in Texas a much more complex and interesting problem. More than 30,000 archaeological sites have been registered with the state, and new ones are discovered regularly. Archaeologists, with the aid of scientists from other disciplines, are bringing more sophisticated techniques to bear on the studies of the clues that prehistoric Texans left. New discoveries and more detailed information open additional dimensions to our knowledge of early man in the state.

The picture of early humans in Texas will not be brought into final focus for decades. But indications are that these first human inhabitants of the state were probably more intelligent, more resourceful and more culturally developed than the often conveyed image of the "squatting savage."

One basic theory remains unchallenged — how these people got to the New World. Early Texans were descendants of those Asian groups that migrated across the Bering Strait during the Ice Ages of the past 50,000 years. At intermittent periods, enough water would accumulate in the massive glaciers worldwide to lower the sealevel several hundred feet. During these periods, the Bering Strait would become a 1,300-mile-wide land bridge between North America and Asia. These early adventurers worked their way southward for thousands of years, eventually getting as far as Tierra del Fuego in Argentina 10,000 years ago. These migrations populated both North and South America in a relatively short time. It is generally accepted that these people walked to the New World, although some scientists suggest that groups may have come by sea.

By land or sea, they brought a paleolithic technology. Their primitive tool kit contained projectile points, scrapers and other simple stone tools. Atlatls, or spear-throwing sticks, were used to launch projectiles. Basically these people were big game hunters and may have followed their prey across the land bridge.

Biologically they were completely modern homo sapiens sapiens. No evidence has been found to indicate that any evolutionary change occurred in the New World. Dressed in modern attire, scientists say, these early Texans would be indistinguishable from those of today.

Four basic periods reflecting cultural advancement of early inhabitants are used by archaeologists in classifying evidence. These periods are the Paleo-Indian (20,000 years ago to 7,000 years ago); Archaic (7,000 years ago to about the time of Christ); Woodland (time of Christ to 800-1,000 years ago), and Neo-American, or Late Prehistoric, (800-1,000 years ago until European contact). Not all early people advanced through all these stages in Texas. Much cultural change was made in adaptation to changes in climate. The Caddo Indians of East Texas, for example, reached the Neo-American stage before French and Spanish explorers made contact in the 16th and 17th centuries. Others, such as the Karankawas of the Gulf Coast, advanced no further

than the Archaic at the same time. Still others advanced and then regressed in the face of a changing climate.

The earliest confirmed evidence indicates that these humans were in Texas between 10,000 and 13,000 years ago. "Midland Minnie," which was identified from only a few pieces of skull, was discovered in Midland County in 1953. Dated by chemical methods, these remains were determined to be 10,000 years old. In 1983, the discoveries of two burial sites dating to about the same period or earlier were announced. Archaeologists with the Texas Department of Highways and Public Transportation uncovered the complete skeleton of a woman in the excavation on a farm-to-market road project near Leander, north of Austin in Central Texas. Material found in the grave site was radiocarbon dated at 10,000 to 13,000 years old. The site also was a well-preserved ceremonial burial with artifacts such as a grinding stone and beads found with the skeleton. A rock, which could have been a primitive headstone, also was found in the grave.

Shortly after the Leander discovery was announced, amateur archaeologists working on an excavation near Waco reported the discovery of a double burial of a man and child. Material from this grave site was radiocarbon dated at 10,000 years, too. In addition, the two skeletons were covered with several large stones, which, along with other evidence, indicated a ceremonial burial. Artifacts — apparently from the High Plains and the Gulf Coast — were found in the grave, indicating the people participated in a wide trade territory.

Paleo-Indians have long been considered successful big game hunters. Artifacts from this period are found across the state but not in great number, indicating they were a small, nomadic population. Some of the artifacts have been found in conjunction with kill sites of large animals. Texas' climate was cooler and much wetter during this period, providing lush grasslands to be grazed by large animals. Early Texans hunted prehistoric bison, which were seven feet tall at the shoulder, and small horses. Although the horse evolved to its modern state in the New World, it had become extinct and had to be returned to the New World in the 16th century by European explorers.

PREHISTORIC Texans used the same hunting tactics for thousands of years. In one area on the Rio Grande in Val Verde County, sites ranging in age from Paleo to Archaic to Pre-Historic indicate that bison were driven over the edge of a cliff to their deaths and then butchered. The ages of the sites vary from hundreds to thousands of years.

Archaeological studies came relatively late to Texas, and the delay probably cost the state a place in the terminology of science. In 1924, a man and a boy walking down the dry bed of Lone Wolf Creek near Colorado City in Mitchell County found the skeleton of an ancient bison eroding from the bank. Within the rib cage of the skeleton were found three projectile points that are described today as "Clovis" points. Large and with a characteristic design, Clovis points are now bench-marks for dating the earliest evidence of man in North America. The Texas discovery could not be dated to the satisfaction of scientists of the day. In 1936, similar points found at a kill site near Clovis, N.M., could be scientifically dated. The New Mexico city is now honored as the namesake of the points. Folsom points, which are smaller and fluted, also are named for a New Mexico community near which the first of these points was found and dated in 1926.

Prior to the discoveries near Leander and Waco, only four or five complete skeletons of Paleo-Indians had been discovered in the New World. These people had long been considered to be nomads with an egali-tarian society. With evidence of ceremonial burials and artifacts indicating broad trade territories, new dimen-sions will be added to the cultural assessment of these early Texans.

For example, the projectile points and other arti-facts found in the Paleo sites of Texas differ significant-ly from those excavated in Northern Mexico sites, indi-cating two distinct cultural traditions within a narrow geographical range.

AS Texas' climate changed at the end of the Ice Age about 7,000 years ago, inhabitants adapted. Ap-parently the state experienced an extended peri-od of warming and drying and a population increase. Archaic Indians accommodated the change by broad-ening cyclical hunting and gathering patterns and by becoming less selective in game. They stalked smaller animals, as well as large beasts, as indicated by the reduced size of the projectile points found at these sites. Their tool kit was expanded to include stone drills, axes and knives used to work bone and wood. And these Tex-ans began to harvest fruits and nuts when in season and exploited rivers for food, as indicated by the fresh-wa-ter mussel shells in ancient garbage heaps. Archaic In-dians also had broad trade territories. Flint from the Alibates quarry in the Panhandle was transported throughout a territory thousands of square miles wide, and chert from the Edwards Plateau was used to make projectile points and other artifacts found in North and East Texas.

Several burial sites from this period also have been excavated. The bodies were buried with tools and some-times dogs. A site near Houston contained dozens of burials, indicating that these early people had returned to the same area over hundreds of years to bury the dead. Dating between 5,000 and 6,000 years old, the site produced artifacts made of chert from near Little Rock, Ark., and sea shells possibly from Florida.

The people were involved in a much wider trade territory than previously thought. At about the time of Christ, the Woodland stage began to emerge in parts of Texas. This period is distinguished by the development of complex, settled societies. The people were less no-madic. While they still ranged widely in search of game, crops and local wild plants provided much of their diets. And the first evidence of social stratification is found. The bow and arrow came into use, and the first pottery is associated with this period. Between 750-800 A.D., Pre-Caddoan Indians in East Texas had formed primitive villages and were building distinctive mounds for burials and for rituals.

Some Indians reached this stage and then reverted when the climate changed, as it did in the Texas Pan-handle and along the Rio Grande. In these areas, evi-dence has been found of agriculture-based communi-ties that ceased to exist.

The Neo-American period, which is best exempli-fied by the highly civilized Caddos of East Texas, is dated between 800-1000 A.D. and the time of the Europe-an contact with New Mexico natives. Early Texans that reached this stage had very complex cultures with well-defined social stratification. They were fully agricul-tural and participated in exotic trade over wide areas.

When the Europeans arrived, they found people in Texas living in cultures that ranged from the very primitive to the highly complex.

Archaeologists often are frustrated by the theories propounded by amateurs and speculators who propose that similarities between cultures in different areas in-dicate a contact. Other questions are raised that simply cannot be answered by the present stage of research and understanding. Some of those will be reviewed here.

One of the most enduring, but unresolved, theories is that Prehistoric Texas was on the route that colonists

of the Olmec or Toltec civilizations in early Mexico fol-lowed to the Mississippi Valley and the Southeast Unit-ed States. There are many similarities between the ear-ly Mexican civilizations and the Mississippi cultures. Both built large ceremonial mounds, had similar social organizations and shared other cultural traits. In Mexi-co, these early tendencies evolved into the massive pyr-amids also characterizing the Maya and Aztec civiliza-tions that greeted early Spaniards. Although some amateurs have found tantalizing evidence of an over-land migration between these New World cultures, ac-ceptable scientific proof has not been established.

The earliest evidence of the presence of humans in Texas also has been clouded by enigmatic finds. In the 1950s, for example, amateur archaeologist R. King Har-ris and other members of the Dallas Archeological Soci-ety found a Clovis projectile point along the shoreline of Lake Lewisville in Denton County before the dam was completed. Radiocarbon dating of material found in the hearths associated with the point ran off the scale of the day. According to these tests, the points were asso-ciated with material that was almost 40,000 years old — much before early humans were in the New World, ac-cording to conventional wisdom. Subsequent investiga-tions in the early 1980s found that the dated samples were contaminated with lignite, a hydrocarbon that would throw the dating far askew. The final evaluation of the hearths, which were restudied when a drought lowered the water level in the lake, was that they were about 10,000 years old. But the sites do represent the first use of a fuel other than wood for a fire in the New World.

Another question not so easily answered is the case of the Malakoff-Trinidad heads found in Henderson County in the 1920s and 1930s. These are three largest ones that have apparent hand-carved human features. They were found in the bottom of a gravel stratum over an eight-year period. And with the exception of the final stone, no scientific archaeological surveys were made of the discovery sites. If the heads were deposited in the bottom of the stratum in which they were found, they indicate that humanity was in Texas — and the New World — 40,000 to 50,000 years ago, again far earlier than thought by many of today's scientists. Because of the lack of a professional survey at the time of discov-ery, this question may never be answered.

Other mysteries also exist. On a West Central Texas hillside, a series of vertical and horizontal lines firmly engraved in sandstone have been deciphered as a form of ancient Celtic line writing in a Celtiberian language. Epigrapher Barry Fell, a marine biologist turned epi-grapher, has been criticized by professional archaeolo-gists for errors and misinterpretation of engravings in rock in other sections of the country. But he holds fast to the theory that these inscriptions were left by Celtic adventurers and traders, giving travel instructions to others. The inscriptions are examples, Fell contends, of a well-developed trade between Europe and the New World long before Columbus or even the Vikings and Irish monks ventured westward.

In another case, a plaque bearing what was inter-preted as ancient Libyan writing was found in the Big Bend in the early 1960s. The plaque itself was lost, but pictures of it have been deciphered by Fell. These, too, verified his contention that even African peoples were trading in the New World long before the usually ac-cepted discoverers of North and South America took to the sea.

THIS curiosity is compounded by an incident men-tioned by Spanish colonizer Jose de Escandon in the middle 18th century when he came upon a tribe of black Indians near the mouth of the Rio Grande. These "Indians" told the explorer that their ancestors had come to the New World by boat from a homeland that must have been Africa. They were identified as Negroids, and the blacks fought with spears and shields unlike those used by other Indians in the area. Escan-don speculated that the blacks were survivors of the wreck of a slave boat or that they had escaped from a slave colony on an island in the Gulf of Mexico. No fur-ther mention is made of this tribe by later colonizers or explorers. But the blacks had intermarried with local Indian women, and chances are that they were ab-sorbed by other bands in the area. Nevertheless, in re-cent years, there has been speculation, based on the Negroid features on some Olmec and Toltec statues, that blacks from Africa visited the New World — and possibly Texas — long before Columbus opened the New World for European colonization.

No definitive answers to these puzzles are expected or obtainable. They stand outside the usual realm of archaeological research. But they still present questions about the prehistory of Texas that should be borne in mind. Studies have found that legends often have a basis in fact. Other enigmas are based on enough evidence to put them a degree beyond rank speculation. But these ideas have yet to rest on the foundation of solid scientific evidence necessary to make them a part of the state's prehistory.

The Spanish Period

SPAIN'S conquest of the New World was one of the first acts of a vigorous, emerging nation. For 700 years, the Spanish fought to oust the Moorish invaders from the Iberian Peninsula. Regional and ethnic divisions hampered the effort, but the marriage of Isabella of Castile and Ferdinand of Aragon unified the country under a single monarchy.

Under Ferdinand's leadership in early 1492, the Spanish army conquered the province of Granada, completing the reconquista. Later in the year, Ferdinand and Isabella took a major stride toward shaping world history by commissioning Christopher Columbus to find a western route to the Far East.

Some historians characterize this voyage and subsequent subjugation of the New World as an extension of the Christian crusades against the Muslims. From the beginning, Columbus' exploration had religious, as well as economic, goals. In a papal bull in 1493, Pope Alexander VI gave Spain the right to develop any new lands that might be discovered west of the longitude 100 leagues west of the Azores and Cape Verde. But the assignment was conditioned on the Spanish making "God's name known there." The ultimate goal of Columbus' voyage was to establish contact with the Great Khan, a mythical figure as it turned out, in the Far East. Initially trade was to be developed, and Christianity was to be taken to the pagans. Ultimately, however, the Spaniards hoped to form an alliance with the powers of the Far East to put the Muslims in pincers and to break their control of the rich overland trade routes through the Middle East and to secure Christian dominance of the Holy Land.

From Columbus' first contact with New World natives, missionaries were in the forefront of the exploration. Early in the conquest, the Spanish crown decreed that the pagans must submit to Christian authority and receive religious instruction. If the natives refused, a "just war" could be initiated against them with enslavement to follow. And the Spanish conquest of Mexico and Central America was accomplished with astonishing speed. Between 1519-21, Hernan Cortez conquered the Aztecs in the Valley of Mexico and partially transformed the sophisticated Indian culture into the image of Christian Spain. The Aztecs of Central Mexico and the Mayans of the Yucatan and Central America, however, were settled, civilized people, much accustomed to following hierarchical leadership and to paying tribute or taxes. Although they stubbornly resisted the Spanish, the ultimate conquest was relatively simple.

Unlike Anglo-Americans, the Spanish had little racial prejudice in the modern sense. Throughout the long struggle with the Moors, the great gulf was between Christians and infidels, not between races. However, dark-skinned people were considered inferior, for most were thought to be infidels. From the initial contact, Spaniards intermixed with Indian women. The only social or religious limitation was the qualification that the women accept Christianity.

Spanish monarchs and religious leaders agonized over the treatment of New World natives. The conquest was bloody, as might be expected in a war. And afterward, other natives resisted conversion to Christianity. Spanish occupation policy also produced atrocities. Throughout the reconquest of the Iberian Peninsula, the Spanish required tribute from the conquered peoples. To reward the conquistadors for the perilous adventure in the New World, an encomienda system was established, in keeping with the practice used throughout the reconquista. The Spaniards were granted land and the use of natives. For this, the grantee was required to protect the Indians, to provide for their needs and to see that they were taught the faith. Too often the system was abused and degenerated into a form of slavery.

By 1540 the concern about treatment of the New World natives became so serious that Charles V suspended expeditions while a junta considered arguments about the proper policy toward treatment of the

Indians. Pope Paul III in 1537 issued a papal bull asserting that the Indians were not "dumb brutes" and should not be enslaved. Bartolome de las Casas, a Dominican missionary with many years of experience in the New World, urged a humane policy. He suggested that priests be given strict parental control while the natives received religious instruction. The mission system that developed reflected some of Las Casas' suggestions. Others disagreed with this argument and harked back to Aristotle's theory of natural slavery. The argument held that some segments of mankind were born to serve a leisure class. The Spaniards, of course, were to be the leisure class.

Official policy of Spanish kings and popes was to treat the New World natives as reasoning human beings. They believed that all humans could be improved with patient instruction. In 1573, an ordinance was promulgated decreeing that "pacification," not "conquest," of the New World was Spain's goal. But policies and pronouncements often did not survive the trip across the Atlantic. The king's policy might always be obeyed, it was said, but it was not always enforced.

Humane treatment of the Indians had more practical sides, too. While England and France had excess populations to colonize the New World, Spain was a relatively sparsely settled nation. Therefore the crown's policy incorporated the Indians as an integral part of the colonization effort. They would be turned into good Spanish citizens. To this end, the mission system was developed with two basic goals: To convert the Indians to Christianity and to make them economically productive citizens. With the protection of the military, the aborigines in an untamed area who expressed a willingness to receive instruction would be congregated at a mission to be taught the faith and a trade as well. When the Indians' training was completed, the mission would be secularized as a church. The missionaries would move to another area. The system worked with varying degrees of success, although the zeal of the Franciscan, Dominican and Jesuit missionaries seldom waned.

"Pacification" of the New World became more difficult as the Spaniards moved north of the Valley of Mexico. The fierce Chichimecas resisted the Spanish yoke as vigorously as they had the Aztecs. These were nomadic Indians whose culture had little resemblance to that of the Aztecs or Mayans. In 1528, two expeditions launched by Cortez from the Rio Panuco crossed the Rio Grande but did not stay. No doubt other explorers briefly probed the region north of the Great River.

AS early as 1519, Alonso Alvarez de Pineda, a captain in the service of Francisco Garay, governor of Jamaica, mapped the coast of Texas. Early historians credited Alvarez de Pineda with exploring the Rio Grande from its mouth to the Brownsville area and with referring to the river as the "Rio de las Palmas." But recent research questions this interpretation. The first recorded exploration of today's Texas was made in the 1530s by Alvar Nunez Cabeza de Vaca, two other Spaniards and a Moorish black slave named "Esteban." They were members of the expedition commanded by Panfilo de Narvaez that left Cuba in 1528 to explore Florida — which included most of the southeastern United States and all the land westward to the Rio Grande at the time. Ill-fated from the beginning, many members of the expedition lost their lives, and others, including Cabeza de Vaca, were shipwrecked on the Texas coast. Cabeza de Vaca and his companions, although separated at intervals, survived and lived with a series of Indian tribes that inhabited much of southwestern and far western Texas. Through a combination of good luck and skill, Cabeza de Vaca gained a reputation as a healer, and after a time he was held in great esteem by many Indian groups. At one point in his wanderings, the Spaniard performed the first recorded medical surgery in the state by removing an arrow head from a man's chest. Wherever the little band of Spaniards went, however, stories circulated about the lands of great wealth to the north — the Seven (Golden) Cities of Cibola. When Cabeza de Vaca was reunited with his countrymen in Mexico in 1536, these tales excited the interest of authorities.

In 1540, Francisco Vazquez de Coronado, governor of New Galicia, was commissioned to lead an exploration of the American Southwest. The quest took him to the land of the Pueblo Indians in New Mexico. Here his interest in riches was further enhanced with tales of Gran Quivira, a land rumored to be even richer than Cibola. Native Americans learned it was best to keep the Europeans away from their homes, so they would suggest vast riches could be found in other areas. So Coronado pursued a fruitless search for the riches across the High Plains of Texas, Oklahoma and Kansas. Missionaries on the expedition found the number of potential souls to save overwhelming and stayed in the upper Rio Grande valley.

While Coronado was investigating Texas' High Plains from the west, Luis Moscoso de Alvarado assumed leadership of Hernando de Soto's expedition when the commander died on the banks of the Mississippi River. In 1542, Moscoso's group ventured as far west as Central Texas before returning to the Mississippi. While sailing for Mexico, the group was shipwrecked for a time at the mouth of the Sabine River. Here they used oil from seeps to caulk their boats, ignoring the claims of local Indians that the petroleum had great medicinal properties. This was the first recorded use of the mineral in the state — the mineral that has become synonymous with Texas.

But an era was ending. Cortez had found great riches that could be easily reaped in the Aztec and Mayan kingdoms. Other conquistadors had been equally successful, and even lesser adventurers had profited within the encomienda system. These vigorous, ambitious men who had fought first to free Spain from the Moors and then to conquer the New World were aging. The Coronado expedition is considered by some historians as the last of the old regime. Certainly the makeup was different. More non-Spaniards participated, and the men were younger, without the battle experience of the older warrior-explorers. And the northern territories were unlike central Mexico in climate, culture and economic potential. Quick wealth was not to be found. A new generation of explorers and settlers would be required to venture into the harsh northern territories.

One of this new breed was Luis de Carvajal, a member of a Jewish family that converted to Christianity. He was given a huge land grant stretching from the Rio Panuco in Mexico to an area near present-day San Antonio. As part of the bargain, he agreed to introduce cattle into the region. Though it is not known if Carvajal ever visited Texas, cattle that he brought into Mexico are thought to have migrated north of the Rio Grande. Carvajal died while imprisoned during the Inquisition for failing to denounce his sister as a Jew.

Spain had no precedents from which to develop an administrative system for the New World colonies. What evolved was cumbersome procedure that stifled initiative and action. The Council of the Indes administered New Spain, as Mexico was called, and viceroys supervised regional affairs. Philip II completely centralized the system upon taking the throne in 1556, however. Several administrative councils became only consulting bodies. Philip made all final decisions on affairs of state, down to the most inconsequential details. Consequently, decisions had to filter through a bureaucracy that stretched across the Atlantic. The process could — and did in some cases — take years. Philip's successors delegated authority to ministers after his death in 1598, but the system remained cumbersome and troublesome.

FORTY years passed after the Coronado and Moscoso expeditions before Fray Agustin Rodriguez, a Franciscan missionary, and Francisco Sanchez Chamuscado, a soldier, led an expedition into Texas and New Mexico. Following the Rio Conchos in Mexico to its confluence with the Rio Grande near present-day Presidio and then turning northwestward in the Great River's valley, the explorers passed through the El Paso area in 1581. Among the Pueblo Indians great material wealth was not found, but the missionary was satisfied with the spiritual potential of the pagans. Father Rodriguez died a martyr. The following year,

Antonio de Espejo led a relief expedition up the Pecos River from the Rio Grande to the Pueblo Indian area only to learn of the missionary's fate.

Permanent colonization of the upper Rio Grande valley was accomplished as the 16th century drew to a close. Juan de Onate was granted the right to develop the area in which the Pueblo Indians lived. In 1598, he blazed a trail across the desert from Santa Barbara, Chihuahua, to intersect the Rio Grande at the Pass of the North — today's El Paso. For the next 200 years, this was the supply route from the interior of Mexico that served the northern colonies. And the El Paso-Juarez area developed as a way station. The first permanent settlement in Texas was established in 1681 after the Pueblo Indians rebelled and drove the Spanish settlers southward. The colonists retreated to the El Paso area, where the missions of Ysleta del Sur and Socorro del Sur — each named for a community in New Mexico — were established. Ysleta pueblo originally was located on the south side of the Rio Grande, but as the river changed course, it ended up on the north bank. Now part of El Paso, the community is considered the oldest European settlement in Texas.

TEXAS was attractive to the Spanish in the 16th and 17th centuries. Small expeditions found trade possibilities, and missionaries had ventured into the territory to instruct the Indians. Frays Juan de Salas and Diego Lopez responded to a request by the Jumano Indians for religious instruction in 1629, and for a brief time the priests lived with the Indians near present-day San Angelo.

Missionary efforts also were made north of the Rio Grande. In 1675, Fernando del Bosque and Fray Juan Larios led an expedition to gain insight into the Coahuiltecan bands in the region. Capt. Juan Dominguez led an expedition that established a mission among the Jumano Indians at the La Junta — the confluence of the Rio Grande and the Rio Conchos. This mission was closed in 1688, and a priest blamed its problems on the military and others who enslaved many Indians to work in the north Mexico mines. But the Spanish crown was preoccupied with affairs in Europe. The colonial wealth also was diverted to these activities — and to extravagant living at court — rather than to investment in development of the New World. Ironically, it was affairs of state in Europe, rather than the resources and natural attractiveness of the territory, that first riveted Spain's attention on Texas. From 1681 to 1697, Spain and France were at war on the Continent, as they had been for much of the 17th century.

Spain's claim to the vast stretch of the New World from Florida to the Pacific Ocean rankled the French. In 1682, an ambitious and courageous Rene Robert Cavalier, Sieur de la Salle, explored the Mississippi to its mouth at the Gulf of Mexico. LaSalle claimed the vast territory for France, cutting the heart out of Spain's North American territories. Two years later, LaSalle returned to the New World with four ships and enough colonists to establish his country's claim in this segment of Spanish America. Some historians think that LaSalle's expedition was blown past the mouth of the Mississippi by a Gulf storm and ended up on the Texas coast by mistake; others think Texas was his planned destination. Nevertheless, though short of supplies because of the loss of two ships, the French colonists established Fort Saint Louis at the head of Lavaca Bay. Hostile Indians, bad weather and disease took their toll on the small enclave, although LaSalle managed three expeditions into the surrounding countryside. Based on these explorations, the French made a weak claim that the Rio Grande was the western boundary of Louisiana Territory. In 1687, LaSalle and a group of soldiers began an overland trip to find French outposts on the Mississippi. Somewhere near present-day Navasota in Grimes County, the great explorer was murdered by one of his men. His grave has never been found.

When Spanish officials heard from Indians about the French colony, a frenzied search for LaSalle was launched. Five sea expeditions combed the Gulf Coast from the Rio Grande to today's Florida. And six land expeditions into Texas' interior provided Spanish officials with the first detailed information about the territory. Finally in 1689, Capt. Alonso de Leon, governor of Coahuila, re-entered Texas at a ford near present-day Eagle Pass and headed eastward. He found the charred remains of Fort Saint Louis at the head of Lavaca Bay. Indians had destroyed the settlement and killed many colonists. DeLeon continued tracking survivors of the ill-fated colony into East Texas.

On this journey, Father Damian Massanet accompanied the official. The priest was fascinated with tales about the "Tejas" Indians of the region. "Tejas" meant friendly, but at the time the term was considered a tribal name. Actually these Indians were members of the Caddo Confederacy that controlled parts of four present states — Texas, Louisiana, Arkansas and Oklahoma. They were the most culturally developed of all Texas Indians. They farmed, had a well-developed leadership structure and traded across a broad area. Unlike other Indians, they had judicial and diplomatic procedures to settle disputes between groups within the confederacy. The Caddo religion also acknowledged one supreme god, which the Spanish felt made them prime candidates for conversion to Christianity. For years, the Tejas had been brought to the attention of the Spanish by the Jumano Indians who traded with them and with the Pueblo Indians of New Mexico.

Usually the Caddos did not let strangers enter their territory. Trade usually was carried on at annual fairs that were held on the periphery of their settlements. But with the French trading with the Caddos' enemies, the East Texas Indians were anxious to develop contacts with Europeans to obtain trade goods, guns and horses. Hence the Spanish were quite welcome.

When a Tejas chief asked Father Massanet to stay and instruct his people in religion, the Spaniards quickly promised to return and establish a mission. The pledge was redeemed in 1690 when the mission San Francisco de las Tejas was founded near present-day Weches in Houston County. A few months later, a second mission, Santisimo Nombre de Maria, was established nearby, only to be washed away by a flood in a few months.

Twin disasters struck this missionary effort. Spanish officials soon lost interest in the French threat. And as was the case with many New World Indians who had no resistance to European diseases, the Tejas soon were felled by an epidemic that killed many. Some Indians blamed the illness on the holy water used for baptism by the priests. Soon the mission languished. It was difficult to supply, being so far from the other Spanish outposts in northern Mexico, and the Caddos remained committed to their native religion. Also the priests often insulted the Indians' leaders and medicine men, and the soldiers were troublesome.

In addition to being the first European settlements in East Texas, the missions also brought ranching to the region. The herds of cattle driven to the area by De Leon were the first organized movement of livestock in Texas.

In 1693, Spanish officials closed the missions, however, leaving the Tejas to the stealthful ministrations of French traders for two decades.

Europeans and Indians

ALTHOUGH Spain had not made a determined effort to settle Texas, great changes were coming to the territory. The French had opened trade with Indians along the Mississippi River and its tributaries and had made contact with Indians on the High Plains. French guns and horses were changing the nature of warfare among the Indians.

Spain introduced horses into Texas and the Southwest. No one is sure when or how the Comanches got mounts. But in the late 17th century they began moving on to the Plains from their Rocky Mountain homelands. On foot, the Comanches were not intimidating. They were short and stocky and somewhat awkward in appearance. They were among the best horsemen in the world, however, and were fierce warriors, spreading terror wherever they went.

The southward movement of the Comanches and their allies on the Great Plains played havoc with the established homelands of several groups of Indians. The Apaches were the first to be displaced. And the Apaches were the first of the fierce Plains Indians to worry the Spanish. In the 1720s, the Apaches moved onto the lower Texas Plains, taking the traditional hunting grounds of the Jumanos and others. The nomadic Coahuiltecan bands were particularly hard hit. Attempts by these Indians to gain Spanish support against the Apaches were fruitless until the late 1720s, and by that time, many of the Apaches' enemies, like the Jumanos, had joined the raiders. As early as 1707, the El Paso area was under siege by the Apaches.

Although the Spanish stayed out of the Indian wars in the beginning of their excursions into Texas, they were soon drawn into the fray. In 1699, the French established a colony on the Mississippi River in Louisiana and began trading with the Indians in East Texas. The Spanish had to respond to the challenge to protect their interests.

Spanish officials became committed to opening Texas for trade and colonization. In 1700, the mission San Juan Bautista was moved to a site on the south side of the Rio Grande near present-day Eagle Pass where two excellent fords provided access across the river. The mission became the gateway to colonial Texas from Mexico, and many figures who shaped the territory's future passed through this portal.

In Europe, Philip V, the grandson of the French king with aspirations to the French throne, ascended to the Spanish throne in 1701, becoming the first of the Bourbon kings. He instituted reforms in the clumsy administrative system, but it remained an impediment to development of the New World frontier.

In 1709, Fray Antonio de San Buenaventura y Olivares made an initial request to establish a mission at San Pedro Springs (today's San Antonio) to minister to the Coahuiltecans, who were suffering at the hands of the Apaches. The request was denied. But the Spanish were xenophobic about the French, and quickly responded to any threat, real or perceived, by their European enemies.

Religious intrigue involving the French spurred the Spanish into action that led to the establishment of permanent missions and the colonization of Texas. Father Francisco Hidalgo had served at the Tejas missions in East Texas in the early 1690s and longed to return. When Spanish officials turned a deaf ear to his request, the priest secretly wrote the French governor of Louisiana in New Orleans seeking help in establishing a mission among the Tejas. Always anxious to open trade with the Spanish, the governor dispatched Louis Juchereau de Saint Denis, an adventurer and explorer, to find the priest and to enter into trade negotiations. While crossing Texas, Saint Denis was impressed with the number of wild cattle that roamed the region. These no doubt were the offspring of the cattle left at the East Texas missions, and the result of De Leon's practice of leaving a cow and a calf at each river crossing while traveling to East Texas in 1689. When Saint Denis arrived at San Juan Bautista, the Spanish were aghast at his temerity. Fears of new French incursions into Texas were fanned. Though Saint Denis vowed he wanted only to open trade — which was strictly forbidden by Spanish colonial policy — he was sent to Mexico City for questioning. Upon release by Spanish authorities, Saint Denis returned to San Juan Bautista, married the commandant's granddaughter and served as a guide for the expedition that established the second set of missions in East Texas.

FATHER Hidalgo's dream of returning to the Tejas was realized when he accompanied Capt. Diego Ramon on the expedition. The mission San Francisco de los Neches was established in 1716 near the site of the old San Francisco de los Tejas mission. Nuestra Senora de Guadalupe was located at the present-day site of Nacogdoches, and Nuestra Senora de los Dolores was placed near present-day San Augustine. Two other missions were located in the area, and another was built across the Sabine River in Louisiana. The East Texas missions did little better on the second try. Saint Denis, who was well-liked by the Indians, planned to stay in the area to set up a trading post. But the suspicious Spanish forced him to leave, to the distress of the Indians. Supplying the missions also was a problem, as it had been in the 1690s. The Indians were unhappy with the trade goods and the delays in receiving supplies. Soon it became apparent that a way station between northern Mexico and the East Texas missions was needed.

In 1718, Spanish officials consented to Fray Olivares' request to found a mission at San Pedro Springs.

Because the Indians of the region often did not get along with each other, other missions soon were established to serve each group. And for a time these missions flourished and each became an early ranching center. But the missions' large herds of cattle and horses soon attracted trouble.

About 1720, the Apaches made their first appearance in the San Antonio area. One settler was killed and scalped and raids on the missions' herds began. Punitive retaliation by the Spanish only outraged the Apaches, and religious authorities opposed the military operations. Attempts to negotiate a peace with the Apaches failed, but the raids subsided between 1726 and 1731.

War broke out between the French and Spanish in Europe, and the East Texas missions were temporarily abandoned a second time in 1717 after a comic-opera incident in which the mission at Nacogdoches was engaged by French soldiers from Natchitoches in present-day Louisiana.

The expulsion from East Texas prompted the Spanish to return with the largest military operation of the period. The Marquis San Miguel de Aguayo, a nobleman of Coahuila, was ordered to launch a retaliatory offensive, but the orders were soon changed. Texas' defenses were to be strengthened. Because of the time lag in receiving orders, Aguayo's expedition did not get into the field until 1721. With 500 men, 4,000 horses and large herds of livestock, he reached San Antonio in April 1721, and after strengthening the presidio there he headed for East Texas.

UNKNOWN to the Spanish in Texas, the French had suffered a financial disaster. John Law, a Scottish banker, had launched an investment scheme that involved the issuance of paper money in France to finance the development of colonies on the Mississippi River. The bubble broke in 1720, and the French government all but abandoned the colonization effort while retrenching to repair the damage to the nation's economy. In some cases, Indians in the Mississippi valley attacked French traders in rebellion against the diminished trade. But Saint Denis had been given command of French troops in Louisiana and tried to arrange a truce with Aguayo to prevent the remanning of Spanish missions and presidios in the region. The ploy did not work. Forts and missions were re-established, and a presidio was built at Los Adaes to keep an eye on the French at Natchitoches. This presidio, which was located near present-day Robeline, La., became the capital of the province of Texas for the next half century.

Aguayo was successful in strengthening the defenses in Texas. He re-established six missions, founded three more. Two new presidios were established, one re-established and a fourth strengthened. When Aguayo left Texas, 269 soldiers were on duty in a territory that previously was defended by only 60 to 70. He also separated the province of Texas from Coahuila for the first time, drawing the boundary along the San Antonio and Medina rivers.

While Texas' eastern frontier was threatened by the French in the 18th century, the greatest problem for the Spanish existed in the thinly populated areas of western Texas. The Comanches began their southward movement from the Northern Plains at the beginning of the century, relentlessly pushing the Apaches and others before them. The Apaches moved westward and southward. Attempts by the Jumano Indians to have missions established in the Big Bend near the junction of the Rio Grande and the Rio Conchos — the Junta de los Rios — were thwarted by hostiles in 1717-18. A mission built near present-day Del Rio suffered a similar fate. And San Juan Bautista, built unfortunately close to one prong of the Comanche trail crossing the Rio Grande, was under constant threat. Only the most adventuresome Spaniard or Mexican braved the hazards of this frontier to attempt colonization, and often the price paid for a display of courage was the settler's life. By the middle 1730s, the Apaches were raiding mercilessly south of the Rio Grande. Monclova and Saltillo were endangered, and the province of Sonora was on the brink of destruction. The Spanish concentrated their defensive efforts south of the river to protect the silver mines and ranches in northern Mexico. The province of Texas was actually "behind enemy lines" for much of the time.

The San Antonio missions felt the Apache wrath. The mission system, which attempted to convert the Indians to Christianity and to "civilize" them, was partially successful in subduing minor tribes. But the Spanish realized that more stable colonization efforts must be made. Mexican Indians, such as the Tlascalans who fought with Cortez against the Aztecs, were brought into Texas to serve as examples of "good" Indians for the wayward natives. In 1731, descendants of the colonists of the Canary Islands were brought to Texas and founded the Villa of San Fernando de Bexar, the first civil jurisdiction in the province and today's San Antonio. But the province remained thinly populated, much to the despair of Spanish officials.

As desperate as was the plight of Texas, the Spanish were more concerned about another area. One of Spain's most successful colonization efforts in the New World came in the Lower Rio Grande Valley. But the history of the effort underscores the lengthy process of decision-making in Spanish Texas. In the late 1730s, officials became concerned over the vulnerability of Seno Mexico — the large area between the Sierra Madre Oriental and the Gulf Coast in Northern Mexico. The area was unsettled, a haven for runaway Indian slaves and marauders, and it was a wide-open pathway for the English or French from the Gulf to the rich silver mines in Durango.

For seven years the search for the right colonizer went on before Jose de Escandon was selected in 1746. A professional military man and successful administrator, Escandon earned a high reputation by subduing Indians in Central Mexico. On receiving the assignment, he launched a broad land survey of the area running from the mountains to the Gulf and from the Rio Panuco in Tamaulipas, Mexico, to the Nueces River in Texas. In 1747, he began placing colonists in settlements throughout the area. Tomas Sanchez received a land grant on the Rio Grande in 1755 from which Laredo developed. And other small Texas communities along the river sprang up as a result of Escandon's well-executed plan. Many old Mexican families in Texas hold title to their land based on grants in this period.

Escandon's colony became the state of Nuevo Santander, named for the founder's home province in Spain. The boundaries extended to the Nueces River, placing the Lower Rio Grande Valley outside of Texas.

Escandon also contributed to the early development of ranching in South Texas. In 1753 he granted Capt. Jose Vasquiz Borrego 433,800 acres of land to develop a ranch. The headquarters was located near the present-day town of San Ygnacio in Zapata County. Other large land grants also helped establish large-scale ranching in the area, although Texas never developed the hacienda concept that was used in Mexico. Ranching helped the economy, but the livestock also attracted Indians.

AS devastating as the Apaches were to Spanish settlements, they were getting the worst of their fight with the Comanches and their allies. By 1747, the Apaches around San Antonio were ready to make peace and said they were ready to enter missions. Attempts to gather them in existing missions failed because other Indians feared and hated them after many years of bloody warfare. In 1757, officials established the mission of San Saba de la Santa Cruz in present-day Menard County. Two years later, the Spanish encountered the Comanches in Texas for the first time. The Comanches, with their allies from the Plains, devastated the mission, killing several priests and Indians. Spanish officials were irate. After much debate they launched a punitive expedition to punish the raiders. Col. Diego Ortiz Parrilla led a mixed army of Mexican soldiers, Lipan Apaches and Spanish soldiers. The force engaged a mixed group of Plains Indians at Spanish Fort on a bend of the Red River in present-day Montague County. Entrenched in a stockade with a crude moat, the Indians fought with French weapons and used disciplined tactics in the field. Abandoned by their allies, the Spanish suffered a humiliating loss, the worst inflicted on them by Texas Indians during the colonial period.

The battle of Spanish Fort was a turning point in Indian warfare. The Plains Indians proved they could adapt to European field tactics. And for a time, they had set aside tribal animosities to present a united front against the colonizers. The Spanish had easily defeated sedentary Indians in Mexico, but the Plains Indians were a different breed, as the defeat of the Spanish proved. Obviously, new tactics were needed if the Spanish were to stay in Texas.

The Demise of Spain

SPAIN'S final 60 years of control of the province of Texas were marked with a few successes and a multitude of failures, all of which could be attributed to a breakdown in the administrative system. Charles III, the fourth of the Bourbon line of kings and generally recognized as an enlightened despot, took the throne in 1759. Soon he launched a series of reforms in the New World. The king's choice of administrators was excellent. In 1765, Jose de Galvez was dispatched to New Spain (an area that then included all of modern Mexico and much of today's American West) with instructions to improve both the economy and the defense.

Galvez initially toured parts of the vast region, gaining first-hand insight into the practical problems of the colony. And there were many that could be traced to Spain's basic concepts of colonial government. Texas, in particular, suffered from the mercantilist economic system that attempted to funnel all colonial trade through ports in Mexico.

In a typical trip, trade goods bound for Texas would enter New Spain at the port of Veracruz. From there they would be shipped to Mexico City and then Saltillo before reaching Texas. At each stop, charges would be added. By the time the goods reached Texas, they would be prohibitively expensive. Texas' economy was limited. Ranching was its foundation, and there were few markets for Texas cattle and horses. The mines in northern Mexico were serviced by haciendas in that region. Texas' market was limited to the army, the missions and the few colonists who lived in the province.

Also, because of the mercantilist approach, trade with the French in Louisiana Territory was strictly forbidden. But Spanish Texans were practical people. When a demand for Texas cattle and horses developed in Louisiana, a healthy smuggling traffic arose. Texas' livestock became a medium of exchange for low-cost trade goods provided by French traders. And government officials in Texas often were bribed to look the other way.

Problems with the Comanches, Apaches and "Nortenos," as the Spanish called some tribes, continued to plague the province, too. The Marquis de Rubi was commissioned to inspect the defenses of the entire northern New Spain frontier from California to Louisiana. Rubi reached Texas in 1767 and was appalled by the deplorable condition of the province's defenses. At San Saba mission, there were not enough horses for each soldier, although each should have had four or five mounts to be properly equipped. Soldiers at Los Adaes had only two guns and two shields for the entire 60-man contingent. Morale was low throughout the province. In some cases, officers were selling equipment and uniforms to soldiers at greatly inflated prices. Rubi recommended sweeping reforms in the defense system. But some changes were based on faulty assumptions.

In 1762, France ceded the Louisiana Territory to Spain in compensation for Spain's help in the losing effort in the Seven Years War in Europe. The politics of the day convinced the French that it was better that this huge — and largely undefined — area be in the hands of the Spanish than the British. For the Spanish in Texas, the cession was a mixed blessing, however. True, the French were no longer an immediate threat on the province's eastern boundary. But the fact lulled Rubi into a false sense of security.

With the need to defend East Texas from the French diminished, Rubi moved to construct Texas' defenses around the needs of the mining and ranching areas in northern Mexico. This meant closing the East Texas missions and presidios and moving the soldiers and colonists to San Antonio to bolster defenses against the Indians. In addition, Rubi moved the presidio San Elizario north of the Rio Grande to defend the El Paso area and abandoned the San Saba mission and presidio, which were inactive anyway. Presidio La Bahia was strengthened, and a military way station was established at Arroyo del Cibola to protect the road between San Antonio and La Bahia. As a practical matter, however, much of Texas was not to be defended; it was, in a sense, "behind enemy lines."

Charles III's well-intentioned reorganization of New Spain took almost a decade. And in the interim, conflicting policies took their toll on good will and attempts to pacify the various Indian groups in Texas.

When Spain undertook the administration of Louisiana Territory, one of the terms of the cession by France was that the region would enjoy certain trading privileges denied to other Spanish dependencies. So although Texas and Louisiana were neighbors, trade between the two provinces was banned. The crown further complicated matters by placing the administration of Louisiana under authorities in Cuba, while Texas remained under the authorities in Mexico City. Officials often acted as if the two Spanish provinces were actually warring foreign countries. This was an intolerable burden on Spanish settlers in East Texas and on French traders who were being integrated into the effort to control the Nortenos, a term which covered a number of Plains Indians in Texas.

The Nortenos, who for a time were allied with the Comanches, warred intermittently against the Spanish after their victory at Spanish Fort in 1759. Nortenos resented treaties between the Spanish and their enemies, the Apaches. Punitive expeditions by the Spanish military only deepened the hostility and prompted retaliation. By the early 1770s, the Osage Indians were encouraged by renegade French traders and the British to raid the Nortenos, who in turn recouped losses of horses and livestock by sacking Spanish settlements.

Several attempts were made by Spanish officials in Texas to make peace with the Nortenos, but the prohibition of trade with Louisiana stymied the efforts. Often the Spanish were not able to produce annual gifts that were promised, and a strict ban on supplying the Indians with guns and munitions hurt the effort. The peace overtures to the Nortenos also damaged relations with the mission Apaches. Rubi's order to close the East Texas missions and forts was not executed until 1773, when Indian depredations again increased around San Antonio. On just a few days' notice, the settlers were ordered to gather up their personal belongings and leave. Many died on the trip across Texas to the new capital at San Antonio. Others were bankrupted when they had to leave behind many possessions acquired during a lifetime. And the incident emphasized another weakness in the Spanish colonial system: Unlike later American settlers, the Spaniards did not have control of their destinies. Too often geopolitical considerations were paramount in the government's colonial policy.

Although the East Texans were offered their choice of unsettled land around San Antonio, the good property had long ago been taken by early colonists. What good land was available was too exposed to Indian raids. The settlers, led by Antonio Gil Y'barbo and Gil Flores, petitioned officials for permission to move back to East Texas. They got approval to go as far as the Trinity River, where in 1774 they set up a fortified village, named Bucareli in honor of the viceroy, on the present-day Walker County line where the Camino Real crossed the river.

WITHOUT a listening post in Louisiana and with communications with the sister colony often officially banned, Texas officials were hard-pressed to keep up with the activities of the Nortenos. When settlers at Bucareli were frightened by Comanche raids in 1778 and 1779 and discouraged by continuing floods that washed away crops, they moved farther east to set up a community at the site of the old Nacogdoches mission. This marked the founding of present-day Nacogdoches. Although the move was not sanctioned initially, Y'barbo later was named lieutenant governor of the province at the settlement and established a clandestine trade and intelligence network with the French traders in Louisiana.

Jose de Galvez' survey of New Spain bore fruit in 1776, when as minister of the Indes he established the Internal Provinces to administer the defense of the northern frontier of New Spain. Under the new arrangement, Texas and Louisiana were ordered to cooperate, which temporarily eased many of the problems.

Not all the changes were welcome, however. Upon becoming commandant general of the Internal Provinces in 1776, Teodoro de Croix decreed that all unbranded livestock in Texas was the property of the crown. Ranchers and missionaries were furious. They complained that they had been unable to conduct semiannual roundups of their stock for years because of the Indian hostilities. De Croix relented to the extent of giving the stockmen four months to brand and mark their cattle and horses, and thereafter they were required to pay fees on their animals. Texas' cattle and horse market improved in 1780 when a concession was granted by the king to allow legal livestock trade with Louisiana.

Bernardo de Galvez, the nephew of Jose and the namesake of Galveston County, was named acting governor of Louisiana in 1777. He had experience as an Indian fighter along the Rio Grande and had an insight into the colonial situation. During the American War for Independence, the younger Galvez occupied the British in Florida, preventing them from concentrating attention on the American revolutionaries. And Galvez had cattle driven from the Gulf Plains and South Texas to supply the Americans along the Mississippi River. The cattle drives were the forerunners of the later livestock movements that played so great a role in the development of Texas after the American Civil War.

During the last two decades of the 18th century, Spain reached the zenith of its power in the northern provinces of New Spain. Operating within Jose de Galvez' recommendations, Charles III reformed the administration of New Spain. Talented, experienced leaders were given control of the new provinces and improvements were made. Although maintaining amicable relations with the various Indian groups in Texas was difficult, the Spanish made accommodations with most of the aborigines. Some of the Apaches remained intractable, and groups within the Comanches sometimes failed to honor treaties made by other Comanche leaders. In 1791, Juan de Ugalde defeated Lipan and Mescalero Apaches in the Lower Rio Grande Valley and brought peace for many years to that region. (Despite the difference in spelling, Uvalde County in South Texas is named for this soldier.)

ONE of the tragedies of the period was the untimely death of the promising young administrator, Bernardo de Galvez. His family had a long record of service to the Spanish crown, and Bernardo in 1785 succeeded his father, Matias, as viceroy of New Spain. Such was the crown's confidence in the new administrator that he retained control of Cuba, the Floridas and Louisiana and gained authority over the Internal Provinces in addition to his other responsibilities. Galvez conceived a policy that maintained peace with the Indians until the turn of the century. Very simply, he gave the Indians the choice between war and peace. Those that chose peace were given annual gifts and, in some cases, old firearms. Indians that chose war were mercilessly pursued. As long as the gifts were forthcoming and frontier-wise administrators were kept in the provinces, relative peace was maintained. But young Galvez died in an epidemic in 1786, and the great promise of his early administration was not fulfilled.

The death of Charles III in 1788 and the beginning of the French Revolution a year later also weakened Spain's hold of the New World dominions. Charles IV was not as good a sovereign as his predecessor, and his choice of ministers was poor. The quality of frontier administrators declined, and relations with Indians soured.

Charles IV's major blunder, however, was to side with French royalty during the revolution, earning Spain the enmity of Napoleon Bonaparte when he assumed control of the government. Spain also allied with England in an effort to thwart Napoleon, and in this losing cause, the Spanish were forced to cede Louisiana back to France. In 1803, Napoleon broke a promise to retain the territory and sold it to the United States. Spain's problems in the New World thereby took on an altogether different dimension. Anglo-Americans cast longing eyes on the vast undeveloped territory of Texas. The available land east of the Mississippi River was being quickly developed as the Americans drove the Indians of the American Southeast westward from their historic homelands.

With certain exceptions for royalists who left the American colonies during the revolution, Spain had maintained a strict prohibition against Anglo or other non-Spanish settlers in their New World territories. But they were unprepared to police the eastern border of Texas after removing the presidios in the 1760s. What had been a provincial line became virtually overnight an international boundary, and an ill-defined one at that.

Spain and France had never set a specific boundary between Texas and Louisiana, and during the colonial period from 1762 to 1803, only a general line was acknowledged. Thomas Jefferson initially tried to claim all of Texas to the Rio Grande as part of the Louisiana Purchase, based on weak French claims tied to LaSalle's explorations. For a period of time, Spanish and American authorities created a no-man's-land between the Sabine River and Arroyo Hondo, which became a refuge for renegades from both nations.

Anglo-Americans began to probe the Spanish frontier. Some settled in East Texas and were tolerated by authorities. Others, however, were thought to have more nefarious designs. Philip Nolan was the first of the American filibusters to test Spanish resolve. Several times, both authorized and unauthorized, he entered Texas to capture wild horses to sell in the United States. But in 1801, the Spanish perceived an attempted armed uprising by Nolan and his followers. He was killed in a battle near present-day Waco, and his company was taken captive to work in the mines of northern Mexico.

In 1806, Anglo-Americans were showing up in the El Paso area. Lt. Zebulon Pike, commissioned by President Jefferson to survey the newly acquired lands of the Louisiana Purchase, was taken into custody in the upper Rio Grande Valley. After a journey into the interior of Mexico, however, he was released and returned to the United States through Texas, becoming the first Anglo-American to write of the geographic features and economic potential of the region.

Spanish officials were beginning to realize that the economic potential of Texas must be developed if the Anglo-Americans were to be neutralized. In the late 18th and early 19th centuries, several attempts were made to find a short route to Sante Fe to open trade with that sister province. Later Moses Austin and Mirabeau Lamar would see the same economic potential in Texas-Santa Fe trade, although it was never realized.

On the continent, Spain's fortunes were at a low ebb. Napoleon was pressuring Charles IV, whose abdication in 1808 the French ruler refused to accept. Ferdinand VII claimed the crown, and Napoleon in the same year placed his brother, Joseph Bonaparte, on the throne. Spain rebelled against this foreign intrusion, and the War for Independence on the Iberian Peninsula was on.

Resistance to Spanish rule had developed in the New World colonies. Liberal ideas from the American and French revolutions had grown popular, despite the crown's attempts to prevent their dissemination. And chaos reigned in the colonies. From the time of Philip II, Spain had been a tightly centralized monarchy with the crown making most decisions. But during the war on the peninsula, three sovereigns — Charles IV, Ferdinand VII and Joseph Bonaparte — often issued edicts simultaneously. The colonials rebelled. Father Miguel Hidalgo ignited the Mexican war for independence on Sept. 16, 1810. And a bloody, decade-long conflict ensued, taking on the trappings of a civil war in many respects. Native Spaniards were fought by Spaniards of Mexican birth. Mestizos — mixed-blood Mexicans — and Indians also joined in the fight for control of the government.

The French control of Spain reached its peak in 1810-1811. England entered the fray on the side of the Spanish, and in 1811, the Spanish parliament — the Cortes — wrote a liberal constitution providing for self-government once control of the peninsula was regained. But Spain was not ready for the liberal government designed by the Cortes, and more disturbances followed as Ferdinand VII regained the throne and dissolved the Cortes.

MEXICO'S war for independence was savage and bloody in the interior provinces, and Texas suffered, as well. In 1811, Capt. Juan Bautista Casas briefly seized Gov. Manuel de Salcedo and military commander Simon de Herrera in the name of King Ferdinand. But the revolt was quickly and bloodily repressed. Later that year, Jose Bernardo Gutierrez de Lara of Revilla (now Guerrero south of Laredo on the Rio Grande) was appointed the diplomatic agent of the Mexican revolutionaries and journeyed to Washington to seek recognition of the newly proclaimed nation. While Gutierrez was warmly received by U.S. officials, he received no formal recognition and no money or arms. In early 1812, the Mexican patriot traveled to Natchitoches, La., where, with the help of U.S. agents, an expedition was organized. Augustus W. Magee, a West Point graduate who had served in the neutral zone between the Sabine and Arroyo Hondo, commanded the troop, which entered Texas in August 1812. This "Republican Army of the North" easily took Nacogdoches, where it gathered recruits, and La Bahia. After withstanding a siege at La Bahia, the army took San Antonio and proclaimed the first Republic of Texas in April 1813. A few months later, the republican forces were bloodily subdued at the Battle of the Medina River. Royalist Gen. Joaquin de Arredondo executed a staggering number of more than 300 republicans, including some Americans, at San Antonio, and a young lieutenant, Antonio Lopez de Santa Anna, was recognized for valor under fire. The Green Flag of the first republic was never recognized by any foreign government. Thinly populated Texas was devastated, however.

Republican furor waned after Ferdinand VII regained the throne, and while Spanish officials in Texas accepted a return to the old order, they knew that more trouble would be forthcoming if the province continued to be neglected. Spain and the United States reached agreement on the eastern boundary of Texas in 1819 in a treaty that provided for the U.S. purchase of Spanish claims to Florida. But the relinquishing of claims to Texas was considered treasonous by some Americans who took matters into their own hands. Dr. James Long led two expeditions into Texas to claim the territory for Americans. The first was successful in capturing Nacogdoches, where many Anglo settlers joined his rebellion. The filibuster returned to the United States briefly, and reentered Texas to complete his conquest. But while attempting to take La Bahia, he was captured by Mexicans, who had gained independence from Spain in 1821. Dr. Long was taken to Mexico City where he died under mysterious circumstances. His wife, Jane, accompanied him on the second expedition and bore the first Anglo-American child to be born in the province, folklore holds. She was a popular figure in the early days of Anglo-American immigration into Texas.

Ferdinand VII was forced to re-assemble the Spanish Cortes in 1820, and a colonization law was passed that welcomed foreigners into Texas, if they pledged loyalty to the Spanish monarchy and to the constitution.

But Spain's role in the history of Texas was over. The Mexicans had gained their independence and would repel an attempted invasion by the king. After almost 300 years, the Spanish had changed the face of Texas, and the Latin nation's culture remains affixed to the state's history. The Anglo-American tide that would sweep across the Southwest was poised at the province's eastern boundary. In only a few years, it would surge across the former Spanish territory.

The Mexican Period

AS Spain's grip on the New World slipped between 1790 and 1820, Texas was almost forgotten, an internal province of little importance. Colonization was ignored, and the Spanish government had larger problems in Europe and in Mexico.

Spain's mercantile economic policy penalized colonists in the area, working to charge them high prices for trade goods and paying low prices for products sent to markets in the interior of New Spain. As a result, settlers had no incentives to come to Texas. Indeed, men of ambition in the province often turned to illegal trade with Louisiana or to smuggling to prosper.

On the positive side, however, Indians of the province had been mollified through annual gifts and by developing a dependence on Spain for trade goods. Ranching flourished. A census in 1803 indicated that there were 100,000 head of cattle in Texas; in 1795, a census also found 69 families living on 45 ranches in the San Antonio area. But aside from a few additional families in Nacogdoches and La Bahia, the province was thinly populated.

When Spain returned the Louisiana Territory to France in the secret treaty of San Ildefonso in 1800, the vulnerability of Texas as a border province again became a concern. In Louisiana, Spain had relaxed its colonization policies. No attempt was made to use the mission system along the Mississippi River. Instead, an immigration policy was adopted that resembled later approaches in Texas. It provided for land grants, commercial privileges and religious toleration for colonists in exchange for a loyalty oath and actual settlement of land.

After Spain gave up Louisiana, Gen. Nemesio Salcedo, commandant-general of the Internal Provinces, allowed former Spanish subjects in Louisiana to settle in Texas. After 1805, other foreigners, under threat of death, were banned.

Several unsuccessful attempts also were made to attract colonists from the interior of Mexico. Gen. Salcedo improved the border defenses when the United States tried to press claims to the Rio Grande as the western boundary of Louisiana.

Texas' major problem was its isolation. Except for the threat of foreign immigration, the province was far removed from the political passions in Spain and Mexico City. The Spanish Cortes, for example, opened colonies to limited self-government in 1812, but the liberalization had little impact on Texas. Federalists and royalists battled for power in Mexico City, but except for a brief flirtation with republicanism after the Magee-Gutierrez expedition in 1813, Texas was unchanged and stagnated. But Spanish and Mexican officials knew that the province must be populated or lost.

Even worse, as the Spanish colonial government declined, Indians recognized its weakness. Annual gifts no longer were distributed. And as important, the Indians found an independent source of weapons and ammunition after American traders in Louisiana Territory began supplying guns and goods in exchange for horses and cattle. Frontier dangers were compounded after Father Hidalgo's 1810 uprising. The private ownership of firearms was prohibited. Indians stepped up raids, and settlers had fewer means of defense.

Therefore, Texas was in a state of suspension, only indirectly by the forces of political and social change that were gripping not only Europe and Mexico, but the North American continent as well. In the United States, currents of dissatisfaction were generated that made Texas very attractive. Federal land policy, agricultural practices and economic disruptions, along with population pressures, were steadily moving the Anglo-Americans westward.

Land policy was a long-standing point of contention between Eastern industrialists and frontiersmen. The industrialists favored high prices and tight credit policies on federal land sold to pioneers. The businessmen feared a reduction in their work force if land policies made settlement of the western lands too inviting. Until 1820, the government opened bidding on land at $2 an acre with a minimum purchase of 640 acres. The purchaser was required to pay down one-quarter of the price in cash, and the balance was due in four annual payments. And cash was scarce on the frontier.

Early in the 19th century, state banks began issuing scrip that was accepted by government land offices for purchases. With the financial panic of 1819, the nation's first major economic depression, these banks were among the first to fail. Many businessmen were ruined, and farmers saw prices drop below the cost of raising crops. The frontier was particularly hard hit.

After 1820, the federal government reduced land prices to $1.25 an acre with an 80-acre minimum purchase and credit policies were relaxed somewhat. Even in those days, Congress "primed the pump" of the nation's economy with a more lenient land policy that would stimulate financial growth. But the price was still high and the required cash was hard to come by.

THE unstable economy made restless Americans look for fresh opportunities. The U.S.-Spanish boundary between the Americans and the rich agricultural lands of East Texas was no barrier to the energetic, nomadic pioneers. Early in the 19th century, they began to filter across the invisible dividing line to squat on New Spain's eastern frontier. Because the boundary was ill-defined until the Adams-Onis treaty of 1819, many Americans thought they were settling in the newly acquired Louisiana Territory of the United States. In 1815, for example, founders of the settlement of Jonesborough in present-day Red River County thought they were in Arkansas. (In fact, in 1824, the community was designated the seat of government of Miller County, Ark., and it was not until Texas attained statehood that the matter of jurisdiction was resolved.) Individual Anglos settled in Southeast Texas and were not disturbed by Spanish authorities. Nacogdoches attracted an undesirable element from the United States, in part because of its proximity to the neutral zone, the no-man's-land between the Sabine River and the Arroyo Hondo before the boundary settlement. As early as 1801 American traders had infiltrated East Texas. By 1804, Anglo families had become numerous enough around Nacogdoches for the Spanish military commander to attempt to expel non-Catholics.

East Texas was particularly attractive to farmers. Over the centuries the Caddo Indians — called Tejas by the Spanish — had cultivated hundreds of acres of land. When the Indians were hit hard by epidemics in the late 18th century, the rich farmland fell into disuse. But it was still cleared, and the open fields between the Sabine and Angelina rivers were quickly settled.

The largest group of early immigrants from the United States was not Anglo, but Indian. As early as 1818, Cherokees from the Southeast United States came to Texas, settling north of Nacogdoches on lands between the Trinity and Sabine rivers. The Cherokees had been among the first U.S. Indians to accept the federal government's offers of resettlement. As American pioneers entered the newly acquired lands of Georgia, Alabama and other areas of the Southeast, the Indians were systematically removed, through legal means or otherwise. The early U.S. policy of attempting to "civilize" and assimilate the Native Americans was changing. Pioneers wanted the Indians' land, and that meant that the native peoples must be moved. Some settled on land provided in Arkansas Territory, but others, like groups of Cherokees, came to Texas, seeking to escape the hostility of the Anglos. And these Cherokees were among the "Five Civilized Tribes" that had adopted agriculture and many Anglo customs in an unsuccessful attempt to get along with their new neighbors.

Alabama and Coushatta tribes had exercised squatters' rights in present Sabine County in the early 1800s, and soon after the Cherokees arrived, groups of Shawnee, Delaware and Kickapoo Indians came from the United States. All sought from the Spanish and Mexican governments title to some of the prime farmland in the region. The presence of the Indians became a factor in the Anglos' disputes with the Mexican government, which attempted, by promising land titles to the Indians, to play the two groups of U.S. immigrants against each other.

After 1820, the second wave of immigrants arrived, larger than the first and of different character. These Anglos were not so interested in agricultural opportunities as in other schemes to quickly recoup their fortunes.

The only group of immigrants expelled by Spanish authorities were Napoleonic exiles who in 1818 attempted to set up the French colony of Champ d'Asile on the present site of Liberty in Liberty County.

Spain, and later Mexico, recognized the danger represented by the unregulated, informal colonization by Americans. The Spanish Cortes' colonization law of 1813 attempted to build a buffer between the eastern frontier and Northern Mexico. The act served as the basis for later Mexican immigration policy through which it was hoped that European and Mexican colonists could be attracted to Texas to dilute the Anglo population. To prevent smuggling, which flourished because of a lack of legal ports, colonies were prohibited within 26 miles — or 10 leagues — of the coast. Also, special permission was required for Americans to settle within 52 miles of the international boundary, although this prohibition often was ignored. As initially envisioned, Americans would be allowed to settle the interior of the vast territory. European and Mexican colonists would be placed along the eastern frontier to limit contact between the Americans and the United States. The Americans already in Texas illegally would be stable if given a stake in the province through land ownership, officials felt.

MOSES Austin, a former Spanish subject who had suffered a severe financial setback in the panic of 1819, applied for the first empresario grant from the Spanish government. With the intercession of Baron de Bastrop, a friend of Austin's from Missouri Territory, Gov. Antonio Maria Martinez approved the request in January 1821. Austin agreed to settle 300 families on land bounded by the Brazos and Colorado rivers on the east and west, by the El Camino Real (the old military road running from San Antonio to Nacogdoches) on the north and by the Gulf Coast, since his grant came before settlement in the area was prohibited. But Austin died in June 1821, leaving the work to his son, Stephen F. Austin.

The younger Austin was uniquely qualified for leadership of the colonial enterprise. Although born in Virginia in 1793, he moved with his parents to Missouri Territory at the age of five. Austin's experiences as a youth gave him an understanding of the disposition of the Spanish and Mexican administrators with whom he dealt. The 27-year-old empresario also was well educated, had served in the Missouri legislature and was appointed judge in Arkansas Territory before coming to Texas. Austin's problems began immediately upon entering Texas when he learned that Mexico had gained independence from Spain. Although his first colonists arrived in December 1821, Austin was told by Gov. Martinez that the provisional government would not recognize the Spanish grant. The new government had to approve the colonization program, Austin learned. So he spent a year in Mexico City, observing the organization of the new government and lobbying for his colonial authorization. On occasion he advised Mexican leaders on the creation of a federal system of government. Finally in January 1823 the Spanish grant was affirmed by the Mexican government.

Mexico's land policy, like Spain's, differed from the U.S. approach. Whereas the United States sold land directly to settlers or to speculators who dealt with the pioneers, the Mexicans retained tight control of the property transfer until predetermined agreements for development were fulfilled. But a 4,428-acre sitio — a square league — and a 177-acre labor could be obtained for only surveying costs and administrative fees as low as $50. The empresario was rewarded with grants of large tracts of land — but only when he fulfilled his quota of families to be brought to the colonies. Considering the prices the U.S. government charged, Texas' land was indeed a bargain — and a major attraction to those Anglo-Americans looking for a new start.

Austin had almost complete civil and military responsibility for his colony. He set up stringent requirements for his colonists, including requiring presentation of affidavits from community leaders at their previous home vouching for their good character and sober work habits. On several occasions, Austin had disreputable characters forcibly removed from his colony. As a consequence of these high standards, Austin attracted many financially stable colonists. And he made some enemies.

Austin was scrupulous in following the terms of his grant. He knew that Mexican officials, like the Spanish, distrusted the intentions of Americans, and the young empresario wanted to give no cause for suspicion. But despite Austin's efforts, the mistrust by officials persisted. They knew that whenever U.S. and Spanish boundaries had met, the Spanish boundaries receded. Florida had been lost in the agreement that set Texas' eastern boundary. Rights in Oregon Territory also had been given to the United States in the same treaty.

Under the Constitution of 1824, Mexicans reversed the U.S. approach to land distribution. The federalist government gave the states responsibility for developing public lands. And colonization policy became even more liberal as the government of Coahuila y Texas, which was the poorest of all the new Mexican states, sought to exploit the economic potential of the region and to build a buffer between Northern Mexico and both the United States and the Plains Indians. The state colonization law of 1825 brought explosive growth to Texas. More than 25 empresarios were commissioned to settle colonists. By 1830, Texas boasted an estimated population of 15,000, with Anglos outnumbering Mexicans by a margin of four to one.

Austin was easily the most successful empresario. After his initial success, Austin was authorized in 1825 to bring 900 more families to Texas, and in 1831, he and his partner, Samuel Williams, received another concession to bring 800 Mexican and European families. Through Austin's efforts, 1,540 land titles were issued to settlers, and the population of his colonies in 1831 was 5,665. The next two most successful empresarios were Green DeWitt and Martin De Leon.

Green DeWitt was authorized in April 1825 to bring 400 families to Texas in an area west of Austin's colony. Mexican officials felt that establishment of towns was important, and in 1825, Gonzales, in present-day Gonzales County, was laid out by surveyor James Kerr. The community was named in honor of Coahuila y Texas Gov. Rafael Gonzales. Because of the danger of Indian raids many of DeWitt's colonists stayed in a small community called Old Station on the Lavaca River near the coast until 1827, when a peace treaty with the Karankawas was signed after a military campaign by joint American and Mexican forces.

DeWitt's colony suffered from other Indian attacks. First the Tonkawas raided because they were being pressed by the Comanches and Wichitas, who had moved into the South Plains. Later the Plains Indians found the horse and cattle herds of the colony lucrative sources of plunder.

DeWitt did not bring 400 families to the province, as

he had contracted, but 166 land titles were issued to settlers who came to Texas through his efforts.

South and west of DeWitt's colony, Martin de Leon, a rancher in Tamaulipas who admired the region during a cattle drive, received a grant from the provincial delegation of San Fernando de Bexar for another colony. Because the Coahuila y Texas legislature was unaware of De Leon's grant, DeWitt's grant overlapped, and there were problems when the two empresarios tried to colonize the same region. De Leon won the dispute because his grant pre-dated DeWitt's and because Mexican citizens were given preference in colonization.

Forty-one Mexican families were settled in the region by De Leon, who in 1824 also founded the city of Guadalupe Victoria, named for the first Mexican president. By 1833, the city had a population of 200.

AUSTIN'S colony flourished, in part because of his understanding of the Mexican character and the necessity for strict adherence to Mexican law. Other empresarios were not so diligent.

In the early years of colonization, the settlers busied themselves by clearing lands, planting crops, building homes and fighting Indians. Many were successful in establishing a subsistence economy. One weakness of the Mexican colonial policy was that it did not provide the factors for a market economy. While towns were established, credit, banks and good roads were not provided by the government. Ports were established at Galveston and Matagorda bays after Mexican independence, but the colonists felt they needed more, particularly one at the mouth of the Brazos. And foreign ships were barred from coastwise trade, which posed a particular hardship since Mexico had few merchant ships.

One attempt to establish a bank failed. When Jose Felix Trespalacios was appointed the political and military chief of Texas in 1822, there was a limited amount of money in circulation in the province. Soldiers and officials were paid irregularly. So Trespalacios set up the Banco Nacional de Texas in San Antonio, which in November 1822 issued to soldiers and officials notes that could be redeemed at face value. Trespalacios had not received prior approval of the central government, which liked the idea. But in late 1822, the government decreed that only two-thirds of the face value of the notes would be redeemed in gold; the rest would be paid in government notes. The value of the Texas bank notes dropped, and the bank failed, leaving, in part, a residual distrust of banks that remained a part of the Texas heritage until the early 20th century.

In eastern Texas and the Austin colony, cotton was planted almost immediately by the new colonists. Four cotton gins were in operation in East Texas by 1826. In 1828, 500 bales of cotton were produced in the Austin colony alone. But in DeWitt colony, the basic crop was corn. Many settlers also raised cattle, hogs and goats for milk.

Although there were complaints about the administration of government, the colonists concentrated on establishing themselves in a new land. Most of the unrest was brought about through a lack of understanding of the Spanish language and an unfamiliarity with the institutions of the government of the fledgling Republic.

Mexican officials, however, distrusted the intentions of the colonists. Most disputes were settled amicably enough, although there undoubtedly was discontent. DeWitt's Old Station near Lavaca Bay was interpreted by some officials as an attempt to develop a way station for smugglers. In fact, James Kerr had misunderstood the 10-league setback requirement for settlements near the coast; he thought the distance began at the outer islands, not on the coast itself.

The first major conflict between the Mexican government and Anglo settlers arose through a misunderstanding. Hayden Edwards received a large land grant around Nacogdoches to be distributed to new colonists. But Edwards misunderstood his charter. He first tried to set himself up as a military commander for the area, which was interpreted by Mexican officials as an attempted revolt. Then the empresario attempted to take land away from long-time Mexican settlers who could not prove title to their property. Many of the families held land under informal grants

made by Gil Y'barbo almost a half-century earlier, and others had not fulfilled the tedious requirements of Spanish land law to get full title. Others had simply lost the documents, of which there was no record in the Spanish archives. Acts more attributable to ignorance than guile were interpreted by Mexican officials as steps toward insurrection. Finally while Hayden Edwards was in the United States on business in 1826, his brother, Benjamin, declared the independence of the Republic of Fredonia and ejected a group of Mexican soldiers from the area.

Most Anglos did not support the revolt. So the Fredonians made a pact with a group of Cherokees to give the Indians the northern half of Texas in exchange for their support in the rebellion. The Mexican army, aided by a contingent of Austin's colonists, quickly put down the revolt. The rebellious leaders fled to the United States. But the insurgency sowed seeds of distrust with Mexican officials. As important in the long run, Anglos from the previously isolated colonies opened communication.

Mexican officials' hope of attracting large numbers of European immigrants never materialized. Government instability, stagnant economy and religious intolerance outweighed whatever attractions Europeans might find in Mexico, and the United States was a more popular place to relocate. Nevertheless, two small colonies of Europeans were settled. James Power and James Hewetson got a special concession to settle an area on the coast between the Lavaca and Nueces rivers. Despite many problems, the town of Refugio, located on the site of the old mission by the same name, was established and almost 200 land titles were issued under this grant. John McMullen and James McGloin got a grant just north of the Power-Hewetson concession and had 84 grants issued to their colonists, most of whom were from Ireland. San Patricio was settled in the McMullen-McGloin colony.

In late 1827, Gen. Manuel Mier y Teran, a soldier, statesman and intellectual, was dispatched by President Victoria on an apparent mission to locate the actual boundary line between the United States and Mexico. In fact, however, Teran was taking the pulse of Texas. Mexican officials could not ignore the nagging threat of American intentions in their northern state.

Although he found no overt rebellion, the tour only reinforced Teran's concern about the developing American influence in Texas. The farther east he traveled, the less Mexican influence he found in the society. In East Texas, only a few long-time Mexican settlers remained, and he noted they were of the poorest classes. From this review of Texas, Teran made three major recommendations: a military occupation of Texas, to provide protection from Indians, but also to isolate the Anglo-American colonies; a counter-colonization program aimed at attracting European and Mexican settlers; and the opening of coastwise trade to develop closer economic ties with the interior of Mexico.

Austin had advocated more coastwise trade to Teran. Most Texas trade went through New Orleans, and Austin, along with Teran, understood that that could become a major problem.

In 1829, Gen. Teran became commandant general of the Eastern Interior Provinces and began to carry out his program, much of which was incorporated in the Law of April 6, 1830, which was obnoxious to most American colonists in Texas. The law went beyond Teran's recommendations by in essence barring further Anglo-American immigration into Texas. Also, it provided for Mexican convict-soldiers, and their families, to be sent to the area, with an option to stay at the end of their terms under favorable circumstances provided by the government.

TERAN reinforced garrisons at San Antonio, La Bahia, Nacogdoches and Velasco. And five new garrisons, three with Nahuatl names to reinforce their Mexican character, were established: Anahuac on Galveston Bay, Tenoxtitlan on the Brazos, Lipantitlan on the Nueces River, Lavaca on the river of the same name, and Teran on the Neches River.

The moving of additional armed forces into Texas concerned the Anglo-Americans, and it was unrest caused by the 1828 election and the military occupation of the state a year later that led to revolution.

Prelude to Revolution

MEXICO'S war for independence had achieved little more than separation from Spain. Sensing that liberal reforms in Spain would reduce the authority of royalists in the New World, Mexican conservatives led the revolt against the mother country. And they achieved early victories in the debate over the form of government the newly independent Mexico should adopt.

The majority of Mexicans had little concept of self-government. The Spanish Constitution of 1812 had provided for election of local officials, but it was not universally implemented. Offsetting this brief experience was a 300-year tradition of authoritarian, centralized colonial government. Since the reign of Phillip II, administration of the Spanish colonies was tightly controlled and slow-moving.

An independent Mexico was torn between advocates of centralist and republican forms of government. Centralists wanted a strong central government with appointed officials at the state and local level who would be under the direction of Mexico City. Federalists supported the election of officials at lower levels, who would run their own administrations. The former royalists won the opening debates, setting Emperor Agustin de Iturbide on the new Mexican throne. But he soon was overthrown and the Constitution of 1824 adopted. Constructing a federal framework of government and making it function smoothly, however, are difficult for a people inexperienced in self-government. The fiercely independent character of the Mexican people often prohibited the acquiescence so necessary to democratic government.

The turbulence experienced in Texas as the Mexicans attempted to set up a representative government was not an isolated experience in the period. Within months after the rebellion in Texas, federalists in California and New Mexico also revolted. But the central government's reaction was not so harsh. Santa Anna's ruthless attempt to crush the Anglo-led rebellion in Texas was motivated as much by the fear of losing the colony to the United States as by the desire to punish the political dissidents. The uprisings in California and New Mexico were settled diplomatically, not with the sword as in Texas.

Friction between the two cultures was inevitable. To settle in Texas, pioneers had to become Mexican citizens and to embrace Roman Catholicism. Most of the Americans were Protestants, if they adhered to any religion, and they were fiercely defensive of the right to religious freedom enjoyed in the United States. Although no more than one-fourth of the Americans ever swore allegiance to the Catholic church, the requirement was a long-standing irritation. Compounding the problem was the fact that to be legal, marriages had to be blessed by a priest. For a decade after the founding of the Austin colony, no priest regularly ministered to the people. A system of contract marriages evolved in which couples took out a bond to have their union blessed by a priest when one was available. Occasionally, couples who found they could not live together would simply destroy the bond to dissolve the marriage if no priest had blessed the union.

Slavery, too, was a point of contention. Mexico prohibited the introduction of slavery after December 1827. Nevertheless, many slaveholders in Austin's colony became nervous at the official rhetoric. Several efforts were made to evade the government policy. Austin got the state legislature to recognize labor contracts under which slaves were technically free but bound themselves to their masters for life. Often entire families were covered by a single contract. While many early Anglo colonists were not slaveholders, they were Southerners, and the ownership of slaves was a cultural institution that they supported. The problem was never settled during the colonial period despite the tensions it generated.

There also was a long delay in getting land titles after the settlers had made the required improvements. And the Mexican court system was cumbersome. Appeals in civil cases and pleadings in criminal cases had to go 700 miles to Saltillo for adjudication, causing interminable and expensive delays in the administration of justice.

Balancing these complaints, however, were many advantages. Taxes, tithes and excises were suspended for several years. Farm implements and household goods could be brought into the colony with no duty charged. Good land was cheap and available for those willing to turn a wilderness into productive farmland.

Austin kept attuned to the settlers' problems, seeking relief from the Mexican government when possible. Many Austin colonists left the United States with a burden of debt brought about by the economic recession. Austin sought relief from the legislature of Coahuila y Texas with the enactment in 1828 of a homestead law that prohibited a person's property from being taken for debt accrued outside Mexico. Based on early Roman and Spanish law, this statute was the forerunner of the homestead protection enjoyed by Texans today.

Mistrust was mutual between Mexican officials and the colonists. As the population grew, the settlers' complaints intensified. Mexican officials' alarm grew in proportion to the population. Hopes of attracting European and Mexican colonists to dilute the burgeoning number of Anglos were not realized. Only a few Irish settlers had been attracted to the San Patricio grant on the Gulf Coast.

Andrew Jackson's election to the American presidency in 1828 further fanned Mexican fears. Jackson was known to covet Texas. The new president reportedly once told a Mexican diplomat that "the United States should never have lost the opportunity to obtain Texas, and that the way to obtain a territory was first to occupy it and, after having possession, treat for it, as had been done in Florida." Indeed, several informal offers to purchase Texas were made by U.S. officials before and after Jackson's election.

The Mexican election of 1828 also was a turning point in the history of the young republic. Self-government had been in effect in parts of Mexico since 1812. Mexico had begun the difficult transition from being an appendage of an absolutist monarchy to a federal republic. Mexicans were transformed from subjects of a crown into citizens in a republic. But the transformation was incomplete. Democracy requires an acquiescence of strongly held individual opinions to the results of the ballot box. But the orderly transfer of power in Mexico was dealt a death blow in 1828 when the legally elected administration of Manuel Gomez Pedraza was overthrown by supporters of Vicente Guerrero, who in turn was ousted by his own vice president Anastasio Bustamante. Mexico's most chaotic political period followed. The pattern of military intervention, coup and countercoup would last a century. Between May 1833 and August 1855, the Mexican presidency changed hands 36 times. The average length of term was only seven and one-half months. As government replaced government and revolt followed rebellion, many Mexicans became disenchanted with the republican experiment. They understood that their quality of life had declined without a strong, well-organized colonial administrative system. The centralist form of government eventually won out.

BUT the Americans who came to Texas were republicans to the core. On his tour of the state in 1827 and 1828, Gen. Manuel Mier y Teran noted that they "carried their constitutions in their pockets." And he feared the Americans' desire for more rights and liberties than the government was prepared to offer would lead to rebellion.

Most of the early Anglo colonists in Texas, however, intended to fulfill their pledge to become good Mexican citizens. But they had made the commitment with the understanding that they would live under a republican form of government as set forth in the Constitution of 1824. The political turmoil following the 1828 presidential election raised doubts in the Americans' minds about the ability of Mexicans to make that form of government function properly.

Unrest increased in Texas when Gen. Teran began reinforcing existing garrisons and establishing new ones. But a major factor in the discontent of Americans came with the decree of April 6, 1830, when the Mexican government in essence banned further Anglo-American immigration into Texas and tried to control slavery.

Austin protested that the prohibition against American immigration would not stop the flow of Anglos into Texas; it would stop only the stable, prosperous Americans from coming to the region. The great empresario had a firm image of the type of colonist he wanted — a Southern gentleman. Austin feared another type of settler: Those " . . . ardent, inexperienced, hot-headed youths piping from college, or ignorant, self-willed 'mobbish' mountaineers and frontiersmen who 'hold to lynch law' and damning those who are in office merely because they are in office would totally ruin us forever."

Austin's predictions about immigration were fulfilled. Legal immigration may have been barred, but illegal entry was not. By 1834, when the law was repealed, it was estimated that the number of Americans and their slaves in Texas totaled 20,700, double the number of four years earlier. By 1836, that number had reached 35,000.

THE first two incidents that inflamed Anglo-American colonists, ironically, were instigated by Americans in the service of the Mexican government. George Fisher, a Serbian by birth but a naturalized American, was ordered by Gen. Teran to set up a customs house at Anahuac on Galveston Bay and to appoint a deputy to a house at Brazoria at the mouth of the Brazos. Fisher tried to require ships leaving the Brazos to stop at Anahuac to pay duties, and in one case, a soldier was wounded when a ship failed to heed the order. In retaliation, Fisher tried to impound goods shipped into the Austin Colony until duties were paid. But Teran removed Fisher from office before further incident. Austin argued that the Americans were not being disloyal or attempting to avoid duties; Fisher's order was simply impractical. Nevertheless, the government abandoned attempts to collect duties in September 1832 and did not resume collection until the spring of 1835.

Col. John Davis Bradburn's problems were more serious. Teran gave him command of the newly established garrison of Anahuac, which was located near the settlement of Atascosito. The small community was one of many settled illegally by Anglo-Americans early in the 19th century. But Mexican authorities had promised to provide the settlers legal titles to their land. In 1831, Francisco Madero was appointed land commissioner to issue the titles. Bradburn detained Madero, arguing that his actions were illegal. The settlement, Bradburn asserted, was too close to the coast. The officer also disbanded a new ayuntamiento established by Madero at Liberty. Madero argued that the Americans settled the land before the Law of April 6, 1830, and the statute did not apply to them. Madero was freed and the titles issued, but complaints about Bradburn continued. He was charged with using the settlers' slaves without compensation to build military structures, with enticing slaves to escape and with arresting colonists and holding them for military trial. William B. Travis was jailed when he tried to represent the claims of a Louisiana slaveholder. An armed revolt ensued that resulted in Bradburn's removal from office. Mexican officials felt that Bradburn's actions had prompted the rebellion, and some ayuntamientos criticized the actions of the insurgents. Although Bradburn was removed from office as a gesture of appeasement, the incidents further kindled the emotions of the settlers — and deepened the concern of the Mexican government.

Thereafter, the colonists began a campaign to drive the Mexican soldiers from Texas, and except for the adroitness of Austin, the settlers would have brought upon themselves severe retribution from the government.

Events in 1830 ended the Texans' usual aloofness to the political maneuverings in Mexico. Gen. Bustamante had replaced Guerrero as president and made himself dictator. Troops rebelled in Veracruz in January 1832, and, led by Santa Anna, were fighting to replace the dictator. Santa Anna, ever an opportunist, declared himself a friend of the republican cause, and Texans backed him. During the engagement at Anahuac, the insurgents who sought release of Travis and other prisoners had declared for Santa Anna. While the revolt at Anahuac was bloodless, Mexican soldiers were killed and injured at Velasco when Texans ran a blockade in an attempt to get aid to the other insurgents. Mexican troops at Nacogdoches also were ousted, although many soldiers were anxious to return to Mexico to fight with Santa Anna and the republic.

Upon hearing the reports of the insurgency in Texas in 1832, Gen. Jose Antonio Mexia brought 400 troops to the state by sea. He was lavishly feted by the Texans and was convinced that there was no rebellion against the government. A supporter of Santa Anna, Mexia returned to Mexico.

Heady with success and with Santa Anna's federalist campaign in Mexico going so well, the Texans felt it was time to petition the government for reforms and to explain their actions. A convention was called in San Felipe, the capital of Austin's colony, in October 1832. With Austin serving as president of the convention, several concerns were expressed to the government. Delegates wanted Texas separated from Coahuila, titles for land in East Texas, encroachments on Indian lands stopped, a militia to defend against Indian attacks, and government-donated land for schools. Mexican officials condemned the meeting, explaining that it was not the proper way to express grievances. Therefore, the concerns were not presented to the government.

Mexican officials, however, were concerned about the "illegal" convention. The proper method of addressing the government, under their system, was to function through the legally constituted ayuntamiento in each colony. For the Americans, the conventions were simply their traditional method of petitioning the government.

Despite the objections of the government, a second convention was called in April of 1833 at San Felipe. This time the radical faction of the colonists controlled, with William H. Wharton serving as president. Nevertheless, the requests of the delegates were essentially the same. They wanted the Law of April 6, 1830, repealed, and they wanted a separation from Coahuila. Serving in his first official capacity in Texas, Sam Houston, a former governor of Tennessee and former congressman, chaired the committee that wrote a sample state constitution. It was based on the Massachusetts' constitution and incorporated few of the features usually found in the constitutions of Mexican states. Austin and two other delegates were selected to present the pleadings to the newly elected Mexican president, Santa Anna.

Austin alone reached Mexico City in October 1833 and presented the petition to Vice President Gomez Farias, who was running the government in the absence of President Santa Anna. A cholera epidemic swept Mexico City — and Texas — at the time, and Austin got no response from Farias. The acting president was preoccupied with other problems and also disagreed with the proposal that Texas be given independent statehood. Distressed by the delay, Austin wrote the ayuntamiento in San Antonio advising it to set up a state government. Upon his resumption of office, Santa Anna met with Austin and agreed with most of the reforms the Texans had requested, except the separation from Coahuila. On the return trip to Texas in December, Austin stopped in Saltillo, where he was arrested. The letter he had written in a huff to San Antonio was interpreted as a call for revolution. Austin was returned to Mexico City and imprisoned.

UNDER Farias' instructions, Col. Juan Nepomuceno Almonte toured Texas in 1834 with a twofold purpose: To assure settlers that the government was moving to implement reforms and to determine the attitude of the colonists. Almonte found no unrest in Texas and advocated most of the reforms that Austin had requested in Mexico City.

Indeed, despite the turmoil, Texas was prospering. By 1834, some 7,000 bales of cotton with a value of $315,000 were shipped to New Orleans. In the middle of the decade, Texas exports, including cotton and beaver, otter and deer skins, amounted to $500,000. Trade ratios were out of balance, however, because $630,000 in manufactured goods were imported. Almonte also found that there was little currency in Texas. Ninety percent of the business transactions were conducted in barter or credit, "which gives the country, in its trading relations, the appearance of a continued fair," he observed.

In 1833 and 1834, the Coahuila y Texas legislature also was diligently trying to respond to the complaints of the Texas colonists. The English language was recognized for official purposes. Religious toleration was approved (Gen. Teran in 1828 had noted that freedom of religion was better than no religion at all, which was the case in Texas at the time). And the court system was revised, providing Texas with an appellate court and trial by jury. Previously, the legislature had approved schools for the colonists, but this measure was not fully implemented because of a lack of funds and low population density. Texas also was divided into three departments, Bexar, Nacogdoches and Brazos, to facilitate administration.

In Mexico City, however, a different scenario was developing. Santa Anna had in essence shared the presidency with Farias, allowing the vice president to enact many federalist reforms that proved unpopular with the church, the wealthy and the military. Santa Anna assumed supreme authority in April 1834, exiled the vice president and began a program of dismantling the federalist government. By October 1835, a centralist government had replaced the federalist, and the Congress was subservient to Santa Anna.

Among the most offensive changes dictated by Santa Anna was the reduction of the militia to one man per each 500 population. The intent was to eliminate possible armed opposition to the emerging centralist government. But liberals in the state of Zacatecas in Central Mexico rebelled. Santa Anna's response was particularly brutal, as he tried to make an example of the rebels. Troops were allowed to sack the state capital after the victory over the insurgents.

Trouble also was brewing closer to the Texans. In March 1833, the Coahuila y Texas legislature moved the state capital from Saltillo to Monclova. The Monclova legislature in 1834 gave the governor authority to sell 400 sitios — or 1.77 million acres of land — to finance the government and to provide for protection. Land speculators jumped at the opportunity to obtain land so cheap.

A year later, the lawmakers criticized Santa Anna's repudiation of federalism. Seeing a chance to regain lost prestige, Saltillo declared for Santa Anna and set up an opposition government. But in the spring of 1835, Santa Anna sent his brother-in-law, Martin Perfecto de Cos, to break up the state government at Monclova.

Texans were appalled by the breakdown in state government, coming on the heels of so many assurances that the political situation was to improve. Texas politics were polarizing. A "war party" advocated breaking away from Mexico altogether, while a "peace party" urged calm and riding out the political storm. Most of the settlers, however, aligned with neither group. And it is said that the passion for rebellion was directly proportional to the stake the individual had in Texas. The long-time settlers wanted to maintain a status quo; newcomers favored revolt.

In January 1835, Santa Anna sent a detachment of soldiers to Anahuac to reinforce the customs office. But duties were being charged irregularly at various ports on the coast. William B. Travis, in an act not supported by all colonists, led a contingent of armed colonists against the Mexican soldiers, who withdrew without a fight.

Although some members of the peace party wrote Gen. Cos, stationed at Matamoros, apologizing for the action, he was not compromising. Cos demanded that members of the group be arrested and turned over to him. The Texans refused.

The committees of correspondence, organized at the Convention of 1832, began organizing another meeting. Because the term "convention" aroused visions of revolution in the eyes of Mexican officials, the gathering at Washington-on-the-Brazos in October 1835 was called a "consultation." But with the break-

down of the state government and with Santa Anna's repeal of the Constitution of 1824, the American settlers felt well within their rights to provide a new framework within which to govern Texas.

Help also came from an unexpected source. Austin was released from prison and arrived in Texas in September 1835. He immediately began agitation for a representative convention to deal with the developing crisis. Austin's long-standing support for patience was at an end. He urged war to protect Texas' rights in the Mexican confederation under the Constitution of 1824.

Fresh from brutally putting down the rebellion in Zacatecas, Santa Anna turned his attention to Texas. Gen. Cos was determined to regarrison the state, and the settlers were equally adamant about keeping soldiers out.

COL. Domingo Ugartechea, headquartered at San Antonio, became concerned about armed rebellion when he heard of the incident at Anahuac. And he recalled a six-pound cannon that had been given DeWitt colonists to fight Indians. Ugartechea ordered Cpl. Casimira de Leon with five men to Gonzales to retrieve the weapon. No problems were expected. But officials at Gonzales refused to surrender the weapon. When the Mexicans reinforced Cpl. De Leon's forces, a call was sent out for volunteers to help the Texans. Dozens responded. On Oct. 2, 1835, the Texans challenged the Mexicans with a "come-and-take-it" flag over the cannon. After a brief skirmish, the Mexicans withdrew, but the first rounds in the Texas Revolution had been fired.

Gen. Cos had entered San Antonio while the Texans were occupied with the affair in Gonzales. When the Mexicans left Gonzales, the volunteer force followed them to San Antonio.

The consultation in Washington-on-the-Brazos created a provisional government with Henry Smith as governor and with an executive council. Austin, despite a lack of military experience, was named commander-in-chief of the army. He immediately went to San Antonio.

Capt. George Collinsworth had captured Goliad and a large store of supplies, which was taken to the Texans besieging San Antonio. Austin remained at the head of the "Army of the People" until mid November when he was sent to the United States to plead the Texans' cause for aid. Edward Burleson assumed command. In early December, a special force of Texans — led by Ben Milam, who died in the battle — assaulted the city, and five days later, Gen. Cos capitulated. The Mexican leader and his troops were furloughed with the understanding they would not fight against the cause of the Constitution of 1824 again, a pledge that Cos broke.

The Texans were euphoric with the string of victories over Mexican forces. It was a euphoria born of overconfidence, it turned out, and led to mistakes that claimed hundreds of lives.

But the Texas Revolution was under way.

End of the Beginning

AS 1836 opened, Texans felt in control of their destiny. The Mexican army had been driven from their soil. Winter was at hand. And the settlers were secure in their land and their liberties.

But tragedy loomed. Easy victories over Mexican forces at Anahuac, Nacogdoches, Goliad, Gonzales and San Antonio in the fall of 1835 had given them a false sense of security. Their frontier independence had served well in forcing Mexicans from their soil. Texans proved their unwillingness to take orders from the Mexican military, but they were not in a mood to take orders from each other either. That independent mood was their undoing, for no government worth the name coordinated the defense of Texas. Consequently, as the Mexican counterattack developed, no one was in charge. In November 1835, the Consultation failed to outline the duties and responsibilities of the provisional government it created. Henry Smith was named governor, and he and the provisional council — one representative from each of the 12 municipalities — were to run the administration. They were antagonists from the beginning. By mid-January the arrangement collapsed, but in the interim much damage was done. With the Mexican military out of Texas, the settlers' primary concern was relieved; the "war" was over.

They had won. The victory's consolidation, however, was a point of contention. Smith supported complete independence for Texas. The council wanted to link up with Mexican liberals to restore the Constitution of 1824. Gen. Jose A. Mexia was to lead a rebellion against the dictator Antonio Lopez de Santa Anna at Tampico. If the Texans could attract the support of the liberal rebels, there was a chance to restore constitutional government in Mexico.

That was the sense of a resolution passed by the Consultation. And the council tried to implement the goal with disastrous results. Sam Houston was commander-in-chief of the Texas forces, but he had little authority. The council, pursuing its intention of gaining Mexican liberal support, conceived the idea of a campaign against Matamoros, the port city across the Rio Grande from present-day Brownsville. Dr. James Grant promoted the plan. He owned property in northern Mexico that had been confiscated by the government. If the dictator were overthrown, Grant could reclaim the land.

The so-called old settlers, however, had lost interest in the conflict. After Gen. Martin Perfecto de Cos had been driven from San Antonio in December 1835, the Texan army had dwindled. Texas volunteers returned home to prepare for spring planting. Their places in the ranks were taken by Americans who flocked to Texas to fight Mexico. On Christmas Day, about 750 men, mostly American volunteers, made up the Texas army. Four hundred men were at San Antonio, 70 at Washington-on-the-Brazos, 80 at Goliad and 200 at Velasco. The provisional government's attempt to establish a regular army failed. It never had more than 80 soldiers, leaving most of the fighting to volunteers.

In late December, the provisional council authorized the Matamoros expedition with a round of comic-opera appointments. First Frank W. Johnson was appointed commander, and when he declined, James W. Fannin was named. Dr. Grant was given the post of commander of the volunteers. Shortly thereafter, Johnson changed his mind, and the council made him commander of the expedition again. Fannin retained his authority, however. Houston was not informed of any of the changes. So the Texas army had four commanders in chief.

DR. Grant and Johnson soon took 300 men and supplies from San Antonio, heading south to set up a command post near Refugio. By Jan. 6, Col. James C. Neill had only 104 men — none Texans — and no clothing or supplies under his command at San Antonio. Fannin, one of the few Texas officers with West Point training, declined to participate in the Matamoros expedition after occupying the old fort at Goliad.

Houston initially planned a line of defense along the San Antonio River, which had strongly fortified positions at Goliad and San Antonio. But with the command split and none of the other three "commanders" willing to take orders, Houston's hands were tied. He visited Refugio but failed to convince Grant and Johnson to abandon plans for attacking Matamoros. Houston was successful in keeping many men from participating. When he left, Grant and Johnson had only about 150 men remaining under their command.

The status of the strongholds along the San Antonio River also was of concern. In mid-January, Houston sent James Bowie to San Antonio to determine if the Alamo was defensible. If not, Bowie had orders to destroy it and withdraw the men and artillery to Gonzales and Copano.

Houston took a furlough to travel to East Texas and meet with the Cherokees. Settlers were concerned about the Indians' intentions. Several chiefs of the Cherokees had met in September 1835 with Mexican officers in San Antonio. The Consultation had approved a "solemn declaration" to recognize Indian claims to ownership of land north of the San Antonio Road and between the Angelina and Sabine rivers. This pledge was repeated in the treaty Houston negotiated in exchange for the Indians' neutrality in the conflict with Mexico. (After the revolution, the treaty was rejected by the Texas Senate, and the Indians later were driven from the land.)

If the Texans' defense was disorganized, few settlers worried. Some thought the Mexicans would not try to re-enter Texas. Others felt the Mexican army would not mount an offensive until spring. The reasons were logical, if wrong. Mexico was experiencing financial problems, and the army was weakened by the continuing civil war between federalists and centralists. The government was disorganized. And the rich buffalo grass on the South Texas prairies was dead, denying fodder for invaders' horses and livestock.

Few Texans counted on the energy and determination of Gen. Antonio Lopez de Santa Anna, the dictator of Mexico. In August 1835, he proclaimed his intention of driving Anglo-American settlers from Texas and of executing any Americans found taking up arms or supporting the rebellion against Mexico. The campaign would be financed through the confiscation of the settlers' property. Preparations for the invasion began in the fall at San Luis Potosi. The army's depleted ranks were filled with conscripts. Forced loans were obtained from the church and other sources, and lenders were given outrageously beneficial terms for some funds. But arrangements were hurried and incomplete. Many of the soldiers were not properly clothed for the march in the cold winter weather. Mayan Indian recruits from the Yucatan, unaccustomed to the northers and other conditions in Northern Mexico, suffered pitiably, for example. Also the army, including officers, was put on half rations from the beginning. And no provision was made for physicans and field hospitals. Nevertheless, about 6,000 men were under arms as the army marched toward Texas.

Racial overtones permeated both sides of the developing conflict. Texans did not trust Mexican-Texans and usually stayed aloof from them. At Refugio, Mexican-Texans complained about abuse from Grant's and Johnson's men. And the Mexican-Texans were dubious about the motives of the Anglos. Many Mexican-Texans were willing to fight for restoration of the Constitution of 1824, but refused to take up arms for an independent Anglo Texas in which they would be a minority. Santa Anna held Anglo frontiersmen in contempt for many years.

As a 19-year-old lieutenant in the Royal Spanish Army, Santa Anna had served in Gen. Joaquin de Arredondo's campaign against republicans after the Gutierrez-Magee rebellion in 1813, which created the first Republic of Texas. Arredondo had been merciless in his retribution, killing more than 300 republicans at San Antonio alone. Santa Anna was revolted by the crude attempts of the Anglo frontiersmen to defend themselves against the best European tactics of the day. And he boasted that he would plant the eagles of Mexico on the banks of the Sabine River and even march to Washington, D.C., to teach the Anglos a lesson in the upcoming campaign.

If Santa Anna had been determined to punish Texas when he began the campaign, he became fanatical when his brother-in-law, Gen. Cos, crossed the Rio Grande with the remnants of his command, which was defeated at San Antonio. Santa Anna ordered Cos to ignore his pledge not to enter Texas again to fight against the Constitution of 1824.

On Feb. 12, Santa Anna's main force crossed the Rio Grande headed for San Antonio. The Mexican battle plan has been debated. But Mexico's national pride had been bruised by the series of defeats the nation's army had suffered in 1835, capped by Gen. Cos' ouster from San Antonio in December. The main body of the army moved northward to San Antonio, but Gen. Jose Urrea was ordered along the coast. Few Texans thought San Antonio — or Bexar as it was generally called — was worth defending. The direct route to the rich Anglo-Texan colonies on the Brazos and Colorado rivers was along the coast. Many strategists anticipated a quick thrust at San Felipe de Austin, the capital of Austin's colony and of Anglo Texas. Mexican strategists, however, did not want to leave a well-defended outpost to their rear during the campaign. And Santa Anna could not leave a pocket of Anglo-Americans behind him when he had pledged to sweep them all from Texas.

The grueling march took Santa Anna 11 days and cost many lives. The weather turned brutal and northers and rain took a heavy toll among the soldiers and animals. Texan scouts also had made the trek more difficult by burning large areas of grassland that the Mexicans had counted on as forage.

WHILE the Mexicans prepared for war through the fall and early winter, the Texans' defensive preparations floundered. On Feb. 11, Gov. Smith sent Col. William Barret Travis to San Antonio to relieve Col. Neill. Immediately a split in command arose. Most of the American defenders were volunteers, who looked to Bowie as their leader. Travis had only a handful of Texas army regulars. So Bowie and Travis agreed to share the command. Almost immediately, Travis began asking for reinforcements. Only 150 men were available to fight, and Travis sought aid from Fannin, from Gov. Smith, from Houston, from the provisional council and from the citizens of the United States. Only a plea to Gonzales was answered.

Aside from the pleas for help, however, activity around San Antonio was leisurely. Discipline was lax, and work on improving the fortifications of the Alamo moved slowly. Indeed, the defenders of San Antonio were fortunate not to have suffered a successful surprise attack on Feb. 22. Santa Anna ordered a surprise attack by Gen. Ramirez y Sesma's cavalry, but a rain-swollen creek scuttled the plan. The Texans would have had their hands full for they were enjoying a fandango celebrating George Washington's birthday at the time, and only 10 men guarded the Alamo. The following morning, however, the forward elements of the Mexican army were spotted by guards at San Antonio and their presence was confirmed by scouts. Quickly the Texans and Americans retreated to the Alamo, which soon was under siege by hundreds of Mexican soldiers whose ranks were being reinforced daily.

Santa Anna left no doubt regarding his attitude toward the Anglo defenders of the Alamo. Upon arrival, he had hoisted a blood-red flag, the traditional Mexican symbol of no quarter, no surrender, no mercy. Travis and Bowie defiantly answered the display with a cannon shot.

Immediately the Mexicans began surrounding the Alamo and bombarding it. Throughout the first night and nights to come, Santa Anna kept up a continual din to destroy the defenders' morale.

On Feb. 24, Bowie took ill and relinquished his share of command to Travis. That evening, Travis penned one of the most stirring appeals for help in the annals of history:

Commandancy of the Alamo—
Bejar, Feby. 24th, 1836
To the people of Texas & all Americans in the world—
Fellow citizens & compatriots—
I am besieged, by a thousand or more of the Mexicans under Santa Anna — I have sustained a continual Bombardment & cannonade for 24 hours & have not lost a man — The enemy has demanded a surrender at discretion, otherwise, the garrison are to be put to the sword, if the fort is taken — I have answered the demand with a cannon shot, & our flag still waves proudly from the walls — I shall never surrender or retreat. Then I call on you in the name of Liberty, of patriotism & everything dear to the American character, to come to our aid, with all dispatch — The enemy is receiving reinforcements daily & will no doubt increase to three or four thousand in four or five days. If this call is neglected, I am determined to sustain myself as long as possible & and die like a soldier who never forgets what is due to his own honor & that of his country — VICTORY OR DEATH.
William Barret Travis,
Lt. Col. comdt.
P.S. The Lord is on our side — When the enemy appeared in sight we had not three bushels of corn — We have since found in deserted houses 80 or 90 bushels and got into the walls 20 or 30 head of Beeves.
Travis.

Within weeks, the plea for help was circulated up the Mississippi Valley and along the eastern seaboard of the United States. It is credited with generating hundreds of volunteers for the Texas cause. But they came far too late to help Travis and his little band of heroes at the Alamo.

The closest garrison of any size to the Alamo was at Goliad under Fannin's command. But Fannin refused several requests from Travis for aid. On Feb. 26, however, he began a relief march, only to have a wagon break down less than a mile from his fort. After a night's reflection on the tactical situation, he turned back.

Near Refugio on Feb. 28, Gen. Urrea fought with remnants of the Matamoros expedition under Johnson, killing several and taking 21 prisoners. The prisoners later were executed by Santa Anna's orders. Johnson escaped to carry word of the engagement to Fannin at Goliad. When news of this battle reached San Antonio, however, Mexican morale soared. The army had suffered nothing but losses, embarrassment and humiliation at the hands of the Texans for a year. Urrea's conquest was seen as a turning point. And on March 3, the general's troops ambushed another remnant of the Matamoros expedition at Agua Dulce Creek, and Dr. Grant and 15 others were killed.

Although the Mexican bombardment of the Alamo continued daily, none of the defenders was killed. In fact, they conducted several successful forays outside the fortress to burn buildings that were providing cover for the Mexican gunners and to gather firewood. Messengers also successfully moved through the Mexican lines at will, and 32 reinforcements from Gonzales under George Kimball and Albert Martin made it into the Alamo without a loss on March 1. But Santa Anna was tightening the perimeter. The last messenger got out on March 3, carrying, among other items, a letter to Jesse Grimes in which Travis asserted to the convention meeting at Washington-on-the-Brazos: "If independence is not declared, I shall lay down my arms, and so will the men under my command. But under the flag of independence, we are ready to peril our lives 100 times a day . . .''

Travis was unaware that the convention had declared Texas' independence from Mexico on March 2 and was engaged in writing a constitution and forming a government for the new republic. Historians disagree over which flag flew over the defenders of the Alamo. Mexican sources have said that Santa Anna was outraged when he saw flying over the fortress a Mexican tri-color, identical to the ones carried by his troops except with the numbers "1 8 2 4" emblazoned upon it. Texas historians have accepted this version because the defenders of the Alamo could not have known that independence had been declared. To the knowledge of the Alamo's defenders, the last official government position taken by Texans was in support of the Constitution of 1824, which the flag symbolized. But the only flag found after the battle, according to historian Walter Lord, was one flown by the New Orleans Grays.

BY March 5 Santa Anna had 4,000 men in camp, a force he felt sufficient to subdue the Alamo. Mexican sources said he was furious that the Texans had held out through 12 days of bombardment and siege. The longer the small band held off the Mexicans, the less would be his glory. Other Mexican commanders felt that major losses in life were not necessary to take the fortress; the defenders could have been starved out eventually. But Santa Anna would not hear of it. His confidence rested in his troops' courage and their training in the best of Napoleonic military tactics. Crude frontiersmen, El Presidente thought, had little chance against this sort of sophisticated armed might.

Santa Anna overlooked the marksmanship of the frontiersmen behind the walls of the Alamo. To a man they had been raised with weapons and trained to hunt. With their long rifles, Davy Crockett and his Tennesseans prided themselves on regularly hitting targets at 200 yards or more. Mexican smooth-bore muskets could carry only 70 yards, and not accurately at that. Faced with the Mexicans' give-no-quarter policy, the defenders of the Alamo would be doubly lethal.

Historians disagree on the date, and in some cases whether the event took place. But legend holds that on March 3 or March 5, Col. Travis called his command together and explained the bleak outlook. He apologized if he had misled them into believing that reinforcements were on the way. But he explained that he had told them that in good faith; he had thought help was coming. Then the young colonel drew a line in the dirt and asked those willing to die for freedom to cross with him. Jim Bowie had his sick bed carried across. Only Louis Rose, a veteran of Napoleon's bitter retreat from Moscow, chose to fight another day. He slipped out of the Alamo that night.

Mexican troops were up well before dawn on March 6 preparing for the final assault on the Alamo. When reminded that there were no doctors or hospital facilities available, Santa Anna reportedly snapped that that was all the better. The troops would know, he said, that it was "not as bad to die as to come out wounded." Twenty-five hundred men in perfect formation surrounded the fortress and on command commenced their attack. During the action, the Mexican bands struck up the deguello, a traditional Spanish march dating back to the battles against the Moors. It signified a no-quarter, throat-cutting, merciless death. The first troops were cut down by the murderous cannon fire from the Alamo's guns and by the precision marksmanship of the frontiersmen's long rifles. Cannon loaded with scrap iron mowed down the Mexican regulars by the squad. There is no doubting the courage of the Mexican soldiers as they faced the lethal fire. At first they would fall back, regroup and attack again. Although the Mexicans were executing perfect Napoleonic maneuvers, they lacked the cannon to give the fortress an appropriate initial bombardment. Also, Mexican commanders were unaware that British army instructions at the time warned that frontal assaults on frontier riflemen behind breastworks could be conducted only with unacceptable casualties. Attempt after attempt at placing scaling ladders was thwarted by the Alamo's cannon and riflemen. But Mexican artillery finally began to have its effect. A wall was breached. The first few Mexican soldiers through the opening were killed. The number of skirmishers soon became too great. The Alamo's huge courtyard was filled with desperate hand-to-hand fighting. Mexicans were armed with bayonets; the defenders used rifle butts and Bowie knives. So frenzied had the Mexican soldiers become that the corpses of defenders were mutilated. Travis died of a bullet wound to the head. Bowie was killed in his sick bed, selling his life dearly with a brace of pistols left for his defense. Crockett's fate is still debated. Some sources say he died in a pile of Mexican soldiers, victims of his rifle and knife. One Mexican officer, Enrique De La Pena, held that Crockett was captured with a few other defenders and executed by Santa Anna.

When the fighting stopped between 8:30 and 9 a.m., all the defenders were dead. Only a few women, children and black slaves survived the assault.

But Travis and his men placed a heavy price indeed on the victory. Almost one-third of the attack force was killed or wounded. And these were the flower of the Mexican army, veterans for the most part. Their deaths in such number set back Santa Anna's timetable. Although recruits were available from the ranks of Mexican-Texans, they had to be trained. The Napoleonic tactics used by the army required highly trained soldiers, and training took time. The fall of the Alamo also brutally shook the old Texans out of their lethargy, and no doubt shamed them, too, for ignoring Travis' appeals for help.

Sam Houston, finally given command of all Texas' army, left the convention at Washington-on-the-Brazos on the day of the fall of the Alamo. On March 11, he arrived at Gonzales to begin organizing the troops. He found just over 370 men at the town, many of whom had been on their way to aid Travis. Two days later, Mrs. Dickinson, the wife of one of the victims of the Alamo, and two slaves arrived with the news of the fall of the fortress. Houston immediately began an evacuation of Gonzales, taking the inhabitants and leaving the town in flames to deny it to the Mexican forces he thought were close behind.

Houston ordered Fannin to abandon the old presidio La Bahia at Goliad and to retreat to Victoria. Fannin had arrived at the fort in late January with more than 400 men. As a former West Pointer, he had a background in military planning. Troops were drilled, and fortifications were reinforced. But Fannin had been indecisive. Travis' pleas for help were refused, and after receiving Houston's orders, Fannin waited for scouting parties to return. Finally, on March 19, he left, but too late. Forward elements of Gen. Urrea's troops caught Fannin's command on an open prairie

near a wooded area. After a short battle, Fannin fortified his position around a broken-down ammunition wagon. Through the night, the Mexican troops were reinforced. After a brief skirmish the following morning, Fannin surrendered.

A controversy surrounded the capitulation. Survivors of Fannin's command later argued that they surrendered with the understanding they would be treated as prisoners of war. Documents indicate, however, that the surrender was unconditional, and the troops were thrown on the mercy of the Mexican commanders. The prisoners were marched to Goliad where they were kept under light restraint. So unconcerned were they that it is said that not one violated the pledge not to attempt an escape. Santa Anna was furious, however, when Gen. Urrea appealed for clemency for the captives. The Mexican leader issued the orders in triplicate for their execution. On March 27, a Palm Sunday, most of the prisoners were divided into groups and marched out of Goliad, thinking they were being transferred to other facilities. When the executions began, many escaped. But about 350 were killed.

In less than a month, Texas' military forces had lost almost 700 men in battle or by execution. Fewer than one in five of these were old settlers, most being American volunteers who had not been in Texas when hostilities began the previous fall. Houston spent almost two weeks on the Colorado River, and on March 26 began a retreat to the Brazos.

Santa Anna had not left San Antonio, but word of the losses soon reached the settlers who began leaving their homes, often in haste. When the Mexican army began pursuit of Houston's forces, Jose Enrique de la Pena, a young staff officer, lamented the fear that the war generated. He blamed the war on a group of promoters. These promoters, the young officer observed, "painted us as savages, as men more ferocious than beasts, to which belief the events of the Alamo, La Bahia and the mission at Refugio unfortunately contributed. No one will disagree with me that provisions should have been made to prevent the war, or that once begun in order to vindicate an injured nation, it should have been carried out in a less disastrous fashion."

But the old Texans finally faced the reality of the conflict. While many ran for safety, others joined Houston for the defense of the Republic. As one soldier noted, "We ask nor expect no quarter in the future." The Texans were on their way to San Jacinto.

San Jacinto and Beyond

SAM Houston spent only a short time at the convention that met March 1, 1836, at Washington-on-the-Brazos. But he may have been the most important man there, for he insisted that the Texans form a coherent government. The Alamo was besieged and in danger, he argued, because there had been no government in Texas.

Attempts to adjourn the convention so the delegates could rush to San Antonio were defeated. Long-winded oratory was discouraged. The convention quickly got down to the business of forming a government. Richard Ellis was named president, and a committee chaired by George Childress wrote a Declaration of Independence, patterned on the one that separated the United States from Great Britain. The declaration was adopted on March 2, and on March 6, the day the Alamo fell, Houston left the convention with full command of all the armed forces in Texas.

Upon arrival at Gonzales, Houston had quickly discerned the Texans' position was untenable. He had only a handful of men, the Alamo had fallen, the settlers were in chaos, and the position was far removed from the Anglo population that was so necessary for supplies and reinforcements. Near midnight, he began the long march to San Jacinto.

By March 17, Houston had reached Burnam's Crossing on the Colorado River, near the present city of LaGrange. Two days later, the small army crossed the river and moved south to Beason's Ford near present-day Columbus. There he began to receive reinforcements. Within a week, the small force had become almost respectable with 1,200-1,400 men in camp.

At the same time Houston reached the Colorado, the convention at Washington-on-the-Brazos was completing work on a constitution for the new Repub-

lic. Only slightly did it differ from the U.S. Constitution. The Texas charter called for a unitary government, rather than dividing the territory into states. And from the Mexican constitution, it prohibited the president from succeeding himself after one three-year term. Ministers of the gospel also were prohibited from holding public office. David Burnet was named interim president of the new government and Lorenzo de Zavala was vice president. Thomas J. Rusk was secretary of war. Upon completion of the work, the new government moved to Harrisburg.

In the excitement of the period, however, important steps were not taken. Stephen F. Austin, serving as Texas' agent in the United States, complained the group was never informed that independence had been declared. William Wharton and Branch T. Archer also were Texas' agents.

Close on Houston's heels was Gen. Joaquin de Ramirez y Sesma who had been dispatched from San Antonio by Santa Anna on March 11 to follow the Texans. Seven hundred and twenty-five men were in Ramirez y Sesma's command, and he sought reinforcements as soon as the Texans were spotted. Heavy rains swelled the river, preventing the Mexicans from crossing.

Houston was criticized for not fighting at this point. But the Texans' commander explained that he would have inevitably suffered casualties and had no means to transport them. Also, the Mexicans could easily be reinforced with numbers far exceeding the small Texan contingent. In addition, word of Fannin's loss had reached the area, and settlers were in full flight. On March 27, Houston moved his men to San Felipe on the Brazos, and left on the following day for Groce's Crossing 20 miles up river, which he reached March 31. The Texans were getting restless for a fight. Moseley

Baker and Wylie Martin and their men, however, refused to follow Houston to Groce's, so they were ordered to defend the river crossings at San Felipe and at Fort Bend.

At Groce's Crossing, the Texans had a respite, offering Houston an opportunity to organize and drill his forces. Most of the volunteers had no military experience. In a battle against well-drilled forces, they would have been at a disadvantage. So Houston attempted to instill military discipline. Up to this point, one of the army's major responsibilities had been the protection of settlers involved in the Runaway Scrape, as the retreat was called. To reinforce discipline, Houston hanged four men accused of raping women and robbing settlers.

Santa Anna had divided his forces after the fall of the Alamo. Gen. Gaona had been ordered to Nacogdoches along a northern route, but he soon was diverted to San Felipe. Ramirez y Sesma had been in pursuit of the main force of the Texas army, and Gen. Jose Urrea was following a path along the coast from Goliad to Brazoria.

Santa Anna initially considered returning to Mexico City after the Alamo fell. The war was over in his mind, and the dictator, fully aware of the fickle political tides that rocked the Mexican government, wanted to consolidate politically his victories on the battlefield. But his general staff talked him out of leaving.

So Santa Anna joined Ramirez y Sesma on April 7, and the Mexicans entered San Felipe on that day. Mexican intelligence informed the dictator that the Texas government was in Harrisburg, and Santa Anna immediately conceived a plan of capturing the rebel leadership to end the war. But he could not cross the Brazos until April 10, when his troops finally gained control of the Fort Bend crossing from Texan sharpshooters. Three days later Ramirez y Sesma arrived, and the Mexicans reached Harrisburg on April 15. But the Texas government was gone, barely escaping advance units of Mexicans who watched them row to a schooner bound for Galveston. Settlers, however, told the Mexicans that Houston was marching toward Lynch's ferry on the San Jacinto River in an attempt to escape to Louisiana. Santa Anna burned Harrisburg and headed toward the ferry.

At Groce's Crossing, Houston was successful in organizing the army. On April 13, using the steamboat Yellow Stone, the army crossed the river, and orders were sent to outlying units to gather at Donoho's. Martin, who had refused to leave the Brazos, again ignored Houston's command to march and took his troops to Nacogdoches to defend against a feared Indian uprising.

The Texas army was impatient for a fight, and there was talk in the ranks that, if action did not develop soon, a new commander should be elected. So prevalent were the rumblings that he would shoot any man who tried to mutiny. But the Texas government also was distressed with the commander-in-chief's tactics. On April 13, Houston received a message from President Burnet:

"This country expects something from you; the government looks to you for action. The time has arrived to determine whether we are to give up the country and make the best of our way out of it or to meet the enemy and make at least one struggle for our boasted independence."

Fifteen miles east of Donoho's was a fork in the road; one leg went to Nacogdoches and the other to Harrisburg. Here one of the great mysteries of the San Jacinto campaign rests. Critics long said that Houston had no intention of fighting the Mexicans, that his plan was to cross into Louisiana where protection of the U.S. Army was available.

Indeed, Gen. Edmund P. Gaines, commander of Fort Jessup near Natchitoches, La., had moved a large body of U.S. troops to the Sabine River by April 1836. Settlers in East Texas feared an Indian uprising while so many men were away fighting the Mexican army. The United States was under a treaty obligation to Mexico to maintain peaceful relations with the Indians. But Gen. Gaines' investigation found the Cherokees and others "more interested in planting corn" than in fighting. Nevertheless the U.S. troops remained on the Sabine until the fall of 1836.

When the Texas army reached the fork in the road, it marched toward Harrisburg, as Houston had indicated he planned to do in a letter written the previous night. Along the road, two Mexican couriers were captured and gave Houston the information he had

hoped for. Santa Anna was leading the small Mexican force that in its haste had moved in front of Houston. Now the Texans had an opportunity to win the war. Throughout the war, Houston's intelligence system had operated efficiently. Scouts, commanded by Erastus "Deaf" Smith, kept the Texans informed of Mexican troop movements. Hendrick Arnold, a free black, was a valuable spy, posing as a runaway slave to enter Mexican camps to gain information.

On April 19, the Texans crossed Buffalo Bayou and made contact with an advance force of Mexican cavalry on April 20. A brief skirmish ensued, and the Texans were ready for more action. But Houston waited. So impressive was the performance of one private, Mirabeau B. Lamar, that Houston promoted him to colonel of the cavalry the next day.

Early on April 21, Gen. Martin Perfecto de Cos reinforced Santa Anna's troop with more than 500 men. Santa Anna complained later that they were recruits and not "picked" veterans that he had requested from Gen. Vicente Filisola, his second in command. Nevertheless, the new troops, who had marched all night, disrupted the camp's routine for a time, but soon all the soldiers and officers settled down for a mid-day rest. Curiously, no sentries were posted, although the Mexicans knew that the small Texas army was no more than a mile away across Peggy McCormick's ranch on the San Jacinto plain.

Houston held a council of war at noon on April 21, with the consensus being that the Texans should attack early the next day. But the men wanted to fight, so about 3 p.m., Houston ordered them to parade and the battle was launched at 4:30 p.m.

A company of Mexican-Texans, commanded by Juan Seguin, had served as the army's rear guard through much of the retreat across Texas and had fought many skirmishes with the Mexican army in the process. Perhaps fearing the Mexican-Texans would be mistaken for Mexican soldiers, Houston had assigned the company to guard duty as the battle approached. But after the men protested, they fought in the battle of San Jacinto.

Historians disagree widely on the number of troops on each side. Houston probably had about 900 while Santa Anna had between 1,100 and 1,300. But the Texans had the decided psychological advantage. Two-thirds of the fledgling Republic's army were "old Texans" who had family and land to defend. They had an investment of years of toil in building their homes. And they were just plain fighting mad about the massacre of men at the Alamo and Goliad. In less than 20 minutes — with strains of "Won't You Come to the Bower" and "Yankee Doodle" mingling with outraged cries of "Remember the Alamo" and "Remember Goliad" — they set the Mexican army to rout. More than 600 Mexicans were killed and hundreds more wounded or captured. Only nine of the Texans died in the fight. The killing frenzy of the Texans lasted until almost sunset.

CRITICS claimed that Houston tried to call a retreat and was guilty of other unworthy conduct during the battle. But the commander had two horses shot from under him and was severely wounded in the encounter. Thomas J. Rusk, secretary of war, however, probably was the most outstanding commander on the field.

But it was not until the following day that Santa Anna, who fled from his forces early in the fight, was captured. Houston had given patrols prophetic advice: "You will find the hero of Tampico, if you find him at all, making his retreat on all fours, and he will be dressed as bad at least as a common soldier." And that was the case. One Texan noticed that a grubby soldier his patrol found in the high grass had a silk shirt under his filthy jacket. Although denying he was an officer, the Mexican was taken back to camp by the patrol, where he was welcomed with cries of "El Presidente! El Presidente!" by other prisoners. Santa Anna introduced himself when taken to the wounded Houston.

Houston quickly got the Mexican dictator to agree to a truce and to order his armies to cease hostilities and withdraw to San Antonio and Victoria. Texas soldiers were ready to execute Santa Anna on the spot for the atrocities at the Alamo and Goliad. But Houston had no intention of killing him. Seeing the Texans' hostility, Santa Anna made quick conciliations, even offering to negotiate an immediate treaty with Houston. But the Texas commander refused, leaving that responsibility to the civil government. Houston soon left for New Orleans to have his wounded ankle treated.

Mexican critics of Gen. Filisola, Santa Anna's

second in command, have argued that he should have ignored the dictator's orders, since they were given under duress, and attacked the Texans. The Italian-born officer had little choice, however, because he was almost out of supplies. The four-ship Texas navy, commanded by Charles E. Hawkins, kept the Gulf clear of Mexican shipping. Supply lines therefore were stretched hundreds of miles overland, and Houston's scorched-earth policy in retreat had denied the Mexicans forage from the land.

President Burnet took charge of Santa Anna, and on May 14 the dictator signed two treaties at Velasco, a public document and a secret one. The public agreement declared that hostilities would cease, that the Mexican army would withdraw to south of the Rio Grande, that prisoners would be released and that Santa Anna would be shipped to Veracruz as soon as possible. In the secret treaty, Santa Anna agreed to recognize Texas' independence, to give diplomatic recognition, to negotiate a commercial treaty and to set the Rio Grande as the new Republic's southern boundary.

Historian Eugene Barker has noted that "The Texas Revolution was not a spontaneous outburst of patriotic indignation against Mexican oppression. Few of the colonists were satisfied with all features of Mexican rule but few also were ready to go to the length of armed rebellion . . ." Some Texas settlers went so far as to oppose the rebellion. Gen. Urrea received almost an enthusiastic welcome when he entered Columbia on April 21. He observed that the settlers felt that many of the rebels were adventurers and were a greater threat to the colonists than the Mexican army. Houston found the names of many Texas Tories among Santa Anna's papers after San Jacinto. He never released the names, but a company of men commanded by Capt. James Kokernot was sent to inform the Tories that they were then supporting a lost cause.

Texas soon faced another military threat, this one from its own army. One historian noted that the disagreement between the military and civilian government over policy and procedure after the revolution brought Texas near the establishment of the very type of military domination that it fought to avoid.

The character of the Texas army was changing rapidly after San Jacinto. Again, the old settlers, who provided two-thirds of the manpower for the fighting force at the time, were ready to go home. Almost immediately, some began drifting off to plant crops or to defend against anticipated Indian raids. These were not professional fighting men, but farmers and shopkeepers who had taken up arms in defense of family and home.

Rusk assumed command of the army when Houston left, and he was detailed to follow the Mexican army out of Texas. Further hostilities were to be avoided, however. But the army soon began to melt away, and neither reinforcements nor supplies were forthcoming. Rusk complained that between the Colorado River and Goliad and San Antonio "There is not a particle of corn or a hoof of cattle." Rusk's officers accused the government of neglecting the army.

Burnet was informed by officers that he was to drop all other matters and give "particular attention" to the army or the army might find it necessary "to pursue at home our most sacred rights."

Burnet denied the charges of neglect and objected to the threat. "When the civil government of a country is compelled to receive a prescription of its duties from an armed force, that government is, if not virtually dissolved, in great danger of being lost in the blazonry of military misrule."

The government's problems deepened in early June when it attempted to release Santa Anna in compliance with the Velasco treaty. Gen. Thomas J. Green, a Texas agent in the United States, arrived with a group of volunteers he had raised. He took the Mexican leader off the ship and held him in army custody despite objections by President Burnet and the cabinet.

By July, the character of the army, and its attitude, changed substantially. Almost three-quarters of the 2,500 men under arms had not been in Texas when the battle of San Jacinto was fought. Most were American volunteers who came to Texas to seek vengeance against the Mexicans for atrocities at Goliad and the Alamo and to take advantage of the large land grants the Republic was giving for military service. But the new army was outraged that the Mexican leaders had not been hanged, although Burnet courageously pointed out that there was no precedent to try or punish a commander for official acts performed during war.

Because of the problems with the new army, Burnet ordered agents in New Orleans to send no more volunteers from the United States. Matters continued to deteriorate, however. Word was received that the Mexican Senate had repudiated Santa Anna's agreements in the treaty of Velasco. Texas agents sent to Matamoros were taken into custody, and it was rumored that Gen. Jose Urrea was marching into Texas with a new army.

IN early July, Gen. Rusk sent Col. Henry Millard to Velasco to discuss various military matters with the president and the cabinet. While in the capital, Millard ordered Maj. Amasa Turner to arrest Burnet and to confiscate the cabinet's archives. Turner instead told Burnet of the order. The outraged president ordered Rusk to dismiss Millard from the rolls of the military and declared "the good people of Texas have been insulted and outraged in the person of the Chief Magistrate; a violent revolution has been attempted, involving the overthrow of the civil authorities and evidently intended to create a military supremacy in the government."

The crisis eased somewhat when attention became riveted on the rumored invasion by Urrea. Burnet ordered the army to prepare for an expedition against Matamoros, and that pacified the officers and men.

But Texas was in deep financial trouble. Debts from the revolution totaled $1,250,000 by the end of August 1836. So in July, Burnet called for an election on the first Monday in September.

Texas had won its independence from Mexico and from a threatened military dictatorship within its own army. But its future was far from assured.

Republic of Texas

SAM Houston was easily the most dominant figure through the nearly 10-year history of the Republic of Texas. While he was roundly criticized for the retreat across Texas during the revolution, the victory at San Jacinto endeared him to most of the new nation's inhabitants.

Houston handily defeated Henry Smith and Stephen F. Austin in the election called in September 1836 by President David G. Burnet and the interim government. Mirabeau B. Lamar was elected vice president, and voters overwhelmingly expressed a desire for annexation to the United States.

Houston was inaugurated on Oct. 22 at the capital in Columbia, which was little more than a frontier village. The first cabinet appointed by the new president represented an attempt to heal old political wounds. Austin was named secretary of state; former provisional governor Henry Smith was secretary of treasury; Thomas J. Rusk, secretary of war; J. Pinckney Henderson, attorney general; Robert Barr, postmaster general, and J. Rhoads Fisher, secretary of navy. The

First Congress of Texas, which convened Oct. 3, named James Collinsworth the chief justice of the Supreme Court.

A host of problems faced the new government. Gen. Santa Anna was still in custody, and public opinion favored his execution. Texas' leadership wisely kept Santa Anna alive, first to keep from giving the Mexicans an emotional rallying point for launching another invasion, which the leader's death would have represented. And second, the Texas leaders hoped that the dictator would keep his promise to work for recognition of Texas, as he promised in the secret Treaty of Velasco. Santa Anna was released in November 1836 and made his way to Washington, D.C. Houston hoped the dictator could convince President Jackson to recognize Texas. Jackson refused to see Santa Anna, who returned to Mexico where he had fallen from power.

Texas suffered a major tragedy in late December 1836 when Austin, the acknowledged "Father of Texas," died of pneumonia after working long hours at the drafty capital at Columbia. The steamboat Yellow Stone ferried his body to Peach Point on the Brazos for burial. This historic steamboat played a major role in Texas history. In April the craft had been used to ferry Houston's army across the Brazos at Groce's Crossing; later the boat transported President Burnet and his cabinet to San Jacinto and carried the government and Santa Anna to Velasco for treaty negotiations. The historic ship sank in Buffalo Bayou in late 1837.

Houston's second major challenge was even more vexing than the problem with Santa Anna. Felix Huston had assumed command of the Texas army when Rusk resigned to take a cabinet post. Huston favored an invasion of Mexico, and the army, made up now mostly of American volunteers, who came to Texas after the battle of San Jacinto, was rebellious and ready to fight. Houston tried to replace Huston as commander with Albert Sidney Johnston, but Huston seriously wounded Johnston in a duel. In May 1837, Huston was asked to Columbia to discuss the invasion. While Huston was away from the troops, Houston sent Rusk to furlough the army without pay — but with generous land grants. Only 600 men were retained in the army.

The Republic's other problems were less tractable. The economy needed attention; Indians still represented a menace; Mexico remained warlike; foreign relations had to be developed, and relations with the United States had to be firmed up.

The economy proved to be the most troublesome. Texas began its experience as a Republic in a boom atmosphere. While most Texans existed in a subsistence economy, raising only enough crops to feed themselves, independence attracted land speculators. Everyone wanted to be in on the beginning of the new nation. But there was little currency in Texas. Some gold and silver Mexican coins were in circulation, but the principal medium of exchange was bank notes from the United States. These notes were in all denominations with no common base. Only the strength of the bank from which they were issued guaranteed the notes.

At the same time the United States also was experiencing an economic boom, but one based on speculation in canals, railroads and land. Foreigners invested heavily in these schemes. In the period 1835-37, nearly 40 million acres of federal land were sold, mostly to speculators, who borrowed from banks to make payments. The number of bank loans soared 500 percent between 1830 and 1837, and many of the institutions made loans without regard to reserves.

By 1836, revenue from federal land sales reached $24 million, and the U.S. Congress opted to distribute the federal surplus among the states on a population basis. The drain of cash from "pet banks" caused a hardship that was intensified when President Andrew Jackson in 1836 required that land payments be made only in hard currency or in notes from banks that paid specie (cash) for their outstanding notes. In May 1837, New York banks stopped paying hard money for their notes or other obligations, and this action precipitated a crisis that resulted in the failure of hundreds of banks. For the next five years, the United States was thrown into the worst economic depression in its history. The economic decline was aggravated when foreign investors withdrew their cash, and a series of crop failures reduced the purchasing power of the major segment of the agricultural economy.

Texas was not affected by the initial decline. But when the depression finally hit the new Republic, it was as devastating as in the United States and lasted longer.

Houston's first administration was plagued by a lack of money. Land was Texas' only asset, and conflicting policies were adopted for use of land. On one hand, land was to be used to back notes issued by the government. On the other hand, generous land grants were to be used to attract immigrants. But when vast amounts of land were given away, the resource was of little use as collateral because it would not hold its value. During the life of the Republic, more than 36.8 million acres of land were alienated by the congresses of Texas. The Republic's Constitution specified that white heads of families living in Texas on March 2, 1836, could receive a First Class headright of a league and a labor — 4,605 acres — of land. Single men could get 1,476 acres. Subsequent headrights were approved for newcomers, and additional grants were available for men who served in the army.

During his first administration, Houston issued $650,000 in interest-bearing notes — so-called "Star Money," because the star of Texas was printed on the backs of the notes — that held their value when redeemed in late 1838. This issue, redeemed before the Panic of 1837 reached Texas, was the only specie issued by the Republic that did not devalue immediately.

The Texas Congress tried to levy some direct taxes, but these were easily evaded. And the taxes were difficult to collect because there simply was little hard cash in Texas. The only source of real revenue was customs collections, and these were paid grudgingly by Texans. The tariffs ranged from one percent on breadstuffs to 50 percent on silk, and custom revenues represented between 50 and 80 percent of the government's income throughout the life of the Republic.

Standing armies are expensive to maintain, so to keep the cost of government down, Houston sought to maintain peaceful relations with the Indians and with Mexico. Frontier defense was to be maintained by local militia. The Congress authorized a line of block houses and trading posts along the frontier, and Houston met personally with the chiefs of several tribes in an effort to maintain peace. But the Texas Senate declined to ratify the treaty Houston had made with the Cherokees and other Indians in East Texas during the revolution, and this hurt the peace efforts. Also many of the trading posts promised to the Indians in agreements were never opened, damaging the government's credibility in the eyes of the Indians.

HOUSTON'S policy of frontier defense relied on ranging companies — the Texas Rangers. Since Stephen F. Austin personally financed a group of 10 men to protect his small colony in 1823, these organizations had been active in Texas. Before the Revolution in 1835, small groups of men had been commissioned to guard the frontier against Indians while other Texans were occupied with the Mexican army. The service of the historic Texas Rangers has been well-documented, and during this period, Capt. Jack Hays was the best-known of these frontier defenders. Also during this era, the six-shooter, one of the most important innovations in weaponry, was introduced into Texas.

Relations with Mexico were stagnant. Mexicans were too involved with internal politics to be concerned with Texas. But they also were adamant about refusing to recognize the independence of the Republic of Texas and about accepting the Rio Grande as any sort of boundary line.

EARLY attempts to gain recognition from England, France and other European countries also were stymied, as the nations waited to see if Texas could remain independent from Mexico.

The greatest disappointment in Houston's first term was the failure to have the Republic annexed to the United States. Henry Morfit, President Jackson's agent, toured the new Republic in the summer of 1836. Although impressed, Morfit reported that Texas' best chance at continued independence lay in the "stupidity of the rulers of Mexico and the financial embarrassment of the Mexican government." He recommended that annexation be delayed. Though U.S. Secretary of State John Forsyth recommended that diplomatic recognition be withheld until others nations led the way, U.S. recognition of Texas' independence came in March 1837, President Jackson's last official act in office. But in June 1837, John Quincy Adams led off the abolitionists' campaign against Texas by denouncing annexation on the floor of the U.S. House. Late that year, Houston withdrew the formal request for annexation. Texas' pride had suffered a severe blow.

Although immigrants were attracted to Texas, the Republic's economy was slow in developing. Almost all manufactured goods had to be imported throughout the history of the Republic, throwing foreign trade out of balance and aggravating the shortage of currency. Most Texans were farmers, eking out an existence for their families. Any surplus crops had to be sold in the immediate neighborhood because transportation facilities were nonexistent. The Republic left most road construction and maintenance to local government. And most of the roads were only cleared trails, muddy to the extent of impassability in wet weather and dusty in dry seasons. Goods had to be hauled by oxcarts or by horse, and fees were high.

The Republic's major rivers never fulfilled the promise of transportation arteries that early explorers expected. Although the Sabine, Red, Trinity and Brazos rivers had steamboat traffic at times, the waterways defied navigation very far inland. The water flow in most of the rivers was seasonal, and at many times, there was simply not enough water to float a craft. Snags, sharp meandering routes along with other obstacles also thwarted navigation, and sand bars at the rivers' mouths were hazardous.

In inland Texas, Preston located on the Red River in present-day Grayson County and Jefferson located near Cypress Bayou in Marion County were major points for river traffic, though much of it was seasonal. Several smaller communities on the lower reaches of other rivers also had water service. The Brazos with heavy cotton farming along its lower reaches was one of the most accessible rivers for water traffic. A small lumbering industry was developing on the rivers, too, with several sawmills in operation around Buffalo Bayou. The lumber was provided for local needs.

In addition to farming, cattle raising already was established in the Republic, and the animals were driven overland to markets in Louisiana. The Coastal Prairies, the Piney Woods and Northeast Texas were the principal centers of cattle ranching in the Republic, as well as South Texas.

San Antonio was the largest town in the Republic, but it was on the frontier and too near Mexico to play a leading role in affairs. The eastern rivers and the coast were the Anglo-American population centers. In April 1837, the capital of the Republic was moved from Columbia to the new city of Houston on Buffalo Bayou. The new capital was named for the hero of San Jacinto and was developed by the brothers A. C. and J. K. Allen near the previous capital of Harrisburg, which was burned by the Mexican army.

Houston's foreign policy achieved initial success when J. Pinckney Henderson negotiated a trade treaty with Great Britain. Although the agreement was short of outright diplomatic recognition, it was progress. In the next few years, France, Belgium, The Netherlands and some German states recognized the new Republic.

Under the constitution, Houston's first term lasted only two years, and he could not succeed himself. The Republic's politics already were dividing along lines of personalities. Houston was a controversial figure, and opponents roundly criticized his drinking habits, along with his policies as president. Lamar, an outspoken opponent of the first president, was the leading candidate to succeed Houston. And Lamar won the election handily when two opponents recruited by Houston's partisans committed suicide.

Lamar brought a different style of government to the Republic of Texas. He was a dreamer, a visionary. Texas, he felt, was in competition with the United States to see which would control the North American continent.

While Houston had been passive, partly out of frugality, in relations with Mexico and Indians, Lamar was more active. He thought Mexico could be forced to accept Texas' independence, and that the borders of the new Republic could be drawn with a sword. Lamar foresaw a Texas empire controlling all the territory to the Pacific Ocean and much of northern Mexico. Indians, the Republic's second president thought, were simply tenants in residence on the land they occupied and had no right to title if white settlers coveted the area.

While Lamar's visions may have been in keeping with those held by many Texans, his administration suffered from economic malaise. Houston was frugal, Lamar a spendthrift. Houston's first term cost Texas only about $500,000, while Lamar and the Congress spent $5 million in the next three years. During Lamar's administration, Texas became afflicted with the so-called "original sin of Americans," as one economist noted — the paper money disease. The government issued paper bills totaling more than $3.5 million in the next three years, leaving a debt of almost $6 million. The notes issued by the government during this period — called "Redbacks" because of the color of the back of the bill — carried no interest and soon depreciated. By the end of Lamar's administration the money was worth only two to three cents on the dollar.

Early in 1839, Lamar gained recognition as the "father of education" in Texas when the Congress granted each of the existing 23 counties three leagues of land to be used for education. Later the allotment was increased to four leagues. Fifty leagues of land also were set aside for development of a university. Despite the lip service paid to education, the government did not have the money for several years to set up a school system. Most education during the Republic was provided by private schools and churches.

Lamar's Indian policies, however, were the most dramatic departure from Houston's. One difference lay in the men's experience. Houston had lived with Cherokees as a child, was adopted as a member of a tribe and advocated Indian rights long before coming to Texas. He was one of the few Anglos who tried to give Indians title to their land rather than place them on reservations. Lamar more accurately reflected the frontier attitude toward the native Americans. His first experience in public life was as secretary to Gov. George Troup of Georgia who successfully opposed the federal government's policy of assimilation of Indians at the time. Indians were simply removed from Georgia.

Texans' concern about Indian's intentions was raised in 1838 when Vicente Cordova, a former official at Nacogdoches, led an uprising of dissident Mexican-Texans, Anglos and Indians in East Texas. Cordova escaped, but Manuel Flores, a Mexican trader, was killed near Austin in 1839. Found on Flores' body were letters urging the Cherokees and other East Texas Indians to take up arms against the white settlers. Texans first tried to negotiate the Cherokees' removal from the region, but in July 1839, the Indians were forcibly ejected from Texas at the battle of the Neches River. Houston's close friend, the aging Cherokee chief Philip Bowles, was killed in the battle while Houston was visiting former President Jackson in Tennessee.

THE most tragic miscalculation in Lamar policy came in March 1840 when a group of Comanches was invited to San Antonio to exchange prisoners. Chief Maguara led 12 other chiefs and dozens of warriors and their families to the city. But they brought only one white girl, who told of harsh treatment at the hands of the Indians. Texas' commissioners, Hugh McLeod and William G. Cooke, and militia commander, William S. Fisher, decided to hold the chiefs until more prisoners were returned. But the Comanches would not be taken prisoner, and the so-called Council House Fight ensued. Many chiefs and warriors were killed and their families captured. Word spread among the Indians of this treachery. In August 1840, an estimated 600 Indians raided Linnville and Victoria near the Gulf Coast in retaliation. Texas' militia under Ranger Ben McCulloch ambushed the raiding party at Plum Creek, killing several of the raiders and recovering horses, livestock and plunder. Later in the year, John H. Moore led a successful campaign against Comanches camped near the present town of Colorado City. The Comanches were Texans' implacable enemies until finally defeated in 1875.

Historians point out that while Lamar's Indian policy was expensive and of questionable morality, it was effective. Large regions of the Republic were cleared of native Americans for immigrants.

To demonstrate his intention to expand the boundaries of the Republic, Lamar wanted the capital moved from Houston. In early 1839, a commission was appointed to select a site to be located near the frontier and named for Stephen F. Austin. Lamar supported the selection of a site on the Colorado River the previous year while on a buffalo hunt. (Historian Eugene C. Barker also noted that Austin had once selected a site in the immediate area for a permanent home that was never built, although this was not connected to Lamar's choice.) Construction of government buildings began in the spring of 1839, and on Oct. 17, 1839, Lamar arrived with an official cavalcade to occupy Austin, the new capital of the Republic. Sam Houston and others never liked the site, feeling it was too vulnerable to attacks by Indians and the Mexican army.

Lamar's foreign policy bore fruit. In 1839, France became the first European nation to extend diplomatic recognition to the newest North American republic. Holland, The Netherlands and Great Britain followed suit in 1840, and Belgium joined the others in 1841. In exchange for Texas' promise to suppress the importation of slaves, Great Britain agreed to mediate Texas' discussions with Mexico. Lamar attempted to bludgeon Mexico into negotiations with the second Texas navy, which took to the seas under the command of Edwin Ward Moore, the "port captain of the Navy." The navy raided Mexican ports and shipping, and for a time it was "rented" to republican rebels in Yucatan, another Mexican state in revolt against the centralist government.

While Lamar was dreaming of empire, Texas' fragile economy collapsed. By the fall of 1840, the boom spirit had completely evaporated, and the economic depression that had swept the United States in 1837 was fully felt in the Republic. Its currency was almost worthless and its credit nonexistent. Lamar had long hoped for a major loan with which to establish a national bank to smooth Texas' economic problems. But most of the world was still gripped by the depression, and Texas could not obtain loans from either the United States or Europe.

Texas also was not attracting as many settlers as was hoped when generous land grants were offered to newcomers. The Fifth Congress revived the empresario program that had been successful for the Mexican government. Immigration companies would be chartered to bring colonists to the Republic. The newcomers would be given free land, and the company would receive blocks of land when immigration quotas were filled.

Several bills chartering companies were considered. The Peters Colony bill was passed in February 1841, setting aside large tracts of land in North Central Texas, running from about the present Dallas-Fort Worth area to the Red River. The Franco-Texiene bill, which would have brought several thousand European immigrants to the Republic, was defeated when concern arose about the impact on the country of such a conclave. Fear of the pro-abolitionist leanings of foreign colonists also may have been a factor.

In 1842, a general colonization law was passed. Henri Castro, a Frenchman, received two grants for settling 600 Europeans, and Henry Francis Fisher and Burchard Miller contracted to bring 1,000 settlers. In 1844, the Fisher-Miller grants were sold to the Adelsverein, a society for promoting German immigration.

LAMAR'S hopes for a $5 million loan were dashed in an incident that would be comical, if not so serious. The French charge d'affaires to Texas, Count Alphonse de Saligny, had many difficulties adjusting to life in frontier Austin. When he refused to pay his hotel bill, innkeeper Richard Bullock cursed him roundly. Saligny was offended, and to placate him, the Texas Congress passed a law against verbally abusing foreign emissaries. Troubles between the count and the innkeeper deepened when Saligny's servant killed some of Bullock's pigs, which were eating grain in the Frenchman's stable. When authorities failed to prosecute Bullock for again cursing him, Saligny demanded his credentials and left Texas. After that, a $5 million loan to Texas by the French government was cancelled. Saligny's brother-in-law was France's minister of finance.

Lamar tried several means of improving the government's finances. In 1839, the Congress authorized the opening of trade with Mexican merchants along the Rio Grande, but this soon soured because Texans were afraid that Mexican agents among the traders were stirring up trouble for settlers with the Indians. Lamar used the authority given in 1839 to launch the Santa Fe expedition in 1841. But this effort ended in disaster.

Lamar tried to reopen negotiations with Mexico. But Bernard Bee in 1839 was not allowed to land in Mexico. James Treat was received by Mexican officials in 1839, probably as a move to keep Texas from backing dissidents in Northern Mexico. In 1841, the Mexican government refused to accept James Webb. This region was almost forgotten by the Mexican government in the political chaos following the Texas Revolution. And the state of limbo was not acceptable to residents near the Rio Grande. In 1839, Antonio Canales, an attorney from Revilla (today's Guerrero), gained support for an independence movement. Canales envisioned a Republic of the Rio Grande separate from Mexico and composed of all the northern Mexican states. Cols. Jose Maria Gonzales of Laredo and Antonio Zapata of Revilla were prominent in the early military successes of Canales. In January 1840, the Republic of the Rio Grande was declared and Laredo was the capital. The movement was short-lived as Mexican centralists defeated its army. Canales capitulated to offers of a commission in the Mexican army, and Gonzales and Zapata, for whom Zapata County is named, were executed. The Lower Rio Grande Valley stayed out of the fight, although many Texans fought in the independence movement.

FROM his seat in Congress, Houston had been a vocal critic of Lamar's administration. Texas' first president became the Republic's third chief executive when Lamar supporters, backing David G. Burnet, could not mount a serious campaign against the hero of San Jacinto.

Houston's second administration was even more frugal than his first. Government expenses were cut to the bone, and by late 1844, income almost matched expenditures. In 1842, Houston had to suspend — not repudiate — the Republic's debt, and he re-entered negotiations with Indian tribes in an attempt to quell the raids on settlements. A series of trading posts were opened along the frontier to pacify the native Americans.

War fever reached a high pitch in Texas in 1842, however, and Houston grew increasingly unpopular because he would not launch an offensive war against Mexico. Texans were irate at the mistreatment of the members of the Santa Fe Expedition who had been captured and marched to Mexico City. In retaliation for the expedition, Mexico, too, caused trouble. In March 1842, Gen. Rafael Vasquez launched guerrilla raids on San Antonio, Victoria and Goliad, but quickly left the Republic. Thirty-five hundred Texas volunteers quickly gathered at San Antonio, demanding that Mexico be punished. Houston urged calm, but the clamor increased when Gen. Adrian Woll with 1,400 men took San Antonio in September 1842. He raised the Mexican flag and declared the reconquest of Texas. Ranger Capt. Jack Hays was camped nearby and within days 600 volunteers had joined him, anxious to drive the Mexican invaders from Texas soil. Gen. Woll withdrew after the Battle of Salado.

Alexander Somervell was commanded by Houston to follow with 700 troops and harass the Mexican army, but Somervell was warned to observe the rules of civilized warfare. Houston wanted no retaliatory raids into Mexico. Somervell reached Laredo in early December 1842 and found no Mexican troops. The Texans sacked Laredo, but Somervell ordered them to return the plunder. Two hundred soldiers were sent home from Laredo, and Somervell continued the expedition, crossing the Rio Grande to find military targets. A few days later, the commander returned home, but 300 soldiers decided to continue the raid under the command of William S. Fisher. On Christmas day, this group attacked the village of Mier, only to be defeated by a Mexican force that outnumbered them 10-to-one.

On a march toward Mexico City, the survivors of the Mier expedition attempted a mass escape. Most were recaptured near Hacienda Salado and taken to Saltillo, the capital of Coahuila. An order to execute all the prisoners was refused by Commandant Gen. Jose Antonio Mejia. The Texans were returned to Hacienda Salado where one in every 10 was ordered by Santa Anna to be executed in atonement for the attempted escape. The prisoners drew beans to determine who would be shot; bearers of black beans were executed. Texans again were outraged by the treatment of prisoners, but the war fever soon subsided. Two major defeats within a year were humiliating enough without attempting a poorly financed offensive war.

Never a fan of the new capital at Austin, Houston took the occasion of the Woll invasion of San Antonio to move the seat of government to Washington-on-the-Brazos where the Seventh Congress convened in November 1842. Houston wanted to permanently move the capital away from the exposed frontier and he gave confidential orders to Col. Thomas I. Smith and Capt. Eli Chandler to remove the Republic's records from Austin. The records were taken at night, but when Austin residents were alerted to the removal by a warning shot from a cannon fired by Mrs. Angelina Eberly, a party led by Mark B. Lewis caught the ox train on Brushy Creek in Williamson County. The so-called Archives War ended without a shot fired, and the records were returned to Austin.

Houston also had problems with the Texas Navy. His recall orders were ignored by Commodore Moore, and finally, Houston asked for international help in returning the "pirates" to Texas. Moore returned voluntarily and asked for a court-martial to clear his name. He was convicted on only two minor charges.

Many free blacks lived in Texas, and some fought in the revolution. The First Texas Congress had provided land grants for them, but in 1840, the Congress passed a punitive law designed to force free blacks to leave Texas. The law was not vigorously enforced, and the Congress approved many exemptions in individual bills. Houston went a step further in his second administration by issuing pardons in advance for free blacks convicted under the law.

While the Republic left most road construction to local government, the Congress did authorize construction of the Central National Road to tie Preston on the Red River in Grayson County to Austin. The road crossed the Trinity River near the confluence of its three forks, and a thriving community grew around a trading post opened by John Neely Bryan. The city is today's Dallas.

Galveston was the Republic's major port of entry, although the new community of Houston was making a bid for leadership. Many public works were considered by the Congresses of Texas to facilitate trade and transportation. None was more bizarre than the suggestion of Houston's aggressive promoters to change the route of the Brazos River to empty into Buffalo Bayou. The bayou was Houston's lifeline to the Gulf, but it periodically ran low. Houston's leadership felt that rerouting the Brazos was reasonable, since the waterway had in ages past emptied into the bayou. The Congress rejected the idea.

As Houston completed his second term, the United States was becoming more interested in annexation.

Texas had seriously flirted with Great Britain and France, and the Americans did not want a rival republic with close foreign ties on the North American continent. Houston orchestrated the early stages of the final step toward annexation. But his successor, Anson Jones, completed the process.

The Republic of Texas' main claim to fame is simply endurance. Its settlers, unlike other Americans who had military help, had cleared a large region of Indians by themselves, had established farms and communities and had persevered through extreme economic hardship. Adroit political leadership had gained the Republic recognition from many foreign countries. And although dreams of empire may have dimmed, Texans had firmly established an identity on a major portion of the North American continent. As Texas prepared to enter the United States, the frontier had been pushed to a line running from Corpus Christi through San Antonio, New Braunfels, Austin, Belton, Waco and Dallas to Preston.

The U.S. presidential campaign of 1844 was to make Texas a part of the Union.

Annexation

ANNEXATION to the United States was not a foregone conclusion for Texans once independence from Mexico was gained in 1836. American volunteers had shed much blood in the Texas Revolution, and patriotic passions flamed high as the Anglo-Texans battled the Mexican army across Texas.

Once the gun smoke settled and negotiations between Texas and the United States began, the road was not smooth. Indeed, on occasion, the Texans resorted to guile. Sam Houston noted that Texas "was more coy than forward" as the negotiations reached a climax.

William H. Wharton was Texas' first representative in Washington. His instructions were to gain diplomatic recognition of the new Republic's independence. After some squabbles, Congress appropriated funds for a minister in Texas, and President Andrew Jackson recognized the new country in one of his last acts in office in March 1837. Later that year, Memucan Hunt replaced Wharton, and although he pursued annexation, President Martin Van Buren rejected the appeal in September 1837. The president noted that annexation of an independent nation was of doubtful constitutionality and that Texas still was nominally at war with Mexico. Annexation could lead to a war between the United States and Mexico with Great Britain possibly siding with the Mexicans.

John Quincy Adams in 1837 argued that annexation was unconstitutional. The congressman mounted a campaign against annexation in the U.S. House in June and July 1838. He claimed the issue was a plan by the Southern slaveholders to strengthen their hand by annexing Texas and dividing it into several states. Texans revolted in 1836, Adams claimed, when Mexico tried to abolish slavery. In late 1838, Houston instructed Texas' minister in Washington to withdraw the annexation proposal, and the Texas Senate approved this action in 1839.

Annexation was in limbo during the presidential term of Mirabeau B. Lamar. He felt that the loss of freedom and independence as a nation was too high a price to pay for Texas to join the United States. Lamar held visions of empire in which Texas would rival the United States for supremacy on the North American continent. However, when Lamar was successful in gaining recognition for Texas by several European countries, the United States' interest in annexation was rekindled.

Great Britain maintained a close relationship with Texas and Mexico and made strenuous efforts to get Mexico to recognize Texas' independence and to develop normal diplomatic relations. This close relationship between Great Britain and Texas raised fears in the United States. Some Americans were concerned that Great Britain might attempt to make Texas part of its empire. Southerners feared for the future of slavery in Texas, which had renounced the importation of slaves as a concession to get a trade treaty with Great Britain. Newspapers noted that U.S. trade with Texas had suffered after the Republic received diplomatic recognition from European nations.

In Houston's second term, Texas began playing coy. Early, Houston suggested to the Texas minister in

Washington that negotiations on annexation could be reopened if chances for success were good. Issac Van Zandt, Texas' minister to Washington, wrote that President John Tyler and the cabinet were anxious to annex Texas but worried about ratification in the U.S. Senate. Houston then suggested dropping the matter, hoping that he would be able to settle matters with Mexico.

U.S. Secretary of State Abel P. Upshur tried to reopen negotiations in October 1843, but Van Zandt said he had no instructions on the question. Texas wanted military protection while negotiations were under way, and this was not forthcoming. Upshur was killed in an accident, and John C. Calhoun replaced him. In the meantime, J. Pinckney Henderson was sent to Washington to help Van Zandt with the negotiations.

In January 1844, Houston again gave Van Zandt instructions to open negotiations, if chances of success were good. The president did not want another failure that could damage negotiations with other countries. Calhoun ordered a naval force to the Gulf and moved U.S. troops to the southwest border, which was the best he could do to provide Texas protection while negotiations were in progress.

On April 11, 1844, Texas and the United States signed a treaty for annexation. Texas would enter the Union as a territory, not a state, under terms of the treaty. The United States would assume Texas' debt up to $10 million and would negotiate with Mexico Texas' southwestern boundary. The treaty was sent to the U.S. Senate for ratification on April 22.

National politics intervened, however. The Whigs came down solidly against annexation and westward expansion. Abolitionists in the party apparently were more afraid of the slavery issue than expansion. The Senate rejected the annexation treaty on June 8 by a vote of 35-16. At least 15 of the opposition votes came from Southern Whig senators who had been counted on for support. Houston suggested to British agents that he was done with annexation after the rejection.

But the annexation of Texas and westward expansion became major issues in the 1844 presidential campaign. Through eight ballots at the Democratic convention, Van Buren failed to receive the necessary two-thirds majority for nomination. On the ninth ballot, his name was withdrawn from consideration, and the convention stampeded to James K. Polk, a supporter of expansion and the party's first "dark horse" nominee. In addition, the Democratic platform included a strong expansion plank, calling for the reoccupation of Oregon and the reannexation of Texas. Polk was elected president in November but would not take office until March 1845.

Great Britain and France increased pressure on Mexico to recognize Texas in hopes that independence would be more attractive to Texans than annexation. But Mexico delayed the decision.

In December 1844, President Tyler declared that the people had spoken on the issue of annexation and resubmitted it to Congress. Several bills were introduced in the U.S. House representing various proposals for annexation. In February 1845, the Congress approved a resolution that would bring Texas into the

Union as a state. Texas would cede its public property — such as forts, barracks and custom houses — to the United States, but it could keep its public lands and must retain its public debt. The territory could be divided into four new states in addition to the original Texas. And the United States would negotiate the Rio Grande boundary claim. Texas had to present a state constitution for congressional approval by Jan. 1, 1846. These terms were much more beneficial to Texas than had been those of the treaty that the Senate rejected in 1844.

Political parties did not develop in the Republic of Texas, and annexation was not a partisan issue. But annexation did set the tone of Texas' politics for more than a century. One editor noted in January 1845, "We are all Democrats in Texas, since the glorious victory of that party, who fearlessly espoused our cause and nailed the 'Lone Star' to the top mast of their noble ship."

British officials asked the Texas government to delay consideration of the U.S. offer for 90 days to attempt to get Mexico to recognize the Republic. The delay did no good. Texans' minds were made up.

President Anson Jones, who succeeded Houston, called the Texas Congress into special session on June 16 and called a convention to write a state constitution into session in Austin on July 4. Mexico finally recognized Texas' independence, but the recognition was rejected. Texas voters overwhelmingly accepted the U.S. proposal and approved the new constitution in a referendum.

On Dec. 29, 1845, the U.S. Congress accepted the state constitution and Texas became a part of the United States.

State officials were elected in December 1845, and on Feb. 19, 1846, the flag of the Republic of Texas was lowered for the last time in Austin and was replaced by the stars and stripes of the United States. J. Pinckney Henderson was sworn in as the first governor of Texas by the speaker of the Texas House.

In an eloquent speech, President Jones reviewed the life of the Republic:

"The lone star of Texas, which ten years since arose amid cloud, over fields of carnage, and obscurely shone for a while, has culminated, and, following an inscrutable destiny, has passed on and become fixed forever in that glorious constellation which all freemen and lovers of freedom in the world must reverence and adore — the American Union. Blending its rays with its sister stars, long may it continue to shine, and may a gracious heaven smile upon this consummation of the wishes of the two republics, now joined together in one. 'May the union be perpetual, and may it be the means of conferring benefits and blessings upon the people of all the States' is my ardent prayer. The final act of this great drama is now performed. The Republic of Texas is no more."

Early Statehood

THE entry of Texas into the Union touched off the War with Mexico, a war that some historians now think was planned by President James K. Polk to obtain the vast American Southwest from Mexico.

Between J. Pinckney Henderson's 1845 election and inauguration as Texas' first governor, U.S. agents tried to get Republic of Texas President Anson Jones to send troops into the contested area between the Nueces River and the Rio Grande — the so-called Nueces Strip. The Republic had claimed the Rio Grande as its southern boundary, but no civil administration was established south of the Nueces River.

Many Texans supported the move, but President Jones flatly refused to initiate any military action after Mexico's attempted recognition of Texas as a nation. Jones was proud of the fact that at the end of his term Texas was at peace with its traditional enemies — the Mexicans and Indians. Jones also argued that if there was to be war with Mexico ". . . the United States Government must take all the responsibility, and all the expense and all the labour of hostile movements upon Mexico . . . Somebody else must break up the state of peace. It shall not be me."

U.S. Gen. Zachary Taylor was sent to Corpus Christi just above the Nueces River in July 1845. In February 1846, just after Texas formally entered the Union, the general was ordered to move troops into the disputed Nueces Strip and to the mouth of the Rio Grande. A month later, Gen. Taylor marched. Mexican officials protested the entry of U.S. troops into the territory, claiming that its status was under negotiation. But Gen. Taylor proceeded to set up a camp at Point Isabel (now Port Isabel) near Brazos Santiago and to fortify a position, under the command of Maj. Jacob Brown, across the Rio Grande from Matamoros. The young officer was killed in a bombardment of the facility in May 1846, and Brownsville is named in his honor.

The U.S. army was in a state of transition at the time. It had last engaged another organized army more than 30 years before during the War of 1812. The military's principal duties in the interim had been to move Indians from the eastern United States to new lands in the west and to fight Indians if they resisted the move. West Point had been under attack in the U.S. Senate, in which the question of the compatibility of a standing army with democratic freedom was debated. The performance of West Point graduates in the ranks of junior officers during the war may have saved the institution.

After Gen. Taylor refused to leave the disputed territory, Mexican President Mariano Paredes declared the opening of a defensive war against the Americans on April 24, 1846. Gen. Anastasio Torrejon crossed the Rio Grande above Matamoros and defeated a small force of U.S. dragoons shortly thereafter. The war with Mexico was under way.

On May 8, U.S. troops moving to relieve Maj. Brown's fort encountered a Mexican force under Gen. Mariano Arista at Palo Alto, about 12 miles from today's Brownsville. Although the Mexican contingent was twice as large as the American, the light artillery tactics of the West Point graduates gave the U.S. forces a victory. The next day the Mexican army was badly mauled at Resaca de la Palma and retreated across the river. Gen. Taylor waited two weeks before crossing the Rio Grande and occupying Matamoros. In the interim, however, he sent news of the military encounters to Washington, and President Polk persuaded Congress to declare war against Mexico on May 13, arguing that American blood had been spilled on American soil. After the initial encounters, the war was fought south of the Rio Grande.

President Polk devised a plan to raise 50,000 volunteers from every section of the United States to fight the war. Texans had long dreamed of carrying a war into the interior of Mexico, and more than 8,000 volunteered for service. About 5,000 Texans actually saw action in Mexico — including Gov. Henderson, who got permission from the Legislature to join the U.S. army during the war. When the Texas Rangers volunteered, they introduced the U.S. army to a new weapon — the six-shooter. The revolvers had been used for several years on the Texas frontier, and the Rangers demanded to be equipped with Colt revolvers when they joined the army. The initial contract to manufacture 1,000 of the weapons rescued Samuel Colt from bankruptcy, and he became a successful gun manufacturer.

Although the actual fighting took place in Mexico, some military activity continued along the lower Rio Grande as the army secured transportation points across the river. In July 1846, Capt. Richard A. Gillespie passed through Laredo and asserted Texas and U.S. sovereignty. For the first time, the American flag flew over the city. A few months later, Mirabeau B. Lamar, serving as a captain in the U.S. forces, established civil administration in Laredo, and for a time the city was in a huge Nueces County that included all of the Lower Rio Grande Valley with Corpus Christi the county seat. In July 1847, the first election in Laredo attracted 40 voters, 37 of whom were Mexicans. Lamar maintained discipline among his 150 troops by banning liquor sales, and regular patrols helped curb Indian activities in the region where 700 persons reportedly had been killed in the previous 20 years.

Steamboat transportation returned to the Rio Grande for the first time since 1831, when Henry Austin left with his ship Ariel. The paddlewheelers provided an important supply link for U.S. forces along the river and in Northern Mexico throughout the war. And important historical figures like Richard King, founder of the King Ranch, and Mifflin Kenedy, another regional rancher, businessman and leader, first came to the

Lower Rio Grande Valley as steamboat operators during the war.

Much farther up the Rio Grande, the war was hardly noticed. Alexander Doniphan led U.S. forces south from Sante Fe, which had been secured by Brig. Gen. Stephen Kearny, in December 1846. After a minor skirmish with Mexican forces just north of present-day El Paso, Doniphan established American jurisdiction in this part of Texas.

U.S. Gen. Winfield Scott brought the war to a close in March 1847 with the capture of Mexico City. When the Treaty of Guadalupe Hidalgo was signed on Feb. 2, 1848, the United States had acquired the American Southwest for development. And in Texas, the Rio Grande became an international boundary, and the borderlands entered a turbulent period. One agreement required the United States to prohibit raids by Plains Indians — primarily the Comanches and Apaches — into the interior of Mexico.

Texas faced many old problems and a few new ones while embarking on the early days of statehood. George T. Wood was elected governor in 1847, succeeding J. Pinckney Henderson who did not seek re-election. The state government, like the Republic, was short of cash. Although Texas kept its public lands, the United States got the customs receipts, which had been the Republic's major source of hard cash. And the state's claim to more than 105,000 square miles of land that included territory in New Mexico, Colorado, Wyoming, Kansas and Oklahoma was under attack in Congress. Wood threatened to go to war with the United States over the disputed land, and he also supported removal of all Indians from Texas' territory.

At the end of the Mexican War, most of Texas north and west of a line drawn from Preston on the Red River through Dallas, Austin and San Antonio to Laredo on the Rio Grande was unexplored territory controlled by Indians. One of the first orders of business in the new state was to explore the vast unknown territory.

THE face of Far West Texas was to change rapidly. In early 1848, gold was discovered at Sutter's Mill in California and within a few months a gold rush across the continent was on. Jack Coffee Hays and a group of Texas Rangers tried to blaze a trail from San Antonio to El Paso in early 1848, but they got lost and almost died of thirst before returning to civilization.

In March 1849, Robert S. Neighbors, John S. Ford and Indian guides set out from Torrey's trading post near today's Waco to find an accessible route to El Paso. They blazed what was called the Upper Trail, which crossed the Pecos River at Horsehead Crossing, and reached El Paso on May 2. On returning along the estimated 500-mile trip, they met wagons already moving west. At the same time, U.S. Army Capt. William Henry Chase Whiting in late May opened the lower El Paso-San Antonio route that ran to the south of Neighbors' trail. Whiting also is the first writer to use the term "Big Bend" for that region of the state. Lt. Francis T. Bryan surveyed both trails.

Ports such as Galveston and Indianola, which was established in 1849 on the west shore of Matagorda Bay, dispatched pioneers along the western trails to California. Many went through San Antonio. By the end of the year, 4,000 people had traveled along the trails through El Paso, which was to develop into a way station for goldseekers and other adventurers. For centuries, the El Paso region had been a major point along the trade route from the interior of Mexico to Santa Fe. The California gold rush established the area along two major trade routes.

U.S. Army Capt. Randolph B. Marcy led a third expedition through unexplored Texas in 1849, covering most of West Central Texas and tying into previously established routes. Marcy's trail later was used by the Butterfield Stage Line. Also during that year, the U.S. War Department established a string of frontier forts running from Fort Duncan at Eagle Pass on the south to Fort Worth on the north. Inexperience in fighting mounted Plains Indians led the army to station infantry at the forts. One Texas editor noted that "The idea of repelling mounted Indians, the most expert horsemen in the world, with a force of foot soldiers, is ridiculous."

One group of German settlers had little trouble with the Comanches, however. John O. Meusebach became leader of the German immigration movement in Texas in 1846. He led a wagon train of some 120 settlers to the site of today's Fredericksburg in May 1846, and a year later, Meusebach made a treaty with Comanche leaders on the San Saba River, which both sides kept. This was the only successful compact between white men and Indians in the state's history.

Germans, rather than Anglos, were the first whites to push into this frontier region after annexation. Germans also migrated to the major cities, like San Antonio and Galveston, and by 1850 there were more people of German birth or parentage in Texas than there were Mexican-Texans.

The eastern part of Texas was flourishing under statehood, as had been expected. The estimated population of 150,000 at annexation grew to 212,592, including 58,161 slaves, at the first U.S. census in 1850. Large plantations were blossoming in the valleys of the Brazos and Trinity Rivers where steamboat transportation to Galveston and Houston was available. Leaders in these areas, however, were worried about the lack of railroad transportation and about a labor shortage. Texas was exporting 500,000 bales of cotton a year in the 1850s, but it was felt that the land could produce three million to five million bales if adequate labor — slave labor — was available.

Although Galveston was the state's major port, Jefferson in Marion County also was a shipping center. A huge log raft on the Red River backed water into Big Cypress Bayou, making Jefferson accessible by steamship. Goods from this northeast Texas city could be shipped to markets along the Mississippi River and to New Orleans.

As the state's population grew, the regions developed distinct population characteristics. The southeast and eastern sections attracted immigrants from the Lower South, the major slaveholding states. Major plantations developed in these areas. North Texas got more Upper Southerners and Midwesterners. These immigrants were mostly small farmers and few owned slaves.

Mexican-Texans had difficulty with the Anglo immigrants. The so-called "cart war" broke out in 1857. Mexican teamsters controlled the transportation of goods from the Gulf coast to San Antonio and could charge much lower rates than their competition. But a campaign of terror was launched by Anglo haulers, especially around Goliad, in an attempt to drive the Mexican-Texans out of business. Intervention by the U.S. and Mexican governments finally brought the situation under control, but it stands as an example of the attitudes held by Anglos toward Mexican-Texans.

Cotton was by far the state's largest money crop. But corn, sweet potatoes, wheat and sugar also were produced. Saw milling and grain milling became the major industries, employing 40 percent of the manufacturing workers.

In the 1849 election, Peter H. Bell defeated incumbent George Wood. Bell's administration was distinguished by settling the land disputes with the federal government. In the Compromise of 1850, Texas gave up claims to lands that are located outside the present borders in exchange for $10 million. The total settlement with the United States, including interest on some delayed funds and compensation for fighting some Indians, amounted to $12 million. That sum was used to pay off the debt of the Republic. Most of the state taxes for several years were remitted to local governments for constructing public buildings, and $2 million was set aside for a school fund during Gov. Elisha M. Pease's administration.

Gov. Bell was the first Texas governor to be elected to a second term, and he resigned in November 1853 to take a seat in Congress. Lt. Gov. James W. Henderson served as chief executive for less than a month before Gov. Pease took office. Henderson's tenure is the shortest of any Texas governor.

Although most Texans probably could be classified as Democrats, political parties were weak during the period of early statehood. Personalities dominated most elections, and Sam Houston was the state's major political figure. Candidates were judged as to whether they were pro-Houston or anti-Houston. Early attempts to formally organize the Democrats failed, and the party had no formal structure on the local level. Statewide conventions were held only to select delegates to national conventions.

After the mid-1850s, however, opposition party victories, particularly the Know-Nothing Party, in local elections prompted Democrats to organize a more formal party structure. The Know-Nothings were a nativist group that arose during the decade. By 1859, the party had disappeared. For most Texans, however, politics were unimportant. Voter turnouts were low. National events began to bear more heavily on the state in the 1850s, and the movement toward support for secession from the Union gained strength.

Secession

TEXAS was far removed from the centers of authority and civilization in the 1850s. Settlers in the new state were more concerned with daily problems, but as the decade passed, the national debate over slavery became a factor in Texas' politics and economic and cultural lives.

Slavery had been a major issue in American politics for decades. The issue cooled somewhat by the Missouri Compromise of 1820 that barred slavery in territory north of a line drawn by the law. But the fear of slavery spreading into the Southwest was used by opponents of Texas' initial efforts to be annexed to the United States. The issue flared anew during the Mexican War. Rep. David Wilmot added a proviso to various fiscal bills in 1846 and 1847 in the U.S. House. It would have barred slavery in any territory gained by the United States by virtue of the Mexican War. Although the House approved the Wilmot Proviso, the Senate never did. Thereafter, however, slavery began to dominate almost all the actions of Congress.

In 1854, Sen. Stephen Douglas, D-Ill., sponsored legislation that in essence repealed the Missouri Compromise by allowing the residents of the territories of Kansas and Nebraska to decide whether they wanted slavery. Since both territories were north of the line drawn against involuntary servitude, abolitionists bitterly opposed the measure. Sam Houston, serving as one of the state's first U.S. Senators, won the undying hatred of Southern Democrats and many Texans by opposing Douglas' legislation. Always a strong Unionist, Houston's vote against the Kansas-Nebraska Act in 1854 cost him any chance of being reappointed to the Senate by the Texas Legislature five years later.

In addition, Texas' population almost tripled in the decade between 1850 and 1860 when 604,215 people were counted, including 182,921 slaves. (Indians were not counted.) Many of these new settlers came from the Lower South and had strong ties to the institution of slavery, even if they were not slaveholders. Population studies indicate that three-quarters of the Texas population and two-thirds of the farmers did not own slaves. But slaveholders controlled 60 to 70 percent of the wealth of the state and produced 90 percent of the cotton. The slaveowning farmers also tightened their grip on state politics during the decade. Studies indicate that in 1850, 41.4 percent of the state's officeholders were from the slaveholding class; a decade later, 51.1 percent of the officeholders also were slaveholders. Politics in antebellum Texas was a mix of democracy and aristocracy. But despite the lack of economic restrictions on free male suffrage, the slaveowning elite dominated politics.

In addition to the political power of the slaveholders, they also provided role models for new immigrants to the state. Land was cheap or free in Texas, as it always had been, and since land ownership was an element of social status, the state represented economic opportunity to newcomers. These new Texans saw slave ownership as another step up the economic ladder, regardless of whether they owned slaves or not. Slave ownership was an economic goal, for with slaves more land could be cultivated and more cotton grown. The attitude was prevalent in areas of Texas where slaveholding was not widespread or even practical. Against this background were the politics of Texas played and the passions for secession from the Union fanned through the 1850s.

Much of the decade of the 1850s was tranquil as Texans went about the business of developing the vast state. Even the frontier areas were relatively peaceful as the U.S. Army became more expert at handling the mounted Plains Indians. With more than 3,000 troops stationed in Texas by 1853, the Indians were quiet. The Texas Legislature even agreed to provide the U.S. government with up to 50,000 acres of land to set up reservations to pacify the state's Indian tribes. Two reservations were set up on the Clear Fork of the Brazos River in West Central Texas. One in Throckmorton County was set aside for the Comanches, and the other in Young County was to accommodate Indians from various other groups. By 1855, these reservations were in operation under the direction of Indian Agent Robert S. Neighbors. Camp Cooper was established near the Comanche Reservation and the Second Cavalry kept peace in the area. Several well-known officers commanded the small post, including Albert Sidney Johnston, Robert E. Lee and John B. Hood. When estab-

lished, these reservations were in advance of the frontier settlement line. But the surrounding country soon was settled. Anglo hostility toward the Indians was fanned when raiding parties began to prey on settlers. Although there was no evidence that reservation Indians were involved, the frontier settlers began to demand removal of the Indians from Texas. By 1858, Neighbors was convinced that the move was necessary, and in August 1859, the reservations were closed and the Indians moved north of the Red River. Settlers quickly claimed the reservation land. The move did not end the Indian raids. Many of the transported Indians felt that the government had acted in bad faith and joined the attacks on settlements in Texas. As the decade drew to a close, the army became less effective in combatting the guerrilla tactics of the Indians, and the breakdown in defense had political repercussions.

In addition to the constant Indian problem, another fact of life was becoming apparent to settlers along the frontier. By 1860, the Texas frontier had moved westward to a line that ran irregularly from Henrietta on the north to Fort Belknap in Young County, Palo Pinto, Brownwood, Llano, Kerrville and Uvalde to Laredo. West of this line was a new land for the settlers from the woodlands of the South and the eastern United States. The treeless prairies and the marked reduction in rainfall posed a new barrier. New farming techniques would be needed to cope with the different environment, and the Indians must be subdued. Cattle ranching would prosper on the prairies, but the industry was in its infancy at the time. The frontier settlers found markets at the military forts and the communities around them. But development of the region had stalled.

In Austin, the 1850s were a relatively progressive period. Relieved of public debt, the state government began to debate economic issues. One of the most important was the development of railroads. One plan that was seriously considered would have made railroad construction a state responsibility. But in 1856, the Legislature decided that private corporations would build the railroad system with generous state aid. Grants of money were used, or the railway lines would be given 16 alternate sections of land (10,240 acres) for each mile of track built. Construction of the first railroad to move cotton and sugar to Galveston — the Buffalo Bayou, Brazos and Colorado Railway — began in 1851, and by 1853, 20 miles of track had been built. By 1860, almost 404 miles of railroad existed, mostly in the Houston-Galveston area.

IN addition, other transportation was available. In North Texas, ox carts were the primary source of transportation for commerce. Although slow, the animals were reliable, especially in dry weather. By 1860, 31 stagecoach lines were operating in Texas, including some tied into intercontinental travel. The Butterfield Line began operation in the state in 1858 running from St. Louis and Memphis through Texas to San Francisco. Mail service between San Antonio and San Diego, Calif., commenced in 1857.

One economic problem that the state government could not and the federal government would not solve was the labor shortage. Cotton raising at the time was labor intensive, and in the minds of the plantation owners, that meant slave labor. Importation of African slaves had been prohibited in the United States in 1808 and in the early days of the Texas Republic. An illegal trade flourished in Texas, however, and hundreds, if not thousands, of the slaves in the state had been imported through this system. But some of the state's leadership saw the reopening of the slave trade as a solution to the labor shortage. More slaves also would bring the price down, and small landowners could afford to acquire involuntary labor. The view was hardly universal, however, because free laborers among the European immigrants saw it as a move to eliminate their jobs or keep wages low. Support for reopening the slave trade also was light among the small farmers of North Texas and the settlers along the frontier.

An outgrowth of the labor problem was strong private support in Texas for the filibuster expeditions to Cuba and Central America in the 1850s. Proponents of slavery thought it would be advantageous to have slave colonies in these areas to supply the labor needs of the state.

Politics quickened in the mid-1850s with the appearance of the Know-Nothing Party, which based its platform on a pro-American, anti-immigrant foundation. Because of the large number of foreign-born settlers, the party attracted many Anglo voters. In 1854, the Know-Nothings elected candidates to city offices in San Antonio, and a year later, the mayor of Galveston was elected with the party's backing. Also in 1855, the Know-Nothings elected 20 representatives and five senators to the Legislature. The successes spurred the Democrats to serious party organization. For the first time, the party nominated statewide candidates at a convention in 1857. Hardin Runnels, a former lieutenant governor and speaker of the Texas House, got the nomination at the convention held in Waco. Sam Houston returned to Texas to seek the governorship as an independent, but he also got Know-Nothing backing. Democrats were organized, however, and Houston was dealt his only election defeat in his political career.

Runnels was a strong states-rights Democrat and irritated many Texans during his administration by advocating reopening the slave trade. His popularity on the frontier also dropped when Indian raids became more severe, and neither the state nor federal governments could stop them.

Most Texans still were ambivalent about secession. The Union was seen as a protector of physical and economic stability. No threats to person or property were perceived in remaining attached to the United States. In 1859, Houston again challenged Runnels and based his campaign on Unionism. Combined with Houston's personal popularity, his position on the secession issue apparently satisfied most voters, for they gave him a solid victory over the more radical Runnels. In addition, Unionists A.J. Hamilton and John H. Reagan won the state's two congressional seats. Texans gave the states-rights Democrats a sound whipping at the polls.

Within a few months, however, events were to change radically the political atmosphere in the state. The defense of slavery was the major concern. But other issues arose that secessionists could use in their arguments for withdrawal from the Union. Shortly after Houston's election, word of John Brown's raid on Harper's Ferry in Virginia reached Texas. States-rights proponents pointed out that it was an example of militant Northerners willing to resort to violence to impose their views on the South. On the frontier, the army could not control Indian raids, and with the later removal of a Republican-controlled Congress to provide essential aid in fighting Indians, the federal government fell into disrepute. On the Texas border, Juan Cortina, a Mexican hero-bandit, captured Brownsville for a time, and rumor had it that he was backed by abolitionists.

Each breakdown in order or failure to provide adequate services, like frontier defense, threw the efficacy of the Union into doubt. Secessionists played on the growing distrust. Then in the summer of 1860, a series of fires in cities around the state aroused fears that an abolitionist plot was afoot and that a slave uprising might be at hand — a traditional concern in a slaveholding society. Vigilantes lynched blacks and Northerners across Texas, and a siege mentality developed. Texans who once viewed the Union as a beneficent protector now wondered if the institution was obsolete. When the election of Republican Abraham Lincoln — though he was not on the ballot in Texas — as president became apparent, secessionists went to work in earnest. Pleas were made to Gov. Houston to call the Legislature into session to consider a secession ordinance. Houston refused, hoping the passions would cool. They did not. Finally, Oran M. Roberts and other secessionist leaders issued a call to the counties to hold elections and send delegates to a convention in Austin to consider the secession ordinance. Ninety-two of 122 counties responded, and on Jan. 28, 1861, the convention convened. Houston called the Legislature into session to try to thwart the convention, but the lawmakers legalized the meeting, noting that the state constitution delegated to the citizens the power to "alter, reform or abolish" their government in any manner they felt expedient. Houston then insisted that any action of the convention must be ratified by voters.

ROBERTS chaired the secession convention, and it quickly passed the secession ordinance on Feb. 1. Only eight delegates voted against it, while 166 supported secession. An election was called for Feb. 23, 1861, and the ensuing campaign was marked by intimidation, intolerance and violence. Opponents of secession were often intimidated — except Gov. Houston, who courageously stumped the state opposing withdrawal from the Union. Houston argued that the convention had overstepped its authority by joining Texas to the Confederacy. The governor declared that if Texas was to leave the Union, it should revert to its status as an independent republic. Only one-fourth of the state's population had been in Texas during the days of independence and the argument carried no weight. On election day, 76 percent of 61,000 voters approved secession, which would become official March 2, 1861, exactly 25 years after Texas had proclaimed its independence from Mexico. However, only Edwin Waller had the distinction of signing both the secession ordinance in 1861 and the Declaration of Independence in 1836.

President Lincoln reportedly sent Gov. Houston a letter offering 50,000 federal troops to keep Texas in the Union. But after a meeting with other Unionists, Houston declined the offer. "I love Texas too well to bring strife and bloodshed upon her," the governor declared. On March 16, Houston refused to take an oath of loyalty to the Confederacy and was replaced in office by Lt. Gov. Edward Clark.

Texas then embarked on one of the darkest periods in its history.

Civil War

TEXAS fared fairly well through the Civil War. The state did not suffer the devastation of its Southern colleagues. Only on a few occasions did Union troops occupy territory in Texas, except in the El Paso area. A manpower shortage did develop as so many men joined the Confederate army or served in the ranks of state troops.

Texas' cotton was important to the Confederate war effort, for it could be transported from Gulf ports when other Southern shipping lanes were blockaded. Some goods became difficult to buy, but unlike other Southern states, Texas still received consumer goods because of the trade that was carried on through Mexico during the war. Public order did break down particularly during the latter part of the war. Army deserters often passed through on the way to Mexico, and with so many men in military service, some communities were left poorly defended or policed. These hardships hardly compared to the damage done by military operations and by the complete social disruption in other states. Texas was virtually without manufacturing facilities prior to the war, however. Several small munitions factories were set up in the state. Bullets were made at the State Land Office in Austin, for example. And the state penitentiary became a major manufacturer of cloth for the Confederacy.

After the secession ordinance was approved by voters, the convention reconvened on March 2, 1861, in Austin. Although the question of joining the Confederacy was not on the ballot, most Texans felt approval was implied. So the convention accepted the provisional government of the Confederacy, and delegates to Montgomery were instructed to apply for statehood. The action was unnecessary since the Confederate Congress already had passed a law admitting Texas as a state.

Military operations began in Texas even before voters approved the secession ordinance. The secession convention appointed a public safety committee to see to preparations for war. The initial goal was to take charge of U.S. army facilities in the state.

Ben McCulloch led a contingent of Texas troops to San Antonio. After brief negotiations, U.S. Maj. Gen. David E. Twiggs surrendered U.S. forces — about 2,700 men scattered across the state — and facilities to the Texans on Feb. 15, 1861. Twiggs was later court-martialed for his action. Like many U.S. army officers, the commander of the Department of Texas was a southern sympathizer and later was given a commission in the Confederate army. On the other hand, Col. Robert E. Lee refused to take an oath of allegiance to the Confederacy before leaving Texas and did not leave the U.S. army until he reached Washington and properly resigned.

Col. William C. Young and Lt. Col. James W. Throckmorton secured three federal posts north of the Red River in May 1861 without firing a shot. Throckmorton, a future governor, was one of many Unionists who opposed secession but fought for Texas in the Confederacy.

Secessionists had argued that the North would not contest the dissolution of the Union. They felt that the great commercial nations of Europe would not allow the North to disrupt the important cotton trade. Therefore early in the war, the Confederate government did not think a large army would be needed. Even if hostilities broke out, it was felt that any war would be short. Most of these arguments were overturned shortly after the firing on Fort Sumter, South Carolina.

Thousands of Texans volunteered for service in the Confederate army as soon as hostilities broke out between the North and South. And after Francis R. Lubbock was elected governor in 1861, he worked to see that the state also fulfilled its manpower quotas under the Confederate conscription law of April 1862. Texans fought in every Confederate campaign in the war. Confederate President Jefferson Davis was highly complimentary of the prowess of Texas soldiers in an address to the troops in Virginia, noting that "The troops from other states have their reputations to gain. The sons of the defenders of the Alamo have theirs to maintain." Units like Hood's Brigade and Terry's Texas Rangers became legendary. Sul Ross, a future governor, fought in more than 130 battles, entering the war a private and emerging as an officer. Although accurate figures are not available, historians estimate that between 70,000 and 90,000 Texans fought for the Confederacy, and between 2,000 and 3,000, including some former slaves, saw service in the Union army.

TEXAS was important to the Confederacy for several reasons. It had a great reservoir of men with some military experience. With more than 400 miles of shoreline, the state could provide important ports, and as the most westerly of the Southern states, Texas held the key to Confederate expansion to the west.

Texas also had some unique problems. It had to defend three of its borders from hostile forces: From the Union on the Gulf coast, from the Mexicans in the borderlands, and from the Indians on the frontier, including along the Red River. Consequently there were tensions between the state and Confederate governments at times during the war. Some Texas governors, like Pendleton Murrah, felt that more manpower should be devoted to frontier defense, and consequently he was not always cooperative with demands from Richmond for additional troops.

Texas' coastline was completely without defenses when the Civil War broke out. Slave labor was used to fortify Sabine Pass, Galveston, Matagorda Island, Aransas Pass and Port Isabel. The work was speeded up when the Union blockade of the Gulf ports reached Texas in July 1861.

On land, Texans participated in one of the war's most ambitious early campaigns. Col. John R. Baylor had taken Union posts in southern New Mexico soon after the war broke out. In late 1861, Gen. Henry H. Sibley was ordered to conduct in the upper Rio Grande Valley a major campaign designed to cut the Union off from California. With 3,000 men, Sibley captured Santa Fe and Albuquerque in early 1862. But the campaign failed when Union soldiers captured the Texans' supply train during the battle of Glorieta Pass in northern New Mexico. Sibley's forces left New Mexico in complete disarray. After the Texans straggled through the El Paso area, Union Col. E.E. Eyre, leading the California Column, occupied the Far West Texas outpost for the remainder of the war. If Gen. Sibley had been successful, the Civil War might have turned out differently. Subsequent campaigns against Union forces in California would have been necessary, but there was support for the Confederate cause in Southern California. And defenses against counterattacks by the Union would have had to be maintained. But with Confederates in control of California's gold, lumber and ports, many of the South's difficulties could have been avoided. The gold would have supported Confederate money; the lumber would have provided ships, and the ports would have opened trade, since the Union could not have blockaded ports on both the Gulf and Pacific coasts. With Sibley's defeat, these opportunities were lost.

One of the most important unsung battles of the Civil War may not have been fought by Americans at all, but by Mexican troops under the command of a native of Texas, Ignacio Zaragoza, at Puebla near Mexico City on May 5, 1862. The French were attempting to place Maximilian on the throne of Mexico. But Gen. Zaragoza defeated the French army at Puebla, delaying the conquest of Mexico for more than a year. Some historians think the French would have supported the Confederate cause if they had gained full control of Mexico at the time. If so, more ports would have been open to Confederate trading, and the character of the Civil War might have changed. Mexico's annual Cinco de Mayo celebration commemorates Zaragoza's victory. He was born near Goliad in 1829.

Texans became disenchanted with the Confederate government early in the war. Gov. Lubbock had to levy direct state taxes for the first time since the Compromise of 1850, and by war's end, the Confederacy had collected more than $37 million in the state. But most of the complaints about the government centered on Brig. Gen. Paul O. Hebert, the Confederate commander of the Department of Texas. In April 1862, Gen. Hebert declared martial law without notifying state officials. Opposition to the South's new conscription law, which exempted persons owning more than 15 slaves among other categories of exemptions, prompted the action. In November 1862, the commander prohibited the export of cotton except under government control, and this proved a disastrous policy. And the final blow came when Gen. Hebert failed to defend Galveston and it fell into Union hands in the fall of 1862.

Maj. Gen. John B. Magruder replaced Hebert and was much more popular. The new commander's first actions were to combat the Union offensive against Texas ports. Sabine Pass had been closed in September 1862 by the Union blockade and Galveston was in Northern hands. On Jan. 1, 1863, Magruder retook Galveston with the help of two "cotton clad" gunboats, the Bayou City and Neptune. Decks of the two steamboats were lined with cotton bales for protection, and sharpshooters proved devastating in battles against the Union fleet. Three weeks later, Magruder used two other cotton clad steamboats to break the Union blockade of Sabine Pass, and two of the state's major ports were reopened.

Late in 1863, the Union launched a major offensive against the Texas coast that was partly successful. On Sept. 8, however, Texas Lt. Dick Dowling and 42 men fought off a 1,500-man Union invasion force at Sabine Pass. In a brief battle, Dowling's command sank two Union gunboats and put the other invasion ships to flight.

Gen. N.J.T. Dana was more successful at the mouth of the Rio Grande. On Nov. 1, 1863, he landed 7,000 troops at Brazos Santiago, and five days later, Union forces entered Brownsville, which had been set on fire by the retreating Confederate Gen. Hamilton Bee.

Union control of Brownsville and the Lower Rio Grande Valley forced the rerouting of the cotton trail across Texas. Brownsville and Matamoros were major shipping points for Southern cotton. The Rio Grande was declared an international river in the Treaty of Guadalupe Hidalgo in 1848, and it could not be legally blockaded by the Union. Texas shippers operated under the Mexican flag, and the region boomed economically from the trade. After the Union took the mouth of the Rio Grande, the cotton trail was shifted up river to Laredo and Eagle Pass where the river could be crossed. Then the cotton was transported overland to Matamoros.

Texas Unionists led by E.J. Davis were active in the Valley, moving as far upriver as Rio Grande City. Col. John S. "Rip" Ford, commanding state troops, finally pushed the Union soldiers out of Brownsville in July 1864, reopening the important port for the Confederacy. Most of the Union troops were withdrawn, however, to be used in an invasion of Texas along the Red River through Louisiana.

Union Maj. Gen. Nathaniel Banks conceived the invasion, planning to mass troops in Louisiana to march into Texas. The plan was thwarted with Confederate victories at the battles of Mansfield, La., and Pleasant Hill, La., in April 1864. Most of Texas never saw a Union soldier during the war. And the ones they might have seen were in the prisoner of war camps operated in Kerr County, at Hempstead or the largest, Camp Ford, near Tyler, which could accommodate 5,000 prisoners.

There was considerable fighting, however, on the Texas frontier. Early in the war, the Confederates tried to man some frontier forts, but the troops were transferred to East Texas in 1864. State attempts to patrol the frontier were not successful in stopping Indian raids. As the defenses grew weaker, the Indians became bolder, raiding in groups numbering in the hundreds rather than in the traditional small bands. Many settlers moved to more secure areas, and the state's frontier receded up to 100 miles eastward in some areas. In many cases, the settlers who remained on the frontier "forted up" in private facilities. Several families would band together for protection, and crude stockades and other breastworks were constructed. Probably the largest of these private forts was Fort Davis in northwest Stephens County where more than 100 people gathered.

As the war dragged on, the mood of Texas changed. Despite the lack of devastation, many families had sacrificed on the home front. With the manpower shortage, many women had to operate plantations and farms with little help. There also was a shortage of consumer goods and prices were greatly inflated. Slaveholders had been exempt from service in many cases, and the homefolks began to feel that they were sacrificing loved ones and suffering hardship so cotton speculators could profit. Public order broke down as refugees flocked to Texas. And slaves from other states were sent to Texas for safekeeping. When the war ended, there were an estimated 400,000 slaves in Texas, more than double the number counted in the 1860 census.

Morale was low in Texas in early 1865. Soldiers at Galveston and Houston began to mutiny. At Austin, Confederate soldiers raided the state treasury in March, and found only $5,000 in specie. Units broke up, and the army simply dissolved before Gen. Lee surrendered at Appomattox in April 1865.

A month earlier, Texas had an opportunity to enter into a separate peace. U.S. Maj. Gen. Lew Wallace, an unofficial representative of Gen. Ulysses S. Grant, met with Confederate Brig. Gen. John E. Slaughter and Col. John S. Ford at Port Isabel on March 10, 1865. Gen. Wallace offered Texas and the Trans-Mississippi Department a separate peace, so Union and Confederate forces could unite in a show of force to the French in Mexico. The offer was presented to the Confederate command in Houston, where it was rejected. U.S. officials were concerned that they would have to enforce the Monroe Doctrine in Mexico, where both the French and English had interests. If the offer had been accepted, Texas possibly could have been spared the agonies of Reconstruction.

The last battle of the Civil War was fought more than a month after Lee's surrender. Col. Ford led a troop of Confederates in the battle of Palmito Ranch near Brownsville on May 11, 1865. After the victory, the troops learned of the surrender.

On June 19, 1865, Gen. Gordon Granger, under the command of Gen. Philip M. Sheridan, arrived in Galveston with 1,800 men to begin the Union occupation of Texas. Gen. Granger proclaimed the emancipation of the slaves. And A.J. Hamilton, a Unionist and former Texas congressman, was named provisional governor of Texas by President Andrew Johnson. Gov. Pendleton Murrah, elected in 1863, fled to Mexico with other Confederate officials, who feared prosecution for their part in the rebellion. Texas was embarked on Reconstruction.

Reconstruction

TEXAS was in turmoil when the Civil War ended. Although thousands of the state's men had died in the conflict, the state was hardly touched by the war. Indian raids had caused as much damage as the skirmishes with the Union army along the Gulf coast and in the Lower Rio Grande Valley.

Even worse, confusion reigned. No one knew what to expect from the conquering Union army. Gov. Pendleton Murrah had tried to call the Legislature into special session to repeal the secession ordinance and to ease Texas' reentry into the Union. But it became apparent that federal authorities would not accept the actions of the Confederate government as legitimate.

As the Confederate army dissolved in April and May 1865, lawlessness prevailed across the state. Confusion seemed to paralyze authorities.

Upon landing at Galveston on June 19, 1865, Union Gen. Gordon Granger dispatched troops to the population centers of the state to restore civil authority. But only a handful of the 50,000 federal troops that came to Texas was stationed in the interior. Most were sent to the Rio Grande as a show of force against the French in Mexico. Clandestine aid was supplied to Mexican President Benito Juarez in his fight against the French and the Mexican royalists.

Texas' frontier, which had suffered an increasing number of Indian raids at the end of the war, got no relief. The federal government banned local militia, fearing that the Confederates would continue to fight a guerrilla war. But the frontier forts were not remanned, and the prohibition against a militia denied settlers a means of self-defense. Provisional Gov. A.J. Hamilton, however, did allow some counties to organize local police forces to work with the military.

The emancipation proclamation issued by Gen. Granger added to the confusion. Thousands of former black slaves were freed. The Union had no plan for providing direction for the freed men. Some stayed on the plantations, but others left immediately, eager to exercise their new freedom. Many blacks migrated to the cities where they felt the federal soldiers would provide protection. Still others traveled the countryside, seeking family members and loved ones from whom they had been separated during the war. Unaccustomed to free blacks, white Texans feared a breakdown in law and order. The status of the newly freed slaves in society also was not defined. And not the least of the problems was the failure of slaveholders to plan for emancipation.

The Freedman's Bureau, authorized by Congress in March 1865, began operation in September 1865 under Gen. E.M. Gregory. It had the responsibility to provide education, relief aid, labor supervision and judicial protection for the newly freed slaves. The bureau was most successful in opening schools for blacks. Education was a priority because 95 percent of the freed slaves were illiterate. The agency also was partially successful in getting blacks back to work on plantations under reasonable labor contracts. But because it was perceived as being involved in partisan politics, many Texans disliked the bureau. It was disbanded in 1870 when President Ulysses S. Grant declared Reconstruction at an end.

Some plantation owners harbored hopes that they would be paid for their property loss when the slaves were freed. In some cases, the slaves were not released from plantations for up to a year. To add to the confusion, some former slaves had the false notion that the federal government was going to parcel out the plantation lands to them. These blacks simply bided their time, waiting for the division of land.

In Washington, President Andrew Johnson tried to pursue Lincoln's ideas for reconstruction. The rebellious states would be brought back into the Union as quickly as possible. As Johnson executed the plan, Congress became enraged. Public opinion in the North required the rebels to be punished for secession.

A.J. Hamilton assumed the provisional governorship on June 22, 1865. He planned to restore civil government as quickly as possible, and soon a series of meetings were held with unionists. Then Hamilton set up a statewide system of voter registration. Prospective voters had to take loyalty oaths to the Union, and former Confederate officials and wealthy planters had to get presidential pardons to regain full civil rights.

Voter registration went slowly, and violence was common. Hamilton interpreted these actions as acts of disloyalty to the Union and delayed calling a constitutional convention as long as possible.

Adding to the confusion was the fact that unionists were split over how the state should be readmitted to the Union. Some unionists who had stayed in Texas during the war had suffered discrimination and intimidation from Confederates, and they wanted revenge. Other unionists had fought for the Confederacy and wanted Reconstruction to be as quick as possible. And a third group had been forced to leave and live in the North. This group had a good idea of what the victors had in mind for the South and Texas.

Under pressure from President Johnson, Hamilton called for an election of delegates to a constitutional convention in January 1866, and the convention convened on Feb. 6, 1866. Hamilton told the parley what was expected: Former slaves were to be given civil rights; the secession ordinance had to be repealed; Civil War debt had to be repudiated; and slavery was to be abolished with the ratification of the Thirteenth Amendment.

Many delegates to the convention were former secessionists, and there was little support for compromise. J.W. Throckmorton, a unionist and one of eight men who had opposed secession in the convention of

1861, was elected chairman of the convention. But a coalition of conservative unionists and Democrats controlled the convention. As a consequence, Texas took limited steps toward appeasing the victorious North. Slavery was abolished, and blacks were given some civil rights. But they still could not vote and were barred from testifying in trials against whites. No action was taken on the Thirteenth Amendment, which abolished slavery, because, the argument went, it already had been ratified. Otherwise the constitution written by the convention followed closely the Constitution of 1845. President Johnson in August 1866 accepted the constitution and declared insurrection over in Texas, the last of the Southern states so accepted under Presidential Reconstruction.

Throckmorton was elected governor in June, when other state and local officials were selected by voters under the new constitution. However, Texans had not learned a lesson from the war. When the Legislature met, a series of laws limiting the rights of blacks were passed. In labor disputes, for example, the employers were to be the final arbitrators. The codes also bound an entire family's labor, not just the head of the household, to an employer. Many of the laws later were overturned by the Freedman's Bureau or military authorities. Funding for black education would be limited to what could be provided by black taxpayers. Since few blacks owned land or had jobs, that provision effectively denied education to black children. The thrust of the laws and the attitude of the lawmakers was clear, however: Blacks simply were not to be considered full citizens.

In addition, the Legislature appointed O.M. Roberts and David G. Burnet, both ardent secessionists, to the U.S. Senate. Neither was seated by Radical Republicans in the upper house.

RADICAL unionists, led by Hamilton, felt that the constitutional convention had not gone far enough in providing full rights of citizenship to blacks. They appealed to federal authorities in Washington, and the Congress in March 1867 responded with a Reconstruction plan of its own. The Southern states were declared to have no legal government, and the former Confederacy was divided into districts to be administered by the military until satisfactory Reconstruction was effected. Texas and Louisiana made up the Fifth Military District under the command of Gen. Philip H. Sheridan.

The freeing of the slaves threw the Texas economy into a crisis. Plantation owners were hard-pressed to attract adequate field labor, especially for harvesting. And since the state's cash economy depended on cotton production, a recession resulted. But in South and West Texas a new industry was developing. In 1866, an estimated 260,000 head of cattle were driven to market outside the state, primarily to Sedalia, Mo. Cattle raising had been basically a hide and tallow industry before the war. But the North and Midwest had developed a taste for beef, and there were thousands of head of wild cattle in Texas for the taking. During the war, herds had not been tended, and unbranded cattle were common across the state. South Texas and the coastal prairies had a long tradition of cattle raising, dating from the Spanish colonial period. Other traditions had come to Northeast Texas and the Piney Woods of East Texas from the eastern United States. And West Central Texas was among the major source areas for cattle for the emerging business.

The great trail drives moved northward to Kansas in 1867 after Texas drovers encountered resistance from farmers in Missouri and Kansas. "Texas fever," which afflicted cattle in these areas, became a problem, killing the native animals although not affecting Texas cattle. The opening of railheads at Abilene, Kan., and other locations gave Texans alternate markets for their herds. But growth of the cattle industry helped offset some of the problems brought on by the labor shortage in the cotton industry.

Gov. Throckmorton clashed often with Gen. Sheridan and Gen. Charles Griffin, commander of the Texas subdistrict of the military district. The governor thought the state had gone far enough in establishing rights for the newly freed slaves and other matters. One federal official noted that Texas resisted Reconstruction so strenuously because it "had not been whipped" in the war. Finally in August 1867, Throckmorton and other state officials were removed from office by Sheridan because they were considered an "impediment to the reconstruction." E.M. Pease, the former two-term governor and a unionist, was named provisional governor by the military authorities.

A new constitutional convention was called by Gen. Winfield S. Hancock, who replaced Sheridan in November 1867. For the first time, blacks were allowed to participate in the elections selecting delegates. Stricter regulations also disenfranchised between 7,000-10,000 former Confederates. A total of 59,633 whites and 49,497 blacks, however, registered for the election. Many whites stayed away from the polls on election day, but the convention call was approved. Delegates gathered on June 1, 1868. The Constitution of 1869 granted full rights of citizenship to blacks, created a system of education, delegated broad powers to the governor and generally reflected the views of the state's unionists. Deliberations got bogged down on partisan political matters, however, and the convention spent $200,000, an unheard-of-sum. At one point, Radical Republicans, arguing that parts of Texas were ungovernable because of the continuing violence, tried to create a State of West Texas, west of the Colorado River, but Congress would not accept dividing the state.

Gov. Pease, disgusted with the convention and the military authorities, resigned in September 1869, and Texas had no chief executive until January 1870, when E.J. Davis took office. The new constitution was approved by voters in November 1869, and Davis was elected governor.

The Republican Party formally organized in Texas in April 1867. Despite internal problems, Radical Republicans, with almost 100 percent support from black voters, controlled the Legislature. Meeting in February 1870, the Legislature passed a series of so-called "obnoxious acts." These created a state militia under the governor's control; created a state police force, also controlled by the governor; postponed the 1870 general election to 1872; enabled the governor to appoint more than 8,500 local officeholders, and granted subsidized bonds for railroad construction at a rate of $10,000 a mile. For the first time, however, a system of public education was created. The law required compulsory attendance of school for four months a year, set aside one-quarter of the state's annual revenue for education and levied a poll tax to support education. Schools also were to be integrated, which enraged many white Texans.

Heavy-handed tactics were used by Radical Republicans in the Senate, where they held only a slim majority. When Democrats and some moderates walked out to break a quorum while considering the militia bill, the Senate leadership had them arrested. Four senators were returned to the capital to give the Senate a quorum, and 10 were jailed for several days while the upper house considered many of the controversial parts of Gov. Davis' program.

Violence was rampant in Texas. One study found that between the close of the Civil War in 1865 and June 1868, 1,035 were murdered in Texas, including 486 blacks, mostly the victims of white violence. Gov. Davis argued that he needed broad police powers to restore order. And despite their unpopularity, the state police and militia — blacks made up 40 percent of the police and a majority of the militia — brought the lawlessness under control in many areas.

The Davis administration was the most unpopular in Texas' history. In fairness, historians have noted that Davis did not feel that whites could be trusted to assure the rights of the newly freed blacks. Therefore many of the governor's actions that have been interpreted as abuses of power were, in the governor's view, his constitutional responsibility. Davis personally was a man of integrity. But he made some bad appointments. His adjutant general, James Davidson, absconded with $37,000 in state funds in 1872, and other officials and legislators were accused of corruption.

State taxes also skyrocketed during the Davis administration and gave moderate Republicans and Democrats a major issue to use against him. E.M. Pease chaired a taxpayers' convention that met in Austin in September 1871 to protest the levies. A.J. Hamilton pointed out that in 1866, state taxes had amounted to 15 cents per $100 worth of property; by 1871, the tax rate had risen to $2.175 per $100 evaluation. Local taxes also rose because communities would offer grants to attract railroads.

Democrats, aided by moderate Republicans, regained control of the Legislature in the 1872 elections — at which Austin also was designated the permanent capital of Texas. In 1873, the lawmakers set about stripping the governor of many of the powers the Radical Republicans had given him.

Through the turbulent period, Texas' economy rebounded. Cotton production had dropped more than

80,000 bales between 1859 and 1869 to 350,629 bales. But by 1873, Texas re-emerged as the leading cotton-producing state. Manufacturing increased with production at 2,399 plants increasing to $11.5 million in 1870 from $6.6 million at 983 plants in 1860. The cattle business that sprang up after the war moved 700,000 head to Kansas in 1871 in the greatest drive in history. So despite the political dissension, Texas was progressing economically.

Gov. Davis also was a champion of frontier defense, which was often neglected by the federal government. Ranger companies were authorized for patrol, but when that proved too expensive, local militia were used by the state. The federal government was slow to re-establish frontier forts. One reason was that Congress was working on a new Indian policy. Another apparently was that federal authorities did not know the situation on the frontier. Gen. Sheridan once answered critics of frontier defense with the charge that more unionists and blacks were being killed by Confederates than were dying at the hands of Indians. He may have been right. An incomplete report from county judges found that between May 1865 and July 1867, 163 persons had been killed by Indians on the frontier, 43 carried into captivity and 24 wounded.

But attempts to pacify Indians on reservations did not ease Texas' plight. The Comanches and Kiowas in particular did not look on Texans as Americans. Texas was a place apart from the rest of the United States in their minds. One Comanche chief insolently told an Indian agent that, if the Great Father did not want the young reservation Indians raiding Texas, Texas should be moved.

The ferocity of the raids was vividly brought home to Gen. William T. Sherman, general in chief of the army, in May 1871. He and a small party were inspecting frontier facilities and traveled from Fort Belknap to Fort Richardson. Shortly after reaching Fort Richardson, survivors of a wagon train that had followed the military party reached the fort. They told a story of brutal murder and torture during an Indian attack at Salt Creek in Young County. Gen. Sherman immediately ordered Col. Ranald Mackenzie to launch a vigorous campaign against the Indians. Three Kiowa chiefs, Santank, Satanta and Big Tree, were arrested on the reservation for the crime, and Satanta and Big Tree were tried in state court. At the request of Indian authorities, Gov. Davis pardoned them after a short time in prison.

Cols. Mackenzie and Nelson A. Miles conducted a vigorous campaign against the Comanche and Kiowa, breaking their backs in the Red River campaign. For the first time, the army pursued the Indians to their previous sanctuaries on the Texas Plains. And in a September 1874 engagement in Palo Duro Canyon, the Indians' horses were killed. Without the animals for transportation, the braves soon reported to the reservations. Texas' Indian problems were at an end.

The political turmoil also ended with the gubernatorial election of 1873 when Richard Coke easily defeated Davis. Davis tried to get federal authorities to keep him in office until April, but President Grant refused to intervene. And in January of 1874, Democrats were in control of state government again. The end of Reconstruction concluded the turbulent Civil War era, although the attitudes that developed during the period lasted well into the 20th century.

Retrenchment

WHEN Gov. Richard Coke and conservative Democrats regained control of state government in 1874, they had power but little else. Texas' economy, unlike that of the rest of the defeated South, was not in ruins. Although there were labor problems, railroads expanded, manufacturing grew and cotton production returned to pre-war levels by 1873. But the economic Panic of 1873 slowed recovery.

Pre-Civil War Texas' economy was based on two factors: slaves and land. After the war, the slaves were free, and land values dropped precipitously. And little hard currency was to be had. Confederate money was worthless, and few Texans had acquired much gold during the war.

Gov. E.J. Davis' administration also was accused of extravagance. But Texans bore a tax burden much lighter than other Southern states.

Railroad construction had resumed after the war, and the total mileage tripled to almost 1,500 miles before the economic panic curtailed work in 1873.

Coke and the Legislature therefore had little choice in financing state government. The Democrats chose to cut state spending dramatically. Although the Davis administration was accused of profligate spending, many Democrats had supported the appropriations. With Davis out of office, however, public education was cut to the bone, the prison system was put on a pay-as-you-go basis by continuing a tragic policy initiated under Davis of leasing convicts to private contractors.

A constitutional convention was called in 1875 to re-write the state constitution, a hated vestige of Radical Republican rule. Again, every avenue to cutting spending at any level of government was explored. Salaries of public officials were slashed. The number of offices was reduced. Judgeships, along with most other offices, were made elective rather than appointive. The Legislature was prohibited from assuming debt beyond $200,000 without a statewide vote. The state road program was curtailed, and the immigration bureau was eliminated. State chartered banks also were prohibited, as they had been in every Texas constitution but one since 1836. Perhaps the worst change was the destruction of the statewide school system. The new charter created a "community system" without a power of taxation, and schools were segregated by race. The constitution, which was approved by voters on Feb. 15, 1876, reflected the public attitudes of the day. Almost half the delegates to the convention were members of the Grange, a new organization that had come to Texas in 1873 to relieve the plight of the farmer. Under Reconstruction, Texans felt they had experienced what government could do to them, not for them. They had borne what they considered a burden of heavy taxation for programs that they neither supported nor approved. And they wanted no repeat performances. Though the United States was in the middle of the Industrial Revolution, the basic law of Texas reflected a world view more in line with 1836.

Despite the basic reactionary character, the charter also was visionary. Following the lead of several other states, the Democrats declared railroads to be common carriers and subject to regulation. But consistent with the desire for keeping government at a minimum, no method for regulation of railroads was provided, and the omission was to fire political debates for a decade and a half.

Another major challenge was the re-establishment of law and order across the state. Since before the Civil War, respect for civil authority had been on the decline in Texas. After the war, the situation deteriorated as thousands of disillusioned and embittered soldiers returned home to suffer under Reconstruction. Indians remained a problem, although the U.S. Army was making progress in taming the frontier. And in the long troublesome Nueces Strip — the land between the Nueces River and the Rio Grande — the Mexican bandit-hero Juan Cortina was again causing trouble. The enigmatic Cortina had served both the Union and Confederacy during the Civil War, and at one time, the Texas Senate approved a pardon for him before the House bowed to a public outcry and let the matter drop. While serving as an official of the Mexican government, however, Cortina also operated a thriving cattle theft business north of the Rio Grande, stealing stock to fulfill meat contracts with Cuba. Anglo ranchers were not safe from the marauders, and many settlers took the law into their own hands, victimizing Mexican-Texans in the process.

To meet the dual challenge of lawlessness and Indian insurrection, Gov. Coke in 1874 re-established the Texas Rangers. Major L. H. McNelly was to lead the Special Force to clean up the borderlands, and Maj John B. Jones commanded the Frontier Battalion, consisting of six companies of 75 Rangers each.

McNelly's force of only 40 men was controversial because it took few prisoners. The Rangers were ordered to kill captives if any attempt was made to free them. But McNelly also developed an excellent intelligence system that kept him a step ahead of the bandits. One of his first acts was to remove the Anglo posse from the field, for many had been used as cover for individuals to settle personal grievances. After a few months in the field, McNelly's force killed 13 Mexican bandits in a running gun battle, and the bodies were displayed on the square at Brownsville as an example for future cattle thieves. Soon the situation was under control, and McNelly moved his operations farther up the Rio Grande to clean out American outlaws operating around Eagle Pass.

Major Jones' task was more difficult. His Frontier Battalion was divided into small groups that continually patrolled the edges of settled Texas to discourage Indian raids. The U.S. Army also put a severe crimp in raids. Cavalry units, under Ranald Mackenzie, relentlessly pursued Indians across the plains. Jones and a group of Rangers fought the last battle against Indians in northern Texas in June 1875 at Lost Valley on the Jack-Young County line. Twenty-seven Rangers, commanded by Jones, engaged 100 Indians for a full day before getting help from Fort Richardson.

Thereafter most Indian raids were concentrated in Far West Texas where U.S. Army Lt. John Bullis and his Negro Seminole Indian Scouts waged a relentless campaign against the Apaches. The last Indian battle in Texas was fought in January 1881 when Capt. George Baylor and a group of Rangers ambushed the remnants of Chief Victorio's Apaches in the Sierra Diablo Mountains.

Also by 1881, every part of Texas had felt the presence of the Rangers. The day of the professional outlaw was coming to an end. Major Jones had quelled feuds in several counties and had reduced the list of wanted criminals in the state. Rampant lawlessness had been reduced to mere sporadic outbursts.

Gov. Coke was re-elected in 1876, but he left office in December of that year for a seat in the U.S. Senate. Lt. Gov. Richard Hubbard replaced him.

Though Texas' population grew substantially after Reconstruction, transportation remained a major problem. The state's rivers were not navigable except for a few miles from the Gulf. Counties were given responsibility for creating and maintaining a road system, and in East Texas, the most populous part of the state, a "firstclass road" was one in which tree stumps were no more than six inches in height. To facilitate construction of much-needed railroads, the Legislature in 1876 established a land-grant system. Railroad companies got 16 alternate sections of land for each mile of track completed, with payment beginning after completion of 10 miles of track. Between 1875 and 1885, one-half of the total railroad mileage built in the 19th century in Texas was completed. In 1877, Texas led all states in railroad construction, and the following year, the construction in Texas exceeded the aggregate for all other states and territories combined. But embarrassed state officials discovered in 1881 that the Legislature had given away eight million more acres of land than was available, and the land-grant law was repealed. More than 32 million acres of land were granted to railroads during the period, however.

As railroads extended across the state, the character of the economy began to change. Farmers began to move from self-contained subsistence agriculture to commercial production. But this meant that they had to purchase many household goods and supplies that they once provided by their own labor. Cash, rather than barter, became the medium of exchange, and in the war-ravaged Confederacy, the need for hard money compounded many problems.

In addition, the construction of railroads spurred other industries. In 1880, Texas & Pacific Railroad alone purchased 500,000 crossties to stimulate lumbering, which became the state's largest manufacturing industry.

Emancipation of the slaves brought about a major realignment of the division of labor in the state. Many owners of large plantations were financially ruined by the loss of slaves and by the drop in land prices. At first, landowners feared there would be a labor shortage, because it was felt that the former slaves would not work for wages. Within a decade, however, most blacks were either employed on farms, had entered into share-cropping agreements or had acquired land. White landowners often would not sell land to blacks or would charge high interest rates for the purchase. Like all small farmers, blacks also got caught in the crop-lien system in which they had to mortgage future crops to buy supplies on credit. Often they still owed money after selling their crops, and a cycle of permanent indebtedness developed. Wage demands of the blacks and a basic prejudice against the former slaves also prompted efforts to attract immigrants into the state. The effort was successful, but landowners also found that many new immigrants worked for others only briefly before acquiring land for themselves. By 1876, 62 percent of the workers were white, with blacks making up only 38 percent. Unlike some other states, Texas did not develop a class of black artisans during the slavery period, so after the war, those blacks not engaged in agricultural work held only menial jobs in either rural or urban areas. A class of independent black businessmen developed only slowly, and most were in service industries like cafes, barbershops and funeral parlors.

Conservative Democrats maintained a firm grip on state politics for almost 20 years after Reconstruction, although dissident political groups arose periodically. The thrust of the Democratic administrations was economy in government and white supremacy. Despite heroic efforts, the state government remained in debt, which served as a continual reminder of the failure of the Confederacy. Texans could not divide the quest of blacks for full civil rights from full social equality. And most white Texans continued to expect subservience from blacks. Efforts had been made to legally discriminate against blacks after the Civil War. In 1866, the Legislature required railroads to provide separate accommodations for black passengers, and the law was not repealed until 1871. Later the lawmakers eliminated state licensing for many businesses in an effort to avoid the antidiscrimination thrust of the federal Civil Rights law of 1875.

IN statewide politics, race was not a major question because the percentage of blacks in the population was declining, although the number of blacks in the state grew. In local politics, however, particularly in East Texas, race was a major factor. Blacks were in the majority in several counties in the so-called Black Belt. Here blacks, along with white Republicans, often controlled local offices. Often white Democrats would use intimidation and violence to discourage black voter participation. As often, black politicians would bend the law. In some counties, specially designed ballots were used for black-supported slates of candidates so illiterate voters could more easily vote a straight ticket. The practice was ended by an 1879 law that required certain types of ballots. As early as 1874 some local Democratic clubs conceived the all-white primary as an instrument for denying blacks participationin local government. Although initial efforts were unsuccessful, the approach continued and finally became state Democratic policy after the turn of the century.

Violence against blacks often was fatal. One source estimates that 500 blacks died in mob violence between 1870 and 1900. Many were victims of lynching after being accused of crimes. On occasion, the victims proved to be innocent.

For 15 years after Reconstruction ended, Texas Democrats could campaign against the Civil War and expect success. During this period, most statewide officeholders and local officials were Confederate veterans. O. M. Roberts, chief justice of the state supreme court, became a compromise candidate for governor when the Democratic convention deadlocked. Roberts, who chaired the secession convention of 1861, was elected for the first of two terms in 1878 and pursued a strict policy of fiscal austerity. He cut spending for public education from one-quarter to one-seventh of state revenues one year and supported a law providing for the sale of stateland at 50-cents an acre. Despite the intent of providing cheap land for immigrants, the law actually encouraged widespread speculation, driving land prices up for farmers.

John Ireland succeeded Roberts as governor and continued the tight fiscal policies. Ireland opposed the liberal land policies of his predecessors and is credited with saving much public land for the state schoolchildren. But cracks were developing in the Democratic dominance of state politics. G. W. (Wash) Jones, a former Democratic lieutenant governor, contested Ireland as an independent in 1882 and polled more than 100,000 votes. It was an impressive showing by a dissident candidate against the entrenched Democrats.

Economic and social problems that began in the 1870s became the major political issues in the 1880s. Democrats were hard-pressed to maintain control of the state government in the turbulent final 20 years of the 19th century.

Economy in Transition

HOLLYWOOD distorted the picture of the Texas economy. While the cowboy and cattle drives are romantic subjects, the fact is that the simple cotton farmer was the backbone of the state's economy well into the 20th century.

But neither the farmer nor the cattleman prospered throughout the last quarter of the 19th century. At the root of their problems was federal monetary policy and the lingering effects of the Civil War.

To finance the war, the Union had gone off the gold standard and had issued paper money — or greenbacks. Throughout the war, paper money could not be redeemed for specie from the national government. The prevailing monetary theory, however, held that this paper was only fiat money without real value. Only a gold-backed currency had intrinsic value. At the end of the war, there were almost $500 million in national bank notes in circulation. Northeastern bankers began to lobby for a return to the gold standard and to hard money. Although the issuance of paper money had brought about a business boom in the Union during the war, inflation also increased. Silver was demonetized in 1873. Congress passed the Specie Resumption Act in 1875 that returned the nation to the gold standard in 1879. Almost immediately a contraction in currency began. Between 1873 and 1891, the amount of national bank notes in circulation declined from $339 million to $168 million.

The reduction in the money supply was devastating in the defeated South. Of the region's major fiscal assets, slaves had been lost altogether and, because of the lack of money, land values plummeted. In 1870, Texas land was valued at an average of $2.62 an acre, compared with the national average of $18.26 an acre. Confederate money was worthless, and gold was scarce. Massachusetts alone had five times more national bank currency in circulation than the entire South.

With the money supply declining and the national economy growing, farm prices dropped. In 1870, a bushel of wheat brought $1, but by 1885, it had dropped to 80 cents. And in the 1890s, wheat was 60 cents a bushel. Except for a brief spurt in the early 1880s, cattle prices followed those of agricultural products.

Credit became an important commodity. And Texas was ill-equipped to meet the challenge. State-chartered banks were prohibited by the constitution, and there were hardly enough national banks to service the state's growing population. To compound the farmers' problems, national banks would not loan money with land as collateral. The credit problem was exacerbated in Texas by growth. In 1870, there were 61,125 farms in the state; 30 years later, the number spiraled to 352,190.

The transition from a self-sufficient agricultural economy to commercial agriculture that the state experienced also strained the farmers' need for credit. Efficient commercial farms needed more land and mechanized equipment. Both were expensive. The war had stripped Texas of its farm implements, and it took time to replace them. In 1860, the value of Texas farm implements per farm was $24 above the national average. For the remainder of the century, however, Texas' average per farm was $50-$60 below the national average, and other regions surpassed the state. Bad weather and poor prices often forced land-owning farmers into tenancy. Between 1880 and 1890, the number of farms in Texas doubled, but the number of tenants tripled. By 1900, almost half the state's farmers were tenants.

The much-criticized crop-lien system was developed following the Civil War to meet the credit needs of small farmers. Merchants would extend credit to farmers throughout the year in exchange for liens on their crops. In most cases cotton was the major cash crop. Critics have blamed the creditors for prohibiting farmers from diversifying. But that is only partly true. Many farmers faithfully planted cotton because it seldom made a complete failure. Through almost any type of bad weather, some cotton would be produced when other crops failed completely. But the result of the crop-lien system, particularly when small farmers did not have enough acreage to operate efficiently, was a state of continual debt and despair.

Furnishing merchants also have been criticized for charging high interest rates for goods that carried premium prices when sold on credit. But many small farmers were not good businessmen, and the merchant's risks were not high.

Cotton was a physically demanding crop to raise. One estimate was that it took 168 man-hours of labor to raise one acre of cotton a year. But many small farmers toiled long hours and then found at the end of the year that their labor had yielded no return. In some cases, they had gone further in debt to the furnishing merchant.

The work ethic held that a man would benefit from his toil. When this apparently failed, farmers looked to the monetary system and the railroads as the causes. Their discontent hence became the source of the agrarian revolt that developed in the 1880s and 1890s.

Farmers, on the other hand, were criticized for thinking of themselves as laborers, rather than investors or capitalists. Across the South, land traditionally had been looked on as a tool, not an investment. Once a piece of land was worn out, the farmer discarded it by moving to the next frontier. But in Texas the familiar land use pattern broke down as the frontier reached the arid plains. Farmers were slow in understanding that new techniques would be needed for dry-land farming, and the periodic droughts, originally thought to be aberrations in the weather, wrought considerable misery before settlers solved the problems of successfully farming land beyond the 98th meridian.

With the defeat of the Indians and the buffalo kill that began in 1874-75, West Texas was opened first to cattlemen and later to farmers. Cattlemen traditionally practiced open-range grazing from Spanish colonial days until the early 1880s. Livestock was allowed to roam over wide areas and was rounded up twice a year. Huge cattle drives following the war had proved successful, and when the High Plains of Texas were cleared of Indians and buffalo, cattle thrived on the rich grasses. Large cattle operations developed. Charles Goodnight established the JA Ranch in the Palo Duro Canyon in the Panhandle in the 1870s, and others soon followed. The huge cattle drives ended about the same time that many states quarantined Texas cattle because of the "Texas Fever" they carried — which was fatal to other domestic livestock. Railroads snaked across Texas in the 1880s, establishing shipping points and eliminating the need for the long drives to out-of-state markets.

Cattle prices improved between 1880 and 1885, but other problems faced stockraisers. In 1883, the Legislature required that stockmen pay grazing fees for state land that their cattle used. Previously this grazing had been free, and many cattleraisers ignored the law or circumvented it by fixing bids to keep fees low. Attempts to prosecute ranchers for conspiring against the law failed because most public officials and jurors in western Texas were either cattlemen or employees of the ranches.

The introduction of barbed wire in the early 1880s brought a revolution to ranching. Texas had long needed a cheap form of fencing. Stone and wooden fences were expensive, and in West Texas the materials simply were not available. Without fences, however, the quality of cattle herds could not be improved. Farmers also needed fences in cattle-raising regions to keep stock from ruining their fields. The new wire was introduced into Texas at Denison in the late 1870s, and in less than 10 years, it had spread across the state. John W. "Bet a Million" Gates, one of the most successful barbed-wire salesmen, dramatically demonstrated the new product by building a corral in downtown San Antonio and wagering that a steer could not break out. The animal didn't, and ranchers bought the wire.

Small range wars developed between open-range cattlemen and fencers as barbed wire moved across the state. Often landowners would block public roads and seal off water holes with their new fences. Fence-cutters would simply snip the wire to remove the barriers. The battles became particularly bitter during droughts when cattle were cut off from water. Finally, Gov. John Ireland called a special session of the Legislature in 1883 to make fence-cutting and the fencing of public lands illegal. Estimates are that more than $20 million in property damage was done by fencecutters, and the adverse publicity surrounding the battles discouraged immigration and land development for a time.

The cattle boom of the 1880s also attracted foreign investment to the state. Thirteen British corporations and eight from Scotland — invested an estimated $25 million in Texas and controlled between them 15 million to 20 million acres of land, primarily on the High Plains and the Rolling Plains. The operations proved generally unprofitable for investors when cattle prices dropped. Drought, bitter winters, cattle thieves and public animosity also took their toll. But the foreign investors are credited with introducing barbed-wire on a large scale, bringing windmills to the region and with improving cattle herds.

One of the largest ranches was created after a disaster in Austin. The state capitol burned in 1881, and the following year, the Legislature gave the Capitol Syndicate three million acres of land to construct a new building. The project was completed in 1888. With the land, the XIT Ranch in the Panhandle was established in 1885, covering parts of nine counties: Dallam, Hartley, Oldham, Deaf Smith, Parmer, Castro, Bailey, Lamb and Hockley. More than 1,500 miles of fence enclosed the ranch, which was operated until 1901 when tracts were sold by the syndicate.

The breakup of the large ranches began in the 1880s and continued after the turn of the century. Small farmers entered the region and purchased the large estates piecemeal. The immigration proved more profitable to the large ranches than cattleraising.

As bleak as the picture was, there were bright spots. After 1860, cottonseed, which had been a waste and a nuisance, developed commercial value. Previously it had been burned or dumped into streams and rivers to the dismay of other Texans. But it was discovered that cottonseed cake could be sold to stock raisers for feed, and the oil became valuable. Cotton presses could be easily moved, and a thriving industry developed. By 1900, cottonseed processing became the second largest industry in Texas, behind lumbering.

Lumbering continued to grow, and by 1890 became the state's largest industry. Improved transportation also allowed wood products to be shipped outside the state as well as to be used within Texas.

In December 1887, the Texas League of Professional Baseball Clubs was organized, and in its inaugural season, Austin, Dallas, Fort Worth, Galveston, Houston and San Antonio fielded teams.

Railroad expansion also continued at a brisk pace. In 1880, there were 3,025 miles of track in operation, and a decade later, the mileage more than doubled to 8,667. In hand with railroad expansion, coal production was initiated in the late 1870s. A mine in Stephens County in West Central Texas produced coal for Fort Griffin and shipped to Fort Worth at a price of $11 a ton, $2 below the eastern price. As coal became available in quantity, the railroads abandoned wood as fuel. In the 1880s, commercial coal production began in Palo Pinto County, and Thurber, near the Palo Pinto-Erath county line, became a major coal production center for the Texas & Pacific Railroad. On the border, Eagle Pass became a coal production center for the Southern Pacific.

Galveston and San Antonio were important trade centers in the last quarter of the century. Galveston was a major cotton-shipping center, and San Antonio was a supply center for the frontier forts. Along the border, El Paso and Laredo became major international trade centers. The Southern Pacific reached El Paso from the west in 1881, and shortly thereafter a northern railroad tied into the Mexican system. Maintenance shops were established at El Paso, and nearby coal mines provided fuel for trains visiting the trade center. Entrepreneur Uriah Lott completed a rail line to Laredo in November 1881, and a few days later, Jay Gould's International and Great Northern Railroad arrived, tying the border community to San Antonio and northern markets. Laredo and its sister city, Nuevo Laredo, marked the arrival of the railroads with a month-long celebration.

Railroad towns blossomed in the wake of construction. Many grew from crew camps. As Jay Gould's Texas & Pacific Railroad moved west from Fort Worth, the cities of Gordon, Eastland, Baird and Abilene were laid out in 1880, and the following year, Sweetwater, Colorado City and Big Spring were established along the route. T&P and Southern Pacific met at Sierra Blanca about 90 miles east of El Paso on Jan.1, 1882, completing connections with the East and West coasts for Texas.

In 1887, the Fort Worth and Denver City Railroad began a diagonal extension across West Texas and the Panhandle. It crossed Childress, Donley, Armstrong, Potter, Hartley and Dallam Counties in the Panhandle and reached Texline on the New Mexico-Texas state line in 1888. The cities of Childress, Clarendon, Amarillo and Dalhart became terminal points for farmers and ranchers. With this extension, most areas of Texas had railroads. But Lubbock on the South Plains and the Lower Rio Grande Valley did not receive rail service until after the turn of the century.

The entry of the Texas & Pacific and the Missouri-Kansas-Texas railroads from the northeast changed trade patterns in the state. Since the days of the Republic, trade generally had flowed to Gulf ports and primarily at Galveston. Jefferson in Northeast Texas served as a gateway to the Mississippi River, but it never carried the volume of trade that was common at Galveston. The earliest railroad systems in the state also were centered around Houston and Galveston, again directing trade southward. With the T&P and Katy lines, North Texas had direct access to markets in St. Louis and the East.

Some problems developed with the railroads, however. In 1882, Jay Gould and Collis P. Huntington, owner of the Southern Pacific, entered into a secret agreement that amounted to creation of a monopoly of rail service in Texas. They agreed to stop competitive track extensions, to divide under a pooling arrangement freight moving from New Orleans and El Paso, to purchase all competing railroads in Texas, and to share the track between Sierra Blanca and El Paso. Railroads owned by the pair soon organized the Texas Traffic Association with its goals of increasing revenues and doing away with abuses and losses. When the courts ordered the association dissolved, the railroads simply reorganized associations based outside Texas.

THE Legislature made weak attempts to regulate railroads, as provided by the state constitution. Gov. Coke had recommended creation of a railroad commission in 1876, but was ignored. Gould thwarted an attempt to create a commission in 1881 with a visit to the state during the Legislative debate. The railroad tycoon subdued the lawmakers' interest with thinly disguised threats that capital would abandon Texas if the state interfered with railroad business. In 1879, the lawmakers did set a maximum rate that railroads could charge for freight and made it unlawful for a rail carrier to discriminate against any person or place. But the laws were loosely enforced.

With the railroads came Texas' first militant labor organizations. The state's traditional agrarian society had little need for unions. Some workers had organized during the days of the Republic. Journeyman printers struck a Houston newspaper in 1839, and groups of artisans organized loosely to seek legislation. Texas' mechanics lien law of 1839 was one of the first protections for workers of its type in North America. Workingmen's associations organized occasionally prior to the Civil War, but they were weak and often did not last long. Only two unions existed in Galveston at the outbreak of the war. Prior to 1870, no outside unions provided aid to Texas workers. In the self-sustaining agricultural economy, unions also were looked upon as "Yankee innovations" and "abominations." After the Civil War, unions became more numerous. The Screwmen's Benevolent Association of Galveston organized in 1866 and lasted into the 20th century after affiliation with a national union. Black dock workers also organized in Galveston, and skilled workers, such as carpenters and bricklayers, struck in major cities.

With the railroads, however, came the militant Knights of Labor. In 1885, the union struck and gained concessions from T&P Railroad, but a year later, another strike turned violent. Troops were called out to protect railroad property, and the strike failed. The unions were heavily criticized for the job action, and the labor movement in Texas remained weak until the state's industrial base developed in the 20th century.

As the 19th century closed, Texas remained an agricultural state, albeit commercial agriculture and not family farms. But the industrial base was growing. Between 1870 and 1900, the per capita value of manufactured goods in the United States rose from $109 to $171. In Texas, these per capita values increased from $14 to $39. But manufacturing values in Texas industry still were only one-half of the annual agricultural values.

But Texas was definitely a state in transition, and there was no better evidence than the tumultuous political upheavals of the last quarter of the 19th century.

The Agrarian Revolt

CONSERVATIVE Texas Democrats maintained control of the state government throughout most of the last quarter of the 19th century. Their ascendancy was based on white supremacy and on the strong emotional rejection of the Radical Republican Reconstruction era. As across most of the United States, Texans had no attraction to burning national issues. Regional and local interests prevailed.

But as the plight of the farmers worsened, strong passions were unleashed that overrode the issues of secession and the Civil War on the national level. A series of third parties with national affiliations arose in Texas that seriously threatened to break the Democrats' grip on the state house and the Legislature.

Texas farmers were not alone in their poverty. The entire South suffered, and the condition was noted by O.H. Kelley, a clerk in the Agricultural Bureau in Washington, on a trip through the region. He was appalled by the Southern farmers' poverty and apathy. To give voice to their plight, he organized the National Grange — the Patrons of Husbandry — in the nation's capital in 1867. The first Texas Grange was established in 1872 at Salado in Bell County. At its peak membership in 1877, the state organization claimed 45,000 members, including 6,000 women, in more than 1,200 local chapters. It had a threefold purpose: To improve the home life of its members; to foster social intercourse to the mutual benefit of all, and to provide economic benefits in dealing with the business world. Grangers were encouraged to participate in politics as citizens, but the organization was not directly involved. Many local Granges and the state organization petitioned the Legislature on various issues, and members felt they had a voice in government through the organization. About half of the 90 delegates to the state constitutional convention of 1875 were Grangers, and they left their mark on the state charter that provided for limited government, restrictions on taxation and debt, and provided a framework for railroad regulation.

The Grange's lasting contribution came through its educational programs. Many of the local meetings were agricultural schools, teaching farmers how to be more efficient. The founding of Texas Agricultural & Mechanical College (now University) in 1876 received strong support from the organization.

But the Grange foundered on two issues. First, it established the Texas Cooperative Association in an effort to circumvent the furnishing merchant who held so many farmers in debt. The goal was to eliminate the middle man and to provide merchandise wholesale to farmers. The state cooperative was to be associated with local cooperatives sponsored by the organization. And this effort attracted many members. Unfortunately, it did not work. The cash-only Grange stores were of no help to farmers who had no cash. And in 1883 and 1884 both the state and local cooperatives suffered severe financial losses because of bad crops and many closed their doors. In addition, as time passed, farmers became more militant and wanted an organization that was more directly involved in politics. State Grange leaders would not abandon the original nonpolitical policy. While most farmers were emotionally tied to the Democratic Party and wanted to work within its framework, others were becoming disenchanted with the "party of the fathers." The Grange's membership began to fall.

The Greenback Party was attractive to many farmers, although the Grange leadership remained loyal to the Democratic Party. The monetary devaluation that was damaging farmers also took its toll on the wages of workers in the industrialized parts of the nation. On the national level, the Greenback Party began activity in 1876 and reached Texas two years later. Although the party supported issues like women's suffrage and an income tax, its basic goal was to provide a greater money supply. Greenbackers opposed the return to the gold standard, supported remonetization of silver and demanded repeal of the national bank law. First and foremost, the party supported an expansion of the currency to eliminate the growing economic hardship of many Americans. In four gubernatorial elections between 1878 and 1884, Greenbackers supplanted Republicans as runners-up to the winning Democrats. In 1882, Greenbacker G.W. "Wash" Jones polled 102,501 votes, the most ever attracted by a dissident party in the state up to that time. In local races, Greenbackers occasionally

were successful, as in the case of the party candidate who was elected mayor of Dallas. The Greenback movement failed, however, when the Democrats usurped some of its platform planks. Farmers also became uncomfortable with some of the radical socialists who gained control of the national party. There was little cultural affinity between the farmers and the socialist of the industrial world. Farmers looked elsewhere for political champion.

In 1877, another farm organization was established. On the J.R. Allen farm in Lampasas County, a group of farmers banded together in the Knights of Alliance with its purpose "to assist the civil officers in maintaining law and order." This group was primarily concerned with curbing livestock thefts. But it had a simple ritual and its literary program was borrowed from the Grange. The Alliance was reorganized in 1879 in Pooville in Parker County, and in the next few years, provided the impetus for the radical politics of the 1890s.

By 1886, the Alliance, led by S.O. Daws and William Lamb, became more radical. At a meeting in Cleburne the organization issued a list of 17 "demands" — in contrast to the Grange's simple petitions — addressed to the state and federal governments. These included demands for fiscal reform, railroad regulation, changes in land policy and the recognition of labor unions. Though some conservative Alliance members were distressed at the apparent split with the Democratic Party, the organization's membership grew tremendously after the meeting. The demands struck a welcome note for many farmers. By the time a second meeting was held in Waco in January 1887 to heal the rift that developed, the Alliance claimed 200,000 members in 3,000 chartered suballiances in Texas.

In Waco, Dr. Charles W. Macune struck a compromise between the divergent elements and took a major step toward spreading the Alliance's influence. He proposed a national system of cooperatives to market farm products and to serve as a purchasing medium for farmers. Within five weeks, Texas lecturers were sent to other states throughout the South. When a national convention was held in Shreveport, La., in October 1887, 10 states that had been organized in eight months were represented.

Democrats easily weathered the early third-party challenges in Texas. Democratic governors continued their policies of fiscal austerity. John Ireland successfully coped with the fence-cutting wars and reversed some of the liberal land policies that were fueling speculation. Lawrence S. "Sul" Ross, elected in 1888, was a popular Confederate veteran who benefited from large monetary settlement with the federal government. Texas was compensated for its costs in fighting Indians and guarding the Mexican border. Ross cut taxes and improved state services.

In 1886, a new breed of Texas politician appeared. James Stephen Hogg was not a Confederate veteran although his father was, and he was not tied to the party policies of the past. As reform-minded attorney general, Hogg had actively enforced the state's few railroad regulatory laws. Through the experience, he became convinced that the state must have a railroad commission. With farmers' support, Hogg was elected governor in 1890, and at the same time, a debate on the constitutionality of a railroad commission was settled when voters amended the constitution to provide for one. Hogg led a group of young Democrats who were step removed from Reconstruction and ties with the Confederate past. These young Democrats launched a brief reform era in state government.

Nationally, the growing power of the emerging corporate interests had become a major political issue. In 1887, Congressman John Reagan of Texas won a 10-year fight to establish the Interstate Commerce Commission to regulate railroads. Two years later, the Texas Legislature passed an anti-trust law, just weeks after Kansas had approved the first such statute in the nation.

Hogg was bitterly opposed in his campaign, but the reform mood of the state was evident. Voters returned only 22 of the 106 members of the Texas House in 1890. The Legislature created the Railroad Commission of Texas in 1891 after an extended debate. A compromise was reached that allowed the first commission to be appointed by the governor, but beginning in 1894, the panel would be elected. Hogg accomplished one of the great political moves of the century by luring Reagan out of the U.S. Senate to serve as the first chairman of the commission, along with commissioners L.L. Foster and William P. McLean. Reagan's long battle to create the ICC gave him an intimate knowledge of railroad operations, and, as the former postmaster general of the Confederacy, he was well-respected by all Texans.

Despite his reputation as a reformer, Hogg accepted the growing use of Jim Crow laws to limit minority access to public services. In 1891, the Legislature responded to public demands and required railroads to provide separate accommodations for blacks and whites.

The stage was being set for one of the major political campaigns in Texas history, however. Farmers did not think that Hogg had gone far enough in his reform program, and they were distressed that Hogg had not appointed a farmer to the railroad commission.

In 1889, Charles Macune, now editor of the Farmers Alliance's national newspaper, the National Economist in Washington, had proposed a radical new monetary system. Under his plan, the federal government would eliminate the farmers' credit pinch, underwriting cooperatives by issuing greenbacks to provide credit for farmers' crops. A more flexible national currency would be created in the process. In addition, the government would store the crops until time for sale and issue "subtreasury" certificates that would serve as legal tender. While the plan contained elements of a modern crop insurance program, it was wildly radical at the time. Texas Democrats had refused to endorse either the subtreasury plan or free silver in their 1890 platform, and to many farmers this was a signal of the party's insensitivity to their plight. Many began to look elsewhere for the solutions to their problems.

The Kansas Farmers Alliance provided the answer in 1888: direct political action through sponsoring slates of candidates. Kansas' success prompted the formation of the People's Party in Texas in August 1891.

The 1892 general election was one of the most spirited in the state's history. Conservative Democrats, after Gov. Hogg's supporters shut them out of the so-called roundhouse convention in Houston, bolted and nominated railroad attorney George Clark for the governorship. Populists for the first time had a presidential candidate, James Weaver, and a gubernatorial candidate, T.L. Nugent.

Texas Republicans also broke ranks. The party's strength centered in the black vote. After the death of former Gov. E.J. Davis in 1883, Norris Wright Cuney, a black, was the party leader. Cuney was considered one of the most astute politicians of the period, and he controlled federal patronage. White Republicans revolted against the black leadership, and these so-called "Lily-whites" nominated Andrew Jackson Houston, son of Sam Houston, for governor. Black Republicans recognized that, alone, their strength was limited, and throughout the latter part of the 19th century, they practiced fusion politics, backing candidates of third parties when they deemed it appropriate. Cuney led the Republicans into a coalition with the conservative Democrats in 1892, backing George Clark.

The election also marked the first time that major Democratic candidates courted the black vote. Gov. Hogg's supporters organized black voter clubs, and the governor got about one-half of the black vote. Black farmers were in a quandary. Their financial problems were the same as those small farmers who backed the Populists. White Populists varied in their sympathy with the racial concerns of the blacks. On the local level, some whites showed sympathy with black concerns about education, voting and law enforcement. Minority farmers also were reluctant to abandon the Republican Party because it was their only political base in Texas.

Hogg was re-elected in 1892 with a 43 percent plurality in a field of five candidates.

During his second term, Hogg continued to try to correct abuses by the railroads. Transportation rates were based in part on railroads' investments. The governor charged during the campaign that railroads had watered their stock, meaning more was sold than necessary for operation. In the previous seven years, Hogg argued, railroad construction had been negligible, but railroad obligations had increased at a rate of $30 million a year. In addition, for rate purposes, railroads claimed outstanding stocks and bonds valued at $455,520,744, while for tax purposes, these same properties were valued at $63,000,000. In 1893, the Legislature gave the railroad commission authority to review new stock sales and to regulate the sales.

Populists continued to run well in state races until 1898. But historians have placed the beginning of the party's demise in the 1896 presidential election in which national Populists fused with the Democrats and supported William Jennings Bryan. This fusion weakened the demand for Macune's subtreasury plan, which would have created a new monetary system, in favor of the Democrats' "free silver" platform plank. Although the Populist philosophy lived on, the party declined in importance after the 1898 elections. Following a depression in the early 1890s, farm prices began to rise after a European crop failure in 1897, and gold discoveries in South Africa, Australia and Alaska helped relieve the currency shortage. Farmers remained active in politics, but most returned to the Democratic Party, which usurped many of the Populists' issues.

But Texas was on the brink of another revolution — an economic revolution that would forever change the face of the state.

Spindletop

SELDOM can a people's history be traced to a single event on a single day. But Texas' entrance into the industrial age can be linked directly to the discovery of oil at Spindletop, three miles from Beaumont, on Jan. 10, 1901. From that day, Texas' progress from a rural, agricultural state to a modern industrial giant has been steady.

The presence of oil near the salt domes along Texas' Gulf Coast had been suspected for many years. Patillo Higgins drilled wells near Spindletop for a decade before his resources were exhausted. In 1900, Higgins leased land to Anthony Lucas to prospect for oil.

Quicksand in the area presented a serious engineering problem to Higgins and to Lucas. But Lucas had experience with similar problems in Louisiana before coming to Texas. A telescoping system of casing, ranging from 12-inch pipe at the surface to four-inch pipe at the bottom of the hole was devised to keep the sand from filling the hole as it was dug. The Lucas No. 1 was spudded-in with a rotary rig in October 1900, and on the afternoon of Jan. 10, blew in. Initial production was estimated between 75,000 and 80,000 barrels of oil per day. Lucas was hardly prepared for the quantity of oil the well produced, and for several days, the oil flowed freely before the drilling crew could bring it under control. Oil was stored in earthen tanks when possible, but much simply was wasted.

Within days, the area was engulfed in Texas' first oil boom. Investors and con men from across the nation descended to enrich themselves in the hysterical activity that followed. Land values skyrocketed. Hundreds of wells were drilled as close together as possible. Little effort was made to stem the flow of oil until a disastrous fire struck the field in March 1901.

Spindletop was not the first oil strike in Texas. Even before Europeans came to the area, oil from seeps had been used by Indians for medicinal purposes. Early Spanish explorers used it as a lubricant and to caulk boats.

Lyne Barret drilled the first commercial well near Nacogdoches in 1866. But there were few uses for his product. Oil also was used to settle dust on public roads. But it was principally used as a lubricant and occasionally as a fuel. Barret's well at Oil Springs was 106 feet deep and produced 10 barrels of oil a day. The field was abandoned and reopened in 1887, though it was never commercially profitable.

Wells also were made in Brown County in 1878 and in Bexar County in 1886 before the first major commercial well was completed at Corsicana in 1894, when oil was struck while the city was drilling a water well. The first well was abandoned, but others soon were drilled. By 1898, Corsicana had 342 wells producing 500,000 barrels of oil a year. Joseph S. Cullinan, a former employee of Standard Oil, arrived in Corsicana in 1897 and developed an integrated oil operation. He constructed the state's first pipeline to serve a refinery he also built. Cullinan also was a champion of conservation, supporting an 1899 law that required abandoned wells to be plugged. He also demonstrated the value of petroleum as a locomotive fuel.

With the development of the Corsicana wells, Texas' oil production in 1900 was 836,000 barrels a year, about one-nineteenth of the total U.S. production.

Spindletop exceeded that production within a few days. In its first year of operation, the well produced 3.2 million barrels of oil. But the price also dropped to three cents a barrel. Desperately needed new markets for oil were soon forthcoming. Railroads were the first to recognize the advantage of the new, inexpensive resource. They soon began converting locomotives from coal to oil. Steamship lines followed suit, and many industries found great cost-saving advantages in fueling boilers with inexpensive oil rather than more expensive coal. Cattlemen even experimented with oil as a possible dip to rid cattle of the ticks that carried so-called Texas Fever, although it caused the animals to get too hot in the summer. These customers supported the industry until automobiles were in widespread use.

Railroad tank cars at first were used to haul oil, but by January 1902, a pipeline had been completed from Spindletop to the Neches River. Soon lines were constructed to points on the Gulf.

Several major oil companies also got their start with Spindletop. Cullinan came from Corsicana and with partners organized the Texas Fuel Co. in 1902 and erected a refinery at Port Arthur. The company grew into Texaco. Likewise, Gulf and Mobil also trace their beginnings to Texas' first major oil strike.

Oil strikes soon followed at Sour Lake and Humble, near Houston. In North Texas, W.T. Waggoner discovered oil in 1904 while drilling for water in Wichita County. The Petrolia Field also opened in 1904, and a few years later, the Electra Field was opened. In 1917, oil was discovered at Ranger in Eastland County. The boom days of Ranger were depicted in the movie "Boom Town," and it is probably the best known of the boom towns. Discoveries followed at Burkburnett, Breckenridge, Mexia and in West Texas.

Texas' oil production grew steadily until it reached 28 million in 1905 and then declined until 1910. Thereafter the growth resumed.

Until 1928, Texas vied with California and Oklahoma for oil production leadership in the United States. But Texas gained a lead that was never relinquished after the discovery of the East Texas Field by C.M. "Dad" Joiner in October 1930. Joiner's Daisy Bradford No. 3, drilled near Kilgore, was the first of 1,000 wells drilled in the field in a six-month period. In the first year, the East Texas Field yielded 100 million barrels of oil. When it was finally defined, the field proved to be 42 miles long, four to eight miles wide and covered 200 square miles. Virtually every acre produced oil.

Natural gas, which was often considered a nuisance and wasted, also was recognized as an important resource. In 1909, Lone Star Gas was organized and ran a pipeline to carry natural gas to Dallas and Fort Worth a year later. Within a few years, the state's major cities had access to this important fuel.

Progressivism

AFTER Jim Hogg left the governor's office in 1895, the reform movement waned. The flurry of passionate political activity during the late 1880s and early 1890s left Texans ready for a respite. Hogg's successor, Charles A. Culberson, was moderately progressive, but the character of the Legislature was changing. In 1890, about half the members were farmers, but by the turn of the century, two-thirds of the lawmakers were lawyers and businessmen. Also, the reform movement had almost brought the railroads to heel, and these were the most obvious extensions of growing corporate power in Texas.

Gov. Culberson's successors, Joseph D. Sayers and S.W.T. Lanham, the last Confederate veteran to serve as governor, were more conservative than Culberson. In 1901, Sayers had to cope with the tragic hurricane that destroyed Galveston in September, killing 6,000 people. In rebuilding from that disaster, Galveston's civic leaders fashioned the commission form of municipal government that was widely copied nationally. Amarillo later refined the system into the council-manager organization that is widely used today. And the great Galveston storm also reinforced arguments by Houston's leadership that an inland port should be built for protection against such tragedies and disruptions of trade. The Houston Ship Channel was soon to be a reality.

The reform spirit in government was not completely dead, however. In 1901, the Legislature prohibited the issuing of railroad passes to public officials. More than 270,000 passes were issued to officials that year, and farmers claimed that the free rides increased their freight rates and influenced public policy as well. In 1903, State Sen. A.W. Terrell got a major election reform law approved, a measure that was further modified two years later. A primary system was established to replace a hodge-podge of practices for nominating candidates that had led to charges of irregularities after each election. And the state, for the first time, imposed the poll tax as a requisite for voting. Historians differ on whether the levy was designed to keep blacks or poor whites from voting. Certainly the poll tax cut election turnouts. Black voter participation dropped from about 100,000 in the 1890s to an estimated 5,000 in 1906. The Democratic State Executive Committee also recommended that county committees limit participation in primaries to whites only, and most accepted the suggestion.

Also in the reform spirit, the Legislature in 1903 prohibited abuse of child labor and set minimum ages at which children could work in certain industries. The action preceded federal child-labor laws by 13 years.

The election of Thomas M. Campbell as governor in 1906 introduced the progressive period in Texas politics. Interest revived in controlling corporate influence. Under Campbell, the state's anti-trust laws were strengthened and a pure food and drug law was passed.

Texas took the lead of states with similar statutes, and the Robertson Insurance Law of 1907 also had a major impact. Life insurance companies were required to invest in Texas 75 percent of their reserves on policies in effect in the state. Less than one percent of the reserves had been invested in Texas prior to the law. Some companies left Texas. But the law was beneficial in the capital-starved economy. Texas' officials also vigorously prosecuted anti-trust cases, notably the Waters-Pierce Oil Co. suit, and the state was developing an anti-business reputation.

In 1904, voters amended the constitution to allow the state to charter banks for the first time in history, and this eased some of the farmers' credit problems. In 1909, the Legislature approved a bank deposit insurance plan that predated the federal program of the 1930s.

The discovery of oil sparked an economic revolution. And other industries flourished. Lumbering entered a period of exceptional growth. In 1901, John H. Kirby organized the Kirby Lumber Co., capitalized with $10 million. The firm's mills developed a capacity to process more than 300 million board-feet of lumber a year. By 1900, Texas mills processed one billion board-feet of lumber a year, and three times in the next 20 years production topped two billion board-feet annually. The peak year was 1907 when almost 2.2 billion board feet were produced. By 1930, 18 million acres of Texas pineland had produced 60 billion board-feet of lumber over a 50-year period.

The growth in lumber production, however, brought problems. Conservationists warned of overcutting as early as the 1880s. W. Goodrich Jones, called the "Father of Texas Forestry," organized the Texas Arbor Day and Forestry Association in 1889, and in 1914, Jones founded the Texas Forestry Association. Its successor, the Texas Forest Service, today is operated by Texas A&M University. After a boom during World War I, lumbering declined in Texas. Only 354 million board-feet were produced in 1932. The state's 14 million to 16 million acre virgin pine forests had been depleted to one million acres.

In addition, lumber companies also operated much like feudal barons. Isolated company towns were built around mills, and workers, about 40 percent of whom were black, were paid in merchandise checks that could be redeemed only at company stores. Union attempts to organize lumber workers were thwarted until the 1930s. Because lumbering was far removed from most of the state's population centers, little interest was aroused by the companies' practices.

With Campbell's election, the progressive era in Texas government was underway. The era is characterized by the attempt to improve both individuals and society through government action. In Texas, with the small corporate influence under acceptable control, attention turned to the moral issue of prohibition. Progressives and prohibitionists joined forces against the conservative establishment to exert a major influence in state government for the next two decades. The period also was dominated by the personality of Joseph W. Bailey, who served as U.S. Senator from 1901 to 1913. Bailey's ethics were called into question when he served as a counsel for oil companies while in the Senate. Although he was cleared of wrongdoing by a legislative investigation, Bailey did not seek re-election in 1912. And voters split along pro-Bailey and anti-Bailey lines for many years thereafter, depending on which side of a political issue the former senator took.

Prohibitionists had long been active in Texas. They had the local-option clause written into the Constitution of 1876, which allowed counties or their subdivisions to be voted dry. In 1887, a prohibition amendment to the constitution had been defeated by a two-to-one margin, and public attention had been turned to other problems. In the early 20th century, the movement gathered strength. Most of Texas already was dry because of local option. When voters rejected a prohibition amendment to the constitution by a slim margin in 1911, the state had 167 dry counties, 61 partially wet ones and 21 totally wet counties. The heavily populated counties, however, were wet. But prohibition continued to be a major issue.

In 1910, Oscar Colquitt, a wet, won a hard-fought campaign. His administration was progressive, but turbulent.

A quiet but significant event also occurred when Lt. Benjamin D. Foulois arrived in San Antonio in 1910 with a crated biplane. The young officer had three orders: assemble the plane; learn to fly it, and teach others to fly the machine. Foulois' arrival in the Texas city marks the beginning of American military aviation. In 1911, he flew the first military mission from Laredo to Eagle Pass in record time, and by 1919, regular patrols of the border were flown.

Problems along the U.S.-Mexico border escalated in 1911. The regime of Mexican President Porfirio Diaz became increasingly unpopular. Francisco Madero challenged Diaz for the presidency in 1910 and was imprisoned for a time during the campaign. He decided that only revolution would remove the unpopular dictator from office. Madero plotted his revolution from hideouts in San Antonio and Dallas and launched his rebellion in early 1911. Soon the revolutionaries controlled some northern Mexican states, including Chihuahua. Juarez and El Paso were major contact points. El Paso residents would stand on rooftops to observe the fighting between revolutionaries and government troops. And some Americans were killed.

A thin line often divided the true revolutionaries and outright bandits. The Lower Rio Grande Valley was particularly hard hit by renegades. After pleas to the federal government got no action, Gov. Colquitt sent state militia and Texas Rangers into the Valley in 1913 to protect Texans after Matamoros fell to the rebels. Unfortunately, the Rangers killed many innocent Mexican-Texans during the operation. In addition to problems caused by the fighting and raids, thousands of Mexican refugees flooded Texas border towns to escape the violence of the revolution.

Texas progressives became prominent nationally in the presidential election of 1912. Several Texans had quietly urged New Jersey Gov. Woodrow Wilson to seek the presidency, and in the precinct caucuses of 1912, progressives gained control of the party. Texas' delegation to the national Democratic convention in Baltimore was instructed to vote for Wilson as long as his name was in nomination. Through 46 ballots, the "Immortal Forty" stuck with Wilson until he received the Democratic nomination. And Texas overwhelmingly supported Wilson at the polls. E. M. House, who had been active behind the scenes in Texas politics since Jim Hogg's second campaign in 1892, became a close personal adviser to President Wilson, and three Texans served in the cabinet: Postmaster General Albert Sidney Burleson, Attorney General Thomas Watt Gregory and Secretary of Agriculture David Houston.

Also in 1912, Texans selected a U.S. Senator at the ballot box for the first time. The Terrell Election Law required a preferential primary for all offices, although the Legislature still officially appointed U.S. Senators.

In 1906 and 1910, incumbents had not been opposed. But when Joseph Bailey declined to seek re-election in 1912, Morris Sheppard received a plurality of the popular vote. Runoffs were not required at the time. In early 1913, Gov. Colquitt recommended that the Legislature honor R.M.Johnson, a newspaper publisher and long-time conservative Democrat, by appointing him to Sen. Bailey's unserved term. Johnson was appointed senator, but served only 26 days. Sheppard's supporters argued that he should get the early appointment to gain valuable seniority over other freshmen senators, and the Legislature agreed.

In 1914, James E. Ferguson entered Texas politics, and for the next three decades, "Farmer Jim" was one of the most dominating and colorful figures on the political stage. A banker in Temple, Ferguson entered the 1914 gubernatorial campaign after a friend turned down the race. Ferguson skirted the prohibition issue by pledging to veto any legislation pertaining to alcoholic beverages. His strength was in the farming community, however. Sixty-two percent of Texas' farmers were tenants, and the candidate pledged to back legislation to limit tenant rents. Ferguson also was a dynamic orator. He easily won the primary and rolled over three opponents in the general election.

Ferguson's first administration was successful. The Legislature passed the law limiting tenants' rents, although it was poorly enforced. And aid to rural schools was improved. In early 1915, the border problems heated up. A Mexican national was arrested in Cameron County carrying a so-called "Plan of San Diego." The document outlined plans to create a rebellion of Mexican-Americans, Indians, Japanese and blacks in Texas and the Southwest. Once all Anglo males over age 16 were eliminated, a new republic controlled by blacks would be created to serve as a buffer between the United States and Mexico. Authorship of the plan has never been determined, but whatever its intent, it started a bloodbath in the Lower Rio Grande Valley. Mexican soldiers participated in raids across the Rio Grande, and Gov. Ferguson sent in the Rangers. Historians differ on the number of people who lost their lives, but a safe assessment would be "hundreds." Tensions were raised so high that Gov. Ferguson and Mexican President Venustiano Carranza met at Nuevo Laredo in November 1915 to improve relations. But the raids continued.

PANCHO Villa raided Columbus, N.M., in early 1916, and two small Texas villages in the Big Bend, Glenn Springs and Bouquillas, also were attacked. In July, President Wilson determined the hostilities were critical and activated the National Guard. Soon 100,000 American troops were stationed along the border. Fort Bliss in El Paso housed 60,000 men, and Fort Duncan near Eagle Pass was home to 16,000 more.

With the exception of Gen. John J. Pershing's pursuit of Villa into Northern Mexico, few American troops crossed into Mexico. But the service along the border gave soldiers basic training that was put to use when the United States entered World War I in 1917.

Gov. Ferguson was easily re-elected in 1916, and he worked well with the Legislature the following year. But after the Legislature adjourned, the governor got into a dispute with the board of regents of the University of Texas. The disagreement culminated with the governor vetoing all appropriations for the school. As the controversy swirled, the Travis County grand jury indicted Gov. Ferguson for misappropriation of funds and for embezzlement. In July 1917, Speaker of the Texas House F. O. Fuller called a special session of the Legislature to consider impeachment of the governor. Although the state constitution provides that only the governor can call special sessions, the attorney general said that it was appropriate for the speaker to call a session on impeachment. The Texas House voted 21 articles of impeachment, and the Senate in August 1917 convicted Ferguson on 10 of the charges. The Senate's judgment not only removed Ferguson from office, but barred him from seeking office again. Ferguson resigned the day before the Senate rendered the decision in an attempt to avoid the prohibition against seeking further office.

Lt. Gov. Will Hobby of Houston became governor. His first order of business was to mobilize Texas to fight in World War I.

War and Reaction

WILL Hobby immediately turned his attention to Texas' war effort after assuming the governorship following Ferguson's removal. Ferguson had appointed a Council of Defense to guide the state's war activities. It helped the Red Cross, conducted war-bond drives and aided in drought relief. The council also became involved in some anti-German and anti-pacifist activities that developed.

Texas participated actively in the war. Almost 200,000 young Texans, including 31,000 blacks, volunteered for military service, and 450 Texas women served in the nurses' corps. Five thousand lost their lives overseas, either fighting or in the influenza epidemics that swept the military. Texas also was a major training ground during the conflict, with 250,000 soldiers getting basic training in the state.

On the negative side, the war frenzy opened a period of intolerance and nativism in the state. German-Texans were suspect because of their national ancestry. A law was passed to prohibit speaking against the war effort. Persons who failed to participate in patriotic activities often were punished. Gov. Hobby even vetoed the appropriation for the German department at the University of Texas.

Ferguson's removal from office was a devastating blow to the state's antiprohibitionists. It was learned that the former governor had received a $156,000 loan from members of the brewers' association while in office. And this provided ammunition for the progressives. Here was an industry that had not been brought under control. With so many young men receiving military training in the state, prohibitionists proposed to prohibit saloons within a 10-mile radius of military posts to protect the soldiers from the temptations of alcohol and vice. One critic said that step alone would dry up 90 percent of the state. The measure was approved in a special session in February 1918, and at the same time, the national prohibition amendment, which had been introduced in Congress by Texas Sen. Morris Sheppard, was ratified by the lawmakers. Women also were given the right to vote in the state primaries at the same session.

Hobby easily won election to a full term as governor in 1918, and progressives and prohibitionists gained control of the Legislature.

Although national prohibition was to become effective in early 1920, the Legislature presented a prohibition amendment to voters in May 1919, and it was approved, bringing prohibition to Texas earlier than to the rest of the nation. At the same time, a women's suffrage amendment was defeated.

Although World War I ended in November 1918, it brought many changes to Texas. Rising prices during the war had increased the militancy of labor unions. Open Shop Associations were organized in many cities. And in 1921, Gov. Hobby declared martial law and called out state troops to end a dock strike in Galveston. Blacks also became more militant after the war. Discrimination against black soldiers led in 1917 to a riot in Houston in which several people were killed.

Federal courts stripped the Texas Railroad Commission of its authority to regulate interstate rates in the "Shreveport case" in 1914. The commission had set up a rate structure for goods entering Texas from Louisiana that had been detrimental to Shreveport merchants. The commission was given additional regulatory responsibility with the approval of a constitutional amendment in 1917 authorizing the state to regulate natural resources. The state also changed a long-standing policy that prohibited companies from operating in more than one field in their industry. Major oil companies needed integrated operations in which they could produce, transport,refine and sell petroleum products, and they lobbied to have the restrictive laws repealed. Finally the lawmakers agreed, and in another move, the Legislature in 1919 also prohibited the waste of natural resources, especially oil, and authorized the railroad commission to regulate pipelines, which carried petroleum. Although the commission approved a rule in 1920 that regulated the spacing of oil wells (Rule 37), little more was done. The oil industry was doing well in Texas, and everyone concerned left well enough alone.

With the election of Mexican President Alvaro Obregon in 1920, the fighting along the U.S.-Mexican border subsided. Although mistrust between the Mexicans and Texans remained for many years, a cohesive

social intercourse developed. In 1919, State Rep. J. T. Canales of Brownsville instigated an investigation of the Texas Rangers' role in the border problems. As a result of the study, the Rangers' manpower was reduced from 1,000 members to 76, and stringent limitations were placed on the agency's activities. Standards for members of the force also were upgraded. Later the Rangers were merged with the highway patrol to form the Department of Public Safety.

Pat M. Neff won the gubernatorial election of 1920, beating former Sen. Bailey. Neff visited 152 counties and made 850 speeches in his campaign. As a former prosecuting attorney in McLennan County, Neff made law and order the major thrust of his administration. Like many governors of the period, Neff was more progressive than the Legislature, and his program often fared poorly. During his administration, however, the state took full responsibility for developing a highway system. And a gasoline tax was imposed. A state park board also was established, and Neff's mother donated 10 acres of land near McGregor for the state's first park. In 1921, a group of West Texans threatened to form a new state because Neff vetoed the creation of a new college in their area. Two years later, Texas Tech College was authorized in Lubbock and opened its doors in 1925.

Neff had problems with the Legislature. Since 1907, it had become the lawmakers' practice not to pass an appropriations bill in the regular session. They were paid $5 a day for the first 60 days of the session, and only $2 a day thereafter. But they received $5 a day in special sessions. In addition, they got travel allowances when returning home between sessions. Neff called the lawmakers into special session the day after the regular session ended in March 1923, but the lawmakers met for only one hour and adjourned, ending what may have been the shortest legislative session anywhere.

Although still predominantly a rural state, Texas cities were growing. In 1900, only 17 percent of the population lived in urban areas; by 1920, that figure had almost doubled to 32 percent. A discontent developed with the growth of the cities. Rural Texans had long seen cities as hotbeds of vice and immorality. Simple rural values were cherished, and it seemed that these values were threatened in a changing world. After World War I, this transition accelerated. In addition, "foreigners" in the state became suspect; nativism reasserted itself. The German-Texans were associated with the enemy in the war, and Mexican-Texans were mostly of the Roman Catholic religion and likened to the troublemakers along the border. Texas was a fertile ground for the new Ku Klux Klan that entered the state in late 1920. The Klan's philosophy was a mixture of patriotism, law-and-order, nativism, white supremacy and Victorian morals. Its influence spread quickly as a cross the state, and reports of Klan violence and murder were rampant.

Prohibition had brought a widespread disrespect for law. Peace officers and other officials often ignored speakeasies, gambling and other vice. The Klan seemed to many Texans to be an appropriate instrument for restoring law and order and for maintaining Victorian morality in towns and cities. By 1922, many of the state's large communities were under direct Klan influence. Between 1922 and 1924 in Dallas, for example, the Klan controlled every public office in city and county government. Opposition was raised, but it was ineffective in the early stages of the development of the Klan.

In 1922, a Klan-backed candidate, Earle Mayfield, was elected to the U.S. Senate from Texas, and the state gained the reputation as the most powerful Klan bastion in the Union. Hiram Wesley Evans of Dallas also was elected imperial wizard of the national Klan in that year.

Gov. Neff never denounced the Klan by name, although he did deplore violence in any form. Once when the governor was out of the state, Lt. Gov. T. Whitfield Davidson ordered the Rangers to investigate a Klan murder. Neff concurred in the order, but soon the investigation was dropped.

After 1922, the Klan became more directly involved in politics and planned to elect the next governor in 1924. Judge Felix Robertson of Dallas got the organization's backing in the Democratic primary. Former governor Ferguson filed to run for the office, but the Texas

Supreme Court ruled that he could not because of the impeachment conviction. So Ferguson placed his wife, Miriam A. Ferguson, on the ballot. Several other prominent Democrats also entered the race.

As soon as Mrs. Ferguson entered the race, she was dubbed "Ma" from the initials of her first and middle names. And she ran a vigorous campaign, although it was her husband's oratory that attracted the crowds, particularly in rural areas. The Fergusons made no secret that Jim would have a big influence on his wife's administration. One campaign slogan was, "Two governors for the price of one." Mrs. Ferguson surprised most observers by finishing second to Robertson in the first primary. And she easily won the runoff when many Texans decided that "Fergusonism" was preferable to the Klan in the governor's office.

Minorities began organizing in Texas to seek their civil rights. The National Association for the Advancement of Colored People opened a Texas chapter in 1912, and by 1919, there were chapters in 31 Texas communities. Similarly, Mexican-Texans formed Orden Hijos de America in 1921, and in 1927, the League of Latin-American Citizens was organized.

The Klan also dominated the Legislature in 1923, and a law passed that year barring blacks from participation in the Democratic primary had been passed. Although blacks had in fact been barred from voting in primaries for years, this law gave Dr. Lawrence A. Nixon, a black dentist from El Paso, the opportunity to go to court to fight the all-white primary. In 1927, the U.S. Supreme Court overturned the statute, but that was only the beginning of several court battles — which were not resolved until 1944, when blacks were finally accorded the right to vote in Democratic primaries.

Disgruntled Democrats and Klansmen tried to beat Mrs. Ferguson in the general election, but although George Butte, the Republican nominee, did better than any other candidate running against a Democrat in many years, Ma Ferguson became governor of Texas. Voters also sent 91 new members to the Texas House, purging it of many of the Klan-backed representatives. After the 1924 election, the Klan's power ebbed rapidly in Texas.

Mrs. Ferguson named Emma Grigsby Meharg as Texas' first woman secretary of state in 1925. The governors Ferguson administration was stormy. Jim was accused of cronyism in awarding highway contracts and in other matters. And "Ma" returned to her husband's practice of liberal clemency for prisoners. In two years, Mrs. Ferguson extended clemency to 3,595 inmates.

Although Jim Ferguson was at his bombastic best in the 1926 Democratic primary, young Attorney General Dan Moody had little trouble winning the nomination and the general election. Texas Republicans in a unique twist held their first primary in 1926 because of Butte's showing against Mrs. Ferguson two years earlier. Political parties were required to hold primaries if they polled more than 100,000 votes in the previous general election.

At age 33, Moody was the youngest person ever to become governor of Texas. Like many of the state's governors, he was more progressive than the Legislature, and much of his program did not pass. Moody was successful in some government reorganization. He also cleaned up the highway department, which had been criticized under the Fergusons, and abandoned the liberal clemency policy for prisoners. And Moody worked at changing Texas' image as an anti-business state. "The day of the political trust-buster is gone," he told one Eastern journalist.

PROGRESSIVES and prohibitionists still had a major influence on the Democratic Party, and 1928 was a watershed year for them. Moody easily won re-nomination and re-election. But the state party was drifting away from the direction of national Democrats. Big-city politicians and political machines controlled by recent immigrants gained influence in the national party. Their political positions and apparent values were foreign to many Texans. When Al Smith, a wet and a Roman Catholic, won the presidential nomination at the national Democratic convention in Houston, Texans were hard-pressed to remain faithful to the "party of the fathers." Moody, who had been considered a potential national figure, ruined his political career trying to straddle the fence, angering both wets and drys, Catholics and Protestants. Former governor Colquitt led an exodus of so-called "Hoovercrats" from the state Democratic convention in 1928, and for the first time in its history, Texas gave its electoral votes to a Republican, Herbert Hoover, in the general election.

Through the 1920s, oil continued to increase in importance in Texas' economy. New discoveries were made at Mexia in 1920, Luling in 1922, Big Lake in Reagan County in 1923, in the Wortham Field in 1924 and in Borger in 1926. But oil still did not dominate the state's economic life.

As late as 1929, meat packing, cottonseed processing and various milling operations exceeded the added value of petroleum refining. And as the 1920s ended, lumbering and food processing shared major economic roles with the petroleum industry. During the decade, Texas grew between 35-42 percent of U.S. cotton and 20-30 percent of the world crop. Irrigation and mechanization opened new areas of Texas to cotton production. In 1918, the U.S. Department of Agriculture reported 50,588 bales of cotton grown on the Texas Plains. Eight years later, more than 1.1 million bales were grown in the region, mostly around Lubbock.

But Texas with the rest of the nation was on the threshhold of a major economic disaster that would have irreversible consequences. The Great Depression was at hand.

Depression and War

TEXAS suffered with the rest of the nation through the Great Depression of the 1930s. Historians have noted that the state's economic collapse was not as severe, however, as that which struck the industrialized states. Texas' economy had sputtered through the decade of the 1920s, primarily because of the fluctuation of the price of cotton and other agricultural products. But agricultural prices were improving toward the end of the decade.

The Fergusons attempted a political comeback in the gubernatorial election of 1930. But Texans elected Ross S. Sterling, the founder of Humble Oil Co. and a successful businessman. Early in the Depression, Texans remained optimistic that the economic problems were temporary, another of the cyclical downturns the nation experienced periodically. Indeed, some Texans even felt that the hardships would be beneficial, ridding the economy of speculators and poor businessmen. Those attitudes gave way to increasing concern as the poor business conditions dragged on.

A piece of good luck turned into a near economic disaster for the state in late 1930. C. M. "Dad" Joiner struck oil near Kilgore, and soon the East Texas oil boom was infull swing. Thousands of wells were drilled. Millions of barrels of new oil flooded the market, making producers and small landowners wealthy. The major oil companies had been caught by surprise by the large discovery. They owned only 20 percent of the producing leases in the region. Independent oil operators discovered the field and did most of the development.

Soon the glut of new oil drove market prices down from $1.10 a barrel in 1930 to 10 cents in 1931. Around the state many wells had to be shut in because they could not produce oil profitably at the low prices. The major companies also saw their reserves in other parts of the state losing value because of the declining prices.

The railroad commission attempted to control production through proration, which assigned production quotas to each well. The first proration order limited each well to about 1,000 barrels a day of production. Proration had two goals: To protect reserves through conservation and to maintain prices by limiting production. In August 1931, the Legislature approved a statute prohibiting the commission from prorating production to market demand. For several months, the railroad commission was hard-pressed to control production, facing resistance from producers as well as adverse court rulings. In February 1931, Gov. Sterling sent state troops into the East Texas Field to maintain order and to force compliance with the proration orders. A federal court later ruled the governor's actions illegal. Gov. Sterling was roundly criticized for sending troops into East Texas. Opponents said the action was taken to aid the major oil companies to the disadvantage of independent producers. Finally, in April 1933, the railroad commission prorated production on the basis, in part, of bottom-hole pressure in each well, and the courts upheld this approach. In Washington, Texas Sen. Tom Connally authored the Hot Oil Act, which involved the federal government in regulation by prohibiting oil produced in violation of state law from being sold in interstate commerce. Thereafter, Texas' producers accepted the concept of proration. Since Texas was the nation's largest oil producer, the railroad commission could set the national price of oil through proration for several decades thereafter.

Despite the problems, the oil boom helped East Texas weather the Depression better than other sections of the state. Farmers were hit particularly hard by 1931. Bumper crops had produced the familiar reduction in prices. Cotton dropped from 18 cents per pound in 1928 to six cents in 1931. That year Louisiana Gov. Huey Long proposed a ban on growing cotton in 1932 to eliminate the surplus. The Louisiana legislature enacted the ban, but Texas was the key state to the plan since it led the nation in cotton production. Gov. Sterling was cool to the idea, but responded to public support of it by calling a special session of the Legislature. The lawmakers passed a cotton acreage limitation bill in 1931, but the law was declared unconstitutional the following year.

Government statistics on unemployment in the period are incomplete, but in February 1932, Gov. Sterling estimated that 300,000 Texans were out of work. Many of them were destitute. One feature of the Depression had become the number of transients drifting from city to city looking for work. Local governments and private agencies tried to provide relief for the unemployed, but the effort was soon overwhelmed by the number of persons needing help. In Houston, blacks and Mexican-Texans were warned not to apply for relief because there was not enough money to take care of whites, and many Hispanics returned to Mexico voluntarily and otherwise. To relieve the local governments, Gov. Sterling proposed a bond program to repay counties for highways they had built and to start a public works program. Texans' long-held faith in self-reliance and rugged individualism was put to a severe test. As optimism faded, attempts were made to find a scapegoat. President Hoover and the Republican Party were the likely choices. The party had taken credit for the economic prosperity that the nation had enjoyed in the 1920s; but it had to assume responsibility for the collapse as well. Many Texans felt guilty about abandoning the Democratic Party in 1928. By 1932, many were looking to the federal government to provide relief from the effects of the Depression.

Texas Congressman John Nance Garner was a presidential candidate when the Democrats held their national convention. To avoid a deadlocked convention, Garner maneuvered the Texans to change strategy. On the fourth ballot, the Texas delegation voted for the eventual nominee, New York Gov. Franklin D. Roosevelt. Garner got the second place on the ticket that swept into office in the general election.

In Texas, Miriam Ferguson was successful in unseating Gov. Sterling in the Democratic primary, winning by about 4,000 votes. Her second administration was less turbulent than the first. State government costs were reduced, and voters approved $20 million in so-called "bread bonds" to help provide relief. In 1933, horse-racing came to the state, authorized through a rider on an appropriations bill. The law was repealed in 1937. Prohibition also was repealed in 1933, although much of Texas remained dry under the local-option laws and the prohibition against open saloons. State government faced a series of financial problems during Mrs. Ferguson's second term. The annual deficit climbed to $14 million, and the state had to default on the interest payments on some bonds. Voters aggravated the situation by approving a $3,000 homestead exemption. Many property owners were losing their homes because they could not pay taxes. And while the exemption saved their homesteads, it worsened the state's financial problems.

Many Texas banks failed during the Depression, as did banks nationally. One of Roosevelt's first actions was to declare a national bank holiday in 1933. Gov. Ferguson closed state banks at the same time, although she had to "assume" authority that was not in the law.

In Washington, Texans played an important role in shaping Roosevelt's New Deal. As vice president, Garner presided over the Senate and maneuvered legislation through the upper house. Texans also chaired six major committees in the House: Sam Rayburn, Interstate and Foreign Commerce; Hatton W. Sumners, Judiciary; Fritz G. Lanham, Public Buildings and Grounds; J.J. Mansfield, Rivers and Harbors, and James P. Buchanan, Appropriations. With this influence, the Texas delegation supported the president's early social programs. In addition, Jesse Jones of Hous-

ton served as director of the Reconstruction Finance Corporation, the Federal Loan Administration and as Secretary of Commerce. Jones was one of the most influential men in Washington and second only to Roosevelt in wielding financial power to effect recovery.

As the New Deal developed, Texas benefited. Almost $1.5 billion was pumped into the state's economy in the early years of President Roosevelt's program. Farmers benefited from higher incomes, though they had restrictions placed on production. Ironically, the Agricultural Adjustment Act fulfilled many of the Populists' demands of a half-century earlier by providing price protection, an expanded money supply and easy farm credit. The Federal Emergency Relief Administration, created in 1933, provided aid for up to 298,000 people a year between 1933 and 1935. And the lumber industry, which had deteriorated in the late 1920s, rebounded, as the Civilian Conservation Corps, created to provide jobs for young people, aided in replanting many acres of depleted forest lands. By 1939, the industry was producing one billion board feet of lumber again, after dropping to almost one-third that volume in 1932.

The aid to farmers and cattlemen was particularly timely because the state began to experience another cycle of drought. Poor conservation practices had left many of the state's farmlands open to erosion. During the Dust Bowl days of the early- and mid-1930s, for example, the weather bureau in Amarillo reported 192 dust storms within a three-year period. Cooperation between state and federal agencies helped improve farmers' conservation efforts and reduced the erosion problem by the end of the decade.

Although the New Deal provided economic relief for many Texans, the state became divided politically over the thrust of the program late in the 1930s. In 1937, the break became most apparent. Frustrated that the U.S. Supreme Court had declared many of the New Deal programs to be unconstitutional, President Roosevelt proposed that the membership of the court be enlarged to allow him to appoint a new majority. Vice-President Garner adamantly opposed the so-called "court-packing" plan, as did many elected officials in Texas. Although public officials' criticism became vitriolic, Roosevelt remained popular with voters, carrying the state in 1940, after Garner left the vice presidency, and in 1944.

MRS. Ferguson did not seek re-election in 1934, and Attorney General James V. Allred was elected. Under his administration, several social welfare programs were initiated, including old-age pensions, teachers' retirement and workmen's compensation. Allred also signed legislation that created the Texas Centennial celebration, marking a century of independence from Mexico. It was hoped that the Centennial would generate jobs and money. Allred was re-elected in 1936.

Some of the New Deal's luster also dimmed when the nation was struck by another recession in 1937. Although Texas' economic condition improved toward the end of the decade, a full recovery was not realized until the beginning of World War II — when the state went through another industrial revolution.

In 1938, voters elected one of the most colorful figures in the state's political history to the governor's office. W. Lee "Pappy" O'Daniel, a flour salesman and leader of a radio hillbilly band, came from nowhere to defeat a field of much better known candidates in the Democratic primary and to easily win the general election. When re-elected two years later, O'Daniel became the first candidate to poll more than one million votes in a Texas election.

But O'Daniel's skills of state did not equal his campaigning ability, and throughout his administration, the governor and the Legislature were in conflict. In early 1941, long-time U.S. Senator Morris Sheppard died, and O'Daniel wanted the office. He appointed Andrew Jackson Houston, Sam Houston's aged son, to fill the vacancy. Houston died after only 24 days in office. O'Daniel won the special election for the post and was elected to a full term in 1942 in a close race with a young congressman, Lyndon B. Johnson.

Lt. Gov. Coke R. Stevenson succeeded O'Daniel and brought a broad knowledge of government to the office. Stevenson was elected to two full terms as governor. Thanks to frugal management and greatly increasing revenues during the war years, he left the state treasury with a surplus in 1947. Voters also solved the continuing deficit problem by approving a pay-as-you-go amendment to the constitution in 1942. It requires the state comptroller to certify that tax revenues will be available to support appropriations. Otherwise the money cannot be spent.

After the Japanese bombed Pearl Harbor on Dec. 7, 1941, Texans were in the forefront of the World War II effort. Texas Sen. Tom Connally, chairman of the Foreign Relations Committee, introduced the resolution declaring war on Japan on Dec. 8.

As in every war fought by the United States after Texas entered the Union, young Texans flocked to military service. More than 750,000 served, including 12,000 women in the auxiliary services. In December 1942, U.S. Secretary of the Navy Frank Knox said Texas contributed the largest percentage of its male population to the armed forces of any state. Thirty Texans won Congressional Medals of Honor in the fighting, and Audie Murphy, a young farm boy from Farmersville, was the most decorated soldier in the war.

Important contributions also were made at home.

Texas was the site of 15 training posts, at which more than one and a quarter million men were trained, and of several prisoner-of-war camps.

Texas industry also flourished. Between mid-1940 and the peak of wartime production activity in November 1943, the number of manufacturing workers in Texas rose from 185,000 to 443,000. New industries that started up during the period included aircraft construction, ordnance and primary metals. Shipbuilders on the Texas Gulf coast employed 96,000 workers, and the aircraft industries employed 82,000. The state's petrochemical industry also expanded.

Between 1919 and 1939, Texas' manufacturing grew at a rate of 4.06 percent a year; in the next 15 years, the growth rate would accelerate to 9.38 percent annually. World War II changed the face of the world, but probably no region was affected more than Texas. The state was on the threshhold of becoming one of the nation's industrial giants.

Post-War Texas

WORLD War II irrevocably changed the face of Texas. During the decade of the 1940s, the state's population switched from predominantly rural to 60 percent urban. The number of manufacturing workers almost doubled. And as had been the dream of Texas leaders for more than a century, the state began to attract out side investment and new industry.

The state's politics became increasingly controlled by conservative Democrats after Gov. Allred left office. In 1946, Beauford H. Jester, a member of the railroad commission, gained the governorship. Under Jester in 1947, the Legislature passed the state's right-to-work law, prohibiting mandatory union membership, and reorganized public education with passage of the Gilmer-Aikin Act.

In 1948, Sen. W. Lee O'Daniel did not seek re-election. Congressman Lyndon Johnson and former Gov. Coke Stevenson vied for the Democratic nomination. In the runoff, Johnson won by a mere 87 votes in the closest — and most hotly disputed — statewide election in Texas' history. Johnson quickly rose to a leadership position in the U.S. Senate, and, with House Speaker Sam Rayburn, gave Texas substantial influence in national political affairs.

During the Jester administration several major constitutional amendments were adopted. Also, one of Texas' greatest tragedies occurred on April 16, 1947, when the French SS Grandcamp exploded at Texas City. This caused 4,000 injuries, with 512 dead. Property damage exceeded $200 million.

Although re-elected in 1948, Jester died in July 1949, the only Texas governor to die in office, and Lt. Gov. Allan Shivers succeeded him. During Shivers' administration, state spending more than doubled, reaching $805.7 million in 1956, as the governor increased appropriations for eleemosynary institutions, school salaries, retirement benefits, highways and old-age pensions. The 51st Legislature met for a total of 177 days in regular and special sessions in 1947, a record at the time.

Shivers broke with tradition, successfully winning three full terms as governor after completing Jester's unexpired term. Shivers also led a revolt by Texas Democrats against the national party in 1952. The governor, who gained both the Democratic and Republican nominations for the office under the law that allowed cross-filing that year, supported Republican Dwight Eisenhower for the presidency. Many Texas Democrats broke with the national party over the so-called "Tidelands issue." Texas claimed land 12 miles out into the Gulf as state lands. The issue was important because revenue from oil and natural gas production from the area supported public education in the state. Major oil companies also backed Texas' position because state royalties on minerals produced from the land were much lower than federal royalties. President Harry S. Truman vetoed legislation that would have given Texas title to the land. Democratic presidential nominee Adlai Stevenson was no more sympathetic to the issue, and Texas gave its electoral votes to Republican Dwight Eisenhower in an election that attracted a two million-vote turnout for the first time in Texas. President Eisenhower signed a measure into law guaranteeing Texas' tidelands.

Scandal struck state government in 1954 when irregularities were discovered in the handling of funds in the veterans' land program in the General Land Office. Land Commissioner Bascom Giles was convicted of several charges and sent to prison. Several insurance companies also went bankrupt in the mid-1950s, prompting a reorganization of the State Board of Insurance in 1957.

In 1954, the U.S. Supreme Court ruled unconstitutional the segregation of schools, and for the next quarter-century, school integration became a major political issue. By the late 1960s, most institutions were integrated, but the state's major cities continued to wage court battles against forced busing of students to attain racial balance. Blacks and Mexican-Texans also made gains in voting rights during the 1950s.

Shivers had easily defeated Ralph W. Yarborough in the Democratic primary in 1952, but the divisions between the party's loyalists and those who bolted ranks to join Republicans in presidential races were growing. Shivers barely led the first 1954 primary over Yarborough and won the nomination with 53 percent of the vote in the runoff. Yarborough ran an equally close race against Price Daniel, a U.S. Senator who sought the governorship in 1956. Upon election as governor, Daniel left the Senate, and Yarborough won a special election to fill the vacancy in 1957. William A. Blakley, whom Yarborough defeated, had been appointed to the Senate seat by Shivers. In 1961, Blakley also was appointed to fill the vacancy created by Sen. Lyndon B. Johnson's election to the vice presidency. Blakley has the distinction of serving in both the Rusk and Houston successions in the Senate. Yarborough beat Blakley for a full term in 1958 and won re-election in 1964 before losing to Lloyd Bentsen in 1970 in the Democratic primary. Although a liberal, Yarborough proved to be unusually durable in Texas' conservative political climate.

The state budget topped $1 billion for the first time in 1958. A year later, a financial crisis gripped state government. Three special sessions were needed for the lawmakers to agree on a record appropriations bill. In 1960, voters approved a constitutional amendment that limited regular sessions to 140 days. The Legislature met for 205 days in regular and special sessions in 1961-62 and levied, over Gov. Daniel's opposition, the state's first broad-based sales tax in 1962.

THROUGH the 1950s and 1960s, Texas' industrial base had expanded and diversified. Petroleum exploration, production, transportation and refining remained the cornerstones, but other industries grew. Attracted by cheap electricity, the aluminum industry came to Texas after World War II. Starting from the base developed during World War II, defense industries and associated high-tech firms, specializing in electronics and computers, centered on the Dallas-Fort Worth area and Houston. One of the most important scientific breakthroughs of the century came in 1959 in Dallas. Jack Kilby, an engineer at Texas Instruments, developed and patented the microchip that became the central part of the computers of the 1980s.

Sen. Lyndon Johnson unsuccessfully sought the Democratic presidential nomination in 1960, and John F. Kennedy subsequently selected the Texan as his running mate. Johnson is credited with keeping several Southern states, including Texas, in the Democratic column in the close election. Kennedy was a Roman Catholic and a liberal, a combination normally rejected by the Southern states. When Johnson left the Senate to assume his new office in 1961, John Tower won a special election that attracted more than 70 candidates and became the first Republican since Reconstruction to serve as a Texas Senator.

During the early 1960s, Harris County was chosen as the site for the National Aeronautics and Space Administration's manned spacecraft center, now the Lyndon B. Johnson Space Center. The acquisition of the facility further diversified Texas' industrial base.

In 1962, John B. Connally, a former aide to Vice President Johnson and Secretary of the Navy under Kennedy, returned to Texas to seek the governorship. Gov. Daniel sought an unprecedented fourth term and was defeated in the Democratic primary. Connally won a close Democratic runoff over Don Yarborough and was elected easily. As governor, Connally concentrated on improving public education and state services and water development. He was re-elected in 1964 and 1966.

One of the major tragedies in the nation's history occurred in Dallas on Nov. 22, 1963, when President Kennedy was assassinated while riding in a motorcade. Gov. Connally also was seriously wounded. Lyndon B. Johnson was administered the oath of the presidency by Federal Judge Sarah T. Hughes of Dallas aboard Air Force One at Love Field. Lee Harvey Oswald was arrested for the murder of the president on the afternoon of the assassination, but Oswald was killed by Dallas nightclub operator Jack Ruby the following day. An extensive investigation into the assassination of President Kennedy was conducted by the Warren Commission. The panel concluded that Oswald was the killer and that he acted alone. Ruby, who was convicted of killing Oswald, died of cancer in the Dallas County jail in 1967 while the case was being appealed.

The assassination damaged the Republican Party in Texas, however. Building strength in Texas' conservative political atmosphere in 1962, eight Republicans, the most in decades, had been elected to the Texas House. And two Republicans — Ed Foreman of Odessa and Bruce Alger of Dallas — served in Congress. All were defeated in the 1964 general election.

In the emotional aftermath of the tragedy, Johnson, who won the presidency outright in a landslide election in 1964, persuaded the Congress to pass a series of civil rights and social welfare programs that changed the face of the nation. Texas was particularly hard hit by the civil rights legislation and a series of lawsuits challenging election practices. During the 1960s, the state constitutional limitation of urban representation in the Legislature was overturned. The poll tax was declared unconstitutional, and the practice of electing officials from at-large districts fell to the so-called "one-man, one-vote" ruling. As a result, more Republican, minority and liberal officials were elected, particularly from urban areas. In 1966, Curtis Graves and Barbara Jordan of Houston and Joe Lockridge of Dallas became the first blacks to serve in the Texas Legislature since 1898.

Lyndon Johnson did not seek re-election in 1968. The nation had become involved in an unpopular war in South Vietnam, and Johnson bowed out of the race in the interest of national unity. Democrats, however, stayed firmly in control of state government. Preston Smith was elected governor, and Ben Barnes gained the lieutenant governorship. Both also were re-elected in 1970. Although state spending continued to increase, particularly on education, the Legislature otherwise was quiet. A minimum-wage law was approved, and public kindergartens were authorized in 1969. At a special session, one of the state's major scandals developed. Gov. Smith allowed the lawmakers to consider special banking legislation supported by Houston banker Frank Sharp. Several public officials were implicated in receiving favors from the banker for seeing that the legislation passed. Texas House Speaker Gus Mutscher and Rep. Tommy Shannon were convicted of conspiracy to accept bribes in a trial held in Abilene. Mutscher subsequently completed his probation, had his rights restored and was elected county judge of Washington County.

But voters in 1972 demanded a new leadership in the state capital. Smith and Barnes were defeated in the Democratic primary, and Dolph Briscoe was elected governor. William P. Hobby Jr., son of the former governor, was elected lieutenant governor. In the fall, Texans gave presidential candidate Richard Nixon the state's electoral votes. Nixon carried 246 counties over Democrat George McGovern and received more than 65 percent of the popular vote, the largest recorded by a Republican in Texas.

The Legislature in 1973 was dominated by a reform atmosphere in the wake of the Sharpstown scandal. Price Daniel Jr., son of the former governor, was selected speaker of the House, and several laws concerning ethics and disclosure of campaign donations and spending were passed. Open meetings and open records statutes also were approved.

By 1970, Texas had become an even more urban state. The census found almost 11.2 million people in the state, ranking it sixth nationally. Three Texas cities, Houston, Dallas and San Antonio, were among the 10 largest in the nation.

Through the first half of the 1970s, several major changes were made in state policy. Liquor-by-the-drink had become legal, the age of majority had been lowered from 20 to 18, giving young people the right to vote, and the state's first Public Utilities Commission was created, hearing its initial case in September 1976.

Texas entered a period of unparalleled prosperity in 1973 when the Organization of Petroleum Exporting Countries boycotted the American market. Severe energy shortages resulted, and the price of oil and natural gas skyrocketed. The federal government had allowed foreign oil to be imported through the 1960s, severely reducing the incentives to find and produce domestic oil. Consequently, domestic producers could not compensate for the loss in foreign oil as a result of the boycott. The Texas Railroad Commission had long complained about the importation of foreign oil, and in 1972, the panel had removed proration controls from wells in the state, allowing 100 percent production. For the rest of the decade, domestic producers mounted a major exploration effort, drilling thousands of wells. Nevertheless, Texas' oil and gas production peaked in 1970 and has been declining since. Newly discovered oil and gas have not replaced the declining reserves. While Texans suffered from the inflation that followed, the state prospered. Tax revenues at all levels of government increased, and state revenues, basically derived from oil and gas taxes, spiraled, as did the state budget.

WITH the new revenue from inflation and petroleum taxes, state spending rose from $2.95 billion in 1970 to $8.6 billion in 1979, and education led the advance, moving from 42 percent of the budget to 51.5 percent. But there was no increase in state tax rates.

It was no surprise that education was one of the major beneficiaries of increased state spending. After World War II, more emphasis was placed on education across the state. Community colleges sprang up in many cities, and a total of 109 colleges were established between the end of the war and 1980. Quantity did not assure quality, however, and Texas' public and higher education seldom were ranked among national leaders.

In 1972, voters approved an amendment authorizing the Legislature to sit as a Constitutional Convention to rewrite the 1876 charter. Judge Robert W. Calvert, former chief justice of the Texas Supreme Court, served as chairman of the Texas Constitutional Revision Commission that held hearings around the state and proposed a new constitution to the Legislature in 1974. But the lawmakers met for several months, spent $5 million and failed to propose anything to be considered by voters. The public was outraged, and in 1975 the Legislature presented the work of the convention to voters in the form of eight constitutional amendments. All were defeated in a special election in November 1975.

Texas voters participated in their first presidential primary in 1976. Jimmy Carter of Georgia won the Democratic primary, and eventually the presidency and Ronald Reagan carried the state's Republicans but lost the party's nomination to President Gerald Ford.

In 1977, Texas farmers joined a national farm protest movement against price levels for their products which, they said, were being sold below the cost of production.

The state proved politically volatile in 1978. First Attorney General John Hill defeated Gov. Dolph Briscoe in the Democratic primary. A political newcomer William P. Clements, upset Hill in the general election giving Texas its first Republican governor since Reconstruction. And also for the first time since Reconstruction, state officials were elected for four-year terms. And a major shakeup occurred in the state's congressional delegation when six members of the U.S. House retired and three more were defeated at the polls. Texas, which usually had strong, experienced representation in Washington, included nine freshmen congressmen in its 24-member delegation.

Bibliography

Books

Adams, Frank Carter, **Texas Democracy: A Centennial History of Politics and Personalities of the Democratic Party 1836-1936, Vol. I**; Democratic Historical Association, Austin, 1936.

Adams, Willena C., editor, **Texas Cities and the Great Depression**; Texas Memorial Museum, Austin, 1973.

Ashcraft, Allan C., **Texas in the Civil War**; Texas Civil War Centennial Commission, Austin, 1962.

Ashford, Gerald, **Spanish Texas: Yesterday and Today**; Jenkins Publishing Co., The Pemberton Press, Austin, 1971.

Barker, Eugene C., editor, **Readings in Texas History**; Southwest Press, Dallas, 1929.

Barker, Eugene C., **The Life of Stephen F. Austin, Founder of Texas, 1793-1836**; Cokesbury Press, Dallas, 1926.

Barksdale, E.C., **The Genesis of the Aviation Industry in North Texas**; Bureau of Business Research, University of Texas, Austin, 1958.

Barnhill, J. Herschel, **From Surplus to Substitution: Energy in Texas**; American Press, Boston, 1983.

Barr, Alwyn, **Black Texans: A History of Negroes in Texas 1528-1971**; Jenkins Publishing Co., The Pemberton Press, Austin, 1973.

Barr, Alwyn, **Reconstruction to Reform: Texas Politics, 1876-1906**; University of Texas Press, Austin, 1971.

Becerra, Francisco, **A Mexican Sergeant's Recollections of the Alamo and San Jacinto**; Jenkins Publishing Co., Austin, 1980.

Bertrand, Louis, and Sir Charles Petrie, **The History of Spain: From the Musulmans to Franco**; Collier Books, New York, 1971.

Binkley, William C., **The Expansionist Movement in Texas 1836-1850**; University of California Publications in History, Vol. 13, University of California Press, Berkeley, 1925.

Binkley, William C., **The Texas Revolution**; Louisiana State University Press, Baton Rouge, 1952 (rpt. Texas State Historical Association, Austin, 1979).

Brown, Norman D., **Hood, Bonnet, and Little Brown Jug**; Texas A&M University Press, College Station, 1984.

Buenger, Walter L., **Secession and the Union in Texas**; University of Texas Press, Austin, 1984.

Campbell, Randolph B., and Richard G. Lowe, **Wealth and Power in Antebellum Texas**; Texas A&M University Press, College Station, 1977.

Casdorph, Paul, **The Republican Party in Texas, 1865-1965**; Jenkins Publishing Co., The Pemberton Press, Austin, 1965.

Castaneda, Carlos E., editor, **The Mexican Side of the Texas Revolution**; P.L. Turner Co., Austin, 1928 (rpt. Graphic Ideas, Inc., Austin, 1970).

Castaneda, Carlos E., **Our Catholic Heritage in Texas, Vols. 1-3**; Von Boeckmann-Jones Co., Austin, 1933-38.

Clarke, Mary Whatley, **Thomas J. Rusk: Soldier, Statesman, Jurist**; Jenkins Publishing Co., The Pemberton Press, Austin, 1971.

Connor, Seymour V., **Adventure in Glory: The Saga of Texas, 1836-1849**; Steck-Vaughn Co., Austin, 1965.

Cotner, Robert C., **James Stephen Hogg: A Biography**; University of Texas Press, Austin, 1959.

Crocket, G.L., **Two Centuries in East Texas**; Southwest Press, Dallas, 1932.

Davis, Ronald L., **Twentieth Century Cultural Life in Texas**; American Press, Boston, 1981.

De la Pena, Jose Enrique, **With Santa Anna in Texas: A Personal Narrative of the Revolution**, Trans. Carmen Perry; Texas A&M University Press, College Station, 1975.

DeLeon, Arnoldo, **The Mexican Image in Nineteenth Century Texas**; American Press, Boston, 1982.

DeLeon, Arnoldo, **The Tejano Community, 1836-1900**; University of New Mexico Press, Albuquerque, 1982.

DeLeon, Arnoldo, **They Called Them Greasers: Anglo Attitudes Toward Mexicans in Texas, 1821-1900**; University of Texas Press, Austin, 1983.

DeVoto, Bernard, **The Year of Decision: 1846**; Little, Brown and Co., Boston, 1943.

Dixon, Sam Houston, and Louis Wiltz Kemp, **The Heroes of San Jacinto**; Anson Jones Press, Houston, 1932.

Dodge, Bertha S., **Cotton: The Plant That Would Be King**; University of Texas Press, Austin, 1984.

Drinnon, Richard, **Facing West: The Metaphysics of Indian-Hating and Empire-Building**; New American Library, New York, 1980.

Durham, George, **Taming the Nueces Strip**; University of Texas Press, Austin, 1982.

Easterlin, Richard A., David Ward, William Bernard, and Reed Ueda, **Immigration**; Belknap Press of Harvard University Press, Cambridge, 1982.

Farber, James, **Texas, C.S.A.: A Spotlight on Disaster**; The Jackson Co., New York, 1947.

Fehrenbach, T.R., **Comanches: The Destruction of a People**; Alfred A. Knopf Co., New York, 1976.

Fehrenbach, T.R., **Lone Star: A History of Texas and the Texans**; MacMillan Co., New York, 1968.

Foner, Eric, **Nothing But Freedom: Emancipation and Its Legacy**; Louisiana State University Press, Baton Rouge, 1983.

Fornell, Earl Wesley, **The Galveston Era: The Texas Crescent on the Eve of Secession**; University of Texas Press, Austin, 1961.

Frantz, Joe B., **Texas: A Bicentennial History**; W. W. Norton & Co., New York, 1976.

Friend, Llerena B., **Sam Houston: The Great Designer**; University of Texas Press, Austin, 1954.

Gambrell, Herbert, **Anson Jones: The Last President of Texas**; Doubleday and Co., Inc., Garden City, N.J., 1948.

Gard, Wayne, **The Chisholm Trail**; University of Oklahoma Press, Norman, 1954.

Goodwyn, Lawrence, **The Populist Moment: A Short History of the Agrarian Revolt in America**; Oxford University Press, New York, 1978.

Gouge, William M., **The Fiscal History of Texas**; Lippincott, Grambo, and Co., Philadelphia, 1852.

Gould, Lewis L., **Progressives and Prohibitionists: Texas Democrats in the Wilson Era**; University of Texas Press, Austin, 1973.

Graham, Philip, **The Life and Poems of Mirabeau Buonaparte Lamar**; University of North Carolina Press, Chapel Hill, 1938.

Grant, Joseph M., and Lawrence L. Crum, **The Development of State Chartered Banking in Texas**; Bureau of Business Research, University of Texas at Austin, 1978.

Green, George Norris, **A Liberal's View of Texas Politics, 1890s-1930s**; American Press, Boston, 1981.

Green, George Norris, **A Liberal View of Texas Politics Since the 1930s**; American Press, Boston, 1981.

Green, George Norris, **The Establishment in Texas Politics: The Primitive Years, 1938-1957**; Greenwood Press, Westport, Conn., 1979.

Gregory, Jack, and Rennard Strickland, **Sam Houston with the Cherokees 1829-1833**; University of Texas Press, Austin, 1967.

Haley, J. Evetts, **The XIT Ranch of Texas and the Early Days of the Llano Estacado**; University of Oklahoma Press, Norman, 1954.

Hanke, Lewis, **Aristotle and the American Indian: A Study of Race Prejudice in the Modern World**; University of Indiana Press, Bloomington, 1959.

Harper, William G., **The Texas Blue Laws**; Exposition Press, Hicksville, N.Y., 1974.

Hawkins, Wallace, **El Sal Del Rey**; Texas State Historical Association, 1947.

Henson, Margaret S., **Anglo American Women in Texas, 1820-1850**; American Press, Boston, 1982.

Hewitt, W. Phil, **Land and Community: European Migration to Rural Texas in the 19th Century**; American Press, Boston, 1981.

Hinkle, Stacy C., **Wings Over the Border: The Army Air Service Armed Patrol of the United States-Mexico Border 1919-1921**; Southwestern Studies, Texas Western Press, El Paso, 1970.

Hogan, William Ransom, **The Texas Republic**; University of Texas Press, Austin, 1969.

Horgan, Paul, **The Great River, Vols. 1-2**; Rinehart & Co., Inc., New York, 1954.

Horsman, Reginald, **Race and Manifest Destiny: The Origins of American Racial Anglo-Saxonism**; Harvard University Press, Cambridge, 1981.

Innes, Hammond, **The Conquistadors**; Alfred A. Knopf, New York, 1969.

Institute of Texan Cultures, **The Indian Texans**; University of Texas at San Antonio, 1970.

Institute of Texan Cultures, **The Spanish Texans**; University of Texas at San Antonio, 1972.

Irby, James A., **Backdoor at Bagdad**; Southwestern Series, Texas Western Press, El Paso, 1968.

James, Marquis, **The Raven: A Biography of Sam Houston**; Blue Ribbon Books, Inc., New York City, 1929.

John, Elizabeth A.H., **Storms Brewed In Other Men's Worlds: The Confrontation of Indians, Spanish and French** in the Southwest, 1540-1795; Texas A&M University Press, College Station, 1975.

Jones, Billy M., The Search for Maturity: Saga of Texas, 1875-1900; Steck-Vaughn Co., Austin, 1965.

Jordan, Terry G., Environment and Environmental Perceptions in Texas; American Press, Boston, 1980.

Jordan, Terry G., Immigration to Texas; American Press, Boston, 1980.

Jordan, Terry G., Trails to Texas: Southern Roots of Western Cattle Ranching; University of Nebraska Press, Lincoln, 1981.

Leckie, William H., The Buffalo Soldiers: A Narative of the Negro Cavalry in the West; University of Oklahoma Press, Norman, 1967.

Lindheim, Milton, The Republic of the Rio Grande; W.M. Morrison, Bookseller, Waco, 1964.

Lockhart, James, and Stuart B. Schwartz, Early Latin America: A History of Colonial Spanish America and Brazil; Cambridge University Press, Cambridge, 1983.

Lord, Walter, A Time to Stand: The Epic of the Alamo; Harpers & Row, New York, 1961 (rpt. University of Nebraska Press, Lincoln, 1978).

Lukes, Edward A., DeWitt Colony of Texas; Jenkins Publishing Co., The Pemberton Press, Austin, 1976.

Malone, Dumas, Jefferson the President: First Term 1801-1805; Little, Brown and Co., Boston, 1970.

Malone, Dumas, Jefferson the President: Second Term 1805-1809; Little, Brown and Co., New York, 1974.

Martin, Roscoe, The People's Party in Texas: A Study in Third Party Politics; University of Texas Press, Austin, 1970.

Maxwell, Robert S., and Robert D. Baker, Sawdust Empire: The Texas Lumber Industry, 1830-1940; Texas A&M University Press, College Station, 1983.

Maxwell, Robert S., Texas Economic Growth, 1890 to World War II: From Frontier to Industrial Giant; American Press, Boston, 1981.

McDonald, Archie P., Texas: All Hail the Mighty State; Eakin Press, Austin, 1983.

McDonald, Archie P., The Trail to San Jacinto; American Press, Boston, 1981.

McDonald, Archie P., Travis; Jenkins Publishing Co., The Pemberton Press, Austin, 1976.

McDonald, Archie P., The Republic of Texas; American Press, Boston, 1981.

McKay, Seth S., and Odie B. Faulk, Texas After Spindletop: Saga of Texas, 1901-1965; Steck-Vaughn Co., Austin, 1965.

Meinig, D.W., Imperial Texas: An Interpretive Essay in Cultural Geography; University of Texas Press, Austin, 1969.

Merk, Frederick, The History of the Westward Movement; Alfred E. Knopf, New York, 1978.

Meyer, Michael C., and Sherman, William L., The Course of Mexican History; Oxford University Press, New York, 1979.

Miller, Hurbert J., Jose de Escandon, Colonizer of Nuevo Santander; New Santander Press, Edinburg, 1980.

Miller, Thomas L., The Public Lands of Texas, 1519-1970; University of Oklahoma Press, Norman, 1972.

Moneyhon, Carl H., Republicanism in Reconstruction Texas; University of Texas Press, Austin, 1980.

Myres, John Myres, The Alamo; E.P. Dutton and Co., 1948 (rpt. University of Nebraska Press, Lincoln, 1973).

Myres, Sandra L., Native Americans of Texas; American Press, Boston, 1981.

Newcomb, W.W. Jr., The Indians of Texas; University of Texas Press, Austin, 1961.

Norman, Mary Anne, The Texas Economy Since World War II; American Press, Boston, 1983.

Nunn, W.C., Texas Under the Carpetbaggers; University of Texas Press, Austin, 1962.

Pettigrew, Thomas E., George M. Fredrickson, Dale T. Knobel, Nathan Glazer and Reed Ueda, Prejudice; Belknap Press of Harvard University Press, Cambridge, 1982.

Pilkington, William T., Imaging Texas: The Literature of the Lone Star State; American Press, Boston, 1981.

Price, Glenn W., Origins of the War with Mexico: Polk-Stockton Intrigue; University of Texas Press, Austin, 1967.

Prindle, David F., Petroleum Politics and the Texas Railroad Commission; University of Texas Press, Austin, 1981.

Procter, Ben H., Not Without Honor: The Life of John H. Reagan; University of Texas Press, Austin, 1962.

Puryear, Pamela A., and Nath Winfield Jr., Sandbars and Sternwheelers: Navagation on the Brazos; Texas A&M University Press, College Station, 1976.

Raat, W. Dirk, editor, Mexico: From Independence to Revolution, 1810-1910; University of Nebraska Press, Lincoln, 1982.

Raat, W. Dirk, Revoltosos; Texas A&M University Press, College Station, 1981.

Ramsdell, Charles William, Reconstruction in Texas; Columbia University Press, New York, 1910 (rpt. University of Texas Press, Austin, 1970).

Red, William Stuart, The Texas Colonists and Religion 1821-1836; E. L. Shettles, Publisher, Austin, 1924.

Reed, S.G., A History of the Texas Railroads; St. Clair Publishing Co., Houston, 1941.

Rice, Lawrence D., The Negro in Texas 1874-1900; Louisiana State University Press, Baton Rouge, 1971.

Richardson, Rupert N., Colonel House: The Texas Years; Hardin-Simmons University Publications in History, Abilene, 1964.

Richardson, Rupert N., Ernest Wallace and Adrian N. Anderson, Texas: The Lone Star State; Prentice-Hall, Inc., Englewood Cliffs, N.J., 1970.

Richardson, Rupert N., The Frontier of Northwest Texas, 1846-1876; The Arthur H. Clark Co., Glendale, Calif., 1963.

Rodriguez, Louis J., Dynamics of Growth: An Economic Profile of Texas; Madrona Press, Austin, 1978.

Rosenbaum, Robert J., Mexican Resistance in the Southwest; University of Texas Press, Austin, 1981.

Rosenbaum, Robert J., The History of Mexican Americans in Texas; American Press, Boston, 1980.

Rutherford, Bruce, Ferguson: The Impeachment of Jim Ferguson; Eakin Press, Austin, 1983.

Samora, Julian, Joe Bernal and Albert Pena, Gunpowder Justice: A Reassessment of the Texas Rangers; Notre Dame Press, South Bend, 1979.

Sibley, Marilyn McAdams, The Port of Houston, A History; University of Texas Press, Austin, 1968.

Sierra, Justo, The Political Evolution of the Mexican People, trans. Charles Ramsdell; University of Texas Press, Austin, 1969.

Silverthorne, Elizabeth, Ashbel Smith of Texas: Pioneer, Patriot, Statesman, 1805-1886; Texas A&M University Press, College Station, 1982.

Smallwood, James, The Great Recovery: The New Deal in Texas; American Press, Boston, 1983.

Smallwood, James, The Struggle for Equality: Blacks in Texas; American Press, Boston, 1983.

Smithwick, Noah, The Evolution of a State or Recollections of Old Texas Days; H.P.N. Gammell, Austin, 1900 (rpt. University of Texas Press, Austin, 1983).

Smyrl, Frank H., Texas in Gray: The Civil War Years, 1861-1865; American Press, Boston, 1983.

Smyrl, Frank H., The Twenty-Eighth Star: Texas During the Period of Early Statehood, 1846-1861; American Press, Boston, 1983.

Sonnichsen, C.L., Pass of the North: Four Centuries on the Rio Grande, Vol. I -1529-1917; Texas Western Press, UT-El Paso, 1968.

Spratt, John Stricklin, The Road to Spindletop: Economic Change in Texas, 1875-1901; SMU Press, Dallas, 1955 (rpt. University of Texas Press, Austin, 1970).

Stambaugh, J. Lee, and Lillian J., The Lower Rio Grande Valley of Texas: Its Colonization and Industrialization, 1518-1953; The Jenkins Co., San Felipe Press, Austin, 1974.

Syers, Ed, Texas: The Beginning 1519-1834; Texian Press, Waco, 1978.

Taylor, Virginia H., The Franco-Texan Land Co.; University of Texas Press, Austin, 1969.

Timmons, W.H., The Anglo-American Advance Into Texas, 1810-1830; American Press, Boston, 1981.

Tinkle, Lon, The Alamo (13 Days to Glory, McGraw-Hill Book Co., New York, 1958); New American Library, New York.

Tolbert, Frank, The Day of San Jacinto; McGraw-Hill Book Co., Inc., New York, 1959.

Utley, Robert M., The Indian Frontier of the American West 1846-1890; University of New Mexico Press, Albuquerque, 1984.

Vigness, David M., The Revolutionary Decades: The Saga of Texas, 1810-1836; Steck-Vaughn Co., Austin, 1965.

Vigness, David M., Spanish Texas, 1519-1810; American Press, Boston, 1983.

Wallace, Ernest, Charles DeMorse: Pioneer Editor and Statesman; Texas Tech Press, Lubbock, 1943.

Wallace, Ernest, and David M. Vigness, Documents of Texas History; The Steck Co., Austin, 1963.

Wallace, Ernest, and E. Adamson Hoebel, The Comanches: Lords of the South Plains; University of Oklahoma Press, Norman, 1952.

Wallace, Ernest, The Howling of Coyotes: Reconstruction Efforts to Divide Texas; Texas A&M University Press, College Station, 1979.

Wallace, Ernest, Ranald S. Mackenzie on the Texas

Frontier; West Texas Museum Association, Lubbock, 1965.

Wallace, Ernest, **Texas in Turmoil: The Saga of Texas: 1849-1875**; Steck-Vaughn Co., Austin, 1965.

Webb, Walter Prescott, and H. Bailey Carroll, editors, **Handbook of Texas, Vols. 1-3**; Texas State Historical Association, Austin, 1952 and 1976.

Webb, Walter Prescott, **The Great Frontier**; University of Texas Press, Austin, 1964.

Webb, Walter Prescott, **The Great Plains**; University of Nebraska Press, Lincoln, 1981.

Webb, Walter Prescott, **The Texas Rangers: A Century of Frontier Defense**; Houghton Mifflin, Boston, 1935 (rpt.University of Texas Press, Austin, 1980).

Weber, David J., **The Mexican Frontier, 1821-1846: The American Southwest Under Mexico**; University of New Mexico Press, Albuquerque, 1982.

Weber, David J., editor, **New Spain's Far Northern Frontier**; University of New Mexico Press, Albuquerque, 1979.

Weddle, Robert S., **San Juan Bautista: Gateway to Spanish Texas**; University of Texas Press, Austin, 1968.

Weddle, Robert S., **Wilderness Manhunt: The Spanish Search for LaSalle**; University of Texas Press, Austin, 1973.

Whisenhunt, Donald W., editor, **Texas: A Sesquicentennial Celebration**; Eakin Press, Austin, 1984.

Whisenhunt, Donald W., editor, **The Depression in the Southwest**; Kennikat Press, Port Washington, N.Y., 1980.

Whisenhunt, Donald W., **The Depression in Texas**; American Press, Boston, 1982.

Whisenhunt, Donald W., **The Depression in Texas: The Hoover Years**; Garland Publishing, Inc., New York, 1983.

Whisenhunt, Donald W., **The Development of Higher Education in Texas**; American Press, Boston, 1983.

White, Dabney, editor, and T. C. Richardson, author, **East Texas: Its History and Its Makers, Vols. I-IV**; Lewis Historical Publishing Co., New York.

Wilkinson, J. B., **Laredo and the Rio Grande Frontier**; Jenkins Publishing Co., Austin, 1975.

Williams, Clayton W. (Ernest Wallace, editor), **Texas' Last Frontier: Fort Stockton and the Trans-Pecos, 1861-1895**; Texas A&M University Press, College Station, 1982.

Williams, Lyle W., **Ranches and Ranching in Spanish Texas**; American Press, Boston, 1982.

Williams, T. Harry, Richard N. Current and Frank Freidel, **A History of the United States (to 1876)**; Alfred A. Knopf, Inc., New York, 1959.

Wilson, James A., **Hide & Horn in Texas: The Spread of Cattle Ranching 1836-1900**; American Press, Boston, 1983.

Wintz, Cary D., **Reconstruction in Texas**; American Press, Boston, 1983.

Wintz, Cary D., **Texas Politics in the Gilded Age, 1873-1890**; American Press, Boston, 1983.

Wright, J. Leitch Jr., **The Only Land They Knew: The Tragic Story of the American Indian in the South**; The Free Press (Division of MacMillan Publishing Co.), New York, 1981.

Wyatt-Brown, Bertram, **Southern Honor: Ethics and Behavior in the Old South**; Oxford University Press, New York, 1982.

Articles

Barker, Eugene C., **"The Annexation of Texas"**; Southwestern Historical Quarterly(SWHQ), Vol. L, No. 1, July 1946.

Barker, Eugene C., **"Land Speculation as a Cause of the Texas Revolution"**; Texas State Historical Quarterly (SWHQ), Vol. X, No. 1, July 1906.

Barker, Eugene C., **"The San Jacinto Campaign"**; SWHQ, Vol. IV, No. 4, April 1901.

Barker, Eugene C., **"The Texan Revolutionary Army"**; SWHQ, Vol. IX, No. 4, April 1906.

Bender, A.B., **"Opening Routes Across West Texas, 1848-1861"**; SWHQ, Vol. XXXVII, No. 2, October 1933.

Bender, A.B., **"The Texas Frontier, 1848-1861, Part II"**; SWHQ Vol. XVI, No. 1, July 1912.

Binkley, William C., **"The Activities of the Texan Revolutionary Army after San Jacinto"**; Journal of Southern History, Vol. VI, August 1940.

Bolton, H.E., **"The Spanish Occupation of Texas, 1519-1690"**; SWHQ, Vol. XVI, No. 1, July 1912.

Caldwell, Edwin L., **"Highlights of the Development of Manufacturing in Texas, 1900-1960"**; SWHQ, Vol. LXVIII, No. 4, April 1965.

Calvert, Robert A., **"Nineteenth-Century Farmers, Cotton, and Prosperity"**; SWHQ, Vol. LXXIII, No. 4, April 1970.

Casdorf, Paul D., **"Norris Wright Cuney and Texas Republican Politics, 1883-1896"**; SWHQ, Vol. LXVIII, No. 4, April 1965.

Cohen, Barry M., **"The Texas-Mexico Border, 1858-1867"**; Texana, Vol. VI, No. 2, Summer 1968.

Cox, Isaac Joslin, **"The Louisiana Texas Frontier"**; SWHQ, Vol. X, No. 1, July 1906.

Crane, M.M., **"Recollections of the Establishment of the Texas Railroad Commission"**; SWHQ, Vol. L, No. 4, April 1947.

Davenport, Harbert, **"Notes on Early Steamboating on the Rio Grande"**; SWHQ, Vol. XLIX, No. 2, October 1945.

Elliott, Claude, **"Union Sentiment in Texas, 1861-65"**; SWHQ, Vol. L, No. 4, April 1947.

Ellis, L. Tuffly, **"Maritime Commerce on the Far Western Gulf, 1861-1865"**; SWHQ, Vol. LXXVII, No. 2, October 1973.

Foner, Eric, **"The New view of Reconstruction"**; American Heritage Magazine, Oct./Nov. 1983, Vol. 34, No. 6.

Gard, Wayne, **"The Fence-Cutters"**; SWHQ, Vol. LI, No. 1, July 1947.

Havins, T.R., **"Texas Fever"**; SWHQ, Vol. LII, No. 2, October 1948.

Holt, R.D., **"The Introduction of Barbed Wire Into Texas and the Fence Cutting War"**; West Texas Historical Association Yearbook (WTHA Yearbook), Vol. VI, June 1930.

Houston, Sam, **"Houston's Last Speech in the United States Senate"**; Texas Almanac of 1860, Galveston News, Galveston, 1860.

Inglis, G. Douglas, **"The Men of Cibola: New Investigations on the Francisco Vazquez de Coronado Expedition"**; Panhandle-Plains Historical Review, Vol. LV, 1982.

Kilgore, Dan, **"Texas Cattle Origins"**; The Cattleman Magazine, January, 1983.

Kingston, Mike, **"Archaeology: A Slow Start in Texas"**; Texas Almanac, 1984-85, Dallas Morning News, Dallas, 1984.

Kingston, Mike, **"A History of the Texas Borderlands"**; Texas Almanac, 1984-85, Dallas Morning News, Dallas, 1984.

Koch, Lena Clara, **"The Federal Indian Policy in Texas, 1845-60"**; SWHQ, Vol. XXVIII, No. 2, April 1925.

Labadie, N.D., **"San Jacinto Campaign"**; Texas Almanac of 1859, Galveston News, Galveston, 1859.

Marshall, Ray, **"Some Reflections on Labor History"**; SWHQ, Vol. LXXV, No. 2, October 1971.

Marshall, Thomas Maitland, **"The Southwestern Boundary of Texas, 1821-1840"**; SWHQ, Vol. XIV, No. 4, April 1911.

Martin, Roscoe C., **"The Grange as a Political Factor in Texas"**; Southwestern Political and Social Science Quarterly, Vol. VI, June 1925-March 1926.

Martin, Roscoe C., **"The Greenback Party in Texas"**; SWHQ, Vol. XXX, No. 3, January 1927.

Myres, Sandra, **"Spanish Cattle Kingdom"**; Texana, Vol. IV, No. 3, Fall 1966.

Neighbours, Kenneth F., **"The Expedition of Maj. Robert S. Neighbors to El Paso in 1849"**; SWHQ, Vol. LVIII, No. 1, July 1954.

Neighbours, Kenneth F., **"Indian Exodus out of Texas in 1859"**; WTHA Yearbook, Vol. XXXVI, 1960.

Neighbours, Kenneth F., **"The Struggle Over the Upper Rio Grande Region in 1850"**; SWHQ, Vol. LXI, No. 4, April 1958.

Norvell, James R ., **"The Railroad Commission of Texas, Its Origin and History"**; SWHQ, Vol. LXVIII, No. 4, April 1965.

Parvin, Bob, **"In Search of the First Texans"**; Texas Parks and Wildlife Magazine, October 1983.

Peterson, Robert L., **"Jay Gould and the Texas Railroad Commission"**; SWHQ, Vol. LVIII, No. 3, January 1955.

Porter, Kenneth Wiggins, **"The Seminole Negro-Indian Scouts, 1870-81"**; SWHQ, Vol. LV, No. 3, January 1952.

Reese, James V., **"The Early History of Labor Organizations in Texas, 1838-1876"**; SWHQ, Vol. LXXII, No. 1, July 1968.

Reese, James V., **"The Evolution of an Early Texas Union: The Screwmans' Benevolent Association of Galveston, 1866-1891"**; SWHQ, Vol. LXXV, No. 2, October 1971.

Rippy, J. Fred, **"British Investments in Texas Land and Livestock"**; SWHQ, Vol. LVIII, No. 3, January 1955.

Smith, Ralph A., **"The Farmers' Alliance in Texas"**; SWHQ, Vol. XLVIII, No. 3, January 1945.

Smith, Ralph A., **"The Grange Movement in Texas, 1873-1900"**; SWHQ, Vol. XLII, No. 4, April 1939.

Smyrl, Frank H., **"Texans in the Union Army, 1861-65"**; SWHQ, Vol. LXV, No. 2, October 1961.

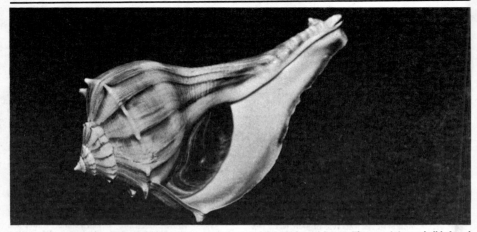

The lightning whelk was added to the list of Texas state symbols by the 70th Legislature. The new state seashell is found only on the Gulf Coast. Photo courtesy the Dallas Museum of Natural History and Aquarium.

State Flags and Other Symbols

Texas often is called the **Lone Star State** because of its state flag with a single star; this also was the **flag of the Republic of Texas.** The following information about the flag and other Texas symbols may be supplemented by information available from the Texas State Library, Austin.

At the Convention of 1836, at Washington-on-the-Brazos, **Lorenzo de Zavala** is reported to have designed a flag for the Republic — a blue field with a white star of five points central, with the letters T E X A S, one letter between each star point. Probably because of the hasty dispersion of the Convention and loss of part of the Convention notes, nothing further was done with the De Zavala recommendation.

The **first official flag of the Republic,** known as **David G. Burnet's flag,** was adopted on Dec. 10, 1836, as the national standard, "the conformation of which shall be an azure ground with a large golden star central." A new national standard was worked out and approved by Mirabeau B. Lamar on Jan. 25, 1839. This flag consisted of a blue perpendicular stripe of the width of one-third of the whole length of the flag with a white star of five points in the center thereof, and two horizontal stripes of equal breadth, the upper stripe white, the lower red, of the length of two-thirds of the whole flag. This is the **Lone Star Flag.**

Six Flags of Texas

Six different flags have flown over Texas during eight changes of sovereignty. The accepted sequence of these flags follows:

Spanish—1519-1685.
French—1685-1690.
Spanish—1690-1821.
Mexican—1821-1836.
Republic of Texas—1836-1845.
United States—1845-1861.
Confederate States—1861-1865.
United States—1865 to the present.

State Flag

The **Lone Star Flag** consists of a blue field with a single white star and white and red horizontal stripes, with white uppermost. This flag was adopted by the Third Congress of the Republic, Jan. 25, 1839, at Houston. Although generally used, the state flag was not officially described and usage rules adopted until 1933. These rules are from Acts of Forty-third Legislature (p. 186, ch. 87).

Flown out-of-doors, the Texas flag must be on flagpole or staff at least 2½ times as long as the flag. It should not be unfurled earlier than sunrise and should not be left out in rain, snow or other inclement weather. It should be flown with the white stripe uppermost except in case of distress. When the flag is displayed against a wall, the blue field should be at the flag's own right (observer's left). The Texas flag should be displayed on all state memorial days; it should fly at every school on every regular school day.

The Texas flag should be on the marching left in a procession in which the flag of the United States is carried; its staff should be behind the staff of the flag of the United States when the two are displayed with crossed staffs. The Texas flag should be underneath the national flag when the two are flown from the same halyard. When flown from separate, adjacent flagpoles, the United States flag and the Texas flag should be of approximately the same size and on flagpoles of equal length, and the United States flag should be on "the flag's own right," i.e., to the observer's left. The Texas flag should never be used for any utilitarian or strictly decorative purpose. No advertising should be placed upon the flag or flagstaff, and no picture of the flag should be used in an advertisement. When the Texas flag is in such condition that it is no longer a suitable emblem for display, it should be destroyed, preferably by burning, "with the spirit of respect and reverence which all Texans owe the emblem."

Texas Flag Pledge

A pledge to the Texas flag also was adopted by the Forty-third Legislature and from 1933 until 1965 that pledge was used. It contained a phrase, "Flag of 1836," which was historically incorrect, as Texas did not have a flag in 1836. On April 3, 1965, Gov. John Connally signed an act of the Fifty-ninth Legislature officially designating the pledge to the Texas flag as follows:

"Honor the Texas flag.
I pledge allegiance to thee,
Texas, one and indivisible."

Texas Flag Salute

There is no official salute to the Texas flag, but most civilians use the same salute as that for the United States flag: right hand over heart.

Other Symbols

State Seal — The seal of the State of Texas consists of "a star of five points, encircled by olive and live oak branches, and the words, 'The State of Texas'." (State Constitution, Art. IV, Sec. 19.) The state seal is a slight modification of the Great Seal of the Republic of Texas, adopted by the Congress of the Republic, Dec. 10, 1836, and readopted with modifications in 1839.

State Citizenship Designation — The people of Texas usually call themselves **Texans.** However, **Texian** was generally used in the early period of history.

State Motto — The state motto of Texas is **"Friendship."** The word, Texas, or Tejas, was the Spanish pronunciation of a Caddo Indian word meaning "friends" or "allies." (Acts of 1930, fourth called session of Forty-first Legislature, p. 105.)

State Tree — The **pecan** is the state tree of Texas. The sentiment that led to its official adoption probably grew out of the request of Gov. James Stephen Hogg that a pecan tree be planted at his grave. (Acts of 1919,

Thirty-sixth Legislature, regular session, p. 155; also Acts of 1927, Fortieth Legislature, p. 234.)

State Stone — Palmwood.

State Flower — The state flower of Texas is the **bluebonnet,** also called **buffalo clover, wolf flower, "el conejo"** (the rabbit). The bluebonnet was adopted as the State Flower, on request of the Society of Colonial Dames in Texas, by the Twenty-seventh Legislature, 1901. (See acts of regular session, p. 232.) The original resolution designated Lupinus subcarnosus as the **state flower,** but a resolution (HCR 44) signed March 8, 1971, by Gov. Preston Smith provided legal status as the state flower of Texas for "Lupinus Texensis and any other variety of bluebonnet."

State Bird — The **mockingbird** (Mimus polyglottos) is the state bird of Texas, adopted by the Legislature at the request of the Texas Federation of Women's Clubs. (Acts of 1927, Fortieth Legislature, regular session, p. 486.)

State Dish — Chili was proclaimed the Texas state dish by the Texas Legislature in 1977.

State Gem — Topaz is the official Texas gem, found in Llano uplift area, especially west to northwest of Mason.

State Grass — Sideoats grama, (Bouteloua curtipendula), a native grass found on many different soils, was designated by the Legislature as the **state grass of Texas** in 1971.

State Seashell — The lightning whelk (Busycon perversum pulleyi) was adopted as the official state seashell by the 70th Legislature on April 2, 1987. One of the few shells that opens on the left side, the lightning whelk is named for its colored stripes. It is found only on the Gulf Coast.

State Holidays — Texas has four state holidays and several special observance days. The four holidays are **Texas Independence Day,** March 2, **San Jacinto Day,** April 21, **Emancipation Day,** June 19, and **Lyndon B. Johnson's Birthday,** August 27. (See index for list of Texas holidays and special observances.)

State Song — The state song of Texas is **"Texas, Our Texas."** The music was written by the late William J. Marsh (who died Feb. 1, 1971, in Fort Worth at age 90), and the words by Marsh and Gladys Yoakum Wright, both of Fort Worth. It was adopted as the result of an award offered by the Legislature. (Acts of 1929, first called session, Forty-first Legislature, p. 286.) Its text follows:

TEXAS, OUR TEXAS

Texas, our Texas! All hail the mighty State!
Texas, our Texas! So wonderful, so great!
Boldest and grandest, withstanding every test;
O empire wide and glorious, you stand supremely blest.

Chorus

God bless you, Texas! And keep you brave and strong.
That you may grow in power and worth, throughout the ages long.

Refrain

Texas, O Texas! Your freeborn single star,
Sends out its radiance to nations near and far.
Emblem of freedom! It sets our hearts aglow.
With thoughts of San Jacinto and glorious Alamo.
Texas, dear Texas! From tyrant grip now free,
Shines forth in splendor your star of destiny!
Mother of Heroes! We come your children true.
Proclaiming our allegiance, our faith, our love for you.

— Words by Gladys Yoakum Wright and William J. Marsh. Music by William J. Marsh.

The adopted song of the University of Texas, **"The Eyes of Texas,"** is also frequently sung at public gatherings. It is usually sung by a standing audience and has a measure of recognition as a state song. Origin of this song is as follows: William Lamdin Prather, president of the University of Texas, 1899-1906, frequently said to the students, "The eyes of Texas are upon you." A university minstrel, as a prank when President Prather was present, sang a song, using this phrase, which had been written by a student, John Lang Sinclair, to the tune of "I've Been Working on the Railroad (Levee)." Gradually it became the adopted song of the University and is popular throughout Texas.

THE EYES OF TEXAS

The eyes of Texas are upon you
All the livelong day.
The eyes of Texas are upon you
You cannot get away.
Do not think you can escape them,
At night or early in the morn,
The eyes of Texas are upon you
Till Gabriel blows his horn.

Belo Corp. Has Grown With Texas

A. H. Belo Corporation, publisher of **The Dallas Morning News** and the **Texas Almanac**, has a history parallel to that of Texas itself. Pioneered in 1842 as the one-page Galveston News, Belo has grown to become a leading southwestern media company, encompassing both newspaper publishing and broadcasting operations across the country.

A. H. Belo Corporation is the oldest continuously operating business in Texas. Founded by Samuel Bangs, a transplanted publisher from Boston, the company was in the publishing business three years before the Republic of Texas achieved statehood. Bangs sold the business within a year of its founding to Wilbur F. Cherry and Michael Cronican, and Cherry soon acquired sole ownership.

Another Massachusetts emigre, Willard Richardson, became editor of the paper a few years later. He campaigned editorially for annexation, fiscal responsibility and railroads. Soon after his campaign began, Texas was annexed to the United States. In 1857, Richardson conceived and founded the **Texas Almanac**, which he hoped would help attract settlers to the new state. Eight years later, he hired A. H. Belo, for whom the company was eventually named.

A. H. Belo, a former Confederate colonel from North Carolina, joined the company as bookkeeper. He was made a full partner in the growing company after only three months and carved out a new life for himself in the Southwest.

Nine years later, George Bannerman Dealey, a 15-year-old English emigrant, was hired as an office boy. Dealey, like A. H. Belo, was full of enthusiasm and energy. He, too, quickly moved up in the company. Working tirelessly, Dealey made his way from office boy to business manager and then to publisher of **The Dallas Morning News**. It was Dealey who chose the then-small settlement of Dallas as a site for a sister publication. Dealey and several other members of the Galveston News' staff relocated to Dallas, and the company prospered and grew.

The Dallas Morning News began publication on October 1, 1885, with a circulation of 5,000 subscribers. After being in operation only two months, **The Dallas Morning News** acquired its first competitor, the **Dallas Herald** (not to be confused with the current **Dallas Times Herald**). Rather than compete with each other for subscribers, the two newspapers combined, keeping the name of **The Dallas Morning News**, but dating itself with the volume number of the former **Dallas Herald**.

In 1906, on the 21st anniversary of **The Dallas Morning News,** Dealey gave a speech that became the motto for the company: "Build The News upon the rock of truth and righteousness. Conduct it always upon the lines of fairness and integrity. Acknowledge the right of the people to get from the newspaper both sides of every important question." Today these words are carved in a three-story-high space above the entrance to **The Dallas Morning News**. The News building, a long-standing dream of Dealey, was completed in 1949, three years after his death.

December 1981 marked the beginning of a new era in A. H. Belo Corporation's history. In that month, the company became a publicly held entity, and its common stock is now traded on the New York Stock Exchange. In May 1987, A. H. Belo Corporation re-incorporated in the State of Delaware, although its headquarters and operations did not move.

While Belo has grown into a multi-faceted media entity, **The Dallas Morning News** remains the flagship of its newspaper business. Growing from that original one-page newspaper in Galveston, **The Dallas Morning News** now has a total daily circulation of more than 388,000. It is the leading newspaper in the Dallas-Fort Worth area, and its growth is evident in the opening in 1985 of its satellite printing plant in Plano, Texas.

In 1963, Belo purchased six daily newspapers — the **Arlington Daily News, Garland Daily News, Grand Prairie Daily News, Irving Daily News, Mid-Cities Daily News** and **Richardson Daily News** — and the weekly **Suburban News,** since renamed **Metrocrest News,** which together form the wholly-owned subsidiary Dallas-Fort Worth Suburban Newspapers, Inc.

Belo entered the television broadcasting business in 1950 with the acquisition of its principal station WFAA-TV, Channel 8, the ABC affiliate in Dallas-Fort Worth. The station had begun broadcasting five months earlier as KBTV-TV.

In 1984 Belo purchased four television stations from Dun & Bradstreet. The company acquired VHF stations KHOU-TV in Houston, KXTV in Sacramento, California, KOTV in Tulsa, Oklahoma and WVEC-TV in Hampton-Norfolk, Virginia.

Belo also was a pioneer in radio in Texas. It began operating a 50-watt radio station, WFAA-AM, on June 26, 1922, which was the first network station in the state. The company sold the last of its radio properties in 1987.

Officers and Directors

Officers of A. H. Belo Corporation are Robert W. Decherd, chairman of the board and chief executive officer; James P. Sheehan, president and chief operating officer; Ward L. Huey Jr., vice chairman of the board and president/broadcast division; Michael J. McCarthy, senior vice president, secretary and general counsel; Walter G. Mullins, vice president/administration; Robert G. Norvell, vice president, treasurer and assistant secretary; and Michael D. Perry, vice president and controller.

Officers of the broadcast division of A. H. Belo Corporation, in addition to Ward L. Huey, president, are Frank B. Davis, vice president/engineering and operations; Herman M. Haag, vice president/news; and Lee R. Salzberger, vice president/administration.

The following are members of the A. H. Belo Corporation board of directors: John W. Bassett Jr., Joe M. Dealey, Robert W. Decherd, Dealey D. Herndon, Ward L. Huey Jr., Lester A. Levy, James M. Moroney Jr., Burl Osborne, Reece A. Overcash Jr., William H. Seay, James P. Sheehan, William T. Solomon, Thomas B. Walker Jr. and J. McDonald Williams.

Officers of **The Dallas Morning News** are Burl Osborne, president and editor; Jeremy L. Halbreich, executive vice president and general manager; Harry M. Stanley Jr., senior vice president/sales and marketing; J. William Cox, senior vice president/administration and finance; Ralph E. Langer, vice president and executive editor; James A. Keeley, vice president/operations; Frank McKnight, vice president/circulation; Harold F. Gaar Jr., vice president/marketing; Barry T. Peckham, vice president and controller; and Grover D. Livingston, vice president/information management.

The principal executives of the five television operating companies are as follows: David T. Lane, president and general manager, WFAA-TV, Dallas-Fort Worth, Texas; Terrence S. Ford, president and general manager, KHOU-TV, Houston, Texas; Allan Howard, vice president and general manager, KXTV, Sacramento, California; J. William Beindorf, vice president and general manager, WVEC-TV, Hampton-Norfolk, Virginia; and Phillip J. Keller, vice president and general manager, KOTV, Tulsa, Oklahoma.

Officers of Dallas-Fort Worth Suburban Newspapers, Inc. are Daniel L. Crowe, president and chief executive officer; James R. Chandler, vice president/production; J. Michael Price, vice president/sales and marketing; David V. Berry, vice president/editorial; Stephen Lynn, vice president and controller; and Roger F. Schneider, vice president/circulation.

Robert W. Decherd

Robert W. Decherd is chairman of the board and chief executive officer of A. H. Belo Corporation and has been a member of the company's board of directors since 1976. He is the son of the late H. Ben Decherd, who served as chairman of the board until his death in 1972.

After graduating from St. Mark's School of Texas in Dallas, Mr. Decherd entered Harvard University. While at Harvard, he became the first Texan to be elected president of The Harvard Crimson, the university's daily student newspaper. Mr. Decherd had worked previously at Dallas-Fort Worth Suburban Newspapers, Inc., and was a stringer for The New York Times. He graduated cum laude from Harvard in 1973. He was elected class orator for the class of 1973 and received the David McCord Award for literary contributions in addition to an honorary freshman scholarship.

Returning to Dallas, Mr. Decherd joined the management training program at **The News** in September 1973. After holding a series of staff positions at The News and Belo, he was elected vice president, corporate administration in 1979.

In February 1980, Mr. Decherd was named executive vice president of **The News**, a position he held until January 1982. Subsequently he was elected executive vice president of A. H. Belo Corporation, chief operating officer and president. He became chairman of the board and chief executive officer effective Jan. 1, 1987.

Ward L. Huey Jr.

Ward L. Huey Jr., vice chairman of the board and president, broadcast division, A. H. Belo Corporation, has an extensive background in broadcast operations and management.

A graduate of Southern Methodist University, Huey joined the WFAA-TV production department in 1960. He rose rapidly through the management ranks, and on Jan. 1, 1975, Huey was named vice president and general manager of Belo Broadcasting Corporation with management responsibilities for all Belo radio and television properties and was also elected to its board of directors. Huey became president and chief executive officer of Belo Broadcasting Corporation on April 27, 1981, and was elected to the board of directors of A. H. Belo Corporation on April 20, 1982. In 1987, he was elected vice chairman of the board and president of the broadcast division of A. H. Belo Corporation. He serves on the A. H. Belo Corporation management committee.

A native of Dallas, Huey is a past chairman of the ABC Television Affiliates Board of Governors, a present member of the board of directors of the Television Bureau of Advertising, the board of directors of the Maximum Service Telecasters, and the board of directors of the Television Operators Caucus. He also is involved in a variety of other professional and civic organizations.

James P. Sheehan

James P. Sheehan joined A. H. Belo Corporation as senior vice president and chief financial officer in February 1982 and was elected to the Board of Directors in April 1982. He became executive vice president of Belo in 1984, and in January 1987 he became president and chief operating officer.

Prior to joining Belo, he spent eight years with United Technologies Corporation and most recently was vice president and controller of the Pratt and Whitney Manufacturing Division.

He also held the positions of director of manufacturing for Otis Elevator North America and controller for Otis Elevator and served on the UTC corporate staff.

Before joining United Technologies, Mr. Sheehan was a financial analyst with Ford Motor Company and accounting manager for Audits and Surveys, Inc.

He received a B.S. from Seton Hall University and an M.B.A. in finance from Wayne State University. From 1967 to 1969 he served in the U.S. Navy.

Burl Osborne

Burl Osborne joined **The Dallas Morning News** as executive editor in October 1980 and added the title of vice president in 1981. In 1983, he was named senior vice president and editor; in 1985, he became president and editor; and he was elected to the board of directors in May 1987.

Mr. Osborne came to **The News** after 20 years with the Associated Press, where he started as a correspondent and editor-reporter, served in a variety of management positions and became managing editor in 1977.

He holds a bachelor's degree in journalism and mathematics from Marshall University, West Virginia, and a master's degree in business from Long Island University.

He serves on the boards of directors of the American Press Institute, American Society of Newspaper Editors, the Amundsen Institute of U.S.-Mexico Studies and the Foundation for American Communications, among others. He is a member of the Pulitzer Prize Board and the Advisory Council of the University of Texas at Austin College of Communications Foundation.

James M. Moroney

James M. Moroney Jr. is the son of the late James M. Moroney and the late Maidie Dealey Moroney. He was born in Dallas, attended Highland Park School and St. John's Military Academy in Delafield, Wis. He graduated from the University of Texas at Austin in 1943. During summer vacations, he worked part-time at radio and television stations WFAA and **The Dallas Morning News.**

During World War II, he entered the U.S. Navy, rising to the rank of lieutenant (jg). He saw much action, including the D-Day landing in Normandy. He was released from active duty in 1946.

Mr. Moroney joined **The News** as a reporter, served as an advertising salesman and worked in the promotion and circulation departments before becoming assistant to the business manager in 1950. He also spent a year at the radio and television stations.

He progressed to assistant treasurer of the corporation and was elected to the board of directors in 1952. In 1955, he was named treasurer, elevated to vice president and treasurer in 1960 and became executive vice president in 1970. In 1973, Mr. Moroney was named president and chief executive officer of Belo Broadcasting Corporation and in 1974 became chairman of the board of that corporation.

In 1980, he was elected to president and chief executive officer of **The Dallas Morning News** and president and chief operating officer of A. H. Belo Corporation.

He was promoted to the position of president and chief executive officer of A. H. Belo Corporation January 1983. In April 1984, he was elected to the additional position of chairman of the board. In January 1985 he relinquished the title of president.

Mr. Moroney retired as an active operating officer of A. H. Belo on Dec. 31, 1986. He currently is a consultant to the corporation and holds the title of chairman of the executive committee.

Joe M. Dealey

Joe M. Dealey, past chairman of the board of the A. H. Belo Corporation, is the son of the late E. M. (Ted) Dealey and the late Clara MacDonald Dealey. A native of Dallas, he graduated from Highland Park High School and, in 1941, from the University of Texas at Austin. By attending the Southwest School of Printing, he learned to operate mechanical equipment in the printing industry. He also worked in the mailing room and photographic laboratory of **The Dallas Morning News.** His permanent employment began Jan. 4, 1942, as a reporter.

In May 1942, Mr. Dealey joined the U. S. Air Force, serving two years as an aircraft mechanic. After attending Officers Training School, he was graduated in 1944 as a second lieutenant. He served as aircraft maintenance officer in the United States and in Berlin until his discharge from service in 1946.

Returning to his previous job as a reporter on **The News,** Mr. Dealey later served as assistant business news editor and assistant to the managing editor. He joined the executive department as assistant secretary in 1950 and was elected to the board of directors in 1952. From 1955 until 1960, he was secretary of the corporation and then president until 1980 when he was named chairman and chief executive officer, following an internal reorganization of the company. On Dec. 31, 1982, he became chairman of the board and held that title until April 1984.

John W. Bassett Jr.

John W. Bassett Jr. is a native of Roswell, N.M., where he practices law. After graduating from Roswell High School, he attended Stanford University, where he majored in economics and received a bachelor's degree in 1960.

Following graduation, he was commissioned as a second lieutenant in the Army and entered active duty at Fort Benning, Ga. He served in the Second Infantry Division there and in the Army Reserves, where he was advanced to first lieutenant.

Mr. Bassett attended the University of Texas School of Law and became an associate editor of The Texas Law Review. Upon graduating with honors in June 1964, he was awarded a bachelor of law degree and became a member of the Order of the Coif, a legal honorary organization.

After passing the Texas and New Mexico Bar examinations in 1964, he practiced law in Roswell.

In 1966, Mr. Bassett was selected as a White House Fellow and for a year served as a special assistant to the attorney general of the United States.

In October 1967, Mr. Bassett returned to private practice with the law firm of Atwood, Malone, Mann and Turner, P.A., in Roswell.

Mr. Bassett was elected to the board of directors of A. H. Belo Corporation in 1979. He also serves as a member of the Board of Education for the State of New Mexico, is a Rotarian and is a member of several boards of directors of local charitable institutions in Roswell.

Dealey D. Herndon

Dealey D. Herndon of Austin was elected to the Board of Directors in 1986. She was born in Dallas and is the daughter of the late H. Ben Decherd and Isabelle Thomason Decherd. She is an honors graduate of Hockaday School and the University of Texas at Austin. She was administrator of Friends of the Governor's Mansion from 1983 to 1984.

Mrs. Herndon has lived in El Paso, Dallas and Austin, where she has been active in civic and non-profit activities for the past eight years. In Dallas, she served on the board of the Dallas County Heritage Society. In Austin, she has been a board member of the Austin Junior League, West Austin Youth Association, the Seton Hospital Development Board and the Pebble Project, a child abuse prevention agency. She served as president of the Austin History Center Association Board. She was treasurer of the St. Andrew's Episcopal School board of trustees and chairman of the Austin High School Excellence Fund.

She currently serves on several statewide boards. She is a board member of the Texas Council on Economic Education and is treasurer of the board of Friends of the Governor's Mansion. She is serving a two-year term on the State Preservation Board, which is charged with preserving the Texas State Capitol.

Lester A. Levy

Lester A. Levy was born and educated in Dallas. He attended the University of Texas at Austin until early 1943, at which time he entered the Air Force. He received his license to practice law during 1943 while in the service. After an honorable discharge in 1946, he joined his father's company, now known as NCH Corporation, while awaiting a semester change in order to take refresher courses at the University of Texas. His father's untimely death caused him to remain with the company, where he is presently chairman of the board of directors.

Mr. Levy was elected to the board of directors of A. H. Belo Corporation in 1985. He has served on the boards of the University of Dallas, Greenhill School, Baylor College of Dentistry, the Lamplighter School, and was co-founder and director of the Winston School. He has also served as a trustee for Temple Emanu-El, Golden Acres Home for the Aged and Special Care and Career Center (formerly Special Care School for Handicapped Children).

Reece A. Overcash

Reece A. Overcash Jr. is chairman and chief executive officer of Associates Corporation of North America, one of the nation's largest independent financial services organizations. He also is senior executive vice president of Gulf + Western, Inc., and president of the firm's financial services group. The Associates is a G+W company.

Mr. Overcash was born and reared in Charlotte, N.C., where he was named as "Man of the Year" in 1972. He earned a degree in commerce from the University of North Carolina and served in the infantry during World War II.

From 1950 to 1952, he was an accountant with a CPA firm in Charlotte. He joined Home Finance Group in 1952 (a predecessor company of American Credit Corp.). Mr. Overcash was named president of American Credit in 1970 and became that company's chief executive officer in 1974. In 1975, he joined The Associates as president and chief operating officer.

He was elected chief executive officer of The Associates in August 1978, and became chairman of the board in August 1979. In March 1983, he also was elected to the G+W offices.

Mr. Overcash is active in many professional, civic and community organizations and serves as director of Duke Power Company, Aancor Holdings, Inc., and a number of other organizations. He was elected to the board of directors of A. H. Belo Corporation in 1983.

William H. Seay

William H. Seay is retired chairman of the board and chief executive officer of Southwestern Life Insurance Company, which is one of the nation's 10 largest stock life insurance companies.

Mr. Seay was born and reared in Dallas. He holds a degree in business administration from the University of Texas and served during World War II as an infantry captain in the Army.

In 1948, he became a partner in the Dallas investment banking firm of Henry, Seay and Black. Eleven years later he joined Universal Life and Accident Insurance Company as vice president, advancing in 1961 to president.

Universal was acquired by Southwestern Life Insurance Company in September 1968, and four months later Mr. Seay was named president and chief executive officer of the parent firm. He continued in that capacity until the transition to a holding-company concept in late 1972.

Mr. Seay is active in many professional, civic and community organizations and serves as director of numerous Dallas-based business firms. He was elected to the board of directors of A. H. Belo Corporation on March 27, 1973.

William T. Solomon

William T. Solomon is chairman, president and chief executive officer of Austin Industries Inc., which is the largest general contractor in Dallas and one of the five largest contractors in the southern half of the United States. Austin Industries is the only major contractor in its markets that is completely employee-owned.

Born and reared in Dallas, Mr. Solomon holds a civil engineering degree from Southern Methodist University and an M.B.A. from Harvard Graduate School of Business.

Mr. Solomon joined Austin full-time in 1967, becoming president and chief executive officer in 1970. The title of chairman was added in 1987.

Mr. Solomon is a member of the boards of directors of Fidelity Union Life Insurance Company, First RepublicBank Dallas, Baylor University Medical Center Foundation, SMU Foundation for Business, SMU Foundation for Science and Engineering, State Fair of Texas, The Texas Water Alliance and the board of trustees of Southern Methodist University. He is a past chairman of the Dallas Chamber of Commerce and serves on the boards of directors of numerous other civic and community organizations. He was elected to the board of directors of A. H. Belo Corporation in 1983.

Thomas B. Walker Jr.

Thomas B. Walker Jr. is a native of Nashville, Tenn. and is a Phi Beta Kappa graduate of Vanderbilt University. During World War II, he served as a lieutenant in the U.S. Navy operating in the Mediterranean, Atlantic and South Pacific areas.

After the war, Mr. Walker joined the Equitable Securities Corporation and moved to Dallas in 1950. He served as senior vice president and director, Equitable Securities (American Express Company) until 1968. In 1968, he became a partner of Goldman, Sachs & Co., and he is a member of the management committee of that firm.

In addition, Mr. Walker is a director of Intermedics, Inc., Sysco Corporation and Transatlantic Fund, Inc., and he is vice chairman of the Board of Trustees of Vanderbilt University. He also is a member of the executive and investment committees of Vanderbilt and is a trustee and member of the investment committee of the Dallas Museum of Art. He was elected to the board of directors of A. H. Belo Corporation in 1982.

J. McDonald Williams

J. McDonald (Don) Williams is a native of Roswell, N.M. He graduated from Abilene Christian University in 1963 and from George Washington University Law School in 1966, both with honors.

He practiced law in Dallas seven years until he joined the Trammell Crow Company in May 1973. He entered the firm as the partner responsible for overseas developments and then was named managing partner in 1977.

Mr. Williams was elected to the board of directors of A. H. Belo Corporation in 1985. He also serves on the boards of First RepublicBank Dallas, N.A., Abilene Christian University, George Washington University, Stanford University School of Business and Southwestern Christian College. He currently serves as chairman of the board of Dallas Challenge, Inc., a non-profit organization assisting youth with chemical dependency problems.

We couldn't be the world's leading insurance agency if we didn't have offices throughout Texas.

Marsh & McLennan offers exceptional service to businesses in Texas and world wide. Our account executives are readily available to study your insurance problems. And they don't have to accept coverages that are "roughly" what you need. With the whole Marsh & McLennan behind them, they can insist on programs that are exactly right for you. Then can call in specialists in every type of coverage. And they have access to all insurance markets to get you the most cost-efficient terms. Give us a call.

Amarillo

Dallas

Fort Worth

Houston

San Antonio

When it comes to insurance, come to the leader.

Marsh & McLennan

Business and Industry

Slower, But Steadier, Growth Expected In Texas

This article was prepared by State Comptroller Bob Bullock and staff members of the Comptroller's Economic Analysis Center: Tom Plaut, Lori McCreary and Dean Ferguson.

Texas and the oil and gas industry have been synonymous since Spindletop ushered in the oil age in 1901. Dramatic increases in the price of oil in 1973-74 and 1979-81 propelled Texas even further as a leader of economic growth and as a magnet for in-migration in the 1970s and early 1980s — with a peak in-migration of more than 400,000 people in 1982.

This good fortune changed rapidly, however. Texas' economy reeled in 1982-83 and again in 1986 as the average world oil price declined by nearly 50 percent — from $27 a barrel in late 1985 to about $15 a barrel in 1986. The oil-patch recession of 1986 saw a loss of more than 100,000 jobs in the state as the decline in the energy industry rippled through the rest of the economy.

At the start of 1986, Texas' unemployment rate was 6.4 percent — slightly below the United States rate of 6.7 percent. But during the winter and spring unemployment grew worse as the state's economy declined. Texas' unemployment rate overtook the U.S. rate in February, then peaked with the highest rate among the 11 largest industrial states, at a record 10.5 percent in June 1986.

In 1987, Texas' economy had regained its footing from the 1986 recession and accelerated its diversification. Oil and gas dependence will continue to give way to a greater reliance on services. Over the next 20 years, the state comptroller's office expects service-producing companies to create three of every four new Texas jobs.

This diversification will make Texas' economy perform more like that of the United States. Both booms and busts in the state will likely be more moderate than those of the past 15 years.

But while overall growth will be slower than in the past, the state will eventually still outpace the nation as a whole, adding new jobs and gaining population at faster rates than the rest of the country.

Agriculture

Texas typically leads the nation in the production of cattle and cotton and, in addition, is a major producer of fresh fruits and vegetables. In 1985, according to the U.S. Department of Agriculture, Texas ranked first in the nation in cash receipts from livestock, with a total of $5.4 billion, and fourth in the nation in crop receipts, with a total of $3.8 billion. The state leads the nation in the number of farms and ranches and in farm and ranch acreage.

Texas has led the nation in cotton production since the late 19th century. Texas' cotton accounts for one-quarter to one-third of all cotton produced in the United States. Much of this cotton crop is exported, with Japan and South Korea being major buyers.

Agriculture in Texas, unlike that in most large agricultural states, is a uniquely diversified industry, producing more than 60 marketable commodities. Besides cattle and cotton, Texas produces significant amounts of grain sorghum (a feed grain), wheat, rice, corn, hay, peanuts, onions, carrots, watermelons, cantaloupe, cabbage, potatoes and grapefruit.

Prices paid for Texas' agricultural products have been depressed in recent years as a result of worldwide production greatly exceeding worldwide consumption. Due to large stocks of commodities in storage and the continued growth in production, the outlook for agricultural prices remains bleak. This is combined with the high operating costs associated with the capital-intensive nature of U.S. agriculture and the national farm debt problem, making it very difficult for the Texas farmer to make a profit or to break even.

Oil and Gas

The precipitous decline of world oil prices in the spring of 1986 threw the Texas economy into recession. Although Texas depends less on oil and gas than in the past, energy is still the state's most important industry. In 1981, oil and gas production, refining, chemicals and energy-related manufacturing accounted for 28 percent of the state's total output of goods and services. By 1986, these businesses made up a hefty 17 percent of the state's economy.

So when oil prices began dropping in early 1986, the energy industry collapsed and pulled the whole Texas economy into recession. The eventual recovery of the energy industry will contribute to the long-term growth prospects of the state. Although state oil and gas employment is expected to decline through 1988, it is expected to slowly increase from 1989 into the next century.

As oil prices increase over the next 20 years — the comptroller projects an average price of $38 per barrel in 2005 — worldwide oil and gas exploration and development activities will increase. Texas will share in this growth.

Energy-related employment in Texas will expand moderately in 1988 and beyond. Texas will remain an important center for oil and gas services, the production of oil-field machinery and other drilling-related manufacturing. Just as New York remained the world's financial capital long after losing its manufacturing base, Houston will remain the world's energy center even though Texas is no longer the major source of oil and gas.

Construction

The 1970s and early 1980s saw Texas' skylines filled with building cranes and rural communities turned into suburbs. The rapid growth of the state's economy and the in-migration of new citizens ignited the construction industry. Texas cities led the nation in both nonresidential and residential construction many times during this boom. Nonresidential construction peaked in 1981 with more than 184.1 million square feet built in one year. Texas' housing starts peaked two years later in 1983 with in excess of 283,000 residences built.

Texas' construction industry was hit in 1986 by the double whammy of a statewide recession and the accumulation of overbuilt markets. Both residential and nonresidential construction plummeted in 1986 as reduced in-migration, slow population and income growth, overbuilding and national tax law changes took their tolls.

The state's construction boom of the last 15 years is unlikely to be repeated in the next two decades. The building industry will grow only modestly and much more slowly than over the past two-and-a-half decades.

In the near term, construction will continue to suffer because of the recent economic slowdown, fewer newcomers and overbuilt markets across the state. Business and industrial construction will turn around in 1988 as excess inventories are absorbed. Homebuilding should rebound in 1989.

Shifts in the construction industry are often more extreme than in the rest of the economy. For example, the comptroller's office expects business construction to drop 35 percent per year from 1985 to 1987 and then increase 7.1 percent yearly from 1987 to 1995, and 3.9 percent annually from 1995 to 2005.

Manufacturing

Texas has a wide range of manufacturing activities. Two manufacturing sectors — oil-field machinery and petrochemicals, along with high-technology and defense-related production — however, dominate Texas manufacturing activities. Both of these areas were hurt in the early 1980s. High-technology employment growth in Texas slowed with the high value of the dollar and the worldwide excess supply in semiconductors. The decline in oil prices in 1986 caused a loss of 19,200 jobs in oil-field machinery, refining and chemicals.

Texas' job losses in manufacturing were expected to ease and then turn around in 1987 as oil prices stabilized and the value of the U.S. dollar declined abroad. A declining dollar stimulates U.S. manufacturing by making domestic goods cheaper relative to imports.

After the Texas manufacturing industry hits bottom in 1987, state manufacturing job growth will recover at nearly double the national rate. From 1987 to 2005, the state comptroller expects manufacturing jobs to grow an average 2.5 percent yearly, nearly double the 1.3 percent U.S. rate. Texas' manufacturing job growth leaders will be high-technology and oil and gas-related industries.

Texas high-technology industries — including electronics, computers, instruments and aerospace equipment — will grow at an average rate of 3.8 percent a year, producing 310,000 new jobs, from 1985 to 2005.

Services

Service-producing industries — including transportation and public utilities, finance, insurance and real estate; services; trade; and government — will create roughly three million jobs over the next 20 years, 76.5 percent of all new jobs in Texas. This represents an average annual growth rate of 2.6 percent.

Texas won't rely as heavily as the U.S. on services for new jobs. Service-producing business will provide 96.3 percent of U.S. job growth to 2005, and a smaller average annual growth rate of 1.7 percent.

In Texas, the largest number of new service-producing jobs will be in wholesale and retail trade. Trade is expected to grow at an average annual rate of 2.8 percent, generating more than one-quarter of all jobs created in Texas over the next 20 years.

Services, including business, health and others, will create more than 915,000 new jobs by 2005 and grow at 2.6 percent per year.

Population

Texas' population is expected to increase from 16.4 million in 1985 to 20.6 million in the year 2000 and 21.6 million in 2005. Growing at this rate, Texas should pass New York to become the nation's second largest state between 1990 and 1995.

From 1985 to 2005, the state's population growth will average 1.4 percent per year. This will be much slower than the 2.5 percent a year averaged from 1970 to 1985. But it is still much higher than the projected national growth rate of 0.8 percent a year over the forecast period.

From 1970 to 1985, 60 percent of the state's population growth was due to newcomers, and 40 percent was caused by natural increase (births exceeding deaths). Over the next 20 years, only 28 percent of the state's population growth will be from new residents. Seventy-two percent will come from births.

Just as the growth in jobs across Texas will outpace the nation as a whole, the state's population will increase at a faster rate than the rest of the U.S. into the next century. A healthy job market will continue to attract young adults to Texas. But the state's population gains over the next 20 years will be due more to large numbers of births than to massive waves of newcomers.

Birth rates for Texas traditionally have been higher than the national average, and this will continue, although the long-term trend in the state and across the country is for a decreasing number of births per capita. Cultural and ethnic factors are important reasons for Texas' higher birth rate, but the key is the large number of women of childbearing age in the state. This number has increased due to vast numbers of in-migrants in the 1970s and early 1980s. And it will increase again with in-migration increases in 1988 through the 1990s.

Death rates have been declining. The Texas death rate per 1,000 population dropped from a post-World War II high of 8.5 in the late 1960s to 7.25 in 1985. The U.S. death rate per 1,000 population was 8.7 in 1984.

Longer life expectancies and declining birth rates will cause Texas' population to age, though, again, not as much as the nation as a whole. The average Texan will continue to be younger than the average American, and the state will feel the effects in somewhat different ways than the rest of the country.

As the U.S. ages, for example, services for the elderly will likely require a larger share of government resources. In Texas, however, the problems associated with an aging population will be less pronounced.

In 1986, there were 4.9 million Texans — 30 percent of the state's population — who were born during the "baby-boom" years from 1946 to 1962. The "boomer" generation has shaped American society from the 1950s to the present.

Boomers are now between 25 and 41 years of age, and in the midst of marrying and having children. Even with the lower birth rates, the large size of that age group has created a mini-baby boom in the 1980s. Between 1985 and 2000, Texas will gain about one million school-age children from five to 17 years of age.

Summary

Texas experienced a severe recession in 1986, losing more than 100,000 jobs, and the state unemployment rate exceeded 10 percent after oil prices dropped almost by half. The effects of this recession were felt in almost all sectors of the state's economy. Weak population and income growth combined with overbuilt construction markets played havoc in the construction industry. Weak real estate and problem energy loans created difficulties for Texas banks and savings and loan institutions. And consumers, worried about a troubled economy or having actual financial difficulties due to the recession, spent less.

The turnaround started slowly in the spring of 1987. The oil-dependent industries declined much more slowly and the non-oil sectors were able to grow and turn the tide for the Texas economy. The year, 1987, was one of transition for Texas, from the recession of 1986 to the more diversified growth expected in 1988 and beyond. Texas will grow because the state remains an attractive place for individuals and industrial location because of its central location in the Sunbelt and relatively low costs of living and doing business.

Economic Regions Of Texas

This article was prepared by State Comptroller Bob Bullock and staff members of the Comptroller's Economic Analysis Center: Tom Pollard, Roy Morey and Rhonda Byrnes.

Since Texas joined the United States under the condition that it could split into five separate states at any time, various methods for dividing the state have been studied.

Texas' great size, together with the cultural, climatic and geological diversity within its borders, provides ample justification for numerous ways of dividing the state into regions.

The availability of natural resources has created regional diversity in wealth and economic development across the state with some cities, like Midland and Odessa, heavily dependent on petroleum for their recent growth. As in the case of oil production, forestry, farming and ranching have been crucial to development of some regions.

Texas' proximity to Mexico has added cultural distinctions to the natural diversity of the state. The Spanish entered Texas from the south via Mexico, settling first at El Paso and then colonizing San Antonio and Nacogdoches. San Antonio prospered as a Spanish settlement. But Nacogdoches, far removed from Mexico and in terrain alien to the Spanish, did not attract as many Spanish settlers. Nacogdoches, therefore, was settled more from neighboring Louisiana and the southern United States than from Mexico and took on a different character than San Antonio. In addition, the plains of North Central Texas received streams of midwestern Americans, while direct immigrants from Europe settled in Central Texas. Even today, these diverse cultures have not completely merged.

Texas can easily be divided into economic regions. The natural and cultural characteristics of a region interact and are influenced by external economic events and changes in available technology to determine a particular region's economic base — those products and services that generate income and employment.

Regional economies differ, so an oil price decline, a peso devaluation, or a change in defense spending affect each region differently.

To more accurately assess the implications of such events for Texas, the Comptroller of Public Accounts divided the state into six economic regions — the Plains, the Metroplex, East Texas, the Gulf Coast, the Central Corridor and the Border. These are compared on a number of economic and demographic factors in Table 1.

The Plains region is the largest and most sparsely populated area of the state and has a petroleum and agricultural-based economy. The Metroplex is almost totally urban with diversified manufacturing and service sectors. East Texas, on the other hand, is primarily a rural region, mostly dependent on producing and processing agricultural commodities, timber, petroleum and coal. The most populous region of Texas, the Gulf Coast, has an economy centered around petroleum production and petrochemical manufacture. The public and private service sectors provide the economic base for the Central Corridor. The Border area is characterized by its economic relationship with Mexico. A more detailed description of each region follows.

The Plains

The economy of the Plains is tied closely to its exhaustible natural resources. The discovery of the West Texas oil fields in the 1930s, the intensive utilization of water from the Ogallala Aquifer for agricultural irrigation, and a strong demand for petroleum and agricultural products have stimulated the rapid economic growth of the Plains for 50 years.

The northern part of the region, from Lubbock north toward Amarillo, has utilized ground water to produce massive quantities of cotton, grain sorghum, wheat, corn and other feed grains. In addition, this area is the United States leader in feedlot cattle production. In 1985, the value of farm production sold from the Plains region was $3.8 billion, 41 percent of the Texas total. In 1984, farm income accounted for 3.4 percent of Plain's total personal income, more than twice the average for other regions of the state.

In 1986, about 67 percent of the oil and 28 percent of the gas produced in Texas came from the Plains region. Oil and gas production dominates the economy of the west central and southwestern portion of this region. Midland and Odessa are the focal points of oil and natural gas production in the Plains.

Recent declines in oil prices have dealt a hard blow to this area. Falling oil prices eliminated about 13,000 petroleum-related jobs in the Plains region between 1982 and 1984 and another 24,000 such jobs since 1984. Total Plains employment fell about 57,000 between 1984 and 1986. However, the region's energy dependence is declining. In 1986, oil and gas-related employment accounted for less than 13 percent of the nonagricultural employment in the Plains region, down from 16 percent in 1984.

In the southeastern part of the Plains, farming becomes smaller scale and less dependent on irrigation. Ranching of cattle, hogs, sheep and goats is more important in this part of the region, and petroleum production is less so. San Angelo and Abilene, in particular, are examples of diversified local economies that are weathering the current downturn in oil and agricultural prices relatively well.

In the short term, the economy of the Plains region will continue to be troubled by problems related to soft demand for agricultural and petroleum products. In the long term, the region faces problems of dependence on petroleum and water, both of which will be in short supply in 40 to 50 years. The development of new techniques in farming and petroleum recovery and the ability to diversify the economy will determine the future economic health of the Plains.

Metroplex

Even though it is in an area with abundant natural resources, the economy of the Metroplex — particularly Dallas and Fort Worth — is dominated by manufacturing, commerce, services and finance.

The Metroplex is the most diversified of the six regional economies. A healthy durable goods manufacturing sector provides almost 14 percent of the region's total employment, the second highest percentage in the state. Of particular importance within this broad category of manufacturing is the production of electronics,

aerospace and military hardware. Defense procurements, primarily for military hardware, totaled more than $6.4 billion or 61 percent of the defense outlays to the state in 1985.

The role of the Metroplex as a trade and financial center is evident from its employment distribution. The region has a higher percentage of its employment in wholesale trade (8.2 percent of total employment) and finance, insurance and real estate (7.9 percent of total employment) than the other regions.

Significant also is the importance of the tourist industry to the economy of the Metroplex. Dallas is one of the most popular tourist destinations in Texas and is the third-ranking convention and trade show host in the nation.

East Texas

The economy of East Texas is based on its natural resources — timber, petroleum and coal. However, manufacturing is emerging as an important source of employment.

Almost all of East Texas is covered by the vegetational region of Texas known as the Piney Woods. This densely forested area has long been a significant source of lumber and wood products. In 1984, East Texas produced 407 million cubic feet of wood, 82 percent of total Texas production. In addition, employment in lumbering and wood-products manufacturing provides about 12,500 jobs in the region.

Mineral resources, centered around Longview, provide significant income and employment in petroleum, coal mining and in related industries. Nearly 12 percent of the crude oil and 13 percent of the natural gas produced in Texas comes from this region. In addition, East Texas accounts for 60 percent of the state's coal production. In 1986, almost 10,000 East Texans were employed in oil and gas extraction and an additional 6,000 worked in the production of oil field equipment and supplies and related construction.

Agricultural production plays a major role in the East Texas economy. As the forests have been cleared in the southern part of the region, the land has been converted to the production of rice, grain sorghum and peanuts. The northern part of the region produces substantial crops of cotton, soybeans and hay. Poultry production has emerged as a significant contributor to the economy of the region, as have cattle and dairy farms.

Gulf Coast

From Beaumont to Corpus Christi, the Gulf Coast has been united economically by the dominance of the petroleum, petrochemical and related industries. However, the Gulf Coast is becoming less dependent on oil as the region's economic base broadens with the growth of aerospace, defense and health industries.

Gulf Coast employment is supplemented by steel production, shipbuilding, commercial fishing, port activity and agriculture. The flat, low-lying coastal plain, with its abundant water supply, produces massive quantities of rice, cotton, flax, grain sorghum, soybeans and various grasses for cattle feed.

The discovery of oil at Spindletop, near Beaumont, in 1901 sparked the first Texas oil boom and the beginning of the oil industry in Texas. Houston, set between the East Texas timber lands and the Gulf of Mexico, became a center for producing oil-drilling equipment, refining oil and transporting petroleum products via rail and sea.

The Gulf Coast accounted for 12 percent of the crude oil and 25 percent of the gas produced in Texas during 1986. In 1985, 45 percent of the state's mining employment and 73 percent of statewide employment in the petroleum refining and petrochemical production industries were in this region.

About 14 percent of total employment in the Gulf Coast is in oil and gas-related industries. This percentage has declined since 1982, as the price of oil has fallen.

The Gulf Coast lost more than 114,000 jobs during the recession in 1982-1983. By the end of 1984, a slow recovery had added nearly 39,000 jobs, but the region's economy remained flat during 1985. However, the steep drop in oil prices that occurred late in 1985 led to another recession. During 1986, nearly 91,000 jobs were lost even though the economy's dependence on oil and gas had lessened.

The Houston metropolitan area, the ninth largest in the nation, represents the most diversified local economy in the region, having built on its importance as a petroleum center. The area's economy has diversified into medical research, biomedical manufacturing and aerospace technology. With diversification, Hous-

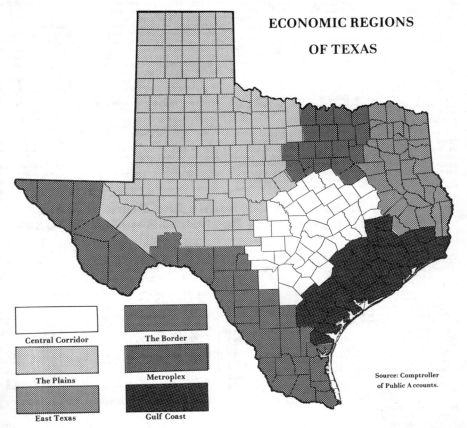

ECONOMIC REGIONS

OF TEXAS

Central Corridor

The Plains

East Texas

The Border

Metroplex

Gulf Coast

Source: Comptroller
of Public Accounts.

ton's economy, and that of the entire Gulf Coast, will provide further growth opportunities for related services.

However, short-term recovery in the region depends on stable oil prices. And long-term prosperity depends on continued expansion into industries other than oil and gas.

Central Corridor

The Central Corridor, like the Metroplex, has prospered independently of its natural resources and geology. The principal economic centers of the region, with the exception of Bryan-College Station in Brazos County, lie along Interstate Highway 35 between Waco and San Antonio.

The economic centers of this region have prospered as a result of spending on public and private services and the operation of military installations in the region.

More than 32 percent of employment in the Central Corridor is in service industries, the largest percentage of any of the regions of the state. Health services, education services and public administration account for more than 26 percent of total regional employment.

This region received $1.1 billion in defense procurements in 1985, 10.2 percent of the state total.

In 1984, government employment represented 25 percent of total employment in the region. Federal and state government employment is more important to the Central Corridor than to any other region of the state.

The Central Corridor, however, does not rely solely on the service sector or government spending. Instead, these sectors serve as a base for a more diversified economy. High-tech employment in the Central Corridor grew by more than 35 percent between 1983 and 1985, an increase of more than 10,000 jobs. Though high-

tech employment declined by 1,700 jobs during 1986, the production of such items as electronic components and computing equipment remains important to the region.

A recent building boom has had a tremendous impact on the Corridor. Of the 153,000 jobs created between 1983 and 1986, 52 percent were in construction, real estate and related finance and service industries. Building leveled off in 1985, and, with parts of the Central Corridor becoming overbuilt, construction employment began to decline in 1986.

Despite recent declines in construction and manufacturing, the Corridor will benefit from two important trends shaping the U.S. economy: the move toward a service-based economy and the growing importance of high-technology manufacturing.

The Border

The Border is delineated as a separate region because of the impact of its economic ties with Mexico. During the 1980s, Mexico's economy has been troubled by high unemployment, inflation and a series of peso devaluations. In 1982, the exchange rate averaged 96 pesos to the dollar. By 1986, the average value of the peso had fallen to 900 per dollar. By early 1987, the value of the peso was even lower, standing at 1,150 to the dollar. This meant a contraction in retail sales to citizens of Mexico all along the border. The result was a loss of jobs in Texas.

But the Border economy continues to grow despite Mexico's problems. Even though since 1983 the economy has become less dependent on retail sales to Mexican nationals, jobs in the region have increased steadily.

During 1986, the region between El Paso and Brownsville gained 5,000 jobs — a growth rate of 1.2

percent. Employment in McAllen grew 4 percent during 1986. Job growth in El Paso, helped by increased defense spending, reached 3 percent. Both in Laredo and Brownsville-Harlingen job growth was 2 percent.

Even with relatively rapid job growth, Border cities have the highest unemployment in the state. During 1986, unemployment in McAllen averaged 20 percent, the highest in the state. All Border communities had unemployment rates in double digits.

Several reasons for the growth in Border employment exist. Citrus orchards destroyed by the devastating freeze of 1983 are beginning to produce again. The population of "winter Texans" — Midwesterners that head to south Texas to escape the cold — is on the rise, stimulating related service-industry jobs.

Another factor in Border employment growth is the rapid expansion of the twin-plant industry, stimulated by the falling peso. Twin-plants in Mexico assemble products from components made by American companies. The products are then shipped back across the border at reduced tariffs for sale in the United States. In 1984-1985, the number of production-sharing plants rose 27 percent. The number of twin-plant workers also

surged, with these workers continuing to shop on the Texas side, despite the falling peso.

Sales tax collections in Border cities during 1985 reflected this growth in commerce. Collections were up nearly 15 percent in McAllen. Taxable sales for the region were up nearly 10 percent during the period compared to an 8.5 percent increase for the state as a whole. While growth in taxable sales slowed somewhat during 1986 in the region, sales declined statewide by 2 percent during this period.

Throughout the region, jobs and income are provided by agriculture irrigated from the Rio Grande and underground aquifers. Together, Hidalgo and Cameron counties, at the southern tip of Texas, contain in excess of one million acres of irrigated cropland.

Although the employment impact is small, oil and gas production contributes substantially to the income of the region. Kleberg County, in the southeastern corner of the region, is a major Texas producer of natural gas. In 1986, mining employed about 2 percent of the workers in the Border region.

The Border is noted also for its high level of local government employment; 23 percent of employment in the region is in the public sector with state and local government alone providing 15 percent.

Table 1. Selected Economic And Demographic Characteristics For The Economic Regions Of Texas

	The Plains	The Metroplex	East Texas	Gulf Coast	Central Corridor	The Border	*STATE TOTAL
TOTAL POPULATION 1985:	1,853,626	3,898,194	1,202,145	4,853,337	2,955,836	1,606,444	16,369,582
Percent Change 1970-1985	17.1%	32.0%	29.0%	34.0%	33.0%	37.0%	45.7%
Percent Living in Metro Areas	56.3	94.0	33.3	91.5	83.3	78.8	81.1
TOTAL PERSONAL INCOME 1984							
(in millions)	$22,950	$56,898	$13,198	$66,896	$34,009	$11,914	$205,584
Percent Farm	3.4%	0.3%	3.0%	0.3%	1.0%	3.5%	1.1%
Percent Non-farm	96.6	99.7	97.0	99.7	99.0	96.5	98.9
Personal Income Per Capita	$12,353	$15,133	$11,115	$13,868	$11,859	$7,501	$12,798
TOTAL EMPLOYMENT 1984:	967,626	2,209,391	519,851	2,455,440	1,459,797	567,692	8,179,797
Percent Farm	7.9%	1.5%	7.8%	1.7%	3.9%	4.8%	3.4%
Percent Nonfarm	92.1	98.5	92.2	98.3	96.1	95.2	96.6
Percent by Type:							
Proprietors	23.0	13.1	22.5	13.5	15.5	15.4	15.6
Private	76.6	88.1	78.2	85.7	71.5	72.2	81.3
Federal Government - Civilian	1.5	1.7	2.2	1.4	4.4	2.7	2.2
Federal Government - Military	2.5	90.4	81.7	91.3	6.4	5.0	2.4
State and Local Government	11.5	7.8	11.1	10.3	13.8	15.4	10.8
TOTAL WAGE AND SALARY							
EMPLOYMENT 1984:	664,186	1,822,969	373,043	2,008,441	1,078,492	429,319	6,376,450
Percent by Industry:							
Agricultural Services, Forestries							
and Fisheries	1.9%	0.5%	1.1%	0.7%	0.7%	4.1%	1.0%
Mining	10.7	1.9	4.1	6.0	1.1	2.7	4.1
Construction	6.4	6.7	6.5	8.7	8.0	5.5	7.4
Manufacturing - Durable Goods	6.3	13.5	15.7	6.5	7.6	4.4	9.0
Manufacturing - Nondurable							
Goods	5.7	6.4	8.3	7.2	4.9	10.5	6.7
Transportation	3.3	4.3	2.4	4.2	2.4	3.1	3.6
Communications	1.7	1.5	1.3	1.3	1.5	1.1	1.4
Utilities	2.0	1.3	2.5	2.1	1.5	2.1	1.8
Wholesale Trade-Durable Goods	3.5	5.5	2.8	4.6	2.9	3.1	4.3
Wholesale Trade-Nondurable							
Goods	2.9	2.7	2.4	2.5	2.1	2.7	2.5
Retail Trade	19.2	18.9	19.0	18.1	20.1	20.1	19.0
Finance, Insurance, Real Estate	4.9	7.9	4.5	6.5	6.5	4.7	6.5
Personal Services	2.1	2.7	1.8	2.4	2.8	2.5	2.5
Business & Repair Services	3.7	6.5	2.8	6.4	5.1	3.5	5.5
Amusement and Recreation	0.9	1.1	0.7	1.0	1.1	0.9	1.0
Health Services	7.6	5.4	8.6	6.9	7.8	6.6	6.8
Legal Services	0.5	0.6	0.4	0.7	0.7	0.5	0.6
Educational Services	9.4	6.1	8.9	7.6	10.7	13.0	8.3
Social Services	1.8	1.2	1.4	1.2	2.2	1.8	1.5
Other Services	1.7	2.5	1.4	2.6	2.5	1.5	2.3
Public Administration	3.9	2.7	3.5	3.0	7.9	5.7	4.0
PERCENT PRODUCTION OF							
SELECTED COMMODITIES:							
Coal—(1985)	0.1%	0.0%	60.1%	6.4%	32.6%	0.7%	100.0%
Crude Oil—(1986)	67.1	1.6	11.6	12.0	4.4	3.3	100.0
Condensate—(1986)	10.4	1.5	18.0	38.6	3.6	28.0	100.0
Natural Gas—(1986)	28.2	3.1	12.8	24.8	3.5	27.7	100.0
Wood—(1984)	0.0	0.0	81.5	18.4	0.0	0.0	100.0
Farm—(1984)	40.7	7.3	12.7	13.5	14.5	11.3	100.0
Defense Procurements—(1985)	4.2	60.7	2.1	20.3	10.2	2.5	100.0

*Totals may not add due to rounding.

SOURCES: United States Department of Commerce, Texas Railroad Commission, Community Services Administration and Texas Forest Service.

Banking In Texas

Texas voters approved constitutional amendments in November 1986 that laid to rest Populist influence in the state's banking system alongside that of Andrew Jackson. The state first outlawed banks and then placed tight restrictions on banking when it was finally legalized in 1905.

Voters, however, now have approved branch banking within counties and out-of-state ownership of Texas banks.

Ironically, despite Texas' attitude toward banks, the first chartered bank west of the Mississippi River was located in the state of Coahuila and Texas. Upon Mexico's gaining independence from Spain in 1822, Jose Felix Trespalacios was named military and political advisor for the region. He determined that the military and political officials were not paid because specie shipments were irregular. As governor in October 1822, Trespalacios promulgated a decree establishing the *Banco Nacional de Texas* in San Antonio. In November 1822, the bank issued scrip that was to be redeemable at face value to pay officials and soldiers. The first notes were sent to the garrison in Goliad to meet the monthly payroll.

History Highlights

The idea of issuing paper money appealed to the Emperor Agustin de Iturbide so much that he made treasury notes legal tender in Mexico, but to be redeemed by the government with only two-thirds specie and one-third paper money. In February 1823, the Texas bank notes were replaced with national notes, which were immediately discounted 33 percent. Holders of the Texas notes successfully sued to get them redeemed at full value in specie, as promised, and though successful, the legal action took several years. The bank soon closed, leaving a distrust in bank notes in Texas.

In April 1835, the legislature of Coahuila and Texas granted a charter to Samuel May Williams for the *Banco de Commercia y Agricultura*. Capitalization of $300,000 was required, and the bank did not open for several years.

Opponents of banking raised the issue during the writing of the constitution of the Republic of Texas. But the charter simply did not mention banking. The notes of out-of-state banks were used as currency for a time, but most of these banks closed in the financial Panic of 1837, leaving many Texans holding worthless paper. Thereafter, the Congress of the Republic banned the circulation of "any note, bill or paper of purported value." And this remained the law until annexation by the United States.

President Mirabeau Lamar in 1838 recommended establishment of a national bank to be the Texas Republic's fiscal agent, but the idea was rejected by Congress.

Andrew Jackson's anti-banking influence was strongly felt when the first State Constitution was written in 1845. From his deathbed in January, he wrote his protege and friend, Sam Houston, urging Texans to repudiate banking in the new constitution. When Jackson died in June, delegates to the constitutional convention wore black crepe armbands in memory of the former president — and prohibited corporate banking in Texas by a 47-7 vote.

Merchants provided primitive banking services for Texas during this period, and the Commercial and Agricultural Bank, chartered during the Mexican period, operated for a time in Galveston. Private banks sprang up, generally unregulated by the state government except for the usury laws.

Andrew Jackson killed the national bank with a veto in 1832, and for the next 30 years, states had no competition in chartering banks. Much of the anti-banking sentiment was in the South. But during the Civil War, the U.S. Congress passed the National Bank Act, which eventually permitted national banks to be established in Texas with capitalization of $50,000. The First National Bank of Galveston, chartered in September 1865, was the first opened in the state under this law.

Texas' Reconstruction Constitution of 1869 omitted the clause prohibiting the state from chartering banks, and the Legislature assumed the authority to do so.

Between 1870 and 1871, 30 banks were chartered by the state, but only eight opened for business. Indeed, branch banking was authorized for several institutions, but was never used. The Texas Banking and Insurance Co. in Galveston received the first state charter on July 1, 1870, but the Island City Savings Bank in Galveston was the first to open its doors.

When the delegates to the constitutional convention of 1875 met, the effects of the financial Panic of 1873 were fresh in their minds. And the prohibition against state-chartered banks was returned to the constitution. Until the turn of the century, private and national banks provided banking services for Texas. Private banks increased from 73 in 1877 to 197 in 1905, and national banks numbered 440 in 1905, with 221 gaining charters after 1900 when the capitalization requirement was reduced to $25,000. National banking also was profitable in the state. The U.S. Comptroller of Currency reported that in the decade ending in 1905, the return on capital in Texas averaged 9.09 percent, while the national average was 7.55 percent.

While Texas prohibited state banks, it was the first state to have a bankers association. The Texas Bankers Association was organized in Lampasas in 1885 and raised the issue of chartering state banks. By that time, Texas was the only state to prohibit these financial institutions. In 1892, the Democratic Party of Texas first added a plank to its platform supporting state banks "under proper restrictions and control for the protection of the depositors and the people." Gov. Jim Hogg proposed a constitutional amendment in 1894 to allow state banking, but the Legislature did not submit the issue to voters for a decade.

Texas' economy was centered in agriculture, and small farmers were starved for credit. National banks could offer little help, for they were prohibited by law from using land as collateral. But Texans also were caught in a political dilemma. Populist sentiment, strong in the state in the 1890s, feared big corporations of any kind, and foreign capitalists were to be tightly controlled, if tolerated at all.

The constitutional amendment of 1904 allowing state-chartered banks carried a strong restraint against branch banking by prohibiting a bank . . . to engage in business in more than one place . . ." This provision has been modified twice in recent years.

In 1980, the provision was amended to authorize banks to establish and operate unmanned teller machines within their home city or county. Such machines may perform all banking functions.

In 1986, the provision was again amended to allow banks, subject to limitations imposed by the Legislature, to establish and operate banking facilities at locations within the bank's home city or county. This amendment also allows banks to branch beyond their city limits across county lines if done so through the purchase and assumption of assets and liabilities of a failed bank domiciled in the state.

Further, implicit recognition of holding-company ownership was contained in the 1986 amendment that provides a bank may not be considered a branch or facility of another bank solely because it is owned or controlled by the same stockholders as the other bank, has common accounting and administrative systems with the other bank, or has a name similar to the other bank's or because of a combination of these factors.

The first provision was intended to keep local money in hometown banks. It was feared that branch banking would funnel money from rural areas to the cities. In practice, the restrictions slowed the accumulation of capital in the state's banks and forced state industrialists in later years to go outside Texas for large loans that could not be handled by local banks.

Texas' first state banking law was passed in 1905, under the direction of State Sen. Thomas B. Love of Dallas. Among other provisions, it allowed banks in communities of under 2,500 population to be chartered with $10,000 capitalization.

State bank charters apparently were available for the asking, and the new Department of Insurance and Banking was to supervise the operations. Between 1905-1913, there were 900 state bank charters issued. By 1910, only 14 of 249 counties had neither a state nor national bank, and the new law was aiding rural areas to get bank services.

Continued on Next Page

Banking—

Continued From Preceding Page

Depositors were given protection when the Legislature mandated in 1909 that all state banks participate in either a Depositors Guaranty Fund or the Bond Security System. This was a state forerunner of the Federal Deposit Insurance Corporation, created in 1934 during the Depression.

One weakness of Texas' system was the failure to regulate state banks. The so-called period of "free banking" ended when the Legislature in 1913 instructed the banking board to exercise its judgment on charters. Authority was given the board to determine the need for a new bank in the area in which the charter was requested and to investigate the integrity of the proposed bank's officers and investors.

The Texas Bankers Association grew during the period, offering various professional and educational services to members. In 1911, the *Texas Bankers Record* was established as the organization's official publication. A year later, the Texas Women Bankers Association was established by TBA and operated until World War I as an educational organization.

On its 75th anniversary in 1986, the name of the association's magazine was changed to *Texas Banking.* Through a period of 101 years, the association has had only two full-time managing officers, William A. Philpott Jr. from 1915-1964 and Sam O. Kimberlin Jr. from 1964 to present.

When the Federal Reserve System was established in 1913, Dallas was selected as the site of one of the 12 reserve banks across the nation. Branch reserve banks were established in Houston, San Antonio and El Paso. The Federal Reserve was established to give the nation a central bank and to provide coordination between banks to solve many of the banking problems of the day.

Hard times hit Texas and state banks in the 1920s and lingered until the Second World War. Between May 1920 and June 1921, wholesale prices nationally dropped 56 percent, the sharpest decline in U.S. history. Cotton prices fell from 36.2 cents a pound in March 1920 to 9.2 cents in April 1921, a 74.6 percent drop. Texas' agriculture-based economy was staggered. It is said with truth that the Great Depression came to Texas a decade earlier than it did to the rest of the nation. Certainly it hit state banks earlier. Between 1920 and 1929, the number of state chartered banks declined by 324, from 1,023 to 699. By 1939, there had been a decline of 636 institutions.

The Depositors Guaranty Fund also reflected the decline. The fund was financed with annual assessments of member banks, but special assessments were necessary when the fund neared insolvency. In its first 11 years of operation from 1910, depositors in 18 liquidated banks had been paid $876,358. No depositor, it was said for a time, ever lost a cent in a Texas state bank. As the state economy declined, however, the guaranty fund banks were sorely pressed to continue to finance the fund with special assessments. When the fund was shut down in 1927, $18 million had been paid to depositors in 138 defunct banks. The fund was declared insolvent in September 1926, and the law was repealed the following year.

Improved roads put bank robbers on wheels, and they became a problem in the late 1920s. In a controversial move, the bankers association offered a $500 reward for dead bank robbers in 1926, and a year later increased it to $5,000. "Not one cent" would be paid for wounded or captured bandits, according to association policy, for they likely would be acquitted or get only short prison terms. And not many bank robbers were caught anyway. Texas Ranger Capt. Frank Hamer called the policy "a perfect murder machine" and said it had ". . . aroused the greed and desire of a small group of men who have more love for money than for human life . . ." But the policy was retained by the bankers group until 1964.

In the late 1920s, state banking officials took steps to shore up some weak banks, to close others and to follow tougher regulatory measures. Consequently, state banks bore up fairly well during the 1930s, but they still faced severe problems. During one period in which depositors made runs on the banks, Gov. Miriam Ferguson "assumed" authority to call a state bank holiday, to coincide with a similar national bank holiday called by President Franklin D. Roosevelt, from March 3-7, 1933. Twenty-one other states already had declared similar bank holidays. (No one complained, but the governor did not have the authority to close Texas banks. The Legislature later ratified Gov. Ferguson's action.)

Most state banking legislation during the 1930s only brought Texas into compliance with national law or allowed the banks to take advantage of federal programs. In 1943 in the midst of World War II, however, Texas banking laws were overhauled.

Women played a large role in Texas banking during the war. In 1942, the Friona State Bank became the first all-woman operated bank in the nation, and during the war, 415 women had officers' positions in Texas banks, including 13 presidencies.

Bank deposits soared and on Dec. 31, 1945, there were 434 national banks in the state with $5.166 billion in deposits and 409 state banks with deposits of $952,200,000. Texas banks were in a good position to take advantage of the post-war boom.

Branch banking had been opposed by Texans from the inception of state-chartered banking. In 1927, Congress prohibited national banks from opening branches in states that prohibited branch banking. But the prohibition began breaking down when federal legislation in 1970 allowed the organization of bank holding companies. By 1972, there were 13 multi-bank and 92 one-bank holding companies in Texas.

By mid-1985, the 11 largest multi-bank holding companies had 463 subsidiaries, but an additional 132 multi-bank holding companies with 390 subsidiaries were in operation.

The 50 largest holding companies owned 597 banks and held 69.1 percent of the deposits in Texas. The 11 largest companies each had more than $1 billion in deposits, with MCorp of Dallas the largest, with deposits of $17.56 billion.

During the 1970s, Texas banks prospered as the price of oil rose and the value of real estate in the booming metropolitan areas increased. But the financial institutions fell on hard times in the mid-1980s with the collapse of worldwide oil prices and the corresponding drop in real estate values. For four years the number of bank failures in Texas doubled each year, reaching 26 in 1986.

In 1986, the Legislature, in special session to deal with an impending budget deficit, authorized interstate ownership of Texas banks and bank holding companies by out-of-state holding companies and ownership of out-of-state banks or holding companies by Texas-based bank holding companies. A new day in Texas banking dawned quickly. On consecutive days in December 1986, Chemical New York Corp. agreed to a friendly buy-out of Houston-based Texas Commerce Bancshares, and RepublicBank Corp. purchased another Dallas-based bank holding company, InterFirst Corp., forming the nation's 12th largest bank — First RepublicBank Corp. — with assets of $35 billion.

Texas banking in the late 1980s was facing an uncertain future. More than 500 new banks were chartered between 1980 and 1986, and a reduction in the almost 1,900 banks operating in the state was expected. With out-of-state banks becoming involved in Texas banking, competition was expected to be keener, loan policies tighter and the range of services greater. Without a rebound in oil prices and improvement in the real estate market, profits were expected to lean more heavily on services rather than loans. Neither Andrew Jackson nor the Populists would approve of the newfound freedom in banking operations.

—MIKE KINGSTON

For Further Reading:

Grant, Joseph M., and Lawrence L. Crum, **The Development of State-Chartered Banking in Texas;** Bureau of Business Research, University of Texas at Austin, 1978.

Gatton, T. Harry, **The Texas Bankers Association: The First Century, 1885-1985;** Texas Bankers Association, Austin, 1984.

Total Deposits and Total Assets of All Insured Commercial Banks in Texas by Counties

Source: Federal Reserve Bank of Dallas as of Dec. 31, 1986
(In thousands of dollars)

County	No. of Banks	Total Deposits	Total Assets	County	No. of Banks	Total Deposits	Total Assets
Anderson	6	$264,912	$297,090	Frio	3	108,272	122,356
Andrews	3	113,394	125,973	Gaines	3	71,417	79,661
Angelina	8	478,305	532,351	Galveston	24	1,273,411	1,464,903
Aransas	3	163,699	179,349	Garza	1	43,836	49,763
Archer	2	35,488	39,037	Gillespie	4	219,960	237,848
Armstrong	1	14,336	15,742	Goliad	1	33,158	37,238
Atascosa	6	160,382	182,780	Gonzales	5	140,537	159,981
Austin	7	219,784	241,208	Gray	4	257,570	294,147
Bailey	2	67,203	75,761	Grayson	17	964,899	1,046,142
Bandera	2	49,393	53,353	Gregg	16	1,099,801	1,198,453
Bastrop	6	186,244	208,471	Grimes	7	132,205	143,471
Baylor	2	52,668	59,667	Guadalupe	7	362,235	401,935
Bee	3	176,342	202,741	Hale	5	268,703	290,788
Bell	18	944,922	1,043,461	Hall	3	51,624	57,150
Bexar	80	8,077,462	9,330,630	Hamilton	3	90,534	99,424
Blanco	3	58,751	65,969	Hansford	3	91,967	107,860
Bosque	6	153,034	167,883	Hardeman	3	66,888	73,032
Bowie	11	524,361	604,242	Hardin	5	167,532	182,859
Brazoria	23	908,651	1,001,205	Harris	259	16,646,827	18,177,143
Brazos	9	781,567	857,128	Harrison	8	350,526	396,395
Brewster	1	47,804	54,806	Haskell	4	78,886	86,682
Briscoe	2	37,496	43,555	Hays	7	269,325	298,074
Brooks	1	38,228	45,324	Hemphill	2	91,839	101,982
Brown	5	283,549	305,438	Henderson	9	326,806	361,635
Burleson	6	157,663	174,664	Hidalgo	25	2,229,127	2,442,191
Burnet	5	290,779	316,473	Hill	7	191,762	213,474
Caldwell	4	138,447	156,146	Hockley	5	283,197	309,366
Calhoun	4	181,290	202,267	Hood	4	186,626	202,386
Callahan	3	77,821	89,522	Hopkins	4	219,943	243,871
Cameron	22	1,374,166	1,506,801	Houston	7	174,249	192,123
Camp	2	84,338	92,449	Howard	4	285,846	323,886
Carson	3	51,897	57,344	Hudspeth	1	5,105	5,774
Cass	6	161,257	180,085	Hunt	11	468,398	514,617
Castro	2	61,945	69,410	Hutchinson	3	102,722	112,229
Chambers	4	104,509	119,441	Irion	1	33,886	39,930
Cherokee	7	262,538	297,850	Jack	3	94,483	104,551
Childress	2	36,042	39,628	Jackson	3	138,088	152,485
Clay	2	60,845	68,206	Jasper	4	151,511	170,976
Cochran	1	32,971	35,865	Jeff Davis	1	10,725	11,736
Coke	2	36,677	40,664	Jefferson	18	2,175,238	2,416,958
Coleman	3	115,141	126,701	Jim Hogg	2	40,873	51,246
Collin	36	1,490,813	1,645,813	Jim Wells	6	276,214	318,986
Collingsworth	2	47,431	52,548	Johnson	12	579,648	633,125
Colorado	5	209,219	249,116	Jones	3	92,822	103,859
Comal	6	282,237	311,606	Karnes	4	107,499	119,947
Comanche	4	156,658	172,298	Kaufman	9	407,778	448,144
Concho	2	24,264	27,289	Kendall	3	154,091	168,756
Cooke	5	250,581	272,964	Kent	1	7,365	8,229
Coryell	6	212,105	234,657	Kerr	6	524,890	585,952
Cottle	1	28,672	36,047	Kimble	2	30,624	35,405
Crane	1	22,683	25,407	Kinney	1	10,619	11,560
Crockett	2	56,071	66,085	Kleberg	3	194,535	224,440
Crosby	3	55,418	62,482	Knox	2	42,516	47,339
Culberson	1	13,314	14,794	La Salle	1	14,614	16,348
Dallam	3	93,334	105,924	Lamar	6	284,148	317,106
Dallas	192	14,777,455	16,603,337	Lamb	6	112,932	127,205
Dawson	2	156,771	177,456	Lampasas	3	118,444	129,701
Deaf Smith	2	161,546	180,503	Lavaca	4	149,535	168,170
Delta	3	49,249	54,661	Lee	5	185,116	204,518
Denton	20	1,132,037	1,225,861	Leon	5	80,909	90,503
DeWitt	8	284,524	313,734	Liberty	9	357,797	395,072
Dickens	1	17,923	19,797	Limestone	7	159,750	176,147
Dimmit	2	50,170	55,460	Lipscomb	2	37,198	40,907
Donley	3	57,066	63,591	Live Oak	5	83,215	96,449
Duval	2	51,602	59,796	Llano	5	163,696	184,769
Eastland	5	138,275	154,833	Lubbock	16	2,047,029	2,341,908
Ector	8	709,155	774,874	Lynn	3	68,679	78,368
Edwards	1	15,177	18,290	McCulloch	2	77,463	85,754
El Paso	29	3,520,483	4,042,265	McLennan	21	1,617,741	1,876,812
Ellis	15	552,522	601,780	McMullen	1	16,587	18,800
Erath	5	270,863	294,281	Madison	3	133,512	146,584
Falls	6	150,295	164,793	Marion	2	45,584	49,025
Fannin	7	182,483	203,685	Martin	2	43,026	48,906
Fayette	9	314,219	347,341	Mason	4	49,265	55,156
Fisher	2	43,061	47,336	Matagorda	4	290,671	333,042
Floyd	2	71,112	80,433	Maverick	2	184,387	200,925
Foard	1	19,092	20,968	Medina	6	103,947	116,680
Fort Bend	13	652,714	710,159	Menard	2	20,677	25,758
Franklin	2	62,723	69,993	Midland	9	1,574,762	1,792,541
Freestone	5	113,303	124,799	Milam	6	195,525	229,780

County		
Mills	2	80,983	90,522
Mitchell	3	76,756	85,821
Montague	5	177,474	194,374
Montgomery	15	818,282	877,069
Moore	3	102,957	116,728
Morris	4	108,758	117,123
Motley	1	6,753	8,053
Nacogdoches	8	458,343	495,702
Navarro	10	452,560	486,489
Newton	1	20,805	22,762
Nolan	3	142,069	159,528
Nueces	25	2,319,749	2,760,403
Ochiltree	2	190,967	214,662
Oldham	1	14,153	16,272
Orange	7	336,484	372,713
Palo Pinto	6	234,545	253,892
Panola	4	164,991	187,459
Parker	6	320,924	354,867
Parmer	3	114,996	131,939
Pecos	3	123,514	135,948
Polk	5	224,557	247,442
Potter	9	1,842,604	2,153,570
Presidio	2	37,984	43,842
Rains	2	52,840	57,630
Randall	3	124,335	135,461
Reagan	2	35,150	40,059
Real	1	9,913	11,504
Red River	4	60,617	64,818
Reeves	2	102,368	116,832
Refugio	2	75,604	96,685
Roberts	1	17,942	20,994
Robertson	4	106,844	119,578
Rockwall	4	107,007	116,308
Runnels	7	143,051	155,192
Rusk	6	365,096	410,047
Sabine	2	63,653	70,658
San Augustine	2	60,173	67,368
San Jacinto	2	25,087	26,814
San Patricio	10	321,307	356,115
San Saba	2	46,688	52,334
Schleicher	1	28,116	33,158
Scurry	3	178,453	199,866
Shackelford	2	61,108	69,407
Shelby	5	165,717	181,287
Sherman	1	46,033	54,305
Smith	18	1,729,115	1,976,715
Somervell	1	26,240	28,267
Starr	2	126,374	139,248
Stephens	2	149,175	160,530
Sterling	1	25,229	29,002
Stonewall	2	20,645	25,602
Sutton	2	46,006	52,465
Swisher	4	105,576	118,969
Tarrant	94	6,382,527	7,009,435
Taylor	13	1,467,859	1,704,294
Terrell	1	16,055	17,589
Terry	2	115,749	127,317
Throckmorton	2	23,717	27,973
Titus	4	276,116	301,085
Tom Green	9	874,198	976,593
Travis	52	5,610,174	6,808,779
Trinity	3	55,720	60,691
Tyler	4	70,831	77,484
Upshur	2	177,279	207,248
Upton	2	36,097	42,311
Uvalde	4	241,674	272,329
Val Verde	4	208,286	228,206
Van Zandt	8	179,285	192,624
Victoria	6	1,214,962	1,396,500
Walker	6	341,745	375,522
Waller	5	106,663	117,178
Ward	2	96,806	112,911
Washington	6	337,358	371,209
Webb	6	1,644,771	1,785,067
Wharton	8	384,835	427,929
Wheeler	4	83,444	95,903
Wichita	11	1,267,344	1,465,439
Wilbarger	3	204,533	227,418
Willacy	2	111,995	125,743
Williamson	22	948,876	1,033,617
Wilson	4	95,958	112,504
Winkler	3	80,930	92,838
Wise	6	190,320	210,719
Wood	7	269,178	298,616
Yoakum	3	67,085	75,807
Young	4	219,932	241,326
Zapata	2	60,679	68,067
Zavala	2	25,577	28,472
TOTAL	**1,949**	**$120,493,496**	**$135,254,280**

The presentation above was derived from the regu-latory Report of Condition, consolidating domestic subsidiaries. Therefore, none of the deposits or assets of foreign branches of domestic banks are included in this tabulation. Listed below are the county totals with data from the Call Report consolidating domestic and foreign subsidiaries. These are:

Total Deposits and Total Assets Consolidation of Domestic and Foreign Subsidiaries

As of December 31, 1986
(In Thousands of Dollars)

County	Total Deposits	Total Assets
Bexar	$9,182,698	$10,832,422
Cameron	1,851,330	2,019,447
Dallas	33,144,504	47,501,784
Harris	35,077,143	49,998,855
Tarrant	10,183,019	12,004,832
Travis	6,127,459	7,490,662
Webb	1,880,427	2,041,172
Total All Counties	$163,426,694	$205,922,262

Texas State Banks

Consolidated Statement, Foreign and Domestic Offices, as of Dec. 31, 1986
Source: Federal Reserve Bank of Dallas

Number of Banks 895

(All figures in thousand dollars)

Assets

Cash and due from banks:
Noninterest-bearing balances and
currency and coin $4,711,626
Interest-bearing balances 3,058,468
Securities 11,633,908
Fed. funds sold and securities purchased
under agreement to resell 7,997,886
Loans and lease financing receivables:
Loans and leases, net of unearned
income 35,601,570
Less: allowance for loan and lease
losses 693,326
Loans and leases, net 34,908,244
Assets held in trading accounts 63,144
Premises and fixed assets
(including capitalized leases) 1,302,340
Other real estate owned 742,116
Investments in unconsolidated
subsidiaries and associated companies. . 34,131
Customers liability on acceptances
outstanding..................... 11,481
Intangible assets................... 5,666
Other assets 1,520,934
Total Assets $65,989,944

Liabilities

Deposits:
In domestic offices................ $57,617,261
Noninterest-bearing 10,735,516
Interest-bearing 46,881,745
In foreign offices, edge & agreement
subsidiaries, IBF's.............. 121,830
Federal funds purchased and securities
sold under agreement to repurchase. ... 2,300,709
Demand notes issued to the U.S. Treasury 341,294
Other borrowed money 125,993
Mortgage indebtedness and obligations
under capitalized leases.............. 91,841
Banks' liability on acceptances executed
and outstanding................... 11,481
Notes and debentures subordinated to
deposits......................... 39,354
Other liabilities..................... 828,842
Total Liabilities $61,478,605

Equity Capital

Perpetual preferred stock............. $697
Common stock 972,335
Surplus 2,300,201
Undivided profits and capital reserves 1,238,128
Total Equity Capital $4,511,361

Total liabilities, limited preferred
stock and equity capital $65,989,966

Texas National Banks

Consolidated Statement, Foreign and Domestic
Offices, as of Dec. 31, 1986

Source: Federal Reserve Bank of Dallas

Number of Banks 1,077

(All figures in thousand dollars)

Assets

Cash and due from banks:	
Noninterest-bearing balances and currency and coin	$11,872,187
Interest-bearing balances	7,646,421
Securities	18,284,717
Fed. funds sold and securities purchased under agreement to resell	14,514,325
Loans and lease financing receivables:	
Loans and leases, net of unearned income 84,348,510	
Less: allowance for loan and lease losses 2,166,061	
Less: allocated transfer risk reserve 35	
Loans and leases, net	82,182,414
Assets held in trading accounts	267,749
Premises and fixed assets (including capitalized leases)	2,426,987
Other real estate owned	1,362,667
Investments in unconsolidated subsidiaries and associated companies	33,636
Customers liability on acceptances outstanding	111,614
Intangible assets	137,228
Other assets	2,557,092
Total Assets	**$141,397,037**

Liabilities

Deposits:		
In domestic offices		$100,593,798
Noninterest-bearing	23,693,199	
Interest-bearing	76,900,599	
In foreign offices, edge & agreement subsidiaries, & IBF's		6,379,391
Noninterest-bearing	21,117	
Interest-bearing	6,358,274	
Federal funds purchased and securities sold under agreement to repurchase		19,705,735
Demand notes issued to the U.S. Treasury		2,887,179
Other borrowed money		1,340,951
Mortgage indebtedness and obligations under capitalized leases		155,147
Banks' liability on acceptances executed and outstanding		111,614
Notes and debentures subordinated to deposits		646,372
Other liabilities		1,588,486
Total Liabilities		**$133,408,673**

Equity Capital

Perpetual preferred stock	$105,148
Common stock	1,737,638
Surplus	2,976,833
Undivided profits and capital reserves . . .	3,168,960
Cumulative foreign currency translation adjustments	−225
Total Equity Capital	**$7,988,354**
Total liabilities, limited preferred stock and equity capital	**$141,397,027**

Texas Bank Resources and Deposits—1905-1986

On Dec. 31, 1986, Texas had a total of 1,972 national and state banks with total deposits of $164,712,280,000 and total resources of $207,386,981,000.

SOURCE: Federal Reserve Bank of Dallas.

(In thousands of dollars)

	National Banks			State Banks			National and State Banks		
Date	No. Banks	Total Resources	Deposits	No. Banks	Total Resources	Deposits	No. Banks	Total Resources	Deposits
Sept. 30, 1905	440	$189,484	$101,285	29	$4,341	$2,213	469	$193,825	$103,498
Nov. 10, 1910	516	293,245	145,249	621	88,103	59,766	1,137	381,348	205,015
Dec. 29, 1920	556	780,246	564,135	1,031	391,127	280,429	1,587	1,171,373	844,564
Dec. 31, 1930	560	1,028,420	826,723	655	299,012	231,909	1,215	1,327,432	1,058,632
Dec. 31, 1940	446	1,695,662	1,534,702	393	227,866	179,027	839	1,923,528	1,713,729
Dec. 31, 1950	442	6,467,275	6,076,006	449	1,427,680	1,338,540	891	7,894,955	7,414,546
Dec. 31, 1955	446	8,640,239	7,983,681	472	2,087,066	1,941,706	918	10,727,305	9,925,387
Dec. 31, 1956	452	8,986,456	8,241,159	480	2,231,497	2,067,927	932	11,217,953	10,309,086
Dec. 31, 1957	457	8,975,321	8,170,271	486	2,349,935	2,169,898	943	11,325,256	10,340,169
Dec. 31, 1958	458	9,887,733	9,049,580	499	2,662,270	2,449,474	957	12,550,007	11,499,054
Dec. 31, 1959	466	10,011,949	9,033,495	511	2,813,006	2,581,404	977	12,824,955	11,614,899
Dec. 31, 1960	468	10,520,690	9,560,668	532	2,997,609	2,735,726	1,000	13,518,299	12,296,394
Dec. 30, 1961	473	11,466,767	10,426,812	538	3,297,588	3,009,499	1,011	14,764,355	13,436,311
Dec. 28, 1962	486	12,070,803	10,712,253	551	3,646,404	3,307,714	1,037	15,717,207	14,019,967
Dec. 30, 1963	519	12,682,674	11,193,194	570	4,021,033	3,637,559	1,089	16,703,707	14,830,753
Dec. 31, 1964	539	14,015,957	12,539,142	581	4,495,074	4,099,543	1,120	18,511,031	16,638,685
Dec. 31, 1965	545	14,944,319	13,315,367	585	4,966,947	4,530,675	1,130	19,911,266	17,846,042
Dec. 31, 1966	546	15,647,346	13,864,727	591	5,332,385	4,859,906	1,137	20,979,731	18,724,633
Dec. 31, 1967	542	17,201,752	15,253,496	597	6,112,900	5,574,735	1,139	23,314,652	20,828,231
Dec. 31, 1968	535	19,395,045	16,963,003	609	7,107,310	6,489,357	1,144	26,502,355	23,452,360
Dec. 31, 1969	529	19,937,396	16,687,720	637	7,931,966	7,069,822	1,166	27,869,362	23,757,542
Dec. 31, 1970	530	22,087,890	18,384,922	653	8,907,039	7,958,133	1,183	30,994,929	26,343,055
Dec. 31, 1971	530	25,137,269	20,820,519	677	10,273,200	9,179,451	1,207	35,410,469	29,999,970
Dec. 31, 1972	538	29,106,654	23,892,660	700	12,101,749	10,804,827	1,238	41,208,403	34,697,487
Dec. 31, 1973	550	32,791,219	26,156,659	716	14,092,134	12,417,693	1,266	46,883,353	38,574,352
Dec. 31, 1974	569	35,079,218	28,772,284	744	15,654,983	13,758,141	1,313	50,734,201	42,530,431
Dec. 31, 1975	584	39,138,322	31,631,199	752	17,740,669	15,650,933	1,336	56,878,991	47,282,132
Dec. 31, 1976	596	43,534,570	35,164,285	761	19,846,695	17,835,078	1,357	63,381,265	52,999,363
Dec. 31, 1977	604	49,091,503	39,828,475	773	22,668,498	20,447,012	1,377	71,760,001	60,275,487
Dec. 31, 1978	609	56,489,274	44,749,491	786	25,987,616	23,190,869	1,395	82,476,890	67,940,360
Dec. 31, 1979	615	65,190,891	50,754,782	807	30,408,232	26,975,854	1,422	95,599,123	77,730,636
Dec. 31, 1980	641	75,540,334	58,378,669	825	35,186,113	31,055,648	1,466	110,726,447	89,434,317
Dec. 31, 1981	694	91,811,510	68,750,678	829	42,071,043	36,611,555	1,523	133,882,553	105,362,233
Dec. 31, 1982	758	104,580,333	78,424,478	841	48,336,463	41,940,277	1,599	152,916,796	120,364,755
Dec. 31, 1983	880	126,914,841	98,103,098	848	55,008,329	47,653,791	1,728	181,923,170	145,758,690
Dec. 31, 1984	999	137,565,365	105,862,656	855	60,361,504	52,855,584	1,854	197,926,869	158,718,240
Dec. 31, 1985	1,058	144,674,908	111,903,178	878	64,349,869	56,392,634	1,936	209,024,777	168,295,812
Dec. 31, 1986	1,077	141,397,037	106,973,189	895	65,989,944	57,739,091	1,972	207,386,981	164,712,280

Leading Texas Commercial Banks, Ranked By Total Domestic Deposits

Table below shows the ranking of Texas banks as of Dec. 31, 1986, according to total domestic deposits.

Source: Federal Reserve Bank of Dallas

Rank	Name and Location of Bank	*Total Deposits (000 dollars)	Rank	Name and Location of Bank	*Total Deposits (000 dollars)
1	RepublicBank Dallas, Dallas	$6,245,182	49	MBank Wichita Falls, Wichita Falls	387,511
2	MBank, Dallas, Dallas	4,896,834	50	Allied Bank West, Houston	385,614
3	Texas Commerce Bank, Houston	4,237,882	51	InterFirst Bank Tyler, Tyler	383,737
4	MBank, Houston, Houston	3,054,383	52	First Victoria National Bank, Victoria	379,532
5	First City National Bank of Houston, Houston	2,812,960	53	Texas American Bank/Dallas, Dallas	376,323
6	Allied Bank of Texas, Houston	2,769,158	54	Broadway National Bank, San Antonio	371,198
7	InterFirst Bank Dallas, Dallas	2,712,250	55	RepublicBank Oak Cliff, Dallas	366,119
8	Texas American Bank/Fort Worth, Fort Worth	1,960,172	56	First City National Bank of Midland, Midland	362,408
9	Frost National Bank of San Antonio, San Antonio	1,573,169	57	Texas Commerce Bank-Arlington, Arlington	355,907
10	InterFirst Bank Austin, Austin	1,306,282	58	First National Bank of Abilene, Abilene	355,791
11	RepublicBank Houston, Houston	1,270,205	59	First State Bank, Denton	344,894
12	National Bank of Commerce of San Antonio, San Antonio	1,095,036	60	First State Bank, Abilene	344,332
13	Texas Commerce Bank-Austin, Austin	1,060,541	61	MBank Waco, Waco	341,554
14	InterFirst Bank Fort Worth, Fort Worth	979,060	62	InterFirst Bank Park Cities, Dallas	340,331
15	Laredo National Bank, Laredo	957,359	63	InterFirst Bank Wichita Falls, Wichita Falls	326,250
16	MBank El Paso, El Paso	927,572	64	First City National Bank of El Paso, El Paso	325,274
17	MBank Fort Worth, Fort Worth	766,909	65	Cullen Center Bank & Trust, Houston	319,709
18	MBank Alamo, San Antonio	755,937	66	American State Bank, Lubbock	314,680
19	First City Bank of Dallas, Dallas	753,310	67	National Bank of Commerce-Heights, Houston	311,336
20	InterFirst Bank Houston, Houston	733,154	68	River Oaks Bank, Houston	310,329
21	RepublicBank First National Midland, Midland	715,720	69	Allied Mercantile Bank, Houston	306,114
22	Texas Commerce Bank-El Paso, El Paso	706,542	70	Interfirst Bank Galveston, Galveston	305,229
23	First City National Bank of Austin, Austin	694,232	71	First City National Bank of Tyler, Tyler	301,765
24	First National Bank of Amarillo, Amarillo	689,261	72	RepublicBank Greenville Ave., Dallas	293,083
25	Allied Bank of Dallas, Dallas	683,676	73	RepublicBank Tyler, Tyler	292,034
26	McAllen State Bank, McAllen	646,392	74	RepublicBank Ridglea, Fort Worth	288,826
27	MBank Corpus Christi, Corpus Christi	636,013	75	Texas Commerce Bank-Beaumont, Beaumont	286,098
28	MBank Preston, Dallas	620,301	76	Texas Commerce Bank-Reagan, Houston	280,159
29	Amarillo National Bank, Amarillo	605,282	77	MBank Abilene, Abilene	274,914
30	National Bank of Fort Sam Houston, San Antonio	582,888	78	InterFirst Bank Irving, Irving	273,613
31	RepublicBank Lubbock, Lubbock	554,450	79	Allied Champions Bank, Harris County	273,564
32	International Bank of Commerce Laredo, Laredo	526,762	80	Charles Schreiner Bank, Kerrville	270,873
33	Victoria Bank & Trust Co., Victoria	523,737	81	First City National Bank of Arlington, Arlington	264,669
34	Allied Bank Memorial, Houston	488,281	82	Central National Bank of San Angelo, San Angelo	256,317
35	First National Bank at Lubbock, Lubbock	485,571	83	InterFirst Bank Harlingen, Harlingen	242,032
36	MBank Austin, Austin	485,075	84	Bank of Dallas, Dallas	240,430
37	Texas Commerce Bank-Dallas, Dallas	479,987	85	MBank Port Arthur, Port Arthur	238,243
38	MBank Brownsville, Brownsville	464,147	86	Texas Commerce Bank-San Angelo, San Angelo	236,381
39	NorthPark National Bank of Dallas, Dallas	441,132	87	Texas Commerce Bank-San Antonio, San Antonio	236,176
40	RepublicBank Waco, Waco	439,348	88	Union National Bank of Laredo, Laredo	235,256
41	First City National Bank Beaumont, Beaumont	424,057	89	Interfirst Bank Corsicana, Corsicana	231,494
42	Texas American Bank/Galleria, Houston	413,443	90	Republicbank Austin, Austin	230,809
43	Texas Commerce Bank-Brownsville, Brownsville	407,681	91	First City Bank-Central Park, San Antonio	229,786
44	RepublicBank San Antonio, San Antonio	403,866	92	InterFirst Bank Conroe, Conroe	229,402
45	Texas Commerce Bank-McAllen, McAllen	399,216	93	Texas Commerce Bank-Las Colinas, Irving	227,986
46	InterFirst Bank San Antonio, San Antonio	398,140	94	Plano Bank & Trust Co., Plano	224,906
47	First City Bank of Corpus Christi, Corpus Christi	396,340	95	Southside State Bank, Tyler	224,654
48	InterFirst Bank Fannin, Houston	394,260	96	MBank Pasadena, Pasadena	222,400
			97	Texas American Bank/Amarillo, Amarillo	221,022

Rank	Name and Location of Bank	*Total Deposits (000 dollars)
98	InterFirst Bank Victoria, Victoria	219,777
99	North Dallas Bank & Trust Co., Dallas	218,648
100	MBank Odessa, Odessa	217,884
101	MBank Sherman, Sherman	215,911
102	First City Bank of Richardson, Richardson	214,632
103	Allied Merchants Bank, Port Arthur	212,036
104	United Bank of Texas, Austin	210,658
105	First City National Bank of Bryan, Bryan	209,410
106	Texas Commerce Bank-Longview, Longview	208,546
107	Longview Bank and Trust Co., Longview	206,521
108	Texas American Bank/McKinney, McKinney	205,293
109	RepublicBank Spring Branch, Houston	202,670
110	Cullen/Frost Bank of Dallas, Dallas	201,978
111	InterFirst Bank El Paso, El Paso	201,798
112	Grand Bank, R. L. Thornton at Grand, Dallas	201,355
113	Texas American Bank/West Side, Fort Worth	198,792
114	Central Bank & Trust, Fort Worth	197,067
115	RepublicBank Garland, Garland	195,336
116	InterFirst Bank University Drive, Fort Worth	192,390
117	MBank Greenway, Houston	191,543
118	First City Bank of Farmers Branch, Farmers Branch	190,897
119	RepublicBank Lufkin, Lufkin	190,732
120	Texas American Bank/Duncanville, Duncanville	190,507
121	Texas American Bank/Austin, Austin	188,417
122	Bank of the Hills, Austin	187,110
123	MBank Westchase, Houston	187,022
124	Allied Bank of Marble Falls, Marble Falls	186,669
125	First Bank & Trust Co. Bryan, Bryan	186,593
126	First State Bank & Trust Co., Mission	184,934
127	South Main Bank, Houston	183,675
128	Texas Commerce Medical Bank, Houston	183,139
129	Allied Northeast Bank, North Richland Hills	183,042
130	Medical Center Bank Houston, Houston	182,820
131	InterFirst Bank Abilene, Abilene	182,430
132	Texas American Bank/Riverside, Fort Worth	181,837
133	Post Oak Bank, Houston	181,302
134	InterFirst Bank Odessa, Odessa	180,733
135	InterFirst Bank Oak Cliff, Dallas	175,429
136	MBank Longview, Longview	174,791
137	Texas American Bank/Levelland, Levelland	170,054
138	National Bank of Commerce-Brooks Field, San Antonio	169,269
139	First State Bank of Uvalde, Uvalde	167,258
140	Citizens National Bank of Henderson, Henderson	166,887
141	InterFirst Bank San Felipe, Houston	166,359
142	Texas Commerce Bank-Corpus Christi, Corpus Christi	164,734
143	RepublicBank Fort Worth East, Fort Worth	164,677
144	Texas Commerce Bank of Fort Worth, Fort Worth	164,502
145	InterFirst Bank Carrollton, Carrollton	159,627
146	Plains National Bank of Lubbock, Lubbock	158,785
147	Texarkana National Bank, Texarkana	158,408
148	American Bank of Commerce, El Paso	157,836
149	United Bank of Waco, Waco	157,185
150	United Bank, Midland	156,517

*Total deposits taken from the Call Report of Condition, Consolidating Domestic Subsidiaries only.

Savings and Loan Associations

Texas on Dec. 31, 1986, had 281 insured savings and loan associations and savings banks, with total assets of $97,343,971. This total included federal- and state-chartered associations, which are members of the Federal Home Loan Bank of Dallas and insured by the Federal Savings and Loan Insurance Corporation.

Details in the following table were supplied by the Federal Home Loan Bank of Dallas, headquarters bank for the district which includes Texas. (In 1983, headquarters were moved to Dallas from Little Rock, Ark.)

Texas Savings and Loan Associations

(Thousands of Dollars)

Year	No. Assns.	Total Assets	+Mortgage Loans	✓Cash	✓Investment Securities	Savings Capital	FHLB Advances and other Borrowed Money	*Net Worth
Dec. 31, 1986	281	$97,343,971	$61,744,402	$9,999,810	...	$80,300,617	$14,538,243	$538,479
Dec. 31, 1985	273	91,798,890	60,866,666	10,426,464	...	72,806,067	13,194,147	3,903,611
Dec. 31, 1984	273	77,544,202	45,859,408	10,424,113	...	61,943,815	10,984,467	2,938,044
Dec. 31, 1983	273	56,684,508	36,243,290	6,678,808	...	46,224,429	6,317,947	2,386,551
Dec. 31, 1982	288	42,505,924	30,013,805	4,713,742	...	34,526,483	5,168,343	1,631,139
Dec. 31, 1981	311	38,343,703	27,717,383	3,294,327	...	30,075,258	4,846,153	1,493,795
Dec. 31, 1980	318	34,954,129	25,238,483	2,512,797	...	25,197,598	2,969,838	1,640,049
Dec. 31, 1979	310	31,280,006	22,830,872	142,721	$1,876,882	22,848,519	2,251,631	1,444,607
Dec. 31, 1978	318	27,933,526	19,765,901	154,027	1,579,440	19,994,347	1,515,045	1,235,096
Dec. 31, 1977	328	24,186,338	16,096,166	196,790	1,344,827	16,908,949	949,231	1,044,611
Dec. 31, 1976	316	19,921,694	13,367,569	167,385	1,000,095	13,876,780	919,404	914,502
Dec. 31, 1975	303	16,540,181	11,452,013	117,097	806,302	11,510,259	1,038,386	834,892
Dec. 31, 1974	295	13,944,524	10,361,847	126,106	795,989	10,483,113	740,725	763,618
Dec. 31, 1973	288	12,629,928	8,919,007	155,901	841,904	9,249,305	459,019	678,086
Dec. 31, 1972	278	10,914,627	7,481,751	140,552	670,622	7,647,906	458,152	589,077
Dec. 31, 1971	272	9,112,590	6,450,730	122,420	509,482	6,335,582	559,953	531,733
Dec. 31, 1970	271	7,706,639	5,998,172	105,604	391,175	5,894,398	473,066	487,308
Dec. 31, 1969	270	7,055,949						

*Net worth includes permanent stock and paid-in surplus general reserves, surplus and undivided profits.
✓Beginning in 1979, cash and investment securities data combined.
+Beginning in 1982, net of loans in process.

State Savings and Loan Associations

There were 218 domestic state-chartered savings and loan associations in Texas as of Dec. 31, 1986, according to the State Savings and Loan Department, including both the associations insured within Federal Savings and Loan System and those not insured. (All except one were insured.) There was one state-chartered foreign association operating in Texas as of Dec. 31, 1986.

Year Ending Dec. 31	Total Assets Domestic Assns.	First Mortgage and Other Loans	Savings Shares Capital	Foreign Assns. Assets
1986	$83,144,528,204	$57,836,464,981	$67,691,635,073	N.A.
1985	78,878,606,765	56,905,601,303	61,098,433,267	N.A.
1984	67,353,905,293	48,779,498,449	53,158,688,383	2,777,705,231
1983	47,001,227,395	36,001,319,622	37,381,969,274	2,737,183,027
1982	35,642,705,010	28,267,050,650	27,180,035,132	2,488,987,112
1981	29,657,222,468	25,194,505,272	22,959,660,206	2,285,379,272
1980	27,132,151,523	23,288,239,156	21,707,038,302	2,258,968,037

Insurance in Texas

The State Board of Insurance reported that, on Aug. 31, 1986, there were 2,285 firms licensed to handle insurance business in Texas, including 807 Texas firms and 1,478 out-of-state companies. Annual premium income of firms operating in Texas caused Dallas and some other cities to rank among the nation's major insurance centers.

Additional details are provided in subsequent tables covering the calendar year 1985.

The former Robertson Law, enacted in 1907 and repealed in 1963, encouraged the establishment of many Texas insurance firms. It required life insurance companies operating in the state to invest in Texas three-fourths of all reserves held for payment of policies written in the state. Many out-of-state firms withdrew from Texas. Later many companies re-entered Texas and the law was liberalized and then repealed.

The State Board of Insurance administers legislation relating to the insurance business. This agency was established in 1957, following discovery of irregularities in some firms and succeeded two previous regulatory groups, established in 1913 and changed in 1927. The governor appoints the three-man board, which appoints a State Insurance Commissioner as executive director of the State Insurance Department.

Insurance Companies in Texas

The following table shows the number and kinds of insurance companies licensed in Texas on Aug. 31, 1986:

	Texas	Out-of-State	Total
Stock Life	323	631	954
Mutual Life	4	84	88
Stipulated Premium Life	67	...	67
Non-profit Life	...	1	1
Stock Fire	5	8	13
Stock Fire and Casualty	109	562	671
Mutual Fire and Casualty	8	76	84
Stock Casualty	9	49	58
Mexican Casualty	...	8	8
Lloyds	86	1	87
Reciprocal Exchanges	13	15	28
Fraternal Benefit Societies	12	27	39
Titles	6	16	22
Non-profit Legal Services	1	...	1

	Texas	Out-of-State	Total
Health Maintenance	24	...	24
Total Legal Reserve	667	1,478	2,145
Statewide Mutual Assessment Life, Health and Accident	2	...	2
Local Mutual Aid Associations	52	...	52
Burial Associations	18	...	18
Exempt Associations	16	...	16
Non-profit Hospital Service	1	...	1
County Mutual Fire	25	...	25
Farm Mutual Fire	26	...	26
Total Mutual Assessment	140	...	140
Grand Total	807	1,478	2,285

LEGAL RESERVE LIFE INSURANCE COMPANIES
Texas Business Only, for Calendar Year 1985:

	Texas	Out-of-State	Total
*Premium income during 1985	$2,155,024,534	$5,406,847,105	$7,561,871,639
*Claims and benefits paid during 1985	$1,775,863,637	$4,263,392,762	$6,039,256,399

*Figures include accident and health premiums and claims which were as follows:
Premiums: Texas companies, $1,205,548,113; Out-of-State companies, $2,629,189,845.
Losses: Texas companies, $1,014,640,942; Out-of-State companies, $1,774,009,153.

MUTUAL FIRE AND CASUALTY INSURANCE COMPANIES
Texas Business Only, for Calendar Year 1985:

	Premiums	Losses
Texas companies	$424,196,534	$324,054,878
Companies of other states	1,418,030,898	919,037,432
Total	$1,842,227,432	$1,243,092,310

LLOYDS INSURANCE
Texas Business Only, for Calendar Year 1985:

	Premiums	Losses
Texas companies	$542,275,702	$384,431,577
Companies of other states	2,073,395	1,476,382
Total	$544,349,097	$385,907,959

RECIPROCAL INSURANCE COMPANIES
Texas Business Only, for Calendar Year 1985:

	Premiums	Losses
Texas companies	$237,819,694	$127,698,158
Companies of other states	148,762,377	93,073,608
Total	$386,582,071	$220,771,766

STOCK FIRE COMPANIES
Texas Business Only, for Calendar Year 1985:

	Premiums	Losses
Texas companies	$1,971,878	$1,678,815
Companies of other states and foreign companies	388,308	194,071
Total	$2,360,186	$1,872,886

FRATERNAL BENEFIT SOCIETIES
Texas Business Only, for Calendar Year 1985:

	Texas	Out-of-State	Total
No. policies issued during 1985	12,472	32,469	44,941
Amount of insurance issued during 1985	$196,638,415	$1,510,348,457	$1,706,986,872
Amount of Premiums received during 1985 (Life and H&A)	27,340,295	82,794,610	110,134,905
Losses and claims paid during 1985 (Life and H&A)	7,077,069	15,216,517	22,293,586
No. policies in force Dec. 31, 1985	272,888	335,140	608,028
Amount of insurance in force Dec. 31, 1985	$905,349,804	$4,676,155,683	$5,581,505,487

STOCK CASUALTY INSURANCE COMPANIES
Texas Business Only, for Calendar Year 1985:

	Premiums	Losses
Texas companies	$7,949,134	$3,111,559
Companies of other states and foreign companies	135,370,961	90,743,149
Total	$143,320,095	$93,854,708

TITLE GUARANTY COMPANIES
Texas Business Only, for Calendar Year 1985:

	Texas	Out-of-State	Total
Premium income	$191,333,077	$292,536,658	$483,869,735
Losses paid	3,933,630	8,868,111	12,801,741

STOCK FIRE AND CASUALTY INSURANCE COMPANIES
Texas Business Only, for Calendar Year 1985:

	Premiums	Losses
Texas companies	$1,457,320,977	$915,164,798
Companies of other states	5,690,257,793	4,070,042,541
Total	$7,147,578,770	$4,985,207,339

Construction Industry

Dollar-wise, the construction industry of Texas enjoyed its second-best volume in history in 1986 despite continuing uncertainties in the state's economy. The 1986 volume of $4,636,310,266 was second only to 1985 when $4,806,998,065 was recorded.

A table below shows the approved Texas construction for 1987. These data were compiled by editors of **Texas Contractor** from official sources.

Comparison of Construction Awards by Years

Source: Texas Contractor

Year	Total Awards	Year	Total Awards	Year	Total Awards
1986	$4,636,310,266	1975	1,737,036,682	1964	1,351,656,302
1985	4,806,998,065	1974	2,396,488,520	1963	1,154,624,634
1984	3,424,721,025	1973	1,926,778,365	1962	1,132,607,006
1983	4,074,910,947	1972	1,650,897,233	1961	988,848,239
1982	3,453,784,388	1971	1,751,331,262	1960	1,047,943,630
1981	3,700,112,809	1970	1,458,708,492	1959	1,122,290,957
1980	3,543,117,615	1969	1,477,125,397	1958	1,142,138,674
1979	3,353,243,234	1968	1,363,629,304	1957	1,164,240,546
1978	2,684,743,190	1967	1,316,872,998	1956	1,220,831,984
1977	2,270,788,842	1966	1,421,312,029	1955	949,213,349
1976	1,966,553,804	1965	1,254,638,051	1954	861,623,224

Approved Texas Construction, 1987

The following is a recapitulation of all approved Texas construction for 1987. The data were compiled by the editors of **Texas Contractor** from official sources.

FEDERAL

General Services Administration	$ 7,000,000
Federal Aviation Administration	80,000,000
Veterans Administration	21,500,000
Soil Conservation Service	33,000,000
Rural Electrification Administration	68,000,000
Department of Agriculture	180,000,000
Department of Defense	240,000,000
Federal Highway Aid	925,000,000
National Aeronautics & Space Administration	2,500,000
U.S. Department of Energy	15,000,000
Total	**$1,572,000,000**

STATE

Highway Construction Funds	$ 975,000,000
State Building Programs	149,629,293
State Colleges and Universities	164,835,383
Total	**$1,289,464,676**

WATER PROJECTS

Bureau of Reclamation	$ 11,419,000
Corps of Engineers	150,000,000
River Authorities	200,000,000
Federal Construction Grants	92,000,000
Total	**$ 453,419,000**

CITIES

Schools, Colleges	$ 169,868,000
Streets, Bridges	241,206,000
Waterworks, Sewers	487,646,000
Apartments, Duplexes and Residences	1,629,596,000
Commercial	2,255,870,000
City Buildings	232,508,000
Total	**$5,016,684,000**

COUNTIES

Roads-County Funds	$ 50,742,000
Road Maintenance	75,382,000
Machinery Purchases	24,928,225
County Buildings	8,543,780
Total	**$ 169,888,305**
GRAND TOTAL 1987 APPROVED CONSTRUCTION	**$8,501,455,981**

Texas Credit Unions

Membership in Texas' 1,079 credit unions has grown by 50 percent during the past decade as credit unions continue to be the fastest-growing segment of the financial industry.

Nationally, there are 16,870 credit unions representing more than $164 billion in assets. Texas remains a leader in the credit union movement: Based on figures compiled by the Texas Credit Union League, Texas credit unions account for more than $12.2 billion and rank second in the nation according to asset size. Texas also has the fourth highest number of credit union members in the country: approximately 3.9 million. Currently, one Texan of every five belongs to a credit union.

Analysis of Awards

The following table analyzes and classifies awards in Texas for the year 1986, as compared with the corresponding year of 1985, as reported by **Texas Contractor**.

	1986		1985	
	No.	Amount	No.	Amount
Engineering Awards	1,760	$2,811,804,095	1,892	$2,517,577,340
Non-Residential Awards	1,330	1,824,506,171	1,378	2,289,420,725
Total	3,090	$4,636,310,266	3,270	$4,806,998,065

ENGINEERING AWARDS

	1986		1985	
	No.	Amount	No.	Amount
Highways, Streets, Airports	1,032	$1,943,051,397	1,146	$2,032,163,918
Waterworks, Sewers, etc.	613	833,991,966	604	415,425,173
Irrigation, Drainage, etc.	77	30,467,136	62	58,385,998
Miscellaneous	38	4,293,596	80	11,602,251
Total	1,760	$2,811,804,095	1,892	$2,517,577,340

NON-RESIDENTIAL CONSTRUCTION AWARDS

	1986		1985	
	No.	Amount	No.	Amount
Educational Bldgs.	346	$618,861,569	308	$606,526,231
Churches, Theaters, etc.	47	55,329,055	46	44,927,631
Hospitals, Hotels, Motels	47	168,846,830	55	84,821,917
Public Bldgs.	447	733,919,006	335	610,381,142
Commercial-Industrial	436	246,675,409	620	941,085,822
Miscellaneous	7	874,302	14	1,677,977
Total	1,330	$1,824,506,171	1,378	$2,289,420,725

In 1986, share (savings) accounts stood at $11.5 billion, up 26 percent from the previous year, and loans amounted to $6.4 billion.

Credit unions are chartered at federal or state levels. The National Credit Union Administration (NCUA) is the regulatory agency for the 666 federally chartered credit unions in Texas. (Elizabeth Burkhart of Houston is one of the 3-member NCUA Board.) The Texas Credit Union Department, Austin, is the regulatory agency for the 413 state-chartered credit unions.

The Texas Credit Union League and Affiliates at 4455 LBJ Freeway, Farmers Branch, Tx. 75244-5998, has been the state association for federal and state chartered credit unions since October 1934.

Employment, by Industries and Counties†

This table shows monthly average employment in third quarter of 1986. This survey is limited to employers who are subject to the Texas Unemployment Compensation Act. Figures provided by Texas Employment Commission.

Counties	1. Total Employment	2. Agriculture	3. Mining	4. Construction	5. Manufacturing	6. Transp., Comm. and Pub. Util.	7. Trade	8. Finance, Ins. and Real Estate	9. Service & Other	10. State Govt.	11. Local Govt.
Anderson	11,846	77	703	333	1,339	366	3,344	444	1,356	2,157	1,727
Andrews	5,069	*	1,840	319	*	240	807	166	755	29	913
Angelina	26,277	245	61	1,358	7,466	1,628	6,278	1,115	4,352	1,222	2,552
Aransas	4,063	78	149	195	434	267	1,394	223	660	109	554
Archer	1,597	112	297	*	*	39	510	88	205	23	323
Armstrong	338	27	*	*	*	6	84	22	98	20	81
Atascosa	5,222	165	568	267	149	361	1,568	245	804	85	1,010
Austin	5,675	87	71	729	636	244	1,666	463	947	73	759
Bailey	1,801	338	*	53	*	154	504	86	298	32	336
Bandera	1,277	23	*	74	49	*	297	89	456	35	254
Bastrop	5,258	60	31	342	875	114	1,446	375	654	131	1,230
Baylor	1,283	18	*	48	*	162	352	88	316	31	268
Bee	6,372	82	503	321	245	204	2,081	291	1,295	103	1,247
Bell	53,090	242	*	3,355	8,083	2,031	14,764	3,040	11,812	505	9,258
Bexar	418,034	2,620	2,326	33,583	41,752	16,857	126,671	35,660	101,370	9,357	47,838
Blanco	1,576	131	*	88	85	*	429	150	461	47	185
Borden	133	15	19	0	*	*	*	*	19	12	68
Bosque	3,120	138	*	123	690	127	823	161	617	44	397
Bowie	25,381	211	*	1,663	4,764	1,031	7,903	1,309	5,059	400	3,041
Brazoria	54,549	615	1,795	5,068	15,335	2,158	11,180	2,061	6,735	2,527	7,075
Brazos	44,530	455	688	2,357	3,125	1,456	10,187	1,869	6,914	14,035	3,444
Brewster	2,533	55	16	75	112	136	621	103	475	579	361
Briscoe	323	*	0	*	*	21	103	33	58	17	91
Brooks	1,737	77	208	15	*	68	496	66	233	43	531
Brown	11,660	32	113	478	3,114	555	2,968	383	2,211	538	1,268
Burleson	2,549	51	250	112	329	87	626	174	302	52	566
Burnet	5,839	36	65	464	1,101	315	1,548	335	1,031	63	881
Caldwell	5,241	74	509	245	424	189	1,261	253	1,384	68	834
Calhoun	8,057	125	132	1,176	3,123	288	1,425	282	458	56	992
Callahan	1,526	*	92	83	79	43	419	86	284	38	402
Cameron	64,020	1,740	57	2,897	9,121	3,202	17,920	3,347	12,417	1,901	11,418
Camp	2,629	300	*	122	729	82	581	170	369	13	263
Carson	4,177	63	178	162	*	85	282	67	2,978	48	314
Cass	6,520	12	129	595	1,513	221	1,429	267	1,003	271	1,080
Castro	2,716	1,077	*	56	162	96	551	91	198	29	456
Chambers	6,357	88	507	826	*	313	1,043	126	2,447	48	959
Cherokee	12,316	471	73	380	3,187	442	2,521	357	2,158	1,619	1,108
Childress	1,660	25	0	102	37	110	599	60	258	136	333
Clay	1,228	16	24	*	91	82	339	55	187	38	396
Cochran	1,008	119	21	*	*	24	143	*	351	17	333
Coke	834	18	171	*	*	*	105	52	185	20	283
Coleman	2,221	13	146	46	249	130	575	119	505	40	398
Collin	56,335	564	*	3,685	11,421	1,286	17,152	3,805	10,961	174	7,287
Collingsworth	894	43	0	5	*	49	198	39	316	30	214
Colorado	5,291	223	256	512	580	257	1,578	227	942	89	627
Comal	14,633	73	*	961	3,291	481	3,857	755	3,330	128	1,757
Comanche	2,974	231	21	106	367	133	911	156	513	44	492
Concho	546	19	0	13	*	*	159	*	180	17	158
Cooke	8,919	86	444	452	2,308	390	2,450	272	900	280	1,337
Coryell	6,771	44	*	638	450	100	1,662	432	818	1,222	1,405
Cottle	607	46	24	19	*	*	164	26	186	35	107
Crane	1,680	18	566	*	90	124	249	35	231	20	347
Crockett	1,350	144	148	25	45	91	416	67	75	37	302
Crosby	2,213	567	*	30	136	58	373	74	539	36	400
Culberson	1,319	28	*	*	*	37	345	23	652	34	200
Dallam	2,132	205	*	104	65	131	777	111	457	46	236
Dallas	1,148,159	5,797	19,919	72,257	193,408	81,392	318,494	123,129	249,967	9,518	74,278
Dawson	3,593	292	375	137	211	184	977	177	456	43	741
Deaf Smith	6,625	1,566	*	285	852	355	1,740	230	625	53	919
Delta	621	*	*	*	*	*	132	47	280	31	131
Denton	58,437	658	41	3,835	11,650	1,728	17,154	1,992	8,648	6,734	5,997
DeWitt	5,615	43	118	136	1,306	197	1,358	373	835	214	1,035
Dickens	448	53	*	*	*	69	93	36	50	19	128
Dimmit	2,501	278	227	71	*	69	495	84	352	59	866
Donley	845	66	*	*	42	20	200	60	162	20	275
Duval	2,799	19	791	*	15	47	386	101	345	52	1,043
Eastland	4,982	*	391	136	907	282	1,171	207	907	84	897
Ector	41,744	132	5,966	2,485	3,652	2,191	12,870	1,756	6,131	781	5,780
Edwards	382	*	0	*	*	*	92	14	139	19	118
Ellis	19,811	150	*	1,234	7,281	1,059	4,067	851	2,607	154	2,408
El Paso	167,903	1,287	*	10,357	35,993	8,779	44,508	9,243	31,164	3,465	23,107

Categories	1	2	3	4	5	6	7	8	9	10	11
Erath.	7,460	96	*	312	1,058	264	2,404	357	1,405	809	755
Falls	3,205	113	0	117	410	114	813	248	691	54	645
Fannin.	4,682	52	*	165	1,073	243	1,134	412	636	93	874
Fayette	7,402	87	244	1,311	709	234	2,264	312	994	102	1,145
Fisher	1,021	61	*	12	*	*	172	46	439	26	265
Floyd.	1,944	463	0	41	124	93	453	81	163	33	493
Foard	464	23	0	*	*	*	65	*	228	8	140
Fort Bend	37,045	716	1,789	1,962	7,304	2,051	7,795	1,568	5,602	2,477	5,781
Franklin	1,250	*	*	25	244	17	267	80	316	29	272
Freestone	3,931	45	*	311	117	566	793	145	1,238	65	651
Frio.	2,559	381	86	39	*	117	682	109	447	67	631
Gaines.	3,319	375	459	129	189	258	858	108	234	23	686
Galveston	66,433	273	475	3,534	9,405	4,618	14,384	4,075	10,884	9,309	9,476
Garza	1,218	79	320	*	19	38	247	35	186	29	265
Gillespie	4,624	48	*	320	530	227	1,530	246	1,183	101	439
Glasscock	290	62	49	0	*	*	36	*	52	6	85
Goliad	1,027	*	11	44	16	*	211	45	291	63	346
Gonzales	5,206	468	69	147	1,051	294	1,304	214	795	82	782
Gray	8,704	152	1,185	340	1,285	397	2,359	366	1,654	96	870
Grayson.	35,222	115	157	1,731	11,662	1,394	8,183	1,645	5,956	215	4,164
Gregg	46,195	230	2,819	2,651	8,236	2,439	14,101	2,575	8,044	339	4,761
Grimes	4,084	118	*	187	544	136	705	187	685	581	941
Guadalupe	14,449	192	85	973	4,400	221	3,528	633	2,015	172	2,230
Hale.	11,943	1,211	*	498	1,974	383	3,824	505	1,891	102	1,555
Hall	1,022	50	*	18	*	*	301	57	314	16	266
Hamilton	1,787	54	*	31	246	76	458	85	537	35	265
Hansford	1,824	350	191	50	*	192	457	89	99	19	377
Hardeman	1,632	*	168	18	*	122	291	76	575	33	349
Hardin	7,667	*	335	474	1,208	285	2,051	295	1,517	133	1,369
Harris	1,247,865	6,966	61,757	91,038	135,089	87,436	336,345	98,327	294,677	28,017	108,213
Harrison	17,648	66	776	385	7,101	652	3,428	745	2,417	213	1,865
Hartley	455	27	*	*	*	*	113	*	140	16	159
Haskell	1,483	47	75	63	47	124	469	79	215	45	319
Hays	16,049	98	7	973	1,654	601	4,345	601	3,219	2,629	1,922
Hemphill	1,305	84	210	23	44	117	237	74	202	24	290
Henderson	10,071	118	289	491	2,254	614	2,526	523	1,518	114	1,624
Hidalgo	83,834	6,505	924	4,106	10,971	2,524	23,591	3,787	12,524	2,958	15,944
Hill	5,536	86	*	425	808	375	1,358	230	1,171	88	995
Hockley	6,720	140	1,590	273	159	329	1,392	198	1,262	40	1,337
Hood	4,966	*	44	313	180	212	1,649	243	1,360	32	933
Hopkins	8,185	88	*	312	1,765	353	3,013	366	1,042	117	1,129
Houston	7,743	74	98	430	1,157	467	1,660	459	1,675	902	821
Howard	10,589	68	916	546	1,423	499	2,710	483	1,598	907	1,439
Hudspeth	728	132	*	*	*	*	75	*	317	46	158
Hunt	19,832	51	0	630	7,445	664	4,069	717	2,164	1,643	2,449
Hutchinson	9,169	63	1,346	1,051	2,072	493	1,618	284	975	62	1,205
Irion	402	17	*	26	*	*	63	*	188	12	96
Jack	1,683	*	362	107	77	157	338	84	153	34	371
Jackson	3,015	119	474	190	71	210	780	156	290	50	675
Jasper	8,167	173	17	437	2,354	231	1,871	332	1,387	136	1,229
Jeff Davis	406	*	0	*	*	*	59	*	153	127	67
Jefferson	97,255	406	1,156	5,166	18,059	7,945	25,490	4,181	20,096	2,992	11,764
Jim Hogg	1,148	122	97	6	*	25	372	*	129	47	350
Jim Wells	9,989	196	1,638	379	231	491	2,760	492	1,946	126	1,730
Johnson	18,659	*	24	1,009	3,900	715	5,539	771	4,016	123	2,562
Jones.	3,816	85	200	122	540	246	1,101	178	415	73	856
Karnes	3,304	58	250	147	349	211	984	164	500	62	579
Kaufman	12,809	139	44	688	2,728	390	3,097	523	2,002	1,474	1,724
Kendall	3,225	57	*	353	245	48	993	238	771	37	483
Kenedy	290	*	*	0	0	0	28	*	229	1	32
Kent	270	*	23	*	*	*	12	*	107	11	117
Kerr	11,696	169	42	707	823	439	3,374	742	3,264	1,034	1,102
Kimble	1,131	*	*	32	163	56	392	49	206	53	180
King	152	*	*	*	0	0	*	0	70	5	77
Kinney.	523	*	0	*	*	*	60	*	297	22	144
Kleberg	8,687	*	509	261	471	270	2,462	275	1,838	1,125	1,476
Knox	1,327	*	77	38	*	20	267	51	546	37	291
Lamar	16,134	81	*	950	5,318	604	3,416	512	3,224	340	1,689
Lamb.	4,507	527	*	157	*	370	1,591	166	960	57	679
Lampasas	2,430	16	*	181	329	68	756	142	461	47	430
La Salle	950	107	23	24	*	24	215	70	134	48	305
Lavaca	4,290	35	217	167	1,314	95	1,098	122	691	83	468
Lee	3,981	64	350	356	375	256	1,161	211	427	306	475
Leon	2,972	77	77	411	*	25	828	218	850	54	432
Liberty	10,378	142	858	551	1,354	425	2,890	655	1,457	139	1,907
Limestone	6,926	39	194	*	657	666	1,298	238	1,393	1,695	746
Lipscomb.	849	*	92	22	*	*	177	119	210	9	220
Live Oak	2,029	38	306	66	*	47	558	92	432	70	420
Llano.	2,503	12	*	192	110	83	760	284	606	54	402
Loving.	25	*	13	0	0	0	0	0	2	0	10
Lubbock	85,779	1,213	251	4,238	7,604	4,283	26,866	5,513	18,172	9,213	8,426
Lynn	1,082	168	*	*	21	*	188	67	257	27	354
McCulloch	2,212	28	90	88	*	103	734	127	589	38	415
McLennan	70,705	532	141	4,064	15,073	3,156	19,121	4,606	15,580	2,249	6,183
McMullen	221	35	35	13	*	*	18	14	40	22	44
Madison	3,157	*	115	97	19	28	871	97	716	732	482
Marion	1,432	*	*	21	287	*	293	*	481	52	298
Martin.	918	72	50	*	9	*	221	46	252	29	239
Mason	688	*	0	29	*	29	241	54	165	24	146
Matagorda.	18,228	438	506	*	773	1,223	2,799	496	10,004	145	1,844

Categories	1	2	3	4	5	6	7	8	9	10	11
Maverick	6,316	289	47	96	1,082	253	1,940	303	513	118	1,675
Medina	5,778	197	54	316	669	172	1,879	194	1,053	119	1,125
Menard	451	*	*	*	*	8	113	*	109	17	204
Midland	42,887	230	9,373	1,595	3,116	2,323	10,735	2,895	7,894	334	4,392
Milam	5,857	165	112	198	*	*	1,165	261	3,020	62	874
Mills	1,075	*	*	26	*	*	204	53	579	21	192
Mitchell	2,193	75	154	70	56	167	625	136	285	50	575
Montague	4,233	18	298	210	900	134	1,062	207	582	67	755
Montgomery	31,737	404	2,076	2,186	2,760	1,212	8,852	1,711	6,035	253	6,248
Moore	6,602	386	316	316	*	472	1,437	161	2,695	47	772
Morris	4,237	26	106	86	1,897	242	598	180	504	65	533
Motley	234	11	*	*	*	9	67	19	47	13	68
Nacogdoches	16,374	*	52	854	3,205	408	4,392	720	2,725	2,154	1,864
Navarro	12,624	109	316	696	2,629	561	3,559	522	2,577	274	1,381
Newton	1,863	*	*	32	655	*	314	*	279	64	519
Nolan	5,241	46	219	224	933	445	1,279	227	771	216	881
Nueces	104,424	667	4,613	7,279	10,717	6,204	29,671	6,282	22,895	2,528	13,568
Ochiltree	3,282	67	850	138	108	256	749	134	383	24	573
Oldham	697	57	86	48	*	7	126	*	165	21	187
Orange	20,795	172	493	1,607	5,660	800	5,141	798	2,648	394	3,082
Palo Pinto	7,129	18	432	186	1,293	448	2,091	301	1,098	126	1,136
Panola	6,226	57	475	1,337	*	214	1,071	186	1,687	61	1,138
Parker	9,944	189	198	609	2,162	490	2,897	445	1,078	105	1,771
Parmer	3,705	527	0	80	*	148	589	88	1,679	24	570
Pecos	5,097	305	786	177	261	475	1,183	296	431	94	1,089
Polk	6,671	45	162	208	1,567	362	1,806	297	953	141	1,130
Potter	58,665	548	1,758	2,911	8,363	4,261	16,861	3,344	11,968	1,204	7,447
Presidio	1,213	*	*	*	*	55	281	56	517	46	258
Rains	1,060	0	0	58	*	*	248	44	497	26	187
Randall	15,232	321	65	970	1,376	368	6,179	742	3,030	1,311	870
Reagan	1,201	*	390	31	*	105	248	53	66	10	298
Real	511	*	*	*	*	*	91	*	278	9	133
Red River	3,129	63	*	43	1,183	107	543	114	412	60	604
Reeves	4,084	763	264	85	81	371	893	144	529	117	837
Refugio	2,574	170	519	*	*	115	651	140	398	39	542
Roberts	219	*	*	0	*	46	46	*	42	5	80
Robertson	2,843	167	14	*	336	148	866	109	561	73	569
Rockwall	5,785	73	*	435	584	236	1,568	224	1,947	49	669
Runnels	3,191	61	204	102	931	155	644	153	370	40	531
Rusk	11,256	33	1,773	732	1,749	1,238	2,069	371	1,728	151	1,412
Sabine	1,726	*	*	36	*	35	342	59	846	31	377
San Augustine	1,539	21	*	27	157	*	386	127	498	52	271
San Jacinto	1,180	*	*	60	142	23	189	156	106	43	461
San Patricio	13,065	813	1,252	1,420	1,096	642	3,395	477	1,291	165	2,514
San Saba	1,417	33	*	64	*	80	426	129	423	30	232
Schleicher	624	*	114	*	*	*	94	32	174	5	205
Scurry	6,334	55	1,949	297	272	364	1,445	208	654	68	1,022
Shackelford	896	*	329	22	39	21	123	49	113	24	176
Shelby	5,189	100	*	181	1,749	163	1,203	298	748	74	673
Sherman	967	161	*	92	*	41	338	*	132	16	187
Smith	60,020	829	1,944	2,987	11,877	2,488	16,292	3,674	12,189	2,381	5,359
Somervell	5,954	*	*	*	*	8	136	52	5,438	34	286
Starr	4,467	417	98	53	*	170	1,183	118	405	102	1,921
Stephens	3,239	20	620	101	425	201	831	172	414	45	410
Sterling	417	37	80	*	*	*	81	*	77	16	126
Stonewall	535	*	92	*	*	24	70	*	188	14	147
Sutton	1,493	55	309	44	90	162	347	68	202	59	247
Swisher	2,081	320	*	35	*	126	698	102	220	34	456
Tarrant	454,470	2,544	3,237	28,613	107,097	24,045	129,019	27,180	90,886	6,524	35,325
Taylor	46,027	272	2,225	2,247	4,925	2,505	13,562	2,410	11,386	2,266	4,229
Terrell	349	*	*	23	4	*	92	*	94	19	117
Terry	3,472	158	630	60	181	232	875	148	409	52	727
Throckmorton	438	29	91	*	*	36	48	32	64	21	117
Titus	9,524	76	*	544	1,968	957	1,981	301	2,135	115	1,447
Tom Green	35,035	323	591	2,018	5,745	3,345	9,260	1,710	6,877	2,138	3,028
Travis	294,066	1,382	616	19,559	34,548	9,720	69,840	23,532	67,905	44,433	22,531
Trinity	1,994	*	*	62	242	75	523	180	518	34	360
Tyler	2,976	*	*	64	679	106	719	99	551	49	709
Upshur	4,395	24	*	185	641	241	1,240	148	979	100	837
Upton	1,416	*	441	43	*	119	254	39	76	28	416
Uvalde	7,141	709	191	291	695	317	2,139	320	1,026	225	1,228
Val Verde	7,458	101	*	372	299	331	2,405	415	1,380	239	1,916
Van Zandt	5,992	149	390	807	521	178	1,576	254	1,052	58	1,007
Victoria	26,817	226	1,461	2,131	2,864	1,285	7,949	1,507	5,489	307	3,598
Walker	16,460	88	*	330	1,525	272	3,394	605	2,302	6,451	1,493
Waller	5,701	337	*	125	706	87	1,435	150	520	1,467	874
Ward	4,198	*	1,131	150	92	452	943	104	340	224	762
Washington	9,959	163	125	569	1,987	242	2,605	617	1,482	989	1,180
Webb	33,203	221	1,526	1,371	1,838	3,571	10,418	1,632	5,424	637	6,565
Wharton	11,327	914	1,018	493	1,190	486	3,336	480	1,655	125	1,630
Wheeler	1,786	79	135	117	30	173	478	69	339	30	453
Wichita	46,065	136	1,954	2,154	8,124	2,498	12,366	2,376	9,859	2,127	4,471
Wilbarger	6,299	293	117	672	661	233	1,344	365	760	957	897
Willacy	3,689	815	28	93	*	176	752	108	667	74	976

Categories	1	2	3	4	5	6	7	8	9	10	11
Williamson.	25,289	348	379	2,199	4,050	873	6,698	1,353	4,725	205	4,459
Wilson	2,488	91	22	183	128	33	800	130	323	76	702
Winkler	2,252	*	495	81	43	151	552	79	198	21	632
Wise	7,124	49	966	260	1,132	687	1,538	539	842	92	1,019
Wood	6,281	61	373	279	980	354	1,557	392	1,248	98	939
Yoakum	3,008	78	1,237	96	67	257	432	72	219	15	535
Young	6,346	68	938	199	1,151	318	1,456	371	942	66	837
Zapata	1,315	0	207	*	*	*	166	88	229	20	605
Zavala	2,140	279	*	30	*	12	387	52	664	84	632

†When there was no employment reported in a county in one of the industry groups, a '0' is shown. When one or two employers comprise 80% or more of the employment for an industry group in a county, a '*' is shown. The employment for that industry is included in 'Service & Other' so as not to reveal information about individual establishments.

*Gross Average Hours and Earnings, 1985 and 1986

The following table shows average weekly hours and earnings for 1985 and 1986 and average hourly earnings for 1986. Comparable figures for previous years appear in earlier editions of the Texas Almanac.

Source: Texas Employment Commission in cooperation with the U.S. Bureau of Labor Statistics.

Industry	Av. Weekly Earnings 1985	Av. Weekly Earnings 1986	Av. Weekly Hours 1985	Av. Weekly Hours 1986	Av. Hourly Earnings 1986
MANUFACTURING . .	$387.69	$399.51	41.2	41.4	$9.65
Durable Goods	386.05	391.35	41.6	41.5	9.43
Lumber and Wood Products	259.85	282.36	38.9	41.1	6.87
Furniture and Fixtures	236.62	240.34	38.6	39.4	6.10
Stone, Clay and Glass Products	381.00	385.42	44.2	43.6	8.84
Primary Metal Industries	422.50	416.40	41.3	40.0	10.41
Fabricated Metal Products	369.46	361.34	41.7	40.6	8.90
Machinery, except Electrical	401.40	411.27	41.9	41.5	9.91
Oilfield Machinery	493.29	470.96	43.5	40.6	11.60
Electric and Electronic Equip. . .	407.12	425.43	41.5	42.5	10.01
Transportation Equipment	530.33	524.03	42.7	42.5	12.33
Instruments, and Related Prod.	317.60	340.05	39.8	40.1	8.48
Miscellaneous Mfg. Industries	268.25	263.61	39.8	39.7	6.64
Nondurable Goods . .	388.95	408.29	40.6	41.2	9.91
Food and Kindred Products	333.56	341.52	41.8	41.7	8.19
Meat Products	279.14	274.44	41.6	40.9	6.71
Malt Beverages . . .	760.38	823.40	46.0	47.9	17.19
Textile Mill Products	283.66	305.54	41.9	43.9	6.96
Apparel and Other Textile Products . . .	192.03	190.17	37.0	36.5	5.21
Paper and Allied Products	436.48	453.53	42.5	43.4	10.45
Printing and Publishing	365.38	383.94	39.5	39.5	9.72
Chemicals and Allied Products	620.43	633.39	42.7	43.0	14.73
Petroleum and Coal Products	615.82	660.77	41.0	43.5	15.19
Petroleum Refining	640.09	687.14	40.9	43.6	15.76
Leather and Leather Products.	208.10	213.50	37.7	38.4	5.56
Other Nondurable Goods.	364.83	381.06	41.6	43.8	8.70
NONMANU- FACTURING					
Mining	483.55	508.80	43.8	42.4	12.00
Oil and Gas Extraction	486.18	512.48	43.8	42.6	12.03
Metal & Bit. Coal and Nonmet. Mn. . .	418.04	458.80	43.5	40.0	11.47
Comm., exc. U.S.P.O.	460.92	483.59	39.7	39.9	12.12
Elec., Gas and Whisle. and San. Svcs. . . .	451.67	445.01	39.9	40.2	11.07
Retail Trade	229.71	226.42	33.1	32.3	7.01
Wholesale Trade . . .	374.12	381.35	39.8	39.6	9.63
Retail Trade	181.72	177.30	30.8	30.0	5.91
Banking	271.87	268.22	38.4	38.1	7.04
Gen Mdse. Stores . . .	178.78	185.66	29.6	29.1	6.38

*Figures cover production workers in manufacturing and mining industries only and nonsupervisory employees in other industry divisions. Earnings' averages include premium pay for overtime, holidays, and for lateshift work.

Texas Unemployment Compensation Fund

This table summarizes the status of the Texas Unemployment Compensation Fund on Aug. 31, 1986, and activities during the fiscal year 1985-86, as reported by the Texas Employment Commission.

Fund Balance Sept. 1, 1985	$9,613,116
Receipts	
Gross Payroll Remittances Allocated	877,998,043
Less Refunds and Returned Checks . . .	−7,500,280
Less Penalties and Interest	−6,664,234
Less Surtax	−30,971,201
Net Payroll Taxes	832,862,328
Interest Earned	4,043,653
FUTA Tax Credits	12,459,720
Transfers from Advance Interest Fund . .	86,600,000
Transfers from Special Adm. Fund	2,434,615
Rent to Amortize State Office Buildings . .	327,257
Benefits Reimbursed by Other States. . . .	11,880,757
From Federal Funds (UCFE, UCX, and ETA-PSE)	15,090,000
Refunds from Reimbursing Employers . .	23,121,043
Total Receipts.	$988,819,373

Disbursements	
Net Benefits Paid Claimants Under State Law (Includes State Share Extended Benefits)	$980,180,274
UCFE, UCX, and ETA-PSE Benefits Paid	15,095,615
Federal Supplemental Compensation . . .	−224,583
Extended Benefits Paid Federal Share	12,588
Benefits Paid Reimbursed by Other States	14,148,881
Reimbursable Benefits Paid	23,903,970
Total Disbursements.	$1,033,116,745
Net Operating Income	−44,297,372
Sub-Total	−34,684,256
FEDERAL ADVANCES	
Title XII Advances	$299,526,749
Less Title XII Repayments	−263,473,604
Net Change in Title XII Advances	$36,053,145
Fund Balance Aug. 31, 1986.	$1,368,889

Texas Civilian Labor Force

Employment in Texas declined to 6,694,900 in December 1986, down from the 6,766,700 in December 1985. Average employment for the 1986 year was 6,410,408.

The following table shows Texas Employment Commission estimates of the civilian labor force in Texas for December 1985 and December 1986 together with the change in the number employed.

Industry	Dec. 1986	Dec. 1985	Change From Dec. 1985
Total Nonagricultural Employment	6,694,900	6,766,700	−71,800
Manufacturing	957,800	996,900	−39,100
Durable Goods	556,500	583,700	−27,200
Lumber, Wood Prod	39,500	41,000	−1,500
Logging Camps, Sawmills, Planing Mills	7,800	7,500	300
Furniture and Fixtures	17,200	17,900	−700
Stone, Clay and Glass Products	45,300	48,800	−3,500
Concrete, Gypsum & Plaster Products	20,900	23,400	−2,500
Primary Metal Ind	29,300	32,700	−3,400
Fabricated Metal Products	75,000	82,000	−7,000
Fabricated Struct. Metal Products	38,700	42,400	−3,700
Machinery, Exc. Elec	111,600	129,400	−17,800
Oilfield Machinery	24,300	37,300	−13,000
Electric and Electronic Equipment	117,400	113,700	3,700
Transportation Equipment	86,600	81,400	5,200
Aircraft & Parts	50,900	42,800	8,100
Inst. & Related Prods	22,100	23,800	−1,700
Misc. Mfg. Ind	12,500	13,000	−500
Nondurable Goods	401,300	413,200	−11,900
Food, Kindred Prod	98,800	100,300	−1,500
Meat Products	27,300	27,000	300
Dairy Products	5,300	5,300	0
Bakery Products	11,100	11,200	−100
Malt Beverages	3,100	3,100	0
Textile Mill Products	4,000	4,500	−500
Apparel, Other Finished Textile Products	52,700	57,500	−4,800
Paper, Allied Prod	23,400	23,100	300
Printing, Publishing	76,400	76,200	200
Newsprs, Misc. Publ.	38,300	38,100	200
Chemicals & Allied Products	73,800	77,300	−3,500
Petroleum & Coal Products	31,000	32,600	−1,600
Petroleum Refining	28,200	29,600	−1,400
Leather & Leather Products	6,800	7,700	−900
Other Nondurable Goods	34,400	34,000	400
Total Nonmanufacturing	5,737,100	5,769,800	−32,700
Mining	191,900	250,500	−58,600
Oil and Gas Extraction	184,500	242,200	−57,700
Metal & Coal & Nonmet. Mnrls., exc. Fuel	7,400	8,300	−900
Construction	397,800	444,400	−46,600

Industry	Dec. 1986	Dec. 1985	Change From Dec. 1985
Transportation and Public Utilities	374,000	383,200	−9,200
Railroad Transportation	21,400	23,000	−1,600
Transportation, Except Railroads	188,300	189,000	−700
Transportation by Air	54,900	48,100	6,800
Communications exc. U.S. Postal Service	86,500	90,400	−3,900
Electric, Gas and Sanitary Services	77,800	80,800	−3,000
Electric Services	45,200	45,800	−600
Gas Production & Distribution	25,300	28,200	−2,900
Wholesale & Retail Trade	1,740,900	1,746,500	−5,600
Wholesale Trade	431,900	444,500	−12,600
Retail Trade	1,309,000	1,302,000	7,000
Building Materials & Garden Supplies	46,800	52,800	−6,000
General Merchandise Stores	184,000	177,600	6,400
Food Stores	241,800	233,800	8,000
Automotive Dealers & Service Stations	144,700	145,100	−400
Apparel & Accessory Stores	89,200	91,100	−1,900
Other Retail Trade	602,500	601,600	900
Finance, Insurance and Real Estate	455,600	447,500	8,100
Banking	102,300	107,500	−5,200
Ins. Carriers, Agents, and Brokers	145,500	137,400	8,100
Other Finance, Ins. & Real Estate	207,800	202,600	5,200
Services	1,383,000	1,362,400	20,600
Hotels & Other Lodging Places	85,000	84,300	700
Personal Services	83,600	82,400	1,200
Business & Repair Services	384,000	379,600	4,400
Amusement, incl. Motion Pictures	49,600	53,400	−3,800
Health Services	362,400	350,700	11,700
Educational Services	73,500	72,300	1,200
Other Services & Misc.	344,900	339,700	5,200
Total Government	1,193,900	1,135,300	58,600
Total Federal Government	192,700	189,500	3,200
Total State Government	251,900	240,600	11,300
Total Local Government	749,300	705,200	44,100

*Estimated number of nonagricultural jobs in Texas without reference to place of residence of workers. Estimates of TEC made in cooperation with Bureau of Labor Statistics, U.S. Department of Labor.

Employment by Industries

This table shows the number of employing establishments, employment and wages paid as reported by the Texas Employment Commission. Wages are estimates based on four times the wages for the third quarter of 1986.

Industry Group	Reporting Units	Employment	Total Wages 1986
All Industries and Federal Agencies	308,178	6,410,408	$126,046,241,508
Industries with Texas UI Coverage only	306,121	6,219,384	121,332,420,440
Agriculture, Forestry, Fisheries	7,655	71,198	878,991,176
Agricultural production—crops	1,406	18,074	192,146,260

Industry Group	Reporting Units	Employment	Total Wages 1986
Agricultural prod. —livestock	1,456	14,574	$ 211,451,544
Agricultural services	4,592	37,360	452,583,580
Forestry	36	639	13,468,536
Fishing, hunting and trapping	165	552	9,341,260

Industry Group	Reporting Units	Employment	Total Wages 1986
Mining	8,421	189,046	6,682,265,984
Metal mining	24	341	8,836,332
Bituminous coal and lignite mining	25	4,057	165,072,032
Oil and gas ext.	8,147	178,448	6,353,327,572
Nonmetallic min., except fuels	225	6,200	155,030,048
Contract Construction	33,185	405,134	8,308,981,484
General building contractors	9,610	89,703	1,900,313,848
Heavy const. contractors	3,281	115,871	2,740,070,536
Special trade contractors	20,294	199,560	3,668,597,100
Manufacturing	18,172	941,220	22,604,327,420
Food and kindred products	1,074	98,435	1,979,432,936
Textile mill products	83	4,218	68,963,656
Apparel and other textile prods.	638	52,347	625,140,896
Lumber and wood products	1,510	37,015	631,368,900
Furniture and fixtures	442	16,999	276,881,644
Paper and allied products	241	23,088	584,471,120
Printing and publishing	3,566	74,889	1,482,378,960
Chemicals and allied products	668	74,285	2,663,768,048
Petroleum and coal products	148	33,638	1,229,358,148
Rubber and misc. plastics prods.	720	31,198	657,314,444
Leather and leather products	147	7,027	86,429,560
Stone, clay and glass products	964	47,452	1,030,692,856
Primary metal inds.	313	27,407	713,608,444
Fabricated metal products	2,141	74,700	1,620,038,584
Mach. (exc. elec.)	3,093	102,797	2,648,484,768
Electric and electronic equip.	839	116,844	3,110,231,356
Transportation equipment	597	83,651	2,470,079,032
Instruments and related prods.	422	22,259	507,461,256
Miscellaneous mfg. industries	566	12,970	218,222,816
Transportation, Communication	10,597	352,939	9,130,673,748
Local, interurban pass. transp.	398	9,170	145,485,820
Trucking and warehousing	4,842	92,251	1,863,175,688
Water transportation	583	15,195	349,380,032
Transportation, air	612	50,448	1,510,577,652
Pipelines (exc. natural gas)	45	4,825	176,818,412
Transportation serv.	2,039	17,662	330,308,988
Communication	1,131	86,386	2,393,414,740
Electric, gas and sanitary serv.	947	77,003	2,361,512,420
Wholesale and Retail Trade	90,873	1,682,295	25,145,418,864
Wholesale trade—durable goods	19,546	263,007	6,855,282,560
Wholesale trade—nondurable	10,031	166,198	3,742,376,580
Building materials and garden supply	3,765	49,038	762,888,468
Gen. mdse. stores	531	158,881	1,791,202,644
Food stores	7,060	233,077	2,839,625,980
Automotive dealers and serv. stas.	10,828	139,596	2,608,700,136
Apparel and access. stores	4,907	81,714	808,613,384
Furniture and home furns. store	5,113	52,240	859,793,836
Eating and drinking places	14,483	403,201	3,147,380,928
Miscellaneous retail	14,609	135,342	1,729,554,348
Finance, Insurance and Real Estate	28,997	439,844	9,851,715,452
Banking	2,208	103,891	2,185,179,472
Credit agencies other than banks	2,503	67,827	1,564,285,196
Security, commodity brokers and services	847	16,007	815,264,196
Insurance carriers	1,128	82,343	1,894,779,564
Ins. agents, brokers and services	6,865	40,505	866,431,480
Real estate	13,379	114,148	2,035,501,356
Combined real estate, insurance	122	453	6,034,604
Holding and other investment offices	1,945	14,670	484,239,584
Service Industries	101,928	1,261,000	22,048,175,448
Hotels, and other lodging places	2,084	85,364	857,002,636
Personal services	8,851	79,345	845,532,032
Business services	19,124	307,411	5,380,721,332
Auto. repair, and garages	7,754	51,577	813,616,072
Miscellaneous repair services	3,745	19,820	367,229,188
Motion pictures	489	10,502	116,702,720
Amusement and recreation services	2,522	47,850	551,165,864
Health services	23,031	372,421	7,058,520,608
Legal services	7,760	48,471	1,535,342,136
Educational services	900	37,673	697,636,772
Social services	3,303	59,826	574,662,732
Museums, botanical, zoological gardens	81	2,254	32,178,128
Membership orgs.	3,890	31,770	449,616,868
Private households	9,347	14,762	120,558,860
Misc. services	9,047	91,954	2,647,689,504
Federal Government	2,057	191,024	4,713,821,068
State and Local Government	5,983	875,901	16,667,011,848
Nonclassified Establishments	310	807	14,859,016

Personal Income by Major Source and Earnings by Major Industry

(Thousands of Dollars)
Source: Bureau of Economic Analysis, Washington, D.C.

Item	1980	1981	1982	1983	1984	1985
Income by Place of Residence						
Total Personal Income	140,543,120	164,336,737	179,856,434	189,067,021	205,834,010	220,715,126
Nonfarm Personal Income	139,449,252	162,207,451	177,595,952	186,477,135	203,514,595	217,866,960
Farm Income	1,093,868	2,129,286	2,260,482	2,589,886	2,319,415	2,848,166
Derivation of Total Personal Income:						
Total Earnings by Place of Work	111,942,716	129,921,202	140,507,684	146,697,517	159,826,343	171,677,738
Net Earnings by Place of Residence	106,298,152	123,102,815	132,960,524	138,882,856	151,266,660	162,095,276
Earnings by Place of Work						
Components of Earnings:						
Wages and Salaries	89,758,050	105,251,143	114,531,387	118,031,769	128,733,810	137,682,463
Other Labor Income	9,221,991	10,697,677	12,058,203	12,481,805	13,032,122	13,792,888
¶Proprietors' Income	12,962,675	13,972,382	13,918,094	16,183,943	18,060,411	20,202,387

Item	1980	1981	1982	1983	1984	1985
‡Farm	618,931	1,682,162	1,763,271	2,111,958	1,847,995	2,372,420
Nonfarm	12,343,744	12,290,220	12,154,823	14,071,985	16,212,416	17,829,967
Earnings by Industry:						
Farm	1,093,868	2,129,286	2,260,482	2,589,886	2,319,415	2,848,166
Nonfarm	110,848,848	127,791,916	138,247,202	144,107,631	157,506,928	168,829,572
Private	95,408,776	110,273,301	118,702,846	122,781,241	134,418,471	143,353,335
**Agricultural Services, Forestry, Fisheries and Other	612,655	633,622	663,645	759,328	752,642	826,122
Mining	6,900,477	9,509,866	10,415,051	9,634,595	10,117,357	10,023,305
Construction	10,891,744	11,661,316	12,579,855	13,092,053	14,323,582	14,627,957
Manufacturing	21,458,017	25,155,882	25,330,215	25,538,180	26,348,452	27,808,262
Nondurable Goods	8,504,590	9,740,981	10,217,590	10,566,866	11,018,452	11,352,507
Durable Goods	12,953,427	15,414,901	15,112,625	13,971,314	15,330,000	16,455,755
Transportation and Public Utilities	9,060,486	10,334,982	10,936,637	11,016,756	11,838,867	12,641,338
Wholesale Trade	9,227,787	10,349,471	11,140,463	10,981,687	11,744,174	12,424,372
Retail Trade	11,801,606	13,250,776	14,438,607	15,652,607	17,040,734	18,190,251
Finance, Insurance and Real Estate	6,386,602	7,116,878	7,966,695	9,399,164	10,640,460	11,956,228
Services	19,069,402	22,260,508	25,231,678	27,706,871	31,612,203	34,855,500
Government and Government Enterprises	15,440,072	17,518,615	19,544,356	21,326,390	23,088,457	25,476,237
Federal, Civilian	3,404,694	3,726,527	3,963,212	4,250,942	4,648,889	5,125,684
Federal, Military	1,976,687	2,308,310	2,552,973	2,653,830	2,739,652	2,958,839
State and Local	10,058,691	11,483,778	13,028,171	14,421,618	15,699,916	17,391,714

†Personal contributions for social insurance are included in earnings by type and industry but excluded from personal income.

‡1978-83 farm proprietors and rental income and residence adjustment reflect revisions which have not been made for previous years.

§Includes the capital consumption adjustment for rental income of persons.

¶Includes the inventory valuation and capital consumption adjustments.

**Other—Wages and salaries of U.S. residents working for international organizations in the U.S.

Per Capita Personal Income

Source: U.S. Department of Commerce

This table shows the per capita personal income in Texas Metropolitan Statistical Areas as reported in the April 1986 Survey of Current Business. All figures are in dollars. These data are based on MSAs as constituted in 1986.

Per capita personal income for the entire state rose from $1,349 in 1950 to $12,575 in 1984. This compared with the U.S. per capita income which rose from $1,496 in 1950 to $12,772 in 1984, according to U.S. Department of Commerce figures.

Metropolitan Statistical Area	1976	1977	1978	1979	1980	1981	1982	1983	1984
TEXAS	$6,158	$6,714	$7,486	$8,478	$9,439	$10,807	$11,378	$11,686	$12,575
Abilene	5,961	6,636	7,242	8,379	9,398	11,076	11,465	11,777	12,175
Amarillo	6,766	7,541	8,121	8,987	9,545	10,769	11,464	11,924	12,666
Austin	5,644	6,743	7,341	8,067	9,065	10,383	11,174	11,937	13,483
Beaumont-Port Arthur	6,553	7,229	8,109	9,018	9,950	11,184	11,784	12,013	12,210
*Brazoria (PMSA)			8,189	9,350	10,188	11,421	12,065	11,860	13,079
Brownsville-Harlingen	3,942	4,375	4,455	4,977	5,506	6,172	6,365	6,654	6,796
Bryan-College Station	4,700	5,606	5,383	5,956	6,740	8,032	8,524	9,085	9,561
Corpus Christi	5,594	6,176	6,733	7,734	8,518	9,850	10,345	10,503	10,923
†Dallas-Fort Worth	6,928	7,752	...	...	...	...	...	...	...
†Dallas (PMSA)	...	...	8,783	10,000	11,179	12,574	13,415	14,222	15,861
Dallas-Fort Worth (CMSA)	...	...	8,585	9,755	10,926	12,302	13,070	13,846	15,272
El Paso	4,692	5,073	5,446	6,051	6,603	7,413	7,753	8,290	8,745
†Fort Worth-Arlington (PMSA)	...	...	8,183	9,262	10,418	11,755	12,384	13,103	14,138
*Galveston-Texas City (PMSA)	6,670	7,180	8,231	9,233	10,370	11,807	12,575	12,323	13,392
*Houston	7,499	8,361	...	...	...	...	...	...	...
*Houston (PMSA)	...	...	...	...	...	...	...	...	14,517
*Houston-Galveston-Brazoria (CMSA)	...	...	9,184	10,348	11,627	13,308	13,755	13,482	14,374
Killeen-Temple	5,578	6,045	6,017	6,373	7,359	8,224	9,187	9,930	10,320
Laredo	3,526	4,026	4,075	4,605	5,321	6,028	6,174	6,017	6,030
Longview-Marshall	6,241	6,829	7,093	7,968	9,028	10,374	10,886	11,008	11,710
Lubbock	5,792	6,642	7,011	7,859	8,674	9,690	10,289	11,123	11,584
McAllen-Edinburg-Mission	3,395	4,003	3,994	4,337	4,939	5,755	5,979	6,012	6,458
Midland	7,982	9,283	10,128	11,671	13,525	16,149	16,805	15,507	15,094
Odessa	6,595	7,506	8,147	8,923	10,203	12,264	12,478	11,512	11,325
San Angelo	6,210	6,927	7,142	7,884	8,899	10,324	11,181	11,580	12,115
San Antonio	5,556	6,035	6,519	7,370	8,346	9,337	9,991	10,569	11,540
Sherman-Denison	5,615	6,297	7,020	8,035	8,768	9,841	10,521	11,148	12,158
Texarkana, Texas-Ark.	5,273	5,912	6,241	6,994	7,633	8,617	9,139	9,557	10,375
Tyler	6,446	7,294	7,422	8,373	9,404	10,854	11,749	12,188	13,296
†Victoria	...	7,000	7,489	8,394	9,498	11,660	12,342	11,928	13,077
Waco	5,854	6,527	6,793	7,495	8,396	9,504	10,252	10,958	11,718
Wichita Falls	6,666	7,186	7,500	8,703	9,857	11,302	11,835	11,970	12,985

*In 1983, Brazoria and Galveston/Texas City were added to the old Houston SMSA and made a Consolidated Metropolitan Statistical Area (CMSA). Brazoria and Galveston/Texas City are independent Primary Metropolitan Statistical Areas (PMSA).

†In 1983, the old Dallas/Fort Worth SMSA was reconstituted. Dallas PMSA consists of Collin, Dallas, Denton, Ellis, Kaufman, Rockwall Counties. The Fort Worth/Arlington PMSA consists of Johnson, Parker and Tarrant Counties. Together they constitute the Dallas/Fort Worth CMSA.

‡Victoria County made an MSA in 1981.

Transportation

Transportation

Texas is a leader among the states in a number of transportation indicators, including total road and street mileage, total railroad mileage and total number of airports. **Texas ranks** second behind California in motor vehicle registrations and in number of general aviation aircraft.

The Texas transportation system includes **273,981 miles of municipal and rural highways, 12,774 miles of railroad line,** approximately **1,603 airports** and **13 major Gulf Coast ports.** Texans own and operate over **14.3 million motor vehicles** and about **23,916 aircraft.**

The transportation industry is a major employer in Texas. Statistics compiled by the Texas Employment Commission indicate that nearly 200,000 Texans are employed in the transportation industry. The largest group — 92,251 — is employed in trucking and warehousing. Railroads employ 21,400, air transportation 50,448 and water transportation 15,195.

The largest state government agency involved in transportation is the **Texas State Department of Highways and Public Transportation.** The **Railroad Commission of Texas** has intrastate authority over railroad safety, truck lines, buses and pipelines. Another state agency with a major role in transportation is the **Texas Aeronautics Commission.**

Texas Highways

Texas has the largest road network in the nation. There are 273,981 miles of roadways in the state, of which 71,560 are maintained by the Texas Department of Highways and Public Transportation. The state-maintained system, however, includes practically all the freeways and other high traffic-carrying highways. With less than three-tenths of the total center-line miles, the state-maintained system carries almost three-fourths of all the miles driven in Texas.

Highway Spending by County, Fiscal 1986

These figures were compiled from the "Supplement to the Annual Financial Report for The Fiscal Year Ended August 31, 1986, Unaudited for the Texas Department of Highways and Public Transportation."

County	Miles Maintained	Construction	Maintenance	Total Spending	County	Miles Maintained	Construction	Maintenance	Total Spending
Anderson	440	$4,728,199	$1,909,979	$6,638,178	Collingsworth	217	357,939	529,947	887,886
Andrews	236	112,476	652,474	764,950	Colorado	282	6,833,457	1,475,627	8,309,084
Angelina	362	8,001,231	2,013,801	10,015,032	Comal	223	5,016,723	963,266	5,979,989
Aransas	73	262,069	327,022	589,091	Comanche	346	1,516,531	1,043,403	2,559,934
Archer	257	617,793	866,491	1,484,284	Concho	202	53,813	664,338	718,151
Armstrong	153	2,979,642	656,078	3,635,720	Cooke	315	18,723,647	1,308,227	20,031,874
Atascosa	391	5,197,770	1,914,362	7,112,132	Coryell	326	1,524,896	938,909	2,463,805
Austin	256	3,161,321	1,374,467	4,535,788	Cottle	196	183,247	501,158	684,405
Bailey	216	381,749	689,267	1,071,016	Crane	135	1,672,144	374,714	2,046,858
Bandera	196	1,385,888	660,613	2,046,501	Crockett	300	588,841	983,684	1,572,525
Bastrop	312	7,834,871	1,172,693	9,007,564	Crosby	253	933,462	714,987	1,648,449
Baylor	215	771,008	852,666	1,623,674	Culberson	286	3,257,604	628,156	3,885,760
Bee	278	1,316,593	829,131	2,145,724	Dallam	288	3,011,736	931,442	3,943,178
Bell	458	6,065,002	2,782,920	8,847,922	Dallas	395	131,136,975	13,725,380	144,862,355
Bexar	604	152,933,820	7,759,674	160,693,494	Dawson	312	292,031	943,758	1,235,789
Blanco	184	713,258	802,413	1,515,671	DeWitt	313	1,053,813	1,059,197	2,113,010
Borden	172	249,805	418,521	668,326	Deaf Smith	270	2,101,082	804,366	2,905,448
Bosque	347	273,829	680,504	954,333	Delta	168	2,716,220	989,208	3,705,428
Bowie	448	9,511,172	2,651,914	12,163,086	Denton	451	13,574,886	3,541,097	17,115,983
Brazoria	428	23,362,708	4,041,886	27,404,594	Dickens	197	151,443	557,062	708,505
Brazos	261	12,979,428	1,324,663	14,304,091	Dimmit	250	1,004,851	534,245	1,539,096
Brewster	290	670,102	580,355	1,250,457	Donley	177	1,680,949	594,880	2,275,829
Briscoe	163	303,380	544,240	847,620	Duval	312	946,630	812,220	1,758,850
Brooks	117	2,766,640	377,250	3,143,890	Eastland	382	1,724,536	1,660,283	3,384,819
Brown	319	3,627,532	1,352,355	4,979,887	Ector	238	4,525,264	1,136,677	5,661,941
Burleson	234	2,612,457	1,197,724	3,810,181	Edwards	240	1,035,775	626,893	1,662,668
Burnet	288	4,418,354	1,211,412	5,629,766	El Paso	320	20,952,911	2,189,230	23,142,141
Caldwell	250	945,506	1,077,681	2,023,187	Ellis	488	7,415,436	3,354,689	10,770,125
Calhoun	174	1,830,783	751,351	2,582,134	Erath	374	2,424,442	1,932,734	4,357,176
Callahan	284	45,635	1,427,152	1,472,787	Falls	341	2,449,036	1,873,719	4,322,755
Cameron	532	12,271,138	3,166,972	15,438,110	Fannin	442	7,038,199	1,494,508	8,532,707
Camp	119	2,890,396	561,924	3,452,320	Fayette	405	17,825,756	1,849,076	19,674,832
Carson	268	362,725	1,454,240	1,816,965	Fisher	274	306,424	706,807	1,013,231
Cass	432	2,752,070	1,682,389	4,434,459	Floyd	300	991,640	776,001	1,767,641
Castro	261	525,475	867,406	1,392,881	Foard	149	0	461,618	461,618
Chambers	242	8,583,053	1,281,804	9,864,857	Fort Bend	352	15,162,049	3,755,272	18,917,321
Cherokee	510	2,209,366	2,450,680	4,660,046	Franklin	131	402,993	833,883	1,236,876
Childress	207	3,279,008	497,156	3,776,164	Freestone	341	2,719,012	1,708,593	4,427,605
Clay	340	4,288,180	1,073,271	5,361,451	Frio	281	4,500,974	1,223,095	5,724,069
Cochran	232	458,320	375,887	834,207	Gaines	275	219,960	769,422	989,382
Coke	172	640,856	617,067	1,257,923	Galveston	253	24,270,352	3,013,540	27,283,892
Coleman	326	2,620,843	980,093	3,600,936	Garza	173	2,551,411	586,015	3,137,426
Collin	519	11,860,693	3,521,559	15,382,252	Gillespie	273	1,307,109	951,477	2,258,586

County	Miles Maintained	Construction	Maintenance	Total Spending	County	Miles Maintained	Construction	Maintenance	Total Spending
Glasscock	137	240,944	398,519	639,463	Nacogdoches ..	395	2,814,815	1,733,878	4,548,693
Goliad	249	1,446,136	741,291	2,187,427	Navarro......	455	15,512,828	2,671,389	18,184,217
Gonzales	399	4,177,895	1,555,053	5,732,948	Newton	274	4,553,809	851,596	5,405,405
Gray	293	1,134,829	1,323,443	2,458,272	Nolan.......	226	6,599,896	1,064,048	7,663,944
Grayson.....	419	14,236,324	2,085,655	16,321,979	Nueces......	399	46,244,149	3,612,634	49,856,783
Gregg	247	4,806,292	2,100,050	6,906,342	Ochiltree	212	122,969	733,304	856,273
Grimes	287	4,519,312	1,185,462	5,704,764	Oldham	114	2,660,067	581,815	3,241,882
Guadalupe ..	347	4,925,177	1,906,841	6,832,018	Orange	183	3,483,494	1,461,388	4,944,882
Hale........	375	7,814,981	1,803,757	9,618,738	Palo Pinto ..	344	601,682	2,332,715	2,934,397
Hall	206	2,080,817	508,928	2,589,745	Panola......	313	7,660,643	1,284,408	8,945,051
Hamilton	287	56,211	788,513	844,724	Parker......	296	1,776,187	2,115,995	3,892,182
Hansford	254	83,475	693,998	777,473	Parmer	253	1,264,419	766,860	2,031,279
Hardeman ...	201	350,363	980,857	1,331,220	Pecos.......	567	1,121,811	2,095,917	3,217,728
Hardin......	236	7,318,792	991,393	8,310,185	Polk........	350	9,485,866	1,433,268	10,919,134
Harris	587	286,818,424	20,908,228	307,726,652	Potter	204	10,944,392	2,092,012	13,036,404
Harrison	430	5,385,944	2,279,398	7,665,342	Presidio.....	271	3,125,156	576,688	3,701,844
Hartley	252	1,577,053	527,278	2,104,331	Rains.......	132	643,020	412,347	1,055,367
Haskell	284	2,001,140	946,898	2,948,038	Randall.....	267	27,297,926	1,214,278	28,512,204
Hays	214	1,525,189	1,339,005	2,864,194	Reagan	159	193,426	406,199	599,625
Hemphill	183	2,276,396	458,956	2,735,352	Real........	148	1,834,785	369,380	2,204,165
Henderson ...	399	3,861,288	2,204,150	6,065,438	Red River ...	371	3,648,962	1,352,632	5,001,594
Hidalgo.....	677	18,963,591	3,968,420	22,932,011	Reeves......	379	2,900,188	1,240,876	4,141,064
Hill	462	3,316,286	2,086,592	5,402,878	Refugio	195	13,244,330	957,733	14,202,063
Hockley	336	585,393	1,157,324	1,742,717	Roberts	116	863,865	365,511	1,229,376
Hood	173	7,754,140	1,244,935	8,999,075	Robertson ...	295	2,971,180	1,346,982	4,318,162
Hopkins.....	380	21,262,081	1,712,424	22,974,505	Rockwall ...	118	5,645,002	1,344,294	6,989,296
Houston	399	413,860	1,517,120	1,930,980	Runnels	329	65,728	927,663	993,391
Howard	279	9,824,553	948,663	10,773,216	Rusk	509	6,538,460	2,210,987	8,749,447
Hudspeth ...	295	9,677,628	727,317	10,404,945	Sabine	222	1,105,758	940,754	2,046,512
Hunt	521	8,524,519	2,393,350	10,917,869	San Augustine .	252	944,913	1,129,134	2,074,047
Hutchinson ..	206	3,877,068	677,464	4,554,532	San Jacinto ..	231	326,294	891,374	1,217,668
Irion	123	123,496	440,413	563,909	San Patricio ..	311	7,846,708	1,617,745	9,464,453
Jack	266	676,063	1,362,953	2,039,016	San Saba	210	615,224	648,958	1,264,182
Jackson	273	2,425,621	1,002,048	3,427,669	Schleicher ...	179	1,143	601,637	602,780
Jasper	322	1,446,233	1,080,970	2,527,203	Scurry	275	6,663,102	1,105,299	7,768,401
Jeff Davis ...	221	2,523,961	493,014	3,016,975	Shackelford ..	175	372,017	827,975	1,199,992
Jefferson	281	26,648,848	2,368,457	29,017,305	Shelby	376	3,995,388	1,678,527	5,673,915
Jim Hogg ...	143	436,037	639,888	1,075,925	Sherman	195	5,834,786	591,837	6,426,623
Jim Wells ...	259	5,862,798	900,759	6,763,557	Smith.......	570	6,755,664	4,154,436	10,910,100
Johnson	344	2,506,422	2,985,496	5,491,918	Somervell ...	92	1,080	540,981	542,061
Jones	411	5,260,231	1,312,907	6,573,138	Starr	231	1,434,663	838,684	2,273,347
Karnes......	332	2,142,504	1,830,324	3,972,828	Stephens	261	1,083,638	1,104,318	2,187,956
Kaufman	416	23,456,298	2,841,021	26,297,319	Sterling	104	82,252	317,423	399,675
Kendall	164	3,052,040	604,900	3,656,940	Stonewall ...	157	217,074	406,463	623,537
Kenedy	47	3,361,835	201,769	3,563,604	Sutton	218	104,211	648,646	752,857
Kent	163	275,630	469,158	744,788	Swisher	269	20,839,469	1,010,520	21,849,999
Kerr	275	1,746,874	1,249,367	2,996,241	Tarrant	491	146,126,237	7,054,812	153,181,049
Kimble	260	2,472,874	803,398	3,276,272	Taylor	375	8,567,530	2,298,183	10,865,713
King	93	493,779	226,275	720,054	Terrell	165	2,029,516	529,851	2,559,367
Kinney......	203	515,652	614,188	1,129,840	Terry	276	793,228	777,368	1,570,596
Kleberg	146	6,494,605	971,386	7,465,991	Throckmorton	170	15,229	749,578	764,807
Knox	214	184,867	894,239	1,079,106	Titus	199	8,886,444	1,405,780	10,292,224
La Salle	194	1,470,028	945,456	2,415,484	Tom Green...	350	10,252,471	2,095,076	12,347,547
Lamar	443	11,237,425	2,175,157	13,412,582	Travis	368	61,869,937	4,759,748	66,629,685
Lamb.......	360	3,865,052	1,331,748	5,196,800	Trinity	208	2,296,609	749,216	3,045,825
Lampasas ...	213	2,488,730	624,318	3,113,048	Tyler	250	5,000,442	945,091	5,945,533
Lavaca	314	1,297,737	1,267,455	2,565,192	Upshur......	330	2,427,806	1,138,760	3,566,566
Lee	194	4,624,990	829,217	5,454,207	Upton	189	2,057,228	354,498	2,411,726
Leon	350	3,258,250	1,713,841	4,972,091	Uvalde	338	1,145,775	702,082	1,847,857
Liberty	353	21,711,984	1,567,417	23,279,401	Val Verde....	310	2,475,820	1,946,257	4,422,077
Limestone ..	372	1,964,785	2,100,011	4,064,796	Van Zandt ..	468	8,869,602	2,586,921	11,456,523
Lipscomb....	197	112,484	636,994	749,478	Victoria	253	10,303,379	1,265,995	11,569,374
Live Oak	341	3,355,432	2,446,064	5,801,496	Walker	290	2,035,089	1,666,251	3,701,340
Llano	229	1,034,480	734,209	1,768,689	Waller	213	7,675,159	2,014,789	9,689,948
Loving	34	3,498	90,881	94,379	Ward	229	1,159,421	650,277	1,809,698
Lubbock	500	26,181,079	3,022,074	29,203,153	Washington ..	265	3,203,547	1,382,753	4,586,300
Lynn	310	401,881	1,104,413	1,506,294	Webb........	319	4,267,269	1,296,827	5,564,096
McCulloch ..	297	1,892,684	770,720	2,663,404	Wharton	385	2,896,769	1,902,917	4,799,686
McLennan ..	507	11,817,890	2,777,380	14,595,270	Wheeler	240	1,854,616	867,279	2,721,895
McMullen ..	159	1,113,477	509,181	1,622,658	Wichita	342	9,452,023	2,209,135	11,661,158
Madison.....	239	5,767,168	1,508,768	7,275,936	Wilbarger ...	295	4,410,924	945,337	5,356,261
Marion	149	4,165,003	779,055	4,944,058	Willacy	218	345,578	729,069	1,074,647
Martin......	239	1,606,157	594,851	2,201,008	Williamson ..	456	15,030,036	2,678,997	17,709,033
Mason	193	260,563	582,855	843,418	Wilson	323	4,326,308	1,145,687	5,471,995
Matagorda ..	320	2,293,777	1,621,788	3,915,565	Winkler	136	245,409	308,636	554,045
Maverick	206	5,545,701	544,926	6,090,627	Wise	350	20,982,809	2,526,038	23,508,847
Medina	307	5,899,567	1,187,675	7,087,242	Wood	415	186,388	2,131,696	2,318,084
Menard	170	265	497,547	497,812	Yoakum.....	196	2,358,808	706,624	3,065,432
Midland.....	265	2,169,652	1,174,711	3,344,363	Young	344	2,068,473	1,395,411	3,463,884
Milam	338	2,670,780	1,654,626	4,325,406	Zapata	120	253,521	364,587	618,108
Mills	206	496,511	848,432	1,344,943	Zavala	266	230,703	736,728	967,431
Mitchell	232	652,864	1,066,506	1,719,370					
Montague ...	339	3,144,030	1,505,394	4,649,424	Totals		$1,925,122,534;	$367,626,018;	$2,292,748,552.
Montgomery .	364	28,239,578	3,629,142	31,868,720	*Nonassigned		1,725,789;	57,550,542;	59,276,331.
Moore	200	787,988	816,992	1,604,980	Grand Total......		71,560; $1,926,848,323;	$425,176,560;	
Morris	135	3,547,285	668,490	4,215,775	$2,352,024,883.				
Motley......	165	105	259,450	259,555	*These funds not assigned to individual county.				

Motor Vehicle Registration, License Fees, By Counties

The following State Department of Highways and Public Transportation table shows, for Jan. 1, 1985, through Dec. 31, 1985, by counties, motor vehicle registrations and license fees. These figures include all types of motor vehicles.

County	Total Vehicles Regis- tered	Total Gross License Fees (Dollars)	Net to County (Dollars)	Net to State (Dollars)	County	Total Vehicles Regis- tered	Total Gross License Fees (Dollars)	Net to County (Dollars)	Net to State (Dollars)
Anderson . . .	35,270	1,544,329	417,774	1,126,555	Cochran	4,324	186,666	184,378	2,289
Andrews . . .	16,490	852,351	313,588	538,763	Coke	4,825	207,226	200,932	6,294
Angelina . . .	60,671	2,717,965	471,934	2,246,031	Coleman . . .	11,328	457,034	348,016	109,018
Aransas	13,469	518,055	265,886	252,169	Collin.	175,170	7,116,899	699,292	6,417,607
Archer	8,881	413,380	313,386	99,995	Collingsworth	4,141	167,947	165,690	2,257
Armstrong . .	2,737	120,037	118,686	1,351	Colorado . . .	20,276	1,194,956	387,108	807,848
Atascosa . . .	22,774	1,054,807	394,184	660,623	Comal	43,666	1,889,002	430,990	1,458,012
Austin	19,658	939,123	387,229	551,894	Comanche . .	12,910	548,747	374,251	174,496
Bailey	7,817	349,136	292,733	56,403	Concho	3,116	110,246	108,710	1,537
Bandera	9,049	361,656	291,251	70,404	Cooke	29,675	1,263,422	405,895	857,527
Bastrop	29,136	1,171,742	405,882	765,860	Coryell.	30,590	1,146,775	409,496	737,278
Baylor	5,792	248,542	217,056	31,486	Cottle.	2,775	104,413	102,885	1,528
Bee	19,519	868,120	378,906	489,215	Crane	5,982	378,661	246,873	131,788
Bell	146,862	5,896,344	664,442	5,231,903	Crockett . . .	4,649	206,892	204,666	2,227
Bexar.	875,359	37,178,924	2,135,858	35,043,067	Crosby	6,766	255,070	244,457	10,613
Blanco	6,321	303,049	218,814	84,234	Culberson . .	2,571	119,663	118,178	1,486
Borden	1,199	73,489	72,949	540	Dallam	7,006	326,994	276,274	50,720
Bosque.	14,805	621,964	379,278	242,686	Dallas	1,656,161	73,912,027	4,049,517	69,862,510
Bowie	73,946	2,913,034	488,297	2,424,737	Dawson	13,669	637,339	375,615	261,724
Brazoria	157,725	6,563,838	643,342	5,920,496	Deaf Smith. .	18,271	959,282	384,985	574,297
Brazos	81,379	3,551,294	497,608	3,053,687	Delta	4,913	182,459	177,816	4,642
Brewster	6,068	239,033	235,573	3,460	Denton.	171,158	6,974,701	732,335	6,242,366
Briscoe	2,692	107,775	106,293	1,482	DeWitt	17,709	732,504	384,216	348,288
Brooks	5,730	241,180	174,292	66,889	Dickens	2,677	96,798	95,396	1,403
Brown	33,402	1,342,359	415,437	926,923	Dimmit	7,242	350,493	249,581	100,912
Burleson . . .	13,487	616,576	362,484	254,092	Donley.	4,545	165,061	162,594	2,467
Burnet	24,615	992,237	365,586	626,651	Duval.	8,567	375,546	305,768	69,778
Caldwell. . . .	19,611	908,799	367,040	541,759	Eastland . . .	19,781	853,578	389,349	464,230
Calhoun. . . .	17,874	700,935	296,719	404,216	Ector	125,649	6,079,580	620,398	5,459,181
Callahan . . .	14,782	596,804	378,169	218,635	Edwards . . .	2,063	86,252	85,191	1,061
Cameron . . .	133,854	5,548,563	615,976	4,932,587	Ellis.	66,848	2,983,610	484,934	2,498,676
Camp.	9,113	439,162	277,326	161,836	El Paso	346,984	14,012,199	1,109,708	12,902,491
Carson	7,419	300,011	267,220	32,790	Erath.	23,881	986,835	395,269	591,566
Cass.	25,724	1,023,520	395,553	627,967	Falls	17,421	1,421,375	382,198	1,039,177
Castro	9,477	441,261	339,785	101,475	Fannin.	22,943	878,807	392,167	486,640
Chambers . . .	21,200	971,948	360,707	611,241	Fayette	20,980	939,365	388,715	550,650
Cherokee . . .	33,549	1,381,348	414,764	966,584	Fisher	5,552	233,569	231,050	2,518
Childress . . .	6,463	244,172	227,461	16,711	Floyd.	8,837	353,093	294,927	58,166
Clay.	8,919	381,187	308,741	72,446	Foard	1,972	85,883	84,854	1,000

Continued on Page 433.

Texas Motor Vehicles, 1917-1986

Motor vehicles registered in Texas during the period April 1 through March 31 of the following year are given for the period 1917-1976. In 1978, the State Department of Highways and Public Transportation went to an annual registration procedure whereby expiration of license plates occurs at staggered intervals throughout the year. Therefore, figures for 1977 and after are for the calendar year ending Dec. 31.

Registration Year	Vehicles Registration	*Percentage of Increase or Decrease	Registration Year	Vehicles Registration	*Percentage of Increase or Decrease	Registration Year	Vehicles Registration	*Percentage of Increase or Decrease
1917.	194,720	. . .	1941.	1,830,821	.60	1965.	6,168,649	3.05
1918.	250,201	28.49	1942.	1,704,295	−6.91	1966.	6,395,770	3.68
1919.	331,721	32.58	1943.	1,624,593	−4.68	1967.	6,651,767	4.00
1920.	430,377	29.74	1944.	1,625,428	.05	1968.	7,016,402	5.48
1921.	470,575	9.34	1945.	1,713,944	5.45	1969.	7,351,437	4.77
1922.	531,608	12.97	1946.	1,943,716	11.82	1970.	7,642,221	3.96
1923.	695,822	30.89	1947.	2,192,654	12.81	1971.	8,086,061	5.81
1924.	840,560	20.80	1948.	2,441,158	11.34	1972.	8,564,582	5.92
1925.	983,420	17.00	1949.	2,784,480	14.06	1973.	9,070,160	5.90
1926.	1,060,716	7.86	1950.	3,132,577	12.50	1974.	9,386,063	3.48
1927.	1,126,982	6.25	1951.	3,285,693	4.89	1975.	9,878,896	5.25
1928.	1,235,162	9.60	1952.	3,373,053	2.66	1976.	10,432,636	5.61
1929.	1,376,427	11.44	1953.	3,551,004	5.28	1977.	11,152,302	9.66
1930.	1,401,748	1.84	1954.	3,781,235	6.48	1978.	11,297,938	1.31
1931.	1,345,436	−4.02	1955.	4,089,718	8.16	1979.	10,085,254	−10.73
1932.	1,237,850	−7.99	1956.	4,220,702	3.20	1980.	11,989,419	18.88
1933.	1,241,848	.32	1957.	4,396,714	4.17	1981.	12,418,020	3.06
1934.	1,358,882	9.42	1958.	4,531,010	3.05	1982.	12,765,555	2.80
1935.	1,426,949	5.01	1959.	4,744,005	4.70	1983.	13,853,020	8.52
1936.	1,537,947	7.78	1960.	4,885,300	2.98	1984.	13,491,236	−2.61
1937.	1,612,533	4.85	1961.	5,206,543	6.58	1985.	13,966,188	3.52
1938.	1,630,040	1.09	1962.	5,456,913	4.81	1986.	14,374,063	2.92
1939.	1,702,507	4.45	1963.	5,721,773	4.85	*Decrease indicated by minus (−) sign.		
1940.	1,802,063	5.85	1964.	5,985,986	4.62			

County	Total Vehicles Registered	Total Gross License Fees (Dollars)	Net to County (Dollars)	Net to State (Dollars)
Fort Bend	127,527	5,353,714	595,534	4,758,179
Franklin	6,268	240,292	201,263	39,029
Freestone	14,900	596,516	378,097	218,419
Frio	8,818	402,143	306,851	95,292
Gaines	12,599	624,371	373,171	251,200
Galveston	165,818	6,549,068	617,128	5,931,940
Garza	4,820	234,869	206,117	28,751
Gillespie	17,027	716,467	381,951	334,516
Glasscock	1,816	81,729	80,945	784
Goliad	5,056	186,242	183,569	2,673
Gonzales	15,780	710,968	379,834	331,134
Gray	30,677	1,446,460	405,588	1,040,872
Grayson	91,898	3,737,894	530,395	3,207,499
Gregg	123,598	5,666,961	511,946	5,155,016
Grimes	14,326	584,325	378,618	205,707
Guadalupe	46,550	2,001,742	436,986	1,564,756
Hale	31,933	1,368,624	411,018	957,606
Hall	4,548	164,558	162,149	2,409
Hamilton	8,028	337,914	286,649	51,264
Hansford	8,203	377,671	302,320	75,351
Hardeman	5,621	277,944	255,137	22,806
Hardin	38,688	1,591,978	426,325	1,165,653
Harris	2,161,162	95,146,067	5,073,068	90,072,999
Harrison	46,771	1,916,039	438,006	1,478,033
Hartley	4,023	184,180	182,271	1,908
Haskell	8,830	315,902	276,251	39,652
Hays	44,149	1,802,981	437,638	1,365,343
Hemphill	5,419	253,029	216,933	36,095
Henderson	50,721	1,980,826	446,298	1,534,528
Hidalgo	196,199	8,816,524	778,153	8,038,371
Hill	25,552	982,297	398,768	583,530
Hockley	22,936	1,086,885	391,318	695,567
Hood	25,112	975,242	343,629	631,613
Hopkins	25,934	1,143,876	402,658	741,218
Houston	18,332	764,105	384,460	379,645
Howard	32,919	1,440,550	415,757	1,024,793
Hudspeth	1,965	98,422	97,318	1,104
Hunt	54,665	2,127,615	465,104	1,662,511
Hutchinson	32,425	1,470,219	408,380	1,061,839
Irion	2,000	106,396	105,254	1,142
Jack	8,879	481,552	354,305	127,248
Jackson	13,789	605,495	376,043	229,452
Jasper	29,366	1,220,065	405,008	815,057
Jeff Davis	1,778	78,411	77,052	1,359
Jefferson	210,026	8,609,967	761,590	7,848,371
Jim Hogg	4,283	201,632	146,700	54,932
Jim Wells	29,073	1,590,735	403,578	1,187,156
Johnson	81,677	3,311,381	527,374	2,784,007
Jones	16,669	754,085	381,403	372,682
Karnes	11,177	502,635	371,431	131,204
Kaufman	43,689	1,759,724	430,797	1,328,927
Kendall	16,398	668,497	322,338	346,160
Kenedy	339	12,212	12,016	196
Kent	1,546	56,904	56,110	794
Kerr	33,218	1,341,017	414,940	926,077
Kimble	4,899	221,295	198,134	23,160
King	433	17,151	16,958	193
Kinney	2,158	81,931	78,945	2,987
Kleberg	23,141	999,772	276,826	722,946
Knox	5,352	224,395	214,094	10,301
Lamar	40,727	1,693,970	429,631	1,264,339
Lamb	15,755	630,657	379,685	250,972
Lampasas	12,290	490,706	360,722	129,984
La Salle	3,416	135,087	133,375	1,712
Lavaca	17,859	722,560	380,873	341,687
Lee	13,957	660,752	370,097	290,654
Leon	11,932	476,500	358,392	118,108
Liberty	45,400	2,150,641	438,033	1,712,609
Limestone	18,090	790,290	384,147	406,143
Lipscomb	4,849	210,384	207,663	2,721
Live Oak	9,587	576,472	367,592	208,880
Llano	13,801	537,296	375,553	161,744
Loving	320	23,434	23,286	148
Lubbock	185,273	7,885,947	727,807	7,158,140
Lynn	6,851	262,187	247,975	14,212
McCulloch	9,084	412,344	323,317	89,026
McLennan	160,212	7,297,037	688,518	6,608,519
McMullen	1,179	50,714	50,166	548
Madison	9,245	398,515	276,978	121,538
Marion	7,956	316,204	262,953	53,252
Martin	5,999	268,725	242,517	26,208
Mason	4,004	149,993	147,988	2,005
Matagorda	34,423	1,493,301	415,022	1,078,279
Maverick	16,933	692,097	257,337	434,760
Medina	23,467	971,590	393,617	577,974
Menard	5,404	676,257	228,073	448,184
Midland	107,183	4,967,527	555,622	4,411,905
Milam	22,023	876,823	390,159	486,664
Mills	4,906	191,462	188,854	2,608
Mitchell	8,943	380,921	308,101	72,821
Montague	19,598	862,252	389,556	472,696
Montgomery	138,124	5,661,566	635,422	5,026,144
Moore	18,436	850,867	347,180	503,687
Morris	15,778	751,052	306,367	444,684
Motley	1,986	71,730	70,709	1,021
Nacogdoches	39,341	1,636,767	423,359	1,213,408
Navarro	34,749	1,549,623	417,487	1,132,135
Newton	8,442	369,515	302,924	66,592
Nolan	16,292	672,675	383,089	289,586
Nueces	228,019	10,135,684	824,605	9,311,079
Ochiltree	12,982	673,734	374,468	299,265
Oldham	2,440	105,495	104,153	1,342
Orange	70,616	2,692,867	470,767	2,222,101
Palo Pinto	26,266	1,084,615	401,444	683,171
Panola	19,678	817,389	386,492	430,898
Parker	51,597	2,125,617	448,273	1,677,344
Parmer	10,925	484,774	362,267	122,506
Pecos	14,763	681,527	376,543	304,984
Polk	26,888	1,130,655	401,836	728,819
Potter	102,577	4,681,435	536,222	4,145,213
Presidio	3,850	148,919	147,140	1,780
Rains	6,290	237,871	200,328	37,543
Randall	81,656	3,259,293	500,357	2,758,936
Reagan	4,505	247,605	206,795	40,810
Real	2,526	107,541	105,988	1,553
Red River	12,896	475,918	358,829	117,089
Reeves	11,766	540,584	371,485	169,099
Refugio	8,025	355,106	236,509	118,597
Roberts	1,692	64,812	64,043	769
Robertson	12,599	486,082	363,368	122,714
Rockwall	20,634	949,252	252,538	696,715
Runnels	13,205	607,826	372,770	235,055
Rusk	36,954	1,563,229	418,858	1,144,372
Sabine	8,461	321,972	254,307	67,665
SanAugustine	7,862	330,492	271,817	58,675
San Jacinto	11,295	478,273	349,747	128,526
San Patricio	45,791	1,977,382	438,777	1,538,605
San Saba	5,931	252,441	242,653	9,788
Schleicher	3,534	141,938	140,131	1,807
Scurry	20,332	978,566	386,128	592,438
Shackelford	4,659	240,888	207,912	32,975
Shelby	21,547	1,029,560	389,445	640,115
Sherman	4,145	184,318	182,146	2,172
Smith	136,967	5,683,272	643,950	5,039,322
Somervell	5,374	214,848	160,148	54,700
Starr	16,952	736,419	390,499	345,920
Stephens	11,564	543,365	359,523	183,842
Sterling	1,667	67,539	66,266	1,273
Stonewall	2,790	130,280	128,967	1,313
Sutton	5,871	338,196	274,067	64,129
Swisher	8,882	356,051	296,463	59,588
Tarrant	990,368	42,799,907	2,303,023	40,496,884
Taylor	114,763	5,155,049	586,535	4,568,513
Terrell	1,625	64,338	63,626	712
Terry	14,564	651,785	377,331	274,455
Throckmortn	2,474	105,327	104,209	1,117
Titus	21,291	894,084	375,490	518,594
Tom Green	87,394	3,662,785	520,399	3,142,386
Travis	467,398	19,684,966	1,372,329	18,312,637
Trinity	10,620	462,860	322,460	140,400
Tyler	15,207	636,555	378,368	258,187
Upshur	23,197	891,387	394,928	496,458
Upton	5,163	350,476	284,750	65,726
Uvalde	18,254	854,533	344,938	509,595
Val Verde	27,845	1,042,360	331,480	710,880
Van Zandt	37,337	1,404,379	416,272	988,107
Victoria	69,442	3,035,440	480,678	2,554,762
Walker	29,699	1,261,620	406,370	855,251
Waller	27,173	1,171,772	399,541	772,232
Ward	14,923	815,571	354,673	460,898
Washington	24,168	1,124,958	396,288	728,670
Webb	63,197	2,953,481	445,469	2,508,012
Wharton	36,920	1,744,593	420,376	1,324,218
Wheeler	7,224	303,116	268,724	34,392
Wichita	118,307	4,998,179	548,485	4,449,694
Wilbarger	15,227	620,792	380,152	240,640
Willacy	11,301	510,207	372,535	137,672
Williamson	94,535	3,898,147	527,473	3,370,673
Wilson	16,075	626,591	378,733	247,858
Winkler	10,556	509,316	276,468	232,848

County	Total Vehicles Registered	Total Gross License Fees (Dollars)	Net to County (Dollars)	Net to State (Dollars)
Wise	34,710	1,769,828	413,253	1,356,575
Wood	30,027	1,206,165	406,865	799,301
Yoakum	9,653	502,329	367,711	134,618
Young	23,834	1,135,060	396,682	738,377
Zapata	6,264	253,414	167,002	86,412
Zavala	6,169	252,478	195,618	56,860

County	Total Vehicles Registered	Total Gross License Fees (Dollars)	Net to County (Dollars)	Net to State (Dollars)
County Totals	13,729,625	594,155,366	99,299,772	494,855,594
State Collections		19,762,534		19,762,534
Grand Totals	13,729,625	613,917,900	99,299,772	514,618,129

Prepared by: State Department of Highways and Public Transportation, Motor Vehicle Division, Austin, TX 78779.

Citizens Helping To Clean Highways

To promote litter-free roadsides around the state, the State Department of Highways and Public Transportation has developed the Adopt-a-Highway Program. Originating in the Tyler District in 1985 and expanding statewide in March 1986, the program provides that each district engineer assign a section of highway, usually two miles or more in length, to each civic or non-profit organization or civic-minded company or corporation taking part in the program. The participating group agrees to remove litter from that section of highway on a regular schedule for a period of a year. The highway department furnishes signs identifying the project and provides safety vests for participating workers.

According to maintenance section engineer Thomas Ohlendorf, the main thrust of the Adopt-a-Highway Program is to make the public more aware of the personal part they can play in keeping the roadsides neat, not only those who participate directly in the pick-up efforts, but also those who drive through and notice the identification signs.

As of April 1987, there were more than 1,300 active Adopt-a-Highway projects picking up trash along 2,600 miles of state highway. For more information, contact your district engineer:

Abilene (Dist. 8), Box 150, 79604; Amarillo (Dist. 4), Box 2708, 79105; Atlanta (Dist. 19), Box 890, 75551; Austin (Dist. 14), Box 15426, 78761; Beaumont (Dist. 20), Box 3468, 77704; Brownwood (Dist. 23), Box 1549, 76804; Bryan (Dist. 17), Box 3249, 77805; Childress (Dist. 25), Box 900, 79201; Corpus Christi (Dist. 16), Box 9907, 78469; Dallas (Dist. 18), Box 3067, 75221; El Paso (Dist. 24), Box 10278, 79994; Fort Worth (Dist. 2), Box 6868, 76115; Houston (Dist. 12), Box 1386, 77251; Lubbock (Dist. 5), Box 771, 79408; Lufkin (Dist. 11), Box 280, 75901.

Odessa (Dist. 6), 3901 E. Hwy. 80, 79761; Paris (Dist. 1), Box 250, 75460; Pharr (Dist. 21), Drawer EE, 78577; San Angelo (Dist. 7), Box 5500, 76902; San Antonio (Dist 15), Box 29928, 78284; Tyler (Dist. 10), Box 2031, 75710; Waco (Dist. 9), Box 1010, 76703; Wichita Falls (Dist. 3), Box 660, 76307; Yoakum (Dist. 13), Box 757, 77995.

Drivers' Licenses

The following report from Texas Department of Public Safety shows the number of drivers' licenses issued during the fiscal year and number of valid licenses at the end of each fiscal year.

Fiscal Year Ending	*Licenses Issued During Year	Valid Licenses at Year's End
Aug. 31, 1986	4,325,742	11,436,780
Aug. 31, 1985	4,677,788	11,241,367
Aug. 31, 1984	4,498,902	11,009,567
Aug. 31, 1983	4,090,602	10,805,539
Aug. 31, 1982	4,281,652	10,463,962
Aug. 31, 1981	3,818,303	9,909,721
Aug. 31, 1980	3,699,543	9,551,683
Aug. 31, 1979	3,616,754	9,189,198
Aug. 31, 1978	3,529,926	8,805,604
Aug. 31, 1977	3,418,606	8,420,678
Aug. 31, 1976	3,233,610	8,127,188
Aug. 31, 1975	2,980,024	7,806,703
Aug. 31, 1974	2,887,456	7,588,372
Aug. 31, 1973	2,807,828	7,334,913
Aug. 31, 1972	2,573,010	7,098,425
Aug. 31, 1971	2,418,170	6,768,319
Aug. 31, 1970	2,321,416	6,420,602
Aug. 31, 1969	3,403,122	6,035,944
Aug. 31, 1968	3,603,082	5,849,126

*Includes renewals during year.

Highway Mileage and Expenditures—1918-1986

Selected years of operation of the State Highway Department, which was established in 1917 and made its first report for fiscal year ended Aug. 31, 1918, is covered by this table:

Fiscal Year	Paved Roads	Total Mileage Maintained	Total Expenditures All Purposes	Fiscal Year	Paved Roads	Total Mileage Maintained	Total Expenditures All Purposes
1918	†	†	$ 1,268,284.82	1965	62,421	62,618	451,909,168.85
1920	†	†	2,411,285.26	1966	63,640	63,718	470,945,064.73
1925	†	†	20,602,264.66	1967	64,486	64,580	562,358,008.43
1930	7,317	18,528	47,331,977.54	1968	65,241	65,335	547,505,442.17
1935	13,285	20,359	35,796,704.45	1969	66,017	66,091	593,923,831.27
1940	19,440	23,434	40,210,347.86	1970	67,139	67,272	674,031,313.81
1945	23,562	25,705	26,955,618.80	1971	67,536	67,651	701,124,133.89
1950	34,200	34,929	115,282,344.55	1972	68,125	68,204	669,939,862.44
1951	39,741	40,368	133,412,463.68	1973	68,463	68,564	646,024,497.30
1952	41,846	42,288	135,668,281.48	1974	69,169	69,268	730,767,580.05
1953	43,877	44,179	160,887,682.32	1975	69,392	69,470	905,008,667.20
1954	46,399	46,676	166,378,588.36	1976	69,613	69,685	820,634,135.48
1955	48,678	48,840	192,826,643.81	1977	69,990	70,020	784,044,000.00
1956	50,697	50,839	212,863,034.52	1978	70,233	70,389	1,013,975,000.00
1957	52,849	52,977	246,009,210.04	1979	71,132	71,212	1,097,793,290.91
1958	54,166	54,367	317,371,972.63	1980	70,605	70,605	1,720,255,170.65
1959	55,750	55,932	411,743,735.10	1981	70,764	70,804	1,675,356,011.20
1960	56,941	57,015	397,185,292.27	1982	70,926	70,933	1,469,004,133.89
1961	58,194	58,286	381,611,493.03	1983	71,060	71,065	1,570,521,630.00
1962	59,305	59,434	384,345,117.74	1984	71,165	71,172	1,515,286,262.00
1963	60,387	60,520	410,897,834.26	1985	71,410	71,418	1,730,400,136.00
1964	61,493	61,604	466,357,175.67	1986	71,555	71,560	2,698,953,833.00
				Total			$28,350,288,166.94

Fiscal Year ended Aug. 31.
†Not reported definitely for these years.

Railroad Mileage Operated By Carrier In Texas, 1985*

Railroad	Miles Operated
Class 1 Railroads**	
Atchison, Topeka & Santa Fe Railway Company	3,349
Burlington Northern Railroad Company	1,313
Kansas City Southern Railway Company	294
Missouri-Kansas-Texas Railroad Company	1,174
St. Louis Southwestern Railway Company	715
Southern Pacific Transportation Company	2,719
Union Pacific Railroad Company	3,289
Total Class 1	12,853
Class 2 Railroads**	
Texas Mexican Railway Company	157
Total Class 2	157
Class 3 Railroads**	
Angelina & Neches River Railroad Company	22
Belton Railroad Company	6
Border Pacific Railroad Company	32
Brownsville and Rio Grande International	10
Galveston, Houston & Henderson Railroad Company	48
Galveston Wharves, Board of Trustees of the	53
Georgetown Railroad Company, Inc.	16
Great Southwest Railroad, Inc.	20
Houston Belt and Terminal Railway Company	58
Moscow, Camden & San Augustine Railroad Company	7
Pecos Valley Southern Railway Company	34
Point Comfort & Northern Railway Company	13
Port Terminal Railroad Association	32
Rockdale, Sandow & Southern Railroad Company	6
Roscoe, Snyder & Pacific Railway Company	3
Sabine River & Northern Railroad Company	30
Texas & Northern Railway Company	8
Texas Central Railroad Company	25
Texas City Terminal Railway Company	6
Texas North Western Railway Company***	71
Texas South-Eastern Railroad Company	18
Texas Transportation Company	1
Weatherford, Mineral Wells & Northwestern Railway Company	23
Western Railroad Company	4
Total Class 3	546
Total Class 1, 2 and 3	13,556

*First main track only, owned and operated or operated under trackage rights.
**Class 1 railroads have annual operating revenues of $50,000,000 or more. Class 2 railroads have annual operating revenues of less than $50,000,000 but more than $10,000,000. Class 3 railroads have annual operating revenues of $10,000,000 or less.
***Not including 38 miles in Oklahoma and Kansas.

Rail Line Abandonments 1984-1986

Carrier	End Points	Miles	Counties
AT&SF..	Wadsworth-Matagorda	7.2	Matagorda
SP.....	Kosmos-Rockport	7.55	Aransas
SP.....	Bay City-Palacios	31.12	Matagorda
SLSW...	Atco-Lime City	16.18	McLennan and Coryell
UP.....	La Pryor-Blewett	22.0	Zavala and Uvalde
Total..		84.05	

Motor Vehicle Accidents, Losses

The following statistics for motor vehicle accidents, deaths and injuries, miles traveled and economic losses are from the Texas Department of Public Safety, Austin.

Year	No. Killed	+No. Injured	No. Fatal	+No. Involving Injury	+No. Non-Injury	+Total	*Number	Deaths per 100 million Miles	✔Economic Loss
				Accidents by Kinds			**Vehicle Miles Traveled**		
1970	3,560	223,000	2,965	124,000	886,000	1,012,965	‡68,031,000,000	5.2	$1,042,200,000
1978	**3,980	178,228	3,468	117,998	††304,830	††426,296	102,624,000,000	3.9	2,430,000,000
1979	4,229	184,550	3,685	122,793	322,336	448,814	101,909,000,000	4.1	2,580,000,000
1980	4,424	185,964	3,863	123,577	305,500	432,940	103,255,000,000	4.3	3,010,000,000
1981	4,701	206,196	4,137	136,396	317,484	458,017	111,036,000,000	4.2	3,430,000,000
1982	4,271	204,666	3,752	135,859	312,159	451,770	‡‡124,910,000,000	3.4	3,375,000,000
1983	3,823	208,157	§§3,328	137,695	302,876	443,899	129,309,000,000	3.0	3,440,000,000
1984	3,913	220,720	3,466	145,543	293,285	442,294	137,280,000,000	2.9	3,795,000,000
1985	3,682	231,009	3,270	151,657	300,531	452,188	143,500,000,000	2.6	3,755,000,000
1986	3,568	234,120	3,121	154,514	298,079	452,593	150,474,000,000	2.4	3,782,000,000

*Vehicle miles traveled since 1964 were estimated on the basis of new data furnished by U.S. Bureau of Public Roads through National Safety Council. Vehicle miles and deaths per 100 million vehicle miles after 1964 cannot, therefore, be compared with previous years.

+In August 1967, amended estimating formula received from National Safety Council. Starting with 1972, actual reported injuries are listed rather than estimates.

‡Vehicle miles traveled estimated by Texas Highway Department starting with 1970. Method of calculation varies from that used for prior years. Vehicle miles and deaths per 100,000,000 vehicle miles for 1969 and before cannot be compared to subsequent years.

✔Economic loss formula last changed 1984.

**Change in counting fatalities. Counted when injury results in death within 90 days of vehicle accident in which the injury occurred.

††Total accidents and non-injury accidents for 1978-84 cannot be compared with years prior to 1978 due to changes in reporting laws.

‡‡Method of calculating vehicle miles traveled revised for 1982 by the Texas State Department of Highways and Public Transportation. Vehicle miles and deaths per 100,000,000 miles cannot be compared to prior years.

§§Change in counting fatalities. Counted when injury results in death within 30 days of vehicle accident in which the injury occurred.

Railroad Operations in Texas

This article was compiled by Edward Kasparik, a former employee of the Texas Railroad Commission.

After a good year in 1984, the large Class 1 railroads in Texas experienced two successive years of decline in freight tonnage and net revenue. In 1985 and particularly in 1986, a troubled state economy and intense competition lowered demand for rail-hauled commodities. In 1986, the last year for which complete information is available, freight tonnage was only 78 percent of the 1984 total. Net revenue declined even more drastically — especially when compared with the peak year of 1981 (see accompanying table). Net revenue in 1986 was adversely impacted by special charges or "writedowns" taken by several of the largest carriers.

Railroad track mileage continues a slow but steady decline. Unlike many other states, however, Texas has not recently experienced major line abandonments.

Throughout the United States, large Class 1 rail-

Statistical History of Railroad Operation in Texas, 1891-1986

The table below shows development and trends of railroad line operations, freight tonnage, operating revenues and expenses in Texas since the Railroad Commission's first report.

Year	Average Miles Operated Included Trackage Rights	Tons Revenue Freight	Railway Operating Revenues	Railway Operating Expenses	Operating Ratio	*Net Reveue From Railway Operations	Freight Revenue	Passenger Revenue	Net From Operations	Freight Revenue Per Ton-Mile
1986.....	12,774	207,679,132	$1,827,330,000	$1,736,580,000	96.9	$90,750,000	$134,532.00	...	$7,834.00	$.0298
1985.....	12,860	217,096,477	2,026,001,000	1,713,245,620	83.9	312,755,380	148,040.00	...	26,816.00	.0300
1984.....	13,071	263,846,292	2,204,659,000	1,848,500,000	83.9	357,197,000	161,980.00	...	33,005.00	.0298
1983.....	12,942.00	245,502,145	2,032,792,000	1,705,625,000	83.8	327,167,000	147,548.00	...	25,824.00	.0296
1982.....	13,017.00	242,451,128	2,138,768,000	1,883,375,000	85.2	225,393,000	145,147.00	...	23,178.00	.0324
1981.....	13,051.00	274,576,260	2,400,252,000	2,055,057,000	81.78	345,195,000	169,528.00	...	32,585.00	.0320
†1980.....	13,075.00	268,445,039	2,064,108,000	1,761,650,000	85.34	304,742,000	151,918.00	...	23,310.00	.0268
†1979.....	13,075.00	239,943,773	1,718,912,000	1,469,238,000	85.47	249,674,000	126,819.00	...	19,096.00	.0243
‡1978.....	13,923.00	241,386,721	1,445,104,000	1,265,949,000	87.60	166,937,000	100,110.00	...	11,990.00	.0216
1977.....	14,554.00	242,267,810	1,314,952,036	993,342,280	75.54	321,609,756	86,994.26	...	22,097.69	.0213
1976.....	14,679.00	206,130,425	1,158,004,603	874,250,182	75.50	283,754,421	75,737.76	...	19,330.64	.0224
1975.....	14,717.00	230,120,781	1,073,029,254	792,786,773	73.88	280,242,481	69,982.79	...	19,042.09	.0196
1974.....	14,712.00	247,320,696	1,048,980,920	794,249,941	75.72	254,730,979	67,805.72	...	17,314.50	.0175
1973.....	14,830.00	253,365,741	928,419,976	699,019,572	75.29	229,400,404	59,512.05	0.15	15,468.67	.0147
1972.....	14,800.00	222,303,703	784,815,674	614,035,456	78.24	170,780,218	50,884.46	0.20	11,539.20	.0149
1971.....	14,909.00	208,878,010	725,469,372	554,682,694	76.46	170,786,678	46,429.13	38.81	11,455.27	.0145
1970.....	14,683.00	211,069,076	655,638,834	504,146,691	76.89	151,492,143	42,245.42	170.71	10,317.52	.0134
1969.....	15,019.00	201,455,133	599,461,296	465,795,906	77.70	133,665,390	37,570.23	206.72	8,899.75	.0130
1968.....	15,039.00	193,822,546	560,178,714	446,936,382	79.78	113,242,332	34,672.47	291.82	7,529.91	.0126
1967.....	15,128.00	183,742,685	517,617,077	411,306,768	79.46	106,310,309	31,432.83	400.93	7,027.39	.0124
1966.....	15,295.00	197,208,761	543,803,770	408,281,725	75.08	135,522,045	32,349.45	522.40	8,860.55	.0117
1965.....	15,214.00	181,553,163	502,191,485	380,412,080	75.75	121,779,405	29,754.73	605.40	8,004.43	.0118
1964.....	15,254.00	173,074,704	462,053,638	366,103,656	79.19	95,949,982	26,875.78	712.94	6,290.15	.0115
1963.....	15,279.00	158,750,736	445,048,337	348,210,665	78.24	96,837,672	25,635.01	791.81	6,337.96	.0120
1962.....	15,389.00	155,728,821	439,606,758	351,277,249	79.54	88,329,509	24,948.34	871.95	5,739.78	.0120
1961.....	15,622.00	157,700,142	429,983,796	344,217,323	80.05	85,766,473	23,915.32	892.94	5,490.11	.0126
1960.....	15,445.00	149,360,161	438,531,081	347,353,628	79.21	91,177,453	26,149.41	937.69	5,903.36	.0121
1959.....	15,600.00	162,985,000	460,813,237	355,981,564	77.25	104,831,673	25,889.59	924.41	6,719.98	.0127
1958.....	15,853.00	152,687,265	449,909,607	338,708,662	75.28	111,200,945	24,908.93	904.14	7,014.50	.0134
1957.....	16,003.00	156,218,472	455,449,879	349,842,282	76.81	105,607,597	24,923.21	1,002.17	6,599.24	.0136
1956.....	16,078.00	163,448,004	451,785,741	354,734,911	78.52	97,050,830	24,502.50	1,089.91	6,036.25	.0131
1955.....	16,151.00	166,742,660	450,865,455	341,963,345	75.85	108,902,110	24,482.83	1,085.84	6,742.75	.0134
1954.....	16,254.00	151,639,475	426,223,548	326,373,490	76.57	99,850,058	22,758.67	1,161.88	6,143.11	.0140
1953.....	16,248.00	163,120,436	474,112,360	359,553,092	75.84	114,559,268	25,489.81	1,238.52	7,050.67	.0147
1952.....	16,249.00	171,536,799	480,598,102	353,835,324	73.62	126,762,778	25,554.16	1,471.58	7,801.27	.0140
1951.....	16,268.00	171,974,878	458,070,697	351,407,963	76.71	106,662,734	24,025.44	1,582.08	6,556.60	.0131
1950.....	16,296.00	155,970,914	420,864,968	310,731,697	73.83	210,133,271	22,021.66	1,366.76	6,758.30	.0132
1949.....	16,326.67	147,769,627	389,948,675	298,378,439	76.52	91,570,236	20,461.53	1,390.79	5,608.63	.0131
1948.....	16,344.72	172,717,282	436,136,261	330,029,402	76.59	106,106,865	22,907.44	1,626.45	6,491.81	.0120
1947.....	16,345.71	163,222,681	372,282,426	280,421,729	75.32	91,860,697	19,005.06	1,727.19	5,619.86	.0079
1946.....	16,365.62	140,735,375	321,208,561	261,245,259	81.33	59,963,302	15,183.86	2,634.56	3,663.98	.0094
1945.....	16,375.97	159,795,571	390,672,459	263,883,854	67.54	126,788,605	17,635.26	4,370.32	7,742.36	.0102
1940.....	17,057.38	69,107,695	144,124,269	110,626,057	76.76	33,498,212	7,028.74	944.72	1,963.85	.0106
1935.....	17,295.66	61,452,202	117,611,146	93,681,088	79.65	23,930,058	5,579.27	802.07	1,383.58	.0112
1930.....	17,569.02	88,942,552	204,371,667	152,169,952	74.46	52,201,715	9,557.06	1,739.55	2,971.24	.0123
1925.....	16,646.53	90,338,397	227,252,064	169,382,692	74.54	57,869,372	10,653.42	2,673.33	3,476.36	.0142
1920.....	16,382.99	77,803,926	235,353,895	234,718,643	99.73	635,252	9,714.47	4,291.77	38.77	.0139
1915.....	16,294.10	54,354,684	107,414,011	85,900,985	79.97	21,513,026	4,504.81	1,809.82	1,320.29	.0100
1910.....	14,339.21	47,084,828	94,731,430	72,524,020	76.56	22,207,410	4,601.92	1,981.27	1,548.72	.0103
1905.....	11,670.65	30,653,070	68,145,132	52,411,748	76.91	15,733,384	4,044.88	1,493.65	1,348.12	.0108
1900.....	9,971.21	22,380,607	47,062,868	35,626,922	75.70	11,435,946	3,537.81	1,106.78	1,167.98	.0096
1895.....	9,353.80	15,591,262	39,387,869	28,864,994	73.28	10,522,875	3,159.04	984.73	1,124.98	.0130
1891.....	8,718.65	10,944,195	35,666,498	28,762,836	80.64	6,903,662	2,956.58	1,081.59	791.83	.0146

*Net revenue before interest and taxes.

†No data available for Rock Island in 1979 and 1980.

‡Beginning in 1978, data no longer reported for Class II and III carriers.

roads have been merging into even larger but fewer mega-railroads of great size and many assets. Concurrently, these same carriers are selling hundreds — sometimes thousands — of miles of light-density branch lines to form new, independent "short-line" railroads. Central Texans witnessed one manifestiation of this trend in 1986 when the Southern Pacific Railroad sold 163 miles of rail line from Giddings-Austin-Marble Falls-Llano to the City of Austin and the Capital Metropolitan Transportation Authority. A new short-line — the Austin & Northwestern Railroad (AU&NW) — now provides daily freight train service over this route, with passenger transit service planned for the future.

The final decision from the Interstate Commerce Commission (ICC) on the merger application of the Atchison, Topeka and Santa Fe Railway Company (AT&SF), the Southern Pacific Transportation Company (SP) and the St. Louis Southwestern Railway Company (SLSW) has not been handed down. If approved, the resulting consolidated carrier would control more than 50 percent of all track mileage in the state, making it the single largest railroad in Texas. In a stunning decision in early 1987, the ICC denied the merger application. At mid-year, however, the commission is considering re-opening the case.

After absorbing the Missouri Pacific (MP) in 1982, the Union Pacific Railroad (UP) filed an application in 1986 with the ICC to acquire the Missouri-Kansas-Texas Railroad (MKT). If approved, the MKT, or "Katy," as it is often called, would disappear as a separate corporate entity. A decision — with or without conditions — is not required until 1989.

Railroad passenger service has dwindled to a few routes. Amtrak continues operating two trains — the Sunset Limited and the Eagle — that connect 18 Texas cities with such points as Los Angeles, Tucson, New Orleans and Chicago. The Texas Mexican Railway (TM) initiated weekend passenger service between Corpus Christi and Laredo in 1986. The Texas State Railroad (TS), owned by the state and operated as a state historical park, offers weekend rides for tourists through the Piney Woods between Rusk and Palestine.

Unlike any other in the state, trains of the TS are powered by steam locomotives.

Although existing passenger train service is limited in the state, much discussion and considerable planning has been invested in proposed high-speed service between the "Texas Triangle" cities of Dallas-Fort Worth, Houston, San Antonio and Austin. Preliminary feasibility studies were initiated by Amtrak in the early 1980s. More recently in 1984, a private consortium of 10 West German companies embarked on a detailed process of economic feasibility studies. The consortium is focusing on a Dallas-Fort Worth to Houston routing.

Amtrak Passengers On/Off at Texas Stations

Station	FY86	FY85	FY84	FY83
San Antonio	29,806	31,145	30,919	29,522
Dallas	25,119	24,304	26,296	24,850
El Paso	16,739	17,130	15,748	15,203
Houston	16,033	15,115	16,940	16,843
Austin	14,277	15,106	13,213	12,851
Fort Worth	12,171	12,226	12,551	12,708
Longview	5,607	5,376	5,574	5,740
Temple	5,133	5,239	5,609	5,254
Texarkana	4,265	4,243	4,318	4,184
Marshall	4,163	3,884	4,497	4,052
Beaumont	3,768	3,566	3,699	4,377
Taylor	3,505	3,772	3,697	3,151
San Marcos	2,445	3,027	2,330	2,132
McGregor	1,904	1,904	1,852	1,750
Alpine	1,849	1,667	1,894	1,810
Cleburne	1,826	1,829	2,669	2,694
Del Rio	1,184	1,201	1,295	1,701
Sanderson	500	582	573	642
Totals	150,294	151,316	153,674	149,464

Source: Amtrak Office of State & Local Services Analysis, Washington, D.C.

Principal Texas Ports

Houston continued to be the leading Texas port in 1985, but the tonnage handled by the state's 27 ports dropped 6.8 percent compared to 1984.

Houston handled 90,669,169 short tons in 1985, according to the Galveston District Corps of Engineers, U.S. Army, a decline of 6.3 percent from the previous year. The state's ports' tonnage dropped to 245,959,297 in 1985 from 263,921,559 in 1984, a decline of 6.8 percent.

Tonnage handled on the Gulf Intracoastal Waterway in Texas increased during 1985. The tonnage handled between the Sabine River and Galveston dropped 3.1 percent to 42,443,030 tons, but increases on the other two segments — Galveston to Corpus Christi and Corpus Christi to the Mexican Border — increased to more than 2 million tons to bring the total tonnage handled on the waterway in 1985 to 67,509,304, a 1.2 percent increase

over the 66,678,903 tons handled in 1984.

Among the 27 ports along the Texas Gulf, several smaller ports registered substantial percentage gains in tonnage handled in 1985. The channel to Liberty increased by 1,834.1 percent, handling a total of 58,486 tons during the year. Double Bayou, with 20,845 tons, showed an increase of 764.2 percent, and Anahuac hiked its tonnage handled to 52,859 tons, a 746.2 percent climb.

Texas City registered the largest tonnage increase, almost 2.8 million tons, to 33,440,917, a 9.1 percent climb. Beaumont suffered the largest tonnage loss, 6.16 million tons, to 26,842,008 tons, an 18.7 percent decline.

Dry cargo handled through the deepwater ports amounted to 28,911,965 tons in 1985, while liquid cargo amounted to 206,846,017 tons, for a total tonnage of 235,757,982.

Receipts, Shipments at Texas Ports

1985 RECEIPTS AND SHIPMENTS
(All figures in short tons)

SABINE PASS HARBOR: **Internal Receipts:** Crude petroleum, 110,733; distillate fuel oil, 26,668; clay, 6,373. **Internal Shipments:** Crude petroleum, 81,864.

ORANGE HARBOR: **Exports:** Distillate fuel oil, 29,770. **Internal Receipts:** Building cement, 208,256; basic chemicals, nec., 169,897; residual fuel oil, 85,608; limestone, 39,190. **Internal Shipments:** Crude petroleum, 16,899.

BEAUMONT HARBOR: **Imports:** Crude petroleum, 8,089,569; residual fuel oil, 289,822; basic chemicals, nec., 232,976; gasoline, 102,634. **Exports:** Wheat, 1,192,400; wheat flour and semolina, 252,829; soybeans, 154,918. **Coastwise Receipts:** Crude petroleum, 1,105,722; gasoline, 102,901; lubricating oils and greases, 75,758. **Coastwise Shipments:** Gasoline, 1,376,841; Crude petroleum, 648,312; liquid sulphur, 481,214; distillate fuel oil, 432,682; residual fuel oil, 316,687; naphtha, 246,477; jet fuel, 204,070; lubricating oils and greases, 81,525. **Internal Receipts:** Crude petroleum, 2,792,409; gasoline, 938,918; iron and steel scrap, 518,679; residual fuel oil, 415,451; distillate fuel oil, 310,725; basic chemicals, nec., 202,102;

naphtha, 192,863; lubricating oils and greases, 110,157; sand and gravel, 103,731; alcohols, 94,287; benzene and toluene, 92,093. **Internal Shipments:** Residual fuel oil, 1,133,704; crude petroleum, 513,631; benzene and toluene, 428,866; basic chemicals, nec., 310,066; lubricating oils and greases, 245,710; asphalt, tar, 221,817; gasoline, 220,452; alcohols, 205,540; naphtha, 179,134; jet fuel, 169,245; distillate fuel oil, 151,964; petroleum and coal prod., nec., 94,757; crude tar, 83,546; iron and steel primary forms, 78,495. **Local:** Gasoline, 93,938.

PORT ARTHUR HARBOR: **Imports:** Crude petroleum, 4,195,236; residual fuel oil, 1,060,520; naphtha, 433,333; basic chemicals, nec., 267,947; building cement, 204,574; coke, pet. coke, 88,252; distillate fuel oil, 56,534; gasoline, 54,819. **Exports:** Coke, pet. coke 768,080; residual fuel oil, 682,962; basic chemicals, nec., 260,628; wheat, 239,567; distillate fuel oil, 207,653; coal and lignite, 150,879; lubricating oils and greases, 114,134; jet fuel, 98,354; paper and paperboard, 61,810. **Coastwise Receipts:** Gasoline, 83,379; crude petroleum, 81,441. **Coastwise Shipments:** Gasoline, 1,161,310. **Internal Receipts:** Residual fuel oil, 227,348; gasoline, 138,777; naphtha, 106,883; distillate fuel oil, 86,696; crude petroleum, 76,214; benzene and toluene, 56,027. **Internal Shipments:**

Residual fuel oil, 1,423,414; basic chemicals, nec., 538,036; coke, pet. coke, 278,249; gasoline, 179,028; petroleum and coal prod., nec., 175,353; building cement, 171,156; lubricating oils and greases, 140,653; distillate fuel oil, 133,056; benzene and toluene, 104,497; jet fuel, 55,804; naphtha, 50,836.

HOUSTON HARBOR: **Imports:** Crude petroleum, 6,758,314; basic chemicals, nec., 2,509,021; residual fuel oil, 2,452,268; iron and steel shapes, 1,685,694; iron and steel pipe, 1,495,365; naphtha, 1,073,634; distillate fuel oil, 865,731; building cement, 695,256; miscellaneous chemical prod., 607,454; liquefied gases, 565,891; alcohols, 554,960; gasoline, 450,482; molasses, 437,045; motor vehicles, parts, equip., 384,095; benzene and toluene, 355,716; clay, 336,508; gypsum, 214,803; machinery, except electrical, 205,640. **Exports:** Wheat, 4,251,162; basic chemicals, nec., 2,835,940; residual fuel oil, 1,178,931; coke, pet. coke, 884,018; sorghum grains, 861,988; plastic materials, 777,626; potassic fertilizers, 535,206; alcohols, 429,942; rice, 425,400; distillate fuel oil, 424,265; lubricating oils and greases, 420,649; tallow, animal fats and oils, 381,166; miscellaneous chemical prod., 350,956; corn, 304,358; machinery, except electrical, 253,280; fertilizers, nec., 251,857; liquefied gases, 228,382; dry sulphur, 212,864. **Coastwise Receipts:** Crude petroleum, 2,148,747; phosphate rock, 787,303; residual fuel oil, 677,150; gasoline, 251,724; commodities, nec., 239,364.

Coastwise Shipments: Gasoline, 2,070,345; residual fuel oil, 1,917,247; distillate fuel oil, 1,640,730; naphtha, 527,379; jet fuel, 349,327; lubricating oils and greases, 341,451; basic chemicals, nec., 258,169; commodities, nec., 221,553; alcohols, 201,743. **Internal Receipts:** Residual fuel oil, 4,297,173; gasoline, 2,731,197; basic chemicals, nec., 1,336,718; distillate fuel oil, 1,104,001; crude petroleum, 1,096,183; jet fuel, 806,606; benzene and toluene, 542,692; naphtha, 473,040; alcohols, 391,857; petroleum and coal prod., nec., 310,142; asphalt, tar, 276,112; iron and steel pipe, 249,989; waste and scrap, nec., 239,093; sodium hydroxide, 233,207; iron and steel scrap, 227,005; lubricating oils and greases, 218,445. **Internal Shipments:** Basic chemicals, nec., 2,736,883; residual fuel oil, 2,144,628; gasoline, 1,530,582; naphtha, 949,511; crude petroleum, 733,623; waste and scrap, nec., 708,652; alcohols, 607,438; lubricating oils and greases, 582,082; sulphuric acid, 558,885; distillate fuel oil, 471,886; liquefied gases, 456,357; benzene and toluene, 428,759; sodium hydroxide, 286,048; limestone, 257,662; liquid sulphur, 201,225; crude tar, 190,040; iron and steel plates, 123,820; petroleum and coal prod., nec., 117,229; jet fuel, 111,793. **Local:** Residual fuel oil, 1,573,493; basic chemicals, nec., 918,554; gasoline, 808,504; distillate fuel oil, 730,035; benzene and toluene, 527,933; alcohols, 429,289; building cement, 410,125; sand and gravel, 296,163; petroleum and coal prod., nec., 215,886.

Tonnage Handled by Texas Ports, 1976-1985

Source: Corps of Engineers, U.S. Army

Table below gives consolidated tonnage handled by ports and moving through Gulf Intracoastal Waterway. All figures are in short tons.

Ports	1985	1984	1983	1982	1981	1980	1979	1978	1977	1976
Brwnsvle	1,442,790	1,481,422	1,338,550	2,200,132	2,810,018	2,569,697	2,508,076	2,163,590	2,130,440	2,584,916
Port Isabel	279,578	257,781	284,758	307,856	313,036	304,964	308,021	245,151	203,702	208,287
Corpus Christi	41,057,313	44,081,109	39,131,318	37,974,192	41,980,354	45,001,096	55,597,104	54,678,296	56,041,113	43,492,959
Freeport	12,918,289	15,122,761	15,671,990	14,989,683	23,357,106	20,131,067	19,983,837	21,712,480	15,332,518	9,710,609
Galveston	7,791,729	11,752,974	10,177,718	9,349,856	11,268,337	9,631,091	8,982,285	7,786,146	9,563,626	7,302,900
Houston	90,669,169	96,777,619	88,706,519	94,649,549	100,966,741	108,937,268	117,550,908	111,936,099	104,291,267	89,897,598
Texas City	33,440,917	30,656,673	35,496,241	33,370,791	27,852,242	25,948,936	35,954,301	34,656,219	33,583,596	28,516,499
Sabine	547,160	605,050	605,108	1,164,632	1,063,238	949,404	867,813	531,491	882,692	677,425
Port Arthur	15,754,931	16,430,368	18,338,237	19,945,958	26,037,529	29,796,633	32,735,633	33,474,523	30,753,732	30,687,203
Beaumont	26,842,008	33,004,372	36,001,675	33,286,791	40,358,920	52,260,728	58,136,896	52,770,276	48,918,843	43,939,073
Orange	648,350	452,488	399,092	279,728	484,942	567,157	631,694	513,009	1,003,331	981,626
Port Lavaca	4,365,748	3,636,922	3,422,854	4,308,436	4,148,664	3,991,089	4,562,702	4,677,509	3,894,810	4,256,320
Anahuac	52,859	6,242	0	31,122	25,276	41,665	14,900	16,219	18,050	31,024
Moss Bluff	0	0	0	128,747	196,402	207,471	290,493	296,833	379,680	279,813
Clear Creek	0	58,726	0	0	0	20,700	103,280	148,182	154,611	195,266
Double Bayou	20,845	2,412	12,915	11,843	26,136	48,554	49,618	48,957	72,731	43,131
Cedar Bayou	218,608	391,946	454,993	404,816	231,485	328,513	361,179	431,047	430,322	570,889
Sweeny	519,417	619,837	629,816	726,684	660,291	673,740	601,435	321,305	414,142	578,986
Palacios	10,116	0	86	54,545	100,293	85,862	88,804	48,080	97,555	42,232
Dickinson	194,932	176,905	16,055	17,921	23,275	19,275	105,573	220,258	93,413	150,776
Aransas Pass	9,649	3,314	959	12,243	9,953	9,113	21,559	6,323	8,359	5,856
Port Mansfld	204,007	57,894	62,871	1,431	115,874	13,432	11,000	10,863	8,969	35,008
Harlingen	692,170	801,003	702,242	862,969	655,127	623,292	666,223	716,122	709,354	586,380
Long Mott	3,414,087	3,674,375	3,342,181	2,744,633	2,930,820	3,303,122	2,807,135	2,819,807	2,564,684	3,238,520
Choc. Byu	4,076,999	3,401,910	2,608,300	3,043,107	4,301,199	2,934,850	3,040,894	3,057,207	2,566,214	2,975,438
Colo. Riv.	480,181	324,075	380,744	392,933	403,016	436,585	458,681	455,448	. . .	. . .
*Other Ports	307,445	143,381	149,118	437,953	848,517	772,349	556,931	520,657	1,198,070	1,046,842

Total . . . . . . 1985, 245,959,297; 1984, 263,921,559; 1983, 257,934,340; 1982, 260,698,551; 1981, 291,168,791; 1980, 309,607,653; 1979, 347,034,688; 1978, 334,262,097; 1977, 315,315,824; 1976, 272,035,576.

Gulf Intracoastal Waterway (Through Traffic)

	1985	1984	1983	1982	1981	1980	1979	1978	1977	1976
Sabine R. to Galv.	42,443,030	43,810,015	40,165,385	38,796,688	43,092,704	41,976,730	42,920,273	43,703,545	45,486,574	41,868,705
Galv. to Corpus Christi	22,937,710	20,991,540	19,340,594	18,975,500	22,692,629	21,142,516	22,436,774	20,433,301	18,796,671	18,159,321
Corpus Christi to Mexico	2,128,564	1,877,348	1,782,427	2,066,270	2,231,646	2,388,221	2,488,372	2,106,132	1,993,577	1,949,616
Total	67,509,304	66,678,903	61,288,406	59,838,458	68,016,979	65,507,467	67,845,419	66,242,978	66,276,822	61,977,642

*Other ports include Rockport, Johnsons Bayou and Channel to Liberty.

TEXAS CITY HARBOR: Imports: Crude petroleum, 12,130,033; residual fuel oil, 327,095; basic chemicals, nec., 281,014; distillate fuel oil, 76,228. **Exports:** Basic chemicals, nec., 588,069; coke, pet. coke, 463,535; potassic fertilizers, 158,796; residual fuel oil, 121,824; alcohols, 74,922; dry sulphur, 53,779. **Coastwise Receipts:** Crude petroleum, 5,669,891; residual fuel oil, 98,911; benzene and toluene, 68,938. **Coastwise Shipments:** Gasoline, 2,062,278; basic chemicals, nec., 882,425; distillate fuel oil, 563,353; alcohols, 108,190; residual fuel oil, 105,472; potassic fertilizers, 60,062. **Internal Receipts:** Crude petroleum, 1,722,282; basic chemicals, nec., 792,162; gasoline, 691,276; benzene and toluene, 493,071; crude tar, 214,542; alcohols, 132,904; naphtha, 106,817; residual fuel oil, 105,695; distillate fuel oil, 77,600. **Internal Shipments:** Basic chemicals, nec., 1,103,985; residual fuel oil, 1,064,985; gasoline, 806,996; distillate fuel oil, 650,898; naphtha, 401,045; alcohols, 236,459; benzene and toluene, 144,804; crude tar, 70,868. **Local:** Basic chemicals, nec., 64,040.

GALVESTON HARBOR: Imports: Bananas and plantains, 214,704; sugar, 145,725; clay, 80,250; iron ores and concentrates, 76,197; iron and steel shapes, 72,091; crude petroleum, 70,508; basic chemicals, nec., 69,280. **Exports:** Wheat, 2,791,254; dry sulphur, 877,282; sorghum grains, 359,076; rice, 178,517; basic chemicals, nec., 85,806; wheat flour and semolina, 77,266. **Coastwise Receipts:** Sugar, 178,763. **Coastwise Shipments:** Liquid sulphur, 1,069,855. **Internal Receipts:** Residual fuel oil, 228,576; distillate fuel oil, 196,874; gasoline, 67,045. **Internal Shipments:** Distillate fuel oil, 36,115; residual fuel oil, 30,942.

FREEPORT HARBOR: Imports: Crude petroleum, 4,386,981; bananas and plantains, 202,549; basic chemicals, nec., 172,219; benzene and toluene, 100,265; residual fuel oil, 82,104. **Exports:** Basic chemicals, nec., 844,960; crude tar, 43,409; rice, 23,657; plastic materials, 22,586; alcohols, 10,212. **Coastwise Receipts:** Crude petroleum, 3,852,026; sulphuric acid, 296,444; basic chemicals, nec., 133,866; residual fuel oil, 71,737; benzene and toluene, 24,172. **Coastwise Shipments:** Basic chemicals, nec., 194,651; gasoline, 17,542; sodium hydroxide, 16,370. **Internal Receipts:** Crude petroleum, 547,303; basic chemicals, nec., 304,954; benzene and toluene, 254,761; sand and gravel, 134,683; crude tar, 54,676; residual fuel oil, 46,941; distillate fuel oil, 45,218; alcohols, 30,100; petroleum and coal prod., nec., 28,089. **Internal Shipments:** Basic chemicals, nec., 434,769; sodium hydroxide, 94,619; gasoline, 51,284; residual fuel oil, 41,777; naphtha, 39,200; benzene and toluene, 37,125; water, 14,674; alcohols, 14,311; crude tar, 13,803. **Local:** Basic chemicals, nec., 40,383.

CORPUS CHRISTI HARBOR: Imports: Crude petroleum, 10,106,165; residual fuel oil, 3,389,421; aluminum ores, concentrates, 1,551,533; naphtha, 897,799; distillate fuel oil, 611,797; basic chemicals, nec., 560,334; clay, 353,713; iron and steel pipe, 160,173. **Exports:** Wheat, 919,142; sorghum grains, 883,299; coke, pet. coke, 431,054; basic chemicals, nec., 390,279; distillate fuel oil, 340,483; residual fuel oil, 291,180; corn, 261,335; coal and lignite, 119,442. **Coastwise Receipts:** Crude petroleum, 1,327,855; residual fuel oil, 465,293. **Coastwise Shipments:** Gasoline, 3,334,439; distillate fuel oil, 2,209,870; crude petroleum, 316,161; basic chemicals, nec., 177,508; jet fuel, 162,496; residual fuel oil, 154,417. **Internal Receipts:** Crude petroleum, 743,818; residual fuel oil, 321,548; gasoline, 263,554; naphtha, 148,962; crude tar, 121,076. **Internal Shipments:** Gasoline, 3,118,568; residual fuel oil, 1,518,227; distillate fuel oil, 1,038,806; basic chemicals, nec., 696,907; jet fuel, 455,146; crude petroleum, 304,421; benzene and toluene, 213,384; sodium hydroxide, 184,774; petroleum and coal prod., nec., 157,190; naphtha, 128,622; alcohols, 118,930. **Local:** Residual fuel oil, 638,506; crude petroleum, 304,144; distillate fuel oil, 243,601; benzene and toluene, 223,706; gasoline, 107,431.

PORT MANSFIELD HARBOR: Internal Receipts: Water, 35,064; machinery, except electrical, 31,022. **Internal Shipments:** Water, 52,823; machinery, except electrical, 32,395; nonmetallic minerals, 14,265.

BROWNSVILLE HARBOR: Imports: Lubricating oils and greases, 104,849; clay, 43,104; basic chemicals, nec., 38,329. **Exports:** Sorghum grains, 142,490; basic chemicals, nec., 57,512. **Internal Receipts:** Gasoline, 358,206; lubricating oils and greases, 96,608; sand and gravel, 93,559. **Internal Shipments:** Residual fuel oil, 286,908; crude petroleum, 186,422.

Gulf Intracoastal Waterway Traffic

From the Sabine River to Brownsville, the **Gulf Intracoastal Waterway** parallels the Texas Gulf Coast for 423 miles. Dimension of the main channel is 12 feet deep by 125 feet wide at bottom. The channel from the Gulf of Mexico through Padre Island and Laguna Madre to the turning basin at Port Mansfield is 14 feet deep, 100 feet wide.

During 1985, the Texas section showed a slight increase over the 1984 tonnage, up from 66,678,903 in 1984 to 67,509,304 in 1985. (These figures include some duplications, total amount of which is not available.)

Principal commodities for 1985 were as follows, with all figures in short tons: Crude petroleum, 11,158,087; residual fuel oil, 11,085,153; basic chemicals, nec., 10,213,969; gasoline, 8,895,652; distillate fuel oil, 3,020,442; naphtha, 2,677,979; benzene and toluene, 2,083,273; sand and gravel, 1,973,637; lubricating oils and greases, 1,394,112; alcohols, 1,334,756; jet fuel, 1,084,988; sodium hydroxide, 1,070,191; waste and scrap, nec., 994,812; unmanufactured shell, 907,599; petroleum and coal prod., nec., 851,622; iron and steel scrap, 847,132; sulphuric acid, 739,955; crude tar, 713,574; nitrogenous fertilizers, 701,663; asphalt, tar, 651,719; liquefied gases, 560,872; coke, pet. coke, 558,421; building cement, 461,357; iron and steel plates, 358,992; iron and steel pipe, 330,259; liquid sulphur, 293,812; iron and steel shapes, 246,337; water, 204,325; kerosene, 185,941; fertilizers, nec., 155,887; limestone, 155,505; iron and steel primary forms, 141,629; nonmetallic minerals, nec., 113,832.

Foreign and Domestic Commerce Through Major Texas Ports

Data in table below represent receipts and shipments for only the 13 major Texas ports in 1985. Total receipts and shipments for these 13 ports amounted to 233,257,884 tons. Total receipts and shipments for all Texas ports amounted to 245,959,297.

Source: U.S. Army Corps of Engineers
(All figures in short tons)

Port	Total	Foreign		Domestic				Local
		Imports	Exports	Coastwise		Internal		
				Receipts	Shipments	Receipts	Shipments	
Sabine Pass	547,160	1,496	...	...	...	147,302	398,362	...
Orange	648,350	1	30,619	...	...	531,559	86,180	...
Beaumont	26,842,008	8,913,195	1,857,581	1,391,577	3,988,713	6,116,421	4,328,278	246,243
Port Arthur	15,754,931	6,436,941	2,726,653	179,577	2,234,897	847,621	3,310,633	18,609
Houston	90,669,169	23,579,259	17,704,676	4,735,156	7,870,188	16,223,239	13,664,112	6,892,539
Texas City	33,440,917	12,915,729	1,682,182	5,874,524	3,789,644	4,427,321	4,649,910	101,407
Galveston	7,791,729	1,044,528	4,798,987	178,763	1,079,855	547,764	139,279	2,553
Freeport	12,918,289	5,027,065	975,832	4,081,801	234,610	1,766,714	791,214	41,053
†Corpus Christi	41,057,313	16,658,117	3,974,675	1,847,929	6,413,052	2,199,387	8,237,886	1,726,267
‡Port Isabel	279,578	...	...	...	...	93,808	185,770	...
‡Brownsville	1,442,790	319,103	201,481	...	19,889	587,404	314,913	...
†Port Aransas (Harbor Island) . . .	1,661,643	1,328,396	...	...	25,481	142,590	165,176	...
Port Mansfield	204,007	...	...	...	...	85,676	118,331	...
Total	**233,257,884**	**76,223,830**	**33,952,686**	**18,289,327**	**25,656,329**	**33,716,797**	**36,390,044**	**9,028,671**

†Combined total for Corpus Christi given in other tables in this chapter; these two totals will not add to the combined total given in other tables, due to duplication in some instances.
‡Combined total for Brownsville given in other tables in this chapter.

Trade Zones Offer Benefits

Information for this article was furnished by the *International Trade Reporter*, **copyright 1979 by The Bureau of National Affairs, Inc., Washington, D.C.**

Foreign-trade-zone status endows a domestic site with certain customs privileges, causing it to be considered to be outside customs territory and therefore available for activities that might otherwise be carried on overseas. Operated as public utilities by qualified corporations, the zones are established under grants of authority from the Foreign Trade Zones Board, which is chaired by the Secretary of Commerce.

Zone facilities are available for operations involving storage, repacking, inspection, exhibition, assembly, manufacturing and other processing. A foreign-trade zone is especially suitable for export processing or manufacturing operations when foreign components or materials with a high U.S. duty are needed to make the end product competitive in markets abroad.

For purely export operations, zones provide accelerated export status in situations where some kind of government credit accrues upon exportation of goods from the U.S., as in the case of excise tax rebates and customs drawbacks. The customs drawback procedure allows recovery of customs duties paid on foreign materials used in the manufacture of a domestic product that is exported. Goods are considered exported for this purpose at the time they enter a zone if they are committed for export. This is controlled by U.S. customs

regulations that treat the entry as 'zone restricted merchandise,' a category of goods that cannot be brought back into U.S. customs territory.

Additional information on the zones is available from each zone manager; from U.S. customs offices; from the executive secretary of the Foreign Trade Zones Board, Dept. of Commerce, Washington, D.C.; or from the nearest Dept. of Commerce district office.

The 16 approved foreign-trade zones in Texas as of April 1986 are as follows: Beaumont/Port Arthur/Orange: Foreign-Trade Zones of Southeast Texas, Inc., 2748 Viterbo Road, Box 9, Beaumont 77705. Brownsville Navigation District, Port of Brownsville, Box 3070, Brownsville 78520. Port of Corpus Christi Authority, Box 1541, Corpus Christi 78403. Dallas/Fort Worth Regional Airport Authority, Drawer DFW, Dallas/Fort Worth Airport 75261.

Also, City of Del Rio, City Manager's Office, Drawer DD, Del Rio 78840. City of Eagle Pass, Box C, City Manager's Office, Eagle Pass 78852. Midlothian Foreign Trade Zone Corp., Two Park Ave., Box 788, Midlothian 76065. El Paso International Airport, El Paso 79925. City of Galveston, Galveston Wharves, Box 328, Galveston 77550. Port of Houston Authority, Box 2562, Houston 77001. Laredo Development Foundation, Box 1435, Laredo 78040. McAllen Trade Zone Inc., 6401 S. 33rd St., McAllen 78501. City of San Antonio, Box 9066, San Antonio 78285. Starr County Industrial Foundation, Drawer H, Rio Grande City 78582.

Foreign Trade, 1920-1985, by Customs Districts

Source: Bureau of Business Research, University of Texas; and U.S. Department of Commerce

(All figures in millions of dollars)

	Exports						Imports					
Year	Total Texas	✔✔Houston	✔Port Arthur	Galveston	Laredo	El Paso	+Dallas-Fort Worth	Total Texas	✔✔***Houston	✔Port Arthur	**Galveston	Laredo	El Paso	+Dallas-Fort Worth
1920 . . .	$832		$113	$649	$56	$14		$55		$9	$31	$10	$5
1930 . . .	555		66	397	82	10		33		2	22	4	5
1940 . . .	290		52	191	39	8		41		2	29	6	4
1950 . . .	1,420		97	992	300	31		312		3	209	76	25
1951 . . .	1,834		117	1,213	456	48		417		4	337	47	25
1952 . . .	1,745.8		141.7	1,167.9	385.4	50.8		509.7		4.8	350.3	91.8	62.8
1953 . . .	1,295.0		146.4	706.9	395.0	46.7		437.6		3.9	337.6	67.3	28.8
1954 . . .	1,321.6		116.4	770.2	393.3	41.7		362.2		5.8	303.5	46.3	40.6
1955 . . .	1,419.1		129.8	835.4	397.7	56.2		430.4		5.7	314.5	69.8	40.4
1956 . . .	2,003.3		230.9	1,192.9	516.3	63.2		489.8		4.6	373.4	70.0	41.8
1957 . . .	2,383.5		255.6	1,503.3	554.8	69.5		494.5		4.8	332.9	88.9	67.9
1958 . . .	2,052.4		224.4	1,214.6	544.4	69.0		574.8		9.4	397.7	102.4	65.3
1959 . . .	2,074.9		252.2	1,306.7	466.3	38.7		642.9		8.3	489.9	100.3	44.5
1960 . . .	2,593.5		318.2	1,715.7	514.2	45.4		618.1		11.0	472.5	93.1	41.5
1961 . . .	2,598.9		321.0	1,729.1	512.2	36.6		626.2		11.1	422.5	135.5	57.1
1962 . . .	2,308.0		364.5	1,425.8	486.0	31.7		676.0		11.1	461.6	146.8	56.5
1963 . . .	2,333.7		346.4	1,428.3	521.4	37.6		731.1		14.1	491.9	174.2	50.9
1964 . . .	3,030.8		462.6	1,822.8	698.2	47.2		815.9		23.6	569.9	174.8	47.6
1965 . . .	3,137.1		452.6	1,857.0	765.5	62.0		858.2		21.7	590.6	188.8	57.1
1966 . . .	3,420.5	$1,315.2	535.0	705.9	806.5	57.9		1,073.7	$586.5	39.4	136.2	227.1	84.5
1967 . . .	3,325.5	1,363.0	431.5	633.1	828.9	69.2		1,116.8	592.4	57.6	168.8	219.7	78.2
1968 . . .	3,640.1	1,522.0	404.3	707.7	930.3	75.8		1,423.9	781.8	47.8	187.1	289.3	117.9
1969 . . .	3,251.1	1,243.1	355.3	603.1	962.7	86.9		1,462.2	763.1	51.5	181.4	321.1	145.1
1970 . . .	4,028.4	1,698.0	458.6	695.2	1,065.2	111.4		1,748.8	956.0	59.6	184.1	369.5	179.6
1971 . . .	4,209.8	2,046.2	388.2	654.7	1,006.6	114.1		2,206.4	1,258.5	85.1	251.2	405.6	206.0
1972 . . .	4,631.3	2,166.3	454.2	700.8	1,155.0	154.9		2,666.3	1,480.3	108.2	254.4	548.9	283.5
1973 . . .	7,926.0	3,694.7	747.5	1,533.1	1,677.4	273.3		3,834.3	1,919.1	344.1	444.2	753.1	373.7
1974 . . .	11,278.0	4,937.8	1,098.6	2,112.4	2,680.9	448.3		7,958.0	3,400.1	1,362.1	1,583.6	1,110.7	501.6
1975 . . .	12,885.3	6,092.5	1,141.3	1,971.3	3,091.5	588.7		8,853.1	3,492.8	1,551.2	2,199.2	1,096.9	513.0
1976 . . .	12,455.2	5,623.5	1,049.0	2,242.9	2,960.1	579.7		12,748.6	4,503.9	3,142.2	3,016.4	1,419.2	666.9
1977 . . .	12,179.5	5,810.7	923.6	2,298.0	2,659.0	488.3		17,523.8	5,742.4	4,424.9	4,826.7	1,746.6	783.2
1978 . . .	15,365.0	7,766.4	1,132.4	2,315.3	3,520.1	630.8		20,680.7	7,539.6	4,594.0	5,452.4	2,035.2	1,059.6
1979 . . .	21,298.3	10,358.4	1,539.4	3,038.7	5,649.8	712.1		28,254.4	9,397.6	7,580.9	7,569.1	2,463.7	1,243.1
1980 . . .	28,320.9	12,148.6	2,013.6	3,627.1	8,301.5	1,753.8	$476.3	34,912.0	10,064.5	9,359.2	10,148.0	2,668.2	1,497.2	$1,174.9
1981 . . .	31,477.2	13,531.9	2,014.5	3,679.0	9,877.2	1,813.2	561.4	36,371.4	12,518.2	7,584.3	10,224.0	3,029.3	1,660.6	1,355.0
¶1982 . . .	27,322.3	. . .	. . .	. . .	. . .	. . .		30,340.2	19,800.8	4,256.2	. . .	3,210.6	1,751.0	1,321.7
¶1983 . . .	22,532.0	. . .	. . .	. . .	. . .	. . .		28,115.7	15,744.4	4,910.4	. . .	4,048.0	1,901.0	1,511.8
1984 . . .	25,097.2	14,672.4	1,653.3	. . .	6,152.1	1,840.0	779.4	32,423.3	17,821.4	5,207.8	. . .	4,929.9	2,301.5	2,162.7
1985 . . .	23,568.7	12,514.9	771.6	. . .	7,222.8	2,095.3	964.1	30,126.3	17,306.4	2,660.8	. . .	5,179.1	2,544.4	2,371.0

*Waterborne trade only. ✔In 1966, Sabine District changed to Port Arthur. ✔✔Houston District added in 1966.
+Dallas/Fort Worth added in 1980.
¶In 1982 and 1983, export trade not listed by individual Customs Districts. Total for Texas only given.
**Beginning in 1982, Galveston imports included with Houston as Galveston/Houston Customs District.

Aviation in Texas

The following was prepared for the Texas Almanac by George B. Dresser, Program Manager, and his staff, Texas Transportation Institute, Texas A&M University, College Station.

Air transportation is a vital and vigorous part of the Texas economy. Texans are major users of air transportation and the state airport system ranks as one of the busiest and largest in the nation. Texas has more than 50 airlines which serve 35 airports and enplane more than 39 million passengers annually. The more than 24,000 registered aircraft are being flown by a resident pilot population of nearly 60,000, utilizing over 1,500 landing facilities.

The Texas Aeronautics Commission (TAC) is the state agency with major responsibility for aeronautics. The TAC was created in 1945 and was directed by the Legislature to encourage, foster and assist in the development of aeronautics within the state, and to encourage the establishment of airports and air navigational facilities. The commission's first annual report of Dec. 31, 1946, stated that Texas had 592 designated airports and 7,756 civilian aircraft.

The TAC is organized into three operational divisions. The Aviation Facilities Development Division has statutory authority to provide engineering and technical services and financial assistance through matching state grants and loans to state agencies authorized to operate airports, and to any governmental entity in this state for the establishment, construction, reconstruction, enlargement or repair of airports, airstrips or air navigational facilities.

The Air Carrier Administration Division conducts the commuter carrier certification program that involves a determination of the applicant's financial, managerial and equipment fitness, traffic pro-forma statements and revenues and expenses. Upon determination of fitness the applicant is issued a certificate to provide scheduled service within Texas.

The Aviation Services and Information Division provides specialized training programs, aeronautical publications and safety information to individuals and groups involved or interested in aviation throughout the state.

Commercial air carriers have experienced strong growth during 1985 and 1986. Nationwide enplanements on commercial air carriers (carriers holding a certificate issued by the Civil Aeronautics Board) increased 11.2 percent from 1984 to 1985 and 9.2 percent from 1985 to 1986. Commercial air carriers operate transport aircraft with more than 60 passenger seats. Commercial air carrier enplanements in Texas increased 10.7 percent from 1984 to 1985 reflecting a lower rate of growth than the nation as a whole; however, Texas with 7 percent of the nation's population accounted for 10.8 per-

Texas Enplaned Passengers—1985

Source: FAA-TAC

This table shows total passenger traffic enplaned at all Texas cities having scheduled air carrier or commuter service during calendar year 1985.

City	Enplanements	City	Enplanements
Abilene	65,221	Lake Jackson	17
Amarillo	441,480	Laredo	12,134
Austin	1,835,012	Longview	23,567
Beaumont-Port Arthur	50,969	Lubbock	565,296
Brownsville	68,604	McAllen	195,161
Brownwood	1,985	Midland-Odessa	637,568
*Clear Lake City	26,452	Paris	869
College Station	462,343	San Angelo	39,022
Corpus Christi	21,055,633	San Antonio	2,155,021
Dallas-Fort Worth	21,055,633	*Sugar Land	6,249
Del Rio	1,642	Temple	7,117
El Paso	1,228,300	Texarkana	26,372
*Galveston	662	Tyler	32,986
Harlingen	370,013	*Victoria	11,897
Houston	9,745,522	Waco	24,042
Killeen	31,559	Wichita Falls	43,565

NOTE: Data obtained from a variety of sources including CAB, TAC, airlines and airports.
*—Service terminated in 1985.

Texas Enplaned Traffic—1985
FAA Certified Carriers

This table shows domestic airline traffic at Texas cities during calendar year 1985, as reported by the Federal Aviation Administration. In addition, U.S. carriers' traffic to foreign destinations is shown.

City	Aircraft Departures	Enplaned Passengers	Air Mail Tons	Cargo Tons	City	Aircraft Departures	Enplaned Passengers	Air Mail Tons	Cargo Tons
DOMESTIC					Mission-McAllen-Edinburg	3,410	194,176	171	193
Amarillo	8,211	441,602	451	275	San Antonio	30,306	2,137,870	6,125	2,278
Austin	29,986	1,828,768	3,121	1,368	Total Domestic	522,455	38,152,612	86,569	153,574
Brownsville-Harlingen-San Benito	7,047	438,617	...	3,331	INTERNATIONAL				
Corpus Christi	6,925	460,359	572	423	Dallas-Fort Worth	3,478	398,216	594	4,353
Dallas-Fort Worth	255,395	20,537,596	51,655	87,954	Houston	3,420	337,646	353	2,157
El Paso	22,443	1,230,127	1,324	2,642	San Antonio	282	24,553	17	107
Houston	138,247	9,679,751	22,653	54,519	Total Intl.	7,180	760,415	964	6,617
Lubbock	10,288	565,690	444	203					
Midland-Odessa	10,197	638,056	53	388	TOTAL	529,635	38,913,027	87,533	160,191

cent of the nation's enplanements. One of every 10 air travelers in the United States boarded at a Texas airport.

In 1985, 38,913,027 passengers were enplaned by U.S. commercial air carriers at 15 Texas airports. As of January 1987 there were 30 U.S. and 12 foreign flag air carriers serving Texas airports.

Texas **ranked second** in the United States after California in aircraft departures and second after California in enplaned passengers by commercial air carriers. More than 93 percent of the state's population lives within 50 miles of an airport with scheduled air passenger service.

Ten cities accounted for the major portion of the enplanements. **Dallas/Fort Worth International Airport, Dallas Love Field, Houston Intercontinental and Houston's William P. Hobby** together accounted for 80 percent of the enplaned passengers on commercial air carriers.

Texas also was served by 17 commuter airlines as of January 1987. Commuter airlines operate small aircraft of 60 seats or less and perform at least five scheduled round trips per week between two or more cities. Commuters provided service from 31 cities and provided the only scheduled service from 16 of these cities as of Dec. 31, 1985. In 1985 commuter airlines enplaned approximately 1.3 million passengers at Texas airports. Since passage of the federal Airline Deregulation Act of 1978 route development activity by commuter airlines has been vigorous in Texas and throughout the nation. Development of successful new commuter markets in Texas has proved to be difficult. Numerous routes have been initiated only to be subsequently abandoned. The most recent trend has been for commuter airlines to associate with major airlines as so-called "code-sharing" partners. The code-sharing commuters provide connecting flights with the major carrier principally at D/FW and at other hub airports. The number of commuter airlines has decreased, and fewer cities are served. However, the level and quality of commuter service continues to improve.

The Texas general aviation fleet, all aircraft except the military and the commercial airlines, consisted of 23,916 registered aircraft as of Dec. 31, 1985. The proportion of the general aviation fleet consisting of single engine airplanes, planes associated with personal or pleasure flying, is decreasing while the proportion consisting of multiengine airplanes, planes associated with

business and executive transportation, is increasing. Business is continuing to increase its use of general aviation aircraft. In 1985, 32 percent of the aircraft hours flown was for executive and business transportation, 24 percent was for personal transportation, 13 percent for instructional flying, 10 percent for commuter and air taxi, 6 percent for aerial application and 14 percent for other purposes. Texas, with 7 percent of the nation's population, has 9 percent of the nation's registered aircraft including 15 percent of the turbine-powered aircraft. The state's 56,949 pilots in 1985 represented 8 percent of the nation's pilots.

Texas leads the nation in the number of aircraft landing facilities, 1,603 as of December 1985, followed by Illinois with 888. These include 1,237 airports, 359 heliports, 5 stolports and 1 seaplane base. The **Texas Aeronautical Facilities Plan** published by the TAC contains a total of 308 airports — 285 existing facilities and 23 proposed new and replacement airports. These airports are needed to meet the forecast aviation demand for the state to the year 2000 and to maximize access by business aircraft to the state's population, business activity, agricultural production value and mineral production value.

Texas Air Traffic

Airline passenger traffic enplaned in Texas by scheduled certificated carriers.

Source: CAB-FAA

Year	Domestic	International	Total
1957	2,699,393	109,165	2,808,558
1958	2,658,897	83,870	2,742,767
1959*	2,750,391	78,150	2,828,541
1960	3,045,391	68,191	3,113,582
1961	3,431,788	72,680	3,505,275
1962*	3,599,658	83,325	3,682,983
1963*	3,914,309	105,150	4,019,459
1964*	4,514,200	108,257	4,622,457
1965	5,635,179	122,510	5,757,689
1966	6,991,148	178,464	7,169,612
1967	7,983,634	189,251	8,172,885
1968	9,286,973	220,026	9,506,999
1969	9,923,696	218,352	10,142,048
1970*	10,039,886	216,805	10,256,691
1971	9,936,887	225,024	10,161,911
1972	11,022,538	232,875	11,255,413
1973	11,954,536	276,325	12,230,861
1974	12,934,999	274,569	13,209,568
1975	12,918,709	264,248	13,182,957
1976	14,218,189	267,151	14,485,340
1977	15,595,237	275,910	15,871,147
1978	17,805,693	435,336	18,241,029
1979	20,966,571	580,223	21,546,794
1980	24,693,080	610,134	25,303,214
1981	26,853,393	596,087	27,449,480
1982	29,031,114	510,674	29,541,788
1983	30,291,548	561,749	30,853,297
1984	34,524,502	606,259	35,130,762
1985	38,152,612	760,415	38,913,027

*Fiscal year July 1 through June 30, all other years calendar.

Ranking of Top 10 States, 1985

Source: FAA

Rank	State	Aircraft Departures
1	California	529,945
2	Texas.	529,643
3	Illinois.	349,768
4	New York	337,064
5	Florida	329,700

Truck, Bus Transportation

The following information was provided to the Texas Almanac by the Texas Motor Transportation Association, Austin:

The Texas truck and bus industry operates nearly 700,000 vehicles and **employs over 700,000 Texans.** In 1986, the industry had a **payroll** totaling nearly **$12 billion.**

In 1986 the industry paid almost $2.5 million daily in state and federal **highway user taxes.** With these highway user taxes, the industry pays for almost one out of every two miles of highways constructed with such funds.

Trucks serve every one of the 2,795 populated cities and towns in Texas, and over 70 percent depend entirely on trucks for their shipping and receiving needs.

In 1986, trucks transported almost all — 98 percent — of fresh fruits and vegetables produced by Texas farmers to the nation's principal markets.

The industry spends in Texas more than $5 billion annually on fuel; nearly $4 billion annually for new trucks, buses and trailers; nearly $425 million annually for tires and tubes; nearly $370 million annually for parts and accessories; and nearly $200 million for lubricating oil, in addition to investing large amounts of money in terminals and related equipment and property.

Top Ten Texas Cities—1985

Source: FAA

City	Aircraft Departures Performed	Percent of Total	Enplaned Passengers	Percent of Total
Dallas-Fort Worth	258,873	49	20,935,812	54
Houston	141,667	27	10,017,397	26
San Antonio	30,588	6	2,162,423	6
Austin	29,986	6	1,828,768	4
El Paso	22,443	4	1,230,127	3
Lubbock.	10,288	2	565,690	1
Midland/Odessa.	10,197	2	638,056	2
Amarillo.	8,211	2	441,602	1
Brownsville-Harlingen-San Benito	7,047	1	438,617	1
Corpus Christi	6,925	1	460,359	1

Total Texas
Aircraft Departures Performed **529,635**
Total Texas
Enplaned Passengers **38,913,027**

Energy

Texas Mineral Production

Texas has maintained its role as one of the leading mining states in the nation and as the top petroleum-producing state in 1986.

Petroleum products were by far the largest money producers. According to Texas Mid-Continent Oil and Gas Association, 813,620,140 barrels of crude oil and condensate were produced at a value of $11,976,488,461 in 1986. There were 5,663,490,598,000 cubic feet of natural gas produced at a value of $8,778,410,427.

Coal production in the state continued its rapid increase. Lignite is by far the most common coal produced, and it is used by 12 plants for the production of steam-generated electricity. In 1986 48,346,000 tons were produced primarily for this purpose. The Bureau of Economic Geology at the University of Texas in Austin estimates 24 billion tons of lignite reserves. This is 70% of the state's oil and gas reserves combined. Two other small bituminous coal operations supply fuel for cement operations near San Antonio and Dallas, but their production is negligible.

Cement was the top-valued construction material, according to the Bureau of Mines, generating $539.6 million in revenue from 9,020,000 short tons produced. Texas also retained its position as a leading **stone**-producing state with 85,061,000 short tons produced valued at $319.7 million. **Sand and gravel** shipments of 64,100,000 short tons were valued at $238.1 million.

In addition, Texas was the leading state in the production of Frasch **sulphur**, shipping 2,612,000 metric tons. But the value was not reported to protect producers' proprietary data.

Total **nonfuel mineral production** for the state in 1986 was $1. billion, according to the Bureau of Mines, slightly less than in 1985 (see table).

Oil and Gas in Texas

Texas' petroleum industry suffered a major depression in 1986 as world oil prices dropped precipitously. Production of crude oil and condensate dropped 5.6 percent from 1985 to 830,597,377 barrels in 1986, and the average price per barrel of oil plummeted to $14.72, reducing revenues to $11,976,488,461, less than half the 1985 total of $23,159,285,664. Natural gas production dropped to 5.66 trillion cubic feet in 1986 at a price of $1.55 per thousand cubic feet, reducing revenues 31 percent to $8,778,410,427. Volumes and revenues were provided by Texas Mid-Continent Oil and Gas Association.

The shock of these price declines was felt throughout the state. New well completions dropped from 31,402 in 1984 to 28,243 in 1985 and then collapsed to 19,736 in 1986. The number of wells plugged rose from 6,651 in 1984 to 7,843 in 1985 and 9,337 in 1986. And the number of

Texas Oil and Gas Production, Amount and Value

Source: U.S. Bureau of Mines

Year	Crude Oil & Condensate Production (thousand bbls.)	Value (Add 000)	Average Price Per Barrel	Natural Gas Production (million cu. ft.)	Value (Add 000)	Average Price (Cents Per MCF)	Year	Crude Oil & Condensate Production (thousand bbls.)	Value (Add 000)	Average Price Per Barrel	Natural Gas Production (million cu. ft.)	Value (Add 000)	Average Price (Cents Per MCF)
1915	24,943	$13,027	$.52	13,324	$2,594	19.5	1973	1,294,671	5,157,623	3.98	8,513,850	1,735,221	20.4
1920	96,868	313,781	3.24	37,063	7,042	19.0	1974	1,262,126	8,773,003	6.95	8,170,798	2,541,118	31.1
1925	144,648	262,270	1.81	134,872	7,040	5.2	1975	1,221,929	9,336,570	7.64	7,485,764	3,885,112	51.9
1930	290,457	288,410	.99	517,880	18,488	3.6	1976	1,189,523	10,217,702	8.59	7,191,859	5,163,755	71.8
1935	392,666	367,820	.94	642,366	13,233	2.1	1977	1,137,880	9,986,002	8.78	7,051,027	6,367,077	90.3
1940	493,209	494,000	1.00	1,063,538	19,356	1.8	1978	1,074,050	9,980,333	9.29	6,548,184	6,515,443	99.5
1945	754,710	914,410	1.21	1,711,401	44,839	2.6	*1979	1,018,094	12,715,994	12.49	7,174,623	8,509,103	118.6
1950	829,874	2,147,160	2.59	3,126,402	146,941	4.7	1980	977,436	21,259,233	21.75	7,115,889	10,673,834	150.0
1955	1,053,297	2,989,330	2.84	4,730,798	378,464	8.0	1981	945,132	32,692,116	34.59	7,050,207	12,598,712	178.7
1960	927,479	2,748,735	2.96	5,892,704	665,876	11.3	1982	923,868	29,074,126	31.47	6,497,678	13,567,151	208.8
1965	1,000,749	2,962,119	2.96	6,636,555	858,396	12.9	1983	876,205	22,947,814	26.19	5,643,183	14,672,275	260.0
1970	1,249,697	4,104,005	3.28	8,357,716	1,203,511	14.4	1984	874,079	25,138,520	28.76	5,864,224	13,487,715	230.0
1971	1,222,926	4,261,775	3.48	8,550,705	1,376,664	16.1	1985	860,300	23,159,286	26.92	5,805,098	12,665,114	218.0
1972	1,301,685	4,536,077	3.48	8,657,840	1,419,886	16.4	1986	813,620	11,976,488	14.72	5,663,491	8,778,410	155.0

*Beginning in 1979 data are from Department of Energy and Texas State Comptroller of Public Accounts.
Note: The production figures of natural gas differ from those found in table entitled "Ultimate Disposition of Texas Natural Gas," which are provided by the Railroad Commission. DOE figures do nto include gas that is vented or flared or used for pressure maintenance and repressuring, but do include non-hydrocarbon gases.

producing wells declined by 10,442 to 200,055 between 1985 and 1986.

In 1986, 15 counties produced more than 10 million barrels of crude oil and condensate, a decline of one county from 1984. The top five producing counties in 1986 were Pecos, 47,412,241 barrels; Ector, 42,897,467; Gaines, 42,641,652; Andrews, 42,595,938, and Yoakum, 35,641,986 barrels.

By Jan. 1, 1987, three Texas counties, Gregg, Ector and Andrews, had produced more than 2 billion barrels of crude oil and condensate, and 11 others had topped 1 billion barrels. Gregg County is the all-time leading producer with 2,956,082,549 barrels, followed by Ector, 2,572,304,080 barrels, and Andrews, 2,216,486,278 barrels.

By late 1986, the Organization of Petroleum Exporting Countries had agreed to limit crude oil production with the effect of stabilizing prices and even increasing them by midway through 1987.

Texas Oil History

Indians found oil seeping from the soils of Texas long before the first Europeans arrived. They told explorers that the fluid had medicinal values. The first record of Europeans using crude oil, however, was the caulking of boats in 1543 by survivors of the DeSoto expedition near Sabine Pass.

Melrose, in Nacogdoches County, was the site in 1866 of the first drilled well to produce oil in Texas. The driller was Lyne T. Barret (whose name has been spelled several ways by historians). Barret used an auger, fastened to a pipe and rotated by a cogwheel driven by a steam engine—a basic principle of rotary drilling that has been used since, although with much improvement.

In 1867 Amory (Emory) Starr and Peyton F. Edwards brought in a well at Oil Springs, in the same area. Other wells followed and Nacogdoches County was the site of Texas' first commercial oil field, pipeline and effort to refine crude. Several thousand barrels of oil were produced there during these years.

Other oil was found in crudely dug wells in Texas,

History of Texas Drilling

Source: Oil and Gas Journal and American Petroleum Institute.

	Wells Completed	Oil Wells	Gas Wells	Stratigraphic & Core Tests	Service Wells	Dry Holes	Percent Dry
1889-1900*	97	71	2			24	24.7
1901-1910*	692	462	9			221	32.0
1911-1920*	2,451	1,682	66			703	28.7
1921-1930*	6,352	3,745	306			2,301	36.2
1931-1940*	9,915	7,404	288	...	...	2,224	22.9
1941-1950*	9,147	5,767	457	...	44	2,901	32.5
1951-1960*	18,439	10,838	814	...	155	6,632	36.0
1961-1970*	11,595	5,798	1,115	367	393	4,121	35.8
1971	7,728	3,880	810	8	449	2,581	33.4
1972	8,088	3,963	943	8	414	2,760	34.1
1973	8,494	3,686	1,475	34	362	2,937	34.6
1974	9,808	4,402	1,843	19	260	3,284	33.5
1975	12,483	6,074	2,135	36	361	3,877	31.1
1976	12,740	5,779	2,443	45	285	4,188	32.9
1977	14,759	6,533	3,064	37	443	4,682	31.7
1978	15,037	6,086	3,292	26	415	5,218	34.7
1979	16,149	6,765	3,609	35	515	5,225	32.4
1980	19,253	9,668	3,684	10	546	5,345	27.8
1981	23,940	13,052	3,807	2	368	6,711	28.0
1982	26,849	13,851	4,345	4	692	7,957	29.6
1983	24,616	13,102	3,317	...	652	7,545	30.6
1984	26,134	14,591	3,242	17	678	7,606	29.1
1985	18,882	11,206	2,215	...	666	5,461	28.9
1986	11,425	6,141	1,326	2	345	3,958	34.6
Total	902,866	486,579	72,122	1,385	13,151	270,642	30.0

*Annual Averages.

Rotary Rigs Actually Making Hole

Source: Hughes Tool Company

Year	Average	Year	Average	Year	Average
1973	376	1978	855.0	1982	989.6
1974	508	1979	770.2	1983	798
1975	637	1980	987.7	1984	850.1
1976	799	1981	1,317.0	1985	677
				1986	311

SOME OF THE THINGS DISCUSSED HERE MIGHT SHOCK YOU.

But not if you follow these tips for working around electricity while working around the house or on the job.

- Keep ladders and trimming tools away from overhead wires.
- Call an expert if your electric meter or fuse box needs to be moved.
- Don't dig if you suspect there are underground wires—call us first.
- Make sure you're clear of all wires when installing an antenna; think about where it might land if it falls during installation.
- Make sure all tools that run on electricity are properly grounded and treat them with respect.

We don't mean to alarm you. But too many people become accident statistics simply because they forget to be cautious around electricity. And that's the shocking truth.

principally in Bexar County, in the latter years of the 19th century. But it was not until June 9, 1894, that Texas had a major discovery. This occurred in the drilling of a water well for the City of Corsicana. Oil caused that well to be abandoned, but a company formed in 1895 drilled several producing wells. The first well-equipped refinery in Texas was built and this plant usually is called the state's first refinery, despite the earlier effort at Nacogdoches. Discovery of the **Powell Field** near Corsicana followed in 1900.

Spindletop, 1901

Jan. 10, 1901, is the most famous date in Texas petroleum history. This is the date that the great gusher erupted in the oil well being drilled at Spindletop, near Beaumont, by a mining engineer, Capt. A. F. Lucas. Thousands of barrels of oil flowed before the well could be capped. This was the first salt dome oil discovery. It created a sensation throughout the world, and encouraged exploration and drilling in Texas that has continued since.

Texas oil production increased from 836,039 barrels in 1900 to 4,393,658 in 1901; and in 1902 Spindletop alone produced 17,421,000 barrels, or 94 per cent of the state's production. Prices dropped to 3c a barrel, an all-time low.

A water-well drilling outfit on the **W. T. Waggoner Ranch** in Wichita County hit oil, bringing in the **Electra**

Marketed Natural Gas Production, Texas and U.S.

This table shows for selected years Texas and United States production of natural gas produced for marketing and Texas percentage of total.

Source: U.S. Department of Energy
(Millions of Cubic Feet)

Year	Texas	U.S.	% Texas
1935	642,366	1,916,595	33.5
1940	1,063,538	2,660,222	40.0
1945	1,711,401	3,918,686	43.7
1950	3,126,402	6,282,060	49.8
1955	4,730,798	9,405,351	50.3
1960	5,892,704	12,771,038	46.1
1965	6,636,555	16,039,753	41.4
1970	8,357,716	21,920,642	38.1
1971	8,550,705	22,493,012	38.0
1972	8,657,840	22,531,698	38.4
1973	8,513,850	22,647,549	37.6
1974	8,170,798	21,600,522	37.8
1975	7,485,764	20,108,611	37.2
1976	7,191,859	19,952,438	36.0
1977	7,051,027	20,025,463	35.2
1978	6,548,184	19,974,033	32.8
1979	6,620,542	19,723,104	33.6
1980	7,252,879	20,378,787	35.5
1981	7,050,207	20,177,701	34.9
1982	6,468,817	18,519,675	34.9
1983	5,938,561	16,822,144	35.3
1984	6,185,021	18,229,638	33.9
1985	6,052,663	17,197,999	35.2

Texas Natural Gas Production and Initial Disposition—1986

Source: Railroad Commission of Texas
(All Gas Volumes in Thousands Cubic Feet)

GAS WELL GAS
Number of Wells, December—46,080

	Volume	Percent of Total
Total Production	4,191,504,832	100.00
Disposition:		
Fuel System & Lease Use	50,308,824	1.2
Gas Lift	10,825,441	.26
Pressure Maintenance and Repressuring	76,032	.02
Transmission Lines	1,465,729,816	34.97
Processing Plants	2,631,552,823	62.78
Carbon Black Plants	865,264	.02
Vented or Flared	1,046,406	.03
Extraction Loss (lease)	31,100,226	.74

CASINGHEAD GAS
Number of Wells, December—194,875

	Volume	Percent of Total
Total Production	1,420,409,034	100.00
Disposition:		
Fuel System and Lease Use	48,457,586	3.41
Pressure Maintenance and Repressuring	5,474,907	.39
Transmission Lines	150,703,479	10.61
Processing Plants	1,558,899,720	109.75
Carbon Black Plants	584,629	.04
Vented or Flared	16,642,706	1.17

Ultimate Disposition of Texas Natural Gas—1986

Source: Railroad Commission of Texas
(All Gas Volumes in Thousands Cubic Feet)

	Volume	Percent of Total
Total Production	5,611,913,866	100.00
Disposition:		
Plant Fuel & Lease Use	420,828,111	7.5
Pressure Maintenance and Repressuring	276,311,341	4.92
Transmission Lines	4,173,780,146	74.37
Cycled	89,845,233	1.60
Carbon Black	2,422,390	.04
Underground Storage	66,961,133	1.19
Vented or Flared	26,191,668	.47
Plant Meter Difference	31,081,047	.55
Acid Gas H2S & CO2	114,968,330	2.05
*Extraction Loss	409,524,465	7.30

*Shrinkage in volume due to removal of liquified hydrocarbons.

Texas Natural Gas Reserves

Source: Committee on Natural Gas Reserves, American Gas Association and Department of Energy
(Millions of Cubic Feet)

Year	Proved Reserves	Percent Annual Change	Year	Proved Reserves	Percent Annual Change	Year	Proved Reserves	Percent Annual Change
1945	78,306,676	—	1961	119,838,711	0.3	1977	62,157,836	−3.8
1946	86,363,459	10.3	1962	119,503,798	−0.3	1978	54,600,235	−12.2
1947	90,025,566	4.2	1963	117,809,376	−1.4	*1979	53,021,000	−.02
1948	95,708,553	6.3	1964	118,855,055	0.9	*1980	50,287,000	−.05
1949	99,170,403	3.6	1965	120,616,760	1.5	*1981	50,469,000	†
1950	102,404,077	3.3	1966	123,609,326	2.5	1982	49,757,000	†
1951	105,653,229	3.2	1967	125,415,064	1.5	1983	50,052,000	†
1952	105,732,763	0.1	1968	119,001,106	−5.1	1984	49,883,000	†
1953	106,529,626	0.8	1969	112,392,622	−5.6	1985	49,035,000	†
1954	105,129,062	−1.3	1970	106,352,993	−5.4			
1955	108,287,548	3.0	1971	101,472,108	−4.6	*These Department of Energy		
1956	112,728,750	4.1	1972	95,042,043	−6.3	figures differ from preceding		
1957	113,084,518	0.3	1973	84,936,502	−10.6	American Petroleum Institute		
1958	115,045,743	1.7	1974	78,540,717	−7.5	figures.		
1959	120,475,783	4.7	1975	71,036,854	−9.6	†Percentage less than one		
1960	119,489,393	−0.8	1976	64,651,410	−9.0	percent.		

Field in 1911. In 1917, came the discovery of the **Ranger Field** in Eastland County. The **Burkburnett Field** in Wichita County was discovered in 1919.

Oil discoveries brought a short era of swindling with oil stock promotion and selling on a nationwide scale. It ended after a series of trials in a federal court.

The **Mexia Field** in Limestone County was discovered in 1920, and the second **Powell Field** in Navarro County in 1924.

Another great area opened in 1921 with discovery of oil in the **Panhandle**, a field which developed rapidly with sensational oil and gas discoveries in Hutchinson and contiguous counties and the booming of Borger.

The **Luling Field** was opened in 1922 and 1925 saw the comeback of **Spindletop** with a production larger than that of the original field. Other fields opened in this period included **Big Lake**, 1923; **Wortham**, 1924-25 and **Yates**, 1926.

In 1925 **Howard County** was opened for production. **Winkler** in West Texas and **Raccoon Bend**, Austin County, were opened in 1927. **Sugar Land** was the most important Texas oil development in 1928. The **Darst Creek**

Field was opened in 1929. In the same year, new records of productive sand thickness were set for the industry at **Van**, Van Zandt County. **Pettus** was another contribution of 1929 in Bee County.

East Texas Field

The East Texas field, biggest of them all, was discovered near Turnertown and Joinerville, Rusk County, by veteran wildcatter **C. M. (Dad) Joiner**, in October 1930. The success of this well—drilled on land condemned many times by geologists of the major companies—was followed by the biggest leasing campaign in history. The field soon was extended to Kilgore, Longview and northward.

The East Texas field brought a large overproduction and a rapid sinking of the price. Private attempts were made to prorate production, but without much success. On Aug. 17, 1931, **Gov. Ross S. Sterling** ordered the National Guard into the field, which he placed under martial law. This drastic action was taken after the Texas Railroad Commission had been enjoined from

U.S. Estimated Proved Reserves of Natural Gas

Source: Department of Energy, Energy Information Administration, "U.S. Crude Oil, Natural Gas, and Natural Gas Liquids Reserves, 1985 Annual Report."

(Billions of Cubic Feet)

Rank, State	Reserves as of Dec. 31, 1985	% of U.S.	Rank, State	Reserves as of Dec. 31, 1985	% of U.S.	Rank, State	Reserves as of Dec. 31, 1985	% of U.S.
1. Texas	49,035	25.36	11. Arkansas	2,019	1.04	21. New York	369	.19
2. *Louisiana	40,151	20.76	12. Utah	1,999	1.03	22. Virginia	235	.12
3. Alaska	33,847	17.50	13. Pennsylvania	1,617	.84	23. Florida	55	.03
4. Oklahoma	16,040	8.30	14. Mississippi	1,360	.70	Other States	76	.04
5. New Mexico	10,900	5.64	15. Ohio	1,331	.69	Total U.S.	193,369	†99.99
6. Wyoming	10,617	5.49	16. Michigan	985	.51			
7. Kansas	9,337	4.83	17. Montana	857	.44	*Includes Alabama Offshore.		
8. California	5,444	2.82	18. Alabama	821	.42	†Does not equal 100% due to rounding.		
9. Colorado	2,881	1.49	19. Kentucky	766	.40			
10. West Virginia	2,058	1.06	20. North Dakota	569	.29			

Receipts By Texas From Tidelands

(Source: General Land Office)

The following table shows receipts from tidelands by the Texas General Land Office to Aug. 31, 1986. It does not include revenue from bays and other submerged area owned by Texas.

From	To	Total	Bonus	Rental	Royalty
6- 9-1922	9-28-1945	$924,363.81	$814,055.70	$61,973.75	$48,334.36
9-29-1945	6-23-1947	296,400.30	272,700.00	7,680.00	16,020.30
6-24-1947	6- 5-1950	7,695,552.22	7,231,755.48	377,355.00	86,441.74
6- 6-1950	5-22-1953	55,095.04		9,176.00	45,919.04
5-23-1953	6-30-1958	54,264,553.11	49,788,639.03	3,852,726.98	623,187.10
7- 1-1958	8-31-1959	771,064.75	—	143,857.00	627,207.75
9- 1-1959	8-31-1960	983,335.32	257,900.00	98,226.00	627,209.32
9- 1-1960	8-31-1961	3,890,800.15	3,228,639.51	68,578.00	593,582.64
9- 1-1961	8-31-1962	1,121,925.09	297,129.88	127,105.00	697,690.21
9- 1-1962	8-31-1963	3,575,888.64	2,617,057.14	177,174.91	781,656.59
9- 1-1963	8-31-1964	3,656,236.75	2,435,244.36	525,315.00	695,677.39
9- 1-1964	8-31-1965	54,654,576.96	53,114,943.63	755,050.12	784,583.21
9- 1-1965	8-31-1966	22,148,825.44	18,223,357.84	3,163,475.00	761,992.60
9- 1-1966	8-31-1967	8,469,680.86	3,641,414.96	3,711,092.65	1,117,173.25
9- 1-1967	8-31-1968	6,305,851.00	1,251,852.50	2,683,732.50	2,370,266.00
9- 1-1968	8-31-1969	6,372,268.28	1,838,118.33	1,491,592.50	3,042,557.45
9- 1-1969	8-31-1970	10,311,030.48	5,994,666.32	618,362.50	3,698,001.66
9- 1-1970	8-31-1971	9,969,629.17	4,326,120.11	726,294.15	4,917,214.91
9- 1-1971	8-31-1972	7,558,327.21	1,360,212.64	963,367.60	5,234,746.97
9- 1-1972	8-31-1973	9,267,975.68	3,701,737.30	920,121.60	4,646,116.78
9- 1-1973	8-31-1974	41,717,670.04	32,981,619.28	1,065,516.60	7,670,534.16
9- 1-1974	8-31-1975	27,321,536.62	5,319,762.85	2,935,295.60	19,066,478.17
9- 1-1975	8-31-1976	38,747,074.09	6,197,853.00	3,222,535.84	29,326,685.25
9- 1-1976	8-31-1977	84,196,228.27	41,343,114.81	2,404,988.80	40,448,124.66
9- 1-1977	8-31-1978	118,266,812.05	49,807,750.45	4,775,509.92	63,683,551.68
9- 1-1978	8-31-1979	100,410,268.68	34,578,340.94	7,318,748.40	58,513,179.34
9- 1-1979	8-31-1980	200,263,803.03	34,733,270.02	10,293,153.80	155,237,379.21
9- 1-1980	8-31-1981	219,126,876.54	37,467,196.97	13,100,484.25	168,559,195.32
9- 1-1981	8-31-1982	250,824,581.69	27,529,516.33	14,214,478.97	209,080,586.39
9- 1-1982	8-31-1983	165,197,734.83	10,180,696.40	12,007,476.70	143,009,561.73
9- 1-1983	8-31-1984	152,755,934.29	32,864,122.19	8,573,996.87	111,317,815.23
9- 1-1984	8-31-1985	140,568,090.79	32,650,127.75	6,844,003.70	101,073,959.34
9- 1-1985	8-31-1986	88,736,086.55	6,365,426.23	4,081,068.05	78,289,592.27
Total		$1,840,426,077.73	$512,414,341.95	$111,284,645.46	$1,216,692,222.02
Recapitulation:					
Inside three-mile line		333,253,591.88	127,526,799.41	31,226,001.06	174,500,791.41
Between three-mile line and three marine-league line		1,504,347,120.27	382,235,458.15	79,920,231.51	1,042,191,430.61
Outside three marine-league line		2,825,365.58	2,652,084.39	173,281.19	0
Totals		$1,840,426,077.73	$512,414,341.95	$111,319,513.76	$1,216,692,222.02

enforcing production restrictions. After the complete shutdown, the Texas Legislature enacted legal prora- tion, the system of regulation still utilized.

The most significant subsequent oil discoveries in Texas were those in West Texas, following a discovery well in Scurry County, Nov. 21, 1948, and later major developments in that region. Many of the leading Texas counties in minerals value are in that section.

Major Fields

Texas fields with estimated ultimate recovery of 100 million barrels of oil or more are in the following list, which gives the name of the field, county and discovery date. Data furnished by Oil and Gas Journal.

Panhandle, Carson-Collingsworth-Gray-Hutchin- son-Moore-Potter-Wheeler, 1910; Thompson (all fields), Fort Bend, 1921; Howard-Glasscock, Howard, 1925; Iatan East, Howard, 1926; Yates, Pecos, 1926; Waddell, Crane, 1927; Van, Van Zandt, 1929; Ward Estes North, Ward, 1929; Cowden North, Ector, 1930; East Texas, Gregg-Rusk, 1930; Sand Hills, Crane, 1930; Conroe, Montgomery, 1931;

Tom O'Connor, Refugio, 1931; Cowden South, Ector, 1932; Greta (all fields), Refugio, 1933; Tomball, Harris, 1933; Means (all fields), Andrews-Gaines, 1934; Anahuac, Chambers, 1935; Goldsmith (all fields), Ector, 1935; Hastings, Brazoria, 1935; Magnet Withers (all fields), Wharton, 1936; Seminole (all fields), Gaines, 1936; Webster, Harris, 1936; Jordan, Crane-Ector, 1937; Slaughter, Cochran, 1937; Wasson (all fields), Gaines, 1937; Dune, Crane, 1938; West Ranch, Jackson, 1938; Key- stone, Winkler, 1939; Diamond M, Scurry, 1940; Hawkins, Wood, 1940; Fullerton (all fields), Andrews, 1941; McEl- roy, Crane, 1941; Oyster Bayou, Chambers, 1941; Welch, Dawson, 1941; Quitman (all fields), Wood, 1942; Anton- Irish, Hale, 1944; TXL (all fields), Ector, 1944; Block 31, Crane, 1945; Levelland, Cochran-Hockley, 1945; Midland Farms (all fields), Andrews, 1945; Andector, Ector, 1946; Dollarhide, Andrews, 1947; Kelly-Snyder, Scurry, 1948; Cogdell Area, Scurry, 1949; Prentice, Yoakum, 1950; Salt Creek, Kent, 1950; Spraberry Trend, Glasscock-Midland, 1952; Lake Pasture, Refugio, 1953; Neches, Anderson- Cherokee, 1953; Fairway, Anderson-Henderson, 1960; Giddings, Lee-Fayette-Burleson, 1971.

Texas Oil Production By Counties

Source: Compiled by Texas Mid-Continent Oil & Gas Association

This table shows the year of oil or gas discovery in each county, total annual and daily crude oil production in 1986 and total crude oil production from date of discovery to Jan. 1, 1987. Counties omitted have not produced oil.

County	Year of Discovery	1986 Crude Production Total Barrels	1986 Crude Production Barrels Per Day	Total Prdn. to Jan. 1, 1987 (bbls.)
Anderson	1929	2,577,782	7,062	274,841,246
Andrews.....	1930	42,595,938	116,701	2,216,486,278
Angelina	1936	15,584	43	376,163
Aransas	1936	749,094	2,052	75,440,951
Archer	1911	3,641,999	9,978	455,931,225
Atascosa ...	1917	1,929,032	5,285	132,940,656
Austin	1915	673,136	1,844	106,203,329
Bastrop.....	1913	177,070	485	10,580,834
Baylor	1924	359,836	986	53,867,735
Bee........	1930	1,000,957	2,742	95,653,695
Bell........	1980			446
Bexar	1889	1,016,518	2,785	29,795,870
Borden	1949	6,801,761	18,635	315,382,449
Bowie	1944	127,586	350	1,831,716
Brazoria ...	1902	6,593,615	18,065	1,204,644,076
Brazos	1942	5,341,469	14,634	44,849,495
Brewster....	1969	—	—	56
Briscoe	1982	—	—	3,554
Brooks	1936	1,012,125	2,773	150,341,660
Brown......	1917	504,007	1,381	48,442,053
Burleson ...	1938	5,795,972	15,879	87,478,082
Caldwell ...	1922	2,109,871	5,781	259,298,183
Calhoun	1935	1,529,851	4,191	87,363,361
Callahan ...	1923	1,352,699	3,706	75,064,649
Cameron....	1944	4,004	11	420,547
Camp	1940	530,288	1,453	20,989,564
Carson	1921	1,054,366	2,889	169,633,665
Cass	1935	1,383,955	3,792	100,687,676
Chambers ...	1916	6,124,355	16,779	861,444,480
Cherokee ...	1926	1,395,997	3,825	60,844,625
Childress ..	1961	4,426	12	1,290,413
Clay	1902	2,476,328	6,785	180,896,566
Cochran	1936	9,214,230	25,245	395,502,826
Coke	1942	2,155,346	5,905	202,642,722
Coleman ...	1902	996,550	2,730	85,643,834
Collin	1963			53,000
Collingsworth .	1936	11,733	32	1,127,938
Colorado....	1932	798,073	2,187	28,151,817
Comanche....	1918	64,510	177	5,631,867
Concho	1940	301,411	826	6,489,327
Cooke	1926	3,508,666	9,613	348,887,902
Coryell	1964	—	—	1,100
Cottle	1955	164,514	451	2,559,329
Crane	1926	22,575,795	61,852	1,472,894,969
Crockett	1925	4,854,525	13,300	294,206,669
Crosby	1955	979,659	2,684	10,898,854
Culberson ..	1953	476,898	1,307	19,799,654
Dallam	1954	(Gas Only)	—	(Gas Only)
Dallas......	1986	68	—	68
Dawson.....	1937	8,157,536	22,349	267,238,485
DeWitt	1930	812,682	2,227	58,488,113
Delta	1984	3,179	9	43,014
Denton	1937	19,564	54	3,275,700
Dickens	1953	196,540	539	4,257,775
Dimmit.....	1943	2,718,075	7,447	76,600,813
Donley	1967	(Gas Only)	—	(Gas Only)
Duval	1905	3,410,094	9,343	545,582,775
Eastland	1917	2,154,947	5,904	143,487,508
Ector	1926	42,897,467	117,527	2,572,304,080
Edwards	1946	11,419	31	393,880
Ellis	1953	12,803	35	756,970
Erath	1917	25,835	71	1,900,208
Falls	1937	61,926	170	611,226
Fannin	1980			13,281
Fayette.....	1943	4,448,818	12,189	51,038,242
Fisher......	1928	3,167,938	8,679	220,522,558
Floyd	1952	6,827	19	105,789
Foard	1929	362,073	992	19,371,081
Fort Bend ...	1919	5,768,941	15,805	627,543,635
Franklin	1936	1,608,287	4,406	161,563,976
Freestone ...	1916	590,827	1,619	37,958,148
Frio	1934	2,529,118	6,929	91,172,844
Gaines	1936	42,641,652	116,826	1,501,914,914
Galveston ...	1922	3,534,247	9,683	420,769,589
Garza	1926	7,905,064	21,658	222,392,536
Glasscock ...	1925	6,852,880	18,775	170,813,806
Goliad......	1930	1,099,428	3,012	70,244,978
Gonzales ...	1902	1,723,964	4,723	23,878,801
Gray	1925	3,541,587	9,703	630,050,902
Grayson	1930	3,501,679	9,594	220,827,911
Gregg	1931	33,913,004	92,912	2,956,082,549
Grimes	1952	514,136	1,409	4,615,616
Guadalupe ..	1922	1,344,526	3,684	183,239,165
Hale	1946	2,966,781	8,128	138,933,578
Hamilton ...	1938	2,355	7	119,597
Hansford....	1937	535,948	1,468	33,036,885
Hardeman ...	1944	3,081,406	8,442	34,562,778
Hardin	1893	3,585,425	9,823	397,612,794
Harris	1905	9,829,565	26,930	1,294,498,931
Harrison	1928	1,835,581	5,029	68,245,852
Hartley	1937	370,787	1,016	1,270,565
Haskell	1929	1,196,071	3,277	101,906,863
Hays	1956	—	—	79
Hemphill....	1955	1,129,486	3,095	24,965,267
Henderson ..	1934	2,491,568	6,826	149,542,597
Hidalgo.....	1934	2,129,848	5,835	51,871,488
Hill	1949	2,952	8	41,007
Hockley	1937	34,034,351	93,245	1,153,646,544
Hood.......	1958	4,039	11	61,407
Hopkins	1936	923,529	2,530	78,868,084
Houston	1934	952,474	2,610	41,919,574
Howard.....	1925	12,413,552	34,010	649,299,026
Hunt	1942	5,644	16	1,848,123
Hutchinson ..	1923	2,428,598	6,654	502,509,282
Irion	1928	3,393,083	9,296	56,687,979
Jack	1923	3,171,569	8,689	178,895,471
Jackson	1934	6,175,729	16,920	638,532,720
Jasper	1928	789,180	2,162	17,281,705
Jeff Davis ..	1980			20,866
Jefferson ...	1901	3,664,566	10,040	482,503,788

County	Year of Discovery	1986 Crude Production Total Barrels	Barrels Per Day	Total Prdn. to Jan. 1, 1987 (bbls.)
Jim Hogg	1922	897,898	2,460	102,499,874
Jim Wells	1933	1,219,219	3,340	453,580,270
Johnson	1962	—	—	194,000
Jones	1926	2,086,051	5,715	200,820,231
Karnes	1930	802,214	2,198	97,824,179
Kaufman	1948	354,230	971	21,771,306
Kenedy	1947	879,614	2,410	29,106,067
Kent	1946	9,370,349	25,672	402,115,109
Kerr	1982	5,633	15	45,925
Kimble	1939	3,860	11	77,654
King	1943	6,508,941	17,833	85,025,162
Kinney	1960	—	—	402
Kleberg	1926	2,637,015	7,225	319,389,586
Knox	1946	1,153,738	3,161	51,259,402
La Salle	1940	464,472	1,273	13,918,203
Lamb	1945	643,638	1,763	25,561,500
Lampasas	1985	—	—	111
Lavaca	1941	1,170,549	3,207	18,093,039
Lee	1939	5,433,251	14,886	70,267,929
Leon	1936	4,025,279	11,028	22,693,553
Liberty	1905	3,519,026	9,641	484,123,928
Limestone	1920	319,806	876	114,926,574
Lipscomb	1956	1,409,760	3,862	42,454,963
Live Oak	1931	2,375,988	6,510	63,550,703
Llano	1978	—	—	647
Loving	1925	1,777,709	4,870	82,505,864
Lubbock	1941	2,571,513	7,045	31,697,019
Lynn	1950	801,345	2,196	13,074,499
Madison	1946	1,675,387	4,590	20,203,059
Marion	1910	469,220	1,286	49,907,000
Martin	1945	8,597,385	23,555	195,804,067
Matagorda	1904	2,173,567	5,955	254,532,068
Maverick	1929	1,303,484	3,571	31,862,176
McCulloch	1938	8,852	24	148,481
McLennan	1902	3,281	9	291,620
McMullen	1919	5,701,325	15,620	61,361,515
Medina	1901	259,915	712	8,354,458
Menard	1941	185,437	508	5,108,048
Midland	1945	9,564,664	26,205	419,185,467
Milam	1921	485,152	1,329	10,362,921
Mills	1982	—	—	28,122
Mitchell	1920	6,276,768	17,197	155,277,554
Montague	1924	2,593,270	7,105	258,227,430
Montgomery	1931	5,792,478	15,870	736,248,163
Moore	1936	849,715	2,328	21,440,427
Motley	1957	132,880	364	8,510,286
Nacogdoches	1866	177,419	486	2,427,670
Navarro	1895	715,365	1,960	209,212,576
Newton	1937	1,072,902	2,940	39,758,418
Nolan	1939	3,754,974	10,288	162,447,502
Nueces	1930	2,817,762	7,720	528,684,783
Ochiltree	1951	3,188,378	8,735	134,021,723
Oldham	1957	758,855	2,079	10,178,912
Orange	1913	2,057,984	5,638	121,669,445
Palo Pinto	1902	442,122	1,211	16,256,327
Panola	1917	1,352,245	3,705	58,483,338
Parker	1942	86,270	236	2,412,367
Parmer	1963	—	—	144,000
Pecos	1926	47,412,241	129,897	1,368,099,349
Polk	1930	1,236,950	3,389	91,419,589
Potter	1925	441,768	1,210	5,372,676
Presidio	1980	15	—	1,873
Rains	1955	—	—	148,762
Reagan	1923	9,134,417	25,026	393,864,907
Red River	1951	89,596	246	1,015,513
Reeves	1939	1,635,959	4,482	58,678,367
Refugio	1928	18,293,919	50,120	1,200,433,879
Roberts	1945	778,046	2,132	37,950,669
Robertson	1944	131,302	360	1,395,366
Runnels	1927	1,995,483	5,467	129,559,494
Rusk	1930	11,832,635	32,418	1,730,171,100
Sabine	1981	186,878	512	759,550
San Augustine	1947	115	—	17,972
San Jacinto	1940	144,888	397	21,393,616
San Patricio	1930	2,769,420	7,588	460,321,539
San Saba	1982	5,150	14	27,916
Schleicher	1937	1,442,963	3,953	75,271,878
Scurry	1923	21,543,554	59,023	1,760,478,236
Shackelford	1910	2,368,730	6,490	158,478,009
Shelby	1917	146,008	400	1,117,912
Sherman	1938	470,595	1,289	2,577,387
Smith	1931	4,037,694	11,062	223,585,276
Somervell	1978	3	—	118
Starr	1929	2,123,987	5,819	257,876,895
Stephens	1916	7,376,322	20,209	261,529,003
Sterling	1947	2,517,546	6,897	56,041,943
Stonewall	1938	3,680,502	10,084	208,422,126
Sutton	1948	136,000	373	5,714,353
Swisher	1981	—	—	6
Tarrant	1969	(Gas Only)	—	(Gas Only)
Taylor	1929	1,686,318	4,620	118,979,491
Terrell	1952	116,775	320	3,179,651
Terry	1940	10,750,440	29,453	327,891,844
Throckmorton	1924	1,879,808	5,150	103,065,877
Titus	1936	1,829,119	5,011	194,473,812
Tom Green	1940	1,832,868	5,022	72,459,135
Travis	1934	3,505	10	699,016
Trinity	1946	162	—	68,652
Tyler	1937	306,727	840	32,182,077
Upshur	1931	737,031	2,019	274,954,743
Upton	1925	12,162,269	33,321	636,689,882
Uvalde	1950	—	—	1,814
Val Verde	1935	874	2	114,436
Van Zandt	1929	3,865,231	10,590	509,375,730
Victoria	1931	1,938,852	5,312	231,124,555
Walker	1934	11,770	32	359,342
Waller	1934	258,776	709	18,534,643
Ward	1928	8,838,718	24,216	636,905,813
Washington	1915	692,341	1,897	18,129,367
Webb	1921	3,191,669	8,744	115,646,807
Wharton	1925	3,997,487	10,952	285,009,035
Wheeler	1921	1,065,343	2,919	84,254,688
Wichita	1910	4,926,749	13,498	769,994,299
Wilbarger	1915	1,727,210	4,732	246,812,008
Willacy	1936	1,662,561	4,555	97,584,066
Williamson	1915	17,598	48	9,329,060
Wilson	1941	1,468,204	4,023	29,702,305
Winkler	1926	7,068,284	19,365	982,960,139
Wise	1942	1,850,309	5,069	81,935,587
Wood	1941	16,273,158	44,584	1,046,587,778
Yoakum	1936	35,641,986	97,649	1,525,599,770
Young	1917	4,149,939	11,370	266,335,233
Zapata	1919	495,926	1,359	41,316,067
Zavala	1937	678,544	1,859	18,114,802
TOTAL		**813,620,140**		**50,946,447,591**

*Since 1970, production figures have been compiled from records of the Railroad Commission of Texas. In prior years, U.S. Bureau of Mines, and State Comptroller reports were the basis of these compilations. The figures in the final column are cumulative of all previously published figures. The change in sources, due to different techniques, may create some discrepancies in year-to-year comparisons among counties.

Rank of Refining States
(Source: The Oil & Gas Journal Survey, March 30, 1987)

Rank	State and Number of Plants	*Crude Oil Capacity	Percent of U.S.
1.	Texas (30)	4,098,700	26.81
2.	California (28)	2,312,593	15.13
3.	Louisiana (18)	2,266,133	14.82
4.	Illinois (7)	924,600	6.05
5.	Pennsylvania (8)	717,200	4.69
6.	Ohio (4)	475,650	3.11
7.	Washington (7)	444,225	2.91
8.	Indiana (4)	425,800	2.79
9.	New Jersey (6)	415,000	2.71
10.	Oklahoma (6)	387,000	2.53
11.	Mississippi (5)	362,300	2.37
12.	Kansas (7)	339,700	2.22
13.	Alaska (6)	225,000	1.47
14.	Minnesota (2)	222,143	1.45
15.	Kentucky (2)	218,900	1.43
16.	Wyoming (6)	165,300	1.08
17.	Utah (6)	154,500	1.01
	All Other States (35)	1,133,530	7.42
	U.S. Total (187)	15,288,274	100.00

*Barrels per calendar day, Jan. 1, 1987.

Nonfuel Mineral Production and Value, 1984, 1985 and 1986

Source: U.S. Bureau of Mines

(Production measured by mine shipments, sales or marketable production, including consumption by producer.)

Mineral—	1984 Production	1984 Value (add 000)	1985 Production	1985 Value (add 000)	*1986 Production	*1986 Value (add 000)
Cement:						
Masonry, thousand short tons	310	$22,360	263	$22,114	220	$18,500
Portland, thousand short tons	10,900	603,200	10,242	532,494	8,800	521,100
Clays, thousand short tons	3,971	27,952	4,107	28,059	5,208	34,410
Gemstones	†	175	†	175	†	†
Gypsum, thousand short tons	2,273	18,536	1,981	17,299	2,193	17,104
Lime, thousand short tons	1,210	66,130	1,192	65,927	1,207	66,775
Salt, thousand short tons	8,142	64,896	8,390	80,434	6,649	46,657
Sand and gravel:						
Construction, thousand short tons	53,200	195,200	§57,800	§198,000	62,600	216,500
Industrial, thousand short tons	2,200	32,400	1,968	29,095	1,500	21,600
Stone:						
Crushed, thousand short tons	79,800	255,000	85,764	306,821	85,000	304,700
Dimension, thousand short tons	47	11,236	37	11,760	61	15,034
Sulphur (Frasch), thousand metric tons	2,772	‡	2,979	‡	2,612	‡
Talc and pyrophyllite, thousand short tons	288	5,000	261	5,245	289	5,637
‡Undistributed	...	415,631	...	435,936	...	395,225
Total Texas Values	...	$1,717,716	...	$1,733,359	...	$1,663,242

*Preliminary. †Not available.
‡Includes asphalt (1985, 1986), fluorspar, gemstones (1986), helium, iron ore, magnesium chloride, magnesium compounds, mica (scrap, 1985), sodium sulphate and sulphur (Frasch). §Estimated.

Nonpetroleum Minerals

The nonpetroleum minerals that occur in Texas constitute a long list. Some are currently mined; some may have a potential for future development; some are minor occurrences only. Although overshadowed by the petroleum, natural gas and natural gas liquids that are produced in the state, many of the nonpetroleum minerals are, nonetheless, important to the economy.

In 1986, they were valued at approximately $2 billion. Texas is annually among the nation's three leading states in value of nonpetroleum mineral production.

Locations of the resource areas of many nonpetroleum minerals are shown on a "Mineral Resources of Texas" map issued by the Bureau of Economic Geology of The University of Texas at Austin. Also available for purchase from the Bureau is a computer-generated, detailed listing of Texas nonpetroleum mineral producers.

The Bureau of Economic Geology, which functions as the state geological survey of Texas, revised the following information about nonpetroleum minerals for this edition of the Texas Almanac. Publications of the bureau, on file in many libraries, contain more detailed information. A catalog of Bureau publications is available free on request from the Bureau (University Station, Box X, Austin, TX 78712-7508; telephone 512 471-1534).

Texas' nonpetroleum minerals are as follows:

ALUMINUM — No aluminum ores are mined in Texas, but three Texas plants process aluminum materials in one or more ways. Plants in San Patricio and Calhoun counties produce aluminum oxide (alumina) from imported raw ore (bauxite), and a plant in Milam County reduces the oxide to aluminum.

ASBESTOS — Small occurrences of amphibole-type asbestos have been found in the state. In West Texas, richterite, a white, long-fibered amphibole, is associated with some of the talc deposits northwest of **Allamoore** in Hudspeth County. Another type, tremolite, has been found in the Llano Uplift of Central Texas where it is associated with serpentinite in eastern Gillespie and western Blanco County. No asbestos is mined in Texas.

ASPHALT (Native) — Asphalt-bearing Cretaceous limestones crop out in Burnet, Kinney, Pecos, Reeves, Uvalde and other counties. The most significant deposit is in southwestern Uvalde County where asphalt occurs naturally in the pore spaces of the Anacacho Limestone. The material is quarried and used extensively as road-paving material. Asphalt-bearing sandstones occur in Anderson, Angelina, Cooke, Jasper, Maverick, Montague, Nacogdoches, Uvalde, Zavala and other counties.

BARITE — Deposits of a heavy, nonmetallic mineral, barite (barium sulphate), have been found in many localities, including Baylor, Brown, Brewster, Culberson, Gillespie, Howard, Hudspeth, Jeff Davis, Kinney, Llano, Live Oak, Taylor, Val Verde and Webb counties. During the 1960s, there was small, intermittent production in the **Seven Heart Gap** area of the **Apache Mountains** in Culberson County, where barite was mined from open pits. Most of the deposits are known to be relatively small, but the Webb County deposit has not been evaluated. Grinding plants, which prepare barite mined outside of Texas for use chiefly as a weighting agent in well-drilling muds and as a filler, are located in Brownsville, Corpus Christi, El Paso, Galena Park, Galveston, Kingsville, Knippa and Pecos.

BASALT (TRAP ROCK) — Masses of basalt — a hard, dark-colored, fine-grained igneous rock — crop out in Kinney, Travis, Uvalde and several other counties along the Balcones Fault Zone, and also in the Trans-Pecos area of West Texas. Basalt is quarried near Knippa in Uvalde County for use chiefly as road-building material and other aggregate and in the production of mineral (rock) wool.

BENTONITE (see Clay).

BERYLLIUM — Occurrences of beryllium minerals at several Trans-Pecos localities have been recognized for several years. Evaluation and development of a beryllium prospect near Sierra Blanca in Hudspeth County, a portion of which is on state-owned land, is now underway. Behoite and other beryllium minerals are associated with fluorspar at this site.

BRINE (see also **Salt, Sodium Sulphate**) — Many wells in Texas produce brine by solution mining of subsurface salt deposits. The annual production of brine has been estimated at over 10 billion gallons, most of which is produced in Andrews, Crane, Ector, Loving, Midland, Pecos, Reeves, Ward and other West Texas counties. These wells in the Permian basin dissolve salt from the Salado Formation, an enormous salt deposit that extends in the subsurface from north of Big Bend northward to Kansas, has an east-west width of 150 to 200 miles, and may have several hundred feet of net salt thickness. The majority of the brine is used in the petroleum industry, but it is also used in water softening, the chemical industry and other uses.

Three Gulf Coast counties, Fort Bend, Duval and Jefferson, have brine stations that produce from salt domes. Approximately 90 percent of the 10 million tons of salt produced in Texas each year are from brining operations.

BUILDING STONE (DIMENSION STONE) — **Granite** and **limestone** currently are quarried for use as dimension stone. The granite quarries are located in Burnet, Gillespie, Llano and Mason counties; the limestone quarries are in Shackelford and Williamson counties. Past production of limestone for use as dimension stone has been reported in Burnet, Gillespie, Jones, Tarrant, Travis and several other counties. There has also been production of **sandstone** in various counties for use as dimension stone.

CEMENT MATERIALS — Texas is the nation's leading producer and consumer of **portland cement**, which is prepared at 13 plants in Bexar, Comal, Dallas, Ector, Ellis, Hays, McLennan, Nolan, and Potter counties. Many of the plants utilize Cretaceous limestones and shales or clays as raw materials for the cement. Such materials occur in the Blacklands, Grand Prairie, Edwards Plateau and Trans-

Pecos areas. On the Texas High Plains, a cement plant near Amarillo uses impure caliche as the chief raw material. Iron oxide, also a constituent of cement, is available from the iron ore deposits of East Texas and from smelter slag. Gypsum, added to the cement as a retarder, is found chiefly in North Central Texas, Central Texas and the Trans-Pecos area.

CHROMIUM — Chromite-bearing rock has been found in several small deposits around the margin of the Coal Creek serpentinite mass in northeastern Gillespie County and northwestern Blanco County. Exploration has not revealed significant deposits. Chromium is processed from out-of-state ores in Cameron and El Paso counties.

CLAYS — Texas has an abundance and variety of ceramic and nonceramic clays and is one of the country's leading producers of clay products.

Almost any kind of clay, ranging from common clay used to make ordinary brick and tile to special clays suitable for manufacture of specialty whitewares, can be used for ceramic purposes. Fire clay suitable for use as refractories occurs chiefly in East and North Central Texas; ball clay, a high-quality plastic ceramic clay, is found locally in East Texas.

Ceramic clay suitable for quality structural clay products such as structural building brick, paving brick and drain tile is especially abundant in East and North Central Texas. Common clay suitable for use in the manufacture of cement and ordinary brick is found in most counties of the state. Many of the Texas clays will expand or bloat upon rapid firing and are suitable for the manufacture of lightweight aggregate, which is used mainly in concrete blocks and highway surfacing.

Nonceramic clays are utilized without firing. They are used primarily as bleaching and adsorbent clays, fillers, coaters, additives, bonding clays, drilling muds, catalysts and potentially as sources of alumina. Most of the nonceramic clays in Texas are bentonites and fuller's earth. These occur extensively in the Coastal Plain and locally in the High Plains and Big Bend areas. Kaolin clays in parts of East Texas are potential sources of such nonceramic products as paper coaters and fillers, rubber fillers and drilling agents. Relatively high in alumina, these clays also are a potential source of metallic aluminum.

COAL (see also Lignite) — Bituminous coal, which occurs in North Central, South and West Texas, was a significant energy source in Texas prior to the large-scale development of oil and gas. During the period from 1895 to 1943, Texas mines produced more than 25 million tons of coal. The mines were inactive for many years, but the renewed interest in coal as a major energy source prompted a reevaluation of Texas' coal deposits. In the late 1970s, bituminous coal production resumed in the state on a limited scale when mines were opened in Coleman, Erath and Webb counties.

Much of the state's bituminous coal occurs in North Central Texas. Deposits are found there in Pennsylvanian rocks within a large area that includes Coleman, Eastland, Erath, Jack, McCulloch, Montague, Palo Pinto, Parker, Throckmorton, Wise, Young and other counties. Before the general availability of oil and gas, underground coal mines near Thurber, Bridgeport, Newcastle, Strawn and other points annually produced significant coal tonnages. Preliminary evaluations indicate substantial amounts of coal may remain in the North Central Texas area. The coal seams there are generally no more than 30 inches thick and are commonly covered by well-consolidated overburden. Ash and sulphur content are high. In 1979, two bituminous coal mines began operations in North Central Texas — one in southern Coleman County and one in northwestern Erath County; the Erath County mine is no longer operating. Coal from the Coleman County mine is used as a fuel by the cement industry.

In South Texas, bituminous coal occurs in the Eagle Pass district of Maverick County, and bituminous cannel coal is present in the Santo Tomas district of Webb County. The Eagle Pass area was a leading coal-producing district in Texas during the late 1800s and early 1900s. The bituminous coal in that area, which occurs in the Upper Cretaceous Olmos Formation, has a high ash content and a moderate moisture and sulphur content. According to reports, Maverick County coal beds range from four to seven feet thick.

The cannel coals of western Webb County occur near the Rio Grande in middle Eocene strata. They were mined for more than 50 years and used primarily as a boiler fuel. Mining ceased from 1939 until 1978, when a surface mine was opened 30 miles northwest of Laredo to produce cannel coal for use as fuel in the cement industry and for export. An educational mine has since been opened in that county. Tests show that the coals of the Webb County Santo Tomas district have a high hydrogen content and yield significant amounts of gas and oil when distilled. They also have a high sulphur content. A potential use might be as a source of various petrochemical products.

Coal deposits in the Trans-Pecos country of West Texas include those in the Cretaceous rocks of the Terlingua area of Brewster County, the Eagle Spring area of Hudspeth

County and the San Carlos area of Presidio County. The coal deposits in these areas are believed to have relatively little potential for development in the near term.

COPPER — Copper minerals have been found in the Trans-Pecos area of West Texas, in the Llano Uplift area of Central Texas and in redbed deposits of North Texas. No copper has been mined in Texas during recent years, and the total copper produced in the state has been relatively small. Past attempts to mine the North Texas and Llano Uplift copper deposits resulted in small shipments, but practically all the copper production in the state has been from the Van Horn-Allamoore district of Culberson and Hudspeth Counties in the Trans-Pecos area. Chief output was from the Hazel copper-silver mine of Culberson County that yielded over 1 million pounds of copper during 1891-1947. Copper ores and concentrates from outside of Texas are processed at smelters in El Paso and Amarillo.

CRUSHED STONE — Texas is among the leading states in the production of crushed stone. Most production consists of limestone; other kinds of crushed stone produced in the state include basalt (trap rock), dolomite, granite, marble, rhyolite, sandstone and serpentinite. Large tonnages of crushed stone are used as aggregate in concrete, as road material and in the manufacture of cement and lime. Some is used as riprap, terrazzo, roofing chips, filter material, fillers and for other purposes.

DIATOMITE (DIATOMACEOUS EARTH) — Diatomite is a very lightweight siliceous material consisting of the remains of microscopic aquatic plants (diatoms). It is used chiefly as a filter and filler; other uses are for thermal insulation, as an abrasive, as an insecticide carrier and as a lightweight aggregate, and for other purposes. The diatomite was deposited in shallow fresh-water lakes that were present in the High Plains during portions of the Pliocene and Pleistocene epochs. Deposits have been found in Armstrong, Crosby, Dickens, Ector, Hartley and Lamb counties. No diatomite is mined in Texas.

DOLOMITE ROCK — Dolomite rock, which consists largely of the mineral dolomite (calcium-magnesium carbonate), commonly is associated with limestone in Texas. Areas in which dolomite rock occurs include Central Texas, the Callahan Divide and parts of the Edwards Plateau, High Plains and West Texas. Some of the principal deposits of dolomite rock are found in Bell, Brown, Burnet, Comanche, Edwards, El Paso, Gillespie, Lampasas, Mills, Nolan, Taylor and Williamson counties. Dolomite rock can be used as crushed stone (although much of Texas dolomite is soft and not a good aggregate material), in the manufacture of lime and as a source of magnesium.

FELDSPAR — Large crystals and crystal fragments of feldspar minerals occur in the Precambrian pegmatite rocks that crop out in the Llano Uplift area of Central Texas — including Blanco, Burnet, Gillespie, Llano and Mason counties — and in the Van Horn area of Culberson and Hudspeth Counties in West Texas. Feldspar has been mined in Llano County for use as roofing granules and as a ceramic material but is not currently mined anywhere within the state.

FLUORSPAR — The mineral fluorite (calcium fluoride), which is known commercially as fluorspar, occurs both in Central and West Texas. In Central Texas, the deposits that have been found in Burnet, Gillespie and Mason Counties are not considered adequate to sustain mining operations. In West Texas, deposits have been found in Brewster, El Paso, Hudspeth, Jeff Davis and Presidio counties. Fluorspar has been mined in the Christmas Mountains of Brewster County and processed in Marathon. Former West Texas mining activity in the Eagle Mountains district of Hudspeth County resulted in the production of approximately 15,000 short tons of fluorspar during the peak years of 1942-1950. No production has been reported in Hudspeth County since that period. Imported fluorspar is processed in Brownsville, Eagle Pass, El Paso and Marathon. Fluorspar is used in the steel, chemical, aluminum, magnesium, ceramics and glass industries and for various other purposes.

FULLER'S EARTH (see Clay).

GOLD — No major deposits of gold are known in Texas. Small amounts have been found in the Llano Uplift region of Central Texas and in West Texas; minor occurrences have been reported on the Edwards Plateau, the Gulf Coastal Plain and North Central Texas. Nearly all of the gold produced in the state came as a by-product of silver and lead mining at Presidio mine, near Shafter, in Presidio County. Additional small quantities were produced as a by-product of copper mining in Culberson County and from residual soils developed from gold-bearing quartz stringers in metamorphic rocks in Llano County. No gold mining has been reported in Texas since 1952. Total gold production in the state, 1889-1952, amounted to more than 8,419 troy ounces according to U.S. Bureau of Mines figures. Most of the production — at least 73 percent and probably more — came from the Presidio mine.

GRANITE — Granites in shades of red and gray and related intrusive igneous rocks occur in the Llano Uplift of Central Texas and in the Trans-Pecos country of West Texas. Deposits are found in Blanco, Brewster, Burnet, El

Paso, Gillespie, Hudspeth, Llano, McCulloch, Mason, Presidio and other counties. Quarries in Burnet, Gillespie, Llano and Mason counties produce Precambrian granite for a variety of uses as **dimension stone** and **crushed stone.**

GRAPHITE — Graphite, a soft, dark-gray mineral, is a form of very high-grade carbon. It occurs in Precambrian schist rocks of the Llano Uplift of Central Texas, notably in Burnet and Llano counties. Crystalline-flake graphite ore formerly was mined from open pits in the Clear Creek area of western Burnet County and processed at a plant near the mine. The mill now occasionally grinds imported material. Uses of natural crystalline graphite are refractories, steel production, pencil leads, lubricants, foundry facings and crucibles and for other purposes.

GRINDING PEBBLES (ABRASIVE STONES) — Flint pebbles, suitable for use in tube-mill grinding, are found in the Gulf Coastal Plain where they occur in gravel deposits along rivers and in upland areas. Grinding pebbles are produced from Frio River terrace deposits near the McMullen-Live Oak county line, but the area is now part of the Choke Canyon Reservoir area.

GYPSUM — Gypsum is widely distributed in Texas. Chief deposits are bedded gypsum in the area east of the High Plains, in the Trans-Pecos country and in Central Texas. It also occurs in salt dome caprocks of the Gulf Coast. The massive, granular variety known as rock gypsum is the kind most commonly used by industry. Other varieties include **alabaster, satin spar** and **selenite.**

Gypsum is one of the important industrial minerals in Texas. Bedded gypsum is produced from surface mines in Culberson, Fisher, Gillespie, Hardeman, Hudspeth, Kimble, Nolan and Stonewall counties. Gypsum also is mined at **Gyp Hill salt dome** in Brooks County, and was formerly mined at **Hockley salt dome** in Harris County. Most of the gypsum is calcined and used in the manufacture of gypsum wallboard, plaster, joint compounds and other construction products. Crude gypsum is used chiefly as a retarder in portland cement and as a soil conditioner.

HELIUM — Texas is a leading producer of this very light, nonflammable, chemically inert gas. Helium is extracted from natural gas of the Panhandle area at the U.S. Bureau of Mines Exell plant near Masterson in Moore County and at two privately owned plants in Hansford County. As a conservation measure, the Bureau of Mines injects the helium that is not sold into the Cliffside gas field near Amarillo for storage. Helium is used in cryogenics, welding, pressurizing and purging, leak detection, synthetic breathing mixtures and for other purposes.

IRON — Iron oxide (limonite, goethite and hematite) and iron carbonate (siderite) deposits occur widely in East Texas, notably in Cass, Cherokee, Marion and Morris counties, and also in Anderson, Camp, Harrison, Henderson, Nacogdoches, Smith, Upshur and other counties. **Magnetite** (magnetic, black iron oxide) occurs in Central Texas, including a deposit at **Iron Mountain** in Llano County. **Hematite** occurs in the Trans-Pecos area and in the Llano Uplift of Central Texas. The extensive deposits of **glauconite** (a complex silicate containing iron) that occur in East Texas and the hematitic and goethitic Cambrian sandstone that crops out in the northwestern Llano Uplift region are potential sources of low-grade iron ore.

Limonite and other East Texas iron ores are mined from open pits in Cherokee and Henderson counties for use in the preparation of **portland cement**, as a weighting agent in well-drilling fluids, as an animal feed supplement and for other purposes. East Texas iron ores also have been mined for use in the iron-steel industry.

KAOLIN (see **Clay**).

LEAD AND ZINC — The lead mineral **galena** (lead sulphide) commonly is associated with zinc and silver. It formerly was produced as a by-product of West Texas silver mining, chiefly from the **Presidio mine** at **Shafter** in Presidio County, although lesser amounts were obtained at several other mines and prospects. Deposits of galena also are known to occur in Blanco, Brewster, Burnet, Gillespie and Hudspeth counties.

Zinc, primarily from the mineral sphalerite (zinc sulphide), was produced chiefly from the **Bonanza** and **Alice Ray mines** in the **Quitman Mountains** of Hudspeth County. In addition, small production was reported from several other areas, including the **Chinati** and **Montezuma mines** of Presidio County and the **Buck Prospect** in the **Apache Mountains** of Culberson County. Zinc mineralization also occurs in association with the lead deposits in Cambrian rocks of Central Texas.

LIGHTWEIGHT AGGREGATE (see **Clay, Diatomite, Perlite, Vermiculite**).

LIGNITE — Lignite, a low-rank coal, is found in belts of Tertiary Eocene strata that extend across the Texas Gulf Coastal Plain from the Rio Grande in South Texas to the Arkansas and Louisiana borders in East Texas. The largest resources and best grades (approximately 6,500 BTU/pound) of lignite occur in the Wilcox Group of strata north of the Colorado River in East and Central Texas.

The near-surface lignite resources, occurring at depths of less than 200 feet in seams of three feet or thicker, are estimated at 23 billion short tons. Recoverable reserves of strippable lignite — those that can be economically mined under current conditions of price and technology — are estimated to be 9 billion to 11 billion short tons.

Additional lignite resources of the Texas Gulf Coastal Plain occur as deep-basin deposits. Deep basin resources, those that occur at depths of 200 to 2,000 feet in seams of five feet or thicker, are comparable in magnitude to near-surface resources. The deep-basin lignites are a potential energy resource that conceivably could be utilized by in situ (in place) recovery methods such as underground gasification.

As with bituminous coal, lignite production was significant prior to the general availability of oil and gas. Remnants of old underground mines are common throughout the area of lignite occurrence. Large reserves of strippable lignite have again attracted the attention of energy suppliers, and Texas is now the nation's 6th leading producer of coal, 99 percent of it lignite. Seven large strip mines are now producing lignite that is burned for mine-mouth electric power generation, and additional mines are planned. One of the currently operating mines is located in Milam County, where part of the electric power is used for alumina reduction. Other mines are in Atascosa, Freestone, Grimes, Harrison, Rusk, Panola, Titus and Hopkins counties, where the power generated supplies municipal, domestic and industrial needs. Another Harrison County strip mine produces lignite that is used to make activated carbon.

LIME MATERIAL — Limestones, which are abundant in some areas of Texas, are heated to produce lime (calcium oxide) at a number of plants in the state. High magnesium limestones and **dolomite** are used to prepare lime at plants in Burnet and Comal counties. The Texas lime plants are located in Bexar, Bosque, Burnet, Comal, Hill, Johnson and Travis counties. Lime is used in soil stabilization, water purification, paper and pulp manufacture, metallurgy, sugar refining, agriculture, construction, removal of sulfur from stack gases and for many other purposes.

LIMESTONE (see also **Building Stone**) — Texas is one of the nation's leading producers of limestone, which is quarried in more than 60 counties. Limestone occurs in nearly all areas of the state with the exception of most of the Gulf Coastal Plain and High Plains. Although some of the limestone is quarried for use as **dimension stone**, most of the output is crushed for uses such as bulk building materials (crushed stone, road base, concrete aggregate), chemical raw materials, fillers or extenders, lime and **portland cement** raw materials, **agricultural limestone** and removal of sulfur from stack gases.

MAGNESITE — Small deposits of magnesite (natural magnesium carbonate) have been found in Precambrian rocks in Llano and Mason counties of Central Texas. There formerly was small-scale mining of magnesite in the area — some of the material was used as **agricultural stone** and as **terrazzo chips.** Magnesite also can be calcined to form magnesia, which is used in metallurgical furnace refractories and other products.

MAGNESIUM — On the Texas Gulf Coast in Brazoria County, **magnesium chloride** is extracted from sea water at a plant in Freeport and used to produce magnesium metal. In West Texas, magnesium-bearing brines of the Permian Basin have been used as a raw material for magnesium metal production at a plant in Scurry County. During World War II, high-magnesium Ellenburger **dolomite** rock from Burnet County was used as magnesium ore at a plant near Austin.

MANGANESE — Deposits of manganese minerals, such as braunite, hollandite and pyrolusite, have been found in several areas, including Jeff Davis, Llano, Mason, Presidio and Val Verde counties. Known deposits are not large. Small shipments have been made from Jeff Davis, Mason and Val Verde counties, but no manganese mining has been reported in Texas since 1954.

MARBLE — Metamorphic and sedimentary marbles suitable for monument and building stone are found in the Llano Uplift and nearby areas of Central Texas and the Trans-Pecos area of West Texas. Gray, white, black, greenish black, light green, brown and cream-colored marbles occur in Central Texas in Burnet, Gillespie, Llano and Mason counties. West Texas metamorphic marbles include the bluish-white and the black marbles found southwest of Alpine in Brewster County and the white marble from **Marble Canyon** north of Van Horn in Culberson County. Marble can be used as **dimension stone, terrazzo** and roofing aggregate and for other purposes.

MERCURY (QUICKSILVER) — Mercury minerals, chiefly **cinnabar,** occur in the Terlingua district and nearby districts of southern Brewster and southeastern Presidio counties. Mining began there about 1894, and from 1905 to 1935, Texas was one of the nation's leading producers of quicksilver. Following World War II, a sharp drop in demand and price, along with depletion of developed ore reserves, caused abandonment of all the Texas mercury mines.

With a rise in the price, sporadic mining took place between 1951-1960. In 1965, when the price of mercury moved to a record high, renewed interest in the Texas mercury districts resulted in the reopening of several mines and the discovery of new ore reserves. By April 1972, however, the price had declined and the mines have reported no production since 1973.

MICA — Large crystals of flexible, transparent mica minerals in igneous pegmatite rocks and mica flakes in metamorphic schist rocks are found in the Llano area of Central Texas and the Van Horn area of West Texas. Most Central Texas deposits do not meet specifications for sheet mica, and although several attempts have been made to produce West Texas sheet mica in Culberson and Hudspeth counties, sustained production has not been achieved. In the early 1980s, a mica quarry began operating in the **Van Horn Mountains** of Culberson and Hudspeth counties to mine mica schist for use as an additive in rotary drilling fluids.

MOLYBDENUM — Small occurrences of molybdenite have been found in Burnet and Llano counties, and wulfenite, another molybdenum mineral, has been noted in rocks in the Quitman Mountains of Hudspeth County. Molybdenum minerals also occur at Cave Peak north of Van Horn in Culberson County, in the **Altuda Mountain** area of northwestern Brewster County and in association with **uranium ores** of the Gulf Coastal Plain.

PEAT — This spongy organic substance forms in bogs from plant remains. It has been found in the Gulf Coastal Plain in several localities including Gonzales, Guadalupe, Lee, Milam, Polk and San Jacinto counties. There has been intermittent, small-scale production of some of the peat for use as a soil conditioner.

PERLITE — Perlite, a glassy igneous rock, expands to a lightweight, porous mass when heated. It can be used as a lightweight aggregate, filter aid, horticultural aggregate and for other purposes. Perlite occurs in Presidio County, where it has been mined in the **Pinto Canyon** area north of the **Chinati Mountains**. No perlite is currently mined in Texas, but perlite mined outside of Texas is expanded at plants in Bexar, Dallas, El Paso, Guadalupe, Harris and Nolan counties.

PHOSPHATE — Rock phosphate is present in Paleozoic rocks in several areas of Brewster and Presidio counties in West Texas and in Central Texas, but the known deposits are not large. In Northeast Texas, sedimentary rock phosphate occurs in thin conglomeratic lenses in Upper Cretaceous and Tertiary rock units; possibly some of these low-grade phosphorites could be processed on a small scale for local use as a fertilizer. Imported phosphate rock is processed at a plant in Brownsville.

POTASH — The potassium mineral **polyhalite** is widely distributed in the subsurface Permian Basin of West Texas and has been found in many wells in that area. During 1927-1931, the federal government drilled a series of potash-test wells in Crane, Crockett, Ector, Glasscock, Loving, Reagan, Upton and Winkler counties. In addition to polyhalite, which was found in all of the counties, these wells revealed the presence of the potassium minerals **carnallite and sylvite** in Loving County and carnallite in Winkler County. The known Texas potash deposits are not as rich as those in the New Mexico portion of the Permian Basin and have not been developed.

PUMICITE (VOLCANIC ASH) — Deposits of volcanic ash occur in Brazos, Fayette, Gonzales, Karnes, Polk, Starr and other counties of the Texas Coastal Plain. Deposits also have been found in the Trans-Pecos area, High Plains and in several counties east of the High Plains. Volcanic ash is used to prepare pozzolan cement, cleansing and scouring compounds and soaps and sweeping compounds; as a carrier for insecticides, and for other purposes. It has been mined in Dickens, Lynn, Scurry, Starr and other counties.

QUICKSILVER (see **Mercury**).

SALT (SODIUM CHLORIDE) (see also **BRINES**)— Salt resources of Texas are virtually inexhaustible. Enormous deposits occur in the subsurface Permian Basin of West Texas and in the salt domes of the Gulf Coastal Plain. Salt also is found in the alkali playa lakes of the High Plains, the alkali flats or **salt lakes** in the Salt Basin of Culberson and Hudspeth Counties and along some of the bays and lagoons of the South Texas Gulf Coast.

Texas is one of the leading salt-producing states. **Rock salt** is obtained from underground mines in salt domes at **Grand Saline** in Van Zandt County and Hockley in Harris County. Only about 10 percent of the salt produced in the state is from rock salt; most of the salt is produced by solution mining as brines from wells drilled into the underground deposits.

SAND, INDUSTRIAL — Sands used for special purposes, due to high silica content or to unique physical properties, command higher prices than common sand. Industrial sands in Texas occur mainly in the Central Gulf Coastal Plain and in North Central Texas. They include abrasive, blast, chemical, engine, filtration, foundry, glass, hydraulic-fracturing (propant), molding and pottery sands. Recent production of industrial sands has been reported in Atascosa, Colorado, El Paso, Hardin, Harris, Liberty, Limestone, McCulloch, Newton, Smith, Somervell and Wood counties.

SAND AND GRAVEL (CONSTRUCTION) — Sand and gravel are among the most extensively utilized resources in Texas. Principal occurrence is along the major streams and in stream terraces. Sand and gravel are important bulk construction materials, used as railroad ballast, base materials and for other purposes.

SANDSTONE — Sandstones of a variety of colors and textures are widely distributed in a number of geologic formations in Texas. Some of the sandstones have been quarried for use as dimension stone in El Paso, Parker, Terrell, Ward and other counties. Crushed sandstone is produced in Freestone, Gaines, Jasper, McMullen, Motley and other counties for use as road-building material, **terrazzo stone**, concrete and other aggregate.

SERPENTINITE — Several masses of serpentinite, which formed from the alteration of basic igneous rocks, are associated with other Precambrian metamorphic rocks of the Llano Uplift. The largest deposit is the Coal Creek serpentinite mass in northern Blanco and Gillespie counties from which **terrazzo chips** have been produced. Other deposits are present in Gillespie and Llano counties. (The features that are associated with surface and subsurface Cretaceous rocks in several counties in or near the Balcones Fault Zone and that are commonly known as "serpentine plugs" are not serpentine at all, but are altered igneous volcanic necks and pipes and mounds of altered volcanic ash — palagonite — that accumulated around the former submarine volcanic pipes.)

SHELL — **Oyster shells** and other shells in shallow coastal waters and in deposits along the Texas Gulf Coast have been produced chiefly by dredging. They were used to a limited extent as raw material in the manufacture of cement, as **concrete aggregate** and road base, and for other purposes. No shell has been produced in Texas since 1981.

SILVER — During the period 1885-1952, the production of silver in Texas, as reported by the U.S. Bureau of Mines, totaled about 33 million troy ounces. For about 70 years, silver was the most consistently produced metal in Texas, although always in moderate quantities. All of the production came from the Trans-Pecos country of West Texas, where the silver was mined in Brewster County (**Altuda Mountain**), Culberson and Hudspeth counties (**Van Horn Mountains** and **Van Horn-Allamoore district**), Hudspeth County (**Quitman Mountains and Eagle Mountains**) and Presidio County (**Chinati Mountains area, Loma Plata mine and Shafter district**). Chief producer was the **Presidio mine** in the Shafter district, which began operations in the late 1800s, and, through September 1942, produced more than 30 million ounces of silver — more than 92 percent of Texas' total silver production. Water in the lower mine levels, lean ores and low price of silver resulted in the closing of the mine in 1942. Another important silver producer was the **Hazel copper-silver mine** in the **Van Horn-Allamoore district** in Culberson County, which accounted for more than 2 million ounces.

An increase in the price of silver in the late 1970s stimulated prospecting for new reserves, and exploration began near the old **Presidio mine**, near the old **Plata Verde mine** in the **Van Horn Mountains district**, at the **Bonanza mine** in the **Quitman Mountains district** and at the old **Hazel mine**. A decline in the price of silver in the early 1980s, however, resulted in reduction of exploration and mine development in the region. There is no current exploration in these areas.

SOAPSTONE (see **Talc and Soapstone**).

SODIUM SULFATE (SALT CAKE) — Sodium sulfate minerals occur in salt beds and brines of the alkali playa lakes of the High Plains in West Texas. In some lakes, the sodium sulfate minerals are present in deposits a few feet beneath the lakebeds. Sodium sulfate also is found in underground brines in the Permian Basin. Current production is from brines and dry salt beds at alkali lakes in Gaines and Terry counties. Past production was reported in Lynn and Ward counties. Sodium sulfate is used chiefly by the detergent and paper and pulp industries. Other uses are in the preparation of glass and other products.

STONE (see **Building Stone; Crushed Stone**).

STRONTIUM — Deposits of the mineral **celestite** (strontium sulfate) have been found in a number of places, including localities in Brown, Coke, Comanche, Fisher, Lampasas, Mills, Nolan, Real, Taylor, Travis and Williamson counties. Most of the occurrences are very minor, and none is currently produced in the state.

SULFUR — Texas is one of the world's principal sulfur-producing areas. The sulfur is mined from deposits of native sulfur, and it is extracted from sour (sulfur-bearing) natural gas and petroleum. Recovered sulfur is a growing industry and accounted for approximately one-half of all 1985 sulfur production in the United States, but less than one-third of Texas production. Native sulfur is found in large deposits in the caprock of some of the salt domes along the Texas Gulf Coast and in some of the surface and subsurface Permian strata of West Texas, notably in Culberson and Pecos counties. Native sulfur obtained from the underground deposits is known as Frasch sulfur, so-called because of Herman Frasch, the chemist who devised the method of drilling wells into the deposits, melting the sulfur with superheated water and forcing the molten sulfur to the surface. Most of the production now goes to the users in molten form.

Frasch sulfur is produced from only one Gulf Coast salt dome in Wharton County and from West Texas underground Permian strata in Culberson County. Operations at several Gulf Coast domes have been closed in recent years. During the 1940s, acidic sulfur earth was produced in the **Rustler Springs district** in Culberson County for use as a fertilizer and soil conditioner. Sulfur is recovered from sour natural gas and petroleum at plants in numerous Texas counties. Sulfur is used in the preparation of fertilizers and organic and inorganic chemicals, in petroleum refining and for many other purposes.

TALC AND SOAPSTONE — Deposits of talc are found in the Precambrian metamorphic rocks of the **Allamoore area** of eastern Hudspeth and western Culberson counties. Soapstone, containing **talc**, occurs in the Precambrian metamorphic rocks of the Llano Uplift area, notably in Blanco, Gillespie and Llano counties. Current production is from surface mines in the Allamoore area. Talc is used in ceramic, roofing, paint, paper, plastic, synthetic rubber and other products.

TIN — Tin minerals have been found in El Paso and Mason Counties. Small quantities were produced during the early 1900s in the **Franklin Mountains** north of El Paso. **Cassiterite** (tin dioxide) occurrences in Mason County are believed to be very minor. The only **tin smelter** in the United States, built at Texas City by the federal government during World War II and later sold to a private company, processes tin concentrates from ores mined outside of Texas, tin residues and secondary tin-bearing materials.

TITANIUM — The titanium mineral rutile has been found in small amounts at the Mueller prospect in Jeff Davis County. Another titanium mineral, ilmenite, occurs in sandstones in Burleson, Fayette, Lee, Starr and several other counties. Deposits that would be considered commercial under present conditions have not been found.

TRAP ROCK (see **Basalt**).

TUNGSTEN — The tungsten mineral scheelite has been found in small deposits in Gillespie and Llano counties and in the **Quitman Mountains** in Hudspeth County. Small deposits of other tungsten minerals have been prospected in the **Cave Peak** area north of Van Horn in Culberson County.

URANIUM — Uranium deposits were discovered in the Texas Coastal Plain in 1954 when abnormal radioactivity was detected in the Karnes County area. A number of uranium deposits have since been discovered within a belt of strata extending more than 250 miles from the middle Coastal Plain southwestward to the Rio Grande.

Various uranium minerals also have been found in other areas of Texas, including the Trans-Pecos, the Llano Uplift and the High Plains. With the exception of small shipments from the High Plains during the 1950s, all the uranium production in Texas has been from the Coastal Plain. Uranium has been obtained from surface mines extending from northern Live Oak County, southeastern Atascosa County, across northern Karnes County and into southern Gonzales County. All mines are now reclaimed. All current uranium production is by in-situ leaching, brought to the surface through wells, and stripped from the solution at several Coastal Plain recovery operations located in Bee, Duval, Jim Hogg, Karnes, Live Oak and Webb counties. Decreased demand and price of uranium since 1980 has brought a sharp decline in operations in Texas.

VERMICULITE — Vermiculite, a mica-like mineral that expands when heated, occurs in Burnet, Gillespie, Llano, Mason and other counties in the Llano region. It has been produced at a surface mine in Llano County. Vermiculite, mined outside of Texas, is exfoliated (expanded) at plants in Dallas, Houston and San Antonio. Exfoliated vermiculite is used for lightweight concrete aggregate, horticulture, insulation and other purposes.

VOLCANIC ASH (see Pumicite).

ZEOLITES — The zeolite minerals clinoptilolite and analcime occur in Tertiary lavas and tuffs in Brewster, Jeff Davis and Presidio counties, in West Texas. Clinoptilolite also is found associated with Tertiary tuffs in the southern Texas Coastal Plain, including deposits in Karnes, McMullen and Webb counties, and currently is produced in McMullen County. Zeolites, sometimes called "molecular sieves," can be used in ion-exchange processes to reduce pollution, as a catalyst in oil cracking, in obtaining high-purity oxygen and nitrogen from air, in water purification and for many other purposes.

ZINC (see **Lead** and **Zinc**).

Utilities in Texas

Because of its large size, population and economic activity, Texas ranks high among the states in the scope of its utilities. It was one of the first states to utilize the telegraph and telephone extensively. A history of telephones in Texas appeared in the 1972-73 Texas Almanac, and other editions record much of the development of utilities.

The following information was prepared through the cooperation of utility firms and their trade associations.

Telephones

Texas had 7,995,170 telephone lines in service on Dec. 31, 1986, served by 66 local-exchange companies. In addition to local service, those companies also provide approximately one-third of the intrastate long distance service in Texas. AT&T and some 50 other competitive carriers provide most of the intrastate and all of the interstate long distance service enjoyed by Texans. Southwestern Bell Corporation — which through its telephone company subsidiary also serves Arkansas, Kansas, New Mexico and Oklahoma — became a separate entity Jan. 1, 1984, the date of divestiture of the Bell System, and is no longer associated with AT&T.

The largest subsidiary of the corporation is Southwestern Bell Telphone Company, which provides local telephone access service to some nine million customers in five states, including Texas.

Also in 1984, the Texas Division of Southwestern Bell Telephone was created, with Dallas selected as its headquarters city.

The Texas Division of Southwestern Bell Telephone serves 6.2 million customers in 549 Texas communities. With some 34,000 employees and an annual payroll of about $1.1 billion, it remains one of the largest nongovernmental employers in the state. State and local operating taxes paid by the company in 1984 totalled over $572 million.

Southwestern Bell handles over 75 million local calls, and provides access for an additional 5 million direct-dialed long distance calls each day. The company serves Texas with over 925,000 miles of cable, including 37,500 miles of fiber optics.

By the end of 1984, Southwestern Bell Telephone's investment in Texas telecommunications facilities totalled over $9 billion.

Major independent telephone companies in Texas and their total access lines as of Dec. 31, 1986 were: General Telephone Company of the Southwest, with 1,024,708 lines; Contel of Texas, with 157,077 lines; Cen-

tral Telephone Co. of Texas, with 117,681 lines; United Telephone Co. of Texas, with 103,272 lines; and Lufkin-Conroe Telephone Exchange, with 56,771. (Because telephone customers can now own the wiring within their premises, as well as all the equipment inside, the industry no longer counts total telephones they serve. Access lines reflect the number of connections the companies provide, and does not equate to number of customers.)

The 66 independent telephone companies in Texas include 24 telephone cooperatives, subscriber-owned systems serving more than 97,000 access lines through 233 exchanges in the state. The Bell System companies serve four out of every five Texans, while the independent companies serve more than half of the state's 250,000 square miles of certified service territory.

In the Houston metro area, Southwestern Bell and five independent telephone companies cooperate to serve 1,300,000 customers, possibly the largest in the nation. On the other hand, **Big Bend Telephone Co.** in West Texas serves about 2,500 subscribers in a service area of 19,000 square miles — roughly equal to the states of Connecticut, Delaware, Massachusetts and Rhode Island combined.

The following table shows the number of telephone access lines on Dec. 31, 1986, in the calling scope of many of Texas' principal cities. Some of the larger cities and towns not shown are included in the metropolitan exchanges of Dallas, Houston, Fort Worth and San Antonio.

Abilene	56,590
Amarillo	91,233
Arlington	97,600
Austin	362,282
Bay City	12,770
Beaumont	63,979
Brownsville-Harlingen	50,057
Cleburne	17,900

Corpus Christi	113,432
Corsicana	12,800
Dallas	970,700
El Paso	202,219
Fort Worth	371,900
Galveston	40,367
Greenville	13,200
Houston	1,375,524
Laredo	33,708
Longview	48,900
Lubbock	106,829
McAllen-Edinburg	42,812
McKinney	12,100
Midland	60,328
Mineral Wells	8,500
Odessa	55,553
Paris	17,700
Port Arthur	31,858
San Antonio Metro	388,596
Temple	21,942
Texas City	25,661
Tyler	56,500
Vernon	6,700
Victoria	27,300
Waco	85,871
Wichita Falls	51,500
Total	**4,943,511**
Total Texas (Actuals)	**6,200,000**

High technology has entered the field of electric meter reading. Hand-held computers like the one held by this TU Electric Co. meter reader are used to record readings. Associated Press Photo.

Electric Utilities

In 1986, utilities serving customers in Texas reported 130 electric power plants (15 not in Texas) with a **total generating capability** of about 62 million (56 million in Texas) kilowatts.

Some of the 130 power plants have several units. For about 380 generating units, the total capability in 1986 was reported as 66 percent natural gas fueled, 31 percent coal and lignite fueled, 2 percent nuclear fueled and 1 percent hydroelectric and other. In addition, about 4 million kilowatts of cogeneration capability was reportedly in operation in Texas.

The nine major investor-owned electric utility companies operating in Texas are: Central Power & Light, El Paso Electric Co., Gulf States Utilities Co., Houston Lighting and Power Co., Southwestern Electric Power Co., Southwestern Public Service Co., Texas-New Mexico Power Co., TU Electric and West Texas Utilities Co.

Also supplying electric power to Texas customers are municipally owned systems, rural electric cooperatives and state and federally financed projects.

As 1987 began, these investor-owned companies had a total investment in plants and facilities to serve Texas customers of about $28 billion. Not included in this amount is a reported balance of about $10 billion for electric construction work in progress at year end 1986.

Location of the **first power plant** in Texas is uncertain. Some authorities believe a plant that began operation on Dec. 17, 1882, in Houston was first; others credit Galveston with the first plant. Either of these would be among the first in the United States, since the initial American plant started in New York City in the summer of 1882.

As late as 1910, Texas electrical operations were mainly limited to isolated municipal and individually owned plants. In 1912 **Texas Power & Light Co.** started building Texas' **first high-voltage transmission line.** It extended from Waco to Fort Worth, with a branch from Hillsboro through Waxahachie to Ferris, where it branched north to Trinity Heights (Dallas) and south to Corsicana.

Rural electrification began after the first transmission lines were constructed. By the early 1930s some 48,000 rural families were receiving service.

Electric Cooperatives

The 77 electric distribution cooperatives operating in Texas were serving over one million rural connections by the end of 1986. The systems, plus two of Texas' three generation and transmission (G&T) cooperatives, were operating more than 250,000 miles of lines extending into all but nine of the 254 counties in Texas. Power produced by the third G&T is relayed through non-cooperatively owned lines to the cooperatives' load centers. Seven additional G&T cooperative federations have no operating facilities but represent their respective member cooperatives in their relations with regulatory bodies and their wholesale power suppliers. Five of the seven have personnel. Altogether, the 85 distribu-

tion and five staffed G&Ts employ 5,520 persons. Average number of consumer units served by the 77 distribution cooperatives, per mile of line: 12.

Gas Utilities

Approximately 300 investor-owned gas companies in Texas are classified as gas utilities and come under the regulatory jurisdiction of the Texas Railroad Commission. Approximately 170 of these companies reported **gas operating revenue** of $10.8 billion in 1985, with **operating expenses** of $10 billion.

In 1985, fixed investment for distribution facilities in Texas was $1.4 billion and for transmission facilities $4.2 billion. Investment in Texas plants in service totaled $6.8 billion. There were 50 investor-owned and 83 municipally owned distribution systems in operation in 1985 serving approximately 1,067 Texas cities.

The eight largest distribution systems — six private and two municipal — served 95 percent of all residential customers. In 1985, there were approximately 3.1 million residential customers, 276,866 small commercial and industrial users, 636 large industrial customers and 10,759 other gas utility customers. The breakdown of distribution sales to these customers was: 67 Mcf per residential customer, 655 Mcf per commercial customer, 313,801 Mcf per industrial customer and 2,365 Mcf for customers in the "other" category. Distribution sales amounted to 609.6 billion cubic feet in 1985.

In addition to industrial sales made by distribution companies, transmission companies reported pipeline-to-industry sales of 1.58 trillion cubic feet and revenue from these sales of $5.3 billion.

In 1985, the average annual residential gas bill in the U.S. was $591. The average annual bill in Texas for the same year was $403, down $42 from the previous year. The State of Texas collected $17 million in **gross receipts taxes** from gas utilities in fiscal year 1986.

There were 46,080 producing gas wells in the state at the end of 1986, up 2,456 from the previous year. New gas well completions during 1986 numbered 3,034, down 1,571 from 1985.

Texas had a total of 130,008 miles of **natural gas pipe lines** in operation in 1985, including 20,559 miles of field and gathering lines, 42,935 miles of **transmission lines** and 66,514 miles of **distribution lines.**

Estimated proved **gas reserves** in the state amounted to 49.04 trillion cubic feet in 1985. Gross production of natural gas, including **casinghead gas,** in 1986 was 5.6 trillion cubic feet. At year end 1986, 24 underground storage reservoirs in the state contained 397.7 billion cubic feet of gas.

Science

Study Benefits Heart Patients

This article was written by Gayle Golden, science writer for The Dallas Morning News.

In November of 1985, two Texas researchers received the Nobel Prize for Physiology or Medicine from the Karolinska Institute in Stockholm, marking the first Nobel Prize honoring scientific work conducted exclusively within a Texas institution.

Joseph L. Goldstein M.D. and *Michael S. Brown* M.D., medical researchers at the University of Texas Health Science Center in Dallas, were honored for pioneering research on how cells remove cholesterol from the bloodstream. Their research, involving more than a decade of close-knit collaboration, revolutionized the treatment and prevention of atherosclerosis — a disease caused by the build-up of cholesterol into bulky plaques on the wall of arteries. Those build-ups inhibit the flow of blood until a clot eventually forms, obstructing an artery and usually causing a heart attack or stroke. Atherosclerosis accounts for half of all deaths in the United States and is higher among those people who eat foods rich in fatty acids, such as beef, eggs or butter.

In the early 1970s, Brown and Goldstein began col-

Nobel Prize

laborating on studies probing how cholesterol is taken up by human cells. In the years before their partnership began, new technologies had already brought the microscopic biological operations of the body's cells into easier view in the laboratory. For years, studies of cell activity progressed through relatively costly and inefficient use of whole animals. But in the late 1960s, scientists developed means of cultivating live cell tissue and cloning genetic material in the laboratory. Those advances were the cornerstone technologies for Brown and Goldstein's research.

Using tissue cultures of a type of human skin cell known as a fibroblast, the two researchers discovered a key to how the body's cells absorb cholesterol. Like all animal cells, fibroblasts need cholesterol to function, and they get the cholesterol from an oily particle known as a low-density lipoprotein — found in the human bloodstream and commonly referred to as an LDL. Brown and Goldstein discovered that cells have special receptors on their surfaces, which trap and absorb the LDLs as they pass alongside the cell. In other words, those receptors act as "doormen" to usher the LDL particles into the cell where the cholesterol can be used to form cell membranes and, in some cases, to help make hormones and bile acids.

Nearly 75 percent of the body's LDL receptors are made in liver cells. The receptors originate inside the cells. Then, they travel to the surface where they sit in coated pits or indentations until they bind with an LDL and bring it back into the cell. Each round trip takes 10 to 15 minutes, and the receptor makes several hundred such round trips in its 30-hour lifespan.

Keeping the cells nourished isn't the only importance the receptors have. As an added benefit, they remove cholesterol from the bloodstream and reduce the chances of atherosclerosis. And so, study of these receptors held an important key to the study of cholesterol-related diseases.

In further research, Brown and Goldstein discovered an important fact about the LDL receptors: The number of receptors on the surface of cells changes, depending on how much cholesterol the cell needs. In other words, when the cell doesn't have much cholesterol, it produces more receptors to take in more LDLs. But, when too much cholesterol is carried into the cell, the gene governing cholesterol suppresses the gene that makes the receptors. As a result, the number of receptors goes down; less cholesterol is carried into the cell; and more LDLs are allowed to float freely in the bloodstream, increasing the chances that cholesterol will be deposited along the walls of arteries.

Studies show that more than 50 percent of people in Western societies, including the United States, have enough LDLs circulating in their bloodstreams to put them at high risk for atherosclerosis. But why some and not others? Is it due strictly to diet? Or are there other factors playing a role? Do those diseases hinge on the body's ability to produce LDL receptors?

Brown and Goldstein probed those questions by studying animals and patients with unusually high cholesterol in their bloodstreams. Their interest settled on a disease known as *familial hypercholesterolemia*, identified in 1939 by Norwegian researcher Carl Muller as an inborn problem with a person's metabolism, which causes high blood cholesterol and heart attacks at a young age. Sometimes, those heart attacks or strokes can occur in childhood or adolescence.

Muller suggested the disease was genetic, related to a dominant trait caused by a mutant gene. Other studies in the 1960s had identified two types of familial hypercholesterolemia: a "heterozygous" form, afflicting those who carry a single faulty gene from one parent, and a "homozygous" form, afflicting those who carry two copies of the mutant gene — one from each parent. Roughly one in 500 persons, in all ethnic groups, have only one of the genes, a condition that leads to heart attacks beginning at age 35. The presence of two faulty genes is less common, occurring to one in a million and causing heart attacks and strokes by age 20.

In research that included isolating and cloning the gene responsible for making the LDL receptor, Brown and Goldstein studied more closely than ever the dynamics of that genetic impairment. They discovered that patients with two mutant genes cannot take up cholesterol for a variety of reasons. In one study of 110 patients, about half could not make any receptors. Other patients made receptors that never reach the cell surfaces. Some made receptors that cannot snare the LDL from the bloodstream. And others made receptors that reach the cell surface, bind with the LDL but cannot find the coated pits to re-enter the cell.

As a result, people with only one of the faulty genes produce half the normal number of receptors. Those with two copies usually make virtually no receptors. In those cases, the cholesterol-packed LDLs circulate through the bloodstream about two and a half times longer than normal.

The faulty gene creates double the trouble, however. In further studies in their own Dallas laboratory and in collaboration with researchers from Japan and London, Brown and Goldstein discovered that animals with the defective LDL gene can actually create more cholesterol-carrying particles than those with normal receptors.

Research Teamwork Rewarded

This article was written by Gayle Golden, science writer for *The Dallas Morning News.*

Texas research received its first homegrown Nobel prize as a result of an unusual, close-knit collaboration between Drs. Joseph L. Goldstein and Michael S. Brown. Their partnership — born nearly 20 years ago and nurtured since 1972 with steady support from the University of Texas Health Science Center in Dallas — is still so close that the team is simply called "Joe-Mike" by their colleagues.

And when they accepted the Nobel Prize for Medicine or Physiology in Stockholm in December 1985, their loyalty to each other broke 85 years of tradition. Customarily, when Nobels are given to two scientists, the senior researcher delivers the after-dinner acceptance speech. Brown and Goldstein shared the lectern.

Goldstein was born April 18, 1940, in Sumter, S.C. In 1962, he earned a bachelor of science at Washington and Lee University in Lexington, Va., and immediately headed to Southwestern Medical School in Dallas. There, in 1966, he was awarded the Ho Din Award, the school's highest academic honor, and earned the respect of faculty who would later lure him back to the medical school.

Brown, a native of New York, was born on April 13, 1941. In 1962, he earned a bachelor of arts degree from the University of Pennsylvania, where he stayed on another four years to complete his medical degree. During his medical studies, he earned the prestigious Frederick L. Packard Prize in Internal Medicine.

The two met at Massachusetts General Hospital in Boston, where they were both interns and residents from 1966 to 1968. They shared a keen interest in medical genetics and metabolic research. Following their residencies, they both went to the National Institutes of Health in Bethesda, Md., where they pursued work that would lay the foundation for their later studies of how cells remove cholesterol from the bloodstream. During that two-year period at NIH from 1968 to 1970, Brown worked as a clinical associate in the Digestive and Hereditary Disease Branch of the National Institute of Arthritis and Metabolic Diseases. Goldstein, meanwhile, was a clinical associate in the National Heart Institute's Laboratory of Biochemical Genetics.

In 1970, with Brown staying in Bethesda to become a guest researcher at the Laboratory of Biochemistry at the National Heart Institute, Goldstein moved to Seat-tle. There, as a special National Institutes of Health fellow in the Division of Medical Genetics at the University of Washington School of Medicine, he investigated the problem of hereditary high cholesterol.

Working with a small group of scientists, Goldstein studied 500 heart patients, admitted to 10 hospitals in Seattle, along with the patients' 2,520 family members. They found that 31 percent of the patients had either high amounts of cholesterol or triglycerides or both, and four percent had a genetic condition called familial hypercholesterolemia. The research linked high cholesterol levels with high mortality, and indicated the connection may be genetically based.

In 1971, Brown moved to Dallas with his wife, Alice, to become a member of the faculty of Southwestern Medical School. One year later, Goldstein joined him, lured back to Southwestern to become head of the Division of Medical Genetics. The two have worked together ever since, along with other collaborators at the UT Health Science Center in Dallas.

"The two of them work together excellently," said Dr. Donald W. Seldin, the chairman of internal medicine at Southwestern who helped lure Goldstein to Dallas. "All the work they've done has been together. Everything. Both are brilliant clinicians."

In addition to the Nobel, the two have won numerous accolades for their work, including the Louisa Gross Horwitz Prize from Columbia University, the Award for Distinguished Research in the Biomedical Sciences from the Association of American Medical Colleges, the Research Achievement Award from the American Heart Association, the V.D. Mattia Award given annually by the Roche Institute of Molecular Biology. Other honors include the Heinrich Weiland Prize, the Pfizer Award from the American Chemical Society, the Albion O. Bernstein M.D. Award from the New York State Medical Society, the Passano Award, the Lounsbery Award from the U.S. National Academy of Sciences, the Gairdner Foundation International Award, the New York Academy of Sciences Award in Biological and Medical Sciences, the Lita Annenberg Hazen Award, the 3M Award from the Federation of American Societies for Experimental Biology and the William Allan Award from the American Society of Human Genetics.

This discovery was made by studying a special breed of rabbits from Japan — known as the "Watanabe heritable hyperlipidemic" rabbits, named after Yoshio Watanabe of Kobe University School of Medicine, who discovered the breed in 1978. Because of a faulty gene, those rabbits produce less than five percent of the normal LDL receptors. From the time of birth, they have a large amount of cholesterol circulating in their bloodstreams, and sometimes have heart attacks by the age of two. Normal rabbits never have heart attacks.

By radioactively tagging LDLs, and injecting the particles into the Watanabe rabbits, the researchers discovered that the animals' cells also could not take up another type of particle — known as an intermediate-density lipoprotein, or IDL. As a result, free-floating IDLs in the bloodstream soon became cholesterol-carrying LDLs. And so, they showed, the genetic impairment actually creates more cholesterol-carrying particles in the bloodstream than normal, leading to an even greater danger of atherosclerosis.

Currently, patients with familial hypercholesterolemia can benefit from two drugs, which Brown and Goldstein's work has helped to identify and explain. One such drug, cholestyramine, has been used by doctors for more than 20 years to lower cholesterol levels in the bloodstream. The other is mevinolin, an experimental drug that is much more powerful. The drugs work by stimulating the production of LDL receptors while preventing cells from making their own cholesterol. When used together, the drugs have shown promising results in patients who have one copy of a faulty receptor gene. Clinical trials conducted at the University of Texas Health Science Center at Dallas, as well as in other laboratories around the world, have so far shown no serious side effects, but the number of patients who have taken the drugs is still quite small.

But the drugs cannot help patients with two of the faulty genes because usually in those cases patients have no way to manufacture any receptors. One answer may be surgery. Three years ago, a team of physicians performed a liver transplant on a six-year-old child from Cumby, Texas, Stormie Jones, who had this condition. The patient could then rely on at least some receptors in the healthy liver. Because of her advanced heart disease, Miss Jones needed a heart transplant as well. Following the surgery, Miss Jones has been free of symptoms from her inherited illness. But she must take drugs to prevent her body from rejecting the transplanted organs.

Brown and Goldstein's research has helped a relatively small number of diseased patients, but, nevertheless, it has had widespread impact.

Because of their work, gains have been made in other areas of science. Organic chemists are fascinated by the LDL receptor's complex structure. Biophysicists have studied the way cholesterol helps form cell membranes. And when Brown and Goldstein discovered the LDL receptors, they changed the way researchers thought about how blood and cells interact. Since then, at least 15 other cell receptors have been identified, including those that transport substances such as iron, vitamin B-12, insulin, growth factors and antibodies.

Finally, their work has enriched the public's understanding of good health by shedding light on the potentially harmful effects of a diet rich in cholesterol. Their studies have shown that cholesterol-rich diets create more LDL in the bloodstream, and that the ability to get rid of that dangerous cholesterol slows with age. In childhood and the early adult years, humans make three or four times the number of LDL receptors they have at birth — partly because they eat so much cholesterol, but also because of hormonal effects. But as age increases, the number of receptors decreases. Most middle-age Americans have enough cholesterol in their blood to put them at risk for atherosclerosis.

Brown and Goldstein say they suspect that a high-cholesterol diet slows production of LDL receptors and thus further hampers the body's ability to sweep cholesterol from the blood. Experiments with rabbits and dogs, fed with cholesterol, show that effect. If initial studies show this to be true for humans, it may be that people should eat much less cholesterol than they do now. Indeed, to avoid atherosclerosis people might need to completely avoid dairy products, including eggs, and severely restrict how much meat or other saturated fats they eat. But Brown and Goldstein say such radical dietary changes aren't necessary for everyone, and that a proper diet depends on a person's genetic make-up.

More recently, Brown and Goldstein have speculated that drugs for stimulating LDL receptors might also help patients whose cholesterol-rich diets have caused dangerous build-up of plaque in their arteries, even though those patients have two normal genes for mak-ing the LDL receptor. Indeed, a recent paper has shown that mevinolin will lower blood cholesterol levels in these people. Mevinolin may not be available for general use until 1988 or 1989, however. Yet if the current studies about the drug are successful, it may prove true the prediction of the Nobel committee when announcing the award to Brown and Goldstein: "It may one day be possible for many people to have their steak and eat it too."

Working with the researchers are several molecular biologists and other researchers at the University of Texas Health Science Center at Dallas, including Drs. Richard G.W. Anderson, David W. Russell, David Bilheimer and Scott Grundy. Collaboration also has come from young researchers from more than a dozen countries, who have come to the Dallas laboratories to work with Brown and Goldstein for periods of two to five years each. These countries include Japan, India, Hong Kong, Germany, Austria, Australia, Ceylon, Spain, Finland, Norway, Taiwan, Romania and Israel.

Biotechnology Moves to the Market

This article was written by Gayle Golden, a science writer for *The Dallas Morning News*.

Since 1980, Texans have turned to biotechnology, both for medical and agricultural applications, as a way of diversifying and strengthening the state's economy.

Their dream is based on scientific techniques developed in the early 1970s, which allow researchers to identify and manipulate genetic material through laboratory cloning. Developed 15 years ago, those technologies can lead to new drugs, more productive plants or perhaps healthier breeds of livestock.

Biotechnology is, however, a broader term when it comes to industrial development. It can refer to producing new ways of diagnosing illness, machines to aid surgeons or improved artificial limbs. In light of scientific breakthroughs in these areas, and in genetic cloning, some experts estimate the market for biotechnology products will expand to between $120 billion and

Biotechnology

$200 billion nationwide by the end of the century.

Currently Texas has only a slim part of the market, with fewer than five percent of all biotechnology companies in the United States. Yet the state's medical and agricultural research amounts to millions of dollars each year. And to tap that, various regions of the state — including Dallas, Houston and San Antonio — have organized local ventures backed by private investors to develop markets for that research. The state also is supporting the effort. In 1985, the Texas Legislature allocated $35 million to state universities as part of an Advanced Technology Research Program, with roughly $11 million given to biotechnology research — funding projects at the Texas A&M Agricultural Experiment Station, Texas A&M University, North Texas State University, University of Houston-University Park and the University of Texas at Austin. Also across the state, a host of smaller biotechnology projects are in progress at several universities. Those projects range from developing soils that can tolerate pesticides to freeze-drying animal tissue to genetically altering cattle to produce low-fat beef.

Houston was one of the first areas to explore the biotechnology potential from research in the Texas Medical Center, where many of the 22 institutions, representing a capital investment of $155 million, conduct research. In 1983, investors formed BCM Technologies, Inc., designed to identify, evaluate and commercialize research from the Baylor College of Medicine. Since then, BCM has negotiated licensing agreements for five projects at the medical school, including a diagnostic test to detect nicotine in a person's system. Company officials think the test will be useful for insurance companies evaluating rates for smokers.

In 1985, BCM formed two separate companies: Cardiovascular System, Inc., which manufactures a machine for purifying and recirculating a patient's blood during surgery, and Oncos, Ltd., a joint venture with Phillips 66 Biosciences Corp., to make test kits for diagnosing cancer. Those cancer diagnostic kits use monoclonal antibodies, which are genetically engineered substances that can interact with cancer cells without disturbing normal cells.

At the University of Texas Health Science Center-Houston, a special Institute for Technology Development and Assessment was established in 1985 to identify and help patent biomedical research. One year later, the institute helped form LifeCell, Inc., with $5 million in venture capital from in and out of Texas, to market a novel technique for freeze-drying animal cells. This technique is primarily useful for scientists who want to study animal cells in the laboratory, but it may one day be used for storing human organs. Already, the method has worked with corneas in animals. The company has also negotiated several licensing agreements for technologies that include dental devices and "genetic probes," or tests that can diagnose disease by identifying the genetic material linked with that disease.

In Dallas, $12 million has been donated from private sources to form the Dallas Biomedical Corporation, a firm designed to help commercialize some of the more than 700 research projects at UT Health Science Center Dallas. The corporation, directed by A. Devon Giacalone, was formed in 1986 largely as a result of a special biotechnology task force established two years earlier by Dallas Mayor A. Starke Taylor to investigate ways of attracting biomedical industries to Dallas.

Within its first year, Dallas Biomedical funded two projects, including a new drug that supresses the immune system enough to prevent transplant patients from rejecting their new organs. The drug, developed by UT Health Science Center Drs. Richard Wasserman and Michael Charley, would have fewer side effects and a shorter dose time than other anti-rejection treatments. Another of Dallas Biomedical's projects is a test to identify people who are genetically predisposed to high cholesterol levels and heart disease. The genetic probe, developed by Drs. Jennifer Cuthbert and Peter Lipsky, grew from the work of UT Health Science Center researchers Joseph Goldstein and Michael Brown, who won the 1985 Nobel Prize in Medicine for identifying the mechanism and the gene responsible for cholesterol metabolism. The corporation also plans to form small companies to bring other products to the market.

Also in Dallas, biotechnology projects are ongoing at the Wadley Institutes, which has applied for a patent on one of several types of cancer-fighting interferon. At North Texas State University, three biologists — Gerard A. O'Donovan, Robert C. Benjamin and David A. Bencini — were awarded $285,000 from the Texas Legislature's Advanced Technology Research Fund to develop a genetically engineered microorganism that would enhance soil's ability to break down pesticides and other undesirable compounds. And at the University of Texas at Dallas, biologists are working with funds from the National Institutes of Health to develop "hybrid toxins," or genetically altered poisons, which may one day be able to attack and kill cancer cells.

San Antonio's effort in biotechnology began in 1983, when business leaders shifted from an emphasis on developing high-tech computer industries to the biosciences — a move that began after San Antonio lost to Austin in the bid for Microelectronics Computer Technology Corporation. The redirected effort received support from Mayor Henry Cisneros' Target 90 project, a citywide effort to organize San Antonio's research into lucrative ventures. In March 1984, business leaders established the Texas Research and Technology Foundation to support the biosciences. The foundation has members from the city's leading research facilities, including Southwest Foundation for Biomedical Research, the Southwest Research Institute, the University of Texas Health Science Center, the University of Texas at San Antonio, Trinity University, St. Mary's University and the University of Texas System.

Soon after the foundation was formed, the UT Board of Regents agreed it would establish an institute for biotechnology in San Antonio if land was available. In 1986, 1,500 acres was donated by Tom Pawel, through the Concord Oil Co. And in early 1987, the group got its biggest financial boost when Dallas billionaire H. Ross Perot donated $15 million to their bioscience effort. An additional $10 million has been raised locally.

In 1986, the foundation published an inventory identifying 42 marketable research projects at the various institutions. Among the chief projects are research on AIDS, work on artificial cells that might reduce the time it takes to heal bone fractures, development of lasers that might diagnose cancer cells and ultrasound images that might improve the fit of artificial limbs. Also, an estimated $10 million each year comes into San Antonio institutions from 40 pharmaceutical companies that use the city's hospitals for conducting clinical trials on drug products.

Austin's technology base has focused more on electronics than biosciences, but that is changing. In 1987, the city's chamber of commerce targeted biotechnology as one of 10 industries to develop over the next decade. The chamber has organized a committee of industry specialists and scientists from the UT-Austin and the nearby UT's Science Park in Smithville, which is investigating the market for Austin.

Texas A&M University in College Station established an Institute of Biosciences and Technology in 1986, and expects a $24 million headquarters to be built by 1990 in the Texas Medical Center in Houston. Another $30 million facility for biotechnology is expected to be built on the main campus as well. The institute will be devoted completely to research and will sponsor work in comparative veterinary medicine, bioengineering and nutrition as well as biotechnology, according to its director Eugene Sander, who is also Texas A&M's vice chancellor for biotechnology development.

Elsewhere around the state, various biotechnology projects are producing interesting results.

In El Paso, local private money has funded research at the University of Texas at El Paso to explore whether biological substances can improve the productivity of oil wells. The researchers discovered a "surfactant," or a soap-like material produced by bacteria, that can be pumped into an oil well to increase its productivity. In 1986, researchers at Texas A&I University

in Kingsville were awarded $285,752 by the National Science Foundation to use monoclonal antibody technology to identify, isolate and the purify proteins that are found in snake venom. The results of their studies will broaden the understanding of venom composition and toxicity.

One of the most concentrated biotechnology efforts in the state has been at the Texas A&M Agricultural Experiment Station in College Station, where biotechnology research amounts to about $13 million each year from federal and state sources. Under the direction of the experiment station's director Neville P. Clarke, the research has focused on eight areas, all of which use genetic engineering techniques. Those areas are to produce plants that can tolerate drought, improve the nutritional value of plants, make enzymes or hormones, control insects with biological materials, diagnose disease, produce safer food, develop vaccines and reproduce livestock more efficiently.

Under Clarke's direction, the projects have been directed to Texas' agricultural needs. For example, researchers are working on ways to detect, and to immunize against, brucellosis — a contagious, fever-causing bacterium that is present in about 2,000 cattle herds in Texas. In unpasteurized dairy products, the infection can be passed to humans.

By studying the genetics of proteins on the surface of the brucellosis cells, researchers are working on vaccines that can enter the cell and kill it from within. If successful, that would be an improvement over current vaccines, which produce antibodies in the animal's bloodstream that are indistinguishable from antibodies caused by the disease itself — a problem for screening infected foods.

Researchers at the experiment station are also working on a way to produce leaner livestock, or "light beef," as it has been coined. Already, the scientists have identified the biochemistry involved in depositing fat in animal muscle and are now studying the genetic properties that control those reactions. The hope is to one day genetically engineer cattle genes that produce less fat.

If "light beef" is successful, it will be because of the ability to add or subtract genetic material to newly conceived embryos. A pioneering company exploiting "embryo transfer" technologies is Granada Genetics, Inc., in Marquez. The company, which grossed $11 million in 1986 and manages yearly research amounting to $8 million, routinely freezes embryos of prime cattle and ships those to breeders across the country. Also, by splitting cells within a week-old embryo, the company has created triplets — all with the identical genetic make-up. The company is also using genetic probes to determine the sex of an embryo. The sex-typing technique may substantially decrease the cost of producing milk if it routinely produces female offspring.

Research Makes Shrimp a Cash Crop

The article below was written by the Texas Almanac staff from information furnished by George W. Chamberlain, Associate Aquaculture Specialist with the Texas A&M University Research and Extension Center in Corpus Christi.

Texas' latest up-and-coming cash crop doesn't grow in the ground. It is a hard-shelled, bug-eyed little critter that swims in the ocean — shrimp.

Up to now, our supply of the luscious crustaceans has been subject to the vagaries of weather, ocean currents and international politics. U.S. demand for shrimp has far outstripped domestic supplies, and we currently import about 75 percent of the shrimp we consume. That demand is expected to continue to rise, with no concomitant increase in supplies from traditional

Aquaculture

shrimping. The U.S. trade deficit for imported shrimp reached a record $1.4 billion in 1986. **Aquaculture,** the cultivation of aquatic plants and animals, could help balance this growing trade deficit.

Texas A&M University conducts what has become the largest non-private shrimp aquaculture research program in the nation. With funding from the federal Sea Grant program, **Dr. Jack Parker** initiated the program in 1969. Parker's research team started by catching juvenile shrimp in bays and transferring them to small "grow-out" ponds to mature to marketable size. Parker's group soon found this method to be impracti-

cal, since it was dependent on the availability of wild shrimp. And they also discovered that a species of shrimp not native to U.S. waters performed better in ponds than did the native shrimp from the Gulf. Of course, the gathering of nonindigenous juvenile shrimp every growing season would be totally unfeasible. The Texas A&M team concluded that, to have a viable industry, they would have to be able to control the entire reproductive cycle.

Progress was slow until a shrimp reproduction laboratory was built in 1980 through a cooperative program between Texas A&M University and Central Power and Light Company. This laboratory quickly demonstrated that the desired species of shrimp could be induced to spawn — albeit sporadically — during any season of the year. This was a critical step toward commercialization.

The risk facing the first commercial shrimp farm in Texas was very high, because it was necessary to build a complex reproduction and larval rearing facility as well as outdoor grow-out ponds. Dr. Parker, who initiated the A&M program, resigned in 1980 to develop this first farm, Laguna Madre Shrimp Farms, near Bayview. After a cautious, pilot-scale beginning, this project was expanded to a mid-1987 size of 520 acres of grow-out ponds and a large, highly productive reproduction and larval-rearing facility. Surplus postlarval shrimp (baby shrimp about half an inch long) are now sold by the Laguna Madre hatchery and others. "A shrimp farmer starting out today can buy his postlarvae and concentrate on the less complicated 'grow out' phase of the operation," says **George W. Chamberlain**, an Aquaculture Specialist for the Texas Agricultural Extension Service in Corpus Christi.

Grow-out ponds in Texas currently range in size from half an acre to 120 acres. As of mid-1987, there were five major commercial farms operating, and there were several pilot projects utilizing saline artesian water. Several more projects were planned or under construction. Chamberlain estimates that Texas shrimp farms produced roughly 400,000 pounds of tails in 1984.

For comparison, in 1987, Florida had one hatchery; South Carolina had three grow-out farms and a research facility; Louisiana had one grow-out farm; California had one shrimp farm; and Hawaii had three.

About 24 Central American, South American and Caribbean countries cultivate shrimp. Ecuador is the acknowledged leader, having exported 62 million pounds of shrimp, most of which was farm-raised, to the U.S. during 1986. The other 23 Latin American shrimp-farming countries produce lesser amounts.

Traditionally, these countries have relied on labor-intensive techniques inappropriate for use in the U.S., i.e., collecting wild postlarvae from the bays and growing them out in ponds. Last year Ecuador and Peru experienced a drastic shortage of wild postlarvae, and shrimp farmers there now realize the importance of hatchery technology. "It is satisfying," says Chamberlain, "to see U.S. hatcheries selling postlarvae to Ecuador, because Ecuador is by far the leader in farm-raised shrimp production and we have had to buy from them for years."

While most of the Texas' shrimp-cultivation facilities are located on the Gulf Coast, there are some experimental projects along the Pecos River in West Texas, hundreds of miles from ocean water. These facilities use water from saline aquifers, but this type of operation is still in the pilot-scale stage of commercial development. "There are many 'ifs,'" says Chamberlain.

"The water must be not only salty, but of the right composition. There has to be enough water and an appropriate place to discharge the water once it has been used in the shrimp ponds. Soil must be impermeable for the construction of leak-proof ponds. Although there are streaks of clay in West Texas, a lot of the soil there is sandy."

Even along the coast, choosing a suitable site for a shrimp hatchery or farm is not simple. Although the composition of sea water is almost constant worldwide and the discharge of salty water back into a salty bay is no problem, there is still the problem of finding clay soil for the ponds along a mostly sandy coastline. The ponds cannot be located in the protected marshes and wetlands, and they cannot be placed where pesticide runoff from agricultural operations will contaminate the water. "By the time you satisfy all those requirements," says Chamberlain, "your choices are very few."

A major worry in the fledging Texas shrimp-farming industry is that shrimp cultivation is increasing rapidly in the world's tropical areas, notably Central and South America and Southeast Asia. Chamberlain says that much of this production is targeted for the U.S. market because the U.S. is the world's leading shrimp consumer. If this increased supply drives shrimp prices down, the profitability of Texas farms could be adversely affected. Whether shrimp farming proves to be a money-maker on the Texas coast or not depends heavily on shrimp prices' remaining fairly stable while advances in technology cause production costs to drop.

"We don't know exactly what the future is going to bring," says Chamberlain. "But unless there is a drastic drop in shrimp prices, we have a strong feeling that the aquaculture industry will continue to expand at a very high rate until at least 1990. What happens after that is hard to predict."

Chamberlain believes that if Texas shrimp farmers can duplicate A&M's research results and the results of commercial shrimp farmers in other parts of the world, Texas will have a new industry on its hands, one with a very bright future.

Plant Resources Center Started Small

This article was written by Georg Zappler, publications editor, Texas Memorial Museum, The University of Texas at Austin.

The rapidly vanishing plant diversity of the forests, prairies, plains, deserts and mountains of Texas, as well as the flora of the Southwest, Mexico and tropical Latin America, have found a permanent refuge among some 1 million plant specimen sheets at the Plant Resources Center at the University of Texas at Austin.

This rich research collection of dried plant materials, ranked fifth in North America, had humble beginnings in 1904. Today's $6 million collection grew from a prize-winning forestry exhibit of less than 2,000 voucher specimens submitted by the state to the Louisiana Purchase Exhibit in 1902.

Botany

The UT Herbarium, initially under the care of Dr. William Bray, experienced a significant period of enrichment when Dr. Mary S. Young was appointed caretaker in 1912. Originally hired in 1910 as lecturer in botany, Dr. Young was soon placed in charge of plant taxonomy (identification and classification of plants) as well as the herbarium collection. From her first days in Austin, she tramped the countryside to collect a full representation of the local flora for use in her lab classes and for preservation in the herbarium. Her collecting excursions, on which she usually took along interested botany students, began to range throughout Central Texas, including trips by train to Granite Mountain, San Marcos, New Braunfels and other locales. However, the unique flora of the Trans-Pecos region intrigued her. With meager funding from the university and accompanied only by a student helper, she spent her summer vacations from 1914 to 1918 exploring and collecting plant materials in the wildest and most undeveloped part of the state. Her ultimate destinations — ranging from Texas' western mountain crags and canyons to the desert scrub of the Big Bend region and the eroded cliffs of the High Plains' eastern escarpment — were far removed from convenient transportation. Dr. Young's solution was to travel with mules,

sometimes with an old wagon. Braving sun and heat, meager rations and bad water, and the mostly unpredictable behavior of her mules, she brought back hundreds of plant specimens for the collection. Until her death in 1919, she added thousands of specimens to the herbarium, not only through her own collecting efforts, but through the exchange of duplicates with individuals and with other herbaria.

The next person to help UT's Herbarium grow significantly was Dr. Benjamin Tharp, a one-time student of Dr. Young's. Inspired by her teaching and example, he became the state's leading plant ecologist. His extensive studies of Texas' uniquely diversified flora led to his publication, in 1939, of the first definitive zonation of the state's different vegetation regions. The arrangement is still in use today. Dr. Tharp saw to the expansion of the herbarium collection, even though the discipline declined at the school before World War II.

In 1953, Dr. Billie L. Turner, the present director of what is now the Plant Resources Center, took over from Dr. Tharp the teaching of taxonomy and the curatorship of the herbarium, which by that time had grown to contain about 150,000 specimens. Under Dr. Turner's leadership as an internationally reputed plant systematist, the collection expanded to become the central resource base upon which all studies on the native flora, as well as the introduced flora of Texas and adjoining regions, have come to depend.

When, in 1974, Dr. C. Longworth Lundell, a leading Texas botanist and a great philanthropist, donated his celebrated collection, valued at $3.6 million to the UT Herbarium, the number of specimens almost doubled — from about 500,000 to more than 900,000. The two herbaria became merged as the Plant Resources Center.

The Lundell sheets, which include many rare and exotic plants, not only beautifully complemented the original holdings of the herbarium, but they also expanded the collection's geographic range into previously only poorly represented areas of tropical Latin America, especially the Yucatan Peninsula and Guatemala, two areas extensively collected by Dr. Lundell.

In 1978, a monument to four-and-a-half centuries of scholarship in the world of leaf, bud and blossom also became part of the Plant Resources Center's holdings.

Dr. and Mrs. Lundell donated their outstanding collection of 5,000 books and manuscripts from many countries and covering the entire history of botany to the university. The library is housed at the Harry H. Ransom Center for the Humanities in a specially built, Williamsburg-style room. Among the library's treasures are a 1547 work in Latin by a German botanist and a large group of 18th century books by Carolus Linnaeus, the father of scientific biological classification. The official archives of the Botanical Society of America, with original manuscripts going back to 1894, also are a part of this invaluable repository.

The Plant Resources Center was relocated to the Main Building in 1984. The center is now completely self-contained on three separate, but adjacent, floors specifically designed for efficient storage and for herbarium operations. The administrative center of the complex is a large room with an ornate ceiling, elegant panelling and tall windows.

An impressive bank of high metal cabinets separated from the administrative area contains specimens of two important plant families — the oak and sunflower groups. The rest of the collection, also arranged by family and numbering more than 900,000 herbarium sheets, is housed on two levels filled from floor to ceiling with special storage cabinets. Cubicles for research and study line the edges of both stack areas. A central area on the lower level serves for the main work of the herbarium. Included are office space, a processing room with press-drying equipment, workroom for preparing herbarium sheets, a sorting area for the handling of interinstitutional loans, and a deep-freeze facility. Collected specimens that come in are either already dried or they are dried in a plant press in the processing area. They are then glued, sewn or taped onto acid-free paper sheets for storage. All pertinent data, such as the collector's name, the exact locality and date of collection, and the scientific name of the specimen are noted on each sheet. These sheets are then stored in an appropriate cabinet depending on the specimen's systematic position. The deep freeze is used to kill insect pests, by freezing infested sheets at minus 40 degrees Celsius for eight or more hours, and also to freeze some seeds for possible germination in the future.

Exchange programs continue to be important to expanding the collection. About 50 institutions exchange duplicate specimens with the Plant Resources Center. For example, in 1985, some 5,000 specimens were added to the collection in this manner. Another activity at the herbarium involves interinstitutional loans, an essential component of worldwide botanical research. In 1985, some 20,000 specimens were received on loan for study purposes, and about 5,000 were sent out. At any given time, the Plant Resources Center usually maintains about 50,000 loan specimens. Modern computerization has added to the research value of the collection. Special programs are being developed by Dr. Guy Nesom, curator of the center, that make it possible to retrieve information on the past and present geographic ranges of a given species. This information can be displayed graphically on a screen by way of a detailed map for any area desired.

The Plant Resources Center is more than a storage depot for dried plants. The research programs that originate here make available to environmental and

Dr. Billie Turner, director of the Plant Resources Center, looks over part of the huge collection of plant samples available for research. Photo courtesy of UT-Austin.

agricultural scientists, as well as the lay public, information on the location of different plant species, their places in the ecosystem, their breeding behavior and their interrelationships, chromosome structure and chemical make-up. All this data is not only of academic interest, but is vitally important for the undertaking of meaningful environmental programs and the development of new varieities of economically important crops, such as sunflowers and pinto beans.

As director of the Plant Resources Center, Professor Turner also is dedicated to saving remnants of the New World's once rich and diverse ecosystems. He believes that about all that can be done is to collect the plant species that are about to disappear. These are preserved as specimens for future study and for viewing by future generations. There also is the hope that the seeds or other reproductive structures of some of the these endangered species could be preserved for propagation in gardens or greenhouses in the future.

Botany Department at UT-Austin Top Rated

This article was written by Georg Zappler, publications editor, Texas Memorial Museum, The University of Texas at Austin.

[Editor's Note: The most recent (1983) survey of 83 graduate departments in botany across the nation has ranked the Department of Botany of the University of Texas at Austin in first place (in a draw with the University of California at Davis). The assessment, made by college professors and called the Lindzey-Jones Report, based its evaluation on 16 criteria. These included the scope, caliber and amount of significant research conducted and published by the faculty and graduate body, the effectiveness of teaching programs, the level of university and outside grant support, and the physical resources of the department, such as plant collections, university and departmental reference libraries, and laboratory space and equipment.]

Created in 1899, the Department of Botany at the University of Texas has held a national reputation for several decades. Its graduates hold positions in most of the nation's most prestigious universities. A faculty of

some 20 professors teaches and trains about 60 graduate students working toward advanced degrees. The department is known for its strength in most of the classical and modern botanical disciplines. Outstanding research has been and is being conducted in the evolutionary systematics and speciation of plants, plant chemistry, cell and membrane biochemistry, plant genetics, cell ultra-structure, physiology, ecology, biotechnology, plant geography and ethnobotany. A uniquely high percentage (about 95 percent) of the faculty is funded by grants from federal sources (such as the National Science Foundation, the U.S. Department of Agriculture, the National Aeronautics and Space Administration and the National Institutes of Health) along with state and private foundation moneys.

Members of the department have received numerous honors for outstanding accomplishments and serve as officers of the major national and international bo tanical societies. Faculty members also serve as editors of the key journals of their disciplines, serve as members of panels for the major federal granting agencies, and have authored many of the "state of the art" textbooks and reference works in the field of botany.

The present success of the botany department has more than fulfilled the hopes of Thomas D. Wooten when in 1892 as president of the board of regents he pleaded for a full professorship in botany, nine years after the creation of the university. In agrarian Texas, Wooten hit a sympathetic chord with the argument, "Botany . . . should be taught by a specialist in charge of a distinct school because it is one of the most practical of the modern sciences . . . Wherever crops are raised or grass grown, wherever farms are cultivated or gardens planted, there the problems solved by the Science of Botany can be put to immediate and practical use . . ."

Actually, the regents had planned for a professor of botany and natural history to be on the original faculty in 1885, but no one was appointed to that position. In fact, the first courses in botany were offered as a sideline by the School of Geology until 1891 when the School of Biology, encompassing botany along with zoology, was created.

The fledgling botany department took wing in 1899, when the School of Biology was separated into two distinct entities: the schools of botany and of animal biology. Botany courses also were offered at the School of Medicine in Galveston as part of the pharmacy program.

By the early 1900s, a full range of offerings in botany had been developed and progress was made in studying the state's vegetation, especially in regard to its relationship to the soils of various regions. The main research effort focused on problems associated with the growth of cotton.

In 1920, the School of Botany became a department and, by 1926, had moved its quarters to the newly completed Biological Laboratories Building and adjoining greenhouses. Bacteriology was added to the curriculum, and with the growth of medical research and the development of food processing, emphasis shifted away from the plant sciences. When the College of Pharmacy moved to the campus in 1927, a joint Department of Botany and Bacteriology was formed.

The death of several key research botanists in the 1940s devastated the department, though the Herbarium under Professor Benjamin Thorp continued to expand.

After World War II, Dr. W. Gordon Whaley led the rejuvenation of the study of botany at UT. This brilliant, 32-year-old plant geneticist and agronomist was recruited in 1946. Whaley was made director of the Cotton Research Investigation Program that was to be expanded into the much broader Plant Research Institute. There, he initiated research in the productivity of maize, arid land use, grass rangeland management and the mechanisms of gene action in hybrid plants. Whaley was appointed chairman when the new Department of Botany was formed in 1949. He hired new members to the faculty with an eye to varied educational backgrounds and research interests. The emphasis on quality and breadth of research set high and lasting standards for the department, which was recognized for steady improvement. By 1965, it was listed eighth in the nation; by 1969, fifth; and, by 1983, first.

The 1950s were exciting times for botany at UT. Basic research activities moved into important new directions, and the department began to take its historically important and continuing role in shaping the university's overall teaching program in the biological sciences. Basic research was expanded, and the department moved into new facilities. An electron microscope laboratory was established as a university facility, and Dr. Whaley began his research into plant cell structures, particularly the Golgi apparatus, an organelle important in cell secretion, until then seen and studied only in animal cells.

In 1962, Dr. Harold C. Bold, an eminent researcher on algae, took over the department chairmanship from Dr. Whaley, who since 1957, had been carrying the responsibilities of the department along with new duties as Dean of the Graduate School. Dr. Whaley held this position for 15 years until his appointment as Ashbel Smith Professor of Cellular Biology. He died unexpectedly in 1983, at age 68.

In 1964, the Plant Research Institute was renamed the Cell Research Institute and became an autonomous research facility still under the direction of Dr. Whaley. Dr. Billie Turner replaced Dr. Bold as department chairman in 1967.

An outstanding faculty was recruited and maintained through these years.

The 1970s witnessed the maturation of much of the research whose groundwork had been laid earlier, as well as the addition of key faculty instrumental in expanding the scope of botanical investigation in the areas of physiology, paleobotany, cell biology, genetics and ecology. Also a number of the "old guard" retired, making room for a new generation of leaders in their respective fields.

An important new facility, a mass spectrometry laboratory for research in phytochemistry, was added to the department. The UT Herbarium received not only the Lundell Library — one of the nation's finest rare book and manuscript collections covering the history of botany — but also the celebrated 400,000-sheet C. L. Lundell Herbarium to add to its already prestigious resources. The integrated herbaria became the Plant Resources Center, now totalling close to one million specimens, with Dr. Billie L. Turner as its director. Another development was the establishment, under the direction of Dr. Marshall C. Johnston, of the Rare Plant Study Center, which, although no longer active, served to stimulate botanical interest across the state in regard to the preservation of Texas' native and endangered plant species.

In 1974, the chairmanship of the department passed to Dr. Theodore Delevoryas, an authority on fossil plants, who had joined the faculty two years earlier. The end of the decade saw the retirement of Dr. Bold from active teaching.

The 1980s began with Dr. Tom J. Mabry's assumption of the departmental chairmanship. Through this period, the department continued to expand its reputation in plant chemistry (Dr. Mabry's specialty), evolutionary and systematic botany, research on algae and fungi (cryptogamic botany), plant physiology, cell biology and ecology. Also, the new discipline of "industrial botany" or plant biotechnology (i.e. the development of commercially important chemicals and other products from plants) has flourished under Dr. Mabry's continuing leadership and holds much promise for the coming years. Dr. Robert P. Adams, a biotechnologist and computer scientist, joined the department in 1981 specifically to help develop new programs in this new field. Dr. Adams is now Director of the Center for Famine and Alternative Agriculture at Baylor University.

Members of the department served as advisors to the National Wildflower Research Center — located just east of Austin and created by Mrs. Lyndon Johnson as her 70th birthday gift to the nation — from its inception. When, in 1984, Dr. David K. Northington, a specialist in the systematics and adaptive mechanisms of flowering plants, was appointed the center's director, he was also invited to join the botany faculty as adjunct professor.

In 1986, Dr. Mabry was succeeded in the department chairmanship by Dr. Stanley J. Roux, a recognized authority in plant physiology.

Another important program development has been the new Plant Cell Biology research facility on the third floor of Painter Hall. The program is under the direction of Dr. R. Malcolm Brown Jr., holder of the recently endowed Johnson and Johnson Centennial Chair in Plant Cell Biology. Dr. Brown (who joined the faculty in 1982) and an international team of scientists, post-doctoral researchers and graduate students are working on the biosynthesis of cellulose — that is, how to produce this essential component of paper, textiles and dozens of other important materials "from scratch" without having to cut down forests or harvest thousands of tons of cotton. Brown and his group have already helped clarify many of the mysteries of cellulose synthesis by studying a common cellulose-producing bacterium easy to grow in lab culture. The Plant Cell Biology unit is equipped with the most advanced optical and analytical processing systems available and includes cell-culture rooms, ultrasonic probes, a complete biochemistry lab, a seminar room and word-processing facilities.

Other work by Dr. Brown's group involves basic research on cloning, or the growth of whole plants from specially prepared single cells. These studies are important to the future of recombinant DNA research, popularly called genetic engineering. This exciting new field, whose practical aims are higher-yielding and disease-resistant crops, is one for which the department has ambitious long-range plans. The newly endowed D. J. Sibley Centennial Professorship in Plant Molecular Genetics has been created specifically for implementing these goals.

The department, through enlightened leadership and scientific excellence, has earned high national recognition. The challenge now is to maintain it.

Mount Livermore Cache Yields Many Mysteries

One mystery is usually enough for archaeologists. A cache of arrowheads found on top of Texas' second highest mountain, however, presents a series of questions that have developed over almost a century. The more it is studied, the more questions the Mount Livermore Cache raises.

Events were set in motion between A.D. 000-1500 when a people living in the Trans-Pecos deposited up to 2,000 arrowheads on Baldy Peak at the exact highest point of Mount Livermore.

There the points rested until a September day in 1895 when two Fort Davis area residents, T.A. Merrill and Charles C. Janes, climbed the rugged mountain on an afternoon outing and discovered a tall cairn — a rock monument. This they dismantled, apparently throwing many of the stones over the edge of a nearby cliff in the process. Beneath the monument they found the cache of arrowheads.

Archaeology

Between 1895 and 1906, Charles' mother, Susan Janes, organized six trips up the mountain looking for additional arrow points. An estimated 1,500 specimens were uncovered and exhibited in Mrs. Janes' private museum in Fort Davis.

The distinctive points, shaped like a tall, tapering pine tree with a wide base that gives the appearance of a cross, were used in defining what has been called the Livermore focus. And the discovery brought national scientific attention to Texas. Newspapers ran stories, and even the Smithsonian Institution sent a scientist to view the discovery. After the initial flurry of activity, however, interest cooled.

Efforts were made to recover arrowheads that had been carried off by relic hunters, and in 1929, Mrs. Janes donated the cache, along with other items of historical interest, to the West Texas Historical and Scientific Society.

Although arrowheads from the cache were displayed at several museums, seven years passed before Dr. J. Charles Kelley, an anthropologist and Curator of Archeology at Sul Ross State Teachers College (now University) in Alpine, did the first scientific study of the points. In 1936, he made a series of notes and photographs of the collection that have been invaluable to later archaeologists.

From his studies, Dr. Kelley postulated that the Livermore people were intrusive Plains dwellers who had visited the Trans-Pecos region between A.D. 900-1200. He attributed a bison-hunting tool kit to them. This interpretation was not well-received at the time, State Archeologist Robert Mallouf said. Many of the materials that Dr. Kelley used in his study were destroyed by a fire, and the next major scientific investigation was not made until 1981.

At this time, the state archeologist took the cache on loan from the Museum of the Big Bend at Sul Ross University in Alpine. The southern Trans-Pecos area had been studied by the Texas Historical Commission since 1973.

Between 1981 and 1986, descriptive records of each point, including detailed measurements, photographs and drawings, were made. Data were computerized to aid in analysis, and the techniques used by prehistoric flint knappers were being identified. The sources of the flint in the eastern Trans-Pecos also were located.

Even before the detailed study began, however, a series of questions perplexed investigators, Mallouf said. First, was the cairn under which the cache was found constructed by the prehistoric peoples or by a later surveyor? "Newspaper articles at the time speak refer to a surveyor," the archaeologist noted. If the prehistoric people built the cairn, or even if they didn't, how did they determine the exact highest point on the mountain to bury their cache of arrowheads? "It (the highest point) certainly isn't apparent from casual observation," Mallouf said.

A 450-year-old cannon from a Spanish shipwreck lies asunder at Texas A&M University after nautical archaeology researchers Jody Simmons, left, and Richard Haiduven split the 6-foot gun open. By sawing the weapon in half, the scholars hope to learn how to clean and preserve the inside of a number of other guns recovered from one of the oldest European shipwrecks in the New World.

Second, how contaminated is the cache? Arrowpoints much later than those from the Livermore focus are now part of the collection. But were these found at the site in the original cache, or have they been placed in the collection by mistake during exhibits at various museums? To determine which points were part of the original collection, efforts have been made to locate early photographs of the cache, but the oldest pictures obtained thus far were taken in the 1930s.

Even with the questions, a construction of the lifestyle of the people who made the Livermore points has been made. They were a nomadic people who were probably indigenous to the Trans-Pecos and lived between A.D. 500-1500. They were hunters, not agriculturalists, but whether they ventured far onto the Plains is questionable. Rarely are Livermore points found north of the Midland-Odessa area.

But Baldy Peak still intrigues. Evidence indicates that the cache was deposited between A.D. 900-1500. The materials are a ritual offering in the strictest sense, Mallouf said. But it is not known if the whole cache was deposited at one time, or if small groups of points were left periodically over a series of years. Also, no burials have been found on the mountain, nor has other ceremonial evidence, such as burned rock, been located.

A full report on the cache was released in late 1987 and is available from the Office of the State Archeologist, Texas Historical Commission, P.O. Box 12276, Austin 78711.

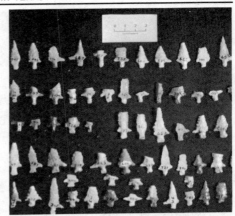

These are but a few of the arrowheads found on Mount Livermore. The distinctive shape used to define the Mount Livermore focus. Photo courtesy State Archeologist.

Unveiling the Panhandle's Buried City

One of Texas' newest archaeological sites also can be classed one of the oldest — and most interesting. The Buried City site southeast of Perryton in Ochiltree County was well-known by early settlers in the 1870s because of the impressive ruins visible above ground. Large mounds covering the ruins of stone dwellings along Wolf Creek and numerous artifacts to be found on the ground around the ruins attracted many visitors. Professor T. L. Eyerly of Canadian Academy in 1907 performed the first scientific excavation. Occasional surveys were made through 1966, but no major excavations probed the ruins.

In the early 1980s, however, Harold D. Courson of Perryton, president of Courson Oil and Gas Company, purchased the site and surrounding property and gave the Texas Historical Commission two conservation easements covering about 50 acres of land. The site also has been added to the National Register of Historic Places and is a State Archeological Landmark protected by the Texas Antiquities Code. Courson financed archaeological excavations in 1985 and 1986 that were directed by David Hughes, a doctoral candidate at the University of Oklahoma. A third excavation was made in conjunction with a Texas Archeological Society field school in the summer of 1987.

State Archeologist Robert Mallouf sees the current investigation of the Buried City as an important step toward understanding these early Plains Indians. After excavations in the early part of the century, he points out, the top two tiers of counties in the Panhandle have been virtually ignored by investigators, as has much of the Plains.

About seven areas of the Buried City including the ruins of about five dwellings have been excavated. None is on the conservation easement. Included in a 900-acre block of land around the easement are between 30 and 40 ruins along Wolf Creek. The latest surveys reveal a different picture of the people who inhabited the site between A.D. 800 and 1500 than earlier investigations had suggested. Previously it was thought that the site was inhabited by people of the Antelope Creek culture who populated much of the Panhandle during this period.

Archaeologist Hughes, however, thinks that the Buried City people were of a different culture, one that developed independently along Wolf Creek through several centuries, though with general Plains Indian characteristics.

Most outstanding of the features of the culture was the massive scale of the dwellings. One house, for example, had up to 650 square feet of floor space, a mansion among prehistoric dwellings.

The architecture, though compared to that of the Pueblo Indians of the Southwest and the Antelope Creek people, appears also to be of local development. Large caliche boulders mined from nearby valley walls were used to outline the rectangular structure. With the stones in place, the inside of the dwelling was dug out to a depth of up to two feet, with the fill being used to construct the one-to-two foot thick exterior walls to a height of up to four feet. Dirt benches, six to eight feet wide, ran along the north and south interior walls of the building, as did another bench across the west end. A center aisle 10 to 12 feet wide included a hearth. Wooden posts, 12 to 18 inches in diameter, were placed in each corner to form supports for the roof. The entrances, always facing east, were eight-to-ten foot long crawlways.

The people must have been energetic, for digging in the hard caliche was a difficult chore. In addition to excavating the houses, the people also dug numerous circular storage pits. These were three to four feet deep and apparently were used until they became rodent infested and then were filled with trash. The job was difficult indeed with only stone and bone tools.

Artifacts such as projectile points, stone knives and bone tools are similar to those produced by other Plains Indians of the period. But the pottery is much different from that of the Antelope Creek people. The Buried City people finished their pottery more smoothly and, in some cases, polished and ornamented it, in contrast to the cord-marked, conical-shaped pottery of the Antelope Creek culture. The pottery of the Buried City people resembles that called Geneceo from southwest Kansas, as do other aspects of the culture.

Though building stone was abundant, the Buried City inhabitants had to travel and trade for flint for tools. Some flint from the Alibates quarry, near present-day Borger, has been found, but Hughes thinks that much of the flint used at the Buried City was from cobbles and pebbles found along the Canadian River. Apparently the Buried City people were not friendly with the Antelope Creek folk who mined the Alibates quarry. Also there is little evidence of trade with Southwestern Indians or Mexico. Some flint appears to have come from a site in Kay County, Oklahoma, and from the Niobrara area between Kansas and Nebraska.

Few burials have been found. Early in the century, archaeologists reported that the dead were laid out on the canyon rim near the village and the bodies were covered with stone cairns (monuments). These graves had been disturbed by local visitors to the site before the latest excavations began.

Farming provided an important part of the Buried City people's diet. They raised corn, and Hughes thinks that squash and beans also were cultivated. These were basic crops of Plains Indians from A.D. 700-800 onward (as they had been in Mexico from about 500 B.C.). The people apparently had a two-tiered system of plots. Crops were planted in the flood plain of the creek, so that in dry weather advantage could be taken of the moisture retained in the sandy bottoms. Other fields

This is a view of the Kit Courson Ruin at the "Buried City" in Ochiltree County. The main room is about 29 feet long and 24.5 feet wide, large by prehistoric standards. Ruins at this site may have been occupied as early as the 12th century A.D. Photo courtesy David T. Hughes.

were planted on higher ground with water diverted along slopes with brush diversions to more widely distribute the rainfall. On the Plains, water from short, heavy rain showers runs off almost immediately unless the flow is impeded. These higher plots were safeguards against heavy rains washing out the lower fields.

In addition to the vegetables, the diet included meat. Bison were hunted as a staple, as were smaller animals, like rodents, rabbits and prairie dogs, and

Warship Located

No feature of the Republic of Texas was more important than its poverty. But the lack of funds has paid dividends for today's Texans. The *Zavala*, a steam-driven warship of the Republic, has been found in a watery grave in Galveston, where it was consigned because the Republic could not pay for its upkeep.

A year-and-a-half project culminated in November 1986 with the discovery of the ship buried in a warehouse district in Galveston. State money is not available to excavate the ship, J. Barto Arnold III, marine archaeologist for the Texas Antiquities Committee said. So private funds have been sought for the work.

Location of the ship was a joint project of the Texas Antiquities Committee and the National Underwater and Marine Agency, a private organization. Several months of research into old charts and other records preceeded the actual field work that turned up the ship. Once the general area of the craft was located, an electronic survey was used to pinpoint the ship. Samples from augering and borings, as well as test pits dug by a backhoe, confirmed the presence of the vessel.

fowl, such as ducks and turkeys, along with fish and mussels.

The climate of the area was probably similar to today's and more attractive for settlement. The region around the site was better watered because of the presence of many springs fed by the Ogallala aquifer. Wolf Creek cut into the upper level of the aquifer and, fed by the springs, flowed the year around.

Hughes thinks that the ruins represent a series of villages, or semi-permanent farmsteads, inhabited over several centuries. At least five groups of structures, with seven or eight dwellings per group, have been identified. Each group could have housed up to 100 people. Each group of dwellings would be inhabited for 20 years until some local resource, such as firewood, was exhausted. Then the people would move along the creek to another site to inhabit for a generation. This trek up and down the creek continued until the area was abandoned about A.D. 1500.

The influence from southwest Kansas on the Buried City people is throught to have come through trade and intermarriage. In small groups such as those at the Buried City, intratribal marriage becomes a problem, Hughes said. Therefore trade ties also could provide an avenue for bringing wives and husbands into the community.

In Hughes' hypothesis, the Buried City people were of Caddoan linguistic stock, and may have been akin to the historic Wichita or Pawnee Indians.

Much interpretive work remains to be done with the information developed from the most recent excavations. But first indications are that the Buried City people developed their own culture in relative isolation. Like today's Texans, they valued their independence.

Culture

The Arts In Texas

The following information on the fine arts in Texas was prepared for the Texas Almanac by Patrice Walker Powell of the Texas Commission on the Arts.

Culture in Texas, as in any market, is a mixture of activity generated by both the commercial and the non-profit sectors.

The commercial sector encompasses Texas-based profit-making businesses including commercial recording artists (such as the legendary Willie Nelson), nightclubs, record companies, private galleries, assorted boutiques which carry fine art collectibles and private dance and music halls. In addition, Texas is becoming an important media center, with Texas-based publications, television and film companies gaining national recognition.

Texas also has extensive cultural resources offered by non-profit organizations that are engaged in charitable, educational and/or humanitarian activities.

The Texas Legislature has authorized seven state agencies to administer cultural services and funds for the public good. The agencies, listed below, fall under the auspices of the Texas Legislature's Cultural and Historical Resources Committee. They are:

State Antiquities Committee, Box 12276, Austin 78711; **Texas Commission on the Arts,** Box 13406, Capitol Sta., Austin 78711; **Texas Film Commission,** Box 12428, Austin 78711; **Texas Historical Commission,** Box 12276, Austin 78711; **Texas Music Commission,** Box 12208, Austin 78711; **Texas State Library and Archives Commission,** Box 12927, Austin 78711; and the **State Preservation Board,** Box 13286, Austin 78711.

Although not a state agency, another organization that provides cultural services to the citizens of Texas is the **Texas Committee on the Humanities,** 1604 Nueces, Austin 78701.

The **Texas Commission on the Arts** was established in 1965 to develop a receptive climate for the arts in Texas, to attract outstanding artists to Texas, to serve as a source of arts information to state government and Texas at large and to expand and enhance the cultural opportunities for all Texans. The commission accomplishes these goals by providing financial, informational and technical assistance.

The agency is headed by an executive director and is organized into four divisions: Administrative, Performing Arts, Visual Arts/Communication Arts and Special Projects/Local Arts Agencies.

The Texas Commission on the Arts provides services and financial assistance to a wide range of non-profit arts organizations. Its clientele includes theaters (professional, civic, children's, ethnic), media (radio, television, film, publications), festivals, music (folk, symphonic, chamber, choral, jazz, opera and new music), visual arts (sculpture, crafts, photography, painting, environmental), dance (modern, ballet, folkloric), schools, presenters of cultural events and services organizations.

Some of Texas' major non-profit arts institutions — orchestras, museums, dance companies, theaters and cultural centers — are listed below. These and others can also be found under the subhead, "Recreation," in the county reports.

Amarillo — Amarillo Symphony Orchestra, Box 2552 (79105).

Austin — Austin Symphony Orchestra, 1101 Red River (78701); Ballet Austin, 1101 River River (78701); Laguna Gloria Art Museum, Box 5568 (78763); Paramount Theatre for the Performing Arts, Box 1205 (78767).

Beaumont — Beaumont Art Museum, 1111 9th St. (77702).

Corpus Christi — Art Museum of South Texas, 1902 N. Shoreline Dr. (78401); Corpus Christi Symphony Orchestra, Box 495 (78403).

Dallas — Dallas Ballet, 1925 Elm (75201); Dallas Opera, 1925 Elm (75201); Dallas Museum of Art, 1717 N. Harwood (75201); Dallas Symphony Orchestra, Box 26207 (75201); Dallas Theatre Center, 3636 Turtle Creek Blvd. (75219); Theatre Three, 2800 Routh (75201).

El Paso — El Paso Museum Of Arts, 1211 Montana Ave. (79902); El Paso Symphony Orchestra, Box 180 (79942).

Fort Worth — Amon Carter Museum Of Western Art, Box 2365 (76101); Fort Worth Art Museum, 1309 Montgomery (76107); Fort Worth Ballet Assn., 6841B Green Oaks Rd. (76116); Fort Worth Opera, 3505 W. Lancaster (76107); Fort Worth Symphony Orchestra, 4401 Trail Lake Dr. (76109); Kimbell Art Museum, Box 9440 (76107); Van Cliburn Foundation, 3505 W. Lancaster (76107).

Houston — Contemporary Arts Museum, 5216 Montrose Blvd. (77006); Houston Ballet Foundation, Box 13150 (77219); Houston Grand Opera, 401 Louisiana (77002); Houston Museum of Fine Arts, Box 6826 (77265); Houston Symphony Orchestra, 615 Louisiana (77002); Nina Vance Alley Theatre, 615 Texas (77002); Society for the Performing Arts, 615 Louisiana (77002); Texas Opera Theatre, 401 Louisiana, 8th Floor (77002); Theatre Under the Stars, 4235 San Felipe (77027).

Midland/Odessa — Midland/Odessa Symphony and Chorale, Box 6266 (79701).

Round Top — James Dick Foundation for the Performing Arts, Box 89 (78954).

San Antonio — Carver Cultural Center, 226 N. Hackberry (78202); Guadalupe Cultural Arts Center, 1300 Guadalupe (78207); McNay Art Institute, Box 6069 (78209); San Antonio Art Institute, Box 6069 (78209); San Antonio Museum Association, Box 2601 (78299-2601); San Antonio Performing Arts Assn., 110 Broadway, Ste. 230 (78205); San Antonio Symphony Orchestra, 109 Lexington Ave., Ste. 207 (78205); Southwest Craft Center, 300 Augusta (78205).

The **Texas Arts Council,** 3939 Bee Caves Rd., Ste. 1A, Austin 78746, promotes, develops and supports local arts agencies. Listed below are the members as of mid-1987:

Abilene—Abilene Cultural Affairs Council, Box 2281 (79604).

Albany—The Old Jail Art Center, Rt. 1, Box 1 (76430).

Amarillo—Amarillo Arts Committee, 1000 S. Polk (79101).

Andrews—Andrews Cultural Affairs Committee, 800 NW 12th Place (79714).

Arlington—Arlington Fine Arts Council, Box 13741 (76013).

Austin—Cultural Arts Program — PARD, Box 1088 (78767).

Beaumont, Orange and Port Arthur—Southeast Texas Arts Council, Box 3925, Beaumont (77704).

Bellaire—Arts Council of Bellaire, Box 862 (77401).

Big Spring—Big Spring Cultural Affairs Council, Box 1391 (79720).

Bonham—FUN, Inc., Box 740 (75418).

Borger—Magic Plains Arts Council, 1314 Lancelot (79007).

Brackettville—Old Quarry Society for the Performing Arts, Box 813 (78832).

Breckenridge—Breckenridge Fine Arts Center, Box 549 (76024).

Brenham—Arts Council of Washington County, 701 Milroy Dr. (77833).

Brownwood—Cultural Affairs Commission, Box 880 (76801).

Burkburnett—Burkburnett Arts Council, Box 652 (76354).

Carrizo Springs—Arts Council of Dimmit County, 414 Pena (78834).

Clifton—Bosque Conservatory of Fine Arts, Box 373 (76634).

College Station—Arts Council of Brazos Valley, 111 University Dr., Ste. 217 (77840).

Columbus—Live Oak Art Club, Box 835 (78934).

Corpus Christi—Corpus Christi Arts Council, 1521 N. Chaparral (78401).

Corsicana—Navarro Council of the Arts, Box 2224 (75110).

Dalhart—Dalhart Fine Arts Assn., 1102 Denver (79022).

Dallas—Division of Cultural Affairs, Majestic Theatre, 1925 Elm, Ste. 600 (75201).

Del Rio—Del Rio Council for the Arts, Box 178 (78841).

Denison—Denison Arts Council, Box 325 (75020).

Denton—Greater Denton Arts Council, 207 S. Bell (76201).

DeSoto—DeSoto Council of Cultural Arts, 1214 Wellington (75116).

Dumas—Quality of Life Committee, 201 S. Bliss (79029).

Duncanville—Duncanville Regional Arts Assn., Box 381014 (75138).

Eagle Pass—Arts Council of Eagle Pass, 1910 Olive (78852).

Edinburg—Upper Valley Council for the Arts, 714 McKee (78539).

El Paso—El Paso Arts Alliance, 333 E. Missouri (79901); El Paso Arts Resources Department, City of El Paso, 2 Civic Center Plaza (79901).

Floydada—Floyd County Arts Assn., Box 73 (79235).

Fort Worth—Arts Council of Fort Worth, One Tandy Center, Ste. 150 (76102).

Friendswood—Friendswood Fine Arts Council, Box 1600 (77546).

Gainesville—Cooke County Arts Council, Box 251 (76240).

Garland—Garland Center for the Performing Arts, Box 469002 (75040).

Granbury—Hood County Arts Council, Box 595 (76048).

Grand Prairie—Grand Prairie Arts Council, Box 1613 (75053).

Harlingen—Harlingen Cultural Arts Center Council, Box 609 (78551).

Hearne—Robertson County Arts Council, Box 203 (77859).

Houston—Cultural Arts Council of Houston, 1950 W. Gray, Ste. 6 (77019).

Huntsville—Huntsville Arts Commission, 1212 Ave. M (77340).

Hurst/Euless/Bedford—Trinity Arts Council, Box 18345, Fort Worth (76118).

Irving—City of Irving Arts Board, 3333 N. McArthur, Ste. 300 (75062); Irving Cultural Affairs Council, same address.

Jacksonville—Jacksonville Council on the Arts, Box 1231 (75766).

Killeen—Vive les Artes Societe, Box 321 (76540).

Lake Jackson—Brazosport Fine Arts Council, 400 College Dr. (77566).

Laredo—Laredo Council for the Arts, Box 790 (78040).

Levelland—Levelland Fine Arts Council, Box 8084 (79338).

Lewisville—Lewisville Cultural Council, Box 416 (75067).

Liberty Hill—Liberty Hill Cultural Affairs Council, Box 158 (78642).

Littlefield—Lamb County Council for the Arts, Box 507 (79339).

Longview—Longview Arts Council, Box 1133 (75606).

Lubbock—Lubbock Cultural Affairs Council, Box 561 (79408).

Lufkin—Angelina County Cultural Affairs Council, Box 1606 (79501).

Marshall—Marshall Regional Arts Council, Box 520 (75671).

Mesquite—Mesquite Arts Council, Box 2104 (75149).

Midland—Midland Arts Assembly, Box 3494 (79702).

Monahans—Ward County Activities Council, 400 E. Fourth (79756).

New Braunfels—Greater New Braunfels Arts Council, Box 1171 (78130).

Odessa—Odessa Cultural Council, Box 7195 (79760).

Orange—(See Beaumont).

Pampa—Pampa Fine Arts Assn., Box 818 (79066).

Paris—Paris Arts Development Council, Box 1096 (75460).

Pasadena—Pasadena Area Cultural Arts Council, Box 3412 (77501).

Pittsburg—Pittsburg/Camp County Arts Council, Box 72 (75686).

Plainview—Plainview Cultural Council, Box 627 (79072).

Plano—Plano Cultural Arts Council, 1076 Collin Creek Mall, 811 N. Central Expwy. (75075).

Port Arthur—(See Beaumont).

Port Lavaca—Calhoun County Arts Council, Box 31 (77979).

Post—Caprock Cultural Assn., Box 37 (79356).

Richardson—Richardson Arts Commission, 411 W. Arapaho (75080).

San Angelo—San Angelo Cultural Affairs Council, Box 2477 (76902).

San Antonio—Arts Council of San Antonio, 227 N. Presa (78205).

Schulenburg—Backstage Inc. Arts Council, Box 66 (78956).

Seagoville—Seagoville Fine Arts Council, Rt. 2, Box 68 (75159).

Sealy—Friends of Arts and Culture in Sealy, Box 1124 (77474).

Sherman—Council for the Arts, Box 1029 (75090).

Snyder—Snyder Cultural Affairs Committee, 2715 48th (79549).

South Padre Island—Rio Grande Valley Council, Box 2189 (78597).

Stephenville—Cross Timbers Fine Arts Council, Box 1172 (76401).

Sugar Land—Fort Bend Arts Council, Sugar Creek Nat'l. Bank, One Sugar Creek Blvd. (77478).

Sweetwater—Sweetwater Cultural Affairs Comm., Box 450 (79556).

Temple—Temple Cultural Activities Center, Box 3292 (76501).

Terrell—Cultural Arts of Terrell, Box 744 (75160).

Texarkana—Texarkana Regional Arts & Humanities Council, Box 1171 (75504).

The Woodlands—The Woodlands Living Arts Council, Box 7411 (77387).

Uvalde—Uvalde Arts Council, Box 1451 (78801).

Vernon—Vernon Council of the Arts, 4107 Bismark (76384).

Victoria—Cultural Council of Victoria, Box 1758 (77902).

Waco—Greater Waco Council for the Arts, 2518 Wooddale Cir. (76710).

Waxahachie—Waxahachie Arts Council, 216 Pensacola Dr. (75165).

Weatherford—Weatherford Performing Arts Council, 801 W. Spring (76086).

West Houston—West Houston Cultural Arts Council, 13302 Alchester Ln. (77079).

Wichita Falls—Wichita Falls Arts Commission, 3702 Cedar Lane (76308).

Poets Laureate

Texas Legislature designates Texas Poets Laureate and alternates. Poetry Society of Texas and Secretary of Senate's office, Austin, supplied this list for recent years.

1975-1976 Mrs. Ethel Osborn Hill, Port Arthur; Dr. Gene Shuford, Denton, alternate.

1976-1977 Mrs. Florice Stripling Jeffers, Burkburnett; Mrs. Vera L. Eckert, San Angelo, alternate.

1977-1978 Mrs. Ruth Carruth, Vernon; Mrs. Joy Gresham Hagstrom, Burkburnett, alternate.

1978-1979 Patsy Stodghill, Dallas; Dorothy B. Elfstroman, Galveston, alternate.

1979-1980 Dorothy B. Elfstroman, Galveston; Ruth Carruth, Vernon, alternate.

1980-1981 Weems S. Dykes, McCamey; Mildred Crabtree Speer, Amarillo, alternate.

1981-1982 No appointment made.

1982-1983 William D. Barney, Fort Worth; Vassar Miller, Houston, alternate.

No appointment made for 1983-84, 1984-85, 1985-86 or 1986-87.

1987-88 Ruth E. Reuther, Wichita Falls.

1988-89 Vassar Miller, Houston.

Completed in 1904, this Carnegie Library building in Cleburne was funded by one of the 34 Carnegie library grants made to Texas towns. Today it houses the Layland Museum. Texas Almanac photo.

Carnegie Boosted Texas Libraries

Philanthropist Andrew Carnegie has been called by one writer the "Santa Claus of Texas Public Libraries." From 1898 to 1917, Carnegie's generosity funded the construction of 34 library buildings in communities across the state.

In the 1880s and 1890s, Texans were increasingly interested in culture and entertainment. Texas women formed literary, social and cultural clubs and founded many schools, museums and churches during this period. However in 1896, Texas had but five public libraries.

When Carnegie began to make funds available for library construction, the women of Texas were ready. In 1898, the Texas Federation of Women's Clubs held its first statewide meeting in Tyler, and the members voted to make the establishment of public libraries their principal project.

Carnegie, who was born in Scotland in 1835, emigrated to Pennsylvania at the age of 13. As a young man, he rose quickly through the ranks of the Pennsylvania Railroad to become head of the railway before he was 25 years of age. In 1865, he set up iron mills in Pittsburgh, switching to steel in 1873. He built a personal fortune, which increased dramatically when he sold his interests to U.S. Steel Corporation in 1901. He spent the last 18 years of his life giving much of his fortune away through various scientific and educational foundations and other entities.

Appropriately, the first Texas town to receive a Carnegie grant was Pittsburg in 1898. Dallas and Fort Worth followed in 1899, with Houston and San Antonio receiving their grants in 1900.

The application process was quite simple. Civic groups or governmental agencies could make formal application for the grants. They would agree to provide a building site and to make annual payments equal to 10 percent of the original building cost for upkeep and operation.

Carnegie personally had to approve the building plans. He favored two-story, Greek Revival-style structures with wooden floors and 16-foot-high embossed metal ceilings. A typical Carnegie building had Corinthian pillars on the front and elevated steps over a split-level basement leading up to the first-floor entrance.

Worldwide, Carnegie donated $41 million for 2,509 libraries. Of these, 1,679 were in 1,500 communities in the United States. Texas received 34 Carnegie grants, which funded the construction of 30 public libraries, one college library, two branch libraries and one lecture hall. Texas towns receiving Carnegie grants were Abilene, Ballinger, Belton, Brownwood, Bryan, Clarksville, Cleburne, Corsicana, Dallas, El Paso, Fort Worth, Franklin, Gainesville, Greenville, Houston, Jefferson, Marshall, Memphis, Palestine, Pecos, Pittsburg, San Antonio, Sherman, Stamford, Sulphur Springs, Temple, Terrell, Tyler, Vernon, Waco and Winnsboro. (Dallas, Houston and San Antonio each received two grants).

Although highly respected, the Carnegie library program was not regarded as an unqualified success. By 1914, when only 24 Carnegie buildings had been finished in Texas, 14 communities were already in default on their operation and maintenance commitments. Some of the towns were simply too small and too poor to furnish the required financial support. In larger cities, however, most Carnegie libraries were very successful. In all, Andrew Carnegie donated $645,000 toward public library construction in Texas, with Vernon receiving the last grant in 1917.

Of the 34 Carnegie Library buildings, 14 are still standing (as of mid-1986): The Ballinger, Stamford and Jefferson structures are the only ones still used as general public libraries, while Palestine's is a genealogy library. Museums are housed in the Carnegie buildings in Belton, Cleburne, Sherman, Terrell and Tyler. Gainesville's is a theater; Bryan's is a city administration building. The Memphis Carnegie building serves as a warehouse, and the facility at Wiley College in Marshall is used as an administration building. The Franklin Carnegie was never used as a library; it was converted to use as a school before completion. It is now owned by the city and is vacant.

Public Libraries

The following information on Texas public libraries was furnished by Dick Getz and Mitchell Gidseg of the Library Development Division, Texas State Library, Austin.

Texas public libraries continue to improve in their efforts to meet the educational, informational and recreational needs of the state's citizens. Perhaps no other public-supported institution directly serves as many Texans as does the public library. The latest statistics, for 1985, reported to the Texas State Library by 455 public libraries across Texas bear this fact out. They show:

• A total of 47,094,739 books were checked out, a figure equivalent to approximately 3.3 books for every person in the state.

• A total of 4,735,953 items other than books were checked out. These items include records, cassettes, magazines, 16 mm films, videocassettes and art prints.

• A total of 10,705,527 answers to reference questions were provided by public libraries, both in the library and over the telephone.

• A total of 4,253,732 persons attended programs at the public library, including "story hour" programs and summer reading club programs for children, as well as cultural, entertainment and adult education programs for adults.

• Audiences totaling 6,938,791 persons viewed films and videocassettes provided by the public library.

The growth in these services has been considerable over the past five years. During this period, from 1980 to 1985, book circulation has increased by 9.5 percent. Circulation of materials other than books increased a dramatic 112.5 percent. The number of reference questions handled by library reference staffs has increased by 45.9 percent. And the number of persons attending programs in libraries has risen by 38.5 percent in the past five years.

All of these services were provided by public libraries with very modest support from tax sources. Total city and county tax support of public libraries in 1985 amounted to only $8.29 per capita, about half the price of an average hardback book. The state of Texas spent approximately 35 cents per capita in 1985 to finance 10 cooperative public library systems, which undertook various projects to develop and improve public library services. The total breakdown of public library funding, by source of funds, was as follows in 1985:

Source	Amount	Percent
Cities	$ 96,460,008	76%
Counties	20,897,163	16%
State	5,199,300	4%
Federal	1,247,272	1%
Other (Private, etc.)	3,587,036	3%
TOTAL	$127,390,779	100%

There is considerable data that suggest this level of support is inadequate to meet the needs of Texas citizens for public library services. Of the 455 libraries reporting for 1985 to the Texas State Library, 66 failed to meet the minimum standards for adequacy of budget, staff, book collection and hours of operation set by the state. Statistics for these 66 libraries show that the typical library in this category serves just under 6,200 population, with a budget from tax sources of less than $11,000 annually and a paid staff consisting of one person working part-time. Clearly, much remains to be done, particularly in less populated areas of the state, to bring library services up to adequate standards. Libraries in urban Texas face a different, but no less critical, problem of coping with rapid population growth and consequent demands for service by new residents. As the major Texas cities grow, new library facilities are needed in suburban areas, along with new library collections and additional staff to provide service at these facilities.

The following table lists all 455 public libraries in Texas, along with statistics on two of the most important services provided to Texas citizens: circulation of library materials (books as well as audiovisual and other materials), and information provided by library staff. Some of the libraries were unable to report the number of reference questions received in 1985. These are listed as "N.A." The following abbreviations are also used in the chart below: L., library; P.L., public library; C.L., county library; Mem. L., memorial library; Mun. L., municipal library, and Com. L., community library.

Library, County	Number Volumes Circulated	Inquiries Handled
Abernathy C.L., Hale	8,014	512
Abilene P.L., Taylor	688,324	184,291
Alamo P.L., Hidalgo	25,929	3,000
Albany, Shackelford C.L., Shackelford	N.A.	0
Alice P.L., Jim Wells	265,253	19,205
Allen P.L., Collin	52,097	N.A.
Alpine P.L., Brewster	53,460	N.A.
Alto, Stella Hill Mem. L., Cherokee	3,555	89
Alvord P.L., Wise	4,842	N.A.
Amarillo P.L., Potter	827,833	277,121
Anahuac, Chambers C.L., Chambers	140,258	5,803
Andrews C. L., Andrews	45,817	2,307
Angleton, Brazoria C.L., Brazoria	826,417	44,256
Anna Com. L., Collin	701	N.A.
Anson P.L., Jones	6,547	0
Aransas Pass P.L., San Patricio	25,725	1,608
Archer City, Archer C.L., Archer	N.A.	0
Arlington P.L., Tarrant	853,171	288,737
Aspermont, Stonewall C.L., Stonewall	17,873	217
Athens, Henderson C. Mem. L., Henderson	86,827	0
Atlanta Mem. L., Cass	12,660	0
Austin P.L., Travis	2,271,227	262,141
Austin, Lake Travis Com. L., Travis	4,080	600
Azle P.L., Tarrant	30,946	7,234
Baird, Callahan C.L., Callahan	7,544	96
Balch Springs P.L., Dallas	37,651	208
Ballinger, Carnegie L., Runnels	11,999	0
Bandera C.L., Bandera	28,439	730
Barksdale, Nueces Canyon P.L., Edwards	8,170	64
Bartlett, Teinert Mem. P.L., Bell	8,447	2,080
Bastrop P.L., Bastrop	61,230	2,611
Bay City P.L., Matagorda	41,352	N.A.

Library, County	Number Volumes Circulated	Inquiries Handled
Baytown, Sterling Mun. L., Harris	733,851	32,544
Beaumont P.L., Jefferson	387,759	35,126
Bedford P.L., Tarrant	261,324	N.A.
Beeville, Bee C. P.L., Bee	58,044	N.A.
Bellaire City L., Harris	135,179	7,396
Bellville P.L., Austin	39,193	1,530
Belton City L., Bell	42,245	3,393
Big Lake, Reagan C.L., Reagan	15,010	675
Big Sandy, Holly Com. L., Wood	3,565	0
Big Spring, Howard C.L., Howard	118,885	12,500
Blanco L., Blanco	3,399	0
Boerne P.L., Kendall	53,167	4,155
Bonham P.L., Fannin	61,794	11,560
Booker, Booker School P.L., Lipscomb	3,965	0
Borger, Hutchinson C.L., Hutchinson	115,468	N.A.
Bowie P.L., Montague	62,104	4,069
Boyd P.L., Wise	1,928	N.A.
Brackettville, Kinney C.P.L., Kinney	6,092	278
Brady, F.M. (Buck) Richards Mem. L., McCulloch	61,791	2,100
Breckenridge P.L., Stephens	8,898	N.A.
Brenham, Nancy Carol Roberts Mem. L., Washington	81,348	4,050
Bridgeport P.L., Wise	49,481	2,500
Brownfield, Kendrick Mem. L., Terry	42,093	3,234
Brownsville, Arnulfo L. Oliveira Mem. L., Cameron	165,933	13,123
Brownwood P.L., Brown	94,773	N.A.
Bryan P.L., Brazos	330,055	21,124
Buda P.L., Hays	8,683	780
Buffalo P.L., Leon	2,610	8
Bullard Com. L., Smith	0	1,200
Buna P.L., Jasper	13,976	205

Library, County	Number Volumes Circulated	Inquiries Handled
Burkburnett L., Wichita	38,695	4,648
Burleson P.L., Johnson	98,847	N.A.
Burnet, Herman Brown Free L., Burnet	118,425	N.A.
Caldwell, Harrie P. Woodson Mem. L., Burleson	17,953	508
Cameron P.L., Milam	29,475	156
Canadian, Hemphill C.L., Hemphill	54,182	2,301
Canton, Van Zandt C.L., Van Zandt	34,779	N.A.
Canyon P.L., Randall	27,099	523
Canyon Lake, Tye Preston Mem. L., Comal	23,118	68
Carrizo Springs, Dimmit C.P.L., Dimmit	22,221	1,585
Carrollton P.L., Dallas	354,283	N.A.
Carthage, Service League L., Panola	31,821	500
Castroville P.L., Medina	16,988	2,140
Cedar Hill P.L., Dallas	34,428	N.A.
Cedar Park P.L., Williamson	21,031	260
Center, Fannie Brown Booth Mem. L., Shelby	15,940	2,170
Centerville, Leon C.L., Leon	1,516	20
Charlotte P.L., Atascosa	2,140	15
Chico P.L., Wise	1,619	0
Childress P.L., Childress	24,705	2,779
Cisco P.L., Eastland	7,719	N.A.
Clarendon, Gabie Betts Burton Mem. L., Donley	15,276	N.A.
Clarksville, Red River C.P.L., Red River	31,990	N.A.
Claude P.L., Armstrong	0	0
Cleburne P.L., Johnson	284,514	N.A.
Cleveland, Austin Mem. L., Liberty	32,721	2,050
Clyde P.L., Callahan	16,724	677
Coleman P.L., Coleman	23,406	878
Colorado City, Mitchell C.P.L., Mitchell	33,373	N.A.
Columbus, Nesbitt Mem. L., Colorado	39,454	5,500
Comanche P.L., Comanche	26,694	N.A.
Comfort P.L., Kendall	17,675	1,024
Commerce P.L., Hunt	18,911	900
Conroe, Montgomery C.L., Montgomery	416,226	56,070
Cooper, Delta C.P.L., Delta	11,930	25
Coppell, W. T. Cozby P.L., Dallas	24,787	634
Copperas Cove P.L., Coryell	76,965	2,253
Corpus Christi, LaRetama P.L., Nueces	816,240	257,054
Corrigan P.L., Polk	16,244	2,763
Corsicana P.L., Navarro	90,374	N.A.
Cotulla, Alexander Mem. L., La Salle	8,342	320
Crane P.L., Crane	40,188	2,000
Crockett P.L., Houston	54,661	2,320
Crosbyton, Crosby C.L., Crosby	35,409	2,593
Cross Plains P.L., Callahan	7,883	375
Crystal City Mem. L., Zavala	6,152	750
Cuero P.L., DeWitt	19,837	74
Daingerfield P.L., Morris	19,053	N.A.
Dalhart, Dallam C.L., Dallam	29,850	900
Dallas County P.L., Dallas	28,332	782
Dallas P.L., Dallas	4,081,187	2,710,130
Dayton, Edmund E. and Nida Smith Jones L., Liberty	13,806	N.A.
Decatur P.L., Wise	41,904	N.A.
Decatur, Wise C. Fed. L. Sys., Wise	0	N.A.
Deer Park P.L., Harris	146,862	9,599
DeLeon P.L., Comanche	0	150
Dell City, G. Grebing P. School L., Hudspeth	10,200	150
Del Rio, Val Verde C.L., Val Verde	102,544	3,034
Denison P.L., Grayson	108,447	4,415
Denton P.L., Denton	222,827	7,643
Denver City, Yoakum C.L., Yoakum	47,506	5,000
DeSoto P.L., Dallas	67,107	10,400
Devine P.L., Medina	12,445	3,337
Diboll, T.L.L. Temple Mem. L., Angelina	42,909	0
Dickinson P.L., Galveston	37,536	1,621
Dimmitt, Rhoads Mem. L., Castro	19,658	N.A.

Library, County	Number Volumes Circulated	Inquiries Handled
Donna P.L., Hidalgo	25,420	4,882
Dublin P.L., Erath	4,730	30
Dumas, Killgore Mem. L., Moore	97,219	0
Duncanville P.L., Dallas	140,546	7,746
Eagle Lake, Eula & David Wintermann L., Colorado	20,372	2,400
Eagle Pass P.L., Maverick	37,363	169
Eastland, Centennial Mem. L., Eastland	3,874	150
Eden P.L., Concho	4,408	40
Edinburg P.L., Hidalgo	105,777	4,836
Edna, Jackson C. Mem. L., Jackson	17,479	N.A.
Eldorado P.L., Schleicher	6,220	390
Electra P.L., Wichita	35,261	1,500
El Paso P.L., El Paso	1,185,983	218,610
Elsa P.L., Hidalgo	22,079	365
Emory, Rains C.P.L., Rains	14,724	100
Ennis P.L., Ellis	34,841	N.A.
Euless P.L., Tarrant	119,034	20,988
Fabens, El Paso C.L., El Paso	31,005	N.A.
Fairfield L., Freestone	21,791	N.A.
Falfurrias, Ed Rachal Mem. L., Brooks	130,075	1,621
Farmers Branch Manske L., Dallas	153,024	N.A.
Farmersville, Charles J. Rike Mem. L., Collin	14,413	620
Ferris P.L., Ellis	2,380	650
Florence P.L., Williamson	6,601	400
Floresville, Wilson C.P.L., Wilson	53,537	N.A.
Floydada, Floyd C.L., Floyd	16,572	1,500
Fort Davis, Jeff Davis C.L., Jeff Davis	10,828	230
Fort Stockton P.L., Pecos	160,486	17,200
Fort Worth P.L., Tarrant	1,705,078	682,201
Franklin, Robertson C.L., Robertson	729	4
Frankston Depot L., Anderson	2,564	304
Fredericksburg, Pioneer Mem. L., Gillespie	83,166	5,616
Friendswood P.L., Galveston	114,816	N.A.
Friona P.L., Parmer	19,537	3,779
Gainesville, Cooke C.L., Cooke	85,999	2,258
Galveston, Rosenberg L., Galveston	242,080	37,752
Garland, Nicholson Mem. L., Dallas	646,895	114,406
Garwood, Veterans Mem. L., Colorado	1,100	75
Gatesville P.L., Coryell	40,500	10,500
Georgetown P.L., Williamson	101,949	N.A.
George West, Live Oak C.L., Live Oak	76,270	2,400
Giddings, Rufus Young King L., Lee	31,234	480
Gilmer, Upshur C.L., Upshur	37,794	892
Gladewater, Lee P.L., Gregg	53,162	320
Glen Rose, Glen Rose-Somervell C.L., Somervell	14,446	N.A.
Gonzales P.L., Gonzales	36,506	6,000
Graham P.L., Young	110,864	6,121
Granbury, Hood C.L., Hood	63,955	20,000
Grand Prairie Mem. L., Dallas	232,575	13,227
Grand Saline P.L., Van Zandt	19,271	620
Grapevine P.L., Tarrant	143,199	1,476
Greenville, W. Walworth Harrison P.L., Hunt	80,159	10,000
Groesbeck, Maffett Mem. L., Limestone	26,500	360
Groves P.L., Jefferson	37,311	3,657
Groveton, Ethel R. Reese P. L., Trinity	7,497	30
Gruver City L., Hansford	5,176	0
Hale Center P.L., Hale	6,123	45
Hallettsville, French Simpson Mem. L., Lavaca	27,837	736
Haltom City P.L., Tarrant	171,390	26,500
Hamilton P.L., Hamilton	23,629	180
Harker Heights Com. L., Bell	13,372	850
Harlingen P.L., Cameron	203,392	12,220
Haskell C.L., Haskell	20,091	0
Hearne, Smith-Welch Mem. L., Robertson	9,832	593
Hebbronville, Jim Hogg C.P.L., Jim Hogg	7,504	N.A.
Hempstead, Waller C.L., Waller	20,146	3,000
Henderson, Rusk C. Mem. L., Rusk	169,762	31,549

Library, County	Number Volumes Circulated	Inquiries Handled
Henrietta, Edwards P.L., Clay	38,436	N.A.
Hereford, Deaf Smith C.L., Deaf Smith	130,774	0
Hewitt Com. L., McLennan	N.A.	N.A.
Higgins P.L., Lipscomb	3,157	295
Highland Park L., Dallas	92,079	N.A.
Hillsboro City L., Hill	30,684	12,845
Hitchcock, Genevieve Miller Hitchcock P.L., Galveston	13,170	N.A.
Hondo P.L., Medina	0	47
Honey Grove, Bertha Voyer Mem. L., Fannin	10,212	262
Houston, Harris C.P.L., Harris	3,136,876	272,711
Houston P.L., Harris	6,384,212	3,278,281
Howe P.L., Grayson	6,522	39
Huntsville P.L., Walker	57,873	13,272
Hurst P.L., Tarrant	344,474	63,649
Hutchins, Atwell P.L., Dallas	6,245	50
Idalou P.L., Lubbock	11,593	820
Imperial P.L., Pecos	9,180	800
Ingleside P.L., San Patricio	23,334	1,413
Iowa Park, Tom Burnett Mem. L., Wichita	16,387	N.A.
Iraan P.L., Pecos	10,235	100
Irving P.L., Dallas	593,863	97,795
Italy, S.M. Dunlap L., Ellis	21,842	0
Jacksboro P.L., Jack	28,220	2,330
Jacksonville P.L., Cherokee	74,581	N.A.
Jasper P.L., Jasper	22,997	1,096
Jayton, Kent C.L., Kent	3,442	8
Jefferson, Carnegie L., Marion	0	0
Jewett P.L., Leon	2,261	0
Johnson City L., Blanco	8,428	N.A.
Jourdanton Com. L., Atascosa	19,377	2,489
Junction, Kimble C.L., Kimble	21,872	1,238
Kaufman C.L., Kaufman	20,466	150
Keller P.L., Tarrant	25,900	N.A.
Kendalia P.L., Kendall	2,811	10
Kenedy, Karnes C.L., Karnes	94,038	2,372
Kermit, Winkler C.L., Winkler	91,145	0
Kerrville, Butt-Holdsworth Mem. L., Kerr	173,288	4,377
Kilgore P.L., Gregg	67,154	1,025
Killeen P.L., Bell	106,554	18,049
Kingsville, Robert J. Kleberg P.L., Kleberg	169,735	3,439
Kirbyville P.L., Jasper	17,679	597
Kountze P.L., Hardin	22,339	4,473
Kyle Com. L., Hays	14,736	0
La Feria, Bailey H. Dunlap Mem. L., Cameron	18,523	4,651
La Grange, Fayette P.L., Fayette	43,225	N.A.
Laguna Vista P.L., Cameron	1,326	0
Lake Dallas, Lake Cities L., Denton	6,103	700
Lake Worth P.L., Tarrant	16,469	N.A.
La Marque P.L., Galveston	56,359	2,059
Lamesa, Dawson C.P.L., Dawson	64,224	N.A.
Lampasas P.L., Lampasas	41,682	3,838
Lancaster, Veterans Mem. L., Dallas	89,386	3,400
Laredo P.L., Webb	76,938	N.A.
League City Helen Hall L., Galveston	168,659	6,147
Leon Valley L., Bexar	34,735	2,674
Leonard P.L., Fannin	3,595	15
Levelland, Hockley C. Mem. L., Hockley	46,240	1,405
Lewisville P.L., Denton	170,827	0
Liberty Mun. L., Liberty	77,556	4,962
Littlefield, Lamb C.L., Lamb	33,674	840
Livingston, Murphy Mem. L., Polk	55,729	3,820
Llano C.P.L., Llano	74,727	N.A.
Lockhart, Dr. Eugene Clark L., Caldwell	31,147	0
Longview, Nicholson Mem. P.L., Gregg	158,523	21,301
Los Fresnos, Ethel Whipple Mem. L., Cameron	31,324	N.A.
Lubbock, City-County L., Lubbock	528,089	32,572
Lufkin, Kurth Mem. L., Angelina	73,603	N.A.
Luling P.L., Caldwell	42,191	0
Lytle P.L., Atascosa	7,770	833
McAllen Mem. L., Hidalgo	442,884	99,539
McAllen, Hidalgo C.L. System, Hidalgo	0	0
McCamey, Upton C.P.L., Upton	26,966	1,500
McKinney Mem. P.L., Collin	105,855	5,600
McLean, Lovett Mem. L., Gray	18,187	0
Madisonville C.L., Madison	17,352	820
Malakoff P.L., Henderson	22,227	600
Mansfield P.L., Tarrant	46,388	8,434
Marfa P.L., Presidio	34,045	931
Marlin P.L., Falls	13,669	N.A.
Marshall P.L., Harrison	73,259	7,509
Mason C. Free L., Mason	11,604	35
Matador, Motley C.L., Motley	10,732	2,202
Mathis P.L., San Patricio	6,147	175
Memphis P.L., Hall	16,455	3,306
Menard P.L., Menard	13,729	N.A.
Mercedes Mem. L., Hidalgo	93,815	5,051
Mertzon, Irion C.L., Irion	0	0
Mesquite P.L., Dallas	242,996	43,378
Mexia, Gibbs Mem. L., Limestone	36,216	6,500
Miami, Roberts C.L., Roberts	5,331	0
Midland C.P.L., Midland	352,199	38,287
Midlothian, A. H. Meadows L., Ellis	19,253	596
Mineola Mem. L., Wood	31,739	1,298
Mineral Wells, Boyce Ditto Mun. L., Palo Pinto	74,655	17,364
Mission, Speer Mem. L., Hidalgo	110,453	0
Monahans, Ward C.L., Ward	102,872	6,126
Morgan's Point L., Bell	1,120	35
Morton, Cochran C.L., Cochran	5,413	0
Mount Calm Regional L., Hill	3,405	0
Mount Pleasant Mun. L., Titus	53,617	3,000
Mt. Vernon, Franklin C.L., Franklin	35,562	1,560
Muenster P.L., Cooke	14,790	N.A.
Muleshoe Area P.L., Bailey	51,685	1,580
Munday, City-County L., Knox	9,778	N.A.
Nacogdoches P.L., Nacogdoches	111,885	12,200
Navasota, Navasota P.L., Grimes	27,008	2,900
Nederland, D. Bob Henson Mem. L., Jefferson	96,041	N.A.
Nederland, Jefferson C.L., Jefferson	95,365	3,325
New Boston P.L., Bowie	26,384	1,142
New Braunfels, Dittlinger Mem. L., Comal	114,405	2,986
Newton C.P.L., Newton	9,220	N.A.
Nocona P.L., Montague	9,175	2,201
North Richland Hills P.L., Tarrant	198,416	16,217
Odem P.L., San Patricio	2,778	59
Odessa, Ector C.L., Ector	505,161	28,219
Olney Com. L., Young	44,827	N.A.
Orange P.L., Orange	164,611	13,373
Ozona, Crockett C.L., Crockett	2,662	10
Paducah, Bicentennial City-County L., Cottle	6,093	0
Paint Rock, H. B. Crozier Mem. L., Concho	1,552	63
Palacios L., Matagorda	27,771	2,000
Palestine P.L., Anderson	113,408	N.A.
Pampa, Lovett Mem. L., Gray	121,190	7,765
Panhandle, Carson C.L., Carson	69,635	N.A.
Paris P.L., Lamar	130,610	15,734
Pasadena P.L., Harris	364,311	30,803
Pearsall, Pearsall P.L., Frio	32,646	800
Perryton, Perry Mem. L., Ochiltree	51,409	4,820
Petersburg P.L., Hale	10,268	17
Pflugerville Com. L., Travis	5,121	0
Pharr Mem. L., Hidalgo	84,178	4,674
Pilot Point Com. L., Denton	15,450	N.A.
Pineland, Arthur Temple Sr. Mem. L., Sabine	36,038	300
Pittsburg, Camp C.L., Camp	42,458	2,000
Plains, Yoakum C.L., Yoakum	37,975	400
Plainview, Unger Mem. L., Hale	54,501	10,840
Plano P.L., Collin	674,163	40,994
Pleasanton P.L., Atascosa	62,210	7,100
Port Aransas P.L., Nueces	22,167	518
Port Arthur P.L., Jefferson	241,767	51,315
Port Isabel P.L., Cameron	12,475	0
Portland, Bell-Whittington P.L., San Patricio	63,472	4,032
Port Lavaca, Calhoun C.L., Calhoun	73,605	N.A.
Port Neches, Effie & Wilton Hebert P.L., Jefferson	67,731	6,570

Library, County	Number Volumes Circulated	Inquiries Handled
Post P.L., Garza	10,319	644
Poteet P.L., Atascosa	18,623	2,685
Presidio, City of, L., Presidio	6,670	20
Quanah, Hardeman C.P.L., Hardeman	18,662	800
Quemado P.L., Maverick	8,382	500
Quitman P.L., Wood	31,782	4,000
Rankin P.L., Upton	13,357	500
Raymondville, Reber Mem. L., Willacy	47,215	3,500
Refugio C.P.L., Refugio	16,403	920
Richardson P.L., Dallas	476,485	58,225
Richland Hills P.L., Tarrant	61,994	6,800
Richmond, Fort Bend C.L., Fort Bend	375,553	22,467
Rio Hondo P.L., Cameron	4,786	215
River Oaks P.L., Tarrant	71,562	125
Roanoke P.L., Denton	2,836	N.A.
Robert Lee, Coke C.L., Coke	10,620	N.A.
Robstown, Nueces C.L., Nueces	39,598	N.A.
Rockdale, Lucy Hill Patterson Mem. L., Milam	23,568	1,169
Rockport, Aransas C.P.L., Aransas	62,954	2,168
Rocksprings, Edwards C. Mem. L., Edwards	2,933	N.A.
Rockwall C.L., Rockwall	38,294	1,298
Rotan P.L., Fisher	8,703	378
Round Rock P.L., Williamson	121,861	7,852
Rowlett P.L., Dallas	18,347	1,327
Rusk, Singletary Mem. L., Cherokee	21,281	650
Sachse P.L., Dallas	7,115	N.A.
Saginaw P.L., Tarrant	20,218	1,683
San Angelo, Tom Green C.L., Tom Green	561,367	31,490
San Antonio P.L., Bexar	2,788,479	N.A.
San Augustine P.L., San Augustine	22,670	1,600
San Benito P.L., Cameron	70,842	5,475
Sanderson, Terrell C.P.L., Terrell	19,539	0
San Marcos P.L., Hays	131,300	6,878
San Saba, Rylander Mem.L., San Saba	27,432	N.A.
Sanger P.L., Denton	3,280	35
Santa Anna City L., Coleman	N.A.	0
Santa Fe Com. L., Galveston	24,021	600
Schertz P.L., Guadalupe	38,456	3,100
Schulenburg P.L., Fayette	12,430	900
Seagoville P.L., Dallas	14,120	N.A.
Sealy, Virgil & Josephine Gordon Mem.L., Austin	23,154	715
Seguin, Seguin-Guadalupe C.P.L., Guadalupe	107,934	0
Seminole, Gaines C.L., Gaines	49,825	747
Seymour, Baylor County Free L., Baylor	20,247	0
Shamrock P.L., Wheeler	19,101	540
Shepherd, Roland Tisinger Mem. L., San Jacinto	16,052	61
Sheridan Youth Mem. L., Colorado	995	0
Sherman, Grayson	232,587	69,311
Silsbee, Hardin	108,798	7,580
Silverton L., Briscoe	620	20
Sinton, San Patricio C.L., San Patricio	0	0
Sinton P.L., San Patricio	30,401	1,186
Slaton City L., Lubbock	16,226	225
Smiley, Stella Ellis Hart L., Gonzales	3,624	167
Smithville P.L., Bastrop	24,438	3,856
Snyder, Scurry C.L., Scurry	82,942	6,250
Sonora, Sutton C.L., Sutton	14,134	1,500
Sour Lake, Alma M. Carpenter P.L., Hardin	7,762	125
Spearman, Hansford C.L., Hansford	23,313	700

Library, County	Number Volumes Circulated	Inquiries Handled
Splendora, Hazel L. McCracken City L., Montgomery	28,487	2,500
Springtown P.L., Parker	4,867	105
Spur, Dickens C. Spur P.L., Dickens	2,851	35
Stamford, Carnegie L., Jones	11,970	762
Stanton, Martin C.L., Martin	8,001	0
Stephenville P.L., Erath	70,170	N.A.
Sterling City, Sterling County P.L., Sterling	573	N.A.
Stratford, Sherman C.L., Sherman	8,487	300
Sulphur Springs P.L., Hopkins	57,253	N.A.
Sunnyvale P.L., Dallas	17,439	476
Sweetwater County-City L., Nolan.	101,450	7,300
Taft P.L., San Patricio	20,954	1,060
Tahoka City-County L., Lynn	5,585	100
Tawakoni Area P.L., Hunt	8,823	145
Taylor P.L., Williamson	0	N.A.
Teague P.L., Freestone	37,818	2,500
Temple P.L., Bell	195,842	29,300
Terrell P.L., Kaufman	61,985	N.A.
Texarkana P.L., Bowie	147,466	3,518
Texas City, Moore Mem. P.L., Galveston	160,208	9,107
The Colony P.L., Denton	41,396	N.A.
Trinity, Blanche K. Werner P.L., Trinity	21,871	N.A.
Tulia, Swisher C.L., Swisher	23,975	1,205
Tyler P.L., Smith	302,935	46,815
Universal City P.L., Bexar	6,487	N.A.
Uvalde, El Progreso Mem. L., Uvalde	96,601	1,350
Van Alstyne P.L., Grayson	12,898	153
Van Horn City-County L., Culberson	8,135	22
Vega, Oldham C.L., Oldham	0	0
Vernon, Carnegie City-County L., Wilbarger	36,537	2,392
Victoria P.L., Victoria	345,750	61,538
Vidor P.L., Orange	65,327	1,500
Waco-McLennan C.L., McLennan.	515,076	170,000
Waelder P.L., Gonzales	854	0
Wallis, Austin C.L., Austin	10,550	118
Warrenton, Fayette C. Bookmobile, Fayette	0	0
Watauga P.L., Tarrant	7,637	N.A.
Waxahachie, Nicholas P. Sims L., Ellis	166,091	N.A.
Weatherford P.L., Parker	116,903	N.A.
Weimar P.L., Colorado	14,775	1,540
Wellington, Collingsworth C.L., Collingsworth	18,632	52
Wells, Rube Sessions Mem. L., Cherokee	6,772	N.A.
Weslaco P.L., Hidalgo	104,251	1,960
Westbank Com. L., Travis	33,606	960
Wharton C.L., Wharton	204,014	12,000
Wheeler P.L., Wheeler	9,571	600
Whitesboro P.L., Grayson	13,697	175
White Settlement P.L., Tarrant	64,500	6,429
Whitewright P.L., Grayson	11,645	N.A.
Wichita Falls, Kemp P.L., Wichita.	215,898	10,125
Wilmer, Elvis Maxine Gilliam Mem. L., Dallas	12,611	N.A.
Wimberley, Village L., Hays	15,927	450
Winnsboro Carnegie L., Wood	15,357	N.A.
Winters P.L., Runnels	5,488	0
Wolfe City P.L., Hunt	8,369	0
Woodville, Allan Shivers L., Tyler	60,509	4,276
Wylie, Rita & Truett Smith L., Collin	13,337	313
Yoakum P.L., De Witt	19,992	720
Yorktown P.L., De Witt	13,367	105
Zapata C.P.L., Zapata	48,092	450

*Newly established library in 1985.
†Figure represents reference questions answered at the central library facility only.

Globe Theater Transplanted

Rising from the mesquite bushes and pump jacks of West Texas, Marjorie Morris' dream of a theater gleams whitely in the Southwestern sun. The octagonal building that has dominated much of Mrs. Morris' life is a replica of Shakespeare's Globe Theatre, which was built on the south bank of the Thames River in London in 1598. The Globe of the Great Southwest, begun in 1958 and opened in 1968, sits on the campus of Odessa College. Plays presented here include not only the same plays that Elizabethan playgoers enjoyed at the original Globe Theatre, but also other period plays, modern dramas, musicals, dance and chamber music, as well as country music revues.

The inspiration for the building of such an unexpected structure came during an English literature class that Mrs. Morris was teaching at Odessa High School in 1948. In preparation for a study of Shakespeare's "Macbeth," the students were researching the design of Elizabethan-era theaters. "One young man asked, 'Why don't we have a Globe Theatre, Mrs. Morris?' " says Marjorie Morris. "And I thought, 'Why not?' " she says. "I thought how exciting it would be to see Shakespeare's plays actually produced on the same kind of stage that was used when they were originally presented."

At first, Mrs. Morris was thinking only of building a stage, not an entire building. To thoroughly research the design of Shakespeare's Globe, Mrs. Morris returned to the college where she had earned her bachelor's degree, North Texas State College (now a university), to work toward her master's degree. The topic of her thesis: "The Proposed Globe Theatre at Odessa, Texas." Mrs. Morris' studies took her to Yale University, the Folger Shakespeare Library in Washington, D.C., the University of Southern California and the University of Birmingham's Extra-Mural School of Shakespeare in Stratford, England.

Upon her return to Odessa, Mrs. Morris was invited to teach at what was then Odessa Junior College (now Odessa College), and she continued to pursue her dream.

Mrs. Morris persuaded Odessa architect J. Ellsworth Powell to provide working drawings of the Globe stage from research she had done for her thesis. "He really put his heart and soul into it," says Mrs. Morris. "I took those drawings all over town, showing them to prospective donors and raising money."

The local newspaper cooperated in the fund drive, publishing articles as well as photographs of donors. Odessa Junior College donated a plot of land for the theater, and in 1958, construction finally began. A wall enclosing the area where the theater would stand was built first to protect the construction site from vandals. Since the name was "Globe of the Great Southwest," architect Powell stipulated that stone for the wall come from Texas and the four closest Southwestern states: New Mexico, Oklahoma, Arizona and Colorado.

To give Odessans a taste of what was in store for them, small-scale performances were given in the open courtyard, with the audience sitting on cushions brought from home. As the fund raising progressed, Mrs. Morris gradually realized that she might be able to raise enough money to build not just a stage but an entire theater.

Architect Powell gladly produced drawings of a complete Globe replica, providing for such non-Elizabethan but essential modern amenities as a roof, air conditioning and heating, allowing for year-round operation.

Construction proceeded in fits and starts over a period of several years: As funds came in, work was done. All during the 1960s, Marjorie Morris juggled her time among fund raising, teaching her college English classes and caring for a sick husband. Since it was to be the Globe of the Great Southwest, not just Odessa, she went all over the state asking for donations. With characteristic understatement, she calls it "quite an undertaking."

Finally in 1968, enough of the Globe was finished to launch an entire season. With festive banners flying from the peak of the roof, West Texas' Elizabethan theater opened its first season with George Bernard Shaw's "Arms and the Man" and concluded with the Globe's first Shakespeare festival, with productions of "A Midsummer Night's Dream" and "The Taming of the Shrew," in the summer of 1969. Charles David McCalley had been hired to provide professional direction, and he remained to guide the fledgling theater through its first ten years. With that first season, a West Texas legend was born.

Built primarily of wood and plaster, the Globe seats 410 and is said to have perfect acoustics. The 1,800-square-foot stage extends out into the audience, creating an intimacy between actors and spectators not experienced with traditional proscenium stages. Rich, British-red carpeting, upholstered seats and London dock lanterns help to produce the illusion of a London theater in the 1600s.

Since its opening, the Globe of the Great Southwest has mounted an annual Odessa Shakespeare Festival. Some of the plays are produced with college and professional talent from the Odessa area, while others are brought in from universities around the state, such as North Texas State University, the University of Texas of the Permian Basin, the University of Texas at El Paso, and Stephen F. Austin State University. In 1985, guest performances included the National Shakespeare Company's highly acclaimed production of "Macbeth," while the 1986 season was highlighted by the national company's "A Comedy of Errors." Other offerings have included modern classics (Tennessee Williams' "The Glass Menagerie"), musicals ("The Boy Friend," "Oklahoma" and "West Side Story," among others) and the avant garde ("The Sand Box" by Edward Albee and "The Bald Soprano" by Eugene Ionesco).

The 1980s have seen the addition of an annual Renaissance Fair, with Elizabethan arts, crafts, food, games and entertainment. "Whenever It Rains," a musical comedy of Odessa's early history, has played to enthusiastic audiences for several years in a row. And several times each year the Globe stage rings with the sounds of country and western music presented by the ongoing Odessa Brand New Opree.

—*MARY G. CRAWFORD*

Texas Institute of Letters

Since 1939, the Texas Institute of Letters has chosen each year outstanding books which are either by Texans or about Texas subjects. Awards have been made for fiction, nonfiction, Southwest history, general information, children's books, poetry and book design. These awards for recent years are listed below:

Year—Author	Title
1984 Max Apple	Free Agents
Celia Morris Eckhardt (co-winner)	Fanny Wright
John Bloom and Jim Atkinson (co-winners)	
	Evidence of Love
William Roger Louis	The British Empire in the Middle East, 1945-1951
Rosemary Catacalos	Again for the First Time
Beverly Lowry	So Far From the Road, So Long Until Morning
Judith MacBain Alter	Luke and the Van Zandt County War
Jeff Unger (co-winner)	Huck at 100
John Davidson (co-winner)	The Man Who Dreamed Luckenbach
Drew Jubera (co-winner)	To Find A Mockingbird: The Search for Harper Lee
Book Design Award: George Lenox	The Other Texas Frontier

The special Barbara McCombs/Lon Tinkle Award for continuing excellence in Texas Letters: Larry McMurtry, Washington, D.C.

Year—Author	Title
1985 Elizabeth W. and Robert A. Fernea	The Arab World: Personal Encounters
Larry McMurtry	Lonesome Dove
Darwin Payne	Owen Wister
Reginald Gibbons	Mr. Walsh's Mare
Paula Paul	Sarah, Sissy Weed and the Ships of the Desert
C. W. Smith	Uncle Dad
Andrew Hudgins	Saints and Strangers
Walter McDonald	Witching on Hardscrabble
Book Design Award: Walter Horton for "Dallas Architecture," published by Texas Monthly Press	
1986 William H. and William N. Goetzmann	The West of the Imagination
Rosalind Wright	Veracruz
Alfred W. Crosby	Ecological Imperialism: The Biological Expansion of Europe, 900-1900
Gail Galloway Adams	Inside Dope
Edward Hirsch	Wild Gratitude
Brenda Bell	Life After Death

Book Design Award: George Lenox and Omega Clay for "The Panoramic Photography of Eugene O. Goldbeck," written by Clyde Burleson and Jessica Hickman.

The special Barbara McCombs/Lon Tinkle Award for continuing excellence in Texas Letters: Elmer Kelton of San Angelo.

Square Dance, starring Jane Alexander and Jason Robards Jr., was filmed in and around Maypearl, Ellis County. Photo courtesy Pacific Arts Pictures.

Texas No Newcomer to Movies

This article was written by Mary G. Crawford, Associate Editor of the Texas Almanac.

Texas has been calling itself the Third Coast of filmmaking — third after the West Coast and the East Coast — since about 1978. That boast, which is challenged by Illinois and Florida, was given credibility at the 1984 Academy Awards ceremony, where films made wholly or partially in Texas captured seven of the top eight Oscars. Movie making is clearly coming of age as an industry in Texas.

The Lone Star State has long been a Hollywood favorite as a film subject and a film setting: Californiabased companies have been filming in Texas since the 1920s. But even before that, there were movie makers in the state. French director Gaston Melies moved his studio from Brooklyn to San Antonio in 1909 and established the Star Film Ranch. After producing several forgettable Westerns, Melies made *The Immortal Alamo*, featuring John Ford's older brother, Francis Ford, as Davy Crockett. Melies himself played Col. Travis, and students from Peacock Military Academy took the roles of soldiers.

Perhaps the earliest attempt to establish a homegrown film industry in Texas was the formation of the Satex Company in Austin in 1913. With $25,000 in assets, Satex remodeled as an old building at Lavaca and 13th Streets to use as a studio and produced their first, and probably only, film, a silent three-reeler titled *Their Lives by a Slender Thread*. It was released by the Warner Company.

Another early and all-but-forgotten film was produced in Texas by famed cattleman Charles Goodnight at his JA Ranch in the Panhandle in 1916. Goodnight staged an old-style buffalo hunt, using Indians, led by a 70-year-old Kiowa named Horse, from the reservation at Fort Sill, Okla. The Wiswall brothers from Denver spent nearly a month shooting the hunt and other footage at the ranch. The resulting film, *Old Texas*, was shown at a cattlemen's association meeting in Denver and was subsequently lost.

Hollywood came to Texas in 1923, when Fox Film Company shot exterior scenes in San Antonio for its seven-reel feature, *The Warrens of Virginia*. The film is memorable mostly because of the tragic death of its star, Martha Mansfield. Near the end of location shooting, her billowy skirt was ignited by a carelessly tossed match, and she died the next day in a San Antonio hospital.

Paramount followed Fox to Texas in 1924, filming *North of the 36th* near Houston.

The year 1925 saw the start of a rash of movies being made near San Antonio, many of them utilizing the military posts of the Alamo City. The classic silent film, *The Big Parade*, starring John Gilbert and Renee Adoree, was produced in San Antonio by legendary director King Vidor in 1925. Battle scenes were shot at Fort Sam Houston.

The first Oscar for best picture was awarded to *Wings*, directed by William Wellman for Paramount in 1927 and filmed at Camp Stanley and Kelly Air Force Base, then called Kelly Field. The cast included Buddy Rogers, Richard Arlen and Clara Bow.

I Wanted Wings, a flag-waving movie starring William Holden, Veronica Lake, Ray Miland and Constance Moore, was filmed at Randolph Field, now known as Randolph Air Force Base, in 1940.

Kyle Field at Texas A&M University was the setting for a 1943 epic entitled, *We've Never Been Licked*, starring Robert Mitchum and Noah Beery Jr. All but forgotten by everyone else, the movie is shown annually at A&M. In his book, *Cowboys and Cadillacs*, author Don Graham quotes an unnamed A&M professor as saying that the title should have been *We've Never Been Liked*.

Another flurry of movie-making in Texas came in the 1950s near Brackettville, 120 miles west of San Antonio. A severe drought and the closing of nearby Fort Clark in 1950 spelled, not disaster, but challenge to Brackettville mayor James T. "Happy" Shahan. Inspired by reports of the movie village of Old Tucson in Arizona, Shahan lured at least four Hollywood films to Brackettville during the 1950s, the best-known being John Wayne's *The Alamo*, for which an Alamo replica was built. Numerous other features have used the Alamo set since then, among them Columbia Pictures' *Two Rode Together* (1961), starring James Stewart, Richard Widmark and Shirley Jones, and 20th Century Fox's *Bandolero* (1968), with Dean Martin, James Stewart and Raquel Welch. And, as Shahan had dreamed, the Alamo set itself became a tourist attraction.

The 1950s also saw the making of several movies in the rugged areas along Texas' border with Mexico. The Eagle Lion film, *The Sundowners*, featuring Robert Preston, Robert Sterling and John Barrymore Jr., was shot in the Davis Mountains in 1950; *Viva Zapata*, with Marlon Brando and Jean Peters, was made near Rio Grande City in 1952; and Marfa was the location for the filming of *Giant* in 1956, with a cast which included Elizabeth Taylor, Rock Hudson and James Dean.

No history of Texas filmmaking would be complete without a mention of two horror films made in the late 1950s by Gordon McLendon's McLendon Radio Pictures: *The Giant Gila Monster* and the now-classic *The Killer Shrews*, which turns up regularly on the late show and which was nominated for a Golden Turkey Award by Harry and Michael Medved in their 1980 book, *The Golden Turkey Awards: The Worst Achievements in Hollywood History*. And who can forget that glory epic, *The Texas Chainsaw Massacre*, made in the Round Rock area in 1973?

There was scattered filmmaking activity throughout the state during the 1960s, including such popular features as *Hud* (1962), filmed in the Panhandle town of Claude and featuring Paul Newman and Patricia Neal, *Bonnie and Clyde*, shot in the North Central Texas area in 1967 with a cast which included Faye Dunaway, and *Viva Max!* (1968), which utilized the original Alamo and starred Peter Ustinov.

The 1970s saw the start of a steady increase in the number of film projects made in Texas, due at least partly to the birth in 1971 of the Texas Film Commission. The commission, created by Gov. Preston Smith, scouts locations for film companies, acts as liaison between the movie-makers and local governmental bodies, furnishes information about equipment and technical personnel available in the state, and generally does whatever it can to smooth the way for out-of-state companies to shoot films in Texas. Film commissions have now been established in several regions of the state (see box) to provide the same types of assistance to film companies that the Texas Film Commission offers statewide.

San Antonio, Floresville and Del Rio were used for the filming of *Sugarland Express* in 1973. In a change from the Southwestern look of most made-in-Texas films up to this time, the futuristic *Logan's Run* was shot in 1975 in ultramodern buildings in Dallas, Houston and Fort Worth. And the modern but Western-flavored *Urban Cowboy*, (1979) was set in Houston.

The 1980s have seen an explosion of filming activity in Texas, not only in theater films, but also in made-for-TV movies, TV series and TV specials. In 1980, the Sissy Spacek film *Raggedy Man* was shot in Maxwell, and the TV series *Dallas* was filmed in (Where else?) Dallas. *The Best Little Whorehouse in Texas* was made around Austin and Hallettsville by Universal in 1981, the same year that saw *The Steeler and the Pittsburgh Kid* produced in Dallas for NBC-TV.

Not only have major Hollywood studios and television production companies been doing more filming in Texas, but there have also been more Texas-based companies making major films, such as Mulberry Square's *Benji*, made in and around McKinney in 1973, several additional *Benji* movies and *Hawmps*, a 1976 comedy based on an experiment of the U.S. military to use camels as pack animals in desert areas of the U.S. in the mid-1850s.

Including features, movies-of-the-week, television series and television specials, 30 film projects were shot in Texas in 1984. Among these were *Alamo Bay*, filmed along the Gulf Coast by famed French director Louis Malle, and *1918* by Horton Foote, shot in the Waxahachie area.

1985 and 1986 each saw 27 Texas film productions. Prominent among the 1986 projects were the pilot for the television series *Houston Knights*, the feature film *Square Dance*, shot around Maypearl, and *Perry Como's Christmas Special*, which featured the San Antonio Symphony Orchestra.

What is the future for filmmaking in Texas? Nothing but opportunity, according to *The Dallas Morning News* Film and Video Board, a panel of six Texas film industry leaders: Joe Camp, president of Mulberry Square Productions; Kim Dawson, president of the Kim Dawson Agency Inc.; Neil Feldman, president of Video Post & Transfer Inc.; Sam Grogg, managing partner of FilmDallas Investment Fund; Richard Kneipper, partner in Jones, Day, Reavis & Pogue; and Fred Kuehnert, president of Houston International Televideo Inc. During a meeting in September 1984, board members generally agreed that because of the need for cable TV to show something besides endless reruns of old Hollywood movies and the increasing numbers of videocassette players being sold, there is a virtually unlimited demand for Texas-made low-budget films.

Film Commissions in Texas

In addition to the following film commissions, which were operating in Texas as of early summer, 1987, many chambers of commerce and convention and visitors' bureaus have employees who specialize in assisting film companies:

Texas Film Commission
   c/o Economic and Development Commission
   Box 12728
   Austin 78711
   (512) 469-9111

El Paso Film Commission
   El Paso Convention & Visitors Bureau
   5 Civic Center Plaza
   El Paso 79901
   (915) 534-0694

Houston Film Commission
   3300 Main Street
   Houston 77002
   (713) 523-5050
   Texas WATS (800) 392-7722
   US WATS (800) 231-7799

Irving Film Commission
   3333 N. MacArthur, Ste. 200
   Irving 75062
   (214) 252-7976

Film Commission of North Texas
   3 Dallas Communications Complex,
   Lock Box N-57
   6311 N. O'Connor Rd.
   Irving 75039
   (214) 869-7657

San Antonio Film Development Bureau
   Box 2277
   San Antonio 78298
   (512) 299-8123
   Texas WATS (800) 292-1010
   US WATS (800) 531-5700

Selected Bibliography

Adams, Lorraine, "Texas running close race for No. 3 on movie scene"; The Dallas Morning News, Aug. 21, 1984, Sec. D, pp. 1, 5.

Adams, Lorraine, "VCRs, cable keys for Texas, film board says", The Dallas Morning News, Sept. 23, 1984, Sec. H, pp. 1, 13.

Austin American-Statesman, "Oscars riding tall in Texas saddles"; Austin, Apr. 11, 1984.

Bowles, Victoria R., "Oscars good advertising for Texas film industry"; San Antonio Light, Apr 11, 1984.

Buchanan, James R., "A Look at the Texas Film Industry"; Texas Business Review, Vol. XLVI, No. 1, Jan. 1972.

Cagle, Eldon Jr., "Lights, Camera, Action & Texas"; Southwest Airlines Magazine, Jan. 1985.

FilmTexas, Vol. 12, No. 2, "Texas Shines on Oscar Night"; Texas Film Commission, Austin, June 1984.

Graham, Don, Cowboys and Cadillacs: How Hollywood Looks at Texas; Texas Monthly Press, Austin, 1983.

Hiller, Terry, "Roll 'em: Texas as the Lone Star Stage"; Fort Worth Star-Telegram, May 6, 1984, Sec. D, p. 6.

Hulbert, Dan, "Texas Yields a Bumper Crop of Movies"; The New York Times, Sept. 2, 1984.

Jones, G. William, "Tinseltown on the Trinity?"; Texas Business, Dec. 1983.

Roberts, Nicki, ed., The Texas Association of Film/Tape Professionals 1987 Directory; TAFTP, Austin, 1987.

Sklar, Robert, Movie-Made America: A Cultural History of American Movies; Vintage Books, New York, 1975.

Medved, Harry and Michael, The Golden Turkey Awards: The Worst Achievements in Hollywood History; G. P. Putnam Sons, New York, 1980.

Smith, Joel, Exec. Dir., Texas Production Manual, 1982-83 Edition; Texas Film Commission, Austin, 1982.

Wuntch, Phillip, "'Amadeus' wins best picture"; The Dallas Morning News, March 26, 1985, Sec. E.

Recreation

Texas State Parks

Texas' expanding system of state parks attracted 20,582,544 visitors in fiscal 1986. The parks offer contrasting attractions, mountains and canyons, forests, spring-fed streams, sandy dunes and saltwater surf.

Most of these parks are listed here. **Texas Parks and Wildlife Department** provided the information. Additional information is available from the Department's Austin headquarters (4200 Smith School Rd., Austin 78744; 1-800-792-1112 within Texas, (512) 389-4890 outside the state), personnel at individual parks or other sources of tourist information.

Abilene State Recreational Area, 19 miles southwest of Abilene in Taylor County, 621 acres. The land was deeded by the city of Abilene in 1933. A part of the official **Texas longhorn herd** is located in the park. In addition to **Lake Abilene, Buffalo Gap,** the original Taylor County seat (1878) and one of the early frontier settlements through which passed the **Butterfield Stage Route** (also called the **Southern Overland Mail Route**), is nearby. Buffalo Gap was on the **Western,** or **Dodge City, Trail,** over which pioneer Texas cattlemen drove herds to Kansas.

Acton State Historic Site, is a .006-acre cemetery plot where **Davy Crockett's** second wife, Elizabeth, was buried in 1860. It is six miles east of Granbury in Hood County.

Adm. Nimitz Museum Historical Park is 9.1 acres in Fredericksburg featuring **Nimitz Steamboat Hotel,** which is now museum; named for Adm. **Chester W. Nimitz** of World War II fame. Nearby is **Kerrville State Park.**

Atlanta State Recreation Area is 1,475 acres located 11 miles northwest of Atlanta in Cass County; adjacent to **Wright Patman Dam and Lake.** Texas acquired the land from the U.S. Army in 1954.

Balmorhea State Recreation Area is 45.9 acres four miles southwest of Balmorhea in Reeves County, deeded in 1935 by private owners. Swimming pool fed by natural spring (**San Solomon Springs**); also provides water to **pupfish refuge** located in park. Nearby are city of **Pecos, Fort Davis National Historic Site,** scenic loop drive through **Davis Mountains** and **Davis Mountains State Park.**

Bastrop State Park is 3,503.7 acres. The park was acquired by deeds from the city of Bastrop and private owners during 1933 to 1935. Site of famous **"Lost Pines,"** isolated timbered area of loblolly pine and hardwoods. Nearby **Lake Bastrop** offers good fishing. State capitol at Austin 30 miles away; 13-mile drive through forest leads to **Buescher State Park.**

Bentsen-Rio Grande State Park, a scenic park, is along the Rio Grande in Hidalgo County. The 587 acres were acquired from private owners in 1944. Park is excellent base from which to tour Rio Grande Valley of Texas and adjacent Mexico; most attractions within 1½ hours' drive. Three miles of hiking trail lead to Rio Grande; provides chance to study unique plants, animals and birds of park. Many species of birds unique to southern United States found here, including **Lichtenstein's oriole, pauraque, groove-billed ani, green jay, Kiskadee flycatcher, red-billed pigeon, elf owl** and **chachalaca.** Park also one of last natural refuges in Texas for cats such as **ocelot** and **jaguarundi.**

Battleship Texas State Historic Site, located in Harris County, eight miles southeast of Houston on U.S. 78 and IH-45 to Texas 225, then east on Texas 225 for 12 miles to Texas 134 for three miles to Park Road 1836. The U.S.S. Texas was moored in the Houston Ship Channel at the **San Jacinto Battleground** on San Jacinto Day, 1948, and is the only survivor of the dreadnought class, a veteran of two world wars and many campaigns. The Battleship is open every day, June 1-Aug. 31, 10:00 a.m.-6:00 p.m.; Sept. 1-May 31, 10:00 a.m.-5:00 p.m. Admission charges: Ages 12 and over, $2.00; 6 to 11, $1.00; under 6, free.

Big Spring State Recreation Area is 370 acres located in Howard County. It was named for a natural spring that was replaced by an artificial spring. The park was deeded by the city of Big Spring in 1934 and 1935. Drive to top of Scenic Mountain provides panoramic view of surrounding country. The "big spring" nearby provided watering place for herds of buffalo, antelope and wild horses. Used extensively also as campsite for early Indians, explorers and settlers. **Prairie dog colony** on mountain.

Blanco State Recreation Area is 104.6 acres along the Blanco River in Blanco County. The land was deeded in 1936 by private owners. Park area was used as campsite by early explorers and settlers. LBJ Ranch and LBJ State Historical Park located less then 30 miles away.

Bonham State Recreation Area is a 261-acre park located near Bonham in Fannin County. It includes a 65-acre lake. The land was acquired in 1933 and 1934 from the city of Bonham. **Sam Rayburn Memorial Library** in Bonham. **Sam Rayburn Home** and **Brushy Creek Reservoir** nearby.

Brazos Bend State Park (formerly **Big Creek Park Site**) in Fort Bend County, seven miles west of Rosharon on FM 762 (approximately 28 miles south of Houston). Total acreage, 4,897. Acquired from private landowners in 1976.

Brazos Island State Recreation Area is 216.6 acres 23 miles northeast of Brownsville in Cameron County. A scenic park, the land was acquired from the Texas General Land Office in 1957. Brownsville, Mexico, **Port Isabel Lighthouse State Historic Structure** and South Padre Island within hour's driving distance; slightly longer drive leads into heart of Rio Grande Valley. Historical spots of surrounding area include two battle sites (**Palo Alto** and **Resaca de la Palma**) from Mexican War, 1846, and battle site of **Palmito Ranch, last land engagement of Civil War,** May 1865. (No development as of 1987.)

Bryan Beach State Recreation Area, is 878 acres near Freeport. Acquired by purchase in 1973 from private sources. (No developed facilities in 1987.)

Buescher State Park, a scenic area, is 1,012 acres near Smithville in Bastrop County. The state was deeded the park by the city of Smithville between 1933 and 1936. **El Camino Real** (King's Highway) once ran near park; road connected **San Antonio de Bexar** with Spanish missions in East Texas and generally followed present-day Texas State Highway 21 and **Old San Antonio Road.** Parkland included in Stephen F. Austin's colonial grant. Scenic park road connects **Buescher State Park** with **Bastrop State Park.**

TEXAS STATE PARKS

TEXAS STATE PARKS	CAMPING	SCREENED SHELTERS	GROUP FACILITY	CAMPSITES ELEC./SEWAGE	CAMPSITES WATER/ELEC.	RESTROOMS	SHOWERS	CABINS	PICNICKING	GROCERIES	FISHING	SWIMMING	WATER SKIING	BOAT RAMP	MUSEUM/EXHIBIT	HISTORIC STRUCTURE	DAY USE ONLY	GROUP TRAILER	TRAILER DUMP STATION	NATURE HIKING TRAILS	MISCELLANEOUS
STATE RECREATION AREAS																					
ABILENE	●	●	P		●	●	●		●					●				●	●	●	L
ARROYO COLORADO	AREA PRESENTLY CLOSED TO PUBLIC PENDING DEVELOPMENT																				
ATLANTA	●		P	●	●	●	●		●		○	○	○	●					●	●	P
BALMORHEA (SAN SOLOMON SPRINGS COURTS)	●					●	●		●			●				●		●			D
BIG SPRING						●	●	●		●							●			●	B
BLANCO	●	●	P		●	●	●		●		○	○		●					●	●	B
BONHAM	●		P GB		●	●	●		●		●	●		●					●	●	B
BRAZOS ISLAND (UNDEVELOPED GULF BEACH)	○								○		○	○									
BRYAN BEACH (UNDEVELOPED GULF BEACH)	○								○		○	○									
CASSELLS BOYKIN	●					●			●		○	○	○	●				●			
CLEBURNE	●	●	GB	●	●	●	●		●	●	●	●		●		●			●	●	
EISENHOWER (MARINA)	●	●	S	●	●	●	●		●		●	●	○	●		●		●	●	●	Z
FAIRFIELD LAKE	●					●	●	●		●		●	●	○	●				●	●	Z
FALCON (AIRSTRIP)	●	●	S	●	●	●	●		●		○	○	○	●					●		
FORT PARKER	●	●	GB	●	●	●	●		●		●	○	○	●					●	●	
GOOSE ISLAND	●		S		●	●	●		●		●	○	○	●					●	●	
JEFF DAVIS*																					
KERRVILLE	●	●	SP	●	●	●	●		●		○	○		●					●	●	E
LAKE ARROWHEAD	●		P		●	●	●		●	●	●	●	●	○	●					●	E
LAKE BOB SANDLIN	AREA PRESENTLY CLOSED TO PUBLIC PENDING DEVELOPMENT																				
LAKE BROWNWOOD	●	●	P	●	●	●	●		●		●	●	○	●					●	●	
LAKE COLORADO CITY	●		S,P		●	●	●		●		●	●	○	●					●		
LAKE CORPUS CHRISTI	●		P		●	●	●		●	●	●	○	○	●					●		B
LAKE LEWISVILLE	●	●	●		●	●	●		●		●	○	○	●		●		●	●	●	
LAKE LIVINGSTON	●	●			●	●	●		●		●	○	○	●		●		●	●	●	C,E,Z
LAKE SOMERVILLE	●		P		●	●	●		●		●	○	○	●					●	●	
LAKE TEXANA	●		P		●	●	●		●		●	●	○						●		
LAKE WHITNEY (AIRSTRIP)	●	●	C	●	●	●	●		●		○	●	○	●					●	●	
LOCKHART	●		S		●	●	●		●		●		●								G,Z
MACKENZIE*	●								●		○	○	○	●			●				G
MARTIN CREEK PARK SITE**	●	●	C	●	●	●	●		●		○	○		●					●	●	Z
MERIDIAN	●					●	●	●	●	●	●	●		●					●	●	LB
POSSUM KINGDOM	●					●	●	●		●	●	●	●	●	●				●		
PURTIS CREEK PARK SITE**	AREA PRESENTLY CLOSED TO PUBLIC PENDING DEVELOPMENT																				
SHELDON									○	●			●		●		●				
TIPS*	●		P		●	●	●		●		●	○									
STATE PARKS																					
BASTROP	●		H GB	●	●	●	●	●	●		●	○	●							●	Z GD
BENTSEN-RIO GRANDE	●		P	●		●	●		●		●	○			●				●	●	P,Z
BRAZOS BEND/HALE RANCH PARK SITE	●	●	S	●	●	●	●		●		●	●							●	●	P
BUESCHER	●	●	S		●	●	●		●		●	●							●	●	P
CADDO LAKE	●	●	S	●	●	●	●	●	●		●	○	○	●					●	●	B
CAPROCK CANYONS	●		P		●	●	●		●		●	●	○	○		●	●		●	●	E,Z
CHOKE CANYON	●		P		●	●	●		●		●	○	○	●		●	●		●	●	
COPPER BREAKS	●		P		●	●	●		●		●	●	○	○		●			●	●	L,E,Z
DAINGERFIELD	●		P		●	●	●	●	●		●	●	●	●		●			●	●	B
DAVIS MOUNTAINS (INDIAN LODGE)	●		P	●	●	●	●		●						●			●	●	●	D
DINOSAUR VALLEY (DINOSAUR FOOTPRINTS)	●		P		●	●	●		●		○	○			●			●	●	●	L
FRANKLIN MOUNTAINS (PEDESTRIAN ACCESS ONLY)	●	●			●	●	●		●		○	○						●	●	●	
GALVESTON ISLAND (SUMMER DRAMA "The Lone Star")	●	●	CS		●	●	●	●	●		●	○	○						●		M,B
GARNER	●	●			●	●	●		●	●	●	○	○							●	Z
GUADALUPE RIVER**	●				●	●	●		●		●	○							●	●	BM
HUNTSVILLE	●	●	P		●	●	●		●	●	●	●	○	○	●				●	●	C,Z,G,B
INKS LAKE	●	●	P		●	●	●		●	●	●	●	●	●		●		●	●	●	B,Z,E
LAKE MINERAL WELLS*	●	●	●		●	●	●		●		●	●	●	●		●					
LONGHORN CAVERN* (DAILY CAVERN TOURS)						●	●		●						●	●		●	●		
MARTIN DIES JR.	●	●	S		●	●	●		●		●	●	○	●					●	●	
McKINNEY FALLS	●	●	●	C,S	●	●	●		●		●	○			●	●			●	●	
MONAHANS SANDHILLS	●					●	●	●		●							●			●	●
MOTHER NEFF	●		X		●	●	●		●		●	○							●	●	

TEXAS STATE PARKS

	CAMPING	SCREENED SHELTERS	GROUP FACILITY	CAMPSITES ELEC./SEWAGE	CAMPSITES WATER/ELEC.	RESTROOMS	SHOWERS	CABINS	PICNICKING	GROCERIES	FISHING	SWIMMING	WATER SKIING	BOAT RAMP	MUSEUM/EXHIBIT	HISTORIC STRUCTURE	DAY USE ONLY	GROUP TRAILER	TRAILER DUMP STATION	NATURE HIKING TRAILS	MISCELLANEOUS
MUSTANG ISLAND	●				●	●	●		●		○	○							●	●	C,Z
PALMETTO	●				●	●	●		●		○	○							●	●	X
PALO DURO CANYON — SUMMER DRAMA "Texas"	●		●	●	●	●	●		●	●	●					●			●	●	RE DD
PEDERNALES FALLS	●				●	●	●		●		○	○							●	●	C,Z
RESACA DE LA PALMA SITE**	AREA PRESENTLY CLOSED TO PUBLIC PENDING DEVELOPMENT																				
RUSK/PALESTINE	●		P	●	●	●	●		●		○								●	●	B
SEA RIM	●				●	●	●		●		○	○		●	●			●	●	●	C,Z
SOUTH LLANO RIVER PARK SITE**	AREA PRESENTLY CLOSED TO PUBLIC PENDING DEVELOPMENT																				
TYLER	●	●	PC	●	●	●	●	●	●	●	●	●							●	●	B
VILLAGE CREEK PARK SITE**	AREA PRESENTLY CLOSED TO PUBLIC PENDING DEVELOPMENT																				
STATE HISTORICAL PARKS																					
ADMIRAL NIMITZ						●									●	●	●				A
CONFEDERATE REUNION GROUNDS			P			●			●		○	○				●				●	
FORT GRIFFIN	●		P		●	●	●		●		○				●	●				●	L
FORT RICHARDSON	●		P	●	●	●	●		●		○				●	●				●	Z
GOLIAD	●	●	S	●	●	●	●		●		○	●			●	●	●		●	●	T,P,Z
GOVERNOR HOGG SHRINE			P			●			●		●				●	●	●				
HUECO TANKS — INDIAN PICTOGRAPHS	●				●	●	●		●		●								●	●	
JIM HOGG						●			●		●				●	●	●			●	
LYNDON B. JOHNSON			S			●			●		○	●			●	●	●				LA
MISSION TEJAS	●		P	●	●	●	●		●		○	○				●				●	
SABINE PASS BATTLEGROUND						●			●		●			●		●	●				
SAN JACINTO BATTLEGROUND — BATTLESHIP TEXAS			P			●			●		○				●	●	●				
SEMINOLE CANYON — INDIAN PICTOGRAPHS	●				●	●	●		●							●				●	●
STEPHEN F. AUSTIN	●	●	S	●	●	●	●		●		○	●			●	●			●	●	G
TEXAS STATE RAILROAD — CONTACT PARK FC*. SCHEDULE OF RUNS						●			●							●	●				
VARNER-HOGG — GUIDED TOURS			P			●			●		●				●	●	●				
WASHINGTON-ON-THE-BRAZOS			P			●			●		●				●	●	●				A,X
STATE NATURAL AREAS/FISHING PIERS																					
COPANO BAY*						●			●		●			●							
ENCHANTED ROCK	●		P		●	●			●									●		●	Z
HILL COUNTRY																					
LOST MAPLES	●				●	●	●		●		○	○				●		●	●	●	C,T,Z
PORT LAVACA*						●			●		●			●							
QUEEN ISABELLA*						●					●										
STATE HISTORIC SITES/STRUCTURES																					
ACTON — BURIAL SITE OF DAVY CROCKETT'S WIFE																●					
CADDOAN MOUNDS						●									●	●	●			●	
EISENHOWER BIRTHPLACE						●									●	●	●				
FANNIN BATTLEGROUND			P			●			●		●					●	●				
FANTHORP INN**	AREA PRESENTLY CLOSED TO PUBLIC PENDING DEVELOPMENT																				
FORT LANCASTER						●									●	●	●				
FORT LEATON						●			●						●	●	●				
FORT McKAVETT						●			●						●	●	●				
FULTON MANSION															●	●	●				
KREISCHE COMPLEX**/MONUMENT HILL						●			●							●				●	
LANDMARK INN — (HOTEL ROOMS)						●			●							●				●	
LIPANTITLAN*	○					●			●												
MAGOFFIN HOME						●									●	●	●				
MATAGORDA ISLAND	○			CT		●				○		○	○			●	●		●	●	C,Z
JOSE ANTONIO NAVARRO						●									●	●	●				
OLD FORT PARKER				·		●									●	●	●				
PORT ISABEL LIGHTHOUSE																●	●				
RANCHO DE LAS CABRAS**	AREA PRESENTLY CLOSED TO PUBLIC PENDING DEVELOPMENT																				
SAM BELL MAXEY HOUSE															●	●	●				
SAN JOSE MISSION						●									●	●	●				
SEBASTOPOL HOUSE	AREA PRESENTLY CLOSED TO PUBLIC PENDING DEVELOPMENT																				
STARR MANSION**															●	●	●				

FACILITIES

* FACILITIES NOT OPERATED BY PARKS AND WILDLIFE
** SITES ARE NOT OFFICIALLY NAMED
○ PERMITTED BUT FACILITIES NOT PROVIDED
● FACILITIES OR SERVICES PROVIDED FOR ACTIVITY

A   AUDITORIUM
B   BOATS FOR RENT
C   GROUP CAMP
CT CHEMICAL TOILETS
D   SCENIC DRIVE
E   EQUESTRIAN TRAIL
G   GOLF
H   GROUP HALL
L   TEXAS LONGHORN HERD
M   MINIATURE GOLF
P   GROUP PICNIC
R   RENTAL HORSES
S   RECREATION HALL
X   OPEN SHELTERS
GB GROUP BARRACKS
Z   PRIMITIVE CAMPING

For information on those park facilities accessible to and usable by the handicapped, ask for park brochure on handicapped facilities.

Caddo Lake State Park, one mile west of Karnack in Harrison County, consists of 480 acres along the 25,400 surface-acre **Caddo Lake.** A scenic area, it was acquired from private owners in 1933-37. Nearby Karnack is childhood home of **Mrs. Lyndon B. Johnson.** Close by is old city of **Jefferson,** famous as commercial center of Northeast Texas during last half of 19th century. Caddo Indian legend attributes formation of **Caddo Lake** to earthquake. Lake originally a natural lake, but dam added in 1914 for flood control; new dam replaced old one in 1971.

Caddoan Mounds State Historic Site in Cherokee County near Alto. Total of 93.5 acres acquired in 1975 by condemnation.

Caprock Canyons State Park, 3.5 miles north of Quitaque off Texas 86 in Briscoe County, has 13,960.6 acres. Purchased in 1975.

Cassells-Boykin State Park, Angelina County, seven miles northeast of Zavalla on **Lake Sam Rayburn.** Total acreage, 265. Acquired in October 1982, by lease from the Department of the Army. Facilities include boat ramp, two-pit toilets, 20 picnic sites, 10 campsites, water well and dump station. No fees are charged.

Choke Canyon State Park: South Shore Unit is a 385-acre park on the 26,000-acre Choke Canyon Reservoir. Located in Live Oak County 4 miles west of Three Rivers off Highway 72, approximately 70 miles equal distance from Corpus Christi and San Antonio. Facilities include picnic sites, campsites with and without electricity, a group shelter and boat ramp with boat dock.

Cleburne State Recreation Area is a 528-acre park located in Johnson County; 75 acres are designated a **wildlife refuge;** 116-acre lake; acquired from the city of Cleburne, Johnson County and private owners in 1935 and 1936. Glen Rose dinosaur tracks found on Paluxy River may be seen at nearby **Dinosaur Valley State Park.**

Confederate Reunion Grounds State Historical Park, located in Limestone County on the Navasota River where it is joined by Jack's Creek, is 78.5 acres in size. The park may be reached by going 6 miles south of Mexia on State Highway 14, then 2.5 miles west on FM 2705.

Copano Bay State Fishing Pier, a 6-acre park with restaurant and fishing pier, is located five miles north of Rockport in Aransas County. Operated by leased concession.

Copper Breaks State Park, 12 miles south of Quanah on Texas 6, was acquired in 1970. Recreation park features rugged scenic beauty on 1,888.7 acres and has a 70-acre lake. Medicine Mounds were important ceremonial sites of Comanche Indians. Nearby **Pease River** was site of battle, 1860, in which **Cynthia Ann Parker** was recovered from Comanches. Portion of official **Texas longhorn herd** maintained at park.

Daingerfield State Park in Morris County is a 551-acre recreational area which includes an 80-surface-acre lake; deeded in 1935 by private owners. This area center of iron industry in Texas; nearby is **Lone Star Steel Co.** On grounds of company is old blast furnace that helped in manufacturing guns and other metal objects for Civil War.

Davis Mountains State Park is 1,869 acres in Jeff Davis County. The scenic area, near Fort Davis, was deeded over many years by private owners. First European, **Antonio de Espejo,** came to area in 1583. Nearby points of interest include **Fort Davis National Historic Site, McDonald Observatory** and scenic loop through **Davis Mountains. Davis Mountains State Park** located halfway between **Carlsbad Caverns** and **Big Bend National Park.** Nearby are scenic **Limpia, Madera, Musquiz** and **Keesey** canyons; **Camino del Rio;** ghost town of **Shafter; Capote Falls; Sul Ross State University** in Alpine; and **Fort Leaton State Historic Site. Indian Lodge,** built by the Civilian Conservation Corps during the early 1930s, has 39 rooms, a restaurant and a swimming pool.

Dinosaur Valley State Park, located near Glen Rose in Somervell County, is a 1,523-acre scenic park. Land was acquired from private owners in 1969 and 1973. Dinosaur tracks and two full-scale dinosaur models on display. There is longhorn herd in park.

Eisenhower State Recreation Area, 457 acres located in Grayson County, was acquired by an Army lease in 1954 and named for the 34th U.S. president, Dwight David Eisenhower. Park located on shores of **Lake Texoma.** First Anglo settlers came to area in 1835 and 1836; **Fort Johnson** was established in area in 1840; **Colbert's Ferry** established on Red River in 1853 and operated until 1931.

Eisenhower Birthplace State Park, a Historic Site, is 3 acres, including the birthplace of **Dwight David Eisenhower,** in Denison, Grayson County. The property was acquired in 1958 from the Sid Richardson Foundation. Restoration of home complete, with furnishings of period and some personal effects of Gen. Eisenhower. His history of World Wars I and II is here. Also crank-type telephone with personal greetings from "Ike." Town of **Denison** established on Butterfield Mail Route in 1858.

Enchanted Rock State Natural Area is 1,643 acres on Big Sandy Creek 18 miles north of Fredericksburg on FM 965. Acquired in 1978 from Nature Conservancy of Texas, Inc. **Enchanted Rock** is huge granite boulder rising 500 feet above ground and covering 640 acres. Indians believed ghost fires flickered at top and were awed by weird creaking and groaning geologists now say resulted from rock's heating by day and contracting in cool night.

Fairfield Lake State Recreation Area is 1,460 acres, six miles northeast of the city of Fairfield in Freestone County. Now open for overnight use, the park is leased from Texas Utilities. Surrounding woods predominantly oak and offer sanctuary for many species of birds and wildlife.

Falcon State Recreation Area is 573 acres located at southern end of **Falcon Lake** at Falcon Heights in Starr and Zapata counties. The park was leased from the International Boundary and Water Commission in 1954. Nearby are Mexico and **Fort Ringgold** in Rio Grande City; **Bentsen-Rio Grande Valley State Park** is 65 miles away.

Fannin Battleground State Historic Site, 9 miles east of Goliad in Goliad County. The park was acquired by legislative enactment in 1965. At this site on March 20, 1836, **Col. J. W. Fannin** surrendered to Mexican **Gen. Jose Urrea** after **Battle of Coleto;** 342 massacred and 28 escaped near what is now **Goliad State Historical Park.** Near Fannin site is **Gen. Zaragoza's Birthplace** and partially restored **Mission Nuestra Senora del Espiritu Santo de Zuniga.** (See also **Goliad State Historical Park** in this list.)

Fanthorp Inn State Historic Site includes a historic structure and 1.4 acres at Anderson in Grimes County; acquired by purchase in 1977 from Edward Buffington. Closed pending development in 1987.

Fort Griffin State Historical Park is 506 acres 15 miles north of Albany in Shackelford County. The state was deeded the land by the county in 1935. A herd of Texas longhorns resides on the park range. On bluff overlooking townsite of Fort Griffin and Clear Fork of Brazos River valley are ruins of **Old Fort Griffin,** restored bakery, replicas of enlisted men's huts. (Townsite is not in park boundaries.) Fort constructed in 1867, deactivated 1881; crumbling ruins of various structures still may be seen. Albany annually holds **"Fandangle"** in commemoration of frontier times.

Fort Lancaster State Historic Site, 81.6-acres located about 33 miles west of Ozona on U.S. 290 in Crockett County, acquired in 1968 by deed from Crockett County; Henry Meadows donated 41 acres in 1975. **Fort Lancaster** established Aug. 20, 1855, to guard San Antonio-El Paso Road and protect movement of supplies and immigrants from Indian hostilities; fort abandoned March 19, 1861, after Texas seceded from Union.

Fort Leaton State Historic Site, four miles east of Presidio in Presidio County on FM 170, was acquired in 1967 from private owners. Consists of 16.5 acres, 5 of which are on site of pioneer trading post. In 1848, **Ben Leaton** built fortified trading post known as **Fort Leaton** near present Presidio. Ben Leaton died in 1851. Partial reconstruction of fort begun in early 1930s and in 1936, Texas Centennial Commission placed marker at site.

Fort McKavett State Historic Site, 80.8 acres acquired in 1967 and 1968 in part from Fort McKavett Restoration, Inc., and Menard County, is located 17 miles west of Menard. Fort built for protection of settlers against Indians in 1852. Originally called **Camp San Saba,** built by War Department as protection for frontier settlers. Camp later renamed for **Capt. Henry McKavett,** killed at Battle of Monterrey, Sept. 21, 1846. Fort abandoned March 1859; reoccupied April 1, 1868; after **Gen. Ranald S. Mackenzie** subdued Indians, fort no longer needed, abandoned June 30, 1883.

Fort Parker State Recreation Area includes 1,485.2 acres south of Mexia in Limestone County. Named for the former fort located near the present park, the site was acquired by deeds from private owners between 1935 and 1937. Nearby point of interest is **Old Fort Parker State Historic Site,** replica of fort erected in 1834 for protection from Indians. Daughter of founder, **Cynthia Ann Parker,** captured by Indians May 19, 1836. She married **Chief Peta Nocona** and mothered **Quanah Parker,** last great Comanche chief, involved in **Battle of Palo Duro.**

Fort Richardson State Historical Park, located one-

half mile south of Jacksboro in Jack County, contains 396.1 acres. Acquired in 1968 from City of Jacksboro. Fort founded in summer of 1866; named **Fort Jacksboro** at that time. April 1867 it was abandoned for site 20 miles farther north; on Nov. 19, 1867, made permanent post at Jacksboro and named for **Israel Richardson. Fort Richardson** part of defensive system against Indians. Expeditions sent from Fort Richardson arrested Indians responsible for **Salt Creek Massacre** in 1871 and fought Comanches in Palo Duro Canyon. Fort abandoned again in May 1878.

Franklin Mountains State Park comprises 16,108 acres in El Paso County. Pedestrian access for day use activities such as hiking, nature study and picnicking is permitted. The site is undeveloped, with no facilities or utilities, and vehicular traffic is prohibited.

Fulton Mansion State Historic Structure is 3.4 miles north of Rockport in Aransas County. Total acreage of 2.3 acquired by purchase from private owner in 1976. Three-story wooden structure, built in 1871-1876, was home of George W. Fulton, prominent in South Texas for economic and commercial influence; mansion derives significance from its innovative construction and Victorian design.

Galveston Island State Park, located approximately six miles southwest of Galveston on FM 3005, is a 1,944-acre site acquired in 1970 from private owners. Offers camping, nature study and fishing amid sand dunes and grassland.

Garner State Park is 1,419.8 acres of recreational facilities in northern Uvalde County. Named for John Nance Garner, U.S. Vice President, 1933-1941, the park was deeded in 1934 by private owners. Nearby is **John Nance "Cactus Jack" Garner Museum** in Uvalde. Nearby also are historic ruins of **Mission Nuestra Senora de la Candelaria del Canon**, founded in 1749; **Camp Sabinal** (a U.S. Cavalry post and later Texas Ranger camp) established 1856; **Fort Inge**, established 1849.

Goliad State Historical Park is 186.6 acres along the San Antonio River in Goliad County. The land was deeded in 1931 by the city and county of Goliad. Nearby are the sites of several battles in the Texas fight for independence from Mexico. The park includes a replica of **Mission Nuestra Senora del Espiritu Santo de Zuniga**, originally established 1722 and settled at its present site in 1749. Park unit contains **Gen. Zaragoza's Birthplace** which is located at **Presidio la Bahia**. He was Mexican national hero who led troops against French at historic Battle of Puebla. Park property also contains ruins of **Mission Nuestra Senora del Rosario**, established 1754, located four miles west of Goliad on U.S. 59. Other nearby points of historical interest are restored **Presidio Nuestra Senora de Loreto de la Bahia**, established 1722 and settled on site in 1749; it is located ¼ mile south of **Goliad State Historical Park** on U.S. 183. Goliad memorial shaft marking common burial site of **Fannin** and victims of **Goliad massacre** (1836) is near Presidio la Bahia. (See also **Fannin Battleground State Historic Site**, above.)

Goose Island State Recreation Area in Aransas County is 307 acres; it was deeded by private owners in 1931-1935. Located here is the tree estimated to be 2,000 years old and listed by American Forestry Association as the **national co-champion live oak**; certified largest live oak in Texas in 1969. **Aransas Wildlife Refuge**, wintering ground for rare and endangered **whooping cranes**, just across St. Charles Bay.

Gov. Hogg Shrine State Historical Park is a 26.7-acre tract in Quitman, Wood County. Named for James Stephen Hogg, first native-born governor of Texas, the park includes a museum housing items which belonged to Hogg. Seventeen acres deeded by the Wood County Old Settlers Reunion Association in 1946; 4.74 acres gift of Miss Ima Hogg in 1970; 3 acres purchased. Old Settlers Reunion held annually in August in this park. **Gov. James Stephen Hogg Memorial Shrine** created in 1941. Gov. Hogg's wedding held in **Stinson Home; Miss Ima Hogg Museum** houses both park headquarters and display of representative history of entire Northeast Texas area.

Guadalupe River State Park in Kendall and Comal counties, 13 miles east of Boerne on Texas 46. Total acreage 1,937.7 on Guadalupe River. Acquired by deed from private owners in 1975. Park has four miles of river frontage with several white-water rapids and is located in middle of 20-mile stretch of Guadalupe River noted for canoeing. It has picnic and camp sites with restroom and shower facilities.

Hill Country State Natural Area (Louise Merrick Unit) in Bandera and Medina counties, nine miles west of Bandera on FM 1077. Total acreage 4,753 acquired by

gift from Louise Merrick in 1976. Park is located in typical Texas Hill Country on West Verde Creek and contains several spring-fed streams.

Hueco Tanks State Historical Park, located 32 miles northeast of El Paso in El Paso County, was obtained from the county in 1969. Featured in this 860.3-acre park are large natural cisterns and site of last great Indian battle in county. Apaches, Kiowas, Comanches and earlier Indian tribesmen camped here and left behind pictographs telling of their adventures. Tanks served as watering place for **Butterfield Overland Mail Route**.

Huntsville State Park is 2,083.2-acre recreational area in Walker County, acquired by deeds from private owners in 1934. **Sam Houston State University** located at nearby Huntsville. **Texas Department of Corrections** also located in Huntsville. At Huntsville is old homestead of Sam Houston **(Steamboat House)** and his grave; homestead contains personal effects of Houston. Park adjoins **Sam Houston National Forest** and encloses **Lake Raven**. Approximately 50 miles away is **Alabama-Coushatta Indian Reservation** in Polk County.

Inks Lake State Park is 1,200.7 acres of recreational facilities along Inks Lake, on the Colorado River, in Burnet County. The park was acquired by deeds from the Lower Colorado River Authority and private owners in 1940. Nearby is **Longhorn Cavern State Park, LBJ Ranch, LBJ State Historical Park, Pedernales Falls State Park** and **Enchanted Rock State Natural Area**. Granite Mountain and quarry at nearby Marble Falls furnished material for Texas state capitol. Deer, turkey and other wildlife abundant. **Buchanan Dam**, largest multi-arch dam in world, located six miles from park.

Jeff Davis State Recreation Area is 37.9 acres southeast of Hillsboro in Hill County. The state acquired the land in 1924 from the Veterans' Administration and leased it to the American Legion until the year 2043. (No park development.)

Jim Hogg State Historical Park is 177.4 acres in East Texas Piney Woods in Cherokee County. A memorial to the state's first native-born governor, James Stephen Hogg, the property was deeded by the city of Rusk in 1941.

Jose Antonio Navarro State Historic Site, on .6 acre in downtown San Antonio, was acquired by donation from San Antonio Conservation Society Foundation in 1975. Has furnished Navarro House complex built about 1848.

Kerrville State Recreation Area is a 517.2-acre area along the Guadalupe River in Kerr County. The land was deeded by the city of Kerrville in 1934. Near the park is the site of **Camp Verde**, scene of an experiment involving the use of **camels** for transportation; the camp was active from 1855 to 1869. **Bandera Pass**, 12 miles south of Kerrville, noted gap in chain of mountains through which passed camel caravans, wagon trains, Spanish conquistadores, immigrant trains. In nearby Fredericksburg is atmosphere of old country of Germany and famous **Nimitz Hotel**. (See **Admiral Nimitz Museum Historical Area**.)

Kreische Complex Park Site located adjacent to **Monument Hill State Historic Site** in LaGrange, Fayette County, is 35.98 acres, acquired by purchase from private owners. Contains Kreische Brewery and house complex built between 1850-1855 on Colorado River; probably first commercial brewery in state. Brewery closed in 1888; it now consists of several intact structures surrounded by ruins in various stages of deterioration. Various out-buildings located on site were associated with brewery and family.

Lake Arrowhead State Recreation Area, south of Wichita Falls in Clay County; this 524-acre park was acquired from city of Wichita Falls in 1970.

Lake Brownwood State Recreation Area in Brown County is 537.5 acres acquired from the Brown County Water Improvement District No. 1 in 1934. Park situated on **Lake Brownwood** near geographical center of Texas.

Lake Colorado City State Recreation Area, 500 acres leased for 50 years from a utility company. It is located in Mitchell County 11 miles southwest of Colorado City.

Lake Corpus Christi State Recreation Area, a 365 land-acre park located in San Patricio, Jim Wells and Live Oak counties, was leased from city of Corpus Christi in 1934. Lake noted for big blue, channel and yellow catfish. Sunfish, bass and crappie also taken. City of Corpus Christi and **Padre Island National Seashore** are nearby.

Lake Lewisville State Park is a 720-acre park located on the reservoir's east central shore. Located north of Dallas in Denton County, the park has campsites, screened shelters, boat ramps, park store and

Engine 500 of the Texas State Railroad waits to board passengers at the Rusk depot for the 24-mile journey through lush woodland to Palestine. Photo Courtesy of the Texas Parks & Wildlife Department.

swimming. Geology of Lake Lewisville directly affects the soils, thus the vegetation. Underlying the east side of the lake is the Eagle Ford Formation, a dark gray to tan shale with marine fossils deposited about 100 million years ago. Lake Lewisville State Park is located on what is called an upland terrace, where silts were deposited on top of shale by the ancient Trinity River.

Lake Livingston State Recreation Area, in Polk County, six miles southwest of Livingston on FM 3126, contains 635.5 acres along Lake Livingston. Acquired by deed from private landowners in 1971. Near ghost town of **Swartwout,** steamboat landing on Trinity River in 1830s and 1840s. Polk County's first commissioners court met there before voters selected Livingston as county seat.

Lake Mineral Wells State Park, located four miles east of the city of Mineral Wells on Highway 180 in Parker County, consists of 2,865 acres encompassing **Lake Mineral Wells.** The city of Mineral Wells donated 1,095 land acres and the 646-acre lake to Texas Parks and Wildlife Department in 1976. The remaining 1,102 acres were transferred from **Fort Wolters Army Post** by the U.S. Government to the State of Texas for use as park land.

Lake Somerville State Recreation Area, in Lee and Burleson counties, was leased from the federal government in 1969. The 5,200-acre park includes many recreational facilities. Many species of wild game observed at park; white-tailed deer, fox, coyote, raccoon, rabbit and quail abundant. Various park areas feature sandy or grassy shallow shorelines ideal for wading or swimming.

Lake Texana State Park (formerly **Palmetto Bend State Park Site**) is 575 acres, seven miles east of Edna on State Highway 111, with camping, boating, fishing, picnicking facilities.

Lake Whitney State Recreation Area is 955 acres along the east shore of **Lake Whitney** in Hill County. Acquired in 1954 by a Department of the Army lease, the state has control until 2003. Located on **Lake Whitney** near ruins of **Towash,** early Texas settlement inundated by Lake Whitney. Towash Village named for chief of Hainai Indians that moved into area in 1835. Park noted for bluebonnets in spring.

Landmark Inn State Historic Site 4.7 acres in Castroville acquired through donation by Miss Ruth Lawler in 1974. **Castroville,** known as **Little Alsace of Texas,** headquarters for group of Alsatian farmers settled there in

1840s. **Landmark Inn** built about 1844 as residence and store for Caesar Monad, mayor of Castroville 1851-1864.

Lipantitlan State Historic Site is five acres east of Orange Grove in Nueces County. The property was deeded by private owners in 1937. Fort constructed here in 1833 by Mexican government; fort fell to Texas forces in 1835. **Lake Corpus Christi State Recreation Area** is nearby.

Lockhart State Recreation Area is 263.7 acres near Lockhart in Caldwell County. The land was deeded by private owners between 1934 and 1937. **Emanuel Episcopal Church** in Lockhart is one of **oldest Protestant churches** in continuous use in Texas. After Comanche raid at Linnville, **Battle of Plum Creek** (1840) was fought in area.

Longhorn Cavern State Park in Burnet County is 639 acres classified as a scenic park. It was acquired in 1932-1937 from private owners. The cave has been used as a shelter since prehistoric times. Among legends about the cave is one that the outlaw Sam Bass hid a $2 million cache of stolen money. Another legend is that the defenders of the Confederacy made gunpowder in the cave during the Civil War, and another story states Gen. Robert E. Lee, while stationed in Texas before the Civil War, chased some Indians into the cave but lost their trail. **Inks Lake State Park** and federal fish hatchery located nearby. Park operated by concession agreement.

Lost Maples State Natural Area consists of 2,174.2 scenic acres in Bandera County, four miles north of Vanderpool on Ranch Road 187. (Formerly **Sabinal Canyon State Park.**) Acquired by purchase from private owners in 1973. Outstanding example of Edwards Plateau flora and fauna, features isolated stand of uncommon Uvalde **bigtooth maple. Golden-cheeked warbler** and **black-capped vireo** have been sighted in park.

Lyndon B. Johnson State Historical Park, in Gillespie County near Stonewall, contains 717.8 acres. Acquired in 1967 with private donations. Statue of **Johnson** unveiled in 1974 ceremonies. Home of **Lyndon B. Johnson** located north bank of Pedernales River across Ranch Road 1 from park; portion of official Texas **longhorn herd** maintained at park. Wildlife exhibit includes turkey, deer and buffalo. Living history demonstrations in progress at restored **Sauer-Beckmann house.** Reconstruction of **Johnson birthplace,** located east of ranch house at end of Park Road 49, open to public. Nearby is family cemetery where former president and relatives are buried. In Johnson City is boyhood home of President Johnson. Near outskirts of Johnson City is cluster of stone barns and buildings constructed by his grandfather, Sam Ealy Johnson Sr., and his brother Tom. (See also National Parks.)

McKinney Falls State Park in Travis County east of Interstate 35 and near Bergstrom AFB is a 632.7-acre park acquired in 1970 from private donation. The headquarters of the Parks and Wildlife Department are at this location.

Mackenzie State Recreation Area in Lubbock County is a 542.2-acre park acquired in 1935 from the city of Lubbock, then leased to that city until 2037. The park was named for Gen. Ranald S. Mackenzie, famous for his campaigns against Indians in West Texas. One of the main features is a colony of native Texas prairie dogs; a section is called "Prairie Dog Town." (Not operated by parks department.)

Magoffin Home State Historic Site, in El Paso County in the city of El Paso; total acreage, 1.5. Purchased jointly by the state of Texas and the city of El Paso in 1976, it is operated by the Texas Parks and Wildlife Department. The Magoffin Home was built in 1875 by pioneer El Pasoan Joseph Magoffin and displays a regional architectural style developed in the Southwest between 1865 and 1880.

Martin Creek Lake State Recreation Area, in Rusk County, 4 miles south of Tatum off State Highway 43. Total acreage 216.4 acres, deeded to the Parks and Wildlife Department by the Texas Utilities Generating Company in 1976. Pending development, approximately 15 acres immediately adjacent to the boat ramp is available for public use. The site is being operated by a concession contract at this time and provides boat ramps and parking area, fishing and picnic supplies and limited picnic sites for day-use visitors. The primary use of the Martin Creek Lake State Park Site is to provide boat ramp access to the reservoir for fishermen.

Martin Dies Jr. State Park, until 1965 the Dam B State Park, is 705-acre recreational area in Jasper and Tyler counties. The land was acquired from the U.S. Army Corps of Engineers by lease in 1964. Park located at edge of Big Thicket. In spring, Dogwood Festival is held at Woodville. Park approximately 30 miles from Alabama-Coushatta Indian Reservation.

Matagorda Island Wildlife Conservation/Park Area, separated from the mainland by San Antonio and Espiru Santo bays, Matagorda Island is one of the barrier islands that border the Gulf and protect the mainland from the great tides and strong wave action of the open ocean. The southwestern tip of the island, consisting of 1,500 acres, is privately owned, and the remainder, which extends approximately 24 miles to the northeast, consists of 24,893 acres of state land and 19,000 acres of federal land. Under a cooperative agreement between the U.S. Department of the Interior and the State of Texas approved in 1983, the entire area of public lands is managed by the Texas Parks and Wildlife Department.

Meridian State Recreation Area in Bosque County is 502.4-acre park including a 73-acre lake. The land was acquired from private owners in 1933-1935. Tonkawa Indians lived in surrounding area before coming of white man; Tawakoni Indians also occupied area prior to 1841. Texas-Santa Fe expedition of 1841 passed through Bosque County near present site of park. Park located on Bee Creek in Bosque Valley is very popular for bream, crappie, catfish and bass fishing. Golden-cheeked warblers nest here annually.

Mission Tejas State Historical Park is a 118-acre park in Houston County. Situated in the Davy Crockett National Forest, the park was acquired from the Texas Forest Service in 1957 by legislative enactment. In the park is a replica of the Mission San Francisco de los Tejas, which was established in 1690; was first mission in east Texas; abandoned due to Indians; re-established 1716 but again abandoned 1719. In 1721, third attempt made and was successful for a while but was abandoned for third and final time in 1730 and moved to San Antonio; renamed San Francisco de la Espada and is today one of four historic mission sites included in the San Antonio Missions National Historical Park.

Monahans Sandhills State Park consists of 3,840 acres of sand dunes in Ward and Winkler counties. The land is leased by the state until 2056. Because water was readily available, dunes used as meeting place by raiding Indians. Burial site of prehistoric Indians in exhibit building adjacent to interpretive center. Odessa meteor crater is nearby.

Monument Hill State Historic Site consists of 4.4 acres

southwest of La Grange in Fayette County. The land was acquired in two parcels — monument and tomb area transferred from Board of Control in 1949; the rest from the Archbishop of San Antonio in 1956. The hill, a historical site, bears a memorial shaft dedicated to Capt. Nicholas Dawson and his men, who fought at Salado Creek in 1842, in Mexican Gen. Woll's invasion of Texas, and to the men of the "black bean lottery" (1843) of the Mier Expedition. Bodies of these heroes were brought to Monument Hill for reburial in 1848. In La Grange, old tree under which Captain Dawson recruited ill-fated expedition still stands.

Mother Neff State Park was the first official state park in Texas. It originated with six acres designated for park purposes by the will of Mrs. I.E. Neff, mother of Pat M. Neff, Governor of Texas from 1921 to 1925. The park now contains 259 acres along the Leon River in Coryell County and is classified as historical park. The additional land was deeded to the state in 1934 by private owners.

Mustang Island State Park is 3,703.6 acres on Gulf of Mexico in Nueces County, 14 miles south of Port Aransas; acquired from private owners in 1972. Mustang Island has a unique and complicated ecosystem, dependent upon the sand dune. The seemingly sterile dunes are the product of wind-deposited sand held in place by stabilizing drought-resistant vegetation. The foundation plants of the dunes are sea oats, beach panic grass and soilbind morning glory. Studies have shown that plants and their progeny can collect enough sand to build a 15-foot dune in three years. The dunes are capable of reducing the destructive might of hurricane-driven waves and protecting bay and mainland areas.

Old Fort Parker State Historic Site, an 11-acre park in Limestone County, was deeded by private owners in 1933. In the park is a replica of Fort Parker stockade, built in 1834 and was site of abduction of Cynthia Ann Parker on May 19, 1836, by Comanche and Kiowa Indians.

Palmetto State Park, a scenic park, is 263.6 acres along the San Marcos River in Gonzales County. The land was deeded in 1934-1937 by private owners. Artesian wells produce distinctive, sulphur-laden water. Nearby Gonzales and Ottine important in early Texas history. Gonzales settled 1825 as center of Green DeWitt's colonies. Nearby is site of Elks' Hospital and Texas Rehabilitation Center.

Palo Duro Canyon State Park, the state's largest, consists of 16,402 acres in Armstrong and Randall counties. The land was deeded by private owners in 1933 and is the scene of the annual production of the drama, Texas. Scenic canyon one million years old and exposes rocks spanning about 200 million years of geological time. Coronado may have visited canyon in 1541. Canyon officially discovered by Capt. R. B. Marcy in 1852. Scene of decisive battle in 1874 between Comanche and Kiowa Indians and U.S. Army troops under Gen. Ranald Mackenzie. Also scene of early ranch undertaking started by Charles Goodnight in 1876.

Pedernales Falls State Park, 4,860 acres in Blanco County about 14 miles east of Johnson City. Acquired from private owners in 1970 along banks of scenic Pedernales River. This area, formerly Circle Bar Ranch, typifies Edwards Plateau with live oaks, deer, turkey and stone hills. Golden-cheeked warbler nests here.

Port Isabel Lighthouse State Historic Structure consists of .6 acre in Port Isabel in Cameron County. It was acquired by purchase from private owners in 1950 and includes a lighthouse constructed in 1852; near battle site of Palmito Ranch (1865); lighthouse remodeled 1952 and is still used. Resort facilities available across Queen Isabella Causeway at South Padre Island.

Port Lavaca State Fishing Pier is a recreational area, acquired by transfer of authority from Texas Highway Department in 1963. It is 1.8 acres on Lavaca Bay in Calhoun County. Main attraction is a 3,200-foot fishing pier made from the former causeway across the bay. Port Lavaca City Park is at base of the pier and offers a boat ramp, camping and picnicking facilities. Operated by leased concession.

Possum Kingdom State Recreation Area in Palo Pinto County is 1,528.7 acres adjacent to Possum Kingdom Lake, in Palo Pinto Mountains and Brazos River Valley. Numerous deer, other wildlife and some cattle of official Texas longhorn herd live in park. The area was acquired from the Brazos River Authority in 1940.

Purtis Creek Park Site in Henderson and Van Zandt counties, three miles north of Eustace on FM 316. Total acreage 1,582.4 acquired in 1976 from private owners. (Closed pending development.)

Queen Isabella State Fishing Pier in Cameron County

was transferred from the Texas State Highway Department in 1973. It is a 5,100-foot lighted fishing pier on seven acres, which connects Port Isabel with South Padre Island. Operated by leased concession.

Rancho de las Cabras State Park Site located in Wilson County. Acquired in 1977 and consists of 99.2 acres. Consists of chapel and three rooms facing walled patio. (Site closed to public.)

Resaca de la Palma State Park Site in Cameron County, three miles northwest of Brownsville, consists of 1,100 acres. Acquired by purchase from private owners in 1978. (Closed to public pending development.)

Rusk/Palestine State Park. Rusk unit located adjacent to Texas State Railroad Rusk Depot with total acreage of 110. Palestine unit located adjacent to Texas State Railroad Palestine Depot with 26 acres. (See also **Texas State Railroad State Historical Park**.)

Sabine Pass Battleground State Historical Park in Jefferson County, southeast of Sabine Pass, contains 56.3 acres, acquired by deed from Kountze County Trust in 1971. **Richard W. Dowling**, with small Confederate force, repelled an attempted 1863 invasion of Texas by Union naval gunboats during Civil War.

Sam Bell Maxey House State Historic Structure in Paris, Lamar County, donated by city of Paris in 1976. Consists of .4 acre. Most of furnishings accumulated by Maxey family included. In March 1971, the Maxey House was officially listed on the National Register of Historic Places.

San Jacinto Battleground State Historical Park is 329.9 acres on which is situated the 570-foot-tall monument erected in honor of Texans who defeated Mexican **Gen. Antonio Lopez de Santa Anna** on April 21, 1836. The site, classified a historical park, is in east Harris County. The 59th Legislature transferred the park to the Texas Parks and Wildlife Department. **The U.S.S. Texas,** another state historical shrine, is moored in the park.

Sea Rim State Park in Jefferson County, 10 miles west of Sabine Pass, contains 15,109.1 acres of marshland with five miles of Gulf beach shoreline, acquired from private owners in 1972. It is prime wintering area for waterfowl; also home of endangered red wolf, American alligator, rare river otter and muskrat.

Sebastopol House State Historic Structure in Seguin, Guadalupe County, was acquired by purchase in 1976 from Seguin Conservation Society, approximately 2.2 acres. Period furnishings are on display in the residence. Pending facility repair and development, not open to public.

Seminole Canyon State Historic Site in Val Verde County, nine miles west of Comstock, contains 2,172.5 acres; acquired by purchase from private owners in 1973. Canyon area contains several important prehistoric Indian pictograph sites. Historic interpretive center open.

Sheldon Wildlife Management Area and Park Site, Harris County on Carpenter's Bayou 20 miles northeast of downtown Houston just north of US 90. Total acreage, 2,503. Acquired by purchase in 1952 from the city of Houston. Facilities include two boat ramps with parking areas and restrooms; five T-head fishing piers and 5.5 miles of levees. Activities include nature study of coastal marshland habitat, bird watching of primarily waterfowl and marsh birds, and fishing with free access to all public facilities during the prescribed mid-February through September fishing season. No rates or charges.

Starr Mansion State Historic Site 3.1 acres in Marshall, Harrison County, not open to the public in 1987.

Stephen F. Austin State Historical Park, is 667.4 acres along the Brazos River in Austin County, named for the "Father of Texas." The area was deeded by the San Felipe de Austin Corporation and the San Felipe Park Association in 1940. Site of township of **San Felipe** was seat of government where conventions of 1832 and 1833 and **Consultation of 1835** held. These led to **Texas Declaration of Independence.** San Felipe was home of **Stephen F. Austin** and other famous early Texans; home of Texas' first Anglo newspaper (the **Texas Gazette**) founded in 1829, postal system of Texas originated here; beginning of **Texas Rangers.**

Texas State Railroad State Historical Park, Anderson and Cherokee counties, between the cities of Palestine and Rusk, adjacent to US 84. Total acreage, 488.7. Acquired by Legislative Act in 1971. Opened for limited runs in summer. See local Parks and Wildlife office for schedules. The railroad was built by the State of Texas to support the state-owned iron works at Rusk. Begun in 1896, the railroad was gradually extended until it reached Palestine in 1909 and established regular rail service between the towns. (See also **Rusk/Palestine State Park**.)

Tips State Recreation Area, 31.3 acres of recreational facilities, is on the Frio River in Live Oak County. The park, a mile west of Three Rivers, was deeded by private owners in 1925 and then leased for 99 years to Three Rivers. Park near site of **first glass factory** in Texas. Privately operated.

Tyler State Park is 985.5 acres, classified as recreational, north of Tyler in Smith County. Included is a 64-acre lake. The land was deeded by private owners in 1934 and 1935. Nearby Tyler famous as **rose capital of world;** there are located **Tyler Junior College** and planetarium, Tyler Rose Garden, Caldwell Children's Zoo and the **Goodman Museum.** Tyler is home of the **Tyler Rose Festival** each fall. **Morton** salt mines in Grand Saline, 40 miles from park.

Varner-Hogg Plantation State Historical Park is 65.2 acres along Varner Creek east of West Columbia in Brazoria County. The land originally was owned by Martin Varner, a member of **Stephen F. Austin's** "Old Three Hundred" colony, but became a later home of Texas governor **James Stephen Hogg.** The state acquired the property in 1956 by a deed from Miss Ima Hogg, daughter of the former governor. First rum distillery in Texas established in 1829 by Varner.

Washington-on-the-Brazos State Historical Park, consists of 154.1 acres southwest of Navasota in Washington County. The land was deeded by private owners in 1916. The land includes the site of the signing in 1836 of the **Texas Declaration of Independence** from Mexico, as well as the site of the later signing of the **Constitution of the Republic of Texas.** In 1842 and 1845, the land included the **capitol of the Republic;** it also included the home of Anson Jones, last president of the Republic of Texas.

Future Parks

The following parks were in the planning stage when this edition of the Texas Almanac went to press:

Lake Houston, South Llano River, Village Creek Park, Arroyo Colorado, Eagle Mountain Lake, Lake Bob Sandlin, Lakeview Park, Davis Hill, Lake Tawakoni and Gorman Falls.

National Parks, Historical Sites, Recreation Areas in Texas

Texas has two national parks, a national seashore, a biological preserve, several historic sites, memorials and recreation areas and 10 national wildlife refuges under supervision of the U.S. Department of Interior. In addition, the state has four national forests (see index) under jurisdiction of U.S. Department of Agriculture.

The number of visitors to national park sites in Texas has fluctuated during the last seven years, partly due to gasoline rationing during 1980 and 1981. For the number of visitors to national parks in Texas since 1980, see table on following page.

Alibates Flint Quarries National Monument consists of 1,079 acres in Potter County. For more than 10,000 years, pre-Columbian Indians dug agatized limestone from the quarries to make projectile points, knives, scrapers and other tools. The area is presently undeveloped and access is by guided tours only. There were 2,210 daily visits made to the area in 1986.

Amistad Recreation Area contains the U.S. portion of

Amistad Reservoir on the Rio Grande. Of 65,000 acres in the area, 43,250 acres are in United States. Limited camping space, and camping from boats permitted on shore. Commercial campgrounds, motels, hotels in area. Open year round. In 1986, there were 95,039 overnight stays reported, and 1,206,670 daily visits.

Big Bend National Park, established in 1944, has spectacular mountain and desert scenery, a variety of unusual geological structures. Located in the great bend of the Rio Grande, the international boundary between United States and Mexico. Park contains 740,118 acres. Numerous campsites are located in park, and the Chisos Mountain Lodge has accommodations for approximately 150 guests. Write for reservations to National Park Concessions, Inc., Big Bend National Park, Texas 79834. Park open year round. There were 221,481 overnight stays in 1986, and 200,620 daily visits.

Big Thicket National Preserve, set at 84,550 acres in Polk, Hardin, Liberty, Tyler, Jasper, Orange and Jefferson counties, was authorized Oct. 11, 1974, to protect biological crossroads of the flora and fauna of the north, south, east and west. Five of the 12 units authorized have developments open to the public as follows: **Turkey Creek Unit,** 7,800 acres, with double-loop, self-guiding nature trail and accessible public information station located on FM 420, 2½ miles east of Highway 69. Also contains a nine-mile hiking trail with accessible ½-mile long spur into a pitcher plant savannah. **Beech Creek Unit,** 4,856 acres, has one-mile loop trail through beech forest. **Hickory Creek Savannah Unit,** 668 acres, with one-mile self-guiding nature trail and ½-mile accessible loop. **Beaumont Unit,** 6,218 acres, has a marked canoe trail available. Waterway corridors open to visitors are: **Little Pine Island Bayou,** connecting Lance Rosier Unit to Beaumont Unit; **Menard Creek Corridor** south and west of Big Sandy Unit to Trinity River; **Neches River** from Dam B south to Beaumont. There were 392 overnight stays recorded in 1986, and 66,660 daily visits.

Chamizal National Memorial, established in 1973, consists of 54.9 acres dedicated to the peaceful settlement of a 99-year-old boundary dispute between the United States and Mexico. Located in the south-central part of El Paso, the park is open year-round from 8:00 a.m. to 5:00 p.m., and from 7:00 p.m. to 11:00 p.m. during performances. It hosts a variety of programs throughout the year, some of which include: The Border Folk Festival (first weekend in October); The Siglo de Oro "Spanish Golden Age Presentation" (February-March); The Border Jazz Festival (May); The Fourth of July — Fiesta of the Arts Celebration; The Zarzuela Festival (July-August); and The Sixteenth of September "Grito" Celebration. All programs are held in the park's quest to commemorate the signing of the Chamizal Treaty through the promotion of intercultural communication, understanding and harmony. There were 194,990 daily visits in 1986.

Fort Davis National Historic Site in Jeff Davis County was a key post in the West Texas defense system, guarding immigrants and tradesmen on the San Antonio-El Paso Road. Fort Davis was manned by black troops for many of the years it was active. These troops, called "Buffalo Soldiers" because of their curly hair, fought with great distinction in the Indian Wars. Henry O. Flipper, the first black graduate of West Point, served at Fort Davis in the 1880s. The 460-acre historic site is located in the Davis Mountains, the second-highest mountain range in the state. The site includes a museum, an auditorium with daily audio-visual programs, restored and refurnished buildings, picnic area and hiking trails. An annual festival is held on the grounds the Saturday of Labor Day weekend. The site was established in 1961. Lodging is available in the nearby community of Fort Davis. Open year round; 63,930 daily visits in 1986.

Guadalupe Mountains National Park, established 1972, consists of 76,293 acres in Hudspeth and Culberson counties. A mountain mass of Permian limestone rises abruptly from the surrounding desert and contains one of the most extensive fossil reefs on record. Deep canyons cut through this exposed fossil reef and provide a rare opportunity for geologic study. Special points of interest are **McKittrick Canyon and Guadalupe Peak, highest in Texas.** Campground near Pine Springs Headquarters area has 24 tent sites plus RV parking, and is hub for 80 miles of trails. Dog Canyon area located one-mile south of Texas-New Mexico state line, at end of NM State Road 137 and County Road 414, contains 18 tent spaces equipped with tables, grills, new comfort station and parking spaces for five self-contained recreational vehicles. Also a new visitor contact station and visitor horse corral. Open year round. Lodging at Van Horn, Texas; White's City or Carlsbad, N.M. There were 22,569 overnight stays in 1986; and 163,310 daily visits.

Lake Meredith Recreation Area, about 35 miles northeast of Amarillo, consists of a reservoir behind **Sanford Dam** on the Canadian River, in Moore, Hutchinson and Potter counties. Occupies 44,951 acres; popular for water-based activities. Marine launching ramps, picnic areas, unimproved campsites. Commercial lodging and trailer hookups available in nearby towns. Open year round. There were 149,063 recorded overnight stays in 1986, and 1,406,700 daily visits.

Lyndon B. Johnson National Historical Park includes the boyhood home of the 36th President of United States, and the Johnson Settlement in Johnson City; free bus tour starting at the LBJ State Park includes the **LBJ Birthplace, old school, cemetery** and close-up exterior look at the **Texas White House.** Site in Blanco and Gillespie counties was established Dec. 2, 1969, and contains 250 acres. Open year round. No camping on site; commercial campground, motels in area. There were 308,140 daily visits in 1986.

Padre Island National Seashore consists of a 67.5-mile stretch of a barrier island along the Gulf Coast; noted for its wide sand beaches, excellent fishing and abundant bird and marine life. Contains 130,355 acres in Kleberg, Willacy and Kenedy counties. Open year round. One paved campground (fee charged) located north of Malaquite Beach, unpaved (primitive) campground area south of beach. Six miles of beach are accessible by regular vehicles (including motor homes) and are open to camping. Fifty-five miles of beach are accessible only by 4x4 vehicles. All 55 miles of beach are also open to camping. Commercial lodging available outside boundaries of National Seashore. There were 80,265 recorded overnight stays in 1986, and 708,930 daily visits.

Palo Alto Battlefield National Historic Site, Brownsville, contains the site of the first of two important Mexican War battles fought on American soil. Gen. Zachary Taylor's victory here made invasion of Mexico possible. There are no federal facilities available at this time. No data available on daily visits.

Rio Grande Wild and Scenic River, is a 191.2-mile strip on the American shore of the Rio Grande in the Chihuahuan Desert that protects the river. It begins in **Big Bend National Park** and continues downstream to the Terrell-Val Verde County line. There are federal facilities in **Big Bend National Park** only. There were 702 daily visits in 1985, with 5,652 overnight stays; there were 820 daily visits in 1986, with 6,467 overnight stays.

San Antonio Missions National Historical Park consists of four Spanish Colonial Missions and two acequias, or irrigation systems, including **Espada Dam** and aqueduct. Each of the four missions — **Concepcion, San Jose, San Juan and Espada** — are open 8-5 CST and 9-6 DST. The park includes 475 acres and is located within the city of San Antonio. Each of the church structures continues to be used as an active parish. For more information, contact San Antonio Missions National Historical Park, 2202 Roosevelt Ave., San Antonio 78210; 512/229-5701. There were 250,410 visits in 1986.

Recreational Visits to National Parks in Texas

This information on National Parks in Texas was furnished by the **National Park Service.** Recreation visits to National Park Service Areas in Texas, by years, numbered 4,170,700 in 1980; 3,968,200 in 1981; 4,747,800 in 1982; 4,664,800 in 1983; 4,800,795 in 1984; 4,539,084 in 1985; and 4,573,390 in 1986. Because of rounding, totals may not add up. There were 97 trails in the National Park Areas in Texas and 409 miles of trails.

Name of Facility	1983	1984	1985	1986
	1,900	2,265	2,202	2,210
Alibates Flint Quarries National Monument, Potter County	1,221,400	1,164,360	1,138,720	1,206,670
Amistad Recreational Area, Rio Grande	164,900	167,670	221,481	200,620
Big Bend National Park	33,400	81,550	77,670	66,660
Big Thicket National Recreation Area	119,600	125,750	149,000	194,990
Chamizal National Monument, El Paso County	71,300	69,010	68,410	63,930
Fort Davis National Historic Site, Jeff Davis County	142,700	151,850	147,750	163,310
Guadalupe Mountains National Park, Hudspeth & Culberson counties	1,844,900	1,944,650	1,597,720	1,406,700
Lake Meredith National Recreational Area, Amarillo	299,500	276,420	287,610	308,140
Lyndon B. Johnson National Historical Park, Johnson City	630,200	613,400	669,080	708,930
Padre Island National Seashore	*	*	702	820
Rio Grande Wild and Scenic River	134,900	205,100	212,170	250,410
**San Antonio Missions National Historical Park				

*In 1983 and 1984, totals were included in Big Bend National Park totals.

**1984 was first full year of visits to this park.

Recreational Special Events

Fairs, festivals and other special events provide year-round recreation in Texas. Some are of national interest and many attract attendance from over the state. Most of them are primarily of local and regional interest.

In addition to those listed here, the recreational paragraph in the county descriptions refers to numerous events.

The list of fairs and expositions below was compiled from information furnished by the **Texas Association of Fairs and Expositions**, 411 W. Front, Tyler 75702; the **Texas State Department of Highways and Public Transportation, Travel and Information Div.**, Box 5064, Austin 78763; the **Texas Tourist Development Agency**, Box 12008, Capitol Sta., Austin 78711; and local chambers of commerce. Specific dates and more information may be obtained from executives listed below or local chambers of commerce.

Fairs, Expositions and Festivals

City—Name of Event, Date, Executive, Address

Abilene—West Texas Fair; Sept.; Sid Saverance; Box 5527 (79608).

Albany—Fort Griffin Fandangle; June; Fandangle Office; Box 185 (76430).

Alvarado—Pioneers and Old Settlers Reunion; Aug.; Otis A. Lane; Box 577 (76009).

Amarillo—Tri-State Fair; Sept.; Lynn M. Griffin; Box 31087 (79120).

Angleton—Brazoria Co. Fair; Oct.; Box 818 (77515).

Athens—Black-Eyed Pea Jamboree; July; Sandra D. Weir; Box 608 (75751).

Athens—Old Fiddlers' Reunion; May; Mary Branton; 110 E. Corsicana (75751).

Austin—Aqua Festival; Aug.; Festival Office; Box 1967 (78767).

Austin—Highland Lakes Bluebonnet Trail; April; Highland Lakes Assn.; Box 1967 (78767).

Austin—Laguna Gloria Fiesta; May; Laguna Gloria Art Museum; 3809 W. 35th (78703).

Bay City—Bay City Rice Festival; Oct.; Box 262 (77414).

Bay City—Matagorda Co. Fair; March; Michael J. Pruett; Box 1803 (77414).

Beaumont—Neches River Festival; April; Festival Office; 745 N. 11th, #200 (77702).

Beaumont—South Texas State Fair; Oct.; Joe Goetschius; Box 3207 (77704).

Bellville—Austin Co. Fair; Oct.; C. W. Brandes; Box 141 (77418).

Belton—Belton Rodeo and Celebration; July; Clarence Griggs; Box 659 (76513).

Big Spring—Howard Co. Fair; Sept.; R. G. Click; Box 2356 (79720).

Boerne—Boerne Berges Fest; June; Richard Baggs; Box 748 (78006).

Boerne—Kendall Co. Fair; Sept.; Mickey George; Box 954 (78006).

Brackettville—Western Horse Races and Barbecue; Sept.; Alamo Village; Box 528 (78832).

Brenham—Washington Co. Fair; Sept.; Douglas Borchardt; Box 105 (77833).

Brownsville—Charro Days; Feb.; LaVerne Hinojosa; Box 1904 (78520).

Caldwell—Burleson Co. Fair; June; Johnny L. Price; Box 634 (77836).

Canyon—"TEXAS" Historical Musical Drama; June; Raymond Raillard; Box 268 (79015).

Clifton—Central Texas Fair & Rodeo; Aug.; Jimmy Burch; Box 562 (76634).

Columbus—Colorado Co. Fair; Sept.; Tom Northrup; 4101 Greenbriar, #305, Houston (77098).

Columbus—Magnolia Homes Tour; May; Chamber of Commerce; Box 343 (78934).

Conroe—Montgomery Co. Fair; March; Stuart Traylor; Box 2347 (77305).

Corpus Christi—Bayfest; Sept.; Festival Office; Box 6683 (78411).

Corpus Christi—Buccaneer Days; April-May; Bob Tucker; Box 30404 (78404).

Dalhart—XIT Rodeo & Reunion; Aug.; XIT; Box 907 (79022).

Dallas—State Fair of Texas; Oct.; Wayne H. Gallagher; Box 26010 (75226).

DeLeon—DeLeon Peach & Melon Festival; Aug.; Betty Terrill; Box 44 (76444).

Decatur—Wise Co. Old Settlers Reunion; July; Don Niblett; 1309 N. Church (76234).

Denton—North Texas State Fair; Aug.; James Roden; Box 1695 (76202).

Edna—Jackson Co. Fair; Sept.-Oct.; Milton Bain; Box 788 (77957).

Ennis—National Polka Festival; May; Martin Zapleta; 310 Shawnee (75119).

Fairfield—Freestone Co. Fair; Aug.; Gene Chavers; Box 640 (75840).

Flatonia—Czhilispiel; Oct.; Chamber of Commerce; Box 651 (78941).

Fredericksburg—Easter Fires Pageant; Easter; Chamber of Commerce; Box 431 (78624).

Fredericksburg—Gillespie Co. Fair; Aug.; Melvin Bonn; Box 526 (78624).

Fredericksburg—Oktoberfest; Oct.; Sherman Durst; Box 222 (78624).

Freer—Freer Rattlesnake Roundup; April; Jesse Hammack; Box 717 (78357).

Galveston—Dickens' Evening on the Strand; Dec.; Galveston Hist. Found.; Drawer 539 (77553).

Gilmer—East Texas Yamboree; Oct.; Box 854 (75644).

Grand Prairie—National Championship Pow-Wow; Sept.; Traders Village; 2602 Mayfield (75051).

Greenville—Hunt Co. Fair; Aug.; Bobby F. Harris; Box 1071 (75401).

Groesbeck—Limestone Co. Fair; June; Bill Freeman; Box 229 (76642).

Hallettsville—Lavaca Co. Fair; Oct.-Nov.; Debbie Garner; Box 69 (77964).

Harlingen—Confederate Air Force Airshow; Oct.; CAF Museum; Box CAF (78550).

Hearne—Robertson Co. Fair; March; Claude Tindle Jr.; Box 246 (77859).

Hempstead—Waller Co. Fair; Sept.; Roy Wiesner; Box 911 (77445).

Hico—Old Settlers Reunion; July; Milton Rainwater; Rt. 3 (76457).

Hidalgo—Border Fest; March; Joe Vera III; Box 309 (78557).

Hondo—Medina Co. Fair; Sept.; Diana Brawner; Box 4 (78861).

Houston—Houston-Harris Co. Fair; Sept.; Donald Schill; Box 41048 (77240).

Houston—The Houston Festival; March; Karen Kerschner; 1950 W. Gray, #6 (77019).

Hughes Springs—Wildflower Trails of Texas; April; Bill McKinney; Rt. 1, Box 178 (75656).

Huntsville—Walker Co. Fair; April; Roy Partin; Box 1817 (77340).

Jefferson—Historical Pilgrimage; May; Chamber of Commerce; 116 W. Austin (75657).

Jefferson—Marion Co. Fair; Sept.; Waymon Moore; 116 W. Austin (75657).

Johnson City—Blanco Co. Fair; Aug.; Camille Coleman; Box 679 (78636).

Kenedy—Bluebonnet Days; April-May; Wade Phelps; Box 724 (78119).

Kerrville—Kerr Co. Fair; June; Sharrin Bacon; Box 842 (78029).

Kerrville—Texas State Arts & Crafts Fair; May; Audie Hamilton; Box 1527 (78028).

Killeen—Central Texas Exposition; March-April; John R. Cowsert; Box 878 (76540).

La Grange—Fayette Co. Fair; Aug.-Sept.; William H. Koehl; Box 544 (78945).

Lamesa—Dawson Co. Fair; Sept.; John J. Hegi; Box 301 (79331).

Laredo—Laredo Frontier Days & Rattlesnake Roundup; May; Elsa Rairie; Box 2245 (78041).

Laredo—Laredo Int'l Fair & Exposition; March; John B. Gilpin; Box 1770 (78044).

Laredo—Washington's Birthday Celebration; Feb.; Chamber of Commerce; Box 790 (78040).

Longview—Gregg Co. Fair and Exposition; Sept.; Billy G. Clay; Box 1124 (75606).

Lubbock—Panhandle-South Plains Fair; Sept.; Steve Lewis; Box 208 (79408).

Luling—Watermelon Thump; June; Mrs. Ann Manford; Box 710 (78648).

Marshall—Central East Texas Fair; Sept.; Jerry A. Martez; Drawer BB (75670).

Mission—Texas Citrus Fiesta; Jan.; Chamber of Commerce; Box 431 (78572).

Mount Pleasant—Titus Co. Fair; Sept.; Bobby C. Wood; Box 1232 (75455).

Nacogdoches—Piney Woods Fair; Oct.; Becky Boren; Box 368 (75963).

Navasota—Grimes Co. Fair; June; Ken Hughes; 217 E. Washington (77868).

New Braunfels—Comal Co. Fair; Sept.; Jan Jachec; Box 223 (78130).

New Braunfels—Wurstfest; Nov.; Tom Purdum; Box 180 (78130).

Odessa—Permian Basin Fair & Exposition; Sept.; Donald D. Thorn; Box 4812 (79760).

Palestine—Anderson Co. Fair; May; W. K. Spaith; Box 228 (75801).

Palestine—Dogwood Trails Festival; March; Chamber of Commerce; Drawer I (75801).

Paris—Red River Valley Fair; Sept.; Rita J. Haynes; Box 964 (75460).

Plantersville—Texas Renaissance Festival; Oct.-Nov.; David Coulam; Rt. 2, Box 219A-1 (77363).

Port Arthur—CavOILcade; Oct.; Chamber of Commerce; Fidelity Tower, #300N (77640).

Port Lavaca—Calhoun Co. Fair; Oct.; Charles L. Ward; Box 42 (77979).

Refugio—Refugio Co. Fair; Oct.; Glenn Naylor; Box 88 (78377).

Rosenberg—Fort Bend Co. Fair; Sept.-Oct.; Leroy Porthum; Box 428 (77471).

San Antonio—Fiesta San Antonio; April; Davis Burnett; 306 N. Presa, #8 (78205).

San Antonio—Texas Folklife Festival; Aug.; Leslie Lea; Box 1226 (78294).

Santa Fe—Galveston Co. Fair & Rodeo; April-May; Connia Webb; Box 889 (77510).

Shamrock—St. Patrick's Day Celebration; March; Chamber of Commerce; Box 588 (79079).

Snyder—Scurry Co. Fair; Sept.; Max Van Roeder; 2605 Ave. M (79549).

Stamford—Texas Cowboy Reunion; July; E. C. Swenson; Box 928 (79553).

Sulphur Springs—Hopkins Co. Fall Festival; Sept.; Jan Sprague; Box 177 (75482).

Sweetwater—Rattlesnake Roundup; March; Chamber of Commerce; Box 1148 (79556).

Texarkana—Four States Fair; Sept.-Oct.; Ralph Shoptaw; Box 1915 (75504).

Tyler—East Texas Fair; Sept.-Oct.; Bob Murdoch; 411 W. Front (75702).

Tyler—Texas Rose Festival; Oct.; Chamber of Commerce; Box 390 (75710).

Waco—Brazos River Festival & Cotton Palace Pageant; April; Chamber of Commerce; Drawer 1220 (76703).

Waco—Heart O'Texas Fair; Oct.; Leon Dollens; Box 7581 (76710).

Waxahachie—Scarborough Faire; May; Faire Office; Box 538 (75165).

Wharton—Wharton Co. Fair & Exposition; April; Patricia Mangum; Box 266 (77488).

Winnsboro—Autumn Trails Festival; Oct.; Chamber of Commerce; 201 W. Broadway (75494).

Woodville—Tyler Co. Dogwood Festival; March; Chamber of Commerce; 507 N. Pine St. (75979).

Yorktown—Western Days; Oct.; Janie Metting; Box 488 (78164).

Livestock Shows

Austin—Austin-Travis Co. Livestock Show; March or April; Dick Engle; Box 15703 (78761).

Donna—South Texas Lamb & Sheep Expo.; Jan.; Jas. C. McQueen; Box 794 (78537).

El Paso—Southwestern International Livestock Show & Rodeo; Feb.; Bernie Ricona; Box 10239 (79993).

Fort Worth—Southwestern Expo. & Fat Stock Show; Jan.-Feb.; W. R. Watt Jr.; Box 150 (76101).

Giddings—Lee Co. Jr. Livestock Show; March; Ruby Weiser; Box 599 (78942).

Houston—Houston Livestock Show & Rodeo; Feb.-March; Dan A. Gattis; Box 20070 (77225).

Mercedes—Rio Grande Valley Livestock Show; March; Frances Cooper; Box 867 (78570).

Pasadena—Pasadena Livestock Show and Rodeo; Sept.; Frank Baker; Box 565 (77501).

San Angelo—San Angelo Stock Show & Rodeo; March; Sheila H. Rathmell; Box 2450 (76902).

Victoria—Victoria Livestock Show; March; Randy Crow; Box 2255 (77902).

State Park Nature/Interpretive and Hiking Trails

Trails in state parks are designated as nature/interpretive trails or hiking trails, and many parks have both. Nature trails usually are less than a mile long with informational stops to explain points of interest. Hiking trails are longer, with some hikes requiring more stamina than others. Only those hiking trails of at least one mile in length are included in the following list. All designated nature trails are included. All trails are through flora native to the area.

Nature/Interpretive Trails

Abilene State Recreation Area: Elm Creek Nature Trail in Taylor County; guide posts and trail brochures available at park identify particular points of interest. Parts of trail are accessible to the handicapped.

Atlanta State Recreation Area: This 2.4-mile nature trail in Cass County winds through an undeveloped area of the park.

Bentsen-Rio Grande Valley State Park: Singing Chapparral Nature Trail in Hidalgo County has informational stops that correspond to park brochure; trail is 1.5 miles long.

Caddo Lake State Park: Forest Nature Trail in Harrison County is a little less than one mile long; numbered stops correspond to brochure explaining features of diversified vegetation.

Copper Breaks State Park: Juniper Ridge Nature Trail in Hardeman County is .5-mile long and a self-guided interpretive route through a portion of rugged breaks of Pease River. Many areas off trail are loose, unstable rock, and users are asked to remain on trail to avoid possible personal injury and to prevent creating further erosion.

Galveston Island State Park: Clapper Rail Nature Trail in Galveston County is a 3-mile trail through salt meadows and marsh; freshwater ponds located in meadows. Trail terminates with observation point overlooking surf and sea. Special features include bird blinds for photography and 1,000-foot boardwalk over marsh. Boardwalk accessible to handicapped.

Goliad State Historical Park: Two trails—the River Trail along San Antonio River, and Aranama Trail through subtropical woodland in Goliad County. Parts of trails are accessible to handicapped. Goliad is located on meeting ground of Gulf Coast Prairie and South Texas Brush Country.

Huntsville State Park: Big Chinquapin Nature Trail in Walker County is 1.3 miles long; bridges and boardwalks have not yet been constructed across marsh, so some wet or muddy spots may be encountered; also must cross a creek or two.

Lake Brownwood State Recreation Area: Texas Oaks Nature Trail in Brown County is just under a mile in length and portions are accessible to handicapped.

Lyndon B. Johnson State Historical Park: This is a 1.4-mile nature trail in Gillespie County, along which are informational stops where recordings of late President Johnson's voice convey message of the trail; trail accessible to the handicapped and passes through a living history exhibit of early 1900 farm life.

McKinney Falls State Park: Smith Rock Shelter Nature Trail in Travis County is just under a mile long; passes Smith Rock Shelter, an Indian campsite, and the remains of the McKinney homestead and mill.

Mission Tejas State Historical Park: Mile-long Tejas Timber Trail in Houston County.

Monahans Sandhills State Park: Short nature trail in Ward and Winkler counties; tracks in sand tell of activity in foreboding, seemingly barren sand dunes.

Palmetto State Park: Palmetto and River nature trails in Gonzales County total about one mile; at one time, this area was called Ottine Swamp; rare plant profusion found in park.

Pedernales Falls State Park: Hill Country Nature Trail in Blanco County .5-mile long; numbered trail markers correspond to interpretive booklet.

Sea Rim State Park: Gambusia Nature Trail in Jefferson County just under mile in length; consists of elevated boardwalk two feet above marsh. Numbered trail markers correspond to interpretive booklet.

Seminole Canyon State Historical Park: A 1.5-mile trail in Val Verde County goes to Fate Bell Shelter Cave, where visitors can see ancient Indian pictographs; climb back up from canyon floor strenuous.

Tyler State Park: Whispering Pines Nature Trail in Smith County is short trail with numbered stops that correspond to interpretive booklet; walk especially beautiful in spring when redbuds and dogwoods bloom.

Hiking Trails

Bastrop State Park: Several miles of undeveloped trails in Bastrop County through **Lost Pines** and other geographically isolated members of plant species.

Bentsen-Rio Grande Valley State Park: A 1.8-mile hiking trail in Hidalgo County lets hikers experience South Texas brushland, Rio Grande and old oxbow lake or resaca.

Caddo Lake State Park: There are 3.2 miles of hiking trails in Harrison County through scenic East Texas forests.

Copper Breaks State Park: Bull Canyon Hiking Trail in Hardeman County is pleasant, fairly easy hike about two miles long.

Daingerfield State Park: Scenic 2.5-mile hiking trail in Morris County; portions of trail are accessible to handicapped.

Davis Mountains State Park: Trail in Jeff Davis County is more than 4 miles long, one-way; begins at park's interpretive center, passes two overlooks on highest ridge and connects with trail leading to **Fort Davis National Historic Site.** Could be several-hour venture.

Dinosaur Valley State Park: Trail in Somervell County is 1.5-miles and goes near best-preserved dinosaur fossil footprints in Texas.

Eisenhower State Recreation Area: Trail 4.2 miles long in Grayson County, traverses entire length of park on Lake Texoma; passes through rugged ravines and grasslands.

Enchanted Rock State Natural Area (Gillespie County): No formally developed trails, but ample opportunity for both hiking and rock climbing.

Fairfield Lake State Recreation Area: Seven-mile hiking trail in Freestone County around **Big Brown Creek Primitive Camping Area.** An out-and-back trail, not a loop.

Garner State Park: Numerous undeveloped hiking trails in Uvalde County; short paved hike-and-bike trail runs along entrance road from park headquarters to main concession area.

Hueco Tanks State Historical Park: Few limited-access trails in El Paso County but many opportunities for climbing and hiking among boulders; **Chihuahuan Desert** scrub vegetation; caves and rock formations displaying **Indian rock art** main attractions.

Huntsville State Park: This 8.5-mile trail in Walker County takes about four hours to hike entire length; five miles are designated for bicyclists and one mile designated for handicapped users.

Inks Lake State Park: Loop trails total about seven miles in Burnet County; primitive camping area available for backpackers.

Jim Hogg State Historical Park: One-mile trail and three-mile trail through typical East Texas Piney Woods in Cherokee County.

Kerrville State Recreation Area: Two trails—.5-mile trail along shore of Flat Rock Lake on Guadalupe River; 2-mile developed trail in Hill Country Unit in Kerr County; several miles of primitive trails where white-tailed deer and wild turkey are common.

Lake Brownwood State Recreation Area (Brown County): System of trails totals 3.5 miles; portions accessible to handicapped recreationists.

Lake Livingston State Recreation Area: System of interconnecting trails in Polk County totals about 4.5 miles along shoreline of Lake Livingston and in East Texas Piney Woods.

Lake Mineral Wells State Park: Five-mile hiking trail in Parker County; some parts require stamina and endurance; others designed primarily for short nature walks.

Lake Somerville State Recreation Area: Somerville Trailway 21-mile system in Lee and Burleson counties; longest single trail in any state park; connects Birch Creek Unit on north with Nails Creek Unit on south; backpacking and equestrian camping. Area open to public, but visitors should be aware of oil and gas exploration in area. Shorter trails loop through post oak woodlands and along lakeshore; each unit has segments designated for the handicapped.

Lost Maples State Natural Area: Ten-mile hiking trail in Bandera County well marked and color coded for easy orientation; several trail loops offer option for distance and degree of difficulty. Eight primitive camping areas with four portable toilets located along trails.

McKinney Falls State Park: Three-mile, surfaced hike and bike trail in Travis County passes along creek through upland woods and back to visitor center.

Cypress trees festooned with moss create a haunted, mysterious air at Caddo Lake. Texas Almanac Photo.

Meridian State Recreation Area (Bosque County): Several small trails interconnecting to form loop around Meridian Lake; 6-mile trail passes interesting features, including scenic overlook of lake and a bee cave. Juniper dominant vegetation furnishing nesting area for **Golden-cheeked warbler.**

Mustang Island State Park: One-mile loop through marsh grass and dunes in Nueces County; trail head located on Park Road 53, just south of park entrance.

Palo Duro Canyon State Park: Trail 4.5 miles up Sunday Canyon past Sleeping Indian, Satanta's Face and turnaround at Lighthouse landmark in Armstrong and Randall counties.

Pedernales Falls State Park: Wolf Mountain Hiking Trail in Blanco County is 7 miles with primitive camping available; trail rugged; hilly terrain along Pedernales River yet easy enough for people in reasonably good physical shape to hike.

Seminole Canyon State Historical Park: Six-mile trail gives hikers look at hot and dry **Chihuahuan Desert** in Val Verde County.

Stephen F. Austin State Historical Park: Two separate trails totaling 2.5 miles in Austin County.

Tyler State Park: Hiking trail 2.5 miles long in Smith County; portions of trail are accessible to handicapped.

Equestrian Trails

Lake Arrowhead State Recreation Area: This is an 80-acre area in Clay and Archer counties designated for horseback riding; visitors must bring own horses.

Lake Mineral Wells State Park: Has 8.5-mile equestrian trail in Parker County; camping available and adequate parking for 20 horse trailers.

Lake Somerville State Recreation Area: Somerville Trailway in Lee and Burleson counties permits horseback riding and equestrian camping.

Palo Duro Canyon State Park: Has 4.5-mile equestrian trail in Armstrong and Randall counties; rental horses are available, or visitors may bring their own.

Recreation Facilities and Visitation Data Corps of Engineers' Lakes Texas 1986

Facilities available for visitors at U.S. Army Corps of Engineers' lakes in Texas, in 1986, are listed below. Since facilities change often, it is best to check at the time of visit.

More than 57 million visitors in 1986 enjoyed the recreational facilities at lakes in Texas under the management of the U.S. Army Corps of Engineers. Lake Texoma, with more than 8 million visitors, led in attendance in Texas.

Name of Reservoir and Stream	Swim Areas	Launch Ramps	Picnic Sites	Camp Sites	Rental Units	Visitation
Addicks & Barker. .	...	...	650	...	...	2,267,500
Aquilla	...	2	...	119	...	112,600
Bardwell	2	7	65	119	...	761,600
Belton	3	19	388	290	7	2,600,000
Benbrook	2	16	144	140	...	2,669,100
Canyon	6	25	175	690	33	2,428,600
Georgetown.	1	3	124	228	...	996,000
Granger	2	5	130	168	...	310,000
Grapevine.	2	18	118	222	...	4,046,100
Hords Creek	1	10	5	187	...	420,300
Lake O' The Pines .	11	29	191	459	12	2,437,300
Lavon	5	25	416	151	...	3,700,500
Lewisville	7	37	317	466	...	7,060,200
Navarro Mills	2	3	...	246	...	1,285,900
O. C. Fisher.	1	16	138	168	...	456,900
Pat Mayse	4	8	...	226	...	552,700
Proctor.	...	6	44	190	...	983,200
Sam Rayburn	7	31	31	844	91	3,287,400
Somerville.	2	12	279	799	...	1,435,800
Stillhouse Hollow . .	2	5	25	142	...	859,500
Texoma.	7	59	355	2,013	318	8,479,100
Town Bluff.	1	14	70	364	46	591,700
Waco.	1	9	60	347	...	4,873,100
Whitney.	3	28	53	575	...	2,419,200
Wright Patman . . .	5	19	255	646	2	2,486,600
Total	77	406	4,033	9,680	509	57,520,900

The National Polka Festival in Ennis opens with a colorful parade headed by this all-female color guard. Texas Almanac Photo.

WOODLAND TRAILS

Below is given brief description of the fifteen Texas Forestry Association's Woodland Trails. For further information, write Texas Forestry Assn., P.O. Box 1488, Lufkin, Texas 75901, or phone (713) 634-5523.

Four-C Trail—Eastern Houston County, 18 miles east of Crockett on Texas 7. Follows old rail tram line along Neches River bottom. Camping. Length, 20 miles.

Bull Creek Trail—Northwestern Polk County, 8.5 miles west of Corrigan on U.S. 287. Winds along banks of Bull Creek. Noted for its large magnolias, oaks, gums and pines. Length, 1½ miles.

Griff Ross Trail—Southern Rusk County, 2.2 miles east of Mount Enterprise on U.S. 84. Follows gentle slope of hill to edge of a forest stream. Donated to TFA by Dr. and Mrs. William F. Ross, Dallas, in memory of his parents, Dr. and Mrs. Griff Ross, Mount Enterprise. No picnicking or camping. Length, ½ mile.

Dogwood Trail—Central Tyler County, 3 miles east of Woodville off U.S. 190. Winding along banks of Theuvenin Creek, trail is noted for dogwood blooms in spring. Length, 1½ miles.

Longleaf Pine Trail—Northeastern Polk County, 3 miles east of Camden on Farm Road 62. Noted for large longleaf pines, many 100 years or older. Features nesting holes of rare red-cockaded woodpecker. Length, 2 miles.

Big Creek Trail—East Central San Jacinto County, west of Shepherd on Forest Service Road 217. Four loops, partially following Big Creek, clear running slope. Camping, picnicking, swimming and showers at Double Lake Recreation Area. Length, 3½ miles.

Moscow Trail—Northern Polk County, 1 mile south of Moscow on U.S. 59. Meanders along banks of Long King Creek, and is noted for tall pines and large variety of other forest growth. Length, 2 miles.

Apolonia Trail—Southeast Grimes County, 8 miles east of Anderson on FM 2819. Three loops provide scene changes from pine forest to post oaks to blackland prairie. Lengths, ¼ mile, 1.1 miles and 1.9 miles.

Sawmill Trail—North Jasper County, off Texas 63 seven miles southeast of Zavalla. One trailhead at Boykin Springs campground and one at Bouton Lake campground, with a spur to abandoned Aldridge Sawmill site. Maintained by U.S. Forest Service. Length, 5½ miles.

Old River Trail—Western Jasper County, 2.9 miles on unpaved road off Farm Road 1747. Follows abandoned railroad into swampy Angelina River bottom land noted for bog flowers, hardwood and other growth. Historic river port of Bevilport is nearby. Length, 1½ miles.

Sylvan Trail—Central Newton County, opposite roadside park on U.S. 190, 4 miles southeast of Newton. Meanders through area noted for picturesque loblolly pines. Location of two old logging railroads. Length, ½ mile.

Yellow Poplar Trail—Northern Marion County, 8.5 miles north of Jefferson on U.S. 59 opposite roadside park. Winds through only stand of yellow poplar in Texas, and includes state champion tree. Nearby historical marker commemorates life of pioneer physician-legislator M. D. Taylor. Length, 1 mile.

Wild Azalea Canyons Trail—Northern Newton County, 4.4 miles north of Newton on Texas 87, then 6.7 miles east on Farm Road 1414, then 1.8 miles on unpaved roads. Inside pocket wilderness noted for longleaf forest, rock cliffs and wild azaleas that bloom each spring. Several trails of varying lengths; trails open only during bloom season, March-April.

The Caverns of Sonora in Sutton County are thought by some veteran cavers to be the most beautiful in the state.

Texas Caves Interesting, Valuable

This article on Texas caves was prepared for the Texas Almanac by William R. Elliott, Ph.D., of the Texas Cave Management Association, Austin.

About 2,000 caves are known in Texas, and many probably remain to be found. The Balcones Escarpment, Edwards Plateau and Stockton Plateau contain numerous limestone caves, while gypsum caves are found in Permian-age rocks in Northwest Texas and in Culberson County. Most of the limestone caves occur in rocks of the Edwards Group or Glen Rose Formation of Cretaceous age, or in the Ellenburger Group of Ordovician age. A few caves around the state occur in unusual rocks, such as clay, caliche, conglomerate, granite and shale.

Commercial caves with lighted paths and educational tours are recommended for the public: **Caverns of Sonora** near Sonora, **Natural Bridge Caverns** near New Braunfels, **Inner Space Cavern** near Georgetown, **Cascade Caverns** and **Cave-Without-A-Name** near Boerne, **Longhorn Cavern** near Burnet and **Wonder Cave** (Wonder World) in San Marcos. These caves have interesting histories and many different types of mineral formations, or speleothems.

Undeveloped caves are explored, mapped and studied by about 300 speleologists, or "cavers," belonging to "grottos" (clubs) located in Austin, San Antonio, San Marcos, College Station, Houston, Galveston, Dallas, Fort Worth, Abilene, Lubbock and Midland. The grottos are affiliated with the **National Speleological Society**. For safety and conservation reasons, persons interested in caving should contact one of these grottos to obtain proper training and equipment. The delicate mineral, biological and cultural contents of caves are easily destroyed by uninformed visitors. The **Texas Cave Management Association**, P.O. Box 310732, New Braunfels 78131, welcomes inquiries from persons interested in Texas caves and cave conservation.

Recent explorations have pushed **Honey Creek Cave** in Comal and Kendall counties to more than 76,000 feet in length, making it the state's longest. The cave is a network of stream passages that demand that a caver have experience and special equipment. **Powell's Cave System** (Jack Pit Cave), a maze of crawlways in Menard County measuring about 75,000 feet, is still being explored. Other long caves include **Caverns of Sonora** in Sutton County (estimated at 20,000 feet), **Indian Creek Cave** in Uvalde County (18,005 feet), **Inner Space Cavern** in Williamson County (14,859 feet), **Cave-Without-A-**Name in Kendall County (14,151 feet), **Airmen's Cave** in Travis County (11,950 feet), **Longhorn Cavern** in Burnet County (9,850 feet), and **Spring Creek Cave** in Kendall County (9,209 feet). Eight other caves longer than 3,000 feet are known.

Deep vertical caves, requiring special equipment and skills to explore, are found mainly in West Texas. **Sorcerer's Cave** in Terrell County (558 feet deep), **Wizard's Well** in Terrell County (388 feet), **Big Tree Cave** in Val Verde County (348 feet), **Devil's Sinkhole** in Edwards County (342 feet), and **Plateau Cave** in Culberson County (340 feet) are but a few. The deepest shafts in these caves are up to 140 feet deep. One water-filled pit, **Jacob's Well** in Hays County, has claimed the lives of numerous sport scuba divers who were not trained and certified as cave divers.

Texas caves contain many natural phenomena of esthetic, scientific and environmental value. Six-thousand-year-old human remains and fossils of extinct ice age animals up to 25,000 years of age have been excavated in several caves and shelter caves by university researchers. These caves are important repositories of natural history. Eyeless crustaceans, insects, millipedes, arachnids and salamanders are sometimes discovered by biologists, adding to our knowledge of animal distribution and evolution. Such creatures are called "troglobites."

Large colonies of the migratory Mexican freetail bat occur in Blanco, Burnet, Comal, Edwards, Mason, Medina and Uvalde counties. The summertime nursery colony in **Bracken Bat Cave**, Comal County, may reach 20 million individuals. Several other species inhabit caves and structures. Bat caves are increasingly protected by private landowners and the state government. The bats are beneficial, eating many tons of insects nightly and providing excrement, or guano, which is mined during the winter, when most bats are gone and sold as fertilizer. Contrary to popular belief, bats are not an important source of rabies. **Bat Conservation International**, with headquarters in Austin, is developing educational programs about bats and bat myths for the public. A research program is aimed at determining the causes of the drastic declines in several valuable bat species in Texas. The organization's address is Brackenridge Field Laboratory, The University of Texas at Austin, Austin 78712.

Politics and Government

Republicans Peck at Democrats' Base

Texas, once a bastion of the Democratic Party, showed more evidence in 1986 that it is becoming a true two-party state. For many years, Republicans have been successful in challenging Democrats at the top of the ticket. In 1986, they maintained presidential-election gains in the state Legislature and Congress and picked up many local offices.

Republican presidential candidates have regularly carried the state, winning three of the past four elections. Republican John Tower served in the U.S. Senate for 23 years, winning four tight statewide races in the process, before retiring. Tower was replaced in 1984 by Democrat-turned-Republican Phil Gramm.

William P. Clements Jr. has stunned political observers in his three statewide campaigns. In 1978, he beat Democrat John Hill, becoming the first Republican in more than a century to win the governorship. Clements' loss to Democrat Mark White Jr. in 1982 was equally surprising, and then the Dallas oilman raised eyebrows the third time in 1986 by becoming only the second former governor to regain the office after being ousted by voters. (See feature, "Texas Governors Fall Often," in this section.)

At one time, statewide Democratic candidates' strategy was to run close to Republicans in the urban areas and then pull away in the solidly Democratic rural areas. Returns show that Clements reversed the procedure. The Republican won only Dallas and Tarrant counties among the state's six major urban areas, but he easily defeated incumbent White in the smaller metropolitan areas and in the rural sections of the state. The voting patterns continued a trend that has built over 20 years. Republicans at the top of the ballot usually run close to their Democratic opposition. Elections also are getting more expensive. The two gubernatorial candidates spent more than $25 million, according to The Dallas Morning News, making the contest the most expensive in Texas history.

In 1984, Republicans won four formerly Democratic congressional seats, but observers credited the performance to the candidates' riding President Ronald Reagan's coattails. The President is very popular in the state. But the four freshman representatives retained their seats in 1986 without help at the top of the ticket. Clements' coattails were not long, for no other statewide Republican candidates were successful. Roy Barrera Jr. did run a closer race than expected against Democratic Attorney General Jim Mattox.) The re-elections of the congressmen allowed Republicans to maintain control of 10 of Texas' 27 seats in the U.S. House of Representatives. Only one change was made in the delegation. Republican Lamar Smith of San Antonio replaced Tom Loeffler of Hunt, who ran an unsuccessful campaign for governor in the Republican primary.

In the Texas Legislature, Republicans gained one seat for a total of 56 in the House and retained their six of 31 seats in the Senate. Democrats hold 94 House seats. Only 22 new representatives were elected, the smallest number in years. Seven lawmakers, five in the primaries and two in the general election, were defeated at the polls, and the others retired. Most observers had expected Republicans to lose seats in the non-presidential year election. Republican State Party Chairman George Strake contended that gains at the state and local levels "perfectly position" the party "to become the majority party in Texas in 1992" after redistricting.

On the local level, however, Republicans made their most substantial gains, picking up almost 150 local and district offices. According to state Republican headquarters, the party now holds 493 local offices, ranging from district judge to constable, up from about 350 in 1984. There are about 3,500 partisan elective local and district offices in the state, according to the Texas Association of Counties, so Republicans hold about 14 percent of the local partisan offices. While Democrats still hold the vast majority of the local offices, the Republicans are pecking away in larger bites in a trend that may prove to be significant. Twenty years ago, Republican candidates for local offices in rural areas were rare and usually unsuccessful.

Also of significance was the election of Democrat Raul Gonzalez of Corpus Christi to the state Supreme Court. He became the first Mexican-American to be elected to statewide office in modern history. Gonzalez had been appointed to the Court of Appeals in Corpus Christi by Gov. Clements and to a vacancy on the Supreme Court by Gov. White before seeking election to a full term.

Party Primaries

Texas political parties have held primary elections since passage of the Terrell Election Law in 1905. It mandated primaries for parties whose gubernatorial candidates received more than 100,000 votes in the previous election. In 1945, the vote requirement was raised to 200,000. Democrats have held primaries each election year since the the law was passed. Republicans held their first primary in 1926 and later held them in 1930, 1934, 1954 and 1958. Since 1962, the party has held primaries each election year and has held a total of 18 primaries since passage of the Terrell law.

Both parties held presidential primaries for the first time in 1976 and have continued the practice, although in slightly different forms. Republican results have been translated directly into delegate votes at the national convention, while Democrats have used a combination primary-convention system to select delegates. Ronald Reagan won the 1984 Republican primary, and Walter Mondale won under the Democratic system.

In 1986, 13.8 percent of the state's 7,951,368 registered voters participated in the Democratic primary, and 6.9 percent voted in the Republican primary.

Texas' late primary elections (moved to May from July in 1960 to accommodate the presidential campaign of Lyndon B. Johnson) has been a concern to the state's political leaders in both parties. Smaller states with earlier primaries, like New Hampshire, have had a more significant impact on the presidential nominations than Texas. Joining with Southern states, Texas has moved its party primaries to the second Tuesday in March beginning in 1988. The impact of the regional vote, according to the strategy, will give the Southern states a greater voice in the selection of presidential nominees and in setting the agenda for the debate of national issues.

Voter Registration

A total of 7,287,173 Texans registered to vote in the 1986 general election and 47.2 percent of them participated in the general election. Fewer persons were registered for the general election than the primaries because the voter lists in each county were purged of those who moved and did not notify voter officials of their new address.

The poll tax was used as a qualification for voting in Texas from 1902 until declared unconstitutional in 1966. The largest number of poll taxes paid under the system was 2,411,679 in 1966, when it was estimated that exemptions for the elderly increased the number of eligible voters to 3,014,597.

Additional information on Texas' political parties and results for selected elections appear on the following pages.

— MIKE KINGSTON

Elections of Texas Governors, 1845-1986

Following are the results of all elections of Texas governors since Texas became a state in 1845. Party prima ies, as well as general elections, are included whenever possible, although Republican totals are not available fc some elections. Prior to 1857, many candidates ran independently; whenever candidates were party nominees, th party is given in parentheses.

1ST ELECTION, 1845

J. P. Henderson	7,853
J. B. Miller	1,673
Scattering	52
Total vote	9,578

2ND ELECTION, 1847

George T. Wood	7,154
J. B. Miller	5,106
N. H. Darnell	1,276
J. J. Robinson	379
Scattering	852
Total vote	14,767

3RD ELECTION, 1849

P. H. Bell	10,319
George T. Wood	8,764
John T. Mills	2,632
Total vote	21,715

4TH ELECTION, 1851

P. H. Bell	13,595
M. T. Johnson	5,262
John A. Greer	4,061
B. H. Epperson	2,971
T. J. Chambers	2,320
Scattering	100
Total vote	28,309

5TH ELECTION, 1853

E. M. Pease	13,091
W. B. Ochiltree	9,178
George T. Wood	5,983
L. D. Evans	4,677
T. J. Chambers	2,449
John Dancy	315
Total vote	35,693

6TH ELECTION, 1855

E. M. Pease	26,336
D. C. Dickson	18,968
M. T. Johnson	809
George T. Wood	226
Total vote	46,339

7TH ELECTION, 1857

H. R. Runnels (Dem.)	32,552
Sam Houston	28,628
Total vote	61,180

8TH ELECTION, 1859

*Sam Houston	36,227
H. R. Runnels (Dem.)	27,500
Scattering	61
Total vote	63,788

*Ran as independent but received the support of the Know-Nothing Party.
Note.—Edward Clark succeeded Sam Houston on March 16, 1861, shortly after Texas seceded from the Union.

9TH ELECTION, 1861

F. R. Lubbock	21,854
Edward Clark	21,730
T. J. Chambers	13,759
Total vote	57,343

10TH ELECTION, 1863

Pendleton Murrah	17,511
T. J. Chambers	12,455
Scattering	1,070
Total vote	31,036

Note.—A. J. Hamilton was named Governor under Reconstruction administration June 17, 1865.

11TH ELECTION, 1866

J. W. Throckmorton	49,277
E. M. Pease	12,168
Total vote	61,445

Note. — E. M. Pease was appointed Governor July 30, 1867.

12TH ELECTION, 1869

E. J. Davis	39,901
A. J. Hamilton	39,092
Hamilton Stuart	380
Total vote	79,373

13TH ELECTION, 1873

Richard Coke (Dem.)	85,549
E. J. Davis (Rep.)	42,633
Total vote	128,182

14TH ELECTION, 1876

Richard Coke (Dem.)	150,581
William Chambers (Rep.)	47,719
Total vote	198,300

Note. — R. B. Hubbard, Lieutenant Governor, succeeded Coke Dec. 1, 1876, when Coke became United States Senator.

15TH ELECTION, 1878

O. M. Roberts (Dem.)	158,933
W. H. Hamman (Greenback)	55,002
A. B. Norton (Rep.)	23,402
Scattering	99
Total vote	237,436

16TH ELECTION, 1880

O. M. Roberts (Dem.)	166,101
E. J. Davis (Rep.)	64,382
W. H. Hamman (Greenback)	33,721
Total vote	264,204

17TH ELECTION, 1882

John Ireland (Dem.)	150,809
G. W. Jones (Greenback)	102,501
J. B. Robertson (I.Dem.)	334
Total vote	253,644

18TH ELECTION, 1884

John Ireland (Dem.)	212,234
Geo. W. Jones (Greenback)	88,450
A. B. Norton (Rep.)	25,557
Total vote	326,241

19TH ELECTION, 1886

L. S. Ross (Dem.)	228,776
A. M. Cochran (Rep.)	65,236
E. L. Dohoney (Prohi.)	19,186
Scattering	102
Total vote	313,300

20TH ELECTION, 1888

L. S. Ross (Dem.)	250,338
Marion Martin (Ind-.Fus.)	98,447
Total vote	348,785

21ST ELECTION, 1890

J. S. Hogg (Dem.)	262,432
W. Flanagan (Rep.)	77,742
E. C. Heath (Prohi.)	2,235
Total vote	342,409

22ND ELECTION, 1892

J. S. Hogg (Dem.)	190,486
George Clark (Dem.)	133,395
T. L. Nugent (Peo.)	108,483
A. J. Houston (Ref.Rep.)	1,322
D. M. Prendergast (Prohi.)	1,605
Scattering	176
Total vote	435,467

23RD ELECTION, 1894

C. A. Culberson (Dem.)	207,167
T. L. Nugent (Peo)	152,731
W. K. Makemson (Rep.)	54,520
J. B. Schmidt (L. W. Rep.)	5,036

24TH ELECTION, 1896

J. M. Dunn (Prohi.)	2,19
Scattering	1,07
Total vote	422,72

C. A. Culberson (Dem.)	298,52
J. C. Kearby (Peo.)	238,69
Randolph Clark (Prohi.)	1,87
Scattering	68
Total vote	539,77

25TH ELECTION, 1898

J. D. Sayers (Dem.)	291,54
Barnett Gibbs (Peo.)	114,95
R. P. Bailey (Prohi.)	2,43
G. H. Royall (Soc. Lab.)	55
Scattering	6
Total vote	409,55

26TH ELECTION, 1900

J. D. Sayers (Dem.)	303,58
R. E. Hanney (Rep.)	112,86
T. J. McMinn (Peo.)	26,86
G. H. Royall (Soc. Lab.)	15
Scattering	6,15
Total vote	449,62

27TH ELECTION, 1902

S. W. T. Lanham (Dem.)	219,07
George W. Burkett (Rep.)	65,70
J. M. Mallett (Peo.)	12,38
G. W. Carroll (Prohi.)	8,70
Scattering	3,2
Total vote	309,15

28TH ELECTION, 1904

S. W. T. Lanham (Dem.)	206,16
J. G. Lowden (Rep.)	56,84
Pat B. Clark (Peo.)	9,36
W. D. Jackson (Prohi.)	4,56
Frank Leitner (Soc. Lab.)	55
W. H. Mills (Soc. Dem.)	2,46
Total vote	279,8

DEMOCRATIC PRIMARY ELECTION, 1906

Previous to the election of 19(all nominations of the Democrat party for state offices had bee made in convention. This campaig was the first held under the Terre election law, which required th Democratic Party (as the law wa first passed) to provide for a tw fold system for nomination of sta and district officers. The primar election was held, but the conven tion vote of each county was to b prorated among the several cand dates for each office on the basis the primary election vote for suc candidates in each of such countie

The popular vote for Governc in the primary of 1906 was as fo lows:

Thomas M. Campbell	90,3
M. M. Brooks	70,0
O. B. Colquitt	68,5
Charles K. Bell	65,1
Total vote	294,1

The law required the conven tion to drop the low man at the en of each ballot and authorized eac county delegation to prorate the r leased vote among the other cand dates according to its choice. O the first convention ballot the pr rated vote was Campbell 213,34 Colquitt 169,934, Bell 163,367 an Brooks 156,318. Brooks was droppe and Colquitt withdrew. Bell als withdrew after finishing but befor announcement of the results of th second ballot which was Campbe 418,656. Bell 257,234.

29TH ELECTION, 1906

. M. Campbell (Dem.) .	148,264
. A. Gray (Rep.)	23,711
W. Pearson (Prohi.) . .	5,252
. C. Edwards (Soc.) . . .	2,958
. S. Dowler (Soc. Lab.) .	260
. W. Atcheson (Reor. Rep.)	5,395
Total vote	185,840

DEMOCRATIC PRIMARY, 1908

In 1907 the primary election law as amended, providing for plural-y nomination of state and district fficers, i.e., leading candidates on, even though they received ss than a majority of all votes ist. The primary of 1908 resulted s follows:

. M. Campbell	202,608
. R. Williams	117,459
Total vote	320,067

30TH ELECTION, 1908

. M. Campbell (Dem.) .	218,956
N. Simpson (Rep.) . . .	73,305
C. Rhodes (Soc.)	8,100
'. B. Cook (Soc. Lab.) . .	234
. C. Heath (Prohi.)	148
Total vote	300,743

DEMOCRATIC PRIMARY, 1910

. B. Colquitt	146,526
'illiam Poindexter	79,711
. V. Davidson	53,187
one Johnson	76,050
Marion Jones	1,906
Total vote	357,380

31ST ELECTION, 1910

. B. Colquitt (Dem.) . . .	174,596
O. Terrell (Rep.)	26,191
edding Andrews (Soc.)	11,538
. J. Houston (Prohi.) . .	6,052
arl Schmitz (Soc. Lab.)	426
Total vote	218,803

DEMOCRATIC PRIMARY, 1912

. B. Colquitt	218,812
'illiam F. Ramsey	177,183
Total vote	395,995

32ND ELECTION, 1912

. B. Colquitt (Dem.) . . .	234,352
d Lasater (Prog.)	15,794
W. Johnson (Rep.) . . .	23,089
. J. Houston (Prohi.) . .	2,356
edding Andrews (Soc.)	25,258
. E. Choate (Soc. Lab.)	308
Total vote	301,157

DEMOCRATIC PRIMARY, 1914

ames E. Ferguson	237,062
homas H. Ball	191,558
Total vote	428,620

33RD ELECTION, 1914

E. Ferguson (Dem.) . .	176,599
M. Etheridge (Prog.)	1,794
ohn W. Philp (Rep.) . . .	11,411
O. Meitzen (Soc.)	24,977
Total vote	214,781

DEMOCRATIC PRIMARY, 1916

ames E. Ferguson	240,561
harles H. Morris.	174,611
. C. Marshall	6,731
Total vote	421,903

34TH ELECTION, 1916

E. Ferguson (Dem.) . .	296,667
. B. Creager (Rep.) . . .	49,118
O. Meitzen (Soc.)	14,580
. W. Lewis (Prohi.)	3,200
Total vote	363,565

Note. — In 1917 Governor Fer-uson was removed from office and cceeded by Lt. Gov. William P. obby.

DEMOCRATIC PRIMARY, 1918

. P. Hobby	461,479

James E. Ferguson	217,012
Total vote	678,491

35TH ELECTION, 1918

W. P. Hobby (Dem.)	148,982
Chas. A. Boynton (Rep.)	26,713
Wm. D. Simpson (Soc.). .	1,660
Total vote	177,355

DEMOCRATIC PRIMARIES, 1920

Note. — In 1918 the primary election law had been amended, re-quiring a majority for nomination for all state and district offices through a double primary election system. In that year, however, only one primary election was neces-sary in the governor's race, as there were but two candidates. The first double primary in the gover-nor's race was in 1920.

First Primary.

Pat M. Neff	149,818
Robert E. Thomason . . .	99,002
Joseph W. Bailey	152,340
Ben F. Looney	48,640
Total vote	449,800

Second Primary.

Pat M. Neff	264,075
Joseph W. Bailey	184,702
Total vote	448,777

36TH ELECTION, 1920

Pat M. Neff (Dem.)	289,188
J. G. Culberson (Rep.) . .	90,217
H. Capers (B. T. Rep.) . .	26,091
T. H. McGregor (Amer.)	69,380
L. L. Rhodes (Soc.)	6,796
Scattering	59
Total vote	481,731

DEMOCRATIC PRIMARY, 1922

Pat M. Neff	318,000
W. W. King.	18,368
Fred S. Rogers.	195,941
Harry T. Warner	57,671
Total vote	589,926

37TH ELECTION, 1922

Pat M. Neff (Dem)	334,199
W. H. Atwell (Rep.)	73,329
Total vote	407,528

DEMOCRATIC PRIMARIES, 1924

First Primary.

Felix D. Robertson	193,508
George W. Dixon	4,035
W. E. Pope	17,136
Joe Burkett	21,720
Mrs. Miriam A. Ferguson	146,424
Lynch Davidson	141,208
V. A. Collins	24,864
T. W. Davidson.	125,011
Thomas D. Barton	29,217
Total vote	703,123

Second Primary.

Mrs. Miriam A. Ferguson	413,751
Felix D. Robertson	316,019
Total vote	729,770

38TH ELECTION, 1924

Mrs. Miriam A. Ferguson (Dem.)	422,558
George C. Butte (Rep.) . .	294,970
Total vote	717,528

DEMOCRATIC PRIMARIES, 1926

First Primary.

Lynch Davidson.	122,449
Mrs. Miriam A. Ferguson	283,482
Mrs. Kate M. Johnston . .	1,029
Dan Moody	409,732
Mrs. Edith E. Wilmans . .	1,580
O. F. Zimmerman	2,962
Total vote	821,234

Second Primary.

Mrs. Miriam A. Ferguson	270,595
Dan Moody	495,723
Total vote	766,318

REPUBLICAN PRIMARY, 1926

Note—First state-wide primary held by Republican party.

H. H. Haines.	11,215
E. P. Scott	4,074
Total vote	15,289

39TH ELECTION, 1926

Dan Moody (Dem.)	233,068
H. H. Haines (Rep.)	31,531
M. A. Smith (Soc.)	908
Total vote	265,507

DEMOCRATIC PRIMARY, 1928

Wm. E. Hawkins.	32,076
Dan Moody	442,080
Louis J. Wardlaw	245,508
Edith E. Wilmans.	18,237
Total vote	737,901

40TH ELECTION, 1928

Dan Moody (Dem.)	582,972
W. H. Holmes (Rep.). . . .	120,504
T. Stedman (Com.)	109
L. L. Rhodes (Soc.).	738
Scattering	2,683
Total vote	707,006

DEMOCRATIC PRIMARIES, 1930

First Primary.

Mrs. Miriam A. Ferguson	242,959
Thomas B. Love	87,068
Paul Loven	2,724
Earle B. Mayfield.	54,459
Barry Miller	54,652
C. C. Moody	4,382
Frank Putnam	2,365
Clint C. Small.	138,934
Ross S. Sterling	170,754
James Young.	73,385
C. E. Walker.	1,760
Total vote	833,442

Second Primary.

Ross S. Sterling	473,371
Mrs. Miriam A. Ferguson	384,402
Total vote	857,773

REPUBLICAN PRIMARY, 1930

George C. Butte	5,001
H. E. Exum	2,773
John F. Grant	1,800
John P. Gaines.	203
Total vote	9,777

41ST ELECTION, 1930

Ross S. Sterling (Dem.) . .	252,738
Wm. E. Talbot (Rep.) . . .	62,224
Total vote	314,962

DEMOCRATIC PRIMARIES, 1932

First Primary.

Roger Q. Evans	3,974
Mrs. Miriam A. Ferguson	402,238
C. A. Frakes.	2,338
J. Ed Glenn	2,089
Tom F. Hunter	220,391
Frank Putnam	2,962
Ross S. Sterling	296,383
M. H. Wolfe	32,241
George W. Armstrong . .	5,312
Total vote	967,928

Second Primary.

Ross S. Sterling	473,846
Mrs. Miriam A. Ferguson	477,644
Total Vote.	951,490

42ND ELECTION, 1932

Mrs. Miriam A. Ferguson (Dem.).	528,986
Orville Bullington (Rep.)	317,807
George C. Edwards (Soc.)	1,866
George W. Armstrong (*J. Dem.)	706
Otho L. Heitt (Liberty) . .	101
Philip L. Howe (Com.) . .	72
Total vote	849,538

*Jackson Democratic party.

DEMOCRATIC PRIMARIES, 1934

First Primary.

C. C. McDonald	206,007
James V. Allred	297,656

Clint C. Small	124,206
Tom F. Hunter	241,339
Edgar Witt	62,208
Edward K. Russell	4,408
Maury Hughes	58,187
Total vote	994,011

Second Primary

James V. Allred	497,808
Tom F. Hunter	457,785
Total vote	995,593

REPUBLICAN PRIMARY, 1934
Note.—This was the third Republican primary.

D. E. Waggoner	13,043

43RD ELECTION, 1934

James V. Allred	421,422
D. E. Wagonner (Rep.). . .	13,534
George C. Edwards (Com.)	1,877
Enoch Hardaway (Com.)	244
Total vote	437,077

DEMOCRATIC PRIMARY, 1936

James V. Allred	553,219
P. Pierce Brooks	33,391
F. W. Fischer	145,877
Tom F. Hunter	239,460
Roy Sanderford	81,170
Total vote	1,053,117

44TH ELECTION, 1936

James V. Allred (Dem.) .	782,083
C. O. Harris (Rep)	58,842
Carl Brannin (Soc.) . .	962
Homer Brooks (Com.) . .	283
Total vote	482,170

DEMOCRATIC PRIMARY, 1938

W. Lee O'Daniel.	573,166
Ernest O. Thompson . . .	231,630
William McCraw	152,278
Tom F. Hunter	117,634
S. T. Brogdon	892
Joseph King.	773
Clarence E. Farmer	3,869
P. D. Renfro.	8,127
Karl A. Crowley	19,153
Clarence R. Miller	667
James A. Ferguson	3,800
Thomas Self.	1,405
Marvin P. McCoy.	1,491
Total vote	1,114,885

45TH ELECTION, 1938

W. Lee O'Daniel (Dem.)	473,526
Alexander Boynton (Rep.)	10,940
Earl E. Miller (Soc.). . . .	398
Homer Brooks (Com.) . .	424
Total vote	485,288

DEMOCRATIC PRIMARY, 1940

W. Lee O'Daniel.	645,646
Ernest O. Thompson . . .	256,923
Harry Hines.	119,121
Mrs. Miriam A. Ferguson	100,578
Jerry Sadler	61,396
Arlon B. Cyclone Davis Jr.	3,625
R. P. Condron	2,001
Total vote	1,189,290

46TH ELECTION, 1940

W. Lee O'Daniel (Dem.)	1,019,338
George C. Hopkins (Rep.)	59,885
Ben H. Lauderdale (Com.)	202
Scattering	113
Total vote	1,079,538

DEMORATIC PRIMARY, 1942

Hal H. Collins	272,469
Alex M. Ferguson.	8,370
Gene S. Porter	4,933
Charles L. Somerville. . .	4,853
Coke R. Stevenson	651,218
Hope Wheeler	9,373
Total vote	951,216

47TH ELECTION, 1942

Coke R. Stevenson (Dem.)	280,735
C. K. McDowell (Rep.). .	9,204
Total vote	289,939

DEMOCRATIC PRIMARY, 1944

Coke R. Stevenson	696,586
Martin Jones	21,379
W. J. Minton	8,537
Alex M. Ferguson.	12,649
Minnie F. Cunningham .	48,039
Gene S. Porter	15,243
Edward L. Carey	4,633
William F. Grimes	9,443
Herbert E. Mills.	6,640
Write-in votes	311
Total vote	823,460

48TH ELECTION, 1944

Coke R. Stevenson (Dem.)	1,007,826
B. J. Peasley (Rep.)	100,287
Total vote	1,108,113

DEMOCRATIC PRIMARIES, 1946
First Primary.

Floyd Brinkley.	4,249
William V. Brown.	3,902
A. J. Burks.	4,881
Chas. B. Hutchison	4,616
Beauford Jester	443,804
Walter Scott McNutt. . . .	4,353
Caso March	20,529
W. J. Minton	2,398
Homer P. Rainey	291,282
Jerry Sadler	103,120
Grover Sellers	162,431
C. R. Shaw	9,764
John Lee Smith	102,961
Reese Turner.	4,914
Total vote	1,163,184

Second Primary.

Beauford H. Jester.	701,018
Homer P. Rainey	335,654
Total vote	1,056,672

49TH ELECTION, 1946

Beauford H. Jester (Dem.).	345,513
Eugene Nolte Jr. (Rep.)	33,231
Total vote	378,744

DEMOCRATIC PRIMARY, 1948

Beauford H. Jester.	642,025
Sumpter W. Stockton . .	21,243
Roger Q. Evans	279,602
Charles B. Hutchison . .	24,441
Holmes A. May.	20,538
Caso March	187,658
W. J. Minton	13,659
Denver S. Whiteley.	16,090
Write-in votes	1
Total vote	1,205,257

50TH ELECTION, 1948

Beauford H. Jester (Dem.).	1,024,160
Alvin H. Lane (Rep.)	177,399
Gerald Overholt (Prohi.)	3,554
Herman Wright (Prog.) .	3,747
Total vote	1,208,860

DEMOCRATIC PRIMARY, 1950

Allan Shivers	829,730
Caso March	195,997
Charles B. Hutchison . . .	16,048
Gene S. Porter	14,728
J. M. Wren.	14,138
Mrs. Benita Louise Marek Lawrence	9,542
Wellington Abbey	6,381
Total vote	1,086,564

51ST ELECTION, 1950

Allan Shivers (Dem.)	833,861
Ralph W. Currie (Rep.) .	39,737
Total vote	374,747

DEMOCRATIC PRIMARY, 1952

Allan Shivers	883,861
Ralph W. Yarborough . .	488,345
Mrs. Allene M. Trayler . .	34,186
Total vote	1,356,392

52ND ELECTION, 1952

*Allan Shivers (Dem.) . . .	1,375,547
*Allan Shivers (Rep.) . . .	468,319
Total vote	1,843,866

*Ran on both Democratic and Republican tickets.

DEMOCRATIC PRIMARIES, 1954
First Primary.

Allan Shivers	668,91
Ralph W. Yarborough . .	645,99
J. J. Holmes.	19,59
Arlon B. Cyclone Davis. .	16,25
Total vote	1,350,75

Second Primary.

Allan Shivers	775,08
Ralph W. Yarborough . .	683,13
Total vote	1,458,22

53RD ELECTION, 1954

Allan Shivers (Dem.) . . .	569,53
Tod R. Adams (Rep.) . . .	66,15
Other.	1,20
Total vote	636,89

DEMOCRATIC PRIMARIES, 1956
First Primary.

Price Daniel	628,91
J. Evetts Haley.	88,77
J. J. Holmes.	10,16
W. Lee O'Daniel.	347,75
Reuben Senterfitt	37,77
Ralph Yarborough.	463,41
Write-in.	7
Total Vote.	1,576,87

Second Primary.

Price Daniel	698,00
Ralph Yarborough.	694,83
Total vote	1,392,83

54TH ELECTION, 1956

Price Daniel (Dem.) . . .	1,350,73
William R. Bryant (Rep.)	261,28
W. Lee O'Daniel (Write-in).	110,23
Other.	1,83
Total vote	1,724,09

DEMOCRATIC PRIMARY, 1958

Price Daniel	799,10
Henry B. Gonzalez	246,96
Joe A. Irwin.	33,64
W. Lee O'Daniel.	238,76
Write-in.	
Total vote	1,317,49

55TH ELECTION, 1958

Price Daniel (Dem.) . . .	695,77
Edward S. Mayer (Rep.)	94,08
Total vote	789,86

DEMOCRATIC PRIMARY, 1960

Jack Cox	619,83
Price Daniel	908,99
Write-in.	
Total vote	1,528,83

56TH ELECTION, 1960

Price Daniel (Dem.) . . .	1,627,69
Wm. M. Steger (Rep.) . .	609,80
Total vote	2,237,50

DEMOCRATIC PRIMARIES, 1962
First Primary.

John Connally	431,49
Price Daniel	248,52
Marshall Formby.	139,09
Edwin A. Walker	138,38
Will Wilson.	171,61
Don Yarborough	317,98
Write-in.	
Total vote	1,447,11

Second Primary.

John Connally	565,17
Don Yarborough	538,92
Total vote	1,104,09

REPUBLICAN PRIMARY, 1962

Jack Cox	99,12
Roy Whittenburg	16,13
Total vote	115,30

57TH ELECTION, 1962

John Connally (Dem.) . .	847,03
Jack Cox (Rep.).	715,02
Jack Carswell (Con.) . . .	7,13
Total vote	1,569,19

DEMOCRATIC PRIMARY, 1964

John Connally	1,125,884
Don Yarborough	471,411
M. T. Banks	22,047
Johnnie Mae Hackworthe	10,955
Total vote	1,630,297

REPUBLICAN PRIMARY, 1964

Jack Crichton	128,146

58TH ELECTION, 1964

John Connally (Dem.)	1,877,793
Jack Crichton (Rep.)	661,675
John C. Williams (Con.)	5,257
Write-in	28
Total vote	2,544,753

DEMOCRATIC PRIMARY, 1966

John Connally	932,641
Stanley C. Woods	291,651
Johnnie Mae Hackworthe	31,105
Write-in votes	3
Total vote	1,255,400

REPUBLICAN PRIMARY, 1966

T. E. Kennerly	49,568

59TH ELECTION, 1966

John Connally (Dem.)	1,037,517
T. E. Kennerly (Rep.)	368,025
Tommye Gillespie (Con.)	10,454
Bard Logan (Conserv.)	9,810
Write-ins	55
Total vote	1,425,861

DEMOCRATIC PRIMARIES, 1968
First Primary.

Preston Smith	386,875
Pat O'Daniel	47,912
John Hill	154,908
Waggoner Carr	257,543
Eugene Locke	218,118
Dolph Briscoe	225,686
Edward L. Whittenburg	22,957
Don Yarborough	421,607
Alfonso Veloz	9,562
Johnnie Mae Hackworthe	5,484
Total vote	1,750,652

Second Primary.

Preston Smith	767,490
Don Yarborough	621,226
Total vote	1,388,716

REPUBLICAN PRIMARY, 1968

Paul Eggers	65,501
John Trice	28,849
Wallace Sisk	10,415
Total vote	104,765

60TH ELECTION, 1968

Preston Smith (Dem.)	1,662,019
Paul Eggers (Rep.)	1,254,333
Total vote	2,916,352

DEMOCRATIC PRIMARY, 1970

Preston Smith	1,011,300

REPUBLICAN PRIMARY, 1970

Paul Eggers	101,875
Roger Martin	7,146
Total vote	109,021

61ST ELECTION, 1970

Preston Smith (Dem.)	1,232,506
Paul Eggers (Rep.)	1,073,831
Other	428
Total vote	2,306,765

DEMOCRATIC PRIMARIES, 1972
First Primary.

Ben Barnes	392,356
Dolph Briscoe	963,397
Frances Farenthold	612,051
Robert E. Looney	10,225
William H. Posey	13,727
Preston Smith	190,709
Gordon F. Wills	10,438
Total vote	2,192,903

Second Primary.

Dolph Briscoe	1,095,168
Frances Farenthold	884,594
Total vote	1,979,762

REPUBLICAN PRIMARIES, 1972
First Primary.

Albert Fay	24,329
Henry C. Grover	37,118
John A. Hall Sr.	8,018
J. A. Jenkins	4,864
Tom McElroy	19,559
David Reagan	20,119
Total vote	114,007

Second Primary.

Albert Fay	19,166
Henry C. Grover	37,842
Total vote	57,008

62ND ELECTION, 1972

Dolph Briscoe (Dem.)	1,633,493
Henry C. Grover (Rep.)	1,533,986
Ramsey Muniz (Raza)	214,118
Deborah Leonard (Soc.)	24,103
Other	3,891
Total vote	3,409,501

DEMOCRATIC PRIMARY, 1974

Dolph Briscoe	1,025,632
Frances Farenthold	437,287
W. H. Posey	31,498
Steve S. Alexander	26,889
Total vote	1,521,306

REPUBLICAN PRIMARY, 1974

Jim Granberry	53,617
Odell McBrayer	15,484
Total vote	69,101

63RD ELECTION, 1974

Dolph Briscoe (Dem.)	1,016,334
Jim Granberry (Rep.)	514,725
Ramsey Muniz (Raza)	93,295
Sherry Smith (Soc)	8,171
S. W. McDonnell (Am.)	22,208
Other	251
Total vote	1,654,984

DEMOCRATIC PRIMARY, 1978

Donald R. Beagle	14,791
Dolph Briscoe	753,309
John Hill	932,345
Ray Allen Mayo	20,249
Preston Smith	92,202
Total vote	1,812,896

REPUBLICAN PRIMARY, 1978

Bill Clements	115,345
Ray Hutchison	38,268
Clarence Thompson	4,790
Total vote	158,403

64TH ELECTION, 1978

John Hill (Dem.)	1,166,919
Bill Clements (Rep.)	1,183,828
Mario C. Compean (Raza)	14,213
Sara Jean Johnston (Soc.)	4,624
Other	115
Total vote	2,369,699

DEMOCRATIC PRIMARY, 1982
First Primary.

David L. Young	25,386
Bob Armstrong	262,189
Mark White	592,658
Don Beagle	15,649
Ray Allen Mayo	20,088
*Buddy Temple	402,693
Total vote	1,318,663

*Temple declined to participate in runoff; White declared winner this race.

REPUBLICAN PRIMARY, 1982

William P. Clements Jr.	246,120
Duke Embs	19,731
Total vote	265,851

65TH ELECTION, 1982

Mark White (Dem.)	1,697,870
William P. Clements Jr. (Rep.)	1,465,937
David Hutzelman (Ind.)	19,143
Bob Poteet (Con.)	8,065
Other	76
Total Vote	3,191,091

DEMOCRATIC PRIMARY, 1986

Sheila Bilyeu	39,370
Andrew C. Briscoe III	248,850
A. Don Crowder	120,999
Bobby Locke	58,936
Ron Slover	38,861
Mark White	589,536
Total vote	1,096,552

REPUBLICAN PRIMARY, 1986

William P. Clements Jr.	318,808
Kent Hance	108,238
Tom Loeffler	117,673
Total Vote	544,719

Following are the vote totals as canvassed by the Republican Party:

William P. Clements Jr.	318,938
Kent Hance	108,583
Tom Loeffler	118,224
Total vote	545,745

66TH ELECTION, 1986

Mark White (Dem.)	1,584,515
William P. Clements Jr. (Rep.)	1,813,779
Theresa Doyle (Lib.)	42,496
Other	670
Total Vote	3,441,460

1986 Primaries
Democratic Primary, 1986

Below are vote counts for contests in the Democratic primary held May 3, 1986, and the primary runoff held June 7, 1986. Included are statewide races; and district races for Congress, state Senate and Courts of Appeals in contested races only. Following these are the results of the Republican primary and primary runoff, which were held on the same dates.

Governor

Shiela Bilyeu	39,370
Andrew C. Briscoe III	248,850
A. Don Crowder	120,999
Bobby Locke	58,936
Ron Slover	38,861
Mark White	589,536
Total vote	1,096,552

Lieutenant Governor

Bill Hobby	761,999
David Young	265,319
Total vote	1,027,318

Attorney General

Jim Mattox	858,315

Railroad Commissioner

P. S. "Sam" Ervin	188,057
W. A. (Bill) MacNaughton	130,349
John C. Pouland	183,508
John Sharp	416,545
Total vote	918,459

Agriculture Commissioner

Noel S. Cowling	187,019
Jim Hightower	827,125
Total vote	1,014,144

Commissioner of the General Land Office

Garry Mauro	796,420

Treasurer

Ann W. Richards	858,977

Comptroller of Public Accounts

Bob Bullock	854,659

Associate Justice, Supreme Court, Place 1

Shirley Butts	249,422
Oscar H. Mauzy	451,225
Sears McGee	184,386
Hugo Touchy	77,602
Total vote	962,635

Associate Justice, Supreme Court, Place 2

Ted Akin	168,291
Jim Brady	303,696
Robert M. Campbell	303,301
Colin Kelly Kaufman	106,504
Total vote	881,792

Associate Justice, Supreme Court, Place 3

Jim Wallace	706,289

Associate Justice, Supreme Court, Place 4 (Unexpired Term)

Jay Gibson	271,512
Raul A. Gonzalez	391,299
John E. Humphreys	177,915
David M. Ivy	100,760
Total vote	941,486

Associate Justice, Court of Criminal Appeals, Place 1

Preston Dial	185,271
Rusty Duncan	243,528
George "Jorge" Martinez	260,664
Paul R. Reagan	200,285
Total vote	889,748

Associate Justice, Court of Criminal Appeals, Place 2

Mike McCormick	729,171

Associate Justice, Court of Criminal Appeals, Place 3

Marvin O. Teague	730,941

COURTS OF APPEALS

Below are results of contested races only in the race for justices of Courts of Appeals in the Democratic Primary, May 3, 1986:

Associate Justice, District 2, Place 4 (Unexpired Term)

David Keltner	32,844
Fred Fick	12,350
Total vote	45,194

Associate Justice, District 2, Place 5

Michael Burkett	21,248
David F. Farris	26,058
Total vote	47,306

Associate Justice, District 8

Jerry Woodard	26,296
Larry Fuller	25,732
Total vote	52,028

CONGRESS

Below are results of contested races only in the race for Congress in the Democratic Primary held May 3, 1986:

District 5

John Bryant	12,715
Gregory A. Witherspoon	912
Total vote	13,627

District 6

Pete Geren	33,849
Leonard Rinaldo	6,200
Total vote	40,049

District 8

Blaine Mann	6,509
Harley Schlanger	2,357
Total vote	8,866

District 10

Nina Butts	11,502
J. J. "Jake" Pickle	49,101
Total vote	60,603

District 12

Elizabeth Arnold	1,869
Jim Wright	18,135
Total vote	20,004

District 13

Doug Seal	23,126
Don Stribling	17,293
Total vote	40,419

District 18

Mickey Leland	17,895
Dorothy F. Stephens	1,706
Total vote	19,601

District 19

Mary Nell Mathis	11,110
Gerald McCathern	18,719
Total vote	29,829

District 21

Davd Hunsicker	6,102
Terry M. Lowry	2,368
Pete Snelson	18,211
Joe Sullivan	5,076
Total vote	31,757

District 24

Martin Frost	19,701
Gardell A. Morehead	1,438
Total vote	21,139

District 25

Mike Andrews	16,678
Curtis Perry II	990
Total vote	17,668

District 26

George Richardson	6,311
David M. Smith	3,355
Total vote	9,666

District 27

Solomon P. Ortiz	44,709
Ken Rich	8,013
Total vote	52,722

STATE SENATE

Below are results in contested races only for State Senate in the Democratic Primary held May 3, 1986:

District 18

Ken Armbrister	33,878
Joe A. Hubenak	25,578
Total vote	59,456

District 19

Tommy Adkisson	14,541
Frank Tejeda	17,190
Total vote	31,731

District 21

Oscar Carillo Sr.	9,428
J. A. "Sporty" Garcia	10,436
Wm. (Billy) Hall Jr.	23,768
Judith Zaffirini	34,029
Total vote	77,661

District 23

Eddie Bernice Johnson	8,539
Dr. Jesse Jones	6,581
Jesse Oliver	8,611
Total vote	23,731

District 27

E. C. Lerma	15,289
Hector Uribe	33,364
Total vote	48,653

DEMOCRATIC PRIMARY RUNOFF, JUNE 7, 1986

Below are the results in the races in the Democratic primary runoff held June 7, 1986:

Railroad Commissioner

P. S. "Sam" Ervin	89,888
John Sharp	344,705
Total vote	434,593

Associate Justice, Supreme Court, Place 1

Shirley Butts	184,017
Oscar H. Mauzy	262,544
Total vote	446,561

Associate Justice, Supreme Court, Place 2

Jim Brady	179,373
Robert M. Campbell	237,195
Total vote	416,568

Associate Justice, Supreme Court, Place 4 (Unexpired Term)

Jay Gibson	209,944
Raul A. Gonzalez	250,009
Total vote	459,953

William P. Hobby Jr. has served as lieutenant governor longer than any predecessor. He took office in 1973 and, at the beginning of the 70th Legislature, had served 14 years.

Associate Justice, Court of Criminal Appeals, Place 1

Rusty Duncan	239,909
George "Jorge" Martinez	188,492
Total vote	428,401

STATE SENATE
District 21

Wm. (Billy) Hall Jr.	19,816
Judith Zaffirini	27,591
Total vote	47,407

District 23

Eddie Bernice Johnson	7,979
Jesse Oliver	6,737
Total vote	14,716

REPUBLICAN PRIMARY, 1986

Below are totals for races in the Republican primary, held May 3, 1986, and the primary runoff, held June 7, 1986. Included are statewide races; and district races for Congress, state Senate, state Supreme Court and Courts of Appeals in contested races only. In races with two columns of figures, the first column contains the votes for that race as reported by the Secretary of State's office and the second column lists the votes as canvassed by the Republican Party.

	Sec. of State	Repub. Party
Governor		
Bill Clements	318,808	318,938
Kent Hance	108,238	108,583
Tom Loeffler	117,673	118,224
Total vote	544,719	545,745
Lieutenant Governor		
Aaron L. Bullock	111,036	111,049
David Davidson	130,201	130,140
Glenn Jackson	81,752	81,806
Virgil E. Mulanax	76,688	76,566
Total vote	399,677	399,561
Attorney General		
Roy R. Barrera Jr.	210,611	210,848
John Roach	87,880	87,355
Ed Walsh	158,401	159,040
Total vote	456,892	457,243
Railroad Commissioner		
Ed Emmett	97,721	97,789
Milton E. Fox	99,748	99,680
John Thomas Henderson	116,280	116,325
Ralph E. Hoelscher	74,321	74,241
Total vote	388,070	388,035
Agriculture Commissioner		
Bill Powers	248,894	249,032
Charles F. "Farmer" Trompler	127,986	127,924
Total vote	376,880	376,956
Commissioner of the General Land Office		
M. D. Anderson Jr.	180,328	180,394
George Collis	96,739	96,755
Grady T. Yarbrough	103,524	103,621
Total vote	380,591	380,770
Associate Justice, Supreme Court, Place 1		
Nathan Lincoln Hecht	144,328	144,443
Charles Ben Howell	228,189	228,167
Total vote	372,517	372,610
Associate Justice, Supreme Court, Place 2		
Nathan E. White Jr.	316,283	316,294

Associate Justice, Supreme Court, Place 4
(Unexpired Term)

John L. Bates	193,163
Bill J. Stephens	168,964
Total vote	362,127

CONGRESS

Below are results in contested races only for U.S. Congress in the Republican primary held on May 3, 1986:

District 2

Louis Dugas	2,058
Julian Gordon	2,882
Total vote	4,940

District 12

Don McNeil	9,279
Clint Young	4,089
Total vote	13,368

District 21

G. Thane Akins	8,103	8,092
Van Archer	14,616	14,592
Lowell "Duke" Embs	376	375
Henry Gandy	5,809	5,788
Lamar Smith	18,390	18,363
Jeff Wentworth	11,781	11,758
Total vote	59,075	58,968

District 24

Bob Burk	8,649
Scott E. Kurth	6,280
Total vote	14,929

District 26

Dick Armey	26,545
Bill Friday	2,917
Clyde Riddle Jr.	1,656
Total vote	31,118

STATE SENATE

Below are results in contested races only for State Senate in the Republican primary held May 3, 1986:

District 19

Joe F. Garcia	2,255
Bill Siebert	7,997
Total vote	10,252

District 21

Bennie Bock	9,954
T. Kellis Dibrell	5,822
Total vote	15,776

COURTS OF APPEALS

Below are results in contested races only for Courts of Appeals in the Republican primary held on May 3, 1986:

Associate Justice, Fifth District, Place 4 (Unexpired Term)

Averil Sweitzer	17,231
Sue Lagarde	41,398
Total vote	58,629

REPUBLICAN PRIMARY RUNOFF, JUNE 7, 1986

Below are the results in the races in the Republican primary runoff held June 7, 1986:

Lieutenant Governor

David Davidson	89,259
Aaron L. Bullock	38,927
Total vote	128,186

Attorney General

Roy R. Barrera Jr.	102,847
Ed Walsh	47,138
Total vote	149,985

Railroad Commissioner

Milton E. Fox	71,155
John Thomas Henderson	56,456
Total vote	127,611

Commissioner of the General Land Office

M. D. Anderson Jr.	79,335
Grady T. Yarbrough	46,558
Total vote	125,893

CONGRESS
District 21

Lamar Smith	18,140
Van Archer	15,709
Total vote	33,849

Gov. Miriam A. Ferguson, left, was the first Texas chief executive to be defeated by voters and then regain the office in a later election. William P. Clements Jr. duplicated Gov. Ferguson's 1932 feat in 1986.

Texas Governors Fall Often

When Gov. Mark White lost the 1986 general election to former Gov. William P. Clements Jr., he became the fifth of the last six Texas governors to be ousted from office by the state's voters. Only John Connally, who served as governor from 1963-1969, escaped embarrassment by the electorate. Texas, in fact, has been hard on governors, sending to defeat 11 (27 percent) of 41 persons who served as chief executive.

The trend began early. George T. Wood, the state's second governor, was defeated in 1849 by Peter Hansbrough Bell, who served two terms.

The Civil War and Reconstruction periods were the most volatile and turbulent in the state's history. Between 1859 and 1873, five governors were ousted from office, one by Reconstruction officials, one by political pressure and three by voters. Another was defeated at the polls and still served almost a full term.

Sam Houston opened the period by defeating incumbent Gov. Hardin R. Runnels in the 1859 general election. Two years earlier, Runnels had dealt Houston his only defeat at the polls in Texas in the gubernatorial race. A failure to solve the intractable problems on the frontier and the general unrest that developed prior to the war made Runnels un-

History Highlights

popular, however, and led to his defeat. Houston, in turn, was forced from office in 1861 when he refused to pledge an oath of allegiance to the Confederacy.

Lt. Gov. Edward Clark served the remaining months of Houston's term but was defeated in his 1861 election bid for a full term by 124 votes by Francis R. Lubbock. The margin of defeat was the narrowest in a Texas gubernatorial race.

Then there was the unusual case of Elisha M. Pease. Twice he was elected governor of Texas, serving from 1853 to 1857. However, in 1866, James W. Throckmorton defeated Pease in the general election. But the military authorities who ran Reconstruction Texas removed Throckmorton from office in 1867 and appointed Pease, who served until 1869. Pease served although defeated by voters.

Reconstruction ended when Democrat Richard Coke defeated the unpopular incumbent Republican Edmund J. Davis in 1873. Davis was the state's only Republican governor until Clements won the office in

1978 and the only governor to serve a four-year term before Dolph Briscoe did a century later.

For more than 50 years, Texas governors generally served their two two-year terms and retired peacefully. Then came the Ferguson era. James E. Ferguson was twice elected governor, but in 1917, he was impeached, convicted and removed from office. He lost a bid to regain the office from William P. Hobby the following year. Ferguson remained active in politics, and in 1924, his wife, Miriam A. "Ma" Ferguson, defeated a Ku Klux Klan-backed opponent to become Texas' first and only woman chief executive. Two years later, she was defeated by the state's attractive young attorney general, Dan Moody.

Four years later, Mrs. Ferguson in a comeback defeated incumbent Ross S. Sterling. In 1932, the Depression was at its height in Texas, and voters wanted a change, any change. Mrs. Ferguson did not seek re-election in 1934, but she was the first Texas governor to be voted out of office and then to regain the post.

For the next 30 years, incumbent governors managed to retain office. But Democrat Price Daniel in 1962 challenged history by attempting to become the first governor to be elected to a fourth two-year term. He failed even to make the Democratic primary runoff that eventually pitted John Connally and Don Yarborough. Connally won and was elected governor in November of 1962.

Preston Smith succeeded Connally in 1969 and served two terms. The Sharpstown scandal struck state government, and though Smith was not involved in influence peddling, voters turned him out in the Democratic primary in 1972, in which he became the second governor not to make the primary runoff. Dolph Briscoe was elected governor in November.

After serving a two-year term, Briscoe was re-elected in 1974 and became the first Texas governor in a century to serve a four-year term after the state constitution was amended in 1972. But Briscoe lost a re-election bid without a runoff in the Democratic primary in 1978 to Attorney General John Hill. But Hill became the first Democrat gubernatorial candidate in more than a century to lose to a Republican when Clements defeated him in the general election.

In 1982, Clements' bid for a second term was thwarted by Democratic Attorney General Mark W. White Jr., who surprised pollsters and political pundits alike in defeating the incumbent.

White was forced to approve tax hikes shortly before the election and had led an unpopular drive for improved public education that made him vulnerable to Clements' comeback bid in the 1986 general election. Thus a new tradition of turning out the incumbent governor was continued.

—*MIKE KINGSTON*

1986 Democratic and Republican Primaries Election Returns for Governor

County—	DEMOCRATIC PRIMARY							REPUBLICAN PRIMARY			
	Sheila Bilyeu	Andrew C. Briscoe III	A. Don Crowder	Bobby Locke	Ron Slover	Mark White	Total Vote (Democratic)	Bill Clements	Kent Hance	Tom Loeffler	Total Vote (Republican)
Anderson	190	1,914	901	526	135	2,559	6,225	549	113	92	754
Andrews	73	424	349	124	55	303	1,328	242	425	76	743
Angelina	354	2,677	1,180	669	351	2,816	8,047	398	165	88	651
Aransas	23	177	79	15	7	346	647	597	116	222	935
Archer	74	447	140	52	386	490	1,589	69	18	16	103
Armstrong	25	138	53	23	214	170	623	17	14	2	33
Atascosa	187	1,472	397	643	67	2,184	4,950	251	39	166	456
Austin	65	425	229	134	55	897	1,805	424	98	116	638
Bailey	18	112	49	20	81	236	516	64	306	12	382
Bandera	86	355	93	118	23	481	1,156	260	39	375	674
Bastrop	246	1,274	716	390	113	3,308	6,047	319	83	156	558
Baylor	53	517	171	41	156	412	1,350	39	7	0	46
Bee	153	1,104	278	215	173	1,806	3,729	278	64	133	475
Bell	204	1,675	788	657	234	3,672	7,230	2,535	539	633	3,707
Bexar	3,783	7,712	1,639	3,631	1,214	35,503	53,482	21,112	2,636	19,402	43,150
Blanco	8	70	19	9	11	171	288	136	21	72	229
Borden	15	94	57	20	4	45	235	9	62	3	74
Bosque	66	1,068	171	99	30	723	2,157	363	27	50	440
Bowie	311	2,872	1,534	1,083	200	5,759	11,759	694	224	73	991
Brazoria	283	1,976	905	629	194	5,434	9,421	3,881	1,132	1,776	6,789
Brazos	168	1,568	403	454	77	3,596	6,266	1,669	826	877	3,372
Brewster	42	375	153	49	41	573	1,233	109	18	227	354
Briscoe	18	155	223	25	185	233	839	9	11	4	24
Brooks	145	755	405	204	98	1,902	3,509	0	0	0	0
Brown	89	1,230	793	156	78	1,433	3,779	387	177	263	827
Burleson	56	504	154	159	41	743	1,657	103	19	16	138
Burnet	61	506	278	156	65	1,312	2,378	650	103	189	942
Caldwell	155	883	242	398	72	2,006	3,756	242	22	73	337
Calhoun	164	1,002	544	276	72	1,959	4,017	161	64	106	331
Callahan	78	853	307	116	74	656	2,084	111	20	21	152
Cameron	865	5,102	2,278	1,051	355	11,393	21,044	2,347	322	473	3,142
Camp	113	653	198	117	49	973	2,103	50	8	14	72
Carson	45	161	64	42	305	297	914	158	365	27	550
Cass	170	1,360	1,008	217	70	2,134	4,959	149	47	21	217
Castro	27	136	111	28	202	388	892	50	614	13	677
Chambers	146	905	427	201	95	1,641	3,415	83	23	51	157
Cherokee	189	2,131	694	237	200	1,557	5,008	448	151	56	655
Childress	36	300	111	63	373	326	1,209	50	17	12	79
Clay	48	532	188	79	306	686	1,839	35	31	2	68
Cochran	28	257	137	74	37	284	817	16	180	8	204
Coke	45	378	158	40	58	384	1,063	28	13	46	87
Coleman	49	338	135	45	29	307	903	198	28	66	292
Collin	70	368	621	86	38	1,858	3,041	10,066	2,667	2,735	15,468
Collingsworth	36	327	134	67	389	420	1,373	14	25	5	44
Colorado	110	886	492	178	136	1,500	3,302	200	34	60	294
Comal	70	201	62	92	30	925	1,380	2,327	342	2,860	5,529
Comanche	75	623	508	146	48	805	2,205	0	0	0	0
Concho	22	117	44	32	14	189	418	27	14	152	193
Cooke	102	430	784	110	80	880	2,386	681	89	86	856
Coryell	120	655	1,198	122	103	1,167	3,365	514	56	144	714
Cottle	33	127	92	61	219	350	882	0	0	0	0
Crane	78	446	234	91	53	305	1,207	25	6	31	62
Crockett	44	296	253	72	21	349	1,035	0	0	0	0
Crosby	42	307	139	58	115	801	1,462	18	120	0	138
Culberson	32	140	89	56	23	337	677	11	2	9	22
Dallam	71	140	67	38	271	262	849	51	39	5	95
Dallas	912	4,678	3,819	894	491	38,152	48,946	64,080	12,759	13,263	90,102
Dawson	99	593	326	103	122	845	2,088	123	557	10	690
Deaf Smith	128	491	387	115	814	1,062	2,997	134	334	13	481
Delta	54	251	252	78	49	628	1,312	9	1	2	12
Denton	134	568	508	142	62	2,598	4,012	5,328	1,481	1,597	8,406
DeWitt	79	661	218	175	30	828	1,991	456	38	201	695
Dickens	39	204	140	59	69	447	958	0	0	0	0
Dimmitt	204	606	204	231	53	1,792	3,090	36	4	17	57
Donley	30	180	88	30	243	219	790	89	23	15	127
Duval	155	1,049	263	568	83	2,252	4,370	16	9	3	28
Eastland	177	1,374	638	128	143	1,023	3,483	304	133	49	486
Ector	177	1,676	527	359	105	2,262	5,106	3,695	1,653	1,139	6,487
Edwards	19	128	32	36	19	106	340	12	5	75	92
El Paso	1,098	3,667	1,358	1,087	613	18,269	26,092	3,579	1,201	1,461	6,241
Ellis	218	1,238	758	452	258	3,229	6,153	1,839	479	461	2,779
Erath	124	978	462	238	56	1,294	3,152	306	61	77	444
Falls	105	758	163	217	127	1,299	2,669	65	11	17	93
Fannin	122	938	956	244	71	1,533	3,864	188	27	37	252
Fayette	103	961	582	274	94	1,356	3,370	464	78	95	637
Fisher	46	302	277	68	22	502	1,217	0	0	0	0
Floyd	65	419	192	131	148	532	1,487	50	201	10	261

County—	DEMOCRATIC PRIMARY							REPUBLICAN PRIMARY			
	Sheila Bilyeu	Andrew C. Briscoe III	A. Don Crowder	Bobby Locke	Ron Slover	Mark White	Total Vote (Democratic)	Bill Clements	Kent Hance	Tom Loeffler	Total Vote (Republican)
Foard	15	1,514	51	9	142	168	1,899	13	1	5	19
Fort Bend	164	1,830	174	207	77	3,749	6,201	4,531	1,363	1,596	7,49(
Franklin	94	484	292	171	52	888	1,981	116	10	10	13(
Freestone	70	619	354	133	128	1,202	2,506	185	37	41	26:
Frio	142	946	155	258	45	1,930	3,476	15	3	21	39
Gaines	77	739	304	128	71	613	1,932	64	273	21	358
Galveston	573	3,340	1,407	782	157	9,824	16,083	2,220	673	750	3,643
Garza	26	203	159	59	27	269	743	60	194	2	256
Gillespie	6	31	21	8	4	226	296	1,160	118	2,237	3,515
Glasscock	17	145	72	20	8	83	345	0	0	0	(
Goliad	102	523	123	107	39	701	1,595	27	2	30	59
Gonzales	124	1,134	376	246	71	1,042	2,993	102	10	49	16)
Gray	31	238	155	93	412	580	1,509	1,547	380	231	2,158
Grayson	179	1,229	1,020	228	120	2,474	5,250	1,649	332	364	2,34:
Gregg	174	3,168	819	174	309	2,563	7,207	2,449	560	540	3,549
Grimes	79	747	276	247	42	1,185	2,576	286	62	86	434
Guadalupe	69	498	93	285	27	1,302	2,274	2,611	404	1,638	4,65:
Hale	85	414	359	139	90	850	1,937	285	1,506	59	1,85(
Hall	26	161	77	24	192	305	785	57	28	10	9:
Hamilton	58	495	241	77	42	632	1,545	164	23	21	208
Hansford	23	152	51	22	215	153	616	209	156	42	40:
Hardeman	47	290	113	26	245	432	1,153	11	14	3	28
Hardin	296	1,357	2,050	361	174	2,576	6,814	169	46	27	24:
Harris	1,225	8,826	2,324	1,179	384	53,984	67,922	50,188	15,229	15,334	80,75)
Harrison	184	1,234	1,149	222	172	3,227	6,188	365	121	25	51)
Hartley	19	91	53	19	193	205	580	67	81	27	17:
Haskell	36	535	274	31	48	312	1,236	0	0	0	(
Hays	204	954	487	308	139	3,296	5,388	805	149	405	1,359
Hemphill	42	179	82	32	288	172	795	124	45	12	18)
Henderson	236	1,855	527	268	256	3,032	6,174	2,122	411	312	2,84:
Hidalgo	1,307	8,886	1,697	757	780	19,917	33,344	2,670	311	650	3,63)
Hill	131	967	448	183	90	1,447	3,266	459	63	78	60(
Hockley	108	844	367	183	88	973	2,563	145	657	11	81:
Hood	76	384	499	206	41	1,020	2,226	767	161	155	1,08:
Hopkins	101	893	582	213	62	1,525	3,376	455	130	144	72:
Houston	136	1,688	814	317	132	1,974	5,061	59	13	11	8:
Howard	224	1,061	774	196	83	1,658	3,996	379	173	117	66:
Hudspeth	23	146	35	33	24	321	582	3	1	3	:
Hunt	208	1,389	1,030	362	197	3,213	6,399	1,139	151	316	1,60(
Hutchinson	63	316	150	78	499	746	1,852	1,002	352	170	1,52:
Irion	45	194	82	43	18	144	526	30	6	56	9:
Jack	35	265	88	96	40	327	851	102	43	20	16:
Jackson	109	824	251	327	85	1,093	2,689	112	13	31	15(
Jasper	224	1,520	867	534	326	2,214	5,685	240	34	26	30(
Jeff Davis	8	74	16	5	5	75	183	48	7	79	13(
Jefferson	906	4,652	7,195	839	981	14,536	29,109	2,195	776	212	3,18:
Jim Hogg	80	387	123	282	48	1,439	2,359	4	0	10	1(
Jim Wells	384	1,584	888	618	307	4,490	8,271	203	76	51	33(
Johnson	95	986	560	159	85	1,899	3,784	1,802	503	483	2,788
Jones	124	734	395	213	147	697	2,310	132	53	21	20(
Karnes	80	663	108	156	39	761	1,807	186	17	66	26:
Kaufman	290	1,457	1,001	308	172	3,221	6,449	665	110	131	90(
Kendall	8	28	12	5	2	198	253	691	100	1,282	2,07:
Kenedy	0	24	11	15	7	111	168	0	0	8	:
Kent	28	172	100	54	46	180	580	0	0	0	
Kerr	25	88	47	24	6	653	843	1,815	212	4,146	6,17:
Kimble	13	130	23	15	6	147	334	89	10	344	44:
King	7	73	34	27	45	36	222	0	0	0	
Kinney	46	264	55	35	19	427	846	17	5	4	2(
Kleberg	105	818	382	120	113	1,437	2,975	220	147	107	47:
Knox	37	186	111	37	82	182	635	32	29	8	6:
Lamar	226	1,220	2,439	512	189	2,686	7,272	299	5	80	38:
Lamb	26	182	302	24	47	398	979	176	986	37	1,19:
Lampasas	89	583	282	79	165	933	2,131	237	23	49	30:
La Salle	45	357	94	130	15	1,124	1,765	0	0	0	
Lavaca	120	1,389	474	156	100	1,245	3,484	260	28	130	41:
Lee	94	636	336	159	118	1,005	2,348	70	17	12	9:
Leon	44	311	774	70	75	713	1,987	257	36	67	36(
Liberty	240	1,657	672	430	458	3,968	7,425	332	154	184	67(
Limestone	118	1,023	279	209	223	1,506	3,358	120	23	23	16:
Lipscomb	23	89	45	30	243	203	633	235	44	203	48:
Live Oak	135	957	280	246	98	859	2,575	122	9	85	21(
Llano	48	340	129	91	20	882	1,510	685	74	592	1,35:
Loving	3	18	8	3	2	13	47	0	0	0	
Lubbock	216	828	679	319	123	4,824	6,989	2,726	18,872	706	22,30:
Lynn	31	261	115	37	29	376	849	33	203	5	24:
McCulloch	33	272	290	37	16	495	1,143	159	17	392	56:
McLennan	672	5,792	1,251	882	544	10,422	19,563	3,626	640	887	5,15:
McMullen	5	50	34	13	1	41	144	0	0	0	
Madison	64	763	236	101	103	794	2,061	62	35	21	11:
Marion	64	284	462	101	42	1,078	2,031	21	5	0	2(

County—	DEMOCRATIC PRIMARY							REPUBLICAN PRIMARY			
	Sheila Bilyeu	Andrew C. Briscoe III	A. Don Crowder	Bobby Locke	Ron Slover	Mark White	Total Vote (Democratic)	Bill Clements	Kent Hance	Tom Loeffler	Total Vote (Republican)
Martin	13	149	75	29	15	179	460	35	146	14	195
Mason	6	65	19	9	6	165	270	60	9	602	671
Matagorda	192	1,759	475	424	176	2,753	5,779	247	76	139	462
Maverick	261	680	443	383	95	2,765	4,627	70	11	27	108
Medina	145	1,666	320	356	73	1,866	4,426	245	31	266	542
Menard	38	173	43	43	10	216	523	21	2	122	145
Midland	55	301	257	111	82	1,071	1,877	4,044	2,819	3,316	10,179
Milam	109	901	484	199	115	1,798	3,606	245	60	64	369
Mills	35	337	205	36	38	302	953	0	0	0	0
Mitchell	66	391	319	70	35	519	1,400	78	31	17	126
Montague	103	1,112	432	147	253	1,076	3,123	60	40	17	117
Montgomery	211	1,557	551	388	141	3,907	6,755	3,980	1,843	1,773	7,596
Moore	78	311	193	88	678	466	1,814	203	111	76	390
Morris	160	884	307	149	108	1,348	2,956	58	17	5	80
Motley	4	65	22	23	63	80	257	15	85	2	102
Nacogdoches	264	2,058	873	397	198	1,821	5,611	397	134	79	610
Navarro	210	1,244	759	205	248	3,019	5,685	385	70	77	532
Newton	107	819	442	121	135	1,358	2,982	79	21	11	111
Nolan	91	642	492	123	64	785	2,197	112	50	55	217
Nueces	718	4,456	2,161	2,185	258	14,014	23,792	4,107	1,157	1,683	6,947
Ochiltree	88	325	209	71	881	422	1,996	143	111	12	266
Oldham	25	113	64	23	214	196	635	8	6	1	15
Orange	393	1,895	3,206	547	297	5,164	11,502	322	116	40	478
Palo Pinto	162	953	518	269	97	1,480	3,479	367	65	61	493
Panola	162	1,672	682	358	78	1,685	4,637	74	4	7	85
Parker	132	982	659	221	69	1,764	3,827	1,304	292	295	1,891
Parmer	31	224	103	34	254	277	923	105	269	14	388
Pecos	100	754	324	181	70	884	2,313	210	55	618	883
Polk	286	1,918	525	359	235	2,324	5,647	215	70	81	366
Potter	216	805	484	214	1,751	2,880	6,350	2,250	1,121	350	3,721
Presidio	32	482	59	66	22	505	1,166	0	0	0	0
Rains	42	353	188	96	188	727	1,594	79	11	11	101
Randall	92	600	439	59	664	1,712	3,566	4,308	3,380	766	8,454
Reagan	50	404	177	42	12	220	905	0	0	0	0
Real	54	278	31	56	36	295	750	21	0	92	113
Red River	116	759	726	151	89	1,314	3,155	40	8	5	53
Reeves	170	1,060	412	249	116	1,836	3,843	0	0	0	0
Refugio	152	736	317	188	57	1,196	2,646	54	6	24	84
Roberts	7	72	46	18	175	94	412	47	10	3	60
Robertson	132	1,104	295	184	179	1,761	3,655	76	20	25	121
Rockwall	10	169	74	27	22	431	733	1,373	574	284	2,231
Runnels	63	399	239	82	28	383	1,194	217	38	147	402
Rusk	193	2,136	1,003	418	191	1,700	5,641	641	129	108	878
Sabine	80	346	264	146	42	496	1,374	195	27	18	240
San Augustine	105	684	280	144	190	1,013	2,416	0	0	0	0
San Jacinto	144	709	211	271	93	1,508	2,936	62	21	28	111
San Patricio	303	1,819	847	447	121	3,497	7,034	545	148	296	989
San Saba	43	414	153	163	60	685	1,518	57	7	28	92
Schleicher	12	123	52	39	9	145	380	45	13	169	227
Scurry	98	701	910	172	64	843	2,788	387	180	76	643
Shackelford	39	432	186	37	31	242	967	11	2	6	19
Shelby	147	1,504	645	263	100	1,766	4,425	58	16	6	80
Sherman	14	100	46	17	231	153	561	73	32	22	127
Smith	111	2,494	543	127	104	2,791	6,170	6,671	1,344	1,305	9,320
Somervell	48	325	163	163	55	482	1,236	30	7	8	45
Starr	163	1,846	126	161	111	2,373	4,780	14	7	1	22
Stephens	92	661	321	189	52	474	1,789	100	25	13	138
Sterling	34	134	72	35	13	112	400	22	6	96	124
Stonewall	48	333	180	52	59	283	955	5	8	14	27
Sutton	35	273	210	49	11	215	793	28	4	63	95
Swisher	37	204	285	39	311	797	1,673	46	58	14	118
Tarrant	943	4,110	1,704	979	486	20,323	28,545	25,756	6,762	6,042	38,560
Taylor	286	2,032	1,018	347	192	3,140	7,015	2,163	823	378	3,364
Terrell	21	128	54	29	13	256	501	0	0	0	0
Terry	64	542	418	55	67	786	1,932	108	569	26	703
Throckmorton	34	302	97	54	64	150	701	0	0	0	0
Titus	134	993	697	207	134	2,271	4,436	252	81	63	396
Tom Green	120	898	366	235	66	2,000	3,685	1,952	371	3,358	5,681
Travis	1,185	6,770	3,548	708	503	33,943	46,657	11,336	2,357	3,486	17,179
Trinity	95	1,828	336	2,518	94	1,149	6,020	0	0	0	0
Tyler	135	800	872	291	126	1,342	3,566	111	12	6	129
Upshur	211	1,785	758	298	262	2,045	5,359	304	40	47	391
Upton	98	554	291	124	45	273	1,385	12	2	12	26
Uvalde	144	1,190	312	396	82	2,096	4,220	170	28	141	339
Val Verde	79	633	138	105	24	1,169	2,148	252	37	437	726
Van Zandt	113	1,832	440	271	192	1,906	4,754	725	76	129	930
Victoria	419	2,018	667	332	162	2,944	6,542	1,372	268	537	2,177
Walker	136	887	404	285	114	1,897	3,723	624	244	257	1,125
Waller	52	645	148	148	58	1,244	2,295	223	64	89	376
Ward	132	907	481	174	136	587	2,417	87	36	45	168
Washington	38	483	463	126	37	1,102	2,249	471	123	181	775
Webb	706	2,075	1,132	708	100	12,183	16,904	287	45	58	390

County—	DEMOCRATIC PRIMARY							REPUBLICAN PRIMARY			
	Sheila Bilyeu	Andrew C. Briscoe III	A. Don Crowder	Bobby Locke	Ron Slover	Mark White	Total Vote (Democratic)	Bill Clements	Kent Hance	Tom Loeffler	Total Vote (Republican)
Wharton	64	920	403	230	107	1,662	3,386	569	111	124	80
Wheeler	49	262	146	85	518	363	1,423	145	171	27	34
Wichita	223	1,405	572	221	648	2,932	6,001	1,672	413	191	2,27
Wilbarger	59	356	127	47	362	586	1,537	107	98	8	21
Willacy	147	1,276	226	171	87	1,839	3,746	46	10	19	7
Williamson	109	732	569	176	63	2,724	4,373	2,690	850	1,149	4,68
Wilson	98	875	157	462	31	1,765	3,388	298	36	194	52
Winkler	50	398	221	110	69	432	1,280	56	30	78	16
Wise	148	1,100	641	319	298	1,755	4,261	298	72	88	45
Wood	86	1,431	373	121	106	1,196	3,313	904	110	226	1,24
Yoakum	106	609	270	193	66	430	1,674	25	155	2	18
Young	71	393	231	88	106	473	1,362	430	147	50	62
Zapata	97	553	221	123	71	1,253	2,318	40	3	5	4
Zavala	99	253	162	232	47	1,612	2,405	0	0	0	4
TOTAL VOTES	39,370	248,850	120,999	58,936	38,861	589,536	1,096,552	318,808	108,238	117,673	544,71
*TOTAL VOTES....								*318,938	*108,583	*118,224	*544,71

*Total votes as canvassed by Republican Party. Vote totals from Secretary of State and from Republican Party do not jibe.

General Election, 1986

Below are given results of the general election held Nov. 4, 1986, for all statewide races, and for those contested congressional, state senate and courts of appeals. These are official returns as canvassed by the State Canvassing Board. Abbreviations used are: (Dem.) Democrat, (Rep.) Republican, (Lib.) Libertarian and (Ind.) Independent.

Governor
Mark White (Dem.)	1,584,515
Bill Clements (Rep.)	1,813,779
Theresa Doyle (Lib.)	42,496
Other	670
Total vote	3,441,460

Lieutenant Governor
Bill Hobby (Dem.)	2,032,781
David Davidson (Rep.)	1,231,858
Bill Howell (Lib.)	47,819
Total vote	3,312,458

Attorney General
Jim Mattox (Dem.)	1,735,820
Roy R. Barrera Jr. (Rep.)	1,588,464
Mike Stephens (Lib.)	41,229
Total vote	3,365,513

Comptroller of Public Accounts
Bob Bullock (Dem.)	2,416,658
George Meeks (Lib.)	267,872
Total vote	2,684,530

State Treasurer
Ann W. Richards (Dem.)	2,425,836
Robert F. Reid (Lib.)	220,024
Total vote	2,645,860

Commissioner of General Land Office
Garry Mauro (Dem.)	1,975,042
M. D. Anderson Jr. (Rep.)	1,180,815
Honey Sue Lanham (Lib.)	62,844
Total vote	3,218,701

Commissioner of Agriculture
Jim Hightower (Dem.)	1,948,736
Bill Powers (Rep.)	1,238,436
Rebecca Reed (Lib.)	64,808
Total vote	3,251,980

Railroad Commissioner
John Sharp (Dem.)	1,738,596
Milton E. Fox (Rep.)	1,328,199
Chloe "Jack" Daniel (Lib.)	65,977
Total vote	3,132,772

Associate Justice, Supreme Court, Place 1
Oscar H. Mauzy (Dem.)	1,734,042
Charles Ben Howell (Rep.)	1,391,895
Total vote	3,125,937

Associate Justice, Supreme Court, Place 2
Robert M. Campbell (Dem.)	1,731,805
Nathan E. White Jr. (Rep.)	1,322,263
Total vote	3,054,068

Associate Justice, Supreme Court, Place 3
Jim Wallace (Dem.)	2,209,278
Wiley H. Rawlins (Lib.)	220,067
Total vote	2,429,345

Associate Justice, Supreme Court, Place 4
Raul A. Gonzalez (Dem.)	1,647,781
John L. Bates (Rep.)	1,452,529
Total vote	3,100,310

Judge, Court of Criminal Appeals, Place 1
Rusty Duncan (Dem.)	2,104,129

Judge Court of Criminal Appeals, Place 2
Mike McCormick (Dem.)	2,098,029

Judge, Court of Criminal Appeals, Place 3
Marvin O. Teague (Dem.)	2,176,576

CONGRESS
Below are results in contested races only for U.S. Congress in the general election, Nov. 4, 1986:

District 2
Charles Wilson (Dem.)	78,529
Julian Gordon (Rep.)	55,986
Sam I. Paradice (Lib.)	3,838
Total vote	138,353

District 3
Steve Bartlett (Rep.)	143,381
Don Gough (Lib.)	2,736
Brent Barnes (Ind.)	6,268
Total vote	152,385

District 4
Ralph Hall (Dem.)	97,540
Thomas Blow (Rep.)	38,578
Total vote	136,118

District 5
John Bryant (Dem.)	57,410
Tom Carter (Rep.)	39,945
Other	749
Total vote	98,104

District 6
Pete Geren (Dem.)	68,270
Joe Barton (Rep.)	86,190
Total vote	154,460

District 7
Harry Kniffen (Dem.)	17,635
Bill Archer (Rep.)	129,673
Roger Plail (Lib.)	1,087
Total vote	148,395

District 8
Blaine Mann (Dem.)	30,617
Jack Fields (Rep.)	66,280
Other	6
Total vote	96,903

District 9
Jack Brooks (Dem.)	73,285
Lisa Duperier (Rep.)	45,834
Total vote	119,119

Eddie Bernice Johnson of Dallas, left, and Judith Zaffirini of Laredo were elected to the state Senate in 1986. With Cyndi Krier of San Antonio, the three women are the most to serve in the upper house at one time in the state's history.

District 10
J. J. Pickle (Dem.)	135,863
Carole K. Rylander (Rep.)	52,000
Total vote	187,863

District 12
Jim Wright (Dem.)	84,831
Don McNeil (Rep.)	38,620
Total vote	123,451

District 13
Doug Seal (Dem.)	45,907
Beau Boulter (Rep.)	84,980
Total vote	130,887

District 14
Greg Laughlin (Dem.)	67,852
Mac Sweeney (Rep.)	74,471
Total vote	142,323

District 16
Ron Coleman (Dem.)	50,590
Roy Gillia (Rep.)	26,421
Total vote	77,011

District 18
Mickey Leland (Dem.)	63,335
Joanne Kuniansky (Ind.)	6,884
Total vote	70,219

District 19
Gerald McCathern (Dem.)	42,129
Larry Combest (Rep.)	68,695
Total vote	110,824

District 21
Pete Snelson (Dem.)	63,779
Lamar Smith (Rep.)	100,346
Jim Robinson (Lib.)	1,432
Other	10
Total vote	165,567

District 22
Susan Director (Dem.)	30,079
Tom DeLay (Rep.)	76,459
Total vote	106,538

District 23
Albert G. Bustamante (Dem.)	68,131
Ken Hendrix (Lib.)	7,001
Total vote	75,132

District 24
Martin Frost (Dem.)	69,368
Bob Burk (Rep.)	33,819
Other	4
Total vote	103,191

District 26
George Richardson (Dem.)	47,651

Richard Armey (Rep.)	101,735
Total vote	149,386

STATE SENATE
Below are results in contested races only for state Senate in the general election, Nov. 4, 1986:

District 6
Gene Green (Dem.)	52,051
Charles George (Write-in)	29
Total vote	52,080

District 10
Bob McFarland (Rep.)	97,690
R. Jerrold Strickler (Lib.)	7,036
Total vote	104,726

District 11
Chet Brooks (Dem.)	54,256
Bob Herman (Rep.)	30,762
Total vote	85,018

District 12
Hugh Parmer (Dem.)	67,299
Reby Cary (Rep.)	47,233
Total vote	114,532

District 16
Ken Gjemre (Dem.)	33,512
John N. Leedom (Rep.)	72,397
Total vote	105,909

District 18
Ken Armbrister (Dem.)	76,723
Bill Livingston (Rep.)	47,771
Total vote	124,494

District 19
Frank Tejeda (Dem.)	44,642
Bill Siebert (Rep.)	26,743
Michael D. Slifer (Lib.)	925
Total vote	72,310

District 21
Judith Zaffirini (Dem.)	59,153
Bennie Bock (Rep.)	54,736
Total vote	113,889

District 23
Eddie Bernice Johnson (Dem.)	61,538
Darrell Castillo (Rep.)	18,832
Total vote	80,370

COURTS OF APPEALS
Below are results in contested races only for Courts of Appeals in the general election, Nov. 4, 1986:

Chief Justice, First District
Frank G. Evans (Dem.)	334,339
Tom D. White (Rep.)	286,205
Total vote	620,544

Associate Justice, First District
James F. (Bud) Warren (Dem.)	368,875
Mike Hjalmarson (Rep.)	241,213
Total vote	610,088

Associate Justice, Second District, Place 2 (unexpired term)
Hal M. Lattimore (Dem.)	173,518
John Narsutis (Rep.)	147,382
Total vote	320,900

Associate Justice, Fifth District, Place 1
Larry Mitchell (Dem.)	173,013
Linda Thomas (Rep.)	254,828
Total vote	427,841

Associate Justice, Fifth District, Place 2
Annette Stewart (Dem.)	214,140
Leonard Hoffman (Rep.)	213,223
Total vote	427,363

Associate Justice, Fifth District, Place 3 (unexpired term)
John L. McCraw Jr. (Dem.)	191,234
James Baker (Rep.)	227,732
Total vote	418,966

Associate Justice, Fifth District, Place 4 (unexpired term)
Cynthia Hollingsworth (Dem.)	209,682
Sue Lagarde (Rep.)	211,217
Total vote	420,899

Associate Justice, Fifth District, Place 6 (unexpired term)
R. T. Scales (Dem.)	189,299
Nathan Hecht (Rep.)	226,778
Total vote	416,077

General Election, 1986

Below are results of the governor's and attorney general's races, Nov. 4, 1986. The first column gives the percer of voter turnout in the race for governor.

County	Voter Turnout	Governor			Attorney General		
		Mark White (Dem.)	Bill Clements (Rep.)	Theresa Doyle (Lib.)	Jim Mattox (Dem.)	Roy R. Barrera Jr. (Rep.)	Mike Stephens (Lib.)
Anderson	48.5	3,929	5,216	104	5,456	3,592	1
Andrews	54.8	727	2,625	68	1,661	1,666	4
Angelina	44.0	6,422	7,639	238	8,370	5,567	34
Aransas	55.2	1,641	2,606	90	2,154	2,091	6
Archer	59.4	1,050	1,661	28	1,628	936	
Armstrong	66.9	270	614	6	413	396	
Atascosa	46.0	2,869	3,659	79	3,269	2,931	4
Austin	55.4	2,069	3,270	35	2,982	2,185	2
Bailey	51.3	660	1,097	21	1,079	641	
Bandera	56.1	871	2,223	61	1,191	1,810	
Bastrop	43.1	4,800	4,403	126	6,111	2,913	1
Baylor	52.8	697	1,004	14	1,122	507	
Bee	48.6	3,367	3,184	90	3,860	2,671	
Bell	49.2	11,692	16,400	368	14,830	12,001	22
Bexar	43.0	98,962	97,390	3,414	74,732	119,252	1,9
Blanco	61.6	849	1,278	19	1,149	960	2
Borden	68.4	105	283	4	228	144	
Bosque	59.4	1,875	2,848	30	2,539	2,014	
Bowie	36.8	7,639	7,451	194	9,926	5,021	22
Brazoria	49.2	17,784	20,680	535	21,011	16,946	39
Brazos	49.4	11,280	13,368	416	12,041	12,440	3
Brewster	51.0	1,120	1,244	54	1,230	1,078	
Briscoe	57.9	356	402	7	521	231	
Brooks	65.8	3,188	870	53	2,841	923	
Brown	50.0	3,007	5,068	124	4,164	3,900	1
Burleson	49.5	1,764	1,757	29	2,277	1,144	
Burnet	60.0	2,961	4,162	71	4,293	2,675	
Caldwell	58.1	3,296	3,212	97	4,223	2,062	1
Calhoun	53.6	2,719	2,794	132	3,646	1,814	1
Callahan	52.4	1,123	2,268	50	1,800	1,520	
Cameron	39.6	19,363	16,548	327	16,663	16,149	22
Camp	45.1	1,498	1,176	12	1,712	784	
Carson	56.4	764	1,660	44	1,264	1,216	
Cass	44.6	3,930	3,374	42	4,814	2,020	
Castro	50.0	1,046	1,108	29	1,255	864	
Chambers	46.8	2,419	2,347	72	3,190	1,510	6
Cherokee	47.9	3,655	5,149	77	4,814	3,547	
Childress	51.9	656	1,060	13	1,031	704	
Clay	50.5	1,420	1,543	29	1,974	915	
Cochran	58.1	613	690	37	869	405	
Coke	55.8	499	742	24	706	488	
Coleman	51.6	1,094	2,050	25	1,704	1,311	
Collin	48.2	15,493	31,410	497	14,983	32,056	6
Collingsworth	55.7	695	875	11	997	457	
Colorado	52.3	2,174	2,776	33	2,995	1,714	
Comal	53.3	3,657	8,793	227	4,360	8,259	1
Comanche	54.3	1,639	2,084	50	2,298	1,292	
Concho	55.9	449	535	24	572	378	
Cooke	55.0	2,737	5,436	110	3,739	4,133	6
Coryell	45.7	2,828	4,286	109	4,389	2,609	
Cottle	46.9	482	331	8	569	191	
Crane	60.2	424	1,275	28	976	617	2
Crockett	40.7	392	684	8	612	424	
Crosby	42.5	1,027	639	15	1,152	472	
Culberson	49.5	470	359	16	508	264	
Dallam	45.1	402	821	19	617	583	
Dallas	47.7	159,151	204,932	4,001	157,716	199,818	5,8
Dawson	44.7	1,469	2,364	34	2,187	1,400	
Deaf Smith	45.9	1,359	2,668	40	1,728	2,221	
Delta	46.0	758	567	6	859	418	
Denton	47.4	16,575	26,267	568	16,843	25,419	6
DeWitt	52.3	1,476	3,206	31	2,206	2,296	
Dickens	51.1	601	339	16	715	185	
Dimmit	42.0	2,117	839	20	2,019	692	
Donley	54.6	431	901	13	660	620	
Duval	45.8	3,183	851	29	2,910	1,052	
Eastland	49.8	1,803	3,557	59	2,079	2,469	
Ector	48.8	7,008	17,848	362	11,802	12,713	3
Edwards	41.4	101	405	5	225	239	
Ellis	48.7	7,123	10,087	249	8,392	8,638	2
El Paso	36.5	37,507	26,884	1,165	35,421	29,016	1,0
Erath	53.7	2,709	3,667	63	3,499	2,744	
Falls	42.5	1,967	2,044	26	2,764	1,158	
Fannin	42.9	2,901	3,022	63	3,711	2,033	
Fayette	56.4	2,081	4,173	48	3,578	2,507	
Fisher	47.1	868	672	15	1,126	398	
Floyd	46.9	880	1,357	10	1,268	860	

County	Voter Turnout	Governor			Attorney General		
		Mark White (Dem.)	Bill Clements (Rep.)	Theresa Doyle (Lib.)	Jim Mattox (Dem.)	Roy R. Barrera Jr. (Rep.)	Mike Stephens (Lib.)
oard	47.8	359	264	3	471	127	0
ort Bend	50.5	18,068	21,039	328	19,451	19,262	367
ranklin	45.2	971	979	16	1,161	674	9
reestone	53.7	2,106	2,550	32	2,616	1,886	28
rio	47.0	2,133	1,554	26	2,109	1,293	13
aines	46.0	818	1,702	57	1,527	978	40
alveston	45.6	27,702	18,653	652	27,475	16,579	577
arza	41.3	322	788	4	599	417	7
illespie	61.9	1,169	4,294	49	1,803	3,562	71
lasscock	64.0	93	344	6	218	193	4
oliad	64.7	890	1,514	24	1,154	952	22
onzales	42.5	1,415	2,689	40	2,242	1,659	20
ray	55.8	1,882	6,083	160	3,274	4,696	110
rayson	49.0	9,228	12,670	292	11,762	9,723	342
regg	48.8	8,716	16,913	332	11,905	11,903	318
rimes	54.8	2,345	2,313	30	3,082	1,328	32
uadalupe	50.8	4,311	8,751	237	5,448	7,531	203
ale	46.3	2,319	4,196	47	3,551	2,800	33
all	47.8	688	710	4	946	393	7
amilton	58.7	1,027	1,566	28	1,438	1,018	15
ansford	60.4	398	1,566	11	816	1,043	11
ardeman	44.2	690	708	6	934	402	4
ardin	32.3	4,321	4,242	175	6,270	2,090	100
arris	44.7	267,685	238,119	4,221	263,607	226,744	6,093
arrison	40.9	6,386	6,042	103	6,786	4,540	101
artley	56.8	429	827	14	607	637	6
askell	46.4	912	1,222	24	1,428	670	9
ays	51.5	7,032	6,749	259	8,001	5,589	282
emphill	54.3	427	1,106	22	681	781	7
enderson	55.2	6,566	9,041	137	8,304	6,808	99
idalgo	36.8	29,532	19,663	408	25,729	21,460	301
ill	46.4	2,626	3,812	51	3,606	2,596	47
ockley	43.0	2,080	2,845	97	2,990	1,910	81
ood	54.3	2,609	4,146	122	3,100	3,621	112
opkins	50.7	3,246	3,415	42	3,901	2,476	31
ouston	46.3	2,540	2,822	46	3,714	1,387	28
oward	53.0	3,525	4,889	132	4,656	3,726	85
udspeth	50.8	286	311	11	374	177	2
unt	46.0	5,975	7,262	159	6,416	6,674	192
utchinson	55.5	2,137	5,613	161	3,625	4,035	117
rion	73.9	238	526	23	362	380	7
ack	49.0	740	1,254	23	1,037	894	12
ackson	60.4	1,695	2,655	26	2,694	1,349	49
asper	36.3	3,046	3,411	154	4,956	1,691	71
eff Davis	52.0	221	333	9	273	268	7
efferson	44.4	34,847	22,500	1,162	43,241	13,507	924
im Hogg	49.5	1,498	475	9	1,329	582	4
im Wells	40.5	5,203	3,335	42	5,264	3,179	42
ohnson	50.1	7,883	11,063	179	8,997	9,582	149
ones	47.8	1,615	2,516	42	2,398	1,635	30
arnes	49.2	1,496	2,131	32	2,009	1,479	16
aufman	45.8	4,756	5,770	123	5,628	4,752	153
endall	59.4	967	3,194	53	1,155	2,952	32
enedy	61.3	141	56	1	123	0	0
ent	46.6	176	227	9	268	116	3
err	57.7	2,792	7,774	128	3,336	7,180	131
imble	58.7	475	899	11	646	672	5
ing	70.4	67	146	3	123	70	4
inney	51.3	405	519	11	501	358	14
leberg	45.1	3,411	2,433	66	3,361	2,375	45
nox	46.1	618	686	16	874	406	5
amar	42.5	4,731	5,098	79	5,727	3,693	58
amb	45.2	1,502	2,439	46	2,426	1,406	17
ampasas	58.3	1,511	2,326	39	2,328	1,300	29
a Salle	61.7	1,576	645	11	1,640	489	8
avaca	54.7	2,159	3,617	46	3,348	2,115	39
ee	55.7	1,473	2,083	23	2,278	1,145	13
eon	46.6	1,530	2,231	20	2,262	1,271	17
iberty	48.4	5,729	5,999	83	7,513	3,675	86
imestone	48.9	2,329	2,542	32	2,928	1,823	11
ipscomb	69.4	462	1,053	23	719	667	14
ive Oak	53.0	1,248	2,200	32	1,926	1,390	34
lano	67.4	1,813	3,243	35	2,746	2,207	17
oving	80.5	28	60	2	38	39	1
ubbock	49.5	18,641	27,241	710	21,522	24,767	469
ynn	56.2	1,057	1,196	32	1,470	613	21
adison	50.0	1,167	1,464	13	1,689	863	6
arion	41.3	1,354	1,089	18	1,557	697	16
artin	45.9	354	791	12	625	467	8
ason	56.1	469	929	5	675	638	8
atagorda	47.5	4,103	4,517	125	5,511	3,014	104
averick	39.7	3,168	1,223	40	2,569	1,427	30

County	Voter Turnout	Governor			Attorney General		
		Mark White (Dem.)	Bill Clements (Rep.)	Theresa Doyle (Lib.)	Jim Mattox (Dem.)	Roy R. Barrera Jr. (Rep.)	Mike Stephens (Lib.)
McCulloch	53.5	1,016	1,366	27	1,292	1,019	1
McLennan	50.0	19,266	24,951	534	26,342	17,824	44
McMullen	56.2	105	244	1	132	200	
Medina	50.6	2,675	3,937	70	3,168	3,260	2
Menard	65.4	422	614	19	521	474	
Midland	51.3	6,381	17,878	344	7,159	16,695	23
Milam	50.8	3,021	2,935	48	3,750	2,058	3
Mills	56.8	529	977	17	848	590	
Mitchell	53.5	964	1,308	26	1,326	914	1
Montague	49.2	2,051	2,878	40	2,772	1,837	2
Montgomery	49.6	14,096	22,013	483	17,788	17,727	48
Moore	51.2	986	2,970	75	1,786	2,164	3
Morris	42.1	2,233	1,379	30	2,531	933	2
Motley	57.4	250	422	6	384	241	
Nacogdoches	43.8	4,242	6,115	129	5,834	4,391	18
Navarro	48.7	4,689	4,516	50	5,023	3,942	3
Newton	37.3	2,011	1,236	86	2,693	489	2
Nolan	46.9	1,507	2,166	71	2,036	1,584	7
Nueces	46.1	34,141	27,282	751	33,187	27,237	72
Ochiltree	58.9	503	2,421	18	1,150	1,565	1
Oldham	68.1	236	476	10	391	297	
Orange	42.8	10,081	6,656	482	13,268	3,707	25
Palo Pinto	51.3	2,679	3,752	70	3,405	2,853	5
Panola	48.4	2,839	3,024	53	3,807	1,814	3
Parker	56.5	5,530	8,808	222	6,924	7,353	21
Parmer	54.8	680	1,482	27	1,087	923	1
Pecos	55.6	1,730	2,572	60	2,472	1,785	5
Polk	46.9	3,439	4,223	151	5,090	2,427	26
Potter	52.3	6,168	11,475	392	7,210	10,345	33
Presidio	32.0	470	442	15	550	244	
Rains	50.6	887	1,014	18	1,107	699	1
Randall	56.3	6,383	17,790	345	7,932	16,271	25
Reagan	48.9	253	732	20	535	427	1
Real	66.2	370	868	15	635	466	1
Red River	38.9	1,842	1,500	14	2,244	846	
Reeves	53.4	2,402	1,986	81	2,824	1,478	5
Refugio	57.2	1,401	1,647	47	1,825	1,091	
Roberts	74.8	135	479	7	298	270	
Robertson	45.1	2,334	1,844	42	3,011	1,024	2
Rockwall	54.1	2,012	4,448	78	2,207	4,098	10
Runnels	50.9	1,018	2,152	51	1,681	1,422	2
Rusk	36.8	3,333	6,431	71	4,995	4,219	11
Sabine	47.4	1,247	1,463	52	1,811	773	1
San Augustine	33.3	1,075	1,057	16	1,443	531	2
San Jacinto	40.5	1,590	1,937	28	2,177	1,113	2
San Patricio	40.5	5,777	6,218	166	6,489	5,033	17
San Saba	56.0	750	940	21	1,073	549	
Schleicher	54.2	281	542	23	413	405	
Scurry	55.0	1,498	3,385	55	2,558	2,253	6
Shackelford	52.7	328	882	11	603	575	
Shelby	42.8	2,985	2,573	35	3,965	1,235	3
Sherman	61.7	313	814	15	581	498	
Smith	52.2	12,717	24,698	450	16,993	19,782	42
Somervell	46.2	554	760	15	715	534	
Starr	31.6	3,750	1,053	17	3,266	1,378	
Stephens	49.4	789	2,036	23	1,374	1,359	1
Sterling	68.9	156	436	33	309	268	
Stonewall	65.2	424	607	17	742	241	1
Sutton	47.1	277	847	20	523	556	1
Swisher	55.5	1,449	898	35	1,743	576	1
Tarrant	50.8	104,196	128,263	2,999	106,805	123,316	3,08
Taylor	50.8	9,275	18,355	462	11,167	16,436	30
Terrell	47.5	264	235	15	318	152	
Terry	39.8	1,384	1,910	31	1,990	1,226	1
Throckmorton	55.9	315	462	4	504	238	
Titus	49.2	3,290	2,688	36	3,876	1,858	2
Tom Green	52.9	7,864	12,944	467	8,920	12,040	41
Travis	56.4	86,152	64,649	2,489	91,096	57,830	2,76
Trinity	40.1	1,673	1,863	36	2,421	952	3
Tyler	43.9	2,077	2,235	91	3,217	990	5
Upshur	44.5	3,393	4,046	60	4,623	2,637	5
Upton	48.0	229	1,074	16	686	525	
Uvalde	47.7	2,332	3,151	65	3,033	2,255	
Val Verde	42.3	3,022	2,663	63	3,180	2,355	
Van Zandt	47.8	3,999	5,776	87	5,023	4,388	2
Victoria	41.6	5,982	11,002	192	8,552	7,557	22
Walker	53.2	4,251	4,674	84	5,266	3,461	5
Waller	47.4	2,626	2,729	55	3,275	1,955	6
Ward	51.0	909	2,402	68	1,870	1,389	5
Washington	56.6	2,933	4,225	55	4,180	2,784	5
Webb	37.4	11,594	3,954	243	8,007	7,560	12
Wharton	47.7	4,136	4,962	101	5,802	3,186	

County	Voter Turnout	Governor			Attorney General		
		Mark White (Dem.)	Bill Clements (Rep.)	Theresa Doyle (Lib.)	Jim Mattox (Dem.)	Roy R. Barrera Jr. (Rep.)	Mike Stephens (Lib.)
Wheeler	56.5	727	1,585	24	1,110	1,053	11
Wichita	46.9	12,392	13,337	364	14,927	10,645	247
Wilbarger	44.2	1,460	1,900	28	2,072	1,224	12
Willacy	39.1	1,846	1,522	27	1,941	1,197	25
Williamson	54.7	12,437	15,516	463	14,518	13,245	434
Wilson	44.5	2,251	2,969	65	2,553	2,488	47
Winkler	48.3	643	1,435	37	1,187	887	24
Wise	49.0	3,086	4,584	92	3,841	3,631	91
Wood	53.7	2,912	4,729	55	3,895	3,501	32
Yoakum	52.7	652	1,521	44	1,256	885	33
Young	52.7	1,674	3,485	44	2,570	2,332	27
Zapata	42.6	1,336	790	13	1,121	957	4
Zavala	42.1	2,288	648	11	1,953	705	10
Total Votes	47.2	1,584,515	1,813,779	42,496	1,735,820	1,588,464	41,229

Other vote in gubernatorial race, 670; other vote in attorney general's race, 0.
Total gubernatorial vote, 3,441,460.
Total attorney general's vote, 3,365,513.

Party Organizations

Democratic State Executive Committee

Chairman, Bob Slagle, Box 1244, Sherman 75090; **Vice Chairman,** Blandina Cardenas-Ramirez, 3246 Swandale, San Antonio 78230; **Vice Chairman For Financial Affairs,** (vacancy); **Secretary,** Ronald E. Luna, 1383 Old Lockhart Rd., Buda 78610; **Treasurer,** Frank Thompson, 6937 Peyton, Houston 77028. **Office Address:** 302 Stokes Bldg., Austin 78701.

National Committee Members: Millie Bruner, Grand Prairie; Billie Carr, Houston; Sue Pate, Bridge City; Gene Rodriquez Jr., San Antonio; Paul G. Gray, Austin; Al Edwards, Houston; Dora Olivo, Rosenberg; Steve Carriker, Roby; Hazel Obey, Austin; Ed Miller, Texarkana; Deborah Bradley, Austin.

District—Member and Address.

1.—Dr. Jeanie Stanley, 1225 Oak Dr., Kilgore 75662; Lamar Yarborough, Rt. 2, Box 225, Beckville 75631.
2.—Mary Elizabeth Jackson, Box 7678, Tyler 75711; Charles P. Elliott, 1407 Cowan, Commerce 75428.
3.—Jeanette Coffield, Box 6057, Jasper 75951; John Henry Tatum II, Box 582, Lufkin 75901.
4.—Bettye R. Smith, 3380 Worcester, Beaumont 77705; Dewey Updegraff, 3633 Hemlock, Orange 77630.
5.—Alta K. Rickett, Rt. 3, Box 2571B, Magnolia 77355; Jim Carter, 1724 18th, Huntsville 77340.
6.—Cora L. Johnson, 10126 Alford Ln., Houston 77041; Terry Bonds, 638 Overbluff, Channelview 77530.
7.—Dianne Richards, 1980 Post Oak, #1600, Houston 77056; Stewart W. Gagnon, 159 Stoney Creek, Houston 77024.
8.—Dr. Louise Young, 8261 Clearsprings Rd., Dallas 75240; Richard Johnston, 4026 Hockaday, Dallas 75229.
9.—Lauri Anderson, Rt. 3, Thornton 76687; Randy Daniel, 110 McDonald, Athens 75751.
10.—Martha Mewhirter, 1221 Wentwood Dr., Irving 75061; Gary Horton, 1815 Briar Meadow, Arlington 76014.
11.—F.G. (Jean) Wortham, 3707 Longwood, Pasadena 77503; Richard Kirkpatrick, 2705 3rd Ave. N., Texas City 77590.
12.—Martha Singleton, 3029 Gardenia Dr., Fort Worth 76119; Lloyd Scurlock, 3717 Kelvin, Fort Worth 76133.
13.—Wilma Oliver, 1712 Blodgett, Houston 77004; Anthony Hall, Box 1562, Houston 77251.
14.—Mary Benavides, 1805 Running Brook, Austin 78733; Patrick Cox, Box 707, Buda 78610.
15.—Francis Frazier, 7102 Camway, Houston 77028; David Patronella, 1706 Seamist, #540, Houston 77008.
16.—Bobbie Holbrook, 6554 Kingsbury, Dallas 75231; Ken Molberg, 5640 Swiss, Dallas 75214.
17.—Rose F. Ramos, 935 Magnolia, Lake Jackson 77566; Edmund L. Cogburn, 5002 Doliver, Houston 77056.
18.—Diana Rhodes, Box 37, Nursery 77976; Vernon Harrison, 518 Land Grant, Richmond 77469.
19.—Ruth Jones, 3811 Willowwood, San Antonio 78219; Gilbert Kissling, 418 E. Huisache, San Antonio 78212.
20.—Lana Peterson, 2208 Post Oak, Portland 78374; Santiago Cantu, 1010 Weber Pkwy., Corpus Christi 78411.
21.—Ninfa Moncada, 1247 E. Crockett, Crystal City 78839; John Taylor, 5 Spyglass, McQueeney 78123.
22.—Nancy Brannon, 1533 Carnation, Lewisville 75067; Harris Worcester, Rt. 2, Box 61, Aledo 76008.
23.—Yvonne Davis, 4036 Shadyhollow, Dallas 75233; Eli Davis, 912 Timber Dell Ln., Dallas 75232.
24.—Clara Lou Sawyer, Rt. 12, Box 100, Llano 78643; Alvan Wells, Box 92, Killeen 76540.
25.—Janet Massey, Box 138, Midland 79702; Gerald Ratliff, 635 S. Jefferson, San Angelo 76902.
26.—Christine Hernandez, Box 9571, San Antonio 78204; John J. Murnin, 319 Montfort, San Antonio 78216.
27.—Rachel G. Perelman, 1860 Price Rd., Brownsville 78521; Mike Sinder, 821 Nolana, McAllen 78504.
28.—Natalie Rothstein, 4230 E. Everglade, Odessa 79762; Leon Cohorn, 209 Highland Dr., Lamesa 79331.
29.—Jesse Carrasco, 3300 Pershing, El Paso 79903; Stanley B. Roberts, 11652 James Watt, El Paso 79936.
30.—Dorthy Wise, 1308 Sunnyside Ln., Wichita Falls 76303; Calvin Gambill, 711 W. California, Seymour 76380.
31.—Angela K. Lamb, Rt. 1, Box 505, Amarillo 79106; Bob Bass, 601 W. 7th, Plainview 79072.

YOUNG DEMOCRATS
Jackie Urbach, Box 12345, Austin 78711; Paul Banda, 520 Linda Dr., #408, San Antonio 78666-8032.

COUNTY CHAIRMAN'S ASSOCIATION
Ron Gay, 2802 Wilderness South, College Station 77840; Karen McLeaish, 4656 Lemonwood, Odessa 79761.

YOUNG DEMOCRATIC CLUBS OF TEXAS
Jackie Urbach, Box 12345, Austin 78711.

Republican State Executive Committee

Chairman, George W. Strake Jr., 712 Main St., Houston 77002; **Vice Chairman,** Diana Denman, Box 6009, San Antonio 78209; **Secretary,** Kay Danks, 7200 W. Rim, Austin 78731; **Treasurer,** Henry Santamaria, 801 Somerset, El Paso 79912, **Office Address:** 1300 Guadalupe, Ste. 205, Austin 78701; **General Counsel,** Leonard Davis, Box 359, Tyler 75710; **Finance Chairman,** William Banowsky, Box 31365, Dallas 75231; **Parliamentarian,** Marguerite Binkley, 1906 Twin Springs, Kingwood 77339.

National Committeeman, Ernest Angelo Jr., 410 N. Main, Midland 79701; **National Committeewoman,** Mrs. Fran Chiles, Box 26162, Fort Worth 76116.

Republicans continued on Page 510.

Republicans continued from Page 509.

District, Member and Address:

1. —William Osborn, 1320 Colgate Dr., Longview; Nancy Gordon, Box 175, Avinger.
2. —Dr. Gene Hightower, Rt. 1, Box 316, Van; Jane Yancey, 1921 Palo Alto Cr., Plano.
3. —J. Matt Dillion, Box 296, Woodville; Marguerete Graves, Box 127, Kirbyville.
4. —Ray Benski, 927 30th St., Nederland; Marguerite Foulk, 3670 Crestwood Dr., Beaumont.
5. —Don Redd, 76 S. Wavy Oak, The Woodlands; Katye Kowierschke, 104 Elkins Lake, Huntsville.
6. —Clymer Wright, 6038 Darkwood, Houston; Wilda Lindstrom, 12843 Eastbrook, Houston.
7. —Walter Jensen, 1927 Chaparral, Houston; Jeanne Wilson, 15202 Morning Pine, Houston.
8. —Bob Driegert, 3 Shadywood Pl., Richardson; Virginia Steenson, 602 Vernet, Richardson.
9. —John Sumlin, 9006 Sugarberry, Dallas; Sarilee Ferguson, 2317 N. 50th, Waco.
10. —James Cribbs, Box 13060, Arlington; Jane Burgland, 3700 Shady Valley Dr., Arlington.
11. —Henry Haney Sr., P.O. Box 547, Dickinson; Gayle West, 4030 Fox Meadow, Pasadena.
12. —William H. Lockard, 6305 Greencastle Crt., Fort Worth; Jane Berberich, 4304 Cadiz, Fort Worth.
13. —Jerry Smith, Box 13608, Houston; Iris Manes, 4939 Glenmeadow, Houston.
14. —Mark Lehman, 1510 W. North Loop, Ste. 1121, Austin; Holly Dechard, 4204 Tallowood, Austin.
15. —Earl Lairson, Box 500017, Houston; Nelda Eppes, 5426 Poinciana, Houston.

16. —Jay Patterson, 5420 LBJ Freeway, Suite 1370, Dallas; Lynne Tweedell, 9911 Coldwater Cir., Dallas.
17. —Bill Borden Jr., 4617 Oakdale, Bellaire; Penny Butler, 819 Briar Ridge, Houston.
18. —Darryl Pool, 1809 Wind Spirit, Round Rock; Ann Ashy, 204 Leisure, Victoria.
19. —Col. B.B. Ford, 829 Canterbury Hill, San Antonio; Mrs. Theo Wickersham, 201 Scott Ave., Universal City.
20. —Lawrence J. Tucker, 3701 Aransas St., Corpus Christi; Leona Knight, 1202 Southbay Dr., Corpus Christi.
21. —H. Pulse Martinez, Box 21, San Antonio; Barbara Schoolcraft, Rt. 3, Box 720, Seguin.
22. —Dunman Perry Jr., Box 640, Mineral Wells; Vivian Millirons, 1016 Stuckert Dr., Burleson.
23. —Dr. Jimmy Morgan, Box 61204, D/FW Airport; Patricia Taylor, 4577 Lynnacre Cr., Dallas.
24. —Marcus Anderson, Box 353, Abilene; Helen Ruland, 2604 N. Beal, Belton.
25. —David Godfrey, Box 994, Midland; Cindy Brockwell, Rt. 5, Box 5171, Boerne.
26. —Jess Young, 111 W. Olmos Dr., San Antonio; Dian Rath, 227 Springwood Ln., San Antonio.
27. —Bob Shepard, Box 1830, Harlingen; Mary Ann Rio Rt. 1, Box 585, McAllen.
28. —John M. Ryan, 4913 92nd St., Lubbock; Janelle Evans, Box 3, Brownfield.
29. —Ronald Ederer, 5925 Cromo, El Paso; Bette Hervey 3920 Hillcrest Dr., El Paso.
30. —Harry Robards, Drawer P, Sherman; Jacque Allen 2206 Clarinda, Wichita Falls.
31. —John E. Kirchhoff, 620 W. 7th, Plainview; Bobbi Nisbet, 2511 Mary Ellen, Pampa.

In addition to Rep. Jim Wright's speakership in the U.S. House, Texans hold other positions of leadership. Sen. Lloyd Bentsen, left, is chairman of the important Senate Finance Committee; Rep. Eligio "Kika" de la Garza, center, chairs the House Agriculture Committee; and Rep. Jack Brooks heads the House Government Operations Committee.

Texans in Congress

Texas is allocated 27 members in the U.S. House of Representatives and two in the U.S. Senate. The salary of members of both houses is $77,400 with limitations on outside income.

The term of office for members of the House is two years, and the terms of all members will expire on Jan. 1, 1989. Senators serve six-year terms. Lloyd Bentsen will serve until Jan. 1989, and Phil Gramm's term will end in 1991.

Addresses and phone numbers of the lawmakers' Washington and district offices are given below. Washngton zip codes are 20515 for members of the House and 20510 for senators.

Senate

Lloyd Bentsen (Dem.)—Washington Office: 703 Hart Senate Office Bldg., (202) 224-5922; District Office: 961 Federal Bldg., Austin, 78701, (512) 482-5834.

Phil Gramm (Rep.)—Washington Office: 370 Russell Senate Office Bldg., (202) 224-2934; District Office:

Federal Bldg., #750, 900 Jackson St., Dallas, 75202 (214) 767-3000.

House

District

1. Jim Chapman (Dem.), Washington Office: 429 Cannon House Office Bldg., (202) 225-3035; District Office: P.O. Box 538, Sulphur Springs, 75482, (214) 88-8682.
2. Charles Wilson (Dem.), Washington Office: 2221 Rayburn House Office Bldg., (202) 225-2401; District Office: 701 North First St., Rm. 201, Lufkin, 75901 (409) 637-1770.
3. Steve Bartlett (Rep.), Washington Office: 1709 Longworth House Office Bldg., (202) 225-4201; District Office: 6600 LBJ Freeway, Suite 4190, Dallas 75240, (214) 767-4848.
4. Ralph Hall (Dem.), Washington Office: 236 Cannon House Office Bldg., (202) 225-6673; District Office: 104 N. San Jacinto, Rockwall, 75087, (214) 722-9118.

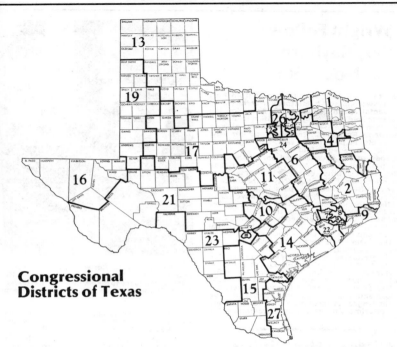

Congressional Districts of Texas

5. **John Bryant (Dem.)**, Washington Office: 412 Cannon House Office Bldg., (202) 225-2231; District Office: 8035 East R. L. Thornton, Dallas, 75228, (214) 767-6554.

6. **Joe Barton (Rep.)**, Washington Office: 1225 Longworth House Office Bldg., (202) 225-2002; District Office: 3509 Hulen, Suite 110, Fort Worth, 76107, (817) 737-7737.

7. **Bill Archer (Rep.)**, Washington Office: 1135 Longworth House Office Bldg., (202) 225-2571; District Office: 7501 Federal Bldg., 515 Rusk, Houston, 77002, (713) 229-2763.

8. **Jack Fields (Rep.)**, Washington Office: 413 Cannon House Office Bldg., (202) 225-4901; District Office: 12605 East Freeway, Suite 320, Houston, 77015, (713) 451-6334.

9. **Jack Brooks (Dem.)**, Washington Office: 2449 Rayburn House Office Bldg., (202) 225-6565; District Office: 230 Federal Bldg., Beaumont, 77701, (409) 839-2508.

0. **J. J. Pickle (Dem.)**, Washington Office: 242 Cannon House Office Bldg., (202) 225-4865; District Office: 763 Federal Bldg., Austin, 78701, (512) 482-5921.

1. **Marvin Leath (Dem.)**, Washington Office: 336 Cannon House Office Bldg., (202) 225-6105; District Office: 206 Federal Bldg., Waco, 76701, (817) 752-9600.

2. **Jim Wright (Dem.)**, Washington Office: 1236 Longworth House Office Bldg., (202) 225-8040; District Office: 536-B Seminary Dr., Fort Worth, 76115, (817) 334-4845.

3. **Beau Boulter (Rep.)**, Washington Office: 124 Cannon House Office Bldg., (202) 225-3706; District Office: 205 East 5th, Amarillo, 79101, (806) 376-2381.

4. **Mac Sweeney (Rep.)**, Washington Office: 1713 Longworth House Office Bldg., (202) 225-2831; District Office: 1908 N. Laurent, Suite 580, Victoria, 77091, (512) 576-6001.

5. **Kika de la Garza (Dem.)**, Washington Office: 1401 Longworth House Office Bldg., (202) 225-2531; District Office: 1418 Beech, McAllen, 78501, (512) 682-5545.

6. **Ron Coleman (Dem.)**, Washington Office: 416 Cannon House Office Bldg., (202) 225-4831; District Office: 146 U.S. Courthouse, El Paso, 79901, (915) 541-7650.

17. **Charles Stenholm (Dem.)**, Washington Office: 1226 Longworth House Office Bldg., (202) 225-6606; District Office: P.O. Box 1237, Stamford, 79553, (915) 773-3623.

18. **Mickey Leland (Dem.)**, Washington Office: 2236 Rayburn House Office Bldg., (202) 225-3816; District Office: 1919 Smith St., Houston, 77002, (713) 739-7339.

19. **Larry Combest (Rep.)**, Washington Office: Longworth House Office Bldg., (202) 225-4005; District Office: Federal Bldg., Suite 613, 1206 Texas Ave., Lubbock, 79401, (806) 763-1611.

20. **Henry Gonzalez (Dem.)**, Washington Office: 2413 Rayburn House Office Bldg., (202) 225-3236; District Office: Federal Bldg., Rm. B-124, 727 E. Durango, San Antonio, 78206, (512) 229-6195.

21. **Lamar Smith (Rep.)**, Washington Office: 507 Cannon House Office Bldg., (202) 225-4236; District Office: 110 San Pedro, Suite 530, San Antonio, 78216, (512) 229-5880.

22. **Tom DeLay (Rep.)**, Washington Office: 1039 Longworth House Office Bldg., (202) 225-5951; District Office: 9000 S.W. Freeway, Suite 205, Houston, 77074, (713) 270-4000.

23. **Albert Bustamante (Dem.)**, 1116 Longworth House Office Bldg., (202) 225-4511; District Office: Federal Bldg., Rm. B-146, 727 E. Durango, San Antonio, 78206, (512) 229-6191.

24. **Martin Frost (Dem.)**, Washington Office: 2459 Rayburn House Office Bldg., (202) 225-3605; District Office: 1319 RepublicBank Tower, 400 S. Zang Blvd., Dallas, 75208, (214) 767-2816.

25. **Mike Andrews (Dem.)**, Washington Office: 322 Cannon House Office Bldg., (202) 225-7508; District Office: Federal Bldg., 515 Rusk, Houston, 77002, (713) 229-2244.

26. **Dick Armey (Rep.)**, Washington Office: 514 Cannon House Office Bldg., (202) 225-7772; District Office: 250 S. Stemmons Freeway, Suite 210, Lewisville, 75067, (214) 221-4527.

27. **Solomon Ortiz (Dem.)**, Washington Office: 1534 Longworth House Office Bldg., (202) 225-7742; District Office: 3649 Leopard, Suite 510, Corpus Christi, 78408, (512) 883-5868.

Jim Wright Follows Garner, Rayburn In U.S. House Role

U. S. Rep. Jim Wright, a Democrat from Fort Worth, was sworn in as the 48th speaker of the House of Representatives in January 1987, becoming the third Texan to hold the prestigious position in the 20th century. John Nance Garner, who served as vice president under Franklin D. Roosevelt, and Sam Rayburn, who held the post for 18 years, the longest tenure in history, preceded Wright.

The speakership is considered one of the most powerful positions in Washington, for the post combines the responsibilities of party spokesman with parliamentary leader. The authority of the office in recent years often reflects the personality and persuasiveness of the holder. House rules have taken much of the authority from the office, placing it in the hands of the party caucuses. Modern speakers have nothing like the unbridled authority of a Henry Clay or Joe Cannon. But they are expected to be political spokesmen, and with the power and prestige of the media, the speaker's effectiveness transcends his parliamentary authority.

Wright graduated in 1941 from Weatherford College and won the Distinguished Flying Cross and the Legion of Merit while flying B-24 bombers in the Pacific in World War II. He won election to the Texas House after the war and served as mayor of Weatherford before entering congressional politics. In 1954, Wright challenged an incumbent congressman and won a bitter primary battle, which was tantamount to election.

History Highlights

As a legislator, Wright considers himself a "Roosevelt Democrat." During the days of the Great Society in the 1960s, he was a strong supporter of economic and social reforms. Some considered him too liberal for the staunchly conservative Texas Democrats. Although unsuccessful in two statewide races for the U.S. Senate, the speaker has had no trouble being re-elected from his Fort Worth district.

Wright appeared uncertain of his personal political goals until the mid-1970s. He seemed caught between two worlds: too liberal for most Texans, but considered unsympathetic to social goals by Northern Democrats. In 1976, however, the congressman defeated Richard Bolling of Missouri by one vote for

John Nance Garner of Uvalde, left, was the first Texan to serve as speaker of the U.S. House. Sam Rayburn of Bonham, right, served 18 years in the post, longer than any other speaker. Associated Press Photos.

Texas Congressman Jim Wright of Fort Worth is presented the gavel by Minority Leader Robert H. Michel after assuming the speakership of the U.S. House of Representatives in January 1987. Photopress International Photo.

the post of majority leader in the House, the major stepping stone to the speakership, and thereafter, he charted a course for national leadership.

Wright's Texan predecessors in the speaker's chair followed essentially the same route. John Nance Garner of Uvalde served as county judge and as a Texas legislator before seeking a new congressional seat in Southwest Texas in 1902. Through much of his early tenure, Republicans controlled the House. Garner, however, became a party whip in 1909 and was considered a leading Democrat by World War I. In 1931, the Uvalde congressman was elected speaker and wrestled with the early problems of the Depression. He won the California presidential primary the following year, and to avoid a party split, Garner joined the national Democratic ticket as Franklin D. Roosevelt's vice-presidential running mate. Though considered a radical in his early years in Washington, Garner became more conservative and split with Roosevelt on many issues. Finally in 1940, he was dropped from the ticket when Roosevelt sought an unprecedented third term. Garner retired to Uvalde where he died in 1967.

Sam Rayburn is considered one of the best political operatives to hold the modern speakership. He apprenticed for the position in the Texas Legislature where he served as speaker in 1911, and the following year, the young politician was elected to Congress where he served for 48 years.

Rayburn served as speaker in three tenures, from 1940-47, from 1949-53, and from 1955-61. He was difficult to categorize politically, being more a middle-of-the-road legislator than a liberal or New Dealer. He was, however, always a party man. Rayburn's speakerships were difficult because the national Democrats were badly divided over many economic and social issues, and he had to use his powers of persuasion to accomplish limited political goals. Historian Randall B. Ripley felt that in view of the split among Democrats, Rayburn's record was "enough to earn . . . a reputation as an incomparable legislative wizard when faced with unfavorable odds."

One major legislative victory credited to Rayburn, however, may have materially changed the course of U.S. history. Through parliamentary maneuvering, he kept the military draft law, which passed the House by only one vote, from being reconsidered and thereby assured U.S. preparedness for World War II.

Rayburn died in 1961.

tate Sen. Chet Brooks of Pasadena, left, and state Rep. Bill Hollowell of Grand Saline were deans of their houses in the 0th Legislature. Sen. Brooks has served since 1967, and Rep. Hollowell has served two tenures in the House, from 1957 to 967 and from 1973 until the present.

Members of Texas Legislature

The Texas Legislature has 181 members—31 in the Senate and 150 in the House of Representatives. Regular essions convene on the second Tuesday of January in odd-numbered years, but the governor may call special essions. Article III of the Texas Constitution deals with the legislative branch.

The following lists are of members of the 70th Legislature, which convened on Jan. 13, 1987, following the Nov. 4, 986, election.

STATE SENATE

Thirty-one members of the State Senate are elected or four-year, **overlapping terms.** Date in parentheses fter each name below indicates expiration of **term of ffice. Chet Brooks** of Pasadena is dean of the Senate. **alary:** The salary of all members of the Legislature, icluding both Senators and Representatives, was set y a constitutional amendment, adopted April 22, 1975, s follows: $600 per month and $30 per diem during leg-lative sessions; **mileage allowance** at same rate pro-ided by law for state employees. The rate of $30 per iem applies during each regular and special session of ie Legislature. The address of senators is Texas Sen-te, P.O. Box 12068, Capitol Station, Austin, Texas 78711.

Senatorial Districts include one or more whole coun-es and some counties have more than one Senator.

President of the Senate is Lt. Gov. William P. Hobby, ouston. Other officers are: **President Pro Tempore,** ay Farabee, Wichita Falls. **Secretary of the Senate,** Bet-' King, Austin. **Sergeant-at-Arms,** Carleton Turner, ustin.

Dist., Name, Address, Term of Office, Occupation.
1—Anderson, Richard, Marshall (1-1-91); attorney.
18—Armbrister, Ken, Victoria (1-1-91); realtor.
14—Barrientos, Gonzalo, Austin (1-1-89); business-man.
3—Blake, Roy, Nacogdoches (1-1-89); insurance-real estate.
11—Brooks, Chet, Pasadena (1-1-91); businessman.
*17—Brown, James E. "Buster," Lake Jackson (1-1-89); attorney.
5—Caperton, Kent, Bryan (1-1-91); attorney.
9—Edwards, Chet, Duncanville (1-1-89); business-man.
30—Farabee, Ray, Wichita Falls (1-1-89); attorney.
22—Glasgow, Bob, Stephenville (1-1-89); attorney.
6—Green, Gene, Houston (1-1-91); printer-at-torney.
*8—Harris, Ike, Dallas (1-1-89); attorney.
*7—Henderson, Don, Houston (1-1-91); attorney-businessman.
23—Johnson, Eddie Bernice, Dallas (1-1-91); agency vice president.
24—Jones, Grant, Abilene (1-1-89); attorney-businessman.
*26—Krier, Cynthia T., San Antonio (1-1-89); attorney.
*16—Leedom, John, Dallas (1-1-91); businessman.

2—Lyon, Ted, Rockwall (1-1-89); attorney.
*10—McFarland, Bob, Arlington (1-1-91); attor-ney.
28—Montford, John, Lubbock (1-1-89); attorney.
4—Parker, Carl, Port Arthur (1-1-89); attorney.
12—Parmer, Hugh, Fort Worth (1-1-91); busi-nessman.
29—Santiesteban, H. Tati, El Paso (1-1-91); attor-ney.
31—Sarpalius, Bill, Amarillo (1-1-89); educator-businessman.
25—Sims, Bill, San Angelo (1-1-91); businessman-rancher.
19—Tejeda, Frank, San Antonio (1-1-91); attorney.
20—Truan, Carlos, Corpus Christi (1-1-89); insur-ance.
27—Uribe, Hector, Brownsville (1-1-91); attorney.
13—Washington, Craig, Houston (1-1-91); attorney.
15—Whitmire, John, Houston (1-1-91); attorney.
21—Zaffirini, Judith, Laredo (1-1-91); communica-tions specialist.
*Republicans; all others are Democrats.

HOUSE OF REPRESENTATIVES

This list shows 150 members of the House of Repre-sentatives in the 70th Legislature. They were elected on Nov. 4, 1986, from districts shown in the list below. **Bill Hollowell** of Grand Saline is the senior House member. Members are elected for 2-year terms. Representatives and senators receive the same salary; see state Senate. Numbers before names denote district. The address of representatives is House of Representatives, P. O. Box 2910, Capitol Station, Austin, Texas 78769.

Speaker, Gib Lewis. **Chief Clerk,** Betty Murray. **Ser-geant-at-Arms,** Ron Hinkle.

Dist., Name, Address, Term of Office, Occupation.
*114—Agnich, Fred, Dallas; businessman.
3—Aikin, A M. III, Greenville; businessman.
106—Arnold, Bill, Grand Prairie; school admin-istrator.
144—Barton, Erwin W., Pasadena; businessman.
119—Beauchamp, Jerry J., San Antonio; insurance, real estate.
34—Berlanga, Hugo, Corpus Christi; businessman.
140—Betts, Weldon, Houston; union officer.
*105—Blackwood, Bill, Mesquite; engineer.
110—Blair, Fred, Dallas; real estate.
66—Burnett, Richardson J., San Angelo; retired FBI.

107—Cain, David H., Dallas; attorney.
*61—Campbell, Ben, Flower Mound; real estate.
78—Carriker, S. A., Roby; farmer-rancher.
*91—Carter, Bill G., Fort Worth; insurance.
35—Cavazos, Eddie, Corpus Christi; real estate.
*112—Ceverha, Bill, Richardson; businessman.
20—Clark, Jerry, Buna; farmer-businessman.
17—Clemons, Billy, Pollok; railroad clerk.
132—Colbert, Paul, Houston; consultant.
23—Collazo, Frank Jr., Port Arthur; businessman.
*126—Connelly, E. Barry, Houston; businessman.
*47—Cooper, Anne, San Marcos; housewife.
*76—Craddick, Tom, Midland; businessman.
25—Criss, Lloyd W. Jr., LaMarque; businessman.
43—Cuellar, Henry, Laredo; attorney, teacher.
42—Cuellar, Renato, Weslaco; businessman.
*125—Culberson, John, Houston; state representative.
137—Danburg, Debra, Houston; attorney.
50—Delco, Wilhelmina R., Austin; legislator.
56—Denton, Betty, Waco; attorney.
142—Dutton, Harold V., Houston; businessman.
33—Earley, Robert, Portland; legislator.
*133—Eckels, Robert, Houston; public relations.
45—Edge, Eldon, Poth; retired schoolman.
146—Edwards, Al, Houston; public relations.
*92—Evans, Charles, Hurst; attorney.
147—Evans, Larry, Houston; attorney.
80—Finnell, Charles, Holliday; attorney.
115—Garcia, Orlando, San Antonio; attorney.
81—Gavin, John, Wichita Falls; insurance.
*67—Geistweidt, Gerald, Mason; rancher-attorney.
58—Gibson, Bruce, Cleburne; attorney-farmer.
*83—Givens, Ron, Lubbock; real estate.
44—Glossbrenner, Ernestine, Alice; teacher.
108—Granoff, Al, Dallas; attorney.
*94—Grusendorf, Kent, Arlington; manufacturer.
51—Guerrero, Lena, Austin; advertising.
139—Hackney, Clint, Houston; attorney.
10—Haley, Bill, Center; teacher.
*109—Hammond, Bill, Dallas; businessman.
*93—Harris, Chris, Arlington; attorney.
*27—Harris, Jack, Pearland; dentist.
68—Harrison, Dudley, Sanderson; car dealer.
*149—Heflin, Talmadge, Houston; businessman.
18—Hightower, Allen R., Huntsville; car salesman.
*150—Hilbert, Paul J., Spring; attorney.
*101—Hill, Anita, Garland; legislator.
*102—Hill, Patricia, Dallas; attorney.
41—Hinojosa, Juan, McAllen; attorney.
5—Hollowell, Bill, Grand Saline; attorney.
*32—Holzheauser, Steve, Inez; veterinarian.
*59—Horn, Jim N., Denton; businessman.
100—Hudson, Samuel W. III, Dallas; attorney.
*79—Hunter, Bob, Abilene; university vice president.
24—Hury, James, Galveston; attorney.
11—Johnson, Cliff, Palestine; real estate.
*60—Johnson, Sam, Plano; home builder.
*71—Jones, Arves E., Fort Worth; investments.
13—Kubiak, Dan, Rockdale; veterinarian
*46—Kuempel, Edmund, Seguin; businessman.
85—Laney, James E., Hale Center; farmer.
111—Larry, Jerald, Dallas; tax consultant.
*97—Leonard, Bob Jr., Fort Worth; investments.
89—Lewis, Gibson D., Fort Worth; businessman.
19—Lewis, Ron E., Mauriceville; real estate.
39—Lucio, Eddie Jr., Brownsville; businessman.
143—Luna, Albert III, Houston; businessman.
116—Luna, Gregory, San Antonio; attorney.
73—McDonald, Nancy, El Paso; nurse.
15—McKinney, Mike, Centerville; doctor.
9—McWilliams, Jim, Hallsville; rancher-businessman.
117—Madla, Frank, San Antonio; insurance.
*99—Marchant, Ken, Carrollton; builder.
148—Martinez, Roman, Houston; investments.
57—Melton, Bob, Gatesville; businessman.
96—Millsap, Mike, Fort Worth; insurance.
124—Morales, Dan, San Antonio; attorney.
40—Moreno, Alejandro Jr., Edinburg; attorney.
72—Moreno, Paul, El Paso; attorney.
4—Oakley, Keith, Terrell; rancher.
113—Ovard, A. R., Dallas; real estate
65—Parker, Jim, Comanche; rancher-attorney.
*123—Patrick, Kae T., San Antonio; businessman.
138—Patronella, David, Houston; attorney.
2—Patterson, L. P., Brookston; farmer-rancher.
*130—Pennington, Randy, Houston; businessman.

State Rep. Gibson "Gib" Lewis of Fort Worth has served as speaker of the Texas House of Representatives since 1983. He served his first term as a legislator in 1971.

74—Perez, Nicholas J., El Paso; attorney.
64—Perry, Rick, Haskell; farmer-rancher.
*122—Pierce, George, San Antonio; public relations.
128—Polumbo, Tony, Houston; real estate.
22—Price, Albert J., Beaumont; pilot.
37—Rangel, Irma, Kingsville; attorney.
*104—Repp, Glenn, Duncanville; engineer.
*49—Richardson, Bob, Austin; attorney.
*52—Riley, Randall, Round Rock; self-employed.
36—Roberts, Ted, Corpus Christi; attorney.
31—Robinson, Phyllis, Gonzales; housewife.
*82—Robnett, Nolan J., Lubbock; real estate-investments.
118—Rodriguez, Ciro, San Antonio; educational specialist.
77—Rudd, Jim D., Brownfield; attorney.
8—Russell, Sam, Mt. Pleasant; attorney.
30—Saunders, Robert, La Grange; businessman.
54—Schlueter, Stan, Salado; real estate.
*121—Schoolcraft, Alan, Universal City; attorney.
62—Seidlits, Curtis L. Jr., Sherman; attorney.
69—Shaw, Larry D., Big Spring; farmer-real estate.
*98—Shea, Gwyn C., Irving; businesswoman.
*127—Shelly, Dan, Crosby; attorney.
53—Shine, Hugh D., Temple; investment consultant.
*136—Smith, Ashley, Houston; attorney.
*14—Smith, Richard, Bryan; real estate.
*48—Smith, Terral R., Austin; attorney.
*86—Smithee, John T., Amarillo; attorney.
*87—Staniswalis, Charles J., Amarillo; real estate.
21—Stiles, Mark, Beaumont; businessman.
120—Sutton, Lou Nelle, San Antonio; businesswoman.
*26—Tallas, Jim, Sugarland; insurance.
*55—Taylor, M.A., Waco; busnessman.
1—Telford, Barry B., DeKalb; businessman.
95—Thompson, Garfield, Fort Worth; retired.
141—Thompson, Senfronia, Houston; attorney.
*135—Toomey, Mike, Houston; attorney.
29—Uher, Donald R., Bay City; attorney.
*16—Valigura, Keith W., Conroe; attorney.
*70—Vowell, Jack, El Paso; investments.
12—Waldrop, Tom C., Corsicana; businessman-rancher.
145—Wallace, Ralph III, Houston; businessman.
38—Warner, Larry, Laguna Vista; attorney.
*88—Waterfield, Richard, Canadian; cattle feeder.
75—Watkins, Gary, Odessa; attorney.
129—Watson, Ed R., Deer Park; oil operator.
84—Whaley, Foster, Pampa; rancher.
63—Williamson, Richard, Weatherford; businessman.
90—Willis, Doyle, Fort Worth; attorney-rancher.
*28—Willy, John, Angleton; real estate.
131—Wilson, Ron, Houston; businessman.
103—Wolens, Steve, Dallas; attorney.
*134—Wright, Brad, Houston; attorney.
*7—Yost, Gerald V., Longview; advertising.
*Republicans; all others are Democrats.

Local Governments

Texas has 254 counties, a number which has not changed since 1931 when Loving County was organized. Loving had 91 population in the 1980 Census, compared with 164 in 1970 and its peak of 285 in 1940. It is the least-populous county in Texas. In contrast, Harris County is the most-populous in Texas and was fifth in the U.S. in 1980 with 2,409,547 population.

Counties range in area from Rockwall's 128 square miles to the 6,169 square miles in Brewster, which is equal to the combined area of the states of Connecticut and Rhode Island.

The Texas Constitution makes a county a legal sub-division of the state. Each county has a commissioners court. It consists of four commissioners, each elected from a commissioner's precinct, and a county judge elected from the entire county. In smaller counties, the county judge retains judicial responsibilities in probate and insanity cases.

Eleven hundred and sixty-eight incorporated Texas municipalities range in size from 15 residents to Houston's 1,705,697 in the 1984 Census Bureau estimates. More than 80 per cent of the state's population lives in cities and towns meeting the U.S. Census Bureau definition of urban areas.

Texas had 269 municipalities with more than 5,000 population in the 1980 Census. Under law, these cities may adopt their own charters by a majority vote. Cities of less than 5,000 population may be chartered only under the general law.

There were 265 home-rule cities on June 1, 1987, most of them cities with over 5,000 residents. Some of these cities now show fewer than 5,000 residents, because population has declined since they adopted their home-rule charters.

Mayors and City Managers of Texas Cities

List below was compiled from questionnaires sent out immediately after the municipal elections in April 1987. Name of city manager is included for those municipalities having that form of government.

Authority by which managers hold their positions is explained by footnotes to which the symbols *, †, ‡ and § refer. If no symbol precedes name of City Manager, it denotes that none was given by Texas Municipal League.

City—	Mayor
Abbott	Ronald E. Kaska
§City Mgr., Harry F. Holland Jr.	
Abernathy	J. Pete Thompson
†City Mgr., Frank Russell	
Abilene	Dale E. Ferguson
*City Mgr., Jim C. Blagg	
¶Ackerly	J. D. Hall
Addison	Jerry Redding
*City Mgr., Ronald Whitehead	
Adrian	Robt. A. Gruhlkey
Agua Dulce	Carl Vajdos
Alamo	Rodolfo Villarreal
City Mgr., Maria A. Espinosa	
Alamo Heights (6616 Broadway, San Antonio 78209)	
. . . .	Wm. D. Balthrope
Alba	Wm. H. Cranford
Albany	Wayne Hogan
City Mgr., Liston F. Todd	
Aledo	Dwight Wilkins
Alice	Octavio Figueroa Jr.
*City Mgr., Roel Valadez	
Allen	Donald Rodenbaugh
*City Mgr., Jon McCarty	
Alma (Rt. 1, Box 109, Ennis 75119)	W. L. Hammonds
Alpine	Paul E. Pierce
‡City Mgr., Thomas A. Longman	
Alto	R. A. Wallace
Altoga (Route 3, McKinney 75069)	Marvin Page
Alton (P.O. Drawer 9004, Mission 78572)	Mike Lopez
Alvarado	John E. Moore
Alvin	Allen Gray
*City Mgr., Richard Hare	
Alvord	Doris S. Bollinger
Amarillo	Glen Parkey
*City Mgr., John Q. Ward	
Ames	Malcolm J. Goudeau Sr.
Amherst	Loyd Pryor
Anahuac	Monroe Kreuzer Jr.
City Mgr., J. R. Nelson	
Andrews	Z. W. Hutcheson
*City Mgr., Len L. Wilson	
Angleton	B. G. Peck
*City Mgr., Clifford Hicks	
Angus (Rt. 3, Box 3060, Corsicana 75110)	Tom Keating
Anna	Jon K. Hendricks
Annetta (Box 191, Aledo 76008)	Olan Usher
Annetta North (632 Quail Ridge, Aledo 76008) . .	Edward K. Hensley
Annetta South (P.O. Box 61, Aledo 76008)	Jack E. Garner
Annona	Carol McNally
Anson	Gene Rodgers
Anthony . . .	Jerry M. Montgomery
City Mgr., Julia J. Frensley	

City—	Mayor
Anton	Louis E. Boothe
City Mgr., Larry Conkin	
Appleby (Rt. 10, Box 5186, Nacogdoches 75961) . . .	N. F. Burt
Aquilla	Larry Maddox
¶Aransas Pass	Robert Watson
*City Mgr., Rick Ewaniszyk	
Archer City	Max Wood Sr.
City Mgr., L. B. Boren Jr.	
¶Arcola	Mike R. Saenz
Argyle	Larry D. Alderson
Arlington	Richard E. Greene
*City Mgr., Bill Kirchhoff	
Arp	Vernon L. Bedair
Asherton . .	Ramon de la Fuente Jr.
¶Aspermont	Jack McGough
Athens	E. Herbert Gatlin Jr.
*City Mgr., Kevin P. Evans	
¶Atlanta	Elston R. Law
*City Mgr., Sidney R. Davis	
Aubrey	Tim Leslie
¶Aurora (P.O. Box 558, Rhome 76078)	O. W. McCarty
Austin	Frank C. Cooksey
*City Mgr., Jorge Carrasco	
¶Austwell	Albert J. Covey
Avery	Walter E. Stinson
Avinger	M. A. Parvino
Azle	C. Y. Rone
Bailey	Jewel A. Mims (Mr.)
Bailey's Prairie (Box 71, Angleton 77515)	W. D. Reed Jr.
Baird	F. A. Payne
Balch Springs . Walter J. Gorzinski	
City Mgr., (Vacancy)	
Balcones Heights (123 Altgelt, San Antonio 78201) . . .	Emil E. Deike
Ballinger	Bill Goetz
*City Mgr., Rudolf A. Hoffman	
Balmorhea . .	Helen K. Humphries	
Bandera	W. D. Smith
Bangs	Tom B. Owens
City Mgr., Jerry W. Gray	
Bardwell	George Grammer
Barry	John W. Braly Sr.
¶Barstow	Angel Abila
Bartlett	Bobby Hill
Bartonville (134B Jeter Road, Argyle 76226) . . .	Jack R. Patterson
Bastrop	David Lock
‡City Mgr., Marvin Patterson	
Bay City	William M. Bell
Bayou Vista (2929 Hwy. 6, #100, Hitchcock 77563)	
. . . .	John F. McWilliams
Bayside	Nell Meier
Baytown	Emmett Hutto
*City Mgr., Fritz Lanham	
Bayview (P.O. Box 1640, Los Fresnos 78566)	James A. Baird

City—	Mayor
Beach City	A. R. Senac
Beasley. . . Ervin Randermann Jr.	
¶Beaumont	Maurice Meyers
*City Mgr., Albert Haines	
Beckville . . . . . Thomas R. Adams	
Bedford	L. Don Dodson
*City Mgr., Jim W. Walker	
Beeville . . . . . Jesse T. DeRusse Jr.	
*City Mgr., Joe B. Montez	
Bellaire . . . . Sam McKinney	
*City Mgr., R. Patrick Lilly	
Bellevue . . . . Wallace Horton	
Bellmead (3015 Bellmead, Waco 76755).	O. B. Lusk
*City Mgr., Harold M. Baker	
¶Bells	A. L. Isom
Bellville . . . . . Abner E. Jackson	
City Mgr., John Mumme	
Belton	Mickey Wade
*City Mgr., Jeff Holberg	
Benavides	Archer Barton
¶Benbrook (P.O. Box 26569, Fort Worth 76126).	Jerry Dunn
‡City Mgr., Ken Neystel	
Benjamin	Buddy Tolson
Berryville (Rt. 1, Box 142, Frankston 75763) . . . . . Erwin H. Berry	
Bertram . . . Johnnie Mae Wheeler	
Beverly Hills (3418 Memorial, Waco 76711). . . . . Joe Frank Holder	
Bevil Oaks (Rt. 1, Box 293, Beaumont 77706) . . . James E. Shults	
Big Lake . . . . H. F. Ritchie	
§City Mgr., Tony Wille	
Big Sandy . . . . . Johnnie L. Baird	
Big Spring . . . . A. C. Mize	
*City Mgr., Mack Wofford	
Big Wells . . . . . . Alvaro Escobedo	
Bishop . . . . Noble Suggs	
City Mgr., Sinoel B. Contreras	
Blackwell . . . . . R. L. Smedley Jr.	
Blanco . . . . Marge Waxler	
Blanket. . . . . Roscoe Blanton	
Bloomburg . . . . Olan Lundy	
Blooming Grove Don von Hoffman	
Blossom . . . . Rickey Thomas	
Blue Mound (1600 Bell, Fort Worth 76131). . . . . Dale Jensen	
¶Blue Ridge . . . . . . Cotton Sagely	
¶Blum. . . . . A. McMillan	
Boerne . . . . Patrick Heath	
§City Mgr., Ronald C. Bowman	
Bogata . . . . . William T. Harbison	
¶Bonham . . . . Roy Floyd	
*City Mgr., Tom Taylor	
Bonney (Rt. 2, Rosharon 77583)	
. . . . Mary M. Coleman	
Booker . . . . Ralph Maxfield	
§City Mgr., Craig Gingerich	
Borger . . . . Frank W. Selfridge	
*City Mgr., James Layton	

City—	Mayor
¶Bovina	Dudley K. Hughes
Bowie	John Middleton
§City Mgr., H. H. Cunningham Jr.	
Boyd	Ronnie T. White
Brackettville	William Mendeke
City Mgr., Charles J. Olsen	
Brady	H. L. Gober Jr.
§City Mgr., James Blankenship	
Brazoria	Joe Ann Miller
City Mgr., K. C. Timmermann	
Breckenridge	Weldon Leonard
*City Mgr., Dwain Tolle	
Bremond	Billy Lee Stelbauer
Brenham	Dorothy Flisowski
*City Mgr., Leonard Addicks	
¶Briarcliff (Briarcliff 1, Spicewood 78669)	Frank Wehking
¶Briaroaks (Box 568, Burleson 76028)	Alan W. Myers
¶Bridge City	John Banken
‡City Mgr., C. R. Nash	
Bridgeport	Walter Hales
Broaddus	W. E. Sheffield
Bronson	Ralph McBride
Bronte	J. T. Henry
Brookshire	Harry K. Searle
Brookside Village (Rt. 3, Box 3440, Pearland 77581)	Phillip W. Rutter
Browndell (P.O. Box 430, Brookeland 75931)	Erma L. Garrett
Brownfield	T. A. Hicks
*City Mgr., R. C. Fletcher	
Brownsboro	Thomas A. Crow
City Mgr., Jack Beall	
Brownsville	Emilio A. Hernandez
*City Mgr., Steve Fitzgibbons (Acting)	
Brownwood	Bert V. Massey II
*City Mgr., Virgil C. Gray	
Bruceville-Eddy (P.O. Drawer A, Bruceville 76630)	Gene McBride
Bryan	Marvin Tate
*City Mgr., E. R. Clark	
¶Bryson	Willard Schlittler
Buckholts	Frances Fuchs
Buckingham (P.O. Box 831452, Richardson 75083)	Frank Malone
Buda	Peter A. Stone
Buffalo	H. L. Burke
Buffalo Gap	O. V. Milstead
¶Bullard	N.A.
Bunker Hill (Box 19404, Houston 77024)	Shirley T. Inman
Burkburnett	Pat Norriss (Mrs.)
*City Mgr., Gary B. Bean	
¶Burke (Rt. 2, Box 122, Diboll 75541)	Zusle Rush Jr.
Burleson	Jerry Boone
*City Mgr., Ron Crabtree	
¶Burnet	Howard R. Benton
†City Mgr., K. A. Taylor	
Burton	James U. Powell
Byers	Billy Ray Jones
Bynum	Roscoe E. Waller
¶Cactus	Leon W. Graham
Caddo Mills	Ron Olson
§City Mgr., Ed Terrell	
Caldwell	William L. Broaddus
¶Callisburg (Rt. 2, Gainesville 76240)	Bobby McDaniel
Calvert	Cooper Wiese
Cameron	Milton J. Schiller
City Mgr., Lanny C. French	
Campbell	Jack White
¶Camp Wood	Austin Dean
Canadian	Therese B. Abraham
†City Mgr., Dean Looper (Acting)	
Caney City (Rt. 2250, Malakoff 75148)	Joe Barron
Canton	Dennis Teal
City Mgr., Gerald Turner	
Canyon	David C. West
*City Mgr., Glen R. Metcalf	
Carbon	Royce McGaha
Carl's Corner (P.O. Box 817, Hillsboro 76645)	Carl Cornelius
Carmine	Jo Littlejohn
Carrizo Springs	Marcelino Castilla Jr.
*City Mgr., Robert Gracia	

City—	Mayor
Carrollton	Milburn R. Gravley
*City Mgr., Mike Eastland	
Carthage	Carson C. Joines
*City Mgr., Charles Thomas	
¶Castle Hills (6915 West Ave., San Antonio 78213)	Dr. H. P. Lundblade
‡City Mgr., David R. Seyfarth	
Castroville	Virginia Suehs
City Mgr., Stevan R. Gallegos	
Cedar Hill	W. S. Permenter
‡City Mgr., Gregory T. Vick	
Cedar Park	Dorthey Duckett
‡City Mgr., Scott Epperson	
Celeste	Solon Milton
Celina	Lloyd Rucker
Center	George W. Ihlo
‡City Mgr., Jeff K. Ellington	
Centerville	Robt. D. Sherbrook
Chandler	Joy Clark
Channing	Ethel Hunnicutt
Charlotte	Ray Wayne Roby
Chateau Woods (10224 Fairview, Conroe 77385)	Arnold Farias
Chester	James G. Casper
Chico	Nobie Tucker
Childress	J. B. Holland
‡City Mgr., David Galligan	
Chillicothe	Frank E. Berngen
¶China	Elaine J. Butler
China Grove (Box 367, Adkins 78101)	John D. Passano
¶Chireno	Orland Strickland
City Mgr., W. Percy Wilson	
¶Christine	Alvie Smith
Cibolo	Sam Bauder
Cisco	Joe Wheatley
§City Mgr., Michael D. Moore	
Clarendon	David Davidson
Clarksville	Gavin Watson Jr.
†City Mgr., Jack Holt	
Clarksville City (Box 1209, Gladewater 75647)	Harvey E. Griffin
City Mgr., Billy F. Silvertooth Jr.	
Claude	Leon James
¶Clay	Mary F. Mack
Clear Lake Shores (931 Cedar Road, Kemah 77565)	George W. Kesseler
Cleburne	J. T. Bass
*City Mgr., Lloyd E. Moss	
Cleveland	Richard Boyett
‡City Mgr., W. N. Petropolis	
Clifton	Kent Westley
Clint	G. Michael Goodwin
Clute	Jerry Adkins
*City Mgr., W. M. Pennington	
Clyde	Don R. Haley
Coahoma	Eleanor Garrett
Cockrell Hill (4125 W. Clarendon, Dallas 75211)	Jan Soroka
City Mgr., Jackie S. Smith	
Coffee City (Box 716, Frankston 75763)	Wayne Phillips
Coldspring	John Benestante
Coleman	J. Hugh Stempel
*City Mgr., Roy McCorkle	
College Station	Larry J. Ringer
*City Mgr., William K. Cole	
Colleyville	J. R. Hubbard
‡City Mgr., C. R. Ballenger	
Collinsville	O. M. Quattlebaum
Colmesneil	Jackie Ruth Brown
Colorado City	Jim Baum
*City Mgr., Brenda Tarter	
¶Columbus	Richard Heffley
†City Mgr., George Purefoy	
¶Comanche	Johnny Livingston
City Mgr., Wade Pyburn	
Combes	Alvice Tucker
City Mgr., Lonnie Bearden	
¶Combine (Rt. 2, Box 231, Seagoville 75159)	Mickey Koller
Commerce	David M. Ayers
*City Mgr., Truitt Gilbreath	
¶Como	Bob Butler
Conroe	Carl Barton Jr.
‡City Mgr., Olen R. Petty	

City—	Mayor
Converse	Bruce Friesenhahn
‡City Mgr., Kent A. Myers	
¶Cool (R. Rte, Box 150, Weatherford 76086)	Billy C. Page
Coolidge	David Glenn McGuire
Cooper	Richard C. Huie
Coppell	Lou Duggan
‡City Mgr., Alan D. Ratliff	
¶Copperas Cove	Jim French
§City Mgr., Mark Roath	
Copper Canyon (400 Woodland Dr., Lewisville 75067)	G. Hugh Meilinger
Corinth (2003 S. Corinth, Denton 76205)	Shirley Spellerberg
Corpus Christi	Betty Turner
*City Mgr., Craig McDowell	
¶Corral City (Rt. 1, Argyle 76226)	J. W. Helton
Corrigan	M. G. Reily
‡City Mgr., Pee Wee Drake	
Corsicana	James H. Gill
*City Mgr., Craig Lonon	
Cottonwood (P.O. Box 348, Kemp 75143)	Tom Anderson
¶Cotulla	W. L. Cotulla
Cove (1202 Maley Rd., Baytown 77520)	Judy S. Leggett
Covington	James E. Jutson
Crandall	Perry Marshak
Crane	Terry L. Schul
§City Mgr., Bill Sanders	
Cranfills Gap	Larry D. Simmons
Crawford	Thomas Frank Golson
¶Creedmoor (Creedmoor Station, Austin 78747)	Joe Click
¶Crockett	Howard Edmiston
*City Mgr., Philip Cook	
Crosbyton	Lance Morris
§City Mgr., Gary Mitchell	
Cross Plains	Frank Robertson
City Mgr., Billy D. Dillard Sr.	
Cross Roads (Rt. 3, Box 435, Aubrey 76227)	Mark A. Coats
Crowell	Robert Kincaid
Crowley	Walton G. Eller
Crystal City	Jose O. Mata
*City Mgr., Jose L. Balderas	
Cuero	John Post
*City Mgr., James C. Morgan	
Cumby	James Strickland
Cuney	Billy Roberts
Cushing	R. C. Pace
City Mgr., Jerry L. Bowers	
Cut and Shoot (Box 7364, Conroe 77303)	Gene Douget
Daingerfield	William L. Thorne
§City Mgr., (Acting) Margie Hargrove	
Daisetta	John W. Moore
Dalhart	Lorraine Wardell
*City Mgr., George Briant	
¶Dallas	Annette Strauss
*City Mgr., Richard Knight	
¶Dalworthington Gardens (2600 Roosevelt Dr., Arlington 76016)	Al Taub
Danbury	Richard Tullos
Darrouzett	Jack Webster
City Mgr., Matt Moore	
Dawson	Robert Holder
Dayton	W. M. Moreau
§City Mgr., Sam M. Barrington	
¶Dayton Lakes (Rt. 1, Box 497, Dayton 77535)	Barry Bailey
Dean (Rt. 5, Box 516, Wichita Falls 76031)	Randall Paden
Decatur	Bobby Wilson
Deer Park	Jimmy Burke
*City Mgr., Floyd O. Socia	
DeKalb	Morris Dunn
DeLeon	Dewey Harris
¶Dell City	Frank D. Gomez
Del Rio	Hugh Williams
*City Mgr., Jeffrey A. Pomeranz	
Denison	Ronnie Cole
*City Mgr., Larry Cruise	
¶Denton	Ray Stephens
*City Mgr., (Lloyd V. Harrell)	

City—	Mayor
¶Denver City	Mike Fears
City Mgr., Paul Grohman	
Deport	Charles Foster
DeSoto	David Doyle
*City Mgr., (Vacancy)	
Detroit	Dale W. Halyard
¶Devers	W. E. Wiser
Devine	Sid R. Malone
City Mgr., R. A. Miller	
Diboll	James P. Simms
‡City Mgr., Vernon Cupit	
Dickens	Bill Scott
¶Dickinson	Joseph F. Molloy
City Mgr., Luther Morgan	
Dilley	Fernando Florez
City Mgr., Rudy Alvarez	
Dimmitt	Wayne Collins
City Mgr., Recford Burrous	
Dodd City	Johnnie Mills
Dodson	Rayburn Hightower
¶Dogwood City (Rt. 2, Box 111A,	
Flint 75762)	Elise Mae Perkins
Domino (Box 298, Queen City	
75572)	Frank Propps
Donna	Hector Casiano
Dorchester (Box 838, Howe	
75059)	Grady Lankford
Double Oak (Box 1396, Lewisville	
75067)	Richard Braud
¶Douglassville	W. A. McCoy
Dripping Springs	Bob Burke
Driscoll	Dan Capehart
Dublin	Jim Leatherwood
‡City Mgr., David Johnson	
Dumas	Mike Salim
*City Mgr., Larry A. Smith	
Duncanville	Russ Kent
*City Mgr., Dan Dodson	
Eagle Lake	Lanny Powers
‡City Mgr., Robert Klockman	
Eagle Pass	Roberto Barrientos
City Mgr., E. P. Rodrigues	
Early (Box 3100, Brownwood	
76801)	Earl W. Rhea
§City Mgr., Tom Byrd	
Earth	R. R. Daniel Jr.
Eastland	Grover Hallmark
*City Mgr., Paul Catoe	
East Mountain (Rt. 1, Box 500,	
Gilmer 75644)	Ralph B. Collins
Easton	E. T. Bell
East Tawakoni (700 Briggs, Lone	
Oak 75453)	Allen Blair
Eastvale (Rt. 3, Box 316, Lewisville	
75056)	William Dorman
Ector	Lynwood E. Hogue
¶Edcouch	E. Jackson
City Mgr., Antonio Barco	
Eden	Thomas F. Kelso
City Mgr., Gerald Prosise	
Edgecliff (1605 Edgecliff Rd., Fort	
Worth 76134)	Art Wright
§City Mgr., (Vacancy)	
Edgewood	Fred Hutchins
Edinburg	P. R. Rudy de la Vina
*City Mgr., John Vidaurri	
Edmonson	Don Ketchum
City Mgr., Franklin Bain	
Edna	Joe D. Hermes
*City Mgr., (Vacancy)	
Edom (Rt. 1, Box 512, Brownsboro	
75756)	Morris Brantley
El Campo	Philip Miller
*City Mgr., Larry W. Keesler	
Eldorado	Bob Lester
Electra	Billy Ray Wright
*City Mgr., Roger L. Dunlap	
Elgin	Kenneth W. Daughtry
§City Mgr., Howard F. Brown	
Elkhart	Garth Moran
City Mgr., Dave Comte	
El Lago (3812 NASA Road 1, Sea-	
brook 77586)	Bill McElwain
¶Elmendorf	Simon R. Tarin
El Paso	Jonathan W. Rogers
§City Mgr., K. E. Beasley	
Elsa	Armando Garza
City Mgr., Ramiro Rosa	
¶Emhouse	Bud Whitehead

City—	Mayor
¶Emory	W. D. McDowell
Enchanted Oaks (Box 517, Mabank	
75147)	Blair Whitelaw
¶Encinal	Alberto M. Ochoa
Ennis	C. T. Abram
*City Mgr., Steve Howerton	
¶Estelline	Don Proffitt
City Mgr., David Galligan	
Euless	Harold D. Samuels
*City Mgr., W. M. Sustaire	
Eureka	Ann Connor
Eustace	Ronnie Sutton
¶Evant	Calvin Burks
Everman	Dean Armes
City Mgr., Bob Hurley	
Fairfield	Monte Cole
Fairview (Collin Co.) (Box 551,	
McKinney 75069)	F. D. Carvajal
Fairview (Wise Co.) (Rt. 1, Box 16A,	
Rhome 76078)	Pearl Carter
Falfurrias	E. Villarreal Jr.
City Mgr., A. C. Rodriguez	
Falls City	Patrick W. Pollok
¶Farmers Branch	John D. Dodd
*City Mgr., Paul M. West	
¶Farmersville	B. J. Harrison
City Mgr., Ron Holifield	
Farwell	Chris Gikas
Fate	W. E. Crawford
Fayetteville	William Graeter
Ferris	Jimmie Birdwell
Flatonia	Leslie J. Greive
Florence	Lee Roy Knauth
Floresville	Roy G. Sanchez
§City Mgr., H. G. Lumbreras	
¶Flower Mound	George O. Coker
‡City Mgr., Steven Lewis	
¶Floydada	Parnell Powell
§City Mgr., Wm. A. Feuerbacher	
Follett	Betty Redelsperger
Forest Hill (6800 Forest Hill Dr.,	
Fort Worth 76140)	
	Donald R. Walker
City Mgr., Ed Badgett	
Forney	Don T. Cates
Forsan	O. W. Scudday
¶Fort Gates (Box 428, Gatesville	
76528)	Dewain Farris
City Mgr., Margie Waters	
Fort Stockton	Joe Shuster
‡City Mgr., Jesse Garcia	
¶Fort Worth	Bob Bolen
*City Mgr., Douglas Harman	
Franklin	Charles Ellison
Frankston	Ronald A. Smith
Fredericksburg	Boyd K. Harper
Freeport	Mark X. Vandaveer
*City Mgr., Earl W. Heath Jr.	
Freer	Malloy A. Hamilton
¶Friendship Village (4500 N. Kings	
Hwy., Texarkana 75501)	
	Gerald Johnson
Friendswood	Ralph L. Lowe
*City Mgr., Annette Brand	
Friona	Clarence Monroe
†City Mgr., Beelee Goodwin	
¶Frisco	Randy Elliott
Fritch	Danny K. Lowe
‡City Mgr., Dan Graves	
Frost	J. O. Williams
¶Fruitvale	Hallie Randall
Fulshear	C. B. Bentley
Fulton	Leslie Cole Sr.
Gainesville	Charles Woolfolk
*City Mgr., William A. Gaither	
Galena Park	Alvin D. Baggett
¶Gallatin	Lem Derrington
Galveston	Janice R. Coggeshall
*City Mgr., Douglas Matthews	
Ganado	Larry Waits
Garden Ridge (Rt. 3, Box 1047, San	
Antonio 78218)	Walter A. Yohey Jr.
Garfield (P.O. Box 460, Del Valle	
78617)	Richard H. Hanshew
Garland	Bill Tomlinson
*City Mgr., James K. Spore	
Garrett (Rt. 3, Box 72, Ennis	
75119)	R. L. Cornelison
¶Garrison	M. H. Stoddard

City—	Mayor
Gary	Walter M. Craft
Gatesville	Creston Brazzil
*City Mgr., Bob Stevens	
Georgetown	Jim Colbert
*City Mgr., Robert Gaylor	
¶George West	Gene Riser
City Mgr., Brad Arvin	
Gholson (Rt. 5, Box 495, Waco	
76705)	H. T. Sexton
¶Giddings	M. Lavonne Droemer
§City Mgr., Larry Pippen	
Gilmer	Jake Dupree
‡City Mgr., James D. Mullins	
Gladewater	E. R. McKain
*City Mgr., Douglas R. Driggers	
Glenn Heights (P.O. Box 1028, De-	
Soto 75115)	Jerry Gallagher
City Mgr., Robert Coffell	
Glen Rose	Marvin W. Cruce
Godley	Larry Richeson
Goldsmith	H. D. Timmons
City Mgr., Betty Fife	
Goldthwaite	Fred Conradt
†City Mgr., Dale Allen	
Goliad	Shirley A. Young
Golinda (Rt. 2, Box 684, Lorena	
76655)	George W. Zinn
Gonzales	Carroll E. Wiley
*City Mgr., Luther Maxey	
¶Goodlow (Box 248, Kerens	
75144)	Willie Washington
Goodrich	Miller Moffett
Gordon	Harold W. Burgett
Goree	George K. Cotton
City Mgr., Jim Cooke	
Gorman	Charles Garrett
Graford	J. D. Tidwell
Graham	Edwin S. Graham III
*City Mgr., Larry M. Fields	
Granbury	Charles E. Baker
†City Mgr., Robt. D. Brockman	
Grandfalls	John Mark Kuhn
Grand Prairie	J. V. Debo III
*City Mgr., Wendel T. Hulse	
Grand Saline	Howard L. Woodall
¶Grandview	Larry Moore
Granger	Dollie Hajda
Granite Shoals (410 N. Sherwood	
Dr., Marble Falls 78654)	
	William B. Haldy Sr.
Grapeland	Dick Murchison
Grapevine	Tom Powers
*City Mgr., Dennis E. Dawson	
¶Grayburg (P.O. Box 23, Sour Lake	
77659)	Johnie Floyd
¶Grays Prairie (Rt. 2, Box 627,	
Scurry 75158)	W. G. Cubley
Greenville	Bill F. Morgan
*City Mgr., William R. Cook	
Gregory	Robert G. Escobedo
Grey Forest (Rt. 15, Box 212, San	
Antonio 78238)	Don Reddout
Groesbeck	Jim Longbotham
Groom	Alfred A. Homer
Groves	Sylvester Moore
*City Mgr., A. R. Kimler	
¶Groveton	Melburn Minter
Gruver	Roy Byrd
‡City Mgr., A. J. Ratliff	
Gun Barrel City (Rt. 8, Hwy. 85, Ma-	
bank 75147)	John Muirhead
Gunter	Foy Wallace
Gustine	Roger L. Oliver
¶Hackberry (Rt. 2, Box 327-AA,	
Frisco 75034)	A. W. Dick
Hale Center	Bob W. Brown
Hallettsville	Troy H. Deavers
Hallsburg (Rt. 7, Box 428, Waco	
76705)	Margie N. Wilbanks
Hallsville	T. Bynum Hatley
Haltom City (Box 14246, Fort Worth	
76117)	Jack O. Lewis
*City Mgr., Mike Groomer	
Hamilton	James H. Soules
§City Mgr., Dennis Jones	
Hamlin	Melvin Scott
Happy	Mary S. Eakes
Hardin	Arley J. Finley
Harker Heights	Danny Hurd
City Mgr., Harold Weiler	

City—	Mayor
Harlingen	Bill Caro
*City Mgr., Gavino D. Sotello	
Hart	Joe D. Bailey
¶Haskell	Abe Turner
City Mgr., Robert Baker	
Haslet	Odie M. Cowart
Hawkins	Douglas Sexton
¶Hawley	Leroy Strickland
Hays (P.O. Box 1258, Buda 78610)	O. Lamont Ramage
¶Hearne	Baylor Carrington
*City Mgr., Jay Williams	
Heath	Dennis Bailey
Hebron (Rt. 3, Box 184, Lewisville 75056)	Stanley Dozier
City Mgr., C. W. Morris	
Hedley	Jon L. Leggitt
Hedwig Village (955 Piney Point Rd., Houston 77024)	Thomas W. Bartlett
Helotes	Vivian Hultz
Hemphill	Ronnie L. Felts
City Mgr., Tommy Neal	
Hempstead	Leroy Singleton
Henderson	Lester Brown
‡City Mgr., Jack Dickerson	
Henrietta	Melvin D. Adams
Hereford	Wesley S. Fisher
*City Mgr., Darwin McGill	
Hewitt	Ernie Emrich
City Mgr., Dennis Woodard	
Hickory Creek (Box 453, Lake Dallas 75065)	Mike Flowers
Hico	W. W. Rutledge Jr.
Hidalgo	Thomas Perez Jr.
City Mgr., Eudocio Garcia	
Higgins	Billy B. Cornett
Highland Park (4700 Drexel Dr., Dallas 75205)	Sam P. Burford Jr.
‡City Mgr., George Patterson	
Highland Village (948 Highland Village, Lewisville 75067)	Jerry W. McKenzie
City Mgr., Joseph Gambill Jr.	
Hill Country Village (116 Aspen Ln., San Antonio 78232)	P. Otis Hibler
Hillcrest Village (Box 1172, Alvin 77512)	Mrs. Joe B. Jansen
Hillsboro	Henry Moore
*City Mgr., Joe Ed Ward	
Hilshire Village (P.O. Box 55233, Houston 77055)	Ronnie Ralston
Hitchcock	C. E. Clifford
Holiday Lakes (Rt. 4, Box 747, Angleton 77515)	Claude Hunter
Holland	G. L. Brisbin
¶Holliday	Elizabeth Gorman
City Mgr., Gary W. Jones	
Hollywood Park (2 Mecca Dr., San Antonio 78232)	Patricia E. Flynn
¶Homer (Rt. 2, Box 319N, Lufkin 75901)	R. A. Noel
Hondo	Anthony L. Hardt
City Mgr., Mike Rhea	
Honey Grove	Theo Avery
City Mgr., Pauline Rodgers	
Hooks	James B. Earnest
Houston	Kathryn J. Whitmire
Howardwick (Box 1143, Clarendon 79226)	Max L. Hennigh
Howe	Ray Bledsoe
§City Mgr., Richard M. Britton	
Hubbard	Don Anderson
§City Mgr., Harvey H. Schronk	
Hudson (Rt. 5, Box 970, Lufkin 75901)	Lloyd W. Bonner
Hudson Oaks	J. Y. McClure
Hughes Springs	Carol H. Leftwich
City Mgr., George K. Fite	
Humble	Haden E. McKay
‡City Mgr., James P. Baker	
Hunters Creek Village (8333 Katy Fwy., Houston 77024)	Cebe Sue Barnett
Huntington	Bobby Weaver
Huntsville	Jane Monday
*City Mgr., Gene Pipes	
Hurst	Bill Souder
*City Mgr., Jim Starr	

City—	Mayor
Hutchins	Joe Ed Wallace Sr.
City Mgr., Steven A. Reed	
¶Hutto	Edmund G. Schmidt
Huxley (Rt. 1, Box 470, Shelbyville 75973)	Larry Vaughn
Idalou	Glen Hunt
Impact (Box 3116, Abilene 79604)	Dallas Perkins
Indian Lake (Rt. 3, Box 699-Z, San Benito 78586)	Nina Rozema
Ingleside	Roy Culver Jr.
City Mgr., Del Lewis	
¶Ingram	Donald Oehler
Iowa Colony (12003 County Road 65, Rosharon 77583)	Maurice Bright
Iowa Park	Timothy W. Hunter
‡City Mgr., James Barrington	
Iraan	S. E. Turpin
City Mgr., Howard Floyd	
Iredell	Ellen L. Bishop
Irving	Robert Pierce
*City Mgr., Jack D. Huffman	
Italy	John P. Goodman
¶Itasca	Carroll C. Curry
City Mgr., David Bowman	
¶Jacinto City (10301 Market St. Rd., Houston 77029)	Mike Blasingame
§City Mgr., Joann Griggs	
Jacksboro	F. C. Heard
‡City Mgr., (Vacancy)	
Jacksonville	R. L. Nichols
*City Mgr., Gordon C. Pierce	
Jamaica Beach (P.O. Box 5264, Galveston 77551)	Philip J. Douglas
¶Jasper	F. R. Lindsey Jr.
*City Mgr., Wayne DuBose	
Jayton	Travis R. Smith
Jefferson	Victor A. Perot
Jersey Village (16501 Jersey Dr., Houston 77040)	Carl A. Norman Jr.
City Mgr., Harry W. Nagel	
Jewett	Joe H. Holmes
Joaquin	Paul Jackson Jr.
Johnson City	Ralph Moss
Jolly (Rt. 2, Box 341, Wichita Falls 76301)	Les Lyde
Jones Creek (Rt. 1, 7207 SFA Rd., Freeport 77541)	Lawrence A. Willis
Jonestown	Deane Armstrong
Josephine	John T. Lemley
Joshua	Steven G. Huneycutt
Jourdanton	Tommy Hon
§City Mgr., Roy Underwood	
Junction	W. K. Blackburn
‡City Mgr., Raymond M. Litton	
Justin	Mark W. Spates
Karnes City	Benhardt Ahrens
Katy	John L. Nelson
Kaufman	Harry H. Holcomb
City Mgr., Norman Smith	
Keene	LeRoy J. Leiske
Keller	Nick Powell
‡City Mgr., Johnny Sartain	
Kemah	Ben Blackledge
Kemp	James R. Main Sr.
Kendleton	Ernest Zomalt
Kenedy	Edgar A. Brown (pro tem)
¶Kenefick (Box 596, Dayton 77535)	Verlon I. Moore Sr.
Kennard	Glenn Westbrook
Kennedale	Steve Radakovich
‡City Mgr., Ted Rowe	
Kerens	O. R. Spurlock
Kermit	O. L. Marshall
‡City Mgr., Randall E. Holly	
Kerrville	Charles F. Johnson
*City Mgr., Glenn D. Brown	
Kilgore	Bob Barbee
*City Mgr., Ronald E. Cox	
¶Killeen	Sidney Young
*City Mgr., Robert M. Hopkins	
Kingsville	Billie G. Gunter
*City Mgr., (Vacancy)	
Kirby (112 Baumann, San Antonio 78219)	Warren Larck
City Mgr., Gerald G. Decker	
Kirbyville	Ed Bradley

City—	Mayor
¶Kirvin	Billie Walthall
Knollwood (100 Collins Dr., Sherman 75090)	Richard Ross Roelke
Knox City	Derrell Marion
City Mgr., Lynward Wilcox	
¶Kosse	W. C. Graeber
Kountze	Walter R. Overstreet
City Mgr., Russell S. Robinson	
Kress	W. F. Reed
Krugerville (Rt. 2, Box 615, Aubrey 76227)	Ricky Stephen Jones
Krum	Joe D. Cates
Kyle	Sandra Martinez
§City Mgr., Douglas E. Dunlap	
Lacoste	George T. Lagleder
Lacy-Lakeview (501 E. Craven, Waco 76705)	J. L. Crawford
Ladonia	Elgin Fowler
La Feria	Jesse F. Byars
City Mgr., Thos. V. Kolterman	
Lago Vista	Olley G. Anderson
City Mgr., Thomas H. Mahon	
La Grange	Charlie Jungmichel
‡City Mgr., J. D. Legler	
La Grulla (P.O. Box 197, Grulla 78548)	Ruben L. Solis
Laguna Vista (Box 105B, Star Route, Port Isabel 78578)	Edna Maye Heinze
La Joya	Rodolfo Farias
City Mgr., Lucrecio Flores Jr.	
Lake Bridgeport (Rt. 2, Box 244F, Bridgeport 76026)	Jeanita Carney
Lake City (Box 177, Mathis 78368)	Oliver W. Skidmore
Lake Dallas	Ronald E. Honse
Lake Jackson	Vick Vickers
*City Mgr., A. A. MacLean	
¶Lake Kiowa (P.O. Box 71, Gainesville 76240)	N.A.
Lakeport (Box 7728, Longview 75607)	Virgil Miller
Lakeside (San Patricio Co. (156 Zenna Dr., Mathis 78368)	Kent S. Abernathy
Lakeside (Tarrant Co.) (Rt. 8, Box 539, Fort Worth 76108)	Rodney Crow
¶Lakeside City (Box 4287, Wichita Falls 76308)	Lee Hickey
Lake Tanglewood (Rt. 7, Box 35-15, Amarillo 79118)	John C. Rickett
¶Lakeview	Russell J. Payne
Lakeway (104 Cross Creek, Austin 78734)	C. E. Smith Jr
Lakewood Village (Box 386, Little Elm 75068)	Brian G. Refoy
¶Lake Worth (6720 Telephone Rd., Fort Worth 76135)	Richard W. Trimble
City Mgr., Linda Ingram	
La Marque	Carlton A. Getty
*City Mgr., Gary Jackson	
Lamesa	Donald R. Bethel
*City Mgr., Paul Feazelle	
Lampasas	Dudley Terry
§City Mgr., Tom Pugh	
Lancaster	Walter D. Arnold II
*City Mgr., Carl Tomerlin	
La Porte	Norman Malone
*City Mgr., Robert T. Herrera	
Laredo	Aldo Tatangelo
*City Mgr., R. Marvin Townsend	
¶Latexo	Winfred E. Alexander
¶La Vernia	Theo F. Gerlich
La Villa	Hector Elizondo
City Mgr., Mary Garza (Acting)	
Lavon	B. G. Robinson
La Ward	Arthur L. Estrada
Lawn	Johnny B. Hudson
League City	Joe L. Lamb
§City Mgr., Paul Nutting	
Leakey	J. H. Chisum
Leander	Pat Bryson (Mrs.
§City Mgr., Reuben Kimball	
Leary (Rt. 5, Box 409, Texarkana 75501)	Elmer E. Line
Lefors	J. W. Frank
¶Leona	F. L. Thompson

City—	Mayor
Leonard	Billy H. Martin
Leon Valley (6400 El Verde Rd., San Antonio 78238)	Irene Baldridge
§City Mgr., Donald R. Manning	
Leroy	W. H. Janes
Levelland	Kenny Willmon
*City Mgr., Gregory Ingham	
Lewisville	Donny Daniel
*City Mgr., Charles R. Owens	
Lexington	Larry W. Nichols
¶Liberty	C. Scott Parker
*City Mgr., Roy Bennett	
¶Lincoln Park (Rt. 1, Box 701, Aubrey 76227)	Roger Pock
¶Lindale	Peyton Jones
Linden	Robert C. Deming
City Mgr., Sammy C. Wells	
Lindsay	Donald L. Metzler
¶Lipan	Gaston Grogan
Little Elm	Jeffery M. Stauffer
Littlefield	Paul D. Bennett
*City Mgr., Jody Butler	
Little River-Academy (Box 521, Little River 76554)	Ronnie White
Live Oak (8001 Shin Oak Dr., San Antonio 78233)	Norm Tremblay
*City Mgr., Douglas G. Faseler	
Liverpool	Allan F. Moore
Livingston	Ben R. Ogletree Jr.
†City Mgr., Sam Gordon	
Llano	John I. Landon
City Mgr., George Rogers	
Lockhart	Maxine R. Goodman
City Mgr., Thomas E. Brymer	
Lockney	Dan B. Smith
Lometa	Mary E. McAnelly
Lone Oak	Harold Slemmons
Lone Star	C. E. Nichols
Longview	Lou Galosy
*City Mgr., C. Ray Jackson	
Loraine	Roy Price
¶Lorena	S. B. Collins
¶Lorenzo	Don C. Nickson
City Mgr., Leon Moore	
¶Los Fresnos	Richard Sparks
City Mgr., Tom Brooks	
¶Los Ybanez (Box 52, Lamesa 79331)	Mary A. Ybanez
Lott	Gordon Broome
Lovelady	Troy R. Driskell
Lowry Crossing (360 Bridgefarmer Rd., McKinney 75069)	Linda S.Terry
Lubbock	R. C. McMinn
*City Mgr., Larry Cunningham	
Lucas (Rt. 7, Box 229, McKinney 75069)	Ann Guzman
Lueders	R. S. Felts
Luella (Rt. 7, Box 231C, Sherman 75090)	Jerry MacNeill
Lufkin	Pitser H. Garrison
*City Mgr., Harvey Westerholm	
Luling	W. S. Hooper
*City Mgr., T. H. Caffall	
Lumberton	Larry Woodall
Lyford	Morris W. Dodd
Lytle	Frank M. Hall
Mabank	B. G. Autry
Madisonville	Joe H. Drew
Magnolia	D. W. Cloyd
Malakoff	Howard Julian
§City Mgr., A. M. Thompson	
Malone	Ben Neal
Manor	Sidney E. Donnell Sr.
§City Mgr., Michael Bamer	
Mansfield	Bobby F. Block
†City Mgr., Clayton W. Chandler	
Manvel	Don Redmon
City Mgr., Jim Mooney	
Marble Falls	Daryl Janicek
†City Mgr., Jack Chaney	
Marfa	Genevieve P. Bassham
¶Marietta	Delton W. Miller
Marion	Felix Arambula Jr.
Marlin	H. B. Stallworth Jr.
†City Mgr., Harold Underwood	
¶Marquez	John Madden
¶Marshall	Sam Birmingham
*City Mgr., Tony Williams	

City—	Mayor
Marshall Creek Estates (P.O. Box 1080, Roanoke 76262)	Bill Sparks
Mart	Babe Aycock
Martindale	Martha E. Holmes
Mason	R. Clinton Schulze
Matador	Gary L. Lancaster
¶Mathis	James T. Knight
Maud	Carrol W. Black
Maypearl	James S. Waller
McAllen	Othal E. Brand Sr.
†City Mgr., Jose Escamilla	
McCamey	John Tucker
McGregor	Felix A. Morris
*City Mgr., A. H. Wolf	
McKinney	Ben Whisenant
*City Mgr., D. E. Paschal Jr.	
McLean	George M. Green
McLendon-Chisholm	Choice Smith
Meadow	Dale Wylie
Meadowlakes (209 Meadowlakes, Marble Falls 78654)	Richard Neill
Meadows (11803 Kirkwood, Stafford 77477)	Sue Troyan
Megargel	Charlie J. Kulhanek
Melissa	Bob Mixon
¶Melvin	J. P. Sparks
Memphis	Kenneth Dale
Menard	W. A. Wilkinson
City Mgr., James F. Cannon	
Mercedes	Norma G. Garcia
*City Mgr., Alan Kamasaki	
Meridian	Hugh Trotter
¶Merkel	Kent Satterwhite
City Mgr., J. A. Sadler	
Mertens	Allen Updegraff
Mertzon	John D. Nicholson
Mesquite	George A. Venner Sr.
*City Mgr., C. K. Duggins	
Mexia	Pat Fain
*City Mgr., Gerald Yarbrough	
Miami	Tom Stribling
Midland	Carroll M. Thomas
†City Mgr., Fred W. Poe	
Midlothian	Maurice Osborn
*City Mgr., Charles M. Pinto	
Midway	Patrick H. Wakefield
¶Milano	Roger Hashem
Mildred (2009 Hamilton Lane, Corsicana 75110)	E. L. Manire Jr.
¶Miles	W. A. Smith
¶Milford	Bobby D. Cooper
¶Miller's Cove (Rt. 3, Box 3, Mt. Pleasant 756455)	Wayne Miller
Millsap	Gail Estep
Mineola	E. M. Bradshaw
Mineral Wells	H. Arthur Zappe
*City Mgr., Sam Phelps	
¶Mingus	Joe Bielinski
Mission	Pat Townsend Jr.
*City Mgr., Mark S. Watson	
Missouri City	John B. Knox
†City Mgr., David A. Harner	
¶Mobeetie	Leona House
Monahans	Richard J. Hoyer
*City Mgr., Jack Forga	
Mont Belvieu	Fred R. Miller
§City Mgr., Ruthie P. Sager	
Montgomery	Donald E. Duncan
¶Monticello (Rt. 3, Box 369, Mt. Pleasant 75455)	Harold J. Smith
¶Moody	Bennie Hargrove
§City Mgr., Charleen Dowell	
Moore Station (Rt. 1, Box 133, Larue 75770)	Matthew W. Wallace
Moran	Mike Jones
Morgan	Harold E. Vandiver Jr.
Morgan's Point (P.O. Box 839, La Porte 77571)	John A. Grimes
Morgan's Point Resort (8 Morgan's Point Blvd., Belton 76513)	Carl P. Brown
†City Mgr., Bill L. Senkel	
Morton	Howell R. Luper
§City Mgr., Albert L. Field	
¶Moulton	Harry Meyer
Mountain City (116 Cedar, Buda 78610)	Beth H. Smith

City—	Mayor
¶Mount Calm	Jack Hawkins
Mount Enterprise	Carl D. Allen
Mount Pleasant	Jerry Boatner
*City Mgr., Van James	
Mount Vernon	Mike Edwards
City Mgr., Jack N. Perrin	
Muenster	Ted Henscheid
Muleshoe	Darrell E. Turner
*City Mgr., Dave Marr Jr.	
¶Mullin	A. C. Spinks
Munday	Doris Dickerson
§City Mgr., W. M. Hertle	
Murchison	Charles Clayton
Murphy (205 N. Murphy Rd., Plano 75074)	Al Wininger
Mustang (P.O. Box 325, Corsicana 75110)	Gene Hobdy Jr.
Mustang Ridge (Creedmoor Rural Sta., Austin 78747)	Alton B. Laws Jr.
Nacogdoches	Judy McDonald
*City Mgr., Jarvis Ammons	
Naples	Howard Belville
¶Nash	Jim Hundley
Nassau Bay (1800 NASA Rd., Houston 77058)	Gerald Allen
*City Mgr., Howard L. Ward	
Natalia	Martin B. Hardison Jr.
¶Navarro	N.A.
Navasota	Hugh Robison
*City Mgr., Al McDonald	
Nazareth	Thomas E. Hoelting
Nederland	Homer E. Nagel
*City Mgr., Howard McDaniel	
Needville	John A. Stern
Nesbitt (Rt. 5, Box 88, Marshall 75670)	Roy A. Nesbitt
Newark	Minor L. Bounds
¶New Berlin (Rt. 6, Box 600, Seguin 78155)	Joyce Wolfe
New Boston	John H. McCoy
New Braunfels	George A. Erben
*City Mgr., Joe A. Michie	
Newcastle	Floyd Gibbs
¶New Chapel Hill (Rt. 25, Box 834, Tyler 75707)	J. T. Pinkerton
New Deal	Terry Martin
New Home	Roy Blevins
¶New Hope (General Delivery, McKinney 75069)	Harold J. Dowell
New London	Charlie McConnico
New Summerfield	Bill Poteet
Newton	Charles M. Glover
¶New Waverly	Delton Ingram
Neylandville (Rt. 1, Box 242, Greenville 75401)	Robert L. Lee
Nixon	W. G. Millington
City Mgr., James E. Talley	
Nocona	Mary Lee Nix
†City Mgr., Tommy Sparks	
Nolanville	Warren Broadstreet
City Mgr., Nancy Ann Miller	
Nome	Hugh R. Ferguson
¶Noonday (P.O. Box 1350, Tyler 75710)	Bennie Smith
Nordheim	H. R. Mutschler
Normangee	J. C. Traylor III
¶North Cleveland (Box 1266, Cleveland 77327)	Woodrow Squiers
Northcrest (613 N. Lacy Dr., Waco 76705)	L. D. Pettey Jr.
¶Northlake (Rt. 2, Justin 76247)	W. T. Yarbrough
¶North Richland Hills (P.O. Box 18609, Fort Worth 76118)	Dan Echols
*City Mgr., Rodger Line	
Novice	J. O. Casey
¶Oak Grove (Rt. 5, Box 177, Kaufman 75142)	Richard H. Harris Jr.
Oakhurst	J. E. Rosier
Oak Leaf (112 Cedar Dr., Red Oak 75154)	James Ezell
Oak Point (P.O. Box 818, Little Elm 75068)	Al Glover
Oak Ridge (Box 1085, Terrell 75160)	James K. Tinsley

City—	Mayor
Oak Ridge North (P.O. Box 7215, The Woodlands 77387)	
. . . . John B. Planchard	
§City Mgr., Kevin G. Kenzenkovic	
¶Oak Valley (P.O. Box 2193, Corsicana 75110)	J. A. Compton
Oakwood	Jack Smith Sr.
O'Brien	Charlene Brothers
¶Odem	Jessie Rodriguez Sr.
Odessa	Don Carter
*City Mgr., John D. Harrison	
O'Donnell	Truett Hodnett
Oglesby	Johnnie Dawson
Old River-Winfree (Box 1169, Mont Belvieu 77580)	Arthur LaFour
City Mgr., Patti McCall	
Olmos Park (119 W. El Prado Dr., San Antonio 78205)	
. . . . Gerald Z. Dubinski	
†City Mgr., A. T. Brainerd	
Olney	Herb Bernhardt
‡City Mgr., Jack N. Northrup	
Olton	Robert C. Dennis
Omaha	B. B. Brown
Onalaska	Robert C. Goodson
Opdyke West (P.O. Box 1179, Levelland 79336)	Leslie Wayne Riggins
¶Orange	James R. Dunaway
*City Mgr., Charles L. Curry	
¶Orange Grove	Truett L. Thomas
City Mgr., Fred H. Hilmer	
Orchard	Eugene L. Demny
Ore City	Albert J. Hiles
¶Overton	Leon Bridges
City Mgr., (Vacancy)	
Ovilla	John Howard
¶Oyster Creek (3210 FM 523, Freeport 77541)	Clifford L. Guidry
City Mgr., Max Pitts	
¶Paducah	Leon Fletcher
§City Mgr., Bill Cartwright St.	
Paint Rock	Billy L. Sims
Palacios	Leonard L. Lamar
Palestine	Jack K. Selden Jr.
*City Mgr., Warren K. Driver	
Palmer	Michael Greenlee
¶Palmhurst (Rt. 1, Box 358, Mission 78572)	Sandford E. Orme
City Mgr., Gary Toothaker	
Palm Valley (Rt. 4, Harlingen 78552)	Bliss B. Clark
Palmview (Rt. 10, Box 598-B, Mission 78572)	Jose Rolando Pena
Pampa	David McDaniel
*City Mgr., Bob Hart	
Panhandle	Leslie L. McNeill
‡City Mgr., Stephen D. Hughes	
Panorama (98 Hiwon Dr., Conroe 77304)	Donald R. Branham
Pantego	H. J. Merbler
‡City Mgr., Robert T. McDaniel	
Paris	Billy Joe Burnett
*City Mgr., Michael E. Malone	
Parker	Frank Tucker
§City Mgr., Betty McMenamy	
Pasadena	John R. Harrison
Pattison	Linda A. Mladenka
Patton Village (P.O. Box 437, Splendora 77327)	Charles G. Bailey
¶Payne Springs (Rt. 2, Box 96, Mabank 75147)	Gary Walsh
Pearland	Tom Reid
*City Mgr., Ronald J. Wicker	
Pearsall	Ruben Leal
§City Mgr., Andres Garza Jr.	
Pecan Gap	John Reid
Pecan Hill (Rt. 2, Box 195E, Waxahachie 75165)	Will Ledbetter
Pecos	Bill H. Hubbs
‡City Mgr., William E. Hopper	
Pelican Bay (1300 Pelican Circle, Azle 76020)	James C. Howard
¶Penelope	Robert E. Tobola
Perryton	Mike R. Richardson
†City Mgr., David Landis	
Petersburg	Jim Fox
§City Mgr., Jesse J. Nave	
Petrolia	Paul Ridinger

City—	Mayor
Petronila (Rt. 3, Box 51, Robstown 78380)	William J. Ordner
Pflugerville	John Mark Franklin
City Mgr., Clarence Bohls	
Pharr	Fidencio R. Barrera
‡City Mgr., Benito Lopez	
Pilot Point	T. Ray Dane
Pine Forest (Box 1004, Vidor 77662)	William G. Elliott
Pinehurst (3640 Mockingbird, Orange 77630)	Grady L. Johnson
§City Mgr., Curtis F. Jeanis	
¶Pine Island (Waller 77484)	N.A.
Pineland	John O. Booker Jr.
Piney Point Village (7745 San Felipe, Houston 77063)	A. Lee Smith
Pittsburg	D. H. Abernathy
†City Mgr., Ned C. Muse	
Plains	T. J. Miller
City Mgr., Ruth Murphree (Acting)	
Plainview	E. V. Ridlehuber
*City Mgr., Jim Jeffers	
Plano	Jack Harvard
*City Mgr., Jerry McGuire (Acting)	
¶Pleak (Rural Route, Richmond 77469)	William J. Poncik
Pleasanton	Danny Qualls
‡City Mgr., Don Savage	
Pleasant Valley (Rt. 2, Box 129, Iowa Park 76367)	Leon T. Little
Plum Grove (Rt. 5, Box 322-G, Cleveland 77327)	Noble Enloe
Point	Bobby Tidwell
¶Pointblank	C. C. McDougle
Point Comfort	Trinidad Rocha Jr.
Ponder	Jo Montague
Port Aransas	Dale Bietendorf
‡City Mgr., Gordon N. Beck	
Port Arthur	Malcolm Clark
*City Mgr., George E. Dibrell	
Port Isabel	Baldemar U. Alaniz
City Mgr., (Vacancy)	
¶Portland	Bobby Whittington
*City Mgr., William H. Lewis	
Port Lavaca	Kenneth D. Lester
*City Mgr., George Shackelford	
Port Neches	Gary C. Graham Sr.
*City Mgr., Charles E. Norwood	
Post	Giles C. McCrary
§City Mgr., W. G. Pool Jr.	
¶Post Oak Bend (General Delivery, Kaufman 75142)	Floyd Kirby
Poteet	Elva Copeland
Poth	Ronald W. Eckel
City Mgr., Carlton R. Pape	
Pottsboro	George E. Cassell
¶Powell	Paul J. Sloan
Poynor	Wilma J. Burgamy
Prairie View	Ronald Leverett
City Mgr., Ulysses R. Bell	
Premont	F. Tino Perez
¶Presidio	H. Gates McHenry
Primera	Ronald D. Harwell
Princeton	Kathy Edwards
§City Mgr., David Harp	
Progreso Lakes (Box 501, Progreso 78579)	William C. Cain
Prosper	F. K. Mullendore
¶Putnam	Winford Fry
Pyote	Darral M. Shirey
Quanah	Charles E. Hurt
Queen City	Jamie W. Rawls
Quinlan	Ben Parrish
¶Quintana (P.O. Box 2379, Freeport 77541)	Mary J. Cornett
Quitaque	Jake Merrell
Quitman	Joe S. Waddleton
Ralls	Kirk A. McLaughlin
¶Rancho Viejo (3461 Carmen, Brownsville 78520)	
. . . . Walter F. Halleman Jr.	
¶Ranger	Raymond Hart
Rangerville (Rt. 4, Box 77, San Benito 78586)	Wayne M. Halbert
¶Rankin	W. R. Stafford
Ransom Canyon	Lee Kitchens
City Mgr., E. Wayne Gentry	
¶Ravenna	N.A.

City—	Mayor
Raymondville	C. M. Crowell
Red Oak	Leon Long
Refugio	Olan J. McBroom
Reklaw	Harlan Crawford
Reno (Lamar Co.) (Route 7, Box 142, Paris 75460)	David S. Lindsey
Reno (Parker Co.) (Rt. 4, Box 270, Azle 76020)	D. A. Creamer
¶Retreat (Rt. 3, Box 2050, Corsicana 75110)	Frances Robinson
Rhome	Clyde Erwin
Rice	Janet Nichols
¶Richardson	Martha E. Ritter
*City Mgr., Bob Hughey	
¶Richland	Guy Lansford
Richland Hills (3201 Diana Dr., Fort Worth 76118)	Paul C. Daniels
City Mgr., James H. Pratt	
Richland Springs	Dean Atchison
Richmond	Hilmar G. Moore
§City Mgr., Jack L. Tyler (Acting)	
Richwood (215 Halbert, Clute 77531)	Thomas W. Jones
Riesel	Burney B. Mullens
Rio Hondo	Robert Roland
City Mgr., Sheryl Paine	
Rio Vista	Jesse James Cortez
Rising Star	H. V. Burk
River Oaks (4900 River Oaks Blvd., Fort Worth 76114)	
. . . . Thomas M. Holland	
City Mgr., W. C. Ray	
Riverside	Verla S. Cook
Roanoke	John Tidwell
¶Roaring Springs	
. . . . Eugene H. Watson	
Robert Lee	Wilson Bryan
Robinson (111 W. Lyndale, Waco 76706)	Randy Cox
¶Robstown	Julio Garcia Jr.
Roby	W. C. Matthies
City Mgr., Jimmy C. Price	
Rochester	Alton L. Byrd
Rockdale	Bill T. Avrett
‡City Mgr., Elizabeth Fenter	
Rockport	C. H. Mills Jr.
City Mgr., Paul Grohman	
Rocksprings	Mary C. Simone
Rockwall	Frank Miller
‡City Mgr., William R. Eisen	
Rocky Mound (Box 795, Pittsburg 75686)	Noble T. Smith
Rogers	W. A. Persky
¶Rolling Meadows (105 McKinnon Dr., Kilgore 75662)	
. . . . E. N. Roberson	
Rollingwood (403 Nixon Dr., Austin 78746)	Travis Phillips
City Mgr., Cindy Selman	
Roma	Jose C. Saenz
§City Mgr., Andy Canales	
Roman Forest (Box 397, New Caney 77357)	Monty M. Miller
Ropesville	Alton Pettiet
Roscoe	Ron Stovall
City Mgr., Don Allen	
Rosebud	Evelyn Longwell
†City Mgr., Cheryie Dunlap	
Rose City (370 Rose City Dr., Vidor 77662)	H. P. Dubuisson
Rose Hill Acres (Box 8285, Lumberton 77711)	David Littleton
Rosenberg	Henry A. Wertheimer
City Mgr., Ed Thatcher	
Ross	James L. Jaska
Rosser	Fred F. Alford Jr.
Rotan	Jerry A. Marshall
§City Mgr., Kenneth R. Vann	
Round Rock	Mike Robinson
‡City Mgr., Jack A. Harzke	
Round Top	Robert P. Sterk
Rowlett	H. C. Ruyle Jr.
*City Mgr., John R. Milford	
Roxton	L. J. Coney
Royse City	Don Becknell
City Mgr., Michael G. Duehring	
Rule	R. C. Langford
Runaway Bay (101 Runaway Bay Dr., Bridgeport 76026)	Jim Bowlin

City—	Mayor
Runge	Daulton Bissett
Rusk	James E. Long
‡City Mgr., Tom Haddock	
Sabinal	Gary Jones (pro tem)
Sachse (Rt. 2, Box 153C, Garland 75040)	Larry Holden
City Mgr., Lloyd Henderson	
¶Sadler	O. L. Woods
Saginaw	Bill Flippo
Saint Hedwig	Albert Strzelczyk
Saint Jo	J. C. Donnell
Saint Paul (745 Parker Rd. Loop, Wylie 75098)	Stuart Wallace
San Angelo	Dick Funk
*City Mgr., Stephen Brown	
San Antonio	Henry G. Cisneros
*City Mgr., Louis J. Fox	
San Augustine	J. W. Richey
‡City Mgr., Alton B. Shaw	
San Benito	Cesar Gonzalez
¶Sanctuary (Azle 76020)	N.A.
San Diego	Amando S. Garcia
San Felipe	Kenneth Currens
Sanford	Jim Gallentine
Sanger	Nel Armstrong
§City Mgr., Steve Shutt	
¶San Juan	Hector Palacios
*City Mgr., Ricardo Gomez	
¶San Leanna (Box 86, Manchaca 78652)	R. W. Kidd
San Marcos	Jim Simpson
*City Mgr., A. C. Gonzalez	
San Patricio (Rt. 2, Box 40, Mathis 78368)	Lonnie Glasscock III
San Perlita	Dorothy Murphy
City Mgr., Marjorie Champagne	
San Saba	Joe Ragsdale
City Mgr., James Reavis	
Sansom Park (5500 Buchanan, Fort Worth 76114)	George Worley
Santa Anna	Thelma Brooker
Santa Fe	Jack L. Long
City Mgr., Mafie McMath	
Santa Rosa	Ruben Ochoa Jr.
Savoy	William Wise
Schertz	Earl W. Sawyer
‡City Mgr., Jimmy G. Gilmore	
Schulenburg	Leo Kopecky
*City Mgr., Robert A. Hoot	
Scotland	Albert Hilbers
Scottsville	John P. Verhalen
Seabrook	Helmut A. Kuehnel
*City Mgr., Lanny S. Lambert	
Seadrift	Donald G. Holder
Seagoville	Neal Wooley
§City Mgr., Joel D. Larkin	
Seagraves	Glenn Lewis
Sealy	Betty Reinbeck
Seguin	Betty Jean Jones
City Mgr., Terry K. Roberts	
Selma (Rt. 20, Box 181B, San Antonio 78218)	Kenneth Fleenor
§City Mgr., Margie Lubianski	
Seminole	Jamiel Aryain
City Mgr., Thomas L. Adams	
Seven Oaks (Rt. 1, Box 833, Livingston 77351)	Viola Jones
Seven Points (P.O. Box 43233, Kemp 75143)	Harold Skinner
Seymour	Nolan Davis
Shady Shores (Box 362, Lake Dallas 75065)	Olive Stephens
Shallowater	Bill Burgett
Shamrock	Douglas O. V. Rives
‡City Mgr., Johnny Rhodes	
Shavano Park (99 Saddletree Rd., San Antonio 78231)	John E. Horner
Shenandoah (801 Maplewood, Spring 77381)	Joe R. McGlaun
City Mgr., Natalie Flores-Kelly	
Shepherd	Victor A. Schrubb
Sherman	G. Dean Gilbert
*City Mgr., T. N. Buie	
Shiner	Arthur T. Ward
¶Shoreacres (619 Shoreacres Blvd., La Porte 77571)	Bill Haiflick
Silsbee	Wesley C. Latham
*City Mgr., Ronald M. Hickerson	

City—	Mayor
Silverton	A. R. Martin
City Mgr., Jerry Patton	
Simonton	Maurice Berkman
Sinton	Darryl Lemke
*City Mgr., Walter W. Hill Jr.	
Skellytown	Wesley L. Russell
Slaton	D. W. Englund
§City Mgr., Jim Estes	
Smiley	Travis C. Griffin Jr.
Smithville	Bill Davison
Smyer	Foy E. Thompson Jr.
Snook	Kim R. Janke
Snyder	Troy D. Williamson
*City Mgr., John Gayle	
Socorro (P.O. Box 17707, El Paso 79917)	Joe S. Carrasco
Somerset	Richard S. Padilla
Somerville	Frank Komar
§City Mgr., David Lozano	
Sonora	Billy C. Gosney
†City Mgr., James E. Dover	
Sour Lake	Charlie Lyons Jr.
City Mgr., Robert Ewart	
South Houston (Box 238, Houston 77587)	Dennis Cordray
Southlake	Johnny H. Westerholm
City Mgr., Lloyd O. Latta Jr.	
Southmayd	Mike Miller
South Padre Island (Box 3410, Port Isabel 78597)	Robert N. Pinkerton
‡City Mgr., Eduardo A. Campirano	
Southside Place (6309 Edloe, Houston 77005)	David Bellamy
City Mgr., Seth M. Young	
Spearman	C. Ralph Blodgett
†City Mgr., James R. Murray	
Splendora	David Aden
¶Spofford	J. B. Herndon
¶Springlake	Harlon Watson
¶Springtown	E. L. Lockhart
Spring Valley (1025 Campbell Rd., Houston 77055)	C. Robert Keeney Jr.
Spur	Dusty Cranford
Stafford	Leonard Scarcella
Stagecoach (Box 364, Tomball 77375)	Timothy L. Rygg
Stamford	Robert Prichard
*City Mgr., Rick Holden	
¶Stanton	Danny Fryar
§City Mgr., Jimmy Mathis	
Star Harbor (P.O. Drawer 949, Malakoff 75148)	Joe C. Gerard
¶Stephenville	David Clayton
‡City Mgr., Kurt J. Ackermann	
Sterling City	Clyde Ross Foster
¶Stinnett	Ronnie E. Griffin
City Mgr., Bruce Titus	
Stockdale	Eugene Stoever
§City Mgr., Carl R. Lambeck	
Stratford	Leland Lewis
City Mgr., Wayland Brown	
Strawn	Mark Mallory
¶Streetman	J. E. Sims
Sudan	Kenneth Wiseman
Sugar Land	Lee Duggan
City Mgr., William H. Lewis	
¶Sulphur Springs	J. O. Walker
*City Mgr., David R. Tooley	
Sundown	Allen Bailey
‡City Mgr., Tommy Phillips	
Sunnyvale (Rt. 2, Box 122, Mesquite 75182)	Robert Williams
§City Mgr., Robert J. Ewalt	
Sunray	Dow Brewer
§City Mgr., Darce Foshee	
Sunrise Beach	Edward W. Houy
Sunset Valley (2 Lone Oak Trail, Austin 78745)	Larry G. Hada
¶Sun Valley (Rt. 2, Box 800, Paris 75460)	Maria Wagnon
Surfside Beach	Burt Strouse
Sweeny	Harry Beverly
City Mgr., Kenneth Lott	
Sweetwater	Rick Rhodes
*City Mgr., David Maddox	
Taft	Herbert O. Grebe Jr.
‡City Mgr., Al Veselka	

City—	Mayor
Tahoka	Jim Solomon
‡City Mgr., Barry Pittman	
¶Talco	Joe B. Morse
Tatum	M. E. Adams
Taylor	Clark Jackson
*City Mgr., Dan Mize	
¶Taylor Lake Village (1202 Kirby, Seabrook 77586)	
	James E. Cumming
¶Teague	Clydell R. Webb
‡City Mgr., Emory Partin	
¶Tehuacana	E. B. Trotter
Temple	John F. Sammons Jr.
*City Mgr., Jack Parker	
Tenaha	George N. Bowers
Terrell	J. R. Briggs Jr.
*City Mgr., Michael H. Talbot	
Terrell Hills (5100 N. New Braunfels, San Antonio 78209)	
	Barbara B. Christian
*City Mgr., M. E. Murphy	
Texarkana	Joe Frost
*City Mgr., Daniel L. Wentzloff	
Texas City	Emmett F. Lowry
Texhoma	Mark H. Freeman
Texline	Doug Antwiler
City Mgr., Bernard Eads	
The Colony	Don Amick
*City Mgr., William M. Hall	
Thompsons	G. W. Longserre
Thorndale	A. J. Lehman
Thornton	Charles M. Peery
Thorntonville (2214 W. 2nd, Monahans 79756)	Harold Callaway
Thrall	James Dvorak
Three Rivers	Louise Shumate
¶Throckmorton	D. K. Weaver
Tiki Island, Village of (1752 Tiki Drive RR2, Tiki Island Village 77551)	Bob Keenan
¶Timbercreek Canyon (Rt. 7, Box 4-5, Amarillo 79118)	Lee E. Weiss
Timpson	Donald E. Amos
Tira (Rt. 7, Box 240, Sulphur Springs 75482)	Coy O. Vicars
Toco (Rt. 1, Brookston 75421)	
	Rocky Thompson
Todd Mission (Rt. 2, Box 650, Plantersville 77363)	George Coulam
Tolar	A. D. Haddock
City Mgr., Howard Nance	
Tomball	Lee Tipton
§City Mgr., Don E. Taylor	
Tom Bean	Billy W. Garner
Tool (Rt. 6, Box 511, Kemp 75143)	Lynn Lee
Toyah	John Newsom
¶Trent	Randy Hunt
City Mgr., Bruce McGlothlin	
Trenton	William E. Dodson
Trinidad	Ernest L. Jenkins
Trinity	Sam R. Barnes
City Mgr., Buddy Drake	
Trophy Club (P.O. Box 1110, Roanoke 76262)	James P. Carter
Troup	Zack Taylor
City Mgr., Kenneth N. Berry	
Troy	Robert L. McKee
Tulia	T. A. Hayhurst
*City Mgr., Marshal Shelton	
Turkey	Hubert Price
Tuscola	Robert Knott
Tye	Violet E. Law
Tyler	James R. Montgomery
*City Mgr., Gary Gwyn	
Uhland (Rt. 1, Box 93, Kyle 78640)	Dan T. Sorrells
Uncertain (1001 Cypress Dr., Karnack 75661)	James E. Delmar
Union Grove (Box 1326, Gladewater 75647)	Mrs. Jessie Boshear
Universal City	Larry Kerkow
*City Mgr., Mike Tanner	
¶University Park (P.O. Box 8005, Dallas 75205)	Don M. Houseman
‡City Mgr., Leland Nelson	
Uvalde	J. D. Goode Jr.
*City Mgr., James Thurmond	
Valentine	Jesus Calderon

Betty Turner (left) of Corpus Christi and Annette Strauss of Dallas joined the ranks of women serving as mayors of Texas cities in the municipal elections in 1986. About eight percent of Texas' 1,125 cities have women mayors.

City—	Mayor
Valley Mills.	Howard Hillin
Valley View.	Preston L. Murray Sr.
Van	V. M. Camper
Van Alstyne	David Schatz
¶Van Horn	Okey D. Lucas
Vega.	Mark J. Groneman
¶Venus	James Flatt
Vernon	George E. Maxon Jr.
*City Mgr., Paul Hawkins	
Victoria	John Blackaller
*City Mgr., James J. Miller	
Vidor	Dru Stephenson
¶Vinton (P.O. Box 1850, Anthony	
88021).	H. Lee Fuller
Waco	David Sibley
*City Mgr., David F. Smith	
Waelder	Zora Schultz
Wake Village (P.O. Box 3776, Texar-	
kana 75501)	John J. Forte
¶Waller.	Danny L. Marburger
¶Wallis	August D. Zurek
Walnut Springs .	John T. McDowell
Warren City (Rt. 2, Box 71,	
Gladewater 75647)	
. . . .	Claude R. Smith
Waskom	Jesse A. George
Watauga (7101 Whitley Rd., Fort	
Worth 76148) Virgil R. Anthony Sr.	
City Mgr., W. E. Keating	
Waxahachie	Gene O'Donnell
*City Mgr., Robert W. Sokoll	
Weatherford. . . .	Sherry Watson
*City Mgr., Kenneth Reneau	
Webster	Dennis Waggett
‡City Mgr., Albert A. Holguin	
Weimar	Tommy Brasher
†City Mgr., F. E. Parks	
¶Weinert.	J. E. Jetton
City Mgr., R. M. Walker	
Wellington . .	Milburn Derryberry
§City Mgr., Glen Taylor	
Wellman	Homer E. Jones
Wells	Horace C. Johnson
Weslaco	Armando Cuellar
*City Mgr., Wai-Lin Lam	

City—	Mayor
¶West	William F. Pareya
Westbrook	C. E. Ranne
West Columbia	
. . . .	Richard D. Gutzman
Westlake (P.O. Box 27, Roanoke	
76262).	Dale L. White
West Lake Hills (911 Westlake Dr.,	
Austin 78746)	Tom H. Taylor
§City Mgr., Richard A. Hargarten	
Westminster. . . .	Richard J. Davis
¶Weston	Kenneth R. Cowan
West Orange (2700 Austin Ave., Or-	
ange 77630) .	Carl K. Thibodeaux
‡City Mgr., Walter Schexnyder	
Westover Hills (5834 Merrymount	
Rd., Fort Worth 76107)	
. . . .	Sam H. Berry
West Tawakoni (Rt. 1, Box 354,	
Quinlan 75474) . . .	David L. Cobb
§City Mgr., Robert E. McKinney	
West University Place (3800 Univer-	
sity Blvd., Houston 77005)	
. . . .	Michael L. Parks
‡City Mgr., R. R. Rockenbaugh	
Westworth Village (311 Burton Hill	
Rd., Fort Worth 76114)	
. . . .	Jodie Colvard
Wharton	Garland Novosad
*City Mgr., C. G. Maclin	
Wheeler	Wanda Herd
¶White Deer	R. W. Standefer
Whiteface	Steve Whittaker
City Mgr., Mary Lou Martin	
Whitehouse. . . .	Richard E. Waller
City Mgr., C. C. Pledger	
White Oak.	Marshall Cline
¶Whitesboro .	Chas. W. Winchester
‡City Mgr., Faye Lynn Anderson	
White Settlement James M. Herring	
*City Mgr., J. E. Keaton	
Whitewright . .	Clarence Tillett Jr.
Whitney	Harry Sims Jr.
Wichita Falls.	Charles Harper
*City Mgr., James B. Berzina	
Wickett.	W. W. Randolph

City—	Mayor
Willis	Carl H. Kleimann
Willow Park	Mark Bumpas
City Mgr., Aref Hassan	
Wills Point . . .	Richard E. Herrin
City Mgr., Wilson Read	
Wilmer	Ann Hester
Wilson	Jackie Bishop
Windcrest (8601 Midcrown, San	
Antonio 78239)	
. . . .	Robert O. Whitmore
Windom	Frank Howell
Windthorst	Howard T. Neeb
Winfield	Jake Narramore
Wink.	Maxie Watts
¶Winnsboro	Lee Ray
City Mgr., Allen Bogard	
Winona	James F. Gray
Winters.	Randy M. Springer
§City Mgr., Charles MacIlvaine	
Wixon Valley (Rt. 2, Box 146, Bryan	
77803).	Donald J. Ballard
Wolfe City	Ronald H. Wensel
Wolfforth	Donald Preston
Woodbranch (P.O. Box 804,	
New Caney 77357) .	Ed C. Vaccaro
Woodcreek (P.O. Box 1570, Wim-	
berley 78676)	Jack Miller
¶Wooded Hills (P.O. Box 1174, Bur-	
leson 76028)	Lanelle Phipps
Woodloch (2626 Woodloch Dr., Con-	
roe 77385).	David Houston
Woodsboro	Roger D. Blaker
Woodson	Bobby Mathiews
Woodville	Thomas C. Knapp
Woodway (P.O. Box 20937, Waco	
76702).	Calvin A. Kent
*City Mgr., Carl S. Dossey	
Wortham	F. B. Covert
Wylie	Charles T. Trimble
Yantis.	Kenneth Heard
Yoakum	M. W. Harbus Jr.
*City Mgr., Mark A. Stubbs	
Yorktown	Leslie Flessner
City Mgr., Milton Ledwig	
Zavalla	John O. Poe

*Cities having charter provision for city manager.
†General law cities adopting plan by election.
‡Cities adopting manager plan by ordinance.
§Cities having officer performing duties of manager. These are city secretaries, city administrators and other paid officials, who are city managers in fact, though not by strict definition of the term. All are places operating under general law.
¶No answer to 1987 questionnaire; data here are the latest available.

Home-Rule Cities

The 265 home-rule cities of Texas are listed below, as reported by the **Texas Municipal League**, Austin, April 1, 1987.

City	Present Form of Government	Present Form Adopted	*First Charter
Abilene	Council-Mgr.	1946	1916
†‡§Addison	...	...	...
Alamo	Mayor-Council	1978	1978
Alamo Heights	Council	1954	1954
Alice	Council-Mgr.	1949	1949
‡Allen	Council-Mgr.		
Alvin	Council-Mgr.	1963	1963
Amarillo	Commission-Mgr.	1913	1913
Andrews	Council-Mgr.	1959	1959
Angleton	Council-Adm.	1967	1967
Anson	Council	1920	1913
Aransas Pass	Council-Mgr.	1951	1951
Arlington	Council-Mgr.	1949	1920
Athens	Council-Mgr.	1966	1960
Atlanta	Council-Mgr.	1968	1968
Austin	Council-Mgr.	1924	1919
Azle	Council-Mgr.	1971	1971
Ballinger	Commission-Mgr.	1963	1963
†‡§Bangs	...	...	...
Baytown	Council-Mgr.	1948	1948
Beaumont	Council-Mgr.	1919	1913
Bedford	Council-Mgr.	1967	1967
Beeville	Council-Mgr.	1951	1951
Bellaire	Council-Mgr.	1949	1949
Bellmead	Council-Mgr.	1961	1955
Belton	Council-Mgr.	1931	1914
†‡§Benbrook	...	...	...
Big Spring	Council-Mgr.	1972	1926
Bonham	Commission-Mgr.	1947	1914
Borger	Commission-Mgr.	1930	1927
†‡§Bowie	...	...	...
†‡§Brady	...	...	...
Breckenridge	Commission-Mgr.	1954	1954
Brenham	Commission-Mgr.	1920	1920
†Bridge City	Council-Mgr.	1974	1974
Brownfield	Council-Mgr.	1954	1954
Brownsville	Commission-Mgr.	1915	1915
Brownwood	Council-Mgr.	1916	1914
Bryan	Council-Mgr.	1917	1917
Burkburnett	Commission-Mgr.	1923	1923
Burleson	Council-Mgr.	1969	1969
Cameron	Council	1956	1956
Canyon	Commission-Mgr.	1959	1959
Carrizo Springs	Council-Mgr.	1959	1959
Carrollton	Council-Mgr.	1961	1961
Carthage	Commission-Mgr.	1948	1948
Cedar Hill	Council-Mgr.	1975	1975
†‡§Center	...	...	...
†Childress	Council-Mgr.	1917	1917
Cisco	Council-Mgr.	1974	1919
Cleburne	Council-Mgr.	1950	1914
†‡§Cleveland	...	...	...
Clute	Council-Mgr.	1967	1957
Coleman	Council-Mgr.	1949	1949
College Station	Council-Mgr.	1952	1952
Colleyville	Council-Mgr.	1977	1977
Colorado City	Council-Mgr.	1948	1948
Commerce	Commission-Mgr.	1954	1954
Conroe	Mayor-Council	1965	1965
Converse	Council-Mgr.	1981	1981
†‡§Coppell	...	...	...
Copperas Cove	Council-Mgr.	1979	1979
Corpus Christi	Council-Mgr.	1945	1926
Corsicana	Commission-Mgr.	1956	1913
Crockett	Council-Adm.	1964	1964
Crystal City	Council-Mgr.	1958	1958
Cuero	Council-Mgr.	1969	1944
†Daingerfield	Council-Mgr.		
Dalhart	Council-Mgr.	1960	1960
Dallas	Council-Mgr.	1931	1889
Dayton	Council-Mgr.	1976	1976
Deer Park	Council-Adm.	1960	1960
De Leon	Commission	1919	1919
Del Rio	Council-Mgr.	1967	1918
Denison	Council-Mgr.	1956	1925
Denton	Council-Mgr.	1959	1914
†‡§Denver City	...	...	...
De Soto	Council-Mgr.	1969	1969
†‡§Dickinson	...	...	...
Donna	Council-Mgr.	1957	1957
Dumas	Commission-Mgr.	1969	1955
Duncanville	Council-Mgr.	1962	1962
Eagle Pass	Council-Mgr.	1964	1918
Eastland	Commission-Mgr.	1919	1919
Edinburg	Commission-Mgr.	1949	1949
Edna	Council-Mgr.	1966	1966
El Campo	Council-Mgr.	1954	1954
Electra	Council	1917	1917
†‡§Elgin	...	...	...
El Paso	Council	1907	1873
†‡§Elsa	...	...	...
Ennis	Commission-Mgr.	1956	1913
Euless	Council-Mgr.	1962	1962
†‡§Everman	...	...	...
Farmers Branch	Council-Mgr.	1956	1956
Flower Mound	Council-Mgr.	1981	1981
Forest Hill	Council-Mgr.	1976	1976
Fort Worth	Council-Mgr.	1925	1919
Freeport	Council-Mgr.	1960	1949
Friendswood	Council-Mgr.	1971	1971
Gainesville	Council-Mgr.	1950	1920
Galena Park	Commission	1946	1946
Galveston	Council-Mgr.	1960	1913
Garland	Council-Mgr.	1951	1951
Gatesville	Council-Mgr.	1966	1966
Georgetown	Council-Mgr.	1970	1970
†George West	Council-Mgr.	...	...
Giddings	Council-Mgr.	1981	1981
Gladewater	Council-Mgr.	1955	1955
Gonzales	Council-Mgr.	1957	1957
Gorman	Commission	1920	1920
Graham	Council-Mgr.	1920	1920
Grand Prairie	Council-Mgr.	1972	1948
Grapevine	Council-Mgr.	1965	1965
Greenville	Council-Mgr.	1953	1921
Groves	Council-Mgr.	1959	1953
Haltom City	Council-Mgr.	1955	1955
Harker Heights	Council-Mgr.	1971	1971
Harlingen	Commission-Mgr.	1927	1927
Hearne	Council-Mgr.	1964	1964
Henderson	Council-Mgr.	1974	1947
Hereford	Council-Mgr.	1952	1952
†‡§Hewitt	...	...	...
Highland Park	Council-Mgr.	1975	1975
†‡§Highland Village	...	...	...
Hillsboro	Council-Mgr.	1962	1915
Hitchcock	Commission	1960	1960
Houston	Council	1946	1913
Humble	Mayor-Ald.	1970	1970
Huntsville	Council-Mgr.	1972	1968
Hurst	Council-Mgr.	1956	1956
‡Ingleside	Council-Mgr.	...	...
Irving	Council-Mgr.	1952	1952
Jacinto City	Council-Mgr.	1980	1980
Jacksonville	Council-Mgr.	1931	1931
Jasper	Council-Mgr.	1967	1964
Katy	Council-Mgr.	1981	1981
Keller	Council-Mgr.	1982	1982
Kerrville	Council-Mgr.	1942	1942
Kilgore	Commission-Mgr.	1960	1960
Killeen	Council-Mgr.	1949	1949
Kingsville	Commission-Mgr.	1951	1916
†‡§La Grange	...	...	...
Lake Jackson	Council-Mgr.	1954	1954
Lake Worth	Council	1965	1965
La Marque	Council-Mgr.	1975	1957
Lamesa	Council-Mgr.	1945	1945
Lancaster	Council-Mgr.	1956	1956
La Porte	Council-Mgr.	1967	1949
Laredo	Council	1921	1921
League City	Council	1962	1962
Levelland	Council-Mgr.	1949	1949
Lewisville	Council-Mgr.	1963	1963
Liberty	Council-Mgr.	1958	1958
Littlefield	Council-Mgr.	1959	1959
‡Live Oak	Council-Mgr.	...	...
Lockhart	Council-Mgr.	1973	1973
Longview	Council-Mgr.	1923	1923
Lubbock	Council-Mgr.	1917	1917
Lufkin	Commission-Mgr.	1919	1919

City	Present Form of Government	Present Form Adopted	*First Charter	City	Present Form of Government	Present Form Adopted	*First Charter
Luling	Council-Mgr.	1977	1977	Rowlett	Council-Mgr.	1979	1979
†McAllen	Commission-Mgr.	1927	1927	San Angelo	Council-Mgr.	1915	1915
‡§McGregor	...	...	...	San Antonio	Council-Mgr.	1951	1914
McKinney	Council-Mgr.	1959	1913	San Benito	Commission-Mgr.	1920	1920
Mansfield	Council-Mgr.	1975	1975	San Juan	Commission-Mgr.	1975	1975
‡§Marble Falls	...	...	...	San Marcos	Council-Mgr.	1967	1967
†Marlin	Council-Mgr.	1915	1915	Santa Fe	Council-Mgr.	1981	1981
Marshall	Commission-Mgr.	1927	1913	Schertz	Council-Mgr.	1974	1974
Mercedes	Commission-Mgr.	1973	1931	Seabrook	Council-Mgr.	1979	1979
Mesquite	Council-Mgr.	1953	1953	Seagoville	Council-Mgr.	1969	1969
Mexia	Commission-Mgr.	1924	1924	Seguin	Mayor-Council	1971	1971
†Midland	Council-Mgr.	1940	1940	Sherman	Council-Mgr.	1915	1915
‡Midlothian	Council-Mgr.			Silsbee	Council-Mgr.	1956	1956
Mineral Wells	Council-Mgr.	1966	1913	Sinton	Council-Mgr.	1966	1966
Mission	Commission-Mgr.	1961	1928	Slaton	Commission	1929	1929
‡Missouri City	Council-Mgr.			Snyder	Council-Mgr.	1952	1952
Monahans	Council-Mgr.	1954	1954	Stamford	Council-Mgr.	1918	1918
Mount Pleasant	Council-Mgr.	1948	1948	Stephenville	Council-Mgr.	1961	1961
Muleshoe	Council-Mgr.	1960	1960	Sugar Land	Council-Mgr.	1981	1981
Nacogdoches	Commission-Mgr.	1929	1929	Sulphur Springs	Commission-Mgr.	1947	1917
Nassau Bay	Council-Mgr.	1973	1973	Sweetwater	Commission-Mgr.	1927	1913
Navasota	Commission-Mgr.	1947	1922	Taylor	Commission-Mgr.	1914	1914
Nederland	Council-Mgr.	1955	1955	Temple	Commission-Mgr.	1922	1922
New Braunfels	Council-Mgr.	1966	1964	Terrell	Council-Mgr.	1973	1913
North Richland Hills	Council-Mgr.	1964	1964	Terrell Hills	Council-Mgr.	1957	1957
Odessa	Council-Mgr.	1969	1945	Texarkana	Council-Mgr.	1960	1917
‡§Olney	...	...	...	Texas City	Commission	1946	1946
Orange	Council-Mgr.	1954	1914	The Colony	Council-Mgr.	1978	1978
Palestine	Commission	1917	1917	‡§Tomball	...	...	...
Pampa	Commission-Mgr.	1927	1927	Tulia	Council-Mgr.	1972	1972
Paris	Council-Mgr.	1948	1919	Tyler	Council-Mgr.	1915	1915
Pasadena	Mayor-Council	1964	1943	Universal City	Council-Mgr.	1972	1972
Pearland	Council-Mgr.	1971	1971	†Uvalde	Council-Mgr.	1951	1934
‡§Pecos	...	...	...	Vernon	Commission-Mgr.	1962	1916
Pharr	Council-Mgr.	1971	1949	Victoria	Council-Mgr.	1957	1915
Plainview	Council-Mgr.	1964	1920	Vidor	Mayor-Council	1969	1969
Plano	Council-Mgr.	1961	1961	Waco	Council-Mgr.	1948	1913
‡§Pleasanton	...	...	...	‡§Watauga	...	...	...
†Port Aransas	Council-Mgr.			Waxahachie	Council-Mgr.	1946	1916
Port Arthur	Council-Mgr.	1932	1915	Weatherford	Commission-Mgr.	1956	1918
‡§Port Isabel	...	...	...	Weslaco	Commission-Mgr.	1927	1927
Portland	Council-Mgr.	1967	1967	West Orange	Council	1956	1956
Port Lavaca	Council-Mgr.	1956	1956	†West University Place	Commission-Mgr.	1940	1940
Port Neches	Council-Mgr.	1967	1955	Wharton	Council-Mgr.	1970	1970
Quanah	Council	1919	1919	White Settlement	Council-Mgr.	1968	1954
Ranger	Commission-Mgr.	1919	1919	Wichita Falls	Council-Mgr.	1920	1913
Raymondville	Commission-Mgr.	1955	1955	‡Woodway	Council-Mgr.		
Richardson	Council-Mgr.	1956	1956	‡§Wylie	...	...	...
Richland Hills	Council-Mgr.	1986	1986	Yoakum	Commission-Mgr.	1915	1915
River Oaks	Council	1949	1949				
Robstown	Council	1948	1948				
Rockdale	Mayor-Council	1978	1978				
‡§Rockport	...	...	...				
‡§Rockwall	...	...	...				
Rosenberg	Council	1960	1956				
‡Round Rock	Council-Mgr.						

*Present (1985) home-rule amendment (Art. XI, Sec. 5) ratified Nov. 5, 1912.
†Has city manager by ordinance.
‡Date present form of charter adopted and date of first charter adoption not available.
§Data on form of government not available.

Councils of Government

The concept of regional planning and cooperation, fostered by enabling legislation in 1965, has spread across Texas since organization of the **North Central Texas Council of Governments** in 1966.

Legal responsibilities of regional councils include making studies and plans to guide the unified development of their areas, elimination of duplication and promotion of economy and efficiency in coordinated area development. They make recommendations to their member governments and may, upon request, assist in implementation of those plans.

Financing is provided by the local governments, the state and the federal government.

A list of the 24 regional councils, the counties served and the executive director as of February 1987, follows:

Alamo Area Council of Governments: Counties — Atascosa, Bandera, Bexar, Comal, Frio, Gillespie, Guadalupe, Karnes, Kendall, Kerr, Medina and Wilson. Executive director, Al Notzon III, 118 Broadway, Ste. 400, San Antonio 78205.

Ark-Tex Council of Governments: Counties — Bowie, Cass, Delta, Franklin, Hopkins, Lamar, Morris, Red River and Titus. Executive director, James D. Goerke, Box 5307, Texarkana, Texas 75505.

Brazos Valley Development Council: Counties — Brazos, Burleson, Grimes, Leon, Madison, Robertson and Washington. Executive director, Glenn J. Cook, Box 4128, Bryan 77805-4128.

Capital Area Planning Council: Counties — Bastrop, Blanco, Burnet, Caldwell, Fayette, Hays, Lee, Llano, Travis and Williamson. Executive director, Richard G. Bean, 2520 IH 35 South, Suite 100, Austin 78704.

Central Texas Council of Governments: Counties — Bell, Coryell, Hamilton, Lampasas, Milam, Mills and San Saba. Executive director, Walton B. Reedy, Box 729, Belton 76513-0729.

Coastal Bend Council of Governments: Counties — Bee, Brooks, Duval, Jim Wells, Kenedy, Kleberg, Live Oak, McMullen, Nueces, Refugio and San Patricio. Executive director, John Buckner, Box 9909, Corpus Christi 78469.

Concho Valley Council of Governments: Counties — Coke, Concho, Irion, Kimble, McCulloch, Mason, Menard, Reagan, Sterling, Sutton and Tom Green. Execu-

ve director, Robert R. Weaver, Box 60050, San Angelo
6906.

Deep East Texas Council of Governments: Counties —
Angelina, Houston, Jasper, Nacogdoches, Newton,
Polk, Sabine, San Augustine, San Jacinto, Shelby, Trinity and Tyler. Executive director, E. Ray Hill, 274 E.
Lamar, Jasper 75961.

East Texas Council of Governments: Counties — Anderson, Camp, Cherokee, Gregg, Harrison, Henderson,
Marion, Panola, Rains, Rusk, Smith, Upshur, Van
Zandt and Wood. Executive director, Glynn Knight,
800 Stone Rd., Kilgore 75662.

Golden Crescent Regional Planning Commission:
Counties — Calhoun, De Witt, Goliad, Gonzales, Jackson, Lavaca and Victoria. Executive director, Patrick
J. Kennedy, Box 2028, Victoria 77902.

Heart of Texas Council of Governments: Counties —
Bosque, Falls, Freestone, Hill, Limestone and McLennan. Executive director, Hugh Davis, 320 Franklin Ave.,
Waco 76701.

Houston-Galveston Area Council: Counties — Austin,
Brazoria, Chambers, Colorado, Fort Bend, Galveston,
Harris, Liberty, Matagorda, Montgomery, Walker,
Waller and Wharton. Executive director, Jack Steele,
Box 22777, Houston 77227.

Lower Rio Grande Valley Development Council:
Counties — Cameron, Hidalgo and Willacy. Executive
director, Robert A. Chandler, 707 Texas Commerce
Bank Bldg., McAllen 78501.

Middle Rio Grande Development Council: Counties —
Dimmit, Edwards, Kinney, La Salle, Maverick, Real,
Uvalde and Zavala. Executive director, Mike M. Paterson, Box 702, Carrizo Springs 78834.

Nortex Regional Planning Commission: Counties —
Archer, Baylor, Childress, Clay, Cottle, Foard, Hardeman, Jack, Montague, Wichita, Wilbarger and Young.
Executive director, Edwin B. Daniel, Box 5144, Wichita
Falls 76307.

North Central Texas Council of Governments: Counties — Collin, Dallas, Denton, Ellis, Erath, Hood, Hunt,
Johnson, Kaufman, Navarro, Palo Pinto, Parker, Rockwall, Somervell, Tarrant and Wise. Executive director,
William J. Pitstick, P.O. Drawer COG, Arlington 76005.

Panhandle Regional Planning Commission: Counties
— Armstrong, Briscoe, Carson, Castro, Collingsworth,
Dallam, Deaf Smith, Donley, Gray, Hall, Hartley,
Hemphill, Lipscomb, Moore, Ochiltree, Oldham,
Parmer, Potter, Randall, Roberts, Swisher and Wheeler. Executive director, Gary Pitner, Box 9257, Amarillo
79105.

Permian Basin Regional Planning Commission:
Counties — Andrews, Borden, Crane, Dawson, Ector,
Gaines, Glasscock, Howard, Martin, Midland, Pecos,
Reeves, Terrell, Upton, Ward and Winkler. Executive
director, Ernest W. Crawford, Box 6391 ATS, Midland
79711.

South East Texas Regional Planning Commission:
Counties — Hardin, Jefferson and Orange. Executive
director, Don Kelly, P.O. Drawer 1387, Nederland 77627.

South Plains Association of Governments: Counties —
Bailey, Cochran, Crosby, Dickens, Floyd, Garza, Hale,
Hockley, King, Lamb, Lubbock, Lynn, Motley, Terry
and Yoakum. Executive director, Jerry D. Casstevens,
Box 2787, Lubbock 79408.

South Texas Development Council: Counties — Jim
Hogg, Starr, Webb and Zapata. Executive director,
Amando Garza Jr., Box 2187, Laredo 78044-2187.

Texoma Regional Planning Commission: Counties —
Cooke, Fannin and Grayson. Executive director, Larry
Cruise, 10000 Grayson Dr., Denison 75020.

West Central Texas Council of Governments: Counties — Brown, Callahan, Coleman, Comanche, Eastland, Fisher, Haskell, Jones, Kent, Knox, Mitchell, Nolan, Runnels, Scurry, Shackelford, Stephens, Stonewall,
Taylor and Throckmorton. Executive director, Brad
Helbert, Box 3195, Abilene 79604.

West Texas Council of Governments: Counties —
Brewster, Culberson, El Paso, Hudspeth, Jeff Davis and
Presidio. Executive director, Justin R. Ormsby, 5th
Floor, Two Civic Center Plaza, El Paso 79999.

COUNTY APPRAISERS

The following list of Chief Appraisers for Texas counties was furnished by Ms. Christine Anderson, Executive
Coordinator, Texas Association of Appraisal Districts, 6633 U.S. 290 East, Suite 203, Austin 78723. It includes the mailing
address for each appraiser and is current to Feb. 1, 1987.

Anderson—Lynda Cromble, Box 279, Palestine 75801
Andrews—David Robinson, 405 N.W. 3rd, Andrews 79714
Angelina—Marvin Hahn Jr., Box 2357, Lufkin 75901
Aransas—Robert Springer, 601 S. Church, Rockport 78382
Archer—Jean James, Box 1141, Archer City 76351
Armstrong—Ron Patterson, Drawer D, Claude 79019
Atascosa—Vernon A. Warren, 1010 Zanderson, Jourdanton 78026
Austin—Allen McKinley, 5 E. Main, Bellville 77418
Bailey—Carl Gilbreath, 104 E. Ave. C, Muleshoe 79347
Bandera—Larry Reagan, Box 1119, Bandera 78003
Bastrop—Lorraine Perry, Drawer 578, Bastrop 78602
Baylor—Grady Hicks, 101 S. Washington, Seymour 76380
Bee—Blaine Luthringer, Box 1262, Beeville 78102
Bell—Tolly Moore, Box 390, Belton 76513
Bexar—Bill Burnette, 535 S. Main, San Antonio 78204
Blanco—Mrs. Hollis Petri, Box 338, Johnson City 78636
Borden—R. D. Lewis, Box 298, Gail 79738
Bosque—David Cooper, Box 393, Meridian 76665
Bowie—Wayne Hawkins, Box 6527, Texarkana 75505
Brazoria—J. R. Gayle Jr., 500 N. Chenango, Angleton 77515
Brazos—Buddy Winn, 1121 Villa Maria Rd., Bryan 77801
Brewster—Jerry Ratcliff, Box 1231, Alpine 79831
Briscoe—Carlye Fleming, Box 728, Silverton 79257
Brooks—Humberto Rivera, Drawer A, Falfurrias 78355
Brown—Alvis Sewalt, 403 Fisk, Brownwood 76801
Burleson—Elizabeth Plagens, Box 1000, Caldwell 77836
Burnet—Alvin C. Williams, Drawer E, Burnet 78611
Caldwell—Joe Rector, Box 59, Lockhart 78644
Calhoun—Keith Matlock, Drawer CC, Port Lavaca 77979
Callahan—Rodney Lewallen, Box 806, Baird 79504
Cameron—Ken Monroe, Box 1010, San Benito 78586
Camp—Vaudene Bennett, Box 739, Pittsburg 75686
Carson—Dianne B. Lavake, Box 970, Panhandle 79068-0970
Cass—Janelle Clements, Box 167, Linden 75563
Castro—Jerry Heller, 204 S.E. 3rd (Rear), Dimmitt 79027
Chambers—Sherwood Blair, Box 1520, Anahuac 77514
Cherokee—S. R. Danner, Box 494, Rusk 75785
Childress—Nadine Parr, Courthouse Box 13, Childress 79201
Clay—A. G. Reis, 101 E. Omega, Henrietta 76365
Cochran—Glen McDaniel, 109 S.E. 1st, Morton 79346
Coke—Patsy Dunn, Box 2, Robert Lee 76945
Coleman—Bill W. Jones, Box 914, Coleman 76834
Collin—Jimmie Honea, 1201 W. 15th, Rm. 136, Plano 75075

Collingsworth—Ann Wauer, Courthouse 1st Floor, Rm. 6, Wellington 79095
Colorado—William Youens Jr., Box 10, Columbus 78934
Comal—Pat Fox (Acting), Box 1222, New Braunfels 78130
Comanche—Nan Owen, Box 6, Comanche 76442
Concho—Eugene Dillard, Box 68, Paint Rock 76866
Cooke—Bill Sherman, 200 W. California, Gainesville 76240
Coryell—Darrell Lisenbe, Box 142, Gatesville 76528
Cottle—Rue Young, Box 459, Paducah 79248
Crane—Mary Lauderback, 511 West 8th, Crane 79731
Crockett—Tom Stokes, Drawer H, Ozona 76943
Crosby—Darla Doss, Box 479, Crosbyton 79322
Culberson—Sally Floyd, Box 550, Van Horn 79855
Dallam—H. V. Stanley, Box 592, Dalhart 79022
Dallas—Foy Mitchell Jr., 1420 W. Mockingbird Ln., Dallas 75247
Dawson—Tom Anderson, Box 797, Lamesa 79331
Deaf Smith—Fred E. Fox, Box 2298, Hereford 79045
Delta—Toyce Phillips, Box 47, Cooper 75432
Denton—Joe Rogers, Box 2816, Denton 76201
DeWitt—Wayne Woolsey, Box 4, Cuero 77954
Dickens—Jerrie Ballard, Box 57, Dickens 79229
Dimmit—Allen Dockery, Box 920, Carrizo Springs 78834
Donley—Charles SoRelle, Box 1220, Clarendon 79226
Duval—Ernesto Molina Jr., Box 809, San Diego 78384
Eastland—Steve Thomas, Box 914, Eastland 76448
Ector—James A. Goodwin, Box 4956, Odessa 79760-4956
Edwards—Sondra Madden, Box 378, Rocksprings 78880
Ellis—Gray Chamberlain, Box 878, Waxahachie 75165
El Paso—Cora Viescas, 1720 Murchison, El Paso 79902
Erath—Jerry Lee, Box 94, Stephenville 76401
Falls—Joyce Collier, Drawer 430, Marlin 76661
Fannin—Cheryl Elmore, 920 N. Center, Bonham 75418
Fayette—James Parker, Box 836, LaGrange 78945
Fisher—Teddy Kral, Box 516, Roby 79543
Floyd—Sheila Faulkenberry, County Courthouse Rm. 107, Floydada 79235
Foard—Jo Ann Vecera, Box 419, Crowell 79227
Fort Bend—Gene Brewer, Drawer 5007, Sugar Land 78487
Franklin—Edward Morrow, Box 720, Mount Vernon 75457
Freestone—Sherrill Minze, Box 675, Fairfield 75840
Frio—Irma Gonzalez, Box 1129, Pearsall 78061
Gaines—Pam Owens, Box 490, Seminole 79360
Galveston—Guy Emanis, Box 3647, Texas City 77592
Garza—Jean Westfall, Drawer F, Post 79356

Gillespie—Olan Tisdale, Box 429, Fredericksburg 78624
Glasscock—Royce Pruit, Box 89, Garden City 79739
Goliad—E. J. Bammert, Box 34, Goliad 77963
Gonzales—Glenda Strackbein, Box 867, Gonzales 78629
Gray—Charles Buzzard, Box 836, Pampa 79066
Grayson—Robert H. Tollison, 205 N. Travis, Sherman 75090
Gregg—Bill Carroll, Box 6700, Longview 75608
Grimes—Bill Sullivan, Box 489, Anderson 77830
Guadalupe—J. Michael Morris, Box 1226, Seguin 78155
Hale—Linda Dobbins, Box 29, Plainview 79072
Hall—Jack Scott, 721 Robertson, Memphis 79245
Hamilton—Doyle Roberts, 119 E. Henry, Hamilton 76531
Hansford—Alice Peddy, Box 567, Spearman 79081-0567
Hardeman—Twila Butler, Box 388, Quanah 79252
Hardin—Edwin Barry, Box 670, Kountze 77625
Harris—K. E. Graeber, Box 920975, Houston 77292
Harrison—David E. Whitmire, Box 818, Marshall 75670
Hartley—Troy Sloan, Box 405, Hartley 79044
Haskell—John L. Grissom, Box 467, Haskell 79521
Hays—Jesse Click, Courthouse Annex, 102 N. LBJ, San Marcos 78666
Hemphill—James McCarley, Box 65, Canadian 79014
Henderson—Jimmy Foreman, Box 430, Athens 75751
Hidalgo—Daniel Boone, Box 632, Pharr 78577
Hill—Shirley Holub, Box 416, Hillsboro 76645
Hockley—Keith Toomire, Box 1090, Levelland 79336
Hood—Ben Griffin, Box 819, Granbury 76048
Hopkins—Tom Witt, Box 753, Sulphur Springs 75482
Houston—Katherine Keith, Box 1125, Crockett 75835
Howard—F. E. Pereira, Box 1441, Big Spring 79721
Hudspeth—John L. Ferrell, Box 186, Sierra Blanca 79851
Hunt—Joe Pat Davis, Box 1339, Greenville 75401
Hutchinson—William Hodge, Box 5065, Borger 79008
Irion—Frances Grice, Box 980, Mertzon 76941
Jack—Doris Ray, Box 850, Jacksboro 76056
Jackson—James Surratt, 106 E. Main, Edna 77957
Jasper—David Luther, 121 N. Austin, Jasper 75951
Jeff Davis—John L. Ferrell, Box 373, Fort Davis 79734
Jefferson—Roland Bieber, Drawer 1176, Nederland 77627
Jim Hogg—Ovidio Garza, Box 459, Hebbronville 78361
Jim Wells—Hector Flores, Box 607, Alice 78333
Johnson—Don Gilmore, 109 N. Main, Cleburne 76031
Jones—John Steele, Box 348, Anson 79501
Karnes—Doris Ahrens, 120 W. Calvert, Karnes City 78118
Kaufman—Jackie Self, Box 819, Kaufman 75142
Kendall—Sue Wiedenfeld, Box 788, Boerne 78006
Kenedy—Carl Maultsby, Box 26510, Austin 78755
Kent—Jarri Parker, Box 167, Jayton 79528
Kerr—Juanita Maples, Box 1885, Kerrville 78029
Kimble—Paul Bierschwale, Box 307, Junction 76849
King—Bama Nell Oliver, Box 117, Guthrie 79236
Kinney—Marcus Tidwell, Box 1377, Brackettville 78832
Kleberg—Adella Arnold, Box 1027, Kingsville 78363
Knox—Oscar Mangis, Box 2, Benjamin 79505
Lamar—Rodney Anderson, 1523 Lamar Ave., Paris 75460
Lamb—Murlene Bilbrey, Box 552, Littlefield 79339
Lampasas—Dana Ripley, Box 175, Lampasas 76550
La Salle—Juanita Lozano, Drawer 0, Cotulla 78014
Lavaca—Diane Munson, Box 386, Hallettsville 77964
Lee—Roy Holcomb, 218 E. Richmond, Giddings 78942
Leon—Tom G. Holmes, Box 536, Centerville 75833
Liberty—L. E. Robinson Jr., Box 712, Liberty 77575
Limestone—Clydene Hyden, Drawer 831, Groesbeck 76642
Lipscomb—Jerry Reynolds, Box 128, Darrouzett 79024
Live Oak—Gayland Wofford, Box MM, George West 78022
Llano—Margie Jung, Box 307, Llano 78643
Loving—Mary Belle Jones, Box 170, Mentone 79754
Lubbock—Dave Kimbrough, Box 10542, Lubbock 79408
Lynn—Dovie Miller, Box 789, Tahoka 79373
McCulloch—Marjorie D. Neal, 104 N. College, Brady 76825
McLennan—Charles Gauer, Box 2297, Waco 76703
McMullen—Mary K. Edwards, Box 38, Tilden 78072
Madison—Dan Singletary, Box 1328, Madisonville 77864
Marion—Linda Rodriguez, Box 690, Jefferson 75657
Martin—Delbert Dickenson, Box 1349, Stanton 79782
Mason—Ann Stapp, Drawer 1119, Mason 76856
Matagorda—Kyle Wilfong, Box 268, Bay City 77414
Maverick—Victor Perry, Box 2628, Eagle Pass 78852
Medina—James Garcia, 1410 Ave. K, Hondo 78861
Menard—Peggy Decker, Box 1058, Menard 76859
Midland—Roland Wilkinson, Box 908002, Midland 79703
Milam—Lynn Gillen, Box 769, Cameron 76520
Mills—Doran Lemke, Box 565, Goldthwaite 76844
Mitchell—Clarence Burt, Box 358, Colorado City 79512
Montague—Wanda Russell, Box 121, Montague 76251
Montgomery—Harold J. Hagan, Box 2233, Conroe 77305
Moore—Joyce Jones, Box 717, Dumas 79029
Morris—Rhonda Hall, Box 563, Daingerfield 75638
Motley—Betty L. Luckett, Box 779, Matador 79244
Nacogdoches—Gary Woods, Box 1893, Nacogdoches 75961
Navarro—Harry Hudson, Box 3118, Corsicana 75110

Newton—Gerald L. Cobb, Drawer X, Newton 75966
Nolan—Patricia Davis, Box 1256, Sweetwater 79556
Nueces—George Moff, Co. Courthouse, Suite 302, Corpus Christi 78401
Ochiltree—Terry Symons, 415 S. Ash, Perryton 79070
Oldham—Jen Carter, Drawer 449, Vega 79092
Orange—Faye Gillet, Box 457, Orange 77630
Palo Pinto—Jackie Samford, Box 250, Palo Pinto 76072
Panola—Jewell Ellis, 1122 West Panola, Carthage 75633
Parker—Larry Hammonds, 118 W. Columbia, Weatherford 76086
Parmer—Ron Procter, Box 56, Bovina 79009
Pecos—Mary Sedlacek, Box 237, Fort Stockton 79735
Polk—Jay V. Snook Jr., Box 305, Livingston 77351
Potter—Jim Nugent, Box 7190, Amarillo 79114-7190
Presidio—John Ferrell, Box 879, Marfa 79843
Rains—Tommy Roberts, Box 71, Emory 75440
Randall—Jim Nugent, Box 7190, Amarillo 79114-7190
Reagan—Christine Gardner, Reagan Co. Courthouse, Big Lake 76932
Real—Fred Thurmond, Box 158, Leakey 78873
Red River—Harold Quillen, Box R, Clarksville 75426
Reeves—Carol K. Markham, Box 1229, Pecos 79772
Refugio—Bettye Kret, Box 156, Refugio 78377
Roberts—Debbie Stribling, Box 476, Miami 79059
Robertson—Sue Sims, Box 818, Calvert 77837
Rockwall—Ray Helm, 106 N. San Jacinto, Rockwall 75087
Runnels—Clayton Brazelton, Box 524, Ballinger 76821
Rusk—Melvin Cooper, Box 7, Henderson 75653-0007
Sabine—Jim Nethery, Box 137, Hemphill 75948
San Augustine—Jamie Doherty, 122 N. Harrison, San Augustine 75972
San Jacinto—Ruth Morrison, Box 117, Coldspring 77331
San Patricio—Kathryn Vermillion, Box 938, Sinton 78387
San Saba—G. P. Adams, Courthouse, San Saba 76877
Schleicher—Ray Ballew, Box 936, El Dorado 76936
Scurry—L. R. Peveler, 2612 College Ave., Snyder 79549
Shackelford—Betty Viertel, Box 565, Albany 76430
Shelby—Harold Robertson, Rt. 5, Box 66, Center 75935
Sherman—Marilyn Albert, Box 239, Stratford 79084
Smith—Michael D. Barnett, 245 South S.E. Loop 323, Tyler 75702
Somervell—Sandra Montgomery, Box 699, Glen Rose 76043
Starr—Ricardo Diaz, Box 137, Rio Grande City 78582
Stephens—Mary Sorrells, Box 351, Breckenridge 76024
Sterling—Linda Low, Box 28, Sterling City 76951
Stonewall—Oscar E. Dickerson, Box 308, Aspermont 79502
Sutton—Rex Ann Friess, 300 E. Oak, Sonora 76950
Swisher—Rose Lee Powell, Box 8, Tulia 79088
Tarrant—Bill Roberts (Interim), 1701 River Run, Suite 200, Fort Worth 76107
Taylor—Richard Petree, Box 1800, Abilene 79604
Terrell—Leta Schlinke, Box 747, Sanderson 79848
Terry—J. O. Burnett Jr., Box 426, Brownfield 79316
Throckmorton—Ruby Dunlap, Box 66, Throckmorton 76083
Titus—Maydelle Renfroe, Box 528, Mount Pleasant 75455
Tom Green—Elvin W. Field, Box 3307, San Angelo 76902
Travis—James Archer, Box 15997, Austin 78761
Trinity—Mark W. Whitmire, Box 950, Groveton 75845
Tyler—Mary F. Mann, Drawer 9, Woodville 75979
Upshur—Louise Stracener, Box 280, Gilmer 75644
Upton—W. J. Campbell Jr., Box 1110, McCamey 79752
Uvalde—Brownie J. Jones, 209 N. High, Uvalde 78801
Val Verde—Lillie Sue Stout, Box 1059, Del Rio 78841
Van Zandt—Ron Groom, N. Hwy. 19, Box 926, Canton 75103
Victoria—Jim Williams, 1611-A E. North, Victoria 77901
Walker—Grover Cook, Box 1798, Huntsville 77340
Waller—Preston Kelly, Box 159, Katy 77492
Ward—Arlice Wittie, Box 905, Monahans 79756
Washington—Charles Gaskamp, Box 681, Brenham 77833
Webb—Ezequiel P. Laurel, Box 719, Laredo 78040
Wharton—Kenneth Wright, Box 1068, Wharton 77488
Wheeler—Marilyn Copeland, Box 349, Wheeler 79096
Wichita—Lanier Wilson, Box 5172, Wichita Falls 76307
Wilbarger—Russell Garrison, Box 1519, Vernon 76384
Willacy—Agustin Colchado, Rt. 2, Box 256, Raymondville 78580
Williamson—Dusty Thames, Box 1085, Georgetown 78626-1085
Wilson—Leon Stoeltje, Box 849, Floresville 78114
Winkler—John R. Oglesby, Box 1219, Kermit 79745
Wise—Ross Fry, Box 509, Decatur 76234
Wood—Carson Wages, Box 951, Quitman 75783
Yoakum—J. D. Brown, Box 748, Plains 79355
Young—Pat Butler, Box 337, Graham 76046
Zapata—Rosalva Villarreal, Box 2315, Zapata 78076
Zavala—Juan Garcia (Acting), 323 W. Zavala, Crystal City 78839

TEXAS COUNTY AND DISTRICT OFFICIALS—TABLE NO. 1

County Seats, County Judges, County Clerks, County Attorneys, County Treasurers, Tax Assessors-Collectors and Sheriffs. See following pages for another table of county and district officials. The officials listed in this table are elected by popular vote.

County	County Seat	County Judge	County Clerk	County Attorney	County Treasurer	Assessor-Collector	Sheriff
Anderson	Palestine	*Jack Rogers	Jo Huddleston	James L. Rex	Virginia Salmon	Betty Broyles	Gary Thomas
Andrews	Andrews	Gary W. Gaston	James Craddock	Ed C. Jones		Louise Williams	Wayne Farmer
Angelina	Lufkin	†Dan Jones	Pauline Grisham	James Anderson Jr.	Frona Lee	Douglas Allen	Michael P. Lawrence
Aransas	Rockport	John D. Wendell	Val Jean Eaton	Gary Southard	Marvine D. Wix	Allena Jones	Robert O. Hewes
Archer	Archer City	B. G. Holder	Jane Adams		Betty Tarno	Charles McDaniel	James J. Harney
Armstrong	Claude	‡Gladys Posey	Kathy Byrd	R. T. Franklin	Bernice Stephenson	Beth Statler	Charles D. Strange
Atascosa	Jourdanton	O. B. Gates	Laquita Hayden	Daniel W. Leedy	John N. Self	Eddie Richter	Tommy Williams
Austin	Bellville	§LeRoy H. Grebe	Dorothy Himly	Linda Elder	Betty Krueger	Kathleen Hayes	T. A. Maddox
Bailey	Muleshoe	Gordon H. Green	Barbara McCamish	Sam L. Darden	Dorothy Turner	Mrs. M. Stevens	Bobby Henderson
Bandera	Bandera	Ray F. Mauer	Vera King		Elizabeth James		Guy V. Pickett
Bastrop	Bastrop	Jimmy Copeland	Shirley Wilhelm	Tony Liebel	Doris Oldfield	Barbara Brinkmeyer	I. R. Hoskins
Baylor	Seymour	Joe Dickson	Doris Swain	Frederick J. Biel	Patricia Coker	Grady Hicks	Wes Hollar
Bee	Beeville	Henry W. Streitman	Julia V. Torres	Pat Ridley		Lulan Fraser	Robt. L. Horn
Bell	Belton	¶John Garth	Vada Sutton		Charles Jones	Tolly Moore	Dan Smith
Bexar	San Antonio	**Tom Vickers	Robert D. Green		Robert D. Green	Rudy A. Garza	Harlon Copeland
Blanco	Johnson City	Charles Scott	Dorothy Uecker	D. C. Myane	Doris Cage	Joyce Koch	Holton Burleson
Borden	Gail	Van L. York	Dorothy Browne		Melissa Ludecke	Norman Sneed	Norman Sneed
Bosque	Meridian	Regina S. Hanson	Patsy O. Mize	Lesa Bennett	Melissa S. Vick	Elva Seidel	Denny Proffitt
Bowie	Boston	††James M. Carlow	Marylene Megason		Margaret Yates	Aleatha Lyle	Thomas Hodge
Brazoria	Angleton	‡‡John W. Damon	Dolly Bailey		Susan Neighbours	Ray Cornett	E. J. King
Brazos	Bryan	§§R. J. Holmgreen	F. J. Boriskie	Jim Kuboviak	Sandie Walker	G. L. Winn	Ronnie Miller
Brewster	Alpine	Tom Connor	Shirley A. Scholl	Val C. Beard	Hortencia Ramos	Jerry Ratcliff	George Jones
Briscoe	Silverton	Fred W. Mercer	Bess McWilliams	S. D. Hale (pro tem)	Janice S. Hill	Fairy L. McWilliams	Richard Roehr
Brooks	Falfurrias	Homer Mora	Calixto Mora	David T. Garcia	Sulema Garza	R. Castellano	R. Castellano
Brown	Brownwood	G. Lee Haney	Margaret Woods	Tanya Cooper	Connie Cline	Rosemary McInnis	W. M. Donahoo
Burleson	Caldwell	Woods A. Caperton	Evelyn M. Henry	J. J. Skrivanek III	Katherine Bravenec	Floy Stephens	A. G. Wilhelm
Burnet	Burnet	D. C. Kincheloe	Millie Williams	Jim M. Cross	Katy Gilmore	J. B. Baker	Weldon Buck
Caldwell	Lockhart	¶¶William J. Ellison	Nina Sells		Amelia Rizzuto	Mattie Robuck	Mike Bading
Calhoun	Port Lavaca	***Alex R. Hernandez	Mary Lois McMahan		Sharron Marek	Annette Baker	A. P. Lacy
Callahan	Baird	Mack Kniffen	Darlene Walker	Robert E. McCool	Dora Hounshell	Wauneta Estes	Bill Skinner
Cameron	Brownsville	†††J. A. Goolsby	Joe G. Rivera	Benjamin Euresti Jr.	M. T. Puckett	Hugh H. Riley	Alex F. Perez
Camp	Pittsburg	Phillip R. Hawkins	Lollis C. Irby	Paul W. Mayben	Virginia Zachary	Brenda Irby	Charles Elwonger
Carson	Panhandle	J. R. Rosellus	Sue Persons	Ed Hinshaw	Peggy Butler	C. L. Sterling	Connie C. Reed
Cass	Linden	Tommy E. Kessler	Wilma O'Rand		Jo Ellen Whatley	Fay Glover	Paul W. Boone
Castro	Dimmitt	Mrs. M. Simpson Jr.	Joy Jones	Jimmy F. Davis	Oleta Raper	Billy W. Hackleman	Lonny Rhynes
Chambers	Anahuac	Oscar Nelson	Norma Rowland		Jimmie Moorhead	Irene Clore	C. E. Morris
Cherokee	Rusk	‡‡‡Emmett Whitehead	Fairy H. Upshaw	E. T. Jenson	Diann Norton	Linda Beard	Allen Horton
Childress	Childress	Dean Decker	Nancy Garrison	Leland Sutton	Elizabeth Kitchens	Elton R. Howard	Claude B. Lane
Clay	Henrietta	Bill Nobles	Kay Brookshire	Ann P. Musgrove	Sue S. Brock	Tom Whitley	Jake Bogard
Cochran	Morton	Robert Yeary	Rita Tyson	R. F. Mitchell	Betty Hudson	Betty Akin	C. G. Richards
Coke	Robert Lee	Aubrey Denman	Effie Hubbard	Bill J. Helwig	Phelan Wrinkle	Maurine D. Vosburg	Marshall Millican
Coleman	Coleman	W. W. Skelton	Glenn Thomas	Joe D. LeMay	Barbara Freeman	Billie Baker	H. F. Fenton
Collin	McKinney	§§§Wm. J. Roberts	Helen Starnes		¶¶¶	Kenneth L. Maun	Terry G. Box
Collingsworth	Wellington	Zook Thomas	Karen Strickland	Charles Darter	Yvonne Brewer	Ann Wauer	John Rainey
Colorado	Columbus	Lester Cranek	Darlene Hayek	E. Woolery-Price	Juanita Renick	Evelyn Thomas	Jim Broussard

*Anderson County Court at Law: Bascom W. Bentley III. †Angelina County Court at Law: Joe Martin. ‡Armstrong County Court at Law: Ronald Patterson. §Austin County Court at Law: Gladys Oakley. ¶Bell County Courts at Law: No. 1, Ed Johnson; No. 2, E. Wayne Bachus. **Bexar County Courts at Law: No. 1, Anthony J. Ferro; No. 2, Charles A. Gonzalez; No. 3, Ray Wietzel; No. 4, Sara Garrahan; No. 5, Tim Johnson; No. 6, Roy Barrera; No. 7, Antonio Jimenez; No. 8, Michael Peden; No. 9, Bonnie Reed. Bexar County Probate Courts: No. 1, Keith Burris; No. 2, T. Armour Ball. ††Bowie County Juvenile Court: Ben Grigson. ‡‡Brazoria County Courts at Law: No. 1, Anthony Willy; No. 2, A. R. Mason; No. 3, James Blackstock. §§Brazos County Courts at Law: No. 1, Claude D. Davis; No. 2, J. D. Langley. ¶¶Caldwell County Court at Law: E. P. Slater. ***Calhoun County Court at Law: Michael M. Fricke. †††Cameron County Courts at Law: No. 1, Noe Robles; No. 2, Adolfo G. Betancourt. ‡‡‡Cherokee County Court at Law: LeRue Dixon. §§§Collin County Courts at Law: No. 1, Curt Henderson; No. 2, Jerry Lewis; No. 3, John O'Keefe Barry. ¶¶¶Office of County Treasurer in Collin County abolished in election Nov. 5, 1985.

County Officials.—Table No. 1: Judges, Clerks, Attorneys, Treasurers, Tax Assessors, Sheriffs.—(Continued.)

County	County Seat	County Judge	County Clerk	County Attorney	County Treasurer	Assessor-Collector	Sheriff
Comal	New Braunfels	*Fred Clark	Rosie Bosenbury	Bill M. Reimer	Betty J. Engelhardt	Gloria K. Clennan	Walter Fellers
Comanche	Comanche	Bobbye Allen	Betty Conway	James L. Edwards	Billie Ruth Rust	Gay Horton	W. G. Garmon
Concho	Paint Rock	C. J. Dankworth	Margaret T. Taylor	John M. Harrod	Dorothy Kirkpatrick	Ernest L. Skeen	Ernest L. Skeen
Cooke	Gainesville	Jim A. Robertson	Frank Scoggin	Janelle Haverkamp	Janet Johnson	Joyce Zwinggi	John S. Aston
Coryell	Gatesville	Douglas H. Smith	Tribble Shepherd	E. E. Powell Jr.	Vesta Leonard	Joan Blanchard	Gerald Kitchens
Cottle	Paducah	Roger Holley	Geneva Bragg	Roy A. Jones	Atha Prater	Rue Young	Frank Taylor
Crane	Crane	Charles Blue	Mary Grimes	James E. Clack	Lena M. Simmons	Raymond Weatherby	Raymond Weatherby
Crockett	Ozona	A. O. Fields	Debbi Puckett	Thomas Cameron	Jim Dudley	Tommy Stokes	Billy Mills
Crosby	Crosbyton	Jerry Robertson	Floyd McGinnes	John L. Barnhill	Joyce M. Whitehead	Buran House	Lavoice Riley
Culberson	Van Horn	John Conoly	Rosalinda Abreo	Stephen L. Mitchell	Carol Shotwell	Mildred M. Straley	Richard E. Upchurch
Dallam	Dalhart	David D. Field	Betty Steele		Francis E. Payne	Patricia Radford	E. H. Little
Dallas	Dallas	†Lee Jackson	Earl Bullock		Bill Melton	John Childs	Jim Bowles
Dawson	Lamesa	‡Glenn R. White	Billie Bingham	Steve Payson	Barbara Stone	Diane Hogg	Bill Horton
Deaf Smith	Hereford	Tom Simons	David Ruland	Roland Saul	Vesta Mae Nunley	Nell Miller	Joe C. Brown Jr.
Delta	Cooper	Fred Potts	Mary E. Preas	C. M. Ederer	Glynana Stockton	Pauline St. Clair	L. C. Talley
Denton	Denton	§Vic Burgess	Marilyn Robinson	Robert W. Post	Claudia Mulkey	Herbert Barnhart	Randy Kaisner
De Witt	Cuero	Ben E. Prause	Ann Drehr	Steven Hale (pro tem)	Walter Wolf	Margaret L. Mueller	Bobby J. McMahan
Dickens	Dickens	H. L. Young	Helen Arrington	Francisco Ponce	Druline Rape	Jerrie Ballard	Doyle King
Dimmit	Carrizo Springs	R. L. Guerra	Mario Z. Garcia	Patrick Slavin	Arturo S. Juarez	Esther Z. Perez	Ben Murray
Donley	Clarendon	W. R. Christal	Fay Vargas		Frieda Gray	Wilma Lindley	Jimmy Thompson
Duval	San Diego	Frank J. Garcia	Oscar Garcia Jr.	Abelardo Garza	Daniel S. Lopez Jr.	Fernando Caballero	Raul S. Serna Jr.
Eastland	Eastland	Scott Bailey	Joann Johnson		Ruth P. Hart	Nancy Trout	Don Underwood
Ector	Odessa	||Jan Fisher	Lucille Wolz	Gary Garrison	Janita Rippy	Lea Taylor	O. A. Brookshire
Edwards	Rocksprings	Neville G. Smart Jr.	Dorothy R. Hatley	Gary C. Gilmer	Jewell V. Merritt	Teresa Sweeten	Robert Don Bates
Ellis	Waxahachie	*James Blakemore	Faye Washington	Mary Lou Shipley	Frances Phillips	Bettye Meador	Barney Boyd
El Paso	El Paso	††Luther Jones	Hector Enriquez Jr.	Joe Lucas	Doris LeBaum	James S. Hicks	Leo Samaniego
Erath	Stephenville	Bill Hailey	Pauline Chandler	Gale Warren	Marilyn Elem	Jennifer Schlicke	David O. Coffee
Falls	Marlin	Bob Cunningham	Ruth H. Wood	Thomas Sehon	Florence Keahey	Randy Chandler	Larry Pamplin
Fannin	Bonham	Jimmy Doyle	Margaret Gilbert	Dan Meehan	Carol Johnson	C. W. Bond Jr.	Sam Patton
Fayette	La Grange	Dan R. Beck	Irene Pratka	John W. Wied		Gordon F. Baker	Vastine Koopman
Fisher	Roby	Marshall Bennett	Bettie Rivers	Rudy V. Hamric	Ilene Hale	Teddy Kral	Mickey A. Counts
Floyd	Floydada	William D. Hardin	Margaret Collier	Kenneth Bain Jr.	Glenna Mae Orman	Jonelle Fawver	Fred A. Cardinal
Foard	Crowell	Charlie Bell	Jana Payne	Marshall Capps	Jan Bond	Loy Hopkins	Loy Hopkins
Fort Bend	Richmond	‡‡J. E. Stavinoha	Dianne Wilson		Kathy Hynson	Marsha P. Gaines	Gus George
Franklin	Mount Vernon	Albert W. Foster	Wanda Johnson	B. F. Hicks	Jeanette O'Neal	Shirley Johnson	W. W. Foster
Freestone	Fairfield	Joe R. Alderman	Doris T. Welch	Robert W. Gage	Patricia Robinson	Patsy Stroud	James R. Sessions Jr.
Frio	Pearsall	Sid Williams III	Mona Hoyle	J. W. Smith Jr.	Elizabeth Sifuentes	Ysabela Pena	Benny C. Sanders
Gaines	Seminole	Max Townsend	Freida Nichols	Joe K. McGill	Linda Clark	Johnnie Stanley	Ed Welch
Galveston	Galveston	§§Ray Holbrook	Mary J. Christensen	Harvey Bazaman	Richard Kirkpatrick	Charles E. Wilson	Joe Max Taylor
Garza	Post	Giles Dalby	Sonny Gossett	Preston Poole	Voda B. Gradine	Ruth Reno	Jim Pippin
Gillespie	Fredericksburg	Jay Weinheimer	Doris Lange	Gerald W. Schmidt	Jeanie B. Crenwelge	Leola Brodbeck	David Nehr
Glasscock	Garden City	W. E. Bednar	Betty Pate	Rick Hamby	Judy Kingston	Royce Pruit	Royce Pruit
Goliad	Goliad	John R. Barnhill	Gail M. Turley	S. G. Paulsgrove	LaNell Oehlke	Neva Thigpen	J. K. McMahan
Gonzales	Gonzales	H. H. Vollentine	Sonny Sievers	R. B. Scheske	Kaye Brzozowski	Norma J. DuBose	Curtis Parsley
Gray	Pampa	Carl Kennedy	Wanda Carter	R. D. McPherson	Scott B. Hahn	Margie Gray	R. H. Jordan

*Comal County Court at Law: Ron Prichard. †Dallas County Courts at Law: No. 1, Michael J. O'Neill; No. 2, Michael J. O'Neill; No. 2, Glenn R. Snyder; No. 3, Anne Packer; No. 4, Robert Day; No. 5, Bob White. County Criminal Courts: No. 1, John J. Orvis; No. 2, John J. Orvis; No. 3, Michael E. Schwille; No. 4, F. Harold Entz; No. 5, Keith T. Dean; No. 6, Berland Brashear; No. 7, John P. McCall; No. 8, John C. Hendrik; No. 9, George B. Shepherd Jr.; No. 10, Randall Isenberg. County Probate Courts: No. 1, Nikki De Shazo; No. 2, Robert E. Price; No. 3, Bill Bedard. County Criminal Courts of Appeal: Kenneth Vaughan; No. 2, Tom Fuller. ‡Dawson County Domestic Relations Court: Denise P. Dyess. §Denton County Courts at Law: No. 1, Wesley Stewart; No. 2, Lon Darley; No. 3, Hollis Godfrey. ||Ector County Courts at Law: No. 1, Carol Gregg; No. 2, George Svanas. **Ellis County Court at Law: Roy A. Scoggins Jr. ††El Paso County Courts at Law: No. 1, Robert J. Galvan; No. 2, John L. Fashing; No. 3, Jack Ferguson; No. 4, D. Clark Hughes; No. 5, Herbert Cooper. ‡‡Fort Bend County Court at Law: No. 1, Thomas R. Culver III; No. 2, Walter McMeans. §§Galveston County Courts at Law: No. 1, John Thoma; No. 2, Ronald L. Wilson. County Probate Court: Jerome Jones.

County Officials.—Table No. 1: Judges, Clerks, Attorneys, Treasurers, Tax Assessors, Sheriffs.—(Continued.)

County	County Seat	County Judge	County Clerk	County Attorney	County Treasurer	Assessor-Collector	Sheriff
Grayson	Sherman	*Horace Groff	Pat Norman	Steve Davidchik	Virginia Hughes	John Ramsey	L. E. Jack Driscoll
Gregg	Longview	†Henry Atkinson Jr.	Mollie Barber	Joe S. Falco Jr.	June Knighten	Bobby Crawford	Bobby Weaver
Grimes	Anderson	Lovett Boggess	Trinston Harris	Elizabeth C. Jandt	Alvina B. Schroeder	Claude Jolly Jr.	Bill Foster
Guadalupe	Seguin	‡Jas. E. Sagebiel	Lizzie M. Lorenz		Larry Jones	Betty Boyd	Melvin L. Harborth
Hale	Plainview	Bill Hollars	Mildred Tucker		Harold N. Martin	Christine Vinson	Charles Tue
Hall	Memphis	James E. Chappell	Phyllis Dunn	John E. Chamberlain	Sandra Braddock	Sherri Smith	T. W. Tippett
Hamilton	Hamilton	Garrett Chappell	Virginia Lovell	Thos. E. White	Karen S. Tyson	Alvin Kaultzsch	Cecil Proctor
Hansford	Spearman	Roy L. McClellan	Amelia C. Johnson	John L. Hutchison	Norma Jean Mackie	Helen Dry	R. L. McFarlin
Hardeman	Quanah	Kenneth McNabb	Loraine White	Stanley Wobbn	Lucille Jobe	Pauline Moore	Chester L. Ingram
Hardin	Kountze	Milton McKinney	Geraldine Collins	Bevil Wright	Henry E. Donelson Jr.	J. McCreight	H. R. Holzapfel
Harris	Houston	§Jon Lindsay	Anita Rodeheaver	Mike Driscoll	Nikki R. Van Hightower	Carl S. Smith	Johnny Klevenhagen
Harrison	Marshall	¶Max A. Sandlin Jr.	Glenn Link		Betty C. Anderson	Marie F. Noland	Bill Oldham
Hartley	Channing	Joe N. Thomas	Grady Belew	Homer A. Davis	Betty Edwards	J. E. Williams Jr.	J. E. Williams Jr.
Haskell	Haskell	B. O. Roberson	Woodrow Frazier	Art Williams	Willie Faye Tidrow	Bobbye Collins	Johnny Mills
Hays	San Marcos	**G. Don Rains	Ronnie Dannelley		Dorothy P. Sims	Ruth Clayton	Alfard Hohman
Hemphill	Canadian	Bob W. Gober	Mrs. G. Vandiver	Charles L. Kessie	Lorene Burton	Gladene Woodside	Billy V. Bowen
Henderson	Athens	††Winston Reagan	Joe Dan Fowler	John Owens	Carolyn Sorrell	Betty Smith	Charlie Fields Jr.
Hidalgo	Edinburg	‡‡J. Edgar Ruiz	William R. Leo		Arturo Soliz	Ciro Trevino	Brig Marmolejo
Hill	Hillsboro	Charles R. Herd	Ruth Pelham	O. T. Beaty	Jewel Burton	Thomas J. Davis	Brent Burton
Hockley	Leveland	Don Avery	Raymond O. Dennis	Gary Goff	Jo Beth Hittson	C. Clevenger	Leroy Schulle
Hood	Granbury	Milton Meyer	Anianette Ables	John Hughes	Buster Damron	Ann Smith	Edwin Tomlinson
Hopkins	Sulphur Springs	Joe R. Pogue	Mary Attlesey	John F. Perry	Betty Green	Jo Ruth Hodge	Mark Bassham
Houston	Crockett	§§Charles English	Dorothy English	Chester V. Hines	Faye Hiroms	Odessa Brown	Claudie Kendrick
Howard	Big Spring	Milton L. Kirby	Margaret Ray	Timothy D. Yeats	Bonnie Franklin	Dorothy W. Moore	A. N. Standard
Hudspeth	Sierra Blanca	Samuel L. Bray	Patricia Bramblett	Roger L. Moore	Pilar R. West	Stella C. Kelcy	Richard I. Love
Hunt	Greenville	¶¶Mike Farris	Jimmy P. Hamilton	Russell Brooks	Allie E. Pearce	Joyce Barrow	Bobby G. Young
Hutchinson	Stinnett	Tom Wicker	Janice Knowles	Wm. D. Smith	Kathy Sargent	Mary L. Henderson	Lon Blackmon
Irion	Mertzon	J. D. Westfall	Jane Ethridge	Tom Davidson	Betty Denis	Joyce Gray	Delmon West
Jack	Jacksboro	Bobbie A. Owen	Patsy Ramzy	M. G. Mask	Ruby Abernathie	Betty Cleveland	W. B. Mathis
Jackson	Edna	L. T. Thedford	Martha Knapp		Toni Wyer	La Verne Ellison	J. H. Reynolds
Jasper	Jasper	Richard H. West	Evelyn Stott	Robert M. Jackson	Brenda Vaughn	Robert C. Pace Jr.	Aubrey E. Cole
Jeff Davis	Fort Davis	Ann Scudday	Peggy Robertson		Fern Fisher	Harvey Adams	Harvey Adams
Jefferson	Beaumont	***R. P. LeBlanc Jr.	Lolita Ramos		Nick Palmarozzi Jr.	Nick Lampson	R. E. Culbertson
Jim Hogg	Hebbronville	H. S. Ramirez	Lilla Pena	E. A. Garza	Cruz G. Ramirez	Margarita R. Vera	Gilberto Ybanez
Jim Wells	Alice	T. L. Harville	Arnoldo Gonzalez	J. Sanchez-Vera	Adan Valadez Jr.	A. Lozano Jr.	Oscar Lopez
Johnson	Cleburne	†††Wayne Bridewell	Robby G. Goodnight	Dale Hanna	D'Will Jones	W. E. Carroll	Eddy Boggs
Jones	Anson	Roy Thorn	Buryl Rye	Eddie L. Meaders	Irene Hudson	M. Lucille Higgs	Mike Middleton
Karnes	Karnes City	Kenneth Pearce	Elizabeth Swize	J. W. Berry	Charlene Blaschke	Ruth Lindsey	R. R. Mutz
Kaufman	Kaufman	Maxine Dunn	Jimmy Graham		Linda Spencer	Donna Sprague	Robert Harris
Kendall	Boerne	Garland A. Perry	Darlene Herrin	Frank Y. Hill Jr.	Joyce F. George	Betty J. Asher	Lee H. D'Spain Jr.
Kenedy	Sarita	J. A. Garcia Jr.	Barbara B. Turcotte	Leo Villarreal	John W. Turcotte	L. G. Weiss	Jas. M. Chandler Jr.
Kent	Jayton	Garth Gregory	Cornella Cheyne	Howard Freemyer	Laverna Harrison	Purvis SoRelle	Purvis SoRelle
Kerr	Kerrville	‡‡‡Danny R. Edwards	Patricia Dye	Gary E. Kersey	Dorothy Hillburn	Doris L. Smith	C. A. Greeson
Kimble	Junction	Wilbur R. Dunk	Louise P. Oliver	Callan Graham	Sue Gibbs	Pat Davis	Pat Davis
King	Guthrie	Hermon Oliver	Evelyn Sursa		Kay Criswell	Jim R. Waller	Jim R. Waller

*Grayson County Courts at Law: No. 1, Richard Pennell; No. 2, Lloyd W. Perkins. †Gregg County Court at Law: John Earl Sharp. ‡Guadalupe County Court at Law: Fred J. Moore. §Harris County Courts at Law: No. 1, Ed Landry; No. 2, Tom Sullivan; No. 3, Jon Allen Hughes; No. 4, Charles Coussons. County Criminal Courts at Law: No. 1, Bill Ragen; No. 2, Don J Hendrix; No. 3, Jimmie Duncan; No. 4, Jack Treadway; No. 5, Neil McKay; No. 6, Bob Musslewhite; No. 7, Shelly P. Hancock; No. 8, Neel Richardson; No. 9, Alfred G. Leal; No. 10, Sherman A. Ross; No. 11, Jack Pickren; No. 12, Joe Terracina; No. 13, Angel Fraga. Probate Courts: No. 1, William Bear; No. 2, Pat Gregory; No. 3, Jim Scanlan. ¶Harrison County Court at Law: J. Ray Kirkpatrick. **Hays County Court at Law: Howard S. Warner II. ††Henderson County Court at Law: Matt Livingston. ‡‡Hidalgo County Courts at Law: No. 1, Juan Partida; No. 2, Jaime Garza; No. 3, Richard H. Garcia. §§Houston County Court at Law: Lynn E. Markham. ¶¶Hunt County Court at Law: Joe Leonard. ***Jefferson County Courts at Law: No. 1, Alfred S. Gerson; No. 3, Harold Plessala; No. 3, Donald J. Floyd. †††Johnson County Court at Law: Tommy Altaras. ‡‡‡Kerr County Court at Law: William L. Baskette Jr.

County Officials.—Table No. 1: Judges, Clerks, Attorneys, Treasurers, Tax Assessors, Sheriffs.—(Continued.)

County	County Seat	County Judge	County Clerk	County Attorney	County Treasurer	Assessor-Collector	Sheriff
Kinney	Brackettville	T. Seargeant	Dolores Raney	Tully Shahan	C. De La Rosa	Norman H. Hooten	Norman H. Hooten
Kleberg	Kingsville	*W. C. McDaniel	Sam D. Deanda	W. A. Ewert Jr.	Sopha N. Fitch	Juanita R. Lara	J. S. Scarborough III
Knox	Benjamin	David N. Perdue	Gloria L. West	B. D. Burnett	Evelyn Balis	Oscar Mangis	Morris E. Nix
Lamar	Paris	Robert A. Burns	Linda Sudduth	Tom D. Wells III	Latricia Miller	Theda Cotton	James W. Parker
Lamb	Littlefield	Wayne Whiteaker	Bill Johnson	C. R. Wilkinson	Lucy M. Moreland	Linda Charlton	Elson D. McNeese
Lampasas	Lampasas	Norris Monroe	Connie Hartmann	Larry W. Allison	Leona Hurst	Glenda Henderson	Gordon Morris
La Salle	Cotulla	L. Martinez Jr.	Nora M. Tyler	Edward Hargrove	Jimmy P. Patterson	Thelma Benavidez	Darwin D. Avant
Lavaca	Hallettsville	W. D. Roznovsky	Henry J. Sitka	James W. Carr	T. M. Grahmann	Mary Lee Supak	Robert E. Wurm
Lee	Giddings	E. W. Kraus	Carol Dismukes	Steven W. Keng	Rose M. Fritsche	Arlene D. Kasper	Joe G. Goodson
Leon	Centerville	Robert L. Gresham	Fonsein Gresham	Gary J. Taylor	Wm. D. Lemons	Louise Wilson	Royce G. Wilson
Liberty	Liberty	†Dempsie Henley	Wanda Barker	A. J. Hartel III	Winn Skidmore	Laverne Zbranek	E. W. Applebe
Limestone	Groesbeck	Ray Seely	Sue Lown	Rex Leach	Imogene Arney	Barbara Rader	Dennis J. Walker
Lipscomb	Lipscomb	Willis V. Smith	Coeta Sperry	Dana A. Ehrlich	Pat Wyatt	Mary W. Gunn	C. J. Babitzke
Live Oak	George West	Jim Huff	Mildred James	W. L. Hardwick	LaVona Stainthorpe	Larry R. Busby	Larry R. Busby
Llano	Llano	W. R. Miller	H. A. Raesener	L. T. DesChamps	LaVerne Miller	Margie Jung	Gale Ligon
Loving	Mentone	Donald C. Creager	Juanita Busby	Michael L. Fostel	Faye Busby	Elgin R. Jones	Elgin R. Jones
Lubbock	Lubbock	†Rodrick L. Shaw	Ann Davidson		Connie Nicholson	Frank A. Stuart	D. L. Keesee
Lynn	Tahoka	J. F. Brandon	C. W. Roberts	J. B. Wright	Cynthia Bryan	George D. McCracken	Clifford Laws
McCulloch	Brady	William M. Day	Rose M. Luttrell	Robert G. Bond	Norma G. Holloway	F. V. Waddill Jr.	Bill Strickland
McLennan	Waco	§Raymond Matkin	Frank Denny		Odessa Wells	Gene Prickette	Jack Harwell
McMullen	Tilden	Claude Franklin Jr.	William K. Hodgin	John L. Oxley	Eris L. White	Mary K. Edwards	Eddie M. Reeves
Madison	Madisonville	Jimmy Fite	Joyce M. Coleman	Tony Hileman	Judy Weathers	Guslyn Hairston	Ed Fannin
Marion	Jefferson	Lola Whelan	Clairece Ford	James L. McGilvray	Peggy McLendon	Sarah Wirt	Walter Thomas
Martin	Stanton	Bob Deavenport	Virginia James	Harold R. Schmidt	H. D. Howard	Leona Louder	Dan Saunders
Mason	Mason	Fritz E. Landers	Beatrice Langehennig		Jane Hoerster	Don K. Grote	Don K. Grote
Matagorda	Bay City	Burt O'Connell	Sarah Vaughn	John C. Dickerson III	Suzanne Kucera	W. B. Wiginton	S. L. Hurta
Maverick	Eagle Pass	Rudolph Bowles Jr.	E. Sumpter	Rolando Menchaca	Manuel Reyes Jr.	Esteban Luna	Tom Bowles
Medina	Hondo	†Donald E. Campsey	Anna Van DeWalle	Hunter Schuehle	Rita L. Moos	Loraine Neuman	Alvin Santleben
Menard	Menard	Otis H. Lyckman	Neva Schmidt	Ben K. Neel	Mickey Crowell	Madelon Highsmith	Floyd Rendon
Midland	Midland	**Wm. B. Anders	Rosenelle Cherry	Mark Dettman	Dee Thompson	Frances Shuffield	Gary Painter
Milam	Cameron	Gene F. Blake	Willie Mae Wieser	Charles E. Lance	Charlie J. Maddox	Porter E. Young Jr.	Leroy Broadus
Mills	Goldthwaite	T. W. Johnson	Walter A. Bryant	D. Lappe (pro tem)	Gloria Marler	Mack Casbeer	Mack Casbeer
Mitchell	Colorado City	Bill F. Carter	Joan Beach	R. L. McKinney	Ann Hallmark	C. C. Burt	Wendell Bryant
Montague	Montague	Jack Winn	Christine Cook	Brian E. Powers	James M. Johnson	Christine Patterson	C. R. Whatley
Montgomery	Conroe	††Alvin L. Stahl	Roy Harris	D. C. Dozier	Martha Gustavsen	John P. Neece Jr.	Joe Corley
Moore	Dumas	‡Jack D. Powell	Rhonnie Mayer	R. A. Ratliff	Phyllis Holmes	Billie Donnell	M. R. Weaver
Morris	Daingerfield	Ronald M. Cowan	Doris McNatt	Charles C. Bailey	Peggy Campbell	Jerry L. Chambliss	Joe E. Skipper
Motley	Matador	Bill J. Whitaker	Lucretia Campbell	Howard Traweek	Joe E. Campbell	Alton Marshall	Alton Marshall
Nacogdoches	Nacogdoches	§§Bob Dunn	Hope Skipper	Bryan Davis	Kay Watkins	Patsy Cates	Joe Evans
Navarro	Corsicana	Gary Bennett	James F. Doolen		E. L. Parrish	Freddy L. Nutt	Jim Hodge
Newton	Newton	Lee Roy Fillyaw	Melba Canty	Edward J. Tracy	Ruth Dickerson	Geraldine A. Kerr	Robert C. Woods
Nolan	Sweetwater	¶¶Terry Julian	Judy Brazelton	Carl M. Anderson	Gayle Biggerstaff	Betty Bryant	Jim Blackley
Nueces	Corpus Christi	***Robert H. Barnes	Marion Uehlinger	Carlos Valdez	Tom Hunt	Richard D. Magee	James T. Hickey
Ochiltree	Perryton	Howard E. Stone	Jane Pletcher	Bruce Roberson	Ginger Hays	Ruby Lee Malaney	Joe Hataway
Oldham	Vega	John P. Gliter	Martha Thompson	R. W. Brainerd	Modean Erwin	Carolyn Slutz	David Medlin
Orange	Orange	†††James D. Stringer	Molly Theriot	Steve Howard	Shirley Lewallen	L. Hryhorchuk	James A. Wade
Palo Pinto	Palo Pinto	Wm. B. Dennison	Bobbie Smith	Bobby Joe Mann	Tanya Fallin	John R. Winters	John L. Turpin
Panola	Carthage	‡‡‡Mike Parker	Roy Cadenhead Jr.	Morris Samford Jr.	Sue Parker	Waymon E. Blair	Tommy J. Harris

*Kleberg County Court at Law: Martin J. Chiuminatto Jr. †Liberty County Court at Law: L. J. Krueger. ‡Lubbock County Courts at Law: No. 1, William C. Dodson; No. 2, Bradley S. Underwood. §McLennan County Courts at Law: No. 1, David L. Hodges; No. 2, Mike Gassaway. †Medina County Court at Law: Joe E. Briscoe. **Midland County Courts at Law: No. 1, Willie B. DuBose; No. 2, James Fitz-Gerald III. ††Montgomery County Courts at Law: No. 1, Suzanne Stovall; No. 2, Jerry Winfree; No. 3, Mason Martin. ‡‡Moore County Court at Law: David G. Lewis. §§Nacogdoches County Court at Law: Jack Yarbrough. ¶¶Nolan County Court at Law: Robert M. Faver. ***Nueces County Courts at Law: No. 1, Robert J. Vargas; No. 2, Hector DePena Jr.; No. 3, Hilda Tagle; No. 4, James E. Klager. †††Orange County Court at Law: Michael W. Shuff. ‡‡‡Panola County Court at Law:

County Officials.—Table No. 1: Judges, Clerks, Attorneys, Treasurers, Tax Assessors, Sheriffs.—(Continued.)

County	County Seat	County Judge	County Clerk	County Attorney	County Treasurer	Assessor-Collector	Sheriff
Parker	Weatherford	*Harris Worcester	Carrie Reed	William Cantrell	Geneva Carter	Judy Spradlin	Billy R. Cain
Parmer	Farwell	Porter Roberts	Bonnie Warren	Charles Aycock	Anne Norton	Hugh Moseley	M. C. Morgan Jr.
Pecos	Fort Stockton	Charles Warnock	Paul W. Yeager	W. C. McDonald Jr.	Garnett McCallister	E. F. Triplett	Bruce Wilson
Polk	Livingston	†Wayne R. Baker	Martha Johnson	Philip Cline	Cheryl Henry	Robert C. Willis	Ted L. Everitt
Potter	Amarillo	‡E. L. Demerson	Sue Daniel	Bill Baumann	Lawrence Youngblood	Maxine Pickett	Jimmy D. Boydston
Presidio	Marfa	Bobby R. Martinez	Ramona Lara		Mario S. Rivera	R. D. Thompson	R. D. Thompson
Rains	Emory	B. D. Chism	Mary Sheppard	L. M. Braziel	Teresa Northcutt	Andrew Roberts	Andrew Roberts
Randall	Canyon	§Charles M. Purcell	Le Roy Hutton		Judy Monk	Carol Autry	Harold D. Hooks
Reagan	Big Lake	Frank Sandel	Hazel S. Carr	Jack P. Schulze	Nancy Ratliff	Christine Gardner	Paul Weatherby
Real	Leakey	J. M. Sanderlin	Rosemary Clark	John A. Daniel	Kathy Brooks	Pearl Brice	James Storey
Red River	Clarksville	L. D. Williamson	Mary Hausler	Thos. H. Fowler	Donna Townes	J. Benningfield	Bob Storey
Reeves	Pecos	¶W. O. Pigman	Catherine Ashley	Scott Johnson	Nina Abila	Jimmie C. Preslar	Raul Florez
Refugio	Refugio	Ginger D. Fagan	Janelle Morgan	Robt. P. McGuill	Betty Greebon	Margie Gregorcyk	Jim Hodges
Roberts	Miami	J. T. Webb	Jackie M. Jackson		Sarah E. Gill	Carol Billingsley	Lando Brown
Robertson	Franklin	Wesley E. Peyton	Mary B. Reagan	Jim McCullough	Virginia Turner	Charlene Bush	Lee S. Hurley
Rockwall	Rockwall	William B. Lofland	Paulette Burks		Richard S. Huff	Doris H. Willess	John McWhorter
Runnels	Ballinger	M. B. Murchison	Linda Bruchmiller	Kendal Granzin	Nora Halfmann	Va Rue McWilliams	Bill Baird
Rusk	Henderson	**Sandra Hodges	Helen Sillick	W. L. Ferguson	Virgil O. Cole	Tommy Haskins Jr.	M. J. Strong
Sabine	Hemphill	Royce C. Smith	Nadine Gary	H. W. Fortson III	Ollie Faye Sparks	Diane Husband	Blan Greer
San Augustine	San Augustine	Jack B. Nichols	Geraldine Smith	Wesley E. Hoyt	Carol W. Vaughn	Mary Lou Alford	N. L. Tindall
San Jacinto	Coldspring	Joe L. McMurrey	Lois Cooksey	Robt. H. Trapp	Charlene Everitt	Ruth G. Morrison	Robert E. Brumley
San Patricio	Sinton	J. M. Edmondson Jr.	Dottie Maley	David Aken	J. J. McWhorter	Davis Vickers	Wayne Hift
San Saba	San Saba	Thomas Bowden	Nila Ruth Barker	David M. Williams	Mada Lee Smith	Billy C. Williams	Billy C. Williams
Schleicher	Eldorado	Johnny F. Griffin	Helen Blakeway	T. Giovannitti	A. G. McCormack	Dorothy M. Evans	Orval Edmiston
Scurry	Snyder	Bobby Goodwin	Beverly Ainsworth	Michael S. Line	Billy W. Thompson	Rona Bley	Keith T. Collier
Shackelford	Albany	Marie Smith	Bobbie L. Cox		Joy Grun	Ben Jack Riley	Ben Jack Riley
Shelby	Center	H. G. Jackson	Peaches Conway	Gary W. Rholes	LaMerle Davis	Harlon Eakin	Paul Ross
Sherman	Stratford	W. S. Frizzell Jr.	Mary Lou Albert	Jack Q. Barton	Linda R. Keener	Zelda Pickens	Tom Wade
Smith	Tyler	††Larry Craig	Lovella Williams	Tim Rudolph	Joyce W. Smith	Harris Oswalt	J. B. Smith
Somervell	Glen Rose	George R. Crump	Mary Morris		Wyneil Whitt	Janet Boren	Frank J. Laramore
Starr	Rio Grande City	‡‡J. M. Martinez Jr.	Juan J. Mills	Heriberto Silva	Aurelio A. Saenz	Maria O. Saenz	Eugenio Falcon
Stephens	Breckenridge	Miller Tuttle	Helen Haddock	Jimmy L. Browning	Nancy Clary	Allena Dover	James N. Cain
Sterling	Sterling City	Robert L. Browne	Diane A. Haar	Drew T. Durham	Beth Kilpatrick	Lloyd J. Brown	Lloyd J. Brown
Stonewall	Aspermont	Ed Wolsch	Betty L. Smith	Isaac Castro	Linda Messick	Joyce Y. McNutt	Zeb Rutherford
Sutton	Sonora	Carla Fields	Erma Lee Turner	David W. Wallace	Joyce H. Chalk	Ann Hill	W. W. Webster
Swisher	Tulia	Jay V. Johnson	Pat Wesley	Donald L. Bookout	Lanelle Dovel	Shirley Whitehead	John Gayler
Tarrant	Fort Worth	§§Roy English	Suzanne Henderson		‡‡‡	June Garrison	Donald Carpenter
Taylor	Abilene	¶¶J. A. Holloway	Janica Lyons		Anna Moore	Lavena Cheek	John Middleton
Terrell	Sanderson	Charles Staveley	Patty Phillips	Marsha Monroe	Ginette Litton	Dalton Hogg	Dalton Hogg
Terry	Brownfield	Herbert Chesshir	Ann Willis	G. Dwayne Pruitt	Bobbie Montgomery	Redelle Davis	Ralph Murry
Throckmorton	Throckmorton	Patricia Harrington	Cathey Mitchell	Clyde Boose	Brenda Rankin	Greg Dunlap	Greg Dunlap
Titus	Mount Pleasant	A. L. Flanagan	Eugenia Roach	Tim Taylor	Cynthia Agan	June Roach	John A. Moss
Tom Green	San Angelo	***Tom C. Massey	Marie Russell	William R. Moore	Billie J. McDaniel	Evelyn A. Vordick	Ernest Haynes
Travis	Austin	†††Bill Aleshire	Dana DeBeauvoir	Ken Oden	Delores Ortega-Carter	Cecelia Burke	Doyne Bailey
Trinity	Groveton	Jimmie Thornton	Elaine Lockhart	Joe W. Bell II	Francis Worsham	Clara Hathorn	Kenneth Moore
Tyler	Woodville	Allen Sturrock	Donece Gregory		Jean Phillips	Barbara Tolbert	Leon Fowler
Upshur	Gilmer	Everett Dean	Rex A. Shaw		Vernon Vick	M. L. Smith	R. D. Jewkes

*Parker County Court at Law: Fred Barker. †Polk County Court at Law: Stephen Phillips. ‡Potter County Courts at Law: No. 1, Morris L. Overstreet; No. 2, Richard Dambold. §Randall County Court at Law: Darrell Carey. ¶Reeves County Court at Law: Lee S. Green. **Rusk County Court at Law: Darrell Hyatt. ††Smith County Courts at Law: No. 1, Milton G. Mell; No. 2, Cynthia Kent. ‡‡Starr County Court at Law: Alex W. Gabert. §§Tarrant County Courts at Law: No. 1, Bill Brigham; No. 2, Doyle Willis Jr. County Criminal Courts at Law: No. 1, Frank Coffey; No. 2, George McManus; No. 3, Billy Mills; No. 4, Pete Perez; No. 5, Jake Cook; No. 6, Rufus Adcock. Probate Courts: Robert M. Burnett and Patrick Ferchill. ¶¶Taylor County Court at Law: John Saringer. ***Tom Green County Court at Law: R. L. Blann. †††Travis County Courts at Law: No. 1, Leslie Taylor; No. 2, Steve Russell; No. 3, Michael J. Schless; No. 4, Guy Herman. ‡‡‡Office of County Treasurer in Tarrant County abolished in election April 2, 1983.

County Officials.—Table No. 1: Judges, Clerks, Attorneys, Treasurers, Tax Assessors, Sheriffs.—(Continued.)

County	County Seat	County Judge	County Clerk	County Attorney	County Treasurer	Assessor-Collector	Sheriff
Upton	Rankin	Peggy Garner	Phyllis Stephens	R. E. Motsenbocker	Doris L. Speed	Glenn Willeford	Glenn Willeford
Uvalde	Uvalde	Wm. R. Mitchell	Eileen Carlisle	David R. White Jr.	Jo S. Noble	Helen Angermiller	Kenneth Kelley
Val Verde	Del Rio	*Sergio Gonzalez Jr.	Maria E. Cardenas	Enrique Fernandez	Clifford Cavender	Wayne H. Hyde	James R. Koog
Van Zandt	Canton	Lester Slaton	Elizabeth Everitt	Tommy Wallace	Shirley Morgan	J. D. Floyd	Travis Shafer
Victoria	Victoria	†Norman D. Jones	Val D. Huvar		Helen R. Walker	Bessie L. Lassmann	Dalton G. Meyer
Walker	Huntsville	Frank J. Robinson	James D. Patton	L. C. Eakin Jr.	Barbara R. McGilberry	Oscar L. Thorne	Darrell White
Waller	Hempstead	§A. M. McCaig	Elva D. Mathis	Randy Cleveland	Elsie C. Stewart	Chrystal Weaver	Ronnie L. Sitton
Ward	Monahans	Richard Sitz	Pat V. Finley	James Reese Jones	Audrey Harris	Edith Porter	D. Hall
Washington	Brenham	Gus F. Mutscher	Gertrude Lehrmann	Richard G. Morales	Rosa Lee Fuchs	Vennie Herzog	Billy W. Rosenbaum
Webb	Laredo	¶Andres Ramos Jr.	Henry Flores		Alberto Martinez	Ezequiel Laurel	Mario Santos Jr.
Wharton	Wharton	I. J. Irvin Jr.	Delfin Marek	Scott Cline	Gus Wessels Jr.	Frank H. Konvicka	R. R. Machala
Wheeler	Wheeler	Wendell Morgan	Margaret Dorman	M. Kent Sims	Jerrie Moore	Jerry D. Hefley	Lonnie Miller
Wichita	Wichita Falls	**Nick Gipson	Vernon Cannon		Mary Lynn Welborn	Miles Graham	Thomas J. Callahan
Wilbarger	Vernon	Bob Arnold	Frances McGee	Kelly Wright	Janice King	JoAnn Bourland	Gerald King
Willacy	Raymondville	Bill Rapp	Lalo Gomez	Lee Price Fernon	Ofelia O. Loya	Emma Ross	Larry G. Spence
Williamson	Georgetown	††Don Wilson	James N. Boydston	Billy R. Stubblefield	Irvin Leschber	Dorothy E. Jones	Jim Boutwell
Wilson	Floresville	W. D. Cox	Richard Bolf	Howard C. Berger	Peggy Jaeggli	Anna D. Gonzales	M. H. Baumann
Winkler	Kermit	Frances Clark	Ruth Godwin	S. Tallaferro	John W. Stout	Patti Franks	Wm. H. Sage
Wise	Decatur	‡‡Willard E. Howell	La Verne Forman	Jean Bishop	Emma Ray	J. C. Stockton	Leroy Burch
Wood	Quitman	Lee E. Williams	Martha R. Bridges		Jane Herring	Fred Morrow	Frank White
Yoakum	Plains	Dallas Brewer	Ruby Bruton		Toni Jones	Wanda Smith	Jimmie Rice
Young	Graham	Jack Q. Neal	LaFonda Taack	Stanley D. Curbo	Wanda Primrose	Jean Hester	Ed Shields
Zapata	Zapata	Angel A. Flores	Arnoldo Flores	A. A. Figueroa Jr.	Jose R. Villarreal	Jaime A. Gonzalez	G. Villarreal
Zavala	Crystal City	Ron Carr	Teresa P. Flores	Pablo Avila	Susie Perez	Martha P. Cruz	Alberto Sanchez

*Val Verde County Court at Law: James M. Simmonds. †Victoria County Courts at Law: No. 1, Jerry J. Garrett; No. 2, Juan Velasquez III. ‡Walker County Court at Law: Ann P. Baker. §Waller County Court at Law: Karl N. Micklitz. ¶Webb County Court at Law: Raul Vasquez. **Wichita County Courts at Law: No. 1, Jim Hogan; No. 2, Tom Bacus. ††Williamson County Court at Law: Tim G. Maresh. ‡‡Wise County Court at Law: Melton D. Cude.

TEXAS COUNTY AND DISTRICT OFFICIALS—TABLE NO.

District Judges, District Clerks, District Attorneys and County Commissioners. See also Table 1.

County	Dist.	District Judge	District Clerk	District Attorney	Comm. Precinct 1	Comm. Precinct 2	Comm. Precinct 3	Comm. Precinct 4
Anderson	3	Wayne Lawrence	Lulu F. Nation	Richard Handorf	Truman Starr	R. O. Browne Sr.	T. L. Beard	J. T. Davis
	87	Sam B. Bournias						
	349	Melvin D. Whitaker						
Andrews	109	James H. Clack	Imogene Tate	James L. Rex	Bill Chesney	W. G. Hathcock	J. W. Moxley	Willard Snow
	159	David Walker						
Angelina	217	David V. Wilson	Jimmie F. Robinson	Gerald Goodwin	Joe Berry	I. D. Henderson Jr.	Jim Nerren	Robert Colwell
Aransas	36	Ronald M. Yeager	Agnes A. Harden	Thos. L. Bridges	Owen H. Booher	Ray Longino	Pete Sanders	Mike Womack
	156	W. Rachel Little John						
	343	A. T. Rodriquez						
Archer	97	Frank J. Douthitt	Jane Adams	Jack McGaughey	Evon Carter	James Berend	Ben Buerger	Duward W. Stone
Armstrong	47	David L. Gleason	Kathy Byrd	Danny Hill	Leo Oles	Tom Adams	Bill Heisler	C. M. Bryant
Atascosa	81	Olin B. Strauss	Sally Starr	Alger H. Kendall	Victor Holguin	E. Mikolajczyk	Freddie Ogden	D. D. Hoover
	218	R. L. Eschenburg II						
Austin	155	Oliver S. Kitzman	Lorri Coody	Charles D. Houston	J. E. Grawunder	Hilbert L. Galle	Everett Tomlinson	L. L. Melnar
Bailey	287	Jack D. Young	Nelda Merriott	Johnny Ackinson	R. L. Scott	Don Seales	Joey R. Kindle	Rudolph Moraw
Bandera	216	Robert R. Barton	Vera King	E. Bruce Curry	Jim Russell	Dan C. Alanis III	A. A. Reed	N. P. Thompson
Bastrop	21	John L. Placke	Peggy Wallick	Chas. D. Penick	Tom Adams	Robert Seidel	Jerry Alexander	Jim Mogonye
	335	Harold R. Towslee						
Baylor	50	David W. Hajek	Doris Swain	Tom Schrandt	G. C. Laney Jr.	James Smajstrla	Jim Richardson	Boyd F. Mayers
Bee	36	Ronald M. Yeager	Margie P. Carter	C. F. Moore	Adam V. Gonzales	Susan Stasny	Santiago Martinez	Henry C. Lohse
	156	W. Rachel Little John						
	343	A. T. Rodriquez						
Bell	27	C. W. Duncan Jr.	Daffy Carpenter	Arthur Eads Jr.	Clifford D. Jones	Robert Shoemaker	Roy Goad	John Oliver
	146	Wm. C. Black						
	169	Stanton B. Pemberton						
	264	Jack W. Prescott						
Bexar	37	John Cornyn III	David J. Garcia	Fred G. Rodriguez	John A. Longoria	Paul Elizondo	Walter Bielstein	Bob Lee
	45	Carol R. Haberman						
	57	John G. Yates						
	73	James C. Onion						
	131	Rose Spector						
	144	Susan Reed						
	150	Fred Biery						

Bexar County Dist. Judges (Con'd.):

Dist.	District Judge
166	Peter Michael Curry
175	P. G. Chavarria Jr.
186	James E. Barlow
187	Patrick Priest
224	Carolyn Spears
225	Emilio M. Garza
226	M. Ted Butler
227	Mike M. Machado
285	David Peeples
288	Raul Rivera
289	Tom Rickhoff
290	David A. Berchelmann

County	Dist.	District Judge	District Clerk	District Attorney	Comm. Precinct 1	Comm. Precinct 2	Comm. Precinct 3	Comm. Precinct 4
Blanco	33	Clayton E. Evans	Dorothy Uecker	Sam Oatman	Charles Jones	Robert Riddell	E. Bergman	Alton Koch
	132	Gene L. Dulaney	Dorothy Browne	Ernie Armstrong	Frank Currey	Larry D. Smith	Vernon Wolf	Hurston Lemons Jr.
	220	James E. Morgan	Diane Wellborn	Andy J. McMullen	Glen Thompson	H. J. Morrison Jr.	Calvin Rueter	J. Paul Howard
Borden	5	Jack E. Carter	Billy Fox	John F. Miller Jr.	Dexter Henry	L. B. Grimes	Dale Barrett	Paul Fannin
Bosque	102	Leon F. Pesek						
Bowie	202	Guy E. Jones						
Brazoria	23	Neil Caldwell	Frances G. Bennett	Jim Mapel	Ronnie Broaddus	G. L. Rouse	Billy J. Plaster	John P. Gayle Jr.
	149	John Rainey						
	239	J. R. Gayle III						
	300	Ogden Bass						
Brazos	85	W. T. McDonald Jr.	Travis E. Nelson	Bill Turner	Bill J. Cooley	Walter Wilcox	Billy Beard	Milton Turner
	272	John Delaney						
	361	Carolyn L. Ruffino						
Brewster	83	Alex R. Gonzalez	Shirley A. Scholl	Phil J. Pollan	Wm. B. Ward	J. W. Pattillo	E. B. Salmon	Abelardo Leyva
Briscoe	110	David C. Cave	Bess McWilliams	John R. Hollums	Shafe Weaver	J. L. Chandler	Beryl L. Long	Bryant Eddleman
Brooks	79	Romeo M. Flores	Rose Martinez	Rolando Ramirez	Jose M. Alaniz	Gustavo Barrera	Jose Garcia	L. E. Wilder
Brown	35	Ernest Cadenhead Jr.	Jan Brown	Steve Ellis	Kenneth L. Boyd	J. D. Chastain	Chester Damron	B. N. Levisay
Burleson	21	John L. Placke	Doris H. Brewer	Charles Sebesta Jr.	F. J. Berran	Don L. Groce	W. J. Stracener	B. E. Schoppe
	335	Harold R. Towslee						
Burnet	33	Clayton E. Evans	Modena R. Curington	Sam Oatman	T. M. Hammond	Carroll McCoy	Kenny Baker	John E. Mead
Caldwell	33	Charles R. Ramsay	Emma J. Schulle	J. L. Van Horn	Jack Schneider	Bobbie Moses	Ronnie Duesterheft	George Glass
	207	Robert T. Pfeuffer						
	274	Fred A. Moore						

District Judges, District Clerks, District Attorneys and County Commissioners. See also Table 1. (Continued)

County	Dist.	District Judge	District Clerk	District Attorney	Comm. Precinct 1	Comm. Precinct 2	Comm. Precinct 3	Comm. Precinct 4
Calhoun	24	C. N. Stevenson	Ollie H. Cuellar	Mark R. Kelly	Leroy Belk	S. L. Mikula	Roy Smith	Oscar F. Hahn
	135	Frank H. Crain						
	267	W. W. Kilgore						
Callahan	42	Donald H. Lane	Cubelle L. Harris	Robert McCool	Eugene Kitchens	Lowell Johnson	F. P. Shackelford	Joe Ingram
Cameron	103	Jane Akin Brasch	Aurora de la Garza	Benjamin Euresti	D. J. Lerma	Miguel Cortinas Jr.	Adolph Thomae Jr.	Tivie Valencia
	107	Gilberto Hinojosa						
	138	Robert Garza						
	197	Darrell B. Hester						
	357	Rogelio Valdez						
Camp	76	Bill D. Moye	Doloria Bradshaw	Chas. M. Cobb	Jack Efurd	Larry Shelton	O. C. Taylor	Curtis Wall
	276	Wm. R. Porter						
	100	John T. Forbis						
Carson	100	John T. Forbis	Sue Persons	David M. McCoy	R. J. Britten	C. F. Smith	Jerry Strawn	Lee Lockridge
Cass	5	Jack E. Carter	Becky Wilbanks	Neal Birmingham	D. J. Rhyne	B. G. Parker	Robt. J. Buzbee	J. H. Clements
	64	Jack R. Miller	Joy Jones	J.F. Davis	Curtis Snitker	Dale Winders	Jeff Robertson	V. Guggemos
Castro	242	Marvin F. Marshall	R. B. Scherer Jr.	Michael R. Little	Kenneth Bettes	S. Desormeaux Jr.	Earl Porter	Paul Lott
	253	W. G. Woods Jr.						
Chambers	344	Carroll E. Wilborn Jr.	Mavis Parrott	Charles Holcomb	R. J. Underwood	Alton Hicks	Joe Henderson	Billy McCutcheon
Cherokee	2	Morris W. Hassell	Nancy Garrison	David M. McCoy	Stanley Terry	Daniel F. Imhof	Irby Teague	H. H. Wilson
Childress	100	John T. Forbis	J. Dan Slagle	Jack McGaughey	G. E. Liggett	Les Lyde	C. F. Copeland	Brice Jackson
Clay	97	Frank J. Douthitt	Rita Tyson	W. G. Tabor Jr.	Billy D. Carter	Frank Davidson	A. W. Coffman	Kenneth Burke
Cochran	286	James K. Walker	Ettie Hubbard	Gerald A. Fohn	George Newby	Billy Joe Luckett	Finis Millican	J. A. Tidwell
Coke	51	Royal Hart	Louise Thompson	Robert McCool	Jack Strickland	Jake McCreary	Vernon Slate	Max Horne
Coleman	35	Ernest Cadenhead Jr.						
	42	Donald H. Lane						
Collin	199	John Roach	Hannah Kunkle	Tom O'Connell	Howard Thornton	Jerry Hoagland	Wallace Webb	Jack Hatchell
	219	Richard A. Schell						
	296	Verla Sue Holland						
	100	John T. Forbis						
Collingsworth	100	John T. Forbis	Karen Strickland	David M. McCoy	Dan Langford	Jimmie Barber	Bill Lowe	Raymond Neeley
Colorado	25	B. B. Schraub	Harvey Vornsand	W. C. Kirkendall	Otto H. Loessin	H. O. Strunk	Jerome C. Wicke	Leon Spanihel
	2025	Gus J. Strauss						
Comal	22	Charles R. Ramsay	Margaret Herbrich	Wm. L. Schroeder	J.L. Evans	Neil Craigmile	Lorenzo Camarillo	Clyde Jacobs Jr.
	207	Robert T. Pfeuffer						
	274	Fred A. Moore						
Comanche	220	James E. Morgan	LaNell Shaw Williams	Andy J. McMullen	Wade Davis	Gene Ward	Brent Daniel	Clyde Brinson
	119	Curt F. Steib		Dick Aicala				
Concho	198	V. Murray Jordan	Margaret T. Taylor	Ronald L. Sutton	Elmo Grounds	O. D. Hight	Dewey Bingham Jr.	John B. Williams
Cooke	235	Larry B. Sullivant	Bobbie Calhoun	Phil L. Adams	Danny Knight	K. D. Alexander	Jerry Lewis	Rosalee Bayer
Coryell	52	Bobby L. Cummings	Carolyn Pollard	Phillip H. Zeigler	Donald K. Fisher	Cloyce Duncan	H. A. Davidson	John A. Hull
Cottle	50	David W. Hajek	Geneva Bragg	Tom Schrandt	Paul Whitener	A. R. Defoor	Lester Moss	Ben Blount
Crane	109	James H. Clack	Mary Grimes	Michael L. Fostel	Gordon Hooper	Billy I. Butler	D. F. Tipton	Dan Blue
Crockett	112	M. Brock Jones Jr.	Debbi Puckett	J. W. Johnson Jr.	S. DeHoyos	Jerry Hill	J. F. Williams	Jesus Castro
Crosby	72	John D. Bevers	Billie Jo Freeman	John L. Barnhill	Nelton Chote	R. W. Self	Herschel Bird	James S. Williams
Culberson	34	William E. Moody	Rosalinda Abreo	Steve W. Simmons	I. M. Navarrette	Oscar Espinoza	John T. Jones	Joel Sanchez
	205	Sam W. Callan						
	210	Sam M. Paxson						
Dallam	69	Bill H. Sheehan	Betty Steele	Barry Blackwell	George R. Reeves	Robert S. Lockhart	Don J. Bowers Jr.	Eulan Sheets
Dallas	14	John M. Marshall	Bill Long	John Vance	Jim Jackson	Nancy Judy	John Wiley Price	Chris V. Semos
	44	Candace Tyson						

Dallas County Dist. Judges (Cont'd.)

191 David Brooks	254 Dee Miller	292 Michael E. Keasler	330 Theo Bedard
192 Harlan Martin	255 Don D. Koons	298 Adolph Canales	Cr. Ron Chapman
193 John Whittington	256 Carolyn Wright	301 Bob O'Donnell	Cr. 2 Larry W. Baraka
194 Ed Kinkeade	265 John Ovard	302 Frances Harris	Cr. 3 Gary R. Stephens
195 Joe Kendall	282 Tom Price	303 Merrill Hartman	Cr. 4 Frances Maloney
203 Thomas B. Thorpe	283 Jack Hampton	304 Harold C. Gaither Jr.	Cr. 5 Pat McDowell
204 Richard D. Mays	291 Gerry H. Meier	305 Catherine J. Stayman	

County	Dist.	District Judge	District Clerk	District Attorney	Comm. Precinct 1	Comm. Precinct 2	Comm. Precinct 3	Comm. Precinct 4
Dawson	106	George H. Hansard	Robert E. L. Smith	Ricky Smith	Rudy Arredondo	Kenneth Clayton	Gene Hendon	Guy Kinnison
Deaf Smith	222	David W. Gulley	Lola Faye Veazey	Roland Saul	William L. Bradly	Austin C. Rose	Troy Don Moore	Johnny Latham
Delta	8	Lanny Ramsay	Mary E. Preas	Frank Long	C. D. Goforth	Gaston Todd	Ardell Allison	Tommy Maddox
Denton	62 16 158 211 362	Jim N. Thompson John K. Narsutis Phillip O. Vick Sam Houston Charles Davis	Lou Anne Morales	Gerald Cobb	Ruth Tansey	Sandy Jacobs	Lee Walker	Don Hill
DeWitt	24 135 267	C. N. Stevenson Frank H. Crain W. W. Kilgore	Gerry Smith	Wiley L. Cheatham	Harold Heyer	P. G. Schaffner	Gilbert Pargmann	Odell White
Dickens	110	David C. Cave	Helen Arrington	John R. Hollums	E. L. Williams	R. J. Bell	Vernon Wright	Darrell Thomason
Dimmit	293	Rey Perez	A. G. Martinez Jr.	Amado Abascal III	Don Urban	Joaquin Salgado	Oscar Alvarado	Osvaldo DeLeon
Donley	100	John T. Forbis	Fay Vargas	David M. McCoy	Steve Reynolds	Clarence Cornell	Buford Holland	Wm. Chamberlain
Duval	229	R. H. Garcia	Antonio Salinas	F. A. Cerda	Alejo C. Garcia	Silifredo Flores	R. M. Barton	Robert S. Lee
Eastland	91	Jim R. Wright	Mary J. Rowch-Brown	Emory C. Walton	R. A. Robinson	Norman Christian	L. T. Owen	Billy Bacon Jr.
Ector	70 161 244 358	Gene Ater Tryon Lewis H. Joseph Connally Bill McCoy	Jackie Sue Barnes	Eric Augesen	Bill Tolbert	Bryan N. Henderson	Gerrid Bowen	Joe E. Hernandez
Edwards	63	George M. Thurmond	Dorothy R. Hatley	Thomas F. Lee	Tony Villarreal	Bobby Cottle	Sydney Bonham	Rex Johnson
Ellis	40	Gene Knize	Billie Fuller	Mary Lou Shipley	David Jones	Ron Gillespie	J. B. Sims	Cliff Womack
El Paso	34 41 65 120 168 171	William E. Moody John McKellips Eduardo S. Marquez Brunson D. Moore Ward L. Koehler Peter S. Peca Jr.	Edie Rubalcaba	S. W. Simmons	Charles C. Hooten	Orlando Fonseca	Rogelio Sanchez	Mary Haynes
		El Paso County Dist. Judges (Cont'd.) 205 Sam W. Callan 210 Sam M. Paxson		El Paso County Dist. Judges (Cont'd.) 243 Herbert E. Marsh Jr. 327 Enrique M. Pena		El Paso County Dist. Judges (Cont'd.) 346 Jose J. Baca		

County	Dist.	District Judge	District Clerk	District Attorney	Comm. Precinct 1	Comm. Precinct 2	Comm. Precinct 3	Comm. Precinct 4
Erath	266	Donald R. Jones	Thomas Pack	John Terrill	Kenneth Robertson	Don Stone	Duane Oakes	Hurrsell Whitefield
Falls	82	Robert M. Stem	Larry R. Hoelscher	Thomas Sehon	E. R. Hardy	Hazel Lewis	E. W. Shaunfield	Shirley A. West
Fannin	6 336	Henry G. Braswell Ray F. Grisham	Eva Lindsey	Dan Meehan	Derrell Hall	Lloyd Flanagan	A. D. McBurnett	Choice Wilson
Fayette	155	Oliver S. Kitzman	Virginia Wied	Charles D. Houston	Arno L. Ruether	Ronald Kneip	Wilbert L. Gross	Royce O. Brauner
Fisher	32	Weldon Kirk	Bettie Hargrove	Norman Arnett	Tommie J. Stuart	B. M. Henderson	Jay R. Hendon	Jimmy Wright
Floyd	110	David C. Cave	Barbara Edwards	John R. Hollums	Sam A. Spence	Floyd Jackson	Thomas Warren	Jack Lackey
Foard	46	Leslie L. Thomas	Jana Payne	Gene Heatly	T. R. Cates	Lloyd Black	Wilson Myers	Dayton Everson
Fort Bend	240 268 328	Chas. A. Dickerson A. Reagan Clark Tom O. Stansbury	Glory Keteler	Sam Dick	Johnnie Pustka	Ben Denham	A. B. Pressley	Bob S. Lutts
Franklin	8 62	Lanny Ramsay Jim N. Thompson	Wanda Johnson	Frank Long	Jearl Cooper	Bobby Elbert	B. F. Ingram	Leon Keith
Freestone	77 87	Putnam K. Reiter Sam B. Bournias	Sue Gregory	Robert W. Gage	Danny T. Willard	W. R. McSwane	Don T. Nesbitt	John J. Stubbs
Frio	81 218	Olin B. Strauss R. L. Eschenburg II	Mildred Burden	Alger H. Kendall	Antonio Moreno Jr.	J. M. Lindsey III	Adolfo Alvarez	Humberto Berrones
Gaines	106	George H. Hansard	Wilma McNew	Ricky Smith	Travis Bagley	Robert Matthews	Otis Johnson	J. W. Allen
Galveston	10 56 122 212 306	Ed J. Harris I. Allan Lerner H. G. Dalehite Jr. Roy Engelke Andrew Z. Baker	V. J. Beninati Jr.	Mike Guarino III	Eddie Barr	Frank T. Carmona	Ron Crowder	Billy J. Pegues
Garza	106	George H. Hansard	Sonny Gossett	Ricky Smith	T. D. Craft	Ted Aten	Tommy Young	Herbert Walls
Gillespie	216	Robert R. Barton	Alberta Geddy	E. Bruce Curry	Dayton F. Herber	James T. McMahon	L. E. Kusenberger	A. L. Hahn
Glasscock	118	James W. Gregg	Betty Pate	Rick Hamby	Wayne Halfmann	Alex Fry	Randell Sherrod	Michael Hoch

District Judges, District Clerks, District Attorneys and County Commissioners. See also Table 1. (Continued)

County	Dist.	District Judge	District Clerk	District Attorney	Comm. Precinct 1	Comm. Precinct 2	Comm. Precinct 3	Comm. Precinct 4
Goliad	24	C. N. Stevenson	Gail M. Turley	Wiley L. Cheatham	W. T. Barnhill	James R. Farley	Edwin Lude	F. F. Post Jr.
	135	Frank H. Crain						
	267	W. W. Kilgore						
Gonzales	25	B. B. Schraub	Patricia Heinemeyer	W. C. Kirkendall	E. R. Breitschopf	J. V. Ochs	Royce Towns	Welly M. Gibson
	2D25	Gus J. Strauss						
Gray	31	Grainger McIlhany	Vickie L. Walls	Guy Hardin	O. L. Presley	Jim Greene	Gerald L. Wright	Ted Simmons
	223	Don E. Cain						
Grayson	15	James Fry	Cyndi Mathis	Steve Davidchik	Carl Thompson	Johnnie McCraw	C. E. Kretsinger	C. E. Short
	59	Joseph M. Joiner						
	336	Ray F. Grisham						
Gregg	124	Alvin Khoury	Ruby Cooper	David Brabham	Elmer Ferguson	Jim Gray	C. B. Young	Jack Bean
	188	Larry Starr						
	307	Wm. C. Martin III						
Grimes	12	Erwin G. Ernst	Wayne Rucker	Latham Boone III	J. P. Brown	Walter V. Borski	Albin Finke	Marcus H. Mallard
	278	Jerry Sandel						
Guadalupe	25	B. B. Schraub	James Behrendt	W. C. Kirkendall	Bobby J. Bulgerin	Monroe Schubert	James M. Brannon	Thomas W. Brown
	2D25	Gus J. Strauss						
	274	Fred A. Moore						
Hale	64	Jack R. Miller	Aliene Wallace	T. D. McEachern	Nina Jo Morris	Homer Roberson	Henry Rieff	James A. Belk
	242	Marvin F. Marshall						
Hall	100	John T. Forbis	Phyllis Dunn	David M. McCoy	Jerry D. Smith	Bobby H. Barbee	Troy Phillips	U. F. Coker Jr.
Hamilton	220	James E. Morgan	La Juan Mizell	Andy J. McMullen	W. O. McCollum Jr.	Ora Dell Tyson	George Kilgo	Garland Short
Hansford	84	J. E. Blackburn	Amelia C. Johnson	Gene Compton	Garland Head	Joe T. Venneman	B. J. Renner	Val Winger
Hardeman	46	Leslie L. Thomas	Loraine White	Gene Heatly	Charles McSpadden	Charles Rine	Charles Taylor	Van Foster
Hardin	88	Earl B. Stover	Aline Harper	R. F. Horka	Andrew Redkey	John Golden	R. P. Douglas	John D. Brown
	356	Britton E. Plunk						
Harris	11	W. N. Blanton Jr.	Ray Hardy	John B. Holmes Jr.	El Franco Lee	James Fonteno	Bob Eckels	E. A. Lyons Jr.
	55	Reagan Cartwright						
	61	R. Shearn Smith						
	80	William R. Powell						
	113	Geraldine Tennant						
	125	Mike O'Brien						
	127	Sharolyn Wood						
	129	Hugo A. Touchy						
	133	Lamar McCorkle						
	151	Alice D. Trevathan						
	152	Jack O'Neill						
	157	Felix Salazar Jr.						
	164	Peter S. Solito						
	165	Kenneth D. Harrison						

Harris County Dist. Judges (Cont'd.)

174 Jon N. Hughes	174 Wyatt H. Heard	248 Woody R. Densen	310 Allen J. Daggett	
176 William M. Hatten	208 Thomas H. Routt	257 Norman R. Lee	311 Bill Elliott	
177 Miron A. Love	209 Michael T. McSpadden	262 Doug Shaver	312 Robert S. Webb III	
178 William T. Harmon	210 Eugene Chambers	263 Charles J. Hearn	313 Robert L. Lowry	
179 I. D. McMaster	228 Ted Poe	269 W. David West	314 Robert B. Baum	
180 Patricia R. Lykos	230 Joe Kegans	270 Ann Cochran	315 Eric G. Andell	
182 Donald K. Shipley	232 A. D. Azios	280 Thomas R. Phillips	333 Davie L. Wilson	
183 Jay W. Burnett	234 Ruby Sondock	281 Louis M. Moore	337 Johnny R. Kolenda	
184 Bob Burdette	245 Henry G. Schuble III	295 Frank O. White	338 Mary Bacon	
185 Carl Walker Jr.	246 John W. Peavy Jr.	308 Bob Robertson	339 Norman Lanford	
189 Richard W. Millard	247 Charles D. Huckabee	309 John D. Montgomery	351 Albert Pruett	

County	Dist.	District Judge	District Clerk	District Attorney	Comm. Precinct 1	Comm. Precinct 2	Comm. Precinct 3	Comm. Precinct 4
Harrison	71	Sam Baxter	Betty Cawood	Bonnie Leggat	James D. Mooney	Wm. D. Power	George K. Brumble	Telly H. Miller
Hartley	69	Bill H. Sheehan	Grady Belew	B. E. Blackwell	J. R. Frantz II	Bob Hunnicutt	James A. Yoder	Ray Snead III
Haskell	39	Charles L. Chapman	Carolyn Reynolds	John Fouts	T. C. Burson	Ronnie Chapman	J. R. Perry	C. A. Turnbow
Hays	22	Charles R. Ramsay	W. H. Moore	Charles Chapman	Rafael Gonzales	Wayne Ford	Craig D. Payne	Oran H. Rippy
	207	Robert T. Pfeuffer						
	274	Fred A. Moore						
Hemphill	31	Grainger McIlhany	Geraldine Vandiver	Guy Hardin	Kenneth Osborne	Don Thomason	L. F. Powledge	Robert Forrest
Henderson	3	Wayne Lawrence	Lela May Garner	Billy Bandy	Jim Blakeney	Fred Box	W. E. McLean	Joe Young
	173	Jack Holland						
Hidalgo	92	Homero Salinas	Pauline G. Gonzalez	Rene Guerra	Samuel Sanchez	Lalo Arcaute	N. Salinas	Leonard Camarillo
	93	John F. Dominguez						
	139	Raul L. Longoria						
	206	Joe B. Evins						
	275	Hector J. Villarreal						
	332	Mario E. Ramirez Jr.						

District Judges, District Clerks, District Attorneys and County Commissioners. See also Table 1. (Continued)

County	Dist.	District Judge	District Clerk	District Attorney	Comm. Precinct 1	Comm. Precinct 2	Comm. Precinct 3	Comm. Precinct 4
Hill	66	Robert G. Dohoney	Virginia Clements	Dan V. Dent	Glynn Thomas	Kenneth Reid	Jim Carmichall	Kenneth R. Davis
Hockley	286	James K. Walker	Jean Leavelle	W. G. Tabor Jr.	Sam Langford	E. L. J. Hensley	J. R. Stanley	Billy W. Thetford
Hood	355	Ralph H. Walton Jr.	Joyce Beckworth	Richard L. Hattox	Joe C. Brown	Melvin Gifford	David Cleveland	Harold Berry
Hopkins	8	Lanny Ramsay	Ola Beckham	Frank Long	Elton Stewart	H. W. Halcomb	Delbert Tulley	Wayne Mobley
	62	Jim N. Thompson						
Houston	3	Wayne Lawrence	Linda Hunt	Donald J. Gordon	George H. Bush	Gene Musick	Otis C. Wooten	Charles Bobbitt
	349	Melvin D. Whitaker						
Howard	118	James W. Gregg	Peggy Crittenden	Rick Hamby	O. L. Brown	Paul H. Allen	W. B. Crooker Jr.	David Barr
Hudspeth	34	William E. Moody	Patricia Bramblett	Steve W. Simmons	Leon Snyder	L. R. Talley	Larry Karr	M. R. Collier
	205	Sam W. Callan						
	210	Sam M. Paxson						
Hunt	196	E. Paul Banner	Ann Prince	F. Duncan Thomas	J. H. Lyon	Henry Hensley	John Mizell	Allen Martin
	354	Richard Bosworth						
Hutchinson	84	J. E. Blackburn	Rena G. Dorsett	Gene Compton	Murry Jennings	Clarence McDaniel	W. D. Shipley	John E. Bayless
	316	Guy Hazlett						
Irion	51	Royal Hart	Jane Ethridge	Gerald Fohn	Mike Dolan	O. Wolfenbarger	Gary McGehee	Steve Elkins
Jack	271	John R. Lindsey	Lella V. Cozart	Patrick M. Morris	Clide Ogle	Linda G. Cranford	Raymond Matlock	J. T. Rumage
Jackson	24	C. N. Stevenson	Dolores Gabrysch	J. A. Henseraling	Miller Rutledge	Lifford Weidner	Edwin E. Hurta Jr.	W. O. Walker
	135	Frank H. Crain						
	267	W. W. Kilgore						
Jasper	1	O'Neal Bacon	Nell Powers	Robert M. Jackson	Edgar W. Lewis	J. C. Sprouse	Holbert H. Jones	Mack Rose
	1-A	Monte Dan Lawlis						
Jeff Davis	83	Alex R. Gonzalez	Peggy Robertson	Phil J. Pollan	J. R. Prude	Chris Lacy	H. L. Kokernot Jr.	Ben F. Gearhart Jr.
Jefferson	58	Ronald L. Walker	John S. Appleman	Tom Maness	N. J. Troy	James A. Smith Jr.	Dave Smith Jr.	Edward Moore
	60	Gary Sanderson						
	136	Jack R. King						
	172	Thomas A. Thomas						
	252	Leonard J. Giblin Jr.						
	279	Robert P. Walker						
	317	James M. Farris						
	Cr.	Lawrence J. Gist						
Jim Hogg	229	R. H. Garcia	Lilia Pena	F. A. Cerda	Primitivo Gonzalez	A. Molina Jr.	Juan M. Perez	Santos Cantu
Jim Wells	79	Romeo M. Flores	Olga Villarreal	Rolando Ramirez	Lucilla DeLeon	Hubert Adami	W. M. Laughlin	
Johnson	18	E. Byron Crosier	Betty Cooke	Dan Boulware	Billy F. Roe	Ron Harmon	Jimmie W. York	Bud Miller
	249	John R. MacLean						
Jones	259	Quay Parker	W. L. McDonald	Jack G. Willingham	W. L. Moore	Jerry Manske	H. R. Hay	Steve Lollar
Karnes	81	Olin B. Strauss	F. A. Ehlinger	Alger H. Kendall	L. B. Hailey Jr.	Tom Dworaczyk	Albert Banduch	Claude Osburn Jr.
	218	R. L. Eschenburg II						
Kaufman	86	Glen M. Ashworth	Sandra Featherston	L. W. Conradt Jr.	George A. Mayfield	John Darden	Ivan Johnson	Barnie Murphy
Kendall	216	Robert R. Barton	Shirley R. Stehling	E. Bruce Curry	David Masters	Gene Vallerie	Victor Phillip	L. Klemstein
Kenedy	105	J. Manuel Banales	Barbara B. Turcotte	Grant Jones	J. E. Errington	L. E. Turcotte Jr.	T. R. Armstrong	Ed Durham
Kent	39	Charles L. Chapman	Cornelia Cheyne	John Fouts	W. H. Parks Sr.	Don Long	Roy H. Parker	Don Trammel
Kerr	198	V. Murray Jordan	Linda Uecker	E. Bruce Curry	Fred Holland	Bill Ray	Victor Lich	H. A. Baldwin
	216	Robert R. Barton						
Kimble	198	V. Murray Jordan	Louise P. Oliver	Ronald L. Sutton	Luke Hagood	Gene Simon	Frank Goodman	Archie K. Lennon
King	50	David W. Hajek	Evelyn Sursa	Tom Schrandt	Jordan Rogers	Royce McLaury	B. J. Tidmore	Owen Brazee
Kinney	63	George M. Thurmond	Dolores Raney	Thomas F. Lee	Joe N. Garza	Rose Mary Slubar	Tim Ward	Billy W. Bizzell
Kleberg	105	J. Manuel Banales	Anita Kislah	Grant Jones	Doyle W. Dreyer	E. S. Roberts	Earl Hubert	Romeo Lomas
Knox	50	David W. Hajek	Gloria L. West	Tom Schrandt	Billy G. Johnston	Bobby J. Roberson	Phillip F. Homer	Lee G. Patterson
Lamar	6	Henry G. Braswell	Tommie Duke	Tom D. Wells III	Yuba Lee	Ronald B. Dockrey		V. E. Easterwood
	62	Jim N. Thompson						
Lamb	154	Pat Boone Jr.	Ray L. Britt	C. R. Wilkinson	A. J. Spain	T. H. Lewis	Emil Macha	Leonard Pierce
Lampasas	27	C. W. Duncan Jr.	Margy Jones	Arthur C. Eads Jr.	D. C. Herring	Wayne Faught	Willard Potts	C. N. Lancaster
La Salle	218	R. L. Eschenburg II	Nora Mae Tyler	Alger H. Kendall	James R. Black	E. P. Alvarado	A. A. Garcia	Carlos B. Gonzalez

District Judges, District Clerks, District Attorneys and County Commissioners. See also Table 1. (Continued)

County	Dist.	District Judge	District Clerk	District Attorney	Comm. Precinct 1	Comm. Precinct 2	Comm. Precinct 3	Comm. Precinct 4
Lavaca	25	B. B. Schraub	Calvin J. Albrecht	W. C. Kirkendall	Jimmie J. Steffek	Eddie Vrana	Daniel Peters	Edward Hermes
	2D25	Gus J. Strauss						
Lee	21	John L. Placke	Adeline Melcher	Steven W. Keng	Elsie Rose	Otto Becker Jr.	W. G. Boyd	Monroe Markert
	335	Harold R. Towslee						
Leon	12	Erwin G. Ernst	Audrey Blake	Latham Boone III	Julian Wakefield	Loyd Richmond	Craig Graham	Curtis Neyland
	87	Sam B. Bournias						
	278	Jerry Sandel						
Liberty	75	Clarence D. Cain	Joy Kay McManus	Michael R. Little	Bobby D. Blake	Lee Groce	Melvin Hunt	Bob Martin
	253	W. G. Woods Jr.						
Limestone	77	Putnam K. Reiter	Mary D. Budde	Pat Simmons	John Rasco	Billy G. Waldrop	Wilmer Little	Jeff Stuver
	87	Sam B. Bournias						
Lipscomb	31	Grainger McIlhany	Coeta Sperry	Guy Hardin	John W. Floyd	Verle Woods	Cecil Wynn	Ross G. Zenor
Live Oak	36	Ronald M. Yeager	Ellen J. McCarley	C. F. Moore	Clem McKinney	Hilbert H. Kopplin	Bill Goodwin	Emilio Garza
	156	V. Rachel Littlejohn						
	343	A. T. Rodriguez						
Llano	33	Clayton E. Evans	Wanda Osbourn	Sam Oatman	W. R. Bauman	Walter Overstreet	Rex King	Leonard Grenwelge
Loving	143	Bob Parks	Juanita Busby	Jack McGowen	Ernest T. Hopper	James J. Wheat	J. E. Wilkinson	Royce Creager
Lubbock	72	John D. Bevers	Wayne LeCroy	Travis Ware	Boyd O. Roberts	Coy E. Biggs	Eliseo Solis	Alton Brazell
	99	Thomas L. Clinton						
	137	Cecil G. Puryear						
	140	Wm. R. Shaver						
	237	John R. McFall						
Lynn	106	George H. Hansard	Joy Laws	Ricky Smith	Eldon Gatlis	Boyd Barnes	Bart Anderson	J. T. Miller
	198	V. Murray Jordan						
McCulloch	19	Bill Logue	Fayrene T. Williams	Ronald L. Sutton	Paul G. Willis	Jackie Behrens	Zane Carroll	Glenn A. Smith
	54	George Allen						
McLennan	74	Derwood Johnson	Joe Johnson	Vic Feazell	Wayne Davis	Jim Lewis	Vince Incardona	Ray Meadows
	170	Joe N. Johnson						
McMullen	36	Ronald M. Yeager	Wm. K. Hodgin	C. F. Moore	Allen Goff	Rodney Swaim Jr.	Herman Smith	Duane W. Atkinson
	156	W. Rachel Littlejohn						
	343	A. T. Rodriguez						
Madison	12	Erwin G. Ernst	Joyce Batson	Latham Boone III	Billy Wilson	Walton Reynolds	Alvin Martin	Milton Wager Jr.
	278	Jerry Sandel						
Marion	115	F. L. Garrison	Syble Blackburn	Tony Hileman	Hollis H. Johnson	Odis A. Powell	J. B. McNeely	George Wolaver
	276	Wm. R. Porter						
Martin	118	James W. Gregg	Virginia James	Rick Hamby	James Biggs	Don L. Tollison	Ronnie Deatherage	E. D. Holcomb.
Mason	33	Clayton E. Evans	Beatrice Langehennig	Sam Oatman	Carl Martin	T. J. Webster	Jesse Dobbs	Michael N. Jordan
Matagorda	23	Neil Caldwell	Paul Hatchett	Daniel W. Shindler	Otha W. Birkner	George Deshotels	F. P. Brhlik	E. R. Vacek.
	130	W. Jack Salyer						
Maverick	293	Rey Perez	D. Trevino	Amado Abascal III	Felix M. Cerna	Rosendo Flores	Eduardo Trevino	Luis S. Minton
Medina	38	Mickey R. Pennington	Jean Marty	Rogelio F. Munoz	David Montgomery	David FitzSimon	Enrique Santos	H. B. Briscoe
Menard	198	V. Murray Jordan	Neva Kothmann	Ronald L. Sutton	Harvey Carriger	Richard Cordes	Ray McGuffin	Tim Childers
Midland	142	Pat M. Baskin	Vivian Wood	Al Schorre	Durward Wright	Guy McCrary	Scott Welch	Winfree L. Brown
	238	Vann Culp						
	318	Barbara G. Culver						
Milam	20	Don G. Humble	Leola L. Komar	Charles E. Lance	V. W. Hauk	Cecil Laywell	Gerald Vinton	Dalton Caffey
Mills	35	Ernest Cadenhead Jr.	Walter A. Bryant	Stephen Ellis	Marvin Lindsay	Lewis D. Watson	Lee Roy Schwartz	Farrel Thorne
Mitchell	32	Weldon Kirk	Bill H. Erwin	Norman Arnett	Edward B. Roach	Johnny Shackelford	Paul B. Hunter	Bill H. Preston.
Montague	97	Frank J. Douthitt	Starr Johnson	J. A. McGaughey	Dwight E. Whitaker	Milton L. Hopkins	Glenn Seay	C. J. Blankenship
Montgomery	9	Lynn Jay Coker	Peggy Stevens	Peter C. Speers III	Oliver H. Hance	Malcolm Purvis Sr.	Ernest E. Chance Sr.	A. V. Sallas
	2D9	John C. Martin						
	221	Lee G. Alworth						
	284	Olen Underwood						
	359	James H. Keeshan						
Moore	69	Bill H. Sheehan	June Mills	Barry E. Blackwell	Jess Starkey	Ernest O. Hanna	J. C. Williams	M. O. Bain.
Morris	76	Bill D. Moye	Reynolds S. Taylor	O. G. Stanley	Robert L. McCain	Rex W. Bass	Forrest A. Clair	Willie G. Smith

District Judges, District Clerks, District Attorneys and County Commissioners. See also Table 1. (Continued)

County	Dist.	District Judge	District Clerk	District Attorney	Comm. Precinct 1	Comm. Precinct 2	Comm. Precinct 3	Comm. Precinct 4
Motley	110	David C. Cave	Lucretia Campbell	John R. Hollums	John M. Russell	Bill D. Washington	Joseph E. Simpson	Thurman F. Watson
Nacogdoches	145	Jack Pierce	Shelby Solomon	Herbert Hancock	Billy Reneau	E. Whitaker	Charles Simmons	Carlyle Goff
Navarro	13	Kenneth A. Douglas	C. O. Curington Jr.	P. C. Batchelor	Betty Armstrong	Joe Graves	Thomas Dyer	Billy Hargrove
Newton	1	O'Neal Bacon	Abbie N. Stark	Bill A. Martin	Joe Bill Powell	Ottis Lewis	Melton G. Jarrell	Gaylon Wood
	1-A	Monte Dan Lawlis						
Nolan	32	Weldon Kirk	Vera Holloman	Norman Arnett	J. T. Johnson	Ernest Shuler	Adrian Barton	Billy Muncy
Nueces	28	Walter Dunham Jr.	Oscar Soliz	Grant Jones	Wm. E. McKinzie	Carl Bluntzer	R. M. Borchard	J. P. Luby
	94	Jack E. Hunter						
	105	J. Manuel Banales						
	117	Robert Blackmon						
	148	Margarito C. Garza						
	214	Mike Westergren						
	319	Max Bennett						
	347	Joaquin Villarreal III						
Ochiltree	84	J. E. Blackburn	Wilma Srof	Bruce Roberson	Jack Kile	Dean Slaughter	Johnie Luthi	Larry Hardy
Oldham	222	David W. Gulley	Martha Thompson	Richard Brainerd	Herb Schroeder	Marvin Axe	Roger Morris Jr.	Grady Skaggs
	128	Patrick A. Clark						
Orange	163	David A. Dunn	Billye Minter	Steve C. Howard	Forrest E. Hudson	Marcelle Adams	Donald E. Cole	Archie B. Smith
	260	Buddie J. Hahn						
Palo Pinto	29	David Cleveland	Helen Slemmons	N. A. Irsfield	David Lee	Jimmy McKee	George Nowak	Almoth Gilbert
Panola	123	Bennie C. Boles	Marie Pike Seale	John Walker	Carl Hendrickson	Lovis O. Nail	Leonard Jones	Lovil Hudson
Parker	43	James O. Mullin	Lana O. Tibbitts	Amy A. Adams	Waymon Wright	Mack Dobbs	Harold Anderson	Mark Riley
Parmer	287	Jack D. Young	Marjorie Watkins	Johnny Actkinson	Ernest Anthony	Tom Ware	Robert White	Raymond McGehee
Pecos	83	Alex R. Gonzalez	Peggy Young	Phil J. Pollan	Gregg McKenzie	M. R. Gonzalez Jr.	Neal Sconiers	Truman W. Grove
	112	M. Brock Jones Jr.		J. W. Johnson Jr.				
Polk	9	Lynn Jay Coker	Nell Lowe	Peter C. Speers III	H. N. Denham	Bobby Smith	James J. Purvis	Paul Harrell
	258	John C. Martin						
	411	Joe Ned Dean		Joe L. Price				
Potter	47	David L. Gleason	Cindy Groomer	Danny Hill	Pat Cunningham	Manny Villasenor	Ray Berry	Will C. Thirkill
	108	Edward B. Nobles						
	181	Samuel C. Kiser						
	251	Naomi Harney						
	320	Don R. Emerson						
Presidio	83	Alex R. Gonzalez	Ramona Lara	Phil J. Pollan	Felipe A. Cordero	Daniel T. Estrada	Ben Benavidez	Samuel F. Cox
Rains	8	Lanny Ramsay	Mary Sheppard	Frank Long	Doris Cochran	Roy Don Shipp	Ralph Middleton	Rayford Briggs
	354	Richard Bosworth						
Randall	47	David L. Gleason	LaQuitta Polvadore	Randall Sherrod	Walter L. Simms	Bill Thomas	Fred Begert	Fred Ritchey
	181	Samuel C. Kiser						
	251	Naomi Harney						
Reagan	83	Alex R. Gonzalez	Hazel S. Carr	Phil J. Pollan	Lester Ratliff	Michael Elkins	Bill Schneemann	Thomas Strube
	112	M. Brock Jones Jr.		J. W. Johnson Jr.				
Real	38	Mickey R. Pennington	Rosemary Clark	Thos. H. Fowler	Lanny Leinweber	Wade Reagor	C. San Miguel	M. Wooldridge
Red River	6	Henry G. Braswell	Clara Gaddis	Jack L. McGowen	H. Drue Pirtle	James Carson	Ben B. Storey	Lane E. Duncan
	102	Leon F. Pesek		Wiley L. Cheatham				
Reeves	143	Bob Parks	Juana Jaquez		Felipe Arredondo	Howard W. Davis	I. Dutchover	Bernardo Martinez
Refugio	24	C. N. Stevenson	Mariliou English		James R. Henry	Clara M. Geistman	James Pfeil	Juan A. Garza
	267	Frank H. Crain						
Roberts	31	W. W. Kilgore	Jackie M. Jackson	Guy Hardin	Wm. H. Clark	Ronnie Gill	Don Morrison	Clyde Hodges
	84	Grainger McIlhany						
Robertson	82	Robert M. Stem	Marjorie D. Hicks	Jimmie McCullough	Tommy C. Singleton	Alvis Bishop	Obia A. Cargill	Sam Abraham
Rockwall	86	Glen M. Ashworth	Marty Bandy	G. Ray Sumrow	Bob Jolly	Barbara Sinclair	David V. Brooks	Wayne Krider
Runnels	119	Curt F. Steib	L. Michalewicz	Dick Alcala	Robert Virden	J. D. Wilson	Gilbert Smith	Marvin Salling
Rusk	4	Donald R. Ross	Pat Endsley	Wm. L. Ferguson	Talmadge Mercer	Harold Kuykendall	Dan Dickeson	Kenneth Ashby
Sabine	1	O'Neal Bacon	Tanya Walker	Bill A. Martin	R. E. Smith	Billy Joe McGee	Eldridge Ellison	Chester D. Cox Sr.
	273	John L. Smith						
San Augustine	1	O'Neal Bacon	Jo Anna Johnson	Bill A. Martin	L. T. Jackson	Herbert Jackson	James J. Craig	Harlon A. Hall
	273	John L. Smith						

District Judges, District Clerks, District Attorneys and County Commissioners. See also Table 1. (Continued)

County	Dist.	District Judge	District Clerk	District Attorney	Comm. Precinct 1	Comm. Precinct 2	Comm. Precinct 3	Comm. Precinct 4
San Jacinto	9; 2D9; 258	Lynn Jay Coker; John C. Martin; Joe Ned Dean	Edna M. Cox	David Walker	Norman J. Streef	Roy Lewis	Donald Cox	Curtis B. Cain
San Patricio	36; 156; 343	Ronald M. Yeager; W. Rachel Littlejohn; A. T. Rodriguez	Patricia Norton	Joe L. Price; Thos. L. Bridges	Joe Zapata	Carl Duncan	Glenn Dorris	Gordon Porter
San Saba	33	Clayton E. Evans	Nila Ruth Barker	Sam Oatman	Ronald G. McBride	Hollis Lord	W. Kuykendall	Bennie L. Lively
Schleicher	51	Royal Hart	Helen Blakeway	Gerald A. Fohn	J. F. Mayo Jr.	Kerry Joy	Priscilla Paxton	Ross Whitten
Scurry	132	Gene L. Dulaney	Polly Underwood	Ernie Armstrong	Duaine Davis	Tommy Pate	C. D. Gray Jr.	Ted Billingsley
Shackelford	259	Quay Parker	Bobbie L. Cox	Jack G. Willingham	Fred J. Coulter	W. S. Jones	H. D. Connally	W. O. McKeever
Shelby	123	Bennie C. Boles	Marsha Singletary	John S. Walker	Charles Williams	Edward Risinger	R. D. Green	V. L. Wedgeworth
Sherman	273; 69	John L. Smith; Bill H. Sheehan	Mary Lou Albert	Barry E. Blackwell	Boyd Spurlock	Wayne Cummings	Dale Hamilton	Veron D. Cotney
Smith	7; 114; 241; 321	W. E. Coats; Galloway Calhoun Jr.; Joe Tunnell; Ruth J. Blake	R. Brad Burger	Jack M. Skeen Jr.	B. J. Payne	G. T. Shamburger	Gene Chandler	A. R. Melontree
Somervell	18; 249	E. Byron Crosier; John R. MacLean	Lovella Williams	Dan Boulware	Elizabeth Hammond	Joe G. Whitworth	Billy C. Miller	Hubert C. Beck
Starr	229	R. H. Garcia	Juan E. Saenz	F. A. Cerda	Jose M. Alvarez	Amando Pena	Eloy Garza	Reynaldo Alaniz
Stephens	90	R. E. Thornton	Juanita Speake	John A. Neal	F. J. Copeland	D. C. Sikes	Ozell Devenport	Carroll Williams
Sterling	51	Royal Hart	Diane A. Haar	Gerald Fohn	Johnny Hughes	Russell Noletubby	Billy R. Bynum	Melvin Foster
Stonewall	39	Charles L. Chapman	Betty L. Smith	John Fouts	John A. Smith	Patsy M. Cumble	J. D. Parker	Robert Branch
Sutton	112	M. Brock Jones Jr.	Erma Lee Turner	J. W. Johnson Jr.	Mike Villanueva	Bill Wade	Bill Keel	Osbauldo Castaneda
Swisher	64; 242	Jack R. Miller; Marvin F. Marshall	Pat Wesley	T. D. McEachern	F. L. McGavock	A. G. House	Roma Boggs	W. C. Weatherred
Tarrant	17; 48; 67; 96; 141; 153; 213; 231	Charles J. Murray; Wm. L. Hughes Jr.; George A. Crowley; Roger J. Walker; James E. Wright; S. C. Farrar Jr.; George S. Kredell; Maryellen Hicks	Tom Hughes	Tim Curry	Dick Andersen	O. L. Watson	Bob Hampton	J. D. Johnson
Tarrant County Dist. Judges (Cont'd.)	233; 236; 297; 322; 323; 324; 325; 342; 348; 352; 360; Cr. 1; Cr. 2; Cr. 3; Cr. 4	Harland Weaver; Albert L. White Jr.; Earl Bates; Frank Sullivan; Scott D. Moore; Brian A. Carper; Robert L. Wright; Joe Bruce Cunningham; Michael D. Schattman; John G. Street; Catherine H. Adamski; Louis E. Sturns; L. Clifford Davis; Don Leonard; Joe Drago III						
Taylor	42; 104; 326; 350	Donald H. Lane; Billy J. Edwards; Aleta Hacker; William A. Thomas Jr.	Rilla Mahoney	Jorge Solis	D. A. Bolls	Don Dudley	John G. Thompson	Neil Fry
Terrell	63	George M. Thurmond	Patty Phillips	Thomas F. Lee	Robert M. Salazar	A. R. Escamilla	W. L. Babb	Lewis Allen
Terry	121	Ray D. Anderson	Betty Frazier	G. D. Pruitt	Harvey Smith	Bill Smith	Delton Gregg	Jimmie Berryhill
Throckmorton	39	Charles L. Chapman	Cathey Mitchell	John Fouts	H. L. Martin	John Jones	Carlton Sullivan	George Seedig
Titus	76; 276	Bill D. Moye; Wm. R. Porter	Bobby LaPrade	Chas. Mac Cobb	Dempsey Johnson	Mike Fields	J. W. Terrell Jr.	Carl R. Ferrell
Tom Green	51; 119; 340	Royal Hart; Curt F. Steib; Randol L. Stout	Sue Bramhall	Gerald Fohn; Dick Alcala	B. C. Dominguez	Mary Burk	E. W. Wilson	David Ryan
Travis	53; 98; 126; 147	Mary P. Williams; Hume Cofer; Joseph H. Hart; Mace B. Thurman Jr.	John Dickson	Ronald Earle	Jimmy Snell	Bruce Todd	Pam Reed	Hank Gonzalez
Travis County Dist. Judges (Cont'd.)	167; 200; 201; 250; 261; 299; 331; 345; 353	Robert D. Jones; Paul R. Davis Jr.; Jerry Dellana; Harley Clark; Peter Lowry; Jon N. Wisser; Robert A. Perkins; Juan Gallardo; Joe Dibrell Jr.						
Trinity	2D9	John Martin	Jorene Legg	Joe L. Price	Lynn Reynolds	Dean Price	Cecil Webb	Wayne Odom

County	Dist.	District Judge	District Clerk	District Attorney	Comm. Precinct 1	Comm. Precinct 2	Comm. Precinct 3	Comm. Precinct 4
Tyler	1-A 88	Monte Dan Lawlis Earl B. Stover	Patricia Brown	Patrick Hardy	Carrol Conner	Arthur M. Barnes	Willis Graham	James R. Jordan
Upshur Upton	115 83 112	F. L. Garrison Alex R. Gonzalez M. Brock Jones Jr.	Horace A. Ray Phyllis Stephens	O. W. Loyd II Phil J. Pollan J. W. Johnson Jr.	Gaddis Lindsey H. W. Vick	Bill Loggins Jr. Genevieve Titsworth	David Loyd Jack Carr	Tommy Eatherton Eugene Kelton
Uvalde Val Verde	38 63	Mickey R. Pennington George M. Thurmond	June Richardson Martha Germany	Rogelio Munoz Thomas F. Lee	A. E. McKinley R. G. Padilla	Gilbert Torres Bob Rodriquez	Austin Schaefer J. L. Leonard	Amaro Cardona Martin Wardlaw
Van Zandt Victoria	294 24 135 267	Richard D. Davis C. N. Stevenson Frank H. Crain W. W. Kilgore	Veta Burns Alice Lee	Tommy W. Wallace George J. Filley III	A. L. Herron Nick Hinojosa	W. A. Warren Jr. Jerry Nobles	Bruce Wilemon John J. Hammack	E. J. Andrews Rex L. Easley
Walker	12 278	Erwin G. Ernst Jerry Sandel	Betty Tackett	Frank Blazek	Sam Park	Cecil Williams	Curtis Ellisor	Joe Malak Jr.
Waller	9 155	Lynn Coker Oliver S. Kitzman	Beverly A. Kluna	Peter C. Spears III Charles D. Houston	Freddie R. Zach	James R. Muse	Richard Frey	Eddie Neuman
Ward Washington	143 21 335	Bob Parks John L. Placke Harold R. Towslee	Betty Love Blondean Kuecker	Jack McGowen Charles Sebesta Jr.	H. A. Collins Joe Renn	Bill Middlebrooks Rudolph Schroeder	J. H. Raglin Gilbert Janner	Bob J. Meek Garrett Spitzer
Webb	49 111 341	Manuel R. Flores A. A. Zardenetta Elma S. Ender	Manuel Gutierrez	Julio A. Garcia	Rosie C. Hinojosa	Judith Gutierrez	Jose L. Rodriguez	Arnulfo Santos
Wharton	23 329	Neil Caldwell Daniel R. Sklar	Roland J. Carlson	Daniel Schindler	Carl Nichols	John J. Girgar Jr.	A. Schoeneberg	C. F. Drapela Jr.
Wheeler Wichita	31 30 78 89	Grainger McIlhany Calvin Ashley Keith Nelson Temple Driver	Paul Topper Dorsey R. Trapp	Guy Hardin Barry L. Macha	E. R. Harrison Dod Wiley Jr.	B. V. Atherton Weldon Nix	Clois Hanner Gordon Griffith	Boyd Hiltbrunner H. C. Greer Jr.
Wilbarger Willacy	46 103 107 138 197 357	Leslie L. Thomas Jane Akin Brasch Gilberto Hinojosa Robert Garza Darrell B. Hester Rogelio Valdez	Annie L. Minyard Iris O. McGlothin	Gene Heatly Lee Price Fernon	O. J. Walker E. Gonzales	Charles Colbert Gene McGee	Glen Turner Alfredo Serrato	Lenville Morris Simon Salinas
Williamson	26 277	William S. Lott John R. Carter	Bonnie Wolbrucek	Ken Anderson	Ron Wood	Wesley O. Foust	Raymond Rister	Jerry L. Mehevec
Wilson	81 218	Olin B. Strauss R. L. Eschenburg II	Jody Gregory	Alger H. Kendall	B. L. Talamantez	Albert Pruski	Billy L. Deagen	C. W. Daniels
Winkler Wise	109 271	James H. Clack John R. Lindsey	Virginia Healy Doris Claborn	Michael L. Fostel Patrick M. Morris	D. Leon Nutt Max I. Weaver	James A. Winn H. N. Nikirk Jr.	J. M. Dawson Chas. F. Wolfe Jr.	W. T. White B. G. Newton
Wood	114 294	Galloway Calhoun Jr. Richard D. Davis	Jo Anna Nelson	Marcus D. Taylor	Glenn Bevill	Sid Cox	Roger Pace	W. B. Woodard
Yoakum Young Zapata Zavala	121 90 49 293	Ray D. Anderson R. E. Thornton Manuel Flores Rey Perez	Mae Barnett George C. Birdwell Arnoldo Flores Rosa E. Mata	Linda Lowrey John A. Neal Julio A. Garcia Amado Abascal III	John Avara Sam Whittenburg Jose Flores Hector Gomez	R. W. Thurston Dois W. Sloan Angel Garza Frank Guerrero	Jim Barron A. D. Bishop David Morales Abelardo Marquez	J. L. Fitzgerald F. H. Green Derly Villarreal Matthew McHazlett

State Government

State government is divided into **executive, legislative and judicial branches** under the Texas Constitution, adopted in 1876. The chief executive is the **Governor** whose term, effective in 1975, is for 4 years, according to a constitutional amendment approved by Texas voters in 1972. Other elected state officials with executive responsibilities include the **Lieutenant Governor, Attorney General, Comptroller of Public Accounts, Treasurer, Commissioner of the General Land Office** and **Commissioner of Agriculture.** The terms of these officials also were increased from 2 to 4 years by the constitutional amendment. Three members of the **Railroad Commis-**sion are elected for 6-year terms.

Except for making numerous appointments, the governor's powers are limited in comparison with those in most states.

The legislative branch is comprised of 31 members of the Senate and 150 members of the House of Representatives.

The judiciary consists of the **Supreme Court** and its co-ordinate **State Court of Criminal Appeals, 14 Courts of Appeals** and more than 330 district courts. Members are elected.

State and Federal Courts

The following lists include U.S. district courts in Texas, Texas district courts, Texas higher courts and administrative judicial districts. The lists were compiled from reports of the Texas Judicial Council and other sources.

The section — Counties, Cities and Towns — shows, alphabetically by counties, judicial districts to which each county is assigned.

Table No. 2 of District and County Officials also shows the district judges by counties.

U.S. District Courts In Texas

Texas is divided into four federal judicial districts, and each district is composed of several divisions. Appeal from all Texas federal district courts is to the **Fifth Circuit Court of Appeals,** New Orleans. Judges are appointed for life and receive a salary of $81,100 annually.

NORTHERN TEXAS DISTRICT

District Judges. — Chief Judge, Robert Porter, Dallas. **Acting Chief Judge,** Barefoot Sanders, Dallas. **Senior Judges,** Joe E. Estes, Dallas and Halbert O. Woodard, Lubbock. **Judges:** Eldon B. Mahon, and David Belew Jr., Fort Worth; Mary Lou Robinson, Amarillo; Jerry Buchmeyer, A. Joe Fish, Sidney A. Fitzwater and Robert B. Maloney, Dallas. **Clerk of District Court:** Nancy Doherty, Dallas. **U.S. Attorney:** Marvin Collins, Dallas (Fort Worth). **U.S. Marshal:** Clint J. Peoples, Dallas. Court is in continuous session in each division of the Northern Texas District. Following are the different divisions of the Northern District and the counties in each division:

Dallas Division

Dallas, Ellis, Hunt, Johnson, Kaufman, Navarro and Rockwall. **Magistrates:** William F. Sanderson Jr. and John B. Tolle, Dallas. **Bankruptcy Judges:** Robert C. McGuire and Harold C. Abramson, Dallas. **Chief Deputy Clerk:** Michael E. Ruhnow.

Fort Worth Division

Comanche, Erath, Hood, Jack, Palo Pinto, Parker, Tarrant and Wise. **Magistrate:** Alex H. McGlinchey, Fort Worth. **Bankruptcy Judge:** Massie Tillman, Fort Worth. **Deputy Clerk in charge:** Faye Ray.

Amarillo Division

Armstrong, Briscoe, Carson, Castro, Childress, Collingsworth, Dallam, Deaf Smith, Donley, Gray, Hall, Hansford, Hartley, Hemphill, Hutchinson, Lipscomb, Moore, Ochiltree, Oldham, Parmer, Potter, Randall, Roberts, Sherman, Swisher and Wheeler. **Magistrate:** Robert R. Sanders, Amarillo. **Bankruptcy Judge:** John C. Akard, Lubbock. **Deputy Clerk in charge:** May Harris.

Abilene Division

Callahan, Eastland, Fisher, Haskell, Howard, Jones, Mitchell, Nolan, Shackelford, Stephens, Stonewall, Taylor and Throckmorton. **Magistrate:** Billy W. Boone, Abilene. **Bankruptcy Judge:** Michael A. McConnell, Fort Worth. **Deputy Clerk in charge:** Georgia Sanders.

San Angelo Division

Brown, Coke, Coleman, Concho, Crockett, Glasscock, Irion, Menard, Mills, Reagan, Runnels, Schleicher, Sterling, Sutton and Tom Green. **Magistrate:** Philip R. Lane, San Angelo. **Bankruptcy Judge:** Massie Tillman, Fort Worth. **Deputy Clerk in charge:** Ann Loyd.

Wichita Falls Division

Archer, Baylor, Clay, Cottle, Foard, Hardeman, King, Knox, Montague, Wichita, Wilbarger and Young. **Magistrate:** Robert K. Roach, Wichita Falls. **Bankruptcy Judge:** Harold C. Abramson, Dallas. **Deputy Clerk in charge:** Nina Hatcher.

Lubbock Division

Bailey, Borden, Cochran, Crosby, Dawson, Dickens, Floyd, Gaines, Garza, Hale, Hockley, Kent, Lamb, Lubbock, Lynn, Motley, Scurry, Terry and Yoakum.

Magistrate: J. Q. Warnick Jr., Lubbock. **Bankruptcy Judge:** John C. Akard, Lubbock. **Deputy Clerk in charge:** Kristy Weinheimer.

WESTERN TEXAS DISTRICT

District Judges. Chief Judge, William S. Sessions, San Antonio. **Judges:** Edward C. Prado, San Antonio; H. F. Garcia, San Antonio; Lucius D. Bunton III, Midland; Harry Lee Hudspeth, El Paso; James R. Nowlin, Austin; Walter S. Smith Jr., Waco. **Senior Judge:** D. W. Suttle, San Antonio. **Clerk of District Court:** Charles W. Vagner, San Antonio. **U.S. Attorney:** Helen Eversburg, San Antonio. **U.S. Marshal:** William J. Jonas Jr., San Antonio. Following are the different divisions of the Western District, and the counties in each division.

San Antonio Division

Atascosa, Bandera, Bexar, Comal, Dimmit, Frio, Gonzales, Guadalupe, Karnes, Kendall, Kerr, Medina, Real and Wilson. Court is in continuous session at San Antonio. **Magistrates:** Robert B. O'Connor, Jamie C. Boyd and Dan A. Naranjo, San Antonio. **Bankruptcy Judges:** R. Glen Ayers and Larry E. Kelly, San Antonio.

Austin Division

Bastrop, Blanco, Burleson, Burnet, Caldwell, Gillespie, Hays, Kimble, Lampasas, Lee, Llano, Mason, McCulloch, San Saba, Travis, Washington and Williamson. Court for the Austin division shall be held at Austin. **Magistrate:** Philip E. Sanders, Austin. **Bankruptcy Judge:** Larry E. Kelly, San Antonio. **Deputy in charge:** Barry Edwards.

El Paso Division

El Paso County only. Court is in continuous session in El Paso. **Magistrates:** Janet Ruesch and Philip T. Cole, El Paso. **Bankruptcy Judge:** Larry E. Kelly, San Antonio. **Deputy in charge:** Lupe E. Martinez.

Waco Division

Bell, Bosque, Coryell, Falls, Freestone, Hamilton, Hill, Leon, Limestone, McLennan, Milam, Robertson and Somervell. Court for the Waco division shall be held at Waco. **Magistrate:** Dennis Green, Waco. **Bankruptcy Judge:** R. Glen Ayres, San Antonio. **Deputy in charge:** Linda D. Wollard.

Del Rio Division

Edwards, Kinney, Maverick, Terrell, Uvalde, Val Verde and Zavala. Court for the Del Rio division shall be held at Del Rio. **Magistrate:** Durwood Edwards, Del Rio. **Bankruptcy Judge:** Larry E. Kelly, San Antonio. **Deputy in charge:** Katherine K. West.

Pecos Division

Brewster, Culberson, Hudspeth, Jeff Davis, Loving, Reeves, Pecos, Presidio, Ward and Winkler. Court for the Pecos division shall be held at Pecos. **Magistrate:** John M. Preston, Pecos. **Bankruptcy Judge:** R. Glen Ayres, San Antonio. **Deputy in charge:** Linda B. Zeman.

Midland-Odessa Division

Andrews, Crane, Ector, Martin, Midland and Upton. Court for the Midland-Odessa Division shall be held at Midland. Court may be held, in the discretion of the court, in Odessa, when courtroom facilities are made available at no expense to the government. **Magistrate:** Darrell F. Smith, Midland. **Bankruptcy Judge:** R. Glen Ayres, San Antonio. **Deputy in charge:** John D. Neil, Midland.

EASTERN TEXAS DISTRICT

District Judges.—Chief Judge, William Wayne Justice, Tyler. **Judges:** Joe J. Fisher, Beaumont; William M. Steger, Tyler; Robert M. Parker, Marshall; Howell Cobb, Beaumont; Sam Hall, Texarkana; Paul N. Brown, Sherman. **Clerk of District Court:** Murray L. Harris, Tyler. **U.S. Attorney:** Robert J. Wortham, Beaumont. **U.S. Marshal:** Keith Gary, Tyler. **Chief U.S. Probation Officer:** Wade E. French, Tyler. **Judge in Bankruptcy** for all divisions of the Eastern District: C. Houston Abel, Tyler. Following are the different divisions of the Eastern District, and the counties in each division:

Tyler Division
Anderson, Cherokee, Gregg, Henderson, Panola, Rains, Rusk, Smith, Van Zandt and Wood. Court in continuous session. **Magistrates:** Judith Guthrie, Tyler; Harry W. McKee, Tyler. **Chief Deputy:** Frank Monges. **Deputy Clerk:** Joy Vandiver.

Beaumont Division
Hardin, Jasper, Jefferson, Liberty, Newton, Orange. Court in continuous session. **Magistrates:** Earl Hines and J. Michael Bradford, Beaumont. **Deputy Clerk:** Bruce Gregory.

Marshall Division
Camp, Cass, Harrison, Marion, Morris, Upshur. Court in continuous session. **Deputy Clerk:** Peggy Anderson.

Sherman Division
Collin, Cooke, Denton and Grayson. Court in continuous session. **Magistrate:** Roger Sanders. **Deputy Clerk:** Sandra Southerland.

Texarkana Division
Bowie, Franklin and Titus. Sessions held as business dictates and as announced by the court. **Magistrate:** Charles Attaway. **Deputy Clerk:** Anita Thomason.

Paris Division
Delta, Fannin, Lamar, Red River and Hopkins. Sessions held as business dictates and as announced by the court.

Lufkin Division
Angelina, Houston, Nacogdoches, Polk, Sabine, San Augustine, Shelby, Trinity, Tyler.

SOUTHERN TEXAS DISTRICT
District Judges.—Chief Judge, John V. Singleton Jr.,

Houston. **Judges:** Carl O. Bue Jr., Ross N. Sterling, George Cire, Gabrielle McDonald, Norman Black, James DeAnda, Lynn N. Hughes and David Hittner, Houston; Hayden W. Head Jr., Corpus Christi; Hugh Gibson, Galveston; Filemon B. Vela, Brownsville; George Kazen, Laredo; Ricardo H. Hinojosa, McAllen. **Senior Judge:** Woodrow B. Seals, Houston. **Clerk of District Court:** Jesse E. Clark, Houston. **U. S. Attorney:** Henry K. Oncken, Houston. **U.S. Marshal:** Basil S. Baker, Houston. **Bankruptcy Judges:** Randolph F. Wheless Jr., Manuel D. Leal and Letitia Z. Clark, Houston. Following are the different divisions of the Southern District and the counties in each division:

Houston Division
Austin, Brazos, Colorado, Fayette, Fort Bend, Grimes, Harris, Madison, Montgomery, San Jacinto, Walker, Waller and Wharton. **Magistrates:** Calvin Botley, H. Lingo Platter, Karen K. Brown and George A. Kett Jr., Houston. **Clerk:** Jesse E. Clark.

Brownsville Division
Cameron and Willacy. **Magistrates:** William Mallett and F. G. Garza (part-time), Brownsville. **Deputy Clerk:** Sofia Anderson.

Corpus Christi Division
Aransas, Bee, Brooks, Duval, Jim Wells, Kenedy, Kleberg, Live Oak, Nueces and San Patricio. **Magistrate:** Eduardo E. deAses, Corpus Christi. **Deputy Clerk:** Sue F. McCall.

Galveston Division
Brazoria, Chambers, Galveston and Matagorda. **Deputy Clerk:** Wilfred H. Bartlett. **Magistrate:** Charles B. Smith (part-time).

Laredo Division
Jim Hogg, LaSalle, McMullen, Webb and Zapata. **Magistrate:** Marcel C. Notzon, Laredo. **Deputy Clerk:** Beatriz Garcia.

Victoria Division
Calhoun, DeWitt, Goliad, Jackson, Lavaca, Refugio and Victoria. **Deputy Clerk:** Thelma Maxine Gammon.

McAllen Division
Hidalgo and Starr. **Magistrates:** William Mallett and Susan R. Williams (part-time), McAllen. **Deputy Clerk:** Juan Barbosa.

State Higher Courts

The state's higher courts are listed below with corrections to July 1, 1985. Notations in parentheses indicate dates of expiration of terms of office. Judges of the Supreme Court, Court of Criminal Appeals and Courts of Appeals are elected to 6-year, overlapping terms. District Court judges are elected to 4-year terms. As of Sept. 1, 1985, the Chief Justice of the Supreme Court and the Presiding Judge of the Court of Criminal Appeals each received $79,310; Justices each received $78,795; Chief Justices of the Courts of Appeals received $71,379; justices received $70,915 from the state. In addition a supplemental amount may be paid by counties but total salary must be at least $1,000 less than that received by Supreme Court justices. District Court judges received $56,135 from the state, plus supplemental pay from various subdivisions. Their total salary must be $1,000 less than that received by Courts of Appeals justices.

The judiciary of the state consists of nine members of the **State Supreme Court;** nine of the **Court of Criminal Appeals;** 80 of the **Courts of Appeals;** 364 of the **State District Courts;** 10 of the **Criminal District Courts;** 146 of the **County Courts at Law;** 12 of the **Probate Courts;** 254 of the **County Courts;** 954 **Justice of the Peace Courts;** and 847 **Municipal Courts.**

Below is given information on only the Supreme Court, Court of Criminal Appeals, Courts of Appeals and state District Courts. Names of county court judges, as well as names of the various district court judges, are given by counties in two tables beginning on page 527.

Supreme Court
Chief Justice, John L. Hill Jr. (12-31-90). **Justices,** Robert M. Campbell (12-31-92); Franklin S. Spears (12-31-90); C. L. Ray (12-31-90); James P. Wallace (12-31-92); Ted Z. Robertson (12-31-88); William W. Kilgarlin (12-31-88); and Raul A. Gonzalez (12-31-88); Oscar Mauzy (12-31-92). **Clerk of Court,** Mary M. Wakefield. **Location of court,** Austin.

Court of Criminal Appeals
Presiding Judge, John F. Onion Jr. (12-31-88). **Justices:** W. C. Davis (12-31-90); Sam Houston Clinton (12-31-90); Michael J. McCormick (12-31-90); Marvin O.

Teague (12-31-92); Chuck Miller (12-31-88); Charles F. Campbell (12-31-88); M. P. Duncan III (12-31-92); Bill White (12-31-90). In 1971, the 62nd Legislature authorized the appointment of two **Commissioners** to assist the Court of Criminal Appeals. In 1977, a constitutional amendment raised the number of judges to eight, doing away with the office of commissioner, effective Jan. 1, 1978. **State's Attorney,** Robert Huttash. **Clerk of Court,** Thomas Lowe. **Location of court,** Austin.

Courts of Appeals
These courts have jurisdiction within their respective supreme judicial districts. A constitutional amendment approved in 1978 raised the number of associate justices for Courts of Appeals where needed. Judges are elected from the district for 6-year terms. Another amendment adopted in 1980 changed the name of the old Courts of Civil Appeals to the **Courts of Appeals** and changed the jurisdiction of the courts. See Art. V, Sec. 6 of the State Constitution.

First District—*Houston. Chief Justice, Frank Evans III (12-31-92). Justices: James F. Warren (12-31-92); Jackson B. Smith (12-31-88); Sam H. Bass Jr. (12-31-88); F. Lee Duggan Jr. (12-31-88); M. B. Cohen (12-31-88); Ben G. Levy (12-31-88); Kenneth M. Hoyt (12-31-90); and D. Camille Dunn (12-31-90). Clerk of court, Kathryn Cox. Counties in the First District are as follows: Austin, Brazoria, Brazos, Burleson, Chambers, Colorado, Fort Bend, Galveston, Grimes, Harris, Trinity, Walker, Waller, Washington.

Second District—Fort Worth: Chief Justice, Howard M. Fender (12-31-88). Justices: David Keltner (12-31-88); David Farris (12-31-88); William E. Burdock (12-31-88); Joe Spurlock II (12-31-88); John Hill (12-31-90); and Hal Lattimore (12-31-90). Clerk of court, Yvonne Palmer. Counties in Second District are as follows: Archer, Clay, Cooke, Denton, Hood, Jack, Montague, Parker, Tarrant, Wichita, Wise, Young.

Third District—Austin: Chief Justice, Bob Shannon (12-31-90). Justices: John Powers (12-31-92); James L. Carroll (12-31-92); Jim Brady (12-31-88); Robert A. Gammage (12-31-88); and Marilyn Aboussie (12-31-88). Clerk of court, Susan K. Bage. Counties in the Third District are as follows: Bastrop, Bell, Blanco, Burnet, Caldwell, Coke, Comal, Concho, Fayette, Hays, Irion, Lampasas, Lee, Llano, McCulloch, Milam, Mills, Runnels, San Saba, Schleicher, Sterling, Tom Green, Travis, Williamson.

Fourth District—San Antonio: Chief Justice, Carlos C. Cadena (12-31-90). Justices: Rudolf S. Esquivel (12-31-92); Shirley W. Butts (12-31-88); Antonio G. Cantu (12-31-88); and Preston H. Dial Jr. (12-31-88). Clerk of court, Herb Schaefer. Counties in the Fourth District are as follows: Atascosa, Bandera, Bexar, Brooks, Dimmit, Duval, Edwards, Frio, Gillespie, Guadalupe, Jim Hogg, Jim Wells, Karnes, Kendall, Kerr, Kimble, Kinney, La Salle, McMullen, Mason, Maverick, Medina, Menard, Real, Starr, Sutton, Uvalde, Val Verde, Webb, Wilson, Zapata, Zavala.

Fifth District—Dallas: Chief Justice, Craig T. Enoch (12-31-88); Justices: Bill J. Stephens (12-31-88); Warren Whitham (12-31-88); Joseph A. Devaney (12-31-88); Charles Ben Howell (12-31-90); Pat McClung (12-31-90); Annette Stewart (12-31-92); Gordon Rowe (12-31-90); Nathan Hecht (12-31-88); James A. Baker (12-31-88); Sue Lagarde (12-31-88); Linda Thomas (12-31-92); and John L. McCraw Jr. (12-31-88). Clerk of Court, Kenneth P. Stripling. Counties in the Fifth District are as follows: Collin, Dallas, Grayson, Hunt, Kaufman, Rockwall, Van Zandt.

Sixth District—Texarkana: Chief Justice, William J. Cornelius (12-31-92). Justices: Charles M. Bleil (12-31-88) and Ben Z. Grant (12-31-90). Clerk of court, Louise Waldrop Lohse. Counties in the Sixth District are as follows: Bowie, Camp, Cass, Delta, Fannin, Franklin, Gregg, Harrison, Hopkins, Hunt, Lamar, Marion, Morris, Panola, Red River, Rusk, Titus, Upshur, Wood.

Seventh District—Amarillo: Chief Justice, Charles L. Reynolds (12-31-90). Justices: Carlton B. Dodson (12-31-92); Richard N. Countiss (12-31-88); and John T. Boyd (12-31-88). Clerk of court, Peggy Culp. Counties in the Seventh District are as follows: Armstrong, Bailey, Briscoe, Carson, Castro, Childress, Cochran, Collingsworth, Cottle, Crosby, Dallam, Deaf Smith, Dickens, Donley, Floyd, Foard, Garza, Gray, Hale, Hall, Hansford, Hardeman, Hartley, Hemphill, Hockley, Hutchinson, Kent, King, Lamb, Lipscomb, Lubbock, Lynn, Moore, Motley, Ochiltree, Oldham, Parmer, Potter, Randall, Roberts, Sherman, Swisher, Terry, Wheeler, Wilbarger, Yoakum.

Eighth District—El Paso: Chief Justice, Max Osborn (12-31-90). Justices: Jerry Woodard (12-31-92); Larry Fuller (12-31-92); and Charles R. Schulte (12-31-88). Clerk of court, Barbara B. Dorris. Counties in the Eighth District are as follows: Andrews, Brewster, Crane, Crockett, Culberson, Ector, El Paso, Gaines, Glasscock, Hudspeth, Jeff Davis, Loving, Martin, Midland, Pecos, Presidio, Reagan, Reeves, Terrell, Upton, Ward, Winkler.

Ninth District—Beaumont: Chief Justice, Martin Dies Jr. (12-31-90). Justices: Jack Brookshire (12-31-88) and Don Burgess (12-31-92). Clerk of court, Shirley Forrest. Counties in the Ninth District are as follows: Angelina, Hardin, Jasper, Jefferson, Liberty, Montgomery, Newton, Orange, Polk, San Jacinto, Tyler.

Tenth District—Waco: Chief Justice, Frank G. McDonald (12-31-88). Justices: Vic Hall (12-31-92) and Bob L. Thomas (12-31-90). Clerk of court, Robert G. Watts. Counties in the Tenth District are as follows: Bosque, Brazos, Coryell, Ellis, Falls, Freestone, Hamilton, Hill, Johnson, Leon, Limestone, McLennan, Madison, Navarro, Robertson, Somervell.

Eleventh District—Eastland: Chief Justice, Austin O. McCloud (12-31-88). Justices: William G. Arnot (12-31-88) and Charles R. Dickenson (12-31-92). Clerk of court, Oleta Moseley. Counties in the Eleventh District are as follows: Baylor, Borden, Brown, Callahan, Coleman, Comanche, Dawson, Eastland, Erath, Fisher, Haskell, Howard, Jones, Knox, Mitchell, Nolan, Palo Pinto, Scurry, Shackelford, Stephens, Stonewall, Taylor, Throckmorton.

Twelfth District—Tyler: Chief Justice, J. W. Summers (12-31-90). Justices: James W. Bass Jr. (12-31-92) and Paul S. Colley (12-31-92). Clerk of court, Barbara A. Holman. Counties in the Twelfth District are as follows: Anderson, Cherokee, Gregg, Henderson, Hopkins, Houston, Kaufman, Nacogdoches, Panola, Rains, Rusk, Sabine, Smith, San Augustine, Shelby, Upshur, Van Zandt, Wood.

Thirteenth District—Corpus Christi: Chief Justice, Paul W. Nye (12-31-88). Justices: Noah O. Kennedy (12-31-88); Norman L. Utter (12-31-88); Robert J. Seerden

(12-31-92); Fortunato P. Benavides (12-31-88); and J. Bonner Dorsey (12-31-90). Clerk of court, Beth Gray. Counties in the Thirteenth District are as follows: Aransas, Bee, Calhoun, Cameron, DeWitt, Goliad, Gonzales, Hidalgo, Jackson, Kenedy, Kleberg, Lavaca, Live Oak, Matagorda, Nueces, Refugio, San Patricio, Victoria, Wharton, Willacy.

Fourteenth District—†Houston: Chief Justice, J. Curtiss Brown (12-31-90). Justices: Paul Pressler (12-31-92); William E. Junell (12-31-92); Paul C. Murphy (12-31-90); Ross A. Sears (12-31-88); George T. Ellis (12-31-88); Joe L. Draughn (12-31-88); Bill Cannon (12-31-88); and Samuel H. Robertson Jr. (12-31-88). Clerk of court, Mary Jane Smart. Counties in the Fourteenth District are as follows: Austin, Brazoria, Brazos, Burleson, Chambers, Colorado, Fort Bend, Galveston, Grimes, Harris, Trinity, Walker, Waller, Washington.

*The location of the First Court of Appeals was changed from Galveston to Houston by the Fifty-fifth Legislature, with the provision that all cases originated in Galveston County be tried in that city and with the further provision that any case may, at the discretion of the court, be tried in either city.

†Because of the heavy workload of the Houston area Court of Appeals, the Sixtieth Legislature, in 1967, provided for the establishment of a Fourteenth Appeals Court at Houston.

Administrative Judicial Districts of Texas

There are nine administrative judicial districts in the state for administrative purposes. An active or retired district judge or an active or retired appellate judge with judicial experience in a district court serves as the Presiding Judge upon appointment by the Governor. They receive extra compensation of $5,000 paid by counties in the respective administrative districts.

The Presiding Judge convenes an annual conference of the judges in the administrative district to consult on the state of business in the courts. This conference is empowered to adopt rules for the administration of cases in the district. The Presiding Judge may assign active or retired district judges residing within the administrative district to any of the district courts within the administrative district. The Presiding Judge of one administrative district may request the Presiding Judge of another administrative district to assign a judge from that district to sit in a district court located in the administrative district of the Presiding Judge making the request.

The Chief Justice of the Supreme Court of Texas convenes an annual conference of the nine Presiding Judges to determine the need for assignment of judges and to promote the uniform administration of the assignment of judges. The Chief Justice is empowered to assign judges of one administrative district for service in another whenever such assignments are necessary for the prompt and efficient administration of justice.

First District—Presiding Judge, Ron Chapman, Dallas: Anderson, Bowie, Camp, Cass, Cherokee, Collin, Dallas, Delta, Ellis, Fannin, Franklin, Grayson, Gregg, Harrison, Henderson, Hopkins, Houston, Hunt, Kaufman, Lamar, Marion, Morris, Nacogdoches, Panola, Rains, Red River, Rockwall, Rusk, Shelby, Smith, Titus, Upshur, Van Zandt and Wood.

Second District—Thomas J. Stovall Jr., Huntsville: Angelina, Bastrop, Brazoria, Brazos, Burleson, Chambers, Fort Bend, Freestone, Galveston, Grimes, Hardin, Harris, Jasper, Jefferson, Lee, Leon, Liberty, Limestone, Madison, Matagorda, Montgomery, Newton, Orange, Polk, Robertson, Sabine, San Augustine, San Jacinto, Trinity, Tyler, Walker, Waller, Washington and Wharton.

Third District—James F. Clawson Jr., Belton: Austin, Bell, Blanco, Bosque, Burnet, Caldwell, Colorado, Comal, Comanche, Coryell, Falls, Fayette, Gonzales, Guadalupe, Hamilton, Hays, Hill, Johnson, Lampasas, Lavaca, Llano, McLennan, Mason, Milam, Navarro, San Saba, Somervell, Travis and Williamson.

Fourth District—Joe E. Kelly, Victoria: Aransas, Atascosa, Bee, Bexar, Calhoun, DeWitt, Dimmit, Frio, Goliad, Jackson, Karnes, LaSalle, Live Oak, Maverick, McMullen, Refugio, San Patricio, Victoria, Webb, Wilson, Zapata and Zavala.

Fifth District—Joe B. Evins, Edinburg: Brooks, Cameron, Duval, Hidalgo, Jim Hogg, Jim Wells, Kenedy, Kleberg, Nueces, Starr and Willacy.

Sixth District—Sam M. Paxson, El Paso: Bandera, Brewster, Crockett, Culberson, Edwards, El Paso, Gillespie, Hudspeth, Jeff Davis, Kendall, Kerr, Kimble, Kinney, Medina, Pecos, Presidio, Reagan, Real, Sutton, Terrell, Upton, Uvalde and Val Verde.

Seventh District—Weldon Kirk, Sweetwater: Andrews, Borden, Brown, Callahan, Coke, Coleman, Concho, Crane, Dawson, Ector, Fisher, Gaines, Garza, Glasscock, Haskell, Howard, Irion, Jones, Kent, Loving, Lynn, McCulloch, Martin, Menard, Midland, Mills, Mitchell, Nolan, Reeves, Runnels, Schleicher, Scurry, Shackelford, Sterling, Stonewall, Taylor, Throckmorton, Tom Green, Ward and Winkler.

Eighth District—Charles J. Murray, Fort Worth: Archer, Clay, Cooke, Denton, Eastland, Erath, Hood, Jack, Montague, Palo Pinto, Parker, Stephens, Tarrant, Wichita, Wise and Young.

Ninth District—Ray D. Anderson, Brownfield: Armstrong, Bailey, Baylor, Briscoe, Carson, Castro, Childress, Cochran, Collingsworth, Cottle, Crosby, Dallam, Deaf Smith, Dickens, Donley, Floyd, Foard, Gray, Hale, Hall, Hansford, Hardeman, Hartley, Hemphill, Hockley, Hutchinson, King, Knox, Lamb, Lipscomb, Lubbock, Moore, Motley, Ochiltree, Oldham, Parmer, Potter, Randall, Roberts, Sherman, Swisher, Terry, Wheeler, Wilbarger and Yoakum.

History of Texas Public Lands

The History of Texas Public Lands was revised for the Texas Almanac by **Commissioner Garry Mauro** and the staff of the General Land Office of Texas. It is a summary of a longer history of the Texas **public domain** in the General Land Office.

The **Texas General Land Office** is one of the oldest governmental entities in the state, dating back to the Republic. The practice of having a commissioner to administer public lands reaches even farther back into Texas history when proprietors of Spanish and Mexican land grants "commissioned" representatives to handle land transactions.

Before the American Revolution, proprietors of the colonies along the eastern seaboard established land offices under the supervision of the commissioned representative to sell land and control squatting or trespassing. Later in Texas, when the Mexican government began issuing land grants for colonization, each empresario colony had a land commissioner to issue individual land titles and settle disputes.

The first General Land Office was established in the **constitution of the Republic of Texas** in 1836, and the first Texas Congress enacted the provision into law in 1837. However, President Sam Houston vetoed the act on the grounds that the office would not be able to function properly until the records of the various empresario colonies, Spanish and Mexican land grants, and the appropriate archives could be properly gathered together. But the new Congress was so anxious to settle land questions that it overrode his veto.

The sale of public lands had been temporarily suspended during the War for Texas Independence from Mexico, and there was a great clamor to open up the public lands again. New settlers were arriving every day and the demand for free or cheap land was tremendous.

Because the new Texas government needed to become stable and productive, it sought to attract and keep these settlers. The Texas Congress enacted generous laws offering large tracts of land to just about anyone who wanted them. For example, all heads of households in Texas as of March 2, 1836, were entitled to a league and a labor of land (about 4,605 acres). Single men could claim a third of a league. In the 10 years Texas existed as a Republic, it alloted 41,570,733 acres to encourage settlement, to reward veterans of the War for Independence, to pay the Republic's debts and to finance its operations.

In 1844, as negotiations proceeded for Texas to join the Union, the resulting treaty stipulated that the U.S. would pay $10 million of the Republic's debts and acquire 175 million acres of the public domain. Opponents to statehood in the U.S. Congress felt that Texas' lands were not worth the assumption of the $10 million debt and refused to make the trade. In the final resolution for annexation, Texas was to keep its public domain and the U.S. was to disclaim any responsibility for Texas' debt. Texas officially came into the Union Dec. 29, 1845, keeping both its debt and its public lands.

When the first **state constitution** was drawn up in July, 1845, it provided no major change in the administration of the Texas public domain. All land titles issued under the laws of Spain, Mexico and the Republic of Texas were recognized. The Commissioner of the General Land Office became one of the elected constitutional officials of the state government.

In the early years of statehood, Texas established the precedent of using its vast public domain for public benefit. The first use was to sell or trade off land to eliminate the huge debt remaining from the War for Independence and early years of the Republic. A west-

ern area of 67 million acres, now part of New Mexico, Colorado, Oklahoma, Kansas and Wyoming, was transferred to the United States by the Texas Legislature on Nov. 25, 1850. Texas received $10 million in government bonds. The state had shed all its debts by 1855 and still had over 98 million acres of open domain. Texas gave away land for internal improvements, homesteads, veterans grants, capitol construction, and for settlement of boundary disputes. More than 32 million acres were given away to promote railroad construction. And 50 million acres were set aside as an **endowment to public schools and colleges.**

By 1898, there was very little remaining unappropriated public land in Texas. The **homestead policy,** which had seen 4.8 million acres of land given away to settlers, was finally abandoned in 1899. The Legislature in 1900 determined that the public schools and the **Permanent School Fund** would receive all unsurveyed land and the few remaining unappropriated public lands. Finally, in 1939, all lakes, bays, islands and the submerged areas off the Texas coast accrued to the School Fund.

The end of the vast unappropriated public domain might have signaled the end of the use of public land for the benefit of all Texans. But when oil was discovered in 1921 on state lands under lease, this remaining public land became a most valuable economic asset to the state. After selling off 91.4 percent of its surface land without reserving mineral rights, Texas finally had established the right to its subsurface minerals in 1895. And the Relinquishment Act of 1919 gave the surface owners of the land rights to participate in the mineral wealth as "agents" of the state. The economic value of the public lands of Texas in the 20th Century thus resulted from the belated development of its mineral ownership.

Today 22.2 million acres are considered to be in the **public domain.** This includes almost 4 million acres of submerged coastal lands, which are bays, inlets and the area from the Texas shoreline to the three marine league line (10.36 miles) in the Gulf of Mexico. In addition, more than one million acres are estimated to make up the state's riverbeds and vacant areas. The University of Texas System holds title to 2,109,000 fee acres and other state agencies or special schools hold title to approximately 3.5 million acres. Texas owns mineral rights alone in approximately 7.4 million covered under the Relinquishment Act, Free Royalty Act and the various sales acts and has outright ownership to approximately 860,000 upland acres, mostly west of the Pecos. Texas has liens on 1.5 million acres of land in the active accounts of the Veterans Land Board and another 1.7 million acres of excess land that are not calculated into any category.

Perhaps the most valuable segment of the Texas public domain is its **coastal submerged land.** And for some time, there was serious question about the state's ownership. The Republic of Texas had proclaimed its Gulf boundaries as three marine leagues, recognized by international law as traditional national boundaries. These boundaries were never seriously questioned when Texas joined the Union in 1845, and Texas continued to claim jurisdiction. A congressional resolution in 1930 authorized the U.S. Attorney General to file suit to establish the offshore lands as properties of the federal government.

The legal question was more important to Texas in the 20th century than it would have been upon entering the Union, since offshore oil and gas production had become a source of tremendous income to the state. Gulf of Mexico leases between the three-mile and the three-marine league limit (the area claimed by the federal government) have brought the state approximately $1.5 billion in revenue since the first oil lease there in 1922. Congress returned the disputed lands to Texas in 1953, and the Supreme Court finally confirmed Texas' ownership to the 1,878,394 acres in 1960. (See Tidelands History in 1972-73 Texas Almanac.)

In 1978, the federal government also granted states a "fair and equitable" share of the revenues from offshore federal leases within three miles of the states' outermost boundary. The states did not receive any such revenue until April 1986 when Congress clarified the meaning of "fair and equitable" through additional legislation. Under the 1986 law, coastal states are entitled to 27 percent of all revenues in perpetuity from federal leases within three miles of the state-federal boundary. In addition, Texas received a one-time settlement to cover the 1978 to 1985 period amounting to $426 million in Fiscal Year 1986 and a deferred payment of $134 million over 15 years.

The General Land Office handles leases and revenue accounting on all lands dedicated to the **Permanent School Fund** and on land owned by various state agencies. The Land Commissioner, two members of the University of Texas Board of Regents and one A&M University Board of Regents member make up the Board for Lease of lands dedicated to the **Permanent University Fund.** Revenue accounting for income from Permanent University Lands is processed by the University of Texas; investment income from the fund is divided approximately two-thirds to one-third between the University of Texas and Texas A&M University, respectively. As of August 31, 1986, the **Permanent University Fund** has a book value of more than $2.6 billion; the **Permanent School Fund** has a book value of more than $5.7 billion.

All activities on state lands are reviewed for their environmental impact, and restrictions are placed in offshore drilling lessons where needed to protect resources.

Veterans Land Program

In 1946, the Legislature created a bond program to aid veterans in purchasing farm land. Up to $1.25 billion in bonding authority has been authorized over the years in a series of constitutional amendments; as of Jan. 1, 1987, $1.05 billion of the bonds had been sold to fund loans.

Loans cannot exceed $20,000, and tracts purchased through the program must be at least five acres. To date, 90,000 veterans have participated in the land program, purchasing more than 4.4 million acres of land.

Veterans Housing Assistance Program

The 68th Legislature created the Veterans Housing Assistance Program, which also is funded through bond proceeds. With the passage of two constitutional amendments, the people of Texas have authorized the selling of $1 billion in bonds to finance the veterans housing program. To date, $750 million in bonds have been sold to fund housing loans.

Eligible veterans may borrow up to $20,000 toward the purchase of a home; the balance of the purchase price is financed through private sector lending institutions. When the low interest veterans loan is combined with private sector interest rates, monthly payments are significantly reduced. Since the program began operation in January 1984, more than 23,700 veterans have been certified as eligible to receive a housing loan.

Veterans Home Improvement Program

In 1986, the Veterans Land Board implemented the Veterans Home Improvement Program, which is funded through the Housing Assistance Program. The Home Improvement Program allows Texas Veterans to borrow between $5,000 and $15,000 to make substantial home repairs and improvements.

To date, 2,200 or more veterans have applied for a Veterans Home Improvement loan. In excess of $6 million has been loaned since the program's inception.

All three programs are administered by the Veterans Land Board, which is chaired by the Texas Land Commissioner. The bonded debt for the programs and all administrative costs are completely financed by the veterans who use the programs; there is no cost to Texas taxpayers. Eligible veterans may participate in each of the three veterans programs.

Details about the programs may be obtained from the Veterans Land Board by calling toll free 1-800-252-VETS.

Public Lands of Texas

Taken from the records of the General Land Office of Texas, the following summary shows the disposition of the public domain. The total area given here differs from the U.S. Census Bureau figure of 171,096,320 given elsewhere in this volume.

	Acres.	Subtotals
Total area to tidewater		172,193,269
Total area to 3-league (10.36-mile) limit		3,997,000
		176,190,269
Grants to promote citizenship and to induce immigration—		
By governments of Spain and Mexico	26,280,000	
Headrights and bounties	36,876,492	
Colonies—(Peter's, Mercer's et al.)	4,494,806	
Homestead donations (pre-emptions)	4,847,136—	72,498,434
Donations to veterans—		
San Jacinto veterans—Act of 1879 and 1881	1,169,382	
Confederate veterans—Act of 1881	1,979,852—	3,149,234
Sold to pay public debts by Republic	1,329,200	
50c Sales scrip act of 1879 and $2 sales scrip act of 1887	1,660,936—	2,990,136
Internal improvements—		
State Capitol Building	3,025,000	
Irrigation, drainage, iron works, Kiamasha Road and sundry	4,088,640—	7,113,640
To acquire transportation facilities—		
Grants to railroads	32,153,878—	32,153,878
For education—		
State University and A&M	2,329,168	
County school purposes	4,229,166	
Eleemosynary institutions	410,600	
Public free school	44,443,744	
Unsold public school land	863,540—	52,276,218
Total surveyed land		170,181,540
Less conflicts (estimated at one half of 1 percent)		850,908
Net as per original surveys		169,330,632
Excess (estimated at approximately 1.1 percent)		1,862,637
River beds and vacancies (estimated)		1,000,000
Submerged coastal areas to three-league limit		3,997,000
Total		176,190,269

Wet and Dry Counties

When approved in local option elections in "wet" precincts of counties, sale of liquor by the drink is permitted in Texas. This resulted from adoption of an amendment to the Texas Constitution in 1970 and subsequent legislation, followed by local option elections. For the first time in more than 50 years liquor by the drink was made legal in Texas.

Below are compilations showing the status of wet and dry counties in Texas as of Aug. 31, 1986. A dagger (†) indicates counties in which the sale of mixed beverages is legal in all or part of the county (91). An asterisk (*) indicates counties wholly wet (36). All others are dry in part (75).

Counties in Which Distilled Spirits Are Legal (174): Anderson, †*Aransas, Archer, Atascosa, †*Austin, †Bandera, *Bastrop, †*Bee, †Bell, †*Bexar, †Blanco, Bosque, †Brazoria, †*Brazos, †*Brewster, Brooks, Brown, Burleson, †Burnet, †Calhoun, Callahan, †*Cameron, †Camp, Carson, Cass, Castro, Chambers, Childress, Clay, Coleman, Collin, †*Colorado, †*Comal, Comanche, Cooke, Crane, †*Culberson, Dallam, †Dallas, Deaf Smith, †Denton, †DeWitt, Dickens, †Dimmit, †Donley, †*Duval, Eastland, †Ector, Edwards, Ellis, †*El Paso, †Falls, Fannin, †Fayette, †*Fort Bend, †Frio, †Galveston, Garza, †Gillespie, †Goliad, Gonzales, Gray, Grayson, Gregg, †Grimes, †Guadalupe, Hall, Hamilton, Hardin, †Harris, Harrison, Haskell, †Hays, †Henderson, †*Hidalgo, Hill, Hood, Howard, †*Hudspeth, Hunt, Hutchinson, †Jackson, Jasper, Jeff Davis, †Jefferson, †*Jim Hogg, †Jim Wells, *Karnes, Kaufman, †*Kendall, Kenedy, †Kerr, Kimble, King, †*Kinney, †Kleberg, †Lamar, Lampasas, †La Salle, †Lavaca, †Lee, Leon, Liberty, Lipscomb, Live Oak, †Llano, †*Loving, †*Lubbock, Marion, †Matagorda, †Maverick, †McCulloch, †McLennan, †Medina, Menard, †Midland, Milam, Mills, Mitchell, †Montgomery, †*Moore, Nacogdoches, †Navarro, Newton, Nolan, †Nueces, †Orange, Palo Pinto, Pecos, †Polk, †Potter, †*Presidio, Rains, †Randall, *Reagan, Red River, †Reeves, Refugio, Robertson, Runnels, San Augustine, San Jacinto, †San Patricio, San Saba, Schleicher, Shelby, †*Starr, Stonewall, †*Sutton, †Tarrant, †Taylor, †Terrell, †Titus, †Tom Green, †*Travis, †Trinity, Upshur, †Upton, Uvalde, †Val Verde, †Victoria, †Walker, †Waller, Ward, †*Washington, †*Webb, †Wharton, †Wichita, Wilbarger, †Willacy, †Williamson, †*Wilson, †Winkler, †*Zapata, †Zavala.

Counties in Which Only Beer Is Legal (15): Baylor, Caldwell, Cherokee, Concho, Dawson, Glasscock, Hartley, Hockley, Irion, Mason, McMullen, Oldham, Sabine, Stephens, Wise.

Counties in Which 14 Percent Beverages Are Legal (2): Limestone, Somervell.

Counties Wholly Dry (62): Andrews, Angelina, Armstrong, Bailey, Borden, Bowie, Briscoe, Cochran, Coke, Collingsworth, Coryell, Cottle, Crockett, Crosby, Delta, Erath, Fisher, Floyd, Foard, Franklin, Freestone, Gaines, Hale, Hansford, Hardeman, Hemphill, Hopkins, Houston, Jack, Johnson, Jones, Kent, Knox, Lamb, Lynn, Madison, Martin, Montague, Morris, Motley, Ochiltree, Panola, Parker, Parmer, Real, Roberts, Rockwall, Rusk, Scurry, Schackelford, Sherman, Smith, Sterling, Swisher, Terry, Throckmorton, Tyler, Van Zandt, Wheeler, Wood, Yoakum, Young.

Texas Main Street Project

To encourage Texas cities to rehabilitate and reuse existing historic buildings, the Texas Historical Commission began the Texas Main Street Project in 1981. The project is primarily a technical assistance program. Each year, five cities are selected to be officially designated Main Street cities. Sponsorship of the project can be by the municipal government, community development corporation, chamber of commerce or downtown organization.

The Texas Main Street Project office provides architectural design assistance and supervision for the Main Street managers, and each city receives a three-day visit by a professional team of consultants who provide immediate and long-term suggestions for the community's revitalization. Other state agencies, including the Texas Economic Development Commission, the Texas Department of Community Affairs, the Texas Department of Agriculture, the Texas Tourist Development Agency and the Governor's Office, provide additional assistance.

Following is a list of Texas Main Street cities as of January 1987, grouped by year of designation. An asterisk before the name denotes a city no longer active in the program. Self-initiated cities are listed last.

1981: *Eagle Pass, Hillsboro, *Navasota, *Plainview, Sequin. 1982: *Gainesville, Georgetown, *Kingsville, *Marshall, McKinney. 1983: Brenham, *Harlingen, Lufkin, *Stamford, Waxahachie. 1984: Belton, *Brownwood, Ennis, *Goliad, Paris. 1985: Corsicana, Cuero, Lampasas, Mineral Wells, Sweetwater. 1986: Greenville, Palestine, Pampa, Pittsburg, San Marcos. 1987: Kilgore, Post, Terrell, Weatherford, Wharton.

Self-initiated cities include: *Alvin, *Athens, Big Spring, *Conroe, Daingerfield, *Edinburg, Floresville, Fort Worth-Polytechnic, Grapevine, Lewisville, *Longview, Port Lavaca, *Sherman, *Sinton, Taylor, Temple, *Tomball, *Uvalde and Wichita Falls.

Health Care

Even though population and knowledge of medicine and health care are increasing, and this field of essential services has greatly expanded in Texas, many small communities of the state have no doctor and must rely upon other places for hospitalization. Houston, Dallas and some other cities are internationally known for their medical centers.

Health care has become the number one concern of Texans, as evidenced by the coverage of health care issues by the Texas media. Rural parts of the state have continued to expand their health care capabilities to care for the growing populations in those areas.

The following information has been supplied chiefly by the **Texas Hospital Association** and the **Texas Department of Health, Bureau of Vital Statistics.**

Hospitals

Texas hospitals employed 215,005 persons in 1985 at a record payroll of more than $4.2 billion. These employees were reported by the 561 hospitals with 86,350 beds registered with the American Hospital Association. One of every 12 U.S. hospitals is located in Texas.

The average length of stay in the 480 short-term, general hospitals was 6.1 days in 1985, compared to 6.8 days in 1975. The length of stay in Texas hospitals was one day less than the U.S. average and the average cost per admission was $2,799, which was 16 percent less than the U.S. average of $3,245. Admissions to short-term, general hospitals totaled 2,234,834 or 92 percent of the total admissions to all Texas hospitals. There were 43,719 RNs, 18,404 LVNs and 4,536 health care professions trainees working in Texas hospitals in 1985.

Allied Health Training

Hospitals are the leading source of allied health education in Texas with over 90 percent of all allied health personnel either completely or partially educated in a clinical, internship or residency situation within the hospital.

The University of Texas system, as well as Texas Woman's University with campuses in all of the major urban areas, are Texas' major providers of health care professionals.

Texas continues to experience a shortage of allied health manpower. Student enrollments and the number of graduates have increased steadily over the past five years. However, there is still a great demand for physical therapists, occupational therapists, respiratory therapists, medical records technicians, medical technologists, radiologic technologists, pharmacists and registered nurses. In the forseeable future, these demands for manpower will continue to exist due largely to the population growth and the expanding requirements for health services.

The Texas Health Careers Program, P.O. Box 15587, Austin, Texas 78761, has free information available for anyone interested in a career in the health field.

Schools of Nursing

There are currently 71 schools of nursing in Texas accredited by the **Board of Nurse Examiners** for the State of Texas. Forty-three offer associate degree programs, 23 offer baccalaureate degree programs and 3 have hospital diploma programs.

The associate degree programs include: **Alvin Junior College** Department of Nursing, Alvin; **Amarillo College** Associate Degree Nursing Program, Amarillo; **Austin Community College**, Austin; **Lee College** Associate Degree Nursing Program, Baytown; **Lamar University** Associate Degree Nursing Program, Beaumont; **How-**

ard County Junior College Associate Degree Nursing Program, Big Spring; Frank Phillips Junior College Associate Degree Nursing Program, Borger; Texas Southmost College School of Nursing, Brownsville; Del Mar College Department of Registered Nurse Education, Corpus Christi; Navarro College School of Nursing, Corsicana; El Centro College Division of Associate Degree Nursing, Dallas; Grayson County College Associate Degree of Nursing Program, Denison; Pan American University Department of Nursing, Edinburg; El Paso Community College Department of Nursing, El Paso; Tarrant County Junior College Department of Nursing, Fort Worth; Cooke County Junior College Department of Nursing, Gainesville; Galveston College, Galveston; Henderson Community College School of Nursing, Henderson; Harris County Hospital District, Houston; Houston Baptist University Associate Degree Nursing Program, Houston; Houston Community College Department of Nursing, Houston; North Harris County College Associate Degree Nursing Program, Houston; Southwestern Adventist College Department of Nursing, Keene; Kilgore College Department of Nursing, Kilgore; Central Texas College School of Nursing, Killeen; Brazosport College Associate Degree Nusing Program, Lake Jackson; Laredo Junior College Department of Nursing, Laredo; Angelina College Division of Nursing, Lufkin; Midland College School of Nursing, Midland; Odessa College Associate Degree Nursing Program, Odessa; Paris Junior College Department of Nursing, Paris; San Jacinto College Department of Nursing Education, Pasadena; Angelo State University Department of Nursing, San Angelo; San Antonio College Department of Nursing, San Antonio; Western Texas College Associate Degree Nursing Program, Snyder; Tarleton State University School of Nursing, Stephenville; Texarkana Community College William Buchanan Department of Nursing, Texarkana; College of the Mainland

Nursing Department, Texas City; Tyler Junior College, Tyler; Victoria College Associate Degree Nursing Program, Victoria; McLennan Community College Department of Nursing, Waco; Wharton County Junior College School of Nursing, Wharton; Midwestern University Department of Nursing, Wichita Falls.

Baccalaureate degree programs include: Abilene Intercollegiate School of Nursing, Abilene; University of Texas School of Nursing at Arlington, Arlington; The University of Texas School of Nursing at Austin, Austin; Lamar University School of Nursing, Beaumont; Mary Hardin-Baylor University Department of Nursing, Belton; West Texas State University School of Nursing, Canyon; Baylor University School of Nursing, Dallas; Dallas Baptist College Division of Nursing, Dallas; Texas Woman's University College of Nursing (which also offers the master's and doctoral degrees in nursing), Denton; The University of Texas School of Nursing at El Paso, El Paso; Texas Christian University Harris College of Nursing, Fort Worth; The University of Texas School of Nursing at Galveston, Galveston; Houston Baptist University School of Nursing, Houston; Texas Woman's University School of Nursing, Houston; University of St. Thomas School of Nursing, Houston; The University of Texas School of Nursing at Houston, Houston; Prairie View A&M University College of Nursing, Houston; Incarnate Word College Department of Nursing, San Antonio; The University of Texas School of Nursing at San Antonio, San Antonio; Texas Tech University School of Nursing, Lubbock; Stephen F. Austin University School of Nursing, Nacogdoches; University of Texas at Tyler School of Nursing, Tyler; Baylor University School of Nursing, Waco.

The hospital diploma programs are: Northwest Texas Hospital School of Nursing, Amarillo; Methodist Hospital School of Nursing, Lubbock; Baptist Memorial Hospital School of Nursing, San Antonio.

LIVE BIRTHS AND DEATHS
(Rates per 1,000 Estimated Population)

Year	Live Births No.	Live Births Rate	Deaths No.	Deaths Rate
1967	203,790	19.2	86,193	8.1
1968	207,191	19.2	92,098	8.5
1969	220,647	20.0	93,336	8.5
1970	230,624	20.6	94,287	8.4
1971	228,983	20.0	94,724	8.3
1972	214,613	18.4	99,275	8.5
1973	209,651	17.8	101,487	8.6
1974	210,787	17.5	99,426	8.3
1975	215,426	17.6	98,354	8.0
1976	218,447	17.5	100,620	8.1
1977	228,871	17.8	100,077	7.8
1978	236,612	18.2	103,670	8.0
1979	254,263	19.0	104,745	7.8
1980	273,433	19.2	108,018	7.6
1981	281,558	19.1	110,498	7.5
1982	297,683	19.5	111,263	7.3
1983	295,178	18.8	114,714	7.3
1984	298,756	18.7	116,755	7.3
1985	308,027	18.8	118,183	7.2

CAUSES OF DEATH

The 10 leading causes of death in Texas in 1985, and the rate per 100,000 population were:

Cause	Deaths	*Rate	% of Total Deaths
All Causes	118,183	721.9	100.0
Heart Disease	40,079	244.8	33.9
Malignant Neoplasms...	24,032	146.8	20.3
Cerebrovascular Diseases...........	8,793	53.7	7.4
Accidents and Adverse Effects......	7,095	43.3	6.0
Bronchitis, Emphysema, Asthma, and Allied Conditions	3,730	22.8	3.2
Pneumonia, Influenza ..	3,521	21.5	3.0
Suicide..............	2,236	13.7	1.9
Homicide...........	2,213	13.5	1.9
Diabetes Mellitus......	1,911	11.7	1.6
Certain Conditions Originating in the Perinatal Period	1,412	8.6	1.2
All Other Causes........	23,161	141.5	19.6

*Rates per 100,000 estimated population

Department of Human Services

The Texas Department of Human Services administers programs which provide financial and medical assistance and social services to those who are eligible. It also is responsible for licensing child care facilities and child placing agencies. The department's headquarters is in Austin but its services are available in all 254 Texas counties.

The Texas Board of Human Services is responsible for adoption of all policies, rules and regulations of the department. (See State Boards and Commissions for membership.)

Department services are provided through 10 administrative regions with two subregions, which correspond to the boundaries of the state's 12 former Health Service Areas. Each region is supervised by a regional administrator. The department's Austin headquarters maintains staff for the development of program policy and provides support functions such as legal, personnel, data processing and fiscal services, which serve all programs.

The department is organized according to client needs. The structure centers around the networks of services — one for families and children and the other for aged and disabled persons.

FAMILIES AND CHILDREN — Services include aid to families with dependent children (AFDC), food stamps, home energy assistance, disaster relief, temporary emergency relief, family self-support services, medically needy services, health screening, day care, family planning, employment services, family violence, protective services for children, licensing, refugee assistance, repatriate services and food services.

Licensing — During fiscal year 1986, the department's Licensing Branch regulated 25,370 child day-care facilities and 4,636 residential 24-hour-care facilities. These facilities had a combined capacity to care for more than 721,000 children. The department also licenses 580 administrators of child care institutions and certified more than 8,650 social workers as meeting educational and experience qualifications.

AGED AND DISABLED — Community care services are provided to enable aged and disabled individuals to live in their own homes. Institutional care services are available for persons who need continuous medical attention and require professional care in nursing homes. The department also provides protective services for aged or disabled adults.

Medical Services — The department purchases

ealth insurance for eligible dependent children, and he aged and disabled persons served by the department. The department also provides matching funds nd technical assistance to county indigent health care rograms.

In addition to providing for inpatient and outatient hospital care, physician services, lab and x-ray services, the department also pays for up to three prescriptions per month for those same recipient groups. Other medical services are health screening, diagnosis and treatment for children receiving **Medicaid**, transortation to and from medical services, and hearing ids for eligible adults. The department also provides ertain dental services, eyeglasses, podiatric services, ome health services, chiropractic services and inome support services.

COSTS/SERVICES

Costs of most programs are shared by the state and ederal governments. Expenditures and services for scal year 1986 are as follows:

FINANCIAL ASSISTANCE: AFDC, $281,285,650; 410,423 ecipients per month. Food stamp value, $758 million; ,304,677 recipients per month. Commodities distributd for child nutrition, $80 million; 1,700,200 children per ay. Refugee assistance payments (100% federal unds), $9.8 million; 1,654 clients per month. Energy as-

sistance payments, $34.2 million; 307,001 households received heating assistance, 308,632 households received cooling assistance. Temporary emergency relief, $1,151,500; 63,697 clients.

MEDICAL PROGRAMS: Purchased health services, $712,021,053; 754,774 Medicaid eligibles. Vendor drugs, $108,391,044; 7,139,216 prescriptions. Medical transportation, $4,629,113; 705,246 one-way trips.

FAMILIES & CHILDREN SERVICES: Protective services for abused and neglected children, $78,789,879; 71,025 investigations, 117,534 clients. Family planning services, $25,314,062; 276,429 clients. Child day care services, $31,899,770; 14,589 children per day. Early periodic screening, diagnosis and treatment, $17,129,599; 80,497 medical screenings, 110,916 dental treatments. Family violence services, $2,498,730; 21,715 residents. Employment services, $7,345,128; 83,709 employment registrants. Licensing of child care facilities, $9,516,228; 30,006 facilities registered or regulated.

AGED & DISABLED SERVICES: Long-term institutional care, $465,091,935; 54,145 clients per month. Intermediate care for the mentally retarded $74,091,804; 8,619 state school clients, 3,822 community facility clients. Community care, $150,537,707; 52,634 clients per month. Adult protective services, $6,676,475; 13,391 investigations, 4,027 clients per month.

State Institutions For Human Services

Texas Department of Mental Health and Mental Retardation, Austin, is responsible for conserving and helping the mentally retarded achieve maximum potential. The department administers state mental hospitals, schools for the mentally retarded, research facilities and human development centers. The department's address is Box 12668, Capitol Station, Austin 78711.

MENTAL HEALTH SERVICES

Austin State Hospital—Austin; 1857; Harold K. Dudey Jr., acting superintendent; 525 patients.

Big Spring State Hospital—Big Spring; 1937; Robert on Rosenberg, acting superintendent; 351 patients.

Kerrville State Hospital—Kerrville; 1950; Dr. Luther J. Ross, superintendent; 549 patients.

Rusk State Hospital—Rusk; 1925; Dr. John V. White, uperintendent; 522 patients.

San Antonio State Hospital—San Antonio; 1896; Dr. . M. Inglis, superintendent; 675 patients.

Terrell State Hospital—Terrell; 1885; Don A. Gilbert, uperintendent; 525 patients.

Vernon State Hospital—Vernon; 1969; Jack Barthold, cting superintendent; 333 patients.

Wichita Falls State Hospital—Wichita Falls; 1922; ichard M. Bruner, superintendent; 500 patients.

STATE SCHOOLS FOR MENTALLY RETARDED

Abilene State School—Abilene; 1901; Bill Waddill, superintendent; 1,000 residents.

Austin State School—Austin; 1917; Dr. B. R. Walker, uperintendent; 700 students.

Brenham State School—Brenham; 1974; Dr. Jimmy . Haskins, superintendent; 560 clients.

Brownwood State School—1970; Don Pagett, superinendent; 240 students.

Corpus Christi State School—Corpus Christi; 1970; r. James G. Armstrong, superintendent; 498 students.

Crockett State School—1953; David Cocoros, superinendent; 100 students.

Denton State School—Denton; 1960; Dr. Jerry Vinent, superintendent; 750 students.

Fort Worth State School—Fort Worth; 1975; Mel ughes, superintendent; 390 students.

Gainesville State School—1916; T. G. Riddle, execuve officer, 250 students.

Lubbock State School—Lubbock; 1969; Lonnie H. Wils, superintendent; 440 students.

Lufkin State School—Lufkin; 1962; Harry G. Heyan, superintendent; 500 students.

Mexia State School—Mexia; 1946; W. H. Lowry, superintendent; 1,011 students.

Richmond State School—Richmond; 1968; Joseph H. merson, superintendent; 1,000 students.

San Angelo State School—Carlsbad; 1969; R. Allen Villiams, superintendent; 700 residents.

San Antonio State School—San Antonio; 1978; Dr. om Deliganis, superintendent; 360 residents.

Travis State School—Austin; 1934; Dr. Victor Hinosa, superintendent; 932 students.

Waco Center for Youth—Waco; 1979; Charles Lockn, director; 100 clients.

STATE CENTERS FOR HUMAN DEVELOPMENT

Amarillo State Center—Amarillo; 1967; Richard D. rowder, director; 350 clients.

Beaumont State Center—Beaumont; 1968; Martin T. Woodard, director; 494 patients.

El Paso State Center—El Paso; 1975; Diane H. Cano, director; 190 patients.

Laredo State Center—Laredo; 1969; Delores V. Rodriguez, director; 830 patients.

Rio Grande State Center—Harlingen; 1962; Aurelio Valdez Jr., director; 190 in-patients. Also operates three mental health centers: Kingsville Community M. H. Center; Laredo Mental Health Center and Cameron-Willacy County MH Center. Also includes Harlingen residential facility and school for mentally retarded.

Texas Research Institute of Mental Sciences—Houston; 1957; Dr. Joseph C. Schoolar, director; 6,000 patients.

COMMUNITY MENTAL HEALTH AND MENTAL RETARDATION CENTERS

Abilene Regional MHMR Center—Abilene; 1971; Russell B. Evans, administrative director; 1,100 patients.

Texas Panhandle Mental Health Authority—Amarillo; 1968; Claire Rigler, executive director; 3,500 clients.

Austin-Travis County MHMR Center—Austin; 1967; John E. Brubaker, administrative director; 7,100 patients.

MHMR of Southeast Texas—Beaumont; 1973; Dr. Roger Pricer, executive director; 6,000 clients.

Central Texas MHMR Center—Brownwood; 1969; Roy A. Cronenberg, executive director; 1,422.

MHMR Authority of Brazos Valley—Bryan-College Station; 1974; Dr. Ann Pye-Shively, executive director; 3,303 clients.

Nueces County MHMR Community Center—Corpus Christi; 1969; Wallace E. Whitworth Jr., executive director; 3,148 patients.

Navarro County MHMR Center—Corsicana; 1969; Julia W. Lang, executive director; 1,000 patients.

Dallas County MHMR Center—Dallas; 1966; James E. Craft, executive director; 12,255 clients.

MHMR Services of Texoma—Denison; 1974; Carl Kelly, executive director; 2,682 clients.

Tropical Texas Center for MHMR—Edinburg; 1967; Marion G. Shirah, executive director; 6,000 patients.

El Paso Center for MHMR Services—El Paso; 1966; Lee W. Yudin, executive director; 5,249 patients.

Tarrant County MHMR Services—Fort Worth; 1969; Loyd Kilpatrick, executive director; 17,000 patients.

Gulf Coast Regional MHMR Center—Galveston; 1968; G. Michael Winburn, executive director; 2,643 patients.

MHMR Authority of Harris County—Houston; 1965; Eugene Williams, executive director; 15,000 patients.

Sabine Valley Regional MHMR Center—Longview; 1970; Ronald R. Cookston, executive director; 5,000 clients.

Lubbock Regional MHMR Center—Lubbock; 1969; Gene Menefee, executive director; 3,400 patients.

Deep East Texas Regional MHMR Services—Lufkin; 1975; Jim McDermott, executive director; 3,404 clients.

North Central Texas MHMR Services—McKinney; 1978; Albert L. Jackson Jr., board chairman; 4,237 clients.

Permian Basin Community Center for MHMR—Midland/Odessa; 1973; Bob Dickson, executive director; 4,000 clients.

Central Plains MHMR Center—Plainview; 1969; Rick Van Hersh, executive director; 2,200 patients.

Concho Valley Center for Human Advancement—San Angelo; 1966; James M. Young, executive director; 1,473 clients.

Bexar County MHMR Center—San Antonio; 1966; George Farias, executive director; 9,546 clients.

Pecan Valley MHMR Center—Stephenville; 1977; Dr. Theresa Mulloy, executive director; 2,500 patients.

Central Counties Center for MHMR Services—Temple; 1967; Dr. Steven B. Schnee, executive director; 6,034 clients.

Northeast Texas MHMR Center—Texarkana; 1967; Joe Bob Hall, executive director; 1,595 patients.

MHMR Regional Center of East Texas—Tyler; 1969; Richard J. DeSanto, executive director; 4,200 patients.

Gulf Bend MHMR Center—Victoria; 1967; Bill Dillard, executive director; 2,800 patients.

Heart of Texas MHMR Center—Waco; 1968; Dean Maberry, executive director; 2,500 patients.

Wichita Falls Community Center for MHMR Services—Wichita Falls; 1969; James E. Snowden, executive director; 2,400 patients.

Leander Rehabilitation Center—Cedar Park; 1969; Fred R. Kaufman, acting director; recreational center serving residents of other department and community MHMR facilities.

YOUTH INSTITUTIONS AND CHEST HOSPITALS

The following institutions are under the direction of the **Texas Youth Commission,** in instances relating to children; and the **State Board of Health** in the case of the chest hospitals.

HOMES FOR DEPENDENT AND NEGLECTED CHILDREN

Corsicana State Home—Corsicana; 1897; Sandra Burnam, superintendent; 66 students.

CORRECTIONAL INSTITUTIONS FOR CHILDREN

Brownwood State School—Brownwood; 1970; Ste Robinson, superintendent; 235 students.

Crockett State School—Crockett; 1947 as **Brady Sta School for Colored Girls;** changed to **Crockett State Scho for Girls;** and in 1975 name changed to present form Robert Drake, superintendent; 112 students.

Gainesville State School—Gainesville; 1916; T. Riddle, superintendent; 252 students.

Gatesville State School for Boys—Gatesville. (Tran ferred to Texas Department of Corrections in 1979.)

Giddings State Home and School—Giddings; 197 Calvin Crenshaw, superintendent; 290 students.

Mountainview School for Boys—Gatesville. (Tran ferred to Texas Department of Corrections in 1975.)

West Texas Children's Home—Pyote; 1966; Johnny Williams, superintendent; 192 students.

In addition, the Texas Youth Council maintains t **Reception Center for Delinquent Girls** at Brownwood, u der administration of the superintendent of the Brow wood State Home and School for Girls. Also, the **Rece tion Center for Delinquent Boys,** maintained und administration of the superintendent of the Gatesvil State Schools for Boys.

CHEST HOSPITALS

East Texas Chest Hospital—Tyler. (Transferred Sept. 1979, to University of Texas System.)

San Antonio State Chest Hospital—San Antonio; 19 Dr. Robert E. Neimes, director; 150 patients.

South Texas Hospital (formerly Harlingen State Che Hospital)—Harlingen; 1954; Dr. Albert L. Gore, directe 125 patients.

Texas Department of Corrections

The Texas Department of Corrections operates the state prison system for adult felony offenders. The headquarters is in Huntsville, with James A. Lynaugh as director. The system maintains more than 100,000 acres of land on 27 units, and houses in excess of 36,000 inmates.

Since 1982, TDC has been under a federal court order to relieve overcrowding and to upgrade various services.

The following summary of current operations deals only with the Texas Department of Corrections. Juvenile offenders are under the jurisdiction of a separate state agency, administered as the **Texas Youth Commission.**

The **Texas Board of Corrections** guides the administration and operation of the department in the areas of policy, planning and budgetary matters; the nine board members are nonsalaried and appointed for 6-year terms by the governor. James A. Lynaugh has served as director since May 11, 1987. Lynaugh had served as prison system finance director from May 1984 to January 20, 1987, when he was named interim director following the resignation of Lane McCotter.

The average number of inmates during fiscal year 1986 was 37,773. Prison population has grown from 18,151 on Aug. 31, 1975, to 20,976 on Aug. 31, 1976, to 20,862 on Aug. 31, 1977, to 24,615 on Aug. 31, 1978, to 25,164 on Aug. 31, 1979, to 28,543 on Aug. 31, 1980, to 30,315 on Aug. 31, 1981, to 34,393 on Aug 31, 1982, to 36,769 on Aug 31, 1983, to 35,772 on Aug. 31, 1984, to 37,320 on Aug. 31, 1985, and to 38,246 on Aug. 31, 1986. Currently, the recidivism rate is approximately 43 percent.

On Aug. 31, 1986, total assets of the department were $631,743,303, including land, buildings and equipment. Total monies appropriated to the department by the Texas Legislature for the 1987 fiscal year amounted to $414,377,252 (this includes $19,337,037 for building programs).

Agriculture and livestock operations are under efficient management and provide a savings to taxpayers. Combined with prison industries and construction projects utilizing inmate labor, this financial effort gives Texas one of the lowest per capita inmate costs to taxpayers in the nation. Costs daily per inmate were: 1986 - $25.07; 1985 - $21.00; 1984 - $17.70; 1983 - $14.57; 1982 - $12.11; 1981 - $9.80; - 1980 - $8.61; 1979 - $7.34; 1978 - $7.15; 1977 - $7.32; 1976 - $5.97; 1975 - $5.20; 1974 - $4.59; 1973 - $3.89 and 1972 - $3.31.

Most treatment programs in the areas of educ tion, recreation, medicine and worship are funded legislative appropriations or other state funds. Supp mental monies to extend these programs are deriv from prison commissary operations.

Cooperative programs in **higher education** are b ing carried out on all units. Junior college progra leading to associate degrees are in effect with Lee C lege, Brazosport College, Alvin College, Central Texas C lege, Blinn College and Trinity Valley Community C lege. Bachelors degrees can be earned through Sa Houston State University, the University of Houstor Clear Lake, Tarleton State University or Stephen F. Aus State University. A Master of Arts degree can be earne at the University of Houston—Clear Lake. During 1985-1986 school year, 11,990 inmates participated in c lege programs. In addition, 1,217 inmates participat in Apprenticeships, Related Training and **Texas A& University Extension Programs** to qualify for cra certificates.

In 1969, an independent school **(Windham School D trict)** was created within the department to offer educ tion in grades 1-12 and special education leading tc G.E.D., or high school diploma. A total of 33,549 inma have received high school or high school equivalen diplomas from 1969 to 1986, and 1986 average mont enrollment involved approximately 12,172 of the inma population.

Approximately 123 courses are offered in varic vocational skills through the Windham School Distr and college programs. Participants in the college a secondary level vocational courses numbered 6,810 s dents during fiscal year 1986.

Rehabilitative programs are also available in fields of physiological and psychiatric health care, v ied recreational programs, legal services, religious tivities, inmate self-help groups, work-release p grams, job placement services, pre-release progra and support programs in conjunction with other sta agencies.

Units

Beto Units, Tennessee Colony, Anderson Coun Agriculture operations include livestock, field crop rabbits, hog feeder slab, fence building, hot house a dog kennels. Industrial operations include a highw sign factory, records conversion and bus repair. Beto is divided into Beto I and Beto II.

Central Unit, Sugar Land, Fort Bend County: Agriculture operations include field and edible crops, livestock, central agriculture commissary, agriculture administrative offices, canning plant, veterinary clinic and a combine operation. Industrial operations include a soap and detergent factory and a transportation warehouse. Other operations include the industrial distribution warehouse and the headquarters for southern area construction activities.

Clemens Unit, Brazoria, Brazoria County: Agriculture operations include field and edible crops, livestock and grain dryer.

Coffield Unit, Tennessee Colony, Anderson County: Agriculture operations include livestock, field and edible crops, feedlot, feed mill, meat packing plant, hog feeder slabs, sawmill and a poultry house. Industrial operations include records conversion, metal fabrication and dump truck bed factory. Other operations include the headquarters for northern area maintenance, asphalt plant and a rock crusher.

Darrington Unit, Rosharon, Brazoria County: Agriculture operations include field and edible crops, livestock and poultry layers. Other operations include tire recapping and a concrete batch plant.

Diagnostic Unit, Huntsville, Walker County: Special operations include testing and classifying of all newly received male inmates in order to assign them to a permanent unit.

Eastham Unit, Lovelady, Houston County: Agriculture operations include field and edible crops, livestock, dairy, gin, feedmill, poultry house, hogs, feeder slab and a brooder slab. Other operations include a garment factory.

Ellis Units, Huntsville, Walker County: Agriculture operations include field and edible crops, livestock, dairy, gin, farrowing barn, stocker cattle and land clearing. Industrial operations include a dental lab, death row garment factory, woodworking shop, shoe factory and bus repair. Other operations include the headquarters for central area maintenance, medical treatment center (acute and intermediate) and the central area region fire and safety office. Ellis is divided into Ellis I and Ellis II.

Ferguson Unit, Midway, Madison County: Agriculture operations include field and edible crops, livestock, swine farrowing and a feeder slab. Other operations include a mop and broom factory and the headquarters for the central area construction program.

Gatesville Unit, Gatesville, Coryell County (Women's Unit): Special operations include a garment factory, regional medical facilities, and the testing and classifying of all newly received female inmates in order to assign them to a permanent unit.

Goree Unit, Huntsville, Walker County: Agriculture operations include a horse breeding program.

Hilltop Unit, Gatesville, Coryell County: Agriculture operations include field and edible crops and a horse breeding program. Industrial operations include records conversion and bus repair. Other operations include a satellite headquarters for northern area maintenance.

Huntsville Unit, Walker County: Industrial operations include prison store, textile mill, mechanical department, print shop. Other operations include regional medical facility, prison rodeo arena, Windham Media Center; headquarters for construction department, maintenance warehouse operations.

Jester Units, Fort Bend County: Agricultural operations include field crops, edible crops, livestock, dairy, poultry house. Pre-release program for males is located on Jester I. Jester is divided into Jester I, Jester II and Jester III.

Mountain View Unit, Gatesville, Coryell County (Women's Unit): Special operations include a braille facility, psychological treatment center and pre-release for female inmates.

Pack Units, Navasota, Grimes County: Agriculture operations include field and edible crops and livestock. Other operations include a stainless steel products factory. Pack is divided into Pack I and Pack II.

Ramsey Units, Rosharon, Brazoria County: Agriculture operations include field and edible crops, livestock, dairy, dehydrator and gin. Other operations include furniture refinishing, operations center for portable buildings crew and the headquarters for southern area maintenance. Ramsey is divided into Ramsey I, Ramsey II and Ramsey III.

Retrieve Unit, Angleton, Brazoria County: Agriculture operations include field and edible crops, livestock and a dairy.

Wynne Unit, Huntsville, Walker County: Agriculture operations include field and edible crops, livestock, dairy and dog kennel program. Industrial operations include a license plate plant, validation sticker plant, mattress factory, corrugated box factory, plastic sign shop, records conversion, transportation department, prison store and laundries. Other operations include the Windham School District's administrative offices and warehouse and headquarters for in-house construction.

Texas Department of Corrections Hospital, Galveston, Galveston County: Special operations include facilities for major surgery, acute care and unique treatment.

Libraries Cooperate With State

The Texas State Documents Depository Program of the Texas State Library is designed to collect and distribute Texas state governmental publications and to promote their use.

The Texas State Publications Clearinghouse office of the Texas State Library in Austin acquires documents from state agencies and state-supported colleges and universities, which it classifies, catalogs and indexes to make them easy to locate. Then it distributes copies of many of those documents to depository libraries around the state.

As of January 1, 1987, there were 47 such centers in Texas, plus one in Chicago and one in Washington, D.C. The Texas libraries are listed below in alphabetical order by city:

Abilene Public Library, 202 Cedar, Abilene 79601; Sul Ross University Library, Alpine 79830; Amarillo Public Library, Box 2171, Amarillo 79189; Univ. of Texas at Arlington Library, Arlington 76019; Legislative Reference Library, Box 12488, Capitol Sta., Austin 78711; Univ. of Texas at Austin, Barker History Center, 2.109 Richardson Hall, Austin 78712; Beaumont Public Library, Box 3827, Beaumont 77704; Lamar University Library, Box 10021, Lamar U. Sta., Beaumont 77710; Pan American Univ. Library, Brownsville Center/80, Brownsville 78520; West Texas State Univ. Library, Box 748, WT Sta., Canyon 79016; Texas A&M Univ. Library, College Station 77843; East Texas State Univ. Library, Commerce 75428.

Also, Corpus Christi Public Library, 805 Comanche, Corpus Christi 78401; Corpus Christi State Univ. Library, 6300 Ocean Dr., Corpus Christi 78412; Dallas Public Library, 1515 Young, Dallas 75201; Southern Methodist Univ., Fondren Library, Dallas 75275; North Texas State Univ. Library, Box 5188, N.T. Sta., Denton 76203; Texas Woman's Univ. Library, Box 23715, TWU Sta.,

Denton 76204; Pan American Univ., 1201 W. University, Edinburg 78539; El Paso Public Library, 501 N. Oregon, El Paso 79901; Univ. of Texas at El Paso Library, El Paso 79968; Fort Worth Public Library, 300 Taylor, Fort Worth 76102; Texas Christian Univ., Burnett Library, Fort Worth 76129; Houston Public Library, 500 McKinney Ave., Houston 77002; Rice Univ. Fondren Library, Box 1892, Houston 77257-1892; Texas Southern Univ. Library, 3201 Wheeler, Houston 77004; Univ. of Houston Library, 4800 Calhoun, Houston 77004; Sam Houston State Univ. Library, Huntsville 77341.

Also, Texas A&I Univ. Library, Kingsville 78363; Laredo State Univ. Library, West End Washington St., Laredo 78040; Texas Tech Univ. Library, Lubbock 79409; Stephen F. Austin State Univ. Library, Nacogdoches 75962; Ector County Library, 321 W. 5th, Odessa 79761; Univ. of Texas of the Permian Basin Learning Resource Center, East University Blvd., Odessa 79762; Prairie View A&M Univ. Library, Prairie View 77445; Univ. of Texas at Dallas Library, Box 643, Richardson 75080; Angelo State Univ., Porter Henderson Library, 2601 West Ave., San Angelo 76909; St. Mary's Univ. Library, One Camino Santa Maria, San Antonio 78284; San Antonio Public Library, Main Branch, 203 S. St. Mary's, San Antonio 78205; Trinity Univ. Library, 715 Stadium Dr., San Antonio 78284; Univ. of Texas at San Antonio Library, 4242 Piedras Dr., Ste. 250, San Antonio 78285; Southwest Texas State Univ. Library, San Marcos 78666; Tarleton State Univ. Library, Stephenville 76402; Univ. of Texas at Tyler Library, 3900 University Blvd., Tyler 75701; Univ. of Houston at Victoria, 2602 N. Ben Jordan, Victoria 77901; Baylor Univ. Texas Collection, Box 6396, Waco 76706; Midwestern Univ. Library, 3400 Taft, Wichita Falls 76308.

Texas State Officials, Boards, Commissions

A list of Texas State officialdom is given on this and following pages, revised to June 1, 1987. Information is given following order: (1) Date of creation of office. (2) Whether elective or appointive. (3) Length of term. (4) Number members, if a board or commission. (5) Name of official (or officials). Dates in parentheses indicate termination appointment. Names of towns in parentheses indicate home of official whose residence is officially in Austin. In som instances the dates of expiration are prior to issuance of this volume; in such instances a holdover term is indicated, no ne appointment having been made at time of publication of the Texas Almanac. Most positions marked "apptv." are appoir ive by the Governor. Where otherwise, appointing authority is designated. Most Advisory Boards are not listed. Salari given were furnished by the Legislative Budget Board and are those effective for the 1987 year.

Accident Board, Industrial—(See **Industrial Accident Board.**)

Accountancy, Texas State Board of Public—(1945 with 2-year terms; reorganized 1959 as nine-member board with 6-yr. overlapping terms; number of members increased to twelve in 1979; expenses paid from fees collected by board; twelve members: Walter D. Davis, Missouri City (1-31-89); James F. Dunn Jr., Houston (1-31-89); Barbara Shimaitis, Katy (1-31-89); Oscar C. Mascorro, San Antonio (1-31-89); Paul W. Hillier Jr., Dallas (1-31-93); S. J. Scott, Dallas (1-31-87); John F. Lanier Jr., Austin (1-31-93); Don Weldon, Ennis (1-31-93); Jarman Bass, Dallas (1-31-91); Dwight L. Kinard, Abilene (1-31-91); R. D. Pattillo, Waco (1-31-91); Nancy Brannon, Lewisville (1-31-91). Executive Director, Bob E. Bradley, 1033 La Posada Dr., Suite 340, Austin 78752-3894 (nonmember) ($47,380).

Adjutant General—(1836 by Republic of Texas; 1905 present office established); apptv.: Maj. Gen. James T. Dennis, Box 5218, Austin 78763 (2-1-87) ($55,826, plus house and utilities).

Adjutant General for Army, Assistant—Gen. Walter J. Dingler, Austin (2-1-87) ($52,324, plus house and utilities).

Adjutant General for Air, Assistant—Brig. Gen. Leroy Thompson, Manchaca (2-1-87) ($52,324, plus house and utilities).

Administrative Judicial Districts of Texas, Presiding Judges of—(Apptv. by Governor); serve terms concurrent with term as District Judge, subject to reappointment if re-elected to bench. No extra compensation: No. 1, Ron Chapman, Dallas; No. 2, Thomas J. Stovall Jr., Seabrook; No. 3, James F. Clawson Jr., Belton; No. 4, Joe E. Kelly, Victoria; No. 5, Joe B. Evins, Edinburg; No. 6, Sam M. Paxson, El Paso; No. 7, Weldon Kirk, Sweetwater; No. 8, Charles J. Murray, Fort Worth; No. 9, Ray D. Anderson, Brownfield.

Adult Probation Commission, Texas—(1977); apptv. as designated; expenses; 6-yr.; nine members: Three judges of district courts and two citizens not employed in criminal justice system to be apptd. by Chief Justice of Texas Supreme Court as follows: B. B. Schraub, 25th District Court, Seguin (6-10-89); Sam W. Callan, 205th District Court, El Paso (6-10-89); Donald Carroll, 7th District Court, Tyler (6-10-85); Max Sherman, Austin (6-10-85); Vice Chairman, Mrs. Diana S. Clark, Dallas (6-10-87). Three judges of district courts and one citizen not employed in the criminal justice system to be apptd. by presiding judge of Texas Court of Criminal Appeals as follows: Chairman, Clarence N. Stevenson, 24th District Court, Victoria (6-10-87); Joe N. Kegans, 230th District Court, Houston (6-10-89); John C. Vance, Associate Justice, 5th Court of Appeals, Dallas (6-10-85); Rev. D. N. Brosnan, San Antonio (6-10-89). Executive Director, Don R. Stiles (nonmember), Box 12427, Austin 78711 ($49,749).

Ad Valorem Tax Rate, Board to Calculate the—(1907); ex officio; term in other office; three members: Gov. William Clements; State Comptroller Robert D. Bullock and State Treasurer Ann Richards.

Aeronautics Commission, Texas—(1945); apptv.; 6-yr.; per diem and expenses; six members: George M. Underwood Jr., Dallas (12-31-86); Stephen E. Cone Jr., Lubbock (2-1-91); Walther Umphrey, Port Arthur (2-1-91); Warren C. Harmon, Bryan (12-31-88); Melvin Phillips, Amarillo (12-31-88); Maxey Grossenbacher, Harlingen (2-1-93). Executive Director, C. A. Wilkins, Box 12607, Capitol Station, Austin 78711 (nonmember) ($49,208).

Aging, Texas Department on—(1965 as **Governor's Committee on Aging**; name changed in 1981 to present form; due to go out of existence 9-1-97 unless continued operation needed); apptv.; 6-yr.; expenses; nine apptv. members: Chmn., R. H. Gibbons, Fort Worth serves at pleasure of Governor; Mary Hazlewood, Amarillo (8-30-91); Jerry Ribnick, Houston (8-30-91); Evelyn Porter, San Antonio (8-30-91); James Roberts, Andrews (8-30-87); Mrs. Willie Lee Glass, Tyler (8-30-87); Rose R. Duvall, Dripping Springs (8-30-87); Eustolio Gonzales, Raymondville (8-30-89); Bert Scheinbrum, Waco (8-30-89); Floyd C. Burnett, Ladonia (8-30-89). Executive Director, O. P. Bobbitt, Box 12786, Capitol Station, Austin 78711 (nonmember) ($42,200).

Air Control Board, Texas—(1965 as six-member board; membership increased to nine in 1967); apptv.; 6-yr.; per diem and expenses; nine members: Dr. D. Jack Killian, Lake Jackson (9-1-85); Dick Whittington, Lockhart (9-1-91); Chmn., John L. Blair, Kountze (9-1-91); William Quortrup, Carrollton (9-1-89); Hubert Oxford III, Beaumont (9-1-89); Dr. Otto Kunze, College Station (9-1-89); Richard H. Moorman IV, Brenham (9-1-87); Bob G. Bailey, Abilene (9-1-87);

Fred Hartman, Baytown (9-1-87). Executive Director, B Stewart, 6330 Highway 290 E., Austin 78723 (nonmembe ($55,517).

Aircraft Pooling Board, State—(1979); apptv.; 6-yr.; fi members — two ex officio: representative of State Aud tor's Office and representative of State Purchasing ar General Services Commission; three apptv. — one by Go ernor, one by Speaker of House of Representatives and or by Lieutenant Governor. Governor's appointee: James Kaster, Austin (1-31-89). Executive Director Fred R. Spie Box 12224, Austin 78711 (nonmember) ($50,985).

A&M University System, Board of Regents of—(See Tex& **A&M University System Board of Regents.**)

Alcohol and Drug Abuse, Texas Commission on—(1953 Texas Commission on Alcoholism; name changed ar membership increased to nine in 1986); apptv.; 6 yrs.; p diem and expenses; nine members: Chmn., Robb Southe land, Austin (6-8-91); Cervando Martinez Jr., San Anton (6-8-91); Calvin Reed, Kress (6-8-91); Jerry P. Cunningha Dallas (6-8-89); Robert W. Harrell, Austin (6-8-89); Marga E. B. Sharpe, Dallas (6-8-87); Jim Clipson Jr., Eagle Lake 8-87); Joshua W. Allen Sr., Beaumont (6-8-87); Nancy W. Pe ry, Odessa (6-8-89). Exec. Dir., Ross Newby, 1705 Guad lupe, Austin 78701 (nonmember) ($44,702).

Alcoholic Beverage Commission, Texas—(1935 as Liqu Control Board; name changed 1970); apptv.; 6-yr.; per die and expenses; administrator appointed by commissio three members: Chmn., Louis M. Pearce Jr., Houst (11-15-91); Morris Atlas, McAllen (11-15-89); J. A. Whitte burg III, Amarillo (11-15-87). Administrator, Sherm McBeath, Box 13127, Capitol Station, Austin 78711 (no member) ($57,474).

Amusement Machine Commission, Texas—(1971 **Vending Commission**; name changed in 1973); apptv.; p diem; 6-yr.; six members — three ex officio: Attorney Ge eral Jim Mattox; James B. Adams, Director Department Public Safety; Sam Kelley, Consumer Credit Commissic er. Three apptv. members: Chairman, Charles M. Bra shaw Sr., Richardson (1-31-91); Perry O. Chrisman, Dall (1-31-89); Ruben Montemayor, San Antonio (1-31-87). E ecutive Director, Jim Lusk, 1606 Headway Circle, Ste. 2 Austin 78754 (nonmember) ($43,157).

Angelina and Neches River Authority, Board of Dire tors—(Est. 1935 as **Sabine-Neches Conservation District**; rec ganized 1950 and name changed to **Neches River Conserv tion District**; changed to present name in 1977; appt expenses; 6-yr.; nine members: Richard Baldwin, Camd (9-5-91); Steve Lilly, Nacogdoches (9-5-85); Salah Cra Henderson (9-5-89); Lila Lee Rehkop, Athens (9-5-89); Joy Swearingen, Nacogdoches (9-5-87); S. D. Griffin, Lufk (9-5-87); Warner A. Dunn, Nacogdoches (9-5-83); Emma Whitehead, Rusk (9-5-91); Horace F. McQueen, Whitehou (9-5-87). Executive Director, William A. Elmore, Box 3& Lufkin 75901 (nonmember).

Animal Health Commission, Texas—(1893 as **Texas Liv stock Sanitary Commission**; reorganized 1955; name chang in 1959, membership increased to nine in 1973; raised twelve in 1983); apptv.; per diem and expenses; 6-yr.; twel members: James D. Sartwell, Houston (9-6-91); James Owen, Tyler (9-6-91); Delvin R. Barrett, Bryan (9-6-91); Jo S. Cargile, San Angelo (9-6-91); Charles Koontz, Olton (9 87); C. E. Knolle, Sandia (9-6-87); Dr. Kenneth Dorris, St phenville (9-6-87); Laurence H. Bostick, Brookshire (9-6-8 Joe E. Chapa Jr., Linn (9-6-89); Florence Rieck, Roosev€ (9-6-89); James L. Snyder, Baird (9-6-89); Mary Nan We Batesville (9-6-89). Executive Director, Dr. John W. H combe, 210 Barton Springs Rd., Austin 78704 (nonmembe ($53,251).

Antiquities Committee, State—(1969 as seven-memb board; membership increased to nine in 1983 with additi of one ex officio and one apptv. member); apptv.; per die and expenses; 2-yr.; nine members—six ex officio, term other office: Chairman Texas Historical Commission; rector State Parks and Wildlife Department; Commissior of General Land Office; State Archeologist; State Engine Director State Department of Highways and Public Trar portation; and Executive Director Texas Department W ter Resources. Three apptv. members: Chmn., Dr. Willia C. Griggs, Houston (1-31-87); Dr. William G. Reeder, Aust (1-31-87); Anne A. Fox, San Antonio (1-31-87).

Architectural Examiners, Texas Board of—(1937 as thr member board; raised to six members in 1951; membersh increased to nine in 1977); apptv.; 6-yr.; per diem and e penses; nine members: James M. Langford, El Paso (1-31-91); Bobbie Joe Wise Jr., San Antonio (1-31-91); Trammel

Crow, Dallas (6-21-85); Ned R. Rosario, Fort Worth (1-31-87); O. E. Schrickel, Arlington (1-31-87); Chmn., Ralph B. Perkins, Wichita Falls (1-31-87); James E. Buie, Longview (1-31-89); Benjamin J. Lednicky, Houston (1-31-89); Nolanda S. Hill, Dallas (1-31-89). Executive Director, Robert H. Norris, 8213 Shoal Creek Blvd., Suite 107, Austin 78751 (nonmember) ($45,320).

Arts, Texas Commission on the—(1965 as Texas Fine Arts Commission; name changed to **Texas Commission on the Arts and Humanities** and membership increased to 18 in 1971; name changed to present form in 1979); apptv.; 6-yr.; expenses; eighteen members: Kenneth Q. Carlile, Marshall (8-31-91); Henry S. Miller Jr., Dallas (8-31-91); Aaronetta Pierce, San Antonio (8-31-91); Kenneth E. Bentsen, Houston (8-31-91); Jeffrey Weiss, Dallas (8-31-91); Margaret S. Mills, Waco (8-31-91); Margaret C. B. Brown, Waco (8-31-87); Chmn., Hugo V. Neuhaus Jr., Houston (8-31-87); Camilla D. Trammell, Houston (8-31-87); Carla Jo C. Francis, Dallas (8-31-87); Beatrice C. Pickens, Amarillo (8-31-87); Edward L. Protz, Galveston (8-31-87); Nancy H. Nelson, Dallas (8-31-89); Louann Temple, Austin (8-31-89); Terrylin G. Neale, Houston (8-31-89); Adan Medrano, San Antonio (8-31-89); Ann K. Stool, Del Rio (8-31-89); Nancy Ann Davis, Fort Worth (8-31-89). Executive Director, Richard E. Huff, 5th Floor, 920 Colorado, Austin 78711 (nonmember) ($44,496).

Arts and Industries, Texas College of—(See **University System of South Texas.**)

Athletic Trainers, Advisory Board of—(1971 as Texas Board of Athletic Trainers; name changed and membership increased to six in 1975; expenses; 6-yr.: Michael K. Stephens, Austin (1-31-91); W. F. Pickard Jr., Bryan (1-31-91); Cash Birdwell, Dallas (1-31-87); Samuel M. Russell, Lewisville (1-31-89); Cynthia L. Raines, El Paso (1-31-89); James G. Murray, Lubbock (1-31-93).

Attorney General, State—(1836 by original Constitution of Republic of Texas, 1876 by present Constitution); elective; (2-yr. by original Constitution; term raised to 4-yr. in 1972, effective 1975: Jim Mattox, Box 12548, Capitol Sta., Austin 78711 (1-1-91) ($73,233).

Attorney, State's—Apptv.: Robert Huttash, Box 12405, Austin 78711 ($56,135).

Auditor, State—(1929); apptv. by Legislative Audit Committee, a joint Senate-House committee; 2-yr.: Lawrence F. Alwin, (Houston), Box 12067, Capitol Sta., Austin 78711 ($66,950).

Automated Information and Telecommunications Council—(1981); apptv.; 2-yr.; expenses; seven members: Three apptd. by governor; two apptd. by Lieutenant Governor and two apptd. by Speaker of House. Governor's appointees: Donald A. Maxwell, College Station (2-1-93); Chmn., Gary L. Hammon, San Antonio (2-1-91); Nancy Norris, Austin (2-1-89). Executive Director, Charles K. Winston Jr., Box 13564, Capitol Sta., Austin 78711 (nonmember) ($49,337).

Bandera County River Authority—(1971); apptv.; 6-yr.; nine members; expenses: Dr. Tom Denyer, Bandera (1-31-91); Connie Taylor, Bandera (1-31-91); Phillip F. Becker, Bandera (1-31-91); Don E. Karr, Bandera (1-31-89); John Cameron, Bandera (1-31-89); Raymond Hicks, Bandera (1-31-87); T. S. Tobin, Bandera (1-31-87); Paul Garrison Jr. (1-31-87); Henry Fisher, Utopia (1-31-89).

Banking Board, State—(1909); two ex officio members, term in other office; one apptd. by Governor for 2 years; three members: Ex officio members — Commissioner of Banking and State Treasurer. Apptv. member: Arthur C. White, Dallas (1-31-89).

Banking Commissioner, State—(1923); apptv. by State Finance Commission; 2-yr.: James L. Sexton, 2601 N. Lamar, Austin 78705 ($79,310). (See also **Finance Commission of Texas.**)

Bar of Texas, State—(1939 as administrative arm of Supreme Court; 30 members elected by membership; 3-yr. terms; expenses paid from dues collected from membership. President, president-elect, vice president and immediate past president serve as ex officio members. Executive Director, Edward O. Coultas, P.O. Box 12487, Austin 78711 (nonmember).

Barber Examiners, State Board of—(1929 as three-member board; membership increased in 1975); apptv.; 6-yr.; $30 per diem and expenses while on duty; six members: Joe W. Turner, Midland (1-31-91); Thelma R. Walker, Fort Worth (1-31-91); Ken Gjemre, Dallas (1-31-87); Vera LeBlanc, Senderland (1-31-87); President, Helen Spears, Dallas (1-31-89); Edward N. Borkland, Austin (1-31-89). Executive Director, Jo King McCrorey, 1300 E. Anderson Lane, Bldg. C., Suite 275, Austin 78752 (nonmember) ($31,518).

Battleship Texas Advisory Board—(1983; supersedes Battleship Texas Commission); apptv.; 6-yr.; nine members: Chmn., Denny G. Hair, Houston (2-1-89); Rosalie L. Kuntz, Pasadena (2-1-89); Mary Catherine Burke, Houston (2-1-89); Robert D. Miller, Houston (2-1-93); Joe S. Cathey, Deer Park (2-1-87); Philip L. Chumlea, Houston (2-1-87); Caroline K. Gregory, Houston (2-1-91); Brig. Gen. Mike P. Cokinos, Beaumont (2-1-91); David A. Jones, Houston (2-1-91).

Blind, Governing Board of the Texas School for the—(1979); apptv.; 6-yr.; nine members; expenses: Dr. Virginia Sowell, Lubbock (1-31-91); Mary G. Behnke, Orange (1-31-91); Don Welch, Dallas (1-31-91); Wandene Coughran, Abilene (1-31-87); Dr. M. Ray Harrington, Dallas (1-31-87); Mrs. Olivia C. Blundell, El Paso (1-31-87); Robert D. Tindle, Austin (1-31-89); Crispin E. Sanchez, Laredo (1-31-89); Dr. Anne L. Corn, Austin (1-31-89). Executive Director, William H. Miller, 1110 W. 45th, Austin 78756 (nonmember).

Blind and Severely Disabled Persons, Texas Committee on Purchases of Products and Services of—(1979); apptv.; 2-yr.; ten members: Robert E. Flaherty, Austin (1-31-85); Ray Vaughn, Austin (1-31-85); Jane D. Pieper, San Antonio (1-31-85); Chmn., Gibson Duterroil, Houston (1-31-85); Marion Truitt, Abilene (1-31-85); Billy J. Killion, Austin (1-31-85); Robert Vassallo, Austin (1-31-85); Dr. Thomas R. Irons, Lubbock (1-31-85); Robert Crieder, Kingswood (1-31-85); Gordon Richardson, Caldwell (1-31-85).

Blind, State Commission for the—(1931 as six-member State Commission for the Blind; raised to nine members in 1979; name changed in 1985); apptv.; 6-yr.; expenses; nine members: Chmn., William C. Conner, Fort Worth (1-1-87); Kyle L. Fulton, Lubbock (2-1-93); C. Robert Keeney Jr., Houston (2-1-93); Walter Musler, San Antonio (1-1-91); Lewis Timberlake, Austin (1-1-91); Dr. Robert Peters, Tyler (1-1-91); John W. Longley, Stamford (1-1-89); Don L. Steelman, Marshall (1-1-89); Ann Masterson, Houston (1-1-89). Executive Director, John C. Wilson, Box 12866, Austin 78711 (nonmember) ($55,105).

Board of—(Note: In most instances, state boards are alphabetized under specific reference word, as **Accountancy, Texas State Board of Public.**)

Brazos River Authority, Directors of—(Organized in 1929 by legislative act as Brazos River Conservation and Reclamation District; name changed to **Brazos River Authority** by Legislature in 1953); apptv.; 6-yr.; expenses; 21 members: Chester R. Upham III, Mineral Wells (2-1-93); William A. Prewitt III, Temple (2-1-87); Brad Crawford, Lubbock (2-1-93); Gary E. Wood, Waco (2-1-93); James C. Atkins Jr., Lake Jackson (2-1-93); Roland Adamson, Richmond (2-1-87); Nelson Durst, Bryan (2-1-87); John M. Wehby, Taylor (2-1-91); Charles Moser, Brenham (2-1-91); Don T. Kearby, Mineral Wells (2-1-91); J. J. Gibson, Guthrie (2-1-91); James H. Mills, Round Rock (2-1-91); Lyndon Olson Sr., Waco (2-1-91); Sidney E. Niblo, Abilene (2-1-91); Paul H. Harvey Jr., Hillsboro (2-1-89); Henry J. Boehm Sr., Brenham (2-1-89); Walter C. Wiese Jr., Calvert (2-1-89); Douglas A. Strain, W. Columbia (2-1-89); President, Glynn A. Williams, Bryan (2-1-89); R. E. Chambers, Wichita Falls (2-1-89); Vice President, Bruce Campbell Jr., Knox City (2-1-89). General Manager, Carson H. Hoge, Box 7555, Waco 76710 (nonmember); Asst. Gen. Manager-Treasurer, Jack Wooley.

Budget Board, Legislative—(1949); 10 members; Ex officio members — Lt. Gov. William P. Hobby; Speaker of House of Representatives; Chairman of Senate Finance and Public Affairs Committees; Chairmen of Appropriations and Revenue, and Ways and Means Committees; and four other members of Legislature. Director, James P. Oliver, Box 12666, Capitol Station, Austin 78711-2666 (nonmember).

Building Code Council, Texas Industrialized—(1985); apptv.; 2-yr.; 12 members: Stanley Kidd, Beaumont (2-1-88); Bob Fowler, Merkel (2-1-88); James S. Walker II, Houston (2-1-88); Bill Bradley, Houston (2-1-86); Jeffry B. Lewis, Houston (2-1-88); Patrick G. Butler, Georgetown (2-1-87); Ben Woody, Wichita Falls (2-1-87); Charles L. Clawson, Arlington (2-1-87); Glenn L. Drennon, Waco (2-1-87); Charles W. Alexander, Irving (2-1-87); Kurt A. J. Monier, San Antonio (2-1-87); Charles D. Kieffer, Dallas (2-1-88).

Caddo Lake Compact Commission—(1979); apptv.; 2-yr.; expenses; two ex officio members—Red River Compact Commissioner and Exec. Dir. of Texas Department of Water Resources. (Apptv. member's function is to negotiate with other states respecting waters of Caddo Lake. See also **Interstate Compact Commission and Canadian River Compact Commissioner.**): Apptv. place on commission vacant at press time.

Canadian River Compact Commissioner—(1951); apptv.; salary and expenses; (his function is to negotiate with other states respecting waters of the Canadian. See also **Interstate Compact Commission and Caddo Lake Compact Commission**): John C. Sims, Lubbock (12-31-91).

Cancer Council, Texas—(1985); 16 members as follows: two ex officio: commissioner of Texas Board of Human Services, chairman of Texas Board of Health; seven each apptd. by Speaker of House of Representatives and Lieutenant Governor; 6-yr.; except legislators and representatives of state agencies; expenses.

Canvassers, State Board of—(1897); two ex officio members, term in other office; one apptd. by Governor for 2-yr. term: Gov. William Clements and Secretary of State Jack M. Rains, ex officio members. Apptv. member: Morris Shapiro, Austin (8-23-87).

Central Colorado River Authority—(See **Colorado River.**)

Chemist, State—(1911); ex officio, indefinite term: Dr. L. R. Richardson, Texas Agricultural Experiment Station, College Station.

Childhood Intervention Services, Interagency Council on Early—(1981); apptv.; 2-yr.; five members — one apptd. by Governor, one each by Department of Health, Department of Mental Health and Mental Retardation, Department of Human Services and Texas Education Agency. Gov.'s apptee: Patricia S. Bizzell, Austin (2-1-87). Acting Administrator, Louise Iscoe, Department of Health, 1100 W. 49th, Austin 78756 (nonmember).

Child Abuse and Neglect Prevention, Council on—(1985); apptv.; 2-yr.; expenses; nine members: Phil D. Strickland, Dallas (9-1-87); Bobbie Mae Matthews, Austin (9-1-87); Emily B. Shelton, Lufkin (9-1-87); Joyce Dorrycott, San Antonio (9-1-87); Peggy B. Smith, Houston (9-1-87); Dr. Rafael R. Garcia, Lubbock (9-1-87); Gretchen B. Denny, Fort Worth (9-1-87); Jane C. Crouch, Hamilton (9-1-87); Michael A. Reilly, Arlington (9-1-87).

Chiropractic Examiners, Texas State Board of—(1949); apptv.; 6-yr.; expenses; nine members: Dr. T. A. Baker, Lake Jackson (8-3-87); Dr. R. E. Hartong, San Antonio (8-3-87); Dr. Jack Christie, Houston (8-3-87); Dr. Sterling H. Pruitt Sr., Fort Worth (8-3-89); Dr. Edmund E. Lacy, Dallas (8-3-89); Dr. Jay H. Perreten, Houston (8-3-89); Dr. V. C. Salyer Jr., Dublin (8-3-91); Dr. Ben H. Procter, Fort Worth (8-3-91); Dr. Dennis Wayne Teal, Canton (8-3-91). Executive Secretary, Edna A. Parsons, 1300 E. Anderson Lane, Bldg. C., Suite 245, Austin 78752 (nonmember) (\$25,338).

Civil Judicial Council, Texas—(See Judicial Council, Texas.)

Coastal Water Authority, Board of Directors of—(1967 as Coastal Industrial Water Authority, Board of Directors of; name changed in 1985); seven members — four to be appointed by mayor of Houston with advice and consent of governing body of Houston; three apptd. by Governor; per diem and expenses; 2-yr. Governor's appointees: Wallace Claypool, Houston (3-31-87); Johnnie G. Jennings, Baytown (3-31-87); Buster E. French, Dayton (3-31-84). Acting Executive Director, Sam B. Dixon, Citicorp Center, 1200 Smith, Suite 2260, Houston 77002 (nonmember).

College and University System, Coordinating Board, Texas—(See Higher Education Coordinating Board, Texas).

Colorado River Authority, Central, Board of Directors—(1935); apptv.; 6-yr.; per diem on duty; nine members: Louis Pittard, Gouldbusk (1-1-91); O. R. Lawlis, Coleman (1-1-91); Jim Bob Thweatt, Coleman (1-1-91); Ross L. Jones, Coleman (1-1-89); Roy D. Young, Burkett (1-1-89); Baker Rudolph, Coleman (1-1-89); Nicholas J. Knox, Burkett (2-1-93); Clifford L. Horn, Talpa (2-1-93); Robert J. Cheaney, Santa Anna (2-1-93). Secretary, Jerri Ann Chambers, Box 964, Coleman 76834 (nonmember).

Colorado River Authority, Lower, Directors of—(1934 as 9-member board; membership increased in 1951 and 1975); apptv.; 6-yr.; \$50 per diem on duty; fifteen members: John K. Dixon, Sunrise Beach (1-1-87); John W. Hancock, El Campo (1-1-87); John W. Jones, Brady (1-1-87); Merritt Schumann, New Braunfels (1-1-87); Milton J. Anderson, Eagle Lake (1-1-87); Marvin Selig, Seguin (1-1-87); Martin E. McLean, Marble Falls (1-1-87); James A. Martin, Austin (1-1-89); Mrs. John Wilson, La Grange (1-1-89); Charles Matus, Johnson City (1-1-89); John M. Scanlan, Austin (1-1-89); Jack Littlejohn, Carmine (1-1-91); Jack B. Miller, San Saba (1-1-91); Cecil Long, Bastrop (1-1-91); Burton B. Letulle, Bay City (1-1-91). General Manager, S. David Freeman, Box 220, Austin 78767 (nonmember).

Colorado River Authority, Upper, Directors of—(1935 as nine-member board; reorganized in 1965); apptv.; 6-yr.; \$50 a day and expenses on duty; indefinite number of members: Harvey D. Glass Jr., Sterling City (1-1-87); Bruce H. Fisher, San Angelo (1-1-87); Brian Richards, Ballinger (2-1-93); Chester L. Wilson, Bronte (2-1-91); Homer J. Hodge, Winters (1-1-85); Victor W. Choate, San Angelo (1-1-85); J. R. Salmon, San Angelo (1-1-89); Cumbie Ivey, Robert Lee (1-1-89); Everett J. Grindstaff, Box 576, Ballinger 76821 (1-1-89).

Commissioner of Agriculture—(1907); elective; (2-yr. by original constitutional provision, term raised to 4-yr. in 1972, effective in 1975): Jim Hightower, Box 12847, Capitol Sta., Austin 78711-2847 (1-1-91) (\$73,233).

Commissioner of Education—(1866 as Superintendent of Public Instruction; 1949 changed to Commissioner of Education by Gilmer-Aikin Law); apptv. by State Board of Education; 4-yr.: W. N. Kirby, 201 E. 11th, Austin 78701 (\$67,362 plus supplement from private sources). See also Education, State Board of.

Commissioner of General Land Office—(1836 by Constitution of Republic of Texas; 1876 by present Constitution); elective; (2-yr. by original Constitutional provision; term raised to 4-yr. in 1972, effective 1975): Garry Mauro, S. F. Austin Bldg., Room 835, Austin 78701 (1-1-91) (\$72,233).

Commissioner of Health—(1879 as State Health Officer; 1955 changed to Commissioner of Health; 1975 changed to Director, Texas Department of Health Resources; 1977 changed to Commissioner, Texas Department of Health); apptv.; 2-yr: Dr. Robert Bernstein, Austin (1-1-87); (\$66,641).

Comptroller of Public Accounts—(1835 by Provisional Government of Texas, 1876 by present Constitution); elective; (2-yr. by original Constitution; term raised to 4-yr. in 1972, effective 1975): Robert D. Bullock, LBJ State Office Bldg., Austin 78774 (1-1-91) (\$73,233).

Concho River Water and Soil Conservation Authority, Lower, Directors of—(1939); 6-yr.; nine members: Howard Loveless, Eden (1-1-87); Leroy Beach, Millersview (1-1-87); Bill J. Mikeska, Eola (1-1-87); T. E. Wells, Paint Rock (1-1-91); Benjamin O. Sims, Paint Rock (1-1-91); E. H. Brosig Jr., Paint Rock (1-1-91); Harvey P. Williams, Eola (1-1-89); Edwin T. Tickle, Paint Rock (1-1-89); N. A. Taylor, Eden (1-1-89).

Conservation Foundation, Texas—(1969 as 12-member board; membership reduced to six in 1979); apptv.; expenses; 6-yr.; six members—three ex officio, term in other office; one apptd. by Governor and one each apptd. by Speaker of House of Representatives and Lieutenant Governor. Governor's appointee: Chmn., George Bristol, Austin (6-13-87), Ex officio members: Executive Director Parks and Wildlife Department; Commissioner of General Land Office and Executive Director of Texas Historical Commission. Executive Director, John Hamilton, 611 S. F. Austin Bldg., Austin 78701 (nonmember) (\$35,947).

Conservatorship Board, State—(1979); apptv.; expenses; 6-yr.; three members: Chairman, Jack N. Roper, Dallas (1-31-85); William M. Noble, Victoria (1-31-83); Frank Junell, San Angelo (1-31-87).

Contracts for Fuel and Public Printing, Board to Approve—(1876); ex officio; term in other office: Gov. William Clements, Secretary of State Jack M. Rains and Comptroller Robert D. Bullock.

Corrections, Texas Board of—(1885 as Texas Prison Board; superseded Superintendent of Penitentiaries est. in 1849; name changed to present form 1957); apptv.; per diem and expenses; nine members: James M. Eller, Bryan (2-15-87); F. L. Stephens, San Angelo (2-15-93); Charles T. Terrell, Dallas (2-15-93); Chmn., Alfred Hughes, Austin (2-15-91); Dennis R. Hendrix, Dallas (2-15-91); Jerry H. Hodge, Amarillo (2-15-91); Thomas R. McDade, Houston (2-15-89); Deralyn R. Davis, Fort Worth (2-15-89); Vice Chmn., Joe LaMantia, McAllen (2-15-89). Director, James A. Lynaugh, Box 99, Huntsville 77340 (nonmember) (\$68,289 and emoluments).

Corrections, Texas Department of—Apptv.; indefinite term: Director, James A. Lynaugh, Huntsville 77340.

Cosmetology Commission, Texas—(1935 as three-member State Board of Hairdressers and Cosmetologists; name changed and membership increased to six apptv. and one ex officio in 1971); apptv.; per diem and expenses; 6-yr.: Ronald McGehee, Bedford (12-31-91); Vice Chmn., Evelyn Hunter, Dallas (12-31-85); Betty Sue Bird, Austin (12-31-87); Sec.-Treasurer, Hope T. Scott, San Antonio (12-31-87); Chmn., Dr. James R. Tarter, Odessa (12-31-89); Ronald B. Jemison, Houston (12-31-89). Ex officio member: Dr. Paul W. Lindsey, Austin. Executive Director, Herbert E. Cohen, 1111 Rio Grande, Austin 78701 (nonmember) (\$34,814).

Counselors, Texas State Board of Examiners of Professional—(1981); apptv.; 6-yr.; expenses; nine members: Chmn. Louis S. Parker Jr., Austin (2-1-87); Vice Chmn., Dr. Jeanie Stanley, Kilgore (2-1-89); Yvonne L. Kohutek, San Antonio (2-1-87); Stephen A. Haberman, Cleveland (2-1-85); Bettye Whitney, Dallas (2-1-87); Dr. Robert L. Smith, Commerce (2-1-91); Carol E. Champion, Brownsville (2-1-89); Katherine Crumley, Shepherd (2-1-89); Ann Karen Barlow, Fort Worth (2-1-89). Executive Secretary, Daniel L. Boone, 1100 W. 49th, Austin 78756-3183 (nonmember).

Court Reporters Certification Board—(1977 as nine-member Texas Reporters Committee; name changed to present form and membership increased to twelve with addition of three citizen members in 1983); apptv. by State Supreme Court; 6-yr.; expenses; twelve members: Ronald C. Bird, San Antonio (12-31-86); Linda Hyde, Austin (12-31-86); Jack B. Moorhead, Houston (12-31-86); Chmn., Joseph H. Hart, Austin (12-31-88); Louise Morse, Austin (12-31-88); Jerry Spence, Big Spring (12-31-88); Charles Griggs, Sweetwater (12-31-90); Judy Kulhanek, Houston (12-31-90); David B. Jackson, Dallas (12-31-90). Citizen members: John M. Keel, Austin (12-31-88); Tom Prentice, Austin (12-31-86); Jean Nipper, Austin (12-31-90). Executive Director, C. Raymond Judice, Box 12066, Capitol Station, Austin 78711 (nonmember).

Credit Commissioner, Consumer—(1969); apptv. by State Finance Commission; 2-yr.: Sam Kelley, Box 2107, Austin 78768 (\$66,360).

Credit Union Commission of Texas—(1949 as 3-member Credit Union Advisory Commission; name changed and number members increased to six in 1969; number members increased to nine in 1981 with addition of three public members); apptv.; 6-yr.; expenses; nine members: Donald G. Storch, Houston (2-15-93); Jimmy Sasser, Edinburg (2-15-93); William H. Inabnett, Wichita Falls (2-15-91); Gerald R. Sheets, Robstown (2-15-91); Jerry A. Deering, Fort Worth (2-15-89); Ada Williams, Dallas (2-15-89). Public members: Horace R. Grace, Killeen (2-15-89); Dennis Morgan, El Campo (2-15-91); Gregg A. Cooke, Dallas (2-15-87). Commissioner, John Hale, 914 E. Anderson Lane, Austin 78752-1699 (nonmember) (\$77,250).

Crime Stoppers Advisory Council—(1981); apptv.; 2-yr.; five members: Mrs. Peggy J. Pickle, Austin (9-1-85); Frank L. Breedlove, Dallas (9-1-85); Richard W. Carter, Arlington (9-1-87); Cary O. Fox, Conroe (9-1-85); Rogelio Martinez, McAllen (9-1-85).

Criminal Justice Coordinating Council—(1983); eleven ex officio members: Director Department Corrections; Executive Director Adult Probation Commission; Executive Director Board of Pardons and Paroles; Executive Director

Prosecutors Coordinating Council; Executive Director Judicial Council; Executive Director Commission on Jail Standards; Director Department Public Safety; Executive Director Criminal Justice Division of Governor's office; Executive Director Texas Youth Commission; Executive Director Juvenile Probation Commission; Executive Director Texas Commission on Law Enforcement; Executive Director State Bar of Texas. Three apptv. members — one each by Governor, Speaker and Lieutenant Governor: Gov.'s apptee: Anita Ashton, Austin.

Criminal Justice Division Advisory Board—(1981); twenty-one members — seven apptd. by Governor; seven apptd. by Lieut. Governor, and seven apptd. by Speaker of House; 2-yr.; expenses. Gov.'s apptees.: Chmn., Omar Harvey, Dallas (9-1-83); Vice Chmn., Joe Greenhill, Austin (9-1-83); James B. Adams, Austin (9-1-83); John B. Holmes Jr., Houston (9-1-83); Barbara G. Culver, Midland (9-1-83); Henry Wade, Dallas (9-1-83); Leonard Hancock, Temple (9-1-83). Director, Gilbert J. Pena, Box 12428, Austin 78711 (nonmember).

Criminal Justice Policy Council—(1983); three ex officio members; eight apptv. — two each by Lieutenant Governor and Speaker of House; four apptd. by Governor. Ex officio members: Governor, Lieutenant Governor and Speaker of House. Gov.'s apptees: Victor Strecher, Huntsville; Cappy Eads, Belton; Mario Santos, Laredo; Myra McDaniel, Austin. (All have indefinite terms.) Executive Director, Rider Scott, Rm. 410, Sam Houston Bldg., 201 E. 14th, Austin 78701 (nonmember) ($53,045).

Deaf, Texas Commission for the—(1971 as six-member board; membership raised to nine in 1979); apptv.; 6-yr.; nine members—three deaf persons, two parents of deaf, two professionals serving deaf and two from general public; expenses: Deaf members: J. Scott Hutchinson, Dallas (1-31-93); William A. Floerke, Taft (1-31-89); N. S. Draughon Jr., Temple (1-31-91). Parents of deaf: Thalia H. Munoz, Rio Grande City (1-31-93); Ann M. Phillips, Dallas (1-31-91). Professionals serving deaf: Melinda F. McKee, Waco (1-31-93); Donald Howard England, Austin (1-31-89). General public members: Jerry A. McCutchin, Coppell (1-31-89); Chmn., Sidney J. Braquet, Houston (1-31-91). Executive Director, Fred Tammen, Box 12904, Capitol Station, Austin 78711 (nonmember) ($36,462).

Deaf, Governing Board of Texas School for the—(1979); 6-yr.; expenses; nine members—three each from workers with deaf, parent of a deaf person and deaf persons: Deaf members: Glynn Whittemore, Houston (1-31-87); Sid Ander, Fort Worth (1-31-91); Robert E. Bevill, Pasadena (1-31-91). Workers with deaf: Marjorie Moore, Brackettville (1-31-87); Ernest R. Fuentes, Austin (1-31-89); Polly P. Walton, Beaumont (1-31-91). Parent of deaf person: Robert Edward Parrish, Dallas (1-31-87); Avril Thompson, Houston (1-31-91); Gayle Lindsey, Austin (1-31-91). Executive Director, Victor H. Galloway, P.O. Box 3538, Austin 78764 (nonmember) ($46,000).

Dental Examiners, Texas State Board of—(1919 as six-member board; increased to nine members in 1971; increased to twelve members in 1981 with addition of three public members); apptv.; 6-yr.; per diem while on duty; twelve members: Dr. Jack T. Clark, Fort Worth (5-10-87); Dr. Brian Babin, Woodville (5-10-87); Dr. Will F. Graham, Borger (5-10-87); Dr. William J. Kemp, Haskell (5-10-91); Dr. Sam H. Rabon, Kingsville (5-10-91); Dr. Terry D. Dickinson, Houston (5-10-91); Dr. L. Jack Bolton, Dallas (5-10-89); Dr. Frank Santos Jr., San Antonio (5-10-89); Dr. R. D. Minatra, Houston (5-10-91). Public members: Clara Hoffman, Dallas (5-10-91); Evelynne Vick, Waco (5-10-89); Lydia E. Torres, Midland (5-10-87). Executive Director, William S. Nail, 411 W. 13th, Suite 503, Austin 78701 (nonmember) ($48,204).

Depository Board, State—(1905); three ex officio; term in other office; one apptd. by Governor for 2-yr. term; four members: Ex officio members — Treasurer Ann Richards, Banking Commissioner James L. Sexton, Comptroller Bob Bullock. Apptv. member: Robert Lee Monaghan, Austin (Midland) (8-22-87).

Developmental Disabilities Planning Council—(1971); twenty-six members; apptv.; 6-yr.; 19 apptv. members, seven ex officio. Ex officio members: Representatives from Department of Mental Health and Mental Retardation; Rehabilitation Commission; Department of Health; Department of Human Services; Texas Education Agency; Texas Commission for the Blind; Texas Commission for the Deaf. Apptv. members: Opal H. Washington, Austin (2-1-89); Ward R. Burke, Lufkin (2-1-89); Patricia McCallum, Seagoville (2-1-89); Diana Fricke, Fort Worth (2-1-89); Dr. James W. Cooper, Corpus Christi (2-1-87); Mary C. Knott, El Paso (2-1-86); Jann E. Steed, Schertz (2-1-91); James McBryde, Abilene (2-1-89); Mary Jane Clark, Pharr (2-1-91); Ronnie N. Alexander, San Antonio (2-1-85); Angela K. Lamb, Amarillo (2-1-91); Jerry G. Hassell, Austin (2-1-91); Debbie Francis, Dallas (2-1-87); Laura R. Guerra, Mercedes (2-1-91); Gary Shreve, Monahans (2-1-87); Gloria Drass, Fort Worth (2-1-91); Mrs. Lee Veenker, Irving (2-1-87); Cathryn D. Bebee, Austin (2-1-91); Dr. Tom Deliganis, San Antonio (2-1-89). Executive Director, Joellen Simmons, 118 E. Riverside Dr., Austin 78704 (nonmember).

Diabetes Council, Texas—(1983); 2-yr.; eleven members

— six from public and five ex officio. Ex officio members: One each from Texas Department of Health, Texas Education Agency, Texas Department of Human Services, Texas Commission for the Blind and Texas Rehabilitation Commission. Public members: David C. Warner, Austin (2-1-87); Linda Russell, Dallas (2-1-87); Dr. Luther B. Travis, Galveston (2-1-85); Carolyn Grubb, Austin (2-1-87); Jacqueline Colvill, Houston (2-1-86); Dr. Maria Luisa Urdanetta, San Antonio (2-1-84).

Dieticians, Texas Board of Examiners of—(1983); apptv.; nine members — three from general public and six licensed dieticians; 6-yr.; per diem and expenses: Gracie Specks, Temple (9-1-91); James T. Moore, Austin (9-1-91); Dr. Johnnie Ruth Stripling, Tyler (9-1-91); Mary Adams, Lubbock (9-1-87); Mrs. Rosario P. Hamilton, San Antonio (9-1-87); Madgelean Bush, Houston (9-1-87); Irma Gutierrez, Laredo (9-1-89); Ronnie A. Nutt, Paris (9-1-89); Mrs. Dale Smith, DeLeon (9-1-89).

Disabilities, Council on—(1983); apptv. as indicated; 2-yr.; 21 members: Four apptd. by Governor, four by Lieutenant Governor, four by Speaker; one member each from Department Human Services, Department Mental Health and Mental Retardation, Department Health, Texas Education Agency, Texas Rehabilitation Commission, Texas Commission for the Deaf, State Commission for the Blind, Texas Department on Aging, Texas Commission on Alcoholism. Gov.'s apptees: Reed Martin, Austin (1-31-87); Amy K. Rosenberg, Austin (1-31-87); Mrs. Joseph Chimelak, Bellaire (1-31-87); Chmn., Bob L. Thomas, Waco (1-31-87).

East Texas State University, Board of Regents of—(1969); apptv.; 6-yr.; nine members: Leon J. Coker Jr., Texarkana (2-15-89); Herman Furlough Jr., Terrell (2-15-89); James L. Toler, Garland (2-15-89); Larry D. Franklin, San Antonio (2-15-91); Raymond B. Cameron, Rockwall (2-15-91); Ted H. Peters, Greenville (2-15-91); W. Ben Munson III, Denison (2-15-87); Peggy M. Wilson, Dallas (2-15-87); Sally R. Lancaster, Dallas (2-15-93). President, Dr. Jerry Morris, ETSU, Commerce 75428 (nonmember).

Economic Development Commission, Texas—(1920 as 5-member Texas Industrial Commission; expanded by Legislature in 1959 to 9-member board; increased to 12 members in 1973 by addition of three rural members; name changed to present form and three members added in 1983); apptv.; 6-yr.; expenses; fifteen members: Hector Gutierrez Jr., Fort Worth (2-15-87); Edward O. Vetter, Dallas (2-15-93); J. A. Koesel Jr., Midland (2-15-87); John F. Sammons Jr., Temple (2-15-87); Edd Hargett, Douglassville (2-15-87); Ed Smith, Houston (2-15-89); William H. Crook, San Marcos (2-15-89); Bob L. Herchert, Fort Worth (2-15-89); Dan Petty, Dallas (2-15-89); Hugh G. Robinson, Dallas (2-15-91); Joe E. Russo, Houston (2-15-91); George McLaughlin, Beaumont (2-15-91); Clyde H. Alexander II, Athens (2-15-91); Al Cisneros, Brownsville (2-15-91); Charles M. Wender, San Antonio (2-15-89). Executive Director, Charles B. Wood, Box 12728, Capitol Station, Austin 78711 (nonmember) ($55,929).

Economy and Efficiency in State Government, Texas Commission on—(1985); 4-yr.; expenses; 15 members apptd. as follows: 5 by Lt. Gov., including two state senators; 5 by Speaker of House, including two state representatives; 5 by Governor. All terms expire and commission will be abolished 9-1-89. Governor's apptees: Joe Christie, Austin; L. W. Gray, Houston; George Beto, Huntsville; John Steen Jr., San Antonio; Curtis N. Leggett, Dallas.

Education Agency, Texas—Legal name of group of educational agencies, including **State Board of Education**, **State Commissioner of Education** and **Advisory Council for Technical-Vocational Education**. See these separate agencies.

Education, State Board of—(1866; re-created 1928 and reformed by Gilmer-Aikin Act, 1949, to consist of 21 elective members, from districts co-extensive with 21 congressional districts at that time; membership increased to 24 with congressional redistricting in 1971, effective 1973; membership increased to 27 with congressional redistricting in 1981, effective 1983; reorganized by special legislative session as 15-member apptv. board in 1984 to become elective board again in 1988); expenses; 15 members; 4-yr.; all terms expire (1-1-89). Figures before names indicate district numbers: (1) Maria Elena Flood, El Paso; (2) Mary Helen Berlanga, Corpus Christi; (3) Pete J. Morales Jr., Devine; (4) Volly C. Bastine Jr., Houston; (5) William V. McBride, San Antonio; (6) Charles Duncan, Houston; (7) Carolyn Crawford, Beaumont; (8) Jack Strong, Longview; (9) Vice-chairman, Rebecca D. Canning, Waco; (10) John Prescott, College Station; (11) Chairman, Jon Brumley, Fort Worth; (12) Geraldine Miller, Dallas; (13) Dr. Emmett Conrad, Dallas; (14) Katherine P. Raines, Cleburne; (15) Paul C. Dunn, Levelland. (See also **Commissioner of Education** who is appointed by this board.)

Education Board, Southern Regional—(1969); apptv.; 4-yr.; four apptv. members and Governor as ex officio member. Apptv. members: Carl Parker, Port Arthur (6-30-84); Wilhelmina Delco, Austin (6-30-85); Max Sherman, Austin (6-30-90); Becky Brooks, Jefferson (6-30-87). Dr. Winfred L. Godwin, President, Southern Regional Education Board, 592 10th St. N. W., Atlanta, Ga. 30318-5790.

Education Board, Legislative—Est. 1984 as temporary advisory board; to expire Jan. 1, 1989; ten members, all ex officio as follows: Lieutenant Governor; Speaker House of Representatives; chairman House Public Education Committee; chairman Senate Education Committee; chairman House Appropriations Committee; chairman Senate Finance Committee; two representatives apptd. by Speaker; two senators apptd. by Lieutenant Governor.

Egg Marketing Advisory Board—(1957); apptv.; 6-yr.; eleven members — two ex officio, nine apptv. Commissioner of Agriculture serves as chairman; one apptd. by head of Poultry Science Department, A&M University. Gov.'s apptees: Ernest A. Mahard Jr., Prosper (9-27-83); Hobart H. Joe, Houston (9-27-83); T. P. Metcalfe, Franklin (9-27-83); D. R. Barrett, Bryan (9-27-85); Kervin E. Jacob, Houston (9-27-85); Edgar H. Burton, Lufkin (9-27-85); James O. Lipscomb, Lockhart (9-27-87); Richard Doty, Corpus Christi (9-27-87); Carl Smith, Flatonia (9-27-87).

Elderly, Coordinating Council on Long-Term Care for the—(1983); apptv. as indicated; 2-yr.; indefinite number of members: Four apptd. by Governor; four by Lieutenant Governor, four by Speaker; one each from Texas Department on Aging, Texas Department of Human Services, Texas Department of Health and Texas Department of Mental Health and Mental Retardation. Gov.'s apptees: A. R. Arriola, Alice (1-31-85); Mrs. Johnnie Cavanaugh, Austin (1-31-85); Rev. Bob Greene, Austin (1-31-85); Dr. David Maldonado, Arlington (1-31-85).

Election Commission, State—(1973); nine members apptv. as indicated: Chairman Democratic State Executive Committee; Chairman Republican State Executive Committee; Chief Justice of Supreme Court; Presiding Judge Court of Criminal Appeals; two persons to be named — one a justice of the Court of Appeals appointed by Chief Justice of Supreme Court; one District Judge appointed by Presiding Judge of Court of Criminal Appeals; two county chairmen — one each from Democratic and Republican parties — named by the parties; Secretary of State.

Employment Commission, Texas—(1936); apptv.; $60,461; 6-yr.; three members: Mary S. Nabers (management), Austin (Brownwood) (2-1-91); Ronald E. Luna (labor), Austin (Buda) (11-21-93); Nancy Barnes (public), Austin (11-21-88). Administrator, William Grossenbacher, 638 TEC Bldg., 101 E. 15th, Austin 78778 (nonmember) ($57,628).

Engineers, State Board of Registration for Professional—(1937 as six-member board; membership increased to nine in 1981 with addition of three members from general public); apptv.; per diem and expenses; 6-yr.; nine members: Ernest D. Dorchester, Midland (9-26-91); Joseph J. Beal, Austin (9-26-91); D. S. Hammett, Dallas (9-26-87); Bill W. Klotz, Houston (9-26-87); Robert Navarro, El Paso (9-26-89); Clay Roming, Eddy (9-26-89). Public members: James K. Newman, Denton (9-26-91); Ron Garrett, Waco (9-26-87); Charles Finnell, Beaumont (9-26-91). Executive Director, Woodrow W. Mize, Drawer 18329, Austin 78760 (nonmember) ($50,676).

Enterprise Zone Board—(1983); apptv.; expenses; 6-yr.; nine members as follows: One member each from Industrial Commission, Texas Employment Commission, Texas Dept. of Community Affairs, one municipal government, one county government, one independent school district, one from small business, one employee and one from general public: Ralph Quintanilla, Austin (2-1-85); Kenyon Clapp, Austin (2-1-85); Henry Cisneros, San Antonio (2-1-85); R. H. Lackner, Brownsville (2-1-87); Santos Saldana, Edinburg (2-1-87); Carlos Carrasco, El Paso (2-1-89); Homer Scott, Mission (2-1-89); Vidal Trevino, Laredo (2-1-89); Karin Richmond, McAllen (2-1-89).

Entomologist, State—(1900); ex officio: Paul W. Jackson, Entomologist at Texas Agricultural Experiment Station, College Station.

Ethics Advisory Commission, State—(1983); 11 members: two ex officio (non-voting) — secretary of state and attorney general; five apptd. by Gov., three from general public and two legal counsels of different major political parties; two apptd. by Lt. Gov., one state senator and one from general public; two apptd. by Speaker of House, one state representative and one from general public; expenses; 2-yr. Governor's apptees: Leonard E. Davis, Tyler (2-1-84); Harold Hammett, Fort Worth (2-1-84); Robert C. McKay, Victoria (2-1-85); William Edward Moody, El Paso (2-1-85); John F. Sutton, Austin (2-1-87).

Evergreen Underground Water Conservation District, Board of Directors—(1965); five members—four elected (two each from Wilson and Atascosa Counties) and one apptd. by Governor; 2-yr.: Mark Connally, Floresville (1-13-85).

Family Practice Residency Advisory Committee—(1977); apptv. as indicated; expenses; 3-yr.; 12 members as follows: One practicing physician apptd. by Texas Osteopathic Medical Assn.; two apptd. by Association of Directors of Family Practice Training Programs; one apptd. by Texas Medical Assn.; two apptd. by Texas Academy of Family Physicians; two administrators of hospitals apptd. by Texas Hospital Assn.; three public members apptd. by Gov.; and the president of the Texas Academy of Family Physicians. Gov.'s apptees: Chmn., Dr. Exalton A. Delco Jr., Austin (8-29-88); Dr. E. J. Mason, Dallas (8-29-84); Georgia S. Hanks, Amarillo (8-29-89).

Finance Commission of Texas—(1923 as **Banking Commis**

sion; reorganized as **Finance Commission** 1943 with nine members: membership increased to twelve in 1983 with addition of three consumer credit members from general public); apptv.; 6-yr.; per diem and traveling expenses. Six members of banking section of commission as follows: Richard H. Skinner, Houston (2-1-91); Carroll N. Sullivan Jr., Georgetown (2-1-91); Gerald H. Smith, Houston (2-1-87); Cullen R. Looney, Edinburg (2-1-87); Scott B. Smith, Denison (2-1-89); Phillip G. Newsom, Ennis (2-1-89). Three members of savings and loan section of commission as follows: D. Gene Phelps, Tomball (2-1-91); R. Dary Scone, Dallas (2-1-93); Ralph D. Reed, College Station (2-1-89). Three members from general public: Alan Lerner, Dallas (2-1-91); Leopoldo Palacios, Pharr (2-1-87); Karen L. Simon, Fort Worth (2-1-89). **Banking Commissioner**, James L. Sexton, 2601 N. Lamar, Austin 78705, appointee of Finance Commission. (See also **Banking Commissioner, State.**)

Firemen's Pension Commissioner—(1937); apptv.; 2-yr.: Hal H. Hood, 503-F Sam Houston Bldg., Austin 78701 (7-1-85) ($31,518).

Fire Fighters' Relief and Retirement Fund, Board of Trustees—(1977); apptv.; expenses; 6-yr.; six members: W. Harold Brodt, Seguin (9-1-87); Joe Rice, Canyon (9-1-89); Marvin R. Setzer Sr., Brazoria (9-1-89); Bobby Joe Looney, Mansfield (9-1-91); J. J. Pruitt, Huffman (9-9-87); Donald Eernisse, Alvin (9-1-91).

Fire Protection Personnel Standards and Education, Commission on—(1969); apptv.; expenses; 6-yr.; nine apptv. members and two ex-officio members: Ex officio members — Commissioner of Higher Education of the Coordinating Board, Texas College and University System, and the Commissioner of the Texas Education Agency. Apptv. members: Ernest A. Emerson, Austin (6-11-89); P. E. Adams, El Paso (6-11-89); Lt. A. J. Bostick Sr., Fort Worth (6-11-89); Mike B. Perez Jr., Laredo (6-11-91); Alcus Greer, Houston (6-11-91); Helen L. Campbell, Austin (6-11-87); Lester W. Tyra Jr., Houston (6-11-91); Chmn., Henry D. Smith, College Station (6-11-87); Rae M. Eastland, Waco (6-11-87). Executive Director, Garland W. Fulbright, 510 S. Congress, Suite 406, Austin 78704 (nonmember) ($31,518).

Forester, State—(1915); apptv. by board of directors of A&M University: Bruce R. Miles, College Station.

Good Neighbor Commission—(1943); apptv.; 6-yr.; expenses; nine members: Paula Montoya, Lubbock (6-18-91); Michael L. Lauderdale, Austin (6-18-91); Sondra Sugerman, San Antonio (6-18-91); Dr. Billy Reagan, Houston (6-18-87); Steve A. Lillard III, Zapata (6-18-87); Dr. Richard Rubottom, Dallas (6-18-87); David L. Garza Jr., Houston (6-18-89); Jose Alvarado Jr., Corpus Christi (6-18-89); Travis Johnson, El Paso (6-18-89). Executive Director, Bob Watson, Box 12007, Capitol Station, Austin 78711 (nonmember) ($43,260).

Governor—(1845 by original Constitution, 1876 by present Constitution); elective; (2-yr. by original constitutional provision, term raised to 4-yr. in 1972, effective 1975): William P. Clements Jr., Austin (Dallas) (1-1-91) ($94,348).

Guadalupe-Blanco River Authority—(1935); apptv.; per diem and expenses on duty; 6-yr.; nine members: Herbert R. Schneider, New Braunfels (2-1-93); Sec.-Treas., Preston A. Stofer, Long Mott (2-1-93); A. C. Schwethelm, Comfort (2-1-87); E. T. Summers Jr., Cuero (2-1-89); Harry E. Gumbert Jr., Wimberley (2-1-89); Kathryn Chenault, Gonzales (2-1-89); Joseph P. Kelly, Victoria (2-1-91); John C. Taylor, McQueeney (2-1-91); Warren P. Kirksey, Lockhart (2-1-91). General Manager, John H. Specht, Box 271, Seguin 78155 (nonmember).

Guadalupe River Authority, Upper—(1939); apptv.; 6-yr.; nine members: Lorita Ann Tipton, Kerrville (2-1-93); Betty Strohacker, Kerrville (11-1-88); William D. Looney, Kerrville (2-1-93); Richard G. Eastland, Hunt (11-1-91); H. Ritman Jons, Kerrville (2-1-87); Charles Schreiner IV, Mountain Home (11-1-88); L. F. E. Koehler, Hunt (11-1-88); T. Beck Gipson, Kerrville (2-1-93); Dr. R. H. Holekamp, Kerrville (11-1-91). General Manager, B. W. Bruns, Box 1278, Kerrville 78029-1278.

Gulf Coast Waste Disposal Authority—(1969); apptv.; 2-yr.; $50 a day and expenses on duty; nine members—three apptv. by Governor, three by County Commissioners Courts of counties in district, and three by Municipalities Waste Disposal Councils of counties in district. Governor's appointees: Rick Ferguson, Winnie (8-31-86); Clyde R. Bickham, Houston (8-31-87); John Unbehagen, Galveston (8-31-86). Gen. Mgr., L. Jack Davis (nonmember), 910 Bay Area Blvd., Houston 77058.

Gulf States Marine Fisheries Commission—(1949); apptv.; 3-yr.; three members: Charles Travis, Executive Director Parks and Wildlife Commission, Austin; Rep. Leroy Wieting, Portland; Leslie E. Casterline Jr., Fulton (3-17-87). Executive Director, Charles H. Lyles, Box 726, Ocean Springs, MS 39564.

Health Coordinating Council, Texas Statewide—(1975); apptv.; 2-yr.; 21 apptv., one ex officio member: Elizabeth Ann Attel, Dallas (9-1-88); Max Brown, Dallas (9-1-88); Lynda Calcote, Abilene (9-1-88); Jose L. Gonzalez, Laredo (9-1-88); Father Robert J. Brooks, Houston (9-1-87); Hon. Lester Cranek, Columbus (9-1-87); James Easter, Houston (9-1-87); James L. Grey, Austin (9-1-87); Marjorie Daniels, Hereford

-1-87); Chmn., Dr. Marion R. Zetzman, Dallas (9-1-88); Dr. Edward A. R. Lord Jr., Houston (9-1-88); Jack L. Campbell, Austin (9-1-88); Lynda Fant Hill, Fort Worth (9-1-87); Dolores Lawless, Beaumont (9-1-87); Hon. Frank Madla, San Antonio (9-1-87); Adrian Arriaga, McAllen (9-1-87); Hon. Buddy Cole, Pilot Point (9-1-87); Melinda Gonzales, Corpus Christi (9-1-88); M. Medesta Smith, Clarksville (9-1-88); Michael C. Waters, Abilene (9-1-88); James L. Caldwell, Austin (9-1-88).

Health and Human Services Coordinating Council—(1975 as nine-member board; membership increased to 19 in 1983); 6-yr.; 19 members. Ex officio members: Governor, Lieutenant Governor, Speaker of House, Chairman Texas Board of Human Services, Chairman Texas Board of Health, Chairman Texas Board of Mental Health and Mental Retardation, Chairman State Board of Education. Two board members of State agencies appointed by Governor: Jerry Kane, Austin (9-1-87); Marshall W. Cooper, Whiteface (9-1-87). Two senators appointed by Lieutenant Governor; two representatives appointed by Speaker; two general public members appointed by Governor: Judith L. Craven, Houston (9-1-87); Arnold N. Sweet, Dallas (9-1-87). Two general public members appointed by Lieutenant Governor: Rebecca Canning, Waco (9-1-85); Helen Farabee, Wichita Falls (9-1-85). Two general public members appointed by Speaker: Sharon Flippen, Austin (9-1-85); Louise Maberry, Orange (9-1-85). Executive Director, Patrice O. Thomas, Box 12428, Austin 78711 (nonmember) ($50,882); Administrative Assistant, Joe Ann Stoker (nonmember).

Health, Texas Board of—(1903 as **State Board of Health**; superseded similar department created in 1891; name changed in 1975 to **Texas Board of Health Resources** and membership increased to 18; name changed in 1977 to present form); apptv.; per diem and expenses on duty; 6-yr.; 18 members: Chmn., Dr. Frank Bryant Jr., San Antonio (2-1-89); Vice Chmn., Dr. Raleigh R. White IV, Temple (2-1-93); *. Max M. Stettner, Lubbock (2-1-89); Dr. Barry D. Cunningham, Round Rock (2-1-89); Dennis K. McIntosh, Seguin (2-1-89); Barbara T. Slover, Fort Worth (2-1-87); Isadore Roosth, Tyler (2-1-85); Dr. Robert D. Moreton, Houston (2-1-85); Joe N. Pyle, San Antonio (2-1-91); Dr. Edward H. Anker, Seguin (2-1-91); R. Jack Ayres Jr., Dallas (2-1-89); Lester Marian Strohmeyer, McAllen (2-1-91); Dr. Jose Roman Jr., El Paso (2-1-91); Larry D. Krupala, Cuero (2-1-93); Lon L. Brewer, Dallas (2-1-93); Dr. Oliver R. Smith, El Paso (2-1-93). Commissioner of Health, Dr. Robert Bernstein, 1100 W. 49th, Austin 78756 (nonmember) ($62,800).

Hearing Aids, Texas Board of Examiners in the Fitting and Dispensing of—(1969); apptv.; 6-yr.; expenses; nine members: William E. Keim, Sugar Land (12-31-87); Richard Durbin, Rowlett (12-31-89); Tom C. Lucenay, Waco (12-31-91); Rev. H. E. Myrick, El Paso (12-31-87); Thomas R. Janes, Fort Worth (12-31-87); George Holland Jr., Lubbock (12-31-91); Dr. Henry M. Carder, Dallas (12-31-89); Carl McGovern, Commerce (12-31-89); President, Gerald W. Brutte, Mexia (12-31-91). Executive Director, Wanda F. Stewart, 105 W. Riverside Dr., Suite 124, Austin 78704 (nonmember) ($23,175).

Higher Education Coordinating Board, Texas—(1953 as temporary board; 1955 as permanent 15-member **Texas Commission on Higher Education**; changed to 18-member board in 1965; name changed to present form in 1987); apptv; 6-yr.; expenses; 18 members: Regina J. Rogers, Houston (8-31-91); Philip G. Warner, Houston (8-31-91); Jack T. Trotter, Houston (8-31-91); Jess Ben Latham III, Amarillo (8-31-91); Dr. Lauro G. Guerra, McAllen (8-31-91); George Hamblett, Dallas (9-1-91); C. F. Guerra Jr., San Antonio (9-1-87); W. K. Barnett, Lubbock (9-1-87); Mrs. Chandler Lindsey, Dallas (9-1-87); Dr. William R. Patterson, Texarkana (9-1-87); Kent R. Hance Sr., Lubbock (9-1-87); William J. Garraway, Houston (9-1-87); Vice Chmn., Harvey Weil, Corpus Christi (9-1-89); John S. Carroll III, El Campo (9-1-89); Eleanor N. Conrad, Dallas (9-1-89); Ray Clymer, Wichita Falls (9-1-89); Mrs. Lee H. Jamail, Houston (9-1-89); Chmn., Larry E. Temple, Austin (9-1-89). Commissioner of Higher Education, Dr. Kenneth H. Ashworth, Box 12788, Austin 78711 (nonmember) ($65,920).

Highway and Public Transportation Commission, Texas—(1917 as State Highway Commission; merged with Mass Transportation Commission and name changed to present form in 1975); apptv.; 6-yr.; ($35,123); three members: Robert H. Dedman, Dallas (2-15-93); Chmn., Robert C. Lanier, Houston (2-15-89); Ray C. Stoker Jr., Odessa (2-15-91).

Highways and Public Transportation, State Engineer-Director for—(1917 as State Highway Engineer; name changed present form in 1975); apptv. by Texas Highway and Public Transportation Commission; indefinite term: Raymond Stotzer Jr., 11th and Brazos, Austin 78701 ($68,701).

Historical Commission, Texas—(1953); apptv.; expenses; 6-yr.; eighteen members: Richard H. Collins, Dallas (1-1-87); Duncan Boeckman, Dallas (1-1-87); Louis P. Terrazas, San Antonio (1-1-87); Karl A. Komatsu, Fort Worth (1-1-93); W. Merriman Morton, El Paso (1-1-91); George Christian, Austin (1-1-91); Lunelle A. Anderson, San Marcos (1-1-91); Dr. Dan Willis, Fort Worth (1-1-91); Mrs. George Ann Carter, Fort Worth (1-1-91); Virginia Long, Kilgore (1-1-91); Chmn., T. R. Fehrenbach, San Antonio (1-1-89);

Richard H. Collins, Dallas (1-1-89); James S. Nabors, Lake Jackson (1-1-87); John M. Bennett, San Antonio (1-1-89); Maxine Flournoy, Alice (1-1-89); Harry A. Golemon, Houston (1-1-87); Martha Gay Ratliff, Austin (1-1-89); Evangeline L. Whorton, Galveston (1-1-89). Executive Director, Curtis Tunnell, Box 12276, Capitol Sta., Austin 78711 (nonmember) ($46,968).

Historical Records Advisory Board, Texas—(1976); apptv.; 3-yr.; nine members: John W. Crain, Dallas (1-23-85); Dr. David B. Gracy II, Austin (1-23-88); Dorman H. Winfrey, Austin (1-23-88); Kent Keeth, Waco (1-23-87); Dr. David J. Murrah, Lubbock (1-23-86); Betty Kissler, San Marcos (1-23-86); A. Jean Shepherd, Baytown (1-23-86); Don Carleton, Austin (1-23-87); Michael Q. Hooks, Austin (1-23-87). **State Historical Records Coordinator**, Dr. David B. Gracy II, State Library, Austin.

Hospital Council, Advisory—(1947); twelve members; State Health Commissioner as ex officio member; T. expenses; apptv. members serve 6-yr. terms: Dr. Joseph T. Ainsworth, Houston (7-17-85); Jessica Harden, Houston (7-17-85); Ray Branson, Midland (7-17-91); Dr. James A. Hallmark, Fort Worth (7-17-85); Margaret Read, Dallas (7-17-87); James E. Bullard, Hereford (7-17-87); Terrie Lynn Brown, Houston (7-17-87); W. B. Lipes, Corpus Christi (7-17-87); O. Ray Hurst, Austin (7-17-89); Kippy Caraway, Houston (7-17-89); Dora Olivo, Rosenberg (7-17-89); Elizabeth L. Kimmel, Houston (7-17-89). Ex officio member, State Commissioner of Health, 1100 W. 49th, Austin.

Housing Agency, Board of Directors of the Texas—(1979); apptv.; expenses; 6-yr.; nine apptv. members: Executive Director Texas Dept. of Community Affairs ex officio member and Chairman of Board. Apptv. members: Kenneth DeJarnett, Garland (1-31-93); Salvador Canchola, El Paso (1-31-87); Perry Bradley, Sulphur Springs (1-31-87); J. Stanley Stephen, Bryan (1-31-89); Melva W. Becnel, Houston (1-31-89); Fred E. Rizk, Houston (1-31-89); Richard Jordan, Austin (1-31-91); W. E. Daniels, Houston (1-31-91); Arthur Navarro, Austin (1-31-91). Executive Administrator, Dan McNeil, Box 13941, Capitol Station, Austin 78711 (nonmember).

Humanities, Texas Commission on the and—(See Arts, Texas Commission on the.)

Humanities, Texas Committee for the—(1972); apptv. and elective by the Committee; 2-yr. for apptv. members; 4-yr. for elective; twenty-two members — four apptv. by Governor as follows: Carol McKay, Fort Worth (12-31-88); Dr. Phyllis Bridges, Denton (12-31-87); Ellena Stone Huckaby, Houston (12-31-87); William P. Wright Jr., Abilene (12-31-87). Executive Director, James F. Veninga, 1604 Nueces, Austin 78701 (nonmember).

Human Rights, State Commission on—(1983); apptv.; 6-yr.; expenses; six members: Mrs. Mallory Robinson, Houston (9-24-91); Maxine Lee, Austin (9-24-91); Alberto H. Magnon Jr., Laredo (9-24-87); Ramiro Casso, McAllen (9-24-87); Chairman, Frank Thompson Jr., Houston (9-24-89); Helen Giddings, Dallas (9-24-89). Executive Director, Bill Hale, Box 13493, Capitol Station, Austin 78711 (nonmember) ($48,204).

Human Services, Texas Board of—(1941 as State Board of Public Welfare; name changed to present form in 1985); apptv.; 6-yr.; per diem and expenses; three members and a commissioner: J. L. Kosberg, Houston (1-20-91); Vicki Garza, Corpus Christi (1-20-89); Robert A. Mosbacher Jr., Houston (2-1-93). **Commissioner**, Marlin W. Johnston, Box 2960, Austin 78769 ($68,289).

Indebtedness, Board of County and District Road Bond—(1932); ex officio; term in other office; three members: Comptroller Robert D. Bullock, Treasurer Ann Richards and State Highway Engineer, M. G. Goode, LBJ State Office Bldg., Austin 78701.

Indian Commission, Texas—(1965); apptv.; 6-yr.; per diem and expenses; three members: W. E. Fifer Jr., El Paso (1-31-87); Mrs. Owanah P. Anderson, Wichita Falls (1-31-91); Don E. Ellyson, Waxahachie (1-31-89). Executive Director, Raymond D. Apodaca, 9434 Viscount, Suite 122, El Paso 79925. (Office will be moved to Austin by Dec. 1, 1985. Address not available at press time.) (nonmember) ($39,346).

Industrial Accident Board—(1913); apptv.; (Chairman, $56,495, others $55,774); 6-yr.; three members: Chmn., Joseph Gagen, Houston (9-1-91); Bobby J. Barnes, Baytown (employee) (9-1-89); N. J. Huestis, Corpus Christi (employer) (9-1-87). Executive Director, William Treacy, Bevington A. Reed Bldg., 200 E. Riverside Dr., Austin 78704 (nonmember apptd. by board) ($52,015).

Industrialized Building Code Council, Texas—(See Building Code Council, Texas Industrialized.)

Insurance, State Board of—(Originally created as **State Board of Insurance Commissioners** in 1927; superseded similar commission of 1913; re-created 1957 to form **State Board of Insurance**); apptv.; 6-yr.; three members at $63,345 each and **State Insurance Commissioner** at $60,873, who serves 2-yr. term and is appointed by board members: David H. Thornberry, Austin (1-31-91); Chmn., Lyndon Olson Jr., Austin (Waco) (1-31-87); James L. Nelson, Austin (1-31-89). **Commissioner**, Tom Bond, State Insurance Bldg., Austin 78786.

Intergovernmental Relations, Texas Advisory Commission on—(1971); apptv.; 6-yr.; 24 apptd. and two ex officio members. Appointed members: Four city officials: Rosalie Brown, Sinton (9-1-87); Anthony Hall, Houston (9-1-89); Emmett Hutto, Baytown (9-1-91); Don R. Windle, Denton (9-1-91). Four county officials: Tom Vickers, San Antonio (9-1-91); Bill Bailey, Pasadena (9-1-85); Joe B. Garcia, Falfurrias (9-1-87); Norman Troy, Beaumont (9-1-89). Two school officials: Kathlyn J. Gilliam, Dallas (9-1-91); Victor Rodrigues, San Antonio (9-1-87). Two federal officials: Joseph Pena, Carrollton (9-1-91); J. Lynn Futch, Temple (9-1-87). Four private citizens: E. C. Green, Denison (9-1-91); Yvonne M. Moore, Austin (9-1-87); Jim D. Dannenbaum, Houston (9-1-89); Mrs. Pic Rivers, Houston (9-1-89). Two from other political subdivisions: Chairman, Fred N. Pfeiffer, San Antonio (9-1-87); Sam Collins, Orange (9-1-89). Three senators appointed by Lt. Governor. Three representatives appointed by Speaker of the House of Representatives. Two ex officio members: Lt. Gov. William P. Hobby and Speaker of the House of Representatives Gib Lewis. Executive Director, Jay G. Stanford, Box 13206, Austin 78711 (nonmember) ($42,848).

Interstate Compact for Supervision of Parolees and Probationers, Texas Administrator—(1951); ex officio: Atty. Gen. Jim Mattox, Austin.

Interstate Co-operation, Texas Commission on—Abolished in 1983.

Interstate Indian Council, Governor's (Texas Representatives)—(1965); designated: Raymond D. Apodaca, El Paso and W. E. Fifer, El Paso.

Interstate Oil Compact Commission, Texas Representative—(1935); ex officio or apptv. according to Governor's choice; per diem and expenses. Ex officio member: Garry Mauro, Land Commissioner, Austin. Apptv. member: Charles A. Moore. (Approximately 150 other appointees serve on various committees.)

Interstate Parole Compact Administrator—(1951); apptv.: Tom W. Bullington, Austin.

Irrigators, Texas Board of—(1979); apptv.; 6-yr.; expenses; six members as follows: Two from general public, four licensed irrigators. General public members: William C. Lucas, Garland (1-31-91); Douglas Hawthorne, Dallas (1-31-87). Licensed irrigators: John Alan Heidman, Dallas (1-31-91); Samuel D. Ousley, Dallas (1-31-89); Herman R. Johnson Sr., Corpus Christi (1-31-89); Hugh Rushing Jr., Austin (1-31-87). Executive Secretary, Joyce Watson, P.O. Box 12337, Capitol Sta., Austin 78711 (nonmember) ($27,192).

Jail Standards, Texas Commission on—(1975); apptv.; 6-yr.; expenses; nine members as follows: Two sheriffs — Joe A. Corley, Conroe (1-31-91); John Klevenhagen, Houston (1-31-91). One county judge — Pat F. O'Rourke, El Paso (1-1-89). One doctor — Dr. Hanes H. Brindley, Temple (1-31-87) and five private citizens — Ronald L. Ramey, Houston (1-31-85); Chmn., Ivy T. Corley, Amarillo (1-31-93); Vice Chmn., Robert J. Uhr, New Braunfels (1-31-89); Fred L. Tinsley, Dallas (1-31-89); Pat Newhouse, Honey Grove (1-31-87). Executive Director, Robert O. Viterna, Box 12985, Austin 78711 (nonmember) ($40,376).

Judicial Conduct, State Commission on—(1965 as nine-member Judicial Qualifications Commission; name changed in 1977 to present form and membership raised to eleven); expenses; 6-yr.; 11 members appointed as follows: Five apptd. by Supreme Court — Chmn., John T. Boyd, Amarillo, Justice, 7th Court of Appeals (11-19-87); William E. Junell, Houston, Justice, 14th Court of Appeals (11-19-89); Raul Longoria, Edinburg, Judge 139th Judicial District Court (11-19-87); S. J. Richburg, Dallas, Justice of the Peace (11-19-85); Elinor Walters, Municipal Court Judge, Seabrook (11-19-89); J. Ray Kirkpatrick, Judge, County Court at Law, Marshall, (11-19-89). Two board members appointed by State Bar — Vice Chmn., Robert H. Parsley, Houston (11-19-87); J. H. Clements, Temple (11-19-87). Four appointed by Governor — Max Emmert III, Odessa (11-19-89); Secretary, Nathan I. Reiter Jr., Texarkana (11-19-87); Scott Taliaferro, Abilene (11-19-85); Lowell Cable, Sulphur Springs (11-19-89). Executive Director, Robert C. Flowers, Box 12265, Capitol Sta., Austin 78711 (non-member) ($56,135).

Judicial Council, Texas—(1929 as Texas Civil Judicial Council; name changed in 1975); ex officio terms vary; apptv. 6-yr.; expenses; 19 members as follows: Six ex officio members: President, Ben Z. Grant, past chairman of House Judiciary Committee; Vice President, John L. Hill Jr., Austin, Chief Justice of Texas Supreme Court; Secretary, Tom G. Davis, Judge, Court of Criminal Appeals, Austin; Rep. Robert Bush, chairman of House Judiciary Committee; Sen. Ray Farabee, past chairman of Senate Jurisprudence Committee; Sen. Oscar Mauzy, chairman of Senate Jurisprudence Committee. Four apptv. members with ex officio qualifications: Sam H. Bass Jr., Justice, First Court of Appeals, Houston (1-1-87); Ray L. McKim, Presiding Judge, Seventh Administrative Judicial District, Odessa (1-1-87); Joe Spurlock II, Justice, Second Court of Appeals, Fort Worth (2-1-91); Charles J. Murray, Presiding Judge, Eighth Administrative Judicial District, Fort Worth (2-1-91). Nine apptv. members: John L. McCraw Jr., McKinney (6-30-91); Robert A. Gammage, Austin (6-30-91); Mark Martin, Dallas (6-30-85); J. Wm. Hartman, Rosenberg (6-30-89); Gene

McLaughlin, Ralls (6-30-89); Charles W. Barrow, Waco (6-30-87); A. W. McNeill, Beaumont (6-30-87); L. E. Frazier, Houston (6-30-87); Curt F. Steib, San Angelo (6-30-89). Executive Director, C. Raymond Judice (nonmember), Box 12066 Capitol Sta., Austin 78711.

Judicial Districts Board—(1985); 12 ex officio member (term in other office); one apptv. (4-yrs.); Ex officio Chmn., Chief Justice of Texas Supreme Court; Presiding Judge, Court of Criminal Appeals; Presiding Judge of eac of nine Administrative Judicial Districts; president of Tex as Judicial Council. Apptee: (appointment pending at pres time).

Judicial Districts of Texas, Administrative, Presiding Judges of—(See **Administrative Judicial Districts**.)

Judicial Qualifications Commission, State—(See Stat Commission on Judicial Conduct.)

Juvenile Probation Commission, Texas—(1981); apptv.; 6 yr.; expenses; nine members — three judges of Distric Courts and six private citizens: Judges: Scott D. Moore Fort Worth (8-31-91); William C. Martin III, Longview (8-3 87); F. P. Benavides, Mission (8-31-89). Citizen members Victoria H. Baldwin, Austin (8-31-91); Margaret E. Dunr San Marcos (8-31-87); Roy E. Turner Sr., Canyon (8-31-91 Lois Carpenter, Midland (8-31-87); Chmn., Marshall W. Coo per, Whiteface (8-31-87); Amos Landry, Beaumont (8-31-89) Executive Director, Bill Anderson, Box 13547, Austin 7871 (nonmember) ($49,749).

Labor and Standards, Commissioner of—(1909); apptv. 2-yr.: Richard L. Morgan, Box 12157, Capitol Sta., Austi 78711 (2-1-87) ($55,002).

Lamar University System, Board of Regents of—(1949) apptv.; 6-yr.; expenses; nine members: Truman Arnold Texarkana (10-4-91); Wayne A. Reaud, Beaumont (10-4-91) Otho Plummer, Beaumont (10-4-91); Joseph D. Deshotel Beaumont (10-4-87); George Dishman Jr., Beaumont (10-4 87); Donna R. Davis, College Station (10-4-87); Lloyd L Hayes, Port Arthur (10-4-89); H. D. Pate, Bridge City (10-4 89); Thomas M. Maes II, Beaumont (10-4-89). President, Dr George McLaughlin, Lamar Sta. Box 10002, Beaumont 7771 (nonmember).

Land Board, School—(1939); one ex officio, term in othe office; two apptd. — one by Governor and one by Attorne General for 2-yr. term; per diem and expenses; ex offic member: Commissioner of General Land Office Garr Mauro. Gov.'s apptee: Lola L. Bonner, Rockport (8-29-87).

Land Board, Veterans—(Est. 1949 as three-member e officio board; reorganized 1956); 4-yr.; per diem and ex penses; three members, one of whom is chairman and e officio member as Commissioner of General Land Office Commissioner Garry Mauro; Jim Sale, Dallas (financ member) (12-29-90); Karl M. May, Waco (veterans affairs (12-29-88). Executive Secretary, Richard Keahey, Land O fice Bldg., Austin 78701 (nonmember) ($57,474).

Land Office—(See **Commissioner of General Land Office.**

Land Surveying, Texas Board of—(1979; formed fror consolidation of membership of Board of Examiners of Li censed Land Surveyors, est. 1977, and State Board of Registra tion for Public Surveyors, est. 1955); apptv.; 6-yr.; 10 member — Commissioner of General Land Office serving by statute three members of general public; two licensed land survey ors; four registered public surveyors, as follows: William C Wilson Jr., San Angelo (1-31-91); Fern Maddera, Levellan (1-31-91); Walter Fortney, Fort Worth (1-31-91); Byron L Simpson, San Antonio (1-31-89); Milton Hanks, Deer Par (1-31-89); Chmn., C. B. Thomson, Junction (1-31-89); D. D Shine, Silsbee (1-31-87); G. W. Gilley, Fort Worth (1-31-87) Executive Secretary, Betty J. Pope, 1106 Clayton, Suit 210W Twin Towers Bldg., Austin 78723 (nonmember ($31,209).

Lands, State Board for Lease of State Park—(1965); 2-yr three members — two ex officio and one apptd. by Attorne General. Ex officio members are Commissioner of Genera Land Office Garry Mauro and Chairman of Parks and Wild life Commission; apptv. member is Judy Sauer, Houston.

Lands, Board for Lease of University—(1929 as three member board; membership increased to four in 1985); e officio; term in other office; four members: Commissione of General Land Office Garry Mauro, Chairman; two mem bers of Board of Regents of University of Texas; one mem ber Board of Regents of A&M University.

Lavaca County Flood Control District—(1960); apptv. 2-yr.; seven members (2 ex officio). Apptv. members Chmn., Robert J. Pesek, Hallettsville (1-1-83); Reynold Ve selka, Hallettsville (1-1-83); Leon Kahanek Jr., Hallettsvill (1-1-84); Alfred Neumeyer Jr., Hallettsville (1-1-84); Rober Gindler, Hallettsville (1-1-84).

Lavaca-Navidad River Authority, Directors of—(1954 a seven-member Jackson County Flood Control District; reorga nized as nine-member board in 1959; name changed t present form in 1969); apptv.; 6-yr.; per diem and expenses nine members: M. H. Brock, Edna (5-1-87); Gene A. Ratliff Edna (5-1-87); Joe Bonnot, Lolita (5-1-87); Cecil D. Fenner Edna (5-1-89); Carl W. Swenson, Ganado (5-1-89); Hans Wit tenburg, Edna (5-1-89); Harry Lee Hafernick, Edna (5-1-91 J. B. Housson, Ganado (5-1-91); Ed Duenow, Lolita (5-1-91 General Manager, W. R. Farquhar Jr., Box 429, Edna 7795 (nonmember).

Law Enforcement Officer Standards and Education, Texas commission on—(1965); expenses; nine apptv. and five ex officio members. Ex officio members: Atty. Gen. Jim Mattox, Director of Public Safety James B. Adams, Commissioner of Education, Executive Director Criminal Justice Division-Governor's Office and Commissioner of Higher Education. Apptv. members: Roger P. Dickey, Abilene (3-30-91); Charles N. Phelps, Bryan (8-30-91); J. R. Sessions Jr., Fairfield (8-30-91); Suzanne Hildebrand, San Antonio (8-30-87); Barto Watson, Humble (8-30-87); Sammy Leach Jr., Lufkin (8-30-87); Walter H. Rankin, Houston (8-30-89); Robert J. Thomas, Tomball (8-30-89); Ruben B. Cisneros, Corpus Christi (8-30-89). Executive Director, Fred Toler, 1606 Headway Circle, Suite 101, Austin 78754 (nonmember) ($47,380).

Law Examiners, State Board of—(1919 as five-member board; revised 1977 to increase membership to nine); apptd. by Supreme Court; 2-yr.; expenses; nine members: Chmn., William E. Collins, Dallas; Vice Chmn., Beverly Tarpley, Abilene; G. R. Garza Jr., Corpus Christi; Warlick Carr, Lubbock; Warren W. Shipman III, Fort Worth; Ralph W. Brite, San Antonio; Raymon Jordan, Houston; Robert M. Roller, Austin; Artie G. Giotes, Waco. Executive Director, Wayne E. Denton, Box 12248, Austin 78711 (nonmember).

Law Library Board, State—(1971); ex officio; expenses; three members: Chief Justice State Supreme Court, Presiding Judge Court of Criminal Appeals and Attorney General. Director, Marian Boner (nonmember), Box 12367, Austin 8711 ($35,226).

Laws, Commission on Uniform State—(1941 as five-member Commissioners to the National Conference on Uniform State Laws; name changed to present form, membership increased to six and term of office raised to six years in 1977); apptv.; 6-yr.; six members: Millard R. Ruud, Austin (9-30-85); E. R. Wood, Dallas (9-30-92); R. F. Dole Jr., Houston (9-30-87); Patrick C. Guillot, Dallas (9-30-87); Stanley Plettman, Beaumont (9-30-89); Peter K. Munson, Sherman (9-30-90).

Legislative Council, Texas—(1949); seventeen members — four senators named by President of Senate; nine representatives named by Speaker; Chairman House Administration Committee; Chairman Senate Administration Committee; President of Senate and Speaker. Executive Director, Robert I. Kelly, Box 12128, Austin 78711 (nonmember).

Legislative Redistricting Board—(1948); five members; ex officio, term in other office: Lt. Gov. William P. Hobby, Speaker of House Gib Lewis, Attorney General Jim Mattox, Comptroller Robert D. Bullock and Commissioner of Land Office Garry Mauro.

Librarian, State—(Originally established in 1839; present office established 1909); apptv.; indefinite term: William D.Gooch, Lorenzo de Zavala Archives and Library Bldg., Austin ($48,410).

Library and Archives Commission, Texas State—(1909 as five-member Library and State Historical Commission; number of members increased to six by Fifty-Third Legislature, 1953; name changed to present form in 1979); apptv.; per diem and expenses on duty; 6-yr.; six members: Aurelia N. McCreless, San Antonio (9-28-91); Price Daniel Sr., Liberty (9-28-91); Ralph W. Yarborough, Austin (9-28-89); T. Frank Glass Jr., Houston (9-28-89); John Ben Shepperd, Odessa (9-28-87); Anne W. Cragg, McAllen (9-28-87). Director, William D. Gooch, State Librarian, Box 12927, Capitol Station, Austin 78711 ($48,410).

Library, State Legislative Reference—(1909); indefinite term: Director, Sally Reynolds, Box 12488, Austin 78711.

Lieutenant Governor, State—(1836 by original Constitution of the Republic of Texas; 1876 by present Constitution); elective; salary same as Senators when acting as President of Senate, Governor's salary when acting as Governor; 2-yr. by original Constitution, term raised to 4-yr. in 1972, effective 1975): William P. Hobby, Box 12068, Capitol Sta., Austin 78711 (1-1-91).

Liquor Control Board—(See **Alcoholic Beverage Commission**.)

Lower Colorado River Authority—(See **Colorado River Authority, Lower**.)

Marine Council, Texas Coastal and—(Abolished by Sunset Commission Sept. 1, 1985.)

Medical Education Board, State Rural—(1973); apptv.; 6-yr.; per diem and expenses; six members: Dr. James W. Caldwell, Rockwall (2-27-92); Leo L. Westerholm, Port Lavaca (2-27-86); Billie Marie Veach, Burnet (2-27-90); Dr. Richard M. Hall, Eden (2-27-90); Chmn., Dr. Sam A. Nixon, Floresville (2-27-88); Lawrence Harmel, Seymour (2-27-88). Executive Director, Duane C. Keeran, Room 310, Southwest Tower Bldg., 211 E. 7th, Austin 78701 (nonmember).

Medical Examiners, Texas State Board of—(1907 as 12-member board; membership raised to 15 in 1981 with addition of three public members); apptv.; 6-yr.; $30 a day on duty; 15 members: Dr. Jesse D. Ibarra Jr., Temple (4-13-87); Dr. Joel D. Holliday, Mesquite (4-13-87); Dr. Charles B. Dryden Jr., Wichita Falls (4-13-87); Dr. John H. Burnett, Dallas (4-13-87); Dr. John C. Bagwell, Dallas (4-13-91); Dr. A. M. Jansa, Houston (4-13-91); Dr. James W. Lively, Corpus Christi (4-13-91); Dr. D. D. Williams, Baytown (4-13-89); Dr. N. E. Dudney, Webster (4-13-89); Dr. Suzanne Ahn, Dallas

(4-13-89); Dr. Robert L. M. Hilliard, San Antonio (4-13-89). Public members: Cindy Jenkins, Stowell (4-13-91); Adele Lucas, Cuero (4-13-87); Bob Crouch, Greenville (4-13-89). (One vacancy). Executive Director, Dr. G. V. Brindley, Box 13562, Capitol Sta., Austin 78711 ($47,586).

Medical District Review Committee—(1977); apptv.; 6-yr.; expenses; 12 members: Dist. 1: Dr. Thomas P. Clarke, Houston (1-15-86); Dr. Homer R. Goehrs, Austin (1-15-86); Dr. Arthur M. Jansa, Houston (1-15-84); Dr. John W. Nichols, Galena Park (1-15-88). Dist. 2: Dr. Phillip E. Williams Jr., Dallas (1-15-84); Dr. Robert G. Haman, Irving (1-15-86); Dr. Clyde Caperton, Bryan (1-15-82). Dist. 3: Dr. Grant F. Begley, Fort Worth (1-15-84); Dr. Wm. G. McGee, El Paso (1-15-86); Dr. Jesse D. Cone, 318 W. Alleghaney, Odessa 79761 (1-15-88). Dist. 4: Dr. Armando Cuellar, Weslaco (1-15-84); Dr. Harold R. High, Cuero (1-15-88).

Mental Health and Mental Retardation, Texas Department of—(1965, superseded Board of Texas State Hospitals and Special Schools); apptv.; 6-yr.; per diem and expenses; nine members: Pattilou Dawkins, Amarillo (1-31-93); Roger Bateman, Corpus Christi (1-31-93); Charles M. Cooper, Dallas (1-31-93); Frank E. Melton, Tyler (1-31-91); Ralph Eads, Houston (1-31-91); Drayton McLane Jr., Temple (1-31-91); Chmn., Richard C. Mills, Waco (1-31-89); Dr. Roberto L. Jimenez, San Antonio (1-31-89); Dr. Grace K. Jameson, Galveston (1-31-89). One vacancy. **Commissioner of Mental Health**, Gary Miller, Box 12668, Capitol Sta., Austin 78711-2668 (nonmember) ($72,615, plus other emoluments).

Midwestern State University, Board of Regents of—(1959); apptv.; 6-yr.; nine members: E. L. Watson, Dallas (2-25-92); Martha W. Hendrickson, Wichita Falls (2-25-92); Jerry K. Estes, Wichita Falls (2-25-92); Edward W. Moran Jr., Wichita Falls (2-25-88); Jack L. Russell, Midland (2-25-88); Harold D. Rogers, Wichita Falls (2-25-88); Larry L. Lambert, Wichita Falls (2-25-90); Margaret Darden, Dallas (2-25-90); Tom Blakeney Jr., Alvin (2-25-90). President, Louis J. Rodriguez, 3400 Taft, Wichita Falls 76308 (nonmember).

Mining Council, Texas—(1975); apptv.; 2-yr.; eleven members, as follows: Three representing state commissions, four mining industry and four general public. State commission members: Mack Wallace, Austin (5-8-83); Robert L. Armstrong, Austin (5-8-83); Dr. H. M. Rollins, Austin (5-8-83). Mining industry members: John H. Montgomery, Fairfield (5-8-83); William R. Kelly, El Paso (5-8-83); Franklin W. Daugherty, Alpine (5-8-83); one vacancy. General public members: James Earl Kellum, Arlington (5-8-83); Ed O. Vetter, Dallas (5-8-83); Linton Barbee, Dallas (5-8-83); George W. Hail Jr., Houston (5-8-83).

Morticians, State Board of—(1903 as State Board of Embalming; 1935 as State Board of Funeral Directors and Embalmers; 1953 as six-member board; membership increased to nine in 1979); apptv.; per diem and expenses; 6-yr.; nine members: James P. Hunter III, Lufkin (1-31-91); Donald H. Taft, Beaumont (1-31-91); Dr. Ray Burchette, Austin (1-31-91); James B. Broussard, Beaumont (1-31-87); George A. Parker, Fort Worth (1-31-87); Margaret Ward, Houston (1-31-87); Rev. William T. Stephenson, Dallas (1-31-89); Henry Thomae Sr., San Benito (1-31-89); John W. Amey, Austin (1-31-89). Executive Secretary, John W. Shocklee, 1513 S. IH-35, Austin 78741 (nonmember) ($35,123).

Motor Vehicle Commission, Texas—(1971 as six-member board; membership increased to nine in 1979); apptv.; 6-yr.; $25 plus expenses; nine members: Eddie Bradley, Amarillo (1-31-91); Erwin Elias, Waco (1-31-91); John R. Cook, Breckenridge (1-31-91); Selma A. Hermann, Alvin (1-31-87); Robert H. Hoy Jr., El Paso (1-31-87); T. M. Demarest Jr., Arlington (1-31-87); John W. Dalton, Houston (1-31-89); Ramsay Gillman, Houston (1-31-89); Vic Salvino, Dallas (1-31-89). Executive Director, Russell Harding, Box 2293, Austin 78768 (nonmember) ($46,350).

Music Commission, Texas—(1985); apptv.; 6-yr.; expenses; nine members: Jarrell McCracken, Waco (2-1-87); Mike Tolleson, Austin (2-1-87); Stephen Mendell, Johnson City (2-1-87); Red Steagall, Azle (2-1-89); Don Ross Malone, Fort Worth (2-1-89); Manuel E. Rangel, San Antonio (2-1-89); Anthony Tomblin, San Marcos (2-1-91); Chmn., Trammell S. Crow Jr., Dallas (2-1-91); Randy McCall, Austin (2-1-91).

National Guard Commander, Texas—(1947); apptv.: Maj. Gen. Willie L. Scott, Austin.

National Guard Armory Board, Texas—(1935 as three-member board; reorganized as six-member board in 1981); 6-yr.; six members — three from general public and three ex officio members of National Guard. Ex officio members: Brig. Gen. Robert W. McDonald, Allen (4-30-91); Brig. Gen. James B. McGoodwin, Fort Worth (4-30-87); Maj. Gen. Charles H. Kone, La Pryor (4-30-89). Public members: V. C. Eissler, Houston (4-30-91); Hal Boyd, Big Spring (4-30-87); Tom E. Chapoton Jr., Austin (4-30-87). Director, Donald J. Kerr, Box 5218, Austin 78763 (nonmember) ($45,011).

Natural Fibers and Food Protein Commission—(1941 as Cotton Research Committee; name changed in 1971 and again in 1975); four ex officio members and seven members apptd. to executive advisory committee by chairman with approval of commission members, to serve 2-yr. terms. Ex officio members serve indefinite term. Dr. Mary Evelyn

Huey, President, Texas Woman's University, Denton; Dr. Lauro F. Cavazos, President, Texas Tech University, Lubbock; Arthur G. Hansen, Chancellor, A&M University System, College Station; President, University of Texas at Austin. Executive Director, Carl Cox, Box 17360 Coit Rd., Dallas 75252 (nonmember) ($49,543).

Neches River Conservation District, Directors of—(See Angelina and Neches River Authority.)

Neches River (Upper) Municipal Water Authority, Board of Directors of—(Est. 1953 as nine-member board; made three-member board in 1959); apptv.; 6-yr.; three members: President, Gordon B. Broyles, Palestine (1-1-87); Lester Hamilton, Palestine (1-1-85); Ben Swinney, Palestine (1-1-89). General Manager, Roy Douglas, Drawer Y, Palestine 75801 (nonmember).

Neches Valley Authority, Lower, Directors of—(1933); apptv. per diem and expenses on duty; 6-yr.; nine members: Joe Broussard II, Beaumont (7-28-89); Dr. William S. Nichols, Woodville (7-28-89); William Doornbos, Nederland (7-28-87); Clyde E. Cole, Silsbee (7-28-87); Ralph A. Leaf, Beaumont (7-28-87); Lee Moore, Port Arthur (7-28-83); F. M. Archer, Woodville (7-28-85); Jack Scott, Port Arthur (7-28-85); Paul Georges, Silsbee (7-28-87). General Manager, J. D. Nixon, Drawer 3464, Beaumont 77704 (nonmember). General Counsel, Josiah Wheat, Box 156, Woodville (nonmember).

Nonresident Violator Compact Administrator—(1981); apptv.; 2-yr.; George Griffin, Austin (2-1-87).

North Texas State University, Board of Regents of—(1949); apptv.; 6-yr.; expenses; nine members: Charles E. Greene, Duncanville (5-22-87); Wayne O. Stockseth, Corpus Christi (5-22-89); Lucille G. Murchison, Dallas (5-22-87); Becky Ann Garth, Temple (5-22-89); J. Jack Hays, Dallas (5-22-89); C. Dean Davis, Austin (5-22-89); Topsy R. Wright, Grand Prairie (5-22-91); B. Craig Raupe, Granbury (5-22-91); E. Bruce Street Sr., Graham (5-22-91). President, Alfred F. Hurley, Board Secretary, Jan Dobbs, Box 13737, NT Station, Denton 76203-3737 (nonmember).

Nueces River Authority—(1935 as Nueces River Conservation and Reclamation District; name changed in 1971); apptv. 6-yr.; per diem and expenses; 21 members: Gus T. Canales, Premont (2-1-87); Joseph W. Taylor, Crystal City (2-1-87); William A. Beinhorn Jr., San Antonio (2-1-87); Stevan R. Gallegos, Castroville (2-1-87); Leslie H. Laffere, Uvalde (2-1-87); Harry J. Schulz, Three Rivers (2-1-87); George A. Finley III, Corpus Christi (2-1-87); Charles S. Carr, Crystal City (2-1-89); George Morrill Jr., Beeville (2-1-89); Salvador Almanza, Poteet (2-1-89); Allen Wood, Corpus Christi (2-1-89); William R. Edwards, Corpus Christi (2-1-89); Edward M. Jones, Ingleside (2-1-91); Jesse Lockhart Jr., Barksdale (2-1-89); Bob Mullen, Alice (2-1-91); James L. Donnell, Fowlerton (2-1-91); George T. Jambers Jr., Whitsett (2-1-91); S. N. Flores, Mathis (2-1-91); James C. Storm, Corpus Christi (2-1-83); Albert A. Ivy, Carrizo Springs (2-1-91); Roy Martin, Cotulla (2-1-91). Executive Director, Con Mims III, Box 349, Uvalde 78801.

Nurse Examiners, State Board of—(1909 as six-member board; reorganized and membership increased to nine in 1981 with addition of three public members); apptv.; per diem and expenses; 6-yr.; nine members: Karen G. Barnes-Cure, Temple (1-31-89); Mrs. Claud B. Jacobs, Yoakum (1-31-89); Elizabeth J. Pryor, Fort Worth (1-31-87); Aimee J. Seamans, San Antonio (1-31-87); Teddy L. Langford, Lubbock (1-31-91); Pauline Barnes, Texarkana (1-31-91). Public members: Karen T. McLeaish, Odessa (1-31-91); Mary E. Jackson, Tyler (1-31-89); Dr. Ruby Lee Morris, Midland (1-31-87). Executive Secretary, Margaret L. Rowland, 1300 E. Anderson Lane, Bldg. C., Suite 225, Austin 78752 (nonmember) ($45,423).

Nurse Examiners, State Board of Vocational—(1951 as nine-member board; membership increased to 12 in 1981); apptv.; 6-yr.; 12 members — one doctor, one registered nurse, one hospital adminstrator, seven licensed vocational nurses and two from general public. Doctor — Dr. Salvador Ortiz-Carrillo, Corpus Christi (9-6-91). Hospital administrator — Victor W. Rhoads, San Angelo (9-6-91). Registered nurse — Adelia D. Miller, Whitehouse (9-6-89). Vocational Nurses: Suzanne Wilkinson, Pampa (9-6-89); Linda Savannah, Fort Worth (9-6-89); Dorothy S. Harris, Victoria (9-6-87); E. Kathleen Franklin, Port Arthur (9-6-87); Lola Marie Mills, San Angelo (9-6-87); Annie Mae Parker, Belton (9-6-91); Sharon Johnson, Taylor (9-6-91). Two from general public — Rafael Acosta, Houston (9-6-89); Lucille Behar, San Antonio (9-6-87). Executive Secretary, Waldeen D. Wilson, 1300 Anderson Lane, Bldg. C., Suite 285, Austin 78752 (nonmember) ($33,166).

Nursing Home Administrators, Texas Board of Licensure for—(1969 as six-member board; membership raised to 11 members in 1979); apptv.; per diem and expenses; 6-yr.; 11 members — nine apptv. and two ex officio. Ex officio members: Commissioner of Human Services and Commissioner of Health. Apptv. members: Lilla O. Hagan, Tyler (1-31-87); Chmn., Dr. Ed Lefeber, Galveston (1-31-87); Mrs. John E. Watson, Houston (1-31-87); Reuben R. McDaniel Jr., Austin (1-31-91); Ray P. Bloebaum, Austin (1-31-91); Jarmese Morris, Houston (1-31-91); Virginia Atkinson, Waco (1-31-89); Velda Phelps-Wasson, Pasadena (1-31-89); Jean Trebert,

Dallas (1-31-89). Executive Director, Dr. Karl E. Bishop 3407 N. Interregional, Austin 78722 (nonmember) ($29,870).

Occupational Therapy, Texas Advisory Board of—(1983), apptv.; six members — three occupational therapists, one assistant occupational therapist and two from general public; 6-yr.; per diem and expenses: Arthur H. Dilley, Austin (2-1-89); Heidi B. Schoenfield, San Antonio (2-1-89); Mrs. Marianne L. Punchard, Mart (2-1-91); Mrs. Peggy Pickens. Houston (2-1-91); Linda Veale, Abilene (2-1-87); Donald S. Thomas, Austin (2-1-87).

Optometry Board, Texas—(1921 as six-member State Board of Examiners in Optometry; revised in 1969 and name changed to present form; again revised in 1981 to increase membership to nine with addition of three from general public); apptv.; per diem; 6-yr.; nine members: Dr. Stanley C. Pearle, Dallas (1-31-91); Dr. William D. Pittman, Mexia (1-31-91); Dr. Gene B. Blackwell, Childress (1-31-89); Dr. James B. Thomas, Galveston (1-31-89); Dr. Barry J. Davis, Port Arthur (1-31-89); Dr. Floyd L. Thornton, Wichita Falls (1-31-93); Dr. Clinton M. DeWolfe, Houston (1-31-93). Public members: Kenneth L. Schorr, Dallas (1-31-91); Marilyn K. Walls, Cleburne (1-31-93). Executive Director, Lois Ewald, 1300 E. Anderson Lane, Suite C-240, Austin 78752 (nonmember) ($32,651).

Pan American University, Board of Regents of—(1965); apptv.; 6-yr.; nine members: Horacio Barrera, Brownsville (8-31-91); Homer H. Scott, Mission (8-31-91); Robert Shepard, Harlingen (8-31-91); K. E. Schaefer, Brownsville (8-31-87); Eddie R. Cano, McAllen (8-31-87); Charles Villasenor, Austin (8-31-87); Lauryn G. White, Dallas (8-31-89); Margaret L. McAllen, Weslaco (8-31-89); Natividad Lopez, Harlingen (8-31-89). President, Miguel A. Nevarez, 1201 W. University, Edinburg 78539 (nonmember).

Pardons and Paroles, Board of—(1893 as Board of Pardon Advisers; changed in 1936 to present name with three members; membership increased to six in 1983); apptv.; 6-yr.; six members at $52,633: Vice Chmn., Albert Neal Pfeiffer, Austin (Elgin) (1-31-89); Chmn., Wendell A. Odom, Austin (Pasadena) (1-31-91); Connie Jackson, Austin (Dallas) (1-31-87); Ruben Torres, Austin (Brownsville) (1-31-89); Winona W. Miles, Austin (1-31-91); Antonio Gil Morales, Austin (Fort Worth) (1-31-87). Executive Director, John W. Byrd, Box 13401, Capitol Station, Austin 78711 (nonmember) ($48,719).

Parks and Wildlife Commission, Texas—(1963 as three-member board; membership increased to six in 1971 and increased to nine in 1983); apptv.; expenses; 6-yr.; nine members: Henry C. Beck III, Dallas (2-1-93); Charles D. Nash Jr., San Marcos (2-1-93); Beatrice C. Pickens, Amarillo (2-1-93); William L. Graham, Amarillo (2-1-89); Richard R. Morrison III, Houston (2-1-89); George R. Bolin, Houston (2-1-89); Chmn., Edwin L. Cox Jr., Dallas (2-1-89); Robert L. Armstrong, Austin (2-1-91); Antonio R. Sanchez Jr., Laredo (2-1-91). Executive Director, Charles Travis, 4200 Smith School Rd., Austin 78744 (nonmember) ($60,461).

Pecos River Compact Commissioner for Texas—(1942); apptv.; 2-yr.; expenses: Billy L. Moody, Fort Stockton (1-23-87) ($16,800).

Pension Boards—For old age, blind and dependent children's assistance, see **Human Services, State Board of**. For unemployment compensation, **Employment Commission, Texas**. For retirement pay to state and municipal employees and teachers, see **Retirement**.

Pension Review Board, State—(1979); apptv.; 6-yr.; nine members — seven apptd. by Governor; one Representative apptd. by Speaker of House; one Senator apptd. by Lieutenant Governor. Governor's apptees.: Dean Gorham, Austin (1-31-87); Chmn., Norman W. Parrish, Houston (1-31-89); Dr. Robert L. Rouse, Lubbock (1-31-89); Frank Eikenburg, Plano (1-31-89); LeRoy M. Hinton, Houston (1-31-91); Vice Chmn., James M. Brelsford, Houston (1-31-91); Peggy S. McAdams, Huntsville (1-31-91). Executive Director, Rita Horwitz, Box 13498, Austin 78711 (nonmember) ($36,668).

Pest Control Board, Texas Structural—(1971 as seven-member board; membership raised to nine in 1979); apptv.; 2-yr.; expenses; nine members — six apptd. by Governor and three ex officio. Ex officio members: Commissioner of Agriculture, Commissioner of Health and head of Entomology Dept., Texas A&M University, College Station. Six apptv. members: Larry A. Esparza, Brownsville (8-30-86); Tommy L. Brown, Fort Worth (8-30-86); Nester M. Macho, Dallas (8-30-88); John P. Mercer, Corpus Christi (8-30-85); Roger P. Maddox, Duncanville (8-30-87); Jim Burns, Houston (8-31-87). Executive Director, David A. Ivie, 1300 E. Anderson Lane, Bldg. C, Ste. 250, Austin 78752 (nonmember) ($45,320).

Pharmacy, Texas State Board of—(1907 as six-member board; membership increased to nine in 1981); apptv.; 6-yr.; nine members: Jerry H. Hodge, Amarillo (8-31-87); R. E. Post Jr., Houston (8-31-87); Virginia M. Bauman, Irving (8-31-87); Georgette Erskine-Hankins, Bedford (8-31-91); Albert Hopkins, Houston (8-31-91); Harold D. Eakman, San Angelo (8-31-91); William H. Pieratt Jr., Giddings (8-31-89); Renee Solis, El Paso (8-31-89); H. Craig Darby, Burleson (8-31-89). Executive Director-Secretary, Fred S. Brinkley Jr., Southwest Tower, Suite 1121, 211 E. 7th, Austin 78701 (nonmember) ($56,238).

Physical Fitness, Commission on—(1971); apptv.; 6-yr.; 15 members: Dr. Richard L. Shorkey, Beaumont (6-13-87); Cissy Woomer, Austin (6-13-87); Dr. Ted L. Edwards, Austin (6-13-87); Chairman, Rollin A. Sininger, Denton (6-13-87); Amanda Bullard, Austin (6-13-87); Vice Chmn., J. Terry Townsend, Austin (6-13-89); Dr. Kenneth H. Cooper, Dallas (6-13-89); A. D. Gearner Jr., Dallas (6-13-89); Dr. William G. Squires Jr., Seguin (6-13-89); Patrice McKinney, Colorado City (6-13-89); Neal Spelce, Austin (6-13-91); William P. Daves, Dallas (6-13-91); Elvin Smith, College Station (6-13-91); R. Lisa Rico Popp, Austin (6-13-91); George F. Dillman, Dallas (6-13-91). Executive Director, A. A. Rooker, 4200 N. Lamar, Suite 110, Austin 78756 (nonmember) ($42,127).

Physical Therapy Examiners, Texas State Board of—(1971); apptv.; nine members; expenses: Cecilia G. Akers, San Antonio (1-31-91); Richard Tinsley, Houston (1-31-91); Patricia K. Winchester, Midlothian (1-31-91); David A. Hardison, Fredericksburg (1-31-87); Barbara Barton, Manchaca (1-31-87); Henry L. Laird, Amarillo (1-31-87); Betty M. Schocke, Galveston (1-31-89); Vernon Wilson Jr., Houston (1-31-89); Robert Hawkins, Bellmead (1-31-89). Executive Director, Lois M. Smith, 1300 E. Anderson Lane, Bldg. C., Suite 260, Austin 78752 (nonmember) ($25,956).

Plumbing Examiners, State Board of—(1947 as six-member board; membership increased to nine in 1981 with provision that one member each must be a master plumber, journeyman plumber, plumbing contractor, licensed sanitary engineer and plumbing inspector; two must be building contractors and two from general public); apptv.; expenses; 6-yr.; nine members: William D. Pickens, Houston (journeyman plumber) (9-5-91); Jay Lee Drymalia, Columbus (contractor-commercial) (9-4-89); Edward A. Tschoepe, San Antonio (sanitary engineer) (9-4-87); Vice Chmn., Edward Lee Smith, San Antonio (master plumber) (9-4-87); William G. Wheeler, Victoria (plumbing inspector) (9-4-87); Chmn., Stanley J. Briers, Seabrook (plumbing contractor) (9-5-91); Ronald Gene Goodnight, Killeen (home building contractor) (9-4-89). Two from general public: Mario Estrada, San Antonio (9-4-89); Joe W. Campbell, Pasadena (9-5-91). Administrator, Lynn Brown, Box 4200, Austin 78765 (nonmember) ($54,487).

Podiatry Examiners, Texas State Board of—(1923 as six-member State Board of Chiropody Examiners; name changed in 1967, made nine-member board in 1981); apptv.; 6-yr.; expenses; nine members: Dr. Thomas F. Eckert, Tyler (7-10-91); Dr. John G. Knecht, Galveston (7-10-91); Pres., Dr. Jerry W. Patterson, San Antonio (7-10-89); Dr. Ben Clark Jr., Dallas (7-10-89); Dr. R. E. Sciolo, Lubbock (7-10-87); Dr. Marion J. Filippone, Houston (7-10-87). Three public members: Mrs. Johnnie Davis, Odessa (7-10-87); Dr. John T. Donohoo, San Antonio (7-10-85); Perry O. Chrisman, Dallas (7-10-89). Executive Director, J. C. Littrell, 411 W. 13th, Suite 504, Austin 78701 (nonmember) (part-time $15,862).

Polygraph Examiners Board—(1965); apptv.; 6-yr.; six members: Eddie Senigaur, Beaumont (6-18-91); William W. Fisher, Houston (6-18-91); William J. Taylor, Round Rock (6-18-87); Charles M. Nelson, Gonzales (6-18-87); Vern L. Thrower, Houston (6-18-89); James E. Hood III, Richardson (6-18-89). System Administrator, Eddie R. Day, Box 4143, Austin 78765 (nonmember) ($28,016).

Preservation Board, State—(1983); 2-yr.; six members: Three ex officio members: Governor, Lieutenant Governor and Speaker of House; three apptv. members — one apptd. by Governor, one senator apptd. by Lieutenant Governor and one representative apptd. by Speaker. Gov.'s apptee: Dealey Herndon, Austin (2-1-89). Office Address: Box 13286, Austin 78711.

Prison Board, Texas—(See Corrections, Texas Board of.)

Private Investigators and Private Security Agencies, Texas Board of—(1969); apptv.; expenses; 6-yr.; eight members — two ex officio and six apptv. Ex officio members: Director, Department of Public Safety and the Attorney General. Apptv. members: Patti Ivey, Robert Lee (1-31-91); Robert D. Sanders, Dallas (1-31-91); Dale O. Simpson, Dallas (1-31-87); Vice Chmn., George A. Smith Jr., Dallas (1-31-87); John W. Snelson, Houston (1-31-89); Chmn., Roland M. Searcy, Bryan (1-31-89). Executive Director, Mrs. Clema D. Sanders, Box 13509, Capitol Sta., Austin 78711 (nonmember) ($39,140).

Produce Recovery Fund Board—(1977 as three-member board; membership increased to six in 1981); apptv.; expenses; 6-yr.; six members — two each from commission merchants, general public and producer representative. Commission merchants: Curt Cargil, Uvalde (1-31-85); N. J. Martino, Houston (1-31-87). Public members: Ronald Osborn, Hereford (1-31-87); Dr. John C. Boling, Raymondville (1-31-83). Producers: Chairman, Wayne A. Showers, McAllen (1-31-85); G. E. Glassford, Laredo (1-31-85).

Property Tax Board, State—(1977 as School Tax Assessment Practices Board; name changed in 1980); apptv.; 6-yr.; six members; expenses: Gerald Winn, Bryan (3-1-91); Chmn., Wm. B. Munson IV, San Antonio (3-1-91); Marvin L. Jones, Spearman (3-1-87); William J. Burnett, San Antonio (3-1-87); Ciro Trevino, Edinburg (3-1-89); Nicholas V. Lampson, Beaumont (3-1-89). Executive Director, Ron Patterson, Box 15900, Austin 78761 (nonmember) ($59,122).

Prosecutors Council, The—(1977 as 4-yr., nine-member Texas Prosecutors' Coordinating Council; name changed to present form, membership makeup changed and terms raised to 6-yr. in 1981); apptv.; expenses; 6-yr.; nine members: Four apptd. by Governor and five prosecutors elected by their peers. Gov.'s apptees: Ken Epley, San Angelo (12-31-89); Dick W. Hicks, Bandera (12-31-85); Claude J. Kelley Jr., Fredericksburg (12-31-87); Joe L. Schott, Castroville (12-31-85). Executive Director, Andy Shuval, Box 13555, Austin 78711 (nonmember) ($54,500).

Psychologists, Texas Board of Examiners of—(1969 as six-member board; membership increased to nine in 1981 with addition of one psychologist's assistant and two members from general public); apptv.; 6-yr.; per diem and expenses; nine members: Dr. Joseph Siegel, Dallas (10-31-87); Dr. J. C. Kobos, San Antonio (10-31-87); Dr. Van Carter Secrest, Fort Worth (10-31-89); Dr. Laurence Abrams, Houston (10-31-89); Dr. Barbara A. Bailey, Austin (10-31-91); Dr. Harold H. LeCrone Jr., Waco (10-31-87). Psychological Associate: Macy Kinzel, Corpus Christi (10-31-87). Public members: Mrs. Sidney S. Smith, Austin (10-31-89); Joe D. Robbins, Irving (10-31-91). Executive Director, Patricia S. Bizzell, 1300 E. Anderson Lane, Bldg. C, Ste. 270, Austin 78752 ($37,595).

Public Building Authority, Texas—(1983); apptv.; 6-yr.; three members; $50 per diem and expenses: Marilyn Jones, San Antonio (2-1-87); Glen Hefner, Houston (2-1-89); Gerald Goff, Austin (2-1-91).

Public Safety Commission—(1935); apptv.; expenses; 6-yr.; three members: Calvin R. Guest, Bryan (12-31-91); Ruben R. Cardenas, McAllen (12-31-89); John Fainter Jr., Austin (12-31-87). Director, Leo E. Gossett, Box 4087, Austin 78773 (nonmember) ($66,641).

Public Utility Commission of Texas—(1975); apptv.; 6-yr.; three members at $60,976: Jo Campbell, Austin (9-1-91); Peggy Rosson, El Paso (8-31-87); Chmn., Dennis L. Thomas, Austin (8-31-89). Executive Director, 7800 Shoal Creek Blvd., Exchange Park Bldg., Suite 400 N, Austin 78757 (nonmember) ($55,620).

Public Utility Counsel—(1983); apptv.; 2-yr.: Geoffrey Gay, Austin (2-1-87) ($60,976).

Public Welfare, State Board of—(Name changed, see Human Services, Texas Board of.)

Purchasing and General Services Commission, State—(Established 1919 as Board of Control; name changed 1979); apptv.; expenses; three members: Chmn., James R. Collier, Houston (1-31-89); Kenneth R. Epley, San Angelo (1-31-91); Ross D. Margraves Jr., Houston (1-31-93). Executive Director, H. A. Foerster, Box 13047, Capitol Station, Austin 78711-3047 (nonmember) ($56,856).

Racing Commission, Texas—(1986); 8 members: 6 apptv., 2 ex officio; 6 years; per diem and expenses. Ex officio members: Chmn. of Public Safety Commission and Comptroller of Public Accounts. (Appointments pending at press time.)

Radiation Advisory Board—(1961 as nine-member board; membership increased to 18 in 1981); apptv.; 6-yr.; expenses; 18 members: Dr. Gordon L. Black, El Paso (4-16-85); Ralph L. Buell, Lake Jackson (4-16-85); Dr. Ben DuBilier, Seguin (4-16-85); Russell F. Cash, Pasadena (4-16-89); Douglas B. Owen, Dallas (4-16-89); Dr. Philip C. Johnson Jr., Houston (4-16-89); Dr. Wm. G. McGee, El Paso (4-16-87); Dr. Dan Hightower, Bryan (4-16-87); Howard Drew, Fort Worth (4-16-85); Dr. Jack S. Krohmer, Georgetown (4-16-87); Dr. Fred J. Bonte, Dallas (4-16-91); George Riddle, Houston (4-16-89); Dr. E. Linn Draper, Beaumont (4-16-89); Robert C. Dunlap Jr., Dallas (4-16-87); Laura Keever, Houston (4-16-89); William G. Hendrick, Austin (4-16-85); Two vacancies.

Radioactive Waste Disposal Authority, Texas Low-Level—(1981); apptv.; 6-yr.; six members; expenses. Membership composed of one medical doctor, one health physicist, one attorney, one geologist and two from general public: Vice Chmn., John E. Simek, Bryan (health physicist) (2-1-89); Dr. Milton J. Guiberteau, Houston (doctor) (2-1-89); Chmn., Dr. William L. Fisher, Austin (geologist) (2-1-87); James P. Allison, Austin (attorney) (2-1-91); Dr. Elbert Wharton, Galveston (public member) (2-1-91); Jim R Phillips, El Paso (public member) (2-1-87). General Manager, Lawrence R. Jacobi Jr., 1300-C E. Anderson Lane, Ste. 175, Austin 78752 (nonmember) ($58,504).

Railroad Commission of Texas—(1891); elective; 6-yr.; ($72,233); three members: Chmn., James E. Nugent, Austin (Kerrville) (12-31-88); Mack Wallace, Austin (Athens) (12-31-90); John Sharp, Austin (Austin) (12-31-92). Drawer 12967, Austin 78711 (nonmember).

Real Estate Commission of Texas—(1949 as six member board; membership increased to nine in 1979); apptv.; per diem and expenses; 6-yr.; nine members: Michael N. Wieland, El Paso (1-31-91); Billie Heffner, Burleson (1-31-91); James N. Johnson, Tyler (1-31-91); Robert T. Martin, Fort Worth (1-31-93); Marsha Shanklin, Victoria (1-31-93); Florence Willess, Dallas (1-31-93); Rachel Perelman, Brownsville (1-31-89); David Cook, Houston (1-31-89); Robert H. Bliss, Dallas (1-31-89). Administrator, Wallace Collins, Box 12188, Capitol Station, Austin 78711 (nonmember) ($48,925).

Real Estate Research Advisory Committee—(1971); apptv.; 6-yr.; nine apptv. and one ex-officio member: Ex officio member represents Texas Real Estate Commission.

Apptv. members: Bill Jennings, Fort Worth (1-31-91); David Stirton, Houston (1-31-91); Frederick D. McClure, San Augustine (1-31-91); Thomas A. Wilder, Euless (1-31-93); Hubert E. Bechtol, Austin (1-31-93); Alberto R. Gonzales, Houston (1-31-93); Patsy Bohannan, Midland (1-31-89); Doris Farmer, Longview (1-31-89); James Fatheree, Richmond (1-31-89). Director, Richard L. Floyd, Texas Real Estate Research Center, Texas A&M, College Station 77843.

Redistricting Board, Legislative—(See Legislative.)

Red River Authority of Texas—(1959); apptv.; 6-yr.; per diem and expenses; nine members: Paul Lyle, Plainview (8-11-91); Rex H. McAnelly, Pampa (8-11-91); Albert B. Wharton III, Vernon (8-11-91); John W. Welch, Telephone (8-11-89); Charles Moorehead, Canadian (8-11-89); Alvin L. Barnes, Wichita Falls (8-11-89); John R. Armstrong, Bonham (8-11-87); Austin T. Guest, Clarksville (8-11-87); Wales Madden III, Amarillo (8-11-87). General Manager, Fred Parkey, 302 Hamilton Bldg., Wichita Falls 76301 (nonmember).

Red River Compact Commissioner—(1949); apptv.; 4-yr.; (his functions are to negotiate with other states respecting waters of the Red. See also Canadian River Compact Commission and Caddo Lake Compact Commission): Nathan A. Reiter Jr., Texarkana (2-1-93) ($22,400).

Rehabilitation Commission, Texas—(1969); apptv.; expenses; 6-yr.; six members: Wendell D. Faulkner, Pecos (8-31-89); Ernestine Washington, Beaumont (8-31-89); Emanuel Bodner, Houston (8-31-91); Dr. Cutberto Garza, Houston (8-31-91); William C. Morrow, Midland (8-31-87); Chmn., Jerry Kane, Corpus Christi (8-31-87). Commissioner, Vernon M. Arrell, 118 E. Riverside Dr., Austin 78704 (nonmember) ($65,199).

Research Laboratory Commission, Texas National—(1986); apptv.; expenses; six yrs.; nine members: Jerome Johnson, Amarillo (2-1-91); Gerald Griffin, Houston (2-1-91); Martin Goland, San Antonio (2-1-91); Dr. Herbert H. Woodson, Austin (2-1-89); Dr. Frank Cotton, College Station (2-1-89); Charles R. Perry, Odessa (2-1-89); Johnnie Lou Avery, Big Spring (2-1-87); Chmn., Peter Flawn, Austin (2-1-93); Dr. Neal Amundson, Houston (2-1-87).

Retirement System, Municipal, Board of Trustees—(1947); apptv.; 6-yr.; expenses; six members: Three executive trustees — Leland D. Nelson, Dallas (1-31-87); Don Cates, Amarillo (1-31-91); Virgil C. Gray, Brownwood (1-31-89); David B. Brinson, Port Arthur (1-31-87); Ernest M. Briones, Corpus Christi (1-31-89); Charles E. Wilson, Waco (1-31-91). Executive Director, Jimmie L. Mormon, Box 2225, Austin 78768 (nonmember).

Retirement System, Texas County and District, Board of Trustees—(1967); apptv.; 6-yr.; nine members: Henry Lee Grimes, Caddo Mills (12-31-89); Carl Smith, Houston (12-31-91); Sam D. Seale, Port Lavaca (12-31-91); Giles W. Dalby, Post (12-31-91); Joan H. Cason, Nacogdoches (12-31-87); Winston C. Reagan, Athens (12-31-87); David Chappell, Corpus Christi (12-31-87); John P. Gayle Jr., West Columbia (12-13-89); Ed Landry, Houston (12-31-89). Executive Director, J. Robert Brown, 400 W. 14th, Austin 78701 (nonmember).

Retirement System of Texas, Employees—(1947); apptv.; 6-yr.; six members; one is apptd. by the Governor, one by the Chief Justice of State Supreme Court and one by Speaker of the House; and three are employee members of the system serving 6-yr. overlapping terms. Apptd. by Governor: Gary R. Rodgers, Austin (8-31-88). Apptd. by Speaker of House: B. L. Parker, Austin (8-31-90). Apptd. by Chief Justice Supreme Court: Jack D. Kyle, Huntsville (8-31-86). Three elected members: Chmn., Marcus L. Yancey Jr., State Highway Department, Austin (8-31-87); Maurice Beckham, Austin (8-31-89); Pamela A. Carley, Austin (8-31-85). Executive Director, Clayton T. Garrison, Box 13207, Capitol Sta., Austin 78711 (nonmember).

Retirement System of Texas, Teacher, Board of Trustees—(1937 as six-member board; membership increased to nine in 1973); expenses; 6-yr.; nine members — two apptd. by State Board of Education, three apptd. by Governor and four TRS members apptd. by Governor after being nominated by popular ballot of the members of the retirement system, one of these four to be a retired member and another to be a member from higher education. Apptd. by Governor from nominees of Retirement System: C. A. Roberson, Fort Worth (8-31-87); Mary W. Kasting, Copperas Cove (8-31-89); Sheila J. Payne, Arlington (8-31-91); Frank Monroe, Dallas (8-31-87) retired member. Apptd. by State Board of Education: Robert R. Ashworth, Amarillo (8-31-85); Dr. George M. Crowson, Houston (8-31-89). Apptd. by Governor: Edward H. Wicker, Beeville (8-31-91); Henry M. Bell Jr., Tyler (8-31-89); Don Houseman, Dallas (8-31-87). Executive Secretary, Bruce Hineman, 1001 Trinity, Austin 78701 (nonmember) ($65,000).

Rio Grande Compact Commissioner for Texas—(1929); apptv.; 2-yr.: Jesse B. Gilmer, El Paso (6-9-89) ($34,200).

Rio Grande Valley Municipal Water Authority—(1969); apptv.; 2-yr.; nine members: W. W. Scurlock, McAllen (4-30-88); Russell F. Klostermann, Raymondville (4-30-89); Roel R. Ramirez, Roma (4-30-89); Charles C. Cardenas, McAllen (4-30-88); Sylvia H. Flores, Mercedes (4-30-88); Connie de la Garza, Harlingen (4-30-89); John W. Topp, Harlin-

gen (4-30-88); Dr. Joseph B. Coutler, Brownsville (4-30-89); Sam Risica, Edinburg (4-30-83).

Road Bond Indebtedness, Board of County and District —(See Indebtedness, Board of County and District Road Bond.)

Runnels County Water Authority—(1955); apptv.; 6-yr.; nine members: President, Arnold Frerich, Rowena (1-1-87); Vice President, Ray Alderman, Winters (1-1-87); Secretary-Treasurer, E. Jerry Holden, Ballinger (2-1-91); Barney C. Puckett, Winters (1-1-85); George A. Ruppert, Rowena (1-1-85); Charles T. Boecking, Ballinger (1-1-89); E. E. Thormeyer, Winters (1-1-89); Elliott J. Kemp, Ballinger (1-1-87); Wesley M. Hays, Winters (1-1-89).

Sabine River Authority—(1949); apptv.; per diem and expenses; 6-yr.; nine members: John W. Cooke, Carthage (7-6-91); Nolton W. Cooke, Bridge City (7-6-91); John H. Butts, San Augustine, (7-6-91); James E. Campbell, Center (7-6-89); R. Earl Lord, Hemphill (7-6-89); Juan D. Nichols, Quitman (7-6-89); William J. Butler, Orange (7-6-87); H. M. Smotherman, Tyler (7-6-87); William Y. Rice, Longview (7-6-87). Executive Vice President and General Manager, John W. Simmons, Box 579, Orange 77630 (nonmember).

Sabine River Compact Commission—(1953); apptv.; five members: One member and chairman apptd. by President of United States without a vote; two from Texas and two from Louisiana. Texas members: Danny Choate, Orange (7-12-92); Jim Tom McMahon, Newton (7-12-89) ($3,700).

San Antonio River Authority—(1937); elected; $100 a meeting and expenses; six from Bexar County and two each from Wilson, Karnes and Goliad Counties; 6-yr.; 12 members: Paul K. Herder, San Antonio (2-1-91); Chmn., Cecil W. Bain, San Antonio (2-1-91); David Evans, San Antonio (2-1-87); Allan B. Polunsky, San Antonio (2-1-87); Walter W. McAllister III, San Antonio (2-1-89); Martha C. McNeel, San Antonio (2-1-89); R. H. Ramsey Jr., Goliad (2-1-89); Vice Chmn., Truett Hunt, Kenedy (2-1-89); Hugh B. Ruckman Jr., Karnes City (2-1-91); J. C. Turner, Floresville (2-1-91); W. W. Lorenz, Stockdale (2-1-89); Mrs. William G. McCampbell Jr., Goliad (2-1-91). General Manager, Fred N. Pfeiffer, Box 9284, San Antonio 78204 (nonmember) ($68,250).

San Jacinto Historical Advisory Board—(1907 as San Jacinto State Park Commission; changed to San Jacinto Battleground Commission and changed again in 1965 to present name); apptv.; 6-yr.; five members — two ex officio: Director, Parks Division, Parks and Wildlife Department and president of San Jacinto Museum of History Assn. Three apptd. by Governor: Mrs. Ward N. Adkins, Houston (9-1-85); Miss Lennie E. Hunt, Houston (9-1-87); Frank W. Calhoun, Houston (9-1-89).

San Jacinto River Authority, Board of Directors of—(1937); apptv.; expenses while on duty; 6-yr.; six members: Vice President, E. Davis Hailey, Conroe (10-16-87); Frank E. Nadolney, Houston (10-16-89); President, D. F. McAdams Jr., Huntsville (10-16-85); Secretary, Oliver Kneisley, Conroe (10-16-87); Varreece Berry, Pasadena (10-16-85); Treasurer, Gilbert M. Turner, Houston (10-16-89). General Manager, Jack K. Ayer, Box 329, Conroe 77305 (nonmember).

Savings and Loan Commissioner—Apptv. by State Finance Commission: Linton Bowman III, Box 1089, Austin 78767 ($77,250).

Secretary of State—(1836 by Constitution of Republic of Texas, 1876 by present Constitution); apptv.: Jack M. Rains, Box 12887, Capitol Station, Austin 78711-2887 ($64,890).

Securities Board, State—(Est. 1957, the outgrowth of several amendments to the Texas Securities Act, originally passed in 1913); act is administered by the Securities Commissioner who is appointed by the board members who have six-year terms; expenses; Chmn., Alan D. Feld, Austin (Dallas) (1-15-91); Robert K. Uttley III, Temple (1-15-89); Hal M. Bateman, Lubbock (1-15-87). Securities Commissioner, Richard D. Latham, Box 13167, Capitol Station, Austin 78711 ($55,929).

Seed and Plant Board, State—(1959); apptv.; 2-yr.; six members: Darwyn Metcalf, Tulia (10-6-86); Kenneth W. Boatwright, Austin (10-6-86); Ray Joe Riley, Hart (10-6-87); Ben Smith, Waller (10-6-86); Vice Chmn., Dr. David Koeppe, Lubbock (10-6-87); Chmn., Dr. E. C. A. Runge, College Station (10-6-87).

Sex Offender Treatment, Interagency Council on—(1983); ex officio and apptv.; 12 members — nine ex officio; three apptv. by Governor. Ex officio members: One each from Texas Department of Corrections, Board of Pardons and Paroles, Texas Adult Probation Commission, Texas Juvenile Probation Commission, Texas Department of Mental Health and Mental Retardation, Texas Youth Commission, Sam Houston State University, Texas Department of Human Services and one member of Governor's office administering criminal justice planning; three apptv. from general public; 6-yr.; expenses. Apptv. members: Collier M. Cole, Dickinson (2-1-91); Michael Cox, Houston (2-1-89); Mrs. Jan Marie Delipsey, Dallas (2-1-89).

Soil and Water Conservation Board, Texas State—(1939); elected by convention in each of five state districts created by State Soil Conservation Act; 2-yr.; per diem and expenses; five members: Dist. 1, J. Frank Gray, Lubbock; Dist. 2, Joe Antilley, Abilene; Dist. 3, C. F. Schendel, Goliad; Dist. 4, Albert Roach, Paris; Dist. 5, Hermon L. Petty, Mineral Wells. Executive Director, Harvey D. Davis, 311 N. 5th, Temple 76503 (nonmember) ($44,908).

Speech Pathology and Audiology, State Committee of Examiners for—(1983); apptv.; nine members — three audiologists, three speech-language pathologists and three from general public; 6-yr.; per diem and expenses: Karen Jones Howard, Abilene (8-31-89); Steven D. Schaefer, Dallas (8-31-89); Dr. Kathryn S. Stream, Denton (8-31-89); Dr. Mary Lovey Wood, Austin (8-31-87); Susan G. N. Dorsett, Stephenville (8-31-87); Sara M. Haynes, Duncanville (8-31-87); Harold G. Beaver, Holland (8-31-87); Carol M. Hering, Austin (8-31-91); Marjorie R. Sanger, Waco (8-31-91).

State Board (Commission, Bureau) of—(Note: in most instances state agencies are alphabetized under key reference word, as, **Accountancy, Texas State Board of Public.**)

State Employee Incentive Commission—(1985); six ex officio: State Auditor; Comptroller; State Treasurer; Admin., Tex. Employment Comm.; Exec. Dir., Tex. Dept. of Labor and Standards; Exec. Dir., Legislative Budget Board. Three public members, apptd. to 2-yr. terms, one each by Gov., Lt. Gov. and Speaker of House. Gov.'s. apptee.: Anita Harris, Greenville (9-1-87).

State-Federal Relations, Division of—(1965); apptv.; term same as Governor's. Director, Henry Gandy, Room 207, Sam Houston Bldg., Austin 78701 ($51,199).

State Railroad, Board of Managers of—(1921; revised 1953); apptv. by Governor; expenses; 6-yr.; three members: Wayne C. Sellers, Palestine; O. V. Mullins, Henderson; Chmn., N. S. Petty, Garland.

State Senior Colleges, Board of Regents of—(See **Texas State University System, Board of Regents of.**)

Stephen F. Austin State University, Board of Regents of—(1969); apptv.; expenses; 6-yr.; nine members: Homer Bryce, Henderson (1-31-87); L. Kelly Jones, Arlington (1-31-93); Peggy W. Wright, Nacogdoches (1-31-93); Morgan M. Stripling, Nacogdoches (1-31-91); Dan Haynes, Burnet, (1-31-91); Richard C. Hile, Jasper (1-31-91); A. N. Rusche, Houston (1-31-89); Willa B. Murphy, Crockett (1-31-89); A. Lavoy Moore, Conroe (1-31-89).

Student Loan Corporation, Texas Guaranteed—(1979); apptv. and ex officio; 6-yr.; eleven members — eight apptd. by Governor; one ex officio, Comptroller of Public Accounts; one apptd. by Commissioner of Higher Education and one apptd. by Chairman of Coordinating Board. Gov.'s. apptees: Gary W. Bruner, Dallas (1-31-87); J. Malon Sutherland, College Station (1-31-93); Wm. H. Schroeder Jr., Lockhart (1-31-89); Hulen M. Davis Sr., Prairie View (1-31-89); John R. Schott, San Marcos (1-31-89); Dr. Robert L. Hardesty, San Marcos (1-31-91); George M. Crews, Bedford (1-31-91); Homero Avila, Donna (1-31-87). Executive Director, Joe L. McCormick, Box 15996, Austin 78761 (nonmember).

Sulphur River Basin Authority Board of Directors—(1985); apptd.; six years; per diem and expenses; six members: Richard R. Morrison Jr., Daingerfield (2-1-87); Bill Jennings, Clarksville (2-1-87); David W. Glass, Paris (2-1-89); Walter Helm, Sulhur Springs (2-1-89); President, Carroll Wheeler, Texarkana (2-1-91); Secretary-Treasurer, Vatra Solomon, Mount Pleasant (2-1-91).

Sunset Advisory Commission—(1977); 10 members: four members of House of Representatives, four members of Senate, one public member apptd. by Speaker of House, one public member apptd. by Lt. Gov.; expenses; 6-yr.

Surplus Property Agency, Texas—(1945 as **Texas State Educational Agency for Surplus Property**; name changed to present form 1949); apptv.; 6-yr.; expenses; nine members: William C. English, Kingsville (3-19-87); Garland P. Ferguson, Gladewater (3-19-87); Raymond R. Brimble, Houston (3-19-89); Charles L. Slaton, Lubbock (3-19-89); Robert A. Lansford, Austin (3-19-89); Chmn., Wm. H. Borchers, New Braunfels (3-19-85); Gerald D. Irons, The Woodlands (3-19-91); A. Max Scheid, Garland (3-19-85); Bruce Wood, Terrell (3-19-87). Executive Director, Marvin J. Titzman, Box 8120, Wainwright Station, San Antonio 78208-0120 (nonmember).

Tax Professional Examiners, Board of—(1977 as **Board of Tax Assessor Examiners**; name changed to present form 1983); apptv.; expenses; 6-yr.; six members: Frances Shuffield, Midland (3-1-87); Joel D. Whitmire, Richmond (3-1-87); E. P. Laurel, Laredo (3-1-89); Ray M. Cornett, Angleton (3-1-89); Michael C. Frazier, Houston (3-1-91); Robert C. Willis, Livingston (3-1-91). Executive Director, Sam H. Smith, Box 15920, Austin 78761 (nonmember) ($38,213).

Tax Board, State—(1905); ex officio; term in other office; no compensation; three members: Comptroller Robert D. Bullock, Secretary of State Jack M. Rains and State Treasurer Ann Richards.

Tax Board, State Property—(See **Property Tax Board, State.**)

Teachers' Professional Practices Commission—(1969); apptv.; expenses; 2-yr.; 15 members: Mazie Mack, Freeport (8-31-86); Edward L. Blake, Texarkana (8-31-88); Jose Salgado, El Paso (8-31-87); Yolanda Villarreal, Corpus Christi (8-31-87); Kathryn White, Arlington (8-31-87); Pete DeHoyos, Del Rio (8-31-87); Jeff Sanders, Uvalde (8-31-87); Mike Sampson, Commerce (8-31-87); Wendell Whittenburg, Sweetwater (8-31-87); Louise Daniel, Amarillo (8-31-87); Marva Miller, Houston (8-31-87); Jack Davidson, Tyler (8-

31-85); Edward Wilson, Abilene (8-31-87); Ron Reaves, San Antonio (8-31-87); Bernard Jackson, Houston (8-31-87).

Teacher Retirement System of Texas, Board of Trustees—(See **Retirement System, Teacher.**)

Technology Training Board—(1985); apptv. by respective organizations; 2-yr.; eight members: three members of Texas Economic Development Commission; two members of State Job Training Coordinating Commission; one member of board of regents of Texas State Technical Institute; one member of Coordinating Board of Texas State College and University System; one member of State Board of Education.

Texas A&I University at Kingsville, Board of Directors of—(See **University System of South Texas.**)

Texas A&M University System, Board of Regents—(1875); apptv.; 6-yr.; expenses; nine members: John Mobley, Austin (2-1-91); L. Lowry Mays, San Antonio (2-1-91); Royce Wisenbaker, Tyler (2-1-91); Dr. John B. Coleman, Houston (1-10-89); Chmn., David G. Eller, Houston (1-10-89); Joe Reynolds, Houston (1-10-89); Wayne Showers, McAllen (2-1-93); Douglas R. DeCluitt, Waco (2-1-93);William A. McKenzie, Dallas (2-1-93). Chancellor, Perry L. Adkisson; Secretary, Valerie P. Nelson, College Station 77843-1123 (nonmembers).

Texas Development Board—(1959); three members: Gov. William Clements, Austin; Chairman Texas Industrial Commission and Chairman of Texas Highway and Public Transportation Commission.

Texas Southern University, Board of Regents of—(1947); expenses; 6-yr.; nine members: Percy F. Creuzot, Houston (2-1-93); Vice Chmn., Randal B. McDonald, Houston (2-1-87); Naomi Andrews, Houston (2-1-87); James C. Belt Jr., Dallas (2-1-91); Milton Carroll, Houston (2-1-91); Andrew R. Melontree, Tyler (2-1-89); Arthur Gaines Jr., Houston (2-1-89); J. Kent Friedman, Houston (2-1-89); Larry R. Veselka, Houston (2-1-91). President (Interim), Dr. Robert Terry, 3100 Cleburne, Houston 77004 (nonmember).

Texas State Board, Commission, Bureau of—(In most instances, agencies are alphabetized under key reference word, as **Pharmacy, Texas State Board of.**)

Texas State Technical Institute, Board of Regents for—(1969); apptv.; expenses; 6-yr.; nine members: Gerald D. Phariss, Seagoville (8-31-89); Ed Aiken Jr., Sweetwater (8-31-89); H. Gene Evans, Waco (8-31-89); G. F. Rhodes, Port Lavaca (8-31-91); Mollie Anna Solomon, Groves (8-31-91); Dr. E. A. Aguilar Jr., El Paso (8-31-91); F. Herman Coleman, Waco (8-31-87); J. A. Besselman, Amarillo (8-31-87); R. T. Dosher Jr., Dallas (8-31-87). President, Jack E. Tompkins, TSTI System, Waco 76705 (nonmember).

Texas State University System, Board of Regents of the—(1911 as **Board of Regents of State Teachers Colleges**; name changed in 1965 to **Board of Regents of State Senior Colleges**; changed again to present form in 1975); apptv.; per diem and expenses; 6-yr.; nine members: John S. Cargile, Del Rio (2-1-93); Jeff Wentworth, San Antonio (2-1-93); W. C. Perry, Waco (2-1-87); Philip G. Warner, Houston (2-1-91); Jack L. Martin, Austin (2-1-91); Edmund M. Longcope, San Antonio (2-1-91); Ruben M. Escobedo, San Antonio (2-1-89); Katherine S. Lowry, Austin (2-1-89); Lee Drain, Dallas (2-1-89). Executive Director, Lamar G. Urbanovsky, 505 Sam Houston Bldg., Austin 78701 (nonmember).

Texas Tech University, Board of Regents of—(1923); apptv.; expenses; 6-yr.; nine members: Gerald Ford, Dallas (1-31-89); Wesley Masters, Amarillo (1-3-89); Larry Johnson, Houston (1-31-89); Wendell Mayes Jr., Austin (1-31-91); Dr. Wm. G. McGee, El Paso (1-31-91); J. Fred Bucy Jr., Dallas (1-31-91); Anne W. Sowell, Fort Worth (1-31-87); Rex P. Fuller, Lubbock (1-31-93); James L. Gulley Jr., Tyler (1-31-93). President, Lauro F. Cavazos, Box 4349, Lubbock 79409 (nonmember).

Texas Woman's University, Board of Regents of—(1901); apptv.; expenses; 6-yr.; nine members: Frances H. Chiles, Fort Worth (1-10-87); Chmn., Margaret E. Davis, Irving (1-10-87); June Page Johnson, Austin (2-1-87); Elizabeth B. Sellers, Houston (1-10-89); LaVonne P. Mason, Austin (1-10-89); Roland Boyd, McKinney (1-10-89); Lavonne Unsell, Fort Worth (2-1-91); Richard White Jr., Houston (2-1-91); Mary Beth Scull, Lubbock (2-1-91). President, Shirley S. Chater, Box 23925, TWU Station, Denton 76204 (nonmember).

Textbook Committee, State—(1929 as **Textbook Advisory Committee**; under Gilmer-Aikin Act of 1949 name changed to present form); apptd. by **State Board of Education** and is recommended by Commissioner of Education; 1-yr.; 15 members: Margaret A. Anderson, El Paso; Anita C. Arnold, San Antonio; Cathy A. Beicker, Seguin; Lou A. Davis, Klein; Billie J. Love, Amarillo; Carol A. Greaney, Galveston; Shirley Heard, Terrell; Georgeann V. Johnston, Hallsville; Carla J. Parrish, Irving; S. Don Rogers, Austin; Arlene H. Ruffin, Dallas; Susan C. Smith, Edinburg; Bill R. Tittle, Abilene; Edwyna Wheadon, Houston; James D. White, Denton.

Tourist Development Board, Texas—(1963 as 6-member board of advisers; made independent board and membership increased to nine members in 1969); apptv.; expenses; 6-yr.; nine members: Gordon Wynne Jr., Wills Point (8-23-87); Mrs. Virginia M. Eggers, Dallas (8-23-87); Mrs. Margaret M. Martin, Austin (8-23-87); Robert Alpert, Dallas

(8-23-91); John Mosty, San Antonio (8-23-91); Gerard J. Inzerillo, Irving (8-23-89); Joe R. Fulton, Corpus Christi (8-23-89); Richard E. Phillips, San Marcos (8-23-89); R. C. Richards Jr., McAllen (8-23-89). Executive Director, Larry Todd, 1032 Stephen F. Austin State Office Bldg., Austin 78711 (nonmember) ($45,732).

Trade Council, Texas World—(1985); expenses; 15 members — three ex officio; term in other office; 12 apptd. by Governor to 2-yr. terms. Ex officio members: Commissioner of Agriculture, Chmn. of Economic Development Commission, Chmn. of Texas Tourist Development Agency. 12 apptees: L. Don Anderson, Lubbock (2-1-87); Archie Bennett Jr., Houston (2-1-87); Diana Natalicio, El Paso (2-1-87); Donald J. Zahn, Dallas (2-1-87); Bob Marbut, San Antonio (2-1-87); Scott Mann III, Austin (2-1-87); Shelby H. Carter, Austin (2-1-87); Steven A. Beede, Houston (2-1-87); Ralph Thomas, Houston (2-1-87); William Moore, Dallas (2-1-87); Robert C. Kelly, Houston (2-1-87); (one vacancy).

Trade Development Authority, Texas World, Board of Directors—(1985); 2-yr.; expenses; nine members: one ex officio: Chairman of Texas World Trade Council. Eight apptd.: David Finney, Fort Worth (2-1-88); Jack Collins, Austin (2-1-88); Dan F. Parman, San Antonio (2-1-88); John H. Keck, Laredo (2-1-88); B. J. McCombs, San Antonio (2-1-88); Edward R. Scott Jr., Amarillo (2-1-88); Charles E. Selecman, Austin (2-1-88); (one vacancy).

Treasurer, State—(1835 by Provisional Government of Texas, 1876 by present Constitution); elective; (2-yr. by original constitutional provision; raised to 4-yr. in 1972, effective 1975): Ann Richards, Box 12608, Capitol Station, Austin 78711 (1-1-91) ($72,233).

Tri-County Municipal Water District—(1955); 2-yr.; apptv.: W. W. Siddons Jr., Hillsboro, director-at-large apptd. by Governor.

Trinity River Authority of Texas—(1955); apptv.; 24 directors — three from Tarrant County, four from Dallas County, two from area-at-large and one each from 15 other districts; per diem and expenses; 6-yr.: Roger Hunsaker, Fort Worth (3-15-87); T. W. Erwin III, Ennis (3-15-87); F. L. Thompson, Leona (3-15-87); John W. Rhea Jr., Dallas (3-15-87); Tommy W. Hollis, Coldspring (3-15-87); Nobel Welch, Terrell (3-15-87); Joe Scott Evans, Groveton (3-15-87); John R. Parten, Madisonville (3-15-87); Vice Pres., Blake Gillen, Corsicana (3-15-91); Mary Ethel Jackson, Buffalo (3-15-91); J. C. Payton, Euless (3-15-91); B. C. Lively, Livingston (3-15-91); Melvin W. Jackson Jr., Dallas (3-15-91); Robert T. Mattox, Crockett (3-15-91); David B. Jenkins, Stowell (3-15-91); Vice President, B. Michael Cummings, Fort Worth (3-15-91); J. L. Conner, Dayton (3-15-89); Mrs. Helen M. Hooper, Palestine (3-15-89); Charles A. Hunter, Dallas (3-15-89); Donald R. Cutler, Duncanville (3-15-89); Howard C. Brants Jr., Fort Worth (3-15-89); Thomas C. Letts, Huntsville (3-15-89); Suel Hill, Fairfield (3-15-89); Bruce Smith, Kemp (3-15-89). General Manager, Danny F. Vance, Box 60, Arlington 76010 (nonmember).

Turnpike (Toll Road) Authority, Texas—(1953 as nine-member board; increased to twelve members in 1971); 6-yr.; twelve members — nine apptv. and three ex officio; ex officio members are three members of the State Highway and Public Transportation Commission (See **Highway Commission** in this list); apptv. members: J. Frank Holt III, Dallas (2-15-87); Chmn., Ed Palm, Fort Worth (2-15-91); Charles R. Matthews, Garland (2-15-93); Richard L. Bischoff, Houston (2-15-91); Robert L. Collins, Houston (2-15-91); Clive Runnels, Houston (2-15-85); C. C. Smitherman, Houston (2-15-89); R. J. Lindley Jr., Houston (2-15-89); Royce B. West, Dallas (2-15-89). Engineer-Manager, H. M. Reily (nonmember); Secretary-Treasurer, Harry Kabler, Box 190369, Dallas 75219 (nonmember).

Uniform State Laws, Commission on—(See **Laws, Commission on Uniform State**.)

University of Houston System, Board of Regents of—(1963); apptv.; expenses; 6-yr.; nine members: Clarence F. Kendall II, Houston (8-31-91); Ralph E. Reamer, Houston (8-31-91); Xavier C. Lemond, Katy (8-31-91); Chester B. Benge Jr., Houston (9-1-87); Chairman, James E. Kolb, Houston (9-1-87); Leonard Rauch, Houston (9-1-87); Mrs. Debbie Hanna, Austin (9-1-89); Jose Molina, Houston (9-1-89); Don A. Sanders, Houston (9-1-89). President, Richard L. Van Horn, 4600 Gulf Fwy., Suite 500, Houston 77023 (nonmember).

University of Texas System, Board of Regents of the—(1881); apptv.; expenses; 6-yr.; nine members: Sam Barshop, San Antonio (2-1-93); Louis A. Beecherl Jr., Dallas (2-1-93); W. A. Moncrief Jr., Fort Worth (2-1-93); Shannon Ratliff, Austin (1-10-91); Chmn., Jack Blanton, Houston (1-10-91); W. F. Roden, Midland (1-10-91); Jess Hay, Dallas (1-10-89); Mario Yzaguirre, Brownsville (1-10-89); Robert B. Baldwin III, Austin (1-10-89). Chancellor, Hans Mark; Secretary, Betty Anne Thedford, 601 Colorado, Austin 78701 (nonmembers).

University System of South Texas, Board of Directors of the—(1929 as **College of Arts & Industries**; name changed in 1967 to **Texas A&I University of Kingsville**; changed to present name in 1977); apptv.; 6-yr.; nine members: Mary Anne Guthrie, Corpus Christi (8-31-91); Mauro Garcia, Falfurrias (8-31-91); C. Ivan Wilson, Corpus Christi (8-31-91); Blas M.

Martinez, Laredo (8-31-89); Gilbert Acuna, Kingsville (8-31-89); Wayne H. King, San Antonio (8-31-89); Mrs. Paul R. Haas, Corpus Christi (8-31-87); Clemente Garcia, Corpus Christi (8-31-87); Mrs. Richard M. Kleberg Jr., Kingsville (8-31-87); Chancellor, Lawrence K. Pettit, Box 1238, Kingsville 78363 (nonmember).

Vehicle Equipment Safety Commissioner—(1965); apptv.: George W. Busby, Department of Public Safety, Austin.

Veterans Commission, Texas—(1927 as **Veterans State Service Office**; reorganized as **Veterans Affairs Commission** 1947 with five members; membership increased to six in 1981 with addition of one disabled veteran as a member; name changed to **Texas Veterans Commission** in 1985); apptv.; 6-yr.; per diem while on duty and expenses; six members: Billy E. Kirby, Clifton (12-31-91); Arturo T. Benavides, Bruni (12-31-89); Robert J. Lyons, Vidor (12-31-87); John E. McKelvey, Electra (12-31-87); Samuel Bier, Austin (disabled veteran member) (12-31-91); Lindon Williams, Baytown (12-31-89). Executive Director, Aubrey L. Bullard, Box 12277, Capitol Station, Austin 78711 (nonmember) ($46,041).

Veterans Land Board—(See **Land Board, Veterans**.)

Veterinary Medical Examiners, Texas Board of—(1911; revised 1953; made nine-member board in 1981); apptv.; expenses on duty; 6-yr.; nine members: Dr. Edward S. Murray, Spur (8-26-87); Mike Levi, Spicewood (8-26-91); Dr. Frank E. Mann Jr., Wharton (8-26-87); Dr. Ed B. Avery, Pearsall (8-26-87); Dr. D. L. K. Frey, Corpus Christi (8-26-85); Dr. Mary E. Mainster, San Antonio (8-26-91); Jim Humphrey, Henrietta (8-26-89); Dr. William L. Anderson, Addison (8-26-89); Dr. Kenneth Dorris, Stephenville (8-26-89). Executive Secretary, Roger D. Shipman, 3810 Medical Pkwy., Ste. 119, Austin 78756 (nonmember) ($42,436).

Water Commission, Texas—(1913 as **State Board of Water Engineers**; name changed in 1962 to **Texas Water Commission**, reorganized and name again changed in 1965 to **Water Rights Commission**; reorganized and name changed to present form in 1977 to perform the judicial function for the **Texas Department of Water Resources**); apptv.; 6-yr.; three members full-time at $51,100: Chmn., Paul Hopkins, Austin (LaMarque) (8-31-89); Ralph Roming, Bovina (8-31-87); John D. Houchins, Houston (8-31-91). Executive Director, Larry Soward ($44,700); Chief Clerk, Mary Ann Hefner (nonmembers), Box 13087, Capitol Sta., Austin 78711.

Water Development Board, Texas—(1957; legislative function for the **Texas Department of Water Resources** 1977); apptv.; per diem and expenses; 6-yr.; six members: Chmn., Louie Welch, Houston (12-31-91); Charles Jenness, Houston (12-31-91); George McCleskey, Lubbock (12-31-87); Glen E. Roney, McAllen (12-31-89); Stuart S. Coleman, Brownwood (12-31-89); Thomas M. Dunning, Dallas (12-31-91). Executive Director, TDWR, Charles E. Nemir, P.O. Box 13087, Capitol Sta., Austin 78711 (nonmember) ($62,200).

Water Resources Planning Commission, Multi-State—(1985); apptv.; 6 yr.; six members: Chmn., T. D. Howell, Marshall (2-1-89); Dr. Idris Traylor Jr., Lubbock (2-1-89); Dr. Judson Williams, El Paso (2-1-91); A. L. Black, Friona (2-1-87); Tom Masterson, Houston (2-1-91); (One vacancy).

Water Well Drillers Board, Texas—(1965 as eight-member board; reorganized 1981 and made nine-member board); apptv.; per diem and expenses; 6-yr.; nine members — six to be water well drillers and three members from general public. Drillers: James Frank Grimes, Dallas (9-15-87); John H. Walker, Alvin (9-15-91); Barry Henderson, Longview (9-15-91); Walton O'Neil Loftis, Midland (9-15-87); M. Don McKinley, Pearsall (9-15-89); Gary D. Grant, Abernathy (9-15-89). Public members: James L. Shawn, III, Austin (9-15-87); Frank Del Rio, Austin (9-15-91); Linda R. Gambill, Seymour (9-15-89). James L. Dyess Jr., TDWR, Box 13087, Capitol Sta., Austin 78711 (nonmember).

West Texas State University, Board of Regents of—(1969); apptv.; 6-yr.; nine members: Dee S. Osborne, Houston (8-31-91); Margo E. Fields, Amarillo (8-31-91); Burk Whittenburg, Amarillo (8-31-91); Chmn., T. Boone Pickens Jr., Amarillo (8-31-87); Tom Christian, Claude (8-31-87); J. R. Walsh Jr., Borger (8-31-87); Nolon Henson Jr., Happy (8-31-89); Mrs. Lennie C. Sims, Wellington (8-31-89); Leo Forrest, Amarillo (8-31-89). President, Ed D. Roach, Box 997, Canyon 79016 (nonmember).

Youth Camp Safety, Advisory Council on—(1973); apptv.; 2-yr.; expenses; 11 members: Ex officio member and chairman, Commissioner of Health Dr. Robert Bernstein. Apptv. members: Mrs. Thomas P. Hubbard, Dallas (12-1-85); Carl Hawkins, Ingram (12-1-85); Mrs. Cordie R. Hines, Dallas (12-1-85); Raymond B. Bean, Dallas (12-1-85); Ann Cunningham, Arlington (12-1-85); Ron Anderson, Kerrville (12-1-85); B. Michael Adams, Henderson (12-1-85); Silas B. Ragsdale Jr., Hunt (12-1-85); Dr. H. Phillip Hook, Tyler (12-1-85); C. Joseph Nelson, Irving (12-1-85); (One vacancy).

Youth Commission, Texas—(1949 as nine-member board; reorganized 1957 and again in 1975); six apptv. members; 6-yr.; per diem on duty: Judge Jorge C. Rangel, Corpus Christi (8-31-87); Chmn., Dr. George Beto, Huntsville (9-1-87); Larry F. York, Austin (8-31-91); Floyd Williams, Houston (8-31-91); Richard Abalos, Odessa (8-31-89); Susan E. Bush, Athens (8-31-89). Executive Director, Ron Jackson, Box 9999, Austin 78766 (nonmember) ($58,916).

Texas State Finances

The 70th session of the Texas Legislature proved to be one of the most traumatic for state spending in recent history. It took a 30-day special session that ended in late July for the lawmakers to agree on a record $38.5 billion budget for the 1988-89 biennium and to increase taxes by a record $5.7 billion to cover the higher cost of government. It was the first time since 1961 that the Legislature failed to pass a budget in regular session.

The fiscal crisis was prompted by a severe drop in crude oil and natural gas prices in 1986 from which the petroleum industry was only beginning to recover in mid-1987. Traditionally, state government receives about one-third of its revenues from the petroleum business and related industries. With the state's economy only beginning to diversify, the heavy economic blow dealt by the drop in petroleum prices threw state government finance into a decline.

One special session was held in the fall of 1986 to provide stopgap financing for the state. But "temporary" taxes levied on sales and gasoline at that time became permanent when it became obvious in 1987 that the petroleum industry was not going to rebound in time to save the state's finances.

Republican Gov. William P. Clements campaigned on a hard-line, no-new-tax platform when defeating incumbent Democrat Mark White in 1986. And the governor maintained that position for a time during the regular session, until it became apparent that tax increases in several categories were going to be necessary. He eventually signed the new taxes into law, however.

As the governor pointed out, Texas is under federal court orders to improve its prison system, its mental institutions and its system of public education.

Among the new or increased taxes approved during the special session are these:

• An increase to 6 cents from 5.25 in the state sales tax with the levy expanded to cover a broader base of goods and services.

• An increase to 6 percent from 5 on the motor vehicle sales tax.

• A permanent increase in the gasoline tax to 15 cents per gallon.

• A temporary increase in the corporate franchise tax to $6.70 from $5.25 per $1,000 of taxable capital and surplus in Texas. The increase is effective until Jan. 1, 1990.

• An increase from 4 to 6 cents per dollar on the hotel tax.

• An increase in the cigarette tax from 20.5 cents per package to 26 cents.

• A temporary 20 percent surtax on the premium taxes paid by insurance companies in 1987 and 1988, with some categories of insurance exempted.

• A new 2.5 percent tax on insurance administrative services.

• And temporary increases of fees for several professions.

State Government Budget, 1987-88 and 1988-89

The state budget was adopted by the 70th Legislature meeting in special session in July 1987. The figures are taken from the appropriations bill, Senate Bill 1. Fiscal year 1988 runs from Sept. 1, 1987 to Aug. 31, 1988, and fiscal year 1989 runs from Sept. 1, 1988 to Aug. 31, 1989.

Fiscal 1988	General Revenue	Other	Total
Article I—Executive and Administrative Departments and Agencies	$1,568,590,000	$4,070,183,975	$5,638,243,484
Article II — Public Health, Hospitals and Youth Institutions	2,090,355,939	2,105,313,059	4,195,668,998
Article III—Education	8,286,713,436	1,062,883,097	9,349,596,533
Article IV—Judiciary	42,684,865	13,470,096	56,154,961
Article VI—Legislature	49,227,307	...	49,227,307
Total, Fiscal Year 1988	$12,037,041,056	$7,251,850,227	$19,288,891,283

Fiscal 1989	General Revenue	Other	Total
Article I—Executive and Administrative Departments and Agencies	$1,457,806,900	$3,748,560,901	$5,206,367,801
Article II — Public Health, Hospitals and Youth Institutions	2,213,090,330	2,252,006,551	4,465,096,881
Article III—Education	8,393,393,681	1,060,071,115	9,453,464,796
Article IV—Judiciary	42,046,281	14,089,096	56,135,377
Article VI—Legislature	54,707,050	...	54,707,050
Total, Fiscal Year 1989	$12,161,044,242	$7,074,727,663	$19,235,771,905
Grand total, 1988-89 Biennium	$24,198,085,298	$14,326,577,890	$38,524,663,188*

*After the appropriations bill was passed, the Legislature approved a further reduction in the appropriations. A total of $177.6 million will be taken from the budgets of the state agencies at some point during the biennium.

State Government Income, 1986

Sources from which cash was received by the state, and amounts for the fiscal year ended Aug. 31, 1986, as reported by the State Comptroller of Public Accounts, Austin, are given below. Due to rounding, totals differ from Comptroller's report of $45,519,742,487 for total revenue and interfund transfers.

Taxes

Ad valorem tax	$12,683
Bedding tax	137,704
Inheritance tax	119,457,147
Oil production tax	769,222,794
Natural and casinghead gas tax	778,703,230
Sulphur tax	4,204,307
Gas utility administration tax	15,873,142
Cement tax	5,853,469
Utilities tax	181,810,406
Telephone tax	36,613,409
Oil and gas well servicing tax	6,403,777
Telegraph tax	113,688
Motor vehicle sales and rental tax	865,963,093
Hotel, motel and miscellaneous excise taxes	65,030,260
Cigarette and tobacco tax	378,715,314
Mixed beverage tax	198,107,356
Liquor tax	51,695,103
Wine tax	7,336,358

Ale tax	2,742,320
Beer tax	87,790,307
Airline beverage tax	351,190
Special motor fuels tax	156,639,017
Motor fuel gasoline tax	854,839,706
Franchise tax	901,046,009
Insurance companies taxes	408,886,583
Coin device machine tax	4,250,978
Limited sales and use tax	4,329,870,820
Total taxes	**$10,231,670,170**

Licenses and Fees

(Only fees totaling more than $1,000,000 revenue are listed individually. Others totaled in a single category.)

Motor vehicle certificates	$22,070,859
Motor vehicle inspection fees	41,324,027
Driver license fees	51,157,102
Driver record information fees	12,800,325
Commercial transportation fees	5,286,304
Motor vehicle safety responsibility violations	7,416,656
City sales tax service fee	18,433,500
Local MTA sales tax service fee	8,429,338
Bank franchise tax service fee	1,458,870
General business filing fees	23,245,607
Coin-operated machine business license fee	1,032,218
Bingo operators/lessors	1,857,586
Manufactured housing certificate of title	1,463,341
Manufactured and industrialized housing inspection fees	1,082,748
Financial institutions regulation	11,442,840
Professional fees	43,217,871
Insurance agents licenses	4,392,318
Insurance dept. fees, miscellaneous	2,509,678
Insurance dept. examination and audit fees	7,724,952
Liquor permit fees	18,358,102
Wine and beer permit fees	5,557,275
Veterans Land Board service fees	1,911,741
Oil and gas well drilling permits	3,289,450
Waste treatment inspection fees	3,394,825
Air pollution control fees	7,455,214
Business fees—agriculture	1,262,911
Agriculture inspection fees	3,176,404
Motorboat registration fees	4,756,217
State park fees	8,700,776
Higher education registration fees	163,322,942
Teacher certification fees	1,411,010
College and university student fees	7,593,996
Administrative fees— higher education	1,956,976
Food and drug fees	1,366,322
Health care facilities fees	2,064,796
Medical examination and registration fees	3,934,074
Health related professional fees	2,199,506
Vital statistics certification and service fees	1,541,628
Radioactive materials and devices or equipment regulation	2,878,370
Waste disposal facilities, generators, transporters	4,018,962
Private institutions license fees	1,344,815
Welfare/MHMR service fees	1,304,328
Marriage licenses	2,261,100
Fees for copies or filing of records	1,106,746

State Bonded Indebtedness

Bonded indebtedness of the State of Texas on Aug. 31, 1986, was $2,813,463,729, according to records of the **State Comptroller of Public Accounts.** Issuance of bonds requires amendment of the Constitution of Texas, authorized in a statewide election.

Outstanding bonded indebtedness, Aug. 31, 1986, consisted of the following:

University of Texas and Texas A&M University Permanent University Fund Bonds	$638,110,000
Higher Education Constitutional Bonds	205,675,860
Veterans Land Fund Bonds	1,458,345,000
Texas Water Development Bonds	353,127,869
Texas Student Loan Bonds	115,705,000
Texas Park Development Bonds	32,500,000
Farm, Ranch Loan Securities Bonds	10,000,000
Total All Bonds	**$2,813,463,729**

Fees with less than $1,000,000 revenue	13,109,365
Sub-total licenses, fees	$535,623,989
Game and fish, licenses and fees	30,734,113
Motor vehicle registration fees	571,247,431
Total license and registration fees	**$1,137,605,533**

Land Income

Land sales, leasing	$5,231,318
Oil and gas royalties	345,723,606
Sand, shell, gravel and timber sales	235,665
Real estate, equipment and commodity sales	34,424,559
Mineral lease, rental and bonus	461,880,793
Surface rental leases and easements	7,996,639
Land reclamation	214,170
Total sales, royalties and rentals	**$855,706,751**

Interest and Dividends

Interest on deposits, state and local	$183,796,041
Interest on securities owned	2,325,352,913
Interest on land sales	69,884,928
Other interest	1,100,714
Interest on loans to college students	13,254,290
Total interest and dividends	**$2,593,388,887**

Miscellaneous Government Revenue

(Sources of $1,000,000 or more. Other categories lumped into one.)

Pay patient collections	$30,189,979
Escheated estates	69,098,595
Alcoholic code beverage money penalty in lieu of cancellation or suspension	1,721,191
Game and fish, water safety and parks violations	1,491,134
Teachers retirement reimbursement from funds outside treasury	58,499,437
Waste disposal violations	1,944,866
Medical assistance cost recovery	2,755,106
Child support collections—state	35,091,768
Arrest fees	4,017,199
Judges retirement contributions	1,566,573
District court suit filing fee	4,222,712
Fees from criminal offenses	7,319,012
Fees from misdemeanor or felony cases	35,278,677
Judgments	4,294,614
Unemployment compensation penalties	6,661,814
Sale of public building bonds	142,282,403
Prison industries sales	5,961,495
Telecommunications service from local funds	2,288,019
Supplies/equipment/services— federal/other	58,514,516
Insurance and damages	3,483,622
Warrants voided by statute of limitations	1,892,550
Repayment of unemployment benefits— local funds	1,594,912
Other miscellaneous government revenue	2,584,180
Local account balance brought into treasury	2,971,488
Reimbursements—third party	17,455,222
Reimbursements—intra-agency	14,185,438
Gain/loss on investments	1,023,328,571
Grants to cities, counties, political subdivisions	5,630,462
Revenue categories, less than $1,000,000 income	5,987,393
Total miscellaneous governmental revenue	**$1,552,312,940**

Federal Funding

Federal grants to highways	$927,162,938
Federal grants to public health	250,026,538
Federal child support collections	5,263,576
Federal grants to public welfare	1,477,661,224
Federal grants to public education	706,640,383
Federal grants, miscellaneous	494,443,747
Federal grants, parks and wildlife	17,257,351
Federal receipts—earned credits	231,016,824
Total federal, county and other aid	**$4,109,472,581**
Total net receipts	**$20,480,156,862**
Interfund transfers	**25,039,585,625**
Total receipts	**$45,519,742,487**

State Government Expenditures, 1986

The following table shows the expenditures by the Texas State Government, giving agencies and purposes of expenditures for the fiscal year ended Aug. 31, 1986, as reported by the State Comptroller of Public Accounts. Due to rounding, total in this compilation differs from the $45,715,399,777.01 reported by the Comptroller's office.

Legislative:

Senate	$9,610,116
House of Representatives	13,314,108
Legislative Council	8,668,965
Legislative Budget Board	2,139,918
Legislative Reference Library	415,896
Commission on Uniform State Laws	38,989
Sunset Advisory Commission	727,196
Auditor	7,346,317
Automated Information System Adv. Council	369,885
Total Legislative	**$42,631,391**

Judicial:

Supreme Court	$2,075,077
Court of Criminal Appeals	2,050,534
Office of Court Administration	1,000,659
State Attorney before Court of Criminal Appeals	266,030
District Courts (Comptroller's Judiciary Section)	29,101,272
Comm. Jud. Conduct	260,145
Law Library	533,936
Texas Prosecutors Coordinating Council	44,080

Courts of Appeals:

First District	$1,496,735
Second District	1,102,123
Third District	1,040,773
Fourth District	1,064,537
Fifth District	2,119,565
Sixth District	556,689
Seventh District	652,778
Eighth District	606,068
Ninth District	447,459
Tenth District	400,404
Eleventh District	518,050
Twelfth District	541,037
Thirteenth District	1,009,869
Fourteenth District	1,542,555
Total Judicial	**$48,430,375**

Executive and Administrative:

Governor's Office	$7,293,158
Attorney General	50,067,602
Purchasing and General Services Comm.	55,555,316
Comptroller of Public Accounts	107,462,636
General Land Office	17,802,268
Library and Archives Commission	7,566,396
Secretary of State	9,044,718
Texas Department on Aging	1,660,641
Treasurer	7,809,958
Securities Board	2,064,962
Commission for the Blind	3,862,415
Good Neighbor Commission	188,184
Employees' Retirement System	133,714,167
Veterans Land Board	4,307,490
Dept. of Community Affairs	9,709,882
Office of State-Federal Relations	778,010
Advisory Commission Intergovernmental Relations	470,875
Commission for Deaf	749,980
Public Building Authority	141,774
Commission on Human Rights	477,185
Department of Highways & Public Transportation	1,772,193
State Property Tax Bd.	4,151,848
Bd. of Tax Professional Examiners	99,132
State Pension Review Board	156,150
Texas Merit System Council	29,629
State Aircraft Pooling Board	4,240,381
Total Executive and Administrative	**$431,176,949**

Protection of Persons and Property:

Adjutant General	$9,146,806
Texas Veterans Commission	1,911,197
Department of Public Safety	154,797,759
National Guard Armory Board	1,674,860
Law Enforcement Officer Standards and Education	2,123,649
Commission on Fire Protection Personnel Standards and Education	210,555
Commission on Jail Standards	350,084
Criminal Justice Policy Council	228,716
Total Protection of Persons and Property	**$170,443,625**

Regulation of Business and Industry:

Real Estate Commission	$2,602,033
Savings and Loan Department	3,082,071
Department of Banking	4,504,077
Department of Labor and Standards	6,155,830
Industrial Accident Board	15,630,018
Board of Insurance	26,133,896
Railroad Commission	33,241,280
Board of Plumbing Examiners	833,099
Alcoholic Beverage Commission	20,403,206
Board of Architectural Examiners	555,648
Board of Registration for Professional Engineers	728,317
Aeronautics Commission	1,421,554
Economic Development Commission	2,657,263
Consumer Credit Commission	960,490
Board of Private Investigators and Private Security Agencies	1,374,875
Polygraph Examiners Board	78,378
Motor Vehicle Commission	361,326
Amusement Machine Commission	780,920
Texas Structural Pest Control Board	448,671
Public Utility Commission	8,554,529
Board of Public Accountancy	2,250,529
Texas Bd. of Land Surveying	160,672
Texas Bd. of Irrigators	90,285
Public Utility Counsel	689,544
Credit Union Department	846,959
Total Regulation of Business and Industry	**$134,545,468**

Conservation of Health and Sanitation:

Department of Health	$115,097,270
Board of Barber Examiners	446,600
Board of Medical Examiners	356,152
Board of Dental Examiners	556,950
Cosmetology Commission	1,274,890
University of Texas System Cancer Center	85,900,545
Board of Nurse Examiners	993,634
Board of Chiropractic Examiners	101,014
Board of Examiners for Hearing Aids	69,373
Board of Podiatry Examiners	55,487
Board of Vocational Nurse Examiners	598,810
Optometry Board	134,211
Board of Pharmacy	1,331,916
Low-Level Radioactive Waste Disposal Authority	1,172,475
Commission on Alcohol and Drug Abuse	2,869,789
Board of Morticians	247,195
Air Control Board	13,208,135
Board of Examiners of Psychologists	220,717
Governor's Commission on Physical Fitness	169,758
Board of Physical Therapy Examiners	134,522
Board of Nursing Home Administrators	280,710
Health Facilities Commission	(−2,006)
Total Conservation of Health and Sanitation	**$225,218,148**

Development and Conservation of Natural Resources:

Department of Agriculture	$21,037,039
Texas Animal Health Commission	12,327,281
Agricultural Extension Service	30,551,329
Agricultural Experiment Station	38,737,331
Veterinary Medical Diagnostic Laboratory	1,738,032
Forest Service	8,189,268
Rodent and Predatory Animal Control	2,170,172
Board of Veterinary Examiners	224,729
Rio Grande Compact Commission	118,316
Water Development Board	5,691,526
Texas Water Commission	32,817,473
Water Well Drillers Board	7,838
Sabine River Compact Commission	28,788
Texas Coastal and Marine Council	24,960
Soil and Water Conservation Board	1,474,578
Red River Compact Commission	28,979

Canadian River Commission	16,453
Pecos River Compact Commission	70,728
Natural Fibers and Food Protein Committee	1,654,946
Total Development and Conservation of Natural Resources	**$156,909,765**

Highway Maintenance and Construction	**$2,428,919,022**

Mental Health and Correctional:

Dept. of Mental Health and Mental Retardation	$44,821,264
Health and Human Services Council	243,838
Commission for Indian Affairs	473,587
Texas Youth Commission	51,074,071
Texas Adult Probation Commission	2,048,256
Texas Juvenile Probation Commission	845,214
Department of Corrections	410,529,921
Board of Pardons and Paroles	26,149,208
Miscellaneous Eleemosynary	476,011,530
Total Mental Health and Correctional	**$1,011,723,303**

Educational:

Governor's Fund	$2,087,159
House of Representatives	87
Commission for the Blind	8,326,546
Department of Community Affairs	903,172
Department of Public Safety	330,894
Savings and Loan Department	1,120
Department of Highways and Public Transportation	2,448,734
Texas Education Agency	5,499,710,750
A&M University System Administration	46,167,651
A&M University Main University	166,269,811
Engineering Experiment Station	5,329,186
Tarleton State University	10,916,948
University of Texas—Arlington	62,623,799
Prairie View A&M University	22,035,553
Texas Transportation Institute	895,938
Engineering Extension Service	2,391,517
Texas Southern University	39,652,397
A&M University at Galveston	7,126,876
Texas State Technical Institute	43,514,965
University of Texas System	56,632,275
University of Texas—Austin	226,439,954
University of Texas Medical Branch—Galveston	156,575,808
University of Texas—El Paso	34,681,429
University of Texas Health Science Center—Dallas	54,161,209
University of Houston — University Park	125,917,996
Texas Woman's University	32,666,112
Texas A&I University	17,214,906
Texas Tech University	79,194,289
Lamar University — Beaumont	30,227,611
Midwestern University	12,448,097
Pan American University	19,393,663
Angelo State University	13,055,873
University of Texas—Tyler	8,999,884
Texas Department on Aging	27,183
Texas Department of Health	3,452,529
Public Utility Commission	1,024,322
Commission on Alcohol and Drug Abuse	191,046
University of Texas—Dallas	26,547,169
Texas Tech Univ. Health Science Center	48,342,068
Advisory Council for Technical/Vocational Education	156,996
University of Texas—Permian Basin	6,901,153
University of Texas—San Antonio	24,042,568
University of Texas Health Science Center—Houston	80,818,034
University of Texas Health Science Center—San Antonio	70,634,635
Pan American Univ. at Brownsville	3,076,978
University of Houston—Clear Lake	15,075,965
Corpus Christi University	10,236,976
Laredo State University	3,316,232
University of South Texas Administration	339,810
East Texas State University	23,872,014
North Texas State University	69,920,313
Sam Houston State University	30,557,185
Southwest Texas State University	44,250,550
S. F. Austin State University	31,218,695

Sul Ross State University	7,930,8
School for the Blind	8,476,2
School for the Deaf	12,055,6
West Texas State University	16,187,0
Board of Regents State University System	283,8
Coordinating Bd. Higher Education	499,063,0
Texas College of Osteopathic Medicine	25,048,5
East Texas State University—Texarkana	3,635,2
University of Houston-Victoria	2,862,5
State Rural Medical Education Board	71,5
University of Houston System	8,418,6
University of Houston—Downtown	11,623,5
UT Health Science Center—Tyler	14,041,9
UT Institute of Texan Cultures	1,940,8
Texas Commission on the Arts	(—65
Southwest Collegiate Institute for Deaf	1,558,2
Comptroller—State Fiscal	12,5
Austin State School	4,1
Texas Youth Commission	(—41
Lamar University System	381,6
Lamar University—Orange	1,813,2
Lamar University—Port Arthur	2,106,8
Texas Historical Commission	9,1
Total Education	**$7,899,868,7**

Parks and Monuments	**$90,630,6**
Public Welfare	**2,543,238,5**
Payment of Public Debt	**1,599,773,9**
State Cost, Employees Retirement	**161,651,8**
State Cost, Social Security	**404,495,1**
Grants to Political Subdivisions and Others	**708,455,1**
State Cost, Teacher Retirement	**736,019,0**
Miscellaneous	**35,685,0**
Total Governmental Expenditures	**$18,829,816,2**
Interfund Transfers	**$26,885,583,5**
Total Expenditures	**$45,715,399,7**

State Government Costs

The yearly cost of state government is shown here. Costs have risen from $127,677 in 1847 to $18,483,139,014 1986. Figures have been rounded out, hence may va slightly from those in other tables.

Fiscal Year Ended	Expenditures	Fiscal Year Ended	Expenditure
1986	$18,483,139,014	1948	$403,983,9
1985	16,186,691,147	1947	319,988,1
1984	14,348,917,194	1946	238,616,4
1983	13,539,476,462	1945	186,493,1
1982	12,074,204,469	1944	142,234,2
1981	11,367,553,831	1943	181,795,9
1980	10,210,907,514	1942	205,741,8
1979	8,600,168,100	1941	166,073,0
1978	7,864,096,032	1940	165,717,6
1977	6,606,979,386	1939	164,323,5
1976	6,203,503,772	1938	157,747,8
1975	5,377,326,615	1937	144,770,2
1974	4,492,958,989	1936	125,693,9
1973	4,041,620,277	1935	111,001,0
1972	3,810,046,333	1934	111,866,2
1971	3,453,207,618	1933	107,922,4
1970	2,954,745,796	1932	95,800,9
1969	2,514,507,766	1931	101,164,4
1968	2,339,869,601	1930	103,137,9
1967	2,060,881,279	1929	84,478,4
1966	1,860,633,769	1928	84,358,9
1965	1,610,278,049	1927	73,563,7
1964	1,574,959,268	1926	66,381,0
1963	1,467,683,645	1925	67,210,1
1962	1,305,846,369	1924	50,919,8
1961	1,200,374,164	1923	66,041,7
1960	1,184,384,437	1922	60,484,2
1959	1,163,593,583	1921	67,223,8
1958	1,027,389,546	1920	34,750,6
1957	872,680,662	1910	10,868,3
1956	805,686,551	1900	5,754,2
1955	777,243,167	1890	4,162,9
1954	706,121,196	1880	2,922,3
1953	662,495,496	1870	660,2
1952	617,210,759	1860	828,7
1951	568,153,444	1850	148,0
1950	527,252,453	1847	127,6
1949	443,776,824		

U.S. Tax Collections in Texas
This information was furnished by the **Internal Revenue Service**

Fiscal Year	Individual Income And Employment Taxes	Corporation Income Taxes	Estate Taxes	Gift Taxes	Excise Taxes	Total U.S. Taxes Collected in Texas
5	$44,090,929,000	$4,808,703,000	$493,405,000	$35,355,000	$4,169,857,000	$53,598,248,000
4	41,497,114,000	5,637,148,000	528,106,000	41,560,000	6,058,110,000	53,762,038,000
3	37,416,203,000	4,750,079,000	494,431,000	19,844,000	5,553,491,000	48,234,047,000
2	36,072,975,000	6,574,940,000	624,559,000	6,789,000	6,880,102,000	50,159,365,000
1	31,692,219,000	7,526,687,000	526,420,000	31,473,000	8,623,799,000	48,400,598,000
0	25,707,514,000	7,232,486,000	453,830,000	23,722,000	4,122,538,000	37,540,089,000
9	22,754,959,000	5,011,334,000	397,810,000	18,267,000	1,680,118,000	29,862,488,000
8	17,876,628,000	5,128,609,000	337,883,000	19,189,000	1,757,045,000	25,119,354,000
7	16,318,652,000	4,135,046,000	422,984,000	182,623,000	1,324,989,000	22,384,294,000
6	11,908,546,000	2,736,374,000	350,326,000	48,804,000	1,320,496,000	16,364,546,000
5	11,512,883,000	2,882,776,000	269,185,000	44,425,000	1,338,713,000	16,047,982,000
4	9,884,442,000	1,989,710,000	259,306,000	43,109,000	1,338,656,000	13,515,223,000
3	8,353,841,000	1,614,204,000	240,470,000	53,329,000	1,511,754,000	11,773,598,000
2	7,125,930,000	1,485,559,000	288,674,000	24,792,000	1,478,340,000	10,403,295,000
1	6,277,877,000	1,229,479,000	179,694,000	31,817,000	1,056,540,000	8,775,407,000
0	6,096,961,000	1,184,342,000	135,694,000	20,667,000	843,724,000	8,281,389,000
9	5,444,372,000	1,180,047,000	158,028,000	23,024,000	810,061,000	7,615,532,000
8	4,721,316,000	935,302,000	138,102,000	24,878,000	821,576,000	6,707,952,000
7	3,616,869,000	1,133,126,000	124,052,000	20,764,000	691,156,000	5,651,336,000
6	3,063,000,000	847,000,000	130,000,000	17,000,000	717,000,000	4,774,000,000
5	2,705,318,000	786,916,000	115,733,000	15,771,000	710,940,000	4,334,678,000
4	2,745,342,000	716,288,000	93,497,000	14,773,000	670,309,000	4,240,209,000
3	2,582,821,000	654,888,000	83,013,000	12,840,000	638,525,000	3,972,087,000
2	2,361,614,000	675,035,000	101,263,000	13,095,000	444,279,000	3,595,287,000
1	2,131,707,000	622,076,000	80,001,000	9,550,000	266,714,000	3,110,047,000
0	2,059,075,000	622,822,000	70,578,000	10,583,000	209,653,000	2,972,712,000
9	1,868,515,000	545,334,000	63,138,000	7,205,000	198,285,000	2,682,478,000
8	1,786,686,000	625,267,000	68,379,000	10,672,000	206,307,000	2,697,309,000
7	1,696,288,000	615,527,000	55,592,000	7,918,000	192,413,000	2,567,739,000

*Beginning in 1976, the fiscal year ending date was changed to Sept. 30, from June 30.

Federal Government in Texas

On this and following pages are brief accounts of activities of the federal government in Texas. Federal tax ections are listed above, and a summary of expenditures is listed elsewhere in the section.

Military Activities

Since 1845 Texas has been one of the leading states in military activities, with its strategic location on the Gulf of xico midway between the East and West Coasts, its generally mild climate and its varied terrain. Back in 1845, ᵛever, it was the **Mexican War**, precipitated by the annexation of Texas by the United States, that made Texas the ᵗer of operations. Between then and the outbreak of the **Civil War** in 1861, U.S. Army forts were established to ᵗect settlers from Indians and to maintain peace in areas still claimed by Mexico.

Fifth U.S. Army

Fifth U.S. Army headquarters, a 3-star command, been located in the historic **Quadrangle** at **Fort Sam ᵘston, San Antonio**, since July 1, 1971, when Fourth ᵈ Fifth Armies merged. With "Readiness" its watchᵈ and mission, Fifth Army commands **U.S. Army ᵉerve (USAR)** units and supervises training and ᵈiness of **Army National Guard (ARNG)** units in its ate area of responsibility — Arkansas, Kansas, Louna, Missouri, Nebraska, New Mexico, Oklahoma ᵈ Texas. Together, the Guard and Reserve form the ᵉerve Components.

The **ARNG** is the only Army resource with dual staas federal and state military force (a unit is never ᵇoth at the same time). The governor is comᵃnder-in-chief of the Texas National and State ᵃrds, while the command function is exercised ough an adjutant general appointed by the governor ᵈ approved by both federal and state legislative auᵗᵉrities. Training is conducted under supervision of Fifth Army commander. Office of the Adjutant Genᵃl, state of Texas, is in Austin. Located there under ᵘrisdiction is the **Command and Control Headquar**, also headquarters of the **49th Armored Division**, one ᵢne major ARNG commands in the Fifth Army area ᵘordinate to the state adjutants general. See also Tex**ᵘard listing.

USAR units in the Fifth Army area fall within nine ᵘor commands, with the following headquartered in ᵃs: **75th Maneuver Area Command, Houston; 90th U.S. ᵘy Reserve Command**, San Antonio; **420th Engineer ᵍade, Bryan**; and **807th Medical Brigade, Seagoville**. ᵉr units range from small detachments to brigades.

Seven USAR schools, under jurisdiction of the 90th, are located in Austin, Beaumont, Dallas, Fort Worth, Houston, Lubbock and San Antonio (Fort Sam Houston).

A Readiness Group at Fort Sam Houston, one of three in the Army area, provides on-the-spot assistance to ARNG/USAR commanders, and reports directly to the Fifth Army commander. Groups provide combat, combat support, combat service support, and maintenance and administrative teams.

One of five continental Armies, Fifth Army is an executive agent for **U.S. Army Forces Command, Fort McPherson, Ga.**, for domestic emergency plans and operations and for specified civil-military programs within the Army area. It also has command responsibility over some 687 military personnel, 283 civilian employees (including 16 student aides) and about 2,900 full-time unit support personnel.

U.S. Army Reserve

The **U.S. Army Reserve (USAR)**, a vital ingredient in the total Army's national defense role, is well represented throughout Texas. Army reservists from all walks of civilian life devote, usually, one weekend a month and two weeks for annual training a year to make themselves and their units ready for mobilization should the need arise.

These citizen-soldiers of Texas are members of 188 separate units that are authorized over 16,532 people and are subordinate to four major Army Reserve commands. These commands are the **90th U.S. Army Reserve Command (ARCOM)**, Fort Sam Houston, San Antonio; **75th Maneuver Area Command (MAC)**, Houston; **420th Engineer Brigade**, Bryan; and the **807th Medical Brigade**, Seagoville. The above unit and personnel totals include some elements of the 95th Division (Training), head-quartered in Oklahoma City, OK.

Except for the 75th MAC, which is located entirely in Houston, these major commands have units in virtually all major metropolitan areas of the state. The Dallas-Fort Worth metroplex has one of the largest concentrations with 38 units stationed in the area.

There are 26 units in San Antonio and others in Amarillo, Austin, Beaumont-Port Arthur, Corpus Christi, El Paso, Houston, Laredo, Lubbock, Texarkana and Wichita Falls. Also, smaller communities such as Abilene, Alice, Bay City, Brownsville, Bryan, Harlingen, Huntsville, McAllen, Midland, Pleasanton, San Marcos, Sinton, Tomball, Tyler, Victoria, Waco and Yoakum are represented with units.

Texas units vary in size and missions, ranging from a 3-person military history detachment to combat engineer brigades to a 1,000-bed hospital unit. There are engineer, supply and service, medical, aviation, transportation, chemical, military police, maintenance, military intelligence, Army Security Agency and judge advocate general units, as well as Army Reserve schools.

Texas Guard

Tracing its history to early frontier days, the Texas Guard is composed of three separate, yet coordinated, entities: The **Texas Army National Guard**, the **Texas Air National Guard** and the **Texas State Guard.**

The Texas State Guard, an all-volunteer backup force, was originally created by the Texas Legislature in 1941. It became an active element of the state military forces in 1965 with a mission of reinforcing the National Guard in state emergencies, and of replacing National Guard units called into federal service. The Texas State Guard, which has a membership of approximately 1,670 personnel, also participates in local emergencies.

When the Guard was reorganized following World War II, the Texas Air National Guard was added. Texas Air National Guard units serve as augmentation units to major Air Force commands, including the Air Defense Command, the Tactical Air Command and the Strategic Air Command.

The Army Guard is available for either national or state emergencies and has been used extensively during hurricanes, tornadoes and floods. Army guardsmen are members of 194 units distributed in 120 cities of Texas.

When called into active federal service, National Guard units come within the chain of command of the Army, Air Force or theater in which they serve. When not in federal service, **Camp Mabry,** in Austin, is the main storage, maintenance and administrative headquarters for the Texas Guard.

The governor of Texas is commander-in-chief of the Texas National and State Guards. This command function is exercized through an **adjutant general** appointed by the governor and approved by both federal and state legislative authority.

The adjutant general is active administrative head of the Guard, and head of the Adjutant General's Department, a state agency, working in conjunction with the National Guard Bureau, a federal agency.

Fort Bliss

Located at El Paso in the vast expanse of West Texas, **Fort Bliss** is the home of the **U.S. Army Air Defense Artillery Center,** largest air defense center in the Free World. Its primary mission is to train individual missilemen and air defense artillery units, which also include foreign military students from as many as 25 countries at one time. Here at Fort Bliss are the key training, development and support activities for the Army's vital guided missile and air defense artillery programs.

Fort Bliss is home of the **U.S. Army Air Defense Artillery School,** the **11th Air Defense Artillery Brigade, U.S. Army Air Defense Board, Range Command, 3d Armored Cavalry Regiment** and the **70th Ordnance Battalion's 2d Platoon, 507th Medical Company (Air Ambulance).** As part of the **Military Assistance to Safety and Traffic (MAST),** the 507th provides emergency air transportation for residents of West Texas and New Mexico to medical facilities in El Paso.

Tenant activities include the **U.S. Army Sergeants Major Academy,** an element of the **U.S. Army Materiel Development and Readiness Command, Army Research Institute, U.S. Army Audit Agency, U.S. Army Special Security Detachment,** and a **Nuclear Weapons Support Detachment.** In addition, the **German Air Force Training Command** and the **German Air Force Air Defense Schoo** are on post through an agreement between the U.S Government and the Federal Republic of Germany.

Fort Bliss and its ranges comprise over 1,125,00 acres extending from Texas' Upper Rio Grande Valle into New Mexico — an area greater than that of Rhod Island. The post's almost 20,000 military personnel an some 8,000 civilian employees receive an annual payro of about $404 million.

Fort Hood

Fort Hood, home of the III Armored Mobile Corps covers 339 square miles in Central Texas just west o Killeen, midway between Waco and Austin.

Named for **Confederate General John Bell Hood,** th "Great Place," as the post is now known throughout th United States Army, is the largest armored installatio in the free world. Originally home of the **Army Tan Destroyer Center** during World War II, Fort Hood toda is the only post in the United States that accommodate two armored divisions and the **Apache Training Brigade**

In addition to the **1st Cavalry Division** and the **2n Armored Division,** the **6th Cavalry Brigade (Air Combat)** the **13th Support Command (Corps),** the **3rd Signal Br gade, 89th Military Police Brigade, 504th Military Intelli gence Brigade,** the **TRADOC Combined Arms Testing Ac tivity (TCATA),** the **Medical Activity (MEDDAC),** th **Dental Activity (DENTAC),** and various other tenant or ganizations are an integral part of Fort Hood. The pos supports more than 190,000 active and retired military their dependents and Department of the Army civi ians. It maintains more than 4,356 buildings, housin facilities for some 24,356 bachelor enlisted servic members and 5,237 family units.

Fort Hood's original site was purchased in 1941 an activated in 1942 as **South Camp Hood.** Since, **North Cam Hood** was established 17 miles north near Gatesville. I 1950, South Camp Hood became a permanent installa tion, redesignated **Fort Hood,** while North Camp Hoo became **North Fort Hood.**

To the west, **Gray Air Force Base** was built by the Ai Force in 1949, on **Killeen Base** which had been estab lished in 1947 as a function of the Defense Atomic Sup port Agency. Both were manned by Air Force personne until the Army assumed operation of Killeen Base i 1952. Fort Hood took charge of the airfield in 1963 an renamed it **Robert Gray Army Airfield.** In 1969, when th Department of Defense closed Killeen Base, it officiall became a subordinate element of Fort Hood, designat ed **West Fort Hood.**

Visitors are welcome at this open post, which boast two museums sponsored by the two divisions and ope daily. Fort Hood also hosts several events during th year, to include Fourth of July and Armed Forces Da celebrations, to which the public is cordially invited.

Fort Sam Houston

Headquarters Fort Sam Houston is the hub of suppor to many tenant commands and activities on the pos including a school that trains thousands of medical per sonnel for Army and other military services.

Fort Sam Houston hosts **Headquarters Fifth U.S Army, Headquarters U.S. Army Health Services Com mand,** (a major Department of the Army Command) the **Academy of Health Sciences, U.S. Army Dental Activ ity** and the **U.S. Army Area Dental Laboratory** and **Head quarters U.S Army Fifth Recruiting Brigade (Southwest).**

Other tenants include the San Antonio field office o the Defense Mapping Agency Topographic Center; th Defense Mapping Agency Inter-American Geodeti Survey; Fort Sam Houston National Cemetery; and th real estate projects office of the Fort Worth Distric Corps of Engineers.

National Guard and Reserve units and high schoo and college ROTC elements throughout South Texa are also among the functions supported by the pos commander.

As part of its support, the command manages Cam Bullis, a 28,000-acre sub-post 20 miles northwest. Nume ous government agencies, including FBI and Air Forc personnel, train there on a year-round basis.

Fort Sam Houston is the birthplace of military avi ation, and that legacy is carried on today by the post 507th Medical Company, a helicopter ambulance uni which transports patients in need of immediate medi cal care. The 507th spearheaded the Defense Depart ment's part in establishing **Military Assistance to Safet and Traffic (MAST)** in 1970. Working with civil authori ties, the pilots and medical aid personnel respond t

edical emergencies to evacuate patients much the
me as wounded soldiers were "MEDEVACed" in
etnam.

Fort Sam Houston is located in the center of the
untry's 10th largest city. With a 3-county population
1,231,700, San Antonio's community calendar is a
cord of year-round civic activities which involve the
st.

Health Services Command

The **U.S. Army Health Services Command (HSC)**,
eadquartered at Fort Sam Houston, San Antonio, op-
ates the largest military medical care system in the
e world.

As one of the Army's largest major commands, HSC
pports the day to day activity of seven Army medical
nters, 30 Army community hospitals, 41 dental activi-
s and laboratories, along with the Academy of Health
iences, the Army Environmental Hygiene Agency,
d three Army installations.

HSC's area of responsibility extends almost halfway
ound the globe and includes the continental United
ites, Alaska, Hawaii, Panama, Puerto Rico, Guam,
hnston Island and the Trust Territory of the Pacific.

HSC's veterinary role is even larger in scope. Com-
and veterinary personnel support, not only the Army,
t also the Navy, Air Force, Marine Corps, and Coast
ard at more than 500 Department of Defense activi-
s. Services include preventive medicine, food inspec-
n, medical research and development, and care of
vernment-owned animals.

The purpose of HSC is to provide health services to
pport the Army during peace and war.

During peacetime, HSC provides medical and den-
care to some 3.5 million beneficiaries. At the same
ne, personnel plan and prepare for their ultimate
ssion of providing medical support to the Army in
mbat.

HSC is also responsible for training of Army medi-
personnel, both officer and enlisted, through the
ademy of Health Sciences. The Academy also devel-
s medical technology and techniques for the battle-
ld of the future.

The command employs approximately 52,000 mili-
y and civilian personnel. Almost half of the work
ce is civilian.

Academy of Health Sciences

The **Academy of Health Sciences**, U.S. Army (AHS) is
major part of the U.S. Army Health Services Com-
nd, and is the largest health sciences school in the
stern world.

Approximately 40,000 resident students per year at-
d its facilities at Fort Sam Houston; the Medical
uipment and Optical School, Aurora, Colorado; the
ool of Aviation Medicine, Fort Rucker, Alabama;
d the Army Medical Department Student Detach-
nt consisting of about 400 officers at over 100 colleges
d universities across the United States, who are
dying to earn their masters or doctorate degrees.
ese physicians and dentists are serving in internship,
idency or fellowship programs with civilian medical
ilities. In addition, approximately 30,000 students
e correspondence courses through the academy
ch year.

Medical students from 22 foreign countries are
ined at the academy. The Allied Training Office at
academy also helps administer security assistance
ining for foreign military personnel at U.S. Army
dical facilities throughout the United States.

Qualified students who successfully complete se-
ted programs of study are eligible for award of col-
e credit from the Academy of Health Sciences. Of the
grams which are affiliated with civilian colleges and
versities, one program results in a bachelor of sci-
ce degree for warrant officers and three result in a
ster's degree for officer students. AHS maintains
duate-level affiliations with **Baylor** and **Tulane Uni-
sities, Texas Wesleyan College**, and undergraduate-
el affiliations with **Regis College** and the **University of
lahoma**.

Historically, the academy dates back to 1920, when
was founded as the **Medical Department Field School** at
rlisle Barracks, Pa. In 1946 it was moved to Fort Sam
uston, where it was known first as **Army Medical Ser-
e School** and then as **Medical Field Service School**. In
2 it moved to its present location at Fort Sam Hous-
and was redesignated Academy of Health Sciences,
. Army.

Brooke Army Medical Center

Brooke Army Medical Center (BAMC) at Fort Sam
Houston, is the successor to Brooke General Hospital
which was established as a post hospital in April 1881.
The second largest of the U.S. Army Health Services
Command's eight medical centers, it has a worldwide
mission of responsibility in every phase of medical education, patient care and medical research.

BAMC operates 692 hospital beds for definitive inpatient treatment, including all phases of surgical,
medical, neuropsychiatric and dental care. It also provides an emergency room, walk-in general medical/
surgical clinic, and clinics in all medical specialties.

Besides an annual inpatient load of 18,600 and outpatient visits of one million, the Center conducts a vast
postgraduate medical education program including internship and resident training in 22 medical specialties.
Graduate resident training is conducted in health care
administration, pharmacy, dietetics, specialized nursing and clinical pastoral education.

The **U.S. Army Institute of Surgical Research**, attached to BAMC for administrative and logistical support, has an international reputation for its outstanding
work in research and treatment of burns. Procedures
developed here are used throughout the world. Teams
flown to scenes of burn cases in the continental U.S. return
patients to the Institute for care in a matter of hours.

U.S. Army Area Dental Laboratory

The **U.S. Army Area Dental Laboratory** at Fort Sam
Houston is one of four throughout HSC providing fixed
and removable dental prosthetic appliances for eligible
beneficiaries in an 8-state area and Panama. It also
provides consultation service to directors of dental services at designated Army installations.

The **Fort Sam Houston Dental Activity (DENTAC)** was
organized in May 1978. The DENTAC operates three
dental clinics with 56 dental treatment rooms to support
over 12,000 active military personnel in the Fort Sam
Houston area. In addition to dental care, the DENTAC
at Fort Sam Houston offers three residency programs.

William Beaumont Army Medical Center

William Beaumont Army Medical Center in El Paso
symbolizes the latest developments in military medicine in the Southwest.

The striking glass and concrete tower standing at
the base of the Franklin Mountains serves the medical
needs of all military services in the tri-state area of
Arizona, New Mexico and West Texas.

The 12-story medical center was dedicated in 1972.
Encompassing over a half-million square feet, the
structure houses departments and clinics providing a
full range of treatment capabilities and physician training in virtually every medical specialty.

The Beaumont mission also includes operation of
the Army's first Residential Treatment Facility for alcoholism and a regional trauma unit. Other activities
include medical clinical investigations, alcohol and
drug abuse prevention and control programs, preventive medicine and mental health.

William Beaumont Army Medical Center is one of
eight major medical centers under the Army's Health
Services Command.

Darnall Army Community Hospital

Opened in 1965, **Darnall Army Hospital** (as it was originally named) at **Fort Hood** was the Army's first permanent 200-300 bed hospital and was known as one of
the most modern in the military. However, the $12-mil-
lion, fully equipped hospital was designed only to provide primary care to 40,000 people, and as Fort Hood
grew and the retiree population increased, the need for
expansion became evident. In 1979, a massive wrap-
around reconstruction and addition project began, and
five years later the hospital had doubled its size.

Darnall is the only Army Medical Department Activity
under the U.S. Army Health Services Command with a new-
born intensive care unit and nuclear medicine service.

Although not a medical center, Darnall does have
an emergency medicine residency program. Additionally, there are training programs in nursing anesthesi-
ology, nursing education training and occupational
specialty training.

Darnall presently supports 38,000 active duty, 50,000
family members, and 93,000 retired personnel and their
families.

Military Aviation

The birth of military aviation took place at San Antonio in 1910, although some earlier flights were made elsewhere. On Feb. 5, 1910, **Benjamin D. Foulois** arrived at Fort Sam Houston and was instructed to teach himself to fly. His first flight was made March 2, 1910. (See Page 164, 1986-87 Texas Almanac, for more details.)

In 1917, during World War I, San Antonio's **Kelly Field** was activated and became one of the world's largest air training fields. It remained open after the war and **Randolph Field** was activated in 1930. During World War II, thousands of pilots, navigators and bombardiers trained at Texas fields.

Present Activities

Air Force bases in Texas in 1985 included:

Bergstrom AFB—7 miles southeast of Austin. 67th Tactical Reconnaissance Wing (host): HQ, 12th Air Force, (Tactical Air Command); 924th Tactical Fighter Group, HQ, 10th Air Force (Reserve).

Brooks AFB—7 miles southeast of San Antonio. Medical research, education and training, (Air Force Systems Command), **Human Systems Division, Occupational and Environmental Lab, USAF School of Aerospace Medicine** and **Air Force Office of Medical Support, Air Force Drug Testing Lab** and **Air Force Human Resources Lab.**

Carswell AFB—7 miles west-northwest of Fort Worth. Bomber and tanker base, **(Strategic Air Command)**; 301 Tactical Fighter Wing (Air Force Reserve).

Dyess AFB—6 miles west-southwest of Abilene. Bomber and tanker base, Hq., 12th Air Division (Strategic Air Command); 96th Bomb Wing **(Strategic Air Command).**

Goodfellow AFB—2 miles southeast of San Angelo. USAF military intelligence personnel training, some DoD-wide cryptological training.

Kelly AFB—5 miles southwest of San Antonio. HQ, San Antonio Air Logistics Center (Air Force Logistics Command). USAF Service Information and News Center. HQ, Electronic Security Command; HQ, A. F. Commissary Service; A. F. Cryptologic Support Center; Joint Electronic Warfare Center; A. F. Electronic Warfare Center; 149th Tactical Fighter Group (Air National Guard); 433d Military Airlift Wing (A. F. Reserve); 1923rd Communications Group; 1827th Electronics Installation Squadron; Defense Reutilization and Marketing Office; Air Force Audit Agency Office.

Lackland AFB—8 miles west-southwest of San Antonio. Air Training Command base. Includes: Basic military training for airmen; precommissioning training for officers; technical training for security police and law-enforcement personnel, patrol dog handlers, instructors, recruiters and social action/drug abuse counselors. Also site of Wilford Hall Medical Center and Defense Language Institute-English Language Center.

Laughlin AFB—6 miles east of Del Rio. Undergraduate pilot training (Air Training Command).

Randolph AFB—20 miles east-northeast of San Antonio. HQ, Air Training Command; HQ Joint Military Medical Command, San Antonio; Instructor Pilot Training, Air Force Military Personnel Center; HQ Air Force Management Engineering Agency; HQ USAF Recruiting Service.

Reese AFB—6 miles west of Lubbock. Undergraduate pilot training (Air Training Command).

Sheppard AFB—4 miles north of Wichita Falls. Technical training center for medical personnel, jet aircraft mechanics and helicopter engine mechanics, accounting and finance specialist training; School of Health Care Sciences; Euro-Nato Joint Jet Pilot Training.

There is also the Tactical Airlift Wing (ANG) at Dallas Naval Air Station that flies the C-130 and the 147th Fighter Interceptor Group (ANG) at Ellington ANGB.

The Air Force Reserve in Texas

The major **U.S. Air Force Reserve** units in Texas are located in San Antonio, Austin and Fort Worth. The units are HQ 10th Air Force (R), Bergstrom AFB (Austin), 433d Military Airlift Wing, Kelly AFB (San Antonio) and the 301st Tactical Fighter Wing, Carswell AFB (Fort Worth). The 924th Tactical Fighter Group is located at Bergstrom AFB.

HQ 10th Air Force (R) is an administrative organization supervising six subordinate wings throughout the United States. The 433d's mission aircraft is the C-5. The 924th flies the F-4. Their primary mission is to maintain a constant state of readiness to be able to augment the tactical forces in the active duty Air Force

on a worldwide basis. The 301st mission aircraft is the F-4.

The Air Force Reserve plays a vital role in helping the active duty Air Force accomplish its mission. With better equipment, more front-line missions and professional people, the Air Force Reserve is a vital part of our nation's defense.

Civil Air Patrol

The Civil Air Patrol (CAP) is a volunteer civilian auxiliary of the Air Force. Southwest Regional headquarters, located at Dallas Naval Air Station, Building 1239, directs CAP activities in Texas, Arizona, Arkansas, Louisiana, Oklahoma and New Mexico. There are 2,918 members of the Texas Wing of the CAP, with headquarters at Bergstrom AFB. Its membership includes 1,103 cadet members (ages 13 to 18) and 1,815 senior members, over 18, from many Texas communities. Mailing address of the Texas Wing is Bldg. 207, Bergstrom AFB, Texas 78743.

Red River Army Depot

Red River Army Depot at Texarkana was activated in August 1941 following a government purchase of 116 farms and ranches, plus wooded acreage. Occupying 56 square miles, it has approximately 1,400 buildings and structures.

Red River's primary mission is to receive, store, recondition and issue all types Army ordnance general supplies and ammunition. It is a major Army maintenance point for rebuilding combat and general purpose vehicles and other types Army ordnance. It has a limited number of military personnel and about 5,600 Civil Service employees.

Corpus Christi Army Depot

Corpus Christi Army Depot (CCAD), activated in 1961, on the **Corpus Christi Naval Air Station**, covers 184 acres, mostly under roof. The Army's only complete overhaul and repair facility for helicopters, the depot repairs UH-1 Huey, AH-Cobra, UH-60 Black Hawk, CH 47D Chinook and other helicopters and components. CCAD also overhauls other U.S. armed forces helicopters for use worldwide.

About 130 job skills in the wage grade area and 80 in the general classification series are used by the approximately 4,100 civilians and 40 assigned military. It is the largest industrial employer in South Texas, with an annual budget of about $277.8 million and an annual payroll of about $122.06 million.

U.S. Navy and Naval Reserve

The most recent figures available show that the U.S. Navy accounted for over $3 billion flowing into the Texas economy in fiscal year 1985. There are 7,482 active-duty military and 2,230 civilian employees stationed throughout the state, but concentrated in four principal locations: Corpus Christi, Kingsville, Beeville and Dallas.

The Chief of Naval Air Training Staff and a major portion of the pilot training pipeline are located at Naval Air Station Corpus Christi. Approximately 400 pilots are trained each year in one of the final phases of carrier flight training. Additional pilot training facilities are found at Naval Air Stations Kingsville and Chase Field (Beeville).

An important facet of the "Navy presence" in Texas as are the approximately 7,400 drilling reservists who serve throughout the state. The largest reserve training site is Naval Air Station Dallas, which is responsible for three reserve aircraft squadrons. VF-201 and VF-202, the two fighter squadrons based in Dallas, operate the F-14 Tomcat fighter aircraft. VR-59, the reserve logistics squadron, transports troops and supplies as part of its mission.

The remainder of the reservists perform their Navy duties at one of 12 Navy and Marine Corps Reserve Centers, the Readiness Center in Houston, or one of three Naval Reserve Facilities located in the major cities throughout the state.

The Navy is also part of the educational opportunities at three major universities in Texas. Naval Reserve Officer Training Corps (NROTC) units are located at the University of Texas at Austin, Rice University and Prairie View A&M. The Merchant Marine and State Maritime Academy in Galveston also has a Navy-sponsored naval science program.

The city of Corpus Christi has begun construction on a naval port facility for the homeporting of a battleship, training carrier and six escort ships. Pending re ease of federal funds, the facility will be completed and operational by 1990. Galveston has also been selected as a Gulf Coast homeport site and is scheduled to construct facilities to support three minesweepers and two rigates.

Marine Corps Reserve

Marine Corps Reserve units are located at Abilene, Amarillo, Austin, Corpus Christi, Dallas (including a Marine Aircraft Group headquarters at NAS, Dallas), El Paso, Galveston, Harlingen, Houston, Lubbock, San Antonio, Texarkana and Waco.

Army and Air Force Exchange Service

Dallas is headquarters for the worldwide **Army and Air Force Exchange Service,** which directs both domestic and overseas operations of the military retail-food-service organization. The Exchange Service is a self-sustaining organization, with minimal tax-dollar support, which employs nearly 70,000 people, including ,400 in Texas.

Approximately 2,400 employees work in the Dallas headquarters, which had operating expenses of $63.7 million in 1986. Through regional offices, the Exchange Service operates Exchange outlets in Texas at Bergstrom AFB (Austin), Fort Bliss (El Paso), Brooks AFB San Antonio), Carswell AFB (Fort Worth), Dyess AFB Abilene), Goodfellow AFB (San Angelo), Fort Hood Killeen), Fort Sam Houston (San Antonio), Kelly AFB San Antonio), Lackland AFB (San Antonio), Laughlin AFB (Del Rio), Randolph AFB (Universal City), Reese AFB (Lubbock) and Sheppard AFB (Wichita Falls). In 986, $11.6 million in exchange funds was expended in exas for AAFES construction projects, while more nan $779 million was spent in Texas for procurement of oods and services.

The Exchange Service operates nearly 16,000 retail, ood, personal services and automotive activities, novie theaters and vending outlets in the United States and foreign areas. These activities generated $5.2 billion in sales during 1986. Earnings from those sales are contributed to the Army and Air Force morale and welfare programs worldwide. AAFES supplies more than 7 million servicemen and women, dependents and retired military personnel with a variety of services and merchandise.

The Exchange Service headquarters moved from New York to Dallas in January, 1967. Employees moved into the $3.5 million office building in Southwest Oak Cliff in late 1967.

U.S. Expenditures in Texas

Below are federal expenditures in Texas for fiscal year 1986, as furnished by the U.S. Bureau of the Census for the Office of Management and Budget. Direct federal expenditures or obligations amounted to $47,581,849,000. In addition, $1,091,112,000 was spent for direct loans and $24,118,377,000 for guaranteed loans and insurance. See also the section on Counties and Cities for federal expenditures by counties.

Item	Expenditure (add 000)
TOTAL EXPENDITURES	$72,791,338
Direct federal expenditures or obligations:	
Total direct expenditures:	
Total expenditures	47,581,849
Defense Department	16,903,309
All other agencies	30,678,540
Grant awards	5,750,357
Salaries and wages:	
Total	7,523,805
Defense Department	4,275,550
Direct payment for individuals:	
Total	20,472,803
Retirement and disability	14,838,894
All other	5,633,909
Procurement contract awards:	
Total	12,692,297
Defense Department	10,833,955
Other federal expenditures or obligations . .	1,142,587
Other federal assistance:	
Direct loans	1,091,112
Guaranteed loans and insurance	24,118,377

Agriculture

Agriculture In Texas

Agribusiness, the combined phases of food and fiber production, processing, transporting and marketing, is a leading Texas industry. Most of the following discussion is devoted to the phase of production on farms and ranches.

Information was provided by Agricultural Extension Service specialists, Texas and U.S. Departments of Agriculture and U.S. Department of Commerce sources and was coordinated by Carl G. Anderson, Extension Marketing Economist, Texas A&M University. All references are to Texas unless otherwise specified.

Agriculture is one of the most important industries in Texas. Many businesses, financial institutions and individuals are involved in providing supplies, credit and services to farmers and ranchers and in processing and marketing agricultural commodities.

Including all its agribusiness phases, agriculture added about $33 billion to the economic activity of the state in 1986. The estimated value of farm assets in Texas — the land, buildings, livestock, machinery, crops, inventory on farms, household goods and farm financial assets — totaled approximately $93 billion in 1986.

Texas agriculture is a strong industry. Receipts from farm and ranch marketings in 1986 were estimated at $9.3 billion. Ten years earlier this figure was $6.3 billion.

The potential for further growth is great. With the increasing demand for food and fiber throughout the world, and because of the importance of agricultural exports to this nation's trade balance, agriculture in Texas is destined to play an even greater role in the future.

Educational and research efforts in the Texas A&M University System are directed toward developing the state's agricultural industry to its fullest potential. The goal is to capitalize on natural advantages that agriculture has in Texas because of the relatively warm climate, productive soils and availability of excellent export and transportation facilities.

The number and nature of Texas farms have changed. The number of farms in Texas has decreased from 418,000 in 1940 to 160,000 in 1986, with an average size of 838 acres. Average value of farm assets, including land and buildings, has increased from $6,196 in 1940 to $463,000 in 1986.

Mechanization of farming continues as new and larger machines replace manpower. Though equipment prices are high, machine power is cheaper than manpower. Tractors, mechanical harvesters and numerous cropping machines have virtually eliminated menial tasks that for many years were traditional to farming.

Revolutionary agricultural chemicals have appeared along with improved plants and animals and methods of handling them. Hazards of farming and ranching have been reduced by better use of weather information, machinery and other improvements; but

Balance Sheet, Texas Farms and Ranches Jan. 1, 1977-85

Source: Economic Indicators of the Farm Sector: State Income and Balance Sheet Statistics, 1985, USDA, ERS.

Table below shows the financial status of Texas farms and ranches as of Jan. 1 of the years 1977 through 1985.

Item	1977	1978	1979	1980	1981	1982	1983	1984	§1985
				— Million dollars —					
Physical Assets:									
Real estate	41,651	46,843	53,615	64,397	73,951	74,528	81,122	89,194	73,738
Nonreal estate:									
Livestock and poultry	2,839	2,866	5,039	5,221	4,646	5,121	4,958	4,897	4,723
Machinery and motor vehicles.	4,091	4,361	4,821	5,878	6,250	6,256	6,216	5,663	5,767
*Crops stored on and off farms	804	1,267	1,225	1,360	1,499	1,805	1,334	1,106	1,494
Household equipment and furnishings	758	764	1,003	1,157	1,430	1,661	1,938	2,601	2,398
Financial assets:									
Deposits and currency	748	949	1,560	1,631	1,724	1,804	1,924	2,025	2,234
U.S. savings bonds	142	226	462	420	407	396	414	409	45
Investments in co-ops	864	981	1,157	1,380	1,481	1,596	1,712	1,861	1,824
TOTAL ASSETS	51,897	58,257	68,882	81,444	91,388	93,167	99,618	107,756	92,646
Liabilities:									
†Real estate debt	4,086	4,276	4,480	5,492	5,795	6,051	6,357	6,483	6,48
Nonreal estate debt:									
†Excluding CCC loans	3,325	3,479	4,643	5,713	6,354	6,383	6,536	6,924	6,66
‡Commodity Credit Corporation loans	61	431	216	66	428	1,147	799	454	97
TOTAL LIABILITIES	7,472	8,186	9,339	11,271	12,577	13,581	13,692	13,861	14,09
Owners' equities	44,425	50,071	59,543	70,173	78,811	79,586	85,926	93,895	78,55
TOTAL CLAIMS	51,897	58,257	68,882	81,444	91,388	93,167	99,618	107,756	92,64

*Includes all crops held on farms and those crops stored off farms by farmers as security for CCC loans.

†Includes debt owed to institutional lenders and to noninstitutional or miscellaneous lenders.

‡Nonrecourse CCC loans secured by crops owned by farmers. These crops are included as assets in this balance sheet.

§Preliminary.

rising costs, labor problems and escalating energy costs have added to the concerns of farmers and ranchers.

Among the major changes in Texas agriculture since World War II are these:

• Farms are fewer, larger, specialized, more expensive to own and operate, but more productive.

• Irrigation is a major factor in crop production.

• Crops and livestock have changed in production areas as in the concentration of cotton on the High Plains and livestock increases in central and eastern Texas.

• Pest and disease control methods are greatly improved. Herbicides are relied upon for weed control.

• Ranchmen and farmers are better educated and informed, more science- and business-oriented.

• Feedlot finishing, commercial broiler production, artificial insemination, improved pastures and brush control, reduced feed requirements and other changes have greatly increased livestock and poultry efficiency.

• Cooperation among farmers in marketing, promotion and other fields has increased.

• Agricultural producers are increasingly dependent on off-the-farm services to supply production inputs such as feeds, chemicals, credit and other essentials.

Agribusiness

Texas farmers and ranchers have developed a dependence upon agribusiness. With many producers specializing in the production of certain crops and livestock, they look beyond the farm and ranch for supplies and services. On the input side, they rely on suppliers of production needs and services and on the output side they need assemblers, processors and distributors.

Since 1940, the proportion of Texans whose livelihood is linked to agriculture has changed greatly.

In 1940, about 23 percent of Texans were producers on farms and ranches, and about 17 percent were suppliers or were engaged in assembly, processing and distribution of agricultural products. The agribusiness alignment in 1986 was less than 2.0 percent on farms and ranches with 20 to 25 percent of the population providing production or marketing supplies and services. The impact of agriculture on the economy of Texas exceeds $33 billion annually.

Cash Receipts

Farm and ranch cash receipts in 1985 totaled $9.3 billion. With estimates of $848.1 million for government payments, $1.1 billion of non-money income and $863.3 million of other farm income are included, realized gross farm income totaled $12.1 billion. With farm production expenses of $9.6 billion and a $2.3 million decrease in farm inventories from the year before, net income totaled $2,486.2 million or $14,046 per farm.

Farm and Ranch Assets

Farm and ranch assets totaled $92.6 billion on Jan. 1, 1986. This was a decrease of 13.9 percent from a year earlier. Value of real estate accounted for most of the decrease. Liabilities totaled $14.1 billion, up 1.7 percent from the previous year. The value of real estate amounted to $73.7 billion, or 80 percent of total assets.

Percent of Income From Products

Livestock and livestock products accounted for 58.5 percent of the cash receipts from farm marketings in 1985 with the remaining 41.5 percent from crops.

From livestock marketings, meat animals accounted for 45.7 percent of total receipts received by farmers and ranchers in 1985. Most of these receipts were from cattle and calf sales. Dairy products made up 5.9 percent of receipts, poultry and eggs 5.7 percent and other livestock 1.2 percent.

From crop receipts, cotton accounted for 10.7 percent, feed crops 11.2 percent, food grains 7.8 percent, vegetables 4.1 percent, oil crops 2.0 percent, fruits and nuts .07 percent, greenhouse/nursery products 4.3 percent, oil crops 1.7 percent, fruit and nuts .6 percent, and other crops 1 percent.

Texas' Rank Among States

Measured by cash receipts for farm and ranch marketings, Texas ranked second in 1985, behind California and ahead of Iowa.

Texas normally leads all other states in numbers of farms and ranches and farm and ranch land, cattle slaughtered, cattle on feed, calf births, sheep and lambs slaughtered, goats, cash receipts from livestock marketings, cattle and calves, beef cows, sheep and lambs, wool production, mohair production and exports of lard and tallow. The state also usually leads in production of cotton, grain sorghum, watermelons and spinach.

A significant change in ranking for Texas in recent times has been in the number of cattle in feedlots. Texas now ranks ahead of Nebraska, Kansas, Colorado and Iowa as the states with the most cattle on feed in commercial feedlots. Nebraska ranked second to Texas in 1985 and Kansas third.

Texas Agricultural Exports

The value of Texas' share of agricultural exports in fiscal year 1985 was $2.031 billion. Cotton accounted for $562.1 million of the exports; feed grains, $384.9 million; wheat and flour, $275.9 million; rice, $110.4 million; tallow and lard, $104.6 million; cottonseed oil, $46.1 million; hides and skins, $202.3 million; meats and meat products, $160.9 million; fruits, $4.8 million; peanuts, $19.9 million; soybeans, $33.7 million; vegetables, $13.7 million; poultry products, $18.6 million; and miscellaneous and other products, $85.1 million.

Texas exports of $2.031 billion of farm and ranch products compares with $2.576 billion in 1984.

Hunting

The management of wildlife as an economic enterprise through leasing for hunting makes a significant contribution to the economy of many counties. Leasing the right of ingress on a farm or ranch for the purpose of hunting is the service marketed. After the leasing, the consumer — the hunter — goes onto the land to seek the harvest of the wildlife commodity. Hunting lease income to farmers and ranchers in 1986 was an estimated $146 million.

The demand for hunting opportunities is growing while the land capable of producing huntable wildlife is decreasing. As a result, farmers and ranchers are placing more emphasis on wildlife management practices to help meet requests for hunting leases.

Irrigation

Texas farmers irrigated approximately 6 million acres of land in 1986. Although some irrigation is practiced in nearly every county of the state, about 68 percent of the total irrigated acreage is in the High Plains of Northwest Texas. Other concentrated areas of irrigation are the Gulf Coast rice-producing area, the Lower Rio Grande Valley, the Winter Garden district of South Texas, the Trans-Pecos area of West Texas and the peanut producing area in North Central Texas centered around Erath, Eastland and Comanche counties. Sprinkler irrigation was used on about 40 percent of the total irrigated acreage, with surface irrigation methods — primarily furrow, border and contour check methods — being used on the remaining 60 percent of the irrigated areas.

Drip, or trickle, irrigation has attracted much attention in recent years for use on tree crops such as citrus, pecans, avocados, peaches and apples. The use

Farm Labor

Source: U.S. Department of Agriculture

Year	*Family Worker Avg. No.	†Hired Worker Avg. No.	‡Total Worker Avg. No.
1955.	323,000	168,000	491,000
1970.	190,000	92,000	282,000
1977.	166,000	83,000	249,000
1978.	155,000	82,000	237,000
1979.	152,000	78,000	230,000
1980.	146,000	77,000	223,000
§1981	154,000	72,500	226,500
1982.	149,000	70,000	219,000
1983.	120,000	85,000	205,000
§§1984	137,500	77,000	214,500
1985.	192,250	82,250	274,500
§§§1986	200,500	70,000	270,500

*Farm operators or members of their families working 15 hours or more, without pay.

†Persons working one or more hours for pay.

‡Persons employed during the last full calendar week ending at least one day before end of month.

§First and second quarters only; survey discontinued thereafter.

§§Third and fourth quarters only, first and second quarter estimates not available.

§§§First and second quarters only, third and fourth quarter estimates not available.

of **drip irrigation** is increasing, with present drip irrigated acreage estimated around 30,000 acres.

The use of sprinkler irrigation is also in an upward trend, increasing to 40 percent in 1986, from about 19 percent in 1969.

Approximately 70 percent of the state's irrigated acreage is supplied with water pumped from wells. Surface water sources supply the remaining area. Declining groundwater levels in several of the major aquifers is a serious problem. As the water level declines, well yields decrease and pumping costs increase. Decreasing groundwater supplies and higher real prices have contributed to decreasing irrigated acreage. However, recent studies of the availability of water in the Ogallala formation, which supplies water for most of the High Plains irrigation, indicate that a viable irrigated agriculture can be expected to continue in the High Plains area much longer than some predictions in the past have indicated.

Rapidly rising fuel costs pose another serious problem for Texas irrigation farmers. More than half of the irrigation pumps in the state are driven with power units which use natural gas as a fuel. Natural gas prices paid by farmers have increased dramatically in recent years. The cost of other fuels used for pumping irrigation water, primarily electricity and diesel, has also increased significantly. Since fuel costs are a major part of the cost of irrigation water, farmers are facing serious management decisions in the use of irrigation for crop production.

Irrigation is an important factor in the productivity of Texas agriculture. The value of crop production from irrigated acreage is approximately 50 to 60 percent of the total value of all crop production, although only about 30 percent of the state's total harvested cropland acreage is irrigated.

Principal Crops

In most years the value of crop production in Texas is almost half of the total value of the state's agricultural output. Cash receipts from farm sales of crops is less because some grain and roughage is fed to livestock on farms where produced.

In 1985, the **leading Texas counties** in cash receipts from crops were Hidalgo, Gaines, Hale, Wharton and Parmer. Receipts from all Texas crops totaled $3.8 billion in 1985.

Cotton accounted for 23 percent of the total crop in 1985 and **wheat** for 15 percent. **Grain sorghum, corn, rice,** cottonseed, peanuts, hay, vegetables and soybeans are other important cash crops.

Cotton

Cotton has been a major crop in Texas for more than a century. Since 1880, Texas has led all states in cotton production, and today the annual Texas cotton harvest amounts to about one-third of total production in the United States. The annual cotton crop has averaged 3.5 million bales since 1980.

Total **value of lint cotton** produced in Texas in 1986 was $566,130,000. Because of low prices and poor yields, the total decreased from $998,380,000 in 1985. **Cottonseed** value was $78,536,000 in 1986, making the total value of crop $644,660,000. In 1985, the cottonseed value was $102,156,000 and the total crop value was $1,100,536,000.

Upland cotton was harvested from 3.45 million acres in 1986, and **American Pima** from 26,200 acres, for a total of 3.476 million acres. Cotton acreage harvested in 1985 totaled 4.669 million. Production amounted to 2.54 million bales in 1986 and 3.945 million in 1985. Counties leading in production of upland cotton are **Gaines, Cameron, Lubbock, Hidalgo** and **Lynn.**

Cotton is the raw material for processing operations at gins, oil mills, compresses and a small number of textile mills in Texas.

Cotton in Texas is machine harvested. Growers in 1985 used **stripper harvesters** to gather 85 percent of the crop and **spindle pickers** to harvest the remaining 15 percent. Field storage of harvested seed cotton is gaining in popularity as gins decline in number. In 1985, 60 percent of the cotton was ginned from modules and 40 percent from trailers. Much of the Texas cotton crop is exported. Japan and South Korea are major buyers.

The state's major cotton-producing areas are tied together by an electronic marketing system. This system is a computer network that links producers through terminals that are usually located at gins to a relatively large number of buyers. The network provides farmers with a centralized market that allows many sellers and buyers to trade with each other on a regular basis.

The first high volume instrument cotton-classing office in the nation was opened at Lamesa in Dawson County in 1980.

Grain Sorghum

Grain sorghum usually ranks second in dollar value. Much of the grain is exported, as well as being used in livestock and poultry feed throughout the state.

In 1986, 3.75 million acres of grain sorghum were harvested, yielding an average of 3,192 pounds per acre, for a total production of 119,700,000 cwt. It was valued at $2.86 per cwt., a total value of $342 million. In

Texas' Export Shares of Agricultural Commodities, 1981-86

Source: Foreign Agricultural Trade of the U.S.

Commodity*	1982	1983	1984	1985	1985 Texas Share of U.S. Exports Percent
	Million Dollars				
Rice	214.4	156.4	153.4	110.4	16.3
Cotton	783.0	387.7	746.5	562.1	28.6
Tallow & Lard	114.0	91.0	112.2	104.6	17.2
Hides & Skins	133.3	129.5	188.2	202.3	15.3
Meats other than Poultry	139.7	122.7	136.4	160.9	13.9
Feed Grains	367.1	369.9	534.5	384.9	5.1
Poultry Products	30.4	22.0	19.5	18.6	5.7
Fruits	39.2	36.1	15.5	4.8	.4
Vegetables	16.9	15.5	17.2	13.7	1.5
Wheat & Flour	540.1	327.1	442.6	275.9	6.1
Soybeans	44.5	81.7	43.6	33.7	.6
Cottonseed Oil	91.0	31.5	36.6	46.1	30.4
Peanuts	23.3	18.5	23.0	19.9	8.4
Nuts	1.7	.9	1.4	.5	.1
†Dairy Products	6.2	6.8	8.6	7.5	1.8
All Other	91.9	101.3	96.4	85.1	—
TOTAL	2,636.7	1,898.6	2,575.6	2,031.0	5.7

*Commodity and related preparations.

†For 1981 and 1982 the USDA changed the variable used to determine export share of dairy products to state fluid milk production.

*Realized Gross Income and Net Income From Farming, Texas, 1958-1985

Year	**Realized Gross Farm Income	Farm Production Expenses	Net Change In Farm Inventories	***Total Net Farm Income	***Total Net Income Per Farm
	Million Dollars				Dollars
1958	$2,666.1	$1,637.5	$17.7	$1,046.3	$3,948.0
1974	6,178.0	5,057.0	−80.3	1,040.7	4,980.0
1975	6,497.4	5,180.3	−106.2	1,210.9	6,407.0
1976	7,029.8	5,926.0	124.8	1,103.8	5,902.7
§1977	7,343.3	6,257.5	−38.4	1,085.8	5,837.6
1978	8,716.4	7,510.7	149.3	1,205.7	6,517.3
1979	11,057.5	9,245.7	−95.6	1,811.7	9,688.2
1980	9,611.4	9,081.1	−542.5	530.4	2,806.3
1981	11,545.7	9,564.7	699.9	1,981.0	10,481.5
1982	11,372.7	9,581.5	−124.3	1,791.2	9,527.7
1983	11,119.0	9,323.0	−563.3	1,796.0	9,604.3
1984	11,983.8	9,923.1	311.5	2,060.7	11,019.8
1985	12,093.1	9,606.9	−2.3	2,486.2	14,046.3

*Details for items may not add to totals because of rounding. Series revised, September, 1981.

**Cash receipts from farm marketings, government payments, value of home consumption and gross rental value of farm dwellings.

***Farm income of farm operators.

§Starting in 1977, farms with production of $1,000 or more used to figure income.

Value of Texas Cotton and Cottonseed

The following table was compiled by Texas Cottonseed Crushers Association from their historical records and reports of U.S. Department of Commerce and Department of Agriculture.

(All Figures in Thousands)

Growth Year	Cotton Production (Bales)	Cotton Value	Cottonseed Production Tons	Cottonseed Value
1968	3,522	$ 344,142	1,490	$ 75,245
1969	2,859	267,207	1,190	49,742
1970	3,210	332,082	1,242	68,310
*1971	2,614	336,666	1,050	59,325
1972	4,277	476,231	1,642	79,850
1973	4,699	1,041,393	1,788	167,178
1974	2,487	420,479	981	116,739
1975	2,393	527,966	909	81,628
1976	3,314	981,970	1,271	124,558
1977	5,500	1,318,447	2,089	133,696
1978	3,819	989,441	1,483	166,096
1979	5,539	1,486,010	2,264	262,624

(All Figures in Thousands)

Growth Year	Cotton Production (Bales)	Cotton Value	Cottonseed Production Tons	Cottonseed Value
1980	3,345	$1,104,576	1,361	$ 161,959
1981	5,663	1,268,863	2,438	207,230
1982	2,723	676,011	1,122	90,882
1983	2,412	694,032	1,002	162,324
1984	3,710	940,234	1,563	157,863
1985	3,945	998,380	1,635	102,156
1986	2,542	566,130	1,061	78,536

*Beginning in 1971, basis for cotton prices was changed from 500 pound gross weight to 480 pound net weight bale; to compute comparable prices for previous years multiply price times 1.04167.

1985, 4.10 million acres were harvested, yielding 3,304 pounds per acre, or 135,464,000 cwt. It was valued at $575,722,000.

Although grown to some extent in all counties where crops are important, the largest concentrations are in the High Plains, Rolling Plains, Blackland Prairie, Grand Prairie, Coastal Prairie, Coastal Bend, Rio Grande Plain and Lower Rio Grande Valley areas. Counties leading in production are **Nueces, Hidalgo, Wharton, Hansford, Moore** and **Deaf Smith.**

Research to develop high-yielding hybrids resistant to diseases and insect damage continues. A leader in this development, **J. Roy Quinby,** is principal author of a history of grain sorghums that appeared in the 1972-73 edition of the Texas Almanac.

Rice

Rice, which is grown in 20 counties on the Coast Prairie of Texas, ranked third in value among Texas crops for a number of years. However, in recent years, cotton, grain sorghum, wheat and corn have outranked rice.

Farms are highly mechanized, producing rice through irrigation and using airplanes for much of the

Heritage Program Links Family, Land

Texas farm and ranch families that have worked and cared for their land for more than a century are recognized and honored through the Texas Department of Agriculture's Family Land Heritage Program.

Initiated in 1974, the program has enrolled 1,900 properties around the state, some of which have been in the same families since the Spanish land grants of the early 1700s. Families honored by the program are of many ethnic backgrounds — German, Czechoslovakian, Italian, black, Hispanic, as well as others.

The oldest property listed in the Family Land Heritage Registry is the Norlecitas Ranch near Hebbronville in South Texas. The ranch was founded in 1740 by Simon de Hinojosa under the authority of King Philip V of Spain.

To be eligible for listing in the registry, the land must meet the following criteria:

● It must have been continuously owned and operated by the same family for 100 years or more.

● The land must be currently productive and either comprise 10 acres or more with sales of $50 or more a year or contain less than 10 acres with sales of at least $250 a year.

● The owners must live in Texas and either live on and work the land or, if living off the historic property, they must actively manage and direct the everyday operation of the farm or ranch.

● The land must never have been rented to someone outside the family, unless the family continued to control and work at least 10 acres of it with sales of at least $50 a year.

planting, fertilizing and application of insecticides and herbicides.

Texas farmers grow long- and medium-grain rice only. The Texas rice industry, which has grown from 110 acres in 1850 to a high of 642,000 in 1954, has been marked by significant yield increases and improved varieties. Record production was in 1981, with 27,239,000 hundredweights harvested. Highest yield was 6,250 pounds per acre in 1986.

Several different types of rice-milling procedures are in use today. The simplest and oldest method produces a product known as **regular milled white rice,** the most prevalent on the market today.

Rice is more valuable if the grains are not broken. In many cases, additional vitamins are added to the grains to produce what is called "enriched rice."

Another process may be used in rice milling to produce a product called **parboiled rice.** After cooking, parboiled rice tends to be fluffy, more separate and plump.

Still another type of rice is **precooked rice,** which is actually milled rice that, after milling, has been cooked. Then the moisture is removed through dehydration process. Precooked rice requires a minimum of preparation time since it needs merely to have the moisture restored to it.

The United States produces only a small part of the world's total rice, but it is one of the leading exporters. American rice is popular abroad and is exported to more than 100 foreign countries.

Rice production was 18,063,000 cwt. in 1986 on 289,000 harvested acres. In 1985, the crop totaled 18,071,000 cwt. on 329,000 acres valued at $133,364,000 or an average of $7.38 per cwt.

Wheat

Wheat for grain is one of the state's most valuable cash crops, usually exceeded in value only by grain sorghum. Wheat pastures also provide considerable winter forage for cattle, which is reflected in value of livestock produced.

Texas wheat growers planted 8,100,000 acres in 1986 and harvested grain from 4,800,000 acres. The yield was 25 bushels per acre for a total production of 120,000,000 bushels valued at $276,000,000. In 1985, farmers planted 8,100,000 acres of wheat and harvested 5,800,000 acres. With a yield of 32 bushels per acre, the 187,200,000 bushels produced were valued at $585,936,000.

Leading wheat-producing counties based on acreage planted are Ochiltree, Deaf Smith, Randall, Dallam, Sherman and Carson. The leading counties, based on total bushels harvested, are as follows: **Deaf Smith, Ochiltree, Hansford, Dallam** and **Parmer.**

Wheat was first grown commercially in Texas near Sherman about 1833. The acreage expanded greatly in North Central Texas after 1850 because of rapid settlement of the state and introduction of the well-adapted Mediterranean strain of wheat. A major family flour industry developed in the Fort Worth-Dallas-Sherman area between 1875 and 1900. Now about half of the state acreage is planted on the High Plains and about a third of this is irrigated. Most of the Texas wheat acreage is of the hard red winter class. Because of the recent development of varieties with improved disease resistance and the use of wheat for winter pasture, there has been a sizable expansion of acreage in Central and South Texas.

Most of all wheat harvested for grain is used in some phase of the milling industry. The better quality hard red winter wheat is used in the production of commercial bakery flour. Lower grades and varieties of soft red winter wheat are used in family flours. By-products of milled wheat are used for feed.

Corn

Interest in corn production throughout the state increased during the 1970s. Once the principal grain crop, corn acreage declined as plantings of grain sorghum increased. Only 500,000 acres were being harvested annually in the mid-1970s when development of new hybrids occurred.

Harvested acreage was 1,330,000 acres in 1986 and 1,490,000 acres in 1985. Yields for the corresponding years were 105 and 112 bushels per acre, respectively.

Most of the acreage and yield increase has occurred in the irrigated High Plains. In recent years, corn has ranked fourth in value among the state's crops. It was valued at $275,576,000 in 1986 and $398,948,000 in 1985.

The leading counties in production for 1985 were Parmer, Castro, Hale, Lamb, Wharton and Dallam.

Rye

Rye is grown mainly on the Northern and Southern High Plains, the Northern Low Plains, Cross Timbers, Blacklands and East Texas areas. Minor acreages are seeded in South Central Texas, the Edwards Plateau and the Upper Coast. Rye is grown primarily as a cover crop and for grazing during the fall, winter and early spring.

In 1986, 100,000 acres of rye were planted, with 10,000 acres harvested, yielding 19 bushels per acre. The crop value was estimated at $380,000 or $2 a bushel. In 1985, 400,000 bushels were harvested from 20,000 acres with a value of $860,000.

Some of the leading rye-producing counties are Eastland, Houston, Henderson, Comanche, Hall and Navarro.

Oats

Oats are grown extensively in Texas for winter pasture, hay, silage, greenchop feeding, and some acreage is harvested for grain.

Texas farmers planted 1,000,000 acres of oats in 1986 and harvested 200,000 acres. The value was $14,700,000, or $1.75 per bushel. In 1985, the harvest value was $29,550,000 on 300,000 acres harvested and 15,000,000 bushels produced.

Almost all oat grain produced in Texas is utilized as feed for livestock within the state. A small acreage is grown exclusively for planting seed.

Leading oat grain-producing counties are Cooke, Collin, McLennan, Falls and Coryell.

Sugar Beets

Sugar beets have been grown on a commercial scale in Texas since 1964 when the first beet sugar factory was built by Holly Sugar Company at Hereford. The leading counties in production in 1985 were Deaf Smith, Castro, Parmer and Randall.

In 1986, 37,000 acres of sugar beets were harvested from 37,200 acres planted, yielding 23.5 tons per acre for total production of 870,000 tons. In 1985, 37,000 acres were harvested from 38,000 acres planted, yielding 22.5 tons per acre for total production of 833,000 tons. Valued at $29.40 per ton, total value was $24,490,000.

Sugar Cane

Sugar cane is grown from seed cane planted in late summer or fall. It is harvested 12 months later and milled to produce raw sugar and molasses. The raw sugar then requires additional refining before it is in final form to be offered to consumers.

The sugar cane grinding mill operated at Santa Rosa, Cameron County, is considered one of the most modern mills in the United States. Texas sugar cane-producing counties are Hidalgo, Cameron and Willacy.

In 1986, 31,000 acres of sugar cane were harvested for sugar and seed, yielding 30.5 tons per acre. This compared with 31,900 acres harvested in 1985, yielding

Cotton Gins By Counties

Source: Texas Cotton Ginners' Assn. and U.S. Department of Commerce

Several counties have cotton gins that did not report the number of bales ginned in 1985. McLennan is the only county with three gins that did not report bales ginned. Those counties with two gins not reporting are: Baylor, Burleson, Concho, Delta, Glasscock, Hardeman, Kent, Lamar, Nolan, Pecos, Taylor, Throckmorton and Young. Counties with one gin not reporting are: Bell, Borden, Bowie, Caldwell, Clay, Coleman, Culberson, Deaf Smith, Denton, Eastland, Fannin, Frio, Hamilton, Houston, Hudspeth, King, Kleberg, McCulloch, Matagorda, Medina, Midland, Reagan, Refugio, Schleicher, Starr, Stonewall, Travis, Uptown, Uvalde, Van Zandt, Walker and Wichita.

Counties	Active Gins Operating During 1985-1986 Crop Year	Running Bales Ginned			Counties	Active Gins Operating During 1985-1986 Crop Year	Running Bales Ginned		
		1985	1984	1983			1985	1984	1983
Bailey	12	50,827	82,177	29,453	Jones	13	86,031	20,120	34,628
Brazoria	3	7,415	6,835	3,945	Kaufman	3	3,362	3,520	3,466
Brazos	5	26,964	23,348	14,747	Knox	4	21,982	16,015	11,575
Briscoe	5	28,484	33,450	17,238	Lamb	24	93,972	197,992	78,148
Cameron	19	151,467	141,720	75,334	Lubbock	26	166,375	223,865	130,324
Castro	10	33,941	61,173	31,497	Lynn	21	183,231	152,255	116,375
Childress	3	19,960	19,143	9,168	Martin	11	96,671	38,272	25,509
Cochran	8	22,384	65,731	33,827	Milam	3	8,069	5,589	7,083
Collin	3	4,544	6,445	5,936	Mitchell	5	38,094	*	17,473
Collingsworth	4	38,220	24,814	19,659	Motley	5	17,011	19,722	9,404
Cottle	4	24,745	25,885	11,056	Navarro	4	12,968	8,592	7,751
Crosby	12	126,590	128,416	77,274	Nueces	12	100,521	74,626	57,155
Dawson	21	125,998	113,439	54,447	Parmer	9	39,821	50,325	19,031
Dickens	3	15,998	15,543	7,425	Reeves	3	22,525	20,616	16,209
Donley	3	15,723	10,228	10,363	Robertson	4	36,379	31,979	20,221
Ellis	6	17,941	12,552	14,241	Runnels	7	34,155	17,691	15,516
El Paso	9	68,645	58,286	51,924	San Patricio	11	127,284	93,742	52,604
Falls	3	5,123	2,840	3,361	Scurry	8	50,159	7,789	32,230
Fisher	7	51,041	17,260	23,215	Swisher	9	26,137	62,482	36,802
Floyd	14	104,370	147,460	71,518	Terry	15	134,932	141,863	110,706
Foard	3	7,753	*	3,989	Tom Green	7	43,493	26,306	24,534
Fort Bend	9	27,487	23,054	19,121	Wharton	5	29,948	25,348	18,890
Gaines	19	168,646	199,849	157,422	Wheeler	3	5,408	3,785	3,733
Garza	3	13,748	13,267	6,942	Wilbarger	6	30,998	18,211	13,061
Hale	24	104,985	232,404	106,432	Willacy	7	159,588	123,206	73,000
Hall	10	55,215	35,636	26,791	Williamson	12	45,350	28,015	37,574
Haskell	9	72,928	47,056	35,366	Yoakum	8	47,638	61,437	52,531
Hidalgo	17	160,241	112,031	58,318	Zavala	4	44,778	44,842	28,623
Hill	5	9,855	7,751	10,203	All Others	—	334,526	210,570	114,837
Hockley	22	130,083	177,869	97,183	Total	597	3,826,734	3,599,491	2,339,164
Howard	9	90,310	11,175	23,409					
Hunt	3	3,697	2,611	1,969	*—None Reported.				

30.1 tons per acre for total production of 961,000 tons. Valued at $20.70 per ton, total value was $19,893,000. Sugar cane was not a commercial crop in Texas for about 50 years following its abandonment in 1923 because of adverse markets.

Hay, Silage and Other Forage Crops

A large proportion of Texas' agricultural land is devoted to forage crop production. This acreage produces forage needs and provides essentially the total feed requirements for most of the state's large domestic livestock population as well as game animals.

Approximately 80 million acres of native rangeland, which is primarily in the western half of Texas, provide grazing for beef cattle, sheep, goats, horses and game animals. An additional 20 million acres are devoted to introduced forage species. Of this total, approximately 16 million acres are established to introduced improved **perennial grasses and legumes** and are harvested by grazing livestock. The average annual acreage of crops grown for hay, silage and other forms of machine harvested forage is over 3 million acres with an estimated value in excess of $500 million.

Hay accounts for the major amount of this production with some **corn** and **sorghum silage** being produced. The most important hay crops are annual and perennial grasses and alfalfa. In 1986, the production of hay was 7,460,000 tons with a value of $436,410,000.

In 1985, hay was harvested from 3,500,000 acres producing an average of 2.34 tons per acre, or 8,175,000 tons valued at $68 per ton, or $555,900,000.

Grass hay production is widely distributed, with some leading counties being **Hopkins, Lamar, Henderson, Van Zandt, Erath, Lamb, McLennan, Ellis** and **Anderson.**

Alfalfa was harvested from 160,000 acres in 1986, yielding 4 tons per acre for total production of 640,000 tons. Value for alfalfa hay crop is included with "all hay." In 1985, 893,000 tons were produced on 190,000 acres, averaging 4.7 tons per acre.

An additional sizable acreage of annual forage crops such as **sudan** and **millet** is grazed, as well as much of the small grain acreage. **Alfalfa, sweetcorn, vetch, arrowleaf clover, grasses** and other forage plants also provide income as seed crops.

Peanuts

Peanuts are grown on approximately 250,000 acres in Texas with some 40 percent of the acreage irrigated.

Yet well over half of the crop is annually produced on acreage that is irrigated. **Texas ranked fourth** nationally in production of peanuts in 1985. Among Texas crops, **peanuts** ranked ninth in value.

Until 1973, essentially all of the Texas acreage was planted to the Spanish types, which were favored because of their earlier maturity and better drought tolerance than other types. The Spanish variety is also preferred for some uses due to its distinctive flavor. Florunner, a runner type, is now planted on a sizable proportion of the acreage where soil moisture is favorable. The variety is later maturing but better yielding than Spanish varieties under good growing conditions. Florunner peanuts have acceptable quality to compete with the Spanish in most products.

Production in 1986 amounted to 391,600,000 pounds of peanuts from 225,000 acres planted and 220,000 acres harvested, or an average of 1,780 pounds per harvested acre valued at 29.4 cents per pound, or $115,130,000. In 1985, the crop value was $107,769,000, or 25.5 cents per pound.

The leading counties in peanut production are **Frio, Comanche, Gaines, Atascosa** and **Eastland.**

Soybeans

Production is largely in the areas of the Upper Coast, irrigated High Plains and the Red River Valley of Northeast Texas. The major counties in soybean production in 1986 were Hale, Lamb, Red River, Chambers and Parmer.

In low rainfall areas, yields have been too low or inconsistent for profitable production under dryland conditions. Soybeans' need for moisture in late summer minimizes economic crop possibilities in the Blacklands and Rolling Plains. In the Blacklands, cotton root rot seriously hinders soybean production. Limited moisture at critical growth stages may occasionally prevent economical yields even in high rainfall areas of Northeast Texas and the Coast Prairie.

Because of day length sensitivity, soybeans should be planted in Texas during the long days of May and June to obtain sufficient vegetative growth for optimum yields. Varieties planted during this period usually cease vegetative development and initiate reproductive processes during the hot, usually dry months of July and August. When moisture is insufficient during the blooming and fruiting period, yields are drastically reduced. In most areas of the state, July and August rainfall is insufficient to permit economical dryland

Cash Receipts By Commodities 1983-85

Source: Texas Crop & Livestock Reporting Service

Commodity	Value			Commodity	Value		
	1983	1984	1985		1983	1984	1985
	—— 1,000 dollars ——				—— 1,000 dollars ——		
All Commodities.....	$9,166,698	$9,469,769	$9,262,540	Carrots	24,842	30,096	22,216
Livestock and products.......	5,521,429	5,900,843	5,438,226	Sweet potatoes....	18,636	16,515	21,251
				Honeydew melons .	15,708	14,535	18,905
Crops, Fruits and others.....	3,645,269	3,568,926	3,824,314	Cucumbers	16,474	18,714	18,275
Livestock and products				Spinach	16,404	15,923	18,045
Cattle and calves ..	4,193,111	4,498,916	4,103,598	Sugarcane.......	16,880	20,767	16,478
Milk, wholesale ...	564,920	536,250	532,680	Broccoli.........	21,434	19,672	14,692
Broilers.........	261,498	294,735	297,078	Oats...........	15,878	8,019	11,240
Eggs...........	178,092	215,182	169,596	Seed, sorghum- sudan crosses ...	9,000	9,000	10,000
Sheep and lambs ..	61,574	71,314	78,164	Sunflowers.......	14,984	4,455	8,690
Hogs...........	93,268	93,569	70,299	Lettuce	9,247	6,521	7,755
Turkeys.........	45,144	55,640	55,640	Tomatoes........	7,905	8,301	4,413
Mohair.........	42,931	48,161	45,885	Barley..........	3,807	5,762	4,176
Wool	15,438	16,100	13,284	Cauliflower	4,497	3,364	2,960
Milk, retail.......	11,063	11,930	12,056	Corn, sweet	3,938	3,053	2,831
*Other	54,390	59,046	59,946	Snap beans.......	2,139	2,363	2,593
Crops				Rye	815	668	628
Cotton lint	932,287	670,506	898,030	†Other crops	73,382	40,750	68,667
Wheat	537,894	495,745	558,974	**Fruits and nuts**			
Sorghum grain....	421,353	407,067	487,407	Pecans..........	38,326	20,744	34,051
Corn	293,904	419,984	390,282	Peaches.........	6,160	5,200	7,000
Rice...........	98,325	167,012	165,021	Oranges.........	24,084	2,720	5,992
Hay...........	126,346	137,910	148,584	Grapefruit.......	26,553	377	1,136
Cottonseed.......	120,939	142,017	94,530	**Other Farm Income**			
Peanuts........	91,134	91,336	87,927	Greenhouse and nursery........	333,000	361,000	400,000
Onions.........	62,112	87,461	54,346	‡Farm forest products.......	52,000	50,000	40,000
Cantaloupes......	39,378	39,965	44,688				
Soybeans........	71,624	78,734	44,447				
Cabbage	34,589	76,983	39,690				
Sugarbeets	22,205	27,357	30,572				
Watermelons	35,707	31,569	29,744				
Potatoes........	27,148	47,355	24,239				
Peppers.........	26,251	29,406	23,839				

*Includes milkfat, turkey eggs, honey bees, equine, goats, goat milk and other poultry and livestock.

†Miscellaneous vegetables, field crops; other berries, fruits and nuts.

‡Includes only sales from farms.

production. The risk of dryland soybean production in the Coast Prairie and Northeast Texas is considerably less when compared to other dryland areas because moisture is available more often during the critical fruiting period.

In 1986, the Texas soybean crop averaged 23 bushels per acre from 190,000 acres harvested. Total production of 4,370,000 bushels was valued at $19,228,000 or $4.40 a bushel. In 1985, 7,250,000 bushels were harvested from 290,000 acres. The crop value was $34,148,000, or $4.71 a bushel.

Sunflowers

Sunflowers constitute one of the most important annual **oilseed crops** in the world. The cultivated types, which are thought to be descendants of the common wild sunflower native to Texas, have been successfully grown in several countries, including Russia, Argentina, Romania, Bulgaria, Uruguay, Western Canada and portions of the northern United States. Extensive trial plantings conducted in the Cotton Belt states since 1968 showed sunflowers have considerable potential as an oilseed crop in much of this area, including Texas. This crop exhibits good cold and drought tolerance, is adapted to a wide range of soil and climatic conditions and tolerates higher levels of hail, wind and sand abrasion than other crops normally grown in the state.

In 1986, about 30,000 acres were planted in sunflowers of which 28,000 were harvested. The yield was 1,300 pounds per acre, and the total crop value was $2,730,000 for 36,400,000 pounds. A crop value of $11,733,000 was realized in 1985. The leading counties in production in 1986 were **Bailey, Floyd, Lamb** and **Parmer.**

Reasons for growing sunflowers include the need for an additional cash crop with low water and plant nutrient requirements, the recent development of sunflower hybrids and interest by food processors in Texas **sunflower oil,** which has a high oleic acid content. Commercial users have found many advantages in this high oleic oil including excellent cooking stability, particularly for use as a deep fat frying medium for potato chips, corn chips and similar products.

Sunflower meal is a high-quality protein source free of nutritional toxins that can be included in rations for swine, poultry and ruminants. The hulls constitute a source of roughage which can also be included in livestock rations.

Forest Products

The non-industrial private forest landowners of East Texas, who own 60 percent of the 11.5 million acres of timberlands, sold timber stumpage with an estimated value of $125 million in 1986. Forest industry landowners had timber stumpage sales of $152 million, with only one-half as much land base as the non-industrial landowners. An estimated $19 million in timber stumpage was sold from the National Forests in Texas. The delivered value of this timber to the processing plants (such as sawmills, papermills and plywood plants) was over $490 million. In 1986, the volume of pine cut in Texas exceeded the growth. Hardwood growth is currently twice the annual harvest.

Pulpwood, sawlogs, and veneer bolts for plywood are the leading timber products, with utility poles, pilings, fence posts, and railroad crossties also providing income to timber growers. Over 450,000 Christmas trees, grown primarily in East Texas but found throughout the state, were sold in the Texas market. In Central Texas some timber is harvested for fuelwood, lumber, veneer, crossties, posts and cedar oil.

In addition to timber production, the forests of Texas provide a multitude of additional products such as wildlife habitat, watershed protection, livestock grazing, and opportunities for outdoor recreation. Minor products include pine straw, edible berries and nuts, wild honey, and decorative plants such as mistletoe.

Texas forests are affected by many problems ranging from urban growth to insect and disease control. Southern pine beetle outbreaks affected many of the poorly-managed stands in 1985 and 1986, driving timber prices down. Regulations restricting control strategies of pine beetle and other pests in national forest wilderness areas threaten the existence of other East Texas forests for timber production and recreation.

Horticultural Specialty Crops

The trend to increased production of horticulture specialty crops continues to rise as transportation costs on long-distance hauling makes the importation of plants from other growing areas increasingly costly. This has resulted in a marked increase in the production of container-grown plants within the state. This increase is noted especially in the production of **bedding plants, foliage plants,** sod and the woody landscape plants.

Texas Fruit-Vegetable Shipments

(Amounts are shown in units of 1,000 hundredweight for rail (RL), truck (TR) and export.)

Commodity	1984 RL	1984 TR	1985 RL	1985 TR	1986 RL	1986 TR
Avocados	0	0	0	0	0	0
Beans	0	1	0	0	0	0
Beets	0	28	0	41	0	72
Broccoli	1	133	0	226	3	245
Broccoli, Expt.	1	0	0	0	0	0
Cabbage	3	3,463	6	3,724	1	4,432
Cabbage, Expt.	0	0	0	0	0	0
Cantaloupes	10	2,611	1	2,766	2	2,773
Cantaloupes, Expt.	0	1	0	0	0	0
Carrots	2	790	48	370	1	938
Cauliflower	0	11	0	5	0	5
Celery	1	213	0	373	0	729
Celery, Expt.	0	0	0	0	0	0
Corn, Sweet	0	14	0	26	0	10
Cucumbers	0	741	0	771	0	898
Eggplant	0	7	0	9	0	5
Grapefruit	0	6	0	109	0	427
Grapefruit, Expt.	0	2	0	0	0	1
Greens	0	171	0	206	0	326
Greens, Expt	0	0	0	0	0	0
Honeydews	3	944	14	866	6	941
Honeydews, Expt.	0	1	0	0	0	0
Lettuce, Iceberg	0	419	0	243	0	317
Lettuce, Ice., Expt.	0	0	0	2	0	0
Lettuce, other	0	0	0	0	0	0
Mixed Citrus	0	0	0	0	0	0
Mixed Misc. Melons	0	0	0	2	0	4
Mixed Vegetables	4	0	1	0	0	0
Mixed Veg., Expt.	1	0	0	0	0	0

Commodity	1984 RL	1984 TR	1985 RL	1985 TR	1986 RL	1986 TR
Okra	0	0	0	11	0	32
Onions, dry	20	4,096	12	3,309	*110	4,693
Onions, dry; Expt.	0	141	0	77	0	105
Onions, green	0	8	0	9	0	14
Oranges	0	3	0	117	0	331
Oranges, Expt.	0	0	0	0	0	0
Parsley	0	25	0	35	0	48
Peaches	0	0	0	0	0	1
Peas, other than green	0	1	0	1	0	1
Peppers, bell	3	775	5	611	3	655
Peppers, bell; Expt.	0	35	0	0	0	0
Peppers, other	0	0	0	17	0	20
Potatoes, table	2	2,722	0	2,167	39	2,478
Potatoes, chipper	0	467	0	526	0	533
Pumpkins	0	0	0	0	0	1
Radishes	0	0	0	0	0	0
Spinach	3	338	4	229	0	299
Spinach, Expt.	16	0	0	0	0	0
Squash	0	29	0	13	0	46
Strawberries	0	0	0	0	0	1
Tangerines	0	0	0	0	0	0
Tomatoes	0	150	0	140	0	180
Tomatoes, cherry	0	7	0	6	0	0
Turnips-Rutabagas	0	9	0	18	0	14
Watermelons	0	2,478	0	2,974	0	2,946
TOTALS	70	20,840	86	19,924	*165	24,421

NOTE: Export data are not complete and should not be interpreted as representing total exports.

*Includes 11 piggyback loads of dry onions.

Plant rental services have become a multimillion dollar business. This comparative newcomer in the plant industry provides the plants for a fee and maintains them in office buildings, shopping malls, public buildings and even in some homes. The response has been great as evidenced by the growth of companies providing these services.

The interest in plants for interior landscapes is confined to no specific age group, as retail nurseries and florist shops report that people of all ages are buying plants.

Extension specialists estimated cash receipts from horticultural specialty crops in Texas to have exceeded $418 million in 1986, making them the **fourth ranking** cash receipts crop. Apparently Texans have decided that they are going to create interesting surroundings by improving their own landscape plantings.

Truck Crops

Some market vegetables are produced in almost all Texas counties, but most of the commercial crop comes from about 200 counties. **Hidalgo County** is the leading Texas county in vegetable acres harvested, followed by **Starr** and **Cameron counties.** Other leading producing counties are: **Frio, Uvalde, Duval, Webb, Hale** and **Zavala.**

Most Texas vegetables are marketed fresh rather than processed.

Nationally, **Texas ranks fourth** in harvested acreage, and value of fresh market vegetables, being exceeded by California, Florida and Arizona. Texas had 5 percent of the harvested acreage, 4.6 percent of the production and 3.8 percent of the value of fresh market vegetables produced in the United States in 1986.

Vegetables leading in value of production usually are **carrots, onions, watermelons, cantaloupes, cabbage and Irish potatoes.** Watermelons led acreage in 1985 and onions accounted for the most value.

Texas growers harvested principal commercial crops valued at $348,179,000 from 197,300 acres in 1985. This compared with $455,487,000 from 211,600 acres in 1984.

Onions

Onions were harvested from 17,300 acres in 1986, valued at $53,047,000. This compared with 21,100 acres in 1985, valued at $54,346,000 in 1985. Hildago County accounted for almost 50 percent of the acreage in Texas in 1985.

Carrots

Carrot production was valued at $18,158,000 in 1986 from 11,600 acres harvested. This compared with 22,432,000 from 13,800 acres harvested in 1985.

The winter carrot production from South Texas accounts for about three-fourths of the total production during the winter season.

Irish Potatoes

In 1986, Texas harvested 16,100 acres of Irish potatoes. Total production amounted to 3,591,000 cwt., valued at $30,951,000. This compared to 19,000 acres valued at $24,239,000 in 1985.

Cantaloupes-Honeydews

Cantaloupes were harvested from 21,000 acres in 1985, and were valued at $44,688,000. This compared with 18,000 acres, valued at $39,965,000 in 1984. Honeydew melons valued at $21,770,000 were harvested from 7,000 acres in 1986. This compared with $18,905,000 from 5,000 acres in 1985.

Cabbage

The 14,000 acres of cabbage harvested in Texas in 1985 brought a value of $39,690,000, compared with 14,400 acres harvested in 1984 with a value of $76,983,000.

Cauliflower

Texas' cauliflower production and value for 1986 were $2,604,000 from 1,000 acres. This compared with 2,960,000 from 1,500 acres in 1985.

Broccoli

Broccoli in 1986 was produced on 6,800 acres with a value of $14,546,000. This compared to 7,300 acres produced in 1985 with a value of $14,692,000. Broccoli is primarily a South Texas crop.

Watermelons

Watermelons were harvested from 44,000 acres in 1985, valued at $29,744,000. This compared with 55,000 acres, valued at $31,569,000 in 1984.

Tomatoes

Commercial production of tomatoes is marketed throughout the year in Texas partly as a result of recent increases in greenhouse production during winter months.

In 1986, tomatoes were harvested from 3,000 acres, valued at $5,784,000. This compared with 3,800 acres valued at $3,853,000 in 1985.

Green Peppers

In 1985, 7,700 acres were harvested for green peppers, valued at $23,839,000. This compared with 8,500 acres valued at $29,406,000 in 1984.

Lettuce

Lettuce was harvested from 2,300 acres and valued at $4,457,000 in 1986. Comparable figures for 1985 were 3,700 acres valued at $7,755,000.

Sweet Potatoes

Sweet potatoes in 1986, were harvested from 7,300 acres with a value of $20,747,000. This compared with 7,700 acres harvested in 1985 with a value of $15,916,000.

Spinach

Spinach production is primarily concentrated in the Winter Garden area of South Texas. The 5,300 acres harvested in 1985 brought $17,315,000. This compared with 4,300 acres valued at $14,519,000 in 1984.

Cucumbers

The cucumber crop in Texas during 1985 was harvested from 6,000 acres valued at $9,720,000. This compared with 6,800 acres valued at $12,786,000 in 1984.

Sweet Corn

Sweet corn in Texas was harvested from 3,800 acres in 1986 and was valued at $1,140,000. This compared with 3,300 acres valued at $2,831,000 in 1985.

Vegetables for Processing

Tomatoes for processing in 1986 were harvested from 3,000 acres valued at $5,784,000. Comparable figures were 3,800 acres valued at $3,853,000 in 1985.

Data for **cucumbers for pickles, snap beans, beets for canning, sweet corn and spinach** used for processing are not published to avoid individual disclosure.

Fruits and Nuts

Texas is noted for producing a wide variety of fruit. The pecan is the only commercial nut crop in the state. The pecan is native to most of the state's river valleys and is the **Texas state tree.** Citrus, practically all produced in the three southernmost counties in the Lower Rio Grande Valley, is the most valuable fruit crop. Texas pecans and Ruby Red grapefruit are famous for their premium quality throughout the nation. Peaches represent the next most important Texas fruit crop, yet there is considerable amount of interest in growing **apples.**

Citrus

Texas ranks with Florida, California and Arizona as one of the four leading states in production of citrus. Most of the Texas production is in Cameron, Hidalgo and Willacy counties of the Lower Rio Grande Valley.

There were 30,600 acres of commercial citrus in Texas in 1985, a 44 percent decrease from the 69,192 acres on Jan. 1, 1983. The December 1983 freeze had a devastating effect on Texas citrus industry.

The number of citrus trees decreased to 3,769,400 since 1983. **Grapefruit acreage** accounted for 62.4 percent of the total citrus acreage in Texas; **oranges**, 37.2 percent; and other citrus, such as lemons, limes, tangelos and tangerines, less than 0.4 percent. Hidalgo County continues to rank No. 1 in citrus with 87.8 percent of the acreage and 88 percent of the trees.

Net acreage of all grapefruit totaled 19,110, down 43 percent from 1983. Ruby Red varieties accounted for 87 percent of the grapefruit acreage; Star Ruby, 11 percent; Pink and White, 2 percent each. The total number of grapefruit trees decreased to 2,450,500, down 54 percent from Jan. 1983. Trees per net acre increased from 120 in 1983 to 128 in 1985.

For oranges, net acreage declined to 11,380, a 54 percent decrease from 1983. Early and mid-season varieties accounted for 55 percent of the orange acreage and Valencia 45 percent. The total number of orange trees declined to 1,303,000, a 52 percent reduction from 1983. Trees per net acre rose from 110 to 114.

The 1986-87 citrus crop was reported at 114,000 tons, a decrease of 23,000 tons produced in 1985-86. Grapefruit production was 1.925 million boxes in 1986-87. In 1985-86, it was .22 million boxes, valued at $2,076,000 or $9.44 a box. The orange crop was .875 million boxes in 1986-87. No value was available. In 1985-86, the orange crop was .310 million boxes valued at $3,166,000, or $10.21 per box.

While grapefruit and oranges account for most of the Texas citrus crop, there are some 110 acres and 15,900 trees of **lemons, limes, tangelos** and **tangerines.** Hardy Satsuma oranges grow in home gardens along the Gulf Coast area.

Tangerines and Tangelos

There is some commercial production of tangerines and tangelos (cross between tangerine and grapefruit) in the Lower Rio Grande Valley and other South Texas areas. There are a few small tangerine orchards in the Laredo and Carrizo Springs-Crystal City area of the Winter Garden. Most of the production is for local consumption or gift boxes. Leading varieties of tangerines are the Clementine and Dancy. Most tangelos are of the Orlando variety.

Lemons

A small acreage is grown in the Lower Rio Grande Valley. Major variety of lemon grown in Texas is the Myers; lemons are sold mostly at roadside stands with a few shipped in gift packs.

Other Fruits and Nuts

Peaches

Primary production areas are East Texas, the Hill Country and the West Cross Timbers. Recently peach production has spread to South and West Texas. Low-chilling varieties for early marketing are being grown in Atascosa, Frio, Webb, Karnes and Duval counties.

The Texas peach crop, damaged by a late freeze, totaled 9,500,000 pounds in 1986 for a value of $3,705,000, or 39 cents per pound. In 1985, 26,000,000 pounds were produced that were valued at $7,280,000, or 28 cents per pound.

The demand for high quality Texas peaches greatly exceeds the supply. Texas ranked 18th nationally in peach production in 1986. Leading Texas counties in production during 1986 were Gillespie, Parker, Montague, Comanche, Limestone and Eastland.

Apples

Small acreages of apples, usually marketed in the state, are grown in a number of counties. The leading counties are Montague and Gillespie, and other producers are Callahan, Collingsworth, Clay, Cass, Donley, Eastland, Hudspeth, Jeff Davis, Lampasas, Parker, San Saba and Young. The crop is harvested and marketed from July to October.

A considerable number of apple trees has been planted in the Hill Country. Most of the trees are new varieties of Red and Golden Delicious types on semi-dwarfing rootstocks. Trees are established in high-density plantings of 100 to 200 trees per acre. Most of the apples are sold at roadside stands or go to nearby markets.

Pears

Well-adapted for home and small-orchard production, the pear is not commercially significant in Texas. Comanche, Parker, Lampasas, Cooke, McCulloch and Eastland counties lead in trees. Fruit usually goes for home consumption or to nearby markets.

Apricots

Not a commercial crop, apricots are grown chiefly in Comanche, Denton, Wilbarger, Parker and Collingsworth counties. Others reporting apricots include Martin, Clay, Young, Lampasas, Gillespie, Anderson, Erath, Wichita and Eastland counties.

Plums

Plum production is scattered over a wide area of the state with the heaviest production in East and Central Texas. The leading counties in production are Smith, Gillespie and Knox. Most of production goes to nearby markets or to processors.

Blackberries

Smith County is a blackberry center, with the Tyler-Lindale area having processed the crop since 1890. There are about 1,500 acres in Smith, Wood, Van Zandt and Henderson counties. The Brazos blackberry is grown as a local market or "pick-your-own" fruit in many sections of the state. Dewberries grow wild in Central and East Texas and are gathered for home use and local sale in May and June.

Strawberries

Atascosa County is the leading commercial area although strawberries are grown for local markets in Wood, Van Zandt and Smith counties in East Texas. The most concentrated production occurs in the Poteet area below San Antonio.

Avocados

Avocados grow on a small acreage in the Lower Rio Grande Valley. Interest in this crop is increasing and production is expected to expand. Lulu is the principal variety.

Pecans

The pecan, the state tree, is one of the most widely distributed trees in Texas. It is native to 150 counties and is grown commercially in some 30 additional counties. The pecan is also widely used as a dual-purpose yard tree. The commercial plantings of pecans has greatly accelerated in Central and West Texas with many of the new orchards being irrigated. Many new pecan plantings are being established under trickle irrigation systems. Two factors that have greatly helped to increase quality and yields have been the development and use of the new USDA pecan varieties and some 40 county and regional pecan grading demonstrations.

The 1986 utilized production totaled 40,000,000 pounds, valued at $38,600,000, or 96.5 cents a pound. In 1985, 78,000,000 pounds, valued at $52,424,000 or 67.2 cents a pound.

Nationally, Texas ranked second in pecan production in 1986. Leading Texas counties in 1984 pecan production were Hood, El Paso, Pecos, San Saba, Mills, Comanche, Wharton and Gonzales.

Livestock and Their Products

Livestock and their products usually account for more than half of the agricultural cash receipts in Texas. The state ranks first nationally in all cattle, beef cattle, cattle on feed, sheep and lambs, wool, goats and mohair. In 1986, it ranked eighth in dairy cows, seventh in broilers, eighth in eggs and 17th in hogs.

Meat animals normally account for around 80 percent of total cash receipts from marketings of livestock and their products. Sales of livestock and products in 1985 totaled $5.4 billion. This compared with $5.9 billion in 1984.

Cattle dominates livestock production in Texas, contributing more than 70 percent of cash receipts from livestock and products each year. The Jan. 1, 1987, inventory of all cattle and calves in Texas totaled 13,400,000 head, valued at $4.56 billion.

Texas sheep raisers have reduced their herd because of increasing production costs. On Jan. 1, 1987, the sheep and lamb inventory stood at 1,930,000 head, compared with 1,810,000 in 1986; 3,214,000 in 1983; 2,400,000 in 1982; and 2,360,000 in 1981. **Sheep and lambs** numbered 3,214,000 on Jan. 1, 1973, down from a high of 10,829,000 in 1943. Sheep and lamb production fell from 148,295,000 pounds in 1973 to 114,980,000 pounds in 1986.

Wool production decreased from 26,352,000 pounds valued at $23,190,000 in 1973 to 16,400,000 pounds valued at $13,284,000 in 1986. The price of wool per pound was 88 cents in 1973, 92 cents in 1984, 82 cents in 1985, and 81 cents in 1986.

Lamb prices averaged $71.60 per cwt. in 1986, compared with $69.60 per cwt. in 1985, and $59.70 in 1984. Average value per head of sheep stock on Jan. 1, 1987 was estimated at $65.00, compared with $58.00 in 1986.

Mohair production in Texas dropped from a 1965 all-time high of 31,584,000 pounds to 9,300,000 pounds in 1979. In 1986, 15,200,000 pounds were produced, an increase from the 13,300,000 pounds in 1985.

In 1965, Mohair was valued at $20,845,000, an average of 66 cents per pound. The value of 1979 production was $47,430,000, or $5.10 per pound. In 1986, production was valued at $48,160,000 or $4.30 per pound.

Beef Cattle

Beef-cattle raising is the most extensive agricultural operation in Texas. In 1985, 44 percent of the total cash receipts from farm and ranch marketings — $4,103,598,000 of $9,262,540,000 — came from cattle and calves. This compared with $4,498,916,000 of

Texas Livestock Numbers And Values

Source: U.S. Department of Agriculture

Class of Livestock	Numbers				Farm Value					
	1985	1986	1987 Preliminary	Number Percent of 1984	Value Per Head			Total Value		
					1985	1986	1987	1985	1986	1987
	Thousands			Pct.	Dollars			1,000 Dollars		
All Cattle	14,100	13,600	13,400	99	$335.00	$335.00	$340.00	$4,723,500	$4,556,000	$4,556,000
*Milk Cows.	314	322	325	101	960.00	920.00	N.A.	301,440	296,240	N.A.
*Beef Cows.	5,586	5,178	5,275	102	N.A.	N.A.	N.A.	N.A.	N.A.	N.A.
†Hogs	415	435	510	117	78.00	70.50	86.50	32,370	30,668	44,115
All Sheep	1,810	1,810	1,930	107	57.50	58.00	65.00	104,075	1,404,980	125,450
Goats.	1,550	1,700	1,670	98	48.30	40.10	46.40	74,865	68,212	77,571
†Chickens	17,400	17,500	17,500	100	1.95	2.00	1.60	33,930	35,000	28,000
†Turkey Hens.	N.A.	N.A.	‡	N.A.	N.A.	N.A.	N.A.	N.A.	N.A.	N.A.
Total Value	...	...	...	...	...	...	...	$5,270,180	$6,391,100	$4,831,136

*Included in "all cattle." †Figures are as of Dec. 1 of preceding year. ‡Turkey figures not released for 1985 to avoid disclosing individual operations. N.A. Not available.

$9,469,769,000 in 1984. Cotton was the next leading commodity.

Nearly all of the 254 counties in Texas derive more revenue from cattle than from any other agricultural commodity, and those that don't usually rank cattle second in importance.

Within the boundaries of Texas are 13 percent of all the cattle in the United States, as are 16 percent of the beef breeding cows, and 12 percent of the calf crop.

The number of all cattle in Texas on Jan. 1, 1987, totaled 13,400,000. This compared with 13,600,000 in 1986.

Calves born on Texas farms and ranches in 1986 totaled 4,950,000, compared with 4,750,000 in 1983.

Receipts of cattle and calves at approximately 153 livestock auctions inspected by the Texas Animal Health Commission totaled 6,108,000 head in 1985. This compared with 7,668,000 in 1984. The number of cattle and calves shipped into Texas totaled 2,920,000 in 1985, and 2,498,000 head in 1984.

Livestock Industries

A large portion of Texas livestock is sold through local auction markets.

In 1985, 153 livestock auctions were reported by the Texas Animal Health Commission. Their receipts in 1986 were 6,368,000 cattle and calves, 362,000 hogs, 944,000 sheep and lambs and 207,000 goats. This com-

Cash Receipts From Farm Marketings 1936-1985

Source: Texas Crop & Livestock Reporting Service

Year	Crop	Livestock and Livestock Production	Total Crops and Livestock	*Government Payments	Total Crops, Livestock and Payments
	1,000 dollars				
1936 . .	$298,361	$186,829	$485,190	$27,121	$512,311
1969 . .	1,202,150	1,851,386	3,053,536	505,248	3,558,784
1970 . .	1,264,766	1,956,991	3,221,757	543,156	3,764,913
1971 . .	1,177,911	2,284,873	3,462,784	468,552	3,931,336
1972 . .	1,463,123	2,614,518	4,077,641	528,567	4,606,208
1973 . .	2,811,135	3,686,236	6,497,371	386,554	6,883,925
1974 . .	2,695,007	2,971,115	5,666,122	80,552	5,746,674
1975 . .	2,759,514	3,076,782	5,836,296	146,562	5,982,858
1976 . .	3,091,434	3,201,974	6,293,408	111,735	6,405,143
1977 . .	3,147,190	3,523,073	6,670,263	157,993	6,828,256
1978 . .	3,015,882	4,628,470	7,644,352	318,843	7,963,195
1979 . .	3,991,103	6,059,942	10,051,045	307,099	10,358,144
1980 . .	3,925,092	5,185,067	9,110,159	231,840	9,341,999
1981 . .	4,371,497	5,448,215	9,819,712	321,365	10,141,077
1982 . .	4,206,582	5,421,060	9,627,642	643,598	10,271,240
1983 . .	3,645,269	5,521,429	9,166,698	1,129,855†	10,296,553
1984 . .	3,568,926	5,900,843	9,469,769	782,441	10,252,210
1985 . .	3,824,314	5,438,226	9,262,540	848,079	10,110,619

*Payments since 1971 were for wheat, cotton, feed grain, sugar beets, wool, mohair, cropland adjustment, rural environmental assistance and Conservation Programs.
†Includes payment-in-kind (PIK) of $661 million.

pared with 6,108,000 cattle and calves, 392,000 hogs, 948,000 sheep and lambs and 188,000 goats in 1985.

During 1986, the commission reported 1,763,373 cattle shipped from Texas to other states and 3,097,893 shipped in, compared with 1,701,586 shipped out and 2,920,197 shipped in during 1985. (Figures exclude cattle shipped direct to slaughter where no health certificates are required.)

Texas, during 1986, shipped out 150,963 sheep and lambs and shipped in 240,038. This compared with 108,041 sheep and lambs shipped out and 355,915 shipped in during 1985.

Feedlot fattening of livestock, mainly cattle, is a major industry in Texas. Texas lots marketed 5,260,000 head of grain-fed cattle in 1986, compared with 5,030,000 head in 1985. In recent years, more cattle have been fed in Texas than in any other state in the United States.

During 1986, there were 148 feedlots with a feeding capacity of 1,000 animals or more. This compared with 152 in 1985.

Federally inspected slaughter plants in Texas numbered 64 in 1987 with 239 state-inspected facilities. This compared with 67 federal and 248 state in 1986. In 1986, the number of head slaughtered in Texas totaled 6,207,000 cattle, 247,000 calves, 993,000 hogs and 562,000 sheep and lambs. This compared with 6,155,000 cattle, 254,000 calves, 1,121,000 hogs, 654,000 sheep and lambs and 101,000 goats in 1985.

Increased feeding of cattle in commercial feedlots has been a major economic development during recent years and has stimulated the establishment and expansion of beef slaughtering plants. Most of this development has been in the Panhandle-Plains area of Northwest Texas. This area alone accounts for more than 70 percent of the cattle fed in the state.

Feedlots with capacities of 1,000 head or more accounted for more than 98 percent of the cattle fed in Texas. Total feedlot marketings in 1986 represented about 23 percent of total U.S. fed cattle marketings.

Large amounts of capital are required for feedlot operations. This has forced many lots to become custom feeding facilities.

Feedlots are concentrated on the High Plains largely because of extensive supplies of sorghum and other feed. Beef breeding herds have increased most in East Texas, where grazing is abundant.

Dairying

Ninety percent of the state's dairy industry is located east of the line from Wichita Falls to Brownwood, to San Antonio to Corpus Christi. Leading counties in milk production are Hopkins, Erath and Johnson, which, combined, produce almost 35 percent of the milk in the state, with Hopkins producing almost 17 percent of the total.

All the milk sold by Texas dairy farmers is marketed under the terms of Federal Marketing Orders. Most Texas dairymen are members of one of four marketing cooperatives. Associated Milk Producers, Inc., is the largest, representing a majority of the state's producers.

Texas dairy farmers received a gross income of $554,370,000 during 1986, compared with $547,524,000 in 1985. Price for milk averaged $13.60 per 100 pounds in 1986, compared with $13.80 in 1985. A total of 3.99 billion pounds of milk was sold to plants and dealers in 1986, bringing $542,640,000 of cash receipts. This compares with 3.86 billion pounds and $532,680,000 in 1985.

The number of milk cows that have calved on Texas farms in 1987 was 325,000 head. This compares with 322,000 head on Jan. 1, 1985. Average production per cow has increased steadily in recent decades. The average production per cow in 1986 was 12,659 pounds. Milk per cow was 12,439 pounds in 1985. Milk production totaled 4,089 million pounds in 1986, compared with 3,968 million pounds in 1985.

There were 8,700 milk-cow operations in Texas in 1986. There was an average of 2,265 commercial milk producing units in Texas in 1986. This compares with 9,200 operations reporting milk cows in 1985 and about 2,438 commercial milk producing units.

Dairy Manufacturing

The major dairy products manufactured in Texas include creamery butter, cheese and condensed, evaporated and dry milk. These data are not available because of the small number of manufacturing plants producing these products.

Frozen Desserts

Production of frozen desserts totaled 126,182,000 gallons in 1985. This compared with 118,496,000 gallons in 1984. Ice cream production in 1985 amounted to 44,898,000 gallons, compared with 53,033,000 gallons in 1984. Ice cream mix produced in Texas in 1985 amounted to 28,438,000 gallons, compared with 27,750,000 gallons in 1984. Ice milk production in Texas amounted to 20,168,000 gallons in 1985, compared with 16,119,000 gallons in 1984. Mellorine in 1985 totaled 4,184,000 gallons. The 1984 production of mellorine was 3,857,000 gallons.

Swine

Texas ranked 17th among the states in number of swine on hand Dec. 1, 1986. Swine producers in the state usually produce about 25 to 30 percent of the pork consumed by the state, or about 800,000 head annually marketed.

Production units vary in size from one to more than 1,100 sows. Although the number of farms producing hogs has steadily decreased, the size of production units has increased. With the trend to larger units, there has been increasing swine production in the Panhandle, South Plains and West Central areas of Texas. The 10 leading counties in 1985 were: Archer, Colorado, Fayette, Harris, Lubbock, Milam, Moore, Rains, Uvalde and Wilson.

Specialization in the swine industry has resulted in a demand for top quality feeder pigs by those farmers who have grain available. To meet this demand, feeder pig marketing associations have been established in the feeder pig producing areas of East and Central Texas. These associations hold feeder pig sales monthly and auction pigs in uniform lots according to grades and weights.

With the establishment of marketing associations capable of shipping slaughter hogs to any point in the United States, and because of the volume of sorghum grain produced in the state, the potential for increased production is tremendous, for both feeder pigs and slaughter hogs.

In 1986, 510,000 head of hogs were marketed in Texas, producing 166,660,000 pounds of pork, valued at $83,053,000 for cash receipts of $81,028,000, or $45.90 per 100 pounds. Comparable figures for 1984 were 435,000 head marketed, 168,950,000 pounds of pork, valued at $73,324,000 with cash receipts of $70,299,000, or $41.60 per 100 pounds.

Goats and Mohair

Goats in Texas numbered 1,670,000 on Jan. 1, 1987, compared with 1,700,000 in 1986. They had a value of $77,571,000 or $46.40 per head in 1987, compared with $68,212,000 or $40.10 per head in 1986.

The goat herd consists largely of Angora goats for mohair production. Angora goats totaled 1,370,000 in 1987, compared with 1,430,000 in 1986. Spanish and others numbered 300,000 in 1987, compared with 270,000 in 1986.

Mohair production during 1986 totaled 15,200,000 pounds, compared with 13,300,000 pounds in 1985. Average price per pound in 1986 was $2.51 from 1,950,000 goats clipped for a total value of $38,152,000. This compared with $3.45 per pound from 1,730,000 goats clipped and total value of $45,885,000 in 1985.

Nearly half of the world's mohair and 97 percent of the U.S. clip is produced in Texas. The leading Texas counties in Angora goats are: Edwards, Val Verde, Sutton, Crockett, Uvalde, Terrell, Kimble, Mason, Mills and Kinney.

Sheep and Wool

Sheep and lambs in Texas numbered 1,930,000 head on Jan. 1, 1987, up from 1,810,000 in 1986.

All sheep were valued at $125,450,000 or $65.00 per head on Jan. 1, 1987, compared with $104,980,000 or $58.00 per head in 1986.

Breeding ewes one year old and over numbered 1,300,000 in 1987, and 1,260,000 in 1986.

Ewe lambs totaled 290,000 head in 1987; 230,000 in

Texas Cattle Marketed, By Size Of Feedlots

Texas Crop and Livestock Reporting Service

	Feedlot Capacity (head)						
Year	Under 1,000	1,000-1,999	2,000-3,999	4,000-7,999	8,000-15,999	16,000 & Over	Total
	— Cattle Marketed — 1,000 head —						
1962 ..	105	87	109	194	*261	—	756
1963 ..	120	111	144	205	185	131	896
1964 ..	118	100	174	223	177	179	971
1965 ..	104	108	205	324	107	246	1,094
1966 ..	163	127	268	359	205	290	1,412
1967 ..	138	126	194	372	343	481	1,654
1968 ..	112	91	138	321	439	869	1,970
1969 ..	111	78	133	303	514	1,567	2,706
1970 ..	98	53	112	281	727	1,867	3,138
1971 ..	99	49	117	304	697	2,397	3,663
1972 ..	98	57	112	308	558	3,175	4,308
1973 ..	99	47	74	210	625	3,357	4,412
1974 ..	85	31	48	189	544	3,002	3,899
1975 ..	50	22	51	134	485	2,325	3,067
1976 ..	60	33	62	170	583	3,039	3,947
1977 ..	146	22	38	206	604	3,211	4,227
1978 ..	80	20	50	242	697	3,826	4,915
1979 ..	54	19	46	227	556	3,543	4,445
1980 ..	51	18	47	226	533	3,285	4,160
1981 ..	50	20	50	220	510	3,110	3,960
1982 ..	55	20	60	210	540	3,190	4,075
1983 ..	100	20	80	130	490	3,580	4,400
1984 ..	60	20	180	150	540	4,140	5,090
1985 ..	70	10	20	170	620	4,140	5,030
1986 ..	—	—	—	—	—	—	5,260

*Marketing from larger size groups included to avoid disclosing individual operations.

Hog Production in Texas

Source: Texas A&M—USDA

Year	Production 1,000 Pounds	Avg. Market Wt. Pounds	Avg. Price Per Cwt. Dollars	Gross Income 1,000 Dollars
1958	262,134	233	$19.50	$44,997
1959	338,343	228	14.40	47,948
1960	288,844	228	14.70	44,634
1961	289,700	229	16.40	49,174
1962	288,815	230	16.30	47,483
1963	282,807	234	15.10	43,685
1964	259,549	240	14.80	43,351
1965	212,404	240	19.80	41,432
1966	234,742	239	22.60	49,992
1967	289,773	240	18.70	51,767
1968	313,515	240	18.10	55,788
1969	325,896	240	21.60	73,027
1970	385,502	241	22.50	75,288
1971	529,986	236	16.60	90,257
1972	449,357	244	24.00	114,730
1973	375,372	242	37.90	148,488
1974	350,811	253	33.30	123,277
1975	271,027	244	43.70	127,323
1976	286,053	247	41.50	118,637
1977	292,290	247	38.00	109,634
1978	303,135	258	43.80	135,006
1979	320,790	261	39.70	125,183
1980	315,827	259	35.90	111,700
1981	264,693	256	41.70	121,054
1982	205,656	256	49.60	112,726
1983	209,621	256	45.20	95,343
1984	189,620	262	45.50	95,657
1985	168,950	266	43.40	75,512
1986	176,660	N.A.	45.90	81,028

1986. Lambs saved numbered 1,130,000 in 1986 and 1,020,000 in 1985. Early lamb crop estimates were discontinued in January, 1983.

Sheep operations in Texas were estimated to be 8,500 in 1986 and 8,800 in 1985.

Texas **wool production** in 1986 was 16,400,000 pounds from 2,260,000 sheep. Value totaled $13,284,000 or 81 cents a pound. This compared with 16,200,000 pounds valued at $13,284,000 or 82 cents a pound in 1985.

Most sheep in Texas are concentrated in the Edwards Plateau area of West Central Texas and nearby counties. The ten leading counties are: Crockett, Concho, Val Verde, Tom Green, Terrell, Kinney, Menard, Gillespie, Schleicher and Pecos. Sheep production is largely dual purpose, for both wool and lamb production.

San Angelo long has been the largest sheep and wool market in the nation and the center for wool and mohair warehouses, scouring plants and slaughterhouses.

Poultry and Eggs

Poultry and eggs annually contribute about 6 percent of the average yearly cash receipts of Texas farmers. In 1986, Texas ranked 7th among the states in broilers produced, 8th in hens and eggs produced and 5th in pullets of laying age.

In 1985, **cash receipts** to producers from production

Texas Sheep and Wool Production

	Sheep		Wool	
Year	*Number	Value	Production (lbs.)	Value
850	100,530	N. A.	131,917	N. A.
860	753,363	N. A.	1,493,363	N. A.
870	1,223,000	$2,079,000	N. A.	N. A.
880	6,024,000	12,048,000	N. A.	N. A.
890	4,752,000	7,128,000	N. A.	N. A.
900	2,416,000	4,590,000	9,630,000	N. A.
910	1,909,000	5,536,000	8,943,000	$1,699,170
920	3,360,000	33,600,000	22,813,000	5,019,000
930	6,304,000	44,758,000	48,262,000	10,135,000
940	10,069,000	49,413,000	79,900,000	23,171,000
950	6,756,000	103,877,000	51,480,000	32,947,000
951	7,119,000	154,962,000	48,712,000	48,225,000
952	6,188,000	114,910,000	46,277,000	26,841,000
953	5,574,000	56,833,000	42,511,000	26,782,000
954	5,331,000	53,829,000	44,220,000	26,090,000
955	5,659,000	57,125,000	45,137,000	19,409,000
956	5,376,000	58,337,000	42,653,000	18,767,000
957	4,749,000	46,769,000	39,409,000	22,069,000
958	4,891,000	85,306,000	38,716,000	15,099,000
959	5,458,000	95,154,000	46,726,000	20,559,000
960	5,938,000	85,801,000	51,980,000	21,832,000
961	6,140,000	72,859,000	52,225,000	23,501,000
962	5,854,000	58,300,000	49,752,000	23,881,000
963	5,538,000	55,175,000	46,602,000	23,767,000
964	5,185,000	47,668,000	38,836,000	20,195,000
965	4,539,000	50,811,000	41,109,000	18,499,000
966	4,795,000	69,587,000	38,777,000	19,001,000
967	4,802,000	67,686,000	36,998,000	15,169,000
968	4,419,000	56,800,000	33,363,000	15,347,000
969	4,029,000	67,284,000	29,717,000	14,561,000
970	3,708,000	73,602,000	30,784,000	11,082,000
971	3,789,000	66,308,000	30,397,000	4,864,000
972	3,524,000	65,194,000	29,430,000	14,126,000
973	3,214,000	64,280,000	26,352,000	23,190,000
974	3,090,000	80,340,000	23,900,000	15,535,000
975	2,715,000	63,803,000	23,600,000	14,868,000
976	2,600,000	81,900,000	22,000,000	17,380,000
977	2,520,000	93,240,000	21,000,000	17,220,000
978	2,460,000	111,930,000	18,500,000	15,355,000
979	2,415,000	152,145,000	19,075,000	18,503,000
980	2,400,000	138,000,000	18,300,000	17,751,000
981	2,360,000	116,820,000	20,500,000	24,600,000
982	2,400,000	100,800,000	19,300,000	16,212,000
983	2,225,000	86,775,000	18,600,000	15,438,000
984	1,970,000	76,830,000	17,500,000	16,100,000
985	1,810,000	104,075,000	16,200,000	13,284,000
986	1,810,000	104,980,000	16,400,000	13,284,000
987	1,930,000	125,450,000	N. A.	N. A.

*Number given here represents all sheep on farms as of Jan. 1; number clipped will vary because of spring and fall clipping.

†Preliminary.

of broilers, eggs, chickens and turkeys totaled $534,010,000, compared with $582,703,000 in 1984.

Gross income from eggs was $196,267,000 in 1986, compared with $169,596,000 in 1985. Eggs produced in 1986 totaled 3.4 billion, compared with 3.1 billion in 1985. Average price received per dozen in 1986 was 70.2 cents, compared with 65 cents in 1985. Leading egg-producing counties are: **Caldwell, Camp, Denton, Fayette, Lavaca, Gonzales, Lubbock, Nacogdoches, Shelby** and **Wharton.**

Broiler production in 1986 totaled 238,600,000 birds, compared with 215,900,000 in 1985. Gross income from broilers in 1986 amounted to $369,353,000, compared with $297,078,000 in 1985. Price per pound averaged 36 cents in 1986 and 32 cents in 1985. Leading broiler-producing counties are: **Camp, Franklin, Gonzales, Nacogdoches, Panola, San Augustine, Shelby, Titus, Upshur** and **Wood.**

Horses

Nationally, Texas ranks as one of the leading states in horse numbers and is the headquarters for many national horse organizations. The largest single horse breed registry in America, the **American Quarter Horse Association,** has its headquarters in Amarillo. The **National Cutting Horse Association** and the **American Paint Horse Association** are both located in Fort Worth. In addition to these national associations, Texas also has active state associations that include **Arabians, Thoroughbreds, Appaloosa** and **Ponies.**

Horses are still used to support the state's giant beef cattle and sheep industries. The largest increase in horse numbers within the state can be found in the urban and suburban areas. Horses are most abundant in the heavily populated areas of the state. State participation activities consist of horse shows, trail rides, play days, rodeos, polo and horse racing. Residential subdivisions have been developed within the state to provide facilities for urban and suburban horse owners.

Angora Goats and Mohair

	Goats		Mohair	
Year	*Number	Farm Value	Production (lbs.)	Value
1900	627,333	$923,777	961,328	$267,864
1910	1,135,000	2,514,000	1,998,000	468,000
1920	1,753,000	9,967,000	6,786,000	1,816,000
1930	2,965,000	14,528,000	14,800,000	4,995,000
1940	3,300,000	10,560,000	18,250,000	9,308,000
1950	2,295,000	13,082,000	12,643,000	9,735,000
1951	2,433,000	23,114,000	12,280,000	14,613,000
1952	2,054,000	17,664,000	11,561,000	11,330,000
1953	1,910,000	12,224,000	11,972,000	10,775,000
1954	2,082,000	13,741,000	13,097,000	9,561,000
1955	2,546,000	14,003,000	16,401,000	13,613,000
1956	2,700,000	18,900,000	17,616,000	14,974,000
1957	2,808,000	17,400,000	18,432,000	15,483,000
1958	2,864,000	25,800,000	20,207,000	14,751,000
1959	3,150,000	26,145,000	23,512,000	22,807,000
1960	3,339,000	29,383,000	23,750,000	21,375,000
1961	3,473,000	29,520,000	25,690,000	22,093,000
1962	3,647,000	30,270,000	26,418,000	19,021,000
1963	3,683,000	25,781,000	28,153,000	25,056,000
1964	3,904,000	29,280,000	28,872,000	27,428,000
1965	4,060,000	28,420,000	31,584,000	20,845,000
1966	4,222,000	28,710,000	28,770,000	15,536,000
1967	3,969,000	20,639,000	26,335,000	10,797,000
1968	3,572,000	17,503,000	25,272,000	11,448,000
1969	3,215,000	22,184,000	20,100,000	13,246,000
1970	2,572,000	19,033,000	17,985,000	7,032,000
1971	2,133,000	12,158,000	14,855,000	4,480,000
1972	1,650,000	10,230,000	10,190,000	8,458,000
1973	1,775,000	15,798,000	9,930,000	18,569,000
1974	1,560,000	22,620,000	8,400,000	11,508,000
1975	1,350,000	17,820,000	8,600,000	15,910,000
1976	1,270,000	25,273,000	8,100,000	24,057,000
1977	1,400,000	35,000,000	8,000,000	22,960,000
1978	1,355,000	44,038,000	8,100,000	37,179,000
1979	1,360,000	61,200,000	9,300,000	47,430,000
1980	1,400,000	64,400,000	8,800,000	30,800,000
1981	1,380,000	53,130,000	10,100,000	35,350,000
1982	1,410,000	57,810,000	10,000,000	25,500,000
1983	1,420,000	53,250,000	10,600,000	42,930,000
1984	1,450,000	82,215,000	11,200,000	48,160,000
1985	1,550,000	74,865,000	13,300,000	45,885,000
1986	1,700,000	68,212,000	15,200,000	38,152,000
†1987	1,670,000	77,571,000	N. A.	N. A.

*Number here represents all goats on farms as of Jan. 1; the number of goats clipped will vary each year, but is usually larger because of spring and fall clipping.

†Preliminary.

Education

Public Schools

Public school enrollment in Texas reached a peak of 2,933,081 in 1985-86, according to **Texas Education Agency.**

The seven largest districts (listed alphabetically) that usually have better than one fourth of the total pupil population are: Austin, Dallas, El Paso, Fort Worth, Houston, San Antonio and Ysleta.

History of Public Education

Public education was one of the primary goals of the early settlers of Texas, who listed the failure to provide education as one of their grievances in the Texas Declaration of Independence from Mexico.

As early as 1838, President Mirabeau B. Lamar's message to the Republic of Texas Congress advocated setting aside public domain for public schools. His interest caused him to be called the "Father of Education in Texas." In 1839 Congress designated three leagues of land to support public schools for each Texas county and 50 leagues for a state university. In 1840 each county was allocated one more league of land.

The Republic, however, did not establish a public school system or university. The **1845 State Constitution** advocated public education, instructing the Legislature to designate at least 10 per cent of the tax revenue for schools. Further delay occurred until **Gov. Elisha M. Pease,** on Jan. 31, 1854, signed the bill **setting up the Texas public school system.**

The public school system was made possible by setting aside $2 million out of $10 million Texas received for relinquishing its claim to land to the north and west of its present boundaries. (See **Compromise of 1850** in historical section.)

During 1854, legislation provided for state apportionment of funds based upon an annual census and required railroads which were granted land to survey alternate sections that were set aside for public school financing. The first **school census** that year showed **65,463 scholastics; state fund apportionment** was 62c per student.

When adopted in 1876, the present **Texas Constitution** provided: "All funds, lands and other property heretofore set apart and appropriated for the support of public schools; all the alternate sections of land reserved by the state of grants heretofore made or that may hereafter be made to railroads, or other corporations, of any nature whatsoever; one half of the public domain of the state, and all sums of money that may come to the state from the sale of any portion of the same shall constitute a perpetual public school fund."

Over 52,000,000 acres of the Texas public domain were allotted for school purposes. (See table, Public Lands of Texas, in chapter on State Government.)

The Constitution also provided for one fourth of occupation taxes and a poll tax of one dollar for school support, and made provisions for local taxation. No provision was made for direct ad valorem taxation for maintenance of an available school fund, but a maximum 20c state ad valorem school tax was adopted in 1883, and raised to 35c in connection with provision of free textbooks in the amendment of 1918.

In 1949, the **Gilmer-Aikin Laws** reorganized the state system of public schools by making sweeping changes in administration and financing. All schools below college level were, prior to 1984, headed by the **State Board of Education,** whose members were elected from congressional districts as set in 1981. Under the new educational reforms of 1984, a new 15-member board was appointed by the governor to replace the existing 27-member elected panel. This board appoints a **State Commissioner of Education** who is executive head of the **Texas Education Agency,** which administers the public school system. Under the law, TEA consists of (1) the State Board of Education, (2) the State Commissioner of Education, (3) the State Department of Education and (4) the State Board of Vocational Education. The personnel of the State Board of Education and the State Board of Vocational Education is the same, the members of the State Board of Education serving ex officio as members of the State Board of Vocational Education when considering matters relating to vocational education.

The funding of Texas public school education con

Enrollment By Grades

(Average Daily Attendance)

1985-86	2,933,081	1980-81	2,639,79▮
1984-85	2,924,000	1979-80	2,605,17▮
1983-84	2,745,338	1978-79	2,589,98▮
1982-83	2,725,009	1977-78	2,576,55▮
1981-82	2,675,168	1976-77	2,555,29▮

The following table shows enrollment by grades for the school years of 1983-84, 1984-85 and 1985-86.

	1983-84	1984-85	1985-8▮
Pre-Kindergarten	15,651	16,228	58,51▮
Kindergarten	242,191	258,162	276,05▮
Grade One	300,795	305,353	320,37▮
Grade Two	265,660	275,432	279,66▮
Grade Three	264,080	262,792	233,09▮
Grade Four	257,556	263,670	263,89▮
Grade Five	258,866	256,443	260,50▮
Grade Six	267,560	264,093	263,12▮
Grade Seven	286,837	279,547	274,96▮
Grade Eight	269,242	278,842	266,01▮
Grade Nine	283,619	296,648	306,31▮
Grade Ten	236,997	246,528	245,71▮
Grade Eleven	205,018	208,964	213,55▮
Grade Twelve	179,748	180,431	180,87▮
TOTAL	3,333,820	3,393,133	3,483,46▮

High School Graduates
Source: Texas Education Agency

1985-86	161,150	1969-70	139,04▮
1984-85	159,343	1968-69	135,34▮
1983-84	161,580	1967-68	127,49▮
1982-83	168,897	1966-67	125,74▮
1981-82	172,099	1965-66	121,08▮
1980-81	171,665	1964-65	121,75▮
1979-80	171,449	1963-64	97,15▮
1978-79	168,518	1962-63	87,64▮
1977-78	167,983	1961-62	86,51▮
1976-77	163,574	1960-61	85,10▮
1975-76	159,855	1959-60	76,50▮
1974-75	159,487	1958-59	71,85▮
1973-74	156,984	1957-58	67,77▮
1972-73	152,172	1956-57	65,13▮
1971-72	153,633	1955-56	64,29▮
1970-71	148,105	1954-55	60,14▮
		1953-54	56,36▮

tinues to be a major issue before the Texas Legislature in the 1980s. The Sixty-fourth (1975) Legislature made major changes in the state's guaranteed **Foundation School Program** with enactment of HB 1126, which provided increased funding for salaries, operating allowance and transportation. This bill also provided state funds for compensatory education and equalization aid and revised the method for determining state aid received by school districts under the Foundation Program.

Major changes continued with the passage of SB 1 during a called special session of the Sixty-fifth (1977) Texas Legislature. The **School Tax Assessment Practices Board** was created to determine, on a statewide basis, the property wealth of school districts. The board was also charged with upgrading professional standards for appraising and assessing school district property taxes.

The Sixty-sixth (1979) Legislature passed SB 350, which increased most categorical programs, including salaries, and lowered the rate used in calculating the districts' share of the Foundation School Program cost. In addition, SB 621 required the establishment of countywide appraisal districts.

House Bill 1060, which was enacted by the 66th Texas Legislature, implements provisions of the Constitutional Amendment (HJR-1) approved by voters in November, 1978. This bill provides for state payments to school districts to replace taxes lost because of state-mandated reduction of ad valorem tax base due to residential timber and agricultural land.

The Sixty-seventh (1981) Legislature passed HB 656, which increased most categorical programs, including salaries, and lowered the rate used in calculating the district's share of the Foundation School Program cost.

Members of the 68th Texas Legislature, in special session, forged a historic education reform bill in the summer of 1984. Known as House Bill 72, the reform action, with a $2.8 billion price tag, came in response to a growing national and statewide concern over declining test scores and deteriorating general literacy in America's schoolchildren over two decades, a deterioration generally reflected in Texas test scores.

The nationally recognized Texas school reform act was formulated by a Select Committee headed by Dallas computer magnate Ross Perot and appointed by Gov. Mark White at the behest of Lt. Gov. Bill Hobby and Speaker of the House Gib Lewis, following failures by the Legislature — and resistance from the voters — to support teacher pay raises or additional public school funding without education reform.

The result was the reform bill of 1984 that provided equalization formulas for state financial aid for public education, raised teacher salaries but tied those raises to teacher performance, and introduced more stringent teacher certification and initiated competency testing for both entering and existing teachers.

Academic achievement was set as a priority in public education with stricter attendance rules, adoption of a no-pass, no-play rule prohibiting students scoring below 70 in each class from participating in sports and other extracurricular activities, and national norm testing through the grades to assure parents of individual schools' performance through a common frame of reference.

A new 10-member oversight panel, the **Legislative Education Board**, would review all aspects of state education policy and school finance.

Higher academic standards had been enacted by the 67th Legislature under H.B. 246 in 1981, which established a statewide curriculum standard for all grades. The reforms of 1984, however, carried a broader price tag and were supported by legislative vote to increase a host of goods, services, gasoline and business franchise taxes — an action that would not have been possible without the education reforms.

Texas has two types of **school districts**, independent and common, each administering local affairs through a board of trustees. Independent school districts deal directly with Texas Education Agency; common districts are supervised by elected county school superintendents and county trustees.

Ad valorem taxes provided most of the financial support for schools by school districts until Jan. 1, 1975, when the 5 cents ad valorem tax for the **available school fund** was abolished. This tax also was a significant source of state support, at a rate not to exceed 35c on each $100 in real and personal property but a constitutional amendment adopted in 1968 provided for gradual phasing out of state ad valorem taxes for all purposes except the tax levied by Sec. 17, Art. VII, for certain institutions of higher learning. Sec. 17, Art. VII, was deleted by a Constitutional amendment adopted in an election Nov. 2, 1982. Other state support comes from designated percentages of several taxes and from the **Permanent School Fund.**

Scholastic Population, Apportionment, 1854-1986

The Texas public school system was established and the permanent fund set up by the Fifth Legislature, Jan. 31, 1854. The first apportionment by the state to public schools was for the school year 1854-55.

Years	Scholastic		Apportionment	
	Age	Population	Per Capita	Amount
1854-55	...	65,463	$0.62	...
1872-73	...	229,568	1.81	$405,518
1880-81	...	266,439	3.00	679,317
1890-91	8-16	545,616	4.00	2,182,464
1900-01	8-17	706,546	4.25	3,002,820
1910-11	7-17	949,006	6.25	5,931,287
1920-21	7-18	1,271,157	14.50	18,431,716
1930-31	6-17	1,562,427	17.50	27,342,473
1940-41	6-17	1,536,910	22.50	34,580,475
1950-51	6-17	1,566,610	60.00	93,996,600
1960-61	6-17	2,249,157	73.00	164,188,461
1970-71	6-17	2,800,500	119.45	287,159,758
1979-80	6-17	3,012,210	309.00	797,805,346
1980-81	...	...	397.00	3,042,476
1981-82	...	...	457.00	3,089,788
1982-83	...	...	525.00	1,401,767,656
1983-84	...	...	480.00	1,304,921,553
1984-85	...	...	225.00	627,870,430
1985-86	...	...	280.00	807,680,617

Scholastic age (6-17 until 1979-80) was determined as follows: A child having attained the age of 6 before Sept. 1 was enumerated for the school year beginning on that date. One having attained the age of 18 prior to Sept. 1 was excluded from the school census. There is no longer a school census. Age requirements are generally from 5 to 21, although for special education, ages range from birth through age 22.

Texas School Salaries

Year	Average Annual Salary, Common School Districts	Average Annual Salary, Independent School Districts	Average Annual Salary, State
1872-73	. . .	. . .	$210.00
1886-87	$218.27	$502.09	244.76
1899-1900	219.05	474.84	260.26
1910-11	320.57	514.22	391.21
1920-21	699.48	1,021.76	895.20
1930-31	781.30	1,274.00	1,079.07
*1940-41	893.00	1,269.00	1,150.00
1950-51	2,967.19	3,250.78	3,215.93
1960-61	. . .	. . .	4,734.00
1970-71	. . .	. . .	8,486.00
1980-81	. . .	. . .	16,724
1981-82	. . .	. . .	18,682
1982-83	. . .	. . .	20,745
1983-84	. . .	. . .	21,418
1984-85	. . .	. . .	24,504
1985-86	. . .	. . .	25,581

*Salaries of both white and Negro teachers included beginning with the school year, 1940-41. Only white teachers' salaries included prior to that year.

School Districts

The following Texas Education Agency table shows the change in the types of school districts in Texas, especially the decline in common school districts in recent years.

Year	Common School Districts*	Independent School Districts	Total
1986-87	10	1,058	1,068
1985-86	10	1,053	1,063
1984-85	10	1,052	1,062
1983-84	10	1,059	1,069
1982-83	10	1,061	1,071
1981-82	12	1,087	1,099
1980-81	12	1,087	1,099
1975-76	118	1,009	1,127
1970-71	188	999	1,187
1965-66	322	1,010	1,332
1960-61	530	1,009	1,539
1955-56	849	1,008	1,857
1950-51	1,558	947	2,505
1945-46	4,461	998	5,459
1940-41	5,319	1,090	6,409
1935-36	5,984	1,015	6,999
1930-31	6,425	1,034	7,459
1910-11 (Largest Count) . .	8,053	546	8,599

*Districts in these columns include Rural High School Districts and Independent School Districts with less than 150 scholastics which are under the county superintendent.

Permanent School Fund

The following table, from the Texas Education Agency, Austin, shows the total value of the Texas permanent school fund and the income earned by years since the fund was established.

Year	*Total Investment Fund	Total Income Earned by P.S.F.
1854	$2,000,000.00	
1880	3,542,126.00	. . .
1898	7,588,712.00	. . .
1899	8,420,588.85	$691,594.85
1900	9,102,872.75	783,142.08
1970	842,217,721.05	34,762,955.32
1971	884,680,139.49	38,107,272.60
1972	927,690,294.64	40,765,514.29
1973	977,970,414.00	44,462,028.00
1974	1,081,492,087.81	50,898,130.46
1975	1,176,441,741.70	61,050,083.01
1976	1,318,313,917.99	67,573,179.43
1977	1,546,151,708.00	84,817,986.33
1978	1,815,364,050.00	104,618,901.41
1979	2,062,710,780.00	130,629,766.02
1980	2,464,579,397.00	163,000,000.00
1981	2,986,784,696.12	217,695,444.70
1982	3,532,013,181.39	270,648,812.76
1983	3,959,923,160.00	698,567,452.76
1984	4,496,345,276.00	359,080,872.00
1985	5,095,802,979.00	417,080,383.00
1986	5,792,619,707.00	†652,030,987.00

*Includes cash — bonds at par and stocks at book value.

†Includes non-recurring extraordinary income of $140,246,302.

Texas School Professional Personnel

This table shows the increase in Texas school professional personnel (teachers, principals, superintendents) from 1872 to 1985-86, according to the Texas Education Agency.

Year	Number	Year	Number
1872	1,890	1973-74	149,139
1875	4,030	1974-75	156,447
1891	10,162	1975-76	164,312
1900	15,019	1976-77	168,857
1910	21,277	1977-78	174,455
1920	31,880	1978-79	179,313
1930	45,474	1979-80	184,278
1940	50,015	1980-81	188,174
1950	54,939	1981-82	190,142
1960-61	91,553	1982-83	194,464
1970-71	139,397	1983-84	197,591
1971-72	142,922	1984-85	201,334
1972-73	145,404	1985-86	207,873

Universities and Colleges of Texas

Table below is from data assembled from these institutions during 1987. Enrollment figures are for the 1986-1987 regular term and the 1986 summer term.

Name of Institution, Location, Ownership, Date of Founding, President	Number in Faculty	Regular Term 1986-87	Summer Session 1986	*Extension
Abilene Christian University—Abilene; private; 1906; William J. Teague	262	4,302	928	N.A.
A&M University, Texas—College Station. (See Texas A&M University System.)				
ALAMO COMMUNITY COLLEGE DISTRICT—Terry Dicianna, Acting Chancellor				
Palo Alto College—San Antonio; district; 1985; Terry Dicianna.	109	1,249	356	. . .
St. Philip's College—San Antonio; state; 1898; Stephen Mitchell, President.	. . .	. . .	. . .	. . .
San Antonio College—San Antonio; state/local; 1925; Max Castillo	858	21,486	11,993	15,163
Alvin Community College—Alvin; state; 1949; Dr. A. Rodney Allbright	196	3,918	3,550	988
Amarillo College—Amarillo; state/local; 1929; Dr. George Miller.	300	5,800	1,200	20,000
Amber University—Garland; private; 1971; Dr. Douglas W. Warner	45	1,000	800	N.A.
American Technological University—Killeen; private; 1973; Dr. L. Harlan Ford	33	564	457	. . .
Angelina College—Lufkin; state; 1968; Dr. Jack W. Hudgins.	100	2,500	1,100	. . .
Angelo State University—San Angelo. (See Texas State University System.)				
Arlington Baptist College—Arlington; Baptist; (1939 as Bible Baptist Seminary; changed to present name in 1965); Dr. Wayne Martin.	20	209	60	. . .

Name of Institution, Location, Ownership, Date of Founding, President	Number in Faculty	Enrollment Regular Term 1986-87	Enrollment Summer Session 1986	*Extension
Austin College—Sherman; Presbyterian, U.S.; 1849; Dr. Harry E. Smith.	112	1,176	250	...
Austin Community College—Austin; state; 1972; Dr. Daniel Angel.	881	18,340	13,964	5,542
Austin Presbyterian Theological Seminary—Austin; Presbyterian, U.S.; 1902 (successor to Austin School of Theology est. 1884); Dr. Jack L. Stotts.	16	257	144	499
Baptist Missionary Association Theological Seminary—Jacksonville; Baptist Missionary; (1955 as North American Theological Seminary); Philip R. Bryan.	11	87	15	...
Baylor College of Dentistry—Dallas; private; 1905; Dr. Richard E. Bradley, President.	221	532	...	...
Baylor College of Medicine—Houston; Baptist until 1969; now private; (Dallas 1903, moved to Houston in 1943); Dr. William T. Butler, President.	3,185	921	...	...
Baylor University—Waco; Southern Baptist (Baptist Convention of Texas); 1845; Dr. Herbert H. Reynolds.	668	11,556	4,487	...
Baylor University School of Nursing—Waco and Dallas; Southern Baptist (Baptist Convention of Texas); (School of Nursing, 1950); Herbert H. Reynolds, dean.	19	122	42	...
Bee County College—Beeville; county; 1965; Dr. Norman E. Wallace.	127	2,143	1,779	1,401
Bible Baptist Seminary—Arlington. (See Arlington Baptist College.).				
Bishop College—Dallas; Baptist; (est. in Marshall in 1881; moved to Dallas in 1961); Dr. Levi Watkins, President.	47	948	325	...
Blinn College—Brenham; state-local; (est. as academy in 1883, junior college 1927); Dr. Walter C. Schwartz.	127	4,144	2,908	...
Brazosport College—Lake Jackson; state; 1948; Dr. W. A. Bass.	85	3,434	2,649	2,003
Cedar Valley College—Lancaster. (See Dallas County Community College District.).				
Central Texas College—Killeen; state junior college; 1967; Chancellor, Dr. Luis M. Morton Jr.	224	16,527	8,628	¶
Cisco Junior College—Cisco; state; (1909 as private institution, became state supported in 1939); Dr. Henry E. McCullough.	60	1,533	1,305	...
Clarendon College—Clarendon; (1898 as church school, 1927 state); Kenneth D. Vaughan.	29	679	290	...
College of the Mainland—Texas City; state/local; 1967; Dr. Larry Stanley.	147	2,901	1,452	...
Collin County Community College District—McKinney; community; 1985; John H. Anthony.	190	3,941	...	477
Concordia Lutheran College—Austin; Lutheran (Missouri Synod); 1926; Dr. Ray F. Martens.	43	464	...	...
Cooke County College—Gainesville; state; (1924 as Gainesville Junior College, name changed); Dr. Luther Bud Joyner.	58	2,261	936	671
Corpus Christi State University—Corpus Christi. (See University System of South Texas.).				
Dallas Baptist University—Dallas; Southern Baptist; (1898 as Decatur Baptist College; moved to Dallas in 1965); Dr. W. Marvin Watson.	98	1,742	828	...
Dallas Christian College—Dallas; Christian; 1949; Gene Shepherd.	22	105	...	...

Name of Institution, Location, Ownership, Date of Founding, President	Number in Faculty	Enrollment Regular Term 1986-87	Summer Session 1986	*Extension
DALLAS COUNTY COMMUNITY COLLEGE DISTRICT—Chancellor, R. Jan LeCroy				
Brookhaven College—Farmers Branch; community; 1978; Dr. Patsy Fulton	270	7,100	5,410	7,500
Cedar Valley—Lancaster; community; 1977; Dr. Floyd S. Elkins	200	2,500	1,010	2,500
Eastfield College—Mesquite; community; 1970; Dan Sundermann	126	8,209	7,000	. . .
El Centro College—Dallas; community; 1966; Dr. Wright Lassiter Jr.	287	5,122	2,008	4,987
Mountain View College—Dallas; community; 1972; Dr. William H. Jordan	173	4,884	3,200	3,237
North Lake—Irving; community; 1977; Dr. James F. Horton Jr.	290	5,483	1,886	5,550
Richland College—Dallas; community; 1972; Dr. Stephen K. Mittelstet.	575	12,835	10,000	9,210
Dallas Theological Seminary—Dallas; private; 1924; Dr. Donald K. Campbell	71	1,196	725	756
‡‡Del Mar College—Corpus Christi; state-local; 1935; Dr. Edwin Biggerstaff	150	13,500	6,000	. . .
Eastfield College—Mesquite. (See Dallas County Community College District.)				
East Texas Baptist University—Marshall; Baptist; (1913 as College of Marshall, changed to East Texas Baptist College in 1944, became University in 1984); Dr. Robert E. Craig.	61	691	124	. . .
‡‡East Texas State University—Commerce; state; (1889 as private institution, 1917 as state); Dr. Jerry Morris.	315	7,135	6,998	. . .
East Texas University Metroplex Commuter Facility—Garland; state; 1976; Dr. Ron Huffstutler, Dean.	8	450	430	N.A
East Texas State University Center at Texarkana—Texarkana; state; 1971; Dr. John F. Moss Jr., Director.	54	1,142	828	. . .
El Centro College—Dallas. (See Dallas County Community College District.)				
El Paso Community College—El Paso; state; 1969; three campuses — Rio Grande, Trans-Mountain and Valle Verde; Dr. Robert Shepack	880	13,833	6,878	4,738
Episcopal Theological Seminary of the Southwest—Austin; Episcopal; 1952; Very Rev. Durstan R. McDonald, Provost	12	67	36	. . .
Frank Phillips College—Borger; state-local; 1948; Dr. Andy Hicks	26	855	520	900
‡‡Galveston College—Galveston; state; 1967; Dr. John Pickelman	105	2,014	1,659	1,512
Grayson County College—Denison; state; 1965; Dr. Jim Williams	140	3,612	1,500	500
Gulf Coast Bible College—Houston. (Moved to Oklahoma in 1985.)				
Hardin College—Wichita Falls. (Branch of Midwestern University.)				
Hardin-Simmons University—Abilene; Southern Baptist; 1891; Dr. Jesse C. Fletcher. . . .	123	1,804	1,098	. . .
Henderson County Junior College—(See Trinity Valley College.)				
Hill College—Hillsboro; public; (1923 as Hillsboro Junior College; name changed in 1962); Dr. William Auvenshine	68	1,483	420	360
Houston Baptist University—Houston; Southern Baptist; 1960; Dr. E. D. Hodo, Pres.; Dr. W. H. Hinton, Chancellor	120	3,305	1,512	. . .
Houston Community College—Houston; state; 1971;	396	38,050	43,824	8,621
Howard College—Big Spring; state; 1945; Dr. Bob E. Riley.	100	1,121	573	392
Howard Payne University—Brownwood; Southern Baptist; 1889; Dr. Don Newbury.	77	980	223	139
Huston-Tillotson College—Austin; United Methodist and United Church of Christ; 1875; Dr. John Q. Taylor King	46	520	213	. . .
Incarnate Word College—San Antonio; Catholic; 1881; Sister Margaret Patrice Slattery, Chancellor; Louis Agnese Jr., Pres.	72	1,576	590	. . .
International Bible College—San Antonio; private; Pentecostal; 1944; Rev. David B. Coote	10	150	. . .	. . .
Jacksonville College—Jacksonville; Baptist; 1899; Don Collins.	30	208	50	29
Jarvis Christian College—Hawkins; Disciples of Christ; 1912; Dr. Charles A. Berry Jr. . . .	50	468	. . .	. . .
Kilgore College—Kilgore; state; 1935; Dr. Stewart H. McLaurin.	140	3,937	1,241	1,693
LAMAR UNIVERSITY SYSTEM—Dr. George McLaughlin, Chancellor				
Lamar University at Beaumont—Beaumont; state; (1923 as junior municipal college, as senior state college Sept., 1951); Dr. Billy J. Franklin	640	11,592	5,026	800
Lamar University at Orange—Orange; state; 1969; Joe Ben Welch	54	934	279	75
Lamar University at Port Arthur—Port Arthur; state; (est. as Port Arthur College, 1909, became part of Lamar University 1975); Dr. W. Sam Monroe.	76	1,453	547	223
Laredo Junior College—Laredo; municipal; 1947; Dr. Roger L. Worsley	184	4,106	2,799	1,284
Laredo State University—Laredo. (See University System of South Texas.)				
Lee College—Baytown; state; 1934; Dr. Vivian Blevins	192	4,416	3,180	3,421
Le Tourneau College—Longview; private; (1946 as LeTourneau Technical Institute; became 4-year college in 1961); Dr. Alvin Austin.	60	675	. . .	. . .
Lon Morris College—Jacksonville; United Methodist; (1854 as Danville Academy; name changed in 1873 to Alexander Institute at Kilgore); Dr. W. Faulk Landrum	33	350	. . .	100
Lubbock Christian College—Lubbock; Church of Christ; 1957; Dr. Steven S. Lemley	90	1,041	163	. . .
Lutheran Concordia College—Austin. (See Concordia Lutheran College.)				
McLennan Community College—Waco; county; 1965; Dr. Wilbur A. Ball	213	5,000	2,500	13,000
McMurry College—Abilene; United Methodist; 1923; Dr. Thomas K. Kim	125	1,703	903	. . .
Mary Hardin-Baylor, University of—Belton; Southern Baptist; 1845; Dr. Bobby E. Parker .	89	1,325	912	2,315
Midland College—Midland; state; 1969; Dr. Jess Parrish	103	3,658	2,166	2,564
Midwestern State University—Wichita Falls; state; (1922 as junior college, 1946 as senior college, 1961 as state college); Dr. Louis J. Rodriguez	179	4,482	3,403	. . .
Mountain View College—Dallas. (See Dallas County Community College District.)				
Navarro College—Corsicana; state; 1946; Dr. Kenneth P. Walker	53	2,092	1,271	. . .
North American Theological Seminary—Jacksonville. (See Baptist Missionary Assn. Theological Seminary.)				
Northeast Texas Community College—Mount Pleasant; state; 1985; Dr. Wayland K. DeWitt	83	1,614	450	1,600
NORTH HARRIS COUNTY COLLEGE DISTRICT—Dr. Joe A. Airola, Chancellor	514	11,342	5,850	1,940
East Campus—Houston; state; 1984; Nellie Thorogood				
†South Campus—Houston; state; 1972; Larry Phillips				
††West Campus—Houston; state; 1988; Roy Lazenby				
North Lake College—Irving. (See Dallas County Community College District.)				

NORTH TEXAS STATE UNIVERSITY

is

"the University of North Texas"

QUALITY. An almost 100-year-old reputation for excellence in teaching and research. Outstanding faculty supported by first-class facilities and instructional equipment. One hundred and twenty-nine undergraduate and graduate majors. Rigorous admission standards that make a degree from North Texas even more desirable.

COST. A state-assisted public institution offering an affordable education and increased financial aid.

LOCATION. Only 45 minutes from Dallas, Fort Worth and other cities in the metroplex.

For information call 817/565-2681 or metro 267-3731 and ask for the admissions office.

Name of Institution, Location, Ownership, Date of Founding, President	Number in Faculty	Enrollment Regular Term 1986-87	Summer Session 1986	*Extension
North Texas State University (Effective May 15, 1988, name changes to University of North Texas)—Denton; state; (1890 as private institution, 1899 as state college; raised to university status in 1961); Dr. Alfred F. Hurley, Chancellor	1,721	21,271	17,078	8
Northwood Institute—Cedar Hill; private; 1966; Dean John Castle	13	205	27	2
Oblate School of Theology—San Antonio; Catholic; (est. in 1903, in present location since 1929; formerly DeMazenod Scholasticate); Rev. Patrick Guidon, O.M.I.	19	140	55	6
Odessa College—Odessa; state; 1946; Dr. Philip T. Speegle	136	4,868	2,396	18,99
Our Lady of the Lake University—San Antonio; Catholic; (as academy for girls 1896, senior college in 1911, raised to university status in 1975); Sister Elizabeth Anne Sueltenfuss	111	1,179	905	1,72
Palo Alto College—San Antonio. (See Alamo Community College District.)				
Pan American University—Edinburg; (est. as state and county Edinburg Junior College in 1927, name changed in 1952; became state senior college in 1965; raised to university status in 1971); Dr. Miguel Nevarez	387	9,984	10,461	. .
Pan American University at Brownsville—Brownsville; state; 1973; Dr. Homer J. Pena	30	1,183	1,431	. .
Panola Junior College—Carthage; state; 1947; Dr. Gary McDaniel	58	1,375	1,052	1,30
Paris Junior College—Paris; state; 1924	90	2,000	800	. .
Paul Quinn College—Waco; African Methodist Episcopal; 1872; Dr. Warren W. Morgan	. . .	464	301	16
Prairie View State University—Prairie View. (See Texas A&M University System.)				
Presbyterian Pan-American School—Kingsville; Presbyterian U.S.; (1912 as Texas-Mexican Industrial Institute; name changed in 1956); Dr. David R. Gifford, Headmaster	19	110	35	. .
Ranger Junior College—Ranger; state; 1926; Dr. Jack Elsom	45	654	466	15
Rice University—Houston; private; 1912; Dr. George B. Rupp	520	4,022	. . .	. .
Richland College—Dallas. (See Dallas County Community College District.)				
Rio Grande Bible Institute and Language School—Edinburg; private; 1946; Dr. Gordon Johnson	18	177	. . .	. .
St. Edwards University—Austin; Catholic; 1885; Dr. Patricia Hayes	129	2,536	846	42
St. Mary's University—San Antonio; Catholic; 1852; Rev. John Leies	145	3,300	. . .	. .
St. Philip's College—San Antonio; state; 1898; Dr. Stephen R. Mitchell	185	5,811	3,500	3,00
Sam Houston State University—Huntsville. (See Texas State University System.)				
San Antonio Community College District—San Antonio. (See Alamo Community College District.)				

SAN JACINTO COLLEGE DISTRICT—Thomas Sewell, Chancellor

Name of Institution, Location, Ownership, Date of Founding, President	Number in Faculty	Regular Term 1986-87	Summer Session 1986	*Extension
Central Campus—Pasadena; state; 1961; Dr. Monte Blue	439	9,329	3,629	. .
North Campus—Houston; state; 1976; Dr. Edwin E. Lehr	71	3,336	1,579	. .
South Campus—Houston; state; 1979; Dr. Parker Williams	184	4,180	2,630	1,05
San Marcos Baptist Academy—San Marcos; Baptist; 1907; Dr. Jack E. Byrom	37	360	200	. .
Schreiner College—Kerrville; Presbyterian, U.S.; 1923; Dr. Sam M. Junkin	48	508	127	. .
Southern Bible College—Houston. (Closed; moved to Joplin, Mo. 1984.)				
Southern Methodist University—Dallas; United Methodist; 1910; Dr. A. Kenneth Pye	667	9,019	3,548	2,40
South Plains College—Levelland; state; 1958; Dr. Marvin L. Baker	195	3,700	1,500	70
‡‡South Texas College of Law—Houston; private; 1923; W. J. Williamson	60	1,186	888	. .
Southwestern Adventist College—Keene; Seventh-Day Adventist; (1894 as Southwestern Junior College); Dr. Marvin Anderson	69	795	159	. .
Southwestern Assemblies of God College—Waxahachie; Assemblies of God; (est. Enid, Okla. in 1927; moved to Waxahachie as Southwestern Bible Institute in 1943); Dr. Paul Savell	27	701	303	16
Southwestern Baptist Theological Seminary—Fort Worth; Southern Baptist; 1909; Dr. Russell H. Dilday Jr.	191	4,341	1,727	98
Southwestern Christian College—Terrell; Church of Christ; (est. as Southern Bible Institute in Fort Worth, moved and name changed in 1950); Dr. Jack Evans Sr.	24	251	. . .	. .
Southwestern Medical School of the University of Texas—Dallas. (See University of Texas Health Science Center at Dallas.)				
Southwestern University—Georgetown; United Methodist; 1840; Dr. Roy B. Shilling Jr.	106	1,119	250	. .
Southwest Collegiate Institute for the Deaf of Howard College—Big Spring; state; 1980; Dr. Ron Brasel	18	100	2	3
Southwest Texas Junior College—Uvalde; state; 1946; Dr. Jimmy Goodson	67	2,216	689	1,24
Southwest Texas State University—San Marcos. (See Texas State University System.)				
Stephen F. Austin State University—Nacogdoches. (See Texas State University System.)				
Sul Ross State University—Alpine. (See Texas State University System.)				
Sul Ross University Uvalde Study Center—Uvalde. (See Texas State University System.)				
Tarleton State University—Stephenville. (See Texas A&M University System.)				

TARRANT COUNTY JUNIOR COLLEGE DISTRICT—Joe B. Rushing, Chancellor

Name of Institution, Location, Ownership, Date of Founding, President	Number in Faculty	Regular Term 1986-87	Summer Session 1986	*Extension
Northeast Campus—Hurst-N. Richland Hills; state; 1965; Dr. Herman L. Crow	346	10,178	3,148	. .
Northwest Campus—Fort Worth; state; 1975; Dr. Michael Saenz	80	4,500	2,000	2,36
South Campus—Fort Worth; state; 1965; Dr. Charles L. McKinney	200	10,400	4,000	6,00
Temple Junior College—Temple; state; 1926; Dr. Marvin R. Felder	106	2,200	900	1,50
Texarkana College—Texarkana; state; 1927; Dr. Carl M. Nelson	220	3,400	2,100	10,00
Texas A&I University—Kingsville. (See University System of South Texas.)				

TEXAS A&M UNIVERSITY SYSTEM—Perry L. Adkisson, Chancellor

Name of Institution, Location, Ownership, Date of Founding, President	Number in Faculty	Regular Term 1986-87	Summer Session 1986	*Extension
Moody College of Marine Sciences and Maritime Resources—Galveston. (See Texas A&M University at Galveston.)				
Prairie View A&M University—Prairie View; state; (1876 as Alta Vista Agricultural College; name changed to Prairie View State Normal School and then to Prairie View Agricultural and Mechanical College; changed to present name in 1973); Dr. Percy A. Pierre	260	4,499	2,229	. .
Tarleton State University—Stephenville; state; (1899; taken over by state in 1917, name changed from John Tarleton Agricultural College in 1949; raised to university in 1973); Dr. Barry B. Thompson	245	4,626	1,612	2,32

Name of Institution, Location, Ownership, Date of Founding, President	Number in Faculty	Enrollment Regular Term 1986-87	Summer Session 1986	*Extension
Texas A&M University—College Station; state; 1876; Dr. Frank E. Vandiver	2,224	36,570	14,720	N.A.
Texas A&M University at Galveston—Galveston; state; (1962 as Texas Maritime Academy, name changed to Moody College of Marine Sciences and Maritime Resources and raised to 4-yr. college 1971; name changed again to present name); Dr. Sammy M. Ray	55	524	415	4
‡‡Texas A&M College of Medicine—College Station; state; 1971; Dr. Robert S. Stone, Dean	71	164	...	...
Texas A&M College of Veterinary Medicine—College Station; state; 1916; Dr. George C. Shelton, Dean	195	1,550	250	800
Texas Baptist Institute and Seminary—Henderson; Missionary Baptist; 1949; Dr. Ray O. Brooks	13	85	...	25
Texas Christian University—Fort Worth; Disciples of Christ; 1873; Chancellor, Dr. William E. Tucker	389	6,919	2,202	...
Texas College—Tyler; Christian Methodist Episcopal; 1894; Dr. David H. Johnson	36	518	300	...
Texas College of Osteopathic Medicine—Fort Worth; state; (1966 as private college, became branch of North Texas State in 1975); Dr. David M. Richards	135	376	...	...
Texas Lutheran College—Seguin; Lutheran; 1891; Dr. Charles H. Oestreich	88	1,363	200	250
Texas Southern University—Houston; state; (1926 as Houston College for Negroes; 1947 as Texas State University for Negroes, name changed to present form in 1951); Dr. Robert Terry	387	7,250	2,768	650
Texas Southmost College.—Brownsville; junior college district; (est. as Brownsville Junior College 1926; name changed in 1949); Dr. Juliet V. Garcia	216	5,454	3,167	282
TEXAS STATE TECHNICAL INSTITUTE—Dr. Jack E. Tompkins, President				
Amarillo Campus—Amarillo; state; 1970; Ron DeSpain, Gen. Mgr.	110	981	952	300
Harlingen Campus—Harlingen; state; 1969; J. Gilbert Leal, Gen. Mgr.	175	2,261	1,380	1,070
Sweetwater Campus—Sweetwater; state; 1970.	44	668	507	...
Waco Campus—Waco; state; (1965 as James Connally Technical Institute; name changed in 1969); Dr. Robert D. Krienke, Gen. Mgr.	390	4,737	2,762	1,159
TEXAS STATE UNIVERSITY SYSTEM—Lamar G. Urbanovsky, Executive Director				
Angelo State University—San Angelo; (est. 1928, became state senior college in 1965); Dr. Lloyd D. Vincent	225	5,806	2,296	740
Sam Houston State University—Huntsville; state; 1879; Dr. Elliott T. Bowers	356	10,486	8,238	...
Southwest Texas State University—San Marcos; state; 1899; Robert L. Hardesty	831	19,775	14,896	26
Stephen F. Austin State University—Nacogdoches; state; 1923; Dr. William R. Johnson	625	12,138	5,260	...
Sul Ross State University—Alpine; state; 1920; Dr. Jack Humphries	155	2,313	2,346	...
Sul Ross University Uvalde Study Center—Uvalde; state; 1973; Dr. Frank Abbott, Dean	12	483	517	...
Texas Tech University—Lubbock; state; 1925; Dr. Lauro F. Cavazos	1,480	23,479	16,421	10,000
Texas Tech University Health Sciences Center—Lubbock; state; 1969; J. Ted Hartman, Dean-Medicine	N.A.	747	...	...
Texas Wesleyan College—Fort Worth; United Methodist; 1891; Dr. Jerry G. Bawcom	101	1,495	1,897	...
†Texas Woman's University—Denton; state; (1901 as College of Industrial Arts; name changed to Texas State College for Women in 1934; changed to present name in 1957); coed in Institute of Health Sciences and Graduate School; Dr. Shirley S. Chater	622	7,966	4,824	65
Texas Woman's University Institute of Health Sciences—Denton; Dr. Carolyn Rozier, Provost. Includes Schools of Health Care Services, Occupational Therapy, Physical Therapy and College of Nursing.				
Texas Woman's University Undergraduate General Divisions—Dr. Wilkes Berry, Provost. Includes Colleges of Humanities and Fine Arts; Natural and Social Sciences; Education; Nutrition, Textiles and Human Development; Health, Physical Education, Recreation and Dance; and School of Library and Information Studies				
Texas Woman's University Graduate School—Denton; Dr. Leslie Thompson, Provost				
Trinity University—San Antonio; private; 1869; Dr. Ronald Calgaard	225	2,717	400	1,000
Trinity Valley Community College—Athens; (formerly Henderson County Junior College); state; 1946; William J. Campion	160	3,960	1,955	1,500
Tyler Junior College—Tyler; state-community; 1926; Dr. Raymond M. Hawkins	336	7,227	2,269	5,189
University of Dallas—Irving; Catholic; 1956; (includes Graduate School of Management); Dr. Robert F. Sasseen	202	2,540	1,150	...
UNIVERSITY OF HOUSTON SYSTEM—Wilbur L. Meier Jr., Chancellor				
University of Houston-Clear Lake—Houston; state; 1975; Dr. Thomas Stauffer, Chancellor	300	6,691	3,781	...
University of Houston-Downtown—Houston; state; (1948 as South Texas College, made branch of University of Houston 1974); Dr. Alexander Schilt, Chancellor	287	7,256	2,410	300
‡‡University of Houston-University Park—Houston; state; (1927 as junior college, 1934 as university; made fully state-supported institution of higher education 1963); Dr. Richard L. Van Horn	1,871	31,114	22,246	...
University of Houston-Victoria—Victoria; state; 1973; Dr. Glenn A. Goerke	28	937	896	2,600
University of North Texas—(See North Texas State University.)				
University of St. Thomas—Houston; Catholic; 1947; Rev. Frank Bredeweg, C.S.B.	135	1,695	750	...
UNIVERSITY SYSTEM OF SOUTH TEXAS—Dr. Lawrence Pettit, Chancellor (formerly Texas A&I University System.)				
Corpus Christi State University—Corpus Christi; state; 1973; Dr. B. Alan Sugg	195	3,880	2,800	...
Laredo State University—Laredo; state; 1979; Dr. Manuel T. Pacheco	51	932	585	...
Texas A&I University—Kingsville; state; 1925; (name changed from South Texas Teachers College in 1929 to Texas College of Arts and Industries; changed to present name in 1967; part of University of South Texas System in 1977); Steven Altman.	207	5,012	5,476	...

Name of Institution, Location, Ownership, Date of Founding, President	Number in Faculty	Regular Term 1986-87	Summer Session 1986	*Extension
UNIVERSITY OF TEXAS SYSTEM—Hans Mark, Chancellor				
University of Texas at Arlington—Arlington; state; (1895 as **Arlington College**, 1917 as state institution; 1923 as **North Texas Agricultural College;** 1949 as **Arlington State;** 1967 to present name); Dr. Wendell H. Nedderman.	1,408	23,245	15,329	18,714
University of Texas at Arlington School of Nursing—Arlington; state; 1976; Dr. Myrna R. Pickard, Dean	60	376	...	...
University of Texas at Austin—Austin; state; 1883; William H. Cunningham.	2,400	47,000	20,000	...
University of Texas at Austin School of Nursing—Austin; state; (1890 as **John Sealy Hospital Training School of Nurses;** present name since 1896); Billye J. Brown, Dean.	52	500	300	1,500
University of Texas at Dallas—Richardson; state; (1969 graduate school only, 1975 university grade); Dr. Robert H. Rutford.	408	7,324	5,029	695
‡‡University of Texas at El Paso—El Paso; state; (1913 as **Texas College of Mines,** 1949 as **Texas Western College;** 1967 present name); Dr. Haskell M. Monroe	640	15,322	8,663	869
University of Texas at El Paso School of Nursing—El Paso. (Enrollment, faculty included with main university above.).				
University of Texas of the Permian Basin—Odessa; state; 1969; Dr. Duane M. Leach	110	1,821	1,187	...
University of Texas at San Antonio—San Antonio; state; 1973; Dr. James W. Wagener	447	12,413	6,426	...
University of Texas at Tyler—Tyler; (1971 as **Tyler State College;** name changed to **Texas Eastern University** in 1975, made branch of UT System in 1979); Dr. George F. Hamm	204	3,642	2,547	...
University of Texas Health Center at Tyler—Tyler; state; (1947 as **East Texas Chest Hospital,** became branch of UT System Sept., 1977); Dr. George A. Hurst, Director.	51	§300	...	1,000
‡THE UNIVERSITY OF TEXAS HEALTH SCIENCE CENTER DALLAS— Dr. Kern Wildenthal, President				
Graduate School of Biomedical Sciences; 1947; Dr. William Neaves, Dean	866	1,519	574	...
School of Allied Health Sciences; 1968; Dr. John W. Schermerhorn, Dean.				
Southwestern Medical School; (est. as private institution in 1943, as branch of University of Texas in 1948); Dr. Kern Wildenthal, Dean				
THE UNIVERSITY OF TEXAS MEDICAL BRANCH AT GALVESTON— Dr. Thomas James, President				
‡‡Graduate School of Biomedical Sciences; 1952; Dr. J. Palmer Saunders, Dean	220	149	119	...
Medical School; 1891; Dr. George T. Bryan, Dean	648	1,683	1,554	...
‡‡School of Allied Health Sciences; 1968; Dr. John G. Bruhn, Dean	70	351	365	...
‡‡School of Nursing; 1890; Dorothy M. Damewood, Dean	44	419	271	...
†‡‡THE UNIVERSITY OF TEXAS SYSTEM CANCER CENTER— Dr. Charles A. LeMaistre, President				
M. D. Anderson Hospital and Tumor Institute—Houston; 1941	422	**1,518	...	...
Science Park—Bastrop County; 1971				
‡THE UNIVERSITY OF TEXAS HEALTH SCIENCE CENTER-HOUSTON— Dr. Roger Bulger, President				
Dental Branch; 1905; Dr. Don Allen, Dean.	756	2,664	1,499	...
Graduate School of Biomedical Sciences; 1963; Dr. R. W. Butcher, Dean.				
Medical School; 1970; Frank Webber, Dean.				
School of Allied Health Sciences; 1973; Judith Craven, Dean.				
School of Nursing; 1972; Dr. Patricia L. Starck, Dean.				
School of Public Health; 1967; Dr. R. A. Stallones, Dean				
Division of Continuing Education; 1958; Dr. Sam A. Nixon, Director				
‡THE UNIVERSITY OF TEXAS HEALTH SCIENCE CENTER AT SAN ANTONIO— Dr. John P. Howe III, President				
Dental School; 1970; Dr. Dominick DePaola, Dean.				
Graduate School of Biomedical Sciences; 1970; Dr. Armand J. Guarino, Dean				
School of Allied Health Sciences; 1976; Dr. Armand J. Guarino, Dean.				
‡Health Science Center; 1972; Dr. John P. Howe III, President.	970	2,174	612	...
Medical School; (est. 1959 as **South Texas Medical School of University of Texas;** 1966 name changed to present form); Dr. Timothy N. Caris, Acting Dean.				
School of Nursing; 1969; Dr. Patty L. Hawken, Dean.				
Vernon Regional Junior College—Vernon; state; 1970; Dr. Joe Mills	48	1,801	1,078	4,561
Victoria College—Victoria; municipal; 1925; Dr. Roland E. Bing	120	3,100	1,250	225
Wayland Baptist University—Plainview; Southern Baptist; 1908; Dr. David L. Jester	107	1,917	1,600	1,634
Weatherford College—Weatherford; county/state; (1869 as branch of **Southwestern University,** 1922 as denominational junior college; 1949 as municipal junior college); Dr. E. W. Mince	76	1,745	738	...
Western Texas College—Snyder; county; 1971; Dr. Harry Krenek	62	1,216	954	...
West Texas State University—Canyon; state; 1910; Dr. Ed D. Roach	324	6,028	4,541	260
Wharton County Junior College—Wharton; state; 1946	120	2,350	867	...
Wiley College—Marshall; United Methodist; 1873; Dr. David L. Beckley	37	442	...	...

*Extension, or Continuing Education enrollment.
†Teaching Hospital and Research Institute.
‡Includes faculty and enrollment at all branches.
¶Included in on-campus enrollment figures.
§Students from other institutions receiving clinical instruction.
**Enrollment figure is for entire fiscal year.
††Opens fall of 1988.
‡‡No reply received to questionnaire. Information repeated from 1986-87 Almanac.

Texas Higher Education

This article was prepared by Janis Monger, public information director for the Texas Higher Education Coordinating Board.

The chairman of the 23-member Select Committee on Higher Education, created two years ago by the 69th Legislature, described 1987 as a "turning point" for higher education in the State of Texas. The 70th Legislature adopted almost all of the Select Committee recommendations to improve quality, access, business management and research opportunities at the state's higher education institutions.

Yet, by mid-summer of 1987 and the middle of a second special session, the Legislature had failed to adopt a state appropriations bill for FY 1988 and FY 1989 to fund higher education and other state agency operations. As of this writing, it appeared the state leadership had agreed to raise more than $5 billion in new taxes to fund a budget containing a small increase in current funding levels for higher education over the next two years. If ultimately adopted by the House and Senate, this increase would restore higher education to 1985 funding levels before the 69th Legislature met in Third Called Special Session in September 1986 and cut general revenue funds for senior colleges by 10.5 percent and for junior colleges by 9 percent.

As lawmakers attempted to find new sources of revenue in the wake of declining oil prices, they looked increasingly to higher education as a resource to facilitate economic diversification and revitalization.

Four new university research programs, an Engineering and Applied Science Recruitment Fund to attract women and ethnic minorities into these fields, and a Texas center for superconductivity at the University of Houston-University Park were all approved by the 70th Legislature in regular session. A hazardous waste alternative center was created at Lamar University in Beaumont, and all institutions were given more control over purchase of research materials and equipment.

Lawmakers were reluctant to create new draws on state revenue for program expansion and new campus construction. They rejected proposals to create a new state-supported law school in South Texas, to expand doctoral-degree granting authority in Texas, to move Corpus Christi State University from a two-year to a four-year institution, and to make Pan American University in Brownsville a free-standing university. They did authorize a name-change for North Texas State University; effective May 1988, the school wil be known as the University of North Texas. Laredo State University succeeded in changing its designation from an upper-level center to an upper-level institution.

Although state lawmakers rejected imposing a four-year moratorium on creating new junior colleges and Texas State Technical Institute branch campuses, they never brought to a vote a proposal to allow local taxpayer elections to expand community colleges into four-year institutions.

The 70th Legislature also defeated a proposal to expand The University of Texas and Texas A&M University boards of regents from nine to 12 members and to group remaining public universities into one of three university systems.

In response to continued forecasts of austere state economic conditions for the remainder of the decade, legislators created an interim committee to study the medical and allied health education delivery system.

The Coordinating Board, Texas College and University System, was renamed the Texas Higher Education Coordinating Board. The 70th Legislature directed the Board to study university funding policies and faculty compensation at peer institutions across the nation.

The Board will develop a five-year master plan for higher education in Texas and update the plan annually. The board must also complete a sunset review of all doctoral programs at public senior institutions by 1992. If state funding is forthcoming, the board will develop a statewide telecommunications network among higher education institutions for integrated teaching and data transmission and computation.

University Research

The Legislature clearly expressed its intent that Texas offer a nationally preeminent state-supported university research program. Lawmakers adopted a four-part research initiative developed by a Select Committee task force led by Dr. Norman Hackerman, president emeritus of Rice University and past president of The University of Texas.

Under the Research Enhancement Program, the Board will allocate state-appropriated funds to each public general academic institution based on the number of full-time equivalent faculty. The institution will develop competitive peer review procedures to award this research money to faculty in any discipline. Funds appropriated under this program will replace money currently distributed by the organized research formula for the public general academic institutions.

The Advanced Research program will provide support for basic research by all faculty members in engineering, math and scientific fields at all public institutions of higher education (including health science centers, community and junior colleges and Texas State Technical Institute). Dr. Hackerman will chair the Coordinating Board's 12-member Research Advisory Committee to recommend research priorities, guidelines and procedures for making awards on the basis of peer review of proposals. A separate committee of nationally eminent scientists will conduct the peer review of research proposals and recommend grant awards.

Faculty members of all public and independent universities and colleges may apply for funds under the new Advanced Technology Program to support research in agriculture, biotechnology, biomedicine, energy, materials science, micro-electronics, aerospace, marine science, aquaculture, telecommunications and manufacturing science. The board will also rely on peer review of proposals to determine the distribution of research grants.

The Coordinating Board will conduct merit reviews of special university research programs now funded by line item appropriations. The new legislation requires that the programs be evaluated for their "intrinsic merit, research performance, and the potential contribution of the research to the development of knowledge and instruction in advanced and emerging technologies and the economic growth of the state."

As of this writing, the 70th Legislature had not determined an initial level of funding for the new research programs. These programs replace the $35 million Texas Advanced Technology Research Program adopted by the 69th Legislature.

Testing and Teacher Education

Concerned about improving the measuring and reporting of college students' academic achievement, the 70th Legislature passed bills mandating diagnostic testing of entering college students and new requirements for reporting first-year academic performance.

Beginning in fall 1989, all entering college students with fewer than 60 credit hours must take a diagnostic test of basic reading, writing and math skills. The test will identify the need for remedial work and, in all but exceptional cases, students must pass this exam before they can enroll in any upper-division course that, upon completion, would give them 60 or more semester credit hours. The test cannot be used to determine college admission. Institutions must provide remedial courses and advising programs for students who do pass a portion of the test.

Institutions must report these test results annually to the Coordinating Board. Separate legislation requires the senior colleges and universities to report back to the high schools and junior colleges on students' first-year academic performance.

The 70th Legislature also voted to require students applying for a teaching certificate after Sept. 1, 1991, to obtain a bachelor's degree in an academic or interdisciplinary academic major other than education. After that date, no more than 18 semester credit hours of education courses at the baccalaureate level may be required for the granting of a Texas teaching certificate. The State Board of Education may adopt rules to permit undergraduates to take more than 18 hours of required education courses for a teaching certificate in early childhood education, special education, English as a second language and bilingual education.

Statewide Enrollment

A total of 762,407 students were enrolled in the 139 Texas public and private institutions of higher education in fall 1986, an increase of 11,969 students or 1.59 percent from the previous year.

Texas' four-year public universities experienced

the second consecutive drop in enrollment in more than 30 years — down .47 percent to 359,343 students from fall 1985 enrollments of 361,052.

The state's public community junior colleges experienced a 4.34 percent enrollment increase since 1985, up 12,553 students to 302,085 in fall 1986. Annual enrollment gains were also reported by the independent community junior colleges. In fall 1986, 1,192 students enrolled at independent community junior colleges compared to 1,151 in fall 1985.

Enrollment for the fall quarter of 1986 was 9,062 at campuses of the Texas State Technical Institute, an increase of 4.56 percent or 395 students compared to the same quarter in 1985.

Public medical and dental institutions reported a 1.41 percent increase in fall 1986 enrollment to 10,802 students compared to 10,652 students in fall 1985. In comparison, enrollment in independent medical and dental institutions dropped 2.7 percent since fall 1985.

Because some institutions have experienced dramatic increases in enrollment while buildings stand empty on other campuses much of the time, the 70th Legislature authorized the Coordinating Board to set enrollment limits for institutions. Coordinating Board Chairman Larry Temple said, "Setting enrollment limits is essential if we are going to stop the runaway construction of unnecessary campus buildings."

The Texas system of public higher education encompasses 24 public four-year universities, five upper-level universities, five upper-level centers, two lower-division centers, 49 community college districts, one technical institute with four campuses, seven medical schools, two dental schools, a school for marine resources and a special institute for the deaf. In 1985, local taxpayers voted to create the Collin County Community College District and Palo Alto College, Alamo Community College District. There has been no expansion of the public higher education system in the past two years.

In the private sector, Texas has 37 independent senior colleges and universities, four junior colleges, one medical school and one dental school.

Tuition

As the state's financial crisis worsened, the 70th Legislature voted to give higher education institutions the latitude to raise graduate school tuition for non-residents to no more than double the current rate.

Resident tuition rates were not increased since, in fall 1985, the Legislature tripled resident tuition — the first increase since 1957 — and set up a graduated schedule of tuition increases capping at $24 per credit hour in 1995. Despite the increases, tuition costs for state residents are at this time among the lowest in the nation.

Out-of-state students and foreign students have paid $120 per semester credit hour since fall 1985. Beginning this fall, non-resident students will pay 100 percent of the cost of their education through a procedure that indexes tuition to an average amount appropriated to general academic teaching institutions in a biennium.

Substantial increases in tuition rates for medical and dental students also were enacted in 1985.

Higher Education Funding

The 70th Legislature voted to replace the current formula system for appropriating money to higher education institutions with a combination "lump sum" appropriation and special incentive and initiative funding programs.

If the Legislature follows this approach in the appropriations bill, in addition to base funding, the Coordinating Board will use special incentive funds to reward institutions meeting goals set by the board in such areas as minority recruitment and retention, raising academic standards, achieving optimum use of college buildings and cutting energy costs. The board will award initiative funds to institutions promoting academic excellence.

History

While there were earlier efforts toward higher education, the first permanent institutions established were these church-supported schools: **Rutersville University,** established in 1840 by Methodist minister Martin Ruter in Fayette County, predecessor of **Southwestern University,** Georgetown, established in 1843; **Baylor University,** now at Waco, but established in 1845 at Independence, Washington County; and **Austin College,** now at Sherman, but founded in 1849 at Huntsville.

Other historic Texas schools of collegiate rank included: **Larissa College,** 1848, at Larissa, Cherokee County; **McKenzie College,** 1841, Clarksville; **Chappell Hill Male and Female Institute,** 1850, Chappell Hill; **Soule University,** 1855, Chappell Hill; **Johnson Institute,** 1852, Driftwood, Hays County; **Nacogdoches University,** 1845, Nacogdoches; **Salado College,** 1859, Salado, Bell County. **Add-Ran College,** established at Thorp Spring in 1873, was the predecessor of present **Texas Christian University,** Fort Worth.

Texas A&M, authorized by the Legislature in 1871, opened its doors in 1876 to become the first publicly supported institution of higher education. In 1881, Texans voted to establish the **University of Texas** in Austin, with a medical branch in Galveston; the Austin institution opened Sept. 15, 1883, the Galveston school in 1891.

In 1901, the 27th Legislature established the **Girls Industrial College** (forerunner of **Texas Woman's University),** which began classes at its campus in Denton in 1903. A campaign to establish a state industrial college for women was led by the State Grange and Patrons of Husbandry. A bill was signed into law on April 6, 1901, creating the college. It was charged with a dual mission, which continues to guide the university today — to provide a liberal education and to prepare young women with a specialized education "for the practical industries of the age." In 1905 the name of the college was changed to the **College of Industrial Arts;** in 1934, it was changed to **Texas State College for Women.** Since 1957 the name of the institution, which is now the largest university for women in the United States, has been the **Texas Woman's University.**

A number of Texas schools were established primarily for **blacks,** although collegiate racial integration is now complete in the state. The black-oriented institutions include state-supported **Prairie View State University,** Prairie View; **Texas Southern University,** Houston; and privately supported **Bishop College,** Dallas; **Huston-Tillotson College,** Austin; **Jarvis Christian College,** Hawkins; **Wiley College,** Marshall; **Paul Quinn College,** Waco; **Mary Allen College,** Crockett; and **Butler** and **Texas Colleges,** Tyler.

Wadley Research Institute, Dallas, and **M. D. Anderson Hospital and Tumor Institute,** Houston, grant graduate degrees although they are not primarily educational institutions.

The following table gives dates of establishment for leading Texas institutions and enrollments, as reported by the schools. In some cases, dates of establishment differ from those given in the preceding discussion because schools use the date when authorization was given, rather than actual date of first classwork.

Statewide Civic Organizations

Listed below are privately supported civic, commercial and other nonprofit statewide organizations in Texas which provided information on questionnaires sent out by the Texas Almanac. Organizations that did not return questionnaires by June 15, 1987, are not included. In some cases regional organizations are included.

Zip codes are given for executive officers or office addresses, where available.

Listing of organizations is alphabetical, according to the key word in the title.

Advertising Agencies, S. W. Assn. of—Pres., Bob Daily, Tulsa, OK; Exec. Dir., Bob Burke. Office Address: 8700 Stemmons Frwy., Ste. 303, Dallas 75247.

Aging, Texas Assn. of Homes for the—Pres., Sandra B. Derrow, 9417 Great Hills Tr., Apt. 3044, Austin 78723; Exec. Dir., Mary Jo Pompeo. Office Address: 6225 Hwy. 290 E, Ste. 204, Austin 78723.

AGRICULTURAL ORGANIZATIONS

Aviation Assn., Texas Agricultural—Pres., Ed Barbour, HCR-1, Box 96-1, Dumas 79029; Exec. Dir., Harry P. Whitworth. Office Address: 1000 Brazos, Ste. 200, Austin 78701.

Cooperative Council, Texas—Pres., Wayne Mengers, Rt. 1, Tynan 78391; Exec. Vice Pres., Billy L. Conner. Office Address: Box 9527, Austin 78766.

Teachers Assn. of Texas, Vocational Agricultural—Pres., Jesse Bradford, 1508 Brookwood, Diboll 75941; Exec. Dir., W. H. Meischen. Office Address: 614 E. 12th, Austin 78701.

Airport Executives, Assn. of Texas—Pres., Kyle Sonnenberg, Box 517, McKinney; Exec. Dir., Ted Willis. Office Address 211 E. 7th, Ste. 1020, Austin 78701.

American Legion, Dept. of Texas—Dept. Cmdr., John W. J. Richter, 302 Goessler, Brenham 77833; Dept.

Adjt., Jimmy D. Lemley. Office Address: Box 789, Austin 78767.

American Legion Auxiliary, Dept. of Texas—Pres., Jane Shultz, 3501 Tanglewood Dr., Bryan; Exec. Dir., Mae Paust. Office Address: 709 E. 10th, Austin 78701.

Anesthesiologists, Texas Society of—Pres., Dr. Law Sone Jr., 3600 Gaston, Ste. 804, Dallas 75246; Exec. Secy., Mary Jones. Office Address: 1905 N. Lamar Blvd., Ste. 107, Austin 78705.

Angus Assn. of America, Texas Red—Pres., Jim Burch, 412 N. Ave. G, Clifton 76634; Secy.-Treas., Dorothy Walker. Office Address: Box 793, Eagle Lake 77434.

Angus Assn., Texas—Pres., Larry Brown, 1024 E. Hopkins, Mexia 76667; Exec. Dir., Julie McMahon. Office Address: 233 N. Judkins, Fort Worth 76111.

Apartment Assn., Texas—Pres., Karl May; Exec. Dir., Jerry Adams. Office Address: 1005 Congress, Ste. 420, Austin 78701.

Apparel Manufacturers Assn., S.W. (SAMA), Div. of Am. Apparel Manufacturers Assn. (AAMA)—Pres., Frank Martino, Box 2306, Denton 76201; Exec. Dir., Jane Stanton. Office Address: Box 585931, Dallas 75258.

Appraisers—(See **Land Managers.**)

ARCHAEOLOGICAL ORGANIZATIONS

Archaeology, Institute of Nautical—Pres., Dr. Donald A. Frey; Exec. Dir., Frederick R. Mayer. Office Address: Drawer AU, College Station 77843.

Archeological Assn., Southern Texas—Office Address: 123 E. Crestline, San Antonio 78201.

Archeological Society, Central Texas—Office Address: 4229 Mitchell Road, Waco 76710.

Archeological Society, Coastal Bend—Office Address: c/o Skip Kennedy, 3413 Cartagena, Corpus Christi 78418.

Archeological Society, Dallas—Office Address: Box 28026, Dallas 75228.

Archeological Society, El Paso—Office Address: Box 4345, El Paso 79914.

Archeological Society, Houston—Office Address: Box 6751, Houston 77265.

Archeological Society, Midland—Office Address: Box 4224, Midland 79704.

Archeological Society, Panhandle—Office Address: Box 814, Amarillo 79105.

Archeological Society, The Texas—Pres., J. Rex Wayland, Box 1580, George West 78022. Office Address: Center for Archaeological Research, Univ. of Tex. at San Antonio, San Antonio 78285.

Archeologists, Council of Texas—Secy.-Treas., Mark Denton, Texas Antiquities Committee, Texas Historical Commission, Box 12276, Austin 78711.

Art Education Assn., Texas—Pres. James M. Clarke, Aldine Independent School Dist., 14910 Aldine-Westfield Rd., Houston 77032. Office Address: 4902 Shatner, Houston 77066.

Assessing Officers, Texas Assn. of—Pres., Arthur Skeen, Midway ISD, 9101 Woodway Dr., Waco 76710; Exec. Dir., Martha Noble Carmean. Office Address: Box 26550, Austin 78755.

Association Executives, Texas Society of—Exec. Dir., Marilyn Monroe, 2550 S. IH-35, Ste. 200, Austin 78704.

Austin College Alumni Assn.—Pres., Susan Cuellar, 16302 Sunset Valley, Dallas 75248.

Auto and Truck Parts Assn., Texas—Pres., Lin Barker, Box 368, Tyler 75710; Exec. Dir., Michael T. Marks. Office Address: 1601 Rio Grande, Ste. 440, Austin 78701.

Automobile Dealers Assn., Texas—Pres., Gene Fondren, 1108 Lavaca, Austin; Chmn. of Board, Jack Coker, Box 1988, Texarkana 75501. Office Address: Box 1028, Austin 78767.

Automotive Service Assn., Independent—Chmn., Richard Cossette, Minneapolis, MN. Exec. Dir., Allen Richey. Office Address: 1901 Airport Frwy., Bedford 76021.

Automotive Wholesalers of Texas—Chmn., G. C. Morris; Exec. Dir., Mrs. Floy Shead. Office Address: 1507 S. IH-35, Austin 78741.

Bank Counsel, Texas Assn. of—Pres., Michael S. Brenan, 450 First City Bank Bldg., San Antonio 78239; Secy.-Treas., Jim Lederer. Office Address: 203 W. Tenth, Austin 78701.

Bankers Assn., Texas—Pres., Lowell Smith Jr., Box 100, Rio Vista 76093; Exec. Dir., Sam Kimberlin Jr. Office Address: 203 W. 10th St., Austin 78701.

Bar of Texas, State—Pres., Joe H. Nagy, Box 1499, Lubbock 79408; Exec. Dir., Larry K. Montgomery. Office Address: Box 12487, Austin 78711.

Baylor Alumni Assn.—Pres., Alton Pearson; Exec. Vice Pres., Dr. James F. Cole. Office Address: Campus Box 378, Waco 76798.

Beefmaster Breeders Universal—Pres., Mickey Johnson, Comanche, OK; Exec. Dir., Gene Kuykendall, 6800 Park Ten Blvd., Ste. 290W, San Antonio 78213.

Beyond Bows and Arrows, Inc.—Pres., Franklin McLemore, 9924 Brockbank Dr., Dallas 75220. Office Address: Box 140343, Dallas 75214.

Big Bend Natural History Association, Inc.—Exec. Dir., Rick L. LoBello, Box 68, Big Bend National Park 79834.

Blindness, Texas Society to Prevent—(See **Prevent Blindness.**)

Blueberry Growers Assn., Texas—Pres., Don Cawthon, Rt. 2, Box 169, Larue 75770; Exec. Dir., Dana Tucker, Box 891, Georgetown 78627.

B'nai B'rith Women, (S.W. Region)—Reg. Dir., Mrs. Marvin Green. Office Address: 4660 Beechnut, #246, Houston 77096.

Boating Trades Assn. of Texas—Pres., Bill Warren; Exec. Dir., Julian O. Read. Office Address: 3811 Turtle Creek Blvd., Ste. 110, Dallas 75219.

Brangus Breeders Assn., Texas—Pres., Dr. Richard Wood, Dallas; Exec. Dir., Mary Perry. Office Address: Box 690750, San Antonio 78269.

Broiler Council, Texas—(See **Poultry Associations.**)

Building and Construction Trade Council, Texas—Pres., R. Harold White; Exec. Sec.-Treas., Jackie W. St. Clair. Office Address: 1106 Lavaca, Ste. 204, Austin 78701.

Building Officials Association of Texas—Pres., Coy Perry, Box 9960, College Station; Exec. Dir., Ted Willis. Office Address: 211 E. 7th, Ste. 1020, Austin 78701.

Business, Natl. Fed. of Independent/Texas—Office Address: 815 Brazos, Ste. 902, Austin 78701.

Business, Texas Association of—Pres., H. Dane Harris, Box 2989, Austin 78769-2989; Exec. Dir., Don G. Kaspar. Office Address: 300 W. 15th, Ste. 300, Austin 78701.

Cattle Raisers Assn., Inc., Texas and Southwestern—Pres., John E. Birdwell, 4901 21st St., Lubbock 79407; Sec.-Gen. Mgr., Don C. King. Office Address: 1301 W. Seventh, Fort Worth 76102.

Celtic Music Assn., Southwest—Pres., Patricia Jump, Box 4474, Dallas 75208.

CHAMBERS OF COMMERCE ASSNS.

East Texas—Pres., John Horton, Box 61, Jacksonville 75766; Exec. Dir., David B. Ross. Office Address: Box 1592, Longview 75606.

Executives, Texas—Pres., Grady L. Elder Jr., 500 Rio Concho Dr., San Angelo 76903. Office Address: 300 W. 15th, Ste. 875, Austin 78701.

Rio Grande Valley—Pres., Carlton Richards, Box 1952, Brownsville 78520; Exec. Vice Pres., C. F. Giles. Office Address: Box 1499, Weslaco 78596.

Texas State—Pres., E. W. Wehman Jr., Drawer W, Pleasanton 78064; Exec. Dir., Pledger C. Cate. Office Address: 300 W. 15th, Ste. 875, Austin 78701.

Christian Church (Disciples of Christ) in the Southwest—Reg. Minister and Pres., James C. Suggs, 2909 Lubbock, Fort Worth 76109; Moderator, J. R. Johnson, Box 228, Hillister 77624.

Christmas Tree Growers Assn., Texas—Pres., Verley G. Spell, Rt. 6, Box 500, Orange 77630; Exec. Sec.-Treas., E. R. Wagoner. Office Address: 1003 Markus, Lufkin 75901.

Churches, Texas Conference of—Pres., Msgr. Robert Rehkemper, Austin; Exec. Dir., Rev. Dr. Frank H. Dietz. Office Address: 2704 Rio Grande, Apt. 9, Austin 78705.

Circulation Management Assn., Texas—Pres., Jerry Hopkins, Box 622, Corsicana 75110; Exec. Dir., Faires Kuykendall. Office Address: Box 1870, Fort Worth 76101.

Citrus and Vegetable Assn., Texas—Pres., R. A. Peterson, Rio Grande City; Exec. Dir., William Weeks. Office Address: 6912 W. Expressway, Harlingen 78552-3701.

City Attorneys Assn., Texas—Pres., David Caylor, No. 2, Civic Center, El Paso 79999; Exec. Dir., Susan Horton. Office Address: 211 E. 7th, Ste. 1020, Austin 78701.

City Management Assn., Texas—Pres., Gary Gwyn, Box 2039, Tyler; Exec. Dir., Gary Watkins. Office Address: 211 E. 7th, #1020, Austin 78701.

City Personnel and Civil Service Officials of Texas,

Assn. of—(Name changed; see **Municipal Personnel Assn., Texas.**)

City Planners Assn. of Texas—Pres., Richard M. Bullock, Box 9909, Corpus Christi; Exec. Dir., Ted Willis. Office Address: 211 E. 7th, Ste. 1020, Austin 78701.

Civil Air Patrol (Texas Wing)—Office Address: Bldg. 207, Bergstrom AFB, TX 78743.

Clerks Assn., Texas Municipal—Pres., Pat Rutherford, Box 26569, Fort Worth; Exec. Dir., Ted Willis. Office Address: 211 E. 7th, Ste. 1020, Austin 78701.

Colleges and Universities, Assn. of Texas—Pres., Dr. Raymond M. Hawkins, Tyler J.C., Box 9020, Tyler 75711; Exec. Dir., Dr. J. R. Woolf. Office Address: UTA Box 19023, Arlington 76019.

Colleges and Universities of Texas, Council of Presidents of the Public Senior—Chmn., Dr. C. Robert Kemble, Lamar Univ. System, Lamar Stn., Box 11900, Beaumont; Exec. Dir., Wanda J. Mills. Office Address: 2609 Coatbridge, Austin 78745-3423.

Colonial Wars in Texas, Society of—Pres., Denis M. Fluker, 8911 Springview Lane, Houston 77080; Exec. Dir., Thomas Bresneher Jr. Office Address: 3207 Top Hill Rd., San Antonio 78209.

Communication Assn., Internatl.—Pres., Dr. L. Edna Rogers, Salt Lake City, UT; Exec. Dir., Robert L. Cox, Box 9589, Austin 78766. Office Address: 8140 Burnet Rd., Austin 78766.

Confederate Research Center—Pres., Dr. Larry Arnold, 7509 Mason Dells Dr., Dallas 75230; Adjutant, Robert L. Johnston, 1401 Harrington Dr., Dallas 75075-2745. Office Address: Hill College, Box 619, Hillsboro 76645.

Conservation Districts, Assn. of Texas Soil and Water—Pres., Waldo Smith, Box 1252, Brenham. Office Address: Box 658, Temple 76503.

CONTRACTORS ASSOCIATIONS

Texas Air Conditioning Contractors Assn.—Pres., Larry Jones, 2226 B. Michigan, Arlington 76013; Exec. Dir., Bexley C. Richard, 940 E. 51st, Austin 78751.

Association of General Contractors of Texas—Highway, Heavy, Utilities & Industrial Branch—Pres., Richard Barth, 210 Barton Springs Rd., Austin 78704; Exec. Dir., Thomas L. Johnson. Office Address: 300 Barton Springs Rd., Austin 78704.

Texas Association of Landscape Contractors—Pres., Len Gallagher, 1512 Cavitt, Bryan 77801; Exec. Dir., Jeff D. Martin. Office Address: 940 E. 51st, Austin 78751.

Texas Council Painting and Decorating Contractors Assn.—Pres., Don Williams; Exec. Dir., Michael Marks. Office Address: 1601 Rio Grande, Ste. 440, Austin 78701.

Associated Plumbing, Heating and Cooling Contractors of Texas, Inc.—Pres., Joe Zimmerman, 6881 S. Gessner, Houston 77036; Exec. Dir., Pat Miller. Office Address: 940 E. 51st, Austin 78751.

Corrections Assn., Texas—Pres., John Byrd, Box 13401, Austin 78711; Exec. Dir., Jeff D. Martin. Office Address: 940 E. 51st, Austin 78751.

COTTON ASSOCIATIONS

Cotton Assn., Texas—Pres., Charles Smith, 1616 Texas Ave., Lubbock 79401; Exec. Vice Pres., H. A. Poteet. Office Address: 100 N. Central Expressway, Ste. 810, Dallas 75137.

Cotton Ginners Assn., Texas—Exec. Vice Pres., J. H. Price. Office Address: 302 E. 11th St., Austin 78701.

Cotton Growers, Inc., Plains—Pres., Myrl D. Mitchell, Box 99, Lenorah 79749; Exec. Vice Pres., Donald A. Johnson. Office Address: 4510 Edgewood, Lubbock 79414.

Cotton Growers Co-operative Assn., Texas—Pres., Paul Underwood, Itasca; Exec. Dir., A. E. Schmidt. Office Address: Box 391, Taylor 76574.

Counseling and Development, Texas Assn. for—Pres., Dr. Ruth Ann White; Exec. Sec., Charlotte McKay. Office Address: 316 W. 12th, Ste. 402, Austin 78701.

Counties, Texas Assn. of (TAC)—Pres., Bill Melton, 303 Records Bldg., Dallas 75202; Exec. Dir., Sam E. Clonts, Box 2131, Austin. Office Address: 400 W. 15th, Ste. 604, Austin 78701.

Courts Assn., Texas Municipal—Pres., Kitty Schild, 1101 N. Mesa, El Paso; Exec. Dir., Ted Willis, 211 E. 7th, #1020, Austin 78701.

CREDIT ASSOCIATIONS

Credit Management Assn. of Texas—Pres., Tommy Langston, Box 2751, Beaumont 77704; Exec. Dir., Pat Miller. Office Address: 940 E. 51st, Austin 78751.

Credit Union League and Affiliates, Texas—Pres., Jack L. Eaker; Chmn. of Board, Jack L. Eaker. Office

Address: 4455 LBJ Freeway, Farmers Branch 75244-5998.

DAUGHTERS ASSOCIATIONS

Of American Colonists, Texas Society—Pres., Mrs. Robert R. Truitt, 901 Oakmont Lane N., Fort Worth 76112.

Of Colonial Wars—Pres., Mrs. Harry E. Rowland Jr., 4521 Northaven, Dallas 75229. Office Address: 6408 Dovenshire Terrace, Fort Worth 76112.

Of the Confederacy, Texas Div. of the United—Pres., Mrs. W. S. McLemore, Box 22, Edgemont 75117; Exec. Dir., Sharon Hardin. Office Address: 112 E. 11th, Austin 78701.

Of 1812, Texas Society, United States—Pres., Mrs. C. J. Holubec, 4706 Willow, Bellaire 77401.

Of the Republic of Texas—Pres. Gen., Henry L. Averitte, 901 Cedar, Palestine 75801. Office Address: 112 E. 11th, Austin 78701.

Dermatological Society, Texas—Pres., Dr. Dennis E. Newton III, 10 Medical Parkway, #205, Dallas 75234; Exec. Dir., Carrie Laymon. Office Address: 1801 N. Lamar Blvd., Austin 78701.

Diabetes and Endocrine Assn., Texas—Exec. Dir., Dr. Eric A. Orzeck. Office Address: 8181 N. Stadium Dr., Houston 77054.

Diabetes Assn., Inc., American (Texas Affiliate, Inc.)—Pres., Dr. Richard Sachson; Exec. Dir., Phillip L. Fry. Office Address: 8140 N. Mopac, Bldg. 1, Ste., 130, Austin 78759.

Discover Texas Assn.—Pres., Jim Battersby, 13538 Hollowview, San Antonio 78232. Office Address: 16607 Blanco Rd., Suite 803, San Antonio 78232.

Donkey and Mule Society, Inc., Am.— Pres., Paul A. Hutchins; Member Services Officer, Betsy Hutchins. Office Address: 2901 N. Elm St., Denton 76201.

Earth Scientists, Society of Independent Professional—Pres., Philip J. McKenna, 910 16th, Ste. 408, Denver, CO 80202; Exec. Sec., Diane Finstrom. Office Address: 4925 Greenville Ave., Ste. 170, Dallas 75206.

Egg Council, Texas—Pres., Hank Novak; Exec. Vice Pres., Bill Powers. Office Address: Ste. 105, 8140 Burnet Rd., Austin 78758.

Electronics Assn., Inc., Texas—Pres., Mike Webber, 5208 Pershing, Fort Worth 76107; Exec. Dir., Arlene Erickson. Office Address: 2708 W. Berry, Fort Worth 76109.

ENGINEERS ASSOCIATIONS

American Society of Civil (Texas Sec.)—Pres., Derrell Johnson, 910 Collier, Fort Worth 76102; Exec. Sec., Fred P. Wagner Jr. Office Address: Box 4250, Lubbock 79409.

Texas Society of Professional—Pres., Earnest F. Gloyna, Dean of Engineering, UT Austin, ECJ 10.310, Austin 78712; Exec. Dir., Gerhardt Schulle, Box 2145, Austin 78768.

Council of Texas, Inc., Consulting—Pres., Conrad S. Hinshaw, 6161 Savoy, Ste. 1199, Houston; Exec. Dir., J. P. Word. Office Address: Suite 402, San Jacinto Bldg., Austin 78701.

Faculty Assn., Texas—Pres., Kenneth Margerison, History Dept., SW Texas State Univ., San Marcos; Exec. Sec.-Treas., Dr. Frances Sage. Office Address: 316 W. 12th, Austin 78701.

Fair Assn., East Texas—Pres., Herbert C. Buie, Box 1116, Tyler; Mgr., Bob Murdoch. Office Address: 411 W. Front, Tyler 75702.

Fair, State of Texas—Pres., Joe M. Dealey, Dallas; Exec. Vice Pres. & Gen. Mgr., Wayne H. Gallagher. Office Address: Box 26010, Dallas 75226.

Fairs and Expositions, Texas Assn. of—Pres., John Emmons, Box 7581, Waco 76710; Sec.-Treas., Ms. Frances Cooper. Office Address: Box 867, Mercedes 78570.

Farm and Ranch Club, East Texas—Pres., Danny Peggram, Box 8, Lindale 75771; Sec.-Treas., Bob Murdoch. Office Address: 411 W. Front, Tyler 75702.

Farmers Union, Texas—Pres., Joe Rankin, Rt. 1, Box 70, Ralls 79357; Vice Pres., Bob Girard. Office Address: Box 7276, Waco 76714-7276.

Fashion Assn., Inc., American—Pres., O. Wade Hampton; Exec. Sec., Bette Hamilton, Box AM586454, Dallas. Office Address: Suite M5F18, Menswear Mart, Dallas 75258.

Finance Officers Assn., Texas Chapter of Municipal—Pres., Suzanne Barnett, Box 110, Sugar Land; Exec. Dir., Ted Willis. Office Address: 211 E. 7th, Ste. 1020, Austin 78701.

Fire Chiefs Assn., Texas—Pres., Curtis Richards,

Box 1971, Amarillo; Exec. Dir., Ted Willis. Office Address: 211 E. 7th, Ste. 1020, Austin 78701.

Firemen's and Fire Marshals' Assn., State—Pres., Tommy Bledsoe, Lone Star Steel FD., Lone Star 75668. Office Address: 2211 S. IH-35, Ste. 209, Austin 78741.

Folklore Society, Texas—Pres., Lou Rodenberger, Star Rte. 1, Box 60, Baird 79504; Exec. Dir., F. E. Abernethy. Office Address: Box 13007, SFA Sta., Nacogdoches 75962-3007.

Food Processors Assn., Texas—Pres., Dave Carter, P.O. Drawer E, Crystal City 78839; Exec. Dir., Al B. Wagner. Office Address: Box 341, College Station 77841.

Foresters, Texas Society of American—Pres., Charles Walker, Texas Forest Service, 508 Pan American Dr., Livingston; Business Mgr., E. R. Wagoner. Office Address: Box 3625, Lufkin 75903.

Forestry Assn., Texas—Pres., John Wood, 1245 E. Ave. L, Silsbee 77656; Exec. Vice Pres., Ron Hufford. Office Address: Box 1488, Lufkin 75901.

Funeral Directors Assn., Inc., Texas—Pres., Charles E. Walker, 801 Teas Rd., Conroe 77303; Exec. Dir., Lee A. Hampton. Office Address: 1513 S. IH-35, Austin 78741.

Future Farmers of America, Texas Assn. of—Pres., Bruce Cobb, Box 13064, Austin 78701; Exec. Sec., Benny Clark. Office Address: 1701 N. Congress Ave., Austin 78701.

Genealogical Society, Texas State—Pres., Trevia Wooster Beverly, 2507 Tannehill, Houston 77008-3052.

Goat Breeders Assn., Am. Angora—Pres., Edwin Hipsher, Rt. 3, Box 175B, Brownwood 76801; Sec.-Treas., Mary Jane Glasscock, Box 195, Rocksprings 78880.

Grange, Texas State—Pres., Clifton Lampman Sr., Rt. 17, Box 126AX, San Antonio 78238; Exec. Dir., James H. Kiles, Luckenbach Rt., Box 6A, Fredericksburg 78624.

Grocers Assn., D-FW—Pres., J. L. Williams, Box 518, Coppell 75019; Exec. Dir., Daisey Fern Nelson. Office Address: 1515 W. Mockingbird, Ste. 113, Dallas 75235.

Hawking Assn., Texas—Pres., Dennis D. Smith, 9027 Post Oak Circle, Dallas 75217.

Health Officials, Texas Assn. of Municipal—Pres., Bill Jackson, Box 860358, Plano; Exec. Dir., Gary Watkins, 211 E. 7th, #1020, Austin 78701.

Health, Physical Education, Recreation and Dance, Texas Assn. for—Pres., Marcella S. Porter, Irving ISD, 901 O'Connor, Irving 75061; Exec. Dir., Quentin A. Christian. Office Address: Box 7578, University Sta., Austin 78713.

Highway 67 Assn., U.S.—Pres., James A. Little, Box 5581, San Angelo 76902; Sec.-Treas., George R. Jordan. Office Address: 401 Rio Concho Dr., San Angelo 76903.

HISTORICAL ASSOCIATIONS

Baptist Historical Society, Texas—Pres., Dr. Charles S. McIlvenne, Lufkin; Sec.-Treas., Dr. Robert L. Philips, Box 2200, Fort Worth 76122.

Catholic Historical Society, Texas—Pres., Dr. Patrick Foley, 1113 Idlewood Ave., Azle 76020-9602. Office Address: Catholic Archives of Texas, c/o Diocese of Austin, Box 13327, Austin 78711.

East Texas—Pres., Joe L. White, E. Texas Oil Museum, Hwy. 259 at Ross, Kilgore 75662; Exec. Dir., Archie P. McDonald. Office Address: Box 6223, SFA Sta., Nacogdoches 75962.

El Paso County Historical Society—Pres., Mary Ann Dodson Dr., 6751 Fiesta Dr., El Paso 79912. Office Address: 603 W. Yandell, El Paso 79902.

Jewish Historical Society, El Paso—Pres., Morris Gafatzan, Texas Commerce Bank Bldg., El Paso 79901; Exec. Dir., Dr. Floyd S. Fierman. Office Address: Temple Mount Sinai, 4408 N. Stanton, El Paso 79901.

Jewish Historical Society, Texas—Pres., Ginger Jacobs, 7060 Brookshire, Dallas 75230; Exec. Sec., Cathy Schechter. Office Address: Box 50501, Austin 78763.

Methodist Historical Society, Texas United—Pres., Rev. John C. Johnson, 215 Zion Hill Rd., Weatherford. Office Address: c/o Roger Loyd, Bridwell Library, SMU, Dallas 75275.

Oral Historical Assn.—Pres., Dr. Monte Lewis, Cisco Jr. Col., Cisco 76437; Exec. Dir., Rebecca Sharpless. Office Address: CSB Box 401, Baylor University, Waco 76798.

Panhandle-Plains Society—Pres., Don Max Vars; Exec. Vice Pres., D. Ryan Smith. Office Address: Box 967 W.T. Station, Canyon 79016.

Permian Historical Society—Pres., Dr. Duane Leache. Office Address: Univ. of Texas of Permian Basin, 4901 E. University Blvd., Odessa 79762-8301.

Texas State—Pres., Dr. James Pohl, Box 1092, San Marcos 78666; Exec. Dir., Dr. Ron C. Tyler. Office Address: 2.306 Sid Richardson Hall, UT Sta., Austin 78712.

West Texas—Pres., Monte Lewis, 1412 Park Dr., Cisco 76437; Exec. Dir., Dr. B. W. Aston. Office Address: Box 152, H-SU, Abilene 79698.

Historical Foundation, The Texas—Pres., J. P. Bryan, 1300 Main, Ste. 1520, Houston; Exec. Dir., Mark L. Tronbridge. Office Address: Box 12243, Austin 78711.

Home Economics Assn., Texas—Pres., Judy S. Knight, Garland ISD, Box 461547, Garland 75046; Exec. Dir., Margaret J. Sloan. Office Address: Box 831, Hurst 76053.

Homefurnishings Assn., Southwest—Exec. Dir., Al Stillman. Office Address: Box 581207, Dallas 75258.

HORSE ASSOCIATIONS

Appaloosa Horse Club, Texas—Pres., Max Wheeler, Rt. 1, Box 47-B, Gordon 76453; Exec. Sec., Cheryl Palmer. Office Address: Box 1449, Burleson 76028.

National Cutting Horse Assn.—Pres., Jim Reno, Box 1820, Kerrville 78028; Exec. Dir., Zack T. Wood Jr. Office Address: Box 12155, Fort Worth 76121.

Miniature Horse Assn., Inc., Am.—Pres., Robert King, N. Salem, IN 46165; Exec. Sec., Tony Greaves. Office Address: Box 129, Burleson 76028.

American Paint—Pres., Dale Fell, 8040 E. Cherry Creek Rd., Franktown, CO 80116; Exec. Sec., Ed Roberts. Office Address: Box 18519, Fort Worth 76118-0519.

American Quarter—Pres., Dr. Gerald A. O'Connor; Exec. Dir., Ronald Blackwell. Office Address: 2701 IH-40 East, Amarillo 79168.

HOSPITAL ASSOCIATIONS

Assn., Texas—Chmn., James J. Farnsworth, 1935 Amelia St., Dallas; Pres., O. Ray Hurst.

Nurses, Texas Society of Professional—Pres., Winnie Lockhart, 1635 North Loop W, Houston; Exec. Dir., Joan Houston.

Independent Colleges and Universities of Texas—Pres., Carol L. McDonald, Box 13105, Austin 78711; Exec. Dir., Dr. Harry Smith. Office Address: 1122 Colorado, Ste. 203, Austin 78701.

INSURANCE ASSOCIATIONS

Advisory Assn., Texas—Chmn. of Exec. Comm., Harold G. Duble; Gen. Mgr., Roy E. Hoga. Office Address: Box 15, Austin 78767.

Independent Agents of Texas—Pres., William R. Black, 126 W. Walker, Breckenridge 76024; Exec. Dir., Ernest Stromberger. Office Address: Box 1663, Austin 78767.

Interior Designers, Texas Chapter of American Society of—Pres., Kathy Ford-Montgomery. Office Address: Box 58525, Dallas 75258.

Jewelers Assn., Inc., Texas—Pres., Arnold Rubin, Fort Worth. Office Address: 504 W. 12th, Austin 78701.

Keep Texas Beautiful, Inc.—Pres., Ebby Halliday Acers, 4455 Sigma Rd., Dallas 75244; Exec. Dir., Mary Ellen Shoop, Box 2251, Austin 78768.

Knights of Columbus, Texas State Council—State Deputy, Ricardo Garcia, Box 355, San Diego 78384; State Exec. Sec., Charles Emery. Office Address: 2500 Columbus Dr., Austin 78746.

Knights of the Order of San Jacinto—Knight-Comdr., Joseph J. Fisher, Box 88, Beaumont 77704. Office Address: 4564 Arcady, Dallas 75205.

Knights of Pythias, Grand Lodge of Texas—Grand Chancellor, John Ellis Jr., Rt. 9, Box 155, Marshall 75670; Grand Sec., Max Williams. Office Address: Box 10071, Longview 75608.

Land Managers and Appraisers, Texas Society of Professional—Pres., Larry Kokel, 2508 Williams, Ste. 202, Georgetown 78628; Exec. Dir., Charles E. Gilliland. Office Address: Box 2996, College Station 77841.

Land Title Assn., Texas—Pres., R. C. von Doenhoff, Box 547, Crockett 75835; Exec. Dir., Catherine Lancaster. Office Address: 220 W. 7th, Ste. 201, Austin 78701.

Language Assn., South Central Modern—Pres., William W. Kibler, Dept. of French, UT-Austin 78712; Exec. Dir., Paul A. Parrish. Office Address: Dept. of English, Texas A&M Univ., College Station 77843.

Lawyers Assn., Texas Young—Pres., Kenneth C. Raney Jr., 2020 LTV Tower, 2001 Ross, Dallas 75201-2916; Coordinator, Sherrie Lacy. Office Address: Box 12487, Capitol Station, Austin 78711.

League of Women Voters of Texas—Pres., Diane B.

Sheridan; Exec. Dir., Joann Lovelace. Office Address: 1212 Guadalupe, Ste. 107, Austin 78701.

Legal Reserve Officials Assn., Texas—Pres., Ronald R. Coleman, 10000 IH-10W, Ste. 308, San Antonio 78730; Exec. Dir., Dave Smith. Office Address: 3724 Jefferson St., Ste. 113, Austin 78731.

Letters, Texas Institute of—Pres., Kaye Northcutt; Sec.-Treas., John Edward Weems. Office Address: Box 8594, Waco 76714-8594.

Libertarian Party of Texas—Chmn., Roger V. Gary. Office Address: 8480 Fredericksburg Rd., Ste. 102, San Antonio 78229.

Library Directors Assn., Texas Municipal—Pres., Mary Kay Snell, Box 2171, Amarillo; Exec. Dir., Ted Willis. Office Address: 211 E. 7th, Ste. 1020, Austin 78701.

Lung Assn. of Texas, Am.—Pres., Donna Richards; Mgng. Dir., Edward Carter. Office Address: 3520 Executive Center Dr., Ste. 6100, Austin 78731.

Magazine Publishers Assn., Texas—Pres., Chris Hearne; Exec. Dir., Karol Rice. Office Address: 1104 W. Ave., No. 101, Austin 78701.

Manufactured Housing Assn., Texas—Pres., Will Ehrle. Office Address: Box 14428, Austin 78761.

Mayors, Councilmembers and Commissioners, Assn. of—Pres., Sandra Pickett, 1829 Sam Houston, Liberty; Exec. Dir., Ted Willis. Office Address: 211 E. 7th, Ste. 1020, Austin 78701.

Meat Packers Assn., S.W.—Pres., Vince Kirchner, Box 249, Richardson 75080; Exec. Dir., Leon N. Kothmann. Office Address: 1333 Corporate Dr., Ste. 213, Irving 75038.

MEDICAL ASSOCIATIONS

Anesthetists, Texas Assn. of Nurse—Pres., Anita D. Johnson, 7206 Glendora, Dallas 75230; Public Information Officer, Henry de la Garza. Office Address: Box 626, Gainesville 76240.

Association, Texas—Pres., David Vanderpool, M.D., 6936 Lupton, Dallas; Exec. Vice Pres., Robert G. Mickey. Office Address: 1801 N. Lamar Blvd., Austin 78701.

Osteopathic Medical Assn., Texas—Pres., Dr. Bill H. Puryear, 4010 E. Belknap, Fort Worth 76111; Exec. Dir., Tex Roberts. Office Address: 226 Bailey, Fort Worth 76107.

Podiatric Medical Assn., Texas—Pres., Dr. Charles E. Hammonds; Exec. Dir., Carolyn F. Schwartz. Office Address: 5017 Bull Creek Rd., Austin 78731.

Thoracic Society, Texas—Pres., Dr. William J. Deaton, 7 Green Lanes, Austin; Chapter Admin., Linda Nichols. Office Address: 3520 Executive Center Dr., Ste. G100, Austin 78731.

Association, Texas Veterinary—Pres., E. T. Skidmore, 2501 N. Main, No. 150, Euless 76039; Exec. Dir., David P. Lancaster. Office Address: 6633 U.S. 290 East, Ste. 201, Austin 78723.

Mental Health Assn. in Texas—Pres., O. S. Chrisman; Exec. Dir., Stella C. Mullins. Office Address: 1111 W. 24th, Austin 78705.

Mesquite, Los Amigos del—Pres., Ms. Rozan Williams; Editor, Paul Hope. Office Address: Box 15551, Austin 78761.

Motorcycle Dealers Assn., Texas—Pres., Jimmy Hall, 4312 Gillis, Houston 78745; Exec. Dir., Michael T. Marks. Office Address: 1601 Rio Grande, Ste. 440, Austin 78701.

Motor Transportation Assn., Texas—Pres., Robert A. Floyd; Chmn., Oran Hardy McAlister II. Office Address: 700 E. 11th, Austin 78767.

Municipal Advisory Council of Texas—Chmn., Bd. of Trustees, Tom Anderlitch, 711 Navarro, Ste. 400, San Antonio 78240; Exec. Dir., Danny Burger. Office Address: Box 2968, Austin 78769-2968.

Municipal Information Officers, Texas Assn. of—Pres., Diana Green, Box 469002, Garland; Exec. Dir., Gary Watkins, 211 E. 7th, #1020, Austin 78701.

Municipal League, Texas—Exec. Dir., Ted Willis. Office Address: 211 E. 7th, Ste. 1020, Austin 78701.

Municipal Personnel Assn., Texas—Pres., Nancy Carney, Box 469002, Garland; Exec. Dir., Ted Willis. Office Address: 211 E. 7th, Ste. 1020, Austin 78701.

Music Educators Assn., Inc., Texas—Pres., David Pennington, 104 Blackfoot Dr., Temple 76501; Exec. Dir., Bill Cormack. Office Address: 807 Stark, Austin 78756.

National Guard Assn. of Texas—Pres., Maj. John W. Cook; Exec. Dir., Lewis O. King. Office Address: Box 10045, Austin 78766.

Neuropsychiatric Assn., Texas—(Succeeded by Texas Dist. Branch of the American Psychiatric Assn.)

New England Women, Tex. Colony #121, Natl. Society

of—Pres., Mrs. Jap Schwartz, 1209 Capetown, Grand Prairie 75050; First Vice Pres., Mary Helen Brengel, 1307 Woodlawn, Dallas 75208.

Newspaper Assn., Texas Daily—Pres., Tucker Sutherland, Box 171150, San Antonio 78217; Exec. Vice Pres., Philip A. Berkebile. Office Address: 1005 Congress, Ste. 495, Austin 78701.

Nurserymen, Texas Assn. of—Pres., Larry Galbreath, Box 70, Harlingen 78550; Exec. Vice Pres., Bill R. Fullingim. Office Address: 7750 S. IH-35, Austin 78745-6621.

Nursing, Texas League for—Pres., Dr. Myrna Pickard, 8301 Anglin Dr., Fort Worth 76119; Exec. Dir., Patty Roberts. Office Address: 11607 Wiginton Dr., Austin 78758.

Office Product Dealers Assn. of Greater Austin—Pres., Hugh Lindsay, Box 1786, Austin 78767; Exec. Dir., Don R. McCullough. Office Address: 940 E. 51st, Austin 78751.

OIL AND GAS ASSOCIATIONS

North Texas—Pres., Robert K. Pace, Box S&P, Wichita Falls; Exec. Vice Pres., Tom Haywood. Office Address: 320 Energy Center Bldg., Wichita Falls 76301.

Texas Mid-Continent—Pres., William H. Abington; Exec. Dir., Richard C. Hudson, 1717 St. James Place, #140, Houston. Office Address: 400 W. 15th, Ste. 500, Austin 78701.

West Central Texas—Pres., Paul R. Galloway Sr., Box 1627, Abilene 79604; Exec. Dir., Morris Burns. Office Address: Box 2332, Abilene 79604.

Optometric Assn., Texas—Pres., Dr. Floyd L. Thornton, 1616 10th, Wichita Falls; Exec. Dir., Stanley Boysen. Office Address: 1016 LaPosada, Ste. 174, Austin 78752.

Parents and Teachers, Texas Congress of—Pres., Mrs. Kathryn Whitfill; Exec. Dir., James L. Crouch. Office Address: 408 W. 11th, Austin 78746.

Parks and Recreation Assn., Texas Municipal—Pres., Ron Parnell, Box 657, Cleburne; Exec. Dir., Ted Willis. Office Address: 211 E. 7th, Ste. 1020, Austin 78701.

Parliamentarians, Texas State Assn. of—Pres., Dennis Clark, 5424 Shirley, Baytown 77521-1740; Exec. Dir., Donna Reed. Office Address: 9318 Faircrest, Dallas 75238.

Peanut Growers' Assn., S.W.—Pres., James P. Neal, Box 253, Pearsall 78061; Mgr., Ross Wilson. Office Address: Box 338, Gorman 76454.

Pediatric Society, Texas—Pres., Dr. William S. Conkling; Adm. Asst., Mary Greene. Office Address: 1801 N. Lamar Blvd., Austin 78701.

Personnel Assn., Texas Municipal—Pres., Ben Blair, Box 2039, Tyler; Exec. Dir., Ted Willis. Office Address: 211 E. 7th, #1020, Austin 78701.

Personnel Consultants, Texas Assn. of—Pres., Ngaire Keene, 8150 N. Central Expressway, No. 701, Dallas 75206; Exec. Dir., Janice E. Meador. Office Address: 722 Fairmont Pkwy., Pasadena 77504.

Pest Control Assn., Inc., Texas—Pres., James Boren, Box 8118, Corpus Christi; Exec. Dir., Don R. McCullough. Office Address: 4302 Airport Blvd., Austin 78722.

PETROLEUM ASSOCIATIONS

Engineers, Society of—Exec. Dir., Dan K. Adamson. Office Address: Box 833836, Richardson 75083-3836.

North Texas Oil & Gas Assn.—Pres., Robert K. Pace, Box S & P, Wichita Falls; Exec. Dir., Tom Haywood. Office Address: 320 Energy Center Bldg., Wichita Falls 76301.

Pharmaceutical Assn., Texas—Pres., Norman S. Anderton III, Box 250, Shallowater 79363; Exec. Dir., Luther R. Parker, Box 14709, Austin 78761. Office Address: 1624 E. Anderson Ln., Austin 78752.

Philosophical Society of Texas—Pres. Joe Greenhill, 1410 United Bank Tower, 400 W. 15th, Austin; Sec., Dorman H. Winfrey. Office Address: Box 12927, Capitol Sta., Austin 78711.

Physical Therapy Assn., Texas (Chap. of Am. Physical Therapy Assn.)—Pres., Susan McPhail, 8299 Cambridge, Apt. 2004, Houston; Exec. Dir., Steve Renfrow. Office Address: 211 E. 7th, Ste. 714, Austin 78701.

Plant Food Inst., Texas—Pres., Gary Fitzgerald, Rt. 2, Box 41, Celina 75009; Exec. Dir., Pat Miller. Office Address: 940 E. 51st, Austin 78751.

Podiatry Assn., Texas—(See Texas Podiatric Medical Assn. under Medical Associations.)

Poetry Society of Texas—Pres., Marvin Hirsh; Cor. Sec., Faye Carr Adams. Office Address: 4244 Skillman, Dallas 75206.

Police Chiefs Assn., Texas—Pres., Jerry Loftin, 7008

Rice Ave., Bellaire; Exec. Dir., Ted Willis. Office Address: 211 E. 7th, Ste. 1020, Austin 78701.

POULTRY ASSOCIATIONS
(Office Address of each one is Box 9589, Austin 8766.)

Texas Allied Assn.—Pres., Charles Yarbrough, Godley; Exec. Vice Pres., Bill Powers.

Texas Broiler Council—Pres., Ralph Simmons; Exec. Vice Pres., Bill Powers. Office Address: 8140 Burnet Rd., Ste. 105, Austin 78758.

Texas Federation—Pres., Joe Conerly, Indian River Internatl., Nacogdoches; Exec. Vice Pres., Bill Powers.

Texas Improvement Assn.—Pres., Bob Sellers, Indian River Internatl., Nacogdoches; Exec. Vice Pres: Bill Powers.

Texas Turkey Federation—Pres., Dick Taylor, Plantation Foods, Waco; Exec. Vice Pres., Bill Powers.

Preservation Texas—Pres., Richard Meyer; Exec. Dir., Anice Read, Box 12832, Austin 78711-2832.

PRESS ASSOCIATIONS
South Texas—Pres., Chip Latcham, Beeville 78102; Exec. Dir., Bill Wilkerson. Office Address: Box 130, Pleasanton 78064.

Texas—Pres., Charles Schulz, Box 1040, Taylor 76574; Exec. Vice Pres., Lyndell Williams. Office Address: 718 W. 5th, Austin 78701.

Texas High School—Dir., Dr. Mary K. Sparks, Dept. of Journalism, TWU, Denton. Office Address: Box 23866, WU, Denton 76204.

West Texas—Pres., Lynn Brisendine, Box 1272, Brownfield 79316; Sec.-Treas., Barbara Craig Kelly. Office Address: 2502 Ivanhoe, Abilene 79605.

Prevent Blindness, Texas Society to (Dallas Br.)—Pres., Ann Musgrave, 4514 Travis, Ste. 315, LB 14, Dallas, 75205; Exec. Dir., Judith M. Todd. Office Address: 610 Fairmount, Dallas 75219.

Producers & Royalty Owners Assn., Texas Ind. (TIPRO)—Pres., Shelby D. Pitts, 500 Meadows Bldg., Dallas 75206; Exec. Vice Pres., Julian G. Martin. Office Address: 1910 InterFirst Tower, Austin 78701.

Psychiatric Physicians, Texas Society of—Pres., Dr. Robert Zapalac, 720 W. 34th, Austin 78705; Adm. Asst., Carrie Laymon, 1801 N. Lamar Blvd., Austin 78701.

Public Employees Assn., Texas—Pres., Bill Warren, 814 22nd, Lubbock 79410; Exec. Dir., Lane A. Ziveley, 19 Martin Lane, Pflugerville 78660.

Public University Presidents and Chancellors, Council of—Pres., Dr. B. Alan Sugg, Corpus Christi State University, 6300 Ocean Dr., Corpus Christi 78712-5599; Exec. Dir., Wanda J. Mills. Office Address: 2609 Coatbridge Dr., Austin 78745-3423.

Public Works Assn., Texas—Pres., Wayne Dickens, Box 2570, Waco; Exec. Dir., Ted Willis. Office Address: 11 E. 7th, Ste. 1020, Austin 78701.

Purchasing Institute, Inc., Natl.—Pres., Earle Hawkes; Las Vegas, NV; Exec. Dir., J. Nelson Slater. Office Address: 201 W. Beltline Rd., Ste. D, Cedar Hill 5104.

Purchasing Managers Assn., Texas Municipal—Pres., Gene Eads, Box 2000, Lubbock; Exec. Dir., Ted Willis. Office Address: 211 E. 7th, Ste. 1020, Austin 78701.

Pythias, Knights of, Grand Lodge of Texas—(See Knights of Pythias.)

Range Management, Texas Sec. of the Society for—Pres., Ron Sosebee, Range and Wildlife Dept., Texas Tech University, Lubbock 79409. Office Address: 1839 York, Denver, CO 80206.

Recreational Vehicle Assn., Texas—Pres., Kenny Peters, 3601 Telephone Rd., Houston 77022; Exec. Dir., Cliff Houy. Office Address: 3355 Bee Cave Rd., Ste. 104, Austin 78746.

Research League, Texas—Pres., Dr. Jared E. Hazleton. Chmn., W. C. McCord, 300 S. St. Paul, Dallas 75201. Office Address: Box 12456, Austin 78701.

Retailers Assn., Texas—Pres., Michael R. Moore. Office Address: 504 W. 12th, Austin 78701.

Roads/Transportation Assn., Texas Good—Chmn., David Glass, Box 626, Paris 75460; Exec. Dir., Eugene W. Robbins. Office Address: 408 Vaughn Bldg., Austin 78701.

Santa Gertrudis Breeders Internatl.—Pres., Dan Wendt; Exec. Dir., W. M. Warren. Office Address: Box 257, Kingsville 78363.

Savings and Loan League, Texas—Pres., W. W.

McAllister III; Exec. Dir., Tom S. King. Office Address: 408 W. 14th, Austin 78701.

SCHOOL ASSOCIATIONS
Boards, Texas Assn. of—Pres., W. D. Hinton, 2501 Johnson, Greenville 75401; Exec. Dir., Orbry D. Holden. Office Address: 406 E. 11th, Austin 78701.

Food Service Assn., Texas—Pres., Marjorie Craft, Dallas ISD, 3700 Ross, Dallas 75204; Exec. Dir., Carole Pfennig. Office Address: 316 W. 12th, Austin 78701.

Public Relations Assn., Texas Chapter, Natl.—Pres., Judy Williams, Aldine ISD, 14910 Aldine-Westfield Rd., Houston 77032; Exec. Sec., Don Agnew. Office Address: Box 8615, Tyler 75711.

Science, Texas Academy of—Pres., Lamar Johnson, Tarleton State Univ., Stephenville 76402; Exec. Sec., William J. Clark. Office Address: Drawer H6, College Station 77844.

Secretaries Assn., Texas Educational—Pres., Frances Passmore, 1101 Ennis Joslin, Corpus Christi 78412; Exec. Officer, Lori Meisner. Office Address: 1101 Trinity, Austin 78701.

Sheep Breeders' Assn., Am. Rambouillet—Pres., Fred Rose, Box 420097, Del Rio 78842; Sec.-Treas., Jo Ann Custer. Office Address: 2709 Sherwood Way, San Angelo 76901.

Sheriffs' Assn. of Texas, Inc.—Pres., Sheriff Royce Wilson, Leon County, Box 278, Centerville 78533; Exec. Dir., Gordon Johnson. Office Address: Box 4488, Austin 78765.

Shorthand Reporters Assn., Texas—Pres., Don Pollock, Bexar County Courthouse, San Antonio, 78205; Exec. Dir., Jeff D. Martin. Office Address: 940 E. 51st, Austin 78751.

Shrimp Assn., The Texas—Pres., Ronald Herndon, Box 1270, Aransas Pass 78336; Exec. Dir., Ralph Rayburn. Office Address: 807 Brazos, #403, Austin 78701.

Shrine Assn., Texas—Pres., John B. Fannin, 8329 Summerwood Dr., Austin 78759; Sec.-Treas., W. A. Spoonts. Office Address: Box 1950, Wichita Falls 76307.

Sign Manufacturers Assn., Texas—Pres., Melvin Sheeton, 1200 E. 3rd, Austin 78702; Exec. Dir., Marcie Funebess. Office Address: 2301-C Central Dr., Ste. 411, Bedford 76021.

Skeet Shooters Assn., Texas—Pres., A. John Sheffield Jr., Box 17, LaPorte 77571. Office Address: Box 680007, San Antonio 78268-0007.

Skeet Shooting Assn., Natl.—Pres., S. Hallock duPont Jr., Vero Beach, FL. Office Address: Box 680007, San Antonio 78268-0007.

Social Workers, Texas Chapter of the Natl. Assn. of—Pres., Sonja R. Berry; Exec. Dir., Susan E. Negreen. Office Address: 810 W. 11th, Austin 78701.

Soft Drink Assn., Texas—Pres., Toby Summers, Coca-Cola Btlg. Co., Box 58, San Antonio 78291; Exec. Dir., Virgil Musick. Office Address: Box 2258, Abilene 79604.

Soil and Water Conservation, Assn. of Texas—Pres., Waldo Smith, Box 1252, Brenham 77833; Advisor, Harvey Davis, Box 658, Temple 76503.

SONS ASSOCIATIONS
Of Confederate Veterans (Texas Div.)—Cmdr., Larry Arnold, 8911 Springview Ln., Houston; Adjt., Robert L. Johnston. Office Address: Box 619, Hillsboro 76645.

Of Hermann in the State of Texas, Grand Lodge of the Order of the—Pres., Louis B. Engelke, 515 S. St. Mary's, San Antonio 78205.

Of Republic of Texas—Pres. Gen., Joe E. Ericson, 1614 Rosebud, Nacogdoches 75961; Admn. Asst., Peggy Cotrone. Office Address: 4564 Arcady, Dallas 75205.

Soybean Assn., Texas—Pres., Bill Sylvester, Rt. 2, Plainview 79072; Exec. Dir., D. Trent Roberts. Office Address: Box 2182, Dallas 75221.

Speech-Language-Hearing Assn., Texas—Pres., Martha McGlothlin, 8414 Stillwood Lane, Austin 78758; Exec. Sec., Banks Miller. Office Address: 6937 N. Interregional Hwy., #100, Austin 78752.

Sportsmen's Clubs of Texas (SCOT)—Pres., Laurin Currie, Box 1568, Austin 78767; Exec. Officer, Alan Allen. Office Address: 311 Vaughn Bldg., Austin 78701.

Surgeons (N. Tex. Chap.), Am. College of—Pres., Dr. James C. Terrell Jr., 150 River North Blvd., Stephenville 76401; Sec., Dr. Michael S. McArthur, 214 E. Houston, Tyler. Office Address: Box 4680 Station A, Dallas 75208.

Surveyors Assn., Texas—Pres., George Sanders, 4800 S. Congress, Austin 78745; Exec. Dir., Don R. McCullough. Office Address: 940 E. 51st, Austin 78751.

Tax Administrators, Texas Assn. of Municipal—Pres.,

Elaine DiFiglia, Box 144, Addison; Exec. Dir., Ted Willis. Office Address: 211 E. 7th, Ste. 1020, Austin 78701.

TEACHERS ASSOCIATIONS
(Also see Faculty Assn.)

Texas Classroom—Pres., Eva Jo Kasinger; 700 Guadalupe, Austin 78701; Exec. Dir., Jeri Stone. Office Address: Box 1489, Austin 78767.

Texas Assn. of College—Pres., Dr. Nelson Thornton, Mktg. & Mgmt., Sam Houston St. Univ., Huntsville; Exec. Dir., Nancy A. Bene. Office Address: 316 W. 12th, Ste. 210, Austin 78701.

English, Texas Joint Council (Teachers of)—Pres., Betty Gray, Klein Oak H.S., 22603 NW Dr., Spring 77389; Exec. Dir., Dr. Marvin Harris. Office Address: East Tex. Baptist Univ., Marshall 75670.

Texas Federation of—Pres., John Cole. Office Address: Box 776, Austin 78767.

Junior College (Teachers) Assn., Texas—Pres., Mary R. Parker, Austin Community College, Box 2285, Austin 78768; Exec. Sec., Charles L. Burnside. Office Address: 7748 Highway 290 West, Ste. 310, Austin 78736.

Texas State—Pres., Charles N. Beard Jr.; Exec. Sec., James T. Butler. Office Address: 316 W. 12th, Austin 78701.

Technology Education, Assn. of Texas—Pres., Melvin L. Oringderff, Cherry Oak Circle, Houston 77088; Exec. Dir., W. A. Mayfield. Office Address: Rt. 25, Box 744, Tyler 75707.

Thoracic Society—Pres., Dr. William J. Deaton, 7 Green Lanes, Austin; Chapter Admin., Linda Nichols. Office Address: 3520 Executive Center Dr., Ste. 6100, Austin 78731.

Tourist Council, Texas—Pres., W. L. Pate Sr., Box 901, Beaumont 77704; Exec. Dir., Randy M. Lee. Office Address: 1806 Rio Grande, Austin 78701.

Travelers Protective Assn. of America (Texas Div.)—Pres., L. A. Bauer Jr., Box 268, Cuero 77951; Exec. Dir., Nathan L. Hutson. Office Address: Box 3383, Waco 7670

Turf Irrigation Assn., Texas—Pres., Howard Coulte 9530 Forestview, Dallas 75243; Exec. Dir., Bexley (Richard. Office Address: 940 E. 51st, Austin 78751.

Turkey Federation, Texas—(See Poultry Associations.

University Professors, Am. Assn. of (Tex. Confe ence)—Pres., Aaron Konstam, Trinity Univ., San Ant nio 78284. Office Address: 312 W. 12th, Ste. 404, Austi 78701.

Urological Society, Texas—Pres., Dr. Steven B. Rob erts, 1017 E. Idel, Tyler 75701; Admin. Asst., Carrie Lay mon. Office Address: 1801 N. Lamar Blvd., Austin 78701

Utility Assn., Texas Municipal—Pres., Richar Sawey, 1000 Throckmorton, Fort Worth; Exec. Dir., Te Willis. Office Address: 211 E. 7th, Ste. 1020, Austin 78701

Veterans of Foreign Wars of U.S., Dept. of Texas— Adjt. Qm., Glen M. Gardner Jr. Office Address: 8503 N IH-35, Austin 78753.

War of 1812 in the State of Texas, Gen. Society of the— Pres., Joseph M. Clark Jr., 4310 Feagan, Houston 77007 Sec.-Treas., Thomas F. Bresnehen Jr. Office Address 3207 Top Hill Rd., San Antonio 78209.

Wars in Texas, The Society of Colonial—Pres., Deni M. Fluker, 8911 Springview Ln., Houston 77080; Exec Dir., Thomas F. Bresnehen Jr. Office Address: 3207 To Hill Rd., San Antonio 78209.

Wheat Producers Assn., Texas—Pres., Rober Graves; Exec. Dir., D. G. Nelson. Office Address: 60 Texas Commerce Bank Bldg., Amarillo 79109.

Women's Clubs, Texas Fed. of—Pres., Carol L. Si vus, 4235 Vantage View, San Antonio 78228; Exec. Dir Margie L. Brown. Office Address: 2312 San Gabrie Austin 78705.

Advertisers' Index

INDEX